1/12

BALDWIN'S

OHIO REVISED CODE

ANNOTATED

Title 31
Domestic Relations—Children
Chapters 3107 to 3111

WEST®

A Thomson Reuters business

Mat# 41243908

DEDICATION

To the Bench and Bar
whose members preserve and protect
the rule of law in American society

*

PREFACE

Baldwin's™ Ohio Revised Code Annotated has been published and maintained since 1921. Through the years, Banks–Baldwin™ met the changing needs of Code users by continuously improving both editorial content and the level of service provided to subscribers. Now published by West in casebound format, *Baldwin's ORC* sets the standard for quality editorial information and user-friendliness. With every content feature known to have value in an annotated Code, and all information presented for maximum user convenience, it is the first state code designed for practice in the 21st century. (Please consult the User's Guide in Volume 1 for additional information.)

This volume contains statutes current through legislation approved by the Governor on or before November 4, 2011, and is kept up to date by means of annual cumulative pocket parts and monthly issues of *Baldwin's Ohio Legislative Service Annotated* (OLS). This system assures the fastest possible availability of the laws, rules, and judicial constructions and the fastest access to the full text of decisions and opinions in *Ohio Official Reports* and in Westlaw electronic research.

Editorial features include:

LEGISLATIVE HISTORY

A complete legislative history, in reverse chronological order, follows each section of law.

UNCODIFIED LAW

Provisions of uncodified law affecting statutory interpretation are printed under related Revised Code sections. See the User's Guide in Volume 1 for a complete explanation of this feature.

HISTORICAL AND STATUTORY NOTES

Editorial notes are inserted where necessary to supplement and clarify legislative history or interpretation; they typically call attention to matters such as endorsements or opinions from the Legislative Service Commission, legislative discrepancies, and statutes repealed and reenacted under the same or different section numbers.

"Pre–1953 H 1 Amendments" are noted in reverse chronological order for each section that existed prior to creation of the Revised Code by 1953 House Bill 1.

Amendment notes summarizing the nature and extent of legislative changes to the Revised Code have been editorially prepared and printed under sections of special interest to the Bench and Bar.

UNIFORM LAWS

Uniform Laws and model acts, as promulgated by the National Conference of Commissioners on Uniform State Laws and adopted by the Ohio General Assembly, contain references to identical or similar provisions in West's *Uni-*

PREFACE

form Laws Annotated®. Uniform Laws Tables specify other jurisdictions that have adopted the same Uniform Laws enacted in Ohio.

COMPARATIVE LAWS

Comparative Laws cite selected references to other state statutes on the same or analogous topic.

COMMENTARY

Where appropriate, commentary from the Ohio Legislative Service Commission, the National Conference of Commissioners on Uniform State Laws, committees of the Ohio State Bar Association, and other professional groups is included to assist in statutory interpretation. In addition, selected Rules of Practice carry Staff Notes from the Supreme Court of Ohio.

CROSS REFERENCES

There is an obvious kinship among various laws included in volumes of *Baldwin's Ohio Revised Code Annotated*. Facilitating full use of these interrelationships, time-saving cross references are provided to related or qualifying constitutional, statutory, and court rule provisions.

OHIO ADMINISTRATIVE CODE REFERENCES

Relevant references are provided to *Baldwin's Ohio Administrative Code*, the complete compilation of state agency rules published by West.

UNITED STATES CODE ANNOTATED

Cross references to federal laws as published in West's *United States Code Annotated®* (U.S.C.A.®) are also provided where deemed relevant or useful.

LIBRARY REFERENCES

A special feature that will appeal to users consists of references to West's Key Numbers ☞, Westlaw® Digest topic numbers, and sections of *Corpus Juris Secundum®* (C.J.S.®). These references open the door to constructions and interpretations of statutory law throughout the country.

RESEARCH REFERENCES

Research References include citations to *Ohio Jurisprudence* (OJur), *American Jurisprudence* (Am Jur), and *American Law Reports* (ALR®). In addition, this feature contains references to West's comprehensive line of practice manuals, handbooks, journals, and other secondary sources on specific subjects of law. References in this category cite pertinent parts of these publications where explanatory text, forms, or other practice and study aids can be found.

LAW REVIEW AND JOURNAL COMMENTARIES

Informative articles and discussions in law reviews and bar journals are highlighted for users by references under this heading.

PREFACE

NOTES OF DECISIONS

Judicial constructions of the Ohio Revised Code, as contained in the annotations, are prepared and reviewed by the Publisher's editorial staff. Our objectives are to provide thorough and authoritative access to caselaw and agency opinions and to assist users in understanding the application and purpose of the statutes as determined by the courts and the agencies.

Coverage of this material in *Baldwin's ORC Annotated* is the most comprehensive available, including: all reported Ohio court decisions; selected unreported Courts of Appeals decisions since 1981; selected decisions of the Court of Claims; federal cases construing or affecting Ohio law; opinions of the Attorney General; and selected decisions from a number of state agencies, among them the Board of Tax Appeals, Civil Rights Commission, Public Utilities Commission, Ohio Ethics Commission, Unemployment Compensation Review Commission, and Board of Commissioners on Grievances & Discipline.

Notes of decisions of State and Federal courts include cases published through November 1, 2011.

Annotations are grouped by subject matter under descriptive headings, or catchlines, which are numbered and indexed alphabetically. The same arrangement and topic numbers will be used in supplementary pocket parts and in the "Case Notes and Journal References" section of *Baldwin's Ohio Legislative Service Annotated*™ (OLS); thus, Baldwin's Code users will always be able to locate quickly annotations to recent decisions construing a particular point of law. Further research beyond the closing dates indicated above can easily be accomplished by consulting first the annual pocket part, then the cumulative Case Notes and Journal References Table in the current year OLS.

All citations of these constructions give the full name of each case, the standard reporter where the case can be found, and complete case history.

GENERAL INDEX, RULES INDEX AND STATUTE INDEXES

The General Index is the most comprehensive, precise, reliable, and usable index to Ohio law ever published. It contains multiple, detailed references to the Ohio and U.S. Constitutions, the Ohio Revised Code, and the Ohio rules of practice.

Each title of the Revised Code carries its own index, found in the volume that concludes that title. When two titles are published in the same volume, the index combines both titles. An index to all rules of practice is found in the last court rule volume.

ANCILLARY RESEARCH AIDS

Other research aids in this set include a User's Guide (in Volume 1); a list of abbreviations; tables of titles and tables of contents; and analyses of chapters and sections.

ADDITIONAL INFORMATION OR RESEARCH ASSISTANCE

For additional information or research assistance call the West reference attorneys at 1-800-REF-ATTY (1-800-733-2889). Contact West's editorial department directly with your questions and suggestions by e-mail at west.editor@ thomson.com. Visit West's home page at west.thomson.com.

PREFACE

ACKNOWLEDGMENT

We express our gratitude and appreciation to members of the Bench and Bar, Ohio's law librarians and law schools, the members and staff of the Ohio Secretary of State's Office, the Legislative Service Commission, and others whose timely suggestions have contributed materially to the successful planning and development of *Baldwin's Ohio Revised Code Annotated*.

THE PUBLISHER

December, 2011

WestlawNext™

THE NEXT GENERATION OF ONLINE RESEARCH

WestlawNext is the world's most advanced legal research system. By leveraging more than a century of information and legal analysis from Westlaw, this easy-to-use system not only helps you find the information you need quickly, but offers time-saving tools to organize and annotate your research online. As with Westlaw.com, WestlawNext includes the editorial enhancements (e.g., case headnotes, topics, key numbers) that make it a perfect complement to West print resources.

- FIND ANYTHING by entering citations, descriptive terms, or Boolean terms and connectors into the WestSearch™ box at the top of every page.

- USE KEYCITE® to determine whether a case, statute, regulation, or administrative decision is good law.

- BROWSE DATABASES right from the home page.

- SAVE DOCUMENTS to folders and add notes and highlighting online.

SIGN ON: next.westlaw.com
LEARN MORE: West.Thomson.com/WestlawNext
FOR HELP: 1–800–WESTLAW (1–800–937–8529)

*

TABLE OF TITLES
BALDWIN'S
OHIO REVISED CODE ANNOTATED

*

ABBREVIATIONS

A	Amended
A B A J	American Bar Association Journal
Abs	Ohio Law Abstract
Admin L Rev	Administrative Law Review, American Bar Association
Akron L. Rev.	Akron Law Review
AFSCME	American Federation of State, County and Municipal Employees
Alb L J Sci & Tech	Albany Law Journal of Science and Technology
ALR	American Law Reports Annotated
ALR2d	American Law Reports Annotated, Second Series
ALR3d	American Law Reports Annotated, Third Series
ALR4th	American Law Reports Annotated, Fourth Series
ALR5th	American Law Reports Annotated, Fifth Series
ALR6th	American Law Reports Annotated, Sixth Series
ALR Fed	American Law Reports Annotated, Federal
ALR Fed2d	American Law Reports Annotated, Federal Second
Am	Amended, Amendment
Am Crim L Rev	American Criminal Law Review
Am Dec	American Decisions
Am Jur	American Jurisprudence
Am Jur 2d	American Jurisprudence, Second Series
Am Jur Legal Forms 2d	American Jurisprudence Legal Forms Second
Am Jur Proof of Facts 2d	American Jurisprudence Proof of Facts Second
Am Jur Proof of Facts 3d	American Jurisprudence Proof of Facts Third
Am L Rec	American Law Record
Am L Reg	American Law Register
Am Rep	American Reports
App	Appellate Court
App	Ohio Appellate Reports
App(2d)	Ohio Appellate Reports, Second Series
App(3d)	Ohio Appellate Reports, Third Series
App R	Rules of Appellate Procedure
Ariz L Rev	Arizona Law Review
Art	Article
Assn	Association
A–TF	Amended and Transferred From
A–TT	Amended and Transferred To
Auth	Authority
B	Weekly Law Bulletin
Babbit's Ohio Mun Serv	Babbit's Ohio Municipal Service
Baldwin's Ohio Sch. L.J.	Baldwin's Ohio School Law Journal
Baldwin's Ohio Sch Serv	Baldwin's Ohio School Service
Bd	Board
Bldg	Building
B.R.	Bankruptcy Reporter
Brook L Rev	Brooklyn L Rev
BTA	Ohio Board of Tax Appeals

ABBREVIATIONS

B U L Rev	Boston University Law Review
Bull	Weekly Law Bulletin
Bus Law	Business Lawyer
Cap. U. L. Rev.	Capital University Law Review
Case W. Res. L. Rev.	Case Western Reserve University Law Review
CC	Ohio Circuit Court Reports
CCA	United States Circuit Court of Appeals
CC(NS)	Ohio Circuit Court Reports, New Series
CCR	Rules of Court of Claims of Ohio
CD	Ohio Circuit Decisions
CFR	Code of Federal Regulations
CF Stds	Court Facility Standards
Ch	Chapter
Cin B Ass'n Rep	Cincinnati Bar Association Report
Cir	Circuit Court
Cities & Villages	Cities and Villages, Ohio Municipal League
CIV DISC	Civil Discovery
Civ R	Rules of Civil Procedure
CJC	Code of Judicial Conduct
C.J.S.	Corpus Juris Secundum
Clev B J	Cleveland Bar Journal
Clev L Rec	Cleveland Law Record
Clev L Reg	Cleveland Law Register
Clev L Rep	Cleveland Law Reporter
Clev–Marshall L Rev	Cleveland–Marshall Law Review
Clev. St. L. Rev.	Cleveland State Law Review
CMR	Court–Martial Reports
Colum Hum Rts L Rev	Columbia Human Rights Law Review
Colum J Gender & L	Columbia Journal of Gender and Law
Colum J L & Soc Probs	Columbia Journal of Law and Social Problems
Columbus B Briefs	Columbus Bar Briefs
Co	Company
COC	Ohio Court of Claims
Comm	Commission
Commr	Commissioner
Com.Pl.	Common Pleas Court
Conf	Conflicting
Const	Constitution
Cornell L Rev	Cornell Law Review
Corp	Corporation
CP	Common Pleas Court
CPR	Code of Professional Responsibility
CRC	Ohio Civil Rights Commission
Crim L J Ohio	Criminal Law Journal of Ohio
Crim R	Rules of Criminal Procedure
CSCR	Cincinnati Superior Court Reports
CSS	Court Security Standards
Ct	Court
D	Ohio Decisions

ABBREVIATIONS

Dayton .... Dayton Reports
Dayton B Briefs .... Dayton Bar Briefs
dba .... doing business as
DC .... District Court
Dept .... Department
Dick L Rev .... Dickinson Law Review
Dist .... District
Div .... Division
Dom Rel .... Domestic Relations Court
Domestic Rel L.J. Ohio ...... Domestic Relations Journal of Ohio
DPID Reg .... Death Penalty Indigent Defense Regulations
DR .... Disciplinary Rules, Code of Professional Responsibility
D Repr .... Ohio Decisions, Reprint
Duq L Rev .... Duquesne Law Review
E .... Enacted
EBR .... Environmental Board of Review (pre 1997)
EBR .... Environmental Review Appeals Commission (1997 and
                               after)
EC .... Ethical Considerations, Code of Professional Responsibility
Ed .... Education
eff. .... Effective
Elections Op .... Ohio Elections Commission Opinions
Envtl L J Ohio .... Environmental Law Journal of Ohio
Envtl Monthly .... Environmental Monthly
ERAC .... Environmental Review Appeals Commission
Ethics Op .... Ohio Ethics Commission Opinions
Evid R .... Ohio Rules of Evidence
ex rel .... on the relation of
Fam L Quar .... Family Law Quarterly, American Bar Association
F .... Form
F. .... Federal Reporter
F.2d .... Federal Reporter, Second Series
F.3d .... Federal Reporter, Third Series
F. Cas .... Federal Cases
Fed .... Federal
Fed Appx .... Federal Appendix
Finley's Ohio Mun Serv   Finley's Ohio Municipal Service
Fla L Rev .... University of Florida Law Review
Forum .... Forum, American Bar Association
F.R.D. .... Federal Rules Decisions
FR Serv .... Federal Rules Service
FR Serv(2d) .... Federal Rules Service, Second Series
F.Supp .... Federal Supplement
F.Supp(2d) .... Federal Supplement, Second Series
GC .... General Code of Ohio
Geo L J .... Georgetown Law Journal
Gotherman's Ohio Mun
    Serv .... Gotherman's Ohio Municipal Service
Gov Bar R .... Supreme Court Rules for the Government of the Bar
Gov Jud R .... Supreme Court Rules for the Government of the Judiciary

XV

ABBREVIATIONS

H ....House Bill
Harv L Rev ....Harvard Law Review
HCR ....House Concurrent Resolution
Health L J Ohio ....Health Law Journal of Ohio
Health Matrix: J. Law-Medi-
    cine ....Health Matrix: Journal of Law-Medicine
HJR ....House Joint Resolution
HR ....House Resolution
HWFB....................Hazardous Waste Facility Board
Inc ....Incorporated
Ind L J ....Indiana Law Journal
Indus Rel Rep ....Industrial Relations Report
Iowa L Rev ....Iowa Law Review
IRC ....Internal Revenue Code
J Fam L ....Journal of Family Law (University of Louisville)
J L & Com ....Journal of Law and Commerce
J L & Educ...............Journal of Law and Education
J.L. & Health.............Journal of Law and Health
J Min L & Pol'y...........Journal of Mineral Law and Policy
J Nat Resources & Envtl
    L......................Journal of Natural Resources and Environmental Law
Joint Legis Ethics Comm ....Joint Legislative Ethics Commission
Jud Cond ....Code of Judicial Conduct
Juv ....Juvenile Court
Juv R ....Rules of Juvenile Procedure
Ky Bench & B.............Kentucky Bench and Bar
Ky L J ....Kentucky Law Journal
Lake Legal Views..........Lake Legal Views, Lake County Bar Association
Law & Fact ....Law & Fact, Cuyahoga County Bar Association
LBA Bull ....Louisville Bar Association News Bulletin
L.Ed. ....Lawyers' Edition, United States Supreme Court Reports
L.Ed.2d ....Lawyers' Edition, United States Supreme Court Reports,
                             Second Series
L.J. Ohio.................Business Law Journal of Ohio
Legal Reference Serv Q .....Legal Reference Services Quarterly
Louisville Law ....Louisville Lawyer
LRA ....Lawyers Reports Annotated
LRA(NS).................Lawyers Reports Annotated, New Series
Ltd ....Limited
May Ed R ....Mayor's Court Education and Procedure Rules
Md L Rev ....Maryland Law Review
Mental Disability L Rep ....Mental Disability Law Reporter
Mercer L Rev ....Mercer Law Review
Mfg ....Manufacturing
Misc.....................Ohio Miscellaneous Reports
Misc(2d) ....Ohio Miscellaneous Reports, Second Series
M J......................Military Justice Reporter
Muni ....Municipal Court
Nat'l L J ....National Law Journal
N D L Rev ....North Dakota Law Review

ABBREVIATIONS

N.D.Ohio	Northern District Ohio
N.E.	Northeastern Reporter
N.E.2d	Northeastern Reporter, Second Series
NEA	National Education Association
Neb L Rev	Nebraska Law Review
N Ky L Rev	Northern Kentucky Law Review
N Ky St L F	Northern Kentucky State Law Forum
NP	Ohio Nisi Prius Reports
NP(NS)	Ohio Nisi Prius Reports, New Series
Nw U L Rev	Northwestern University Law Review
O	Ohio Reports
OAC	Baldwin's Ohio Administrative Code
OAG	Opinions of the Ohio Attorney General
OAPSE	Ohio Association of Public School Employees
OBR	Ohio Bar Reports
OCA	Ohio Courts of Appeals Reports
O Const	Ohio Constitution
O Constr. & Code J.	Ohio Construction and Code Journal
OCRC	Ohio Civil Rights Commission
OEA	Ohio Education Association
OFD	Ohio Federal Decisions
OFT	Ohio Federation of Teachers
Ohio	Ohio Reports
Ohio App	Ohio Appellate Reports
Ohio App.2d	Ohio Appellate Reports, Second Series
Ohio App.3d	Ohio Appellate Reports, Third Series
Ohio B Ass'n Serv Letter	Ohio Bar Association Service Letter
Ohio C.C.	Ohio Circuit Court Reports
Ohio C.C.N.S.	Ohio Circuit Court Reports, New Series
Ohio C.D.	Ohio Circuit Decisions
Ohio Civ Prac J	Ohio Civil Practice Journal
Ohio Ct.Cl.	Ohio Court of Claims
Ohio Com.Pl.	Ohio Common Pleas Court
Ohio Dec.	Ohio Decisions
Ohio Dec. Reprint	Ohio Decisions, Reprint
Ohio F.Dec.	Ohio Federal Decisions
Ohio L Rep	Ohio Law Reporter
Ohio Law.	Ohio Lawyer
Ohio Law Abs.	Ohio Law Abstract
Ohio Misc.	Ohio Miscellaneous Reports
Ohio Misc.2d	Ohio Miscellaneous Reports, Second Series
Ohio N.P.	Ohio Nisi Prius Reports
Ohio N.P.N.S.	Ohio Nisi Prius Reports, New Series
Ohio N.U. L. Rev.	Ohio Northern University Law Review
Ohio Sch Boards Ass'n J	Ohio School Boards Association Journal
Ohio St.	Ohio State Reports
Ohio St.2d	Ohio State Reports, Second Series
Ohio St.3d	Ohio State Reports, Third Series
Ohio St B Ass'n Rep	Ohio State Bar Association Report

ABBREVIATIONS

Ohio St.L.J.	Ohio State Law Journal
Ohio Tax Rev	Ohio Tax Review
Ohio Trial	Ohio Trial, Ohio Academy of Trial Lawyers Education Foundation
OJur 3d	Ohio Jurisprudence, Third Series
OLS	Baldwin's Ohio Legislative Service Annotated
OMR	Baldwin's Ohio Monthly Record
OO	Ohio Opinions
OO(2d)	Ohio Opinions, Second Series
OO(3d)	Ohio Opinions, Third Series
Or L Rev	Oregon Law Review
ORC	Baldwin's Ohio Revised Code
OS	Ohio State Reports
OS(2d)	Ohio State Reports, Second Series
OS(3d)	Ohio State Reports, Third Series
OSLJ	Ohio State Law Journal
OS Unrep	Ohio State Unreported
O.Supp.	Ohio Supplement
Otto	Otto's Supreme Court Reports
Pa B A Q	Pennsylvania Bar Association Quarterly
Pa Law	Pennsylvania Lawyer
Pa St B Ass'n Bull	Pennsylvania State Bar Association Bulletin
PBR	Personnel Board of Review
PConf	Possibly or Partially Conflicting
Pepp L Rev	Pepperdine Law Review
Prob	Probate Court
Prob & Trust J	Probate and Trust Journal
Prob. L.J. Ohio	Probate Law Journal of Ohio
Civ Discovery Edition	PRO/GRAM Civil Discovery Edition
Civ Litig Edition	PRO/GRAM Civil Litigation Edition
PUCO	Public Utilities Commission of Ohio
R	Repealed
RBR	Reclamation Board of Review (pre 1997)
RBR	Reclamation Commission (1997 and after)
RC	Ohio Revised Code
R–E	Repealed and Reenacted
RPC	Rules of Professional Conduct
RRD	RC 119.032 rule review date(s)
Rep R	Supreme Court Rules for the Reporting of Opinions
RS	Revised Statutes of Ohio
S	Senate Bill
St Mary's L J	St. Mary's Law Journal
SCR	Senate Concurrent Resolution
S.Ct.	United States Supreme Court Reporter
SCt R	Rules of Practice of the Supreme Court of Ohio
S.D.Ohio	Southern District Ohio
SERB	State Employment Relations Board
Shingle	The Shingle, Philadelphia Bar Association
SJR	Senate Joint Resolution
SR	Senate Resolution

ABBREVIATIONS

Stat	Statutes
State Employment Rel Board Q	State Employment Relations Board Quarterly
Sub	Substitute
Sup R	Rules of Superintendence for Courts of Ohio
TC	Tax Court (United States)
Temp L Q	Temple Law Quarterly
Temp L Rev	Temple Law Review
TF	Transferred From
Title Topics	Title Topics, Ohio Land Title Association
TJS	Trial Court Jury Use and Management Standards
Tol B Ass'n News	Toledo Bar Association Newsletter
Tort L.J. Ohio	Tort Law Journal of Ohio
Traf R	Ohio Traffic Rules
Trial	Trial, Association of Trial Lawyers of America
TT	Transferred To
Twp	Township
UCBR	Unemployment Compensation Board of Review (pre 1997)
UCBR	Unemployment Compensation Review Commission (1997 and after)
UCC	Uniform Commercial Code
U. Cin. L. Rev.	University of Cincinnati Law Review
U Colo L Rev	University of Colorado Law Review
UCRC	Unemployment Compensation Review Commission
U. Dayton L. Rev.	University of Dayton Law Review
U Pa L Rev	University of Pennsylvania Law Review
U Pitt L Rev	University of Pittsburgh Law Review
U Rich L Rev	University of Richmond Law Review
U.S.	United States Supreme Court Reports
USC	United States Code
USCA	United States Code Annotated
USLW	United States Law Week
USP.Q.	United States Patent Quarterly
USP.Q.2d	United States Patent Quarterly, Second Series
U. Tol. L. Rev.	University of Toledo Law Review
v	versus
v	volume, Ohio Laws
VCC R	Rules of Court of Claims of Ohio, Victims of Crime Compensation Section
Vill L Rev	Villanova Law Review
W	Withdrawn
W	Wright's Ohio Supreme Court Reports
Wall.	Wallace's Supreme Court Reports
Wake Forest L Rev	Wake Forest Law Review
Washburn L J	Washburn Law Journal
WL	Westlaw reference number
W.L.B.	Weekly Law Bulletin
WLG	Weekly Law Gazette
WLJ	Western Law Journal
WLM	Western Law Monthly

ABBREVIATIONS

TABLE OF CONTENTS

Title 31—Domestic Relations–Children

(Chapters 3107 to 3111)

*

CITE THIS BOOK

OHIO REV. CODE ANN. § 3107.01 (Baldwin 2011)

*

BALDWIN'S OHIO REVISED CODE ANNOTATED

Title XXXI

DOMESTIC RELATIONS—CHILDREN

(Chapters 3107 to 3111 appear in this volume.)

CHAPTER 3107

ADOPTION

GENERAL PROVISIONS

1

ADOPTION

Comparative Laws

Uniform Adoption Act

Table of Jurisdictions Wherein Act Has Been Adopted.

For text of Uniform Act, and variation notes and annotation materials for adopting jurisdictions, see Uniform Laws Annotated, Master Edition, Volume 9, Pt. IA.

Jurisdiction	Statutory Citation
Alaska	AS 25.23.005 to 25.23.240.
Arkansas	A.C.A. § 9–9–201 to 9–9–224.
North Dakota	NDCC 14–15–01 to 14–15–23.

Comparative Laws

Ariz.—A.R.S. § 8-101 et seq.
Ark.—A.C.A. § 9-9-201 et seq.
Fla.—West's F.S.A. § 63.012 et seq.
Ga.—O.C.G.A. § 19-8-1 et seq.
Idaho—I.C. § 16-1501 et seq.
Ill.—ILCS 750 50/1 et seq.
Ind.—West's A.I.C. 31–19–2–1 et seq.
Iowa—I.C.A. § 600.1 et seq.
Ky.—Baldwin's KRS 199.470 et seq.
Mass—M.G.L.A. c. 210, § 1 et seq
Me.—18-A M.R.S.A. § 9–101 et seq.
Mich.—M.C.L.A. § 710.21 et seq.

Minn.—M.S.A. § 259.21 et seq.
Mo.—V.A.M.S. § 453.010 et seq.
N.C.—G.S. § 48-1-100 et seq.
Neb.—R.R.S.1943, § 43–101 et seq.
N.J.—N.J.S.A. 9:3-37 et seq.
N.Y.—McKinney's Domestic Relations Law § 109 et seq.
Tenn.—T.C.A. § 36-1-101 et seq.
Tex.—V.T.C.A. Family Code § 162.001 et seq.
Wis.—W.S.A. 48.81 et seq.
W.Va.—Code, 48–22–101 et seq.

Cross References

Children, see 3109.01 et seq.
Confidentiality of adoption files, courts, Sup R 55
Custody of children, notice of dispositional hearing to prospective adoptive parent, see 2151.424
Department of job and family services, division of social administration; care and placement of children; interstate compact on placement of children, see 5103.12 to 5103.17, 5103.20 to 5103.27
Designation of heir-at-law, see 2105.15

Hearsay exceptions, statements regarding declarant's own adoption, Evid R 804
Parentage, see 3111.01 et seq.
Parental duty of support, see 3103.031
Placement for adoption of children from other states, see 2151.39
Powers and duties of county children services board, see 5153.16
Registering adoptions; access of adopted individual to birth certificate, see 3705.12
Wills, status of pretermitted heirs, see 2107.34

Ohio Administrative Code References

Adoption assistance for children in permanent and temporary custody, see OAC Ch 5101:2–47

AdoptOhio agency, services and responsibilities, see OAC Ch 5101:2–48

Department of job and family services, child care agencies, boarding homes, and child care institutions, see OAC Ch 5101:2–5 to Ch 5101:2–9

Subsidized adoptions, see OAC Ch 5101:2–44

Temporary or permanent custody and placement of children, interstate placements by individuals and courts, see OAC Ch 5101:2–42

GENERAL PROVISIONS

3107.01 Definitions

As used in sections 3107.01 to 3107.19 of the Revised Code:

(A) "Agency" means any public or private organization certified, licensed, or otherwise specially empowered by law or rule to place minors for adoption.

(B) "Attorney" means a person who has been admitted to the bar by order of the Ohio supreme court.

(C) "Child" means a son or daughter, whether by birth or by adoption.

(D) "Court" means the probate courts of this state, and when the context requires, means the court of any other state empowered to grant petitions for adoption.

(E) "Foster caregiver" has the same meaning as in section 5103.02 of the Revised Code.

(F) "Identifying information" means any of the following with regard to a person: first name, last name, maiden name, alias, social security number, address, telephone number, place of employment, number used to identify the person for the purpose of the statewide education management information system established pursuant to section 3301.0714 of the Revised Code, and any other number federal or state law requires or permits to be used to identify the person.

(G) "Minor" means a person under the age of eighteen years.

(H) "Putative father" means a man, including one under age eighteen, who may be a child's father and to whom all of the following apply:

(1) He is not married to the child's mother at the time of the child's conception or birth;

(2) He has not adopted the child;

(3) He has not been determined, prior to the date a petition to adopt the child is filed, to have a parent and child relationship with the child by a court proceeding pursuant to sections 3111.01 to 3111.18 of the Revised Code, a court proceeding in another state, an administrative agency proceeding pursuant to sections 3111.38 to 3111.54 of the Revised Code, or an administrative agency proceeding in another state;

(4) He has not acknowledged paternity of the child pursuant to sections 3111.21 to 3111.35 of the Revised Code.

(2000 S 180, eff. 3–22–01; 2000 H 448, eff. 10–5–00; 1997 H 352, eff. 1–1–98; 1997 H 408, eff. 10–1–97; 1996 H 274, eff. 9–18–96; 1996 H 419, eff. 9–18–96; 1976 H 156, eff. 1–1–77)

Uncodified Law

1996 H 419, § 5: See Uncodified Law under 3107.06.

Historical and Statutory Notes

Ed. Note: Former 3107.01 repealed by 1976 H 156, eff. 1–1–77; 1973 S 1; 1953 H 1; GC 8004–1; Source—GC 10512–9.

Pre–1953 H 1 Amendments: 124 v S 65

Amendment Note: 2000 S 180 substituted "3111.18" for "3111.19", "3111.38" for "3111.20" and "3111.54" for "3111.29" in division (B)(3); and substituted "3111.25" for "3111.211" and "3111.821" for "5101.314" in division (B)(4).

Amendment Note: 2000 H 448 added new division (E) and redesignated former divisions (E) through (G) as new divisions (F) through (H).

Amendment Note: 1997 H 352 substituted "5101.314" for "2105.18" in division (G)(4).

Amendment Note: 1997 H 408 deleted former division (G); and redesignated former division (H) as new division (G). Prior to deletion, former division (G) read:

"(G) 'Private child placing agency,' 'private non-custodial agency,' and 'public children services agency' have the same meanings as in section 2151.011 of the Revised Code."

Amendment Note: 1996 H 274 added division (H)(4).

Amendment Note: 1996 H 419 rewrote this section, which previously read:

"As used in sections 3107.01 to 3107.19 of the Revised Code, unless the context otherwise requires:

"(A) 'Child' means a son or daughter, whether by birth or by adoption;

"(B) 'Court' means the probate courts of this state, and when the context requires, means the court of any other state empowered to grant petitions for adoption;

"(C) 'Minor' means a person under the age of eighteen years;

"(D) 'Agency' means any public or private organization certified, licensed, or otherwise specially empowered by law or rule to place minors for adoption."

Cross References

Age of majority, see 3109.01

Conditions for juvenile court approving parent's agreement for childs' adoption, identifying information defined, see 5103.151

Department of human resources, division of social administration, placing of children, see 5103.16

Duty of parents to support children of unemancipated minor children, see 3109.19

Jurisdiction of juvenile court, see 2151.23

Jurisdiction of probate court, see 2101.24

Persons required to report injury or neglect; procedures on receipt of report, see 2151.421

Ohio Administrative Code References

Adoption administrative falsification procedures, see OAC 5101:2–33–13

AdoptOhio, adoption, see OAC Ch 5101:2–48

Research References

ALR Library

28 ALR 6th 349, Requirements and Effects of Putative Father Registries.

Encyclopedias

OH Jur. 3d Decedents' Estates § 802, Beneficiaries Indicated in General Terms--Gift to "Children," "Issue," "Heirs," and the Like.

OH Jur. 3d Family Law § 870, Generally; Definitions.

OH Jur. 3d Family Law § 873, Jurisdiction.

OH Jur. 3d Family Law § 878, Who May be Adopted.

OH Jur. 3d Family Law § 882, Putative Father Registry.

OH Jur. 3d Family Law § 884, Agency's Consent.

OH Jur. 3d Trusts § 124, Adopted Child as Within Class.

Forms

Ohio Forms Legal and Business § 28:2, Definitions.

Ohio Forms Legal and Business § 28:17, Introduction.

Ohio Jurisprudence Pleading and Practice Forms § 6:40, Court.

Ohio Jurisprudence Pleading and Practice Forms § 96:1, Definitions.

Ohio Jurisprudence Pleading and Practice Forms § 96:2, Introduction.

Ohio Jurisprudence Pleading and Practice Forms § 96:3, Who May be Adopted.

Ohio Jurisprudence Pleading and Practice Forms § 96:32, Confidentiality.

Ohio Jurisprudence Pleading and Practice Forms § 96:75, Permanent Surrender of Child.

Treatises and Practice Aids

Sowald & Morganstern, Baldwin's Ohio Practice Domestic Relations Law § 3:9, Judicial Parentage Action--Initial Procedure.

Carlin, Baldwin's Ohio Prac. Merrick-Rippner Probate Law § 3:2, Statutory.

Carlin, Baldwin's Ohio Prac. Merrick-Rippner Probate Law § 99:2, History.

Carlin, Baldwin's Ohio Prac. Merrick-Rippner Probate Law § 99:5, Parties--Who May be Adopted--Statutory Provisions.

Carlin, Baldwin's Ohio Prac. Merrick-Rippner Probate Law § 99:28, Papers and Records--Accounting.

Carlin, Baldwin's Ohio Prac. Merrick-Rippner Probate Law § 99:30, Statutorily Required Consent.

Carlin, Baldwin's Ohio Prac. Merrick-Rippner Probate Law § 99:32, Parties Giving Consent--Putative Father.

Carlin, Baldwin's Ohio Prac. Merrick-Rippner Probate Law § 99:38, Consent Not Required--Statutory Scheme.

Carlin, Baldwin's Ohio Prac. Merrick-Rippner Probate Law § 99:54, Inheritance Rights of Adoptees--"Stranger to the Adoption" Doctrine.

Carlin, Baldwin's Ohio Prac. Merrick-Rippner Probate Law § 110:31, Parentage Act--Continuing Jurisdiction to Modify or Revoke Judgment.

Adrine & Ruden, Ohio Domestic Violence Law § 10:7, Relationships Covered--Persons Who Have a Child in Common.

Law Review and Journal Commentaries

Adoption and Religious Control, Rita E. Hauser. 54 A B A J 771 (August 1968).

Adoption Laws of Ohio: a Critical and Comparative Study, William Yost. 21 Clev St L Rev 1 (September 1972).

Adoption Reform in Ohio, Note. 24 Clev St L Rev 146 (Winter 1975).

Adoption Rights of Natural Parents and Those of Non-parents in Adoption Proceedings, Note. 14 J Fam L 318 (1975).

Adoptions and Their Legal Consequences, John H. Woehrmann. 34 Clev B J 161 (July 1963).

Advertising for Adoption Placement: Gray Market Activities in a Gray Area of Constitutional Protection, Comment. 25 Duq L Rev 129 (Fall 1986).

Cohabitants And Constructive Trusts—Comparative Approaches, Robert L. Stenger. 27 J Fam L 373 (1989).

The Emergence Of Wrongful Adoption As A Cause Of Action, Note. 27 J Fam L 475 (1989).

Family Law—Ohio's Statutory Requirement of Legal Guardian Consent to Adoption and Its Effect on the Jurisdiction of the Probate Court, Note. 36 Ohio St L J 451 (1975).

The Historical Background of the American Law of Adoption, Stephen B. Presser. 11 J Fam L 443 (1972).

The Interracial Adoption Implications of Drummond v Fulton County Department of Family and Children Services, Comment. 17 J Fam L 117 (1978–79).

The Law of Adoption in Ohio, Beverly E. Sylvester. 2 Cap U L Rev 23 (1973).

Ohio House Bill 419: Increased Openness in Adoption Records Law, Wendy L. Weiss. 45 Clev St L Rev 101 (1997).

Race And Child Placement: The Best Interests Test And The Cost Of Discretion, Twila L. Perry. 29 J Fam L 51 (1990–91).

Racial Matching and the Adoption Dilemma: Alternatives for the Hard to Place, Note. 17 J Fam L 333 (1978–79).

The Revised Law of Adoption in Ohio, Beverly E. Sylvester. 7 Cap U L Rev 219 (1977).

Symposium: The Implications of Welfare Reform for Children. 60 Ohio St L J 1177 (1999).

Transracial Adoption: A Critical View Of The Courts' Present Standards, Note. 28 J Fam L 303 (1990).

Notes of Decisions

1. In general

Goal of adoption statutes is to protect best interests of children, which is best accomplished in cases where adoption is necessary by providing child with permanent and stable home and ensuring that adoption process is completed in expeditious manner. In re Adoption of Zschach (Ohio, 06-06-1996) 75 Ohio St.3d 648, 665 N.E.2d 1070, reconsideration denied 76 Ohio St.3d 1410, 666 N.E.2d 569, certiorari denied 117 S.Ct. 582, 519 U.S. 1028, 136 L.Ed.2d 513. Adoption ☞ 3

No breach of contract suit by adoptive parents against an adoption agency is recognized in Ohio and nowhere in the statutes dealing with adoptions has the general assembly expressly created any cause of action for damages in such a situation; the only cause of action by adoptive parents against adoption agencies sounds in fraud. Allen v. Childrens Services (Cuyahoga 1990) 58 Ohio App.3d

41, 567 N.E.2d 1346, motion overruled 54 Ohio St.3d 709, 561 N.E.2d 944.

"Adoption" is not a custody proceeding and may only become one at such time that a guardian, as opposed to a guardian ad litem, is appointed to protect the child's best interest. In re Adoption of Reams (Franklin 1989) 52 Ohio App.3d 52, 557 N.E.2d 159, dismissed 50 Ohio St.3d 707, 553 N.E.2d 684. Adoption ☞ 1

The main purpose of adoption is to find homes for children, not children for families. (See also In re Harshey, 40 App(2d) 157, 318 NE(2d) 544 (1974).) In re Harshey (Cuyahoga 1975) 45 Ohio App.2d 97, 341 N.E.2d 616, 74 O.O.2d 120. Adoption ☞ 1

The adoption of children exists in this country only by virtue of statute. There is no common law adoption. Belden v. Armstrong (Summit 1951) 93 Ohio App. 307, 113 N.E.2d 693, 51 O.O. 62. Adoption ☞ 1

Adoption is purely statutory, and statutory provisions should be strictly complied with. In re Privette (Franklin 1932) 45 Ohio App. 51, 185 N.E. 435, 12 Ohio Law Abs. 652, 38 Ohio Law Rep. 90. Adoption ☞ 1

Adoption is a function which requires the exercise of the judicial power which is vested in the courts of Ohio pursuant to O Const Art IV §4.

State ex rel. Portage County Welfare Dept. v. Summers (Ohio 1974) 38 Ohio St.2d 144, 311 N.E.2d 6, 67 O.O.2d 151.

The statutes of Ohio do not require, as a condition of the adoption of a minor child, either that child be a citizen of the United States, or that its natural parents, or either of them, be citizens. 1920 OAG p 1038.

2. Federal provisions

The district court had authority, under the Hague Convention on Civil Aspects of International Child Abduction, to determine the merits of an abduction claim, but not the merits of the underlying child custody claim. Anderson v. Acree (S.D.Ohio, 12-11-2002) 250 F.Supp.2d 872, subsequent determination 250 F.Supp.2d 876. Child Custody ☞ 816

Even assuming equitable tolling could delay the commencement of the one-year period, for purposes of provision of Hague Convention on Civil Aspects of International Child Abduction under which the court "shall," without considering whether child is settled in new environment, order the child's return if a period of less than one year has elapsed from the date of the wrongful removal or retention, equitable tolling was not warranted, where father clearly had been aware of the child's whereabouts long before he filed his petition for the child's return. Anderson v. Acree (S.D.Ohio, 12-11-2002) 250 F.Supp.2d 872, subsequent determination 250 F.Supp.2d 876. Child Custody ☞ 808

3. Jurisdiction

Since putative father's action to determine parentage was pending in juvenile court when prospective stepfather filed in the probate court his petition to adopt minor son of his fiancee, the probate court was required to stay the proceedings pending the juvenile court determination, and probate court was then required to give effect to the juvenile court's determination of the existence of a parent-child relationship between putative father and child and to find that putative father's status was that of "father." In re Adoption of G.B. (Ohio App. 3 Dist., Seneca, 10-18-2010) No. 13-10-01, 2010-Ohio-5059, 2010 WL 4055551, Unreported. Adoption ☞ 9.1

Stepfather's failure to file a certified copy of child's birth certificate with his petition to adopt child did not deprive the trial court of subject matter jurisdiction; statute that referred to the filing of a certified copy of child's birth certificate did not require the birth certificate to be filed with the adoption petition and it did not designate a date upon which the birth certificate was required to be filed, stepfather filed a certified copy of child's birth certificate after father objected to the lack of birth certificate, and father was not prejudiced by stepfather's failure to file the birth certificate with his adoption petition. In re Adoption of Reed (Ohio App. 4 Dist., Scioto, 04-17-2006) No. 05CA3048,

2006-Ohio-2094, 2006 WL 1115464, Unreported. Adoption ☞ 11

Kentucky was child's home state under Uniform Child Custody Jurisdiction Act (UCCJA) at time adoption proceedings were commenced in Ohio, where child was born in Kentucky and had resided with prospective adoptive parents in Ohio for less than four months when original adoption petition was filed and natural parents had filed custody action in Kentucky within six-month period after child left Kentucky for last time. In re Adoption of Asente (Ohio, 08-23-2000) 90 Ohio St.3d 91, 734 N.E.2d 1224, 2000-Ohio-32, reconsideration denied 90 Ohio St.3d 1431, 736 N.E.2d 27. Child Custody ☞ 736

Probate court has duty of making adoption ruling based on all evidence presented to it, and such evidence can include testimony of natural parent. In re Adoption of Lassiter (Ohio App. 2 Dist., 02-24-1995) 101 Ohio App.3d 367, 655 N.E.2d 781, dismissed, appeal not allowed 73 Ohio St.3d 1410, 651 N.E.2d 1308. Adoption ☞ 7.8(2)

While natural parents entrusted with the permanent custody of their children may deprive a probate court of jurisdiction to enter a decree of adoption by withholding their consent to the adoption, the refusal of consent to an adoption by a "certified agency" as defined in RC 3107.01(C) does not impair the jurisdiction of the probate court to fully hear and determine an adoption proceeding. (See also In re Harshey, 45 App(2d) 97, 341 NE(2d) 616 (1975).) In re Harshey (Cuyahoga 1974) 40 Ohio App.2d 157, 318 N.E.2d 544, 69 O.O.2d 165. Adoption ☞ 7.7

Original and exclusive jurisdiction over adoption proceedings is vested specifically in the probate court. In re Adoption of Barkhurst (Ohio App. 12 Dist., Butler, 09-04-2002) No. CA2002-04-081, 2002-Ohio-4711, 2002 WL 31009205, Unreported, appeal not allowed 97 Ohio St.3d 1471, 779 N.E.2d 237, 2002-Ohio-6347. Adoption ☞ 10

Original and exclusive jurisdiction over adoption proceedings is vested specifically in the probate court pursuant to RC Ch 3107. State ex rel. Portage County Welfare Dept. v. Summers (Ohio 1974) 38 Ohio St.2d 144, 311 N.E.2d 6, 67 O.O.2d 151.

The refusal of consent to an adoption by a "certified organization," as defined in RC 3107.01(C), does not impair the jurisdiction of the probate court, but the recommendations and the reports, filed pursuant to RC 3107.05 and 3107.10, are to be considered, in conjunction with all other evidence adduced in the proceeding, by the court in deciding the issues presented by RC 3107.09. State ex rel. Portage County Welfare Dept. v. Summers (Ohio 1974) 38 Ohio St.2d 144, 311 N.E.2d 6, 67 O.O.2d 151.

By this section, exclusive jurisdiction is conferred upon probate court in proceedings for adoption. Eastman v Brewer, 20 Abs 597 (App, Cuyahoga 1935).

4. Consent

Unwed father was putative father, for purposes of determining whether his alleged failure to register with the putative father registry obviated necessity of his consent to child's adoption, where father had not been determined to have parent-child relationship with child through court proceeding prior to date wife's husband filed petition to adopt. In re Adoption of A.N.L. (Ohio App. 12 Dist., Warren, 08-16-2005) No. CA2004-11-131, No. CA2005-04-046, 2005-Ohio-4239, 2005 WL 1949678, Unreported. Adoption ⬅ 7.2(3)

Probate court cannot decree an adoption, unless mother of child files written consent with court, and mother may withdraw such consent any time before decree. State ex rel Scholder v Scholder, 2 Abs 471, 22 OLR 608 (App, Summit 1924).

Whether or not father was served with notice of hearing on proposed adoption of child by mother's husband, father's consent to adoption was sufficient consideration for agreement whereby mother waived back child support in return for father's consent; by consenting, father waived right to raise any justifiable causes as to why he did not pay support or visit child in year immediately preceding filing of adoption petition. Eckliff v. Walters (Ohio App. 11 Dist., 09-15-2006) 168 Ohio App.3d 727, 861 N.E.2d 843, 2006-Ohio-4817. Child Support ⬅ 456

Agreement between biological parents to exchange a consent to adoption for forgiveness of arrearages in current child support is an enforceable agreement. Eckliff v. Walters (Ohio App. 11 Dist., 09-15-2006) 168 Ohio App.3d 727, 861 N.E.2d 843, 2006-Ohio-4817. Adoption ⬅ 7.5; Child Support ⬅ 456

Evidence of whether father believed that waiver of back child support was legal was irrelevant in proceeding to recover alleged child support arrearage for period up to date that child was adopted by mother's husband with father's consent; it was legal to waive back support in an agreement involving child support obligor's consent to adoption. Eckliff v. Walters (Ohio App. 11 Dist., 09-15-2006) 168 Ohio App.3d 727, 861 N.E.2d 843, 2006-Ohio-4817. Adoption ⬅ 7.5; Child Support ⬅ 456; Child Support ⬅ 483

In proceeding to collect back child support, evidence supported trial court's finding that oral agreement existed whereby father's child support arrearage would be waived in return for consenting to adoption of child by mother's husband; evidence indicated that mother told father two day prior to signing consent to adopt that if father signed consent there would be no back or future child support involved. Eckliff v. Walters (Ohio App. 11 Dist., 09-15-2006) 168 Ohio App.3d 727, 861 N.E.2d 843, 2006-Ohio-4817. Child Support ⬅ 456

Consent to adoption is not required of putative father who fails to register within thirty days of child's birth if he is still a putative father when petition for adoption is filed, but if a putative father judicially establishes parentage prior to the filing of

adoption petition, he ceases to be a putative father and his consent is required based on parent and child relationship with minor. In re Adoption of Baby Boy Brooks (Ohio App. 10 Dist., 03-21-2000) 136 Ohio App.3d 824, 737 N.E.2d 1062, appeal not allowed 89 Ohio St.3d 1433, 730 N.E.2d 383. Adoption ⬅ 7.2(3)

Refusal of consent to an adoption by an individual or agency having permanent custody of a child, does not deprive the court of jurisdiction, but raises the issues of the best interest and welfare of the child. In re Haun (Ohio Prob. 1971) 31 Ohio Misc. 9, 277 N.E.2d 258, 58 O.O.2d 336, 60 O.O.2d 154, affirmed 31 Ohio App.2d 63, 286 N.E.2d 478, 60 O.O.2d 163.

Where parents, by contract, surrender the permanent custody and control of their child to an approved child care agency with authority to give consent to the adoption of such child under GC 1352–12 (RC 5103.15), such approved child care agency is the only one authorized to give consent to adoption, as long as the contract of permanent surrender remains in force, and is a necessary party to a proceeding to adopt such child. In re Bolling's Adoption (Cuyahoga 1948) 83 Ohio App. 1, 82 N.E.2d 135, 52 Ohio Law Abs. 572, 38 O.O. 122. Adoption ⬅ 7.1; Adoption ⬅ 11; Adoption ⬅ 15

The consent of the juvenile court is merely a statutory condition that must be met in some cases before an adoption can proceed. In re Adoption of Barkhurst (Ohio App. 12 Dist., Butler, 09-04-2002) No. CA2002-04-081, 2002-Ohio-4711, 2002 WL 31009205, Unreported, appeal not allowed 97 Ohio St.3d 1471, 779 N.E.2d 237, 2002-Ohio-6347. Adoption ⬅ 10

An order stating that the consent of a natural parent to the adoption of her child is not necessary is a "final appealable order" within the meaning of RC 2505.02 since such an order affects a substantial right, and a court therefore cannot vacate a consent order sua sponte. In re Adoption of Daniel B, No. L–93–306, 1994 WL 374196 (6th Dist Ct App, Lucas, 6–15–94).

Mother of illegitimate child has right to withdraw her consent to adoption of her child at any time before court acts upon such consent and in so doing dismisses the petition for the adoption of the child and deprives the court of proceeding further with the case. In re Adoption of Rubin, 33 Abs 108 (Prob, Belmont 1941).

5. Inheritance

Contract to receive child by adoption and as apprentice, to be maintained, clothed, educated, and treated like natural child of persons receiving child, does not show intention to adopt child as heir. Sisson v. Irish (Cuyahoga 1926) 23 Ohio App. 462, 155 N.E. 168, 4 Ohio Law Abs. 768, 6 Ohio Law Abs. 470. Adoption ⬅ 21; Descent And Distribution ⬅ 26; Labor And Employment ⬅ 926

Contract to receive child by adoption and as apprentice, containing no tangible rights with respect to heirship in existence at time of contract and no reference to property which might come into possession or ownership at later date, cannot be specifically enforced. Sisson v. Irish (Cuyahoga 1926) 23 Ohio App. 462, 155 N.E. 168, 4 Ohio Law Abs. 768, 6 Ohio Law Abs. 470.

6. Right to counsel

Approval by the court of the permanent surrender of a child is purely an administrative matter, and not in the nature of an adversary proceeding; the court has no duty to advise the mother of her right to counsel or to appoint a lawyer for her in the event of indigency. In re K. (Ohio Juv. 1969) 31 Ohio Misc. 218, 282 N.E.2d 370, 60 O.O.2d 134, 60 O.O.2d 388.

No action to recover damages for breach of a contract of marriage will lie where the parties are related as first cousins. Reed v. Reed (Ohio 1892) 49 Ohio St. 654, 29 W.L.B. 48, 32 N.E. 750. Breach Of Marriage Promise ☞ 7; Marriage ☞ 10

3107.011 Representation by agency or attorney; false statements

(A) A person seeking to adopt a minor shall utilize an agency or attorney to arrange the adoption. Only an agency or attorney may arrange an adoption. An attorney may not represent with regard to the adoption both the person seeking to adopt and the parent placing a child for adoption.

Any person may informally aid or promote an adoption by making a person seeking to adopt a minor aware of a minor who will be or is available for adoption.

(B) A person seeking to adopt a minor who knowingly makes a false statement that is included in an application submitted to an agency or attorney to obtain services of that agency or attorney in arranging an adoption is guilty of the offense of falsification under section 2921.13 of the Revised Code.

(2006 S 238, eff. 9–21–06; 1996 H 419, eff. 9–18–96)

Historical and Statutory Notes

Amendment Note: 2006 S 238 designated division (A) and added division (B).

Ohio Administrative Code References

Application process and preservice training, see OAC 5101:2–48–09
Approval of a foster home for adoptive placement, see OAC 5101:2–48–11
Completion of the homestudy report, see OAC 5101:2–48–12

Foster caregiver adoption process of a foster child who has resided with the caregiver for at least twelve consecutive months, see OAC 5101:2–48–11.1

Library References

Adoption ☞4, 6.
Infants ☞17.
Westlaw Topic Nos. 17, 211.

C.J.S. Adoption of Persons §§ 10 to 21, 27 to 45, 140.
C.J.S. Infants §§ 6, 8 to 9.

Research References

Encyclopedias

OH Jur. 3d Family Law § 879, Who May Arrange Adoptions.
OH Jur. 3d Family Law § 902, Investigation.

Forms

Ohio Forms Legal and Business § 28:17, Introduction.

Treatises and Practice Aids

Carlin, Baldwin's Ohio Prac. Merrick-Rippner Probate Law § 99:27, Papers and Records--Assessor.

Notes of Decisions

Relative, person "arranging" adoption 1

1. **Relative, person "arranging" adoption**

A grandmother who arranges the adoption of her grandchild with a prospective adoptive parent vio- lates RC 3107.011 and in such a case it is beyond the trial court's discretion to impose a penalty and to exclude the interested person as a prospective adoptive parent based on the grandmother's viola- tion. In re Adoption of Baby Doe (Ohio App. 9 Dist., Summit, 04-14-1999) No. 19279, 1999 WL 241379, Unreported.

3107.012 Application for adoption by foster caregiver seeking to adopt foster child

(A) A foster caregiver may use the application prescribed under division (B) of this section to obtain the services of an agency to arrange an adoption for the foster caregiver if the foster caregiver seeks to adopt the foster caregiver's foster child who has resided in the foster caregiver's home for at least six months prior to the date the foster caregiver submits the application to the agency.

(B) The department of job and family services shall prescribe an application for a foster caregiver to use under division (A) of this section. The application shall not require that the foster caregiver provide any information the foster caregiver already provided the department, or undergo an inspection the foster caregiver already underwent, to obtain a foster home certificate under section 5103.03 of the Revised Code.

(C) An agency that receives an application prescribed under division (B) of this section from a foster caregiver authorized to use the application shall not require, as a condition of the agency accepting or approving the application, that the foster caregiver undergo a criminal records check under section 2151.86 of the Revised Code as a prospective adoptive parent. The agency shall inform the foster caregiver, in accordance with division (G) of section 2151.86 of the Revised Code, that the foster caregiver must undergo the criminal records check before a court may issue a final decree of adoption or interlocutory order of adoption under section 3107.14 of the Revised Code.

(2008 H 7, eff. 4-7-09; 2000 H 448, eff. 10–5–00)

Historical and Statutory Notes

Ed. Note: Former 3107.012 amended and reco- dified as 3107.014 by 2000 H 448, eff. 10–5–00; 1998 H 446, eff. 8–5–98; 1996 H 419, eff. 9–18–96.

Amendment Note: 2008 H 7 substituted "six" for "twelve" in division (A).

Library References

Adoption ⬤⁓11.
Infants ⬤⁓17, 226.
Westlaw Topic Nos. 17, 211.

C.J.S. Adoption of Persons §§ 10 to 14, 41, 80 to 83.
C.J.S. Infants §§ 6, 8 to 9, 43, 73 to 92.

Research References

Encyclopedias

OH Jur. 3d Family Law § 876, Who May Adopt-- Foster Parents.
OH Jur. 3d Family Law § 902, Investigation.

Forms

Ohio Forms Legal and Business § 28:24, Introduc- tion.

Treatises and Practice Aids

Carlin, Baldwin's Ohio Prac. Merrick-Rippner Pro- bate Law § 99:22, Types of Placement--Indepen- dent Adoptions.
Carlin, Baldwin's Ohio Prac. Merrick-Rippner Pro- bate Law § 99:27, Papers and Records--Assessor.

3107.013 Information about adoption

An agency arranging an adoption pursuant to an application submitted to the agency under section 3107.012 of the Revised Code for a foster caregiver seeking to adopt the foster caregiver's foster child shall provide the foster caregiver information about adoption, including information about state adoption law, adoption assistance available pursuant to section 5153.163 of the Revised Code and Title IV–E of the "Social Security Act," 94 Stat. 501, 42

U.S.C.A. 670 (1980), as amended, the types of behavior that the prospective adoptive parents may anticipate from children who have experienced abuse and neglect, suggested interventions and the assistance available if the child exhibits those types of behavior after adoption, and other adoption issues the department of job and family services identifies. The agency shall provide the information to the foster caregiver in accordance with rules the department of job and family services shall adopt in accordance with Chapter 119. of the Revised Code.

(2001 S 27, eff. 3–15–02; 2000 H 448, eff. 10–5–00)

Historical and Statutory Notes

Ed. Note: Former 3107.013 amended and recodified as 3107.015 by 2000 H 448, eff. 10–5–00; 1999 H 471, eff. 7–1–00; 1996 H 419, eff. 6–20–96.

Amendment Note: 2001 S 27 rewrote this section which prior thereto read:

"An agency arranging an adoption pursuant to an application submitted to the agency under section 3107.012 of the Revised Code for a foster caregiver seeking to adopt the foster caregiver's foster child shall offer to provide the foster caregiver information about adoption, including information about state adoption law, adoption assistance available pursuant to section 5153.163 of the Revised Code and Title IV–E of the "Social Security Act," 94 Stat. 501, 42 U.S.C.A. 670 (1980), as amended, and other adoption issues the department of job and family services identifies. If the foster caregiver informs the agency that the foster caregiver wants the information, the agency shall provide the information to the foster caregiver in accordance with rules the department of job and family services shall adopt in accordance with Chapter 119. of the Revised Code."

Administrative Code References

Postfinalization services, see OAC 5101:2–48–18

Library References

Infants ⟲17, 226.
Westlaw Topic No. 211.

C.J.S. Adoption of Persons §§ 10 to 14, 41.
C.J.S. Infants §§ 6, 8 to 9, 43, 73 to 92.

3107.014   Home study assessor; qualifications, registry

(A) Except as provided in division (B) of this section, only an individual who meets all of the following requirements may perform the duties of an assessor under sections 3107.031, 3107.032, 3107.082, 3107.09, 3107.101, 3107.12, 5103.0324, and 5103.152 of the Revised Code:

(1) The individual must be in the employ of, appointed by, or under contract with a court, public children services agency, private child placing agency, or private noncustodial agency;

(2) The individual must be one of the following:

(a) A professional counselor, social worker, or marriage and family therapist licensed under Chapter 4757. of the Revised Code;

(b) A psychologist licensed under Chapter 4732. of the Revised Code;

(c) A student working to earn a four-year, post-secondary degree, or higher, in a social or behavior science, or both, who conducts assessor's duties under the supervision of a professional counselor, social worker, or marriage and family therapist licensed under Chapter 4757. of the Revised Code or a psychologist licensed under Chapter 4732. of the Revised Code. Beginning July 1, 2009, a student is eligible under this division only if the supervising professional counselor, social worker, marriage and family therapist, or psychologist has completed training in accordance with rules adopted under section 3107.015 of the Revised Code.

(d) A civil service employee engaging in social work without a license under Chapter 4757. of the Revised Code, as permitted by division (A)(5) of section 4757.41 of the Revised Code;

(e) A former employee of a public children services agency who, while so employed, conducted the duties of an assessor.

(3) The individual must complete training in accordance with rules adopted under section 3107.015 of the Revised Code.

(B) An individual in the employ of, appointed by, or under contract with a court prior to September 18, 1996, to conduct adoption investigations of prospective adoptive parents may perform the duties of an assessor under sections 3107.031, 3107.032, 3107.082, 3107.09, 3107.101, 3107.12, 5103.0324, and 5103.152 of the Revised Code if the individual complies with division (A)(3) of this section regardless of whether the individual meets the requirement of division (A)(2) of this section.

(C) A court, public children services agency, private child placing agency, or private noncustodial agency may employ, appoint, or contract with an assessor in the county in which a petition for adoption is filed and in any other county or location outside this state where information needed to complete or supplement the assessor's duties may be obtained. More than one assessor may be utilized for an adoption.

(D) Not later than January 1, 2008, the department of job and family services shall develop and maintain an assessor registry. The registry shall list all individuals who are employed, appointed by, or under contract with a court, public children services agency, private child placing agency, or private noncustodial agency and meet the requirements of an assessor as described in this section. A public children services agency, private child placing agency, private noncustodial agency, court, or any other person may contact the department to determine if an individual is listed in the assessor registry. An individual listed in the assessor registry shall immediately inform the department when that individual is no longer employed, appointed by, or under contract with a court, public children services agency, private child placing agency, or private noncustodial agency to perform the duties of an assessor as described in this section. The director of job and family services shall adopt rules in accordance with Chapter 119. of the Revised Code necessary for the implementation, contents, and maintenance of the registry, and any sanctions related to the provision of information, or the failure to provide information, that is needed for the proper operation of the assessor registry.

(2006 S 238, eff. 9–21–06; 2000 H 448, eff. 10–5–00)

Historical and Statutory Notes

Ed. Note: 3107.014 is former 3107.012, amended and recodified by 2000 H 448, eff. 10–5–00; 1998 H 446, eff. 8–5–98; 1996 H 419, eff. 9–18–96.

Amendment Note: 2006 S 238 rewrote this section. See *Baldwin's Ohio Legislative Service Annotated*, 2006, page 3/L–1574, or the OH–LEGIS or OH–LEGIS–OLD database on Westlaw, for prior version of this section.

Amendment Note: 2000 H 448 inserted "5103.0324" in divisions (A) and (B); added new division (A)(2)(e); and substituted "3107.015" for "3107.013" in division (A)(3).

Amendment Note: 1998 H 446 substituted "in the employ of, appointed by," for "employed by" and inserted "court," in division (A)(1); substituted "division (A)(5) of section 4757.41" for "division (E) of section 4757.16" in division (A)(2)(d); rewrote division (B); and added division (C). Prior to amendment, division (B) read:

"(B) An individual employed by a court prior to the effective date of this section to conduct home studies of prospective adoptive parents may conduct home studies under section 3107.031 of the Revised Code if the individual complies with division (A)(3) of this section."

Cross References

Powers and duties of committee, see 5103.40
Child welfare training program objectives, see 5103.30

Probate courts, appointment of assessors, see 2101.11

Ohio Administrative Code References

Assessor roles and responsibilities, see OAC 5101:2–48–06

Library References

Infants ⬥17.
Westlaw Topic No. 211.

C.J.S. Adoption of Persons §§ 10 to 14, 41.
C.J.S. Infants §§ 6, 8 to 9.

Research References

Encyclopedias

OH Jur. 3d Family Law § 902, Investigation.

Treatises and Practice Aids

Carlin, Baldwin's Ohio Prac. Merrick-Rippner Probate Law § 99:27, Papers and Records--Assessor.

3107.015 Training programs for assessors

The director of job and family services shall adopt rules in accordance with Chapter 119. of the Revised Code governing the training an individual must complete for the purpose of division (A)(3) of section 3107.014 of the Revised Code. The training shall include courses on adoption placement practice, federal and state adoption assistance programs, and post adoption support services.

(2006 S 238, eff. 9–21–06; 2000 H 448, eff. 10–5–00)

Historical and Statutory Notes

Ed. Note: 3107.015 is former 3107.013, amended and recodified by 2000 H 448, eff. 10–5–00; 1999 H 471, eff. 7–1–00; 1996 H 419, eff. 6–20–96.

Amendment Note: 2006 S 238 substituted "The" for "Not later than ninety days after June 20, 1996, the" and substituted "training" for "education programs" in the first sentence; and substituted "training" for "education programs" in the second sentence.

Amendment Note: 2000 H 448 substituted "June 20, 1996" for "the effective date of this section" and "3107.014" for "3107.012".

Amendment Note: 1999 H 471 substituted "director of job and family services" for "department of human services".

Ohio Administrative Code References

Assessor roles and responsibilities, see OAC 5101:2–48–06
Postfinalization services, see OAC 5101:2–48–18

Library References

Infants ⟰17.
Westlaw Topic No. 211.

C.J.S. Adoption of Persons §§ 10 to 14, 41.
C.J.S. Infants §§ 6, 8 to 9.

Research References

Encyclopedias

OH Jur. 3d Family Law § 902, Investigation.

Forms

Ohio Jurisprudence Pleading and Practice Forms § 96:20, Home Study.

3107.016 Schedule of training

The department of job and family services shall develop a schedule of training that meets the requirements established in rules adopted pursuant to section 3107.015 of the Revised Code. The schedule shall include enough training to provide all agencies equal access to the training. The department shall distribute the schedule to all agencies.

(2006 S 238, eff. 9–21–06; 2000 H 448, eff. 10–5–00)

Historical and Statutory Notes

Amendment Note: 2006 S 238 rewrote this section, which prior thereto read:

"The department of job and family services shall develop a schedule of education programs that meet the requirements established in rules adopted pursuant to section 3107.015 of the Revised Code. The schedule shall include enough programs to provide all agencies equal access to the programs. The department shall distribute the schedule to all agencies."

Library References

Infants ⟰17.
Westlaw Topic No. 211.

C.J.S. Adoption of Persons §§ 10 to 14, 41.

C.J.S. Infants §§ 6, 8 to 9.

3107.017   Standardized form for disclosure of information

The department of job and family services shall develop a standardized form for the disclosure of information about a prospective adoptive child to prospective adoptive parents. The information disclosed shall include all background information available on the child. The department shall distribute the form to all agencies.

(2001 S 27, eff. 3–15–02)

Library References

Adoption ☞9.1.   C.J.S. Adoption of Persons §§ 10 to 14, 41, 46, 77.
Infants ☞17.   C.J.S. Infants §§ 6, 8 to 9.
Westlaw Topic Nos. 17, 211.

3107.018   Adoption assistance loans

(A) A prospective adoptive parent may apply to the department of job and family services for a loan from the state adoption assistance loan fund created under section 5101.143 of the Revised Code. Subject to available funds, the department may approve a state adoption assistance loan application, in whole or in part, or deny the application. In reviewing a loan application submitted to the department, the department shall consider the financial need of the prospective adoptive parent in determining whether to approve a loan application, in whole or in part, or deny the application. If the department approves a loan application, in whole or in part, and the child being adopted resides in Ohio, the department shall loan a prospective adoptive parent not more than three thousand dollars from the state adoption assistance loan fund. If the department approves a loan application, in whole or in part, and the child being adopted does not reside in Ohio, the department shall loan a prospective adoptive parent not more than two thousand dollars from the state adoption assistance loan fund.

(B) A prospective adoptive parent who receives a loan under division (A) of this section shall use that loan for only a disbursement listed under division (C) of section 3107.055 of the Revised Code or an expense related to adopting from the public child welfare system.

(C) This section applies to adoptions arranged by an attorney or by any public or private organization certified, licensed, or otherwise specially empowered by law or rule to place minors for adoption.

(2008 H 562, eff. 6–24–08)

Cross References

Adoption assistance loan fund, see 5101.143

3107.02   Persons who may be adopted

(A) Any minor may be adopted.

(B) An adult may be adopted under any of the following conditions:

(1) If the adult is totally or permanently disabled;

(2) If the adult is determined to be a mentally retarded person;

(3) If the adult had established a child-foster caregiver, kinship caregiver, or child-stepparent relationship with the petitioners as a minor, and the adult consents to the adoption;

(4) If the adult was, at the time of the adult's eighteenth birthday, in the permanent custody of or in a planned permanent living arrangement with a public children services agency or a private child placing agency, and the adult consents to the adoption;

(5) If the adult is the child of the spouse of the petitioner, and the adult consents to the adoption.

(C) When proceedings to adopt a minor are initiated by the filing of a petition, and the eighteenth birthday of the minor occurs prior to the decision of the court, the court shall require the person who is to be adopted to submit a written statement of consent or objection to the adoption. If an objection is submitted, the petition shall be dismissed, and if a consent is submitted, the court shall proceed with the case, and may issue an interlocutory order or final decree of adoption.

(D) Any physical examination of the individual to be adopted as part of or in contemplation of a petition to adopt may be conducted by any health professional authorized by the Revised Code to perform physical examinations, including a physician assistant, a clinical nurse specialist, a certified nurse practitioner, or a certified nurse-midwife. Any written documentation of the physical examination shall be completed by the healthcare professional who conducted the examination.

(E) An adult who consents to an adoption pursuant to division (B)(4) of this section shall provide the court with the name and contact information of the public children services agency or private child placing agency that had permanent custody of or a planned permanent living arrangement with that adult. The petitioner shall request verification from the agency as to whether the adult was or was not in the permanent custody of or in a planned permanent living arrangement with that agency at the time of the adult's eighteenth birthday and provide the verification to the court.

(F) As used in this section:

(1) "Kinship caregiver" has the same meaning as in section 5101.85 of the Revised Code.

(2) "Mentally retarded person" has the same meaning as in section 5123.01 of the Revised Code.

(3) "Permanent custody" and "planned permanent living arrangement" have the same meanings as in section 2151.011 of the Revised Code.

(2011 H 92, eff. 9-30-11; 2006 S 238, eff. 9-21-06; 2002 S 245, eff. 3-31-03; 2000 H 448, eff. 10-5-00; 1984 H 71, eff. 9-20-84; 1981 H 1; 1976 H 156)

Historical and Statutory Notes

Ed. Note: Former 3107.02 repealed by 1976 H 156, eff. 1-1-77; 1953 H 1; GC 8004-2; Source—GC 10512-10; see now 3107.03 for provisions analogous to former 3107.02.

Pre-1953 H 1 Amendments: 124 v S 65

Amendment Note: 2011 H 92 substituted "or" for "and" in division (B)(1); deleted "as defined in section 5123.01 of the Revised Code" at the end of division (B)(2); inserted ", kinship caregiver," in division (B)(3); inserted "or in a planned permanent living arrangement with" in divisions (B)(4) and (E); added division (B)(5); inserted "or a

planned permanent living arrangement with" in division (E); and added divisions (F), (F)(1), (F)(2), and (F)(3).

Amendment Note: 2006 S 238 added division (B)(4) and (E); and made other nonsubstantive changes.

Amendment Note: 2002 S 245 added division (D).

Amendment Note: 2000 H 448 substituted "caregiver" for "parent" in division (B)(3); and made changes to reflect gender neutral language.

Cross References

Department of job and family services, division of social administration; care and placement of children; interstate compact on placement of children, see 5103.12 to 5103.17, 5103.20 to 5103.27

Designation of heir-at-law, see 2105.15

Placement for adoption of children from other states, see 2151.39

Powers and duties of county children services board, see 5153.16

Ohio Administrative Code References

AdoptOhio, adoption, see OAC Ch 5101:2-48

Library References

Adoption ⟨key⟩5, 9.1, 13.
Westlaw Topic No. 17.

C.J.S. Adoption of Persons §§ 22 to 27, 46 to 47, 77, 93 to 102.

Research References

Encyclopedias

OH Jur. 3d Decedents' Estates § 802, Beneficiaries Indicated in General Terms--Gift to "Children," "Issue," "Heirs," and the Like.
OH Jur. 3d Family Law § 875, Who May Adopt.
OH Jur. 3d Family Law § 878, Who May be Adopted.
OH Jur. 3d Family Law § 909, Final Decree or Interlocutory Order.
OH Jur. 3d Family Law § 910, Dismissal.
OH Jur. 3d Trusts § 124, Adopted Child as Within Class.

Forms

Ohio Forms Legal and Business § 28:20, Adult Adoptions.
Ohio Forms Legal and Business § 28:24, Introduction.
Ohio Forms Legal and Business § 28:25, Form Drafting Principles.
Ohio Forms Legal and Business § 28:27, Consent to Adoption--By Adult or Minor Over Age of 12.
Ohio Jurisprudence Pleading and Practice Forms § 96:3, Who May be Adopted.
Ohio Jurisprudence Pleading and Practice Forms § 96:4, Who May Adopt.

Ohio Jurisprudence Pleading and Practice Forms § 96:55, Adult Adoption--Final Order.

Treatises and Practice Aids

Carlin, Baldwin's Ohio Prac. Merrick-Rippner Probate Law § 3:5, Subject Matter--Specific Areas--Inter Vivos Trusts.
Carlin, Baldwin's Ohio Prac. Merrick-Rippner Probate Law § 17:3, Designation--Contrast With Adoption.
Carlin, Baldwin's Ohio Prac. Merrick-Rippner Probate Law § 99:4, Parties--Who May Petition to Adopt.
Carlin, Baldwin's Ohio Prac. Merrick-Rippner Probate Law § 99:5, Parties--Who May be Adopted--Statutory Provisions.
Carlin, Baldwin's Ohio Prac. Merrick-Rippner Probate Law § 15:28, Adopted Child.
Carlin, Baldwin's Ohio Prac. Merrick-Rippner Probate Law § 44:16, Liberal Construction--Gifts to a Class: Construction Problems.
Carlin, Baldwin's Ohio Prac. Merrick-Rippner Probate Law § 99:54, Inheritance Rights of Adoptees--"Stranger to the Adoption" Doctrine.
Carlin, Baldwin's Ohio Prac. Merrick-Rippner Probate Law App B SPF 19.1, Final Order of Adoption of Adult.

Notes of Decisions

Adoption of adult   3
Eligibility to adopt   2
Rights of adoptee   1

---

1. Rights of adoptee

An adult who is adopted pursuant to RC 3107.02(B)(3), and thus is a "child" by definition under RC 3107.01(A), has the same status and the same rights as a person who is a minor at the time of adoption.   Solomon v. Central Trust Co. of Northeastern Ohio, N.A. (Ohio 1992) 63 Ohio St.3d 35, 584 N.E.2d 1185.

2. Eligibility to adopt

Under RC 3107.03(B), an unmarried adult in Ohio is an eligible person to adopt those persons specified in RC 3107.02.   In re Adoption of Charles B. (Ohio 1990) 50 Ohio St.3d 88, 552 N.E.2d 884.   Adoption ☞ 4

While an unmarried adult in Ohio is eligible to adopt, the right is permissive and not absolute as both RC 3107.02 and 3107.03 use the verb "may." In re Adoption of Charles B. (Ohio 1990) 50 Ohio St.3d 88, 552 N.E.2d 884.   Adoption ☞ 4

3. Adoption of adult

Relationship involving emotional support, guidance, love, and affection existed between birth father and adult child, during child's minority and into his majority, such that father would be permitted to adopt child, who had previously been adopted by step-father pursuant to birth father's consent.   Matter of Huskins (Ohio Com.Pl., 11-21-1997) 89 Ohio Misc.2d 13, 692 N.E.2d 1105. Adoption ☞ 13

Evidence that petitioners and an eighteen-year-old orphan had developed strong emotional ties, mutual affection for each other, and a showing that petitioners' children and the adult orphan had developed a sibling relationship is insufficient to support a petition for the adoption of an adult based upon a child-foster parent or child-stepparent relationship established during the minority of such adult where there is no evidence that petitioners contributed financial support, provided schooling, medical care, or a residence to the adult orphan. In re Adoption of Huitzil (Butler 1985) 29 Ohio App.3d 222, 504 N.E.2d 1173, 29 O.B.R. 267.

3107.03   Persons who may adopt

The following persons may adopt:

(A) A husband and wife together, at least one of whom is an adult;

(B) An unmarried adult;

(C) The unmarried minor parent of the person to be adopted;

(D) A married adult without the other spouse joining as a petitioner if any of the following apply:

(1) The other spouse is a parent of the person to be adopted and supports the adoption;

(2) The petitioner and the other spouse are separated under section 3103.06 or 3105.17 of the Revised Code;

(3) The failure of the other spouse to join in the petition or to support the adoption is found by the court to be by reason of prolonged unexplained absence, unavailability, incapacity, or circumstances that make it impossible or unreasonably difficult to obtain either the support or refusal of the other spouse.

(1996 H 419, eff. 9–18–96; 1976 H 156, eff. 1–1–77)

Historical and Statutory Notes

Ed. Note: 3107.03 is analogous to former 3107.02, repealed by 1976 H 156, eff. 1–1–77.

Ed. Note: Former 3107.03 repealed by 1976 H 156, eff. 1–1–77; 1969 S 49; 1953 H 1; GC 8004–3; Source—GC 10512–11; see now 3107.05 for provisions analogous to former 3107.03.

Pre–1953 H 1 Amendments: 124 v S 65

Amendment Note: 1996 H 419 substituted "supports," "support," and "support" for "consents to," "consent to," and "consent," respectively, in divisions (D)(1) and (3).

Cross References

Department of job and family services, placing of children, assumption of responsibility for expenses, see 5103.16

Designation of heir-at-law, see 2105.15

Parent and child relationship, definition and establishment, see 3111.01, 3111.02

Powers and duties of county children services board, see 5153.16

Ohio Administrative Code References

AdoptOhio, adoption, see OAC Ch 5101:2–48
Eligibility of adoptive parents for subsidized adoption, see OAC 5101:2–44–06

Library References

Adoption ☜4.
Westlaw Topic No. 17.
C.J.S. Adoption of Persons §§ 15 to 21, 27.

Research References

Encyclopedias

OH Jur. 3d Family Law § 875, Who May Adopt.
OH Jur. 3d Family Law § 902, Investigation.
OH Jur. 3d Family Law § 909, Final Decree or Interlocutory Order.

Forms

Ohio Forms Legal and Business § 28:17, Introduction.
Ohio Forms Legal and Business § 28:30, Consent to Commencement of Adoption Proceeding by Spouse.
Ohio Jurisprudence Pleading and Practice Forms § 96:4, Who May Adopt.
Ohio Jurisprudence Pleading and Practice Forms § 96:21, Home Study--Report.

Ohio Jurisprudence Pleading and Practice Forms § 96:29, Adoption Period.

Treatises and Practice Aids

Sowald & Morganstern, Baldwin's Ohio Practice Domestic Relations Law § 2:73, Cohabitation Agreements--Limitations.
Carlin, Baldwin's Ohio Prac. Merrick-Rippner Probate Law § 18:2, Inheritance Rights of Illegitimate Child--Statutory Provisions.
Carlin, Baldwin's Ohio Prac. Merrick-Rippner Probate Law § 99:3, Jurisdiction.
Carlin, Baldwin's Ohio Prac. Merrick-Rippner Probate Law § 99:4, Parties--Who May Petition to Adopt.
Carlin, Baldwin's Ohio Prac. Merrick-Rippner Probate Law § 99:8, Suitability of Adoptive Parents--Best Interests of Child.

Law Review and Journal Commentaries

An Alternative Placement for Children in Adoption Law: Allowing Homosexuals the Right to Adopt, Comment. 18 Ohio N U L Rev 631 (1992).

In Re Adoption Of Charles B.—A Tough Act To Follow, Note. 24 Akron L Rev 447 (Fall 1990).

In Whose Best Interests: Sexual Orientation and Adoption Law, William C. Duncan. 31 Cap U L Rev 787 (2003).

Open Adoption in Kentucky: Public Attitudes, the Present Law, and Proposed Changes, Elizabeth Lewis Rompf and John H. Rompf, Jr. III Ky Children's Rts J 11 (Spring 1993).

The Opportunities, Or Lack Thereof, For Homosexual Adults To Adopt Children—*In re Adoption of Charles B*, 50 Ohio St. 3d 88, 553 N.E.2d 884 (1990), Note. 16 U Dayton L Rev 471 (Winter 1991).

Race And Child Placement: The Best Interests Test And The Cost Of Discretion, Twila L. Perry. 29 J Fam L 51 (1990–91).

The Right of the Thwarted Father to Veto the Adoption of His Child, Comment. 62 U Cin L Rev 1695 (Spring 1994).

Notes of Decisions

Ethnic heritage   4
Jurisdiction   1
Natural parent adoption   2
Stepparent   5
Unmarried adult   3

-----

1.   Jurisdiction

Jurisdiction in adoption cases and in cases of placement of minors is vested in the probate court by RC 3107.02 as to the former, and RC 5103.16 as to the latter. In re McTaggart (Cuyahoga 1965) 2 Ohio App.2d 214, 207 N.E.2d 562, 31 O.O.2d 336, on rehearing 4 Ohio App.2d 359, 212 N.E.2d 663, 33 O.O.2d 447.

A probate court has jurisdiction to hear and determine an adoption proceeding relating to a minor child notwithstanding the fact that the custody of such child is at the time within the continuing jurisdiction of a divorce court. In re Adoption of Biddle (Ohio 1958) 168 Ohio St. 209, 152 N.E.2d 105, 6 O.O.2d 4, on remand 163 N.E.2d 188, 81 Ohio Law Abs. 529.

2.   Natural parent adoption

The natural parent of a legitimate child may not seek to adopt his natural child to terminate the other natural parent's parental rights. In re Adoption of Kohorst (Paulding 1992) 75 Ohio App.3d 813, 600 N.E.2d 843, motion overruled 65 Ohio St.3d 1466, 602 N.E.2d 1174.

3.   Unmarried adult

Under RC 3107.03(B), an unmarried adult in Ohio is an eligible person to adopt those persons specified in RC 3107.02. In re Adoption of Charles B. (Ohio 1990) 50 Ohio St.3d 88, 552 N.E.2d 884. Adoption ☜ 4

While an unmarried adult in Ohio is eligible to adopt, the right is permissive and not absolute as both RC 3107.02 and 3107.03 use the verb "may." In re Adoption of Charles B. (Ohio 1990) 50 Ohio St.3d 88, 552 N.E.2d 884. Adoption ☜ 4

The concepts of homosexuality and adoption are so inherently mutually exclusive and inconsistent, if not hostile, that the legislature never considered it necessary to enact an express ineligibility provision; however, homosexuals are ineligible to adopt as a matter of law. In re Adoption of Charles B, No. CA–3382 (5th Dist Ct App, Licking, 10–28–88), reversed by 50 OS(3d) 88, 552 NE(2d) 884 (1990).

4.   Ethnic heritage

Ethnic heritage of a child and prospective adoptive parents may be considered as a factor in adoption placements, but may not be used as the sole or determinative criterion; the opportunity to adopt a child may not be denied merely because the prospective adoptive parents are Caucasian and the child is African–American. In re Moorehead (Montgomery 1991) 75 Ohio App.3d 711, 600 N.E.2d 778.

5.   Stepparent

Adoption of children by stepfather was in their best interest; there was evidence that children were being raised in loving and stable environment, and visitations with natural father had been confusing and disconcerting to them, and at hearing both children expressed desire to terminate their relationship with natural father and to be raised by stepfather. In re Adoption of Deems (Ohio App. 3 Dist., 11-12-1993) 91 Ohio App.3d 552, 632 N.E.2d 1347, cause dismissed 70 Ohio St.3d 1451, 639 N.E.2d 460. Adoption ☜ 13

Trial court's finding that stepfather's adoption of child was in child's best interest was not against manifest weight of the evidence; county children's services board recommended that adoption proceed, child's maternal grandmother and her mother testified that child considered stepfather to be her father, that he spent time playing with her and taking her various places, and provided healthy, stable home for child. In re Adoption of Cline (Trumbull 1993) 89 Ohio App.3d 450, 624 N.E.2d 1083. Adoption ☜ 13

3107.031   Home study

Except as otherwise provided in this section, an assessor shall conduct a home study for the purpose of ascertaining whether a person seeking to adopt a minor is suitable to adopt. A written report of the home study shall be filed with the court at least ten days before the petition for adoption is heard.

A person seeking to adopt a minor who knowingly makes a false statement that is included in the written report of a home study conducted pursuant to this section is guilty of the offense of falsification under section 2921.13 of the Revised Code, and such a home study shall not be filed with the court. If such a home study is filed with the court, the court may strike the home study from the court's records.

The report shall contain the opinion of the assessor as to whether the person who is the subject of the report is suitable to adopt a minor, any multiple children assessment required under section 3107.032 of the Revised Code, and other information and documents specified in rules adopted by the director of job and family services under section 3107.033 of the Revised Code. The assessor shall not consider the person's age when determining whether the person is suitable to adopt if the person is old enough to adopt as provided by section 3107.03 of the Revised Code.

An assessor may request departments or agencies within or outside this state to assist in the home study as may be appropriate and to make a written report to be included with and attached to the report to the court. The assessor shall make similar home studies and reports on behalf of other assessors designated by the courts of this state or another place.

Upon order of the court, the costs of the home study and other proceedings shall be paid by the person seeking to adopt, and, if the home study is conducted by a public agency or public employee, the part of the cost representing any services and expenses shall be taxed as costs and paid into the state treasury or county treasury, as the court may direct.

On request, the assessor shall provide the person seeking to adopt a copy of the report of the home study. The assessor shall delete from that copy any provisions concerning the opinion of other persons, excluding the assessor, of the person's suitability to adopt a minor.

This section does not apply to a foster caregiver seeking to adopt the foster caregiver's foster child if the foster child has resided in the foster caregiver's home for at least six months prior to the date the foster caregiver submits an application prescribed under division (B) of section 3107.012 of the Revised Code to the agency arranging the adoption.

(2008 H 7, eff. 4-7-09; 2006 S 238, eff. 9–21–06; 2000 H 448, eff. 10–5–00; 1999 H 471, eff. 7–1–00; 1996 H 274, eff. 9–18–96; 1996 H 419, eff. 9–18–96)

Historical and Statutory Notes

Ed. Note: 3107.031 is former 3107.12, amended and recodified by 1996 H 419, eff. 9–18–96; 1984 H 84, eff. 3–19–85; 1978 S 340; 1976 H 156.

Amendment Note: 2008 H 7 substituted "six" for "twelve" in the last undesignated paragraph.

Amendment Note: 2006 S 238 added the second paragraph; inserted ", any multiple children assessment required under section 3107.032 of the Revised Code," and substituted "3107.033" for "3107.032" in the first sentence of the third paragraph.

Amendment Note: 2000 H 448 substituted "Except as otherwise provided in this section, an" for "an"; and added the last paragraph.

Amendment Note: 1999 H 471 substituted "director of job and family services" for "department of human services" in the second paragraph.

Amendment Note: 1996 H 274 deleted "Except when a stepparent adopts a stepchild," from the beginning of the first paragraph.

Amendment Note: 1996 H 419 rewrote this section, which formerly read:

"(A) An investigation shall be made by the department of human services, an agency, or other person appointed by the court into the conditions and antecedents of a minor sought to be adopted and of the petitioner, for the purpose of ascertaining whether the adoptive home is a suitable home for the minor and whether the proposed adoption is in the best interest of the minor. If the minor is in the custody of the department or an agency, the department or agency shall perform the investigation.

"(B) A written report of the investigation as described in division (C) of this section shall be filed with the court at least ten days before the petition for adoption is heard.

"(C) The report of the investigation shall contain, in addition to any other information that the court requires regarding the petitioner or the minor sought to be adopted, the following information:

"(1) The physical and mental health, emotional stability, and personal integrity of the petitioner and the ability of the petitioner to provide for the needs of the minor;

"(2) The physical, mental, and developmental condition of the minor;

"(3) The minor's family background, including names and identifying data regarding the biological or other legal parents, and, except when the adoption is by a stepparent or grandparent, the social and medical histories described in division (D) of this section, to the extent that they can be prepared;

"(4) The reasons for the minor's placement with persons other than his biological or other legal parents, their attitude toward the proposed adoption, and the circumstances under which the minor came to be placed in the home of the petitioner;

"(5) The attitude of the minor toward the proposed adoption in any case in which the minor's age makes this feasible;

"(6) The recommendation of the investigator as to the granting or denial of the petition for adoption.

"(D)(1) The department of human services shall prescribe, and shall supply for purposes of an investigation pursuant to division (A) of this section, forms for the taking of the social and medical histories of the biological parents of minors sought to be adopted.

"(2) Except when an adoption is by a stepparent or grandparent, the department, an agency, and any other person appointed by a court to make an investigation pursuant to division (A) of this section, to the extent possible, shall record the social and medical histories of the biological parents of the minor sought to be adopted, using the forms prescribed pursuant to division (D)(1) of this section. The investigator shall not include on the forms the names of the biological parents or other ancestors of the minor, or any identifying data that would allow a person, except the court or the investigator, to determine the identity of the biological parents or other ancestors.

"(3) The social history of the biological parents of a minor sought to be adopted shall describe and identify the ethnic, racial, religious, marital, physical characteristics, educational, cultural, talent and hobby, and work experience background of the biological parents of the minor. The medical history of the biological parents of a minor sought to be adopted shall identify major diseases, malformations, allergies, ear or eye defects, major conditions, and major health problems of the biological parents that are or may be congenital or familial. These histories may include other social and medical information relative to the biological parents, and shall include social and medical information relative to the minor's other ancestors.

"The social and medical histories may be obtained through interviews with the biological parents or other persons, and from any available records if a parent or any legal guardian of a parent consents to the release of information contained in a record. If the investigator considers it necessary, it may request that a parent undergo a medical examination. In obtaining social and medical histories of a biological parent, an investigator shall inform the biological parent, or a person other than a biological parent who provides information pursuant to this section, of the purpose and use of the histories and of his right to correct or expand the histories at any time.

"(4) A biological parent, or a person other than a biological parent who provided information in the preparation of the social and medical histories of the biological parents of a minor, may cause, in accordance with this division, the histories to be corrected or expanded to include different or additional types of information. A biological parent or such a person may cause the histories to be corrected or expanded at any time prior or subsequent to the adoption of the minor, including, but not limited to, at any time after the minor becomes an adult. A biological parent may cause the histories to be corrected or expanded even if he did not provide any information to the investigator at the time the histories were prepared.

"To cause the histories to be corrected or expanded, a biological parent or such a person shall provide the information that he wishes to have included, or shall specify the information that he wishes to have corrected, to one of the following, whichever is appropriate under the circumstances:

"(a) subject to division (D)(4)(b) of this section, if the biological parent or person knows the investigator that prepared the histories, to the investigator;

"(b) if the biological parent or person does not know the investigator that prepared the histories, if he ascertains that the investigator has ceased to exist, or if an investigator other than the department of human services refuses to assist him, to the clerk of the court involved in the adoption or, if that court is not known, to the department of health.

"If an investigator receives information from a biological parent or such a person pursuant to division (D)(4)(a) of this section and is willing to assist the biological parent or person, it shall determine whether the information is of a type that divisions (D)(2) and (3) of this section permit to be included in the histories and, to the best of its ability, whether the information is accurate. If it determines the information is of a permissible type and accurate, the investigator shall cause the histories to be corrected or expanded to reflect the information. If, at the time the information is received, the histories have been filed with the court as required by division (D)(6) of this section, the clerk of the court shall cooperate with the investigator in the correcting or expanding of the histories.

"If the department of health or a clerk receives information from a biological parent or such a person pursuant to division (D)(4)(b) of this section, it shall determine whether the information is of a type that divisions (D)(2) and (3) of this section permit to be included in the histories and, to the best of its ability, whether the information is accurate. If a clerk determines the information is of a permissible type and accurate, he shall cause the histories to be corrected or expanded to reflect the information. If the department of health so determines, the clerk of the court involved shall cooperate with the department in the correcting or expanding of the histories.

"(5) An investigator shall comply, to the extent possible, with division (D)(3) of this section, but neither the failure of the investigator to obtain all or any part of the information mentioned in that division nor the refusal of a biological parent to supply information shall invalidate, delay, or otherwise affect the adoption.

"(6) An investigator shall file, as part of the report required by division (B) of this section, the social and medical histories of the biological parents prepared, to the extent possible, pursuant to divisions (D)(2) and (3) of this section. The court promptly shall provide a copy of the social and medical histories filed with it to the petitioner. No interlocutory order or final decree of adoption shall be entered by a court, in a case involving the adoption of a minor, if either the histories of his

biological parents have not been so filed or the copy of the histories has not been so provided.

"(E) The department of human services, an agency, or a person, when required to make an investigation pursuant to division (A) of this section, may request departments or agencies within or outside this state to make or assist in the investigation as may be appropriate and to make a written report which shall be included with and attached to the report to the court. The department, an agency, or a person appointed to make an investigation pursuant to division (A) of this section shall make similar investigations and reports on behalf of departments, agencies, or persons designated by the courts of this state or another place.

"(F) Upon order of the court, the costs of the investigation and other proceedings shall be paid by the petitioner, and, if the investigation is conducted by a public agency or public employee, the part of the cost representing any services and expenses shall be taxed as costs and paid into the state treasury or county treasury, as the court may direct."

Cross References

Availability of adoption records, see 149.43
Certificate of adoption for person born in foreign country, inspection, see 3705.12
Courts, confidentiality of adoption files, Sup R 55
Placement of child for adoption, criteria, see 5103.16

Placing of child in public or private institution, agreements to be in writing, social and medical histories required, see 5103.15
Probate courts, appointment of assessors, see 2101.11

Ohio Administrative Code References

Adoption administrative falsification procedures, see OAC 5101:2–33–13
Adoption placement requirements pursuant to the Multiethnic Placement Act, see OAC 5101:2–48–13
Agency adoption policy and recruitment plan, see OAC 5101:2–48–05
Agency adoption review procedures, see OAC 5101:2–48–24
Approval of a foster home for adoptive placement, see OAC 5101:2–48–11

Completion of adoption homestudy updates and amendments, see OAC 5101:2–48–12.1
Completion of the homestudy report, see OAC 5101:2–48–12
Foster caregiver adoption process of a foster child who has resided with the caregiver for at least twelve consecutive months, see OAC 5101:2–48–11.1
Prefinalization services, see OAC 5101:2–48–17
Soliciting and releasing adoptive homestudies and related material for consideration of placement, see OAC 5101:2–48–19

Library References

Adoption ⬡9.1, 13.
Westlaw Topic No. 17.

C.J.S. Adoption of Persons §§ 46 to 47, 77, 93 to 102.

Research References

Encyclopedias

OH Jur. 3d Family Law § 902, Investigation.

Forms

Ohio Forms Legal and Business § 28:43, Introduction.
Ohio Jurisprudence Pleading and Practice Forms § 96:20, Home Study.
Ohio Jurisprudence Pleading and Practice Forms § 96:21, Home Study--Report.

Ohio Jurisprudence Pleading and Practice Forms § 96:25, Order to Redo or Supplement Report or History--Appointment of Different Assessor.

Treatises and Practice Aids

Carlin, Baldwin's Ohio Prac. Merrick-Rippner Probate Law § 99:27, Papers and Records--Assessor.
Carlin, Baldwin's Ohio Prac. Merrick-Rippner Probate Law App B SPF 18.1, Judgment Entry Setting Hearing and Ordering Notice.

Law Review and Journal Commentaries

Deboer v Schmidt: Disregarding the Child's Best Interests in Adoption Proceedings, Note. 23 Cap U L Rev 1099 (1994).

The Interracial Adoption Implications of Drummond v Fulton County Department of Family and Children Services, Comment. 17 J Fam L 117 (1978–79).

Racial Matching and the Adoption Dilemma: Alternatives for the Hard to Place, Note. 17 J Fam L 333 (1978–79).

S.B. 340: Disclosure of Social and Medical History of the Biological Parents of an Adopted Child, Note. 4 U Dayton L Rev 533 (Summer 1979).

Will *Palmore v. Sidoti* Preclude the Use of Race as a Factor in Denying an Adoption?, Note. 24 J Fam L 497 (1985–86).

Wrongful Adoption: Adoption Agency Held Liable for Fraudulent Representations: *Burr v. Stark County Board of Commissioners*, Note. 56 U Cin L Rev 343 (1987).

Notes of Decisions

Agency   1
Costs   6
Ethnic heritage   3
Guardian ad litem   4
Investigator   2
Report   5

___

1. Agency

The refusal of consent to an adoption by a "certified organization," as defined in RC 3107.01(C), does not impair the jurisdiction of the probate court, but the recommendations and the reports, filed pursuant to RC 3107.05 and 3107.10, are to be considered, in conjunction with all other evidence adduced in the proceeding, by the court in deciding the issues presented by RC 3107.09. State ex rel. Portage County Welfare Dept. v. Summers (Ohio 1974) 38 Ohio St.2d 144, 311 N.E.2d 6, 67 O.O.2d 151.

2. Investigator

Where natural father refuses to consent to adoption of his child by a third party, bifurcated procedure is followed; first, hearing on issue of necessity of consent is held, and in second stage, court determines whether adoption is in best interest of child after home study investigation. In re Adoption of Cline (Trumbull 1993) 89 Ohio App.3d 450, 624 N.E.2d 1083. Adoption ☞ 13

The failure of the human services department to include the name of the investigator on its report prior to an adoption hearing is merely a clerical oversight and not error. In re Adoption of Howell (Lawrence 1991) 77 Ohio App.3d 80, 601 N.E.2d 92, motion overruled 62 Ohio St.3d 1508, 583 N.E.2d 1320.

When authorized by the probate court under RC 5103.16 to make an investigation of a proposed placement, or when appointed by a probate court under RC 3107.04 and 3107.05 to act as the next friend of a child being adopted, a child welfare board has the duty to carry out the court's request. 1962 OAG 2747.

3. Ethnic heritage

Ethnic heritage of a child and prospective adoptive parents may be considered as a factor in adoption placements, but may not be used as the sole or determinative criterion; the opportunity to adopt a child may not be denied merely because the prospective adoptive parents are Caucasian and the child is African–American. In re Moorehead (Montgomery 1991) 75 Ohio App.3d 711, 600 N.E.2d 778.

Order denying adoption reversed where such order was based on the fact that the adopting father was Caucasian, his wife Japanese, the natural mother of English descent, and the natural father Puerto Rican. In re Adoption of Baker (Cuyahoga 1962) 117 Ohio App. 26, 185 N.E.2d 51, 90 Ohio Law Abs. 125, 22 O.O.2d 459.

4. Guardian ad litem

Appointment of guardian ad litem for minor who was subject of adoption proceedings was not required, since interest of child in adoption is protected by appointment of agency or persons who inquire into conditions and antecedents of person sought to be adopted and of petitioner for adoption. In re Adoption of Carnes (Portage 1983) 8 Ohio App.3d 435, 457 N.E.2d 903, 8 O.B.R. 560. Infants ☞ 78(1)

5. Report

The probate judge has primary responsibility for deciding whether to allow an adoption but great weight should be given the report and investigation made under RC 3107.12. In re Adoption of Labo (Shelby 1988) 47 Ohio App.3d 57, 546 N.E.2d 1384.

In granting or denying an application for adoption, great weight should be accorded to the report and recommendation of the next friend appointed pursuant to RC 3107.04. In re Adoption of Baker (Cuyahoga 1962) 117 Ohio App. 26, 185 N.E.2d 51, 90 Ohio Law Abs. 125, 22 O.O.2d 459.

A reviewing court is without authority to require filing, as a part of the transcript, a so-called "next friend's report" to the probate court. In re Adoption of Kane (Stark 1952) 91 Ohio App. 327, 108 N.E.2d 176, 48 O.O. 407.

6. Costs

The adopting parents of an illegitimate child are liable only for the cost of the adoption proceeding, and not for expenses incurred by the child welfare board for prenatal care or delivery or for the care of the mother and child after birth. 1955 OAG 5956.

3107.032   Multiple children assessment

(A) Except as provided in division (C) of this section, each time a person seeking to adopt a minor or foster child will have at least five children residing in the prospective adoptive home after the minor or foster child to be adopted is placed in the home, an assessor, on behalf of an agency or attorney arranging an adoption pursuant to sections 3107.011 or 3107.012 of the Revised Code, shall complete a multiple children assessment during the home study. The multiple children assessment shall evaluate the ability of the person seeking to adopt in meeting the needs of the minor or foster child to be adopted and continuing to meet the needs of the children residing in the home. The assessor shall include the multiple children assessment in the written report of the home study filed pursuant to section 3107.031 of the Revised Code.

(B) The director of job and family services shall adopt rules in accordance with Chapter 119. of the Revised Code necessary for an assessor to complete a multiple children assessment.

(C) This section does not apply to an adoption by a stepparent whose spouse is a biological or adoptive parent of the minor to be adopted.

(2006 S 238, eff. 9–21–06)

Historical and Statutory Notes

Ed. Note: Former RC 3107.032 amended and recodified as RC 3107.033 by 2006 S 238, eff. 9–21–06; 1999 H 471, eff. 7–1–00; 1996 H 419, eff. 6–20–96.

Cross References

Custody of files, investigators, clerks and appointees, appropriation, action in court of appeals, limitation of contempt power, see 2101.11

Ohio Administrative Code References

Agency adoption policy and recruitment plan, see OAC 5101:2–48–05
Application process and preservice training, see OAC 5101:2–48–09
Approval of a foster home for adoptive placement, see OAC 5101:2–48–11
Completion of the homestudy report, see OAC 5101:2–48–12

Foster caregiver adoption process of a foster child who has resided with the caregiver for at least twelve consecutive months, see OAC 5101:2–48–11.1
Prefinalization services, see OAC 5101:2–48–17

Research References

Encyclopedias

OH Jur. 3d Family Law § 902, Investigation.
OH Jur. 3d Family Law § 903, Investigation--Written Report.

Forms

Ohio Jurisprudence Pleading and Practice Forms § 96:20, Home Study.

3107.033   Rules for conducting home study

Not later than June 1, 2009, the director of job and family services shall adopt rules in accordance with Chapter 119. of the Revised Code specifying both of the following:

(A) The manner in which a home study is to be conducted and the information and documents to be included in a home study report, which shall include, pursuant to section 3107.034 of the Revised Code, a summary report of a search of the uniform statewide automated child welfare information system established in section 5101.13 of the Revised Code and a report of a check of a central registry of another state if a request for a check of a central registry of another state is required under division (A) of section 3107.034 of the Revised Code. The director shall ensure that rules adopted under this section align the home study content, time period, and process with any foster care home study content, time period, and process required by rules adopted under section 5103.03 of the Revised Code.

(B) A procedure under which a person whose application for adoption has been denied as a result of a search of the uniform statewide automated child welfare information system established in section 5101.13 of the Revised Code as part of the home study may appeal the denial to the agency that employed the assessor who filed the report.

(2008 H 7, eff. 4-7-09; 2008 S 163, eff. 8–14–08; 2006 S 238, eff. 9–21–06)

Uncodified Law

2008 S 163, § 6, eff. 8–14–08, reads:

Until the Uniform Statewide Automated Child Welfare Information System established under section 5101.13 of the Revised Code is implemented statewide by all public children services agencies as described in section 5153.02 of the Revised Code, agencies or persons required to include a summary report pursuant to section 3107.033 or 5103.18 of the Revised Code shall request a check of the Ohio Central Registry of Abuse and Neglect from the Department of Job and Family Services regarding any prospective foster parent and any person eighteen years of age or older who resides with the prospective foster parent or regarding any prospective adoptive parent and any person eighteen years of age or older who resides with the prospective adoptive parent, whichever is applicable, to enable the agency or person to check any child abuse and neglect registry maintained by any state in which the prospective foster parent, the prospective adoptive parent, or the person eighteen years of age or older who resided with the prospective foster parent or prospective adoptive parent has resided in the preceding five years. After the Uniform Statewide Automated Child Welfare Information System established under section 5101.13 of the Revised Code is implemented statewide by all public children services agencies as described in section 5153.02 of the Revised Code, all private agencies, as defined in section 5103.02 of the Revised Code, shall request a check of that System by the Department of Job and Family Services until the private agency can access the System and conduct its own search.

Historical and Statutory Notes

Ed. Note: RC 3107.033 is former RC 3107.032, amended and recodified by 2006 S 238, eff. 9–21–06; 1999 H 471, eff. 7–1–00; 1996 H 419, eff. 6–20–96.

Amendment Note: 2008 H 7 substituted "June" for "January" and "2009" for "2008" in the first undesignated paragraph; added the last sentence in division (A); and made a nonsubstantive change.

Amendment Note: 2008 S 163 added the phrase "and a report of a check of a central registry of another state if a request for a check of a central registry of another state is required under division (A) section 3107.034 of the Revised Code" to the end of division (A).

Amendment Note: 2006 S 238 rewrote this section, which prior thereto read:

"Not later than ninety days after June 20, 1996, the director of job and family services shall adopt rules in accordance with Chapter 119. of the Revised Code specifying the manner in which a home study is to be conducted and the information and documents to be included in a home study report."

Amendment Note: 1999 H 471 substituted "June 20, 1996" for "the effective date of this section" and "director of job and family services" for "department of human services".

Cross References

Custody of files, investigators, clerks and appointees, appropriation, action in court of appeals, limitation of contempt power, see 2101.11

Powers and duties of department in certification of institutions for children, see 5103.03

Ohio Administrative Code References

Adoption agency staffing, see OAC 5101:2–48–06

Adoption inquiry, see OAC 5101:2–48–08

Adoption placement requirements pursuant to the Multiethnic Placement Act, see OAC 5101:2–48–13

Agency adoption policy, agency recruitment plan, and bi-annual comprehensive assessment report, see OAC 5101:2–48–05

Application process and preservice training, see OAC 5101:2–48–09

Approval of a foster home for adoptive placement, see OAC 5101:2–48–11

Completion of the homestudy report, see OAC 5101:2–48–12

Foster caregiver adoption process of a foster child who has resided with the caregiver for at least twelve consecutive months, see OAC 5101:2–48–11.1

Prefinalization services, see OAC 5101:2–48–17

Release of identifying and nonidentifying information, see OAC 5101:2–48–20

Library References

Adoption ☞9.1, 13.

Infants ☞17.

3107.034 Abuse and neglect determination summary report

(A) Whenever a prospective adoptive parent or a person eighteen years of age or older who resides with a prospective adoptive parent has resided in another state within the five-year period immediately prior to the date on which a criminal records check is requested for the person under division (A) of section 2151.86 of the Revised Code, the administrative director of an agency, or attorney, who arranges the adoption for the prospective adoptive parent shall request a check of the central registry of abuse and neglect of this state from the department of job and family services regarding the prospective adoptive parent or the person eighteen years of age or older who resides with the prospective adoptive parent to enable the agency or attorney to check any child abuse and neglect registry maintained by that other state. The administrative director or attorney shall make the request and shall review the results of the check before a final decree of adoption or an interlocutory order of adoption making the person an adoptive parent may be made. Information received pursuant to the request shall be considered for purposes of this chapter as if it were a summary report required under section 3107.033 of the Revised Code. The department of job and family services shall comply with any request to check the central registry that is similar to the request described in this division and that is received from any other state.

(B) The summary report of a search of the uniform statewide automated child welfare information system established in section 5101.13 of the Revised Code that is required under section 3107.033 of the Revised Code shall contain, if applicable, a chronological list of abuse and neglect determinations or allegations of which the person seeking to adopt is subject and in regards to which a public children services agency has done one of the following:

(1) Determined that abuse or neglect occurred;

(2) Initiated an investigation, and the investigation is ongoing;

(3) Initiated an investigation and the agency was unable to determine whether abuse or neglect occurred.

(C) The summary report required under section 3107.033 of the Revised Code shall not contain any of the following:

(1) An abuse and neglect determination of which the person seeking to adopt is subject and in regards to which a public children services agency determined that abuse or neglect did not occur;

(2) Information or reports the dissemination of which is prohibited by, or interferes with eligibility under, the "Child Abuse Prevention and Treatment Act," 88 Stat. 4 (1974), 42 U.S.C. 5101 et seq., as amended;

(3) The name of the person who or entity that made, or participated in the making of, the report of abuse or neglect.

(D)(1) An application for adoption may be denied based on a summary report containing the information described under division (B)(1) of this section, when considered within the totality of the circumstances. An application that is denied may be appealed using the procedure adopted pursuant to division (B) of section 3107.033 of the Revised Code.

(2) An application for adoption shall not be denied solely based on a summary report containing the information described under division (B)(2) or (3) of this section.

(2008 S 163, eff. 8–14–08; 2006 S 238, eff. 9–21–06)

Historical and Statutory Notes

Amendment Note: 2008 S 163 added new division (A); redesignated former divisions (A) to (C) as (B) to (D); substituted "(B)" for "(A)" in the reference "to division (B)(1) of this section" in division (D)(1); and substituted "(B)" for "(A)" in the reference "to division (B)(2) or (3) of this section" in division (D)(2).

Ohio Administrative Code References

Access/confidentiality of child abuse and neglect information contained in the uniform statewide automated child welfare information system, see OAC 5101:2–33–22

Approval of a foster home for adoptive placement, see OAC 5101:2–48–11

Completion of the homestudy report, see OAC 5101:2–48–12

Foster caregiver adoption process of a foster child who has resided with the caregiver for at least twelve consecutive months, see OAC 5101:2–48–11.1

Research References

Encyclopedias

OH Jur. 3d Family Law § 902.5, Summary Report.

3107.04 Venue; caption of petition for adoption

(A) A petition for adoption shall be filed in the court in the county in which the person to be adopted was born, or in which, at the time of filing the petition, the petitioner or the person to be adopted or parent of the person to be adopted resides, or in which the petitioner is stationed in military service, or in which the agency having the permanent custody of the person to be adopted is located.

(B) If the court finds in the interest of justice that the case should be heard in another forum, the court may stay the proceedings or dismiss the petition in whole or in part on any conditions that are just, or certify the case to another court.

(C) The caption of a petition for adoption shall be styled, "In the matter of adoption of _____". The person to be adopted shall be designated in the caption under the name by which he is to be known if the petition is granted.

(1976 H 156, eff. 1–1–77)

Historical and Statutory Notes

Ed. Note: Former 3107.04 repealed by 1976 H 156, eff. 1–1–77; 1975 S 145; 1953 H 1; GC 8004–4; Source—GC 10512–12; see now 3107.11 for provisions analogous to former 3107.04.

Pre–1953 H 1 Amendments: 124 v S 65

Cross References

Department of job and family services, division of social administration; care and placement of children; interstate compact on placement of children, see 5103.12 to 5103.17, 5103.20 to 5103.27

Powers and duties of county children services board, see 5153.16

Library References

Adoption ☞10, 11.
Westlaw Topic No. 17.
C.J.S. Adoption of Persons §§ 78 to 83.

Research References

Encyclopedias

OH Jur. 3d Family Law § 532, Jurisdiction of Probate Court.

OH Jur. 3d Family Law § 898, Additional Filing Requirements.

Forms

Ohio Jurisprudence Pleading and Practice Forms § 96:7, Venue.

Treatises and Practice Aids

Carlin, Baldwin's Ohio Prac. Merrick-Rippner Probate Law § 3:24, Adoption--Form.

Carlin, Baldwin's Ohio Prac. Merrick-Rippner Probate Law § 99:25, Papers and Records--Petition.

Notes of Decisions

Jurisdiction   1

_____

1. Jurisdiction

Stepfather's failure to file a certified copy of child's birth certificate with his petition to adopt child did not deprive the trial court of subject matter jurisdiction; statute that referred to the filing of a certified copy of child's birth certificate did not require the birth certificate to be filed with the adoption petition and it did not designate a date upon which the birth certificate was required to be filed, stepfather filed a certified copy of child's birth certificate after father objected to the lack of birth certificate, and father was not prejudiced by stepfather's failure to file the birth certificate with his adoption petition. In re Adoption of Reed (Ohio App. 4 Dist., Scioto, 04-17-2006) No. 05CA3048, 2006-Ohio-2094, 2006 WL 1115464, Unreported. Adoption ⬅ 11

Court of Appeals had general subject matter jurisdiction to consider petition for writ of habeas corpus filed by prospective adoptive parents, seeking to compel child's biological father to return physical custody of child to them, even though a juvenile court of a different county had exercised jurisdiction over custody of child in the context of a parentage proceeding, since jurisdictional priority rule did not apply to give juvenile court exclusive jurisdiction over matter; although issues were similar in both cases, the habeas corpus cause of action in the Court of Appeals case was not the same as the cause of action in the juvenile court. In re G.T.B. (Ohio, 04-19-2011) 128 Ohio St.3d 502, 947 N.E.2d 166, 2011-Ohio-1789. Habeas Corpus ⬅ 624

Where the mother of a baby and two adoptive parents are Lucas county residents and the baby is born in Lucas county, the Wood county probate court has no jurisdiction over the adoption of the baby. In re Adoption of Murphy (Wood 1988) 53 Ohio App.3d 14, 557 N.E.2d 827.

3107.05   Petition; documents to be filed with clerk

(A) A petition for adoption shall be prepared and filed according to the procedure for commencing an action under the Rules of Civil Procedure. It shall include the following information:

(1) The date and place of birth of the person to be adopted, if known;

(2) The name of the person to be adopted, if known;

(3) The name to be used for the person to be adopted;

(4) The date of placement of a minor and the name of the person placing the minor;

(5) The full name, age, place, and duration of residence of the petitioner;

(6) The marital status of the petitioner, including the date and place of marriage, if married;

(7) The relationship to the petitioner of the person to be adopted;

(8) That the petitioner has facilities and resources suitable to provide for the nurture and care of the person to be adopted, and that it is the desire of the petitioner to establish the relationship of parent and child with the person to be adopted;

(9) A description and estimate of value of all property of the person to be adopted;

(10) The name and address, if known, of any person whose consent to the adoption is required, but who has not consented, and facts that explain the lack of the consent normally required to the adoption.

(B) A certified copy of the birth certificate of the person to be adopted, if available, and ordinary copies of the required consents, and relinquishments of consents, if any, shall be filed with the clerk.

(1976 H 156, eff. 1–1–77)

Historical and Statutory Notes

Ed. Note: 3107.05 is analogous to former 3107.03, repealed by 1976 H 156, eff. 1–1–77.

Ed. Note: Former 3107.05 repealed by 1976 H 156, eff. 1–1–77; 1969 S 49; 1953 H 1; GC 8004–5;

Source—GC 10512–13; see now 3107.12 for provisions analogous to former 3107.05.

Pre–1953 H 1 Amendments: 124 v S 65

Cross References

Birth certificates, see 3705.10 to 3705.15
Commencement of action, service of process, Civ R 3 to 4.6

Fee for filing petition for adoption, see 2101.16

Library References

Adoption ☞11.
Westlaw Topic No. 17.
C.J.S. Adoption of Persons §§ 80 to 83.

Research References

Encyclopedias

OH Jur. 3d Family Law § 897, Petition.
OH Jur. 3d Family Law § 898, Additional Filing Requirements.

Forms

Ohio Jurisprudence Pleading and Practice Forms § 96:8, Petition Contents.

Treatises and Practice Aids

Klein, Darling, & Terez, Baldwin's Ohio Practice Civil Practice § 3:1, Commencement; Venue--In General.
Klein, Darling, & Terez, Baldwin's Ohio Practice Civil Practice § 4:4, Form of Summons.
Klein, Darling, & Terez, Baldwin's Ohio Practice Civil Practice § 1:22, Civ. R. 1(C): Exceptions--The Proviso--Effect of Statute Providing for Procedure by General or Specific Reference to All Statutes Governing Procedure in Civil Actions.

Carlin, Baldwin's Ohio Prac. Merrick-Rippner Probate Law § 99:3, Jurisdiction.
Carlin, Baldwin's Ohio Prac. Merrick-Rippner Probate Law § 99:22, Types of Placement--Independent Adoptions.
Carlin, Baldwin's Ohio Prac. Merrick-Rippner Probate Law § 99:25, Papers and Records--Petition.
Carlin, Baldwin's Ohio Prac. Merrick-Rippner Probate Law § 99:31, Parties Giving Consent--Biological Parents.
Carlin, Baldwin's Ohio Prac. Merrick-Rippner Probate Law § 99:57, Requirements in Independent Adoptions.
Carlin, Baldwin's Ohio Prac. Merrick-Rippner Probate Law § 99:58, Finalization of Independent Adoptions and Stepparent Adoptions--Form.
Carlin, Baldwin's Ohio Prac. Merrick-Rippner Probate Law App B SPF 18.0, Petition for Adoption of Minor.

Law Review and Journal Commentaries

The Right of the Thwarted Father to Veto the Adoption of His Child, Comment. 62 U Cin L Rev 1695 (Spring 1994).

Notes of Decisions

Consent   6
Custody affidavit   2
Denial of petition   4
Duties of petitioners   5
"Person" defined   1
Placement date   3

------

1. "Person" defined

Word "person" as used in statute is to be construed as having meaning ordinarily given that word, to wit, a "human being."   1944 OAG 6716.

2. Custody affidavit

Grandparents seeking to adopt their grandchild are not required to file an affidavit of custody since adoption proceedings do not determine custody.

In re Adoption of Howell (Lawrence 1991) 77 Ohio App.3d 80, 601 N.E.2d 92, motion overruled 62 Ohio St.3d 1508, 583 N.E.2d 1320.

RC 3107.05 does not require that a custodial affidavit be filed in conjunction with a petition for adoption.   In re Adoption of Reams (Franklin 1989) 52 Ohio App.3d 52, 557 N.E.2d 159, dismissed 50 Ohio St.3d 707, 553 N.E.2d 684.   Adoption ☞ 11

3. Placement date

In an adoption proceeding initiated by the child's grandparents, the placement date is determined to be the date that she was left in the care of the grandparents, which was considered to be a temporary placement since no adoption was intended at the time.   In re Adoption of Howell (Lawrence

1991) 77 Ohio App.3d 80, 601 N.E.2d 92, motion overruled 62 Ohio St.3d 1508, 583 N.E.2d 1320.

4. Denial of petition

After conducting a hearing pursuant to RC 3107.09, the probate court improperly denies a petition for adoption of a four-year-old boy in the custody of the county welfare department, when the court finds that the petitioners meet all the requirements of suitability as adoptive parents, but denies the petition for adoption on the grounds that the granting of the adoption would violate the integrity of a waiting list allegedly maintained by the welfare department, where at the adoption hearing there was no evidence establishing the existence or administration of such a waiting list and no evidence that the waiting list contained suitable applicants ready, willing, and able to adopt the child in question. In re Harshey (Cuyahoga 1975) 45 Ohio App.2d 97, 341 N.E.2d 616, 74 O.O.2d 120.

A petition for adoption, duly filed in accordance with RC 3107.03, is not properly dismissed without a hearing on the merits merely upon a finding by the probate court that a certified agency has not consented to the adoption as required in RC 3107.06. (See also In re Harshey, 45 App(2d) 97, 341 NE(2d) 616 (1975).) In re Harshey (Cuyahoga 1974) 40 Ohio App.2d 157, 318 N.E.2d 544, 69 O.O.2d 165.

5. Duties of petitioners

Stepfather's failure to file a certified copy of child's birth certificate with his petition to adopt child did not deprive the trial court of subject matter jurisdiction; statute that referred to the filing of a certified copy of child's birth certificate did not require the birth certificate to be filed with the adoption petition and it did not designate a date upon which the birth certificate was required to be filed, stepfather filed a certified copy of child's birth certificate after father objected to the lack of birth certificate, and father was not prejudiced by stepfather's failure to file the birth certificate with his adoption petition. In re Adoption of Reed (Ohio App. 4 Dist., Scioto, 04-17-2006) No. 05CA3048, 2006-Ohio-2094, 2006 WL 1115464, Unreported. Adoption ☞ 11

After original adoption was vacated for failure to notify birth father, simply notifying father of original petition for adoption, rather than requiring that petitioner file of a new adoption petition prior to such notification, did not prejudice father, where he received notice within five months of original filing and sought to enforce his rights shortly thereafter. In re Adoption of Goldberg (Ohio App. 12 Dist., Warren, 03-05-2003) No. CA2002-09-091, No. CA2002-09-099, No. CA2002-10-109, 2003-Ohio-1015, 2003 WL 833085, Unreported, appeal not allowed 98 Ohio St.3d 1567, 787 N.E.2d 1231, 2003-Ohio-2242. Adoption ☞ 15

The requirements of RC 5103.16 relating to the duty of parents applying to probate court for approval of a proposed placement for adoption do not apply to a situation where prospective adoptive parents in accordance with RC 3107.03 have duly petitioned for the adoption of a child whose permanent custody has been entrusted to the county welfare department. (See also In re Harshey, 45 App(2d) 97, 341 NE(2d) 616 (1975).) In re Harshey (Cuyahoga 1974) 40 Ohio App.2d 157, 318 N.E.2d 544, 69 O.O.2d 165. Adoption ☞ 6

The adopting parents of an illegitimate child are liable only for the cost of the adoption proceeding and not for expenses incurred by the child welfare board for prenatal care or delivery or for the care of the mother and child after birth. 1955 OAG 5956.

6. Consent

Consent of parent was required for pre-adoptive placement of child with nonrelatives. In re Taylor (Ohio App. 5 Dist., Tuscarawas, 10-15-2004) No. 04AP040032, 2004-Ohio-5643, 2004 WL 2375908, Unreported. Adoption ☞ 7.2(1)

Dismissal of particular petition for child's adoption does not invalidate biological mother's consent to adoption executed in connection therewith; prior statutory references to applicability of consent to one adoption petition only were deleted during legislative revisions, applicable statutes do not place time limit on effectiveness of consent, consent is viable until the court grants a motion to withdraw it, and consent to adoption and petition for adoption must be two separate legal documents. In re Adoption of Koszycki (Ohio App. 1 Dist., 05-14-1999) 133 Ohio App.3d 434, 728 N.E.2d 437. Adoption ☞ 7.5

Consent to adoption and petition for adoption must be two separate legal documents. In re Adoption of Koszycki (Ohio App. 1 Dist., 05-14-1999) 133 Ohio App.3d 434, 728 N.E.2d 437. Adoption ☞ 7.5; Adoption ☞ 11

Biological mother's consent to child's adoption survived dismissal of prospective adoptive parents' first petition for adoption and could be used in support of their second petition. In re Adoption of Koszycki (Ohio App. 1 Dist., 05-14-1999) 133 Ohio App.3d 434, 728 N.E.2d 437. Adoption ☞ 7.5

Where a mother, as sole parent, files an "application for placement" and a written waiver and consent to adoption in the probate court to place her newborn baby with a married couple whose identity she did not know but who were procured by an intermediary at her request with adoption in mind, appears in person before such court for approval of such placement, and the probate court, after an independent investigation of the proposed placement by a qualified person, determines that it is in the best interest of the child and approves of record the proposed placement, and the child is delivered to the married couple pursuant to the order of the court, the mother, as petitioner in a habeas corpus action filed in the court of common pleas to regain custody of her child, is estopped from claiming that the probate court was without jurisdiction by reason of an insufficient application in not identifying by names the placement parents; and a finding by the court of common pleas of lack of such jurisdiction is reversible error. In re McTaggart (Cuyahoga 1965) 4 Ohio App.2d 359, 212 N.E.2d 663, 33 O.O.2d 447.

In an adoption proceeding, written consent of child to the adoption was not required to be filed of record by former statutes, and where record disclosed that such consent was given, it was presumed that consent was legally executed. In re Dickman's Estate (Mercer 1946) 81 Ohio App. 281, 79 N.E.2d 172, 37 O.O. 125. Adoption ☞ 7.1

3107.051 Submission of petition for adoption

(A) Except as provided in division (B) of this section, a person seeking to adopt a minor, or the agency or attorney arranging the adoption, shall submit a petition for the minor's adoption no later than ninety days after the date the minor is placed in the person's home. Failure to file a petition within the time provided by this division does not affect a court's jurisdiction to hear the petition and is not grounds for denying the petition.

(B) This section does not apply if any of the following apply:

(1) The person seeking to adopt the minor is the minor's stepparent;

(2) The minor was not originally placed in the person's home with the purpose of the person adopting the minor;

(3) The minor is a "child with special needs," as defined by the director of job and family services in accordance with section 5153.163 of the Revised Code.

(1999 H 471, eff. 7–1–00; 1996 H 419, eff. 9–18–96)

Historical and Statutory Notes

Amendment Note: 1999 H 471 substituted "director of job and family services" for "department of human services" in division (B)(3).

Library References

Adoption ☞9.1.
Westlaw Topic No. 17.
C.J.S. Adoption of Persons §§ 46, 77.

Research References

Encyclopedias

OH Jur. 3d Family Law § 897, Petition.

Forms

Ohio Forms Legal and Business § 28:24, Introduction.

Ohio Jurisprudence Pleading and Practice Forms § 96:8, Petition Contents.

Treatises and Practice Aids

Carlin, Baldwin's Ohio Prac. Merrick-Rippner Probate Law § 99:25, Papers and Records--Petition.

3107.055 Accounting; disbursements

(A) Notwithstanding section 3107.01 of the Revised Code, as used in this section, "agency" does not include a public children services agency.

(B) An agency or attorney, whichever arranges a minor's adoption, shall file with the court a preliminary estimate accounting not later than the time the adoption petition for the minor is filed with the court. The agency or attorney, whichever arranges the adoption, also shall file a final accounting with the court before a final decree of adoption is issued or an interlocutory order of adoption is finalized for the minor. The agency or attorney shall complete and file accountings in a manner acceptable to the court.

An accounting shall specify all disbursements of anything of value the petitioner, a person on the petitioner's behalf, and the agency or attorney made and has agreed to make in connection with the minor's permanent surrender under division (B) of section 5103.15 of the Revised Code, placement under section 5103.16 of the Revised Code, and adoption under this chapter. The agency or attorney shall include in an accounting an itemization of each expense listed in division (C) of this section. The itemization of the expenses specified in divisions (C)(3) and (4) of this section shall show the amount the agency or attorney charged or is going to charge for the services and the actual cost to the agency or attorney of providing the services. An accounting shall indicate whether any expenses listed in division (C) of this section do not apply to the adoption proceeding for which the accounting is filed.

The agency or attorney shall include with a preliminary estimate accounting and a final accounting a written statement signed by the petitioner that the petitioner has reviewed the accounting and attests to its accuracy.

(C) No petitioner, person acting on a petitioner's behalf, or agency or attorney shall make or agree to make any disbursements in connection with the minor's permanent surrender, placement, or adoption other than for the following:

(1) Physician expenses incurred on behalf of the birth mother or minor in connection with prenatal care, delivery, and confinement prior to or following the minor's birth;

(2) Hospital or other medical facility expenses incurred on behalf of the birth mother or minor in connection with the minor's birth;

(3) Expenses charged by the attorney arranging the adoption for providing legal services in connection with the placement and adoption, including expenses incurred by the attorney pursuant to sections 3107.031, 3107.032, 3107.081, 3107.082, 3107.09, 3107.101, and 3107.12 of the Revised Code;

(4) Expenses charged by the agency arranging the adoption for providing services in connection with the permanent surrender and adoption, including the agency's application fee and the expenses incurred by the agency pursuant to sections 3107.031, 3107.032, 3107.09, 3107.101, 3107.12, 5103.151, and 5103.152 of the Revised Code;

(5) Temporary costs of routine maintenance and medical care for a minor required under section 5103.16 of the Revised Code if the person seeking to adopt the minor refuses to accept placement of the minor;

(6) Guardian ad litem fees incurred on behalf of the minor in any court proceedings;

(7) Foster care expenses incurred in connection with any temporary care and maintenance of the minor;

(8) Court expenses incurred in connection with the minor's permanent surrender, placement, and adoption;

(9) Living expenses not exceeding three thousand dollars for the birth mother that are incurred during pregnancy through the sixtieth day after the date the minor is born and paid by the petitioner to the birth mother through the attorney or agency arranging the minor's adoption.

(D) If a court determines from an accounting that an amount that is going to be disbursed for an expense listed in division (C) of this section is unreasonable, the court may order a reduction in the amount to be disbursed. If a court determines from an accounting that an unreasonable amount was disbursed for an expense listed in division (C) of this section, the court may order the person who received the disbursement to refund to the person who made the disbursement an amount the court orders.

If a court determines from an accounting that a disbursement for an expense not permitted by division (C) of this section is going to be made, the court may issue an injunction prohibiting the disbursement. If a court determines from an accounting that a disbursement for an expense not permitted by division (C) of this section was made, the court may order the person who received the disbursement to return it to the person who made the disbursement.

If a court determines that a final accounting does not completely report all the disbursements that are going to be made or have been made in connection with the minor's permanent surrender, placement, and adoption, the court shall order the agency or attorney to file with the court an accounting that completely reports all such disbursements.

The agency or attorney shall file the final accounting with the court not later than ten days prior to the date scheduled for the final hearing on the adoption. The court may not issue a final decree of adoption or finalize an interlocutory order of adoption of a minor until at least ten days after the agency or attorney files the final accounting.

(E) This section does not apply to an adoption by a stepparent whose spouse is a biological or adoptive parent of the minor.

(2008 H 7, eff. 4-7-09; 2006 S 238, eff. 9–21–06)

Historical and Statutory Notes

Ed. Note: RC 3107.055 is former RC 3107.10, amended and recodified by 2006 S 238, eff. 9–21–06; 2005 H 66, eff. 6–30–05; 1999 H 471, eff. 7-1-00; 1996 H 274, eff. 9–18–96; 1996 H 419, eff. 9–18–96; 1986 H 428, eff. 12–23–86; 1978 H 832; 1976 H 156.

Amendment Note: 2008 H 7 added division (C)(9).

Amendment Note: 2006 S 238 inserted "3107.032," and "3107.101," in divisions (C)(3) and (C)(4).

Amendment Note: 2005 H 66 deleted division (E) and redesignated former division (F) as new division (E). Prior to amendment, former division (E) read:

"(E) At the conclusion of each adoption proceeding, the court shall prepare a summary of the proceeding, and on or before the tenth day of each month, send copies of the summaries for all proceedings concluded during the preceding calendar month to the department of job and family services. The summary shall contain:

"(1) A notation of the nature and approximate value or amount of anything paid in connection with the proceeding, compiled from the final accounting required by division (B) of this section and indicating the category of division (C) of this section to which any payment relates;

"(2) If the court has not issued a decree because of the requirements of division (D) of this section, a notation of that fact and a statement of the reason for refusing to issue the decree, related to the financial data summarized under division (E)(1) of this section;

"(3) If the adoption was arranged by an attorney, a notation of that fact.

"The summary shall contain no information identifying by name any party to the proceeding or any other person, but may contain additional narrative material that the court considers useful to an analysis of the summary."

Amendment Note: 1999 H 471 substituted "job and family" for "human" in the introductory paragraph in division (E).

Amendment Note: 1996 H 274 substituted "may" for "shall" in the fourth paragraph in division (D).

Amendment Note: 1996 H 419 rewrote this section, which prior thereto read:

"(A) The petitioner in any proceeding for the adoption of a minor shall file, before the petition is heard, a full accounting in a manner acceptable to the court of all disbursements of anything of value made or agreed to be made by or on behalf of the petitioner in connection with the placement or adoption of the minor. The accounting shall show any payments made or to be made by or on behalf of the petitioner in connection with the placement or adoption.

"(B) A petitioner shall not make or agree to make any disbursements in connection with the placement or adoption of a minor other than for the following:

"(1) Physician expenses incurred in connection with prenatal care and confinement or in connection with the birth of the minor to be adopted;

"(2) Hospital expenses incurred in connection with the birth of the minor to be adopted;

"(3) Attorneys' fees incurred in providing legal services in connection with the placement of the minor to be adopted or in connection with legal services provided to initiate and pursue the adoption proceedings;

"(4) Agency expenses incurred for providing services in connection with the adoption or in connection with placement services provided by an agency under section 5103.16 of the Revised Code;

"(5) Temporary costs of routine maintenance and medical care for a minor required under section 5103.16 of the Revised Code if the person seeking to adopt the minor refuses to accept placement of the minor.

"(C) The court shall review and approve, prior to the entry of any decree of adoption, all expenses made or agreed to be made by a petitioner in connection with the adoption of a minor. The court shall not issue a decree of adoption if after a hearing it determines that any of the expenses incurred by the petitioner were unreasonable or were for services other than those permitted under division (B) of this section or if after a hearing it determines that the petitioner has failed to report all of the expenses incurred in connection with the placement or adoption of the minor.

"(D) At the conclusion of each adoption proceeding, the court shall prepare a summary of the proceeding, and on or before the tenth day of each month, send copies of the summaries for all proceedings concluded during the preceding calendar month to the department of human services. The summary shall contain:

"(1) A notation of the nature and approximate value or amount of anything paid in connection with the proceeding, compiled from the accounting required by division (A) of this section and indicating the category of division (B) of this section to which any payment relates;

"(2) If the court has not issued a decree because of the requirements of division (C) of this section, a notation of that fact and a statement of the reason for refusing to issue the decree, related to the financial data summarized under division (D)(1) of this section;

"(3) If placement in the petitioners' home was privately arranged under section 5103.16 of the Revised Code, a notation of that fact.

"The summary shall contain no information identifying by name any party to the proceeding or any other person, but may contain additional narrative material that the court considers useful to an analysis of the summary.

"(E) This section does not apply to an adoption by a stepparent whose spouse is a biological or adoptive parent of the minor."

Cross References

Job and family services department, report on summaries submitted, see 2151.416

Placing of children, assumption of responsibility for expenses, see 5103.16

Library References

Adoption ⬤⇒6, 7.5, 13.
Westlaw Topic No. 17.

C.J.S. Adoption of Persons §§ 28 to 47, 56, 70 to 73, 93 to 102, 140.

Research References

Encyclopedias

OH Jur. 3d Family Law § 899, Accounting by Petitioner.

Treatises and Practice Aids

Carlin, Baldwin's Ohio Prac. Merrick-Rippner Probate Law § 99:2, History.

Carlin, Baldwin's Ohio Prac. Merrick-Rippner Probate Law § 19:14, Uniform Parentage Act-Surrogacy Agreement.
Carlin, Baldwin's Ohio Prac. Merrick-Rippner Probate Law § 99:31, Parties Giving Consent--Biological Parents.
Carlin, Baldwin's Ohio Prac. Merrick-Rippner Probate Law § 99:39, Consent Not Required--Noncommunication and Nonsupport.

Notes of Decisions

Accounting   1
Attorneys' fees   2
Contracts   3

1. Accounting

Although an accounting is mandatory before the adoption petition is heard, its late filing is not reversible error when the child had been placed with her natural grandparents and the mother had shown no prejudicial effect. In re Adoption of Howell (Lawrence 1991) 77 Ohio App.3d 80, 601 N.E.2d 92, motion overruled 62 Ohio St.3d 1508, 583 N.E.2d 1320.

2. Attorneys' fees

RC 3107.10 does not prohibit adoptive parents from paying the legal expenses of the birth mother, but the attorney must, in accordance with DR 5-107(A), disclose their intention to his client, the birth mother, before he accepts such payment. In re Adoption of Infant Girl Banda (Franklin 1988) 53 Ohio App.3d 104, 559 N.E.2d 1373.

3. Contracts

Since surrogate mother and mother's husband breached surrogacy contract by obtaining custody of children born as result of surrogacy and since surrogacy contract was enforceable, surrogate mother and her husband were liable for restitution of monies paid by biological father, as well as attorney fees, pursuant to section of surrogacy contract providing that, in event of breach by surrogate mother and her husband, mother and husband shall be liable for any and all monies expended on their behalf, plus attorney fees. J.F. v. D.B. (Ohio App.

9 Dist., 03-15-2006) 165 Ohio App.3d 791, 848 N.E.2d 873, 2006-Ohio-1175, appeal allowed 110 Ohio St.3d 1438, 852 N.E.2d 187, 2006-Ohio-3862, affirmed in part, reversed in part 116 Ohio St.3d 363, 879 N.E.2d 740, 2007-Ohio-6750. Children Out-of-wedlock ⬤⇒ 22

Indemnification provision in surrogacy contract providing that, in the event that custody of children was awarded to surrogate mother and mother's husband, biological father would be indemnified by surrogate mother and her husband for any and all monies biological father was required to pay for child support, did not violate public policy; this was not abrogation of obligation to support offspring of coital relationship but recognition that, since surrogate was not a parent, if surrogate mother and her husband decided to obtain custody of children, they would become legal parents and surrogacy agreement would terminate, and biological father would be treated as merely the sperm donor and not the parent. J.F. v. D.B. (Ohio App. 9 Dist., 03-15-2006) 165 Ohio App.3d 791, 848 N.E.2d 873, 2006-Ohio-1175, appeal allowed 110 Ohio St.3d 1438, 852 N.E.2d 187, 2006-Ohio-3862, affirmed in part, reversed in part 116 Ohio St.3d 363, 879 N.E.2d 740, 2007-Ohio-6750. Children Out-of-wedlock ⬤⇒ 22; Contracts ⬤⇒ 108(2)

Surrogacy contract between biological father, egg donor, surrogate mother, and surrogate mother's husband, under which surrogate mother would be implanted with fertilized embryos in exchange for compensation and under which surrogate mother and husband agreed to not attempt to form a parent-child relationship, did not violate Ohio's public policy against private agreements to forgo parental rights; at time the parties entered the contract, surrogate mother and her husband were not the children's parents, so they had no parental rights to contract away, and fact that they later obtained custody of children in another state's court did not retroactively grant them the status of parents at time they signed or breached the con-tract. J.F. v. D.B. (Ohio App. 9 Dist., 03-15-2006) 165 Ohio App.3d 791, 848 N.E.2d 873, 2006-Ohio-1175, appeal allowed 110 Ohio St.3d 1438, 852 N.E.2d 187, 2006-Ohio-3862, affirmed in part, reversed in part 116 Ohio St.3d 363, 879 N.E.2d 740, 2007-Ohio-6750. Contracts ☞ 108(2)

CONSENTS AND PUTATIVE FATHER REGISTRY

3107.06 Consents required

Unless consent is not required under section 3107.07 of the Revised Code, a petition to adopt a minor may be granted only if written consent to the adoption has been executed by all of the following:

(A) The mother of the minor;

(B) The father of the minor, if any of the following apply:

(1) The minor was conceived or born while the father was married to the mother;

(2) The minor is his child by adoption;

(3) Prior to the date the petition was filed, it was determined by a court proceeding pursuant to sections 3111.01 to 3111.18 of the Revised Code, a court proceeding in another state, an administrative proceeding pursuant to sections 3111.38 to 3111.54 of the Revised Code, or an administrative proceeding in another state that he has a parent and child relationship with the minor;

(4) He acknowledged paternity of the child and that acknowledgment has become final pursuant to section 2151.232, 3111.25, or 3111.821 of the Revised Code.

(C) The putative father of the minor;

(D) Any person or agency having permanent custody of the minor or authorized by court order to consent;

(E) The minor, if more than twelve years of age, unless the court, finding that it is in the best interest of the minor, determines that the minor's consent is not required.

(2008 H 7, eff. 4-7-09; 2000 S 180, eff. 3–22–01; 1997 H 352, eff. 1–1–98; 1996 H 274, eff. 9–18–96; 1996 H 419, eff. 9–18–96; 1988 H 790, eff. 3–16–89; 1986 H 476; 1982 H 245; 1976 H 156)

Uncodified Law

1996 H 419, § 5, eff. 6–20–96, reads: The amendment made by this act to sections 3107.06 and 3107.07 of the Revised Code concerning a putative father, as defined in section 3107.01 of the Revised Code, consenting to his child's adoption apply only if the child is born on or after January 1, 1997. Whether a putative father's consent to the adoption of his child born prior to January 1, 1997, is required shall be determined in accordance with sections 3107.06 and 3107.07 of the Revised Code as those sections exist immediately prior to their amendment by this act.

Historical and Statutory Notes

Ed. Note: Former 3107.06 repealed by 1976 H 156, eff. 1–1–77; 1975 S 145; 1969 S 49; 130 v S 155; 129 v 498; 126 v 392; 1953 H 1; GC 8004–6; Source—GC 10512–14; see now 3107.07 and 3107.09 for provisions analogous to former 3107.06.

Pre–1953 H 1 Amendments: 124 v S 65

Amendment Note: 2008 H 7 deleted former division (E); and redesignated former division (F) as new division (E).

Amendment Note: 1997 H 352 rewrote division (B)(4), which prior thereto read:

"(4) He acknowledged paternity of the child pursuant to section 2105.18 of the Revised Code."

Amendment Note: 1996 H 274 added division (B)(4).

Amendment Note: 1996 H 419 rewrote division (B); added new division (C); redesignated former divisions (C) through (E) as divisions (D) through (F), respectively; and deleted former section (F). Prior to amendment and deletion, divisions (B) and (F) read:

"(B) The father of the minor, if the minor was conceived or born while the father was married to the mother, if the minor is his child by adoption, or if the minor has been established to be his child by a court proceeding;

"(F) Subject to division (B) of section 3107.07 of the Revised Code, the putative father, if he:

"(1) Is alleged to be the father of the minor in proceedings brought under sections 3111.01 to 3111.19 of the Revised Code at any time before the placement of the minor in the home of the petitioner;

"(2) Has acknowledged the child in a writing sworn to before a notary public at any time before the placement of the minor in the home of the petitioner;

"(3) Has signed the birth certificate of the child as an informant as provided in section 3705.09 of the Revised Code;

"(4) Has filed an objection to the adoption with the agency having custody of the minor or the department of human services at any time before the placement of the minor in the home of the petitioner, or with the probate court or the department of human services within thirty days of the filing of a petition to adopt the minor or its placement in the home of the petitioner, whichever occurs first."

Comparative Laws

Ariz.—A.R.S. § 8-106 et seq.
Ark.—A.C.A. § 9-9-206 et seq.
Fla.—West's F.S.A. § 63.062 et seq.
Idaho—I.C. § 16-1503, 16-1504.
Ill.—ILCS 750 50/8 et seq.
Ind.—West's A.I.C. 31–19–9–1 et seq.
Iowa—I.C.A. § 600.7.
Ky.—Baldwin's KRS 199.500.
Mass.—M.G.L.A. c. 210, § 2 et seq.
Me.—18-A M.R.S.A. § 9–302.

Mich.—M.C.L.A. § 710.43 et seq.
Minn.—M.S.A. § 259.24.
Mo.—V.A.M.S. § 453.040, 453.050.
N.C.—G.S. § 48-3-601 et seq.
N.Y.—McKinney's Domestic Relations Law § 111.
Okl.—10 Okl.St.Ann. § 7503–2.1.
Tenn.—T.C.A. § 36-1-108 et seq.
Tex.—V.T.C.A. Family Code § 162.010, 162.011.

Cross References

Custody of child by public agency, see 2151.38
Department of job and family services, division of social administration, placing of children; interstate compact on placement of children, see 5103.12 to 5103.17, 5103.20 to 5103.27

Jurisdiction of juvenile court, see 2151.23
Placement of children from other states, see 2151.39
Powers and duties of county children services board, see 5153.16

Library References

Adoption ☞7.1 to 7.2(3).
Westlaw Topic No. 17.
C.J.S. Adoption of Persons §§ 49 to 57, 59 to 61.

Research References

ALR Library

28 ALR 6th 349, Requirements and Effects of Putative Father Registries.
84 ALR 5th 191, Natural Parent's Indigence as Precluding Finding that Failure to Support Child Waived Requirement of Consent to Adoption--Factors Other Than Employment Status.
83 ALR 5th 375, Natural Parent's Indigence Resulting from Unemployment or Underemployment as Precluding Finding that Failure to Support Child Waived Requirement of Consent to Adoption.
82 ALR 5th 443, Comment Note: Natural Parent's Indigence as Precluding Finding that Failure to Support Child Waived Requirement of Consent to Adoption--General Principles.

Encyclopedias

OH Jur. 3d Family Law § 881, Who Must Consent.
OH Jur. 3d Family Law § 882, Putative Father Registry.
OH Jur. 3d Family Law § 890, Who Need Not Consent--Construction of Statute.
OH Jur. 3d Family Law § 916, Appeal.

Forms

Ohio Forms Legal and Business § 28:24, Introduction.
Ohio Forms Legal and Business § 28:27, Consent to Adoption--By Adult or Minor Over Age of 12.
Ohio Forms Legal and Business § 28:28, Consent of Parent of Adult to Adoption of Adult.
Ohio Forms Legal and Business § 28:29, Consent of One Spouse to Adoption of Other Spouse.
Ohio Jurisprudence Pleading and Practice Forms § 96:7, Venue.
Ohio Jurisprudence Pleading and Practice Forms § 96:11, Consent Required.
Ohio Jurisprudence Pleading and Practice Forms § 96:12, Consent Not Required.
Ohio Jurisprudence Pleading and Practice Forms § 96:43, Temporary and Permanent Custody.
Ohio Jurisprudence Pleading and Practice Forms § 96:48, Acknowledgment of Natural Parent.
Ohio Jurisprudence Pleading and Practice Forms § 96:75, Permanent Surrender of Child.
Am. Jur. Pl. & Pr. Forms Adoption § 93, Person Other Than Natural Parent--Child.

Treatises and Practice Aids

Klein, Darling, & Terez, Baldwin's Ohio Practice Civil Practice § 24:12, Intervention of Right--Nonstatutory Intervention of Right--"The Applicant Claims an Interest Relating to the Property or Transaction Which is the Subject of the Action"--Interest...

Sowald & Morganstern, Baldwin's Ohio Practice Domestic Relations Law § 3:49, Related Issues--Adoption.

Carlin, Baldwin's Ohio Prac. Merrick-Rippner Probate Law § 6:4, Action--Parties.

Carlin, Baldwin's Ohio Prac. Merrick-Rippner Probate Law § 99:3, Jurisdiction.

Carlin, Baldwin's Ohio Prac. Merrick-Rippner Probate Law § 99:8, Suitability of Adoptive Parents--Best Interests of Child.

Carlin, Baldwin's Ohio Prac. Merrick-Rippner Probate Law § 99:14, Types of Placement--Agency Adoptions--Termination of Parental Rights.

Carlin, Baldwin's Ohio Prac. Merrick-Rippner Probate Law § 99:15, Types of Placement--Agency Adoptions--Through Juvenile Court.

Carlin, Baldwin's Ohio Prac. Merrick-Rippner Probate Law § 99:21, Types of Placement--Stepparent, Guardian, and Grandparent Adoptions.

Carlin, Baldwin's Ohio Prac. Merrick-Rippner Probate Law § 99:30, Statutorily Required Consent.

Carlin, Baldwin's Ohio Prac. Merrick-Rippner Probate Law § 99:31, Parties Giving Consent--Biological Parents.

Carlin, Baldwin's Ohio Prac. Merrick-Rippner Probate Law § 99:32, Parties Giving Consent--Putative Father.

Carlin, Baldwin's Ohio Prac. Merrick-Rippner Probate Law § 99:34, Parties Giving Consent--Agency.

Carlin, Baldwin's Ohio Prac. Merrick-Rippner Probate Law § 99:35, Parties Giving Consent--Adoptee.

Carlin, Baldwin's Ohio Prac. Merrick-Rippner Probate Law § 99:36, Method of Giving Consent.

Carlin, Baldwin's Ohio Prac. Merrick-Rippner Probate Law § 99:38, Consent Not Required--Statutory Scheme.

Carlin, Baldwin's Ohio Prac. Merrick-Rippner Probate Law § 99:39, Consent Not Required--Noncommunication and Nonsupport.

Carlin, Baldwin's Ohio Prac. Merrick-Rippner Probate Law § 99:40, Consent Not Required--Putative Father.

Carlin, Baldwin's Ohio Prac. Merrick-Rippner Probate Law § 99:41, Consent Not Required--Parent Who Has Relinquished Rights.

Carlin, Baldwin's Ohio Prac. Merrick-Rippner Probate Law § 99:51, Attacking Adoption Orders--Appeal.

Carlin, Baldwin's Ohio Prac. Merrick-Rippner Probate Law § 107:13, Authority Following Certification.

Carlin, Baldwin's Ohio Prac. Merrick-Rippner Probate Law § 108:24, Agreements for Temporary and Permanent Custody.

Carlin, Baldwin's Ohio Prac. Merrick-Rippner Probate Law § 109:80, Disposition of Abused, Neglected, or Dependent Child--Permanent Custody.

Carlin, Baldwin's Ohio Prac. Merrick-Rippner Probate Law App B SPF 18.3, Consent to Adoption--Form.

Giannelli & Yeomans, Ohio Juvenile Law § 45:8, Permanent Custody--Defined.

Law Review and Journal Commentaries

Adoption—Consent—A Court May Enter a Final Decree of Adoption without the Consent of a Certified Child Welfare Agency When the Adoption Is in the Child's Best Interest, Note. 41 U Cin L Rev 704 (1972).

Awarding Child Support Against the Impoverished Parent: Straying from Statutory Guidelines and Using SSI in Setting the Amount, Note. 83 Ky L J 653 (1994–95).

Family Law—Ohio's Statutory Requirement of Legal Guardian Consent to Adoption and Its Effect on the Jurisdiction of the Probate Court, Note. 36 Ohio St L J 451 (1975).

Judicial Review of Adoption Agency Decisions, Note. 25 Case W Res L Rev 650 (Spring 1975).

The Law of Adoption in Ohio, Beverly E. Sylvester. 2 Cap U L Rev 23 (1973).

Lehr v Robertson: Putting the Genie Back in the Bottle: the Supreme Court Limits the Scope of the Putative Father's Right to Notice, Hearing, and Consent in the Adoption of His Illegitimate Child, Note. 15 U Tol L Rev 1501 (Summer 1984).

Seeking the wisdom of Solomon: Defining the rights of unwed fathers in newborn adoptions, Scott A. Resnik. 20 Seton Hall Legis J 363 (1996).

Termination of Parental Rights in Adoption Cases: Focusing on the Child, Comment. 14 J Fam L 547 (1975–76).

Notes of Decisions

In general 2
Agency or institution consent 9
Best interest of child 5
Communication with child 7
Consent must be voluntary 8
Due process 1
Establishment of paternity 10
Jurisdiction of court 3

Objections to adoption 14
Power and authority of court 4
Putative father, generally 11
Registration by putative father 12
Support and maintenance of child 6

Withdrawal of consent   13

---

1. Due process

Probate court violated mother's due process rights by granting the adoption petition; during pendency of mother's appeal of order granting permanent custody of child to county social services agency and terminating mother's parental rights, trial court overruled both agency's and mother's motions to vacate adoption decree, thereby, in essence, divesting mother of her right to appeal underlying permanent custody award. In re Adoption of V.N.M. (Ohio App. 5 Dist., Licking, 05-23-2005) No. 04CA109, 2005-Ohio-2555, 2005 WL 1208855, Unreported. Adoption ☞ 16; Constitutional Law ☞ 4395; Infants ☞ 244.1

Due process did not require that birth mother be appointed counsel in child's stepmother's petition to adopt child; case was not initiated by state, but by third party, case was instituted as adoption petition in probate court, not termination of parental rights in juvenile court, and, although state played role by removing child from birth mother and placing her with birth father, state did not seek to terminate birth mother's parental rights. In re Adoption of Drake (Ohio App. 12 Dist., Clermont, 02-03-2003) No. CA2002-08-067, 2003-Ohio-510, 2003 WL 231298, Unreported. Adoption ☞ 13; Constitutional Law ☞ 4395

2. In general

Mortmain statute did not apply to invalidate charitable bequest by testamentary trust to three named hospitals made within one year of settlor's death, given that settlor did not have "issue," as required by statute; settlor had no lineal descendents, and heirs seeking to invalidate trust provision were nephew, great nieces and nephews, and purpose of mortmain statute was to protect testator's children from effects of undue influence in obtaining charitable bequests. Bank One Trust Co., NA v. Miami Valley Hosp. (Ohio App. 2 Dist., Montgomery, 08-29-2003) No. 19703, 2003-Ohio-4590, 2003 WL 22026337, Unreported. Charities ☞ 4

Child's paternal grandmother had no right to intervene in proceeding to adopt, even though she had been granted visitation rights by order from the domestic relations court. In re Adoption of Hilliard (Ohio App. 3 Dist., 08-25-2003) 154 Ohio App.3d 54, 796 N.E.2d 46, 2003-Ohio-4471. Adoption ☞ 11

Father of child has same adoption rights with respect to adoption of child as mother, with few narrowly defined exceptions. Bryant v. Hacker (Ohio App. 1 Dist., 12-24-1996) 116 Ohio App.3d 860, 689 N.E.2d 609. Adoption ☞ 7.2(1)

Finding that parent's consent to adoption is unnecessary is final, appealable order. In re Adoption of Hudnell (Ohio App. 4 Dist., 08-06-1996) 113 Ohio App.3d 296, 680 N.E.2d 1055. Adoption ☞ 15

Natural parent may relinquish or consent to give up rights and duties of parentage. Belsito v. Clark (Ohio Com.Pl. 1994) 67 Ohio Misc.2d 54, 644 N.E.2d 760. Infants ☞ 154.1; Infants ☞ 155

RC 2151.353, permitting the state to receive permanent custody of a "dependent child" whose parent is jailed, does not conflict with RC 3107.07; where the child is a "dependent child" under RC 2151.04 the state has authority to obtain permanent custody under RC 2151.353, and once parental rights have been terminated under RC Ch 2151, it is provided by RC 3107.06(D) that this parent's consent to adoption is no longer necessary. In re Dillard (Montgomery 1988) 48 Ohio App.3d 263, 549 N.E.2d 213.

The main purpose of adoption is to find homes for children, not children for families. (See also In re Harshey, 40 App(2d) 157, 318 NE(2d) 544 (1974).) In re Harshey (Cuyahoga 1975) 45 Ohio App.2d 97, 341 N.E.2d 616, 74 O.O.2d 120. Adoption ☞ 1

Strict statutory compliance with RC 3107.06(B) is required. (See also In re Harshey, 45 App(2d) 97, 341 NE(2d) 616 (1975).) In re Harshey (Cuyahoga 1974) 40 Ohio App.2d 157, 318 N.E.2d 544, 69 O.O.2d 165.

RC 5103.16 is intended to provide a measure of judicial control over so-called "independent" placements for adoption, not conducted under the aegis of an authorized agency such as the county welfare department, and such measure of control can be accomplished by requiring, inter alia, that parents of a child seeking to make such an independent placement for adoption personally apply to and appear before the proper probate court for approval of the placement. (See also In re Harshey, 45 App(2d) 97, 341 NE(2d) 616 (1975).) In re Harshey (Cuyahoga 1974) 40 Ohio App.2d 157, 318 N.E.2d 544, 69 O.O.2d 165.

The legality of a placement of a child with persons other than his parents is governed by the statute in effect at the time such placement is made. In re Adoption of Wright (Ohio Prob. 1968) 15 Ohio Misc. 354, 240 N.E.2d 923, 44 O.O.2d 509.

Order denying adoption reversed where such order was based on the fact that the adopting father was Caucasian, his wife Japanese, the natural mother of English descent, and the natural father Puerto Rican. In re Adoption of Baker (Cuyahoga 1962) 117 Ohio App. 26, 185 N.E.2d 51, 90 Ohio Law Abs. 125, 22 O.O.2d 459.

A consent to adoption required by section may be obtained prior to the time the petition to adopt is filed; sno exclusive method of executing such consent is defined by statute, and, where the consent is in writing, verified or acknowledged and filed in the court, compliance with the terms of the statute is accomplished. In re Burdette (Summit 1948) 83 Ohio App. 368, 83 N.E.2d 813, 38 O.O. 429.

Statute is mandatory, and must be followed strictly in order to effect a legal adoption. Martin v.

Fisher (Mercer 1927) 25 Ohio App. 372, 158 N.E. 287, 5 Ohio Law Abs. 596.

Consent of the juvenile court was required before legal custodians could adopt minor children, because custodians were not authorized by court to consent to the adoption. In re Adoption of Barkhurst (Ohio App. 12 Dist., Butler, 09-04-2002) No. CA2002-04-081, 2002-Ohio-4711, 2002 WL 31009205, Unreported, appeal not allowed 97 Ohio St.3d 1471, 779 N.E.2d 237, 2002-Ohio-6347. Adoption ☞ 7.3

When the natural parents of children sought to be adopted are living and under no legal disability to assume parental custody over the same, their written consent to the adoption proceedings is a necessary statutory requirement of GC 8025 (Repealed). 1921 OAG p 955.

A department of human services does not act in a "wanton or reckless manner" by its decision to place a foster child for adoption in a home other than that of the foster parents. Jay T v Williams County Human Services Dept, No. 94WM000007, 1995 WL 19112 (6th Dist Ct App, Williams, 1–20–95).

3. Jurisdiction of court

Parental consent generally is a jurisdictional prerequisite to adoption of parent's child by another. In re Adoption of McNutt (Ohio App. 4 Dist., 09-27-1999) 134 Ohio App.3d 822, 732 N.E.2d 470. Adoption ☞ 7.2(1)

Parental consent to adoption order is jurisdictional prerequisite which, if absent, allows order to be attacked as void. In re Adoption of Zschach (Ohio, 06-06-1996) 75 Ohio St.3d 648, 665 N.E.2d 1070, reconsideration denied 76 Ohio St.3d 1410, 666 N.E.2d 569, certiorari denied 117 S.Ct. 582, 519 U.S. 1028, 136 L.Ed.2d 513. Adoption ☞ 7.7

Valid consent to adoption is jurisdictional prerequisite to issuance of adoption order. In re Adoption of Zschach (Ohio, 06-06-1996) 75 Ohio St.3d 648, 665 N.E.2d 1070, reconsideration denied 76 Ohio St.3d 1410, 666 N.E.2d 569, certiorari denied 117 S.Ct. 582, 519 U.S. 1028, 136 L.Ed.2d 513. Adoption ☞ 7.7

Parental consent to an adoption is a jurisdictional prerequisite which, if absent, allows adoption to be attacked as void in a habeas corpus proceeding. Barnebey v. Zschach (Ohio, 03-08-1995) 71 Ohio St.3d 588, 646 N.E.2d 162. Adoption ☞ 7.7; Habeas Corpus ☞ 534

Parental consent to adoption is generally a jurisdictional prerequisite. Celestino v. Schneider (Lucas 1992) 84 Ohio App.3d 192, 616 N.E.2d 581. Adoption ☞ 7.7

The required consent for an adoption may be executed any time from seventy-two hours after the birth of a child to be adopted until the time the adoption petition is granted, and there is no jurisdictional defect if the required consent is not executed prior to the hearing on the adoption petition or prior to the close of the petitioner's case; thus, where the guardian of children sought to be adopted gives her written consent well before the adoption petition is granted, the trial court has jurisdiction to grant the adoption petition even though the consent was not given prior to the close of the petitioner's case. In re Adoption of Jordan (Preble 1991) 72 Ohio App.3d 638, 595 N.E.2d 963.

The continuing jurisdiction in a divorce action of the court of common pleas, domestic relations division, to determine the custody of a minor child does not deprive the court of common pleas, probate division, of jurisdiction in adoption proceedings relating to that child. Syversten v. Carrelli (Cuyahoga 1979) 67 Ohio App.2d 105, 425 N.E.2d 930, 21 O.O.3d 418. Courts ☞ 475(15)

RC 3107.06 does not mandate that the ongoing jurisdiction of a Kentucky juvenile court bars the issuance of an adoption order by the probate division of an Ohio court of common pleas. In re Johnson (Hamilton 1978) 56 Ohio App.2d 265, 382 N.E.2d 1176, 10 O.O.3d 278.

While the consent required by RC 3107.06 is not a prerequisite for granting jurisdiction to the probate court in an adoption proceeding, compliance with the statute is. In re Dickhaus (Ohio Com.Pl. 1974) 41 Ohio Misc. 1, 321 N.E.2d 800, 70 O.O.2d 24.

A probate court is without jurisdiction to hear a case, and properly dismisses a petition for adoption of a child in the custody of a natural parent, where the natural parent has not consented to the adoption as required in RC 3107.06(B). (See also In re Harshey, 45 App(2d) 97, 341 NE(2d) 616 (1975).) In re Harshey (Cuyahoga 1974) 40 Ohio App.2d 157, 318 N.E.2d 544, 69 O.O.2d 165. Adoption ☞ 7.7; Adoption ☞ 10

While natural parents entrusted with the permanent custody of their children may deprive a probate court of jurisdiction to enter a decree of adoption by withholding their consent to the adoption, the refusal of consent to an adoption by a "certified agency" as defined in RC 3107.01(C) does not impair the jurisdiction of the probate court to fully hear and determine an adoption proceeding. (See also In re Harshey, 45 App(2d) 97, 341 NE(2d) 616 (1975).) In re Harshey (Cuyahoga 1974) 40 Ohio App.2d 157, 318 N.E.2d 544, 69 O.O.2d 165. Adoption ☞ 7.7

A probate court has jurisdiction to hear and determine an adoption proceeding relating to a minor child notwithstanding the fact that the custody of such child is at the time within the continuing jurisdiction of a divorce court. In re Adoption of Biddle (Ohio 1958) 168 Ohio St. 209, 152 N.E.2d 105, 6 O.O.2d 4, on remand 163 N.E.2d 188, 81 Ohio Law Abs. 529.

Where, in divorce proceedings, one parent is awarded custody of child, consent of that parent, under GC 10512–11 (RC 3107.03), together with consent of court granting divorce, is sufficient consent to adoption of such child, and once such court has granted consent, it loses jurisdiction of child, and subsequent vacation of such consent is ineffective to revest jurisdiction or to prevent adoption.

In re Stromberg's Adoption (Montgomery 1944) 58 N.E.2d 88, 41 Ohio Law Abs. 133.

While courts in one state will enforce a valid custody decree of foreign court rendered in divorce action, in so far as it determines the status of the child at the time it was issued, yet such courts may, if they have jurisdiction, change such award upon facts which have arisen subsequent to the first decree, without consent of such foreign court. In re Adoption of Wyant (Henry 1942) 72 Ohio App. 249, 51 N.E.2d 221, 40 Ohio Law Abs. 164, 27 O.O. 105.

Where a minor child has been awarded to his mother in divorce proceedings, and the mother remarries, her husband adopting the child, the court which granted the divorce loses jurisdiction over the child to make an order affecting its future custody by virtue of GC 10512–11 (RC 3107.03), but still retains jurisdiction of the parties interested in the modification of the support order. Kosen v. Kosen (Cuyahoga 1942) 42 N.E.2d 778, 36 Ohio Law Abs. 156, 23 O.O. 449, appeal dismissed 140 Ohio St. 131, 42 N.E.2d 647, 23 O.O. 459.

A decree of adoption which only shows consent of one of the natural parents, where the statute requires both unless the other is accounted for, is not subject to collateral attack to defeat the right to be the heir of the foster parent; compliance with the requirement is not jurisdictional and is presumed. Taylor v Bushnell, 29 CC(NS) 497, 35 CD 642 (1919).

An Ohio probate court is without jurisdiction to act in adoption proceedings where parties in interest are nonresidents of the state of Ohio, and a former decree unrevoked of a court of another state has awarded the custody of said minor to a foster parent. Such court originally determining such matters has a continuing jurisdiction in the same. 1921 OAG p 955.

4. Power and authority of court

Statutory requirement that juvenile court give its consent to adoption where court has jurisdiction over child and child's guardian is not authorized to give consent does not give court greater power and involvement in adoption proceeding than guardian or agency would have. State ex rel. Hitchcock v. Cuyahoga Cty. Court of Common Pleas, Probate Div. (Ohio App. 8 Dist., 10-07-1994) 97 Ohio App.3d 600, 647 N.E.2d 208. Adoption ☞ 7.1; Infants ☞ 226

A probate court errs in stating it will uphold the denial of consent to adoption by a human services department absent an abuse of discretion by such department, since this constitutes an impermissible delegation of judicial power to the department; the court must independently determine whether an adoption should be granted. In re Adoption of Yoder (Tuscarawas 1989) 62 Ohio App.3d 820, 577 N.E.2d 692, motion overruled 45 Ohio St.3d 710, 545 N.E.2d 905.

While the consent required by RC 3107.06 is not a prerequisite for granting jurisdiction to the pro-bate court in an adoption proceeding, compliance with the statute is. In re Dickhaus (Ohio Com.Pl. 1974) 41 Ohio Misc. 1, 321 N.E.2d 800, 70 O.O.2d 24.

Except in those instances specified in GC 8004–6 (RC 3107.06), a probate court had no power to make a final decree or interlocutory order of adoption of a child where it affirmatively appears that there was not filed with the court a written consent to the adoption by the living mother of such child; and the requirement of such a consent was not dispensed with in an instance where a juvenile court had previously made a valid determination that such child was "neglected." In re Ramsey (Ohio 1956) 164 Ohio St. 567, 132 N.E.2d 469, 58 O.O. 431.

RC 3107.06(D) may not operate to divest the probate court of its necessary judicial power to fully hear and determine an adoption proceeding. State ex rel. Portage County Welfare Dept. v. Summers (Ohio 1974) 38 Ohio St.2d 144, 311 N.E.2d 6, 67 O.O.2d 151.

5. Best interest of child

Probate court was not required to hold hearing, upon filing by incompetent adjudicated father's co-guardians of objections to petition for child's adoption, to consider reasons for such objections and to consider best interest of subject child, where hearing was not required by statute and father's consent to adoption was required and had been denied. In re Adoption of Law (Ohio App. 3 Dist., Allen, 02-13-2006) No. 1-05-64, 2006-Ohio-600, 2006 WL 319141, Unreported. Adoption ☞ 7.7; Adoption ☞ 13

First step of adoption involves determining whether parental consent is required, and the second step requires a determination of whether the adoption is in the best interest of the child. In re Adoption of S.R.A. (Ohio App. 10 Dist., 09-21-2010) 189 Ohio App.3d 363, 938 N.E.2d 432, 2010-Ohio-4435. Adoption ☞ 4; Adoption ☞ 7.2(1)

Even where a probate court finds that the natural father's consent to an adoption is not necessary, a determination of what is in the child's best interests is still required prior to termination of parental rights. In re Adoption of Jones (Medina 1990) 70 Ohio App.3d 576, 591 N.E.2d 823.

Where evidence shows that the social services agency has no substantial reasons for withholding the answer and consent required by RC 3107.06, the court will order the answer and consent filed when the court determines it is in the best interest of the child, but if substantial reasons exist for withholding such answer and consent, and the court is satisfied that it is not in the best interest of the child to require it, the petition for adoption will be denied. In re Dickhaus (Ohio Com.Pl. 1974) 41 Ohio Misc. 1, 321 N.E.2d 800, 70 O.O.2d 24.

The refusal of an agency to consent to an adoption does not deprive the probate court of jurisdiction even when such refusal is not arbitrary, unreasonable, or capricious, and is but an element for consideration in the probate court's determination of the qualifications of the adoptive parents and the best interests of the child. In re Haun (Cuyahoga 1972) 31 Ohio App.2d 63, 286 N.E.2d 478, 60 O.O.2d 163. Adoption ☞ 7.1

6. Support and maintenance of child

Evidence did not support finding in adoption proceeding that biological mother failed to provide for her children's maintenance and support during year preceding filing of adoption petition, as required to allow adoption to proceed without mother's consent, given the non-monetary support that mother provided during her frequent, regularly scheduled visits with children; mother cooked for children when they visited her apartment, or brought pizzas to visitations, and she provided entertainment and brought photo albums and crafts to the visitations, which she allowed children to keep. In re Adoption of L.C.H. (Ohio App. 4 Dist., Scioto, 02-19-2010) No. 09CA3318, No. 09CA3319, No. 09CA3324, 2010-Ohio-643, 2010 WL 628428, Unreported, appeal not allowed 125 Ohio St.3d 1450, 927 N.E.2d 1129, 2010-Ohio-2510. Adoption ☞ 7.4(6)

A natural father's consent is required for adoption by a stepparent where the father has justifiable cause to fail to provide maintenance and support to his children due to a spinal cord injury which severely limits his earning ability. In re Richison (Ohio App. 2 Dist., Montgomery, 06-11-1999) No. 17488, 1999 WL 375587, Unreported.

Fact of incarceration in a penal institution does not constitute a willful failure to properly support and maintain a child so as to vitiate statutory requirement of consent by both natural parents prior to entry of a decree of adoption; although the act that resulted in the imprisonment was voluntary and thus results in a voluntary reduction in income which need not result in a reduction of child support, imprisonment, in and of itself, is not a voluntary lack of support. In re Adoption of C.L.B. (Ohio App. 3 Dist., 10-25-2010) 191 Ohio App.3d 64, 944 N.E.2d 1190, 2010-Ohio-5190. Adoption ☞ 7.4(6)

Evidence supported finding that father's failure to provide support for child for one year prior to maternal grandmother's filing of petition to adopt child was justified, and thus father's consent to adoption was required; a domestic relations court order, which granted temporary custody of child to grandmother, provided that "no child support will be ordered," and thus father was relieved of his duty of support. In re Adoption of W.K.M. (Ohio App. 2 Dist., 05-05-2006) 166 Ohio App.3d 684, 852 N.E.2d 1264, 2006-Ohio-2326. Adoption ☞ 7.4(6)

Domestic relations court's order, awarding temporary custody of child to maternal grandmother and stating that no child support from father would be ordered due to his incarceration, superseded father's statutory duty of child support and provided justifiable cause for his failure to support child during the year prior to grandmother's filing of

adoption petition, and thus father's consent was required for the adoption. In re Adoption of W.K.M. (Ohio App. 2 Dist., 05-05-2006) 166 Ohio App.3d 684, 852 N.E.2d 1264, 2006-Ohio-2326. Adoption ☞ 7.4(6); Child Support ☞ 24

Probate court's order finding that child's father had justifiable cause for failing to support the child for one year prior to filing of maternal grandmother's adoption petition, such that probate court could not grant the adoption petition without father's consent, was a final, appealable order. In re Adoption of W.K.M. (Ohio App. 2 Dist., 05-05-2006) 166 Ohio App.3d 684, 852 N.E.2d 1264, 2006-Ohio-2326. Adoption ☞ 15

Evidence supported finding that mother failed to provide for the maintenance and support of her children, without justifiable cause, during the one year prior to maternal aunt and uncle filing petitions to adopt children, and thus mother's consent was not required for adoption; mother gave son a computer game for his birthday and gave the children clothing and toys for Christmas, maternal aunt and uncle requested $200.00 per week from mother for support of the children, mother never paid any support to aunt and uncle, and mother was employed or able to seek employment during the applicable time period. In re Adoption of James (Ohio Com.Pl., 10-03-2003) 126 Ohio Misc.2d 7, 799 N.E.2d 669, 2003-Ohio-5953. Adoption ☞ 7.4(6)

Father's duty to support child did not begin until date administrative parentage determination became final, nearly a month after mother and stepfather petitioned to adopt child, and, therefore, father's earlier failure to support child did not obviate need to obtain father's consent to adoption. In re Adoption of Hudnell (Ohio App. 4 Dist., 08-06-1996) 113 Ohio App.3d 296, 680 N.E.2d 1055. Adoption ☞ 7.4(6); Children Out-of-wedlock ☞ 21(2)

A father who has supported his illegitimate child must receive notice of an application for adoption; where the father has not been notified until after the thirty-day objection period of RC 3107.06(F)(4), his objection is timely if filed within thirty days of his notice of the proceedings. In re Adoption of Holt (Hamilton 1991) 75 Ohio App.3d 450, 599 N.E.2d 812.

The one-year period of nonsupport prescribed by RC 3107.07(A) which obviates the requirement to obtain parental consent to an adoption pursuant to RC 3107.06 commences on the date that parentage has been judicially established. In re Adoption of Sunderhaus (Ohio 1992) 63 Ohio St.3d 127, 585 N.E.2d 418, rehearing denied 63 Ohio St.3d 1442, 589 N.E.2d 46. Adoption ☞ 7.4(6)

In proceeding for adoption of child of divorced parents, on ground that father had consented to adoption, and on ground that mother had willfully failed to properly support and maintain child for more than two years prior to filing of petition for adoption, burden of proof was on petitioners.

Adoption of Stephen (Darke 1952) 111 N.E.2d 762, 64 Ohio Law Abs. 289. Adoption ☞ 13

Under statute providing that no final decree of adoption shall be made unless by consent of parents or unless both parents have willfully failed to support the child for over two years, mere failure, in and of itself, to pay support of minor children does not constitute willfulness. Poet v. Rosinski (Cuyahoga 1951) 102 N.E.2d 19, 60 Ohio Law Abs. 513, appeal dismissed 155 Ohio St. 510, 99 N.E.2d 320, 44 O.O. 460. Adoption ☞ 7.4(6)

Probate court's finding that mother had justifiable cause for her failure to support her daughter was against the manifest weight of the evidence, and thus mother's consent to adoption was not required, where mother worked full-time as a cashier making $8 or $9 an hour, her husband was also working full-time, making approximately $650 per week, and mother and her husband purchased a house during the year immediately preceding the filing of the petitions for adoption. In re Adoption of Barkhurst (Ohio App. 12 Dist., Butler, 09-04-2002) No. CA2002-04-081, 2002-Ohio-4711, 2002 WL 31009205, Unreported, appeal not allowed 97 Ohio St.3d 1471, 779 N.E.2d 237, 2002-Ohio-6347. Adoption ☞ 7.4(6)

A natural parent's consent to her daughter's adoption is required in light of the contention that the mother failed to provide any monetary support or in kind support for her daughter where the justifiable reason is that the mother has no job and earns no income other than a $512 monthly SSI benefit. In re Adoption of Way (Ohio App. 4 Dist., Washington, 01 09 2002) No. 01CA23, 2002-Ohio-117, 2002 WL 59629, Unreported.

7. Communication with child

Clear and convincing evidence supported finding that biological father had not failed to communicate with child for one year prior to the date stepfather filed his petition to adopt child, and thus father's consent to adoption was required; father attempted to visit child but mother denied his requests, father spoke with mother regarding child at the visitation exchange for their other children, and father saw child at a school play and waved to her but child was grabbed by mother when father got close to child. In re Adoption of Blausenhauer (Ohio App. 5 Dist., Guernsey, 04-17-2009) No. 08 CA 32, 2009-Ohio-1853, 2009 WL 1040301, Unreported. Adoption ☞ 7.8(5)

Application of civil procedure rule which provides that an action is not commenced unless service is effectuated within one year of filing complaint is inconsistent with consent provision within adoption statute, as would support finding that rule does not apply to adoptions; consent provision is an objective determination of abandonment providing that a parent's consent to an adoption is not required if parent fails to communicate with child for period of at least one year prior to filing of adoption petition, and objectivity is lost if one-year abandonment period begins sometime after filing petition, as a parent who opposes an adoption is likely to attempt to contact child after petition is filed. In re Adoption of Goldberg (Ohio App. 12 Dist., Warren, 03-05-2003) No. CA2002-09-091, No. CA2002-09-099, No. CA2002-10-109, 2003-Ohio-1015, 2003 WL 833085, Unreported, appeal not allowed 98 Ohio St.3d 1567, 787 N.E.2d 1231, 2003-Ohio-2242. Adoption ☞ 9.1

Pursuant to the explicit language of RC 3107.07, failure by a parent to communicate with his or her child is sufficient to authorize adoption without that parent's consent only if there is a complete absence of communication for the statutorily defined one-year period. In Matter of Bryant (Ohio App. 4 Dist., Washington, 12-09-1997) No. 97CA635, 1997 WL 766460, Unreported.

A natural unmarried father who was in the physical presence of his child twice within the one-year period immediately preceding the filing of a petition for adoption by the mother's husband constitutes communication with the child and the consent of the natural father in order to effect the adoption is required. In re Adoption of Doe, No. H-93-11, 1993 WL 434681 (6th Dist Ct App, Huron, 10-29-93).

Evidence established that mother communicated with her children in the one-year period prior to maternal aunt and uncle filing petitions to adopt children, and thus mother's consent to adoption of children was required; mother visited each child once, for a period of a few hours, when the child was at maternal grandmother's residence, and mother purchased holiday presents and clothing that maternal grandmother gave to the children. In re Adoption of James (Ohio Com.Pl., 10-03-2003) 126 Ohio Misc.2d 7, 799 N.E.2d 669, 2003-Ohio-5953. Adoption ☞ 7.4(2.1)

Biological father's consent to adoption by stepfather was required, where in the year before the filing of the adoption petition, biological father communicated with the child by telephone at least three times and paid for some birthday gifts and for karate lessons. In re Adoption of Williams (Ohio Prob., 02-04-2002) 117 Ohio Misc.2d 39, 766 N.E.2d 637, 2002-Ohio-1034. Adoption ☞ 7.8(5)

Judgment entry on issue of whether child's biological father had been in communication with child during year prior to filing of petition for child's adoption by husband of child's mother was partial final judgment; while final and appealable when entered, it was appealable alternatively 30 days after court rendered final order on all issues in case. In re Adoption of Eblin (Ohio App. 3 Dist., 03-24-1998) 126 Ohio App.3d 774, 711 N.E.2d 319, appeal allowed 82 Ohio St.3d 1482, 696 N.E.2d 1088, cause dismissed 83 Ohio St.3d 1454, 700 N.E.2d 617. Adoption ☞ 15

Accidental meeting between father and child was "communication" for purposes of adoption statutes requiring parent's consent unless parent has failed without justifiable cause to communicate with child during the year preceding the adoption petition. In re Adoption of Hudnell (Ohio App. 4 Dist.,

08-06-1996) 113 Ohio App.3d 296, 680 N.E.2d 1055. Adoption ☞ 7.4(2.1)

The consent of the natural father is not required in an adoption proceeding under RC 3107.06 and 3107.07 where (1) the father abandoned the mother and child when the child was three; (2) the mother was granted a divorce eight months later and retained full custody of the child; (3) the natural father did not contact the mother until three years after the divorce, after the petitioner had filed the adoption petition, although the mother and the petitioner did not marry until five months later; and (4) the father refused to consent to the adoption; the court's consideration of only one of two dates for calculation of the requisite one-year period during which the parent fails without justifiable cause to communicate with the minor or to provide for the maintenance and support is error, as the entire one-year period should be examined, not just a portion. In re Adoption of Jones (Medina 1990) 70 Ohio App.3d 576, 591 N.E.2d 823.

A probate court could conclude that a petitioner has not carried his burden on the issue of "justifiable cause" for his failure to communicate with his child in RC 3107.07(A) where the natural father establishes prior to the filing of the petition that he was an alcoholic with suicidal tendencies, that once in recovery the father secured employment and tried to contact his ex-wife to arrange for visits with and support payments to the child, that he made contact through an attorney rather than to have a face-to-face confrontation with his ex-wife, and that his ex-wife largely rebuffed his advances, failed to encourage visitation, and employed the adoption process largely as a means of severing his parental rights; the term "justifiable cause" in RC 3107.07 is not a readily defined term and must be determined from the surrounding circumstances of each case. In re Adoption of Jones (Medina 1990) 70 Ohio App.3d 576, 591 N.E.2d 823.

8. Consent must be voluntary

Valid consent to adoption is one which has been freely, knowingly, and voluntarily given with full understanding of adoption process and consequences of one's actions. In re Adoption of Zschach (Ohio, 06-06-1996) 75 Ohio St.3d 648, 665 N.E.2d 1070, reconsideration denied 76 Ohio St.3d 1410, 666 N.E.2d 569, certiorari denied 117 S.Ct. 582, 519 U.S. 1028, 136 L.Ed.2d 513. Adoption ☞ 7.5

When public agency subjects natural parent, who is minor, single, and unrepresented by counsel, to undue influence, and as result of that undue influence, parent signs agreement permanently surrendering her child, parent's consent to agreement is invalid and custody of child remains with parent. In re Adoption of Zschach (Ohio, 06-06-1996) 75 Ohio St.3d 648, 665 N.E.2d 1070, reconsideration denied 76 Ohio St.3d 1410, 666 N.E.2d 569, certiorari denied 117 S.Ct. 582, 519 U.S. 1028, 136 L.Ed.2d 513. Adoption ☞ 7.5

The consent of a natural parent to an adoption must be of the parent's own volition, free from duress or other extraordinary circumstances, and with full understanding of the adoption process. In re Adoption of Infant Girl Banda (Franklin 1988) 53 Ohio App.3d 104, 559 N.E.2d 1373. Adoption ☞ 7.5

The acceptance of attorney fees from adoptive parents by the attorney of the natural mother does not invalidate the consent of the natural mother where she was fully informed of such fees and where the consent was not induced by coercion or undue influence. In re Adoption of Infant Girl Banda (Franklin 1988) 53 Ohio App.3d 104, 559 N.E.2d 1373.

Consent to adoption is voluntary where both consenting parents have attained the age of majority, attend college, and are fully aware of their rights to retain the child and the consequences of signing the consent form. Morrow v. Family & Community Services of Catholic Charities, Inc. (Ohio 1986) 28 Ohio St.3d 247, 504 N.E.2d 2, 28 O.B.R. 327.

9. Agency or institution consent

A petition for adoption, duly filed in accordance with RC 3107.03 is not properly dismissed without a hearing on the merits merely upon a finding by the probate court that a certified agency has not consented to the adoption as required in RC 3107.06. (See also In re Harshey, 45 App(2d) 97, 341 NE(2d) 616 (1975).) In re Harshey (Cuyahoga 1974) 40 Ohio App.2d 157, 318 N.E.2d 544, 69 O.O.2d 165.

Where adoptive parents clearly meet all of the agency's standards concerning maturity, stability, financial ability to carry responsibility, and love of the child, and where the agency placed the child with the adoptive parents from birth to the present time as foster parents, the denial of agency consent based solely upon the age of the adoptive parents is unreasonable, arbitrary, and capricious, and violates the spirit of the whole adoption system while holding to the letter of part of it. In re Haun (Cuyahoga 1972) 31 Ohio App.2d 63, 286 N.E.2d 478, 60 O.O.2d 163.

A child, surrendered by its parents into the permanent custody of an institution established for the purpose of aiding, caring for and placing children in homes, under a written agreement pursuant to RC 5103.15, which agreement provides that the institution may appear in any legal proceeding for the adoption of such child and consent to the child's adoption, continues as an heir of its parents, either natural or adoptive, until such time as the child has been legally adopted pursuant to RC Ch 3107. Maurer v. Becker (Ohio 1971) 26 Ohio St.2d 254, 271 N.E.2d 255, 55 O.O.2d 486. Adoption ☞ 21

An answer and consent signed and verified by the executive secretary of the child welfare board is sufficient compliance with RC 3107.06 to authorize the court to enter a decree of adoption. In re Adoption of Wyatt (Ohio Prob. 1965) 4 Ohio Misc. 47, 210 N.E.2d 925, 33 O.O.2d 27.

Where the parents of a child make an agreement surrendering such child into the permanent custody of an association or institution of this state, established for the purposes of aiding, caring for, and placing children in homes, and approved and certified by the division of social administration of the department of public welfare, in writing on a form prescribed and furnished by such division, and authorizes the association or institution to appear in any proceeding for the legal adoption of such child and consent to its adoption without fraud or misrepresentation, and the association or institution accepts, the agreement is irrevocable except with the consent of the association or institution even though one of the parents was a minor. Kozak v. Lutheran Children's Aid Soc. (Ohio 1955) 164 Ohio St. 335, 130 N.E.2d 796, 58 O.O. 125.

The consent to adoption of a county child welfare board required under RC 3107.06 can be given by a majority of a quorum of the board, but not by the executive secretary to the board. OAG 65–24.

Under the provisions of GC 8025 (Repealed), a New York society can give the legal consent to the adoption in Ohio of a child, if and when said society has received the certificate mentioned in GC 1352–1 (RC 5103.03) and has fully complied with the provisions of GC 1677 (Repealed). 1922 OAG p 518.

10. Establishment of paternity

Administrative proceeding initiated by Child Support Enforcement Agency (CSEA), resulting in issuance of administrative order establishment of paternity and finding that parent-child relationship existed between adjudicated father and child, was sufficient to establish paternity, for purposes of statutes establishing requirements for consent to adoption. In re Adoption of Law (Ohio App. 3 Dist., Allen, 02-13-2006) No. 1-05-64, 2006-Ohio-600, 2006 WL 319141, Unreported. Adoption ⟲ 7.2(3)

The probate court was required to refrain from proceeding with stepfather's petition to adopt child while biological father's paternity proceeding was pending in juvenile court. In re Adoption of P.A.C. (Ohio, 07-22-2010) 126 Ohio St.3d 236, 933 N.E.2d 236, 2010-Ohio-3351, reconsideration denied 126 Ohio St.3d 1592, 934 N.E.2d 939, 2010-Ohio-4880. Adoption ⟲ 9.1

One year period of nonsupport which obviates requirement to obtain parent's consent to adoption by another commences on date of the paternity adjudication. In re Adoption of McNutt (Ohio App. 4 Dist., 09-27-1999) 134 Ohio App.3d 822, 732 N.E.2d 470. Adoption ⟲ 7.4(6)

Paternity was established, within meaning of adoption statute requiring father's consent, when administrative determination of parentage was made, even though order did not become final for 30 days. In re Adoption of Hudnell (Ohio App. 4 Dist., 08-06-1996) 113 Ohio App.3d 296, 680 N.E.2d 1055. Adoption ⟲ 7.2(3)

Prescriptive one-year period after which natural father may be deemed to have abandoned child so that natural father's consent is not necessary to

child's adoption commences running not upon birth of child, but upon determination of paternity, so that father's actions regarding communication and support were to be analyzed from date of declaration of paternity, where father's parentage action was filed and determined prior to filing of adoption petition. In re Adoption of Sherry (Ohio App. 9 Dist., 12-20-1995) 107 Ohio App.3d 830, 669 N.E.2d 551. Adoption ⟲ 7.2(3)

The natural father of a child, the subject of an adoption proceeding, who, as an active member of the armed forces is stationed in another state, is not entitled to notice of the proposed placement or adoption of his child where the father is not married to the mother of the child, has made no attempt to acknowledge his paternity prior to an untimely filed objection to the adoption, and where there is no evidence that the father was prevented from timely filing an adoption due to fraud or legal disability. In re Adoption of Baby Girl Hudnall (Franklin 1991) 71 Ohio App.3d 376, 594 N.E.2d 45.

11. Putative father, generally

Putative father was a necessary party to adoption proceeding brought by prospective stepfather, seeking to adopt minor son of his fiancee and, as such, consent of putative father was necessary for the adoption, where putative father's action to determine parentage was pending in juvenile court when prospective stepfather filed his adoption petition in the probate court, adoption proceeding should, therefore, have been stayed, juvenile court adjudicated putative father's paternity, and probate court was required to give effect to the juvenile court's determination. In re Adoption of G.B. (Ohio App. 3 Dist., Seneca, 10-18-2010) No. 13-10-01, 2010-Ohio-5059, 2010 WL 4055551, Unreported. Adoption ⟲ 7.2(3); Adoption ⟲ 9.1; Adoption ⟲ 11

Putative father's argument with respect to constitutionality of state's putative father statutory scheme was not properly before trial court on putative father's motion to vacate adoption, where putative father failed to serve copy of his motion upon Attorney General as required by statute. In re Adoption of Coppersmith (Ohio App. 2 Dist., 08-24-2001) 145 Ohio App.3d 141, 761 N.E.2d 1163, 2001-Ohio-1484. Adoption ⟲ 2

Putative father was entitled, under circumstances of the case, to opportunity to amend his motion to vacate child's adoption, to allege unconstitutionality of state's putative father statutory scheme and properly to serve the Attorney General as required by statute; putative father was child's biological parent, child was adopted by step-parent without his knowledge, after notice by publication, putative father moved to vacate adoption on ground of insufficient notice, and step-parent argued application of allegedly unconstitutional statute purporting to obviate notice requirement. In re Adoption of Coppersmith (Ohio App. 2 Dist., 08-24-2001) 145 Ohio App.3d 141, 761 N.E.2d 1163, 2001-Ohio-1484. Adoption ⟲ 2; Adoption ⟲ 16

Putative father's failure to strictly comply with time limits of statute due to misleading notice sent out by court did not preclude his filing of objection to adoption within time frame set out in notice and delay was excusable due to putative father's incarceration. In re Adoption of Bowes (Ohio App. 11 Dist., 08-07-1995) 105 Ohio App.3d 574, 664 N.E.2d 963. Adoption ☞ 7.2(3)

Mother's notification to putative father concerning proposed adoption satisfied due process, justifying dismissal of putative father's untimely objection to adoption; putative father was not entitled to additional notice from probate court of child's placement with adoptive parents, absent evidence that putative father had participated in rearing of child or had otherwise provided any care or support, and there was no evidence that putative father was prevented from filing objection because of either fraud or legal disability. In re Adoption of Baby Boy Dearing (Ohio App. 9 Dist., 10-26-1994) 98 Ohio App.3d 197, 648 N.E.2d 57, dismissed, appeal not allowed 71 Ohio St.3d 1492, 646 N.E.2d 467. Adoption ☞ 12; Constitutional Law ☞ 4395

Probate court order allowing adoption to proceed without putative father's consent was a final, appealable order as an order that affected a substantial right made in a special proceeding. In re Adoption of Greer (Ohio, 09-21-1994) 70 Ohio St.3d 293, 638 N.E.2d 999, 1994-Ohio-69. Adoption ☞ 15

To preserve right to withheld consent to child's adoption and avoid finding that requirement of father's consent shall be excused, putative father who has signed birth certificate must file objection to adoption with court, department or agency having custody of child, but his objection need not be filed within 30 days of earlier of date of filing of adoption petition or placement of child. In re Adoption of Greer (Ohio, 09-21-1994) 70 Ohio St.3d 293, 638 N.E.2d 999, 1994-Ohio-69. Adoption ☞ 7.3

Unless statutory requirement to consent of adoption is excused by virtue of failure of putative father to file objection, a putative father who has signed birth certificate as informant has statutory right to withhold consent to adoption of that child, thereby barring child's adoption by another. In re Adoption of Greer (Ohio, 09-21-1994) 70 Ohio St.3d 293, 638 N.E.2d 999, 1994-Ohio-69. Adoption ☞ 7.2(3)

A probate court's failure to consider a putative father's objection to adoption which is filed before entry of the final decree of adoption is not erroneous where the putative father's objection is not filed within thirty days of placement of the minor as set forth in RC 3107.06(F); thus, the putative father's consent was not necessary in order for the court to proceed with the adoption. In re Adoption of Hall (Franklin 1991) 72 Ohio App.3d 503, 595 N.E.2d 473.

Where notice of an adoption petition sent to a putative father states that any objections must be filed on or before the hearing date, rather than within thirty days of the filing of the adoption

petition, and the putative father files objections to the adoption eleven days prior to the hearing, it is a violation of due process for the trial court to find the putative father's consent unnecessary for failure to timely object. In re Adoption of Greer, No. 5–92–34 (3d Dist Ct App, Hancock, 3–16–93).

12. Registration by putative father

Adjudicated father's failure to register as putative father was irrelevant to determination of whether his consent to child's adoption was required, where adjudication of paternity established existence of parent-child relationship. In re Adoption of Law (Ohio App. 3 Dist., Allen, 02-13-2006) No. 1-05-64, 2006-Ohio-600, 2006 WL 319141, Unreported. Adoption ☞ 7.2(3)

Evidence supported trial court determination that prospective adoptive parents failed to establish that putative father willfully abandoned birth mother of child, which would have allowed adoptive parents to proceed with adoption of child without the consent of putative father; birth mother testified that father attempted to make doctor's appointments for her, that after she moved out of house with father he moved into a house next door to her, that she continued to see and talk to father, that father attempted to talk to her after the parties obtained mutual protective orders against each other, and father gave birth mother money while he was in jail and registered with the putative father registry. In re Adoption of Baby F. (Ohio App. 10 Dist., Franklin, 04-13-2004) No. 03AP-1092, No. 03AP-1132, 2004-Ohio-1871, 2004 WL 771575, Unreported, appeal not allowed 102 Ohio St.3d 1486, 810 N.E.2d 968, 2004-Ohio-3069. Adoption ☞ 7.4(2.1)

If a child's putative father fails to register within the statutory 30–day period, then his child may be adopted by another person without his consent; in fact, he is not even entitled to notice of the pending adoption proceeding. In re Adoption of Coppersmith (Ohio App. 2 Dist., 08-24-2001) 145 Ohio App.3d 141, 761 N.E.2d 1163, 2001-Ohio-1484. Adoption ☞ 7.3

Consent to adoption is not required of putative father who fails to register within thirty days of child's birth if he is still a putative father when petition for adoption is filed, but if a putative father judicially establishes parentage prior to the filing of adoption petition, he ceases to be a putative father and his consent is required based on parent and child relationship with minor. In re Adoption of Baby Boy Brooks (Ohio App. 10 Dist., 03-21-2000) 136 Ohio App.3d 824, 737 N.E.2d 1062, appeal not allowed 89 Ohio St.3d 1433, 730 N.E.2d 383. Adoption ☞ 7.2(3)

13. Withdrawal of consent

Clear and convincing evidence established that birth mother's consent to adoption of child was given under circumstances constituting duress, and thus, affidavit purporting to give mother's consent to adoption was invalid and adoption decree was void as lacking requisite valid parental consent to adoption; mother believed it was very dangerous for her daughter, as a Vietnamese–American child born out of wedlock, to remain in Vietnam, and mother's "consent" to adoption was result of duress caused by her concern for life of child, and mother signed adoption consent affidavit, written in English, without legal advice and with limited understanding as to its consequences. In re Adoption of Baby Girl E. (Ohio App. 10 Dist., Franklin, 07-14-2005) No. 04AP932, 2005-Ohio-3565, 2005 WL 1652344, Unreported, stay granted 106 Ohio St.3d 1475, 832 N.E.2d 60, 2005-Ohio-3953, appeal not allowed 107 Ohio St.3d 1423, 837 N.E.2d 1208, 2005-Ohio-6124. Adoption ☞ 7.5

Revocation of a natural parent's consent to adoption is not shown where, after repeated questioning, the custodial parent testifies that it may be in the child's best interest to become reacquainted with the noncustodial parent before the child decides whether he wants to be adopted by a stepparent. In re Adoption of Carletti (Muskingum 1992) 78 Ohio App.3d 244, 604 N.E.2d 243, motion overruled 65 Ohio St.3d 1457, 602 N.E.2d 253.

A petition in habeas corpus seeking to revoke a natural parent's consent to an adoption will be denied where the issues raised have already been determined in an action to revoke consent and an appeal from such action. McGinty v. Jewish Children's Bureau (Ohio 1989) 46 Ohio St.3d 159, 545 N.E.2d 1272.

Approval by the court of the permanent surrender of a child is purely an administrative matter, and not in the nature of an adversary proceeding; the court has no duty to advise the mother of her right to counsel or to appoint a lawyer for her in the event of indigency. In re K. (Ohio Juv. 1969) 31 Ohio Misc. 218, 282 N.E.2d 370, 60 O.O.2d 134, 60 O.O.2d 388.

Where a mother, as sole parent, files an "application for placement" and a written waiver and consent to adoption in the probate court to place her newborn baby with a married couple whose identity she did not know but who were procured by an intermediary at her request with adoption in mind, appears in person before such court for approval of such placement, and the probate court, after an independent investigation of the proposed placement by a qualified person determines that it is in the best interest of the child and approves of record the proposed placement, and the child is delivered to the married couple pursuant to the order of the court, the mother, as petitioner in a habeas corpus action filed in the court of common pleas to regain custody of her child, is estopped from claiming that the probate court was without jurisdiction by reason of an insufficient application in not identifying by names the placement parents; and a finding by the court of common pleas of lack of such jurisdiction is reversible error. In re McTaggart (Cuyahoga 1965) 4 Ohio App.2d 359, 212 N.E.2d 663, 33 O.O.2d 447.

Consent to adoption by the mother of a child is necessary in order to confer jurisdiction to enter the adoption order, and the lack of such consent

may be asserted in a habeas corpus proceeding. In re Martin (Cuyahoga 1957) 140 N.E.2d 623, 76 Ohio Law Abs. 219.

Where one of the parents had been awarded divorce and custody of child, and other parent had failed or refused to support such child for two consecutive years prior to proceeding to adopt child, the consent, under the statute, of former to such adoption is sufficient, notwithstanding failure of court which awarded such divorce and custody to approve such consent; and as the consents prescribed by subdivisions (a) and (d) of the second provision of the statute are cumulative, consent complying with former subdivision need not comply with latter. In re Adoption of Wyant (Henry 1942) 72 Ohio App. 249, 51 N.E.2d 221, 40 Ohio Law Abs. 164, 27 O.O. 105.

An interlocutory order of adoption is erroneously entered after the putative father of the minor child who signed the birth certificate objects to the adoption, and consequently, a mother's motion to withdraw her consent to the adoption is not time barred pursuant to RC 3107.09. In re Adoption of Zschach, Nos. 1994CA-14+, 1994 WL 728626 (5th Dist Ct App, Fairfield, 12–19–94), reversed by 75 Ohio St.3d 648 (1996).

Mother of illegitimate child has right to withdraw her consent to an adoption of her child at any time before the court acts upon such consent and in so doing dismisses the petition for the adoption of the child and deprives the court of proceeding further with the case. In re Adoption of Rubin, 33 Abs 108 (Prob, Belmont 1941).

Consent to the adoption of an illegitimate child may be withdrawn by the mother. In re O— (Ohio Juv. 1964) 199 N.E.2d 765, 95 Ohio Law Abs. 101, 28 O.O.2d 165.

Placement of an illegitimate child for adoption and subsequent withdrawal of consent thereto by the mother does not of itself warrant a finding that the child is neglected. In re O—(Ohio Juv. 1964) 199 N.E.2d 765, 95 Ohio Law Abs. 101, 28 O.O.2d 165.

Consent of the mother in writing at the time of the decree, if she is accessible, is necessary to a decree for adoption by petition; and her previous consent may be revoked at any time before decree. State ex rel Scholder v Scholder, 22 LR 608 (1924).

A mother who is a minor under twenty-one years of age may lawfully give her consent to the adoption of her child, under this section, and may also surrender such child under GC 1352-12 and 1352-13 (RC 5103.15 and 5103.16). 1930 OAG 1584.

14. Objections to adoption

Putative father's attempt to condition his consent to adoption upon his retention of permanent visitation rights was not written objection to adoption, required to preserve his right to contest adoption. In re Adoption of Zschach (Ohio, 06-06-1996) 75 Ohio St.3d 648, 665 N.E.2d 1070, reconsideration denied 76 Ohio St.3d 1410, 666 N.E.2d 569, certiorari denied 117 S.Ct. 582, 519 U.S. 1028, 136 L.Ed.2d 513. Adoption ☞ 7.3

The filing of the acknowledgement of paternity pursuant to RC 2105.18 accompanied by the filing of an objection to adoption pursuant to RC 3107.06(F)(4) is sufficient to place the father within the purview of RC 3107.07(A) as a parent and not within RC 3107(B). In re Adoption of Dickson, No. 94–CA–57, 1995 WL 495450 (5th Dist Ct App, Fairfield, 5–19–95).

Verbal objections made over the telephone by a putative father to the department of human services do not constitute the "filing" of an objection satisfying RC 3107.06. In re Adoption of Eckleberry, No. 94APF10–1523, 1995 WL 311409 (10th Dist Ct App, Franklin, 5–11–95).

A putative father who fails to preserve his rights to contest an adoption by filing an objection within the time limits prescribed by RC 3107.06 has no parental rights and, as such, is due no process. In re Adoption of Eckleberry, No. 94APF10–1523, 1995 WL 311409 (10th Dist Ct App, Franklin, 5–11–95).

3107.061 Adoption of child without putative father's consent

A man who has sexual intercourse with a woman is on notice that if a child is born as a result and the man is the putative father, the child may be adopted without his consent pursuant to division (B) of section 3107.07 of the Revised Code.

(1996 H 419, eff. 6–20–96)

Library References

Adoption ☞7.2(3), 7.3.
Westlaw Topic No. 17.
C.J.S. Adoption of Persons §§ 56 to 58, 62.

Research References

Encyclopedias

OH Jur. 3d Family Law § 881, Who Must Consent.

Forms

Ohio Forms Legal and Business § 28:24, Introduction.

Ohio Jurisprudence Pleading and Practice Forms § 96:9, Putative Father Registry.

Treatises and Practice Aids

Carlin, Baldwin's Ohio Prac. Merrick-Rippner Probate Law § 6:4, Action--Parties.

Carlin, Baldwin's Ohio Prac. Merrick-Rippner Probate Law § 99:30, Statutorily Required Consent.

Carlin, Baldwin's Ohio Prac. Merrick-Rippner Probate Law § 99:32, Parties Giving Consent--Putative Father.

Carlin, Baldwin's Ohio Prac. Merrick-Rippner Probate Law § 99:38, Consent Not Required--Statutory Scheme.

Law Review and Journal Commentaries

Ohio House Bill 419: Increased Openness in Adoption Records Law, Wendy L. Weiss. 45 Clev St L Rev 101 (1997).

3107.062 Putative father registry

The department of job and family services shall establish a putative father registry. To register, a putative father must complete a registration form prescribed under section 3107.065 of the Revised Code and submit it to the department. The registration form shall include the putative father's name; the address or telephone number at which he wishes to receive, pursuant to section 3107.11 of the Revised Code, notice of a petition to adopt the minor he claims as his child; and the name of the mother of the minor.

A putative father may register before or not later than thirty days after the birth of the child. No fee shall be charged for registration.

On receipt of a completed registration form, the department shall indicate on the form the date of receipt and file it in the putative father registry. The department shall maintain registration forms in a manner that enables it to access a registration form using either the name of the putative father or of the mother.

(1999 H 471, eff. 7–1–00; 1996 H 274, eff. 9–18–96; 1996 H 419, eff. 9–18–96)

Historical and Statutory Notes

Amendment Note: 1999 H 471 substituted "job and family" for "human" in the first paragraph.

Amendment Note: 1996 H 274 substituted "not later than thirty days" for ", to the extent provided by division (B)(1) of section 3107.07 of the Revised Code," in the second paragraph.

Cross References

Availability of state government public records, public records defined, see 149.43

Personal information systems, right to inspection of putative father registry, see 1347.08

Uniform Interstate Family Support Act, bases for jurisdiction over nonresident, see 3115.03

Ohio Administrative Code References

Putative father registry, see OAC 5101:2–48–02

Library References

Adoption ☞7.2(3).
Westlaw Topic No. 17.
C.J.S. Adoption of Persons § 56.

Research References

ALR Library

5 ALR 6th 193, Construction and Application of Interstate Compact on the Placement of Children.

Encyclopedias

OII Jur. 3d Defamation & Privacy § 183, Exceptions.

OH Jur. 3d Family Law § 882, Putative Father Registry.

OH Jur. 3d Family Law § 889, Who Need Not Consent.

OH Jur. 3d Family Law § 1228, Restrictions on Use of Information; Confidentiality.

OH Jur. 3d Family Law § 1247, Access to Information; Restrictions on Use and Confidentiality.

Forms

Ohio Jurisprudence Pleading and Practice Forms § 48:7, Public Records.

Ohio Jurisprudence Pleading and Practice Forms § 96:9, Putative Father Registry.

Treatises and Practice Aids

Klein, Darling, & Terez, Baldwin's Ohio Practice Civil Practice § 4.3:23, Primary Ohio Long-Arm Provisions in General--The Various Ohio Long-Arm Provisions.

Sowald & Morganstern, Baldwin's Ohio Practice Domestic Relations Law § 23:28, UIFSA--Long-Arm Provisions.

Carlin, Baldwin's Ohio Prac. Merrick-Rippner Probate Law § 6:4, Action--Parties.

Carlin, Baldwin's Ohio Prac. Merrick-Rippner Probate Law § 99:30, Statutorily Required Consent.

Carlin, Baldwin's Ohio Prac. Merrick-Rippner Probate Law § 99:32, Parties Giving Consent--Putative Father.

Carlin, Baldwin's Ohio Prac. Merrick-Rippner Probate Law § 99:34, Parties Giving Consent--Agency.

Carlin, Baldwin's Ohio Prac. Merrick-Rippner Probate Law § 99:38, Consent Not Required--Statutory Scheme.

Carlin, Baldwin's Ohio Prac. Merrick-Rippner Probate Law § 99:40, Consent Not Required--Putative Father.

Carlin, Baldwin's Ohio Prac. Merrick-Rippner Probate Law App B SPF 18.3, Consent to Adoption--Form.

Hennenberg & Reinhart, Ohio Criminal Defense Motions F 2:44, Motion for Sanctions for Violations of R.C. Chapter 149 [Public Records Act]--Discovery Demands and Motions.

Hennenberg & Reinhart, Ohio Criminal Defense Motions F 2:46, Motion to Inspect Public Records--Discovery Demands and Motions.

Gotherman & Babbit, Ohio Municipal Law § 6:12, Exceptions to General Rule.

Law Review and Journal Commentaries

A National Putative Father Registry. Mary Beck, 36 Cap. U. L. Rev. 295 (Winter 2007).

Ohio House Bill 419: Increased Openness in Adoption Records Law, Wendy L. Weiss. 45 Clev St L Rev 101 (1997).

Unmarried Fathers and Adoption: "Perfecting" or "Abandoning" an Opportunity Interest. Laura Oren, 36 Cap. U. L. Rev. 253 (Winter 2007).

Notes of Decisions

---

1. Time period for registration

If a child's putative father fails to register within the statutory 30–day period, then his child may be adopted by another person without his consent; in fact, he is not even entitled to notice of the pending adoption proceeding. In re Adoption of Coppersmith (Ohio App. 2 Dist., 08-24-2001) 145 Ohio App.3d 141, 761 N.E.2d 1163, 2001-Ohio-1484. Adoption ☞ 7.3

3107.063   Request to search registry

A mother or an agency or attorney arranging a minor's adoption may request at any time that the department of job and family services search the putative father registry to determine whether a man is registered as the minor's putative father. The request shall include the mother's name. On receipt of the request, the department shall search the registry. If the department determines that a man is registered as the minor's putative father, it shall provide the mother, agency, or attorney a certified copy of the man's registration form. If the department determines that no man is registered as the minor's putative father, it shall provide the mother, agency, or attorney a certified written statement to that effect. The department shall specify in the statement the date the search request was submitted. No fee shall be charged for searching the registry.

Division (B) of section 3107.17 of the Revised Code does not apply to this section.

(1999 H 471, eff. 7–1–00; 1996 H 274, eff. 9–18–96; 1996 H 419, eff. 9–18–96)

Historical and Statutory Notes

Amendment Note: 1999 H 471 substituted "job and family" for "human" in the first paragraph.

Amendment Note: 1996 H 274 deleted "Not sooner than thirty one days after the birth of a minor," from the beginning of, and inserted "at any time" in, the first sentence in the first paragraph; and made other nonsubstantive changes.

Library References

Adoption ☞7.2(3).
Westlaw Topic No. 17.
C.J.S. Adoption of Persons § 56.

Research References

Encyclopedias

OH Jur. 3d Family Law § 882, Putative Father Registry.

Forms

Ohio Forms Legal and Business § 28:24, Introduction.

Ohio Jurisprudence Pleading and Practice Forms § 96:9, Putative Father Registry.

3107.064   Required search of registry prior to adoption; exceptions

(A) Except as provided in division (B) of this section, a court shall not issue a final decree of adoption or finalize an interlocutory order of adoption unless the mother placing the minor for adoption or the agency or attorney arranging the adoption files with the court a certified document provided by the department of job and family services under section 3107.063 of the Revised Code. The court shall not accept the document unless the date the department places on the document pursuant to that section is thirty-one or more days after the date of the minor's birth.

(B) The document described in division (A) of this section is not required if any of the following apply:

(1) The mother was married at the time the minor was conceived or born;

(2) The parent placing the minor for adoption previously adopted the minor;

(3) Prior to the date a petition to adopt the minor is filed, a man has been determined to have a parent and child relationship with the minor by a court proceeding pursuant to sections 3111.01 to 3111.18 of the Revised Code, a court proceeding in another state, an administrative agency proceeding pursuant to sections 3111.38 to 3111.54 of the Revised Code, or an administrative agency proceeding in another state;

(4) The minor's father acknowledged paternity of the minor and that acknowledgment has become final pursuant to section 2151.232, 3111.25, or 3111.821 of the Revised Code;

(5) A public children services agency has permanent custody of the minor pursuant to Chapter 2151. or division (B) of section 5103.15 of the Revised Code after both parents lost or surrendered parental rights, privileges, and responsibilities over the minor.

(2000 S 180, eff. 3–22–01; 1999 H 471, eff. 7–1–00; 1997 H 352, eff. 1–1–98; 1996 H 274, eff. 9–18–96; 1996 H 419, eff. 9–18–96)

Historical and Statutory Notes

Amendment Note: 2000 S 180 substituted "3111.18" for "3111.19", "3111.38" for "3111.20" and "3111.54" for "3111.29" in division (B)(3); and substituted "3111.25" for "3111.211" and "3111.821" for "5101.314" in division (B)(4).

Amendment Note: 1999 H 471 substituted "job and family" for "human" in division (A).

Amendment Note: 1997 H 352 rewrote division (B)(4), which prior thereto read:

"(4) The minor's father acknowledged paternity of the minor pursuant to section 2105.18 of the Revised Code."

Amendment Note: 1996 H 274 added the second sentence in division (A); added division (B)(4); and redesignated former division (B)(4) as division (B)(5).

Library References

Adoption ☞7.2(3), 13.
Westlaw Topic No. 17.

C.J.S. Adoption of Persons §§ 46 to 47, 56, 93 to 102.

Research References

Encyclopedias

OH Jur. 3d Family Law § 882, Putative Father Registry.

Forms

Ohio Forms Legal and Business § 28:24, Introduction.
Ohio Jurisprudence Pleading and Practice Forms § 96:9, Putative Father Registry.

Treatises and Practice Aids

Carlin, Baldwin's Ohio Prac. Merrick-Rippner Probate Law § 19:4, Legitimation--Historical Provisions.
Carlin, Baldwin's Ohio Prac. Merrick-Rippner Probate Law § 99:32, Parties Giving Consent--Putative Father.
Carlin, Baldwin's Ohio Prac. Merrick-Rippner Probate Law § 99:34, Parties Giving Consent--Agency.

Notes of Decisions

Putative father registration   1

1. Putative father registration

Notice to a putative father of a pending adoption is not required if the he fails to register on the putative father registry. In re K.M.S. (Ohio App. 2 Dist., Miami, 09-09-2005) No. 05CA17, 2005-Ohio-4739, 2005 WL 2179297, Unreported. Adoption ☞ 12

Putative father's consent to child's adoption by mother's husband was not required; adoption stat-

ute provided that putative father's consent to adoption of child was not required if he failed to register as child's putative father within 30 days of child's birth, and husband filed certified written statement from Department of Job and Family Services that no man was registered on putative father registry as child's father, as required by statute. In re K.M.S. (Ohio App. 2 Dist., Miami, 09-09-2005) No. 05CA17, 2005-Ohio-4739, 2005 WL 2179297, Unreported. Adoption ☞ 7.2(3)

3107.065 Rules, registration form, and informational campaign for registry

Not later than ninety days after the effective date of this section, the director of job and family services shall do both of the following:

(A) Adopt rules in accordance with Chapter 119. of the Revised Code governing the putative father registry. The rules shall establish the registration form to be used by a putative father under section 3107.062 of the Revised Code.

(B) Establish a campaign to promote awareness of the putative father registry. The campaign shall include informational materials about the registry.

(1999 H 471, eff. 7–1–00; 1996 H 419, eff. 6–20–96)

Historical and Statutory Notes

Amendment Note: 1999 H 471 substituted "director of job and family services" for "department of human services" in the introductory paragraph.

Library References

Adoption ☞7.2(3).
Infants ☞17.
Westlaw Topic Nos. 17, 211.

C.J.S. Adoption of Persons §§ 10 to 14, 41, 56.
C.J.S. Infants §§ 6, 8 to 9.

Research References

Encyclopedias

OH Jur. 3d Family Law § 882, Putative Father Registry.

3107.066   Prior law applicability

(A) Notwithstanding the provisions of the versions of former sections 3107.06 and 3107.07 of the Revised Code that, pursuant to Section 5 of Am. Sub. H.B. 419 of the 121st general assembly, apply regarding a putative father's consent to the adoption of any child born prior to January 1, 1997, on and after the effective date of this section, both of the following apply:

(1) The references in division (F)(4) of former section 3107.06 of the Revised Code to the department of human services are repealed, and division (F)(4) of that former section shall be considered as reading, and shall be applicable, as follows: "Has filed an objection to the adoption with the agency having custody of the minor at any time before the placement of the minor in the home of the petitioner, or with the probate court within thirty days of the filing of a petition to adopt the minor or its placement in the home of the petitioner, whichever occurs first."

(2) The references in division (B) of former section 3107.07 of the Revised Code to the department of human services are repealed, and division (B) of that former section shall be considered as reading, and shall be applicable, as follows: "The putative father of a minor if the putative father fails to file an objection with the court or the agency having custody of the minor as provided in division (F)(4) of section 3107.06 of the Revised Code, or files an objection with the court or agency and the court finds, after proper service of notice and hearing, that he is not the father of the minor, or that he has willfully abandoned or failed to care for and support the minor, or abandoned the mother of the minor during her pregnancy and up to the time of her surrender of the minor, or its placement in the home of the petitioner, whichever occurs first."

(B) As used in this section:

(1) "Former section 3107.06 of the Revised Code" means the version of that section that was in effect immediately prior to September 18, 1996, and that was amended by Am. Sub. H.B. 419 of the 121st general assembly.

(2) "Former section 3107.07 of the Revised Code" means the version of that section that was in effect immediately prior to September 18, 1996, and that was amended by Am. Sub. H.B. 419 of the 121st general assembly.

(2008 S 163, eff. 8–14–08)

3107.07   Consents not required

Consent to adoption is not required of any of the following:

(A) A parent of a minor, when it is alleged in the adoption petition and the court, after proper service of notice and hearing, finds by clear and convincing evidence that the parent has failed without justifiable cause to provide more than de minimis contact with the minor or to provide for the maintenance and support of the minor as required by law or judicial decree for a period of at least one year immediately preceding either the filing of the adoption petition or the placement of the minor in the home of the petitioner.

(B) The putative father of a minor if either of the following applies:

(1) The putative father fails to register as the minor's putative father with the putative father registry established under section 3107.062 of the Revised Code not later than thirty days after the minor's birth;

(2) The court finds, after proper service of notice and hearing, that any of the following are the case:

(a) The putative father is not the father of the minor;

(b) The putative father has willfully abandoned or failed to care for and support the minor;

(c) The putative father has willfully abandoned the mother of the minor during her pregnancy and up to the time of her surrender of the minor, or the minor's placement in the home of the petitioner, whichever occurs first.

(C) Except as provided in section 3107.071 of the Revised Code, a parent who has entered into a voluntary permanent custody surrender agreement under division (B) of section 5103.15 of the Revised Code;

(D) A parent whose parental rights have been terminated by order of a juvenile court under Chapter 2151. of the Revised Code;

(E) A parent who is married to the petitioner and supports the adoption;

(F) The father, or putative father, of a minor if the minor is conceived as the result of the commission of rape by the father or putative father and the father or putative father is convicted of or pleads guilty to the commission of that offense. As used in this division, "rape" means a violation of section 2907.02 of the Revised Code or a similar law of another state.

(G) A legal guardian or guardian ad litem of a parent judicially declared incompetent in a separate court proceeding who has failed to respond in writing to a request for consent, for a period of thirty days, or who, after examination of the written reasons for withholding consent, is found by the court to be withholding consent unreasonably;

(H) Any legal guardian or lawful custodian of the person to be adopted, other than a parent, who has failed to respond in writing to a request for consent, for a period of thirty days, or who, after examination of the written reasons for withholding consent, is found by the court to be withholding consent unreasonably;

(I) The spouse of the person to be adopted, if the failure of the spouse to consent to the adoption is found by the court to be by reason of prolonged unexplained absence, unavailability, incapacity, or circumstances that make it impossible or unreasonably difficult to obtain the consent or refusal of the spouse;

(J) Any parent, legal guardian, or other lawful custodian in a foreign country, if the person to be adopted has been released for adoption pursuant to the laws of the country in which the person resides and the release of such person is in a form that satisfies the requirements of the immigration and naturalization service of the United States department of justice for purposes of immigration to the United States pursuant to section 101(b)(1)(F) of the "Immigration and Nationality Act," 75 Stat. 650 (1961), 8 U.S.C. 1101(b)(1)(F), as amended or reenacted.

(K) Except as provided in divisions (G) and (H) of this section, a juvenile court, agency, or person given notice of the petition pursuant to division (A)(1) of section 3107.11 of the

Revised Code that fails to file an objection to the petition within fourteen days after proof is filed pursuant to division (B) of that section that the notice was given;

(L) Any guardian, custodian, or other party who has temporary custody of the child.

(2008 H 7, eff. 4-7-09; 1999 H 176, eff. 10–29–99; 1998 H 484, eff. 3–18–99; 1996 H 274, eff. 9–18–96; 1996 H 419, eff. 9–18–96; 1986 H 428, eff. 12–23–86; 1980 S 205; 1977 H 1; 1976 H 156)

Uncodified Law

1996 H 419, § 5: See Uncodified Law under 3107.06.

Historical and Statutory Notes

Ed. Note: 3107.07 contains provisions analogous to former 3107.06, repealed by 1976 H 156, eff. 1–1–77.

Ed. Note: Former 3107.07 repealed by 1976 H 156, eff. 1–1–77; 1953 H 1; GC 8004–7; Source— GC 10512–17.

Pre–1953 H 1 Amendments: 124 v S 65

Amendment Note: 2008 H 7 deleted "finds" after "court", inserted "finds by clear and convincing evidence" after "hearing," and substituted "provide more than de minimis contact" for "communicate" after "cause to" in division (A); and made a non-substantive change.

Amendment Note: 1999 H 176 substituted "(A)(1)" for "(A)(2)" in division (K).

Amendment Note: 1998 H 484 added division (L).

Amendment Note: 1996 H 274 deleted ", or for reasons beyond his control, other than lack of knowledge of the minor's birth, is not able to register within that time period and fails to register not later than ten days after it becomes possible to register" from the end of division (B)(1).

Amendment Note: 1996 H 419 rewrote divisions (B) and (C); added divisions (E), (F), and (K); redesignated former divisions (E) through (H) as (G) through (J), respectively; and made changes to reflect gender neutral language throughout. Prior to amendment, divisions (B) and (C) read:

"(B) The putative father of a minor if the putative father fails to file an objection with the court, the department of human services, or the agency having custody of the minor as provided in division (F)(4) of section 3107.06 of the Revised Code, or files an objection with the court, department, or agency and the court finds, after proper service of notice and hearing, that he is not the father of the minor, or that he has willfully abandoned or failed to care for and support the minor, or abandoned the mother of the minor during her pregnancy and up to the time of her surrender of the minor, or its placement in the home of the petitioner, whichever occurs first;

"(C) A parent who has relinquished his right to consent under section 5103.15 of the Revised Code;"

Cross References

Department of job and family services, division of social administration, placing of children; interstate compact on placement of children, see 5103.12 to 5103.17, 5103.20 to 5103.237

Married persons to support self, spouse and children, duration of duty to support, see 3103.03

Support of children, see 3109.05

Library References

Adoption ⇐7.3 to 7.4(6).
Westlaw Topic No. 17.
C.J.S. Adoption of Persons §§ 56 to 58, 62 to 68.

Research References

ALR Library

28 ALR 6th 349, Requirements and Effects of Putative Father Registries.

5 ALR 6th 193, Construction and Application of Interstate Compact on the Placement of Children.

84 ALR 5th 191, Natural Parent's Indigence as Precluding Finding that Failure to Support Child Waived Requirement of Consent to Adoption-- Factors Other Than Employment Status.

83 ALR 5th 375, Natural Parent's Indigence Resulting from Unemployment or Underemployment as

Precluding Finding that Failure to Support Child Waived Requirement of Consent to Adoption.

82 ALR 5th 443, Comment Note: Natural Parent's Indigence as Precluding Finding that Failure to Support Child Waived Requirement of Consent to Adoption--General Principles.

Encyclopedias

OH Jur. 3d Family Law § 874, Jurisdiction--Effect of Continuing Jurisdiction in Other Actions.

OH Jur. 3d Family Law § 881, Who Must Consent.

Law Review and Journal Commentaries

Adoption—Abandonment and Failure to Support as Grounds for Dispensing With the Natural Parent's Consent, Note. 14 J Fam L 139 (1975).

Awarding Child Support Against the Impoverished Parent: Straying from Statutory Guidelines and Using SSI in Setting the Amount, Note. 83 Ky L J 653 (1994–95).

Children Born Out Of Wedlock And Nonsupport—Valid Statutory Grounds For Termination Of Parental Rights?, Note. 25 J Fam L 755 (1986–87).

Contested Adoptions, Glenn E. Forbes. 12 Lake Legal Views 9 (February 1989).

Defining the "Best Interests": Constitutional Protections in Involuntary Adoptions, Erwin Chemerinsky. 18 J Fam L 79 (1979–80).

Intercountry Adoption: A Need for Mandatory Medical Screening, Comment. 11 J L & Health 243 (1996–97).

Lehr v Robertson: Putative Fathers Revisited, Note. 11 Ohio N U L Rev 385 (1984).

Lehr v Robinson: Putting the Genie Back in the Bottle: the Supreme Court Limits the Scope of the

Putative Father's Right to Notice, Hearing, and Consent in the Adoption of His Illegitimate Child, Comment. 15 U Tol L Rev 1501 (Summer 1984).

Looking Beyond the United States: How Other Countries Handle Issues Related to Unwed Fathers in the Adoption Process. Cynthia R. Mabry, 36 Cap. U. L. Rev. 363 (Winter 2007).

A National Putative Father Registry. Mary Beck, 36 Cap. U. L. Rev. 295 (Winter 2007).

Ohio adoption conundrum: What constitutes "communication" and "support"? Thomas W. Landon, 20 Ohio Law 12 (July/August 2006).

Protecting the Putative Father's Rights After Stanley v Illinois: Problems In Implementation, Note. 13 J Fam L 115 (1973–74).

Seeking the wisdom of Solomon: Defining the rights of unwed fathers in newborn adoptions, Scott A. Resnik. 20 Seton Hall Legis J 363 (1996).

Termination of Parental Rights in Adoption Cases: Focusing on the Child, Comment. 14 J Fam L 547 (1975–76).

Notes of Decisions

---

1. Due process

Where notice of hearing on adoption petition did not clearly notify birth parents that hearing would address both issues of consent and best interest of child, due process required a separate hearing on best interest of child. In re C.M.W. (Ohio App. 12 Dist., Madison, 12-20-2004) No. CA2004-09-031, 2004-Ohio-6935, 2004 WL 2937632, Unreported. Adoption ☞ 12; Constitutional Law ☞ 4395

For purposes of statute allowing adoption without parental consent in certain circumstances and placing on petitioner the burden of proving not only his allegations of parent's failure to support, but also his allegations of the lack of justifiable cause, any alteration in allocation of burden of proof may offend due process. In re A.M.W. (Ohio App. 9 Dist., 02-20-2007) 170 Ohio App.3d 389, 867 N.E.2d 471, 2007-Ohio-682. Adoption ☞ 7.8(1); Constitutional Law ☞ 4395

If the court opts to hold more than one hearing on an adoption petition, i.e., one hearing on issue of consent and a second hearing on the best interests of the child, statute requiring notice of filing of adoption petition and of time and place of hearing requires service of notification of the date and time of all hearings on a biological parent whose consent is statutorily unnecessary. In re Adoption of Walters (Ohio, 01-17-2007) 112 Ohio St.3d 315, 859 N.E.2d 545, 2007-Ohio-7. Adoption ☞ 12

In cases in which a party proves by clear and convincing evidence at the adoption hearing that the parent's consent is unnecessary by statute, the due process rights of the parent have been protected once that parent has been given notice of the hearing. In re Adoption of Walters (Ohio, 01-17-2007) 112 Ohio St.3d 315, 859 N.E.2d 545, 2007-Ohio-7. Constitutional Law ☞ 4395

Publication notice identifying date and time of joint hearing on petitions for adoption of children by mother's husband, alleging that biological father's consent to adoptions was unnecessary because he had failed to communicate with or support children for one year, did not violate father's right to due process, though notice referenced only consent portion of adoption hearing and not best interests of children portion, given that, because father had received notice that court would be taking evidence as to whether his parental rights should be terminated, there was no need for any additional requirement that father be given notice that it would consider both consent and best interests of children at hearing. In re Adoption of Walters (Ohio, 01-17-2007) 112 Ohio St.3d 315, 859 N.E.2d 545, 2007-Ohio-7. Adoption ☞ 12; Constitutional Law ☞ 4395

Publication notice identifying date and time of joint hearing on petitions for adoption of children by mother's husband, alleging that biological father's consent to adoptions was unnecessary because he had failed to communicate with or support children for one year, complied with statute requiring notice of filing of adoption petition and of time and place of hearing, though notice did not specifically declare that a best interests hearing would be held, as statute did not require that specific reference be made in notice to both the consent and best interests portions of the hearing; overruling, In re C.M.W., 2004 WL 2937632. In re Adoption of Walters (Ohio, 01-17-2007) 112 Ohio St.3d 315, 859 N.E.2d 545, 2007-Ohio-7. Adoption ☞ 12

2. Effective assistance of counsel

Counsel's failure to provide biological father's medical records to the trial court did not prejudice father, in proceeding to allow stepfather to adopt children without father's consent, and thus was not ineffective assistance; father failed to describe the medical records with specificity or claim that he provided the medical records to his trial counsel.

In re Adoption of Randall G. (Ohio App. 6 Dist., Lucas, 03-14-2003) No. L-02-1340, No. L-02-1341, 2003-Ohio-1412, 2003 WL 1473698, Unreported. Adoption ☞ 13

3. In general

Evidence supported finding that county children's services board unreasonably withheld their consent to foster parents' adoption petitions; the sole reason the board objected to the petitions was because foster parents were not blood relatives of the children, and the board failed to consider other factors such as the relationship between foster parents and the children, the nurturing home environment foster parents had provided for the children, the relationships between the children and foster parents' biological children and the developmental progress the children had achieved while under the primary care of foster parents. In re Jeffrey A. (Ohio App. 6 Dist., Lucas, 10-03-2008) No. L-08-1006, 2008-Ohio-5135, 2008 WL 4444316, Unreported, appeal not allowed 120 Ohio St.3d 1459, 898 N.E.2d 971, 2008-Ohio-6813. Adoption ☞ 13

Letter from co-guardians of incompetent adjudicated father, responding to prospective adoptive parents' request for consent to adopt child, complied with statutory requirement of written response within 30 days, preserving adjudicated father's right to consent; following prospective adoptive parents' letter to adjudicated father's co-guardians, which requested that co-guardians consent to child's adoption, co-guardians responded in writing through their attorney, stating that they would not consent to adoption at that time and that they would object to any petition for adoption. In re Adoption of Law (Ohio App. 3 Dist., Allen, 02-13-2006) No. 1-05-64, 2006-Ohio-600, 2006 WL 319141, Unreported. Adoption ☞ 7.2(3); Guardian And Ward ☞ 29

Death of child's biological father during pendency of step-father's appeal from dismissal of his petition for step-parent adoption obviated statutory requirement that his consent to adoption be obtained. In re Adoption of Rader (Ohio App. 11 Dist., Trumbull, 04-05-2004) No. 2003-T-0066, 2004-Ohio-1709, 2004 WL 721149, Unreported. Adoption ☞ 7.2(1)

Error, if any, in trial court's failure to strike adoptive parents' response, on timeliness basis, to mother's objections to magistrate's decision that mother's consent to adoption of her children was not required, was harmless, where mother failed to explain how she was prejudiced by failure. In re Adoption of C.P. (Ohio App. 9 Dist., Lorain, 09-17-2003) No. 03CA008268, No. 03CA008269, 2003-Ohio-4905, 2003 WL 22136288, Unreported. Adoption ☞ 15

Application of civil procedure rule which provides that an action is not commenced unless service is effectuated within one year of filing complaint is inconsistent with consent provision within adoption statute, as would support finding that rule does not apply to adoptions; consent provision is an objective determination of abandonment providing that a parent's consent to an adoption is not required if parent fails to communicate with child for period of at least one year prior to filing of adoption petition, and objectivity is lost if one-year abandonment period begins sometime after filing petition, as a parent who opposes an adoption is likely to attempt to contact child after petition is filed. In re Adoption of Goldberg (Ohio App. 12 Dist., Warren, 03-05-2003) No. CA2002-09-091, No. CA2002-09-099, No. CA2002-10-109, 2003-Ohio-1015, 2003 WL 833085, Unreported, appeal not allowed 98 Ohio St.3d 1567, 787 N.E.2d 1231, 2003-Ohio-2242. Adoption ☞ 9.1

When an issue concerning parenting of a minor is pending in the juvenile court, a probate court must refrain from proceeding with the adoption of that child, and the determination of a parent-child relationship in the juvenile court proceeding must be given effect in the stayed adoption proceeding. In re Adoption of G.V. (Ohio, 07-22-2010) 126 Ohio St.3d 249, 933 N.E.2d 245, 2010-Ohio-3349, reconsideration denied 126 Ohio St.3d 1592, 934 N.E.2d 939, 2010-Ohio-4880, reconsideration denied 127 Ohio St.3d 1247, 937 N.E.2d 1285, 2010-Ohio-4879, certiorari denied 131 S.Ct. 1610, 179 L.Ed.2d 501. Adoption ☞ 9.1; Children Out–of–wedlock ☞ 68

The probate court was required to refrain from proceeding with stepfather's petition to adopt child while biological father's paternity proceeding was pending in juvenile court. In re Adoption of P.A.C. (Ohio, 07-22-2010) 126 Ohio St.3d 236, 933 N.E.2d 236, 2010-Ohio-3351, reconsideration denied 126 Ohio St.3d 1592, 934 N.E.2d 939, 2010-Ohio-4880. Adoption ☞ 9.1

Minor child generally may be adopted only when the child's parent has given written consent. In re A.M.W. (Ohio App. 9 Dist., 02-20-2007) 170 Ohio App.3d 389, 867 N.E.2d 471, 2007-Ohio-682. Adoption ☞ 7.2(1)

Parental consent generally is a jurisdictional prerequisite to adoption of parent's child by another. In re Adoption of McNutt (Ohio App. 4 Dist., 09-27-1999) 134 Ohio App.3d 822, 732 N.E.2d 470. Adoption ☞ 7.2(1)

Termination of natural parent's right to object to adoption of child is very serious matter, requiring strict adherence to controlling statute. In re Adoption of Kuhlmann (Ohio App. 1 Dist., 12-07-1994) 99 Ohio App.3d 44, 649 N.E.2d 1279. Adoption ☞ 7.3

Probate court's judgment to dispense with parent's consent to adoption will not be reversed as being against "manifest weight of the evidence" if it is supported by some competent, credible evidence. In re Adoption of Kuhlmann (Ohio App. 1 Dist., 12-07-1994) 99 Ohio App.3d 44, 649 N.E.2d 1279. Adoption ☞ 15

The one-year time requirement of RC 3107.07(A) is not to be applied to RC 3107.07(B). In re Adoption of Hart (Lucas 1989) 62 Ohio App.3d 544, 577 N.E.2d 77, motion overruled 45 Ohio St.3d 704, 543 N.E.2d 810.

RC 3107.07(A) does not impose any new duty nor does it remove any vested right. In re Adoption of McDermitt (Ohio 1980) 63 Ohio St.2d 301, 408 N.E.2d 680, 17 O.O.3d 195.

4. Construction and application

Any exception to the statutory requirement of parental consent to an adoption must be strictly construed so as to protect the right of natural parents to raise and nurture their children. In re Adoption of C.L.B. (Ohio App. 3 Dist., 10-25-2010) 191 Ohio App.3d 64, 944 N.E.2d 1190, 2010-Ohio-5190. Adoption ☞ 7.3

Statute governing situations in which a natural parent's consent to adoption is not required must be strictly construed so as to protect the rights of natural parents to raise and nurture their children, since adoption severs completely the relationship between the children and their natural noncustodial parent. In re Adoption of A.J.Y. (Ohio Com.Pl., 09-16-2010) 160 Ohio Misc.2d 4, 937 N.E.2d 1109, 2010-Ohio-5726. Adoption ☞ 3; Adoption ☞ 7.3

5. "Best interest" of child

A bifurcated procedure is required where the natural parent of a minor child refuses to consent to adoption of that child by a third party whereby (1) initially, the probate court determines the issue of necessity of consent, (2) a judgment on the issue of consent only is filed, and (3) in the second stage, the best interest of the child standard is utilized; failure to conduct a hearing on the issue of whether the proposed adoption is in the best interest of the child is error. Matter of Adoption of Zachary H. (Ohio App. 6 Dist., Williams, 03-07-1997) No. WM 96-013, 1997 WL 103808, Unreported.

Even when an individual's consent to adoption is deemed unnecessary, he or she is still entitled to notice of the best-interest hearing and has an overriding interest in being heard on the issue of best interest of the child. In re Adoption of S.R.A. (Ohio App. 10 Dist., 09-21-2010) 189 Ohio App.3d 363, 938 N.E.2d 432, 2010-Ohio-4435. Adoption ☞ 12; Adoption ☞ 13

If all other requirements are met, decision following consent phase of adoption, in which the probate court determines that consent was not required, is a "final appealable order," even though the probate court has not reached the best interest phase. In re Adoption of S.R.A. (Ohio App. 10 Dist., 09-21-2010) 189 Ohio App.3d 363, 938 N.E.2d 432, 2010-Ohio-4435. Adoption ☞ 15

Natural father who did not consent to adoption of his child was given reasonable opportunity to present evidence concerning child's best interest at final hearing; notice of hearing was sent and received by counsel for father on at least two, if not three, separate occasions, and father did not proffer testimony of witnesses he claimed he would have called if he had had notice of hearing. In re Adoption of Cline (Trumbull 1993) 89 Ohio App.3d 450, 624 N.E.2d 1083. Adoption ☞ 12; Adoption ☞ 13

Even after court determines that consent of natural parent is not necessary for child's adoption, court must still determine whether adoption is in best interest of child. Celestino v. Schneider (Lucas 1992) 84 Ohio App.3d 192, 616 N.E.2d 581. Adoption ☞ 13

Even where a probate court finds that the natural father's consent to an adoption is not necessary, a determination of what is in the child's best interests is still required prior to termination of parental rights. In re Adoption of Jones (Medina 1990) 70 Ohio App.3d 576, 591 N.E.2d 823.

A finding that the consent of a natural parent is not required for an adoption under RC 3107.07(A) does not constitute consent to the adoption but merely "provides for cutting off the statutory right of a parent to withhold his consent to the adoption of the child," leaving all other parental rights and obligations intact. Therefore, the exclusion of a natural parent from the final hearing on whether or not adoption is in the best interest of the child renders meaningless the requirement of RC 3107.11 that a natural parent who has lost the right to withhold consent to the adoption be given notice of the time and place of the best interest hearing, and an adoption under such circumstances must be reversed. In re Adoption of Jorgensen (Hancock 1986) 33 Ohio App.3d 207, 515 N.E.2d 622.

The marriage of a natural parent and the subsequent bringing of a minor into the home with the stepparent will not initiate ab initio the placement of a minor for the purposes of RC 3107.07(A). In determining whether a placement pursuant to RC 3107.07(A) has occurred, a court should consider the facts of each particular case while remaining mindful that the paramount concern is the best interest of the child. In re Adoption of Kreyche (Ohio 1984) 15 Ohio St.3d 159, 472 N.E.2d 1106, 15 O.B.R. 304. Adoption ☞ 7.4(2.1); Adoption ☞ 7.4(6)

6. Placement

Evidence supported finding that children were placed with maternal step-grandmother on the date a permanent managing conservatorship was granted to grandmother, rather that the date grandmother first obtained physical custody of the children, for the purpose of determining whether mother's consent to adoption was required based on whether mother had provided support or communicated with children in the year preceding the children's placement; the Texas Department of Protective and Regulatory Services maintained jurisdiction over the children until grandmother was granted a conservatorship. In re Crandall (Ohio App. 1 Dist., Hamilton, 03-02-2007) No. C-060770, 2007-Ohio-855, 2007 WL 625009, Unreported. Adoption ☞ 6; Adoption ☞ 7.4(1)

Definition of "placement," for purposes of statute providing that parent's consent to child's adoption was not required when parent had failed to communication with child, without justifiable cause, for over one year immediately preceding child's placement in home of adoption petitioner, could not be taken from juvenile statute defining "placement for adoption," as juvenile statute explicitly provided definitions of terms used in juvenile delinquency, abuse, dependency, and neglect cases. In re Adoption of G.W. (Ohio App. 9 Dist., Lorain, 03-23-2005) No. 04CA008609, 2005-Ohio-1274, 2005 WL 663002, Unreported. Adoption ☞ 7.4(1)

A probate court errs in considering only one of two dates specified by RC 3107.07(A) regardless of policy implications where the statute contemplates the calculation of the requisite year from either the filing of the adoption petition or the placement of the child in the petitioner's home; RC 1.02(F) does not apply to alter the meaning of a provision where the statutory language is plain and unambiguous or if application of the rule would render a passage senseless. In re Adoption of Jones (Medina 1990) 70 Ohio App.3d 576, 591 N.E.2d 823.

7. Failure to support—In general

Evidence did not support finding in adoption proceeding that biological mother failed to provide for her children's maintenance and support during year preceding filing of adoption petition, as required to allow adoption to proceed without mother's consent, given the non-monetary support that mother provided during her frequent, regularly scheduled visits with children; mother cooked for children when they visited her apartment, or brought pizzas to visitations, and she provided entertainment and brought photo albums and crafts to the visitations, which she allowed children to keep. In re Adoption of L.C.II. (Ohio App. 4 Dist., Scioto, 02-19-2010) No. 09CA3318, No. 09CA3319, No. 09CA3324, 2010-Ohio-643, 2010 WL 628428, Unreported, appeal not allowed 125 Ohio St.3d 1450, 927 N.E.2d 1129, 2010-Ohio-2510. Adoption ☞ 7.4(6)

Support order from child support enforcement agency requiring biological mother, as obligor, to pay zero dollars support for her children, and naming mother's husband as obligee, did not supersede mother's duty to support her children, and thus, mother's failure to provide support could properly serve as basis for allowing adoption to proceed without mother's consent; order was outdated by mother's dramatic increase in her income less than one month after agency issued its support order, and husband had no right to be named obligee because he did not have custody of children. In re Adoption of L.C.H. (Ohio App. 4 Dist., Scioto, 02-19-2010) No. 09CA3318, No. 09CA3319, No. 09CA3324, 2010-Ohio-643, 2010 WL 628428, Unreported, appeal not allowed 125 Ohio St.3d 1450, 927 N.E.2d 1129, 2010-Ohio-2510. Adoption ☞ 7.4(6); Child Support ☞ 189

Biological mother's failure to pay child support to father, the child's custodial parent, did not demonstrate a failure on her part to support the child for purposes of adoption statute, and thus, biological mother's consent was a necessary precondition to stepmother's adoption of child; at the time of biological parents' divorce, the domestic relations court issued an order requiring no child support from mother, which remained an applicable judicial order for purposes of determining whether biological mother had failed to support the child under exception to consent provision of adoption statute, and evidence indicated that mother did provide limited support during her supervised visits, yet record was silent as to whether father and stepmother ever requested support. In re Adoption of Collene (Ohio App. 3 Dist., Crawford, 11-10-2008) No. 3-08-08, 2008-Ohio-5827, 2008 WL 4853583, Unreported. Adoption ☞ 7.4(6)

Mother's lack of knowledge of court order requiring her to pay $50 per month in child support for her minor children did not excuse mother's failure to pay any support in the year leading up to father's and stepmother's petition to allow stepmother to adopt the children, and thus father and stepmother were not required to obtain mother's consent to the adoption; mother had an independent statutory duty to provide support even apart from the court order. In re Adoption of J.M.N. (Ohio App. 2 Dist., Clark, 08-29-2008) No. 08-CA-23, No. 08-CA-24, 2008-Ohio-4394, 2008 WL 3990828, Unreported. Adoption ☞ 7.4(6)

Failure by father or Child Support Enforcement Agency (CSEA) to pursue mother for court-ordered child support payments did not excuse mother's failure to support children, for purposes of termination of mother's parental rights in a proceeding to allow stepmother to adopt the children without mother's consent; duty to pay support was owed to the children, rather than to father, and mother did not make a conscious decision that father did not require support. In re Adoption of J.M.N. (Ohio App. 2 Dist., Clark, 08-29-2008) No. 08-CA-23, No. 08-CA-24, 2008-Ohio-4394, 2008 WL 3990828, Unreported. Adoption ☞ 7.4(6)

Maternal step-grandmother was only required to prove one of the statutory factors for granting an adoption without parental consent before the court could determine that mother's consent to adoption was not required, and thus mother's act of providing maintenance and support in the year preceding grandmother's petition did not prohibit the court from ruling that mother's consent to adoption was not required due to her failure to provide support in the year preceding child's placement with grandmother; the consent for adoption statute was written in the disjunctive, and thus the court need only find that mother failed to provide support or communicate with child during the year preceding the filing of the adoption petition or during the first-year period. In re Crandall (Ohio App. 1 Dist., Hamilton, 03-02-2007) No. C-060770, 2007-Ohio-855, 2007 WL 625009, Unreported. Adoption ☞ 7.4(6)

Biological father provided maintenance and support to child within one year of filing of stepfather's petition for stepparent adoption, and thus biological father's consent to adoption was necessary, although biological father did not pay any support through Child Support Enforcement Agency (CSEA) during year preceding filing of petition; biological father saw child every other weekend and provided child with food, clothing, and toys. Gorski v. Myer (Ohio App. 5 Dist., Stark, 05-23-2005) No. 2005CA00033, 2005-Ohio-2604, 2005 WL 1242168, Unreported, appeal not allowed 106 Ohio St.3d 1556, 836 N.E.2d 581, 2005-Ohio-5531. Adoption ☞ 7.4(6)

For purposes of determining mother's level of child maintenance in father's new wife's action seeking to adopt father's children without mother's consent, mother was not entitled to credit for money used for maintenance of children that came from mother's medical malpractice settlement during marriage of father and mother, where settlement money was awarded to father as part of property division in father's and mother's divorce proceedings. In re Adoption of C.S. (Ohio App. 2 Dist., Montgomery, 11-05-2004) No. 20557, No. 20558, No. 20559, 2004-Ohio-5933, 2004 WL 2526380, Unreported. Adoption ☞ 7.4(6)

The one-year limitations period within the statute governing parental consent to adoption, which stated that a biological parent's consent to adoption was not required when the parent had failed to communicate with the child or provide maintenance and support for the child for a period of at least one year prior to the filing of the adoption petition, was not tolled by restraining order that prevented mother from having physical contact with child; the restraining order did not prohibit mother from communicating with child through letters or cards. In re Adoptions of Doyle (Ohio App. 11 Dist., Ashtabula, 08-06-2004) No. 2003-A-0071, No. 2003-A-0072, 2004-Ohio-4197, 2004 WL 1778821, Unreported. Adoption ☞ 7.4(4)

Natural father's nonmonetary contributions of clothing, shoes, and diapers to his child should have been considered by trial court in adoption proceeding to determine whether father made maintenance and support payments for child for at least one year prior to the filing of grandparents' adoption petition, and thus whether father's consent was required as a prerequisite to child's adoption. In re Adoption of McNutt (Ohio App. 4 Dist., 09-27-1999) 134 Ohio App.3d 822, 732 N.E.2d 470. Adoption ☞ 7.4(6)

Evidence did not support finding in adoption proceeding that natural father failed to provide for his child's maintenance and support during year preceding filing of grandparents' adoption petition; child frequently returned from her visits with father with new clothes and shoes, father's mother and sister testified that father purchased items that child needed, father did not make contributions to child's maintenance and support only in an effort to thwart grandparents' adoption petition, and father provided child with necessities in course of exercising his visitation privileges with her. In re Adoption of McNutt (Ohio App. 4 Dist., 09-27-1999) 134 Ohio App.3d 822, 732 N.E.2d 470. Adoption ☞ 7.8(4)

One-year period of nonsupport which obviates requirement to obtain parent's consent to adoption by another commences on date of the paternity adjudication. In re Adoption of McNutt (Ohio

App. 4 Dist., 09-27-1999) 134 Ohio App.3d 822, 732 N.E.2d 470. Adoption ⌖ 7.4(6)

Natural father waived on appeal right to assert jurisdictional defect in maternal grandparents' adoption petition, where father conceded that he had a duty to support his child during year preceding the filing of petition. In re Adoption of McNutt (Ohio App. 4 Dist., 09-27-1999) 134 Ohio App.3d 822, 732 N.E.2d 470. Adoption ⌖ 15

Natural mother's two payments of $10 each in October and November 1994 constituted support and maintenance of child, for purposes of October 1995 hearing on whether her consent to stepmother's adoption petition was required, even though payments were made to child support agency in wrong county and receipt of payments was delayed by nearly a year. In re Fetzer (Ohio App. 3 Dist., 02-05-1997) 118 Ohio App.3d 156, 692 N.E.2d 219, dismissed, appeal not allowed 78 Ohio St.3d 1513, 679 N.E.2d 309. Adoption ⌖ 7.4(6)

So long as natural parent complies with duty to support child for any period during the one year immediately preceding adoption petition, then she has not failed to support for purposes of statute listing circumstances in which natural parent's consent to adoption is not required. In re Fetzer (Ohio App. 3 Dist., 02-05-1997) 118 Ohio App.3d 156, 692 N.E.2d 219, dismissed, appeal not allowed 78 Ohio St.3d 1513, 679 N.E.2d 309. Adoption ⌖ 7.4(6)

Natural parent's consent to minor child's adoption would be required if he or she provided maintenance and support for, and communicated with, child within one year prior to filing of adoption petition. In re Adoption of Wagner (Ohio App. 11 Dist., 01-21-1997) 117 Ohio App.3d 448, 690 N.E.2d 959, appeal not allowed 78 Ohio St.3d 1516, 679 N.E.2d 311. Adoption ⌖ 7.2(1)

Nonconsenting parent should not be allowed to thwart operation of statute making his consent to adoption unnecessary if he has failed to pay child support or communicate with child for one year prior to petition by making one or two token support payments just prior to adoption petition. In re Serre (Ohio Com.Pl., 02-20-1996) 77 Ohio Misc.2d 29, 665 N.E.2d 1185. Adoption ⌖ 7.4(5); Adoption ⌖ 7.4(6)

Although natural father's income was not enough to allow him to make full support payments, two partial support payments totalling $70 within week of stepfather's filing of adoption petition were insufficient to require natural father's consent to petition; payments equalled about one percent of natural father's income, and natural father made no attempt to seek reduction of support order. In re Serre (Ohio Com.Pl., 02-20-1996) 77 Ohio Misc.2d 29, 665 N.E.2d 1185. Adoption ⌖ 7.4(6)

Child who was subject of adoption petition had been legitimized by natural father, as required to commence period of nonsupport permitting court to approve adoption without consent of natural parent. In re Adoption of Lassiter (Ohio App. 2 Dist., 02-24-1995) 101 Ohio App.3d 367, 655

N.E.2d 781, dismissed, appeal not allowed 73 Ohio St.3d 1410, 651 N.E.2d 1308. Adoption ⌖ 7.4(6)

Legitimation of child granted pursuant to code section in effect at time of legitimation was sufficient to trigger one-year period of nonsupport found in subsequently adopted code section which obviated need to obtain parental consent to adoption, as language in new code section did not change or modify law, but merely clarified it. In re Adoption of Lassiter (Ohio App. 2 Dist., 02-24-1995) 101 Ohio App.3d 367, 655 N.E.2d 781, dismissed, appeal not allowed 73 Ohio St.3d 1410, 651 N.E.2d 1308. Adoption ⌖ 7.4(6)

Father assumed duty of supporting son, and one-year period of nonsupport obviating need to obtain parental consent to adoption began to run, when father acknowledged paternity and trial court granted legitimacy. In re Adoption of Lassiter (Ohio App. 2 Dist., 02-24-1995) 101 Ohio App.3d 367, 655 N.E.2d 781, dismissed, appeal not allowed 73 Ohio St.3d 1410, 651 N.E.2d 1308. Adoption ⌖ 7.4(6)

Probate court order finding that natural father's consent was not required for son's adoption, due to natural father's failure to support son for one year prior to adoption petition, was final appealable order. In re Adoption of Lassiter (Ohio App. 2 Dist., 02-24-1995) 101 Ohio App.3d 367, 655 N.E.2d 781, dismissed, appeal not allowed 73 Ohio St.3d 1410, 651 N.E.2d 1308. Adoption ⌖ 15

In deciding whether natural parent has failed to provide support and maintenance for at least one year prior to the filing of adoption petition, such that parent's consent is not prerequisite to adoption, court's inquiry is not whether parent can be held in contempt for failing to provide support, but whether parent's failure to support as ordered is of such magnitude as to be the equivalent of abandonment. Celestino v. Schneider (Lucas 1992) 84 Ohio App.3d 192, 616 N.E.2d 581. Adoption ⌖ 7.4(6)

Any contribution toward child support, no matter how meager, satisfies maintenance and support requirements of adoption provision and preserves natural parent's consent as jurisdictional prerequisite to child's adoption. Celestino v. Schneider (Lucas 1992) 84 Ohio App.3d 192, 616 N.E.2d 581. Adoption ⌖ 7.4(6)

The one partial payment that father made on his court-ordered child support obligation, in amount of $36, qualified as "support and maintenance" for purposes of adoption petition filed by natural mother's new husband; trial court could not dispense with natural father's consent as prerequisite to adoption, on theory that father had failed to provide support and maintenance. Celestino v. Schneider (Lucas 1992) 84 Ohio App.3d 192, 616 N.E.2d 581. Adoption ⌖ 7.4(6)

A probate court does not err when it concludes that a payment of one-week support after notice of intention to file an adoption petition and immediately before the petition is filed is not support within the meaning of RC 3107.07(A). In re Adoption of Carletti (Muskingum 1992) 78 Ohio App.3d

244, 604 N.E.2d 243, motion overruled 65 Ohio St.3d 1457, 602 N.E.2d 253.

In an adoption wherein the natural grandparents seek to adopt their granddaughter whose father is deceased and whose mother has not seen or supported her in three years, it is in the best interest of the child to have a guardian ad litem, and the trial court's failure to appoint one is error. In re Adoption of Howell (Lawrence 1991) 77 Ohio App.3d 80, 601 N.E.2d 92, motion overruled 62 Ohio St.3d 1508, 583 N.E.2d 1320.

A trial court's finding that a child's natural father's consent to the child's adoption is not required on the ground that the father failed to provide for the maintenance and support of the child as required by law or judicial decree for a period of at least one year immediately preceding the filing of the adoption petition is erroneous where it is shown that the father made payments through the bureau of support totaling $130 during the one year preceding the filing of the adoption petition. Vecchi v. Thomas (Montgomery 1990) 67 Ohio App.3d 688, 588 N.E.2d 186. Adoption ⌫ 7.4(6)

The one-year period of nonsupport prescribed by RC 3107.07(A) which obviates the requirement to obtain parental consent to an adoption pursuant to RC 3107.06 commences on the date that parentage has been judicially established. In re Adoption of Sunderhaus (Ohio 1992) 63 Ohio St.3d 127, 585 N.E.2d 418, rehearing denied 63 Ohio St.3d 1442, 589 N.E.2d 46. Adoption ⌫ 7.4(6)

A father's duty of support includes "necessaries," such as expenses for pregnancy and confinement of the mother attendant to the birth of a child. In re Adoption of Youngpeter (Hancock 1989) 65 Ohio App.3d 172, 583 N.E.2d 360.

In calculating the one-year lack of support and communication by a natural father that is a condition of adoption without a natural parent's consent, the time before the adjudication of an illegitimate child's paternity may be considered. In re Adoption of Taylor (Medina 1989) 61 Ohio App.3d 500, 573 N.E.2d 156, motion overruled 43 Ohio St.3d 712, 541 N.E.2d 78.

RC 2151.353, permitting the state to receive permanent custody of a "dependent child" whose parent is jailed, does not conflict with RC 3107.07; where the child is a "dependent child" under RC 2151.04 the state has authority to obtain permanent custody under RC 2151.353, and once parental rights have been terminated under RC Ch 2151, it is provided by RC 3107.06(D) that this parent's consent to adoption is no longer necessary. In re Dillard (Montgomery 1988) 48 Ohio App.3d 263, 549 N.E.2d 213.

Where a man establishes himself as a child's father in a paternity action brought pursuant to RC Ch 3111, the father's duty to support the child is retroactive to birth of the child for determining the father's failure to support the child for purposes of RC 3107.07(A). In re Adoption of Foster (Van Wert 1985) 22 Ohio App.3d 129, 489 N.E.2d 1070, 22 O.B.R. 331.

Where the record indicates that a nonconsenting parent made some contribution, although meager, to the support of her children within the one year immediately preceding the filing of the adoption proceedings, the parent will not be held to have abandoned her parental responsibilities and it is not error for the trial court to find that the parent's consent can not be dispensed with. In re Adoption of Salisbury (Franklin 1982) 5 Ohio App.3d 65, 449 N.E.2d 519, 5 O.B.R. 161.

RC 3107.07 must be strictly construed to protect the rights of the natural parents; thus, so long as the nonconsenting parent complies with his duty to support the child for any period during the one year immediately preceding the filing of the petition, the parent has not failed to provide support for one year and has not abandoned his parental responsibilities to the extent that he will be deemed to have forfeited his parental rights. In re Adoption of Anthony (Franklin 1982) 5 Ohio App.3d 60, 449 N.E.2d 511, 5 O.B.R. 156.

In order to properly support and maintain her child within the meaning of RC 3107.06, a mother has a duty to give personal care and attention to that child and, if able to do so, to provide financial support for the child, even though the child is being properly supported and maintained by someone else, and whether such mother has legal custody and actual possession of the child, either such custody or such possession, or neither such custody nor such possession. In re Adoption of Lewis (Ohio 1966) 8 Ohio St.2d 25, 222 N.E.2d 628, 37 O.O.2d 376.

Small sporadic payments for support of children does not constitute such support as to make the consent of the payor thereof a prerequisite to adoption. In re Adoptions of Zinsmeister (Ohio Prob. 1961) 178 N.E.2d 849, 87 Ohio Law Abs. 129.

Satisfaction of a mother's child support obligation by her parents who are under no duty to so satisfy constitutes the provision of maintenance and support to require the mother's consent for adoption of her child by her former husband and his present wife. In re Wells (Ohio App. 7 Dist., Belmont, 09-25-2001) No. 00 BA 49, 2001-Ohio-3411, 2001 WL 1199875, Unreported.

The failure of the natural father to pay weekly child support payments to his son does not constitute failure to provide for his maintenance and support under RC 3107.07(A) where the father provides the son with clothes, toys and meals during visitation periods. In re Adoption of Pinkava, No. L–88–034 (6th Dist Ct App, Lucas, 1–13–89).

The involuntary withholding of one support payment from the wages of the natural father in the previous year is not sufficient support to require the consent of the natural father to the adoption of his child under RC 3107.07(A). In re Adoption of Thomas, No. CA–3311 (5th Dist Ct App, Licking, 12–22–87).

Where a child's natural father is disabled and cannot work, supporting the child on social security disability payments alone does not constitute a failure to support under RC 3107.07, and the consent of the natural father is required for adoption. In re Adoption of Davis, No. 402 (4th Dist Ct App, Pike, 10–21–87).

The payment of three partial weekly support payments and one full payment three days prior to the filing of an adoption petition is sufficient to maintain the requirement of consent of the natural parent to the adoption petition. In re Adoption of Mackall, No. 1365 (9th Dist Ct App, Medina, 4–24–85).

Where a non-custodial parent chooses a particular life style that prevents her from being able to provide for the maintenance and support of her minor child for at least one year, such parent's consent to the adoption of the child is not required. In re Adoption of Adolphson, No. 82–C–19 (7th Dist Ct App, Columbiana, 3–4–83).

Where the natural father made a lump sum payment of child support, accruing over a fourteen month period, three days before the stepfather filed a petition for adoption, such payment is sufficient to require the consent of the natural father to the adoption petition where the natural father has been in communication with his child. In re Adoption of Wallace, No. 82–CA–24 (5th Dist Ct App, Muskingum, 7–20–82).

Where the natural father has made four weeks of child support payments and has visited with his children once during the year immediately preceding the filing of an adoption petition by the child's stepfather, the natural father's consent to the adoption may not be dispensed with under RC 3107.07. Anthony v Arick, No. 81AP–907 (10th Dist Ct App, Franklin, 5–13–82).

8. —— Justifiable cause, failure to support

Father had justifiable cause for failing to visit his minor daughter and, therefore, father's consent for daughter's adoption was required, where child's mother continually thwarted his attempts to visit and provide support, and father was pursuing visitation through juvenile court. In re M.E.M. (Ohio App. 11 Dist., Lake, 09-17-2010) No. 2010-L-020, 2010-Ohio-4430, 2010 WL 3666981, Unreported. Adoption ☞ 7.4(4); Adoption ☞ 7.4(6)

Mother who sought to avoid termination of her parental rights, in connection with a petition to allow stepmother to adopt children without mother's consent, failed to establish that her failure to provide support for children was justified by an inability to provide such support; mother had been employed off and on since she was ordered to pay support, mother testified that she believed she had overcome an alcohol abuse problem, and mother stated that she would have paid support had she known of court order requiring her to do so. In re Adoption of J.M.N. (Ohio App. 2 Dist., Clark, 08-29-2008) No. 08-CA-23, No. 08-CA-24, 2008-Ohio-4394, 2008 WL 3990828, Unreported. Adoption ☞ 7.4(6)

Credible evidence supported the trial court's determination that father's failure to provide support for child for one year was justifiable, and thus father's consent to stepfather's adoption of child was required; witnesses testified that child resided with father for two months during the year in which he allegedly failed to provide support for child, during that year father enlisted in the Navy and relied on representations from Navy financial officers that the Navy would be withholding his child support payments, and child attended father's graduation from Navy boot camp and saw father when he was home on holiday leave. In re Adoption of Reed (Ohio App. 4 Dist., Scioto, 04-17-2006) No. 05CA3048, 2006-Ohio-2094, 2006 WL 1115464, Unreported. Adoption ☞ 7.8(4)

Natural father did not have justifiable cause for failure to support his child for period of at least one year immediately preceding stepfather's petition for adoption, thus rendering his consent to adoption unnecessary; natural father did not pay support for more than one year preceding petition, no person or judicial entity told him dismissal of contempt action brought by county child support enforcement agency against him for failure to pay support terminated support order, and fact that mother may have requested dismissal to increase stepfather's chance of adopting child did not affect father's support obligation. In re Adoption of Rodabaugh (Ohio App. 3 Dist., Hancock, 03-27-2006) No. 5-05-33, 2006-Ohio-1419, 2006 WL 759707, Unreported. Adoption ☞ 7.4(6)

Father's failure to provide maintenance and support for child for one year prior to filing of adoption petition by mother's husband was not justified, and thus, father's consent to adoption was not necessary; father was employed, with a sufficient salary, but failed to provide maintenance or support, and, although father argued that he failed to communicate with child because of contentious relationship with mother, father expressly acknowledged he was aware he could send maintenance and support without court order, and father admitted mother did not prevent him from providing maintenance and support. In re Caudill (Ohio App. 4 Dist., Jackson, 07-21-2005) No. 05CA4, 2005-Ohio-3927, 2005 WL 1802850, Unreported. Adoption ☞ 7.4(6)

Evidence in proceedings for step-parent adoption of biological father's failure to support children, including his admission to making no child support payments whatsoever during one-year period despite his awareness that child support "was an issue," and to making no attempt to communicate or have any contact with children during such period, considered together with lack of evidence of justification for failure to provide support, was sufficient to support termination of his parental rights on grounds of non-support. In Matter of Adoption of Lasky (Ohio App. 11 Dist., Portage, 03-31-2005) No. 2004-P-0087, No. 2004-P-0088, No. 2004-P-0089, 2005-Ohio-1565, 2005 WL 737414, Unreported. Adoption ☞ 7.4(6); Infants ☞ 178

Admission of minor child's biological father that he borrowed an unknown amount of money at some point during the relevant period did not require finding, in step-parent adoption proceeding, that father had sufficient means to support child, such that his consent to adoption was not required due to his failure without justifiable cause to support child. In re Ewart (Ohio App. 4 Dist., Ross, 01-10-2005) No. 04CA2796, 2005-Ohio-116, 2005 WL 77097, Unreported. Adoption ☞ 7.4(6)

Finding that minor child's biological father was justified in failing to support child, such that his consent to step-parent adoption was required, was supported by competent, credible evidence, including his testimony that he substantially complied with the court-ordered support payments for child until his employment was terminated because he did not have a GED, that he applied for numerous jobs but his efforts were hampered by his lack of education and transportation, and that he eventually found employment with a fast food restaurant, as well as two recent pay stubs showing deductions for support payments. In re Ewart (Ohio App. 4 Dist., Ross, 01-10-2005) No. 04CA2796, 2005-Ohio-116, 2005 WL 77097, Unreported. Adoption ☞ 7.8(4)

Absence of court order requiring parents to provide support for minor child did not render parent's failure to support child justifiable, as would make parents' consent to maternal grandparents' adoption of child necessary, and thus cause was remanded for determination of whether parents' failure to support child could be justified on economic basis alone. In re Adoption of Moore (Ohio App. 5 Dist., Fairfield, 05-25-2004) No. 03 CA 74, 2004-Ohio-2802, 2004 WL 1192075, Unreported. Adoption ☞ 15

Evidence supported trial court's findings that ex-wife failed to provide any financial support to her child and that her failure to pay was without justifiable cause, and thus, ex-wife did not have right to withhold her consent to adoption of her daughter by the child's step-mother pursuant to statute providing that consent to adoption is not required of a parent of a minor when the court finds that the parent has failed without justifiable cause to provide for support of the minor; although ex-wife had been diagnosed with fibromyalgia and osteoarthritis, she was not disabled or otherwise unable to work, and although ex-wife claimed to have purchased items for child, she never gave the items to child. In re Adoption of D.P. (Ohio App. 9 Dist., Summit, 08-06-2003) No. 21470, 2003-Ohio-4150, 2003 WL 21804666, Unreported. Adoption ☞ 7.4(6)

Reversal and remand of trial court order which found that mother's failure to provide support for child for one year was without justifiable cause was required, in paternal grandmother's proceeding to adopt child without the consent of mother; trial court relied on mother's failure to provide any support to child after mother received a lump sum payment of over $6,000.00, and mother received the lump sum payment outside of the one year period the court was required to analyze for grandmother's

petition. In re Placement for Adoption Of C.E.T (Ohio App. 2 Dist., Montgomery, 07-11-2003) No. 19566, 2003-Ohio-3783, 2003 WL 21658682, Unreported. Adoption ☞ 15

Biological father failed to establish that his failure to pay child support for over one year was justified, in stepfather's proceeding to adopt children without biological father's consent; father asserted that he was unable to pay child support due to a leg injury but failed to present any evidence, such as medical records, to justify his failure to pay support. In re Adoption of Randall G. (Ohio App. 6 Dist., Lucas, 03-14-2003) No. L-02-1340, No. L-02-1341, 2003-Ohio-1412, 2003 WL 1473698, Unreported. Adoption ☞ 7.8(5)

Natural father had justifiable cause in failing to support children, such that his consent was required before step-father's adoptions of children could proceed, where mother and step-father rejected natural father's attempts to give gifts to his children, to provide them with medical coverage, and to make a payment toward their living expenses, during six months prior to filing of adoption petitions. In re Adoption of Lawrence Stojkov (Ohio App. 11 Dist., Trumbull, 02-14-2003) No. 2002-T-0151, No. 2002-T-0152, 2003-Ohio-705, 2003 WL 352763, Unreported. Adoption ☞ 7.4(6)

While sincere voluntary effort to cure illness or improve lifestyle may be viewed as justifiable cause for failure to pay child support, natural father's four-month stay in a drug rehabilitation facility does not excuse non-support where he has failed to pay support before his commitment or after his release. Matter of Adoption of Stidham (Ohio App. 2 Dist., Montgomery, 09-25-1998) No. 16930, 1998 WL 656567, Unreported.

A mother's refusal to accept payment for the child's tuition is justifiable cause for the natural father's failure to support his child and his consent to adoption by the mother's current husband is necessary where in addition the court fails to schedule a hearing to determine the amount of support which results in the father being unable to make any payments to the child support enforcement agency which would not accept payment without a court order. Adoption of Williams (Ohio App. 5 Dist., Muskingum, 06-04-1998) No. CT97-0038, 1998 WL 346853, Unreported.

There was insufficient evidence that the limited contact between biological father and his minor child in year preceding adoption petition was not justifiable given father's limitations, as required to support finding that father's consent was not required for adoption by child's stepfather; biological father was in prison during relevant period, mother admitted that she never provided a forwarding address and would not have allowed visits, and she did not deny that the father did not have her phone number. In re Adoption of C.L.B. (Ohio App. 3 Dist., 10-25-2010) 191 Ohio App.3d 64, 944 N.E.2d 1190, 2010-Ohio-5190. Adoption ☞ 7.4(4)

Whether or not father was served with notice of hearing on proposed adoption of child by mother's husband, father's consent to adoption was sufficient consideration for agreement whereby mother waived back child support in return for father's consent; by consenting, father waived right to raise any justifiable causes as to why he did not pay support or visit child in year immediately preceding filing of adoption petition. Eckliff v. Walters (Ohio App. 11 Dist., 09-15-2006) 168 Ohio App.3d 727, 861 N.E.2d 843, 2006-Ohio-4817. Child Support ☞ 456

Probate court's order finding that child's father had justifiable cause for failing to support the child for one year prior to filing of maternal grandmother's adoption petition, such that probate court could not grant the adoption petition without father's consent, was a final, appealable order. In re Adoption of W.K.M. (Ohio App. 2 Dist., 05-05-2006) 166 Ohio App.3d 684, 852 N.E.2d 1264, 2006-Ohio-2326. Adoption ☞ 15

Evidence supported finding that mother failed to provide for the maintenance and support of her children, without justifiable cause, during the one year prior to maternal aunt and uncle filing petitions to adopt children, and thus mother's consent was not required for adoption; mother gave son a computer game for his birthday and gave the children clothing and toys for Christmas, maternal aunt and uncle requested $200.00 per week from mother for support of the children, mother never paid any support to aunt and uncle, and mother was employed or able to seek employment during the applicable time period. In re Adoption of James (Ohio Com.Pl., 10-03-2003) 126 Ohio Misc.2d 7, 799 N.E.2d 669, 2003-Ohio-5953. Adoption ☞ 7.4(6)

To preserve the right to consent to the adoption of his or her children, a natural parent must justify his or her failure to support for substantially the entire one-year period preceding the petition for adoption; it is not enough to show that some time during the year a failure to support was justified, but it must instead be demonstrated that no modicum of support reasonably could have been provided at any time during the year. In re Adoption of Kilbane (Ohio App. 8 Dist., 10-01-1998) 130 Ohio App.3d 203, 719 N.E.2d 1012. Adoption ☞ 7.4(6)

Stepfather established by clear and convincing evidence that his stepchildren's biological father had failed to support the children without justifiable cause for one-year statutory period preceding stepfather's petition for adoption, and thus biological father's consent was not required for proposed adoption; biological father did not make any support payments until just prior to filing of adoption petition, and his claim that he was unemployed through most of year was contradicted by other evidence in record. In re Adoption of Kilbane (Ohio App. 8 Dist., 10-01-1998) 130 Ohio App.3d 203, 719 N.E.2d 1012. Adoption ☞ 7.8(4)

Finding that natural father failed, without justifiable cause, to provide maintenance and support for his minor child, so that his consent to child's adoption by stepfather was not necessary, was supported

by evidence that father was obligated to pay $150 per week, or $7,800 per year, in child support, that father's total income for year in question was $13,443.81, that father paid total of $329.40, or less than three percent of his income, in support for his two children, and that father failed to obtain employment commensurate with his level of education. In re Adoption of Wagner (Ohio App. 11 Dist., 01-21-1997) 117 Ohio App.3d 448, 690 N.E.2d 959, appeal not allowed 78 Ohio St.3d 1516, 679 N.E.2d 311. Adoption ☞ 7.8(5)

Under statute providing that natural parent's consent to adoption is not required where that parent has failed, without justifiable cause, to support child for period of "at least one year," trial court was not required to limit its review to period of one year. Dallas v. Dotson (Ohio App. 9 Dist., 08-14-1996) 113 Ohio App.3d 484, 681 N.E.2d 464, dismissed, appeal not allowed 77 Ohio St.3d 1515, 674 N.E.2d 370. Adoption ☞ 7.4(6)

Natural mother's alleged ignorance of law requiring her to support child was not justifiable cause for nonsupport of child, for purposes of mother's right to object to adoption of child. In re Adoption of Kuhlmann (Ohio App. 1 Dist., 12-07-1994) 99 Ohio App.3d 44, 649 N.E.2d 1279. Adoption ☞ 7.4(6)

Once failure of natural parent to provide support has been proven by petitioner seeking adoption, court must then decide whether failure was justified, and such determination will not be disturbed on appeal unless against manifest weight of evidence. In re Adoption of Kuhlmann (Ohio App. 1 Dist., 12-07-1994) 99 Ohio App.3d 44, 649 N.E.2d 1279. Adoption ☞ 7.4(6); Adoption ☞ 15

In determining whether failure to support child is justified, so as to permit parent to object to adoption, parent who is willing to support but unable to do so may have "justification," but parent who is unwilling but able to support does not. In re Adoption of Kuhlmann (Ohio App. 1 Dist., 12-07-1994) 99 Ohio App.3d 44, 649 N.E.2d 1279. Adoption ☞ 7.4(6)

Evidence, which indicated that at one time mother was homeless and unable to pay any support, but that she was not indigent during one-year period prior to adoption petition, failed to establish "justification" for mother's nonpayment of support, and thus, mother was precluded from objecting to adoption; evidence indicated that mother worked briefly for temporary employment service, and then worked at another job where she received at least two raises, one of which was merit raise. In re Adoption of Kuhlmann (Ohio App. 1 Dist., 12-07-1994) 99 Ohio App.3d 44, 649 N.E.2d 1279. Adoption ☞ 7.8(4)

Natural father had not shown facially justifiable cause for terminating employment, and his consent to adoption was consequently not required by virtue of his having failed to make court-ordered support payments, even though he claimed that he had left work to help his parents in operation of their farm, and former wife and children would have continued to be supported if they had remained in farm residence where they were being provided for during marriage. In re Adoption of Deems (Ohio App. 3 Dist., 11-12-1993) 91 Ohio App.3d 552, 632 N.E.2d 1347, cause dismissed 70 Ohio St.3d 1451, 639 N.E.2d 460. Adoption ☞ 7.4(6)

Evidence supported finding that natural father was without "justifiable cause" for failure to support child during one-year period prior to adoption petition and, thus, his consent was not required for adoption; natural father was experiencing financial hardship but it was clear from fairly significant support paid for his other two children and fact that he was able to pay attorney fees for both divorce and bankruptcy proceedings that he had some discretionary income which he could have divided among his three children and contributed toward support of child who was to be adopted. In re Adoption of Cline (Trumbull 1993) 89 Ohio App.3d 450, 624 N.E.2d 1083. Adoption ☞ 7.8(4)

Determination of whether justifiable cause for natural parent's failure to pay child support has been proven by clear and convincing evidence, for purposes of determining whether natural parent's consent to adoption is required, can be disturbed on appeal only if determination is against manifest weight of the evidence; hence, judgment will not be overturned if supported by some competent and credible evidence. In re Adoption of Cline (Trumbull 1993) 89 Ohio App.3d 450, 624 N.E.2d 1083. Adoption ☞ 15

Monies involuntarily intercepted from father's federal income tax refund, and then used to support child, constituted "support" for purposes of statute obviating necessity for parental consent to adoption in cases of parent's unjustifiable failure to provide "maintenance" and "support" for child for period of one year prior to filing of adoption petition; fact that money was derived from interception of income tax refund, rather than from voluntary payment or withholding from wages, did not render payment something other than payment for support of maintenance, regardless of degree of voluntariness involved. In re Adoption of Kessler (Huron 1993) 87 Ohio App.3d 317, 622 N.E.2d 354. Adoption ☞ 7.4(6)

If petitioner for adoption presents evidence that natural parent has failed to support child for one-year period, parent must justify his or her failure to support for substantially entire one-year period to avoid nonconsensual adoption; it is not enough to show that sometime during year failure to support was justified; it must be demonstrated that no modicum of support reasonably could have been provided at any time during year. In re Adoption of Kessler (Huron 1993) 87 Ohio App.3d 317, 622 N.E.2d 354. Adoption ☞ 7.4(6)

Assuming that father failed to provide support for his child for one-year period necessary to obviate necessity of father's consent to child's adoption by another, failure could not be deemed unjustifiable where father was unemployed and was unable to find new employment, outside of temporary job that lasted six weeks; there was no evidence as to

amount father earned during time period from temporary job or from other jobs or of his ability to pay support. In re Adoption of Kessler (Huron 1993) 87 Ohio App.3d 317, 622 N.E.2d 354. Adoption ☞ 7.4(6)

A stepmother petitioning to adopt her stepchild has the burden of proving that the natural mother's failure to provide support is unjustifiable after the natural mother comes forward with some evidence justifying her failure to provide support. In re Adoption of Dues (Montgomery 1990) 69 Ohio App.3d 498, 591 N.E.2d 257.

A natural father's duty to support a child arises at birth, particularly where he acknowledges paternity, and where the natural father unjustifiably fails to communicate with or support a child for one year prior to the filing of an adoption petition, his consent to the adoption of his illegitimate child is unnecessary. In re Adoption of Taylor (Medina 1989) 61 Ohio App.3d 500, 573 N.E.2d 156, motion overruled 43 Ohio St.3d 712, 541 N.E.2d 78.

The question of whether a natural parent's failure to support his or her child has been proven by the petitioner by clear and convincing evidence to have been without justifiable cause is a determination for the probate court, and will not be disturbed on appeal unless such determination is against the manifest weight of the evidence. In re Adoption of Bovett (Ohio 1987) 33 Ohio St.3d 102, 515 N.E.2d 919. Adoption ☞ 15

Under RC 3107.07(A), the probate court shall determine the issue of justifiable cause by weighing the evidence of the natural parent's circumstances for the statutory period for which he or she failed to provide support. The court shall determine whether the parent's failure to support the child for that period as a whole (and not just a portion thereof) was without justifiable cause. In re Adoption of Bovett (Ohio 1987) 33 Ohio St.3d 102, 515 N.E.2d 919. Adoption ☞ 7.4(6)

A natural mother collecting public assistance and cohabiting with an employed man is not unable to pay $5 weekly support for her child in the custody of paternal grandparents; the lack of payment is thus unjustifiable. In re Adoption of Lay (Ohio 1986) 25 Ohio St.3d 41, 495 N.E.2d 9, 25 O.B.R. 66.

The question of whether justifiable cause for failure to pay child support has been proven by clear and convincing evidence in a particular case is a determination for the probate court and will not be disturbed on appeal unless such determination is against the manifest weight of the evidence. In re Adoption of Masa (Ohio 1986) 23 Ohio St.3d 163, 492 N.E.2d 140, 23 O.B.R. 330. Adoption ☞ 15

A natural father has justifiable cause for failure to support his child, within the meaning of RC 3107.07(A), if the mother has denied visitation and refused some of his tendered contributions toward support of the child. In re Adoption of Foster (Van Wert 1985) 22 Ohio App.3d 129, 489 N.E.2d 1070, 22 O.B.R. 331.

Absent an allegation that the natural parent failed to communicate with his child, in order for the natural parent to maintain his right to avoid an adoption of his child by withholding consent, the natural parent must pay the full amount of support required by judicial decree for at least one of the twelve months immediately preceding the filing of the adoption petition or else show "justifiable cause" for failure to pay for at least one of those months. In re Adoption of Burton (Warren 1981) 3 Ohio App.3d 251, 444 N.E.2d 1061, 3 O.B.R. 283. Adoption ☞ 7.4(6).

Where petition for adoption alleged that the mother "has not supported" child "for two consecutive years," but does not allege that mother "has failed or refused to support the child" for such length of time, as prescribed by statute, and there is no proof of a failure or refusal to support, it is reversible error for court to render decree of adoption without mother's consent thereto, and court's finding that mother is not a proper person to have custody of the child is unjustifiable where court ruled that testimony relative to mother's reputation was incompetent and evidence as to her moral qualifications was very limited. In re Goodfleisch (Franklin 1943) 73 Ohio App. 17, 53 N.E.2d 913, 40 Ohio Law Abs. 432, 27 O.O. 542.

Children's legal custodian's refusal to accept child support from father was justifiable cause for father's failure to support children, and thus father's consent was required before children could be adopted by maternal aunt and uncle. In re Adoption of Morelli (Ohio App. 7 Dist., Jefferson, 09-19-2002) No. 02 JE 5, No. 02 JE 6, 2002-Ohio-5045, 2002 WL 31114885, Unreported, stay granted 97 Ohio St.3d 1426, 777 N.E.2d 845, 2002-Ohio-5854, appeal not allowed 97 Ohio St.3d 1471, 779 N.E.2d 237, 2002-Ohio-6347. Adoption ☞ 7.4(6)

Petitioner for adoption has the burden of proving, by clear and convincing evidence, that the natural parent has failed to support the child and that this failure was without justifiable cause. In re Adoption of Barkhurst (Ohio App. 12 Dist., Butler, 09-04-2002) No. CA2002-04-081, 2002-Ohio-4711, 2002 WL 31009205, Unreported, appeal not allowed 97 Ohio St.3d 1471, 779 N.E.2d 237, 2002-Ohio-6347. Adoption ☞ 7.8(1)

A mother's consent is required for the adoption of her natural daughter by the child's paternal grandparents who claim the mother had failed without justiciable cause to provide child support where a juvenile court has relieved the mother of her general statutory duty of support as well as any judicially-decreed duty until further order and so a failure to support cannot be used against her. In re Adoption of Stephens (Ohio App. 2 Dist., Montgomery, 12-21-2001) No. 18956, 2001-Ohio-7027, 2001 WL 1636284, Unreported, appeal not allowed 94 Ohio St.3d 1471, 762 N.E.2d 1017.

In adoption proceedings where a natural father, unemployed for three years, is willing yet unable to provide support for his children, the failure to support is justified and his consent to the adoption is necessary. In re Rickus, No. CA–7089 (5th Dist Ct App, Stark, 8–24–87).

Where a putative father sends two checks totalling thirty dollars for the support of a child just prior to the filing of a petition for adoption and where this constitutes the only support ever offered or given, a finding that the putative father has failed to care for and support the minor child is justified and renders his consent to the adoption unnecessary. In re Adoption of Rouleau, No. 1058 (4th Dist Ct App, Ross, 8–31–84).

A finding that the natural mother has failed without justifiable cause to support the child for a one-year period prior to the filing of a step-parent adoption petition is not proven by clear and convincing evidence where the record indicates that the mother visited and provided support payments, as well as in-kind maintenance, during at least part of the one-year period, and the mother presented unrebutted evidence that she was attending school full time during part of the period, which impacted on her ability to be gainfully employed, and that her physical and mental well being and her ability to work were impaired as a result of injuries sustained in an assault by the natural father. In re Adoption of Cutlip, Nos. 00COA01383 and 00COA01384, 2001 WL 197924 (5th Dist Ct App, Ashland, 2–26–01).

Where natural father deposited child support payments into an escrow account pursuant to approval of the court of another state, such a failure to pay child support directly to the mother constitutes "justifiable cause" under RC 3107.07(A). In re Adoption of Howard, No. 81–02–0013 (12th Dist Ct App, Butler, 1–13–82).

9. —— Incarceration, failure to support

Biological father failed to maintain and support child for the year immediately preceding adoption petition, and thus, father's consent to adoption was not required; father had worked for 89 days when he was not incarcerated but he never sent any portion of his earnings for support, choosing instead to support his drug habit, and he did not ask about support obligations while incarcerated in other states. In re Adoption of Devin Scott S. (Ohio App. 6 Dist., Lucas, 07-25-2003) No. L-03-1067, 2003-Ohio-3985, 2003 WL 21716339, Unreported. Adoption ☞ 7.4(6)

Evidence was sufficient to support trial court's finding that mother's failure to support her child for a period of at least one year was justified, and thus, mother's consent to step-mother's adoption of the child was required; mother was incarcerated for over six months of the statutory period, she did not have any meaningful employment during the period, any money she received was from the natural father, and during the periods when mother was not incarcerated she was continuously using drugs. In re Adoption of Zachary Steven S. (Ohio App. 6 Dist., Lucas, 07-25-2003) No. L-03-1056, 2003-Ohio-3981, 2003 WL 21716338, Unreported. Adoption ☞ 7.4(6)

Prospective adoptive parents did not establish, by clear and convincing evidence, that mother failed, without justifiable cause, to provide for maintenance and support for child for one year prior to the adoption petition, and absent such showing, mother's consent to adoption was required; mother sent cards, letters, and clothing to the child, and mother's expenditures of minimal amounts on nonessential items while incarcerated did not necessitate a finding that she failed to support child. In re Adoption of Rodgers (Ohio App. 11 Dist., Trumbull, 03-17-2003) No. 2002-T-0171, 2003-Ohio-1424, 2003 WL 1473635, Unreported. Adoption ⚎ 7.4(6)

A trial court's conclusion that a father has abandoned his daughter is erroneous where, although he failed to provide financial support to her because he had been incarcerated since her birth, he had regular visits with her while incarcerated, and following his release he takes a more active role in her life by caring for her during her visits with his parents, he finds employment that will permit him to financially support her, and he indicates willingness to begin paying child support. Burbaugh v. Handshoe (Ohio App. 3 Dist., Marion, 08-15-2000) No. 9-2000-01, 2000 WL 1201291, Unreported.

Stepfather presented no evidence to contradict evidence that biological father attempted to provide support for his minor child from prison, by contacting the Child Support Enforcement Agency (CSEA) to have it withhold funds, as required to show that father's incarceration was not a justifiable cause of his failure to pay support in year preceding adoption petition, so as to allow adoption without father's consent. In re Adoption of C.L.B. (Ohio App. 3 Dist., 10-25-2010) 191 Ohio App.3d 64, 944 N.E.2d 1190, 2010-Ohio-5190. Adoption ⚎ 7.4(6)

Domestic relations court's order, awarding temporary custody of child to maternal grandmother and stating that no child support from father would be ordered due to his incarceration, superseded father's statutory duty of child support and provided justifiable cause for his failure to support child during the year prior to grandmother's filing of adoption petition, and thus father's consent was required for the adoption. In re Adoption of W.K.M. (Ohio App. 2 Dist., 05-05-2006) 166 Ohio App.3d 684, 852 N.E.2d 1264, 2006-Ohio-2326. Adoption ⚎ 7.4(6); Child Support ⚎ 24

Trial court was not bound or required to find that natural father's incarceration was justifiable cause for nonsupport, so as to require his consent to adoption. Dallas v. Dotson (Ohio App. 9 Dist., 08-14-1996) 113 Ohio App.3d 484, 681 N.E.2d 464, dismissed, appeal not allowed 77 Ohio St.3d 1515, 674 N.E.2d 370. Adoption ⚎ 7.4(6)

The fact of incarceration in a penal institution does not constitute a willful failure to properly support and maintain a child, within the meaning of RC 3107.06(B)(4), so as to vitiate the requirement of consent by both natural parents prior to the entry of a decree of adoption. In re Schoeppner's Adoption (Ohio 1976) 46 Ohio St.2d 21, 345 N.E.2d 608, 75 O.O.2d 12. Adoption ⚎ 7.4(6)

Evidence in adoption proceeding supported finding that natural father failed to provide support for son without justifiable cause for one year prior to stepfather's petition for adoption, and thus natural father's consent for adoption was not required; although natural father was incarcerated, and divorce order effectively relieved him of support payments until after his release from prison, it was father's own violent acts towards his family which caused subsequent lack of support for son. Frymier v. Crampton (Ohio App. 5 Dist., Licking, 07-08-2002) No. 02 CA 8, 2002-Ohio-3591, 2002 WL 1489563, Unreported. Adoption ⚎ 7.4(2.1)

10. —— Judicial determination of paternity, failure to support

Biological father of out-of-wedlock child was not subject to a support obligation, for the purpose of statute that authorized another party to adopt child without the biological parent's consent after one year of nonsupport, and thus statute did not apply to obviate requirement to obtain parental consent to child's adoption by stepfather, where there had been no final judicial determination of paternity. In re Adoption of Pushcar (Ohio App. 11 Dist., Lake, 09-23-2005) No. 2005-L050, 2005-Ohio-5114, 2005 WL 2372761, Unreported, appeal allowed 108 Ohio St.3d 1436, 842 N.E.2d 62, 2006-Ohio-421, affirmed 110 Ohio St.3d 332, 853 N.E.2d 647, 2006-Ohio-4572, reconsideration denied 111 Ohio St.3d 1495, 857 N.E.2d 1231, 2006-Ohio-6171. Adoption ⚎ 7.2(3); Adoption ⚎ 7.4(6)

Father's duty to support child did not begin until date administrative parentage determination became final, nearly a month after mother and stepfather petitioned to adopt child, and, therefore, father's earlier failure to support child did not obviate need to obtain father's consent to adoption. In re Adoption of Hudnell (Ohio App. 4 Dist., 08-06-1996) 113 Ohio App.3d 296, 680 N.E.2d 1055. Adoption ⚎ 7.4(6); Children Out–of–wedlock ⚎ 21(2)

Prescriptive one-year period after which natural father may be deemed to have abandoned child so that natural father's consent is not necessary to child's adoption commences running not upon birth of child, but upon determination of paternity, so that father's actions regarding communication and support were to be analyzed from date of declaration of paternity, where father's parentage action was filed and determined prior to filing of adoption petition. In re Adoption of Sherry (Ohio App. 9 Dist., 12-20-1995) 107 Ohio App.3d 830, 669 N.E.2d 551. Adoption ⚎ 7.2(3)

An unmarried parent is subject to the support obligation to which RC 3107.07(A) refers only where a paternity determination has been rendered pursuant to RC 3111.08(B) or 3111.12. In re Adoption of Sunderhaus (Ohio 1992) 63 Ohio St.3d 127, 585 N.E.2d 418, rehearing denied 63 Ohio St.3d 1442, 589 N.E.2d 46. Adoption ⚎ 7.4(6)

Where there has been no judicial determination of parentage, the acknowledged natural father of a child born out of wedlock, who has signed the birth certificate, has no legal obligation to support his child and cannot be found to have violated a legal duty, thereby dispensing with his consent in an adoption proceeding. Amstutz v Braden, No. L–85–191 (6th Dist Ct App, Lucas, 12–27–85).

11. —— Willful failure, failure to support

Willful failure to fulfill common-law duty of support for substantial period of time prior to filing of adoption petition can result in determination that putative father's consent to adoption is not required. In re Adoption of Bowes (Ohio App. 11 Dist., 08-07-1995) 105 Ohio App.3d 574, 664 N.E.2d 963. Adoption ⚘ 7.4(6)

There was some competent credible evidence to support trial court's finding that putative father had cared for and had not willfully failed to support child under statutory provision allowing putative father to object to adoption where testimony showed that putative father's income was between $0 and $6,000 per year since child's birth, and that father had provided repair and other in kind services to child's mother and had been incarcerated part of time since child's birth. In re Adoption of Bowes (Ohio App. 11 Dist., 08-07-1995) 105 Ohio App.3d 574, 664 N.E.2d 963. Adoption ⚘ 7.8(4)

Willful abandonment and failure to support a child will be found where (1) the father provides no support to the mother of the child either before or after the birth; (2) the father does not pay for the expenses of the birth; and (3) although the mother, child, and father temporarily reside in the father's parents' home, the father fails to support the child and continues to date another woman. In re Adoption of Hart (Lucas 1989) 62 Ohio App.3d 544, 577 N.E.2d 77, motion overruled 45 Ohio St.3d 704, 543 N.E.2d 810.

Where a divorce court decreed that the mother assume financial responsibility for the children and imposed no legal obligation upon the father for their support, the failure of the father to pay support was not the willful failure to perform a legal duty, so long as the mother was willing and able to provide the required support; and the adoption of the children cannot be granted without the consent of the father. In re Adoption of McCoy (Ohio Com.Pl. 1972) 31 Ohio Misc. 195, 287 N.E.2d 833, 60 O.O.2d 356. Adoption ⚘ 7.4(4)

Where a couple petition for adoption of their grandson, who has lived in their home during his mother's separation and divorce from his father, and in their custody since her death, claiming that the consent of the father is not required because of willful failure to support the child for more than two years immediately preceding filing the petition, as specified in RC 3107.06, the burden of proving such willful failure is not sustained by evidence that the petitioners, financially able to support the child without hardship, had never requested any payment from the father, although he had told them on numerous occasions to call on him if they needed

any money for the boy's care, and he did maintain an interest otherwise in his son's welfare, even seeking to have the boy live in his own home. In re Adoption of Wright (Ohio Prob. 1968) 15 Ohio Misc. 354, 240 N.E.2d 923, 44 O.O.2d 509.

A parent may be found to have "willfully failed" to support, within the meaning of RC 3107.06, where such parent, knowing of the duty and being able to provide such support, voluntarily and intentionally fails to do so. In re Adoption of Lewis (Ohio 1966) 8 Ohio St.2d 25, 222 N.E.2d 628, 37 O.O.2d 376.

The words, "willfully failed to properly support and maintain," as used in RC 3107.06 in regard to circumstances in which consent of a parent to adoption of a child is not necessary, imply more than a mere failure to provide financial support; such failure must be intentional. In re Adoption of Earhart (Miami 1961) 117 Ohio App. 73, 190 N.E.2d 468, 23 O.O.2d 156.

Payment by a divorced father under a $25 per week support order of only $1,500 over a two and one-half year period constituted willful failure to support such children within the meaning of RC 3107.06. In re Adoptions of Zinsmeister (Ohio Prob. 1961) 178 N.E.2d 849, 87 Ohio Law Abs. 129.

Evidence that the mother of a child born out of wedlock paid nothing for the support of the child does not establish "willful failure" to support, nor can any inference be drawn therefrom to that effect where there is positive evidence that the mother was not financially able to contribute to the support of the child, and the petitioner for adoption, with whom the child was placed, never requested or expected any assistance, payment or contribution by the mother. In re Adoption of Peters (Lucas 1961) 113 Ohio App. 173, 177 N.E.2d 541, 17 O.O.2d 141.

A father has not "willfully failed to properly support" his minor child for a period of more than two years, where for almost fourteen months of such time he fulfills his obligations of support, and does furnish some, but not enough, "support" for nine months more and there is no evidence of a willful failure to furnish enough "support," and the consent of the father to the adoption of such child is necessary. In re Adoption of De Vore (Franklin 1959) 111 Ohio App. 1, 167 N.E.2d 381, 83 Ohio Law Abs. 14, 13 O.O.2d 376.

A parent, who for more than seven years prior to the filing of a petition for the adoption of her child has refused to contribute to the support of such child except for occasional Christmas presents, has "willfully failed to properly support and maintain" such child; and the consent of such parent to the adoption is not required. In re Adoption of Krisher (Fairfield 1958) 107 Ohio App. 109, 157 N.E.2d 123, 7 O.O.2d 465. Adoption ⚘ 7.4(6)

Natural parents who placed a child with the sister of the mother several hours after its birth and permitted such sister and her husband to care for such child and did not contribute to its support did not "willfully fail" to support such child within the meaning of GC 8004–6 (RC 3107.06). Adoption of

Wedl (Ohio Prob. 1952) 114 N.E.2d 311, 65 Ohio Law Abs. 231.

In a proceeding for adoption, instituted by the filing of such petition, where the evidence discloses that a nonconsenting parent willfully neglected to properly support and maintain such child for a period of time far in excess of two years, and where there is no evidence to show that the petitioners for adoption are not suitably qualified to support and maintain the child, or that the adoption is not for the best interests of the child, or that the child is not suitable for adoption, the consent of such nonconsenting parent is not required and the adoption will be granted. In re Adoption of Shaw (Brown 1950) 91 Ohio App. 347, 108 N.E.2d 236, 48 O.O. 427.

Where a father has signed the birth certificate as an informant, making him the child's putative father, a decision of the juvenile court finding that consent to adoption is not needed is unlawful in that it violates RC 3107.07 by failing to find that the party is not the natural father or that he willfully abandoned or failed to care for and support the minor. In re Adoption of Hilary Marie B, No. WM–96–014, 1996 WL 715453 (6th Dist Ct App, Williams, 12–13–96).

12. —— Putative father, failure to support

Natural father's single payment of $20 for child support in year preceding filing of adoption petition by putative father did not constitute maintenance and support required to make natural father's consent to adoption necessary; payment was less than half of natural father's child support obligation for a single week. In re Adoption of Knight (Ohio App. 10 Dist., 11-29-1994) 97 Ohio App.3d 670, 647 N.E.2d 251. Adoption ⬥ 7.4(6)

Natural father's payment, in year preceding filing of adoption petition by putative father, of $300 to child's psychologist for counseling to work on problem of child's fear of visiting natural father, did not constitute maintenance and support required to make natural father's consent to adoption necessary. In re Adoption of Knight (Ohio App. 10 Dist., 11-29-1994) 97 Ohio App.3d 670, 647 N.E.2d 251. Adoption ⬥ 7.4(6)

Evidence that putative father neither paid nor offered to pay natural mother's medical bills associated with pregnancy was insufficient to establish that father had abandoned mother, and, thus, that mother could place child for adoption without father's consent, where no evidence showed that father was made aware of medical bills or that mother would have accepted his assistance, and all indications were that mother and her parents would have refused any assistance. In re Adoption of Klonowski (Stark 1993) 87 Ohio App.3d 352, 622 N.E.2d 376. Adoption ⬥ 7.4(6)

Willful failure by a putative father of a child born out of wedlock to support the child for a substantial period of time prior to the filing of an adoption petition can result in the conclusion that the consent of this putative father is not required for the adoption. In re Adoption of Youngpeter (Hancock 1989) 65 Ohio App.3d 172, 583 N.E.2d 360. Adoption ⬥ 7.4(6)

A putative father's payment of medical bills attendant to a child's birth within one year of the filing of a petition for adoption qualifies as "support" for purposes of the duty of support of a minor child; since the putative father's duty of support is met, his consent is required for adoption. In re Adoption of Youngpeter (Hancock 1989) 65 Ohio App.3d 172, 583 N.E.2d 360.

A putative father has no legal duty to support his child until the duty is established in a paternity action; therefore, where paternity proceedings have not been instituted, failure to support, pursuant to RC 3107.07(A), does not provide a basis for determining that the father's consent to adoption is not required. In re Adoption of Sunderhaus, No. CA89–12–176 (12th Dist Ct App, Butler, 10–15–90), affirmed by 63 OS(3d) 127, 585 NE(2d) 418 (1992).

13. —— Gifts, failure to support

Gift card of $125 for clothing store and $60 that father sent to child, respectively, for Christmas and her birthday constituted "maintenance and support," for purposes of exception dispensing with requirement of written consent to adoption when parent has failed to provide for maintenance and support for a period of at least one year immediately preceding filing of adoption petition, and, thus, father's consent to stepfather's adoption of child was required; father's monetary gifts to child evidenced his intent not to abandon child, gift card was from a clothing store, which enabled child to purchase clothing, an undeniable necessary, and the cash gift provided means by which child might attain additional comforts. In re Adoption of M.B. (Ohio App. 9 Dist., Summit, 03-16-2011) No. 25304, 2011-Ohio-1215, 2011 WL 899638, Unreported, motion to certify allowed 128 Ohio St.3d 1555, 949 N.E.2d 42, 2011-Ohio-2905. Adoption ⬥ 7.4(6)

Gifts that biological mother provided her children at Christmas and clothes and shoes she provided them when school started were not sufficient to meet mother's parental obligation to support her child, as required to show that mother supported her children during year preceding filing of adoption petition, such as to require mother's consent for adoption. In re Adoption of L.C.H. (Ohio App. 4 Dist., Scioto, 02-19-2010) No. 09CA3318, No. 09CA3319, No. 09CA3324, 2010-Ohio-643, 2010 WL 628428, Unreported, appeal not allowed 125 Ohio St.3d 1450, 927 N.E.2d 1129, 2010-Ohio-2510. Adoption ⬥ 7.4(6)

Mother did not provide support and maintenance for children, and because mother failed, without justifiable cause, to provide for the children, mother's consent to the adoption was not required; mother did not provide regular contributions to help pay for food, clothing, and shelter for the children, the purchases made for the children were in the nature of gifts rather than maintenance and support, and the occasional meal at fast food restaurant and some small toys did not equate to the provision of maintenance and support. Garner v. Greenwalt (Ohio App. 5 Dist., Stark, 11-17-2008) No. 2007 CA 00296, 2008-Ohio-5963, 2008 WL 4918231, Unreported, appeal not allowed 120 Ohio St.3d 1528, 901 N.E.2d 246, 2009-Ohio-614. Adoption ☞ 7.4(6)

Evidence supported finding that mother unjustifiably failed to support children, and thus mother's consent to step-grandmother's petition to adopt children was not required; grandmother testified that mother never paid medical support for the children, as ordered by the court, mother disputed that statement but did not provide any evidence to establish that she had paid the support, and mother's occasional purchases and gifts did not constitute maintenance. In re Crandall (Ohio App. 1 Dist., Hamilton, 03-02-2007) No. C-060770, 2007-Ohio-855, 2007 WL 625009, Unreported. Adoption ☞ 7.4(6); Adoption ☞ 7.8(5)

Assuming that biological father's gifts to children constituted "support" within scope of statute governing termination of parental rights for non-support, such gifts did not compel finding that biological father had attempted to support children, where such gifts were made outside of one-year statutory period cited in petition for step-parent adoption. In Matter of Adoption of Lasky (Ohio App. 11 Dist., Portage, 03-31-2005) No. 2004-P-0087, No. 2004-P-0088, No. 2004-P-0089, 2005-Ohio-1565, 2005 WL 737414, Unreported. Adoption ☞ 7.4(6); Infants ☞ 155

Mother failed to preserve for review claim that trial court erred in finding that providing clothing, toys, and a money card did not constitute support for her children, so as to allow for adoption of her children without her consent, where magistrate initially made decision in case, and mother failed to file written objections to finding that mother had not provided for maintenance and support of the children. In re Adoption of C.P. (Ohio App. 9 Dist., Lorain, 09-17-2003) No. 03CA008268, No. 03CA008269, 2003-Ohio-4905, 2003 WL 22136288, Unreported. Adoption ☞ 15

Grandmother failed to establish in adoption petition that non-consenting mother did not have justifiable cause for failure to pay child support or for failure to spend time with children, and thus grandmother's adoption was barred; mother presented six witnesses that testified grandmother refused to allow mother to see children or to give gifts to children, and mother's minimal income precluded her from providing support for children. In re Adoption of A.P.L. (Ohio App. 2 Dist., Montgomery, 08-22-2003) No. 19772, 2003-Ohio-4433, 2003 WL 21995325, Unreported. Adoption ☞ 7.8(5)

Evidence supported finding that mother's failure to provide support to her children for requisite one-year period was without justifiable cause, even though she did send some gifts to children, and thus mother's consent to adoption of children by children's paternal grandmother and grandmother's husband was not required; mother knew she had a child support obligation, mother had discretionary

funds available to pay support but spent her money on immaterial luxuries, and gifts were of no value to children. In re Minich (Ohio App. 11 Dist., Trumbull, 05-30-2003) No. 2003-T-0010, No. 2003-T-0011, 2003-Ohio-2817, 2003 WL 21263874, Unreported. Adoption ☞ 7.4(6)

Purchasing Christmas presents and including the child on a medical insurance policy at work are not sufficient to require consent of the putative father for adoption by the child's stepfather. Matter of Hilary Marie B. (Ohio App. 6 Dist., Williams, 09-19-1997) No. WM-97-013, 1997 WL 586741, Unreported.

In a step-parent adoption petition, consent of the natural father is necessary where he provides $200.00 in support in the year preceding the adoption petition; whether some funds deposited by the father's mother were a gift to her son or wages earned by her son is of no consequence where the funds were deposited in his name with the Bureau of Support. In Matter of Adoption of Alexander (Ohio App. 2 Dist., Darke, 09-29-1995) No. 1366, 1995 WL 570555, appeal not allowed 75 Ohio St.3d 1412, 661 N.E.2d 760.

Gifts to a child from child's natural parent do not qualify as "support" for purposes of determining whether parent has failed to provide maintenance and support for his child for at least one year prior to the filing of an adoption petition, such that parent's consent is not prerequisite to the child's adoption. In re Adoption of McNutt (Ohio App. 4 Dist., 09-27-1999) 134 Ohio App.3d 822, 732 N.E.2d 470. Adoption ☞ 7.4(6)

When a child possesses sufficient clothes and toys, a natural father's purchase of clothing and toys for child may not constitute "maintenance" or "support" sufficient to preserve the father's right to prevent an adoption, under statute obviating requirement that natural parent of child consent to child's adoption when parent fails to provide maintenance or support for child for one year prior to filing of adoption petition. In re Adoption of McNutt (Ohio App. 4 Dist., 09-27-1999) 134 Ohio App.3d 822, 732 N.E.2d 470. Adoption ☞ 7.4(6)

A child can be adopted under RC 3107.07(A) without the consent of a natural parent if the parent failed without just cause to pay child support even though the parent communicated with the child and sent gifts; interference by the child's stepfather with the father's telephone calls and written correspondence with his child are held insufficient cause for the father's failure to pay support in light of the court's conclusion that "ultimately it was [the child's] own choice to discontinue contact" because of the father's lack of "real interest." In re Adoption of Labo (Shelby 1988) 47 Ohio App.3d 57, 546 N.E.2d 1384.

The purchase of toys and clothes valued at approximately $133 is insufficient to fulfill a natural parent's duty of support where the gifts are not requested and they provide no real value of support because the child has sufficient toys and clothes; consequently, the consent of the natural parent is not required in an action for adoption. In re Adoption of Strawser (Franklin 1987) 36 Ohio App.3d 232, 522 N.E.2d 1105.

14. —— Health insurance, failure to support

Alleged payments made by natural father for provision of health coverage for minor child did not constitute "maintenance and support," for purposes of statute permitting adoption of child without natural parent's consent if parent has failed to support child without justifiable cause for year prior to adoption petition, where father failed to reveal existence of health coverage to child's mother, child derived no benefit from payments as result of father's concealment, and earlier health insurance card that mother did receive from father was rejected when she attempted to use it. In re Adoption of Wagner (Ohio App. 11 Dist., 01-21-1997) 117 Ohio App.3d 448, 690 N.E.2d 959, appeal not allowed 78 Ohio St.3d 1516, 679 N.E.2d 311. Adoption ⬤ 7.4(2.1)

Natural father's purchase of health insurance for child, in year preceding filing of adoption petition by putative father, did not constitute maintenance and support required to make natural father's consent to adoption necessary, where natural father did not reveal existence of insurance to child or child's mother, and insurance thus did not benefit child. In re Adoption of Knight (Ohio App. 10 Dist., 11-29-1994) 97 Ohio App.3d 670, 647 N.E.2d 251. Adoption ⬤ 7.4(6)

The fact that a natural father places his child on a medical insurance policy through his employer at a cost of $6 per month is insufficient to constitute care and support of the child pursuant to RC 3107.07(B) where the nominal contribution is neither used nor within the knowledge of the child's natural mother for two or three years prior to the filing of an adoption petition. In re Adoption of Strawser (Franklin 1987) 36 Ohio App.3d 232, 522 N.E.2d 1105. Adoption ⬤ 7.4(6)

Father's claim that he provided health insurance for children during one year period prior to filing of petition for adoption by child's maternal aunt and uncle did not constitute maintenance and support, for purposes of establishing that father's consent was not required for adoption, where father did not reveal existence of health insurance to aunt and uncle. In re Adoption of Morelli (Ohio App. 7 Dist., Jefferson, 09-19-2002) No. 02 JE 5, No. 02 JE 6, 2002-Ohio-5045, 2002 WL 31114885, Unreported, stay granted 97 Ohio St.3d 1426, 777 N.E.2d 845, 2002-Ohio-5854, appeal not allowed 97 Ohio St.3d 1471, 779 N.E.2d 237, 2002-Ohio-6347. Adoption ⬤ 7.4(1)

Where a natural father pays three premiums of $173 toward health insurance coverage for himself and his child for a few months, but fails to reveal the existence of the health insurance to the child or the child's mother and as a result the health insurance never benefits the child, the insurance payments do not constitute sufficient support and maintenance of the child to make the natural father's consent necessary for the child's proposed

adoption. In re Adoption of Knight, No. 94APF06-875, 1994 WL 672999 (10th Dist Ct App, Franklin, 11-29-94).

Diapers, toys, clothing and medical insurance constitute maintenance and support within the meaning of RC 3107.07 and there was evidence to show natural mother provided support, however meager, to child within one year of adoption petition filing. In re Adoption of Mills, No. CA93-04-036, 1993 WL 430473 (12th Dist Ct App, Warren, 10-25-93).

15. —— Burden of proof, failure to support

Trial court applied an incorrect standard or burden of proof in determining that father's consent to maternal great-grandmother's adoption of his two minor children was not necessary; trial court erroneously required father to prove that his failure to support and communicate with the children was justified, when the burden of proving that the failure to support and communicate was without justifiable cause properly belonged to maternal great-grandmother and her husband. In re Adoption of B.G. (Ohio App. 6 Dist., Erie, 10-12-2010) No. E-10-024, No. E-10-025, 2010-Ohio-5025, 2010 WL 4027668, Unreported. Adoption ⬤ 7.8(1)

Trial court finding that mother failed, without justifiable cause, to provide support or maintenance for child for one year prior to the adoption petition being filed was not against the manifest weight of the evidence, even though mother spent nine months in drug rehabilitation centers; mother exchanged sex for drugs or money for three months out of the 12 months prior to filing of adoption petition, but failed to use any of the money to support child. In re Adoption of Haylett (Ohio App. 11 Dist., Portage, 05-07-2004) No. 2003-P-0093, No. 2003-P-0103, 2004-Ohio-2306, 2004 WL 1043430, Unreported. Adoption ⬤ 7.4(6)

Evidence supported finding that biological father had failed to provide support and maintenance to child for one year prior to step-father filing his petition to adopt child, and thus biological father's consent to adoption was not required; father had not paid child support in the one year time period before step-father petitioned to adopt child, he had not filed any motions to pay child support, father was employed and earned approximately $53,000.00 per year, magistrate found that mother did not interfere with support by father, and father's gift of a hockey jersey was insufficient to fulfill his duty of support and maintenance. In re Adoption of Diego Esteban Breckenridge (Ohio App. 10 Dist., Franklin, 04-22-2004) No. 03AP-1166, 2004-Ohio-2145, 2004 WL 894604, Unreported. Adoption ⬤ 7.4(6)

Biological father failed to establish that the trial court impermissibly shifted the burden of proof from stepfather to biological father, in stepfather's action to adopt children with biological father's consent; the burden of proof remained with stepfather to establish that biological father failed to communicate or failed to provide support for the children for one year, once stepfather established either situation, biological father had the burden of producing evidence that his failure to communicate or failure to provide support was justified. In re Adoption of Randall G. (Ohio App. 6 Dist., Lucas, 03-14-2003) No. L-02-1340, No. L-02-1341, 2003-Ohio-1412, 2003 WL 1473698, Unreported. Adoption ☞ 7.8(1)

Counsel's stipulation to allegation that biological father failed to communicate with his children for one year and failed to provide any support for the children for one year did not prejudice father by causing the trial court to shift the burden of proof to father to establish any justification for the failures, as alleged by father in stepfather's proceeding to adopt children without the consent of father; there was no evidence that the trial court shifted the burden of proof to father on the issue, or that the stipulations caused the trial court to do so. In re Adoption of Randall G. (Ohio App. 6 Dist., Lucas, 03-14-2003) No. L-02-1340, No. L-02-1341, 2003-Ohio-1412, 2003 WL 1473698, Unreported. Adoption ☞ 13

Assuming, arguendo, that stepmother who sought to adopt her two stepchildren perpetrated fraud upon the court by falsely claiming that she attempted to notify biological mother of adoption petition, biological mother failed to show that adoptions would not have been granted but for such fraud, and thus, one-year statute of limitations for mother's challenge to adoptions was not tolled, where mother failed to pay child support as ordered by custody agreement between mother and father for year preceding filing of petition, and mother had not seen children in two years and did not prove that letters, gifts, and money orders that she allegedly sent in year prior to adoption were actually sent to or received at home of father and stepmother. In re Adoption of Miller (Ohio App. 3 Dist., Logan, 02-19-2003) No. 8-02-22, No. 8-02-23, 2003-Ohio-718, 2003 WL 354941, Unreported. Adoption ☞ 16

The party petitioning for adoption without a biological parent's consent has the burden of proving, by clear and convincing evidence, that the biological parent failed to support or to communicate with the child during the requisite one-year period and that there was no justifiable cause for the failure of support or communication; once the petitioner has met his or her burden of proof, the burden of going forward with evidence shifts to the biological parent to show some facially justifiable cause for the failure, although the burden of proof remains at all times with the petitioner, who must establish the lack of justifiable cause by clear and convincing evidence. In re Adoption of C.L.B. (Ohio App. 3 Dist., 10-25-2010) 191 Ohio App.3d 64, 944 N.E.2d 1190, 2010-Ohio-5190. Adoption ☞ 7.8(1)

In stepfather's action seeking to adopt children and asserting that father's consent was not required, once stepfather established that father had failed to support children for at least one year, burden of going forward with evidence shifted to father to

show some facially justifiable cause, but burden of demonstrating that failure of support was without justifiable cause remained with stepfather. In re A.M.W. (Ohio App. 9 Dist., 02-20-2007) 170 Ohio App.3d 389, 867 N.E.2d 471, 2007-Ohio-682. Adoption ☞ 7.8(1)

Before probate court can reach issue of whether natural parent had justifiable cause for not supporting or communicating with child, for purposes of determining whether natural parent's consent to adoption petition is necessary, it is incumbent upon petitioner to show, by clear and convincing evidence, that natural parent failed to support or communicate with child for requisite one-year period. In re Fetzer (Ohio App. 3 Dist., 02-05-1997) 118 Ohio App.3d 156, 692 N.E.2d 219, dismissed, appeal not allowed 78 Ohio St.3d 1513, 679 N.E.2d 309. Adoption ☞ 7.8(5)

Once adoption petitioner has established, by clear and convincing evidence, that natural parent has failed to support or communicate with child for at least one year, burden of going forward with evidence shifts to natural parent to show some facially justifiable cause for failure; however, burden of proof remains with petitioner. In re Fetzer (Ohio App. 3 Dist., 02-05-1997) 118 Ohio App.3d 156, 692 N.E.2d 219, dismissed, appeal not allowed 78 Ohio St.3d 1513, 679 N.E.2d 309. Adoption ☞ 7.8(5)

Once party who has filed adoption petition has established failure of minor child's natural parent to either provide support for, or communicate with, child, burden of going forward with evidence shifts to natural parent to show some facially justifiable cause for such failure. In re Adoption of Wagner (Ohio App. 11 Dist., 01-21-1997) 117 Ohio App.3d 448, 690 N.E.2d 959, appeal not allowed 78 Ohio St.3d 1516, 679 N.E.2d 311. Adoption ☞ 7.8(1)

When adoption petition has been filed so that natural parent faces termination of his or her parental rights, burden of proof is on petitioner to establish by clear and convincing evidence that natural parent failed to communicate with or support, without justifiable cause, his or her minor child during one-year period prior to adoption petition. In re Adoption of Wagner (Ohio App. 11 Dist., 01-21-1997) 117 Ohio App.3d 448, 690 N.E.2d 959, appeal not allowed 78 Ohio St.3d 1516, 679 N.E.2d 311. Adoption ☞ 7.8(5)

Once petitioner for adoption has established by clear and convincing evidence that natural parent has failed to support child for requisite one-year period, burden of going forward with evidence shifts to natural parent to show some facially justifiable cause for that failure, though burden of proof remains with petitioner. Dallas v. Dotson (Ohio App. 9 Dist., 08-14-1996) 113 Ohio App.3d 484, 681 N.E.2d 464, dismissed, appeal not allowed 77 Ohio St.3d 1515, 674 N.E.2d 370. Adoption ☞ 7.8(5)

Party alleging that need for parent's consent to adoption has been obviated by nonsupport has burden to prove by clear and convincing evidence that parent has failed to support child for requisite one-year period. In re Adoption of Hudnell (Ohio App. 4 Dist., 08-06-1996) 113 Ohio App.3d 296, 680 N.E.2d 1055. Adoption ☞ 7.8(4)

Once adoption petitioner has established, by clear and convincing evidence, that natural parent has failed to support or communicate with child for at least one year, burden of going forward with evidence shifts to natural parent to show some facially justifiable cause for such failure; however, burden of proof remains with petitioner. In re Serre (Ohio Com.Pl., 02-20-1996) 77 Ohio Misc.2d 29, 665 N.E.2d 1185. Adoption ☞ 7.8(1)

Burden is on party seeking adoption to prove by clear and convincing evidence that putative parent willfully failed to monetarily support child. In re Adoption of Bowes (Ohio App. 11 Dist., 08-07-1995) 105 Ohio App.3d 574, 664 N.E.2d 963. Adoption ☞ 7.8(4)

Petitioner seeking adoption without natural parent's consent must prove by clear and convincing evidence that natural parent has not only failed to support child for statutory period but that failure was without justifiable cause; furthermore, petitioner had burden of proving that natural parent's failure to provide support is not justified after natural parent provides some evidence to justify failure to provide support. In re Adoption of Lassiter (Ohio App. 2 Dist., 02-24-1995) 101 Ohio App.3d 367, 655 N.E.2d 781, dismissed, appeal not allowed 73 Ohio St.3d 1410, 651 N.E.2d 1308. Adoption ☞ 7.4(6)

Probate court's finding, in support of conclusion that one year of nonsupport obviated need for father's approval of son's adoption, that father had at least some income but still did not pay any support was not against manifest weight of evidence. In re Adoption of Lassiter (Ohio App. 2 Dist., 02-24-1995) 101 Ohio App.3d 367, 655 N.E.2d 781, dismissed, appeal not allowed 73 Ohio St.3d 1410, 651 N.E.2d 1308. Adoption ☞ 7.8(4)

Probate court's determination regarding justifiable cause for failing to support minor child as would toll one-year period of nonsupport obviating need to obtain parental consent to adoption will not be disturbed on appeal unless it is against manifest weight of evidence. In re Adoption of Lassiter (Ohio App. 2 Dist., 02-24-1995) 101 Ohio App.3d 367, 655 N.E.2d 781, dismissed, appeal not allowed 73 Ohio St.3d 1410, 651 N.E.2d 1308. Adoption ☞ 15

Once petitioner seeking adoption has proven by clear and convincing evidence the failure to support child within required one-year period, natural parent has burden of going forward with some evidence to show that failure was justified; burden of proof remains with petitioner. In re Adoption of Kuhlmann (Ohio App. 1 Dist., 12-07-1994) 99 Ohio App.3d 44, 649 N.E.2d 1279. Adoption ☞ 7.8(1)

Petitioner seeking adoption has burden of establishing, by clear and convincing evidence, natural parents' noncompliance with either support requirement or communication with child requirement. In re Adoption of Kuhlmann (Ohio App. 1 Dist.,

12-07-1994) 99 Ohio App.3d 44, 649 N.E.2d 1279. Adoption ☞ 7.8(3.1)

Adoption petitioner, seeking to establish that consent of natural parent is not required because natural parent has neglected support obligation, is required to prove at adoption hearing that natural parent's failure to support was without justifiable cause. In re Adoption of Deems (Ohio App. 3 Dist., 11-12-1993) 91 Ohio App.3d 552, 632 N.E.2d 1347, cause dismissed 70 Ohio St.3d 1451, 639 N.E.2d 460. Adoption ☞ 7.4(6)

Once adoption petitioner, seeking to establish that consent of natural parent is not required because natural parent has failed to support child, has shown by clear and convincing evidence that natural parent has failed to support child for at least one-year period, burden of going forward with evidence shifts to natural parent to show some facially justifiable cause for failure, with ultimate burden of proof remaining with petitioner. In re Adoption of Deems (Ohio App. 3 Dist., 11-12-1993) 91 Ohio App.3d 552, 632 N.E.2d 1347, cause dismissed 70 Ohio St.3d 1451, 639 N.E.2d 460. Adoption ☞ 7.8(1)

Because cases in which consent to adoption may not be required may involve termination of fundamental parental rights, burden of proof is on petitioner seeking adoption to establish by clear and convincing evidence that natural parent failed to support, without justifiable cause, minor child during one-year period prior to adoption petition; then, once petitioner has established a failure, burden of going forward with evidence is on natural parent to show some facially justifiable cause for the failure. In re Adoption of Cline (Trumbull 1993) 89 Ohio App.3d 450, 624 N.E.2d 1083. Adoption ☞ 7.8(1); Adoption ☞ 7.8(4)

Burden of proving abandonment is upon natural mother who seeks to place child for adoption without putative father's consent. In re Adoption of Klonowski (Stark 1993) 87 Ohio App.3d 352, 622 N.E.2d 376. Adoption ☞ 7.8(1)

Petitioner for adoption who seeks to utilize statute in lieu of parent's consent to adoption has burden of proving by clear and convincing evidence that natural parent has not only failed to support child for statutory period but that such failure was without justifiable cause. In re Adoption of Kessler (Huron 1993) 87 Ohio App.3d 317, 622 N.E.2d 354. Adoption ☞ 7.8(4)

Burden is on parties petitioning to adopt child to demonstrate that natural parent's consent is not prerequisite to adoption, on ground that natural parent has failed to provide support and maintenance for at least one year before petition was filed. Celestino v. Schneider (Lucas 1992) 84 Ohio App.3d 192, 616 N.E.2d 581. Adoption ☞ 7.8(1)

Pursuant to RC 3107.07(A), the petitioner for adoption has the burden of proving, by clear and convincing evidence, both (1) that the natural parent has failed to support the child for the requisite one-year period, and (2) that this failure was without justifiable cause. Once the petitioner has established, by clear and convincing evidence, that the natural parent has failed to support the child for at least the requisite one-year period, the burden of going forward with the evidence shifts to the natural parent to show some facially justifiable cause for such failure. The burden of proof, however, remains with the petitioner. In re Adoption of Bovett (Ohio 1987) 33 Ohio St.3d 102, 515 N.E.2d 919.

Pursuant to RC 3107.07(A), the petitioner for adoption has the burden of proving, by clear and convincing evidence, that the natural parent has failed to support the child for the requisite one-year period and that this failure was without justifiable cause. In re Adoption of Masa (Ohio 1986) 23 Ohio St.3d 163, 492 N.E.2d 140, 23 O.B.R. 330. Adoption ☞ 7.8(4)

In addressing the RC 3107.07(A) requirement that the failure to communicate or support must be without justifiable cause, the trial court may place no burden upon the nonconsenting parent to establish that his failure was justifiable. In re Adoption of Anthony (Franklin 1982) 5 Ohio App.3d 60, 449 N.E.2d 511, 5 O.B.R. 156.

The showing of a mere failure to make payment for the support and maintenance of a child will not support a finding that such failure was willful, and the burden of proof of such willfulness is on the petitioner charging such failure. In re Adoption of Baker (Hardin 1955) 100 Ohio App. 146, 136 N.E.2d 147, 60 O.O. 137.

When evidence of failure to pay child support is shown, the burden of proof shifts to the parent not paying child support to go forward with evidence to show that such lack of support was not willful. In re Adoption of Bitner, No. 81–CA–77 (7th Dist Ct App, Mahoning, 2–24–82).

16. Waiver of back support for consent

In proceeding to collect back child support, evidence supported trial court's finding that oral agreement existed whereby father's child support arrearage would be waived in return for consenting to adoption of child by mother's husband; evidence indicated that mother told father two day prior to signing consent to adopt that if father signed consent there would be no back or future child support involved. Eckliff v. Walters (Ohio App. 11 Dist., 09-15-2006) 168 Ohio App.3d 727, 861 N.E.2d 843, 2006-Ohio-4817. Child Support ☞ 456

Evidence of whether father believed that waiver of back child support was legal was irrelevant in proceeding to recover alleged child support arrearage for period up to date that child was adopted by mother's husband with father's consent; it was legal to waive back support in an agreement involving child support obligor's consent to adoption. Eckliff v. Walters (Ohio App. 11 Dist., 09-15-2006) 168 Ohio App.3d 727, 861 N.E.2d 843, 2006-Ohio-4817. Adoption ☞ 7.5; Child Support ☞ 456; Child Support ☞ 483

Agreement between biological parents to exchange a consent to adoption for forgiveness of arrearages in current child support is an enforceable agreement. Eckliff v. Walters (Ohio App. 11 Dist., 09-15-2006) 168 Ohio App.3d 727, 861 N.E.2d 843, 2006-Ohio-4817. Adoption ☞ 7.5; Child Support ☞ 456

17. Failure to communicate—In general

The tolling provision in the Servicemembers Civil Relief Act applied to one-year provision in amended statute allowing for adoption of minor child without natural parent's consent based on finding that natural parent's attempts to communicate with child constituted no more than de minimis contact during one-year period preceding filing of petition; record indicated that the natural parent was deployed to Japan only seven days after requisite statutory time period commenced. In re Adoption of W.C. (Ohio App. 12 Dist., 08-09-2010) No. CA2010-02-020, 2010 -Ohio- 3688, 2010 WL 3101879, Unreported. Adoption ☞ 7.4(1); Armed Services ☞ 34.11(1)

Amended statute, which permitted adoption of minor child without natural father's consent when natural father's contact with child was not more than de minimis, rather than nonexistent, during statutory one-year period, was substantive, rather than merely remedial, and, thus, state constitution's retroactivity clause barred retroactive application of statute to entire one-year period preceding stepfather's petition for adoption, where one-year period commenced approximately 5 months before amended statute was enacted. In re Adoption of W.C. (Ohio App. 12 Dist., 08-09-2010) No. CA2010-02-020, 2010 -Ohio- 3688, 2010 WL 3101879, Unreported. Adoption ☞ 3

Notwithstanding natural father's failure to raise issue below, father did not waive on appeal application of tolling provision in Servicemembers Civil Relief Act (SCRA) to de minimis contact standard in amended statute allowing adoption without natural parent's consent, where parent failed during one-year period preceding date of proposed adoption to have more than de minimis contact with child, as the tolling provision of SCRA was mandatory. In re Adoption of W.C. (Ohio App. 12 Dist., 08-09-2010) No. CA2010-02-020, 2010 -Ohio- 3688, 2010 WL 3101879, Unreported. Adoption ☞ 15; Armed Services ☞ 34.11(1)

Clear and convincing evidence supported finding that biological father had not failed to communicate with child for one year prior to the date stepfather filed his petition to adopt child, and thus father's consent to adoption was required; father attempted to visit child but mother denied his requests, father spoke with mother regarding child at the visitation exchange for their other children, and father saw child at a school play and waved to her but child was grabbed by mother when father got close to child. In re Adoption of Blausenhauer (Ohio App. 5 Dist., Guernsey, 04-17-2009) No. 08 CA 32, 2009-Ohio-1853, 2009 WL 1040301, Unreported. Adoption ☞ 7.8(5)

Biological father of child born out of wedlock did not fail to "communicate" with child for period of one year so as to permit stepfather's adoption of two-year-old child without biological father's consent, even if visitation did not occur, where father paid child support for the child, sent birthday card to child, made telephone calls to mother or stepfather attempting to schedule visitation, and traveled from out of stay to visit child but could not reach stepfather by phone. In re Adoption of Campbell (Ohio App. 5 Dist., Guernsey, 04-22-2008) No. 07 CA 43, 2008-Ohio-1916, 2008 WL 1810231, Unreported. Adoption ⟜ 7.4(1)

In reviewing trial court's finding that mother's consent to adoption of minor children by grandmother was not required due to failure to communicate with children, Court of Appeals would look to actual language of journal entry in mother's criminal case, not mother's recollection of what was said by trial judge who issued judicial release in criminal case, when determining limitations that were placed on mother concerning communication with children; court spoke only through its journal, not through oral pronouncements. In re Kr.E. (Ohio App. 9 Dist., Lorain, 09-18-2006) No. 06CA008891, 2006-Ohio-4815, 2006 WL 2661053, Unreported. Adoption ⟜ 7.4(4)

Evidence supported finding that birth parents' failure to communicate with child or pursue visitation for one year prior to adoption petition was the result of their own lack of motivation, and thus, their consent was not required; during the one year before petition was filed, birth parents never sent cards or gifts to child, did not take part in child's medical treatment even though child had cancer and a bone disease, and were not involved in child's education. In re C.M.W. (Ohio App. 12 Dist., Madison, 12-20-2004) No. CA2004-09-031, 2004-Ohio-6935, 2004 WL 2937632, Unreported. Adoption ⟜ 7.4(1)

Trial court's finding that mother failed to communicate with children within twelve-month period prior to grandmother's petition for adoption was not against manifest weight of evidence; grandmother's journal containing record of events supported her claim that mother made no attempt to contact children, while there was no evidence to support mother's claim that she had made telephone calls, or sent cards or gifts. In re Adoption of Sours (Ohio App. 3 Dist., Wyandot, 07-08-2003) No. 16-02-16, No. 16-02-17, 2003-Ohio-3583, 2003 WL 21529922, Unreported. Adoption ⟜ 7.8(5)

The issue of what constituted failure to communicate, for the purpose of statute which provided for adoption of child without consent of the biological parent based on the parent's failure to communicate with the child for one year, was not preserved for appellate review, in action challenging adoption; biological father stipulated in the trial court that he had not had contact with his children for one year, and the trial court thus never addressed the issue of what constituted a communication. In re Adoption of Randall G. (Ohio App. 6 Dist., Lucas, 03-14-2003) No. L-02-1340, No. L-02-1341, 2003-Ohio-1412, 2003 WL 1473698, Unreported. Adoption ⟜ 15

Pursuant to the explicit language of RC 3107.07, failure by a parent to communicate with his or her child is sufficient to authorize adoption without that parent's consent only if there is a complete absence of communication for the statutorily defined one-year period. In Matter of Bryant (Ohio App. 4 Dist., Washington, 12-09-1997) No. 97CA635, 1997 WL 766460, Unreported.

Where a natural father's testimony stating he sent cards and packages to his children in the one-year period immediately preceding the filing of a petition for adoption conflicts with the children's testimony they did not recall receiving the alleged card and packages, the natural father failed to communicate with his children for a one-year period and the consent of the natural father is unnecessary for the adoption. In re Doe (Ohio App. 6 Dist., Huron, 12-30-1993) No. H-93-12, 1993 WL 551530, Unreported.

Judgment entry on issue of whether child's biological father had been in communication with child during year prior to filing of petition for child's adoption by husband of child's mother was partial final judgment; while final and appealable when entered, it was appealable alternatively 30 days after court rendered final order on all issues in case. In re Adoption of Eblin (Ohio App. 3 Dist., 03-24-1998) 126 Ohio App.3d 774, 711 N.E.2d 319, appeal allowed 82 Ohio St.3d 1482, 696 N.E.2d 1088, cause dismissed 83 Ohio St.3d 1454, 700 N.E.2d 617. Adoption ⟜ 15

Uncontested facts established that father failed to communicate with child for one-year statutory period, for purposes of dispensing with father's consent to adoption of child by stepfather. In re Doe (Ohio App. 9 Dist., 10-15-1997) 123 Ohio App.3d 505, 704 N.E.2d 608, stay denied 80 Ohio St.3d 1470, 687 N.E.2d 298, dismissed, jurisdictional motion overruled 81 Ohio St.3d 1443, 690 N.E.2d 15. Adoption ⟜ 7.4(2.1)

Natural father did not communicate with child during requisite one-year period preceding adoption petition filed by mother's husband where letters and cards sent to child by father through father's mother were never received by child and never read. In re Adoption of Hedrick (Ohio App. 8 Dist., 04-29-1996) 110 Ohio App.3d 622, 674 N.E.2d 1256. Adoption ⟜ 7.4(2.1)

Statute making nonconsenting parent's consent to adoption unnecessary if he has failed to pay child support or communicate with child for one year prior to petition must be strictly construed to protect interests of natural parent. In re Serre (Ohio Com.Pl., 02-20-1996) 77 Ohio Misc.2d 29, 665 N.E.2d 1185. Adoption ⟜ 7.4(2.1); Adoption ⟜ 7.4(6)

Two-part responsibility upon parent is imposed by statute, in order to avoid termination of right to object to adoption: to provide support and to communicate with child. In re Adoption of Kuhlmann (Ohio App. 1 Dist., 12-07-1994) 99 Ohio App.3d 44, 649 N.E.2d 1279. Adoption ⟜ 7.4(2.1); Adoption ⟜ 7.4(6)

Statute citing circumstances in which natural parent's consent to adoption is not required imposes dual responsibility upon "non-petitioning" natural parent to both communicate with minor child and provide maintenance and support. In re Adoption of Cline (Trumbull 1993) 89 Ohio App.3d 450, 624 N.E.2d 1083. Adoption ☞ 7.4(2.1); Adoption ☞ 7.4(6)

In an adoption wherein the natural grandparents seek to adopt their granddaughter whose father is deceased and whose mother has not seen or supported her in three years, it is in the best interest of the child to have a guardian ad litem, and the trial court's failure to appoint one is error. In re Adoption of Howell (Lawrence 1991) 77 Ohio App.3d 80, 601 N.E.2d 92, motion overruled 62 Ohio St.3d 1508, 583 N.E.2d 1320.

Pursuant to the explicit language of RC 3107.07(A), failure by a parent to communicate with his or her child is sufficient to authorize adoption without that parent's consent only if there is a complete absence of communication for the statutorily defined one-year period. In re Adoption of Holcomb (Ohio 1985) 18 Ohio St.3d 361, 481 N.E.2d 613, 18 O.B.R. 419. Adoption ☞ 7.4(2.1)

Adoption without a parent's consent is authorized by the failure of the parent to communicate with his child only if the failure to communicate is complete, tantamount to a complete abandonment of current interest in the child. Matter of Adoption of Hupp (Cuyahoga 1982) 9 Ohio App.3d 128, 458 N.E.2d 878, 9 O.B.R. 192.

RC 3107.07 requires that, in order for there to be a failure of communication, there must have been a complete absence of communication for a period of at least one year immediately prior to the filing of the petition. In re Adoption of Anthony (Franklin 1982) 5 Ohio App.3d 60, 449 N.E.2d 511, 5 O.B.R. 156.

In the phrase "communicate with the minor child or to provide maintenance and support of the minor" the word "or" cannot be construed to mean "and." In re Adoption of McDermitt (Ohio 1980) 63 Ohio St.2d 301, 408 N.E.2d 680, 17 O.O.3d 195.

The two-year requirement of RC 3107.06(B)(4) is not tolled by fact that child was living away from parents by agreement with them, or merely because parents made telephone calls discussing return of child or because parents were in financial difficulty for a portion of the period and unable to contribute to child's support. In re Adoption of Sargent (Ohio Com.Pl. 1970) 28 Ohio Misc. 261, 272 N.E.2d 206, 57 O.O.2d 135, 57 O.O.2d 494.

The phrase in RC 3107.06, "properly support and maintain," implies personal care and attention by the parent having custody as well as mere financial support. (See also In re Biddle, 81 Abs 529, 163 NE(2d) 190 (App, Franklin 1959).) In re Adoption of Biddle (Ohio 1958) 168 Ohio St. 209, 152 N.E.2d 105, 6 O.O.2d 4, on remand 163 N.E.2d 188, 81 Ohio Law Abs. 529.

The trial court correctly holds that a parent's written consent to adoption is required where the parent made repeated attempts to exercise his visitation rights and was thwarted in each instance by some objection raised or limitation placed thereon by the custodial parent. In re Adoption of Meagley, No. 1–83–45 (3d Dist Ct App, Allen, 5–14–84).

18. —— Communication defined, failure to communicate

Father's ten minute telephone conversation with child approximately two months before child's stepfather petitioned to adopt child constituted "communication" under statute providing that parent's consent to child's adoption is not required when that parent has failed without justifiable cause to communicate with child for period of at least one year immediately preceding filing of adoption petition, and, thus, father's consent to adoption was required. In re K.L.K.-F. (Ohio App. 2 Dist., Miami, 05-29-2009) No. 08-CA-46, 2009-Ohio-2543, 2009 WL 1515728, Unreported. Adoption ☞ 7.4(2.1)

Evidence supported trial court's finding that mother failed to communicate with minor children during one-year period before filing of grandmother's adoption petition, as would support conclusion that mother's consent was not required, although mother testified that she briefly saw children at grandfather's funeral; evidence indicated that visits facilitated by father occurred before relevant period, mother did not attempt to communicate with children through cards, letters, telephone calls, or gifts during one-year period, grandmother disputed that children were at funeral home, and alleged brief contact at funeral home did not constitute communication. In re Kr.E. (Ohio App. 9 Dist., Lorain, 09-18-2006) No. 06CA008891, 2006-Ohio-4815, 2006 WL 2661053, Unreported. Adoption ☞ 7.4(1)

Biological mother's "chance encounter" with her child at county fair, during which she interacted with child for approximately 10 minutes and presented him with a stuffed animal she won at the fair, was a "communication" within the context of the adoption statute so as to require her consent to adoption, in adoption proceeding initiated by child's stepmother. In re Vaughn (Ohio App. 5 Dist., Guernsey, 10-25-2004) No. 04CA06, 2004-Ohio-5657, 2004 WL 2381869, Unreported. Adoption ☞ 7.4(1)

Evidence supported trial court finding of a lack of communication between biological father and child during the 365 days immediately prior to stepfather's filing of petition to adopt child without obtaining the consent of biological father; biological father conceded that he was not in the physical presence of child for over one year, a period of just over one year existed between the time when father sent child gifts, and infant child's babbling into the telephone did not constitute communication with biological father. In re Adoption of Cutright (Ohio App. 4 Dist., Ross, 07-15-2003) No. 03CA2696, 2003-Ohio-3795, 2003 WL 21660034, Unreported, appeal not allowed 101 Ohio St.3d 1453, 803 N.E.2d 401, 2004-Ohio-462. Adoption ☞ 7.8(5)

Sending of a birthday card along with photographs and a letter during the year preceding adoption adequately supports a finding of communication for purposes of RC 3107.07 and preserves the natural father's right not to consent to adoption of his daughter by her stepfather. In re Christie (Ohio App. 9 Dist., Wayne, 03-12-1997) No. 96CA0049, 1997 WL 119556, Unreported.

Mother's mere presentation to child of Christmas card from child's father constituted a "communication" from father, for purposes of statute under which a prospective adoptive parent is not required to obtain parent's consent if parent has failed without justifiable cause to communicate with the minor for one-year period, even if child refused to accept card. In re Adoption of Peshek (Ohio App. 2 Dist., 06-01-2001) 143 Ohio App.3d 839, 759 N.E.2d 411. Adoption ☞ 7.4(2.1)

Court of Appeals was required to follow precedent of State Supreme Court in *In re Adoption of Holcomb* in determining whether an arguably de minimis communication from father to child constituted a "communication" under statute providing that a person who seeks to adopt child is not required to obtain parent's consent if parent has failed without justifiable cause to communicate with child for one-year period, though Court of Appeals was not of Supreme Court's view that a complete absence of communication was necessary in order to satisfy statute. In re Adoption of Peshek (Ohio App. 2 Dist., 06-01-2001) 143 Ohio App.3d 839, 759 N.E.2d 411. Courts ☞ 91(1)

Accidental meeting between father and child was "communication" for purposes of adoption statutes requiring parent's consent unless parent has failed without justifiable cause to communicate with child during the year preceding the adoption petition. In re Adoption of Hudnell (Ohio App. 4 Dist., 08-06-1996) 113 Ohio App.3d 296, 680 N.E.2d 1055. Adoption ☞ 7.4(2.1)

Essence of "communication," for purposes of statute allowing adoption without consent of noncustodial parent if parent failed without justifiable cause to communicate with child for over one year preceding adoption petition, is the passing of thought from mind of one person to mind of another; message not received or successfully passed to mind of another is not communicated, nor does unsuccessful attempt to communicate constitute communication. In re Adoption of Hedrick (Ohio App. 8 Dist., 04-29-1996) 110 Ohio App.3d 622, 674 N.E.2d 1256. Adoption ☞ 7.4(2.1)

Natural father's motion to show cause to enforce his visitation rights was not "communication with the child," for purposes of statute making nonconsenting parent's consent to adoption unnecessary if he has failed to pay child support or communicate with child for one year prior to petition. In re Serre (Ohio Com.Pl., 02-20-1996) 77 Ohio Misc.2d 29, 665 N.E.2d 1185. Adoption ☞ 7.4(2.1)

Clear and convincing evidence exists to support a trial court's conclusion that a natural mother failed to communicate with her two sons for the requisite one-year period prior to the children's guardian's filing an adoption petition; the mother saw her children only once at a school Christmas program and the only interaction between the mother and the children consisted of a wave, a smile, or a nod, which does not constitute communication within the meaning of RC 3107.07(A) since a wave, smile, or nod does not convey information. In re Adoption of Jordan (Preble 1991) 72 Ohio App.3d 638, 595 N.E.2d 963. Adoption ☞ 7.4(2.1); Adoption ☞ 7.8(5)

Telephone conversations between a mother and minor child constitute communication of a parent with a child within the purview of RC 3107.07(A) and therefore the consent of such mother is required for the adoption of such child. In re Adoption of Kreyche, No. 1258 (11th Dist Ct App, Portage, 3–18–83), affirmed by 15 OS(3d) 159, 15 OBR 304, 472 NE(2d) 1106 (1984).

19. —— Justifiable cause, failure to communicate

Biological father's failure to communicate with or provide support for child for a period of one year prior to stepfather's filing of a petition for adoption was not justified, even though father alleged that he was unemployed, and thus father's consent to adoption was unnecessary; father stipulated to the fact that he had not communicated with child or provided any support for the year immediately prior to the filing of the petition for adoption, after father's visitation with child was terminated he did not attempt to resolve the problem with the agency or seek help from the court, father had previously been successful on representing himself before the court, so an attorney was not necessary to resolve the issue, and during the short periods of time that father was employed he failed to provide any support to child. In re Adoption of M.E. (Ohio App. 6 Dist., Erie, 06-05-2009) No. E-08-081, 2009-Ohio-2604, 2009 WL 1579085, Unreported. Adoption ☞ 7.2(3)

Petition to allocate parental rights and responsibilities filed by a predominately absent biological father satisfied the communication requirement of statute, authorizing adoption of child without consent of parent who has failed without justifiable cause to communicate with that child for period of at least one year immediately preceding filing of adoption petition; unwed father wished to assume responsibility for child, and as result, he filed petition to allocate parental rights and responsibilities, mother received notice of petition and a pending hearing, and with knowledge of the pending petition, mother married shortly thereafter and stepfather immediately filed a petition for adoption. In re A.J.B. (Ohio App. 12 Dist., Butler, 05-11-2009) No. CA2008-12-306, 2009-Ohio-2200, 2009 WL 1278433, Unreported. Adoption ☞ 7.2(3)

Mother's failure to communicate with minor children during one-year period before grandmother filed adoption petition was not justified, and thus mother's consent to adoption was not required, although court orders in criminal and juvenile cases generally prohibited mother from associating with one child and visiting with other children, and although grandmother would not agree to visitation; court orders did not prohibit communication by cards, letters, or telephone calls, and grandmother did not significantly interfere with all possible means of communication. In re Kr.E. (Ohio App. 9 Dist., Lorain, 09-18-2006) No. 06CA008891, 2006-Ohio-4815, 2006 WL 2661053, Unreported. Adoption ☞ 7.4(4)

Natural father's failure to communicate with his children for one year period preceding filing of adoption petition by stepfather was not justified, and thus, natural father's consent to adoption was unnecessary; while natural father alleged that a no contact order prohibited him from having contact with child or her mother during such time period, natural father failed to show that order prohibited all communication, and understanding by the parties that order prohibited all communication may have been incorrect. In re K.K. (Ohio App. 9 Dist., Lorain, 03-29-2006) No. 05CA008849, No. 05CA008850, 2006-Ohio-1488, 2006 WL 786504, Unreported. Adoption ☞ 7.4(4)

Evidence supported trial court's finding that children's biological father failed, without justifiable cause, to communicate with children and to provide for support of children for period of at least one year before filing of adoption petition by children's stepfather, and thus biological father's consent to adoption was not necessary, although custody order prohibited biological father from having parenting time, and although biological father testified he had medical condition which caused him to be unable to work; evidence indicated that custody order did not prohibit communication, and biological father did not send cards or letters. In re Amanda W. (Ohio App. 6 Dist., Lucas, 03-03-2006) No. L-05-1305, No. L-05-1306, 2006-Ohio-977, 2006 WL 513911, Unreported. Adoption ☞ 7.4(4); Adoption ☞ 7.4(6)

Record supported finding that failure of children's natural mother to have any communication with the children or to provide support for the children was justifiable, and thus natural mother's consent was required before stepmother could adopt the children; natural mother was prohibited by court order from having any communication with her children, as she was a mentally ill person subject to involuntary hospitalization. In re Mitchell Children (Ohio App. 5 Dist., Licking, 09-15-2005) No. 2005-CA-68, 2005-Ohio-4841, 2005 WL 2245686, Unreported. Adoption ☞ 7.4(4)

Child's natural father had justifiable cause for his failure to communicate or provide support to child within applicable one year period, and, as such, father's consent to child's adoption by her maternal grandmother and step-grandfather was required; all credible evidence confirmed that grandmother never gave father her contact information when she relocated out of state, and, when father contacted grandmother's ex-husband to obtain grandmother's

contact information, ex-husband refused to assist him in locating child. In re Adoption of Geis (Ohio App. 7 Dist., Harrison, 08-16-2005) No. 05 HA 574, 2005-Ohio-4378, 2005 WL 2033270, Unreported, appeal not allowed 107 Ohio St.3d 1411, 836 N.E.2d 1230, 2005-Ohio-5859. Adoption ☞ 7.4(6)

Father failed to preserve for appeal in adoption proceeding issue of whether "placement" of child had occurred for purposes of statute providing that parent's consent to child's adoption is not required when parent had failed to communication with child, without justifiable cause, for over one year immediately preceding child's placement in home of adoption petitioner, as he failed to assert argument and he failed to file a transcript to support any challenge to findings of fact in lower court, as required by rule. In re Adoption of G.W. (Ohio App. 9 Dist., Lorain, 03-23-2005) No. 04CA008609, 2005-Ohio-1274, 2005 WL 663002, Unreported. Adoption ☞ 15

Evidence in proceedings on stepfather's petitions to adopt children established that natural father's failure to communicate with children for more than one year was without justifiable cause, and thus natural father's consent to adoption was not required, even though mother obtained two civil protection orders (CPOs) against natural father; first CPO did not name children as protected persons, father continued to visit children after issuance of first CPO, father later terminated visitation without explanation, father made no attempts to communicate with children between expiration of first CPO and issuance of second CPO, and father's actions caused second CPO to be issued. In re Adoption of Corl (Ohio App. 5 Dist., Licking, 02-23-2005) No. 2004CA96, 2005-Ohio-736, 2005 WL 428036, Unreported. Adoption ☞ 7.4(4)

Trial court could require mother's consent to adoption, even though mother had failed to communicate with child for more than one year, after court found that there was justifiable cause for the lack of communication. In re Adoption of Linder (Ohio App. 3 Dist., Paulding, 12-20-2004) No. 11-04-07, 2004-Ohio-6962, 2004 WL 2940869, Unreported. Adoption ☞ 7.4(1)

Father's new wife failed to establish that consent of children's mother was not required, and thus wife was not entitled to adopt father's children without consent of the mother; although mother had no contact with children for over one year immediately preceding wife's filing of adoption petition, father and paternal grandmother had interfered with mother's ability to communicate with children by restricting mother's contact with children, and mother did not attempt further telephone contact with children because such attempts would have been futile. In re Adoption of C.S. (Ohio App. 2 Dist., Montgomery, 11-05-2004) No. 20557, No. 20558, No. 20559, 2004-Ohio-5933, 2004 WL 2526380, Unreported. Adoption ☞ 7.4(4)

Trial court finding that mother failed, without justifiable cause, to communicate with child for one year prior to the adoption petition being filed was not against the manifest weight of the evidence; mother admitted she did not contact child for statutory period but alleged father interfered with her ability to contact child, father admitted interference, but vast majority, if not all, of father's interference occurred prior to statutory period. In re Adoption of Haylett (Ohio App. 11 Dist., Portage, 05-07-2004) No. 2003-P-0093, No. 2003-P-0103, 2004-Ohio-2306, 2004 WL 1043430, Unreported. Adoption ⟶ 7.4(4)

Mother's failure to communicate with her child for one year period preceding filing of adoption petition by father's wife was not justified, and thus, mother's consent to adoption was unnecessary; although mother's visitation privileges had been discontinued by court order during this time period, she was still free to contact child in other ways, and if mother was uncertain as to meaning of court order, she could have contacted her counsel or court to inquire as to its parameters. In re Adoption of Mineer (Ohio App. 4 Dist., Adams, 02-10-2004) No. 03CA768, 2004-Ohio-656, 2004 WL 257674, Unreported, appeal not allowed 102 Ohio St.3d 1412, 806 N.E.2d 563, 2004-Ohio-1763. Adoption ⟶ 7.4(4)

Natural father's consent for adoption was not required due to his failure to communicate with daughter without justifiable cause for one year prior to stepfather's petition for adoption; although natural father was in the armed forces, he failed to take advantage of numerous opportunities to visit his daughter or at the least communicate with her by telephone or mail. In re Adoption of Harris (Ohio App. 5 Dist., Tuscarawas, 12-04-2003) No. 2003-AP-090072, 2003-Ohio-6788, 2003 WL 22952748, Unreported. Adoption ⟶ 7.4(1)

Father's alcoholism and belief it would be futile to ask mother if he could visit with child did not justify his failure to communicate with child for one year, for purposes of determining whether stepfather could pursue adoption of child absent father's consent, even though father did not have mother's most recent address, where father had mother's cellular phone number at all times, and he was aware of mother's prior address. In re Adoption of S.N.C. (Ohio App. 9 Dist., Medina, 11-19-2003) No. 03CA0075-M, 2003-Ohio-6121, 2003 WL 22715623, Unreported. Adoption ⟶ 7.4(1)

Trial court was not required to find that mother failed without justifiable cause to communicate with her children to find that her consent to the adoption of her children was not required, where court found that mother, without justifiable cause, failed to provide for the maintenance and support of the children. In re Adoption of C.P. (Ohio App. 9 Dist., Lorain, 09-17-2003) No. 03CA008268, No. 03CA008269, 2003-Ohio-4905, 2003 WL 22136288, Unreported. Adoption ⟶ 13

Evidence established that justifiable cause existed to explain biological father's failure to communicate with child for a period of one year immediately prior to step-father filing a petition to adopt child, and thus biological father's consent to step-father's petition to adopt child was required; biological father and child lived more than one thousand miles apart, biological father made plans to take mother and child to a family wedding during the one year period immediately prior to step-father filing his petition for adoption but mother cancelled the plans shortly before the wedding and told biological father that she would be out of town with child, and biological father and mother discussed mother and child taking a trip to visit biological father but the trip never materialized. In re Adoption of Cutright (Ohio App. 4 Dist., Ross, 07-15-2003) No. 03CA2696, 2003-Ohio-3795, 2003 WL 21660034, Unreported, appeal not allowed 101 Ohio St.3d 1453, 803 N.E.2d 401, 2004-Ohio-462. Adoption ⟶ 7.4(2.1)

Mother's decision to expend financial resources to pursue legal rights with other children she had not seen in three or four months, rather than with daughters, supported determination that mother's failure to provide support for or to communicate with daughters for period of one year prior to grandmother filing adoption petition was not justifiable. In re Adoption of Sours (Ohio App. 3 Dist., Wyandot, 07-08-2003) No. 16-02-16, No. 16-02-17, 2003-Ohio-3583, 2003 WL 21529922, Unreported. Adoption ⟶ 7.4(6)

Father's refusal to allow mother to visit children at his residence was not justification for mother's failure to communicate with child for period of one year prior to paternal grandmother filing petition for adoption; father's refusal merely eliminated one location in which visitation could occur, and mother had previously visited child at grandmother's residence. In re Adoption of Sours (Ohio App. 3 Dist., Wyandot, 07-08-2003) No. 16-02-16, No. 16-02-17, 2003-Ohio-3583, 2003 WL 21529922, Unreported. Adoption ⟶ 7.4(2.1)

There was clear and convincing evidence that biological mother failed without justifiable cause to communicate with children for period of at least one year, thus supporting finding that mother's consent to adoption of children by children's maternal grandmother was not required; mother offered no evidence, other than her testimony, that she called children and sent them cards, which testimony was contradicted by grandmother and grandmother's companion. In re Adoption of Gabrielle Ann M. (Ohio App. 6 Dist., Lucas, 06-06-2003) No. L-03-1037, No. L-03-1043, 2003-Ohio-2906, 2003 WL 21299929, Unreported. Adoption ⟶ 7.8(4)

Clear and convincing evidence established that biological father, without justifiable cause, failed to communicate with his child for at least one year prior to moment that child's stepfather petitioned to adopt child, thus rendering biological father's consent to adoption unnecessary; testimony of child's stepfather, biological mother, maternal grandparents, and biological father's sister tended to show that biological father failed to communicate with child for approximately three years prior to date in which hearing was held to determine applicability of statute under which stepfather asserted his right to adopt child without biological father's consent. In re Adoption of TMP (Ohio App. 2 Dist., Champaign, 05-09-2003) No. 2003 CA 1, 2003-Ohio-2404, 2003 WL 21060852, Unreported. Adoption ☞ 7.4(2.1)

Biological father's failure to communicate with child during one-year period prior to filing of petition for step-parent adoption had justifiable cause, for purposes of determining necessity of biological father's consent to adoption, where adoption decree, later rescinded, had been in effect during such one-year period, terminating his parental rights. In re Adoption of Copas (Ohio App. 12 Dist., Fayette, 05-05-2003) No. CA2002-10-024, 2003-Ohio-2224, 2003 WL 2012632, Unreported. Adoption ☞ 7.4(4)

When adoption petitioner seeks to dispense with natural parent's consent based on the latter's alleged failure to communicate with child during one-year period, nonconsenting parent has the burden of going forward with evidence to show some facially justifiable cause for failure to communicate, but the ultimate burden of proof remains with petitioner. In re Adoption of A.J.Y. (Ohio Com.Pl., 09-16-2010) 160 Ohio Misc.2d 4, 937 N.E.2d 1109, 2010-Ohio-5726. Adoption ☞ 7.8(1)

Stepfather who sought to adopt child failed to meet his burden of proving by clear and convincing evidence that presumed father's consent to child's adoption was not required under statute providing that natural parent's consent to adoption was not required if he failed without justifiable cause to communicate with or support child for at least one year immediately preceding filing of adoption petition, as requisite one-year period set forth in statute could not begin to run until there had been a judicial ascertainment of paternity, which was a matter unresolved when stepfather filed adoption petition. In re Adoption of Pushcar (Ohio, 09-20-2006) 110 Ohio St.3d 332, 853 N.E.2d 647, 2006-Ohio-4572, reconsideration denied 111 Ohio St.3d 1495, 857 N.E.2d 1231, 2006-Ohio-6171. Adoption ☞ 7.8(5)

Mother who relied on statute permitting adoption to proceed without consent of a natural parent when that parent failed without justifiable cause to communicate with or support child for at least one year immediately preceding filing of adoption petition to divest presumed father of his parental rights carried obligation of establishing presumed father's paternity. In re Adoption of Pushcar (Ohio, 09-20-2006) 110 Ohio St.3d 332, 853 N.E.2d 647, 2006-Ohio-4572, reconsideration denied 111 Ohio St.3d 1495, 857 N.E.2d 1231, 2006-Ohio-6171. Adoption ☞ 7.4(6)

The ability of a court to dispense with a natural parent's consent to adoption on statutory ground that parent failed without justifiable cause to communicate with or support child for at least one year immediately preceding filing of adoption petition is dependent upon the establishment of the parent-child relationship. In re Adoption of Pushcar (Ohio, 09-20-2006) 110 Ohio St.3d 332, 853 N.E.2d 647, 2006-Ohio-4572, reconsideration denied 111 Ohio St.3d 1495, 857 N.E.2d 1231, 2006-Ohio-6171. Adoption ☞ 7.4(6)

Under statute providing that consent to adoption is not required where parent has failed without justifiable cause to communicate with child or to provide for maintenance and support of child, there is no requirement for adoption petitioner to show both parent's failure to support child and parent's failure to communicate with minor child, as statute is written in the disjunctive. In re Adoption of Ford (Ohio App. 3 Dist., 04-17-2006) 166 Ohio App.3d 161, 849 N.E.2d 330, 2006-Ohio-1889. Adoption ☞ 7.4(1); Adoption ☞ 7.4(6)

Person who seeks to adopt a child without the consent of one of child's parents has the burden under governing statute of proving by clear and convincing evidence that the parent has failed without justifiable cause to communicate with the minor or to provide for the maintenance and support of the minor as required by law or judicial decree for a period of at least one year immediately preceding either the filing of the adoption petition or the placement of the minor in the home of the petitioner. In re Adoption of Peshek (Ohio App. 2 Dist., 06-01-2001) 143 Ohio App.3d 839, 759 N.E.2d 411. Adoption ☞ 7.8(1)

Evidence that child's biological father had not had contact with child for one year prior to filing of petition to dispense with his consent to child's adoption by mother's husband was less than clear and convincing and could not form basis for granting petition, where biological father contended that he had attempted to contact child from prison but that his efforts were continually frustrated by child's mother, and where trial court improperly placed burden of proving justifiable cause for failure to communicate on biological father. In re Adoption of Eblin (Ohio App. 3 Dist., 03-24-1998) 126 Ohio App.3d 774, 711 N.E.2d 319, appeal allowed 82 Ohio St.3d 1482, 696 N.E.2d 1088, cause dismissed 83 Ohio St.3d 1454, 700 N.E.2d 617. Adoption ☞ 7.8(4)

"Failure to communicate" portion of the statute providing that consent to adoption is not required where parent has failed without justifiable cause to communicate with child is an objective standard, and courts should not read into the phrase such qualifiers as "meaningfully," "substantially," "significantly," or "regularly." In re Doe (Ohio App. 9 Dist., 10-15-1997) 123 Ohio App.3d 505, 704 N.E.2d 608, stay denied 80 Ohio St.3d 1470, 687 N.E.2d 298, dismissed, jurisdictional motion overruled 81 Ohio St.3d 1443, 690 N.E.2d 15. Adoption ☞ 7.4(2.1)

Natural mother did not have justifiable cause for failure to communicate with son in year prior to stepmother's filing of adoption petition, and therefore her consent to adoption was not necessary; although father and stepmother did not make any effort to voluntarily allow natural mother to visit son, nothing was done to conceal child's whereabouts, natural mother never attempted to contact son either in person or through any written communication, and she never attempted to establish any visitation rights to her son until after adoption petition was filed. In re Fetzer (Ohio App. 3 Dist., 02-05-1997) 118 Ohio App.3d 156, 692 N.E.2d 219, dismissed, appeal not allowed 78 Ohio St.3d 1513, 679 N.E.2d 309. Adoption ☞ 7.4(2.1)

Natural mother waived any objection to probate court's jurisdiction to hear issue, in stepmother's adoption proceeding, of whether natural mother had failed without justifiable cause to communicate with child, where mother orally stipulated that communication issue was to be determined by probate court and produced evidence on that issue at hearing. In re Fetzer (Ohio App. 3 Dist., 02-05-1997) 118 Ohio App.3d 156, 692 N.E.2d 219, dismissed, appeal not allowed 78 Ohio St.3d 1513, 679 N.E.2d 309. Adoption ☞ 15

Natural parent's failure to either support or communicate with his or her minor child within year prior to filing of adoption petition would abrogate need for parent's consent to adoption if trial court also decided that such failure was without justifiable cause. In re Adoption of Wagner (Ohio App. 11 Dist., 01-21-1997) 117 Ohio App.3d 448, 690 N.E.2d 959, appeal not allowed 78 Ohio St.3d 1516, 679 N.E.2d 311. Adoption ☞ 7.4(1)

For purposes of statute allowing adoption without consent of noncustodial parent if parent failed without justifiable cause to communicate with child for over one year preceding adoption petition, term "communicate" must be given its ordinary and accepted meaning. In re Adoption of Hedrick (Ohio App. 8 Dist., 04-29-1996) 110 Ohio App.3d 622, 674 N.E.2d 1256. Adoption ☞ 7.4(2.1)

In examining whether noncustodial parent's failure to communicate with child within requisite one-year period preceding adoption petition was justified, court is not restricted to focusing only on events occurring during period; court must also examine preceding events bearing on parent's failure to communicate with child. In re Adoption of Hedrick (Ohio App. 8 Dist., 04-29-1996) 110 Ohio App.3d 622, 674 N.E.2d 1256. Adoption ☞ 7.4(2.1)

Natural father did not have justifiable cause for failing to communicate with child during requisite one-year period preceding adoption petition filed by mother's husband even though father's mother, through whom father sent letters and cards to child at undisclosed address, did not forward letters and cards for fear that her contact with child would be cut off. In re Adoption of Hedrick (Ohio App. 8 Dist., 04-29-1996) 110 Ohio App.3d 622, 674 N.E.2d 1256. Adoption ☞ 7.4(2.1)

Natural father failed to show justifiable cause for his failure to communicate with his child, and thus his consent to child's adoption was not necessary; mother testified that she concealed her residence from father because he had threatened her and physically abused her in the past but that she agreed to father's supervised visitations with child

in another place, and child's registration in school under petitioner's surname in order to conceal her whereabouts did not preclude father from contacting child through child's grandmother. In re Serre (Ohio Com.Pl., 02-20-1996) 77 Ohio Misc.2d 29, 665 N.E.2d 1185. Adoption ☞ 7.4(2.1); Adoption ☞ 7.4(4)

No justifiable cause existed for a natural mother's failure to communicate with her two children for over a one-year period despite the mother's claim that interference from the children's guardian kept her from visiting the children, as the mother cited only one occasion where she called about a month before the adoption petition was filed to arrange a time to see her children, but according to the mother, the guardian hung up on her, since this one incident does not constitute significant interference with communication between the mother and her children and the guardian reaction was justified because the natural mother became abusive on the phone; moreover, no other instances existed where the mother attempted to visit her children even though she knew their address and phone number and worked only 200 yards from where the children were living, and she never tried to speak to her children on the phone. In re Adoption of Jordan (Preble 1991) 72 Ohio App.3d 638, 595 N.E.2d 963.

A probate court could conclude that a petitioner has not carried his burden on the issue of "justifiable cause" for his failure to communicate with his child in RC 3107.07(A) where the natural father establishes prior to the filing of the petition that he was an alcoholic with suicidal tendencies, that once in recovery the father secured employment and tried to contact his ex-wife to arrange for visits with and support payments to the child, that he made contact through an attorney rather than to have a face-to-face confrontation with his ex-wife, and that his ex-wife largely rebuffed his advances, failed to encourage visitation, and employed the adoption process largely as a means of severing his parental rights; the term "justifiable cause" in RC 3107.07 is not a readily defined term and must be determined from the surrounding circumstances of each case. In re Adoption of Jones (Medina 1990) 70 Ohio App.3d 576, 591 N.E.2d 823.

The consent of the natural father is not required in an adoption proceeding under RC 3107.06 and 3107.07 where (1) the father abandoned the mother and child when the child was three; (2) the mother was granted a divorce eight months later and retained full custody of the child; (3) the natural father did not contact the mother until three years after the divorce, after the petitioner had filed the adoption petition, although the mother and the petitioner did not marry until five months later; and (4) the father refused to consent to the adoption; the court's consideration of only one of two dates for calculation of the requisite one-year period during which the parent fails without justifiable cause to communicate with the minor or to provide for the maintenance and support is error, as the entire one-year period should be examined, not just a portion. In re Adoption of Jones (Medina 1990) 70 Ohio App.3d 576, 591 N.E.2d 823.

Where a mother refuses to permit visitation by a father on one occasion, and fails to provide the father with the child's name and address, the father did not completely fail to communicate with the child for purposes of ascertaining whether his consent is required for adoption of the child by the mother's new husband. In re Adoption of Youngpeter (Hancock 1989) 65 Ohio App.3d 172, 583 N.E.2d 360.

A natural father's duty to support a child arises at birth, particularly where he acknowledges paternity, and where the natural father unjustifiably fails to communicate with or support a child for one year prior to the filing of an adoption petition, his consent to the adoption of his illegitimate child is unnecessary. In re Adoption of Taylor (Medina 1989) 61 Ohio App.3d 500, 573 N.E.2d 156, motion overruled 43 Ohio St.3d 712, 541 N.E.2d 78.

Where a woman with custody of children moves them to California and refuses to give their address or telephone number to the father despite the urgings of the domestic relations judge, and where the repeated efforts of the father, the post office, and the telephone company to locate the woman and the children are unsuccessful, a petition by the woman's new husband to adopt the children and eliminate the father's parental rights without his consent, based on an assertion that the father failed without justifiable cause to communicate and failed to pay child support, must be granted without regard to the father's opposition where he had not gone back to court and succeeded at having the support obligation halted, even though (1) mail he sent to the children was returned on at least two occasions, (2) he had paid support in a timely manner until the woman disappeared, and (3) the woman made no attempt to collect any money after taking the children away from their father: "interference" with visitation rights is not an "excuse" for unilateral refusal to pay support. In re Adoptions of Bruce (Montgomery 1989) 56 Ohio App.3d 126, 564 N.E.2d 1110.

A child can be adopted under RC 3107.07(A) without the consent of a natural parent if the parent failed without just cause to pay child support even though the parent communicated with the child and sent gifts; interference by the child's stepfather with the father's telephone calls and written correspondence with his child are held insufficient cause for the father's failure to pay support in light of the court's conclusion that "ultimately it was [the child's] own choice to discontinue contact" because of the father's lack of "real interest." In re Adoption of Labo (Shelby 1988) 47 Ohio App.3d 57, 546 N.E.2d 1384.

Where the record discloses that neither the custodial parent nor the party seeking to adopt has provided current address or telephone information concerning the children to a non-consenting parent residing thousands of miles distant, justifiable cause for lack of communication is established, and an adoption order based upon a contrary finding will reversed. In re Adoption of Holcomb (Ohio 1985) 18 Ohio St.3d 361, 481 N.E.2d 613, 18 O.B.R. 419.

In RC 3107.07(A), providing that consent to an adoption is not required of a parent of a minor when the court finds that the parent has failed without justifiable cause to communicate with the minor "or" to provide for the maintenance and support of the minor, the word "or" should be read "and." In re Adoption of Taylor (Ohio Com.Pl. 1977) 55 Ohio Misc. 15, 380 N.E.2d 370, 7 O.O.3d 167, 9 O.O.3d 350. Adoption ☞ 7.4(6)

Under RC 3107.07(A) the consent to an adoption is not required of a parent who has been found by the court to have failed without justifiable cause to communicate with or support the minor for a period of at least one year either immediately preceding the filing of the adoption petition or immediately preceding the placement of the minor in the home of the petitioner, and the words "whichever occurs first" are deemed to refer or pertain to such parent's failure during either period rather than to the relative dates of filing and placement. In re Adoption of Taylor (Ohio Com.Pl. 1977) 55 Ohio Misc. 15, 380 N.E.2d 370, 7 O.O.3d 167, 9 O.O.3d 350. Adoption ☞ 7.4(6)

A mother who does not have custody of her child has a duty to give some personal care and attention to that child even though the child is being properly supported and maintained by his father, so that where she knows of her duty to give some personal care and attention to her child, is able to do so, and completely fails to give any care or attention to such child, such failure may justify a finding that she willfully failed to properly "maintain the child" within the meaning of those words as used in RC 3107.06(B)(4). Johnson v. Varney (Ohio 1965) 2 Ohio St.2d 161, 207 N.E.2d 558, 31 O.O.2d 316. Adoption ☞ 7.4(6)

A father's unsuccessful attempts to communicate with his child, for one year immediately preceding either the filing of the adoption petition or the placement of the minor in the home of petitioner, qualifies as justifiable cause for not communicating with the minor. In re Adoption of Shipman (Ohio App. 3 Dist., Crawford, 08-31-2001) No. 3-01-11, 2001-Ohio-2257, 2001 WL 997532, Unreported.

Probate court's denial of Civ R 60(B) motion to vacate adoption order is not error when record shows clear and convincing evidence that father lacked a justifiable cause for failing to communicate with child during year immediately preceding adoption. In re Adoption of Linn, No. 64243 (8th Dist Ct App, Cuyahoga, 4–29–93).

That natural father received annual earnings between $3,000 and $4,000 from public assistance and sporadic employment does not constitute justifiable cause for failure to pay any child support or communicate with his child pursuant to RC 3107.07. In re Adoption of Bitner, No. 81–CA–77 (7th Dist Ct App, Mahoning, 2–24–82).

20. —— Incarceration, failure to communicate

Father's incarceration on felony conviction did not constitute a disability that prevented him from maintaining contact with his child over a period of one year nor otherwise serve as grounds for contesting child's adoption absent his consent under no-contact provisions of adoption statute; father had no contact with child five months prior to his incarceration, and father was capable of contacting persons outside prison during his incarceration. In re Adoption of T.M. (Ohio App. 6 Dist., Sandusky, 09-30-2009) No. S-09-010, 2009-Ohio-5194, 2009 WL 3132282, Unreported. Adoption ☞ 7.4(1)

Trial court finding that incarcerated father failed without justifiable cause to communicate with his child was not an abuse of discretion, for the purpose of stepfather's petition to adopt father's child without father's consent; father failed to file an objection to the petition or explain the circumstances surrounding his failure to communicate with the court before the court conducted a hearing on the matter and entered an order granting the adoption. In re Adoption of S.L.C. (Ohio App. 2 Dist., Miami, 12-29-2005) No. 05-CA-32, 2005-Ohio-7067, 2005 WL 3610305, Unreported. Adoption ☞ 7.8(4)

Biological father's consent to stepfather's adoption of child was not required pursuant to statute providing that consent is unnecessary when biological father had failed, without justifiable cause, to provide maintenance and support and to communicate with child for period of at least one year immediately preceding filing of adoption petition, where biological father's criminal behavior caused court in domestic proceeding to enter order prohibiting biological father from having contact with child and biological father made only two $5.25 child support payments during relevant time period as result of state wage withholding of his prison wages. Askew v. Taylor (Ohio App. 5 Dist., Stark, 10-12-2004) No. 2004CA00184, 2004-Ohio-5504, 2004 WL 2315190, Unreported. Adoption ☞ 7.4(6)

The one-year limitations period within the statute governing parental consent to adoption, which stated that a biological parent's consent to adoption was not required when the parent had failed to communicate with the child or provide maintenance and support for the child for a period of at least one year prior to the filing of the adoption petition, was not tolled by mother's incarceration; mother's incarceration did not prevent her from communicating with the children. In re Adoptions of Doyle (Ohio App. 11 Dist., Ashtabula, 08-06-2004) No. 2003-A-0071, No. 2003-A-0072, 2004-Ohio-4197, 2004 WL 1778821, Unreported. Adoption ☞ 7.4(1)

Evidence supported trial court finding that mother's failure to communicate with her children for one year was without justifiable cause, and thus mother's consent to step-mother's adoption of children was not required; even though mother was incarcerated and there was a restraining order preventing mother from having physical contact with child, mother was not prevented from communicating with the children through cards and letters. In re Adoptions of Doyle (Ohio App. 11 Dist., Ashtabula, 08-06-2004) No. 2003-A-0071, No. 2003-A-0072, 2004-Ohio-4197, 2004 WL 1778821, Unreported. Adoption ☞ 7.4(4)

A natural mother has justifiable cause for failure to communicate with her child where (1) the mother is incarcerated and the child is separated from the mother at birth, (2) the mother provides a suitable home for her child during her absence, and (3) a conflict arises with the child's temporary custodians who will not cooperate with the mother's attempts to enforce visitation or to find out about her child's well-being. In re Adoption of Peyton Ashley F. (Ohio App. 6 Dist., Lucas, 10-13-2000) No. L-00-1146, 2000 WL 1513690, Unreported, stay denied 90 Ohio St.3d 1471, 738 N.E.2d 383, dismissed, appeal not allowed 90 Ohio St.3d 1481, 738 N.E.2d 1254.

A natural father's incarceration which prevents him from seeking his child's whereabouts is justiciable cause for failure to communicate for a period of one year immediately preceding the filing of an adoption petition by the child's stepfather. In re Adoption of Cockerham (Ohio App. 5 Dist., Stark, 01-27-1997) No. 1996 CA 0247, 1997 WL 118267, Unreported.

Clear and convincing evidence supported conclusion that biological father did not communicate with child for at least one year prior to mother's husband filing petition to adopt child, such that father's consent to adoption of child by mother's husband was not required; mother and her husband testified that they did not receive any communication from father's mother for child, contrary to father's claim that he had sent child letters via his mother while he was incarcerated, and biological father did not produce any evidence to show justifiable cause, such as interference, for his failure to communicate. In re Adoption of Ford (Ohio App. 3 Dist., 04-17-2006) 166 Ohio App.3d 161, 849 N.E.2d 330, 2006-Ohio-1889. Adoption ☞ 7.8(4)

Where a stepfather and the custodial parent make a concerted effort to thwart an incarcerated father's efforts to communicate with his children by refusing to accept his calls and returning his letters to his children unopened, the father's failure to communicate with his children is justified and even though the stepfather and the custodial parent believe their actions are in the children's best interest, they cannot prohibit communication and then claim the benefits of their efforts under RC 3107.07(A). In re Adoption of Lauck (Summit 1992) 82 Ohio App.3d 348, 612 N.E.2d 459, motion overruled 65 Ohio St.3d 1499, 605 N.E.2d 952.

The consent of a natural parent who fails to communicate with or provide support to her children for a full year prior to the filing of an adoption petition is required where such failure to communicate or support is due to the incarceration of the natural parent. In re Adoption of Thompson, No. 27–CA–87 (5th Dist Ct App, Fairfield, 1–7–88).

21. —— Discouragement of communication, failure to communicate

Justifiable cause existed for lack of communication between father and child, under statute providing that parent's consent to child's adoption is not required when that parent has failed without justifiable cause to communicate with child for period of at least one year immediately preceding filing of adoption petition, and, thus, father's consent to adoption of child by her stepfather was required; mother significantly discouraged communication between father and child, including instructing child's daycare provider not to allow father to speak to child, and refusing to allow child to attend party upon learning that father would be present. In re K.L.K.-F. (Ohio App. 2 Dist., Miami, 05-29-2009) No. 08-CA-46, 2009-Ohio-2543, 2009 WL 1515728, Unreported. Adoption ☞ 7.4(2.1)

Probate court's conclusion that step-father had failed to show, by clear and convincing evidence, that father's consent to the adoption was not required was not against the manifest weight of the evidence; because of his meager financial resources, there was justifiable cause for father's failure to support his child in the year preceding the petition for adoption, and mother had significantly discouraged communication, thus justifying father's failure to communicate with his son. In re Adoption of H.M.F. (Ohio App. 2 Dist., Montgomery, 04-17-2009) No. 22805, 2009-Ohio-1947, 2009 WL 1114222, Unreported. Adoption ☞ 7.8(5)

Clear and convincing evidence supported finding that mother failed to communicate with child for a period of one year without justifiable cause, and thus mother's consent to stepmother's petition to adopt child was not necessary; mother testified that she felt uncomfortable visiting child in father and stepmother's house so she stopped attending visitation, mother never sought to modify the visitation schedule, and father and stepmother never discouraged the visits with mother. In re Adoption of Delong (Ohio App. 3 Dist., Hancock, 03-16-2009) No. 5-08-48, 2009-Ohio-1150, 2009 WL 654310, Unreported. Adoption ☞ 7.4(1)

In context of determining whether a natural parent's consent to adoption may be dispensed with for failure to communicate with the child, the standard of proof to establish justifiable cause for a noncustodial parent's failure to communicate is significant interference between the noncustodial parent and the child, or significant discouragement of such communication. In re Adoption of A.J.Y. (Ohio Com.Pl., 09-16-2010) 160 Ohio Misc.2d 4, 937 N.E.2d 1109, 2010-Ohio-5726. Adoption ☞ 7.4(4)

Natural mother's relocation with child on multiple occasions over a nine-year period, coupled with her failure to file notices of intent to relocate and her use of four different surnames during that period, caused significant interference in, or significant discouragement of, communication between noncustodial father and child, such that child could

not be adopted without father's consent despite his failure to communicate with child in the one-year period immediately preceding the filing of adoption petition. In re Adoption of A.J.Y. (Ohio Com.Pl., 09-16-2010) 160 Ohio Misc.2d 4, 937 N.E.2d 1109, 2010-Ohio-5726. Adoption ☞ 7.4(4)

Significant interference by custodial parent with communication between child and noncustodial parent or significant discouragement of such communication is required to establish justifiable cause to excuse noncustodial parent's failure to communicate with child for one year, and make noncustodial parent's consent a prerequisite to adoption. In re Serre (Ohio Com.Pl., 02-20-1996) 77 Ohio Misc.2d 29, 665 N.E.2d 1185. Adoption ☞ 7.4(4)

Significant interference by a custodial parent with communication between the noncustodial parent and the child, or significant discouragement of such communication, is required to establish justifiable cause for the noncustodial parent's failure to communicate with the child. The question of whether justifiable cause exists in a particular case is a factual determination for the probate court and will not be disturbed upon appeal unless such determination is unsupported by clear and convincing evidence. In re Adoption of Holcomb (Ohio 1985) 18 Ohio St.3d 361, 481 N.E.2d 613, 18 O.B.R. 419. Adoption ☞ 13; Adoption ☞ 15

Justifiable cause for a noncustodial parent's failure to communicate with his child exists where the custodial parent interfered to a significant degree with communication between the noncustodial parent and the child, and a showing is made that the failure was neither voluntary nor intentional. Matter of Adoption of Hupp (Cuyahoga 1982) 9 Ohio App.3d 128, 458 N.E.2d 878, 9 O.B.R. 192.

22. —— Burden of proof, failure to communicate

Although the burden of proof is on the adoption petitioner to show by clear and convincing evidence that the respondent parent has failed to communicate with the child, such that respondent parent's consent to adoption is not required, the respondent parent has the burden of going forward to show justifiable cause for a failure to communicate. In re Adoption of Ford (Ohio App. 3 Dist., 04-17-2006) 166 Ohio App.3d 161, 849 N.E.2d 330, 2006-Ohio-1889. Adoption ☞ 7.8(1); Adoption ☞ 7.8(4)

Biological father's consent to adoption by stepfather was required, where in the year before the filing of the adoption petition, biological father communicated with the child by telephone at least three times and paid for some birthday gifts and for karate lessons. In re Adoption of Williams (Ohio Prob., 02-04-2002) 117 Ohio Misc.2d 39, 766 N.E.2d 637, 2002-Ohio-1034. Adoption ☞ 7.8(5)

Face-to-face encounter between child and his biological father, in which the two exchanged conversation, hugged, and interacted by playing ball and in which father identified himself as child's father, constituted a "communication" for purposes of statute requiring father's consent to adoption if he had communicated with child within the year prior to filing of adoption petition. In re Adoption of Tscheiner (Ohio App. 1 Dist., 12-22-2000) 141 Ohio App.3d 527, 752 N.E.2d 292. · Adoption ☞ 7.2(3)

Trial court erroneously placed burden of proof, on issue of whether child's biological father communicated with child during statutory one-year period prior to filing of adoption petition by child's mother's husband, on biological father; trial court required biological father, who had been incarcerated during statutory period on conviction related to domestic violence against child's mother, to prove that there was justifiable cause for his failure, if any, to communicate with child from prison. In re Adoption of Eblin (Ohio App. 3 Dist., 03-24-1998) 126 Ohio App.3d 774, 711 N.E.2d 319, appeal allowed 82 Ohio St.3d 1482, 696 N.E.2d 1088, cause dismissed 83 Ohio St.3d 1454, 700 N.E.2d 617. Adoption ☞ 7.8(1)

Although the nonconsenting parent is responsible for articulating a justifiable cause for failure to communicate with child, in action to dispense with parent's consent to adoption, no burden is placed upon nonconsenting parent to establish that the failure to communicate was justifiable. In re Doe (Ohio App. 9 Dist., 10-15-1997) 123 Ohio App.3d 505, 704 N.E.2d 608, stay denied 80 Ohio St.3d 1470, 687 N.E.2d 298, dismissed, jurisdictional motion overruled 81 Ohio St.3d 1443, 690 N.E.2d 15. Adoption ☞ 7.8(1)

Clear and convincing evidence did not establish that father's failure to communicate with his child for one-year period was unjustified, as required for stepfather to adopt child without father's consent, where mother and stepfather failed to appear at meeting to discuss father's visitation rights, and father thereafter sought relief in courts to enforce and augment his visitation rights. In re Doe (Ohio App. 9 Dist., 10-15-1997) 123 Ohio App.3d 505, 704 N.E.2d 608, stay denied 80 Ohio St.3d 1470, 687 N.E.2d 298, dismissed, jurisdictional motion overruled 81 Ohio St.3d 1443, 690 N.E.2d 15. Adoption ☞ 7.8(5)

Trial judge's comment, in contested adoption proceeding, that burden of proof switched to noncustodial parent after petitioner proved by clear and convincing evidence a lack of communication without justifiable cause was harmless error where noncustodial parent was provided full and fair hearing and judge as trier of fact had sufficient evidence to satisfy petitioner's burden of proof. In re Adoption of Hedrick (Ohio App. 8 Dist., 04-29-1996) 110 Ohio App.3d 622, 674 N.E.2d 1256. Adoption ☞ 15

Adoption petitioner offered competent, credible testimony showing natural father's failure to communicate with child without justifiable cause and thus burden of going forward shifted to father to show some facially justifiable cause for such failure. In re Serre (Ohio Com.Pl., 02-20-1996) 77 Ohio Misc.2d 29, 665 N.E.2d 1185. Adoption ☞ 7.8(1); Adoption ☞ 7.8(4)

A petitioner for adoption has the burden of proving, by clear and convincing evidence, that the natural parent has failed to communicate with the child for one year, and that there was no justifiable cause for this failure. In re Adoption of Gibson (Ohio 1986) 23 Ohio St.3d 170, 492 N.E.2d 146, 23 O.B.R. 336. Adoption ☞ 7.8(4); Adoption ☞ 7.8(5)

The party petitioning for adoption has the burden of proving, by clear and convincing evidence, that the parent failed to communicate with the child during the requisite one-year period and that there was no justifiable cause for the failure of communication. In re Adoption of Holcomb (Ohio 1985) 18 Ohio St.3d 361, 481 N.E.2d 613, 18 O.B.R. 419. Adoption ☞ 7.8(5)

23. "To provide more than de minimis" construed

Qualifying phrase "to provide more than de minimis" in adoption statute, allowing adoption of a minor child without biological parent's consent if the parent has failed to provide more than de minimis contact with the child or to provide for the maintenance and support of the child as required by law or judicial decree for a period of at least one year immediately preceding the filing of the adoption petition, pertains only to the biological parent's contact with the minor child and does not modify a biological parent's maintenance and support of the minor child. In re Adoption of O.N.C. (Ohio App. 3 Dist., 10-25-2010) 191 Ohio App.3d 72, 944 N.E.2d 1196, 2010-Ohio-5187. Adoption ☞ 7.4(1); Adoption ☞ 7.4(6)

24. Putative father—In general

Notice and petition for adoption sent to putative father failed to satisfy putative father's right to due process of law, and thus father's consent to adoption was not excused based on father's failure to file objections to the petition within 14 days; the notice did not inform father of the limited time period for filing objections to the petition for adoption, and the notice might have misled father to believe that he could assert his parental rights and object to the adoption at the scheduled adoption hearing. In re Adoption of Baby F. (Ohio App. 10 Dist., Franklin, 04-13-2004) No. 03AP-1092, No. 03AP-1132, 2004-Ohio-1871, 2004 WL 771575, Unreported, appeal not allowed 102 Ohio St.3d 1486, 810 N.E.2d 968, 2004-Ohio-3069. Adoption ☞ 7.3; Adoption ☞ 11; Adoption ☞ 12; Constitutional Law ☞ 4395

Finding that putative father's consent to adoption of child was not necessary was plain error, where finding was based on portion of statute that related to need for consent of parents, rather than on portion of statute that related to need for consent of putative father; error affected fairness of proceeding, as putative father had been given notice that adoption petition involved portion of statute that related to putative fathers, and portion of statute on consent of parent had no applicability to putative fathers. In re Adoption of R.C.A. (Ohio App. 2 Dist., Montgomery, 02-07-2003) No. 19509,

2003-Ohio-607, 2003 WL 262568, Unreported. Adoption ☞ 7.1; Adoption ☞ 15

Paternity was established, within meaning of adoption statute requiring father's consent, when administrative determination of parentage was made, even though order did not become final for 30 days. In re Adoption of Hudnell (Ohio App. 4 Dist., 08-06-1996) 113 Ohio App.3d 296, 680 N.E.2d 1055. Adoption ☞ 7.2(3)

Administrative determination of parentage was "court proceeding," within meaning of adoption statute requiring consent of father whose parentage is established in court proceeding. In re Adoption of Hudnell (Ohio App. 4 Dist., 08-06-1996) 113 Ohio App.3d 296, 680 N.E.2d 1055. Adoption ☞ 7.2(3)

Where putative father fails to demonstrate full commitment to responsibilities of parenthood, state should not be compelled to listen to his opinion of where child's best interests lie. In re Adoption of Zschach (Ohio, 06-06-1996) 75 Ohio St.3d 648, 665 N.E.2d 1070, reconsideration denied 76 Ohio St.3d 1410, 666 N.E.2d 569, certiorari denied 117 S.Ct. 582, 519 U.S. 1028, 136 L.Ed.2d 513. Adoption ☞ 7.4(1)

Putative father was not entitled to notice and hearing before probate court's finalization of adoption that deprived him of right to visitation; father's constitutionally protected interests were adequately safeguarded in being given opportunity to object to adoption of his putative child, but failing to object and thereby demonstrate his full commitment to responsibilities of parenthood. In re Adoption of Zschach (Ohio, 06-06-1996) 75 Ohio St.3d 648, 665 N.E.2d 1070, reconsideration denied 76 Ohio St.3d 1410, 666 N.E.2d 569, certiorari denied 117 S.Ct. 582, 519 U.S. 1028, 136 L.Ed.2d 513. Adoption ☞ 12; Adoption ☞ 13

Putative father had common-law duty to support his child for purposes of father's right to object to adoption of child by another, even if there had been no specific court-ordered support of child. In re Adoption of Bowes (Ohio App. 11 Dist., 08-07-1995) 105 Ohio App.3d 574, 664 N.E.2d 963. Adoption ☞ 7.2(3); Adoption ☞ 7.4(6)

It is quality of relationship between putative parent and child, and not amount of money spent on child by putative parent, which determines whether putative father has acquired parental interest in child for purposes of statute section requiring consent of person with parental interest in child to adoption of child. In re Adoption of Bowes (Ohio App. 11 Dist., 08-07-1995) 105 Ohio App.3d 574, 664 N.E.2d 963. Adoption ☞ 7.2(3); Adoption ☞ 7.4(6)

To preserve right to withheld consent to child's adoption and avoid finding that requirement of father's consent shall be excused, putative father who has signed birth certificate must file objection to adoption with court, department or agency having custody of child, but his objection need not be filed within 30 days of earlier of date of filing of adoption petition or placement of child. In re

Adoption of Greer (Ohio, 09-21-1994) 70 Ohio St.3d 293, 638 N.E.2d 999, 1994-Ohio-69. Adoption ☞ 7.3

Unless statutory requirement to consent of adoption is excused by virtue of failure of putative father to file objection, a putative father who has signed birth certificate as informant has statutory right to withhold consent to adoption of that child, thereby barring child's adoption by another. In re Adoption of Greer (Ohio, 09-21-1994) 70 Ohio St.3d 293, 638 N.E.2d 999, 1994-Ohio-69. Adoption ☞ 7.2(3)

Probate court order allowing adoption to proceed without putative father's consent was a final, appealable order as an order that affected a substantial right made in a special proceeding. In re Adoption of Greer (Ohio, 09-21-1994) 70 Ohio St.3d 293, 638 N.E.2d 999, 1994-Ohio-69. Adoption ☞ 15

Trial court's conclusion that putative father abandoned natural mother during term of her pregnancy, and, thus, that mother could place child for adoption without putative father's consent, was against manifest weight of evidence and was unsupported by clear and convincing evidence; evidence overwhelmingly demonstrated that it was mother that forsook all contact with father, and that father's attempts to reconcile his relationship with mother were met with resistance, threats, and deceit. In re Adoption of Klonowski (Stark 1993) 87 Ohio App.3d 352, 622 N.E.2d 376. Adoption ☞ 7.8(5)

A probate court's failure to consider a putative father's objection to adoption which is filed before entry of the final decree of adoption is not erroneous where the putative father's objection is not filed within thirty days of placement of the minor as set forth in RC 3107.06(F); thus, the putative father's consent was not necessary in order for the court to proceed with the adoption. In re Adoption of Hall (Franklin 1991) 72 Ohio App.3d 503, 595 N.E.2d 473.

RC 3107.07(A), which sets forth the circumstances under which the consent of a parent is not required in an adoption proceeding, does not apply to an acknowledged natural father of a child who was not married to the mother of the child at the time of the child's birth and who has not been established to be the child's father in a paternity proceeding under RC Ch 3111; rather, the provisions of RC 3107.07(B) apply. In re Adoption of Toth (Summit 1986) 33 Ohio App.3d 265, 515 N.E.2d 950.

Where a man establishes himself as a child's father in a paternity action brought pursuant to RC Ch 3111, the father's duty to support the child is retroactive to birth of the child for determining the father's failure to support the child for purposes of RC 3107.07(A). In re Adoption of Foster (Van Wert 1985) 22 Ohio App.3d 129, 489 N.E.2d 1070, 22 O.B.R. 331.

The filing of the acknowledgement of paternity pursuant to RC 2105.18 accompanied by the filing of an objection to adoption pursuant to RC

3107.06(F)(4) is sufficient to place the father within the purview of RC 3107.07(A) as a parent and not within RC 3107(B). In re Adoption of Dickson, No. 94–CA–57, 1995 WL 495450 (5th Dist Ct App, Fairfield, 5–19–95).

A putative father as that term is used in RC 3107.07 is not a "father" or "parent" as those words are used in RC 3107.06, 3111.01, and 5103.15. In re Adoption of Eckleberry, No. 94APF10–1523, 1995 WL 311409 (10th Dist Ct App, Franklin, 5–11–95).

Where there has been no judicial determination of parentage, the acknowledged natural father of a child born out of wedlock, who has signed the birth certificate, has no legal obligation to support his child and cannot be found to have violated a legal duty, thereby dispensing with his consent in an adoption proceeding. Amstutz v Braden, No. L–85–191 (6th Dist Ct App, Lucas, 12–27–85).

Where a putative father sends two checks totalling thirty dollars for the support of a child just prior to the filing of a petition for adoption and where this constitutes the only support ever offered or given, a finding that the putative father has failed to care for and support the minor child is justified and renders his consent to the adoption unnecessary. In re Adoption of Rouleau, No. 1058 (4th Dist Ct App, Ross, 8–31–84).

25. ——— Adjudicated father, putative father

Statute governing circumstances under which consent of legal parent to child's adoption is not required, rather than statute governing circumstances under which consent of a putative father to child's adoption is not required, governed issue of whether adjudicated father's consent to child's adoption was required in adoption proceeding in probate court, though adjudicated father was a putative father at time adoption petition was filed, as probate court was required to consider juvenile court's determination of parentage made while probate case was stayed, and, after adjudicated father's paternity had been established, probate court correctly proceeded with adoption case and consideration of whether adjudicated father's consent was required. In re Adoption of G.V. (Ohio App. 6 Dist., Lucas, 11-30-2009) No. L-09-1160, 2009-Ohio-6338, 2009 WL 4447562, Unreported, appeal allowed 124 Ohio St.3d 1474, 921 N.E.2d 246, 2010-Ohio-354, motion to dismiss denied 124 Ohio St.3d 1519, 923 N.E.2d 620, 2010-Ohio-1075, affirmed 126 Ohio St.3d 249, 933 N.E.2d 245, 2010-Ohio-3349, reconsideration denied 126 Ohio St.3d 1592, 934 N.E.2d 939, 2010-Ohio-4880, reconsideration denied 127 Ohio St.3d 1247, 937 N.E.2d 1285, 2010-Ohio-4879, certiorari denied 131 S.Ct. 1610, 179 L.Ed.2d 501, stay granted 126 Ohio St.3d 1576, 934 N.E.2d 350, 2010-Ohio-4615. Adoption ☞ 7.3

Prospective adoptive parents were not unfairly burdened with having to seek consent of multiple classifications of fathers, as child's legal father at time adoption petition was filed executed permanent surrender of his parental rights, in which he stated that he was not child's biological father, and the only person whose consent prospective adoptive parents would potentially need would be that of adjudicated father. In re Adoption of G.V. (Ohio App. 6 Dist., Lucas, 11-30-2009) No. L-09-1160, 2009-Ohio-6338, 2009 WL 4447562, Unreported, appeal allowed 124 Ohio St.3d 1474, 921 N.E.2d 246, 2010-Ohio-354, motion to dismiss denied 124 Ohio St.3d 1519, 923 N.E.2d 620, 2010-Ohio-1075, affirmed 126 Ohio St.3d 249, 933 N.E.2d 245, 2010-Ohio-3349, reconsideration denied 126 Ohio St.3d 1592, 934 N.E.2d 939, 2010-Ohio-4880, reconsideration denied 127 Ohio St.3d 1247, 937 N.E.2d 1285, 2010-Ohio-4879, certiorari denied 131 S.Ct. 1610, 179 L.Ed.2d 501, stay granted 126 Ohio St.3d 1576, 934 N.E.2d 350, 2010-Ohio-4615. Adoption ☞ 7.2(3)

Adjudicated father's failure to register as putative father was irrelevant to determination of whether his consent to child's adoption was required, where adjudication of paternity established existence of parent-child relationship. In re Adoption of Law (Ohio App. 3 Dist., Allen, 02-13-2006) No. 1-05-64, 2006-Ohio-600, 2006 WL 319141, Unreported. Adoption ☞ 7.2(3)

Statute section governing consent of putative fathers, rather than section applicable to consent of one whose status as parent had been legally adjudicated, was appropriate to apply to issue of whether putative father's consent was required for adoption of minor child. In re Adoption of Bowes (Ohio App. 11 Dist., 08-07-1995) 105 Ohio App.3d 574, 664 N.E.2d 963. Adoption ☞ 7.2(3)

26. ——— Registration, putative father

Evidence supported trial court determination that father's consent to adoption was not required, where father was child's putative father, and father failed to register with the putative father registry. In re Adoption of Osoro (Ohio App. 5 Dist., Stark, 12-30-2008) No. 2008 CA 00163, 2008-Ohio-6925, 2008 WL 5412814, Unreported, appeal not allowed 121 Ohio St.3d 1429, 903 N.E.2d 327, 2009-Ohio-1296. Adoption ☞ 7.2(3)

Statute, which provided that a putative father's consent to adoption was not required if the putative father failed to register with the Ohio putative father registry no later than 30 days after the child's birth, was not unconstitutional as applied to father and did not deprive father of his due process rights; father had never seen child, father sought to protect his opportunity to develop a relationship with child, and the putative father registry was constitutionally adequate to protect father's opportunity to develop a relationship with child. In re Adoption of Osoro (Ohio App. 5 Dist., Stark, 12-30-2008) No. 2008 CA 00163, 2008-Ohio-6925, 2008 WL 5412814, Unreported, appeal not allowed 121 Ohio St.3d 1429, 903 N.E.2d 327, 2009-Ohio-1296. Adoption ☞ 7.2(3); Constitutional Law ☞ 4395

Notice to a putative father of a pending adoption is not required if the he fails to register on the putative father registry. In re K.M.S. (Ohio App. 2 Dist., Miami, 09-09-2005) No. 05CA17,

2005-Ohio-4739, 2005 WL 2179297, Unreported. Adoption ☞ 12

Putative father's consent to child's adoption by mother's husband was not required; adoption statute provided that putative father's consent to adoption of child was not required if he failed to register as child's putative father within 30 days of child's birth, and husband filed certified written statement from Department of Job and Family Services that no man was registered on putative father registry as child's father, as required by statute. In re K.M.S. (Ohio App. 2 Dist., Miami, 09-09-2005) No. 05CA17, 2005-Ohio-4739, 2005 WL 2179297, Unreported. Adoption ☞ 7.2(3)

Putative father, who failed to properly register with state's putative father registry, did not have right to participate in hearing to determine if adoption was in best interest of child. In re Adoption of A.N.L. (Ohio App. 12 Dist., Warren, 08-16-2005) No. CA2004-11-131, No. CA2005-04-046, 2005-Ohio-4239, 2005 WL 1949678, Unreported. Adoption ☞ 13

Putative father's consent to adoption of child was not required, where father failed to register as child's putative father with state's putative father registry within 30 days after child's birth. In re Adoption of A.N.L. (Ohio App. 12 Dist., Warren, 08-16-2005) No. CA2004-11-131, No. CA2005-04-046, 2005-Ohio-4239, 2005 WL 1949678, Unreported. Adoption ☞ 7.2(3)

Evidence supported trial court determination that prospective adoptive parents failed to establish that putative father willfully abandoned birth mother of child, which would have allowed adoptive parents to proceed with adoption of child without the consent of putative father; birth mother testified that father attempted to make doctor's appointments for her, that after she moved out of house with father he moved into a house next door to her, that she continued to see and talk to father, that father attempted to talk to her after the parties obtained mutual protective orders against each other, and father gave birth mother money while he was in jail and registered with the putative father registry. In re Adoption of Baby F. (Ohio App. 10 Dist., Franklin, 04-13-2004) No. 03AP-1092, No. 03AP-1132, 2004-Ohio-1871, 2004 WL 771575, Unreported, appeal not allowed 102 Ohio St.3d 1486, 810 N.E.2d 968, 2004-Ohio-3069. Adoption ☞ 7.4(2.1)

Genuine issue of material fact as to whether consent of non-resident birth father, who complied with his state's putative father registry statute, was required for the adoption placement within state precluded summary judgment in adoption petitioners' favor in adoption proceedings. In re Adoption of Lichtenberg (Ohio App. 12 Dist., Warren, 03-05-2003) No. CA2002-11-125, 2003-Ohio-1014, 2003 WL 868306, Unreported, appeal not allowed 98 Ohio St.3d 1567, 787 N.E.2d 1231, 2003-Ohio-2242. Judgment ☞ 181(15.1)

Consent of biological father was not required for adoption of child by stepfather, since biological father had failed to register on putative father registry or otherwise safeguard his right to object to the adoption before adoption petition was filed. In re Adoption of P.A.C. (Ohio App. 1 Dist., 09-02-2009) 184 Ohio App.3d 88, 919 N.E.2d 791, 2009-Ohio-4492, stay granted 123 Ohio St.3d 1470, 915 N.E.2d 1253, 2009-Ohio-5704, appeal allowed 123 Ohio St.3d 1522, 918 N.E.2d 525, 2009-Ohio-6487, reversed 126 Ohio St.3d 236, 933 N.E.2d 236, 2010-Ohio-3351, reconsideration denied 126 Ohio St.3d 1592, 934 N.E.2d 939, 2010-Ohio-4880. Adoption ☞ 7.2(3)

Even assuming that, before adoption, unmarried putative father had visited child on weekly basis and had provided exclusive financial support for child, putative father did not have "developed relationship" with child before adoption, and thus, it did not violate putative father's substantive due process rights to apply statute providing that a putative father's consent to adoption is not required if putative father fails to register with registry of putative fathers not less than 30 days after child's birth. In re Cameron (Ohio App. 1 Dist., 08-15-2003) 153 Ohio App.3d 687, 795 N.E.2d 707, 2003-Ohio-4304. Adoption ☞ 7.3; Constitutional Law ☞ 4395

Putative father, who brought motion to set aside judgment granting adoption, was not required to serve Attorney General with copy of complaint challenging constitutionality of statute providing that a putative father's consent to adoption is not required if putative father fails to register with registry of putative fathers not less than 30 days after child's birth; statutory requirement of serving Attorney General with notice of constitutional challenge applied only to declaratory judgment actions. In re Cameron (Ohio App. 1 Dist., 08-15-2003) 153 Ohio App.3d 687, 795 N.E.2d 707, 2003-Ohio-4304. Constitutional Law ☞ 958; Declaratory Judgment ☞ 257

If a child's putative father fails to register within the statutory 30–day period, then his child may be adopted by another person without his consent; in fact, he is not even entitled to notice of the pending adoption proceeding. In re Adoption of Coppersmith (Ohio App. 2 Dist., 08-24-2001) 145 Ohio App.3d 141, 761 N.E.2d 1163, 2001-Ohio-1484. Adoption ☞ 7.3

Consent to adoption is not required of putative father who fails to register within thirty days of child's birth if he is still a putative father when petition for adoption is filed, but if a putative father judicially establishes parentage prior to the filing of adoption petition, he ceases to be a putative father and his consent is required based on parent and child relationship with minor. In re Adoption of Baby Boy Brooks (Ohio App. 10 Dist., 03-21-2000) 136 Ohio App.3d 824, 737 N.E.2d 1062, appeal not allowed 89 Ohio St.3d 1433, 730 N.E.2d 383. Adoption ☞ 7.2(3)

27. —— Written objection, putative father

Putative father's attempt to condition his consent to adoption upon his retention of permanent visitation rights was not written objection to adoption, required to preserve his right to contest adoption.

In re Adoption of Zschach (Ohio, 06-06-1996) 75 Ohio St.3d 648, 665 N.E.2d 1070, reconsideration denied 76 Ohio St.3d 1410, 666 N.E.2d 569, certiorari denied 117 S.Ct. 582, 519 U.S. 1028, 136 L.Ed.2d 513. Adoption ☞ 7.3

Nothing short of written objection to adoption proceeding suffices to preserve putative father's right to contest adoption. In re Adoption of Zschach (Ohio, 06-06-1996) 75 Ohio St.3d 648, 665 N.E.2d 1070, reconsideration denied 76 Ohio St.3d 1410, 666 N.E.2d 569, certiorari denied 117 S.Ct. 582, 519 U.S. 1028, 136 L.Ed.2d 513. Adoption ☞ 7.3

28. Petition for adoption

A petition, in the proceeding for the adoption of a child, which does not allege that the parents "willfully" failed to properly support and maintain their child, is not in compliance with the requirements of RC 3107.06, and fails to state a good cause of action. In re Gates' Adoption (Shelby 1948) 84 Ohio App. 269, 85 N.E.2d 597, 53 Ohio Law Abs. 315, 39 O.O. 379.

29. Withholding consent

County children services agency did not unreasonably withhold consent to relatives' petition to adopt minor child in proceeding in which the adoption petition of foster parents was granted, in view of child's bond with foster parents, certain concerns with relatives' home study report, the recommendations of the guardian ad litem and caseworker, and child's desires. In re Adoption of I.C. (Ohio App. 6 Dist., Lucas, 03-11-2011) No. L-10-1157, 2011-Ohio-1145, 2011 WL 857002, Unreported. Adoption ☞ 7.1

30. Final appealable order

Judgment that the consent of a natural parent is not required for the adoption of a minor by another is a final order subject to appellate review. In re Doe (Ohio App. 9 Dist., 10-15-1997) 123 Ohio App.3d 505, 704 N.E.2d 608, stay denied 80 Ohio St.3d 1470, 687 N.E.2d 298, dismissed, jurisdictional motion overruled 81 Ohio St.3d 1443, 690 N.E.2d 15. Adoption ☞ 15

Finding that party's consent to adoption is not required is final appealable order. In re Adoption of Wagner (Ohio App. 11 Dist., 01-21-1997) 117 Ohio App.3d 448, 690 N.E.2d 959, appeal not allowed 78 Ohio St.3d 1516, 679 N.E.2d 311. Adoption ☞ 15

Finding that parent's consent to adoption is unnecessary is final, appealable order. In re Adoption of Hudnell (Ohio App. 4 Dist., 08-06-1996) 113 Ohio App.3d 296, 680 N.E.2d 1055. Adoption ☞ 15

A ruling by the court that the consent of a natural parent is not required in an adoption proceeding filed pursuant to RC Ch 3107 is a final appealable order, since it constitutes "an order affecting a substantial right made in a special proceeding" within the meaning of RC 2505.02. In re Adoption of Jorgensen (Hancock 1986) 33 Ohio App.3d 207, 515 N.E.2d 622.

3107.071 Parental consent required despite voluntary permanent custody surrender agreement; exceptions

If a parent enters into a voluntary permanent custody surrender agreement under division (B)(2) of section 5103.15 of the Revised Code on or after the effective date of this section, the parent's consent to the adoption of the child who is the subject of the agreement is required unless all of the following requirements are met:

(A) In the case of a parent whose child, if adopted, will be an adopted person as defined in section 3107.45 of the Revised Code:

(1) The parent does all of the following:

(a) Signs the component of the form prescribed under division (A)(1)(a) of section 3107.083 of the Revised Code;

(b) Checks either the "yes" or "no" space provided on the component of the form prescribed under division (A)(1)(b) of section 3107.083 of the Revised Code and signs that component;

(c) If the parent is the mother, completes and signs the component of the form prescribed under division (A)(1)(c) of section 3107.083 of the Revised Code.

(2) The agency provides the parent the opportunity to sign, if the parent chooses to do so, the components of the form prescribed under divisions (A)(1)(d), (e), and (f) of section 3107.083 of the Revised Code;

(3) The agency files with the juvenile and probate courts the form prescribed under division (A)(1) of section 3107.083 of the Revised Code signed by the parent, provides a copy of the form signed by the parent to the parent, and keeps a copy of the form signed by the parent in the agency's records.

The court shall keep a copy of the form signed by the parent in the court records.

(B) In the case of a parent whose child, if adopted, will be an adopted person as defined in section 3107.39 of the Revised Code:

(1) The parent does both of the following:

(a) Signs the component of the form prescribed under division (B)(1)(a) of section 3107.083 of the Revised Code;

(b) If the parent is the mother, completes and signs the component of the form prescribed under division (B)(1)(b) of section 3107.083 of the Revised Code.

(2) The agency provides the parent the opportunity to sign, if the parent chooses to do so, the components of the form prescribed under divisions (B)(1)(c), (d), and (e) of section 3107.083 of the Revised Code at the time the parent enters into the agreement with the agency;

(3) The agency files the form signed by the parent with the juvenile and probate courts, provides a copy of the form signed by the parent to the parent, and keeps a copy of the form signed by the parent in the agency's records.

The court shall keep a copy of the form signed by the parent in the court records.

(1999 H 471, eff. 7–1–00; 1996 H 419, eff. 9–18–96)

Historical and Statutory Notes

Amendment Note: 1999 H 471 deleted "by the department of human services" after "prescribed" in divisions (A)(1)(a) and (B)(1)(a); and made other nonsubstantive changes.

Ohio Administrative Code References

Acceptance of permanent custody by permanent surrender, see OAC 5101:2–42–09

Library References

Adoption ⬅7.3.
Westlaw Topic No. 17.
C.J.S. Adoption of Persons §§ 56 to 58, 62.

Research References

Encyclopedias

OH Jur. 3d Family Law § 881, Who Must Consent.
OH Jur. 3d Family Law § 889, Who Need Not Consent.
OH Jur. 3d Family Law § 914, Forwarding of Adoption Information.

Forms

Ohio Forms Legal and Business § 28:24, Introduction.
Ohio Jurisprudence Pleading and Practice Forms § 96:11, Consent Required.

Ohio Jurisprudence Pleading and Practice Forms § 96:12, Consent Not Required.

Treatises and Practice Aids

Carlin, Baldwin's Ohio Prac. Merrick-Rippner Probate Law § 99:36, Method of Giving Consent.
Carlin, Baldwin's Ohio Prac. Merrick-Rippner Probate Law § 99:38, Consent Not Required--Statutory Scheme
Carlin, Baldwin's Ohio Prac. Merrick-Rippner Probate Law § 99:44, Hearing of Petition--Notice.

3107.08   Execution of consent

(A) The required consent to adoption may be executed at any time after seventy-two hours after the birth of a minor, and shall be executed in the following manner:

(1) If by the person to be adopted, in the presence of the court;

(2) If by a parent of the person to be adopted, in accordance with section 3107.081 of the Revised Code;

(3) If by an agency, by the executive head or other authorized representative, in the presence of a person authorized to take acknowledgments;

(4) If by any other person, in the presence of the court or in the presence of a person authorized to take acknowledgments;

(5) If by a juvenile court, by appropriate order.

(B) A consent which does not name or otherwise identify the prospective adoptive parent is valid if it contains a statement by the person giving consent that it was voluntarily executed irrespective of disclosure of the name or other identification of the prospective adoptive parent. (1996 H 419, eff. 9–18–96; 1976 H 156, eff. 1–1–77)

Historical and Statutory Notes

Ed. Note: Former 3107.08 repealed by 1976 H 156, eff. 1–1–77; 1975 S 145; 1953 H 1; GC 8004–8; Source—GC 10512–16.

Pre–1953 H 1 Amendments: 124 v S 65

Amendment Note: 1996 H 419 added division (A)(2); redesignated former divisions (A)(2) through (4) as (A)(3) through (5), respectively; substituted "acknowledgments" for "acknowledge-ments" in divisions (A)(3) and (4); deleted "except a minor" following "If by any other person" in division (A)(4); added "juvenile" in division (A)(5); deleted former division (A)(5), which read: "(5) If by a minor parent, pursuant to section 5103.16 of the Revised Code"; substituted "adoptive" for "adopting" twice in division (B); and made a nonsubstantive change.

Cross References

County children services board, powers and duties, see 5153.16

Department of job and family services, division of social administration; care and placement of children; interstate compact on placement of children, see 5103.12 to 5103.17, 5103.20 to 5103.237

Notaries public and commissioners, acknowledgments, see 147.01 et seq.

Library References

Adoption ☞7.5.
Westlaw Topic No. 17.
C.J.S. Adoption of Persons §§ 56, 70 to 73.

Research References

Encyclopedias

OH Jur. 3d Family Law § 886, Execution of Consent.

Forms

Ohio Forms Legal and Business § 28:24, Introduction.
Ohio Forms Legal and Business § 28:25, Form Drafting Principles.
Ohio Forms Legal and Business § 28:26, Consent to Adoption.
Ohio Forms Legal and Business § 28:27, Consent to Adoption--By Adult or Minor Over Age of 12.

Ohio Jurisprudence Pleading and Practice Forms § 96:14, Execution of Consent.

Treatises and Practice Aids

Carlin, Baldwin's Ohio Prac. Merrick-Rippner Probate Law § 99:22, Types of Placement--Independent Adoptions.
Carlin, Baldwin's Ohio Prac. Merrick-Rippner Probate Law § 99:36, Method of Giving Consent.
Carlin, Baldwin's Ohio Prac. Merrick-Rippner Probate Law § 99:37, Withdrawal of Consent.
Carlin, Baldwin's Ohio Prac. Merrick-Rippner Probate Law App B SPF 18.3, Consent to Adoption--Form.

Notes of Decisions

Nature of consent   2
Time of consent   1

_____

1. Time of consent

The required consent for an adoption may be executed any time from seventy-two hours after the birth of a child to be adopted until the time the adoption petition is granted, and there is no jurisdictional defect if the required consent is not executed prior to the hearing on the adoption petition or prior to the close of the petitioner's case; thus, where the guardian of children sought to be adopted gives her written consent well before the adoption petition is granted, the trial court has jurisdiction to grant the adoption petition even though the consent was not given prior to the close of the petitioner's case. In re Adoption of Jordan (Preble 1991) 72 Ohio App.3d 638, 595 N.E.2d 963.

2. Nature of consent

Mother was not prejudiced by consent to adoption form that indicated child's "name after adoption" would include his present surname rather than that of adoptive parents, in absence of evidence mother was confused as to the identity of child at issue. In re Adoption of Jimenez (Ohio App. 2 Dist., 09-24-1999) 136 Ohio App.3d 223, 736 N.E.2d 477, appeal allowed 88 Ohio St.3d 1427, 723 N.E.2d 1114, appeal dismissed as improvidently allowed 90 Ohio St.3d 1214, 735 N.E.2d 898, 2000-Ohio-42. Adoption ☜ 7.5

Statute regarding execution of biological mother's consent to child's adoption does not require that a petition be filed prior to the execution and does not require that the consent to adopt provide a name or identify the adoptive parent, as long as it contains a statement that it is voluntarily executed irrespective of such disclosure. In re Adoption of Koszycki (Ohio App. 1 Dist., 05-14-1999) 133 Ohio App.3d 434, 728 N.E.2d 437. Adoption ☜ 7.5

Consent to adoption of minor child was freely given by natural parents, for purpose of probate court's subject-matter jurisdiction to enter final order of adoption; natural parents had attained age of majority and had completed all but one semester of college, adoption of child had been considered even prior to its birth, both parents were before court of law and were fully aware of their rights to retain child and were fully aware that by signing consent form they were permanently surrendering their rights to child, and there was no evidence that they did not understand consequences of their actions. Morrow v. Family & Community Services of Catholic Charities, Inc. (Ohio 1986) 28 Ohio St.3d 247, 504 N.E.2d 2, 28 O.B.R. 327. Adoption ☜ 7.5

3107.081 Conditions for court acceptance of parental consent

(A) Except as provided in divisions (B), (E), and (F) of this section, a parent of a minor, who will be, if adopted, an adopted person as defined in section 3107.45 of the Revised Code, shall do all of the following as a condition of a court accepting the parent's consent to the minor's adoption:

(1) Appear personally before the court;

(2) Sign the component of the form prescribed under division (A)(1)(a) of section 3107.083 of the Revised Code;

(3) Check either the "yes" or "no" space provided on the component of the form prescribed under division (A)(1)(b) of section 3107.083 of the Revised Code and sign that component;

(4) If the parent is the mother, complete and sign the component of the form prescribed under division (A)(1)(c) of section 3107.083 of the Revised Code.

At the time the parent signs the components of the form prescribed under divisions (A)(1)(a), (b), and (c) of section 3107.083 of the Revised Code, the parent may sign, if the parent chooses to do so, the components of the form prescribed under divisions (A)(1)(d), (e), and (f) of that section. After the parent signs the components required to be signed and any discretionary components the parent chooses to sign, the parent, or the attorney arranging the adoption, shall file the form and parent's consent with the court. The court or attorney shall give the parent a copy of the form and consent. The court and attorney shall keep a copy of the form and consent in the court and attorney's records of the adoption.

The court shall question the parent to determine that the parent understands the adoption process, the ramifications of consenting to the adoption, each component of the form prescribed under division (A)(1) of section 3107.083 of the Revised Code, and that the minor and adoptive parent may receive identifying information about the parent in accordance with section 3107.47 of the Revised Code unless the parent checks the "no" space provided on the component of the form prescribed under division (A)(1)(b) of section 3107.083 of the Revised Code or has a denial of release form filed with the department of health under section 3107.46 of the Revised Code. The court also shall question the parent to determine that the parent's consent to the adoption and any decisions the parent makes in filling out the form prescribed under division (A)(1) of section 3107.083 of the Revised Code are made voluntarily.

(B) The parents of a minor, who is less than six months of age and will be, if adopted, an adopted person as defined in section 3107.45 of the Revised Code, may consent to the minor's adoption without personally appearing before a court if both parents do all of the following:

(1) Execute a notarized statement of consent to the minor's adoption before the attorney arranging the adoption;

(2) Sign the component of the form prescribed under division (A)(1)(a) of section 3107.083 of the Revised Code;

(3) Check either the "yes" or "no" space provided on the component of the form prescribed under division (A)(1)(b) of section 3107.083 of the Revised Code and sign that component.

At the time the parents sign the components of the form prescribed under divisions (A)(1)(a) and (b) of section 3107.083 of the Revised Code, the mother shall complete and sign the component of the form prescribed under division (A)(1)(c) of that section and the attorney arranging the adoption shall provide the parents the opportunity to sign, if they choose to do so, the components of the form prescribed under divisions (A)(1)(d), (e), and (f) of that section. At the time the petition to adopt the minor is submitted to the court, the attorney shall file the parents' consents and forms with the court. The attorney shall give the parents a copy of the consents and forms. At the time the attorney files the consents and forms with the court, the attorney also shall file with the court all other documents the director of job and family services requires by rules adopted under division (D) of section 3107.083 of the Revised Code to be filed with the court. The court and attorney shall keep a copy of the consents, forms, and documents in the court and attorney's records of the adoption.

(C) Except as provided in divisions (D), (E), and (F) of this section, a parent of a minor, who will be, if adopted, an adopted person as defined in section 3107.39 of the Revised Code, shall do all of the following as a condition of a court accepting the parent's consent to the minor's adoption:

(1) Appear personally before the court;

(2) Sign the component of the form prescribed under division (B)(1)(a) of section 3107.083 of the Revised Code;

(3) If the parent is the mother, complete and sign the component of the form prescribed under division (B)(1)(b) of section 3107.083 of the Revised Code.

At the time the parent signs the components prescribed under divisions (B)(1)(a) and (b) of section 3107.083 of the Revised Code, the parent may sign, if the parent chooses to do so, the components of the form prescribed under divisions (B)(1)(c), (d), and (e) of that section. After the parent signs the components required to be signed and any discretionary components the parent chooses to sign, the parent, or the attorney arranging the adoption, shall file the form and parent's consent with the court. The court or attorney shall give the parent a copy of the form and consent. The court and attorney shall keep a copy of the form and consent in the court and attorney's records of the adoption.

The court shall question the parent to determine that the parent understands the adoption process, the ramifications of consenting to the adoption, and each component of the form prescribed under division (B)(1) of section 3107.083 of the Revised Code. The court also shall question the parent to determine that the parent's consent to the adoption and any decisions the parent makes in filling out the form are made voluntarily.

(D) The parent of a minor who is less than six months of age and will be, if adopted, an adopted person as defined in section 3107.39 of the Revised Code may consent to the minor's adoption without personally appearing before a court if the parent does all of the following:

(1) Executes a notarized statement of consent to the minor's adoption before the attorney arranging the adoption;

(2) Signs the component of the form prescribed under division (B)(1)(a) of section 3107.083 of the Revised Code;

(3) If the parent is the mother, completes and signs the component of the form prescribed under division (B)(1)(b) of section 3107.083 of the Revised Code.

At the time the parent signs the components of the form prescribed under divisions (B)(1)(a) and (b) of section 3107.083 of the Revised Code, the attorney arranging the adoption shall provide the parent the opportunity to sign, if the parent chooses to do so, the components of the form prescribed under divisions (B)(1)(c), (d), and (e) of that section. At the time the petition to adopt the minor is submitted to the court, the attorney shall file the parent's consent and form with the court. The attorney shall give the parent a copy of the consent and form. At the time the attorney files the consent and form with the court, the attorney also shall file with the court all other documents the director of job and family services requires by rules adopted under division (D) of section 3107.083 of the Revised Code to be filed with the court. The court and attorney shall keep a copy of the consent, form, and documents in the court and attorney's records of the adoption.

(E) If a minor is to be adopted by a stepparent, the parent who is not married to the stepparent may consent to the minor's adoption without appearing personally before a court if the parent executes consent in the presence of a person authorized to take acknowledgments. The attorney arranging the adoption shall file the consent with the court and give the parent a copy of the consent. The court and attorney shall keep a copy of the consent in the court and attorney's records of the adoption.

(F) If a parent of a minor to be adopted resides in another state, the parent may consent to the minor's adoption without appearing personally before a court if the parent executes consent in the presence of a person authorized to take acknowledgments. The attorney arranging the adoption shall file the consent with the court and give the parent a copy of the consent. The court and attorney shall keep a copy of the consent in the court and attorney's records of the adoption.

(1999 H 471, eff. 7–1–00; 1996 H 274, eff. 9–18–96; 1996 H 419, eff. 9–18–96)

Historical and Statutory Notes

Amendment Note: 1999 H 471 deleted "by the department of human services" after "prescribed" in divisions (A)(2), (B)(2), (C)(2), and (D)(2); substituted "director of job and family services" for "department of human services" in the final paragraphs in divisions (B) and (D); and made other nonsubstantive changes.

Amendment Note: 1996 H 274 substituted "At the time the petition to adopt the minor is submit-

ted to the court" for "Not later than two business days after the parents execute consent and sign the components of the form required to be signed and any discretionary components the parents choose to sign" in the final paragraph in division (B); and for "Not later than two business days after the parents execute consent and signs the components of the form required to be signed and any discretionary components the parent chooses to sign" in the final paragraph in division (D).

Library References

Adoption ⟨key⟩7.5, 13.
Westlaw Topic No. 17.

C.J.S. Adoption of Persons §§ 46 to 47, 56, 70 to 73, 93 to 102.

Research References

Encyclopedias

8 Am. Jur. Proof of Facts 2d 481, Undue Influence in Obtaining Parent's Consent to Adoption of Child.
OH Jur. 3d Family Law § 881, Who Must Consent.
OH Jur. 3d Family Law § 886, Execution of Consent.
OH Jur. 3d Family Law § 914, Forwarding of Adoption Information.

Forms

Ohio Jurisprudence Pleading and Practice Forms § 96:14, Execution of Consent.

Ohio Jurisprudence Pleading and Practice Forms § 96:15, Court's Acceptance of Parental Consent.

Treatises and Practice Aids

Carlin, Baldwin's Ohio Prac. Merrick-Rippner Probate Law § 99:31, Parties Giving Consent--Biological Parents.
Carlin, Baldwin's Ohio Prac. Merrick-Rippner Probate Law § 99:37, Withdrawal of Consent.
Carlin, Baldwin's Ohio Prac. Merrick-Rippner Probate Law App B SPF 18.3, Consent to Adoption--Form.

Law Review and Journal Commentaries

Ohio House Bill 419: Increased Openness in Adoption Records Law, Wendy L. Weiss. 45 Clev St L Rev 101 (1997).

Notes of Decisions

Condition on consent   1-2
   Criminal nonsupport effect   1
   Parent's right to withdraw it   2

Criminal nonsupport effect, condition on consent
1
Parent's right to withdraw it, condition on consent
2

Procedural issues   4
Voluntary consent   3

---

1. Condition on consent—Criminal nonsupport effect

Biological father's consent to adoption of his minor daughter in exchange for state's agreement to reduce two felony charges of nonsupport to one misdemeanor count of nonsupport was not unconscionable; state had valid interest in pursuing those who fail to support their children, prosecution's consulting with mother in reaching agreement did not render it abusive, as mother was also victim of father's nonsupport, and, through advice of his own counsel, father was fully aware of his options and their consequences. In re Adoption of Gatley (Ohio App. 10 Dist., 09-21-2000) 138 Ohio App.3d 878, 742 N.E.2d 728. Adoption ☞ 7.5

2. —— Parent's right to withdraw it, condition on consent

Mother's consent to place son for adoption was invalid, where attorney for prospective adoptive parents had previously conveyed misimpression that mother would retain right to withdraw consent within six months for any reason at all, magistrate judge inaccurately stated withdrawal of consent would depend on "good cause shown" rather than best interests of child, and magistrate did not question mother to determine her understanding of adoption process and of ramifications of consent. In re Adoption of Jimenez (Ohio App. 2 Dist., 09-24-1999) 136 Ohio App.3d 223, 736 N.E.2d 477, appeal allowed 88 Ohio St.3d 1427, 723 N.E.2d 1114, appeal dismissed as improvidently allowed 90 Ohio St.3d 1214, 735 N.E.2d 898, 2000-Ohio-42. Adoption ☞ 7.5

3. Voluntary consent

Biological mother failed to establish that her consent to stepmother's adoption of children was procured by duress or undue influence, which would have provided grounds for invalidating biological mother's consent to adoption, even though mother was involved in a divorce from an abusive spouse and had a history of health problems; when the consent to adoption was executed, mother was an adult, she had a high school diploma, there was no evidence that the consents were rushed, there was no evidence that mother was not alert or was unaware of what she was signing, and there was no evidence that anyone acted in a way that compromised the exercise of mother's free will. In re Adoption of Hockman (Ohio App. 11 Dist., Portage, 01-14-2005) No. 2004-P-0079, No. 2004-P-0080, 2005-Ohio-140, 2005 WL 89387, Unreported. Adoption ☞ 7.5

Trial court abused its discretion in invalidating biological mother's written consent to stepmother's

adoption of children, where biological mother failed to establish that her consent was procured by fraud, duress or undue influence. In re Adoption of Hockman (Ohio App. 11 Dist., Portage, 01-14-2005) No. 2004-P-0079, No. 2004-P-0080, 2005-Ohio-140, 2005 WL 89387, Unreported. Adoption ☞ 7.5

Competent and credible evidence supported finding that birth parents' consent to adoption of child was voluntarily made without undue influence; court assessor met with birth parents and testified they did not seem confused about their options and they did not express doubts about placing child for adoption, hospital social worker testified that birth parents indicated that they were placing child for adoption voluntarily, birth parents were 24 and 23 years old when they placed child for adoption, and both birth parents stated under oath in court that it was their intention to place child for adoption and that they made the decision freely and voluntarily. In re Adoption of Baby Doe (Ohio App. 10 Dist., Franklin, 02-17-2004) No. 03AP-917, 2004-Ohio-689, 2004 WL 292066, Unreported, motion for delayed appeal denied 101 Ohio St.3d 1486, 805 N.E.2d 538, 2004-Ohio-1293, appeal not allowed 102 Ohio St.3d 1412, 806 N.E.2d 563, 2004-Ohio-1763. Adoption ☞ 7.8(3.1)

4. Procedural issues

Stepmother was not required to provide biological mother with a time-stamped copy of mother's signed consent to adoption, as a condition precedent for the adoption; statute did not require that a time-stamped copy of consent to adoption be provided to a biological mother when a stepparent was adopting the child. In re Adoption of Hockman (Ohio App. 11 Dist., Portage, 01-14-2005) No. 2004-P-0079, No. 2004-P-0080, 2005-Ohio-140, 2005 WL 89387, Unreported. Adoption ☞ 7.1

Birth parents failed to establish that the probate court committed prejudicial error by violating its own procedural rules regarding the adoption process; magistrate's explanations during consent to adoption hearing were proper and were made to make sure that birth parents understood the permanent nature of their decision, and the failure to wait the full 15 days after filing of the replacement application before child was placed with adoptive parents did not warrant reversal of adoption since parents declined any postponement of the adoption and adoptive parents' home study was approved. In re Adoption of Baby Doe (Ohio App. 10 Dist., Franklin, 02-17-2004) No. 03AP-917, 2004-Ohio-689, 2004 WL 292066, Unreported, motion for delayed appeal denied 101 Ohio St.3d 1486, 805 N.E.2d 538, 2004-Ohio-1293, appeal not allowed 102 Ohio St.3d 1412, 806 N.E.2d 563, 2004-Ohio-1763. Adoption ☞ 15

3107.082 Assessor's meeting with parent prior to parent's consent to adoption

Not less than seventy-two hours prior to the date a parent executes consent to the adoption of the parent's child under section 3107.081 of the Revised Code, an assessor shall meet in person with the parent and do both of the following unless the child is to be adopted by a stepparent or the parent resides in another state:

(A) Provide the parent with a copy of the written materials about adoption prepared under division (C) of section 3107.083 of the Revised Code, discuss with the parent the adoption process and ramifications of a parent consenting to a child's adoption, and provide the parent the opportunity to review the materials and to ask questions about the materials, discussion, and related matters;

(B) Unless the child, if adopted, will be an adopted person as defined in section 3107.39 of the Revised Code, inform the parent that the child and the adoptive parent may receive, in accordance with section 3107.47 of the Revised Code, identifying information about the parent that is contained in the child's adoption file maintained by the department of health unless the parent checks the "no" space provided on the component of the form prescribed under division (A)(1)(b) of section 3107.083 of the Revised Code or signs and has filed with the department a denial of release form prescribed under section 3107.50 of the Revised Code.

(1999 H 471, eff. 7-1-00; 1996 H 419, eff. 9-18-96)

Historical and Statutory Notes

Amendment Note: 1999 H 471 deleted "by the department of human services" after "prepared" in division (A).

Cross References

Probate courts, appointment of assessors, see
  2101.11

Library References

Adoption ⚖7.5.
Westlaw Topic No. 17.
C.J.S. Adoption of Persons §§ 56, 70 to 73.

Research References

Encyclopedias

OH Jur. 3d Family Law § 886, Execution of Consent.

Forms

Ohio Forms Legal and Business § 28:24, Introduction.

Ohio Jurisprudence Pleading and Practice Forms
  § 96:20, Home Study.

Treatises and Practice Aids

Carlin, Baldwin's Ohio Prac. Merrick-Rippner Probate Law § 99:14, Types of Placement--Agency Adoptions--Termination of Parental Rights.

3107.083 Form authorizing release of information

Not later than ninety days after June 20, 1996, the director of job and family services shall do all of the following:

(A)(1) For a parent of a child who, if adopted, will be an adopted person as defined in section 3107.45 of the Revised Code, prescribe a form that has the following six components:

(a) A component the parent signs under section 3107.071, 3107.081, or 5103.151 of the Revised Code to indicate the requirements of section 3107.082 or 5103.152 of the Revised Code have been met. The component shall be as follows:

"Statement Concerning Ohio Law and Adoption Materials

By signing this component of this form, I acknowledge that it has been explained to me, and I understand, that, if I check the space on the next component of this form that indicates that I authorize the release, the adoption file maintained by the Ohio Department of Health, which contains identifying information about me at the time of my child's birth, will be released, on request, to the adoptive parent when the adoptee is at least age eighteen but younger than age twenty-one and to the adoptee when he or she is age twenty-one or older. It has also been explained to me, and I understand, that I may prohibit the release of identifying information about me contained in the adoption file by checking the space on the next component of this form that indicates that I do not authorize the release of the identifying information. It has additionally been explained to me, and I understand, that I may change my mind regarding the decision I make on the next component of this form at any time and as many times as I desire by signing, dating, and having filed with the Ohio Department of Health a denial of release form or authorization of release form prescribed and provided by the Department of Health and providing the Department two items of identification.

By signing this component of this form, I also acknowledge that I have been provided a copy of written materials about adoption prepared by the Ohio Department of Job and Family Services, the adoption process and ramifications of consenting to adoption or entering into a voluntary permanent custody surrender agreement have been discussed with me, and I have been provided the opportunity to review the materials and ask questions about the materials and discussion.

Signature of biological parent: _____

Signature of witness: _____

Date: . . . ."

(b) A component the parent signs under section 3107.071, 3107.081, or 5103.151 of the Revised Code regarding the parent's decision whether to allow identifying information about the parent contained in an adoption file maintained by the department of health to be released to the parent's child and adoptive parent pursuant to section 3107.47 of the Revised Code. The component shall be as follows:

"Statement Regarding Release of Identifying Information

The purpose of this component of this form is to allow a biological parent to decide whether to allow the Ohio Department of Health to provide an adoptee and adoptive parent identifying information about the adoptee's biological parent contained in an adoption file maintained by the Department. Please check one of the following spaces:

___YES, I authorize the Ohio Department of Health to release identifying information about me, on request, to the adoptive parent when the adoptee is at least age eighteen but younger than age twenty-one and to the adoptee when he or she is age twenty-one or older.

___NO, I do not authorize the release of identifying information about me to the adoptive parent or adoptee.

Signature of biological parent: _____

Signature of witness: _____

Date: . . . ."

(c) A component the parent, if the mother of the child, completes and signs under section 3107.071, 3107.081, or 5103.151 of the Revised Code to indicate, to the extent of the mother's knowledge, all of the following:

(i) Whether the mother, during her pregnancy, was a recipient of the medical assistance program established under Chapter 5111. of the Revised Code or other public health insurance program and, if so, the dates her eligibility began and ended;

(ii) Whether the mother, during her pregnancy, was covered by private health insurance and, if so, the dates the coverage began and ended, the name of the insurance provider, the type of coverage, and the identification number of the coverage;

(iii) The name and location of the hospital, freestanding birth center, or other place where the mother gave birth and, if different, received medical care immediately after giving birth;

(iv) The expenses of the obstetrical and neonatal care;

(v) Whether the mother has been informed that the adoptive parent or the agency or attorney arranging the adoption are to pay expenses involved in the adoption, including expenses the mother has paid and expects to receive or has received reimbursement, and, if so, what expenses are to be or have been paid and an estimate of the expenses;

(vi) Any other information related to expenses the department determines appropriate to be included in this component.

(d) A component the parent may sign to authorize the agency or attorney arranging the adoption to provide to the child or adoptive parent materials, other than photographs of the parent, that the parent requests be given to the child or adoptive parent pursuant to section 3107.68 of the Revised Code.

(e) A component the parent may sign to authorize the agency or attorney arranging the adoption to provide to the child or adoptive parent photographs of the parent pursuant to section 3107.68 of the Revised Code.

(f) A component the parent may sign to authorize the agency or attorney arranging the adoption to provide to the child or adoptive parent the first name of the parent pursuant to section 3107.68 of the Revised Code.

(2) State at the bottom of the form that the parent is to receive a copy of the form the parent signed.

(3) Provide copies of the form prescribed under this division to probate and juvenile courts, public children services agencies, private child placing agencies, private noncustodial agencies, attorneys, and persons authorized to take acknowledgments.

(B)(1) For a parent of a child who, if adopted, will become an adopted person as defined in section 3107.39 of the Revised Code, prescribe a form that has the following five components:

(a) A component the parent signs under section 3107.071, 3107.081, or 5103.151 of the Revised Code to attest that the requirement of division (A) of section 3107.082 or division (A) of section 5103.152 of the Revised Code has been met;

(b) A component the parent, if the mother of the child, completes and signs under section 3107.071, 3107.081, or 5103.151 of the Revised Code to indicate, to the extent of the mother's knowledge, all of the following:

(i) Whether the mother, during her pregnancy, was a recipient of the medical assistance program established under Chapter 5111. of the Revised Code or other public health insurance program and, if so, the dates her eligibility began and ended;

(ii) Whether the mother, during her pregnancy, was covered by private health insurance and, if so, the dates the coverage began and ended, the name of the insurance provider, the type of coverage, and the identification number of the coverage;

(iii) The name and location of the hospital, freestanding birth center, or other place where the mother gave birth and, if different, received medical care immediately after giving birth;

(iv) The expenses of the obstetrical and neonatal care;

(v) Whether the mother has been informed that the adoptive parent or the agency or attorney arranging the adoption are to pay expenses involved in the adoption, including expenses the mother has paid and expects to receive or has received reimbursement for, and, if so, what expenses are to be or have been paid and an estimate of the expenses;

(vi) Any other information related to expenses the department determines appropriate to be included in the component.

(c) A component the parent may sign to authorize the agency or attorney arranging the adoption to provide to the child or adoptive parent materials, other than photographs of the parent, that the parent requests be given to the child or adoptive parent pursuant to section 3107.68 of the Revised Code.

(d) A component the parent may sign to authorize the agency or attorney arranging the adoption to provide to the child or adoptive parent photographs of the parent pursuant to section 3107.68 of the Revised Code.

(e) A component the parent may sign to authorize the agency or attorney arranging the adoption to provide to the child or adoptive parent the first name of the parent pursuant to section 3107.68 of the Revised Code.

(2) State at the bottom of the form that the parent is to receive a copy of the form the parent signed.

(3) Provide copies of the form prescribed under this division to probate and juvenile courts, public children services agencies, private child placing agencies, private noncustodial agencies, and attorneys.

(C) Prepare the written materials about adoption that are required to be given to parents under division (A) of section 3107.082 and division (A) of section 5103.152 of the Revised Code. The materials shall provide information about the adoption process, including ramifications of a parent consenting to a child's adoption or entering into a voluntary permanent custody surrender agreement. The materials also shall include referral information for professional counseling and adoption support organizations. The director shall provide the materials to assessors.

(D) Adopt rules in accordance with Chapter 119. of the Revised Code specifying the documents that must be filed with a probate court under divisions (B) and (D) of section 3107.081 of the Revised Code and a juvenile court under divisions (C) and (E) of section 5103.151 of the Revised Code.

(1999 H 471, eff. 7–1–00; 1996 H 419, eff. 6–20–96)

Historical and Statutory Notes

Amendment Note: 1999 H 471 substituted "June 20, 1996" for "the effective date of this section" and "director of job and family services" for "department of human services" in the introductory paragraph; substituted "Job and Family" for "Human" in the form in division (A)(1); and substituted "director" for "department" in division (C).

Cross References

Assessor's meeting with birth parent prior to parent's consenting to adoption, written materials, see 5103.152

Conditions for juvenile court approving parent's agreement for child's adoption, form, see 5103.151

Ohio Administrative Code References

Acceptance of permanent custody by permanent surrender, see OAC 5101:2–42–09
Release of identifying and nonidentifying information, see OAC 5101:2–48–20

Soliciting and releasing adoptive homestudies and related material for consideration of placement, see OAC 5101:2–48–19

Library References

Adoption ☞7.5.
Health ☞397.
Westlaw Topic Nos. 17, 198H.

C.J.S. Adoption of Persons §§ 56, 70 to 73.
C.J.S. Health and Environment §§ 24, 74.

Research References

Encyclopedias

OH Jur. 3d Family Law § 886, Execution of Consent.
OH Jur. 3d Family Law § 912, Records and Papers--Open Adoption.
OH Jur. 3d Family Law § 913, Records and Papers--Inspection.
OH Jur. 3d Family Law § 914, Forwarding of Adoption Information.

Forms

Ohio Forms Legal and Business § 28:24, Introduction.
Ohio Jurisprudence Pleading and Practice Forms § 96:11, Consent Required.
Ohio Jurisprudence Pleading and Practice Forms § 96:15, Court's Acceptance of Parental Consent.

Ohio Jurisprudence Pleading and Practice Forms § 96:20, Home Study.
Ohio Jurisprudence Pleading and Practice Forms § 96:27, Permanent Custody Surrender Agreement--Juvenile Court Approval.
Ohio Jurisprudence Pleading and Practice Forms § 96:35, Authorization by Biological Parent or Sibling.

Treatises and Practice Aids

Carlin, Baldwin's Ohio Prac. Merrick-Rippner Probate Law § 99:49, Interlocutory and Final Orders.
Carlin, Baldwin's Ohio Prac. Merrick-Rippner Probate Law § 108:24, Agreements for Temporary and Permanent Custody.

Law Review and Journal Commentaries

Ohio House Bill 419: Increased Openness in Adoption Records Law, Wendy L. Weiss. 45 Clev St L Rev 101 (1997).

3107.084 Withdrawal of consent

(A) A consent to adoption is irrevocable and cannot be withdrawn after the entry of an interlocutory order or after the entry of a final decree of adoption when no interlocutory order has been entered. The consent of a minor is not voidable by reason of the minor's age.

(B) A consent to adoption may be withdrawn prior to the entry of an interlocutory order or prior to the entry of a final decree of adoption when no interlocutory order has been entered if the court finds after hearing that the withdrawal is in the best interest of the person to be adopted and the court by order authorizes the withdrawal of consent. Notice of the hearing shall be given to the petitioner, the person seeking the withdrawal of consent, and the agency placing the minor for adoption.

(1996 H 419, eff. 9–18–96)

Historical and Statutory Notes

Ed. Note: 3107.084 is former 3107.09, amended and recodified by 1996 H 419, eff. 9–18–96, 1976 H 156, eff. 1–1–77.

Amendment Note: 1996 H 419 amended this section by substituting "the minor's age" for "his minority" at the end of division (A).

Library References

Adoption ☞7.6.
Westlaw Topic No. 17.
C.J.S. Adoption of Persons §§ 56, 74 to 76.

Research References

Encyclopedias

8 Am. Jur. Proof of Facts 2d 481, Undue Influence in Obtaining Parent's Consent to Adoption of Child.

OH Jur. 3d Family Law § 888, Withdrawal of Consent.

Forms

Ohio Forms Legal and Business § 28:25, Form Drafting Principles.

Ohio Jurisprudence Pleading and Practice Forms § 96:16, Withdrawal of Consent.

Ohio Jurisprudence Pleading and Practice Forms § 96:22, Home Study--Social and Medical History.

Ohio Jurisprudence Pleading and Practice Forms § 96:52, Application--Approval of Placement.

Treatises and Practice Aids

Carlin, Baldwin's Ohio Prac. Merrick-Rippner Probate Law § 99:31, Parties Giving Consent--Biological Parents.

Carlin, Baldwin's Ohio Prac. Merrick-Rippner Probate Law § 99:36, Method of Giving Consent.

Carlin, Baldwin's Ohio Prac. Merrick-Rippner Probate Law § 99:37, Withdrawal of Consent.

Notes of Decisions

Agency consent   1
Burden of proof   2
Denial of petition   5
Grounds for revocation   3
Minor parent   4
Timing of withdrawal   6

---

1. Agency consent

The refusal of consent to an adoption by a "certified organization," as defined in RC 3107.01(C), does not impair the jurisdiction of the probate court, but the recommendations and the reports, filed pursuant to RC 3107.05 and 3107.10, are to be considered, in conjunction with all other evidence adduced in the proceeding, by the court in deciding the issues presented by RC 3107.09. State ex rel. Portage County Welfare Dept. v. Summers (Ohio 1974) 38 Ohio St.2d 144, 311 N.E.2d 6, 67 O.O.2d 151.

2. Burden of proof

Biological mother failed to establish that her consent to stepmother's adoption of children was procured by fraud, which would have provided grounds for invalidating biological mother's consent to adoption; mother only alleged that her consent was not knowingly, intelligently, and voluntarily given since she did not understand the consequences of signing the consent forms. In re Adoption of Hockman (Ohio App. 11 Dist., Portage, 01-14-2005) No. 2004-P-0079, No. 2004-P-0080, 2005-Ohio-140, 2005 WL 89387, Unreported. Adoption ⊕ 7.5

Evidence supported finding that it was in child's best interest to remain with adoptive parents, in proceeding initiated by birth parents to withdraw consent to adoption; adoptive parents were married, had home, and adoptive mother stayed home with the children, birth parents were not married, birth father was on community control for a prior drug trafficking conviction, birth mother was recovering from filing bankruptcy due to a prior relationship, and child had resided with adoptive parents for six months and was bonded to them. In re Adoption of Baby Doe (Ohio App. 10 Dist., Franklin, 02-17-2004) No. 03AP-917, 2004-Ohio-689, 2004 WL 292066, Unreported, motion for delayed appeal denied 101 Ohio St.3d 1486, 805 N.E.2d 538, 2004-Ohio-1293, appeal not allowed 102 Ohio St.3d 1412, 806 N.E.2d 563, 2004-Ohio-1763. Adoption ⊕ 7.6(2)

Biological mother who signed adoption consent form had burden to establish duress or undue influence by clear and convincing evidence. In re Rabatin (Geauga 1992) 83 Ohio App.3d 836, 615 N.E.2d 1099. Adoption ⊕ 7.8(3.1)

Once a natural mother has entered her consent to an adoption in open court, any claim of duress or undue influence must be established by clear and convincing evidence. In re Adoption of Infant Boy (Allen 1989) 60 Ohio App.3d 80, 573 N.E.2d 753. Adoption ⊕ 7.8(3.1)

3. Grounds for revocation

Trial court abused its discretion in invalidating biological mother's written consent to stepmother's adoption of children, where biological mother failed to establish that her consent was procured by fraud, duress or undue influence. In re Adoption of Hockman (Ohio App. 11 Dist., Portage, 01-14-2005) No. 2004-P-0079, No. 2004-P-0080, 2005-Ohio-140, 2005 WL 89387, Unreported. Adoption ⊕ 7.5

Biological mother failed to establish that her consent to stepmother's adoption of children was procured by duress or undue influence, which would have provided grounds for invalidating biological mother's consent to adoption, even though mother was involved in a divorce from an abusive spouse and had a history of health problems; when the consent to adoption was executed, mother was an adult, she had a high school diploma, there was no evidence that the consents were rushed, there was no evidence that mother was not alert or was unaware of what she was signing, and there was no evidence that anyone acted in a way that compromised the exercise of mother's free will. In re Adoption of Hockman (Ohio App. 11 Dist., Portage, 01-14-2005) No. 2004-P-0079, No. 2004-P-0080, 2005-Ohio-140, 2005 WL 89387, Unreported. Adoption ⊕ 7.5

Fact that the natural mother has had a change of heart about the adoption is insufficient grounds for her to revoke her consent. In re Adoption of Jimenez (Ohio App. 2 Dist., 09-24-1999) 136 Ohio App.3d 223, 736 N.E.2d 477, appeal allowed 88 Ohio St.3d 1427, 723 N.E.2d 1114, appeal dismissed as improvidently allowed 90 Ohio St.3d 1214, 735 N.E.2d 898, 2000-Ohio-42. Adoption ⊕ 7.6(2)

Letter to psychologist who conducted court-ordered psychological evaluations in connection with mother's motion to withdraw consent to adoption, in which attorney for prospective adoptive parents stated that mother had been "vindictive, hateful, hostile, and spiteful" since filing her motion, was not prejudicial to mother; psychologist testified that he was not influenced by letter's tone and that he customarily received such letters when acting as an independent examiner. In re Adoption of Jimenez (Ohio App. 2 Dist., 09-24-1999) 136 Ohio App.3d 223, 736 N.E.2d 477, appeal allowed 88 Ohio St.3d 1427, 723 N.E.2d 1114, appeal dismissed as improvidently allowed 90 Ohio St.3d 1214, 735 N.E.2d 898, 2000-Ohio-42. Adoption ⊕ 7.8(2)

In ruling on mother's motion to withdraw consent to adoption, judge could not rely on out-of-court-room conversation in which an individual allegedly told judge that mother, after signing consent to adoption, had said that "I just signed my baby away." In re Adoption of Jimenez (Ohio App. 2 Dist., 09-24-1999) 136 Ohio App.3d 223, 736 N.E.2d 477, appeal allowed 88 Ohio St.3d 1427, 723 N.E.2d 1114, appeal dismissed as improvidently allowed 90 Ohio St.3d 1214, 735 N.E.2d 898, 2000-Ohio-42. Adoption ⊕ 13

A change of heart on the part of a natural mother who consented to an adoption is insufficient ground to revoke her consent. In re Adoption of Infant Boy (Allen 1989) 60 Ohio App.3d 80, 573 N.E.2d 753.

A court considering a motion to withdraw consent to an adoption cannot properly consider the best interests of the various family members. In re Adoption of Infant Boy (Allen 1989) 60 Ohio App.3d 80, 573 N.E.2d 753.

4. Minor parent

A minor parent may consent to the adoption of her child, and such consent may not be withdrawn after the entry of an interlocutory order, or after the final decree, of adoption. In re Burdette (Summit 1948) 83 Ohio App. 368, 83 N.E.2d 813, 38 O.O. 429. Adoption ⊕ 7.6(3)

5. Denial of petition

After conducting a hearing pursuant to RC 3107.09, the probate court improperly denies a petition for adoption of a four-year-old boy in the custody of the county welfare department, when the court finds that petitioners meet all the requirements of suitability as adoptive parents, but denies the petition for adoption on the grounds that the granting of the adoption would violate the integrity of a waiting list allegedly maintained by the welfare department, where at the adoption hearing there was no evidence adduced establishing the existence or administration of such a waiting list and no evidence that the waiting list contained suitable applicants ready, willing, and able to adopt the child in question. (See also In re Harshey, 40 App(2d) 157, 318 NE(2d) 544 (1974).) In re Harshey (Cuyahoga 1975) 45 Ohio App.2d 97, 341 N.E.2d 616, 74 O.O.2d 120.

6. Timing of withdrawal

One year limitations period for a biological parent to challenge the validity of written consent to adoption, rather than statute that provided that consent to adoption could be withdrawn prior to the entry of an interlocutory order or prior to the entry of a final decree if the court found that it was in the best interest of the person to be adopted, applied to proceeding challenging the validity of biological mother's consent to stepmother's adoption of children. In re Adoption of Hockman (Ohio App. 11 Dist., Portage, 01-14-2005) No. 2004-P-0079, No. 2004-P-0080, 2005-Ohio-140, 2005 WL 89387, Unreported. Adoption ☞ 9.1

Mother's consent to place son for adoption was invalid, where attorney for prospective adoptive parents had previously conveyed misimpression that mother would retain right to withdraw consent within next six months for any reason at all, magistrate judge inaccurately stated withdrawal of consent would depend on "good cause shown" rather than best interests of child, and magistrate did not question mother to determine her understanding of adoption process and of ramifications of consent. In re Adoption of Jimenez (Ohio App. 2 Dist., 09-24-1999) 136 Ohio App.3d 223, 736 N.E.2d 477, appeal allowed 88 Ohio St.3d 1427, 723 N.E.2d 1114, appeal dismissed as improvidently allowed 90 Ohio St.3d 1214, 735 N.E.2d 898, 2000-Ohio-42. Adoption ☞ 7.5

Mother was not entitled to continuance, in hearing on her motion to withdraw consent to adoption, in order to permit her counsel to participate in in camera inspection of medical records of prospective adoptive parents' biological child; hearing had already extended over an eight month period, and

trial court could have reasonably concluded that any interest counsel had in participating in inspection was outweighed by court's interest in prompt disposition of matter. In re Adoption of Jimenez (Ohio App. 2 Dist., 09-24-1999) 136 Ohio App.3d 223, 736 N.E.2d 477, appeal allowed 88 Ohio St.3d 1427, 723 N.E.2d 1114, appeal dismissed as improvidently allowed 90 Ohio St.3d 1214, 735 N.E.2d 898, 2000-Ohio-42. Adoption ☞ 13

Consent to adoption is viable until the court grants a motion to withdraw it, which must be filed before the entry of an interlocutory order or the entry of a final order of adoption. In re Adoption of Koszycki (Ohio App. 1 Dist., 05-14-1999) 133 Ohio App.3d 434, 728 N.E.2d 437. Adoption ☞ 7.5

Biological mother's consent to adoption was not product of fraud or undue influence; thus, she was not allowed to withdraw her consent after final order of adoption. In re Adoption of Zschach (Ohio, 06-06-1996) 75 Ohio St.3d 648, 665 N.E.2d 1070, reconsideration denied 76 Ohio St.3d 1410, 666 N.E.2d 569, certiorari denied 117 S.Ct. 582, 519 U.S. 1028, 136 L.Ed.2d 513. Adoption ☞ 7.5; Adoption ☞ 7.6(2)

An interlocutory order of adoption is erroneously entered after the putative father of the minor child who signed the birth certificate objects to the adoption, and consequently, a mother's motion to withdraw her consent to the adoption is not time barred pursuant to RC 3107.09. In re Adoption of Zschach, Nos. 1994CA-14+, 1994 WL 728626 (5th Dist Ct App, Fairfield, 12-19-94), reversed by 75 Ohio St.3d 648 (1996).

The condition of RC 3107.09(B) that consent to adoption may be withdrawn upon a finding that the withdrawal is in the best interests of the child applies after an application for placement has been filed pursuant to RC 5103.16 and the consent has been executed in compliance with RC 3107.08, even though no adoption petition has yet been filed. In re Adoption of Frank, No. 85CA54 (2d Dist Ct App, Greene, 3-11-86).

3107.085   Temporary custody—Repealed

(1996 H 274, eff. 8-8-96; 1996 H 419, eff. 9-18-96)

HISTORY OF BIOLOGICAL PARENTS

3107.09   Social and medical histories of biological parents

(A) The department of job and family services shall prescribe and supply forms for the taking of social and medical histories of the biological parents of a minor available for adoption.

(B) An assessor shall record the social and medical histories of the biological parents of a minor available for adoption, unless the minor is to be adopted by the minor's stepparent or grandparent. The assessor shall use the forms prescribed pursuant to division (A) of this section. The assessor shall not include on the forms identifying information about the biological parents or other ancestors of the minor.

(C) A social history shall describe and identify the age; ethnic, racial, religious, marital, and physical characteristics; and educational, cultural, talent and hobby, and work experience background of the biological parents of the minor. A medical history shall identify major diseases, malformations, allergies, ear or eye defects, major conditions, and major health problems of the biological parents that are or may be congenital or familial. These histories may include other social and medical information relative to the biological parents and shall include social and medical information relative to the minor's other ancestors.

The social and medical histories may be obtained through interviews with the biological parents or other persons and from any available records if a biological parent or any legal guardian of a biological parent consents to the release of information contained in a record. An assessor who considers it necessary may request that a biological parent undergo a medical examination. In obtaining social and medical histories of a biological parent, an assessor shall inform the biological parent, or a person other than a biological parent who provides information pursuant to this section, of the purpose and use of the histories and of the biological parent's or other person's right to correct or expand the histories at any time.

(D) A biological parent, or another person who provided information in the preparation of the social and medical histories of the biological parents of a minor, may cause the histories to be corrected or expanded to include different or additional types of information. The biological parent or other person may cause the histories to be corrected or expanded at any time prior or subsequent to the adoption of the minor, including any time after the minor becomes an adult. A biological parent may cause the histories to be corrected or expanded even if the biological parent did not provide any information to the assessor at the time the histories were prepared.

To cause the histories to be corrected or expanded, a biological parent or other person who provided information shall provide the information to be included or specify the information to be corrected to whichever of the following is appropriate under the circumstances:

(1) Subject to division (D)(2) of this section, if the biological parent or other person knows the assessor who prepared the histories, to the assessor;

(2) If the biological parent or person does not know the assessor or finds that the assessor has ceased to perform assessments, to the court involved in the adoption or, if that court is not known, to the department of health.

An assessor who receives information from a biological parent or other person pursuant to division (D)(1) of this section shall determine whether the information is of a type that divisions (B) and (C) of this section permit to be included in the histories. If the assessor determines the information is of a permissible type, the assessor shall cause the histories to be corrected or expanded to reflect the information. If, at the time the information is received, the histories have been filed with the court as required by division (E) of this section, the court shall cooperate with the assessor in correcting or expanding the histories.

If the department of health or a court receives information from a biological parent or other person pursuant to division (D)(2) of this section, it shall determine whether the information is of a type that divisions (B) and (C) of this section permit to be included in the histories. If a court determines the information is of a permissible type, the court shall cause the histories to be corrected or expanded to reflect the information. If the department of health so determines, the court involved shall cooperate with the department in the correcting or expanding of the histories.

An assessor or the department of health shall notify a biological parent or other person in writing if the assessor or department determines that information the biological parent or other person provided or specified for inclusion in a history is not of a type that may be included in a history. On receipt of the notice, the biological parent or other person may petition the court involved in the adoption to make a finding as to whether the information is of a type that may be included in a history. On receipt of the petition, the court shall issue its finding without holding a hearing. If the court finds that the information is of a type that may be included in a history, it shall cause the history to be corrected or expanded to reflect the information.

(E) An assessor shall file the social and medical histories of the biological parents prepared pursuant to divisions (B) and (C) of this section with the court with which a petition to adopt the biological parents' child is filed. The court promptly shall provide a copy of the social and medical histories filed with it to the petitioner. In a case involving the adoption of a minor by any person other than the minor's stepparent or grandparent, a court may refuse to issue an interlocutory order or final decree of adoption if the histories of the biological parents have not been so filed, unless the assessor certifies to the court that information needed to prepare the histories is unavailable for reasons beyond the assessor's control.

(1999 II 471, eff. 7–1–00; 1996 II 419, eff. 9–18–96)

Historical and Statutory Notes

Ed. Note: Former 3107.09 amended and recodi-fied as 3107.084 by 1996 H 419, eff. 9–18–96; 1976 H 156, eff. 1–1–77.

Ed. Note: Prior 3107.09 repealed by 1976 H 156, eff. 1–1–77; 1969 S 49; 1953 H 1; GC 8004–9;

Source—GC 10512–18; see now 3107.14 for provi-sions analogous to former 3107.09.

Pre–1953 H 1 Amendments: 124 v S 65

Amendment Note: 1999 H 471 substituted "job and family" for "human" in division (A).

Cross References

Adoption registration, contents of file, see 3705.12
Placement of child in institution, custody agree-ment, see 5103.15

Probate courts, appointment of assessors, see 2101.11

Ohio Administrative Code References

Requirement of "Social and Medical History", see OAC 5101:2–48–03

Library References

Adoption ☞13.
Health ☞396.
Westlaw Topic Nos. 17, 198H.

C.J.S. Adoption of Persons §§ 16 to 17, 93 to 102.
C.J.S. Health and Environment § 24.

Research References

Encyclopedias

OH Jur. 3d Family Law § 904, Investigation--Social and Medical Histories.
OH Jur. 3d Family Law § 909, Final Decree or Interlocutory Order.

Forms

Ohio Forms Legal and Business § 28:25, Form Drafting Principles.
Ohio Forms Legal and Business § 28:31, Withdraw-al of Consent to Adoption.
Ohio Jurisprudence Pleading and Practice Forms § 96:16, Withdrawal of Consent.
Ohio Jurisprudence Pleading and Practice Forms § 96:22, Home Study--Social and Medical Histo-ry.
Ohio Jurisprudence Pleading and Practice Forms § 96:25, Order to Redo or Supplement Report or History--Appointment of Different Assessor.
Ohio Jurisprudence Pleading and Practice Forms § 96:34, Birth Record.
Ohio Jurisprudence Pleading and Practice Forms § 96:43, Temporary and Permanent Custody.
Ohio Jurisprudence Pleading and Practice Forms § 96:52, Application--Approval of Placement.
Ohio Jurisprudence Pleading and Practice Forms § 96:75, Permanent Surrender of Child.

Treatises and Practice Aids

Carlin, Baldwin's Ohio Prac. Merrick-Rippner Pro-bate Law § 99:3, Jurisdiction.
Carlin, Baldwin's Ohio Prac. Merrick-Rippner Pro-bate Law § 99:8, Suitability of Adoptive Parents--Best Interests of Child.
Carlin, Baldwin's Ohio Prac. Merrick-Rippner Pro-bate Law § 99:21, Types of Placement--Steppar-ent, Guardian, and Grandparent Adoptions.
Carlin, Baldwin's Ohio Prac. Merrick-Rippner Pro-bate Law § 99:29, Papers and Records--Confi-dentiality
Carlin, Baldwin's Ohio Prac. Merrick-Rippner Pro-bate Law § 99:31, Parties Giving Consent Bio logical Parents.
Carlin, Baldwin's Ohio Prac. Merrick-Rippner Pro-bate Law § 99:33, Parties Giving Consent--Minor Parent.
Carlin, Baldwin's Ohio Prac. Merrick-Rippner Pro-bate Law § 99:34, Parties Giving Consent--Agen-cy.
Carlin, Baldwin's Ohio Prac. Merrick-Rippner Pro-bate Law § 99:36, Method of Giving Consent.
Carlin, Baldwin's Ohio Prac. Merrick-Rippner Pro-bate Law § 99:37, Withdrawal of Consent.
Carlin, Baldwin's Ohio Prac. Merrick-Rippner Pro-bate Law § 99:49, Interlocutory and Final Or-ders.

Carlin, Baldwin's Ohio Prac. Merrick-Rippner Probate Law § 108:24, Agreements for Temporary and Permanent Custody.

Carlin, Baldwin's Ohio Prac. Merrick-Rippner Probate Law § 110:15, Visitation Right of Noncustodial Parent and Others.

Notes of Decisions

Jurisdiction to determine paternity   1

----

1. Jurisdiction to determine paternity

A final decree of adoption does not patently and unambiguously divest a juvenile court of jurisdiction to determine paternity solely for the limited purpose of allowing the putative father to establish that he is the biological father so that he can exercise his statutory rights to provide information regarding his social and medical history for placement in the child's adoption records. State ex rel. Furnas v. Monnin (Ohio, 10-30-2008) 120 Ohio St.3d 279, 898 N.E.2d 573, 2008-Ohio-5569. Adoption ☞ 14

Adoptive parents who, after final decree of adoption was entered in probative court, sought writ of prohibition to prevent juvenile court judge from proceeding in parentage action and to order him to dismiss case and to vacate all orders entered in the case were required to establish that (1) judge was about to exercise judicial or quasi-judicial power, (2) the exercise of that power was unauthorized by law, and (3) denying the writ would result in injury for which no other adequate remedy existed in the ordinary course of law. State ex rel. Furnas v. Monnin (Ohio, 10-30-2008) 120 Ohio St.3d 279, 898 N.E.2d 573, 2008-Ohio-5569. Prohibition ☞ 3(1); Prohibition ☞ 10(2)

3107.091   Biological parent may add medical and social history to records concerning an adopted person

(A) As used in this section, "biological parent" means a biological parent whose offspring, as a minor, was adopted and with respect to whom a medical and social history was not prepared prior or subsequent to the adoption.

(B) A biological parent may request the department of job and family services to provide the biological parent with a copy of the social and medical history forms prescribed by the department pursuant to section 3107.09 of the Revised Code. The department, upon receipt of such a request, shall provide the forms to the biological parent, if the biological parent indicates that the forms are being requested so that the adoption records of the biological parent's offspring will include a social and medical history of the biological parent.

In completing the forms, the biological parent may include information described in division (C) of section 3107.09 of the Revised Code, but shall not include identifying information. When the biological parent has completed the forms to the extent the biological parent wishes to provide information, the biological parent shall return them to the department. The department shall review the completed forms, and shall determine whether the information included by the biological parent is of a type permissible under divisions (B) and (C) of section 3107.09 of the Revised Code and, to the best of its ability, whether the information is accurate. If it determines that the forms contain accurate, permissible information, the department, after excluding from the forms any information the department deems impermissible, shall file them with the court that entered the interlocutory order or final decree of adoption in the adoption case. If the department needs assistance in determining that court, the department of health, upon request, shall assist it.

The department of job and family services shall notify the biological parent in writing if it excludes from the biological parent's social and medical history forms information deemed impermissible. On receipt of the notice, the biological parent may petition the court with which the forms were filed to make a finding as to whether the information is permissible. On receipt of the petition, the court shall issue its finding without holding a hearing. If the court finds the information is permissible, it shall cause the information to be included on the forms.

Upon receiving social and medical history forms pursuant to this section, a court shall cause them to be filed in the records pertaining to the adoption case.

Social and medical history forms completed by a biological parent pursuant to this section may be corrected or expanded by the biological parent in accordance with division (D) of section 3107.09 of the Revised Code.

Access to the histories shall be granted in accordance with division (D) of section 3107.17 of the Revised Code.

(1999 H 471, eff. 7–1–00; 1996 H 419, eff. 9–18–96)

Historical and Statutory Notes

Ed. Note: 3107.091 is former 3107.121, amended and recodified by 1996 H 419, eff. 9–18–96; 1984 H 84, eff. 3–19–85.

Amendment Note: 1999 H 471 substituted "job and family" for "human" in the first and third paragraphs in division (B).

Amendment Note: 1996 H 419 amended this section (former 3107.121) by substituting "the biological parent" and "the biological parent's" for "he," "him," and "his" throughout the section; substituting "3107.09" for "3107.12" throughout the section; substituting "information" for "data as described in division (D)(2) of that section" in the first sentence of the second paragraph of division (B); substituting "information the department deems impermissible" for "impermissible information" and "divisions (B) and (C) of section 3107.09" for "divisions (D)(2) and (3) of section 3107.12" in the second paragraph of division (B); adding the third paragraph of division (B); deleting "the clerk of" preceding "a court shall cause them to be filed" in the fourth paragraph of division (B); and substituting "division (D) of section 3107.09" for "division (D)(4) of section 3107.12" in the fifth paragraph of division (B).

Cross References

Adoption registration, contents of file, see 3705.12
Availability of adoption records, see 149.43
Courts, confidentiality of adoption files, Sup R 55

Ohio Administrative Code References

Requirement of "Social and Medical History", see
  OAC 5101:2–48–03

Library References

Adoption ☞13.
Health ☞396.
Westlaw Topic Nos. 17, 198H.

C.J.S. Adoption of Persons §§ 46 to 47, 93 to 102.
C.J.S. Health and Environment § 24.

Research References

Encyclopedias

OH Jur. 3d Family Law § 904, Investigation--Social and Medical Histories.
OH Jur. 3d Family Law § 909, Final Decree or Interlocutory Order.

Forms

Ohio Jurisprudence Pleading and Practice Forms § 96:25, Order to Redo or Supplement Report or History--Appointment of Different Assessor.
Ohio Jurisprudence Pleading and Practice Forms § 96:32, Confidentiality.

Ohio Jurisprudence Pleading and Practice Forms § 96:34, Birth Record.
Ohio Jurisprudence Pleading and Practice Forms § 96:76, Request for Notification.

Treatises and Practice Aids

Carlin, Baldwin's Ohio Prac. Merrick-Rippner Probate Law § 99:34, Parties Giving Consent--Agency.
Carlin, Baldwin's Ohio Prac. Merrick-Rippner Probate Law § 110:20, Parentage Act--Jurisdiction and Venue.

Notes of Decisions

Jurisdiction to determine paternity   1

----

1. Jurisdiction to determine paternity

A final decree of adoption does not patently and unambiguously divest a juvenile court of jurisdiction to determine paternity solely for the limited purpose of allowing the putative father to establish that he is the biological father so that he can exercise his statutory rights to provide information regarding his social and medical history for placement in the child's adoption records.   State ex rel. Furnas v. Monnin (Ohio, 10-30-2008) 120 Ohio St.3d 279, 898 N.E.2d 573, 2008-Ohio-5569.   Adoption ☞ 14

ACCOUNTING TO COURT

3107.10 Out of county adoption; notice and information sharing

(A)(1) A public children services agency arranging an adoption in a county other than the county where that public children services agency is located, private child placing agency, or private noncustodial agency, or an attorney arranging an adoption, shall notify the public children services agency in the county in which the prospective adoptive parent resides within ten days after initiation of a home study required under section 3107.031 of the Revised Code.

(2) After a public children services agency has received notification pursuant to division (A)(1) of this section, both the public children services agency arranging an adoption in a county other than the county where that public children services agency is located, private child placing agency, private noncustodial agency, or attorney arranging an adoption, and the public children services agency shall share relevant information regarding the prospective adoptive parent as soon as possible after initiation of the home study.

(B) A public children services agency arranging an adoption in a county other than the county where that public children services agency is located, private child placing agency, or private noncustodial agency, or an attorney arranging an adoption, shall notify the public children services agency in the county in which the prospective adoptive parent resides of an impending adoptive placement not later than ten days prior to that placement. Notification shall include a description of the special needs and the age of the prospective adoptive child and the name of the prospective adoptive parent and number of children that will be residing in the prospective adoptive home when the prospective adoptive child is placed in the prospective adoptive home.

(C) An agency or attorney sharing relevant information pursuant to this section is immune from liability in a civil action to recover damages for injury, death, or loss to person or property allegedly caused by any act or omission in connection with sharing relevant information unless the acts or omissions are with malicious purpose, in bad faith, or in a wanton or reckless manner.

(D) The director of job and family services shall adopt rules in accordance with Chapter 119. of the Revised Code necessary for the implementation and execution of this section, including, but not limited to, a definition of "relevant information" for the purposes of division (A) of this section.

(E) This section does not apply to an adoption by a stepparent whose spouse is a biological or adoptive parent of the minor to be adopted.

(2006 S 238, eff. 9–21–06)

Historical and Statutory Notes

Ed. Note: Former RC 3107.10 amended and recodified as RC 3107.055 by 2006 S 238, eff. 9–21–06; 2005 H 66, eff. 6–30–05; 1999 H 471, eff. 7–1–00; 1996 H 274, eff. 9–18–96; 1996 H 419, eff. 9–18–96; 1986 H 428, eff. 12–23–86; 1978 H 832; 1976 H 156.

Ed. Note: Prior 3107.10 repealed by 1976 H 156, eff. 1–1–77; 1953 H 1; GC 8004–10; Source— GC 10512–19; see now 3107.14 for provisions analogous to former 3107.10.

Pre–1953 H 1 Amendments: 124 v S 65

Ohio Administrative Code References

Approval of a foster home for adoptive placement, see OAC 5101:2–48–11

Completion of the homestudy report, see OAC 5101:2–48–12

Foster caregiver adoption process of a foster child who has resided with the caregiver for at least twelve consecutive months, see OAC 5101:2–48–11.1

Pre-adoptive staffing, matching and placement procedures, see OAC 5101:2–48–16

Soliciting and releasing adoptive homestudies and related material for consideration of placement, see OAC 5101:2–48–19

Research References

Encyclopedias

14 Am. Jur. Proof of Facts 2d 727, Legitimation of Child by Father Seeking Custody of Child.

22 Am. Jur. Trials 347, Child Custody Litigation.

OH Jur. 3d Family Law § 899, Accounting by Petitioner.

OH Jur. 3d Family Law § 902, Investigation.

OH Jur. 3d Family Law § 903, Investigation--Written Report.

Forms

Ohio Forms Legal and Business § 28:32, Introduction.

Ohio Forms Legal and Business § 28:36, Promise to Adopt.

Ohio Jurisprudence Pleading and Practice Forms § 96:17, Accounting to Court.

Ohio Jurisprudence Pleading and Practice Forms § 96:44, Independent Placement of Children.

Ohio Jurisprudence Pleading and Practice Forms § 96:78, Petitioner's Account.

Treatises and Practice Aids

Carlin, Baldwin's Ohio Prac. Merrick-Rippner Probate Law § 3:2, Statutory.

Carlin, Baldwin's Ohio Prac. Merrick-Rippner Probate Law § 99:3, Jurisdiction.

Carlin, Baldwin's Ohio Prac. Merrick-Rippner Probate Law § 19:14, Uniform Parentage Act-Surrogacy Agreement.

Carlin, Baldwin's Ohio Prac. Merrick-Rippner Probate Law § 99:22, Types of Placement--Independent Adoptions.

Carlin, Baldwin's Ohio Prac. Merrick-Rippner Probate Law § 99:28, Papers and Records--Accounting.

Carlin, Baldwin's Ohio Prac. Merrick-Rippner Probate Law § 99:31, Parties Giving Consent--Biological Parents.

Carlin, Baldwin's Ohio Prac. Merrick-Rippner Probate Law App B SPF 18.9, Petitioner's Account.

3107.101 Prospective home visits

(A) Not later than seven days after a minor to be adopted is placed in a prospective adoptive home pursuant to section 5103.16 of the Revised Code, the assessor providing placement or post placement services in the prospective adoptive home shall begin monthly prospective adoptive home visits in that home, until the court issues a final decree of adoption. During the prospective adoptive home visits, the assessor shall evaluate the progression of the placement in the prospective adoptive home. The assessor shall include the evaluation in the prefinalization assessment required under section 3107.12 of the Revised Code.

(B) During the prospective home visit required under division (A) of this section, the assessor shall make face-to-face contact with the prospective adoptive parent and the minor to be adopted. The assessor shall make contact, as prescribed by rule under division (C) of this section, with all other children or adults residing in the prospective adoptive home.

(C) The director of job and family services shall adopt rules in accordance with Chapter 119. of the Revised Code necessary for the implementation and execution of this section.

(D) This section does not apply to an adoption by a stepparent whose spouse is a biological or adoptive parent of the minor to be adopted.

(2008 H 7, eff. 4-7-09; 2006 S 238, eff. 9-21-06)

Historical and Statutory Notes

Amendment Note: 2008 H 7 substituted "begin monthly" for "conduct a" after "home shall", substituted "visits" for "visit", and deleted "every thirty days," after "that home," in the first sentence of division (A).

Cross References

Custody of files, investigators, clerks and appointees, appropriation, action in court of appeals, limitation of contempt power, see 2101.11

Ohio Administrative Code References

Prefinalization services, see OAC 5101:2–48–17

Research References

Encyclopedias

OH Jur. 3d Family Law § 903, Investigation--Written Report.

Treatises and Practice Aids

Carlin, Baldwin's Ohio Prac. Merrick-Rippner Probate Law § 99:27, Papers and Records--Assessor.

COURT PROCEEDINGS

3107.11 Hearing and notice

(A) After the filing of a petition to adopt an adult or a minor, the court shall fix a time and place for hearing the petition. The hearing may take place at any time more than thirty days after the date on which the minor is placed in the home of the petitioner. At least twenty days before the date of hearing, notice of the filing of the petition and of the time and place of hearing shall be given by the court to all of the following:

(1) Any juvenile court, agency, or person whose consent to the adoption is required by this chapter but who has not consented;

(2) A person whose consent is not required as provided by division (A), (G), (H), or (I) of section 3107.07 of the Revised Code and has not consented;

(3) Any guardian, custodian, or other party who has temporary custody or permanent custody of the child.

Notice shall not be given to a person whose consent is not required as provided by division (B), (C), (D), (E), (F), or (J) of section 3107.07, or section 3107.071, of the Revised Code. Second notice shall not be given to a juvenile court, agency, or person whose consent is not required as provided by division (K) of section 3107.07 of the Revised Code because the court, agency, or person failed to file an objection to the petition within fourteen days after proof was filed pursuant to division (B) of this section that a first notice was given to the court, agency, or person pursuant to division (A)(1) of this section.

(B) Upon the filing of a petition for adoption that alleges that a parent has failed without justifiable cause to provide more than de minimis contact with the minor or to provide for the maintenance and support of the minor, the clerk of courts shall send a notice to that parent with the following language in boldface type and in all capital letters:

"A FINAL DECREE OF ADOPTION, IF GRANTED, WILL RELIEVE YOU OF ALL PARENTAL RIGHTS AND RESPONSIBILITIES, INCLUDING THE RIGHT TO CONTACT THE MINOR, AND, EXCEPT WITH RESPECT TO A SPOUSE OF THE ADOPTION PETITIONER AND RELATIVES OF THAT SPOUSE, TERMINATE ALL LEGAL RELATIONSHIPS BETWEEN THE MINOR AND YOU AND THE MINOR'S OTHER RELATIVES, SO THAT THE MINOR THEREAFTER IS A STRANGER TO YOU AND THE MINOR'S FORMER RELATIVES FOR ALL PURPOSES. IF YOU WISH TO CONTEST THE ADOPTION, YOU MUST FILE AN OBJECTION TO THE PETITION WITHIN FOURTEEN DAYS AFTER PROOF OF SERVICE OF NOTICE OF THE FILING OF THE PETITION AND OF THE TIME AND PLACE OF HEARING IS GIVEN TO YOU. IF YOU WISH TO CONTEST THE ADOPTION, YOU MUST ALSO APPEAR AT THE HEARING. A FINAL DECREE OF ADOPTION MAY BE ENTERED IF YOU FAIL TO FILE AN OBJECTION TO THE ADOPTION PETITION OR APPEAR AT THE HEARING."

(C) All notices required under this section shall be given as specified in the Rules of Civil Procedure. Proof of the giving of notice shall be filed with the court before the petition is heard.

(2008 H 7, eff. 4-7-09; 1999 H 176, eff. 10–29–99; 1998 H 484, eff. 3–18–99; 1996 H 419, eff. 9–18–96; 1986 H 428, eff. 12–23–86; 1978 H 832; 1976 H 156)

Historical and Statutory Notes

Ed. Note: 3107.11 is analogous to former 3107.04, repealed by 1976 H 156, eff. 1–1–77.

Ed. Note: Former 3107.11 repealed by 1976 H 156, eff. 1–1–77; 130 v H 202; 1953 H 1; GC

8004–11; Source—GC 10512–20; see now 3107.14 and 3107.19 for provisions analogous to former 3107.11.

Pre–1953 H 1 Amendments: 124 v S 65

Amendment Note: 2008 H 7 added new division (B); and redesignated former division (B) as division (C).

Amendment Note: 1999 H 176 deleted former division (A)(1); redesignated former divisions (A)(2) through (A)(4) as new divisions (A)(1) through (A)(3); deleted "The notice to the department of human services shall be accompanied by a copy of the petition." from the beginning of the final paragraph in division (A); and substituted "(A)(1)" for "(A)(2)" in the final paragraph in

division (A). Prior to deletion, former division (A)(1) read:

"(1) The department of human services."

Amendment Note: 1998 H 484 added division (A)(4).

Amendment Note: 1996 H 419 added "juvenile" to division (A)(2); substituted "consent is not required as provided by division (A), (G), (H), or (I) of section 3107.07 of the Revised Code and has not consented." for "consent is dispensed with upon any ground mentioned in divisions (A), (E), (F), and (G) of section 3107.07 of the Revised Code, but who has not consented." in division (A)(3); and added the second and third sentences of the second paragraph of division (A)(3).

Cross References

Department of job and family services, division of social administration; care and placement of children; interstate compact on placement of children, see 5103.12 to 5103.17, 5103.20 to 5103.27

Service and filing of pleadings and other papers subsequent to original complaint, Civ R 5

Library References

Adoption ⟊12, 13.
Westlaw Topic No. 17.
C.J.S. Adoption of Persons §§ 46 to 47, 84 to 102.

Research References

ALR Library

28 ALR 6th 349, Requirements and Effects of Putative Father Registries.

Encyclopedias

OH Jur. 3d Family Law § 882, Putative Father Registry.
OH Jur. 3d Family Law § 890, Who Need Not Consent--Construction of Statute.
OH Jur. 3d Family Law § 901, Time, Place, and Notice of Hearing.
OH Jur. 3d Process § 50, Proceedings in Which Service of Process by Publication Authorized.

Forms

Ohio Jurisprudence Pleading and Practice Forms § 96:12, Consent Not Required.
Ohio Jurisprudence Pleading and Practice Forms § 96:18, Notice and Hearing.

Treatises and Practice Aids

Klein, Darling, & Terez, Baldwin's Ohio Practice Civil Practice § 4:4, Form of Summons.
Carlin, Baldwin's Ohio Prac. Merrick-Rippner Probate Law § 99:3, Jurisdiction.
Carlin, Baldwin's Ohio Prac. Merrick-Rippner Probate Law § 99:8, Suitability of Adoptive Parents--Best Interests of Child.
Carlin, Baldwin's Ohio Prac. Merrick-Rippner Probate Law § 99:31, Parties Giving Consent--Biological Parents.
Carlin, Baldwin's Ohio Prac. Merrick-Rippner Probate Law § 99:38, Consent Not Required--Statutory Scheme.
Carlin, Baldwin's Ohio Prac. Merrick-Rippner Probate Law § 99:43, Hearing of Petition--Date.
Carlin, Baldwin's Ohio Prac. Merrick Rippner Pro bate Law § 99:44, Hearing of Petition--Notice.
Carlin, Baldwin's Ohio Prac. Merrick-Rippner Probate Law App B SPF 18.1, Judgment Entry Setting Hearing and Ordering Notice.

Notes of Decisions

"Best–interest" test 2
Hearing 4
Notice 1
Temporary custody 3

---

1. Notice

Biological father received proper notice of step-father's petition for adoption of child, where biolog-

ical father was served by certified mail with notice of filing of petition and hearing on petition. Askew v. Taylor (Ohio App. 5 Dist., Stark, 10-12-2004) No. 2004CA00184, 2004-Ohio-5504, 2004 WL 2315190, Unreported. Adoption ⟊ 12

Trial court lacked jurisdiction over biological father, in proceeding initiated by step-father to adopt step-son, where step-father provided notice of the hearing by publication, and there was less than 20 days between the date of the last publication of notice and the date of the hearing. In re Adoption of Chapman (Ohio App. 4 Dist., Ross, 01-22-2004) No. 03CA2722, 2004-Ohio-254, 2004 WL 102796, Unreported. Adoption ☞ 12

Publication notice identifying date and time of joint hearing on petitions for adoption of children by mother's husband, alleging that biological father's consent to adoptions was unnecessary because he had failed to communicate with or support children for one year, complied with statute requiring notice of filing of adoption petition and of time and place of hearing, though notice did not specifically declare that a best interests hearing would be held, as statute did not require that specific reference be made in notice to both the consent and best interests portions of the hearing; overruling, In re C.M.W., 2004 WL 2937632. In re Adoption of Walters (Ohio, 01-17-2007) 112 Ohio St.3d 315, 859 N.E.2d 545, 2007-Ohio-7. Adoption ☞ 12

Publication notice identifying date and time of joint hearing on petitions for adoption of children by mother's husband, alleging that biological father's consent to adoptions was unnecessary because he had failed to communicate with or support children for one year, did not violate father's right to due process, though notice referenced only consent portion of adoption hearing and not best interests of children portion, given that, because father had received notice that court would be taking evidence as to whether his parental rights should be terminated, there was no need for any additional requirement that father be given notice that it would consider both consent and best interests of children at hearing. In re Adoption of Walters (Ohio, 01-17-2007) 112 Ohio St.3d 315, 859 N.E.2d 545, 2007-Ohio-7. Adoption ☞ 12; Constitutional Law ☞ 4395

Among protections accorded natural parent where adoption of child is proposed are right to adequate notice and opportunity to be heard before any parental rights which may exist are terminated. State ex rel. Smith v. Smith (Ohio, 04-10-1996) 75 Ohio St.3d 418, 662 N.E.2d 366, 1996-Ohio-215. Adoption ☞ 12; Adoption ☞ 13

Even if probate court makes determination that parent's consent to adoption is not required, court must still go on to make determination that adoption is in best interest of child, and parent whose consent to adoption has been found unnecessary still must be given notice of the best-interest hearing. In re Adoption of Kuhlmann (Ohio App. 1 Dist., 12-07-1994) 99 Ohio App.3d 44, 649 N.E.2d 1279. Adoption ☞ 12; Adoption ☞ 13

Biological mother was presumed to have actual notice of adoption and to have effectively waived notice requirement where mother signed adoption consent form which contained waiver of notice of hearing on petition for adoption and mother presented no evidence showing that she was unable to read or otherwise could not understand consent

form. In re Rabatin (Geauga 1992) 83 Ohio App.3d 836, 615 N.E.2d 1099. Adoption ☞ 7.8(1)

Trial court's failure to notify Department of Human Services prior to hearing on petition filed by grandparents seeking to adopt grandchild was not prejudicial error where natural mother placed child with grandparents, and Department of Human Services was not involved in adoption. In re Adoption of Howell (Lawrence 1991) 77 Ohio App.3d 80, 601 N.E.2d 92, motion overruled 62 Ohio St.3d 1508, 583 N.E.2d 1320. Adoption ☞ 15

Section which provides for notice of the adoption hearing to be given to the parent of the child does not require the issuance of a summons to such parent; GC 10501–21 (RC 2101.26, 2101.27, 2101.28), as amended, eff. 9–29–45, provides for the manner in which notice is to be given. In re Burdette (Summit 1948) 83 Ohio App. 368, 83 N.E.2d 813, 38 O.O. 429.

2. "Best–interest" test

An adoption proceeding is a two-step process involving a "consent" phase and a "best-interest" phase; thus, a trial court errs when it fails to hold a best-interest hearing even though parental consent was not required for the adoption since the natural parents have an overriding interest in being heard on the issue of whether the proposed adoption would be in the child's best interest. In re Adoption of Jordan (Preble 1991) 72 Ohio App.3d 638, 595 N.E.2d 963.

A finding that the consent of a natural parent is not required for an adoption under RC 3107.07(A) does not constitute consent to the adoption but merely "provides for cutting off the statutory right of a parent to withhold his consent to the adoption of the child," leaving all other parental rights and obligations intact. Therefore, the exclusion of a natural parent from the final hearing on whether or not adoption is in the best interest of the child renders meaningless the requirement of RC 3107.11 that a natural parent who has lost the right to withhold consent to the adoption be given notice of the time and place of the best interest hearing, and an adoption under such circumstances must be reversed. In re Adoption of Jorgensen (Hancock 1986) 33 Ohio App.3d 207, 515 N.E.2d 622.

3. Temporary custody

There was no competent, credible evidence showing that due process rights of foster parents were violated by county department of human services' decision to place foster child with different couple for purposes of permanent adoption; there was testimony that adoptive parents had taken child with understanding that custody was temporary, until child was returned to birth mother or placed with another couple, and county had policies prohibiting adoption by couple that was fertile or had more than one adopted or natural child. Tingley v. Williams Cty. Dept. of Human Serv. (Ohio App. 6 Dist., 01-20-1995) 100 Ohio App.3d 385, 654 N.E.2d 148, dismissed, appeal not allowed 72 Ohio St.3d 1528, 649 N.E.2d 838, certiorari denied 116

S.Ct. 773, 516 U.S. 1071, 133 L.Ed.2d 725. Constitutional Law ⟳ 4404; Infants ⟳ 226

Where a final decree of adoption is vacated due to a defect in service, a prior order granting temporary custody to the adoptive parents remains in full force and effect precluding the need for a new temporary custody order; thus, a trial court errs in failing to dismiss a subsequent duplicative temporary custody petition. In re Knipper (Hamilton 1987) 39 Ohio App.3d 35, 528 N.E.2d 1319. Adoption ⟳ 16

4. Hearing

The trial court's failure to provide father with notice and the opportunity to be heard on the issue of whether stepfather's adoption of child was in child's best interest violated due process, even though the court had previously determined that father's consent to adoption was not required; trial court was required to conduct a best interest hearing, and father was one of several classes of persons that were entitled to 20 days notice of a hearing to determine the merits of the adoption petition and contest the best interest finding. In re Adoption of S.L.C. (Ohio App. 2 Dist., Miami, 12-29-2005) No. 05-CA-32, 2005-Ohio-7067, 2005 WL 3610305, Unreported. Adoption ⟳ 12; Adoption ⟳ 13; Constitutional Law ⟳ 4395

Putative father, who failed to properly register with state's putative father registry, did not have right to participate in hearing to determine if adoption was in best interest of child. In re Adoption of A.N.L. (Ohio App. 12 Dist., Warren, 08-16-2005) No. CA2004-11-131, No. CA2005-04-046, 2005-Ohio-4239, 2005 WL 1949678, Unreported. Adoption ⟳ 13

Evidence regarding biological father's attempts to contact child prior to hearing to determine suitability of mother's husband as adoptive parent was irrelevant and, thus, inadmissible at the suitability hearing. Kasunic v. Koenig (Ohio App. 8 Dist., Cuyahoga, 08-22-2002) No. 80762, 2002-Ohio-4281, 2002 WL 1933248, Unreported. Adoption ⟳ 9.1

Trial court did not consider suitability hearing to be a mere formality, in proceedings commenced by mother's husband to adopt child, where child's biological father was served with notice of the hearing and was provided with opportunity to participate, trial court heard and considered evidence presented by husband regarding his suitability to parent child, and court affirmatively indicated to father that it would receive any relevant evidence he had. Kasunic v. Koenig (Ohio App. 8 Dist., Cuyahoga, 08-22-2002) No. 80762, 2002-Ohio-4281, 2002 WL 1933248, Unreported. Adoption ⟳ 9.1; Adoption ⟳ 12

For purposes of adoption statute requiring notice of filing of adoption petition and of time and place of hearing, although a court may choose to hold separate hearings on consent and the best interests

of the child, there is no requirement to do so; one hearing to address both requirements is sufficient, provided notice of the adoption hearing pursuant to the statute is afforded the biological parent. In re Adoption of Walters (Ohio, 01-17-2007) 112 Ohio St.3d 315, 859 N.E.2d 545, 2007-Ohio-7. Adoption ⟳ 12; Adoption ⟳ 13

If the court opts to hold more than one hearing on an adoption petition, i.e., one hearing on issue of consent and a second hearing on the best interests of the child, statute requiring notice of filing of adoption petition and of time and place of hearing requires service of notification of the date and time of all hearings on a biological parent whose consent is statutorily unnecessary. In re Adoption of Walters (Ohio, 01-17-2007) 112 Ohio St.3d 315, 859 N.E.2d 545, 2007-Ohio-7. Adoption ⟳ 12

Former foster parents' dilatory filing of complaint which sought writ of prohibition preventing probate court from holding finalization hearing in adoption of former foster child by third parties warranted dismissal of prohibition; juvenile court order endeavoring to stop adoption proceedings was filed approximately one month before adoption proceedings but complaint in prohibition was not filed until two and a half hours before adoption hearing was to commence. State ex rel. Hitchcock v. Cuyahoga Cty. Court of Common Pleas, Probate Div. (Ohio App. 8 Dist., 10-07-1994) 97 Ohio App.3d 600, 647 N.E.2d 208. Prohibition ⟳ 24

It is not abuse of discretion for a trial court in an adoption proceeding to grant a motion to reopen such case, after the hearing but before judgment, for the submission of a so-called "stipulation of facts," the contents of which are admitted to be substantially true and which evidence goes to the heart of the only issue before the court. In re Adoption of Earhart (Miami 1961) 117 Ohio App. 73, 190 N.E.2d 468, 23 O.O.2d 156.

Appointment of a next friend under statute throws out a protecting arm of the court in the best interests of the minor and does not deny to one contesting an adoption the right of cross-examination. In re Todhunter's Adoption (Franklin 1941) 35 N.E.2d 992, 33 Ohio Law Abs. 567.

Trial court did not consider suitability hearing to be a mere formality, in proceedings commenced by mother's husband to adopt child, where child's biological father was served with notice of the hearing and was provided with opportunity to participate, trial court heard and considered evidence presented by husband regarding his suitability to parent child, and court affirmatively indicated to father that it would receive any relevant evidence he had. Kasunic v. Koenig (Ohio App. 8 Dist., Cuyahoga, 08-22-2002) No. 80762, 2002-Ohio-4281, 2002 WL 1933248, Unreported. Adoption ⟳ 9.1; Adoption ⟳ 12

3107.12   Prefinalization assessment and report

(A) Except as provided in division (B) of this section, an assessor shall conduct a prefinalization assessment of a minor and petitioner before a court issues a final decree of adoption or finalizes an interlocutory order of adoption for the minor. On completion of the assessment, the assessor shall prepare a written report of the assessment and provide a copy of the report to the court before which the adoption petition is pending.

The report of a prefinalization assessment shall include all of the following:

(1) The adjustment of the minor and the petitioner to the adoptive placement;

(2) The present and anticipated needs of the minor and the petitioner, as determined by a review of the minor's medical and social history, for adoption-related services, including assistance under Title IV–E of the "Social Security Act," 94 Stat. 501 (1980), 42 U.S.C.A. 670, as amended, or section 5153.163 of the Revised Code and counseling, case management services, crisis services, diagnostic services, and therapeutic counseling.

(3) The physical, mental, and developmental condition of the minor;

(4) If known, the minor's biological family background, including identifying information about the biological or other legal parents;

(5) The reasons for the minor's placement with the petitioner, the petitioner's attitude toward the proposed adoption, and the circumstances under which the minor was placed in the home of the petitioner;

(6) The attitude of the minor toward the proposed adoption, if the minor's age makes this feasible;

(7) If the minor is an Indian child, as defined in 25 U.S.C.A. 1903(4), how the placement complies with the "Indian Child Welfare Act of 1978," 92 Stat. 3069, 25 U.S.C.A. 1901, as amended;

(8) If known, the minor's psychological background, including prior abuse of the child and behavioral problems of the child;

(9) If applicable, the documents or forms required under sections 3107.032, 3107.10, and 3107.101 of the Revised Code.

The assessor shall file the prefinalization report with the court not later than twenty days prior to the date scheduled for the final hearing on the adoption unless the court determines there is good cause for filing the report at a later date.

The assessor shall provide a copy of the written report of the assessment to the petitioner with the identifying information about the biological or other legal parents redacted.

(B) This section does not apply if the petitioner is the minor's stepparent, unless a court, after determining a prefinalization assessment is in the best interest of the minor, orders that an assessor conduct a prefinalization assessment.

(C) The director of job and family services shall adopt rules in accordance with Chapter 119. of the Revised Code defining "counseling," "case management services," "crisis services," "diagnostic services," and "therapeutic counseling" for the purpose of this section.

(2006 S 238, eff. 9–21–06; 2001 S 27, eff. 3–15–02; 2000 H 448, eff. 10–5–00; 1999 H 471, eff. 7–1–00; 1998 H 446, eff. 8–5–98; 1996 H 274, eff. 9–18–96; 1996 H 419, eff. 9–18–96)

Historical and Statutory Notes

Ed. Note: Former 3107.12 amended and recodified as 3107.031 by 1996 H 419, eff. 9–18–96; 1984 H 84, eff. 3–19–85; 1978 S 340; 1976 H 156.

Ed. Note: Prior 3107.12 repealed by 1976 H 156, eff. 1–1–77; 1953 H 1; GC 8004–12; Source— GC 10512–21; see now 3107.14 for provisions analogous to former 3107.12.

Pre–1953 H 1 Amendments: 124 v S 65

Amendment Note: 2006 S 238 added division (A)(9) and made other nonsubstantive changes.

Amendment Note: 2001 S 27 added new division (A)(8); added the last sentence of division (A); and rewrote division (B) which prior thereto read:

"(B) This section does not apply if the petitioner is the minor's stepparent, unless a court, after determining a prefinalization assessment is in the best interest of the minor, orders that an assessor conduct a prefinalization assessment. This section also does not apply if the petitioner is the minor's foster caregiver and the minor has resided in the petitioner's home as the foster caregiver's foster child for at least twelve months prior to the date the petitioner submits an application prescribed under division (B) of section 3107.012 of the Revised Code to the agency arranging the adoption."

Amendment Note: 2000 H 448 added the last sentence in division (B)

Amendment Note: 1999 H 471 substituted "director of job and family services" for "department of human services" in division (C).

Amendment Note: 1998 H 446 designated new division (A) and inserted "Except as provided in division (B) of this section," in the first paragraph therein; redesignated former divisions (A) through (G) as new divisions (A)(1) through (A)(7); added new division (B); designated new division (C); and made other nonsubstantive changes.

Amendment Note: 1996 H 274 deleted "Except in the case of a stepparent adopting a stepchild," from the beginning of the first paragraph.

Cross References

Probate courts, appointment of assessors, see 2101.11

Ohio Administrative Code References

Prefinalization services, see OAC 5101:2–48–17

Library References

Adoption ⟐13.
Westlaw Topic No. 17.
C.J.S. Adoption of Persons §§ 46 to 47, 93 to 102.

Research References

Encyclopedias

OH Jur. 3d Family Law § 902, Investigation.
OH Jur. 3d Family Law § 903, Investigation--Written Report.

Forms

Ohio Jurisprudence Pleading and Practice Forms § 96:24, Prefinalization Assessment.
Ohio Jurisprudence Pleading and Practice Forms § 96:25, Order to Redo or Supplement Report or History--Appointment of Different Assessor.
Ohio Jurisprudence Pleading and Practice Forms § 96:32, Confidentiality.
Ohio Jurisprudence Pleading and Practice Forms § 96:43, Temporary and Permanent Custody.
Ohio Jurisprudence Pleading and Practice Forms § 96:51, Application--Investigation.
Ohio Jurisprudence Pleading and Practice Forms § 96:60, Entry--Ordering Investigation.
Ohio Jurisprudence Pleading and Practice Forms § 96:73, Social and Medical History.
Ohio Jurisprudence Pleading and Practice Forms § 96:75, Permanent Surrender of Child.
Ohio Jurisprudence Pleading and Practice Forms § 96:76, Request for Notification.

Treatises and Practice Aids

Carlin, Baldwin's Ohio Prac. Merrick-Rippner Probate Law § 99:4, Parties--Who May Petition to Adopt.

Carlin, Baldwin's Ohio Prac. Merrick-Rippner Probate Law § 99:8, Suitability of Adoptive Parents--Best Interests of Child.
Carlin, Baldwin's Ohio Prac. Merrick-Rippner Probate Law § 99:22, Types of Placement--Independent Adoptions.
Carlin, Baldwin's Ohio Prac. Merrick-Rippner Probate Law § 99:27, Papers and Records--Assessor.
Carlin, Baldwin's Ohio Prac. Merrick-Rippner Probate Law § 99:28, Papers and Records--Accounting.
Carlin, Baldwin's Ohio Prac. Merrick-Rippner Probate Law § 99:29, Papers and Records--Confidentiality.
Carlin, Baldwin's Ohio Prac. Merrick-Rippner Probate Law § 99:31, Parties Giving Consent--Biological Parents.
Carlin, Baldwin's Ohio Prac. Merrick-Rippner Probate Law § 99:44, Hearing of Petition--Notice.
Carlin, Baldwin's Ohio Prac. Merrick-Rippner Probate Law § 99:47, Hearing of Petition--Determination by Court.
Carlin, Baldwin's Ohio Prac. Merrick-Rippner Probate Law § 99:49, Interlocutory and Final Orders.
Carlin, Baldwin's Ohio Prac. Merrick-Rippner Probate Law App B SPF 18.1, Judgment Entry Setting Hearing and Ordering Notice.

Notes of Decisions

Stepparent assessment   1

___

1. Stepparent assessment
Trial court did not abuse its discretion in refusing to appoint guardian ad litem for subject child, in proceedings to dispense with biological mother's consent to step-parent adoption, where trial court was statutorily required to assess child and stepparent to determine whether adoption was in child's best interests, and appointment of guardian ad litem was not statutorily mandated. In re Adoption

of Haylett (Ohio App. 11 Dist., Portage, 02-18-2005) No. 2004-P-0063, 2005-Ohio-696, 2005 WL 407526, Unreported. Infants ☞ 78(1)

3107.121 Biological parent may add medical and social history to records concerning adopted person—Repealed

(1996 H 419, eff. 9–18–96; 1984 H 84, eff. 3–19–85)

Historical and Statutory Notes

Ed. Note: Former 3107.121 amended and recodified as 3107.091 by 1996 H 419, eff. 9–18–96.

3107.13 Residence in adoptive home

(A) A final decree of adoption shall not be issued and an interlocutory order of adoption does not become final, until the person to be adopted has lived in the adoptive home for at least six months after placement by an agency, or for at least six months after the department of job and family services or the court has been informed of the placement of the person with the petitioner, and the department or court has had an opportunity to observe or investigate the adoptive home, or in the case of adoption by a stepparent, until at least six months after the filing of the petition, or until the child has lived in the home for at least six months.

(B) In the case of a foster caregiver adopting a foster child or person adopting a child to whom the person is related, the court shall apply the amount of time the child lived in the foster caregiver's or relative's home prior to the date the foster caregiver or relative files the petition to adopt the child toward the six-month waiting period established by division (A) of this section.

(2000 H 448, eff. 10–5–00; 1999 H 471, eff. 7–1–00; 1996 H 419, eff. 9–18–96; 1986 H 428, eff. 12–23–86; 1980 S 205; 1976 H 156)

Historical and Statutory Notes

Ed. Note: Former 3107.13 repealed by 1976 H 156, eff. 1–1–77; 1971 S 267; 132 v S 326; 129 v 1566; 1953 H 1; GC 8004–13; Source—GC 10512–23; see now 3107.15 for provisions analogous to former 3107.13.

Pre–1953 H 1 Amendments: 124 v S 65

Amendment Note: 2000 H 448 substituted "caregiver" for "parent" throughout the section.

Amendment Note: 1999 H 471 substituted "job and family" for "human" in division (A).

Amendment Note: 1996 H 419 designated division (A) and added division (B).

Cross References

Residency requirements for public school attendance, see 3313.64

Library References

Adoption ☞14.
Westlaw Topic No. 17.

C.J.S. Adoption of Persons §§ 103 to 108, 130 to 135, 140.

Research References

ALR Library

69 ALR 5th 1, Grandparents' Visitation Rights Where Child's Parents Are Deceased, or Where Status of Parents is Unspecified.
36 ALR 5th 395, Adopted Child as Within Class Named in Testamentary Gift.
37 ALR 5th 237, Adopted Child as Within Class Named Deed or Inter Vivos Trust Instrument.

Encyclopedias

OH Jur. 3d Decedents' Estates § 548, Illegitimate Children.
OH Jur. 3d Family Law § 908, Probationary Period.

Forms

Ohio Jurisprudence Pleading and Practice Forms § 96:29, Adoption Period.

Ohio Jurisprudence Pleading and Practice Forms § 96:30, Effect of Adoption.

Treatises and Practice Aids

Carlin, Baldwin's Ohio Prac. Merrick-Rippner Probate Law § 44:16, Liberal Construction--Gifts to a Class: Construction Problems.

Carlin, Baldwin's Ohio Prac. Merrick-Rippner Probate Law § 44:23, Words and Phrases--Grandchildren.

Carlin, Baldwin's Ohio Prac. Merrick-Rippner Probate Law § 99:49, Interlocutory and Final Orders.

Carlin, Baldwin's Ohio Prac. Merrick-Rippner Probate Law § 99:53, Inheritance Rights of Adoptees.

Carlin, Baldwin's Ohio Prac. Merrick-Rippner Probate Law § 99:54, Inheritance Rights of Adoptees--"Stranger to the Adoption" Doctrine.

Carlin, Baldwin's Ohio Prac. Merrick-Rippner Probate Law App B SPF 18.7, Final Decree of Adoption (Without Interlocutory Order).

Law Review and Journal Commentaries

Inheritance Rights of Adopted Children: A Review of Recent Cases, Angela G. Carlin. 3 Prob L J Ohio 52 (March/April 1993).

Symposium: The Implications of Welfare Reform for Children. 60 Ohio St L J 1177 (1999).

Notes of Decisions

Death of adoptive parent 2
Decree vacated 1

1. Decree vacated

An order vacating a final decree of adoption pursuant to Civ R 60(B) is a final appealable order. In re Adoption of Davis, No. 851 (4th Dist Ct App, Ross, 1-4-82).

2. Death of adoptive parent

Where a child is placed in a prospective adoptive home but the father dies before the child has resided therein for six months and hence the adoption has not been completed, the child is not entitled to social security benefits. Spiegel v. Flemming (N.D.Ohio 1960) 181 F.Supp. 185, 89 Ohio Law Abs. 562, 13 O.O.2d 225.

3107.14 Court's discretion; final decree or interlocutory order

(A) The petitioner and the person sought to be adopted shall appear at the hearing on the petition, unless the presence of either is excused by the court for good cause shown.

(B) The court may continue the hearing from time to time to permit further observation, investigation, or consideration of any facts or circumstances affecting the granting of the petition, and may examine the petitioners separate and apart from each other.

(C) If, at the conclusion of the hearing, the court finds that the required consents have been obtained or excused and that the adoption is in the best interest of the person sought to be adopted as supported by the evidence, it may issue, subject to division (C)(1)(a) of section 2151.86, section 3107.064, and division (E) of section 3107.09 of the Revised Code, and any other limitations specified in this chapter, a final decree of adoption or an interlocutory order of adoption, which by its own terms automatically becomes a final decree of adoption on a date specified in the order, which, except as provided in division (B) of section 3107.13 of the Revised Code, shall not be less than six months or more than one year from the date the person to be adopted is placed in the petitioner's home, unless sooner vacated by the court for good cause shown. In determining whether the adoption is in the best interest of the person sought to be adopted, the court shall not consider the age of the petitioner if the petitioner is old enough to adopt as provided by section 3107.03 of the Revised Code.

In an interlocutory order of adoption, the court shall provide for observation, investigation, and a further report on the adoptive home during the interlocutory period.

(D) If the requirements for a decree under division (C) of this section have not been satisfied or the court vacates an interlocutory order of adoption, or if the court finds that a person sought to be adopted was placed in the home of the petitioner in violation of law, the court shall dismiss the petition and may determine the agency or person to have temporary or permanent custody of the person, which may include the agency or person that had custody prior to the filing of the petition or the petitioner, if the court finds it is in the best interest of the person as supported by the evidence, or if the person is a minor, the court may certify the case to the juvenile court of the county where the minor is then residing for appropriate action and disposition.

(E) The issuance of a final decree or interlocutory order of adoption for an adult adoption under division (A)(4) of section 3107.02 of the Revised Code shall not disqualify that adult for services under section 2151.82 or 2151.83 of the Revised Code.

(2008 H 7, eff. 4-7-09; 2008 S 163, eff. 8–14–08; 2006 S 238, eff. 9–21–06; 2000 H 448, eff. 10–5–00; 1998 H 446, eff. 8–5–98; 1996 H 419, eff. 9–18–96; 1984 H 84, eff. 3–19–85; 1976 H 156)

Historical and Statutory Notes

Ed. Note: 3107.14 contains provisions analogous to former 3107.08 to 3107.12, repealed by 1976 H 156, eff. 1–1–77.

Ed. Note: Former 3107.14 repealed by 1976 H 156, eff. 1–1–77; 130 v H 202; 1953 H 1; GC 8004–14; Source—GC 10512–22; see now 3107.17 for provisions analogous to former 3107.14.

Pre–1953 H 1 Amendments: 124 v S 65

Amendment Note: 2008 H 7 substituted "the person to be adopted is placed in the petitioner's home" for "of the issuance of the order" after "from the date" in the first sentence of division (C).

Amendment Note: 2008 S 163 added the (a) to "subject to division (C)(1)(a)" in division (C).

Amendment Note: 2006 S 238 designated division (D) and added division (E).

Amendment Note: 2000 H 448 substituted "(C)" for "(B)" after "subject to division" in division (C).

Amendment Note: 1998 H 446 inserted "division (B)(1) of section 2151.86," in the first paragraph in division (C); and made other nonsubstantive changes.

Amendment Note: 1996 H 419 substituted "as supported by the evidence, it may issue, subject to section 3107.064, division (E) of section 3107.09 of the Revised Code," for "it may issue, subject to division (D)(6) of section 3107.12 of the Revised Code" in division (C); added "except as provided in division (B) of section 3107.13 of the Revised Code," preceding "shall not be less than six months or more than one year" in division (C); added the second sentence in the first paragraph of division (C); added "as supported by the evidence," preceding "or if the person is a minor" in division (D); and made other nonsubstantive changes.

Cross References

Prohibition: 3107.65(B)

Adoption, recognition of decrees from other countries, see 3107.18

Department of job and family services, division of social administration, placing of children, see 5103.16

Powers and duties of county children services board, see 5153.16

Residency requirements for public school attendance, see 3313.64

Ohio Administrative Code References

Temporary or permanent custody and placement of children, interstate placements by individuals and courts, see OAC Ch 5101:2–42

Library References

Adoption ☞13, 14, 16.
Westlaw Topic No. 17.

C.J.S. Adoption of Persons §§ 46 to 47, 93 to 108, 119 to 135, 140.

Research References

Encyclopedias

OH Jur. 3d Family Law § 532, Jurisdiction of Probate Court.

OH Jur. 3d Family Law § 890, Who Need Not Consent--Construction of Statute.

OH Jur. 3d Family Law § 901, Time, Place, and Notice of Hearing.

OH Jur. 3d Family Law § 906, Hearing.

OH Jur. 3d Family Law § 909, Final Decree or Interlocutory Order.

OH Jur. 3d Family Law § 910, Dismissal.

Forms

Ohio Forms Legal and Business § 28:17, Introduction.

Ohio Jurisprudence Pleading and Practice Forms § 96:26, Open Adoption--Judicial Determination.

Ohio Jurisprudence Pleading and Practice Forms § 96:29, Adoption Period.

Treatises and Practice Aids

Carlin, Baldwin's Ohio Prac. Merrick-Rippner Probate Law § 99:2, History.

Carlin, Baldwin's Ohio Prac. Merrick-Rippner Probate Law § 99:3, Jurisdiction.

Carlin, Baldwin's Ohio Prac. Merrick-Rippner Probate Law § 99:8, Suitability of Adoptive Parents--Best Interests of Child.

Carlin, Baldwin's Ohio Prac. Merrick-Rippner Probate Law § 99:22, Types of Placement--Independent Adoptions.

Carlin, Baldwin's Ohio Prac. Merrick-Rippner Probate Law § 99:23, Illegal Placement.

Carlin, Baldwin's Ohio Prac. Merrick-Rippner Probate Law § 99:31, Parties Giving Consent--Biological Parents.

Carlin, Baldwin's Ohio Prac. Merrick-Rippner Probate Law § 99:45, Hearing of Petition--Procedure--Persons Present.

Carlin, Baldwin's Ohio Prac. Merrick-Rippner Probate Law § 99:47, Hearing of Petition--Determination by Court.

Carlin, Baldwin's Ohio Prac. Merrick-Rippner Probate Law § 99:48, Hearing of Petition--Continuance.

Carlin, Baldwin's Ohio Prac. Merrick-Rippner Probate Law § 99:49, Interlocutory and Final Orders.

Carlin, Baldwin's Ohio Prac. Merrick-Rippner Probate Law § 99:50, Dismissal of Petition.

Carlin, Baldwin's Ohio Prac. Merrick-Rippner Probate Law § 107:12, Certification from Probate Court.

Carlin, Baldwin's Ohio Prac. Merrick-Rippner Probate Law § 110:14, Modification of Decree Allocating Parental Rights and Responsibilities for Care of Children.

Carlin, Baldwin's Ohio Prac. Merrick-Rippner Probate Law App B SPF 18.5, Interlocutory Order of Adoption.

Carlin, Baldwin's Ohio Prac. Merrick-Rippner Probate Law App B SPF 18.6, Final Decree of Adoption (After Interlocutory Order).

Carlin, Baldwin's Ohio Prac. Merrick-Rippner Probate Law App B SPF 18.7, Final Decree of Adoption (Without Interlocutory Order).

Giannelli & Yeomans, Ohio Juvenile Law § 34:11, Certification or Transfer from Another Court.

Law Review and Journal Commentaries

Belsito v Clark: Ohio's Battle with "Motherhood," Dawn Wenk. 28 U Tol L Rev 247 (Fall 1996).

Child's Relationship with Biological Father's Family Not Precluding Adoption by Stepfather,

Pamela J. MacAdams. 4 Domestic Rel J Ohio 41 (May/June 1992).

Notes of Decisions

In general   2
Approval of placement, jurisdiction   3
Constitutional issues   1
Decree, jurisdiction   4
Disposition of child if petition dismissed   5

---

1. Constitutional issues

The trial court's failure to provide father with notice and the opportunity to be heard on the issue of whether stepfather's adoption of child was in child's best interest violated due process, even though the court had previously determined that father's consent to adoption was not required; trial court was required to conduct a best interest hearing, and father was one of several classes of persons that were entitled to 20 days notice of a hearing to determine the merits of the adoption petition and contest the best interest finding. In re Adoption of S.L.C. (Ohio App. 2 Dist., Miami, 12-29-2005) No. 05-CA-32, 2005-Ohio-7067, 2005 WL 3610305, Unreported. Adoption ☞ 12; Adoption ☞ 13; Constitutional Law ☞ 4395

Due process did not require that birth mother be appointed counsel in child's stepmother's petition to adopt child; case was not initiated by state, but by third party, case was instituted as adoption petition in probate court, not termination of parental rights in juvenile court, and, although state played role by removing child from birth mother and placing her with birth father, state did not seek to terminate birth mother's parental rights. In re

Adoption of Drake (Ohio App. 12 Dist., Clermont, 02-03-2003) No. CA2002-08-067, 2003-Ohio-510, 2003 WL 231298, Unreported. Adoption ☞ 13; Constitutional Law ☞ 4395

Publication notice identifying date and time of joint hearing on petitions for adoption of children by mother's husband, alleging that biological father's consent to adoptions was unnecessary because he had failed to communicate with or support children for one year, did not violate father's right to due process, though notice referenced only consent portion of adoption hearing and not best interests of children portion, given that, because father had received notice that court would be taking evidence as to whether his parental rights should be terminated, there was no need for any additional requirement that father be given notice that it would consider both consent and best interests of children at hearing. In re Adoption of Walters (Ohio, 01-17-2007) 112 Ohio St.3d 315, 859 N.E.2d 545, 2007-Ohio-7. Adoption ☞ 12; Constitutional Law ☞ 4395

Publication notice identifying date and time of joint hearing on petitions for adoption of children by mother's husband, alleging that biological father's consent to adoptions was unnecessary because he had failed to communicate with or support children for one year, complied with statute requiring notice of filing of adoption petition and of time and place of hearing, though notice did not specifically declare that a best interests hearing would be held, as statute did not require that specific reference be made in notice to both the consent and best interests portions of the hearing; overruling, *In re C.M.W.*, 2004 WL 2937632. In re Adoption of Walters (Ohio, 01-17-2007) 112 Ohio St.3d 315, 859 N.E.2d 545, 2007-Ohio-7. Adoption ⌬ 12

Failure to notify natural mother that investigation report had been filed in stepmother's adoption action did not violate natural mother's due process rights; no statutory authority required service of report on parties involved, and report was primarily for use of court in assessing quality of adoptive home. In re Fetzer (Ohio App. 3 Dist., 02-05-1997) 118 Ohio App.3d 156, 692 N.E.2d 219, dismissed, appeal not allowed 78 Ohio St.3d 1513, 679 N.E.2d 309. Adoption ⌬ 12; Constitutional Law ⌬ 4395

If biological father fails to accept responsibilities of parenthood, no continuing constitutionally protected interest will be recognized from mere existence of biological link. In re Adoption of Zschach (Ohio, 06-06-1996) 75 Ohio St.3d 648, 665 N.E.2d 1070, reconsideration denied 76 Ohio St.3d 1410, 666 N.E.2d 569, certiorari denied 117 S.Ct. 582, 519 U.S. 1028, 136 L.Ed.2d 513. Children Out–of–wedlock ⌬ 1

Even if probate court makes determination that parent's consent to adoption is not required, court must still go on to make determination that adoption is in best interest of child, and parent whose consent to adoption has been found unnecessary still must be given notice of the best-interest hearing. In re Adoption of Kuhlmann (Ohio App. 1 Dist., 12-07-1994) 99 Ohio App.3d 44, 649 N.E.2d 1279. Adoption ⌬ 12; Adoption ⌬ 13

Ethnic heritage of a child and prospective adoptive parents may be considered as a factor in adoption placements, but may not be used as the sole or determinative criterion; the opportunity to adopt a child may not be denied merely because the prospective adoptive parents are Caucasian and the child is African–American. In re Moorehead (Montgomery 1991) 75 Ohio App.3d 711, 600 N.E.2d 778.

RC 3107.14(D), to the extent that it allows a probate court to award permanent custody of a child to a nonparent without a determination that the parent has relinquished custody or that the parent is unsuitable, is an unconstitutional infringement of the parent's fundamental interest in the custody of the child. In re Adoption of Mays (Hamilton 1986) 30 Ohio App.3d 195, 507 N.E.2d 453, 30 O.B.R. 338. Constitutional Law ⌬ 4395; Constitutional Law ⌬ 4396; Infants ⌬ 132

2. In general

Trial court order finding that finalization of child's adoption by her step-father was in child's best interest, but which did not actually finalize adoption, was not final and appealable; although order was entered in special proceeding, biological father's substantial right was not affected by order as waiting until order was finalized to appeal would not foreclose biological father's chance of obtaining appropriate appellate relief. In re Brianna D.

(Ohio App. 6 Dist., Lucas, 09-29-2004) No. L-04-1139, 2004-Ohio-5402, 2004 WL 2260118, Unreported. Adoption ⌬ 15

Probate court did not abuse its discretion in considering wishes of child to be adopted by mother's husband, despite fact that child's biological paternal grandparents had taken active role in child's life; child testified that she very much wanted to be adopted by husband, she resisted visitation with paternal grandparents in Florida because she missed her life in Ohio, and fact that relationship with grandparents did not outweigh her interest in being with her family and friends and social activities could speak to nature of relationship with paternal grandparents. In re Adoption of B.G. (Ohio App. 10 Dist., Franklin, 10-29-2002) No. 02AP-810, 2002-Ohio-5910, 2002 WL 31417928, Unreported. Adoption ⌬ 13

A bifurcated procedure is required where the natural parent of a minor child refuses to consent to adoption of that child by a third party whereby (1) initially, the probate court determines the issue of necessity of consent, (2) a judgment on the issue of consent only is filed, and (3) in the second stage, the best interest of the child standard is utilized; failure to conduct a hearing on the issue of whether the proposed adoption is in the best interest of the child is error. Matter of Adoption of Zachary H. (Ohio App. 6 Dist., Williams, 03-07-1997) No. WM 96-013, 1997 WL 103808, Unreported.

Natural mother had an adequate legal remedy to contest adoption by filing a motion in probate court during pendency of adoption proceedings alleging that consent to adoption was invalid; therefore, natural mother was not entitled to a writ of habeas corpus. Barnebey v. Zschach (Ohio, 03-08-1995) 71 Ohio St.3d 588, 646 N.E.2d 162. Habeas Corpus ⌬ 280

The natural parent of a legitimate child may not seek to adopt his natural child to terminate the other natural parent's parental rights. In re Adoption of Kohorst (Paulding 1992) 75 Ohio App.3d 813, 600 N.E.2d 843, motion overruled 65 Ohio St.3d 1466, 602 N.E.2d 1174.

An adoption proceeding is a two-step process involving a "consent" phase and a "best-interest" phase; thus, a trial court errs when it fails to hold a best-interest hearing even though parental consent was not required for the adoption since the natural parents have an overriding interest in being heard on the issue of whether the proposed adoption would be in the child's best interest. In re Adoption of Jordan (Preble 1991) 72 Ohio App.3d 638, 595 N.E.2d 963.

Under RC 3107.14, adoption matters must be decided on a case-by-case basis through the able exercise of discretion by the trial court giving due consideration to all known factors in determining what is the best interest of the person to be adopted. In re Adoption of Charles B. (Ohio 1990) 50 Ohio St.3d 88, 552 N.E.2d 884. Adoption ⌬ 13

A natural parent cannot be the sole adoptive parent of a natural child even with the consent of other natural parent as a matter of law. In re Adoption of Graham (Ohio Com.Pl. 1980) 63 Ohio Misc. 22, 409 N.E.2d 1067, 16 O.O.3d 347, 17 O.O.3d 341.

Prospective adoptive parents could not adopt child of whom they did not have legal placement. In re Stephenson (Ohio App. 5 Dist., Fairfield, 09-06-2002) No. 02CA37, 2002-Ohio-4751, 2002 WL 31026988, Unreported. Adoption ☞ 4

The function of RC 5103.16 is to prevent black-market adoptions which is not the case where a mother moves her child into the prospective adoptive home to parties who have agreed to adopt the child and would also care for the child until the adoption process is completed. In re Adoption of a Child by Michael S. and Shirley S, No. H–98–009, 1998 WL 769788 (6th Dist Ct App, Huron, 11–6–98).

3. Approval of placement, jurisdiction

Court's decision to allow adoption was presumptively proper, where investigator's report favorably indicated that adoptive parents could provide loving, stable environment in which child would thrive in every realm of life and court entered final order of adoption following interlocutory decree and investigator's report. In re Rabatin (Geauga 1992) 83 Ohio App.3d 836, 615 N.E.2d 1099. Adoption ☞ 15

For purposes of statute which provides that final decree of adoption may not be issued until child has lived in adoptive home for at least six months, date on which adoption petition was filed could be used as start of six-month period where child's natural mother had placed child with paternal grandparents, there was no indication that mother intended to place child in grandparents' home for adoption, and grandparents later sought to adopt child after mother failed to support or contact child for several years. In re Adoption of Howell (Lawrence 1991) 77 Ohio App.3d 80, 601 N.E.2d 92, motion overruled 62 Ohio St.3d 1508, 583 N.E.2d 1320. Adoption ☞ 13

A trial court's conclusion that the placement of a child with foster parents for purposes of adoption is not in the child's best interest because of the issue of confidentiality is against the manifest weight of the evidence where all the evidence of record is positive to the adoption and the investigator's report recommends the placement; "confidentiality" was never demonstrated to be a necessary factor in evaluating the suitability of either any adoption or specifically this adoption and there was no evidence presented to the court to indicate that the lack of confidentiality would cause problems at the present or a future date. In re Reichenbach (Portage 1991) 71 Ohio App.3d 730, 595 N.E.2d 399.

The trial court's denial of a child's placement with foster parents for purposes of adoption based on the fact that the foster parents established a relationship with the child and that the placement would diminish the integrity of the foster care system is against the manifest weight of the evidence where (1) no specific policy prohibiting such a placement was put into evidence via judicial notice or otherwise, (2) no testimony indicated that the best interests of the child were offended, and (3) the facts of the case do not support the contention that the foster parents were using the foster care system to adopt a child, since during the five years they had fostered fourteen children they had never sought to adopt any of them as they had three children of their own and did not seek to adopt the present child until they became aware that the child's grandmother was searching for adoptive parents for her. In re Reichenbach (Portage 1991) 71 Ohio App.3d 730, 595 N.E.2d 399.

Where adoptive parents clearly meet all of the agency's standards concerning maturity, stability, financial ability to carry responsibility, and love of the child, and where the agency placed the child with the adoptive parents from birth to the present time as foster parents, the denial of agency consent based solely upon the age of the adoptive parents is unreasonable, arbitrary, and capricious, and violates the spirit of the whole adoption system while holding to the letter of part of it. In re Haun (Cuyahoga 1972) 31 Ohio App.2d 63, 286 N.E.2d 478, 60 O.O.2d 163.

The legality of a placement of a child with persons other than his parents is governed by the statute in effect at the time such placement is made. In re Adoption of Wright (Ohio Prob. 1968) 15 Ohio Misc. 354, 240 N.E.2d 923, 44 O.O.2d 509.

The probate court no longer has authority to approve an illegal placement of a child in the best interest of said child. In re Boyd's Adoption (Ohio Prob. 1962) 185 N.E.2d 331, 89 Ohio Law Abs. 202.

RC 5103.16 and 2151.04 effect by implication a partial repeal of RC 3107.08, and by such sections it is required that the parents of a child apply to the probate court for placement of the child for adoption prior to the placement. In re Boyd's Adoption (Ohio Prob. 1962) 185 N.E.2d 331, 89 Ohio Law Abs. 202.

Within the meaning of RC 3107.09, a child is "legally placed in the home of the petitioner" when such child was brought there voluntarily by the parent immediately after birth and so maintained there after such parent was subsequently awarded legal custody in a divorce action, and under such circumstances the probate court is the "proper court" to determine whether the placement was "beneficial to the child." In re Adoption of Biddle (Ohio 1958) 168 Ohio St. 209, 152 N.E.2d 105, 6 O.O.2d 4, on remand 163 N.E.2d 188, 81 Ohio Law Abs. 529.

Though the division of social administration of the department of public welfare is not a necessary party to adoption proceedings, its responsibility for enforcing certain laws concerning placement or adoption causes it to be a person in interest entitled to notice of an illegal placement and thus a proper party to such proceedings. 1962 OAG 2747.

Under RC 5103.16 probate courts may approve the proposed placement of children under the procedures set forth in that statute; probate courts may also, under RC 3107.08, during an adoption proceeding, and upon a finding that the child being adopted was placed in the home of the petitioner in violation of the laws relating to the placement of children, determine whether the placement is for the best interest of the child and either approve or disapprove it. 1962 OAG 2747.

4. Decree, jurisdiction

When parental consent for adoption is required and is denied, probate court cannot then approve adoption based on best interest of child because court lacks jurisdiction to proceed. In re Adoption of Baby Boy Brooks (Ohio App. 10 Dist., 03-21-2000) 136 Ohio App.3d 824, 737 N.E.2d 1062, appeal not allowed 89 Ohio St.3d 1433, 730 N.E.2d 383. Adoption ☞ 7.7

A trial judge fails to base his adoption decisions on a consideration of the best interests of the children involved when he denies foster parents' petition for adoption based on a consideration of the children's biological grandparents' visitation rights. In re Adoption of Ridenour (Ohio 1991) 61 Ohio St.3d 319, 574 N.E.2d 1055.

After conducting a hearing pursuant to RC 3107.09, the probate court improperly denies a petition for adoption of a four-year-old boy in the custody of the county welfare department, when the court finds that petitioners meet all the requirements of suitability as adoptive parents, but denies the petition for adoption on the grounds that the granting of the adoption would violate the integrity of a waiting list allegedly maintained by the welfare department, where at the adoption hearing there was no evidence adduced establishing the existence or administration of such a waiting list and no evidence that the waiting list contained suitable applicants ready, willing, and able to adopt the child in question. (See also In re Harshey, 40 App(2d) 157, 318 NE(2d) 544 (1974).) In re Harshey (Cuyahoga 1975) 45 Ohio App.2d 97, 341 N.E.2d 616, 74 O.O.2d 120.

Where evidence shows that the social services agency has no substantial reasons for withholding the answer and consent required by RC 3107.06, the court will order the answer and consent filed when the court determines it is in the best interest of the child, but if substantial reasons exist for withholding such answer and consent, and the court is satisfied that it is not in the best interest of the child to require it, the petition for adoption will be denied. In re Dickhaus (Ohio Com.Pl. 1974) 41 Ohio Misc. 1, 321 N.E.2d 800, 70 O.O.2d 24.

The refusal of an agency to consent to an adoption does not deprive the probate court of jurisdiction even when such refusal is not arbitrary, unreasonable, or capricious, and is but an element for consideration in the probate court's determination of the qualifications of the adoptive parents and the best interests of the child. In re Haun (Cuyahoga

1972) 31 Ohio App.2d 63, 286 N.E.2d 478, 60 O.O.2d 163. Adoption ☞ 7.1

It is not an abuse of discretion for a trial court in an adoption proceeding to grant a motion to reopen such case, after the hearing but before judgment, for the submission of a so-called "stipulation of facts," the contents of which are admitted to be substantially true and which evidence goes to the heart of the only issue before the court. In re Adoption of Earhart (Miami 1961) 117 Ohio App. 73, 190 N.E.2d 468, 23 O.O.2d 156.

A probate court has jurisdiction to hear and determine an adoption proceeding relating to a minor child notwithstanding the fact that the custody of such child is at the time within the continuing jurisdiction of a divorce court. In re Adoption of Biddle (Ohio 1958) 168 Ohio St. 209, 152 N.E.2d 105, 6 O.O.2d 4, on remand 163 N.E.2d 188, 81 Ohio Law Abs. 529.

In proceeding involving validity of decree of adoption, court of appeals must rely wholly on record before it. McClain v. Lyon (Morrow 1926) 24 Ohio App. 279, 156 N.E. 529, 6 Ohio Law Abs. 60. Adoption ☞ 15; Appeal And Error ☞ 671(1)

Adoption proceedings are wholly statutory, and statutes must be clearly followed to give probate court jurisdiction to decree adoption. McClain v. Lyon (Morrow 1926) 24 Ohio App. 279, 156 N.E. 529, 6 Ohio Law Abs. 60. Adoption ☞ 1; Courts ☞ 202(1)

Under GC 8030 and 8030–1 (Repealed), where probate court was without jurisdiction in first instance in adoption proceedings, such proceedings were not merely voidable, but were void. McClain v. Lyon (Morrow 1926) 24 Ohio App. 279, 156 N.E. 529, 6 Ohio Law Abs. 60.

Where a child is placed in a prospective adoptive home but the father dies before the child has resided therein for six months and hence the adoption has not been completed, the child is not entitled to social security benefits. Spiegel v. Flemming (N.D.Ohio 1960) 181 F.Supp. 185, 89 Ohio Law Abs. 562, 13 O.O.2d 225.

The refusal of consent to an adoption by a "certified organization," as defined in RC 3107.01(C), does not impair the jurisdiction of the probate court, but the recommendations and the reports, filed pursuant to RC 3107.05 and 3107.10, are to be considered, in conjunction with all other evidence adduced in the proceeding, by the court in deciding the issues presented by RC 3107.09. State ex rel. Portage County Welfare Dept. v. Summers (Ohio 1974) 38 Ohio St.2d 144, 311 N.E.2d 6, 67 O.O.2d 151.

5. Disposition of child if petition dismissed

Lack of agency involvement or court approval of initial placement of child with adoptive parent did not require dismissal of adoption petition, where biological parents were active participants in placement, contacting adoptive parent as "a friend" after they engaged in unsuccessful negotiations to place child with three sets of prospective adoptive parents. In re Adoption of Zschach (Ohio, 06-06-1996) 75 Ohio St.3d 648, 665 N.E.2d 1070, reconsideration denied 76 Ohio St.3d 1410, 666 N.E.2d 569, certiorari denied 117 S.Ct. 582, 519 U.S. 1028, 136 L.Ed.2d 513. Adoption ⬅ 13

Upon rendering a judgment denying a petition for adoption, the court must certify the cause to the juvenile court in the county in which the child is residing, for appropriate action and disposition. In re Adoption of Peters (Lucas 1961) 113 Ohio App. 173, 177 N.E.2d 541, 17 O.O.2d 141. Adoption ⬅ 15

Where, in an action to vacate an adoption decree upon the ground that the next friend of the child fraudulently concealed the fact that the child was mentally defective, the court sustained a motion to quash service upon the next friend, the action to vacate was not terminated in its entirety, and hence the order was not final. In re Adoption of Sladky (Franklin 1958) 109 Ohio App. 120, 161 N.E.2d 554, 81 Ohio Law Abs. 264, 10 O.O.2d 304.

Where probate court denies decree for adoption, section requires that the cause be certified to juvenile court for appropriate action, but probate judge, even though in the county he was also juvenile judge, may not proceed from the adoption hearing directly to his capacity as juvenile judge and dispose of question of custody in absence of evidence submitted to him as juvenile judge relating to custody or in absence of stipulation that the evidence offered in the adoption proceeding was to be submitted to juvenile court. In re Sparto's Adoption (Darke 1948) 82 N.E.2d 328, 52 Ohio Law Abs. 189.

A declaration or finding in a proceeding begun by an adopting father under provisions of GC 10512–21 (RC 3107.12), that an adoption is null and void on grounds therein set forth, operates prospectively only and does not cut off rights acquired by the adopted child prior to such declaration. In such case, in an action under GC 10509–95 (RC 2123.01) to determine who is entitled to next estate of inheritance of adopting mother, who died prior to such declaration without issue or surviving spouse, the adopted child is entitled to the next estate of inheritance of the deceased adopting mother. Steiner v. Rainer (Mahoning 1941) 69 Ohio App. 6, 42 N.E.2d 684, 23 O.O. 306.

The certification of a cause from the probate court to the juvenile court under the provisions of section does not constitute a complaint against the parents that the child which was the subject of the adoption proceedings is a dependent, delinquent or neglected child, and a judgment by the juvenile

court finding that such child is a dependent child, made without the filing of a complaint against the parents, is void ab initio for lack of jurisdiction. State ex rel. Clark v. Allaman (Ohio 1950) 154 Ohio St. 296, 95 N.E.2d 753, 43 O.O. 190.

The provision of former section (part of the Adoption Code), that "if for any reason whatsoever the petition shall be dismissed or the court shall deny or revoke its interlocutory order of adoption or deny a final decree of adoption... the cause shall be certified to the juvenile court of the county where the child is then residing for appropriate action and disposition by such court," authorizes and requires the juvenile court, upon receiving such certification, to make proper investigation within its statutory jurisdiction to determine who has the responsibility for the care of such child. State ex rel. Clark v. Allaman (Ohio 1950) 154 Ohio St. 296, 95 N.E.2d 753, 43 O.O. 190.

Where a petition for the adoption of an illegitimate child was filed in the probate court and the child's mother gave her consent in writing to such adoption, but the petitioners withdrew their petition before any action thereon was taken, the court, upon issuing an order that the petition be withdrawn and the cause dismissed, is without authority to certify the cause to the juvenile court for disposition under section in such case; there was no proper basis for certification from the probate court to the juvenile court; and, no complaint having been filed charging the child to be a dependent child or any other form of complaint originating in the juvenile court, that court was without jurisdiction to determine that the child was a dependent child or to make an order depriving the mother of custody and committing the child to the custody of a detention home. State ex rel. Clark v. Allaman (Montgomery 1950) 87 Ohio App. 101, 90 N.E.2d 394, 57 Ohio Law Abs. 17, 42 O.O. 330, affirmed 154 Ohio St. 296, 95 N.E.2d 753, 43 O.O. 190.

Under the provisions of section upon a proper certification of the case to the juvenile court, jurisdiction is conferred upon such court to determine the custody of the child. State ex rel. Sparto v. Williams (Darke 1949) 86 Ohio App. 377, 86 N.E.2d 501, 55 Ohio Law Abs. 341, 41 O.O. 474.

Where a child is placed for adoption and the mother's consent is subsequently withdrawn, a certification of the case to the juvenile court upon dismissal of the petition does not of itself give the juvenile court jurisdiction to determine the child's custody. In re O—(Ohio Juv. 1964) 199 N.E.2d 765, 95 Ohio Law Abs. 101, 28 O.O.2d 165.

3107.141 Order to redo or supplement report or history; appointment of different assessor

After an assessor files a home study report under section 3107.031, a social and medical history under section 3107.09, or a prefinalization assessment report under section 3107.12 of the Revised Code, or the department of job and family services files a social and medical history under section 3107.091 of the Revised Code, a court may do either or both of the following if the court determines the report or history does not comply with the requirements governing the report or history or, in the case of a home study or prefinalization assessment report, does not enable the court to determine whether an adoption is in the best interest of the minor to be adopted:

(A) Order the assessor or department to redo or supplement the report or history in a manner the court directs;

(B) Appoint a different assessor to redo or supplement the report or history in a manner the court directs.

(1999 H 471, eff. 7–1–00; 1998 H 446, eff. 8–5–98)

Historical and Statutory Notes

Amendment Note: 1999 H 471 substituted "job and family" for "human" in the introductory paragraph.

Library References

Adoption ☞13.
Westlaw Topic No. 17.
C.J.S. Adoption of Persons §§ 46 to 47, 93 to 102.

Research References

Encyclopedias

OH Jur. 3d Family Law § 902, Investigation.

Forms

Ohio Jurisprudence Pleading and Practice Forms § 96:25, Order to Redo or Supplement Report or History--Appointment of Different Assessor.

Treatises and Practice Aids

Carlin, Baldwin's Ohio Prac. Merrick-Rippner Probate Law § 99:27, Papers and Records--Assessor.

3107.15   Effects of final decree

(A) A final decree of adoption and an interlocutory order of adoption that has become final as issued by a court of this state, or a decree issued by a jurisdiction outside this state as recognized pursuant to section 3107.18 of the Revised Code, shall have the following effects as to all matters within the jurisdiction or before a court of this state, whether issued before or after May 30, 1996:

(1) Except with respect to a spouse of the petitioner and relatives of the spouse, to relieve the biological or other legal parents of the adopted person of all parental rights and responsibilities, and to terminate all legal relationships between the adopted person and the adopted person's relatives, including the adopted person's biological or other legal parents, so that the adopted person thereafter is a stranger to the adopted person's former relatives for all purposes including inheritance and the interpretation or construction of documents, statutes, and instruments, whether executed before or after the adoption is decreed, which do not expressly include the person by name or by some designation not based on a parent and child or blood relationship;

(2) To create the relationship of parent and child between petitioner and the adopted person, as if the adopted person were a legitimate blood descendant of the petitioner, for all purposes including inheritance and applicability of statutes, documents, and instruments, whether executed before or after the adoption is decreed, and whether executed or created before or after May 30, 1996, which do not expressly exclude an adopted person from their operation or effect;

(3) Notwithstanding division (A)(2) of this section, a person who is eighteen years of age or older at the time the person is adopted, and the adopted person's lineal descendants, are not included as recipients of gifts, devises, bequests, or other transfers of property, including transfers in trust made to a class of persons including, but not limited to, children, grandchildren, heirs, issue, lineal descendants, and next of kin, for purposes of inheritance and applicability of statutes, documents, and instruments, whether executed or created before or

after May 30, 1996, unless the document or instrument expressly includes the adopted person by name or expressly states that it includes a person who is eighteen years of age or older at the time the person is adopted.

(B) Notwithstanding division (A) of this section, if a parent of a child dies without the relationship of parent and child having been previously terminated and a spouse of the living parent thereafter adopts the child, the child's rights from or through the deceased parent for all purposes, including inheritance and applicability or construction of documents, statutes, and instruments, are not restricted or curtailed by the adoption.

(C) Notwithstanding division (A) of this section, if the relationship of parent and child has not been terminated between a parent and that parent's child and a spouse of the other parent of the child adopts the child, a grandparent's or relative's right to companionship or visitation pursuant to section 3109.11 of the Revised Code is not restricted or curtailed by the adoption.

(D) An interlocutory order of adoption, while it is in force, has the same legal effect as a final decree of adoption. If an interlocutory order of adoption is vacated, it shall be as though void from its issuance, and the rights, liabilities, and status of all affected persons that have not become vested are governed accordingly.

(2002 H 509, eff. 3–14–03; 2000 S 180, eff. 3–22–01; 1996 S 129, eff. 5–30–96; 1976 H 156, eff. 1–1–77)

Uncodified Law

2002 H 509, § 3, eff. 3–14–03, reads:

No liability shall arise against any one of the following that, prior to the effective date of this section, authorized or was otherwise responsible for a distribution or other payment or a transfer of property that is inconsistent with division (A)(3) of section 3107.15 of the Revised Code, as amended by this act:

(1) A fiduciary under a trust instrument, will, or other document;

(2) A bank, savings and loan association, credit union, or society for savings, in connection with written contracts described in sections 2131.10 and 2131.11 of the Revised Code;

(3) A registering entity, as defined in division (H) of section 1709.01 of the Revised Code, for a transfer-on-death made pursuant to Chapter 1709. of the Revised Code.

Historical and Statutory Notes

Ed. Note: 3107.15 contains provisions analogous to former 3107.13, repealed by 1976 H 156, eff. 1–1–77.

Amendment Note: 2002 H 509 added division (A)(3).

Amendment Note: 2000 S 180 substituted "May 30, 1996" for "the effective date of this amendment" in divisions (A) and (A)(2); added new division (C); and redesignated former division (C) as new division (D).

Amendment Note: 1996 S 129 inserted "or a decree issued by a jurisdiction outside this state as recognized pursuant to section 3107.18 of the Revised Code" and "whether issued before or after the effective date of this amendment" in division (A); inserted "and whether executed or created before or after the effective date of this amendment" in division (A)(2); and made changes to reflect gender neutral language and other nonsubstantive changes throughout.

Cross References

Descent and distribution, see 2105.06
Dower, see 2103.01 et seq.
Estate tax, see 5731.01 et seq.

Ohio Administrative Code References

Acceptance of permanent custody by permanent surrender, see OAC 5101:2–42–09

Library References

Adoption ⚘14, 20 to 24.
Westlaw Topic No. 17.

C.J.S. Adoption of Persons §§ 103 to 108, 130 to 135, 137 to 138, 140 to 145, 152 to 154, 156 to 164.

Research References

ALR Library

61 ALR 6th 1, Adoption of Child by Same-Sex Partners.

71 ALR 5th 99, Grandparents' Visitation Rights Where Child's Parents Are Living.

36 ALR 5th 395, Adopted Child as Within Class Named in Testamentary Gift.

Encyclopedias

OH Jur. 3d Constitutional Law § 488, Distinction Between Statutes Dealing With Substantive or Vested Rights and Remedies.

OH Jur. 3d Decedents' Estates § 33, Law at Time of Intestate's Death as Controlling.

OH Jur. 3d Decedents' Estates § 93, Children of Intestate and Their Descendants; Adopted Children.

OH Jur. 3d Decedents' Estates § 522, "Issue"--As Including Illegitimate or Adopted Children.

OH Jur. 3d Decedents' Estates § 529, "Grandchildren".

OH Jur. 3d Decedents' Estates § 542, as Including Adopted Children.

OH Jur. 3d Decedents' Estates § 549, Adopted Children.

OH Jur. 3d Decedents' Estates § 802, Beneficiaries Indicated in General Terms--Gift to "Children," "Issue," "Heirs," and the Like.

OH Jur. 3d Decedents' Estates § 1654, Allowance to Children.

OH Jur. 3d Family Law § 877, Who May Adopt--Effect of Sexual Orientation of Adoptive Parents.

OH Jur. 3d Family Law § 909, Final Decree or Interlocutory Order.

OH Jur. 3d Family Law § 922, Effect on Grandparent Visitation.

OH Jur. 3d Family Law § 925, Inheritance by Child from or Through Natural Parents.

OH Jur. 3d Family Law § 1172, Effect of Child's Adoption on Visitation.

OH Jur. 3d Trusts § 124, Adopted Child as Within Class.

Forms

Ohio Forms Legal and Business § 24:96, Drafting Will.

Ohio Forms Legal and Business § 28:17, Introduction.

Ohio Forms Legal and Business § 24:181, Child or Children--"Adopted" as Included in Word "Children".

Ohio Jurisprudence Pleading and Practice Forms § 123:7, Distribution Among Beneficiaries.

Ohio Jurisprudence Pleading and Practice Forms § 96:30, Effect of Adoption.

Ohio Jurisprudence Pleading and Practice Forms § 96:33, Foreign Decrees.

Treatises and Practice Aids

Sowald & Morganstern, Baldwin's Ohio Practice Domestic Relations Law § 18:9, The Impact of Adoption.

Sowald & Morganstern, Baldwin's Ohio Practice Domestic Relations Law § 21:6, Development of Statutory Requirements.

Sowald & Morganstern, Baldwin's Ohio Practice Domestic Relations Law § 3:36, Effect of Judgment--Allocation of Parental Rights and Responsibilities, Visitation, and Companionship Rights--Relatives and Nonparents.

Carlin, Baldwin's Ohio Prac. Merrick-Rippner Probate Law § 3:5, Subject Matter--Specific Areas--Inter Vivos Trusts.

Carlin, Baldwin's Ohio Prac. Merrick-Rippner Probate Law § 6:6, Probate Court Proceedings.

Carlin, Baldwin's Ohio Prac. Merrick-Rippner Probate Law § 17:2, Designation--Effect.

Carlin, Baldwin's Ohio Prac. Merrick-Rippner Probate Law § 17:3, Designation--Contrast With Adoption.

Carlin, Baldwin's Ohio Prac. Merrick-Rippner Probate Law § 19:8, Uniform Parentage Act--Support Order.

Carlin, Baldwin's Ohio Prac. Merrick-Rippner Probate Law § 44:5, Action for Construction--Direction of the Testator as to Interpretation of a Will.

Carlin, Baldwin's Ohio Prac. Merrick-Rippner Probate Law § 99:3, Jurisdiction.

Carlin, Baldwin's Ohio Prac. Merrick-Rippner Probate Law § 99:8, Suitability of Adoptive Parents--Best Interests of Child.

Carlin, Baldwin's Ohio Prac. Merrick-Rippner Probate Law § 107:6, Probate Powers.

Carlin, Baldwin's Ohio Prac. Merrick-Rippner Probate Law § 15:28, Adopted Child.

Carlin, Baldwin's Ohio Prac. Merrick-Rippner Probate Law § 15:29, Designated Heir.

Carlin, Baldwin's Ohio Prac. Merrick-Rippner Probate Law § 30:27, Adopted Child.

Carlin, Baldwin's Ohio Prac. Merrick-Rippner Probate Law § 44:16, Liberal Construction--Gifts to a Class: Construction Problems.

Carlin, Baldwin's Ohio Prac. Merrick-Rippner Probate Law § 44:23, Words and Phrases--Grandchildren.

Carlin, Baldwin's Ohio Prac. Merrick-Rippner Probate Law § 44:25, Words and Phrases--Heirs or Children.

Carlin, Baldwin's Ohio Prac. Merrick-Rippner Probate Law § 44:30, Words and Phrases--Per Stirpes.

Carlin, Baldwin's Ohio Prac. Merrick-Rippner Probate Law § 99:21, Types of Placement--Stepparent, Guardian, and Grandparent Adoptions.

Carlin, Baldwin's Ohio Prac. Merrick-Rippner Probate Law § 99:31, Parties Giving Consent--Biological Parents.

Carlin, Baldwin's Ohio Prac. Merrick-Rippner Probate Law § 99:34, Parties Giving Consent--Agency.

Carlin, Baldwin's Ohio Prac. Merrick-Rippner Probate Law § 99:39, Consent Not Required--Noncommunication and Nonsupport.

Carlin, Baldwin's Ohio Prac. Merrick-Rippner Probate Law § 99:40, Consent Not Required--Putative Father.

Carlin, Baldwin's Ohio Prac. Merrick-Rippner Probate Law § 99:49, Interlocutory and Final Orders.

Carlin, Baldwin's Ohio Prac. Merrick-Rippner Probate Law § 99:53, Inheritance Rights of Adoptees.

Carlin, Baldwin's Ohio Prac. Merrick-Rippner Probate Law § 99:54, Inheritance Rights of Adoptees--"Stranger to the Adoption" Doctrine.

Carlin, Baldwin's Ohio Prac. Merrick-Rippner Probate Law § 99:55, Inheritance Rights of Adoptees--Effect of Testamentary Language.

Carlin, Baldwin's Ohio Prac. Merrick-Rippner Probate Law § 110:15, Visitation Right of Noncustodial Parent and Others.

Carlin, Baldwin's Ohio Prac. Merrick-Rippner Probate Law § 110:30, Parentage Act--Enforcement of Support Order.

Carlin, Baldwin's Ohio Prac. Merrick-Rippner Probate Law § 110:35, Civil Support Proceedings--Liability for Child Support.

Carlin, Baldwin's Ohio Prac. Merrick-Rippner Probate Law § 30:242, Miscellaneous Trust Provision--Disinheriting an Adopted Child or Including an Adult Adopted Child--Form.

Bogert - the Law of Trusts and Trustees § 182, Construction--Beneficiaries and Their Interests.

Restatement (2d) of Property, Don. Trans. § 25.4, Gifts to "Children"-Adopted Children.

Restatement (2d) of Property, Don. Trans. § 25.5, Gifts to "Children"-Child Adopted by Another.

Law Review and Journal Commentaries

Advanced Directives in Same–Sex Relationships. Marc L. Stolarsky, 19 Prob. L. J. Ohio 132 (January/February 2009).

Belsito v Clark: Ohio's Battle with "Motherhood," Dawn Wenk. 28 U Tol L Rev 247 (Fall 1996).

Browsing Among the Later Probate Authorities, Harry L. Deibel. 22 Ohio St B Ass'n Rep 243 (1949).

The Effect of a Step Parent Adoption on a Grandchild's Remainder Interest in a Trust. Richard W. Burke and Michael P. Morley, 18 Prob. L. J. Ohio 221 (July/August 2008).

Grandparent Visitation Rights in Ohio After Grandchild Adoption: Is It Time to Move in a New Direction?, Note. 46 Clev St L Rev 385 (1998).

In re Adoption of Ridenour, Note. 18 Ohio N U L Rev 719 (1992).

Inheritance from an Adopted Child, Robert R. Augsburger. 1 W Reserve U L Rev 133 (1949).

Inheritance Rights of Adopted Children: A Review of Recent Cases, Angela G. Carlin. 3 Prob L J Ohio 52 (March/April 1993).

An Interpretation of Ohio Law on Maternal Status in Gestational Surrogacy Disputes: Belsito v. Clark, Note. 21 U Dayton L Rev 229 (Fall 1995).

Little Red Riding Hood is Missing—Grandparent Visitation Not Authorized After Stepparent Adoption, Richard L. Innis. 7 Domestic Rel J Ohio 17 (March/April 1995).

Probate Litigation Issues and Trends. Kerin Lyn Kaminski, 19 Prob. L. J. Ohio 160 (March/April 2009).

Right of Adopted Child to Inherit Through its Adoptive Parents, John P. McMahon. 7 Ohio St L J 441 (September 1941)

A Surrogacy Agreement that Could Have and Should Have Been Enforced: *R.R. v. M.H.*, 689 N.E.2d 790 (Mass. 1998), Note. 24 U Dayton L Rev 513 (Spring 1999).

There's More than the Wolf Keeping Little Red Riding Hood from Her Grandparents, Hon. Russell A. Steiner. 5 Domestic Rel J Ohio 93 (November/December 1993).

Who Are the Grantor's Issue? Martin C. Boron, 18 Prob. L. J. Ohio 218 (July/August 2008).

Wills Can Be Made "Unbreakable," Ellis V. Rippner. 6 Clev–Marshall L Rev 336 (May 1957).

Notes of Decisions

In general 1
As issue or lineal descendant, child's right to inherit 3
Child's right to inherit 2-5
  In general 2
  As issue or lineal descendant 3
  From and through natural parent 4
  Trusts 5
Death of adopted child 6
From and through natural parent, child's right to inherit 4
Rights of adopting parents 7
Trusts, child's right to inherit 5

Visitation 8

———

1. In general

Amendments to statutes that created right of grandparent, and other relative, visitation after adoption by stepparent, could not be applied retroactively to children adopted prior to amendments' effective date and, thus, juvenile court did not have authority to grant paternal grandmother and paternal aunt visitation with children after children's father died, and mother's new husband, as stepfather, adopted children; amendments did not include language suggesting they were to be applied retroactively, and adoptive father's duty to support children, and children's right to compel that duty, were vested duties and rights. In re Busdiecker (Ohio App. 12 Dist., Warren, 05-19-2003) No. CA2002-10-104, 2003-Ohio-2556, 2003 WL 21135496, Unreported. Child Custody ⬯ 6

The juvenile court's authority to order payment of back child support is not defeated by subsequent adoption of the child; however, the court errs by ordering the father to pay support for five months after the child is adopted by the mother's husband. Black v. Hart (Ohio App. 9 Dist., Summit, 06-05-1996) No. 17524, 1996 WL 304284, Unreported.

A final decree of adoption does not patently and unambiguously divest a juvenile court of jurisdiction to determine paternity solely for the limited purpose of allowing the putative father to establish that he is the biological father so that he can exercise his statutory rights to provide information regarding his social and medical history for placement in the child's adoption records. State ex rel. Furnas v. Monnin (Ohio, 10-30-2008) 120 Ohio St.3d 279, 898 N.E.2d 573, 2008-Ohio-5569. Adoption ⬯ 14

Adoption statutes terminate all relationships held through the parent whose rights were terminated. In re Adoption of Hilliard (Ohio App. 3 Dist., 08-25-2003) 154 Ohio App.3d 54, 796 N.E.2d 46, 2003-Ohio-4471. Adoption ⬯ 20

Biological father's child support obligation terminated upon issuance of interlocutory order of adoption pursuant to petition filed by the adoptive father, where final order eventually issued; applicable statutes provided that interlocutory order had same force and effect as final order and that final order had effect of terminating all parental rights and responsibilities of biological father, including support obligation. In re Scheehle (Ohio App. 10 Dist., 09-09-1999) 134 Ohio App.3d 167, 730 N.E.2d 472. Child Support ⬯ 33

Adoption of child by adult who was not child's stepparent would terminate parental rights of biological parent by operation of law, in accordance with unambiguous language and meaning of adoption statutes, notwithstanding that unmarried adult seeking to adopt child was lesbian partner of child's biological mother and was otherwise eligible to adopt child. In re Adoption of Doe (Ohio App. 9 Dist., 12-16-1998) 130 Ohio App.3d 288, 719 N.E.2d 1071, appeal not allowed 85 Ohio St.3d 1467, 709 N.E.2d 173, reconsideration denied 86 Ohio St.3d 1408, 711 N.E.2d 234. Adoption ⬯ 4; Adoption ⬯ 20

Best interest of the child test pertains to adoption process, not to legal effects of adoption on parental rights. In re Adoption of Doe (Ohio App. 9 Dist., 12-16-1998) 130 Ohio App.3d 288, 719 N.E.2d 1071, appeal not allowed 85 Ohio St.3d 1467, 709 N.E.2d 173, reconsideration denied 86 Ohio St.3d 1408, 711 N.E.2d 234. Adoption ⬯ 13; Adoption ⬯ 20

Adoption of child born out of wedlock by mother's spouse did not relieve child's biological father of support obligations incurred and unpaid prior to child's adoption, even though no support obligation was reduced to judgment prior to child's adoption

and child was emancipated at time she brought action for support; biological father's obligation commenced at child's birth and continued until her adoption, and child's right to pursue support for such time period was not extinguished by her adoption. Hudgins v. Mitchell (Ohio App. 9 Dist., 06-17-1998) 128 Ohio App.3d 403, 715 N.E.2d 213. Child Support ⬯ 33

Adoption terminates all legal relationships between adopted person and natural family, making adopted person stranger to former relatives. Sawyer v. Lebanon Citizens Natl. Bank (Ohio App. 12 Dist., 07-31-1995) 105 Ohio App.3d 464, 664 N.E.2d 571, dismissed, appeal not allowed 74 Ohio St.3d 1476, 657 N.E.2d 783. Adoption ⬯ 20

Mother was not entitled to writ of prohibition to prevent juvenile court judge from proceeding with father's parentage action, based on foreign adoption decree, since foreign adoption law did not require notice to father before adoption of child out-of-wedlock and therefore may not have been enforced under comity as being repugnant to state law, jurisdiction was not divested even if action was barred on res judicata grounds, and inadequacy of postjudgment appeal was not established. State ex rel. Smith v. Smith (Ohio, 04-10-1996) 75 Ohio St.3d 418, 662 N.E.2d 366, 1996-Ohio-215. Prohibition ⬯ 3(3); Prohibition ⬯ 10(2)

Putative paternal grandparents were not qualified to seek court-ordered right to visit their putative biological grandchild, until alleged paternity of grandchild was established by putative father filing legitimation petition or by paternity action to determine if putative father was father of child. In re Martin (Ohio, 02-09-1994) 68 Ohio St.3d 250, 626 N.E.2d 82. Children Out–of–wedlock ⬯ 20.4

Even if putative father was father of child, putative paternal grandparents were not entitled to court-ordered right to visit child who had been adopted by maternal grandparents, as statute which provides that adoption of child terminates all legal relationships between adopted child and his relatives does not distinguish between adoption by strangers and nonstrangers. In re Martin (Ohio, 02-09-1994) 68 Ohio St.3d 250, 626 N.E.2d 82. Children Out–of–wedlock ⬯ 20.9

The common law rule known as "stranger to the adoption" was abrogated as to wills, including trusts established by wills, as of the effective date of GC 8004–13, even though the doctrine remained viable as to trust instruments until the amendments to former RC 3107.13 effective in 1972. Central Trust Co. of Northern Ohio, N.A. v. Smith (Ohio 1990) 50 Ohio St.3d 133, 553 N.E.2d 265. Adoption ⬯ 3; Wills ⬯ 497(5); Wills ⬯ 682(1)

Given the absence of an expression by the general assembly to the contrary, RC 3107.15 shall be applied prospectively only, and subsequent to its effective date, January 1, 1977, to those documents, statutes, and instruments, whether executed before or after an adoption is decreed, which do not expressly exclude the adopted person from the laws' or instruments' operation and effect. Ohio Citizens Bank v. Mills (Ohio 1989) 45 Ohio St.3d 153, 543 N.E.2d 1206.

Following an adoption, RC 3107.15(A)(1) does not operate in a retroactive manner to relieve the payor spouse of all past due child support arrearages not reduced to judgment prior to adoption. Bercaw v. Bercaw (Ohio 1989) 45 Ohio St.3d 160, 543 N.E.2d 1197. Child Support ☞ 33

Where a final decree of adoption is vacated due to a defect in service, a prior order granting temporary custody to the adoptive parents remains in full force and effect precluding the need for a new temporary custody order; thus, a trial court errs in failing to dismiss a subsequent duplicative temporary custody petition. In re Knipper (Hamilton 1987) 39 Ohio App.3d 35, 528 N.E.2d 1319. Adoption ☞ 16

The "stranger to the adoption" doctrine is not a rule of construction which should be given effect. Cleveland Trust Co. v. Schumacher (Ohio Com.Pl. 1973) 35 Ohio Misc. 118, 298 N.E.2d 913, 64 O.O.2d 394.

A child adopted in a foreign state or country may take under local statutes of descent and distribution, if such foreign state or country had jurisdiction to fix his status with respect to his adoptive parents, but this rule of international comity is subject to the condition that the law, with regard to adoption, of the state in which the real and personal property is situated, does not differ essentially from the law of the state in which the adoption was had, so that local public policy is not violated by recognizing and giving effect to the adoption proceedings of the foreign state or country. National City Bank of Cleveland v. Judkins (Ohio Com.Pl. 1964) 8 Ohio Misc. 119, 219 N.E.2d 456, 37 O.O.2d 200. Adoption ☞ 25

3107.13 is constitutional. In re Millward's Estate (Ohio 1957) 166 Ohio St. 243, 141 N.E.2d 462, 2 O.O.2d 61.

GC 5334 (RC 5731.09), prescribing exemptions from succession taxes, and GC 5335 (RC 5731.12), prescribing rates of such taxes as applicable to certain categories of persons named therein, are not in pari materia with section, relating to the adoption of children and the inheritable rights of such children. In re Friedman's Estate (Ohio 1950) 154 Ohio St. 1, 93 N.E.2d 273, 42 O.O. 97.

2. Child's right to inherit—In general

Former RC 3107.13 provided that a legally adopted child, for all purposes under laws of this state, including laws and wills governing inheritance and succession, shall have the same status and rights as a natural born child of the adoptive parents. Central Trust Co. of Northern Ohio, N.A. v. Smith (Ohio 1990) 50 Ohio St.3d 133, 553 N.E.2d 265. Adoption ☞ 21; Wills ☞ 497(5)

Where a testator uses the term "heirs of the body" as a term of limitation in a class gift to exclude adopted beneficiaries, such term in the absence of contrary intent constitutes an express exclusion of adopted persons under RC 3107.15.

Tootle v. Tootle (Ohio 1986) 22 Ohio St.3d 244, 490 N.E.2d 878, 22 O.B.R. 420. Wills ☞ 506(5)

With respect to instruments executed after the effective date, in 1951, of the provisions of GC 8004–13 (RC 3107.13), children adopted by children of the testator are to be included in a class gift to his "grandchildren," in the absence of other language within the same instrument evidencing a contrary intent. Conkle v. Conkle (Coshocton 1972) 31 Ohio App.2d 44, 285 N.E.2d 883, 60 O.O.2d 144.

A child, surrendered by its parents into the permanent custody of an institution established for the purpose of aiding, caring for and placing children in homes, under a written agreement pursuant to RC 5103.15, which agreement provides that the institution may appear in any legal proceeding for the adoption of such child and consent to the child's adoption, continues as an heir of its parents, either natural or adoptive, until such time as the child has been legally adopted pursuant to RC Ch 3107. Maurer v. Becker (Ohio 1971) 26 Ohio St.2d 254, 271 N.E.2d 255, 55 O.O.2d 486. Adoption ☞ 21

A bequest to grandchildren of the testatrix should be construed to include the adopted children of a child of the testatrix, where the adoptions occurred between the time of the execution of the will and the death of the testatrix, she knew and approved of the adoptions, and, having the ability to change the will, the testatrix failed to do so. Weitzel v. Weitzel (Ohio Prob. 1968) 16 Ohio Misc. 105, 239 N.E.2d 263, 45 O.O.2d 55, 45 O.O.2d 83.

A child adopted in a foreign state or country may take under local statutes of descent and distribution, if such foreign state or country had jurisdiction to fix his status with respect to his adoptive parents, but this rule of international comity is subject to the condition that the law with regard to adoption of the state in which the real and personal property is situated, does not differ essentially from the law of the state in which the adoption was had, so that local public policy is not violated by recognizing and giving effect to the adoption proceedings of the foreign state or country. National City Bank of Cleveland v. Judkins (Ohio Com.Pl. 1964) 8 Ohio Misc. 119, 219 N.E.2d 456, 37 O.O.2d 200. Adoption ☞ 25

Where an adoptive parent has obtained a decree of adoption and taken the adopted child into his own home, his presumptive heirs, personal representatives, as well as himself, are estopped thereafter from asserting the adoption was invalid due to an irregularity in the adoption proceedings, which is not jurisdictional. National City Bank of Cleveland v. Judkins (Ohio Com.Pl. 1964) 8 Ohio Misc. 119, 219 N.E.2d 456, 37 O.O.2d 200. Adoption ☞ 14

A legally adopted child's right of inheritance is governed by the law in effect at the time of the parent's death and not by the law in effect at the time of the adoption. In re Millward's Estate (Ohio 1957) 166 Ohio St. 243, 141 N.E.2d 462, 2 O.O.2d 61. Adoption ☞ 3

Validity of an adoption proceeding cannot be collaterally attacked in a proceeding to determine heirship. Wachuta v. Wachuta (Ohio Com.Pl. 1954) 122 N.E.2d 677, 69 Ohio Law Abs. 324, 55 O.O. 293.

Where, in providing for his "heirs at law" after a life interest, a testator indicates his intention that such heirs should be determined at the date of the expiration of such life interest, then the statutory law in effect at the expiration of such life interest should be applied in determining such heirs of the testator unless by the provisions of the will or surrounding circumstances a contrary intention is indicated, even though such statutory law will permit an adopted child of the testator's daughter to take and the statutory law in effect at the testator's death would not have permitted such adopted child to take and even though such adopted child was not either born or adopted until long after the testator's death. Tiedtke v. Tiedtke (Ohio 1952) 157 Ohio St. 554, 106 N.E.2d 637, 47 O.O. 411. Wills ⊕ 506(5)

Where a testator bequeathed property to "each of my then living grandchildren, whether born prior or subsequent to my decease," there is a presumption, in the absence of any language in the will to the contrary, that the testator intended only the blood children of his children to partake of his bounty. Third Nat. Bank & Trust Co. v. Davidson (Ohio 1952) 157 Ohio St. 355, 105 N.E.2d 573, 47 O.O. 257.

An adopted child's right to inherit is governed by the statutes in force at the time of decedent's death and not those in force at the time he was adopted. Staley v. Honeyman (Miami 1950) 98 N.E.2d 429, 59 Ohio Law Abs. 203, affirmed 157 Ohio St. 61, 104 N.E.2d 172, 47 O.O. 67. Adoption ⊕ 3

In a proceeding to determine heirship in an administration of decedent's estate, where issue is validity of a judgment of adoption, an attack on such judgment on ground that court rendering it had no jurisdiction is a collateral attack, and in such case, where a complete record of adoption proceeding was made according to statute, original papers in the proceeding were not admissible in determination of heirship proceeding as a part of record of former proceeding, and such original papers could not be used to impeach record of adoption proceeding. In re Dickman's Estate (Mercer 1946) 81 Ohio App. 281, 79 N.E.2d 172, 37 O.O. 125.

An adopted child is entitled to the same rights as a child begotten in lawful wedlock, including the right to have a will revoked. Surman v. Surman (Ohio 1926) 114 Ohio St. 579, 151 N.E. 708, 4 Ohio Law Abs. 276, 24 Ohio Law Rep. 374. Adoption ⊕ 20; Wills ⊕ 229

Where granddaughter of testator was adopted by daughter of testator in New York, effect of such adoption obviously being governed by law of that state, right of inheritance is determinable by law in force at time of foster parents' death, and child had right of inheritance from foster parent, as she would under Ohio law, and she takes one-third of estate as granddaughter of testator and one-third as granddaughter through adoption of testator, to wit, adopted daughter of daughter of testator. Hollister v. Witherbee (Ohio Com.Pl. 1937) 2 Ohio Supp. 345, 24 Ohio Law Abs. 312, 9 O.O. 37.

Since GC 10503–18 (RC 2105.21) provides for disposition of estates of a husband and wife who died within three days of each other as though they had survived each other, their adopted child of the age of ten years would be entitled to a year's allowance and an allowance of property not deemed assets from the estate of each. Harrison v. Hillegas (Ohio Prob. 1939) 1 Ohio Supp. 160, 28 Ohio Law Abs. 404, 13 O.O. 523. Descent And Distribution ⊕ 52(1)

Adopted daughter held entitled to the share her deceased adopting parent would have inherited, the same as if she were a natural child of such parent. Shearer v Gasstman, 15 Abs 103 (Prob, Franklin 1933).

An adopted child inherits no interest in the estate of a relative of the adopting parent in which as a child of the blood he would be entitled to share. Hollencamp v Greulich, 27 NP(NS) 344 (1928).

In a suit to determine heirs for the purpose of distributing a decedent's estate under the laws of intestate succession, the doctrine of equitable adoption does not apply if there is no evidence of a purported contract or agreement to adopt, and the trial court's order of escheat to the state was proper. Boulger v Unknown Heirs of Robertson, No. 951 (4th Dist Ct App, Ross, 7–1–83).

3. —— As issue or lineal descendant, child's right to inherit

Adoption of grandchild by stepmother terminated relationship between grandchild and grandparents and relationship between great grandchildren and grandparents, and thus grandchild and great grandchildren could not maintain wrongful death beneficiary claims following death of grandparents in automobile accident. Turvey v. Ocheltree (Ohio App. 5 Dist., Tuscarawas, 07-29-2005) No. 2005 AP 01 0002, 2005-Ohio-4114, 2005 WL 1897848, Unreported, appeal not allowed 107 Ohio St.3d 1683, 839 N.E.2d 404, 2005-Ohio-6480. Death ⊕ 31(8)

Adopted daughter cannot participate in distribution of an estate where testator limited estate to brother's "issue." Reinhard v. Reinhard (Franklin 1936) 23 Ohio Law Abs. 306.

Order of adoption creates parent-child relationship for all purposes, including inheritances, regardless of date of instrument under which gifts are given; effects of adoption apply retroactively to any instrument which does not expressly exclude adopted person. Fifth Third Bank v. Crosley (Ohio Com.Pl., 06-21-1996) 79 Ohio Misc.2d 10, 669 N.E.2d 904, affirmed 1997 WL 770159. Adoption ⊕ 20; Adoption ⊕ 21; Adoption ⊕ 22

Terms such as child, children, grandchild, heirs of body, issue, or heirs appearing in will or trust exclude adopted child, absent contrary intention

within instrument itself. Fifth Third Bank v. Crosley (Ohio Com.Pl., 06-21-1996) 79 Ohio Misc.2d 10,
669 N.E.2d 904, affirmed 1997 WL 770159. Trusts
☞ 124; Wills ☞ 497(5); Wills ☞ 498

Class gifts to "only lawful issue of blood of
Trustor" unambiguously excluded adopted children
from class of beneficiaries. Fifth Third Bank v.
Crosley (Ohio Com.Pl., 06-21-1996) 79 Ohio
Misc.2d 10, 669 N.E.2d 904, affirmed 1997 WL
770159. Trusts ☞ 124

Class gift to settlor's "lawful issue... includ[ing]
children, grandchildren and more remote descendants" included settlor's adopted grandchildren;
there was no express prohibition against adoptees
being included in class of beneficiaries. Fifth Third
Bank v. Crosley (Ohio Com.Pl., 06 21 1996) 79
Ohio Misc.2d 10, 669 N.E.2d 904, affirmed 1997
WL 770159. Trusts ☞ 124

Adopted children of testator's son were "issue"
of testator, entitled to share in class gift to "each of
my (testator's) issue per stirpes" upon termination
of testamentary trust. Fifth Third Bank v. Crosley
(Ohio Com.Pl., 06-21-1996) 79 Ohio Misc.2d 10,
669 N.E.2d 904, affirmed 1997 WL 770159. Wills
☞ 682(1)

When a settlor established a trust in 1924 which,
by subsequent modification in 1933, left property to
the "lawful issue" of his son or their "surviving
heirs of the body," the settlor's intent was to limit
devolution of his property to blood relatives, even
though two children adopted by the settlor's son
after the settlor's death were thereby excluded, and
under such facts, the 1932 adoption statute does
not create a presumption of inclusion for adopted
children even though no affirmative statement of
exclusion is embodied in the trust instrument; and
an adopted child is deemed to be excluded from a
class of beneficiaries under a trust where the settlor
was a stranger to the adoption and had not otherwise manifested an intent to include adopted children. National City Bank of Cleveland v. Mitchell
(Cuyahoga 1968) 13 Ohio App.2d 141, 234 N.E.2d
916, 42 O.O.2d 262. Trusts ☞ 124

A testamentary provision for "lineal descendants
of my blood" furnishes "other clear identification,"
as required by RC 3107.13(B), of the children of
testator's predeceased son, without naming them,
so as to enable them to succeed to a designated
portion of testator's estate, although such children
were previously adopted by nonrelatives. Saintignon v. Saintignon (Darke 1966) 5 Ohio App.2d 133,
214 N.E.2d 124, 34 O.O.2d 243.

RC 3107.13 enables adopted children to inherit
through an adopting parent, and one who can
inherit through another is a lineal descendant of
the testator, even though adopted. Schneider v.
Dorr (Ohio Prob. 1965) 3 Ohio Misc. 103, 210
N.E.2d 311, 32 O.O.2d 391.

Where a testator who died in 1925 provided for a
life estate for his children with a remainder to their
"living issue," and said testator's son died in 1952, a
child of said son adopted in 1912 was included
within the meaning of "living issue." Cook v.

Crabill (Greene 1959) 110 Ohio App. 45, 164
N.E.2d 425, 82 Ohio Law Abs. 164, 12 O.O.2d 220.

Where a devise is made to a devisee with a
provision that in the event of his death leaving
issue, his issue shall take his share, an adopted child
may take as such "issue." Graves v. Graves (Ohio
Prob. 1956) 155 N.E.2d 540, 79 Ohio Law Abs. 262.

Where testator's only lineal descendant was his
granddaughter, who had been adopted by her stepfather who had married the testator's daughter-in-
law after the death of the testator's son, the testator
died without issue or the lineal descendant of issue,
and charitable bequests executed within a year of
testator's death are valid. Campbell v. Musart Soc.
of Cleveland Museum of Art (Ohio Prob. 1956) 131
N.E.2d 279, 72 Ohio Law Abs. 46, 2 O.O.2d 517.

The succession of an adopted child of a child of a
decedent in the estate of the latter is not taxable
under the provisions of RC 5731.09 and 5731.12 as
passing to a person as a lineal descendant of such
decedent. In re Friedman's Estate (Ohio 1950)
154 Ohio St. 1, 93 N.E.2d 273, 42 O.O. 97.

**4. ——— From and through natural parent, child's
right to inherit**

Introduction of evidence that patient's minor
daughter was adopted by her stepfather after patient's death was prejudicial error in patient's estate's medical malpractice action, as status of
daughter was fixed at time of patient's death, before his daughter's adoption, and child's statutory
rights derived from and through patient were not
restricted by child's subsequent adoption. Ulmer v.
Ackerman (Allen 1993) 87 Ohio App.3d 137, 621
N.E.2d 1315, dismissed, jurisdictional motion overruled 67 Ohio St.3d 1434, 617 N.E.2d 685. Appeal
And Error ☞ 1050.1(6); Death ☞ 60

A child who becomes vested in interest, but not
in possession, of an expectant estate in land limited
to the "heirs of the body" as a natural descendant
and survivor of the grantee of an estate in fee tail
prior to his adoption by others does not have his
right as the vested owner of such expectant estate
cut off by reason of the adoption statute. Eisenmann v. Eisenmann (Ohio Com.Pl. 1976) 52 Ohio
Misc. 119, 370 N.E.2d 788, 6 O.O.3d 449. Adoption ☞ 20

Under RC 3107.13 a child adopted by his stepfather before his natural father's death may inherit
through his natural father from estate of the latter's
mother. First Nat. Bank of East Liverpool v. Col-
lar (Ohio Com.Pl. 1971) 27 Ohio Misc. 88, 272
N.E.2d 916, 56 O.O.2d 302. Adoption ☞ 21

A child, surrendered by its parents into the permanent custody of an institution established for the
purpose of aiding, caring for and placing children in
homes, under a written agreement pursuant to RC
5103.15, which agreement provides that the institution may appear in any legal proceeding for the
adoption of such child and consent to the child's
adoption, continues as an heir of its parents, either
natural or adoptive, until such time as the child has
been legally adopted pursuant to RC Ch 3107.

Maurer v. Becker (Ohio 1971) 26 Ohio St.2d 254, 271 N.E.2d 255, 55 O.O.2d 486. Adoption ☞ 21

RC 3107.13, although generally denying adopted child legal status of child of his natural parents, expressly prevents debarring of such child from taking under will of natural parent, when he is identified by name or otherwise clearly identified as intended beneficiary. Seeley v. Bedillion (Ohio Com.Pl. 1969) 23 Ohio Misc. 4, 260 N.E.2d 639, 51 O.O.2d 128, 52 O.O.2d 14.

The provisions of RC 3107.13 preclude an adopted child, who has again been adopted subsequent to the deaths of the first adopting parents and prior to the death of an ancestor of a first adopting parent, from inheriting under the statute of descent and distribution through the first adopting parent from the first adopting parent's ancestor who died subsequent to the second adoption. Evans v. Freter (Tuscarawas 1969) 20 Ohio App.2d 8, 251 N.E.2d 513, 49 O.O.2d 4.

Under the provisions of former RC 3107.13, for the purpose of inheritance to, through, and from a legally adopted child, such child shall be treated the same as if he were the natural child of his adopting parents, and shall cease to be treated as the child of his natural parents for the purposes of intestate succession; such child's right of inheritance is governed by the law in effect at the time of the parent's death and not by the law in effect at the time of the adoption. In re Millward's Estate (Ohio 1957) 166 Ohio St. 243, 141 N.E.2d 462, 2 O.O.2d 61. Adoption ☞ 2; Statutes ☞ 278.31

A legally adopted child may not inherit from an intestate natural parent. In re Millward's Estate (Ohio 1957) 166 Ohio St. 243, 141 N.E.2d 462, 2 O.O.2d 61. Adoption ☞ 21

An adopted child cannot take under the statute of descent and distribution from a parent of his natural parent. Frantz v. Florence (Ohio Com.Pl. 1954) 131 N.E.2d 630, 72 Ohio Law Abs. 222.

Where testator's only lineal descendant was his granddaughter, who had been adopted by her stepfather who had married the testator's daughter-in-law after the death of the testator's son, the testator died without issue or the lineal descendant of issue, and charitable bequests executed within a year of testator's death are valid. Campbell v. Musart Soc. of Cleveland Museum of Art (Ohio Prob. 1956) 131 N.E.2d 279, 72 Ohio Law Abs. 46, 2 O.O.2d 517.

An adopted child may inherit collaterally through his adoptive parent as well as from such parent. Staley v. Honeyman (Miami 1950) 98 N.E.2d 429, 59 Ohio Law Abs. 203, affirmed 157 Ohio St. 61, 104 N.E.2d 172, 47 O.O. 67. Adoption ☞ 21

By terms of statute reciting that adopted child shall be capable of inheriting property expressly limited by will or by operation of law to child, heir or next of kin of adopting parent, adopted child was enabled to inherit property through as well as from his adopting parent whether property passed by will or by operation of law. Flynn v. Bredbeck (Ohio 1946) 147 Ohio St. 49, 68 N.E.2d 75, 33 O.O. 243. Adoption ☞ 21

An adopted child is entitled to inherit not only from adopting parent, but also through such parent from a deceased sister of the adopting parent. White v. Meyer (Cuyahoga 1940) 66 Ohio App. 549, 37 N.E.2d 546, 33 Ohio Law Abs. 151, 21 O.O. 38.

Foster children can inherit from their foster parents, but they cannot inherit through them; and, where a man dies intestate, leaving no wife or children, the foster children of his deceased sister are not entitled to share in his estate. Pickering v. Koesling (Cuyahoga 1928) 30 Ohio App. 201, 164 N.E. 537, 6 Ohio Law Abs. 507, 27 Ohio Law Rep. 18.

Where children of a deceased mother have been adopted by their natural grandparents and one of the grandparents dies, such children cannot inherit from their grandmother and adopted mother in a two-fold capacity but take only as children of the adopting grandmother, because in such a situation the smaller interest receivable by them will be merged in the larger, so that the most they can receive is the larger of the two interests. Paul v. Paul (Ohio Prob. 1940) 2 Ohio Supp. 349, 31 Ohio Law Abs. 453, 17 O.O. 392. Adoption ☞ 21

By the terms of RC 3107.15, if a parent of a child dies without the relationship of parent and child having been previously terminated, and a spouse of the living parent thereafter adopts the child, the child's rights through the deceased parent to survivor's benefits under RC Ch 145 are not restricted or curtailed by the adoption, notwithstanding RC 145.45(B)(4). OAG 79–079.

5. —— Trusts, child's right to inherit

Statute providing that in order for a testator's or settlor's transfer to "lineal descendants" to be effective with respect to a person adopted as an adult, the instrument must expressly include the adopted person by name or must expressly state that it includes a person who is adopted as an adult, was substantive rather than remedial, and thus, statute violated Ohio Constitution's prohibition of retroactive statutes, as applied to a testamentary trust executed before enactment of statute, which trust did not expressly include by name the son that, as an adult, was adopted by testator's grandson, nor did it expressly state that it included a person adopted as an adult; statute limited testator's right under Ohio Constitution to create a testamentary trust as a means of protecting property. Bank One Trust Co. N.A. v. Reynolds (Ohio App. 2 Dist., 08-17-2007) 173 Ohio App.3d 1, 877 N.E.2d 342, 2007-Ohio-4197. Statutes ☞ 278.31; Wills ☞ 3

Adult children adopted by son of grantor of irrevocable trust were not entitled to partake in the distribution of grantor's trust estate; statutes in effect when trust agreement was signed did not permit the legal adoption of adults and only permitted the adoption of persons under the age of 21, the adults adopted by son of grantor were 32 and 54 years old when they were adopted, and state in which son adopted adult children did not allow the adoption of adults when grantor signed trust agreement. Fifth Third Bank v. Harris (Ohio Prob., 06-24-2003) 127 Ohio Misc.2d 1, 804 N.E.2d 1044, 2003-Ohio-7361. Trusts ☞ 124

Irrevocable trust for benefit of minor children created with proceeds from wrongful death of their natural mother did not terminate on subsequent adoption of children; interests of children in trust vested when shares of all beneficiaries were adjusted in wrongful death proceeding and children were proper beneficiaries. Sawyer v. Lebanon Citizens Natl. Bank (Ohio App. 12 Dist., 07-31-1995) 105 Ohio App.3d 464, 664 N.E.2d 571, dismissed, appeal not allowed 74 Ohio St.3d 1476, 657 N.E.2d 783. Adoption ☞ 20; Trusts ☞ 61(1)

An adopted grandchild is entitled to share in a trust as a beneficiary where the grandchild is adopted after the death of the settlor but before the eldest biological grandchild reaches the age of thirty, the time at which the trustee is directed to begin payments from the trust corpus and the time at which the class of beneficiaries closes. Bank One, Youngstown, N.A. v. Heltzel (Trumbull 1991) 76 Ohio App.3d 524, 602 N.E.2d 412, motion overruled 63 Ohio St.3d 1458, 590 N.E.2d 753.

A testator who creates a trust that provides for termination at the death of a life beneficiary and distribution of trust assets to the "then living children" of the beneficiary is presumed to know that the legislative definition of children will be determined at the time the class closes and that the definition may include adult adoptees even though adult adoptions were not authorized at the time the trust was created. Solomon v. Central Trust Co. of Northeastern Ohio, N.A. (Ohio 1992) 63 Ohio St.3d 35, 584 N.E.2d 1185. Evidence ☞ 65

Where there is no specific language in a trust provision of a will prohibiting an adopted child from taking under the trust, a child adopted by a trust beneficiary, after the testator's death, may take under the term of the instrument as a member of the class of "then living children" of the beneficiary, even though the adoptee was an adult at the time of his adoption. Solomon v. Central Trust Co. of Northeastern Ohio, N.A. (Ohio 1992) 63 Ohio St.3d 35, 584 N.E.2d 1185. Wills ☞ 682(1)

Repeal of "stranger to the adoption" doctrine in RC 3107.13 applied to trust modified after its effective date. Cleveland Trust Co. v. Schumacher (Ohio Com.Pl. 1973) 35 Ohio Misc. 118, 298 N.E.2d 913, 64 O.O.2d 394.

Provisions of RC 3107.13, as in effect since 1951, which establish rights of adopted children to inherit, do not create presumption that settlor of inter vivos trust created in 1930 intended to include adopted child as beneficiary where settlor is stranger to adoption proceedings and did not otherwise express intention to include adopted children. Central Trust Co. v. Bovey (Ohio 1971) 25 Ohio St.2d 187, 267 N.E.2d 427, 54 O.O.2d 297.

The intention of settlor of an inter vivos trust created in 1930, in providing gift of portion of corpus of trust to "child or children... surviving the daughter then dying," should be determined in light of law existing at time of creation of the trust; an adopted child will not be deemed to be "child... surviving the daughter..." of settlor where, under law of intestacy at time of creation of trust applicable by analogy, term "child" included only blood relatives. Central Trust Co. v. Bovey (Ohio 1971) 25 Ohio St.2d 187, 267 N.E.2d 427, 54 O.O.2d 297.

When a settlor established a trust in 1924 which, by subsequent modification in 1933, left property to the "lawful issue" of his son or their "surviving heirs of the body," the settlor's intent was to limit devolution of his property to blood relatives, even though two children adopted by the settlor's son after the settlor's death were thereby excluded, and under such facts, the 1932 adoption statute does not create a presumption of inclusion for adopted children even though no affirmative statement of exclusion is embodied in the trust instrument; and an adopted child is deemed to be excluded from a class of beneficiaries under a trust where the settlor was a stranger to the adoption and had not otherwise manifested an intent to include adopted children. National City Bank of Cleveland v. Mitchell (Cuyahoga 1968) 13 Ohio App.2d 141, 234 N.E.2d 916, 42 O.O.2d 262. Trusts ☞ 124

Where it was determined in action to construe will that upon the death of a life tenant leaving no surviving children, the principal and income should be divided among the testator's heirs, and the life tenant died leaving an adopted child surviving, such adopted child takes the corpus of the trust. Tiedtke v. Tiedtke (Lucas 1951) 91 Ohio App. 442, 108 N.E.2d 578, 49 O.O. 36, appeal denied 156 Ohio St. 187, 101 N.E.2d 500, 46 O.O. 58, affirmed 157 Ohio St. 554, 106 N.E.2d 637, 47 O.O. 411.

Rights of adopted children to take under trust deed antedating adoption were fixed by statute in effect when they were adopted, not statute as subsequently amended. Rodgers v. Miller (Franklin 1932) 43 Ohio App. 198, 182 N.E. 654, 12 Ohio Law Abs. 23, 36 Ohio Law Rep. 310. Adoption ☞ 3; Trusts ☞ 124

Under trust deed, adopted children of settlor's deceased son held not entitled to take as "children" or "issue" of settlor's deceased child. Rodgers v. Miller (Franklin 1932) 43 Ohio App. 198, 182 N.E. 654, 12 Ohio Law Abs. 23, 36 Ohio Law Rep. 310. Trusts ☞ 124

6. Death of adopted child

An adoption terminates any right of the relatives of the natural mother to inherit from the adopted child, and where the adopting parent is deceased, the heirs of such adopting parent will take. (See also Vodrey v Quigley, 74 Abs 29, 139 NE(2d) 108 (Prob, Columbiana 1956).) Vodrey v. Quigley (Columbiana 1956) 143 N.E.2d 162, 75 Ohio Law Abs. 65.

Where a child has been validly adopted, a blood relative is deprived of all rights of intestate succession, regardless of whether the natural parents were alive at the time of such adoption. Vodrey v. Quigley (Ohio Prob. 1956) 139 N.E.2d 108, 74 Ohio

Law Abs. 29, affirmed 143 N.E.2d 162, 75 Ohio Law Abs. 65.

Where adopted child dies intestate, leaving no spouse or issue, his property passes to his blood kin and not to his kin by adoption, even though such property was inherited by the adopted child from his adopting mother and brother by adoption and is identifiable as identical. National Bank of Lima v. Hancock (Allen 1948) 85 Ohio App. 1, 88 N.E.2d 67, 40 O.O. 30.

Although the adopted child of a childless couple dies before the adopting parents, if it leaves issue the issue or its devisee inherits to the exclusion of collaterals. The primary purpose of GC 8029 and 8030 (Repealed) being to make the child the same as a natural child, unless it dies first without issue. Kroff v. Amrhein (Ohio 1916) 94 Ohio St. 282, 114 N.E. 267, 14 Ohio Law Rep. 204.

Where adopted child dies before his adopting parent, the issue of the adopted child inherits from the adopting parent. Kroff v. Amrhein (Ohio 1916) 94 Ohio St. 282, 114 N.E. 267, 14 Ohio Law Rep. 204.

7. Rights of adopting parents

Where an adoptive parent has obtained a decree of adoption and taken the adopted child into his own home, his presumptive heirs, personal representatives, as well as himself, are estopped thereafter from asserting the adoption was invalid due to an irregularity in the adoption proceedings, which is not jurisdictional. National City Bank of Cleveland v. Judkins (Ohio Com.Pl. 1964) 8 Ohio Misc. 119, 219 N.E.2d 456, 37 O.O.2d 200. Adoption ☞ 14

The natural mother and adoptive father of a decedent are entitled to share equally in his estate. Mancino v. Smith (Ohio Prob. 1964) 201 N.E.2d 93, 95 Ohio Law Abs. 51, 30 O.O.2d 282.

That an adopting parent perpetrated a fraud by adopting a child, and then using such child's estate for its support, even if true, would not invalidate the adoption or change the application of the laws of descent and distribution. Vodrey v. Quigley (Ohio Prob. 1956) 139 N.E.2d 108, 74 Ohio Law Abs. 29, affirmed 143 N.E.2d 162, 75 Ohio Law Abs. 65. Adoption ☞ 14; Adoption ☞ 23

Since a presumption of law arises from a decree of adoption that all provisions of law relating thereto have been complied with and such exists until overcome by proof to the contrary adopting parents are entitled to custody of their adopted child, to the exclusion of all other persons, until some lawful reason for a change in the child's custody is made to appear by competent evidence. Martin v. Fisher (Mercer 1927) 25 Ohio App. 372, 158 N.E. 287, 5 Ohio Law Abs. 596.

Adopting parents allowed to recover for the wrongful death of adopted child. Ransom v. New York, C. & St. L.R. Co. (Ohio 1915) 93 Ohio St. 223, 112 N.E. 586, 13 Ohio Law Rep. 514, 13 Ohio Law Rep. 566.

8. Visitation

Juvenile court was required to afford to aunt, who had been found in contempt for violating terms of its visitation order, option to purge herself of contempt; precedent made clear that law required court to provide aunt option to purge herself of contempt, and choice presented to aunt was consistent with need to compel obedience to court order, was necessary to remedy aunt's actions, and was generally appropriate under facts of case. In re Stevenson (Ohio App. 3 Dist., Mercer, 02-13-2006) No. 10-05-17, 2006-Ohio-607, 2006 WL 319240, Unreported, appeal not allowed 109 Ohio St.3d 1508, 849 N.E.2d 1028, 2006-Ohio-2998. Child Custody ☞ 854

Aunt's adoption of child did not divest juvenile court of jurisdiction to continue with proceeding in which aunt was found in contempt for violating terms of visitation order; court issued judgment entry granting brother right to visit child months before probate court entered its final decree of adoption, and aunt violated terms of visitation schedule, and brother initiated contempt proceeding, well before probate court granted adoption, and thus, since all events leading to contempt proceeding occurred before adoption ever transpired, fact that juvenile court did not find aunt in contempt until after adoption was inconsequential. In re Stevenson (Ohio App. 3 Dist., Mercer, 02-13-2006) No. 10-05-17, 2006-Ohio-607, 2006 WL 319240, Unreported, appeal not allowed 109 Ohio St.3d 1508, 849 N.E.2d 1028, 2006-Ohio-2998. Adoption ☞ 21; Child Custody ☞ 855

Juvenile court's finding, in proceeding brought by paternal grandmother and paternal aunt for visitation with children following death of children's father, that mother and father were never married did not require reversal of juvenile court's denial of visitation, even though mother stated in her affidavit that she was married to children's father, and magistrate had found mother and father were married, where father's paternity was not disputed, his paternal rights had never been terminated prior to his death, and finding of marriage was not germane to ultimate issue of whether statutes on visitation by persons other than parents applied retroactively. In re Busdiecker (Ohio App. 12 Dist., Warren, 05-19-2003) No. CA2002-10-104, 2003-Ohio-2556, 2003 WL 21135496, Unreported. Child Custody ☞ 922(6)

The legislature has not provided the juvenile court with the authority to grant visitation rights to biological grandparents following an adoption of a grandchild by a stepparent even where the parental rights of the grandparents' child have been terminated through death. Matter of Apple (Ohio App. 2 Dist., Miami, 09-21-1994) No. 93-VA-59, 1994 WL 515116, Unreported.

Statute providing that effect of an adoption was to terminate all legal relationships between the adopted child and adopted child's relatives barred juvenile court, after child's adoption, from continuing its prior order of visitation in favor of adoptive mother's former husband, pursuant to statute governing visitation rights to "any other person other than a parent" after a divorce; adoption statute sought to transform the child's collection of relationships and, in effect, give the child a new identity. In re L.H. (Ohio App. 2 Dist., 06-19-2009) 183 Ohio App.3d 505, 917 N.E.2d 829, 2009-Ohio-3046. Child Custody ☞ 182

Trial court lacked jurisdiction to grant post-adoption visitation rights to child's biological, paternal grandmother, though she had been previously granted visitation rights and the court pointed out that it would be in best interests of the child to continue the visitation, given that the parental rights of child's biological father were terminated and child was adopted by her step-father. In re Adoption of Hilliard (Ohio App. 3 Dist., 08-25-2003) 154 Ohio App.3d 54, 796 N.E.2d 46, 2003-Ohio-4471. Child Custody ☞ 313

Trial court lacked authority to grant paternal grandparents visitation with children of divorced parents after the children were adopted by their stepfather subsequent to their father's death; while a statute preserved the right of grandparent visitation when a surviving spouse remarried, it did not provide for the preservation of visitation rights after an adoption by a stepparent. Foor v. Foor (Ohio App. 12 Dist., 04-26-1999) 133 Ohio App.3d 250, 727 N.E.2d 618. Child Custody ☞ 313

A trial court has no authority to grant grandparents' visitation rights following a stepparent adoption. Foor v. Foor (Ohio App. 12 Dist., 04-26-1999) 133 Ohio App.3d 250, 727 N.E.2d 618.

Biological father's allegations, that appeal was not complete, beneficial, and speedy, and thus was not adequate remedy to prevent Court of Common Pleas from granting visitation to biological mother following issuance of adoption decree that terminated her parental rights, and that irreparable harm to child and to relationship between biological father would result should visitation proceedings not be stopped, stated cause of action in complaint seeking writ of prohibition. State ex rel. Kaylor v. Bruening (Ohio, 10-22-1997) 80 Ohio St.3d 142, 684 N.E.2d 1228, 1997-Ohio-350. Prohibition ☞ 20

Although Court of Common Pleas had basic statutory jurisdiction to grant visitation to biological parent, it was patently and unambiguously divested by adoption statute of jurisdiction to proceed on biological mother's motions relating to visitation following adoption decree terminating her parental rights, and writ of prohibition preventing Court from doing so thus was appropriate. State ex rel. Kaylor v. Bruening (Ohio, 10-22-1997) 80 Ohio St.3d 142, 684 N.E.2d 1228, 1997-Ohio-350. Child Custody ☞ 312; Prohibition ☞ 10(2)

Relatives of parents whose parental rights are terminated have no standing to assert visitation rights. Farley v. Farley (Licking 1992) 85 Ohio App.3d 113, 619 N.E.2d 427. Child Custody ☞ 409

Juvenile court does not have authority to grant paternal grandparents visitation rights with grandchild after grandchild has been adopted by stepfather. Krnac v. Starman (Medina 1992) 83 Ohio App.3d 578, 615 N.E.2d 344, dismissed, jurisdictional motion overruled 66 Ohio St.3d 1485, 612 N.E.2d 1241. Child Custody ☞ 313

A domestic relations court which granted a divorce retains jurisdiction for the purposes of granting visitation rights as required by the best interest of any children born as issue of the marriage regardless of the existence or venue of a subsequent stepparent adoption proceeding. Bente v. Hill (Clermont 1991) 73 Ohio App.3d 151, 596 N.E.2d 1042, dismissed, jurisdictional motion overruled 62 Ohio St.3d 1422, 577 N.E.2d 1105. Child Custody ☞ 313; Child Custody ☞ 404; Divorce ☞ 154

Even if juvenile court had authority to set postadoption terms and conditions in granting permanent custody of children to county children services board, it could not require that visitation by biological grandparents continue following adoption of children by stranger. In re Adoption of Ridenour (Ohio 1991) 61 Ohio St.3d 319, 574 N.E.2d 1055. Infants ☞ 230.1

Maternal grandparents could be granted visitation with their grandchildren where grandchildren were adopted by paternal grandmother and her husband; court was permitted to grant visitation on case by case basis, considering all relevant facts and taking best interests of children as guiding principle. In re Pennington (Scioto 1988) 55 Ohio App.3d 99, 562 N.E.2d 905. Child Custody ☞ 313

Where a child's parent dies, the surviving parent remarries, and the surviving parent's new spouse adopts the child, a court may grant visitation rights to relatives of the deceased parent pursuant to RC 3109.11 over the objections of the child's parents, notwithstanding RC 3107.15. In re Thornton (Franklin 1985) 24 Ohio App.3d 152, 493 N.E.2d 977, 24 O.B.R. 241.

RC 3107.15 does not prohibit an order pursuant to RC 3109.05, granting visitation rights to a biological paternal grandparent after adoption of a child by a stepfather, when the biological father's whereabouts are unknown. Welsh v. Laffey (Butler 1984) 16 Ohio App.3d 110, 474 N.E.2d 681, 16 O.B.R. 117.

The power of the court to order visitation and companionship rights to relatives under RC 3109.11 is not divested or terminated by the adoption of the child of a deceased parent by a stepparent, pursuant to RC 3107.13, and such adoption is merely a factor which the court must consider in determining the best interest of the child under RC 3109.11. Graziano v. Davis (Mahoning 1976) 50 Ohio App.2d 83, 361 N.E.2d 525, 4 O.O.3d 55.

3107.16 Appeals; finality of decree

(A) Appeals from the probate court are subject to the Rules of Appellate Procedure and, to the extent not in conflict with those rules, Chapter 2505. of the Revised Code. Unless there is good cause for delay, appeals shall be heard on an expedited basis.

(B) Subject to the disposition of an appeal, upon the expiration of one year after an adoption decree is issued, the decree cannot be questioned by any person, including the petitioner, in any manner or upon any ground, including fraud, misrepresentation, failure to give any required notice, or lack of jurisdiction of the parties or of the subject matter, unless, in the case of the adoption of a minor, the petitioner has not taken custody of the minor, or, in the case of the adoption of a minor by a stepparent, the adoption would not have been granted but for fraud perpetrated by the petitioner or the petitioner's spouse, or, in the case of the adoption of an adult, the adult had no knowledge of the decree within the one-year period.

(1996 H 419, eff. 9–18–96; 1986 H 412, eff. 3–17–87; 1976 H 156)

Historical and Statutory Notes

Amendment Note: 1996 H 419 added the second sentence to division (A).

Library References

Adoption ☞14 to 16.
Westlaw Topic No. 17.
C.J.S. Adoption of Persons §§ 103 to 135, 140.

Research References

Encyclopedias

OH Jur. 3d Family Law § 934, Collateral Attack on Adoption--Time Limit on Attack.

Forms

Ohio Forms Legal and Business § 28:36, Promise to Adopt.
Ohio Jurisprudence Pleading and Practice Forms § 96:31, Appealability.
Ohio Jurisprudence Pleading and Practice Forms § 96:44, Independent Placement of Children.
Ohio Jurisprudence Pleading and Practice Forms § 96:48, Acknowledgment of Natural Parent.

Treatises and Practice Aids

Carlin, Baldwin's Ohio Prac. Merrick-Rippner Probate Law § 99:30, Statutorily Required Consent.
Carlin, Baldwin's Ohio Prac. Merrick-Rippner Probate Law § 99:31, Parties Giving Consent--Biological Parents.
Carlin, Baldwin's Ohio Prac. Merrick-Rippner Probate Law § 99:36, Method of Giving Consent.
Carlin, Baldwin's Ohio Prac. Merrick-Rippner Probate Law § 99:37, Withdrawal of Consent.
Carlin, Baldwin's Ohio Prac. Merrick-Rippner Probate Law § 99:51, Attacking Adoption Orders--Appeal.

Notes of Decisions

Challenge of decree 3
Constitutional issues 1
Fraud 4
Habeas corpus 2
Paternity 5

_____

1. Constitutional issues

One-year limitations period governing motion to vacate adoption order was not unconstitutional as applied to mother who claimed that she was not given notice of petition for adoption filed by father's wife and that her whereabouts were allegedly reasonably ascertainable, where mother learned of adoption less than seven months after it was finalized but waited more than four years to file motion, and mother admitted that she underwent name change but she failed to report her name change to Child Support Enforcement Agency. In re Adoption of A.C. (Ohio App. 8 Dist., Cuyahoga, 04-14-2011) No. 95612, 2011-Ohio-1809, 2011 WL 1419640, Unreported. Adoption ☞ 3; Adoption ☞ 16

Father would not have prevailed in setting aside adoption if he had been named, and thus, denial of his motion for relief from adoption order was not an abuse of discretion, although mother purposefully failed to provide Probate Court with father's name and address when her husband sought to adopt child, where father became aware of the fraud five to six years prior to his attempt to set aside adoption, at that time he agreed to limit his involvement to visitation only, and it could not be said that father would have reacted any differently when the adoption was granted. In re McCandlish (Ohio App. 5 Dist., Fairfield, 12-16-2002) No. 02CA71, 2002-Ohio-6979, 2002 WL 31819640, Unreported. Adoption ☞ 16

Father's failure to raise at trial court level the issue of constitutionality of statute governing appeals from adoption decrees and finality of such decrees constituted a waiver of that issue on appeal. In re McCandlish (Ohio App. 5 Dist., Fairfield, 12-16-2002) No. 02CA71, 2002-Ohio-6979, 2002 WL 31819640, Unreported. Adoption ☞ 15

Statute providing that decrees of adoption are uncontestable after one year was not unconstitutional as applied to biological mother, where mother freely and knowingly signed adoption consent form which contained waiver of notice of hearing on petition for adoption, mother had actual notice of adoption proceedings, and mother had adequate posttermination opportunity to contest adoption placement, since she learned of adoption decree at least one month before expiration of one year period. In re Rabatin (Geauga 1992) 83 Ohio App.3d 836, 615 N.E.2d 1099. Adoption ☞ 2

RC 3107.16(B) is unconstitutional insofar as it bars a biological parent from attacking a decree of adoption more than one year after it is issued, where the adopting parents failed to use reasonable diligence in their efforts to locate the biological parent's address. In re Adoption of Knipper (Hamilton 1986) 30 Ohio App.3d 214, 507 N.E.2d 436, 30 O.B.R. 371.

Adoption, jurisdiction of Supreme Court, review of state court's interpretation of state law. O'Connell v. Kirchner (U.S.Ill. 1995) 115 S.Ct. 891, 513 U.S. 1303, 130 L.Ed.2d 873.

Adoption, federal due process rights of adoptive parents and child, habeas corpus ordering surrender of custody. O'Connell v. Kirchner (U.S.Ill. 1995) 115 S.Ct. 891, 513 U.S. 1303, 130 L.Ed.2d 873.

2. Habeas corpus

Where a natural mother alleges that she has been unlawfully deprived of her child upon signing a permanent surrender agreement, pursuant to RC 5103.15, in response to undue pressure, a writ of habeas corpus seeking the return of the child is proper where an informal request for the vacation of a court entry consenting to the permanent surrender agreement has been denied rendering a formal motion for vacation futile, and the appeal process from a formal denial is an inadequate remedy at law where an expeditious resolution is required to challenge a possible adoption and a speedy permanent placement of the child is sought. Marich v. Knox County Dept. of Human Services/Children Services Unit (Ohio 1989) 45 Ohio St.3d 163, 543 N.E.2d 776, rehearing denied 45 Ohio St.3d 715, 545 N.E.2d 909.

Where the natural parent of minor children was not represented by counsel during neglect, dependency and temporary custody proceedings but was represented by counsel at the parental rights termination and permanent custody proceedings, such parent is barred from bringing a habeas corpus action more than one year after the final decrees of adoption were issued for the minor children. Beard v Williams County Dept of Social Services,

No. WMS–83–3 (6th Dist Ct App, Williams, 7–15–83).

3. Challenge of decree

Adjudicated father failed to show that juvenile court's judgment awarding child support to mother should be reversed, and that result of such reversal would be negation of final decrees of adoption issued by probate court, on ground that juvenile court purposefully delayed issuing child support decision in order to influence probate court's decision to grant stepfather's adoption of minor children, where nothing in record suggested any purposeful impropriety in trial court's handling of proceedings, and reversal would not impact adoption decrees as they were issued by separate court and statute prohibited any person from questioning decree after one year. G.A. v. G.L. (Ohio App. 6 Dist., Erie, 09-30-2009) No. E-08-061, 2009-Ohio-5184, 2009 WL 3132926, Unreported, appeal not allowed 124 Ohio St.3d 1476, 921 N.E.2d 247, 2010-Ohio-354. Adoption ☞ 16; Children Out–of–wedlock ☞ 67; Children Out–of–wedlock ☞ 73

Evidence supported finding that granting foster parents' petitions to adopt children was in the best interest of the children; the children suffered from neurological problems as a result of their cocaine exposure, foster parents regularly help the children perform physical exercises to help their motor skill development, they transport them to weekly speech therapy classes, the children bonded with foster parents' biological children, foster parents expressed a desire to help the children maintain a relationship with their great-grandparents, and the guardian ad litem (GAL) recommended that foster parents be allowed to adopt the children. In re Jeffrey A. (Ohio App. 6 Dist., Lucas, 10-03-2008) No. L-08-1006, 2008-Ohio-5135, 2008 WL 4444316, Unreported, appeal not allowed 120 Ohio St.3d 1459, 898 N.E.2d 971, 2008-Ohio-6813. Adoption ☞ 13

Clear and convincing evidence established that birth mother's consent to adoption of child was given under circumstances constituting duress, and thus, affidavit purporting to give mother's consent to adoption was invalid and adoption decree was void as lacking requisite valid parental consent to adoption; mother believed it was very dangerous for her daughter, as a Vietnamese–American child born out of wedlock, to remain in Vietnam, and mother's "consent" to adoption was result of duress caused by her concern for life of child, and mother signed adoption consent affidavit, written in English, without legal advice and with limited understanding as to its consequences. In re Adoption of Baby Girl E. (Ohio App. 10 Dist., Franklin, 07-14-2005) No. 04AP932, 2005-Ohio-3565, 2005 WL 1652344, Unreported, stay granted 106 Ohio St.3d 1475, 832 N.E.2d 60, 2005-Ohio-3953, appeal not allowed 107 Ohio St.3d 1423, 837 N.E.2d 1208, 2005-Ohio-6124. Adoption ☞ 7.5

Assuming that evidence of unwillingness of child's father to comply with parameters of visitation ordered in biological mother's action for visitation with child amounted to newly discovered evidence in proceedings for step-parent adoption, such evidence was not grounds for granting biological mother relief from judgment from judgment granting adoption petition, where visitation proceeding was collateral matter and evidence with respect to visitation was not relied on in making best interest determination. In re Adoption of Haylett (Ohio App. 11 Dist., Portage, 02-18-2005) No. 2004-P-0063, 2005-Ohio-696, 2005 WL 407526, Unreported. Adoption ☞ 16

One year limitations period for a biological parent to challenge the validity of written consent to adoption, rather than statute that provided that consent to adoption could be withdrawn prior to the entry of an interlocutory order or prior to the entry of a final decree if the court found that it was in the best interest of the person to be adopted, applied to proceeding challenging the validity of biological mother's consent to stepmother's adoption of children. In re Adoption of Hockman (Ohio App. 11 Dist., Portage, 01-14-2005) No. 2004-P-0079, No. 2004-P-0080, 2005-Ohio-140, 2005 WL 89387, Unreported. Adoption ☞ 9.1

Biological mother failed to establish that her consent to stepmother's adoption of children was procured by duress or undue influence, which would have provided grounds for invalidating biological mother's consent to adoption, even though mother was involved in a divorce from an abusive spouse and had a history of health problems; when the consent to adoption was executed, mother was an adult, she had a high school diploma, there was no evidence that the consents were rushed, there was no evidence that mother was not alert or was unaware of what she was signing, and there was no evidence that anyone acted in a way that compromised the exercise of mother's free will. In re Adoption of Hockman (Ohio App. 11 Dist., Portage, 01-14-2005) No. 2004-P-0079, No. 2004-P-0080, 2005-Ohio-140, 2005 WL 89387, Unreported. Adoption ☞ 7.5

One year statute of limitations applied to biological mother's challenge to the adoptions of her children by their stepmother, where she received notice of the adoptions one month after the adoptions were finalized. In re Adoption of Miller (Ohio App. 3 Dist., Logan, 02-19-2003) No. 8-02-22, No. 8-02-23, 2003-Ohio-718, 2003 WL 354941, Unreported. Adoption ☞ 16

Court of Appeals was prohibited from considering biological mother's constitutional challenge to statute limiting a biological parent's right to challenge adoption, where mother failed to provide the attorney general with notice of constitutional challenge. In re Adoption of Miller (Ohio App. 3 Dist., Logan, 02-19-2003) No. 8-02-22, No. 8-02-23, 2003-Ohio-718, 2003 WL 354941, Unreported. Constitutional Law ☞ 958

Natural father's contention, on appeal of adoption order, that record contained no clear and convincing evidence of marriage between child's mother and stepfather, was assigned and briefed but was not addressed at trial, and thus Court of Appeals was not required to address it, but would do so, since matter of adoption was so important. In re Adoption of Lassiter (Ohio App. 2 Dist., 02-24-1995) 101 Ohio App.3d 367, 655 N.E.2d 781, dismissed, appeal not allowed 73 Ohio St.3d 1410, 651 N.E.2d 1308. Adoption ☞ 15

Judgment that consent of natural father was not required for adoption of child by third party was not a final appealable order and, thus, natural father's dismissal of his former appeal on consent ruling was not res judicata regarding consent. In re Adoption of Cline (Trumbull 1993) 89 Ohio App.3d 450, 624 N.E.2d 1083. Adoption ☞ 15

Statute providing that decree of adoption is uncontestable after one year applied to biological mother's motion for relief from judgment, not rule of civil procedure governing relief from judgment or order on ground of fraud or misrepresentation, where mother had signed adoption consent form which gave her actual notice of adoption proceedings. In re Rabatin (Geauga 1992) 83 Ohio App.3d 836, 615 N.E.2d 1099. Adoption ☞ 16

Where a putative father receives notice of adoption proceedings after they have been instituted, but before the final decree is rendered, and is given an opportunity to contest the adoption, neither RC 3107.16(B) nor In re Adoption of Knipper, 30 App(3d) 214, 30 OBR 371, 507 NE(2d) 436 (Hamilton 1986), apply. In re Adoption of Hart (Lucas 1989) 62 Ohio App.3d 544, 577 N.E.2d 77, motion overruled 45 Ohio St.3d 704, 543 N.E.2d 810.

An adoption decree, defective because it violated a biological parent's due process rights, may be vacated more than four years after the decree was journalized under Civ R 60(B)(5). In re Adoption of Knipper (Hamilton 1986) 30 Ohio App.3d 214, 507 N.E.2d 436, 30 O.B.R. 371.

4. Fraud

Biological mother failed to establish that her consent to stepmother's adoption of children was procured by fraud, which would have provided grounds for invalidating biological mother's consent to adoption; mother only alleged that her consent was not knowingly, intelligently, and voluntarily given since she did not understand the consequences of signing the consent forms. In re Adoption of Hockman (Ohio App. 11 Dist., Portage, 01-14-2005) No. 2004-P-0079, No. 2004-P-0080, 2005-Ohio-140, 2005 WL 89387, Unreported. Adoption ☞ 7.5

Trial court abused its discretion in invalidating biological mother's written consent to stepmother's adoption of children, where biological mother failed to establish that her consent was procured by fraud, duress or undue influence. In re Adoption of Hockman (Ohio App. 11 Dist., Portage, 01-14-2005) No. 2004-P-0079, No. 2004-P-0080, 2005-Ohio-140, 2005 WL 89387, Unreported. Adoption ☞ 7.5

Stepmother who sought to adopt her two step-children did not perpetrate fraud on the court when she claimed that she was unable to locate children's' biological mother, and thus, one-year statute of limitations for biological mother's challenge to the adoptions was not tolled; although stepmother had a two-year-old address of biological mother, she had moved, was living out of state at time petitions were filed, and no evidence was produced to show that mother notified stepmother or children of her current address, although stepmother had two-year-old addresses for members of mother's family, family members had since moved, and although stepmother could have tried to locate family members through a few phone calls, such lack of diligence did not rise to the level of fraud. In re Adoption of Miller (Ohio App. 3 Dist., Logan, 02-19-2003) No. 8-02-22, No. 8-02-23, 2003-Ohio-718, 2003 WL 354941, Unreported. Adoption ☞ 16

Father would not have prevailed in setting aside adoption if he had been named, and thus, denial of his motion for relief from adoption order was not an abuse of discretion, although mother purposefully failed to provide Probate Court with father's name and address when her husband sought to adopt child, where father became aware of the fraud five to six years prior to his attempt to set aside adoption, at that time he agreed to limit his involvement to visitation only, and it could not be said that father would have reacted any differently when the adoption was granted. In re McCandlish (Ohio App. 5 Dist., Fairfield, 12 16 2002) No. 02CA71, 2002-Ohio-6979, 2002 WL 31819640, Unreported. Adoption ☞ 16

Biological mother's consent to adoption was not product of fraud or undue influence; thus, she was not allowed to withdraw her consent after final order of adoption. In re Adoption of Zschach (Ohio, 06-06-1996) 75 Ohio St.3d 648, 665 N.E.2d 1070, reconsideration denied 76 Ohio St.3d 1410, 666 N.E.2d 569, certiorari denied 117 S.Ct. 582, 519 U.S. 1028, 136 L.Ed.2d 513. Adoption ☞ 7.5; Adoption ☞ 7.6(2)

Biological father's cause of action for fraudulent adoption accrued, for limitations purposes, when he discovered that biological mother of child had placed child for adoption, rather than when court decided that his consent to adoption was not required; elements of cause of action for fraud were established when father was on notice that child might be his and that he could lose his parental rights. Copeland v. Delvaux (Lucas 1993) 89 Ohio App.3d 1, 623 N.E.2d 569, dismissed, jurisdictional motion overruled 67 Ohio St.3d 1510, 622 N.E.2d

657. Limitation Of Actions ☞ 100(2); Limitation Of Actions ☞ 100(12)

Injury, in action for fraudulent adoption, is loss of parenthood. Copeland v. Delvaux (Lucas 1993) 89 Ohio App.3d 1, 623 N.E.2d 569, dismissed, jurisdictional motion overruled 67 Ohio St.3d 1510, 622 N.E.2d 657. Fraud ☞ 25; Limitation Of Actions ☞ 99(1)

Biological mother's claim of fraud in securing her consent to adoption was not sufficient to exempt her from one-year limitation applicable to challenges to adoption decrees, even if adoptive parents' financial and personal situation may have changed after expiration of one-year period; there was no evidence that mother was unable to understand adoption consent form when she signed it, there was no evidence of fraud or misrepresentation at time of adoption, and there was no evidence of adverse conditions which mother alleged were found by court's investigator. In re Rabatin (Geauga 1992) 83 Ohio App.3d 836, 615 N.E.2d 1099. Adoption ☞ 16

RC 3107.16(B) does not permit the court to vacate adoption decrees of three children on the basis of fraud and compensatory damages including all past child support filed by a stepparent who is a quadriplegic and claims he was fraudulently induced to marry his caretaker who (1) begins to ingratiate herself to him, (2) manages his money which consists of monthly annuity payments of over $10,000, (3) leaves her first husband and moves into the gentleman's home, (4) immediately spends large amounts of money and initiates a sexual relationship, and (5) ceases to provide the necessary care and admits that she had married only for her children and their security; furthermore, the relationship turns hostile and the husband fears for his life and is transported to the hospital while his wife and one man with whom she is having an affair destroy the husband's property, including the wheelchair ramps to the house, and the court's basis for upholding the adoption and child support order is that the nature of this action is based upon a promise of marriage or upon an obligation dependent upon, or growing out of, a contract of marriage and is not cognizable by law. Joslyn v Reynolds, No. 3169–M, 2001 WL 1194869 (9th Dist Ct App, Medina, 10–10–01).

5. Paternity

Knowledge of a mother regarding the paternity of her child whom she has put up for adoption cannot be imputed to the prospective adoptive parents. In re Adoption of Hart (Lucas 1989) 62 Ohio App.3d 544, 577 N.E.2d 77, motion overruled 45 Ohio St.3d 704, 543 N.E.2d 810.

3107.161 Contested adoption; factors considered; best interest of child

(A) As used in this section, "the least detrimental available alternative" means the alternative that would have the least long-term negative impact on the child.

(B) When a court makes a determination in a contested adoption concerning the best interest of a child, the court shall consider all relevant factors including, but not limited to, all of the following:

(1) The least detrimental available alternative for safeguarding the child's growth and development;

(2) The age and health of the child at the time the best interest determination is made and, if applicable, at the time the child was removed from the home;

(3) The wishes of the child in any case in which the child's age and maturity makes this feasible;

(4) The duration of the separation of the child from a parent;

(5) Whether the child will be able to enter into a more stable and permanent family relationship, taking into account the conditions of the child's current placement, the likelihood of future placements, and the results of prior placements;

(6) The likelihood of safe reunification with a parent within a reasonable period of time;

(7) The importance of providing permanency, stability, and continuity of relationships for the child;

(8) The child's interaction and interrelationship with the child's parents, siblings, and any other person who may significantly affect the child's best interest;

(9) The child's adjustment to the child's current home, school, and community;

(10) The mental and physical health of all persons involved in the situation;

(11) Whether any person involved in the situation has been convicted of, pleaded guilty to, or accused of any criminal offense involving any act that resulted in a child being abused or neglected; whether the person, in a case in which a child has been adjudicated to be an abused or neglected child, has been determined to be the perpetrator of the abusive or neglectful act that is the basis of the adjudication; whether the person has been convicted of, pleaded guilty to, or accused of a violation of section 2919.25 of the Revised Code involving a victim who at the time of the commission of the offense was a member of the person's family or household; and whether the person has been convicted of, pleaded guilty to, or accused of any offense involving a victim who at the time of the commission of the offense was a member of the person's family or household and caused physical harm to the victim in the commission of the offense.

(C) A person who contests an adoption has the burden of providing the court material evidence needed to determine what is in the best interest of the child and must establish that the child's current placement is not the least detrimental available alternative.

(1996 S 292, eff. 11–6–96; 1996 H 419, eff. 9–18–96)

Uncodified Law

1996 S 292, § 4, eff. 11–6–96, reads: The repeal by this act of division (C) of section 3107.161 of the Revised Code shall not be construed to change the public policy of this state regarding the status of a child in a contested adoption and whether the child may be represented by independent counsel as the public policy existed immediately prior to the enactment of Am. Sub. H.B. 419 of the 121st General Assembly.

Historical and Statutory Notes

Amendment Note: 1996 S 292 added division (A); redesignated former division (A) as division (B); added division (B)(1); redesignated former divisions (A)(1) through (A)(10) as divisions (B)(2) through (B)(11); redesignated former division (B) as division (C); and deleted former division (C), which previously read:

"(C) A child in a contested adoption has full party status and may be represented by independent counsel."

Library References

Adoption ☞4.
Westlaw Topic No. 17.
C.J.S. Adoption of Persons §§ 15 to 21, 27.

Research References

Encyclopedias

OH Jur. 3d Family Law § 907, Determination.

Forms

Ohio Forms Legal and Business § 28:17, Introduction.

Ohio Jurisprudence Pleading and Practice Forms § 96:19, Notice and Hearing--Best Interest of Child Standard--Contested Case.

Treatises and Practice Aids

Carlin, Baldwin's Ohio Prac. Merrick-Rippner Probate Law § 99:8, Suitability of Adoptive Parents--Best Interests of Child.

Carlin, Baldwin's Ohio Prac. Merrick-Rippner Probate Law § 99:31, Parties Giving Consent--Biological Parents.

Carlin, Baldwin's Ohio Prac. Merrick-Rippner Probate Law § 99:37, Withdrawal of Consent.

Carlin, Baldwin's Ohio Prac. Merrick-Rippner Probate Law § 99:39, Consent Not Required--Noncommunication and Nonsupport.

Notes of Decisions

Best Interests 1
Review 4
Statutory factors 2
Wishes of child 3

---

1. Best interests

Trial court acted within its discretion by determining that the adoption of two minor children by their stepfather was in the children's best interests, even though it would sever ties with their biological father and his family; the children, who were nine and eleven years old, had not seen their biological father or his family in six years, biological father had provided no support for the children for five years, children had a loving family relationship with mother and stepfather, and stepfather had a strong parental bond with both children. In re Adoption of Kat. P. (Ohio App. 5 Dist., Fairfield, 08-04-2010) No. 10CA16, No. 10CA17, 2010-Ohio-3623, 2010 WL 3046997, Unreported. Adoption ☞ 4

The trial court's failure to provide father with notice and the opportunity to be heard on the issue of whether stepfather's adoption of child was in child's best interest violated due process, even though the court had previously determined that father's consent to adoption was not required; trial court was required to conduct a best interest hearing, and father was one of several classes of persons that were entitled to 20 days notice of a hearing to determine the merits of the adoption petition and contest the best interest finding. In re Adoption of S.L.C. (Ohio App. 2 Dist., Miami, 12-29-2005) No. 05-CA-32, 2005-Ohio-7067, 2005 WL 3610305, Unreported. Adoption ☞ 12; Adoption ☞ 13; Constitutional Law ☞ 4395

Trial court's findings in connection with petition for step-parent adoption were sufficient to support judgment granting petition, where trial court specifically found that child had been out of her biological mother's custody for two-and-one-half years at time of best interest hearing, child was well adjusted to her home, school, and community, and stepmother was best able to provide safe, stable environment for child. In re Adoption of Haylett (Ohio App. 11 Dist., Portage, 02-18-2005) No.

2004-P-0063, 2005 Ohio 696, 2005 WL 407526, Unreported. Adoption ☞ 4

Stepfather's adoption of child was in child's best interests; evidence submitted at the hearing showed that child did not wish to have any contact with her biological father, given child's age there was little likelihood of father establishing any sort of relationship with child, order from domestic relations court which forbade father from having contact with child would apparently continue after father's probation ended, and adoption would promote stability of family unit, as stepfather had already adopted child's half-sister and was father of another child with child's mother. In re Adoption of Tucker (Ohio App. 11 Dist., Trumbull, 03-14-2003) No. 2002-T-0154, 2003-Ohio-1212, 2003 WL 1193776, Unreported. Adoption ☞ 4

Evidence was sufficient to support finding that granting stepfather's adoption petition was not in children's best interests, even though stepfather provided a loving and supportive environment for children to live and go to school and children were thriving and well-adjusted under the care of stepfather, and father had failed to pay child support for several years; father made attempts to remain in contact with children by traveling from Texas to Ohio, and older child consistently expressed a desire to see father. In re B.M.S. (Ohio App. 10 Dist., 02-17-2011) 192 Ohio App.3d 394, 949 N.E.2d 111, 2011 Ohio 714, appeal not allowed 128 Ohio St.3d 1516, 948 N.E.2d 451, 2011-Ohio-2686. Adoption ☞ 13

Evidence supported finding that it was in children's best interest to be adopted by their foster parents, rather than their great aunt; children's guardian ad litem recommended adoption by foster parents, witnesses testified as to their observations of positive interactions between foster parents and children, children never spent any overnights with aunt, foster parents were active in children's school, and there was evidence that children were well-adjusted to their foster home, their school, and their community. In re Adoption Cotner (Ohio App. 12 Dist., Fayette, 09-30-2002) No. CA2002-02-004, No. CA2002-02-005,

2002-Ohio-5145, 2002 WL 31155151, Unreported. Adoption ☞ 13

2. Statutory factors

Trial court did not err in determining that it was in child's best interest to be adopted by her foster parents, rather than by relatives who were also petitioning for adoption; county children's services agency indicated that the relatives had not been approved through the matching conference process, agency also indicated that child was doing well, happy and thriving in her placement with foster parents, trial court clearly stated it had considered the statutory factors, and trial court acknowledged that relative placement was a factor to consider in determining a child's best interest, but found that other factors outweighed child's blood ties to relatives. In re Adoption of I.C. (Ohio App. 6 Dist., Lucas, 03-11-2011) No. L-10-1157, 2011-Ohio-1145, 2011 WL 857002, Unreported. Adoption ☞ 13

Burden of production of evidence relating to child's best interest, in proceedings on petition for step-parent adoption, was upon child's biological father, as party opposing petition for adoption, with burden of proof shifting only with respect to statutory factor requiring that adoption be least detrimental available alternative for safeguarding child's growth and development. In re Adoption of Brianna Marie D. (Ohio App. 6 Dist., Lucas, 02-22-2005) No. L-04-1367, 2005-Ohio-797, 2005 WL 435167, Unreported, appeal not allowed 105 Ohio St.3d 1564, 828 N.E.2d 118, 2005-Ohio-2447. Adoption ☞ 13

Judgment granting petition for step-parent adoption was required clearly to indicate that probate court considered statutory factors relevant to determining child's best interests and include court's rationale for finding that adoption was in those interests. In re Adoption of Brianna Marie D. (Ohio App. 6 Dist., Lucas, 02-22-2005) No. L-04-1367, 2005-Ohio-797, 2005 WL 435167, Unreported, appeal not allowed 105 Ohio St.3d 1564, 828 N.E.2d 118, 2005-Ohio-2447. Adoption ☞ 13

Trial court did not abuse its discretion in granting petition for step-parent adoption, despite biological mother's presentation of significant evidence regarding her progress in treatment for drug and alcohol addiction, where court considered such evidence, as well as other relevant statutory factors, in reaching its conclusion that granting petition for adoption was in child's best interest. In re Adoption of Haylett (Ohio App. 11 Dist., Portage, 02-18-2005) No. 2004-P-0063, 2005-Ohio-696, 2005 WL 407526, Unreported. Adoption ☞ 4

Trial court was required to consider the statutory factors to determine whether granting step-mother's petition to adopt child, without mother's consent, was in child's best interest. In re Adoption of Haylett (Ohio App. 11 Dist., Portage, 05-07-2004) No. 2003-P-0093, No. 2003-P-0103, 2004-Ohio-2306, 2004 WL 1043430, Unreported. Adoption ☞ 4

Trial court complied with statutory requirements in determining whether contested adoption was in child's best interests; there was evidence before

court regarding child's age, her wishes, length of separation between biological father and child, stability of child's current placement with her mother and stepfather, importance of stability for child, child's interaction with her family, and her current adjustment, and court discussed sexual abuse charges against father and its view that father's continued denial of responsibility for those acts was troubling. In re Adoption of Tucker (Ohio App. 11 Dist., Trumbull, 03-14-2003) No. 2002-T-0154, 2003-Ohio-1212, 2003 WL 1193776, Unreported. Adoption ☞ 13

Trial court, in determining whether granting stepfather's adoption petition would be in children's best interests following determination that father's consent was not necessary for adoption, properly considered father's reasons for not paying child support, and did not, by doing so, improperly revisit the issue of whether father's nonpayment was justifiable for purposes of determining whether his consent was needed; father's willingness to support his children financially was relevant to trial court's consideration of the relationship among the parties and of the need for permanency, stability, and continuity of those relationships, all proper factors under statute governing best interests determination. In re B.M.S. (Ohio App. 10 Dist., 02-17-2011) 192 Ohio App.3d 394, 949 N.E.2d 111, 2011-Ohio-714, appeal not allowed 128 Ohio St.3d 1516, 948 N.E.2d 451, 2011-Ohio-2686. Adoption ☞ 13

3. Wishes of child

Probate court did not abuse its discretion in allowing mother's husband to adopt child, potentially terminating relationship with child's paternal grandparents; child was aware of differences that would accrue with adoption, and child wanted adoption, child's family unit was very significant in her life, and day-to-day influence in her life from adoptive father outweighed not insubstantial benefits accruing to her through her continuing relationship with grandparents. In re Adoption of B.G. (Ohio App. 10 Dist., Franklin, 10-29-2002) No. 02AP-810, 2002-Ohio-5910, 2002 WL 31417928, Unreported. Adoption ☞ 4

Probate court did not abuse its discretion in considering wishes of child to be adopted by mother's husband, despite fact that child's biological paternal grandparents had taken active role in child's life; child testified that she very much wanted to be adopted by husband, she resisted visitation with paternal grandparents in Florida because she missed her life in Ohio, and fact that relationship with grandparents did not outweigh her interest in being with her family and friends and social activities could speak to nature of relationship with paternal grandparents. In re Adoption of B.G. (Ohio App. 10 Dist., Franklin, 10-29-2002) No. 02AP-810, 2002-Ohio-5910, 2002 WL 31417928, Unreported. Adoption ☞ 13

4. Review

On appeal of a decision in a proceeding on a petition for adoption, an appellate court will reverse a probate court's best-interest determination only upon a finding of an abuse of discretion. In re B.M.S. (Ohio App. 10 Dist., 02-17-2011) 192 Ohio App.3d 394, 949 N.E.2d 111, 2011-Ohio-714, appeal not allowed 128 Ohio St.3d 1516, 948 N.E.2d 451, 2011-Ohio-2686. Adoption ⬡ 15

RECORDS

3107.17   Confidentiality; records; access to histories of biological parents; rights of parties concerning proposed correction or expansion; procedures

(A) All hearings held under sections 3107.01 to 3107.19 of the Revised Code shall be held in closed court without the admittance of any person other than essential officers of the court, the parties, the witnesses of the parties, counsel, persons who have not previously consented to an adoption but who are required to consent, and representatives of the agencies present to perform their official duties.

(B)(1) Except as provided in divisions (B)(2) and (D) of this section and sections 3107.39 to 3107.44 and 3107.60 to 3107.68 of the Revised Code, no person or governmental entity shall knowingly reveal any information contained in a paper, book, or record pertaining to an adoption that is part of the permanent record of a court or maintained by the department of job and family services, an agency, or attorney without the consent of a court.

(2) An agency or attorney may examine the agency's or attorney's own papers, books, and records pertaining to an adoption without a court's consent for official administrative purposes. The department of job and family services may examine its own papers, books, and records pertaining to an adoption, or such papers, books, and records of an agency, without a court's consent for official administrative, certification, and eligibility determination purposes.

(C) The petition, the interlocutory order, the final decree of adoption, and other adoption proceedings shall be recorded in a book kept for such purposes and shall be separately indexed. The book shall be a part of the records of the court, and all consents, affidavits, and other papers shall be properly filed.

(D) All forms that pertain to the social or medical histories of the biological parents of an adopted person and that were completed pursuant to section 3107.09 or 3107.091 of the Revised Code shall be filed only in the permanent record kept by the court. During the minority of the adopted person, only the adoptive parents of the person may inspect the forms. When an adopted person reaches majority, only the adopted person may inspect the forms. Under the circumstances described in this division, an adopted person or the adoptive parents are entitled to inspect the forms upon requesting the clerk of the court to produce them.

(E)(1) The department of job and family services shall prescribe a form that permits any person who is authorized by division (D) of this section to inspect forms that pertain to the social or medical histories of the biological parents and that were completed pursuant to section 3107.09 or 3107.091 of the Revised Code to request notice if any correction or expansion of either such history, made pursuant to division (D) of section 3107.09 of the Revised Code, is made a part of the permanent record kept by the court. The form shall be designed to facilitate the provision of the information and statements described in division (E)(3) of this section. The department shall provide copies of the form to each court. A court shall provide a copy of the request form to each adoptive parent when a final decree of adoption is entered and shall explain to each adoptive parent at that time that an adoptive parent who completes and files the form will be notified of any correction or expansion of either the social or medical history of the biological parents of the adopted person made during the minority of the adopted person that is made a part of the permanent record kept by the court, and that, during the adopted person's minority, the adopted person may inspect the forms that pertain to those histories. Upon request, the court also shall provide a copy of the request form to any adoptive parent during the minority of the adopted person and to an adopted person who has reached the age of majority.

(2) Any person who is authorized to inspect forms pursuant to division (D) of this section who wishes to be notified of corrections or expansions pursuant to division (D) of section 3107.09 of the Revised Code that are made a part of the permanent record kept by the court

shall file with the court, on a copy of the form prescribed by the department of job and family services pursuant to division (E)(1) of this section, a request for such notification that contains the information and statements required by division (E)(3) of this section. A request may be filed at any time if the person who files the request is authorized at that time to inspect forms that pertain to the social or medical histories.

(3) A request for notification as described in division (E)(2) of this section shall contain all of the following information:

(a) The adopted person's name and mailing address at that time;

(b) The name of each adoptive parent, and if the adoptive person is a minor at the time of the filing of the request, the mailing address of each adoptive parent at that time;

(c) The adopted person's date of birth;

(d) The date of entry of the final decree of adoption;

(e) A statement requesting the court to notify the person who files the request, at the address provided in the request, if any correction or expansion of either the social or medical history of the biological parents is made a part of the permanent record kept by the court;

(f) A statement that the person who files the request is authorized, at the time of the filing, to inspect the forms that pertain to the social and medical histories of the biological parents;

(g) The signature of the person who files the request.

(4) Upon the filing of a request for notification in accordance with division (E)(2) of this section, the clerk of the court in which it is filed immediately shall insert the request in the permanent record of the case. A person who has filed the request and who wishes to update it with respect to a new mailing address may inform the court in writing of the new address. Upon its receipt, the court promptly shall insert the new address into the permanent record by attaching it to the request. Thereafter, any notification described in this division shall be sent to the new address.

(5) Whenever a social or medical history of a biological parent is corrected or expanded and the correction or expansion is made a part of the permanent record kept by the court, the court shall ascertain whether a request for notification has been filed in accordance with division (E)(2) of this section. If such a request has been filed, the court shall determine whether, at that time, the person who filed the request is authorized, under division (D) of this section, to inspect the forms that pertain to the social or medical history of the biological parents. If the court determines that the person who filed the request is so authorized, it immediately shall notify the person that the social or medical history has record kept by the court, and that the forms that pertain to the records may be inspected in accordance with division (D) of this section.

(2006 S 238, eff. 9–21–06; 1999 H 471, eff. 7–1–00; 1996 H 419, eff. 9–18–96; 1984 H 84, eff. 3–19–85; 1978 H 832, S 340; 1976 H 156)

Historical and Statutory Notes

Ed. Note: 3107.17 contains provisions analogous to former 3107.14, repealed by 1976 H 156, eff. 1–1–77.

Amendment Note: 2006 S 238 deleted "a placement under section 5103.16 of the Revised Code or to" after "pertaining to" in division (B)(1); and substituted "an" for "a placement or" after "pertaining to" twice in division (B)(2).

Amendment Note: 1999 H 471 substituted "job and family" for "human" in divisions (B)(1), (B)(2), (E)(1), and (E)(2).

Amendment Note: 1996 H 419 rewrote division (B); deleted "probate" preceding "court" in divisions (C) and (E)(1); substituted "section 3107.09 or 3107.091 of the Revised Code" for "division (D)

of section 3107.12 or section 3107.121 of the Revised Code" in division (D); substituted "section 3107.09 or 3107.091 of the Revised Code to request notice if any correction or expansion of either such history, made pursuant to division (D) of section 3107.09 of the Revised Code" for "division (D) of section 3107.12 or section 3107.121 of the Revised Code to request that he be notified if any correction or expansion of either such history, made pursuant to division (D)(4) of section 3107.12 of the Revised Code" in division (E)(1); substituted "division (D) of section 3107.09 of the Revised Code" for "division (D)(4) of section 3107.12 of the Revised Code" in division (E)(2); and made changes to reflect gender neutral language throughout the section.   Prior to amendment, former division (B) read:

"(B) All papers, books, and records pertaining to a placement under section 5103.16 of the Revised Code or an adoption, whether part of the permanent record of the court or of a file in the department of human services or in an agency, are, except as provided in division (D) of this section, subject to inspection only upon consent of the court."

Comparative Laws

Idaho—I.C.   § 16-1511.
Ill.—ILCS 750 50/18.
Ind.—West's A.I.C. 31–19–19–1 et seq.
Iowa—I.C.A.   § 600.24.
Ky.—Baldwin's KRS 199.570.
Mass.—M.G.L.A.   c.   210, § 5c.

Me.—18-A M.R.S.A. § 9–310.
Mo.—V.A.M.S.   § 453.120.
N.C.—G.S.   § 48-9-101 et seq.
N.J.—N.J.S.A.   9:3-51.
Wis.—W.S.A.   48.93.

Cross References

Penalty: 3107.99
Prohibition: 3107.65(A)
Availability of adoption records, see 149.43
Courts, confidentiality of adoption files, Sup R 55
Jurisdiction of juvenile court, see 2151.23
Maternity hospital record of children given out or adopted, see 3711.08

Personal information systems; rights of subjects, or possible subjects, to inspection, see 1347.08
Probate court, record and index of adoptions, see 2101.12

Ohio Administrative Code References

Adoptive family case record, see OAC 5101:2–48–22
Preservation of adoptive child case record, see OAC 5101:2–48–23

Requirement of "social and medical history", see OAC 5101:2–48–03

Library References

Adoption ⟜13.
Infants ⟜17.
Records ⟜32.
Westlaw Topic Nos. 17, 211, 326.
C.J.S. Adoption of Persons §§ 10 to 14, 41, 46 to 47, 93 to 102.

C.J.S. Bankruptcy §§ 830 to 834.
C.J.S. Infants §§ 6, 8 to 9.
C.J.S. Records §§ 80, 82 to 88.

Research References

ALR Library

103 ALR 5th 255, Restricting Access to Judicial Records of Concluded Adoption Proceedings.

Encyclopedias

OH Jur. 3d Defamation & Privacy § 183, Exceptions.
OH Jur. 3d Family Law § 882, Putative Father Registry.
OH Jur. 3d Family Law § 906, Hearing.
OH Jur. 3d Family Law § 911, Records and Papers.
OH Jur. 3d Family Law § 913, Records and Papers--Inspection.
OH Jur. 3d Family Law § 1434, Recordkeeping Requirements.

Forms

Ohio Forms Legal and Business § 28:18, Placement of Children in Independent Adoptions.

Ohio Jurisprudence Pleading and Practice Forms § 96:6, Open Adoption--Prohibitions.
Ohio Jurisprudence Pleading and Practice Forms § 96:32, Confidentiality.
Ohio Jurisprudence Pleading and Practice Forms § 96:76, Request for Notification.

Treatises and Practice Aids

Carlin, Baldwin's Ohio Prac. Merrick-Rippner Probate Law § 30:27, Adopted Child.
Carlin, Baldwin's Ohio Prac. Merrick-Rippner Probate Law § 99:29, Papers and Records--Confidentiality.
Carlin, Baldwin's Ohio Prac. Merrick-Rippner Probate Law § 99:45, Hearing of Petition--Procedure--Persons Present.
Hastings, Manoloff, Sheeran, & Stype, Ohio School Law § 44:5, Scope.

Law Review and Journal Commentaries

Ohio House Bill 419: Increased Openness in Adoption Records Law, Wendy L. Weiss. 45 Clev St L Rev 101 (1997).

The Open Adoption Records Movement: Constitutional Cases And Legislative Compromise, Note. 26 J Fam L 395 (1987–88).

A Reasonable Approach to the Adoptee's Sealed Record Dilemma, Michael L. Hanley. 2 Ohio N U L Rev 542 (1975).

Secrecy and genetics in adoption law and practice, Demosthenes A. Lorandos. 27 Loy U Chi L J 277 (1996).

Notes of Decisions

Confidentiality 2
Contempt 1
Record keeping 3

1. Contempt

Trial court did not improperly rely on testimony of adoptive mother, regarding adopted child's attachment issues, in reaching its determination not to order adoptive parents to pay child support, sought by county that assumed custody of child after adoption failed; court simply acknowledged conflicting views on issue, and record demonstrated no undue reliance by court. Wood Cty. Dept. of Job & Family Serv. v. Pete F. (Ohio App. 6 Dist., Wood, 11-10-2005) No. WD-05-023, 2005-Ohio-6006, 2005 WL 3008904, Unreported. Infants ☞ 228(1)

Contempt proceedings ex parte are a proper means for a court to protect the secrecy of adoption records. State ex rel. Wolff v. Donnelly (Ohio 1986) 24 Ohio St.3d 1, 492 N.E.2d 810, 24 O.B.R. 1.

2. Confidentiality

Trial court did not abuse its discretion in preserving confidentiality of adoption records of county that facilitated adoption of child, in proceeding brought by county that assumed custody of child after adoption failed, in which county sought child support from adoptive parents and adoption records of child; court gave determinative weight to public policy concern to not creating a "chilling effect" on future adoptions of troubled children, and court expressly ruled in such a way to preserve the greater public good. Wood Cty. Dept. of Job & Family Serv. v. Pete F. (Ohio App. 6 Dist., Wood, 11-10-2005) No. WD-05-023, 2005-Ohio-6006, 2005 WL 3008904, Unreported. Records ☞ 32

Trial court's order permitting counsel to inspect and discover contents of adoption records would be affirmed, where actual documents at issue were not before Court of Appeals, and thus it could not be determined whether trial court abused its discretion in permitting counsel to inspect their contents; in absence of adequate record, validity of trial court's

action had to be presumed. Cochran v. Northeast Ohio Adoption Serv. (Portage 1993) 85 Ohio App.3d 750, 621 N.E.2d 470. Appeal And Error ☞ 907(1)

More specific statute concerning county department of human services records pertaining particularly to adoptions and placements was applicable to issue whether adoption records were confidential and not discoverable, rather than more general statute providing that records required to be kept by such agency be confidential, and open to inspection to other persons only upon written permission of executive secretary. Cochran v. Northeast Ohio Adoption Serv. (Portage 1993) 85 Ohio App.3d 750, 621 N.E.2d 470. Statutes ☞ 223.4

The department of health is under no particular statutory duty to ensure the confidentiality of any adoption records in the possession of local registrars; rather, under RC 3107.17, the department is only obligated to maintain the confidentiality of its own records, and it is not responsible for any adoption records kept by local registrars. Grothouse v. Ohio Dept. of Health (Franklin 1992) 80 Ohio App.3d 258, 608 N.E.2d 1183.

3. Record keeping

Proposed placements by a probate court under RC 5103.16 are "other adoption proceedings" as that phrase is used in RC 3107.14 and, therefore, all papers that are a part of the record in such placement proceedings should be separately recorded and indexed, and kept in the manner provided for under RC 3107.14. 1962 OAG 2747.

Proceedings in adoption cases should be separately recorded in a book kept for that purpose and separately indexed and should not be journalized or generally recorded. 1959 OAG 652.

A probate court may make up the record required by RC 2101.12, 3107.14, 5123.37, 5123.38, and 5731.48 by microfilming or other duplication process authorized by RC 9.01, provided the originals are maintained on file and until they are eventually destroyed in accordance with RC 149.38. 1955 OAG 5667.

3107.18 Recognition of decrees of other jurisdictions and countries

(A) Except when giving effect to such a decree would violate the public policy of this state, a court decree terminating the relationship of parent and child, or establishing the relationship by adoption, issued pursuant to due process of law by a court of any jurisdiction outside this state, whether within or outside the United States, shall be recognized in this state, and the rights and obligations of the parties as to all matters within the jurisdiction of this state, including, without limitation, those matters specified in section 3107.15 of the Revised Code, shall be determined as though the decree were issued by a court of this state. A decree or certificate of adoption that is issued under the laws of a foreign country and that is verified and approved by the immigration and naturalization service of the United States shall be recognized in this state. Nothing in this section prohibits a court from issuing a final decree of adoption or interlocutory order of adoption pursuant to section 3107.14 of the Revised Code for a person the petitioner has adopted pursuant to a decree or certificate of adoption recognized in this state that was issued outside the United States.

(B) If a child born in a foreign country is placed with adoptive parents or an adoptive parent in this state for the purpose of adoption and if the adoption previously has been finalized in the country of the child's birth, the adoptive parent or parents may bring a petition in the probate court in their county of residence requesting that the court issue a final decree of adoption or an interlocutory order of adoption pursuant to section 3107.14 of the Revised Code. In a proceeding on the petition, proof of finalization of the adoption outside the United States is prima-facie evidence of the consent of the parties who are required to give consent even if the foreign decree or certificate of adoption was issued with respect to only one of two adoptive parents who seek to adopt the child in this state.

(C) At the request of a person who has adopted a person pursuant to a decree or certificate of adoption recognized in this state that was issued outside the United States, the court of the county in which the person making the request resides shall order the department of health to issue a foreign birth record for the adopted person under division (A)(4) of section 3705.12 of the Revised Code. The court may specify a change of name for the child and, if a physician has recommended a revision of the birth date, a revised birth date. The court shall send to the department with its order a copy of the foreign adoption decree or certificate of adoption and, if the foreign decree or certificate of adoption is not in English, a translation certified as to its accuracy by the translator and provided by the person who requested the order.

(2000 S 173, eff. 10–10–00; 1996 H 274, eff. 9–18–96; 1996 H 419, eff. 9–18–96; 1996 H 266, eff. 5–15–96; 1976 H 156, eff. 1–1–77)

Historical and Statutory Notes

Amendment Note: 2000 S 173 substituted "3107.14" for "3701.14"; and made other nonsubstantive changes.

Amendment Note: 1996 H 274 deleted "of common pleas" before "of the county" in division (C).

Amendment Note: 1996 H 419 designated division (A); added the second and third sentences to division (A); and added divisions (B) and (C).

Amendment Note: 1996 H 266 designated division (A) and added the second and third sentences therein; and added divisions (B) and (C).

Cross References

Adoption registration, issuance of foreign birth record on receipt of order, see 3705.12

Interstate compact on placement of children, see 5103.22 et seq.

Placement of children from other states, see 2151.39

Library References

Adoption ⚎25.
Westlaw Topic No. 17.

C.J.S. Adoption of Persons §§ 139, 155.
C.J.S. Conflict of Laws § 57.

Research References

Encyclopedias

OH Jur. 3d Family Law § 915, Foreign Decrees; Effect.

OH Jur. 3d Family Law § 1172, Effect of Child's Adoption on Visitation.

OH Jur. 3d Health & Sanitation § 68, Births--Records for Adopted Persons.

OH Jur. 3d Trusts § 124, Adopted Child as Within Class.

Forms

Ohio Jurisprudence Pleading and Practice Forms § 96:30, Effect of Adoption.

Ohio Jurisprudence Pleading and Practice Forms § 96:33, Foreign Decrees.

Ohio Jurisprudence Pleading and Practice Forms § 96:34, Birth Record.

Treatises and Practice Aids

Sowald & Morganstern, Baldwin's Ohio Practice Domestic Relations Law § 3:49, Related Issues--Adoption.

Carlin, Baldwin's Ohio Prac. Merrick-Rippner Probate Law § 3:5, Subject Matter--Specific Areas--Inter Vivos Trusts.

Carlin, Baldwin's Ohio Prac. Merrick-Rippner Probate Law § 99:6, Parties--Who May be Adopted--Foreign Child.

Carlin, Baldwin's Ohio Prac. Merrick-Rippner Probate Law § 44:16, Liberal Construction--Gifts to a Class: Construction Problems.

Carlin, Baldwin's Ohio Prac. Merrick-Rippner Probate Law § 99:52, Foreign Adoptions.

Carlin, Baldwin's Ohio Prac. Merrick-Rippner Probate Law § 99:53, Inheritance Rights of Adoptees.

Carlin, Baldwin's Ohio Prac. Merrick-Rippner Probate Law § 99:54, Inheritance Rights of Adoptees--"Stranger to the Adoption" Doctrine.

Carlin, Baldwin's Ohio Prac. Merrick-Rippner Probate Law § 110:19, Parentage Act--Effect.

Law Review and Journal Commentaries

Intercountry Adoption: A Need for Mandatory Medical Screening, Comment. 11 J L & Health 243 (1996–97).

Notes of Decisions

Exceptions to recognition of foreign decree   1

_____

1. Exceptions to recognition of foreign decree

Parent and child relationship could not be established between husband and wife's child for purposes of establishing husband's child support obligation pursuant to a divorce, even though husband adopted child in another country; parent and child relationship could only be established on basis of foreign adoption of child by husband, and court could not recognize foreign adoption without verification and approved by the Immigration and Naturalization Service. Walsh v. Walsh (Ohio App. 11 Dist., 09-24-2001) 146 Ohio App.3d 48, 764 N.E.2d 1103, 2001-Ohio-4315. Adoption ☞ 20

Refusal of trial court to recognize adoption of wife's child by husband for purposes of establishing husband's child support obligation subsequent to divorce was supported by evidence and was not against the manifest weight of the evidence, where court considered documents provided by wife from country where adoption was granted, and documents from Immigration and Naturalization Service (INS) regarding support of alien relative, and there was no evidence that INS had verified and approved adoption. Walsh v. Walsh (Ohio App. 11 Dist., 09-24-2001) 146 Ohio App.3d 48, 764 N.E.2d 1103, 2001-Ohio-4315. Adoption ☞ 20

Trial court's failure to recognize foreign adoption of wife's child by husband in divorce proceeding on principles of comity was not unreasonable, arbitrary, or unconscionable, given that state law prohibited recognition of adoption without verification and approval by Immigration and Naturalization Service (INS). Walsh v. Walsh (Ohio App. 11 Dist., 09-24-2001) 146 Ohio App.3d 48, 764 N.E.2d 1103, 2001-Ohio-4315. Adoption ☞ 20

Foreign adoption of wife's child by husband failed to meet statutory requirements for recognition, where adoption had not been verified and approved by the Immigration and Naturalization Service. Walsh v. Walsh (Ohio App. 11 Dist., 09-24-2001) 146 Ohio App.3d 48, 764 N.E.2d 1103, 2001-Ohio-4315. Adoption ☞ 25

Mother was not entitled to writ of prohibition to prevent juvenile court judge from proceeding with father's parentage action, based on foreign adoption decree, since foreign adoption law did not require notice to father before adoption of child out-of-wedlock and therefore may not have been enforced under comity as being repugnant to state law, jurisdiction was not divested even if action was barred on res judicata grounds, and inadequacy of postjudgment appeal was not established. State ex rel. Smith v. Smith (Ohio, 04-10-1996) 75 Ohio St.3d 418, 662 N.E.2d 366, 1996-Ohio-215. Prohibition ☞ 3(3); Prohibition ☞ 10(2)

Recognition and effectiveness of foreign adoption decree are subject to condition that decree not be repugnant to laws of state. State ex rel. Smith v. Smith (Ohio, 04-10-1996) 75 Ohio St.3d 418, 662 N.E.2d 366, 1996-Ohio-215. Adoption ☞ 25

3107.19   Information forwarded to human services department

If the adopted person was born in this state or outside the United States, the court shall forward all of the following to the department of health within thirty days after an adoption decree becomes final:

(A) A copy of the adopted person's certificate of adoption;

(B) The form prescribed under division (A)(1) of section 3107.083 of the Revised Code, if a parent filled out and signed the form pursuant to section 3107.071, 3107.081, or 5103.151 of the Revised Code;

(C) A statement of whether the adopted person is an adopted person as defined in section 3107.39 or 3107.45 of the Revised Code.

If the adopted person was born in another state of the United States, the court shall forward a copy of the adopted person's certificate of adoption to that state's vital statistics office within thirty days after an adoption decree becomes final.

(1999 H 176, eff. 10–29–99; 1996 H 419, eff. 9–18–96; 1986 H 428, eff. 12–23–86; 1976 H 156)

Historical and Statutory Notes

Ed. Note: 3107.19 is analogous to provisions of former 3107.11, repealed by 1976 H 156, eff. 1–1–77.

Amendment Note: 1999 H 176 deleted "Within thirty days after an adoption decree becomes final, the court shall forward a copy of the decree to the department of human services of this state for statistical purposes." from the beginning of the introductory paragraph; and substituted "within thirty days after an adoption decree becomes final" for "at the time of forwarding the adoption decree

to the department of human services" in the introductory and final paragraphs.

Amendment Note: 1996 H 419 rewrote this section, which prior thereto read:

"Within thirty days after an adoption decree becomes final, the clerk of the court shall prepare an application for a birth record of the adopted person and forward the application to the appropriate vital statistics office of the place, if known, where the adopted person was born, and forward a copy of the decree to the department of human services of this state for statistical purposes."

Comparative Laws

Ark.—A.C.A. § 9-9-219.
Mich.—M.C.L.A. § 710.67.

Cross References

Adoption registration, items sent by probate court, see 3705.12

Library References

Records ⬤32.
Westlaw Topic No. 326.

C.J.S. Bankruptcy §§ 830 to 834.
C.J.S. Records §§ 80, 82 to 88.

Research References

Encyclopedias

OH Jur. 3d Family Law § 914, Forwarding of Adoption Information.
OH Jur. 3d Health & Sanitation § 68, Births-- Records for Adopted Persons.

Forms

Ohio Jurisprudence Pleading and Practice Forms § 96:1, Definitions.
Ohio Jurisprudence Pleading and Practice Forms § 96:32, Confidentiality.

Ohio Jurisprudence Pleading and Practice Forms § 96:34, Birth Record.

Treatises and Practice Aids

Carlin, Baldwin's Ohio Prac. Merrick Rippner Probate Law § 99:2, History.
Carlin, Baldwin's Ohio Prac. Merrick-Rippner Probate Law § 99:49, Interlocutory and Final Orders.
Carlin, Baldwin's Ohio Prac. Merrick-Rippner Probate Law App B SPF 18.7, Final Decree of Adoption (Without Interlocutory Order).

Law Review and Journal Commentaries

Intercountry Adoption: A Need for Mandatory Medical Screening, Comment. 11 J L & Health 243 (1996–97).

ACCESS TO ADOPTION RECORDS BY ADOPTEES

3107.38   Adoptee's written request or petition to see adoption file

(A) As used in this section:

(1) "Adoption file" means the file maintained by the department of health under section 3705.12 of the Revised Code.

(2) "Items of identification" include a motor vehicle driver's or commercial driver's license, an identification card issued under sections 4507.50 to 4507.52 of the Revised Code, a marriage application, a social security card, a credit card, a military identification card, or an employee identification card.

(B) An adopted person whose birth occurred in this state and whose adoption was decreed prior to January 1, 1964, may do either or both of the following:

(1) Submit a written request to the department of health for the department to provide the adopted person with a copy of the contents of the adopted person's adoption file. The request shall provide the adopted person's address, notarized signature, and be accompanied by two items of identification of the adopted person. If the adopted person submits such a request, the fee required by section 3705.241 of the Revised Code is paid, and the department has an adoption file for the adopted person, the department shall mail to the adopted person, at the address provided in the request, a copy of the contents of the adopted person's adoption file.

(2) File a petition pursuant to section 3107.41 of the Revised Code for the release of information regarding the adopted person's name by birth and the identity of the adopted person's biological parent and biological sibling.

(1996 H 419, eff. 9–18–96)

Cross References

Adoption registration, release of file contents, see   Fees for copying adoption file, contents, see
   3705.12   3705.241

Library References

Records ☜32.   C.J.S. Bankruptcy §§ 830 to 834.
Westlaw Topic No. 326.   C.J.S. Records §§ 80, 82 to 88.

Research References

Forms

Ohio Jurisprudence Pleading and Practice Forms
   § 96:37, Request to Department for Adoption
   Information--Adoptee.

3107.39   Definitions

As used in sections 3107.39 to 3107.44 of the Revised Code:

(A) "Adopted person" means a person who, as a minor, was adopted and who, prior to September 18, 1996, became available or potentially available for adoption. For the purpose of this division, a person was available or potentially available for adoption prior to September 18, 1996, if, prior to that date, either of the following occurred:

(1) At least one of the person's biological parents executed consent to person's adoption;

(2) A probate court entered a finding that the consent of at least one of the person's biological parents to the person's adoption was not needed as determined pursuant to section 3107.07 of the Revised Code.

(B) "Adopted sibling" means an adopted person who has a biological sibling.

(C) "Agency" means any public or private organization that is certified by the department of job and family services to place minors for adoption.

(D) "Biological parent" means a parent, by birth, of an adopted person.

(E) "Biological sibling" means a sibling, by birth, of an adopted person.

(F) "Effective release" means a release that is filed by a biological parent or biological sibling of an adopted person, and with respect to which a withdrawal of release has not been filed by that biological parent or biological sibling.

(G) "File of releases" means the file that is established by the department of health pursuant to division (C) of section 3107.40 of the Revised Code.

(H) "Final decree of adoption" includes an interlocutory order of adoption that has become final.

(I) "Identifying information" has the same meaning as in section 3107.01 of the Revised Code.

(J) "Offspring" means a child, by birth, of a person.

(K) "Petition for release of information" means the petition filed in a probate court in accordance with section 3107.41 of the Revised Code.

(L) "Release" means the form that is filed, pursuant to division (B) of section 3107.40 of the Revised Code, by a biological parent or biological sibling with the department of health and that contains the information, statement, and matter required by division (B)(3) of that section.

(M) "Withdrawal of release" means the form that is filed, pursuant to division (D) of section 3107.40 of the Revised Code, by a biological parent or biological sibling with the department of health and that contains the information, statement, and matter required by division (D)(3) of that section.

(1999 H 471, eff. 7–1–00; 1996 H 419, eff. 9–18–96; 1988 H 790, eff. 3–16–89; 1984 H 84)

Historical and Statutory Notes

Amendment Note: 1999 H 471 substituted "September 18, 1996" for "the effective date of this amendment" twice in the introductory paragraph in division (A); and substituted "job and family" for "human" in division (C).

Amendment Note: 1996 H 419 rewrote this section, which prior thereto read:

"As used in sections 3107.39 to 3107.44 of the Revised Code:

"(A) 'Adopted person' means a person who, as a minor, was adopted pursuant to a final decree of adoption entered by a court.

"(B) 'Agency' means any public or private organization that is certified by the department of human services to place minors for adoption.

"(C) 'Biological parent' means a parent, by birth, of an adopted person and, for purposes of section 3107.40 of the Revised Code, includes a parent, by birth, of a minor who has been placed for adoption.

"(D) 'Biological sibling' means a sibling, by birth, of an adopted person and, for purposes of section 3107.40 of the Revised Code, includes a sibling, by birth, of a minor who has been placed for adoption.

"(E) 'Effective release' means a release that is filed by a biological parent or biological sibling of an adopted person, and with respect to which a withdrawal of release has not been filed by that biological parent or biological sibling.

"(F) 'File of releases' means the file that is established by the department of health pursuant to division (C) of section 3107.40 of the Revised Code.

"(G) 'Final decree of adoption' includes an interlocutory order of adoption that has become final.

"(H) 'Identifying information' means information that is described in either of the following categories:

"(1) Information that is likely to assist an adopted person in identifying his name by birth or one or both of his biological parents and that is described in any of the following categories:

"(a) The information is contained in the copy of the adopted person's original birth record that is obtained by an agency pursuant to an order of a probate judge to the department of health to provide the agency with a copy of the person's original birth record.

"(b) If the probate court in which the petition for release of identifying information is filed is the court that entered the final decree of adoption in the adoption proceedings pertaining to the adopted person, the information is contained in the adoption records of that court. Such information includes, but is not limited to, the addresses of the adopted person's biological parents at the time of the entry of the decree.

"(c) The information is contained in a release filed by a biological parent of the adopted person and is obtained by an agency pursuant to division (B)(2) of section 3107.41 of the Revised Code.

"(d) The information is contained in a probate court's or agency's records and relates to any deceased biological parent of the adopted person.

"(2) If the adopted person's original birth record contains the name of only one of his biological parents, a statement that informs the adopted person of this fact.

"'Identifying information' does not include information that pertains to a biological sibling of the adopted person.

"(I) 'Offspring' means a child, by birth, of a person.

"(J) 'Adopted sibling' means a sibling, by birth, of a person who has been adopted or in relation to whom an adoption petition has been filed.

"(K) 'Petition for release of information' means the petition filed in a probate court in accordance with section 3107.41 of the Revised Code.

"(L) 'Release' means the form that is filed, pursuant to division (B) of section 3107.40 of the Revised Code, by a biological parent or biological sibling with the department of health and that contains the information, statement, and matter required by division (B)(3) of that section.

"(M) 'Withdrawal of release' means the form that is filed, pursuant to division (D) of section 3107.40 of the Revised Code, by a biological parent or biological sibling with the department of health and that contains the information, statement, and matter required by division (D)(3) of that section."

Cross References

Assessor's meeting with birth parent prior to parent's consenting to adoption, adopted person defined, see 5103.152

Conditions for juvenile court approving parent's agreement for child's adoption, adopted person defined, see 5103.151

Probate court, procedure; adoption information, fees, see 2101.16

Library References

Records ☞32.
Westlaw Topic No. 326.

C.J.S. Bankruptcy §§ 830 to 834.
C.J.S. Records §§ 80, 82 to 88.

Research References

Encyclopedias

OH Jur. 3d Family Law § 914, Forwarding of Adoption Information.

Forms

Ohio Forms Legal and Business § 28:18, Placement of Children in Independent Adoptions.

Ohio Jurisprudence Pleading and Practice Forms § 48:7, Public Records.

Ohio Jurisprudence Pleading and Practice Forms § 96:1, Definitions.

Ohio Jurisprudence Pleading and Practice Forms § 96:11, Consent Required.

Ohio Jurisprudence Pleading and Practice Forms § 96:15, Court's Acceptance of Parental Consent.

Ohio Jurisprudence Pleading and Practice Forms § 96:20, Home Study.

Ohio Jurisprudence Pleading and Practice Forms § 96:27, Permanent Custody Surrender Agreement--Juvenile Court Approval.

Ohio Jurisprudence Pleading and Practice Forms § 96:32, Confidentiality.

Ohio Jurisprudence Pleading and Practice Forms § 96:41, Nonpublic Records.

Ohio Jurisprudence Pleading and Practice Forms § 96:42, Unauthorized Release of Information.

Treatises and Practice Aids

Carlin, Baldwin's Ohio Prac. Merrick-Rippner Probate Law § 99:1, Defined.

Carlin, Baldwin's Ohio Prac. Merrick-Rippner Probate Law § 99:29, Papers and Records--Confidentiality.

Carlin, Baldwin's Ohio Prac. Merrick-Rippner Probate Law § 99:49, Interlocutory and Final Orders.

Carlin, Baldwin's Ohio Prac. Merrick-Rippner Probate Law App B SPF 18.6, Final Decree of Adoption (After Interlocutory Order).

Carlin, Baldwin's Ohio Prac. Merrick-Rippner Probate Law App B SPF 18.7, Final Decree of Adoption (Without Interlocutory Order).

Law Review and Journal Commentaries

Ohio House Bill 419: Increased Openness in Adoption Records Law, Wendy L. Weiss. 45 Clev St L Rev 101 (1997).

3107.40 Release of identifying information; consent of biological parents or siblings; procedures; withdrawal of release

(A) The department of health shall prescribe a form that permits any biological parent to authorize the release of identifying information, in accordance with section 3107.41 of the

Revised Code, to the biological parent's offspring and a form that permits any biological sibling to authorize the release of specified information, in accordance with section 3107.41 of the Revised Code, to the biological sibling's adopted sibling. The forms shall be designed in a manner that permits the biological parent or biological sibling, whichever is applicable, to supply the information, statement, and matter required by division (B)(3) of this section. The department shall prepare written instructions that explain to biological parents and biological siblings the manner in which the applicable form is to be completed; the information, statement, and matter required by division (B)(3) of this section; and the manner in which the completed form is to be filed by a biological parent or biological sibling with the department.

The department shall provide copies of the forms and the instructions to agencies located in, and to the probate courts of, this state. Upon request of any biological parent or biological sibling, the department shall provide the parent or sibling with a copy of the applicable form and the instructions. If an agency or a probate court has copies of the applicable form and the instructions available, the agency or probate court shall provide, upon request, a copy of the applicable form and the instructions to any biological parent or biological sibling.

(B)(1) Any biological parent or biological sibling who wishes to obtain a copy of the applicable form prescribed and the instructions prepared by the department pursuant to division (A) of this section, may obtain them from the department or from an agency located in, or a probate court of, this state, if the agency or probate court has copies of the form and instructions available.

(2) Any biological parent who wishes to authorize the release of identifying information, in accordance with section 3107.41 of the Revised Code, to the biological parent's offspring, and any biological sibling who wishes to authorize the release of specified information, in accordance with section 3107.41 of the Revised Code, to the biological sibling's adopted sibling shall file with the department, on a copy of the applicable form prescribed by it pursuant to division (A) of this section, a release that contains the information, statement, and matter required by division (B)(3) of this section. A release may be filed with the department at any time.

(3) A release shall contain at least the following:

(a) For a biological parent:

(i) The complete name of the biological parent who is filing the release, at the time of its filing with the department and at the time the adoption petition for the biological parent's offspring was filed, if the biological parent knows when the petition was filed;

(ii) The complete name and date of birth, as set forth in the original birth record, of the offspring of the biological parent to whom the biological parent authorizes the release of identifying information in accordance with section 3107.41 of the Revised Code;

(iii) A statement authorizing the release of identifying information, in accordance with section 3107.41 of the Revised Code, to that offspring;

(iv) The written signature of the biological parent, the biological parent's residential mailing address, and the date upon which the release is filed with the department.

(b) For a biological sibling:

(i) The complete name of the biological sibling who is filing the release, at the time of its filing with the department and at the time the adoption petition for the biological sibling's adopted sibling was filed, if the biological sibling knows when the petition was filed;

(ii) The complete name and date of birth, as set forth in the original birth record, of the adopted sibling to whom the biological sibling authorizes the release of the specified information in accordance with section 3107.41 of the Revised Code;

(iii) A statement authorizing the release of the information specified in the release, in accordance with section 3107.41 of the Revised Code, to that adopted sibling;

(iv) The signature of the biological sibling, the biological sibling's residential mailing address, and the date upon which the release is filed with the department.

(4)(a) A release of a biological parent also may contain information that is not required by division (B)(3)(a) of this section and that the biological parent wishes to reveal, in accordance with section 3107.41 of the Revised Code, to the biological parent's offspring. This information shall not include information pertaining to the other biological parent of the offspring or information pertaining to a biological sibling of the offspring.

(b) A release of a biological sibling also may contain information that is not required by division (B)(3)(b) of this section and that the biological sibling wishes to reveal, in accordance with section 3107.41 of the Revised Code, to the biological sibling's adopted sibling. This information shall not include information pertaining to either biological parent of the adopted person or information pertaining to any biological sibling of the adopted person other than the sibling filing the release.

(C) The department shall establish and maintain a file of releases that shall be organized in the manner described in this section and be used in accordance with section 3107.41 of the Revised Code. If any biological parent or biological sibling files with the department a release that has been completed in accordance with the applicable provisions of division (B) of this section, the department shall accept it and place it in the file of releases in accordance with this division.

The department shall place each release accepted pursuant to this division in the file of releases in alphabetical order, according to the surname of the offspring or adopted sibling to whom it pertains, as set forth in the release. The department shall maintain an index to the file of releases that shall list each offspring and each adopted sibling in alphabetical order, according to the surname set forth in the release. The department also shall maintain a separate, alphabetical index to the file of releases that shall list each biological parent and each biological sibling who files a release according to the biological parent's or biological sibling's name at the time of the filing of the release or, if the release indicates that the biological parent or biological sibling had a different name at the time of the filing of an adoption petition, according to the biological parent's or biological sibling's name at that time; and that shall cross-reference each biological parent and each biological sibling listing to the listing of the biological parent's offspring or biological sibling's adopted sibling, whichever is applicable, that is contained in the other index to the file of releases.

(D)(1) The department of health shall prescribe a form that permits any biological parent or biological sibling who has filed a release with the department pursuant to division (B) of this section to withdraw the release. The form shall be designed in a manner that permits the biological parent or biological sibling to supply the information, statement, and matter required by division (D)(3) of this section. Upon request of any biological parent or biological sibling who has filed a release with the department pursuant to division (B) of this section, the department shall provide a copy of the form to the biological parent or biological sibling.

(2) At any time after filing a release with the department, a biological parent or biological sibling may withdraw the release by filing with the department, on a form prescribed by it pursuant to division (D)(1) of this section, a withdrawal of release that contains the information, statement, and matter required by division (D)(3) of this section.

(3) A withdrawal of release shall contain all the following:

(a) The information that the biological parent set forth in the release in accordance with divisions (B)(3)(a)(i) and (ii) of this section, or that the biological sibling set forth in the release in accordance with divisions (B)(3)(b)(i) and (ii) of this section, whichever is applicable;

(b) A statement withdrawing the authorization of the biological parent to release identifying information, in accordance with section 3107.41 of the Revised Code, to the biological parent's offspring, or withdrawing the authorization of the biological sibling to release specified information, in accordance with section 3107.41 of the Revised Code, to the biological sibling's adopted sibling, whichever is applicable;

(c) The written signature of the biological parent or biological sibling, the biological parent's or biological sibling's residential mailing address, and the date upon which the withdrawal of release is filed with the department.

(4) If any biological parent or biological sibling who previously filed a release with the department, files with the department a withdrawal of release that has been completed in accordance with division (D)(3) of this section, the department shall accept the withdrawal of release and place it in the file of releases together with and attached to the release previously filed by the biological parent or biological sibling. Upon request of the biological parent or biological sibling, the department shall provide the biological parent or biological sibling with a copy of the withdrawal of release.

Upon the withdrawal of a release, the department shall note in the index to the file of releases that lists each biological parent and biological sibling who files a release, the fact that the biological parent or biological sibling has filed the withdrawal of release. This notation shall be placed in the index next to the biological parent's or biological sibling's name and the cross-reference to the listing of the biological parent's offspring or the biological sibling's adopted sibling in the other index to the file of releases.

(1996 H 419, eff. 9–18–96; 1988 H 790, eff. 3–16–89; 1984 H 84)

Historical and Statutory Notes

Amendment Note: 1996 H 419 deleted divisions (A)(1) and (2) and redesignated division (A)(3) as division (A); rewrote divisions (B)(3)(a)(i) and (B)(3)(b)(i); and made changes to reflect gender neutral language. Prior to amendment, divisions (A)(1) and (2), (B)(3)(a)(i) and (B)(3)(b)(i), respectively, read:

"(A)(1) The department of human services shall prescribe the procedure to be used by agencies for informing the biological parents of their right to file a form that permits them to authorize the release of identifying information to their offspring, in accordance with section 3107.41 of the Revised Code. The procedure shall include instructions for advising the biological parents of their right to authorize the release of identifying information at the time of the transfer of permanent custody, in accordance with section 5103.15 or Chapter 2151. of the Revised Code, or when a consent to adoption is filed, whichever occurs first.

"(2) A probate court that is acting upon an application filed pursuant to section 5103.16 of the Revised Code shall prescribe the procedure for notification of the biological parents of their right to file a form that permits them to authorize the release of identifying information to their offspring, in accordance with section 3107.41 of the Revised Code."

"(i) The complete name of the biological parent who is filing the release, at the time of its filing with the department; and, if prior to the filing of the release, an adoption petition has been filed or a final decree of adoption entered relative to the offspring described in division (B)(3)(a)(ii) of this section, and the biological parent is aware of the adoption proceedings, the complete name of that biological parent at the time of the filing of that adoption petition [.]"

"(i) The complete name of the biological sibling who is filing the release, at the time of its filing with the department and, if prior to the filing of the release, an adoption petition has been filed or a final decree of adoption entered regarding the adopted sibling described in division (B)(3)(b)(ii) of this section and the biological sibling is aware of the adoption proceedings, the complete name of that biological sibling at the time of the filing of the adoption petition [.]"

Cross References

Availability of public records, see 149.43
Courts, confidentiality of adoption files, Sup R 55
Probate court, procedure; adoption information, fees, see 2101.16

Registration of adoption, original birth record no longer a public record, see 3705.12

Ohio Administrative Code References

Release of identifying and nonidentifying information, see OAC 5101:2–48–17

Library References

Health ⟾397.
Records ⟾32.
Westlaw Topic Nos. 198H, 326.

C.J.S. Bankruptcy §§ 830 to 834.
C.J.S. Health and Environment §§ 24, 74.
C.J.S. Records §§ 80, 82 to 88.

Research References

Encyclopedias

OH Jur. 3d Family Law § 913, Records and Papers--Inspection.

Forms

Ohio Forms Legal and Business § 28:18, Placement of Children in Independent Adoptions.

Ohio Jurisprudence Pleading and Practice Forms § 96:1, Definitions.

Ohio Jurisprudence Pleading and Practice Forms § 96:35, Authorization by Biological Parent or Sibling.

Law Review and Journal Commentaries

Ohio House Bill 419: Increased Openness in Adoption Records Law, Wendy L. Weiss. 45 Clev St L Rev 101 (1997).

3107.41   Rights of an adult who believes he is an adopted person; birth record; procedures

(A)(1) Any person who is twenty-one years of age or older and who believes he is an adopted person may file a petition for the release of information regarding his name by birth, and the identity of his biological parents and biological siblings, as follows:

(a) If the person is a resident of this state, the petition shall be filed in the probate court of the county in which he resides or in the probate court that entered the final decree of adoption in the adoption proceedings pertaining to him;

(b) If the person is not a resident of this state, the petition shall be filed in the probate court that entered the final decree of adoption in the adoption proceedings pertaining to him, or, if the person does not know which probate court entered that decree, in the probate court of any county.

(2) The petition shall be accompanied by the fee that the probate court has fixed pursuant to division (E) of section 2101.16 of the Revised Code.

(B)(1) Upon the filing of a petition for the release of such information and the payment of the fee fixed by the probate court, the probate judge to whom the petition is assigned shall do each of the following:

(a) Appoint the agency that was involved in the adoption proceeding to perform the tasks described in divisions (B)(2), (C), and (D) of this section, or if no agency was involved in the proceeding, it is not possible to determine the agency involved, or the court determines that it is not feasible for the agency involved in the proceeding to perform those tasks, appoint any agency to perform those tasks;

(b) Issue an order to the department of health that requires it to provide the agency appointed pursuant to division (B)(1)(a) of this section with a copy of the original birth record of the petitioner or with the identity of the court involved in the petitioner's adoption if the department does not possess the original birth record of the petitioner;

(c) Give a certified copy of the order issued pursuant to division (B)(1)(b) of this section to the appointed agency;

(d) Require the appointed agency to perform the tasks described in division (B)(2) of this section within the time that the judge shall prescribe, which time shall be no later than ninety days from the date of appointment or as extended by the judge for good cause shown.

(2)(a) An agency appointed pursuant to division (B)(1) of this section shall present, by mail or in another reasonable manner, the certified copy of the order issued pursuant to division (B)(1) of this section to the department of health. Upon receipt of the order, the department shall provide the agency with a copy of the original birth record of the petitioner, if any. If the department possesses no original birth record of the petitioner, it shall inform the agency, in writing, of this fact and shall provide the agency with the identity of the court that was involved in the petitioner's adoption, and the agency, upon receipt of this information, shall present, by mail or in another reasonable manner, a copy of the order issued pursuant to division (B)(1) of this section and a copy of the information provided by the department to that court and shall request the court to provide the agency with a copy of the original birth record of the petitioner. Upon receipt of the copy of the order and the copy of the information provided by the department, the court shall provide the agency with a copy of the original birth record of the petitioner, if any. If the court possesses no copy of the original birth record of the petitioner, it shall inform the agency of this fact, and, if the court determines that the petitioner was born outside of this state, the department also shall inform the agency of the petitioner's state of birth and shall provide the agency with any pertinent information contained in its file that normally is noted on a birth record in this state.

(b) If the agency receives a copy of the petitioner's original birth record, it shall inspect the record. If the agency determines, upon the inspection, that the petitioner is not an adopted person, it shall report this determination to the probate court in writing. If it determines, upon the inspection, that the petitioner is an adopted person, it shall contact the department of health and request the department to determine whether the file of releases contains a release or releases filed by one or both of the petitioner's biological parents and authorizing the release of identifying information to him, to determine whether the file of releases contains a release or releases filed by any biological sibling of the petitioner and authorizing the release of specified information to him, to determine whether a withdrawal of release also has been filed with respect to any such release, and to provide the agency with a copy of each release with respect to which a withdrawal of release has not been filed. If the agency determines, upon the inspection, that the petitioner is an adopted person, the agency also shall review its records to determine whether they indicate that one or both of the petitioner's biological parents as indicated on the petitioner's original birth record are deceased.

Upon receipt of an agency's request as described in this division, the department of health shall search the file of releases to determine whether it contains a release or releases filed by one or both of the petitioner's biological parents and authorizing the release of identifying information to him, to determine whether it contains a release or releases filed by any biological sibling of the petitioner and authorizing the release of specified information to him, and to determine whether a withdrawal of release also has been filed with respect to any such release. The department promptly shall inform the agency, in writing, of its findings and provide the agency with a copy of each such release with respect to which a withdrawal of release has not been filed.

(c) If the department of health informs an agency either that the file of releases does not contain a release or releases filed by one or both of the petitioner's biological parents that authorize the release of identifying information to him and does not contain a release or releases filed by any biological sibling of the petitioner that authorize the release of specified information to him or that it contains at least one such release but a withdrawal of release has been filed that negates each such release, the agency shall report its determination that the petitioner is an adopted person and the findings of the department to the probate court, in writing, and shall attach to the report the copy of the petitioner's original birth record. If the department informs the agency that the file of releases contains a release or releases filed by one or both of the petitioner's biological parents that authorize the release of identifying information to him for which no withdrawal has been filed or contains a release or releases filed by any biological sibling of the petitioner for which no withdrawal has been filed, and provides the agency with a copy of each such release, the agency shall report its determination that the petitioner is an adopted person and the findings of the department to the probate court, in writing, and shall attach to the report the copy of the petitioner's original birth record and the copy of each release provided by the department. In either case, if the agency after its review of records, has determined that one or both of the petitioner's biological parents as indicated on the petitioner's original birth record are deceased, the agency also shall report that fact to the probate court, in writing, and shall identify the deceased parent or parents.

If the department informs the agency that it possesses no original birth record of the petitioner, the agency shall report that fact and the identity of the court that was involved in the petitioner's adoption, as provided by the department, to the probate court, in writing; if the court that was involved in the adoption informs the agency that it possesses no copy of the original birth record of the petitioner, the agency also shall report that fact to the probate court, in writing; and if the court that was involved in the adoption informs the agency that the petitioner was born outside of this state, the agency also shall report that fact and the identity of the other state to the probate court, in writing.

(d) An agency shall perform all tasks required of it by division (B)(2) of this section within the time prescribed by the probate judge pursuant to division (B)(1)(d) of this section.

(C) Upon receipt of an agency's report submitted pursuant to division (B)(2) of this section, the probate judge shall review the records of the court to determine whether they indicate that one or both of the petitioner's biological parents as indicated on the petitioner's original birth record are deceased, and shall do whichever of the following is appropriate:

(1) If the agency determined that the petitioner is not an adopted person, or if no original birth record was possessed by the department of health and no copy of such record was possessed by the court that was involved in the petitioner's adoption, the judge shall enter an order dismissing the petition, which order shall state the reason for the dismissal.

(2) If the agency determined that the petitioner is an adopted person, if the department of health informed the agency either that the file of releases does not contain a release or releases filed by one or both of the petitioner's biological parents that authorize the release of identifying information to him and does not contain a release or releases filed by any biological sibling that authorizes the release of specified information to him or that the file of releases contains at least one such release but a withdrawal of release has been filed that negates each such release, if the agency did not inform the court that it had determined that one or both of the petitioner's biological parents as indicated on the petitioner's original birth record were deceased, and if the court did not determine that one or both of the petitioner's biological parents as indicated on that record were deceased, the judge shall order that the petition remain pending until withdrawn by the petitioner and order the department of health to note its pendency in the file of releases according to the surname of the petitioner as set forth in his original birth record; shall inform the petitioner that he is an adopted person and, if known, of the county in which the adoption proceedings occurred; shall inform the petitioner that information regarding his name by birth and the identity of his biological parents and biological siblings may not be released at that time because the file of releases at that time does not contain an effective release that authorizes the release of any such information to him; and shall inform the petitioner that, upon the subsequent filing of a release by or the death of either of his biological parents, or the subsequent filing of a release by any of his biological siblings, the petition will be acted upon within thirty days of the filing in accordance with division (E) of this section.

(3) If the agency determined that the petitioner is an adopted person and either the agency informed the court that it had determined that one or both of the petitioner's biological parents as indicated on the petitioner's original birth record were deceased or the court determined that one or both of the petitioner's biological parents as indicated on that record were deceased, the judge shall proceed as follows:

(a) The judge shall inform the petitioner that he is an adopted person and, if known, of the county in which the adoption proceedings occurred;

(b) The judge shall inform the petitioner that one or both of his biological parents, whichever is applicable, is deceased, provided that the information provided under this requirement shall not identify either biological parent of the petitioner;

(c) If two biological parents were indicated on the petitioner's original birth record, if only one of those biological parents is deceased, and if an effective release of the surviving biological parent that authorizes the release of identifying information to the petitioner was provided the agency by the department of health, the judge shall comply with division (C)(4) of this section in relation to the surviving biological parent, and the judge may enter an order granting the petition in relation to the deceased biological parent and requiring the agency and the department of health to release identifying information in relation to the deceased biological parent, subject to the limitations of division (D)(2) of this section and within the time prescribed by the judge;

(d) If two biological parents were indicated on the petitioner's original birth record, if only one of those biological parents is deceased, and if either no effective release of the surviving biological parent that authorizes the release of identifying information to the petitioner is contained in the file of releases or such an effective release is contained in the file but the judge does not enter an order of a type described in division (C)(3)(c) of this section, the judge shall inform the petitioner that one of his biological parents is deceased, shall order that the petition remain pending until withdrawn by the petitioner and order the department of health to note its pendency in the file of releases according to the surname of the petitioner as set forth in his original birth record, and shall inform the petitioner that upon the subsequent filing of a release by or the death of the surviving biological parent, the petition will be acted on in accordance with division (E) of this section;

(e) If two biological parents were indicated on the petitioner's original birth record and both of them are deceased or if only one biological parent was indicated on that record and is deceased, the judge may enter an order granting the petition in relation to each such deceased biological parent and requiring the agency and the department of health to release identifying information in relation to each such deceased biological parent to the petitioner, subject to the limitations of division (D)(2) of this section and within the time prescribed by the judge; if the judge does not enter such an order the petition shall be dismissed;

(f) The judge shall comply with division (C)(4)(d) of this section in relation to any biological sibling of the petitioner who has filed a release that authorizes the release of information to the petitioner and that has not been withdrawn.

(4) If the agency determined that the petitioner is an adopted person and the department of health provided the agency with a copy of each release that authorizes the release of identifying information or specified information to him, the judge shall do each of the following that applies:

(a) Enter an order granting the petition in relation to each biological parent who has filed a release that has not been withdrawn;

(b) Inform the petitioner that he is an adopted person and, if known, of the county in which the adoption proceedings occurred;

(c) In relation to a biological parent:

(i) Require the agency to release identifying information to the petitioner, subject to the limitations of division (D)(2) of this section and within the time prescribed by the judge;

(ii) If an effective release of only one of the petitioner's biological parents that authorizes the release of information to him is contained in the file of releases and either the agency has informed the court that it has determined that the other biological parent is deceased or the court has determined that the other biological parent is deceased, comply with division (C)(3) of this section in relation to the deceased biological parent;

(iii) If an effective release of only one of the petitioner's biological parents that authorizes the release of identifying information to him is contained in the file of releases, if the agency has not informed the court that it has determined that the other biological parent is deceased, and if the court has not determined that the other biological parent is deceased, order that the petition remain pending as to the other biological parent until withdrawn by the petitioner and order the department of health to note its pendency in the file of releases according to the surname of the petitioner as set forth in his original birth record, and inform the petitioner that, upon the subsequent filing of a release by or the death of that biological parent or the filing of a release by any biological sibling, the petition will be acted upon within thirty days of the filing in accordance with division (E) of this section.

(d) In relation to a biological sibling:

(i) If the agency or the court has determined that each biological parent indicated on the petitioner's original birth record is deceased or has filed a release authorizing the release of identifying information to the petitioner that has not been withdrawn, enter an order granting the petition in relation to the biological sibling, require the agency to release the information specified in the biological sibling's release to the petitioner, subject to the limitations of division (D)(2) of this section and within the time prescribed by the judge;

(ii) Order that the petition remain pending until withdrawn by the petitioner and order the department of health to note its pendency in the file of releases according to the surname of the petitioner as set forth in his original birth record, and inform the petitioner that, upon the subsequent filing of a release by any biological sibling or biological parent whose effective release is not contained in the file, the petition will be acted upon within thirty days in accordance with division (E) of this section.

(D)(1) Each agency that is required by an order of a probate judge entered under division (C)(3) or (4) of this section to release information to a petitioner shall do both of the following:

(a) Gather all the information that is subject to the order that it is permitted to release;

(b) Subject to the limitations of division (D)(2) of this section and within the time prescribed by the judge, release to the petitioner the information that is subject to the order that it is permitted to release.

(2)(a) Except as otherwise provided in this division, if a biological parent of a petitioner is deceased or an effective release of a biological parent of a petitioner is contained in the file of releases, and an agency is required by an order of a probate judge entered under division (C)(3) or (4) of this section to release identifying information pertaining to that biological parent to the petitioner, the agency shall not release to the petitioner any identifying information pertaining to a surviving biological parent who filed a withdrawal of release, a surviving biological parent who did not file a release, or a deceased biological parent other than in the circumstances described in division (C)(3) of this section, or any information pertaining to a biological sibling of the petitioner. The agency shall release identifying information pertaining to any biological parent of the petitioner who the probate court's or agency's records indicates is deceased in accordance with an order to do so issued under division (C)(3) of this section, and if a biological sibling has filed an effective release, shall release the information specified in the release, in accordance with any order issued under division (C)(4) of this section requiring the release.

(b) Except as otherwise provided in this division, if an effective release of a biological sibling of a petitioner is in the file of releases and an agency is required by an order of a probate judge entered under division (C)(4) of this section to release information specified in the release of that biological sibling to the petitioner, the agency shall not release to the petitioner any information pertaining to a biological sibling of the petitioner who filed a withdrawal of release or who did not file a release, or any identifying information pertaining to a biological parent of the petitioner. The agency shall release identifying information pertaining to any biological parent of the petitioner who the probate court's or agency's records indicate is deceased in accordance with an order to do so issued under division (C)(3) of this section, and shall release identifying information pertaining to any biological parent who has filed an effective release, in accordance with any order issued by a probate judge under division (C)(4) of this section requiring the release of identifying information.

(E) The petition of a petitioner to whom no information is released in relation to a biological parent in accordance with an order entered pursuant to division (C)(2) of this section, or in accordance with division (C)(3) or (4) of this section, shall remain pending until withdrawn by the petitioner. The petition of a petitioner to whom identifying information is released concerning only one biological parent in accordance with an order entered pursuant to division (C)(3) or (4) of this section shall remain pending as to the other biological parent and as to biological siblings until withdrawn by the petitioner. At the same time as it enters the order under division (C)(2), (3), or (4) of this section, the probate court in which the petition is pending shall order the department of health promptly to provide both the agency appointed pursuant to division (B)(1) of this section and the court with a copy of each release that subsequently is filed by one or both of the petitioner's biological parents, or by the petitioner's other biological parent, whichever is applicable, or by a biological sibling of the petitioner, and that authorizes the release of identifying information to the petitioner, and promptly to notify the agency and the court of the death of a surviving biological parent as indicated on the petitioner's original birth record for whom no identifying information had been released relative to the petition for release, of which the department gains knowledge. Upon receipt of a copy of any such release or of notice of the death of any such biological parent, the probate judge, within thirty days of the date on which the release was filed with the department or the date on which the department gained knowledge of the death, shall do each thing listed in divisions (C)(3)(a) to (f) or (4)(a) to (d) of this section that applies.

Any petitioner who has filed a petition with the probate court that is to remain pending under this division and who wishes to update it with respect to a new mailing address may inform the department in writing, through the court, of the new address. The court shall promptly file the writing with the department and provide the department with the petitioner's name as set forth in his original birth record. The department shall attach the writing to the notation of pendency of the petition contained in the file of releases. Any petitioner who has filed a petition with the probate court that is to remain pending under this division may file a written withdrawal of the petition with the court at any time. Upon the filing of such a withdrawal, the court shall enter an order dismissing the petition, and shall notify both the agency appointed pursuant to division (B)(1) of this section and the department of health of the withdrawal, and upon receipt of such a notice, the department does not have to provide copies of any subsequently filed releases to the agency or the court, as otherwise would be required by this division.

(F) An agency that performs any task described in this division relative to or in connection with a petition for the release of identifying information filed under this section may be reimbursed a reasonable portion of the fee charged for the filing of that petition, in accordance with division (D) of section 2101.16 of the Revised Code, for any services it renders in performing any such task.

(1989 S 46, eff. 1–1–90; 1988 H 790; 1984 H 84)

Cross References

Adoption information, jurisdiction of probate court, see 2101.24
Availability of public records, see 149.43
Certificate of adoption for person born in foreign country, inspection; registration of adoption, new birth record issued, see 3705.12
Courts, confidentiality of adoption files, Sup R 55
Department of job and family services, division of social administration; care and placement of

children; interstate compact on placement of children, see 5103.12 to 5103.17, 5103.20 et seq.
Placement of children from other states, see 2151.39
Powers and duties of county children services board, see 5153.16
Probate court, procedure, adoption information, fees, see 2101.16
Registration of births, see 3705.09

Library References

Health ☞397.
Records ☞32 to 34, 58.
Westlaw Topic Nos. 198H, 326.
C.J.S. Bankruptcy §§ 830 to 834.

C.J.S. Health and Environment §§ 24, 74.
C.J.S. Records §§ 77 to 80, 82 to 88, 102 to 105, 123 to 124, 136 to 137.

Research References

Encyclopedias

OH Jur. 3d Family Law § 913, Records and Papers--Inspection.

Forms

Ohio Jurisprudence Pleading and Practice Forms § 96:1, Definitions.
Ohio Jurisprudence Pleading and Practice Forms § 96:34, Birth Record.
Ohio Jurisprudence Pleading and Practice Forms § 96:35, Authorization by Biological Parent or Sibling.

Ohio Jurisprudence Pleading and Practice Forms § 96:36, Adult Adopted Person's Petition for Information.
Ohio Jurisprudence Pleading and Practice Forms § 96:37, Request to Department for Adoption Information--Adoptee.
Ohio Jurisprudence Pleading and Practice Forms § 96:42, Unauthorized Release of Information.

Treatises and Practice Aids

Carlin, Baldwin's Ohio Prac. Merrick-Rippner Probate Law § 99:29, Papers and Records--Confidentiality.

Law Review and Journal Commentaries

The only Americans legally prohibited from knowing who their birth parents are: A rejection of privacy rights as a bar to adult adoptees' access to original birth and adoption records. Susan Whittaker Hughes, 55 Clev. St. L. Rev. 429 (2007).

Notes of Decisions

Consent to discovery   1

Privileged Communications And Confidentiality ☞ 265

---

1. Consent to discovery

Assuming that counsel for adoptee promised in open court, in wrongful adoption action brought by adoptee's parents against Department of Human Services (DHS), that adoptee would consent to disclosure of his confidential medical information if bifurcated trial reached damages phase, such promise did not amount to blanket waiver of privilege against disclosure of such information during liability phase, where adoptee was not a complaining party, but had been joined by DHS as third-party defendant for sole purpose of compelling him to disclose medical information, and had thus not put his medical condition at issue. Sirca v. Medina Cty. Dept. of Human Serv. (Ohio App. 9 Dist., 08-08-2001) 145 Ohio App.3d 182, 762 N.E.2d 407.

Fact that adoptee's adoptive parents may have had in their possession and disclosed to Department of Human Services (DHS) certain of adoptee's medical and mental health treatment records did not imply adoptee's consent to discovery by DHS of records pertaining to adoptee's treatment after reaching age of majority, in context of parents' action against DHS for wrongful adoption; nothing in record established what medical records, if any, adoptee's parents disclosed to DHS or that parents obtained any of adoptee's medical records after adoptee reached majority, or rebutted possibility that adoptee consented to release of certain medical records and not others. Sirca v. Medina Cty. Dept. of Human Serv. (Ohio App. 9 Dist., 08-08-2001) 145 Ohio App.3d 182, 762 N.E.2d 407. Privileged Communications And Confidentiality ☞ 265; Privileged Communications And Confidentiality ☞ 323

3107.42   Records declared not public

(A) The following records are not public records subject to inspection or copying under section 149.43 of the Revised Code:

(1) The file of releases;

(2) The indices to the file of releases;

(3) Releases and withdrawals of releases in the file of releases, and information contained in them;

(4) Probate court and agency records pertaining to proceedings under sections 3107.39 to 3107.44 of the Revised Code.

(B) No adopted person who is the subject of personal information contained in a record listed in division (A) of this section may inspect or copy all or part of any such record. (1984 H 84, eff. 3–19–85)

Cross References

Availability of public records, see 149.43
Courts, confidentiality of adoption files, Sup R 55

Personal information systems, rights of subjects or possible subjects to inspection, see 1347.08

Library References

Records ☞32.
Westlaw Topic No. 326.

C.J.S. Bankruptcy §§ 830 to 834.
C.J.S. Records §§ 80, 82 to 88.

Research References

Encyclopedias

OH Jur. 3d Defamation & Privacy § 183, Exceptions.

Forms

Ohio Jurisprudence Pleading and Practice Forms § 48:7, Public Records.
Ohio Jurisprudence Pleading and Practice Forms § 96:41, Nonpublic Records.

Treatises and Practice Aids

Carlin, Baldwin's Ohio Prac. Merrick-Rippner Probate Law § 99:29, Papers and Records--Confidentiality.
Hennenberg & Reinhart, Ohio Criminal Defense Motions F 2:44, Motion for Sanctions for Violations of R.C. Chapter 149 [Public Records Act]--Discovery Demands and Motions.

Hennenberg & Reinhart, Ohio Criminal Defense Motions F 2:46, Motion to Inspect Public Records--Discovery Demands and Motions.

Gotherman & Babbit, Ohio Municipal Law § 6:12, Exceptions to General Rule.

Hastings, Manoloff, Sheeran, & Stype, Ohio School Law § 44:5, Scope.

Hastings, Manoloff, Sheeran, & Stype, Ohio School Law § 44:2.30, Public Records--Statutory Exclusions.

3107.43   Revealing information without statutory authority; penalty

(A) No employee or officer of the department of health shall knowingly reveal whether any release or withdrawal of release is included in the file of releases, knowingly provide a copy of any release or withdrawal of release in the files of releases, or knowingly reveal any information contained in any release or withdrawal of release in the file of releases, to any person unless authorized to do so by sections 3107.39 to 3107.44 of the Revised Code.

(B)(1) No agency, officer of an agency, or employee of an agency shall knowingly reveal any information regarding the name by birth of an adopted person or the identity of an adopted person's biological parents or biological siblings to a person who filed a petition for the release of such information unless a probate judge has entered an order under division (C)(3) or (4) of section 3107.41 of the Revised Code requiring the agency, officer, or employee to release such information to the petitioner.

(2) No agency required to release information regarding the name by birth of an adopted person or the identity of an adopted person's biological parents or biological siblings to a petitioner by an order entered by a probate judge under division (C)(3) or (4) of section 3107.41 of the Revised Code, officer of such an agency, or employee of such an agency shall knowingly reveal any information in violation of division (D)(2) of section 3107.41 of the Revised Code.

(C) Whoever violates this section is guilty of a minor misdemeanor.

(1984 H 84, eff. 3–19–85)

Cross References

Personal information systems, civil cause of action for harm done, criminal penalties, see 1347.10, 1347.99

Library References

Health ☞984.

Records ☞31.

Westlaw Topic Nos. 198H, 326.

C.J.S. Criminal Law §§ 587 to 591.

C.J.S. Health and Environment § 89.

C.J.S. Records §§ 89 to 111, 117.

Research References

Forms

Ohio Jurisprudence Pleading and Practice Forms § 96:42, Unauthorized Release of Information.

Treatises and Practice Aids

Carlin, Baldwin's Ohio Prac. Merrick-Rippner Probate Law § 99:29, Papers and Records--Confidentiality.

3107.44   Rights of adult who believes he is adopted; release of information to petitioner; immunity from liability

No agency, officer of an agency, or employee of an agency that releases any information to a petitioner pursuant to an order entered by a probate judge under division (C)(3) or (4) of section 3107.41 of the Revised Code is liable in damages in a civil action to any person for injury, death, or loss allegedly arising from the release of the information to the petitioner, or is criminally liable for the release of the information to the petitioner, if the agency, officer, or employee makes a good·faith effort to comply with division (D) of section 3107.41 of the Revised Code in its release of that information.

(1984 H 84, eff. 3–19–85)

Cross References

Civil liabilities of officers and employees, see 9.86

Library References

Health ☞367.
Infants ☞17.
Westlaw Topic Nos. 198H, 211.
C.J.S. Adoption of Persons §§ 10 to 14, 41.

C.J.S. Health and Environment §§ 9, 16 to 26, 44
to 45.
C.J.S. Infants §§ 6, 8 to 9.

Research References

Forms

Ohio Jurisprudence Pleading and Practice Forms
§ 48:7, Public Records.
Ohio Jurisprudence Pleading and Practice Forms
§ 96:1, Definitions.
Ohio Jurisprudence Pleading and Practice Forms
§ 96:32, Confidentiality.
Ohio Jurisprudence Pleading and Practice Forms
§ 96:41, Nonpublic Records.

Ohio Jurisprudence Pleading and Practice Forms
§ 96:42, Unauthorized Release of Information.

Treatises and Practice Aids

Carlin, Baldwin's Ohio Prac. Merrick-Rippner Probate Law § 99:1, Defined.
Carlin, Baldwin's Ohio Prac. Merrick-Rippner Probate Law § 99:29, Papers and Records--Confi-
dentiality.

ACCESS TO ADOPTION RECORDS BY BIRTH PARENTS AND SIBLINGS

3107.45 Definitions

As used in sections 3107.45 to 3107.53 of the Revised Code:

(A) "Adopted person" means a person who, as a minor, was adopted but is not an "adopted person" as defined in section 3107.39 of the Revised Code.

(B) "Adoption file" means the file maintained by the department of health under section 3705.12 of the Revised Code.

(C) "Adoptive parent" means a person who adopted an adopted person.

(D) "Authorization of release form" means the form prescribed under division (A)(2) of section 3107.50 of the Revised Code.

(E) "Birth parent" means the biological parent of an adopted person.

(F) "Birth sibling" means a biological sibling of an adopted person.

(G) "Denial of release form" means either of the following:

(1) The component of the form prescribed under division (A)(1)(b) of section 3107.083 if the birth parent checked the "no" space provided on that component.

(2) The form prescribed under division (A)(1) of section 3107.50 of the Revised Code.

(H) "Effective denial of release form" means a denial of release form that has not been rescinded by an authorization of release form pursuant to division (B) of section 3107.46 of the Revised Code.

(I) "Final decree of adoption" includes an interlocutory order of adoption that has become final.

(J) "Identifying information" has the same meaning as in section 3107.01 of the Revised Code.

(K) "Items of identification" include a motor vehicle driver's or commercial driver's license, an identification card issued under sections 4507.50 to 4507.52 of the Revised Code, a marriage application, a social security card, a credit card, a military identification card, or an employee identification card.

(1996 H 419, eff. 9–18–96)

Cross References

Conditions for juvenile court approving parent's agreement for child's adoption, adopted person defined, see 5103.151

Fees for copying adoption file, adoption records fund, see 3705.241

Ohio Administrative Code References

Forms used in the system of vital statistics, see OAC 3701–5–02

Library References

Records ⟿32.
Westlaw Topic No. 326.

C.J.S. Bankruptcy §§ 830 to 834.
C.J.S. Records §§ 80, 82 to 88.

Research References

Encyclopedias

OH Jur. 3d Family Law § 886, Execution of Consent.
OH Jur. 3d Family Law § 914, Forwarding of Adoption Information.

Forms

Ohio Jurisprudence Pleading and Practice Forms § 96:11, Consent Required.
Ohio Jurisprudence Pleading and Practice Forms § 96:15, Court's Acceptance of Parental Consent.
Ohio Jurisprudence Pleading and Practice Forms § 96:27, Permanent Custody Surrender Agreement--Juvenile Court Approval.

Ohio Jurisprudence Pleading and Practice Forms § 96:32, Confidentiality.

Treatises and Practice Aids

Carlin, Baldwin's Ohio Prac. Merrick-Rippner Probate Law § 99:49, Interlocutory and Final Orders.
Carlin, Baldwin's Ohio Prac. Merrick-Rippner Probate Law App B SPF 18.6, Final Decree of Adoption (After Interlocutory Order).
Carlin, Baldwin's Ohio Prac. Merrick-Rippner Probate Law App B SPF 18.7, Final Decree of Adoption (Without Interlocutory Order).

Law Review and Journal Commentaries

Ohio House Bill 419: Increased Openness in Adoption Records Law, Wendy L. Weiss. 45 Clev St L Rev 101 (1997).

3107.46   Denial or authorization of release form;   rescinding of form

(A) A birth parent who did not check, pursuant to section 3107.071, 3107.081, or 5103.151 of the Revised Code, the "no" space provided on the component of the form prescribed pursuant to division (A)(1)(b) of section 3107.083 of the Revised Code may sign, date, and have filed with the department of health a denial of release form prescribed under section 3107.50 of the Revised Code.   A birth parent who signs an authorization of release form under division (B) of this section may rescind that form by signing, dating, and having filed with the department of health a denial of release form prescribed under section 3107.50 of the Revised Code.   If, at the time of submitting the denial of release form, the birth parent provides the department two items of identification, the department shall file the form in the adoption file of the adopted person indicated on the form.

(B) If an adoption file contains a birth parent's denial of release form, the birth parent may rescind that form by signing, dating, and having filed with the department of health an authorization of release form.   If, at the time of submitting the authorization of release form, the birth parent provides the department two items of identification, the department shall file the form in the adoption file of the adopted person indicated on the form.

(C) After a birth parent submits a denial of release form or an authorization of release form under this section, the department of health shall provide the birth parent a copy of the form.

(D) A birth parent may rescind an authorization of release form pursuant to division (A) of this section and rescind a denial of release form pursuant to division (B) of this section as many times as the birth parent wishes.

(1996 H 419, eff. 9–18–96)

Adoption registration, release of file contents, see
    3705.12

Library References

Records ☞32, 35.
Westlaw Topic No. 326.

C.J.S. Bankruptcy §§ 830 to 834.
C.J.S. Records §§ 80, 82 to 88, 102 to 105, 111.

Research References

Encyclopedias

OH Jur. 3d Family Law § 913, Records and Pa-
pers--Inspection.

Forms

Ohio Jurisprudence Pleading and Practice Forms
    § 96:15, Court's Acceptance of Parental Consent.

Ohio Jurisprudence Pleading and Practice Forms
    § 96:27, Permanent Custody Surrender Agree-
    ment--Juvenile Court Approval.
Ohio Jurisprudence Pleading and Practice Forms
    § 96:34, Birth Record.
Ohio Jurisprudence Pleading and Practice Forms
    § 96:35, Authorization by Biological Parent or
    Sibling.

3107.47 Adoptee or adoptee's parents requesting copy of adoption file

(A) An adopted person age twenty-one or older, or an adoptive parent of an adopted person at least age eighteen but under age twenty-one, may submit a request to the department of health for a copy of the contents of the adopted person's adoption file. If the adopted person includes with the request the adopted person's notarized signature and copies of two items of identification, or the adoptive parent includes with the request the adoptive parent's notarized signature and copies of two items of identification, the department shall do the following:

(1) If there is not an effective denial of release form for either birth parent in the adopted person's adoption file and the fee required by section 3705.241 of the Revised Code is paid, provide the adopted person or adoptive parent a copy of the contents of the adopted person's adoption file;

(2) If there is an effective denial of release form for each birth parent in the adopted person's adoption file, refuse to provide the adopted person or adoptive parent a copy of the contents of the adopted person's adoption file;

(3) If there is an effective denial of release form for only one of the birth parents in the adopted person's adoption file and the fee required by section 3705.241 of the Revised Code is paid, provide the adopted person or adoptive parent a copy of the contents of the adopted person's adoption file with all identifying information about the birth parent for whom there is an effective denial of release form deleted.

(B) If an adopted person or adoptive parent is denied a copy of the contents of the adopted person's adoption file or receives a copy of the contents with identifying information about one of the birth parents deleted, the department of health shall inform the adopted person or adoptive parent that it will notify the adopted person or adoptive parent if the department subsequently receives an authorization of release form from one or both birth parents and the adopted person or adoptive parent submits to the department a request to be notified. An adopted person or adoptive parent who submits a request to be notified shall provide the department the adopted person's or adoptive parent's address and notify the department of any change of address. An adopted person or adoptive parent who subsequently decides not to be notified may submit a statement with the department for the department not to notify the adopted person or adoptive parent.

The department shall notify the adopted person or adoptive parent if the department receives an authorization of release form from one or both birth parents and the adopted person or adoptive parent submitted a request to be notified and has not subsequently submitted a statement not to be notified. If the adopted person or adoptive parent contacts the department after being notified and indicates a desire to receive the information the department may provide, the department shall provide the adopted person or adoptive parent information in accordance with division (A) of this section.

(1996 H 419, eff. 9–18–96)

Cross References

Prohibition: 3107.65(A)
Adoption registration, release of file contents, see 3705.12
Assessor's meeting with birth parent prior to parent's consenting to adoption, identifying information about parent, see 5103.152

Fees for copying adoption file, contents, see 3705.241

Ohio Administrative Code References

Forms used in the system of vital statistics, see OAC 3701–5–02

Library References

Records ☞32, 33.
Westlaw Topic No. 326.

C.J.S. Bankruptcy §§ 830 to 834.
C.J.S. Records §§ 77 to 78, 80, 82 to 88.

Research References

Encyclopedias

OH Jur. 3d Family Law § 911, Records and Papers.
OH Jur. 3d Family Law § 913, Records and Papers--Inspection.

Forms

Ohio Jurisprudence Pleading and Practice Forms § 96:6, Open Adoption--Prohibitions.
Ohio Jurisprudence Pleading and Practice Forms § 96:20, Home Study.

Ohio Jurisprudence Pleading and Practice Forms § 96:27, Permanent Custody Surrender Agreement--Juvenile Court Approval.
Ohio Jurisprudence Pleading and Practice Forms § 96:34, Birth Record.
Ohio Jurisprudence Pleading and Practice Forms § 96:37, Request to Department for Adoption Information--Adoptee.
Ohio Jurisprudence Pleading and Practice Forms § 96:42, Unauthorized Release of Information.

3107.48　Adoptee's request that health department assist birth parents or siblings in finding adoptee's name by adoption

(A) An adopted person age twenty-one or older may submit a request with the department of health for the department to assist the adopted person's birth parent or birth sibling in finding the adopted person's name by adoption pursuant to section 3107.49 of the Revised Code. The adopted person shall submit the request on a form prescribed by the department under section 3107.51 of the Revised Code. If the adopted person provides all the information required by section 3107.51 of the Revised Code on the form, the department shall file it in the adopted person's adoption file and assist the birth parent or birth sibling in finding the adopted person's name by adoption unless the adopted person rescinds the request pursuant to division (B) of this section.

(B) An adopted person who has requested under division (A) of this section that the department of health assist the adopted person's birth parent or birth sibling in finding the adopted person's name by adoption pursuant to section 3107.49 of the Revised Code may rescind the request and prohibit the department from assisting the birth parent or birth sibling in finding the adopted person's name by adoption pursuant to section 3107.49 of the Revised Code. The department shall remove the request from the adopted person's adoption file and destroy the request to rescind the request if the adopted person does both of the following:

(1) Makes a written request to the department;

(2) Provides to the department the adopted person's residence address, notarized signature, and two items of identification of the adopted person.

(C) An adopted person may submit requests under division (A) of this section and rescind requests under division (B) of this section as many times as the adopted person wishes.

(1996 H 419, eff. 9–18–96)

Cross References

Adoption registration, contents of file, see 3705.12

Ohio Administrative Code References

Forms used in the system of vital statistics, see
  OAC 3701–5–02

Library References

Records ☞33, 34.
Westlaw Topic No. 326.
C.J.S. Records §§ 77 to 79, 87, 102 to 105.

Research References

Encyclopedias

OH Jur. 3d Family Law § 913, Records and Papers--Inspection.

Forms

Ohio Jurisprudence Pleading and Practice Forms
  § 96:34, Birth Record.

Ohio Jurisprudence Pleading and Practice Forms
  § 96:38, Request to Department for Adoption
  Information--Birth Parent or Sibling.
Ohio Jurisprudence Pleading and Practice Forms
  § 96:39, Request to Department for Adoption
  Information--Assist Birth Parent or Sibling.

3107.49 Birth parent or sibling's request for assistance in finding adoptee's name by adoption

(A) A birth parent, or birth sibling age twenty-one or older, may submit a request to the department of health for assistance in finding an adopted person's name by adoption. The department shall examine the adopted person's adoption file to determine the adopted person's name by adoption and provide the birth parent or birth sibling with the adopted person's name by adoption if all of the following are the case:

(1) The adopted person's adoption file contains a request submitted by the adopted person under division (A) of section 3107.48 of the Revised Code that the department assist the birth parent or birth sibling in finding the adopted person's name by adoption;

(2) The adopted person was the child of the birth parent or sibling of the birth sibling before the adoption;

(3) In the case of a request by a birth parent, the court that issued the adopted person's final decree of adoption sends the department, in accordance with division (B) of this section, a notice stating that the birth parent's parental rights concerning the adopted person were not involuntarily terminated pursuant to Chapter 2151. of the Revised Code;

(4) The request is in writing and includes the birth parent's or birth sibling's residence address and notarized signature, one or more items of identification of the birth parent or birth sibling, and the adopted person's name and date of birth as it appears on the original birth record;

(5) The department has an adoption file for the adopted person and is able to determine the adopted person's name by adoption from the file's contents.

(B) If a birth parent requests assistance from the department of health in finding an adopted person's name by adoption, the department shall request the court that issued the adopted person's final decree of adoption to determine whether the birth parent's parental rights concerning the adopted person were involuntarily terminated pursuant to Chapter 2151. of the Revised Code. The department shall provide to the court any information the department has and the court needs to make the determination. On request from the department, the court shall make the determination. After making the determination, the court shall send a notice to the department stating whether the birth parent's parental rights were so involuntarily terminated.

(C) If a birth parent or birth sibling does not know all the information about the adopted person that the department needs to be able to find the adopted person's adoption file, the department shall, if it is known which court issued the adopted person's final decree of adoption, ask the court to find the information about the adopted person from its records. The department shall provide to the court any information the department receives from the birth parent or birth sibling that the court needs to find the information. On the department's request, the court shall provide to the department any information the court has that will aid the department in finding the adopted person's adoption file.

(D) If a birth parent or birth sibling is denied assistance in finding an adopted person's name by adoption because the adopted person's adoption file does not contain a request submitted by the adopted person under division (A) of section 3107.48 of the Revised Code, the department shall inform the birth parent or birth sibling that it will notify the birth parent or birth sibling if the adopted person subsequently submits a request under division (A) of section 3107.48 of the Revised Code and the birth parent or birth sibling submits to the department a request to be notified. A birth parent or birth sibling who submits a request to be notified shall provide the department the birth parent's or birth sibling's address and shall notify the department of any change of address. A birth parent or birth sibling who subsequently decides not to be notified may submit a statement with the department for the department not to notify the birth parent or birth sibling. The department shall notify the birth parent or birth sibling if the adopted person submits a request under division (A) of section 3107.48 of the Revised Code and the birth parent or birth sibling has submitted a request to be notified and not subsequently submitted a statement not to be notified.

(1996 H 419, eff. 9–18–96)

Cross References

Adoption registration, release of file contents, see
   3705.12

Library References

Records ⬥33, 34.
Westlaw Topic No. 326.
C.J.S. Records §§ 77 to 79, 87, 102 to 105.

Research References

Encyclopedias

OH Jur. 3d Family Law § 911, Records and Papers.
OH Jur. 3d Family Law § 913, Records and Papers--Inspection.

Forms

Ohio Jurisprudence Pleading and Practice Forms
   § 96:34, Birth Record.

Ohio Jurisprudence Pleading and Practice Forms
   § 96:38, Request to Department for Adoption Information--Birth Parent or Sibling.
Ohio Jurisprudence Pleading and Practice Forms
   § 96:39, Request to Department for Adoption Information--Assist Birth Parent or Sibling.
Ohio Jurisprudence Pleading and Practice Forms
   § 96:42, Unauthorized Release of Information.

Law Review and Journal Commentaries

The only Americans legally prohibited from knowing who their birth parents are: A rejection of privacy rights as a bar to adult adoptees' access to original birth and adoption records. Susan Whittaker Hughes, 55 Clev. St. L. Rev. 429 (2007).

3107.50   Denial of release form; authorization of release form

(A) Not later than ninety days after the effective date of this section, the department of health shall prescribe the following forms:

(1) A denial of release form to be used by a birth parent under division (A) of section 3107.46 of the Revised Code. The form shall explain that the birth parent may rescind the denial of release at any time by signing, dating, and having filed with the department of health an authorization of release form pursuant to division (B) of section 3107.46 of the Revised Code.

(2) An authorization of release form to be used by a birth parent under division (B) of section 3107.46 of the Revised Code. The form shall state that the birth parent may rescind

the authorization of release at any time by signing, dating, and having filed with the department of health a denial of release form pursuant to division (A) of that section.

(B) On request of a birth parent, the department shall provide a copy of a denial of release form or authorization of release form to the birth parent.

(1996 H 419, eff. 6–20–96)

Cross References

Assessor's meeting with birth parent prior to parent's consenting to adoption, denial of release form, see 5103.152

Library References

Records ⊖35.
Westlaw Topic No. 326.
C.J.S. Records §§ 87, 102 to 105, 111.

Research References

Forms

Ohio Jurisprudence Pleading and Practice Forms § 96:20, Home Study.

Ohio Jurisprudence Pleading and Practice Forms § 96:39, Request to Department for Adoption Information--Assist Birth Parent or Sibling.

3107.51 Form for adoptee's requesting assistance for birth parents or siblings finding adoptee's name by adoption

(A) Not later than ninety days after the effective date of this section, the department of health shall prescribe a form with which an adopted person may make a request under division (A) of section 3107.48 of the Revised Code. The form shall require all of the following information:

(1) The residence address of the adopted person;

(2) The adopted person's name and date of birth as it appears on the adopted person's new birth record;

(3) The notarized signature of the adopted person;

(4) Any other information considered necessary by the department.

(B) The form shall include instructions that explain how it is to be completed and filed with the department. The department shall include on the form information that advises the adopted person that the adopted person may, in accordance with division (B) of section 3107.48 of the Revised Code, rescind the request at any time, and shall include instructions on how to do so.

(C) On request of an adopted person, the department shall provide the adopted person with a copy of the form.

(1996 H 419, eff. 6–20–96)

Library References

Records ⊖34.
Westlaw Topic No. 326.
C.J.S. Records §§ 78 to 79, 87, 102 to 105.

Research References

Forms

Ohio Jurisprudence Pleading and Practice Forms § 96:39, Request to Department for Adoption Information--Assist Birth Parent or Sibling.

3107.52 Records not public

(A) The department of health's records pertaining to proceedings under sections 3107.45 to 3107.53 of the Revised Code are not public records subject to inspection or copying under section 149.43 of the Revised Code.

(B) No person who is the subject of personal information contained in a record listed in division (A) of this section may inspect or copy all or part of any such record except pursuant to section 3107.47 of the Revised Code.

(1996 H 419, eff. 9–18–96)

Cross References

Availability of state government public records, public records defined, see 149.43

Library References

Health ☞396 to 397.
Records ☞32, 33.
Westlaw Topic Nos. 198H, 326.

C.J.S. Bankruptcy §§ 830 to 834.
C.J.S. Health and Environment §§ 24, 74.
C.J.S. Records §§ 77 to 78, 80, 82 to 88.

Research References

Encyclopedias

OH Jur. 3d Defamation & Privacy § 183, Exceptions.
OH Jur. 3d Family Law § 913, Records and Papers--Inspection.

Forms

Ohio Jurisprudence Pleading and Practice Forms § 96:32, Confidentiality.

Treatises and Practice Aids

Hennenberg & Reinhart, Ohio Criminal Defense Motions F 2:44, Motion for Sanctions for Viola-

tions of R.C. Chapter 149 [Public Records Act] Discovery Demands and Motions.
Hennenberg & Reinhart, Ohio Criminal Defense Motions F 2:46, Motion to Inspect Public Records--Discovery Demands and Motions.
Gotherman & Babbit, Ohio Municipal Law § 6:12, Exceptions to General Rule.
Hastings, Manoloff, Sheeran, & Stype, Ohio School Law § 44:5, Scope.
Hastings, Manoloff, Sheeran, & Stype, Ohio School Law § 44:2.30, Public Records--Statutory Exclusions.

3107.53 No liability for release of information

No officer or employee of the department of health who releases any information contained in an adopted person's adoption file or provides a copy of the contents of an adopted person's adoption file to a person who requests the copy pursuant to section 3107.47 or 3107.49 of the Revised Code is liable in damages in a civil action to any person for injury, death, or loss allegedly arising from the release to the person or is criminally liable for the release if the officer or employee releases the information or copy in accordance with section 3107.47 or 3107.49 of the Revised Code.

(1996 H 419, eff. 9–18–96)

Library References

Health ☞367.
Westlaw Topic No. 198H.

C.J.S. Health and Environment §§ 9, 16 to 26, 44 to 45.

Research References

Encyclopedias

OH Jur. 3d Family Law § 911, Records and Papers.

Forms

Ohio Jurisprudence Pleading and Practice Forms § 96:32, Confidentiality.

Ohio Jurisprudence Pleading and Practice Forms § 96:42, Unauthorized Release of Information.

OPEN ADOPTIONS

3107.60 Definitions

As used in sections 3107.60 to 3107.68 of the Revised Code:

(A) "Agency," "attorney," and "identifying information" have the same meanings as in section 3107.01 of the Revised Code.

(B) "Nonidentifying information" means one of the following:

(1) In relation to a birth parent, any information that is not identifying information, including all of the following:

(a) A birth parent's age at the time the birth parent's child is adopted;

(b) The medical and genetic history of the birth parents;

(c) The age, sex, and medical and genetic history of an adopted person's birth sibling and extended family members;

(d) A person's heritage and ethnic background, educational level, general physical appearance, religion, occupation, and cause of death;

(e) Any information that may be included in a social and medical history as specified in divisions (B) and (C) of section 3107.09 of the Revised Code.

(2) In relation to an adoptive parent, subject to a determination made pursuant to division (E) of section 3107.66 of the Revised Code, any information that is not identifying information, including all of the following:

(a) An adoptive parent's age at the time of adoption;

(b) An adoptive sibling's age at the time of adoption;

(c) The heritage, ethnic background, religion, educational level, and occupation of the adoptive parent;

(d) General information known about the well-being of the adoptee before and after the adoption.

(2008 H 7, eff. 4-7-09; 1996 H 419, eff. 9–18–96)

Historical and Statutory Notes

Amendment Note: 2008 H 7 rewrote division (B); redesignated former divisions (B)(1), (B)(2), (B)(3), (B)(4), and (B)(5) as divisions (B)(1)(a), (B)(1)(b), (B)(1)(c), (B)(1)(d), and (B)(1)(e), respectively; and added new divisions (B)(2), (B)(2)(a), (B)(2)(b), (B)(2)(c), and (B)(2)(d). Prior to amendment, division (B) read:

"(B) 'Nonidentifying information' means any information that is not identifying information, including all of the following:"

Library References

Adoption ⟸6.
Westlaw Topic No. 17.
C.J.S. Adoption of Persons §§ 28 to 45, 140.

Research References

Forms

Ohio Jurisprudence Pleading and Practice Forms § 96:23, Profiles of Prospective Adoptive Parents.

Ohio Jurisprudence Pleading and Practice Forms § 96:32, Confidentiality.

Treatises and Practice Aids

Carlin, Baldwin's Ohio Prac. Merrick-Rippner Probate Law § 99:28, Papers and Records--Accounting.

Carlin, Baldwin's Ohio Prac. Merrick-Rippner Probate Law § 99:29, Papers and Records--Confidentiality.

Law Review and Journal Commentaries

Ohio House Bill 419: Increased Openness in
Adoption Records Law, Wendy L. Weiss. 45 Clev
St L Rev 101 (1997).

3107.61 Profiles of prospective adoptive parents shown to birth parent

At the request of a birth parent who voluntarily chooses to have a child placed for adoption,
the agency or attorney arranging the child's placement and adoption may provide the birth
parent profiles of prospective adoptive parents who an assessor has recommended pursuant to
a home study under section 3107.031 of the Revised Code be approved to adopt a child. At
the request of the birth parent, the agency or attorney may include identifying information
about a prospective adoptive parent in the profile if the prospective adoptive parent agrees to
the inclusion of the identifying information. If a birth parent chooses a prospective adoptive
parent from a profile, the agency or attorney shall give that prospective adoptive parent priority
when determining with whom the agency or attorney will place the child.

(1996 H 419, eff. 9 18 96)

Ohio Administrative Code References

Child study inventory, see OAC 5101:2-48-21
Provision of information to adoptive family, see
    OAC 5101:2-48-15

Library References

Adoption ⊕6.
Westlaw Topic No. 17.
C.J.S. Adoption of Persons §§ 28 to 45, 140.

Research References

Forms

Ohio Jurisprudence Pleading and Practice Forms
    § 96:23, Profiles of Prospective Adoptive Par-
    ents.

Law Review and Journal Commentaries

Ohio House Bill 419: Increased Openness in
Adoption Records Law, Wendy L. Weiss. 45 Clev
St L Rev 101 (1997).

3107.62 Nonbinding open adoption option

An agency or attorney arranging a child's adoptive placement shall inform the child's birth
parent and prospective adoptive parent that the birth parent and prospective adoptive parent
may enter into a nonbinding open adoption in accordance with section 3107.63 of the Revised
Code.

(1996 H 274, eff. 9–18–96; 1996 H 419, eff. 9–18–96)

Historical and Statutory Notes

Amendment Note: 1996 H 274 deleted "or
3107.64" after "3107.63".

Ohio Administrative Code References

Provision of information to adoptive family, see
    OAC 5101:2-48-15

Library References

Adoption ☜6.
Westlaw Topic No. 17.
C.J.S. Adoption of Persons §§ 28 to 45, 140.

Research References

Encyclopedias

OH Jur. 3d Family Law § 912, Records and Papers--Open Adoption.

Forms

Ohio Jurisprudence Pleading and Practice Forms § 96:5, Open Adoption.

Treatises and Practice Aids

Carlin, Baldwin's Ohio Prac. Merrick-Rippner Probate Law § 99:28, Papers and Records--Accounting.

Law Review and Journal Commentaries

Ohio House Bill 419: Increased Openness in Adoption Records Law, Wendy L. Weiss. 45 Clev St L Rev 101 (1997).

3107.63 Birth parent requesting open adoption of child voluntarily placed for adoption

(A) A birth parent who voluntarily chooses to have the birth parent's child placed for adoption may request that the agency or attorney arranging the child's adoptive placement provide for the birth parent and prospective adoptive parent to enter into an open adoption with terms acceptable to the birth parent and prospective adoptive parent. Except as provided in division (B) of this section, the agency or attorney shall provide for the open adoption if the birth parent and prospective adoptive parent agree to the terms of the open adoption.

(B) An agency or attorney arranging a child's adoptive placement may refuse to provide for the birth parent and prospective adoptive parent to enter into an open adoption. If the agency or attorney refuses, the agency or attorney shall offer to refer the birth parent to another agency or attorney the agency or attorney knows will provide for the open adoption.
(1996 H 419, eff. 9–18–96)

Library References

Adoption ☜6.
Westlaw Topic No. 17.
C.J.S. Adoption of Persons §§ 28 to 45, 140.

Research References

Encyclopedias

OH Jur. 3d Family Law § 912, Records and Papers--Open Adoption.

Forms

Ohio Jurisprudence Pleading and Practice Forms § 96:5, Open Adoption.

Law Review and Journal Commentaries

Ohio House Bill 419: Increased Openness in Adoption Records Law, Wendy L. Weiss. 45 Clev St L Rev 101 (1997).

3107.64 Birth parent requesting open adoption of child involuntarily placed for adoption—Repealed

(1996 H 274, eff. 8–8–96; 1996 H 419, eff. 9–18–96)

3107.65 Prohibitions in open adoptions

(A) No open adoption shall do any of the following:

(1) Provide for the birth parent to share with the prospective adoptive parent parental control and authority over the child placed for adoption or in any manner limit the adoptive parent's full parental control and authority over the adopted child;

(2) Deny the adoptive parent or child access to forms pertaining to the social or medical histories of the birth parent if the adoptive parent or child is entitled to them under section 3107.17 of the Revised Code;

(3) Deny the adoptive parent or child access to a copy of the contents of the child's adoption file if the adoptive parent or child is entitled to them under section 3107.47 of the Revised Code;

(4) Deny the adoptive parent, child, birth parent, birth sibling, or other relative access to nonidentifying information that is accessible pursuant to section 3107.66 of the Revised Code or to materials, photographs, or information that is accessible pursuant to section 3107.68 of the Revised Code;

(5) Provide for the open adoption to be binding or enforceable.

(B) A probate court may not refuse to approve a proposed placement pursuant to division (D)(1) of section 5103.16 of the Revised Code or to issue a final decree of adoption or interlocutory order of adoption under section 3107.14 of the Revised Code on the grounds that the birth parent and prospective adoptive parent have entered into an open adoption unless the court issues a finding that the terms of the open adoption violate division (A) of this section or are not in the best interest of the child. A probate court may not issue a final decree of adoption or interlocutory order of adoption that nullifies or alters the terms of an open adoption unless the court issues a finding that the terms violate division (A) of this section or are not in the best interest of the child.

(C) Subject to divisions (A) and (B) of this section, an open adoption may provide for the exchange of any information, including identifying information, and have any other terms. All terms of an open adoption are voluntary and any person who has entered into an open adoption may withdraw from the open adoption at any time. An open adoption is not enforceable. At the request of a person who has withdrawn from an open adoption, the court with jurisdiction over the adoption shall issue an order barring any other person who was a party to the open adoption from taking any action pursuant to the open adoption.

(1996 H 274, eff. 9–18–96; 1996 H 419, eff. 9–18–96)

Historical and Statutory Notes

Amendment Note: 1996 H 274 deleted "or relative" after "birth parent" in division (A)(1), and deleted ", or relative of the child to be adopted and prospective adoptive parent," after "adoptive parent" in division (B).

Library References

Adoption ⊕6, 13.
Health ⊕396.
Records ⊕32.
Westlaw Topic Nos. 17, 198H, 326.
C.J.S. Adoption of Persons §§ 28 to 47, 93 to 102, 140.

C.J.S. Bankruptcy §§ 830 to 834.
C.J.S. Health and Environment § 24.
C.J.S. Records §§ 80, 82 to 88.

Research References

Encyclopedias

OH Jur. 3d Family Law § 912, Records and Papers--Open Adoption.

Forms

Ohio Jurisprudence Pleading and Practice Forms § 96:5, Open Adoption.

Ohio Jurisprudence Pleading and Practice Forms § 96:6, Open Adoption--Prohibitions.
Ohio Jurisprudence Pleading and Practice Forms § 96:26, Open Adoption--Judicial Determination.

Treatises and Practice Aids

Carlin, Baldwin's Ohio Prac. Merrick-Rippner Probate Law § 99:28, Papers and Records--Accounting.

Law Review and Journal Commentaries

Ohio House Bill 419: Increased Openness in Adoption Records Law, Wendy L. Weiss. 45 Clev St L Rev 101 (1997).

3107.66 Written request for information on adoption

(A) As used in this section:

(1) "Adopted person" includes both an "adopted person" as defined in section 3107.39 of the Revised Code and an "adopted person" as defined in section 3107.45 of the Revised Code.

(2) "Adoptive parent" means a person who adopted an adopted person.

(3) "Birth parent" means the biological parent of an adopted person.

(4) "Birth sibling" means a biological sibling of an adopted person.

(B) An adopted person age eighteen or older, an adoptive parent of an adopted person under age eighteen, or an adoptive family member of a deceased adopted person may submit a written request to the agency or attorney who arranged the adopted person's adoption, or the probate court that finalized the adopted person's adoption, for the agency, attorney, or court to provide the adopted person, adoptive parent, or adoptive family member information about the adopted person's birth parent or birth sibling contained in the agency's, attorney's, or court's adoption records that is nonidentifying information. Except as provided in division (C) of this section, the agency, attorney, or court shall provide the adopted person, adoptive parent, or adoptive family member the information sought within a reasonable amount of time. The agency, attorney, or court may charge a reasonable fee for providing the information.

A birth parent of an adopted person eighteen years of age or older, a birth sibling age eighteen or older, or a birth family member of a deceased birth parent may submit a written request to the agency or attorney who arranged the adopted person's adoption, or the probate court that finalized the adoption, for the agency, attorney, or court to provide the birth parent, birth sibling, or birth family member information about the adopted person or adoptive parent contained in the agency's, attorney's, or court's adoption records that is nonidentifying information. Except as provided in division (C) of this section, the agency, attorney, or court shall provide the birth parent, birth sibling, or birth family member the information sought within a reasonable amount of time. The agency, attorney, or court may charge a reasonable fee for providing the information.

(C) An agency or attorney that has permanently ceased to arrange adoptions is not subject to division (B) of this section. If the adoption records of such an agency or attorney are held by a probate court, person, or other governmental entity pursuant to section 3107.67 of the Revised Code, the adopted person, adoptive parent, adoptive family member, birth parent, birth sibling, or birth family member may submit the written request that otherwise would be submitted to the agency or attorney under division (B) of this section to the court, person, or other governmental entity that holds the records. On receipt of the request, the court, person, or other governmental entity shall provide the information that the agency or attorney would have been required to provide within a reasonable amount of time. The court, person, or other governmental entity may charge a reasonable fee for providing the information.

(D) Prior to providing nonidentifying information pursuant to division (B) or (C) of this section, the person or governmental entity providing the information shall review the record to ensure that all identifying information about any person contained in the record is deleted.

(E) An agency, attorney, person, or other governmental entity may classify any information described in division (B)(2) of section 3107.60 of the Revised Code as identifying information and deny the request made under division (B) or (C) of this section if the agency, attorney, court, person, or other governmental entity determines that the information could lead to the identification of the adoptive parent. This determination shall be done on a case-by-case basis.

(2008 H 7, eff. 4-7-09; 2006 S 238, eff. 9–21–06; 1996 H 419, eff. 9–18–96)

Historical and Statutory Notes

Amendment Note: 2008 H 7 inserted "eighteen years of age or older" after "adopted person" in the first sentence of the second paragraph in division (B); and added division (E).

Amendment Note: 2006 S 238 rewrote division (A), which prior thereto read:

"(A) As used in this section, 'adopted person,' 'adoptive parent,' 'birth parent,' and 'birth sibling' have the same meanings as in section 3107.45 of the Revised Code."

Cross References

Prohibition: 3107.65(A)

Library References

Adoption ⚫6.
Infants ⚫17.
Records ⚫33.
Westlaw Topic Nos. 17, 211, 326.

C.J.S. Adoption of Persons §§ 10 to 14, 28 to 45, 140.
C.J.S. Infants §§ 6, 8 to 9.
C.J.S. Records §§ 77 to 78.

Research References

Encyclopedias

OH Jur. 3d Family Law § 912, Records and Papers--Open Adoption.

Forms

Ohio Jurisprudence Pleading and Practice Forms § 96:6, Open Adoption--Prohibitions.

Ohio Jurisprudence Pleading and Practice Forms § 96:40, Request for Nonidentifying Information to Agency or Attorney--Adoptee.

Treatises and Practice Aids

Carlin, Baldwin's Ohio Prac. Merrick-Rippner Probate Law § 99:29, Papers and Records--Confidentiality.

Law Review and Journal Commentaries

Ohio House Bill 419: Increased Openness in Adoption Records Law, Wendy L. Weiss. 45 Clev St L Rev 101 (1997).

3107.67 Agency or attorney providing probate court with adoption records upon permanently ceasing to arrange adoptions

(A) For the purpose of division (C) of section 3107.66 of the Revised Code, an agency or attorney that arranged an adoption shall provide the probate court that finalized the adoption with the agency's or attorney's records of the adoption when the agency or attorney permanently ceases to arrange adoptions.

If an agency permanently ceases to arrange adoptions because the person operating the agency has died or become incapacitated or the attorney ceases to arrange adoptions because the attorney has died or become incapacitated, the person responsible for disposing of the agency's or attorney's records shall provide the court with the adoption records. If no one is responsible for disposing of the records, the person responsible for administering the estate or managing the resources of the attorney or the person who operated the agency shall provide the court with the adoption records.

If the attorney who permanently ceases to arrange adoptions is in practice with another attorney, the attorney may provide the adoption records to the other attorney rather than the court if the other attorney agrees to act in the place of the first attorney for the purpose of section 3107.66 of the Revised Code. The person responsible for the practice of the first attorney shall provide the adoption records to the probate court that finalized the adoption when the practice no longer includes an attorney who agrees to act in the first attorney's place for the purpose of section 3107.66 of the Revised Code.

(B) A probate court that receives adoption records under division (A) of this section may transfer the records to a person or governmental entity that voluntarily accepts the records. If the court finds a person or governmental entity that accepts the adoption records, the court shall maintain a directory for the purpose of informing a person seeking the records where the records are held.

(1996 H 419, eff. 9–18–96)

Library References

Adoption ☞6.
Infants ☞17.
Records ☞13.
Westlaw Topic Nos. 17, 211, 326.

C.J.S. Adoption of Persons §§ 10 to 14, 28 to 45, 140.
C.J.S. Infants §§ 6, 8 to 9.
C.J.S. Records §§ 37 to 39.

Research References

Forms

Ohio Jurisprudence Pleading and Practice Forms
§ 96:40, Request for Nonidentifying Information to Agency or Attorney--Adoptee.

3107.68   Birth parent providing information and photographs

A birth parent who signs the component of the form prescribed pursuant to division (A)(1)(d), or (B)(1)(c), of section 3107.083 of the Revised Code shall provide the materials the birth parent requests be given to the birth parent's child or adoptive parent to the agency or attorney arranging the adoption. At the request of the birth parent's child or adoptive parent, the agency or attorney shall provide the materials to the child or adoptive parent.

A birth parent who signs the component of the form prescribed pursuant to division (A)(1)(e), or (B)(1)(d), of section 3107.083 of the Revised Code shall provide the photographs of the birth parent that the birth parent requests be given to the birth parent's child or adoptive parent to the agency or attorney arranging the adoption. At the request of the birth parent's child or adoptive parent, the agency or attorney shall provide the photographs to the child or adoptive parent.

If a birth parent has signed the component of the form prescribed pursuant to division (A)(1)(f), or (B)(1)(e), of section 3107.083 of the Revised Code authorizing the agency or attorney that arranged the adoption of the birth parent's child to provide the child or adoptive parent the first name of the birth parent, the agency or attorney may provide the birth parent's first name to the child or adoptive parent at the request of the child or adoptive parent.

An agency or attorney arranging a child's adoption shall provide the adoptive parent the child's social security number.

(1996 H 419, eff. 9–18–96)

Cross References

Prohibition: 3107.65(A)

Ohio Administrative Code References

Provision of information to adoptive family, see
OAC 5101:2–48–15

Library References

Adoption ☞6.
Infants ☞17.
Westlaw Topic Nos. 17, 211.

C.J.S. Adoption of Persons §§ 10 to 14, 28 to 45, 140.
C.J.S. Infants §§ 6, 8 to 9.

Research References

Encyclopedias

OH Jur. 3d Family Law § 912, Records and Papers--Open Adoption.

Forms

Ohio Jurisprudence Pleading and Practice Forms
§ 96:6, Open Adoption--Prohibitions.

Ohio Jurisprudence Pleading and Practice Forms § 96:23, Profiles of Prospective Adoptive Parents.

Ohio Jurisprudence Pleading and Practice Forms § 96:32, Confidentiality.

Ohio Jurisprudence Pleading and Practice Forms § 96:35, Authorization by Biological Parent or Sibling.

PENALTIES

3107.99   Penalties

Whoever violates division (B)(1) of section 3107.17 of the Revised Code is guilty of a misdemeanor of the third degree.

(1996 H 419, eff. 9–18–96)

Library References

Health ☞984.
Records ☞31.
Westlaw Topic Nos. 198H, 326.

C.J.S. Criminal Law §§ 587 to 591.
C.J.S. Health and Environment § 89.
C.J.S. Records §§ 89 to 111, 117.

Law Review and Journal Commentaries

DNA Dragnets: Constitutional Aspects of Mass DNA Identification Testing, Comment. 28 Cap U L Rev 479 (2000).

CHAPTER 3109

CHILDREN

GENERAL PROVISIONS

Cross References

Adoption, see 3107.01 et seq.
Domestic violence, criminal sanctions, see 2919.25 to 2919.271
Juvenile court, see 2151.01 et seq.
Neglect, abandonment, or domestic violence, see 3113.01 et seq.
Non-spousal artificial insemination, see 3111.30 et seq.

School child, treatment by city or general health district board of health only on request of parent or guardian, see 3709.22
Uniform Interstate Family Support Act, duties and powers of responding tribunal, see 3115.16

Ohio Administrative Code References

Abused and neglected children, supportive services for, see OAC Ch 5101:2–39

Collection of past due support by federal tax refund offset, see OAC Ch 5101:1–30

GENERAL PROVISIONS

3109.01　Age of majority

All persons of the age of eighteen years or more, who are under no legal disability, are capable of contracting and are of full age for all purposes.
(1973 S 1, eff. 1–1–74;　1953 H 1;　GC 8005–1;　Source—GC 8023)

Historical and Statutory Notes

Pre–1953 H 1 Amendments: 124 v S 65

Cross References

Anatomical gifts, age requirement, see 2108.02

Disability assistance program, eligibility requirements, see 5115.05

Duty of married person to support self, spouse, and children, wife to assist, see 3103.03

"Legal disability" defined, see 2131.02

Minor can consent to diagnosis and treatment of drug-related condition, parents not liable for payment unless consent, see 3719.012

Minor's contract for life insurance, see 3911.08

Parental duty of support continuing beyond age of majority where child attending high school, see 3105.21, 3111.13, 3111.20, 3113.04, 3113.31

Persons who may marry, see 3101.01

Prohibitions regarding purchase of liquor, see 4301.63 et seq.

Seventeen-year-olds may donate blood, see 2108.21

Small loans, assignment of wages by minor invalid without consent of parent or guardian, see 1321.31

Voters, age requirements, see O Const Art V §1; 3503.011

Who may make a will, see 2107.02

Library References

Infants ⟐1, 46.
Westlaw Topic No. 211.
C.J.S. Infants §§ 1 to 3, 209 to 213, 253, 268, 275.

Research References

ALR Library

162 ALR 1084, Power of Court in Divorce or Separation Suit to Provide for Support Of, or Aid To, Adult Child, or to Continue Provision for Support After Child Attains Majority.

Encyclopedias

OH Jur. 3d Family Law § 786, Termination of Minority.

OH Jur. 3d Family Law § 979, Child Support Judgments or Orders--Period During Which Duty Owed.

OH Jur. 3d Family Law § 1014, Child's Emancipation or Majority; Duty to Disabled Adult Children.

OH Jur. 3d Family Law § 1141, Continuation of Support Beyond Age of Majority.

OH Jur. 3d Family Law § 1142, Effect of Child's Mental or Physical Disability.

OH Jur. 3d Family Law § 1143, Agreements to Extend Support Beyond Child's Majority.

OH Jur. 3d Limitations & Laches § 99, Minority.

OH Jur. 3d Public Welfare § 155, Income and Other Requirements.

Forms

Ohio Forms Legal and Business § 2:1, Definition--General Background.

Ohio Forms Legal and Business § 28:2, Definitions.

Ohio Forms Legal and Business § 29:1, Introduction.

Ohio Forms Legal and Business § 28:46, Introduction.

Ohio Forms Legal and Business § 28:75, Support of Children.

Ohio Forms Legal and Business § 24:198, Minor.

Ohio Jurisprudence Pleading and Practice Forms § 22:8, Capacity of Minors and Incompetent Persons.

Treatises and Practice Aids

Sowald & Morganstern, Baldwin's Ohio Practice Domestic Relations Law § 7:1, Nature of Marriage and Annulment.

Sowald & Morganstern, Baldwin's Ohio Practice Domestic Relations Law § 7:6, Statutory Grounds--Underage Marriage.

Sowald & Morganstern, Baldwin's Ohio Practice Domestic Relations Law § 16:1, Jurisdiction.

Sowald & Morganstern, Baldwin's Ohio Practice Domestic Relations Law § 2:16, Capacity to Marry--Legal Age.

Sowald & Morganstern, Baldwin's Ohio Practice Domestic Relations Law § 23:23, Full Faith and Credit for Child Support Orders Act--Choice of Law.

Sowald & Morganstern, Baldwin's Ohio Practice Domestic Relations Law § 27:20, Subject Matter Jurisdiction--Loss of Subject Matter Jurisdiction--Assumption by Juvenile Court.

Carlin, Baldwin's Ohio Prac. Merrick-Rippner Probate Law § 19:4, Legitimation--Historical Provisions.

Carlin, Baldwin's Ohio Prac. Merrick-Rippner Probate Law § 19:8, Uniform Parentage Act--Support Order.

Carlin, Baldwin's Ohio Prac. Merrick-Rippner Probate Law § 62:2, Person Under the Age of 18.

Carlin, Baldwin's Ohio Prac. Merrick-Rippner Probate Law § 110:3, Criminal Jurisdiction--Proceedings for Nonsupport.

Carlin, Baldwin's Ohio Prac. Merrick-Rippner Probate Law § 19:10, Uniform Parentage Act--Procedure in Action to Determine Father-Child Relationship.

Carlin, Baldwin's Ohio Prac. Merrick-Rippner Probate Law § 108:20, Juvenile Court Jurisdiction--Consent for Child to Marry.

Carlin, Baldwin's Ohio Prac. Merrick-Rippner Probate Law § 110:20, Parentage Act--Jurisdiction and Venue.

Carlin, Baldwin's Ohio Prac. Merrick-Rippner Probate Law § 110:35, Civil Support Proceedings--Liability for Child Support.

Carlin, Baldwin's Ohio Prac. Merrick-Rippner Probate Law § 110:36, Civil Support Proceedings--Determination of Amount of Support Under Child Support Guidelines.

White, Ohio Landlord Tenant Law § 2:22, Description of the Parties--Mental Capacity.

Kuehnle & Levey, Ohio Real Estate Law and Practice § 20:18, Conveyancing--Grantors--Capacity--Individuals--Minors and Persons Incarcerated.

Law Review and Journal Commentaries

Annual Survey of Family Law, 1990 Volume 12, compiled by the International Society On Family Law. (Ed. note: articles from Australia, Belgium, Canada, China, Czechoslovakia, England, France, Germany, Greece, Israel, Italy, Jamaica, Japan, Netherlands, Pakistan, Poland, Scotland, South Africa, Spain, Sweden, USSR, United States.) 28 J Fam L 397 (1989–90).

Annual Survey of Family Law, compiled by The International Society On Family Law. (Ed. note: Articles on family law from 23 countries.) 29 J Fam L 277 (1990–91).

Child Custody Jurisdiction in Ohio—Implementing the Uniform Child Custody Jurisdiction Act, Comment. 12 Akron L Rev 121 (Summer 1978).

Children—The Innocent Victims of Family Breakups: How the Family Law Attorney, the Courts, and Society Can Protect Our Children, Michael J. Albano. 26 U Tol L Rev 787 (Summer 1995).

Deceptions, delusions and spin doctors in family court litigation, Dennis W. Mattingly. (Ed. note: The author, a domestic relations magistrate, recounts war stories of lying litigants, and urges mediation of domestic disputes). 18 Ohio Law 12 (May/June 2004).

Dividing the Child: *Shea v. Metcalf*, 712 A.2d 887 (Vt. 1998), Note. 24 U Dayton L Rev 543 (Spring 1999).

Fragmenting and Reassembling the World: Of Flying Squirrels, Augmented Persons, and Other Monsters, Michael H. Shapiro. (Ed. note: The moral dimensions of abortion, genetic engineering, and other products of modern technology are explored.) 51 Ohio St L J 331 (1990).

Human Cloning Symposium. 32 U Tol L Rev 321 (Spring 2001).

Judge's Column, Hon. Francine M Bruening. (Ed. note: Judge Bruening discusses the pending Ohio Parenting Act.) 20 Lake Legal Views 1 (June 1997).

The Lawyer Turns Peacemaker—with mediation emerging as the most popular form of alternate dispute resolution, the quest for common ground could force attorneys to reinterpret everything they do in the future, Richard C. Reuben. 82 A B A J 54 (August 1996).

Ligation Litigation, Brian Murphy, Leo C. Downing. 25 J Fam L 729 (1986–87).

Litigation Results—Count on a CPA, Keith J. Libman. 67 Clev B J 12 (October 1996).

What Lawyers Should Know About the New Age of Majority, Stanley J. Aronoff. 46 Ohio St B Ass'n Rep 1551 (10–7–73).

Notes of Decisions

In general **2**
Alcohol purchasing under age 21 **11**
Change of age of majority **10**
Constitutional issues **1**
Disaffirming contracts **9**
Educational issues **7**
Emancipation defined **3**
Emancipation, support decree **6**
Personal injury action **8**
Retroactive application, support decree **5**
Support decree **4-6**
   In general **4**
   Emancipation **6**
   Retroactive application **5**

---

1. Constitutional issues

The amendment to RC 3109.01 changing the age of majority from twenty-one years to eighteen years is constitutional and applies to an injured person who is eighteen years of age on the effective date of the amendment. Durham v. Anka Research Ltd. (Hamilton 1978) 60 Ohio App.2d 239, 396 N.E.2d 799, 14 O.O.3d 222.

The effect of a statutory amendment reducing the age of majority from twenty-one to eighteen in shortening the period of limitations governing the actions of minors is remedial in nature and does not violate O Const Art II §28, prohibiting retroactive laws, provided a reasonable time is still permitted to bring the action. Ledwell v. May Co. (Ohio Com.Pl. 1977) 54 Ohio Misc. 43, 377 N.E.2d 798, 7 O.O.3d 138, 8 O.O.3d 347. Statutes ☞ 278.32

Statute, as amended (110 v 125) effective 7–18–23, raising the age of majority of females from eighteen to twenty-one years, is unconstitutional to the extent that it attempted to divest females who had attained the age of eighteen before such date of the right to convey real estate. Gigger v. Kelly (Ohio Com.Pl. 1923) 24 Ohio N.P.N.S. 499.

The amendment to RC 3109.01 changing the age of majority from twenty-one years to eighteen years is constitutional and applies to an injured person who reached eighteen years of age after the effective date of the amendment. Scheer v. Air–Shields, Inc. (Hamilton 1979) 61 Ohio App.2d 205, 401 N.E.2d 478, 15 O.O.3d 321.

2. In general

Due to legal disability from being subject of guardianship, surviving 19-year-old child did not reach age of majority, and thus, he was a "minor" for purposes of statute providing for family allowance for children of parents who die leaving minor children and no surviving spouse. In re Estate of Davis (Ohio App. 2 Dist., Greene, 05-14-2010) No. 2010-CA-1, 2010-Ohio-2131, 2010 WL 1931982, Unreported. Executors And Administrators ⊆ 180; Guardian And Ward ⊆ 30(1); Infants ⊆ 1

Time in which to bring a claim to establish paternity is five years longer than period of father's duty to support, which expires when child reaches age 18. Snider v. Lillie (Ohio App. 1 Dist., 10-17-1997) 131 Ohio App.3d 444, 722 N.E.2d 1036, dismissed, appeal not allowed 81 Ohio St.3d 1452, 690 N.E.2d 546. Children Out–of–wedlock ⊆ 38

A statutory amendment lowering the age of majority from twenty-one to eighteen operates prospectively from its effective date to remove the disability of minority of all persons who are eighteen to twenty-one years of age on such effective date. Ledwell v. May Co. (Ohio Com.Pl. 1977) 54 Ohio Misc. 43, 377 N.E.2d 798, 7 O.O.3d 138, 8 O.O.3d 347. Limitation Of Actions ⊆ 72(1)

Persons under the age of legal capacity to contract may become a "guest," within the meaning of RC 4515.02, so that a child who rides in an automobile, without any consideration for such ride having been received by its owner, is a "guest" although neither parent nor guardian consented to such ride. Kemp v. Parmley (Ohio Com.Pl. 1967) 17 Ohio Misc. 23, 243 N.E.2d 779, 46 O.O.2d 18, affirmed 16 Ohio St.2d 3, 241 N.E.2d 169, 45 O.O.2d 67.

Statute of limitations on minor patients' medical malpractice claims was tolled or suspended until patients reached the age of majority, such that their re-filed complaint was neither re-filed beyond applicable time limitations nor subject to savings statute and, thus, complaint could be properly dismissed without prejudice pursuant to stipulation of dismissal signed by all parties. Butler v. Harper (Ohio App. 9 Dist., Summit, 09-25-2002) No. 21051, 2002-Ohio-5029, 2002 WL 31114898, Unreported. Limitation Of Actions ⊆ 72(1); Limitation Of Actions ⊆ 130(5)

RC 737.15 and 737.16 permit the appointment of otherwise qualified persons of the age of eighteen to the offices of village marshal, deputy marshal, policeman, night watchman and special policeman. OAG 78–058.

RC 509.01 and 505.49 permit the appointment of otherwise qualified persons of the age of eighteen to township police positions, unless, in the operation of a police district, pursuant to RC 505.48 et seq., the board of trustees under RC 505.49 has

acted by a two-thirds vote to establish a higher age requirement. OAG 78–058.

RC 311.04 permits the appointment of an otherwise qualified person of the age of eighteen to the office of deputy sheriff. OAG 78–058.

RC 124.41 requires that all persons originally appointed as policemen or policewomen in a city or civil service township police department be at least twenty-one years of age. OAG 78–058.

An employee who leaves work to take her child to the hospital after receiving a telephone call, though the child is above the age of majority, is fired without just cause by the employer. While a parent has no legal obligation to care for a child past majority, under some circumstances such care is normal and expected from a parent and is not to be penalized as an unexcused absence. In re Shupe, UCRC B2002–00578 (10–20–2004).

3. Emancipation defined

Child was not "emancipated," as required for father to be relieved of child support obligation, despite evidence that child withdrew from high school in district in which father lived after father sold home and moved out-of-state and then child re-enrolled at age eighteen by listing address of friend; child continued to live with mother and mother continued to provide for child financially. Demcho v. Demcho (Ohio App. 9 Dist., Medina, 09-15-2004) No. 03CA0105-M, 2004-Ohio-4868, 2004 WL 2047363, Unreported. Child Support ⊆ 393

The terms "emancipation" and "majority" with regard to status of a child are not synonymous; emancipation generally refers to freeing of a child from parental control, and majority refers to the "age of majority." Risser v. Risser (Ohio App. 3 Dist., 09-24-2007) 173 Ohio App.3d 430, 878 N.E.2d 1073, 2007-Ohio-4936, appeal not allowed 117 Ohio St.3d 1406, 881 N.E.2d 274, 2008-Ohio-565. Infants ⊆ 9; Parent And Child ⊆ 16

"Emancipation" is the entire surrender by parent of right to care, custody, and earnings of minor child as well as renunciation of parental duties. Swanson v. Swanson (Ohio App. 2 Dist., 02-09-1996) 109 Ohio App.3d 231, 671 N.E.2d 1333. Child Support ⊆ 386; Infants ⊆ 9; Parent And Child ⊆ 16

4. Support decree—In general

By stating that a parent must provide child support for "the parties' two minor children," the parties' pre–1974 divorce decree implicitly provides a duration for the support obligation which is the age of twenty-one, the statutorily defined age of majority at the time the decree was entered. Quillen v. Deaton (Ohio App. 12 Dist., Butler, 02-02-1998) No. CA97-07-147, 1998 WL 42234, Unreported, appeal not allowed 81 Ohio St.3d 1527, 692 N.E.2d 1027.

Ex-husband's child support obligation continued past daughter's 18th birthday, as provided for under Missouri law in Missouri child support order, despite Ohio law providing for termination of support when child reaches age 18. Emig v. Massau (Ohio App. 10 Dist., 11-16-2000) 140 Ohio App.3d 119, 746 N.E.2d 707. Child Support ☞ 391

Determination of whether a child support obligation in a pre–1974 divorce decree was altered by statutory amendments lowering of the age of majority depends on whether the decree, explicitly or implicitly, enumerated the duration of the obligation; if it did, the lowering of the age of majority did not change that obligation, but if it did not, the lowering of the age of majority meant that the support obligation ended when the child or children at issue reached the age of eighteen. Cox v. Cox (Ohio App. 1 Dist., 12-04-1998) 130 Ohio App.3d 609, 720 N.E.2d 946. Child Support ☞ 293

A court errs in overruling a father's motion for return of overpayment of child support where the magistrate uses an incorrect termination date for the support obligation as the twenty-first birthday of the youngest child when the order should have terminated when each child reached age eighteen. Cox v. Cox (Ohio App. 1 Dist., 12-04-1998) 130 Ohio App.3d 609, 720 N.E.2d 946.

Parents' common-law duty to support their child continued after child's majority, where child had been blind and mentally impaired, and therefore fully disabled, continuously since birth. Abbas v. Abbas (Ohio App. 7 Dist., 06-23-1998) 128 Ohio App.3d 513, 715 N.E.2d 613. Child Support ☞ 390

Minor's employment does not terminate child support obligation as a matter of law, and mere capability of minor child to earn money on his or her own behalf is no ground for termination or reduction of child support order. Swanson v. Swanson (Ohio App. 2 Dist., 02-09-1996) 109 Ohio App.3d 231, 671 N.E.2d 1333. Child Support ☞ 295; Child Support ☞ 375; Child Support ☞ 386

Determination of whether obligation to provide child support pursuant to divorce decree entered prior to statutory amendment lowering age of majority from 21 to 18 is affected by amendment depends upon whether decree, explicitly or implicitly, enumerates duration of obligation of support; if it does, obligation is not changed by lowering of age; if it does not, lowering means that support obligation ends when child reaches age 18. Motley v. Motley (Ohio App. 9 Dist., 03-22-1995) 102 Ohio App.3d 67, 656 N.E.2d 995. Child Support ☞ 392

Where divorce decree did not include enumeration of duration of husband's child support obligation, but only provided that it would continue until further order of court, obligation ended when each child reached age 18, even though original divorce decree was entered prior to statutory amendment lowering age of majority from 21 to 18. Motley v. Motley (Ohio App. 9 Dist., 03-22-1995) 102 Ohio App.3d 67, 656 N.E.2d 995. Child Support ☞ 392

Where the parties to a separation agreement agree that the obligation to make child support payments will terminate when the child reaches the "age of majority," the obligation to make support payments terminates when the child reaches his or her eighteenth birthday unless the parties specify some other definition of the phrase "age of majority." In re Dissolution of Marriage of Lazor (Ohio 1991) 59 Ohio St.3d 201, 572 N.E.2d 66. Child Support ☞ 390

After a man is adjudged a putative father and ordered to pay support until the child is eighteen, pursuant to former RC 3111.17, if the man acknowledges paternity under RC 2105.18, he assumes the obligation imposed by RC 3103.03 to support the child throughout its minority, as minority is defined by RC 3109.01, subject to subsequent amendments to RC 3109.01 and 3103.03. Zweifel v. Price (Franklin 1985) 24 Ohio App.3d 101, 493 N.E.2d 300, 24 O.B.R. 171.

Common-law duty imposed on parents to support their minor children may be found by a court of domestic relations having jurisdiction of the matter to continue beyond age of majority if the children are unable to support themselves because of mental or physical disabilities which existed before attaining the age of majority. Castle v. Castle (Ohio 1984) 15 Ohio St.3d 279, 473 N.E.2d 803, 15 O.B.R. 413. Child Support ☞ 111

A court in Ohio has no authority to compel a divorced husband to continue paying support for his disabled child who has reached the age of majority. Maphet v. Heiselman (Clermont 1984) 13 Ohio App.3d 278, 469 N.E.2d 92, 13 O.B.R. 343.

The statutory change in the age of majority operates prospectively only and does not affect the provisions of pre–1974 support decrees. Price v. Price (Darke 1983) 12 Ohio App.3d 42, 465 N.E.2d 922, 12 O.B.R. 129.

RC 3105.10 clothes courts with jurisdiction to incorporate into a court order an agreement to support a child of the parties beyond the age of that child's majority, and such an order may be enforced by contempt proceedings. Bugay v. Bugay (Summit 1977) 53 Ohio App.2d 285, 373 N.E.2d 1263, 7 O.O.3d 336.

The statutory change in the age of majority has no application to pre–1974 support decrees incorporating parental separation agreements. Rosenfeld v. Rosenfeld (Ohio 1976) 47 Ohio St.2d 12, 351 N.E.2d 181, 1 O.O.3d 8.

The statutory change in the age of majority has no application to pre–1974 support decrees. Nokes v. Nokes (Ohio 1976) 47 Ohio St.2d 1, 351 N.E.2d 174, 1 O.O.3d 1.

Where the language of a court order in a divorce action fixes support "until majority," after January 1, 1974, such support order—no matter when made—will terminate as to any child who has attained age eighteen; where the court order fixes support until age twenty-one, such order will be ineffective after January 1, 1974, as to any child who has reached eighteen; where a property settlement agreement provides for payment until majority, a motion to terminate support as to an eighteen-year-old should be sustained after January 1, 1974;

where a property settlement agreement provides for payment until age twenty-one, the court may continue to enforce such order. Istnick v. Istnick (Ohio Com.Pl. 1973) 37 Ohio Misc. 91, 307 N.E.2d 922, 66 O.O.2d 244.

Father's duty to support his minor child does not stop when such child has arrived at the age of eighteen years. Rutter v. Rutter (Ohio Com.Pl. 1970) 24 Ohio Misc. 7, 261 N.E.2d 202, 53 O.O.2d 32. Child Support ☞ 375

Separation agreement incorporated into divorce decree in which wife agrees to provide for support of child of parties after it arrives at age of eighteen years, does not relieve husband from duty of providing for such child. Rutter v. Rutter (Ohio Com. Pl. 1970) 24 Ohio Misc. 7, 261 N.E.2d 202, 53 O.O.2d 32. Child Support ☞ 47

Determination of the age at which a person becomes an adult for the purpose of enforcing the provisions of the reciprocal support act, depends upon the state in which the child is living and the state in which the father is living, and not in the state in which the original divorce was granted. Burney v. Vance (Ohio Com.Pl. 1969) 17 Ohio Misc. 307, 246 N.E.2d 371, 46 O.O.2d 427.

The uniform support act covers children who are minors, and under RC 3115.22 is in addition to and not in substitution of any other remedies authorized by law. Burney v. Vance (Ohio Com.Pl. 1969) 17 Ohio Misc. 307, 246 N.E.2d 371, 46 O.O.2d 427. Child Support ☞ 500

RC 3109.01 which effectuates a change of the age of majority to eighteen effective January 1, 1974 has no effect upon pre–1974 child support decrees. Coleman v Coleman, No. L–82–005 (6th Dist Ct App, Lucas, 5–7–82).

In an action to extend child support provisions to cover the children from age eighteen to twenty-one, the trial court does have authority to entertain the motion to modify the original divorce decree and extend the time of the husband's support obligation. Kufrin v Kufrin, No. 42926 (8th Dist Ct App, Cuyahoga, 4–23–81).

5. —— Retroactive application, support decree

Statute that changed age of majority from 21 years of age to 18 years of age could not be applied retroactively to divorce decree to so as to terminate father's obligation to pay child support when parties' youngest child reached 18 years of age, instead of 21, even though divorce decree did not contain language that specifically referred to children reaching age of 21; decree specified father would provide support for "minor children," and age of majority was 21 when decree was entered. Sandy v. Sandy (Ohio App. 5 Dist., Stark, 08-09-2004) No. 2003CA00322, 2004-Ohio-4341, 2004 WL 1846109, Unreported. Child Support ☞ 6; Child Support ☞ 392

Juvenile Court lacked jurisdiction to order retroactive child support, in paternity proceedings, when the first claim for support was made after the child reached the age of majority and the duty to support

had elapsed. Carnes v. Kemp (Ohio App. 3 Dist., Auglaize, 11-03-2003) No. 2-03-10, 2003-Ohio-5884, 2003 WL 22473582, Unreported, stay denied 101 Ohio St.3d 1419, 802 N.E.2d 152, 2004-Ohio-123, motion to certify allowed 101 Ohio St.3d 1465, 804 N.E.2d 39, 2004-Ohio-819, appeal allowed 101 Ohio St.3d 1466, 804 N.E.2d 40, 2004-Ohio-819, motion granted 103 Ohio St.3d 1419, 814 N.E.2d 63, 2004-Ohio-4504, reversed 104 Ohio St.3d 629, 821 N.E.2d 180, 2004-Ohio-7107. Children Out-of-wedlock ☞ 67

6. —— Emancipation, support decree

Trial court did not abuse its discretion in determining that father's child support obligation terminated on date child graduated from high school, and that father was not required to pay support through the entire month in which child graduated, as the common law duty imposed on father to support minor child terminated when child became emancipated, either reaching the age of majority or graduating from high school, such that parties' child became emancipated on date of his graduation. He v. Zeng (Ohio App. 5 Dist., Licking, 05-11-2010) No. 2009-CA-00060, 2010-Ohio-2095, 2010 WL 1918797, Unreported, appeal not allowed 126 Ohio St.3d 1601, 935 N.E.2d 47, 2010-Ohio-4928. Child Support ☞ 393

Father was not required to pay for emancipated child's college education, as parties' divorce decree did not obligate father to pay for it. He v. Zeng (Ohio App. 5 Dist., Licking, 05-11-2010) No. 2009-CA-00060, 2010-Ohio-2095, 2010 WL 1918797, Unreported, appeal not allowed 126 Ohio St.3d 1601, 935 N.E.2d 47, 2010-Ohio-4928. Child Support ☞ 119

The trial court does not err in finding that a nineteen-year-old daughter is not emancipated and, accordingly, properly denies a motion by the father for termination of child support where the evidence in the record shows that (1) the daughter is a full-time college student, (2) the father and mother pay for nearly all of her expenses including tuition, room, and board, (3) the daughter lives on campus but returns to her mother's home during the summer and on breaks, (4) the daughter works part-time in a public service related area as a requirement to maintain her scholarship, and (5) there is no indication that the mother has renunciated her right to the care and custody of the daughter nor that the daughter has taken affirmative steps to release herself from parental control. Smyers v. Abramovich (Ohio App. 9 Dist., Summit, 03-07-2001) No. 20124, 2001 WL 222962, Unreported.

A high school student who learns he is not eligible for graduation and (1) has already attained the age of majority, (2) has no intentions of returning to high school after summer recess, and (3) begins working full-time is no longer continuously attending high school and is an emancipated child for whom a parent owes no duty to pay support pursuant to a child support order. Hiltbrand v. Hiltbrand (Ohio App. 5 Dist., Tuscarawas,

07-02-1999) No. 1998AP0115, 1999 WL 547962, Unreported.

Parents can agree to provide post-divorce support for emancipated children by way of an annuity to provide for the children's college education. Strong v. Strong (Ohio App. 6 Dist., Lucas, 02-28-1997) No. L-96-044, 1997 WL 89105, Unreported.

Stipulation in divorce decree that husband would continue to pay child support for child who had already reached the age of majority was irrelevant to the issue of whether husband was obligated to pay child support after child was emancipated, where child had reached the age of majority at the time of the stipulation but was living at home and still attending high school, which indicated that he was not emancipated. Risser v. Risser (Ohio App. 3 Dist., 09-24-2007) 173 Ohio App.3d 430, 878 N.E.2d 1073, 2007-Ohio-4936, appeal not allowed 117 Ohio St.3d 1406, 881 N.E.2d 274, 2008-Ohio-565. Child Support ☞ 52; Child Support ☞ 386

Child was not "emancipated" on 18th birthday, and thus former husband's child support obligation ended upon child's 18th birthday, even though child was still in high school at that time, and parties agreed to extend child support until later date, where separation agreement provided for termination of child support upon alternative contingencies, namely either child reaching 18 or becoming emancipated, emancipation was not defined by agreement, and child was not self-supporting on 18th birthday. Jack v. Jack (Ohio App. 7 Dist., 09-20-2000) 139 Ohio App.3d 814, 745 N.E.2d 1101, 2000-Ohio-2553. Child Support ☞ 50; Parent And Child ☞ 16

Court lacked authority to order biological father to provide present and future child support to child who had reached age of majority and was emancipated, even though paternity action had been timely filed within five years after child reached age 18. Snider v. Lillie (Ohio App. 1 Dist., 10-17-1997) 131 Ohio App.3d 444, 722 N.E.2d 1036, dismissed, appeal not allowed 81 Ohio St.3d 1452, 690 N.E.2d 546. Children Out–of–wedlock ☞ 21(2); Children Out–of–wedlock ☞ 67

With respect to present and future child support, once child reaches age of majority and becomes emancipated, court is without power to provide child with support, child has no legal right to be supported, and the court no longer has the power to order a parent to pay child support. Snider v. Lillie (Ohio App. 1 Dist., 10-17-1997) 131 Ohio App.3d 444, 722 N.E.2d 1036, dismissed, appeal not allowed 81 Ohio St.3d 1452, 690 N.E.2d 546. Child Support ☞ 103; Child Support ☞ 390

Marriage of minor child is an act of emancipation that terminates obligations of domestic relations order as a matter of law. Swanson v. Swanson (Ohio App. 2 Dist., 02-09-1996) 109 Ohio App.3d 231, 671 N.E.2d 1333. Child Support ☞ 387; Infants ☞ 10

To extent that emancipation relieves parent of duty of support, it does so only with respect to parent's duty to support minor child; emancipation is irrelevant to any duty of support that may exist after child reaches age of majority. Swanson v. Swanson (Ohio App. 2 Dist., 02-09-1996) 109 Ohio App.3d 231, 671 N.E.2d 1333. Child Support ☞ 386

Emancipation discharges parent from obligation to support minor child, but only so long as minor child is competent to support himself or herself. Swanson v. Swanson (Ohio App. 2 Dist., 02-09-1996) 109 Ohio App.3d 231, 671 N.E.2d 1333. Child Support ☞ 386

Emancipation applies only to minor children. Swanson v. Swanson (Ohio App. 2 Dist., 02-09-1996) 109 Ohio App.3d 231, 671 N.E.2d 1333. Parent And Child ☞ 16

A father is obligated to support a child until she reaches majority at age eighteen, at which time she becomes legally emancipated despite a separation agreement stating that the father's support would end when the child graduated high school or became emancipated, whichever came first, where the child graduates one month before her eighteenth birthday. Dudziak v. Dudziak (Cuyahoga 1992) 81 Ohio App.3d 361, 611 N.E.2d 337.

Age of majority in effect at time of entry of dissolution decree that contained child support obligation controlled determination of child's emancipation based on attainment of age of majority. Bauer v. Bauer (Franklin 1989) 57 Ohio App.3d 24, 566 N.E.2d 185. Child Support ☞ 392

A parent owes no duty of support to an emancipated epileptic child who is capable of being self-supporting. Cooksey v. Cooksey (Erie 1988) 55 Ohio App.3d 135, 562 N.E.2d 934.

Where the age of legal majority is reduced by the legislature, a party to a divorce settlement, under which he is bound to support minor children until they become emancipated, is relieved of any obligation beyond that age designated by the new act. Allison v. Allison (Warren 1975) 44 Ohio App.2d 230, 337 N.E.2d 666, 73 O.O.2d 243.

A father is primarily responsible for the support of his minor children, and that support continues under the law of Ohio until the child is twenty-one years of age or is otherwise emancipated. Burney v. Vance (Ohio Com.Pl. 1969) 17 Ohio Misc. 307, 246 N.E.2d 371, 46 O.O.2d 427.

7. Educational issues

A trial court's extension of support beyond a child's eighteenth birthday violates the terms of the couple's 1978 divorce agreement and reliance on present day RC 3109.05(E) is misplaced as that section's language, requiring support issued pursuant to this section to continue past the age of majority so long as the child is in high school, was enacted years after the divorce decree was issued and is not controlling. Wendling v. Wendling (Ohio App. 8 Dist., Cuyahoga, 02-08-1996) No. 68837, 1996 WL 50825, Unreported, dismissed, appeal not allowed 76 Ohio St.3d 1420, 667 N.E.2d 24.

A high school that has been recognized by another state and accredited by non-Ohio entities need not also have been approved by the state of Ohio in order to be a "recognized and accredited" high school as contemplated by child support statute providing that parental duty of support shall continue beyond age of majority as long as child continuously attends "any" recognized and accredited high school; in choosing adjective of "any," the legislature manifested its intent that the phrase "recognized and accredited high school" was to be construed expansively. Davis v. Davis (Ohio, 10-10-2007) 115 Ohio St.3d 180, 873 N.E.2d 1305, 2007-Ohio-5049. Child Support ☞ 393

Out-of-state home schooling program in which adult child enrolled was a "recognized and accredited" high school, as contemplated by statute providing that parental duty of support shall continue beyond age of majority as long as child continuously attends "any" recognized and accredited high school, and thus, former husband, as the child support obligor, was required to continue to pay child support despite child's age of majority and enrollment in school that was recognized by another state and accredited by non-Ohio entities. Davis v. Davis (Ohio, 10-10-2007) 115 Ohio St.3d 180, 873 N.E.2d 1305, 2007-Ohio-5049. Child Support ☞ 393

Evidence supported finding that former husband was responsible for payment of tuition, room, board, and books necessary for child's college education based on cost of attendance at state college in state where former husband and former wife entered into separation agreement, subject to credit for student loan which child used to purchase vehicle, even though child attended out-of-state college, where parties did not contemplate attendance at school out of state and parties did not discuss specific limitations and financial expectations surrounding education of child at time of agreement, and child and former wife acquiesced in such payments. Jack v. Jack (Ohio App. 7 Dist., 09-20-2000) 139 Ohio App.3d 814, 745 N.E.2d 1101, 2000-Ohio-2553. Child Support ☞ 202

There could be no "meeting of the minds" between child, former wife, and former husband, as required to establish contract to modify former husband's obligation to financially support child's college education, where child was unaware of exact language contained within original separation agreement between former wife and former husband. Jack v. Jack (Ohio App. 7 Dist., 09-20-2000) 139 Ohio App.3d 814, 745 N.E.2d 1101, 2000-Ohio-2553. Child Support ☞ 239

Withdrawal from high school by child who was in custody of former husband on day child turned 18 years of age terminated wife's duty to pay child support, and divested trial court of jurisdiction to order wife to pay child support or to modify child support agreement; child's subsequent enrollment in vocational school did not resurrect order, as

obligation continues after age 18 only if child continuously attends high school. Gleason v. Gleason (Ohio App. 4 Dist., 08-27-1998) 129 Ohio App.3d 563, 718 N.E.2d 512. Child Support ☞ 293; Child Support ☞ 390; Child Support ☞ 470

If child does not continuously attend high school on a full-time basis after turning 18, parent's duty to provide child support ends, and trial court loses subject matter jurisdiction. Gleason v. Gleason (Ohio App. 4 Dist., 08-27-1998) 129 Ohio App.3d 563, 718 N.E.2d 512. Child Support ☞ 103; Child Support ☞ 120

During child's minority, domestic relations court has jurisdiction to alter provisions of its decree which relate to college education of child upon proper motion of or consent of parties but once child reaches age of majority, court is without jurisdiction to modify those provisions without consent of child of the parties. Rohrbacher v. Rohrbacher (Lucas 1992) 83 Ohio App.3d 569, 615 N.E.2d 338. Child Support ☞ 293; Child Support ☞ 304

An order in a divorce action that a father pay a child's room, board, and college tuition beyond the child's eighteenth birthday is reversible error. Verplatse v. Verplatse (Hancock 1984) 17 Ohio App.3d 99, 477 N.E.2d 648, 17 O.B.R. 161.

Where, as part of a valid agreement, a husband agrees to provide college education for his children and further agrees to keep in effect insurance policies on his life in which such children are beneficiaries, and where such agreement is incorporated in a decree divorcing the husband from his wife, such decree becomes binding upon the husband even though the performance required by the decree may extend beyond the minority of the children. Grant v. Grant (Erie 1977) 60 Ohio App.2d 277, 396 N.E.2d 1037, 14 O.O.3d 249. Child Support ☞ 52; Child Support ☞ 54

The juvenile court has jurisdiction to require the father of a child whose custody had been given to the mother in a divorce decree to support said child after he has reached his eighteenth birthday, but before he attains the age of twenty-one years, where such continued support beyond the age of eighteen is intended for the purpose of a college education for said child. Calogeras v. Calogeras (Ohio Juv. 1959) 163 N.E.2d 713, 82 Ohio Law Abs. 438, 10 O.O.2d 441.

8. Personal injury action

A plaintiff in a personal injury action who was injured in an accident occurring prior to January 1, 1974, while he was under the age of 21, must litigate his claim within two years after the January 1, 1974 amendment to RC 3109.01, lowering the age of majority to 18 years, or within two years after his eighteenth birthday, whichever is later. Cook v. Matvejs (Ohio 1978) 56 Ohio St.2d 234, 383 N.E.2d 601, 10 O.O.3d 384. Limitation Of Actions ☞ 72(1)

A plaintiff in a personal injury action who was injured in an accident occurring prior to January 1, 1974, while he was under the age of twenty-one, must litigate his claim within two years after the January 1, 1974, amendment to RC 3109.01, lowering the age of majority to eighteen years. Dickerson v. Ferrell (Richland 1976) 53 Ohio App.2d 160, 372 N.E.2d 619, 7 O.O.3d 161. Limitation Of Actions ⚬= 72(1)

Mother of hockey player, who supported her son's participation in ice hockey and was at the ice rink at the time of his injury, was barred under Ohio law under the doctrine of estoppel by acquiescence from disaffirming the release signed by both hockey player and his father. Mohney v. USA Hockey, Inc. (N.D.Ohio, 12-14-1999) 77 F.Supp.2d 859, affirmed in part, reversed in part 5 Fed.Appx. 450, 2001 WL 223852, on remand 300 F.Supp.2d 556. Estoppel ⚬= 92(2)

When a minor reaches her majority and the probate court grants the request to terminate her guardianship the probate court loses jurisdiction over any matter pertaining to her including a personal injury claim from an automobile accident which occurs during minority. In re Layshock (Ohio App. 7 Dist., Mahoning, 12-28-2001) No. 00-C.A.-198, 2001-Ohio-3381, 2001 WL 1667872, Unreported.

9. Disaffirming contracts

At time the parties entered into surrogacy contract, surrogate mother's legal status was as a disinterested third party, akin to a caretaker, and fact that surrogate mother and mother's husband, who kept children born as result of surrogacy, later obtained custody of children in Pennsylvania court did not retroactively grant surrogate mother and her husband the status of parents at time they signed or breached surrogacy contract with biological father; as such, when surrogate mother and her husband contracted with biological father, surrogate mother and her husband did not contract away any parental rights and, therefore, surrogacy contract did not violate public policy on that basis. J.F. v. D.B. (Ohio App. 9 Dist., 03-15-2006) 165 Ohio App.3d 791, 848 N.E.2d 873, 2006-Ohio-1175, appeal allowed 110 Ohio St.3d 1438, 852 N.E.2d 187, 2006-Ohio-3862, affirmed in part, reversed in part 116 Ohio St.3d 363, 879 N.E.2d 740, 2007-Ohio-6750. Contracts ⚬= 108(2)

Minor, who had been two months shy of his 18th birthday when he co-signed loan from credit union for his sister's purchase of vehicle from him, did not attempt to disaffirm the loan contract within reasonable time after he reached age 18, and thus, the contract was enforceable against him; minor waited until more than three years after his 18th birthday to disaffirm the loan contract, by which time credit union had sued him to collect on the loan. Muller v. CES Credit Union (Ohio App. 5 Dist., 06-24-2005) 161 Ohio App.3d 771, 832 N.E.2d 80, 2005-Ohio-3251. Infants ⚬= 58(1)

Contracts for "necessities," as exception to general rule that a contract with a minor is voidable at the minor's election upon reaching majority or a reasonable time thereafter, are contracts for food, medicine, clothes, shelter, or personal services usu-

ally considered reasonably essential for preservation and enjoyment of life. Muller v. CES Credit Union (Ohio App. 5 Dist., 06-24-2005) 161 Ohio App.3d 771, 832 N.E.2d 80, 2005-Ohio-3251. Infants ⚬= 58(1)

Contracts of a minor are voidable at the minor's election upon reaching majority or a reasonable time thereafter. Muller v. CES Credit Union (Ohio App. 5 Dist., 06-24-2005) 161 Ohio App.3d 771, 832 N.E.2d 80, 2005-Ohio-3251. Infants ⚬= 58(1)

To maintain action on contract for necessaries made with minor, transaction must be fair and reasonable, made in good faith by plaintiff, and without knowledge of defendant's lack of capacity to contract; "necessaries" are defined as food, medicine, clothing, shelter or personal services usually considered reasonably essential for preservation and enjoyment of life. Parkwood OB/GYN Inc. v. Hess (Ohio Mun., 03-30-1995) 70 Ohio Misc.2d 32, 650 N.E.2d 533. Infants ⚬= 50

Although medical services provided to minor constituted "necessary" services, medical clinic was precluded from recovering on contract for services, since clinic knew minor's date of birth when services were rendered and therefore had knowledge of minor's incapacity to contract. Parkwood OB/GYN Inc. v. Hess (Ohio Mun., 03-30-1995) 70 Ohio Misc.2d 32, 650 N.E.2d 533. Infants ⚬= 50

Contracts of minor are voidable at minor's election upon reaching majority or reasonable time thereafter; only exceptions are those authorized by law, those entered in performance of legal duty, and those for purchase of necessities. Parkwood OB/GYN Inc. v. Hess (Ohio Mun., 03-30-1995) 70 Ohio Misc.2d 32, 650 N.E.2d 533. Infants ⚬= 58(1)

A minor can void a contract whether or not she is married. Bramley's Water Conditioning v. Hagen (Portage 1985) 27 Ohio App.3d 300, 501 N.E.2d 38, 27 O.B.R. 356.

Infant before or within reasonable time after coming of age may disaffirm contract not for necessaries. Infant who, on attaining majority, elected to disaffirm contract for purchase of automobile, made disaffirmance effective by returning car to seller without notifying seller's assignee. Hoffman v. Edson Co. (Cuyahoga 1929) 37 Ohio App. 262, 173 N.E. 307, 7 Ohio Law Abs. 388. Infants ⚬= 58(2)

A minor can withdraw from contract without placing other party in statu quo, where it is impossible to do so. Eagle Dairy Co. v. Dylag (Cuyahoga 1929) 33 Ohio App. 113, 168 N.E. 754, 7 Ohio Law Abs. 358, 30 Ohio Law Rep. 361. Infants ⚬= 58(2)

Infant misrepresenting his age upon purchasing automobile may plead minority to avoid contract and may recover payments made without any diminution. Summit Auto Co. v. Jenkins (Summit 1925) 20 Ohio App. 229, 153 N.E. 153, 4 Ohio Law Abs. 50, 24 Ohio Law Rep. 392.

Where minor purchases an automobile, giving notes in part payment therefor, and continues to use it and make payments thereon for more than six months after attaining majority, it is too late to disaffirm his contract of purchase, and he is bound thereby. Herschede Motor Car Co. v. Bangham (Ohio Com.Pl. 1926) 26 Ohio N.P.N.S. 232.

Under this section, no minor can make a valid contract unless it be for necessaries, or for some other purpose which law permits. No provision permits a minor parent to contract away a child. GC 10512–11 (RC 3107.03) permits parent to give consent to adoption, and GC 1352–12 (RC 5103.15) permits parents to place children with state department of public welfare, and while no age is mentioned in these sections, consent of minor parents is sufficient because these sections place no limitation as to age of parents. As contracting away a child is not an adoption case, or a placement with department of public welfare, this section would thereby restrict minor parent from making contract in question. In re Swentosky, 25 Abs 601 (Prob, Tuscarawas 1937).

10. Change of age of majority

It is error for trial court to dismiss action for divorce on ground that plaintiff is a minor, being a female under twenty-one years of age at time of trial, where she was of legal age at time of filing the action, and subsequent thereto but before trial, the legislature amended the statute, changing the age of majority of females from eighteen to twenty-one years. Tigner v. Tigner (Hamilton 1923) 19 Ohio App. 297, 2 Ohio Law Abs. 571.

Ex-father's child support obligation, pursuant to divorce decree entered prior to statutory amendments that lowered age of majority from twenty-one to eighteen, terminated when youngest child reached age eighteen, where decree did not state a duration for support order but referred to parties' "minor children." Cox v. Cox (Ohio App. 1 Dist., 12-04-1998) 130 Ohio App.3d 609, 720 N.E.2d 946. Child Support ☞ 392

A deed by female persons over the age of eighteen but under twenty-one years of age, executed at a time when the amendment of this section, changing the majority of females from eighteen to twenty-one was effective, is voidable and may be set aside. Coleman v. Coleman (Hamilton 1935) 51 Ohio App. 221, 200 N.E. 197, 19 Ohio Law Abs. 661, 4 O.O. 172.

Legislature acted within its power in passing statute increasing age of majority of females from eighteen to twenty-one years and the statute is not retroactive. Pickering v. Peskind (Cuyahoga 1930) 43 Ohio App. 401, 183 N.E. 301, 13 Ohio Law Abs. 312, 31 Ohio Law Rep. 439. Infants ☞ 4

Right of action for tort, by female who became eighteen on January 7, 1923, then accrued and being a property right, could not be taken away by statute becoming effective July 18, 1923, increasing age of majority of females to twenty-one years.

Pickering v. Peskind (Cuyahoga 1930) 43 Ohio App. 401, 183 N.E. 301, 13 Ohio Law Abs. 312, 31 Ohio Law Rep. 439. Constitutional Law ☞ 2754; Constitutional Law ☞ 4389; Infants ☞ 4; Limitation Of Actions ☞ 6(7)

The amendment to the statute, fixing age of majority of females at twenty-one, is not retroactive and does not affect existing rights of property of women who became eighteen years of age prior to the date the amendment became effective. Pickering v. Peskind (Cuyahoga 1930) 43 Ohio App. 401, 183 N.E. 301, 13 Ohio Law Abs. 312, 31 Ohio Law Rep. 439. Infants ☞ 4

In an action to extend child support provisions to cover the children from age eighteen to twenty-one, the trial court does have authority to entertain the motion to modify the original divorce decree and extend the time of the husband's support obligation. Kufrin v Kufrin, No. 42926 (8th Dist Ct App, Cuyahoga, 4–23–81).

The 1974 amendment to RC 3109.01 lowering the age of majority to eighteen years will be applied so that a pre–1974 support order will terminate upon the child reaching the age of eighteen years, absent a separation agreement provision concerning termination of support at a different time. Colvin v Colvin, No. 10120 (2d Dist Ct App, Montgomery, 3–5–87).

11. Alcohol purchasing under age 21

A state's decision to limit the consumption of alcoholic beverages to persons twenty-one years and older is a lawful exercise of a state's police power and is rationally related to a legitimate state interest in keeping inexperienced and young drivers from driving on the streets of Ohio while under the influence of alcohol. State v. Powers (Ohio App. 3 Dist., Marion, 10-16-1998) No. 9-98-08, No. 9-98-09, No. 9-98-10, 1998 WL 720694, Unreported.

No cause of action exists against liquor permit holder on part of a voluntarily intoxicated patron who is "underage" pursuant to statute but who has attained the age of majority, or on part of patron's representative, for patron's self-inflicted injury or death which is due to intoxication. Klever v. Canton Sachsenheim, Inc. (Ohio, 09-15-1999) 86 Ohio St.3d 419, 715 N.E.2d 536, 1999-Ohio-117. Intoxicating Liquors ☞ 295

Nineteen-year-old motorist who sustained fatal injuries in single-vehicle accident which occurred while motorist was driving after becoming intoxicated at wedding reception was not protected by Dramshop Act, and thus, motorist's representative could not maintain wrongful death action under Dramshop Act against club which had hosted reception and served alcohol to motorist. Klever v. Canton Sachsenheim, Inc. (Ohio, 09-15-1999) 86 Ohio St.3d 419, 715 N.E.2d 536, 1999-Ohio-117. Intoxicating Liquors ☞ 295; Intoxicating Liquors ☞ 297

3109.02 Veteran's exception

Any person who is eligible for a loan under the Servicemen's Readjustment Act of 1944, any amendments thereto or re-enactment thereof, the Veterans Readjustment Assistance Act of

1952, any amendments thereto or re-enactment thereof, the Act of September 2, 1958, Public Law 85–857, 72 Stat. 1105, any amendments thereto or re-enactment thereof, or the Veterans' Readjustment Benefits Act of 1966, any amendments thereto or re-enactments thereof, whether or not he or his spouse is a minor, may, in his name and without any order of court or the intervention of a guardian or trustee, execute any instruments, take title to real property, borrow money thereon, and do all other acts necessary to secure to him all rights and benefits under said acts, or any regulations thereunder, in as full and ample manner as if he and his spouse had attained the age of eighteen years. No person eligible for such loan, or his spouse, is, by reason only of such minority, incompetent to acquire title to property by contract or to borrow thereon; and no instrument made in connection with acquiring title to real estate or making such loan shall be voidable on the grounds of minority of such person or his spouse.

Any person who has qualified under said acts or any regulations thereunder and has secured a loan and taken title to real property thereunder is capable of disposing of such property by deed or other conveyance, notwithstanding the fact that he or his spouse is a minor, and no such deed or other conveyance shall be voidable on the grounds of minority of such person or his spouse.

(1973 S 1, eff. 1–1–74; 132 v H 909; 125 v 99; 1953 H 1; GC 8005–2; Source—GC 8023–1)

Historical and Statutory Notes

Pre–1953 H 1 Amendments: 124 v S 65

Library References

Armed Services ⟷31, 108, 123.
Infants ⟷46, 51.
Westlaw Topic Nos. 34, 211.

C.J.S. Armed Services §§ 1, 162, 309 to 312.
C.J.S. Infants §§ 209 to 213, 253, 268, 270 to 275.

Research References

Encyclopedias

OH Jur. 3d Family Law § 797, Statutory Exceptions; Loans.

Treatises and Practice Aids

White, Ohio Landlord Tenant Law § 2:22, Description of the Parties--Mental Capacity.

Notes of Decisions

Unimproved lots   1

1. Unimproved lots

The spouse of a serviceman, who is a minor and who joins with her husband in executing a promissory note in payment of the purchase price of three unimproved lots, as a separate consideration for same and apart from the consideration paid for an adjacent dwelling house purchased concurrently although constituting one transaction, upon arriving at her majority, may disaffirm her legal obligation of liability on such note. Lambright v. Heck

(Wood 1949) 86 Ohio App. 456, 93 N.E.2d 45, 42 O.O. 64.

Where one "who is eligible for a loan under the Servicemen's Readjustment Act of 1944" purchases a dwelling house and three unimproved lots adjacent, and who obtains a loan under the act on the lot improved with a dwelling house, and who in the same transaction executes a promissory note in payment of the purchase price of three unimproved lots, the provisions of the act have no application in determining the validity of the promissory note. Lambright v. Heck (Wood 1949) 86 Ohio App. 456, 93 N.E.2d 45, 42 O.O. 64.

PARENTAL RIGHTS AND RESPONSIBILITIES

3109.03 Equal rights of parents to parental rights and responsibilities toward children

When husband and wife are living separate and apart from each other, or are divorced, and the question as to the parental rights and responsibilities for the care of their children and the place of residence and legal custodian of their children is brought before a court of competent jurisdiction, they shall stand upon an equality as to the parental rights and responsibilities for the care of their children and the place of residence and legal custodian of their children, so far as parenthood is involved.

(1990 S 3, eff. 4–11–91; 1953 H 1; GC 8005–3; Source—GC 8032)

Historical and Statutory Notes

Pre–1953 H 1 Amendments: 124 v S 65

Cross References

Action for divorce, annulment, or legal separation, custody and support of children, see 3105.21

Husband and wife are natural guardians of minor children, see 2111.08

Provision for allocation of parental rights and responsibilities in separation agreement attached to petition for dissolution of marriage, see 3105.63

Library References

Child Custody ⬅24.
Parent and Child ⬅1 to 2.5.
Westlaw Topic Nos. 76D, 285.

C.J.S. Divorce § 994.
C.J.S. Parent and Child §§ 1 to 12, 40 to 54, 68, 201.

Research References

Encyclopedias

OH Jur. 3d Family Law § 1056, Parent's Equality in Allocation.

Forms

Ohio Forms Legal and Business § 28:1, Introduction.

Ohio Forms Legal and Business § 28:46, Introduction.

Ohio Jurisprudence Pleading and Practice Forms § 101:37, Allocation of Parental Rights and Responsibilities.

Treatises and Practice Aids

Sowald & Morganstern, Baldwin's Ohio Practice Domestic Relations Law § 15:9, Best Interest

Standard--Interactions and Interrelationships With Others.

Sowald & Morganstern, Baldwin's Ohio Practice Domestic Relations Law § 7:19, Relief Incident to Annulment--Children of an Annulled Marriage--Child Support and Custody.

Sowald & Morganstern, Baldwin's Ohio Practice Domestic Relations Law § 21:29, Criminal Sanctions.

Sowald & Morganstern, Baldwin's Ohio Practice Domestic Relations Law § 21:31, Custody to Non-Parent.

Sowald & Morganstern, Baldwin's Ohio Practice Domestic Relations Law § 25:30, Motions Regarding Temporary Relief--Motion for Allocation of Parental Rights and Responsibilities Pendente Lite.

Law Review and Journal Commentaries

Bankruptcy Reform Act of 1994—What the Bankruptcy Code Giveth, Domestic Relations Courts (and Congress) Taketh Away, C.R. "Chip" Bowles. 8 Domestic Rel J Ohio 17 (March/April 1996).

Child custody disputes between lesbians: Legal strategies and their limitations, Nicole Berner. 10 Berkeley Women's L J 31 (1995).

The Child Dependency Exemption And Divorced Parents: What Is "Custody"?, David J. Benson. 18 Cap U L Rev 57 (Spring 1989).

Children—The Innocent Victims of Family Breakups: How the Family Law Attorney, the Courts, and Society Can Protect Our Children, Michael J. Albano. 26 U Tol L Rev 787 (Summer 1995).

Custody Disputes Following the Dissolution of Interracial Marriages: Best Interests of the Child or Judicial Racism?, Colleen McKinley. 19 J Fam L 97 (1980–81).

Difficult Situations, Mary Kay Kisthardt and Barbara Handschu. 29 Nat'l L J 12 (5–10–2004).

Enforcement Of Surrogate Mother Contracts: Case Law, The Uniform Acts, and State and Federal Legislation, James T. Flaherty. 36 Clev St L Rev 223 (1988).

Granting Custody to Third Party. Pamela J. MacAdams, 14 Domestic Rel J Ohio 65 (July/August 2002).

Judges' Column, Hon. Francine Bruening. (Ed. note: Judge Bruening discusses the Child Support Reorganization Act of House Bill 352, effective 1–1–98.) 21 Lake Legal Views 1 (June 1998).

Report of the Family Law Committee (Uniform Child Custody Jurisdiction Act). 49 Ohio St B Ass'n Rep 611 (5–17–76).

Standard of Proof in Proceedings to Terminate Parental Rights, Note. 31 Clev St L Rev 679 (1982).

Notes of Decisions

Assistance of counsel   2
Child support   3
Constitutional issues   1
Divorced parents   9

Full faith and credit   5
Habeas corpus   11
Interests of child   12
Jurisdiction   7

---

1. Constitutional issues

Investigatory stop of child custody detainee's vehicle was justified by reasonable suspicion, and thus comported with Fourth Amendment; at time that detective requested uniformed officers to make stop, he had seen order granting custody of daughter to other parent, had observed detainee come out of home with two children, and reasonably believed that detainee was unlawfully interfering with custody. Krantz v. City of Toledo Police Dept. (C.A.6 (Ohio), 09-20-2006) No. 05-3636, 197 Fed.Appx. 446, 2006 WL 2706510, Unreported. Arrest ⊜ 60.2(10)

Father was not denied a fair trial in custody determination by trial court's refusal to permit his child to be cross-examined during evidentiary hearing, where remand from previous appeal of trial court's award of custody to maternal grandparents was limited to requiring trial court to allow cross-examination of guardian ad litem. Rife v. Morgan (Ohio App. 2 Dist., 10-18-1995) 106 Ohio App.3d 843, 667 N.E.2d 450. Child Custody ⊜ 924

Father in custody proceeding was not prejudiced by trial court's failure to rule on motions to allow newly discovered evidence and for finding of contempt against child's maternal grandmother, and thus was not denied a fair trial, where trial court recognized that it had not yet ruled upon motions and matter had been remanded to trial court from earlier appeal only for purpose of allowing father to cross-examine guardian ad litem. Rife v. Morgan (Ohio App. 2 Dist., 10-18-1995) 106 Ohio App.3d 843, 667 N.E.2d 450. Child Custody ⊜ 923(1)

Father in custody proceeding was not prejudiced by trial court's implicit overruling of father's motion to remove guardian ad litem for child, and thus was not denied a fair trial, where father did not explain how he was prejudiced and matter had been remanded to trial court from earlier appeal only for purpose of allowing father to cross-examine guardian ad litem. Rife v. Morgan (Ohio App. 2 Dist., 10-18-1995) 106 Ohio App.3d 843, 667 N.E.2d 450. Child Custody ⊜ 923(1)

Father in custody proceeding was not prejudiced by trial court's failure to rule on pro se motions for findings of contempt against school, social worker, and children's home after remand from earlier appeal to allow father opportunity to cross-examine guardian ad litem, and thus was not denied a fair trial, where father did not explain how he was prejudiced, motions did not implicate limited purpose of remand, and there was no reason to conclude that trial court would not eventually rule on motions. Rife v. Morgan (Ohio App. 2 Dist.,

10-18-1995) 106 Ohio App.3d 843, 667 N.E.2d 450. Child Custody ⊜ 923(1)

Appellate court, on appeal after remand to allow father in custody proceeding to cross-examine guardian ad litem, would not address argument by father that trial court had denied him a fair trial by withholding the record of its discussions with child; discussion appeared to be germane to prior appeal from court's original judgment, and any problem with securing record should have been addressed during pendency of prior appeal. Rife v. Morgan (Ohio App. 2 Dist., 10-18-1995) 106 Ohio App.3d 843, 667 N.E.2d 450. Child Custody ⊜ 907

There is no substantive federal constitutional right to physical possession of a child; a parent's right to custody or visitation with a child, however, is a constitutionally protected liberty interest that cannot be interfered with absent due process of law. Scarso v. Cuyahoga County Dept. of Human Services (N.D.Ohio 1989) 747 F.Supp. 381, affirmed in part and remanded 917 F.2d 1305.

Natural parents have a constitutionally-protected liberty interest in the care and custody of their children. In re Barker (Ohio App. 12 Dist., Butler, 07-29-2002) No. CA2001-12-293, 2002-Ohio-3871, 2002 WL 1758378, Unreported. Constitutional Law ⊜ 4391

2. Assistance of counsel

Sixth Amendment right to effective assistance of counsel did not apply to child custody proceedings. Spirito v. Partridge (Ohio App. 2 Dist., Greene, 10-21-2005) No. 04-CA0118, 2005-Ohio-5589, 2005 WL 2697259, Unreported. Child Custody ⊜ 500

Sixth Amendment right to effective assistance of counsel did not apply to child custody proceedings. In re Logwood (Ohio App. 5 Dist., Guernsey, 07-11-2005) No. 2004-CA-38, 2005-Ohio-3639, 2005 WL 1682732, Unreported. Child Custody ⊜ 500

Mother did not have a constitutional right to effective assistance of counsel during proceeding on father's motion for legal custody of child and mother's motion to suspend father's visitation; there was no constitutional right to counsel in a civil case between individual parents. In re Rosier Lemmon (Ohio App. 5 Dist., Stark, 03-15-2004) No. 2003 CA 00306, 2004-Ohio-1290, 2004 WL 540299, Unreported. Child Custody ⊜ 500

A trial court commits reversible error when a husband is not provided with opportunity to be heard as to the issues of property division and child custody at his divorce trial under circumstances that (1) he is present in the courtroom without counsel while seated in the back of the room, (2) he waves his arms in objection and the trial judge requests that the defendant either stop waving his arms or leave the courtroom, and (3) the defendant verbally objects to a particular statement, to which the judge responds, "Just be quiet. I'm taking testimony up here at this time," after which trial continues without defendant's participation and proceeds to grant judgment in favor of the plaintiff following her presentation of evidence. Skaggs v. Skaggs (Ohio

App. 3 Dist., Marion, 06-23-1995) No. 9-94-60, 1995 WL 368838, Unreported.

Father was not denied fair trial in custody determination proceedings by being denied right to proceed pro se; father claimed right to proceed pro se as cocounsel, father was represented by counsel throughout proceedings, father ignored instructions to file papers only through his attorney, trial court recognized obligation to rule on all motions filed by counsel, and father did not indicate how he was prejudiced by failure of court to rule on several pro se motions. Rife v. Morgan (Ohio App. 2 Dist., 10-18-1995) 106 Ohio App.3d 843, 667 N.E.2d 450. Attorney And Client ☞ 62

Father was not prejudiced by minimal participation of mother's counsel in evidentiary hearing in custody determination, despite mother's apparent agreement that custody should be with maternal grandparents, and thus, he was not denied a fair trial or due process of law. Rife v. Morgan (Ohio App. 2 Dist., 10-18-1995) 106 Ohio App.3d 843, 667 N.E.2d 450. Child Custody ☞ 923(1); Constitutional Law ☞ 4396

Father was not denied due process in custody determination by trial court's appointment of counsel for guardian ad litem without affording father an opportunity to be heard, where guardian ad litem was to be subjected to cross-examination. Rife v. Morgan (Ohio App. 2 Dist., 10-18-1995) 106 Ohio App.3d 843, 667 N.E.2d 450. Child Custody ☞ 500; Constitutional Law ☞ 4396

Father who lost custody of his child was not denied a fair trial or equal protection by trial court's failure to obtain complete record of prior proceedings to resolve authenticity objection to report used by father's counsel on cross-examination of guardian ad litem, where father's counsel convinced trial court that document was authentic and counsel was allowed to use report. Rife v. Morgan (Ohio App. 2 Dist., 10-18-1995) 106 Ohio App.3d 843, 667 N.E.2d 450. Constitutional Law ☞ 3463; Constitutional Law ☞ 4003; Evidence ☞ 382

3. Child support

Father was not entitled to child support credit to cover visitation travel expenses, although mother was given a $231 credit to cover such expenses when father initially had custody of child following divorce and new visitation order placed additional burdens on father, as father was in a more tenable financial position to cover the costs associated with his travel to and from Virginia in order to see child. Pellettiere v. Pellettiere (Ohio App. 2 Dist., Montgomery, 10-09-2009) No. 23141, 2009-Ohio-5407, 2009 WL 3246751, Unreported. Child Support ☞ 350

Former husband's payment of child support arrears on the day before the contempt hearing did not divest the court of its contempt power, and contempt sanctions of imprisonment and fine thus were permissible to uphold the dignity of the court. In re Contemnor Caron (Ohio Com.Pl., 04-27-2000) 110 Ohio Misc.2d 58, 744 N.E.2d 787. Child Support ☞ 444

Former husband purged himself of civil contempt by making his lump-sum delinquent payment of child support on the day before the contempt hearing. In re Contemnor Caron (Ohio Com.Pl., 04-27-2000) 110 Ohio Misc.2d 58, 744 N.E.2d 787. Child Support ☞ 445

Former husband's failure to pay child support for several years was criminal contempt of court immediately before his forced payment of child support on the day before the contempt hearing. In re Contemnor Caron (Ohio Com.Pl., 04-27-2000) 110 Ohio Misc.2d 58, 744 N.E.2d 787. Child Support ☞ 444

A sentence of thirty days in jail was warranted for criminal contempt by a former husband for failing to pay child support for several years. In re Contemnor Caron (Ohio Com.Pl., 04-27-2000) 110 Ohio Misc.2d 58, 744 N.E.2d 787. Child Support ☞ 444

A proposed settlement of child support and custody disputes was not in the best interests of the child; the former husband was five-and-one-half years delinquent in child support, and the former wife waived a major portion of the court-ordered entitlements for the benefit of the child. In re Contemnor Caron (Ohio Com.Pl., 04-27-2000) 110 Ohio Misc.2d 58, 744 N.E.2d 787. Child Custody ☞ 35; Child Support ☞ 44

The best interests of a child demand that the father pay to the mother, for the benefit of the child, all monies and expenses previously ordered by the court. In re Contemnor Caron (Ohio Com. Pl., 04-27-2000) 110 Ohio Misc.2d 58, 744 N.E.2d 787. Child Support ☞ 430

Former husband was required to comply with child support orders until paternity claim was resolved. In re Contemnor Caron (Ohio Com.Pl., 04-27-2000) 110 Ohio Misc.2d 58, 744 N.E.2d 787. Child Support ☞ 375

Trial court lacked jurisdiction to order ex-husband to pay child support for period preceding filing of divorce action. Jackson v. Jackson (Ohio App. 2 Dist., 05-26-2000) 137 Ohio App.3d 782, 739 N.E.2d 1203. Child Support ☞ 150

Trial court did not abuse its discretion by ordering that commencement of former wife's child support obligation begin at time when all three children of couple began residing with former husband, even though husband had been designated as residential parent for two of children eight months earlier. Bowen v. Bowen (Ohio App. 9 Dist., 02-09-1999) 132 Ohio App.3d 616, 725 N.E.2d 1165, dismissed, appeal not allowed 86 Ohio St.3d 1402, 711 N.E.2d 231. Child Support ☞ 150

A custodial parent is not entitled to reimbursement for child support from the non-custodial parent where no support order is made or requested at the time custody is awarded. Bowen v. Bowen (Ohio App. 9 Dist., 02-09-1999) 132 Ohio App.3d 616, 725 N.E.2d 1165, dismissed, appeal not allowed 86 Ohio St.3d 1402, 711 N.E.2d 231. Child Support ☞ 55

Evidence supported trial court's determination that father should pay entire amount of child support owed under dissolution decree, even though child had moved in with her boyfriend; mother testified that she used money received to pay child's expenses, and child testified that she remained dependent upon mother for support after she left her mother's home. Swanson v. Swanson (Ohio App. 2 Dist., 02-09-1996) 109 Ohio App.3d 231, 671 N.E.2d 1333. Child Support ☞ 487

A custodial parent is not entitled to reimbursement for child support from the noncustodial parent where no support order is made or requested at the time custody is awarded. Meyer v. Meyer (Ohio 1985) 17 Ohio St.3d 222, 478 N.E.2d 806, 17 O.B.R. 455. Child Support ☞ 55

Where a wife abandons her husband without any aggression on his part and takes her children to another state, the husband cannot be compelled to support such children under the uniform enforcement of support laws where he retains a domicile in Ohio, earns his living in Ohio, and apparently is ready, willing and able to support his children in Ohio. Buliox v. Buliox (Ohio Com.Pl. 1962) 185 N.E.2d 802, 90 Ohio Law Abs. 251, 21 O.O.2d 30.

4. Unmarried parents

Statute, which applied to issues of parenting rights between a husband and wife who were living separate and apart from each other or were divorced, did not apply to afford father equal parenting rights over child, in father's action to establish visitation with child; the statute only applied to husbands and wives who were separated or were divorced, and statute did not refer to unmarried parents, such as mother and father. In re Frank Brown (Ohio App. 3 Dist., Seneca, 05-11-2009) No. 13-08-46, 2009-Ohio-2192, 2009 WL 1272642, Unreported. Children Out-of-wedlock ☞ 20.9

Doctrine of res judicata applied to bar collateral attack on findings contained in agreed entry between former same-sex partners, in which parties agreed to share custody of child borne by partner, and, thus, agreed entry affirmatively established that partner who did not bear child was a proper person for the care, training, and education of child, for purposes of declaratory judgment action brought by partner who bore child seeking determination on trial court's authority to enforce agreed entry, as neither party appealed or challenged agreed entry. Morris v. Hawk (Ohio App. 5 Dist., 02-10-2009) 2009 -Ohio- 656, 2009 WL 350915. Children Out-Of-Wedlock ☞ 20.4

At time the parties entered into surrogacy contract, surrogate mother's legal status was as a disinterested third party, akin to a caretaker, and fact that surrogate mother and mother's husband, who kept children born as result of surrogacy, later obtained custody of children in Pennsylvania court did not retroactively grant surrogate mother and her husband the status of parents at time they signed or breached surrogacy contract with biological father; as such, when surrogate mother and her husband contracted with biological father, surrogate

mother and her husband did not contract away any parental rights and, therefore, surrogacy contract did not violate public policy on that basis. J.F. v. D.B. (Ohio App. 9 Dist., 03-15-2006) 165 Ohio App.3d 791, 848 N.E.2d 873, 2006-Ohio-1175, appeal allowed 110 Ohio St.3d 1438, 852 N.E.2d 187, 2006-Ohio-3862, affirmed in part, reversed in part 116 Ohio St.3d 363, 879 N.E.2d 740, 2007-Ohio-6750. Contracts ☞ 108(2)

Statute specifying that husband and wife who are divorced or living separate and apart shall stand upon equality as to parental rights and responsibilities and shall have equal rights to custody in absence of agreement or binding court order does not deal with rights of putative father who has neither acknowledged paternity nor supported the child. State v. Hill (Ohio, 03-05-1996) 75 Ohio St.3d 195, 661 N.E.2d 1068, reconsideration denied 75 Ohio St.3d 1453, 663 N.E.2d 333, certiorari denied 117 S.Ct. 241, 519 U.S. 895, 136 L.Ed.2d 170, denial of post-conviction relief affirmed 1997 WL 727587, dismissed, appeal not allowed 81 Ohio St.3d 1468, 690 N.E.2d 1288. Children Out-of-wedlock ☞ 20.2

Although parents who are suitable persons generally have paramount right to custody of their minor children, rights and interests of natural parents are not absolute. In re Hiatt (Adams 1993) 86 Ohio App.3d 716, 621 N.E.2d 1222. Child Custody ☞ 22

A trial court abuses its discretion when it awards the father custody of the two minor children of the unmarried couple where (1) the mother supported the couple and children through part-time employment during the eight years they were together but the father was not regularly employed and rarely spent quality time with the children; (2) the father took the children on vacation to Florida and, after the mother informed him over the telephone that she wished to terminate their relationship, he refused to let the mother see them or often even to speak to them on the telephone; and (3) once in Florida, the father changed his residence, found employment, enrolled the children in school, affiliated with a church, and began to spend time with the children. In re Markham (Meigs 1990) 70 Ohio App.3d 841, 592 N.E.2d 896, dismissed, jurisdictional motion overruled 60 Ohio St.3d 702, 573 N.E.2d 118.

When the alleged natural father of an illegitimate child, who has participated in the nurturing process of the child, files a complaint seeking custody of the child under RC 2151.23(A)(2), and the mother admits that he is the natural father of the child, the natural father has equality of standing with the mother with respect to the custody of the child, and the court shall determine which parent shall have the legal custody of the child, taking into account what would be in the best interests of the child. In re Byrd (Ohio 1981) 66 Ohio St.2d 334, 421 N.E.2d 1284, 20 O.O.3d 309. Children Out-of-wedlock ☞ 20.4

The father of a child born out of wedlock is not entitled to visitation with such child over the objections of the mother, who has legal custody, unless he clearly establishes that such would be in the best interests of the child. In re Connolly (Franklin 1974) 43 Ohio App.2d 38, 332 N.E.2d 376, 72 O.O.2d 194. Children Out–of–wedlock ☞ 20.9

5. Full faith and credit

Where a court of another state has awarded custody of a minor child pursuant to a valid in personam order, and there is no evidence of a subsequent change in circumstances affecting the best interests of the child, the courts of this state will give full faith and credit to that order. Williams v. Williams (Ohio 1975) 44 Ohio St.2d 28, 336 N.E.2d 426, 73 O.O.2d 121.

6. Moral conduct of parents

A mother's having surreptitiously relocated a child is one of several factors for a court to consider in making a custody determination and it does not err in vacating a child custody portion of a divorce decree which awards sole custody to the father where evidence is insufficient to support a granting of permanent custody to either parent and the court has heard very little evidence concerning the best interests of the child. Eichenberger v. Eichenberger (Ohio App. 10 Dist., Franklin, 10-24-1995) No. 95APF04-456, 1995 WL 632059, Unreported, appeal not allowed 75 Ohio St.3d 1425, 662 N.E.2d 27.

A court's inquiry into the moral conduct or standards of a custodial parent is limited to a determination of the effect of such conduct on the child. In re Rex (Seneca 1981) 3 Ohio App.3d 198, 444 N.E.2d 482, 3 O.B.R. 226.

7. Jurisdiction

Mother's appearance before court, after having raised issue, did not waive the defense of lack of personal jurisdiction as to father's motion for reallocation of parental rights and responsibilities. Alestock v. Bomestar (Ohio App. 5 Dist., Stark, 11-08-2004) No. 2004CA00001, 2004-Ohio-7317, 2004 WL 3563903, Unreported. Child Custody ☞ 601; Child Custody ☞ 607

Father was not required to file a transcript of the evidence submitted to magistrate in connection with his motion for reallocation of parental rights and responsibilities against mother, where father objected to magistrate's order concerning personal jurisdiction as a matter of law, not a finding of fact. Alestock v. Bomestar (Ohio App. 5 Dist., Stark, 11-08-2004) No. 2004CA00001, 2004-Ohio-7317, 2004 WL 3563903, Unreported. Child Custody ☞ 907

An Ohio juvenile court, in a dependency proceeding pursuant to RC 2151.27 et seq., has no jurisdiction to interfere with a mother's legal custody of her children, in the absence of proof and a finding of unfitness of such parent, merely for the purpose of releasing such children to the officers of the court of a foreign state, and the court need not give full faith and credit to a Michigan decree where that decree was obtained by the husband in an ex parte custody determination, subsequent to a divorce decree, in which the Michigan court had no personal jurisdiction over the nonresident wife. In re Messner (Huron 1969) 19 Ohio App.2d 33, 249 N.E.2d 532, 48 O.O.2d 31.

The Lucas County court of common pleas, division of domestic relations, is a court of competent jurisdiction to determine care, custody, and control of minor children. Witkorowski v. Witkorowski (Lucas 1951) 89 Ohio App. 424, 102 N.E.2d 896, 46 O.O. 259. Child Custody ☞ 920

8. Married parents

When a divorce is denied, the parties are still married and they have equal rights as to custody of minor children, and both are responsible for care and support, and, until such time as a separate complaint or application is made to a court of competent jurisdiction, the provisions of RC 3109.03 and 3109.04 may not be invoked. Holderle v. Holderle (Franklin 1967) 11 Ohio App.2d 148, 229 N.E.2d 79, 40 O.O.2d 305.

9. Divorced parents

Visitation rights as to children of divorced parents must be considered without regard to the child's religious training, for all Christian denominations stand on the same footing in the eye of the law. Angel v. Angel (Ohio Com.Pl. 1956) 140 N.E.2d 86, 74 Ohio Law Abs. 531, 2 O.O.2d 136.

Trial court was justified in awarding custody of children eleven, ten, and six to the father because of the mother's emotional instability. Herzog v. Herzog (Montgomery 1955) 132 N.E.2d 754, 72 Ohio Law Abs. 22.

Where in a divorce action in which neither party is found to be unsuited for custody, custody is awarded to the mother, and the court pursuant to agreement of the parties orders that the child continue to reside with the paternal grandparents, and each party thereafter seeks modification of the order, the agreement is waived and the court must award physical custody to the mother in the absence of a showing that she is not suitable. La Ferier v. Garey (Lucas 1954) 98 Ohio App. 37, 128 N.E.2d 168, 57 O.O. 157.

Custody of minor children in a divorce proceeding may be given to the father's sister, even though the divorce was granted for his aggression, where the mother's health is such that she should not have the children. Peterson v. Peterson (Ohio Com.Pl. 1954) 123 N.E.2d 546, 69 Ohio Law Abs. 459, 55 O.O. 134.

The remarriage of divorced parents terminates the jurisdiction of the divorce court over the custody of their minor children. Lockard v. Lockard (Ohio Com.Pl. 1951) 102 N.E.2d 747, 63 Ohio Law Abs. 549, 49 O.O. 163.

Where the natural parents of a minor child are divorced, custody of the child being given to the mother, and the mother remarries and her husband adopts the child, and then the mother and adoptive father are divorced, and custody is awarded to the adoptive father, and the natural father seeks custody, and prior to hearing the mother and adoptive father are remarried, the court loses jurisdiction over the custody of the child. Lockard v. Lockard (Ohio Com.Pl. 1951) 102 N.E.2d 747, 63 Ohio Law Abs. 549, 49 O.O. 163.

Under the provisions of GC 8032 (RC 3109.03), when the parents are divorced and the question as to the custody of their child is before the court, the parents "stand upon an equality as to the care, custody and control" of their child. Ludy v. Ludy (Franklin 1948) 84 Ohio App. 195, 82 N.E.2d 775, 53 Ohio Law Abs. 47, 39 O.O. 241, rehearing denied 84 N.E.2d 120, 53 Ohio Law Abs. 47.

10. Tender years doctrine

While RC 3109.03 eliminates the presumption that the mother is the proper custodian of a child of tender years, the age of the child and the child's relationship with the mother are factors to be considered under RC 3109.04(C); and a trial court's failure to consider the child's tender years constitutes an abuse of discretion. Berry v Berry, No. CA88–11–081 (12th Dist Ct App, Clermont, 3–12–90).

11. Habeas corpus

On the evidence in a habeas corpus action the court will permit two boys to remain with their father rather than being given to their mother or separated. Trout v. Trout (Ohio Com.Pl. 1956) 136 N.E.2d 474, 73 Ohio Law Abs. 91, appeal dismissed 167 Ohio St. 476, 149 N.E.2d 728, 5 O.O.2d 156.

12. Interests of child

The welfare of the child is considered when the question of custody of such child arises between the parents who stand on an equality, or when the parents are found to be unfit and the court is required to grant custody to a third person. Ludy v. Ludy (Franklin 1948) 84 Ohio App. 195, 82 N.E.2d 775, 53 Ohio Law Abs. 47, 39 O.O. 241, rehearing denied 84 N.E.2d 120, 53 Ohio Law Abs. 47. Child Custody ⟞ 76

13. Voluntary relinquishment

Parents may waive their right to custody of their children, and are bound by an agreement to do so. In re Bonfield (Ohio, 12-13-2002) 97 Ohio St.3d 387, 780 N.E.2d 241, 2002-Ohio-6660. Child Custody ⟞ 35

Parents' agreement to grant custody to a third party is enforceable subject only to a judicial determination that the custodian is a proper person to assume the care, training, and education of the child. In re Bonfield (Ohio, 12-13-2002) 97 Ohio St.3d 387, 780 N.E.2d 241, 2002-Ohio-6660. Child Custody ⟞ 35

Natural parent has paramount right to custody of his or her child as against nonparent, but exception exists providing that abandonment, contractual relinquishment, or total inability to provide support may be a forfeiture of natural parent's paramount right to custody. Miller v. Miller (Hocking 1993) 86 Ohio App.3d 623, 621 N.E.2d 745. Child Custody ⟞ 22

Whether relinquishing custody should be forfeiture of right of custody of parent is question of fact, and any contractual custody arrangement is not necessarily as matter of law a relinquishment of right of custody; there are situations where parent might make contractual arrangement for care and custody of child that cannot be construed to be forfeiture of custodial rights. Miller v. Miller (Hocking 1993) 86 Ohio App.3d 623, 621 N.E.2d 745. Child Custody ⟞ 35; Child Custody ⟞ 68; Child Custody ⟞ 509

14. Uniform child custody jurisdiction act

Intent of legislature in adopting Uniform Child Custody Jurisdiction Act (UCCJA) was to avoid jurisdictional conflict and to promote cooperation between state courts in custody matters so that decree is rendered in state that can best decide best interest of child. Justis v. Justis (Ohio, 04-01-1998) 81 Ohio St.3d 312, 691 N.E.2d 264, 1989-Ohio-626. Child Custody ⟞ 703

The Uniform Child Custody Jurisdiction Act was adopted to resolve jurisdictional disputes between two states, each of which could properly exercise jurisdiction over a child's custody. Daerr v. Daerr (Medina 1987) 41 Ohio App.3d 206, 534 N.E.2d 1229.

The Uniform Child Custody Jurisdiction Act, RC 3109.21 to RC 3109.37, is a body of substantive law affecting a court's authority to determine matters of custody and support, and therefore it may not be applied retroactively. Overbee v. Overbee (Hamilton 1986) 31 Ohio App.3d 179, 509 N.E.2d 960, 31 O.B.R. 345.

3109.04 Court awarding parental rights and responsibilities; shared parenting; modifications; best interests of child; child's wishes

(A) In any divorce, legal separation, or annulment proceeding and in any proceeding pertaining to the allocation of parental rights and responsibilities for the care of a child, upon hearing the testimony of either or both parents and considering any mediation report filed pursuant to section 3109.052 of the Revised Code and in accordance with sections 3127.01 to 3127.53 of the Revised Code, the court shall allocate the parental rights and responsibilities for the care of the minor children of the marriage. Subject to division (D)(2) of this section, the court may allocate the parental rights and responsibilities for the care of the children in either of the following ways:

(1) If neither parent files a pleading or motion in accordance with division (G) of this section, if at least one parent files a pleading or motion under that division but no parent who filed a pleading or motion under that division also files a plan for shared parenting, or if at least one parent files both a pleading or motion and a shared parenting plan under that division but no plan for shared parenting is in the best interest of the children, the court, in a manner consistent with the best interest of the children, shall allocate the parental rights and responsibilities for the care of the children primarily to one of the parents, designate that parent as the residential parent and the legal custodian of the child, and divide between the parents the other rights and responsibilities for the care of the children, including, but not limited to, the responsibility to provide support for the children and the right of the parent who is not the residential parent to have continuing contact with the children.

(2) If at least one parent files a pleading or motion in accordance with division (G) of this section and a plan for shared parenting pursuant to that division and if a plan for shared parenting is in the best interest of the children and is approved by the court in accordance with division (D)(1) of this section, the court may allocate the parental rights and responsibilities for the care of the children to both parents and issue a shared parenting order requiring the parents to share all or some of the aspects of the physical and legal care of the children in accordance with the approved plan for shared parenting. If the court issues a shared parenting order under this division and it is necessary for the purpose of receiving public assistance, the court shall designate which one of the parents' residences is to serve as the child's home. The child support obligations of the parents under a shared parenting order issued under this division shall be determined in accordance with Chapters 3119., 3121., 3123., and 3125. of the Revised Code.

(B)(1) When making the allocation of the parental rights and responsibilities for the care of the children under this section in an original proceeding or in any proceeding for modification of a prior order of the court making the allocation, the court shall take into account that which would be in the best interest of the children. In determining the child's best interest for purposes of making its allocation of the parental rights and responsibilities for the care of the child and for purposes of resolving any issues related to the making of that allocation, the court, in its discretion, may and, upon the request of either party, shall interview in chambers any or all of the involved children regarding their wishes and concerns with respect to the allocation.

(2) If the court interviews any child pursuant to division (B)(1) of this section, all of the following apply:

(a) The court, in its discretion, may and, upon the motion of either parent, shall appoint a guardian ad litem for the child.

(b) The court first shall determine the reasoning ability of the child. If the court determines that the child does not have sufficient reasoning ability to express the child's wishes and concern with respect to the allocation of parental rights and responsibilities for the care of the child, it shall not determine the child's wishes and concerns with respect to the allocation. If the court determines that the child has sufficient reasoning ability to express the child's wishes or concerns with respect to the allocation, it then shall determine whether, because of special circumstances, it would not be in the best interest of the child to determine the child's wishes and concerns with respect to the allocation. If the court determines that, because of special circumstances, it would not be in the best interest of the child to determine the child's wishes and concerns with respect to the allocation, it shall not determine the child's wishes and concerns with respect to the allocation and shall enter its written findings of fact and opinion in the journal. If the court determines that it would be in the best interests of the child to determine the child's wishes and concerns with respect to the allocation, it shall proceed to make that determination.

(c) The interview shall be conducted in chambers, and no person other than the child, the child's attorney, the judge, any necessary court personnel, and, in the judge's discretion, the attorney of each parent shall be permitted to be present in the chambers during the interview.

(3) No person shall obtain or attempt to obtain from a child a written or recorded statement or affidavit setting forth the child's wishes and concerns regarding the allocation of parental

rights and responsibilities concerning the child. No court, in determining the child's best interest for purposes of making its allocation of the parental rights and responsibilities for the care of the child or for purposes of resolving any issues related to the making of that allocation, shall accept or consider a written or recorded statement or affidavit that purports to set forth the child's wishes and concerns regarding those matters.

(C) Prior to trial, the court may cause an investigation to be made as to the character, family relations, past conduct, earning ability, and financial worth of each parent and may order the parents and their minor children to submit to medical, psychological, and psychiatric examinations. The report of the investigation and examinations shall be made available to either parent or the parent's counsel of record not less than five days before trial, upon written request. The report shall be signed by the investigator, and the investigator shall be subject to cross-examination by either parent concerning the contents of the report. The court may tax as costs all or any part of the expenses for each investigation.

If the court determines that either parent previously has been convicted of or pleaded guilty to any criminal offense involving any act that resulted in a child being a neglected child, that either parent previously has been determined to be the perpetrator of the neglectful act that is the basis of an adjudication that a child is a neglected child, or that there is reason to believe that either parent has acted in a manner resulting in a child being a neglected child, the court shall consider that fact against naming that parent the residential parent and against granting a shared parenting decree. When the court allocates parental rights and responsibilities for the care of children or determines whether to grant shared parenting in any proceeding, it shall consider whether either parent or any member of the household of either parent has been convicted of or pleaded guilty to a violation of section 2919.25 of the Revised Code or a sexually oriented offense involving a victim who at the time of the commission of the offense was a member of the family or household that is the subject of the proceeding, has been convicted of or pleaded guilty to any sexually oriented offense or other offense involving a victim who at the time of the commission of the offense was a member of the family or household that is the subject of the proceeding and caused physical harm to the victim in the commission of the offense, or has been determined to be the perpetrator of the abusive act that is the basis of an adjudication that a child is an abused child. If the court determines that either parent has been convicted of or pleaded guilty to a violation of section 2919.25 of the Revised Code or a sexually oriented offense involving a victim who at the time of the commission of the offense was a member of the family or household that is the subject of the proceeding, has been convicted of or pleaded guilty to any sexually oriented offense or other offense involving a victim who at the time of the commission of the offense was a member of the family or household that is the subject of the proceeding and caused physical harm to the victim in the commission of the offense, or has been determined to be the perpetrator of the abusive act that is the basis of an adjudication that a child is an abused child, it may designate that parent as the residential parent and may issue a shared parenting decree or order only if it determines that it is in the best interest of the child to name that parent the residential parent or to issue a shared parenting decree or order and it makes specific written findings of fact to support its determination.

(D)(1)(a) Upon the filing of a pleading or motion by either parent or both parents, in accordance with division (G) of this section, requesting shared parenting and the filing of a shared parenting plan in accordance with that division, the court shall comply with division (D)(1)(a)(i), (ii), or (iii) of this section, whichever is applicable:

(i) If both parents jointly make the request in their pleadings or jointly file the motion and also jointly file the plan, the court shall review the parents' plan to determine if it is in the best interest of the children. If the court determines that the plan is in the best interest of the children, the court shall approve it. If the court determines that the plan or any part of the plan is not in the best interest of the children, the court shall require the parents to make appropriate changes to the plan to meet the court's objections to it. If changes to the plan are made to meet the court's objections, and if the new plan is in the best interest of the children, the court shall approve the plan. If changes to the plan are not made to meet the court's objections, or if the parents attempt to make changes to the plan to meet the court's objections, but the court determines that the new plan or any part of the new plan still is not in the best interest of the children, the court may reject the portion of the parents' pleadings or deny their motion requesting shared parenting of the children and proceed as if the request in the pleadings or the motion had not been made. The court shall not approve a plan under this division unless it determines that the plan is in the best interest of the children.

(ii) If each parent makes a request in the parent's pleadings or files a motion and each also files a separate plan, the court shall review each plan filed to determine if either is in the best interest of the children. If the court determines that one of the filed plans is in the best interest of the children, the court may approve the plan. If the court determines that neither filed plan is in the best interest of the children, the court may order each parent to submit appropriate changes to the parent's plan or both of the filed plans to meet the court's objections, or may select one of the filed plans and order each parent to submit appropriate changes to the selected plan to meet the court's objections. If changes to the plan or plans are submitted to meet the court's objections, and if any of the filed plans with the changes is in the best interest of the children, the court may approve the plan with the changes. If changes to the plan or plans are not submitted to meet the court's objections, or if the parents submit changes to the plan or plans to meet the court's objections but the court determines that none of the filed plans with the submitted changes is in the best interest of the children, the court may reject the portion of the parents' pleadings or deny their motions requesting shared parenting of the children and proceed as if the requests in the pleadings or the motions had not been made. If the court approves a plan under this division, either as originally filed or with submitted changes, or if the court rejects the portion of the parents' pleadings or denies their motions requesting shared parenting under this division and proceeds as if the requests in the pleadings or the motions had not been made, the court shall enter in the record of the case findings of fact and conclusions of law as to the reasons for the approval or the rejection or denial. Division (D)(1)(b) of this section applies in relation to the approval or disapproval of a plan under this division.

(iii) If each parent makes a request in the parent's pleadings or files a motion but only one parent files a plan, or if only one parent makes a request in the parent's pleadings or files a motion and also files a plan, the court in the best interest of the children may order the other parent to file a plan for shared parenting in accordance with division (G) of this section. The court shall review each plan filed to determine if any plan is in the best interest of the children. If the court determines that one of the filed plans is in the best interest of the children, the court may approve the plan. If the court determines that no filed plan is in the best interest of the children, the court may order each parent to submit appropriate changes to the parent's plan or both of the filed plans to meet the court's objections or may select one filed plan and order each parent to submit appropriate changes to the selected plan to meet the court's objections. If changes to the plan or plans are submitted to meet the court's objections, and if any of the filed plans with the changes is in the best interest of the children, the court may approve the plan with the changes. If changes to the plan or plans are not submitted to meet the court's objections, or if the parents submit changes to the plan or plans to meet the court's objections but the court determines that none of the filed plans with the submitted changes is in the best interest of the children, the court may reject the portion of the parents' pleadings or deny the parents' motion or reject the portion of the parents' pleadings or deny their motions requesting shared parenting of the children and proceed as if the request or requests or the motion or motions had not been made. If the court approves a plan under this division, either as originally filed or with submitted changes, or if the court rejects the portion of the pleadings or denies the motion or motions requesting shared parenting under this division and proceeds as if the request or requests or the motion or motions had not been made, the court shall enter in the record of the case findings of fact and conclusions of law as to the reasons for the approval or the rejection or denial. Division (D)(1)(b) of this section applies in relation to the approval or disapproval of a plan under this division.

(b) The approval of a plan under division (D)(1)(a)(ii) or (iii) of this section is discretionary with the court. The court shall not approve more than one plan under either division and shall not approve a plan under either division unless it determines that the plan is in the best interest of the children. If the court, under either division, does not determine that any filed plan or any filed plan with submitted changes is in the best interest of the children, the court shall not approve any plan.

(c) Whenever possible, the court shall require that a shared parenting plan approved under division (D)(1)(a)(i), (ii), or (iii) of this section ensure the opportunity for both parents to have frequent and continuing contact with the child, unless frequent and continuing contact with any parent would not be in the best interest of the child.

(d) If a court approves a shared parenting plan under division (D)(1)(a)(i), (ii), or (iii) of this section, the approved plan shall be incorporated into a final shared parenting decree granting the parents the shared parenting of the children. Any final shared parenting decree shall be issued at the same time as and shall be appended to the final decree of dissolution, divorce, annulment, or legal separation arising out of the action out of which the question of the allocation of parental rights and responsibilities for the care of the children arose.

No provisional shared parenting decree shall be issued in relation to any shared parenting plan approved under division (D)(1)(a)(i), (ii), or (iii) of this section. A final shared parenting decree issued under this division has immediate effect as a final decree on the date of its issuance, subject to modification or termination as authorized by this section.

(2) If the court finds, with respect to any child under eighteen years of age, that it is in the best interest of the child for neither parent to be designated the residential parent and legal custodian of the child, it may commit the child to a relative of the child or certify a copy of its findings, together with as much of the record and the further information, in narrative form or otherwise, that it considers necessary or as the juvenile court requests, to the juvenile court for further proceedings, and, upon the certification, the juvenile court has exclusive jurisdiction.

(E)(1)(a) The court shall not modify a prior decree allocating parental rights and responsibilities for the care of children unless it finds, based on facts that have arisen since the prior decree or that were unknown to the court at the time of the prior decree, that a change has occurred in the circumstances of the child, the child's residential parent, or either of the parents subject to a shared parenting decree, and that the modification is necessary to serve the best interest of the child. In applying these standards, the court shall retain the residential parent designated by the prior decree or the prior shared parenting decree, unless a modification is in the best interest of the child and one of the following applies:

(i) The residential parent agrees to a change in the residential parent or both parents under a shared parenting decree agree to a change in the designation of residential parent.

(ii) The child, with the consent of the residential parent or of both parents under a shared parenting decree, has been integrated into the family of the person seeking to become the residential parent.

(iii) The harm likely to be caused by a change of environment is outweighed by the advantages of the change of environment to the child.

(b) One or both of the parents under a prior decree allocating parental rights and responsibilities for the care of children that is not a shared parenting decree may file a motion requesting that the prior decree be modified to give both parents shared rights and responsibilities for the care of the children. The motion shall include both a request for modification of the prior decree and a request for a shared parenting order that complies with division (G) of this section. Upon the filing of the motion, if the court determines that a modification of the prior decree is authorized under division (E)(1)(a) of this section, the court may modify the prior decree to grant a shared parenting order, provided that the court shall not modify the prior decree to grant a shared parenting order unless the court complies with divisions (A) and (D)(1) of this section and, in accordance with those divisions, approves the submitted shared parenting plan and determines that shared parenting would be in the best interest of the children.

(2) In addition to a modification authorized under division (E)(1) of this section:

(a) Both parents under a shared parenting decree jointly may modify the terms of the plan for shared parenting approved by the court and incorporated by it into the shared parenting decree. Modifications under this division may be made at any time. The modifications to the plan shall be filed jointly by both parents with the court, and the court shall include them in the plan, unless they are not in the best interest of the children. If the modifications are not in the best interests of the children, the court, in its discretion, may reject the modifications or make modifications to the proposed modifications or the plan that are in the best interest of the children. Modifications jointly submitted by both parents under a shared parenting decree shall be effective, either as originally filed or as modified by the court, upon their inclusion by the court in the plan. Modifications to the plan made by the court shall be effective upon their inclusion by the court in the plan.

(b) The court may modify the terms of the plan for shared parenting approved by the court and incorporated by it into the shared parenting decree upon its own motion at any time if the court determines that the modifications are in the best interest of the children or upon the request of one or both of the parents under the decree. Modifications under this division may be made at any time. The court shall not make any modification to the plan under this division, unless the modification is in the best interest of the children.

(c) The court may terminate a prior final shared parenting decree that includes a shared parenting plan approved under division (D)(1)(a)(i) of this section upon the request of one or both of the parents or whenever it determines that shared parenting is not in the best interest of the children. The court may terminate a prior final shared parenting decree that includes a shared parenting plan approved under division (D)(1)(a)(ii) or (iii) of this section if it determines, upon its own motion or upon the request of one or both parents, that shared parenting is not in the best interest of the children. If modification of the terms of the plan for shared parenting approved by the court and incorporated by it into the final shared parenting decree is attempted under division (E)(2)(a) of this section and the court rejects the modifications, it may terminate the final shared parenting decree if it determines that shared parenting is not in the best interest of the children.

(d) Upon the termination of a prior final shared parenting decree under division (E)(2)(c) of this section, the court shall proceed and issue a modified decree for the allocation of parental rights and responsibilities for the care of the children under the standards applicable under divisions (A), (B), and (C) of this section as if no decree for shared parenting had been granted and as if no request for shared parenting ever had been made.

(F)(1) In determining the best interest of a child pursuant to this section, whether on an original decree allocating parental rights and responsibilities for the care of children or a modification of a decree allocating those rights and responsibilities, the court shall consider all relevant factors, including, but not limited to:

(a) The wishes of the child's parents regarding the child's care;

(b) If the court has interviewed the child in chambers pursuant to division (B) of this section regarding the child's wishes and concerns as to the allocation of parental rights and responsibilities concerning the child, the wishes and concerns of the child, as expressed to the court;

(c) The child's interaction and interrelationship with the child's parents, siblings, and any other person who may significantly affect the child's best interest;

(d) The child's adjustment to the child's home, school, and community;

(e) The mental and physical health of all persons involved in the situation;

(f) The parent more likely to honor and facilitate court-approved parenting time rights or visitation and companionship rights;

(g) Whether either parent has failed to make all child support payments, including all arrearages, that are required of that parent pursuant to a child support order under which that parent is an obligor;

(h) Whether either parent or any member of the household of either parent previously has been convicted of or pleaded guilty to any criminal offense involving any act that resulted in a child being an abused child or a neglected child; whether either parent, in a case in which a child has been adjudicated an abused child or a neglected child, previously has been determined to be the perpetrator of the abusive or neglectful act that is the basis of an adjudication; whether either parent or any member of the household of either parent previously has been convicted of or pleaded guilty to a violation of section 2919.25 of the Revised Code or a sexually oriented offense involving a victim who at the time of the commission of the offense was a member of the family or household that is the subject of the current proceeding; whether either parent or any member of the household of either parent previously has been convicted of or pleaded guilty to any offense involving a victim who at the time of the commission of the offense was a member of the family or household that is the subject of the current proceeding and caused physical harm to the victim in the commission of the offense; and whether there is reason to believe that either parent has acted in a manner resulting in a child being an abused child or a neglected child;

(i) Whether the residential parent or one of the parents subject to a shared parenting decree has continuously and willfully denied the other parent's right to parenting time in accordance with an order of the court;

(j) Whether either parent has established a residence, or is planning to establish a residence, outside this state.

(2) In determining whether shared parenting is in the best interest of the children, the court shall consider all relevant factors, including, but not limited to, the factors enumerated in division (F)(1) of this section, the factors enumerated in section 3119.23 of the Revised Code, and all of the following factors:

(a) The ability of the parents to cooperate and make decisions jointly, with respect to the children;

(b) The ability of each parent to encourage the sharing of love, affection, and contact between the child and the other parent;

(c) Any history of, or potential for, child abuse, spouse abuse, other domestic violence, or parental kidnapping by either parent;

(d) The geographic proximity of the parents to each other, as the proximity relates to the practical considerations of shared parenting;

(e) The recommendation of the guardian ad litem of the child, if the child has a guardian ad litem.

(3) When allocating parental rights and responsibilities for the care of children, the court shall not give preference to a parent because of that parent's financial status or condition.

(G) Either parent or both parents of any children may file a pleading or motion with the court requesting the court to grant both parents shared parental rights and responsibilities for the care of the children in a proceeding held pursuant to division (A) of this section. If a pleading or motion requesting shared parenting is filed, the parent or parents filing the pleading or motion also shall file with the court a plan for the exercise of shared parenting by both parents. If each parent files a pleading or motion requesting shared parenting but only one parent files a plan or if only one parent files a pleading or motion requesting shared parenting and also files a plan, the other parent as ordered by the court shall file with the court a plan for the exercise of shared parenting by both parents. The plan for shared parenting shall be filed with the petition for dissolution of marriage, if the question of parental rights and responsibilities for the care of the children arises out of an action for dissolution of marriage, or, in other cases, at a time at least thirty days prior to the hearing on the issue of the parental rights and responsibilities for the care of the children. A plan for shared parenting shall include provisions covering all factors that are relevant to the care of the children, including, but not limited to, provisions covering factors such as physical living arrangements, child support obligations, provision for the children's medical and dental care, school placement, and the parent with which the children will be physically located during legal holidays, school holidays, and other days of special importance.

(H) If an appeal is taken from a decision of a court that grants or modifies a decree allocating parental rights and responsibilities for the care of children, the court of appeals shall give the case calendar priority and handle it expeditiously.

(I)(1) Upon receipt of an order for active military service in the uniformed services, a parent who is subject to an order allocating parental rights and responsibilities or in relation to whom an action to allocate parental rights and responsibilities is pending and who is ordered for active military service shall notify the other parent who is subject to the order or in relation to whom the case is pending of the order for active military service within three days of receiving the military service order.

(2) On receipt of the notice described in division (I)(1) of this section, either parent may apply to the court for a hearing to expedite an allocation or modification proceeding so that the court can issue an order before the parent's active military service begins. The application shall include the date on which the active military service begins.

The court shall schedule a hearing upon receipt of the application and hold the hearing not later than thirty days after receipt of the application, except that the court shall give the case calendar priority and handle the case expeditiously if exigent circumstances exist in the case.

The court shall not modify a prior decree allocating parental rights and responsibilities unless the court determines that there has been a change in circumstances of the child, the child's residential parent, or either of the parents subject to a shared parenting decree, and that modification is necessary to serve the best interest of the child. The court shall not find past, present, or possible future active military service in the uniformed services to constitute a change in circumstances justifying modification of a prior decree pursuant to division (E) of this section. The court shall make specific written findings of fact to support any modification under this division.

(3) Nothing in division (I) of this section shall prevent a court from issuing a temporary order allocating or modifying parental rights and responsibilities for the duration of the parent's active military service. A temporary order shall specify whether the parent's active military service is the basis of the order and shall provide for termination of the temporary order and resumption of the prior order within ten days after receipt of notice pursuant to division (I)(5) of this section, unless the other parent demonstrates that resumption of the prior order is not in the child's best interest.

(4) At the request of a parent who is ordered for active military service in the uniformed services and who is a subject of a proceeding pertaining to a temporary order for the allocation or modification of parental rights and responsibilities, the court shall permit the parent to participate in the proceeding and present evidence by electronic means, including communication by telephone, video, or internet to the extent permitted by the rules of the supreme court of Ohio.

(5) A parent who is ordered for active military service in the uniformed services and who is a subject of a proceeding pertaining to the allocation or modification of parental rights and responsibilities shall provide written notice to the court, child support enforcement agency, and the other parent of the date of termination of the parent's active military service not later than thirty days after the date on which the service ends.

(J) As used in this section:

(1) "Abused child" has the same meaning as in section 2151.031 of the Revised Code.

(2) "Active military service" means service by a member of the uniformed services in compliance with military orders to report for combat operations, contingency operations, peacekeeping operations, a remote tour of duty, or other active service for which the member is required to report unaccompanied by any family member, including any period of illness, recovery from injury, leave, or other lawful absence during that operation, duty, or service.

(3) "Neglected child" has the same meaning as in section 2151.03 of the Revised Code.

(4) "Sexually oriented offense" has the same meaning as in section 2950.01 of the Revised Code.

(5) "Uniformed services" means the United States armed forces, the army national guard, and the air national guard or any reserve component thereof, or the commissioned corps of the United States public health service.

(K) As used in the Revised Code, "shared parenting" means that the parents share, in the manner set forth in the plan for shared parenting that is approved by the court under division (D)(1) and described in division (L)(6) of this section, all or some of the aspects of physical and legal care of their children.

(L) For purposes of the Revised Code:

(1) A parent who is granted the care, custody, and control of a child under an order that was issued pursuant to this section prior to April 11, 1991, and that does not provide for shared parenting has "custody of the child" and "care, custody, and control of the child" under the order, and is the "residential parent," the "residential parent and legal custodian," or the "custodial parent" of the child under the order.

(2) A parent who primarily is allocated the parental rights and responsibilities for the care of a child and who is designated as the residential parent and legal custodian of the child under an order that is issued pursuant to this section on or after April 11, 1991, and that does not provide for shared parenting has "custody of the child" and "care, custody, and control of the child" under the order, and is the "residential parent," the "residential parent and legal custodian," or the "custodial parent" of the child under the order.

(3) A parent who is not granted custody of a child under an order that was issued pursuant to this section prior to April 11, 1991, and that does not provide for shared parenting is the "parent who is not the residential parent," the "parent who is not the residential parent and legal custodian," or the "noncustodial parent" of the child under the order.

(4) A parent who is not primarily allocated the parental rights and responsibilities for the care of a child and who is not designated as the residential parent and legal custodian of the child under an order that is issued pursuant to this section on or after April 11, 1991, and that does not provide for shared parenting is the "parent who is not the residential parent," the "parent who is not the residential parent and legal custodian," or the "noncustodial parent" of the child under the order.

(5) Unless the context clearly requires otherwise, if an order is issued by a court pursuant to this section and the order provides for shared parenting of a child, both parents have "custody of the child" or "care, custody, and control of the child" under the order, to the extent and in the manner specified in the order.

(6) Unless the context clearly requires otherwise and except as otherwise provided in the order, if an order is issued by a court pursuant to this section and the order provides for shared parenting of a child, each parent, regardless of where the child is physically located or with whom the child is residing at a particular point in time, as specified in the order, is the "residential parent," the "residential parent and legal custodian," or the "custodial parent" of the child.

(7) Unless the context clearly requires otherwise and except as otherwise provided in the order, a designation in the order of a parent as the residential parent for the purpose of determining the school the child attends, as the custodial parent for purposes of claiming the child as a dependent pursuant to section 152(e) of the "Internal Revenue Code of 1986," 100 Stat. 2085, 26 U.S.C.A. 1, as amended, or as the residential parent for purposes of receiving public assistance pursuant to division (A)(2) of this section, does not affect the designation pursuant to division (L)(6) of this section of each parent as the "residential parent," the "residential parent and legal custodian," or the "custodial parent" of the child.

(M) The court shall require each parent of a child to file an affidavit attesting as to whether the parent, and the members of the parent's household, have been convicted of or pleaded guilty to any of the offenses identified in divisions (C) and (F)(1)(h) of this section.

(2011 H 121, eff. 6-9-11; 2007 H 119, eff. 6–30–07; 2006 S 260, eff. 1–2–07; 2004 S 185, eff. 4–11–05; 2000 S 180, eff. 3–22–01; 1994 H 415, eff. 11–9–94; 1993 S 115, eff. 10–12–93; 1990 S 3, H 514, H 591; 1983 H 93; 1981 S 39, H 71; 1977 S 135; 1975 H 370, H 1; 1974 H 740, H 233; 131 v H 745; 1953 H 1; GC 8005–4; Source—GC 8033)

Historical and Statutory Notes

Pre–1953 H 1 Amendments: 124 v S 65

Amendment Note: 2011 H 121 rewrote divisions (I), (J)(2), and (J)(5), which prior thereto read:

"(I) Upon receipt of an order to active military service in the uniformed services, a parent who is subject to an order allocating parental rights and responsibilities or in relation to whom an action to allocate parental rights and responsibilities is pending and who is ordered to active military service shall notify the other parent who is subject to the order or in relation to whom the case is pending of the order to active military service within three days of receiving the military service order. Either parent may apply to the court for a hearing to expedite an allocation or modification proceeding. The application shall include the date on which the active military service begins.

"The court shall schedule a hearing upon receipt of the application and hold the hearing not later than thirty days after receipt of the application, except that the court shall give the case calendar priority and handle the case expeditiously if exigent circumstances exist in the case.

"The court shall not modify a prior decree allocating parental rights and responsibilities unless the court determines that there has been a change in circumstances of the child, the child's residential parent, or either of the parents subject to a shared parenting decree, and that modification is necessary to serve the best interest of the child. The court may consider active military service in the uniformed services in determining whether a change in circumstances exists under this section and shall make specific written findings of fact to support any modification under this division.

"Upon application by either parent, the court may modify a prior decree allocating parental rights and responsibilities after the parent's active military service has been terminated, hearing testimony and making specific written findings of fact to support the modification.

"Nothing in this division shall prevent a court from issuing a temporary order allocating or modifying parental rights and responsibilities for the duration of the parent's active military service.

"(2) 'Active military service' means the performance of active military duty by a member of the uniformed services for a period of more than thirty days.

"(5) 'Uniformed services' means the United States armed forces, army national guard and air national guard when engaged in active duty for training, or the commissioned corps of the United States public health service."

Amendment Note: 2007 H 119 added new division (I); redesignated former divisions (I) through (L) as new divisions (J) through (L) and division (M), respectively; rewrote new division (J); and substituted "(L)(6)" for "(K)(6)" in new divisions (K) and (L)(7). Prior to amendment and redesignation, former division (I) read:

"(I) As used in this section:

"(1) 'Abused child' has the same meaning as in section 2151.031 of the Revised Code, and 'neglected child' has the same meaning as in section 2151.03 of the Revised Code.

"(2) 'Sexually oriented offense' has the same meaning as in section 2950.01 of the Revised Code."

Amendment Note: 2006 S 260 rewrote the second paragraph of division (C); rewrote division (F)(1)(h); rewrote division (I); added new division

(L). Prior to amendment, the second paragraph of division (C) read:

"If the court determines that either parent previously has been convicted of or pleaded guilty to any criminal offense involving any act that resulted in a child being a neglected child, that either parent previously has been determined to be the perpetrator of the neglectful act that is the basis of an adjudication that a child is a neglected child, or that there is reason to believe that either parent has acted in a manner resulting in a child being a neglected child, the court shall consider that fact against naming that parent the residential parent and against granting a shared parenting decree. When the court allocates parental rights and responsibilities for the care of children or determines whether to grant shared parenting in any proceeding, it shall consider whether either parent has been convicted of or pleaded guilty to a violation of section 2919.25 of the Revised Code involving a victim who at the time of the commission of the offense was a member of the family or household that is the subject of the proceeding, has been convicted of or pleaded guilty to any other offense involving a victim who at the time of the commission of the offense was a member of the family or household that is the subject of the proceeding and caused physical harm to the victim in the commission of the offense, or has been determined to be the perpetrator of the abusive act that is the basis of an adjudication that a child is an abused child. If the court determines that either parent has been convicted of or pleaded guilty to a violation of section 2919.25 of the Revised Code involving a victim who at the time of the commission of the offense was a member of the family or household that is the subject of the proceeding, has been convicted of or pleaded guilty to any other offense involving a victim who at the time of the commission of the offense was a member of the family or household that is the subject of the proceeding and caused physical harm to the victim in the commission of the offense, or has been determined to be the perpetrator of the abusive act that is the basis of an adjudication that a child is an abused child, it may designate that parent as the residential parent and may issue a shared parenting decree or order only if it determines that it is in the best interest of the child to name that parent the residential parent or to issue a shared parenting decree or order and it makes specific written findings of fact to support its determination."

Prior to amendment, division (F)(1)(h) read:

"(h) Whether either parent previously has been convicted of or pleaded guilty to any criminal offense involving any act that resulted in a child being an abused child or a neglected child; whether either parent, in a case in which a child has been adjudicated an abused child or a neglected child, previously has been determined to be the perpetrator of the abusive or neglectful act that is the basis of an adjudication; whether either parent previously has been convicted of or pleaded guilty to a violation of section 2919.25 of the Revised Code involving a victim who at the time of the commission of the offense was a member of the family or household that is the subject of the current proceeding; whether either parent previously has been convicted of or pleaded guilty to any offense involving a victim who at the time of the commission of the offense was a member of the family or household that is the subject of the current proceeding and caused physical harm to the victim in the commission of the offense; and whether there is reason to believe that either parent has acted in a manner resulting in a child being an abused child or a neglected child;"

Prior to amendment, division (I) read:

"(I) As used in this section, 'abused child' has the same meaning as in section 2151.031 of the Revised Code, and 'neglected child' has the same meaning as in section 2151.03 of the Revised Code."

Amendment Note: 2004 S 185 substituted "3127.01 to 3127.53" for "3109.21 to 3109.36" in division (A).

Amendment Note: 2000 S 180 substituted "Chapters 3119., 3121., 3123., and 3125.," for "section 3113.215" in division (A)(2); inserted "court-approved parenting time rights or" and deleted "approved by the court" after "companionship rights" in division (F)(1)(f); substituted "parent's" for "parent his or her" and "parenting time" for "visitation" in division (F)(1)(i); deleted "division (B)(3) of" after "enumerated" and substituted '3119.23" for "3113.215" in division (F)(2); and made changes to reflect gender neutral language.

Amendment Note: 1994 H 415 rewrote division (E)(2); substituted "the parent with which the children will be physically located during legal holidays, school holidays, and other days of special importance" for "visitation" in division (G); inserted "and described in division (K)(6)" in division (J); substituted "each" for "the" and inserted ", regardless of where the child is physically located or" in division (K)(6); and rewrote division (K)(7). Prior to amendment, divisions (E)(2) and (K)(7) read:

"(2) In addition to a modification authorized under division (E)(1) of this section:

"(a) Both parents under a shared parenting decree jointly may modify the terms of the plan for shared parenting approved by the court and incorporated by it into the shared parenting decree. Modifications under this division may be made in relation to a final decree at any time and may be made in relation to a provisional decree issued prior to April 11, 1991, at any time prior to sixty days after the date of issuance of the provisional decree. The modifications to the plan shall be filed jointly by both parents with the court, and the court shall include them in the plan, unless they are not in the best interest of the children, in which case the court may reject the modifications. Modifications jointly submitted by both parents under a shared parenting decree shall be effective upon their inclusion by the court in the plan. A modification to a provisional plan issued prior to April 11, 1991, that is made under this division does not affect or extend the ninety-day period during which

the provisional plan may be terminated upon motion of either parent or the court itself.

"(b) The court may modify the terms of the plan for shared parenting approved by the court and incorporated by it into the shared parenting decree upon the request of one or both of the parents under the decree. Modifications under this division may be made in relation to a final decree at any time and may be made in relation to a provisional decree issued prior to April 11, 1991, at any time prior to sixty days after the date of issuance of the provisional decree. The court shall not make any modification to the plan under this division, unless the modification is in the best interest of the children and, if the plan was approved under division (D)(1)(a)(i) of this section, unless both parents agree to the modification. A modification to a provisional plan issued prior to April 11, 1991, that is made under this division does not affect or extend the ninety-day period during which the provisional plan may be terminated upon motion of either parent or the court itself, as described in divisions (E)(2)(c), (d), and (e) of this section.

"(c) The court shall terminate a provisional shared parenting decree issued prior to April 11, 1991, if either parent or the court itself makes a motion to terminate the provisional decree at any time prior to the expiration of ninety days after the date of its issuance. The court itself may make a motion to terminate a provisional decree only if it has reason to believe that the plan incorporated into the provisional decree is not in the best interest of the children and that it cannot be modified so as to be in the best interest of the children or if it has reason to believe that shared parenting itself is not in the best interest of the children. If the court has reason to believe that the plan incorporated into the provisional decree is not in the best interest of the children but that it can be modified so as to be in the best interest of the children, the plan may be modified in accordance with division (E)(2)(a) or (b) of this section regardless of whether the sixty-day period that normally applies in relation to modification of provisional decrees under those divisions has expired. If a provisional decree is terminated under this division, the court shall proceed in accordance with division (E)(2)(e) of this section. If neither parent nor the court itself makes a motion to terminate a provisional decree prior to the expiration of the ninety-day period, the provisional decree immediately and without need for further action shall become final on the ninetieth day after the date of its issuance, subject to modification or termination authorized by this section. Division (E)(2)(c) of this section does not apply in relation to a final shared parenting decree.

"(d) The court may terminate a prior final shared parenting decree that includes a shared parenting plan approved under division (D)(1)(a)(i) of this section upon the request of one or both of the parents or whenever it determines that shared parenting is not in the best interest of the children. The court may terminate a prior final shared parenting decree that includes a shared parenting plan approved under division (D)(1)(a)(ii) or (iii) of this section if it determines, upon its own motion or upon the request of one or both parents, that shared parenting is not in the best interest of the children. If modification of the terms of the plan for shared parenting approved by the court and incorporated by it into the final shared parenting decree is attempted under division (E)(2)(a) of this section and the court rejects the modifications, it may terminate the final shared parenting decree if it determines that shared parenting is not in the best interest of the children.

"(e) Upon the termination of a provisional shared parenting decree issued prior to April 11, 1991, or a prior final shared parenting decree under division (E)(2)(c) or (d) of this section, the court shall proceed and issue a modified decree for the allocation of parental rights and responsibilities for the care of the children under the standards applicable under divisions (A), (B), and (C) of this section as if no decree for shared parenting had been granted and as if no request for shared parenting ever had been made."

"(7) Unless the context clearly requires otherwise and except as otherwise provided in the order, if an order is issued by a court pursuant to this section and the order provides for shared parenting of a child, the parent with whom the child is not to reside at a particular point in time, as specified in the order, is the 'parent who is not the residential parent,' the 'parent who is not the residential parent and legal custodian,' or the 'noncustodial parent' of the child at that point in time."

Amendment Note: 1993 S 115 substituted "April 11, 1991" for "the effective date of this amendment" in division (E); changed a reference to section 3109.05(A) to a reference to section 3113.215(B)(3) in the first paragraph of division (F)(2); and substituted "April 11, 1991" for "the effective date of this amendment" in division (K).

Cross References

Boards of education, residency for attendance purposes, acceptance of certain tuition requirements, enforcement, see 3313.64

Criminal interference with custody, see 2919.23

Dismissal of petition or approval of agreement, see 3105.65

Divorce, annulment, and legal separation actions, custody and support of children, see 3105.21, Civ R 75

Juvenile courts, exercise of jurisdiction in custody matters, see 2151.23

Report of investigations conducted by court made available to all parties, see 2317.39

Separation agreements, petition for dissolution, shared parenting plan, see 3105.63

Taking of child into custody by juvenile court, Juv R 6

Tuition exemption, qualified former spouse of fire fighter or law enforcement officer killed in line of duty, see 3333.26

Library References

Child Custody ⬤1 to 662.
Westlaw Topic No. 76D.
C.J.S. Adoption of Persons §§ 140 to 141, 143.

C.J.S. Divorce §§ 976 to 978, 980 to 986, 988 to 1041, 1050 to 1076.
C.J.S. Parent and Child §§ 55 to 155, 157, 203.

Research References

ALR Library

21 ALR 6th 577, Effect of Parent's Military Service Upon Child Custody.

70 ALR 5th 377, Custodial Parent's Relocation as Grounds for Change of Custody.

80 ALR 5th 1, Child Custody and Visitation Rights Arising from Same-Sex Relationship.

124 ALR 5th 203, Religion as Factor in Child Custody Cases.

99 ALR 5th 475, Restrictions on Parent's Child Visitation Rights Based on Parent's Sexual Conduct.

71 ALR 5th 99, Grandparents' Visitation Rights Where Child's Parents Are Living.

15 ALR 5th 692, Continuity of Residence as Factor in Contest Between Parent and Nonparent for Custody of Child Who Has Been Residing With Nonparent--Modern Status.

Encyclopedias

69 Am. Jur. Proof of Facts 3d 281, Grandparent Visitation and Custody Awards.

114 Am. Jur. Proof of Facts 3d 275, Obtaining Child Custody from Citizen Parent and Parent Who Immigrated by Marriage to U.S.

22 Am. Jur. Trials 347, Child Custody Litigation.

OH Jur. 3d Constitutional Law § 524, Evidence, Argument, and Witnesses.

OH Jur. 3d Evidence & Witnesses § 362, Composite Reports of Experts.

OH Jur. 3d Family Law § 226, Who is "Parent" Under Statutes.

OH Jur. 3d Family Law § 359, Decree of Dissolution.

OH Jur. 3d Family Law § 530, Effect of Failure of Proof on Jurisdiction.

OH Jur. 3d Family Law § 534, Jurisdiction of Juvenile Court--Certification to Juvenile Court.

OH Jur. 3d Family Law § 581, Investigation Where Minor Children Involved.

OH Jur. 3d Family Law § 582, Report of Investigation; Cross-Examination.

OH Jur. 3d Family Law § 583, Expenses of Investigation as Costs.

OH Jur. 3d Family Law § 678, Judgment Order for Disposition, Care, and Maintenance of Children.

OH Jur. 3d Family Law § 704, Motions for Relief--Timing of Motion.

OH Jur. 3d Family Law § 723, Effect of Death of Person Awarded Custody.

OH Jur. 3d Family Law § 727, Child Custody.

OH Jur. 3d Family Law § 742, Parties.

OH Jur. 3d Family Law § 745, Discovery and Hearing.

OH Jur. 3d Family Law § 839, Procedure for Appointment of Representative.

OH Jur. 3d Family Law § 1034, Equal Rights of Parents to Their Children.

OH Jur. 3d Family Law § 1035, Relinquishment of Custody and Control to Other Parent.

OH Jur. 3d Family Law § 1038, Denial of Custody Where One Parent is Convicted of Killing the Other.

OH Jur. 3d Family Law § 1041, Relinquishment of Child to Grandparent Through Power of Attorney.

OH Jur. 3d Family Law § 1056, Parent's Equality in Allocation.

OH Jur. 3d Family Law § 1057, Allocation Primarily to One Parent.

OH Jur. 3d Family Law § 1058, Allocation to Both Parents.

OH Jur. 3d Family Law § 1060, Effect of Parent Neglecting or Abusing Child.

OH Jur. 3d Family Law § 1061, Court-Ordered Investigation of Parents.

OH Jur. 3d Family Law § 1063, Determination of Preference.

OH Jur. 3d Family Law § 1064, Determination of Preference--In-Chambers Interview.

OH Jur. 3d Family Law § 1066, Factors for Determining the Child's Best Interest, Generally.

OH Jur. 3d Family Law § 1068, Parent's Immoral Conduct.

OH Jur. 3d Family Law § 1070, Parent's Religious Practices.

OH Jur. 3d Family Law § 1078, Where Parents Make Joint Request.

OH Jur. 3d Family Law § 1079, Where Parents Submit Separate Plans.

OH Jur. 3d Family Law § 1080, Where Only One Parent Files Shared Parenting Plan.

OH Jur. 3d Family Law § 1081, Incorporation of Shared Parenting Plan Into Decree.

OH Jur. 3d Family Law § 1082, Factors for Determining Whether Shared Parenting is in the Children's Best Interest.

OH Jur. 3d Family Law § 1083, Request for Shared Parenting Plan.

OH Jur. 3d Family Law § 1088, Motion to Modify Shared Decree.

OH Jur. 3d Family Law § 1089, Motion to Modify Decree to Become Shared Decree.

OH Jur. 3d Family Law § 1091, Preference for Residential Parent.

OH Jur. 3d Family Law § 1092, Change of Circumstances.

OH Jur. 3d Family Law § 1098, Termination of Prior Final Shared Parenting Decree.

OH Jur. 3d Family Law § 1099, Effect of Termination of Provisional or Prior Final Decree.

OH Jur. 3d Family Law § 1148, Setting Parenting-Time Schedule.

OH Jur. 3d Family Law § 1176, Mediation Report and Costs.

OH Jur. 3d Family Law § 1248, Generally; Contempt.

OH Jur. 3d Family Law § 1332, Generally; Jurisdiction.

OH Jur. 3d Family Law § 1536, on Certification from Another Court.

OH Jur. 3d Family Law § 1541, Child Custody.

OH Jur. 3d Family Law § 1549, on Certification from Common Pleas.

OH Jur. 3d Family Law § 1761, Generally; Abuse of Discretion Standard.

OH Jur. 3d Family Law § 1803, Discretion of Trial Court.

Forms

Ohio Forms Legal and Business § 27:64, Custody of Children.

Ohio Forms Legal and Business § 27:65, Shared Parenting.

Ohio Jurisprudence Pleading and Practice Forms § 101:9, Investigation.

Ohio Jurisprudence Pleading and Practice Forms § 101:19, Continuing Jurisdiction.

Ohio Jurisprudence Pleading and Practice Forms § 101:29, Petition and Separation Agreement

Ohio Jurisprudence Pleading and Practice Forms § 101:37, Allocation of Parental Rights and Responsibilities.

Ohio Jurisprudence Pleading and Practice Forms § 101:42, Best Interest of Child Standard.

Ohio Jurisprudence Pleading and Practice Forms § 101:43, Exercise of Jurisdiction.

Ohio Jurisprudence Pleading and Practice Forms § 101:49, Modification of Parental Rights Orders.

Ohio Jurisprudence Pleading and Practice Forms § 101:50, Termination of Shared Parenting Order.

Ohio Jurisprudence Pleading and Practice Forms § 101:125, Shared Parenting Plan.

Ohio Jurisprudence Pleading and Practice Forms § 101:129, Motion for Modification of Allocation of Parental Rights and Responsibilities--Integration Into Another Household.

Treatises and Practice Aids

Klein, Darling, & Terez, Baldwin's Ohio Practice Civil Practice § 1:100, Modern Courts Amendment of 1968 as Limiting Scope of Application of Civil Rules.

Klein, Darling, & Terez, Baldwin's Ohio Practice Civil Practice § 60:13, Procedural Alternatives to Civ. R. 60(B) Motion--In General.

Klein, Darling, & Terez, Baldwin's Ohio Practice Civil Practice § 60:34, Effect of Statutory Limitations on Modification of Judgments.

Klein, Darling, & Terez, Baldwin's Ohio Practice Civil Practice § 60:58, Civ. R. 60(B)(4)--No Longer Equitable that Judgment Should Have Prospective Application--Limitation to Events Subsequent to Judgment.

Sowald & Morganstern, Baldwin's Ohio Practice Domestic Relations Law § 8:6, Parental Rights and Child Support.

Sowald & Morganstern, Baldwin's Ohio Practice Domestic Relations Law § 10:3, Dissolution Versus Divorce.

Sowald & Morganstern, Baldwin's Ohio Practice Domestic Relations Law § 11:6, Preliminary Considerations--Jurisdiction--Parental Rights and Responsibilities.

Sowald & Morganstern, Baldwin's Ohio Practice Domestic Relations Law § 15:1, Allocating Parental Rights.

Sowald & Morganstern, Baldwin's Ohio Practice Domestic Relations Law § 15:3, Jurisdiction--In General.

Sowald & Morganstern, Baldwin's Ohio Practice Domestic Relations Law § 15:6, Best Interest Standard--In General.

Sowald & Morganstern, Baldwin's Ohio Practice Domestic Relations Law § 15:8, Best Interest Standard--Wishes and Concerns of Child.

Sowald & Morganstern, Baldwin's Ohio Practice Domestic Relations Law § 15:9, Best Interest Standard--Interactions and Interrelationships With Others.

Sowald & Morganstern, Baldwin's Ohio Practice Domestic Relations Law § 16:1, Jurisdiction.

Sowald & Morganstern, Baldwin's Ohio Practice Domestic Relations Law § 16:3, 1990 Senate Bill 3--In General.

Sowald & Morganstern, Baldwin's Ohio Practice Domestic Relations Law § 16:4, Election Abolished.

Sowald & Morganstern, Baldwin's Ohio Practice Domestic Relations Law § 16:5, Ascertaining the Wishes and Concerns of the Child.

Sowald & Morganstern, Baldwin's Ohio Practice Domestic Relations Law § 16:6, Written or Recorded Statements from Child.

Sowald & Morganstern, Baldwin's Ohio Practice Domestic Relations Law § 16:7, Investigations and Examinations.

Sowald & Morganstern, Baldwin's Ohio Practice Domestic Relations Law § 16:8, Previous Child Neglect or Child Abuse.

Sowald & Morganstern, Baldwin's Ohio Practice Domestic Relations Law § 17:2, UCCJA--Applicability.

Sowald & Morganstern, Baldwin's Ohio Practice Domestic Relations Law § 17:8, UCCJA--Jurisdiction--Continuing Jurisdiction And/Or Concurrent Jurisdiction.

Sowald & Morganstern, Baldwin's Ohio Practice Domestic Relations Law § 20:8, Continuing Jurisdiction--In General.

Sowald & Morganstern, Baldwin's Ohio Practice Domestic Relations Law § 21:3, Parenting Time--Jurisdiction--In General.

Sowald & Morganstern, Baldwin's Ohio Practice Domestic Relations Law § 21:6, Development of Statutory Requirements.

Sowald & Morganstern, Baldwin's Ohio Practice Domestic Relations Law § 24:3, Jurisdiction.

Sowald & Morganstern, Baldwin's Ohio Practice Domestic Relations Law § 3:35, Effect of Judgment--Allocation of Parental Rights and Responsibilities, Visitation, and Companionship Rights--As Between Parents.

Sowald & Morganstern, Baldwin's Ohio Practice Domestic Relations Law § 3:60, Complaint for Custody, Support, and Visitation--Form.

Sowald & Morganstern, Baldwin's Ohio Practice Domestic Relations Law § 31:7, Findings of Fact and Conclusions of Law--Request by a Party; Required by Law.

Sowald & Morganstern, Baldwin's Ohio Practice Domestic Relations Law § 37:2, Mental Health Experts in General--Mental Health Reports.

Sowald & Morganstern, Baldwin's Ohio Practice Domestic Relations Law § 6:12, Planning for Post-Decree Mediation.

Sowald & Morganstern, Baldwin's Ohio Practice Domestic Relations Law § 6:14, Arbitration.

Sowald & Morganstern, Baldwin's Ohio Practice Domestic Relations Law § 9:39, Effect of Signed Agreement--Modification.

Sowald & Morganstern, Baldwin's Ohio Practice Domestic Relations Law § 11:45, Judgment Entry--Divorce Before a Magistrate With Children--Form.

Sowald & Morganstern, Baldwin's Ohio Practice Domestic Relations Law § 15:11, Best Interest Standard--Adjustment to Environment.

Sowald & Morganstern, Baldwin's Ohio Practice Domestic Relations Law § 15:12, Best Interest Standard--Health of All Persons.

Sowald & Morganstern, Baldwin's Ohio Practice Domestic Relations Law § 15:13, Best Interest Standard--Facilitation of Visitation.

Sowald & Morganstern, Baldwin's Ohio Practice Domestic Relations Law § 15:14, Best Interest Standard--Payment of Child Support.

Sowald & Morganstern, Baldwin's Ohio Practice Domestic Relations Law § 15:15, Best Interest Standard--Domestic Violence, Abuse, or Neglect.

Sowald & Morganstern, Baldwin's Ohio Practice Domestic Relations Law § 15:16, Best Interest Standard--Denial of Visitation.

Sowald & Morganstern, Baldwin's Ohio Practice Domestic Relations Law § 15:17, Best Interest Standard--Residence Out of State.

Sowald & Morganstern, Baldwin's Ohio Practice Domestic Relations Law § 15:19, Procedure for Allocating Parental Rights--In General.

Sowald & Morganstern, Baldwin's Ohio Practice Domestic Relations Law § 15:20, Procedure for Allocating Parental Rights--Interviewing the Child.

Sowald & Morganstern, Baldwin's Ohio Practice Domestic Relations Law § 15:21, Procedure for Allocating Parental Rights--Interview Procedure.

Sowald & Morganstern, Baldwin's Ohio Practice Domestic Relations Law § 15:33, Procedure for Allocating Parental Rights--Abuse, Neglect, or Domestic Violence.

Sowald & Morganstern, Baldwin's Ohio Practice Domestic Relations Law § 15:34, Procedure for Allocating Parental Rights--Investigation and Report.

Sowald & Morganstern, Baldwin's Ohio Practice Domestic Relations Law § 15:35, Procedure for Allocating Parental Rights--Expert Witnesses.

Sowald & Morganstern, Baldwin's Ohio Practice Domestic Relations Law § 15:36, Sole Residential Parent.

Sowald & Morganstern, Baldwin's Ohio Practice Domestic Relations Law § 15:37, Shared Parenting--In General.

Sowald & Morganstern, Baldwin's Ohio Practice Domestic Relations Law § 15:39, Shared Parenting--Shared Parenting Plan.

Sowald & Morganstern, Baldwin's Ohio Practice Domestic Relations Law § 15:40, Shared Parenting--Joint Request and Plan--In General.

Sowald & Morganstern, Baldwin's Ohio Practice Domestic Relations Law § 15:42, Shared Parenting--Joint Request and Plan--Joint Plan for Specific Times--Form.

Sowald & Morganstern, Baldwin's Ohio Practice Domestic Relations Law § 15:44, Shared Parenting--Separate Requests Separate Proposed Plans.

Sowald & Morganstern, Baldwin's Ohio Practice Domestic Relations Law § 15:45, Shared Parenting--Separate Requests--One Proposed Plan.

Sowald & Morganstern, Baldwin's Ohio Practice Domestic Relations Law § 15:47, Shared Parenting--Best Interest in Shared Parenting.

Sowald & Morganstern, Baldwin's Ohio Practice Domestic Relations Law § 15:48, Shared Parenting--Shared Parenting Decree.

Sowald & Morganstern, Baldwin's Ohio Practice Domestic Relations Law § 15:51, Shared Parenting--Child Support in Shared Parenting.

Sowald & Morganstern, Baldwin's Ohio Practice Domestic Relations Law § 15:54, Award to Third Party--By the Court.

Sowald & Morganstern, Baldwin's Ohio Practice Domestic Relations Law § 15:55, Award to Third Party--By the Court--Jurisdiction.

Sowald & Morganstern, Baldwin's Ohio Practice Domestic Relations Law § 15:57, Modifying Allocation of Parental Rights--In General.

Sowald & Morganstern, Baldwin's Ohio Practice Domestic Relations Law § 15:60, Modifying Allocation of Parental Rights--De Facto Custody.

Sowald & Morganstern, Baldwin's Ohio Practice Domestic Relations Law § 15:63, Modifying Allocation of Parental Rights--Sanctions for Frivolous Motions.

Sowald & Morganstern, Baldwin's Ohio Practice Domestic Relations Law § 15:64, Modifying Allocation of Parental Rights--Shared Parenting.

Sowald & Morganstern, Baldwin's Ohio Practice Domestic Relations Law § 15:66, Guardian Ad Litem--Procedure.

Sowald & Morganstern, Baldwin's Ohio Practice Domestic Relations Law § 15:71, Guardian Ad Litem--Testimony by Guardian Ad Litem.

Sowald & Morganstern, Baldwin's Ohio Practice Domestic Relations Law § 15:75, Custody in Juvenile Court Proceedings.

Sowald & Morganstern, Baldwin's Ohio Practice Domestic Relations Law § 15:76, Custody in Juvenile Court Proceedings--Entry Certifying to Juvenile Court--Form.

Sowald & Morganstern, Baldwin's Ohio Practice Domestic Relations Law § 16:10, Change of Circumstances--In General.

Sowald & Morganstern, Baldwin's Ohio Practice Domestic Relations Law § 16:13, Change of Circumstances--Cohabitation or Remarriage of Residential Parent--Same Sex Relationships.

Sowald & Morganstern, Baldwin's Ohio Practice Domestic Relations Law § 16:16, Best Interest Standard.

Sowald & Morganstern, Baldwin's Ohio Practice Domestic Relations Law § 16:17, Modification of Prior Decrees to Shared Parenting.

Sowald & Morganstern, Baldwin's Ohio Practice Domestic Relations Law § 16:18, Modification of Shared Parenting Plan Submitted Jointly.

Sowald & Morganstern, Baldwin's Ohio Practice Domestic Relations Law § 16:19, Appellate Review.

Sowald & Morganstern, Baldwin's Ohio Practice Domestic Relations Law § 16.21, Motion to Modify Parental Rights and Responsibilities--Change of Circumstances--Form.

Sowald & Morganstern, Baldwin's Ohio Practice Domestic Relations Law § 18:19, Procedure--Effect of Support on Visitation.

Sowald & Morganstern, Baldwin's Ohio Practice Domestic Relations Law § 18:21, Modifying Visitation or Parenting Time Orders--Jurisdiction.

Sowald & Morganstern, Baldwin's Ohio Practice Domestic Relations Law § 18:22, Modifying Parenting Time--Basis for Modification.

Sowald & Morganstern, Baldwin's Ohio Practice Domestic Relations Law § 18:23, Modifying Parenting Time--Evidentiary Considerations.

Sowald & Morganstern, Baldwin's Ohio Practice Domestic Relations Law § 21:11, Enforcement of Parenting Time--Motion to Modify Parental Rights.

Sowald & Morganstern, Baldwin's Ohio Practice Domestic Relations Law § 21:14, Enforcement of Parenting Time--Interview of Child.

Sowald & Morganstern, Baldwin's Ohio Practice Domestic Relations Law § 21:18, Practical Methods--Mediation.

Sowald & Morganstern, Baldwin's Ohio Practice Domestic Relations Law § 21:23, Enforcement Problems--Drug Use or Alcohol Abuse.

Sowald & Morganstern, Baldwin's Ohio Practice Domestic Relations Law § 25:21, Motions Regarding Parties--Motion to Appoint Guardian Ad Litem.

Sowald & Morganstern, Baldwin's Ohio Practice Domestic Relations Law § 25:30, Motions Regarding Temporary Relief--Motion for Allocation of Parental Rights and Responsibilities Pendente Lite.

Sowald & Morganstern, Baldwin's Ohio Practice Domestic Relations Law § 25:32, Motions for Study and Guidance of Parties--Motion for Psychological Evaluation.

Sowald & Morganstern, Baldwin's Ohio Practice Domestic Relations Law § 25:33, Motions for Study and Guidance of Parties--Motion for Investigation.

Sowald & Morganstern, Baldwin's Ohio Practice Domestic Relations Law § 25:41, Motions Regarding Court Proceedings--Motion for Findings by Court.

Sowald & Morganstern, Baldwin's Ohio Practice Domestic Relations Law § 26:22, Physical and Mental Examinations.

Sowald & Morganstern, Baldwin's Ohio Practice Domestic Relations Law § 26:23, Motion for a Medical/Psychiatric Exam--Form.

Sowald & Morganstern, Baldwin's Ohio Practice Domestic Relations Law § 27:38, Jurisdiction Over Children.

Sowald & Morganstern, Baldwin's Ohio Practice Domestic Relations Law § 37:20, Privileged Communication--State Law Privileges--Guardian Ad Litem.

Sowald & Morganstern, Baldwin's Ohio Practice Domestic Relations Law § 37:22, Privileged Communication--Civil Rules.

Sowald & Morganstern, Baldwin's Ohio Practice Domestic Relations Law § 37:23, Privileged Communication--Allocation of Parental Rights Proceedings.

Sowald & Morganstern, Baldwin's Ohio Practice Domestic Relations Law § 37:32, Privileged Communication--Waiver--Custody and Visitation.

Snyder & Giannelli, Baldwin's Ohio Practice Evidence R 702, Testimony by Experts.

Carlin, Baldwin's Ohio Prac. Merrick-Rippner Probate Law § 67:2, Termination--Discretionary--Court; Removal.

Carlin, Baldwin's Ohio Prac. Merrick-Rippner Probate Law § 99:3, Jurisdiction.

Carlin, Baldwin's Ohio Prac. Merrick-Rippner Probate Law § 107:3, Divorce or Alimony Involving Care or Custody of Children.

Carlin, Baldwin's Ohio Prac. Merrick-Rippner Probate Law § 107:4, Custody and Support of Children: Certified from Common Pleas Court.

Carlin, Baldwin's Ohio Prac. Merrick-Rippner Probate Law § 61:11, Caretaker Authorization Affidavit--Grandparent and Grandchild.

Carlin, Baldwin's Ohio Prac. Merrick-Rippner Probate Law § 67:10, Termination of Guardianship--Minor.

Carlin, Baldwin's Ohio Prac. Merrick-Rippner Probate Law § 107:11, Certification from Common Pleas Court.

Carlin, Baldwin's Ohio Prac. Merrick-Rippner Probate Law § 107:13, Authority Following Certification.

Carlin, Baldwin's Ohio Prac. Merrick-Rippner Probate Law § 109:46, Adjudicatory Hearings--Child's Right to Guardian Ad Litem.

Carlin, Baldwin's Ohio Prac. Merrick-Rippner Probate Law § 109:79, Disposition of Abused, Neglected, or Dependent Child--Legal Custody.

Carlin, Baldwin's Ohio Prac. Merrick-Rippner Probate Law § 110:13, Jurisdiction Over Child Custody Matters--Determination of Custody.

Carlin, Baldwin's Ohio Prac. Merrick-Rippner Probate Law § 110:14, Modification of Decree Allocating Parental Rights and Responsibilities for Care of Children.

Carlin, Baldwin's Ohio Prac. Merrick-Rippner Probate Law § 110:15, Visitation Right of Noncustodial Parent and Others.

Carlin, Baldwin's Ohio Prac. Merrick-Rippner Probate Law § 109:115, Modification of Dispositional Orders in Abuse, Neglect, and Dependency Proceedings.

Carlin, Baldwin's Ohio Prac. Merrick-Rippner Probate Law § 109:120, Appeals--Juvenile Court Judgments--Appeals from Custody Determinations.

Carlin, Baldwin's Ohio Prac. Merrick-Rippner Probate Law § 109:135, Motion to Certify Case to Juvenile Court--Form.

Adrine & Ruden, Ohio Domestic Violence Law § 15:2, Custody and Visitation Issues; Background Information.

Adrine & Ruden, Ohio Domestic Violence Law § 15:4, General Statutory and Court Trends.

Adrine & Ruden, Ohio Domestic Violence Law § 15:5, Ohio's Legislative Response to Domestic Violence.

Adrine & Ruden, Ohio Domestic Violence Law § 15:6, Ohio's Judicial Response to Domestic Violence.

Adrine & Ruden, Ohio Domestic Violence Law § 15:7, Presenting Evidence of Domestic Violence in Custody and Visitation Proceedings; Practice Pointers.

Adrine & Ruden, Ohio Domestic Violence Law § 16:1, Introduction.

Adrine & Ruden, Ohio Domestic Violence Law § 7:13, Collateral Effects of a Guilty Plea or of Being Found Guilty--Custody and Visitation.

Adrine & Ruden, Ohio Domestic Violence Law § 12:16, Remedies--Protected Party Concerns.

Adrine & Ruden, Ohio Domestic Violence Law § 15:12, Consideration of Domestic Violence as a Best-Interest Factor--In Custody Decisions; Recent Case Law.

Adrine & Ruden, Ohio Domestic Violence Law § 15:13, Consideration of Domestic Violence as a Best-Interest Factor--Findings of Fact that Support a Court Decision.

Adrine & Ruden, Ohio Domestic Violence Law § 15:14, Shared Parenting Considerations.

Adrine & Ruden, Ohio Domestic Violence Law § 15:16, Presenting Evidence of Domestic Violence--Use of Experts; Generally.

Adrine & Ruden, Ohio Domestic Violence Law § 15:18, Presenting Evidence of Domestic Violence--Use of Mental Health Professionals and Other Experts.

Adrine & Ruden, Ohio Domestic Violence Law § 15:19, Presenting Evidence of Domestic Violence--Use of a Guardian Ad Litem.

Adrine & Ruden, Ohio Domestic Violence Law § 15:22, Presenting Evidence of Domestic Violence--Role of the Attorney--Specific Trial Concerns.

Adrine & Ruden, Ohio Domestic Violence Law § 15:23, Mediation in Domestic Violence Cases.

Adrine & Ruden, Ohio Domestic Violence Law § 15:24, Other Issues that Impact Custody and Visitation Awards.

Adrine & Ruden, Ohio Domestic Violence Law § 16:12, Evidentiary Considerations Involving Independent Documentation.

Giannelli & Yeomans, Ohio Juvenile Law § 2:2, Exclusive Original Jurisdiction.

Giannelli & Yeomans, Ohio Juvenile Law § 2:3, Concurrent Jurisdiction.

Giannelli & Yeomans, Ohio Juvenile Law § 13:2, Issuance to Proper Parties.

Giannelli & Yeomans, Ohio Juvenile Law § 36:2, Issuance to Proper Parties.

Giannelli & Yeomans, Ohio Juvenile Law § 45:4, Dispositional Alternatives.

Giannelli & Yeomans, Ohio Juvenile Law § 45:7, Legal Custody.

Giannelli & Yeomans, Ohio Juvenile Law § 54:4, Final Order Requirement.

Giannelli & Yeomans, Ohio Juvenile Law § 54:6, Stay of Proceedings.

Giannelli & Yeomans, Ohio Juvenile Law § 34:11, Certification or Transfer from Another Court.

Giannelli & Yeomans, Ohio Juvenile Law § 43:13, Reasonable Efforts Determination.

Law Review and Journal Commentaries

Allocation of Dependency Tax Exemptions to Noncustodial Parents: When and Why, Pamela J. MacAdams. 4 Domestic Rel J Ohio 65 (July/August 1992).

Arbitration as an Alternative to Divorce Litigation: Redefining the Judicial Role. Andre R. Imbrogno, 31 Cap U L Rev 413 (2003).

Artificial insemination: In the child's best interest? 5 Alb L J Sci & Tech 321 (1996).

The best interest test and child custody: Why transgender should not be a factor in custody determinations. Note, 16 Health Matrix: J Law–Medicine 209 (Winter 2006).

A Case Study in Divorce Law Reform and Its Aftermath, Robert E. McGraw, Gloria J. Sterin and Joseph M. Davis. 20 J Fam L 443 (1981–82).

Child Custody Determination—A Better Way!, Sheldon G. Kirshner. 17 J Fam L 275 (1978–79).

Child custody disputes between lesbians: Legal strategies and their limitations, Nicole Berner. 10 Berkeley Women's L J 31 (1995).

Child Custody Standards, Barbara Handschu and Mary Kay Kisthardt. 29 Nat'l L J 16 (10–27–2003).

The Child Dependency Exemption And Divorced Parents: What Is "Custody"?, David J. Benson. 18 Cap U L Rev 57 (Spring 1989).

Children And Cults: A Practical Guide, Susan Linda. 29 J Fam L 591 (May 1991).

Children At Risk In The Politics Of Child Custody Suits: Acknowledging Their Needs For Nurture, Arlene Browand Huber. 32 J Fam L 33 (Winter 1994).

Children—The Innocent Victims of Family Breakups: How the Family Law Attorney, the Courts, and Society Can Protect Our Children, Michael J. Albano. 26 U Tol L Rev 787 (Summer 1995).

The Child's Advocate—Changing Roles in Changing Times, Ilana Horowitz Ratner. 7 Domestic Rel J Ohio 1 (January/February 1995).

Confessions of a Judicial Activist, Hon. Ronald L. Solove. [Ed. note: Judge Solove discusses and advocates custody mediation.] 54 Ohio St L J 797 (1993).

Custodial Rights in Non–Traditional Families. Pamela J. MacAdams, 20 Domestic Rel. J. Ohio 53 (July/August 2008).

Custody Case Basics, Hon. Michael V. Brigner. 47 Dayton B Briefs 15 (December 1997).

Custody and the Cohabitating Parent, Note. 20 J Fam L 697 (1981–82).

Custody Disputes Following the Dissolution of Interracial Marriages: Best Interests of the Child or Judicial Racism?, Colleen McKinley. 19 J Fam L 97 (1980–81).

Custody in Ohio—A New Concept for an Age–Old Problem, V. Sinclair Lewis. 3 Domestic Rel J Ohio 57 (May/June 1991).

Custody of Children—Child's Right of Choice under Ohio G.C. Section 8033, Comment. 7 Ohio St L J 246 (March 1941).

Custody Rights Of Gay And Lesbian Parents, Comment. 36 Vill L Rev 1665 (1991).

Deceptions, delusions and spin doctors in family court litigation, Dennis W. Mattingly. (Ed. note: The author, a domestic relations magistrate, recounts war stories of lying litigants, and urges mediation of domestic disputes). 18 Ohio Law 12 (May/June 2004).

Dividing the Child: Shea v. Metcalf, 712 A.2d 887 (Vt. 1998), Note. 24 U Dayton L Rev 543 (Spring 1999).

Divorce And Amended Section 152(e) Of The Internal Revenue Code: Do State Courts Have

The Power To Allocate Dependency Exemptions?, Note. 29 J Fam L 901 (August 1991).

Divorce child custody mediation: In order to form a more perfect disunion? Ben Barlow, 52 Clev St L Rev 499 (2004–05)

Divorce Reform, Ohio Style, Alan E. Norris. 47 Ohio St B Ass'n Rep 1031 (9–16–74).

Family, Church And State: An Essay On Constitutionalism And Religious Authority, Carol Weisbrod. 26 J Fam L 741 (1987–88).

Gay Parents: A Legal Oxymoron In Ohio?, Comment. 18 Cap U L Rev 277 (Summer 1989).

Grandparent Visitation: Can the Parent Refuse?, Kathleen S. Bean. 24 J Fam L 393 (1985–86).

Granting Custody to Third Party. Pamela J. MacAdams, 14 Domestic Rel J Ohio 65 (July/August 2002).

Illinois Court Overturns Mandatory Parent Education Class, Paul J. Buser. 18 Lake Legal Views 8 (August 1995).

In all its Variations, the Father's Rights Movement is Saying One Thing... Make Room for Daddy, Stephanie B. Goldberg. 83 A B A J 48 (February 1997).

Informed Consent to the Medical Treatment of Minors: Law and Practice. Lawrence Schlam and Joseph P. Wood, M.D., 10 Health Matrix: J Law-Medicine 141 (Summer 2000).

In Whose Best Interests? Legal Standards on Relocation of the Custodial Parent, Karen Tapp. III Ky Children's Rts J 19 (Spring 1993).

Interference with Visitation as an Independent Tort, Note. 24 J Fam L 481 (1985–86).

Interminable Child Neglect/Custody Cases: Are There Better Alternatives?, Sheila Reynolds and Roy B. Lacoursiere. 21 J Fam L 239 (1982–83).

Irreconcilable Differences: When Children Sue Their Parents For "Divorce", Note. 32 J Fam L 67 (1993–94).

The Issue of Stability in the Modification of Custody Decisions: Factor or Determinant?, Constance W. Cole. 29 Vill L Rev 1095 (1983–84).

Joint Custody: A Jaundiced View, Gary N. Skoloff. 20 Trial 52 (March 1984).

Joint Custody: A View From the Bench, Hon. Jerry Hayes. 2 Domestic Rel J Ohio 71 (September/October 1990).

Joint Custody and the Right to Travel: Legal and Psychological Implications, Paula M. Raines. 24 J Fam L 625 (1985–86).

Joint Custody: Constitutional Imperatives, Holly L. Robinson. 54 U Cin L Rev 27 (1985).

Joint Custody: Recent Research and Overloaded Courtrooms Inspire New Solutions to Custody Disputes, Diane Trombetta. 19 J Fam L 213 (1980–81).

Judge's Column, Hon. Francine M. Bruening. (Ed. note: Judge Bruening goes through RC 3109.04 step-by-step in this guide for practitioners.) 17 Lake Legal Views 1 (June 1994).

Judicial Activism in Domestic Relations Cases, Hon. V. Michael Brigner. (Ed. note: Judge Brigner lists the powers of a judge hearing custody, support, and visitation matters.) 45 Dayton B Briefs 22 (January 1996).

Keeping Kids Out of Court. (Ed. note: Arbitration of custody disputes, but courts reserve the right to review awards.) 19 Nat'l L J B8 (May 5, 1997).

Legal Separation Proceedings, Dawn S. Garrett. 50 Dayton B Briefs 18 (February 2001).

Legal Standard to Be Applied in Custody Litigation Between Parent and Non-Parent, Pamela J. MacAdams. 15 Domestic Rel J Ohio 33 (May/June 2003).

Out of State Move as Change in Circumstances—Eaches Court Requires More, James R. Kirkland. 9 Domestic Rel J Ohio 79 (September/October 1997).

Parenting Order Must not be Based on Future Possibilities, Pamela J. MacAdams. 4 Domestic Rel J Ohio 28 (March/April 1992).

The Plight of the Interstate Child in American Courts, Leona Mary Hudak. 9 Akron L Rev 257 (Fall 1975).

The Power Of State Courts To Award The Federal Dependency Exemption Upon Divorce, David J. Benson. 16 U Dayton L Rev 29 (Fall 1990).

Practice Pointer—In Camera Interviews—Parents Have No Right to Access Transcript; Courts Not Required to Make Findings of Fact, Lynn B. Schwartz. 7 Domestic Rel J Ohio 84 (November/December 1995).

Primary Caretaker Doctrine, Stanley Morganstern. 1 Domestic Rel J Ohio 2 (September/October 1989).

The Proper Role of Psychology in Child Custody Disputes, Thomas R. Litwack, Gwendolyn L. Gerber and C. Abraham Fenster. 18 J Fam L 269 (1979–80).

Pro–Rating Child Support for Shared Parenting, James R. Kirkland. 6 Domestic Rel J Ohio 82 (November/December 1994).

Protecting The Interests Of Children In Divorce Mediation, Gary Paquin. 26 J Fam L 279 (1987–88).

Psychological Parents vs. Biological Parents: The Courts' Response to New Directions in Child Custody Dispute Resolution, Note. 17 J Fam L 545 (1978–79).

Reframing Child Custody Decisionmaking, Naomi R. Cahn. 58 Ohio St L J 1 (1997).

Relocation Battles, Barbara Handschu and Mary Kay Kisthardt. 29 Nat'l L J 11 (7–12–2004).

Relocation Issues—Part II—The Law in Selected States, Hon. Cheryl S. Karner. 5 Domestic Rel J Ohio 57 (July/August 1993).

Relocation of the Children After the Divorce, Hon. Cheryl S. Karner. 64 Law & Fact 6 (January–February 1990).

Remedies for Parental Kidnapping in Federal Court: A Comment Applying the Parental Kidnapping Prevention Act in Support of Judge Edwards, Joan M. Krauskopf. 45 Ohio St L J 429 (1984).

Representation for Children in Custody Decisions: All That Glitters Is Not Gault, Donald N. Bersoff. 15 J Fam L 27 (1976–77).

Rethinking Joint Custody, Elizabeth Scott and Andre Derdeyn. 45 Ohio St L J 455 (1984).

Shared Parenting—Modification Easier After 11–9–94, Richard L. Innis. 6 Domestic Rel J Ohio 81 (November/December 1994).

Should the Ill Effects of Environmental Tobacco Smoke Exposure Affect Child–Custody Decisions?, Note. 32 J Fam L 115 (1993–94).

Smoking And Parenting: Can They Be Adjudged Mutually Exclusive Activities?, Note. 42 Case W Res L Rev 1025 (Summer 1992).

State Intervention in the Family: Making a Federal Case Out of It, Martin Guggenheim. 45 Ohio St L J 399 (1984).

A Surrogacy Agreement that Could Have and Should Have Been Enforced: *R.R. v. M.H.*, 689 N.E.2d 790 (Mass. 1998), Note. 24 U Dayton L Rev 513 (Spring 1999).

Tax Tips—Award of Dependency Exemptions, Stanley Morganstern. 3 Domestic Rel J Ohio 89 (July/August 1991).

Termination of Parental Rights in Adoption Cases: Focusing on the Child, Comment. 14 J Fam L 547 (1975–76).

Trial Court May Not Adopt Its Own Shared Parenting Plan, Pamela J. MacAdams. 5 Domestic Rel J Ohio 76 (September/October 1993).

Troxel v. Granville: Another Elusive Evaluation of Parental Rights?, Tracy M. Frey. 32 U Tol L Rev 387 (Spring 2001).

Unhappy Families: Special Considerations In Custody Cases Involving Handicapped Children, Note. 24 J Fam L 59 (1985–86).

Visitation Interference: Legal Solutions for Fathers, Hon. V. Michael Brigner. 49 Dayton B Briefs 19 (November 1999).

The Voice of a Child: Independent Legal Representation of Children in Private Custody Disputes When Sexual Abuse Is Alleged, Kerin S. Bischoff. 138 U Pa L Rev 1383 (May 1990).

Within The Best Interests Of The Child: The Factor Of Parental Status In Custody Disputes Arising From Surrogacy Contracts, Irma S. Russell. 27 J Fam L 585 (1988–89).

Would Abolishing the Natural Parent Preference in Custody Disputes Be in Everyone's Best Interest?, Note. 29 J Fam L 539 (1990–91).

Yes Parents, There is a Privelege Protecting Your Counseling Record, Mag. Elaine M. Stoermer. 50 Dayton B Briefs 12 (December 2000).

"You Get the House. I Get the Car. You Get the Kids. I Get Their Souls." The Impact of Spiritual Custody Awards on the Free Exercise Rights of Custodial Parents, Comment. 138 U Pa L Rev 583 (December 1989).

Notes of Decisions

---

1. In general

Trial court lacked subject matter jurisdiction to modify child custody as it related to parties' youngest child who had turned 18 and was emancipated. Schumann v. Schumann (Ohio App. 8 Dist., 11-10-2010) 190 Ohio App.3d 824, 944 N.E.2d 705, 2010-Ohio-5472. Child Custody ⇐ 601

Trial court's post-dissolution journal entry establishing child visitation schedule for former husband and former wife, in recognition of child's move out of former wife's home and into former husband's home, was plainly a temporary document put into place pending further orders of the court, and thus could not be construed as an intentional relinquishment, waiver, or abandonment of former wife's existing parental rights; journal entry did not set forth determination from trial court regarding "best interests" of child, it did not allocate parental rights and responsibilities for care of child, and did not designate parent as residential parent. Schumann v. Schumann (Ohio App. 8 Dist., 11-10-2010) 190 Ohio App.3d 824, 944 N.E.2d 705, 2010-Ohio-5472. Child Custody ⇐ 325

Competent evidence existed to support trial court's finding that grant of legal custody of children born out-of-wedlock to father was in children's best interests, in father's action against mother for determination of custody of children, notwithstanding that mother had been primary caregiver, where other evidence indicated that mother had told father she had miscarriage during her pregnancy with first child, that father had little contact with first child for first two years due to behavior of mother, and that mother's allegations of child abuse on part of father were unfounded. Cireddu v. Clough (Ohio App. 11 Dist., Lake, 11-05-2010) No. 2010-L-008, 2010-Ohio-5401, 2010 WL 4398750, Unreported, appeal not allowed 128 Ohio St.3d 1413, 942 N.E.2d 385, 2011-Ohio-828, reconsideration denied 128 Ohio St.3d 1485, 946 N.E.2d 242, 2011-Ohio-2055. Children Out–of–wedlock ⇐ 20.3

Trial court did not abuse its discretion in finding mother to be in contempt of court for not complying with court order providing father with parenting time and requiring mother to provide all necessary transportation for such parenting time to occur, in action by father against mother with regard to custody of children born out-of-wedlock, notwithstanding mother's assertions that she withheld visitation because she believed that child abuse had occurred, where mother admitted to non-compliance with court order. Cireddu v. Clough (Ohio App. 11 Dist., Lake, 11-05-2010) No. 2010-L-008, 2010-Ohio-5401, 2010 WL 4398750, Unreported, appeal not allowed 128 Ohio St.3d 1413, 942 N.E.2d 385, 2011-Ohio-828, reconsideration denied 128 Ohio St.3d 1485, 946 N.E.2d 242, 2011-Ohio-2055. Children Out–of–wedlock ⇐ 20

Former client's children did not have a contractual relationship with former client's attorneys and thus lacked cause of action for legal malpractice against attorneys, who represented former client in connection with motion by her former husband to enforce shared parenting and separation agreement. Haas v. Bradley (Ohio App. 9 Dist., Lorain, 08-17-2005) No. 04CA008541, 2005-Ohio-4256, 2005 WL 1963013, Unreported. Attorney And Client ⇐ 26

Statute providing that, in any divorce, legal separation, or annulment proceeding and in any proceeding pertaining to the allocation of parental rights and responsibilities for the care of a child, court shall allocate the parental rights and responsibilities for the care of the minor children of the marriage was applicable to custody dispute between maternal grandmother and paternal grandparents, given that the parents had previously granted legal custody and allocated parental rights and responsibilities of one of their two children to maternal grandmother and of their other child to paternal grandparents in prior consent judgment entries. Thomas v. Moothart (Ohio App. 3 Dist., Hancock, 07-15-2003) No. 5-02-56, 2003-Ohio-3724, 2003 WL 21648102, Unreported, appeal not allowed 100 Ohio St.3d 1486, 798 N.E.2d 1094, 2003-Ohio-5992. Child Custody ⇐ 275

Action between mother and paternal grandparents of minor children concerning legal custody of children fell within coverage of statute involving custody disputes between parent and non-parent, not statute governing custody determinations involving divorcing parties, and thus trial court was required to examine parental unsuitability before custody could be awarded to nonparent. Ives v. Ives (Ohio App. 9 Dist., Lorain, 07-02-2003) No. 02CA008176, 2003-Ohio-3505, 2003 WL 21508795, Unreported. Child Custody ⟳ 279

In proceedings to terminate father's parental rights, father did not have standing to appeal order denying children's grandmother's motion to intervene. In re Cunningham Children (Ohio App. 5 Dist., Stark, 05-27-2003) No. 2003CA00054, 2003-Ohio-2805, 2003 WL 21260017, Unreported. Infants ⟳ 242

Stepfather was joined as party in parental rights proceedings, which gave him right to appeal trial court's order that he undergo psychological evaluation, and thus, stepfather failed to establish essential element for issuance of writ of prohibition against trial court. Lutton v. O'Malley (Ohio App. 8 Dist., Cuyahoga, 03-13-2003) No. 82001, 2003-Ohio-1176, 2003 WL 1090719, Unreported. Prohibition ⟳ 3(3)

Ohio was child's home state for purposes of custody proceedings, and thus Ohio trial court had proper jurisdiction over child, although father, who was an enrolled member of Indian tribe, had previously filed complaint in tribal court in North Carolina seeking custody, as at the time mother filed her complaint in Ohio trial court, child, who was born in Ohio, had resided there with mother since her birth and was less than six months old. In re Absher Children (Ohio App. 12 Dist., 02-05-2001) 141 Ohio App.3d 118, 750 N.E.2d 188, 2001-Ohio-4197, dismissed, appeal not allowed 91 Ohio St.3d 1489, 745 N.E.2d 437. Child Custody ⟳ 736; Indians ⟳ 136

Former husband's payment of child support arrears on the day before the contempt hearing did not divest the court of its contempt power, and contempt sanctions of imprisonment and fine thus were permissible to uphold the dignity of the court. In re Contemnor Caron (Ohio Com.Pl., 04-27-2000) 110 Ohio Misc.2d 58, 744 N.E.2d 787. Child Support ⟳ 444

Former husband purged himself of civil contempt by making his lump-sum delinquent payment of child support on the day before the contempt hearing. In re Contemnor Caron (Ohio Com.Pl., 04-27-2000) 110 Ohio Misc.2d 58, 744 N.E.2d 787. Child Support ⟳ 445

Former husband's failure to pay child support for several years was criminal contempt of court immediately before his forced payment of child support on the day before the contempt hearing. In re Contemnor Caron (Ohio Com.Pl., 04-27-2000) 110 Ohio Misc.2d 58, 744 N.E.2d 787. Child Support ⟳ 444

A sentence of thirty days in jail was warranted for criminal contempt by a former husband for failing to pay child support for several years. In re Contemnor Caron (Ohio Com.Pl., 04-27-2000) 110 Ohio Misc.2d 58, 744 N.E.2d 787. Child Support ⟳ 444

Former spouses' court-approved shared parenting agreement was "initial decree," within meaning of statutes setting forth standards for determining initial custody orders and later modifications; consequently, showing of changed circumstances was necessary to justify later change in custody. Miller v. Miller (Ohio App. 3 Dist., 11-20-1996) 115 Ohio App.3d 336, 685 N.E.2d 319. Child Custody ⟳ 555

Where Kentucky court initially awards custody of child to mother, and where mother and child subsequently move to Ohio and reside in Ohio for nearly two years, Ohio becomes "home state" within meaning of Uniform Child Custody Jurisdiction Act. In re Reynolds (Hamilton 1982) 2 Ohio App.3d 309, 441 N.E.2d 1141, 2 O.B.R. 341. Child Custody ⟳ 736

There is no provision in RC 3109.04 for a "physical custodian" and a trial court errs as a matter of law by awarding "physical custody" of a child to a parent without statutory authority. In re Ghadr, Nos. 95CA22 and 96CA6, 1997 WL 133299 (4th Dist Ct App, Hocking, 3–19–97).

Any person has standing to bring an action for child custody under RC 2151.23; such a person need not be a parent, need not have established paternity and need not have legitimized the child. Harris v Hopper, No. L–81–187 (6th Dist Ct App, Lucas, 1–15–82).

2. Hearing for deaf party

Jury question was presented as to state court's violation of ADA retaliation provision where hearing-impaired parent involved in child custody proceeding had filed administrative complaint alleging court's inadequate accommodation of his disability, and court subsequently presented parent with choice between going forward with hearing when scheduled and waiving any claim against state, or preserving such claim at risk of long delay in proceedings. Popovich v. Cuyahoga County Court of Common Pleas, Domestic Relations Div. (C.A.6 (Ohio), 01-10-2002) 276 F.3d 808, certiorari denied 123 S.Ct. 72, 537 U.S. 812, 154 L.Ed.2d 15. Civil Rights ⟳ 1431

Eleventh Amendment barred hearing-impaired parent's action alleging that state court violated ADA by failing to provide him with adequate accommodation during child custody proceeding, insofar as action relied on equal protection theory; since disability is not a suspect category, Congress did not validly abrogate states' Eleventh Amendment immunity when, in non-employment discrimination provision of ADA, it attempted to enforce Fourteenth Amendment's Equal Protection Clause. Popovich v. Cuyahoga County Court of Common Pleas, Domestic Relations Div. (C.A.6 (Ohio), 01-10-2002) 276 F.3d 808, certiorari denied 123 S.Ct. 72, 537 U.S. 812, 154 L.Ed.2d 15. Constitutional Law ⟳ 4866; Federal Courts ⟳ 265

In analyzing safeguards needed in child custody proceedings, Due Process Clause requires balancing of private interests at stake, government's interest, and risk that procedures used will lead to erroneous decisions. Popovich v. Cuyahoga County Court of Common Pleas, Domestic Relations Div. (C.A.6 (Ohio), 01-10-2002) 276 F.3d 808, certiorari denied 123 S.Ct. 72, 537 U.S. 812, 154 L.Ed.2d 15. Constitutional Law ⊕ 4396

3. Initial allocation of rights and responsibilities and "best interest"—In general

Trial court issued sufficient findings to support its decision to deny wife's proposed plan for shared parenting; trial court found the parties had a history of trouble communicating and setting aside their differences and disagreements, recognized wife's "burdensome" drive, but found the best interest of the child best served by designating husband legal custodian and residential parent while basically splitting time with each parent, further found the children were well adjusted to attending school near father's home in addition to their participation in church and sporting activities there, and recognized the guardian ad litem (GAL) did not recommend shared parenting. Huffman v. Huffman (Ohio App. 5 Dist., Richland, 10-13-2009) No. 08-CA-93, 2009-Ohio-5511, 2009 WL 3326636, Unreported. Child Custody ⊕ 511

Father's complaint sought original residential parent designation as opposed to modification of existing decree in that there was no past decree allocating parental rights and responsibilities in the first place, thus limiting the custody determination to one considering out-of-wedlock child's best interests notwithstanding any detriment that a change in existing arrangement would occasion. In re Colvin (Ohio App. 5 Dist., Guernsey, 07-23-2008) No. 08-CA-000005, 2008-Ohio-3927, 2008 WL 2972644, Unreported. Children Out–of–wedlock ⊕ 20.3

For purposes of determining child custody incident to divorce, husband's use of child's custodial account was not factor weighing against award of custody, where husband testified that he closed account at issue and used funds to pay expenses for child, including household expenses, clothing, food, daycare, and doctor visits, and wife was awarded one-half of value of account at issue. Wingard v. Wingard (Ohio App. 2 Dist., Greene, 12-30-2005) No. 2005-CA-09, 2005-Ohio-7066, 2005 WL 3610302, Unreported. Child Custody ⊕ 48

Wife properly was permitted to utilize a third party for day care of child, rather than husband who worked out of his home; husband had a very unstructured work schedule where he was frequently out of town on travel, husband could not devote his full attention to child's needs, and husband's mother watched child whenever he was not home. Bechara v. Essad (Ohio App. 7 Dist., Mahoning, 06-11-2004) No. 03MA34, 2004-Ohio-3042, 2004 WL 1325636, Unreported. Child Custody ⊕ 100

Evidence supported trial court's designation of former wife as children's residential parent and legal custodian in divorce proceedings, even though former wife lived with man who had been convicted of attempted gross sexual imposition; children did not like former husband's live-in girlfriend, children reported incidents of physical abuse by former hus-band, children all stated they wanted to live with mother, children were afraid to visit former husband, and former husband failed to pay temporary child support. Tallman v. Tallman (Ohio App. 6 Dist., Fulton, 02-27-2004) No. F-03-008, 2004-Ohio-895, 2004 WL 368146, Unreported. Child Custody ⊕ 41; Child Custody ⊕ 58; Child Custody ⊕ 78

Trial court's award of custody of nonmarital child to natural father, rather than mother, was warranted, even though mother had been primary caregiver, and child spent much time with father's girlfriend; mother's status as primary care-giver was not due greater weight than other factors, father had a strong support network, including girlfriend and family, father was a full-time student and earned money to support child, while mother was 17 but had not finished the ninth grade and had a problem attending school. Wooten v. Casey (Ohio App. 4 Dist., Gallia, 01-05-2004) No. 03CA15, 2004-Ohio-55, 2004 WL 35814, Unreported. Children Out–of–wedlock ⊕ 20.3

Trial court fully complied with analysis mandated by statute when it determined that awarding legal custody of nonmarital child to biological father instead of biological mother was in child's best interest, where court applied all statutory factors to determine child's best interests, and court further examined whether shared parenting would be in child's best interests, and in doing so, court concluded that child be placed into legal custody of father with companionship to mother on specific dates and times. In re Knight (Ohio App. 11 Dist., Trumbull, 12-31-2003) No. 2002-T-0158, 2003-Ohio-7222, 2003 WL 23097094, Unreported. Children Out–of–wedlock ⊕ 20.3

There was no error of law or other defect on face of magistrate's decision granting legal custody of children to wife and designating her residential parent, and thus, trial court's adoption and incorporation of decision in final divorce decree was not abuse of discretion; magistrate addressed required statutory factors in making determination of what was in best interests of children. Calhoun Brannon v. Brannon (Ohio App. 11 Dist., Trumbull, 12-31-2003) No. 2003-T-0019, 2003-Ohio-7216, 2003 WL 23097091, Unreported. Child Custody ⊕ 504

Trial court's designation of former wife as child's sole residential parent, disregarding magistrate's recommendation that former husband be designated sole residential parent, was not in child's best interest, was abuse of discretion, and was against manifest weight of the evidence, where trial court failed to address issues raised in magistrate's decision, including past drug activity of former wife's live-in boyfriend, credibility of former wife and her boyfriend, and fact that former wife allowed child to have contact with man alleged to have sexually abused former wife. Sickle v. Sickle (Ohio App. 9 Dist., Wayne, 10-29-2003) No. 03CA0013, 2003-Ohio-5788, 2003 WL 22439848, Unreported. Child Custody ⊕ 504; Child Custody ⊕ 511

Evidence supported trial court order, which found that designating mother as the residential parent was in the children's best interests, in divorce proceeding; the trial court considered psychological testing of both parents, and testimony from both parents and witnesses regarding each parent's caretaking abilities. Stan v. Stan (Ohio App. 12 Dist., Preble, 10-20-2003) No. CA2003-01-001, 2003-Ohio-5540, 2003 WL 22382973, Unreported. Child Custody ☞ 469

Whether trial court's finding that mother was willful and vindictive was supported by the evidence was irrelevant to determination that awarding father custody was in the best interests of the child, where court weighed all of the evidence presented and considered all statutory factors. Prusia v. Prusia (Ohio App. 6 Dist., Lucas, 04-18-2003) No. L-02-1165, 2003-Ohio-2000, 2003 WL 1904410, Unreported. Child Custody ☞ 511

Trial court did not abuse its discretion in adopting magistrate's decision and declining to hear additional testimony on matter of allocation of parental rights and responsibilities; trial court clearly explained basis for its decision, as it explained that it could not accept former wife's unsupported assertions of change in children's circumstances, that it could find no binding precedent which would compel it to hear additional evidence, and that wife was free to file motion to modify allocation of parental rights and responsibilities. Frankart v. Frankart (Ohio App. 3 Dist., Seneca, 04-01-2003) No. 13-02-39, 2003-Ohio-1662, 2003 WL 1699821, Unreported. Child Custody ☞ 504

Weight of evidence that mother had unstable residency, a promiscuous lifestyle which she believed was appropriate, had reported physical abuse to her other child, and poor employment history, together with police reports as to home problems and recommendation of guardian ad litem, supported finding that best interests of nonmarital child was to grant custody to father, subject to visitation and participation by mother. Korosy v. Barker (Ohio App. 5 Dist., Stark, 11-04-2002) No. 2002CA00076, 2002-Ohio-6072, 2002 WL 31492289, Unreported. Children Out–of–wedlock ☞ 20.3

In child-custody disputes, the *Perales* suitability test is distinguishable from the best-interest test; under the best-interest test, the court looks for the best situation available to the child and places the child in that situation, whereas the suitability test requires a detriment to the child be shown before the court takes him or her away from an otherwise suitable parent. In re B.P. (Ohio App. 4 Dist., 12-22-2010) 191 Ohio App.3d 518, 946 N.E.2d 818, 2010-Ohio-6458. Child Custody ☞ 76

Trial court has broad discretion in cases relating to custody of children for it is in the best position to gain knowledge of the parties and it is delegated with the authority to decide disputes of fact and weigh testimony and credibility of witnesses. Sayre v. Hoelzle-Sayre (Ohio App. 3 Dist., 04-06-1994) 100 Ohio App.3d 203, 653 N.E.2d 712, appeal allowed 70 Ohio St.3d 1426, 638 N.E.2d 88, appeal dismissed as improvidently allowed 72 Ohio St.3d 1218, 651 N.E.2d 430, 1995-Ohio-274. Child Custody ☞ 7; Child Custody ☞ 467

Permanent custody order was "judgment," for purposes of rule requiring court to issue written findings of fact and conclusions of law supporting judgment, regardless of when order was entered. State ex rel. Papp v. James (Ohio, 06-01-1994) 69 Ohio St.3d 373, 632 N.E.2d 889, 1994-Ohio-86. Child Custody ☞ 511

RC 3109.04(B) requires findings of a change in circumstance upon modification of a final custody decree only, and not upon modification of an interlocutory custody order. Schoffner v. Schoffner (Auglaize 1984) 19 Ohio App.3d 208, 483 N.E.2d 1190, 19 O.B.R. 352.

4. —— Agreement of parties, initial allocation of rights and responsibilities and "best interest"

Substantial competent and credible evidence supported the trial court's refusal to terminate shared parenting plan; guardian ad litem recommended that the plan not be terminated, the witnesses seemed to agree that the children were well adjusted and relatively well behaved, children were not discipline problems, parents communicated reasonably well through email, and children were doing well under the plan. McGraw v. McGraw (Ohio App. 4 Dist., Scioto, 08-06-2010) No. 09CA3327, 2010-Ohio-3956, 2010 WL 3298708, Unreported. Child Custody ☞ 576, Child Custody ☞ 616

Custody of frozen embryos of former wife and former husband following parties' divorce was controlled by contract between former wife, former husband, and fertility clinic that was entered into prior to the marriage, as trial court lacked authority or jurisdiction to interfere in a contract made between parties and fertility clinic, which was not a party to the divorce action. Karmasu v. Karmasu (Ohio App. 5 Dist., Stark, 09-30-2009) No. 2008 CA 00231, 2009-Ohio-5252, 2009 WL 3155062, Unreported. Child Custody ☞ 35; Child Custody ☞ 274.5

Mediated settlement agreement between husband and wife concerning child custody incident to divorce was valid and thus enforceable, despite husband's claims after the fact that he was not aware that the agreements reached during mediation were binding, where husband had been in business for 17 years, which required him to negotiate and enter into contracts, and husband knew he could leave the negotiations during the mediation session. Fichthorn v. Fichthorn (Ohio App. 5 Dist., Guernsey, 09-28-2009) No. 09-CA-10, 2009-Ohio-5138, 2009 WL 3111922, Unreported. Child Custody ☞ 419

Trial court did not abuse its discretion in awarding custody of children to mother; the trial court methodically reviewed the statutory factors and the recommendation of the guardian ad litem, and concluded that it was in the best interest of the children to name mother as their residential parent and legal guardian, and, as for father's shared parenting request, the court found that the parties were unable to communicate with one another and certainly would not be able to make joint decisions with respect to the children. Garritano v. Pacella (Ohio App. 6 Dist., Lucas, 06-19-2009) No. L-07-1171, 2009-Ohio-2928, 2009 WL 1719365, Unreported. Child Custody ☞ 127; Child Custody ☞ 421; Child Custody ☞ 511

Trial court had jurisdiction to adopt shared parenting plan executed by unmarried mother and father, despite mother's contention that child was not a resident of state, was not dependent, and did not otherwise require court's protection; no other court was a more appropriate forum, and motion for shared parenting plan stated that parties jointly requested that the plan be adopted and approved, that parties acknowledged the court's jurisdiction and venue, and that they waived service of process. Pearl v. Porrata (Ohio App. 3 Dist., Mercer, 12-08-2008) No. 10-07-24, 2008-Ohio-6353, 2008 WL 5124584, Unreported. Children Out–of–wedlock ☞ 20.13

Trial court's finding that unmarried mother signed shared parenting agreement with father was not against the manifest weight of the evidence, on mother's motion to dismiss for want of jurisdiction father's motion for temporary custody of child after mother allegedly absconded with child in violation of shared parenting plan; father testified that mother signed the agreement, mother admitted during cross-examination that her signature was on the agreement, school secretary testified that mother had a copy of the agreement with her when she attempted to remove parties' child from school, and trial court found father's testimony to be more credible than mother's. Pearl v. Porrata (Ohio App. 3 Dist., Mercer, 12-08-2008) No. 10-07-24, 2008-Ohio-6353, 2008 WL 5124584, Unreported. Children Out–of–wedlock ☞ 20.8

Probate court did not have jurisdiction to consider mother's application for guardianship over the person of her eighteen-year-old autistic son due to previous order from domestic relations court concerning terms of the shared parenting agreement, even though the terms of such agreement were not a part of the probate court record; regardless of the terms of the agreement, the existence of the prior parenting agreement concerning the autistic son required the probate court to defer jurisdiction. In re Campbell (Ohio App. 7 Dist., Mahoning, 03-31-2006) No. 05 MA 10, 2006-Ohio-1764, 2006 WL 890999, Unreported. Mental Health ☞ 109

Trial court correctly considered all relevant factors in determining child's best interests, in proceeding in which court granted relief from previous divorce decree establishing parental rights and responsibilities and designated father as residential parent, after mother moved to city other than that specified in separation agreement; magistrate indicated that he considered wishes and concerns child expressed during in camera interview, and magistrate considered that child was adapted to life in city specified in agreement, where her extended family from both sides was located, while she had

no connection to city where her mother had moved. Day v. Day (Ohio App. 3 Dist., Seneca, 11-14-2005) No. 13-05-17, 2005-Ohio-6032, 2005 WL 3031009, Unreported. Child Custody ☞ 526

Provision of statute prohibiting court from modifying parental rights unless certain requirements are met was not applicable in proceeding in which trial court granted relief from previous divorce decree establishing parental rights and responsibilities and designated father as residential parent, after mother moved to city other than that specified in separation agreement; court found that mother failed to adhere to terms of agreement, and once portion of decree had been vacated, court was required to make initial determination of parental rights, and thus, court did not make modification of parental rights. Day v. Day (Ohio App. 3 Dist., Seneca, 11-14-2005) No. 13-05-17, 2005-Ohio-6032, 2005 WL 3031009, Unreported. Child Custody ☞ 526

In divorce action in which husband sought shared parenting plan, evidence supported trial court's findings that both parties had shown they were likely to honor and facilitate court-approved parenting time rights, that the parties had successfully cooperated and made joint decisions, and that the parties had the ability to cooperate and make decisions jointly with respect to the children. Swain v. Swain (Ohio App. 4 Dist., Pike, 08-06-2005) No. 05CA740, 2005-Ohio-4321, 2005 WL 1995388, Unreported. Child Custody ☞ 472

Trial court acted within its discretion when it allowed consent agreement as to parenting plan to be reduced to judgment before both parties had actually signed it, even though former wife claimed she was under the influence of medication when she entered agreement and only later realized it was against her interest; medication claim was not raised to trial court, and court had gone to great length to gain assurances that agreement was entered voluntarily. Killa v. Killa (Ohio App. 7 Dist., Mahoning, 02-06-2004) No. 03MA101, 2004-Ohio-566, 2004 WL 234746, Unreported. Child Custody ☞ 521

Evidence supported the trial court's determination that father, who donated sperm for child's conception and signed an agreement relinquishing his parental rights, had not relinquished his parental rights to mother and her former same-sex domestic partner; the agreement signed by father relinquished his parental rights to mother only, as there was no contract between father and mother's former domestic partner. In re Mullen (Ohio App. 1 Dist., 12-31-2009) 185 Ohio App.3d 457, 924 N.E.2d 448, 2009-Ohio-6934, stay granted 124 Ohio St.3d 1505, 922 N.E.2d 968, 2010-Ohio-799, appeal allowed 125 Ohio St.3d 1413, 925 N.E.2d 1001, 2010-Ohio-1893, affirmed 129 Ohio St.3d 417, 953 N.E.2d 302, 2011-Ohio-3361. Children Out–of–wedlock ☞ 15

Competent evidence supported the trial court's determination that mother did not contractually relinquish some of her parental rights as to child conceived with donated sperm in favor of shared custody with former same-sex domestic partner, even though mother had executed a general durable power of attorney and a health-care power of attorney that gave domestic partner the ability to make school, health, and other decisions for child; the documents that gave domestic partner parental decision-making powers were given at mother's discretion, and mother always retained the unilateral right to revoke them, and mother repeatedly refused to enter into a legally enforceable shared-custody agreement with domestic partner when presented with the option to do so. In re Mullen (Ohio App. 1 Dist., 12-31-2009) 185 Ohio App.3d 457, 924 N.E.2d 448, 2009-Ohio-6934, stay granted 124 Ohio St.3d 1505, 922 N.E.2d 968, 2010-Ohio-799, appeal allowed 125 Ohio St.3d 1413, 925 N.E.2d 1001, 2010-Ohio-1893, affirmed 129 Ohio St.3d 417, 953 N.E.2d 302, 2011-Ohio-3361. Children Out-of-wedlock ⊖ 20.8

Parents may waive their right to custody of their children and are bound by an agreement to do so. In re Bonfield (Ohio, 08-28-2002) 96 Ohio St.3d 218, 773 N.E.2d 507, 2002-Ohio-4182, opinion superseded on reconsideration 97 Ohio St.3d 387, 780 N.E.2d 241, 2002-Ohio-6660. Child Custody ⊖ 35

The parents' agreement to grant custody to a third party is enforceable subject only to a judicial determination that the custodian is a proper person to assume the care, training, and education of the child. In re Bonfield (Ohio, 08-28-2002) 96 Ohio St.3d 218, 773 N.E.2d 507, 2002-Ohio-4182, opinion superseded on reconsideration 97 Ohio St.3d 387, 780 N.E.2d 241, 2002-Ohio-6660. Child Custody ⊖ 35

The duty owed by the courts to children under the doctrine of parens patriae cannot be severed by agreement of the parties in a domestic relations action. Kelm v. Kelm (Ohio, 07-05-2001) 92 Ohio St.3d 223, 749 N.E.2d 299, 2001-Ohio-168. Child Custody ⊖ 9; Child Custody ⊖ 35

Agreed entry awarding temporary and permanent custody of children was interlocutory prior to its integration as part of final divorce decree and thus court, in determining custody provision of final decree, was required to apply "best interest of child" standard, and it had discretion to accept, reject or modify parties' agreement; statute authorizing change of custody only upon showing of changed circumstances was applicable only where parties sought to modify prior, final custody decree. Frost v. Frost (Franklin 1992) 84 Ohio App.3d 699, 618 N.E.2d 198, motion overruled 66 Ohio St.3d 1489, 612 N.E.2d 1245. Child Custody ⊖ 36; Child Custody ⊖ 76

A trial court that approved a separation agreement, thereafter adopted as a part of the judgment in a divorce, alimony and custody action, which agreement contained a provision regarding the custody of a minor child, is not bound by the terms of that agreement in a subsequent hearing on a motion to modify the provisions of the judgment entry.

Bastian v. Bastian (Cuyahoga 1959) 160 N.E.2d 133, 81 Ohio Law Abs. 408, 13 O.O.2d 267.

An agreement between husband and wife, parties to a divorce action, that the custody of their child should be given to a third person, is enforceable, subject only to judicial determination that the custodian was in every way a proper person to have the care of the child. Rowe v. Rowe (Franklin 1950) 97 N.E.2d 223, 58 Ohio Law Abs. 497, 44 O.O. 224. Child Custody ⊖ 35

The juvenile court errs where it fails to make the requisite findings under RC 3109.04(E)(1)(a) in determining the reallocation of parental rights and responsibilities and where the court's journal entry does not even reference RC 3109.04. In re Surdel (Ohio App. 9 Dist., Lorain, 10-03-2001) No. 01CA007783, 2001-Ohio-1407, 2001 WL 1162830, Unreported.

A court must consider the factors listed in RC 3109.04(C) and make an independent original determination of custody, not merely adopt the provisions of a separation agreement in a divorce action, and a court's failure to do so is an abuse of discretion. Clark v Clark, No. 11021 (2d Dist Ct App, Montgomery, 1-18-89).

In the event of a dissolution of marriage, as contrasted with divorce, child custody is determined by whatever separation agreement is approved by the court and incorporated into its dissolution decree, the parties having the right to amend the agreement prior to or during the hearing on the petition for dissolution. Davidson v Davidson, No. 4-79-7 (3d Dist Ct App, Defiance, 2-20-80).

5. ⸺ Appeal, initial allocation of rights and responsibilities and "best interest"

Father was precluded from challenging on appeal the trial court's order adopting magistrate's decision designating mother as children's residential parent and legal custodian, as father did not raise this issue in an objection to magistrate's decision or argue plain error in his merit brief. Allgeier v. Allgeier (Ohio App. 12 Dist., Clinton, 11-01-2010) No. CA2009-12-019, 2010-Ohio-5313, 2010 WL 4340650, Unreported. Child Custody ⊖ 904; Child Custody ⊖ 908

Father waived his appellate argument that trial court erred in not permitting him to submit proposed findings of fact and conclusions of law because he was a pro se litigant, in child custody modification proceeding, where father failed to object to the court's ruling. Smith v. Quigg (Ohio App. 5 Dist., Fairfield, 03-22-2006) No. 2005-CA-002, 2006-Ohio-1495, 2006 WL 786856, Unreported. Child Custody ⊖ 904

Court of Appeals was required to presume regularity of trial court's findings as to parental fitness and its award of custody and visitation, in action on wife's complaint for divorce, and to affirm trial court's award of custody to husband, in absence of transcript of final hearing before trial court. Kinney v. Kinney (Ohio App. 10 Dist., Franklin,

06-14-2005) No. 04AP-1146, 2005-Ohio-2959, 2005 WL 1394786, Unreported. Child Custody ☞ 920

Appellate court would not review former husband's challenge regarding trial court's judgment that child lacked sufficient reasoning ability to express wishes and concerns as to custody in divorce proceedings, where husband did not provide court with transcript of in camera hearing with child. Francis v. Francis (Ohio App. 2 Dist., Montgomery, 04-18-2003) No. 19367, 2003-Ohio-1940, 2003 WL 1901302, Unreported. Child Custody ☞ 907

Former wife waived on appeal any error in admission or consideration of child's guidance counselor's testimony in child custody proceeding, where wife did not raise an objection to testimony. Dyslin v. Marks (Ohio App. 5 Dist., Stark, 04-07-2003) No. 2002CA00300, 2003-Ohio-1855, 2003 WL 1857108, Unreported. Child Custody ☞ 904

A Civ R 35(A) order for further psychological examination is a final appealable order and affects a substantial right when made in a custody and divorce proceeding. Wayne M. Shoff v. Andrea J. Shoff (Ohio App. 10 Dist., Franklin, 07-27-1995) No. 95APF01-8, 1995 WL 450249, Unreported.

The issue of credit for child support that is raised for the first time in an objection to a referee's report should not be reviewed by an appellate court. Myers v. Mantia (Ohio App. 2 Dist., Miami, 06-22-1994) No. 93-CA-44, 1994 WL 277859, Unreported.

Husband could not be heard to complain on appeal that trial court abused its discretion by accepting a stipulation as to custody that the parties entered into prior to trial and that was not subject of objection at trial. Phillis v. Phillis (Ohio App. 5 Dist., 11-14-2005) 164 Ohio App.3d 364, 842 N.E.2d 555, 2005-Ohio-6200. Child Custody ☞ 904

"Abuse of discretion," such as will permit appellate court to disturb custody decision of divorce court, connotes more than error of law or judgment; it implies that divorce court's attitude is unreasonable, arbitrary or unconscionable. Marshall v. Marshall (Ohio App. 3 Dist., 01-15-1997) 117 Ohio App.3d 182, 690 N.E.2d 68. Child Custody ☞ 921(1)

Appellate court must uphold custody decision absent an abuse of discretion and, therefore, may not independently review the weight of the evidence in the majority of cases. Miller v. Miller (Ohio App. 3 Dist., 11-20-1996) 115 Ohio App.3d 336, 685 N.E.2d 319. Child Custody ☞ 921(1)

Award of custody supported by substantial amount of credible and competent evidence will not be reversed on appeal as being against weight of evidence; finding of error in law is legitimate ground for reversal, but difference of opinion on credibility of witnesses and evidence is not. Davis v. Flickinger (Ohio, 02-12-1997) 77 Ohio St.3d 415, 674 N.E.2d 1159, 1997-Ohio-260. Child Custody ☞ 922(2)

Trial court's judgment in custody matters enjoys presumption of correctness. Butler v. Butler (Ohio App. 3 Dist., 12-05-1995) 107 Ohio App.3d 633, 669 N.E.2d 291. Child Custody ☞ 920

When award of custody is supported by some competent, credible evidence, that award will not be reversed by reviewing court as being against the weight of the evidence. Evans v. Evans (Ohio App. 12 Dist., 10-02-1995) 106 Ohio App.3d 673, 666 N.E.2d 1176, dismissed, appeal not allowed 75 Ohio St.3d 1448, 663 N.E.2d 330. Child Custody ☞ 922(1)

When there is no evidence to the contrary, appellate court will presume that trial court considered all relevant factors in determining custody. Evans v. Evans (Ohio App. 12 Dist., 10-02-1995) 106 Ohio App.3d 673, 666 N.E.2d 1176, dismissed, appeal not allowed 75 Ohio St.3d 1448, 663 N.E.2d 330. Child Custody ☞ 920

Trial court's decision in custody matters will be reversed only upon a showing of abuse of discretion. Evans v. Evans (Ohio App. 12 Dist., 10-02-1995) 106 Ohio App.3d 673, 666 N.E.2d 1176, dismissed, appeal not allowed 75 Ohio St.3d 1448, 663 N.E.2d 330. Child Custody ☞ 921(1)

Trial court's decision concerning custody in divorce cannot be reversed by reviewing court absent abuse of discretion. Rowe v. Franklin (Ohio App. 1 Dist., 06-28-1995) 105 Ohio App.3d 176, 663 N.E.2d 955, appeal not allowed 74 Ohio St.3d 1464, 656 N.E.2d 1299. Child Custody ☞ 921(1)

Abuse of discretion standard for reviewing trial court's decision in child custody matters means that discretion which trial court enjoys in custody matters should be accorded the utmost respect, and, consequently, it is improper for appellate court to independently review weight of the evidence in the majority of cases. Sayre v. Hoelzle-Sayre (Ohio App. 3 Dist., 04-06-1994) 100 Ohio App.3d 203, 653 N.E.2d 712, appeal allowed 70 Ohio St.3d 1426, 638 N.E.2d 88, appeal dismissed as improvidently allowed 72 Ohio St.3d 1218, 651 N.E.2d 430, 1995-Ohio-274. Child Custody ☞ 921(1)

A permanent custody award supported by substantial evidence will not be reversed on appeal as being against the weight of the evidence. Bechtol v. Bechtol (Ohio 1990) 49 Ohio St.3d 21, 550 N.E.2d 178, rehearing denied 49 Ohio St.3d 718, 552 N.E.2d 952, opinion corrected 51 Ohio St.3d 701, 554 N.E.2d 899.

Where a court of appeals finds that a trial court's adoption of a referee's report in a custody proceeding constitutes an abuse of discretion, it is error for the appellate court to independently weigh the evidence and rule on the custody motion; instead, the appellate court must remand the case for a new trial. Miller v. Miller (Ohio 1988) 37 Ohio St.3d 71, 523 N.E.2d 846, clarification denied 43 Ohio St.3d 710, 540 N.E.2d 728.

An appeal from an order regarding the custody of a child is conditional upon giving bond. Call v. Call (Franklin 1958) 107 Ohio App. 516, 160 N.E.2d 307, 81 Ohio Law Abs. 243, 9 O.O.2d 54.

On the evidence in a habeas corpus action the court will permit two boys to remain with their father rather than being given to their mother or separated. Trout v. Trout (Ohio Com.Pl. 1956) 136 N.E.2d 474, 73 Ohio Law Abs. 91, appeal dismissed 167 Ohio St. 476, 149 N.E.2d 728, 5 O.O.2d 156.

On an appeal where the appellant had supplied only a few pages of the transcript, the appellate court could not determine whether there had been an abuse of discretion by the trial court. The partial transcript did not demonstrate that there was not sufficient evidence to support the basis for the trial court's decision. A reviewing court will not disturb an exercise of discretion unless the above is plain and manifestly shown, and the complaining party's rights have been prejudiced. Guard v Guard, No. 1123 (11th Dist Ct App, Ashtabula, 6–10–83).

Where custody of minor children is originally granted to the maternal grandparents and a subsequent court order grants custody to the father, both awards of custody constitute final, appealable orders and, therefore, preclude the mother from asserting assignments of error in a proceeding which is not a timely appeal of those orders. Torbeck v Torbeck, No. C–810827 (1st Dist Ct App, Hamilton, 7–21–82).

6. —— Relative advantages of each parent, initial allocation of rights and responsibilities and "best interest"

Trial court's denial of ex-husband's motion for change of residential parent was supported by some competent, credible evidence; there was no indication of any imbalance on behalf of ex-wife in the record, both parties demonstrated an inability to communicate well with one another regarding the children's needs and visitation, ex-wife took the children to their numerous medical appointments and treatments, and, although informed of the dates and times of the medical appointments, ex-husband never attended the children's appointments and was skeptical that the children had any special needs or medical issues, and children were well-adjusted in ex-wife's home. Gore v. Gore (Ohio App. 6 Dist., Ottawa, 05-08-2009) No. OT-08-015, 2009-Ohio-2158, 2009 WL 1263508, Unreported. Child Custody ⬥ 577

Record supported trial court's determination, in a proceeding on father's motion for modification of child custody, that it was not in the best interest of the children to be placed with either father or mother, where a court–appointed investigator, in a written report, expressed concerns about both parents' ability to provide the children with a safe and stable home, expressed concerns over father's prior conviction for corruption of a minor, stated that father's home was in a dilapidated state and was dirty and littered, and, inter alia, stated that although the cupboards of father's home were well stocked, the refrigerator held a bare minimum of food. Horn v. Frazier (Ohio App. 5 Dist., Licking, 01-07-2009) No. 08 CA 000068, 2009-Ohio-51, 2009 WL 50608, Unreported. Child Custody ⬥ 552

Granting mother legal custody of child was in child's best interests, in initial custody determination between unmarried parents, even though father desired to spend as much time as possible with child; child was less than one year old and had resided with mother since his birth. In re Stose (Ohio App. 5 Dist., Stark, 10-20-2008) No. 2008CA00049, 2008-Ohio-5457, 2008 WL 4650725, Unreported. Children Out–of–wedlock ⬥ 20.3

Evidence supported finding that it was not in the best interests of the children to reallocate parental rights and responsibilities to name former husband as the sole residential parent of children, in post-divorce proceeding on father's motion to modify original custody award under which mother was named sole residential parent and legal custodian of the parties' children; the children were well adjusted, both parents had been flexible in allowing the other parent to have time outside of the court-ordered parenting time and both had at times denied the other additional time with the children, and there were no allegations of abuse or neglect. Cichanowicz v. Cichanowicz (Ohio App. 3 Dist., Crawford, 09-22-2008) No. 3-08-04, 2008-Ohio-4779, 2008 WL 4292724, Unreported. Child Custody ⬥ 577

In divorce action in which husband sought shared parenting plan, evidence supported trial court's finding that husband encouraged the children to talk about wife and that husband had the ability to encourage the sharing of love and affection between both children and wife. Swain v. Swain (Ohio App. 4 Dist., Pike, 08-06-2005) No. 05CA740, 2005-Ohio-4321, 2005 WL 1995388, Unreported. Child Custody ⬥ 472

Trial court's decision in divorce proceedings, granting custody of minor child to husband rather than wife, was not against the manifest weight of the evidence, even though wife was the primary caretaker, and guardian ad litem recommended grant of custody to wife; neither home was markedly better than the other, there was great animosity between the parties, and husband's lifestyle was more stable than wife's. Broadbent v. Broadbent (Ohio App. 3 Dist., Union, 06-27-2005) No. 14-04-52, 2005-Ohio-3227, 2005 WL 1503961, Unreported. Child Custody ⬥ 44; Child Custody ⬥ 48; Child Custody ⬥ 51

Evidence supported magistrate's designation of mother as residential parent and legal custodian for out-of-wedlock child, in child custody proceeding; magistrate found that each parent was capable of caring for child, and that mother was more mature and parent-like. In re Vodila (Ohio App. 5 Dist., Stark, 02-07-2005) No. 2004CA00249, 2005-Ohio-496, 2005 WL 299844, Unreported. Children Out–of–wedlock ⬥ 20.8

Substantial evidence supported trial court's determination to award custody of child to its mother; court followed the statutory procedures for determining the child's best interest while struggling to reconcile testimony, that father was a good father, with evidence that he engaged in inappropriate sexual conduct with a female minor. Krayterman v. Krayterman (Ohio App. 12 Dist., Butler, 05-24-2004) No. CA2003-05-108, 2004-Ohio-2592, 2004 WL 1144400, Unreported. Child Custody ⊙ 467

Evidence supported trial court decision to name mother as residential parent and legal guardian of child, even though guardian ad litem recommended granting father custody of child; the guardian ad litem's recommendation was neutral and the guardian stated how difficult the custody decision was, family counselor recommended that mother receive custody of child, and the trial court found that child was healthy, well-nourished child. Charles H.H. v. Marie S. (Ohio App. 6 Dist., Lucas, 06-13-2003) No. L-02-1312, 2003-Ohio-3094, 2003 WL 21384879, Unreported. Child Custody ⊙ 421

Evidence was sufficient to support trial court's finding in custody dispute that mother was willful and vindictive; guardian ad litem and psychologist recounted a number of times where mother interpreted doctor's letters to invent reasons why father could not have companionship with his child, including preventing him from seeing his father on Christmas. Prusia v. Prusia (Ohio App. 6 Dist., Lucas, 04-18-2003) No. L-02-1165, 2003-Ohio-2000, 2003 WL 1904410, Unreported. Child Custody ⊙ 469

Trial court considered the non-exclusive statutory factors in determining that designating mother as custodial and residential parent was in child's best interest, where court found that child was well adjusted to his mother's home and to his daycare arrangements, court considered that both parents wanted to be custodial and residential parent, appeared to be in good physical and mental health, neither party had criminal convictions for abuse or neglect of a child, and neither party was currently denying the other parenting time, court noted its concerns about father's extremely negative opinion of mother, and that mother was a competent and effective parent and appeared to be more committed to fostering a positive relationship for her child with both parents than was father. Barnett-Soto v. Soto (Ohio App. 9 Dist., Medina, 02-05-2003) No. 02CA0011-M, 2003-Ohio-535, 2003 WL 245825, Unreported. Child Custody ⊙ 48; Child Custody ⊙ 51; Child Custody ⊙ 84

Order entered in custody action by father that named mother as child's sole residential and legal custodian was not abuse of discretion despite mother's convictions for domestic violence and child endangerment arising from altercation with father; record also reflected that father had failed to make child support payments, and there was evidence presented that both parents had a good relationship with child and were both active in her upbringing and that both wished to be the residential parent. Bonar v. Boggs (Ohio App. 7 Dist., Jefferson, 12-20-2002) No. 01JE33, 2002-Ohio-7173, 2002 WL 31859445, Unreported. Child Custody ⊙ 58; Child Custody ⊙ 61; Child Custody ⊙ 85

Evidence, though conflicting, was sufficient to support best interests finding in divorce action that husband, rather than wife, qualified as residential parent for the minor children; while wife's witnesses testified that she acted appropriately with the children, several other witnesses testified that they observed wife take out her anger and frustration on the boys by being overly rough with the children or refusing to help the children when they were hurt, wife admitted that husband and the boys had a bond and that husband acted lovingly towards them, and husband testified that he engaged in feeding, clothing, and bathing the children prior to the separation and since the separation he has taken a cardiopulmonary resuscitation (CPR) class and a cooking class. Saltzman v. Saltzman (Ohio App. 3 Dist., Wyandot, 11-27-2002) No. 16-02-10, 2002-Ohio-6490, 2002 WL 31667314, Unreported. Child Custody ⊙ 469

Psychological well-being of the parties is an important factor in determining the best interest of the children in custody proceedings. Yazdani-Isfehani v. Yazdani-Isfehani (Ohio App. 4 Dist., 12-26-2006) 170 Ohio App.3d 1, 865 N.E.2d 924, 2006-Ohio-7105. Child Custody ⊙ 62

Wife's residence with her parents, and her parents' strong commitment to child, were relevant to determination of best interests of child and to award of custody in action for divorce. Davis v. Wilson (Ohio App. 12 Dist., 09-22-1997) 123 Ohio App.3d 19, 702 N.E.2d 1227. Child Custody ⊙ 76

Trial court is not required to make finding that one of child's parents is unsuitable before it may consider child's relationship with his or her grandparents as one factor in its best interest analysis in rendering award of custody incident to divorce proceeding. Davis v. Wilson (Ohio App. 12 Dist., 09-22-1997) 123 Ohio App.3d 19, 702 N.E.2d 1227. Child Custody ⊙ 511

Trial court did not abuse its discretion in refusing to grant husband sole custody of child, where either parent would have been fit person for custody. deLevie v. deLevie (Franklin 1993) 86 Ohio App.3d 531, 621 N.E.2d 594, dismissed, jurisdictional motion overruled 67 Ohio St.3d 1409, 615 N.E.2d 1043. Child Custody ⊙ 48

An award of custody to a father will be upheld as in the best interest of the child where the mother is irresponsible with money, lacks control over her impulses, and has poor judgment. Apgar v. Apgar (Cuyahoga 1984) 21 Ohio App.3d 193, 486 N.E.2d 1181, 21 O.B.R. 206.

The welfare of the child is considered when the question of custody of such child arises between the parents who stand on an equality, or when the parents are found to be unfit and the court is required to grant custody to a third person. Ludy v. Ludy (Franklin 1948) 84 Ohio App. 195, 82 N.E.2d 775, 53 Ohio Law Abs. 47, 39 O.O. 241, rehearing denied 84 N.E.2d 120, 53 Ohio Law Abs. 47. Child Custody ⊙ 76

7. —— Child's "best interest" generally, initial allocation of rights and responsibilities and "best interest"

Trial court was not authorized to unilaterally change parties' submitted parenting plan without determining that the changed portion was not in the children's best interest and without allowing the parties the opportunity to make the appropriate change, in divorce proceedings. Collins v. Collins (Ohio App. 3 Dist., Marion, 05-16-2011) No. 9-10-53, 2011-Ohio-2339, 2011 WL 1944276, Unreported. Child Custody ☞ 141; Child Custody ☞ 147

Trial court did not abuse its discretion in finding that it was in children's best interests to have father as their residential parent with mother exercising extended parenting time; father was flexible and willing to compromise as to the children's care if mother would stay close as opposed to moving away, whereas mother's wishes were unstable and wavering, giving custody to father did not require the children to transition to a new residence or neighborhood, mother was described as jealous, suspicious, and paranoid, and was viewed as telling incredulous stories, as being untruthful, or as being almost delusional, mother's claims regarding father's anger and substance abuse problems were found to be exaggerated or fabricated, father was more likely to facilitate visitation, and mother intended to establish a residence out of state. Manshadi v. Mossayebi (Ohio App. 7 Dist., Mahoning, 03-22-2011) No. 10 MA 2, 2011-Ohio-1469, 2011 WL 1118715, Unreported. Child Custody ☞ 210

Substantial evidence supported trial court's judgment adopting magistrate's decision that it was in best interests of child born out-of-wedlock for mother to be designated residential parent and legal custodian of child; mother was more likely than adjudicated father to honor and facilitate visitation rights approved by court, given father's initially steadfast position that mother should have no contact with child until child was older, father only grudgingly conceded after being further questioned on the subject that he would permit mother to have contact with child if it was court-ordered, child had a great relationship with her older half-sister and the two children shared a room in mother's home, and father admitted to self-medicating with a prescription drug. Pahl v. Haugh (Ohio App. 3 Dist., Hancock, 03-21-2011) No. 5-10-27, 2011-Ohio-1302, 2011 WL 947016, Unreported. Children Out–of–wedlock ☞ 20.3

Evidence established that it served child's best interests for mother to be awarded residential parent and legal custodian status, in child custody action involving child who was born out of wedlock; evidence showed that child's misbehavior over the summers in which he was entrusted to father's care was directly related to lack of supervision, and, despite visitation schedule, father would allow child to determine whether he wanted to visit his mother. Ensell v. Ensell (Ohio App. 7 Dist., Jefferson, 11-26-2010) No. 09 JE 14, 2010-Ohio-5942, 2010 WL 4939996, Unreported. Children Out–of–wedlock ☞ 20.3

Finding that it was in best interests of minor children to name father as custodial parent, in divorce proceeding, was supported by sufficient evidence, including evidence that father had stronger financial status to provide for children, that mother had mental health issue, that mother lived in dangerous area, and that mother had permitted children to put rocks in their mouths. Shaw v. Shaw (Ohio App. 6 Dist., Huron, 09-17-2010) No. H-09-023, 2010-Ohio-4380, 2010 WL 3610250, Unreported. Child Custody ☞ 58; Child Custody ☞ 62; Child Custody ☞ 63

Grant of child custody to father in divorce proceedings was in best interests of child; guardian ad litem advised against shared parenting because of communication difficulties between parents, child expressed fear concerning mother's future actions toward father, there was evidence that mother had an explosive temper, father had removed children from home on several occasions because of mother's temper, supervised visits between mother and child became infrequent after temporary protection order was issued against mother. Bristow v. Bristow (Ohio App. 12 Dist., Butler, 07-26-2010) No. CA2009-05-139, 2010-Ohio-3469, 2010 WL 2892759, Unreported. Child Custody ☞ 134; Child Custody ☞ 421

Trial court's prior order, granting equal parenting time of minor child during divorce proceedings was not a "shared parenting decree" that allocated parental rights and responsibilities for care of child, and, thus, court was not required to modify order only if it found substantial change in circumstances of child, but, instead, was simply required to make allocation that was in best interests of child; court's grant of equal parenting time was simply an interlocutory and temporary order issued during pendency of action for divorce. Daniels v. Daniels (Ohio App. 3 Dist., Paulding, 02-23-2009) No. 11-08-10, 2009-Ohio-784, 2009 WL 427525, Unreported. Child Custody ☞ 324

Evidence supported finding that shared parenting would not be in best interest of child; parents were unable to cooperate or communicate with one another regarding child, when child left father's care, he was disrespectful to mother and other adults, suggesting father did not encourage respectful relationships, there may have been abuse or domestic violence within marriage, mother was better able to provide son with structured environment and deal with son's educational and separate needs, and trial court spoke to child to determine his wishes and concerns and had benefit of parental investigation report detailing several statutory best interest factors and providing assessment of living arrangements, parties' employment, and caretaking. Seng v. Seng (Ohio App. 12 Dist., Clermont, 12-22-2008) No. CA2007-12-120, 2008-Ohio-6758, 2008 WL 5330000, Unreported. Child Custody ☞ 127; Child Custody ☞ 421; Child Custody ☞ 472

Declining to adopt shared parenting plan was not abuse of discretion; trial court made its determination in best interest of child, and trial court was not unreasonable, arbitrary or unconscionable when it declined to adopt shared parenting agreement. Seng v. Seng (Ohio App. 12 Dist., Clermont, 12-22-2008) No. CA2007-12-120, 2008-Ohio-6758, 2008 WL 5330000, Unreported. Child Custody ⊚ 123; Child Custody ⊚ 511

Evidence supported finding that father was a suitable parent, thus supporting order granting father, rather than maternal grandparent and stepgrandfather, custody of child; father had a well-established, devoted relationship with child, although his strained relationship with his in-laws had sometimes interfered with their time together, grandparents had been dishonest with father in an effort to limit his involvement in child's life, and father held a steady job, could provide appropriate housing and care for child, did not have a drug or alcohol abuse problem, and responded well to anger management classes. Holbrook v. Holbrook (Ohio App. 2 Dist., Montgomery, 05-02-2008) No. 22320, 2008-Ohio-2079, 2008 WL 1921639, Unreported. Child Custody ⊚ 279

Shared parenting plan was not in best interest of parties' child, where parties were unable to communicate with respect to child other than by notes left by husband in child's suitcase. Wingard v. Wingard (Ohio App. 2 Dist., Greene, 12-30-2005) No. 2005-CA-09, 2005-Ohio-7066, 2005 WL 3610302, Unreported. Child Custody ⊚ 127

Trial court did not abuse its discretion by including provision in divorce judgment that required that wife, who was awarded custody of parties' two children, not smoke in presence of children or otherwise expose children to secondhand smoke; secondhand smoke was "relevant factor" and "physical health factor" trial court was mandated to consider under statute on awarding parental rights and responsibilities. Day v. Day (Ohio App. 5 Dist., Ashland, 08-22-2005) No. 04 COA 74, 2005-Ohio-4343, 2005 WL 2002249, Unreported. Child Custody ⊚ 528

Trial court did not abuse its discretion, in proceedings for divorce, in finding overriding reasons, apart from statutory factors considered by it, warranting award of custody of parties' child to husband, where testimony of child's caregiver, police witness, social worker, and wife's neighbors established that wife abused and neglected child, and court was not limited to statutory "best interests" factors in awarding custody. Shaffer v. Shaffer (Ohio App. 3 Dist., Paulding, 08-01-2005) No. 11-04-22, 2005-Ohio-3884, 2005 WL 1797739, Unreported. Child Custody ⊚ 76; Child Custody ⊚ 469

Sufficient evidence supported award of custody of out-of-wedlock child to father; father was child's primary caretaker when child lived with him, father had plan for caring for child, and he had a substantial relationship with the child, mother had been reluctant to facilitate visitation between child and father, and other children of mother had history in foster care and being removed from her care due to her repeated drug abuse. In re Jump (Ohio App. 5 Dist., Holmes, 06-15-2005) No. 04CA011, 2005-Ohio-3287, 2005 WL 1519297, Unreported. Children Out–of–wedlock ⊚ 20.3

Sufficient competent and credible evidence supported conclusion that it was in child's best interest to be placed with her paternal grandparents; case worker testified that county representative had contacted her to tell her grandparents' home was sufficient and criminal background check was also sufficient, that paternal grandparents were the only ones who consistently maintained that they were interested in taking the child, and that they had also indicated willingness to work with mother until she was able to take child back. In re Volheim (Ohio App. 5 Dist., Fairfield, 01-31-2005) No. 2004-CA-53, 2005-Ohio-369, 2005 WL 267651, Unreported. Infants ⊚ 222

Trial court's findings with respect to best interest of child, in proceedings for allocation of parental rights and responsibilities incident to divorce, were sufficient to support its conclusion that shared parenting was not in child's best interest; court found that child had good relationship with both parties, loved and wanted to spend time with both of them, but was frustrated with parenting schedule alternating time with each parent on daily basis and, if required to choose with whom he would prefer to spend more time, would probably choose mother. Kellogg v. Kellogg (Ohio App. 10 Dist., Franklin, 12-30-2004) No. 04AP-382, 2004-Ohio-7202, 2004 WL 3090184, Unreported, appeal not allowed 105 Ohio St.3d 1546, 827 N.E.2d 328, 2005-Ohio-2188. Child Custody ⊚ 511

Change of custody from unwed mother to father was in child's best interest; father was the parent most likely to facilitate visitation, mother did not believe that child should have contact with father until she was old enough to express a desire to do so, mother effectively relinquished her role as residential parent by moving from her parents' home to college housing, and as between father and maternal grandparents, it was in child's best interest to have father provide for her day-to-day care, and advantages of granting custody to father outweighed the disadvantages of removing child from the care of her maternal grandparents. Gaines v. Pelzl (Ohio App. 2 Dist., Greene, 04-23-2004) No. 2003-CA-60, 2004-Ohio-2043, 2004 WL 869549, Unreported. Children Out–of–wedlock ⊚ 20.10

Substantial amount of credible and competent evidence supported determination that awarding custody of minor child to father was in the best interest of child. Ream v. Ream (Ohio App. 5 Dist., Licking, 04-14-2003) No. 02-CA-000071, 2003-Ohio-2144, 2003 WL 1962332, Unreported. Child Custody ⊚ 467

Statute governing awards of parental rights and responsibilities, which limits court's power to alter prior decree which allocated parental rights and responsibilities only to situations in which change in circumstances of child or parents has occurred since prior decree, did not apply to trial court's award of custody of child to father, as no prior decree establishing custody or paternity existed, and thus court correctly determined custody based on best interests of child. In re Mefford (Ohio App. 2 Dist., Greene, 01-24-2003) No. 2002CA37, 2003-Ohio-313, 2003 WL 164811, Unreported. Child Custody ☞ 76; Child Custody ☞ 555

Award of custody of child to father was not against manifest weight of the evidence; father had not had any incidents of domestic violence for several years, had taken classes in anger management, and had been sober for several years, mother had negative parenting behavior, including having child sleep in same bed with her and another man and leaving child in car for ten minutes while she went into a bar, child and father had good relationship, and father had stable home and employment. In re Mefford (Ohio App. 2 Dist., Greene, 01-24-2003) No. 2002CA37, 2003-Ohio-313, 2003 WL 164811, Unreported. Child Custody ☞ 48; Child Custody ☞ 60; Child Custody ☞ 61; Child Custody ☞ 66

An initial grant of custody requires application of the best interest of the child standard and in a case where there is no order for support after paternity is established, and therefore no "prior decree" which grants custody of the parties' child to either party, the trial court properly applies the best interest standard. David W. v. Amy S. (Ohio App. 6 Dist., Huron, 02-23-1996) No. H-95-029, 1996 WL 76054, Unreported.

A child custody case that involves no prior paternity adjudication or support order does not require a showing of a change in circumstances and custody is awarded to the father in the best interest of the child. Barker v. Helton (Ohio App. 12 Dist., Butler, 09-11-1995) No. CA94-11-207, 1995 WL 540423, Unreported.

Allocating transportation responsibilities to nonresidential parent in parenting-time order is not inherently unfair. Gregory v. Gregory (Ohio App. 2 Dist., 08-10-2007) 172 Ohio App.3d 822, 877 N.E.2d 333, 2007-Ohio-4098. Child Custody ☞ 213

Parenting time order allocating transportation responsibilities to husband, as nonresidential parent, was not an abuse of discretion, in absence of demonstration by husband that transportation was an undue burden for him or that the parties lived far apart. Gregory v. Gregory (Ohio App. 2 Dist., 08-10-2007) 172 Ohio App.3d 822, 877 N.E.2d 333, 2007-Ohio-4098. Child Custody ☞ 213

Testimony from wife's brother and brother-in-law regarding incidents of alleged domestic violence by husband toward wife was relevant when determining allocation of parental rights and responsibilities in divorce action. Barry v. Barry (Ohio App. 8 Dist., 09-28-2006) 169 Ohio App.3d 129, 862 N.E.2d 143, 2006-Ohio-5008. Child Custody ☞ 451

The preeminent purposes of the Uniform Child Custody Jurisdiction Act (UCCJA) are avoiding jurisdictional competition and conflict with the courts of other states and assuring that the state with the optimum access to the relevant facts makes the custody determination, thus protecting the best interests of the child. State ex rel. Seaton v. Holmes (Ohio, 11-19-2003) 100 Ohio St.3d 265, 798 N.E.2d 375, 2003-Ohio-5897. Child Custody ☞ 703

A proposed settlement of child support and custody disputes was not in the best interests of the child; the former husband was five-and-one-half years delinquent in child support, and the former wife waived a major portion of the court-ordered entitlements for the benefit of the child. In re Contemnor Caron (Ohio Com.Pl., 04-27-2000) 110 Ohio Misc.2d 58, 744 N.E.2d 787. Child Custody ☞ 35; Child Support ☞ 44

The best interests of a child demand that the father pay to the mother, for the benefit of the child, all monies and expenses previously ordered by the court. In re Contemnor Caron (Ohio Com. Pl., 04-27-2000) 110 Ohio Misc.2d 58, 744 N.E.2d 787. Child Support ☞ 430

Former husband's assertion that he and former wife would be unable to cooperate to advance child's best interests, without more, was insufficient to render shared parenting against child's best interests, given overwhelming contrary testimony from experts, child's step-father, and former wife, based on experts' interviews with both parents and with child. In re Marriage of Shore (Ohio App. 8 Dist., 08-18-1999) 135 Ohio App.3d 374, 734 N.E.2d 395, dismissed, appeal not allowed 87 Ohio St.3d 1459, 720 N.E.2d 541. Child Custody ☞ 472

Divorce courts have discretion in matters of child custody, in accordance with statutory elements, standards and factors focusing on best interests of child. Marshall v. Marshall (Ohio App. 3 Dist., 01-15-1997) 117 Ohio App.3d 182, 690 N.E.2d 68. Child Custody ☞ 7; Child Custody ☞ 76

Irrespective of terminology involved, ultimate goal of court in considering request to modify child custody decree is the same: to determine what is best for the child. Waggoner v. Waggoner (Ohio App. 9 Dist., 05-08-1996) 111 Ohio App.3d 1, 675 N.E.2d 541, dismissed, appeal not allowed 77 Ohio St.3d 1445, 671 N.E.2d 1284. Child Custody ☞ 554

Since there was no prior formal award of custody, trial court's judgment entry awarding legal custody of child to father was an initial award of custody, as opposed to modification of prior custodial arrangement, and as such, no showing of change of circumstances was required and trial court properly applied the best interest standard. In re Wells (Ohio App. 12 Dist., 12-26-1995) 108 Ohio App.3d 41, 669 N.E.2d 887. Children Out-of-wedlock ☞ 20.10

Where child custody determination in habeas corpus proceeding is simply between child's natural parents, and neither party has judicial order awarding custody, court will determine what custody award will be in child's best interests. Pegan v. Crawmer (Ohio, 07-24-1996) 76 Ohio St.3d 97, 666 N.E.2d 1091, 1996-Ohio-419. Habeas Corpus ☞ 532(1)

Trial court is bound to consider best interests of child when determining which parent should have custody of minor child in divorce proceeding. Rowe v. Franklin (Ohio App. 1 Dist., 06-28-1995) 105 Ohio App.3d 176, 663 N.E.2d 955, appeal not allowed 74 Ohio St.3d 1464, 656 N.E.2d 1299. Child Custody ☞ 76

Under RC 3109.04 as presently constituted, the custodian of a child is selected with reference to the best interest of the child. Thrasher v. Thrasher (Summit 1981) 3 Ohio App.3d 210, 444 N.E.2d 431, 3 O.B.R. 240.

Under the provisions of GC 8033 (RC 3109.04), when the question of custody arises between the parents, "the court shall decide which one of them shall have the care, custody and control of such offspring, taking into account that which would be for their best interests." Ludy v. Ludy (Franklin 1948) 84 Ohio App. 195, 82 N.E.2d 775, 53 Ohio Law Abs. 47, 39 O.O. 241, rehearing denied 84 N.E.2d 120, 53 Ohio Law Abs. 47.

Trial court's finding that it was in children's best interests for husband to be designated residential and custodial parent of children was not against manifest weight of the evidence, although children related well to wife, and although wife was physically healthy, was capable of caring for children, and was established in her home and community; evidence indicated that husband was capable of caring for children, husband was established in his home and community, and children were integrated into husband's extended family, while wife preferred that children be integrated into her fiance's extended family. Graves v. Graves (Ohio App. 9 Dist., Medina, 07-24-2002) No. 3242-M, 2002-Ohio-3740, 2002 WL 1626144, Unreported. Child Custody ☞ 467

Substantial competent, credible evidence supported finding that the award of residential custody of parties' three minor children to wife was in children's best interest; statutory factors were carefully considered, husband had been found guilty of domestic violence towards wife, although wife had history of depression, at time of hearing she was in good health, and wife's interaction and interrelationship with children was good while husband's interaction and interrelationship with children was questionable. Grimm v. Grimm (Ohio App. 7 Dist., Jefferson, 06-19-2002) No. 01 JE 6, 2002-Ohio-3208, 2002 WL 1396799, Unreported. Child Custody ☞ 61; Child Custody ☞ 62; Child Custody ☞ 467

8. —— Child's wishes and interview with judge, initial allocation of rights and responsibilities and "best interest"

Evidence in post-divorce action for reallocation of parental rights and responsibilities was sufficient to support finding of a change in circumstances since initial custody decree, although child had always expressed a desire to live with mother; there was evidence child's desire to live with her mother, as well as a feeling of detachment from her father, had only intensified as child had matured over 10-year period following divorce, and child was able to clearly articulate her reasons for wanting to live with mother, as well as her reasons for not wanting to live with father. Pellettiere v. Pellettiere (Ohio App. 2 Dist., Montgomery, 10-09-2009) No. 23141, 2009-Ohio-5407, 2009 WL 3246751, Unreported. Child Custody ☞ 557(2); Child Custody ☞ 566

Trial court did not abuse its discretion by finding, on father's motion to modify custody, that a change in circumstance had occurred sufficient to warrant modification of order in divorce proceeding that designated mother as child's residential parent; child stated that he wished to live with his father, child was one month shy of eight at time of hearing on father's motion and had matured from toddler-hood to boyhood since original designation of residential parent, he now attended school and participated in extracurricular activities, and mother had remarried and had other young children with her new husband. Wilson v. Wilson (Ohio App. 4 Dist., Lawrence, 09-11-2009) No. 09CA1, 2009-Ohio-4978, 2009 WL 3043967, Unreported. Child Custody ☞ 576

Trial court ensured under applicable statute that seven-year-old child possessed sufficient reasoning ability to express his wishes regarding father's post-divorce motion to modify custody, where record reflected that the magistrate spoke with the child and found him to be bright and articulate, and record contained no evidence to suggest otherwise. Wilson v. Wilson (Ohio App. 4 Dist., Lawrence, 09-11-2009) No. 09CA1, 2009-Ohio-4978, 2009 WL 3043967, Unreported. Child Custody ☞ 654

Statute providing that, in determining child's best interest for purposes of making allocation of the parental rights and responsibilities for care of the child, the court shall interview in chambers any or all of the involved children regarding their wishes was not applicable in contempt proceeding, seeking to hold ex-wife in contempt for failure to abide by court's visitation order; contempt proceeding was not an original proceeding for the allocation of parental rights and responsibilities as contemplated by statute. Forrester v. Forrester (Ohio App. 2 Dist., Greene, 09-30-2005) No. 2004 CA 81, 2005-Ohio-5230, 2005 WL 2403955, Unreported. Child Custody ☞ 871

In divorce action in which husband sought shared parenting plan, evidence supported trial court's finding that oldest child's wishes favored adopting the shared parenting plan; trial judge conducted an in camera interview with child and found that his wishes favored a shared parenting arrangement. Swain v. Swain (Ohio App. 4 Dist., Pike, 08-06-2005) No. 05CA740, 2005-Ohio-4321, 2005 WL 1995388, Unreported. Child Custody ☞ 427

Trial court did not abuse its discretion in questioning child with respect to child's preferences as to allocation of parental rights and responsibilities in connection with final judgment of divorce, despite court's failure specifically to ask child how much time he wished to spend with each parent or to present child with alternative parenting schedules, where court was aware from previous discussions with guardian ad litem that child was dissatisfied with the existing parenting schedule, questioned child about his concerns, asked detailed questions about time he spent with each parent, and asked him with which parent he would prefer to spend greater amount of time. Kellogg v. Kellogg (Ohio App. 10 Dist., Franklin, 12-30-2004) No. 04AP-382, 2004-Ohio-7202, 2004 WL 3090184, Unreported, appeal not allowed 105 Ohio St.3d 1546, 827 N.E.2d 328, 2005-Ohio-2188. Child Custody ⇨ 506

Statute governing conduct of interviews with minor children in custody proceedings regarding their wishes and concerns with respect to allocation of parental rights and responsibilities did not require trial court, in fashioning final judgment of divorce, to ask child how much time he would like to spend with each parent, or to present child with alternative parenting schedules from which to choose; statute did not specify particular course of action to be followed by trial court during the interview, nor did it require court to ask specific questions or pose questions in particular manner. Kellogg v. Kellogg (Ohio App. 10 Dist., Franklin, 12-30-2004) No. 04AP-382, 2004-Ohio-7202, 2004 WL 3090184, Unreported, appeal not allowed 105 Ohio St.3d 1546, 827 N.E.2d 328, 2005-Ohio-2188. Child Custody ⇨ 506

Trial court was not required to enter written findings concerning child's wishes and concerns, in proceedings for allocation of parental rights and responsibilities incident to divorce, where court did not determine that child had sufficient reasoning ability to express his wishes and concerns with respect to the allocation of parental rights, but that it would not be in child's best interest to determine those wishes and concerns because of special circumstances. Kellogg v. Kellogg (Ohio App. 10 Dist., Franklin, 12-30-2004) No. 04AP-382, 2004-Ohio-7202, 2004 WL 3090184, Unreported, appeal not allowed 105 Ohio St.3d 1546, 827 N.E.2d 328, 2005-Ohio-2188. Child Custody ⇨ 511

Fact that trial court listed other factors that it considered, in addition to 11-year-old child's wishes, did not translate to a failure to give child's expressed wishes appropriate weight on motion to modify custody. Ebinger v. Ebinger (Ohio App. 12 Dist., Warren, 09-07-2004) No. CA2003-10-100, No. CA2003-10-103, 2004-Ohio-4784, 2004 WL 2003948, Unreported. Child Custody ⇨ 659

Trial court's question to minor child, as to whether he wanted to live with mother or father, before court determined child did not have maturity to understand circumstances did not render court's interview and maturity finding unlawful, in hearing on father's motion to modify parenting agreement; question was posed to child in context of determining if he possessed sufficient reasoning ability to

make his choice, and child's answers to court's questions supported court's finding. Keller v. Keller (Ohio App. 4 Dist., Jackson, 11-26-2003) No. 02CA19, No. 03CA3, 2003-Ohio-6462, 2003 WL 22860832, Unreported, appeal not allowed 102 Ohio St.3d 1421, 807 N.E.2d 366, 2004-Ohio-2003. Child Custody ⇨ 654

Trial court was required to interview child to determine his wishes as to parent with which he wanted to reside once mother moved for court to interview child, even though guardian ad litem indicated child had expressed differing opinions, thus, requiring remand for interview child. In Re Brazile (Ohio App. 1 Dist., Hamilton, 12-06-2002) No. C-010694, 2002-Ohio-6652, 2002 WL 31728896, Unreported. Child Custody ⇨ 506; Child Custody ⇨ 924

The trial court is obligated to conduct an in camera interview with the children with respect to their wishes regarding custody upon the request of one of the parties prior to entry of the final decree. Bauer v. Bauer (Ohio App. 12 Dist., Warren, 06-30-1997) No. CA97-01-003, 1997 WL 368371, Unreported.

In designating the residential parent, a court abuses discretion in adopting the findings and recommendations of the referee over the preference of the minor children to live with their mother in light of a repetitive theme throughout the proceedings of her activities with other men and her failure to be a "dutiful" wife and mother with respect to (1) her employment outside the home, (2) fewer "home cooked meals," (3) the husband being forced to take a more active role in the care of their children and home, and (4) failure to attend and meet the standards of the husband's church; the law imposes no religious standards for wives and mothers, and such evidence has no relevance other than to paint the wife and mother in a bad light. Sellman v. Sellman (Ohio App. 4 Dist., Highland, 09-26-1996) No. 95CA888, 1996 WL 557553, Unreported.

In allocating parental rights and responsibilities it is discretionary with the judge in the absence of a motion from any of the parties to interview minor children in chambers; however, when either party moves the court to interview the children in chambers, it is mandatory that the judge conduct the interview. Troll v. Troll (Ohio App. 7 Dist., Belmont, 01-17-1996) No. 94-B-17, 1996 WL 19079, Unreported.

Evidence did not support trial court's finding in child custody dispute that father did not attempt to influence children, who had expressed desire to live with mother at temporary custody hearing; father did not call children and did not attempt to set up visitation after hearing, one child felt that father did not return her phone calls because of child's statement that she wanted to stay with mother, and father told another child that he did not know why child bothered to call after what she had said in court. In re Custody of Harris (Ohio App. 2 Dist., 07-14-2006) 168 Ohio App.3d 1, 857 N.E.2d 1235, 2006-Ohio-3649, on subsequent appeal

2006-Ohio-3746, 2006 WL 2037323. Child Custody ⊂⟶ 78

Although process involving sealing transcript of trial court's in camera interviews with minor children in child custody proceedings requires a party to "blindly" raise an assignment of error on the in camera interview issue, it still allows for appellate review while protecting the best interests of the child. Myers v. Myers (Ohio App. 5 Dist., 01-09-2007) 170 Ohio App.3d 436, 867 N.E.2d 848, 2007-Ohio-66. Child Custody ⊂⟶ 908

Trial court acted within its discretion when it decided, on its own initiative, not to interview children in chambers regarding their wishes as to custody in divorce action; interview was not required since neither party requested that court interview children. Barry v. Barry (Ohio App. 8 Dist., 09-28-2006) 169 Ohio App.3d 129, 862 N.E.2d 143, 2006-Ohio-5008. Child Custody ⊂⟶ 506

Trial court allocating parental rights and responsibilities must, pursuant to statute, interview child if either party requests interview; interview is discretionary only if no party requests it. Badgett v. Badgett (Ohio App. 7 Dist., 07-15-1997) 120 Ohio App.3d 448, 698 N.E.2d 84. Child Custody ⊂⟶ 427

Trial court must make record of any in camera interview with children involved in custody proceedings, to be kept under seal for review on appeal; audio recording, video recording, or stenographic record must be made, and no other person other than child and court personnel authorized by judge may be present with judge in chambers. Donovan v. Donovan (Ohio App. 12 Dist., 04-29-1996) 110 Ohio App.3d 615, 674 N.E.2d 1252. Child Custody ⊂⟶ 427

Upon mother's motion in custody proceeding, trial court was required to appoint guardian ad litem for child before it could interview child. State ex rel. Papp v. James (Ohio, 06-01-1994) 69 Ohio St.3d 373, 632 N.E.2d 889, 1994-Ohio-86. Infants ⊂⟶ 78(1)

Mother was not entitled to writ of mandamus to compel trial court in custody proceeding to appoint guardian ad litem for child; although mother had clear right to have trial court appoint guardian ad litem for child it sought to privately interview in custody proceedings, appeal was adequate remedy for violation of that right. State ex rel. Papp v. James (Ohio, 06-01-1994) 69 Ohio St.3d 373, 632 N.E.2d 889, 1994-Ohio-86. Mandamus ⊂⟶ 4(4)

In determining the best interests of the child one factor to be considered is her wish to live with her father; where both parents live in the same school district, have homes and jobs to provide ample support for their children, and neither has any emotional problems, the trial court's naming the father as the residential parent is not arbitrary, capricious, or unreasonable. Williams v. Williams (Hardin 1992) 80 Ohio App.3d 477, 609 N.E.2d 617.

In a case in which both unmarried parents of two minor children seek custody after their relationship ends, a trial court errs in interviewing the children in chambers out of the presence of the parties and off the record where the children are eight and six years of age. In re Markham (Meigs 1990) 70 Ohio App.3d 841, 592 N.E.2d 896, dismissed, jurisdictional motion overruled 60 Ohio St.3d 702, 573 N.E.2d 118.

An award of custody of the eldest minor child of the marriage to the former husband is proper despite the child's election of the former wife as custodian where substantial evidence negated the child's election, including evidence that the home where the former wife was the caretaker was unsanitary and that she periodically left the children unattended, including the youngest who was handicapped; the paramount consideration is always the best interest of the child, and the child's election is only one factor to be considered in the trial court's custody determination, which is to be given the utmost deference. Thornton v. Thornton (Wyandot 1990) 70 Ohio App.3d 317, 590 N.E.2d 1375.

RC 3109.04(C) requires the court to determine whether it is in the child's best interests to allow him to elect to choose his custodial parent, not whether the choice made by the child is in his best interests under RC 3109.04(C). Buckles v. Buckles (Franklin 1988) 46 Ohio App.3d 102, 546 N.E.2d 950.

A child's choice of custodian, made pursuant to RC 3109.04(A), is not binding on the court, but is merely one factor for the court to consider in determining the best interests of the child. In re Brazell (Ohio Com.Pl. 1986) 27 Ohio Misc.2d 7, 499 N.E.2d 925, 27 O.B.R. 68.

Where one child is of an age to make a choice, such election does not mean that siblings must also be placed with same parent. Glimcher v. Glimcher (Franklin 1971) 29 Ohio App.2d 55, 278 N.E.2d 37, 58 O.O.2d 37.

Failure of trial court to consider preference of child over ten years of age in determining question of custody, is reversible error. Holland v. Holland (Cuyahoga 1947) 75 N.E.2d 489, 49 Ohio Law Abs. 237.

The statute is mandatory insofar as it allows children ten years of age or more to choose parent with whom they prefer to live, except that court shall determine their custodian when parent so selected is unfitted by reason of moral depravity, habitual drunkenness or incapacity. Dailey v. Dailey (Ohio 1945) 146 Ohio St. 93, 64 N.E.2d 246, 32 O.O. 29. Child Custody ⊂⟶ 78

Privilege of child to choose parent with which he wishes to live exists only where court finds that both parents have capacity to properly care for child. Godbey v. Godbey (Hamilton 1942) 70 Ohio App. 450, 44 N.E.2d 810, 36 Ohio Law Abs. 511, 25 O.O. 184.

Trial court's failure to interview dependent child in permanent child custody proceeding to clarify child's feelings was not erroneous, given that child's wishes are only one of several factors to be considered and child was of tender age. In re Bradford

(Ohio App. 10 Dist., Franklin, 08-08-2002) No. 01AP-1151, 2002-Ohio-4013, 2002 WL 1813406, Unreported, appeal not allowed 97 Ohio St.3d 1470, 779 N.E.2d 236, 2002-Ohio-6347. Infants ⟲ 207

A letter which states a child's preference for custodial parent, which is addressed to the attorney of a party, rather than to the court, does not constitute a valid election under RC 3109.04(A). McFiggen v McFiggen, No. 46996 (8th Dist Ct App, Cuyahoga, 2-2-84).

The wishes of a child twelve years of age or older is a factor the court must consider, but not controlling upon it. Fisk v Fisk, No. CA85-03-009 (12th Dist Ct App, Preble, 8-12-85).

A court does not commit error by assuming that a four-year-old child lacks the reasoning capacity to express her own wishes without questioning her, or by failing to make a record of its interviews with two older children, as RC 3109.04 indicates that the interviews are to be confidential and are not to be disclosed to the parents. Linger v Linger, No. 92-CA-120, 1993 WL 274318 (5th Dist Ct App, Licking, 6-30-93).

Court is bound by this section to consider preference expressed by child over ten years of age as to which of divorced parents child desires to live with, and failure so to do is reversible error. Mollencamp v Mollencamp, 18 Abs 90 (App, Franklin 1934).

9. —— Constitutional issues, initial allocation of rights and responsibilities and "best interest"

Trial court order in child custody action was "ambiguous, confusing, and not certain in itself," as it purported both to modify custody and to terminate shared parenting plan, and thus order was void for vagueness and Court of Appeals lacked jurisdiction to consider mother's appeal from the order. Clyburn v. Gregg (Ohio App. 4 Dist., Ross, 09-21-2010) No. 09CA3115, 2010-Ohio-4508, 2010 WL 3722260, Unreported. Child Custody ⟲ 661; Child Custody ⟲ 902

Federal habeas jurisdiction was not available to review state court child-custody determination. Jacobson v. Summit County Children Services Bd (C.A.6 (Ohio), 10-25-2006) No. 05-4397, 202 Fed. Appx. 88, 2006 WL 3039795, Unreported. Habeas Corpus ⟲ 532(1)

Former husband was not denied due process of law when trial court dismissed his motion to modify custody/parental rights and responsibilities for lack of jurisdiction without completing evidentiary hearing, even though it would have been prudent to complete the hearing, trial court did schedule an evidentiary hearing where eight witnesses testified on husband's behalf, and there was no indication that husband would have proffered any evidence to exclude California as having jurisdiction in matter. Nick A.V. v. Laurie Anne F. (Ohio App. 6 Dist., Huron, 01-14-2005) No. H-04-004, 2005-Ohio-132,

2005 WL 78515, Unreported. Child Custody ⟲ 779; Constitutional Law ⟲ 4396

Mother did not have a constitutional right to effective assistance of counsel during proceeding on father's motion for legal custody of child and mother's motion to suspend father's visitation; there was no constitutional right to counsel in a civil case between individual parents. In re Rosier Lemmon (Ohio App. 5 Dist., Stark, 03-15-2004) No. 2003 CA 00306, 2004-Ohio-1290, 2004 WL 540299, Unreported. Child Custody ⟲ 500

Separation agreement incorporated into divorce decree was not invalid on grounds of no meeting of minds or informed consent; although Chinese husband argued that he had limited understanding of English, no understanding of law, and he did not understand terms of agreement when he agreed to them, transcript of final hearing indicated that court questioned him at length regarding terms, he understood what was being asked of him, he understood terms of agreement, and he was represented by counsel. Zamonski v. Wan (Ohio App. 2 Dist., Montgomery, 02-21-2003) No. 19392, 2003-Ohio-780, 2003 WL 366756, Unreported. Divorce ⟲ 11.5

Mother failed to preserve for appeal issue of whether statute limiting court's power to alter prior decree which allocated parental rights and responsibilities only to situations in which change in circumstances of child or parents has occurred since prior decree was unconstitutional, as mother failed to raise issue before trial court. In re Mefford (Ohio App. 2 Dist., Greene, 01-24-2003) No. 2002CA37, 2003 Ohio 313, 2003 WL 164811, Unreported. Child Custody ⟲ 904

Language contained in summons and mother's motion for temporary orders was insufficient as a means of providing father with notice that hearing would result in final judgment on issues of custody, child support, and visitation of parties' minor child, and thus, father was denied his constitutional right to due process when hearing was transformed into final hearing on merits of case. Wyatt v. Decsi (Ohio App. 9 Dist., Summit, 12-18-2002) No. 21072, 2002-Ohio-6993, 2002 WL 31828821, Unreported. Child Custody ⟲ 410; Child Support ⟲ 180; Constitutional Law ⟲ 4396

Rooker Feldman doctrine did not require district court to abstain from consideration of claims for prospective declaratory relief of custodial parents of minor children, who alleged that ex parte custody procedures followed by judge of county domestic relations court violated their due process rights, since some claims did not require reversal of specific decisions made by state court or substantive review of merits of decisions made by that court, and other claims may not have implicated merits of such decisions, depending upon how parents put on their proof. Butterfield v. Steiner (S.D.Ohio, 09-05-2002) No. C2-01-1224, 2002 WL 31159304, Unreported. Courts ⟲ 509

A court's decision to require the residential parent to live close enough to the non-residential parent to facilitate visitation deals with the custody of the parties' children and does not prohibit either party from travelling state to state or relocating; the residential parent is merely prohibited from taking the children with her if she decides to relocate and the prohibition does not violate the residential parent's right to travel. Alvari v. Alvari (Ohio App. 4 Dist., Lawrence, 02-02-2000) No. 99CA05, 2000 WL 133849, Unreported.

A residential parent is in contempt of court for changing the religious practice of the parties' minor child in violation of a previously issued standard order of visitation which conditions any change in the child's religious practices on agreement of the parents and approval of the court; the visitation order does not unconstitutionally prohibit either parent the freedom to choose a religion or to enjoy the right to expose their child to such religion. Cappelli v. Cappelli (Ohio App. 7 Dist., Mahoning, 11-16-1998) No. 97 CA 15, 1998 WL 811346, Unreported, dismissed, appeal not allowed 85 Ohio St.3d 1441, 708 N.E.2d 208.

Application of statute governing allocation and modification of parental rights and responsibilities to dismiss for lack of jurisdiction, due to son's emancipation, father's claims on motion to show cause that mother had failed to timely honor his request for records related to the parties' son did not implicate the state constitution's impairment of contracts clause, where statute was enacted prior to divorce decree in which mother agreed to provide copies of the children's educational records to the father upon request, and thus statute did not impair vested contractual rights. Flanagan v. Flanagan (Ohio App. 9 Dist., 11-26-2007) 174 Ohio App.3d 77, 880 N.E.2d 962, 2007-Ohio-6209. Child Custody ⚖ 4; Child Custody ⚖ 855; Constitutional Law ⚖ 2759

Requirement that the trial court's in camera interviews of minor children in child custody proceedings be recorded is designed to protect the due process rights of the parents; due process protection is achieved by sealing the transcript of the in camera interview and making it available only to the courts for review. Myers v. Myers (Ohio App. 5 Dist., 01-09-2007) 170 Ohio App.3d 436, 867 N.E.2d 848, 2007-Ohio-66. Constitutional Law ⚖ 4396

Due process rights of the parents must be balanced against the best interests of the child in a child custody proceeding. Myers v. Myers (Ohio App. 5 Dist., 01-09-2007) 170 Ohio App.3d 436, 867 N.E.2d 848, 2007-Ohio-66. Constitutional Law ⚖ 4396

Trial court's sua sponte revocation of former wife's residential-parent status violated former wife's due process rights; revocation did not arise out of emergency situation or occur in response to motion filed by former wife or former husband, revocation followed former wife's request that in camera interview of children be rescheduled, and former wife received no notice of proposed change in custody or of what she had done wrong. Myers

v. Myers (Ohio App. 5 Dist., 01-09-2007) 170 Ohio App.3d 436, 867 N.E.2d 848, 2007-Ohio-66. Child Custody ⚖ 576; Child Custody ⚖ 606; Constitutional Law ⚖ 4396

Overriding concern of courts in child custody cases must be the best interests of the child, which may, at times, conflict with the due process rights of the parents. Myers v. Myers (Ohio App. 5 Dist., 01-09-2007) 170 Ohio App.3d 436, 867 N.E.2d 848, 2007-Ohio-66. Child Custody ⚖ 76

Appellate court, in determining whether mother's due process rights were violated by trial court's consideration of report of child's guardian ad litem (GAL), which was filed with trial court on day before trial began, would follow provisions of specific statute providing for GAL's report to be made available to parent not less than five days before trial upon written request, rather than statute governing reports generally, which did not govern GAL reports, as father's pending motion was for reallocation of parental rights and responsibilities. Wilburn v. Wilburn (Ohio App. 9 Dist., 11-06-2006) 169 Ohio App.3d 415, 863 N.E.2d 204, 2006-Ohio-5820. Child Custody ⚖ 916

Trial court did not abuse its discretion in denying mother's motion for appointment of counsel for child, in proceeding in which father sought reallocation of parental rights and responsibilities; child was not a party to the case, nor was child required to be made a party, and there was no conflict between child's desires and recommendations of guardian ad litem (GAL) appointed for child, in that child wished to remain with her mother and GAL recommended that mother retain custody of child. Wilburn v. Wilburn (Ohio App. 9 Dist., 11-06-2006) 169 Ohio App.3d 415, 863 N.E.2d 204, 2006-Ohio-5820. Infants ⚖ 90

Mother's due process rights were not violated due to trial court's reliance on report of child's guardian ad litem, which was filed with trial court on day before trial began on father's motion seeking reallocation of parental rights and responsibilities, as neither GAL nor trial court were required by statute to provide mother or her counsel with a copy of report, absent a written request for report prior to trial, and neither mother nor her counsel made such request, at beginning of trial judge commented to parties that he had received report, and mother and her counsel had plenty of opportunity during 30-week span of trial to obtain and review report. Wilburn v. Wilburn (Ohio App. 9 Dist., 11-06-2006) 169 Ohio App.3d 415, 863 N.E.2d 204, 2006-Ohio-5820. Child Custody ⚖ 616; Constitutional Law ⚖ 4396

Within the framework of the governing statutes, the overriding principle in custody cases between a parent and nonparent is that natural parents have a fundamental liberty interest in the care, custody, and management of their children; this interest is protected by the Due Process Clause of the Fourteenth Amendment to the United States Constitution and by Due Process Clause of Ohio Constitution. In re Hockstok (Ohio, 12-27-2002) 98 Ohio

St.3d 238, 781 N.E.2d 971, 2002-Ohio-7208, modified 98 Ohio St.3d 1476, 784 N.E.2d 709, 2003-Ohio-980. Child Custody ⇐ 42; Constitutional Law ⇐ 4396

Biological or adoptive parent's fundamental due process right to make decisions concerning the care, custody and control of one's children does not embrace the right to have all decisions recognized or approved in law. In re Bonfield (Ohio, 12-13-2002) 97 Ohio St.3d 387, 780 N.E.2d 241, 2002-Ohio-6660. Constitutional Law ⇐ 4391; Constitutional Law ⇐ 4395

Enforcement of parties' prior agreement, embodied in shared parenting agreement incident to divorce, that their child would attend religious school was within trial court's discretion, and therefore not in violation of former husband's constitutional rights. In re Marriage of Shore (Ohio App. 8 Dist., 08-18-1999) 135 Ohio App.3d 374, 734 N.E.2d 395, dismissed, appeal not allowed 87 Ohio St.3d 1459, 720 N.E.2d 541. Child Custody ⇐ 228; Constitutional Law ⇐ 1408

Provision of modified shared parenting plan governing selection of religious school to be attended by parties' child did not articulate preference for either party's religious beliefs over that of the other, and was not based on either party's religious beliefs; former husband was given primary physical custody of child, and former wife was given right to select three schools, from which former husband would select school to be attended by child, with former wife given right to choose should former husband fail or refuse to do so. In re Marriage of Shore (Ohio App. 8 Dist., 08-18-1999) 135 Ohio App.3d 374, 734 N.E.2d 395, dismissed, appeal not allowed 87 Ohio St.3d 1459, 720 N.E.2d 541. Child Custody ⇐ 141; Child Custody ⇐ 227

Findings in support of determination that it was in best interests of children for custody to be awarded to their maternal uncle, rather than their father, following their mother's death necessarily also tended to prove that father was unsuitable to have custody, and implicit finding of unsuitability precluded father from establishing violation of his fundamental right under State and Federal Constitutions to custody of his children as against third parties. Baker v. Baker (Ohio App. 9 Dist., 08-21-1996) 113 Ohio App.3d 805, 682 N.E.2d 661, appeal not allowed 77 Ohio St.3d 1525, 674 N.E.2d 376. Child Custody ⇐ 42; Child Custody ⇐ 271

Father in custody dispute with children's maternal uncle, which fell within statute allowing award of custody to relative other than parent when in best interest of child, was not similarly situated to parent involved in custody dispute under statute establishing jurisdiction of juvenile courts over various matters, which required explicit finding of unsuitability before awarding custody to any nonparent, as opposed to only relatives, and father's right to equal protection of law was therefore not violated by lack of explicit finding of unsuitability in connection with award of custody to maternal uncle. Baker v. Baker (Ohio App. 9 Dist.,

08-21-1996) 113 Ohio App.3d 805, 682 N.E.2d 661, appeal not allowed 77 Ohio St.3d 1525, 674 N.E.2d 376. Child Custody ⇐ 42; Constitutional Law ⇐ 3738

Former husband's federal action against his former wife, seeking declaration that state divorce decree was void as a violation of due process, was not a core domestic relations case to which domestic relations exception to federal jurisdiction applied; action did not seek declaration of marital or parental status, but instead presented a constitutional claim in which it was incidental that the underlying action involved a divorce. Catz v. Chalker (C.A.6 (Ohio), 04-16-1998) 142 F.3d 279, opinion amended on denial of rehearing 243 F.3d 234. Federal Courts ⇐ 8

10. —— Custody while case is pending, effect, initial allocation of rights and responsibilities and "best interest"

Since ex-wife had already voluntarily placed her child in custody of paternal great-grandmother, ex-wife's motion for custody did not constitute an "original" custody determination and, therefore, her motion would be treated as one for custody modification, and change of circumstances test applied, and court was not required to make a parental unsuitability finding in determining whether child's custody arrangement should be modified. Anderson v. Anderson (Ohio App. 12 Dist., Warren, 10-26-2009) No. CA2009-03-033, 2009-Ohio-5636, 2009 WL 3416024, Unreported. Child Custody ⇐ 579

Placement of child in custody of paternal grandparents was not in best interest of child, insofar as child's conception resulted from father's criminal sex offenses perpetrated on sixteen-year-old mother, which charges were still pending. In re Goff (Ohio App. 11 Dist., Portage, 12-12-2003) No. 2001-P-0144, 2003-Ohio-6768, 2003 WL 22952808, Unreported. Infants ⇐ 222

Direct adverse impact of custodial mother's conduct on child was standard that applied when making initial custody determination some 18 months after parties separated and mother assumed custody; interests in refraining from moving child between parents are same as in postdecree modification decisions. Rowe v. Franklin (Ohio App. 1 Dist., 06-28-1995) 105 Ohio App.3d 176, 663 N.E.2d 955, appeal not allowed 74 Ohio St.3d 1464, 656 N.E.2d 1299. Child Custody ⇐ 48; Child Custody ⇐ 84

Provision of Hague Convention on Civil Aspects of International Child Abduction, under which the court "shall," without considering whether child is settled in new environment, order the child's return if a period of less than one year has elapsed from the date of the wrongful removal or retention, is not a statute of limitations which could be subject to equitable tolling. Anderson v. Acree (S.D.Ohio, 12-11-2002) 250 F.Supp.2d 872, subsequent determination 250 F.Supp.2d 876. Child Custody ⇐ 808; Child Custody ⇐ 814

11. —— **Discretion of court, initial allocation of rights and responsibilities and "best interest"**

Trial court acted within its discretion in concluding that the harm likely to be caused by a change of environment in relocating children to Ohio outweighed the advantages of the change, if any, thus supporting order denying father's motion to modify shared parenting decree that had named mother children's residential parent; children had previously lived in Ohio, but, children had since relocated out of state with mother, and, as the party seeking modification of custody, father was required to show a change in circumstances warranting modification, and children's familiarity with an alternate placement, Ohio, did not establish a changed circumstance. Gillum v. Gillum (Ohio App. 2 Dist., Montgomery, 05-27-2011) No. 24401, 2011-Ohio-2558, 2011 WL 2084148, Unreported. Child Custody ☞ 576

Trial court abused its discretion in dismissing for lack of jurisdiction father's motion to renew his motion for reallocation of parental rights and responsibilities; when father filed his initial motion for reallocation of parental rights and responsibilities, he also filed an affidavit, commonly known as a Uniform Child Custody Jurisdiction Act (UCCJA) affidavit, which was a statement informing the court that no other court had taken jurisdiction over child, but father did not file a new UCCJA affidavit with respect to his motion to renew his motion for reallocation of parental rights, and father's failure to file another UCCJA affidavit did not divest court of jurisdiction. Dole v. Dole (Ohio App. 5 Dist., Holmes, 03-18-2011) No. 10CA013, 2011-Ohio-1314, 2011 WL 977053, Unreported. Child Custody ☞ 769

Evidence supported trial court's designation of mother as child's primary residential parent; mother had been the primary caregiver of child for all of child's life, child was integrated into the community, attended school and church functions with mother, and had been well cared for by her maternal grandparents during his mother's hospitalization and convalescence following an alleged assault, and, while child's visitation with father was arguably hindered at times by the maternal grandparents at mother's direction, this action was initiated because of questions and allegations that father had assaulted mother and caused her head injury. Ott v. Ott (Ohio App. 6 Dist., Huron, 01-28-2011) No. H-10-007, 2011-Ohio-356, 2011 WL 319955, Unreported. Child Custody ☞ 210

Trial court acted within its discretion in divorce action when it named husband residential parent and legal custodian of children, even though wife had handled 90 percent of parenting duties before she stabbed husband in chest in presence of children, and even though husband's decision to leave children with his parents for six months after he was stabbed was probably based more on convenience than necessity; wife's conduct in stabbing husband in presence of children was horrific. Thompson v. Thompson (Ohio App. 12 Dist., But-

ler, 01-18-2011) No. CA2010-03-052, 2010-Ohio-158, 2011 WL 282424, Unreported. Child Custody ☞ 58; Child Custody ☞ 61

Because no motion for shared parenting with an accompanying plan was filed with the trial court, shared parenting was not an issue before the court, and, to the extent sufficient evidence was presented for the court to make a determination regarding the children's best interests, it possessed the discretion to allocate parental rights and responsibilities. Rymers v. Rymers (Ohio App. 11 Dist., Lake, 12-23-2010) No. 2009-L-160, 2010-Ohio-6439, 2010 WL 5550227, Unreported. Child Custody ☞ 414

Trial court did not abuse its discretion by concluding mother's shared parenting plan was not in the best interest of the children or by concluding that it was in the best interest of children that father be named the residential parent and legal custodian for the children, where, although diagnosed with a schizophrenic mood disorder, mother refused to seek treatment and denied that she was out of touch with reality, mother's behavior had caused significant stress for the children, mother was unable to focus on the needs and lives of her children, and both children wished to live with father in the home they knew and the stable environment that father provided. Vaughan v. Vaughan (Ohio App. 9 Dist., Medina, 12-06-2010) No. 10CA0014-M, 2010-Ohio-5928, 2010 WL 4927629, Unreported. Child Custody ☞ 62; Child Custody ☞ 78; Child Custody ☞ 147

12. —— **Education and school performance, initial allocation of rights and responsibilities and "best interest"**

Trial court's modification of the shared parenting plan to make father the residential parent of out-of-wedlock child for school purposes and its adoption of equal parenting time was not an abuse of discretion; the guardian ad litem (GAL) and the family court evaluator testified that a weekly rotation, where child spent one week with mother and then one week with father, would be beneficial to child, that mother was too involved in child's school, and they both recommended enrolling child in a new school for a fresh start. Ankney v. Bonos (Ohio App. 9 Dist., Summit, 11-15-2006) No. 23178, 2006-Ohio-6009, 2006 WL 3304343, Unreported. Children Out–of–wedlock ☞ 20.10

Even if trial court erred in including general language, in settlement entry regarding parties' parenting rights, allowing mother access to all records relating to child's health care and other records maintained for child, rather than using more specific language limiting access to medical and school records, error was harmless, where child's psychological records maintained by school counselor would be school records accessible to mother even under narrower language father sought to include in settlement entry, and father never asked trial court to make finding that it would not be in child's best interests for mother to review child's psychological records. Lucas v. Reese (Ohio App. 4 Dist., Athens, 07-20-2005) No. 05CA2, 2005-Ohio-3846,

2005 WL 1791583, Unreported. Child Custody ☞ 923(1)

Although settlement entry in child custody dispute did not include father's requirement that mother provide child with state-certified tutor when needed during summers child spent with mother, agreement could be interpreted as so requiring and, thus, it was not unreasonable for trial court to refuse to add term "state-certified" to modify term "tutor" in settlement entry filed by mother's attorney; agreement required mother to provide academic tutoring or other services needed by child and, if tutoring by state-certified tutor was necessary for child to complete her course requirements, services of state-certified tutor would be necessary services mother would be responsible for providing under agreement. Lucas v. Reese (Ohio App. 4 Dist., Athens, 07-20-2005) No. 05CA2, 2005-Ohio-3846, 2005 WL 1791583, Unreported. Child Custody ☞ 36

Trial court did not abuse its discretion in not naming husband residential parent and legal custodian of children during school year; judgment entry indicated trial court followed recommendation of guardian ad litem when allocating parenting time, trial court noted custody decision was close call because both parties were suitable parents, and children, who had been living with wife, were doing well in their current school district. Schoren v. Schoren (Ohio App. 6 Dist., Huron, 04-29-2005) No. H-04-019, 2005-Ohio-2102, 2005 WL 1010016, Unreported. Child Custody ☞ 146; Child Custody ☞ 147; Child Custody ☞ 421

Trial court's decision to terminate divorced parties' shared parenting plan and award custody of both children to father was not against the manifest weight of the evidence; mother had, at various times, denied father orally agreed upon parenting time, teachers at children's school believed that father was much more involved and interested in children's academic progress than mother, mother continued to smoke in her home even though it adversely effected the health of one child who had asthma, children lived in fear of mother's new husband, and new husband assaulted father in front of the children. Matis v. Matis (Ohio App. 9 Dist., Medina, 01-12-2005) No. 04CA0025-M, 2005 Ohio 72, 2005 WL 53432, Unreported. Child Custody ☞ 469

Divorced mother waived all but plain error on claim that trial court improperly considered hearsay evidence regarding observations by minor children's teachers during proceeding in which court terminated parties' shared parenting plan and awarded custody of both children to father, where mother failed to object to the teachers' testimony during the proceeding. Matis v. Matis (Ohio App. 9 Dist., Medina, 01-12-2005) No. 04CA0025-M, 2005-Ohio-72, 2005 WL 53432, Unreported. Child Custody ☞ 904

Juvenile court's findings of fact supported denial of father's motion to modify shared parenting plan and name father residential parent for school purposes; although court did not express its findings with respect to all statutory factors, court considered relevant factors, including child's adjustment to his home, school, and community, the child's interaction and interrelationship with his parents, the mother's failure to completely comply with the shared parenting plan, and the general well-being of the child in his current living situation. In re Jacobberger (Ohio App. 11 Dist., Geauga, 12-10-2004) No. 2003-G-2538, 2004-Ohio-6937, 2004 WL 2937402, Unreported. Child Custody ☞ 576

Evidence supported trial court's findings that modification of shared parenting plan to name father residential parent for school purposes was not in best interests of child; although there was evidence that child's grades improved when child received father's assistance with homework, proposed change would disrupt child's well-established routine and require change of schools, child was progressing well under current shared parenting plan, and guardian ad litem stated that change proposed could be detrimental to child's progress in school. In re Jacobberger (Ohio App. 11 Dist., Geauga, 12-10-2004) No. 2003-G-2538, 2004-Ohio-6937, 2004 WL 2937402, Unreported. Child Custody ☞ 576

Designating husband as residential parent for school enrollment purposes, under shared parenting plan implemented in divorce action, was not an abuse of discretion, where spouses and child had lived in husband's home during the marriage and husband intended to continue living in the home after the divorce. Wei v. Shen (Ohio App. 12 Dist., Butler, 11-24-2003) No. CA2002-12-300, 2003 WL 22763865, Unreported. Child Custody ☞ 147

Fact that wife paid day-care expenses was not a relevant factor for determining, in divorce action which implemented a shared parenting plan, which spouse should be designated as residential parent for purposes of school enrollment. Wei v. Shen (Ohio App. 12 Dist., Butler, 11-24-2003) No. CA2002-12-300, 2003 WL 22763865, Unreported. Child Custody ☞ 147

Trial court's failure to include provision in judgment entry incorporating shared parenting agreement that parties could change children's school without court approval did not constitute abuse of discretion, insofar as trial court advised father that anything that was mutually agreed upon could be changed without coming to court. Dobran v. Dobran (Ohio App. 7 Dist., Mahoning, 03-24-2003) No. 02 CA 14, 2003-Ohio-1605, 2003 WL 1689584, Unreported. Child Custody ☞ 528

Issue of whether custody of parties' children would change if wife moved from children's present school district was not ripe for judicial review on wife's appeal from divorce judgment that granted custody of children to her with condition that husband would become residential parent if she moved from current school district. Ferris v. Ferris (Ohio App. 4 Dist., Meigs, 03-11-2003) No. 02CA4,

2003-Ohio-1284, 2003 WL 1227326, Unreported. Child Custody ☞ 916

Trial court had jurisdiction in child support proceeding, under statutory provisions permitting under certain circumstances a support award above and beyond standard amount, to order that noncustodial parent pay portion of child's private school tuition, even though public schools were available. Smith v. Null (Ohio App. 4 Dist., 01-29-2001) 143 Ohio App.3d 264, 757 N.E.2d 1200, 2001-Ohio-2386. Child Support ☞ 118

Quality of education parties' children would receive at school operated by wife's church was legitimate consideration in determining residential custody, and consideration thereof did not amount to improper consideration of wife's religious affiliation, where public school children would attend while in husband's custody offered programs for gifted students and wide curriculum, and where court expressed concerns with church-operated school's below-average class sizes, problems with teacher staffing, lack of teacher experience, lack of curriculum, and sheltered lifestyle. Arthur v. Arthur (Ohio App. 5 Dist., 10-22-1998) 130 Ohio App.3d 398, 720 N.E.2d 176. Child Custody ☞ 46

Post-divorce motions filed by mother and father to determine child's school district dealt with allocation of parental rights and responsibilities for care of child, and thus fell within scope of statute governing court's allocation of such rights and responsibilities. Badgett v. Badgett (Ohio App. 7 Dist., 07-15-1997) 120 Ohio App.3d 448, 698 N.E.2d 84. Child Custody ☞ 105

In a change of custody dispute initiated by the child's father in response to the child's school situation, father's remarriage, attractive home, and affluent lifestyle do not outweigh the stability in the child's life by maintaining custody with the mother; where the child attends summer school and is returned from the third to the second grade, there is no evidence to suggest that transfer to a school in the father's district would resolve whatever problems in school the child may experience or produce advantages for the child that outweigh the harm involved. Averill v. Bradley (Ohio App. 2 Dist., Montgomery, 12-14-2001) No. 18939, 2001-Ohio-6982, 2001 WL 1597881, Unreported.

13. —— Expert testimony required or not, initial allocation of rights and responsibilities and "best interest"

There was no competent and credible evidence in the record that unwed mother exhibited signs of either Munchausen Syndrome by Proxy or Parental Alienation Syndrome, and therefore, trial court abused its discretion to the extent it considered either Munchausen Syndrome by Proxy or Parental Alienation Syndrome when determining best interest of child in custody action; the only witness qualified to testify called mother's actions "situationally appropriate" and not signs of Parental Alienation Syndrome, no affirmative evidence was offered to show that mother had Parental Alienation Syndrome, and father offered no evidence

that mother either falsified or caused child's health problems. Rice v. Lewis (Ohio App. 4 Dist., Scioto, 04-10-2009) No. 08CA3238, 2009-Ohio-1823, 2009 WL 1027544, Unreported. Children Out-of-wedlock ☞ 20.3

The trial court's denial of wife's request for a psychological evaluation of the parties' child was not an abuse of discretion, during divorce proceeding; wife requested the evaluation on the last day of hearings, a psychological evaluation and testimony relative to it had already been presented, and the entire matter had been heard over a period of four months. Ward v. Ward (Ohio App. 5 Dist., Stark, 02-21-2006) No. 2005CA00118, 2006-Ohio-851, 2006 WL 438685, Unreported. Child Custody ☞ 425

For purposes of statute providing that an order made in special proceeding that affects substantial right constitutes a final appealable order, trial court's order that denied husband's request to have parties and children undergo independent psychological evaluations by expert of husband's choice in divorce action did not affect a "substantial right"; neither statute governing medical, psychological, and psychiatric examinations in child custody proceedings nor civil procedure rule governing physical and mental examinations of parties during discovery gave father right to select professional who would conduct examination. Yazdani-Isfehani v. Yazdani-Isfehani (Ohio App. 4 Dist., 12-26-2006) 170 Ohio App.3d 1, 865 N.E.2d 924, 2006-Ohio-7105. Child Custody ☞ 902

In custody cases where the best interests of the child are at issue, RC 3109.04 does not require that expert testimony be presented. Mohrman v. Mohrman (Sandusky 1989) 57 Ohio App.3d 33, 565 N.E.2d 1283. Child Custody ☞ 475

14. —— Findings of fact and conclusions of law, initial allocation of rights and responsibilities and "best interest"

Evidence was sufficient to support finding that husband had engaged in domestic violence against wife, which was relevant to child custody determination in divorce proceedings; wife testified that husband had slammed her against a sofa, at which time their son appeared and referred to the incident as the time husband put "Mommy in a timeout," and wife testified to another incident where husband repeatedly accelerated and slammed on the brakes of vehicle in the middle of the road to scream at wife. Ruble v. Ruble (Ohio App. 12 Dist., Madison, 07-05-2011) No. CA2010-09-019, 2011-Ohio-3350, 2011 WL 2611797, Unreported. Child Custody ☞ 48

Although trial court failed to make an express finding in its judgment entry that the harm likely to be caused by a change of environment was outweighed by the advantages of the change of environment to the child, the record demonstrated that trial court engaged in the statutorily required advantages-versus-harm balancing test in arriving at its decision to change custody of the parties' child from mother to father, and credible and competent evidence existed to support the trial court's determination; while the trial court found that child was developing well and had no health, learning or behavioral issues, it placed great emphasis on mother's ongoing failure to facilitate companionship and a relationship with and between child and father, and determined that a change of environment would allow for the better facilitation of companionship and relationship with both of the parents. Schneider v. Schneider (Ohio App. 11 Dist., Trumbull, 01-21-2011) No. 2010-T-0012, 2011-Ohio-252, 2011 WL 320906, Unreported. Child Custody ☜ 637; Child Custody ☜ 659

Trial court considering child custody as part of divorce was not per se prohibited from adopting and incorporating by reference mother's proposed findings of fact and conclusions of law rather than drafting its own entry. Mummey v. Mummey (Ohio App. 7 Dist., Noble, 09-07-2010) No. 10 NO 371, 2010-Ohio-4243, 2010 WL 3503501, Unreported. Child Custody ☜ 511

Trial court considered the statutory custody factors when it designated ex-wife as the residential parent and legal custodian of their son; there was no requirement that trial court expressly and separately address each best-interest factor, court reviewed the psychological evaluations of the parties, the evaluator recommended that ex-wife be given custody, and the court found that the analysis and recommendation made by the evaluating psychologist was a strong one. Wise v. Wise (Ohio App. 2 Dist., Montgomery, 03-19-2010) No. 23424, 2010-Ohio-1116, 2010 WL 1038393, Unreported. Child Custody ☜ 421; Child Custody ☜ 511

15. —— Guardian ad litem, initial allocation of rights and responsibilities and "best interest"

Guardian ad litem (GAL) fees in case involving allocation of parental rights were in the nature of support, rather than court costs, based on language of the agreed judgment entry so stating and the duties performed by GAL, which were to protect the best interests of the minor children, and, as such, trial court did not err as a matter of law in conducting a contempt proceeding against unwed mother for her failure to pay her portion of the GAL fees pursuant to the judgment entry; majority of GAL fees were generated due to protracted custody battle between mother and father, allegations were made that mother was not meeting children's medical and developmental needs, and GAL was actively involved in all aspects of the investigation and litigation. Raleigh v. Hardy (Ohio App. 5 Dist., Licking, 09-10-2009) No. 08 CA 0140, 2009-Ohio-4829, 2009 WL 2933727, Unreported. Children Out-of-wedlock ☜ 69(7); Infants ☜ 83

Trial court's finding that unwed mother did not meet her burden in establishing her inability to pay was not an abuse of discretion in contempt proceeding brought against mother for nonpayment of guardian ad litem (GAL) fees, which were in nature of support, in allocation of parental rights action;

mother stated that she had only recently gained sporadic employment, but court doubted mother's credibility and trustworthiness. Raleigh v. Hardy (Ohio App. 5 Dist., Licking, 09-10-2009) No. 08 CA 0140, 2009-Ohio-4829, 2009 WL 2933727, Unreported. Children Out-of-wedlock ☜ 69(7)

Trial court did not abuse its discretion by permitting the guardian ad litem to advocate in the best interests of the children and recommend that the children be placed with husband without providing a written report and recommendation prior to trial in dissolution action; no written request for the guardian ad litem's report was made by either party, guardian was present at trial and was subject to cross-examination but was not called to the stand by either party, and, at trial, the parties stipulated to the timing of the submission of the report of the guardian ad litem. Lawson v. Lawson (Ohio App. 5 Dist., Licking, 01-13-2009) No. 08-CA-37, 2009-Ohio-248, 2009 WL 153439, Unreported. Child Custody ☜ 421

Juvenile court had authority to allow guardian ad litem to represent juvenile at hearing on mother's motion seeking judicial release of her delinquent child and approve guardian ad litem's fees for services provided at the hearing, even though guardian ad litem's appointment arose from domestic relations court in prior child custody proceedings between mother and father, where, by filing her motion in the juvenile court asking it to accept jurisdiction of custody and all other issues regarding the child then pending, mother essentially consented to the juvenile court's appointment of guardian ad litem. In re Kovacic (Ohio App. 11 Dist., Lake, 12-26-2008) No. 2008-L-101, 2008-Ohio-6882, 2008 WL 5389712, Unreported. Infants ☜ 83; Infants ☜ 205

Evidence supported conclusion that children's guardian ad litem (GAL) properly fulfilled her duties and was not biased against mother, in proceeding commenced by mother to reallocate parental rights and responsibilities, and, thus, mother's due process rights were not violated; while GAL did not state in her report that mother was a good mother, such evidence was before trial court via GAL's testimony, and, while GAL's report did not include investigation of father's home, the GAL did visit father's home, and she testified that she did not file supplemental report after completing home investigations because she did not find anything during investigations to change her recommendation. Brunip v. Nickerson (Ohio App. 7 Dist., Columbiana, 09-30-2008) No. 07-CO-42, 2008-Ohio-5052, 2008 WL 4416456, Unreported, appeal not allowed 120 Ohio St.3d 1525, 901 N.E.2d 245, 2009-Ohio-614. Child Custody ☜ 616; Constitutional Law ☜ 4396

Order requiring former husband to pay all costs of guardian ad litem and psychological examination while ordering parties to split other court costs was supported by trial court's findings that husband requested both guardian ad litem and psychological evaluation, husband later asked court not to pursue some of those issues, and husband had financial resources to pay for those costs. Fisher v. Fisher (Ohio App. 3 Dist., Henry, 10-24-2005) No. 7-05-03, 2005-Ohio-5615, 2005 WL 2709526, Unreported. Child Custody ☞ 942; Infants ☞ 83

Guardian ad litem's investigation was sufficient to support report supporting trial court's determination that residential and legal custody of child born out of wedlock be awarded to father; despite mother's claim that guardian ad litem was improperly influenced by fact that mother's boyfriend was an ex-convict, guardian ad litem interviewed numerous individuals before making recommendation, guardian ad litem attempted to contact mother's boyfriend but was unsuccessful, and guardian ad litem recommended that parents share custody and only listed as a "consideration" that father should be the residential parent if mother continued to allow ex-convict boyfriend to reside in her home. John A.L. v. Sheri B. (Ohio App. 6 Dist., Lucas, 10-07-2005) No. L-04-1250, 2005-Ohio-5357, 2005 WL 2471040, Unreported. Children Out–of–wedlock ☞ 20.4

Trial court's failure to require guardian ad litem, who was appointed to interview divorcing parties and their child, to submit written report and trial court's failure to conduct hearing providing parties with opportunity to cross-examine guardian violated due process and was abuse of discretion, where guardian was essentially performing function of investigator, who was required by statute to file report and be subject to cross-examination. Schill v. Schill (Ohio App. 11 Dist., Geauga, 09-24-2004) No. 2002-G-2465, 2004-Ohio-5114, 2004 WL 2803230, Unreported. Child Custody ☞ 421; Child Custody ☞ 500; Constitutional Law ☞ 4386

Trial court did not meet with children before allocating parental rights and responsibilities, and thus trial court was not required to appoint a guardian ad litem for children, even though mother requested one. Feltz v. Feltz (Ohio App. 3 Dist., Mercer, 08-09-2004) No. 10-04-04, 2004-Ohio-4160, 2004 WL 1771072, Unreported. Infants ☞ 78(7)

Trial court acted within its discretion when it entered child custody award, even though court failed to follow the recommendation of the guardian ad litem; court considered all statutory factors, determined that former wife had the more appropriate parenting skills, and court was not bound by guardian's recommendation. Baker v. Baker (Ohio App. 6 Dist., Lucas, 02-06-2004) No. L-03-1018, 2004-Ohio-469, 2004 WL 226092, Unreported. Child Custody ☞ 421

Trial court was entitled to accept report of guardian ad litem when making custody determination as part of divorce proceedings; although mother alleged that guardian ad litem only performed a "minimal, perfunctory investigation," record indicated that guardian ad litem issued five reports which evidenced a solid working knowledge of facts and issues presented. Ream v. Ream (Ohio App. 5 Dist., Licking, 04-14-2003) No. 02-CA-000071, 2003-Ohio-2144, 2003 WL 1962332, Unreported. Child Custody ☞ 421

When financial affidavits of a party in a child custody proceeding generally indicate financial distress, but the trial court finds some inconsistencies in the financial affidavits, a hearing on the issue would be more appropriate than concluding that the party was not indigent and was not entitled to some accommodation when determining how the guardian ad litem (GAL) would get paid. Myers v. Myers (Ohio App. 5 Dist., 01-09-2007) 170 Ohio App.3d 436, 867 N.E.2d 848, 2007-Ohio-66. Infants ☞ 80(1)

Under statute allowing appointment of guardian ad litem (GAL) when court conducts in camera interview of children in custody proceeding and under local rule governing deposit of GAL fees, trial court is required to determine that request for GAL has been waived only when a person fails to post reasonable amount of bond within reasonable amount of time; person's financial circumstances are used to determine what is reasonable. Myers v. Myers (Ohio App. 5 Dist., 01-09-2007) 170 Ohio App.3d 436, 867 N.E.2d 848, 2007-Ohio-66. Infants ☞ 80(1)

Former wife was not ordered to post reasonable amount of bond within reasonable time when trial court required former wife to post $500 bond within 30 days regarding fees of guardian ad litem (GAL) in proceeding involving revocation of former wife's residential-parent status and court's in camera interview of minor children, and thus former wife's failure to post bond in compliance with order did not result in waiver of request for GAL, although former wife's income figures were inconsistent; income figures indicated limited financial circumstances, and former wife's affidavit showed that former wife was barely making it financially. Myers v. Myers (Ohio App. 5 Dist., 01-09-2007) 170 Ohio App.3d 436, 867 N.E.2d 848, 2007-Ohio-66. Infants ☞ 80(1)

Mother waived her right of access to report of child's guardian ad litem, in proceeding commenced by father seeking reallocation of his parental rights and responsibilities, as she failed to provide a written request for report as required by statute and rule, she failed to request a recess on first day of trial to review report, she did not obtain a copy of report during pendency of trial, and she did not cross-examine GAL regarding report. Wilburn v. Wilburn (Ohio App. 9 Dist., 11-06-2006) 169 Ohio App.3d 415, 863 N.E.2d 204, 2006-Ohio-5820. Child Custody ☞ 616

"Adoption" is not a custody proceeding and may only become one at such time that a guardian, as opposed to a guardian ad litem, is appointed to protect the child's best interest. In re Adoption of Reams (Franklin 1989) 52 Ohio App.3d 52, 557 N.E.2d 159, dismissed 50 Ohio St.3d 707, 553 N.E.2d 684. Adoption ☞ 1

A court may make minor children of a pending divorce parties to the action and appoint a guardian ad litem to represent them where the interests of the minor children are or may be substantially different from either or both of the parents. Barth

v. Barth (Ohio Com.Pl. 1967) 12 Ohio Misc. 141, 225 N.E.2d 866, 39 O.O.2d 83, 41 O.O.2d 166.

16. —— **Guardianship effect, initial allocation of rights and responsibilities and "best interest"**

Trial court did not abuse its discretion by granting divorced mother permission to travel outside the country with minor child; trial court denied mother permission to travel to her home country of Kyrgyzstan or any neighboring country due to civil unrest, and father was incarcerated and unable to care for child. Moore v. Moore (Ohio App. 5 Dist., Licking, 08-11-2005) No. 04CA112, 2005-Ohio-4152, 2005 WL 1924348, Unreported. Child Custody ☞ 261

Termination of a guardianship of seven months' duration, where the mother has not contracted away her rights, should be determined pursuant to a good cause test not a best interest standard. In re Spriggs, No. 89–CA–1803 (4th Dist Ct App, Scioto, 4–24–90).

17. —— **Habeas corpus, initial allocation of rights and responsibilities and "best interest"**

Husband was not entitled to seek habeas corpus relief from judgment entered in divorce action granting permanent custody of minor child to wife, as he had an adequate remedy by way of appeal. Evans v. Klaeger (Ohio, 12-01-1999) 87 Ohio St.3d 260, 719 N.E.2d 546, 1999-Ohio-55, reconsideration denied 87 Ohio St.3d 1495, 722 N.E.2d 527. Habeas Corpus ☞ 280

Habeas corpus relief is exception rather than general rule in child custody actions. Pegan v. Crawmer (Ohio, 07-24-1996) 76 Ohio St.3d 97, 666 N.E.2d 1091, 1996-Ohio-419. Habeas Corpus ☞ 532(1)

To prevail on petition for writ of habeas corpus in child custody case, petitioner must establish that child is being unlawfully detained, and petitioner has superior legal right to custody of child. Pegan v. Crawmer (Ohio, 07-24-1996) 76 Ohio St.3d 97, 666 N.E.2d 1091, 1996-Ohio-419. Habeas Corpus ☞ 532(1)

Former wife, by being able to bring contempt motion before trial court concerning former husband's alleged failure to comply with custody order, had adequate remedy at law, and thus former wife's habeas corpus petition would be dismissed, although former husband had appealed judgment containing custody order and had obtained stay of non-custody order contained in that judgment. Williams v. Williams (Ohio App. 11 Dist., Trumbull, 08-14-2002) No. 2002-T-0105, 2002-Ohio-4224, 2002 WL 1902571, Unreported. Habeas Corpus ☞ 280

18. —— **Immorality of parent, initial allocation of rights and responsibilities and "best interest"**

A court's inquiry into the moral conduct or standards of a custodial parent is limited to a determination of the effect of such conduct on the child.

Whaley v. Whaley (Lawrence 1978) 61 Ohio App.2d 111, 399 N.E.2d 1270, 15 O.O.3d 136; In re Rex (Seneca 1981) 3 Ohio App.3d 198, 444 N.E.2d 482, 3 O.B.R. 226.

Trial court was required to consider whether shared parenting plan proposed by cohabiting, same sex partners was in the best interest of child, in light of evidence of benefits from having two caregivers, legally responsible for child's welfare, as well as evaluation conducted by clinical psychologist concluding that both partners were effective parents, committed to child's well being. In re J.D.M. (Ohio App. 12 Dist., Warren, 10-11-2004) No. CA2003-11-113, No. CA2004-04-035, No. CA2004-04-040, 2004-Ohio-5409, 2004 WL 2272063, Unreported. Children Out–of–wedlock ☞ 20.3

In proceeding on petition of cohabiting, same sex partners for shared custody of child, trial court was required to make a conclusive finding as to who was child's mother and which partner was assuming parental rights. In re J.D.M. (Ohio App. 12 Dist., Warren, 10-11-2004) No. CA2003-11-113, No. CA2004-04-035, No. CA2004-04-040, 2004-Ohio-5409, 2004 WL 2272063, Unreported. Children Out–of–wedlock ☞ 20.4

Lack of a present controversy between cohabiting, same sex partners was not an impediment to consideration of petition seeking entry of shared custody agreement for child. In re J.D.M. (Ohio App. 12 Dist., Warren, 10-11-2004) No. CA2003-11-113, No. CA2004-04-035, No. CA2004-04-040, 2004-Ohio-5409, 2004 WL 2272063, Unreported. Children Out of wedlock ☞ 20.4

Trial court was not required to structure parenting time schedule so as to prevent child, who was born during mother's wedlock to step-father but conceived as result of premarital relationship with natural father, from being left with step-father, even though step-father was an alcoholic, where step-father's alcoholism did not pose a danger to child. Bates v. Gould (Ohio App. 4 Dist., Highland, 02-02-2004) No. 03CA12, 2004-Ohio-571, 2004 WL 235199, Unreported. Children Out–of–wedlock ☞ 20.9

Award of child custody to mother was warranted as to child born during mother's wedlock to step father but conceived as result of premarital relationship with natural father, even though mother's new husband was an alcoholic and was allegedly violent; step-father's alcoholism did not adversely impact child, no evidence indicated that step-father was violent, and Court of Appeals had to presume that statutory factors were considered, absent findings of fact and conclusions of law. Bates v. Gould (Ohio App. 4 Dist., Highland, 02-02-2004) No. 03CA12, 2004-Ohio-571, 2004 WL 235199, Unreported. Children Out–of–wedlock ☞ 20.3; Children Out–of–wedlock ☞ 20.11

Evidence supported trial court's denial of former husband's motion to show cause, which alleged that former wife denied his visitation rights with child;

record contained no evidence that former wife interfered with former husband's visitation rights, child was afraid of her father and did not want to see him, and both the child's counselor and the court-appointed social worker had recommended that former husband participate in the child's counseling, but former husband refused. Oleksy v. Oleksy (Ohio App. 8 Dist., Cuyahoga, 10-23-2003) No. 82646, 2003-Ohio-5657, 2003 WL 22413671, Unreported. Child Custody ☞ 870

Evidence of mother's sexual promiscuity, lack of stable housing, and relationships with six separate live-in men in five-year period was sufficient to support conclusion, in child custody proceeding, that best interests of child were to be with her father. Stout v. Korosy (Ohio App. 5 Dist., Stark, 06-09-2003) No. 2002CA00361, 2003-Ohio-3084, 2003 WL 21378609, Unreported. Child Custody ☞ 41; Child Custody ☞ 48; Child Custody ☞ 53; Child Custody ☞ 56

Provision of divorce judgment ordering that wife, who was awarded custody of parties' minor children, keep children away from man with whom wife was romantically involved until a psychologist determined that being in that man's presence would not harm the children was not abuse of discretion, where children expressed fear of that man to guardian ad litem, and wife admitted during her testimony that children saw a gun belonging to that man when he stayed at wife's residence for two weeks. Ferris v. Ferris (Ohio App. 4 Dist., Meigs, 03-11-2003) No. 02CA4, 2003-Ohio-1284, 2003 WL 1227326, Unreported. Child Custody ☞ 528

Where the issue is the appropriate residential parent for the youngest child whose father is not the husband in the divorce action it is reasonable to restrict the evidence to events and circumstances that affect the child within his lifetime; evidence of the mother's past sexual misconduct to show that she is not an appropriate residential parent is irrelevant. Eitel v. Eitel (Ohio App. 4 Dist., Pickaway, 08-23-1996) No. 95CA11, 1996 WL 482703, Unreported, appeal not allowed 77 Ohio St.3d 1525, 674 N.E.2d 376, reconsideration denied 78 Ohio St.3d 1415, 675 N.E.2d 1252.

Upon remand, in proceedings on cohabiting same-sex partners' petition for allocation of parental rights and responsibilities with respect to one partner's biological and adopted children, trial court was required to exercise its discretion in giving due consideration to all known factors in determining best interest of subject children. In re Bonfield (Ohio, 12-13-2002) 97 Ohio St.3d 387, 780 N.E.2d 241, 2002-Ohio-6660. Child Custody ☞ 42; Child Custody ☞ 310

Cohabiting, unmarried female same-sex partner of children's biological and adoptive mother was not children's "parent" for purposes of entering into shared parenting agreement. In re Bonfield (Ohio, 12-13-2002) 97 Ohio St.3d 387, 780 N.E.2d 241, 2002-Ohio-6660. Child Custody ☞ 274

Trial court's award of child custody to husband, in divorce action, was not improperly based on immorality of wife's admitted adultery; trial court was aware of the "direct adverse impact" test, under which the court could consider moral principles when awarding child custody but only in relation to the direct or probable effect of the wife's nonmarital sexual conduct on the children, and trial court's findings emphasized the harmful effects of wife's lifestyle, rather than the immorality of her affairs. Anderson v. Anderson (Ohio App. 7 Dist., 03-12-2002) 147 Ohio App.3d 513, 771 N.E.2d 303, 2002-Ohio-1156. Child Custody ☞ 53

The "direct adverse impact" test, under which the court could consider moral principles when awarding child custody, but only in relation to the direct or probable effect of the parent's conduct on the child, could also be applied in a divorce action when determining nonresidential parent's visitation rights, where the nonresidential parent had admitted to adultery. Anderson v. Anderson (Ohio App. 7 Dist., 03-12-2002) 147 Ohio App.3d 513, 771 N.E.2d 303, 2002-Ohio-1156. Child Custody ☞ 192

Trial court's visitation order in divorce action, prohibiting any unrelated male individual from being present during wife's visitation, was improper, even if wife had committed adultery during the marriage and during a previous marriage; trial court had not considered whether presence of an unrelated male individual would have a direct adverse impact on the children, and the broad prohibition of "any" male individual from being present during visitation was not tailored to fit the specific concern the trial court was attempting to address. Anderson v. Anderson (Ohio App. 7 Dist., 03-12-2002) 147 Ohio App.3d 513, 771 N.E.2d 303, 2002-Ohio-1156. Child Custody ☞ 219

Trial court properly excluded evidence of ex-wife's alleged extramarital affairs in divorce proceeding involving custody dispute, where ex-husband failed to establish a connection between ex-wife's alleged extra-marital affairs and child's well-being. Arnold v. Arnold (Ohio App. 12 Dist., 11-01-1999) 135 Ohio App.3d 465, 734 N.E.2d 837. Child Custody ☞ 451

Evidence was insufficient to support determination that sexual orientation of former husband, who had custody of child of marriage and who was living in openly homosexual relationship, had directly and adversely affected child since prior custody decision, as would warrant modification of parental rights and responsibilities on that basis; investigator recommended that child continue to live with husband, psychologist did not make any recommendation regarding custody and did not find that child had been adversely affected, and no witnesses testified that husband's sexual orientation had adversely affected child. Inscoe v. Inscoe (Ohio App. 4 Dist., 06-16-1997) 121 Ohio App.3d 396, 700 N.E.2d 70. Child Custody ☞ 637

Parent's sexual orientation, standing alone, has no relevance to decision concerning allocation of parental rights and responsibilities. Inscoe v. Inscoe (Ohio App. 4 Dist., 06-16-1997) 121 Ohio

App.3d 396, 700 N.E.2d 70. Child Custody ⊙ 53;
Child Custody ⊙ 562

In determining whether parental nonmarital sexual conduct is having direct harmful effect on child, as will give that conduct relevance in connection with allocation of parental rights and responsibilities, primary focus should be on child's present physical and psychological welfare and developmental potential; unless accompanied by clearly adverse collateral consequences, moral impact should be ignored. Inscoe v. Inscoe (Ohio App. 4 Dist., 06-16-1997) 121 Ohio App.3d 396, 700 N.E.2d 70. Child Custody ⊙ 55

Former judge, who had entered visitation order in connection with divorce proceeding, was properly precluded from testifying, at hearing on subsequent motion for modification of parental rights and responsibilities, with regard to whether he was aware of former husband's sexual orientation at time of prior hearing; matter in question was one judge had learned solely in his official capacity as judge, and husband, who stated that his sexual orientation was discussed at prior hearing, failed to show that no other witness could testify about judge's awareness. Inscoe v. Inscoe (Ohio App. 4 Dist., 06-16-1997) 121 Ohio App.3d 396, 700 N.E.2d 70. Witnesses ⊙ 71

Order limiting the overnight stays of former spouses' romantic friends was straightforward and comprehensible and provided adequate notice to the parties as to the scope and nature of the mandate. Dilworth v. Dilworth (Ohio App. 2 Dist., 11-08-1996) 115 Ohio App.3d 537, 685 N.E.2d 847. Child Custody ⊙ 659

Order preventing former spouses from having romantic guests stay overnight when the children were present modified custody provisions of divorce decree, despite trial court's statement that order served merely to remind former spouses of trial court's policy concerning parental conduct. Dilworth v. Dilworth (Ohio App. 2 Dist., 11-08-1996) 115 Ohio App.3d 537, 685 N.E.2d 847. Child Custody ⊙ 659

Trial court was required to consider, and to enter findings concerning, statutory factors for determining best interests of children before it could adopt magistrate's order preventing former spouses from having romantic guests stay overnight when the children were present. Dilworth v. Dilworth (Ohio App. 2 Dist., 11-08-1996) 115 Ohio App.3d 537, 685 N.E.2d 847. Child Custody ⊙ 562; Child Custody ⊙ 652; Child Custody ⊙ 659

Awarding custody of child to father based on mother's move to pursue career, attending law school, and engaging in sexual conduct with recently separated man, resulting in pregnancy, was an abuse of discretion absent showing that mother's conduct had direct adverse impact on best interests of child. Rowe v. Franklin (Ohio App. 1 Dist., 06-28-1995) 105 Ohio App.3d 176, 663 N.E.2d 955, appeal not allowed 74 Ohio St.3d 1464, 656 N.E.2d 1299. Child Custody ⊙ 53; Child Custody ⊙ 67

Although court is not obligated to wear blinders as to parent's morals, including sexual conduct, when determining best interests of child in custody dispute, consideration of parent's life-styles and moral values is limited to determination of direct or probable effect of parental conduct on physical, mental, emotional, and social development of child. Rowe v. Franklin (Ohio App. 1 Dist., 06-28-1995) 105 Ohio App.3d 176, 663 N.E.2d 955, appeal not allowed 74 Ohio St.3d 1464, 656 N.E.2d 1299. Child Custody ⊙ 55

The award of custody of male children to a father who admits to a past homosexual liaison is improper where the mother is fit to be granted custody despite her recent drug use. Glover v. Glover (Brown 1990) 66 Ohio App.3d 724, 586 N.E.2d 159, motion overruled 55 Ohio St.3d 715, 563 N.E.2d 725.

In making an initial award of custody, the trial court is bound to consider the best interests of the child. A court is not required to find that the mother's lesbian relationship will have an adverse impact on the child in order to award custody to the father; rather, the court need only consider the effects of the mother's relationship upon the child. Mohrman v. Mohrman (Sandusky 1989) 57 Ohio App.3d 33, 565 N.E.2d 1283.

A court's inquiry into moral conduct of custodial parent in a dependent/neglect action is limited to a determination of the effect such conduct has on the child. In re Burrell (Ohio 1979) 58 Ohio St.2d 37, 388 N.E.2d 738, 12 O.O.3d 43.

Evidence that a woman, while separated from but still married to her husband, openly consorted with another man, permitting him to frequent her apartment in the small hours of the morning and sleep there on occasion, will support a finding that she is, thereby, unfit to retain custody of a minor child of the parties and that custody of such child should be in the husband. Bingham v. Bingham (Hamilton 1968) 14 Ohio App.2d 202, 237 N.E.2d 620, 43 O.O.2d 403.

Trial court did not abuse its discretion, in action for divorce and ancillary relief, in awarding custody of parties' child to wife, despite evidence that wife had used marijuana in the past; trial court considered all statutory factors relevant to custody and found credible wife's testimony that she had not used marijuana for the two years prior to trial, and husband lived out of state and had accrued substantial arrearage in child support by time of trial. Syslo v. Syslo (Ohio App. 6 Dist., Lucas, 09-30-2002) No. L-01-1273, 2002-Ohio-5205, 2002 WL 31166937, Unreported, appeal not allowed 98 Ohio St.3d 1477, 784 N.E.2d 711, 2003-Ohio-974, certiorari denied 124 S.Ct. 468, 540 U.S. 983, 157 L.Ed.2d 373, on subsequent appeal 2005-Ohio-4870, 2005 WL 2249583. Child Custody ⊙ 41; Child Custody ⊙ 60; Child Custody ⊙ 87

Cohabitation cannot be the sole determining factor in denying custody to a parent. Williams v Williams, No. 85AP-293 (10th Dist Ct App, Franklin, 8-27-85).

There are three possible rules to apply in an initial custody determination when the party seeking custody is cohabiting with a person not his or her spouse: (1) it is an automatic disqualification; (2) it is but one factor to consider in "best interests"; (3) it is not to be considered at all, absent specific proof of harm to the child. Wilder v Wilder, No. 84AP–604 (10th Dist Ct App, Franklin, 2–5–85).

19. —— Moving or relocation, initial allocation of rights and responsibilities and "best interest"

Sufficient evidence supported conclusion that modification of residential custody of child from mother to father was in child's best interest; mother had relocated to another state following her marriage, and had been permitted temporarily to take child with her, but child had spent a substantial portion of her time with her paternal grandparents, who played a significant role in raising her, child had close relationship with both extended families, child's paternal grandmother had been her primary caregiver, custody investigator recommended that father be granted residential custody of child, and mother had interfered with father's parenting time after relocating with child. Brammer v. Meachem (Ohio App. 3 Dist., Marion, 02-07-2011) No. 9-10-43, 2011-Ohio-519, 2011 WL 378809, Unreported. Child Custody ⟳ 577

Evidence supported trial court's decision awarding legal custody of child to father and naming father as child's primary residential parent; naming father as primary residential parent maintained child's home, school, and community ties, as well as child's relationship with supporting relatives, while mother testified that she planned to move out of state. Branum v. Branum (Ohio App. 6 Dist., Ottawa, 01-28-2011) No. OT-10-019, 2011-Ohio-361, 2011 WL 322400, Unreported. Child Custody ⟳ 83; Child Custody ⟳ 85; Child Custody ⟳ 210

Trial court did not abuse its discretion in making husband the sole residential parent and legal custodian of children if wife did not move from Idaho to Ohio; trial court reasoned that wife's contempt for husband and her fear that he might hit her or the children would negatively impact husband's relationship with the children, and, to support this reasoning, the trial court pointed to evidence that children did not timely return husband's telephone calls and he rarely spoke with them. Lumley v. Lumley (Ohio App. 10 Dist., Franklin, 12-31-2009) No. 09AP-556, 2009-Ohio-6992, 2009 WL 5174121, Unreported. Child Custody ⟳ 48; Child Custody ⟳ 57; Child Custody ⟳ 260

When determining that it was in children's best interests for wife to be designated the sole residential parent and legal custodian as long as she relocated to Ohio from Idaho, trial court did not disfavor wife because of her non-residency, but, rather, sought an arrangement conducive for both parents to actively participate in the raising of their children; trial court made its custody determination based on multiple considerations, not just wife's out-of-state residency, and trial court found it troubling that travel between Columbus and Idaho Falls required both great expense and significant time, making it impossible for husband to be even marginally involved in his children's lives. Lumley v. Lumley (Ohio App. 10 Dist., Franklin, 12-31-2009) No. 09AP-556, 2009-Ohio-6992, 2009 WL 5174121, Unreported. Child Custody ⟳ 260

Magistrate's decision, upon terminating parties' shared parenting plan and granting mother sole custody with permission to relocate, to use financial documentation from time period child support was intended to cover, commencing when the child relocated to California, rather than current data in calculating father's modified child support obligation under guidelines was justified, as either party could move to modify child support if he or she felt that amount of support was no longer proper. Kemp v. Kemp (Ohio App. 5 Dist., Stark, 11-16-2009) No. 2009-CA-00035, 2009-Ohio-6089, 2009 WL 3838256, Unreported. Child Support ⟳ 356

Order determining that it would be in child's best interest to modify the parties' shared parenting plan if mother chose to relocate out of state was not an abuse of discretion; child did not want to move, and child had extended family and friends in the area but knew no one in Colorado, where mother sought to relocate. Picciano v. Lowers (Ohio App. 4 Dist., Washington, 07-23-2009) No. 08CA38, 2009-Ohio-3780, 2009 WL 2351760, Unreported. Child Custody ⟳ 130; Child Custody ⟳ 150

Former husband's relocation to Illinois with the parties' children did not constitute a material change in circumstances warranting modification of child custody to award former wife more visitation with the children; there was no evidence that the relocation itself caused any adverse effects on the children's well-being or their relationship with former wife, their natural mother, and relocation actually brought the children closer to their mother. Thebeau v. Thebeau (Ohio App. 4 Dist., Lawrence, 09-10-2008) No. 07CA34, 2008-Ohio-4751, 2008 WL 4278127, Unreported. Child Custody ⟳ 577

In divorce action in which husband sought shared parenting plan, evidence supported trial court's finding that both husband and wife had jobs in the area and had no plans to establish an out-of-state residence. Swain v. Swain (Ohio App. 4 Dist., Pike, 08-06-2005) No. 05CA740, 2005-Ohio-4321, 2005 WL 1995388, Unreported. Child Custody ⟳ 472

Fact that husband, enlisted in the military, had been deployed overseas was not a proper consideration for Court of Appeals in determining whether trial court abused its discretion in granting custody of minor child to husband in divorce proceedings, where husband had not yet been deployed at time of custody hearing, and the deployment was not in the record of proceedings before the trial court. Broadbent v. Broadbent (Ohio App. 3 Dist., Union,

06-27-2005) No. 14-04-52, 2005-Ohio-3227, 2005 WL 1503961, Unreported. Child Custody ⬤ 907

Awarding custody of non-marital child to mother in proceeding to establish custody was in child's best interests, even though child would need to relocate to Las Vegas; effect that relocation would have on child was not sole dispositive factor. Figley v. Heather Corp (Ohio App. 9 Dist., Wayne, 05-25-2005) No. 04CA0054, 2005-Ohio-2566, 2005 WL 1225936, Unreported. Children Out–of–wedlock ⬤ 20.3

Trial court did not abuse its discretion when it denied mother's request to relocate with her children out of state; because mother's proposed move would have negative impact on children by virtually severing their relationship with their father, proposed relocation constituted change of circumstances, and testimony of parties supported finding that it would not be in children's best interest to relocate. Valentine v. Valentine (Ohio App. 12 Dist., Butler, 05-16-2005) No. CA2004-01-024, 2005-Ohio-2366, 2005 WL 1131748, Unreported. Child Custody ⬤ 261

Trial court acted within its discretion in refusing to grant former husband's motion for civil contempt against former wife in proceedings to terminate shared-parenting agreement; trial court found that while wife's moving child out of state without notice to husband indicated a lack of commitment to keeping the husband involved with the parties' child, wife's actions were not actionable contempt. Lopez v. Lopez (Ohio App. 10 Dist., Franklin, 03-17-2005) No. 04AP-508, 2005-Ohio-1155, 2005 WL 615651, Unreported. Child Custody ⬤ 852

Given change of circumstances caused by former wife's remarriage and move to another state, child's best interest was served by modifying parenting time but not modifying parental rights and responsibilities; psychologist did not think it was in child's best interest to be moved into father's household, child indicated she wanted to continue to live with former wife and wanted midweek visitation changed so that child would not miss softball practice, and child also indicated she wanted to alternate weeks with former wife and former husband during the summer. (Per Bryant, J., with two Judges concurring in judgment only.) Miller v. Miller (Ohio App. 3 Dist., Henry, 05-10-2004) No. 7-03-09, 2004-Ohio-2358, 2004 WL 1049158, Unreported. Child Custody ⬤ 568; Child Custody ⬤ 577

In deciding former wife's motion to relocate minor child to another state, trial court had no authority to prevent relocation; however, if visitation schedule were not modified, former wife would be required to comply with existing visitation schedule or face charges of contempt. (Per Bryant, J., with two Judges concurring in judgment only.) Miller v. Miller (Ohio App. 3 Dist., Henry, 05-10-2004) No. 7-03-09, 2004-Ohio-2358, 2004 WL 1049158, Unreported. Child Custody ⬤ 261

Unwed mother's actions of moving out of her parents' home to a college dormitory, leaving her child behind to be raised by her parents, constituted a change in circumstances justifying modification of custody; by moving, mother delegated day-to-day child care responsibilities to her mother and essentially relinquished her role as child's residential parent, mother saw child at her parents' house one or two weekends a month, and father now had more direct contact with child through his visitation than mother did on her visits home. Gaines v. Pelzl (Ohio App. 2 Dist., Greene, 04-23-2004) No. 2003-CA-60, 2004-Ohio-2043, 2004 WL 869549, Unreported. Children Out–of–wedlock ⬤ 20.10

Trial court did not abuse its discretion by awarding primary custody of child to mother and allowing her to move out-of-state; although mother had moved numerous times, mother provided a reasonable explanation for each of the moves and it did not indicate that mother would fail to facilitate visitation. Chirico v. Chirico (Ohio App. 2 Dist., Montgomery, 06-20-2003) No. 19722, 2003-Ohio-3238, 2003 WL 21419242, Unreported. Child Custody ⬤ 261

Determination that child's best interest was served by naming father, who had remarried and moved to Ohio, residential parent during school year was not against manifest weight of the evidence in proceeding to modify prior joint custody order; child, who had moved from mother's home in Florida to live with father while mother finished military training and technical school, had had a difficult time adjusting to her new school in Ohio, but father, with help of a school counselor, diligently worked to integrate child into his community, and child enjoyed a close relationship with her stepsister and stepmother. Dyslin v. Marks (Ohio App. 5 Dist., Stark, 04-07-2003) No. 2002CA00300, 2003-Ohio-1855, 2003 WL 1857108, Unreported. Child Custody ⬤ 564; Child Custody ⬤ 567; Child Custody ⬤ 568

Child's custody would be transferred from that of ex-wife to that of ex-husband since modification of custody was in child's best interest and there had been change of circumstances; ex–wife decided to move to Texas with child, did not tell ex-husband about this until after the decision to move had been made, and this move would adversely affect ex-husband's opportunity for visitation, and there was evidence that ex-wife had made significant decisions about child's life without ex-husband's input. Kubin v. Kubin (Ohio App. 12 Dist., 09-18-2000) 140 Ohio App.3d 367, 747 N.E.2d 851. Child Custody ⬤ 642

Mere fact that possession schedule established by court on former wife's application for modification of shared parenting plan required child to travel extensively by plane did not render schedule adverse to child's best interests, absent any showing of actual harm to child resulting from his travels. In re Marriage of Shore (Ohio App. 8 Dist., 08-18-1999) 135 Ohio App.3d 374, 734 N.E.2d 395, dismissed, appeal not allowed 87 Ohio St.3d 1459, 720 N.E.2d 541. Child Custody ⬤ 213

A trial court's award of custody of the parties' minor child to the father constitutes an abuse of discretion where the mother is the primary caretaker of the child and the court fails to consider the child's tender years, which is a relevant factor meriting consideration in determining the child's best interest, and additionally, the court improperly relies on possible future circumstances which are placed before the court through the testimony of a clinical psychologist who recommends that the father be awarded custody because he is concerned with the mother's financial and emotional instability caused by her having to relocate and find a job with limited employment qualifications. Seibert v. Seibert (Clermont 1990) 66 Ohio App.3d 342, 584 N.E.2d 41, motion overruled 53 Ohio St.3d 705, 558 N.E.2d 60.

If the best interests of the child will be served, custody will be awarded to nonresidents, either in an original custody award or in a modification of a standing custody award; a nonresident or one intending to become a nonresident will not be deprived of custody of a child merely because of her nonresidence. In re Marriage of Barber (Cuyahoga 1983) 8 Ohio App.3d 372, 457 N.E.2d 360, 8 O.B.R. 485.

Trial court did not abuse its discretion when finding that modification of child custody in favor of noncustodial parent was not in the children's best interests, even though witness testified that custodial parent married her ex-husband and children were not attending school, noncustodial parent indicated that custodial parent moved to an undisclosed location and did not bring children to an ordered visitation, and professional opined that children should have visitation with noncustodial parent. In re Surdel (Ohio App. 9 Dist., Lorain, 09-04-2002) No. 02CA007980, 2002-Ohio-4529, 2002 WL 2010201, Unreported. Child Custody ⬥ 554; Child Custody ⬥ 567; Child Custody ⬥ 568; Child Custody ⬥ 569

On noncustodial parent's motion to modify child custody, custodial parent's change of residence to an undisclosed location was a material change of circumstances that warranted a further inquiry into the best interests of the children. In re Surdel (Ohio App. 9 Dist., Lorain, 09-04-2002) No. 02CA007980, 2002-Ohio-4529, 2002 WL 2010201, Unreported. Child Custody ⬥ 568

Trial court did not abuse its discretion by failing to find wife in contempt for failure to file a notice of intention to relocate; court found that notice had been given, and without a transcript of the hearing, appellate court assumed that the trial court properly considered the evidence and credibility of the witnesses. Murray v. Murray (Ohio App. 5 Dist., Licking, 05-03-2002) No. 01-CA-00084, 2002-Ohio-2505, 2002 WL 925257, Unreported. Child Custody ⬥ 852; Child Custody ⬥ 920

20. —— Nonparent as custodian, initial allocation of rights and responsibilities and "best interest"

Trial court's determination that mother was a suitable parent was against the manifest weight of the evidence, in action in which father sought custody of child upon mother's incarceration; record clearly demonstrated, by a preponderance of the evidence, mother's total inability to provide care or support for child, given mother's history of drug abuse and failed drug treatment efforts, mother's criminal record, mother's failure to respond favorably to criminal sanctions, mother's likelihood of recidivism, mother's complete reliance upon her parents, child's maternal grandparents, to provide child's care to such extent that family members, family friends, and neighbors considered the grandparents to be child's parents, and mother did not even bother to enter an appearance in the very custody action in which the trial court determined that mother was a suitable parent. In re Schwendeman (Ohio App. 4 Dist., Washington, 02-07-2006) No. 05CA18, No. 05CA25, 2006-Ohio-636, 2006 WL 327831, Unreported. Children Out–of–wedlock ⬥ 20.10

Denial of motion seeking continuance, on first day of trial in dependency proceedings to award legal custody of child to relatives, based on mother's failure to appear was not abuse of discretion; there had been at least five continuances since filing and hearing date, mother was aware of date of final hearing, mother had not responded to attorney's diligent efforts to contact her in months prior to hearing, and attorney could not provide explanation for mother's absence. In re I.R. (Ohio App. 10 Dist., Franklin, 12-13-2005) No. 04AP-1296, 2005-Ohio-6622, 2005 WL 3416146, Unreported. Infants ⬥ 204

Evidence in child protection proceedings with respect to child's best interests did not support modification of custody award to remove child from legal custody of his maternal aunt and award legal custody of child to child's paternal aunt, despite request of child's paternal grandfather that custody be awarded to paternal aunt, where mother's parental rights had not been terminated, mother wished child to remain in custody of his maternal aunt, mother's wishes were mandatory factor to be considered, trial court failed to consider mother's wishes, and paternal grandfather's wishes were not mandatory factor. In Matter of Mouser (Ohio App. 3 Dist., Logan, 05-09-2005) No. 8-04-34, 2005-Ohio-2244, 2005 WL 1077532, Unreported. Infants ⬥ 230.1

Finding that award of legal custody of dependant infant to paternal aunt and uncle, rather than to paternal grandfather who already had custody of older sibling, would be in best interest of infant was not abuse of discretion; though both parties presented good and viable options for placement, grandfather's smoking risked aggravation of infant's pre-asthmatic condition, and aunt and uncle appeared to have more realistic understanding of infant's developmental levels. In re M.S. (Ohio App. 9 Dist., Summit, 01-05-2005) No. 22158, 2005-Ohio-10, 2005 WL 19441, Unreported. Infants ⬥ 222

Trial court did not abuse its discretion, in dependency proceeding, in adopting magistrate's decision that grant of legal custody of child to foster parents was in child's best interest, given testimony of social worker that child had a bond with foster parents but not father's sister who also sought custody, and testimony of caseworker that mother-daughter relationship had developed between child and foster mother. In re Sellers (Ohio App. 5 Dist., Richland, 12-08-2004) No. 03 CA 95, 2004-Ohio-6595, 2004 WL 2827811, Unreported, appeal not allowed 105 Ohio St.3d 1517, 826 N.E.2d 315, 2005-Ohio-1880. Infants ⟜ 230.1

Trial court did not err by finding that award of child custody to father would be detrimental to child and that award of custody to child's maternal grandparents would be in child's best interests, where child resided with mother until she died, child had never resided with father, father's wife was victim of domestic violence assaults committed by father, and father was unemployed, whereas grandparents actively supported child's education, took child to counseling following mother's death, and provided organized home with reasonable rules. Christopher A.L. v. Heather D.R. (Ohio App. 6 Dist., Huron, 08-13-2004) No. H-03-040, 2004-Ohio-4271, 2004 WL 1802987, Unreported. Child Custody ⟜ 276; Child Custody ⟜ 279

Denial of mother's motion for reallocation of parental rights and responsibilities was not abuse of discretion; original order placing custody of child with paternal grandmother was not "temporary" and mother failed to establish sufficient change in circumstances. Kenney v. Kenney (Ohio App. 12 Dist., Warren, 07-26-2004) No. CA2003-07-078, 2004-Ohio-3912, 2004 WL 1662280, Unreported. Child Custody ⟜ 579

Trial court order granting paternal aunt and uncle legal custody of children in a custody proceeding incident to a dependency action was not an abuse of discretion, even though children were bonded to their foster parents; aunt and uncle had a positive home study and were willing to do whatever was necessary to care for the children, and children were bonded to grandmother. In re Mitchell (Ohio App. 11 Dist., Lake, 08-01-2003) No. 2002-L-078, No. 2002-L-079, 2003-Ohio-4102, 2003 WL 21782611, Unreported. Child Custody ⟜ 271; Infants ⟜ 230.1

Although mother alleged that trial court erred in failing to find mother was entitled to companionship with her daughter over a non-parent, record indicated that trial court did not grant "companionship" to a non-parent. Ream v. Ream (Ohio App. 5 Dist., Licking, 04-14-2003) No. 02-CA-000071, 2003-Ohio-2144, 2003 WL 1962332, Unreported. Child Custody ⟜ 907

Competent, credible evidence in custody dispute between biological father and mother's ex-husband supported trial court's finding that biological father abandoned child, who was conceived as result of mother's extra-marital affair with father while she was married; father was aware of mother's pregnancy and that the child could be his, father failed to inquire as to results of paternity test, despite evidence indicating his belief that child was his, father

told mother's ex-husband that he did not want to know the outcome of the test, and father made no effort to contact or support child until he resumed a relationship with mother, a period of more than seven years. Dawson v. Stout (Ohio App. 3 Dist., Union, 03-31-2003) No. 14-02-17, 2003-Ohio-1575, 2003 WL 1617974, Unreported. Children Out-of-wedlock ⟜ 20.3

The domestic relations court was not without jurisdiction to award custody of a child to a nonparent, or to hold a hearing to aid in that determination, despite the U.S. Supreme Court's decision in Troxel v. Granville (2000), 530 U.S. 57, 120 S.Ct. 2054, 147 L.Ed.2d 49, which did not, against the father's arguments, stand for the proposition that custody must be given to the parent; rather, its narrow holding was that the best interest standard as applied it to a broad visitation statute did not give sufficient deference to parental prerogatives. State ex rel. State ex rel. Reeves v. O'Malley (Ohio App. 8 Dist., Cuyahoga, 06-01-2001) No. 78900, 2001 WL 664137, Unreported, as amended nunc pro tunc.

A court is not obligated to find parents unfit before awarding custody to the child's grandmother where the child (1) has adjusted to life at his grandmother's house, (2) is participating in school and community activities and (3) the grandmother is making an effort to preserve the child's relationships with the father and his extended family. Wright v. Wright (Ohio App. 8 Dist., Cuyahoga, 10-19-1995) No. 67884, 1995 WL 614500, Unreported.

In a child custody case arising out of a parentage action between a natural parent of the child and a nonparent, trial court must make a parental unsuitability determination on the record before awarding legal custody of child to nonparent. In re Hockstok (Ohio, 12 27 2002) 98 Ohio St.3d 238, 781 N.E.2d 971, 2002-Ohio-7208, modified 98 Ohio St.3d 1476, 784 N.E.2d 709, 2003-Ohio-980. Child Custody ⟜ 511

Custody proceedings between a parent and a nonparent, unlike those between two parents, pose the possibility of terminating a parent's rights in favor of one who is not a parent. In re Bonfield (Ohio, 12-13-2002) 97 Ohio St.3d 387, 780 N.E.2d 241, 2002-Ohio-6660. Child Custody ⟜ 42

Juvenile court's exclusive responsibility to determine the custody of any child not a ward of another court of the state cannot be avoided merely because a petitioner for allocation of parental rights and responsibilities is not a "parent" under the statutory definition of the term. In re Bonfield (Ohio, 12-13-2002) 97 Ohio St.3d 387, 780 N.E.2d 241, 2002-Ohio-6660. Child Custody ⟜ 270

Shared parenting plan that designated grandfather, mother, and father each as residential parent and legal custodian was void ab initio; court cannot give non-parent parental status. Konicek v. Konicek (Ohio App. 9 Dist., 01-24-2001) 144 Ohio App.3d 105, 759 N.E.2d 801. Child Custody ⟜ 149

Following death of mother to whom trial court had awarded custody in divorce proceeding, dispute over custody of children between father and children's maternal uncle fell within coverage of statute allowing custody to be awarded to relative other than parent "when it is in the best interest of the child," rather than under statute establishing jurisdiction of juvenile courts to determine custody of child not ward of another court of state. Baker v. Baker (Ohio App. 9 Dist., 08-21-1996) 113 Ohio App.3d 805, 682 N.E.2d 661, appeal not allowed 77 Ohio St.3d 1525, 674 N.E.2d 376. Child Custody ☞ 271; Child Custody ☞ 405

Evidence supported trial court's decision that it was in best interests of 11–year–old child to remain with nonparents who had cared for her since she was a week old; guardian ad litem, court investigator and psychologist all testified that nonparents should be granted custody with liberal visitation by biological father. Reynolds v. Goll (Ohio, 03-04-1996) 75 Ohio St.3d 121, 661 N.E.2d 1008, 1996-Ohio-153. Child Custody ☞ 468

Trial court's finding of abandonment by and unsuitability of biological father was supported by competent evidence; court heard extensive testimony over two days which supported that father had abandoned his daughter by leaving her under care of another family with very limited visitation and no financial support other than medical insurance. Reynolds v. Goll (Ohio, 03-04-1996) 75 Ohio St.3d 121, 661 N.E.2d 1008, 1996-Ohio-153. Child Custody ☞ 469

Evidence supported award of custody of child to stepmother, rather than to cousin of mother and her husband; stepmother had attended many parenting skills training classes, and was a licensed foster home provider; by contrast, cousin and her husband ignored recommendations that child be taken to particular school and to day-care, and did not comply with court order requiring them to attend parenting skills training classes. In re Whaley (Athens 1993) 86 Ohio App.3d 304, 620 N.E.2d 954. Child Custody ☞ 272

Where both parents had voluntarily relinquished custody of child, and child custody proceeding involved only competing claims of nonparents to custody, court did not have to make a finding of parental unsuitability prior to awarding custody to stepmother. In re Whaley (Athens 1993) 86 Ohio App.3d 304, 620 N.E.2d 954. Child Custody ☞ 272

Custody may not be awarded to a nonparent without a judicial finding that the custodial parent is unsuitable. Truitt v. Truitt (Preble 1989) 65 Ohio App.3d 126, 583 N.E.2d 331. Child Custody ☞ 42

As between a parent and non-parent, a parent may be denied custody only if a preponderance of the evidence indicates abandonment, contractual relinquishment of custody, total inability to provide care or support, or that the parent is otherwise unsuitable so that an award of custody to the parent would be detrimental to the child, and although RC

3109.04(C) does not apply to temporary custody orders, the factors enumerated therein are factors which the court may consider in determining the suitability or unsuitability of the parent. In re Custody of Carpenter (Greene 1987) 41 Ohio App.3d 182, 534 N.E.2d 1216. Child Custody ☞ 42; Child Custody ☞ 465

A parent's consent to guardianship over his child by the child's grandparents constitutes a forfeiture of the parent's rights to custody to the extent that a later change-of-custody motion may be decided according to the best interests of the child, and without a finding of the parent's unsuitability. Masitto v. Masitto (Ohio 1986) 22 Ohio St.3d 63, 488 N.E.2d 857, 22 O.B.R. 81.

In a child custody dispute brought under RC 3109.04 between the child's parent and a nonparent, a suitable parent has a paramount right to custody so long as such custody causes no detriment to the child. Thrasher v. Thrasher (Summit 1981) 3 Ohio App.3d 210, 444 N.E.2d 431, 3 O.B.R. 240. Child Custody ☞ 42

Where court found natural parent of child had renounced custody she had forfeited her right to paramount custody, and court could award custody to a third party if a preponderance of the evidence indicated abandonment, contractual release of custody, inability to support or other unsuitability. In re Young (Ohio 1979) 58 Ohio St.2d 90, 388 N.E.2d 1235, 12 O.O.3d 93.

Natural paternity alone is insufficient to support a claim in habeas corpus where the child is well cared for by grandparents and the natural parent abandoned the child and for nine years did nothing for her. Hughes v. Scaffide (Ohio 1979) 58 Ohio St.2d 88, 388 N.E.2d 1233, 12 O.O.3d 92.

Insofar as Civ R 75(P), which requires the court to find, prior to committing a child to a relative, that both parents are unsuitable to have custody, abridges the child's statutory right under RC 3109.04 to be committed to a relative where commitment to a parent would be contrary to the child's best interest, such rule is invalid under the provisions of O Const Art IV §5. Boyer v. Boyer (Ohio 1976) 46 Ohio St.2d 83, 346 N.E.2d 286, 75 O.O.2d 156, certiorari denied 97 S.Ct. 245, 429 U.S. 889, 50 L.Ed.2d 172. Courts ☞ 80(1)

In determining who shall have the care, custody, and control of a child under eighteen years of age, even though the child's parents are not found to be unfit or unsuitable, the court may commit the child to a relative of the child where the court finds that custody to neither parent is in the best interest of the child. Boyer v. Boyer (Ohio 1976) 46 Ohio St.2d 83, 346 N.E.2d 286, 75 O.O.2d 156, certiorari denied 97 S.Ct. 245, 429 U.S. 889, 50 L.Ed.2d 172. Child Custody ☞ 271

Under RC 3109.04, common pleas court has no authority to award custody of minor child to its grandmother unless it has found that "neither parent is a suitable person to have custody," and such lack of authority may not be obviated by describing commitment as "physical" rather than "legal" custody. Baxter v. Baxter (Ohio 1971) 27 Ohio St.2d 168, 271 N.E.2d 873, 56 O.O.2d 104.

An award of custody of a child in a divorce action is conclusive only as to the parties to such action, and the remedy of habeas corpus is available to obtain such child where a party other than the parties to the divorce action is involved; and it is not necessary to apply to the court which originally awarded custody of such child. In re Howland (Highland 1961) 115 Ohio App. 186, 184 N.E.2d 228, 20 O.O.2d 277.

The welfare of the child is considered when the question of custody of such child arises between the parents who stand on an equality, or when the parents are found to be unfit and the court is required to grant custody to a third person. Ludy v. Ludy (Franklin 1948) 84 Ohio App. 195, 82 N.E.2d 775, 53 Ohio Law Abs. 47, 39 O.O. 241, rehearing denied 84 N.E.2d 120, 53 Ohio Law Abs. 47. Child Custody ☞ 76

A court may not award custody of children to any other person than their parents unless a finding is made of the unfitness of the parents to have their children's custody as provided by this section. Luebkeman v. Luebkeman (Montgomery 1945) 75 Ohio App. 566, 61 N.E.2d 638, 43 Ohio Law Abs. 17, 31 O.O. 319.

A woman has not contractually given up her paramount right to custody where (1) she and her brother orally agree to have her artificially inseminated so that she can bear a child for the HIV-positive brother and his lifetime companion to raise, (2) the brother asks his sister to sign a unilateral declaration unconditionally relinquishing custody of the child the day before it is born while the sister is on medication for an abscessed tooth, and (3) the brother arguably misleads his sister as to the significance of what she is signing. Decker v. Decker (Ohio App. 3 Dist., Hancock, 09-28-2001) No. 5-01-23, 2001-Ohio-2279, 2001 WL 1167475, Unreported, stay denied 93 Ohio St.3d 1486, 758 N.E.2d 186, appeal not allowed 94 Ohio St.3d 1411, 759 N.E.2d 787.

RC 3105.21(B) affords a domestic relations court authority to determine custody of a child, as between his parents and another relative, even though that court has dismissed the parent's divorce action; if after dismissing the divorce action, the domestic relations court elects to certify the matter of custody to juvenile court, under RC 3105.21(B) and 3109.04 the domestic relations court must specifically find custody in neither parent to be in the child's best interest, or all jurisdiction over the matter is lost. State ex rel. Easterday v. Zieba (Ohio 1991) 58 Ohio St.3d 251, 569 N.E.2d 1028.

Where a mother grants voluntary temporary custody to an infant's paternal grandparents, the proper standard to be used by the court in determining an award of custody upon the filing of a petition by the mother is the fitness of the mother, not the best interests of the child standard in RC 3109.04(B). In re Curry, No. 89AP–550 (10th Dist Ct App, Franklin, 11–21–89).

Where a child's mother has been determined to be an unsuitable parent, the father gives physical custody of the child to the maternal grandmother, the child undergoes brain surgery and is left with a soft skull, and the mother's boyfriend has a propensity for violence, an award of custody of the child to the maternal grandmother is proper despite the lack of a finding that the child's father is an unsuitable parent where such award of custody to a nonparent is in the best interest of the child. Mannering v Mannering, No. 559 (4th Dist Ct App, Jackson, 5–3–89).

A court must make a finding of parental unsuitability prior to assuming jurisdiction under RC 3109.04 to award permanent custody of a child to a nonparent relative. Fronk v Arison, No. 1167 (11th Dist Ct App, Ashtabula, 10–26–84).

A complainant who is not a parent of the minor child does not have standing to bring an action under RC 3109.04. Young v Young, No. 29–CA–92 (5th Dist Ct App, Fairfield, 4–26–93).

21. —— Paternity issues, initial allocation of rights and responsibilities and "best interest"

Trial court was not precluded from considering husband's request for paternity testing in considering award of custody in context of divorce. Saluppo v. Saluppo (Ohio App. 9 Dist., Summit, 05-31-2006) No. 22680, 2006-Ohio-2694, 2006 WL 1479633, Unreported. Child Custody ☞ 424

Exclusion as the father through genetic testing constitutes clear and convincing evidence that overcomes the presumption of paternity created under RC 3111.03 and where the defendant is excluded as the father there is no minor issue of the marriage and RC 3109.04 no longer provides the court of common pleas with subject matter jurisdiction to make a ruling on custody; instead the issue of custody becomes subject matter exclusive to the juvenile court pursuant to RC 2151.23, and consequently, the "best interest of the child" standard in determining custody does not apply. Thompson v. Thompson (Ohio App. 4 Dist., Highland, 08-10-1995) No. 94CA859, 1995 WL 481480, Unreported.

Pursuant to a parentage action where the issue of who would have custody of the child is never before the court or addressed in an agreement between the parties, it is error for the trial court to address issues of child support and visitation without first making a determination as to which parent will have custody. State ex rel. Ellen v. Deal (Ohio App. 10 Dist., Franklin, 12-27-1994) No. 94APF04-549, 1994 WL 723377, Unreported.

Where an unmarried mother leaves a child less than two years old with the child's maternal grandmother in an inappropriate environment and the mother does not disclose her location for six months and does not return until eight or nine months passed, and upon returning the mother institutes a paternity action but does not address the custody of the child, a trial court properly determines the custody of the child under the best interest of the child standard used in initial custody determinations when presented with the respective custody motions of the adjudged father and natural mother of the child. In re Webster, No. 92CA1559, 1993 WL 373784 (4th Dist Ct App, Athens, 9–14–93).

Finding in original divorce decree that child born during parties' marriage was former husband's child was res judicata as to father's motion to have himself declared as not the child's biological father because DNA (deoxyribonucleic acid) test results indicated that father and child were not genetically linked. Van Dusen v. Van Dusen (Ohio App. 10 Dist., 01-28-2003) 151 Ohio App.3d 494, 784 N.E.2d 750, 2003-Ohio-350. Divorce ⟳ 172

Issue of whether any subsequent application for cash public assistance by either husband and wife would result in change of circumstances, for purposes of modifying custodial rights to their children, did not present a justiciable controversy in divorce action, so that court lacked jurisdiction to include as part of divorce decree provision under which any future application would constitute such a change of circumstances. Stewart v. Stewart (Ohio App. 4 Dist., 09-07-1999) 134 Ohio App.3d 556, 731 N.E.2d 743. Child Custody ⟳ 521

Legal custodians of child, who obtained custody from child's mother, were in privity with mother, and so were barred by res judicata from litigating issue of paternity of child that had been decided in divorce decree. Broxterman v. Broxterman (Ohio App. 1 Dist., 03-15-1995) 101 Ohio App.3d 661, 656 N.E.2d 394. Children Out–of–wedlock ⟳ 33; Divorce ⟳ 172

Legal parentage, not to be confused with biological parentage, must be established before the issue of custody can properly be decided where the child is the product of artificial insemination of a married woman by a man not her husband. In re Adoption of Reams (Franklin 1989) 52 Ohio App.3d 52, 557 N.E.2d 159, dismissed 50 Ohio St.3d 707, 553 N.E.2d 684. Adoption ⟳ 7.1

A judgment establishing paternity and imposing a duty to support on the father may also imply a determination of custody to the mother, so that a motion to determine custody filed years later by the father should be determined according to the standards for change in custody set forth in RC 3109.04(B)(1). In re Brazell (Ohio Com.Pl. 1986) 27 Ohio Misc.2d 7, 499 N.E.2d 925, 27 O.B.R. 68.

A judgment in a paternity action has the effect of a prior determination of custody; therefore, a subsequent change of custody pursuant to a petition by the natural father must be based on a finding of changed circumstances. In re Yates (Franklin 1984) 18 Ohio App.3d 95, 481 N.E.2d 646, 18 O.B.R. 458.

When the alleged natural father of an illegitimate child, who has participated in the nurturing process of the child, files a complaint seeking custody of the child under RC 2151.23(A)(2), and the mother admits that he is the natural father of the child, the natural father has equality of standing with the mother with respect to the custody of the child, and the court shall determine which parent shall have the legal custody of the child, taking into account what would be in the best interests of the child. In re Byrd (Ohio 1981) 66 Ohio St.2d 334, 421 N.E.2d 1284, 20 O.O.3d 309. Children Out–of–wedlock ⟳ 20.4

The mother of an illegitimate child has a right of custody that is superior to that of the putative father. In re H. (Ohio Com.Pl. 1973) 37 Ohio Misc. 123, 305 N.E.2d 815, 66 O.O.2d 178, 66 O.O.2d 368.

In a husband's action for divorce, in which the wife's cross-petition raises the issue of the paternity of her child, a finding by the trial court that the evidence is insufficient to prove that the husband is not the father of the child is a determination that the child was conceived by the parties as husband and wife, and it is the duty of such court to make an order for the disposition, care and maintenance of the child. Whitecotton v. Whitecotton (Lucas 1955) 103 Ohio App. 149, 144 N.E.2d 678, 3 O.O.2d 210. Child Custody ⟳ 511; Child Support ⟳ 214

22. —— "Primary caregiver" preference and "Tender years" doctrine, initial allocation of rights and responsibilities and "best interest"

It was not an abuse of trial court's discretion for court to designate wife as the custodial and residential parent; wife had acted as the child's primary custodial parent and caregiver, and during that time the child had been healthy, normal, well-adjusted and happy, and, although wife was found in contempt of court for failing to obey the parenting time order, the child's guardian ad litem recommended that wife be awarded custody of the child, wife was in the process of applying for a "green card," wife intended to remain in Ohio, and she had family located in the Cincinnati area. Pickel v. Ghouati (Ohio App. 2 Dist., Montgomery, 04-03-2009) No. 23026, 2009-Ohio-1644, 2009 WL 903299, Unreported. Child Custody ⟳ 44; Child Custody ⟳ 57; Child Custody ⟳ 260

In divorce action in which husband sought shared parenting plan, evidence supported trial court's finding that youngest child was almost 16 months old when the first agreed shared parenting order went into place and was 27 months old when the court first adopted the shared parenting plan, and thus child spent almost one-half of his life in care of both husband and wife. Swain v. Swain (Ohio App. 4 Dist., Pike, 08-06-2005) No. 05CA740, 2005-Ohio-4321, 2005 WL 1995388, Unreported. Child Custody ⟳ 472

Grant of custody of infant daughter, who was born out-of-wedlock, to biological father was not abuse of discretion, given evidence that father was more likely to foster mother-child relationship than mother was to encourage father-child relationship. Goodrich v. Larrick (Ohio App. 5 Dist., Muskingum, 01-21-2005) No. 2004 CA 0032,

2005-Ohio-250, 2005 WL 136319, Unreported. Children Out–of–wedlock ☞ 20.3

Evidence supported finding that custodial unwed mother's motive for relocating was to frustrate father's visitation, supporting conclusion that relocation constituted change in circumstances; though mother argued that move allowed her to be with her fiance, obtain better employment, and enroll child in better school, evidence showed that fiance was still defendant in divorce at time of move, mother held three different jobs in three months at new location and did not consult with father about move that occurred while father's custody motion was pending, there was no evidence on quality of schools, there was history of visitation problems, and move disrupted child's relationship with maternal grandmother who played significant role in raising her. In re Seitz (Ohio App. 11 Dist., Trumbull, 09-26-2003) No. 2002-T-0097, 2003-Ohio-5218, 2003 WL 22234850, Unreported. Children Out–of–wedlock ☞ 20.10

That trial court did not award mother custody of minor child did not establish court disregarded or failed to consider the primary caregiver doctrine; court found that "'both parties were involved in the daily care of the child,'" and, without an affirmative record demonstration to the contrary, it is presumed trial court considered mother's role in upbringing of child in determining appropriate award of custody. Ream v. Ream (Ohio App. 5 Dist., Licking, 04-14-2003) No. 02-CA-000071, 2003 Ohio 2144, 2003 WL 1962332, Unreported. Child Custody ☞ 511; Child Custody ☞ 920

Trial court was not required to make a finding as to which party was child's primary caregiver in making a custody decision in the best interest of the child. Prusia v. Prusia (Ohio App. 6 Dist., Lucas, 04-18-2003) No. L-02-1165, 2003-Ohio-2000, 2003 WL 1904410, Unreported. Child Custody ☞ 511

Custody of the parties' daughter granted to the natural father is within the court's discretion after considering (1) the mother's limited contact with the child over the previous two years, (2) the mother's decision to abscond with the child to North Carolina where the mother is residing, (3) most of the child's extended family, including the maternal grandparents, live in Ohio, and (4) the active role played by the father's present wife in helping him raise his daughter. Michael v. Chesnut (Ohio App. 2 Dist., Greene, 05-16-1997) No. 96-CA-72, 1997 WL 254142, Unreported.

Being the primary caretaker of the children does not lead to a presumption that the particular parent should be the residential parent but should be considered with other statutory factors; in addition, where there is documentation that an obligor is under a duty to support two other children, the trial court must consider such obligation when calculating the current child support obligation. Matter of Kunkle v. Lupardus (Ohio App. 11 Dist., Portage, 03-28-1997) No. 96-P-0014, 1997 WL 158104, Unreported.

Substantial amount of credible and competent evidence supported trial court's decision to name former wife primary caregiver of parties' child in connection with divorce proceeding; wife had been child's primary caregiver before divorce, and social worker, psychologist, and psychology trainee all gave opinion testimony that wife should continue to be primary caregiver. Badovick v. Badovick (Ohio App. 8 Dist., 05-26-1998) 128 Ohio App.3d 18, 713 N.E.2d 1066. Child Custody ☞ 470; Evidence ☞ 571(1)

Ohio courts must give due consideration to which parent was primary caregiver in fashioning custody award. Marshall v. Marshall (Ohio App. 3 Dist., 01-15-1997) 117 Ohio App.3d 182, 690 N.E.2d 68. Child Custody ☞ 44

A trial court abuses its discretion when it awards the father custody of the two minor children of the unmarried couple where (1) the mother supported the couple and children through part-time employment during the eight years they were together but the father was not regularly employed and rarely spent quality time with the children; (2) the father took the children on vacation to Florida and, after the mother informed him over the telephone that she wished to terminate their relationship, he refused to let the mother see them or often even to speak to them on the telephone; and (3) once in Florida, the father changed his residence, found employment, enrolled the children in school, affiliated with a church, and began to spend time with the children. In re Markham (Meigs 1990) 70 Ohio App.3d 841, 592 N.E.2d 896, dismissed, jurisdictional motion overruled 60 Ohio St.3d 702, 573 N.E.2d 118.

The primary caretaker doctrine, although not a dispositive rule in Ohio, is a factor that can properly be considered when reviewing other statutory factors relating to custody. Roth v. Roth (Lucas 1989) 65 Ohio App.3d 768, 585 N.E.2d 482. Child Custody ☞ 44

When forming a custody order, a trial court should give due consideration to which parent performed the role of primary caregiver. Bechtol v. Bechtol (Ohio 1990) 49 Ohio St.3d 21, 550 N.E.2d 178, rehearing denied 49 Ohio St.3d 718, 552 N.E.2d 952, opinion corrected 51 Ohio St.3d 701, 554 N.E.2d 899. Child Custody ☞ 44

The primary caregiver doctrine is part of the best interest of the child and is included in the language of RC 3109.04(C)(3), "the child's interaction and interrelationship with his parents." Thompson v. Thompson (Washington 1987) 31 Ohio App.3d 254, 511 N.E.2d 412, 31 O.B.R. 538. Child Custody ☞ 44

A trial court commits reversible error by presuming that a mother is entitled to custody of a child of tender years. Charles v. Charles (Franklin 1985) 23 Ohio App.3d 109, 491 N.E.2d 378, 23 O.B.R. 175.

To determine the best interests of a child of tender years in an original award of custody, it is within the sound discretion of the trial court to strongly consider which parent was the primary caretaker of the child, in addition to considering the factors set forth in RC 3109.04(C). In re Maxwell (Darke 1982) 8 Ohio App.3d 302, 456 N.E.2d 1218, 8 O.B.R. 409.

Under statute, one parent is not preferred over other, and court is authorized to award custody to either parent, taking into account that which would be for best interests, and while courts, in awarding custody of children of tender years, most times prefer mother over father, where circumstances warrant, it is always in furtherance of what court conceives to be for children's best interests. Riggs v. Riggs (Franklin 1954) 124 N.E.2d 835, 69 Ohio Law Abs. 263. Child Custody ☞ 26

While RC 3109.03 eliminates the presumption that the mother is the proper custodian of a child of tender years, the age of the child and the child's relationship with the mother are factors to be considered under RC 3109.04(C); and a trial court's failure to consider the child's tender years constitutes an abuse of discretion. Berry v Berry, No. CA88–11–081 (12th Dist Ct App, Clermont, 3–12–90).

Where custody of a minor child was originally awarded to the child's mother, subsequently the child's father obtained custody with the mother's consent, and later the mother filed a motion to return custody of the child to her, the trial court erred in granting such motion based solely on the tender years doctrine. Kiskis v Kiskis, No. 330 (4th Dist Ct App, Meigs, 12–1–83).

23. —— **Procedural issues and hearings and evidence generally, initial allocation of rights and responsibilities and "best interest"**

Father's due process rights were not violated when magistrate denied his request for recess to use the restroom, in child custody action involving child who was born out of wedlock; although father claimed on appeal that his reason for requesting a recess was to provide rebuttal testimony, the transcript of the proceeding demonstrated otherwise. Ensell v. Ensell (Ohio App. 7 Dist., Jefferson, 11-26-2010) No. 09 JE 14, 2010-Ohio-5942, 2010 WL 4939996, Unreported. Children Out–of–wedlock ☞ 20.4; Constitutional Law ☞ 4392

Trial court did not abuse its discretion in overruling mother's motion for continuance to permit her to obtain new counsel after the court had allowed prior counsel to withdraw in child custody action; mother had filed at least five requests for continuances, the matter had been pending for over two and one-half years, counsel's reasons for withdrawing included failure to pay her fee and client conduct, and court had directed there would be no more continuances when it had granted the previous continuance. Moore v. Lanning (Ohio App. 5 Dist., Fairfield, 03-29-2010) No. 2009-CA-46, 2010-Ohio-1395, 2010 WL 1234414, Unreported. Child Custody ☞ 502

Trial court did not abuse its discretion by denying mother's motion to recess child custody hearing until the next day, upon reconvening after recess until noon on day of hearing; matter had not been set for a two-day hearing, judge had another case scheduled for 9:00 am the following day, judge's schedule was very full, and the matter would not run over to the second day unless the parties were unable to complete the trial on the first day. Moore v. Lanning (Ohio App. 5 Dist., Fairfield, 03-29-2010) No. 2009-CA-46, 2010-Ohio-1395, 2010 WL 1234414, Unreported. Child Custody ☞ 502

Trial court abused its discretion in denying unwed mother's motion for a continuance to find another attorney to represent her, in custody and visitation action brought by father, where mother throughout the action had alleged the father may have sexually abused the parties' child, mother allegedly discovered shortly before hearing on motion for continuance that her attorney had previously represented the father in a case in which father was accused of sexually molesting a young relative, mother's allegation was credible, mother's attorney had failed to disclose to mother that he had represented father in the prior action, other motions were pending and scheduled to be heard at the hearing, and mother was not prepared to argue the other pending motions on her own. Rice v. Lewis (Ohio App. 4 Dist., Scioto, 03-11-2010) No. 09CA3307, 2010-Ohio-1077, 2010 WL 1006657, Unreported. Children Out–of–wedlock ☞ 20.4

Trial court acted within its discretion in designating mother the residential parent of child in a proceeding to allocate parental rights, even though father argued that trial court did not appropriately consider mother's physical and mental health and that mother was the least likely to honor court-approved visitation rights and had expressed an intention to relocate to another state; trial court carefully considered all of the evidence that was both favorable and unfavorable to mother, trial court also had to weigh negative testimony concerning father, and trial court considered additional factors, such as child's greater bond with mother. Reinhart v. Allen (Ohio App. 3 Dist., Seneca, 10-05-2009) No. 13-08-42, 2009-Ohio-5277, 2009 WL 3165585, Unreported. Child Custody ☞ 511

Magistrate and trial court were not required to find a change in circumstances concerning the parties' shared parenting order in order to grant former husband's motion to modify parental rights and find it was in the best interest of one of the parties' children to reside with former husband, where former wife did not voice clear opposition to former husband's motion, and former wife acceded to the child primarily living with former husband. Sahr v. Sahr (Ohio App. 5 Dist., Fairfield, 08-12-2009) No. 09 CA 3, 2009-Ohio-4055, 2009 WL 2469544, Unreported. Child Custody ☞ 576

Statute governing modification of prior decrees allocating parental rights and responsibilities did not apply to determine which parent of children born out-of-wedlock should be awarded custody of children, in proceeding filed by father to obtain legal custody of children, though prior judgment entry existed awarding mother child support from father, as no prior custody decree had been issued, in that issue of custody was never litigated in child support proceeding but, instead, court in that proceeding applied statutory presumption that mother was custodial parent. DeWitt v. Myers (Ohio App. 2 Dist., Clark, 02-20-2009) No. 08-CA-86, 2009-Ohio-807, 2009 WL 440628, Unreported. Children Out–of–wedlock ☜ 20.3; Children Out–of–wedlock ☜ 20.10

Modification of father's parenting time due to mother's requested relocation to another state was not a modification of parental rights and responsibilities that was subject to changed circumstances test or test as to whether harm likely to be caused by change of environment was outweighed by advantages of change of environment to child, both of which are set forth in child custody statutes; rather, modification of father's parenting time was a modification of father's visitation, such that best interest test set forth in visitation statute applied. Campana v. Campana (Ohio App. 7 Dist., Mahoning, 02-20-2009) No. 08 MA 88, 2009-Ohio-796, 2009 WL 428580, Unreported. Child Custody ☜ 577

Record showed that trial court's denial of father's motion for modification of child custody was based in part on findings that father was in contempt of court, which was an impermissible ground for modification of custody, where trial court listed father's filing of a false and misleading parenting proceeding affidavit and father's failure to disclose his prior conviction for corruption of a minor as reasons for its denial of the motion for modification, and those factors were also the basis for the contempt findings. Horn v. Frazier (Ohio App. 5 Dist., Licking, 01-07-2009) No. 08 CA 000068, 2009-Ohio-51, 2009 WL 50608, Unreported. Child Custody ☜ 552

Ex-husband was not entitled to act as pro se co-counsel while simultaneously being represented by counsel, in proceedings on his motions to modify parental rights and responsibilities and to modify child support, even though ex-husband was a licensed attorney, since trial court had authority to manage its own courtroom; he interrupted his own attorney during depositions and, in some instances, instructed a deponent on how or when to answer, and obstructed reasonable discovery requests by filing countless motions to quash and by failing to produce documents.. Klayman v. Luck (Ohio App. 8 Dist., Cuyahoga, 11-13-2008) No. 91298, No. 91317, 2008-Ohio-5876, 2008 WL 4885043, Unreported, appeal not allowed 121 Ohio St.3d 1451, 904 N.E.2d 901, 2009-Ohio-1820, reconsideration denied 122 Ohio St.3d 1413, 907 N.E.2d 1195, 2009-Ohio-2751. Attorney and Client ☜ 62; Child Custody ☜ 650; Child Support ☜ 340

Wife's medical records were subject to in camera inspection by trial court prior to their release to husband in order to determine existence of physician-patient privilege or whether privilege was outweighed by other rights or considerations, during contested child custody proceedings in underlying divorce action; husband's blanket discovery request for release of medical records was overly broad on its face, sufficient to support wife's burden of showing that requested information would not lead to

discovery of relevant admissible evidence. Sweet v. Sweet (Ohio App. 11 Dist., Ashtabula, 12-29-2005) No. 2004-A-0062, 2005-Ohio-7060, 2005 WL 3610481, Unreported. Privileged Communications And Confidentiality ☜ 276

Possibility that defendant's domestic violence conviction could be used against him when allocating parental rights were there to be a custody dispute over defendant's son was not type of collateral disability that could give viability to appeal of such conviction that was otherwise rendered moot by defendant's completion of sentence; conviction for domestic violence was only one of many factors to be considered by the trial court when making a determination as to whom custody of a minor child should be awarded, and defendant's argument was purely speculative, as there was no evidence in the record that a custody dispute over defendant's son had arisen. State v. Moore (Ohio App. 2 Dist., Montgomery, 08-19-2005) No. 20772, 2005-Ohio-4518, 2005 WL 2083059, Unreported. Criminal Law ☜ 1131(4)

Mother was not entitled to relief from divorce custody judgment, which designated father residential parent and legal guardian of children and granted mother visitation; although mother claimed she was in emotional turmoil at time of final divorce hearing and father misrepresented matters relevant to determination of custody in original proceeding, no operative facts indicated mother's condition was such as to render her incompetent for purposes of service or comprehending her legal rights or obligations, and mother failed to establish fraud, misrepresentation, or misconduct on part of father. Walsh v. Walsh (Ohio App. 11 Dist., Geauga, 06-24-2005) No. 2004-G-2587, 2005-Ohio-3264, 2005 WL 1503707, Unreported. Child Custody ☜ 526

Former husband's two-month delay in requesting transcript of custody proceedings before magistrate to which he had filed objections did not constitute flagrant, substantial disregard for court rule requiring that transcript be requested within three days after filing of objections, where former husband's statement to court that he could not afford $4,000 cost of preparing transcript at time he filed his objections was unchallenged. O'Brien v. O'Brien (Ohio App. 10 Dist., Franklin, 06-21-2005) No. 04AP-1157, 2005-Ohio-3101, 2005 WL 1432315, Unreported. Child Custody ☜ 504

Trial court abused its discretion in denying continuance and dismissing husband's objections to magistrate's decision with respect to child custody and support, based upon husband's violation of local rule of court requiring party objecting to magistrate's decision to request transcript within three days of filing of objections, where delay did not constitute flagrant, substantial disregard for court rules, husband had no apparent history of asking for continuances, nothing indicated that continuance at issue was requested solely for purpose of delay, wife did not claim prejudice in seeking dismissal, and any financial prejudice from delay was suffered by husband. O'Brien v. O'Brien

(Ohio App. 10 Dist., Franklin, 06-21-2005) No. 04AP-1157, 2005-Ohio-3101, 2005 WL 1432315, Unreported. Child Custody ☞ 502; Child Custody ☞ 504

Former wife's motion, denominated motion for modification of child support, was actually initial request for child support, where trial court never issued formal support order, either upon finalization of decree of divorce or upon modification of shared parenting agreement, and parties' agreement with respect to child support was never explicitly made subject to any order of support. Kosovich v. Kosovich (Ohio App. 11 Dist., Lake, 06-17-2005) No. 2004-L-044, 2005-Ohio-3084, 2005 WL 1423435, Unreported. Child Support ☞ 187

Father had an adequate legal remedy to correct domestic relations court's alleged abuse of discretion in refusing to accept a proposed "agreed judgment entry/decree of divorce" executed by father and mother, and thus father was not entitled to writ of mandamus compelling trial judge to accept the proposed agreement, despite father's contention that absence of a transcript of hearing at which trial judge allegedly ordered him to file a shared parenting plan rendered appeal an inadequate remedy; father could prepare statement of the evidence to make up for the lack of a transcript. State ex rel. Cummings v. Squire (Ohio App. 10 Dist., Franklin, 06-02-2005) No. 04AP-899, 2005-Ohio-2713, 2005 WL 1302992, Unreported. Mandamus ☞ 4(4)

Father who sought writ of mandamus compelling trial judge in divorce action to accept a proposed "agreed judgment entry/decree of divorce" executed by father and mother did not have a clear legal right to have domestic relations court enter judgment based on the agreement of the parties; court was required to determine that the agreement was in the best interest of the parties' child. State ex rel. Cummings v. Squire (Ohio App. 10 Dist., Franklin, 06-02-2005) No. 04AP-899, 2005-Ohio-2713, 2005 WL 1302992, Unreported. Child Custody ☞ 36; Child Support ☞ 45

Non-marital child's father, as appellant, failed to satisfy his burden on appeal to support claim that trial court employed gender bias against him and in favor of mother in proceeding to establish custody, where father did not support accusation of gender bias with anything more than his distaste for outcome, and father did not direct appellate court's attention to any statement, reasoning, or circumstance that would have supported his accusation. Figley v. Heather Corp (Ohio App. 9 Dist., Wayne, 05-25-2005) No. 04CA0054, 2005-Ohio-2566, 2005 WL 1225936, Unreported. Children Out–of–wedlock ☞ 20.11

Wife was not improperly denied access to report issued by family services coordinator regarding factors associated with child custody determinations in divorce proceedings, even though report could only be examined at the courthouse during regular office hours; there was no requirement that parties be provided copy of report, and trial court provided notice to wife that report was available at the courthouse for review. Goodman v. Goodman (Ohio App. 3 Dist., Marion, 03-14-2005) No. 9-04-37, 2005-Ohio-1091, 2005 WL 579154, Unreported. Child Custody ☞ 421

Recommendations contained in family services coordinator's report regarding factors associated with child custody determinations were not improper in divorce proceedings, where report contained sufficient facts from which the trial court could draw a proper conclusion, and trial court did not rely exclusively on the report in reaching its conclusions. Goodman v. Goodman (Ohio App. 3 Dist., Marion, 03-14-2005) No. 9-04-37, 2005-Ohio-1091, 2005 WL 579154, Unreported. Child Custody ☞ 421

Ohio court with jurisdiction over former husband's motion to reallocate parental rights and responsibilities, based on the parties' residence in that state, was not required to ascertain if a pending proceeding existed in the New Mexico court that had granted the parties' divorce. Rodriguez v. Frietze (Ohio App. 4 Dist., Athens, 12-17-2004) No. 04CA14, 2004-Ohio-7121, 2004 WL 3001067, Unreported, appeal not allowed 105 Ohio St.3d 1519, 826 N.E.2d 316, 2005-Ohio-1880. Child Custody ☞ 748

Mother's challenge on appeal to trial court's conclusion that award of custody of mother's child to grandparents was in child's best interest raised issue of law for which entire transcript of hearing was not necessary for appellate review. In re Self (Ohio App. 5 Dist., Stark, 12-13-2004) No. 2004CA00199, 2004-Ohio-6822, 2004 WL 2913567, Unreported, appeal not allowed 105 Ohio St.3d 1518, 826 N.E.2d 315, 2005-Ohio-1880. Child Custody ☞ 907

Former wife's appeal from ex parte orders with respect to transportation of children to particular extracurricular events according to schedule specified in shared parenting plan was not rendered moot by completion of events to which challenged orders applied, where appeal presented issue capable of repetition and avoiding review. Yoel v. Yoel (Ohio App. 11 Dist., Lake, 11-19-2004) No. 2003-L-123, 2004-Ohio-6174, 2004 WL 2647577, Unreported. Child Custody ☞ 911

Award of custody of parties' children to ex-husband was not abuse of discretion; ex-husband elicited testimony from ex-wife, her adult daughter, and himself in his case-in-chief, and utilized report of court-ordered child custody evaluator in eliciting all of his witnesses' testimony, and, since ex-wife was not entitled to have evaluator's report stricken, it was not error for ex-husband to elicit lay testimony by way of report, and lay witnesses called by both parties presented factual testimony supporting custody award. Jeskey v. Jeskey (Ohio App. 5 Dist., Muskingum, 09-13-2004) No. CT2003-0038, 2004-Ohio-5002, 2004 WL 2260698, Unreported. Child Custody ☞ 421; Child Custody ☞ 467

Trial court did not abuse its discretion in refusing to allow ex-wife to add to her witness list mental health counselor, whom ex-wife claimed was rebuttal witness intended to challenge custody evaluation report submitted by court-ordered child custody evaluator; evaluator was trial court's witness, statute required report be provided to all counsel not less than seven days before trial, and, because of this time constraint, ex-wife should have anticipated her need to call mental health counselor to testify in rebuttal and submitted counselor's name as potential witness on her list. Jeskey v. Jeskey (Ohio App. 5 Dist., Muskingum, 09-13-2004) No. CT2003-0038, 2004-Ohio-5002, 2004 WL 2260698, Unreported. Child Custody ⚖ 423

Ex-wife failed to preserve for appeal her right to object to non-appearance at trial of court-ordered child custody evaluator, in divorce proceeding; while magistrate's order requiring payment of evaluator's fee prior to trial by party wishing evaluator to testify was inappropriate, ex-wife failed to object to this order or notify trial court that she would be unable to pay fee, and ex-wife could have filed motion asking that evaluator's fee be taxed as costs in action, pursuant to statute and rule, but did not do so. Jeskey v. Jeskey (Ohio App. 5 Dist., Muskingum, 09-13-2004) No. CT2003-0038, 2004-Ohio-5002, 2004 WL 2260698, Unreported. Child Custody ⚖ 904

Unwed father's first custody motion, which was dismissed, was not "the prior decree" within meaning of statute providing that trial court is required to base its finding of changed circumstances, justifying modification of custody, on facts that have arisen since the prior decree; statute's reference to the "prior decree" meant the prior decree that allocated parental rights, and trial court filed that decree when it designated mother as the residential parent, and trial court's later dismissal of father's first motion for a change of custody, at his request, did not constitute a decree that allocated parental rights. Gaines v. Pelzl (Ohio App. 2 Dist., Greene, 04-23-2004) No. 2003-CA-60, 2004-Ohio-2043, 2004 WL 869549, Unreported. Children Out-of-wedlock ⚖ 20.10

Regardless of whether case was a modification of child custody situation or an initial custody determination, award of custody to child's father was not against manifest weight of evidence; nine-year-old child desired to live with his father, and child got along well with father's household members and had comfortable relationships with everyone in the home. Esaw v. Esaw (Ohio App. 7 Dist., Belmont, 06-25-2003) No. 02BA6, 2003-Ohio-3485, 2003 WL 21504116, Unreported. Child Custody ⚖ 75; Child Custody ⚖ 78

Competent, credible evidence indicating that father deliberately feigned lack of knowledge of mother's location in order to effect service by publication in county where mother no longer resided supported finding that mother did not receive notice of custody hearing. In re Calhoun (Ohio App. 2 Dist., Montgomery, 05-16-2003) No. 19713, 2003-Ohio-2521, 2003 WL 21127798, Unreported. Child Custody ⚖ 410

In a custody dispute, a trial court fails to comply with Civ R 53 where it chooses to adopt the referee's report without any modification even though the report contains no findings of fact on the issue of allocation of parental rights and responsibilities upon which the court can independently determine the best interest of the children and analyze the custody issue. Jordan v. Jordan (Ohio App. 4 Dist., Scioto, 06-06-1996) No. 95CA2333, 1996 WL 310039, Unreported.

Awarding sole custody of children to mother was warranted; father attempted to manipulate children about custody issue, father's choice not to see children after temporary custody hearing was punitive and not in children's best interest, and father failed to pay child support even though he could afford to pay his obligation. In re Custody of Harris (Ohio App. 2 Dist., 07-14-2006) 168 Ohio App.3d 1, 857 N.E.2d 1235, 2006-Ohio-3649, on subsequent appeal 2006-Ohio-3746, 2006 WL 2037323. Child Custody ⚖ 68; Child Custody ⚖ 78

Wife's failure to file an answer in husband's action seeking divorce did not preclude her from contesting issues or from presenting evidence, and thus trial court was required to reset case on contested docket after wife appeared at hearing intending to contest issues, including division of property and custody of children; performance of trial court's independent judicial duties to divide the marital and separate property equitably and to allocate parental rights and responsibilities consistent with the best interests of the children does not lend itself to judgment by default. Rue v. Rue (Ohio App. 2 Dist., 09-29-2006) 169 Ohio App.3d 160, 862 N.E.2d 166, 2006-Ohio-5131. Child Custody ⚖ 534; Divorce ⚖ 160

Failure of husband to verify habeas corpus petition that he filed in Court of Appeals to contest trial court's award of custody of parties' minor daughter to wife in divorce action precluded any entitlement to relief. Evans v. Klaeger (Ohio, 12-01-1999) 87 Ohio St.3d 260, 719 N.E.2d 546, 1999-Ohio-55, reconsideration denied 87 Ohio St.3d 1495, 722 N.E.2d 527. Habeas Corpus ⚖ 673

Unexcused absence of mother who voluntarily left courtroom after being summoned to the stand as father's witness did not afford her grounds to object to the proceeding of the hearing on father's motion for modification of child custody decree, and, consequently, trial court did not abuse its discretion by holding the hearing despite mother's absence. Sayre v. Hoelzle-Sayre (Ohio App. 3 Dist., 04-06-1994) 100 Ohio App.3d 203, 653 N.E.2d 712, appeal allowed 70 Ohio St.3d 1426, 638 N.E.2d 88, appeal dismissed as improvidently allowed 72 Ohio St.3d 1218, 651 N.E.2d 430, 1995-Ohio-274. Child Custody ⚖ 655

Cross-examination testimony by stepmother about alleged domestic violence committed by father was properly excluded in child custody case as irrelevant to question whether stepmother or cousin of mother should have custody of child, as father no longer resided with stepmother; moreover, although evidence might have been relevant to issue whether father's motion for visitation should have been granted, it was beyond scope of cross-examination, as direct examination did not address question of father's visitation. In re Whaley (Athens 1993) 86 Ohio App.3d 304, 620 N.E.2d 954. Child Custody ☞ 451; Witnesses ☞ 269(2.1)

A statement by the court in its judgment entry that it carefully considered all the evidence presented to the referee and made an independent review of the facts shows that the referee's decision was not merely "rubber-stamped." Roach v. Roach (Montgomery 1992) 79 Ohio App.3d 194, 607 N.E.2d 35.

Excluding testimony and report of maternal grandparents' expert related to child's best interests was not abuse of discretion in child custody modification proceeding involving natural father and grandparents, where grandparents had four months to provide father with report but did not send it to father's counsel until night before hearing. Harrold v. Collier (Ohio App. 9 Dist., Wayne, 07-31-2002) No. 02CA0005, 2002-Ohio-3864, 2002 WL 1758392, Unreported. Child Custody ☞ 632

24. —— Psychological and related investigations and evaluations, initial allocation of rights and responsibilities and "best interest"

Trial court did not abuse its discretion in designating mother as children's sole residential parent and legal custodian, in child custody proceeding; both the custody investigator and doctor who performed psychological evaluations on the parties recommended that mother be awarded sole custody of the children, based primarily on father's unresolved psychological issues, father failed to shield children from his hostility toward parties' divorce and mother's decision to end the marriage, father had no appreciation for the children's need for their mother, he had no insight into how his behavior was negatively impacting children, and some of his behavior was abusive and erratic. Cwik v. Cwik (Ohio App. 1 Dist., Hamilton, 02-04-2011) No. C-090843, 2011-Ohio-463, 2011 WL 346173, Unreported, appeal not allowed 128 Ohio St.3d 1515, 948 N.E.2d 451, 2011-Ohio-2686. Child Custody ☞ 48; Child Custody ☞ 58; Child Custody ☞ 421

Trial court's decision designating ex-wife as the residential parent and legal custodian of their son was not contrary to manifest weight of the evidence; guardian ad litem's recommendation was based on his objection to ex-wife's move to Mississippi, and he recommended shared parenting if ex-wife moved back but recommended ex-husband have sole custody if ex-wife stayed in Mississippi, psychological evaluations offered the court an independent and considered perspective of parties as potential parents, and evaluator concluded, based on his observations and the results of standard psychological evaluations completed by parties, that child's best interest was with ex-wife. Wise v. Wise (Ohio App. 2 Dist., Montgomery, 03-19-2010) No.

23424, 2010-Ohio-1116, 2010 WL 1038393, Unreported. Child Custody ☞ 421

Evidence supported trial court's decision to designate husband as sole residential parent and legal custodian of child in divorce action; evidence indicated that there was wide gap between wife's actual functional capacities and her inflated estimation of her own abilities, particularly when addressing child's health issues, wife initiated treatments for child that were unnecessary, and wife displayed consistent lack of credibility given that she overstated her professional qualifications and educational achievements, grossly inflated her resume and work history, and portrayed herself as related to Greek royalty. Wilson v. Wilson-Michelakis (Ohio App. 10 Dist., Franklin, 02-04-2010) No. 09AP-81, 2010-Ohio-370, 2010 WL 383616, Unreported. Child Custody ☞ 469

Competent, credible evidence supported trial court's decision to award custody to husband; clinical psychologist's evaluation of husband was that he was a pretty normal functioning individual and he noted no significant problems with husband, and, regarding his evaluation of wife, psychologist was concerned about her difficulty cognitively and her perceptions and mistrust/suspicion of people in her life, and a general way of describing her symptoms was paranoia, specifically related to adult relations, husband had not seen his children for several months because of wife's conduct, and wife had prior felony conviction for domestic violence and conviction for violation of a civil protection order as well. Lawson v. Lawson (Ohio App. 5 Dist., Licking, 01-13-2009) No. 08-CA-37, 2009-Ohio-248, 2009 WL 153439, Unreported. Child Custody ☞ 469

Trial court acted within its discretion in not sua sponte ordering a psychological or psychiatric evaluation of father after a hearing on father's complaint for allocation of parental rights as to their out-of-wedlock child, even though mother pointed to testimony of her daughter from a prior relationship that father, inter alia, had disciplined the daughter by placing duct tape on her face; mother was aware of the alleged instances of abuse and could have requested a psychological or psychiatric evaluation of father prior to the hearing. In re S.M.K. (Ohio App. 2 Dist., Miami, 12-19-2008) No. 2008 CA 17, 2008-Ohio-6733, 2008 WL 5273344, Unreported. Children Out–of–wedlock ☞ 20.4

Failure to order full and complete psychological custody evaluation of parties and parties' children did not constitute abuse of discretion on parties' motions for sole custody at end of same year in which divorce judgment was entered under which parties agreed to care for children pursuant to court-approved shared parenting plan; potential harm of order outweighed any possible benefit, and court pointed out that children's guardian ad litem, appointed to be advocate for children, upon concluding her investigation, did not recommend psychological evaluations. Mangan v. Mangan (Ohio App. 2 Dist., Greene, 07-18-2008) No. 07-CA-100,

2008-Ohio-3622, 2008 WL 2809225, Unreported. Child Custody ⟜ 616

Father lacked standing to assert negligence or professional malpractice against his child's psychologist for making custody recommendation in mother's favor, regardless of whether he had retained and paid for psychologist's counseling services in the past; absent physician-patient relationship between himself and psychologist, father was not entitled to recover damages for injuries based on psychologist's duty owed strictly to the minor child. Silvers v. Bardenstein (Ohio App. 8 Dist., Cuyahoga, 08-18-2005) No. 85971, 2005-Ohio-4309, 2005 WL 1994941, Unreported. Health ⟜ 750

Trial court did not abuse its discretion, in proceedings on wife's complaint for divorce, in designating wife as children's residential parent, despite expert testimony that wife's psychological evaluation suggested that she suffered from hysteria, depression, psychothenia, schizophrenia, introversion, and neurosis, and evidence that wife had unilaterally withdrawn from therapy for such ailments, where wife's mental stability was not determinative of issue of custody, but merely one factor to be considered, and trial court considered all applicable factors in reaching its decision. Puls v. Puls (Ohio App. 2 Dist., Montgomery, 03-25-2005) No. 20487, 2005-Ohio-1373, 2005 WL 678931, Unreported, on subsequent appeal 2005-Ohio-6839, 2005 WL 3502148. Child Custody ⟜ 62

Wife did not waive privilege as to medical and/or mental health records related to her son from prior marriage by requesting custody of child born during subsequent marriage at issue in divorce proceeding, although son's health was relevant to child's best interest in determining custody, as son would be member of household and influence on child if wife was granted custody of child, record belied husband's contention that son sexually and/or physically abused child such that there was no affirmative showing of direct link between son's medical and mental health and child's best interest. Schill v. Schill (Ohio App. 11 Dist., Geauga, 09-24-2004) No. 2002-G-2465, 2004-Ohio-5114, 2004 WL 2803230, Unreported. Privileged Communications And Confidentiality ⟜ 265; Privileged Communications And Confidentiality ⟜ 323

Wife waived privilege as to her own medical and/or mental health records by requesting custody of child in divorce proceeding, given that mental and physical health of parents is of major importance in determining custody. Schill v. Schill (Ohio App. 11 Dist., Geauga, 09-24-2004) No. 2002-G-2465, 2004-Ohio-5114, 2004 WL 2803230, Unreported. Privileged Communications And Confidentiality ⟜ 265; Privileged Communications And Confidentiality ⟜ 323

Trial court denial of wife's request that husband and the children be ordered to submit to psychological evaluations was not an abuse of discretion, during divorce proceeding; wife did not request the psychological evaluations until after the third full day of the divorce hearing, and evidence showed that the children were already in counseling. Weaver v. Weaver (Ohio App. 5 Dist., Licking, 08-09-2004) No. 2003CA00096, 2004-Ohio-4212, 2004 WL 1784595, Unreported. Child Custody ⟜ 425

Husband failed to preserve for appellate review his claim that the trial court erred when it ordered both parties to divorce trial to submit to psychological evaluations; husband failed to object to the order requiring the evaluations, he never sought to vacate the order, and the order was entered during trial. Brewer v. Brewer (Ohio App. 5 Dist., Licking, 07-01-2004) No. 2003CA00087, 2004-Ohio-3531, 2004 WL 1486781, Unreported. Divorce ⟜ 179

Mother waived right to claim on appeal from grant of child custody to grandmother that trial court abused its discretion by admitting counselor's report, where mother failed at trial to object to report and stipulated that it would be entered into evidence. In re Beireis (Ohio App. 12 Dist., Clinton, 03-29-2004) No. CA2003-01-001, 2004-Ohio-1506, 2004 WL 602291, Unreported, appeal not allowed 102 Ohio St.3d 1473, 809 N.E.2d 1159, 2004-Ohio-2830. Child Custody ⟜ 904; Child Custody ⟜ 918

Admitting court-appointed psychologist's report was not abuse of discretion in proceeding in which child's custody was granted to grandmother; although mother did not receive report until morning of trial, mother objected and stated that 45 minutes was needed to prepare for cross-examination, psychologist was not questioned until after one and one-half hour lunch break, all parties to action received report at same time, and all parties were aware that court ordered such evaluation. In re Beireis (Ohio App. 12 Dist., Clinton, 03-29-2004) No. CA2003-01-001, 2004-Ohio-1506, 2004 WL 602291, Unreported, appeal not allowed 102 Ohio St.3d 1473, 809 N.E.2d 1159, 2004-Ohio-2830. Child Custody ⟜ 421

In divorce action, trial court complied both with statute allowing court to appoint investigator regarding custody issues and with local rule based on statute; trial court considered investigator's report in making findings of fact, but also stated that court considered all of the evidence admitted during trial, observed parties and witnesses, and assessed their credibility. Martin v. Martin (Ohio App. 3 Dist., Marion, 02-23-2004) No. 9-03-47, 2004-Ohio-807, 2004 WL 324862, Unreported. Child Custody ⟜ 511

Report prepared by court-appointed investigator regarding factors associated with child custody determinations could include investigator's recommendations. Martin v. Martin (Ohio App. 3 Dist., Marion, 02-23-2004) No. 9-03-47, 2004-Ohio-807, 2004 WL 324862, Unreported. Child Custody ⟜ 421

Trial court did not abuse its discretion in awarding custody of child to father, even though father had a history of mental illness, and drug and alcohol abuse, where father was medication-compliant, his court-ordered drug screen result was negative, and father's psychiatrist testified and reported no barriers to his ability to take care of child. Simmons v. Willett (Ohio App. 5 Dist., Morgan, 07-08-2003) No. 02 CA 8, 2003-Ohio-3677, 2003 WL 21569718, Unreported. Child Custody ☞ 60; Child Custody ☞ 62; Child Custody ☞ 469

Court-appointed psychologist's evaluation in divorce proceeding was not proximate cause of former husband's agreement to the shared parenting plan naming former wife the primary residential parent, and thus, psychologist was not liable for husband's damages in malpractice or negligence action due to inaccurate evaluation of wife's stability; husband's draft proposal for the parenting agreement was dated prior to any evaluation by the psychologist, and there was no rebuttal to evidence that the husband did not rely on the evaluation in formulating his decision to propose his wife as the primary residential parent. McCleery v. Leach (Ohio App. 11 Dist., Lake, 04-14-2003) No. 2001-L-195, 2003-Ohio-1875, 2003 WL 1871005, Unreported. Health ☞ 696

Court-appointed psychologist who served as such during the divorce proceeding to aid the trial court in allocating parental rights and responsibilities was entitled to absolute immunity in suit filed against him for psychological malpractice and negligence by former husband, regardless of whether psychologist's court imposed duty was to produce an evaluation or to testify; in being ordered to conduct a psychological examination and evaluation of the parties to the divorce, psychologist was acting as an arm of the court and only carrying out a duty imposed upon him by the court order. McCleery v. Leach (Ohio App. 11 Dist., Lake, 04-14-2003) No. 2001-L-195, 2003-Ohio-1875, 2003 WL 1871005, Unreported. Health ☞ 768

Mother waived claim that trial court erred by considering child's custodial preferences as set forth in psychological evaluation of the child, where mother failed to object to the admission of evaluation into evidence or to the psychologist's testimony at trial. Lynch v. Lynch (Ohio App. 6 Dist., Huron, 03-07-2003) No. H-02-022, 2003-Ohio-1039, 2003 WL 876566, Unreported. Child Custody ☞ 904

Father was not prejudiced by trial court's alleged error in custody proceedings of limiting cross-examination of mother on matters related to her therapy, where information that father sought was subsequently introduced through mother's psychologist's testimony. Barnett-Soto v. Soto (Ohio App. 9 Dist., Medina, 02-05-2003) No. 02CA0011-M, 2003-Ohio-535, 2003 WL 245825, Unreported. Child Custody ☞ 923(1)

Responsibility of determining what specific parenting structure will serve a child's best interests rests with the trial court, not a psychologist's report and recommendation; psychologist's report or recommendation is but one factor that a court should consider. Dannaher v. Newbold (Ohio App. 10

Dist., 03-04-2004) 2004-Ohio-1003, 2004 WL 396993. Child Custody ☞ 421

The trial court's decision to disregard the testimony of psychologist, who opined that mother suffered from mental illness, was not an abuse of discretion, in proceeding to terminate shared parenting plan; evidence introduced at the hearing, including evidence that psychologist was not mother's treating physician and that psychologist gave too much weight to the oldest children's complaints about mother, supported the trial judge's conclusion that psychologist's opinion was unconvincing. H.R. v. L.R. (Ohio App. 10 Dist., 04-07-2009) 181 Ohio App.3d 837, 911 N.E.2d 321, 2009-Ohio-1665. Evidence ☞ 571(2)

Statute governing medical, psychological, and psychiatric examinations in child custody proceedings does not afford the party seeking such an examination the right to select the professional who will conduct the examination. Yazdani-Isfehani v. Yazdani-Isfehani (Ohio App. 4 Dist., 12-26-2006) 170 Ohio App.3d 1, 865 N.E.2d 924, 2006-Ohio-7105. Child Custody ☞ 424; Child Custody ☞ 425

Statute governing medical, psychological, and psychiatric examinations in child custody proceedings places the decision to order an investigation clearly within the trial court's sound discretion. Yazdani-Isfehani v. Yazdani-Isfehani (Ohio App. 4 Dist., 12-26-2006) 170 Ohio App.3d 1, 865 N.E.2d 924, 2006-Ohio-7105. Child Custody ☞ 424; Child Custody ☞ 425

Assertions by counsel for maternal grandparents that trial court had manipulated custody investigation were completely unsupported by record, in proceeding on parents' request for return of custody of child who had been adjudicated abused and dependent and whose legal custody had been granted maternal grandparents; counsel suggested that trial court had had inappropriate discussions with court-appointed custody investigator, but counsel, in cross-examining custody investigator, was unable to unearth any irregularities, and trial court's threat to impose sanctions was not proof of impropriety by trial court. In re James (Ohio App. 1 Dist., 09-16-2005) 163 Ohio App.3d 442, 839 N.E.2d 39, 2005-Ohio-4847, appeal allowed 108 Ohio St.3d 1413, 841 N.E.2d 318, 2006-Ohio-179, reversed 113 Ohio St.3d 420, 866 N.E.2d 467, 2007-Ohio-2335, reconsideration denied 114 Ohio St.3d 1484, 870 N.E.2d 734, 2007-Ohio-3699. Infants ☞ 246

Trial court's appointment of independent custody investigator, rather than clinical psychologist who had worked with parties, to conduct custody investigation on parents' request for return of custody of child who had been adjudicated abused and dependent and whose legal custody had been granted maternal grandparents, was not only within trial court's discretion, but appropriate under the circumstances; trial court deliberately appointed custody investigator who was not familiar with parties or case in any way to help trial court determine what would be in child's best interest. In re James

(Ohio App. 1 Dist., 09-16-2005) 163 Ohio App.3d 442, 839 N.E.2d 39, 2005-Ohio-4847, appeal allowed 108 Ohio St.3d 1413, 841 N.E.2d 318, 2006-Ohio-179, reversed 113 Ohio St.3d 420, 866 N.E.2d 467, 2007-Ohio-2335, reconsideration denied 114 Ohio St.3d 1484, 870 N.E.2d 734, 2007-Ohio-3699. Infants ☞ 208

Parties to a domestic relations proceeding may choose to submit a psychologist's report to the court without conducting an evidentiary hearing and without considering the psychologist's oral testimony. Beaver v. Beaver (Ohio App. 4 Dist., 05-25-2001) 143 Ohio App.3d 1, 757 N.E.2d 41, 2001-Ohio-2399. Child Custody ☞ 421

Wife was not entitled to introduce testimony of licensed social worker as an expert witness in proceedings to determine which party should be son's custodial parent; social worker only briefly met with son for five minutes, social worker met with husband on only two occasions in context of counseling with parties' daughter, and trial court heard testimony from all parties involved and also conducted in camera interview with son and daughter. Donovan v. Donovan (Ohio App. 12 Dist., 04-29-1996) 110 Ohio App.3d 615, 674 N.E.2d 1252. Evidence ☞ 512

Statute and rule which provide for admission of court-ordered investigation reports involving child custody and divorce matters and permit cross-examination of the parties concerning contents of reports import the use of such reports as testimony. Sayre v. Hoelzle-Sayre (Ohio App. 3 Dist., 04-06-1994) 100 Ohio App.3d 203, 653 N.E.2d 712, appeal allowed 70 Ohio St.3d 1426, 638 N.E.2d 88, appeal dismissed as improvidently allowed 72 Ohio St.3d 1218, 651 N.E.2d 430, 1995-Ohio-274. Child Custody ☞ 421; Evidence ☞ 333(1)

Divorce court was within its discretion to disregard psychologist's recommendation and base its child custody decision on other evidence. Frost v. Frost (Franklin 1992) 84 Ohio App.3d 699, 618 N.E.2d 198, motion overruled 66 Ohio St.3d 1489, 612 N.E.2d 1245. Evidence ☞ 571(1)

Custody investigation reports as to the character, earning ability, financial worth, past conduct and family relations of both parties to the action are to be made available to each party's counsel at least seven days before trial under Civ R 75 and five days under RC 3109.04. Roach v. Roach (Montgomery 1992) 79 Ohio App.3d 194, 607 N.E.2d 35.

Custody investigation reports on both parties' backgrounds are to be admitted into evidence subject to cross-examination of the investigator about the contents of the report so due process rights are protected. Roach v. Roach (Montgomery 1992) 79 Ohio App.3d 194, 607 N.E.2d 35.

In a custody dispute where the noncustodial parent undergoes a court-ordered psychological evaluation, the trial court does not abuse its discretion by declining to order the noncustodial parent's second wife to undergo an evaluation as well. In re Reynolds (Hamilton 1982) 2 Ohio App.3d 309, 441 N.E.2d 1141, 2 O.B.R. 341. Child Custody ☞ 418

Where a court in a child custody hearing authorizes a custodial investigation and bases its decision entirely on the findings therefrom while excluding other available evidence, such decision is invalid. Hillard v. Hillard (Butler 1971) 29 Ohio App.2d 20, 277 N.E.2d 557, 58 O.O.2d 14.

Trial court was justified in awarding custody of children eleven, ten, and six to the father because of the mother's emotional instability. Herzog v. Herzog (Montgomery 1955) 132 N.E.2d 754, 72 Ohio Law Abs. 22.

Competent and credible evidence supported finding that, although wife had a history of depression, she was in good health at time of hearing and able to provide for the care and sustenance of the parties' three minor children, a finding that supported award of residential custody of children to wife; wife's psychologist and her mental health case manager both testified that wife was able to provide care and sustenance for children, and nurse for parties' terminally ill child testified that she had no concerns regarding wife's care for the child. Grimm v. Grimm (Ohio App. 7 Dist., Jefferson, 06-19-2002) No. 01 JE 6, 2002-Ohio-3208, 2002 WL 1396799, Unreported. Child Custody ☞ 469

Competent and credible evidence supported finding that wife's hospitalization for depression was result of husband's manipulations, a factor that supported awarding residential custody of parties' three minor children to wife; evidence included wife's testimony that she and husband fought often, he told her their child's terminal illness was her fault, lied to doctor about wife which led to her hospitalization, and the delay in her release, wife's mother testified that as wife was being led to a police car in handcuffs to be taken to the hospital, husband, who had previously been arrested for domestic violence towards wife said, "now she knows how I felt when I had handcuffs behind my back going to jail," and while wife was in hospital, husband moved children and most of parties' possessions out of their home and into his parents' home. Grimm v. Grimm (Ohio App. 7 Dist., Jefferson, 06-19-2002) No. 01 JE 6, 2002-Ohio-3208, 2002 WL 1396799, Unreported. Child Custody ☞ 469

The power of the court to order psychological evaluations of parties to a custody dispute under RC 3109.04 is advisory and not mandatory. Heyob v Newman, No. 638 (4th Dist Ct App, Highland, 12-8-87).

In a custody hearing, it is within the discretion of the trial court to refuse to consider an investigative report prepared by the county welfare department. Garza v Garza, No. S-81-28 (6th Dist Ct App, Sandusky, 5-14-82).

Pursuant to RC 3109.04, a trial court is required to review the mental and physical health of all parties concerned in addressing issues of parental rights and responsibilities and it does not abuse discretion in ordering a mental health counseling facility to disclose medical records where a case presents an ongoing issue regarding a parent's visitation and companionship rights with the parties' minor children and whether the visitation would be in the children's best interests. Smith v Smith, No. 94–B–55, 1997 WL 467554 (7th Dist Ct App, Belmont, 8–8–97).

25. —— Racial matters, initial allocation of rights and responsibilities and "best interest"

Where mother appealed the award of custody of minor child to the father claiming the court used race as a determinative factor, the court of appeals found that the determinative factors were other than race. Hayes v Hayes, No. CA–5551 (5th Dist Ct App, Stark, 7–29–81).

26. —— Religion, initial allocation of rights and responsibilities and "best interest"

Modification of shared parenting plan which established possession schedule giving former wife possession of child on all secular and religious holidays was abuse of court's discretion, absent any showing that child would suffer harm from contact with former husband on such occasions; court's modifications both deprived former husband of any opportunity to teach child his religious traditions, which differed from those of former wife, and removed child from contact with extended family on both sides during holidays, as former wife lived out of state and minimized contact with members of her family. In re Marriage of Shore (Ohio App. 8 Dist., 08-18-1999) 135 Ohio App.3d 374, 734 N.E.2d 395, dismissed, appeal not allowed 87 Ohio St.3d 1459, 720 N.E.2d 541. Child Custody ☞ 637

Parent may not be denied custody on basis of his or her religious practices unless such practices adversely affect mental or physical well-being of child. Arthur v. Arthur (Ohio App. 5 Dist., 10-22-1998) 130 Ohio App.3d 398, 720 N.E.2d 176. Child Custody ☞ 46

A parent may not be denied custody of a child on the basis of the parent's religious practices unless there is probative evidence that those practices will adversely affect the mental or physical health of the child; evidence that the child will not be permitted to participate in certain social or patriotic activities is not sufficient to prove possible harm. Pater v. Pater (Ohio 1992) 63 Ohio St.3d 393, 588 N.E.2d 794. Child Custody ☞ 46

A court may not restrict a noncustodial parent's right to expose his or her child to religious beliefs, unless the conflict between the parents' religious beliefs is affecting the child's general welfare. Pater v. Pater (Ohio 1992) 63 Ohio St.3d 393, 588 N.E.2d 794. Child Custody ☞ 104; Constitutional Law ☞ 1408

A court may consider the parents' religious convictions in awarding custody as those convictions relate to the determination of what is in the best interests of the child; the court does not thereby violate the parties' constitutional rights. Klamo v. Klamo (Butler 1988) 56 Ohio App.3d 15, 564 N.E.2d 1078.

In deciding the custody of minor children, the court may consider the religious practices of a parent in making the custody determination without violating the parent's constitutional right to the free exercise of religion; the parent may be found unsuitable after such consideration without a finding of actual harm to the children. Birch v. Birch (Ohio 1984) 11 Ohio St.3d 85, 463 N.E.2d 1254, 11 O.B.R. 327.

The provisions of a separation agreement, dealing with the promise of the mother to see to it that the daughter placed in her custody be reared in the Catholic faith and attend a school affiliated with the Catholic church, cannot be enforced by judicial decree. Hackett v. Hackett (Lucas 1958) 150 N.E.2d 431, 78 Ohio Law Abs. 485. Child Custody ☞ 35

27. —— "Residential parent" rights and duties, initial allocation of rights and responsibilities and "best interest"

Trial court's decision to designate wife as the residential parent and legal custodian of child was supported by competent, credible evidence; court's decision was based upon the inability of husband to communicate and cooperate with wife in regard to child without verbally abusing or threatening her, his inability to comply with court orders including child support and visitation time, and the guardian ad litem's positive testimony of wife as a parent. Strauss v. Strauss (Ohio App. 8 Dist., Cuyahoga, 08-04-2011) No. 95377, 2011-Ohio-3831, 2011 WL 3359920, Unreported. Child Custody ☞ 48

Trial court acted within its discretion in designating wife as the residential parent and legal custodian of the parties' minor children upon divorce; trial court heard testimony describing manner in which husband had physically abused wife in presence of children and threatened the children, and other evidence showed that wife was the children's primary caregiver and was more likely to facilitate visitation. Ruble v. Ruble (Ohio App. 12 Dist., Madison, 07-05-2011) No. CA2010-09-019, 2011-Ohio-3350, 2011 WL 2611797, Unreported. Child Custody ☞ 48; Child Custody ☞ 58

In initial child custody case involving parents who were never married, trial court did not abuse its discretion in designating biological father as the residential parent and legal custodian of child; the critical issue to the trial court was which parent was most likely to honor and facilitate court-approved parenting time, rights or visitation and companionship rights, and the court found that biological mother had put forth little effort, if any, to ensure that father had companionship with child, noted that father provided the transportation involved even after mother moved child to Ohio, and clearly believed that mother's husband had a hostile attitude toward father and was critical of him. Hartman v. Eggar (Ohio App. 5 Dist., Fairfield, 12-16-2010) No. 09 CA 0055, 2010-Ohio-6357, 2010 WL 5480652, Unreported. Children Out-of-wedlock ☞ 20.3

Evidence supported finding in divorce proceeding that it was in the best interests of parties' minor daughter to designate wife as the child's sole residential parent; court considered guardian ad litem's report recommending that wife be designated the sole residential parent and husband's failure to pay temporary child support, and although husband alleged that wife's paramour had abused the child, the court recognized that the allegations had been investigated and were found to be unsubstantiated. Albert v. Albert (Ohio App. 2 Dist., Montgomery, 12-10-2010) No. 24000, 2010-Ohio-6112, 2010 WL 5140594, Unreported. Child Custody ☞ 210

Trial court did not have authority to impose, in essence, a shared parenting plan by designating each parent the minor child's residential parent when the child was in that parent's physical custody, where there was no evidence that either parent requested shared parenting or filed a shared parenting plan; court was statutorily required to designate one of the parents the child's residential parent. Preston v. Preston (Ohio App. 4 Dist., 08-05-2010) No. 09CA26, 2010 -Ohio- 3711, 2010 WL 3159217, Unreported. Child Custody ☞ 414

Trial court's designation of adjudicated father as child's residential parent and legal custodian was not against manifest weight of the evidence; child had alleged that mother's older son had sexually abused her, but mother did not take child's allegations seriously enough, and, in fact, still did not fully believe child's story, which upset child, child, who had been residing with father, his wife, and wife's grandson, who was same age as child, since sex abuse allegations surfaced, was well adjusted to her home, school, and community life, and she had close and loving relationship with father, his wife, and her grandson. Pyburn v. Woodruff (Ohio App. 2 Dist., Clark, 11-06-2009) No. 2009-CA-10, 2009-Ohio-5872, 2009 WL 3683658, Unreported. Children Out–of–wedlock ☞ 20.3

Trial court could not designate husband the residential parent of children during school year and wife the residential parent during the summer months when allocating parental rights and responsibilities in a divorce case in which neither party asked for shared parenting or filed a shared parenting plan; trial court was required to designate either husband or wife. Cuvar v. Cuvar (Ohio App. 2 Dist., Greene, 08-14-2009) No. 08CA0056, No. 08CA0059, 2009-Ohio-4114, 2009 WL 2489221, Unreported. Child Custody ☞ 414

Trial court acted within its discretion in a divorce proceeding in designating wife as the residential parent of child, even though husband argued that the primary rationale for trial court's decision was the sibling bond between child and child's sister, who was mother's first child, and that wife was no longer the primary custodian of sister; sibling relationship was only one factor considered by trial court, trial court found that child's interaction and interrelationship with wife was very good, noted that child had adjusted to living with wife throughout most of the parties' separation, and found that husband's desire to split parenting time equally was

not feasible. Cross v. Cross (Ohio App. 12 Dist., Preble, 03-23-2009) No. CA2008-07-015, 2009-Ohio-1309, 2009 WL 737382, Unreported. Child Custody ☞ 210

Trial court acted within its discretion in a custody-modification proceeding in concluding that it was in child's best interest for former husband to be designated as the residential parent for purposes of school placement, even though former husband had several weekdays off and would able to visit the school that child would attend if former wife were the residential parent; if child attended that school, child would only see former husband on weekend evenings after he returned from work, and trial court found that designating former husband as the residential parent would best allow child frequent contact with both parents. Ralston v. Ralston (Ohio App. 3 Dist., Marion, 02-17-2009) No. 9 08 30, 2009 Ohio 679, 2009 WL 376753, Unreported. Child Custody ☞ 576

Record supported trial court's conclusion that designation of father as residential parent and legal custodian was in out-of-wedlock child's best interest, even though mother argued that trial court did not properly consider evidence of defendant's abusive behavior toward child and mother's daughter from a prior relationship; there was no evidence that defendant's discipline was ongoing, excessive, or for prolonged periods of time, trial court concluded that it appeared that the mother's lack of discipline resulted in father responding with inappropriate discipline, and mother had previously lost custody of her daughter due to the poor condition of her household. In re S.M.K. (Ohio App. 2 Dist., Miami, 12-19-2008) No. 2008 CA 17, 2008-Ohio-6733, 2008 WL 5273344, Unreported. Children Out–of–wedlock ☞ 20.3

Trial court acted within its discretion in adopting husband's shared parenting plan, thereby deciding against designating wife as residential parent or legal guardian, incident to divorce; parties were able to cooperate and make joint decisions respecting the children, parties were able to encourage the sharing of love, affection, and contact between the children and other parent, there was no history of or potential for child abuse, spousal abuse, other domestic violence or parental kidnapping by either parent, and parents were in rather close geographic proximity to each other. Dietrich v. Dietrich (Ohio App. 8 Dist., Cuyahoga, 11-06-2008) No. 90565, 2008-Ohio-5740, 2008 WL 4812439, Unreported. Child Custody ☞ 127; Child Custody ☞ 130; Child Custody ☞ 134

Evidence was sufficient in divorce action to support finding that it was in child's best interests to designate mother residential parent under sole custody order, allow her to relocate, and issue modified standard visitation schedule, despite father's contention that order would not allow him to maintain child's Muslim culture; guardian ad litem report recommended that mother be the residential parent, there was evidence mother was child's primary caregiver even though she was employed while father was unemployed, there was evidence mother's family lived where she wished to relocate while father's family lived in another state, court considered child's adjustment to his home, school, and community, court found father to be a difficult witness and was concerned about father's credibility, and clinical counselor's report found that child was in danger of psychological and emotional damage due to father's behavior. Najmi v. Najmi (Ohio App. 9 Dist., Lorain, 09-02-2008) No. 07CA009293, 2008-Ohio-4405, 2008 WL 4023719, Unreported. Child Custody ☞ 210; Child Custody ☞ 261; Child Custody ☞ 421

Evidence supported trial court's order awarding wife custody of parties' children and designating her as residential parent incident to divorce; court-appointed psychologist and guardian ad litem recommended that wife be given residential status, which recommendation was supported by wife's expert witness, a licensed psychologist, and, although husband and his expert testified that any tension experienced by children during visits with husband was attributable to wife's attempts to alienate children from him, the trial court conducted in-camera interview with children and was free to place more weight on testimony of wife and her witnesses. Hamilton v. Hamilton (Ohio App. 2 Dist., Montgomery, 07-25-2008) No. 22005, 2008-Ohio-3711, 2008 WL 2861705, Unreported. Child Custody ☞ 421; Child Custody ☞ 469

Trial court properly considered whether the harm suffered by out-of-wedlock child outweighed the benefit of granting father's request to modify child custody award, which named mother the primary residential parent and awarded father visitation, to award father custody; trial court recognized that mother and child would miss one another when they were not together, and considered the impact on the child and all parties involved, but determined that the loss of mother as the residential parent was outweighed by the advantages of the change. C.G. v. C.L. (Ohio App. 8 Dist., Cuyahoga, 06-26-2008) No. 90341, 2008-Ohio-3135, 2008 WL 2536058, Unreported. Children Out–of–wedlock ☞ 20.10

Trial court's designation of father as residential parent was not an abuse of discretion in divorce proceeding; although court recognized that both parents were loving and nurturing, record contained evidence that mother engaged in reckless behavior which included consumption of alcohol, a conviction for driving under the influence (DUI), and mixing alcohol with antidepressants, and there was testimony mother interfered with father's parenting time. Lanfranc v. Lanfranc (Ohio App. 5 Dist., Licking, 09-08-2005) No. 05CA11, 2005-Ohio-4715, 2005 WL 2175155, Unreported, appeal not allowed 108 Ohio St.3d 1437, 842 N.E.2d 63, 2006-Ohio-421. Child Custody ☞ 51; Child Custody ☞ 57; Child Custody ☞ 60

Trial court did not abuse its discretion, in action for divorce, in designating husband child's residential parent and awarding wife visitation in accordance with modified version of its standard schedule, where trial court considered all statutory and other relevant factors in determining child's best interest; wife intended to relocate out of state and was unwilling to live in close proximity to husband, husband had greater interaction with child, was highly suitable role model, and kept child on consistent schedule at school, and wife had previously left child unattended and failed to comply with rules and schedule of child's school. Caldas v. Caldas (Ohio App. 2 Dist., Montgomery, 08-19-2005) No. 20691, 2005-Ohio-4493, 2005 WL 2077783, Unreported. Child Custody ☞ 48; Child Custody ☞ 51; Child Custody ☞ 261

Trial court order naming former wife as sole residential parent and legal custodian of parties' minor children on conditional basis that former wife not move out-of-state was abuse of discretion; ambiguous language employed by trial court created uncertainty as to which of parties was custodial or residential parent, and made it impossible for Court of Appeals to determine, from framework of record, whether former wife or former husband was residential parent. Wyatt v. Wyatt (Ohio App. 11 Dist., Portage, 05-13-2005) No. 2004-P-0045, 2005-Ohio-2365, 2005 WL 1131766, Unreported. Child Custody ☞ 261; Child Custody ☞ 522

Trial court did not abuse its discretion, in proceedings on complaint for divorce, in granting wife residential parent status with respect to parties' three children, despite fact that wife was on bond pending deportation as illegal alien, where no evidence was presented that wife was unfit mother, family service coordinator testified and reported that husband repeatedly encouraged children to say negative things about wife during his visits, civil protective order had been issued against husband based on domestic violence finding, and wife had been children's primary caregiver from birth and had appropriate and varied discipline techniques, while husband told family service coordinator that he did not discipline the children. Caceres v. Caceres (Ohio App. 3 Dist., Marion, 04-25-2005) No. 9-04-60, 2005-Ohio-1915, 2005 WL 940858, Unreported. Child Custody ☞ 33

Trial court did not abuse its discretion in designating former husband residential parent of parties' minor child, where magistrate considered appropriate factors related to child's best interest, psychologist's report indicating that former wife suffered from fixed delusions and severe personality and parenting deficit, report of guardian ad litem, relationship between child and both parents, and parents' ability to assist child with her schoolwork. Wilkerson v. Wilkerson (Ohio App. 12 Dist., Butler, 03-21-2005) No. CA2004-02-043, No. CA2004-02-046, 2005-Ohio-1236, 2005 WL 637783, Unreported. Child Custody ☞ 147

Evidence in divorce proceedings supported trial court's finding that wife was unlikely to facilitate the parent/child relationship between father and child, thus supporting trial court's designating husband as residential parent of child; wife sent child to live with maternal grandparents for ten months against husband's wishes, father's phone calls to child during this time were not always answered or returned, mother was seeking full time employment out-of-state, and family services report stated that mother was unlikely to facilitate the father/child relationship. Goodman v. Goodman (Ohio App. 3 Dist., Marion, 03-14-2005) No. 9-04-37, 2005-Ohio-1091, 2005 WL 579154, Unreported. Child Custody ☞ 48; Child Custody ☞ 57

Change of daughter's residential parent from mother to father, once shared parenting plan became unworkable due to mother's relocation to distant city, was not abuse of discretion; ruling permitted child to remain in place and school where she had lived most of her life. O'Neil v. Presler (Ohio App. 4 Dist., Pickaway, 01-13-2005) No. 04CA2, 2005-Ohio-246, 2005 WL 130193, Unreported. Child Custody ☞ 576

Trial court abused its discretion in modifying legal and residential custody from mother to father, where court erroneously found that ex-wife only objected to modified custody arrangement after ex-husband sought to reduce his child support obligation and court arbitrarily and unreasonably relied upon such finding to support its award of custody to ex-husband. Cowan v. Cowan (Ohio App. 4 Dist., Washington, 11-12-2004) No. 04CA5, 2004-Ohio-6119, 2004 WL 2616410, Unreported. Child Custody ☞ 552

Granting mother custody of child was not abuse of discretion, where all relevant factors were nearly equal as between mother and father and there was no reason to uproot child from her mother's residence, especially in light of child's improved academic progress while she was living with mother. Ruark v. Smith (Ohio App. 10 Dist., Franklin, 12-16-2003) No. 03AP-498, 2003-Ohio-6831, 2003 WL 22956018, Unreported. Child Custody ☞ 25; Child Custody ☞ 88

Trial court reasonably ordered that former husband, rather than former wife, would be child's residential parent under shared parenting arrangement, where former husband remained in same school district in which child had previously attended school, and former wife had moved out of the district. Fee v. Fee (Ohio App. 12 Dist., Butler, 12-15-2003) No. CA2002-11-274, 2003-Ohio-6781, 2003 WL 22946425, Unreported. Child Custody ☞ 147

Even though change of custody was not pursuant to court order, non-residential parent was entitled to credit, against the amount of earlier medical expenses ordered to be reimbursed by her to residential parent, for child support payments made to residential parent while non-residential parent had physical custody of children with full knowledge and consent of residential parent; failure to permit credit would provide windfall to residential parent and deny children the benefit of support they were entitled to receive. Johnson v. Johnson (Ohio App. 3 Dist., Union, 12-15-2003) No. 14-03-32, 2003-Ohio-6710, 2003 WL 22939480, Unreported. Child Support ☞ 454

As trial court designated former wife as residential parent of children, and such decision was not

abuse of discretion, statute allowing trial court to certify proceedings to juvenile court if it determined best interest of the children would not be served by designating either party as residential parent was not applicable. Mills v. Mills (Ohio App. 11 Dist., Trumbull, 12-05-2003) No. 2002-T-0102, 2003-Ohio-6676, 2003 WL 22928461, Unreported. Courts ☞ 486; Infants ☞ 196

Ohio courts had jurisdiction to adjudicate the custody of mother's two children, in child custody dispute between mother in Ohio and father in North Carolina; Ohio was the "home state" of the children since the children had lived in Ohio on a permanent basis for the past four years, their schools, friends, and physicians were located in Ohio, and mother lived in Ohio. Taylor v. Taylor (Ohio App. 3 Dist., Crawford, 11-24-2003) No. 3-03-22, 2003-Ohio-6298, 2003 WL 22770053, Unreported. Child Custody ☞ 736

Substantial credible and competent evidence supported designation of father as residential parent of parties' child; record indicated neither parent had been primary caregiver, child's daily contact was with paternal relatives, mother was involved with potentially abusive men, mother went on drinking binges, and father provided majority of parenting during period between parties' separation and mother's relocation. Lowry v. Lowry (Ohio App. 5 Dist., Guernsey, 04-24-2003) No. 02CA13, 2003-Ohio-2121, 2003 WL 1958030, Unreported. Child Custody ☞ 41; Child Custody ☞ 48; Child Custody ☞ 60

Determination that designation of former wife as residential parent was in child's best interests was supported by findings that child had close bond with wife and half sister, wife was no longer suffering from depression since separation, wife was more likely than husband to honor visitation, and husband was in arrears on child support. Francis v. Francis (Ohio App. 2 Dist., Montgomery, 04-18-2003) No. 19367, 2003-Ohio-1940, 2003 WL 1901302, Unreported. Child Custody ☞ 48; Child Custody ☞ 62; Child Custody ☞ 84

Failure to find that former husband was primary caregiver of child, for purposes of determining whether husband or wife would be residential parent, was not abuse of discretion, despite evidence that child alternated equally between parties during period of separation, where wife, who did not work outside home during marriage, was primarily responsible for child's care prior to separation. Francis v. Francis (Ohio App. 2 Dist., Montgomery, 04-18-2003) No. 19367, 2003-Ohio-1940, 2003 WL 1901302, Unreported. Child Custody ☞ 44

Father was appropriate party to be awarded status of residential parent of nonmarital child, since father's relationship with his wife was more stable and permanent than mother's relationship with her boyfriend, mother had consistent pattern of living in various homes with different boyfriends, and mother was apparently relying on her boyfriend as sole means of economic support. In re Meyer (Ohio App. 12 Dist., Warren, 01-13-2003) No.

CA2002-05-048, 2003-Ohio-83, 2003 WL 103431, Unreported. Children Out–of–wedlock ☞ 20.3

Court could not allocate responsibilities for the care of the children primarily to one parent without designating that parent as the residential parent since RC 3109.04 is directory rather than discretionary. In re Clark (Ohio App. 8 Dist., Cuyahoga, 03-25-1999) No. 74663, 1999 WL 166018, Unreported.

Former wife was not entitled to transcripts of trial court's in camera interviews of minor children in child custody proceeding in which trial court revoked former wife's residential-parent status. Myers v. Myers (Ohio App. 5 Dist., 01-09-2007) 170 Ohio App.3d 436, 867 N.E.2d 848, 2007-Ohio-66. Child Custody ☞ 942

Husband's failure to comply with local rule governing mandatory parenting seminar precluded husband from being named sole residential parent and legal custodian in divorce action. Barry v. Barry (Ohio App. 8 Dist., 09-28-2006) 169 Ohio App.3d 129, 862 N.E.2d 143, 2006-Ohio-5008. Child Custody ☞ 48

Trial court was required to provide basis for designating wife as the sole residential parent and legal custodian of the minor children in divorce action. Derrit v. Derrit (Ohio App. 11 Dist., 09-09-2005) 163 Ohio App.3d 52, 836 N.E.2d 39, 2005-Ohio-4777. Child Custody ☞ 511

Former husband's proposed move out of state with children amounted to change of circumstances requiring trial court to inquire, upon former wife's motion for modification of parental rights and responsibilities originally established in judgment of divorce, into whether change of custody would be in children's best interests, where children had close relationships with members of extended family resident in state on both sides of the family and no connection with state to which former husband proposed to move, and where proposed move would undoubtedly impact children's ability to continue their family relationships. Zinnecker v. Zinnecker (Ohio App. 12 Dist., 05-10-1999) 133 Ohio App.3d 378, 728 N.E.2d 38. Child Custody ☞ 568; Child Support ☞ 290

Change of residence on part of residential parent that has no direct impact on child amounts to slight or inconsequential change in circumstances, while move that directly impacts child in some demonstrable way constitutes substantive change sufficient to meet threshold showing, on nonresidential parent's motion for modification of parental rights and responsibilities, that change of circumstances has occurred warranting further inquiry to determine whether change of custody is in best interest of child. Zinnecker v. Zinnecker (Ohio App. 12 Dist., 05-10-1999) 133 Ohio App.3d 378, 728 N.E.2d 38. Child Custody ☞ 568; Child Support ☞ 270; Child Support ☞ 290

Although a party exercising visitation rights might gain temporary physical control over the child for that purpose, such control does not constitute "child custody" because the legal authority to make fundamental decisions about the child's welfare remains with the custodial party and because the child eventually must be returned to the more permanent setting provided by that party. Braatz v. Braatz (Ohio, 03-24-1999) 85 Ohio St.3d 40, 706 N.E.2d 1218, 1999-Ohio-203. Child Custody ☞ 226

Wife could not be allowed to satisfy her child support arrearages in two years, at time of sale of marital home two years after effective date of division of marital assets in divorce proceeding, despite fact that husband was being allowed to reside with minor children in home for that period before sale of home, where trial court's decision to let husband and children reside in home was based on parties' desire to avoid further disruptions in children's lives. McQuinn v. McQuinn (Ohio App. 12 Dist., 04-08-1996) 110 Ohio App.3d 296, 673 N.E.2d 1384. Child Support ☞ 462

Where a divorce decree, voluntarily agreed to by both parties, gives legal custody of minor children to their father but leaves the immediate care and control with their mother, it is not error for the domestic relations court to approve a change of schools requested by the mother, since the immediate welfare of the children is in her hands. Majnaric v. Majnaric (Summit 1975) 46 Ohio App.2d 157, 347 N.E.2d 552, 75 O.O.2d 250.

Where evidence conclusively shows that mother of minor child is not suitable person to have custody of such child, and where an award of custody to mother would constitute abuse of discretion, it is erroneous, as a matter of law, for common pleas court to award "physical" custody of child to grandmother and "legal" custody to mother; under such circumstances court of appeals is not required to remand cause for new trial but may order custody awarded to father. Baxter v. Baxter (Ohio 1971) 27 Ohio St.2d 168, 271 N.E.2d 873, 56 O.O.2d 104. Child Custody ☞ 51; Child Custody ☞ 924

Evidence that it was in the child's best interest to be in the residential care of her mother was sufficient to support award to mother of residential care of daughter, where father vacated residence prior to daughter's birth and never returned, mother owned residence and it was an appropriate place to raise daughter, daughter had good relationship with stepsiblings, and father lived with girlfriend which made his living arrangements contingent on the strength of that relationship. Clantz v. Clantz (Ohio App. 5 Dist., Ashland, 09-30-2002) No. 02COA005, 2002-Ohio-5291, 2002 WL 31185868, Unreported. Child Custody ☞ 68; Child Custody ☞ 76

If a child is not the ward of any other court, trial court has jurisdiction over custody proceedings where the trial court's state has been the child's home state within six months before commencement of the proceeding, the child has developed significant connections with the state by virtue of the former residence, and the plaintiff, who acknowledges that he is the child's natural father, resides in the state. Harris v Hopper, No. L–81–187 (6th Dist Ct App, Lucas, 1–15–82).

28. —— Split custody and each parent with a child, initial allocation of rights and responsibilities and "best interest"

Evidence supported trial court's finding that shared parenting was in child's best interests, in divorce proceedings that involved child custody dispute; psychologist testified that the parties appeared to have a very loving, caring relationship with their daughter, and that child had a healthy bond with both parties, and other evidence showed that parties had the ability to cooperate with one another, and although husband's brother was a registered sex offender, trial court ordered that child not be permitted to have contact with husband's brother. Rainey v. Rainey (Ohio App. 12 Dist., Clermont, 08-29-2011) No. CA2010-10-083, 2011-Ohio-4343, 2011 WL 3820611, Unreported. Child Custody ☞ 472; Evidence ☞ 571(1)

Evidence supported finding that a shared parenting plan was in child's best interest, in divorce proceeding, even though husband and wife could not communicate well; child was well cared for in husband's care, child's paternal grandparents lived near father, child was well-adjusted in mother and father's homes, neither party suffered from any physical issues, except for one instance, the parties had been able to cooperate in exchanging child on alternating four or five day periods, neither party had denied the other party parenting time, and both parties resided close to each other in state. Eddy v. Eddy (Ohio App. 7 Dist., Harrison, 08-24-2011) No. 10-HA-05, 2011-Ohio-4315, 2011 WL 3820123, Unreported. Child Custody ☞ 147

Trial court did not abuse its discretion in ordering split custody of parties' four minor children in divorce action, with wife having residential custody of parties' daughters and husband having residential custody of parties' sons; although split custody arrangements are not generally encouraged, in case sub judice sons had interests outside school which were best furthered by their residence with husband, and visitation schedule gave all children substantial time with their nonresidential parents. Arthur v. Arthur (Ohio App. 5 Dist., 10-22-1998) 130 Ohio App.3d 398, 720 N.E.2d 176. Child Custody ☞ 27

In the absence of compelling evidence to the contrary, it is in the best interests of siblings to grow up in an environment in which they may interact and share experiences with one another. Kasten v Kasten, No. CA87-02-011 (12th Dist Ct App, Warren, 11-23-87).

The election of one child, aged twelve years, to live with his mother should not determine the custody of another, younger child but it is a factor the trial judge may consider in deciding what arrangement will best serve the interest of the younger child. Brown v Long, No. 8469 (2d Dist Ct App, Montgomery, 7-27-84).

29. —— Sufficiency of evidence, initial allocation of rights and responsibilities and "best interest"

Wife put forth sufficient evidence to establish a prima facie case that she was entitled to sole custody of the couple's children, for purposes of husband's motion to dismiss for insufficiency of evidence; children had continuously lived with wife since the date of separation, and during that time, wife had made all decisions pertinent to the children's lifestyles and general well-being, husband had been voluntarily uninvolved in the children's day-to-day routine as well as personally removed from all parental decision-making, wife had a steady job, income, insurance, and stable residence in which to care for the children, and husband, while employed, had had his hours cut and had been evicted from his apartment. Rymers v. Rymers (Ohio App. 11 Dist., Lake, 12-23-2010) No. 2009-L-160, 2010-Ohio-6439, 2010 WL 5550227, Unreported. Child Custody ☞ 509

30. —— "Unsuitability" of parent, initial allocation of rights and responsibilities and "best interest"

Finding that it was in best interests of minor children to name father as custodial parent, in divorce proceeding, was supported by sufficient evidence, including evidence that father had stronger financial status to provide for children, that mother had mental health issue, that mother lived in dangerous area, and that mother had permitted children to put rocks in their mouths. Shaw v. Shaw (Ohio App. 6 Dist., Huron, 09-17-2010) No. H-09-023, 2010-Ohio-4380, 2010 WL 3610250, Unreported. Child Custody ☞ 58; Child Custody ☞ 62; Child Custody ☞ 63

Grant of child custody to father in divorce proceedings was in best interests of child; guardian ad litem advised against shared parenting because of communication difficulties between parents, child expressed fear concerning mother's future actions toward father, there was evidence that mother had an explosive temper, father had removed children from home on several occasions because of mother's temper, supervised visits between mother and child became infrequent after temporary protection order was issued against mother. Bristow v. Bristow (Ohio App. 12 Dist., Butler, 07-26-2010) No. CA2009-05-139, 2010-Ohio-3469, 2010 WL 2892759, Unreported. Child Custody ☞ 134; Child Custody ☞ 421

Trial court's allocation of father as the custodial parent of out-of-wedlock child was not an abuse of discretion; both parents loved child and were capable parents, and mother's mental health issues and past history of denying father visitation with child weighed against designating her as the custodial parent. McCarty v. Hayner (Ohio App. 4 Dist., Jackson, 08-25-2009) No. 08CA8, 2009-Ohio-4540, 2009 WL 2783427, Unreported. Children Out-of-wedlock ☞ 20.3

Evidence was sufficient, in action by unmarried parents each seeking legal custody of minor child, to support finding that it was in best interest of child for father to be designated residential parent and legal custodian; father had ongoing relationship on non-working weekends despite four-hour distance, mother was unable to adequately help child with school-work because of her own reading deficiency, father was willing to help with school, mother's house was in disarray and she had lived with a man on drugs, father had a stable home, good salary, and stay-at-home wife, while the child's very mild preference for being with mother could be given little weight as being immature, since based on factors like tutoring, which would also be available with father, and a wish to skip attending religious services. Dunn v. Marcum (Ohio App. 2 Dist., Clark, 06-19-2009) No. 08-CA-112, 2009-Ohio-3015, 2009 WL 1800609, Unreported. Children Out–of–wedlock ☞ 20.3

The trial court, after child was adjudicated an abused, neglected, or dependent child and mother had remedied the circumstances that led to the adjudication, was not required to make a separate finding that mother was unsuitable before awarding custody of child to maternal grandparents; abuse, neglect, or dependency adjudications implicitly involved a determination of the unsuitability of the child's parents. In re Sorgen (Ohio App. 11 Dist., Lake, 08-11-2006) No. 2005-L-121, 2006-Ohio-4180, 2006 WL 2337557, Unreported. Infants ☞ 210

Trial court finding that it was in the best interest of child to remain in the custody of maternal grandparents was not an abuse of discretion; father's actions and mental health issues formed the basis of the finding of neglect and continued to place child at risk, and mother refused to separate from father and minimized the issues that formed the basis of the neglect finding. In re Sorgen (Ohio App. 11 Dist., Lake, 08-11-2006) No. 2005-L-121, 2006-Ohio-4180, 2006 WL 2337557, Unreported. Infants ☞ 231

Trial court did not abuse its discretion in designating unmarried father as child's residential parent and legal custodian; court found child had contact with her paternal and maternal relatives on regular basis, that child was six years old and enrolled in school, that each parent wanted to visit child on regular basis, that neither parent had been convicted of, or committed, any offense which resulted in neglect or abuse of child, and that unmarried mother did not notify unmarried father of her intent to take child to another state, had left state and left child in father's care, and had previously disappeared so there was not way to contact her. Pennycuff v. Thompson (Ohio App. 3 Dist., Seneca, 03-27-2006) No. 13-05-48, 2006-Ohio-1410, 2006 WL 759738, Unreported. Children Out–of–wedlock ☞ 20.3

Trial court finding that it was in the best interest of child for husband to be named the residential parent was not against the manifest weight of the evidence, during divorce proceeding; guardian ad litem and independent psychologist recommended that husband be designated the residential parent, guardian ad litem found husband more credible than wife and found wife's flight from the marital residence and her refusal to let husband know where she and child had gone indicated she was not being a responsible caregiver. Ward v. Ward (Ohio App. 5 Dist., Stark, 02-21-2006) No. 2005CA00118, 2006-Ohio-851, 2006 WL 438685, Unreported. Child Custody ☞ 57; Child Custody ☞ 421

Once trial court had determined mother had not abandoned her children and was not otherwise unsuitable for custody, analysis of the best interests of the children became immaterial in her action to regain custody, which had temporarily been granted to the children's grandparents. In re Custody of C.E. (Ohio App. 2 Dist., Champaign, 11-04-2005) No. 2005-CA-11, 2005-Ohio-5913, 2005 WL 2978938, Unreported. Child Custody ☞ 554

Trial court's decision naming father, rather than mother, as residential parent and legal custodian of child born out of wedlock was not against the manifest weight of the evidence; evidence showed mother was allowing ex-convict boyfriend to be paroled to her home, mother was an overly strict disciplinarian to young child, communication between mother and father had broken down, mother failed to cooperate with terms of shared parenting agreement, and mother was not truthful with regard to her living situation. John A.L. v. Sheri B. (Ohio App. 6 Dist., Lucas, 10-07-2005) No. L-04-1250, 2005-Ohio-5357, 2005 WL 2471040, Unreported. Children Out–of–wedlock ☞ 20.3

Allegations of child abuse and neglect, not leading to conviction or to removal of child from wife's care, were relevant consideration, in proceedings for divorce, in determining best interests of child with respect to custody. Shaffer v. Shaffer (Ohio App. 3 Dist., Paulding, 08-01-2005) No. 11-04-22, 2005-Ohio-3884, 2005 WL 1797739, Unreported. Child Custody ☞ 58; Child Custody ☞ 451

Trial court could not award maternal grandparents custody of child absent finding that mother was unfit parent. In re Self (Ohio App. 5 Dist., Stark, 12-13-2004) No. 2004CA00199, 2004-Ohio-6822, 2004 WL 2913567, Unreported, appeal not allowed 105 Ohio St.3d 1518, 826 N.E.2d 315, 2005-Ohio-1880. Child Custody ☞ 279

Father was not a suitable parent for the children, and thus, maternal grandmother, as opposed to father, was entitled to custody; father smoked marijuana in front of his children, he taught his son how to break into vehicles to steal tools, and, although he did not have a valid driver's license, father transported his children without proper child restraints in a work van with expired tags and no vehicle insurance, and father ignored child when child objected to father's association with certain friends which made the child uncomfortable. Radka v. McFall (Ohio App. 9 Dist., Lorain, 09-29-2004) No. 04CA008438, 2004-Ohio-5181, 2004 WL 2241753, Unreported. Child Custody ☞ 271

Juvenile court was required to determine that child's father, as the natural parent of child, was unsuitable to have custody of child before awarding legal custody to child's maternal aunt and uncle, in juvenile court case in which child's maternal aunt and uncle, her paternal grandmother, and her father all moved for legal custody after the County Department of Children and Family Services obtained emergency custody of child from child's mother. In re C.R. (Ohio App. 8 Dist., Cuyahoga, 08-26-2004) No. 82891, 2004-Ohio-4465, 2004 WL 1899219, Unreported, stay granted 104 Ohio St.3d 1443, 819 N.E.2d 1125, 2004-Ohio-7119, motion to certify allowed 105 Ohio St.3d 1436, 822 N.E.2d 809, 2005-Ohio-531, certified question answered 108 Ohio St.3d 369, 843 N.E.2d 1188, 2006-Ohio-1191, reconsideration denied 109 Ohio St.3d 1483, 847 N.E.2d 1227, 2006-Ohio-2466. Infants ⟳ 222

Wife properly was designated as child's residential parent; husband had used the child to get what he wanted, husband had not fostered telephone contact between wife and child nor had he sought wife's input on matters affecting child's care, and wife had better fostered the love and affection between husband and child while also complying with court ordered parenting time. Bechara v. Essad (Ohio App. 7 Dist., Mahoning, 06-11-2004) No. 03MA34, 2004-Ohio-3042, 2004 WL 1325636, Unreported. Child Custody ⟳ 48; Child Custody ⟳ 51; Child Custody ⟳ 57

Credible evidence supported trial court's finding that natural mother was unsuitable because she abandoned child, for purpose of proceeding in which child custody was granted to grandmother; mother left child in grandmother's care for period of more than seven months and did not attempt to visit or communicate with child during this period. In re Beireis (Ohio App. 12 Dist., Clinton, 03-29-2004) No. CA2003-01-001, 2004-Ohio-1506, 2004 WL 602291, Unreported, appeal not allowed 102 Ohio St.3d 1473, 809 N.E.2d 1159, 2004-Ohio-2830. Child Custody ⟳ 280

Evidence supported trial court designation of mother as residential parent of out-of-wedlock child; father never told mother when he was incarcerated for 30 days for passing a bad check, father lied to mother about his whereabouts during his incarceration, father enrolled child in school without mother's permission, father took child out of state without telling mother or getting her permission, and father was uncooperative in dealing with parenting issues or communicating with mother. Kauble v. Pfeiffer (Ohio App. 3 Dist., Marion, 12-22-2003) No. 9-03-36, 2003-Ohio-6988, 2003 WL 22994559, Unreported. Children Out–of–wedlock ⟳ 20.9

Father's misdemeanor disorderly conduct conviction did not bar his designation as residential parent and legal custodian. Prusia v. Prusia (Ohio App. 6 Dist., Lucas, 04-18-2003) No. L-02-1165, 2003-Ohio-2000, 2003 WL 1904410, Unreported. Child Custody ⟳ 61

Parental suitability, rather than best interest, applies as threshold determination in a proceeding for custody between a parent and nonparent; best interest standard is premised on idea that both parents in a divorce-related custody dispute are suitable, and thus, child's best interest becomes only relevant consideration in dispute between parents, which cannot be said in a dispute between a parent

and a nonparent. In re Daily (Ohio App. 4 Dist., Athens, 02-12-2003) No. 02CA31, 2003-Ohio-787, 2003 WL 368105, Unreported. Child Custody ⟳ 42; Child Custody ⟳ 76

Awarding sole custody of children to mother was warranted; father attempted to manipulate children about custody issue, father's choice not to see children after temporary custody hearing was punitive and not in children's best interest, and father failed to pay child support even though he could afford to pay his obligation. In re Custody of Harris (Ohio App. 2 Dist., 07-14-2006) 168 Ohio App.3d 1, 857 N.E.2d 1235, 2006-Ohio-3649, on subsequent appeal 2006-Ohio-3746, 2006 WL 2037323. Child Custody ⟳ 68; Child Custody ⟳ 78

Whether a parent smokes is a proper factor to consider when making child custody determinations. Pierce v. Pierce (Ohio App. 7 Dist., 09-21-2006) 168 Ohio App.3d 556, 860 N.E.2d 1087, 2006-Ohio-4953, appeal not allowed 112 Ohio St.3d 1491, 862 N.E.2d 117, 2007-Ohio-724. Child Custody ⟳ 48

Designation of former husband as residential parent was not abuse of discretion; former wife and her fiancé each had pack-a-day smoking habit, child's doctor told former husband that some of child's illnesses, such as ear infections, were linked to secondhand smoke, former husband did not smoke, and other factors did not weigh in favor of naming either parent as residential parent. Pierce v. Pierce (Ohio App. 7 Dist., 09-21-2006) 168 Ohio App.3d 556, 860 N.E.2d 1087, 2006-Ohio-4953, appeal not allowed 112 Ohio St.3d 1491, 862 N.E.2d 117, 2007-Ohio-724. Child Custody ⟳ 147

When determining custody of a child between a parent and a non-parent in an original custody dispute, custody may not be awarded to a non-parent without a finding of parental unsuitability; to demonstrate unsuitability, it must be shown by a preponderance of the evidence that the parent contractually relinquished custody of the child, that the parent has become totally incapable of supporting or caring for the child, or that an award of custody to the parent would be detrimental to the child. In re Sean T. (Ohio App. 6 Dist., 10-28-2005) 164 Ohio App.3d 218, 841 N.E.2d 838, 2005-Ohio-5739. Child Custody ⟳ 42; Child Custody ⟳ 465

A parent should be given only one unsuitability determination, which should come at the time of the legal custody hearing; after such a determination has established, or taken away, a parent's fundamental custodial rights, the focus must shift from the rights of the parents to the rights of the child. In re Hockstok (Ohio, 12-27-2002) 98 Ohio St.3d 238, 781 N.E.2d 971, 2002-Ohio-7208, modified 98 Ohio St.3d 1476, 784 N.E.2d 709, 2003-Ohio-980. Child Custody ⟳ 511

The Supreme Court of the United States has ruled that (1) smoking is not a fundamental right, (2) judicial notice is taken of the health-destructive effects of cigarettes and secondhand smoke, (3) both present harm and possible future harm from secondhand smoke is a real and substantial danger to non-smokers, and (4) secondhand smoke cannot be imposed involuntarily upon people because it is detrimental to their health. In re Julie Anne (Ohio Com.Pl., 08-27-2002) 121 Ohio Misc.2d 20, 780 N.E.2d 635, 2002-Ohio-4489. Environmental Law ☞ 285; Evidence ☞ 14

The Supreme Court of the United States has ruled that (1) the constitutional right to privacy is not absolute, (2) the state has an "urgent interest" in the welfare of the child and a "duty of the highest order" to protect the child, (3) along with parental rights come reciprocal responsibilities, and (4) when the interests of the parent and the child conflict to the point where the child is threatened with harm the state has an obligation to protect the welfare of the child. In re Julie Anne (Ohio Com.Pl., 08-27-2002) 121 Ohio Misc.2d 20, 780 N.E.2d 635, 2002-Ohio-4489. Constitutional Law ☞ 1226; Infants ☞ 13; Parent And Child ☞ 1

Courts take judicial notice that a superabundance of authoritative scientific evidence irrefutably demonstrates that secondhand smoke is a real and substantial danger to the health of children because it causes and aggravates serious diseases in children. In re Julie Anne (Ohio Com.Pl., 08-27-2002) 121 Ohio Misc.2d 20, 780 N.E.2d 635, 2002-Ohio-4489. Evidence ☞ 14

"Unsuitability" of parent to have custody of child does not necessarily connote any moral or character weakness, but rather, is designed to indicate that contractual relinquishment of custody, abandonment, complete inability to provide care or support, or that parental custody would be detrimental to child, has been proved by preponderance of evidence. Baker v. Baker (Ohio App. 9 Dist., 08-21-1996) 113 Ohio App.3d 805, 682 N.E.2d 661, appeal not allowed 77 Ohio St.3d 1525, 674 N.E.2d 376. Child Custody ☞ 465

After wife, husband, and child's maternal grandmother agreed during pendency of wife's divorce action to terminate agreement under which grandmother had been named child's guardian shortly after being born out of wedlock prior to the marriage, trial court was required to make a finding of husband's unsuitability as parent, as opposed to determining best interests of child, in deciding husband's third-party claim against grandmother for permanent custody of child, since paramount right of custody reverted back to child's parents with agreement to terminate guardianship. Lee v. Lee (Ohio App. 4 Dist., Meigs, 07-03-2002) No. 02CA2, 2002-Ohio-3554, 2002 WL 1561051, Unreported. Child Custody ☞ 68

Though biological father was determined to be a suitable parent, placing child with nonparent relative was in the best interest of the child, since, under RC 3109.04, parental unsuitability is not a required finding for placing with a nonparent. Downing v Lella, No. CA2000–11–237, 2001 WL 1023655 (12th Dist Ct App, Butler, 9–10–01).

31. —— **Visitation, initial allocation of rights and responsibilities and "best interest"**

Trial court acted within its discretion in divorce action when it named wife as residential and custodial parent of minor child, even though wife had been diagnosed with obsessive compulsive disorder; wife's disorder manifested itself primarily in frequent hand-washing and occasional need to double-check whether appliances had been turned off, wife testified that her obsessive compulsive disorder did not interfere with her job or her parenting and was not made worse by caring for child, and husband, who saw child shortly after she was born, did not see her again for more than nine months, notwithstanding temporary visitation order which gave him right to do so. Brewer v. Brewer (Ohio App. 2 Dist., Darke, 03-18-2011) No. 2010 CA 17, 2011-Ohio-1275, 2011 WL 944433, Unreported. Child Custody ☞ 62; Child Custody ☞ 68

Magistrate's temporary order permitting father to exercise his six-week summer visitation with child at pre-trial hearing on father's motion to modify parenting time was not a final, appealable order. Long v. Long (Ohio App. 3 Dist., Union, 10-04-2010) No. 14-10-01, 2010-Ohio-4817, 2010 WL 3836168, Unreported. Child Custody ☞ 902

The trial court's adoption of the local rule "long distance" visitation schedule once child attained school age was not an abuse of discretion, in divorce proceeding; father lived in Ohio and mother and child lived in South Carolina, and the schedule provided child with a stable routine, given the travel time and expense involved in visitation. Parker v. Parker (Ohio App. 10 Dist., Franklin, 08-10-2006) No. 05AP-1171, 2006-Ohio-4110, 2006 WL 2300797, Unreported. Child Custody ☞ 210

Trial court order that rejected husband's proposed shared parenting plan, in which child would spend nine days per month in Ohio with husband, was not unreasonable or an abuse of discretion, in divorce proceeding; trial court determined that requiring child to travel from South Carolina to Ohio every month was too much for child to handle at her young age, and child's babysitter and mother testified that child was so irritable and tired after visits to Ohio that she required several days to adjust. Parker v. Parker (Ohio App. 10 Dist., Franklin, 08-10-2006) No. 05AP-1171, 2006-Ohio-4110, 2006 WL 2300797, Unreported. Child Custody ☞ 147

Trial court's failure to interview 10-year-old son of divorced parents regarding his wishes with respect to visitation, or to appoint a guardian ad litem to represent child's interests, required reversal of trial court's ruling on mother's petition to suspend father's visitation, where mother moved the trial court to interview son and to appoint guardian ad litem. Dolub v. Chmielewski (Ohio App. 9 Dist., Summit, 09-07-2005) No. 22405, 2005-Ohio-4662, 2005 WL 2140564, Unreported. Child Custody ☞ 654; Child Custody ☞ 923(3); Infants ☞ 78(7)

In divorce action in which husband sought shared parenting plan, evidence supported trial court's finding that both husband and wife observed the agreed temporary custody order and that neither had continuously or willfully denied the other parent's right to parenting time. Swain v. Swain (Ohio App. 4 Dist., Pike, 08-06-2005) No. 05CA740, 2005-Ohio-4321, 2005 WL 1995388, Unreported. Child Custody ☞ 472

Trial court order suspending mother's visitation rights with dependent child was not against the manifest weight of the evidence and was not an abuse of discretion; mother violated the trial court's prior judgment entry by missing three or more scheduled visits with child within a three month period, mother had missed numerous visits with child prior to the judgment entry, mother was unemployed, mother was not current on her child support obligation, mother failed to comply with a court ordered drug and alcohol assessment, mother had previously had her parental rights to another child terminated, and guardian ad litem petitioned to have mother's visitation rights suspended. In re Shackelford (Ohio App. 3 Dist., Seneca, 06-06-2005) No. 13-04-50, 2005-Ohio-2778, 2005 WL 1322762, Unreported. Infants ☞ 230.1

Trial court did not abuse its discretion, in proceedings on former husband's motion to show cause, in refusing to find former wife in contempt for failing to abide by interim visitation order and visitation schedule in shared parenting plan, where child at issue was 16 years old and independently decided not to visit with former husband, and mother testified that she encouraged child to see former husband, offered to drive him to and from former husband's house, and desired that child have a relationship with former husband. Cherwin v. Cherwin (Ohio App. 8 Dist., Cuyahoga, 04-28-2005) No. 84875, 2005-Ohio-1999, 2005 WL 991706, Unreported. Child Custody ☞ 853

After denying former husband's request for shared parenting on expert's recommendation that shared parenting would be problematic, trial court's grant of extended child visitation to husband, such that husband's visitation accounted for more than half of the children's time, was against the manifest weight of the evidence; expert did not recommend extended visitation as an alternative to shared parenting, and expansion of visitation relieved husband of responsibilities of shared parenting while depriving wife of capacity to make decisions which, as residential parent, she alone had authority to make. Livesay v. Livesay (Ohio App. 2 Dist., Montgomery, 12-03-2004) No. 20504, 2004-Ohio-6785, 2004 WL 2903876, Unreported, appeal not allowed 105 Ohio St.3d 1472, 824 N.E.2d 542, 2005-Ohio-1186. Child Custody ☞ 421; Child Custody ☞ 471

Clear and convincing evidence supported finding that mother was in contempt for violation of shared parenting plan which provided for father to receive visitation; for the four months from daughter's 13th birthday to date of contempt hearing, father did not receive visitation with daughter, and mother testified that she did not affirmatively compel daughter to visit father. Caldwell v. Caldwell (Ohio App. 4 Dist., Gallia, 04-02-2003) No. 02CA17,

2003-Ohio-1752, 2003 WL 1795247, Unreported. Child Custody ☞ 854

State domestic relations court had jurisdiction to modify out-of-state order establishing former husband's visitation in connection with divorce, where children, together with their mother and stepfather, had resided in state for two years at time of modification, giving rise to substantial evidence in state regarding children's present and future care, protection, and personal relationships, and where neither children nor any contestant still resided in state which had issued original order. Boeckmann v. Baker (Ohio App. 2 Dist., Greene, 01-31-2003) No. 2002 CA 72, 2003-Ohio-456, 2003 WL 203579, Unreported. Child Custody ☞ 733

Maternal grandparents of dependent children should have been allowed to intervene, pursuant to joinder statute, in custody proceedings initiated by county children services agency; fact that grandparents were previously granted legal custody of the children established a colorable claim of a custody or visitation right, as required by the statute. In re Fusik (Ohio App. 4 Dist., Athens, 08-19-2002) No. 02CA16, 2002-Ohio-4410, 2002 WL 1978880, Unreported. Infants ☞ 200

A court errs in denying a noncustodial parent's right of visitation where there is no independent proof through a psychological evaluation and through a report of a guardian ad litem that visitation with the father would jeopardize the child's safety, welfare, and well-being. Kreuzer v. Kreuzer (Ohio App. 2 Dist., Greene, 08-01-1997) No. 96-CA-131, 1997 WL 432224, Unreported.

Evidence did not support trial court's finding in child custody dispute that father did not attempt to influence children, who had expressed desire to live with mother at temporary custody hearing; father did not call children and did not attempt to set up visitation after hearing, one child felt that father did not return her phone calls because of child's statement that she wanted to stay with mother, and father told another child that he did not know why child bothered to call after what she had said in court. In re Custody of Harris (Ohio App. 2 Dist., 07-14-2006) 168 Ohio App.3d 1, 857 N.E.2d 1235, 2006-Ohio-3649, on subsequent appeal 2006-Ohio-3746, 2006 WL 2037323. Child Custody ☞ 78

Standard visitation was not warranted in divorce action in absence of specific findings as to why equal-time recommendation of therapist, who evaluated parties pursuant to court order, was not ordered; therapist's recommendation was only evidence on the record as to appropriate visitation schedule. Barry v. Barry (Ohio App. 8 Dist., 09-28-2006) 169 Ohio App.3d 129, 862 N.E.2d 143, 2006-Ohio-5008. Child Custody ☞ 511

Trial court was entitled to enforce agreed judgment entry submitted by husband and wife and thus was not required to independently address issue of husband's visitation with younger children in divorce action; court asked at brief divorce hearing whether parties had agreed concerning parenting, wife's attorney stated that parties had submitted agreed judgment entry that took care of parental rights, and neither husband nor his attorneys disagreed with statement of wife's attorney. Kevdzija v. Kevdzija (Ohio App. 8 Dist., 04-06-2006) 166 Ohio App.3d 276, 850 N.E.2d 734, 2006-Ohio-1723. Child Custody ⟋ 203

Court cannot issue a visitation order that promotes one faith over another. In re Marriage of Shore (Ohio App. 8 Dist., 08-18-1999) 135 Ohio App.3d 374, 734 N.E.2d 395, dismissed, appeal not allowed 87 Ohio St.3d 1459, 720 N.E.2d 541. Child Custody ⟋ 185

Maintaining close family ties with extended family members is in a child's best interest, and such ties are one of the factors required to be considered in ascertaining child's best interests in connection with custody and visitation dispute. In re Marriage of Shore (Ohio App. 8 Dist., 08-18-1999) 135 Ohio App.3d 374, 734 N.E.2d 395, dismissed, appeal not allowed 87 Ohio St.3d 1459, 720 N.E.2d 541. Child Custody ⟋ 85; Child Custody ⟋ 179

Court may consider the extraordinary costs associated with visitation and the need and capacity of the child for an education in determining whether departure from the child support figure calculated in accordance with the statutory schedule and worksheet is warranted. In re Marriage of Shore (Ohio App. 8 Dist., 08-18-1999) 135 Ohio App.3d 374, 734 N.E.2d 395, dismissed, appeal not allowed 87 Ohio St.3d 1459, 720 N.E.2d 541. Child Support ⟋ 149

Uniform Child Custody Jurisdiction Act provisions requiring that each party in a parentage proceeding must file an affidavit containing certain enumerated information did not apply to stepfather's motion for visitation with ex-wife's child by previous marriage, where stepfather was not seeking custody of child. Shannon v. Shannon (Ohio App. 9 Dist., 08-13-1997) 122 Ohio App.3d 346, 701 N.E.2d 771. Child Custody ⟋ 769

Trial court has considerable discretion to decide domestic relations issues, including visitation; discretion requires only that decisions not be unreasonable, arbitrary or unconscionable. Jacobs v. Jacobs (Ohio App. 9 Dist., 04-19-1995) 102 Ohio App.3d 568, 657 N.E.2d 580. Child Custody ⟋ 176; Divorce ⟋ 184(5)

Possibility that parties could seek further modification of child visitation order did not justify imposition of midweek visitation which trial court expressly found to be "unfair." Jacobs v. Jacobs (Ohio App. 9 Dist., 04-19-1995) 102 Ohio App.3d 568, 657 N.E.2d 580. Child Custody ⟋ 577

Custody must be an issue before the Uniform Child Custody Jurisdiction Act (UCCJA) can apply; an out-of-state support order cannot be certified under UCCJA even when the order concerns visitation rights. Snelling v. Gardner (Franklin 1990) 69 Ohio App.3d 196, 590 N.E.2d 330.

The father of a child born out of wedlock is not entitled to visitation with such child over the objections of the mother, who has legal custody, unless he clearly establishes that such would be in the best

interests of the child. In re Connolly (Franklin 1974) 43 Ohio App.2d 38, 332 N.E.2d 376, 72 O.O.2d 194. Children Out–of–wedlock ⟋ 20.9

Custodial parent's failure to bring children to a meeting with noncustodial parent did not constitute material change of circumstances required to modify child custody order, as noncustodial parent was not awarded visitation rights in divorce decree, and court order that provided him with an opportunity to visit children neither altered divorce decree nor implemented visitation rights. In re Surdel (Ohio App. 9 Dist., Lorain, 09-04-2002) No. 02CA007980, 2002-Ohio-4529, 2002 WL 2010201, Unreported. Child Custody ⟋ 569

32. Modification of rights and responsibilities and "change in circumstances"—In general

Sufficient evidence existed to prove a change in circumstances which warranted a reallocation of parental rights, where mother's boyfriend had a criminal history, mother was financially dependent on him, mother had not made significant improvements in making decisions based on child's welfare and best interests, and mother had been involved in a violent attack wherein an acquaintance broke into her home and beat her with a shotgun while child was in the home. Wartman v. Livengood (Ohio App. 5 Dist., Stark, 11-29-2010) No. 2009CA00284, 2010-Ohio-6005, 2010 WL 5071111, Unreported. Children Out–of–wedlock ⟋ 20.10

Trial court's modification of parties' shared parenting plan as to afford father greater time with child represented not just a change in a term of the plan but reallocated the parental rights and responsibilities of the parties in manner as to require a finding that a change in circumstances had occurred since entry of original decree; overruling *Hunter v. Bachman*, 2004 WL 2244125; *Ankney v. Bonos*, 2006 WL 3304343. Gunderman v. Gunderman (Ohio App. 9 Dist., Medina, 08-03-2009) No. 08CA0067-M, 2009-Ohio-3787, 2009 WL 2356811, Unreported. Child Custody ⟋ 576

Former wife's affidavit in support of motion to reallocate parental rights and responsibilities failed to allege change in circumstances; some issues occurred prior to court's prior order were fully litigated, and more recent issues were in the nature of contempt allegations, not changes in circumstances. Kraft v. Hetrick (Ohio App. 5 Dist., Stark, 07-27-2009) No. 2008-CA-00235, 2009-Ohio-3665, 2009 WL 2217726, Unreported. Child Custody ⟋ 555; Child Custody ⟋ 557(2); Child Custody ⟋ 609

Evidence supported conclusion that no change in circumstances had occurred since father had been appointed children's residential parent and mother had been awarded companionship rights, as necessary to warrant reallocation of parental rights and responsibilities naming mother as children's residential parent, or, in the alternative, to establish a shared parenting plan; father and children still lived in same home, children attended the same daycare, and children continued to spend significant time with their paternal grandparents, as they had before mother's and father's divorce, and father had smoked before divorce. Brunip v. Nickerson (Ohio App. 7 Dist., Columbiana, 09-30-2008) No. 07-CO-42, 2008-Ohio-5052, 2008 WL 4416456, Unreported, appeal not allowed 120 Ohio St.3d 1525, 901 N.E.2d 245, 2009-Ohio-614. Child Custody ⚖ 559; Child Custody ⚖ 577

Evidence supported trial court's order denying mother's motions for reallocation of parental rights; mother claimed that a change in circumstances had occurred since entry of custody order in that father's home was in foreclosure and child was scratched and developed cold sores while in father's care, but father showed that, although he lost his job, he was employed at time of hearing on mother's motion and was establishing payment plan with mortgagee, and, although child was scratched by family's kitten, the scratches healed, and child developed cold sores due to illness. Van Scoder v. Van Scoder (Ohio App. 3 Dist., Paulding, 09-22-2008) No. 11-08-06, 2008-Ohio-4780, 2008 WL 4292723, Unreported. Child Custody ⚖ 563; Child Custody ⚖ 565

The trial court's failure to find maternal grandparents in contempt of court due to their alleged failure to abide by order that required grandparents to comply with father's wishes regarding religious training for his out-of-wedlock child was not an abuse of discretion. Smith v. Quigg (Ohio App. 5 Dist., Fairfield, 03-22-2006) No. 2005-CA-002, 2006-Ohio-1495, 2006 WL 786856, Unreported. Children Out-of-wedlock ⚖ 20

The trial court's failure to hold maternal grandparents in contempt of court due to their alleged failure to abide by a court order that required grandparents to comply with the wishes of father regarding the religious training for child was not an abuse of discretion, during child custody modification proceeding in which maternal and paternal grandparents sought custody of out-of-wedlock child; four orders were entered by the court after the order that addressed the religious training of child and none of the subsequent orders contained any language regarding religious training. Smith v. Quigg (Ohio App. 5 Dist., Fairfield, 03-22-2006) No. 2005-CA-001, 2006-Ohio-1494, 2006 WL 786855, Unreported. Children Out-of-wedlock ⚖ 20

Paternal grandparents failed to establish that the trial court demonstrated preferential treatment for maternal grandparents' religion or that the court interfered with paternal grandparents' ability to practice their own religion, during child custody modification proceeding in which maternal and paternal grandparents sought custody of out-of-wedlock child; the court made extensive findings of fact regarding the child's best interest, the issue of religion was only one factor considered by the court, and the court's order granted paternal grandparents visitation with child and required child to be with them to celebrate their religion's only holiday. Smith v. Quigg (Ohio App. 5 Dist., Fairfield, 03-22-2006) No. 2005-CA-001, 2006-Ohio-1494, 2006 WL 786855, Unreported. Children Out-of-wedlock ⚖ 20.10

Trial court was not required to find change in circumstances prior to terminating shared parenting plan originally entered incident to divorce and designating former husband child's custodial parent, where court found that termination was in child's best interest. Williamson v. Williamson (Ohio App. 2 Dist., Clark, 11-26-2003) No. 2003 CA 30, 2003-Ohio-6540, 2003 WL 22888291, Unreported. Child Custody ⚖ 576

Former wife was not entitled to modification of parental rights and responsibilities, where her affidavit failed to aver the occurrence of a change in the circumstances of the child or the child's residential parent, the former husband. Vocaire v. Beltz (Ohio App. 5 Dist., Stark, 11-10-2003) No. 2003CA00215, 2003-Ohio-6015, 2003 WL 22664190, Unreported. Child Custody ⚖ 609

Neither child's tardiness to school nor former husband's failure to visit child constituted a change in circumstance warranting a modification of parenting plan, for purposes of former husband's motion for reallocation of parental rights and responsibilities; former wife did not interfere with visitation, and tardiness was not a change in circumstances. Oleksy v. Oleksy (Ohio App. 8 Dist., Cuyahoga, 10-23-2003) No. 82646, 2003-Ohio-5657, 2003 WL 22413671, Unreported. Child Custody ⚖ 552; Child Custody ⚖ 569

Evidence was sufficient to support finding that a sufficient change in circumstances occurred to warrant modification of residential parent and legal custodian status of mother, and such modification was in children's best interest; mother had moved with the four children to a two bedroom home, at times, ten persons lived in such residence, as mother had remarried a man with children, mother severely interfered with father's visitation with children, prevented communication between father and children, had continually conducted herself and her comments so as to surround the children with an atmosphere of animosity toward father and his wife, the older children wanted to live with father, and children had adjusted well to father's wife and their home. Fetty v. Fetty-Omaits (Ohio App. 5 Dist., Tuscarawas, 02-04-2003) No. 2002 AP 07 0053, 2003-Ohio-661, 2003 WL 302399, Unreported. Child Custody ⚖ 566; Child Custody ⚖ 567; Child Custody ⚖ 568; Child Custody ⚖ 569

Psychologist's proposed expert testimony regarding correlation between deviant personality test scores and domestic violence was not "relevant" evidence that could be admitted on behalf of former wife regarding former husband's motion to modify custody, and thus trial court's error of refusing to qualify psychologist as an expert was harmless, where there was no evidence that former wife was a victim of domestic violence. Harley v. Harley (Ohio App. 4 Dist., Athens, 01-15-2003) No. 02CA25, 2003-Ohio-232, 2003 WL 146014, Unreported. Child Custody ⚖ 923(4); Evidence ⚖ 510

A finding that a change in circumstances had occurred was required to modify an award of custody and if the statutory factors required for such modification are not found, the court may not look only to the best interests of the child or children in making that modification. In re Kilkenny (Ohio App. 2 Dist., Greene, 02-11-2000) No. 99CA77, 2000 WL 145924, Unreported.

A change in circumstances required for modification of custody decree must be of substance, not slight or inconsequential. Brammer v. Brammer (Ohio App. 3 Dist., 05-31-2011) 194 Ohio App.3d 240, 955 N.E.2d 453, 2011-Ohio-2610, stay denied 129 Ohio St.3d 1442, 951 N.E.2d 1041, 2011-Ohio-4221. Child Custody ⬦ 556

Statute governing a modification of child custody based upon a change in circumstances does not require that the child suffer adverse consequences. LaBute v. LaBute (Ohio App. 3 Dist., 12-01-2008) 179 Ohio App.3d 696, 903 N.E.2d 652, 2008-Ohio-6190. Child Custody ⬦ 555

Changes of substance were present in child's life with respect to father's motion to reallocate shared parental rights set out in divorce decree by making him the residential parent; mother had married and divorced multiple times, had moved multiple times, and had various financial difficulties including two bankruptcies, and result of those circumstances was that parties' child, who had chromosomal disorder that affected her ability to communicate verbally, was forced to change schools on a frequent basis, which allegedly interfered with her ability to progress in her education. LaBute v. LaBute (Ohio App. 3 Dist., 12-01-2008) 179 Ohio App.3d 696, 903 N.E.2d 652, 2008-Ohio-6190. Child Custody ⬦ 576

Father's request for custody of his two out-of-wedlock children sought to modify a prior child custody award, and did not constitute an initial child custody determination, and thus the trial court was required to apply the change of circumstances test; there was an implied child custody order by virtue of the fact that father was ordered to pay child support when his paternity was established, and the exceptions to the application of the change in circumstances test did not apply since a significant amount of time had passed since the child support order and the motion for custody and father did not have a relationship with child prior to the entry of the support order. In re Johnson (Ohio App. 4 Dist., 03-06-2006) 166 Ohio App.3d 632, 852 N.E.2d 1223, 2006-Ohio-1125. Children Out-of-wedlock ⬦ 20.10

Pursuant to statute, trial court cannot order modification of custody decree without evidence that change in circumstances has occurred and that child's best interest is served by modification; change in circumstances requirement fosters continuity and stability in child's life, and also serves court's interest by discouraging relitigation of same issues. Waggoner v. Waggoner (Ohio App. 9 Dist., 05-08-1996) 111 Ohio App.3d 1, 675 N.E.2d 541,

dismissed, appeal not allowed 77 Ohio St.3d 1445, 671 N.E.2d 1284. Child Custody ⬦ 553

Mere possibility of change in circumstances in the future will not ordinarily suffice to support modification of child custody decree. Waggoner v. Waggoner (Ohio App. 9 Dist., 05-08-1996) 111 Ohio App.3d 1, 675 N.E.2d 541, dismissed, appeal not allowed 77 Ohio St.3d 1445, 671 N.E.2d 1284. Child Custody ⬦ 555

In deciding whether change in circumstances sufficient to warrant modification of child custody decree exists, court is required by statute to weigh harm against advantages that would likely result from change; implicit in balancing test is recognition that disruption in child's regular residence and care is harmful, and to balance that harm, court must be able to justify risk in part through change in circumstances requirement. Waggoner v. Waggoner (Ohio App. 9 Dist., 05-08-1996) 111 Ohio App.3d 1, 675 N.E.2d 541, dismissed, appeal not allowed 77 Ohio St.3d 1445, 671 N.E.2d 1284. Child Custody ⬦ 553

In determining whether change of circumstances has occurred so as to warrant change in custody initially established by decree allocating parental rights and responsibilities, trial judge, as trier of fact, must have wide latitude in considering all issues and evidence before him or her which support such change. Davis v. Flickinger (Ohio, 02-12-1997) 77 Ohio St.3d 415, 674 N.E.2d 1159, 1997-Ohio-260. Child Custody ⬦ 555

Statute governing modification of decrees allocating parental rights and responsibilities, while requiring that change in circumstances justifying change of custody be change of substance and not slight or inconsequential, does not require "substantial" change in circumstances; word "substantial" does not appear in statute, and intent of statute is to spare children from constant tug of war between their parents and provide stability to custodial status of children. Davis v. Flickinger (Ohio, 02-12-1997) 77 Ohio St.3d 415, 674 N.E.2d 1159, 1997-Ohio-260. Child Custody ⬦ 556

Court cannot modify prior decree that allocates parental rights and responsibilities for care of child, including parental rights to continuing contact with that child, unless it finds that change in circumstances has occurred and that modification is necessary to serve best interest of child. Jacobs v. Jacobs (Ohio App. 9 Dist., 04-19-1995) 102 Ohio App.3d 568, 657 N.E.2d 580. Child Custody ⬦ 553

Modification of visitation order to impose court's standard visitation schedule is not per se just and reasonable, as court must consider whether there has been change of circumstances and whether modification is in best interest of child. Jacobs v. Jacobs (Ohio App. 9 Dist., 04-19-1995) 102 Ohio App.3d 568, 657 N.E.2d 580. Child Custody ⬦ 577

Trial court's use of term "substantial" in its findings in support of denial of mother's motion for change of custody did not indicate that trial court improperly required mother to demonstrate "substantial" change of circumstances rather than simply a change of circumstances. Clyborn v. Clyborn (Ohio App. 3 Dist., 02-16-1994) 93 Ohio App.3d 192, 638 N.E.2d 112. Child Custody ⬥ 659

Under "best interest of the child" test, custody will not be modified unless party can prove that change of custody will be in best interest of child, and mere assertion that it will not be detrimental is insufficient. Miller v. Miller (Hocking 1993) 86 Ohio App.3d 623, 621 N.E.2d 745. Child Custody ⬥ 554

There must be some substantial change of circumstance that is significant to question of child custody before reexamination of best interest of child is appropriate. Perz v. Perz (Lucas 1993) 85 Ohio App.3d 374, 619 N.E.2d 1094, motion overruled 67 Ohio St.3d 1423, 616 N.E.2d 506. Child Custody ⬥ 553

Modification of parental rights is not warranted unless there is some competent credible evidence to effect that there has been change in circumstances, modification is in best interest of child, and any harm likely to be caused by change in environment is outweighed by advantages. Holm v. Smilowitz (Athens 1992) 83 Ohio App.3d 757, 615 N.E.2d 1047. Child Custody ⬥ 552

By adopting one party's judgment entry modifying children's custody in the absence of an agreement of the parents or a finding that the statutory factors justify a change, a domestic relations court exceeds its authority. Zigmont v. Toto (Cuyahoga 1988) 47 Ohio App.3d 181, 547 N.E.2d 1208, cause dismissed 38 Ohio St.3d 715, 533 N.E.2d 783.

The family reunification law set forth in RC 2151.414 has no relevance and does not apply to motions for a change of custody under RC 3109.04; RC 2151.414 is limited to matters pertaining to a motion for permanent custody of a child by a county department, board, or certified organization that has temporary custody of the child. Miller v. Miller (Ohio 1988) 37 Ohio St.3d 71, 523 N.E.2d 846, clarification denied 43 Ohio St.3d 710, 540 N.E.2d 728.

The grant of final custody after a temporary custody order is issued pending a final divorce decree does not constitute a modification of an existing order; therefore, the provisions of RC 3109.04(B) are inapplicable. Thompson v. Thompson (Washington 1987) 31 Ohio App.3d 254, 511 N.E.2d 412, 31 O.B.R. 538.

A judgment in a paternity action has the effect of a prior determination of custody; therefore, a subsequent change of custody pursuant to a petition by the natural father must be based on a finding of changed circumstances. In re Yates (Franklin 1984) 18 Ohio App.3d 95, 481 N.E.2d 646, 18 O.B.R. 458.

The prohibition of RC 3109.04(B)(1) against modification of a prior custody decree unless there has been a change in circumstances applies when the prior decree was rendered under the provisions of RC 3105.21(B) upon the failure of proof of the causes in a complaint for divorce. Dickrede v.

Dickrede (Allen 1984) 14 Ohio App.3d 292, 470 N.E.2d 925, 14 O.B.R. 349.

A parent seeking a transfer of custody must establish that: (1) the circumstances of the child or the custodial parent have changed since the original custody order was entered; (2) the child's best interests will be served by the modification; and (3) the present environment of the child poses a significant danger to "his physical health or his mental, moral, or emotional development and the harm likely to be caused by a change in environment is outweighed by the advantages of the change." Stone v. Stone (Warren 1983) 9 Ohio App.3d 6, 457 N.E.2d 919, 9 O.B.R. 6.

Under former RC 3109.04(B) (now RC 3109.04(B)(1)), facts "unknown to the court at the time of the prior decree" may include facts known to the adverse party, but not the court, at the time of the prior decree. Wyss v. Wyss (Franklin 1982) 3 Ohio App.3d 412, 445 N.E.2d 1153, 3 O.B.R. 479.

In a custody action subsequent to the original custody order, the trial court does not abuse its discretion by limiting the evidence to events which occurred after the original custody order was made. In re Reynolds (Hamilton 1982) 2 Ohio App.3d 309, 441 N.E.2d 1141, 2 O.B.R. 341.

Where a court in a change-of-custody action determines it is no longer equitable that a judgment continue to have prospective application, it may change such, notwithstanding RC 3109.04(B) and even though none of the exceptions in that statute exist. Sexton v. Sexton (Morrow 1978) 60 Ohio App.2d 339, 397 N.E.2d 425, 14 O.O.3d 297. Child Custody ⬥ 552

A court of common pleas does not have absolute discretion to change a previous award of custody of a minor child; such a change must be based on a finding of a "change of conditions." McVay v. McVay (Columbiana 1974) 44 Ohio App.2d 370, 338 N.E.2d 772, 73 O.O.2d 415. Child Custody ⬥ 555

In a change-of-custody proceeding initiated by motion in a divorce action as between the parents of the children, it is not necessary for the court to determine a parent is unfit to be a custodian prior to ordering change of custody, but only that a change of circumstances occurring since the prior order of the court justifies such change of custody for the best interests of the children. Beamer v. Beamer (Seneca 1969) 17 Ohio App.2d 89, 244 N.E.2d 775, 46 O.O.2d 118. Child Custody ⬥ 553

Court is not warranted in modifying a previous order fixing custody of children where there is neither a change of conditions nor a discovery of material facts existent at the time of entering previous order and then unknown to court; but upon proof of such change or discovery of material facts, court is empowered to make an order of modification when warranted by evidence. Dailey v. Dailey (Ohio 1945) 146 Ohio St. 93, 64 N.E.2d 246, 32 O.O. 29.

No change of circumstances supported divorced father's motion for modification of parental rights regarding his minor son and daughter, although son had expressed an interest in living with father; general breakdown in communication between father and mother did not constitute a change in circumstances, nor did father's unsuccessful attempt to make phone contact with his daughter or father's attempt to informally obtain after-school visits with the son and daughter. Kager v. Kager (Ohio App. 5 Dist., Stark, 06-17-2002) No. 2001CA00316, 2002-Ohio-3090, 2002 WL 1343266, Unreported. Child Custody ☞ 555

In an action for custody modification, a showing that the child would be better off with the non-custodial parent is not sufficient; there must be a change in circumstances before the change of custody can be considered. Cummins v Voorheis, No. 1325 (4th Dist Ct App, Scioto, 6–10–81).

Where the only prior custody decree is the one at the time of the divorce, the noncustodial parent may attempt to show a change of circumstances occurring since the original decree under RC 3109.04(B). Hlutke v Hlutke, No. 3000 (9th Dist Ct App, Lorain, 11–5–80).

In order to effect a change of custody it is incumbent upon the trial court to find pursuant to RC 3109.04 that it is in the child's interest to change custody and that the advantages of a change in environment outweigh the harm likely to be caused thereby. Smith v Smith, No. CA98–04–005, 1998 WL 857523 (12th Dist Ct App, Fayette, 12–14–98).

33. ——— Age and maturity of child, modification of rights and responsibilities and "change in circumstances"

Language in the agreed judgment entry and shared parenting plan, stating that the parties agreed to revisit the matter of the child's residence upon the child reaching age 12, did not constitute an agreement that the child reaching the age of twelve would necessarily constitute a change of circumstances warranting custody modification. Pryor v. Hooks (Ohio App. 9 Dist., Summit, 12-15-2010) No. 25294, 2010-Ohio-6130, 2010 WL 5141353, Unreported. Child Custody ☞ 574

Evidence was sufficient to establish that termination and not modification of shared parenting agreement was necessary to serve best interest of child; both parents, as well as the guardian ad litem, were in favor of terminating the agreement, and their son was approaching school age, making the shared parenting plan unworkable since they resided in different school districts. In re Illig (Ohio App. 3 Dist., Seneca, 03-02-2009) No. 13-08-26, 2009-Ohio-916, 2009 WL 500600, Unreported. Child Custody ☞ 526

Evidence was sufficient to support trial court's finding that award of residential custody of teenage son to husband was in son's best interests; parties did not agree regarding discipline and permissible activities for their children, son adamantly did not want to reside with his mother, and she apparently was unable to control son's conduct. Hayman v. Hayman (Ohio App. 12 Dist., Butler, 01-13-2003)

No. CA2001-10-250, No. CA2001-11-268, 2003-Ohio-76, 2003 WL 103413, Unreported. Child Custody ☞ 48; Child Custody ☞ 51; Child Custody ☞ 75; Child Custody ☞ 78

A combination of facts including (1) the child's age of twelve years, (2) the child's preference to reside primarily with his father, and (3) the long history of difficulty between the parties is sufficient for a finding of a change of circumstances in order for the court to address its decision to change residential parents. Khulenberg v. Davis (Ohio App. 12 Dist., Butler, 08-25-1997) No. CA96-07-143, 1997 WL 527647, Unreported.

Change in child's age is alone not dispositive of right to modify prior child custody decree. Waggoner v. Waggoner (Ohio App. 9 Dist., 05-08-1996) 111 Ohio App.3d 1, 675 N.E.2d 541, dismissed, appeal not allowed 77 Ohio St.3d 1445, 671 N.E.2d 1284. Child Custody ☞ 555

Change in age of child subject to custody decree, without more, is not sufficient factor to permit modification of decree for change in circumstances. Davis v. Flickinger (Ohio, 02-12-1997) 77 Ohio St.3d 415, 674 N.E.2d 1159, 1997-Ohio-260. Child Custody ☞ 555

Passage of time during significant portion of child's life, i.e., from age of 11 months to age of five and one-half years, combined with other pertinent factors, particularly child's relationship with her parents, relative stability of each parent's life, and fact that mother had had two incidents of unruly behavior requiring involvement by police from time of original custody order, supported finding of changed circumstances requiring further inquiry by trial court into redetermination of parental rights and responsibilities. Butler v. Butler (Ohio App. 3 Dist., 12-05-1995) 107 Ohio App.3d 633, 669 N.E.2d 291. Child Custody ☞ 555

Passage of time, alone, is not sufficient to find change of circumstances and relitigate issue of custody. Butler v. Butler (Ohio App. 3 Dist., 12-05-1995) 107 Ohio App.3d 633, 669 N.E.2d 291. Child Custody ☞ 555

Change in circumstances supporting modification of visitation order generally should not be predicated upon change in child's age, but child's age is properly considered as relevant factor in determination of child's best interests. Jacobs v. Jacobs (Ohio App. 9 Dist., 04-19-1995) 102 Ohio App.3d 568, 657 N.E.2d 580. Child Custody ☞ 577

Passage of children from infancy to early adolescence was sufficient "change of circumstance" to warrant inquiry into question of whether interests of children would best be served by their remaining with custodial parent, or by changing custody. Perz v. Perz (Lucas 1993) 85 Ohio App.3d 374, 619 N.E.2d 1094, motion overruled 67 Ohio St.3d 1423, 616 N.E.2d 506. Child Custody ☞ 553

The passage of children from infancy to early adolescence is a sufficient change of circumstances to warrant an inquiry into the question of whether the interests of the children would best be served by remaining with the current custodial parent, or by a change in custody; thus, a trial court's refusal to make a determination as to the best interests of the children on a motion for a change of custody constitutes an abuse of discretion. Perz v Perz, No. L–92–183 (6th Dist Ct App, Lucas, 3–19–93).

34. —— Appeal, modification of rights and responsibilities and "change in circumstances"

Former husband waived appellate review of his contentions that magistrate failed to adhere to rules of contract construction in modifying terms of shared parenting agreement and failed to make requisite finding of change in circumstances, by failing to object thereto before trial court. Pierson v Pierson (Ohio App. 12 Dist., Warren, 10-03-2005) No. CA2004-04-042, 2005-Ohio-5295, 2005 WL 2416816, Unreported. Child Custody ☞ 904

On appeal from grant of ex-husband's motion to terminate shared parenting plan, ex-wife waived right to claim all but plain error with respect to trial court's admission of evidence of automobile accident involving child and of resulting child endangerment citation issued to ex-wife, where ex-wife failed to object to such evidence at trial. Basford v. Basford (Ohio App. 7 Dist., Noble, 03-26-2004) No. 03-NO-310, 2004-Ohio-1539, 2004 WL 610773, Unreported. Child Custody ☞ 904

Mother, who alleged that manner in which trial court considered and applied evidence with respect to its child custody and child support determinations was an abuse of discretion and that such determinations were against the manifest weight of the evidence, failed to provide a complete transcript of trial court proceedings, and thus, Court of Appeals presumed omitted portions of record supported trial court's findings and conclusions. Napper v. Napper (Ohio App. 3 Dist., Allen, 05-28-2003) No. 1-02-82, 2003-Ohio-2719, 2003 WL 21224230, Unreported. Child Custody ☞ 920; Child Support ☞ 555

Trial court could not sustain father's objection to magistrate's findings of fact in child support action that father was voluntarily unemployed and that his support obligation should be calculated based on prior income, since father failed to file a transcript of proceedings or an affidavit of the evidence presented at the magistrate hearing. McClain v. Taylor (Ohio App. 9 Dist., Medina, 01-22-2003) No. 02CA0027-M, 2003-Ohio-248, 2003 WL 149793, Unreported. Child Support ☞ 211

Trial court's error in summarily overruling former husband's objections to magistrate's recommended custody decision, on ground that transcript was not timely filed, was not rendered harmless by fact that the transcript was currently before the Court of Appeals, as Court of Appeals was precluded from determining the appeal on the evidence contained in transcript, which had not been before trial court. Shull v. Shull (Ohio App. 3 Dist., 12-08-1999) 135 Ohio App.3d 708, 735 N.E.2d 496, 1999-Ohio-950. Child Custody ☞ 923(1)

Trial court's order that parties to proceeding for modification of custody provisions of divorce decree undergo physical and psychological testing did not affect substantial right and was not immediately appealable; trial court had broad discretion to order testing, tests ordered were not intrusive, and blanket assertion that order was final and appealable did not demonstrate that appeal from final custody determination would not adequately afford meaningful or effective remedy. Montecalvo v. Montecalvo (Ohio App. 11 Dist., 01-25-1999) 126 Ohio App.3d 377, 710 N.E.2d 379, motion dismissed 85 Ohio St.3d 1455, 708 N.E.2d 1010. Divorce ☞ 177

Determination of trial judge as to whether "change of circumstances" warranting change in custody has occurred should not be disturbed on appeal absent abuse of discretion. Davis v. Flickinger (Ohio, 02-12-1997) 77 Ohio St.3d 415, 674 N.E.2d 1159, 1997-Ohio-260. Child Custody ☞ 921(4)

Father's claims that home study report and doctor's report did not indicate that he was unfit for custody of his child was not an issue for appeal of trial court's decision on remand from prior appeal to maintain custody with maternal grandparents; reports were before trial court in connection with original decision awarding custody and any contentions as to those reports should have been raised in earlier appeal. Rife v. Morgan (Ohio App. 2 Dist., 10-18-1995) 106 Ohio App.3d 843, 667 N.E.2d 450. Child Custody ☞ 914

Trial court did not abuse its discretion in overruling mother's motion for change of custody of parties' three daughters; there was evidence to support trial court's determination that change in circumstances had not occurred, and no evidence to show that modification of custody would be in best interest of children. Clyborn v. Clyborn (Ohio App. 3 Dist., 02-16-1994) 93 Ohio App.3d 192, 638 N.E.2d 112. Child Custody ☞ 553

Decisions concerning change of custody of minor children will not be reversed absent showing that trial court abused its discretion. Perz v. Perz (Lucas 1993) 85 Ohio App.3d 374, 619 N.E.2d 1094, motion overruled 67 Ohio St.3d 1423, 616 N.E.2d 506. Child Custody ☞ 921(4)

In proceeding on motion for change of custody, judgment that defers issue of child support for future determination is not "final appealable order." Kouns v. Pemberton (Lawrence 1992) 84 Ohio App.3d 499, 617 N.E.2d 701, motion overruled 66 Ohio St.3d 1489, 612 N.E.2d 1245. Child Custody ☞ 902

The denial of a motion for modification of a custody order will not be reversed on the ground that the conditions described in RC 3109.04 exist unless the evidence compels that conclusion. Pryer v. Pryer (Hardin 1984) 20 Ohio App.3d 170, 485 N.E.2d 268, 20 O.B.R. 205.

35. —— Child's "best interest" generally, modification of rights and responsibilities and "change in circumstances"

Evidence supported conclusion that it was in children's best interests for custody of children to be modified such that adjudicated father, rather than mother, be designated as children's residential parent; one of parties' two children, who was 11, expressed a strong desire to live with father, there was evidence that children were having trouble adjusting to their new school located in town about 30 miles away from town children had lived in their entire lives, and mother failed to take child to doctor to get an immunization booster shot, despite being notified of the need to do so several times within the span of three years. Wallace v. Willoughby (Ohio App. 3 Dist., Shelby, 06-20-2011) No. 17-10-15, 2011-Ohio-3008, 2011 WL 2449009, Unreported. Children Out–of–wedlock ☞ 20.10

Trial court acted within its discretion in modifying child custody order as to name father the child's legal custodian and residential parent, where trial court received evidence showing the differences between parties in relation to child, specifically with respect to the manner in which mother relied upon medical providers to address child's behavior, which trial court identified as a change of circumstances warranting modification, trial court entered findings concerning the child's more ideal living conditions while in father's custody, which went to the required best interests finding, and trial court considered issues related to many of factors enumerated in custody statute. Mackowiak v. Mackowiak (Ohio App. 12 Dist., Fayette, 06-20-2011) No. CA2010-04-009, 2011-Ohio-3013, 2011 WL 2448997, Unreported, stay denied 129 Ohio St.3d 1503, 955 N.E.2d 386, 2011-Ohio-5358. Child Custody ☞ 555; Child Custody ☞ 559

Regardless of whether the e-mail sent by ex-husband to ex-wife was threatening, there was sufficient evidence to support trial court's finding that the e-mail showed ex-husband's lack of parenting and decision-making skills, and parenting skills were a relevant consideration when determining child's best interests for the purposes of custody modification; psychologist stated that the e-mail was an extremely improper communication. Eitutis v. Eitutis (Ohio App. 11 Dist., Lake, 06-10-2011) No. 2009-L-121, 2011-Ohio-2838, 2011 WL 2415369, Unreported. Child Custody ☞ 552

Evidence supported finding that modification of child custody was necessary to serve the best interests of the children, in post-divorce child custody modification proceeding; the court found that both of the children had a greater opportunity to develop healthy relationships with friends, relatives and others while residing with father, and the guardian ad litem recommended that father be designated the residential and custodial parent of the children. Scarberry v. Scarberry (Ohio App. 2 Dist., Clark, 06-10-2011) No. 10-CA-0091, 2011-Ohio-2829, 2011 WL 2410234, Unreported. Child Custody ☞ 554

Evidence did not support finding that it was in the best interest of children to modify parental rights and responsibilities such that the parents no longer equally cared for the children, and, instead, designating mother as residential parent for school purposes, who planned to move with children to other state to pursue job promotion; although mother testified that schools in other state could provide better services to special needs child, the only evidence that schools were better was mother's testimony, and father presented evidence regarding plan in place at child's present school to address his special needs, and children had developed strong ties to their current community where the majority of their extended family lived, and there was no evidence that father was incapable of taking the lead in handling the children's education and medical issues. Brammer v. Brammer (Ohio App. 3 Dist., 05-31-2011) 194 Ohio App.3d 240, 955 N.E.2d 453, 2011-Ohio-2610, stay denied 129 Ohio St.3d 1442, 951 N.E.2d 1041, 2011-Ohio-4221. Child Custody ☞ 637; Child Custody ☞ 642

Remand of trial court's judgment modifying parenting-time schedule was required in order for trial court to make a determination based on the best interest of the child. Hart v. Hart (Ohio App. 9 Dist., Summit, 05-25-2011) No. 25426, 2011-Ohio-2501, 2011 WL 2040926, Unreported. Child Custody ☞ 924

Substantial evidence supported magistrate's determination that it was in child's best interest to designate father as the residential parent and legal custodian of child; father would be the parent more likely to honor and facilitate court-approved parenting time and visitation, mother was cooperative with facilitating father's visitation so long as she was in control when it took place, mother violated temporary visitation orders when she took child out of town on father's scheduled weekend and denied him visitation, and mother was resistant to communicating with father and letting him be involved in making decisions about child's medical care. Crow v. Baughman (Ohio App. 3 Dist., Hancock, 03-14-2011) No. 5-10-28, 2011-Ohio-1170, 2011 WL 861687, Unreported. Child Custody ☞ 51; Child Custody ☞ 57

Awarding custody of child to father was in the best interests of the child, where mother was involved with men who had criminal histories, father was more likely to comply with court-ordered companionship, and mother had not made significant improvements in her lifestyle based on child's welfare or best interests. Wartman v. Livengood (Ohio App. 5 Dist., Stark, 11-29-2010) No. 2009CA00284, 2010-Ohio-6005, 2010 WL 5071111, Unreported. Children Out–of–wedlock ☞ 20.10

Father failed to establish a change in circumstances necessary to modify parental rights and responsibilities order, which had designated mother as the residential parent; despite mother's violation of order prohibiting the hosting of overnight guests, the minor child loved both parents, desired that her parents get along, had had no consequential changes in health, and had remained an engaging, active young girl who enjoyed being with both parents, and mother's circumstances had actually improved since imposition of the disputed parental rights order, in that she had secured full-time employment, relocated to a larger apartment, and obtained appropriate babysitting services. A.P. v. J.Z. (Ohio App. 6 Dist., Wood, 11-12-2010) No. WD-09-063, 2010-Ohio-5502, 2010 WL 4546709, Unreported. Child Custody ⚬⟿ 577

Substantial evidence supported conclusion that modifying custody decree naming mother as child's residential parent and legal guardian to name father as child's residential parent and legal guardian was in child's best interests, following mother's relocation to another state; child had on-going, wholesome relationship with numerous family and friends in the local area and was integrated into father's and grandfather's home, and mother had unilaterally and without justification withheld child from father and his family for an extended period of time in effort to compel father's compliance with mother's will, and she willfully denied father parenting time in breach of court order. Long v. Long (Ohio App. 3 Dist., Union, 10-04-2010) No. 14-10-01, 2010-Ohio-4817, 2010 WL 3836168, Unreported. Child Custody ⚬⟿ 568; Child Custody ⚬⟿ 569

Evidence supported trial court's finding that reallocation of parental rights and responsibilities from mother to father, subsequent to divorce judgment naming mother residential parent of parties' three minor children, was in best interests of child being treated for mitochondrial disease; child had lived in mother's home with older sibling who also suffered from and ultimately died from mitochondrial disease, father testified that atmosphere in mother's home was dominated by the thought of illness and death while father encouraged child to behave as a normal child, guardian ad litem believed that child's best interests would be served by her living with father, doctor described mother as being overly vigilant about child's care, and mother was not as conducive to facilitating visitation as father. D.M. v. J.M. (Ohio App. 9 Dist., 08-18-2010) 189 Ohio App.3d 723, 940 N.E.2d 591, 2010-Ohio-3852. Child Custody ⚬⟿ 576

Since trial court did not abuse its discretion in determining that mother who sought modification of prior allocation of parental rights and responsibilities failed to show that a substantive change in circumstances had occurred, it had no need to consider the children's best interests. Sites v. Sites (Ohio App. 4 Dist., Lawrence, 06-03-2010) No. 09CA19, 2010-Ohio-2748, 2010 WL 2391647, Unreported, appeal not allowed 126 Ohio St.3d 1600, 935 N.E.2d 46, 2010-Ohio-4928. Child Custody ⚬⟿ 659

Considering all the evidence before it since parties' divorce, trial court properly found change of circumstances of the child had occurred, so as to require it to address the child's best interests on father's motion to modify custody; child's stepfather was not helpful in facilitating visitation and contact, child's mother had been found in contempt

in failing to inform court of address change, and she failed to provide father with his five weeks of summer visitation until ordered by court, and child reported that her stepfather stuck her with a fork. Gomez v. Gomez (Ohio App. 7 Dist., Noble, 09-11-2009) No. 08 NO 356, 2009-Ohio-4809, 2009 WL 2917963, Unreported. Child Custody ⚬⟿ 558; Child Custody ⚬⟿ 569

Trial court abused its discretion in determining that best interest of the child was for unwed father to be the residential parent, given that there was no indication in record that child had adjusted to father's home, community, or future pre-school and father had failed to pay child support for extended periods of the child's life. Rice v. Lewis (Ohio App. 4 Dist., Scioto, 04-10-2009) No. 08CA3238, 2009-Ohio-1823, 2009 WL 1027544, Unreported. Children Out–of–wedlock ⚬⟿ 20.3

It is only after final judgment allocating parental rights and responsibilities that court must comply with statutory requirements for modification of child custody; in effect, when court modifies temporary custody order, court need only apply best interest standard. Williams v. Williams (Ohio App. 11 Dist., Trumbull, 07-30-2004) No. 2002-T-0101, 2004-Ohio-3992, 2004 WL 1713283, Unreported. Child Custody ⚬⟿ 550

Trial court was not required to consider child's best interests in child custody proceeding, where father failed to first make threshold showing that change in circumstances had occurred, as necessary for modification of child custody to occur. Venuto v. Pochiro (Ohio App. 7 Dist., Mahoning, 05-21-2004) No. 02 CA 225, 2004-Ohio-2631, 2004 WL 1152055, Unreported. Child Custody ⚬⟿ 554

Awarding residential custody to natural father, on father's motion to modify, was in best interests of two minor children; mother suffered from mental and emotional problems, mother refused to comply with visitation order, and mother failed to secure therapeutic treatment for the children as called for by experts and court order. Allen v. Murphy (Ohio App. 5 Dist., Tuscarawas, 05-17-2004) No. 2003AP100081, 2004-Ohio-2578, 2004 WL 1124953, Unreported. Children Out–of–wedlock ⚬⟿ 20.10

While trial court could have considered predecree evidence in determining the best interests of the children in modification of custody proceeding, it was not required to consider such evidence, and thus, trial court did not abuse its discretion when it precluded unwed father from putting on evidence of mother's suicide attempt that had taken place prior to the last custody decree. Font v. Morris (Ohio App. 3 Dist., Mercer, 05-10-2004) No. 10-03-21, 2004-Ohio-2354, 2004 WL 1049130, Unreported. Children Out–of–wedlock ⚬⟿ 20.10

Substantial competent, credible evidence supported trial court's finding that modification of custody was necessary to serve best interest of the children and that the harm that would result from change of custody from unwed father to mother would be outweighed by the benefit from the result of the change; father was not involved in children's schooling, father obstructed mother's visitation with children when he had custody, father had left the children asleep in car in freezing temperatures when children were not appropriately dressed, and children had adjusted well to being placed with mother. Font v. Morris (Ohio App. 3 Dist., Mercer, 05-10-2004) No. 10-03-21, 2004-Ohio-2354, 2004 WL 1049130, Unreported. Children Out–of–wedlock ⟶ 20.10

Trial court did not abuse its discretion in determining that granting custody to wife was in best interest of children, where older child had a slightly strained relationship with husband due to husband's disciplinary tactics, both husband and wife failed to consistently honor court-approved visitation rights, and husband failed to pay child support as agreed upon by the parties without a court order. Pengov v. Pengov (Ohio App. 11 Dist., Geauga, 12-12-2003) No. 2002-G-2485, 2003-Ohio-6755, 2003 WL 22952829, Unreported. Child Custody ⟶ 57; Child Custody ⟶ 85

Trial court properly considered primary caregiver factor when considering whether to change daughter's residential parent, although court did not specifically mention factor, where court noted that daughter would not have to change school systems or school activities because of a change, and court found that any harm would be greatly outweighed by best interests of daughter. Rosebrugh v. Rosebrugh (Ohio App. 11 Dist., Ashtabula, 08-22-2003) No. 2002-A-0002, 2003-Ohio-4595, 2003 WL 22038538, Unreported. Child Custody ⟶ 659

Magistrate did not fail to consider relevant factors in determining best interests of the child when modifying prior custody order to designate father as residential parent; magistrate's findings demonstrated that she considered all of the relevant factors, including wishes of parents, child's reluctance to express his wishes to the court, fact that the child was only in preschool, mother's past pattern of failing to honor father's court-approved visitation either in person or by phone, father's child support arrearages and reasons for failure to pay, and fact that mother relocated to Maryland but both parents had family in state. Mollica v. Mollica (Ohio App. 9 Dist., Medina, 07-23-2003) No. 02CA0079-M, 2003-Ohio-3921, 2003 WL 21697333, Unreported. Child Custody ⟶ 659

Although trial court did not apply three part analysis set forth in statute for determining whether to modify custody, the failure to do so was harmless error in custody dispute between maternal grandmother, who had been granted legal custody of one of parents' two children in prior consent judgment, and paternal grandparents, who had been granted legal custody of the other child in prior consent judgment; maternal grandmother did not support her complaint for custody of the other child by specifying that change in circumstances had occurred, and even if grandmother had been successful in showing a change in circumstances, she would have failed three-part test because court found that it was not in best interest of children to modify prior custody agreements. Thomas v. Moothart

(Ohio App. 3 Dist., Hancock, 07-15-2003) No. 5-02-56, 2003-Ohio-3724, 2003 WL 21648102, Unreported, appeal not allowed 100 Ohio St.3d 1486, 798 N.E.2d 1094, 2003-Ohio-5992. Child Custody ⟶ 923(5)

Trial court error in failing to consider evidence that mother abused a child in the past warranted reversal of child custody order; the trial court was required to hear evidence regarding changed circumstances since the last child custody order and evidence probative of the best interests of the child before entering a child custody order, and evidence of possible child abuse was probative of whether granting mother custody was in the best interests of the children. In re Ballard (Ohio App. 2 Dist., Montgomery, 06-20-2003) No. 19511, 2003-Ohio-3233, 2003 WL 21419169, Unreported. Child Custody ⟶ 632; Child Custody ⟶ 923(4)

Trial court was required to find that death of children's mother, who was co-residential parent with father and primary residential parent under divorce decree, constituted change of circumstances before making determination whether father was unsuitable to retain custody of children, and if so, whether custody of children with maternal grandparents was in best interests of children. In re Guardianship of Kutz (Ohio App. 12 Dist., Fayette, 06-09-2003) No. CA2002-07-012, No. CA2002-07-013, No. CA2002-07-015, 2003-Ohio-2924, 2003 WL 21305252, Unreported. Child Custody ⟶ 579

Trial court's order modifying existing custody decree to name former husband residential parent of child during school year met statutory requirements for modifying such decrees, and thus, order was valid, where court found that, since issuance of joint parenting orders, substantial changes in circumstances occurred, modification of orders was necessary to serve best interests of child, and harm likely to be caused by change of environment was outweighed by advantages of change of environment to child. Dyslin v. Marks (Ohio App. 5 Dist., Stark, 04-07-2003) No. 2002CA00300, 2003-Ohio-1855, 2003 WL 1857108, Unreported. Child Custody ⟶ 576

Finding that awarding custody of nonmarital child to biological father was in child's best interest was not abuse of discretion, in light of trial court's consideration of pertinent issues with regard to both father and mother under best interest analysis. Noonan v. Edson (Ohio App. 12 Dist., Butler, 04-07-2003) No. CA2002-04-088, 2003-Ohio-1767, 2003 WL 1795576, Unreported. Children Out–of–wedlock ⟶ 20.3

Even though consideration of a single factor in isolation may suggest a certain result in a child custody determination, it is incumbent on the trial court to consider all of the factors and determine what, on the whole, is in the best interest of a child. Lynch v. Lynch (Ohio App. 6 Dist., Huron, 03-07-2003) No. H-02-022, 2003-Ohio-1039, 2003 WL 876566, Unreported. Child Custody ⟶ 76

Evidence was sufficient to support finding that changing residential custodian of parties' four children from mother to father was in children's best interest; although children expressed a desire to stay with mother, both parents had a healthy interaction with children, and although a prior domestic violence charge existed against father, charge was an isolated incident, mother did not live in children's school district, court was concerned over children's mental health due to long drawn out litigation, mother's mental health, and her state of unemployment, and court believed that father was more likely to honor and facilitate court-approved parenting time in light of mother's history of willful interference with father's visitation rights. Bland v. Bland (Ohio App. 9 Dist., Summit, 02-26-2003) No. 21228, 2003-Ohio-828, 2003 WL 470180, Unreported. Child Custody ☞ 552; Child Custody ☞ 560; Child Custody ☞ 564; Child Custody ☞ 566; Child Custody ☞ 569

Juvenile court abused its discretion in its order on father's motion to modify legal custody by considering the best interests factors only as a basis to find that a change in circumstances occurred, but did not apply such factors to determine whether modification was in child's best interest. In re S.G. (Ohio App. 8 Dist., Cuyahoga, 01-16-2003) No. 80952, 2003-Ohio-161, 2003 WL 125122, Unreported. Child Custody ☞ 553

Juvenile court's refusal to admit evidence relevant to the best interests factors in hearing on motion to modify legal custody was abuse of discretion. In re S.G. (Ohio App. 8 Dist., Cuyahoga, 01-16-2003) No. 80952, 2003-Ohio-161, 2003 WL 125122, Unreported. Child Custody ☞ 632

Trial court erred by entering an order on father's motion to modify custody that, after finding that a change in circumstances had occurred, mother and her family had been noncomplying with previous orders for visitation and psychological testing, and mother's custody of child was to be terminated, reinstated mother as legal custodian on best interests grounds, where best interests finding was based on lack of evidence which court had a duty to obtain, on "medical" opinion of a guardian ad litem who thought that child would have been harmed by removal from mother's home, and on hypothetical and ex parte questions asked of psychologist off record, court refused to admit relevant evidence, mother and grandfather, a party to matter, apparently suffered from poor physical and mental health, and mother's family fought vigorously over five year period to deny father his rights to child. In re S.G. (Ohio App. 8 Dist., Cuyahoga, 01-16-2003) No. 80952, 2003-Ohio-161, 2003 WL 125122, Unreported. Child Custody ☞ 659

Evidence supported trial court's determination that change of parental environment was not in child's best interest, and thus father was not entitled to grant of motion to reallocate parental rights and responsibilities, even though mother had suffered from depression and had interfered with visitation schedule; child services worker testified that mother worked well with child and set limits, mother reported that father had history of emotional abuse and assaultive behaviors toward mother in the presence of child, child did not express concern for her future safety and well-being with mother, and father was behind on child support payments. Riggle v. Riggle (Ohio App. 9 Dist., Wayne, 10-16-2002) No. 02CA0015, 2002-Ohio-5553, 2002 WL 31313710, Unreported. Child Custody ☞ 552; Child Custody ☞ 560; Child Custody ☞ 564; Child Custody ☞ 569

In considering a change of custody RC 3109.04 requires only a finding of a "change of circumstances" before a trial court can determine the best interest of the child and a court that bases its finding upon a substantial change of circumstances errs. Willis v. Willis (Ohio App. 8 Dist., Cuyahoga, 05-22-1997) No. 70937, 1997 WL 272377, Unreported.

Statutory requirement of a change in circumstances for modification of custody decree does not require that the change be substantial nor does the change have to be quantitatively large; rather, the change must have a material effect on the child. Brammer v. Brammer (Ohio App. 3 Dist., 05-31-2011) 194 Ohio App.3d 240, 955 N.E.2d 453, 2011-Ohio-2610, stay denied 129 Ohio St.3d 1442, 951 N.E.2d 1041, 2011-Ohio-4221. Child Custody ☞ 556

When a trial court is asked to modify a custody decree, the initial determination to be made by the court is whether there has been a change in circumstances of the child or the residential parent since the prior court order; this finding should be made prior to weighing the child's best interest. Brammer v. Brammer (Ohio App. 3 Dist., 05-31-2011) 194 Ohio App.3d 240, 955 N.E.2d 453, 2011-Ohio-2610, stay denied 129 Ohio St.3d 1442, 951 N.E.2d 1041, 2011-Ohio-4221. Child Custody ☞ 659

Evidence did not support finding that it was in the best interest of children to modify parental rights and responsibilities such that the parents no longer equally cared for the children, and, instead, designating mother, who planned to move with children to other state to pursue job promotion, as residential parent for school purposes; although mother testified that schools in other state could provide better services to special needs child, the only evidence that schools were better was mother's testimony, and father presented evidence regarding plan in place at child's present school to address his special needs, and children had developed strong ties to their current community where the majority of their extended family lived, and there was no evidence that father was incapable of taking the lead in handling the children's education and medical issues. Brammer v. Brammer (Ohio App. 3 Dist., 05-31-2011) 194 Ohio App.3d 240, 955 N.E.2d 453, 2011-Ohio-2610, stay denied 129 Ohio St.3d 1442, 951 N.E.2d 1041, 2011-Ohio-4221. Child Custody ☞ 637; Child Custody ☞ 642

Juvenile court in which child's mother moved for modification of custody, following award of custody to child's parental grandmother and step-grandfather, could not entertain mother's motion for a new hearing regarding parental suitability that would be separate and apart from her pending motion to modify custody; rather, mother's arguments that juvenile court incorrectly applied a best-interests-of-the-child standard instead of a parental suitability standard in initial custody determination had to be made in context of pending motion for modification of custody. In re O.H.W. (Ohio App. 12 Dist., 02-19-2008) 175 Ohio App.3d 349, 887 N.E.2d 354, 2008-Ohio-627. Child Custody ⚘ 512

After the legal custody determination is made, the best-interest-of-the-child standard should be used for any custody modification petitions filed by a natural parent. In re Hockstok (Ohio, 12-27-2002) 98 Ohio St.3d 238, 781 N.E.2d 971, 2002-Ohio-7208, modified 98 Ohio St.3d 1476, 784 N.E.2d 709, 2003-Ohio-980. Child Custody ⚘ 554

Term "shall," as used in statute enumerating factors to be considered in determining children's best interest, is mandatory and requires trial court to consider such factors in entering or modifying an order allocating parental rights and responsibilities. Dilworth v. Dilworth (Ohio App. 2 Dist., 11-08-1996) 115 Ohio App.3d 537, 685 N.E.2d 847. Child Custody ⚘ 75; Child Custody ⚘ 554

When elder of two children whose custody has previously been awarded to divorced parent becomes ten years of age and thereafter chooses as custodian the other parent who is not disqualified by unfitness, there is a change of conditions as to the younger child and it is for the court to determine whether it is for the best interest of the children to be separated and to fix custody of the younger child accordingly. Dailey v. Dailey (Ohio 1945) 146 Ohio St. 93, 64 N.E.2d 246, 32 O.O. 29. Child Custody ⚘ 555

Trial court did not abuse its discretion in custody modification proceeding by finding that it was in child's best interests that mother continue as child's residential parent; child had a half-brother that resided with mother, child's half-brother testified that he loved child and that he helped with her homework and played games with child, child's maternal grandmother testified that child, mother, and mother's husband have a good relationship, and guardian ad litem testified child wanted to go back to living with mother. In re Firth (Ohio App. 7 Dist., Columbiana, 09-27-2002) No. 01-CO-23, 2002-Ohio-5219, 2002 WL 31168826, Unreported. Child Custody ⚘ 554; Child Custody ⚘ 566

36. —— Child's wishes and interview with judge, modification of rights and responsibilities and "change in circumstances"

Trial court did not abuse its discretion in determining that a material change had occurred in the circumstances of the children, for purposes of determining whether custody of children should be modified such that adjudicated father, rather than mother, be designated as children's residential parent; one of parties' two children, who was 11, expressed a great desire to reside with father, and

his desire was so strong that mother allowed child to live with father for three months, children were enrolled in three different schools within a span of nine months, and when mother relocated with children to town approximately 30 miles from place they had lived their entire lives, they were removed from their extended families, with whom they were close. Wallace v. Willoughby (Ohio App. 3 Dist., Shelby, 06-20-2011) No. 17-10-15, 2011-Ohio-3008, 2011 WL 2449009, Unreported. Children Out–of–wedlock ⚘ 20.10

There was no evidence that juvenile court did not properly consider minor child's wishes and concerns after it conducted an in camera interview with the child, who was born out-of-wedlock, and thus juvenile court did not abuse its discretion by dismissing mother's motion for change of custody from father to mother; record established that the juvenile court was fully aware of the statutory procedure and considered the appropriate factors. Stevenson v. Kotnik (Ohio App. 11 Dist., Lake, 05-27-2011) No. 2010-L-063, 2011-Ohio-2585, 2011 WL 2120092, Unreported. Children Out–of–wedlock ⚘ 20.10

Fact that child had reached age 12 and expressed his desire to live with ex-wife because he liked the warmer climate and had more fun in Arizona did not constitute changed circumstances, as required for modification of prior custody order designating husband as the residential parent under shared parenting plan; the change in circumstances required for modification had to be a change of substance. Pryor v. Hooks (Ohio App. 9 Dist., Summit, 12-15-2010) No. 25294, 2010-Ohio-6130, 2010 WL 5141353, Unreported. Child Custody ⚘ 576

Trial court did not err in refusing to conduct an interview of the parties' children in custody action; wife, who resided with children in Idaho, wanted the trial court to conduct a telephone conference with the children, and instead of offering to send the children to the trial court's Ohio chambers, wife contemplated setting up neutral location at which children could speak with the court from Idaho, and despite wife's promise to find a neutral location for the children, the trial court could not control the children's environment to eliminate the possibility of "off-stage" coaching or pressure. Lumley v. Lumley (Ohio App. 10 Dist., Franklin, 12-31-2009) No. 09AP-556, 2009-Ohio-6992, 2009 WL 5174121, Unreported. Child Custody ⚘ 506

Trial court acted within its discretion in choosing not to conduct in camera interview of child for purposes of making child custody decision incident to parties' divorce proceedings; neither party requested such an interview and, in the absence of a request from the parents, the trial court had discretion in determining whether such an interview would be helpful, and child was six years old at the time of the hearing, and the court cited his young age as the basis for its decision not to interview him. White v. White (Ohio App. 2 Dist., Clark, 08-21-2009) No. 2009 CA 17, 2009-Ohio-4311, 2009 WL 2602341, Unreported. Child Custody ⚘ 427

Trial court was not required, when considering former husband's motion for legal custody of his youngest child with former wife, to interview the parties' children at former husband's request; trial court did not find a change of circumstances that would warrant custody modification and, thus, did not need to address the children's best interests. Cravens v. Cravens (Ohio App. 12 Dist., Warren, 04-13-2009) No. CA2008-02-033, 2009-Ohio-1733, 2009 WL 975579, Unreported. Child Custody ☞ 654

Neither magistrate nor trial court was required by statute to interview children, though mother had filed motion seeking such interview, in suit she commenced seeking reallocation of parental rights and responsibilities, as both magistrate and trial court had determined that no change in circumstances had occurred, before court could reach determination of children's best interests it first had to find a change in circumstances had occurred, statute mandating that court interview children upon parental request applied when court was determining best interests of children, and, absent a finding of change in circumstances, there was no reason for court to consider testimony and evidence as to children's best interests. Brunip v. Nickerson (Ohio App. 7 Dist., Columbiana, 09-30-2008) No. 07-CO-42, 2008-Ohio-5052, 2008 WL 4416456, Unreported, appeal not allowed 120 Ohio St.3d 1525, 901 N.E.2d 245, 2009-Ohio-614. Child Custody ☞ 654

Trial judge's failure to conduct in-chambers interview of children on parties' motions for sole custody at end of same year in which divorce judgment was entered under which parties agreed to care for children pursuant to court-approved shared parenting plan was error, as trial court had no discretion but was subject to clear statutory directive. Mangan v. Mangan (Ohio App. 2 Dist., Greene, 07-18-2008) No. 07-CA-100, 2008-Ohio-3622, 2008 WL 2809225, Unreported. Child Custody ☞ 654

Statute requiring trial court in a custody dispute to make certain determinations as to the child's wishes following an interview of the child in chambers did not apply in custody dispute between biological father and deceased mother's surviving husband, to whom mother was married at time she gave birth to child; statute only applied to proceedings pertaining to the allocation of parental rights between the two natural parents of a child. Lorence v. Goeller (Ohio App. 9 Dist., Lorain, 06-01-2005) No. CIV.A. 04CA008556, 2005-Ohio-2678, 2005 WL 1283713, Unreported. Children Out–of–wedlock ☞ 20.4

Trial court's failure to conduct in camera interview with children in child custody proceeding, after father had requested such interview, was reversible error, where statute mandated that trial court interview children at request of either party. Church v. Church (Ohio App. 7 Dist., Noble, 11-18-2004) No. 03 NO 314, 2004-Ohio-6215, 2004 WL 2659250, Unreported. Child Custody ☞ 923(1)

Substantial change in child's circumstances occurred, as required for modification of child custody, where ex-wife was designated as residential parent and child's legal custodian, child expressed desire to reside with ex-husband, and child resided with ex-husband during school year. Cowan v. Cowan (Ohio App. 4 Dist., Washington, 11-12-2004) No. 04CA5, 2004-Ohio-6119, 2004 WL 2616410, Unreported. Child Custody ☞ 566

Terminating shared parenting plan and awarding child custody to ex-husband was not abuse of discretion, where ex-wife placed child in automobile with intoxicated boyfriend and automobile accident subsequently occurred, child attended numerous schools and was excessively absent from school while living with ex-wife, and judge was concerned that child's stated wish to live with ex-wife was mere repetition of what he had heard, rather than what he wanted. Basford v. Basford (Ohio App. 7 Dist., Noble, 03-26-2004) No. 03-NO-310, 2004-Ohio-1539, 2004 WL 610773, Unreported. Child Custody ☞ 576

Trial court considered relevant factors when deciding whether to change daughter's residential parent to father, although teenage daughter stated preference to live with mother; court noted that daughter's dislike of father's girlfriend was main reason for preference and that dislike was based partially on minor or disciplinary reasons, court noted that mother made bad financial decisions, court considered daughter's adjustment to home and community, and there was no child support order for court to consider. Rosebrugh v. Rosebrugh (Ohio App. 11 Dist., Ashtabula, 08-22-2003) No. 2002-A-0002, 2003-Ohio-4595, 2003 WL 22038538, Unreported. Child Custody ☞ 659

Trial court did not abuse its discretion by determining that child's preference to live with his mother, as indicated during an in camera interview, was to be accorded little weight in determining that a change in custody from a shared parenting scheme to father as residential custodian was in child's best interest, where, although child expressed a preference to live with his mother, he also expressed a wish to reside with his father, and the court considered any parent-specific reasons for child's preferences, as well as fact that at least one parent engaged in a discussion with child about the in-camera interview. Lynch v. Lynch (Ohio App. 6 Dist., Huron, 03-07-2003) No. H-02-022, 2003-Ohio-1039, 2003 WL 876566, Unreported. Child Custody ☞ 566

Fact that no record was made of court's in-camera interview with child at issue in custody dispute was not error, where mother, who requested the in-camera interview, did not request that a record of such interview be made. Lynch v. Lynch (Ohio App. 6 Dist., Huron, 03-07-2003) No. H-02-022, 2003-Ohio-1039, 2003 WL 876566, Unreported. Child Custody ☞ 506

In considering a motion for reallocation of parental rights and responsibilities, though passage of time alone is insufficient to find a change of circumstances to relitigate the issue of custody, the passage of time during a significant developmental portion of a child's life, combined with other pertinent factors, such as the child's expressed desires to reside with the mother, supports the finding of a change of circumstances. Boone v. Kaser (Ohio App. 5 Dist., Tuscarawas, 08-28-2001) No. 2001AP050050, 2001 WL 1011453, Unreported.

In a mother's motion for change in custody with respect to her daughter who is nearly nine at the time of hearing on the motion, a trial court commits reversible error by excluding the testimony of the child without first conducting a voir dire examination to determine the child's competency to testify; in addition, the mother's failure to proffer what her daughter's testimony would have been had she been allowed to testify does not preclude the mother from raising the issue on appeal without having to resort to the plain error rule. Baird v. Gillispie (Ohio App. 2 Dist., Miami, 01-21-2000) No. 99-CA-12, 2000 WL 43493, Unreported.

The expressed desire of a child who is nearly ten years old to reside with his mother is insufficient to warrant separation from his father who has had custody since the child was two years old where (1) the child suffers from attention deficit disorder and hyperactivity and is prescribed Ritalin, (2) when not taking Ritalin he is disruptive at school and unable to learn, (3) the mother refuses to give the medication while the child is staying with her for a short period so the father takes the medication to his son's school for it to be administered, and (4) the child's relationship with his father is normal and healthy. Basinger v. Basinger (Ohio App. 11 Dist., Trumbull, 04-30-1999) No. 98-T-0080, 1999 WL 266606, Unreported.

A court properly conducts an in camera interview of a child now fifteen years old who has lived with her father for ten years and presently chooses to live with her mother and stepfather where the court determines that (1) the child is capable of expressing her wishes in an intelligent and rational manner, (2) she chooses to live with her mother and stepfather so that she might foster a better relationship with them and her half siblings, (3) she finds it difficult to participate in after school activities because of the location of her private school, (4) due to her father's and stepmother's jobs and lifestyles her interaction with them is very limited, and (5) her father is planning to move to Arizona. Zygela v. Euler (Ohio App. 6 Dist., Lucas, 12-05-1997) No. L-97-1123, 1997 WL 770972, Unreported.

A father's continued payment of child support while he has extended summer visitation with his son is not inappropriate; in addition, a court is within its discretion in finding that an eight-year-old child lacks sufficient reasoning ability to make an informed choice with respect to who would be his residential parent. Dicke v. Dicke (Ohio App. 3 Dist., Allen, 11-07-1995) No. 1-95-23, 1995 WL 657112, Unreported.

Trial court which performed in camera interview of child in connection with motion seeking modifi-

cation of parental rights and responsibilities established by order in divorce action did not abuse its discretion by failing to ask child ultimate question regarding whether he would prefer to live with his mother or his father; method of questioning did not violate letter or spirit of statute, and judge asked questions sufficient to ascertain child's wishes and concerns with respect to allocation of rights and responsibilities. Inscoe v. Inscoe (Ohio App. 4 Dist., 06-16-1997) 121 Ohio App.3d 396, 700 N.E.2d 70. Child Custody ☞ 654

Trial court which had conducted in camera interview of minor child, in connection with motion for modification of parental rights and responsibilities established by prior order in divorce action, erred by sealing interview from parties; no statutory basis exists for denying parents access to transcript of their child's in camera interview. Inscoe v. Inscoe (Ohio App. 4 Dist., 06-16-1997) 121 Ohio App.3d 396, 700 N.E.2d 70. Infants ☞ 133

Trial court considering parents' post-divorce cross-motions to determine child's school district was statutorily obligated to appoint guardian ad litem for child, where mother requested interview of child and filed motion for appointment of guardian. Badgett v. Badgett (Ohio App. 7 Dist., 07-15-1997) 120 Ohio App.3d 448, 698 N.E.2d 84. Infants ☞ 78(1)

Trial court considering parents' post-divorce cross-motions to determine child's school district was statutorily obligated to interview child, even though neither party filed written motion requesting interview, where mother's counsel orally requested an interview, and counsel objected several times to lack of interview. Badgett v. Badgett (Ohio App. 7 Dist., 07-15-1997) 120 Ohio App.3d 448, 698 N.E.2d 84. Child Custody ☞ 506

Statute prohibiting use in custody and visitation proceedings of statements and affidavits purporting to set forth child's preference concerning allocation of parental responsibilities also applied in mandamus proceeding which arose out of custody proceeding; harm to child from demand that he choose between his parents was valid concern in any proceeding. State ex rel. Papp v. James (Ohio, 06-01-1994) 69 Ohio St.3d 373, 632 N.E.2d 889, 1994-Ohio-86. Mandamus ☞ 168(3)

Record should have been made of trial court's in-chambers interview of children on issue of change of custody following divorce; statute listing persons allowed to be present at interview requires that court stenographer and/or other recording device be present upon timely request; overruling *Crabbs v Crabbs*, 1992 WL 195417. Patton v. Patton (Licking 1993) 87 Ohio App.3d 844, 623 N.E.2d 235. Child Custody ☞ 650; Trial ☞ 23

Issues involving child custody and visitation are peculiarly within the very broad discretion of the trial court since the knowledge obtained through contact with and observation of the parties cannot be conveyed to a reviewing court through the printed word and therefore, a court is required to find a change of circumstances subsequent to the prior custody award to allow a change of custody and although a child's arrival at the statutory age accompanied by his election of the parent who does not presently have custody and would not be deemed unfit is a change of circumstances, a trial court is permitted to deny the wishes of the child when conditions surrounding the custody change indicate it is not in the best interests of the child and the benefit of the custody change would not outweigh the harm caused by such change. Bawidamann v. Bawidamann (Montgomery 1989) 63 Ohio App.3d 691, 580 N.E.2d 15.

To determine the best interests of a child in an action where one parent is seeking to modify custody, where both parents are deemed fit, and where the child has expressed a preference or election pursuant to RC 3109.04 the trial court must look to the totality of the circumstances surrounding the change and therefore, where a trial court finds that a father's allegation of an unhealthy environment provided by his children's mother is untrue and that the father has exerted a subtle manipulative power over his children and that his actions are based more on his desire for revenge than for the well being of the children, the court does not abuse its discretion in finding that custody of the children should remain with the mother, even though both parents are fit to have custody and the children elect to live with their father. Bawidamann v. Bawidamann (Montgomery 1989) 63 Ohio App.3d 691, 580 N.E.2d 15.

In a proceeding to vacate a prior custody decree pursuant to Civ R 60(B), a trial court may use its sound discretion in deciding whether to allow a child under eleven years of age to testify, pursuant to RC 3109.04(C)(2), regarding the child's preferred custodian. Wade v. Wade (Wayne 1983) 10 Ohio App.3d 167, 461 N.E.2d 30, 10 O.B.R. 220.

A trial court may consider the factors set out in RC 3109.04 when ruling on a motion for relief from judgment of a custody decree pursuant to Civ R 60(B); specifically, the expressed desire of a nine-year-old child to live with her mother is insufficient to meet the requirement of a change in circumstances as set forth in RC 3109.04. Wade v. Wade (Wayne 1983) 10 Ohio App.3d 167, 461 N.E.2d 30, 10 O.B.R. 220.

In an action seeking a change of child custody, a presumption is created by RC 3109.04 favoring retention of the current custodian; such presumption is especially strong if the children are twelve or older, and want to stay with the current custodial parent. Kraus v. Kraus (Cuyahoga 1983) 10 Ohio App.3d 63, 460 N.E.2d 680, 10 O.B.R. 73.

Circumstances short of a parent being found unfit may necessitate the denial of a change of custody where the child expresses a preference or makes an election pursuant to RC 3109.04 because the change may not be in the best interests of the child. Venable v. Venable (Cuyahoga 1981) 3 Ohio App.3d 421, 445 N.E.2d 1125, 3 O.B.R. 498. Child Custody ☞ 566

Where both parents are fit and suitable and a child has expressed a preference, the court may still deny a change of custody upon a determination that the change is not in the best interest of the child. Venable v. Venable (Cuyahoga 1981) 3 Ohio App.3d 421, 445 N.E.2d 1125, 3 O.B.R. 498.

A change of circumstance sufficient to justify a change of custody exists where a child over the age of eleven expresses a strengthening desire to live with her noncustodial parent. In re Reynolds (Hamilton 1982) 2 Ohio App.3d 309, 441 N.E.2d 1141, 2 O.B.R. 341.

Upon hearing of a motion for change of custody of a child now fifteen years old previously granted to the father, the expression of the child of the preference to live with his mother is a sufficient change in conditions to require consideration of the motion, and the child's preference between parents should be a major factor in the determination of what will be in his best interest. In re Custody of Smelser (Ohio Com.Pl. 1969) 22 Ohio Misc. 41, 257 N.E.2d 769, 51 O.O.2d 31, 51 O.O.2d 75.

Court did not err in refusing to change custody of fourteen-year-old daughter from father to mother, even though daughter requested such change, where mother had carried on adulterous relationship with individual whom she subsequently married. Watson v. Watson (Columbiana 1956) 146 N.E.2d 443, 76 Ohio Law Abs. 348.

In proceeding for change of custody of eight year old child awarded to father by divorce decree, wherein evidence established abuse and misuse of child by father's present wife, denial of change of custody on ground that child in conference with trial judge stated she desired to stay with father had effect of making 8 year old child choose between her parents though she was not capable of being sworn as a witness, and was prejudicially erroneous. Newman v. Newman (Cuyahoga 1951) 104 N.E.2d 707, 61 Ohio Law Abs. 438. Child Custody ☞ 558; Child Custody ☞ 566; Child Custody ☞ 923(4)

When a child in custody of divorced parent by virtue of a previous order of court arrives at age of ten years and, in court proceeding involving modification of previous order, chooses as custodian the other parent who is not unfitted for charge by reason of moral depravity, etc., there is a change of conditions requiring modification of previous order. Dailey v. Dailey (Ohio 1945) 146 Ohio St. 93, 64 N.E.2d 246, 32 O.O. 29.

Burden of proof is upon the parent seeking modification of decree awarding custody of child, at the child's election, to the other parent, to show unfitness of such other parent. Schwalenberg v. Schwalenberg (Columbiana 1940) 65 Ohio App. 217, 29 N.E.2d 617, 18 O.O. 397.

In a wrongful death action brought by the administrator of the estate of a divorced woman who did not have custody of her children, a federal trial court does not err by refusing to instruct the jury that when the children reached the age of twelve an Ohio court could let them choose under RC

3109.04 which parent to live with; the administrator's argument that it is "reasonable and probable that... each... would have selected the mother" is unfounded, and the proposed change would require the jury to speculate. Bowman v. Koch Transfer Co. (C.A.6 (Ohio) 1988) 862 F.2d 1257.

Modification of custody order to grant child's legal and residential custody to father was in child's best interest; trial court interviewed child in chambers, found her to be a "very bright" and "remarkably mature child," during interview, child indicated that she wished to live with her father, and at time of interview, child was already living with her father, and was 17 1/2 years old. Douglass Makni v. Makni (Ohio App. 4 Dist., Pike, 09-24-2002) No. 01CA680, 2002-Ohio-5098, 2002 WL 31131877, Unreported. Child Custody ⚬⟶ 554; Child Custody ⚬⟶ 566

Court's disregard of a child's preference to remain in the father's custody is reasonable pursuant to RC 3109.04 which eliminates the child's ability to choose a residential parent; custody to the mother is in the child's best interest where the trial court believes the child's stated wish to stay with his father is the product of the control the father holds over the child and the child's version of what occurred during supervised visits with the mother is contradicted by neutral observers. Bates v Bates, No. 2000–A–0058, 2001 WL 1560915 (11th Dist Ct App, Ashtabula, 12–7–01).

A twelve-year-old child's election to live with the noncustodial parent must be granted unless there is a finding that it is detrimental to the child's best interests, and a court does not abuse its discretion in modifying custody of minor children when the evidence supports a finding that modification is necessary to serve the minors' best interests. Collins v Collins, No. 42688 (8th Dist Ct App, Cuyahoga, 3–19–81).

Court has no jurisdiction to modify or vacate a prior order "sua sponte" where no motion to change custody is pending and where no notice is given to the parties; in addition, a change of custody cannot be based solely upon the expressed wishes of a nine-and-one-half-year-old child. In re Remmer, No. 52712 (8th Dist Ct App, Cuyahoga, 7-2-87).

Courts have traditionally defined the phrase "change in circumstances" in RC 3109.04 to denote an event, occurrence, or situation which has a material and adverse effect upon the child, and that requirement of a change in circumstances of either the residential parent or the child is to prevent the continued relitigation of issues previously raised and considered by the trial court; and although the former RC 3109.04 permitted a court to allow any child who was twelve years of age or older to choose the parent with whom he wants to live, under the amended version of RC 3109.04 a change in the child's wishes and concerns regarding a residential parent standing alone is not a change of circumstances, though it is one factor in determining whether there has been such a change. Moyer

v Moyer, No. 96APF05–659, 1996 WL 729859 (10th Dist Ct App, Franklin, 12–17–96).

While a court is not bound by the preference of a ten-year-old child when ruling on a motion for change of custody, RC 3109.04 does not preclude the court from considering it. Gordon v Gordon, No. 1334 (4th Dist Ct App, Athens, 10–19–87).

It is improper to grant a change of custody solely on the expressed wishes of a nine-year-old child, although the child's preference may be a consideration; the requisite statutory factors should be investigated and weighed. In re Remmer, No. 52712 (8th Dist Ct App, Cuyahoga, 7–2–87).

37. —— Constitutional issues, modification of rights and responsibilities and "change in circumstances"

Custodial mother, who was defendant in non-custodial father's civil rights suit, was not a "state actor," and thus, father could not maintain his civil rights suit against mother to challenge constitutionality of state laws governing custody determinations, where mother was simply involved in the custody dispute and was subject to the same laws that father was contesting. Galluzzo v. Champaign County Court of Common Pleas (C.A.6 (Ohio), 01-31-2006) No. 04-3527, 168 Fed.Appx. 21, 2006 WL 229801, Unreported, rehearing en banc denied, certiorari denied 127 S.Ct. 949, 549 U.S. 1124, 166 L.Ed.2d 724. Civil Rights ⚬⟶ 1326(4)

Non-custodial father's civil rights suit against custodial mother, seeking declaration that state laws governing custody determinations were unconstitutional, lacked case and controversy as required for federal court jurisdiction, and thus his lawsuit was inappropriate means to challenge Ohio's parental custody laws and procedures, where father had dropped all of his fact-based claims, and sought only a general declaration that the Ohio statute and rule were unconstitutional. Galluzzo v. Champaign County Court of Common Pleas (C.A.6 (Ohio), 01-31-2006) No. 04-3527, 168 Fed.Appx. 21, 2006 WL 229801, Unreported, rehearing en banc denied, certiorari denied 127 S.Ct. 949, 549 U.S. 1124, 166 L.Ed.2d 724. Declaratory Judgment ⚬⟶ 124.1

The trial court's failure to provide notice to mother of out-of-wedlock child of its intent to address at pre-trial conference the merits of father's motion for modification of the allocation of parental rights violated mother's due process rights; mother was not afforded notice or an opportunity to be heard before the court terminated the parties' shared parenting plan, granted father legal custody, eliminated mother's parenting time, and ordered mother to pay child support. In re Murphy (Ohio App. 5 Dist., Stark, 10-24-2005) No. 2005CA00109, 2005-Ohio-5656, 2005 WL 2746296, Unreported. Children Out–of–wedlock ⚬⟶ 20.10; Constitutional Law ⚬⟶ 4396

Mother's due process right to confront and cross-examine witnesses was not violated in change-of-custody proceeding when trial court conducted unsworn, in camera interviews with child and relied on information obtained in those interviews to make determination that father should be child's residential parent and legal custodian; trial court's questioning of child covered issues related to child's preference regarding his custody and child's best interest, subjects of trial court's discussions with child were same as those raised and discussed in open court, and no new evidence was introduced into trial court's deliberations as result of interviews with child. Jackson v. Herron (Ohio App. 11 Dist., Lake, 08-05-2005) No. 2003-L-145, 2005-Ohio-4046, 2005 WL 1861965, Unreported. Child Custody ☞ 654; Trial ☞ 38

Awarding child custody to child's maternal grandparents did not deny father due process; although father argued he had fundamental right to make decisions concerning care and custody of his child, parent only has paramount right to custody when such custody is not detrimental to child, and court made clear finding that award of custody to father would be detrimental to child. Christopher A.L. v. Heather D.R. (Ohio App. 6 Dist., Huron, 08-13-2004) No. H-03-040, 2004-Ohio-4271, 2004 WL 1802987, Unreported. Child Custody ☞ 275; Constitutional Law ☞ 4396

Trial court's retroactive determination of amount of child support former wife should have paid under magistrate's temporary child support order during pendency of proceedings on former husband's motion for modification of parenting plan was not impermissible retroactive modification of support order and did not violate due process, where magistrate's temporary support order specifically stated amount was to be determined in future, no request was ever made for amount to be determined prior to hearing on former husband's motion, former wife had ample time to prepare for hearing and to prepare her finances to accommodate support, and, at hearing, both former wife and former husband were afforded the opportunity to present evidence regarding their incomes, including their incomes during the pendency. U.S.C.A. Const. Amend. 14. Tate v. Wells (Ohio App. 3 Dist., Van, 08-09-2004) No. 15-04-06, 2004-Ohio-4161, 2004 WL 1770420, Unreported. Child Support ☞ 364; Constitutional Law ☞ 4396

Trial court's immediate and unscheduled ruling on former wife's motion to modify visitation at a contempt hearing, in the absence of former husband, was a violation of due process and an abuse of discretion. Vocaire v. Beltz (Ohio App. 5 Dist., Stark, 11-10-2003) No. 2003CA00215, 2003-Ohio-6015, 2003 WL 22664190, Unreported. Child Custody ☞ 859; Child Custody ☞ 871; Constitutional Law ☞ 4494

Statute governing custody determinations arising out of divorce action was inapplicable, and trial court appropriately considered statutory requirements for other custody determinations in deciding to modify custody of nonmarital child, which had originally been awarded to maternal grandparents, in favor of biological father; since original placement father had married, obtained employment, cleared support arrearage, and attended parenting and anger classes, trial court considered such fac-

tors sufficient changes in circumstances to warrant custody reconsideration, and trial court was bound by Constitutional imperatives preferring natural parent in raising of child absent certain factors. In re Hollowell (Ohio App. 5 Dist., Stark, 11-18-2002) No. 2002CA00127, 2002-Ohio-6405, 2002 WL 31649171, Unreported. Children Out–of–wedlock ☞ 20.10

Statute requiring child's parents to demonstrate a change in circumstances for either the child or the maternal grandparents, who had been granted legal custody of child adjudicated abused and dependent, in order for court to modify custody, violated parents' right to due process and, as such, was unconstitutional; grandparents had only legal custody of child, which was non-permanent custody award, fact that trial court awarded parents supervised visitation with child and ordered them to pay child support to grandparents indicated that grandparents' custody of child was only temporary, and grandparents repeatedly stated that they did not view their custody of child as permanent. In re James (Ohio App. 1 Dist., 09-16-2005) 163 Ohio App.3d 442, 839 N.E.2d 39, 2005-Ohio-4847, appeal allowed 108 Ohio St.3d 1413, 841 N.E.2d 318, 2006-Ohio-179, reversed 113 Ohio St.3d 420, 866 N.E.2d 467, 2007-Ohio-2335, reconsideration denied 114 Ohio St.3d 1484, 870 N.E.2d 734, 2007-Ohio-3699. Constitutional Law ☞ 4396; Infants ☞ 132

A smoker has a constitutional right of privacy to treat his health in whatever manner he chooses, but this right does not include the right to inflict health-destructive secondhand smoke upon other persons, especially children who have no choice in the matter. In re Julie Anne (Ohio Com.Pl., 08-27-2002) 121 Ohio Misc.2d 20, 780 N.E.2d 635, 2002-Ohio-4489. Constitutional Law ☞ 1225

An order changing child custody for no reason other than the vacation of the original decree, by virtue of Civ R 60(B), would violate the express prohibition by O Const Art IV §5(B) of modification of substantive rights by operation of procedural rules, inasmuch as a change of custody must be based upon a finding either that a condition described at RC 3109.04(B) exists or that a de facto change has already taken place; consequently, a motion to vacate a custody decree will be treated as a motion for modification of custody when appropriate. Tatom v. Tatom (Montgomery 1984) 19 Ohio App.3d 198, 482 N.E.2d 1339, 19 O.B.R. 306.

Trial court's consideration, in custody modification motion filed by former husband, of former wife's sexual orientation in determining that former wife's sudden change in sexual orientation had contributed to former wife becoming systematically isolated from outside world did not violate former wife's rights under Equal Protection Clause of Fourteenth Amendment, since trial court did not consider issue of sexual orientation to be determinative. In re Marriage of Faulhaber (Ohio App. 11 Dist., Portage, 06-28-2002) No. 2001-P-0110, 2002-Ohio-3380, 2002 WL 1401066, Unreported. Child Custody ☞ 562; Constitutional Law ☞ 3440

Modification of shared parenting plan and denial former wife's motion to move child to Utah was not restriction on parties' right to travel, where decision merely dealt with child's residence for purposes of school attendance, and visitation with former wife if she moved to Utah, and it did not prohibit either party from traveling state to state. Martin v. Martin (Ohio App. 9 Dist., Summit, 03-13-2002) No. 20567, 2002-Ohio-1110, 2002 WL 388902, Unreported, appeal not allowed 96 Ohio St.3d 1467, 772 N.E.2d 1203, 2002-Ohio-3910. Child Custody ⟶ 261

38. —— Dangerous environment and actual acts, modification of rights and responsibilities and "change in circumstances"

Former wife's drug addiction, termination from employment at hospital for theft of drugs, and loss of housing that resulted in cohabitation with boyfriend constituted a change of circumstances authorizing trial court to consider former husband's motion seeking custody of children. Bowker v. Bowker (Ohio App. 5 Dist., Delaware, 09-02-2011) No. 10CAF110085, 2011-Ohio-4524, 2011 WL 3930295, Unreported. Child Custody ⟶ 552; Child Custody ⟶ 559; Child Custody ⟶ 565

Mother of child born out-of-wedlock failed in her burden of establishing that second hand smoke, father's use of profanity, and child's diet of fast food constituted a change of circumstances warranting a change in custody from father to mother, where record was silent as to whether father was a heavy smoker and whether he smoked in the child's presence at the time he assumed custody, record was equally silent as to any evidence of a change in this habit, and record was also silent as to both a baseline and a change in father's use of profanity and sources of nutrition for the child. Stevenson v. Kotnik (Ohio App. 11 Dist., Lake, 05-27-2011) No. 2010-L-063, 2011-Ohio-2585, 2011 WL 2120092, Unreported. Children Out-of-wedlock ⟶ 20.10

Trial court did not abuse its discretion by terminating mother's designation as residential parent and legal custodian and committing children to the custody of maternal grandmother, on grandmother's third-party motion to modify custody of grandchildren respectively determined in mother's two prior divorce actions, where court learned mother had resumed her relationship with violent former spouse who had beaten mother in front of children, and that mother had exposed her children to sexually inappropriate situations, encouraged violence between the children, and verbally abused the children, and the court followed recommendations of parenting specialist. Williams v. Gonzalez (Ohio App. 1 Dist., Hamilton, 08-27-2010) No. C-090483, No. C-090484, 2010-Ohio-3993, 2010 WL 3365741, Unreported. Child Custody ⟶ 558; Child Custody ⟶ 559; Child Custody ⟶ 616

A change in circumstances had occurred, as required for modification of child custody, where mother, who was the residential parent and legal custodian, was arrested for possession of marijuana and driving under the influence of alcohol, mother served 11 days in jail, mother's driver's license was suspended for five years, forcing child to depend on extended family members or friends for his transportation needs, child had not had behavior problems in school until after his mother was jailed, and mother and child had moved four times in the four years since the prior custody decree had been entered. Kirchhofer v. Kirchhofer (Ohio App. 9 Dist., Wayne, 08-16-2010) No. 09CA0061, 2010-Ohio-3797, 2010 WL 3210756, Unreported. Child Custody ⟶ 559; Child Custody ⟶ 568

Order awarding custody of the parties children to husband was not an abuse of discretion, in divorce proceeding; the children witnessed mother's boyfriend assault mother, mother and boyfriend continued to reside together, and mother alleged that the children had been abused in husband's home but county department of jobs and family services conducted an investigation and found no evidence of abuse. Isaacs v. Isaacs (Ohio App. 5 Dist., Tuscarawas, 09-08-2009) No. 2008AP11071, 2009-Ohio-4768, 2009 WL 2914253, Unreported. Child Custody ⟶ 41; Child Custody ⟶ 48; Child Custody ⟶ 58

Trial court acted within its discretion in modifying a shared parenting plan to designate mother the residential parent; trial court found that there had been changes in the circumstances of the children and mother and father since the parties entered into the original shared parenting plan and that substantial issues had arisen, including alleged abuse and neglect by father, and trial court considered the best interests of the children by analyzing the statutory best-interest factors, noting, inter alia, one child's need for stability and consistent medical treatment and father's history of refusing to acknowledge the child's need for treatment and medication. Leeth v. Leeth (Ohio App. 12 Dist., Preble, 08-24-2009) No. CA2009-02-004, 2009-Ohio-4260, 2009 WL 2581399, Unreported. Child Custody ⟶ 576; Child Custody ⟶ 659

Evidence supported trial court's decision in divorce proceeding to designate father as child's residential parent, due to concerns that mother's child from prior relationship posed a danger to child; mother's child had range of psychological, emotional, and behavioral problems, mother's child had exhibited violent behavior toward friends, family members, and animals, problem behaviors of mother's child included urinating on the floor,inappropriate spitting, licking, and touching, smearing feces on a toilet, and stealing money, and while mother's child had been hospitalized against for psychological problems, and mother argued that he was permanently institutionalized, there was no evidence indicating how long he would be hospitalized or what would happen to him upon his release. Kniszek v. Kniszek (Ohio App. 7 Dist., Jefferson, 06-26-2009) No. 08 JE 30, 2009-Ohio-3249, 2009 WL 1914393, Unreported. Child Custody ⟶ 210

Evidence supported modifying allocation of parental rights in favor of father so as to name father residential parent; acts arising from mother and stepfather's marital difficulties, and evidence relating thereto, constituted change in circumstances, magistrate cited domestic violence reports between mother and her husband and argument between mother and older daughter, which resulted in mother grabbing her daughter by the chin, pulling her hair, and choking her, magistrate had opportunity to view credibility and demeanor of witnesses, and magistrate considered all relevant statutory factors in determining best interests of children. Theurer v. Foster-Theurer (Ohio App. 12 Dist., Warren, 03-30-2009) No. CA2008-06-074, No. CA2008-06-083, 2009-Ohio-1457, 2009 WL 806715, Unreported. Child Custody ⟜ 558

Evidence supported trial court's decision in divorce proceeding to designate wife as residential parent and legal custodian, although wife failed to pay temporary child support to husband and owed arrearage; evidence indicated that husband abused alcohol and used marijuana and crack cocaine. Fricke v. Fricke (Ohio App. 3 Dist., Allen, 09-18-2006) No. 1-06-18, 2006-Ohio-4845, 2006 WL 2664219, Unreported. Child Custody ⟜ 48; Child Custody ⟜ 60

Trial court's finding that husband had propensity to cause conflict with regard to parenting time, and therefore, that wife was more likely than husband to facilitate parenting time, as justification for designating wife primary residential parent, was supported by evidence that husband had threatened to have police go to children's school to make sure that wife had no contact with children. Saluppo v. Saluppo (Ohio App. 9 Dist., Summit, 05-31-2006) No. 22680, 2006-Ohio-2694, 2006 WL 1479633, Unreported. Child Custody ⟜ 469

Changing residential parent from mother, who had been designated residential parent under consent judgment entry setting out shared parenting arrangement, to father was not an abuse of discretion; trial court considered all necessary statutory factors and found that mother began drinking in excess, father showed he had children's best interests at heart, and he provided satisfactory care for children and seemed most likely to facilitate visitation. Wygant v. Wygant (Ohio App. 3 Dist., Wyandot, 04-03-2006) No. 16-05-16, 2006-Ohio-1660, 2006 WL 846270, Unreported. Child Custody ⟜ 576

Trial court order that modified the parties' shared parenting plan by changing child's school district and re-allocating parenting time, which resulted in father having primary custody of child during the school year, was not an abuse of discretion; stepmother was available to drive child to school, father was available to pick up child or spend time with him after school, if child resided with mother he would sometimes have to ride for an hour on the bus and would go to daycare many afternoons, and mother had health issues. Blaker v. Wilhelm (Ohio App. 6 Dist., Wood, 01-28-2005) No. WD-04-003, 2005-Ohio-317, 2005 WL 196761, Unreported. Child Custody ⟜ 576

Trial court did not abuse its discretion in modifying custody of minor child born out-of-wedlock to

grant custody to father, where child expressed a desire to live with father, alleged domestic violence between her mother and her mother's boyfriend, was afraid of mother's boyfriend, and feared for mother's safety, and mother did not take advantage of her right to visitation while father had temporary custody of child. McClay v. Reed (Ohio App. 5 Dist., Guernsey, 12-29-2004) No. 2004CA-4, 2004-Ohio-7304, 2004 WL 3563008, Unreported. Children Out-of-wedlock ⟜ 20.10

Change of circumstances had occurred since time of initial custody order, warranting modification of custody of child born out-of-wedlock, where child alleged domestic violence between her mother and her mother's boyfriend, and suddenly did not want to be near her mother's boyfriend, child had matured during the eight years she resided with her mother, and could better articulate her needs and wishes as well as her fears. McClay v. Reed (Ohio App. 5 Dist., Guernsey, 12-29-2004) No. 2004CA-4, 2004-Ohio-7304, 2004 WL 3563008, Unreported. Children Out-of-wedlock ⟜ 20.10

Evidence supported juvenile court's decision that grant of legal custody to father, rather than mother, was in children's best interest; although father was unemployed and behind in mortgage payments, mother lived with man who threatened to drown one of her children, mother lived in four different school districts in three years, mother was unemployed, mother suffered from anxiety and depression, mother had been under court order limiting her visitation with children, and mother had trouble controlling her anger. In re Pasco (Ohio App. 7 Dist., Jefferson, 09-01-2004) No. 04JE1, No. 04JE2, 2004-Ohio-4825, 2004 WL 2029322, Unreported. Child Custody ⟜ 51

Police officers' testimony that they responded to calls while on duty and found father highly intoxicated was relevant in child custody proceeding to issue of credibility of father, who testified that he had successfully completed court-ordered alcohol treatment program, and to issue of father's suitability as parent. Christopher A.L. v. Heather D.R. (Ohio App. 6 Dist., Huron, 08-13-2004) No. H-03-040, 2004-Ohio-4271, 2004 WL 1802987, Unreported. Child Custody ⟜ 451

Modification of child custody order, removing child from mother's custody and granting residential custody of child to father, was in best interests of child; mother moved a great deal and had had ten addresses since dissolution of marriage, child spent considerable time with maternal grandparents who provided food and shelter, mother had pattern of abusive and unstable relationships, child stated that he did not feel safe and stable in his mother's care, father had always satisfied support obligations, maintained health insurance and exercised visitation, father had stable employment and relationships, and child would have stable home with father. In re Rutan (Ohio App. 3 Dist., Union, 08-02-2004) No. 14-03-52, 2004-Ohio-4022, 2004 WL 1718160, Unreported. Child Custody ⟜ 552

Evidence supported finding that child's best interests would be served by a change in residential custody from divorced father to mother; father had been experiencing depression, he had serious difficulties with controlling his anger, and he had been convicted of several misdemeanor offenses involving his former girlfriend. Hostetter v. Cotton (Ohio App. 5 Dist., Licking, 06-30-2004) No. 03CA94, 2004-Ohio-3524, 2004 WL 1486264, Unreported. Child Custody ☞ 576

Divorced father's depression and incidents of domestic violence and subsequent probation were a "change of circumstances" in his life, for purposes of mother's motion to modify allocation of parental rights to designate her sole residential parent. Hostetter v. Cotton (Ohio App. 5 Dist., Licking, 06-30-2004) No. 03CA94, 2004-Ohio-3524, 2004 WL 1486264, Unreported. Child Custody ☞ 576

Awarding child custody to divorcing husband was not abuse of discretion, where child heard incident in which wife repeatedly kicked husband in groin and issue as to mother's mental and emotional health had not been resolved. Clark v. Clark (Ohio App. 7 Dist., Noble, 03-24-2004) No. 03NO308, 2004-Ohio-1577, 2004 WL 615708, Unreported. Child Custody ☞ 61; Child Custody ☞ 62

Criminal background and violent history of former wife's new spouse had an adverse impact on minor child, warranting a modification of previous shared parenting agreement, where grandmother testified that child became fearful of going home to former wife, new spouse had engaged in inappropriate sexual activity with minor children, new spouse's former wife characterized him as a violent man and related how she contacted law enforcement more than a dozen times during their marriage, and daughter of new spouse's prior girlfriend testified she had been hit by new spouse. Keller v. Keller (Ohio App. 4 Dist., Jackson, 11-26-2003) No. 02CA19, No. 03CA3, 2003-Ohio-6462, 2003 WL 22860832, Unreported, appeal not allowed 102 Ohio St.3d 1421, 807 N.E.2d 366, 2004-Ohio-2003. Child Custody ☞ 576

There was no change in circumstances so as to warrant modification of shared parenting plan, which provided equal time between mother and father, so as to designate father as sole residential parent; the record neither showed that mother's drug use was something that had arisen since the trial court's previous custody determination nor that it had had any detrimental impact on the child, and mother's multiple misdemeanor convictions, while occurring since the previous decree, had not been shown to have any effect on the child. Leonard v. Yenser (Ohio App. 3 Dist., Mercer, 08-11-2003) No. 10-2003-01, 2003-Ohio-4251, 2003 WL 21904773, Unreported. Child Custody ☞ 576

Evidence was sufficient to support trial court's finding that a change in circumstances had occurred since the separation agreement named mother as residential parent under joint custody arrangement, and thus, supported changing the designation from mother to father; in approximately two years mother had moved three times, resulting in children changing schools three times, children's step-father disciplined them with a belt and stated he would do it again if he felt justified, children had severe dental problems and mother had not provided dental care children required, children had episodes of head lice, and court found that as many as three packs of cigarettes were being smoked around children per day. Silverman v. Silverman (Ohio App. 4 Dist., Hocking, 06-27-2003) No. 03CA2, 2003-Ohio-3757, 2003 WL 21652183, Unreported. Child Custody ☞ 576

A single offense does not constitute a "history" of domestic violence relative to custody determination. Bland v. Bland (Ohio App. 9 Dist., Summit, 02-26-2003) No. 21228, 2003-Ohio-828, 2003 WL 470180, Unreported. Child Custody ☞ 61

Evidence was sufficient to support finding that trial court considered father's domestic violence charge when it modified the existing order to award residential custody of parties' four children to father; court noted that father was only charged once with domestic violence, the charge was in the past, and it was an isolated event that appeared to have been resolved. Bland v. Bland (Ohio App. 9 Dist., Summit, 02-26-2003) No. 21228, 2003-Ohio-828, 2003 WL 470180, Unreported. Child Custody ☞ 659

Evidence was sufficient to support finding that harm likely to be caused by a change of environment resulting from changing residential custodian of parties' four children from mother to father was outweighed by the advantages of the change of environment to the children; court found that parties' three sons, ages 12, 14, and 16 were more in need of a positive, involved, and caring father during their teen years. Bland v. Bland (Ohio App. 9 Dist., Summit, 02-26-2003) No. 21228, 2003-Ohio-828, 2003 WL 470180, Unreported. Child Custody ☞ 552

Evidence was sufficient to support finding that custodial mother's relationship with an abusive boyfriend was not a change in circumstance which would support father's motion for change in custody; mother acted appropriately and ended relationship, and nothing indicated that mother intentionally subjected children or herself to the abuse. Dunlop v. Dunlop (Ohio App. 2 Dist., Montgomery, 10-25-2002) No. 19313, 2002-Ohio-5828, 2002 WL 31398674, Unreported. Child Custody ☞ 558; Child Custody ☞ 567

Custody of a child will not be changed merely on a showing by the nonresidential parent that he can provide a better environment than the residential parent. Steele v. Wyatt (Ohio App. 12 Dist., Butler, 12-04-2000) No. CA2000-02-011, 2000 WL 1782324, Unreported.

Modification of a shared parenting plan and change of custody to the child's father is warranted where (1) the mother leaves her three-year-old child in the care of her present husband who falls asleep while taking care of the child, (2) dog feces are found in the child's bedroom and on her sheets and toys at the mother's home, (3) police become involved in the mother's fighting with her present husband, and (4) the mother changes her residence at least six times over a period of two years. Dedic v. Dedic (Ohio App. 9 Dist., Wayne, 01-27-1999) No. 98CA0008, 1999 WL 33445, Unreported.

Change of custody is awarded to the father based upon testimony concerning (1) the child not being fed or cared for by the mother, (2) the presence of cockroaches in the home and dirty dishes stacked high in the kitchen, and (3) bruises on the child's body. Rhoads v. Rhoads (Ohio App. 4 Dist., Highland, 08-24-1998) No. 97 CA 944, 1998 WL 548759, Unreported.

In a motion to modify custody, the trial court does not err in concluding that the teenaged child's best interest is served by continuing to have the child remain in the father's custody, and apparently disbelieved testimony by the teenager that the father used drugs, made threats about using plastic explosives to blow up people, and that the child slept on a mattress on the floor in a house with no heat, when the court also considered the father's contrary testimony and evidence that since the child had voluntarily moved in with his mother, his grades and school attendance were very poor. Clutter v. Reidy (Ohio App. 7 Dist., Jefferson, 06-20-1996) No. 95-JE-20, 1996 WL 342194, Unreported.

Danger posed to children by secondhand smoke is both a relevant factor and a physical health factor that a family court is mandated to consider under statutory "best interests of the child" analysis for visitation and custody matters. In re Julie Anne (Ohio Com.Pl., 08-27-2002) 121 Ohio Misc.2d 20, 780 N.E.2d 635, 2002-Ohio-4489. Child Custody ☞ 81

When determining best interests of the child in visitation and custody matters, family court has a statutory duty to consider on its own initiative the serious risk of harm of secondhand smoke to children. In re Julie Anne (Ohio Com.Pl., 08-27-2002) 121 Ohio Misc.2d 20, 780 N.E.2d 635, 2002-Ohio-4489. Child Custody ☞ 81

When conducting "best interests of the child" analysis for visitation and custody matters, family courts have an unqualified duty to consider the dangers of secondhand smoke to all children, regardless of the condition of their health. In re Julie Anne (Ohio Com.Pl., 08-27-2002) 121 Ohio Misc.2d 20, 780 N.E.2d 635, 2002-Ohio-4489. Child Custody ☞ 81

In light of its duties under parens patriae doctrine and "best interests of the child" statute, family court would, on its own initiative in child custody and visitation proceeding, restrain mother and father under the penalty of contempt from allowing any person, including themselves, to smoke tobacco anywhere in the presence of minor child, given the scientific evidence demonstrating that secondhand smoke constituted a real and substantial danger to health of children. In re Julie Anne (Ohio Com. Pl., 08-27-2002) 121 Ohio Misc.2d 20, 780 N.E.2d

635, 2002-Ohio-4489. Child Custody ☞ 81; Child Custody ☞ 103; Child Custody ☞ 223

Physical altercation between custodial parent's spouse and spouse's child was not a change of circumstance necessary for a reallocation of parental rights and responsibilities; the spouse was not the residential parent, and the record did not indicate whether the children witnessed the altercation or were at home during it. Saal v. Saal (Ohio App. 9 Dist., 10-17-2001) 146 Ohio App.3d 579, 767 N.E.2d 750, 2001-Ohio-1518. Child Custody ☞ 567

Evidence supported determination that modification of custody from father to mother was in the children's best interest and that advantages of such a change in custody outweighed any harm likely to result from change of custody; father admitted to several drinking incidents at hearing before the magistrate even though father claimed he had stopped drinking at original custody hearing, father was cited for pedestrian intoxication on a highway despite previously completing a alcohol rehabilitation program, father was angrily confronted by a friend's wife after she found her husband and father drunk in father's bedroom with father undressed to his underwear, father had not seen his alcohol counselor in six months, and children had been tardy and absent many times while they were in father's custody. Sallee v. Sallee (Ohio App. 12 Dist., 04-23-2001) 142 Ohio App.3d 366, 755 N.E.2d 941. Child Custody ☞ 637

Unsubstantiated allegation that former wife's current husband committed sexual abuse against former wife's children did not alone warrant change of custody to former husband; rather, unsubstantiated allegations of sexual abuse by their stepfather was only one factor that court could consider when determining whether change in circumstances had occurred. Stover v. Plumley (Ohio App. 4 Dist., 08-23-1996) 113 Ohio App.3d 839, 682 N.E.2d 683. Child Custody ☞ 558; Child Custody ☞ 637

Trial court did not abuse its discretion in modifying custody order so as to designate father residential parent to child; evidence showed that child was underdeveloped in several respects for her age, that mother's temperament was volatile and had caused her to be involved in two physical altercations, and that father would provide stable environment for child, and trial court specifically stated that it considered statutory factors in reaching its determination that it was in child's best interest to designate father as residential parent. Butler v. Butler (Ohio App. 3 Dist., 12-05-1995) 107 Ohio App.3d 633, 669 N.E.2d 291. Child Custody ☞ 554

Child's best interests would be served by natural father retaining custody, where child was found wandering in street while in custody of mother, mother had been convicted of theft, and mother had been convicted of child endangering with respect to one of her other children. Pegan v. Crawmer (Ohio, 07-24-1996) 76 Ohio St.3d 97, 666 N.E.2d 1091, 1996-Ohio-419. Children Out-of-wedlock ☞ 20.3

Trial court which modified child custody decree by designating father as the residential parent and legal custodian of children complied with statute governing modification of custody by concluding that harm to the children, if they stayed with mother, was outweighed by the advantages of giving custody to father. Sayre v. Hoelzle-Sayre (Ohio App. 3 Dist., 04-06-1994) 100 Ohio App.3d 203, 653 N.E.2d 712, appeal allowed 70 Ohio St.3d 1426, 638 N.E.2d 88, appeal dismissed as improvidently allowed 72 Ohio St.3d 1218, 651 N.E.2d 430, 1995-Ohio-274. Child Custody ☜ 554

When modifying child custody decree, trial court must make some finding that the harm is outweighed by the advantages of changing the environment. Sayre v. Hoelzle-Sayre (Ohio App. 3 Dist., 04-06-1994) 100 Ohio App.3d 203, 653 N.E.2d 712, appeal allowed 70 Ohio St.3d 1426, 638 N.E.2d 88, appeal dismissed as improvidently allowed 72 Ohio St.3d 1218, 651 N.E.2d 430, 1995-Ohio-274. Child Custody ☜ 552

Deficient proficiency results on exams taken by children who were home-schooled by parent, alone, may constitute grounds for change of custody as custody may be modified in situations where child's development will be affected by condition in his present environment. Sayre v. Hoelzle-Sayre (Ohio App. 3 Dist., 04-06-1994) 100 Ohio App.3d 203, 653 N.E.2d 712, appeal allowed 70 Ohio St.3d 1426, 638 N.E.2d 88, appeal dismissed as improvidently allowed 72 Ohio St.3d 1218, 651 N.E.2d 430, 1995-Ohio-274. Child Custody ☜ 552

Improvement in mother's emotional state since she was allegedly "coerced" to relinquish custody of her children to father did not warrant modification in custody; change in circumstances of the child or residential parent was required. Clyborn v. Clyborn (Ohio App. 3 Dist., 02-16-1994) 93 Ohio App.3d 192, 638 N.E.2d 112. Child Custody ☜ 555

Evidence supports awarding custody of minor children of a marriage to the former husband despite the former wife's assertion that she was the primary caretaker where the trial court finds that she had not fulfilled her duties as caretaker because (1) the home was filthy and unsanitary based on results of investigations of a state agency finding (a) a dead mouse and dog feces on the floor where the youngest child, who was handicapped, played; (b) dirty bedroom and linens of the former wife; and (c) children's clothing scattered around the house; (2) the general impression that the children were left unattended, even the youngest child, and their conduct was unrestrained; (3) the former wife's failure to obtain CPR certification to properly care for the youngest child; and (4) the former wife's failure to participate in family outings and activities; the trial court further found that the former wife failed to recognize that there were problems and was thus unmotivated to remedy them. Thornton v. Thornton (Wyandot 1990) 70 Ohio App.3d 317, 590 N.E.2d 1375.

Competent and credible evidence supported trial court finding that change in circumstances had occurred due to former wife changing her name and religion and taking up residence with a convicted sex offender, as would support former husband's motion for permanent change of custody, although court-appointed psychologist recommended that change of circumstances did not occur; psychologist was not aware that former wife's new roommate was convicted sex offender who had served time in jail. In re Marriage of Faulhaber (Ohio App. 11 Dist., Portage, 06-28-2002) No. 2001-P-0110, 2002-Ohio-3380, 2002 WL 1401066, Unreported. Child Custody ☜ 637

Where a child frequently exhibits inappropriate behavior and such behavior is attributable to the environment provided by the custodial parent, a court is justified in granting a motion for change of custody. Circelli v Petrunak, No. 47847 (8th Dist Ct App, Cuyahoga, 6–7–84).

A change of custody is awarded to the father even though he had little contact with the child for seven years after the divorce, where it is shown that during the time the mother had custody, she tried to commit suicide, and she had failed to work with the son concerning problems in school; here, the advantage of a change outweighs the harm caused by a change. Krueck v Walters, No. L–81–064 (6th Dist Ct App, Lucas, 10–2–81).

A court may change custody from the mother to the father when the mother shows an inability to provide a stable environment for the child; this outweighs the benefits the child could receive by remaining with her mother and continuing in a fluctuating lifestyle. Cholewa v Cholewa, No. 42942 (8th Dist Ct App, Cuyahoga, 3–19–81).

In a custody action, evidence showing that a mother was living with men to whom she was not married, drank excessively and used marijuana, is only relevant if it can be demonstrated that such conduct has an adverse impact on the best interests of the child. Horsley v Horsley, No. 803 (4th Dist Ct App, Ross, 7–14–81).

39. —— Dangerous environment claim and false allegations of abuse, modification of rights and responsibilities and "change in circumstances"

Trial court did not abuse its discretion in determining that mother failed to show a substantive change in circumstances warranting modification of prior allocation of parental rights and responsibilities; fact that father sometimes requested his daughter to shorten her phone call with mother so that she could do her homework did not entirely support mother's claim that father had interfered with her visitation and communication with the children, there was no evidence to substantiate mother's claim that father lived in deplorable conditions, there was no evidence that any disciplinary measures father used adversely and materially affected children, although father was evicted from his residence, eviction followed and may have been a result of mother's failure to pay accumulated child support, father found a new residence, and mother failed to show that father's lack of job stability materially and adversely affected the children. Sites v. Sites (Ohio App. 4 Dist., Lawrence, 06-03-2010) No. 09CA19, 2010-Ohio-2748, 2010 WL 2391647, Unreported, appeal not allowed 126 Ohio St.3d 1600, 935 N.E.2d 46, 2010-Ohio-4928. Child Custody ☞ 637

Former husband's unsupported allegation that former wife had physically abused parties' child was insufficient to demonstrate change of circumstances warranting modification of allocation of parental rights and responsibilities, absent any evidence of pattern of physical abuse, and in light of former wife's testimony that she was concerned that parties' teen-aged daughter was involved with controlling boyfriend three years her senior, where question of relative credibility of parties was for resolution by trier of fact. Adams v. Adams (Ohio App. 4 Dist., Washington, 08-23-2005) No. 05CA2, 2005-Ohio-4588, 2005 WL 2100539, Unreported. Child Custody ☞ 637

Evidence established the existence of a change in circumstances supporting grant of motion filed by mother, the non-residential parent, for modification of child custody order that had placed children with father; children had been in physical custody of mother for two years upon suggestion of municipal court and children's services that children not reside with father who was accused of committing sexual abuse, and mother had physical custody of children with the full knowledge and consent of father. Johnson v. Johnson (Ohio App. 3 Dist., Union, 12-15-2003) No. 14-03-32, 2003-Ohio-6710, 2003 WL 22939480, Unreported. Child Custody ☞ 558; Child Custody ☞ 560

Evidence was sufficient to support finding that change in residential parent was in best interests of daughter; evidence included mother's driving under the influence conviction, boyfriend's mental health problems, mother's bad financial decisions, and father's ability to provide stable residence. Rosebrugh v. Rosebrugh (Ohio App. 11 Dist., Ashtabula, 08-22-2003) No. 2002-A-0002, 2003-Ohio-4595, 2003 WL 22038538, Unreported. Child Custody ☞ 637

Trial court could consider effect of mother's boyfriend on daughter when considering whether to change residential parent of daughter; daughter stated that she did not like him, there was testimony he had mental health problems, and mother testified that he had been arrested several times for assault and menacing but that she still allowed him in house. Rosebrugh v. Rosebrugh (Ohio App. 11 Dist., Ashtabula, 08-22-2003) No. 2002-A-0002, 2003-Ohio-4595, 2003 WL 22038538, Unreported. Child Custody ☞ 567

Ex-wife's unsubstantiated allegations that ex-husband abused children was a change of circumstances warranting change of custody from ex-wife to ex-husband. Beekman v. Beekman (Ohio App. 4 Dist., 10-25-1994) 96 Ohio App.3d 783, 645 N.E.2d 1332. Child Custody ☞ 555

Unsubstantiated allegations of sexual abuse by noncustodial parent are a change of circumstances that may be grounds on which to modify a prior custody award. Beekman v. Beekman (Ohio App. 4 Dist., 10-25-1994) 96 Ohio App.3d 783, 645 N.E.2d 1332. Child Custody ☞ 555

A trial court errs in granting an ex-husband's motion to modify custody by awarding him custody of the minor children of the marriage where (1) there is conflicting evidence concerning the amount of time and care that the mother gave to the children; (2) after the divorce the mother and children lived first with her parents, while she worked in Chillicothe, and later with her sister and brother-in-law in Bainbridge, while she worked in Columbus; and (3) because her job required her to work later hours, she often stayed overnight in Columbus; the ex-husband's showing that the children would be "better off" with him is insufficient to support modification of a prior custody decree absent a showing that the children's present environment endangers significantly their physical health or mental, moral, or emotional development and that the harm likely to result from the change in environment is outweighed by the advantages of the proposed change. Well v. Well (Ross 1990) 70 Ohio App.3d 606, 591 N.E.2d 843, motion overruled 59 Ohio St.3d 720, 572 N.E.2d 696.

Pursuant to former RC 3109.04(B)(1)(c), a party seeking a modification of custody must show that some action by the custodial parent presently endangers the child or, with a reasonable degree of certainty, will manifest itself and endanger the child in the future if the child is not removed from his or her present environment immediately. Gardini v. Moyer (Ohio 1991) 61 Ohio St.3d 479, 575 N.E.2d 423, rehearing denied 62 Ohio St.3d 1419, 577 N.E.2d 663. Child Custody ☞ 552

40. —— Disabled adult child, modification of rights and responsibilities and "change in circumstances"

Trial court that awarded custody of parties' fully disabled adult child pursuant to divorce retained jurisdiction to modify its custody order and child support awarded therein, where award of custody amounted to recognition by court of fact that child was under permanent legal disability due to extent of his physical and mental disabilities. Abbas v. Abbas (Ohio App. 7 Dist., 06-23-1998) 128 Ohio App.3d 513, 715 N.E.2d 613. Child Custody ☞ 550; Child Custody ☞ 601; Child Support ☞ 232

41. —— Education and school performance, modification of rights and responsibilities and "change in circumstances"

Even if parties' agreement with respect to the custody of the children had not eliminated the need for trial court to make change of circumstances finding necessary for modification of child custody, children's purported behavioral problems did not constitute a change of circumstances necessary to support father's motion seeking primary physical custody of children, where son's behavioral problems were not new since parties' divorce, and trial court was presented with evidence from school officials and others that mother had been very proactive in dealing with these problems. Klein v. Botelho (Ohio App. 2 Dist., Montgomery, 08-19-2011) No. 24393, 2011-Ohio-4165, 2011 WL 3655169, Unreported. Child Custody ☞ 564; Child Custody ☞ 571

Evidence supported finding that a change in circumstances sufficient to warrant modification of child custody had occurred since the entry of the last custody order; since mother had been designated the residential parent and legal custodian of the children, the children had experienced educational difficulties and suffered from neglect of their health and dental care needs. Scarberry v. Scarberry (Ohio App. 2 Dist., Clark, 06-10-2011) No. 10-CA-0091, 2011-Ohio-2829, 2011 WL 2410234, Unreported. Child Custody ☞ 556

Trial court did not abuse its discretion in reallocating the designation of residential parent and legal custodian from ex-wife to ex-husband; ex-wife first obtained custody of child when he was only three years old, and upon child's entering kindergarten, he began to suffer academically and socially, to the concern of both the school and ex-husband, psychologist opined that there was sufficient cause to be concerned that, under ex-wife's care, child had not been getting the attention he needed in terms of his academic and social development, change in custody was in child's best interest, and the harm likely to be caused by a change of environment was outweighed by the advantages of the change of environment. Kurfess v. Gibbs (Ohio App. 6 Dist., Lucas, 06-03-2011) No. L-09-1295, 2011-Ohio-2698, 2011 WL 2175039, Unreported. Child Custody ☞ 555

Evidence supported conclusion that no change in circumstances had occurred with respect to parties' oldest child, for whom father had been designated residential parent, as necessary to warrant a reallocation of parental rights and responsibilities sought by mother under shared parenting plan; child's "D" grade-point average and fact that father had permitted child to drink beer, when weighed against the estranged relationship between mother and child, did not constitute a change in circumstances sufficient to warrant a reallocation of parental rights. Vella v. Vella (Ohio App. 7 Dist., Jefferson, 03-09-2011) No. 10 JE 7, 2011-Ohio-1182, 2011 WL 862037, Unreported. Child Custody ☞ 576

Denial of mother's request to change to her custody of child, whose legal custody after dependency determination had previously been transferred from paternal grandparents to father, was not an abuse of discretion, although child had expressed a desire to live with mother, where father had been custodial parent for five years, mother failed to disclose to father that a relative had attempted to sexually abuse child at home of paternal grandparents, child was well adjusted to her home, school, and community with father, father had allowed visitation for mother in excess of court order many times, mother would not allow extra time to him if granted custody, and mother owed

$3442.15 in child support. In re Taylor G. (Ohio App. 6 Dist., Lucas, 04-21-2006) No. L-05-1197, 2006-Ohio-1992, 2006 WL 1047474, Unreported. Infants ☞ 231

Decision to modify shared parenting plan in best interest of minor children, to designate former husband as the residential parent for school purposes, was not arbitrary, unreasonable, or unconscionable; court found that former husband's living arrangements were stable, while former wife's residence and living arrangements "fluctuate wildly," former wife had uncertain relationship with her current husband, including his attempted suicide and his arrests for domestic violence, and uncertain future plans with respect to relocating out of state, former wife acknowledged former husband was a good father, and her decisions reduced amount and quality of time children spent with former husband. Tener v. Tener-Tucker (Ohio App. 12 Dist., Warren, 07-25-2005) No. CA2004-05-061, 2005-Ohio-3892, 2005 WL 1798273, Unreported. Child Custody ☞ 576

Trial court's decision to modify shared parenting arrangement to designate ex-husband as residential parent for school purposes was supported by evidence; trial court discussed child's interrelationship and interaction with his parents and others, child's adjustment to home, school, and community, as well as recommendation of guardian ad litem, child's wishes, parents' wishes concerning child's care, and mother's move out of state. Ebinger v. Ebinger (Ohio App. 12 Dist., Warren, 09-07-2004) No. CA2003-10-100, No. CA2003-10-103, 2004-Ohio-4784, 2004 WL 2003948, Unreported. Child Custody ☞ 576

Modification of 50/50 parenting schedule to designate mother as child's residential parent was in best interests of child, insofar as 50/50 parenting schedule was not conducive to child's school schedule. Wholf v. Wholf (Ohio App. 11 Dist., Geauga, 07-23-2004) No. 2003-G-2501, 2004-Ohio-3931, 2004 WL 1663508, Unreported. Child Custody ☞ 576

Ex-wife was provided with notice that ex-husband sought to terminate shared parenting plan based on more than child's school attendance, where, in motion for change of custody, ex-husband indicated that child's school attendance was only one reason why he filed motion and that there were other facts that would establish change in circumstances. Basford v. Basford (Ohio App. 7 Dist., Noble, 03-26-2004) No. 03-NO-310, 2004-Ohio-1539, 2004 WL 610773, Unreported. Child Custody ☞ 610

On ex-husband's motion to terminate shared parenting plan, trial court did not abuse its discretion by denying ex-wife's request to supplement record with child's hospital records, where, in motion, ex-husband stated that one reason he sought change in custody was child's school attendance problems and ex-wife had over one month to assemble medical records she wished to submit to explain why child missed school. Basford v. Basford (Ohio App. 7 Dist., Noble, 03-26-2004) No. 03-NO-310,

2004-Ohio-1539, 2004 WL 610773, Unreported. Child Custody ☞ 650

Guardian ad litem's request to trial court for forensic evaluation regarding custody and visitation was proper and based on showing of good cause in former husband's action to modify custody, since neither former husband nor former wife responded to requests for scholastic achievement and adjustment records, custodial parent failed to respond to numerous requests for explanation regarding child's large number of absences from school, and there was allegation that former husband had struck one of the children. Citta-Pietrolungo v. Pietrolungo (Ohio App. 8 Dist., Cuyahoga, 06-26-2003) No. 81943, No. 82069, 2003-Ohio-3357, 2003 WL 21469770, Unreported. Child Custody ☞ 613

Fact that trial court did not consider the impact of a change of schools upon child when making its determination to change residential custody was not error, where no evidence was offered to show that a change of schools would have had any impact on the best interest of the child. Lynch v. Lynch (Ohio App. 6 Dist., Huron, 03-07-2003) No. H-02-022, 2003-Ohio-1039, 2003 WL 876566, Unreported. Child Custody ☞ 637

Trial court did not err by failing to include in its judgment in divorce proceedings an order that child attend a particular private school, even though parents verbally stipulated that such school would be appropriate; nothing indicated that parents agreed that such school was the only school that child could attend, and record revealed that mother wanted the option of a public school alternative. Dannaher v. Newbold (Ohio App. 10 Dist., 03-04-2004) 2004-Ohio-1003, 2004 WL 396993. Child Custody ☞ 105

Trial court's determination that a reallocation of shared parental rights making father the residential parent was not in child's best interests was supported by some credible evidence and therefore did not constitute an abuse of discretion, where trial court noted testimony of child's current teachers that she was making progress, as well as testimony that child showed no signs of an adverse effect from the numerous changes in her life. LaBute v. La-Bute (Ohio App. 3 Dist., 12-01-2008) 179 Ohio App.3d 696, 903 N.E.2d 652, 2008-Ohio-6190. Child Custody ☞ 637

Modification of shared parenting plan to permit former wife to select religious school for child which was outside former husband's religious tradition was not against child's best interests and was not abuse of discretion; there was no evidence that child experienced conflict as result of former wife's choice of schools, that differences between religious traditions of former wife and former husband would harm child, or that former husband's life with child or his own individual religious freedoms were impacted by former wife's choice of schools, and court adequately took into account statutory factors relevant to child's best interests. In re Marriage of Shore (Ohio App. 8 Dist., 08-18-1999) 135 Ohio App.3d 374, 734 N.E.2d 395, dismissed,

appeal not allowed 87 Ohio St.3d 1459, 720 N.E.2d 541. Child Custody ☞ 637

Expert testimony, in proceedings on former wife's application for modification of shared parenting plan, concerning whether child's primary residence should be with former husband in state or former wife out of state was not relevant to, or determinative of, issue of whether attending religious school preferred by former wife was in child's best interests. In re Marriage of Shore (Ohio App. 8 Dist., 08-18-1999) 135 Ohio App.3d 374, 734 N.E.2d 395, dismissed, appeal not allowed 87 Ohio St.3d 1459, 720 N.E.2d 541. Evidence ☞ 508

Trial court's decision to grant father's motion for modification of custody by designating father as the residential parent and legal custodian of children was clearly substantiated based on school psychologist's evaluation of children who were home-schooled by mother and who had deficient proficiency results on exams, and testimony by father. Sayre v. Hoelzle-Sayre (Ohio App. 3 Dist., 04-06-1994) 100 Ohio App.3d 203, 653 N.E.2d 712, appeal allowed 70 Ohio St.3d 1426, 638 N.E.2d 88, appeal dismissed as improvidently allowed 72 Ohio St.3d 1218, 651 N.E.2d 430, 1995-Ohio-274. Child Custody ☞ 637

A trial court does not abuse its discretion in modifying a prior custody order when there is some evidence to support the trial court's finding of a change in circumstances in that the children's schooling is very poor while in the mother's custody and the father can offer a better educational environment, which is in the children's best interests. Paparodis v Paparodis, No. 88-CA-119 (7th Dist Ct App, Mahoning, 3-23-89)

42. —— **Expert testimony, modification of rights and responsibilities and "change in circumstances"**

Trial court's determination that termination of shared parenting plan and designation of husband as child's residential parent was in child's best interest was not based upon unsubstantiated claims with respect to wife's mental health and was not abuse of discretion, despite court's failure to hear testimony of wife's treating psychologist, where wife testified as to her own mental health history, indicating that she had twice attempted suicide, expert evaluation stated that wife had history of depression, suicidal ideation and attempt, and mental health treatment, and wife's treating psychologist did not disclose wife's medical records at husband's request. Wiesman v. Wiesman (Ohio App. 12 Dist., Butler, 12-08-2003) No. CA2002-08-193, No. CA2003-01-002, 2003-Ohio-6544, 2003 WL 22887918, Unreported, appeal not allowed 102 Ohio St.3d 1423, 807 N.E.2d 367, 2004-Ohio-2003. Child Custody ☞ 637

Professional testimony need not be presented on the issue of the probable relative harm and advantages to be caused by a change in custody. Stone v. Stone (Warren 1983) 9 Ohio App.3d 6, 457 N.E.2d 919, 9 O.B.R. 6. Child Custody ☞ 637

43. —— **Consideration of facts that arose before prior decree, modification of rights and responsibilities and "change in circumstances"**

Statutory provision that precluded a trial court from modifying a prior divorce decree allocating parental rights unless it found a change in circumstance based on facts that arose since the prior decree or that were unknown to the court at time of prior decree did not prevent court from considering facts that had arisen before prior decrees in making its change-in-circumstances determination on maternal grandmother's third-party motion to modify custody of grandchildren respectively determined in mother's two prior divorce actions, where custody was uncontested in both prior divorce cases, and the challenged facts were not known to the court at the time of the prior decrees. Williams v. Gonzalez (Ohio App. 1 Dist., Hamilton, 08-27-2010) No. C-090483, No. C-090484, 2010-Ohio-3993, 2010 WL 3365741, Unreported. Child Custody ☞ 557(3)

44. —— **Findings of fact and conclusions of law, modification of rights and responsibilities and "change in circumstances"**

Father was not entitled to reversal of trial court grant of modification order awarding mother shared parental rights on the basis of his contention that trial court committed legal error when it failed to make express findings concerning its determination that the advantages of altering the original allocation of parental rights outweighed the likely harm, where father did not cite any authority supporting this claim, and there was no authority for this proposition in the statute. Cameron v. Cameron (Ohio App. 9 Dist., Medina, 08-08-2011) No. 10CA0064-M, 2011-Ohio-3884, 2011 WL 3427216, Unreported. Child Custody ☞ 922(5)

Trial court's decision to reallocate parental rights and designate father as the residential parent of the parties' two minor sons was not an abuse of discretion or against the manifest weight of the evidence, even though father worked full time, where trial court applied the evidence adduced at trial to each and every factor in the statutory list of relevant factors, and the majority of the factors were either neutral in respect to both parties, or weighed against mother and in favor of father, particularly mother's pattern of denying father parenting time. Malone v. Malone (Ohio App. 3 Dist., Seneca, 05-02-2011) No. 13-10-39, 2011-Ohio-2096, 2011 WL 1642915, Unreported. Child Custody ☞ 569

Sufficient evidence supported trial court's finding that father was more likely than mother to honor and facilitate court-approved parenting time rights, for purposes of determining whether modification of residential custody from mother to father was in child's best interests; mother did not notify court of her intent to relocate with child to another state prior to doing so, and mother had failed to comply with parenting time schedule on several occasions. Brammer v. Meachem (Ohio App. 3 Dist., Marion,

02-07-2011) No. 9-10-43, 2011-Ohio-519, 2011 WL 378809, Unreported. Child Custody ☞ 638

Trial court's use and citation to custody investigator's report in support of its decision that modification of residential custody of child from father to mother was in child's best interests was proper, as investigator's report contained numerous facts, all of which were supported by the record, and it was clear from trial court's judgment entry that it did not rely solely on the investigator's report in making its best interest determination. Brammer v. Meachem (Ohio App. 3 Dist., Marion, 02-07-2011) No. 9-10-43, 2011-Ohio-519, 2011 WL 378809, Unreported. Child Custody ☞ 616

Finding that change in circumstances did not exist, as required for reallocation of parental rights and responsibilities, was not against manifest weight of evidence, in post-divorce proceeding concerning competing motions of mother and father for such modification, notwithstanding allegations of alleged deterioration in communication between parties, as well as poor sleeping arrangements for children and child abuse at mother's house, or that father moved further away from mother; father's move did not change amount of time that children spent with him, allegations of abuse were unsubstantiated, issue of sleeping arrangements related more to shared parenting plan than to custody, and terrible relationship between parties did not further deteriorate since implementation of shared parenting plan. Depascale v. Finocchi (Ohio App. 7 Dist., Mahoning, 09-30-2010) No. 08 MA 216, 2010-Ohio-4869, 2010 WL 3904163, Unreported. Child Custody ☞ 576

Magistrate in a divorce proceeding made appropriate findings of fact and conclusions of law in recommending that trial court adopt husband's shared parenting plan, where the magistrate found that shared parenting would ensure that both parents would have frequent and continuing contact with the children, that exchanging the children would not be a problem, that neither parent had continuously or willfully denied the other parent parenting time, and, inter alia, that the magistrate had considered all of the parties' evidence, that she had set forth the relevant factors in making findings of fact, and that the husband's shared parenting plan should be adopted because it was in the children's best interests. Clouse v. Clouse (Ohio App. 3 Dist., Seneca, 03-23-2009) No. 13-08-40, 2009-Ohio-1301, 2009 WL 737778, Unreported, appeal not allowed 122 Ohio St.3d 1521, 913 N.E.2d 457, 2009-Ohio-4776. Child Custody ☞ 504

The trial court made sufficient findings of fact, during child custody modification proceeding in which maternal and paternal grandparents sought custody of out-of-wedlock child, even though many of the findings of fact were mere recitations of evidence; the court made extensive conclusions of law regarding the standard for awarding legal custody to a non-parent and also enumerated the factors to be considered in determining the best interest of the child, and the court set out each factor and then itemized the pertinent facts of the case which bore on each factor. Smith v. Quigg (Ohio App. 5 Dist., Fairfield, 03-22-2006) No. 2005-CA-001, 2006-Ohio-1494, 2006 WL 786855, Unreported. Children Out–of–wedlock ⬥ 20.10

Wife waived appellate review of her claim that husband's proposed shared parenting plan was untimely filed, in action for divorce, by failing to object to allegedly untimely filing. Swain v. Swain (Ohio App. 4 Dist., Pike, 01-06-2005) No. 04CA726, 2005-Ohio-65, 2005 WL 43948, Unreported. Child Custody ⬥ 904

Trial court's factual findings and legal conclusions were inadequate to support its adoption of husband's proposed shared parenting plan, in action for divorce, where court offered no factual findings or legal conclusions other than conclusory statement that it found husband's shared parenting plan to be in children's best interest. Swain v. Swain (Ohio App. 4 Dist., Pike, 01-06-2005) No. 04CA726, 2005-Ohio-65, 2005 WL 43948, Unreported. Child Custody ⬥ 511

Trial court abused its discretion by failing to determine that shared parenting plan proffered by husband was in the best interest of children and failing to make findings of fact and conclusions of law, where wife, prior to final hearing, withdrew her agreement to participate in the shared parenting plan originally submitted, and asked to be appointed as the sole residential parent. Feltz v. Feltz (Ohio App. 3 Dist., Mercer, 08-09-2004) No. 10-04-04, 2004-Ohio-4160, 2004 WL 1771072, Unreported. Child Custody ⬥ 35; Child Custody ⬥ 511

Finding that there was not change in circumstances sufficient to warrant modification of prior custody decree naming mother of out-of-wedlock child as residential parent, or approval of shared parenting plan, was not abuse of discretion; although mother had been in jail for 30 days for violation of terms of probation stemming from conviction for underage consumption of alcohol, mother completed jail sentence approximately five months prior to hearing on motion to change residential parent status, since time of release mother returned to status quo and found employment and underwent drug and alcohol counseling, and mother was seeking proper medical attention for child. Duer v. Moonshower (Ohio App. 3 Dist., Van, 08-02-2004) No. 15-03-15, 2004-Ohio-4025, 2004 WL 1718234, Unreported. Children Out–of–wedlock ⬥ 20.10

Trial court's single use of term "substantial," in concluding that father had failed to show "substantial change of circumstances," did not indicate that it applied heightened burden of proof on father to show change of circumstances warranting reallocation of parental rights and responsibilities, in child custody proceeding. Venuto v. Pochiro (Ohio App. 7 Dist., Mahoning, 05-21-2004) No. 02 CA 225, 2004-Ohio-2631, 2004 WL 1152055, Unreported. Child Custody ⬥ 659

Trial court could not reallocate residential and legal custody of child, upon father's motion for a change of custody, without making express findings relevant to a change in circumstances or the best interests of child. Schaeffer v. Schaeffer (Ohio App. 1 Dist., Hamilton, 04-23-2004) No. C-020721, No. C-030255, No. C-020722, No. C-030385, No. C-020723, 2004-Ohio-2032, 2004 WL 869359, Unreported. Child Custody ⬥ 659

Modifying parental rights and responsibilities was abuse of discretion in child custody proceeding, where trial court failed to make findings related to change in circumstances or best interests of children. Engelmann v. Engelmann (Ohio App. 11 Dist., Ashtabula, 03-29-2004) No. 2003-A-0020, 2004-Ohio-1530, 2004 WL 609901, Unreported. Child Custody ⬥ 659

On motion to modify child's residential placement, trial court erred by failing to enter in record findings of fact and conclusions of law as to reasons mother's proposed shared parenting plan was approved; court merely stated that it adopted mother's plan. Stroud v. Lyons (Ohio App. 11 Dist., Ashtabula, 12-12-2003) No. 2002-A-0050, 2003-Ohio-6773, 2003 WL 22952597, Unreported. Child Custody ⬥ 659

Wife was not entitled to findings of fact and conclusions of law on trial court's ruling on her objections to magistrate's decision in child custody proceeding, where wife did not file a request for findings of fact and conclusions of law until after she filed her objections to the magistrate's decision. Ream v. Ream (Ohio App. 5 Dist., Licking, 04-14-2003) No. 02-CA-000071, 2003-Ohio-2144, 2003 WL 1962332, Unreported. Child Custody ⬥ 511

Pursuant to the terms of a joint custody agreement between the parties, husband is obligated to pay not only the costs of the children's private school education but also, in years where there is a tuition waiver due to husband's position at work, he must pay child support in the agreed upon amount of $350 per month, per child, despite additional financial obligations husband incurs. Neiheiser v. Neiheiser (Ohio App. 8 Dist., Cuyahoga, 01-13-2000) No. 75184, 2000 WL 23116, Unreported, appeal not allowed 88 Ohio St.3d 1516, 728 N.E.2d 403.

In case in which father petitioned to modify parenting time, domestic relations court could not certify the case to the juvenile court based on a finding it made, on evidence presented in proceedings on the petition, that one of the children may have been sexually abused by an unknown perpetrator, and, therefore, jurisdiction never vested in juvenile court, where there was no complaint, indictment, or information that contained allegations of abuse, neglect, or dependency, and the domestic relations court did not obtain the juvenile court's consent prior to transfer and did not make a finding that the parents were unsuitable. Thompson v. Valentine (Ohio App. 12 Dist., 08-30-2010) 189 Ohio App.3d 661, 939 N.E.2d 1289, 2010-Ohio-4075. Courts ⬥ 488(1)

Custodial parent's failure to immunize her children was not a change of circumstance necessary for a reallocation of parental rights and responsibilities; her decision not to immunize arose prior to the relevant court order regarding custody, even though the children contracted the mumps following the order. Saal v. Saal (Ohio App. 9 Dist., 10-17-2001) 146 Ohio App.3d 579, 767 N.E.2d 750, 2001-Ohio-1518. Child Custody ⟶ 558

Custodial parent's failure to alert medical staff that her child was not immunized for tetanus or to administer a homeopathic remedy to prevent tetanus was not a change of circumstance necessary for a reallocation of parental rights and responsibilities; since nothing indicated that the child suffered a tetanus infection, the parent's conduct did not materially affect the child. Saal v. Saal (Ohio App. 9 Dist., 10-17-2001) 146 Ohio App.3d 579, 767 N.E.2d 750, 2001-Ohio-1518. Child Custody ⟶ 558

Mother who has been awarded custody of her children in previous court proceeding is entitled to be informed of reasons behind an order divesting her of such custody rendered by court or its appointed referee. Currens v. Currens (Hamilton 1970) 26 Ohio App.2d 215, 270 N.E.2d 362, 55 O.O.2d 360.

Failure of trial court, in its modification of a child custody order, to make a specific finding that harm caused by the change of environment outweighs the advantages of the change does not constitute reversible error, where the record indicates that the trial court properly applied the statutory criteria. Douglass Makni v. Makni (Ohio App. 4 Dist., Pike, 09-24-2002) No. 01CA680, 2002-Ohio-5098, 2002 WL 31131877, Unreported. Child Custody ⟶ 923(4)

45. —— Guardian ad litem, modification of rights and responsibilities and "change in circumstances"

In proceeding to modify shared parenting agreement, trial court could order ex-wife to pay half of the guardian ad litem's fees, even without any evidence of her ability to pay being introduced; ex-wife did not cite to any authority to establish that the trial court was required to find that she was able to pay the guardian ad litem's fees, and she never raised the issue of her ability, or lack thereof, to pay in her brief. Swanson v. Schoonover (Ohio App. 8 Dist., Cuyahoga, 05-12-2011) No. 95213, No. 95517, No. 95570, 2011-Ohio-2264, 2011 WL 1797231, Unreported. Child Custody ⟶ 945

The trial court's failure to adopt the guardian ad litem's (GAL) recommendations for a smoke-free environment at father's home and the parents' attendance of parenting classes was not an abuse of discretion, in proceeding to modify the allocation of parental rights concerning out-of-wedlock child; the trial court was not obligated to follow the GAL's recommendations. Ankney v. Bonos (Ohio App. 9 Dist., Summit, 11-15-2006) No. 23178, 2006-Ohio-6009, 2006 WL 3304343, Unreported. Children Out–of–wedlock ⟶ 20.4

Trial court order that failed to grant father independent parenting time with his out-of-wedlock child, but granted paternal grandparents regularly scheduled visitation, was not an abuse of discretion, in child custody modification proceeding that granted maternal grandparents legal custody of child; the trial court found that father had abandoned child, that he had shared parenting duties with paternal grandparents, and that father could visit child when he was at paternal grandparents' house. Smith v. Quigg (Ohio App. 5 Dist., Fairfield, 03-22-2006) No. 2005-CA-002, 2006-Ohio-1495, 2006 WL 786856, Unreported. Children Out–of–wedlock ⟶ 20.10

The trial court's failure to remove the guardian ad litem was not an abuse of discretion, during child custody modification proceeding in which maternal and paternal grandparents sought custody of out-of-wedlock child, even though paternal grandparents argued that he did not appropriately discharge his duties and did not act fairly; the guardian ad litem's report discussed religion, child's interactions with maternal and paternal grandparents, the corporal punishment administered by paternal grandmother, child's report of sexual abuse by paternal grandmother, and father's lack of commitment for being child's caregiver. Smith v. Quigg (Ohio App. 5 Dist., Fairfield, 03-22-2006) No. 2005-CA-001, 2006-Ohio-1494, 2006 WL 786855, Unreported. Infants ⟶ 82

Trial court was not required to interview children and appoint guardian ad litem (GAL), in proceeding in which mother sought to modify child custody; statute required court to interview children and appoint GAL only when it considered best interest of children in making its custody determination, and since mother failed to show change in circumstances, which was first prong of test to determine whether court should grant motion to modify custody, court did not reach best interest determination, as second prong of test. Walsh v. Walsh (Ohio App. 11 Dist., Geauga, 06-24-2005) No. 2004-G-2587, 2005-Ohio-3264, 2005 WL 1503707, Unreported. Child Custody ⟶ 654; Infants ⟶ 78(7)

Fact that the "tender years" doctrine is no longer law in Ohio does not mean a guardian ad litem cannot consider the tender years of a child in evaluating child custody situation. Stark v. Haser (Ohio App. 5 Dist., Delaware, 09-02-2004) No. 03CAF11057, 2004-Ohio-4641, 2004 WL 1945581, Unreported. Child Custody ⟶ 421

Guardian ad litem's use of the term "tender years" did not establish that he used the tender years doctrine, which was no longer the law, as the basis of his recommendation in child custody action; instead, guardian's use of the term "tender years" was an adjective to describe the child, as opposed to a doctrine of law. Stark v. Haser (Ohio App. 5 Dist., Delaware, 09-02-2004) No. 03CAF11057, 2004-Ohio-4641, 2004 WL 1945581, Unreported. Child Custody ⟶ 421

Record did not support mother's claim that trial court did not consider deficiencies of guardian ad litem's report, in ruling on mother's motion for reallocation of parental rights and responsibilities; nothing in record indicated that trial court was unaware of scope of report. Kenney v. Kenney (Ohio App. 12 Dist., Warren, 07-26-2004) No. CA2003-07-078, 2004-Ohio-3912, 2004 WL 1662280, Unreported. Child Custody ☞ 616

Trial court order, which equitably divided the guardian ad litem fees in divorce case between husband and wife, was proper; court found that husband was voluntarily underemployed and had previously earned income of approximately $80,000.00 per year, and there was a large disparity in the incomes of the parties. Brewer v. Brewer (Ohio App. 5 Dist., Licking, 07-01-2004) No. 2003CA00087, 2004-Ohio-3531, 2004 WL 1486781, Unreported. Infants ☞ 83

Statements and actions of father's counsel at trial abrogated and waived father's previous pro se request for appointment of guardian ad litem for child, to be present at in camera interview with child, in child custody proceeding; father failed to file brief or identify guardian ad litem issue in any other fashion prior to trial, when given another opportunity to raise issue father's counsel stated only that father was seeking reallocation of parental rights and responsibilities, and, when asked about in camera interview with child, father's counsel stated that father encouraged such interview, without raising guardian ad litem issue. Venuto v. Pochiro (Ohio App. 7 Dist., Mahoning, 05-21-2004) No. 02 CA 225, 2004-Ohio-2631, 2004 WL 1152055, Unreported. Infants ☞ 80(2)

Order in child custody proceeding directing child's guardian ad litem to deliver certain passports to counsel for former wife was supported by legitimate concern that former husband could abscond with minor child, as parties had been married in New Zealand and husband had previously absconded with child, traveling throughout the United States for an eight-month period. Jancuk v. Jancuk (Ohio App. 7 Dist., Mahoning, 03-15-2004) No. 95-CA-246, No. 99-CA-91, No. 96-CA-206, No. 96-CA-258, 2004-Ohio-1374, 2004 WL 550785, Unreported. Child Custody ☞ 530

Trial court did not abuse its discretion, on parents' request for return of custody of child who had been adjudicated abused and dependent and whose legal custody had been granted maternal grandparents, in denying grandparents' motion for appointment of guardian ad litem for child; grandparents brought motion at later stage of proceedings, and only after independent, court-appointed custody investigator had submitted report to trial court recommending that parents be given custody of child, trial court's decision was supported by existence of many evaluations and investigations that had already been conducted in case, and custody investigator "operated almost as a guardian ad litem would operate." In re James (Ohio App. 1 Dist., 09-16-2005) 163 Ohio App.3d 442, 839 N.E.2d 39, 2005-Ohio-4847, appeal allowed 108 Ohio St.3d 1413, 841 N.E.2d 318, 2006-Ohio-179, reversed 113 Ohio St.3d 420, 866 N.E.2d 467, 2007-Ohio-2335, reconsideration denied 114 Ohio St.3d 1484, 870 N.E.2d 734, 2007-Ohio-3699. Infants ☞ 205

Civ R 75(B)(2) leaves the appointment of a guardian ad litem for the child in a change of custody proceeding to the sound discretion of the trial court. Stone v. Stone (Warren 1983) 9 Ohio App.3d 6, 457 N.E.2d 919, 9 O.B.R. 6. Infants ☞ 78(1)

46. —— Immorality of parent, modification of rights and responsibilities and "change in circumstances"

Evidence supported finding that a substantial change in circumstances had occurred, warranting modification of child custody; mother had multiple sexual partners in child's presence, she did not maintain a clean home, mother's boyfriend injured child, child feared mother's boyfriend, and mother repeatedly chose her relationship with boyfriend over her relationship with child. Thomas v. Thomas (Ohio App. 2 Dist., Clark, 06-17-2011) No. 2009 CA 88, 2011-Ohio-2977, 2011 WL 2436912, Unreported. Child Custody ☞ 562; Child Custody ☞ 567

Testimony related to ex-wife's childhood abuse was not admissible in child custody modification case; sexual abuse that occurred during ex-wife's childhood would have been previously addressed in the initial determination of custody, and any sexual abuse that occurred during ex-wife's childhood was known prior to the judgment entry of divorce, and information related to sexual abuse in ex-wife's past had not arisen since the prior decree and, therefore, was not relevant to the current proceedings. Eitutis v. Eitutis (Ohio App. 11 Dist., Lake, 06-10-2011) No. 2009-L-121, 2011-Ohio-2838, 2011 WL 2415369, Unreported. Child Custody ☞ 632

Evidence supported reallocation of parental rights and responsibilities by changing residential parent designation for parties' two younger children from mother to father under shared parenting plan; change of circumstances had occurred, in that mother began cohabiting with her boyfriend at some point after parties entered into shared parenting agreement, mother's cohabitation with her boyfriend proved to be a polarizing force in the family dynamic, which mother conceded when she testified that boyfriend offered to leave their home when parties' older child was scheduled to stay with her, and children's best interest would be served by reallocation of parental rights, in that boyfriend's presence interfered with children's relationship with both parents and their older brother. Vella v. Vella (Ohio App. 7 Dist., Jefferson, 03-09-2011) No. 10 JE 7, 2011-Ohio-1182, 2011 WL 862037, Unreported. Child Custody ☞ 576

Reallocation of parental rights and responsibilities under order designating mother as the sole residential parent and legal custodian to make father the residential parent was not in out-of-wedlock child's best interests, despite mother's conviction for unlawful sexual conduct with a minor other than child; neither mother's probation officer nor the guardian ad litem expressed concerns with mother caring for child, mother's actions after her conviction, including seeking mental health counseling, taking medication for her bipolar condition, abstaining from alcohol, and attending Alcoholics Anonymous, all indicated that mother appreciated the gravity of her behavior and intended to do whatever was necessary to be a healthy, balanced individual capable of adequately caring for her child, child was thriving with mother as the residential parent, father had an overt and aggressively negative attitude about mother, and father's disregard of both companionship and child support orders suggested that father lacked insight concerning child's best interests. Neighbor v. Jones (Ohio App. 9 Dist., Summit, 06-30-2010) No. 25050, 2010-Ohio-3003, 2010 WL 2622940, Unreported. Children Out–of–wedlock ☞ 20.10

Trial court in proceeding on unmarried father's motion to modify the allocation of parental rights and responsibilities was required to consider whether mother's conviction of unlawful sexual conduct with a minor constituted a change in circumstances, and whether, in light of the nature of the offense, it was in child's best interest to remain in mother's custody; mother's criminal conviction was not a mere lifestyle choice that could be deemed irrelevant except insofar as it had a direct or probable effect on the child. Neighbor v. Jones (Ohio App. 9 Dist., Summit, 07-23-2008) No. 24032, 2008-Ohio-3637, 2008 WL 2814311, Unreported. Children Out–of–wedlock ☞ 20.10

A former wife's new baby and intimate relationship with the opposite sex do not amount to a change of substance and do not constitute a sufficient change of circumstance in the former wife's life to warrant reexamination of the custody issue or award of custody to the former husband. Marshall v. Marshall (Ohio App. 3 Dist., Allen, 09-08-1998) No. 97 10 0067, 1998 WL 725941, Unreported.

A court need not classify certain conduct as a "wicked sin" or "mere indiscretion;" the best test to determine a change of custody for reasons of morality is whether the residential parent's conduct has had a direct or probable adverse impact on the welfare of the child. Jasper v. Jasper (Ohio App. 1 Dist., Hamilton, 09-13-1995) No. C-940481, 1995 WL 540110, Unreported, dismissed, appeal not allowed 75 Ohio St.3d 1404, 661 N.E.2d 753.

A mother's lesbian relationship bears upon her fitness and ability to provide proper parenting where she allows her children to be exposed to her sexual orientation and activities and the relationship alienates the children and unnecessarily competes with the children's time with their mother so that custody is awarded to the father. Phillips v. Phillips (Ohio App. 12 Dist., Preble, 03-20-1995) No. CA94-03-005, 1995 WL 115426, Unreported.

Evidence in child custody modification proceeding supported finding that, since the parties' divorce, circumstances in the living arrangements and familial relationship of the children had gone through "substantial changes"; since the divorce, mother had started cohabitating with a man she subsequently married, and father was cohabitating with a woman in Connecticut, and had changed residences. Clark v. Smith (Ohio App. 3 Dist., 12-08-1998) 130 Ohio App.3d 648, 720 N.E.2d 973. Child Custody ☞ 637

Trial court could order former spouses not to have overnight romantic guests when children were present, despite former wife's contention that the order was impermissibly based on notions of morality, where overnight visits had adverse impact on the children. Dilworth v. Dilworth (Ohio App. 2 Dist., 11-08-1996) 115 Ohio App.3d 537, 685 N.E.2d 847. Child Custody ☞ 562

Where an action seeking a change of custody is filed, based on the fact that the custodial parent (the mother) has allowed her boyfriend to live in the marital home, an order of change of custody is erroneous where the evidence does not clearly show that the boyfriend's presence has an adverse impact on the children's physical, mental, emotional, or moral development. Kraus v. Kraus (Cuyahoga 1983) 10 Ohio App.3d 63, 460 N.E.2d 680, 10 O.B.R. 73.

Where a custodial parent is married to the person with whom she previously lived and there is no evidence that the child was materially adversely affected by the paramour relationship, change of custody may not be properly ordered as a penalty for the past misconduct of the custodial parent. Wyss v. Wyss (Franklin 1982) 3 Ohio App.3d 412, 445 N.E.2d 1153, 3 O.B.R. 479.

In light of the needs of a child for a stable environment, the modification of a prior custody order under RC 3109.04(B) can only be made where the harm caused by the change is outweighed by the advantage of such change. In re Rex (Seneca 1981) 3 Ohio App.3d 198, 444 N.E.2d 482, 3 O.B.R. 226.

A court's inquiry into the moral conduct or standards of a custodial parent is limited to a determination of the effect of such conduct on the child. Whaley v. Whaley (Lawrence 1978) 61 Ohio App.2d 111, 399 N.E.2d 1270, 15 O.O.3d 136.

In light of the needs of a child for a stable environment, the modification of a prior custody order under RC 3109.04(B) can only be made where the harm caused by the change is outweighed by the advantages of such change. Whaley v. Whaley (Lawrence 1978) 61 Ohio App.2d 111, 399 N.E.2d 1270, 15 O.O.3d 136.

The custody of an illegitimate child will not be taken from the mother and awarded to the father merely upon the basis that the wife has contracted an interracial marriage. In re H. (Ohio Com.Pl. 1973) 37 Ohio Misc. 123, 305 N.E.2d 815, 66 O.O.2d 178, 66 O.O.2d 368.

Court did not err in refusing to change custody of fourteen-year-old daughter from father to mother, even though daughter requested such change, where mother had carried on adulterous relationship with individual whom she subsequently married. Watson v. Watson (Columbiana 1956) 146 N.E.2d 443, 76 Ohio Law Abs. 348.

Where there is reliable, probative, and credible evidence that the parties' minor child's emotional problems were the result of the parties' rancorous marriage relationship, and was not the result of the wife's living with a male companion, a new trial court hearing to change custody will not be granted. Mann v Mann, No. 45157 (8th Dist Ct App, Cuyahoga, 7–21–83).

The trial court did not err in granting custody to the mother, even though there was evidence that she was cohabitating with a man subsequent to her divorce; alleged immoral conduct must be shown to have a direct or probable adverse impact on the welfare of the child in order to justify a change of custody. Mann v Mann, No. 45157 (8th Dist Ct App, Cuyahoga, 7–21–83).

Where the custodial parent engaged in nonmarital sexual conduct, the trial court erred in ordering a change of custody absent any evidence that such conduct had a direct adverse impact on the child, especially where there is no indication that the child lacked proper care. In re Demangone, No. 81–CA–38 (2d Dist Ct App, Greene, 7–30–82).

A court cannot change the custody of a child to punish a parent whom the court believes has behaved immorally. DeMangone v DeMangone, No. 81–CA–38 (2d Dist Ct App, Greene, 2–22–82).

In a custody action, evidence showing that a mother was living with men to whom she was not married, drank excessively and used marijuana, is only relevant if it can be demonstrated that such conduct has an adverse impact on the best interests of the child. Horsley v Horsley, No. 803 (4th Dist Ct App, Ross, 7–14–81).

The trial court did not err in granting a change of custody from the custodial parent who had two sequential common law marriages, to the non-custodial parent who was established in a sound second marriage; a court's inquiry into the moral conduct of the custodial parent is limited to the determination of the affect of such conduct on the child. Zubay v Zubay, No. 79–C–48 (7th Dist Ct App, Columbiana, 11–26–80).

Where a custodial mother openly engages in homosexual activities in the presence of her minor daughter, a change of custody is in order because such activities endanger the child's physical health and mental, moral, and emotional development. Haton v Haton, No. WD–80–30 (6th Dist Ct App, Wood, 11–21–80).

Where a mother neglects to give her child corrective shoes for the prevention of scolosis, and where the child is afraid of the mother's new live-in boyfriend, a change of custody is in the best interest of the child. In re Lambeth, No. 78CA168 (7th Dist Ct App, Mahoning, 8–27–79).

Where the custodial mother establishes a lesbian household, there has been a substantial change in the circumstances of the children warranting a

modification of a prior custody decree. Starnes v Starnes, No. 5029 (5th Dist Ct App, Stark, 6–19–79).

Where a custodial mother violates a court order granting custody so long as no male person shall be in the mother's house between midnight and 7:00 a.m., and in fact she admits sleeping in bed with four different men during the time, the court will award a change of custody due to the effect on the child. Wallace v Wallace, No. 81–C–32 (7th Dist Ct App, Columbiana, 2–26–82).

47. —— "Integration" into one parent's family, modification of rights and responsibilities and "change in circumstances"

There was credible, competent evidence upon which the magistrate could find lack of interaction and interrelationship between child and unwed mother's family in Arizona; at most, the record contained mother's affirmative statements that child had relationships with these individuals, but there was no evidence as to the extent of the relationships, and none of mother's Arizona family members testified at the hearing nor did mother present, for example, any pictures showing child and these individuals spending time together. Cotterill v. Turner (Ohio App. 3 Dist., Hancock, 10-26-2009) No. 5-09-22, 2009-Ohio-5657, 2009 WL 3416001, Unreported. Children Out–of–wedlock ☞ 20.8

Trial court acted within its discretion in refusing to modify child custody, under which father originally was designated the children's residential parent and legal custodian, by adopting mother's shared parenting plan; children were doing well in current living arrangement with father, guardian ad litem testified that parents were unable to communicate and that proposed shared parenting plan would be disruptive, and mother was able to be with the children a substantial amount of time due to her work at children's school. Lough v. Lough (Ohio App. 5 Dist., Licking, 01-06-2005) No. 03CA93, No. 03CA104, 2005-Ohio-79, 2005 WL 66576, Unreported. Child Custody ☞ 576

A motion for change of custody from a father is granted the mother where the court analyzes evidence including testimony from both parents and a teacher sufficient to find that the circumstances of the children had changed in the four-month long time period that the father leaves the children with their mother to go on a camping trip and to find a new babysitter, and that the children had become integrated into their mother's homelife and family. Wirt v. Wirt (Ohio App. 9 Dist., Wayne, 04-10-1996) No. 95CA0041, 1996 WL 170362, Unreported.

It is not in the best interest of a child to change her residential parent when the evidence presented at trial indicates that the child is living a happy, well-adjusted life with her father, step -brother and -sister, that the child is bonded closely with her step-brother, that the step-sister's alcohol abuse has not affected the child's mental state and that the father, rather than the mother, would be the most likely to facilitate visitation with the child. Kreimes

v. Schmidt (Ohio App. 6 Dist., Erie, 09-23-1994) No. E-93-80, 1994 WL 518133, Unreported, dismissed, appeal not allowed 71 Ohio St.3d 1464, 644 N.E.2d 1387.

Trial court, in overruling paternal grandmother's objections to court order that vacated prior order giving grandmother temporary custody of child, did not abuse its discretion in not awarding custody to paternal grandmother, even though grandmother alleged she was child's primary caretaker and primary attachment figure; physician testified that even if grandmother were the primary attachment figure for child, child would have been able to establish another primary attachment figure without significant trauma. Vance v. Vance (Ohio App. 2 Dist., 01-24-2003) 151 Ohio App.3d 391, 784 N.E.2d 172, 2003-Ohio-310. Child Custody ⟋ 473

While mother of illegitimate child had sole physical custody of child for a year and a half following child's birth, albeit with at least one interruption, mother did not have de facto residential custody of child for purposes of custody determination. In re Wells (Ohio App. 12 Dist., 12-26-1995) 108 Ohio App.3d 41, 669 N.E.2d 887. Children Out–of–wedlock ⟋ 20.3

In a child custody action between a mother and stepmother, custody may not be awarded to the nonparent without a showing of parental unsuitability by a preponderance of the evidence, not merely determining if the best interests of the children would be served; therefore, an award of custody to the stepmother instead of the mother, who remarried after leaving her husband and their two children, is based upon the detrimental effect living with the mother would have on the children, not on society's judgment of her, since the children do not view their natural mother as a parental figure and are integrated into the stepmother's community. In re Dunn (Auglaize 1992) 79 Ohio App.3d 268, 607 N.E.2d 81, dismissed, jurisdictional motion overruled 65 Ohio St.3d 1416, 598 N.E.2d 1168.

Evidence that five-year-old child interacted well with former wife's fiancé, and guardian ad litem's concern that former husband would be less likely to honor and facilitate companionship with former wife or to encourage former wife to be involved in child's school work and activities, supported designation of former wife as residential parent, upon termination of shared parenting plan. Ferrell v. Ferrell (Ohio App. 7 Dist., Carroll, 06-11-2002) No. 01 AP 0763, 2002-Ohio-3019, 2002 WL 1376039, Unreported. Child Custody ⟋ 637

Evidence supported finding that five-year-old child had adjusted equally well to both of his homes and respective communities, as element for designating residential parent upon termination of shared parenting plan; child enjoyed good relationship with former wife's fiancé, looked up to him, and enjoyed golfing with him, guardian ad litem found that the child was happy and well-adjusted child and that both parties deserved credit, and former wife had purchased a home where she intended to continue to live, after moving with child

four times since the divorce. Ferrell v. Ferrell (Ohio App. 7 Dist., Carroll, 06-11-2002) No. 01 AP 0763, 2002-Ohio-3019, 2002 WL 1376039, Unreported. Child Custody ⟋ 637

Evidence supported finding that both parties appeared to recognize the importance of maintaining close ties for five-year-old child with members of his extended maternal and paternal families, as element for designating residential parent upon termination of shared parenting plan; child's aunt and paternal grandmother lived in same city a s former wife, former wife testified that she had no problem with maintaining relationships for child with his paternal relatives, she testified that after she picked up child from former husband's home, she and child would stop and visit with her mother and sometimes her sisters, and she testified that she invites family to visit at her home. Ferrell v. Ferrell (Ohio App. 7 Dist., Carroll, 06-11-2002) No. 01 AP 0763, 2002-Ohio-3019, 2002 WL 1376039, Unreported. Child Custody ⟋ 637

Where a custodial parent deliberately delays psychological testing ordered by the court pursuant to a motion for change of custody, it is not error for the referee to consider the integration of the child into the custodial parent's family during this period and a denial of change of custody based on a referee's recommendation citing this integration as a favorable factor is proper. Bartholomew v Bartholomew, No. CA–7133 (5th Dist Ct App, Stark, 8–24–87).

Where a custodial parent moves out of state upon remarriage and integration into the noncustodial parent's family takes place as a result of the children residing with the noncustodial parent until the custodial parent obtains mandatory court approval to move the children out of state, the children's integration into the noncustodial parent's family is voluntary and with the consent of the custodial parent. Brown v Schrull, No. 4139 (9th Dist Ct App, Lorain, 4–22–87).

Integration with consent does not require consent to change custody, only consent to the placement and retention that constitutes integration. Tighe v Tighe, No. 11844 (9th Dist Ct App, Summit, 3–27–85).

Where custodial parent permits the child to visit with non-custodial parent in excess of court ordered visitation rights to such an extent that the child becomes integrated with the family of the non-custodial parent, trial court does not abuse its discretion in changing custody pursuant to RC 3109.04. Morris v Morris, No. 970 (11th Dist Ct App, Geauga, 3–31–82).

48. —— Moving or relocation, modification of rights and responsibilities and "change in circumstances"

Impending relocation of mother to different state due elimination of her job at current location and a job promotion opportunity in the other state was a substantial change having a material effect on children and constituted a change in circumstances supporting the need to modify a prior decree allocating parental rights and responsibilities for the care of the children equally between her and children's father. Brammer v. Brammer (Ohio App. 3 Dist., 05-31-2011) 194 Ohio App.3d 240, 955 N.E.2d 453, 2011-Ohio-2610, stay denied 129 Ohio St.3d 1442, 951 N.E.2d 1041, 2011-Ohio-4221. Child Custody ⟐ 576

Mother's mere intention or desire to relocate did not constitute the requisite change in circumstances for a change in custody, and thus trial court abused its discretion in granting father's motion to modify parental rights; no actual relocation had taken place and mother testified she would not move without child. In re Dissolution of Marriage of Kelly (Ohio App. 7 Dist., Carroll, 05-27-2011) No. 09 CA 863, 2011-Ohio-2642, 2011 WL 2175221, Unreported. Child Custody ⟐ 568

Change in mother's work schedule that caused her to be unavailable to care for child much of time, together with mother's move, which resulted in change of school districts, did not amount to change in circumstances in the time since prior agreed order that warranted modification of custody to father; mother still cared for child most of time, mother worked overnight, and therefore worked mostly while child slept, and mother slept while child was at school, mother got child ready for school and took her to bus stop each morning, and relocation alone did not qualify as change in circumstances. In re A.N. (Ohio App. 2 Dist., Greene, 05-20-2011) No. 2010 CA 83, No. 2011 CA 7, 2011-Ohio-2422, 2011 WL 1936030, Unreported. Children Out-of-wedlock ⟐ 20.10

Substantial evidence supported conclusion that a change in circumstances had occurred since entry of initial custody decree naming mother as child's residential parent and legal guardian, as required to justify a modification of the custody decree sought by father; mother, who had relocated to another state with child and her new husband, admitted that she had denied father access to child for a two-month period, which clearly interfered with father's visitation with child, and mother's relocation with child disrupted the familial relationships that child had cultivated since his birth. Long v. Long (Ohio App. 3 Dist., Union, 10-04-2010) No. 14-10-01, 2010-Ohio-4817, 2010 WL 3836168, Unreported. Child Custody ⟐ 568; Child Custody ⟐ 569

Trial court did not abuse its discretion by finding that record did not contain any change in circumstances warranting modification or reallocation of parental rights and responsibilities for care of child; divorced father's claim that child would be better off with him was not sufficient to support a change of custody, there was nothing in the record to indicate that mother's move had a materially adverse effect upon child, and, according to father's own testimony, child was excelling academically and considered gifted. Welch v. Schudel (Ohio App. 3 Dist., Van, 03-01-2010) No. 15-09-13, 2010-Ohio-715, 2010 WL 702294, Unreported. Child Custody ⟐ 552; Child Custody ⟐ 568

Increase in time that former husband, who was non-residential parent, spent with children after former husband moved closer to children's residence did not constitute a "change in circumstances" of the children, for purposes of statute governing modification of parental rights and responsibilities, and thus former husband was not entitled to modification of residential parent status or adoption of shared parenting plan. Barto v. Barto (Ohio App. 3 Dist., Hancock, 10-27-2008) No. 5-08-14, 2008-Ohio-5538, 2008 WL 4694520, Unreported. Child Custody ⟐ 568

Former husband's motion to transfer residential parent status, or, in the alternative, for adoption of shared parenting plan was not frivolous, and thus award of attorney fees to former wife as sanction was unwarranted; although former husband was unable to prove that requisite change in circumstances had occurred, he was able to prove that some changes in circumstances of children had occurred, as he moved and was able to spend significantly more time with children. Barto v. Barto (Ohio App. 3 Dist., Hancock, 10-27-2008) No. 5-08-14, 2008-Ohio-5538, 2008 WL 4694520, Unreported. Costs ⟐ 2

Prior judgment entry journalizing settlement agreement between former husband and wife, in which husband, a resident of Alabama, was designated primary residential parent, did not require Ohio to exercise continuing jurisdiction for purposes of wife's motion to modify custody, where judgment entry did not address issue of jurisdiction and was merely ancillary to original agreed order regarding custody in order to remedy inadequate visitation provisions in original order. Harris v. Harris (Ohio App. 11 Dist., Trumbull, 11-15-2005) No. 2004-T-0057, No. 2004-T-0107, 2005-Ohio-6077, 2005 WL 3047500, Unreported. Child Custody ⟐ 739; Child Custody ⟐ 745

Former wife was not entitled to evidentiary hearing on whether Ohio had jurisdiction to adjudicate change of custody motion with respect to child living with husband in Alabama; record before magistrate contained sufficient facts to determine question of jurisdiction, evidence was not disputed, and wife was allowed 30 days to respond to husband's motion to dismiss and to introduce testimonial evidence but chose not to do so, and there was no evidence indicating that wife requested hearing. Harris v. Harris (Ohio App. 11 Dist., Trumbull, 11-15-2005) No. 2004-T-0057, No. 2004-T-0107, 2005-Ohio-6077, 2005 WL 3047500, Unreported. Child Custody ⟐ 779

Evidence in proceedings on wife's motion to modify shared parenting plan to accommodate her relocation out of state with parties' minor child was sufficient to demonstrate change in circumstances; evidence established that wife's job was being relocated out of state, that her salary and benefits would greatly increase were she to relocate, that she would lose her job if she did not relocate, that her job was "niche" position which only existed in one other company in the country and said company was not located in Ohio, and that wife had attempted and failed to secure new employment in Ohio affording income comparable to that she would earn by following her job out of state. Lempner v. Lempner (Ohio App. 9 Dist., Lorain, 08-31-2005) No. 04CA008580, 2005-Ohio-4543, 2005 WL 2087834, Unreported. Child Custody ⚯ 576

Finding former wife in contempt for moving from county in contravention of shared parenting plan and awarding former husband attorney fees as part of costs taxable to wife was not an abuse of discretion; former wife admitted she knew she violated court agreement. Tener v. Tener-Tucker (Ohio App. 12 Dist., Warren, 07-25-2005) No. CA2004-05-061, 2005-Ohio-3892, 2005 WL 1798273, Unreported. Child Custody ⚯ 852; Child Custody ⚯ 943

Father's claim that reallocation of parental rights was warranted because mother had moved their out-of-wedlock child out of school district and that he could accommodate child's after-school activities was rendered moot when school district allowed child to continue attending same school. McCage v. Dingess (Ohio App. 5 Dist., Licking, 10-13-2004) No. 03CA111, 2004-Ohio-5692, 2004 WL 2391678, Unreported. Children Out–of–wedlock ⚯ 20.11

Restricting mother's parenting time with non-marital child to county in which father's motion for reallocation of parental rights and responsibilities had been filed and to contiguous counties was warranted; evidence indicated that mother did not return child to father when ordered to do so, mother did not take child to school when ordered to do so, and mother did not take child to therapy during time period she previously had child with her. Haney v. Corbett (Ohio App. 5 Dist., Delaware, 09-02-2004) No. 04CAF01005, 2004-Ohio-4642, 2004 WL 1945642, Unreported. Children Out–of–wedlock ⚯ 20.10

Even if trial court abused its discretion when it issued ex parte order requiring mother of non-marital child to relocate to Ohio to maintain custody, any issue concerning that error became moot once mother moved back to Ohio, obtained custody, and matter of father's request for reallocation of parental rights and responsibilities was scheduled for hearing. Haney v. Corbett (Ohio App. 5 Dist., Delaware, 09-02-2004) No. 04CAF01005, 2004-Ohio-4642, 2004 WL 1945642, Unreported. Children Out–of–wedlock ⚯ 20.11

Child's time with mother in New York prior to overturning on appeal of order granting mother's initial motion for reallocation of parental rights did not constitute substantial change in circumstances necessary to warrant modification. Kenney v. Kenney (Ohio App. 12 Dist., Warren, 07-26-2004) No. CA2003-07-078, 2004-Ohio-3912, 2004 WL 1662280, Unreported. Child Custody ⚯ 552

Mother violated terms of divorce decree when she first took child with her to California to establish residency and to enroll child in school there and also violated decree when she took child with her to New York, and thus mother was subject to contempt, even though mother intended to return child from California if her relocation motion was denied, and legitimately believed that relevant parenting order would be stayed, where divorce decree forbade mother from removing child from court's jurisdiction for purposes of establishing residency before securing permission. Schaeffer v. Schaeffer (Ohio App. 1 Dist., Hamilton, 04-23-2004) No. C-020721, No. C-030255, No. C-020722, No. C-030385, No. C-020723, 2004-Ohio-2032, 2004 WL 869359, Unreported. Child Custody ⚯ 853

Mother's motion to relocate with child to California was rendered moot in light of mother's acknowledgement that she no longer had employment in California and now resided in New York, which was where she now wanted to move child; economic advantages that arguably justified move to California no longer existed, and court would not issue an advisory opinion on some potential future move. Schaeffer v. Schaeffer (Ohio App. 1 Dist., Hamilton, 04-23-2004) No. C-020721, No. C-030255, No. C-020722, No. C-030385, No. C-020723, 2004-Ohio-2032, 2004 WL 869359, Unreported. Child Custody ⚯ 917

Trial court finding that a change in circumstances had occurred due to mother's relocation out of state with child, which entitled the court to modify the parties' allocation of parental rights and responsibilities in their divorce decree, was not an abuse of discretion; evidence established that mother relocated out of state prior to the court hearing and only moved back to state to comply with the court's temporary order. Lyall v. Lyall (Ohio App. 5 Dist., Muskingum, 03-25-2004) No. CT2003-0044, 2004-Ohio-1565, 2004 WL 614990, Unreported. Child Custody ⚯ 568

Some competent, credible evidence supported trial court's decision to grant ex-husband's motion to adopt mediation memorandum related to shared parenting plan, in which parties agreed that children would begin residing in specified county by specified date; parties agreed to binding resolution of issue by mediation, ex-wife admitted at hearing that she signed agreement providing that she would relocate with children to specified county by specified date and that she failed to do so, and there was no evidence ex-wife was coerced into making agreement with ex-husband. Engelmann v. Engelmann (Ohio App. 11 Dist., Ashtabula, 03-29-2004) No. 2003-A-0020, 2004-Ohio-1530, 2004 WL 609901, Unreported. Child Custody ⚯ 419

Mother's intended move to Washington did not constitute a change in circumstance requiring trial court to terminate shared parenting plan; interstate moves did not require termination of such plans necessarily. Murphy v. Murphy (Ohio App. 5 Dist., Knox, 06-27-2003) No. 02CA000040, 2003-Ohio-3860, 2003 WL 21674965, Unreported. Child Custody ⚯ 576

Former husband, who filed motion to modify shared parenting decree following former wife changing residence of child to another state, had burden of establishing statutory elements for modification of original shared parenting plan, although parenting plan restricted parties' ability to relocate with child, since former husband was party that was seeking modification. Willoughby v. Masseria (Ohio App. 11 Dist., Geauga, 05-12-2003) No. 2002-G-2437, 2003-Ohio-2368, 2003 WL 21054787, Unreported. Child Custody ⟨⟩ 633

Issue of whether custody of parties' children would change if wife moved from children's present school district was not ripe for judicial review on wife's appeal from divorce judgment that granted custody of children to her with condition that husband would become residential parent if she moved from current school district. Ferris v. Ferris (Ohio App. 4 Dist., Meigs, 03-11-2003) No. 02CA4, 2003-Ohio-1284, 2003 WL 1227326, Unreported. Child Custody ⟨⟩ 916

Provision of divorce judgment that husband would become residential parent if wife moved from children's current school district exceeded trial court's jurisdictional powers by ruling on future events that might or might not occur. Ferris v. Ferris (Ohio App. 4 Dist., Meigs, 03-11-2003) No. 02CA4, 2003 Ohio 1284, 2003 WL 1227326, Unreported. Child Custody ⟨⟩ 528

Wife waived argument, asserted on appeal from divorce judgment that awarded her custody of parties' children, that trial court violated her rights as custodial parent by ordering that children continue to attend school in current school district, where wife failed to object to trial court's announcement of that order and failed to make her argument to trial court. Ferris v. Ferris (Ohio App. 4 Dist., Meigs, 03 11 2003) No. 02CA4, 2003 Ohio 1284, 2003 WL 1227326, Unreported. Child Custody ⟨⟩ 904

Denial of mother's motion to relocate to different county did not constitute constructive modification of shared parenting plan; order had no effect on mother's custody of children. Kolb v. Kolb (Ohio App. 9 Dist., Lorain, 01-29-2003) No. 02CA008045, 2003-Ohio-359, 2003 WL 187577, Unreported. Child Custody ⟨⟩ 568

Fact that child had reached school age, and that former wife had moved to another county, established changed circumstances warranting modification of child custody, so that former wife would have custody only during summer, but if she relocated to Stark County, the two-week alternating shared parenting arrangement would resume; child was well-adjusted to elementary school in Stark County, and it did not appear there was any adverse impact on child from having to wake up at 5:00 a.m. on school days to accommodate former husband's work schedule. Butcher v. Butcher (Ohio App. 5 Dist., Stark, 12-16-2002) No. 2002CA00214, 2002-Ohio-7011, 2002 WL 31831417, Unreported. Child Custody ⟨⟩ 552; Child Custody ⟨⟩ 568; Child Custody ⟨⟩ 576

Evidence was sufficient to support trial court's finding that, although mother had moved children six times, the number was not excessive and did not constitute a change in circumstance that would support change in custody; two of the moves were necessary to extract mother and children from an abusive relationship, children were happy and well-adjusted despite the moves, and children had been attending same school for two years and would have continued at same school even after moving into new housing secured by mother. Dunlop v. Dunlop (Ohio App. 2 Dist., Montgomery, 10-25-2002) No. 19313, 2002-Ohio-5828, 2002 WL 31398674, Unreported. Child Custody ⟨⟩ 568

A trial court order restricting any move of the minor children to within 50 miles from the parties current home infringes upon the custodial parent's constitutionally protected freedom to live where she chooses. Smeltzer v Smeltzer, No. 92-C-50, 1993 WL 488235 (7th Dist Ct App, Columbiana, 11-24-93).

In determining whether to modify custody in case in which custodial parent expresses a desire to move to another state, a court may consider the fact that a relocation of the child would remove him or her from a supportive network of family and friends as a factor in finding that a change of circumstances has occurred. Brammer v. Brammer (Ohio App. 3 Dist., 05-31-2011) 194 Ohio App.3d 240, 955 N.E.2d 453, 2011-Ohio-2610, stay denied 129 Ohio St.3d 1442, 951 N.E.2d 1041, 2011-Ohio-4221. Child Custody ⟨⟩ 568

A court may consider any attendant circumstances surrounding a residential parent's relocation that affect the child's welfare in determining whether a change in circumstances has occurred as to support a motion for a change of custody. Brammer v. Brammer (Ohio App. 3 Dist., 05-31-2011) 194 Ohio App.3d 240, 955 N.E.2d 453, 2011-Ohio-2610, stay denied 129 Ohio St.3d 1442, 951 N.E.2d 1041, 2011-Ohio-4221. Child Custody ⟨⟩ 568

The relocation of the residential parent, in and of itself, does not constitute a change in circumstances as to support a motion for change of custody. Brammer v. Brammer (Ohio App. 3 Dist., 05-31-2011) 194 Ohio App.3d 240, 955 N.E.2d 453, 2011-Ohio-2610, stay denied 129 Ohio St.3d 1442, 951 N.E.2d 1041, 2011-Ohio-4221. Child Custody ⟨⟩ 568

Impending relocation of mother to different state due to elimination of her job at current location and a job promotion opportunity in the other state was a substantial change having a material effect on children and constituted a change in circumstances supporting the need to modify a prior decree allocating parental rights and responsibilities for the care of the children equally between her and children's father. Brammer v. Brammer (Ohio App. 3 Dist., 05-31-2011) 194 Ohio App.3d 240, 955 N.E.2d 453, 2011-Ohio-2610, stay denied 129 Ohio St.3d 1442, 951 N.E.2d 1041, 2011-Ohio-4221. Child Custody ⟨⟩ 576

Ex-wife's relocation with children, over whom she had primary custody under shared parenting plan, 172 miles away from ex-husband was "change in circumstances" for purposes of ex-husband's motion to modify plan so as to award him sole parental rights and responsibilities. Rohrbaugh v. Rohrbaugh (Ohio App. 7 Dist., 02-11-2000) 136 Ohio App.3d 599, 737 N.E.2d 551. Child Custody ☞ 568

Evidence supported trial court's finding, in denying ex-husband's motion to modify shared parenting plan to award him sole custody, that ex-wife's relocation with children 172 miles away from ex-husband was to gain job security; ex–wife presented evidence that previous employer was undergoing major reorganization that resulted in loss of jobs by employees of greater seniority, that she was sole earner and that her job provided her and her children with health insurance coverage, and that she did not think it wise to wait until her position was terminated. Rohrbaugh v. Rohrbaugh (Ohio App. 7 Dist., 02-11-2000) 136 Ohio App.3d 599, 737 N.E.2d 551. Child Custody ☞ 642

Divorce court's custody order, which focused on wife's failure to return with children to Ohio, contrary to court's order, as basis for awarding custody to husband, was abuse of discretion, where wife was primary caretaker, where she had moved with children, only in response to husband's admitted physical abuse, in order to be near her relatives, and where wife had not attempted to secret children from husband or otherwise to frustrate his visitation rights. Marshall v. Marshall (Ohio App. 3 Dist., 01-15-1997) 117 Ohio App.3d 182, 690 N.E.2d 68. Child Custody ☞ 44; Child Custody ☞ 50

Trial court abused its discretion by modifying custody of child by changing custodial parent from wife to husband after dissolution of marriage, where only evidence supporting its conclusion was filing of motion to remove child from state, which reflected desire to leave state and had to be filed according to local rule. Masters v. Masters (Ohio, 04-27-1994) 69 Ohio St.3d 83, 630 N.E.2d 665, 1994-Ohio-483. Child Custody ☞ 568

Filing of motion to remove child from state that merely reflects mother's desire to leave state does not on its own constitute "substantial change" in circumstances under statute governing child custody. Masters v. Masters (Ohio, 04-27-1994) 69 Ohio St.3d 83, 630 N.E.2d 665, 1994-Ohio-483. Child Custody ☞ 555

Where movement out of state by the custodial parent in order to obtain employment will result in no more than an increase in travel costs and time to the noncustodial parent, the trial court erred in refusing to grant the custodial parent permission to leave the state. Schwartz v. Schwartz (Lake 1982) 8 Ohio App.3d 311, 456 N.E.2d 1272, 8 O.B.R. 419.

Where the custodial parent disrupts the residence of her children for a period of two weeks, such a disruption is not sufficient evidence to grant a change of custody under RC 3109.04. Wyss v. Wyss (Franklin 1982) 3 Ohio App.3d 412, 445 N.E.2d 1153, 3 O.B.R. 479.

Where the custodial parent moves out of state and the children resettle with a new stepparent and enroll in a new school, sufficient change of circumstance does not exist to allow a court to change custody of the children to an in-state parent. Vincenzo v. Vincenzo (Lake 1982) 2 Ohio App.3d 307, 441 N.E.2d 1139, 2 O.B.R. 339. Child Custody ☞ 568

Fact that mother took children out of state and moved twice thereafter while not disclosing place of residence to husband justified trial court's awarding custody to husband. Ross v. Ross (Ohio 1980) 64 Ohio St.2d 203, 414 N.E.2d 426, 18 O.O.3d 414.

When a remarried mother removes children in her custody from the country of their father's residence to a foreign country, there is a sufficient change of conditions to warrant a court's modifying its original order to change the custody of the children from the mother to the father. Wallace v. Wallace (Lorain 1974) 49 Ohio App.2d 31, 358 N.E.2d 1369, 3 O.O.3d 105. Child Custody ☞ 568

Residential parent's proposed move across the country with child, which had not been disclosed to the court or to the nonresidential parent when the initial child custody order had been entered, was a "change in circumstances," as element for modification of child custody. Duning v. Streck (Ohio App. 12 Dist., Warren, 06-24-2002) No. CA2001-06-061, No. CA2001-06-062, 2002-Ohio-3167, 2002 WL 1358683, Unreported. Child Custody ☞ 568

Evidence supported a modification of parental responsibilities making the former wife the primary residential parent after the former husband moved to another state. Brenneman v. Brenneman (Ohio App. 6 Dist., Wood, 05-24-2002) No. WD-01-052, 2002-Ohio-2630, 2002 WL 1290842, Unreported. Child Custody ☞ 637

In making its decision to grant custody to the father, the trial court errs by placing undue emphasis on the fact that the mother left Ohio and established residence out of state under circumstances where (1) the mother is the primary caregiver, (2) she leaves the marital home because of spousal abuse, (3) she provides the father with an address and telephone number and does not thwart any efforts at visitation, and (4) the father elects not to visit even though he had vacation time. Marshall v Marshall, No. CA96-05-0033, 1997 WL 22859 (3d Dist Ct App, Allen, 1-15-97).

Where there is no substantive evidence presented as to living conditions or schooling, removal of a child to another state is justification for a change of custody; however, mere contemplation of removal is not justification for modification. Evick v Evick, No. 81CA39 (7th Dist Ct App, Mahoning, 1–25–82).

The fact that the father is planning to move out of state and that the mother is now a fit parent for the child is not sufficient in itself to warrant a change in custody under RC 3109.04(B). Gooch v Mathews, No. 1479 (5th Dist Ct App, Tuscarawas, 6–9–81).

49. —— **"Best interests" of child relative to moving or relocation, modification of rights and responsibilities and "change in circumstances"**

Any error in modifying shared parenting plan from ex-husband and ex-wife alternating weekly as residential parent and legal custodian to sole custody for ex-husband was not plain error, where ex-wife's circumstances had changed, in that her work schedule and propensity for moving her residence had created instability in the lives of her children, and stability in ex-husband's living arrangements was conducive to the children's best interests. Rutherford v. Rutherford (Ohio App. 11 Dist., Portage, 09-03-2010) No. 2009-P-0086, 2010-Ohio-4195, 2010 WL 3492892, Unreported. Child Custody ☞ 904

Trial court did not abuse its discretion by modifying magistrate's order, in proceedings on father's motion to modify shared parenting plan, to allow father to exercise parenting time during child's spring break, even though mother was moving to Hawaii; before magistrate's order, parenting plan had provided that father was entitled to parenting time during his son's week-long fall break each year parties had successfully honored the arrangement, and there was no showing that continued practice would not be in child's best interest while residing in Hawaii. Koeppen v. Swank (Ohio App. 12 Dist., Butler, 07-27-2009) No. CA2008-09-234, 2009-Ohio-3675, 2009 WL 2232106, Unreported. Child Custody ☞ 652

Competent, credible evidence supported trial court's conclusion that designating father as residential parent was in child's best interests, in proceeding in which court granted relief from previous divorce decree establishing parental rights and responsibilities, after mother moved to city other than that specified in separation agreement; extended family on both sides resided in city specified in separation agreement, and child had no family other than her mother in area where mother relocated, and there was evidence in record that mother intended to move at time she entered into initial agreement, and that she hid fact from father and from court. Day v. Day (Ohio App. 3 Dist., Seneca, 11-14-2005) No. 13-05-17, 2005-Ohio-6032, 2005 WL 3031009, Unreported. Child Custody ☞ 526

Trial court abused its discretion, in proceedings on wife's motion to modify shared parenting plan to accommodate her relocation out of state with parties' minor child, in finding that harm of relocation was outweighed by benefits of relocation, without first making any finding or conclusion with respect to child's best interests. Lempner v. Lempner (Ohio App. 9 Dist., Lorain, 08-31-2005) No. 04CA008580, 2005-Ohio-4543, 2005 WL 2087834, Unreported. Child Custody ☞ 659

Mother's proposed relocation with two of four children to different county 210 miles away from where father and siblings resided was not in best interests of children; other than maternal grandmother, children had no family in area in which

they would relocate, children enjoyed close relationships with father, paternal relatives and friends in current area, children were successful in current school and were active in extracurricular activities, and mother provided no evidence of benefit to children or occupational opportunities for her by relocating to proposed community. Kolb v. Kolb (Ohio App. 9 Dist., Lorain, 01-29-2003) No. 02CA008045, 2003-Ohio-359, 2003 WL 187577, Unreported. Child Custody ☞ 568

Trial court did not abuse its discretion, in proceeding on motion to modify the shared parenting plan, by finding that it was in children's best interests to modify designation of residential parent for school purposes from father to mother; children would have been required to change schools if father's designation as residential parent was maintained due to his recent move. Porter v. Porter (Ohio App. 9 Dist., Summit, 11-06-2002) No. 21040, 2002-Ohio-6038, 2002 WL 31466445, Unreported. Child Custody ☞ 576

Relocation of the residential parent due to the current husband's job transfer and increased employment opportunities for wife is not legal basis for finding a change of circumstances where the move is not for the improper purpose of interfering with visitation even though the child will not be able to see the father, grandparents, or cousins as often as before absent proof that harm from the move will exceed the normal expected problems of moving; having held there is thus no change of circumstances whatever from the move, the court refuses to proceed to consider what action is in the best interest of the child. Thatcher v. Thatcher (Ohio App. 3 Dist., Mercer, 10-06-1997) No. 10-97-08, 1997 WL 619808, Unreported.

Where a mother has left the state taking a child and the court enters a shared parenting order that the child be returned to Cuyahoga County and reside with the mother if she returns also, but reside with the father if the mother elects to not return, this order does not violate the mother's "constitutional right to travel;" the order concerns the child's best interests and residence, interferes with no one's travel, and it is essential here to remove this child from the negative atmosphere of the mother's efforts to alienate the child from her father. Marsala v Marsala (Ohio App. 8 Dist., Cuyahoga, 07-06-1995) No. 67301, 1995 WL 396360, Unreported.

Former husband's intention to relocate out of state, without more, was insufficient change in circumstances, and had insufficient impact upon child's best interest, to warrant modification of shared-parenting plan to designate former husband child's permanent residential parent and legal custodian. Patton v. Patton (Ohio App. 3 Dist., 03-06-2001) 141 Ohio App.3d 691, 753 N.E.2d 225, 2001-Ohio-2117. Child Custody ☞ 568

Divorce court may consider nonresidence of one of the spouses in determining what custody award will be in best interests of child, but nonresidence alone should not deprive parent of custody. Marshall v. Marshall (Ohio App. 3 Dist., 01-15-1997) 117 Ohio App.3d 182, 690 N.E.2d 68. Child Custody ☞ 87

Mother seeking to relocate minor children pursuant to terms of divorce decree as modified failed to meet her burden of establishing that relocation was in children's best interests, where mother failed to rebut conclusion of expert approved by both parties that children's present residence offered accessibility of day-to-day contact with persons significant to children and that relocation would disrupt children's relationships with their father and other family members. Rozborski v. Rozborski (Ohio App. 8 Dist., 12-02-1996) 116 Ohio App.3d 29, 686 N.E.2d 546. Child Custody ☞ 260

Moving party bears burden of establishing, according to statutory guidelines, whether requested relocation is in best interest of child. Rozborski v. Rozborski (Ohio App. 8 Dist., 12-02-1996) 116 Ohio App.3d 29, 686 N.E.2d 546. Child Custody ☞ 554

A court may consider a parent's move from Ohio in determining the best interests of the child but this should not be the only factor depriving a parent of custody. Rowe v. Franklin (Ohio App. 1 Dist., 06-28-1995) 105 Ohio App.3d 176, 663 N.E.2d 955, appeal not allowed 74 Ohio St.3d 1464, 656 N.E.2d 1299.

Finding that modification of custody to make father residential parent was in child's best interest was supported by evidence that child did not establish strong interpersonal relationships with her maternal relatives in Utah, child's ties to North Carolina, where father lived, predated her move with mother to Utah, child had frequent social interaction with children in North Carolina, mother continuously and willfully interfered with father's visitation rights and was not likely to honor his visitation rights in future, and father indicated that he desired that mother have access to child. Holm v. Smilowitz (Athens 1992) 83 Ohio App.3d 757, 615 N.E.2d 1047. Child Custody ☞ 637

A party seeking modification of a custody and visitation order to delete the restriction against the removal of the child from the county and to change the noncustodial parent's visitation rights from frequent weekday and weekend contact to a long-distance visitation schedule bears the burden of affirmatively demonstrating by a preponderance of the evidence that the changes sought are in the best interests of the child pursuant to consideration of the factors set forth in RC 3109.04(C)(1) through RC 3109.04(C)(5). Powe v. Powe (Ohio Com.Pl. 1987) 38 Ohio Misc.2d 5, 525 N.E.2d 845.

The removal of a child from the state by his custodial parent is a factor that may be considered if it adversely affects the best interests of the child to the extent set forth by RC 3109.04(B)(3), but it does not per se require a change in custody or shift the burden of proof. Schmidt v. Schmidt (Franklin 1982) 7 Ohio App.3d 175, 454 N.E.2d 970, 7 O.B.R. 221.

In a change of custody action, the removal of the child from the state by his custodial parent is a factor that may be considered if it adversely affects the best interests of the child to the extent set forth by RC 3109.04(B)(3), but it does not per se require a change in custody or shift the burden of proof. Schmidt v. Schmidt (Franklin 1982) 7 Ohio App.3d 175, 454 N.E.2d 970, 7 O.B.R. 221.

Finding that changing custody of child from father to mother would not be for best interest of child and that child would be immediately removed from this state is equivalent to finding that mother lacked capacity to care properly for child within territorial jurisdiction of court. Godbey v. Godbey (Hamilton 1942) 70 Ohio App. 450, 44 N.E.2d 810, 36 Ohio Law Abs. 511, 25 O.O. 184.

Evidence established that it was in best interest of the two children to modify custody by granting legal custody to former husband; trial court interviewed the children, the children, while living with former husband pursuant to temporary custody order, had adjusted well to former husband's home, they were doing well at school, and they had improved their grades, former husband would better facilitate visitation orders, and former wife had at least discussed moving to another state with the children. Truax v. Regal (Ohio App. 9 Dist., Summit, 09-18-2002) No. 20902, 2002-Ohio-4867, 2002 WL 31060383, Unreported. Child Custody ☞ 637

Shared parenting plan that was incorporated into divorce decree did not include express or implied prohibition against relocating children to another state, and therefore mother did not have the burden, in seeking modification of plan so as to permit her to relocate with children to Arizona, to show that relocation was in best interest of children; while plan stated parties' intention that plan be based on parties' living within Northeast Ohio area, it also included provisions addressing a possible relocation. Harbottle v. Harbottle (Ohio App. 9 Dist., Summit, 09-18-2002) No. 20897, 2002-Ohio-4859, 2002 WL 31060237, Unreported. Child Custody ☞ 261; Child Custody ☞ 452

Residential parent's proposed across-the-country move with child was not in child's best interest, and thus, modification of child custody was warranted; other than the residential parent, all of child's relatives resided in southwest Ohio, many of those relatives had taken an active role in child's life, the nonresidential parent had never been separated from the child for more than a few weeks, and in light of residential parent's fraudulent conduct in obtaining child custody order without disclosing that she had accepted a job offer which would require a cross-country move, the residential parent was not more likely to facilitate court-approved parenting time rights or visitation. Duning v. Streck (Ohio App. 12 Dist., Warren, 06-24-2002) No. CA2001-06-061, No. CA2001-06-062, 2002-Ohio-3167, 2002 WL 1358683, Unreported. Child Custody ☞ 554; Child Custody ☞ 568

Sufficient evidence supported finding that child's best interests would be served by denial of former wife's motion to move child to Utah, and modification of shared parenting plan to designate former husband's residence as child's residence for school purposes, even though former wife's desire to move was change in circumstances, parties appeared to have shared responsibility for child's care equally since divorce, child had special bond with former wife, and former wife was capable of providing comfortable home for child in Utah, where former wife, former husband, representative of Family Court Services, guardian ad litem, and stepmother each testified, child had relationship with former husband and stepmother, child had good relationships with friends and teachers in Ohio, guardian ad litem recommended that child stay in Ohio county, and child had substantial family ties in Ohio county. Martin v. Martin (Ohio App. 9 Dist., Summit, 03-13-2002) No. 20567, 2002-Ohio-1110, 2002 WL 388902, Unreported, appeal not allowed 96 Ohio St.3d 1467, 772 N.E.2d 1203, 2002-Ohio-3910. Child Custody ⚬ 261

Where there is evidence that the mother is moving to another state to be near a male friend, and that the child reacts unfavorably to the friend, such facts represent a change in circumstances, so it is not necessary that the court find the custodial parent unfit, but only that the court find the best interest of the child requires a change of custody. Hahner v Hahner, No. 7–166 (11th Dist Ct App, Lake, 3–31–80).

In an action for permission to remove a child from the jurisdiction and the noncustodial father, the court determined that the mutual benefit of the father/child visitation right is more in the child's best interests than the mother's change of residence. Jamison v Jamison, No. C–800829 (1st Dist Ct App, Hamilton, 11–10–81).

The removal of a child to another state which affects the best interest of the child constitutes sufficient reason to justify a change of custody pursuant to RC 3109.04(B). Evick v Evick, No. 81 CA 39 (7th Dist Ct App, Mahoning, 1–25–82).

50. ——— Negative effect of moving or relocation, modification of rights and responsibilities and "change in circumstances"

Substantial evidence supported conclusion in child custody modification hearing that the harm likely to be caused by the change of environment for the child if mother were permitted to retain custody and relocate with child was outweighed by the benefits of the change of environment for child if custody decree were modified to award father residential custody, and, thus, trial court was justified in modifying custody decree naming mother as child's residential parent and legal guardian to name father as child's residential parent and legal guardian; child had been integrated into both his paternal and maternal extended families in the local area, and had acclimated well to his local school, and potential harm would be caused to child by a weekly eight-hour car trip for child to facilitate father's visitation. Long v. Long (Ohio App. 3 Dist., Union, 10-04-2010) No. 14-10-01,

2010-Ohio-4817, 2010 WL 3836168, Unreported. Child Custody ⚬ 568

Evidence was sufficient to establish that harm likely to be caused by a change of child's environment, through termination and not modification of shared parenting agreement, was outweighed by advantages of the change in environment, where parents resided in different school districts, making shared parenting difficult, child would benefit from simplified custody arrangement to add consistency to his routine, mother did not have an outside job, mother had fiance and other children in house, while father was alone, and guardian ad litem believed mother was much more likely to communicate with father and be flexible with visitation issues, was the more nurturing parent, and would make the better residential parent. In re Illig (Ohio App. 3 Dist., Seneca, 03-02-2009) No. 13-08-26, 2009-Ohio-916, 2009 WL 500600, Unreported. Child Custody ⚬ 526

Trial court was not required to weigh harm caused by former wife's move with child from Ohio to North Carolina, in former husband's action to modify shared parenting plan so that child would be relocated to Ohio, since former husband had burden of demonstrating that harm of continued primary residence with former wife was outweighed by its advantages. Willoughby v. Masseria (Ohio App. 11 Dist., Geauga, 05-12-2003) No. 2002-G-2437, 2003-Ohio-2368, 2003 WL 21054787, Unreported. Child Custody ⚬ 568

Substantial amount of competent and credible evidence supported trial court's determination that "change of circumstances" occurred, as would support former husband's motion to modify custody; evidence indicated that child had fallen behind in her academic skills, former wife's frequent changes of residence and of care providers had resulted in abruptly discontinued relationships with caregivers and friends in child's life, and former wife had personality disorder marked by extreme defensiveness. Harley v. Harley (Ohio App. 4 Dist., Athens, 01-15-2003) No. 02CA25, 2003-Ohio-232, 2003 WL 146014, Unreported. Child Custody ⚬ 559; Child Custody ⚬ 568

A custodial parent's multiple moves, from Ohio to Oklahoma to Ohio to Indiana, coupled with the introduction of several different men into the child's life and environment, demonstrate a material change of circumstances justifying a modification of the custody order and placement of the child with the other, more stable parent. Johnson v. Johnson (Ohio App. 2 Dist., Clark, 08-11-2000) No. 00CA0004, 2000 WL 1133243, Unreported.

The pending remarriage and relocation of a custodial parent coupled with the loss to the child of contact with the child's local support network including grandparents can be factors justifying a change in custody. Franklin v Franklin, No. CA–8696 (2d Dist Ct App, Montgomery, 9–12–84).

51. —— Nonparent as custodian, modification of rights and responsibilities and "change in circumstances"

Evidence was sufficient to establish that ex-wife was a suitable parent, in child custody contest between ex-wife and paternal uncle and aunt following death of ex-husband who had been designated the residential parent and legal custodian; ex-wife possessed a fundamental right to the custody of her children, as non-parents paternal uncle and aunt had the burden to demonstrate ex-wife's unsuitability, and there was evidence that ex-wife was employed as a nurse, that she was capable of financially supporting the children, that no child in ex-wife's custody had ever been adjudicated as neglected, dependent or abused, that though she had not physically visited with the children for three years she had maintained a relationship with them by telephone, and that ex-husband did not always report his change of address to ex-wife, which interfered with her ability to visit the children. Scavio v. Ordway (Ohio App. 3 Dist., Shelby, 03-15-2010) No. 17-09-07, 2010-Ohio-984, 2010 WL 893662, Unreported. Child Custody ☞ 23; Child Custody ☞ 271; Child Custody ☞ 452

Trial court finding that father and paternal grandparents were in contempt, and order requiring them to pay fees and costs totaling $105,540.37, was not an abuse of discretion, in child custody modification proceeding in which maternal grandparents were awarded legal custody of father's out-of-wedlock child; trial court found that due to the contemptuous acts of father and paternal grandparents the maternal grandparents were required to take drastic, prolonged court action, and that all activity and expenses after the initial visitation order were the result of father and paternal grandparents' conduct. Smith v. Quigg (Ohio App. 5 Dist., Fairfield, 03-22-2006) No. 2005-CA-002, 2006-Ohio-1495, 2006 WL 786856, Unreported. Children Out–of–wedlock ☞ 20.1; Children Out–of–wedlock ☞ 20.12

Issue of who should have legal custody of father's out-of-wedlock child, whose mother had previously died, came down to choice between the maternal and paternal grandparents, not between father and maternal grandparents, and decision to award custody to maternal grandparents was not an abuse of discretion; father had relinquished his parental rights to paternal grandparents in previously dismissed adoption proceeding, had relinquished child's caretaking to paternal grandparents and intended to continue to do so, and had physically and emotionally abused child, maternal grandparents had statutorily protected right not possessed by paternal grandparents to be directly involved with child because of mother's death, and trial court concluded, based on five pages of findings, child's best interest lay with maternal grandparents on every statutory factor. Smith v. Quigg (Ohio App. 5 Dist., Fairfield, 03-22-2006) No. 2005-CA-002, 2006-Ohio-1495, 2006 WL 786856, Unreported. Children Out–of–wedlock ☞ 20.10

Trial court order granting custody of child to maternal grandparents was not an abuse of discretion, during child custody modification proceeding in which maternal and paternal grandparents sought custody of out-of-wedlock child; paternal grandmother administered corporal punishment to child, child alleged that paternal grandmother had sexually abused him, the grandparents practiced different religions and disagreed over child's religious upbringing, and the court analyzed every statutory factor and concluded on every factor that it was in child's best interest to place him with maternal grandparents. Smith v. Quigg (Ohio App. 5 Dist., Fairfield, 03-22-2006) No. 2005-CA-001, 2006-Ohio-1494, 2006 WL 786855, Unreported. Children Out–of–wedlock ☞ 20.10

Nine-month delay between hearing on child custody dispute and issuance of magistrate's decision awarding custody to paternal uncle and aunt did not render decision stale, where maternal grandmother and aunt challenging decision only asserted that circumstances of parties and children may have changed, but offered no specific examples to suggest what circumstances changed and did not show how delay prejudiced parties or children. In re R.N. (Ohio App. 10 Dist., Franklin, 08-24-2004) No. 04AP-130, 2004-Ohio-4420, 2004 WL 1879061, Unreported. Child Custody ☞ 511

Finding that it was in orphaned children's best interest to award custody to paternal uncle and aunt, rather than maternal grandmother and aunt, was not against manifest weight of evidence; although children had lived with maternal grandmother and aunt for past five years and were happy and healthy, children's extended stay with maternal grandmother and aunt resulted in large part from protracted custody litigation, children bonded with paternal uncle and aunt during limited time with them, and paternal uncle and aunt were fit to raise children and could provide more traditional family. In re R.N. (Ohio App. 10 Dist., Franklin, 08-24-2004) No. 04AP-130, 2004-Ohio-4420, 2004 WL 1879061, Unreported. Child Custody ☞ 271; Child Custody ☞ 276

In recommending that custody of orphaned children be granted to paternal uncle and aunt, rather than maternal grandmother and aunt, magistrate properly considered statutory factors, where magistrate examined children's interactions with all parties, parties' ages and employment status, children's physical and emotional health, and communication between parties. In re R.N. (Ohio App. 10 Dist., Franklin, 08-24-2004) No. 04AP-130, 2004-Ohio-4420, 2004 WL 1879061, Unreported. Child Custody ☞ 271; Child Custody ☞ 276

Even if trial court erred in child custody dispute between maternal grandmother and aunt and paternal uncle and aunt by applying statute governing modification of existing decree allocating parental rights and responsibilities, rather than statute applicable to custody disputes between nonparents, no prejudice resulted, where court ultimately addressed best interest of orphaned children and considered appropriate statutory factors. In re R.N.

(Ohio App. 10 Dist., Franklin, 08-24-2004) No. 04AP-130, 2004-Ohio-4420, 2004 WL 1879061, Unreported. Child Custody ☞ 923(1); Child Custody ☞ 923(5)

Granting legal custody of child, who had been adjudicated a dependent child, to her paternal grandmother, rather than mother, was in the child's best interest; child did not always want to visit mother and usually exhibited some behavioral problems upon her return from visiting mother, child developed rash while in mother's care despite numerous discussions and written instructions to mother regarding how to keep the rash from occurring or to properly treat rash, and child was well-adjusted in her grandmother's home. In re A.W.-G. (Ohio App. 12 Dist., Butler, 05-10-2004) No. CA2003-04-099, 2004-Ohio-2298, 2004 WL 1040696, Unreported. Infants ☞ 222

Preponderance of the evidence, as opposed to clear and convincing evidence, was appropriate standard for granting legal custody of child to paternal grandmother in dependency proceeding; clear and convincing evidence was standard in permanent custody proceeding, legal custody where parental rights were not terminated was not as drastic a remedy as permanent custody, and mother retained residual parental rights, such as visitation. In re A.W.-G. (Ohio App. 12 Dist., Butler, 05-10-2004) No. CA2003-04-099, 2004-Ohio-2298, 2004 WL 1040696, Unreported. Infants ☞ 222

Credible evidence supported trial court's finding that placing child, whom mother had left in grandmother's care without attempt to visit or communicate for seven months, in grandmother's custody was in child's best interest; although guardian ad litem concluded that mother should be given custody, counselor and psychologist concluded that custody should be given to grandmother, who cared for child while child was abandoned by mother. In re Beireis (Ohio App. 12 Dist., Clinton, 03-29-2004) No. CA2003-01-001, 2004-Ohio-1506, 2004 WL 602291, Unreported, appeal not allowed 102 Ohio St.3d 1473, 809 N.E.2d 1159, 2004-Ohio-2830. Child Custody ☞ 473

Competent, credible evidence supported trial court order granting legal custody of child to foster parents, rather than grandmother; grandmother told one witness that she would not be involved in child's life but only intended to give child back to child's father, who was in prison, and the evidence on whether child was happier with grandmother or with foster parents conflicted. In re Huffer (Ohio App. 2 Dist., Clark, 11-07-2003) No. 2002 CA 96, 2003-Ohio-5964, 2003 WL 22532923, Unreported. Child Custody ☞ 473

Juvenile court's order denying children's grandmother's motion to intervene in proceedings to terminate father's parental rights did not prevent grandmother from obtaining requested relief, and thus order was not a final appealable order, where father filed a motion for change of custody to grandmother, and trial court had statutory authority to grant custody to a relative. In re Cunningham

Children (Ohio App. 5 Dist., Stark, 05-27-2003) No. 2003CA00054, 2003-Ohio-2805, 2003 WL 21260017, Unreported. Infants ☞ 242

Substantial evidence supported trial court's decision to return to parents custody of child who had been adjudicated abused and dependent and whose legal custody had been granted maternal grandparents; since time grandparents took custody of child, parents had each made extensive efforts to improve their relationship and their situation, they remained married throughout their difficulties, they had participated in over 23 sessions with a parenting specialist, and they had had another child, whom they had parented without incident. In re James (Ohio App. 1 Dist., 09-16-2005) 163 Ohio App.3d 442, 839 N.E.2d 39, 2005-Ohio-4847, appeal allowed 108 Ohio St.3d 1413, 841 N.E.2d 318, 2006-Ohio-179, reversed 113 Ohio St.3d 420, 866 N.E.2d 467, 2007-Ohio-2335, reconsideration denied 114 Ohio St.3d 1484, 870 N.E.2d 734, 2007-Ohio-3699. Infants ☞ 231

Unsuitability determination was not constructively made when mother failed to appeal award of legal custody to her parents, and thus mother's motion to modify award was governed by parental unsuitability standard, rather than by best-interest-of-the-child standard. In re Hockstok (Ohio, 12-27-2002) 98 Ohio St.3d 238, 781 N.E.2d 971, 2002-Ohio-7208, modified 98 Ohio St.3d 1476, 784 N.E.2d 709, 2003-Ohio-980. Child Custody ☞ 511; Child Custody ☞ 554

Evidence that former husband believed, at change of custody hearing at which custody was awarded to child's maternal grandmother, that he would be able to obtain change in custody in the future when he stopped working third shift and began working first shift, did not establish that former husband had not relinquished his right to custody. Wilburn v. Wilburn (Ohio App. 2 Dist., 06-15-2001) 144 Ohio App.3d 279, 760 N.E.2d 7. Child Custody ☞ 637

Allegations that former husband had sexually abused child, made by maternal grandmother who had custody of child, did not establish change of circumstances, as element of former husband's request for change of custody, where grandmother's suspicions were not unfounded; child had made sexual comments, had imitated sexual acts with her dolls and with other children, and had told stories about things former husband and former husband's stepson had said, done, or taught to her, and a young child would not commonly have knowledge of such things. Wilburn v. Wilburn (Ohio App. 2 Dist., 06-15-2001) 144 Ohio App.3d 279, 760 N.E.2d 7. Child Custody ☞ 637

Father had no justiciable concern in whether trial court discharged guardian ad litem after determination was made to maintain custody with maternal grandparents. Rife v. Morgan (Ohio App. 2 Dist., 10-18-1995) 106 Ohio App.3d 843, 667 N.E.2d 450. Child Custody ☞ 903

Trial court's determination that best interest of children warranted continuation of custody with paternal grandparents, rather than change of custody to mother, was supported by evidence; evidence indicated that mother originally consented to grandparents having custody, that she had not paid much, if anything, in support, that children had lived with grandparents for about ten years, and that children had received lower grades when they lived with their parents during three-month trial period, although both children said they wanted to live with mother. Miller v. Miller (Hocking 1993) 86 Ohio App.3d 623, 621 N.E.2d 745. Child Custody ☞ 473

Trial court's finding that mother contractually relinquished custody of child to paternal grandparents, thus requiring application of best interest standard to determine whether mother was entitled to change of custody, was supported by evidence; evidence indicated that both children had lived with paternal grandparents since infancy and that mother and her ex-husband had filed a motion to award custody to paternal grandparents. Miller v. Miller (Hocking 1993) 86 Ohio App.3d 623, 621 N.E.2d 745. Child Custody ☞ 473

Where the natural father placed his infant daughter in the care of nonrelatives during and after the natural mother's protracted final illness, that father's paramount right to custody may be terminated only upon a finding of unsuitability. Reynolds v. Goll (Lorain 1992) 80 Ohio App.3d 494, 609 N.E.2d 1276.

Where a parent or parents have consented to a change of custody to a nonparent and this change of custody was effected by way of a judicially approved contractual agreement, the parent or parents have relinquished the paramount right to custody and the proper test on a motion to change custody by a parent or parents is the best interest of the child pursuant to RC 3109.04(B). In re Whiting (Ottawa 1990) 70 Ohio App.3d 183, 590 N.E.2d 859. Child Custody ☞ 35

Where the parents of a child voluntarily grant custody of a child to other family members, a change of the child's circumstances is required to be shown where the mother seeks to regain custody of the child; a change in the mother's circumstances is insufficient. In re Whiting (Ottawa 1990) 70 Ohio App.3d 183, 590 N.E.2d 859.

A parent's consent to guardianship over his child by the child's grandparents constitutes a forfeiture of the parent's rights to custody to the extent that a later change-of-custody motion may be decided according to the best interests of the child, and without a finding of the parent's unsuitability. Masitto v. Masitto (Ohio 1986) 22 Ohio St.3d 63, 488 N.E.2d 857, 22 O.B.R. 81.

Where possession of a child over 14 years has been voluntarily relinquished by a father to a blood relative under an agreement where possession is not to be taken away and where the child has been properly reared and is content and the child is well adjusted, the wishes of the child raise a presumption that the child's best interest will be served by not being changed, in the absence of showing that such change would be beneficial to the child's welfare. Ex parte Justice (Ohio Com.Pl. 1956) 135 N.E.2d 285, 72 Ohio Law Abs. 323. Child Custody ☞ 566

A common pleas court has no authority in a divorce proceeding, after having first awarded custody of a child to its mother, to later change the legal custody of that child when under eighteen from its mother to its grandmother, where the child has not been abandoned by the mother and it does not find that the mother is not "a suitable person to have custody" of such child, notwithstanding that it determines that the mother is not as suitable as the grandmother and that changing such custody to the grandmother will be for the child's best interest. Grandon v. Grandon (Ohio 1955) 164 Ohio St. 234, 129 N.E.2d 819, 57 O.O. 462.

Where a minor child was entrusted to friends because the mother was unfit, and the father subsequently remarried and reclaimed the child, a court may not award custody to any person other than the father except upon a finding of the father's unfitness. Garabrandt v. Garabrandt (Ohio Com. Pl. 1953) 114 N.E.2d 919, 65 Ohio Law Abs. 380, 51 O.O. 319.

Even where the circumstances have changed, and a previously unfit mother is now better suited to take care of her children, the court does not have to remove custody from the grandmother because the mere fact that a natural parent is fit, though it is certainly one factor that may enter into judicial consideration, does not automatically entitle the natural parent to custody of her child since the best interests and welfare of that child are of paramount importance. Hanson v Hanson, No. 519 (7th Dist Ct App, Monroe, 9–28–79).

52. ——— Poisoning of child's relationship with other parent, modification of rights and responsibilities and "change in circumstances"

Trial court did not abuse its discretion in terminating mother and father's shared parenting plan and naming father as the residential and custodial parent of the parties' two youngest children; two doctors testified that mother had engaged in parental alienation and one testified that a change of custody of the children would be less harmful to them than the continued alienation. Rooney v. Rooney (Ohio App. 5 Dist., Stark, 06-01-2010) No. 2009CA00256, 2010-Ohio-2439, 2010 WL 2186026, Unreported. Child Custody ☞ 576

Evidence supported finding that mother had been source of animosity between parties on subject of father's role in child's life, as a consideration in modifying shared parenting plan to increase father's parenting time; mother had enrolled child in baseball program using the surname of her new husband rather than father's, mother and husband had requested father to relinquish his parental rights, and mother had allowed husband to tell father that father had "no say" in child's participation in family counseling and that child did not have to speak to father when he called. Koeppen v. Swank (Ohio

App. 12 Dist., Butler, 07-27-2009) No. CA2008-09-234, 2009-Ohio-3675, 2009 WL 2232106, Unreported. Child Custody ⚖ 576

Trial court acted within its discretion when it found that change of circumstance had occurred, as would support motion to change custody that was filed by father of nonmarital child; trial court found that mother had engaged in pattern of behavior which was detrimental to child's well-being and that mother had attempted to alienate child from her father because of mother's animosity toward father. In re Jones (Ohio App. 12 Dist., Butler, 09-08-2003) No. CA2002-10-256, 2003-Ohio-4748, 2003 WL 22071508, Unreported. Children Out–of–wedlock ⚖ 20.10

Where evidence shows that after initial decree residential parent is not living up to court's presumption and is attempting to poison relationship between ex-spouse and child, this is a change of circumstances that warrants modification of prior custody decree. Beekman v. Beekman (Ohio App. 4 Dist., 10-25-1994) 96 Ohio App.3d 783, 645 N.E.2d 1332. Child Custody ⚖ 555

53. —— Privileged communications, modification of rights and responsibilities and "change in circumstances"

Former wife waived issue on appeal regarding whether the trial court was required to conduct an in camera inspection of her medical records from drug dependency program, which she was compelled to produce, to determine whether records were relevant to issues in child custody dispute, where wife did not file a brief in opposition to motion to compel release of records, did not request such inspection, and did not argue, in the alternative, that some of the records were not causally or historically related to the claims at issue in custody dispute. Gill v. Gill (Ohio App. 8 Dist., Cuyahoga, 01-16-2003) No. 81463, 2003-Ohio-180, 2003 WL 132447, Unreported. Child Custody ⚖ 904

Former wife who sought custody of her child, subjected herself to extensive investigation of all factors relevant to an award of permanent custody, which included her mental and physical health, and thus, she waived her physician-patient privilege, which covered medical records related to wife's treatment in inpatient drug dependency program, by filing counterclaim seeking child custody and by introducing into evidence letters from her treating physicians. Gill v. Gill (Ohio App. 8 Dist., Cuyahoga, 01-16-2003) No. 81463, 2003-Ohio-180, 2003 WL 132447, Unreported. Privileged Communications And Confidentiality ⚖ 265

By seeking custody of parties' children during divorce proceeding, wife made her mental and physical condition an element to be considered by the trial court in awarding custody, and thus waived physician-patient privilege with respect to communications concerning her condition; however, only those communications, including medical records, that related causally or historically to the conditions relevant to divorce proceeding could be discovered.

Neftzer v. Neftzer (Ohio App. 12 Dist., 12-18-2000) 140 Ohio App.3d 618, 748 N.E.2d 608. Privileged Communications And Confidentiality ⚖ 265

The doctor-patient privilege established by RC 2317.02(B) is effective in an action for modification of child custody, and a private physician or psychologist retained by the movant for modification cannot be deposed with respect to treatment administered before the filing of the motion unless the privilege is waived. Brown v Long, No. 8469 (2d Dist Ct App, Montgomery, 7–27–84).

54. —— Psychological and related investigations and evaluations, modification of rights and responsibilities and "change in circumstances"

Trial court did not abuse its discretion in finding that a change in circumstances had occurred so as to warrant a change in custody, where both parents remarried, a new residence and new school system created an entirely new environment for the children, the children began exhibiting changes in attitudes and behavior toward their father around the time their stepfather entered their lives, and the mental and physical health of the children deteriorated while they resided with their mother. Malone v. Malone (Ohio App. 3 Dist., Seneca, 05-02-2011) No. 13-10-39, 2011-Ohio-2096, 2011 WL 1642915, Unreported. Child Custody ⚖ 555; Child Custody ⚖ 567; Child Custody ⚖ 568

There was no evidence to suggest that any of the parties involved in proceeding pertaining to mother's motion to modify prior allocation of parental rights and responsibilities had mental health issues that required evaluation, and thus trial court did not abuse its discretion by overruling mother's motion for psychological evaluation. Sites v. Sites (Ohio App. 4 Dist., Lawrence, 06-03-2010) No. 09CA19, 2010-Ohio-2748, 2010 WL 2391647, Unreported, appeal not allowed 126 Ohio St.3d 1600, 935 N.E.2d 46, 2010 Ohio 4928. Child Custody ⚖ 617

Unpreserved alleged error in trial court's admission of expert testimony that was not based on facts personally known to witness or facts admitted into evidence at trial did not rise to the level of plain error, at hearing on mother's and father's motions for reallocation of parental rights and responsibilities; the admission of the testimony did not seriously affect the basic fairness, integrity, or public reputation of the judicial process. Rooney v. Rooney (Ohio App. 5 Dist., Stark, 06-01-2010) No. 2009CA00256, 2010-Ohio-2439, 2010 WL 2186026, Unreported. Child Custody ⚖ 904

Trial court did not abuse its discretion by concluding that it was not in child's best interest to terminate shared parenting plan; child's guardian ad litem (GAL) opined that much of conflict that arose between mother and father was result of their immaturity and would hopefully improve with time, GAL specified that mother and father had been able to agree on most parenting issues and that there were no issues which might cause her to question either mother's or father's ability to parent, and social worker, who conducted assessment for court, shared GAL's opinion that both mother and father displayed lack of maturity but were making their shared parenting plan work overall. Sindelar v. Gall (Ohio App. 9 Dist., Summit, 05-05-2010) No. 25022, 2010-Ohio-1960, 2010 WL 1780146, Unreported. Child Custody ☞ 637

Trial court did not abuse its discretion in admitting psychological report in child custody case; court had appointed a psychologist to perform a psychological and custody and companionship evaluation of the parties and specifically stated the written evaluations would be admissible as evidence, and statute permitted court to order an investigative report and that such reports would be available to all parties and subject to cross-examination. Moore v. Lanning (Ohio App. 5 Dist., Fairfield, 03-29-2010) No. 2009-CA-46, 2010-Ohio-1395, 2010 WL 1234414, Unreported. Child Custody ☞ 451

Trial court was, at minimum, required to conduct in-camera inspection of mother's medical records prior to ruling on father's subpoena directed to director of records of medical center, seeking discovery of such records, which evidence was highly relevant to the issue of mother's mental health and more general question of her fitness as a parent, in child custody action in which both mother and father sought custody of their children. In re Kelleher (Ohio App. 7 Dist., Jefferson, 06-16-2009) No. 08-JE-31, No. 08-JE-34, No. 08-JE-32, No. 08-JE-33, 2009-Ohio-2960, 2009 WL 1743678, Unreported. Child Custody ☞ 423

Change of circumstances occurred since entry of trial court's order designating mother as residential parent, and thus, modification of child custody was warranted, such that father would be designated as residential parent; mother and her husband interfered with father's visitation, mother refused to agree to change in parenting schedule when father's work schedule changed to weekends, child's behavior changed in that he had started banging his head on hard surfaces, mother did not seek medical evaluation of child, there was evidence that mother's husband might have given child alcohol, and father was the parent more likely to honor court-approved parenting time. Gossard v. Miller (Ohio App. 3 Dist., Wyandot, 05-09-2005) No. 16-04-15, 2005-Ohio-2252, 2005 WL 1077050, Unreported. Child Custody ☞ 576

Trial court's consideration of fact that ex-husband had sought appropriate medical treatment for child, who had been diagnosed with Tourette's Syndrome and attention deficit hyperactivity disorder (ADHD) since prior parenting order, was appropriate in determining whether child's diagnosis constituted change of circumstances warranting further consideration of child's best interests, in custody modification proceeding in which ex-wife sought to be re-named child's residential parent; diagnosis was relevant to change of circumstances inquiry since, as result of receiving appropriate treatment, child's present circumstance had changed very little, and, absent appropriate treatment, child's diagnosis

alone might have been change of circumstances warranting further consideration of ex-wife's motion. Kubin v. Kubin (Ohio App. 12 Dist., Clermont, 03-07-2005) No. CA2004-02-009, 2005-Ohio-947, 2005 WL 516522, Unreported. Child Custody ☞ 576

Child's diagnosis of Tourette's Syndrome and attention deficit hyperactivity disorder (ADHD) since prior parenting order, standing alone, did not constitute change of circumstances warranting further consideration of child's best interests, in custody modification proceeding in which ex-wife sought to be re-named child's residential parent; evidence indicated child had exhibited symptoms of Tourette's Syndrome and ADHD as early as age three, his symptoms remained mild and were not causing functional or social impairment or physical discomfort according to physician's evaluation, and, although child's homework took him longer to complete than it likely should, child continued to do well in school. Kubin v. Kubin (Ohio App. 12 Dist., Clermont, 03-07-2005) No. CA2004-02-009, 2005-Ohio-947, 2005 WL 516522, Unreported. Child Custody ☞ 576

Evidence supported finding that changing child's residential parent status from mother, who sought permission to relocate out of state with child, to father was in child's best interests; child's father and both sets of grandparents resided within state, expert testified that father's profile presented no emotional or psychological problems, that mother's profile suggested the possibility of an addictive disorder, and that mother reported a tendency toward impulsiveness and anger proneness under conditions of conflict, and father was employed and mother was not employed. Lyall v. Lyall (Ohio App. 5 Dist., Muskingum, 03-25-2004) No. CT2003-0044, 2004-Ohio-1565, 2004 WL 614990, Unreported. Child Custody ☞ 565; Child Custody ☞ 568; Child Custody ☞ 642

Trial court was not required to conduct hearing before granting guardian ad litem's motion for reconsideration of request that parties submit to forensic psychological evaluation regarding former husband's motion to modify custody, where trial court had all necessary information to determine whether to reconsider its prior ruling to vacate its previous order. Citta-Pietrolungo v. Pietrolungo (Ohio App. 8 Dist., Cuyahoga, 06-26-2003) No. 81943, No. 82069, 2003-Ohio-3357, 2003 WL 21469770, Unreported. Child Custody ☞ 650

Costs of psychological examinations for parents and their child, in connection with ex-wife's motion to reduce visitation or for supervised visitation, properly were taxed evenly between ex-wife and ex-husband; the psychological examinations were an integral part of the "investigation" required by the court before the motion for supervised visitation could be determined pursuant to statute providing that court could cause an investigation to be made as to the character, family relations, past conduct, earning ability, and financial worth of each parent and court could tax as costs all or any part of the expenses for each investigation. Tinnel v. Tinnel

(Ohio App. 6 Dist., Huron, 03-21-2003) No. H-02-040, 2003-Ohio-1403, 2003 WL 1464081, Unreported. Child Custody ⚬ 940

Trial court did not impermissibly consider child's custodial preferences as set forth in a written psychological evaluation of child in custody modification proceeding; court's references in its findings of fact as to the preference expressed by child to psychologist were set forth in context of court's in camera interview with child, which revealed that court reached its conclusion concerning child's preference as to a custodial parent, and reached a determination to give any expressed preference "little weight," based upon that interview and not upon evaluation. Lynch v. Lynch (Ohio App. 6 Dist., Huron, 03-07-2003) No. H-02-022, 2003-Ohio-1039, 2003 WL 876566, Unreported. Child Custody ⚬ 659

Trial court's order requiring psychological evaluations of all parties before deciding specifics of hotly contested visitation issues did not affect former wife or her son's substantial rights, and thus order was not appealable. Harness v. Harness (Ohio App. 4 Dist., 06-04-2001) 143 Ohio App.3d 669, 758 N.E.2d 793, 2001-Ohio-2433. Child Custody ⚬ 923(3)

Evidentiary hearing was required, in former wife's action for modification of custody order, to permit cross-examination of psychologist whose report on results of his post-trial examination of former husband apparently formed sole basis of trial court's modification of custody order, where report cast former husband's parenting skills in very positive light, and court did not indicate how former husband's alleged deficiencies affected his ability to function and to parent, or how such deficiencies amounted to change in circumstances sufficient to warrant custody modification. Beaver v. Beaver (Ohio App. 4 Dist., 05-25-2001) 143 Ohio App.3d 1, 757 N.E.2d 41, 2001-Ohio-2399. Child Custody ⚬ 650

Any error in admitting posthearing psychological report into evidence, under seal, without allowing cross-examination of its author, in connection with motion for modification of parental rights and responsibilities established by order in divorce action, was harmless, where copies of report were ultimately released to parties, and report did not change result of case. Inscoe v. Inscoe (Ohio App. 4 Dist., 06-16-1997) 121 Ohio App.3d 396, 700 N.E.2d 70. Child Custody ⚬ 923(4)

Trial court did not err in considering home study report as evidence in the absence of sworn testimony in proceeding regarding modification of child custody decree, given that statutes and rule authorized trial court to consider court-ordered investigation reports as evidence. Sayre v. Hoelzle-Sayre (Ohio App. 3 Dist., 04-06-1994) 100 Ohio App.3d 203, 653 N.E.2d 712, appeal allowed 70 Ohio St.3d 1426, 638 N.E.2d 88, appeal dismissed as improvidently allowed 72 Ohio St.3d 1218, 651 N.E.2d 430, 1995-Ohio-274. Child Custody ⚬ 632

It is within the sound discretion of the court to decline to order a home investigation of both parties before ordering a change of custody. Stone v. Stone (Warren 1983) 9 Ohio App.3d 6, 457 N.E.2d 919, 9 O.B.R. 6. Child Custody ⚬ 615

Upon a motion to modify custody provisions of a divorce decree, a court is not limited to any particular line of inquiry, nor is it bound by strict legal rules governing the introduction of evidence, and while hearsay evidence alone is insufficient to support a modification of a custody order, the court may properly consider reports of court-appointed social workers. Woodruff v. Woodruff (Ohio Com. Pl. 1965) 7 Ohio Misc. 87, 217 N.E.2d 264, 36 O.O.2d 165. Child Custody ⚬ 632

The trial court errs where it grants a motion for a change of custody without the required findings of a change of circumstance. No. CA2000–10–030, 2001 WL 1112036 (12th Dist Ct App, Brown, 9–24–01), In re Tuepker.

55. —— Racial matters, modification of rights and responsibilities and "change in circumstances"

Trial court did not act unreasonably, arbitrarily or unconscionably in divorce proceedings in denying husband's request to modify the standard parenting order with respect to early return of children to wife on Sunday evenings for church purposes; contrary to husband's contention that court gave him "less [parenting time] than the Standard Order of Parenting," court modified the standard parenting time guidelines in such a manner as to increase husband's parenting time by delaying return time on weekday nights by one hour during the year school year and two hours during the summer, and court attempted to accommodate husband's desire for additional weekend time by permitting an early Friday pick-up, thereby adding an hour or more parenting time for husband. Daugherty v. Daugherty (Ohio App. 12 Dist., Butler, 08-08-2005) No. CA2004-04-097, 2005-Ohio-4056, 2005 WL 1864142, Unreported. Child Custody ⚬ 147

The custody of an illegitimate child will not be taken from the mother and awarded to the father merely upon the basis that the wife has contracted an interracial marriage. In re H. (Ohio Com.Pl. 1973) 37 Ohio Misc. 123, 305 N.E.2d 815, 66 O.O.2d 178, 66 O.O.2d 368.

56. —— Remarriage effect, modification of rights and responsibilities and "change in circumstances"

Trial court finding that a change in circumstances had occurred, warranting modification of the parties' shared parenting plan, was not against the manifest weight of the evidence; former wife had remarried, her husband was an alcoholic who refused to get treatment, she had been involved in domestic disturbances with her new husband, she had three additional children, and she had started working evenings. Bracy v. Bracy (Ohio App. 3 Dist., Allen, 08-04-2008) No. 1-08-15,

2008-Ohio-3888, 2008 WL 2954717, Unreported. Child Custody ☞ 576

Evidence supported trial court's finding of changed circumstances supporting reallocation of former husband's and wife's parental rights and responsibilities under decree previously naming former wife the sole residential parent and legal custodian of both children; parties had each remarried, had an additional child, and moved more than once. Wine v. Wine (Ohio App. 5 Dist., Delaware, 03-04-2005) No. 04 CA F 10 068, 2005-Ohio-975, 2005 WL 519021, Unreported, appeal not allowed 106 Ohio St.3d 1463, 830 N.E.2d 1170, 2005-Ohio-3490. Child Custody ☞ 552; Child Custody ☞ 567; Child Custody ☞ 568

Father failed to show change in circumstances of sufficient substance to warrant modification of parties' shared parenting agreement by increasing father's parenting time from 33 percent to 53 percent, where changes that had occurred since agreement was entered into were slight and inconsequential; both parents had remarried, mother and her husband had child, father and his wife were expecting child, father's job allowed him more free time, mother had changed employment, and child was almost nine years old and remained active in sports. Bauer v. Bauer (Ohio App. 12 Dist., Clermont, 05-19-2003) No. CA2002-10-083, 2003-Ohio-2552, 2003 WL 21135483, Unreported. Child Custody ☞ 571

Trial court properly considered former husband's remarriage as factor in determining best interests of child in proceeding to modify prior custody order; court found that child's relationship with stepmother was described as close, stepmother characterized relationship with child as more like a big sister, and court concluded that child had appropriate interaction and interrelationships with each parent and with her stepparents, but that child's relationship with stepmother appeared to be more bonded than with stepfather, by virtue of having been placed with stepmother for a greater period of time. Dyslin v. Marks (Ohio App. 5 Dist., Stark, 04-07-2003) No. 2002CA00300, 2003-Ohio-1855, 2003 WL 1857108, Unreported. Child Custody ☞ 567

Non-custodial parent's alleged ability to provide his children with a better home environment than the custodial parent after her remarriage did not constitute a change of circumstance necessary for a reallocation of parental rights and responsibilities. Saal v. Saal (Ohio App. 9 Dist., 10-17-2001) 146 Ohio App.3d 579, 767 N.E.2d 750, 2001-Ohio-1518. Child Custody ☞ 565

A residential parent's remarriage may be considered a change of circumstance supporting a reallocation of parental rights and responsibilities, if hostility erupts between the residential parent and new spouse and the nonresidential parent. Saal v. Saal (Ohio App. 9 Dist., 10-17-2001) 146 Ohio App.3d 579, 767 N.E.2d 750, 2001-Ohio-1518. Child Custody ☞ 567

A court does not have the power under the statutes respecting custody of minor children of divorced parents to place restrictions concerning the right of such divorced parent to remarry, the necessity to have a relative reside in the home of such parent to whom custody is awarded, and restrict such parent in the choice of school to which the children shall be sent. Selby v. Selby (Summit 1952) 124 N.E.2d 772, 69 Ohio Law Abs. 257.

It was in child's best interest for custody to be transferred from ex-wife to ex-husband, on motion for allocation of parental rights and responsibilities; child had her own bedroom at ex-husband's house, whereas she had to share her room with half-siblings at ex-wife's house, and child was prohibited from answering the phone when the caller I.D. identified the phone call as coming from ex-husband. Wilson v. Wetter (Ohio App. 12 Dist., Butler, 06-17-2002) No. CA2001-10-253, 2002-Ohio-3877, 2002 WL 1327464, Unreported. Child Custody ☞ 552; Child Custody ☞ 569

57. —— Residential parent, modification of rights and responsibilities and "change in circumstances"

Evidence was sufficient to support trial court's finding that a modification of its prior joint child custody order was not necessary to serve the best interest of two minor children, even though there might have been some negatives in father's household based on marital problems between husband and his wife; children were flourishing both in and out of school since father had become the residential parent, and children had expressed a desire to remain in the same school district. Musgrove n/k/a Owen v. Musgrove (Ohio App. 2 Dist., Montgomery, 09-02-2011) No. 24640, 2011-Ohio-4460, 2011 WL 3890305, Unreported. Child Custody ☞ 576

Evidence supported finding that there had been no change in circumstances that warranted modification of parental rights and responsibilities, in post-divorce action to modify child custody; the fact that son had a stronger bond with father since father had become child's residential parent was an intended result of the trial court's decision to award custody to father, and thus did not constitute a change of circumstances warranting modification of child custody, child's desire to reside with mother was not a substantial change in circumstances, and child's development of a strong sibling relationship with half-brother was not a fact that had arisen since the prior decree. Baxter v. Baxter (Ohio App. 9 Dist., Lorain, 08-15-2011) No. 10CA009927, 2011-Ohio-4034, 2011 WL 3567246, Unreported. Child Custody ☞ 576

Trial court acted within its discretion by adopting magistrate's recommendation for shared parenting plan on mother's motion to modify judgment by which father was designated the residential parent and legal custodian for the parties' four children; trial court was required to accept all of the magistrate's findings of fact as true, magistrate made factual findings and considered statutory best interest factors as applied to the findings. Cameron v. Cameron (Ohio App. 9 Dist., Medina, 08-08-2011)

No. 10CA0064-M, 2011-Ohio-3884, 2011 WL 3427216, Unreported. Child Custody ☞ 575

Evidence supported trial court's decision to designate mother of non-marital child as child's residential parent and legal custodian, although mother's living arrangements were somewhat unstable given that she had moved four times since child's birth; evidence indicated that mother was child's caregiver, child, who was three years old, had strong and stable relationship with mother, and child had bonded with her two-half brothers, who also resided with mother. Althammer v. Pottorf (Ohio App. 12 Dist., Clermont, 08-01-2011) No. CA2010-11-090, 2011-Ohio-3764, 2011 WL 3274086, Unreported. Children Out–of–wedlock ☞ 20.3

Trial court did not exceed the scope of appellate court's remand when it held hearings to determine the children's best interests with respect to ex-husband's motion to reallocate parental rights and responsibilities; appellate court determined that a change in circumstances had occurred, and thus, the trial court was required to accept this issue as finally settled, appellate court intended its remand order to include a further hearing given the nature of ex-husband's modification motion, and next step in the modification statute was to determine the children's best interests. Gomez v. Gomez (Ohio App. 7 Dist., Noble, 06-09-2011) No. 10-NO-375, 2011-Ohio-2843, 2011 WL 2410484, Unreported. Child Custody ☞ 924

In action to reallocate parental rights and responsibilities, trial court did not abuse its discretion in concluding that a change in custody, namely designating ex husband as residential parent, was not in the children's best interests; ex-husband had strained relationship with ex-wife's current husband, ex-husband had anger management problems, children were well adjusted in their current residence with ex-wife and her husband, ex-husband was not forthcoming in providing information to the guardian ad litem (GAL) and was disrespectful toward the GAL, and GAL recommended that children remain in ex-wife's custody and that designating ex-husband as the residential parent would not be in their best interest. Gomez v. Gomez (Ohio App. 7 Dist., Noble, 06-09-2011) No. 10-NO-375, 2011-Ohio-2843, 2011 WL 2410484, Unreported. Child Custody ☞ 554

Order modifying child custody to designate father as the residential parent and legal custodian of the children was not against the manifest weight of the evidence; the trial court found mother's witnesses were not credible, and that the harm likely to be caused by a change in the children's environment resulting from a modification of the prior decree was outweighed by the advantages of the change in environment to the children. Scarberry v. Scarberry (Ohio App. 2 Dist., Clark, 06-10-2011) No. 10-CA-0091, 2011-Ohio-2829, 2011 WL 2410234, Unreported. Child Custody ☞ 555

Agreed order pursuant to which father was granted parenting time in accordance with standard order of parenting time and which did not expressly designate mother as child's residential parent and legal custodian constituted de facto designation of mother as child's residential parent and legal custodian, and thus, father's complaint for custody was not original custody proceeding and he was required to prove change in circumstances to warrant modification of custody. In re A.N. (Ohio App. 2 Dist., Greene, 05-20-2011) No. 2010 CA 83, No. 2011 CA 7, 2011-Ohio-2422, 2011 WL 1936030, Unreported. Children Out–of–wedlock ☞ 20.4; Children Out–of–wedlock ☞ 20.10

Trial court acted within its discretion by adopting magistrate finding that designating father as residential parent for school enrollment purposes under shared parenting agreement was in child's best interest, even though father resided in marital residence that was up for sale by court order, and mother had prepaid rent for six months on an apartment; father testified he would remain in the area of the school district after sale of marital home, child had lived in the area since birth, attended swim classes, dance classes, and gymnastics, and preschool in the area, and mother had already been in the apartment, which was outside the area, for five of the six prepaid months, and was to pay rent on month-to-month basis thereafter. Allen v. Allen (Ohio App. 12 Dist., Warren, 03-28-2011) No. CA2010-11-107, 2011-Ohio-1478, 2011 WL 1137148, Unreported. Child Custody ☞ 147

Evidence supported trial court's finding that change in the circumstances having a material effect on nine-year-old nonmarital child had occurred, as would support father's request to modify custody by changing child's residential parent from mother to father; evidence indicated that child had significantly matured since issuance of existing custody decree eight years earlier, mother was no longer in committed relationship that was in existence when decree was entered, and father had become a responsible father despite being young teenager when child was born. Dodson v. Bullinger (Ohio App. 3 Dist., Van, 12-20-2010) No. 15-10-06, 2010-Ohio-6263, 2010 WL 5296950, Unreported. Children Out–of–wedlock ☞ 20.10

Evidence supported trial court's finding that it was in nonmarital child's best interest to modify custody by changing residential parent from mother to father, even though father had been convicted of drug paraphernalia offense; evidence indicated that father's limited driving privileges following conviction allowed him to pick up child, mother allowed her former boyfriend to take child on most weekends that boyfriend had visitation with his children, mother lived with male "friend" who did not pay rent, and mother did not involve father in decision to begin medicating child regarding attention deficit hyperactivity disorder (ADHD). Dodson v. Bullinger (Ohio App. 3 Dist., Van, 12-20-2010) No. 15-10-06, 2010-Ohio-6263, 2010 WL 5296950, Unreported. Children Out–of–wedlock ☞ 20.10

58. —— Split custody and each parent with a child, modification of rights and responsibilities and "change in circumstances"

Evidence supported trial court's finding that harm likely to be caused by a change of environment was outweighed by the advantage that a change of environment would have on son of former husband and wife, thus supporting reallocation of parental rights and responsibilities, giving father custody of son while leaving daughter in custody of mother, under decree previously naming former wife the sole residential parent and legal custodian of both children; although son was thriving in mother's care, mother's move out of state would separate children from father, and son had much to gain from living with father and remaining in the state. Wine v. Wine (Ohio App. 5 Dist., Delaware, 03-04-2005) No. 04 CA F 10 068, 2005-Ohio-975, 2005 WL 519021, Unreported, appeal not allowed 106 Ohio St.3d 1463, 830 N.E.2d 1170, 2005-Ohio-3490. Child Custody ☞ 552; Child Custody ☞ 568

Evidence supported trial court's finding that separation of siblings was in the best interest of children, thus supporting trial court's reallocation of former husband's and wife's parental rights and responsibilities, giving father custody of son while leaving daughter in custody of mother, under decree previously naming former wife the sole residential parent and legal custodian of both children; mother's move out of state would separate children from father, daughter had unique bond with mother while son had much to gain from living with father, and guardian ad litem supported separation of the children. Wine v. Wine (Ohio App. 5 Dist., Delaware, 03-04-2005) No. 04 CA F 10 068, 2005-Ohio-975, 2005 WL 519021, Unreported, appeal not allowed 106 Ohio St.3d 1463, 830 N.E.2d 1170, 2005-Ohio-3490. Child Custody ☞ 552; Child Custody ☞ 568; Child Custody ☞ 616

Custody modification was unwarranted, despite mother's contention that younger child's relationship with elder sibling deteriorated after each parent was designated residential parent of one child, where younger child was acclimated to father's home, school, and community, child was performing well at school, children were close despite seven-year age difference, children were together every weekend and one night every week under custody provisions of divorce decree, and father was not shown to be unsuitable to have custody. Miller v. Miller (Ohio App. 3 Dist., 11-20-1996) 115 Ohio App.3d 336, 685 N.E.2d 319. Child Custody ☞ 552

59. —— Standard of living improvement and its effect, modification of rights and responsibilities and "change in circumstances"

Evidence supported finding that child's interests were better served in mother's custody, thus supporting order changing residential custody from father, who was also child's legal custodian under original custody order, to mother; father failed to request findings and conclusions of law in response to issuance of general judgment, but record did show that guardian ad litem testified at hearing recommending placement of child, who had Fragile X Syndrome, with mother due to the conditions of her home, which was spacious, newer, and clean, which was more ideally suited to child's special needs. Crites v. Dingus (Ohio App. 4 Dist., Athens, 12-24-2008) No. 07CA38, 2008-Ohio-7039, 2008 WL 5456382, Unreported. Child Custody ☞ 638

Evidence was sufficient to support finding that changing residential parent status from mother to father was in children's best interest; children were comfortable in both homes and were equally adjusted to both homes and communities, eight-year-old child did not state a preference regarding where she wanted to live, it was unclear whether six-year-old child had sufficient reasoning ability to express her wishes and concerns, both parents were likely to facilitate companionship with other parent, father was more likely to provide a stable environment for children, was more likely to use reasonable discipline with children, and had proven himself to be more motivated to meet the educational and particularly medical needs of the children. Silverman v. Silverman (Ohio App. 4 Dist., Hocking, 06-27-2003) No. 03CA2, 2003-Ohio-3757, 2003 WL 21652183, Unreported. Child Custody ☞ 576

Assuming, arguendo, that change of circumstances had been demonstrated, father's claim that he could have provided a better living environment for children constituted insufficient grounds to determine that a change of custody from mother to father would have been in the best interest of the children, where children were happy and doing well at home and in school, and the guardian ad litem recommended that mother retain custody if she became employed and obtained independent housing, which she accomplished. Dunlop v. Dunlop (Ohio App. 2 Dist., Montgomery, 10-25-2002) No. 19313, 2002-Ohio-5828, 2002 WL 31398674, Unreported. Child Custody ☞ 559; Child Custody ☞ 564

In proceeding by mother for modification of an order granting custody of three minor sons to father, fact that shortly prior to the hearing maternal grandparents purchased a residence, that maternal grandmother testified that if custody were given to mother, she would furnish home for mother and children and would furnish financial support if needed of $60 per week, that there was no binding obligation on part of grandparents, and that the claimed changed conditions were prospective in character were to be considered by trial judge in determining whether evidence showed sufficient change to warrant modification. Harper v. Harper (Greene 1954) 98 Ohio App. 359, 129 N.E.2d 471, 57 O.O. 389. Child Custody ☞ 637

60. —— Support order, modification of rights and responsibilities and "change in circumstances"

The trial court's determination that the date former wife was served with former husband's motion to modify child support was the effective date of former husband's new child support obligation, rather than an earlier date that corresponded with when former husband started the administrative process seeking a reduction, was not an abuse of discretion; the combined gross income of the parties was over $150,000 per year, and thus former husband was required to seek administrative review to modify child support. L.B. v. T.B. (Ohio App. 2 Dist., Montgomery, 07-08-2011) No. 24441, 2011-Ohio-3418, 2011 WL 2671915, Unreported. Child Support ☞ 364

Trial court, which granted custody of children to husband after the trial and ended husband's child support obligation, properly ordered that any child support paid by husband after the date of the trial be applied against any arrearage owed by husband under the earlier temporary order, which named wife as residential parent and legal custodian of children and ordered husband to pay child support; effect of the trial court's order was the diminution of any arrearage owed by husband under the previous temporary child support order. Maag v. Maag (Ohio App. 9 Dist., Summit, 08-25-2004) No. 21771, 2004-Ohio-4451, 2004 WL 1882776, Unreported. Child Support ☞ 454

Trial court in child custody case ruled on issue of whether father was in arrears on his child support obligations, where judgment, which designated father as residential parent, stated that father's child support was terminated effective July 31, 2002, and the child support enforcement agency was to lift his wage withholding order once his current support obligation was paid in full. Bland v. Bland (Ohio App. 9 Dist., Summit, 02-26-2003) No. 21228, 2003-Ohio-828, 2003 WL 470180, Unreported. Child Support ☞ 496

Award of $202.03 per month in child support in shared parenting arrangement was proper, where obligor earned 71 percent of parties' combined incomes, children lived with obligor 50 percent of the time, and 71 percent of total child support obligation, less 50 percent deviation, was $2424.34. Muzechuk v. Muzechuk (Ohio App. 5 Dist., Tuscarawas, 05-14-2002) No. 2001 AP 090089, 2002-Ohio-2527, 2002 WL 999300, Unreported. Child Support ☞ 140(1)

While a domestic relations court which grants a divorce has continuing jurisdiction over all matters pertaining to child custody and support, it has no authority to retroactively modify the total amount due and payable under its prior order for support of minor children in an action involving a change of custody. Kuntz v Kuntz, No. 78AP–831 (10th Dist Ct App, Franklin, 7–5–79).

61. —— Time period considered, modification of rights and responsibilities and "change in circumstances"

Statute governing modification of parenting time or visitation, and not statute governing allocation of parental rights and responsibilities for care of children, governed former wife's motion to modify husband's overnight parenting schedule. Banfield

v. Banfield (Ohio App. 12 Dist., Clermont, 07-25-2011) No. CA2010-09-066, No. CA2010-09-068, 2011-Ohio-3638, 2011 WL 2989883, Unreported. Child Custody ☞ 3

Relevant time period for determination of whether change of circumstances had occurred as would warrant change in child custody began with trial court's prior judgment entry, and not from time that motion for change of custody was made. Jackson v. Herron (Ohio App. 11 Dist., Lake, 08-05-2005) No. 2003-L-145, 2005-Ohio-4046, 2005 WL 1861965, Unreported. Child Custody ☞ 555

Delay of approximately ten months between end of trial and entering of decision did not prejudice mother of non-marital child and thus did not amount to prejudicial error in father's modification action that resulted in father being designated residential parent and legal custodian; mother gave child to father after first day of trial with note stating that he could have custody, and father was subsequently awarded temporary custody. Haney v. Corbett (Ohio App. 5 Dist., Delaware, 09-02-2004) No. 04CAF01005, 2004-Ohio-4642, 2004 WL 1945642, Unreported. Children Out–of–wedlock ☞ 20.11

Evidence admissible under RC 3109.04(B) may be excluded by limiting admissible evidence to activities which occurred within a reasonable time immediately preceding a change of custody hearing, especially when its probative value is outweighed by considerations of undue delay. Schmidt v. Schmidt (Franklin 1982) 7 Ohio App.3d 175, 454 N.E.2d 970, 7 O.B.R. 221.

In a custody action subsequent to the original custody order, the trial court does not abuse its discretion by limiting the evidence to events which occurred after the original custody order was made. In re Reynolds (Hamilton 1982) 2 Ohio App.3d 309, 441 N.E.2d 1141, 2 O.B.R. 341.

In proceeding seeking modification of decree awarding custody of a child, at child's election, it is not error for court to refuse evidence of parent's habits earlier than one year immediately preceding the hearing, as this matter rests in the sound discretion of the trial court. Schwalenberg v. Schwalenberg (Columbiana 1940) 65 Ohio App. 217, 29 N.E.2d 617, 18 O.O. 397.

In a change of custody hearing, trial court does not commit prejudicial error in hearing upon remand by admitting evidence concerning matters which preceded the previous hearing. Gooch v Mathews, No. CA–1571 (5th Dist Ct App, Tuscarawas, 4–9–82).

62. —— "Unfitness" of parent as factor, modification of rights and responsibilities and "change in circumstances"

Evidence supported trial court's finding that husband did not provoke wife into stabbing husband in chest in presence of children, as would support trial court's conclusion that it was in children's best interest to name husband residential parent and legal custodian of children in divorce action; evidence indicated that wife told police officer who responded to wife's 911 call that wife "lost it" and stabbed husband, and wife had opportunity to, but did not, tell police officer that wife had been acting in self-defense or in response to serious provocation from husband when she stabbed husband. Thompson v. Thompson (Ohio App. 12 Dist., Butler, 01-18-2011) No. CA2010-03-052, 2010-Ohio-158, 2011 WL 282424, Unreported. Child Custody ☞ 469

Any error in modifying shared parenting plan from ex-husband and ex-wife alternating weekly as residential parent and legal custodian to sole custody for ex-husband was not plain error, where ex-wife's circumstances had changed, in that her work schedule and propensity for moving her residence had created instability in the lives of her children, and stability in ex-husband's living arrangements was conducive to the children's best interests. Rutherford v. Rutherford (Ohio App. 11 Dist., Portage, 09-03-2010) No. 2009-P-0086, 2010-Ohio-4195, 2010 WL 3492892, Unreported. Child Custody ☞ 904

Upon custodial mother's incarceration, any detrimental effects caused by the change of child's environment, from maternal grandparents' home to father's home, and father's need to utilize daycare services did not constitute the type of detriment required to render father unsuitable to parent, and thus, maternal grandparents' motion for custody of child, in opposition to father's motion to change custody to himself, was appropriately denied, in deference to father's essential and basic civil right, as against third parties, to raise his child. In re Schwendeman (Ohio App. 4 Dist., Washington, 02-07-2006) No. 05CA18, No. 05CA25, 2006-Ohio-636, 2006 WL 327831, Unreported. Children Out–of–wedlock ☞ 20.10

Trial court order that precluded wife from having any contact with any children, absent special written permission, was not an abuse of discretion, during divorce proceeding; wife was convicted of eight counts of endangering children based on her conduct with her own children and with other children in the home, videotapes from the endangerment hearings showed multiple incidents of violence and mistreatment of the children under wife's care, counsel for the children testified that the children suffered from post-traumatic stress syndrome from years of abuse by wife, and wife's probation officer stated that wife never took responsibility for her actions. Weaver v. Weaver (Ohio App. 5 Dist., Licking, 08-09-2004) No. 2003CA00096, 2004-Ohio-4212, 2004 WL 1784595, Unreported. Child Custody ☞ 216

Competent, credible evidence supported trial court's finding of changed circumstances so as to warrant change of custody from unwed father to mother; father moved from an apartment to a trailer that was valued at $600, mother testified that the times she had been to father's trailer it had been dark, there had been garbage in the trailer, and that she could smell a foul odor outside, father was unemployed, and father had chronic health problems. Font v. Morris (Ohio App. 3 Dist., Mercer, 05-10-2004) No. 10-03-21, 2004-Ohio-2354, 2004 WL 1049130, Unreported. Children Out–of–wedlock ☞ 20.10

Evidence in shelter care hearing supported trial court's finding that award of legal custody of child to father, rather than mother, was in child's best interest; case manager testified that drugs had been sold at mother's home, that domestic violence had occurred in child's presence, that child had not begun to learn age appropriate skills, that child flourished in father's custody, that child had become attached to father, that mother had only recently begun to apply herself to attempt to complete her case plan, father testified to child's growth under his care, and mother testified that she had been diagnosed as bipolar, had been charged with writing bad checks, and with possession of illegal drugs. In re Law (Ohio App. 5 Dist., Tuscarawas, 01-09-2004) No. 2003AP0645, 2004-Ohio-117, 2004 WL 60485, Unreported. Infants ☞ 231

Trial court determination that designating husband as residential parent and legal custodian for the parties' three children was in the best interests of the children was not an abuse of discretion, in divorce proceeding; mother had difficulty completing daily tasks, she lied to husband about their business, she hid mail, she did not get the children immunized for school, she did not deal with stress in a straightforward manner, and she had her telephone service cut off after she moved away from husband. Gehring v. Gehring (Ohio App. 12 Dist., Warren, 01-12-2004) No. CA2003-03-038, 2004-Ohio-95, 2004 WL 47688, Unreported. Child Custody ☞ 48

In custody dispute between two parents, to extent both parents were presumed suitable, it was unnecessary for court to enter into suitability or unfitness analysis in determining that child's best interest would be served by modification of custody, and thus former husband's substantive due process rights were not violated by lack of inquiry into parental unfitness before modifying custody. Winfield v. Winfield (Ohio App. 11 Dist., Lake, 12-12-2003) No. 2002-L-010, 2003-Ohio-6771, 2003 WL 22952773, Unreported. Child Custody ☞ 653; Constitutional Law ☞ 4396

Former husband's failure to bring claim to trial court's attention, that statutes setting forth procedure for modifying child custody decree and setting forth factors to consider in determining child's best interest were unconstitutional for lack of requirement of inquiry into parental unfitness, operated as waiver of claim on appeal. Winfield v. Winfield (Ohio App. 11 Dist., Lake, 12-12-2003) No. 2002-L-010, 2003-Ohio-6771, 2003 WL 22952773, Unreported. Child Custody ☞ 904

Fact that trial court, in determining that awarding custody to father was in child's best interest on motion to modify shared parenting agreement, made a finding of fact indicating that since parties' divorce, mother had eight pregnancies by five men and five abortions, had over 20 jobs as an adult, and was presently 34 years old did not indicate that trial court impermissibly applied reproval of mother standard; rather, fact was one of many that trial court used to determine stability of each of party's households. Lynch v. Lynch (Ohio App. 6 Dist., Huron, 03-07-2003) No. H-02-022, 2003-Ohio-1039, 2003 WL 876566, Unreported. Child Custody ☞ 659

No evidence existed to support magistrate's finding, in decision that recommended granting father's motion for change in custody, that mother failed to support her children; mother testified at hearing that she was employed as a health care provider working approximately 40 hours per week, she secured her own residence prior to the hearing on motion, and no evidence was presented to dispute testimony. Dunlop v. Dunlop (Ohio App. 2 Dist., Montgomery, 10-25-2002) No. 19313, 2002 Ohio 5828, 2002 WL 31398674, Unreported. Child Custody ☞ 637

RC 3109.04(D)(2) is unconstitutionally broad in that it applies a best interests of the child standard as a basis to grant custody to a nonparent rather than an "unfitness" or "unsuitability" of the parents standard, and thereby violates the due process clause of the Fourteenth Amendment to the United States Constitution by infringing on the fundamental right of parents to make decisions concerning the care, custody and control of their children. Esch v. Esch (Ohio App. 2 Dist., Montgomery, 02-23-2001) No. 18489, 2001 WL 173198, Unreported.

Trial court, in determining whether paternal grandmother should be granted custody of child, properly applied standard of whether a preponderance of the evidence supported finding that child's biological parents abandoned child, contractually relinquished custody, and demonstrated a total inability to provide care or support for child, or were otherwise unsuitable. Vance v. Vance (Ohio App. 2 Dist., 01-24-2003) 151 Ohio App.3d 391, 784 N.E.2d 172, 2003 Ohio 310. Child Custody ☞ 279

Even if trial court erred in custody proceeding by finding that paternal grandmother had violated court order by not returning child to mother, and thus violation could not be used as evidence to establish it was not in child's best interests to award grandmother custody, such error was harmless; to award custody to grandmother would have first required the determination that mother was unsuitable, and such evidence was irrelevant to such determination. Vance v. Vance (Ohio App. 2 Dist., 01-24-2003) 151 Ohio App.3d 391, 784 N.E.2d 172, 2003-Ohio-310. Child Custody ☞ 923(5)

Trial court abuses its discretion when it uses document filed in compliance with local rule as only evidence to remove child from mother's custody. Masters v. Masters (Ohio, 04-27-1994) 69 Ohio St.3d 83, 630 N.E.2d 665, 1994-Ohio-483. Child Custody ☞ 467

In a change-of-custody proceeding initiated by a motion in a divorce action, as between the parents of the children, it is not necessary for the court to determine a parent is unfit to be a custodian prior to ordering change of custody, but only that the change of circumstances occurring since the prior order of the court justifies such change of custody for the best interests of the children. Beamer v. Beamer (Seneca 1969) 17 Ohio App.2d 89, 244 N.E.2d 775, 46 O.O.2d 118. Child Custody ☞ 553

Where a minor child was entrusted to friends because the mother was unfit, and the father subsequently remarried and reclaimed the child, a court may not award custody to any person other than the father except upon a finding of the father's unfitness. Garabrandt v. Garabrandt (Ohio Com. Pl. 1953) 114 N.E.2d 919, 65 Ohio Law Abs. 380, 51 O.O. 319.

Where a child's mother has been determined to be an unsuitable parent, the father gives physical custody of the child to the maternal grandmother, the child undergoes brain surgery and is left with a soft skull, and the mother's boyfriend has a propensity for violence, an award of custody of the child to the maternal grandmother is proper despite the lack of a finding that the child's father is an unsuitable parent where such award of custody to a nonparent is in the best interest of the child. Mannering v Mannering, No. 559 (4th Dist Ct App, Jackson, 5–3–89).

63. —— Visitation generally, modification of rights and responsibilities and "change in circumstances"

Error in consideration of statute governing allocation of parental rights and responsibilities for care of children on former wife's motion to modify husband's overnight parenting schedule, rather than statute governing modification of parenting time or visitation, was harmless, where trial court referred to facts that corresponded with "best interests of the child" factors, including interactions between child and husband, child's adjustment to current schedule, and benefits child received as result of overnight parenting time. Banfield v. Banfield (Ohio App. 12 Dist., Clermont, 07-25-2011) No. CA2010-09-066, No. CA2010-09-068, 2011-Ohio-3638, 2011 WL 2989883, Unreported. Child Custody ☞ 923(4)

Remand was necessary for trial court to correct its entry of divorce judgment with respect to father's child visitation schedule to accurately reflect the stipulation of the parties that father would, during summer vacation, have the children until Monday's at 5 p.m., which the trial court, in fact, approved at the hearing; trial court's final judgment afforded father visitation until mother finished working on Mondays, without providing a set time. Kindig v. Kindig (Ohio App. 3 Dist., Allen, 10-04-2010) No. 1-10-13, 2010-Ohio-4805, 2010 WL 3836136, Unreported. Child Custody ☞ 924

Trial court acted within its discretion in divorce proceedings by cautiously granting visitation between mother and child on alternating weekends; although mother had made progress as a positive parental figure, mother had had temporary protection order and domestic violence charges against her arising out of her explosive temper, and there remained concern for mother's ability to manage her temper. Bristow v. Bristow (Ohio App. 12 Dist., Butler, 07-26-2010) No. CA2009-05-139, 2010-Ohio-3469, 2010 WL 2892759, Unreported. Child Custody ☞ 210

Trial court error, if any, in adopting portions of the magistrate's decision that relied on exhibits that were not formally admitted into evidence was harmless, in a judgment entry of divorce in which the court adopted the magistrate's recommendation that parental rights and responsibilities be allocated to the mother but modified the magistrate's findings on visitation; father conceded that the email in question listed his email address, but father stated that he could not remember sending any of the emails to mother, and, even if the emails were disregarded, the magistrate heard enough testimony from father to substantiate the factual conclusion that a tumultuous relationship existed between the parties. Kong v. Kong (Ohio App. 8 Dist., Cuyahoga, 07-08-2010) No. 93120, 2010-Ohio-3180, 2010 WL 2681835, Unreported. Child Custody ☞ 923(1)

Evidence supported the trial court's downward deviation from its own visitation guidelines by modifying the magistrate's initial decision to grant father only three weeks of visitation during summer vacation; father had been diagnosed with depression but he refused to take his medicine, and father refused to give child her medicine for diagnosed attention deficit disorder. Kong v. Kong (Ohio App. 8 Dist., Cuyahoga, 07-08-2010) No. 93120, 2010-Ohio-3180, 2010 WL 2681835, Unreported. Child Custody ☞ 504

Trial court acted within its discretion by entering order modifying father's parenting time with out-of-wedlock child, despite father's contention that a reduction in his visitation was based only on an in-camera interview with the child and the guardian ad litem's report. Midkiff v. Kuzniak (Ohio App. 7 Dist., Mahoning, 06-04-2010) No. 09-MA-104, 2010-Ohio-2531, 2010 WL 2249851, Unreported. Children Out–of–wedlock ☞ 20.10

Father's failure, in appellate brief, to point to pertinent parts of the record of hearing on mother's motion to modify father's visitation as to their out-of-wedlock child precluded appellate review of his argument that the trial court limited his ability to examine witnesses and present evidence in the hearing. Midkiff v. Kuzniak (Ohio App. 7 Dist., Mahoning, 06-04-2010) No. 09-MA-104, 2010-Ohio-2531, 2010 WL 2249851, Unreported. Children Out–of–wedlock ☞ 20.11

Trial court acted within its discretion by declining to issue an order to compel mother of out-of-wedlock child to produce tax returns upon father's discovery request, on mother's motion to modify father's visitation; no issues dealing with the child tax credit were pending before the court, and issues of potential errors on the tax returns were irrelevant. Midkiff v. Kuzniak (Ohio App. 7 Dist., Ma-

honing, 06-04-2010) No. 09-MA-104, 2010-Ohio-2531, 2010 WL 2249851, Unreported. Children Out–of–wedlock ☞ 20.10

Father of child born out of wedlock had sufficient notice of what would be addressed at hearing on various pending motions in child custody and child support case, specifically, that the issue of modifying father's visitation time was to be considered, and thus, order reducing father's parenting time was not reversible on the basis of father's contention that trial court did not respond to his purported motion asking the court what it would address at that hearing. Midkiff v. Kuzniak (Ohio App. 7 Dist., Mahoning, 06-04-2010) No. 09-MA-104, 2010-Ohio-2531, 2010 WL 2249851, Unreported. Children Out–of–wedlock ☞ 20.11

There was competent, credible evidence to support the magistrate's finding that unwed father would be more likely to honor and facilitate court-approved visitation; mother did not inform father of her intention of moving to Arizona, father attempted to contact mother concerning the move, but mother ignored his contacts until several weeks later, father allowed maternal grandmother visitation, and father was reasonable not to allow grandmother to take child to a family gathering, given grandmother's criminal record and grandmother's and grandmother's husband's excessive drinking. Cotterill v. Turner (Ohio App. 3 Dist., Hancock, 10-26-2009) No. 5-09-22, 2009-Ohio-5657, 2009 WL 3416001, Unreported. Children Out–of–wedlock ☞ 20.8

Father was not entitled to child support credit to cover visitation travel expenses, although mother was given a $231 credit to cover such expenses when father initially had custody of child following divorce and new visitation order placed additional burdens on father, as father was in a more tenable financial position to cover the costs associated with his travel to and from Virginia in order to see child. Pellettiere v. Pellettiere (Ohio App. 2 Dist., Montgomery, 10-09-2009) No. 23141, 2009-Ohio-5407, 2009 WL 3246751, Unreported. Child Support ☞ 350

Magistrate abused his discretion by failing to include overnight visits with father when he ordered a visitation schedule after deciding to award custody of child to mother, where mother, father, and a psychologist all testified that the overnight visits between father and child were successful, and mother even stated her willingness to increase the number of overnight visits as child got older. In re Kruthaupt (Ohio App. 1 Dist., Hamilton, 03-27-2009) No. C-080405, 2009-Ohio-1372, 2009 WL 804932, Unreported. Child Custody ☞ 210

Trial court order that failed to grant father independent parenting time with his out-of-wedlock child, but granted paternal grandparents regularly scheduled visitation, was not an abuse of discretion, in child custody modification proceeding that granted maternal grandparents legal custody of child; the trial court found that father had abandoned child, that he had shared parenting duties with paternal grandparents, and that father could visit child when he was at paternal grandparents' house. Smith v. Quigg (Ohio App. 5 Dist., Fairfield, 03-22-2006) No. 2005-CA-002, 2006-Ohio-1495, 2006 WL 786856, Unreported. Children Out–of–wedlock ☞ 20.10

For purposes of determining child custody incident to divorce, husband's occasional non-compliance with custody and visitation agreement did not amount to willful denial of wife's visitation rights, where husband testified that occasional delays in making child available for exchange were attributable to construction work in progress on his route, and "couple of occasions" on which husband failed to make child available for visitation resulted from parties' inability to communicate rather than from willful denial of visitation. Wingard v. Wingard (Ohio App. 2 Dist., Greene, 12-30-2005) No. 2005-CA-09, 2005-Ohio-7066, 2005 WL 3610302, Unreported. Child Custody ☞ 57

Magistrate appropriately considered "some concern" over wife's mental health, in resolving custody and visitation issues incident to divorce, where wife testified that she missed seven months of work due to depression because of her father's terminal illness and husband's announcement that he wanted a divorce, and that husband placed child in daycare during that time, although wife disagreed with that decision. Wingard v. Wingard (Ohio App. 2 Dist., Greene, 12-30-2005) No. 2005-CA-09, 2005-Ohio-7066, 2005 WL 3610302, Unreported. Child Custody ☞ 62; Child Custody ☞ 201

Magistrate's decision allowing visitation to occur between child and child's father in residence shared by father with his parents did not exceed scope of review to be conducted on remand for consideration of conditions of father's exercise of visitation rights, despite implication in such decision that other persons, including child's paternal grandfather, could be present in residence during visitation, where presence of others during scheduled visitation was implicit in inquiry into circumstances under which father could exercise his visitation rights given his physical disabilities. Arnold v. Arnold (Ohio App. 4 Dist., Athens, 09-27-2005) No. 04CA36, 2005-Ohio-5272, 2005 WL 2416378, Unreported. Child Custody ☞ 924

Trial court did not abuse its discretion in modifying former husband's visitation with child to permit visitation in residence shared by former husband and his parents, despite prohibition in original divorce decree of visitation between child and child's paternal grandfather, where modification was necessary to facilitate former husband's visitation with child due to former husband's disability and caretaking needs; former husband was confined to wheelchair, required constant care, and could not afford handicapped-accessible transportation to supervised visitation center. Arnold v. Arnold (Ohio App. 4 Dist., Athens, 09-27-2005) No. 04CA36, 2005-Ohio-5272, 2005 WL 2416378, Unreported. Child Custody ☞ 577

Ex-wife was in contempt of court's visitation order; many visits were missed, and there was ample evidence which, if believed, supported conclusion that ex-wife had not been cooperative with the visitation, observations of staff at the supervised visitation center were inconsistent with ex-wife's claims that she unequivocally encouraged children to visit ex-husband, and children's alleged reactions to modifications in visitation arrangements clearly paralleled ex-wife's substantial apprehension about moving toward supervised visitation away from the center and, ultimately, unsupervised visitation, in accordance with the court's orders. Forrester v. Forrester (Ohio App. 2 Dist., Greene, 09-30-2005) No. 2004 CA 81, 2005-Ohio-5230, 2005 WL 2403955, Unreported. Child Custody ☞ 854

Visitation order which granted father parenting time with parties' out-of-wedlock child every other weekend and alternate Monday and Thursday over nights was not against manifest weight of evidence, in that it was based on mutual agreement between parties. McCage v. Dingess (Ohio App. 5 Dist., Licking, 10-13-2004) No. 03CA111, 2004-Ohio-5692, 2004 WL 2391678, Unreported. Children Out–of–wedlock ☞ 20.9

Modification of parenting schedule to give father more equal parenting time with parties' out-of-wedlock child was not warranted, where father failed to show substantial change in child's circumstances or that modification would be in child's best interests, and relationship between mother and father was not amicable such that they could cooperate and make decisions jointly with respect to child. McCage v. Dingess (Ohio App. 5 Dist., Licking, 10-13-2004) No. 03CA111, 2004-Ohio-5692, 2004 WL 2391678, Unreported. Children Out–of–wedlock ☞ 20.10

Provision of shared parenting agreement regarding summer weekdays that former husband worked merely extended a right of visitation to former wife, which she was not required to exercise, rather than ordering her to provide childcare. Barnes v. Barnes (Ohio App. 2 Dist., Darke, 02-13-2004) No. 1613, 2004-Ohio-675, 2004 WL 260991, Unreported. Child Custody ☞ 141

In determining whether to modify father's visitation with nonmarital child, trial court should have made best-interest determination pursuant to factors in statute governing granting parenting time to parent, not statute governing allocating parental rights and responsibilities. In re Jones (Ohio App. 12 Dist., Butler, 09-08-2003) No. CA2002-10-256, 2003-Ohio-4748, 2003 WL 22071508, Unreported. Children Out–of–wedlock ☞ 20.10

Trial court's failure to include provision in judgment entry incorporating shared parenting agreement that was read into record that mother was limited to two trips to Canada with children, and only for purposes of visiting family, did not constitute abuse of discretion; parties did not clearly agree that mother would be limited to two trips per year, and, while parties did agree that trips were to visit family, father did not include such restriction in proposed judgment. Dobran v. Dobran (Ohio App. 7 Dist., Mahoning, 03-24-2003) No. 02 CA 14, 2003-Ohio-1605, 2003 WL 1689584, Unreported. Child Custody ⟳ 528

Grandmother never obtained prior to her motion for intervention, through statute, court order, or other means, any legal right to custody or visitation with her grandson, nor any legal interest in the care and custody of her grandson, which would have allowed her to intervene as of right in child protection matter; grandmother's claimed interest in her grandson's welfare or desire for custody and in visitation were not legally protectable, and grandmother made no attempts to become involved in child's life until trial court granted permanent custody to county department of job and family services. In re Hoffman (Ohio App. 5 Dist., Stark, 03-03-2003) No. 2002CA0419, No. 2002CA0422, 2003-Ohio-1241, 2003 WL 1193770, Unreported. Infants ⟳ 200

Appropriate and applicable standard for considering questions of modification of visitation is set forth in statute governing parenting time rights rather than statute that sets forth the specific rules for determining when a court may modify a custody decree. Flynn v. Flynn (Ohio App. 10 Dist., Franklin, 03-06-2003) No. 02AP-801, 2003-Ohio-990, 2003 WL 759174, Unreported. Child Custody ⟳ 577

Any error committed by trial court in failing to specifically refer to the visitation best-interest factors, when making its decision to prohibit four of mother's family members from having contact with children during mother's visitation, was harmless, where many of the visitation best-interest factors had analogues within the custody best-interest factors, trial court analyzed matter under the custody best-interest factors, and trial court's judgment evinced consideration of the relevant visitation factors. Troyer v. Troyer (Ohio App. 7 Dist., 06-28-2010) 2010 -Ohio- 3276, 2010 WL 2749051. Child Custody ⟳ 923(3)

Trial court limited mother's visitation not out of moral or religious concerns but, rather, out of concerns for the safety and welfare of the children, which was a best-interest factor recognized by visitation statute, and, thus, trial court was not required to find a direct adverse impact upon children for purposes of restraining four of mother's family members from having contact with children during mother's visitation. Troyer v. Troyer (Ohio App. 7 Dist., 06-28-2010) 2010 -Ohio- 3276, 2010 WL 2749051. Child Custody ⟳ 219

Trial court limited mother's visitation not out of moral or religious concerns, but rather out of concerns for the safety and welfare of the children, which was a best-interest factor recognized by visitation statute, and thus, trial court was not required to find a direct adverse impact upon children for purposes of restraining four of mother's family members from having contact with children during mother's visitation; although trial court did not specifically cite to the visitation best interest factors, its judgment, along with the magistrate's deci-

sion which it adopted, did evince consideration of the relevant factors. Troyer v. Troyer (Ohio App. 7 Dist., 06-28-2010) 2010 -Ohio- 3276, 2010 WL 2749051. Child Custody ⟳ 219; Child Custody ⟳ 511

Competent and credible evidence established that it was not in children's best interest to have contact with their maternal uncle during their limited visitation with mother, thus supporting issuance of restraining order prohibiting such contact, in action in which father sought allocation of parental rights and responsibilities; evidence showed that the uncle had a history of sexually abusing young children in the same religious community in which mother resided. Troyer v. Troyer (Ohio App. 7 Dist., 06-28-2010) 188 Ohio App.3d 543, 936 N.E.2d 102, 2010-Ohio-3276. Child Custody ⟳ 219

Competent and credible evidence established that it was not in children's best interest to have contact with their maternal uncle during their limited visitation with mother, thus supporting issuance of restraining order prohibiting such contact, in action in which father sought allocation of parental rights and responsibilities; evidence showed that the uncle had a history of mental health issues, namely a psychotic episode that lasted for several days and was witnessed by young children in the community, including some under the age of ten, the uncle threatened life of sheriff three separate times, and he broke into the home of children's paternal grandfather and assaulted grandfather. Troyer v. Troyer (Ohio App. 7 Dist., 06-28-2010) 188 Ohio App.3d 543, 936 N.E.2d 102, 2010-Ohio-3276. Child Custody ⟳ 219

Competent and credible evidence established that it was not in children's best interest to have contact with their maternal uncle during their limited visitation with mother, thus supporting issuance of restraining order prohibiting such contact, in action in which father sought allocation of parental rights and responsibilities; there was testimony that the uncle acted maliciously towards his brother in the presence of the brother's young children, and uncle admitted holding another brother down on the ground in freezing temperatures throughout the night while the brother had a psychotic episode. Troyer v. Troyer (Ohio App. 7 Dist., 06-28-2010) 188 Ohio App.3d 543, 936 N.E.2d 102, 2010-Ohio-3276. Child Custody ⟳ 219

Competent and credible evidence established that it was not in children's best interest to have contact with their maternal grandfather during their limited visitation with mother, thus supporting issuance of restraining order prohibiting such contact, in action in which father sought allocation of parental rights and responsibilities; evidence showed that grandfather abused his authority as bishop of local religious community by preventing father from having contact with children for a period of nine months during which he missed the birth of his second child, and other witnesses testified about how they too had been prevented from seeing their loved ones under similar circumstances. Troyer v. Troyer (Ohio App. 7 Dist., 06-28-2010) 188 Ohio App.3d

543, 936 N.E.2d 102, 2010-Ohio-3276. Child Custody ☞ 533; Child Custody ☞ 916

Former husband's threat to reduce time children spent with former wife was not sufficient to establish significant change of circumstance that would warrant modifying custody regarding shared parenting plan. Lindman v. Geissler (Ohio App. 5 Dist., 04-23-2007) 171 Ohio App.3d 650, 872 N.E.2d 356, 2007-Ohio-2003. Child Custody ☞ 576

Former wife's petition to transfer jurisdiction over child custody matters from court of state in which dissolution was originally entered, and for modification of visitation and child support originally established in dissolution decree, did not place parenting determination at issue, and Uniform Child Custody Jurisdiction Act (UCCJA) was therefore inapplicable. In re Monroe (Ohio App. 7 Dist., 03-24-1999) 133 Ohio App.3d 294, 727 N.E.2d 953. Child Custody ☞ 702; Child Custody ☞ 706; Child Support ☞ 502

Modification of child visitation is governed by statute that specifically addresses visitation rights, rather than by statute that governs child custody, i.e., "parental rights and responsibilities." Braatz v. Braatz (Ohio, 03-24-1999) 85 Ohio St.3d 40, 706 N.E.2d 1218, 1999-Ohio-203. Child Custody ☞ 577

Trial court acted within its discretion in refusing to find former husband in contempt for his technical violation of custody order from divorce proceeding in picking up parties' children at former wife's home on evening which was not one of his scheduled visitation nights, where former wife was in hospital that evening, children were left at home without adult present, and children telephoned former husband. Brooks v. Brooks (Ohio App. 10 Dist., 12-24-1996) 117 Ohio App.3d 19, 689 N.E.2d 987. Child Custody ☞ 970

An extended visitation order at issue was not the equivalent of a formal modification of a prior custody decree. State ex rel. Scordato v. George (Ohio 1981) 65 Ohio St.2d 128, 419 N.E.2d 4, 19 O.O.3d 318.

The mere statement of a twelve-year-old child of divorced parents that she did not want to see her father again was insufficient evidence to justify a complete refusal to permit such father to visit her, and a statement by the mother's counsel that defendant had been guilty of misconduct toward his stepdaughter was of no probative value. Marsh v. Marsh (Franklin 1954) 126 N.E.2d 468, 69 Ohio Law Abs. 539.

64. —— Visitation interference, modification of rights and responsibilities and "change in circumstances"

Contempt imposed against father in child visitation dispute was civil, not criminal, contempt, and thus double jeopardy principles did not apply to prohibit additional sanctions, where contempt was designed to remedy the effects of father's contempt in failing to comply with grandparents' visitation award. Estate of Harrold v. Collier (Ohio App. 9 Dist., Wayne, 07-26-2010) No. 09CA0060, 2010-Ohio-3457, 2010 WL 2892262, Unreported. Child Custody ☞ 854; Double Jeopardy ☞ 34

Unwed father was not in contempt of court when he scheduled a vacation with child during mother's visitation time because mother did not tell father that the child could not go, but father did appear to take advantage of mother by not offering to let her make up her lost visitation time, and as such, trial court would make mother whole by granting her extra visitation time. Wooten v. Schwaderer (Ohio App. 3 Dist., Union, 06-30-2008) No. 14-08-13, 2008-Ohio-3221, 2008 WL 2582913, Unreported. Children Out–of–wedlock ☞ 20

Although father was not required to move for modification of visitation schedule in order for trial court to modify the schedule to father's benefit on wife's motion for modification, the trial court acted outside its discretion by modifying the schedule without basing its decision on whether the modification was in the best interest of the children, requiring reversal and remand, even though trial court found that mother had interfered with father's visitation. Taylor v. Hamlin-Scanlon (Ohio App. 9 Dist., Summit, 04-23-2008) No. 23873, 2008-Ohio-1912, 2008 WL 1808366, Unreported. Child Custody ☞ 554; Child Custody ☞ 610; Child Custody ☞ 924

Evidence in proceedings on husband's complaint for divorce was sufficient to support designation of husband as child's residential parent and legal custodian, where some concern as to wife's mental health was appropriate, husband's occasional non-compliance with existing custody and visitation agreement did not amount to willful denial of wife's visitation rights, husband's use of child's custodial account was not factor weighing against award of custody, and husband was sufficiently familiar with child's health needs and took appropriate steps to deal with them. Wingard v. Wingard (Ohio App. 2 Dist., Greene, 12-30-2005) No. 2005-CA-09, 2005-Ohio-7066, 2005 WL 3610302, Unreported. Child Custody ☞ 48; Child Custody ☞ 57; Child Custody ☞ 62; Child Custody ☞ 81

Evidence supported trial court's determination that its custody modification, which changed the residential custodian from divorced wife to former husband, served the best interests of the parties' children; trial court found that husband was clearly the parent who would honor and facilitate parenting time and companionship rights, and found that wife would not honor parenting time. Valentine v. Valentine (Ohio App. 12 Dist., Butler, 11-21-2005) No. CA2004-12-314, 2005-Ohio-6163, 2005 WL 3096587, Unreported. Child Custody ☞ 569

Trial court did not abuse its discretion in finding a change of circumstances warranting modification of the residential custodian from divorced wife to former husband; trial court noted that, despite its attempts to foster parental cooperation through court orders, admonitions, and contempt citations, wife had interfered in husband's parenting time and the children were being negatively impacted by the parents' ongoing difficulties. Valentine v. Valentine (Ohio App. 12 Dist., Butler, 11-21-2005) No. CA2004-12-314, 2005-Ohio-6163, 2005 WL 3096587, Unreported. Child Custody ☞ 552; Child Custody ☞ 569

Designating husband as sole residential parent was not against manifest weight of evidence in divorce proceeding; although wife argued she was better trained and experienced in child welfare, witnesses testified as to wife's harsh forms of discipline and refusal to let father have his parenting time. Jackson v. Copeland-Jackson (Ohio App. 3 Dist., Paulding, 10-12-2004) No. 11-04-05, 2004-Ohio-5426, 2004 WL 2283193, Unreported. Child Custody ☞ 51; Child Custody ☞ 57; Child Custody ☞ 58

In determining children's best interest and awarding custody to husband in divorce proceeding, trial court properly considered statutory factors of which parent was likely to honor visitation, whether child was abused by parent, and whether residential parent denied other parent parenting time, where husband experienced resistance from wife when he attempted to see children, wife's family would not allow husband to take children when he arrived to pick them up for visitation, wife refused to allow husband to speak to children over telephone, and wife hit child with belt. Jackson v. Copeland-Jackson (Ohio App. 3 Dist., Paulding, 10-12-2004) No. 11-04-05, 2004-Ohio-5426, 2004 WL 2283193, Unreported. Child Custody ☞ 57; Child Custody ☞ 58

Father failed to meet burden of showing change in circumstances necessitating reallocation of parental rights and responsibilities in child custody proceeding; father asserted that mother was frustrating his visitation with child, constituting change in circumstances, but trial court did not so find, record reflected that certain events, including child's illness, hindered "by the book" visitation, on which father insisted, and father's inflexible compliance with visitation schedule was unrealistic. Venuto v. Pochiro (Ohio App. 7 Dist., Mahoning, 05-21-2004) No. 02 CA 225, 2004-Ohio-2631, 2004 WL 1152055, Unreported. Child Custody ☞ 569

Divorced mother failed to establish a change of circumstances warranting modification of child custody order, despite her allegation that father obstructed and interfered with her visitation rights; record reflected that father caused little, if any, interference with mother's visitation rights, that mother routinely exercised her visitation rights, and that father only denied her requests for additional time beyond existing court order. Hinton v. Hinton (Ohio App. 4 Dist., Washington, 05-28-2003) No. 02CA54, 2003-Ohio-2785, 2003 WL 21255919, Unreported. Child Custody ☞ 638

Evidence was sufficient to support finding that a change in circumstances existed warranting a change in custody; after the parties were divorced, and mother was designated as residential parent, mother continuously interrupted father's visitation and companionship with the children in contravention of the court-ordered schedule. Bland v. Bland (Ohio App. 9 Dist., Summit, 02-26-2003) No. 21228, 2003-Ohio-828, 2003 WL 470180, Unreported. Child Custody ☞ 569

It is in the best interest of a fourteen-year-old child with Down's Syndrome to be removed from the custody of his mother who has been his primary caretaker since birth and to designate the father as legal custodian and residential parent where it is found that (1) the mother has willfully denied the father's visitation rights and (2) the father is the parent more likely to facilitate visitation. Deimling v. Messer (Ohio App. 12 Dist., Clermont, 03-16-1998) No. CA97-07-070, 1998 WL 117208, Unreported.

The court may award custody to a mother who previously interfered with visitation rights and who is accused of immoral conduct where the court considers all relevant factors concerning the best interests of the child, there is no evidence that the mother's alleged immoral conduct had any impact on the one and one-half year old child, and an intention is stated to tolerate no further interference with visitation. McDonald v. Johnston (Ohio App. 3 Dist., Allen, 11-22-1995) No. 1-95-37, 1995 WL 695086, Unreported.

Evidence that on some occasions former husband might not have been entitled to visitation under the visitation schedule, and that former husband had failed to pick up child at scheduled time or had canceled visitation on some occasions, established that maternal grandmother, who had custody of child, did not interfere with visitation to such degree as to constitute change of circumstances, as element of former husband's request for change of custody. Wilburn v. Wilburn (Ohio App. 2 Dist., 06-15-2001) 144 Ohio App.3d 279, 760 N.E.2d 7. Child Custody ☞ 637

Evidence supported determination that mother's interference with visitation constituted a "change in circumstances" warranting custody modification, despite father's child support arrearages, and even though guardian ad litem had found that the children were thriving while living with mother; father was currently paying child support and diligently working on reducing his arrearages, he had been forced to seek court intervention to enjoy visitation on at least three separate occasions while mother had custody, and the children were of relatively tender years, and had shown great flexibility in adjusting to new environments. Clark v. Smith (Ohio App. 3 Dist., 12-08-1998) 130 Ohio App.3d 648, 720 N.E.2d 973. Child Custody ☞ 637

Evidence in child custody modification proceeding supported determination that father did not interfere with visitation between mother and children, despite incident in which father's cohabitant took the children to Kentucky to see her brother's graduation, during which time mother could not reach them; father testified that he attempted to call mother and let her know the children would be out of town. Clark v. Smith (Ohio App. 3 Dist.,

12-08-1998) 130 Ohio App.3d 648, 720 N.E.2d 973. Child Custody ⬚ 637

Custodial parent's interference with visitation by a noncustodial parent may be considered as part of a "change in circumstances" which would allow for modification of custody. Clark v. Smith (Ohio App. 3 Dist., 12-08-1998) 130 Ohio App.3d 648, 720 N.E.2d 973. Child Custody ⬚ 555

Custodial parent's interference with visitation by noncustodial parent may be considered "change of circumstances" which would allow for modification of custody. Mitchell v. Mitchell (Ohio App. 2 Dist., 03-20-1998) 126 Ohio App.3d 500, 710 N.E.2d 793. Child Custody ⬚ 555

For purposes of custodial parent's request that noncustodial parent be sanctioned for filing motion for modification of custody lacking basis in law or fact, custodial parent's alleged denial of visitation to noncustodial parent, supported by evidence in record, constituted "change of circumstances" sufficient, standing alone, to provide legal basis for noncustodial parent's motion. Mitchell v. Mitchell (Ohio App. 2 Dist., 03-20-1998) 126 Ohio App.3d 500, 710 N.E.2d 793. Child Custody ⬚ 555

Trial court's modification of original custody decree to designate father of child born out of wedlock as child's residential parent was supported by substantial evidence; mother requested complete termination of father's visitation rights, mother and her new husband were hostile to child's father, child entered kindergarten subsequent to issuance of original decree, and mother and new husband refused to modify visitation agreement to permit father to spend time with child under child's new school schedule. Davis v. Flickinger (Ohio, 02-12-1997) 77 Ohio St.3d 415, 674 N.E.2d 1159, 1997-Ohio-260. Children Out–of–wedlock ⬚ 20.10

Request by mother of minor child born out of wedlock for complete termination of father's visitation rights could be considered by trial court in evaluating best interest of child as required by custody statute, as such request added to hostility between child's parents and demonstrated mother's disregard for best interest of child. Davis v. Flickinger (Ohio, 02-12-1997) 77 Ohio St.3d 415, 674 N.E.2d 1159, 1997-Ohio-260. Children Out–of–wedlock ⬚ 20.9

Trial court could consider, in determining whether to modify custodial status of child born out of wedlock, change in circumstances created by maturing of child; child entered kindergarten subsequent to original decree, and residential parent was unwilling to provide any substitute arrangements that would enable nonresidential parent to spend as much time with child as before child was in kindergarten. Davis v. Flickinger (Ohio, 02-12-1997) 77 Ohio St.3d 415, 674 N.E.2d 1159, 1997-Ohio-260. Children Out–of–wedlock ⬚ 20.10

Trial court could consider, in determining whether to modify custodial status of child born out of wedlock, issue of which parent was more likely to honor and facilitate visitation, and factor that issue into best interest of child. Davis v. Flickinger (Ohio, 02-12-1997) 77 Ohio St.3d 415, 674 N.E.2d 1159, 1997-Ohio-260. Children Out–of–wedlock ⬚ 20.10

A trial court is without authority to modify a mother's custody because of her failure to encourage or implement regular visitation with grandparents pursuant to a court's visitation order. Truitt v. Truitt (Preble 1989) 65 Ohio App.3d 126, 583 N.E.2d 331. Child Custody ⬚ 872

Child custody may not be altered as a sanction for contempt of court. Truitt v. Truitt (Preble 1989) 65 Ohio App.3d 126, 583 N.E.2d 331. Child Custody ⬚ 552

Termination of a mother's custody for her bitterness and uncooperativeness regarding a grandparent's visitation order is unwarranted. Truitt v. Truitt (Preble 1989) 65 Ohio App.3d 126, 583 N.E.2d 331.

Modification of a custody order is not among the available sanctions under RC 2705.05(A) as punishment for contempt; a trial court may not as a sanction for contempt of court arising from a custodial parent's interference with a noncustodial parent's visitation rights transfer the authority to the noncustodial parent to grant permission to a minor child to apply for a driver's license or to participate in extracurricular school activities as these changes actually modify custody, which is not a sanction authorized by RC 2705.05(A). Fry v. Fry (Paulding 1989) 64 Ohio App.3d 519, 582 N.E.2d 11.

Custody of children may not be changed merely as a sanction for contempt of a court order. Sontag v Sontag, No. C–800223 (1st Dist Ct App, Hamilton, 4–15–81).

The denial of visitation by the custodial parent to the noncustodial parent is not sufficient grounds to justify a change in custody under RC 3109.04(B). In re Lehman, No. 87AP020012 (5th Dist Ct App, Tuscarawas, 7–20–87).

Pursuant to a motion for change of custody hearing, a custodial parent's prior citation for contempt in violating the visitation rights of the other parent is not sufficient to establish a change of circumstances under RC 3109.04(B). Mundschenk v Mundschenk, No. 81AP–406 (10th Dist Ct App, Franklin, 3–25–82).

65. —— Procedural issues, hearings, evidence generally, modification of rights and responsibilities and "change in circumstances"

Trial court abused its discretion in issuing a conditional shared parenting order in a proceeding to determine child custody, where neither mother nor father had requested a conditional shared parenting plan or filed a proposed shared parenting plan. Kish v. Dobos (Ohio App. 5 Dist., Delaware, 09-16-2009) No. 08 CAF 10 0058, 2009-Ohio-4895, 2009 WL 2973504, Unreported. Child Custody ⬚ 414

Trial court, in a proceeding on father's motion for modification of child custody, which arose in trial court, specifically the Domestic Relations Division of the Court of Common Pleas, subsequent to a parentage action, was required to certify the case to the juvenile court for further proceedings after trial court determined that it was not in the best interest of the children to be placed with either father or mother, given the written report of a court-appointed investigator that essentially indicated that neither parent was a suitable placement for the children. Horn v. Frazier (Ohio App. 5 Dist., Licking, 01-07-2009) No. 08 CA 000068, 2009-Ohio-51, 2009 WL 50608, Unreported. Courts ☞ 486

Trial court abused its discretion in finding former wife in contempt of court based on its determination that she violated the parties' visitation schedule; the parties never reached a formal long-term agreement regarding visitation, the trial court never imposed the court's shared parenting time schedule on the parties, and the trial court never imposed any specific visitation obligations upon wife. Malson v. Berger (Ohio App. 9 Dist., Summit, 12-30-2005) No. 22800, 2005-Ohio-6987, 2005 WL 3556411, Unreported. Child Custody ☞ 854

Trial court's consideration, in hearing on complaint for modification of custody of minor child born out-of-wedlock, of licensed counselor's testimony regarding veracity of child's statements was not plain error, where counselor specifically testified that even if child fabricated allegations of domestic violence between child's mother and mother's boyfriend entirely, counselor's recommendation to place child with father would not change; mother suffered no prejudice from admission of testimony because outcome would not have been different. McClay v. Reed (Ohio App. 5 Dist., Guernsey, 12-29-2004) No. 2004CA-4, 2004-Ohio-7304, 2004 WL 3563008, Unreported. Children Out–of–wedlock ☞ 20.11

Trial court's error, if any, in admitting hearsay testimony of father and his current wife in hearing on complaint for modification of custody of child born out-of-wedlock was harmless, where trial court heard the same testimony from child's licensed counselor, whose testimony was properly admitted, from child's guardian ad litem, and perhaps from child herself; error did not affect the outcome of the case. McClay v. Reed (Ohio App. 5 Dist., Guernsey, 12-29-2004) No. 2004CA-4, 2004-Ohio-7304, 2004 WL 3563008, Unreported. Children Out–of–wedlock ☞ 20.11

Trial court was required to consider threshold question of change in circumstances prior to ruling on cross-motions for reallocation of parental rights. Loudermilk v. Lynch (Ohio App. 11 Dist., Ashtabula, 09-30-2004) No. 2002-A-0044, No. 2002-A-0045, 2004-Ohio-5299, 2004 WL 2803411, Unreported. Child Custody ☞ 555

Dismissal of ex-husband's post-dissolution motions to show cause and motion to modify child support, in which he sought to enforce his visitation rights with children and to reduce his support obligation, was appropriate under rule governing dismissal of actions; ex-husband had notice of possibility of dismissal through his presence at hearing, and he was given opportunity to explain his reasons for being in default of order that parties' prepare judgment entry, both at hearing and through objections to magistrate's decision, but he did not do so. Riedel v. Riedel (Ohio App. 9 Dist., Medina, 08-25-2004) No. 03CA0087-M, 2004-Ohio-4458, 2004 WL 1888409, Unreported. Child Custody ☞ 850; Child Support ☞ 469

Trial court did not require father, who sought to modify prior child custody decree as to out-of-wedlock child, to meet higher burden of proof than that required by statute providing that court shall not modify prior custody decree unless it finds that change in circumstances has occurred; although court's judgment entry used phrase "substantial change in circumstance," court went on to state that it did not find any change in circumstances required under statute, and case law demonstrated that court must examine whether change in circumstances is of sufficient import to warrant modification of prior custody decree. Duer v. Moonshower (Ohio App. 3 Dist., Van, 08-02-2004) No. 15-03-15, 2004-Ohio-4025, 2004 WL 1718234, Unreported. Children Out–of–wedlock ☞ 20.10

Ex-wife had standing to file appeal from order granting ex-husband's motion to remove attorney retained by ex-wife to represent child in proceeding to modify parental rights and determine child support; parents may assert their child's rights to counsel because of unique nature of parent/child relationship. Jennings-Harder v. Yarmesch (Ohio App. 8 Dist., Cuyahoga, 07-29-2004) No. 83984, 2004-Ohio-3960, 2004 WL 1688538, Unreported. Child Custody ☞ 903; Child Support ☞ 538

Trial court's order granting ex-husband's motion to remove attorney retained by ex-wife to represent child in proceeding to modify parental rights and determine child support was final and appealable, where order involved substantial right and was made in special proceeding. Jennings-Harder v. Yarmesch (Ohio App. 8 Dist., Cuyahoga, 07-29-2004) No. 83984, 2004-Ohio-3960, 2004 WL 1688538, Unreported. Child Custody ☞ 902; Child Support ☞ 537

Magistrate, and trial court in adopting magistrate's decision in its entirety, abused discretion afforded in child custody cases in denying former husband's motion for reallocation of parental rights and responsibilities without first conducting evidentiary hearing to determine whether change of circumstances had occurred. Green v. Green (Ohio App. 3 Dist., Union, 01-20-2004) No. 14-03-29, 2004-Ohio-185, 2004 WL 77881, Unreported. Child Custody ☞ 500; Child Custody ☞ 504

Even if factual findings regarding former wife's payment of her credit card debt without aid from former husband and regarding children's adjustment to wife's home and their school were in error, such findings did not amount to reversible error in proceeding designating wife as residential parent. Mills v. Mills (Ohio App. 11 Dist., Trumbull,

12-05-2003) No. 2002-T-0102, 2003-Ohio-6676, 2003 WL 22928461, Unreported. Child Custody ⊗ 922(3)

There was no record to support former husband's claim that statements of his minor children qualified under any hearsay exception, and thus statements were inadmissible in proceedings to determine whether husband or former wife would be residential parent; husband failed to supply transcript or record of proceedings. Mills v. Mills (Ohio App. 11 Dist., Trumbull, 12-05-2003) No. 2002-T-0102, 2003-Ohio-6676, 2003 WL 22928461, Unreported. Child Custody ⊗ 451; Child Custody ⊗ 907

Magistrate Court lawfully entered nunc pro tunc order, which corrected misspelling and typographical errors in modification of parenting agreement order; Magistrate Court had authority to enter nunc pro tunc orders, and correction of typographical errors was a correct use of such orders. Keller v. Keller (Ohio App. 4 Dist., Jackson, 11-26-2003) No. 02CA19, No. 03CA3, 2003-Ohio-6462, 2003 WL 22860832, Unreported, appeal not allowed 102 Ohio St.3d 1421, 807 N.E.2d 366, 2004-Ohio-2003. Child Custody ⊗ 661

Former husband's letter to Magistrate Court, inquiring as to status of case concerning modification of parenting agreement, was not an unlawful ex parte contact; case had been pending for over a year, and communication simply demonstrated a concern over resolution of case. Keller v. Keller (Ohio App. 4 Dist., Jackson, 11-26-2003) No. 02CA19, No. 03CA3, 2003-Ohio-6462, 2003 WL 22860832, Unreported, appeal not allowed 102 Ohio St.3d 1421, 807 N.E.2d 366, 2004-Ohio-2003. Child Custody ⊗ 650

Fifteen-month interval between conclusion of hearing and issuance of modified parenting plan, as sought by former husband, did not prejudice former wife, even though former wife claimed decision referred to nonexistent witnesses, confused some names of witnesses, and overlooked some testimony; mistakes did not create any real prejudice, and testimony was not overlooked, but rather not credited. Keller v. Keller (Ohio App. 4 Dist., Jackson, 11-26-2003) No. 02CA19, No. 03CA3, 2003-Ohio-6462, 2003 WL 22860832, Unreported, appeal not allowed 102 Ohio St.3d 1421, 807 N.E.2d 366, 2004-Ohio-2003. Child Custody ⊗ 923(4)

Magistrate Court did not act egregiously in delaying its disposition of former wife's request for a new trial, after court modified parenting plan, where new trial was made as part of a multi-pronged motion, and it appeared that the trial court had simply overlooked the request for new trial. Keller v. Keller (Ohio App. 4 Dist., Jackson, 11-26-2003) No. 02CA19, No. 03CA3, 2003-Ohio-6462, 2003 WL 22860832, Unreported, appeal not allowed 102 Ohio St.3d 1421, 807 N.E.2d 366, 2004-Ohio-2003. Child Custody ⊗ 660

Trial court which dismissed, for lack of jurisdiction, motion to modify child custody and support

order issued by other county, did not have authority to reinstate matter, and thus mother who brought motion was not entitled to writ of mandamus compelling court to reinstate matter; county that originally obtained jurisdiction retained exclusive jurisdiction over matter. State ex rel. Allen v. Burney (Ohio App. 8 Dist., Cuyahoga, 09-29-2003) No. 83066, 2003-Ohio-5253, 2003 WL 22251784, Unreported. Child Custody ⊗ 600; Child Support ⊗ 320; Courts ⊗ 472.5

Former husband's motion to reinstate his prior motion to modify child support was nullity, where motion was equivalent of motion for reconsideration and was made after final judgment. Grubic v. Grubic (Ohio App. 8 Dist., Cuyahoga, 07-10-2003) No. 82462, 2003-Ohio-3680, 2003 WL 21570497, Unreported, appeal not allowed 100 Ohio St.3d 1507, 799 N.E.2d 186, 2003-Ohio-6161. Child Support ⊗ 340

Trial court was not required to conduct hearing on parties' financial ability to pay before ordering that former wife pay one-half of cost of retainer fee for forensic examination for custody and visitation purposes that was sought by guardian ad litem regarding former husband's motion to modify custody, since trial court was in position to make factual determination from prior record and orders. Citta-Pietrolungo v. Pietrolungo (Ohio App. 8 Dist., Cuyahoga, 06-26-2003) No. 81943, No. 82069, 2003-Ohio-3357, 2003 WL 21469770, Unreported. Child Custody ⊗ 943

Medical and psychological evaluation of wife's new husband was not relevant to issues in controversy pending before trial court, and therefore former husband was not entitled to order for such evaluation; pending matters were designation of airport to exchange companionship of children, contempt against former husband for failure to provide health insurance and pay medical bills, and contempt against former wife for failure to notify former husband of her relocation and modification of visitation necessitated thereby. Beatley v. Beatly (Ohio App. 5 Dist., Delaware, 05-14-2003) No. 02CAF11050, 2003-Ohio-2510, 2003 WL 21121843, Unreported. Child Custody ⊗ 617; Child Custody ⊗ 850; Child Support ⊗ 476

Former husband did not have burden to show change of circumstances and to show that modification was in best interests of children, in former husband's motion that sought parenting time during periods former wife would have children with baby-sitter, even though former husband moved for a modification of terms of divorce decree regarding parenting time, since former husband was actually seeking clarification regarding right of first refusal, which was an issue not addressed in divorce decree. Lassiter v. Lassiter (Ohio App. 1 Dist., Hamilton, 05-09-2003) No. C-020494, No. C-020370, No. C-020128, 2003-Ohio-2333, 2003 WL 21034193, Unreported. Child Custody ⊗ 526; Child Custody ⊗ 633

Former husband waived issue on appeal of trial court's failure to rule on husband's motion to change custody of parties' daughter, where husband's objection to magistrate's decision did not specifically address issue. McCain v. McCain (Ohio App. 5 Dist., Stark, 04-28-2003) No. 2002CA00267, 2003-Ohio-2179, 2003 WL 1983747, Unreported. Child Custody ⬱ 904

Order finding mother in contempt for not permitting or facilitating communication between father and children, and for not providing father with updated names and information concerning children's health care providers, was abuse of discretion, where mother had not violated existing order; neither initial judgment and decree of divorce, nor subsequent orders modifying decree, contained any provisions dealing with communications between non-residential parent and children, and provision of divorce decree stating that each party shall have full access to all school, medical, and health records of minor children, did not require either party to provide to other party names or other pertinent information concerning children's care-providers. Ryan v. Ryan (Ohio App. 2 Dist., Greene, 04-25-2003) No. 2002-CA-87, 2003-Ohio-2087, 2003 WL 1949792, Unreported. Child Custody ⬱ 853

By suspending mother's sentence for contempt for violation of visitation order, trial court allowed mother to purge herself of contempt through compliance with court's order. Caldwell v. Caldwell (Ohio App. 4 Dist., Gallia, 04-02-2003) No. 02CA17, 2003-Ohio-1752, 2003 WL 1795247, Unreported. Child Custody ⬱ 873

Trial court's denial to grant a stay of execution of judgment modifying residential custodian of parties' four children from mother to father was not abuse of discretion, where trial court indicated the desire to end litigation and have the parenting plan go into effect, and informed mother that she had an appeal issue. Bland v. Bland (Ohio App. 9 Dist., Summit, 02-26-2003) No. 21228, 2003-Ohio-828, 2003 WL 470180, Unreported. Child Custody ⬱ 661

Assuming, arguendo, that custody order issued by juvenile court one year after divorce decree which initially determined custody was "prior decree" from which trial court should have determined whether a change of circumstances occurred to warrant modification of custody, trial court still had right to review any facts that were unknown to court at time of prior decree, and thus, if juvenile court did not know about any of facts that occurred after divorce, but before its order, trial court could have properly considered those facts as well. Bland v. Bland (Ohio App. 9 Dist., Summit, 02-26-2003) No. 21228, 2003-Ohio-828, 2003 WL 470180, Unreported. Child Custody ⬱ 557(3)

"Prior decree" from which the trial court was to determine whether change in circumstances occurred as would warrant modification of custody was the divorce decree, even though a subsequent custody decree had apparently issued by the juvenile court, where parties never filed a copy of the juvenile court order, rendering reviewing court unable to determine whether the purported order was

the "prior decree." Bland v. Bland (Ohio App. 9 Dist., Summit, 02-26-2003) No. 21228, 2003-Ohio-828, 2003 WL 470180, Unreported. Child Custody ⬱ 557(1)

Mother's alleged filing of false affidavit and misstating that a consent decree entered into approximately 12 years ago was in effect at date of child custody modification hearing, when, in truth, a new consent decree had been entered into approximately four years ago, did not attempt to defile the court or impede operation of justice, and thus, such actions did not constitute a fraud on the court. Short v. Short (Ohio App. 6 Dist., Fulton, 01-31-2003) No. F-02-021, 2003-Ohio-489, 2003 WL 220450, Unreported. Child Custody ⬱ 661

Pursuant to RC 3109.04 the trial court is not required to find a change in circumstances before terminating a shared parenting plan; on the other hand, before a trial court can modify a shared parenting plan, a change of circumstances must be found. Massengill v. Massengill (Ohio App. 2 Dist., Montgomery, 03-23-2001) No. 18610, 2001 WL 283001, Unreported.

Clear intent of statute requiring a change of circumstances for modification of a prior decree allocating parental rights and responsibilities is to spare children from a constant tug of war between their parents who would file a motion for change of custody each time the parent out of custody thought he or she could provide the child a better environment; the statute is an attempt to provide some stability to the custodial status of the children, even though the parent out of custody may be able to prove that he or she can provide a better environment. Fisher v. Hasenjager (Ohio, 10-25-2007) 116 Ohio St.3d 53, 876 N.E.2d 546, 2007-Ohio-5589. Child Custody ⬱ 555

Trial court did not abuse its discretion or err as a matter of law in finding it lacked jurisdiction over former husband's motion for custody and support as to child born to mother five months prior to five-year marriage to former husband but shown by paternity testing at time of their divorce not to be former husband's; trial court found that former husband's pleadings did not reach the factual and legal threshold required for former husband to intervene in mother's paternity proceeding against alleged biological father. Strope v. Wells (Ohio App. 5 Dist., 04-23-2007) 171 Ohio App.3d 658, 872 N.E.2d 363, 2007-Ohio-1962. Children Out-of-wedlock ⬱ 20.4; Children Out-of-wedlock ⬱ 34

Former wife was required to satisfy statutory factors governing modification of custody before court could modify terms of shared-parenting plan, although plan allowed former wife to request immediate hearing if former husband altered daycare arrangement; former husband never altered children's after-school arrangement. Lindman v. Geissler (Ohio App. 5 Dist., 04-23-2007) 171 Ohio App.3d 650, 872 N.E.2d 356, 2007-Ohio-2003. Child Custody ⬱ 576

After minor parent, involved in child custody proceeding in which that parent's parent, i.e., grandparent, was made a party because the parent was a minor at onset of proceeding, reaches age of majority, trial court may remove grandparent as party, if grandparent has not taken an action which gives rise to independent legal interest or rights in the proceeding. In re H.W. (Ohio, 06-27-2007) 114 Ohio St.3d 65, 868 N.E.2d 261, 2007-Ohio-2879. Child Custody ☞ 409

Trial court did not abuse its discretion in custody proceeding involving biological parents and paternal grandmother, in finding that physician's testimony, that mother was a suitable parent and awarding custody to mother would not be detrimental to child, was credible and persuasive; physician had interviewed all of the parties in the matter and had conducted a thorough report and evaluation of the custody situation. Vance v. Vance (Ohio App. 2 Dist., 01-24-2003) 151 Ohio App.3d 391, 784 N.E.2d 172, 2003-Ohio-310. Child Custody ☞ 473

An allocation of custody and visitation rights remains subject to future modification by the trial court and, thus, the doctrine of res judicata should not be applied strictly in cases involving child custody and visitation. Kelm v. Kelm (Ohio, 07-05-2001) 92 Ohio St.3d 223, 749 N.E.2d 299, 2001-Ohio-168. Child Custody ☞ 532; Child Custody ☞ 550

Mistaken finding of fact regarding child custody modification, erroneously stating the date of the parties' divorce, was not relevant to the custody determination. Clark v. Smith (Ohio App. 3 Dist., 12-08-1998) 130 Ohio App.3d 648, 720 N.E.2d 973. Child Custody ☞ 923(4)

Mistaken finding of fact regarding child custody modification, erroneously stating that a shared-parenting plan was adopted in the divorce decree, was not prejudicial error; trial court was aware that mother was the residential parent and that father was granted visitation by the original divorce decree. Clark v. Smith (Ohio App. 3 Dist., 12-08-1998) 130 Ohio App.3d 648, 720 N.E.2d 973. Child Custody ☞ 923(4)

Requirement by referee that former wife, who sought modification of decree which awarded custody of children to former husband, show "change of circumstances substantial enough to warrant this modification" did not impose impermissibly heavy burden of proof on wife. Waggoner v. Waggoner (Ohio App. 9 Dist., 05-08-1996) 111 Ohio App.3d 1, 675 N.E.2d 541, dismissed, appeal not allowed 77 Ohio St.3d 1445, 671 N.E.2d 1284. Child Custody ☞ 633

Generally, prior notice of change of custody ought to be given to both parties so that they have enough time to make arrangements and expedite transfers; however, where it appears that demonstrated recalcitrance of one party may interfere with orderly transfer, court might permit a more summary transfer. Beekman v. Beekman (Ohio App. 4 Dist., 10-25-1994) 96 Ohio App.3d 783, 645 N.E.2d 1332. Child Custody ☞ 606

Trial court's order granting father's motion for change in parental rights and responsibilities met requirements of statute governing such motions, despite fact trial court viewed motion as motion to modify disposition and failed to include specific statutory language in order and, thus, order was valid where referees report, adopted by trial court, contained sufficient facts to find that change in circumstances had occurred, that modification would be in best interests of child, and that harm of changing child's environment was outweighed by benefits of changing environment. In re Kennedy (Ohio App. 3 Dist., 04-19-1994) 94 Ohio App.3d 414, 640 N.E.2d 1176. Child Custody ☞ 652; Child Custody ☞ 659

Domestic relations court did not delegate to magistrate, on motion for allocation of parental rights and responsibilities, the determination of whether order transferring custody of children from ex-wife to ex-husband should have immediate effect or whether it should be interim order, given that clerical error prevented order from being properly designated as interim order, clerical error was corrected, and order was then properly designated; magistrate did not make determination and did not issue decision since the decision was properly adopted and validly issued by court. Wilson v. Wetter (Ohio App. 12 Dist., Butler, 06-17-2002) No. CA2001-10-253, 2002-Ohio-3877, 2002 WL 1327464, Unreported. Child Custody ☞ 652

Marital dissolution granted in California pursuant to wife's petition did not constitute a prior decree that required Ohio trial court in husband's divorce action to apply statutory factors regarding modification of custody, since California court did not have jurisdiction over parental rights and responsibilities concerning children. Graves v. Graves (Ohio App. 9 Dist., Medina, 07-24-2002) No. 3242-M, 2002-Ohio-3740, 2002 WL 1626144, Unreported. Child Custody ☞ 717

Testimony concerning former husband's reputation for truthfulness was of no consequence and was irrelevant in proceeding on modification of child custody, where trial court refused to determine the veracity of or rely on allegations allegedly attacking former husband's truthfulness. Brenneman v. Brenneman (Ohio App. 6 Dist., Wood, 05-24-2002) No. WD-01-052, 2002-Ohio-2630, 2002 WL 1290842, Unreported. Witnesses ☞ 361(1)

A motion for relief from judgment pursuant to Civ R 60(B) has no application to an action for a change of custody under RC 3109.04. Mundschenk v Mundschenk, No. 81AP-406 (10th Dist Ct App, Franklin, 3-25-82).

66. —— Evidence, modification of rights and responsibilities and "change in circumstances"

No compelling reason existed to modify parenting time to allow father equal parenting time with minor children, and thus trial court's decision to deny father's motion to modify parenting time was not against manifest weight of evidence; children expressed unwillingness to play certain extracurricular activities proposed by father, father signed children up for extracurricular activities without consulting with mother, children failed to complete their homework on weeknights spent with father, father withheld prescribed medication from child when child was with father, and evidence established that it was physically and mentally detrimental to withhold child's medication. Franklin-Rengan v. Rengan (Ohio App. 2 Dist., Montgomery, 05-27-2005) No. 20705, 2005-Ohio-2763, 2005 WL 1322569, Unreported, appeal not allowed 106 Ohio St.3d 1556, 836 N.E.2d 581, 2005-Ohio-5531, reconsideration denied 107 Ohio St.3d 1701, 840 N.E.2d 205, 2005-Ohio-6763. Child Custody ☞ 577

Trial court's introduction of notes taken in previous hearings, into evidence in hearing on complaint for modification of custody of child born out-of-wedlock, did not constitute plain error, where transcript revealed that witnesses at the hearing repeated in some form or fashion most of the information in the notes, and were subject to cross-examination; record did not suggest that had the notes not been read into the record, the outcome of the case would have been different. McClay v. Reed (Ohio App. 5 Dist., Guernsey, 12-29-2004) No. 2004CA-4, 2004-Ohio-7304, 2004 WL 3563008, Unreported. Children Out–of–wedlock ☞ 20.11

Trial court's decision modifying shared parenting plan in child custody proceedings, making father residential parent for school purposes and granting father final authority regarding child's education and medical treatment, was not against the manifest weight of the evidence; mother failed to present any evidence consistent with her assertions that child had developmental difficulties, alleged problems only exhibited themselves while child was in mother's care, and mother was interfering with the relationship between father and child. Nigro v. Nigro (Ohio App. 9 Dist., Lorain, 11-24-2004) No. 04CA008461, 2004-Ohio-6270, 2004 WL 2674587, Unreported. Child Custody ☞ 576

Father could not challenge on appeal the evidentiary rulings made by the magistrate and approved by the trial court in child custody action since rule required that any objection to a finding of fact be supported by a transcript of all the evidence submitted to the magistrate and father failed to comply with this rule in that he failed to file transcript of the magistrate's hearing for trial court to review when ruling on his objections to magistrate's decision. Stark v. Haser (Ohio App. 5 Dist., Delaware, 09-02-2004) No. 03CAF11057, 2004-Ohio-4641, 2004 WL 1945581, Unreported. Child Custody ☞ 904

Trial court's consideration of transcripts of children's in-chambers interviews with magistrate, which were not certified, file-stamped, or recorded on docket sheet, was harmless error in child custody proceeding, given that transcripts of magistrate's hearing provided sufficient evidence to support trial court's grant of custody to father; parents were unmarried and no prior court order was issued related to custody such that parties stood on equal footing before court and transcript of hearing revealed that mother did not allow children to telephone father, that mother drank every day and

stayed out late at bars, and that mother had impression that children wanted to live with father. Francis v. Westfall (Ohio App. 7 Dist., Jefferson, 08-24-2004) No. 03-JE-20, No. 03-JE-21, 2004-Ohio-4543, 2004 WL 1931779, Unreported. Child Custody ☞ 923(1)

Trial court error, if any, in allowing counsel for father to question mother as if on cross-examination was harmless, in proceeding to determine legal custody of child; the facts elicited from mother's testimony had previously been introduced into evidence through the guardian ad litem's report, and mother chose to testify and to present her case. In re Rosier Lemmon (Ohio App. 5 Dist., Stark, 03-15-2004) No. 2003 CA 00306, 2004-Ohio-1290, 2004 WL 540299, Unreported. Child Custody ☞ 923(1)

Allowing parties in child custody dispute to present additional evidence, but failing to consider it when reviewing magistrate's decision to modify custody to name former husband residential parent, was unreasonable and constituted abuse of discretion; additional evidence submitted potentially did not support magistrate's findings that former wife's relocation was for purposes of interfering with husband's visitation and that move to another state was detrimental to child. Clifton v. Clifton (Ohio App. 3 Dist., Union, 12-22-2003) No. 14-03-07, 2003-Ohio-6993, 2003 WL 22995014, Unreported. Child Custody ☞ 652

In addressing motion to modify child's residential placement, trial court properly held hearing to determine which parenting plan was in child's best interest; although parents preliminarily agreed to waive presentation of evidence and to submit joint shared parenting plan, mother filed her own plan and father did not submit his own plan until one year later such that it appeared allocation of parental rights and responsibilities was contested, and parents had previously been unable to make joint decisions regarding child. Stroud v. Lyons (Ohio App. 11 Dist., Ashtabula, 12-12-2003) No. 2002-A-0050, 2003-Ohio-6773, 2003 WL 22952597, Unreported. Child Custody ☞ 650

Trial court abused its discretion in modifying prior decree that designated father as primary residential parent for educational purposes to designating father as primary residential parent and legal custodian, even though trial court treated modification as nunc pro tunc entry; mother was never given opportunity to challenge father's request, there was no evidence that modification was in child's best interests, trial court granted motion on day of filing without first holding hearing, and attempted nunc pro tunc entry altered respective position of parents in fundamental manner. Criado v. Truesdell (Ohio App. 11 Dist., Ashtabula, 12-12-2003) No. 2002-A-0035, 2003-Ohio-6681, 2003 WL 22931377, Unreported. Child Custody ☞ 526; Child Custody ☞ 650

Without transcript, Court of Appeals could not find that trial court's decision designating former wife as residential parent of parties' children was against manifest weight of evidence or that trial court abused its discretion in determining that designating former wife as residential parent was in children's best interest. Mills v. Mills (Ohio App. 11 Dist., Trumbull, 12-05-2003) No. 2002-T-0102, 2003-Ohio-6676, 2003 WL 22928461, Unreported. Child Custody ☞ 907

Trial court, in overruling paternal grandmother's objections to court order that vacated prior court order allowing grandmother temporary custody of child, and designating mother sole residential custodian, considered all evidence from hearing that resulted in prior order being vacated; trial court's decision referenced all of the relevant motions and memoranda filed by the parties. Vance v. Vance (Ohio App. 2 Dist., 01-24-2003) 151 Ohio App.3d 391, 784 N.E.2d 172, 2003-Ohio-310. Child Custody ☞ 511

Evidence supported trial court's determination that former wife had not shown change of circumstances sufficient to warrant modification of decree which awarded custody of all six children to former wife; much the same evidence had been before court when it last decided custody two years previously, and evidence of bitterness between parties did not demonstrate change in circumstances, as situation had been ongoing since dissolution of marriage. Waggoner v. Waggoner (Ohio App. 9 Dist., 05-08-1996) 111 Ohio App.3d 1, 675 N.E.2d 541, dismissed, appeal not allowed 77 Ohio St.3d 1445, 671 N.E.2d 1284. Child Custody ☞ 637

Best interest of the child test for modification of custody is a weight of the evidence question and, if judgment of trial court is supported by competent probative evidence, Court of Appeals must affirm trial court's decision. Miller v. Miller (Hocking 1993) 86 Ohio App.3d 623, 621 N.E.2d 745. Child Custody ☞ 922(5)

In considering a motion for change of custody, it is error for a court to exclude evidence of circumstances occurring after a specified date, where relevant evidence is thereby excluded. Van Hook v. Van Hook (Summit 1985) 26 Ohio App.3d 188, 499 N.E.2d 365, 26 O.B.R. 408.

Evidence regarding former wife's relationship with her daughter, including questions about whether daughter smoked at age 15 and whether daughter became pregnant before age 18, were not relevant when determining residential parent for five-year-old child upon termination of shared parenting plan, where former husband did not tie such evidence to any impact on five-year-old child. Ferrell v. Ferrell (Ohio App. 7 Dist., Carroll, 06-11-2002) No. 01 AP 0763, 2002-Ohio-3019, 2002 WL 1376039, Unreported. Child Custody ☞ 632

Evidence supported finding that former husband would be less likely to honor and facilitate companionship with former wife or to encourage former wife to be involved in child's school work and activities, as element for designating residential parent upon termination of shared parenting plan; former wife complained of former husband's stubbornness and refusal to compromise on several

visitation issues and complained that former husband was non-communicative regarding child's activities, and former husband did not provide daycare provider with former wife's name and address. Ferrell v. Ferrell (Ohio App. 7 Dist., Carroll, 06-11-2002) No. 01 AP 0763, 2002-Ohio-3019, 2002 WL 1376039, Unreported. Child Custody ☞ 637

67. —— Timeliness of hearing, modification of rights and responsibilities and "change in circumstances"

Trial court order, which denied father's motion to reallocate parental rights and name father as the sole residential parent of child, adequately complied with statute, which required a determination that a change in circumstances had occurred and that modification was in the best interest of the child before the residential parent or legal custodian of a child could be modified; father was the temporary residential parent at the time of the hearing. Wood v. Wood (Ohio App. 11 Dist., Trumbull, 03-19-2010) No. 2009-T-0082, 2010-Ohio-1154, 2010 WL 1052267, Unreported. Child Custody ☞ 659

Thirty-month delay from the time of father's filing of his motion for the reallocation of parental rights and responsibilities to the time of the hearing on motion did not prejudice father, given the numerous motions and related matters that were filed, a clear example of "the wheels of justice grind[ing] exceedingly slow, but grind[ing] exceedingly fine." Edwards v. Edwards (Ohio App. 5 Dist., Fairfield, 08-18-2008) No. 07CA52, 2008-Ohio-4418, 2008 WL 4052894, Unreported. Child Custody ☞ 923(4)

Trial court abused its discretion when it summarily overruled former husband's objections to magistrate's decision recommending denial of his motion for change of custody, on ground that transcript was not timely filed, where court did not set any type of deadline for former husband to produce transcript, and there was no hearing date or any articulation of a reasonable time to allow lengthy transcript of proceedings to be prepared. Shull v. Shull (Ohio App. 3 Dist., 12-08-1999) 135 Ohio App.3d 708, 735 N.E.2d 496, 1999-Ohio-950. Child Custody ☞ 921(1)

Court referee did not abuse her discretion in limiting time for hearing on father's motion to modify custody to one and one-half hours per party, where a number of depositions were submitted into evidence, both mother and another witness testified at length as to merits of father's motion, and there was no indication in record of what any additional evidence presented by mother might have shown. Holm v. Smilowitz (Athens 1992) 83 Ohio App.3d 757, 615 N.E.2d 1047. Child Custody ☞ 651

68. —— Remand, modification of rights and responsibilities and "change in circumstances"

Remand was necessary of trial court order overruling grandmother's objections to magistrate's opinion denying grandmother's motion to change legal custody of teenaged child to herself from mother, who had requested to live with grandmother after divorce due to difficult relationship with child, for trial court to consider magistrate's in camera interviews of child as to with whom child wished to reside; unlike the other transcripts, the transcripts of the multiple in camera interviews were not available until after the trial court entered its judgment awarding custody to child's mother. In re Hatch (Ohio App. 3 Dist., Hancock, 11-10-2008) No. 5-07-46, 2008-Ohio-5822, 2008 WL 4831410, Unreported. Child Custody ☞ 924

Trial court's failure, in denying mother's motion for reallocation of parental rights with respect to child whose legal custody had been transferred to maternal grandmother over a decade before, to apply best interest test in denying motion, or to make clear what factors supported its decision, required reversal and remand for trial court to actually state in its journal that its judgment was in child's best interests and explain reasons underlying that judgment. In re Bell (Ohio App. 7 Dist., Noble, 12-12-2005) No. 04 NO 321, 2005-Ohio-6603, 2005 WL 3388209, Unreported. Child Custody ☞ 659; Child Custody ☞ 924

Remand was required for a determination of whether the trial court was required to analyze whether a change in circumstances mandated a change in custody; record was insufficient to allow the Court of Appeals to determine whether child custody proceeding was an original custody proceeding or whether than had been a prior child custody order, which would have required the trial court to apply change in circumstances standard. In re Ballard (Ohio App. 2 Dist., Montgomery, 06-20-2003) No. 19511, 2003-Ohio-3233, 2003 WL 21419169, Unreported. Child Custody ☞ 924

Trial court arbitrarily and unreasonably journalized judgment entry reinstating allocation format of divorce decree regarding parenting time, and thus remand to trial court was warranted for purpose of holding hearing on former husband's motion that sought clarification of decree regarding right of first refusal for periods of parenting time if former wife would otherwise use babysitter, since entry was complete turnaround from what had earlier occurred in case, no motion to modify court's prior holding on issue was pending, and hearing on right of first refusal, which court had earlier stated would be set as soon as possible, was never held. Lassiter v. Lassiter (Ohio App. 1 Dist., Hamilton, 05-09-2003) No. C-020494, No. C-020370, No. C-020128, 2003-Ohio-2333, 2003 WL 21034193, Unreported. Child Custody ☞ 526

69. Shared parenting and joint custody—In general

Trial court's order that father's shared parenting plan as amended go into effect, with several exceptions, and instruction to father's counsel to prepare a judgment order in accordance with court's decision, in contravention of requirements of custody statute providing that if trial court objects to portions of a submitted shared parenting plan, it may request that the party file a modified shared parenting plan to address its concerns, constituted plain error, in proceeding commenced by father to reallocate parental rights and responsibilities by modifying residential custody of child from mother to him; court never explicitly determined that shared parenting plan was in child's best interest, and assuming that court did find that shared parenting plan was in child's best interest, it was required to approve the plan, but if court found that no plan was in child's best interest, it was required to order each parent to submit appropriate changes to father's plan. Elson v. Plokhooy (Ohio App. 3 Dist., Shelby, 06-20-2011) No. 17-10-24, 2011-Ohio-3009, 2011 WL 2448955, Unreported. Child Custody ☞ 904

Mother waived challenge on appeal to trial court's adoption and journalization of parenting plan agreement submitted by father; parties agreed on record to terms of shared parenting plan, mother's counsel offered to draft and file agreement with court but failed to do so, father's attorney then submitted proposed order and served mother with copy, and mother failed to make any objections at hearing to terms of plan and failed to make any objections to father's proposed order. Eckstein v. Eckstein (Ohio App. 12 Dist., Warren, 04-11-2011) No. CA2010-10-097, 2011-Ohio-1724, 2011 WL 1346843, Unreported. Child Custody ☞ 904; Child Custody ☞ 918

Trial court did not abuse its discretion in designating mother as children's legal custodian and residential parent, as mother appeared to have been children's primary caretaker during the marriage and seemed best suited to care for children, guardian ad litem recommended mother as legal custodian and residential parent, mother had stable and relatively secure full-time employment and worked during the day when children were in school, when mother was unavailable, her mother assisted her in caring for children, and father admitted being "flat broke," and his schedule as a truck driver required him to work second shift, resulting in him essentially seeking the children only on weekends. Ussher v. Ussher (Ohio App. 2 Dist., Champaign, 03-25-2011) No. 2009-CA-49, 2011-Ohio-1440, 2011 WL 1102991, Unreported. Child Custody ☞ 44; Child Custody ☞ 67; Child Custody ☞ 421

Trial court did not have authority to impose, in essence, a shared parenting plan by designating each parent the minor child's residential parent when the child was in that parent's physical custody, where there was no evidence that either parent requested shared parenting or filed a shared parenting plan; court was statutorily required to designate one of the parents the child's residential parent. Preston v. Preston (Ohio App. 4 Dist., 08-05-2010) No. 09CA26, 2010-Ohio-3711, 2010 WL 3159217, Unreported. Child Custody ☞ 414

Evidence was sufficient to establish a change in circumstances warranting modification of child custody award, which named mother the primary residential parent and awarded father visitation, to award father custody of their out-of-wedlock child; evidence showed that mother had steadfastly and without just excuse denied father and the child all rights of companionship and contact, that mother purposefully denied father access to the child's medical providers, that mother lacked stable housing and drifted between hotels and homeless shelters, that mother persisted in making unfounded and baseless allegations that child had been sexually abused by father, and that mother demonstrated a profound lack of insight into the child's needs. C.G. v. C.L. (Ohio App. 8 Dist., Cuyahoga, 06-26-2008) No. 90341, 2008-Ohio-3135, 2008 WL 2536058, Unreported. Children Out–of–wedlock 20.10

The trial court's designation of wife as the residential parent of the children for school registration purposes under shared parenting decree was not against the weight of the evidence or an abuse of discretion, in divorce proceeding; magistrate found that wife was more nurturing and patient, that husband was heavy-handed and almost obsessive about things, and that son's negative impressions of wife were motivated by an attempt to please husband. Brewer v. Brewer (Ohio App. 5 Dist., Licking, 07-01-2004) No. 2003CA00087, 2004-Ohio-3531, 2004 WL 1486781, Unreported. Child Custody 147

Evidence supported finding that mother had entered into shared parenting agreement voluntarily; mother entered into agreement with her attorney present, terms of agreement were reviewed line by line with both parties to agreement, agreement made no mention of genetic testing of putative father, mother was aware at time of entering into agreement that there were other men who could potentially be child's father, and putative father's paternity had never been confirmed through genetic testing. Thomas v. Cruz (Ohio App. 9 Dist., Lorain, 11-12-2003) No. 03CA008247, 2003-Ohio-6011, 2003 WL 22657864, Unreported. Children Out–of–wedlock 20.8

Ohio was not children's home state, and thus trial court lacked jurisdiction to modify child custody order from foreign state; children had not been with former husband in Ohio for six months prior to filing of judgment entry modifying custody, and children had been with former wife, their legal custodian, for two to three month periods during time spent with husband. Louck v. Louck (Ohio App. 3 Dist., Marion, 11-10-2003) No. 9-03-35, 2003-Ohio-5999, 2003 WL 22533679, Unreported. Child Custody 736

Trial court order denying husband's proposed shared parenting plan was not an abuse of discretion, in divorce proceeding; trial court found that husband and wife lacked the ability to cooperate and make shared parenting decisions on behalf of child, and father filed his proposed shared parenting plan a day before the hearing on the allocation of parental rights. Howell v. Howell (Ohio App. 2 Dist., Clark, 09-12-2003) No. 2002 CA 60, 2003-Ohio-4842, 2003 WL 22110309, Unreported. Child Custody 127; Child Custody 410

In a child custody dispute California is the proper forum to consider a motion for reallocation of parental rights and responsibilities where (1) California is the home state of the minor child who has resided in the state for six years, (2) the child's medical and educational records are available in California, and (3) California has a closer connection than Ohio with the child's mother and family. Eichenberger v. Eichenberger (Ohio App. 10 Dist., Franklin, 04-24-2001) No. 00AP-948, 2001 WL 410276, Unreported, appeal not allowed 93 Ohio St.3d 1416, 754 N.E.2d 262.

A trial court is required to develop a shared parenting order pursuant to the father's motion where the child (1) has become acquainted and accustomed to the father's home, (2) has developed friendships with neighbors in the father's community and school district, (3) has a large extended family in the area, (4) has no friends or extended family within the state where the mother plans to move, and (5) would be required to adjust to a new school, neighbors, friends, and community. Thieken v. Spoerl (Ohio App. 12 Dist., Butler, 05-20-1996) No. CA95-11-186, 1996 WL 263583, Unreported.

Alleged financial hardship in former wife's home was not sufficient to establish significant change of circumstance that would warrant modifying custody regarding shared-parenting plan; there was no evidence that former wife's financial situation had significantly changed from time of inception of party's original agreement to time of hearing on motion to modify custody. Lindman v. Geissler (Ohio App. 5 Dist., 04-23-2007) 171 Ohio App.3d 650, 872 N.E.2d 356, 2007-Ohio-2003. Child Custody 576

Cohabiting, unmarried female same-sex partner of children's mother was not a "parent," for purposes of entering into a shared parenting agreement. In re Bonfield (Ohio, 08-28-2002) 96 Ohio St.3d 218, 773 N.E.2d 507, 2002-Ohio-4182, opinion superseded on reconsideration 97 Ohio St.3d 387, 780 N.E.2d 241, 2002-Ohio-6660. Child Custody 125; Child Custody 274

During divorce proceeding, trial court is required to allocate parental rights and responsibilities for care of minor children pursuant to statute, and has two options when doing so. Court may designate one parent as residential parent and legal custodian who bears primary rights and responsibilities for care of the children; or court may issue shared parenting order requiring parents to share all or some aspects of physical and legal care of the children. Arthur v. Arthur (Ohio App. 5 Dist., 10-22-1998) 130 Ohio App.3d 398, 720 N.E.2d 176. Child Custody 100; Child Custody 152

Competent, credible evidence supported trial court's determination that shared parenting agreement was fair and reasonable and in best interest of children; record indicated that in addition to parties' own joint plan and trial court's observation of parties, trial court had before it detailed psychological evaluations of both parties and children. Evans

v. Evans (Ohio App. 12 Dist., 10-02-1995) 106 Ohio App.3d 673, 666 N.E.2d 1176, dismissed, appeal not allowed 75 Ohio St.3d 1448, 663 N.E.2d 330. Child Custody ⬥ 141; Child Custody ⬥ 472; Evidence ⬥ 571(1)

Award of shared parenting was not an abuse of discretion; trial court could reasonably have concluded from evidence presented at hearing, including husband's testimony regarding his sobriety and his alcoholism rehabilitation program, that husband's alcoholism was not an appropriate reason to deny shared custody, and husband's demanding work schedule did not require that he be denied shared custody, given testimony that husband would seek other employment, if necessary, to preserve relationship with children and feasibility of tailoring parenting arrangement to accommodate husband's work schedule. Harris v. Harris (Ohio App. 2 Dist., 08-11-1995) 105 Ohio App.3d 671, 664 N.E.2d 1304. Child Custody ⬥ 134; Child Custody ⬥ 139

Trial court did not have to reject husband's shared parenting plan based on his omission of statutorily required elements, as those issues had already been addressed by trial court in final decree of divorce issued before court adopted shared parenting plan. Harris v. Harris (Ohio App. 2 Dist., 08-11-1995) 105 Ohio App.3d 671, 664 N.E.2d 1304. Child Custody ⬥ 511

Trial court erred in granting shared parenting on terms not set forth in shared-parenting plan submitted to court by one party or other. McClain v. McClain (Summit 1993) 87 Ohio App.3d 856, 623 N.E.2d 242. Child Custody ⬥ 141

"Shared parenting" of children by divorced couples means that parents literally share some, or all, of aspects of physical and legal care of their children. Snouffer v. Snouffer (Meigs 1993) 87 Ohio App.3d 89, 621 N.E.2d 879. Child Custody ⬥ 120

Pursuant to Civ R 75(P) and RC 3109.04, it is mandatory for the trial court to award custody of minor children to one of the parents where a divorce is granted, unless neither parent is a suitable person to have custody. McVay v. McVay (Columbiana 1974) 44 Ohio App.2d 370, 338 N.E.2d 772, 73 O.O.2d 415. Child Custody ⬥ 22

Evidence was sufficient in divorce action to support award of custody of son to husband, although wife was awarded custody of daughter; trial court had before it the report of the psychologist and the guardian ad litem's recommendation, held an in camera hearing with son, and had discretion to approve a shared parenting plan. Burson v. Burson (Ohio App. 5 Dist., Stark, 08-05-2002) No. 2001CA00282, 2002-Ohio-4207, 2002 WL 1881162, Unreported. Child Custody ⬥ 467

70. —— Arbitration agreements for disputes, shared parenting and joint custody

A mother is entitled to reimbursement of daycare costs that she would not have had if the former spouse had exercised his summer visitation pursuant to the parties' shared parenting agreement

which states "The father shall be solely responsible for the payment of childcare expenses during the children's period of residence with him." Freed v. Freed (Ohio App. 2 Dist., Greene, 07-07-2000) No. 99 CA 102, 2000 WL 896285, Unreported.

Matters of child custody and parental visitation were not subject to arbitration in a domestic relations case, notwithstanding parties' agreement that any future disputes regarding child custody or visitation would be submitted to arbitration; only a court was empowered to resolve disputes relating to child custody and visitation. Kelm v. Kelm (Ohio, 07-05-2001) 92 Ohio St.3d 223, 749 N.E.2d 299, 2001-Ohio-168. Child Custody ⬥ 419

Former wife did not, by virtue of her acquiescence to original shared parenting plan that contained an agreement to arbitrate any future custody and visitation disputes, waive her right to challenge plan's arbitration provision; to hold that former wife waived her right to challenge arbitration agreement and to permit arbitration of parties' child custody and visitation disputes would have impermissibly prevented trial court from fulfilling its role as parens patriae in serving the best interests of the children. Kelm v. Kelm (Ohio, 07-05-2001) 92 Ohio St.3d 223, 749 N.E.2d 299, 2001-Ohio-168. Child Custody ⬥ 419

Former wife's failure to challenge parties' agreement to arbitrate custody and visitation disputes in previous divorce action did not deprive trial court of jurisdiction to consider her subsequent motion to modify or terminate the shared parenting plan, under the doctrine of res judicata; arbitration clause impermissibly interfered with trial court's continuing responsibility to protect the best interests of the children. Kelm v. Kelm (Ohio, 07-05-2001) 92 Ohio St.3d 223, 749 N.E.2d 299, 2001-Ohio-168. Child Custody ⬥ 532

Dispute over mother's relocation involved matter of child custody that was not arbitrable, even though parties' shared parenting agreement provided for arbitration of parties' disputes. Pulfer v. Pulfer (Ohio App. 3 Dist., 03-28-1996) 110 Ohio App.3d 90, 673 N.E.2d 656, dismissed, appeal not allowed 77 Ohio St.3d 1412, 670 N.E.2d 1001. Alternative Dispute Resolution ⬥ 119

71. —— 'Best interests" of children, shared parenting and joint custody

Trial court reasonably concluded that the parties had an inability to communicate and cooperate and to make decisions jointly with respect to their minor children and that it was not in the children's best interest that shared parenting be ordered; father had been children's stay-at-home parent their entire lives and was comfortable with and capable of continuing to provide care, he did not harbor as much anger as mother, shared parenting arrangement proposed by mother was designed primarily to accommodate her work schedule and would have involved frequent exchanges of children, and guardian ad litem thought it was in children's best interest to minimize transfers between parents as they had inability to communicate and cooperate and make decisions jointly with respect to children. Henderson v. Henderson (Ohio App. 2 Dist., Clark, 10-10-2008) No. 2007 CA 124, 2008-Ohio-5360, 2008 WL 4599607, Unreported. Child Custody ☞ 127; Child Custody ☞ 133; Child Custody ☞ 421

Trial court did not abuse its discretion in terminating shared parenting plan originally entered into incident to divorce, where magistrate conducted in camera interview with parties' 16-year-old child, in which child indicated that he no longer desired to stay overnight with former husband, and magistrate entered requisite finding that it considered statutory factors relevant to child's best interests and concluded that shared parenting was no longer in child's best interests. Cherwin v. Cherwin (Ohio App. 8 Dist., Cuyahoga, 04-28-2005) No. 84875, 2005-Ohio 1999, 2005 WL 991706, Unreported. Child Custody ☞ 566; Child Custody ☞ 571; Child Custody ☞ 654; Child Custody ☞ 659

Trial court did not abuse its discretion in refusing to weight former wife's ability to place child on school bus in the mornings and prepare home-cooked breakfast as heavily as other factors in determining that termination of shared parenting plan and placement of child with former husband as residential parent was in child's best interests. Wiesman v. Wiesman (Ohio App. 12 Dist., Butler, 12-08-2003) No. CA2002-08-193, No. CA2003-01-002, 2003-Ohio-6544, 2003 WL 22887918, Unreported, appeal not allowed 102 Ohio St.3d 1423, 807 N.E.2d 367, 2004-Ohio 2003. Child Custody ☞ 659

Substantial evidence supported trial court's determination in divorce proceedings that child's best interests would be served by rejecting shared parenting proposal and by designating mother as child's residential parent and legal custodian; parents were unable to communicate or cooperate regarding the best interests of child, current shared custody arrangement exacerbated hostilities between parents, child was more adjusted and comfortable in mother's home, father demonstrated obsessive and controlling tendencies regarding child and had been violent toward mother, father had interfered with mother's contact with child, parents lived 40 miles apart, and transportation schedule for shared parenting would prevent child from participating in extracurricular activities. Dannaher v. Newbold (Ohio App. 10 Dist., 03-04-2004) 2004-Ohio-1003, 2004 WL 396993. Child Custody ☞ 148

Trial court's erroneous finding that no change of circumstances occurred was harmless in context of father's motion to reallocate shared parental rights set out in divorce decree so as to make him the residential parent, where trial court proceeded despite that finding to consider whether a change of custody was in best interests of child. LaBute v. LaBute (Ohio App. 3 Dist., 12-01-2008) 179 Ohio App.3d 696, 903 N.E.2d 652, 2008-Ohio-6190. Child Custody ☞ 923(4)

Evidence established that shared parenting was no longer in child's best interests; shared parenting

had been ordered when child was three years old and parents were living in California, child was now 11 and father was living in Ohio while mother was living in Maryland, an 11–year–old child had more complex needs than a three-year-old child, the child's needs would grow even more complex during his teenage years, and parents had little or no contact with respect to child's needs because of their commitment to their new families. Meyer v. Anderson (Ohio App. 2 Dist., Miami, 06-07-2002) No. 01CA53, 2002-Ohio-2782, 2002 WL 1251449, Unreported. Child Custody ☞ 576

72. —— Child support, shared parenting and joint custody

Former husband's contention, on judicial review of administrative determination modifying his child support obligation, that his designation as residential parent relieved him of any child support obligation pursuant to statute was barred by res judicata, where former husband agreed to pay child support as part of shared parenting plan incorporated into decree of dissolution. Teiberis v. Teiberis (Ohio App. 9 Dist., Lorain, 03-09-2005) No. 04CA008482, 2005-Ohio-999, 2005 WL 544827, Unreported. Child Support ☞ 225; Child Support ☞ 240

In child custody proceedings, father had no standing to appeal juvenile court's failure to address mother's request for recalculation of child support. In re Jacobberger (Ohio App. 11 Dist., Geauga, 12-10-2004) No. 2003-G-2538, 2004-Ohio-6937, 2004 WL 2937402, Unreported. Child Support ☞ 538

Trial court was not required to offset former husband's child support obligation by former wife's obligation under shared parenting plan on 50/50 basis. Tonti v. Tonti (Ohio App. 10 Dist., Franklin, 05-18-2004) No. 03AP-494, No. 03AP-728, 2004-Ohio-2529, 2004 WL 1109840, Unreported, appeal not allowed 103 Ohio St.3d 1478, 816 N.E.2d 254, 2004-Ohio-5405. Child Support ☞ 165

Trial court did not abuse its discretion in modifying husband's child support obligation; shared parenting agreement did not require change in factual situation of children, and husband's income had substantially increased. Bailey v. Bailey (Ohio App. 5 Dist., Stark, 04-19-2004) No. 2003CA00319, 2004-Ohio-2004, 2004 WL 858741, Unreported. Child Support ☞ 240; Child Support ☞ 258

Former wife was not entitled to deviation from guideline child support based on her claim that under shared parenting plan child spent greater amount of time with her, in light of evidence that when child was in custody of former wife he was in care of day care provider or his grandparents during her work day, and, as a result, child spent roughly equal amount of time with both parties. Warner v. Warner (Ohio App. 3 Dist., Union, 09-29-2003) No. 14-03-10, 2003-Ohio-5132, 2003 WL 22229412, Unreported. Child Support ☞ 148

Former husband ordered to pay child support under shared parenting plan was not entitled to an automatic credit for time child resided with him. McAninch v. McAninch (Ohio App. 3 Dist., Union, 10-18-2002) No. 14-02-10, 2002-Ohio-5580, 2002 WL 31323246, Unreported. Child Support ☞ 165

The parent in a shared parenting plan with the greater child support obligation, after being given credit for the time that the child lives with him or her, is the obligor parent, and the obligor parent is required to pay as child support only the difference between his or her greater obligation and the other parent's lesser obligation. Leis v. Leis (Ohio App. 2 Dist., Miami, 06-20-1997) No. 96-CA-20, 1997 WL 335145, Unreported.

A residential parent is entitled to a reduction of the child support obligation in proportion to the time the children reside with the parent. Beard v. Beard (Ohio App. 11 Dist., Portage, 04-04-1997) No. 96-P-0011, 1997 WL 184766, Unreported.

Father could not have child support obligation reduced by 36%, to reflect percentage of time that he had physical custody of children under agreed upon shared parenting agreement; statute already covered method of computing child support in those situations. LaLiberte v. LaLiberte (Ohio App. 9 Dist., 07-12-1995) 105 Ohio App.3d 207, 663 N.E.2d 974. Child Support ☞ 236; Child Support ☞ 356

Trial court which adopted shared-parenting plan granting residential status to father during school year and to mother during summer months could properly determine that strict application of child support guidelines would be inappropriate and accordingly deny child support to father under circumstances that parties stipulated that cost of children's parochial education would be shared in proportion to their relative incomes, both parties were required to carry medical insurance for children, and parties were required to share cost of clothing, school supplies and other ordinary expenses. Eickelberger v. Eickelberger (Ohio App. 12 Dist., 02-22-1994) 93 Ohio App.3d 221, 638 N.E.2d 130. Child Support ☞ 148

Court of common pleas had jurisdiction to modify child support award contained within agreed joint custody plan pursuant to wife's motion based upon husband's increased income and Uniform Child Support Guidelines which were adopted after original plan, despite husband's lack of consent. Santantonio v. Santantonio (Lorain 1993) 88 Ohio App.3d 201, 623 N.E.2d 670, motion overruled 67 Ohio St.3d 1506, 622 N.E.2d 653. Child Support ☞ 239; Child Support ☞ 356

Former RC 3113.215(B)(4), which required a trial court to modify a joint custody support order that was ten per cent less than the amount set by the child support guidelines, is an exception to former RC 3109.04(B)(2)(b), which prohibited a court from modifying a joint custody support order without the consent of both custodians. Martin v. Martin (Ohio 1993) 66 Ohio St.3d 110, 609 N.E.2d 537.

73. —— Conflicting plans, shared parenting and joint custody

Shared parenting arrangement was not appropriate in divorce action; older child, who was only child in favor of arrangement, reached age of majority before final decree, wife did not believe that shared parenting arrangement would be in younger child's best interest, and younger child was hesitant about arrangement. Kinney v. Kinney (Ohio App. 5 Dist., Stark, 10-24-2005) No. 2004CA00378, 2005-Ohio-5712, 2005 WL 2806667, Unreported. Child Custody ☞ 123; Child Custody ☞ 143

Custody modification statute requiring party seeking modification to show change in circumstances since time of prior order affecting custody applied to ex parte order placing child in husband's custody at time of wife's arrest, and not original temporary order in which wife was granted custody. In re Logwood (Ohio App. 5 Dist., Guernsey, 07-11-2005) No. 2004-CA-38, 2005-Ohio-3639, 2005 WL 1682732, Unreported. Child Custody ☞ 555

Judgment entry, requiring father to pay for all uninsured medical expenses for two of three children, and then requiring father to pay 84.5% of the balance of uncovered costs for all the children, was contradictory, requiring remand for clarification. Dobran v. Dobran (Ohio App. 7 Dist., Mahoning, 03-24-2003) No. 02 CA 14, 2003-Ohio-1605, 2003 WL 1689584, Unreported. Child Custody ☞ 522; Child Custody ☞ 924

Trial court's decision to accept shared parenting plan presented to court by father rather than plan presented by mother on motion to reallocate parental rights was not to penalize mother for refusing to accept father's plan; rather, court found that father's plan was equitable and prevented mother from further interrupting father's time with children, and court believed that continued litigation would have further contributed to a deteriorating relationship between children and father. Bland v. Bland (Ohio App. 9 Dist., Summit, 02-26-2003) No. 21228, 2003-Ohio-828, 2003 WL 470180, Unreported. Child Custody ☞ 659

There was no evidence of meeting of the minds of mother and father as to shared parenting plan, and thus mother was entitled to relief from judgment which incorporated shared parenting plan; mother disputed that she ever agreed to the shared parenting plan, neither mother nor her attorney signed judgment entry or the shared parenting plan, and there was no transcript of hearing at which mother allegedly agreed to plan. Marquitta C. v. Anthony S. (Ohio App. 6 Dist., Lucas, 12-20-2002) No. L-02-1042, 2002-Ohio-7108, 2002 WL 31846297, Unreported. Child Custody ☞ 526

Trial court did not abuse its discretion in divorce proceeding by ordering a shared parenting plan under which mother had possession of children during the school year and husband had possession of the children during the summer, where husband had acquiesced in wife's making of almost all of the decisions regarding the children until wife filed for divorce, but had opposed wife on almost every issue since that time, wife had a strict and organized approach to raising children, and husband had a laissez-faire approach to parenting. Mason v. Mason (Ohio App. 8 Dist., Cuyahoga, 11-07-2002) No. 80368, No. 80407, 2002-Ohio-6042, 2002 WL 31478901, Unreported, appeal not allowed 98 Ohio St.3d 1511, 786 N.E.2d 62, 2003-Ohio-1572. Child Custody ⟢ 147

A trial court abuses its discretion at a hearing on a shared parenting plan in denying a motion for a new trial where after settlement negotiations lasted until midnight the night before the hearing, and the ex-wife was not informed until the trial had begun that the ex-husband had not accepted the agreement, and arrived at the courthouse after the hearing had already concluded, since the law clearly establishes both parents should be given the opportunity to present evidence at a hearing for an order of shared parenting and the ex-wife was denied the right to a fair trial because she was refused the chance to present evidence at the hearing. Nash v. Nash (Ohio App. 9 Dist., Lorain, 12-04-1996) No. 96CA006433, 1996 WL 724760, Unreported.

Agreed entry in proceeding commenced by putative father of child born out-of-wedlock seeking to establish parent-child relationship, stating that mother and paternal grandparents agreed to share in parenting of child, and that mother was to retain custody of child, was not a "shared parenting plan" between mother and grandparents, for purposes of determining legal standard applicable to grandparents' subsequent motion seeking custody of child; mother and grandparents, as nonparents, could not enter into a shared parenting agreement as a matter of law, as statute governing such agreements provided that they were to be between parents. Purvis v. Hazelbaker (Ohio App. 4 Dist., 02-19-2009) 181 Ohio App.3d 167, 908 N.E.2d 489, 2009-Ohio-765, on subsequent appeal 191 Ohio App.3d 518, 946 N.E.2d 818, 2010-Ohio-6458. Child Custody ⟢ 276; Child Custody ⟢ 579; Children Out–of–wedlock ⟢ 20.4

Agreed entry in proceeding commenced by putative father of child born out-of-wedlock seeking to establish parent-child relationship, stating that mother and paternal grandparents agreed to share in parenting of child, and that grandparents were to have visitation with child, did not constitute a contractual relinquishment of mother's paramount right to custody, and, thus, unsuitability/unfitness standard, rather than change-in-circumstances/best-interest standard applied to grandparents' subsequent motion for custody of child; while the agreed entry indicated that the parties agreed to share in the "parenting" of the child, express terms of entry also stated that mother was to retain custody of child and grandparents were awarded 'visitation, and grandparents did not argue that mother had contractually relinquished her rights under the terms of the agreed entry, but, rather, they contested matter solely on issue of mother's suitability. Purvis v. Hazelbaker (Ohio App. 4 Dist., 02-19-2009) 181 Ohio App.3d 167, 908 N.E.2d 489,

2009-Ohio-765, on subsequent appeal 191 Ohio App.3d 518, 946 N.E.2d 818, 2010-Ohio-6458. Child Custody ⟢ 276; Children Out–of–wedlock ⟢ 20.4

Where both parties submit shared parenting plans, court may determine that one of the submitted plans is in the best interest of the children and adopt that plan verbatim; however, barring adoption of one of the submitted plans, court may only make suggestions for modification of the plans to the parties, and if the parties do not make appropriate changes, or if the court is not satisfied with the changes that are resubmitted following the suggestions for modification, then the court may deny the request for shared parenting of the children. Bowen v. Bowen (Ohio App. 9 Dist., 02-09-1999) 132 Ohio App.3d 616, 725 N.E.2d 1165, dismissed, appeal not allowed 86 Ohio St.3d 1402, 711 N.E.2d 231. Child Custody ⟢ 141

Trial court acted within its discretion in adopting shared parenting plan in which child would reside with former husband during school year and with former wife during summer months, rather than wife's plan, under which child would have resided with wife and husband would have been permitted alternating weekend visitation and extended visitation during summer months. Donovan v. Donovan (Ohio App. 12 Dist., 04-29-1996) 110 Ohio App.3d 615, 674 N.E.2d 1252. Child Custody ⟢ 147

Trial court did not abuse its discretion in refusing to grant shared parenting, in view of parties' unwillingness to agree on basic decisions regarding child's upbringing, most notably in area of religious education. deLevic v. deLevic (Franklin 1993) 86 Ohio App.3d 531, 621 N.E.2d 594, dismissed, jurisdictional motion overruled 67 Ohio St.3d 1409, 615 N.E.2d 1043. Child Custody ⟢ 127

74. —— Constitutional issues, shared parenting and joint custody

Trial court did not violate ex-husband's right to due process when court failed to permit him to introduce evidence in support of his emergency motion regarding school enrollment, alleging that parties' children had special needs which could only be met through their attendance at private school; since parties' shared parenting plan, stating that children would be enrolled in public schools, was incorporated into parties' divorce decree and ex-husband did not appeal from that decree, res judicata barred any attack by ex-husband on validity of shared parenting plan, and since language of plan was unambiguous, court did not err in refusing to admit further evidence. King v. King (Ohio App. 9 Dist., Medina, 08-24-2005) No. 05CA0008-M, 2005-Ohio-4365, 2005 WL 2020621, Unreported. Child Custody ⟢ 532; Child Custody ⟢ 650; Constitutional Law ⟢ 4391

Shared parenting order requiring custodial parent to request court order prior to relocating children concerned residence and visitation of children, and did not unconstitutionally prohibit custodial parent from travelling; custodial parent was never ordered to stay in county, and in fact agreed to stay there as part of shared parenting plan. Rozborski v. Rozborski (Ohio App. 8 Dist., 12-02-1996) 116 Ohio App.3d 29, 686 N.E.2d 546. Child Custody ⟜ 260; Constitutional Law ⟜ 1286

"Parent," for the purposes of RC 3109.04 includes only the natural or adoptive parents of a child and a partner in a same-sex female relationship (1) is neither the natural nor the adoptive parent of any of five children, two by adoption and three by artificial insemination, which the partners are raising, (2) is not entitled to an award of parental rights or shared parenting, and (3) is not denied the constitutional right to direct the upbringing of her children by dismissal of the petition for allocation of parental rights and responsibilities; although one partner's decision to co-parent her children with the other partner in a same-sex female relationship may be protected from interference by the state she is not entitled to the benefit of laws that are at present clearly inapplicable to such a "familial" arrangement. In re Ray, Nos. C-000436+, 2001 WL 127666 (1st Dist Ct App, Hamilton, 2–16–01).

75. —— Court-appointed experts, shared parenting and joint custody

Trial court does not err by submitting its chosen shared parenting plan to psychologist for review. Donovan v. Donovan (Ohio App. 12 Dist., 04-29-1996) 110 Ohio App.3d 615, 674 N.E.2d 1252. Child Custody ⟜ 418

76. —— Creation after initial decree issued, shared parenting and joint custody

Record in a divorce proceeding supported a determination that adoption of husband's shared parenting plan was in the children's best interests, even though wife presented testimony that husband had a drinking problem, that husband had difficulty controlling his anger, and, inter alia, that the children would sometimes act in an abnormal or aggressive way after returning from husband's scheduled parenting time; testimony was also presented that husband had twice been evaluated for and cleared of having alcohol-control problems, that husband was a very involved parent, and, inter alia, that the children liked the shared parenting schedule. Clouse v. Clouse (Ohio App. 3 Dist., Seneca, 03-23-2009) No. 13-08-40, 2009-Ohio-1301, 2009 WL 737778, Unreported, appeal not allowed 122 Ohio St.3d 1521, 913 N.E.2d 457, 2009-Ohio-4776. Child Custody ⟜ 147

On motion by non-residential parent for equal parenting time with child, which was treated by trial court as motion for shared parenting, trial court erred by failing to address statutorily required issue of whether change of substance in circumstances of child or residential parent occurred. Buckingham v. Buckingham (Ohio App. 2 Dist., Darke, 04-16-2004) No. 1626, 2004-Ohio-1942, 2004 WL 830054, Unreported, on subsequent appeal 2004-Ohio-5275, 2004 WL 2245196. Child Custody ⟜ 659

To modify divorce decree in order to implement shared parenting plan, trial court must determine that such modification is in best interest of child and that there has been a change in circumstances. Neel v. Neel (Ohio App. 8 Dist., 07-25-1996) 113 Ohio App.3d 24, 680 N.E.2d 207, dismissed, appeal not allowed 77 Ohio St.3d 1514, 674 N.E.2d 369. Child Custody ⟜ 553

Trial court could not modify custody provisions of divorce decree to provide for shared parenting plan, absent change of circumstances and showing that such modification was in best interest of child, particularly as parties' relationship had deteriorated to such an extent that cooperation between them was highly unlikely. Neel v. Neel (Ohio App. 8 Dist., 07-25-1996) 113 Ohio App.3d 24, 680 N.E.2d 207, dismissed, appeal not allowed 77 Ohio St.3d 1514, 674 N.E.2d 369. Child Custody ⟜ 553

77. —— Discretion of court, shared parenting and joint custody

Trial court did not abuse its discretion in disqualifying individual as a witness in child custody modification proceeding since witness, who would purportedly testify on the issue of whether ex-husband would ever harm child, had not seen ex-husband with child for over 7 years; only testimony regarding the time frame from the last custody order forward was relevant to the issues before the court. Kurfess v. Gibbs (Ohio App. 6 Dist., Lucas, 06-03-2011) No. L-09-1295, 2011-Ohio-2698, 2011 WL 2175039, Unreported. Child Custody ⟜ 653

Trial court did not abuse its discretion in denying father's motion for shared parenting, as parties appeared to be incapable of cooperating or communicating with each other, they had called the police on each other numerous times, and they had regular disputes about visitation and about medications necessary for their older child, who had special medical needs. Ussher v. Ussher (Ohio App. 2 Dist., Champaign, 03-25-2011) No. 2009-CA-49, 2011-Ohio-1440, 2011 WL 1102991, Unreported. Child Custody ⟜ 127

Trial court abused its discretion in ordering shared parenting, absent a motion by either husband or wife requesting shared parenting. Stephens v. Stephens (Ohio App. 5 Dist., Stark, 10-12-2010) No. 2009CA00295, 2010-Ohio-4964, 2010 WL 4008163, Unreported. Child Custody ⟜ 576

Trial court failed to properly apply statutory standard for determining allocation of parental rights and responsibilities in divorce proceeding, in case in which wife filed motion to adopt proposed shared parenting plan, where trial court did not consider proposed shared parenting plan, court made no findings of fact or conclusions of law regarding its rejection of proposed plan or its decision to deny motion for adoption of a shared parenting plan, court designated wife as residential parent of children but failed to further designate her as legal custodian, and divorce decree was internally inconsistent in adopting parties' separation agreement but not proposed shared parenting plan. Young v.

Young (Ohio App. 9 Dist., Wayne, 08-09-2010) No. 09CA0067, 2010-Ohio-3658, 2010 WL 3075601, Unreported. Child Custody ☞ 511

Trial court did not abuse its discretion in granting father shared parenting of parties' child; child's guardian ad litem recommended shared parenting and stated that, despite mother's opposition to sharing decision-making with father, she found the parties regularly changed parenting time to accommodate father's job schedule, did not disagree about major medical decisions for their child, and never stopped communicating with one another, both parents lived within a 15-minute drive of each other, both parents' residences were comfortable and safe for child, and child was well cared for, safe, loved and thriving physically at father's house. Halliday v. Halliday (Ohio App. 8 Dist., Cuyahoga, 06-10-2010) No. 92116, 2010-Ohio-2597, 2010 WL 2333021, Unreported. Child Custody ☞ 127; Child Custody ☞ 130; Child Custody ☞ 421

Trial court acted within its discretion in divorce action in denying husband's request for shared parenting and naming wife residential parent and legal custodian of the children, even though husband was invested in children's lives; evidence indicated that husband and wife were not in harmony in decision-making process, as was shown by wife's failure to keep husband informed as to children's activities and appointments. Johnson v. Johnson (Ohio App. 12 Dist., Butler, 03-29-2010) No. CA2009-06-177, 2010-Ohio-1283, 2010 WL 1176656, Unreported. Child Custody ☞ 127

Trial court, in approving mother's shared parenting plan with amendments, complied with statute requiring trial court, when approving shared parenting plan where only one parent submits a proposed parenting plan, to enter in record findings of fact and conclusions of law and reasons for approval; while trial court did not make explicit findings of fact concerning father's objections to mother's plan, father raised no objections to facts contained in mother's plan, but, rather objected to legal conclusions drawn from facts, and, while additional explanation by trial court might have been helpful, trial court's reasons for approving mother's amended plan and determining that this plan was in child's best interest could be discerned from record. Reed v. Hinkle (Ohio App. 10 Dist., Franklin, 08-20-2009) No. 09AP-136, 2009-Ohio-4217, 2009 WL 2579487, Unreported. Child Custody ☞ 511

Trial court determination that no change in circumstances had occurred was an abuse of discretion, in proceeding to terminate the parties' shared parenting agreement; the child's residential parent and custodian had changed from the time the parties had entered into the original shared parenting decree, as did the parties' visitation arrangement and support, and the court had granted an emergency ex parte order which contravened the shared parenting agreement. Sims v. Durant (Ohio App. 5 Dist., Fairfield, 12-05-2008) No. 2008-CA-27, 2008-Ohio-6442, 2008 WL 5159899, Unreported. Child Custody ☞ 576

Trial court's findings supported its decision to continue father's original child support obligation, though magistrate had modified parents' shared parenting plan to provide for father to have possession of child for more time than mother; there was substantial disparity in household incomes of mother and father, with mother's income being far less than father's, it was father who made voluntary decision to move an hour away from mother, creating transportation difficulties for mother, it was reasonable that father shoulder small part of additional costs that he caused mother, and fact that father was designated residential parent for school purposes under modified shared parenting plan and might have child for more time than mother did not necessarily mean that mother should be obligor of child support. Kilgore v. Kilgore (Ohio App. 11 Dist., Ashtabula, 11-03-2008) No. 2008-A-0006, No. 2008 A 0008, 2008 Ohio 5858, 2008 WL 4877151, Unreported, appeal not allowed 121 Ohio St.3d 1440, 903 N.E.2d 1223, 2009-Ohio-1638. Child Support ☞ 250; Child Support ☞ 258; Child Support ☞ 277

Trial court acted outside its discretion in denying mother's motion for a continuance of trial on modification of parental rights, which mother sought in order to obtain substitute counsel after terminating her original counsel, even though trial court had issued a scheduling order expressly indicating that no continuance would be granted; trial had been set for only three months and mother had not previously requested a continuance, mother was not attempting to delay proceedings, a short continuance would not have caused inconvenience to the parties other than having to reschedule, the case did not involve allegations regarding the child's safety, trial court agreed to permit counsel's withdrawal, and without the continuance mother was forced to proceed pro se. Swanson v. Swanson (Ohio App. 8 Dist., Cuyahoga, 09-25-2008) No. 90472, 2008-Ohio-4865, 2008 WL 4356124, Unreported. Child Custody ☞ 651

Mother was prejudiced by having to represent herself pro se at trial on modification of child custody, which mother was forced to do after trial court denied her motion for continuance in order to obtain counsel, and therefore, reversal of judgment placing child in father's custody was required; mother failed to object to a considerable amount of hearsay evidence at trial, and expressed, during the trial, her lack of knowledge of the evidentiary and procedural rules. Swanson v. Swanson (Ohio App. 8 Dist., Cuyahoga, 09-25-2008) No. 90472, 2008-Ohio-4865, 2008 WL 4356124, Unreported. Child Custody ☞ 923(4)

Any error in allowing Family Court Services representative to testify regarding 12 police reports filed against husband and that wife had obtained two civil protection orders against husband did not prejudice husband with respect to child custody determination; police reports were not admitted into evidence, and order naming wife primary residential custodian of children with continuous visitation for husband was supported by trial court's consideration of independent relevant factors, including guardian ad litem's recommendation that shared parenting was not in best interests of children because parties could not get along, and that wife had been primary caregiver of children. Saluppo v. Saluppo (Ohio App. 9 Dist., Summit, 05-31-2006) No. 22680, 2006-Ohio-2694, 2006 WL 1479633, Unreported. Child Custody ☞ 923(1)

Trial court did not abuse its discretion when it determined that shared parenting plan was not in best interests of child and awarded custody of child to mother, in divorce proceeding; numerous witnesses testified that father had anger management issues, father's therapist testified that father suffered in addition from obsessive compulsive disorder, which was being treated with psychiatric medications, and GAL testified he did not believe parents could implement shared parenting plan, and that shared parenting plan was not in best interests of child. Vujovic v. Vujovic (Ohio App. 9 Dist., Medina, 08-03-2005) No. 04CA0083-M, 2005-Ohio-3942, 2005 WL 1819527, Unreported. Child Custody ☞ 469; Child Custody ☞ 472

Trial court's failure to compel release of mother's psychological records was not an abuse of discretion in proceeding in which father filed motion for shared parenting plan; father was aware of any of mother's potential mental health issues long before he filed for custody, and father gave no explanation for delay in filing his motion to compel. Steven D.C. v. Carrie Anne P. (Ohio App. 6 Dist., Huron, 07-29-2005) No. H-04-029, No. H-04-023, 2005-Ohio-3858, 2005 WL 1793770, Unreported. Child Custody ☞ 425

Trial court's designation of mother as daughter's residential parent and legal custodian was not an abuse of discretion, in proceeding in which father filed motion for shared parenting plan; court treated parties equally, and, although court recognized that both parties had loving and affectionate relationship with daughter, that both parties participated in her daily care, and that neither parties' home was inappropriate for daughter, court found that father had not demonstrated ability to communicate effectively to make joint decisions for daughter and that shared parenting was not in her best interest. Steven D.C. v. Carrie Anne P. (Ohio App. 6 Dist., Huron, 07-29-2005) No. H-04-029, No. H-04-023, 2005-Ohio-3858, 2005 WL 1793770, Unreported. Child Custody ☞ 122; Child Custody ☞ 123; Child Custody ☞ 127

Shared parenting plan which named wife residential parent and legal custodian of children but which allocated parenting time equally between both parties was not abuse of discretion, even though parties did not request shared parenting time, in view of guardian ad litem's recommendation that shared parenting time was in best interests of children. Shultz v. Shultz (Ohio App. 5 Dist., Stark, 07-18-2005) No. 2004CA00306, 2005-Ohio-3640, 2005 WL 1682585, Unreported. Child Custody ☞ 414; Child Custody ☞ 421

Trial court did not abuse its discretion, in proceedings on wife's complaint for divorce, in denying husband's motion for shared parenting, based upon its finding that wife and husband could not cooperate on matters concerning their children, where psychological expert witness testified that shared parenting arrangement was not feasible due to parties' distrust and anger with each other and inability to work together, wife testified that she was afraid of husband, as evidenced by civil protection order, but would do what was necessary to comply with parenting order, and court did not rule out possibility of shared parenting in future. Puls v. Puls (Ohio App. 2 Dist., Montgomery, 03-25-2005) No. 20487, 2005-Ohio-1373, 2005 WL 678931, Unreported, on subsequent appeal 2005-Ohio-6839, 2005 WL 3502148. Child Custody ☞ 472

Divorce court's approval of wife's shared parenting plan was abuse of discretion, though husband had submitted no competing plan, where court made no findings of fact or conclusions of law as to reasons for approval. Phillips v. Phillips (Ohio App. 5 Dist., Stark, 01-14-2005) No. 2004CA00105, No. 2004CA00005, 2005-Ohio-231, 2005 WL 121657, Unreported. Child Custody ☞ 511

Former husband's contention that trial court abused its discretion when it disregarded parties' in-court shared parenting agreement and added language to shared parenting plan that was not part of in-court agreement was moot, where trial court had, on remand while appeal was pending, entered order that reflected agreement between parties as to custody. Holt v. Holt (Ohio App. 11 Dist., Trumbull, 08-27-2004) No. 2002-T-0147, 2004-Ohio-4536, 2004 WL 1921974, Unreported. Child Custody ☞ 917

Trial court did not abuse its discretion when it denied husband's request for shared parenting; parties were not able to cooperate in matters affecting other areas of their own lives, and wife specifically stated that she did not believe she could cooperate with husband for the purposes of shared parenting. Bechara v. Essad (Ohio App. 7 Dist., Mahoning, 06-11-2004) No. 03MA34, 2004-Ohio-3042, 2004 WL 1325636, Unreported. Child Custody ☞ 127

Trial court lacked authority to compel husband and wife to submit shared parenting plan. Debevec v. Debevec (Ohio App. 11 Dist., Portage, 06-04-2004) No. 2002-P-0126, 2004-Ohio-2927, 2004 WL 1238609, Unreported. Child Custody ☞ 120

Trial court had authority to enforce shared parenting agreement, even though child's putative father was determined not to be child's biological father, where evidence established that parent and child relationship existed between putative father and child; putative father was listed as father on child's birth certificate, mother and putative father went to Child Support Enforcement Agency (CSEA) and signed acknowledgement of paternity, administrative order that required putative father to pay child support and provide health insurance for child indicated that basis of support duty was acknowledgement of paternity filed with central paternity registry, and there was no evidence either party had attempted to rescind acknowledgment of paternity. Thomas v. Cruz (Ohio App. 9 Dist., Lorain, 11-12-2003) No. 03CA008247, 2003-Ohio-6011, 2003 WL 22657864, Unreported. Children Out–of–wedlock ☞ 20.9

Trial court did not abuse its discretion in implementing shared parenting plan, which required former wife to turn child over to former husband, who due to his work schedule was out of town approximately 57 percent of the time, when he returned from business travel, where there was no evidence that trial court failed to consider all statutory factors in awarding custody, and record showed that court took into consideration that parties were cooperating and abiding by shared parenting plan before trial court implemented plan. Warner v. Warner (Ohio App. 3 Dist., Union, 09-29-2003) No. 14-03-10, 2003-Ohio-5132, 2003 WL 22229412, Unreported. Child Custody ☞ 148; Child Custody ☞ 505

Trial court did not abuse its discretion in divorce action in granting husband 50 percent parenting time while refusing to adopt husband's shared parenting plan; trial court concluded that husband's plan, under which children would spend alternating weeks with each parent, involved frequent movement because husband and wife would live in different school districts. Petersen v. Petersen (Ohio App. 5 Dist., Ashland, 08-05-2003) No. 02COA059, 2003-Ohio-4189, 2003 WL 21805614, Unreported. Child Custody ☞ 147; Child Custody ☞ 210

Evidence supported conclusion that ex-husband could not cooperate with ex-wife with respect to a shared parenting plan, and award of sole physical custody of child to ex-wife was proper, in dissolution proceeding; guardian ad litem testified that hostility and anger between parties would make shared parenting an unreasonable option and would not be in child's best interest, and ex-wife testified as to threats made to her by ex-husband, his extreme anger during marriage, that she had filed for protection order during pendency of divorce proceedings, and that ex-husband had pushed her through mirror, and punched hole in child's nursery door. Ketchum v. Ketchum (Ohio App. 7 Dist., Columbiana, 05-16-2003) No. 2001 CO 60, 2003-Ohio-2559, 2003 WL 21134713, Unreported. Child Custody ☞ 469; Child Custody ☞ 472

Mother of out-of-wedlock child failed to demonstrate that juvenile court abused its discretion in ordering shared parenting, in accordance with recommendation of the guardian ad litem; even though mother had been the primary caregiver and there was evidence that father did not always fully understand extent of child's medical difficulties, report of guardian ad litem reflected that parties communicated well with each other concerning child, father lived with child for first ten months after his birth and had extensive visitation with minor child up to date of trial, and there was no evidence to suggest that father had taken any action which would in any way have harmed child. Giaquinta v. Anderson (Ohio App. 5 Dist., Stark, 02-24-2003) No. 2002CA00283, 2003-Ohio-844,

2003 WL 490034, Unreported. Children Out–of–wedlock ☞ 20.9

The choice of proposing shared parenting is on the parties, not the court, and a trail judge has no authority to force shared parenting where it has not been requested; a previous temporary custody plan, although evidence of the factors in RC 3109.04(L) is not a "formal request." Torch v. Torch (Ohio App. 5 Dist., Tuscarawas, 06-19-1996) No. 95AP060041, 1996 WL 363429, Unreported.

Trial court did not abuse its discretion by modifying shared parenting plan, which named unwed mother as the school placement parent, so as to name father as the school placement parent, even though doing so was contrary to guardian ad litem's recommendation; mother's relocation constituted a change in circumstances, and mother, without asking the court to modify the parenting plan, had terminated father's weeknight visits, father lost the continual and routine contact he had with his son on a weekly basis regardless of whether mother made up for missed visits, and father fostered his son's relationship with mother, but mother had resisted father's relationship with his son. Geier v. Swank (Ohio App. 10 Dist., 02-23-2010) 186 Ohio App.3d 497, 928 N.E.2d 1162, 2010-Ohio-627. Children Out–of–wedlock ☞ 20.10

Trial court abused its discretion when it named both mother and father of out-of-wedlock child as the residential parent and legal custodian of child, where the evidence established, and the court agreed, that shared parenting was against child's best interest. Andrew P. v. Jessy Z. (Ohio App. 6 Dist., 08-15-2008) 177 Ohio App.3d 837, 896 N.E.2d 220, 2008-Ohio-4124. Children Out–of–wedlock ☞ 20.9

Trial court has broad authority to order shared parenting, and its decision in that regard is discretionary. Donovan v. Donovan (Ohio App. 12 Dist., 04-29-1996) 110 Ohio App.3d 615, 674 N.E.2d 1252. Child Custody ☞ 121

Statute governing allocation of parental rights and responsibilities for care of children upon divorce allows the trial court, in the exercise of its sound discretion, to designate one parent as the residential parent and legal custodian of the child and divide other rights accordingly, or to allocate rights to both parents under a shared parenting plan. Snyder v. Snyder (Ohio App. 2 Dist., Clark, 06-07-2002) No. 2002-CA-6, 2002-Ohio-2781, 2002 WL 1252835, Unreported. Child Custody ☞ 7; Child Custody ☞ 120; Child Custody ☞ 320

Trial court did not abuse its discretion in declining to order shared parenting in divorce action, and in awarding custody of parties' child to wife, where award of custody to either party would have been appropriate, neither party submitted shared parenting plan as required by the court, and consideration of statutory factors indicated that shared parenting was not in child's best interest; parties were unable to agree as to visitation or to communicate effectively concerning child's interests and needs, and child had close relationship with his half-sibling, who was mother's child. Snyder v. Snyder (Ohio App. 2 Dist., Clark, 06-07-2002) No. 2002-CA-6, 2002-Ohio-2781, 2002 WL 1252835, Unreported. Child Custody ⬚ 76; Child Custody ⬚ 123

78. —— Filing request with court as prerequisite, shared parenting and joint custody

Unmarried mother and father's joint motion for adoption of a shared parenting plan constituted a de facto complaint commencing a child custody action; motion contained the language of a complaint, and trial court proceeded to accept filings from the parties, issue orders, and set and conduct hearings in the matter. Pearl v. Porrata (Ohio App. 3 Dist., Mercer, 12-08-2008) No. 10-07-24, 2008-Ohio-6353, 2008 WL 5124584, Unreported. Children Out–of–wedlock ⬚ 20.4

Trial court was precluded from creating shared parenting plan, and was required to make determination as to which parent would be residential parent and allocate parental rights and responsibilities for care of child, where neither parent requested shared parenting plan, and both sought to be named residential parent. Schmidli v. Schmidli (Ohio App. 7 Dist., Belmont, 06-19-2003) No. 02 BE 63, 2003-Ohio-3274, 2003 WL 21443742, Unreported. Child Custody ⬚ 120

A satisfactory shared parenting plan must be filed with the court for adoption, and otherwise, the court will not adopt any plan. Bowen v. Bowen (Ohio App. 9 Dist., 02-09-1999) 132 Ohio App.3d 616, 725 N.E.2d 1165, dismissed, appeal not allowed 86 Ohio St.3d 1402, 711 N.E.2d 231. Child Custody ⬚ 142

Trial court in divorce action could not adopt shared parenting plan that was not submitted by either party, and that, while derived from a plan submitted by former wife, was nonetheless a product of court's own creation. Bowen v. Bowen (Ohio App. 9 Dist., 02-09-1999) 132 Ohio App.3d 616, 725 N.E.2d 1165, dismissed, appeal not allowed 86 Ohio St.3d 1402, 711 N.E.2d 231. Child Custody ⬚ 142

Statutory requirement that shared parenting plan must be filed at least 30 days prior to hearing on parental rights and responsibilities is directory, not mandatory, although statutory deadline does implicate party's right to due process; although trial court may relieve party of statutory deadline and grant party's request to file shared parenting plan within 30 days prior to hearing, other party must have adequate opportunity to respond to plan. Harris v. Harris (Ohio App. 2 Dist., 08-11-1995) 105 Ohio App.3d 671, 664 N.E.2d 1304. Child Custody ⬚ 409; Constitutional Law ⬚ 4396; Statutes ⬚ 227

Where neither party files a written motion or a shared parenting plan pursuant to RC 3109.04, a request for shared parenting is denied. Bache v Bache, No. 92–AP–090071 (5th Dist Ct App, Tuscarawas, 5–6–93).

A court may not award joint custody of a child to his parents where the parents have not requested or consented to joint custody, and an award of joint custody without the consent of the parties will be reversed. Mani v Mani, No. CA–7861 (5th Dist Ct App, Stark, 12–11–89).

Where a joint custody plan is not submitted by either parent and there is no mutual consent by the parents to a joint custody agreement ordered by the court, the provisions of the joint custody statute are not applicable and the trial court errs in awarding joint custody. Monroe v Presgraves, No. CA–2847 (5th Dist Ct App, Licking, 10–29–82).

79. —— Recommendation of guardian ad litem, shared parenting and joint custody

In adopting shared parenting plan on father's motion to modify parental rights and responsibilities, trial court did not abuse its discretion by resolving the conflicts in the evidence in favor of guardian ad litem's recommendation over that of the child's counselor, where, in addition to discussions with the parents and stepmother, guardian ad litem had investigated a variety of other sources, including mother's counselor, her probation officer, her father, the Child Support Enforcement Agency, child's school, and father's parents as well as his doctor, while child's counselor, on the other hand, had conducted just ten sessions with child and a couple involving his parents and stepmother, and trial court was statutorily required to consider the recommendation of the guardian ad litem when evaluating request for shared parenting. Kirchhofer v. Kirchhofer (Ohio App. 9 Dist., Wayne, 08-16-2010) No. 09CA0061, 2010-Ohio-3797, 2010 WL 3210756, Unreported. Child Custody ⬚ 616

80. —— Modification, shared parenting and joint custody

A request for a guardian ad litem must ordinarily be made before a court interviews the child in child custody proceeding; however, where mother requested the court appoint a guardian ad litem at the objections hearing, the children's wishes, as expressed to the magistrate, conflicted with the trial court's ultimate decision to maintain father as the residential parent for school purposes and, in light of the children's wishes and their respective ages and under the unique facts presented, the absence of a guardian ad litem, who could have fully and independently investigated the situation, called into question one important factor of the trial court's decision, remand was required, under plain error doctrine, of trial court order denying mother's request for modification of shared parenting plan to be named sole residential parent in order for trial court to appoint a guardian ad litem before conducting hearing to ascertain the children's best interests, even though mother may have waived statutory right to appointment by failing to request appointment prior to magistrate's interview of children. Cochran v. Cochran (Ohio App. 4 Dist., Lawrence, 03-29-2011) No. 10CA15, 2011-Ohio-1644, 2011 WL 1233199, Unreported. Child Custody ⬚ 904; Child Custody ⬚ 924; Infants ⬚ 79

Evidence supported conclusion that a change in circumstances had occurred since entry of shared parenting plan, as necessary to support modification of plan to designate mother as child's residential parent for school purposes; father deliberately prevented contact or communication between mother and the child, child's paternal grandmother, rather than father, acted as primary caregiver for child while child resided with him in South Carolina, and the majority, if not all, of child's major procedures and surgeries, necessitated by child having been born with severe congenital heart disease, had been performed by doctors in Ohio, because the facility in South Carolina where father lived lacked a pediatric surgeon capable of performing the heart catheterization needed by the child, and she was therefore required to return to Ohio for treatment. Sutton v. Sutton (Ohio App. 2 Dist., Montgomery, 03-25-2011) No. 24108, 2011-Ohio-1439, 2011 WL 1102998, Unreported. Child Custody ☞ 576

Evidence supported conclusion that it was in child's best interest to modify shared parenting plan to designate mother as child's residential parent for school purposes; child expressed desire to remain primarily in mother's custody, while child had good interaction with both parents, she was more bonded to mother, child had lived with mother for an entire summer and was well-adjusted to arrangement, father had purposefully denied mother's right to have contact with child, and mother was more likely to facilitate father's parenting time. Sutton v. Sutton (Ohio App. 2 Dist., Montgomery, 03-25-2011) No. 24108, 2011-Ohio-1439, 2011 WL 1102998, Unreported. Child Custody ☞ 576

Statutory requirement that there be a change in circumstances to support modification of a shared-parenting decree did not apply to parties' child custody proceeding, as trial court did not modify a shared-parenting decree, but, rather, entered an original custody decree designating mother as children's sole residential parent and legal custodian, and, in doing so, it vacated the interim agreed entry that provided for shared parenting. Cwik v. Cwik (Ohio App. 1 Dist., Hamilton, 02-04-2011) No. C-090843, 2011-Ohio-463, 2011 WL 346173, Unreported, appeal not allowed 128 Ohio St.3d 1515, 948 N.E.2d 451, 2011-Ohio-2686. Child Custody ☞ 401; Child Custody ☞ 576

Trial court did not abuse its discretion, in post-divorce proceeding, by finding that modifications of shared parenting time, so as to alter exchange dates, eliminate mid-week parenting time, and designate father as residential parent for school and health decisions, were in minor children's best interests; modifications reduced change of either parent being untimely for exchange, reduced conflict and interaction between parties in presence of children, and eliminated power struggles over medical and school decisions. Depascale v. Finocchi (Ohio App. 7 Dist., Mahoning, 09-30-2010) No. 08 MA 216, 2010-Ohio-4869, 2010 WL 3904163, Unreported. Child Custody ☞ 576

Any error in modifying shared parenting plan from ex-husband and ex-wife alternating weekly as residential parent and legal custodian to sole custody for ex-husband was not plain error, where ex-wife's circumstances had changed, in that her work schedule and propensity for moving her residence had created instability in the lives of her children, and stability in ex-husband's living arrangements was conducive to the children's best interests. Rutherford v. Rutherford (Ohio App. 11 Dist., Portage, 09-03-2010) No. 2009-P-0086, 2010-Ohio-4195, 2010 WL 3492892, Unreported. Child Custody ☞ 904

Modification of parental rights and responsibilities to adopt shared parenting plan suggested by father was in best interests of child, where mother, who was child's residential parent and legal custodian, was arrested for possession of marijuana and driving under the influence of alcohol, child's maternal grandfather had been child's main caregiver over the years and had generally spent more time with child than mother, and, although child was more bonded with his mother than his father, child had a good relationship with father and got along well with his stepmother. Kirchhofer v. Kirchhofer (Ohio App. 9 Dist., Wayne, 08-16-2010) No. 09CA0061, 2010-Ohio-3797, 2010 WL 3210756, Unreported. Child Custody ☞ 552; Child Custody ☞ 559

Trial court's modification of shared parenting order so as to change location for parties to exchange children was subject to statute requiring that modification be in best interests of children, rather than statute requiring that change in circumstances be shown and that such modification be in best interests of children, notwithstanding that parenting order provided that plan could not be altered absent showing of change in circumstances; terms of parenting order could not supersede trial court's statutory authority. Bonner v. Bonner (Ohio App. 2 Dist., Darke, 02-26-2010) No. 2009 CA 10, 2010-Ohio-742, 2010 WL 703517, Unreported. Child Custody ☞ 577

Trial court's modification of shared parenting order to change location for parties to exchange children was in children's best interest, under statute providing that court could modify terms of parenting plan upon request by party where modification would be in best interest of children, where mother failed to appear at appropriate time to exchange children on holiday, and children witnessed altercation between father and mother's boyfriend at such location. Bonner v. Bonner (Ohio App. 2 Dist., Darke, 02-26-2010) No. 2009 CA 10, 2010-Ohio-742, 2010 WL 703517, Unreported. Child Custody ☞ 577

Trial court, in increasing father's parenting time with son under shared parenting plan, substantially complied with statute governing modification of parenting time pursuant to shared parenting plan, even though court did not expressly reference statutory factors, in setting forth reasoning and factual basis for decision, discussing wishes of parents and son, son's relationship with parents, parties' psychological issues, and mother interference with father's parenting time with respect to parties' daughter.

Lake v. Lake (Ohio App. 11 Dist., Portage, 02-19-2010) No. 2009-P-0015, 2010-Ohio-588, 2010 WL 597120, Unreported. Child Custody ⇔ 659

Evidence supported order modifying shared parenting plan as to designate private social services company as location at which parties were to exchange child, where evidence showed that father had history of volatility during exchanges, even at a police station, and designated location was a business designed to counsel and accommodate peaceful exchanges. Holeski v. Holeski (Ohio App. 11 Dist., Portage, 11-13-2009) No. 2009-P-0007, 2009-Ohio-6036, 2009 WL 3807168, Unreported. Child Custody ⇔ 576

Trial court did not abuse its discretion in determining it was in the child's best interest to modify the parties' shared parenting plan to an alternating weekly schedule; child, who had been in kindergarten, exhibited confusion during the school year as to whether she should ride the bus or wait for ex-husband to pick her up at school, and the "week-on/week-off" schedule would alleviate child's confusion. Herdman v. Herdman (Ohio App. 3 Dist., Marion, 01-26-2009) No. 9-08-32, 2009-Ohio-303, 2009 WL 161716, Unreported. Child Custody ⇔ 576

Evidence was insufficient to support finding that child's circumstances had measurably changed or that mother's changed circumstances, which included attending school and the birth of additional children, adversely affected child so as to support modifying custody order and making father the residential parent; fact that child was now old enough to attend school did not constitute a changed circumstance warranting modification of custody. Pazin v. Pazin (Ohio App. 7 Dist., Columbiana, 12-31-2008) No. 07-CO-43, 2008-Ohio-6975, 2008 WL 5427970, Unreported. Child Custody ⇔ 637

Order denying former husband's motion to modify the parties' shared parenting plan to grant former husband an extra overnight of parenting time every other weekend was not an abuse of discretion; the court found that granting the extra overnight would have a "chilling effect" on parents seeking to be flexible and cooperative regarding agreements in shared parenting plan, as former husband's motion to modify was filed after former wife began allowing former husband the extra overnight with child. Ryan v. Ryan (Ohio App. 7 Dist., Belmont, 12-04-2008) No. 07-BE-48, 2008-Ohio-6358, 2008 WL 5124568, Unreported, appeal not allowed 121 Ohio St.3d 1474, 905 N.E.2d 654, 2009-Ohio-2045. Child Custody ⇔ 576

Remand of trial court's order granting mother's request for modification of child support, which order changed the terms of a shared parenting plan by increasing father's support obligations, was required in order for trial court to set forth statutorily mandated findings as to why the modification was in the child's best interest. Laver v. Laver (Ohio App. 3 Dist., Henry, 11-24-2008) No. 7-08-01,

2008-Ohio-6068, 2008 WL 4965168, Unreported. Child Support ⇔ 559

Father moved to modify a term of the shared parenting plan, not to re-allocate parental rights and responsibilities, and thus, trial court should have based its decision on whether to enjoin or restrict mother from applying for a passport on child's behalf based on the best interest of the child, and not whether there had been an adequate change in circumstances since the shared plan went into effect. Van Osdell v. Van Osdell (Ohio App. 12 Dist., Warren, 11-10-2008) No. CA2007-10-123, 2008-Ohio-5843, 2008 WL 4839667, Unreported. Child Custody ⇔ 577

Imposition of default parenting grid in lieu of provisions of shared-parenting plan (SPP) was in best interests of children in proceeding to modify parenting schedule, although grid was rigid, and although parties' jobs as pilot and flight attendant were not traditional nine-to-five occupations; grid granted parties equal amount of time with children, SPP was resulting in former wife having on average four less parenting days than former husband per month, and grid allowed for more structure in children's lives. Kauza v. Kauza (Ohio App. 12 Dist., Clermont, 11-03-2008) No. CA2008-02-014, 2008-Ohio-5668, 2008 WL 4766862, Unreported. Child Custody ⇔ 576

No change of circumstance occurred since entry of original decree granting residential parent status to unwed father, with mother having visitation rights, and, as such, trial court did not need to make a determination as to whether modification of parental rights to one of shared parenting would be in the best interest of child; although child had expressed a desire to spend more time with his mother, that was not necessarily a change in circumstances, it appeared that the child had been coached by mother prior to coming to court, and child's opportunity to have contact with his half-brother existed at time of court's prior custody order. Wooten v. Schwaderer (Ohio App. 3 Dist., Union, 06-30-2008) No. 14-08-13, 2008-Ohio-3221, 2008 WL 2582913, Unreported. Children Out–of–wedlock ⇔ 20.10

Trial court in child custody modification proceedings acted within its discretion in excluding evidence of matters that took place before the parties entered into their original shared parenting plan; mother had not filed any objections to the plan and had not appealed from it, and trial court permitted evidence as to all of the requisite elements. In re D.M. (Ohio App. 8 Dist., Cuyahoga, 11-22-2006) No. 87723, 2006-Ohio-6191, 2006 WL 3378429, Unreported, appeal not allowed 113 Ohio St.3d 1468, 864 N.E.2d 654, 2007-Ohio-1722. Child Custody ⇔ 650

The best interest test, rather than the parental suitability test, applied to child custody modification proceeding involving father and maternal grandmother, where father, mother, and grandmother had previously entered into a shared parenting/joint custody agreement, the custody agreement was adopted by the court and constituted an original child custody determination, and father consented to the agreement. In re DeLucia v. West (Ohio App. 7 Dist., Mahoning, 12-21-2005) No. 05-MA-5, 2005-Ohio-6933, 2005 WL 3536486, Unreported. Child Custody ☞ 571

Domestic court did not abuse its discretion in modifying parties' shared parenting agreement to name mother as the primary residential parent and residential parent for school purposes; court found father failed to establish that he could provide child with a stable home environment in Colorado, father's failure to pay child support and failure to provide child's medical insurance coverage were also important factors in the court's decision, and finally, the court reasoned that child had formed strong familial relationships with relatives in Ohio and had established medical relationship with health care providers in Ohio. In re Shelton (Ohio App. 11 Dist., Lake, 11-18-2005) No. 2004-L-134, 2005-Ohio-6148, 2005 WL 3096534, Unreported. Child Custody ☞ 571

Trial court should have designated mother as obligor and father as obligee on child support worksheet, in proceeding on mother's motion for clarification of child care payments and father's motion for child support; shared parenting plan expressly provided that father was residential parent, and plan was approved and adopted by trial court. Lindman v. Lindman (Ohio App. 5 Dist., Delaware, 09-06-2005) No. 04CAF09065, 2005-Ohio-4708, 2005 WL 2174617, Unreported. Child Support ☞ 146

Trial court did not abuse its discretion in finding mother failed to show change in circumstances warranting modification of prior custody order, which designated father residential parent and legal guardian and granted mother visitation, to provide for shared parenting of children; although mother argued eldest daughter, who provided some care for younger children at father's residence, suffered from psychological problems, and that father's residence was in state of disrepair, father's residence was in same state of repair it had been at time of original decree, nothing in record established condition of residence posed risk to children, and nothing in record showed any problems arising from daughter's babysitting of other children. Walsh v. Walsh (Ohio App. 11 Dist., Geauga, 06-24-2005) No. 2004-G-2587, 2005-Ohio-3264, 2005 WL 1503707, Unreported. Child Custody ☞ 557(2); Child Custody ☞ 564

Evidence that modification of shared parenting plan to grant child's mother standard order of visitation was in child's best interest was sufficient to support such modification, where testimony of guardian ad litem established that child was frequently tardy at or absent from school while in mother's custody. In re Hodge (Ohio App. 2 Dist., Montgomery, 06-24-2005) No. 20898, 2005-Ohio-3177, 2005 WL 1490446, Unreported. Children Out–of–wedlock ☞ 20.10

The fact that children presently resided in the same city as father was not a sufficient change in circumstance to warrant a modification of the previous allocation of parental rights and responsibilities and grant father's request for shared parenting with mother. Gordon v. Liberty (Ohio App. 11 Dist., Portage, 06-10-2005) No. 2004-P-0059, 2005-Ohio-2884, 2005 WL 1383962, Unreported. Child Custody ☞ 568

Statutory provisions for modification and termination of parental rights and responsibilities under shared parenting decrees should be viewed as existing independently; thus, where trial court terminated prior shared-parenting decree, statutory provisions governing termination were implicated for appellate review, even though, in terminating shared-parenting decree, the trial court arguably also modified the decree because it made a basic or fundamental change to the underlying shared-parenting agreement. Lopez v. Lopez (Ohio App. 10 Dist., Franklin, 03-17-2005) No. 04AP-508, 2005-Ohio-1155, 2005 WL 615651, Unreported. Child Custody ☞ 576; Child Custody ☞ 916

A sufficient change of circumstances existed to warrant modification of the parties' shared parenting plan; the shared parenting plan was entered into by the parties when child was a toddler, and child was now old enough to begin school. Blaker v. Wilhelm (Ohio App. 6 Dist., Wood, 01-28-2005) No. WD-04-003, 2005-Ohio-317, 2005 WL 196761, Unreported. Child Custody ☞ 576

Statute governing the modification of a prior decree allocating parental rights and responsibilities did not include a presumption favoring retaining the mother as a primary parent. Rodriguez v. Frietze (Ohio App. 4 Dist., Athens, 12-17-2004) No. 04CA14, 2004-Ohio-7121, 2004 WL 3001067, Unreported, appeal not allowed 105 Ohio St.3d 1519, 826 N.E.2d 316, 2005-Ohio-1880. Child Custody ☞ 634

Reallocation of parental rights and responsibilities so as to make former husband the residential parent was proper, despite former wife's allegations of rape and domestic violence, since these were highly controverted and uncorroborated. Rodriguez v. Frietze (Ohio App. 4 Dist., Athens, 12-17-2004) No. 04CA14, 2004-Ohio-7121, 2004 WL 3001067, Unreported, appeal not allowed 105 Ohio St.3d 1519, 826 N.E.2d 316, 2005-Ohio-1880. Child Custody ☞ 637

Statutory factors applicable to determination of whether shared parenting is in the best interest of children are not applicable upon motion seeking modification of shared parenting plan. In re Jacobberger (Ohio App. 11 Dist., Geauga, 12-10-2004) No. 2003-G-2538, 2004-Ohio-6937, 2004 WL 2937402, Unreported. Child Custody ☞ 576

Father's proposed modification of shared parenting plan, seeking to be named residential parent for school purposes, was governed by section of statute governing modification of previously allocated parental rights and responsibilities, and required threshold finding of change of circumstances before considering child's best interests; modification would substantially change the allocation of the parties' parental rights by significantly decreasing mother's time with the child. In re Jacobberger (Ohio App. 11 Dist., Geauga, 12-10-2004) No. 2003-G-2538, 2004-Ohio-6937, 2004 WL 2937402, Unreported. Child Custody ☞ 576

Father failed to show change in circumstances warranting modification of shared parenting agreement by naming father residential parent for school purposes, where changes in child's life since inception of plan had not been detrimental to welfare of the child, and guardian ad litem stated that drastic change such as that proposed could be detrimental to child's progress in school. In re Jacobberger (Ohio App. 11 Dist., Geauga, 12-10-2004) No. 2003-G-2538, 2004-Ohio-6937, 2004 WL 2937402, Unreported. Child Custody ☞ 576

Evidence supported trial court's grant of mother's request that shared parenting plan be modified to increase her weekend possession time; mother's new work schedule would allow her to spend weekend time with child, guardian ad litem testified that additional family time with mother's new family would be beneficial for child, and court attempted to otherwise compensate father for his reduced weekend possession time. In re Jacobberger (Ohio App. 11 Dist., Geauga, 12-10-2004) No. 2003-G-2538, 2004-Ohio-6937, 2004 WL 2937402, Unreported. Child Custody ☞ 576

Shared parenting decree that was incorporated into both original divorce decree and nunc pro tunc decree was a final, appealable order, and thus shared parenting plan was permanent, unless modification occurred in future, even though court stated that parenting allocation was temporary. Riley v. Riley (Ohio App. 11 Dist., Portage, 09-30-2004) No. 2002-P-0125, 2004-Ohio-5302, 2004 WL 2803229, Unreported. Child Custody ☞ 531(1)

Trial court's judgment entry that modified shared parenting plan, which had been incorporated into divorce decree, was a final, appealable order, even though entry stated that former husband would be temporary residential parent and legal custodian until close of school year. Riley v. Riley (Ohio App. 11 Dist., Portage, 09-30-2004) No. 2002-P-0125, 2004-Ohio-5302, 2004 WL 2803229, Unreported. Child Custody ☞ 902

Before trial court could modify shared parenting decree and reallocate residential parent status and legal custody to former husband, trial court was required to conduct evidentiary hearing and make findings that reallocation was in best interest of child; neither former husband nor former wife made motion to modify shared parenting plan, and court reviewed only report of guardian ad litem (GAL) before electing to modify decree. Riley v. Riley (Ohio App. 11 Dist., Portage, 09-30-2004) No. 2002-P-0125, 2004-Ohio-5302, 2004 WL 2803229, Unreported. Child Custody ☞ 650; Child Custody ☞ 659

Before trial court could modify shared parenting decree and reallocate residential parent status and legal custody to former husband, trial court was required to make independent evaluation as to reasoning ability of child and wishes of child; trial court granted former husband's motion for in-camera interview of child, and court was statutorily required to determine reasoning ability of child before conducting interview. Riley v. Riley (Ohio App. 11 Dist., Portage, 09-30-2004) No. 2002-P-0125, 2004-Ohio-5302, 2004 WL 2803229, Unreported. Child Custody ☞ 654

Former wife and former husband were not entitled to access to court-ordered psychological reports as well as opportunity to cross-examine psychologist at a hearing prior to court modifying shared parenting agreement; modification was not based on reports. Riley v. Riley (Ohio App. 11 Dist., Portage, 09-30-2004) No. 2002-P-0125, 2004-Ohio-5302, 2004 WL 2803229, Unreported. Child Custody ☞ 617; Child Custody ☞ 650

While trial court abused its discretion by failing to hold evidentiary hearing before modifying shared parenting agreement, trial court's error did not constitute plain error. Riley v. Riley (Ohio App. 11 Dist., Portage, 09-30-2004) No. 2002-P-0125, 2004-Ohio-5302, 2004 WL 2803229, Unreported. Child Custody ☞ 904

In modifying shared parenting plan, trial court was not required to find change in circumstances, where modification did not reallocate parental rights but, instead, retained parties' parental rights as residential parent and legal custodian during time children resided with that parent, designated father as residential parent for school enrollment purposes, adopted father's suggested parenting plan which implied equal parenting time for both parents, and ordered mother to pay child support. Hunter v. Bachman (Ohio App. 9 Dist., Lorain, 09-29-2004) No. 04CA008421, 2004-Ohio-5172, 2004 WL 2244125, Unreported. Child Custody ☞ 576

Modifying shared parenting plan so as to grant ex-wife primary residential parenting responsibility and permitting mother to relocate with children to California was in children's best interest, where children were living in economically stressed circumstances, ex-wife could improve her economic circumstances if she moved to California, and move to California would give children opportunity for more stable and less impoverished upbringing. Valentyne v. Ceccacci (Ohio App. 8 Dist., Cuyahoga, 08-12-2004) No. 83725, 2004-Ohio-4240, 2004 WL 1799180, Unreported. Child Custody ☞ 576

Ex-husband failed to show change in circumstances, as required for modification of shared parenting plan; although ex-wife attempted to keep child on holiday, this was not based upon hostility between parties but on child's wishes, ex-wife allowed ex-husband to spend more time with child than provided for in shared parenting plan, and fact that both parties remarried did not show change in circumstances. Fox v. Fox (Ohio App. 3 Dist.,

Hancock, 06-28-2004) No. 5-03-42, 2004-Ohio-3344, 2004 WL 1433553, Unreported. Child Custody ⬅ 576

Trial court did not abuse its discretion by finding that no change in circumstance warranted modification of existing shared parenting order, despite divorced mother's claims that child's father had no regard for child's needs, that he refused to facilitate court-approved parenting time, engaged in spousal abuse in front of child, and exposed child to potential abuse by transporting child in car while under suspension and while under the influence of alcohol; several of mother's allegations involved events that occurred prior to the issuance of the original custody order and therefore could not constitute a change in circumstance, father was found not guilty of criminal charges arising out of the spousal abuse incident, and there was no evidence that father was ever cited for driving under suspension with child in the car. Kinney v. Kinney (Ohio App. 7 Dist., Belmont, 06-03-2004) No. 03 BE 7, 2004-Ohio-2935, 2004 WL 1240385, Unreported. Child Custody ⬅ 557(1); Child Custody ⬅ 637; Child Custody ⬅ 659

Modification of father's weeknight visitation with child, requiring him to both pick up and drop off child at mother's residence, which was located approximately one-and-one-half hours from father's residence, was in child's best interests, in child custody proceeding; it was not in child's best interests for her to be traveling in car for this period of time. Venuto v. Pochiro (Ohio App. 7 Dist., Mahoning, 05-21-2004) No. 02 CA 225, 2004-Ohio-2631, 2004 WL 1152055, Unreported. Child Custody ⬅ 577

Trial court improperly modified the child care provisions of the shared parenting plan without a finding on best interests of the children. Tonti v. Tonti (Ohio App. 10 Dist., Franklin, 05-18-2004) No. 03AP-494, No. 03AP-728, 2004-Ohio-2529, 2004 WL 1109840, Unreported, appeal not allowed 103 Ohio St.3d 1478, 816 N.E.2d 254, 2004-Ohio-5405. Child Custody ⬅ 659

Trial court did not act unreasonably, arbitrarily, or unconscionably in modifying parties' shared parenting plan and designating father as child's residential parent for school placement purposes; seven-year-old child repeatedly stated that he wished to live with his father, and trial court found child had sufficient reasoning ability to express his wishes and concerns, even though child "seemed immature and somewhat uncomfortable with the process." (Per Kline, J., with two judges concurring in judgment only). In re Beekman (Ohio App. 4 Dist., Pike, 03-04-2004) No. 03CA710, 2004-Ohio-1066, 2004 WL 432235, Unreported. Child Custody ⬅ 576

Trial court may modify the terms of a shared parenting plan based solely upon the best interest of the child, without a preliminary determination into whether there was change in circumstances of the child, his residential parent, or either of the parents subject to the shared-parenting decree. (Per

Kline, J., with two judges concurring in judgment only). In re Beekman (Ohio App. 4 Dist., Pike, 03-04-2004) No. 03CA710, 2004-Ohio-1066, 2004 WL 432235, Unreported. Child Custody ⬅ 576

Record supported finding that termination of parties' shared parenting agreement was necessary to serve best interest of child; trial court found child had difficulty adjusting to school prior to receiving treatment for Attention Deficit with Hyperactivity Adjustment Disorder (ADHD), that child needed structured home, that former wife's home was more structured than former husband's, that parties experienced difficulty agreeing on parenting styles, and that husband often acted unilaterally, without consulting wife, regarding child's ADHD. Winfield v. Winfield (Ohio App. 11 Dist., Lake, 12-12-2003) No. 2002-L-010, 2003-Ohio-6771, 2003 WL 22952773, Unreported. Child Custody ⬅ 576

Statutes setting forth procedure for modifying child custody decree and setting forth factors to consider in determining child's best interest did not treat former husband any differently than they treated former wife in wife's motion to modify child custody, and thus were not violative of husband's equal protection rights. Winfield v. Winfield (Ohio App. 11 Dist., Lake, 12-12-2003) No. 2002-L-010, 2003-Ohio-6771, 2003 WL 22952773, Unreported. Child Custody ⬅ 4; Constitutional Law ⬅ 3738

Former husband's due process rights were not violated by failure of statutes setting forth procedure for modifying child custody decree and setting forth factors to consider in determining child's best interest to admit to presumption of joint custody, where parties had entered into shared parenting agreement. Winfield v. Winfield (Ohio App. 11 Dist., Lake, 12-12-2003) No. 2002-L-010, 2003-Ohio-6771, 2003 WL 22952773, Unreported. Child Custody ⬅ 4; Constitutional Law ⬅ 4396

Proposed modification of shared parenting agreement that sought to substantially change allocation of parties' parental rights and responsibilities by increasing divorced father's parenting time from 33 percent to 53 percent was governed by section of statute that governed modification of previously allocated parental rights and responsibilities, and required threshold finding of change of circumstances before considering child's best interests, rather than by provision of statute on allocation of parental rights, which required only that court take into account child's best interest. Bauer v. Bauer (Ohio App. 12 Dist., Clermont, 05-19-2003) No. CA2002-10-083, 2003-Ohio-2552, 2003 WL 21135483, Unreported. Child Custody ⬅ 571

Trial court was not required to find a change in circumstances to modify custody order in case, and was only required to find that a change in custody was in child's best interest, where custody issue involved termination of a prior shared parenting plan. Lynch v. Lynch (Ohio App. 6 Dist., Huron, 03-07-2003) No. H-02-022, 2003-Ohio-1039, 2003 WL 876566, Unreported. Child Custody ⬅ 576

The trial court adequately found a change of circumstances warranting modification of mother and father's shared parenting plan, in proceeding to modify parental rights; both parents filed motions to modify or terminate the shared parenting agreement, the guardian ad litem report established that the parties' employment times had changed, and father failed to follow through with counseling, as previously ordered by the court. In re Wright (Ohio App. 5 Dist., Stark, 02-03-2003) No. 2002CA00184, 2003-Ohio-546, 2003 WL 245677, Unreported. Child Custody ☞ 560

Former wife was not entitled to relief from shared parenting plan authorized by judgment modifying child support pursuant to plan, despite fact that former wife allegedly did not authorize plan; evidence indicated wife assented to shared parenting plan, so there was no alternative to plan, and trial court made specific finding that shared parenting plan was in best interest of children. Trump v. Trump (Ohio App. 5 Dist., Stark, 01-21-2003) No. 2002CA00213, 2003-Ohio-266, 2003 WL 152833, Unreported. Child Custody ☞ 661; Child Support ☞ 342

Evidence was insufficient to support wife's contention on appeal of divorce action that shared parenting plan was not in child's best interest; trial court reviewed proposed shared parenting plan, trial testimony, and guardian ad litem's report when determining shared parenting plan, and wife failed to include guardian ad litem's report in the record on appeal. Jagusch v. Jagusch (Ohio App. 9 Dist., Medina, 01-22-2003) No. 02CA0036-M, 2003-Ohio-243, 2003 WL 149697, Unreported. Child Custody ☞ 511; Child Custody ☞ 907

Father did not have burden of proving changed circumstances as basis for trial court's modification of shared parenting plan; rather, because mother filed motions for custody and to vacate prior judgment incorporating shared-parenting plan, mother had burden of showing that current parenting plan was not in child's best interests. In Re Brazile (Ohio App. 1 Dist., Hamilton, 12-06-2002) No. C-010694, 2002-Ohio-6652, 2002 WL 31728896, Unreported. Child Custody ☞ 526

Order modifying shared parenting plan to increase amount of time mother had custody of child during school year and increasing amount of time father had custody during summer months, rather than giving mother custody on her motion for custody and motion to vacate prior judgment validating allegedly forged shared parenting plan, did not indicate that trial court ignored fact that child spent significant time with mother, but was based on determination child's best interests were best served by maintaining shared parenting plan with some modifications, in view of evidence that child had lived with mother and father at various times. In Re Brazile (Ohio App. 1 Dist., Hamilton, 12-06-2002) No. C-010694, 2002-Ohio-6652, 2002 WL 31728896, Unreported. Child Custody ☞ 526

Evidence supported magistrate's decision recommending that shared parenting plan be modified to designate father as residential parent; mother denied father court-ordered companionship with child, mother kept child in after-school care program for extended period of time, and father's work schedule was more flexible such that child would have more time with parent if he lived with father. In re Lemon (Ohio App. 5 Dist., Stark, 11-12-2002) No. 2002 CA 00098, 2002-Ohio-6263, 2002 WL 31546216, Unreported. Child Custody ☞ 576

Trial court's determination, upon former husband's motion to modify child custody so that former wife would no longer be residential parent, that shared parenting would not be in best interest of children was not an abuse of discretion; the former spouses had failed to behave civilly to each other, with former wife allegedly attempting to alienate children from former husband and former husband allegedly blocking former wife's telephone calls, failing to pass on notices of school events, and failing to take children to activities in which former wife had enrolled them. Klausing v. Overholt (Ohio App. 3 Dist., Van, 10-23-2002) No. 15-02-06, 2002-Ohio-5746, 2002 WL 31374698, Unreported. Child Custody ☞ 576

A trial court errs in granting a husband's motion to modify a transportation provision of the parties' shared parenting agreement regarding visitation where (1) he appears with counsel and the wife appears without counsel and is deprived of adequate opportunity to present her case, (2) there is no evidence that the modification was necessary to serve the best interest of the child, and (3) the court's decision is wrongly based on its finding that the husband was fully employed which itself was based on his unsworn, unsubstantiated assertion. Schoettle v. Bering (Ohio App. 12 Dist., Brown, 04-22-1996) No. CA95-07-011, 1996 WL 189027, Unreported.

A mother's modified version of a shared parenting plan is in the children's best interest where it establishes continuity and a routine to follow by having the children reside with the mother every weeknight during the school year and reside overnight with the father during the summer months. Yunker v. Yunker (Ohio App. 12 Dist., Clermont, 02-20-1996) No. CA95-07-041, 1996 WL 71497, Unreported.

A trial court may modify a shared parenting decree without the approval of both or either parent when it concludes that it is in the best interests of the child and a change of circumstance has occurred. Davis v. Davis (Ohio App. 2 Dist., Montgomery, 06-24-1994) No. 14184, 1994 WL 277903, Unreported.

Trial court order in child custody and child support modification proceeding was ambiguous and confusing, and thus was void for uncertainty and was not a final appealable order; order specifically denied former wife's motion to modify the parties' shared parenting plan, which granted former husband unsupervised visitation with the children, but also stated that the current parenting order was "working" and would remain in effect, even though the current parenting order was a temporary order that provided that former husband's visitation with the children would be supervised visitation. Brown v. Brown (Ohio App. 4 Dist., 07-15-2009) 183 Ohio App.3d 384, 917 N.E.2d 301, 2009-Ohio-3589. Child Custody ⟐ 902; Child Support ⟐ 537

The domestic relations court's exercise of jurisdiction to modify a decree allocating parental rights and responsibilities is not automatic; the General Assembly has restricted the exercise of judicial authority with respect to modification of such a decree unless a court finds, based on facts that have arisen since the time of the decree or were unknown to it at that time, not only that a change has occurred in circumstances of the child, the child's residential parent, or either parent subject to a shared-parenting decree, but also that the modification of the prior custody decree is necessary to serve the best interest of the child. Hanna v. Hanna (Ohio App. 10 Dist., 07-15-2008) 177 Ohio App.3d 233, 894 N.E.2d 355, 2008-Ohio-3523. Child Custody ⟐ 576

Designation of residential parent and legal custodian cannot be a term of shared-parenting plan and cannot be modified under statute permitting modification of the terms of a shared-parenting plan without a change of circumstances if doing so is in child's best interests; a plan is statutorily different from a decree or an order and is not used by a court to designate the residential parent or legal custodian. Fisher v. Hasenjager (Ohio, 10-25-2007) 116 Ohio St.3d 53, 876 N.E.2d 546, 2007-Ohio-5589. Child Custody ⟐ 147; Child Custody ⟐ 576

Trial court is precluded from modifying prior decree allocating parental rights and responsibilities unless it finds, based on facts that have arisen since time of decree or were unknown to it at that time, not only that change has occurred in circumstances of child, child's residential parent, or either parent subject to shared parenting decree, but also that modification of prior custody decree is necessary to serve best interest of child. In re Brayden James (Ohio, 05-30-2007) 113 Ohio St.3d 420, 866 N.E.2d 467, 2007-Ohio-2335, reconsideration denied 114 Ohio St.3d 1484, 870 N.E.2d 734, 2007-Ohio-3699. Child Custody ⟐ 554; Child Custody ⟐ 555; Child Custody ⟐ 557(3); Child Custody ⟐ 576

Intent of statute precluding trial court from modifying prior decree allocating parental rights and responsibilities unless it finds, based on facts that have arisen since time of decree or that were unknown to it at that time, that change has occurred in circumstances of child, child's residential parent, or either parent subject to shared parenting decree, and finds that modification of prior custody decree is necessary to serve best interest of child, is to spare children from constant tug of war and to attempt to provide some stability to custodial status of children, even though out-of-custody parent may be able to prove that he or she can provide a "better" environment. In re Brayden James (Ohio, 05-30-2007) 113 Ohio St.3d 420, 866 N.E.2d 467, 2007-Ohio-2335, reconsideration denied 114 Ohio St.3d 1484, 870 N.E.2d 734, 2007-Ohio-3699. Child Custody ⟐ 554; Child Custody ⟐ 555; Child Custody ⟐ 557(3); Child Custody ⟐ 576

Trial court did not abuse its discretion when it determined that the modification of shared parenting plan to designate mother as the sole residential parent and legal custodian was in the best interest of child born out-of-wedlock; father had deviated from shared parenting order without taking appropriate steps to obtain court approval, mother testified that when father picked up or dropped off child for parenting time he would denigrate mother, call her obscene names, and flip her off in front of child, and counselor testified that she did not have any concern about mother's ability to care for child. Fisher v. Hasenjager (Ohio App. 3 Dist., 08-14-2006) 168 Ohio App.3d 321, 859 N.E.2d 1022, 2006-Ohio-4190, appeal allowed 112 Ohio St.3d 1406, 858 N.E.2d 817, 2006 Ohio 6447, reversed 116 Ohio St.3d 53, 876 N.E.2d 546, 2007-Ohio-5589. Children Out-of-wedlock ⟐ 20.10

The provisions in a shared parenting plan that allocate the parental rights and responsibilities of a child between his or her parents are "terms" of the plan, within meaning of statutory subsection governing modification of the terms of shared parenting plans, and thus, under that subsection, a trial court may modify such a plan to designate a parent the residential parent and legal custodian, either on its own motion or on the request of one or both parents, solely on its determination that the modifications are in the best interest of the child. Fisher v. Hasenjager (Ohio App. 3 Dist., 08-14-2006) 168 Ohio App.3d 321, 859 N.E.2d 1022, 2006-Ohio-4190, appeal allowed 112 Ohio St.3d 1406, 858 N.E.2d 817, 2006-Ohio-6447, reversed 116 Ohio St.3d 53, 876 N.E.2d 546, 2007-Ohio-5589. Child Custody ⟐ 576

General Assembly's use of the word "terms," in statute permitting court to modify the terms of a shared parenting plan, shows its intent to allow trial courts to modify all provisions incorporated in a shared parenting plan. Fisher v. Hasenjager (Ohio App. 3 Dist., 08-14-2006) 168 Ohio App.3d 321, 859 N.E.2d 1022, 2006-Ohio-4190, appeal allowed 112 Ohio St.3d 1406, 858 N.E.2d 817, 2006-Ohio-6447, reversed 116 Ohio St.3d 53, 876 N.E.2d 546, 2007-Ohio-5589. Child Custody ⟐ 576

When the proposed modifications to a shared parenting plan change the allocation of parental rights and responsibilities, are substantial modifications, or substantially change the parental rights and responsibilities, trial courts are able to make such modifications to the terms of the shared parenting plan, either on its own motion or on the request of one or both of the parents, as long as the modifications are in the best interest of the child. Fisher v. Hasenjager (Ohio App. 3 Dist., 08-14-2006) 168 Ohio App.3d 321, 859 N.E.2d 1022, 2006-Ohio-4190, appeal allowed 112 Ohio St.3d 1406, 858 N.E.2d 817, 2006-Ohio-6447, reversed 116 Ohio St.3d 53, 876 N.E.2d 546, 2007-Ohio-5589. Child Custody ⟐ 576

Trial court modified, rather than terminated, parents' shared parenting plan when it named mother as the residential parent and legal custodian of child born out-of-wedlock, where both mother and father had moved to be designated the sole residential parent and legal custodian, not to terminate the shared parenting plan, and trial court stated that all other orders not in conflict therewith "shall remain in full force and effect," and, on motion for clarification, confirmed that mother's first right of refusal to provide child care to child, which was part of shared parenting plan, was still in full force and effect. Fisher v. Hasenjager (Ohio App. 3 Dist., 08-14-2006) 168 Ohio App.3d 321, 859 N.E.2d 1022, 2006-Ohio-4190, appeal allowed 112 Ohio St.3d 1406, 858 N.E.2d 817, 2006-Ohio-6447, reversed 116 Ohio St.3d 53, 876 N.E.2d 546, 2007-Ohio-5589. Children Out–of–wedlock ☞ 20.10

Trial court was required to consider, upon former husband's motion for reallocation of parental rights and responsibilities under shared-parenting plan, whether change in circumstances of child, residential parent, or either of the parents had occurred since prior decree, where former wife was child's residential parent and legal custodian at time of hearing. Patton v. Patton (Ohio App. 3 Dist., 03-06-2001) 141 Ohio App.3d 691, 753 N.E.2d 225, 2001-Ohio-2117. Child Custody ☞ 555

Evidence of changed circumstances since adoption of shared parenting plan incident to divorce, while sufficient to support modification of plan, was insufficient to justify trial court's sua sponte modification of plan in manner not contemplated by either former spouse and not supported by any evidence in hearing record concerning statutory factors applicable to determination of children's best interests; both former spouses wanted sole custody, court modified plan to provide for custody changing each school year, and court's modification did not address dispute as to which school children should attend, which originally brought matter before court. Bunten v. Bunten (Ohio App. 3 Dist., 02-26-1998) 126 Ohio App.3d 443, 710 N.E.2d 757. Child Custody ☞ 637

Evidence that both parties to shared parenting plan had remarried since original divorce decree was effected, with attendant changes in obligations to children and step-children, that former wife had left full-time employment outside home to stay with children and work as day-care provider, and that children were reaching school age, making original arrangement in which former spouses alternated as "residential" parent on month-to-month basis detrimental to stability of children's educations, was sufficient to establish change in circumstances warranting modification of shared parenting plan. Bunten v. Bunten (Ohio App. 3 Dist., 02-26-1998) 126 Ohio App.3d 443, 710 N.E.2d 757. Child Custody ☞ 637

Unless modification of child custody decree is sought from shared parenting order, statutory change in circumstances requirement relates to circumstances of child or residential parent. Waggon-er v. Waggoner (Ohio App. 9 Dist., 05-08-1996) 111 Ohio App.3d 1, 675 N.E.2d 541, dismissed, appeal not allowed 77 Ohio St.3d 1445, 671 N.E.2d 1284. Child Custody ☞ 555

Fact that trial court, in addition to finding shared parenting agreement fair, reasonable and in best interest of children, also found that there had been no change in circumstance that would support a motion to modify did not invalidate trial court's finding that plan served children's best interests. Evans v. Evans (Ohio App. 12 Dist., 10-02-1995) 106 Ohio App.3d 673, 666 N.E.2d 1176, dismissed, appeal not allowed 75 Ohio St.3d 1448, 663 N.E.2d 330. Child Custody ☞ 511

Evidence established that it was in best interest of the two children to modify custody by granting legal custody to former husband; trial court interviewed the children, the children, while living with former husband pursuant to temporary custody order, had adjusted well to former husband's home, they were doing well at school, and they had improved their grades, former husband would better facilitate visitation orders, and former wife had at least discussed moving to another state with the children. Truax v. Regal (Ohio App. 9 Dist., Summit, 09-18-2002) No. 20902, 2002-Ohio-4867, 2002 WL 31060383, Unreported. Child Custody ☞ 637

Shared parenting plan that was incorporated into divorce decree did not include express or implied prohibition against relocating children to another state, and therefore mother did not have the burden, in seeking modification of plan so as to permit her to relocate with children to Arizona, to show that relocation was in best interest of children; while plan stated parties' intention that plan be based on parties' living within Northeast Ohio area, it also included provisions addressing a possible relocation. Harbottle v. Harbottle (Ohio App. 9 Dist., Summit, 09-18-2002) No. 20897, 2002-Ohio-4859, 2002 WL 31060237, Unreported. Child Custody ☞ 261; Child Custody ☞ 452

Trial court properly concluded that modification of shared parenting plan to designate former husband children's residential parent was in children's best interest, where magistrate fully considered all statutory factors relevant to such conclusion, noting those favorable to former wife as well as those favorable to former husband, and where evidence indicated that former wife was driving without valid drivers' license, had used alcohol in the past when upset, continued to drink, had tested positive for cocaine during year prior to hearing, and was having trouble controlling older child, and that younger child's attendance record at school was progressively declining. Pickett v. Pickett (Ohio App. 11 Dist., Lake, 06-21-2002) No. 2001-L-136, 2002-Ohio-3128, 2002 WL 1357163, Unreported. Child Custody ☞ 554; Child Custody ☞ 559

A request by a party to a shared parenting agreement that it be modified from the children living six months with each parent to them living with the mother the entire year except for six weeks in the summer when they would live with their father is governed by RC 3109.04(E)(1)(a) rather than RC 3109.04(E)(2)(b) since the proposed modification of the agreement substantially changes the allocation of the parties' parental rights and responsibilities, and therefore "change of circumstances" is the appropriate standard, and age of the children alone is not a sufficient factor to find a change of circumstances, since if age was sufficient there would be no reason to impose this requirement as children always grow older. Fisher v Campbell, No. CA96–11–248, 1997 WL 349013 (12th Dist Ct App, Butler, 6–23–97).

81. —— Moral and religious issues, shared parenting and joint custody

A father's proclivity to cross-dressing is not evidence that he would not be a fit, loving, and capable parent and a shared parenting plan in such case is proper where it establishes (1) the mother as residential parent for nine months, (2) the father as residential parent for three months, and (3) a provision for modification once the child becomes school age. Mayfield v. Mayfield (Ohio App. 5 Dist., Tuscarawas, 08-14-1996) No. 96AP030032, 1996 WL 489043, Unreported.

In a custody dispute involving parties raised as Jehovah Witnesses, a plan of shared parenting in accordance with the recommendations of a court-appointed psychologist is adopted by the trial court in light of the court's continuing jurisdiction and in view of evidence presented by the father who has left the religious sect that (1) the church "shuns" those who have left, (2) family members are restricted in the kinds of interaction they can have with a former church member, and (3) such disfellowship will interfere with his relationship with the children unless he is made the residential parent. Reier v. Reier (Ohio App. 2 Dist., Darke, 06-21-1996) No. 1372, 1996 WL 339943, Unreported.

Former wife's unrelenting refusal to place child's needs above her own religious convictions clearly justified modifying custody from shared parenting plan to sole custody in favor of former husband. Holder v. Holder (Ohio App. 2 Dist., 05-11-2007) 171 Ohio App.3d 728, 872 N.E.2d 1239, 2007-Ohio-2354. Child Custody ☞ 576

Prohibiting former wife from taking child to religious activities at former wife's church during her visitation was unwarranted in post-divorce proceeding that modified custody from shared parenting plan to sole custody in favor of former husband; former wife and child were bonded, child was well-adjusted for the most part and was doing well in school, and ongoing conflict between two households that child experienced did not affect child's general welfare to extent that would warrant curtailing former wife's fundamental right to communicate her religious convictions to child. Holder v. Holder (Ohio App. 2 Dist., 05-11-2007) 171 Ohio App.3d 728, 872 N.E.2d 1239, 2007-Ohio-2354. Child Custody ☞ 577

Trial court's judgment that benefits of reallocation of parental rights and responsibilities out-

weighed harm likely to be caused by change of environment was not against weight of evidence, as would support former husband's motion for permanent change in custody, even though children were doing well in school and were getting along with former wife's new roommate, where former wife's life had undergone many changes, including changes to name, religion, and sexual orientation, and roommate was a convicted sex offender. In re Marriage of Faulhaber (Ohio App. 11 Dist., Portage, 06-28-2002) No. 2001-P-0110, 2002-Ohio-3380, 2002 WL 1401066, Unreported. Child Custody ☞ 637

82. —— Parent's refusal to consider, as factor in custody, shared parenting and joint custody

Trial court was not required to adopt parties' proposed shared parenting plan that had been implemented pending divorce and subsequently recommended by guardian ad litem, where wife testified at trial that she did not feel shared parenting was appropriate, plans proposed by each party at divorce proceeding were very different, wife's plan more closely followed typical plan associated with allocation of residential parent and traditional visitation schedule, testimony at trial indicated that parties had great difficulty cooperating with each other, and husband was awarded more visitation than normally allotted under standard visitation orders. Huelskamp v. Huelskamp (Ohio App. 3 Dist., 12-28-2009) 185 Ohio App.3d 611, 925 N.E.2d 167, 2009-Ohio-6864. Child Custody ☞ 141; Child Custody ☞ 421

Evidence supported trial court's grant of parenting time to father who had previously enjoyed shared parenting; court noted that it had never seen so much conflict between parents in such a short amount of time, father and stepmother's aversion to accommodating changes created conflict, and court devised a visitation schedule that sought to minimize exposure to such conflict. Winkler v. Winkler (Ohio App. 10 Dist., Franklin, 05-13-2003) No. 02AP-937, No. 02AP-1267, 2003-Ohio-2418, 2003 WL 21060867, Unreported. Child Custody ☞ 577

Court substantially complied with statute requiring a review of a shared parenting plan proposed by father to determine if plan was in children's best interests, even though court did not explicitly review his plan, where trial court found the parties unable to cooperate and jointly make decisions concerning their children, and thus, a shared parenting plan was not in the children's best interest. Winkler v. Winkler (Ohio App. 10 Dist., Franklin, 05-13-2003) No. 02AP-937, No. 02AP-1267, 2003-Ohio-2418, 2003 WL 21060867, Unreported. Child Custody ☞ 511

Evidence was sufficient to support trial court's findings that shared parenting was not appropriate in case; mother and father did not have the ability to cooperate and make decisions jointly regarding their children, both parents somewhat lacked the ability to encourage contact, love, and affection between the children and the other parent, and guardian ad litem report indicated that shared parenting was not in the best interest of the children and existing plan should have been terminated. Winkler v. Winkler (Ohio App. 10 Dist., Franklin, 05-13-2003) No. 02AP-937, No. 02AP-1267, 2003-Ohio-2418, 2003 WL 21060867, Unreported. Child Custody ☞ 127; Child Custody ☞ 421

A trial court abuses its discretion by trying to require a mother to accept joint custody and by considering her failure to agree to joint custody as a material factor in the court's decision to award sole custody to the father. Ellars v. Ellars (Franklin 1990) 69 Ohio App.3d 712, 591 N.E.2d 783. Child Custody ☞ 50; Child Custody ☞ 141

83. —— Presumption, shared parenting and joint custody

Evidence at divorce trial was sufficient to support award of visitation to father and allocation of parental rights to mother, rather than shared parenting, despite father's contention that temporary order of shared parenting was working; court considered statutory factors, found that mother was child's primary caregiver and was more likely to honor and facilitate parenting time and visitation, and court found that father's attitude of inflexibility and unwillingness to work out parenting time unless in writing impaired the parties' ability to cooperate and make joint decisions. Mummey v. Mummey (Ohio App. 7 Dist., Noble, 09-07-2010) No. 10 NO 371, 2010-Ohio-4243, 2010 WL 3503501, Unreported. Child Custody ☞ 133; Child Custody ☞ 134

Evidence supported the trial court's determination that the presumption in favor of shared parenting was rebutted, in divorce proceeding; the magistrate's findings of fact characterized the relationship between father and mother as "tumultuous," the magistrate found that father wrote "vile" messages on the walls of the residence, and that he had been "stalking" mother, father had been diagnosed with depression but he refused to take his medicine, and father refused to give child her medicine for diagnosed attention deficit disorder. Kong v. Kong (Ohio App. 8 Dist., Cuyahoga, 07-08-2010) No. 93120, 2010-Ohio-3180, 2010 WL 2681835, Unreported. Child Custody ☞ 456

84. —— Procedural issues, shared parenting and joint custody

Former husband waived his appellate argument that alleged the trial court erred when it dismissed his shared parenting termination motion without hearing from the guardian ad litem or receiving his report into evidence, where counsel for former husband failed to request the admission of the guardian ad litem's report in the trial court. Rice v. Rice (Ohio App. 5 Dist., Delaware, 06-23-2011) No. 10 CA F 11 0091, 2011-Ohio-3099, 2011 WL 2520149, Unreported. Child Custody ☞ 904

Trial court acted within its discretion in ordering father to pay for mother's family counseling, in action on opposing motions to modify shared parenting plan, where evidence showed that father was responsible for mother's fragile emotional state fol-

lowing divorce, and father had the financial resources to afford the counseling. Holeski v. Holeski (Ohio App. 11 Dist., Portage, 11-13-2009) No. 2009-P-0007, 2009-Ohio-6036, 2009 WL 3807168, Unreported. Child Custody ☞ 661

Remand of trial court's order selecting father's proposed shared parenting plan, rather than mother's, was required in order for trial court to comport with statutory requirements by stating findings of fact and conclusions of law as to the reasons trial court approved father's and rejected mother's. Spence v. Spence (Ohio App. 11 Dist., Portage, 05-02-2008) No. 2007-P-0070, 2008-Ohio-2127, 2008 WL 1934424, Unreported. Child Custody ☞ 924

On remand, the trial court was required to clarify the shared parenting plan between the parties; the parties filed proposed shared parenting plans that were almost identical with the exception of possession times, parties later agreed on possession times and stipulated to the same, and the trial court addressed possession times and failed to address the rest of the issues in the proposed shared parenting plans. Yasinow v. Yasinow (Ohio App. 8 Dist., Cuyahoga, 03-23-2006) No. 86467, 2006-Ohio-1355, 2006 WL 728736, Unreported. Child Custody ☞ 924

Trial court was not required to serve former husband with copy of order dismissing motion for shared parenting due to failure by husband's attorney to prepare and submit shared parenting order after motion was initially granted; rather, service was required to be made on husband's attorney. Spirito v. Partridge (Ohio App. 2 Dist., Greene, 10-21-2005) No. 04-CA0118, 2005-Ohio-5589, 2005 WL 2697259, Unreported. Child Custody ☞ 410; Child Custody ☞ 521

Denying former wife's request for continuance of hearing on request to modify shared parenting plan, to appoint guardian ad litem, was not an abuse of discretion, where wife's request for continuance was made on day of hearing, nearly seven months after her first motion for appointment of a guardian ad litem. Tener v. Tener-Tucker (Ohio App. 12 Dist., Warren, 07-25-2005) No. CA2004-05-061, 2005-Ohio-3892, 2005 WL 1798273, Unreported. Child Custody ☞ 651

Court of Appeals lacked jurisdiction to consider, on mother's appeal from judgment entry adopting magistrate's decision denying her motion for reallocation of parental rights and other related motions, issue of whether mother had been properly served in connection with hearing on father's motion for reallocation of parental rights, as mother presented argument that she had not been properly served to trial court in motion to set aside judgment entry adopting magistrate's decision terminating parties' shared parenting plan and designating father as residential parent and legal custodian of child, trial court specifically ruled that mother had been properly served, and mother had not appealed from ruling. In re K.X. (Ohio App. 10 Dist., Franklin, 07-26-2005) No. 04AP-949, 2005-Ohio-3791, 2005 WL 1745311, Unreported. Child Custody ☞ 661

Parents who voluntarily relinquished custody of their child to custodian without intervention of any state agency were not entitled to reunification plan. In re Bailey (Ohio App. 1 Dist., Hamilton, 06-17-2005) No. C-040014, No. C-040479, 2005-Ohio-3039, 2005 WL 1413269, Unreported, appeal not allowed 107 Ohio St.3d 1423, 837 N.E.2d 1208, 2005-Ohio-6124. Infants ☞ 155

Once trial court was divested of subject matter jurisdiction over matters relating to custody of child after one-year period following entry of order granting legal custody to child's great aunt and uncle had lapsed, it was not "a court that had jurisdiction to make parenting determination related to child" under Uniform Child Custody Jurisdiction Act. In re N.W. (Ohio App. 8 Dist., Cuyahoga, 05-19-2005) No. 85468, 2005-Ohio-2466, 2005 WL 1190728, Unreported. Children Out–of–wedlock ☞ 20.13

Unwed father waived his appellate argument that alleged that the trial court's adoption and approval of his second proposed shared parenting plan, which was effective upon father's relocation out of state, was erroneous as a matter of law, where father failed to raise the alleged error in his objection to the magistrate's opinion. In re Vodila (Ohio App. 5 Dist., Stark, 02-07-2005) No. 2004CA00249, 2005-Ohio-496, 2005 WL 299844, Unreported. Children Out–of–wedlock ☞ 20.11

Trial court did not abuse its discretion in considering husband's untimely filed shared parenting plan, in action for divorce, where wife was given adequate opportunity to respond thereto at hearing. Swain v. Swain (Ohio App. 4 Dist., Pike, 01-06-2005) No. 04CA726, 2005-Ohio-65, 2005 WL 43948, Unreported. Child Custody ☞ 147; Child Custody ☞ 500

Reasons for trial court's denial of wife's proposed shared parenting plan were not apparent from record in proceedings on complaint for divorce, where trial court clearly indicated evidence relied upon by it with respect to each factor in best interests determination, but made no findings of fact, entered no conclusions of law, and did not expressly adopt specific reasons offered by magistrate. Erwin v. Erwin (Ohio App. 3 Dist., Union, 04-04-2004) No. 14-04-37, 2005-Ohio-1603, 2004 WL 3254669, Unreported. Child Custody ☞ 907

Trial court was required to include in its order granting divorce and rejecting wife's proposed shared parenting plan specific, delineated findings of fact and conclusions of law with respect to its conclusions as to children's best interests, where its reasons for rejecting wife's shared parenting plan were not apparent from record. Erwin v. Erwin (Ohio App. 3 Dist., Union, 04-04-2004) No. 14-04-37, 2005-Ohio-1603, 2004 WL 3254669, Unreported. Child Custody ☞ 511

Trial court's erroneous sua sponte request that parties to child custody proceeding submit proposed shared parenting plans was harmless, where neither party objected at hearing, or prior to or concurrent with submission of such plans. Loudermilk v. Lynch (Ohio App. 11 Dist., Ashtabula, 09-30-2004) No. 2002-A-0044, No. 2002-A-0045, 2004-Ohio-5299, 2004 WL 2803411, Unreported. Child Custody ☞ 923(2)

In proceeding to modify shared parenting plan, trial court's finding that mother unilaterally reduced father's parenting time was not inconsistent with finding that neither parent continuously or willfully denied other parenting time in accordance with order of court, where no definite court order existed in regard to what specific time each parent was entitled to have with children. Hunter v. Bachman (Ohio App. 9 Dist., Lorain, 09-29-2004) No. 04CA008421, 2004-Ohio-5172, 2004 WL 2244125, Unreported. Child Custody ☞ 659

Former wife was not operating under duress when she entered into settlement agreement with husband and paternal grandparents, in which husband was named child's residential parent, in presence of court; wife had voluntarily released her attorney on day of hearing despite admonishment from court that she would be representing herself that day, husband was not involved in wife's decision to terminate attorney, and wife affirmatively stated that she had read agreement and stipulation, that she had been given opportunity to negotiate settlement terms, and that she agreed with terms. Gabel v. Gabel (Ohio App. 3 Dist., Marion, 08-16-2004) No. 9-04-13, 2004-Ohio-4292, 2004 WL 1812824, Unreported. Child Custody ☞ 35

Denial of former wife's motion for continuance of final hearing on husband's motion to modify custody was not abuse of discretion; litigation had already been lengthy and protracted, wife had three months notice of final hearing, two continuances were granted in order to complete discovery, wife did not request continuance until one day prior to final hearing, several witnesses, including experts, had been subpoenaed, attorneys, court, and other parties were prepared for hearing on that day. Gabel v. Gabel (Ohio App. 3 Dist., Marion, 08-16-2004) No. 9-04-13, 2004-Ohio-4292, 2004 WL 1812824, Unreported. Child Custody ☞ 651

Wife waived right to claim on appeal from custody determination in divorce proceeding that hospital's assessment of her alcohol use was privileged and constituted expert report, where wife failed to raise such specific arguments in trial court. Klausman v. Klausman (Ohio App. 9 Dist., Summit, 06-30-2004) No. 21718, 2004-Ohio-3410, 2004 WL 1461356, Unreported. Child Custody ☞ 904

Hospital's assessment of wife's alcohol use could not be excluded from divorce proceeding based on wife's claim that assessment was not court ordered, where record indicated to contrary in that wife admitted that assessment was performed pursuant to referral by Family Court Services (FCS) for counseling and for evaluation related to child custody challenge. Klausman v. Klausman (Ohio App. 9 Dist., Summit, 06-30-2004) No. 21718, 2004-Ohio-3410, 2004 WL 1461356, Unreported. Child Custody ☞ 451

Trial court was required to hold evidentiary hearing before granting former wife sole custody of parties' minor child; there was no indication in record that trial court took any testimony or admitted any evidence beyond former wife's assertions that parties agreed to submit entry granting sole custody to wife, and parties were not able to reach agreement on shared parenting. Kelm v. Kelm (Ohio App. 10 Dist., Franklin, 03-04-2004) No. 03AP-472, 2004-Ohio-1004, 2004 WL 396325, Unreported. Child Custody ☞ 500

Former wife could not claim, on motion to vacate court's implementation of shared parenting plan, that trial court unlawfully permitted former spouses to enter into settlement agreement concerning parenting plan without presence of guardian ad litem, where former wife fully participated in settlement without guardian, agreement was entered voluntarily, and both parties and the court had read the guardian's report. Killa v. Killa (Ohio App. 7 Dist., Mahoning, 02-06-2004) No. 03MA101, 2004-Ohio-566, 2004 WL 234746, Unreported. Child Custody ☞ 526

Former husband's failure to timely object to magistrate's findings in post-divorce proceedings that change of circumstances occurred such that termination of shared parenting agreement was warranted, that evidence did not support dismissal of his contempt motion, and that husband was required to pay child support prohibited husband from raising alleged errors on appeal (Per Evans, J., with two judges concurring in the result). Brown v. Brown (Ohio App. 4 Dist., Adams, 01-05-2004) No. 02CA749, 2004-Ohio-330, 2004 WL 135848, Unreported. Child Custody ☞ 904; Child Support ☞ 539

Former husband's failure to timely object to magistrate's allowance of alleged hearsay testimony in post-divorce proceeding over shared parenting agreement, and his failure to file with trial court transcript of magistrate's hearing and evidence submitted during hearing, prohibited consideration of alleged error on appeal, even though transcripts had been included with record on appeal. (Per Evans, J., with two judges concurring in the result). Brown v. Brown (Ohio App. 4 Dist., Adams, 01-05-2004) No. 02CA749, 2004-Ohio-330, 2004 WL 135848, Unreported. Child Custody ☞ 904

Trial court erred in failing to state its reasons for denying unwed father's shared parenting plan pursuant to statute requiring the trial court to enter findings of fact and conclusions of law as to the reasons for the approval or refusal of shared parenting plan. In re Minnick (Ohio App. 12 Dist., Madison, 08-11-2003) No. CA2003-01-001, 2003-Ohio-4245, 2003 WL 21905088, Unreported. Children Out–of–wedlock ☞ 20.4

Unwed father was deprived of due process because he did not receive adequate notice that mother's shared parenting plan, which was submitted at close of custody hearing, would be considered by the trial court, and trial court erred in adopting mother's shared parenting plan which was not time-ly filed in compliance with statute requiring that a motion for shared parenting be filed at least 30 days prior to hearing; trial court's comments about submitting proposed entries did not give father any indication that the trial court would allow mother to submit a shared parenting plan after the hearing, and father was not given any opportunity after the submission of the plan to respond to its contents. In re Minnick (Ohio App. 12 Dist., Madison, 08-11-2003) No. CA2003-01-001, 2003-Ohio-4245, 2003 WL 21905088, Unreported. Children Out–of–wedlock ☞ 20.4; Constitutional Law ☞ 4396

Trial court was not required to make explicit findings concerning other statutory best interest factors before rejecting shared parenting plan, in dissolution proceeding; it was obvious that trial court had accepted parties' inability to cooperate as overriding factor in rejecting shared parenting plan, and thus any further discussion of other best interest factors would have been superfluous. Ketchum v. Ketchum (Ohio App. 7 Dist., Columbiana, 05-16-2003) No. 2001 CO 60, 2003-Ohio-2559, 2003 WL 21134713, Unreported. Child Custody ☞ 511

A referee's interim report is by nature incomplete and indicates that there is to be a final report at some future time and a domestic relations court abuses discretion when it denies a father's motion for shared parenting on the basis of this report where the order is stamped as a final appealable order but the referee states within the report that it is interim. Thieken v. Spoerl (Ohio App. 12 Dist., Butler, 08-07-1995) No. CA94-11-201, 1995 WL 470535, Unreported.

Testimony of former same-sex partner who had borne child while partners were in relationship was inadmissible under parol evidence rule for purposes of determining her intention to terminate co-custodial status of parties vis-a-vis child if they separated, as agreed entry, in which parties agreed to share custody, clearly contemplated that it was to be in effect until child finished high school or turned 18, and that trial court would retain jurisdiction to resolve any future disputes. Morris v. Hawk (Ohio App. 5 Dist., 02-10-2009) 180 Ohio App.3d 837, 907 N.E.2d 763, 2009-Ohio-656. Evidence ☞ 450(2)

Minor child did not have an independent legal right, separate and apart from his parents, to commence or maintain an action requesting court to modify prior custody decree and grant shared custody, and thus child lacked standing to file objections to magistrate's decision that resolved and dismissed father's motion requesting shared parenting, after father withdrew his objections; child's status as a party was contingent upon one or both of the minor child's parents bringing and maintaining the action and the court's exercise of its continuing jurisdiction in the matter. Hanna v. Hanna (Ohio App. 10 Dist., 07-15-2008) 177 Ohio App.3d 233, 894 N.E.2d 355, 2008-Ohio-3523. Child Custody ☞ 605; Infants ☞ 72(1)

Minor child was not prejudiced by trial court's failure to rule on his objections to magistrate's decision that resolved and dismissed father's motion to modify prior child custody decree and grant shared custody, after father withdrew his objections, since child's limited interest in expressing his wishes concerning custody, though important, was no longer at issue once father decided to forgo his motion and withdraw his own objections. Hanna v. Hanna (Ohio App. 10 Dist., 07-15-2008) 177 Ohio App.3d 233, 894 N.E.2d 355, 2008-Ohio-3523. Child Custody ⇒ 923(4)

In choosing shared parenting plan in divorce proceeding, trial court was not required to issue findings of fact pertaining to in camera interview it conducted with parties' children, where there were no special circumstances. Donovan v. Donovan (Ohio App. 12 Dist., 04-29-1996) 110 Ohio App.3d 615, 674 N.E.2d 1252. Child Custody ⇒ 511

Wife's due process rights were not violated by divorce court's consideration of husband's motion for shared parenting, filed on day of custody hearing, or by manner in which custody hearing was conducted, as wife was not thereby prejudiced; husband's alternative request for shared parenting was filed more than 30 days before hearing and indicated that specific terms would be discussed at hearing, both parties had requested sole custody and wife was thus undoubtedly prepared to address relative strengths and weaknesses of parties' parenting skills, wife had more than two months between first and second days of hearing to further prepare case against shared parenting, and trial court did not adopt plan initially submitted by husband but gave wife ample opportunity to present her own plan once it decided that shared parenting was in best interests of children. Harris v. Harris (Ohio App. 2 Dist., 08-11-1995) 105 Ohio App.3d 671, 664 N.E.2d 1304. Child Custody ⇒ 410; Child Custody ⇒ 500; Constitutional Law ⇒ 4396

Trial court should not have rejected wife's shared parenting plan based on plan's incorporation of referee's recommendation as to child support and inclusion of items provided elsewhere or not customary in jurisdiction, as wife's plan addressed issues relevant to care of children which were not outside scope of shared parenting plan contemplated by statute, and trial court's own failure to follow statutory procedure in issuing final decree of divorce, which resolved some issues related to child custody and support, before adopting shared parenting plan made it uncertain which provisions parties needed to include in proposals requested by court. Harris v. Harris (Ohio App. 2 Dist., 08-11-1995) 105 Ohio App.3d 671, 664 N.E.2d 1304. Child Custody ⇒ 511

Statute providing that courts shall allocate parental rights and responsibilities for care of minor children of marriage terminating in divorce "upon hearing the testimony of either or both parents" precluded court from adopting shared parenting plan submitted by former wife without holding hearing and entertaining objections to plan by former husband. Snouffer v. Snouffer (Meigs 1993) 87 Ohio App.3d 89, 621 N.E.2d 879. Child Custody ⇒ 500

Trial court's denial of mother's motion to hold father in contempt for alleged violations of private agreement that was incorporated into shared parenting plan, without first hearing evidence regarding the motion, was abuse of discretion in proceedings in which both parties sought to modify shared parenting plan. Harbottle v. Harbottle (Ohio App. 9 Dist., Summit, 09-18-2002) No. 20897, 2002-Ohio-4859, 2002 WL 31060237, Unreported. Child Custody ⇒ 871

Trial court's orders regarding schooling of child, entered after former wife had violated shared parenting plan by removing child from the school he had been enrolled in pursuant to the plan, were proper sua sponte orders, rather than improper ex parte orders; former husband did not file any motion to obtain the orders, there was no indication that either former husband or his counsel prepared the orders, and appellate court would not assume that trial court and former husband's counsel engaged in improper ex parte contacts. Millstein v. Millstein (Ohio App. 8 Dist., Cuyahoga, 09-12-2002) No. 79617, No. 80185, No. 80188, No. 79754, No. 80186, No. 80963, No. 80184, No. 80187, 2002-Ohio-4783, 2002 WL 31031676, Unreported, appeal not allowed 98 Ohio St.3d 1462, 783 N.E.2d 521, 2003-Ohio-644. Child Custody ⇒ 872; Child Custody ⇒ 920

85. —— Termination, shared parenting and joint custody

Substantial change in circumstances was not necessary to terminate shared parenting plan; under provision of child custody statute concerning termination of a shared parenting plan, trial court was only required to determine whether termination of shared parenting plan was in the best interests of the children. Toler v. Toler (Ohio App. 2 Dist., Clark, 07-15-2011) No. 10-CA-69, 2011-Ohio-3510, 2011 WL 2739642, Unreported. Child Custody ⇒ 576

Error in requiring mother to establish a substantial change in circumstances in support of motion to terminate shared parenting plan was harmless, where trial court found that termination of shared parenting plan was not in the best interests of the children, which was a sufficient, independent basis for denying the motion to terminate shared parenting plan. Toler v. Toler (Ohio App. 2 Dist., Clark, 07-15-2011) No. 10-CA-69, 2011-Ohio-3510, 2011 WL 2739642, Unreported. Child Custody ⇒ 923(4)

Evidence was sufficient to establish that termination of shared parenting plan was not in the best interests of the children, thus supporting order denying mother's motion to terminate shared parenting plan; although parties did have a period of time where they experienced some small difficulties getting along, those issues were minor, and evidence showed that children were well adjusted and enjoyed a loving relationship with both parents. Toler v. Toler (Ohio App. 2 Dist., Clark, 07-15-2011) No. 10-CA-69, 2011-Ohio-3510, 2011 WL 2739642, Unreported. Child Custody ⇒ 576

Motion seeking complete termination of shared parenting should not have been overruled based on failure to argue or find change in circumstances, as was required for a motion to modify custody; father requested a complete termination of all aspects of shared parenting, which had been implemented as part of divorce decree, and trial court should have applied custody statute governing termination of shared parenting and utilized only the "best interests" test, as clearly provided under statute. Kougher v. Kougher (Ohio App. 7 Dist., 06-29-2011) 2011-Ohio-3411, 2011 WL 2671824. Child Custody ☞ 576

Former husband was required to demonstrate a change in circumstances before the court would permit an in camera interview between the court and the children, in former husband's post-divorce action that sought to terminate shared parenting. Rice v. Rice (Ohio App. 5 Dist., Delaware, 06-23-2011) No. 10 CA F 11 0091, 2011-Ohio-3099, 2011 WL 2520149, Unreported. Child Custody ☞ 576

Evidence supported finding that former husband failed to establish a change in circumstances that warranted terminating shared parenting, in post-divorce child custody modification proceeding. Rice v. Rice (Ohio App. 5 Dist., Delaware, 06-23-2011) No. 10 CA F 11 0091, 2011-Ohio-3099, 2011 WL 2520149, Unreported. Child Custody ☞ 576

Trial court terminated, rather than modified, parties' shared parenting plan for child born out-of-wedlock, and, thus, trial court was charged with finding that the termination of the shared parenting plan was in child's best interest; magistrate found a change of circumstances had occurred and determined that modification of the allocation of parental rights was in child's best interest and terminated parties' shared parenting plan and designated father as sole custodian and residential parent and awarded mother standard visitation, and trial court overruled mother's objections and ordered that the shared parenting plan be terminated. Poshe v. Chisler (Ohio App. 11 Dist., Lake, 03-11-2011) No. 2010-L-017, 2011-Ohio-1165, 2011 WL 901001, Unreported. Children Out–of–wedlock ☞ 20.10

Trial court did not abuse its discretion in terminating the shared parenting decree, because the parties could neither effectively communicate nor cooperate with one another. Curry v. Curry (Ohio App. 10 Dist., Franklin, 12-30-2010) No. 10AP-437, 2010-Ohio-6536, 2010 WL 5550702, Unreported. Child Custody ☞ 576

Trial court did not rely on false allegations when terminating the shared parenting decree and reallocating the parties' parental rights and responsibilities; allegation that mother abused drugs did not enter into trial court's consideration when it reallocated parental rights, since it explicitly found that mother did not abuse drugs, and evidence established that father did not misrepresent his marital status to the magistrate. Curry v. Curry (Ohio App. 10 Dist., Franklin, 12-30-2010) No. 10AP-437,

2010-Ohio-6536, 2010 WL 5550702, Unreported. Child Custody ☞ 637; Child Custody ☞ 659

Trial court acted within its discretion by finding that change in custody of child born out of wedlock was in the child's best interest, which change terminated an agreed entry granting mother primary physical custody and award mother and father shared legal and physical custody in alternating weeks; mother had demanding school and work schedule and a new baby and left child in care of grandfather who had been accused of sexual molestation, mother failed to attend to child's medical and hygiene needs, father and his girlfriend had positive relationship with child and were active in her life, and child desired to spend more time with father. Preece v. Stern (Ohio App. 12 Dist., Madison, 03-08-2010) No. CA2009-09-019, 2010-Ohio-857, 2010 WL 764210, Unreported. Children Out–of–wedlock ☞ 20.10

Evidence was sufficient to support trial court's finding that a change in circumstances had occurred to justify termination of an agreed parenting entry granting mother primary custody of child born out of wedlock, in order to split legal and physical custody equally between mother and father; mother took on additional work and school hours, had a new baby, failed to attend to child's medical and hygiene needs, child was in maternal grandfather's care seven hours a day and grandfather had been accused of sexual molestation. Preece v. Stern (Ohio App. 12 Dist., Madison, 03-08-2010) No. CA2009-09-019, 2010-Ohio-857, 2010 WL 764210, Unreported. Children Out–of–wedlock ☞ 20.10

Trial court did not abuse its discretion by terminating the parties' shared parenting plan and by designating ex-husband as the children's residential parent; guardian ad litem explained that she based her recommendation to designate ex-husband as the residential parent not on ex-wife's relocation, but based upon the children's school performance and child's behavioral improvement due to consistency with his medication, and ex-wife's relocation to a distant city would render shared parenting impractical. In re J.L.R. (Ohio App. 4 Dist., Washington, 10-29-2009) No. 08CA17, 2009-Ohio-5812, 2009 WL 3634403, Unreported. Child Custody ☞ 576; Child Custody ☞ 616

Evidence was sufficient to support termination of shared parenting plan and naming father sole residential parent of out-of-wedlock child; child's reaching age of compulsory school attendance, coupled with mother's move out of county, made shared parenting agreement impractical. Francis v. McDermott (Ohio App. 2 Dist., Darke, 08-21-2009) No. 1753, 2009-Ohio-4323, 2009 WL 2612609, Unreported. Children Out–of–wedlock ☞ 20.10

Evidence established that trial court conducted thorough de novo review of record in adopting magistrate's recommended ruling to terminate shared parenting plan and name father sole residential parent of out-of-wedlock child; decision of trial court stated that court conducted de novo review of magistrate's findings and conclusions of law, thereafter, court stated "after giving due consideration to all the above, including a review of the pleadings and testimony, the court affirms the decision of the magistrate," and so mother's argument that trial court made no reference to any independent evaluation of 803-page transcript of proceedings was rebutted by above statements of trial court. Francis v. McDermott (Ohio App. 2 Dist., Darke, 08-21-2009) No. 1753, 2009-Ohio-4323, 2009 WL 2612609, Unreported. Children Out–of–wedlock ☞ 20.10

Best interest of children was only criterion required for termination of shared parenting plan. In re E.M.W. (Ohio App. 2 Dist., Champaign, 06-19-2009) No. 08-CA-25, 2009-Ohio-3016, 2009 WL 1803812, Unreported. Child Custody ☞ 576

Best interest of children supported termination of shared parenting agreement and designation of mother as primary residential parent; mother wanted to be awarded sole custody of children while father wanted to maintain current arrangement, mother had more time to spend with children and was more nurturing, more involved in care of children, was in better position to provide stability and consistency during school year, and was more willing to communicate with father over issues with children, and father's separation from wife caused level of instability, particularly because children were part of reason for separation. In re E.M.W. (Ohio App. 2 Dist., Champaign, 06-19-2009) No. 08-CA-25, 2009-Ohio-3016, 2009 WL 1803812, Unreported. Child Custody ☞ 576

Trial court's failure to explain its reasoning for finding a change in circumstances, or to analyze the best interest factors, before terminating an agreed parenting entry, and establishing shared parenting, was an abuse of discretion, and required remand for further clarification, even though it found that child had some medical problems and hygiene issues, and mother's change in work schedule dictated that grandfather had to watch child seven hours a day, where trial court couched issues in terms of father's concerns but did not explain why they specifically constituted a change in circumstance. Preece v. Stern (Ohio App. 12 Dist., Madison, 06-01-2009) No. CA2008-09-024, No. CA2008-12-029, 2009-Ohio-2519, 2009 WL 1509168, Unreported. Child Custody ☞ 924

Trial court acted within its discretion in terminating a shared parenting plan and designating former husband as the residential parent for child; former husband and former wife had agreed that former husband would become child's residential parent when child, who was breast feeding when the shared parenting plan was executed, was no longer physically dependent on former wife, child was no longer even bottle feeding and wore diapers only at bedtime when she stayed with former husband, and former wife displayed increased hostility that clearly frustrated cooperation between the parties as to both medical care and visitation issues. Surgenavic v. Surgenavic (Ohio App. 7 Dist., Mahoning, 03-05-2009) No. 08 MA 29, 2009-Ohio-1028, 2009 WL 582575, Unreported. Child Custody ☞ 576

Evidence in child custody modification proceedings, following mother's move out of state with child, supported juvenile court's findings that there was a change in circumstances, and that modification was in child's best interests, thus supporting termination of shared parenting agreement and designation of father as the sole residential and custodial parent; child had very good relationship with father and father's family, child was well-adjusted to his home and community, mother's life was marked by changes in employment and housing, and father was more inclined to honor court-approved parenting time rights than mother. In re D.M. (Ohio App. 8 Dist., Cuyahoga, 11-22-2006) No. 87723, 2006-Ohio-6191, 2006 WL 3378429, Unreported, appeal not allowed 113 Ohio St.3d 1468, 864 N.E.2d 654, 2007-Ohio-1722. Child Custody ☞ 576

Order terminating shared parenting plan without explicit findings of change in circumstances was not abuse of discretion; evidence in record indicated change in circumstances in view of deterioration of child's relationship with husband, child's adjustment to community and school, and effect of parents' relationship on child. Fisher v. Fisher (Ohio App. 3 Dist., Henry, 10-24-2005) No. 7-05-03, 2005-Ohio-5615, 2005 WL 2709526, Unreported. Child Custody ☞ 576; Child Custody ☞ 659

Trial court did not abuse its discretion in terminating shared parenting plan originally entered into incident to divorce, and designating former husband as children's sole residential parent, where court found requisite change of circumstances, considered harm to children likely to be caused by change of environment outweighed by advantages of change to children, and considered all relevant statutory factors in determining that modification of custody was in children's best interest. Lawrence v. Lawrence (Ohio App. 11 Dist., Lake, 06-30-2005) No. 2004-L-089, No. 2004-L-142, 2005-Ohio-3406, 2005 WL 1538104, Unreported. Child Custody ☞ 576

Evidence of change of circumstances was sufficient to support termination of shared parenting plan originally entered into incident to divorce, and designation of former husband as children's sole residential parent, where former wife demonstrated deep anger toward or hatred of former husband and his family, interfered with communication and visitation between minor children and former husband, and encouraged minor children to lie to former husband. Lawrence v. Lawrence (Ohio App. 11 Dist., Lake, 06-30-2005) No. 2004-L-089, No. 2004-L-142, 2005-Ohio-3406, 2005 WL 1538104, Unreported. Child Custody ☞ 576

Trial court did not act arbitrarily, unreasonably or unconscionably when it refused to order psychological evaluations, in proceeding in which court terminated shared parenting plan and designated father as residential parent and legal custodian of child; court heard testimony from three counselors, a guardian ad litem, and numerous other witnesses, and thus, court had an ample basis for making decision about child's best interests. Bowers v. Bowers (Ohio App. 2 Dist., Darke, 06-30-2005) No.

1655, 2005-Ohio-3327, 2005 WL 1531308, Unreported. Child Custody ☞ 617

Trial court's decision terminating shared parenting plan and granting custody of child to father was not against manifest weight of evidence; court found that father would be more likely to facilitate visitation, that mother made unsubstantiated allegations of sexual abuse against father, that father was deprived of any meaningful visitation with child for several months, that father had significantly participated in raising child, that record failed to contain any indication that child was exposed to dangers while in father's home or custody, and that there was evidence that child's anxiety was caused by violence to which he had been exposed in his mother's home. Bowers v. Bowers (Ohio App. 2 Dist., Darke, 06-30-2005) No. 1655, 2005-Ohio-3327, 2005 WL 1531308, Unreported. Child Custody ☞ 576

Trial court's failure specifically to discuss in its order denying former wife's motion for termination of shared parenting agreement certain issues pertaining to children did not indicate that trial court failed to consider all factors relevant to children's best interest. Ross v. Ross (Ohio App. 12 Dist., Preble, 06-13-2005) No. CA2004-07-009, 2005-Ohio-2922, 2005 WL 1385225, Unreported. Child Custody ☞ 659

Trial court did not abuse its discretion in denying former wife's motion to terminate shared parenting agreement, where agreement continued to be in children's best interest; former husband denied former wife's allegation that he verbally and emotionally abused her in front of the children, sleeping arrangements at former husband's home were adequate, and agreement established routine for children that was not overly disruptive, especially given close proximity of homes of former wife and former husband. Ross v. Ross (Ohio App. 12 Dist., Preble, 06-13-2005) No. CA2004-07-009, 2005-Ohio-2922, 2005 WL 1385225, Unreported. Child Custody ☞ 576

Trial court was not required to set out, in its order terminating shared parenting plan originally entered into incident to divorce, all statutory factors considered by it in reaching conclusion that shared parenting was no longer in child's best interests, especially where evidence at trial established that child and former husband did not have close relationship, that child no longer wished to abide by shared parenting plan's strict custody schedule, and that since entry of shared parenting plan, child had entered into social obligations, including a job, that made his life less structured. Cherwin v. Cherwin (Ohio App. 8 Dist., Cuyahoga, 04-28-2005) No. 84875, 2005-Ohio-1999, 2005 WL 991706, Unreported. Child Custody ☞ 659

Evidence supported trial court's finding that shared-parenting plan was not in the best interest of child, thus supporting termination of shared-parenting plan; parties' geographical proximity was not conducive to shared parenting, and mother's surreptitious relocation of child was not in spirit of shared-parenting agreement. Lopez v. Lopez (Ohio App. 10 Dist., Franklin, 03-17-2005) No. 04AP-508, 2005-Ohio-1155, 2005 WL 615651, Unreported. Child Custody ☞ 576

Facts merited termination of shared parenting agreement between father and mother, and entry of order awarding custody of child to mother; change in circumstances since entry of shared parenting agreement had occurred due in part to fact child had gotten older, and mother had moved to location 90 minutes from father's home. Gillam v. Gillam (Ohio App. 10 Dist., Franklin, 02-15-2005) No. 04AP-555, 2005-Ohio-583, 2005 WL 351877, Unreported. Child Custody ☞ 576

Trial court's decision to terminate divorced parties' shared parenting plan and award custody of both children to father was not against the manifest weight of the evidence; mother had, at various times, denied father orally agreed upon parenting time, teachers at children's school believed that father was much more involved and interested in children's academic progress than mother, mother continued to smoke in her home even though it adversely effected the health of one child who had asthma, children lived in fear of mother's new husband, and new husband assaulted father in front of the children. Matis v. Matis (Ohio App. 9 Dist., Medina, 01-12-2005) No. 04CA0025-M, 2005-Ohio-72, 2005 WL 53432, Unreported. Child Custody ☞ 469

Divorced mother had adequate notice that the trial court was considering termination of the parties' shared parenting plan; both parties filed and served written motions to modify the shared parenting plan, and counsel for both parties were served with a "Magistrate's Order Post Decree Prerial" entry, which explicitly noted that father was requesting a "Modification of Designation of Residential Parent and Legal Custodian." Matis v. Matis (Ohio App. 9 Dist., Medina, 01-12-2005) No. 04CA0025-M, 2005-Ohio-72, 2005 WL 53432, Unreported. Child Custody ☞ 410 Matis v. Matis (Ohio App. 9 Dist., Medina, 01-12-2005) No. 04CA0025-M, 2005-Ohio-72, 2005 WL 53432, Unreported. Child Custody ☞ 410

Finding that shared parenting plan was not in child's best interest and granting ex-husband sole custody was not abuse of discretion, where ex-husband testified that he primarily took care of getting child to school and frequently made dinners, ex-wife admitted that ex-husband was more involved in helping child with school work, ex-wife admitted that she drove child after drinking alcohol, and ex-wife was diagnosed with chemical dependency. Klausman v. Klausman (Ohio App. 9 Dist., Summit, 06-30-2004) No. 21718, 2004-Ohio-3410, 2004 WL 1461356, Unreported. Child Custody ☞ 51; Child Custody ☞ 58; Child Custody ☞ 60; Child Custody ☞ 137; Child Custody ☞ 139

After dispute as to reallocation of parental rights was referred to mediation, trial court erred by granting ex-husband's motion for ruling without giving ex-wife opportunity to respond, where parties agreed to mediation after judge stated that judge would try to "get mediation this week" and that if he could not he would fix parties up with further hearing, judge expressed concern with being able to determine best interest of child based on limited evidence presented prior to mediation, no hearing or response from ex-wife was received before judge granted ex-husband's motion and designated him as residential parent, court failed to delineate basis for finding that termination of shared parenting plan was in child's best interest, and court's procedure appeared to be in derogation of local rules. Stillings v. Stillings (Ohio App. 3 Dist., Union, 06-28-2004) No. 14-03-54, 2004-Ohio-3342, 2004 WL 1433533, Unreported. Child Custody ☞ 650; Child Custody ☞ 659

Former husband's motion, denominated "motion for change of custody" and seeking order designating him as child's primary residential parent, was reasonably construed by trial court as motion for termination of shared parenting plan originally entered incident to divorce; concept of "residential parent" was inconsistent with implementation of a shared parenting plan. Williamson v. Williamson (Ohio App. 2 Dist., Clark, 11-26-2003) No. 2003 CA 30, 2003-Ohio-6540, 2003 WL 22888291, Unreported. Child Custody ☞ 609

On former wife's motion to amend or dissolve shared parenting plan, with respect to which court determined to keep shared parenting plan in effect, trial court erred in treating both former husband and former wife as residential parents for purposes of child support, where parties' shared parenting plan established that former husband was residential parent, who had no order to pay child support, and nothing in record indicated court ever terminated such status; even if trial court had ended former husband's status, there was no indication why court reduced former husband's putative child support obligation under worksheet, requiring remand. Shaffer v. Shaffer (Ohio App. 11 Dist., Trumbull, 09-30-2003) No. 2002-T-0172, 2003-Ohio-5223, 2003 WL 22235377, Unreported. Child Support ☞ 240; Child Support ☞ 357

Change of circumstances existed to modify or terminate shared parenting decree to designate father as sole residential parent; mother had frequent changes of address, mother exposed child to a sexually charged and possibly dangerous environment, mother refused to let father know of her whereabouts, and mother had refused to allow father to visit or take custody of child at different times. Myers v. Myers (Ohio App. 7 Dist., 06-30-2003) 153 Ohio App.3d 243, 792 N.E.2d 770, 2003-Ohio-3552. Child Custody ☞ 576

Trial court, prior to modifying or terminating shared parenting decree, was not required to find a change of circumstances; trial court was only required to find that it was in best interests of child to modify or terminate decree. Myers v. Myers (Ohio App. 7 Dist., 06-30-2003) 153 Ohio App.3d 243, 792 N.E.2d 770, 2003-Ohio-3552. Child Custody ☞ 576

Evidence supported finding in custody proceeding involving biological parents and paternal grandmother that shared parenting agreement between biological parents be terminated and that mother be granted sole custody of child. Vance v. Vance (Ohio App. 2 Dist., 01-24-2003) 151 Ohio App.3d 391, 784 N.E.2d 172, 2003-Ohio-310. Child Custody ☞ 473

A joint custody plan can only work so long as both parents continue to hold to the proposition that joint custody is in the best interest of all parties; thus, if either parent concludes that joint custody is no longer viable, the court may terminate joint custody upon request. Blair v. Blair (Tuscarawas 1986) 34 Ohio App.3d 345, 518 N.E.2d 950. Child Custody ☞ 141; Child Custody ☞ 576

Where joint custody is terminated pursuant to the request of the parties, the court is empowered to issue a modified custody decree based on the best interest of the child just as if no decree for joint custody had ever been requested or granted. Blair v. Blair (Tuscarawas 1986) 34 Ohio App.3d 345, 518 N.E.2d 950. Child Custody ☞ 576

Trial court did not abuse its discretion by failing to adopt guardian ad litem's recommendation that former husband be designated as residential parent upon termination of shared parenting plan, where guardian qualified her recommendation by stating that "either parent would provide 'the child' with a loving, safe environment," that "I cannot emphasize enough how close a call this decision is on my part," and that guardian would have "no serious objection" to designating former wife as residential parent. Ferrell v. Ferrell (Ohio App. 7 Dist., Carroll, 06-11-2002) No. 01 AP 0763, 2002-Ohio-3019, 2002 WL 1376039, Unreported. Child Custody ☞ 616

Evidence established that former wife was involved in addressing five-year-old child's eye disorder, as element for designating residential parent upon termination of shared parenting plan; former wife made special arrangements with school district as recommended by ophthalmologist, former wife went with former husband to speak with specialist regarding child's eye condition, and doctor had told former wife that change in child's eyeglass prescription was minor and that she could wait to get it filled. Ferrell v. Ferrell (Ohio App. 7 Dist., Carroll, 06-11-2002) No. 01 AP 0763, 2002-Ohio-3019, 2002 WL 1376039, Unreported. Child Custody ☞ 637

Eleven-year-old child's desire to live with his father in Ohio, presumably expressed with an understanding that a move from his mother's home in Maryland would take him from his friends and to a new school, supported the juvenile court's designation of father as residential parent, upon termination of shared parenting. Meyer v. Anderson (Ohio App. 2 Dist., Miami, 06-07-2002) No. 01CA53, 2002-Ohio-2782, 2002 WL 1251449, Unreported. Child Custody ☞ 566

Proper issue on termination of joint custody, where both agree it should be terminated is best interest of the child under RC 3109.04(C). Shrider v Shrider, No. 87AP–229 (10th Dist Ct App, Franklin, 7–14–87).

86. —— Violations, shared parenting and joint custody

Trial court did not abuse its discretion in concluding that it was in best interests of child born out-of-wedlock to terminate parents' shared parenting plan and designate father as child's sole residential parent and legal custodian; record was replete with instances in which mother violated shared parenting agreement and made derogatory and profane statements in public and in front of child, and under shared parenting agreement, child was not to have unsupervised contact with her maternal grandmother, who had an extensive criminal record, yet father and others had observed maternal grandmother alone with child. Poshe v. Chisler (Ohio App. 11 Dist., Lake, 03-11-2011) No. 2010-L-017, 2011-Ohio-1165, 2011 WL 901001, Unreported. Children Out–of–wedlock ☞ 20.10

Clear and convincing evidence showed that ex-wife disobeyed a lawful court order by failing to abide by the terms of the shared parenting agreement regarding vacation and regular summer visitation, and, as a result, ex-wife would be held in contempt for disobeying the court order; however unreasonable ex-wife found the midnight pick-up time to be, ex-husband made his vacation request according to shared parenting plan, and ex-wife failed to communicate her disapproval of ex-husband's stated pick-up time or suggest alternate exchange time, and, thus, when ex-wife denied ex-husband's vacation, she disobeyed the shared parenting plan. Rapp v. Pride (Ohio App. 12 Dist., Butler, 07-06-2010) No. CA2009-12-311, 2010-Ohio-3138, 2010 WL 2653628, Unreported. Child Custody ☞ 854

Given ex-wife's denial of ex-husband's rightful parenting time and vacation, the trial court's decision to order make-up time was not arbitrary, unreasonable, or unconscionable, and did not constitute an abuse of discretion. Rapp v. Pride (Ohio App. 12 Dist., Butler, 07-06-2010) No. CA2009-12-311, 2010-Ohio-3138, 2010 WL 2653628, Unreported. Child Custody ☞ 874

Trial court's determination that mother was in contempt for denying father part of his summer and holiday visitation, and for interfering with his telephone communication with children, was proper, in divorce proceeding regarding father's motion for contempt, inasmuch as father was entitled to such parenting time and phone calls, and violations were not technical, in that mother changed plans for visitation and exchange on her own without father's agreement, and many of father's phone calls were of two minutes' duration. Bonner v. Bonner (Ohio App. 2 Dist., Darke, 02-26-2010) No. 2009 CA 10, 2010-Ohio-742, 2010 WL 703517, Unreported. Child Custody ☞ 854

Evidence supported finding that mother was in contempt of court for violating the shared parenting plan; mother admitted that she denied father his scheduled visitation with the children on more than one occasion. Mann v. Mendez (Ohio App. 9 Dist., Lorain, 06-22-2005) No. 04CA008562, 2005-Ohio-3114, 2005 WL 1460045, Unreported. Child Custody ☞ 854

Ex-husband was not in contempt of parties' shared parenting plan for failing to pay for child's private school tuition once child reached first grade, given that, under terms of parties' plan, parties did not have agreement to send children to private school. Roberts v. Roberts (Ohio App. 12 Dist., Butler, 06-06-2005) No. CA2004-04-081, No. CA2004-04-087, 2005-Ohio-2792, 2005 WL 1324726, Unreported. Child Support ☞ 444

Evidence in proceeding to modify shared parenting plan supported finding that mother unilaterally reduced father's parenting time; mother, with no notice to father and no discussion, took children for holiday and refused to return them to father. Hunter v. Bachman (Ohio App. 9 Dist., Lorain, 09-29-2004) No. 04CA008421, 2004-Ohio-5172, 2004 WL 2244125, Unreported. Child Custody ☞ 569

Trial court finding that mother was in contempt due to her failure to comply with shared parenting plan agreement was not an abuse of discretion; mother violated the shared parenting plan by not allowing paternal grandmother holiday visitation with child and by not allowing grandmother to have telephone contact with child during times designated by the parenting plan for telephone contact. In re M.M. (Ohio App. 2 Dist., Montgomery, 04-09-2004) No. 20026, 2004-Ohio-1812, 2004 WL 758387, Unreported. Child Custody ☞ 852

Trial court acted within its inherent authority and discretion to enforce its lawful order, a shared parenting plan, when it imposed $1000 fine on mother for first offense finding of contempt. Caldwell v. Caldwell (Ohio App. 4 Dist., Gallia, 04-02-2003) No. 02CA17, 2003-Ohio-1752, 2003 WL 1795247, Unreported. Child Custody ☞ 874

Evidence supported trial court's finding in custody proceeding that paternal grandmother had violated court order by not returning child to mother, and thus violation of order was evidence to support finding it was not in child's best interests for grandmother to have custody and that shared parenting arrangement between biological parents should be terminated; several periods of time existed that grandmother had physical custody in clear violation of the court order for child to be with mother. Vance v. Vance (Ohio App. 2 Dist., 01-24-2003) 151 Ohio App.3d 391, 784 N.E.2d 172, 2003-Ohio-310. Child Custody ☞ 473

Wife could not be found in contempt of shared parenting agreement before shared parenting decree was entered. Evans v. Evans (Ohio App. 12 Dist., 10-02-1995) 106 Ohio App.3d 673, 666 N.E.2d 1176, dismissed, appeal not allowed 75 Ohio St.3d 1448, 663 N.E.2d 330. Child Custody ☞ 852

87. Custody or visitation issues in proceedings other than divorce—Death of undivorced parents

Where husband and wife have been divorced and custody of their minor child under ten years of age awarded the mother, upon the mother's death, such custody does not devolve upon the father, nor upon probate court of the father's residence, but is still exclusively under control of the court granting the divorce. In re Hampshire (Ohio App. 5 Dist. 1922) 17 Ohio App. 139.

RC 3109.04(A) deals exclusively with divorce and is not applicable in a custody action brought by children's grandmother after the children's parents were killed in an airplane accident. In re Caneen, No. 654 (7th Dist Ct App, Monroe, 3–23–89).

88. —— Habeas corpus, custody or visitation issues in proceedings other than divorce

In a case where a foreign decree of dissolution stipulates that the father gives up custody and visitation rights in exchange for the mother's agreement to forego child support payments, the father's motion to adopt the foreign decree is granted and Ohio is the proper forum to litigate the issue of custody where it is the child's home state. Kirby v. Nakanishi (Ohio App. 8 Dist., Cuyahoga, 12-20-1995) No. 68671, 1995 WL 753944, Unreported.

Although filing of bankruptcy petition stays equitable distribution in divorce case of debtor's interest in marital assets, certain aspects of divorce case, such as dissolution of marriage and child custody issues, are not stayed. State ex rel. Miley v. Parrott (Ohio, 11-06-1996) 77 Ohio St.3d 64, 671 N.E.2d 24, 1996-Ohio-350. Bankruptcy ⬅ 2401

Trial court was obligated to reactivate divorce case after bankruptcy court lifted automatic stay affecting Chapter 12 debtor-husband; order inactivating divorce case stated that case would stay inactive until judge "is advised in writing of the stay having been lifted," trial court was advised in writing that bankruptcy court had lifted stay for divorce case, trial court would not be subject to contempt for violating stay after bankruptcy court expressly modified and lifted stay, and divorce case would not be better resolved after conclusion of bankruptcy proceedings. State ex rel. Miley v. Parrott (Ohio, 11-06-1996) 77 Ohio St.3d 64, 671 N.E.2d 24, 1996-Ohio-350. Bankruptcy ⬅ 2401

Automatic stay may be lifted or modified for cause. State ex rel. Miley v. Parrott (Ohio, 11-06-1996) 77 Ohio St.3d 64, 671 N.E.2d 24, 1996-Ohio-350. Bankruptcy ⬅ 2422.5(1)

Though husband had insufficient contacts with Ohio to provide Ohio court with in personam jurisdiction for purposes of division of property and support, Ohio had jurisdiction under Ohio statutes to make custody determination, where mother and child were present in Ohio; very presence of child in Ohio, meeting requirements of the Uniform Child Custody Jurisdiction Act (UCCJA) made clear the necessity of custody order. Schroeder v. Vigil-Escalera Perez (Ohio Com.Pl., 11-09-1995) 76 Ohio Misc.2d 25, 664 N.E.2d 627. Child Custody ⬅ 732

Although divorce action was completed, jurisdiction over paternity action that was brought as postdecree motion was proper in Court of Domestic Relations, not solely in Juvenile Court, since other postdecree matters were still pending. Broxterman v. Broxterman (Ohio App. 1 Dist., 03-15-1995) 101 Ohio App.3d 661, 656 N.E.2d 394. Courts ⬅ 475(15)

Common pleas courts which have already issued orders concerning parental rights and responsibilities do not lose jurisdiction after the death of the custodial parent and must resolve the case in the best interests of the children under RC 3109.04. In re Dunn (Auglaize 1992) 79 Ohio App.3d 268, 607 N.E.2d 81, dismissed, jurisdictional motion overruled 65 Ohio St.3d 1416, 598 N.E.2d 1168.

Pursuant to RC 2151.23(A), the juvenile court has jurisdiction to determine the custody of a child alleged to be abused, neglected, or dependent, when that child is not the ward of any court in this state; this jurisdiction includes children subject to a divorce decree granting custody pursuant to RC 3109.04. In re Poling (Ohio 1992) 64 Ohio St.3d 211, 594 N.E.2d 589. Infants ⬅ 196

Although a Florida dissolution decree obtained by parties who lived in Ohio both before and after its issuance says it "shall be construed and governed" in accordance with Florida law, in later proceedings in Ohio court Ohio law presumably controls any change of custody for a child who resides in Ohio, while Florida law controls the meaning of the decree and the agreement it incorporates. Zigmont v. Toto (Cuyahoga 1988) 47 Ohio App.3d 181, 547 N.E.2d 1208, cause dismissed 38 Ohio St.3d 715, 533 N.E.2d 783.

A court, in ordering dismissal of a complaint for divorce at a party's request, may not issue an order of child custody and support as "terms and conditions" of dismissal under Civ R 41(A)(2), since the purpose of that provision is to permit an order that leaves the parties as if the action had not been brought. Lilly v. Lilly (Montgomery 1985) 26 Ohio App.3d 192, 499 N.E.2d 21, 26 O.B.R. 412.

Where the domestic relations division of a common pleas court concludes a divorce action with judgment entries including one finding that custody of a child to neither parent is in the child's best interest and certifies its findings to the juvenile court for further proceedings pursuant to RC 3109.04(A), the certification order is a final appealable order. Robinson v. Robinson (Franklin 1984) 19 Ohio App.3d 323, 484 N.E.2d 710, 19 O.B.R. 496.

When a parent having legal custody of minor children takes up residence with such children outside the state, an Ohio court has continuing jurisdiction to modify the original custody order. Murck v. Murck (Cuyahoga 1976) 47 Ohio App.2d 292, 353 N.E.2d 917, 1 O.O.3d 355.

Where a court, having acquired jurisdiction over a child by virtue of a divorce action between the child's parents, certifies the matter of the child's custody to a juvenile court, the consent of the juvenile court having been first obtained, the juvenile court has exclusive jurisdiction over the child's custody by virtue of RC 3109.06 and 2151.23(D) and a finding of unfitness of the parents or that there is no suitable relative to have custody is not a necessary prerequisite to such certification, and while such certification shall be deemed to be the complaint in the juvenile court, it does not constitute a complaint in the juvenile court that such child is dependent or neglected and those dispositions provided for under RC 2151.353, 2151.354, and 2151.355 are not applicable to the disposition of such a child, disposition thereof being subject to and controlled by RC 3109.04. In re Height (Van Wert 1975) 47 Ohio App.2d 203, 353 N.E.2d 887, 1 O.O.3d 279. Courts ☞ 472.1

Where a child, whose original custody was determined by an out-of-state court, presently resides in Ohio, a court of this state has jurisdiction to determine whether it is in the best interests of the child to give full faith and credit to the out-of-state order. Purcell v. Purcell (Hamilton 1975) 47 Ohio App.2d 258, 353 N.E.2d 882, 1 O.O.3d 316. Judgment ☞ 815

Where a court of another state has awarded custody of a minor child pursuant to a valid in personam order, and there is no evidence of a subsequent change in circumstances affecting the best interests of the child, the courts of this state will give full faith and credit to that order. Williams v. Williams (Ohio 1975) 44 Ohio St.2d 28, 336 N.E.2d 426, 73 O.O.2d 121.

When a mother having legal custody of a minor child is domiciled in another state with such child, an Ohio court does not have continuing jurisdiction to modify the original custody order, but if such child resides in Ohio, even though he may be domiciled in another state with the parent having legal custody, the courts of Ohio will have continuing jurisdiction to hear a motion for modification of custody. Heiney v. Heiney (Columbiana 1973) 40 Ohio App.2d 571, 321 N.E.2d 611, 69 O.O.2d 519.

When a divorce is denied, the parties are still married and they have equal rights as to custody of minor children, and both are responsible for care and support, and, until such time as a separate complaint or application is made to a court of competent jurisdiction, the provisions of RC 3109.03 and 3109.04 may not be invoked. Holderle v. Holderle (Franklin 1967) 11 Ohio App.2d 148, 229 N.E.2d 79, 40 O.O.2d 305.

An award of custody of a child in a divorce action is conclusive only as to the parties to such action, and the remedy of habeas corpus is available to obtain such child where a party other than the parties to the divorce action is involved; and it is not necessary to apply to the court which originally awarded custody of such child. In re Howland (Highland 1961) 115 Ohio App. 186, 184 N.E.2d 228, 20 O.O.2d 277.

RC 3105.20 does not deny the court of common pleas in any matter concerning domestic relations the exercise of "its full equity powers and jurisdiction," but there must be a statutory basis upon which to exercise those powers before they may be put into execution. Haynie v. Haynie (Ohio 1959) 169 Ohio St. 467, 159 N.E.2d 765, 8 O.O.2d 476.

A probate court has jurisdiction to hear and determine an adoption proceeding relating to a minor child notwithstanding the fact that the custody of such child is at the time within the continuing jurisdiction of a divorce court. (See also In re Biddle, 81 Abs 529, 163 NE(2d) 190 (App, Franklin 1959).) In re Adoption of Biddle (Ohio 1958) 168 Ohio St. 209, 152 N.E.2d 105, 6 O.O.2d 4, on remand 163 N.E.2d 188, 81 Ohio Law Abs. 529.

A common pleas court has no jurisdiction to make any order respecting the care and custody or visitation with minor children unless in the prayer of the petition the plaintiff asks for a divorce or alimony. Crum v. Howard (Ohio Com.Pl. 1956) 137 N.E.2d 654, 73 Ohio Law Abs. 111, 1 O.O.2d 399. Child Custody ☞ 404

Where the natural parents of a minor child are divorced, custody of the child being given to the mother, and the mother remarries and her husband adopts the child, and then the mother and adoptive father are divorced, and custody is awarded to the adoptive father, and the natural father seeks custody, and prior to hearing the mother and adoptive father are remarried, the court loses jurisdiction over the custody of the child. Lockard v. Lockard (Ohio Com.Pl. 1951) 102 N.E.2d 747, 63 Ohio Law Abs. 549, 49 O.O. 163.

The remarriage of divorced parents terminates the jurisdiction of the divorce court over the custody of their minor children. Lockard v. Lockard (Ohio Com.Pl. 1951) 102 N.E.2d 747, 63 Ohio Law Abs. 549, 49 O.O. 163.

A domestic relations court has jurisdiction under RC 3105.21(B) to determine custody despite dismissal of a divorce action for lack of prosecution. State ex rel. Easterday v. Zieba (Ohio 1991) 58 Ohio St.3d 251, 569 N.E.2d 1028.

RC 3105.21(B) affords a domestic relations court authority to determine custody of a child, as between his parents and another relative, even though that court has dismissed the parent's divorce action; if after dismissing the divorce action, the domestic relations court elects to certify the matter of custody to juvenile court, under RC 3105.21(B) and 3109.04 the domestic relations court must specifically find custody in neither parent to be in the child's best interest, or all jurisdiction over the matter is lost. State ex rel. Easterday v. Zieba (Ohio 1991) 58 Ohio St.3d 251, 569 N.E.2d 1028.

Where a trial court feels an award of custody to either parent at the time of granting a divorce is not in the best interests of the child, an order indicating that one of the parties has temporary possession of a minor child for one year is not a final appealable order under Civ R 55(b). Shun v

Shun, No. 43075 (8th Dist Ct App, Cuyahoga, 8–6–81).

Since an award of custody pendente lite to the father on a motion for temporary custody is not a custody decree, the award can be modified without a showing of changed circumstance. Garnet v Garnet, No. 80CA31 (7th Dist Ct App, Mahoning, 3–2–81).

A domestic relations court has continuing jurisdiction over the issue of child custody although the divorce decree did not address the issue of custody. Huxley v Huxley, No. 1903 (9th Dist Ct App, Wayne, 5–23–84).

89. —— **Juvenile court and custody of abused, neglected or dependent children, custody or visitation issues in proceedings other than divorce**

In case in which father petitioned to modify parenting time, domestic relations court could not certify the case to the juvenile court based on a finding it made, on evidence presented in proceedings on the petition, that one of the children may have been sexually abused by an unknown perpetrator, and therefore, jurisdiction never vested in juvenile court, notwithstanding juvenile court's exclusive jurisdiction over cases concerning allegations of child abuse, where there was no complaint, indictment, or information that contained allegations of abuse, neglect, or dependency, and the domestic relations court did not obtain the juvenile court's consent prior to transfer, and did not make a finding that the parents were unsuitable. Thompson v. Valentine (Ohio App. 12 Dist., 08-30-2010) No. CA2009-09-231, 2010 -Ohio- 4075, 2010 WL 3386235, Unreported. Courts ☜ 488(1)

Juvenile court's order denying foster parents' motion for legal custody of child, along with their motions to intervene and to stay the removal of child from their home, which were filed after it was determined that child would spend three days a week with biological relatives who were willing to adopt him, was not a final appealable order, since the denial of the motions did not affect foster parents' substantial rights; child had not been permanently awarded to the County Children's Services Board at the time the motions were filed and, until such time, the wishes or rights of the foster parents were mere expectancies. In re Fell (Ohio App. 5 Dist., Guernsey, 05-16-2005) No. 2004-CA-39, 2005-Ohio-2415, 2005 WL 1163260, Unreported. Infants ☜ 242

Paternal grandparents' due process rights were violated at hearing on guardian ad litem's motion to change paternal grandparents' visitation with children to supervised visitation; paternal grandparents were not given right to rebut allegations of court's witness that children were exposed to unsafe conditions at paternal grandparents' residence, and paternal grandparents were not given opportunity to present evidence. In re Byerly (Ohio App. 11 Dist., Portage, 02-06-2004) No. 2001-P-0158, No. 2001-P-0159, 2004-Ohio-523, 2004 WL 231804, Un-

reported. Child Custody ☜ 650; Constitutional Law ☜ 4396

Father, who appeared pro se in neglect and dependency proceedings concerning his children, was not entitled to polygraph examination at court's expense; there was no provision within the law for polygraph examination to be court ordered or admissible in civil proceedings. In re Tracy (Ohio App. 2 Dist., Miami, 07-03-2003) No. 2002CA41, No. 2002CA66, No. 2002CA64, No. 2002CA67, No. 2002CA65, 2003-Ohio-3781, 2003 WL 21658665, Unreported. Infants ☜ 208; Infants ☜ 212

Motion filed by father in neglect and dependency proceedings upon entry of magistrate's decision, which, among other things, granted custody of his children to mother with certain protective conditions and barred father from visitation or contact with children, which motion appeared to be a motion to set aside criminal sentence, was not appropriate vehicle for father to seek relief from magistrate's decision; there was no criminal case and no criminal sentence had issued. In re Tracy (Ohio App. 2 Dist., Miami, 07-03-2003) No. 2002CA41, No. 2002CA66, No. 2002CA64, No. 2002CA67, No. 2002CA65, 2003-Ohio-3781, 2003 WL 21658665, Unreported. Infants ☜ 206

Court of Appeals could not review father's objections, filed pro se, to magistrate's order in neglect and dependency proceedings barring father, who had been previously adjudicated sexual predator, from having any contact or visitation with his children, where magistrate entered order not as new condition, but merely as a reiteration of father's parole conditions stemming from prior criminal proceedings against father; Court of Appeals had no jurisdiction to alter father's conditions of parole that were entered by a trial court following criminal case against father. In re Tracy (Ohio App. 2 Dist., Miami, 07-03-2003) No. 2002CA41, No. 2002CA66, No. 2002CA64, No. 2002CA67, No. 2002CA65, 2003-Ohio-3781, 2003 WL 21658665, Unreported. Infants ☜ 248.1

Father was not entitled to subpoena mother in conjunction with his filing of objections to magistrate's decision in neglect and dependency proceedings, which, among other things, granted custody to mother with certain protective conditions and barred father from visitation or contact with children, where Court of Appeals found no meritorious objection on which to hold a hearing. In re Tracy (Ohio App. 2 Dist., Miami, 07-03-2003) No. 2002CA41, No. 2002CA66, No. 2002CA64, No. 2002CA67, No. 2002CA65, 2003-Ohio-3781, 2003 WL 21658665, Unreported. Infants ☜ 206

Where a domestic relations court seeks to transfer a case to juvenile court pursuant to the juvenile court's jurisdiction over cases concerning abused, neglected, or dependent child, it must make finding that it is in the best interest of child for neither parent to be designated residential parent and legal custodian of the child in order for jurisdiction to vest in the juvenile court. Thompson v. Valentine (Ohio App. 12 Dist., 08-30-2010) 189 Ohio App.3d

661, 939 N.E.2d 1289, 2010 -Ohio- 4075. Courts ☞ 487(1)

Juvenile court may not award legal custody to nonparent unless it first determines that both of the child's parents are unsuitable. Davis v. Wilson (Ohio App. 12 Dist., 09-22-1997) 123 Ohio App.3d 19, 702 N.E.2d 1227. Child Custody ☞ 510

Juvenile court's exercise of jurisdiction over child custody and abuse complaint filed by mother and grandmother was subject to terms of Uniform Child Custody Jurisdiction Act (UCCJA), given that there was pending divorce and custody proceeding in Kentucky. In re Simons (Ohio App. 2 Dist., 03-07-1997) 118 Ohio App.3d 622, 693 N.E.2d 1111. Child Custody ☞ 748

Father had standing to assert on appeal that trial court erred in not granting legal custody of children to one of his relatives rather than granting permanent custody to county children services agency, even though none of relatives had appealed, where by granting permanent custody to agency, father lost residual parental rights, privileges and obligations. In re Hiatt (Adams 1993) 86 Ohio App.3d 716, 621 N.E.2d 1222. Infants ☞ 242

While there is no statutory mandate that factors for determining best interest of child in custody disputes arising from divorce actions be considered in custody proceedings incident to dependency action, juvenile courts should consider totality of circumstances, including those factors, to extent they are applicable. In re Pryor (Athens 1993) 86 Ohio App.3d 327, 620 N.E.2d 973. Infants ☞ 154.1

Failure of common pleas court to make finding that natural parents were unfit custodians of child did not preclude certification of child custody case to juvenile court, where case was certified pursuant to statute giving juvenile court discretion whether to accept certification, rather than statute pursuant to which juvenile court must accept certification based on finding that it is in best interest of child for neither parent to have custody. In re Whaley (Athens 1993) 86 Ohio App.3d 304, 620 N.E.2d 954. Courts ☞ 487(1)

Because RC 2151.23 is a jurisdictional statute without any substantive law test, the common-law parental-suitability test is to be applied when a nonparent seeks custody of a child; the "best-interest" test of RC 3109.04 applies only to divorce-custody proceedings. Reynolds v. Goll (Lorain 1992) 80 Ohio App.3d 494, 609 N.E.2d 1276.

When a juvenile court makes a custody determination under RC 2151.23 and 2151.353, it must do so in accordance with RC 3109.04. In re Poling (Ohio 1992) 64 Ohio St.3d 211, 594 N.E.2d 589.

An order placing children in custody of children's services is in error absent a finding of unsuitability of the mother and consideration of the best interest of the children. Truitt v. Truitt (Preble 1989) 65 Ohio App.3d 126, 583 N.E.2d 331. Infants ☞ 154.1

In exercising its jurisdiction under RC 2151.23(A)(2) to determine custody of children, a juvenile court must rely on the standards in RC 3109.04. In re Brazell (Ohio Com.Pl. 1986) 27 Ohio Misc.2d 7, 499 N.E.2d 925, 27 O.B.R. 68.

When a case concerning a child is transferred or certified from another court, such certification does not constitute a complaint in the juvenile court that such a child is neglected, dependent, or abused, and those dispositions provided for under RC 2151.353 pertaining to neglected, dependent, or abused children, including an award of permanent custody to a county welfare department which has assumed the administration of child welfare, are not applicable to such a child, disposition thereof being subject to and controlled by RC 3109.04. In re Snider (Defiance 1984) 14 Ohio App.3d 353, 471 N.E.2d 516, 14 O.B.R. 420. Infants ☞ 197; Infants ☞ 222

In a RC 2151.23(A)(2) child custody proceeding between a parent and a nonparent, the hearing officer may not award custody to the nonparent without first making a finding of parental unsuitability—that is, without first determining that a preponderance of the evidence shows that the parent abandoned the child, that the parent contractually relinquished custody of the child, that the parent has become totally incapable of supporting or caring for the child, or that an award of custody to the parent would be detrimental to the child. In re Perales (Ohio 1977) 52 Ohio St.2d 89, 369 N.E.2d 1047, 6 O.O.3d 293. Child Custody ☞ 42

To the extent that RC 3109.04 proceedings may grant custody in the "best interest" of the child without a finding of parental unsuitablity, it is error to apply the "best interest" test of custody provided for in RC 3109.04 proceedings to a case involving proceedings under RC 2151.23. In re Perales (Ohio 1977) 52 Ohio St.2d 89, 369 N.E.2d 1047, 6 O.O.3d 293.

Where a juvenile court grants the temporary custody of a minor child, with the consent of his parents, to a non-relative, after the father had unrestricted custody pursuant to a divorce decree, RC 3109.04(B) and 3109.04(C), as effective September 23, 1974, are not applicable to prevent the court's consideration of a motion filed by the father, in the same court, for the restoration of custody. Leininger v. Leininger (Fulton 1975) 48 Ohio App.2d 21, 355 N.E.2d 508, 2 O.O.3d 15. Child Custody ☞ 6; Child Custody ☞ 578

RC 3109.04 is applicable to a proceeding for change of custody under the Juvenile Court Act. In re Custody of Smelser (Ohio Com.Pl. 1969) 22 Ohio Misc. 41, 257 N.E.2d 769, 51 O.O.2d 31, 51 O.O.2d 75.

Except when the question of custody is incidental to the separation of parents, their right to custody cannot be taken away unless the grounds as recognized by statute, in general that the child is dependent, neglected or delinquent or that the parent is unfit, are present to support a proper exercise of the police power. Holderle v. Holderle (Franklin 1967) 11 Ohio App.2d 148, 229 N.E.2d 79, 40 O.O.2d 305. Child Custody ☞ 8

A juvenile court which acquires jurisdiction of a minor child of persons who are subsequently divorced has exclusive jurisdiction of such minor, and the common pleas court wherein such divorce is granted has no jurisdiction to make any order respecting the custody of such child. Patton v. Patton (Muskingum 1963) 1 Ohio App.2d 1, 203 N.E.2d 662, 30 O.O.2d 49.

Where a neglected child proceeding is instituted in the juvenile court by a parent of such child, and a divorce action is later instituted by such parent, the juvenile court has exclusive original jurisdiction to determine whether the child is neglected, the power to determine his custody and the authority to place the child with a relative. In re Small (Darke 1960) 114 Ohio App. 248, 181 N.E.2d 503, 19 O.O.2d 128.

RC 3109.04 is not applicable to a neglected child proceeding under RC 2151.27. In re Small (Darke 1960) 114 Ohio App. 248, 181 N.E.2d 503, 19 O.O.2d 128.

Petitioner, who allegedly had resided with biological mother and acted as child's co-custodian for several years, was not the natural or adoptive parent of child to be deemed a parent within meaning of statutory section governing the best interests of child test used in child custody cases, and thus, was not entitled to award of parental rights under statute giving juvenile courts exclusive jurisdiction to determine custody of child who is not a ward of another court of state. In re Jones (Ohio App. 2 Dist., Miami, 05-10-2002) No. 2000 CA 56, 2002-Ohio-2279, 2002 WL 940195, Unreported. Child Custody ☞ 274

As used in 4507.07, "custody" refers to any relationship in which a person stands in loco parentis to a minor, whether or not that person has legal custody of the minor. OAG 72–087.

90. —— Probation, custody or visitation issues in proceedings other than divorce

Municipal court order modifying visitation as part of defendant's probation was void as matters of visitation are within the sole jurisdiction of courts of common pleas, and even assuming the defendant agreed to supervised visitation as part of a plea agreement, a party can not agree to submit a court's subject matter jurisdiction and, as a result, the municipal court could not enforce the new conditions because it lacked the subject matter jurisdiction to do so. City of Rocky River v. Taylor (Ohio App. 8 Dist., Cuyahoga, 02-17-2000) No. 75621, No. 75661, 2000 WL 193234, Unreported.

A residential parent's motion to terminate visitation and the motion of the nonresidential parent to set specific visitation times do not concern custodial issues, and a court errs by granting a motion to modify custody in a case where testimony and evidence do not rise to the level of a substantial change of circumstance but rather indicate the nonresidential parent's increasing demand for additional visitation. David v. Flickinger (Ohio App. 5 Dist., Tuscarawas, 09-19-1995) No. 94AP110077, 1995 WL 557132, Unreported, appeal allowed 75

Ohio St.3d 1410, 661 N.E.2d 758, reversed 77 Ohio St.3d 415, 674 N.E.2d 1159, 1997-Ohio-260.

Without a shared parenting plan, a change in circumstances of the non-custodial parent may not be considered changed circumstances pursuant to RC 3109.04 and thus a change in the visitation schedule does not affect custody and consequently does not warrant a change therein. Yasher v. Yasher (Ohio App. 8 Dist., Cuyahoga, 03-24-1994) No. 65545, 1994 WL 97694, Unreported.

Child's change in age from two and one-half years to nine years, father's desire to spend more time with child, and parties' de facto modification of holiday visitation schedule did not constitute changed circumstances warranting modification of father's visitation schedule as set forth in agreement upon marital dissolution. Jacobs v. Jacobs (Ohio App. 9 Dist., 04-19-1995) 102 Ohio App.3d 568, 657 N.E.2d 580. Child Custody ☞ 574; Child Custody ☞ 577

Change in nonresidential parent's circumstances is relevant in proceeding to modify visitation schedule only if prior decree was shared parenting decree. Jacobs v. Jacobs (Ohio App. 9 Dist., 04-19-1995) 102 Ohio App.3d 568, 657 N.E.2d 580. Child Custody ☞ 577

Trial court erred in failing to consider uncontroverted testimony of child's treating psychologist, on father's motion to modify visitation schedule, as statute required consideration of physical and mental health of all persons involved and testimony was only evidence submitted on child's mental health. Jacobs v. Jacobs (Ohio App. 9 Dist., 04-19-1995) 102 Ohio App.3d 568, 657 N.E.2d 580. Child Custody ☞ 614

Trial court's failure to determine that modification of visitation schedule was in child's best interests was erroneous on father's motion for modification of divorce decree. Jacobs v. Jacobs (Ohio App. 9 Dist., 04-19-1995) 102 Ohio App.3d 568, 657 N.E.2d 580. Child Custody ☞ 924

Parties' agreement to modify prior visitation schedule may be sufficient change of circumstances to justify court's modification of schedule to conform with that agreement, provided it is in best interest of child; agreement, however, should not be used as change in circumstances that justifies discontinuation of entire visitation schedule without reference to parties' mutually demonstrated desires. Jacobs v. Jacobs (Ohio App. 9 Dist., 04-19-1995) 102 Ohio App.3d 568, 657 N.E.2d 580. Child Custody ☞ 574; Child Custody ☞ 577

The factors set forth in RC 3109.04(C) with respect to determining the child's best interest in custody cases apply equally to visitation cases. The trial court must weigh these and other relevant factors in determining the child's best interest in visitation cases. In re Whitaker (Ohio 1988) 36 Ohio St.3d 213, 522 N.E.2d 563. Child Custody ☞ 178

Specific rules for determining when a court may modify custody decree are not equally applicable to modification of visitation rights. Appleby v. Appleby (Ohio 1986) 24 Ohio St.3d 39, 492 N.E.2d 831, 24 O.B.R. 81. Child Custody ☞ 577

Trial court enjoys a broader measure of discretion in setting visitation than in awarding or modifying custody; although domestic relations practitioners and judges routinely consider visitation modification in the context of the presence or absence of changed circumstances, there is no requirement that they do so. Roudebush v. Roudebush (Franklin 1984) 20 Ohio App.3d 380, 486 N.E.2d 849, 20 O.B.R. 485. Child Custody ☞ 577

91. Emergency and temporary orders—In general

Father was not required to raise issue of mother's alleged immoral conduct and its potential impact on children prior to magistrate's decision granting temporary custody of children to mother, or prior to final divorce hearing, in order to preserve right to present such evidence at hearing. Lanfranc v. Lanfranc (Ohio App. 5 Dist., Licking, 09-08-2005) No. 05CA11, 2005-Ohio-4715, 2005 WL 2175155, Unreported, appeal not allowed 108 Ohio St.3d 1437, 842 N.E.2d 63, 2006-Ohio-421. Child Custody ☞ 500

RC 3109.04(B)(1) does not apply to a parent's motion to extinguish an award of custody to a nonparent that is temporary both in its denomination and in terms of the length of time elapsing between the award and the parent's motion to terminate the award. In re Custody of Carpenter (Greene 1987) 41 Ohio App.3d 182, 534 N.E.2d 1216. Child Custody ☞ 550

In a proceeding to award temporary custody of a child, the governing principle is the best interest of the child under RC 3109.04; limitation of examination concerning events in the child's life before the proceeding began is therefore prejudicial error. Mercer v Channell, No. 509 (4th Dist Ct App, Jackson, 5–14–86).

92. —— Appeal, emergency and temporary orders

While the better practice in child custody proceedings would be for a court to explicitly find a "change of circumstances" before delving into the issue of the best interests of the child, Court of Appeals will affirm a decision modifying shared parenting plan where the factual findings of the court support a finding of changed circumstances; explicit language is preferable, but not necessary. Nigro v. Nigro (Ohio App. 9 Dist., Lorain, 11-24-2004) No. 04CA008461, 2004-Ohio-6270, 2004 WL 2674587, Unreported. Child Custody ☞ 659; Child Custody ☞ 922(5)

Emergency order temporarily designating father as residential parent was interlocutory in nature and, therefore, not immediately appealable. Brooks v. Brooks (Ohio App. 10 Dist., 12-24-1996) 117 Ohio App.3d 19, 689 N.E.2d 987. Child Custody ☞ 902

93. —— Findings of fact and conclusions of law, emergency and temporary orders

Magistrates are not required to issue findings of fact and conclusions of law when, during pendency

of divorce action, they make temporary award of child custody to parent who has been convicted of offense involving family member that resulted in physical harm to that victim; rather, statute that requires findings and conclusions when custody is awarded to such parent applies only to final decrees. State ex rel. Thompson v. Spon (Ohio, 11-10-1998) 83 Ohio St.3d 551, 700 N.E.2d 1281, 1998-Ohio-298. Child Custody ☞ 511

94. —— Appeal, shared parenting: joint custody, emergency and temporary orders

Mother waived appellate review of trial court's sua sponte request that parties in custody proceeding submit proposed shared parenting plans, by failing timely to object to such request. Loudermilk v. Lynch (Ohio App. 11 Dist., Ashtabula, 09-30-2004) No. 2002-A-0044, No. 2002-A-0045, 2004-Ohio-5299, 2004 WL 2803411, Unreported. Child Custody ☞ 904

Court of Appeals' decision holding that modification made by the trial court crossed the line separating an adjustment of visitation from a modification of custody, in that it essentially created a shared parenting plan, and that none of the reasons cited by trial court in support of its order were sufficient to justify change of custody was the law of the case since neither party appealed from Court of Appeals' decision, and thus, trial court's order, on remand, again directing the parties to equally divide parenting time on a month-to-month basis could not stand. Buckingham v. Buckingham (Ohio App. 2 Dist., Darke, 09-30-2004) No. CIV.A. 1644, 2004-Ohio-5275, 2004 WL 2245196, Unreported. Child Custody ☞ 924

Court of Appeals lacked jurisdiction to review order granting divorce and adopting shared parenting plan, where order expressly retained jurisdiction as to wife's retirement account, pending evaluation thereof. Crise v. Crise (Ohio App. 9 Dist., Lorain, 06-23-2004) No. 03CA008375, 2004-Ohio-3250, 2004 WL 1397632, Unreported. Child Custody ☞ 902; Divorce ☞ 1207

Husband waived his right to appeal the amount of parenting time he was provided with child, in divorce proceeding, where father entered into an agreement with wife that allocated parental rights, responsibilities, and parenting time, and the trial court spent a considerable amount of time making sure that the parties understood the effect of the agreement. Miller v. Miller (Ohio App. 3 Dist., Marion, 03-01-2004) No. 9-03-38, 2004-Ohio-923, 2004 WL 370406, Unreported. Child Custody ☞ 918

Fact that trial judge signed magistrate's decision recommending modification of shared parenting plan two days before same was filed did not prevent mother from filing objections to magistrate's decision, where notice contained in magistrate's decision advised mother of right to file objections and, at hearing, magistrate stated that hearing would be held before judge if objections were filed and mother responded "okay." In re Lemon (Ohio App. 5 Dist., Stark, 11-12-2002) No. 2002 CA 00098,

2002-Ohio-6263, 2002 WL 31546216, Unreported. Child Custody ☞ 652

Wife waived for appellate review claim that trial court erred in denying her motion to set aside shared parenting agreement, where wife failed to raise objection before trial court. Evans v. Evans (Ohio App. 12 Dist., 10-02-1995) 106 Ohio App.3d 673, 666 N.E.2d 1176, dismissed, appeal not allowed 75 Ohio St.3d 1448, 663 N.E.2d 330. Child Custody ☞ 904

Plain-error doctrine did not apply to wife's claim that trial court erred in denying her motion to set aside shared parenting agreement absent any indication in record that there had been a miscarriage of justice or that wife was prejudiced by trial court's decision to adopt shared parenting agreement. Evans v. Evans (Ohio App. 12 Dist., 10-02-1995) 106 Ohio App.3d 673, 666 N.E.2d 1176, dismissed, appeal not allowed 75 Ohio St.3d 1448, 663 N.E.2d 330. Child Custody ☞ 904

95. —— Modification, emergency and temporary orders

Change of circumstances standard for modifying prior custody decree does not apply to temporary orders with issue of custody pending. Schmidli v. Schmidli (Ohio App. 7 Dist., Belmont, 06-19-2003) No. 02 BE 63, 2003-Ohio-3274, 2003 WL 21443742, Unreported. Child Custody ☞ 555

Trial court's denial of grandmother's motion to terminate temporary custody of her grandchildren in foster care with County Children's Services Board was interlocutory in nature and, therefore, was not a final appealable order. In re Tartt (Ohio App. 3 Dist., Logan, 03-07-2003) No. 8-02-20, No. 8-02-21, 2003-Ohio-1026, 2003 WL 832581, Unreported. Infants ☞ 242

A two-year interval between a grant of temporary child custody to a relative and the parent's attempt to regain custody is insufficient to find that the parent has relinquished her parental rights and so the court does not err in concluding that the natural parent is a suitable parent who has not relinquished legal custody of her daughter. In re Wilson (Ohio App. 2 Dist., Miami, 04-30-1999) No. 98-CA-19, 1999 WL 252799, Unreported.

RC 3109.04(B)(1) does not apply to a parent's motion to extinguish an award of custody to a non parent that is temporary both in its denomination and in terms of the length of time elapsing between the award and the parent's motion to terminate the award. In re Custody of Carpenter (Greene 1987) 41 Ohio App.3d 182, 534 N.E.2d 1216. Child Custody ☞ 550

An interlocutory order regarding child custody entered pursuant to Civ R 75(M) is by its very nature temporary and may be modified upon the entering of the final divorce decree; RC 3109.04(A), rather than RC 3109.04(B), applies to the final determination of custody as well as such inherently temporary orders. Spence v. Spence (Franklin 1981) 2 Ohio App.3d 280, 441 N.E.2d 822, 2 O.B.R. 310.

Where a mother grants voluntary temporary custody to an infant's paternal grandparents, the proper standard to be used by the court in determining an award of custody upon the filing of a petition by the mother is the fitness of the mother, not the best interests of the child standard in RC 3109.04(B). In re Curry, No. 89AP–550 (10th Dist Ct App, Franklin, 11–21–89).

RC 3109.04(B) does not apply where a parent files to obtain custody after an award of temporary custody to a non-parent. An agreement to allow temporary custody is not a knowing surrender of parents' natural right to preferential treatment in a custody proceeding. In re Carpenter, No. 87–CA–3 (2d Dist Ct App, Greene, 7–27–87).

96. Retroactive or prospective effect of amendments

Admissible evidence in proceedings for modification of shared parenting plan with respect to child born to parties several years after their divorce when they resumed living together, demonstrating that harm likely to be caused by change of environment was far outweighed by advantages of change of environment to child, was sufficient to support modification of plan to name former husband as child's residential and custodial parent; former wife pled guilty to criminal trespass after incident occurring during former husband's visitation with child, during which former wife struck former husband, and former wife was in willful contempt of court for failure to abide by parenting plan and interference with former husband's visitation. Scaffidi v. Scaffidi (Ohio App. 9 Dist., Medina, 08-31-2005) No. 04CA0068-M, 2005-Ohio-4546, 2005 WL 2087795, Unreported. Children Out–of–wedlock ☞ 20.10

Custody modification statute, which required proof of change of circumstances, did not apply to father's motion for return of custody from maternal grandparents, to whom father, while minor, had previously relinquished custody of out of wedlock child. Culp v. Burkhart (Ohio App. 5 Dist., Tuscarawas, 08-13-2004) No. 04AP010006, 2004-Ohio-4425, 2004 WL 1879659, Unreported. Children Out–of–wedlock ☞ 20.10

Although courts must give due consideration to which parent was primary caregiver in fashioning custody award in divorce proceeding, no presumptive quality is to be given to primary caregiver doctrine, assuming that it applies, in custody modification proceeding. Holm v. Smilowitz (Athens 1992) 83 Ohio App.3d 757, 615 N.E.2d 1047. Child Custody ☞ 44; Child Custody ☞ 634

Although the current version of RC 3109.04 was not in effect at the time the complaint was filed, and the court mistakenly applied it and its criteria for a best interest of the child determination anyway, this error does not require reversal where there was no prejudice and the decision was proper under the prior statute. Williams v. Williams (Hardin 1992) 80 Ohio App.3d 477, 609 N.E.2d 617.

RC 3109.04(B) and 3109.04(C), effective September 23, 1974, affect substantial vested rights of parents and their children and will not be applied retroactively. Leininger v. Leininger (Fulton 1975) 48 Ohio App.2d 21, 355 N.E.2d 508, 2 O.O.3d 15. Child Custody ⚷ 6

97. Arbitration, generally

Matters of child custody may only be decided by trial court and are not subject to arbitration despite any agreement entered into by parties. Pulfer v. Pulfer (Ohio App. 3 Dist., 03-28-1996) 110 Ohio App.3d 90, 673 N.E.2d 656, dismissed, appeal not allowed 77 Ohio St.3d 1412, 670 N.E.2d 1001. Alternative Dispute Resolution ⚷ 119

98. Attorney fees

Mother was entitled to recover attorney fees when, after the trial court dismissed father's motion to renew his motion for re-allocation of parental rights and responsibilities, father withdrew his pending contempt motion which had been scheduled to be heard that day; court and opposing counsel were prepared to go forward with the contempt motion, and father could have proceeded with the show cause motion and, if the court found mother in contempt, it could consider that fact in the future. Dole v. Dole (Ohio App. 5 Dist., Holmes, 03-18-2011) No. 10CA013, 2011-Ohio-1314, 2011 WL 977053, Unreported. Child Custody ⚷ 943

Sanctions were not warranted for mother's filing of motion to modify parental rights and responsibilities, despite mother's failure to allege or demonstrate a change of circumstances, where divorce decree purported to permit modification without a change of circumstances, parties' agreement opened the door to litigating matters that predated the entry of the divorce decree, and neither father nor the trial court raised the issue of whether the parties lacked the authority to waive the change-of-circumstances requirement until after the hearing. Eastwood v. Eastwood (Ohio App. 9 Dist., Summit, 12-30-2010) No. 25310, 2010-Ohio-6492, 2010 WL 5550706, Unreported. Costs ⚷ 2

Trial court acted within its discretion in awarding mother attorney fees in action to modify shared parenting plan; among other findings, trial court cited examples of father's egregious and litigious time-consuming conduct throughout proceedings, in addition to father's far greater income and earning capacity. Holeski v. Holeski (Ohio App. 11 Dist., Portage, 11-13-2009) No. 2009-P-0007, 2009-Ohio-6036, 2009 WL 3807168, Unreported. Child Custody ⚷ 943

Imposition of $3,000 in attorney fees to be paid within six months from date of judgment entry, as a purge condition for mother's contemptuous conduct in interfering with father's visitation rights involving out-of-wedlock child, was reasonable and capable of compliance, despite mother's unemployed status at the time, where mother had previously been gainfully employed and she was able-bodied and capable of full-time employment. C.G. v. C.L. (Ohio App. 8 Dist., Cuyahoga, 06-26-2008) No. 90341, 2008-Ohio-3135, 2008 WL 2536058, Unreported. Children Out–of–wedlock ⚷ 20

Trial court did not abuse its discretion in awarding husband attorney fees associated with husband's motions to find wife in contempt of court, where record showed that wife repeatedly sought to prevent husband from exercising his scheduled parenting time awarded by trial court's prior orders. Day v. Day (Ohio App. 5 Dist., Ashland, 08-22-2005) No. 04 COA 74, 2005-Ohio-4343, 2005 WL 2002249, Unreported. Child Custody ⚷ 943

Former wife was not entitled to award of her full attorney fees incurred in prosecuting her motions for modification of child custody and child support and defending against former husband's motion for contempt, absent any indication that failure to award fees would prevent her from litigating her rights or protecting her interests, where itemization submitted by former wife's counsel failed to detail which fees were attributable to each motion, former wife was entitled to some fees incurred in defending against contempt motion, but trial court did not make requisite findings as to former husband's ability to pay before awarding fees incurred in connection with former wife's motions. Cherwin v. Cherwin (Ohio App. 8 Dist., Cuyahoga, 04-28-2005) No. 84875, 2005-Ohio-1999, 2005 WL 991706, Unreported. Child Custody ⚷ 949; Child Custody ⚷ 955; Child Support ⚷ 609; Child Support ⚷ 615

Ohio court lacked jurisdiction over former wife's complaint for reallocation of parental rights, and thus her complaint was frivolous, for purposes of determining former husband's entitlement to award of attorney fees, where parties had obtained their divorce in Texas, the children's domicile was not in Ohio, and wife learned that alleged abuse of children by stepmother was parental discipline shortly after filing the complaint. Caudell v. McKenzie (Ohio App. 5 Dist., Fairfield, 12-20-2004) No. 04CA26, 2004-Ohio-7095, 2004 WL 2988300, Unreported. Costs ⚷ 194.44

Former husband was not entitled to award of attorney fees following denial of former wife's motion for relief from agreed judgment entry of divorce, which established shared parenting plan with former husband as residential parent for school purposes, based on genetic test results showing zero percent probability of former husband being father of child; there was no basis for award of attorney fees merely because party was successful in defending against motion for relief from judgment. Blystone v. Blystone (Ohio App. 10 Dist., Franklin, 10-23-2003) No. 03AP-247, 2003-Ohio-5667, 2003 WL 22415636, Unreported. Child Custody ⚷ 943

Trial court did not lose jurisdiction to consider former husband's motions for attorney fees after former wife filed a voluntary dismissal of her motion for shared parenting of parties' minor daughter. Curtis v. Curtis (Ohio App. 1 Dist., 12-08-2000) 140 Ohio App.3d 812, 749 N.E.2d 772, dismissed, appeal not allowed 91 Ohio St.3d 1489, 745 N.E.2d 437. Child Custody ⚷ 943

Court of Appeals' inability to determine how the trial court arrived at a $7,926 award of attorney fees to former husband, in light of the evidence that his attorney fees during custody dispute exceeded $22,000, required remand to the trial court for a recalculation of the fees on the basis of the evidence of record. Curtis v. Curtis (Ohio App. 1 Dist., 12-08-2000) 140 Ohio App.3d 812, 749 N.E.2d 772, dismissed, appeal not allowed 91 Ohio St.3d 1489, 745 N.E.2d 437. Child Custody ⬌ 949

Expert testimony of attorney was inadmissible, in hearing on attorney fee requests made pursuant to cross-motions for custody of children, to determine whether former wife's motion for change of custody was warranted under existing law or could be supported by good-faith argument for extension, modification, or reversal of existing law. Mitchell v. Mitchell (Ohio App. 2 Dist., 03-20-1998) 126 Ohio App.3d 500, 710 N.E.2d 793. Child Custody ⬌ 952

It is not an abuse of discretion to award an ex-wife her reasonable attorney fees incurred in resisting a motion to modify custody. Cohen v. Cohen (Lake 1983) 8 Ohio App.3d 109, 456 N.E.2d 581, 8 O.B.R. 143.

There is no statute and no provision for attorney fees to be awarded to custodial parent who resists a motion to visit brought by grandparents. Midkiff v Midkiff, No. CA86–10–025 (12th Dist Ct App, Madison, 7–20–87).

A court has the power to order a husband to pay his ex-wife's attorney's fees in post divorce decree proceedings involving the custody of the parties' child. Roberts v Roberts, No. 47635 (8th Dist Ct App, Cuyahoga, 5–24–84).

99. Ethics of divorce attorneys

Elihu Root's observation is worth recalling, that "About half the practice of a decent lawyer consists of telling... clients they are d——— fools and should stop... [that]the law lets you do it but don't. It's a rotten thing to do." Stivison v. Goodyear Tire & Rubber Co. (Ohio App. 4 Dist., Hocking, 05-06-1996) No. 95CA13, 1996 WL 230037, Unreported, appeal allowed 77 Ohio St.3d 1447, 671 N.E.2d 1285, reversed 80 Ohio St.3d 498, 687 N.E.2d 458, 1997-Ohio-321.

100. Federal provisions

Trial court lacked jurisdiction over father's motion to find mother in contempt for denying visitation, based on claim that mother moved with children to Pennsylvania without informing father, where neither parties nor children resided in Ohio; rather, trial court was required to determine whether it had continuing jurisdiction over issues of child custody under Uniform Child Custody Jurisdiction Act. Pearson v. Pearson (Ohio App. 4 Dist., Meigs, 09-13-2005) No. 04CA6, 2005-Ohio-4909, 2005 WL 2268207, Unreported. Child Custody ⬌ 730; Child Custody ⬌ 733; Child Custody ⬌ 745

Juvenile court's order returning child custody to mother did not constitute "parenting determination," within meaning of Uniform Child Custody Jurisdiction Act (UCCJA), and thus, order did not constitute initial and binding custody decree as to

parties' future entitlement to custody, as alleged by mother, where return of custody occurred before father's paternity was established, custody determination was only between mother and Department of Children's Services, and mother and father were married after paternity was established. In re Sklenchar (Ohio App. 7 Dist., Mahoning, 08-18-2004) No. 04MA55, 2004-Ohio-4405, 2004 WL 1874572, Unreported. Child Custody ⬌ 717; Infants ⬌ 231

Alabama was child's home state under Uniform Child Custody Jurisdiction Act (UCCJA), where both mother and father had equal parenting rights once father's domestic violence complaint against mother was dismissed, father had physical child custody for approximately five years, and child resided with father in Alabama for more than six consecutive months prior to time instant child custody action was brought. In re Sklenchar (Ohio App. 7 Dist., Mahoning, 08-18-2004) No. 04MA55, 2004-Ohio-4405, 2004 WL 1874572, Unreported. Child Custody ⬌ 736

Trial court denial of maternal grandparents' motion to intervene in child dependency proceeding was an abuse of discretion; trial court had previously granted grandparents temporary custody of child, Juvenile Rule provided that temporary custody meant legal custody, and statute provided that a person with legal custody to a child should be joined in a dependency proceeding. In re Perez (Ohio App. 5 Dist., Tuscarawas, 05-24-2004) No. 2003AP120091, 2004-Ohio-2707, 2004 WL 1171689, Unreported. Infants ⬌ 200

Denying mother's request to continue hearing on father's motion to show cause why mother should not have been held in contempt for her denial of telephone contact and visitation was abuse of discretion, where mother lived in another state, she did not receive notice until five days prior to hearing, no evidence suggested that request for continuance was dilatory, purposeful or contrived, or sought solely to delay proceedings, continuance motion, made three days after receiving notice, was not untimely, no evidence suggested that granting a continuance would have inconvenienced or prejudiced parties, witnesses, or opposing counsel, and Uniform Child Custody Jurisdiction Act required court to give a nonresident party at least 20 days notice before scheduling any hearing in state involving a parenting proceeding. In re Zak (Ohio App. 11 Dist., Lake, 04-18-2003) No. 2001-L-216, No. 2001-L-217, No. 2001-L-218, 2003-Ohio-1974, 2003 WL 1904049, Unreported. Child Custody ⬌ 871

Juvenile court was authorized to exercise jurisdiction over parties' minor children in interstate custody dispute, where children were born in state and lived there until one year prior to custody proceedings in case, mother, who was residential custodian, filed a petition to register a foreign judgment and suit seeking modification of the out-of-state order in her state of residence, children had a significant connection to state, as their natural father, grandparents, and other family members lived in state, their guardians ad litem, supervisors for father's in-state visits were in state, substantial evidence concerning children's present and/or future protection and relationships was available in state, and mother alleged that she denied visitation based on abuse that took place in state. In re Zak (Ohio App. 11 Dist., Lake, 04-18-2003) No. 2001-L-216, No. 2001-L-217, No. 2001-L-218, 2003-Ohio-1974, 2003 WL 1904049, Unreported. Child Custody ☞ 730; Child Custody ☞ 735; Child Custody ☞ 737

Issue of whether custody of parties' children would change if wife moved from children's present school district was not ripe for judicial review on wife's appeal from divorce judgment that granted custody of children to her with condition that husband would become residential parent if she moved from current school district. Ferris v. Ferris (Ohio App. 4 Dist., Meigs, 03-11-2003) No. 02CA4, 2003-Ohio-1284, 2003 WL 1227326, Unreported. Child Custody ☞ 916

Doctrine of res judicata barred maternal relatives' motion to intervene, motion for custody, and motion for visitation of child involved in child protection matter, where relatives had failed to appeal denial of first motion, and second motion was attempt to relitigate same issues. In re Hoffman (Ohio App. 5 Dist., Stark, 03-03-2003) No. 2002CA0419, No. 2002CA0422, 2003-Ohio-1241, 2003 WL 1193770, Unreported. Infants ☞ 232

Domestic relations court had personal jurisdiction over former husband in connection with modification of out-of-state order establishing visitation incident to divorce, where former husband filed motion for reinstatement of visitation in such court. Boeckmann v. Baker (Ohio App. 2 Dist., Greene, 01-31-2003) No. 2002 CA 72, 2003-Ohio-456, 2003 WL 203579, Unreported. Child Custody ☞ 742

The term "parenting determination" as used in RC 3109.25(A) relates to the decision of custody matters, while a child support determination does not determine parenthood or paternity, but is rather an equitable determination. Drucker v. Drucker (Ohio App. 8 Dist., Cuyahoga, 08-17-2000) No. 77601, 2000 WL 1176514, Unreported.

The mere fact that Ohio court has basic statutory jurisdiction to determine child custody matters in legal separation and divorce cases does not preclude a more specific statute like the Uniform Child Custody Jurisdiction and Enforcement Act (UCCJEA) from patently and unambiguously divesting the court of such jurisdiction. Rosen v. Celebrezze (Ohio, 03-05-2008) 117 Ohio St.3d 241, 883 N.E.2d 420, 2008-Ohio-853. Child Custody ☞ 743; Statutes ☞ 223.4

When the Ohio version of the Uniform Child Custody Jurisdiction Act conflicts with the Parental Kidnapping Prevention Act (PKPA), the PKPA prevails. State ex rel. Morenz v. Kerr (Ohio, 11-22-2004) 104 Ohio St.3d 148, 818 N.E.2d 1162, 2004-Ohio-6208. Child Custody ☞ 702

The Ohio civil procedure rule pertaining to continuing jurisdiction does not confer jurisdiction in Ohio over post-decree child custody matters when jurisdiction is otherwise lacking under the Parental

Kidnapping Prevention Act (PKPA) or the Uniform Child Custody Jurisdiction Act (UCCJA). State ex rel. Seaton v. Holmes (Ohio, 11-19-2003) 100 Ohio St.3d 265, 798 N.E.2d 375, 2003-Ohio-5897. Child Custody ☞ 745

Insofar as the Ohio version of the Uniform Child Custody Jurisdiction Act (UCCJA) conflicts with the federal Parental Kidnapping Prevention Act (PKPA), the PKPA prevails, under preemption principles. State ex rel. Seaton v. Holmes (Ohio, 11-19-2003) 100 Ohio St.3d 265, 798 N.E.2d 375, 2003-Ohio-5897. Child Custody ☞ 707

Under the Uniform Child Custody Jurisdiction Act (UCCJA) and the Parental Kidnapping Prevention Act (PKPA), a state court that has rendered an initial custody decree has exclusive jurisdiction over the ongoing custody dispute if that state has continuing jurisdiction. State ex rel. Seaton v. Holmes (Ohio, 11-19-2003) 100 Ohio St.3d 265, 798 N.E.2d 375, 2003-Ohio-5897. Child Custody ☞ 745

Trial court properly applied Uniform Child Custody Jurisdiction Act (UCCJA) and Parental Kidnapping Protection Act (PKPA) to jurisdictional conflict in proceedings to adopt child who was born in another state. In re Adoption of Asente (Ohio, 08-23-2000) 90 Ohio St.3d 91, 734 N.E.2d 1224, 2000-Ohio-32, reconsideration denied 90 Ohio St.3d 1431, 736 N.E.2d 27. Adoption ☞ 10

West Virginia court from which divorce decree originated maintained continuing jurisdiction with respect to child custody and visitation issues, where hearing was held in West Virginia court on former husband's motion to modify child support and order entered thereon two months before former wife filed petition to transfer jurisdiction to Ohio. In re Monroe (Ohio App. 7 Dist., 03-24-1999) 133 Ohio App.3d 294, 727 N.E.2d 953. Child Custody ☞ 745

In determining jurisdiction under Uniform Child Custody Jurisdiction Act (UCCJA), two-step process is used in which court first determines if Ohio has jurisdiction, and then determines whether Ohio should exercise that jurisdiction. In re Skrha (Ohio App. 8 Dist., 11-14-1994) 98 Ohio App.3d 487, 648 N.E.2d 908. Child Custody ☞ 746

Uniform Child Custody Jurisdiction Act (UCCJA) acts to statutorily ensure same type of recognition of interstate continuing custody jurisdiction as is afforded intrastate continuing custody jurisdiction. Boehn v. Shurtliff (Ohio App. 6 Dist., 09-17-1993) 90 Ohio App.3d 363, 629 N.E.2d 478. Child Custody ☞ 745

Grandparents without any legal right to custody of or visitation with grandchildren, obtained through statute, court order, or other legal means, have no right under RC 3109.28 to intervene in a proceeding to terminate the parents' rights to the children. In re Schmidt (Ohio 1986) 25 Ohio St.3d 331, 496 N.E.2d 952, 25 O.B.R. 386.

In a dispute over visitation rights, an Ohio court may retain jurisdiction, even though the defendant and children reside in another state, where the parties have recently entered into a consent order in the court, thereby indicating that they consider family ties to Ohio to be strong. Willis v. Willis (Ohio Com.Pl. 1985) 25 Ohio Misc.2d 1, 495 N.E.2d 478, 25 O.B.R. 50.

Custody decree rendered by juvenile court in Ohio was binding on grandmother who had taken children from Ohio to Louisiana, given fact that both Ohio and Louisiana had adopted the Uniform Child Custody Jurisdiction Act, R.C. §3109.01 et seq., and given fact that record indicated that grandmother was properly served; thus, mother could enforce custody decree through Louisiana courts and issuance of an extraordinary writ of habeas corpus was unnecessary and duplicative. In re Davis (Ohio 1985) 18 Ohio St.3d 226, 480 N.E.2d 775, 18 O.B.R. 285. Child Custody ☞ 788; Habeas Corpus ☞ 232

A custody decree or court determination that is entitled to recognition in Ohio under Uniform Child Custody Jurisdiction Act includes a finding of child neglect and dependency by another state's court. Squires v. Squires (Preble 1983) 12 Ohio App.3d 138, 468 N.E.2d 73, 12 O.B.R. 460. Child Custody ☞ 723

The Uniform Child Custody Jurisdiction Act, as adopted in Ohio, is applicable to and must be complied with in a guardianship termination proceeding. In re Wonderly's Guardianship (Ohio 1981) 67 Ohio St.2d 178, 423 N.E.2d 420, 21 O.O.3d 111. Guardian And Ward ☞ 25

The presence of a child and one spouse in Illinois is not enough, in and of itself, to give an Illinois court jurisdiction under the Due Process Clause over the other spouse such that an Ohio court is bound by its custody decree. Pasqualone v. Pasqualone (Ohio 1980) 63 Ohio St.2d 96, 406 N.E.2d 1121, 17 O.O.3d 58. Child Custody ☞ 732

The district court had authority, under the Hague Convention on Civil Aspects of International Child Abduction, to determine the merits of an abduction claim, but not the merits of the underlying child custody claim. Anderson v. Acree (S.D.Ohio, 12-11-2002) 250 F.Supp.2d 872, subsequent determination 250 F.Supp.2d 876. Child Custody ☞ 816

Maternal grandparents of dependent children should have been allowed to intervene, pursuant to joinder statute, in custody proceedings initiated by county children services agency; fact that grandparents were previously granted legal custody of the children established a colorable claim of a custody or visitation right, as required by the statute. In re Fusik (Ohio App. 4 Dist., Athens, 08-19-2002) No. 02CA16, 2002-Ohio-4410, 2002 WL 1978880, Unreported. Infants ☞ 200

A writ of habeas corpus is a "custody decree" or "custody determination" within the meaning of RC 3109.21(B) and (D), and therefore a Louisiana court may choose to enforce an Ohio writ of habeas corpus, pursuant to the uniform child custody jurisdiction law. Davis v Davis, Nos. 47377 and 47378 (8th Dist Ct App, Cuyahoga, 4–19–84).

Where a final judgment denying a change of custody has been entered and the court has only a visitation motion before it, it is violative of due process for the court to subsequently sua sponte change the custody order since notice of the proposed action was not provided to the parties involved. In re Remmer, No. 52712 (8th Dist Ct App, Cuyahoga, 7–2–87).

RC 3109.23(C) must be interpreted to require "at least twenty days before any hearing in this state" from the time the notice of the hearing is "served, mailed [or] delivered." Sontag v Sontag, No. C–800223 (1st Dist Ct App, Hamilton, 4–15–81).

An Ohio court has authority to modify a New Jersey court decree as to visitation with children residing in Ohio even where the decree lacks sufficient finality to entitle it to full faith and credit as to child support and alimony. Auberry v Auberry, No. 13966 (9th Dist Ct App, Summit, 2–15–89).

101. States' sovereign rights in domestic relations—In general

Federal court abstention under the *Younger* abstention doctrine is generally appropriate in matters of family relations such as child custody. Meyers v. Franklin County Court of Common Pleas (C.A.6 (Ohio), 08-07-2001) No. 99-4411, 23 Fed.Appx. 201, 2001 WL 1298942, Unreported, on subsequent appeal 81 Fed.Appx. 49, 2003 WL 22718238. Federal Courts ☞ 47.1

Existence of pending state temporary custody commitment proceeding supported District Court's abstention under the *Younger* abstention doctrine, in action against juvenile court and court officers brought by parents of minor child, alleging defendants violated parents' constitutional rights by granting temporary custody of child to county agency without full evidentiary hearing, where state proceeding implicated important state interests. Meyers v. Franklin County Court of Common Pleas (C.A.6 (Ohio), 08-07-2001) No. 99-4411, 23 Fed. Appx. 201, 2001 WL 1298942, Unreported, on subsequent appeal 81 Fed.Appx. 49, 2003 WL 22718238. Federal Courts ☞ 47.1

Federal courts have no jurisdiction to resolve domestic relations disputes involving child custody. Evans v. Klaeger (C.A.6 (Ohio), 06-12-2001) No. 00-4353, 12 Fed.Appx. 326, 2001 WL 700825, Unreported. Federal Courts ☞ 8

102. —— Federal involvement, states' sovereign rights in domestic relations

Disabled father's daughter failed to allege that delays in custody litigation purportedly caused by a state court's failure to accommodate his disability caused her to be deprived of his companionship for a period of five years, as required to recover on her Americans with Disabilities Act (ADA) associational discrimination claim against the state court; her complaint did not allege that she had been denied his companionship as a result of the proceedings in the custody case, but rather, because she was removed from his home as the result of a protective order issued in a separate case and based on allegations of domestic violence committed against her mother. Popovich v. Cuyahoga County Court of Common Pleas, Domestic Relations Div. (C.A.6 (Ohio), 09-27-2005) No. 04-3734, 150 Fed.Appx. 424, 2005 WL 2374236, Unreported, certiorari denied 126 S.Ct. 1319, 546 U.S. 1176, 164 L.Ed.2d 58. Civil Rights ⊗ 1025

Disabled father's daughter, who claimed that delays in custody litigation caused by a state court's failure to accommodate his disability deprived her of his companionship for a period of five years, failed to allege that she had suffered an injury cognizable under the Americans with Disabilities Act (ADA), and thus lacked standing to sue the

state court on an associational discrimination theory; she had not been denied access to or participation in any of the public services covered by the statute. Popovich v. Cuyahoga County Court of Common Pleas, Domestic Relations Div. (C.A.6 (Ohio), 09-27-2005) No. 04-3734, 150 Fed.Appx. 424, 2005 WL 2374236, Unreported, certiorari denied 126 S.Ct. 1319, 546 U.S. 1176, 164 L.Ed.2d 58. Civil Rights ⊗ 1332(6)

The domestic relations exception to federal jurisdiction applies only where a plaintiff positively sues in federal court for divorce, alimony, or child custody. Catz v. Chalker (C.A.6 (Ohio), 04-16-1998) 142 F.3d 279, opinion amended on denial of rehearing 243 F.3d 234. Federal Courts ⊗ 8

3109.041 Shared parenting modification to decree entered before specific authority in law

(A) Parties to any custody decree issued pursuant to section 3109.04 of the Revised Code prior to April 11, 1991, may file a motion with the court that issued the decree requesting the issuance of a shared parenting decree in accordance with division (G) of section 3109.04 of the Revised Code. Upon the filing of the motion, the court shall determine whether to grant the parents shared rights and responsibilities for the care of the children in accordance with divisions (A), (D)(1), (E)(1), and (I) of section 3109.04 of the Revised Code.

(B) A custody decree issued pursuant to section 3109.04 of the Revised Code prior to April 11, 1991, that granted joint care, custody, and control of the children to the parents shall not be affected or invalidated by, and shall not be construed as being affected or invalidated by, the provisions of section 3109.04 of the Revised Code relative to the granting of a shared parenting decree or a decree allocating parental rights and responsibilities for the care of children on and after April 11, 1991. The decree issued prior to April 11, 1991 shall remain in full force and effect, subject to modification or termination pursuant to section 3109.04 of the Revised Code as that section exists on and after April 11, 1991.

(C) As used in this section, "joint custody" and "joint care, custody, and control" have the same meaning as "shared parenting."

(2007 H 119, eff. 6–30–07; 1990 S 3, eff. 4–11–91; 1981 S 39, H 71)

Historical and Statutory Notes

Amendment Note: 2007 H 119 substituted "April 11, 1991" for "the effective date of this amendment" throughout the section; and added the reference to section 3109.04(I) in division (A).

Library References

Child Custody ⊗6.
Westlaw Topic No. 76D.

C.J.S. Parent and Child §§ 55 to 56, 58 to 62, 77, 82 to 83, 90 to 127, 132 to 155.

Research References

Treatises and Practice Aids

Sowald & Morganstern, Baldwin's Ohio Practice Domestic Relations Law § 15:1, Allocating Parental Rights.

Sowald & Morganstern, Baldwin's Ohio Practice Domestic Relations Law § 16:17, Modification of Prior Decrees to Shared Parenting.

Law Review and Journal Commentaries

Dividing the Child: *Shea v. Metcalf*, 712 A.2d 887 (Vt. 1998), Note. 24 U Dayton L Rev 543 (Spring 1999).

Notes of Decisions

In general 1
Discretion of court 2
Effective date 3
Out–of–state child 4

---

1. In general

To modify divorce decree in order to implement shared parenting plan, trial court must determine that such modification is in best interest of child and that there has been a change in circumstances. Neel v. Neel (Ohio App. 8 Dist., 07-25-1996) 113 Ohio App.3d 24, 680 N.E.2d 207, dismissed, appeal not allowed 77 Ohio St.3d 1514, 674 N.E.2d 369. Child Custody ☞ 553

Trial court could not modify custody provisions of divorce decree to provide for shared parenting plan, absent change of circumstances and showing that such modification was in best interest of child, particularly as parties' relationship had deteriorated to such an extent that cooperation between them was highly unlikely. Neel v. Neel (Ohio App. 8 Dist., 07-25-1996) 113 Ohio App.3d 24, 680 N.E.2d 207, dismissed, appeal not allowed 77 Ohio St.3d 1514, 674 N.E.2d 369. Child Custody ☞ 553

2. Discretion of court

Trial court did not abuse its discretion in terminating mother and father's shared parenting plan and naming father as the residential and custodial parent of the parties' two youngest children; two doctors testified that mother had engaged in parental alienation and one testified that a change of custody of the children would be less harmful to them than the continued alienation. Rooney v. Rooney (Ohio App. 5 Dist., Stark, 06-01-2010) No. 2009CA00256, 2010-Ohio-2439, 2010 WL 2186026, Unreported. Child Custody ☞ 576

Custody award was abuse of discretion where there was no evidence that court had considered

and rejected party's motion and proposed plan for shared parenting. Frost v. Frost (Franklin 1992) 84 Ohio App.3d 699, 618 N.E.2d 198, motion overruled 66 Ohio St.3d 1489, 612 N.E.2d 1245. Child Custody ☞ 120; Child Custody ☞ 141

3. Effective date

Statute authorizing "shared parenting" custody decrees was applicable to divorce case pending on its effective date. Frost v. Frost (Franklin 1992) 84 Ohio App.3d 699, 618 N.E.2d 198, motion overruled 66 Ohio St.3d 1489, 612 N.E.2d 1245. Child Custody ☞ 6

A mediation provision in a joint custody decree of September 30, 1986 is enforceable pursuant to RC 3109.041; however, the parties waive their right to have nonpayment of medical expenses submitted to mediation where one of the parties files a motion for contempt with the court and the other party fails to request mediation and actively participates in the proceedings. Dugach v Dugach, No. 93–L–073, 1995 WL 237040 (11th Dist Ct App, Lake, 3–31–95).

4. Out–of–state child

Where a mother has left the state taking a child and the court enters a shared parenting order that the child be returned to Cuyahoga County and reside with the mother if she returns also, but reside with the father if the mother elects to not return, this order does not violate the mother's "constitutional right to travel;" the order concerns the child's best interests and residence, interferes with no one's travel, and it is essential here to remove this child from the negative atmosphere of the mother's efforts to alienate the child from her father. Marsala v. Marsala (Ohio App. 8 Dist., Cuyahoga, 07-06-1995) No. 67301, 1995 WL 396360, Unreported.

3109.042 Designation of residential parent and legal custodian

An unmarried female who gives birth to a child is the sole residential parent and legal custodian of the child until a court of competent jurisdiction issues an order designating another person as the residential parent and legal custodian. A court designating the residential parent and legal custodian of a child described in this section shall treat the mother and father as standing upon an equality when making the designation.

(1997 H 352, eff. 1–1–98)

Library References

Children Out-of-Wedlock ☞20 to 20.3.
Westlaw Topic No. 76H.
C.J.S. Children Out-of-Wedlock §§ 7 to 9, 32 to 38.

Research References

Encyclopedias

OH Jur. 3d Family Law § 1041, Relinquishment of Child to Grandparent Through Power of Attorney.
OH Jur. 3d Family Law § 1056, Parent's Equality in Allocation.

OH Jur. 3d Guardian & Ward § 88, Form, Notice, and Execution.

Treatises and Practice Aids

Sowald & Morganstern, Baldwin's Ohio Practice Domestic Relations Law § 3:10, Judicial Parentage Action--Parties.

Sowald & Morganstern, Baldwin's Ohio Practice Domestic Relations Law § 3:35, Effect of Judgment--Allocation of Parental Rights and Responsibilities, Visitation, and Companionship Rights--As Between Parents.

Sowald & Morganstern, Baldwin's Ohio Practice Domestic Relations Law § 15:60, Modifying Allocation of Parental Rights--De Facto Custody.

Carlin, Baldwin's Ohio Prac. Merrick-Rippner Probate Law § 110:13, Jurisdiction Over Child Custody Matters--Determination of Custody.

Carlin, Baldwin's Ohio Prac. Merrick-Rippner Probate Law § 110:14, Modification of Decree Allocating Parental Rights and Responsibilities for Care of Children.

Carlin, Baldwin's Ohio Prac. Merrick-Rippner Probate Law § 110:29, Parentage Act--Judgment Determining Existence of Parent-Child Relationship.

Adrine & Ruden, Ohio Domestic Violence Law § 10:11, Parties Authorized to File for Civil Protection Orders.

Adrine & Ruden, Ohio Domestic Violence Law § 15:24, Other Issues that Impact Custody and Visitation Awards.

Hastings, Manoloff, Sheeran, & Stype, Ohio School Law § 23:2, Admission Requirements and Tuition Liability--Statutory Requirements in General.

Notes of Decisions

Domestic violence, consideration   2
Procedural issues   3
Unfitness of parent as factor   1

----

1. Unfitness of parent as factor

In initial child custody case involving parents who were never married, trial court did not abuse its discretion in designating biological father as the residential parent and legal custodian of child; the critical issue to the trial court was which parent was most likely to honor and facilitate court-approved parenting time, rights or visitation and companionship rights, and the court found that biological mother had put forth little effort, if any, to ensure that father had companionship with child, noted that father provided the transportation involved even after mother moved child to Ohio, and clearly believed that mother's husband had a hostile attitude toward father and was critical of him. Hartman v. Eggar (Ohio App. 5 Dist., Fairfield, 12-16-2010) No. 09 CA 0055, 2010-Ohio-6357, 2010 WL 5480652, Unreported. Children Out–of–wedlock ☞ 20.3

Trial court did not err in naming wife residential parent and legal custodian of children; although there was testimony presented indicating wife's troubled past, including battle with alcohol and drugs, which ultimately led to her arrest and conviction for forging prescriptions, there was testimony describing her ongoing treatment and continued success in rehabilitation, something that had caused her to change immensely, wife was primary caretaker for children prior to rehabilitation, and children had spent significant amount of time bonding with her extended family, and husband admitted that wife had become "supermom," and that children were happy when they were with her. Kranz v. Kranz (Ohio App. 12 Dist., Warren, 05-26-2009) No. CA2008-04-054, 2009-Ohio-2451, 2009 WL 1460097, Unreported. Child Custody ☞ 469

Trial court's consideration of transcripts of children's in-chambers interviews with magistrate, which were not certified, file-stamped, or recorded on docket sheet, was harmless error in child custody proceeding, given that transcripts of magistrate's hearing provided sufficient evidence to support trial court's grant of custody to father; parents were unmarried and no prior court order was issued related to custody such that parties stood on equal footing before court and transcript of hearing revealed that mother did not allow children to telephone father, that mother drank every day and stayed out late at bars, and that mother had impression that children wanted to live with father. Francis v. Westfall (Ohio App. 7 Dist., Jefferson, 08-24-2004) No. 03-JE-20, No. 03-JE-21, 2004-Ohio-4543, 2004 WL 1931779, Unreported. Child Custody ☞ 923(1)

Trial court acted within its discretion in entering order in divorce proceeding naming husband as primary residential parent of parties' child; husband, although currently unemployed, seemed to be more focused on child, and had considerable family support in caring for child, while wife seemed less mature and more focused on her social life, and trial court relied on reports of guardian ad litem (GAL) and psychologist who determined that, while both parties might be appropriate parents, husband would be better suited to be named residential parent. Thomas v. Thomas (Ohio App. 7 Dist., Columbiana,   11-25-2003)   No.   03   CO   9, 2003-Ohio-6393, 2003 WL 22838715, Unreported. Child Custody ☞ 147

Evidence supported determination that mother was not capable of meeting child's financial and emotional needs, in proceedings to determine custody of child between mother and paternal grandparents; mother was minor herself and without high school diploma or suitable employment opportunities, mother was pregnant with second child and was on unpaid maternity leave, mother was ineligible for most forms of public assistance, and none of money that she had saved went to pay for care and support of son. In re Ratliff (Ohio App. 11 Dist., Portage,   11-29-2002)   No.   2001-P-0142,   No. 2001-P-0143, 2002-Ohio-6586, 2002 WL 31716783, Unreported. Child Custody ☞ 279; Child Custody ☞ 281

Trial court's finding that circumstances had not changed from time mother agreed to let child's paternal grandparents take custody of child and time of hearing on habeas corpus petition to have child returned to her did not demonstrate application of a "change of circumstances" standard in determining custody of child between mother and paternal grandparents; rather, comment was in context of determining that mother was still unfit to parent child at time of hearing. In re Ratliff (Ohio App. 11 Dist., Portage, 11-29-2002) No. 2001-P-0142, No. 2001-P-0143, 2002-Ohio-6586, 2002 WL 31716783, Unreported. Child Custody ☞ 279; Habeas Corpus ☞ 799

That child's mother was pregnant by another man who lived with mother did not support determination that mother was unfit to parent child, in proceedings to determine custody of child between mother and paternal grandparents, to whom mother had previously relinquished custody; however, court could consider mother's second pregnancy in context of determining whether mother would be able to financially and emotionally support two children. In re Ratliff (Ohio App. 11 Dist., Portage, 11-29-2002) No. 2001-P-0142, No. 2001-P-0143, 2002-Ohio-6586, 2002 WL 31716783, Unreported. Child Custody ☞ 279

Trial court's determination to award custody of child to child's paternal grandparents, to whom mother had previously relinquished custody, on mother's petition for writ of habeas corpus seeking return of child to her custody and on grandparents' petition for custody, was based on considerations regarding mother's suitability to parent child, and was not improperly based on best interest of child. In re Ratliff (Ohio App. 11 Dist., Portage, 11-29-2002) No. 2001-P-0142, No. 2001-P-0143, 2002-Ohio-6586, 2002 WL 31716783, Unreported. Child Custody ☞ 279; Habeas Corpus ☞ 532(1)

2. Domestic violence, consideration

Trial court did not abuse its discretion in considering evidence regarding several incidents of domestic violence occurring in home where child's mother lived with his grandmother and her husband, together with evidence of alcohol abuse, in proceedings to determine custody of child between mother and paternal grandparents, to whom mother had previously relinquished custody. In re Ratliff (Ohio App. 11 Dist., Portage, 11-29-2002) No. 2001-P-0142, No. 2001-P-0143, 2002-Ohio-6586, 2002 WL 31716783, Unreported. Child Custody ☞ 279

Evidence that child's maternal grandmother and her husband smoked in home where mother lived, and the absence of any testimony that either would quit smoking if child came to live with them, supported determination that mother lacked insight into son's asthmatic condition, as basis for determination of custody of child between mother and paternal grandparents, to whom mother had previously relinquished custody. In re Ratliff (Ohio App. 11 Dist., Portage, 11-29-2002) No. 2001-P-0142, No. 2001-P-0143, 2002-Ohio-6586, 2002 WL 31716783, Unreported. Child Custody ☞ 279

Mother's unemployment status and lack of income were proper factors for trial court to consider, in proceedings to determine custody of child between mother and paternal grandparents, to whom mother had previously relinquished custody. In re Ratliff (Ohio App. 11 Dist., Portage, 11-29-2002) No. 2001-P-0142, No. 2001-P-0143, 2002-Ohio-6586, 2002 WL 31716783, Unreported. Child Custody ☞ 279

3. Procedural issues

Legal father's action against mother to be declared child's father, and for designation as child's custodial parent and legal custodian, was not paternity action, for purposes of biological father's motion to intervene; execution of acknowledgement of paternity with mother conclusively established legal father as child's father after acknowledgement of paternity became final, and legal father was essentially seeking custody of child and parenting rights. Clark v. Malicote (Ohio App. 12 Dist., Clermont, 04-18-2011) No. CA2010-07-049, 2011 Ohio 1874, 2011 WL 1458696, Unreported. Children Out-of-wedlock ☞ 12; Children Out-of-wedlock ☞ 20.4

Court did not abuse its discretion, in action by unmarried parents each seeking legal custody of minor child, in granting father legal custody, although it would require child to move nearly 300 miles away from his original home, family, and friends; child also had friends and step-siblings in father's town, he enjoyed spending time there, he had a good relationship with father, father could provide for his care best, and the mother was granted standard visitation with the father ordered to meet her half-way to exchange the child for visits. Dunn v. Marcum (Ohio App. 2 Dist., Clark, 06-19-2009) No. 08-CA-112, 2009-Ohio-3015, 2009 WL 1800609, Unreported. Children Out-of-wedlock ☞ 20.3; Children Out-of-wedlock ☞ 20.9

Statute governing modification of prior decrees allocating parental rights and responsibilities did not apply to determine which parent of children born out-of-wedlock should be awarded custody of children, in proceeding filed by father to obtain legal custody of children, though prior judgment entry existed awarding mother child support from father, as no prior custody decree had been issued, in that issue of custody was never litigated in child support proceeding but, instead, court in that proceeding applied statutory presumption that mother was custodial parent. DeWitt v. Myers (Ohio App. 2 Dist., Clark, 02-20-2009) No. 08-CA-86, 2009-Ohio-807, 2009 WL 440628, Unreported. Children Out-of-wedlock ☞ 20.3; Children Out-of-wedlock ☞ 20.10

Unmarried mother was not harmed by any procedural errors in trial court's adoption of magistrate's decision awarding custody to father, or entry of interim order declaring father to be residential parent, even if such errors rendered the orders in question legal nullities; trial court previously entered temporary order naming father the temporary residential parent, and nullification of subsequent orders would therefore leave child in father's custody, rather than cause custody to revert to mother. Goeller v. Moore (Ohio App. 10 Dist., Franklin, 01-27-2005) No. 04AP-394, 2005-Ohio-292, 2005

WL 174809, Unreported. Children Out–of–wedlock 20.11

Mother waived for appellate review claim that award of legal custody to nonmarital child's father was not supported by substantial amount of credible and competent evidence, where mother failed to raise any objection to trial court concerning content and/or sufficiency of evidence on which magistrate relied in rendering his decision. In re Knight (Ohio App. 11 Dist., Trumbull, 12-31-2003) No. 2002-T-0158, 2003-Ohio-7222, 2003 WL 23097094, Unreported. Children Out–of–wedlock 20.11

Trial court fully complied with analysis mandated by statute when it determined that awarding legal custody of nonmarital child to biological father instead of biological mother was in child's best interest, where court applied all statutory factors to determine child's best interests, and court further examined whether shared parenting would be in child's best interests, and in doing so, court concluded that child be placed into legal custody of father with companionship to mother on specific dates and times. In re Knight (Ohio App. 11 Dist., Trumbull, 12-31-2003) No. 2002-T-0158, 2003-Ohio-7222, 2003 WL 23097094, Unreported. Children Out–of–wedlock 20.3

Mother waived claim that trial court erred by not considering suitability of child's paternal grandparents, as basis for determination to award grandparents custody, where she failed to present any legal authority in support of claim, and pointed to no evidence in record showing that grandparents were not suitable. In re Ratliff (Ohio App. 11 Dist., Portage, 11-29-2002) No. 2001-P-0142, No. 2001-P-0143, 2002-Ohio-6586, 2002 WL 31716783, Unreported. Child Custody 908

Trial court was not required to conduct evidentiary hearing on grandparent's objections to magistrate's determination that mother was fit to parent child, in proceedings to determine custody of child between mother and paternal grandparents, to whom mother had previously relinquished custody. In re Ratliff (Ohio App. 11 Dist., Portage, 11-29-2002) No. 2001-P-0142, No. 2001-P-0143, 2002-Ohio-6586, 2002 WL 31716783, Unreported. Child Custody 504

Juvenile court magistrate did not patently and unambiguously lack jurisdiction to proceed on child custody matter, where mother was an unmarried female who gave birth to out-of-wedlock child, and there was no allegation or evidence that the child was a ward of another state court. State ex rel. Mosier v. Fornof (Ohio, 06-10-2010) 126 Ohio St.3d 47, 930 N.E.2d 305, 2010-Ohio-2516. Courts 175

3109.043 Temporary order regarding allocation of parental rights and responsibilities while action pending

In any proceeding pertaining to the allocation of parental rights and responsibilities for the care of a child, when requested in the complaint, answer, or counterclaim, or by motion served with the pleading, upon satisfactory proof by affidavit duly filed with the clerk of the court, the court, without oral hearing and for good cause shown, may make a temporary order regarding the allocation of parental rights and responsibilities for the care of the child while the action is pending.

If a parent and child relationship has not already been established pursuant to section 3111.02 of the Revised Code, the court may take into consideration when determining whether to award parenting time, visitation rights, or temporary custody to a putative father that the putative father is named on the birth record of the child, the child has the putative father's surname, or a clear pattern of a parent and child relationship between the child and the putative father exists.

(2006 H 136, eff. 5–17–06)

Research References

Treatises and Practice Aids

Sowald & Morganstern, Baldwin's Ohio Practice Domestic Relations Law § 3:35, Effect of Judgment--Allocation of Parental Rights and Responsibilities, Visitation, and Companionship Rights--As Between Parents.

Carlin, Baldwin's Ohio Prac. Merrick-Rippner Probate Law § 19:4, Legitimation--Historical Provisions.

Carlin, Baldwin's Ohio Prac. Merrick-Rippner Probate Law § 19:6, Uniform Parentage Act--Jurisdiction of Action to Determine Father-Child Relationship.

Carlin, Baldwin's Ohio Prac. Merrick-Rippner Probate Law § 19:10, Uniform Parentage Act--Procedure in Action to Determine Father-Child Relationship.

Carlin, Baldwin's Ohio Prac. Merrick-Rippner Probate Law § 99:49, Interlocutory and Final Orders.

Carlin, Baldwin's Ohio Prac. Merrick-Rippner Probate Law § 109:41, Prehearing Procedures in Juvenile Court--Temporary Orders Pending Hearing.

Carlin, Baldwin's Ohio Prac. Merrick-Rippner Probate Law § 110:13, Jurisdiction Over Child Custody Matters--Determination of Custody.

Carlin, Baldwin's Ohio Prac. Merrick-Rippner Probate Law § 110:29, Parentage Act--Judgment

Determining Existence of Parent-Child Relationship.

3109.05 Support orders; medical needs

(A)(1) In a divorce, dissolution of marriage, legal separation, or child support proceeding, the court may order either or both parents to support or help support their children, without regard to marital misconduct. In determining the amount reasonable or necessary for child support, including the medical needs of the child, the court shall comply with Chapter 3119. of the Revised Code.

(2) The court, in accordance with Chapter 3119. of the Revised Code, shall include in each support order made under this section the requirement that one or both of the parents provide for the health care needs of the child to the satisfaction of the court, and the court shall include in the support order a requirement that all support payments be made through the office of child support in the department of job and family services.

(3) The court shall comply with Chapters 3119., 3121., 3123., and 3125. of the Revised Code when it makes or modifies an order for child support under this section.

(B) The juvenile court has exclusive jurisdiction to enter the orders in any case certified to it from another court.

(C) If any person required to pay child support under an order made under division (A) of this section on or after April 15, 1985, or modified on or after December 1, 1986, is found in contempt of court for failure to make support payments under the order, the court that makes the finding, in addition to any other penalty or remedy imposed, shall assess all court costs arising out of the contempt proceeding against the person and require the person to pay any reasonable attorney's fees of any adverse party, as determined by the court, that arose in relation to the act of contempt and, on or after July 1, 1992, shall assess interest on any unpaid amount of child support pursuant to section 3123.17 of the Revised Code.

(D) The court shall not authorize or permit the escrowing, impoundment, or withholding of any child support payment ordered under this section or any other section of the Revised Code because of a denial of or interference with a right of parenting time granted to a parent in an order issued under this section or section 3109.051 or 3109.12 of the Revised Code or companionship or visitation granted in an order issued under this section, section 3109.051, 3109.11, 3109.12, or any other section of the Revised Code, or as a method of enforcing the specific provisions of any such order dealing with parenting time or visitation.

(2000 S 180, eff. 3–22–01; 1999 H 471, eff. 7–1–00; 1997 H 352, eff. 1–1–98; 1993 H 173, eff. 12–31–93; 1993 S 115; 1992 S 10; 1990 S 3, H 514, H 591, H 15; 1988 H 708; 1987 H 231; 1986 H 509; 1984 H 614; 1981 H 694, H 71; 1974 H 233; 1971 H 163, H 544; 1953 H 1; GC 8005–5; Source—GC 8034)

Historical and Statutory Notes

Ed. Note: Former RC 3109.05(E) related to the duration of support orders. See now RC 3119.86 for provisions analogous to former RC 3109.05(E).

Pre–1953 H 1 Amendments: 124 v S 65

Amendment Note: 2000 S 180 substituted "Chapter 3119" for "sections 3113.21 to 3113.219" in division (A)(1) and (A)(2); rewrote division (A)(3); substituted "3123.17" for "3113.219"; rewrote division (D); and deleted division (E). Prior to amendment or deletion divisions (A)(3), (D), and (E) read:

"(3) Each order for child support made or modified under this section shall include as part of the order a general provision, as described in division (A)(1) of section 3113.21 of the Revised Code, requiring the withholding or deduction of income or assets of the obligor under the order as described in division (D) or (H) of section 3113.21 of

the Revised Code, or another type of appropriate requirement as described in division (D)(3), (D)(4), or (H) of that section, to ensure that withholding or deduction from the income or assets of the obligor is available from the commencement of the support order for collection of the support and of any arrearages that occur; a statement requiring both parents to notify the child support enforcement agency in writing of their current mailing address; current residence address, current residence telephone number, current driver's license number, and any changes to that information, and a notice that the requirement to notify the agency of all changes to that information continues until further notice from the court. The court shall comply with sections 3113.21 to 3113.219 of the Revised Code when it makes or modifies an order for child support under this section.

"(D) The court shall not authorize or permit the escrowing, impoundment, or withholding of any child support payment ordered under this section or any other section of the Revised Code because of a denial of or interference with a right of companionship or visitation granted in an order issued under this section, section 3109.051, 3109.11, 3109.12, or any other section of the Revised Code, or as a method of enforcing the specific provisions of any such order dealing with visitation.

"(E) Notwithstanding section 3109.01 of the Revised Code, if a court issues a child support order under this section, the order shall remain in effect beyond the child's eighteenth birthday as long as the child continuously attends on a full-time basis any recognized and accredited high school or the order provides that the duty of support of the child continues beyond the child's eighteenth birthday. Except in cases in which the order provides that the duty of support continues for any period after the child reaches age nineteen, the order shall not remain in effect after the child reaches age nineteen. Any parent ordered to pay support under a child support order issued under this section shall continue to pay support under the order, including during seasonal vacation periods, until the order terminates."

Amendment Note: 1999 H 471 substituted "job and family" for "human" in division (A)(2).

Amendment Note: 1997 H 352 substituted "division of child support in the department of human services" for "child support enforcement agency" in division (A)(2); deleted "on or after December 31, 1993," before "shall include", substituted "income" for "wages" twice and "(D)(3), (D)(4)" for "(D)(6), (D)(7)", and inserted "current residence telephone number, current driver's license number,", in division (A)(3); inserted "or the order provides that the duty of support of the child continues beyond the child's eighteenth birthday" and added the second sentence in division (E); and made other nonsubstantive changes.

Amendment Note: 1993 H 173 rewrote division (A)(3) before the first semi-colon, which previously read:

"(3) Each order for child support made or modified under this section on or after December 1, 1986, shall be accompanied by one or more orders described in division (D) or (H) of section 3113.21 of the Revised Code, whichever is appropriate under the requirements of that section".

Amendment Note: 1993 S 115 rewrote division (A)(1), which previously read:

"(A)(1) In a divorce, dissolution of marriage, legal separation, or child support proceeding, the court may order either or both parents to support or help support their children, without regard to marital misconduct. In determining the amount reasonable or necessary for child support, including the medical needs of the child, the court shall comply with sections 3113.21 to 3113.219 of the Revised Code and shall consider all relevant factors, including, but not limited to, all of the following:

"(a) The financial resources and the earning ability of the child;

"(b) The relative financial resources, other assets and resources, and needs of the residential parent and of the parent who is not the residential parent, when a decree for shared parenting is not issued;

"(c) The standard of living and circumstances of each parent and the standard of living the child would have enjoyed had the marriage continued;

"(d) The physical and emotional condition and needs of the child;

"(e) The financial resources, other assets and resources, and needs of both parents, when a decree for shared parenting is issued;

"(f) The need and capacity of the child for an education, and the educational opportunities that would have been available to him had the circumstances requiring a court order for his support not arisen;

"(g) The earning ability of each parent;

"(h) The age of the child;

"(i) The responsibility of each parent for the support of others;

"(j) The value of services contributed by the residential parent."

Comparative Laws

Ariz.—A.R.S.   § 25-320.
Ark.—A.C.A.   § 9-12-312.
Conn.—C.G.S.A.   § 46b-84.
Ga.—O.C.G.A.   § 19-6-17.
Ill.—ILCS 750 5/505.
Ind.—West's A.I.C. 31–16–6–1 et seq.
Ky.—Baldwin's KRS 403.210.
La.—LSA-C.C.   art. 227.
Mass.—M.G.L.A.   c.   208, § 28.

Mich.—M.C.L.A.   § 552.151 et seq.
Mo.—V.A.M.S.   § 452.340.
Neb.—R.R.S.1943, § 42–364 et seq.
N.J.—N.J.S.A.   2A:34-23.
N.M.—NMSA 1978, § 40–4–7.
Wash.—West's RCWA 26.09.100.
Wis.—W.S.A.   767.25.
W.Va.—Code, 48–12–101 et seq.

Cross References

Contempt action for failure to pay support, see 2705.031, 2705.05
Criminal interference with custody, see 2919.23
Criminal nonsupport of dependents, see 2919.21

Department of job and family services, division of social administration, care and placement of children, see 5103.12 to 5103.17

Failure to support minor, consent to adoption not required, see 3107.07

Interfering with action to issue or modify support order, see 2919.231

Juvenile courts, exercise of jurisdiction in child support matters, see 2151.23

Lottery winner must state under oath whether or not he is in default of support order, see 3770.071

Parents to support child committed by juvenile court, see 2151.36

Powers and duties of county children services board, see 5153.16

Procedures for collection of past-due child support from state income tax refunds, see 5747.121

Reciprocal enforcement of support, see 3115.01 et seq.

Reciprocal enforcement of support, suspension of visitation rights, see 3115.21

Relief pending appeal of child support order, Civ R 75

Wage assignments for support of spouse or children, see 1321.33

Library References

Child Custody ⟶874.
Child Support ⟶11, 109 to 114, 397, 425, 496.
Westlaw Topic Nos. 76D, 76E.
C.J.S. Divorce §§ 976 to 980, 982, 1043 to 1044, 1049, 1100, 1132 to 1133.

C.J.S. Parent and Child §§ 166, 171, 180, 200 to 201, 203 to 205.

Research References

ALR Library

2003 ALR 5th 9, Laches or Acquiescence as Defense, So as to Bar Recovery of Arrearages of Permanent Alimony or Child Support.

71 ALR 5th 99, Grandparents' Visitation Rights Where Child's Parents Are Living.

69 ALR 5th 1, Grandparents' Visitation Rights Where Child's Parents Are Deceased, or Where Status of Parents is Unspecified.

98 ALR 3rd 1146, Propriety of Decree in Proceeding Between Divorced Parents to Determine Mother's Duty to Pay Support for Children in Custody of Father.

162 ALR 1084, Power of Court in Divorce or Separation Suit to Provide for Support Of, or Aid To, Adult Child, or to Continue Provision for Support After Child Attains Majority.

Encyclopedias

OH Jur. 3d Family Law § 360, Decree of Dissolution--In Cases Involving Minor Children.

OH Jur. 3d Family Law § 730, Modification of Child Support Order as Sanction for Violation of Visitation Rights.

OH Jur. 3d Family Law § 1124, Certification of Support to Juvenile Court.

OH Jur. 3d Family Law § 1129, Provision for Withholding or Deduction of Wages.

OII Jur. 3d Family Law § 1152, Residential Parent's Duty Regarding Visitation.

OH Jur. 3d Family Law § 1167, Motion to Prevent Notice of Relocation to Nonresidential Parent.

OH Jur. 3d Family Law § 1207, Interfering With Action to Issue or Modify Support Order.

OH Jur. 3d Family Law § 1230, Payment of Support by Obligor to Child Support Enforcement Agency.

OH Jur. 3d Family Law § 1255, Suspension of Support for Denial of Visitation.

OH Jur. 3d Family Law § 1296, Awarding Expenses, Costs, Interest, and Attorney's Fees.

OII Jur. 3d Family Law § 1536, on Certification from Another Court.

Forms

Ohio Forms Legal and Business § 27:66, Support of Children.

Ohio Forms Legal and Business § 28:75, Support of Children.

Treatises and Practice Aids

Katz & Giannelli, Baldwin's Ohio Practice Criminal Law § 109:10, Nonsupport.

Katz & Giannelli, Baldwin's Ohio Practice Criminal Law § 109:13, Interfering With Support Actions.

Sowald & Morganstern, Baldwin's Ohio Practice Domestic Relations Law § 9:9, Elements of Agreement--Allocation of Parental Rights and Responsibilities.

Sowald & Morganstern, Baldwin's Ohio Practice Domestic Relations Law § 19:2, Jurisdiction Over Child Support.

Sowald & Morganstern, Baldwin's Ohio Practice Domestic Relations Law § 19:8, Medical Support.

Sowald & Morganstern, Baldwin's Ohio Practice Domestic Relations Law § 19:9, Computation Requirements: Information for the Child Support Worksheet.

Sowald & Morganstern, Baldwin's Ohio Practice Domestic Relations Law § 20:1, Statutory History--The Advent of Withholding.

Sowald & Morganstern, Baldwin's Ohio Practice Domestic Relations Law § 20:8, Continuing Jurisdiction--In General.

Sowald & Morganstern, Baldwin's Ohio Practice Domestic Relations Law § 21:6, Development of Statutory Requirements.

Sowald & Morganstern, Baldwin's Ohio Practice Domestic Relations Law § 22:7, Establishing Support Order.

Sowald & Morganstern, Baldwin's Ohio Practice Domestic Relations Law § 24:1, Election of Remedy.

Sowald & Morganstern, Baldwin's Ohio Practice Domestic Relations Law § 24:3, Jurisdiction.

Sowald & Morganstern, Baldwin's Ohio Practice Domestic Relations Law § 24:8, Visitation.

Sowald & Morganstern, Baldwin's Ohio Practice Domestic Relations Law § 3:33, Attorney Fees and Costs.

Sowald & Morganstern, Baldwin's Ohio Practice Domestic Relations Law § 4:15, Support Obligations Upon Divorce--Spousal Support--Initial Award.

Sowald & Morganstern, Baldwin's Ohio Practice Domestic Relations Law § 7:19, Relief Incident to Annulment--Children of an Annulled Marriage--Child Support and Custody.

Sowald & Morganstern, Baldwin's Ohio Practice Domestic Relations Law § 9:11, Elements of Agreement--Child Support--In General.

Sowald & Morganstern, Baldwin's Ohio Practice Domestic Relations Law § 13:22, The Statutory Factors--(N)--Any Other Factor.

Sowald & Morganstern, Baldwin's Ohio Practice Domestic Relations Law § 14:36, Requirements for Modification--Other Circumstances.

Sowald & Morganstern, Baldwin's Ohio Practice Domestic Relations Law § 15:14, Best Interest Standard--Payment of Child Support.

Sowald & Morganstern, Baldwin's Ohio Practice Domestic Relations Law § 16:17, Modification of Prior Decrees to Shared Parenting.

Sowald & Morganstern, Baldwin's Ohio Practice Domestic Relations Law § 18:11, Procedure--Relocation Notices, Access to Records, Day Care Facilities, and School Activities.

Sowald & Morganstern, Baldwin's Ohio Practice Domestic Relations Law § 18:19, Procedure--Effect of Support on Visitation.

Sowald & Morganstern, Baldwin's Ohio Practice Domestic Relations Law § 19:14, Parenting Time.

Sowald & Morganstern, Baldwin's Ohio Practice Domestic Relations Law § 19:17, Modification of Prior Orders--Jurisdiction.

Sowald & Morganstern, Baldwin's Ohio Practice Domestic Relations Law § 19:26, Contempt.

Sowald & Morganstern, Baldwin's Ohio Practice Domestic Relations Law § 19:30, Arrearages--Interest on Arrearages.

Sowald & Morganstern, Baldwin's Ohio Practice Domestic Relations Law § 20:24, Contempt and Show Cause Procedures--Attorney Fees.

Sowald & Morganstern, Baldwin's Ohio Practice Domestic Relations Law § 20:31, Contempt Defenses--Emancipation.

Sowald & Morganstern, Baldwin's Ohio Practice Domestic Relations Law § 20:32, Contempt Defenses--Denial of Visitation Rights.

Sowald & Morganstern, Baldwin's Ohio Practice Domestic Relations Law § 20:43, Reduction to Judgment and Execution--In General.

Sowald & Morganstern, Baldwin's Ohio Practice Domestic Relations Law § 21:10, Enforcement of Parenting Time--Equitable Circumstances.

Sowald & Morganstern, Baldwin's Ohio Practice Domestic Relations Law § 21:26, Civil Sanctions.

Sowald & Morganstern, Baldwin's Ohio Practice Domestic Relations Law § 21:30, Effect of Inability to Pay Support on Parenting Time.

Sowald & Morganstern, Baldwin's Ohio Practice Domestic Relations Law § 23:16, In-State Remedies--Determination of Support.

Sowald & Morganstern, Baldwin's Ohio Practice Domestic Relations Law § 25:29, Motions Regarding Temporary Relief--Motion for Temporary Child Support.

Sowald & Morganstern, Baldwin's Ohio Practice Domestic Relations Law § 25:56, Post-Decree Motions--Motion to Modify.

Sowald & Morganstern, Baldwin's Ohio Practice Domestic Relations Law § 25:57, Motions Regarding Attorneys--Motion for Attorney Fees.

Sowald & Morganstern, Baldwin's Ohio Practice Domestic Relations Law § 27:21, Subject Matter Jurisdiction--Jurisdiction for Child Support.

Carlin, Baldwin's Ohio Prac. Merrick-Rippner Probate Law § 99:3, Jurisdiction.

Carlin, Baldwin's Ohio Prac. Merrick-Rippner Probate Law § 110:1, Criminal Jurisdiction.

Carlin, Baldwin's Ohio Prac. Merrick-Rippner Probate Law § 99:21, Types of Placement--Stepparent, Guardian, and Grandparent Adoptions.

Carlin, Baldwin's Ohio Prac. Merrick-Rippner Probate Law § 109:11, Service of Summons.

Carlin, Baldwin's Ohio Prac. Merrick-Rippner Probate Law § 110:15, Visitation Right of Noncustodial Parent and Others.

Carlin, Baldwin's Ohio Prac. Merrick-Rippner Probate Law § 110:31, Parentage Act--Continuing Jurisdiction to Modify or Revoke Judgment.

Carlin, Baldwin's Ohio Prac. Merrick-Rippner Probate Law § 110:35, Civil Support Proceedings--Liability for Child Support.

Carlin, Baldwin's Ohio Prac. Merrick-Rippner Probate Law § 110:36, Civil Support Proceedings--Determination of Amount of Support Under Child Support Guidelines.

Carlin, Baldwin's Ohio Prac. Merrick-Rippner Probate Law § 109:135, Motion to Certify Case to Juvenile Court--Form.

Employment Coordinator Compensation § 42:589, Ohio; Employer's Payment of Court Costs and Attorney's Fees in a Contempt Action.

Law Review and Journal Commentaries

Abusing the Power to Regulate: The Child Support Recovery Act of 1992, Comment. (Ed. note: Federal encroachment into traditional fields of State criminal law is discussed.) 46 Case W Res L Rev 935 (Spring 1996).

Agreement to Provide College Education—Clear, Unambiguous Language Required, Lynn B. Schwartz. 8 Domestic Rel J Ohio 40 (May/June 1996).

Ascertaining Self–Employment Income, Elaine M. Stoermer. 48 Dayton B Briefs 17 (October 1998).

Awarding Child Support Against the Impoverished Parent: Straying from Statutory Guidelines and Using SSI in Setting the Amount, Note. 83 Ky L J 653 (1994–95).

Bankruptcy Basics—DISCHARGE... A Simple Word, Not Easily Found, And is the Meaning Plain?, Thomas R. Noland. (Ed. note: The author explains the effect of discharging a debt in bankruptcy court.) 47 Dayton B Briefs 18 (June 1998).

Bankruptcy Reform Act of 1994—What the Bankruptcy Code Giveth, Domestic Relations Courts (and Congress) Taketh Away, C.R. "Chip" Bowles. 8 Domestic Rel J Ohio 17 (March/April 1996).

Business Owner's Compensation and Valuation, Robert G. Turner, Jr. 11 Domestic Rel J Ohio 24 (March/April 1999).

BWC and Self–Insured Employer Liability for Spousal and Child Support, C. Jeffrey Waite. 11 Domestic Rel J Ohio 17 (March/April 1999).

A Case Study in Divorce Law Reform and Its Aftermath, Robert E. McGraw, Gloria J. Sterin and Joseph M. Davis. 20 J Fam L 443 (1981–82).

The Child Dependency Exemption And Divorced Parents: What Is "Custody"?, David J. Benson. 18 Cap U L Rev 57 (Spring 1989).

Child Support Deviation Calculation, David K. Ross. 17 Lake Legal Views 9 (December 1994).

Children—The Innocent Victims of Family Breakups: How the Family Law Attorney, the Courts, and Society Can Protect Our Children, Michael J. Albano. 26 U Tol L Rev 787 (Summer 1995).

Completed Child Support Worksheet Must be Made Part of Court Record, Pamela J. MacAdams. 5 Domestic Rel J Ohio 1 (January/February 1993).

Deceptions, delusions and spin doctors in family court litigation, Dennis W. Mattingly. (Ed. note: The author, a domestic relations magistrate, recounts war stories of lying litigants, and urges mediation of domestic disputes). 18 Ohio Law 12 (May/June 2004).

Dividing the Child: *Shea v. Metcalf*, 712 A.2d 887 (Vt. 1998), Note. 24 U Dayton L Rev 543 (Spring 1999).

Divorce Reform, Ohio Style, Alan E. Norris. 47 Ohio St B Ass'n Rep 1031 (9–16–74).

Family Law: Construing Ohio Revised Code § 3109.05, Note. 4 Cap U L Rev 283 (1975).

Family Law: Ohio's New Child Support Guidelines: Amended Substitute House Bill Number 591, 1990 Ohio Legis. Serv. 5–546 (Baldwin), Note. 16 U Dayton L Rev 521 (Winter 1991).

The Federal Income Tax Consequences of the Legal Obligation of Parents to Support Children, Note. 47 Ohio St L J 753 (1986).

Grandparent Visitation: The Best Interests of the Grandparent, Child, and Society, Erica L. Strawman. 30 U Tol L Rev 31 (Fall 1998).

Guidelines in Alimony and Support for Ohio, Hon. John R. Milligan. 52 Ohio St B Ass'n Rep 2009 (12–3–79).

Illinois Court Overturns Mandatory Parent Education Class, Paul J. Buser. 18 Lake Legal Views 8 (August 1995).

Informed Consent to the Medical Treatment of Minors: Law and Practice. Lawrence Schlam and Joseph P. Wood, M.D., 10 Health Matrix: J Law-Medicine 141 (Summer 2000).

Into the Red to Stay in the Pink: The Hidden Cost of Being Uninsured. Hugh F. "Trey" Daly III, Leslie M. Oblak, Robert W. Seifert, and Kimberly Shellenberger, 12 Health Matrix: J Law-Medicine 39 (Winter 2002).

Judges' Column, Hon. Francine Bruening. (Ed. note: Judge Bruening discusses the Child Support Reorganization Act of House Bill 352, effective 1–1–98.) 21 Lake Legal Views 1 (June 1998).

Judicial Activism in Domestic Relations Cases, Hon. V. Michael Brigner. (Ed. note: Judge Brigner lists the powers of a judge hearing custody, support, and visitation matters.) 45 Dayton B Briefs 22 (January 1996).

The Lawyer Turns Peacemaker—with mediation emerging as the most popular form of alternate dispute resolution, the quest for common ground could force attorneys to reinterpret everything they do in the future, Richard C. Reuben. 82 A B A J 54 (August 1996).

Learning From Social Sciences: A Model For Reformation of the Laws Affecting Stepfamilies, David R. Fine and Mark A. Fine. 97 Dick L Rev 49 (Fall 1992).

Litigation Results—Count on a CPA, Keith J. Libman. 67 Clev B J 12 (October 1996).

Little Red Riding Hood is Missing—Grandparent Visitation Not Authorized After Stepparent Adoption, Richard L. Innis. 7 Domestic Rel J Ohio 17 (March/April 1995).

The New Child Support Act—1993 S.B. 115, Richard L. Innis. 5 Domestic Rel J Ohio 73 (September/October 1993).

Nobody Gets Married for the First Time Anymore—A Primer on the Tax Implications of Support Payments in Divorce, C. Garrison Lepow. 25 Duq L Rev 43 (Fall 1986).

Ohio's Child Support Guidelines Revisited, Hon. Lillian M. Kern. 3 Ohio Law 12 (January/February 1989).

Ohio's Mandatory Child Support Guidelines: Child Support or Spousal Maintenance?, Note. 42 Case W Res L Rev 297 (1992).

Origins and Development of the Law of Parental Child Support, Donna Schuele. 27 J Fam L 807 (1988–89).

Parents Who Abandon or Fail to Support their Children and Apportionment of Wrongful Death Damages, Note. 27 J Fam L 871 (1988–89).

Pathfinder: Economic Effects of Divorce on Women, Barbara Laughlin. 14 Legal Reference Serv Q 57 (1995).

Paying for Children's Medical Care: Interaction Between Family Law and Cost Containment, Walter J. Wadlington. 36 Case W Res L Rev 1190 (1985–86).

The Plain Meaning of the Automatic Stay in Bankruptcy: The Void/Voidable Distinction Revisited, Timothy Arnold Barnes. 57 Ohio St L J 291 (1996).

The Power Of State Courts To Award The Federal Dependency Exemption Upon Divorce, David J. Benson. 16 U Dayton L Rev 29 (Fall 1990).

Practice Pointer—Determining Child Support Where the Parties' Combined Income is Over $150,000: Or Where the Maximum is Really the Minimum, Diane M. Palos. 16 Domestic Rel J Ohio 45 (May/June 2004).

The Presumption of Paternity in Child Support Cases: A Triumph of Law over Biology, Comment. 70 U Cin L Rev 1151 (Spring 2002).

The Reasonableness of Attorney's Fees to be Awarded in Domestic Proceedings, William K. McCarter and Sean A. McCarter. 19 Lake Legal Views 10 (September 1996).

The Significance Of A Divorced Father's Remarriage In Adjudicating A Motion To Modify His Child Support Obligations, Marvin M. Moore. 18 Cap U L Rev 483 (Winter 1989).

Standard of Proof in Proceedings to Terminate Parental Rights, Note. 31 Clev St L Rev 679 (1982).

Support Obligations Beyond Majority, Stanley Morganstern. 6 Domestic Rel J Ohio 33 (May/June 1994).

Tax Consequences of Attorney Fees, Awards, and Payments, Stanley Morganstern. 4 Domestic Rel J Ohio 29 (March/April 1992).

Total of Spousal Support Deducted from Payor's Gross in Child Support Computation, Pamela J. MacAdams. 5 Domestic Rel J Ohio 42 (May/June 1993).

Validity of Agreements Between Parties to Suspend Support Payments, Pamela J. MacAdams. 3 Domestic Rel J Ohio 12 (January/February 1991).

Notes of Decisions

1. Constitutional issues

Father was given meaningful opportunity to be heard regarding contempt charges and thus was not denied due process of law by County Children Service Enforcement Agency's alleged failure to provide a proper audit of the amount owed and the trial court's reliance upon the Agency's testimony at contempt hearing, where father was personally served with complaint, appeared at hearing with his attorney, and testified on his own behalf. McKinnis v. Parlier (Ohio App. 12 Dist., Clermont, 06-14-2004) No. CA2003-06-050, 2004-Ohio-3010, 2004 WL 1300160, Unreported. Child Support ☞ 474; Child Support ☞ 489; Child Support ☞ 491; Constitutional Law ☞ 4396

Requiring divorced father to pay one-half of his minor child's parochial school tuition did not violate the religious freedom provision of the State Constitution or the Establishment Clause of the United States Constitution, where child had attended parochial school prior to divorce; it was mother's right, as custodial parent, to determine whether child would attend a parochial school, and primary purpose of court's order was to assist mother in financing child's education, not to advance religion. Worthen v. Worthen (Ohio App. 2 Dist., Clark, 10-18-2002) No. 2002 CA 33, 2002-Ohio-5587, 2002 WL 31341597, Unreported. Child Custody ☞ 105; Child Support ☞ 118; Constitutional Law ☞ 1409

A defendant is not exposed to double jeopardy when criminally convicted for child non-support following his civil contempt citation in the divorce proceedings. State v. Yacovella (Ohio App. 8 Dist., Cuyahoga, 02-01-1996) No. 69487, 1996 WL 38898, Unreported, dismissed, appeal not allowed 76 Ohio St.3d 1420, 667 N.E.2d 23.

Court of Appeals would decline, on wife's appeal from child support provisions of divorce decree, to create a novel fundamental right on minor children's part to paid attendance at a private school or college of their choice or on wife's part to be reimbursed for paying children's private school or future college tuition. Bardes v. Todd (Ohio App. 1 Dist., 10-13-2000) 139 Ohio App.3d 938, 746 N.E.2d 229, stay denied 90 Ohio St.3d 1492, 739 N.E.2d 817, motion for delayed appeal denied 91 Ohio St.3d 1411, 740 N.E.2d 1111, dismissed, appeal not allowed 91 Ohio St.3d 1445, 742 N.E.2d 144, reconsideration denied 91 Ohio St.3d 1484, 744 N.E.2d 1196, cause dismissed 91 Ohio St.3d 1454, 742 N.E.2d 658, reconsideration denied 91 Ohio St.3d 1468, 744 N.E.2d 190, dismissed, appeal not allowed 93 Ohio St.3d 1427, 755 N.E.2d 352, motion denied 93 Ohio St.3d 1475, 757 N.E.2d 773, certiorari denied 122 S.Ct. 355, 534 U.S. 955, 151 L.Ed.2d 268. Child Support ☞ 117; Child Support ☞ 119

Reviewing court's application of amended versions of child support statutes to post-dissolution proceeding did not violate constitutional prohibition on retroactive legislation since amendments did not impose new duty upon ex-husband, but instead merely altered how already existing general duty of support codified by former statute could be enforced. Smith v. Smith (Ohio App. 12 Dist., 03-24-1997) 119 Ohio App.3d 15, 694 N.E.2d 476. Child Support ☞ 6

Statute providing for enforcement of child support orders past child's age of majority is remedial, not substantive, and thus does not violate constitutional prohibition against retroactive laws. Swanson v. Swanson (Ohio App. 2 Dist., 02-09-1996) 109 Ohio App.3d 231, 671 N.E.2d 1333. Child Support ☞ 6; Child Support ☞ 460; Statutes ☞ 278.32

After a child has reached the age of majority and support money yet unpaid and owing is reduced to a lump-sum judgment during a civil proceeding, the judgment becomes a debt for which imprisonment is prohibited pursuant to O Const Art I §15. Bauer v. Bauer (Franklin 1987) 39 Ohio App.3d 39, 528 N.E.2d 964. Child Support ☞ 497; Constitutional Law ☞ 1106

Judicial enforcement of a separation agreement incorporated into a divorce decree calling for the parent without custody to pay tuition for his child's religious education does not offend O Const Art I §7, which concerns freedom of religion. Rand v. Rand (Ohio 1985) 18 Ohio St.3d 356, 481 N.E.2d 609, 18 O.B.R. 415. Constitutional Law ☞ 1409

Judicial enforcement of a separation agreement that requires the noncustodial parent to pay tuition for his children's education at a religiously oriented school does not constitute unconstitutional state support of such religiously oriented school under either the Establishment or Free Exercise Clauses of the US Constitution, or the religious freedom provision of the Ohio Constitution. Rand v Rand, No. 47712 (8th Dist Ct App, Cuyahoga, 6-28-84), affirmed by 18 OS(3d) 356, 18 OBR 415, 481 NE(2d) 609 (1985).

A decree in a divorce action, ordering the payment of money for the support of a minor child, is not a judgment for the payment of money nor is it a debt within the constitutional inhibition against imprisonment for debt, but is in the nature of an order for the payment of alimony, and contempt will lie for willful failure to comply with its terms. Slawski v. Slawski (Lucas 1934) 49 Ohio App. 100, 195 N.E. 258, 18 Ohio Law Abs. 515, 1 O.O. 201.

There is no substantive federal constitutional right to physical possession of a child; a parent's right to custody or visitation with a child, however, is a constitutionally protected liberty interest that cannot be interfered with absent due process of law. Scarso v. Cuyahoga County Dept. of Human Services (N.D.Ohio 1989) 747 F.Supp. 381, affirmed in part and remanded 917 F.2d 1305.

A suit against state officials for injunctive and declaratory relief for violations of Social Security Act requirements at 42 USC 651 to 669 that states adopt plans for child support enforcement to remain eligible for aid to families with dependent children funds is not barred by US Const Am 11. Carelli v. Howser (S.D.Ohio 1990) 733 F.Supp. 271, reversed 923 F.2d 1208, rehearing denied. Federal Courts ☞ 272

RC 3109.05, in allowing visitation rights to grandparents, does not violate the Equal Protection Clause by treating divorced parents differently than married parents because divorced parents are not a suspect classification and because it promotes a legitimate state interest in protecting the best interests of children. Andrews v Andrews, No. CA88–03–035 (12th Dist Ct App, Butler, 11–28–88).

Where defendant is unemployed and his sole income is from aid to dependent children, an order to pay child support for an illegitimate child does not violate 42 USC 601 or the Supremacy Clause of the US Constitution. Goode v Wilburn, No. 1542 (4th Dist Ct App, Lawrence, 3–25–82).

2. In general

Evidence of money former wife paid out-of-pocket for children's medical expenses was insufficient to support reimbursement from former husband for such expenses; former wife failed to submit any medical bills or other documentation from health care providers as evidence of her out-of-pocket expenses, and only provided self-prepared audit sheets indicating the medical expenditures. Onyshko v. Onyshko (Ohio App. 11 Dist., Portage, 03-12-2010) No. 2008-P-0035, 2010-Ohio-969, 2010 WL 891335, Unreported. Child Support ☞ 487

Natural mother's relocation with child on multiple occasions over a nine-year period, coupled with her failure to file notices of intent to relocate and her use of four different surnames during that period, caused significant interference in, or significant discouragement of, communication between noncustodial father and child, such that child could not be adopted without father's consent despite his failure to communicate with child in the one-year period immediately preceding the filing of adoption petition. In re Adoption of A.J.Y. (Ohio Com.Pl., 09-16-2010) 160 Ohio Misc.2d 4, 937 N.E.2d 1109, 2010-Ohio-5726. Adoption ☞ 7.4(4)

Both common and statutory law mandate that a biological parent, absent a court order to the contrary, provide sufficient support for his or her child. Trump v. Trump (Ohio App. 9 Dist., 11-17-1999) 136 Ohio App.3d 123, 736 N.E.2d 39. Child Support ☞ 23

In the absence of a court order specifically addressing child support in the context of a divorce or dissolution, the custodial parent is required to support the child. Trump v. Trump (Ohio App. 9 Dist., 11-17-1999) 136 Ohio App.3d 123, 736 N.E.2d 39. Child Support ☞ 59

Father's argument that he did not want child and would have elected either abortion or adoption did not release him from his obligation to pay child support. Bryant v. Hacker (Ohio App. 1 Dist., 12-24-1996) 116 Ohio App.3d 860, 689 N.E.2d 609. Children Out–of–wedlock ☞ 21(2)

Child support is a duty and obligation imposed by statute and common law. Hamilton v. Hamilton (Ohio App. 6 Dist., 10-27-1995) 107 Ohio App.3d 132, 667 N.E.2d 1256, appeal not allowed 75 Ohio St.3d 1425, 662 N.E.2d 27. Child Support ☞ 20

Medical expenses are child support. Rohrbacher v. Rohrbacher (Lucas 1992) 83 Ohio App.3d 569, 615 N.E.2d 338. Child Support ☞ 113

Trial court abused its discretion by setting up savings account for child born out-of-wedlock to be funded by father and be disbursed as court ordered, where account was not based on child's current needs or support. Bailey v. Mitchell (Cuyahoga 1990) 67 Ohio App.3d 441, 587 N.E.2d 358. Children Out–of–wedlock ☞ 67

Obligation of father to support his minor children after his divorce is granted is obligation cast upon him by law and not by decree of divorce. Verplatse v. Verplatse (Hancock 1984) 17 Ohio App.3d 99, 477 N.E.2d 648, 17 O.B.R. 161. Child Support ☞ 58

Under Ohio law, the duty of support runs from parent to child, and not directly from noncustodial parent to custodial parent. In re Baker (Bkrtcy. N.D.Ohio, 12-17-2002) 294 B.R. 281. Child Support ☞ 23

Under Ohio law, an overpayment of child support still retains its character as a support obligation. In re Baker (Bkrtcy.N.D.Ohio, 12-17-2002) 294 B.R. 281. Child Support ☞ 425

3. Agreement of the parties

Trial court's order that required husband to pay child support in the amount of $781 until child's 19th birthday misstated stipulations submitted by husband and wife which indicated husband had completely satisfied his child support obligation with the exception of $781, and thus required remand, where due to stipulations made by husband and wife, issue of modifying child support was not before the court. Vengrow v. Vengrow (Ohio App. 9 Dist., Summit, 06-09-2010) No. 24907, 2010-Ohio-2568, 2010 WL 2298823, Unreported. Child Support ☞ 240; Child Support ☞ 559

Trial court's failure to issue an order indicating husband was entitled to a credit toward his child support obligations in the amount of $4,469.90 based on his overpayment of child support required remand, where husband and wife stipulated to the overpayment based upon the facts before them at child support modification hearing. Vengrow v. Vengrow (Ohio App. 9 Dist., Summit, 06-09-2010) No. 24907, 2010-Ohio-2568, 2010 WL 2298823, Unreported. Child Support ☞ 456; Child Support ☞ 559

Father was not required to pay for emancipated child's college education, as parties' divorce decree did not obligate father to pay for it. He v. Zeng (Ohio App. 5 Dist., Licking, 05-11-2010) No. 2009-CA-00060, 2010-Ohio-2095, 2010 WL 1918797, Unreported, appeal not allowed 126 Ohio St.3d 1601, 935 N.E.2d 47, 2010-Ohio-4928. Child Support ☞ 119

Pursuant to divorce decree, former wife was not entitled to be reimbursed from former husband for child's orthodontia care in the absence of an agreement between the parties that child needed such treatment. Onyshko v. Onyshko (Ohio App. 11 Dist., Portage, 03-12-2010) No. 2008-P-0035, 2010-Ohio-969, 2010 WL 891335, Unreported. Child Support ☞ 456

Annual $100 deductible for child's uncovered orthodontia expenses, provided for in shared parenting plan, did not apply to orthodontia bill incurred as lump sum and covering treatment over several years. Cherwin v. Cherwin (Ohio App. 8 Dist., Cuyahoga, 04-28-2005) No. 84875, 2005-Ohio-1999, 2005 WL 991706, Unreported. Child Support ☞ 50

Trial court did not abuse its discretion, in proceedings on former wife's motions for modification of child custody and support, in finding former husband in contempt for failing to pay his portion of child's orthodontia bill, as established by agreed judgment entry, where orthodontia expenses were not unnecessarily incurred, former husband failed to exercise his option under shared parenting agreement to get second opinion with respect to child's need for orthodontia, and shared parenting agreement provided that in event of disagreement former wife's reasonable opinion would prevail. Cherwin v. Cherwin (Ohio App. 8 Dist., Cuyahoga, 04-28-2005) No. 84875, 2005-Ohio-1999, 2005 WL 991706, Unreported. Child Support ☞ 444

Trial court did not abuse its discretion, in proceedings on wife's complaint for divorce, in omitting from final settlement agreement incorporated into judgment of divorce language relevant to spousal and child support, where language at issue, although agreed to by parties, precluded wife from seeking increase in spousal or child support and precluded husband from seeking decrease, and trial court's modification maintained basic framework of parties' agreement. Mulholland v. Mulholland (Ohio App. 1 Dist., Hamilton, 03-18-2005) No. C-030931, 2005-Ohio-1196, 2005 WL 628490, Unreported. Child Support ☞ 223; Divorce ☞ 939

Trial court did not abuse its discretion, by determining that child support obligation specified in parents' settlement agreement was not in best interest of child, and by setting the obligation in accordance with child support guidelines, where the proposed obligation calculated by the parties in the settlement agreement was generated by a faulty computer software program, and the proposed obligation did not comply with the guidelines. Montague v. Simms (Ohio App. 5 Dist., Stark, 04-21-2003) No. 2002CA00244, 2003-Ohio-2038, 2003 WL 1919053, Unreported. Child Support ☞ 51

Judgment entry read into record, incorporating shared parenting agreement, did not erroneously modify term of shared parenting agreement allegedly giving father first right to take children for non-emergency medical treatment; rather, agreement as read into record stated that either father or mother would have right to take children for non-emergency medical treatment when other parent was unable to do so, that mother's right was superior to paternal grandmother, and that mother had primary responsibility for health care. Dobran v. Dobran (Ohio App. 7 Dist., Mahoning, 03-24-2003) No. 02 CA 14, 2003-Ohio-1605, 2003 WL 1689584, Unreported. Child Custody ☞ 524

Separation agreement incorporated into divorce decree was not invalid on grounds of no meeting of minds or informed consent; although Chinese husband argued that he had limited understanding of English, no understanding of law, and he did not understand terms of agreement when he agreed to them, transcript of final hearing indicated that court questioned him at length regarding terms, he understood what was being asked of him, he understood terms of agreement, and he was represented by counsel. Zamonski v. Wan (Ohio App. 2 Dist., Montgomery, 02-21-2003) No. 19392, 2003-Ohio-780, 2003 WL 366756, Unreported. Divorce ☞ 11.5

Although parties had entered into a consent decree approximately four years earlier that mother was to have custody of daughter and was to be responsible for all of daughter's expenses, apportioning responsibility, based on parties' incomes, to father for 72.6% of mother's legal bill, for costs relating to mother's recent motion for transfer of custody, and for daughter's medical and psychological bills incurred while daughter was in mother's custody was not abuse of discretion, where custody of daughter had been transferred to father six months prior to mother's motion, court noted that no one party was to blame in case and each party was a parent to child, and daughter's medical costs were extraordinary. Short v. Short (Ohio App. 6 Dist., Fulton, 01-31-2003) No. F-02-021, 2003-Ohio-489, 2003 WL 220450, Unreported. Child Custody ☞ 942; Child Custody ☞ 943; Child Support ☞ 358(2)

To the extent that surrogate mother and her husband had obtained custody of the children born as result of surrogacy, they had to indemnify biological father for any court-ordered expenses associated with that custody, as they agreed to do under indemnification provisions of surrogacy contract; indemnification provision of surrogacy contract was recognition that, since surrogate was not a parent, if surrogate mother and her husband decided to obtain custody of children, they would become legal parents and surrogacy agreement would terminate, and biological father would be treated as merely the sperm donor and not the parent. J.F. v. D.B. (Ohio App. 9 Dist., 03-15-2006) 165 Ohio App.3d 791, 848 N.E.2d 873, 2006-Ohio-1175, appeal allowed 110 Ohio St.3d 1438, 852 N.E.2d 187, 2006-Ohio-3862, affirmed in part, reversed in part 116 Ohio St.3d 363, 879 N.E.2d 740, 2007-Ohio-6750. Children Out-of-wedlock ☞ 22

Lesbian mother's agreement, to accept full financial responsibility for children in exchange for father impregnating mother, was circumstance "which ought reasonably to relieve father" of child support obligation between date of birth and date amicable and cooperative parenting arrangement broke down and, thus, trial court's refusal to order child support to commence at birth was not an abuse of discretion. Myers v. Moschella (Ohio App. 1 Dist., 06-26-1996) 112 Ohio App.3d 75, 677 N.E.2d 1243. Children Out-of-wedlock ☞ 22; Children Out-of-wedlock ☞ 67

A domestic relations court may enforce the provisions of an agreement incorporated to a divorce decree that a parent provide financial support for an incompetent adult child, notwithstanding the fact that the child is an adult at the time the decree is issued and may utilize the child support guidelines to determine the appropriate amount of support. O'Connor v. O'Connor (Franklin 1991) 71 Ohio App.3d 541, 594 N.E.2d 1081, motion overruled 62 Ohio St.3d 1409, 577 N.E.2d 362.

Children remained "third-party beneficiaries" of separation agreement which created benefits for them, even after agreement was merged into divorce decree; merger did not alter agreement, but rather, only affected enforcement and ability to alter agreement. Wolfinger v. Ocke (Shelby 1991) 72 Ohio App.3d 193, 594 N.E.2d 139. Contracts ☞ 187(1)

Parties to separation agreement may not abrogate right of minor child of marriage to be supported by either parent. In re Dissolution of Marriage of Lazor (Ohio 1991) 59 Ohio St.3d 201, 572 N.E.2d 66. Child Support ☞ 47

The parties to a separation agreement may not abrogate the right of a minor child of the marriage to be supported by either parent; prior to the effective date of RC 3113.215 to 3113.218, the parties could, however, agree to allocate the support obligation between themselves in a manner analogous to an indemnity agreement. In re Dissolution of Marriage of Lazor (Ohio 1991) 59 Ohio St.3d 201, 572 N.E.2d 66.

A child's right to insurance policy proceeds is vested by a separation agreement providing that a husband "shall keep or cause to be kept" a life insurance policy with his child as "primary, irrevocable beneficiary"; this right is enforceable in equity and cannot be defeated by the husband's failure to maintain the policy as required. Thomas v. Studley (Cuyahoga 1989) 59 Ohio App.3d 76, 571 N.E.2d 454.

Where parents of a child continue their disputes and animosity toward each other after the dissolution of their marriage and such conflict causes their child psychological problems, the parents' agreement to share medical expenses of the child includes the costs of the child's psychological treatment. Sterbling v. Sterbling (Clermont 1987) 35 Ohio App.3d 68, 519 N.E.2d 673. Child Support ☞ 44

A parent may agree to extend his obligation to support a child beyond the parent's death, in which case the support obligation becomes a charge, against the estate; language in the agreement that it is binding on the parties' estates, heirs, executors, and administrators is sufficient to bind the estate. Gilford v. Wurster (Lorain 1983) 24 Ohio App.3d 77, 493 N.E.2d 258, 24 O.B.R. 145.

Where a separation agreement provides that a parent will pay for education costs at a school to be agreed on by both parties, upon the death of a party, that party's discretion to agree on a choice of schools is to be exercised by the court. Gilford v. Wurster (Lorain 1983) 24 Ohio App.3d 77, 493 N.E.2d 258, 24 O.B.R. 145.

The court must be satisfied that the child support provision in a separation agreement represents compliance with the husband's duty of support. Scholler v. Scholler (Ohio 1984) 10 Ohio St.3d 98, 462 N.E.2d 158, 10 O.B.R. 426. Child Support ☞ 45

Where a court accepts as fair and reasonable an agreement of the parties that a husband support his children beyond the age of majority the court may enforce it within the provisions of RC 3105.10. Bugay v. Bugay (Summit 1977) 53 Ohio App.2d 285, 373 N.E.2d 1263, 7 O.O.3d 336.

An agreement between a father and a mother (formerly husband and wife) of minor children, whereby the father, in consideration of his executing and delivering to the wife a written consent to the adoption of the children by their stepfather, is released from his obligation under the decree of divorce to support such children, is valid as between the parties, even though the adoption never takes place and the mother is subsequently divorced from the stepfather; and the mother cannot recover from the father for herself a lump-sum judgment for the installments of such child support award which otherwise would have been payable. Tressler v. Tressler (Defiance 1972) 32 Ohio App.2d 79, 288 N.E.2d 339, 61 O.O.2d 85. Child Support ☞ 47

The full equity powers and jurisdiction lodged in the court of common pleas by RC 3105.21 extend to orders made for the disposition, care, maintenance and support of minor children, so that in a divorce action, the court in making an order for the disposition, care, maintenance and support of minor children of the parties, may incorporate in its decree the terms of an agreement entered into between such parties that the husband support a child past the age of majority even though the court, in the absence of an agreement of the parties, would not have the power to make the resultant decree. Robrock v. Robrock (Ohio 1958) 167 Ohio St. 479, 150 N.E.2d 421, 5 O.O.2d 165.

Written agreement between debtor and his ex-spouse is persuasive evidence of their intent in imposing payment obligation on debtor, whether to require payment as nondischargeable support or as part of equalization of distribution of marital assets, and an unambiguous agreement creates a substantial obstacle for party challenging its express terms to overcome. In re Loper (10th Cir.BAP (Okla.), 09-08-2005) 329 B.R. 704. Bankruptcy ☞ 3365(12); Bankruptcy ☞ 3366

When debtor and ex-spouse's divorce was by agreement, question as to whether obligation arising under that agreement is in nature of nondischargeable "alimony, maintenance or support" obligation is resolved by determining: (1) shared intent of parties as to nature of obligation at time it arose; and (2) whether obligation had actual effect of providing support. In re Loper (10th Cir.BAP

(Okla.), 09-08-2005) 329 B.R. 704. Bankruptcy ⟜ 3365(12); Bankruptcy ⟜ 3366

A cost-of-living clause in a separation agreement providing for automatic increases in child support is valid, as the ability of a domestic relations court to modify for a change of circumstances exists despite the clause. Gui v Brown, No. CA–6392 (5th Dist Ct App, Stark, 11–26–84).

In an action for arrearages, the trial court rightly denied the right to recover past obligations where the parties had mutually agreed to discharge the continuing obligation to pay support in exchange for a waiver of a continuing visitation right; in an action to reinstate both child support payments and visitation rights, the party seeking reinstatement will not be denied such based on the previous mutual agreement, as the child has an interest in future payments; therefore, such an agreement is binding on both parties as to past obligations, but is not binding on the court as to future payments. In re Dissolution of Marriage of Saltis v Frisby, No. 10345 (9th Dist Ct App, Summit, 1–27 82).

Where the trial court enters a divorce order incorporating a separation agreement in which the plaintiff-mother waived all rights to child support in exchange for which the father waived his visitation rights, said order may be modified to establish a child support obligation without a finding of a change of circumstances. Botticello v Botticello, No. 7372 (2d Dist Ct App, Montgomery, 1–7–82).

A once unemployed mother now earning $520 per month is not grounds for a reduction of child support since the possibility of the mother's employment could have been reasonably expected such that it is not a change of circumstances, and further, because such contingency was not in the agreement. Swartz v Swartz, No. 948 (11th Dist Ct App, Geauga, 9–30–81).

Where a separation agreement states that child-support payments shall terminate as each child becomes emancipated, and further provides that the modification will either be agreed upon or submitted to the court, the matter must be submitted to the court as a changing circumstance. McFadden v McFadden, No. 80AP–626 (10th Dist Ct App, Franklin, 7–28–81).

4. Attorney fees

Trial court acted within its discretion in awarding mother attorney fees in the amount of $1,312.50, as the prevailing party in contempt proceedings brought against father for non-payment of child support, which had been ordered in earlier divorce proceedings; in a post-divorce contempt of court proceeding, an award of reasonable attorney fees to the party filing the successful contempt action was mandated, trial court had been informed of breakdown of attorney's time and services rendered, trial court had denied request of mother's counsel to appear telephonically and was thereby aware of counsel's travel expenses, and trial court was familiar with the case. Gruber v. Gruber (Ohio App. 6 Dist., Ottawa, 08-12-2011) No. OT-10-003,

2011-Ohio-4049, 2011 WL 3568273, Unreported. Child Support ⟜ 603

Ex-husband's counsel was entitled to attorney fees in contempt proceeding brought against ex-wife for failure to facilitate visitation and failure to pay children's medical bills, as required by court order. Hanzlik v. Hanzlik (Ohio App. 11 Dist., Portage, 07-23-2010) No. 2009-P-0089, 2010-Ohio-3462, 2010 WL 2892631, Unreported. Child Custody ⟜ 943; Child Support ⟜ 603

County child support enforcement agency's request of $500 in attorney fees upon obtaining contempt judgment against ex-husband for failure to pay child support was not de facto reasonable under local rule allowing up to $500 in attorney fees upon a finding of contempt in a domestic relations matter; under the plain language of statute requiring a contemnor to pay reasonable attorney fees of any adverse party in a contempt proceeding based on failure to pay child support, the trial court had the responsibility to determine whether the amount of requested fees was reasonable. Roush v. Brown (Ohio App. 12 Dist., Butler, 05-26-2009) No. CA2008-11-275, 2009-Ohio 2446, 2009 WL 1456530, Unreported. Child Support ⟜ 603

Trial court did not abuse its discretion in reducing magistrate's award of attorney fees to former wife, from $5,346 to $2,218, upon finding that former husband was in contempt for failure to pay spousal support; the change of circumstances that warranted the reduction of former husband's spousal support obligation was ultimately ignored in magistrate's award of attorney's fees to former wife, and former wife's need did not outweigh former husband's ability to pay. Goldberg v. Goldberg (Ohio App. 8 Dist., Cuyahoga, 04-20-2006) No. 86590, No. 86588, 2006-Ohio-1948, 2006 WL 1044812, Unreported. Divorce ⟜ 1143; Divorce ⟜ 1162; Divorce ⟜ 1168(2); Divorce ⟜ 1170(8)

Awarding amount of attorney fees requested by father, on father's motion for contempt and to compel minor child's maternal aunt and uncle, as the residential parents of the child, to pay child's medical bills, was an abuse of discretion, where only evidence regarding reasonableness of attorney fees was father's testimony that the "almost $2,600.00 in legal fees to get $700.00 worth of bills paid" was reasonable, and there was no indication that trial court distinguished between time spent in regard to contempt motion, on which father prevailed, and time spent in regard to his motion for an accounting of child support payments, on which he did not prevail. Willett v Willett (Ohio App. 9 Dist., Summit, 02-02-2005) No. 22167, 2005-Ohio-342, 2005 WL 236178, Unreported. Child Support ⟜ 609

Trial court was required by statute to impose attorney fees on ex-husband upon finding him in contempt for failure to make court-ordered child support payments. Flynn v. Sender (Ohio App. 8 Dist., Cuyahoga, 11-24-2004) No. 84406,

2004-Ohio-6283, 2004 WL 2676742, Unreported. Child Support ☞ 603

Order granting mother attorney fees of $495 to defend father's motion for relief from judgment requiring him to pay child support was not abuse of discretion, where father's income was substantially greater than mother's, and attorney fees were not unreasonable, based on amount of time spent to represent mother and attorney's hourly rate. Demcho v. Demcho (Ohio App. 9 Dist., Medina, 09-15-2004) No. 03CA0105-M, 2004-Ohio-4868, 2004 WL 2047363, Unreported. Child Support ☞ 603; Child Support ☞ 609

Father waived claim that trial court should have denied mother's oral motion for attorney fees, at hearing on father's motion for relief from judgment requiring him to pay child support, where father failed to object to motion. Demcho v. Demcho (Ohio App. 9 Dist., Medina, 09-15-2004) No. 03CA0105-M, 2004-Ohio-4868, 2004 WL 2047363, Unreported. Child Support ☞ 539

The Court of Appeals could not review wife's appellate argument that husband had assets available to pay wife's attorney fees, in post-divorce proceeding to modify husband's child support obligation; wife failed to raise the argument in the trial court, and she failed to ascertain that the trial transcript on the issue of attorney fees was included in the appellate record. Nickoloff v. Nickoloff (Ohio App. 9 Dist., Lorain, 07-07-2004) No. 03CA008415, 2004-Ohio-3565, 2004 WL 1496852, Unreported. Child Support ☞ 539; Child Support ☞ 542

Trial court did not abuse its discretion, in proceedings on former husband's motion to modify child support and tuition, in awarding attorney fees to former wife, where former husband was found in contempt for failure to continue to pay his tuition obligations during pendency of his motion. Mencini v. Mencini (Ohio App. 8 Dist., Cuyahoga, 06-17-2004) No. 83638, No. 83820, 2004-Ohio-3125, 2004 WL 1364402, Unreported. Child Support ☞ 603

Former husband waived for appellate review any complaint against trial court's order awarding former wife attorney fees for bringing contempt action against husband for his failure to adhere to divorce decree, where husband failed to object at trial. Bergman v. Bergman (Ohio App. 10 Dist., Franklin, 02-10-2004) No. 03AP-570, 2004-Ohio-584, 2004 WL 249607, Unreported. Divorce ☞ 1217

Trial court made requisite findings to support its order awarding former wife attorney fees for bringing contempt action against former husband for failure to comply with terms of divorce decree; upon finding husband in contempt for failure to pay child support, trial court was required to order husband, as party in contempt, to pay wife's attorney fees relating to contempt proceedings. Bergman v. Bergman (Ohio App. 10 Dist., Franklin, 02-10-2004) No. 03AP-570, 2004-Ohio-584, 2004 WL 249607, Unreported. Divorce ☞ 1170(8)

Court of Appeals was unable to evaluate merits of former husband's appeal, contesting trial court's order awarding wife attorney fees for bringing action resulting in contempt order entered against husband for failing to comply with divorce decree, absent hearing transcript and evidentiary materials. Bergman v. Bergman (Ohio App. 10 Dist., Franklin, 02-10-2004) No. 03AP-570, 2004-Ohio-584, 2004 WL 249607, Unreported. Divorce ☞ 1241

Former wife was entitled to attorney fees incurred in action in which former husband was found in contempt of court for failure to pay child support and child's medical expenses. Oleksy v. Oleksy (Ohio App. 8 Dist., Cuyahoga, 10-23-2003) No. 82646, 2003-Ohio-5657, 2003 WL 22413671, Unreported. Child Support ☞ 603

Upon finding that former husband was in contempt for failing to pay child support, trial court was required to order husband to pay former wife reasonable attorney's fees. Sinnott v. Sinnott (Ohio App. 10 Dist., Franklin, 08-28-2003) No. 02AP-1277, 2003-Ohio-4571, 2003 WL 22020815, Unreported. Child Support ☞ 603

Trial court did not abuse its discretion by awarding to wife only those attorney fees attributable to wife's prosecution of contempt actions against husband for failure to pay child support, rather than to all post-divorce issues between parties, where court noted that some of wife's fees apparently were result of duplicate filings, issues in case were not particularly difficult or unique, many disputes were eventually resolved by joint stipulation of parties, both parties had adequate resources from which to pay their own fees, wife's expert witness as to fees was not particularly helpful in establishing that fees were reasonable and necessary, and court found that fees incurred by wife other than those related to contempt actions would have been incurred in normal course of the divorce proceedings. Schafer v. Schafer (Ohio App. 6 Dist., Lucas, 04-11-2003) No. L-02-1120, 2003-Ohio-1867, 2003 WL 1861435, Unreported. Child Support ☞ 603; Divorce ☞ 1162

Trial court did not abuse its discretion in awarding wife only $350 out of claimed $2,750 in attorney fees following finding of contempt against husband for failure to pay child support, where majority of fees incurred were not incurred in connection with contempt claim. Huff v. Huff (Ohio App. 9 Dist., Summit, 03-19-2003) No. 20934, 2003-Ohio-1304, 2003 WL 1240392, Unreported. Child Support ☞ 609

Elihu Root's observation is worth recalling, that "About half the practice of a decent lawyer consists of telling... clients they are d——— fools and should stop... [that]the law lets you do it but don't. It's a rotten thing to do." Stivison v. Goodyear Tire & Rubber Co. (Ohio App. 4 Dist., Hocking, 05-06-1996) No. 95CA13, 1996 WL 230037, Unreported, appeal allowed 77 Ohio St.3d 1447, 671 N.E.2d 1285, reversed 80 Ohio St.3d 498, 687 N.E.2d 458, 1997-Ohio-321.

Reversal of order finding former husband in contempt of court for failing to reimburse former wife for medical expenses as required by marital dissolution judgment required reversal of order that required former husband to pay former wife's attorney fees regarding contempt motion; claim for attorney fees was derivative of contempt motion. Kirk v. Kirk (Ohio App. 3 Dist., 06-25-2007) 172 Ohio App.3d 404, 875 N.E.2d 125, 2007-Ohio-3140. Child Support ⟜ 559

Under terms of divorce decree, ex-wife could recover attorney fees incurred in instituting contempt proceedings to enforce ex-husband's obligation to pay one half of costs of parties' child's education, notwithstanding ex-husband's contention that amount he owed was in dispute; even if amount was in dispute, there was no dispute that ex-husband had failed to pay any portion of child's educational expenses during relevant period. Wesselman v. Wesselman (Butler 1993) 88 Ohio App.3d 338, 623 N.E.2d 1300. Child Support ⟜ 603

While award of attorney fees to wife in divorce proceeding may have been reasonable, trial court's failure to do so did not constitute abuse of discretion, given that Court of Appeals increased wife's sustenance alimony award from $2,700 to $3,500 and trial court awarded to wife portion of bonus to which husband was entitled through his employment. Kaechele v. Kaechele (Franklin 1992) 83 Ohio App.3d 468, 615 N.E.2d 273. Divorce ⟜ 1147

An award of attorney fees is improper where the court fails to determine (1) the time and labor involved, (2) the fee customarily charged in the locality, and (3) the nature and length of the professional relationship with the client. Hockenberry v. Hockenberry (Henry 1992) 75 Ohio App.3d 806, 600 N.E.2d 839.

Two parties, in a noncommercial transaction, may lawfully contract to require the payment by the unsuccessful party in a subsequent suit between them, of the prevailing party's attorney fees. Nottingdale Homeowners' Ass'n, Inc. v. Darby (Ohio 1987) 33 Ohio St.3d 32, 514 N.E.2d 702.

Where a husband moving for a reduction in child support does not come to the hearing on his motion, an award of attorney fees to the wife without a showing of necessity but based instead on the husband's failure to prosecute is not an abuse of discretion. Harpole v. Harpole (Medina 1986) 27 Ohio App.3d 289, 500 N.E.2d 915, 27 O.B.R. 334.

A clause in a separation agreement requiring the party in default to pay the other party's attorney fees in an enforcement action is not enforceable. Snyder v. Snyder (Cuyahoga 1985) 27 Ohio App.3d 1, 499 N.E.2d 320, 27 O.B.R. 1.

A noncustodial parent may not recover attorney fees upon successfully defending, on procedural grounds only, a post-decree enforcement action for child support, where procedural errors by the party seeking enforcement were not the result of bad faith. Montgomery County Welfare Dept. v. Bobo

(Montgomery 1984) 21 Ohio App.3d 69, 486 N.E.2d 222, 21 O.B.R. 74.

The awarding of attorney fees in proceedings on a motion after a decree of divorce is within the sound discretion of the trial court, and a showing of necessity is not a prerequisite to an award. Rand v. Rand (Ohio 1985) 18 Ohio St.3d 356, 481 N.E.2d 609, 18 O.B.R. 415.

Where post-divorce proceedings to enforce the support obligation of the noncomplying noncustodial parent are necessary, it is not an abuse of discretion for the court to award attorney fees to the complainant spouse regardless of her ability to pay such fees. Rand v Rand, No. 47712 (8th Dist Ct App, Cuyahoga, 6-28-84), affirmed by 18 OS(3d) 356, 18 OBR 415, 481 NE(2d) 609 (1985).

A trial court has authority, after the entry of a divorce decree, to enter an order requiring the divorced husband to pay reasonable expense money to his former wife to enable her to pay attorney fees incurred in post-decree proceedings relative to the support of the minor children of the marriage. Blum v. Blum (Ohio 1967) 9 Ohio St.2d 92, 223 N.E.2d 819, 38 O.O.2d 224.

Where a divorced wife obtains an order modifying a support order and the defendant husband appeals and loses such appeal, the court is authorized to grant her an allowance for reasonable expenses in connection with such appeal. Ward v. Ward (Montgomery 1956) 104 Ohio App. 105, 140 N.E.2d 906, 74 Ohio Law Abs. 408, 4 O.O.2d 177.

Debtor's obligation to his ex-wife for attorney fees awarded by state court in post-divorce custody proceedings was nondischargeable in bankruptcy, as being in nature of "domestic support obligation," where fees, which were awarded following determination by state court that debtor, in attempt to induce his ex-wife to dismiss her custody claims, had threatened that he would otherwise outspend her in effort to preserve their previously agreed shared parenting plan, were meant to compensate wife for legal expenses that she incurred as result of debtor's behavior, which detracted from her ability to support children. In re Gruber (Bkrtcy. N.D.Ohio, 07-12-2010) 436 B.R. 39. Bankruptcy ⟜ 3365(9)

Determination of dischargeability of debtor's obligation to his former wife for attorney fees awarded by state court in post-divorce custody proceedings, as allegedly being in nature of "domestic support obligation," had to be made in accordance with federal bankruptcy, and not state, law; the label attached to obligation by state law, while relevant, was not necessarily controlling. In re Gruber (Bkrtcy.N.D.Ohio, 07-12-2010) 436 B.R. 39. Bankruptcy ⟜ 3366

Father who was found in contempt for failure to comply with child support order was required by statute to pay mother's attorney's fees, and thus trial court did not err by failing to make findings regarding his ability to pay, which were required by other statute regarding award of attorney's fees in divorce or legal separation proceedings. Harper v.

Harper (Ohio App. 10 Dist., Franklin, 08-22-2002) No. 01AP-1314, 2002-Ohio-4320, 2002 WL 1938319, Unreported. Child Support ☞ 603; Child Support ☞ 615

Father who was in contempt for failure to pay medical expenses as required by child support agreement did not object to award of $4,500 in attorney's fees to mother on the basis that the evidence did not establish that mother incurred that amount in fees, and thus waived the argument on appeal. Harper v. Harper (Ohio App. 10 Dist., Franklin, 08-22-2002) No. 01AP-1314, 2002-Ohio-4320, 2002 WL 1938319, Unreported. Child Support ☞ 539

Ex-husband, who was held in contempt for failing to pay child support arrearages as ordered by court, properly was ordered to pay ex-wife's attorney fees pursuant to statute providing that, if any person required to pay child support is found in contempt for failure to make support payments, the court shall require the person to pay any reasonable attorney fees of any adverse party; at the contempt hearing, ex-husband stipulated that the attorney fees incurred by ex-wife in relation to the contempt motion were both necessary and reasonable. Miller v. Miller (Ohio App. 12 Dist., Butler, 07-29-2002) No. CA2001-06-138, 2002-Ohio-3870, 2002 WL 1758374, Unreported. Child Support ☞ 603

The provisions of RC 3109.05(C) awarding costs and attorney fees are mandatory where there is a finding of contempt for failure to pay child support. Holyak v Holyak, No. 411 (7th Dist Ct App, Harrison, 5–22–89).

Where a request for an increase in support is met with resistance and litigation is required, the expense of such litigation is in the nature of additional child support necessary for the child to have the standard of living commensurate with the parent's income. Hummer v Hummer, No. 86AP–293 (10th Dist Ct App, Franklin, 8–28–86).

5. Bankruptcy—In general

Forgiveness of indebtedness by medical practitioners who had provided services to former Chapter 7 debtor's children did not affect debtor's obligation, pursuant to terms of divorce decree, to pay childrens' medical expenses, so that evidence of medical providers' forgiveness of indebtedness was properly excluded as irrelevant in proceeding brought to determine dischargeability of debtor's debt. Bratton v. Frederick (Ohio App. 3 Dist., 01-31-1996) 109 Ohio App.3d 13, 671 N.E.2d 1030. Bankruptcy ☞ 3404

Chapter 7 trustee could not avoid, as preferential transfer, federal government's prepetition seizure of tax refund payable to debtor, for transfer to local child support agency and ultimately to debtor's ex-spouse for delinquent child support, upon theory that ex-spouse had assigned support rights to local agency prepetition; under Ohio law, funds were paid to local agency not as assignee of ex-spouse, but as trustee on ex-spouse's behalf. In re Sanks

(Bkrtcy.N.D.Ohio, 05-29-2001) 265 B.R. 566. Bankruptcy ☞ 2602.1

Under Ohio law, payments by debtor to child support enforcement agency are not an assignment, but are funds held in trust for benefit of custodial parent. In re Sanks (Bkrtcy.N.D.Ohio, 05-29-2001) 265 B.R. 566. Child Support ☞ 430

Debts arising from a property settlement are not encompassed within the discharge exception for those debts contained in a divorce decree or separation agreement which are for the maintenance and support of debtor's child or former spouse. In re Luman (Bkrtcy.N.D.Ohio, 04-14-1999) 238 B.R. 697. Bankruptcy ☞ 3365(1)

Adjustment of Chapter 13 debtor's obligation under marital separation agreement to make college assistance payments for children's education pursuant to marital separation agreement was not appropriate where debtor's financial position had improved from time of separation agreement when he was unemployed until time of petition filing when debtor was earning $3,000 per month and was remarried to wife who also worked. Matter of Bush (Bkrtcy.S.D.Ohio 1993) 154 B.R. 69. Bankruptcy ☞ 3705

Chapter 13 debtor's obligation under marital separation agreement to make college assistance payments for his children's educations fell within the exception to discharge for support; payments were intended to be support, and they were not overly burdensome on debtor. Matter of Bush (Bkrtcy. S.D.Ohio 1993) 154 B.R. 69. Bankruptcy ☞ 3365(13)

Bankruptcy court has authority to adjust and alter amount of payments owed for spousal and child support if it finds the payments to be unreasonably burdensome to Chapter 13 debtor; however, it is only appropriate to make such a modification if original state court award was unreasonable or if there has been detrimental change in financial circumstances from time divorce decree was entered to time of petition filing. Matter of Bush (Bkrtcy.S.D.Ohio 1993) 154 B.R. 69. Bankruptcy ☞ 3705

In determining whether an award of support in a divorce decree is necessary or excessive and subject to discharge in a former husband's bankruptcy proceedings, the bankruptcy court will consider the circumstances considered by Ohio domestic relations courts in deciding what amounts to award as alimony and child support, such as those listed in RC 3105.18 and 3109.05. In re Angel (Bkrtcy. S.D.Ohio 1989) 105 B.R. 825.

A monthly support award of $2000 is considered "manifestly excessive" by the federal bankruptcy court when the former husband charged with paying it is now disabled and has a monthly income of just $778; the court will review the former husband's budget and decide to what extent the support payment should be adjusted. In re Skaggs (Bkrtcy.S.D.Ohio 1988) 91 B.R. 1018.

6. —— Jurisdiction, bankruptcy

Federal and state courts have concurrent jurisdiction to hear questions of dischargeability arising out of alimony and child support exception. In re Baker (Bkrtcy.S.D.Ohio, 04-25-1996) 195 B.R. 883. Bankruptcy ⟳ 2062

Where state court has not yet determined property interests involved, it is appropriate for bankruptcy court to defer to that state court for determination of dischargeability under alimony and child support exception. In re Baker (Bkrtcy.S.D.Ohio, 04-25-1996) 195 B.R. 883. Bankruptcy ⟳ 2062

In general, federal courts defer to state courts in domestic relations matters, but this deference is limited to matters where the matter is more suitably handled by state courts. In re Baker (Bkrtcy. S.D.Ohio, 04-25-1996) 195 B.R. 883. Federal Courts ⟳ 8

State and federal courts have concurrent jurisdiction to determine whether debt is excepted from discharge under spousal and child support exception. Matter of Tremaine (Bkrtcy.S.D.Ohio, 09-28-1995) 188 B.R. 380. Bankruptcy ⟳ 2060.1

In proceedings to determine dischargeability under child and spousal support exception where bankruptcy court and state court have concurrent jurisdiction to determine issue, general rule is that court in which issue is first presented, or capable of presentation, through proper filings and proceedings will continue proceedings to conclusion. Matter of Tremaine (Bkrtcy.S.D.Ohio, 09-28-1995) 188 B.R. 380. Bankruptcy ⟳ 2062

Bankruptcy court would abstain, in favor of state domestic relations court, from determining whether debts owed to Chapter 7 debtor's former wife were nondischargeable under spousal support exception, in light of related proceeding pending in state court system, appearance of forum shopping by debtor, and lack of finality caused by debtor's pursuit of state court appellate proceedings that diminished, if not eliminated, any meaningful determination of dischargeability by bankruptcy court; appellate proceeding had reached advanced stages in state court system, but had not finally established amount of divorce decree debts, and absence of finality in amount of obligations precluded determination of nature of debt. Matter of Tremaine (Bkrtcy. S.D.Ohio, 09-28-1995) 188 B.R. 380. Federal Courts ⟳ 47.5

7. —— Attorney fees, bankruptcy

Even assuming that debtor's obligation to his ex-wife for attorney fees awarded by state court in post-divorce custody proceedings was not in nature of "domestic support obligation," this debt, as one arising out litigation between parties on whether to modify the joint parenting plan agreed to in connection with their divorce, was obligation incurred "in connection with" divorce decree, as required for it to be excepted from discharge as debt to former spouse that was not in nature of domestic support obligation, and that was incurred "in the course of a divorce or separation or in connection with a separation agreement, divorce decree or other or-

der of a court of record." In re Gruber (Bkrtcy. N.D.Ohio, 07-12-2010) 436 B.R. 39. Bankruptcy ⟳ 3367(1)

Attorney fees which may be viewed as inextricably intertwined with the litigation of nondischargeable support qualify for nondischargeability under dischargeability actions. In re McLaughlin (Bkrtcy. N.D.Ohio, 02-01-2005) 320 B.R. 661. Bankruptcy ⟳ 3365(9)

Attorney fees for services to obtain or enforce child support are entitled to priority. In re McLaughlin (Bkrtcy.N.D.Ohio, 02-01-2005) 320 B.R. 661. Bankruptcy ⟳ 2951

Attorney fees incurred in prosecution of state court child support action were entitled to priority treatment, since co-claimant obligee had not agreed to different treatment of entire priority proof of claim, state court found debtor in contempt for failure to pay child support, state court judgment mandated payment of attorney fees to enforce debtor's child support obligations, and state court had construed attorney fees related to enforcement of child support obligations as support obligations. In re McLaughlin (Bkrtcy.N.D.Ohio, 02-01-2005) 320 B.R. 661. Bankruptcy ⟳ 2951

8. —— Overpayments, bankruptcy

A custodial parent is not entitled to reimbursement for child support from the noncustodial parent where no support order is made or requested at the time custody is awarded. Meyer v. Meyer (Ohio 1985) 17 Ohio St.3d 222, 478 N.E.2d 806, 17 O.B.R. 455. Child Support ⟳ 55

Even though creditor-father may have been dilatory in seeking to enforce his legal rights by obtaining an order staying the garnishment of his wages after he was made the residential parent of the parties' child, this delay did not excuse Chapter 7 debtor-mother from dissipating those funds to which she was not otherwise entitled; debtor was clearly aware of the court order terminating creditor's obligation to pay child support and, having wrongfully kept creditor's money, debtor did not come to the court with clean hands and so was not entitled to equitable relief. In re Baker (Bkrtcy. N.D.Ohio, 12-17-2002) 294 B.R. 281. Bankruptcy ⟳ 2125

Creditor-father's child support overpayments to Chapter 7 debtor-mother, made when, due to an administrative delay, his wages continued to be garnished for child support even after he was made the residential parent of the parties' child, fell within the discharge exception for alimony, maintenance, or "support"; such overpayments were made pursuant to the parties' original order for child support, so that creditor was under a legal duty to make them. In re Baker (Bkrtcy.N.D.Ohio, 12-17-2002) 294 B.R. 281. Bankruptcy ⟳ 3365(13)

A man whose earnings from an apparently failing business in which he is a partner have dropped from $35,000 per year to $18,000 and who has taken cash advances against future salary in order to meet support obligations under a divorce decree will not be granted relief in his bankruptcy proceedings, on the ground changed circumstances have lessened his ability to pay support or the ground that ordered support is excessive, with respect to obligations to pay $150 weekly child support, $200 weekly alimony, medical insurance, the former wife's auto costs for two years, half the children's tuition at a private school, and an additional $2000 per year for five years; the court considers that "there is no indication" the former husband, "an apparently able-bodied, middle-aged man is incapable of earning a respectable income." In re Angel (Bkrtcy.S.D.Ohio 1989) 105 B.R. 825.

Where a former husband's income has declined dramatically since a divorce decree and now amounts to $1321 monthly, from which he claims to spend $1285 monthly on necessities exclusive of the $600 monthly support he was ordered to pay his former wife, and where the former wife has income of $400 monthly and monthly expenses of $625, the bankruptcy court will find it "manifestly unreasonable under traditional concepts of support" to make the former husband pay the support decreed; instead, the former husband is found able to pay $80 weekly henceforth by effecting economies, and the remainder of the obligation is held subject to his discharge in bankruptcy. In re Caughenbaugh (Bkrtcy.S.D.Ohio 1988) 92 B.R. 255.

9. ⸺ Arrearages, bankruptcy

Chapter 13 debtor's right to payment of past-due child support was part of her bankruptcy estate. In re Davis (Bkrtcy.S.D.Ohio, 05-06-1994) 167 B.R. 104. Bankruptcy ⸺ 2553

Absent showing that current needs of child support payee are unmet, Chapter 13 plan providing for 100 percent payment of arrearages over life of plan is acceptable. In re Walter (Bkrtcy.N.D.Ohio 1993) 153 B.R. 38. Bankruptcy ⸺ 3705

Because child support obligations are typically nondischargeable, in instances where Chapter 13 plan calls for less than full payment of arrearages, relief from automatic stay may be available to allow payee or appropriate governmental agency to pursue only those amounts not provided for in plan. In re Walter (Bkrtcy.N.D.Ohio 1993) 153 B.R. 38. Bankruptcy ⸺ 2422.5(7)

The fact that a man and woman remarry ten years after they divorced has no effect on the arrearage for child support that he owes her and that she had assigned to the county while she collected aid to dependent children during the time that the couple was divorced. In re Lhamon (Bkrtcy.N.D.Ohio 1991) 139 B.R. 849.

Any part of a support award that is not "manifestly unreasonable under traditional concepts of support" and that is owing but unpaid from the entry of the state court divorce decree until commencement of the former husband's federal bankruptcy case will not be affected by the former husband's discharge in bankruptcy; he remains responsible for the arrearage and must make arrangements with his former wife for payment. In re Caughenbaugh (Bkrtcy.S.D.Ohio 1988) 92 B.R. 255.

Seven years of child support arrearages cannot be discharged in bankruptcy even where the husband ceased payment because the wife began receiving $465 each month for the children from her next husband's social security, and she then gave the children to her mother to raise yet only gave her mother $150 each month for doing so. In re Troxell (Bkrtcy.S.D.Ohio 1986) 67 B.R. 328.

An obligation for child support arrearages will be discharged in bankruptcy, as between the debtor and the mother, where the obligation arose by agreement in settlement of a paternity proceeding in which the debtor denied paternity, and where no evidence of paternity is before the bankruptcy court. Matter of Gray (Bkrtcy.S.D.Ohio 1984) 41 B.R. 759.

10. ⸺ Non-dischargeability of support, bankruptcy

Former Chapter 7 debtor's obligation to pay legal and travel expenses incurred by his ex-wife in enforcing support obligations of parties' divorce decree was likewise in nature of "support," so as not to be dischargeable in bankruptcy. Bratton v. Frederick (Ohio App. 3 Dist., 01-31-1996) 109 Ohio App.3d 13, 671 N.E.2d 1030. Bankruptcy ⸺ 3365(3); Bankruptcy ⸺ 3365(9)

Former Chapter 7 debtor's obligation, pursuant to terms of divorce decree, to procure medical insurance for his children and to pay for certain medical expenses was in nature of "child support," so as not to be dischargeable in bankruptcy. Bratton v. Frederick (Ohio App. 3 Dist., 01-31-1996) 109 Ohio App.3d 13, 671 N.E.2d 1030. Bankruptcy ⸺ 3365(8)

Chapter 7 case filed by above-median income debtors was not subject to being dismissed, on ability to pay theory, as abuse of provisions of that chapter, where, even if debtor-husband's child support obligation of $507 per month was removed as expense, based on fact that this obligation had been suspended during debtor-husband's unemployment, debtors still had substantial shortfall in their monthly budget. In re Sorrell (Bkrtcy.S.D.Ohio, 01-26-2007) 359 B.R. 167. Bankruptcy ⸺ 2253

The case law discussing whether debts are "actually in the nature of alimony, maintenance or support" is applicable and useful precedent in determining whether such debts should receive priority treatment. In re McLaughlin (Bkrtcy.N.D.Ohio, 02-01-2005) 320 B.R. 661. Bankruptcy ⸺ 2951

Statutory exception to discharge for debts for alimony, maintenance or support in connection with separation agreement, divorce decree or other order of court is broad enough to include award of past child support made by court of competent jurisdiction. In re Smith (Bkrtcy.S.D.Ohio, 09-24-2001) 273 B.R. 138. Bankruptcy ⸺ 3365(13)

Adversary proceeding brought by debtor for determination as to dischargeability of his obligation for past child support between time that he was adjudicated to be father of children and time, some years later, that he was ordered to provide support was premature, prior to determination by state court as to whether he had any obligation for such past child support; bankruptcy court was in no position to determine question of dischargeability in absence of specific award. In re Smith (Bkrtcy. S.D.Ohio, 09-24-2001) 273 B.R. 138. Bankruptcy ⟲ 3397

In proceeding to avoid, as preferential transfer, a prepetition seizure of tax refund by Internal Revenue Service (IRS) to satisfy debtor-taxpayer's past due child support obligation, Chapter 7 trustee had burden of showing that debt in question was assigned to another entity, as required under statutory exception to general nonavoidability of debtor's support payments. In re Sanks (Bkrtcy.N.D.Ohio, 05-29-2001) 265 B.R. 566. Bankruptcy ⟲ 2726.1(2)

Nondebtor spouse who seeks to hold a debt nondischargeable under the discharge exception for alimony, maintenance, or support must, at a minimum, establish that the following three elements are met: (1) debt(s) must have arisen "in connection" with a separation agreement, divorce decree, or other order of a court of record; (2) underlying debt(s) must actually be owed to the former spouse or child; and (3) debt(s) owed to the former spouse must actually be in the "nature of alimony or support." In re Luman (Bkrtcy.N.D.Ohio, 04-14-1999) 238 B.R. 697. Bankruptcy ⟲ 3365(1)

Purpose of third step of the *Calhoun* test for determining whether payments by debtor pursuant to divorce decree are in the nature of nondischargeable support, which requires court to examine whether amount of support provision is so excessive so as to be manifestly unreasonable under the traditional concepts of support, is to prevent a debtor from effectively contracting away his or her right and opportunity for a fresh start under the Bankruptcy Code. In re Luman (Bkrtcy.N.D.Ohio, 04-14-1999) 238 B.R. 697. Bankruptcy ⟲ 3365(12); Bankruptcy ⟲ 3366

In determining whether a debtor's assumption of debt pursuant to a divorce decree is in the nature of nondischargeable alimony, maintenance, or support, bankruptcy courts consider such relevant factors as the following: (1) disparity of earning power between the parties; (2) need for economic support and stability, (3) presence of minor children; (4) marital fault; (5) nature of the obligations assumed; (6) structure and language of parties' agreement or court's decree; (7) whether other lump sum or periodic payments were also provided; (8) length of the marriage; (9) age, health, and work skills of the parties; (10) whether obligation terminates upon the death or remarriage of the parties; (11) adequacy of support absent the debt assumption; and (12) evidence of negotiations or other understandings as to intended purposes of the assumption. In re Luman (Bkrtcy.N.D.Ohio, 04-14-1999) 238 B.R. 697. Bankruptcy ⟲ 3365(4)

Under third step of *Calhoun* test for determining whether payments made by a debtor pursuant to a divorce decree are in the nature of nondischarge-able support, Chapter 7 debtor's assumption of credit card debt in the amount of $20,451.73 was not manifestly unreasonable under traditional concepts of support; debtor's annual income was approximately $32,000, it was feasible that debtor could actually experience a positive monthly cash flow if extra income were imputed to debtor and debtor would reduce some of his questionable expenses, such as an expenditure for cable television, and nondebtor spouse was the residential parent of parties' child. In re Luman (Bkrtcy.N.D.Ohio, 04-14-1999) 238 B.R. 697. Bankruptcy ⟲ 3365(4); Bankruptcy ⟲ 3365(7)

Although a "hold harmless" provision in a separation agreement or divorce decree is strong evidence of an intent to create a support obligation, the lack thereof does not necessarily indicate that the underlying obligation is not in the nature of support, for nondischargeability purposes. In re Luman (Bkrtcy.N.D.Ohio, 04-14-1999) 238 B.R. 697. Bankruptcy ⟲ 3365(11)

Provision in divorce judgment requiring husband to hold wife harmless from husband's business debts was intended as nondischargeable "support" for parties' children. In re Sanders (Bkrtcy. N.D.Ohio, 09-13-1995) 187 B.R. 588. Bankruptcy ⟲ 3365(11)

Joint marital debts that Chapter 7 debtor assumed under divorce judgment entry came within discharge exception for support, where former wife's retention of house was necessary as support for minor children, nonpayment of debts could result in attachment of house by creditors, former wife lacked sufficient income to enable her to pay marital debts, and hold harmless provision of entry stated that bankruptcy filing should not be undertaken if it would affect former wife's right of ownership in house. In re Chapman (Bkrtcy.N.D.Ohio, 06-23-1995) 187 B.R. 573. Bankruptcy ⟲ 3365(4); Bankruptcy ⟲ 3365(6); Bankruptcy ⟲ 3365(11)

Merely because spousal and child support were otherwise provided for in divorce judgment entry did not establish that Chapter 7 debtor's assumption of marital debts under decree was not intended to provide support, and that discharge exception for support was inapplicable. In re Chapman (Bkrtcy. N.D.Ohio, 06-23-1995) 187 B.R. 573. Bankruptcy ⟲ 3365(4)

Calhoun test for determining whether debt is nondischargeable child support obligation did not apply to order entered for sole purpose of designating rights and obligations of unmarried parents with respect to their minor child. In re Kidd (Bkrtcy. S.D.Ohio, 02-14-1995) 177 B.R. 876. Bankruptcy ⟲ 3365(13)

"Right to receive," as expressed in Ohio statute exempting from claims of creditors right to receive spousal support, child support, allowance or other maintenance to extent necessary to support person or his dependents, includes payments previously ordered, but not yet due, as well as payments due, but not paid as of date of bankruptcy filing; because parent to whom arrearage is owed has first responsibility to use arrearages for benefit of child, arrearages may be held exempt from claims of creditors to extent such usage is reasonably necessary support, determination which is factual issue requiring an evidentiary hearing. In re Davis (Bkrtcy.S.D.Ohio, 05-06-1994) 167 B.R. 104. Exemptions ⬡ 37

To determine if college assistance payments for children's education are dischargeable, courts must examine whether intent of state court or the parties was to create a support obligation, whether the support provision has actual effect of providing necessary support, whether amount of support is so excessive as to be unreasonable under traditional concepts of support, and if amount of support is unreasonable what part should be characterized as nondischargeable in bankruptcy. Matter of Bush (Bkrtcy.S.D.Ohio 1993) 154 B.R. 69. Bankruptcy ⬡ 3365(13)

Support payments do not have to be in form of monthly payments to be considered nondischargeable "support." In re Oberley (Bkrtcy.N.D.Ohio 1993) 153 B.R. 179. Bankruptcy ⬡ 3365(13)

Medical expenses incurred due to birth of debtor's child were nondischargeable as "support." In re Oberley (Bkrtcy.N.D.Ohio 1993) 153 B.R. 179. Bankruptcy ⬡ 3365(13)

In determining whether debt is nondischargeable as "support," courts are required to determine if debt is so high that it is considered unreasonable under "traditional concepts of support." In re Oberley (Bkrtcy.N.D.Ohio 1993) 153 B.R. 179. Bankruptcy ⬡ 3365(13)

Debtor's obligation to pay $5 per week to county department of human services for child's past medical expenses was not unreasonable burden on debtor, and, accordingly, obligation could be found nondischargeable as "support," even though it would take debtor over 200 years to pay off entire debt based on weekly payments of $5. In re Oberley (Bkrtcy.N.D.Ohio 1993) 153 B.R. 179. Bankruptcy ⬡ 3365(13)

A retroactive $15 per week child support obligation imposed on the father in a paternity suit begun when the child was aged sixteen years cannot be discharged in the father's bankruptcy action. In re Smith (Bkrtcy.N.D.Ohio 1992) 139 B.R. 864.

An $11,000 obligation resulting from the compromise of a paternity action is a support payment to the child that cannot be discharged in the father's bankruptcy action where the amount was based on analysis of what would have been required for support had a declaration of paternity applied from the date of birth to the time of the agreement and from certain medical expenses relating to the birth. In re Wilson (Bkrtcy.S.D.Ohio 1989) 109 B.R. 283. Bankruptcy ⬡ 3365(13)

Unpaid child support that accrued before the support obligation ended and that would have supported the children if paid when due is a debt that cannot be discharged in the father's bankruptcy. In re Matyac (Bkrtcy.S.D.Ohio 1989) 102 B.R. 125.

The Bankruptcy Code at 11 USC 523(a)(5) is apparently devised to prevent a debtor from discharging in bankruptcy obligations to support his former wife and children imposed on him under the divorce decree even if the "support" is in the form of paying a debt jointly owed by the man and woman to a third party; thus, a debtor's agreement to hold his former wife harmless on joint debts cannot be discharged in bankruptcy to the extent his agreement is found to be "in payment of alimony, maintenance or support." In re Shelton (Bkrtcy.S.D.Ohio 1988) 92 B.R. 268.

An obligation imposed on a father under a divorce decree to maintain medical insurance covering children is considered an obligation of support and thus cannot be discharged in his bankruptcy proceedings. In re Shelton (Bkrtcy.S.D.Ohio 1988) 92 B.R. 268.

A party claiming that an award in a divorce decree constitutes "support" has the burden of proving it is support money even though the parties termed it such in the separation agreement; thus, absent evidence of the parties' intentions and of a former wife's assets, education, and needs, a bankruptcy court will not find an award of $4000 monthly for 126 months to be "support" payments that cannot be discharged in the former husband's bankruptcy proceedings. In re Skaggs (Bkrtcy.S.D.Ohio 1988) 91 B.R. 1018.

Where a separation agreement provides that a laborer earning more than $28,000 yearly pay a $4,700 second mortgage on the home of the wife and children while she pays the first mortgage, taxes, and other expenses, and where the wife's new husband maintains his own separate residence, the first husband's obligation is "support" for shelter, at least for the minor children, is not unreasonable in relation to his income, and as a result is not discharged by his bankruptcy. In re Mizen (Bkrtcy. N.D.Ohio 1987) 72 B.R. 251.

A father who signed private school tuition contracts with his wife, was thereafter divorced by her, was sued by her and lost a judgment for the tuition amount, and who soon afterward filed for bankruptcy, is relieved of liability for the wife's judgment where the divorce decree provided for support and did not mention the contracts, and there is no proof the state court awarding the judgment considered the sum to be support. In re Motley (Bkrtcy. N.D.Ohio 1987) 69 B.R. 406.

11. Federal non-bankruptcy involvement

Trial court acted within its discretion in refusing to place former husband's funds from refinancing of marital residence in escrow to protect former wife from any future failure of former husband to pay child support, in contempt action arising from nonpayment of child support; former husband had claimed that child support payments garnished from former husband's paychecks were less than amount ordered due to federal law that barred garnishment of more than 50 percent of employee's wages. Duncan v. Duncan (Ohio App. 9 Dist., Summit,

01-28-2004) No. 21593, 2004-Ohio-326, 2004 WL 133169, Unreported. Child Support ☞ 496

While federal law is controlling in determining dischargeability of debt as alleged support obligation, state law may be used as source of guidance in developing federal standards for determining nature of debt. Bratton v. Frederick (Ohio App. 3 Dist., 01-31-1996) 109 Ohio App.3d 13, 671 N.E.2d 1030. Bankruptcy ☞ 3366

Trial court did not abuse its discretion in temporarily suspending child support while it was waiting for continuation of hearing on former husband's motion to terminate child support; court suspended payments because child's needs were being met by government during child's tenure with Federal Job Corps. In re Owens (Ohio App. 2 Dist., 08-12-1994) 96 Ohio App.3d 429, 645 N.E.2d 130. Child Support ☞ 375

Ohio domestic relations court had jurisdiction to consider propriety of representative payee's expenditure of Social Security Administration funds received on behalf of child whose father was disabled; Social Security Administration had no interest in funds once they were paid, and state court jurisdiction was not precluded by statute or nature of particular case. Catlett v. Catlett (Clermont 1988) 55 Ohio App.3d 1, 561 N.E.2d 948, motion overruled 39 Ohio St.3d 730, 534 N.E.2d 357. Courts ☞ 489(1)

The domestic relations exception to federal jurisdiction applies only where a plaintiff positively sues in federal court for divorce, alimony, or child custody. Catz v. Chalker (C.A.6 (Ohio), 04-16-1998) 142 F.3d 279, opinion amended on denial of rehearing 243 F.3d 234. Federal Courts ☞ 8

12. Imprisonment effect

A child support obligor who is incarcerated and loses his ability to work as the result of his criminal acts is voluntarily underemployed because the criminal act and its consequences are treated as being voluntary. Foley v. Foley (Ohio App. 11 Dist., Lake, 06-29-2001) No. 2000-L-121, 2001 WL 735738, Unreported.

Imprisonment because of criminal conduct is "voluntary" and, as such, will no longer be considered a "change in circumstances" justifying modification of a child support obligation; contempt proceedings should not go forward while the man is already jailed, however. Richardson v Ballard, 113 App(3d) 552, 681 NE(2d) 507 (Butler 1996).

13. Income of obligor

Trial court did not abuse its discretion in declining to impute income to ex-husband for child support modification purposes; ex-husband voluntarily left a job paying more than $67,000.00 annually for one paying less than $45,000.00, trial court utilized the lower figure for ex-husband's guidelines worksheet income, ex-husband stated that he was not fired from the higher-paying job but simply left for unspecified personal reasons, and, since statute did not provide an explicit definition of "underemployment," appellate court was not inclined to substi-

tute its judgment regarding ex-husband's income level for that of the trial court in these circumstances. Pace v. Pace (Ohio App. 5 Dist., Tuscarawas, 08-02-2010) No. 10 AP 02 0008, 2010-Ohio-3573, 2010 WL 3011083, Unreported. Child Support ☞ 259; Child Support ☞ 557(4)

Income could not be imputed to wife, who was unemployed, for purposes of determining husband's future obligation to pay child support, in divorce action, where wife's unemployment was not voluntary. Zbydnowski v. Zbydnowski (Ohio App. 8 Dist., Cuyahoga, 07-08-2010) No. 93863, 2010-Ohio-3198, 2010 WL 2690589, Unreported. Child Support ☞ 90

Trial court's denial of husband's request for evidentiary hearing and for limited discovery regarding wife's income was not an abuse of discretion, as to determination of husband's child support obligation pursuant to trial court's reserved jurisdiction after issuance of divorce decree; husband had ample opportunity during discovery to depose wife regarding her income, trial court, which had issued posttrial order finding wife in contempt and sentencing her to 30 days in jail unless she complied with court order to submit documentation regarding her income, must have believed the documents submitted by wife satisfied the purge order since no jail time was ordered for wife, and the case involved years of discovery and litigation and a 33-day trial. Halliday v. Halliday (Ohio App. 8 Dist., Cuyahoga, 07-08-2010) No. 93763, 2010-Ohio-3194, 2010 WL 2690504, Unreported. Child Support ☞ 182; Child Support ☞ 210

Trial court substantially complied with requirement of issuing findings of fact and conclusions of law regarding former husband's child support obligation, where journal entry stated that trial court considered the parties' tax returns in determining the child support obligation, and trial court attached a child support worksheet indicating how the support was calculated. Halliday v. Halliday (Ohio App. 8 Dist., Cuyahoga, 07-08-2010) No. 93763, 2010-Ohio-3194, 2010 WL 2690504, Unreported. Child Support ☞ 215

Trial court's decision to impute $20,000 of income to wife on review of spousal award was not arbitrary, even though court found wife to have been a stay-at-home mom who had not worked, except part time, where divorce decree, which reflected an agreement entered into by the parties, stated at the time the court reviewed the spousal award in 24 months, it would consider the wife's income if it was greater than $20,000 per year, or impute no less than $20,000 per year of income to wife. Vengrow v Vengrow (Ohio App. 9 Dist., Summit, 06-09-2010) No. 24907, 2010-Ohio-2568, 2010 WL 2298823, Unreported. Divorce ☞ 614; Divorce ☞ 628(1)

Trial court in divorce proceeding did not abuse its discretion in computing former husband's income for child support purposes; former husband was self employed and his income was not easily determined given that certain tax returns were not provided to the court. Onyshko v. Onyshko (Ohio App. 11 Dist., Portage, 03-12-2010) No. 2008-P-0035, 2010-Ohio-969, 2010 WL 891335, Unreported. Child Support ☞ 339(3)

Trial court did not abuse its discretion in proceeding on divorced mother's motion to modify father's child support obligation by including in father's income the entire amount derived by father's current wife from office building owned by wife and occupied by father's medical practice; building was purchased by father and wife jointly and then deeded to wife for tax reasons. Lyons v. Bachelder (Ohio App. 5 Dist., Morrow, 09-08-2005) No. 2004AP0017, 2005-Ohio-4966, 2005 WL 2300226, Unreported. Child Support ☞ 265

Evidence at hearing on divorced mother's motion to modify father's child support obligation did not support father's contention that $19,869 amount that trial court included in father's income for particular year, representing half of the contribution of father's medical practice toward father's pension, actually represented half of the practice's contribution toward the pensions of all employees, and that half of the contribution toward his own pension was only $9,934; exhibit to father's appellate brief with which he supported his contention was not introduced in the trial court. Lyons v. Bachelder (Ohio App. 5 Dist., Morrow, 09-08-2005) No. 2004AP0017, 2005-Ohio-4966, 2005 WL 2300226, Unreported. Child Support ☞ 542

Trial court did not abuse its discretion in modifying husband's child support obligation; shared parenting agreement did not require change in factual situation of children, and husband's income had substantially increased. Bailey v. Bailey (Ohio App. 5 Dist., Stark, 04-19-2004) No. 2003CA00319, 2004-Ohio-2004, 2004 WL 858741, Unreported. Child Support ☞ 240; Child Support ☞ 258

Money former husband received for minor work he had done for company was properly included in his annual salary, for purposes of determining child support award; although husband claimed income was nonrecurring, his W-2s for two years indicated that he received an average of $25,117 in income from company, and husband did not testify that income would cease. Gerlach v. Gerlach (Ohio App. 10 Dist., Franklin, 03-30-2004) No. 03AP-22, No. 03AP-872, 2004-Ohio-1607, 2004 WL 625686, Unreported. Child Support ☞ 89

Money former husband received from his company for travel/entertainment expenses was properly included in his annual salary, for purposes of determining child support award; husband provided no documentation for expenses, and his own accountant testified that husband should have documentation to support these expenses. Gerlach v. Gerlach (Ohio App. 10 Dist., Franklin, 03-30-2004) No. 03AP-22, No. 03AP-872, 2004-Ohio-1607, 2004 WL 625686, Unreported. Child Support ☞ 99

Loans former husband received from his company over and above his salary and shareholder distributions were properly included in his annual salary, for purposes of determining child support award; husband testified that he used loans to pay personal expense, husband was majority shareholder of company and did not need approval to loan himself monies, and there was no written documentation to show that he was obligated to repay company for loans. Gerlach v. Gerlach (Ohio App. 10 Dist., Franklin, 03-30-2004) No. 03AP-22, No. 03AP-872, 2004-Ohio-1607, 2004 WL 625686, Unreported. Child Support ☞ 99

Former husband's claims that trial court erred in failing to add former wife's spousal support award to her salary in calculating child support, and in determining that husband's child support obligation was higher than minimum total child support obligation for parents with combined annual income greater than $150,000, were moot, since trial court's amended order reduced total child support obligation to minimum and added wife's spousal support award to her salary. Gerlach v. Gerlach (Ohio App. 10 Dist., Franklin, 03-30-2004) No. 03AP-22, No. 03AP-872, 2004-Ohio-1607, 2004 WL 625686, Unreported. Child Support ☞ 552

Finding that husband was not voluntarily underemployed was not abuse of discretion, for purpose of calculating husband's child support obligation following divorce, where, following his job termination, husband obtained plumber's license and was trying hard to earn good income. Arnott v. Arnott (Ohio App. 9 Dist., Summit, 04-30-2003) No. 21291, 2003-Ohio-2152, 2003 WL 1983819, Unreported, motion granted 99 Ohio St.3d 1525, 793 N.E.2d 496, 2003-Ohio-4303, appeal not allowed 99 Ohio St.3d 1545, 795 N.E.2d 683, 2003-Ohio-4671. Child Support ☞ 88

Refusing to impute income to husband based on his inflated income estimate on automobile credit application was not abuse of discretion, for purpose of calculating husband's child support obligation following divorce, where husband testified that his gross receipts were less than listed on application and that he inflated income on application in order to be approved for loan. Arnott v. Arnott (Ohio App. 9 Dist., Summit, 04-30-2003) No. 21291, 2003-Ohio-2152, 2003 WL 1983819, Unreported, motion granted 99 Ohio St.3d 1525, 793 N.E.2d 496, 2003-Ohio-4303, appeal not allowed 99 Ohio St.3d 1545, 795 N.E.2d 683, 2003-Ohio-4671. Child Support ☞ 201

Refusing to impute to husband full time wage of $55 per hour was not abuse of discretion, for purpose of calculating husband's child support obligation following divorce, where husband did not testify that he earned that rate on full time basis and husband testified that business was sometimes slow and that some jobs were billed on flat fee. Arnott v. Arnott (Ohio App. 9 Dist., Summit, 04-30-2003) No. 21291, 2003-Ohio-2152, 2003 WL 1983819, Unreported, motion granted 99 Ohio St.3d 1525, 793 N.E.2d 496, 2003-Ohio-4303, appeal not allowed 99 Ohio St.3d 1545, 795 N.E.2d 683, 2003-Ohio-4671. Child Support ☞ 201

Evidence supported court's determination that divorced father could afford to pay one-half of his minor child's parochial school tuition, despite father's contention that he had incurred credit card debt furnishing his new residence, and had a monthly deficit of $1,563.15; court had examined evidence regarding the financial situation of both mother and father, and mother worked three jobs to provide for herself and her two children. Worthen v. Worthen (Ohio App. 2 Dist., Clark, 10-18-2002) No. 2002 CA 33, 2002-Ohio-5587, 2002 WL 31341597, Unreported. Child Support ☞ 201

An obligor who deliberately redirects part of his income to his new wife to avoid child support obligations perpetrates a fraud upon the court which consequently awards retroactive support payments to remedy the results of the scheme to defraud the court. Leffel v. Leffel (Ohio App. 2 Dist., Clark, 10-24-1997) No. 97-CA-20, 1997 WL 666102, Unreported.

Trial court's decision to impute to father his "potential" income for purposes of child support was not per se abuse of discretion. In re Yeauger (Union 1992) 83 Ohio App.3d 493, 615 N.E.2d 289. Child Support ☞ 89

For purposes of comparing parties' prospective standards of living to determine whether divorce obligations are dischargeable, each party's projected income should be measured by his or her realistic earning potential, not by lifestyle or other choices which restrict income. In re Findley (Bkrtcy. N.D.Ohio, 03-02-2000) 245 B.R. 526. Bankruptcy ☞ 3367(3)

Evidence did not support defendant's affirmative defense of inability to pay, in prosecution for failure to pay child support; evidence showed that defendant kept large amounts of cash at home, and that defendant told ex-wife in e-mail that he would keep his money for himself and his children. State v. Roders (Ohio App. 9 Dist., Summit, 07-31-2002) No. 20962, 2002-Ohio-3867, 2002 WL 1758903, Unreported. Child Support ☞ 663

Magistrate's decision that father only owed mother $45.41 for medical expenses of their children and attorney fees was against the manifest weight of the evidence; mother presented uncontradicted evidence indicating that medical bills totaled $4,468.97 and that she had paid $2,458.12, and on two occasions, father admitted to not paying the medical expenses despite receiving bills from mother. Geschke v. Smercina (Ohio App. 8 Dist., Cuyahoga, 07-25-2002) No. 79409, 2002-Ohio-3768, 2002 WL 1729907, Unreported. Child Support ☞ 487

14. Jurisdiction

Trial court was without jurisdiction to extend terms of husband's spousal obligation, where trial court retained jurisdiction in the original divorce decree only to modify spousal support payments in regard to the amount, but not the duration. Vengrow v. Vengrow (Ohio App. 9 Dist., Summit, 06-09-2010) No. 24907, 2010-Ohio-2568, 2010 WL 2298823, Unreported. Divorce ☞ 623

Trial court had subject matter jurisdiction to prosecute Georgia defendant for criminal nonsupport of child who resided in Ohio and who suffered consequences of defendant's nonsupport in Ohio. State v. Coley (Ohio App. 1 Dist., Hamilton, 10-15-2004) No. C-040031, 2004-Ohio-5498, 2004 WL 2315024, Unreported. Criminal Law ☞ 97(.5)

Trial court lacked personal jurisdiction over father to enter child support order against him, due to defective service of process of motion to set support; docket sheet showed that father was served with motion to set child support by ordinary mail only, rather than by certified mail, or express mail, as required by rule, so continuing jurisdiction of juvenile court was not invoked, and, due to failure to provide notice, any subsequent order based on void order was nullity. In re Brandon P. (Ohio App. 6 Dist., Lucas, 04-11-2003) No. L-02-1230, 2003-Ohio-1861, 2003 WL 1861564, Unreported. Child Support ☞ 180

Where domestic relations court has previously entered child support order in divorce case and child who is beneficiary of that support order is subsequently found to be delinquent in juvenile court, domestic relations court and juvenile court have concurrent jurisdiction to entertain motions regarding that support order. Machaterre v. Looker (Ohio App. 6 Dist., Lucas, 01-17-2003) No. L-02-1155, 2003-Ohio-220, 2003 WL 139772, Unreported. Child Support ☞ 173

Trial court had subject matter jurisdiction to award child support arrearages to mother once child had reached age of majority. In re Buechter (Ohio App. 2 Dist., Miami, 10-18-2002) No. 2002-CA-22, 2002-Ohio-5598, 2002 WL 31341567, Unreported, motion to certify allowed 98 Ohio St.3d 1407, 781 N.E.2d 1017, 2003-Ohio-60, cause dismissed 98 Ohio St.3d 1481, 784 N.E.2d 1183, 2003-Ohio-1076. Child Support ☞ 460

Missouri modification of child support order was entitled to full faith and credit in Ohio, despite ex-husband's claim that Missouri court did not have jurisdiction, as ex-husband was afforded a full opportunity to litigate question of personal jurisdiction when he entered his initial, limited appearance before Missouri court to contest that issue, and ex-husband thereafter failed to appeal in Missouri from Missouri trial court's determination that it could exercise personal jurisdiction over him, such that Missouri court's resolution of issue of personal jurisdiction was res judicata. Emig v. Massau (Ohio App. 10 Dist., 11-16-2000) 140 Ohio App.3d 119, 746 N.E.2d 707. Child Support ☞ 506(2)

Domestic relations court's jurisdiction includes the determination and subsequent modification of child support. Trump v. Trump (Ohio App. 9 Dist., 11-17-1999) 136 Ohio App.3d 123, 736 N.E.2d 39. Child Custody ☞ 601; Child Support ☞ 11; Child Support ☞ 232

A trial court that enters a decree for child support has continuing jurisdiction over matters relating to child support and has full power to enforce its decree, to modify it as the parties' changing circumstances require, and to order the payment of support arrearages. Jefferies v. Stanzak (Ohio

App. 12 Dist., 10-18-1999) 135 Ohio App.3d 176, 733 N.E.2d 305. Child Support ☞ 232; Child Support ☞ 440

Domestic relations court has continuing jurisdiction to enforce a prior child support order by reducing an overpayment of child support to a judgment or granting a credit in favor of the obligor. Jefferies v. Stanzak (Ohio App. 12 Dist., 10-18-1999) 135 Ohio App.3d 176, 733 N.E.2d 305. Child Support ☞ 454

Four years after dissolution of parties' marriage, Court of Common Pleas did not have jurisdiction to decide parentage and ultimately award child support for child conceived after dissolution through artificial insemination. Bailey v. Bailey (Ohio App. 4 Dist., 02-29-1996) 109 Ohio App.3d 569, 672 N.E.2d 747. Children Out–of–wedlock ☞ 15

In order for trial court to maintain continuing jurisdiction over issue of child support, there must have been minor child either born or conceived prior to entry of final judgment in dissolution. Bailey v. Bailey (Ohio App. 4 Dist., 02-29-1996) 109 Ohio App.3d 569, 672 N.E.2d 747. Child Support ☞ 232

Court of Appeals could not say that domestic relations court abused its discretion in suspending father's child support obligation, notwithstanding statute prohibiting court from authorizing or permitting withholding of child support payment based on denial of or interference with visitation rights; mother took children to her native England, out of reach of American courts, with specific intent of denying father and children their mutual rights of companionship, children were being adequately supported, and it was in best interest of children that father had financial resources to pursue his rights of companionship in English courts. Miller v. Miller (Ohio App. 6 Dist., 11-19-1993) 92 Ohio App.3d 340, 635 N.E.2d 384, motion overruled 69 Ohio St.3d 1424, 631 N.E.2d 164. Child Custody ☞ 874

Judgment in form of child support and alimony can be awarded as part of valid divorce decree where court obtains jurisdiction over real or personal property of defendant and, in essence, transforms nature of award to in rem or quasi in rem. Meadows v. Meadows (Hancock 1992) 73 Ohio App.3d 316, 596 N.E.2d 1146. Child Support ☞ 173; Divorce ☞ 590

Insufficient minimum contacts exist with Ohio to warrant assumption of personal jurisdiction over a father in a child support action where the parties are married and reside in California, the mother removes herself and the children to Ohio and obtains a divorce in an Ohio court, the father has only briefly visited Ohio twice to visit his children, and he owns no property in Ohio. Meadows v. Meadows (Hancock 1992) 73 Ohio App.3d 316, 596 N.E.2d 1146.

A domestic relations court which granted a divorce retains jurisdiction for the purposes of granting visitation rights as required by the best interest of any children born as issue of the marriage re-gardless of the existence or venue of a subsequent stepparent adoption proceeding. Bente v. Hill (Clermont 1991) 73 Ohio App.3d 151, 596 N.E.2d 1042, dismissed, jurisdictional motion overruled 62 Ohio St.3d 1422, 577 N.E.2d 1105. Child Custody ☞ 313; Child Custody ☞ 404; Divorce ☞ 154

The failure to support one's minor children constitutes a tortious act or omission in Ohio conferring in personam jurisdiction; thus, in personam jurisdiction exists over a nonresident mother whose children are in the care of guardians who are receiving aid to dependent children for purposes of a support action brought against the mother by a county bureau of support. Wayne Cty. Bur. of Support v. Wolfe (Wayne 1991) 71 Ohio App.3d 765, 595 N.E.2d 421.

Transfer of jurisdiction of a case concerning enforcement of an order for child support is within the discretion of the court to refuse, even though the desired transferee court consents to the transfer. Bieniek v. Bieniek (Medina 1985) 27 Ohio App.3d 28, 499 N.E.2d 356, 27 O.B.R. 29.

In any case where a court of common pleas has made an award of custody or an order for support, or both, of minor children, that court may certify the case to the juvenile court of any county in the state for further proceedings. Pylant v. Pylant (Huron 1978) 61 Ohio App.2d 247, 401 N.E.2d 940, 15 O.O.3d 407. Courts ☞ 483

The authority vested in a court by 3109.05, in extreme circumstances, includes the authority to give relief, through a just modification of an order of support, to a parent continuously or repeatedly prevented from exercising a right to visit a child by the child's refusal to visit with him; but such jurisdiction should not be exercised until the court first considers whether to make the child a party pursuant to Civ R 75(B)(2). Foster v. Foster (Franklin 1974) 40 Ohio App.2d 257, 319 N.E.2d 395, 69 O.O.2d 250. Child Support ☞ 306; Child Support ☞ 324

Court has jurisdiction and duty to require father to pay adequate support for his minor children whether or not there was an express reservation of continuing jurisdiction in original divorce decree; and where original divorce decree made no order of support, though it approved provisions of separation agreement, modification of support payments may be made without showing changed circumstances. Gilmore v. Gilmore (Ohio Com.Pl. 1971) 28 Ohio Misc. 161, 275 N.E.2d 646, 57 O.O.2d 272. Child Support ☞ 59

When the question of custody only comes before a court, under the authority granted in 2151.23(A)(2), that court has jurisdiction to include in the award of custody an order for the support of such child. Kolody v. Kolody (Summit 1960) 110 Ohio App. 260, 169 N.E.2d 34, 13 O.O.2d 25.

Court of Appeals lacked jurisdiction to hear former husband's appeal of portion of trial court's non-final order which reinstated former wife's voluntarily dismissed motion for modification of child support and established the original date of filing of that motion as the retroactivity date for purposes of adjusting child support. Fisher v. Fisher (Ohio App. 10 Dist., Franklin, 05-21-2002) No. 01AP-1041, 2002-Ohio-3086, 2002 WL 1020152, Unreported. Child Support ☞ 537

This section confers jurisdiction to hear a motion for modification of a foreign decree of child support when the child is an Ohio resident. Bowden v Bowden, No. L–84–212 (6th Dist Ct App, Lucas, 12–14–84).

A court has no jurisdiction to modify a visitation decree where the party was not served pursuant to Civ R 75(I). Jenkins v Jenkins, No. 1504 (4th Dist Ct App, Lawrence, 12–9–81).

RC 3109.05 does not impliedly permit the retroactive application of a support order to a time prior to the institution of the divorce proceedings, because the trial court lacks jurisdiction to retroactively apply an award of child support to a time prior to the court's subject matter jurisdiction; to maintain an action for support prior to a court order for child support, one must file an action based on the common law seeking compensation for necessaries furnished to the minor child. Liggins v Liggins, No. 796 (4th Dist Ct App, Ross, 11–9–81).

Where the father received no notice pursuant to the rules of procedure that the continuing jurisdiction of the court had been invoked to modify his visitation rights, the court of appeals will reverse because the father is entitled to attend such a hearing with a clear understanding of its purpose. Harris v Harris, No. 1593 (2d Dist Ct App, Clark, 10–22–81).

While a domestic relations court which grants a divorce has continuing jurisdiction over all matters pertaining to child custody and support, it has no authority to retroactively modify the total amount due and payable under its prior order for support of minor children in this action involving a change of custody. Kuntz v Kuntz, No. 78AP-831 (10th Dist Ct App, Franklin, 7–5–79).

15. Modification of support—In general

Trial court did not err by denying father's motion to increase child support on the grounds of a change in circumstance; father's failure to provide trial court with a transcript of magistrate's proceeding precluded the trial court from conducting a proper review of magistrate's factual findings as to whether a change of circumstance had occurred which would have justified a modification of mother's child support obligation. Pagonis v. Steele (Ohio App. 9 Dist., Summit, 09-22-2010) No. 25189, 2010-Ohio-4459, 2010 WL 3676997, Unreported. Children Out–of–wedlock ☞ 67

Fact that divorced father was found to be indigent for purposes of obtaining appointed counsel and transcripts at court expense did not constitute a judicial determination that he was unable to pay child support, so as to warrant excusing him from his child support obligation; determinations of indigency for purposes of counsel and court fees were

made liberally so as to preserve the due process right to access to the courts, and were not conclusive as to father's ability to pay child support. U.S.C.A. Const.Amend. 14. Evans v. Evans (Ohio App. 10 Dist., Franklin, 09-27-2005) No. 04AP-816, No. 04AP-1208, 2005-Ohio-5090, 2005 WL 2364976, Unreported. Child Support ☞ 617

Divorced father who sought modification of his child support obligation based, in part, on his allegations that he was disabled due to a fall from a roof was not prejudiced by trial court's refusal to consider deposition and letter from his family physician as to the extent of his injuries and work restrictions; medical conclusions in deposition and letter were entirely duplicative of earlier letter from same physician that was admitted into evidence. Evans v. Evans (Ohio App. 10 Dist., Franklin, 09-27-2005) No. 04AP-816, No. 04AP-1208, 2005-Ohio-5090, 2005 WL 2364976, Unreported. Child Support ☞ 558(4)

Trial court did not abuse its discretion in ordering effective date of mother's child support obligation, on modification of custody from mother to father, to be same date that father's support obligation terminated. Dadosky v. Dadosky (Ohio App. 4 Dist., Pike, 06-27-2005) No. 04CA732, 2005-Ohio-3496, 2005 WL 1594861, Unreported. Child Support ☞ 364

Provision of divorce decree relieving husband of duty to pay child support was subject to modification. Layne-Burnett v. Burnett (Ohio App. 2 Dist., Montgomery, 05-20-2005) No. 20660, 2005-Ohio-2510, 2005 WL 1207963, Unreported. Child Support ☞ 232

Modification of child support as to parties' out-of-wedlock child became effective as of date motion was filed. McCage v. Dingess (Ohio App. 5 Dist., Licking, 10-13-2004) No. 03CA111, 2004-Ohio-5692, 2004 WL 2391678, Unreported. Children Out–of–wedlock ☞ 64

Wife failed to establish that the trial court erroneously shifted the burden of proof onto her to prove that a substantial change of circumstances warranting a modification of child support had not occurred, in post-divorce proceeding to reduce husband's child support obligation; magistrate and trial court records established that the burden of proof was correctly placed upon husband. Nickoloff v. Nickoloff (Ohio App. 9 Dist., Lorain, 07-07-2004) No. 03CA008415, 2004-Ohio-3565, 2004 WL 1496852, Unreported. Child Support ☞ 336

Record supported finding that former husband's standard of living had increased since entry of child support order, and that former wife was paying expenses related to parties' son's college tuition, for purposes of determining whether modification of child support was warranted; at time of divorce, husband's stock in family business was valued at $200,000, and just over two years after divorce, husband received well over one million dollars from sale of business, and court heard evidence regarding wife's expenses for son's college tuition. Rex v. Rex (Ohio App. 8 Dist., Cuyahoga, 03-04-2004) No.

82864, 2004-Ohio-997, 2004 WL 396369, Unreported. Child Support ☞ 339(3); Child Support ☞ 339(4)

Trial court properly attributed to former husband income received at last full-time job for purposes of imputing former husband's income in making post-divorce modification to child support obligation, although former husband attributed end of employment to problems flowing from his medical condition, because evidence indicated both that former husband was capable of earning same amount as he was previously making and that former husband's health did not prevent him from resuming such employment. Graham v. Graham (Ohio App. 10 Dist., Franklin, 01-28-2003) No. 02AP-720, 2003-Ohio-351, 2003 WL 178881, Unreported. Child Support ☞ 260

Former husband's allegedly inequitable conduct in evading discovery requests while former husband and former wife each were seeking modification of former husband's child support obligation was not related to his request for a credit for child support overpayments he had made under valid court orders, and thus, unclean hands doctrine did not preclude former husband from receiving credit for overpayments. Offenberg v. Offenberg (Ohio App. 8 Dist., Cuyahoga, 01-23-2003) No. 78885, No. 79425, No. 78886, No. 79426, 2003-Ohio-269, 2003 WL 152814, Unreported. Child Support ☞ 350

Trial court acted within its discretion in denying mother's request to have an attorney appointed to represent her in proceeding to modify father's child support obligation, where trial court found that mother was not indigent. Church v. Gadd (Ohio App. 11 Dist., Geauga, 12-20-2002) No. 2001-G-2398, 2002-Ohio-7129, 2002 WL 31866165, Unreported. Child Support ☞ 340

A trial court did not abuse its discretion in an action to modify a child support order by finding a substantial change in circumstances justifying a ninety-two per cent increase in the father's obligation where his gross income has increased twenty-five per cent and his teenage daughter's financial needs have increased since the divorce due to her involvement in extra-curricular high-school activities, and her driving expenses and increased clothing costs over the previous three years. Holt v. Troha (Ohio App. 2 Dist., Greene, 08-02-1996) No. 96-CA-19, 1996 WL 430866, Unreported.

A trial court abuses its discretion when it orders the suspension of a child support obligation for a period of eighteen months due to the residential parent's noncompliance with the visitation schedule. Roberts v. Roberts (Ohio App. 10 Dist., Franklin, 07-20-1995) No. 95APF01-33, 1995 WL 432612, Unreported.

Former wife's voluntary decision to quit her guidance counseling job and take another one that paid $15,000 less but was in a community closer to her home and children did not warrant imputing potential income to her in determining whether to modify her $550 monthly child support obligation, where she was still working as a counselor and was earning the most she could in the closer community. Shank v. Shank (Ohio App. 3 Dist., 08-04-1997) 122 Ohio App.3d 189, 701 N.E.2d 439, appeal not allowed 80 Ohio St.3d 1471, 687 N.E.2d 299. Child Support ☞ 259; Child Support ☞ 260

Requiring wife to pay first $100 of extraordinary medical expenses per year per child rather than first $150, with balance to be paid 20% by wife and 80% by husband, did not violate local rule stating that custodial parent would pay ordinary health care expenses not exceeding $150 per year per child, and in fact any deviation from local rule benefitted husband by excusing him from paying any portion of first $100 of uninsured extraordinary expenses. Shaffer v. Shaffer (Ohio App. 3 Dist., 02-09-1996) 109 Ohio App.3d 205, 671 N.E.2d 1317. Child Support ☞ 149

Former husband's failure to pay past due and owing college expenses and medical expenses, as required under separation agreement and modification order, justified contempt finding; former husband's motion to modify filed after contempt proceeding was instituted was not viable defense and husband offered no evidence of alleged inability to pay. Rohrbacher v. Rohrbacher (Lucas 1992) 83 Ohio App.3d 569, 615 N.E.2d 338. Child Support ☞ 459; Child Support ☞ 487

Generally, changed circumstances relied upon to obtain modification of child support order must not have been within knowledge or contemplation of court when decree was entered, and must be substantial. Osborne v. Osborne (Meigs 1992) 81 Ohio App.3d 666, 611 N.E.2d 1003. Child Support ☞ 234; Child Support ☞ 235

Modification of award of child support normally requires two-step determination: determination whether there has been change of circumstance and, if so, redetermination of amount of child support. Osborne v. Osborne (Meigs 1992) 81 Ohio App.3d 666, 611 N.E.2d 1003. Child Support ☞ 340

To modify a child support agreement, the court must go through a two-step analysis: (1) determining if there has been a change in circumstances, and (2) if so, reanalyzing the amount of support necessary. Dudziak v. Dudziak (Cuyahoga 1992) 81 Ohio App.3d 361, 611 N.E.2d 337. Child Support ☞ 233; Child Support ☞ 350

Incarceration of a child support obligor, standing alone, does not warrant a finding of change of circumstances; arrearages accrued during the incarceration of the obligor can be paid after release by way of a supplement to the original order. Cole v. Cole (Erie 1990) 70 Ohio App.3d 188, 590 N.E.2d 862.

Denial of modification of child support despite the incarceration of the obligor does not constitute cruel and unusual punishment as continuation of the support order does not constitute a fine, nor is the denial a violation of equal protection as a support order may remain in force on one who is voluntarily unemployed; incarceration is the result of a voluntary willful act. Cole v. Cole (Erie 1990) 70 Ohio App.3d 188, 590 N.E.2d 862.

The intentional act of a parent which results in incarceration is not voluntary, and a motion for termination or modification of support because of this change in circumstances is justifiable; a father's incarceration bears a close resemblance to a situation where an employer terminates an individual's employment. Peters v. Peters (Warren 1990) 69 Ohio App.3d 275, 590 N.E.2d 777, motion overruled 57 Ohio St.3d 711, 568 N.E.2d 697.

To modify child support, court must apply two-step analysis that determines whether change of circumstances exists and, if so, redetermines appropriate amount of child support under statutes and under child support guidelines. Miller v. Barker (Cuyahoga 1989) 64 Ohio App.3d 649, 582 N.E.2d 647. Child Support ☞ 233; Child Support ☞ 356

A modification of an existing support order is justified where the moving party demonstrates a substantial change of circumstances which renders unreasonable an order which was once reasonable; evidence constituting a substantial change of circumstances justifying modification of an original support order includes the wife's fraudulent misrepresentation that the child she was carrying at the time of marriage was that of her husband and the results of blood test excluding the moving party as the father. Carson v. Carson (Brown 1989) 62 Ohio App.3d 670, 577 N.E.2d 391, motion overruled 46 Ohio St.3d 716, 546 N.E.2d 1334.

Public policy underlying statutory provision for modification of child support is that parental relationships and obligations continue after parents divorce each other and that children have right to expect same support and care they could have reasonably expected if their parents had remained married. Colizoli v. Colizoli (Ohio 1984) 15 Ohio St.3d 333, 474 N.E.2d 280, 15 O.B.R. 458. Child Support ☞ 290

In an action for modification of child support, the "relevant factors" set out in RC 3109.05 must be considered, and an order of modification based solely upon evidence of the supporting parent's resources and needs is improperly granted. Cooper v. Cooper (Van Wert 1983) 10 Ohio App.3d 143, 460 N.E.2d 1137, 10 O.B.R. 194.

Evidence of the inflation rate and its effect on the financial resources of the parents and the needs of the child may be considered within the entire context of proving the existence of changes in circumstances necessary to justify modification of an existing support order. Bright v. Collins (Franklin 1982) 2 Ohio App.3d 421, 442 N.E.2d 822, 2 O.B.R. 514. Child Support ☞ 236

In order to justify an increase in an existing support order, there must be a finding supported by evidence that either (1) the amount necessary for child support is greater than it was at the time of the original order, or (2) a greater amount is reasonable in view of the parents' increased resources. Bright v. Collins (Franklin 1982) 2 Ohio App.3d 421, 442 N.E.2d 822, 2 O.B.R. 514. Child Support ☞ 254; Child Support ☞ 274

The determination of child support must be achieved in two steps: first, the monetary amount necessary for the child's support in the standard of living he would have enjoyed had the marriage continued, including the child's educational needs and opportunities, must be established; then, the support obligation must be divided equitably between the parents in proportions reasonable under all circumstances, including the financial resources and needs of both parents. In many instances it would be unreasonable to require the parents to pay the full amount necessary to support the child in the standard of living he would have enjoyed had the marriage continued. Cheek v. Cheek (Franklin 1982) 2 Ohio App.3d 86, 440 N.E.2d 831, 2 O.B.R. 95.

To determine child support, the monetary amount necessary for the support of the children in a standard of living commensurate with the incomes of their parents should first be established; then the proportionate share of the child support so established that each parent equitably should bear should be set. In re Machmer (Franklin 1981) 2 Ohio App.3d 84, 440 N.E.2d 829, 2 O.B.R. 93. Child Support ☞ 62

Where the evidence shows the father's income has increased by 50 per cent in the past five years and the mother's income has increased by 250 per cent, the trial court erred by not finding a substantial change in circumstances. In re Machmer (Franklin 1981) 2 Ohio App.3d 84, 440 N.E.2d 829, 2 O.B.R. 93.

3109.05 applies to modification proceedings as well as original proceedings. Martin v. Martin (Summit 1980) 69 Ohio App.2d 78, 430 N.E.2d 962, 23 O.O.3d 102.

RC 3109.05 does not permit an automatic termination of support if visitation privileges are denied without cause, but requires a determination based upon evidence as to what, if any, modification of support is just, which necessarily includes an evaluation of the needs of a child for support against the right of a parent to visit with such child and a balancing of the equities involved. Foster v. Foster (Franklin 1974) 40 Ohio App.2d 257, 319 N.E.2d 395, 69 O.O.2d 250.

Upon a motion to modify custody provisions of a divorce decree, a court is not limited to any particular line of inquiry, nor is it bound by strict legal rules governing the introduction of evidence, and, while hearsay evidence alone is insufficient to support a modification of a custody order, the court may properly consider reports of court-appointed social workers. Woodruff v. Woodruff (Ohio Com. Pl. 1965) 7 Ohio Misc. 87, 217 N.E.2d 264, 36 O.O.2d 165. Child Custody ☞ 632

An order of a divorce court increasing the support payments required of a father for the declared purpose of "the support of the children" is a valid order, notwithstanding one of the children is a high school graduate, intends to acquire a college education, has had part-time employment and saves some of his earnings toward a college education. Ford v. Ford (Miami 1959) 109 Ohio App. 495, 167 N.E.2d 787, 12 O.O.2d 67. Child Support ⬤ 293

Where the circumstances of a non-custodial parent have improved subsequent to the divorce, and child support costs have increased, fault should not be attributed to the custodial parent because she chose to take a lower paying job in order to be able to live with her parents. Pitcher v Pitcher, No. 83AP–530 (10th Dist Ct App, Franklin, 2–28–84).

A motion to terminate a child support decree will be denied where a man marries a pregnant woman with full knowledge of her condition, because the law conclusively presumes that he is father of the child, and even a failure to permit or admit blood tests to disprove paternity is not in error. Humphrey v Humphrey, No. C–800312 (1st Dist Ct App, Hamilton, 5–6–81).

Where trial court merely recites that the statutory factors set forth in RC 3109.05 have been considered without a specific showing of the basis upon which a modification of a child support order is made, the judgment of the trial court will be reversed and remanded for a showing of such a basis. Coleman v Coleman, No. L–82–005 (6th Dist Ct App, Lucas, 5–7–82).

16. —— Benefits paid by third party, modification of support

Federal preemption principles did not serve to preclude downward modification of child support arrearage payments derived from Social Security withholdings; trial court had jurisdiction to enter order governing payment of child support arrearage, state-imposed obligation did not conflict with discretionary decision by Social Security Administration to withhold even more money, nor did trial court's withholding notice act as an obstacle to any federal purpose. Wortham v. Wortham (Ohio App. 2 Dist., Montgomery, 09-24-2010) No. 23831, 2010-Ohio-4524, 2010 WL 3722775, Unreported. Child Support ⬤ 442

Social security payments received by a child for a parent's disability should be considered in calculating child support where the disabled parent is the obligee. Edmonds v. Edmonds (Ohio App. 4 Dist., Athens, 09-19-1994) No. 93CA1604, 1994 WL 514890, Unreported, appeal not allowed 71 Ohio St.3d 1466, 644 N.E.2d 1388.

Disabled parent is entitled to a full credit in his or her child support obligation for Social Security payments received by a minor child due to the parent's disability. Williams v. Williams (Ohio, 05-17-2000) 88 Ohio St.3d 441, 727 N.E.2d 895, 2000-Ohio-375, reconsideration denied 89 Ohio St.3d 1443, 731 N.E.2d 688. Child Support ⬤ 165

Social Security payments made on a minor child's behalf, due to a parent's disability, are not mere gratuities from the federal government, nor do they constitute earnings by the child, for child support purposes; instead, the payments arise simply because the obligor has paid into the Social Security

system and was found to be disabled. Williams v. Williams (Ohio, 05-17-2000) 88 Ohio St.3d 441, 727 N.E.2d 895, 2000-Ohio-375, reconsideration denied 89 Ohio St.3d 1443, 731 N.E.2d 688. Child Support ⬤ 106

Social Security payments made on a minor child's behalf, due to a parent's disability, are tantamount to earnings by the disabled parent, for purposes of determining parent's child support obligation. Williams v. Williams (Ohio, 05-17-2000) 88 Ohio St.3d 441, 727 N.E.2d 895, 2000-Ohio-375, reconsideration denied 89 Ohio St.3d 1443, 731 N.E.2d 688. Child Support ⬤ 106

Granting a disabled parent a credit for Social Security benefits does not retroactively modify the disabled parent's monthly child support obligation; it merely changes the source of the payments. Williams v. Williams (Ohio, 05-17-2000) 88 Ohio St.3d 441, 727 N.E.2d 895, 2000-Ohio-375, reconsideration denied 89 Ohio St.3d 1443, 731 N.E.2d 688. Child Support ⬤ 165; Child Support ⬤ 364

Social security payments for a child's benefit must be considered in connection with child support payments ordered to be made by the parent whose retirement triggers the payments, but this does not justify crediting the entire monthly benefit amount to child support, nor is the determination of necessary child support unaffected by the receipt of the benefits; the proper method is to deduct all or part of the benefit amount from the guideline-determined necessary support based on the child's best interest and equity to both parents. McNeal v. Cofield (Franklin 1992) 78 Ohio App.3d 35, 603 N.E.2d 436.

A domestic relations court does not abuse its discretion in ordering a representative payee to place in trust for the benefit of a child the excess social security funds not needed for her current needs. Catlett v. Catlett (Clermont 1988) 55 Ohio App.3d 1, 561 N.E.2d 948, motion overruled 39 Ohio St.3d 730, 534 N.E.2d 357.

An Ohio domestic relations court may consider the propriety of a representative payee's expenditure of social security disability benefits received on behalf of a child. Catlett v. Catlett (Clermont 1988) 55 Ohio App.3d 1, 561 N.E.2d 948, motion overruled 39 Ohio St.3d 730, 534 N.E.2d 357.

Social security payments received on behalf of a minor child as a result of a parent's disability may be credited toward that parent's support obligation commencing at such time as the benefit is received and not exceeding the monthly support obligation set forth in the decree of divorce, and such credit is not a retroactive modification of a child support order, but is merely a credit against the arrearage. Pride v. Nolan (Hamilton 1987) 31 Ohio App.3d 261, 511 N.E.2d 408, 31 O.B.R. 546. Child Support ⬤ 454

When an obligor's estate is bound to pay child support after the obligor's death, social security death benefits paid to the child should be credited against the support obligation. Gilford v. Wurster

(Lorain 1983) 24 Ohio App.3d 77, 493 N.E.2d 258, 24 O.B.R. 145.

Social security benefits which a handicapped child receives under the supplemental security income program do not alter the noncustodial parent's obligation for his support nor constitute a change of circumstances warranting a modification of child support order. Oatley v. Oatley (Lucas 1977) 57 Ohio App.2d 226, 387 N.E.2d 245, 11 O.O.3d 260. Child Support ⇒ 296

Seven years of child support arrearages cannot be discharged in bankruptcy even where the husband ceased payment because the wife began receiving $465 each month for the children from her next husband's social security, and she then gave the children to her mother to raise yet only gave her mother $150 each month for doing so. In re Troxell (Bkrtcy.S.D.Ohio 1986) 67 B.R. 328.

The receipt by a child of supplemental security income neither alters the father's obligation nor constitutes a change of circumstances warranting a modification of support. Justice v Justice, No. CA–3250 (5th Dist Ct App, Licking, 6–24–87).

Where a minor child is receiving veterans administration benefits payable to the custodial parent for the support of such child due to the death of the child's stepfather, the noncustodial parent is not entitled to offset the amount of such benefits against the noncustodial parent's obligation to pay child support. Houser v Houser, No. CA–2887 (5th Dist Ct App, Licking, 9–24–82).

The trial court did not err when it declined to hold the appellee in contempt of court for child support arrearages as it chose to credit the social security benefits received on behalf of the minor children to the arrearage that accrued after the social security disability payments began; since the monies received exceeded the amount owed under the child support order, the trial court did not err in refusing to reduce the alleged arrearage to judgment. Yuhasz v Yuhasz, No. 42193 (8th Dist Ct App, Cuyahoga, 11–28–80).

Child support benefits received upon a parent's retirement may be credited against the parent's child support obligation because a credit for social security child support payments on retirement merely reflects the fact that the amounts due have been paid, and in no respect alters the obligation of the parent or the award to the children. Curnutte v Delarino, No. 2974 (9th Dist Ct App, Lorain, 9–3–80).

Where a father who has been ordered to make child support payments becomes totally and permanently disabled, and unconditioned Social Security payments for the benefit of minor children are paid to the divorced mother, the father is entitled to credit such payments by the government against his liability for child support under the divorce decree, but the father is entitled to credit, however, only up to the extent of his obligation for monthly payments of child support, but not exceeding it; the excess paid each month must be regarded under the divorce decree as a gratuity to the children. Loucks

v Loucks, No. 18619 (6th Dist Ct App, Ottawa, 6–13–80).

17. ——— Change in parental rights and responsibilities, modification of support

Former husband was not entitled to an increased credit for health insurance that he provided for his minor children; only evidence husband submitted with respect to health care expenditures was that he provided health insurance for the children at a cost of $90 per month for one year, and magistrate was under no obligation to assist husband in eliciting information regarding his financial expenditures. Unger v. Unger (Ohio App. 12 Dist., Brown, 12-30-2004) No. CA2003-10-013, 2004-Ohio-7136, 2004 WL 3015751, Unreported. Child Support ⇒ 339(5)

Where the custodial parent does not provide child support and the child resides with the noncustodial parent who provides full support in kind while the child attends high school, the custodial parent is not entitled to support arrearage for such time as full support is provided by the noncustodial parent; since the noncustodial parent is providing child support, the amount he was ordered to pay should be credited to the arrearage for that time. Peterson v. Hunt (Ohio App. 3 Dist., Allen, 10-15-1998) No. 1-98-25, 1998 WL 720690, Unreported.

A child who temporarily leaves the home of a parent will not be considered emancipated for child support purposes if the child remains dependant on a parent for care and attends high school on a full-time basis. Matter of Siefker v. Siefker (Ohio App. 3 Dist., Putnam, 10-23-1997) No. 12-97-09, 1997 WL 658995, Unreported.

False testimony of an adverse party in a divorce proceeding, that the husband was the father of a child fourteen years before, does not warrant a finding of fraud upon the court; this is intrinsic fraud, time-barred by the one-year statute of limitations of Civ 60(B)(3). Still v. Still (Ohio App. 4 Dist., Gallia, 06-25-1996) No. 95CA15, 1996 WL 362259, Unreported.

Denial of an obligor's motion to terminate his child support obligation for his nineteen-year-old severely handicapped child is error where the court fails to recognize the child's ability to support himself from a trust fund in excess of $200,000 received as settlement of a medical malpractice action that occurred after the child's parents divorced. Mitchell v. Mitchell (Ohio App. 6 Dist., Erie, 09-23-1994) No. E-93-77, 1994 WL 518183, Unreported.

Former husband's court-ordered child support obligation for daughter who was initially placed in custody of his former wife did not terminate merely because custody of daughter was transferred to husband. Lytle v. Lytle (Ohio App. 10 Dist., 12-15-1998) 130 Ohio App.3d 697, 720 N.E.2d 1007, dismissed, appeal not allowed 85 Ohio St.3d 1464, 709 N.E.2d 171. Child Support ⇒ 396

When support is paid in accordance with child support order, courts are reluctant to order a refund to obligor because of facts and circumstances learned after support has been paid; to avoid that prospect, support orders should require obligee to notify obligor of any change in circumstances underlying the support order. Swanson v. Swanson (Ohio App. 2 Dist., 02-09-1996) 109 Ohio App.3d 231, 671 N.E.2d 1333. Child Support ☞ 223; Child Support ☞ 230; Child Support ☞ 364

Trial court could not order ex-husband to visit his multihandicapped child as a form of child support; determination of child support obligation was governed by comprehensive statutory scheme that did not provide for visitation as a form of support. Hamilton v. Hamilton (Ohio App. 6 Dist., 10-27-1995) 107 Ohio App.3d 132, 667 N.E.2d 1256, appeal not allowed 75 Ohio St.3d 1425, 662 N.E.2d 27. Child Custody ☞ 175; Child Support ☞ 223

Reduction in former husband's income as result of voluntary resignation to start his own company was not shown to be substantial change of circumstances and, therefore, did not entitle former husband to modification of child support; trial court could conclude that former husband failed to give adequate weight to duty to support children. Woloch v. Foster (Ohio App. 2 Dist., 11-23-1994) 98 Ohio App.3d 806, 649 N.E.2d 918. Child Support ☞ 259

Child who was ordered out of his mother's home and then enrolled in Federal Job Corps program was not yet emancipated, for purposes of determining whether former husband's child support obligation continued; mother continued to provide child with money and assistance, child went to live with his father and then his uncle upon leaving his mother's home, and mother provided child with money for long-distance phone calls when child was in program, and paid for his bus ticket when he left program. In re Owens (Ohio App. 2 Dist., 08-12-1994) 96 Ohio App.3d 429, 645 N.E.2d 130. Child Support ☞ 386; Child Support ☞ 395

Trial court's adding on remand only $500 to $2,200 sustenance alimony award already determined by Court of Appeals to be inadequate was abuse of discretion, where trial court, on remand, adopted Court of Appeals' findings and determined wife's monthly expenses to be approximately $4,000; consideration of award to wife of portion of bonus to which husband was entitled through his employment, which was more in nature of division of property, did not render alimony award reasonable. Kaechele v. Kaechele (Franklin 1992) 83 Ohio App.3d 468, 615 N.E.2d 273. Divorce ☞ 1322(1)

Where a consent order is entered which changes the custody of minor children but such change never takes place, the trial court, in subsequently considering child support, has jurisdiction to award a lesser amount to the de facto custodial parent other than that set forth in a prior order. Ollangg v. Ollangg (Franklin 1979) 64 Ohio App.2d 17, 410 N.E.2d 789, 18 O.O.3d 11.

RC 3109.05 does not permit an automatic termination of support if visitation privileges are denied without cause, but requires a determination based upon evidence as to what, if any, modification of support is just, which necessarily includes an evaluation of the needs of a child for support against the right of a parent to visit with such child and a balancing of the equities involved. Foster v. Foster (Franklin 1974) 40 Ohio App.2d 257, 319 N.E.2d 395, 69 O.O.2d 250.

Child support order did not terminate on death of children's mother, and thus father had duty by judicial decree to support his children, even though juvenile court never ordered that support be paid to grandparents or aunt and uncle who had custody of children, where neither party requested modification of support order. In re Adoption of Morelli (Ohio App. 7 Dist., Jefferson, 09-19-2002) No. 02 JE 5, No. 02 JE 6, 2002-Ohio-5045, 2002 WL 31114885, Unreported, stay granted 97 Ohio St.3d 1426, 777 N.E.2d 845, 2002-Ohio-5854, appeal not allowed 97 Ohio St.3d 1471, 779 N.E.2d 237, 2002-Ohio-6347. Child Support ☞ 375

Trial court's order that downward deviation from Ohio Child Support Guidelines be retroactive to date on which father moved to modify child support obligation was abuse of discretion in proceeding in which mother moved successfully to modify shared parenting plan to permit her to relocate with parties' children to Arizona, where trial court based deviation solely on father's estimated transportation costs were he to exercise his visitation rights three times per year without hearing any evidence on what it would actually cost to fly children round trip from Arizona. Harbottle v. Harbottle (Ohio App. 9 Dist., Summit, 09-18-2002) No. 20897, 2002-Ohio-4859, 2002 WL 31060237, Unreported. Child Support ☞ 364

A child support order will not be amended retroactively on the ground that minor children who lived with their mother at the time of a joint custody order took up residence with their father less than a month thereafter, where it is found that the order for payment of child support to the mother was made in contemplation of the children living with the father. Palladino v Palladino, No. 48378 (8th Dist Ct App, Cuyahoga, 12–27–84).

18. —— Dependency tax exemptions, modification of support

Trial court did not abuse its discretion in finding ex-wife in contempt for refusing to sign and return tax documents for dependency exemption and granting attorney fees in favor of ex-husband in the amount of $3,000.00; ex-wife had received at least two written requests from ex-husband, with forms enclosed, to sign and return tax documents for the dependency exemption, ex-wife had simply refused to sign them, and there was no rationalization for such refusal. Pace v. Pace (Ohio App. 5 Dist., Tuscarawas, 08-02-2010) No. 10 AP 02 0008, 2010-Ohio-3573, 2010 WL 3011083, Unreported. Child Support ☞ 444

Any error the trial court made in determining that provision of divorce decree relating to payment of motorcycle racing expenses of parties' two sons was indefinite but not ambiguous and that husband's obligations were not limited to expenses incurred in connection with races in which husband participated was harmless; court denied the wife's motion that husband be held in contempt for failure to reimburse her for the racing expenses and any interpretation the trial court gave the racing expenses provision of the prior divorce decree was advisory only. Bond v. Bond (Ohio App. 2 Dist., Miami, 12-23-2004) No. 04CA8, 2004-Ohio-7253, 2004 WL 3561212, Unreported. Child Support ☞ 558(4)

Trial court properly considered all relevant statutory factors in awarding former husband only two of the parties' three children as federal income tax exemptions, and thus Court of Appeals would not substitute its judgment for that of trial court on issue. Gerlach v. Gerlach (Ohio App. 10 Dist., Franklin, 03-30-2004) No. 03AP-22, No. 03AP-872, 2004-Ohio-1607, 2004 WL 625686, Unreported. Child Support ☞ 557(3)

Father waived his appellate argument that he was entitled to the income tax exemption for out-of-wedlock child because granting mother the exemption might result in mother qualifying for the earned income credit, in child custody case, where father failed to raise the issue in the trial court, and the issue was speculative. Kauble v. Pfeiffer (Ohio App. 3 Dist., Marion, 12-22-2003) No. 9-03-36, 2003-Ohio-6988, 2003 WL 22994559, Unreported. Children Out–of–wedlock ☞ 20.11

Father was not entitled to the income tax exemption for out-of-wedlock child, where mother was designated as the residential parent of child. Kauble v. Pfeiffer (Ohio App. 3 Dist., Marion, 12-22-2003) No. 9-03-36, 2003-Ohio-6988, 2003 WL 22994559, Unreported. Children Out–of–wedlock ☞ 20.9

Former wife should have been ordered to amend her tax return, since she inappropriately took child dependency tax exemption, which should have been awarded to former husband, who was gainfully employed. Avery v. Avery (Ohio App. 2 Dist., Greene, 09-19-2003) No. 2002 CA 121, No. 2003 CA 1, No. 2002 CA 105, 2003-Ohio-4975, 2003 WL 22159477, Unreported, appeal not allowed 101 Ohio St.3d 1421, 802 N.E.2d 153, 2004-Ohio-123. Child Support ☞ 141

Trial court abused its discretion by ordering that tax dependency exemption alternate between the custodial parent and non-residential parent as the record and transcript did not reveal any evidence regarding any tax savings that would result from awarding the tax dependency exemption to one parent or the other. Pentzer v. Thomas (Ohio App. 12 Dist., Fayette, 02-14-2000) No. CA99-09-026, 2000 WL 190019, Unreported.

An award of the dependency tax exemption to a wife who does not have custody is error where the parents have comparable incomes in the same tax bracket. Wolfangel v. Wolfangel (Ohio App. 9 Dist., Summit, 05-24-1995) No. 16868, 1995 WL 312697, Unreported, appeal not allowed 74 Ohio St.3d 1422, 655 N.E.2d 741.

When determining whether awarding dependency tax exemption to nonresidential parent would produce a net tax savings for the parents, a trial court should review all pertinent factors, including the parents' gross incomes, the exemptions and deductions to which the parents are otherwise entitled, and the relevant federal, state and local income tax rates. Corple v. Corple (Ohio App. 7 Dist., 09-26-1997) 123 Ohio App.3d 31, 702 N.E.2d 1234. Child Support ☞ 141

Trial court abused its discretion in divorce proceeding by awarding husband, who was nonresidential parent, the dependency tax exemption for parties' minor child, where record did not indicate that trial court found net tax savings to parties or that best interest of child was furthered in awarding exemption to husband. Corple v. Corple (Ohio App. 7 Dist., 09-26-1997) 123 Ohio App.3d 31, 702 N.E.2d 1234. Child Support ☞ 141

Husband's challenge to trial court's failure to award him income tax exemptions for minor children of marriage in judgment of divorce was waived by husband's failure to object to referee's report on this issue. Shaffer v. Shaffer (Ohio App. 3 Dist., 02-09-1996) 109 Ohio App.3d 205, 671 N.E.2d 1317. Child Support ☞ 539

Trial court did not err in splitting children's tax exemptions between father and mother even though father, pursuant to shared-parenting plan, was residential parent of children for nine months of year. Eickelberger v. Eickelberger (Ohio App. 12 Dist., 02-22-1994) 93 Ohio App.3d 221, 638 N.E.2d 130. Child Support ☞ 141

Dependency exemption provided by Internal Revenue Code may be awarded to noncustodial parent when that allocation would produce net tax savings for parents, thereby furthering best interest of child. Singer v. Dickinson (Ohio 1992) 63 Ohio St.3d 408, 588 N.E.2d 806. Child Support ☞ 141

As alternative to contempt to enforce award of dependency tax exemption, court may consider that exemption when considering parents' financial resources; where noncustodial parent would experience greater tax benefit from exemption he should generally receive it, and when custodial parent refuses to surrender exemption at order of court, noncustodial parent's support obligation may be reduced accordingly. Esher v. Esher (Medina 1989) 63 Ohio App.3d 394, 579 N.E.2d 222. Child Support ☞ 351; Child Support ☞ 467

Since a trial court may properly award the dependency exemption to either parent in the best interest of the child, even where the parents were never married, the dependency exemption is a matter concerning the duty of support pursuant to RC 3109.05, and not the division of property, and accordingly, the trial court retains jurisdiction over the award of this exemption during the minority of the child. Esber v. Esber (Medina 1989) 63 Ohio App.3d 394, 579 N.E.2d 222.

In an action for the modification of child support, a trial court errs in ruling that it lacks jurisdiction to allocate the child dependency tax exemption and therefore, on remand, the court must consider the tax exemption issue and determine whether the exemption benefits the children best in the hands of their custodial mother or their noncustodial father and then whether any increase or decrease in support is necessary. Esber v. Esber (Medina 1989) 63 Ohio App.3d 394, 579 N.E.2d 222.

Although a contempt of court action in a state court could be used to force an unwilling parent to part with his tax exemption when the court considers that an award of the tax exemption to the other parent would be in the best interest of the child, as an alternative solution the court may consider the tax exemption when considering the financial resources of the parents pursuant to RC 3109.05 and where the noncustodial parent would experience the greater tax benefit from the exemption, he should generally receive the exemption since the additional disposable income generated can be considered for additional child support, and when the custodial parent refuses to surrender the exemption at the order of the court, the court may reduce the noncustodial parent's support obligation accordingly. Esber v. Esber (Medina 1989) 63 Ohio App.3d 394, 579 N.E.2d 222.

Where there was no provision in divorce decree concerning which parent was entitled to claim dependency exemptions for minor children, trial court could consider whether noncustodial parent's inability to claim dependency exemption would result in a substantial reduction in income so as to warrant reduction of child support obligation. Mettler v. Mettler (Ross 1988) 61 Ohio App.3d 14, 572 N.E.2d 127. Child Support ☞ 250; Child Support ☞ 351

The tax exemption for dependent children awarded to the custodial parent as part of the division of property may not be subsequently modified by a court. Mettler v. Mettler (Ross 1988) 61 Ohio App.3d 14, 572 N.E.2d 127.

Tax exemptions for children are "marital property," notwithstanding the fact that the separation agreement incorporated within the dissolution decree treats the exemptions as a component of child support; therefore, a court lacks subject matter jurisdiction to subsequently modify the award of the exemptions. In re Lee (Ohio Com.Pl. 1989) 58 Ohio Misc.2d 4, 567 N.E.2d 1350.

The child support guidelines, C P Sup R 75, do not address the issue of tax exemptions; accordingly, there is no provision for taking into account the tax exemptions and the tax ramifications of child support in considering at what level to place child support. In re Lee (Ohio Com.Pl. 1989) 58 Ohio Misc.2d 4, 567 N.E.2d 1350.

As part of the division of marital property in a divorce proceeding, a domestic relations court may award the dependency exemption permitted in 26 USC 151, to the noncustodial parent. Such an order does not conflict with 26 USC 152, nor with the Sixteenth Amendment to the US Constitution. Hughes v. Hughes (Ohio 1988) 35 Ohio St.3d 165,

518 N.E.2d 1213, certiorari denied 109 S.Ct. 124, 488 U.S. 846, 102 L.Ed.2d 97.

Where a taxpayer's former wife is the lessee of real estate and pays her ex-husband a fixed rental, she is entitled to be credited with the lodging support for the minor children in determining whether the wife or husband has provided more than one-half support of the children for purposes of federal income tax dependency exemptions, since she has the right to use and possession of the property. Klofta v. U. S. (N.D.Ohio 1970) 333 F.Supp. 781, 64 O.O.2d 291.

An award of the dependency tax exemption to the noncustodial parent which appears in the property division section of the divorce decree is not properly linked to the amount of the child support obligation, nor is it to be modified upon modification of child support. Kozloski v Kozloski, No. CA87–10–141 (12th Dist Ct App, Butler, 6–30–88).

19. —— Guidelines, modification of support

Trial court did not abuse its discretion, in proceedings on former wife's motion for modification of child support, by increasing former husband's child support obligation, where modification was supported by sufficient evidence of change in circumstances resulting from termination of shared parenting plan, pursuant to which former husband had paid child support in less than guidelines amount and recalculated worksheet indicated child support obligation more than ten percent higher than amount former husband had been obliged to pay under shared parenting plan. Cherwin v. Cherwin (Ohio App. 8 Dist., Cuyahoga, 04-28-2005) No. 84875, 2005-Ohio-1999, 2005 WL 991706, Unreported. Child Support ☞ 236; Child Support ☞ 239

Father waived for appellate review the issue of whether the trial court erred in using 2001 tax returns as basis to deviate from child support guidelines in postdissolution change of custody and child support proceeding, where father knew the court intended to use the parties' tax returns and failed to object prior to court's final judgment. Carter v. Carter (Ohio App. 9 Dist., Summit, 01-22-2003) No. 21156, 2003-Ohio-240, 2003 WL 150090, Unreported. Child Support ☞ 539

Trial court acted within its discretion by not applying changes to child support guidelines, which allowed spousal support to be considered, to divorce judgment that was filed after effective date of changes, although child support statutes could be applied retroactively, where changes became effective after court conducted final hearing. Taylor v. Taylor (Ohio App. 7 Dist., Belmont, 12-12-2002) No. 01-BA-17, 2002-Ohio-6884, 2002 WL 31812684, Unreported. Child Support ☞ 144

Motion for modification of child support requires trial court to decide whether movant has demonstrated substantial change of circumstances; if substantial change of circumstances is demonstrated, court should make modification appropriate to statutory factors. Woloch v. Foster (Ohio App. 2

Dist., 11-23-1994) 98 Ohio App.3d 806, 649 N.E.2d 918. Child Support ⟨⟩ 234; Child Support ⟨⟩ 236

Trial court which adopted shared-parenting plan granting residential status to father during school year and to mother during summer months could properly determine that strict application of child support guidelines would be inappropriate and accordingly deny child support to father under circumstances that parties stipulated that cost of children's parochial education would be shared in proportion to their relative incomes, both parties were required to carry medical insurance for children, and parties were required to share cost of clothing, school supplies and other ordinary expenses. Eickelberger v. Eickelberger (Ohio App. 12 Dist., 02-22-1994) 93 Ohio App.3d 221, 638 N.E.2d 130. Child Support ⟨⟩ 148

A trial court errs when it orders a divorced mother to pay child support in accordance with the child support guidelines based on her income from a prior year without the benefit of evidence of the individualized criteria set forth in RC 3109.05. Carter v. Carter (Clermont 1989) 62 Ohio App.3d 167, 574 N.E.2d 1154. Child Support ⟨⟩ 146

Although the child support guidelines set forth in CP Sup R 75 are intended to be used by a court to indicate the appropriate level of child support to be ordered, the court still retains broad discretion to deviate from the guidelines if it substantiates its decision by stating its findings of fact; consequently, a child support order which deviates more than forty per cent from the guidelines may not be an abuse of discretion where the child support obligor incurs increased necessary living expenses due to relocation and remarriage. Hurdelbrink v. Hurdelbrink (Lucas 1989) 45 Ohio App.3d 5, 544 N.E.2d 700, motion overruled 44 Ohio St.3d 715, 542 N.E.2d 1112.

Although fact that level of child support called for by application of new guidelines would exceed by ten-percent level of child support provided for in preguidelines dissolution decree would be sufficient to justify increase in child support, father was entitled to evidentiary hearing on issue because guidelines were merely guidelines and did not supplant statutory requirement that court consider all relevant factors in determining amount reasonable or necessary for child support. Wogoman v. Wogoman (Miami 1989) 44 Ohio App.3d 34, 541 N.E.2d 128. Child Support ⟨⟩ 340; Child Support ⟨⟩ 356

The guidelines set forth in CP Sup R 75 are just that—guidelines; they are not intended to supplant the requirement in RC 3109.05 that courts must consider all relevant factors in determining the amount reasonable or necessary for child support, including the factors expressly stated in the statute. Wogoman v. Wogoman (Miami 1989) 44 Ohio App.3d 34, 541 N.E.2d 128.

In considering amount which is reasonable and necessary to support a child when a change of circumstances has occurred, needs of child must first be determined, guided by statutory factors, and determination of amount found to be necessary

must be tempered by ascertaining the amount of child support which is reasonable in view of the overall financial picture of the parents and of the child. Zacek v. Zacek (Franklin 1983) 11 Ohio App.3d 91, 463 N.E.2d 391, 11 O.B.R. 143. Child Support ⟨⟩ 254; Child Support ⟨⟩ 274; Child Support ⟨⟩ 290

The child support guidelines are not a mathematical straitjacket, and the refusal of a domestic relations court to consider evidence supporting deviation from the guidelines constitutes an abuse of discretion. Oyer v Oyer, No. CA88–03–007 (12th Dist Ct App, Madison, 9–19–88).

On a motion to reduce a child support obligation, where the trial court finds a change of circumstances but orders only a minimal reduction in support not in conformity with the support guidelines, the modification order will be remanded for computation in accordance with the guidelines, absent findings of fact warranting the deviation. Kozloski v Kozloski, No. CA87–10–141 (12th Dist Ct App, Butler, 6–30–88).

The use of child support guidelines to obtain calculation of child support level, without prorating custodial parent's proportion and without considering other factors, is an abuse of discretion. Johnson–Wagner v Wagner, No. CA2304 (2d Dist Ct App, Clark, 6–29–87).

When using child support guidelines, court must compute formula correctly. Further, a prior agreement regarding child support adjustments cannot bind the court or the parties for future child support which continues to be subject to the court's jurisdiction. Gross v Gross, No. 49018 (8th Dist Ct App, Cuyahoga, 5–30–85).

The trial court erred in ordering child support modification based solely upon the cost of living index without actual evidence of increased costs of child care expenses. Nichols v Nichols, No. 992 (11th Dist Ct App, Geauga, 5–28–82).

Where a judgment for child support is tied to the consumer price index, and the father seeks credit for overpayment of his obligation, the trial court erred by allowing the credit because the child is the true party in interest and the child's needs have increased, and further, the father has the ability to pay the increased support. Firebaugh v Firebaugh, No. L–81–016 (6th Dist Ct App, Lucas, 8–28–81).

The adoption of the child support guidelines found in CP Sup R 75 has extinguished the burden of demonstrating a change of circumstances in order to obtain modification of a child support order. Andreas v Andreas, No. CA–7559 (5th Dist Ct App, Stark, 11–7–88).

20. —— Income and expense statements, modification of support

Evidence supported finding that there was a change of circumstances to warrant recalculation of former husband's child support obligation; husband's incarceration, which was the result of his voluntary criminal actions, did not constitute a change in circumstances, however former wife's substantial increase in her income constituted a change in circumstances warranting the reduction of former husband's support obligation. L.B. v. T.B. (Ohio App. 2 Dist., Montgomery, 07-08-2011) No. 24441, 2011-Ohio-3418, 2011 WL 2671915, Unreported. Child Support ⟁ 277

Any error resulting from trial court using a child support guideline worksheet that omitted spousal support mother received from father as additional annual income to her, or that failed to reflect father's child support expenses, was harmless and did not require remand, where the record on appeal included a complete worksheet used by trial court in earlier decree, and the imputed incomes therein had not changed. Longo v. Longo (Ohio App. 11 Dist., Geauga, 06-30-2010) No. 2008-G-2874, No. 2009-G-2901, 2010-Ohio-3045, 2010 WL 2636843, Unreported. Child Support ⟁ 558(2); Child Support ⟁ 559

Trial court was not required to rely on statutory child support guideline worksheet or the basic child support guideline schedule to determine amount of father's child support obligation, where parties' combined gross income was over $150,000, and trial court determined that the applicable child support schedule was insufficient to meet the needs and standard of living the parties had established for themselves and their children. Longo v. Longo (Ohio App. 11 Dist., Geauga, 06-30-2010) No. 2008-G-2874, No. 2009-G-2901, 2010-Ohio-3045, 2010 WL 2636843, Unreported. Child Support ⟁ 145

Trial court acted within its discretion when it conducted a hearing on mother's motion to modify child support without the benefit of father's income and expense statement; mother never filed a motion to compel father to complete the document, and mother's motion was based on her lack of income such that she was not prejudiced by the trial court holding the scheduled hearing without father's income and expense statement. Calhoun v. Calhoun (Ohio App. 8 Dist., Cuyahoga, 05-27-2010) No. 93369, 2010-Ohio-2347, 2010 WL 2106488, Unreported, appeal not allowed 127 Ohio St.3d 1462, 938 N.E.2d 364, 2010-Ohio-6008. Child Support ⟁ 340

21. —— Remarriage, modification of support

Upward deviation from child support worksheet in former husband's child support obligation, which resulted in obligation equalling nearly 68% of husband's earnings, was abuse of discretion. Julian v. Julian (Ohio App. 9 Dist., Summit, 03-24-2004) No. 21616, 2004-Ohio-1430, 2004 WL 574161, Unreported. Child Support ⟁ 159

Although trial court could consider benefit former husband received as a result of remarriage in determining whether to deviate from child support worksheet figure, nothing in the record supported trial court's determination former husband was saving at least $350.00 due to remarriage so as to support deviation in that amount. Julian v. Julian (Ohio App. 9 Dist., Summit, 03-24-2004) No. 21616,

2004-Ohio-1430, 2004 WL 574161, Unreported. Child Support ⟁ 148

A trial court's consideration of the income of a divorced father's new wife for the purpose of determining the amount of income the divorced father could pay in child support did not deny the new wife due process by taking her income without affording her notice or an opportunity to be heard since as she is not required to make child support payments for her husband, either directly or indirectly, she has not suffered any loss of property; court's decision was based on the rational conclusion that the divorced father's marriage to a wage-earning spouse will provide him with additional money for child support that might otherwise be required for his personal household expenses. Esber v. Esber (Medina 1989) 63 Ohio App.3d 394, 579 N.E.2d 222. Child Support ⟁ 265; Child Support ⟁ 324; Child Support ⟁ 340; Constitutional Law ⟁ 4410

In a modification of child support action, a trial court's determination of the amount of child support a divorced father should pay is reasonable and will not be disturbed based on a divorced father's argument that the court should not have considered all of his new wife's income, but only the amount of her income he actually received where the new wife's income was not the trial court's sole consideration but in addition, the court noted that the divorced father was trying to hide his true financial status. Esber v. Esber (Medina 1989) 63 Ohio App.3d 394, 579 N.E.2d 222. Child Support ⟁ 356

Remarriage of the custodial parent may be considered in determining whether to reduce the supporting parent's obligation. Snyder v. Snyder (Cuyahoga 1985) 27 Ohio App.3d 1, 499 N.E.2d 320, 27 O.B.R. 1.

RC 3109.05(E) requires that a court, in determining the "financial resources and needs of the noncustodial parent," consider the father's remarriage and its resulting new obligations, together with the other factors delineated in RC 3109.05, before either granting or denying a change in a previous child support order. Martin v. Martin (Summit 1980) 69 Ohio App.2d 78, 430 N.E.2d 962, 23 O.O.3d 102. Child Support ⟁ 255; Child Support ⟁ 260

The trial court did not abuse its discretion by its subsequent modification of a support order in favor of the plaintiff-wife, since the defendant-husband failed to show how the fact of his former wife's remarriage justified alteration in the reapportionment of child support obligations. Jeffries v Jeffries, No. 45634 (8th Dist Ct App, Cuyahoga, 5–19–83).

In an action appealing an order to increase child support, the court may consider the income of the father's present wife in determining his present ability to pay increased child support. Pearson v Pearson, No. 44880 (8th Dist Ct App, Cuyahoga, 12–23–82).

22. —— **Retroactivity, modification of support**

Retroactive modification of child support obligation to date of divorce hearing was not abuse of discretion, where obligee perpetrated fraud by including daycare expenses in child support calculation worksheet when she never intended to use formal daycare. Hanes v. Hanes (Ohio App. 3 Dist., Hancock, 04-29-2003) No. 5-02-55, 2003-Ohio-2131, 2003 WL 1960934, Unreported. Child Support ☞ 364

While existing child support orders may be modified retroactively, an order establishing retroactive child support obligations ancillary to a divorce proceeding is invalid. Trump v. Trump (Ohio App. 9 Dist., 11-17-1999) 136 Ohio App.3d 123, 736 N.E.2d 39. Child Support ☞ 150; Child Support ☞ 364

Custodial parent was not entitled to retroactive child support, where no support order was issued at time he was awarded custody subsequent to divorce and no motion seeking support was pending. Hannas v. Hannas (Ohio App. 11 Dist., 09-29-1997) 123 Ohio App.3d 378, 704 N.E.2d 294. Child Support ☞ 459

Evidence that husband committed fraud in misrepresenting amount of his annual income justified making order for increased child support effective from date of dissolution decree, rather than date from filing of motion of increase; if support figure could be retroactively ordered only to date of wife's motion, husband would still retain benefits of fraud he perpetrated upon wife and the court between dates of dissolution decree and wife's motion, which anomalous result would not be sanctioned. Osborne v. Osborne (Meigs 1992) 81 Ohio App.3d 666, 611 N.E.2d 1003. Child Support ☞ 460

Absent some special circumstance, an order of a trial court modifying child support should be retroactive to the date such modification was first requested; the effective date of modification must coincide with some significant event in the litigation, and an arbitrary date may not be employed. State, ex rel. Draiss, v. Draiss (Medina 1990) 70 Ohio App.3d 418, 591 N.E.2d 354.

When a father who has custody of a child and a court-ordered obligation of support transfers the child to the custody of its mother, the obligation of support remains, so that the mother's motion for support, made after a lapse of time since the transfer, is not to be denied as a motion for a retroactive order or modification. Royse v. Royse (Ohio Com. Pl. 1984) 23 Ohio Misc.2d 5, 491 N.E.2d 397, 23 O.B.R. 113.

A trial court does not abuse its discretion by ordering an increase in child support to be retroactive to the date the motion for modification was filed, since disposition of such motions often takes a substantial length of time. Murphy v. Murphy (Franklin 1984) 13 Ohio App.3d 388, 469 N.E.2d 564, 13 O.B.R. 471.

A trial court has jurisdiction to modify a support order as to future installments, whether or not the right is reserved in the decree; but it has no such jurisdiction to modify unpaid installment support payments which have accrued if the child for whose benefit support was awarded was living and not emancipated at the time of the accrual, unless the right to retrospective modification was specifically reserved in the decree. Wedebrook v. Wedebrook (Ohio Com.Pl. 1977) 51 Ohio Misc. 81, 367 N.E.2d 937, 5 O.O.3d 342. Child Support ☞ 232; Child Support ☞ 460

Child support order could be made retroactive to day that the first hearing was held regarding the appropriate amount of child support. Surface v. Grottla Kennedy (Ohio App. 2 Dist., Clark, 04-19-2002) No. 2001 CA 94, 2002-Ohio-1894, 2002 WL 628647, Unreported. Child Support ☞ 150

Retroactive child support order was improper, as it was not supported by required statutory findings and was unclear; order made no findings concerning father's or mother's incomes for years within retroactive term, father owed no "arrearages," as there was no prior order requiring support that father failed to pay, and amount of father's retroactive obligation was unclear. Woods v. Mt. Castle (Ohio App. 2 Dist., Clark, 04-19-2002) No. 01CA-0050, 2002-Ohio-1878, 2002 WL 628888, Unreported. Child Support ☞ 494; Child Support ☞ 496

23. —— **Sole responsibility/waiver, modification of support**

A proposed settlement of child support and custody disputes was not in the best interests of the child; the former husband was five-and-one-half years delinquent in child support, and the former wife waived a major portion of the court-ordered entitlements for the benefit of the child. In re Contemnor Caron (Ohio Com.Pl., 04-27-2000) 110 Ohio Misc.2d 58, 744 N.E.2d 787. Child Custody ☞ 35; Child Support ☞ 44

In an action seeking modification of a child support order, the initial determination is whether the order can (rather than should) be modified, requiring a finding of a substantial change in circumstances; in the unusual circumstance where one parent has expressly agreed to assume sole responsibility for the future support of the parties' children, if that parent later seeks to modify the order, the question is whether his circumstances have changed so much that he can no longer provide the entire support of the children; factors to be considered in such a determination include his assets which may be used to satisfy the support obligation, his income, his ability to earn extra income, and whether he can free up financial resources for the support of the children by limiting his own standard of living. Bahgat v. Bahgat (Franklin 1982) 8 Ohio App.3d 291, 456 N.E.2d 1239, 8 O.B.R. 386.

A court may reinstate an order for support and visitation rights, though the parties to the divorce signed an affidavit stating their intent to terminate the support and relinquish certain visitation rights. Green v. Green (Ohio Com.Pl. 1972) 31 Ohio Misc. 69, 286 N.E.2d 328, 60 O.O.2d 216. Child Custody ☞ 203; Child Support ☞ 45

Where a noncustodial mother inherits sixty thousand dollars, the trial court does not abuse its discretion in denying the father's motion for child support, notwithstanding that the father was ordered to pay support before he gained custody, where the father does not show that he is unable to provide for his children's needs and where the court finds that the mother desires use of the money for her own purposes. Griffith v Griffith, No. CA–84–07–078 (12th Dist Ct App, Butler, 12–17–84).

In an action for arrearages, the trial court rightly denied the right to recover past obligations where the parties had mutually agreed to discharge the continuing obligation to pay support in exchange for a waiver of a continuing visitation right; in an action to reinstate both child support payments and visitation rights, the party seeking reinstatement will not be denied such based on the previous mutual agreement, as the child has an interest in future payments; therefore, such an agreement is binding on both parties as to past obligations, but is not binding on the court as to future payments. In re Dissolution of Marriage of Saltis v Frisby, No. 10345 (9th Dist Ct App, Summit, 1–27–82).

Trial court may order defendant-father to pay child support when plaintiff-mother's waiver of child support is conditioned upon defendant-father's refraining from exercising visitation and evidence that visitation was requested and exercised by defendant is shown. Botticello v Botticello, No. 7372 (2d Dist Ct App, Montgomery, 1–7–82).

Where the trial court enters a divorce order incorporating a separation agreement in which the plaintiff-mother waived all rights to child support in exchange for which the father waived his visitation rights, said order may be modified to establish a child support obligation without finding of a change of circumstances. Botticello v Botticello, No. 7372 (2d Dist Ct App, Montgomery, 1–7–82).

Where a mother waives her right to child support payments in exchange for father's foregoing of his visitation rights, the mother may not subsequently demand a lump sum judgment for the unpaid child support. Church v Church, No. 80X23 (4th Dist Ct App, Washington, 8–12–81).

An action for child support arrearages accumulated over sixteen years was rightly denied, in that the trial court found that the plaintiff-mother was estopped from asserting such claim in that she had waived the right to child support payments to avoid contact with the defendant-father, who had waived his visitation rights to avoid the child support payments. Long v Long, No. 9590 (9th Dist Ct App, Summit, 10–22–80).

24. —— Unemployment, modification of support

Trial court imputation of income to husband, for the purpose of calculating husband's child support obligation, was not an abuse of discretion; husband's health did not prevent him from working full time, husband had worked as a veterinarian for zoo, animal park, and in private practice, husband's veterinarian license was in good standing, husband had failed to file an income tax return for over 15 years, and the court found that the various "trusts" in which husband associated all of his prior assets were a sham in order to avoid taxation. Temple v. Temple (Ohio App. 8 Dist., Cuyahoga, 01-13-2005) No. 83758, No. 83797, 2005-Ohio-92, 2005 WL 77085, Unreported, appeal not allowed 106 Ohio St.3d 1413, 830 N.E.2d 346, 2005-Ohio-3154. Child Support ☞ 88; Child Support ☞ 89

Former husband's unsubstantiated assertions that he had injured his back, lost his job, and received workers' compensation benefits were insufficient to establish impossibility as defense to contempt for failing to pay child support. Montgomery v. Montgomery (Ohio App. 4 Dist., Scioto, 12-14-2004) No. 03CA2923, No. 03CA2925, 2004-Ohio-6926, 2004 WL 2940915, Unreported. Child Support ☞ 444

Trial court was not unreasonable in finding that former wife was currently unable to find suitable employment, in determining former husband's spousal support obligations; trial court considered wife's various medical problems requiring significant physical therapy, considered that wife was attending school to improve skills for future employment, and that wife was primary custodian of parties' child. Avery v. Avery (Ohio App. 2 Dist., Greene, 09-19-2003) No. 2002 CA 121, No. 2003 CA 1, No. 2002 CA 105, 2003-Ohio-4975, 2003 WL 22159477, Unreported, appeal not allowed 101 Ohio St.3d 1421, 802 N.E.2d 153, 2004-Ohio-123. Divorce ☞ 576; Divorce ☞ 580; Divorce ☞ 584

As former wife's unemployment benefits had run out before end of year, trial court did not abuse its discretion in not using annualized amount in determining former husband's child support obligations. Avery v. Avery (Ohio App. 2 Dist., Greene, 09-19-2003) No. 2002 CA 121, No. 2003 CA 1, No. 2002 CA 105, 2003-Ohio-4975, 2003 WL 22159477, Unreported, appeal not allowed 101 Ohio St.3d 1421, 802 N.E.2d 153, 2004-Ohio-123. Child Support ☞ 99

Remand was required for trial court to recalculate cost of child care for the parties' children, which father was responsible for paying, for the summer that father was unemployed, where father took care of the children for most of that summer. Kouris v. Kouris (Ohio App. 8 Dist., Cuyahoga, 04-10-2003) No. 81237, 2003-Ohio-1831, 2003 WL 1849158, Unreported. Child Support ☞ 559

Father's retirement was voluntary, and thus, denial of father's motion to modify child support based on his reduced income from retirement and part-time employment was not abuse of discretion, even though father retired to avoid disciplinary action due to his own misconduct. Combs v. Combs (Ohio App. 12 Dist., Warren, 01-21-2003) No. CA2001-11-102, 2003-Ohio-198, 2003 WL 138708, Unreported. Child Support ☞ 259

Imputation of a $36,000 annual salary to a husband who is capable of working as an attorney is an abuse of discretion absent evidence that he is voluntarily underemployed and failed to look for work within his profession; whether defendant should be required to obtain work outside his area of expertise is a factual determination depending on whether it appears he will be unable to find work as an attorney, or whether temporary work outside his profession will interfere with looking for a job. English v. Rubino (Ohio App. 8 Dist., Cuyahoga, 04-04-1996) No. 68901, 1996 WL 157342, Unreported.

Trial court did not abuse its discretion in reducing amount of child support owed by former husband, where evidence supported finding that former husband was not voluntarily terminated from his employment, but that he resigned in order to avoid involuntary termination and to obtain favorable severance package. Hardman v. Hardman (Ohio App. 11 Dist., 04-07-2006) 166 Ohio App.3d 479, 851 N.E.2d 523, 2006-Ohio-1793. Child Support ☞ 259

Evidence supported trial court's finding concerning child support and imputing income in divorce action that wife's loss of income production capacity was involuntary and due to family obligations, although husband encouraged wife to get steady job; wife did not obtain full-time job because youngest child was not in school full-time and oldest child required frequent transportation to doctor's appointments, and cost of daycare would have negated any income from full-time employment. Kevdzija v. Kevdzija (Ohio App. 8 Dist., 04-06-2006) 166 Ohio App.3d 276, 850 N.E.2d 734, 2006-Ohio-1723. Child Support ☞ 88

Income decrease resulting from obligor's voluntary unemployment or underemployment may be rejected by court as substantial change of circumstances for modification of child support. Woloch v. Foster (Ohio App. 2 Dist., 11-23-1994) 98 Ohio App.3d 806, 649 N.E.2d 918. Child Support ☞ 259

Reduction of child support obligor's income as result of voluntary choice does not necessarily demonstrate voluntary underemployment; test is not only whether change is voluntary, but also whether it was made with due regard to obligor's income-producing abilities and duty to provide for continuing needs of children. Woloch v. Foster (Ohio App. 2 Dist., 11-23-1994) 98 Ohio App.3d 806, 649 N.E.2d 918. Child Support ☞ 259

A parent has a duty dictated by public policy to take care of his children and a parent will not be totally excused from paying child support without any showing of good faith in making some payment; absent such a showing, failure to pay may be punished by imprisonment. Allen v. Allen (Columbiana 1988) 59 Ohio App.3d 54, 571 N.E.2d 139.

A court may reduce the amount of life insurance to be maintained for the benefit of a minor child where it is shown that the insured party has since been unemployed, as the unemployment of the payor/spouse constitutes a change of circumstances sufficient to allow the modification of child support provisions originally set forth in a separation agreement. Linehan v. Linehan (Cuyahoga 1986) 34 Ohio App.3d 124, 517 N.E.2d 967.

Voluntary termination of employment at the request of a parent's new spouse does not constitute an inability to support and therefore does not constitute a change of circumstances justifying the modification or termination of an earlier support order. Boltz v. Boltz (Summit 1986) 31 Ohio App.3d 214, 509 N.E.2d 1274, 31 O.B.R. 484. Child Support ☞ 259

When seeking a decrease in or termination of child support, a party fails to show that the loss of his job constituted a material change in circumstances where the period of unemployment was not more than a year and the party failed to show: (1) that he quit for good cause, (2) that he was laid off because of lack of work; or (3) that chances for new employment were highly unlikely. Smith v. Smith (Ohio Com.Pl. 1983) 12 Ohio Misc.2d 22, 467 N.E.2d 913, 12 O.B.R. 495.

It is an abuse of discretion to order that a noncustodial parent, without disabilities, who has been out of the employment market for twelve years, must pay child support whether or not employed. Zaller v Zaller, No. 10–035 (11th Dist Ct App, Lake, 6–29–84).

In a paternity action, an order to pay child support is properly made when trial court considers all factors listed under RC 3109.05 even though defendant is unemployed and supported totally by the federal aid to dependent children program. Goode v Wilburn, No. 1542 (4th Dist Ct App, Lawrence, 3–25–82).

Where the father has been laid off from his job, it is not an abuse of discretion to deny a motion for modification of child support because the fact that he would not be held in contempt to pay while he remains unemployed prevents unnecessary hardship on the appellant. Szymkowiak v Calabrese, No. L–81–008 (6th Dist Ct App, Lucas, 10–16–81).

A court may suspend support payment obligations when the father loses his job; the change in the financial condition of a parent may warrant a modification of the support decree. In re Dissolution of Marriage of Sandor, No. 10043 (9th Dist Ct App, Summit, 7–1–81).

25. Procedural issues

Divorced father was not prejudiced by a delay of 28 months between the submission of evidence at hearing on mother's motion to modify father's child support obligation and magistrate's issuance of decision, even though such delay was unreasonable. Lyons v. Bachelder (Ohio App. 5 Dist., Morrow, 09-08-2005) No. 2004AP0017, 2005-Ohio-4966, 2005 WL 2300226, Unreported. Child Support ☞ 341; Child Support ☞ 558(3)

Former husband waived appellate consideration of his claim of evidentiary error in trial court's refusal to admit particular insurance check into evidence in proceedings on former wife's motion for modification of child support, where former husband never proffered check into evidence. Cherwin v. Cherwin (Ohio App. 8 Dist., Cuyahoga,

04-28-2005) No. 84875, 2005-Ohio-1999, 2005 WL 991706, Unreported. Child Support ☞ 539

Trial court did not abuse its discretion, in proceedings on former wife's motions for modification of child custody and child support incident to divorce, in refusing to admit into evidence copy of fourth check issued by former husband's insurance company to cover child's orthodontia expenses, where former wife's counsel requested at deposition and at trial that former husband produce all insurance checks issued to cover orthodontia expenses, former husband produced three such checks, and fourth check was apparently purposely not disclosed earlier in proceedings, permitting impeachment of former wife's testimony that only three checks were issued. Cherwin v. Cherwin (Ohio App. 8 Dist., Cuyahoga, 04-28-2005) No. 84875, 2005-Ohio-1999, 2005 WL 991706, Unreported. Child Support ☞ 477

Dismissal of husband's appeal of the denial of his motion to set aside child support order was required, where husband filed the motion under the case number of child's juvenile delinquency case, rather than under the number for the child support case. In re D.H. (Ohio App. 8 Dist., Cuyahoga, 07-15-2004) No. 83996, 2004-Ohio-3734, 2004 WL 1575378, Unreported. Child Support ☞ 545

Former husband's failure to raise claim before trial court, that since parties divided parenting time equally, deviation from worksheet's amount of child support was warranted, could not be raised for first time on appeal. Gerlach v. Gerlach (Ohio App. 10 Dist., Franklin, 03-30-2004) No. 03AP-22, No. 03AP-872, 2004-Ohio-1607, 2004 WL 625686, Unreported. Child Support ☞ 539

Former wife waived judicial review of her contention that magistrate failed to consider fact that she was unemployed, lacked work experience, and had no means to pay any amount of child support in setting her child support obligation, by failing to provide trial court with transcript of evidentiary hearing upon which magistrate's decision and permanent order was based. Banks v. Banks (Ohio App. 2 Dist., Montgomery, 10-31-2003) No. 19873, 2003-Ohio-5845, 2003 WL 22462030, Unreported. Child Support ☞ 211

Dismissal of father's appeal of his child support obligation was warranted, even though the trial court affirmed the magistrate's child support determination, where the trial court's orders never specified the relief granted and thus never terminated the action. In re McCoy (Ohio App. 4 Dist., Athens, 03-24-2003) No. 02CA33, 2003-Ohio-1524, 2003 WL 1563790, Unreported. Child Support ☞ 545

Former wife who filed motion for relief from judgment regarding order terminating former husband's child support obligation was required to state the section of rule providing for such relief that allegedly applied to former wife's case. Machaterre v. Looker (Ohio App. 6 Dist., Lucas, 01-17-2003) No. L-02-1155, 2003-Ohio-220, 2003 WL 139772, Unreported. Child Support ☞ 409

Trial court acted within its discretion in denying a continuance in the interest of its own docket, even though both parties requested a continuance, where both motions were filed on day before hearing on father's petition to modify child support. Church v. Gadd (Ohio App. 11 Dist., Geauga, 12-20-2002) No. 2001-G-2398, 2002-Ohio-7129, 2002 WL 31866165, Unreported. Child Support ☞ 340

Interlocutory orders regarding child support that are merged into a divorce decree may be enforced by the obligor who may be awarded any amount overpaid under the temporary order. Garrett v. Garrett (Ohio App. 10 Dist., Franklin, 10-19-2000) No. 99AP-1050, No. 99AP-1306, 2000 WL 1537901, Unreported, dismissed, appeal not allowed 91 Ohio St.3d 1470, 744 N.E.2d 192, dismissed, appeal not allowed 91 Ohio St.3d 1472, 744 N.E.2d 193, dismissed, appeal not allowed 91 Ohio St.3d 1524, 747 N.E.2d 250, dismissed, appeal not allowed 91 Ohio St.3d 1526, 747 N.E.2d 251.

A trial court's assertion that it is not required to record child support proceedings unless requested by a party is erroneous and contrary to the requirements of Civ R 53(D)(2). Moyers v. Moyers (Ohio App. 11 Dist., Ashtabula, 06-18-1999) No. 98-A-0080, 1999 WL 418007, Unreported.

Former wife's supplemental motion to show cause, which sought finding of contempt regarding former husband's failure to pay his share of medical expenses, was ripe for review; judgment of marital dissolution set forth 30-day period in which former husband was required to reimburse former wife after bills for medical expenses were presented to former husband, and motion was filed more than 30 days after bills were presented to former husband. Kirk v. Kirk (Ohio App. 3 Dist., 06-25-2007) 172 Ohio App.3d 404, 875 N.E.2d 125, 2007-Ohio-3140. Child Support ☞ 472

Local rule providing party with 14 days in which to respond to any motion precluded court from conducting hearing on former wife's supplemental motion to show cause, which asserted that former husband violated provision of marital dissolution judgment that required former husband to pay part of medical expenses, prior to expiration of 14-day period, where record did not show that former husband waived right to 14-day response period. Kirk v. Kirk (Ohio App. 3 Dist., 06-25-2007) 172 Ohio App.3d 404, 875 N.E.2d 125, 2007-Ohio-3140. Child Support ☞ 489

Issue of whether trial court failed to conduct independent review of magistrate's decision before adopting that decision was moot on appeal in former wife's proceeding that resulted in finding former husband in contempt of court for violating provision of marital dissolution judgment that required former husband to pay part of medical expenses; contempt finding had been reversed on appeal. Kirk v. Kirk (Ohio App. 3 Dist., 06-25-2007) 172 Ohio App.3d 404, 875 N.E.2d 125, 2007-Ohio-3140. Child Support ☞ 552

Doctrine of laches did not bar Ohio court from recognizing and enforcing Indian divorce decree, which required former husband to pay child and spousal support, even though former husband had previously obtained a divorce judgment from a Canadian court, and former husband claimed he was materially prejudiced due to his reliance on the Canadian judgment; Indian court held that Canadian judgment had no legal validity in India, and record did not support former husband's claim of prejudice. Kalia v. Kalia (Ohio App. 11 Dist., 12-20-2002) 151 Ohio App.3d 145, 783 N.E.2d 623, 2002-Ohio-7160, appeal not allowed 98 Ohio St.3d 1566, 787 N.E.2d 1231, 2003-Ohio-2242. Child Support ☞ 525; Divorce ☞ 1442(5)

Once a marriage is over, either through divorce or dissolution, the parents' obligations to support their minor children become subject to court order. Trump v. Trump (Ohio App. 9 Dist., 11-17-1999) 136 Ohio App.3d 123, 736 N.E.2d 39. Child Support ☞ 58

Unappealed entry of juvenile court, finding that ex-husband owed no arrearage on support payments for child born to the parties after their divorce decree was entered, was res judicata, and therefore domestic relations court lacked authority, in ruling on husband's motion for return of overpayment of support paid under divorce decree, to find that he still owed $2,500 in support for the child born after the marriage. Cox v. Cox (Ohio App. 1 Dist., 12-04-1998) 130 Ohio App.3d 609, 720 N.E.2d 946. Child Support ☞ 235

Trial court did not abuse its discretion in ordering father to provide health insurance for child if it was available to him at reasonable cost, even absent investigation to determine whether father had satisfactory health insurance coverage; based upon history of case, trial court already knew that father had health care coverage. Yost v. Unanue (Ohio App. 5 Dist., 02-12-1996) 109 Ohio App.3d 294, 671 N.E.2d 1374. Child Support ☞ 158

Appellate courts should exercise great restraint when asked to reverse or modify child support orders for reasons that are fact sensitive. Swanson v. Swanson (Ohio App. 2 Dist., 02-09-1996) 109 Ohio App.3d 231, 671 N.E.2d 1333. Child Support ☞ 557(1)

Appeal was adequate remedy at law after trial court refused to dismiss mother's motion to modify child support, in alleged violation of parties' agreement to mediate postdivorce disputes before resorting to court action, making mandamus and prohibition unavailable to husband to challenge court's interlocutory decision; although husband claimed that appeal would not be complete, beneficial and speedy, reviewing court could determine that trial judge erred in proceeding on postdivorce motion without parties first resorting to mediation and could vacate any support modification order. State ex rel. Hunter v. Patterson (Ohio, 05-29-1996) 75 Ohio St.3d 512, 664 N.E.2d 524, 1996-Ohio-203. Mandamus ☞ 4(4); Prohibition ☞ 3(5)

Statutory right to interest on delinquent child-support payments upon judicial finding that support order had not been paid did not apply to support order that was neither issued nor modified on or after effective date specified in statute. Dunbar v. Dunbar (Ohio, 03-02-1994) 68 Ohio St.3d 369, 627 N.E.2d 532, 1994-Ohio-509. Interest ☞ 22(1)

Failure to include child support worksheet in record on appeal required reversal and remand for completion of worksheet. McClain v. McClain (Summit 1993) 87 Ohio App.3d 856, 623 N.E.2d 242. Child Support ☞ 559

An action by the state to collect money paid by ADC to a mother for the past support of her children differs from the mother's own action to enforce present and future support; thus, an action for present and future action is not barred by res judicata. Crittendon v. Crittendon (Summit 1992) 82 Ohio App.3d 484, 612 N.E.2d 759.

A referee's report need not recite all the evidence, or absence of evidence, regarding each and every factor mentioned in RC 3109.05 and 3113.215. Smith v. Smith (Scioto 1991) 75 Ohio App.3d 679, 600 N.E.2d 396. Reference ☞ 83

A defendant who fails to avail himself of the opportunity to defend against his former wife's motion for child support modification and custody determination, to challenge an alleged error in the admission of bureau of support records, and to bring the objection to the trial court's attention waives that objection. Hostetler v. Kennedy (Wayne 1990) 69 Ohio App.3d 299, 590 N.E.2d 793.

A trial court modifying child support sufficiently complies with a request for findings of fact and conclusions of law where it appends a prior decision of the court which determined the facts of the case and set out the law applicable to the case and the circumstances contemplated by the prior decision have not changed. Riepenhoff v. Riepenhoff (Jackson 1990) 64 Ohio App.3d 135, 580 N.E.2d 846.

The rules of superintendence are merely internal housekeeping rules, to be used as guidelines to facilitate the administration of justice and although they do not give any rights to individual defendants, to the extent that they are applied in an action for the determination of child support, they should be applied correctly and not used as a substitute for the judicial discretion mandated by RC 3109.05. Esber v. Esber (Medina 1989) 63 Ohio App.3d 394, 579 N.E.2d 222.

A motion for child support necessarily raises the issue of the medical needs of the child; a motion expressly pertaining to medical needs is not a prerequisite to consideration of the issue. Gorman v. Gorman (Franklin 1986) 28 Ohio App.3d 85, 501 N.E.2d 1234, 28 O.B.R. 128.

A court, in ordering dismissal of a complaint for divorce at a party's request, may not issue an order of child custody and support as "terms and conditions" of dismissal under Civ R 41(A)(2), since the purpose of that provision is to permit an order that leaves the parties as if the action had not been brought. Lilly v. Lilly (Montgomery 1985) 26 Ohio App.3d 192, 499 N.E.2d 21, 26 O.B.R. 412.

Where there is evidence that a woman has borne, during wedlock, illegitimate children by a man other than her husband, the husband lacks standing either under RC Ch 3111 or the common law to bring an action against the alleged natural father for past necessaries furnished to the children. Weinman v. Larsh (Ohio 1983) 5 Ohio St.3d 85, 448 N.E.2d 1384, 5 O.B.R. 138.

In an action to determine support under RC 3109.05, the burden of going forward with necessary evidence may vary depending on the circumstances of the case, but generally each party is responsible for bringing forth evidence as to his or her needs. Factors about which neither party adduces evidence may be deemed by the trial court to have no significance. Cheek v. Cheek (Franklin 1982) 2 Ohio App.3d 86, 440 N.E.2d 831, 2 O.B.R. 95. Child Support ⮌ 337

A petition by a minor child, alleging that a defendant wrongfully induced the plaintiff's father to abandon his family thereby (1) depriving the plaintiff of his father's affection, companionship and guidance and (2) bringing unwanted attention and unwarranted publicity causing embarrassment, humiliation and loss of social standing to the plaintiff, is subject to demurrer on the ground that it fails to state a cause of action. Kane v. Quigley (Ohio 1964) 1 Ohio St.2d 1, 203 N.E.2d 338, 30 O.O.2d 1.

Laches did not apply to bar divorced husband's motion to set aside child support obligations because of newly discovered DNA evidence; unrefuted results of genetic testing indicated that divorced husband was not child's father, former wife must have known that there was at least a possibility that divorced husband was not father but she did not present any testimony to that effect during paternity adjudication, and divorced husband paid support for a child that was not his for nearly two decades. Poskarbiewicz v. Poskarbiewicz (Ohio App. 6 Dist., Lucas, 03-22-2002) No. L-01-1305, 2002-Ohio-3666, 2002 WL 445058, Unreported. Child Support ⮌ 220

Trial court should not have used catchall provision of rule governing relief from judgment as basis for granting divorced husband's motion to set aside child support obligations because of newly discovered DNA evidence; equity and newly discovered evidence provisions of rule were applicable, but husband was not entitled to relief under those provisions, where he submitted the DNA evidence after paying support for nearly two decades. Poskarbiewicz v. Poskarbiewicz (Ohio App. 6 Dist., Lucas, 03-22-2002) No. L-01-1305, 2002-Ohio-3666, 2002 WL 445058, Unreported. Child Support ⮌ 220

Portion of trial court's order that vacated judgment increasing former husband's monthly child support obligation was a final, appealable order. Fisher v. Fisher (Ohio App. 10 Dist., Franklin, 05-21-2002) No. 01AP-1041, 2002-Ohio-3086, 2002 WL 1020152, Unreported. Child Support ⮌ 537

Child support obligor's repeated appeals from non-final orders and attempts to cast himself as prevailing party in case where he was consistently defeated warranted imposition of $3000 in sanctions, which he was required to pay to obligee, where obligor, who was an attorney, filed appeal under circumstances that suggested he knew it would be dismissed for lack of final appealable order, and that appeal would afford him further delay. Nwabara v. Willacy (Ohio App. 8 Dist., Cuyahoga, 03-21-2002) No. 79416, No. 79717, 2002-Ohio-1279, 2002 WL 451092, Unreported, appeal not allowed 96 Ohio St.3d 1465, 772 N.E.2d 1202, 2002-Ohio-3910. Child Support ⮌ 602

It is error for a court to modify a child support order to exclude a child because of the non-paternity of the payor, when the issue of paternity is first raised by oral motion at a hearing to determine whether there has been a change in circumstances sufficient to warrant modification of the original decree. Hines v Hines, No. C–830772 (1st Dist Ct App, Hamilton, 7–25–84).

26. Remedies—In general

Former husband's payment of an additional $25 per month to be applied toward his child support arrearage was not sufficient to purge contempt citation arising from his failure to pay support, absent evidence establishing that the arrearages were indeed satisfied. Montgomery v. Montgomery (Ohio App. 4 Dist., Scioto, 12-14-2004) No. 03CA2923, No. 03CA2925, 2004-Ohio-6926, 2004 WL 2940915, Unreported. Child Support ⮌ 445

Former husband, who had been held in contempt for failing to pay child support, did not purge himself of that contempt citation even if he did satisfy his child support arrearage at time of citation, where he did not pay his child support in a timely manner for the remaining period that the support was owed. Montgomery v. Montgomery (Ohio App. 4 Dist., Scioto, 12-14-2004) No. 03CA2923, No. 03CA2925, 2004-Ohio-6926, 2004 WL 2940915, Unreported. Child Support ⮌ 445

Requirement that father pay county for services rendered in connection with child's birth did not constitute a double recovery for county, even though father had already paid restitution to county for mother's welfare fraud, as mother's welfare fraud restitution payments were separate from father's obligations. McKinnis v. Parlier (Ohio App. 12 Dist., Clermont, 06-14-2004) No. CA2003-06-050, 2004-Ohio-3010, 2004 WL 1300160, Unreported. Child Support ⮌ 55

In prosecution for nonsupport of dependents in which defendant was ordered to pay past due child support in the form of restitution, defendant was entitled to a hearing in the trial court to determine the proper amount of restitution. State v. Hubbell (Ohio App. 2 Dist., Darke, 01-30-2004) No. 1617, 2004-Ohio-398, 2004 WL 190066, Unreported. Sentencing And Punishment ⮌ 2192

Husband properly was ordered to pay $271 to wife for his step-daughter's prescription; wife was required to pay $271 for prescription medicine for her daughter out of her own funds because husband had removed wife's children from the prescription coverage that his health insurance provided, wife testified that husband did not tell her that he canceled the coverage until after the bill was incurred, and wife had incurred the costs due to husband's actions and she was due reimbursement. Jackson v. Jackson (Ohio App. 2 Dist., Greene, 12-24-2003) No. 2003CA36, 2003-Ohio-7095, 2003 WL 23011368, Unreported. Child Support ☞ 113

Ohio Department of Aging was entitled to indemnification from former employee for the amount of child support arrearage the Department paid to mother of former employee's child; former employee acknowledged that the amount paid by Department represented the child-support arrearage he owed at the time he received a lump-sum payment from the Public Employees Retirement System. White v. Department of Aging (Ohio Ct.Cl., 02-19-2003) No. 2001-01027, 2003-Ohio-966, 2003 WL 1084699, Unreported, adopted 2003-Ohio-1993, 2003 WL 1904625. States ☞ 60.2

Neither repealed statute that formerly imposed interest requirement on child support arrearages nor statute permitting assessment of interest on any unpaid amount of child support pursuant to statute that was itself not yet in effect provided basis for awarding former wife interest on child support arrearage. Galluzzo v. Galluzzo (Ohio App. 2 Dist., Champaign, 11-27-2002) No. 2001CA16, 2002-Ohio-6524, 2002 WL 31682009, Unreported. Child Support ☞ 453

Although parent-spouse cannot escape his or her parental obligations from the time of physical separation to the commencement of formal divorce proceedings, the proper remedy for non-payment is to be found with the juvenile court. Trump v. Trump (Ohio App. 9 Dist., 11-17-1999) 136 Ohio App.3d 123, 736 N.E.2d 39. Child Support ☞ 469

If the adjudicated father unreasonably failed to seek relief from child support order earlier, a court may properly decide that the reasonable time period for equitable relief from the order has expired. Dunkle v. Dunkle (Ohio App. 4 Dist., 11-08-1999) 135 Ohio App.3d 669, 735 N.E.2d 469. Child Support ☞ 323; Children Out-of-wedlock ☞ 21(1)

Divorced mother was entitled to recover aggregate total of medical bills incurred by children, not merely out-of-pocket expenses, from father, regardless of whether expenses were covered by insurance procured by mother's new spouse; father failed to pay for any of children's medical expenses, prompting mother to acquire insurance for children and to incur uninsured out-of-pocket medical costs, and father was responsible under separation agreement for all medical, dental, hospital and surgical expenses that exceeded $15 per occurrence. Stracker v. Stracker (Ohio App. 9 Dist., 04-13-1994) 94 Ohio App.3d 261, 640 N.E.2d 611. Child Support ☞ 448

A nonresident custodial parent has a right to pursue an action for child support against the non-

custodial parent in a court of competent jurisdiction in this state when the noncustodial parent is a resident of Ohio and the parties' foreign divorce decree and child custody order do not address the issue of support. Haskins v. Bronzetti (Ohio 1992) 64 Ohio St.3d 202, 594 N.E.2d 582. Child Support ☞ 507

A defendant who fails to avail himself of the opportunity to defend against his former wife's motion for child support modification and custody determination, to challenge an alleged error in the admission of bureau of support records, and to bring the objection to the trial court's attention waives that objection. Hostetler v. Kennedy (Wayne 1990) 69 Ohio App.3d 299, 590 N.E.2d 793.

Uniform Reciprocal Enforcement of Support Act does not authorize suspension of support order by reason of denial or interference with visitation rights. Brown v. Brown (Warren 1984) 16 Ohio App.3d 26, 474 N.E.2d 613, 16 O.B.R. 28. Child Support ☞ 501(1)

Father could not excuse his failure to pay child support required by separation agreement merely because of mother's denial of visitation rights. Flynn v. Flynn (Madison 1984) 15 Ohio App.3d 34, 472 N.E.2d 388, 15 O.B.R. 57. Child Support ☞ 44

Where circumstances indicate an inability on the part of the noncustodial parent to pay child support, such parent cannot be deprived of his right of visitation solely by reason of his inability to pay. Johnson v. Johnson (Summit 1977) 52 Ohio App.2d 180, 368 N.E.2d 1273, 6 O.O.3d 170. Child Custody ☞ 188

A parent having custody of minor children who is able to fully support such children, and has done so, may not utilize criminal prosecution under 2919.21 as a means of enforcing the obligation of the other parent to contribute to the support of their minor children. State v. Oppenheimer (Franklin 1975) 46 Ohio App.2d 241, 348 N.E.2d 731, 75 O.O.2d 404. Child Support ☞ 653

There is no duty on the father of minor children to make support payments to the mother as decreed by another court pursuant to the uniform reciprocal enforcement of support act, where the father has obtained a prior order of custody and the mother has removed the children from the jurisdiction of the court contrary to such order. State of N. J. v. Morales (Franklin 1973) 35 Ohio App.2d 56, 299 N.E.2d 920, 64 O.O.2d 175.

Compliance with common pleas court order fixing amount of support payments for minor child of divorced parents is a bar to prosecution for nonsupport in juvenile court. State v. Holl (Auglaize 1971) 25 Ohio App.2d 75, 266 N.E.2d 587, 54 O.O.2d 114.

The uniform support act covers children who are minors, and under 3115.22 is in addition to and not in substitution of any other remedies authorized by law. Burney v. Vance (Ohio Com.Pl. 1969) 17 Ohio Misc. 307, 246 N.E.2d 371, 46 O.O.2d 427. Child Support ☞ 500

Where a wife abandons her husband without any aggression on his part and takes her children to another state, the husband cannot be compelled to support such children under the uniform enforcement of support laws where he retains a domicile in Ohio, earns his living in Ohio, and apparently is ready, willing and able to support his children in Ohio. Buliox v. Buliox (Ohio Com.Pl. 1962) 185 N.E.2d 802, 90 Ohio Law Abs. 251, 21 O.O.2d 30.

The payee of an installment child-support order or judgment, issued in conjunction with a divorce decree, is not precluded by a statutory limitation of time, by laches, or by loss of jurisdiction by the court making the order, from having unpaid and delinquent installments thereon reduced to a "lump-sum judgment," upon which execution may be lawfully levied, because fourteen years elapsed since the last payment on the order was due or because the court lost custodial jurisdiction of the child when he reached the age of twenty-one. Smith v. Smith (Ohio 1959) 168 Ohio St. 447, 156 N.E.2d 113, 7 O.O.2d 276.

Where for many years the plaintiff in a divorce proceeding failed to enforce installment payments of support money for a minor child, ordered in a decree granting a divorce to plaintiff, the unpaid installments become vested when due, and the court has no power to reduce the amount found to be due where the evidence does not indicate any intention on the part of the plaintiff to waive, relinquish, or abandon her rights under the support order. Brunner v. Williams (Franklin 1955) 100 Ohio App. 144, 135 N.E.2d 908, 60 O.O. 136.

Although matters concerning divorce and alimony have been excepted from federal court jurisdiction based on diversity of the parties' state citizenship since Barber v Barber, 62 US 582, 16 LEd(2d) 226(1859), this rule does not bar a husband's claim in federal court that the former wife intentionally inflicted emotional distress on him by taking their child to another state and denying him visitation rights, or that she interfered with his employment by writing letters to his employer; the court may also hear his counterclaim for enforcement of a state judgment concerning arrearages in alimony and child support. Drewes v. Ilnicki (C.A.6 (Ohio) 1988) 863 F.2d 469.

In a federal suit based on diversity of citizenship the principle that federal courts will not hear domestic relations disputes does not apply where the claim is that an employer who withheld wages to satisfy an Ohio court's support order converted the funds instead of turning them over to the Cuyahoga support enforcement agency; the federal court will not be delving into the plaintiff's domestic affairs here, the level or appropriateness of the support payments is not at issue, the state court's orders are not questioned, and it is merely alleged that the employer converted withheld wages. Ungrady v. Burns Intern. Sec. Services, Inc. (N.D.Ohio 1991) 767 F.Supp. 849.

Where an indigent individual is ordered to appear and show cause why he should not be held in contempt for failure to pay support, and where the penalty that may be inflicted includes incarceration, due process requires that the indigent be informed he has a right to appointed counsel, and that such counsel be appointed on request before an appearance to show cause is required. Johnson v. Zurz (N.D.Ohio 1984) 596 F.Supp. 39. Constitutional Law ☞ 4494

The fact that children to whom a support order relates have reached the age of majority does not prevent a finding that a debt based on arrearages cannot be discharged in the obligor's bankruptcy proceedings. In re Ridgway (Bkrtcy.N.D.Ohio 1989) 108 B.R. 154.

A court may recognize the defense of laches in an action for past due child support; however, the obligor must prove he was materially prejudiced. The court will not infer prejudice from the mere lapse of time or inconvenience in having to meet an obligor. Garrison v Garrison, No. 10256 (2d Dist Ct App, Montgomery, 6–5–87).

A court may not use its contempt power to force a public employees retirement system member to withdraw money from PERS in order to pay child support arrearages since PERS moneys are exempt from execution, attachment, garnishment, or other process of law. Baecker v Baecker, No. CA–9810 (2d Dist Ct App, Montgomery, 11–6–86).

A court cannot order withholding of funds from a member of the public employees retirement system until he has requested a refund or is entitled to receive retirement benefits, and a court cannot compel a party to a child support action to make such a request to pay arrearages. Baecker v Baecker, No. CA–9810 (2d Dist Ct App, Montgomery, 11–6–86).

Trial court may order defendant-father to pay child support when plaintiff-mother's waiver of child support is conditioned upon defendant-father's refraining from exercising visitation and evidence that visitation was requested and exercised by defendant is shown. Botticello v Botticello, No. 7372 (2d Dist Ct App, Montgomery, 1–7–82).

27. ——— Contempt, remedies

Trial court did not err in refusing to find mother in contempt for failing to pay child support, even though magistrate found mother acknowledged not making the payments pursuant to support order, and that mother would have difficulty finding employment due to a criminal conviction for nonsupport, because the trial court could not conduct a proper review of the magistrate's factual findings, where the record did not contain a Child Support Enforcement Agency (CSEA) audit that would have enabled the court to determine whether or not father's prior support arrearages had been completely offset, and father failed to provide a transcript of the underlying proceeding in support of his objection to magistrate's findings. Pagonis v. Steele (Ohio App. 9 Dist., Summit, 09-22-2010) No. 25189, 2010-Ohio-4459, 2010 WL 3676997, Unreported. Children Out–of–wedlock ☞ 69(7)

Father could not be held in contempt for failing to comply with order to pay child support arrearages, and failing to stay current on his child support obligations, when on two separate occasions trial court determined father had complied with the terms set out to purge his contempt, and contempt order that attempted to regulate future conduct would be void and of no effect. Davis-Wright v. Wright (Ohio App. 4 Dist., Highland, 08-20-2010) No. 09CA1, 2010-Ohio-3984, 2010 WL 3328661, Unreported. Child Support ☞ 445

Father could not be held in contempt for failing to report to jail as ordered after being granted an extension to pay lump sum amount on child support arrearages in order to purge himself of contempt, because fundamental fairness should have protected father from being jailed for failing to do an act the trial court did not order him to do until a week after the date set for that act had already expired. Davis-Wright v. Wright (Ohio App. 4 Dist., Highland, 08-20-2010) No. 09CA1, 2010-Ohio-3984, 2010 WL 3328661, Unreported. Child Support ☞ 444; Child Support ☞ 445

The finding of contempt by the trial court did not violate ex-wife's due process rights, and trial court did not err by setting purge terms that required compliance with an established order; trial court adopted the parties' agreement, which dealt with the fact that ex-wife admitted she was in willful contempt of court order which required ex-wife to pay for children's medical bills, ex-wife purged herself of contempt for her willful failure to facilitate visitation between ex-husband and the minor children, and she paid $1,083.35 to ex-husband that she owed for medical bills, thus purging herself of that contempt. Hanzlik v. Hanzlik (Ohio App. 11 Dist., Portage, 07-23-2010) No. 2009-P-0089, 2010-Ohio-3462, 2010 WL 2892631, Unreported. Child Custody ☞ 854; Child Support ☞ 444; Child Support ☞ 445; Constitutional Law ☞ 4494

Trial court did not abuse its discretion for failing to find father in contempt for failing to comply with child support order during the time when the issue of his child support obligation was pending before the court, where there was confusion regarding father's child support figure. Onyshko v. Onyshko (Ohio App. 11 Dist., Portage, 03-12-2010) No. 2008-P-0035, 2010-Ohio-969, 2010 WL 891335, Unreported. Child Support ☞ 444

Trial court order requiring paternal grandparents to pay all of maternal grandparents' legal fees, all guardian ad litem fees, all expert fees, the cost of all psychological evaluations, the costs of depositions and transcriptions, and for the parenting classes both maternal and paternal grandparents attended, which totaled $105,540.37, was not an abuse of discretion, during child custody modification proceeding in which maternal and paternal grandparents sought custody of out-of-wedlock child; the trial court determined that the contemptuous conduct of paternal grandparents arose after the issuance of the original visitation order granting maternal grandparents visitation, that paternal grandparents' contemptuous conduct gave rise to the entire action, and that paternal grandparents had a "track record" of total disdain for any court order and believed that their wishes outweighed a court order. Smith v. Quigg (Ohio App. 5 Dist., Fairfield, 03-22-2006) No. 2005-CA-001, 2006-Ohio-1494, 2006 WL 786855, Unreported. Children Out-of-wedlock ☞ 20.12

Trial court abused its discretion in finding former husband in contempt for his failure to pay his portion of expenses for child's eyeglasses, as set out in shared parenting plan, where former wife never showed former husband applicable bills or requested reimbursement. Cherwin v. Cherwin (Ohio App. 8 Dist., Cuyahoga, 04-28-2005) No. 84875, 2005-Ohio-1999, 2005 WL 991706, Unreported. Child Support ☞ 444

Husband was in contempt of trial court's orders in divorce proceeding requiring him to pay the horse-related expenses of one minor child and the uninsured medical expenses and private tuition of both children; the language in the court's orders did not provide restrictions upon husband's payment of those expenses, and the orders did not require husband's approval of the expenses as a condition of his payment. O'Brien v. O'Brien (Ohio App. 5 Dist., Delaware, 11-02-2004) No. 2003-CA-F12069, 2004-Ohio-5881, 2004 WL 2496808, Unreported. Child Support ☞ 444

Former husband did not substantially comply with "spirit and terms" of post-divorce court order relating to care plan for parties' adult disabled child which provided for shared responsibilities and duties of each parent, and thus, finding husband in contempt was not abuse of discretion, where husband admitted that he did not comply with order, in that he failed to provide a yearly calendar on November 1st of each year to former wife detailing his 44 weekends of care for daughter, failed to care for daughter for the required 14 day periods per year from 1998 through 2001, failed to administer prescribed medications to daughter, failed to provide a home telephone number to wife, and failed to pay respite care to wife. Robinson v. Robinson (Ohio App. 9 Dist., Summit, 09-24-2003) No. 21440, 2003-Ohio-5049, 2003 WL 22188536, Unreported. Child Custody ☞ 852

Magistrate's contempt order constituted a final, appealable order regarding former wife's motion to show cause that alleged that former husband was in contempt of court for failing to pay child and spousal support, since order found former husband was in contempt of court and imposed a sanction of jail time, which would be automatically carried out if former husband did not appear at scheduled compliance hearing. McCree v. McCree (Ohio App. 7 Dist., Mahoning, 03-25-2003) No. 01 CA 228, 2003-Ohio-1600, 2003 WL 1656845, Unreported. Child Support ☞ 537; Divorce ☞ 1207

Former husband purged himself of civil contempt by making his lump-sum delinquent payment of child support on the day before the contempt hearing. In re Contemnor Caron (Ohio Com.Pl.,

04-27-2000) 110 Ohio Misc.2d 58, 744 N.E.2d 787. Child Support ⬥ 445

Former husband's payment of child support arrears on the day before the contempt hearing did not divest the court of its contempt power, and contempt sanctions of imprisonment and fine thus were permissible to uphold the dignity of the court. In re Contemnor Caron (Ohio Com.Pl., 04-27-2000) 110 Ohio Misc.2d 58, 744 N.E.2d 787. Child Support ⬥ 444

Former husband's failure to pay child support for several years was criminal contempt of court immediately before his forced payment of child support on the day before the contempt hearing. In re Contemnor Caron (Ohio Com.Pl., 04-27-2000) 110 Ohio Misc.2d 58, 744 N.E.2d 787. Child Support ⬥ 444

Trial court acted within its discretion in refusing to find former husband in contempt for his alleged violation of divorce decree in not making any payment toward certain medical bill of parties' child; decree required former wife to provide former husband with "such information as could be submitted to former husband's insurance carrier," and former husband testified that he had needed "explanation of benefits" form from former wife's insurer showing what portion of bill was paid and what claims were denied in order to submit bill for payment to his insurance carrier. Brooks v. Brooks (Ohio App. 10 Dist., 12-24-1996) 117 Ohio App.3d 19, 689 N.E.2d 987. Child Support ⬥ 459

Former husband could not be found in contempt of court's order directing him to pay one half of children's uninsured medical expenses, where husband never received actual notice or notice by service of court's order. Sancho v. Sancho (Ohio App. 3 Dist., 10-17-1996) 114 Ohio App.3d 636, 683 N.E.2d 849. Child Support ⬥ 474

Former husband could be found in contempt for failure to remain current on medical payments and failure to maintain dental insurance for children in violation of separation agreement incorporated in judgment. Woloch v. Foster (Ohio App. 2 Dist., 11-23-1994) 98 Ohio App.3d 806, 649 N.E.2d 918. Child Support ⬥ 456

Former husband's failure to pay past due and owing college expenses and medical expenses, as required under separation agreement and modification order, justified contempt finding; former husband's motion to modify filed after contempt proceeding was instituted was not viable defense and husband offered no evidence of alleged inability to pay. Rohrbacher v. Rohrbacher (Lucas 1992) 83 Ohio App.3d 569, 615 N.E.2d 338. Child Support ⬥ 459; Child Support ⬥ 487

In a contempt action brought by a wife against her ex-husband for failure to pay child support, the ex-husband's defense of laches does not prevent a trial court's willful contempt finding against him, even though the wife's action is brought eleven years after the children became emancipated and twenty years after the divorce, custody, and support decree was entered, where the husband never successfully disputes that his ex-wife did not know or had never learned of his address in another state or any other particulars about his existence there and never indicates how the delay in enforcing the support order has materially or legally prejudiced him. Johnson v. Johnson (Portage 1991) 71 Ohio App.3d 713, 595 N.E.2d 388. Child Support ⬥ 451

A wife's action against her ex-husband for contempt for failure to pay child support is a civil contempt proceeding in which proof of willfulness is not a prerequisite. Johnson v. Johnson (Portage 1991) 71 Ohio App.3d 713, 595 N.E.2d 388.

A trial court may not use its contempt powers to seek to enforce a prior child support order by ordering monthly installments to retire arrearages after the children have become emancipated. Crigger v. Crigger (Franklin 1991) 71 Ohio App.3d 410, 594 N.E.2d 67. Child Support ⬥ 496

RC 3105.10 clothes courts with jurisdiction to incorporate into a court order an agreement to support a child of the parties beyond the age of that child's majority, and such an order may be enforced by contempt proceedings. Bugay v. Bugay (Summit 1977) 53 Ohio App.2d 285, 373 N.E.2d 1263, 7 O.O.3d 336.

Finding former husband guilty of contempt for failing to maintain health insurance for children and for failing to appear as ordered for contempt hearing was not an abuse of discretion, where husband failed to establish it was impossible for him to attend the prior hearing or impossible for him to afford to maintain health insurance for children. Heid v. Heid (Ohio App. 5 Dist., Stark, 08-12-2002) No. 2002 CA 00113, 2002-Ohio-4271, 2002 WL 1922759, Unreported. Child Support ⬥ 444

Ex-wife was not in contempt for permitting liens to be placed on parties' commercial property; while ex-wife allowed the liens to arise, there was no evidence that she failed to remove the liens which were placed against the property, all of the liens had been fully satisfied by date that ex-husband's contempt motion was filed with and heard by court, and ex-wife was unable to comply with the provision that she not allow liens to be placed against the property since she had yearly, pretax income of $20,000 and ex-husband failed to pay the spousal support as ordered during the time that the liens were placed against the property. Miller v. Miller (Ohio App. 12 Dist., Butler, 07-29-2002) No. CA2001-06-138, 2002-Ohio-3870, 2002 WL 1758374, Unreported. Divorce ⬥ 1106

28. —— Prison, remedies

Contempt citation against father as a result of his failure to pay child support, ordering him to serve an additional three days in jail, in addition to the 79 days remaining on previously imposed 90-day sentence, constituted a final appealable order, even though father was given an opportunity to purge that contempt, because the court expected its contempt citations to be self-executing in that, if father did not purge himself of contempt, he was, pursuant to court's order, to appear at county jail for incarceration, and thus, no further proceedings were necessary or contemplated before sentence was to be imposed. Davis-Wright v. Wright (Ohio App. 4 Dist., Highland, 08-20-2010) No. 09CA1, 2010-Ohio-3984, 2010 WL 3328661, Unreported. Child Support ☞ 537

Evidence did not warrant defendant's requested jury instruction on affirmative defense of inability to pay child support obligation, in prosecution for non-support charged as failure to provide support as established by a court order to another person whom the offender is obligated by law to support, where, although evidence established that defendant was destitute, arguably as result of his health condition, defendant made no attempt to seek relief from the court-ordered support obligation he was accused of failing to pay in order to avoid potential criminal liability for not paying support. State v. Jones (Ohio App. 2 Dist., Montgomery, 08-27-2004) No. 20162, 2004-Ohio-4519, 2004 WL 1909137, Unreported. Child Support ☞ 667

Trial court's failure to make requisite statutory findings on the record to support its imposition of prison term for defendant's conviction for two counts of non-support, failure to provide support as established by a court order to another person whom the offender is obligated by law to support necessitated remand for resentencing; although trial court expressly found that defendant, a first-time offender, was not amenable to community control sanctions, it made no reference to the purposes and principles of sentencing set out in sentencing statute, its findings in that regard, or any reason for its findings. State v. Jones (Ohio App. 2 Dist., Montgomery, 08-27-2004) No. 20162, 2004-Ohio-4519, 2004 WL 1909137, Unreported. Criminal Law ☞ 1181.5(8); Sentencing And Punishment ☞ 373

A sentence of thirty days in jail was warranted for criminal contempt by a former husband for failing to pay child support for several years. In re Contemnor Caron (Ohio Com.Pl., 04-27-2000) 110 Ohio Misc.2d 58, 744 N.E.2d 787. Child Support ☞ 444

Before a person can be incarcerated for failure to pay child support and arrearages pursuant to a trial court's order, it is first necessary that a judge review and approve the referee's written report with his factual determination that the person has not purged himself of his contempt sentence by making a substantial effort to seek work by a certain date. State ex rel. Burns v. Haines (Montgomery 1989) 55 Ohio App.3d 168, 563 N.E.2d 52.

29. Support award—In general

Trial court was required to allocate child support between husband and wife consistent with each party's pro-rata share of total income, and thus, order requiring that husband pay 100% of total child support obligation was reversible error. Pruitt v. Pruitt (Ohio App. 8 Dist., Cuyahoga, 08-25-2005) No. 84335, 2005-Ohio-4424, 2005 WL 2046422, Unreported, appeal not allowed 108 Ohio St.3d 1417, 841 N.E.2d 320, 2006-Ohio-179, certio-

rari denied 127 S.Ct. 71, 549 U.S. 814, 166 L.Ed.2d 25. Child Support ☞ 87

Former husband's failure to request child support during divorce, when he was awarded custody of son, did not prevent former husband from seeking child support payments in the future; former husband was only prevented from seeking reimbursement for child support. Baddam-Reddy v. Baddam-Reddy (Ohio App. 8 Dist., Cuyahoga, 06-30-2005) No. 85038, 2005 Ohio-3432, 2005 WL 1541080, Unreported, appeal not allowed 107 Ohio St.3d 1423, 837 N.E.2d 1208, 2005-Ohio-6124. Child Custody ☞ 531(1); Child Support ☞ 55

Former husband's entry into financial agreement and promissory note with child's orthodontist constituted independent basis for enforcement of provision of shared parenting plan requiring him to pay portion of child's orthodontia bill, where agreement set out total amount due and estimated amount that would be covered by insurance, and thus made former husband aware of amount of uncovered expenses prior to his execution of agreement and note. Cherwin v. Cherwin (Ohio App. 8 Dist., Cuyahoga, 04-28-2005) No. 84875, 2005-Ohio-1999, 2005 WL 991706, Unreported. Child Support ☞ 456

Trial court order granting husband $2,651.88 for child support relative to his step-daughter was an abuse of discretion, in divorce proceeding; wife had a court order to receive child support, the order was not modified in any way, and an award of child support could not be retroactively modified. Weaver v. Weaver (Ohio App. 5 Dist., Licking, 08-09-2004) No. 2003CA00096, 2004-Ohio-4212, 2004 WL 1784595, Unreported. Child Support ☞ 364

It is proper for a trial court to order a custodial parent to pay child support to the noncustodial parent where the parents have equal time with the child. Prusia v. Prusia (Ohio App. 6 Dist., Lucas, 04-18-2003) No. L-02-1165, 2003-Ohio-2000, 2003 WL 1904410, Unreported. Child Support ☞ 70

Trial court abused its discretion by calculating child support using the shared parenting form, even though parties had equal parenting time with child, where father was named legal custodian and residential parent. Prusia v. Prusia (Ohio App. 6 Dist., Lucas, 04-18-2003) No. L-02-1165, 2003-Ohio-2000, 2003 WL 1904410, Unreported. Child Support ☞ 146

Former wife was entitled to award of child support retroactive to date trial court entered decree for divorce, where wife had requested child support in complaint for divorce, and trial court expressly reserved jurisdiction over issue of child support. Brittingham v. Brittingham (Ohio App. 12 Dist., Brown, 02-24-2003) No. CA2002-04-009, 2003-Ohio-812, 2003 WL 434590, Unreported. Child Support ☞ 150

A child support order does not survive the death of the payor parent unless the payor parent consents to continuation of child support after his death and so a trial court abuses discretion by ordering the obligor to maintain life insurance as security for his child support obligation. Whitt v. Whitt (Ohio App. 5 Dist., Fairfield, 12-24-1998) No. 98CA12, 1999 WL 3938, Unreported.

Common law rules that the father is the head of the family and that death terminates his obligation of child support are based on outdated social and sexual stereotypes; the modern trend is for a divorce court to mandate that the obligor designate the child as the beneficiary on the parent's life insurance policy to ensure that the child receive support during minority in the event the obligor parent dies before the child reaches majority. Webb v. Webb (Ohio App. 2 Dist., Montgomery, 12-31-1997) No. 16371, 1997 WL 797719, Unreported.

The best interests of a child demand that the father pay to the mother, for the benefit of the child, all monies and expenses previously ordered by the court. In re Contemnor Caron (Ohio Com. Pl., 04-27-2000) 110 Ohio Misc.2d 58, 744 N.E.2d 787. Child Support ☞ 430

Former husband was required to comply with child support orders until paternity claim was resolved. In re Contemnor Caron (Ohio Com.Pl., 04-27-2000) 110 Ohio Misc.2d 58, 744 N.E.2d 787. Child Support ☞ 375

Finding of domestics relations court, on ex-husband's motion for return of overpayment of child support, that support order was in-gross order that ex-husband was required to pay in fall until youngest child reached age of emancipation, was not abuse of discretion, where divorce decree failed to specify support obligation as to each child. Cox v. Cox (Ohio App. 1 Dist., 12-04-1998) 130 Ohio App.3d 609, 720 N.E.2d 946. Child Support ☞ 391

In determining child support obligations, trial court was statutorily required to issue separate orders regarding health insurance for children. Cuyahoga Cty. Support Enforcement Agency v. Lozada (Ohio App. 8 Dist., 07-10-1995) 102 Ohio App.3d 442, 657 N.E.2d 372. Child Support ☞ 158

Shared-parenting order in divorce action was not improper on theory it encouraged excessive entanglement between parties in requiring parties to cooperate and communicate by sharing expenses. Eickelberger v. Eickelberger (Ohio App. 12 Dist., 02-22-1994) 93 Ohio App.3d 221, 638 N.E.2d 130. Child Custody ☞ 127

Juvenile court was required by statute to consider father's finances as they related to determination of future support payments for child who was born out-of-wedlock and was receiving Aid to Families with Dependent Children (AFDC). Gilpen v. Justice (Fayette 1993) 85 Ohio App.3d 86, 619 N.E.2d 94, motion overruled 67 Ohio St.3d 1410, 615 N.E.2d 1044. Children Out–of–wedlock ☞ 67

Divorce court is required to consider financial resources and earning ability of child, including interest income earned on child's accumulated assets, when setting amount of child support. Frost

v. Frost (Franklin 1992) 84 Ohio App.3d 699, 618 N.E.2d 198, motion overruled 66 Ohio St.3d 1489, 612 N.E.2d 1245. Child Support ☞ 105; Child Support ☞ 107

Court of Appeals would set sustenance alimony award pursuant to 1986 divorce at $3,500 per month, where trial court had determined wife's monthly expenses to be approximately $4,000, wife suggested award in amount of $3,500, and husband offered no suggestion other than trial court's award of $2,700, which was found by Court of Appeals to constitute abuse of discretion. Kaechele v. Kaechele (Franklin 1992) 83 Ohio App.3d 468, 615 N.E.2d 273. Divorce ☞ 1322(1)

Although trial court is required by statute in fixing child support under guidelines to consider financial resources and earning ability of minor child, including social security benefits paid either to child or child's representative payee, it is unreasonable to permit one parent to receive windfall and be totally relieved of child support obligation which would otherwise be allocated to that parent under child support guidelines solely because of social security benefits to or for benefit of minor child. McNeal v. Cofield (Franklin 1992) 78 Ohio App.3d 35, 603 N.E.2d 436. Child Support ☞ 146

Nonresident custodial parent had right to pursue action against resident noncustodial parent for child support in court of competent jurisdiction in state, where foreign divorce decree and child custody order did not address issue of support. Haskins v. Bronzetti (Ohio 1992) 64 Ohio St.3d 202, 594 N.E.2d 582. Child Support ☞ 507

In a case in which the unmarried parents of two minor children both seek custody after the relationship between the parties has terminated, a trial court does not err in making a child support determination without an evidentiary hearing where the judge met with counsel for the parties and requested information about the party's incomes; this information coupled with the testimony presented at the hearing was a sufficient basis on which the court could make its determination and a further hearing was not necessary. In re Markham (Meigs 1990) 70 Ohio App.3d 841, 592 N.E.2d 896, dismissed, jurisdictional motion overruled 60 Ohio St.3d 702, 573 N.E.2d 118.

It is an abuse of discretion for a trial court to order a father to put money into a savings account which is set up by the court and which is for his son to be disbursed as the court may order where this order does not serve as support for the current needs of the child. Bailey v. Mitchell (Cuyahoga 1990) 67 Ohio App.3d 441, 587 N.E.2d 358.

Court-ordered support is for benefit of children, rather than custodial parent, and cannot be waived by parents. Nelson v. Nelson (Lake 1990) 65 Ohio App.3d 800, 585 N.E.2d 502. Child Support ☞ 8; Child Support ☞ 47

In the absence of factors making it inequitable, the right to interest under RC 1343.03(A) on unpaid child support accrues on the date each installment becomes due, and runs until paid; such interest may be included in a lump-sum judgment for child support arrearages. Allen v. Allen (Summit 1990) 62 Ohio App.3d 621, 577 N.E.2d 126.

Proper amount of child support is that amount necessary to maintain for children standard of living they would have enjoyed had marriage continued, and amount includes consideration of financial resources and needs of both custodial and noncustodial parent. Birath v. Birath (Franklin 1988) 53 Ohio App.3d 31, 558 N.E.2d 63, motion overruled 39 Ohio St.3d 730, 534 N.E.2d 357. Child Support ⊕ 62; Child Support ⊕ 70

The amount of child support necessary is the amount needed to maintain for the children the standard of living they would have had if the marriage had continued, with consideration given to other factors like the financial resources and needs of the custodial and the noncustodial parents. Birath v. Birath (Franklin 1988) 53 Ohio App.3d 31, 558 N.E.2d 63, motion overruled 39 Ohio St.3d 730, 534 N.E.2d 357. Child Support ⊕ 62; Child Support ⊕ 70

Deviation from the child support guidelines, set forth in C P Sup R 75, by using a father's net income where the father's living expenses are substantially higher than the mother's due to geographic differences does not constitute an abuse of discretion. Booth v. Booth (Ohio 1989) 44 Ohio St.3d 142, 541 N.E.2d 1028.

A family maintenance provision, where no portion of the amount is specifically fixed as child support, incorporated within a divorce decree in order to take advantage of tax benefits, may not be reduced by the amount intended by the parties as child support upon the death or the emancipation of the child, where the provision provides for a reduction or termination of the support only if the receiving spouse reaches a certain income level. Rittgers v. Rittgers (Fairfield 1986) 38 Ohio App.3d 115, 528 N.E.2d 571.

Known and reasonably anticipated medical needs of a child must be provided for in every support order, and it is not sufficient for a trial court to assume, as a basis for its order, that payments for medical expenses made voluntarily by one parent will continue. Gorman v. Gorman (Franklin 1986) 28 Ohio App.3d 85, 501 N.E.2d 1234, 28 O.B.R. 128.

A loss of income to a supporting parent does not require a proportional reduction in his support obligation. Snyder v. Snyder (Cuyahoga 1985) 27 Ohio App.3d 1, 499 N.E.2d 320, 27 O.B.R. 1.

An automatic escalator clause in a child support decree is improper if not based on future earning capability or future needs of the child. Royse v. Royse (Ohio Com.Pl. 1984) 23 Ohio Misc.2d 5, 491 N.E.2d 397, 23 O.B.R. 113.

In determining if there has been a material change in circumstances justifying an increase in child support, a trial court may consider changes in the: (1) take-home pay of the parties, (2) cost-of-living index, and (3) other support obligations of the parties. Neukam v. Neukam (Ohio Com.Pl.

1983) 13 Ohio Misc.2d 4, 468 N.E.2d 391, 13 O.B.R. 76. Child Support ⊕ 236

Trial court order holding father responsible for his daughter's medical bills incurred in giving birth to illegitimate child was not erroneous on ground that natural father of illegitimate child was obligated, pursuant to public policy of state, to pay such expenses, where in accordance with decretal support order as modified, father was responsible for all medical, dental, optical and hospital expenses of child in excess of $50 during any one year. Nuckols v. Nuckols (Wood 1983) 12 Ohio App.3d 94, 467 N.E.2d 259, 12 O.B.R. 400. Child Support ⊕ 149

Where a husband and wife are divorced, the duty to support minor children is governed by RC 3109.05, so that a wife may be required to contrib ute to the support of her minor children who are in the custody of their father. Hacker v. Hacker (Fairfield 1981) 5 Ohio App.3d 46, 448 N.E.2d 831, 5 O.B.R. 50. Child Support ⊕ 60

In determining the amount of child support which is reasonable and necessary under RC 3109.05(A), the trial court first must determine the child's needs, after considering all relevant factors, including those listed in RC 3109.05(A); the determination of need must then be tempered by ascertaining the amount which is reasonable in view of the overall financial condition of the parents and the child. Bright v. Collins (Franklin 1982) 2 Ohio App.3d 421, 442 N.E.2d 822, 2 O.B.R. 514.

Minor children are third party beneficiaries of provisions in a divorce decree granting support payments for their benefit, and such benefits may not be modified by the parties to the detriment of the minors. Rhoades v. Rhoades (Hamilton 1974) 40 Ohio App.2d 559, 321 N.E.2d 242, 69 O.O.2d 488. Child Support ⊕ 242

Where a husband and wife are divorced, the duty to support a minor child is governed by 3109.05 and not 3103.03, so that a wife may be required to assume the support of her child who is in the custody of another. Hill v. Hill (Hamilton 1973) 40 Ohio App.2d 1, 317 N.E.2d 250, 69 O.O.2d 1.

Where a noncustodial mother inherits sixty thousand dollars, the trial court does not abuse its discretion in denying the father's motion for child support, notwithstanding that the father was ordered to pay support before he gained custody, where the father does not show that he is unable to provide for his children's needs and where the court finds that the mother desires use of the money for her own purposes. Griffith v Griffith, No. CA-84-07-078 (12th Dist Ct App, Butler, 12-17-84).

A cost-of-living clause in a separation agreement providing for automatic increases in child support is valid, as the ability of a domestic relations court to modify for a change of circumstances exists despite the clause. Gui v Brown, No. CA-6392 (5th Dist Ct App, Stark, 11-26-84).

It is an abuse of discretion to order that a noncustodial parent, without disabilities, who has been out of the employment market for twelve years, must pay child support whether or not employed. Zaller v Zaller, No. 10–035 (11th Dist Ct App, Lake, 6–29–84).

Inflation alone will not justify a modification in a support award, but where the custodial parent has experienced increased food, fuel, and educational expenses, and the noncustodial parent has received a pay raise sufficient to cover the increase in support, a modification is justified under RC 3109.05. Frierott v Frierott, No. 2–82–18 (3d Dist Ct App, Auglaize, 1–10–84).

Where a minor child uses the surname of her stepfather but no legal steps have been taken to change such child's surname, the use of the surname does not relieve the noncustodial parent's obligation to pay child support. Houser v Houser, No. CA–2887 (5th Dist Ct App, Licking, 9–24–82).

In a divorce proceeding, take-home pay is not the equivalent of "relative earning abilities of the parties" for purposes of awarding a property settlement nor is take-home pay the determinative factor in arriving at an order for child support. Hanney v Hanney, No. OT–81–25 (6th Dist Ct App, Ottawa, 5–7–82).

An order to pay child support is proper only if the trial court determines the appropriateness of the amount of child support by considering the required factors under RC 3109.05. Botticello v Botticello, No. 7372 (2d Dist Ct App, Montgomery, 1–7–82).

The court defines dental, optical and pharmaceutical services as medical expenses, but optical expenses include only those services provided by an opthalmologist and not glasses furnished by an optometrist. Minick v Minick, No. OT–81–3 (6th Dist Ct App, Ottawa, 8–14–81).

Although RC 3109.05 requires that the financial resources and needs of both the custodial and noncustodial parent be considered in determining a reasonable child-support amount, it is an abuse of discretion to require the mother to pay twenty-three per cent of her meager $110 per week income for child support. Logsdon v Logsdon, No. 80AP–919 (10th Dist Ct App, Franklin, 7–21–81).

Where a court of appeals does not have testimony concerning the amount required to support the children, the need of the father for additional support for the children, and the needs of the mother, an award of forty-five dollars per month child support is deemed as adequate and not an abuse of discretion. Adams v Adams, No. 81AP–233 (10th Dist Ct App, Franklin, 5–28–81).

Where the non-custodial parent is ordered to pay child support, to have an abuse of discretion in such a case, there must be a showing of a combination of circumstances where there is an inability to contribute even a nominal amount by the person out of custody, coupled with a showing that the person in custody has an ability to support without help. McCauley v McCauley, No. 79AP–727 (10th Dist Ct App, Franklin, 1–29–80).

30. —— College expenses, support award

Former husband's failure to pay for child's college expenses for fall and summer semesters did not constitute contempt of divorce decree, which required him to pay for child's college tuition, books, and room and board, though former husband's failure to pay constituted noncompliance with decree, as former husband had paid $80,675.02 for tuition, books, and room and board and for numerous miscellaneous expenses, including suite fees, apartment rent, meals, telephone bills, electric bills, internet bills, permit fees, housing deposits, and computer-related expenses, former husband paid these miscellaneous expenses even though they did not qualify for payment under divorce decree, and it was impossible to compute how much more former husband had paid than he was required to pay, and whatever additional amount, if any, that he owed, could not be quantified. Wolf v. Wolf (Ohio App. 1 Dist., Hamilton, 06-18-2010) No. C-090587, 2010-Ohio-2762, 2010 WL 2473277, Unreported. Child Support 444

Former wife was entitled to award of costs and attorney fees incurred to prosecute motion for contempt against husband based on his refusal to pay costs of child's college education and books, in express violation of unambiguous provision in settlement agreement incorporated into parties' divorce decree requiring him to do so. Blazic v. Blazic (Ohio App. 1 Dist., Hamilton, 08-26-2005) No. C-040414, No. C-040440, 2005-Ohio-4417, 2005 WL 2044954, Unreported. Child Support 603

Trial court lacked authority to modify unambiguous provision in settlement agreement incorporated into parties' divorce decree requiring husband to pay child's college expenses, including books, by ordering that husband was not required to pay for child's books, on wife's motion for contempt based on husband's failure to pay for books. Blazic v. Blazic (Ohio App. 1 Dist., Hamilton, 08-26-2005) No. C-040414, No. C-040440, 2005-Ohio-4417, 2005 WL 2044954, Unreported. Child Support 496

Provision in settlement agreement incorporated into parties' divorce decree that husband would pay child's college expenses, limited to tuition, room and board, and books until he obtained bachelor's decree was clear and unambiguous, and thus, husband's refusal to pay tuition and books at private college where child was attending simply because child was earning low grades, without seeking to modify settlement agreement, warranted finding of contempt. Blazic v. Blazic (Ohio App. 1 Dist., Hamilton, 08-26-2005) No. C-040414, No. C-040440, 2005-Ohio-4417, 2005 WL 2044954, Unreported. Child Support 52; Child Support 444

A child support obligation that remains in effect beyond a child's eighteenth birthday until graduation from high school does not apply to the child's attendance at a community college for attainment of college credits towards a high school diploma. Chowdhury v. Fitzgerald (Ohio App. 5 Dist.,

Guernsey, 03-27-1997) No. 96 CA 43, 1997 WL 219172, Unreported.

A child support obligation is in effect as long as a child who is eighteen is attending high-school and completes his graduation requirements six weeks after full-time high-school has let out for the summer. O'Brien v. O'Brien (Ohio App. 12 Dist., Clermont, 04-28-1997) No. CA96-11-101, 1997 WL 208133, Unreported.

A trial court's extension of support beyond a child's eighteenth birthday violates the terms of the couple's 1978 divorce agreement and reliance on present day RC 3109.05(E) is misplaced as that section's language, requiring support issued pursuant to this section to continue past the age of majority so long as the child is in high school, was enacted years after the divorce decree was issued and is not controlling. Wendling v. Wendling (Ohio App. 8 Dist., Cuyahoga, 02-08-1996) No. 68837, 1996 WL 50825, Unreported, dismissed, appeal not allowed 76 Ohio St.3d 1420, 667 N.E.2d 24.

Judgment for payment of a child's college expenses provided for in a separation agreement should not be considered child support and collection thereof should not be made through the Child Support Enforcement Agency. Chester v. Baker (Ohio App. 5 Dist., Licking, 08-10-1995) No. 95 CA 7, 1995 WL 497602, Unreported, dismissed, appeal not allowed 74 Ohio St.3d 1482, 657 N.E.2d 1376.

An obligor is not entitled to a credit towards child support where a child receives a full college tuition scholarship and the separation agreement that provides child support of $225 per month per child and continues as to that child until graduation from college is a binding contract, and the parties did not contemplate and provide in the agreement for one of the children receiving a scholarship. Urban v. Spriestersbach (Ohio App. 3 Dist., Seneca, 02-28-1995) No. 13-94-26, 1995 WL 81975, Unreported.

A divorce decree that contains a provision that the husband has the college education obligation for the parties' child providing he is financially able to pay it fails to specify an objective standard to be used to determine when the husband is "financially able" and is vague and unenforceable. Hartlieb v. Hartlieb (Ohio App. 8 Dist., Cuyahoga, 02-03-1994) No. 64635, 1994 WL 30427, Unreported.

Foreign divorce decree issued by Indian court, requiring former husband to pay child support for his daughter, did not violate public policy on ground it required former husband to support his daughter beyond the age of 18, and thus the decree could be enforced in Ohio on the basis of comity; Indian court ordered former husband to pay a lump-sum amount within two months of the date of its decree, or else he would be in arrears at certain monthly rate from 1986, former husband's daughters were still minors in 1986, and it was not unreasonable to expect former husband to support his children. Kalia v. Kalia (Ohio App. 11 Dist., 12-20-2002) 151 Ohio App.3d 145, 783 N.E.2d 623,

2002-Ohio-7160, appeal not allowed 98 Ohio St.3d 1566, 787 N.E.2d 1231, 2003-Ohio-2242. Child Support ☞ 525

Trial court had jurisdiction in child support proceeding, under statutory provisions permitting under certain circumstances a support award above and beyond standard amount, to order that noncustodial parent pay portion of child's private school tuition, even though public schools were available. Smith v. Null (Ohio App. 4 Dist., 01-29-2001) 143 Ohio App.3d 264, 757 N.E.2d 1200, 2001-Ohio-2386. Child Support ☞ 118

Ex-husband's child support obligation continued past daughter's 18th birthday, as provided for under Missouri law in Missouri child support order, despite Ohio law providing for termination of support when child reaches age 18. Emig v. Massau (Ohio App. 10 Dist., 11-16-2000) 140 Ohio App.3d 119, 746 N.E.2d 707. Child Support ☞ 391

Withdrawal from high school by child who was in custody of former husband on day child turned 18 years of age terminated wife's duty to pay child support, and divested trial court of jurisdiction to order wife to pay child support or to modify child support agreement; child's subsequent enrollment in vocational school did not resurrect order, as obligation continues after age 18 only if child continuously attends high school. Gleason v. Gleason (Ohio App. 4 Dist., 08-27-1998) 129 Ohio App.3d 563, 718 N.E.2d 512. Child Support ☞ 293; Child Support ☞ 390; Child Support ☞ 470

Voluntary contributions by child support obligor to education of adult children are not an appropriate consideration in calculation of child support obligations, and do not entitle obligor to reduction in child support obligations. State ex rel. Scioto Cty. Child Support Enforcement Agency v.Gardner (Ohio App. 4 Dist., 07-25-1996) 113 Ohio App.3d 46, 680 N.E.2d 221. Child Support ☞ 236; Child Support ☞ 293; Child Support ☞ 302

Father's obligation to pay child support, under dissolution decree, continued until daughter completed her high school education, even though she already had attained age of majority. Swanson v. Swanson (Ohio App. 2 Dist., 02-09-1996) 109 Ohio App.3d 231, 671 N.E.2d 1333. Child Support ☞ 393

Trial court did not abuse its discretion in requiring father to pay child support under dissolution decree until adult child graduated from high school, even though child could have graduated from high school a year earlier than she did, where additional year of high school prepared child for job. Swanson v. Swanson (Ohio App. 2 Dist., 02-09-1996) 109 Ohio App.3d 231, 671 N.E.2d 1333. Child Support ☞ 393

Statute providing for postmajority enforcement of child support orders did not operate retroactively as to father, where, when dissolution decree was entered, statute governing duty to support children required parents to continue paying child support for children attending high school. Swanson v.

Swanson (Ohio App. 2 Dist., 02-09-1996) 109 Ohio App.3d 231, 671 N.E.2d 1333. Child Support ⚬ 6

Court is generally without jurisdiction to order a parent to support a child once that child reaches age of majority. Troha v. Troha (Ohio App. 2 Dist., 06-28-1995) 105 Ohio App.3d 327, 663 N.E.2d 1319. Child Support ⚬ 103

Courts are generally without jurisdiction to order parents to support children who have attained age of majority except where parties have entered into separation agreement that provides their child with support beyond age of majority and agreement is incorporated into divorce or dissolution decree. Tapp v. Tapp (Ohio App. 2 Dist., 06-14-1995) 105 Ohio App.3d 159, 663 N.E.2d 944, dismissed, appeal not allowed 74 Ohio St.3d 1418, 655 N.E.2d 738. Child Support ⚬ 23; Child Support ⚬ 44

Court of Common Pleas had proper jurisdiction to enforce a separation agreement pursuant to which husband agreed to pay for daughter's college education. Tapp v. Tapp (Ohio App. 2 Dist., 06-14-1995) 105 Ohio App.3d 159, 663 N.E.2d 944, dismissed, appeal not allowed 74 Ohio St.3d 1418, 655 N.E.2d 738. Child Support ⚬ 52

Ex-husband unreasonably withheld approval of his daughter's choice of college under separation agreement, incorporated into dissolution decree, rendering ex-husband responsible for payment of all expenses incurred by or for daughter's college education in four-year undergraduate program, where only college program he approved was that of a community college which only provided a two-year program. Tapp v. Tapp (Ohio App. 2 Dist., 06-14-1995) 105 Ohio App.3d 159, 663 N.E.2d 944, dismissed, appeal not allowed 74 Ohio St.3d 1418, 655 N.E.2d 738. Child Support ⚬ 52

Trial court lacked jurisdiction to order former husband to maintain trust fund for child's college education after former husband won lottery, even though former husband had voluntarily established trust fund; there was no separation agreement or any other enforceable agreement by which former husband had agreed to fund trust for child's college education. Pratt v. McCullough (Ohio App. 12 Dist., 01-30-1995) 100 Ohio App.3d 479, 654 N.E.2d 372, appeal not allowed 72 Ohio St.3d 1540, 650 N.E.2d 481. Child Support ⚬ 393

In determining whether parent has duty to support mentally or physically disabled child beyond age of 18, court must make factual determination as to whether child is so physically or mentally disabled as to be incapable of maintaining himself or herself. In re Owens (Ohio App. 2 Dist., 08-12-1994) 96 Ohio App.3d 429, 645 N.E.2d 130. Child Support ⚬ 111

Parent's obligations to pay medical expenses of child ceases at time child obtains age of majority and is not enrolled fulltime in accredited high school unless separation agreement incorporated into decree of divorce or dissolution provides otherwise. Rohrbacher v. Rohrbacher (Lucas 1992) 83 Ohio App.3d 569, 615 N.E.2d 338. Child Support ⚬ 114

A child who enters the United States coast guard academy on a full scholarship with stipend for the pursuit of a baccalaureate is a full-time college student for the purposes of a support order provision which requires child support payments to continue during college study. Howard v. Howard (Clermont 1992) 80 Ohio App.3d 832, 610 N.E.2d 1152.

Domestic relations court had authority to give effect to former husband's agreement which was incorporated in divorce decree and required him to support incompetent adult child, although domestic relations court never had jurisdiction over child. O'Connor v. O'Connor (Franklin 1991) 71 Ohio App.3d 541, 594 N.E.2d 1081, motion overruled 62 Ohio St.3d 1409, 577 N.E.2d 362. Child Support ⚬ 44

A domestic relations court may enforce the provisions of an agreement incorporated to a divorce decree that a parent provide financial support for an incompetent adult child, notwithstanding the fact that the child is an adult at the time the decree is issued and may utilize the child support guidelines to determine the appropriate amount of support. O'Connor v. O'Connor (Franklin 1991) 71 Ohio App.3d 541, 594 N.E.2d 1081, motion overruled 62 Ohio St.3d 1409, 577 N.E.2d 362.

While domestic relations court in divorce, dissolution, legal separation or child support proceeding has authority to order either or both parents to aid or support their children, the court does not have power to make decree regarding support of minor children beyond date when child reaches age of majority. Crigger v. Crigger (Franklin 1991) 71 Ohio App.3d 410, 594 N.E.2d 67. Child Support ⚬ 103; Child Support ⚬ 390

A trial court's broad interpretation of the word "tuition" as used in a parties' separation agreement to include the undergraduate fee and the general fee listed on a university fee statement for purposes of the amount of tuition an ex-husband is required to pay as part of his child support is not unreasonable, arbitrary, or unconscionable; the general fee is a fee assessed against all students for admission into college and is not an optional fee. Baker v. Baker (Wood 1990) 68 Ohio App.3d 402, 588 N.E.2d 944.

A trial court did not abuse its discretion in limiting college costs paid by a former husband to those specific items mentioned in the separation agreement; room and board is not included in an obligation to pay "costs of such items as tuition, fees, and books." Uram v. Uram (Summit 1989) 65 Ohio App.3d 96, 582 N.E.2d 1060. Child Support ⚬ 52

A divorced father's support obligations self-terminate when his child turns eighteen, even though the child has not yet graduated from high school, where the divorce decree incorporating the parties' separation agreement provides for support to continue during the child's minority and no lawful motion to continue support until graduation from high school has been made; therefore, a trial court properly denies the father's motion to terminate his child support obligations, since such motion in reality constitutes a request for an advisory opinion. Behrisch v. Behrisch (Summit 1989) 62 Ohio App.3d 164, 574 N.E.2d 1152.

Father had no duty to provide continued support for his epileptic son, after son graduated from high school; there was evidence that extent of disability did not prevent son from being employable, and he in fact held a part-time job. Cooksey v. Cooksey (Eric 1988) 55 Ohio App.3d 135, 562 N.E.2d 934. Child Support ⚫ 111

A divorce decree requiring one parent to pay a child's tuition expenses at a designated university may reasonably be interpreted to require payment of an equivalent amount toward tuition costs of another university which the child and custodial parent choose. Evans v. Brown (Franklin 1985) 23 Ohio App.3d 97, 491 N.E.2d 384, 23 O.B.R. 163.

Where a separation agreement provides that the father shall pay the cost of a child's college education, and the agreement is silent as to whether that education must be at a public or private institution, the father is required to pay the full cost of the child's college education at the private institution attended. Rand v Rand, No. 47712 (8th Dist Ct App, Cuyahoga, 6-28-84), affirmed by 18 OS(3d) 356, 18 OBR 415, 481 NE(2d) 609 (1985).

A domestic relations court retains jurisdiction over parties in a divorce, dissolution, or separation proceeding to continue or to modify support payments for a mentally or physically disabled child, who was so disabled before he or she attained the statutory age of majority, as if the child were still an infant. Castle v. Castle (Ohio 1984) 15 Ohio St.3d 279, 473 N.E.2d 803, 15 O.B.R. 413. Child Support ⚫ 232; Child Support ⚫ 390

The court that granted a divorce has no subject matter jurisdiction to provide for the support of a child of the divorced parties once the child reaches the age of majority. Maphet v. Heiselman (Clermont 1984) 13 Ohio App.3d 278, 469 N.E.2d 92, 13 O.B.R. 343.

Where the children of a marriage have reached the age of majority, the trial court cannot enforce an existing child support order by exercising its contempt power; however, the child support obligee may collect any support arrearage by garnishment, attachment, or execution on the lump sum judgments previously granted. Thompson v. Albers (Clermont 1981) 1 Ohio App.3d 139, 439 N.E.2d 955, 1 O.B.R. 446.

RC 3105.10 clothes courts with jurisdiction to incorporate into a court order an agreement to support a child of the parties beyond the age of that child's majority, and such an order may be enforced by contempt proceedings. Bugay v. Bugay (Summit 1977) 53 Ohio App.2d 285, 373 N.E.2d 1263, 7 O.O.3d 336.

The statutory change in the age of majority can have no application to the subject decretal support obligations because such change, in and of itself, has no effect on pre–1974 support decrees. Nokes

v. Nokes (Ohio 1976) 47 Ohio St.2d 1, 351 N.E.2d 174, 1 O.O.3d 1.

Determination of the age at which a person becomes an adult for the purpose of enforcing the provisions of the reciprocal support act, depends upon the state in which the child is living and the state in which the father is living, and not in the state in which the original divorce was granted. Burney v. Vance (Ohio Com.Pl. 1969) 17 Ohio Misc. 307, 246 N.E.2d 371, 46 O.O.2d 427.

An order of a divorce court increasing the support payments required of a father for the declared purpose of "the support of the children" is a valid order, notwithstanding one of the children is a high school graduate, intends to acquire a college education, has had part-time employment and saves some of his earnings toward a college education. Ford v. Ford (Miami 1959) 109 Ohio App. 495, 167 N.E.2d 787, 12 O.O.2d 67. Child Support ⚫ 293

In a divorce action, it is not abuse of discretion as a matter of law for the trial court, having jurisdiction of the parties, to order payments by the father for the college education of minor children electing to matriculate in an accredited college. Mitchell v. Mitchell (Ohio 1960) 170 Ohio St. 507, 166 N.E.2d 396, 11 O.O.2d 281.

Where as part of a valid agreement, a husband agrees to provide a college education for his children and further agrees to keep in effect insurance policies on his life in which such children are beneficiaries, and where such agreement is incorporated in a decree divorcing the husband from his wife, such decree becomes binding on the husband even though the performance required by the decree may extend beyond the minority of the children. Robrock v. Robrock (Ohio 1958) 167 Ohio St. 479, 150 N.E.2d 421, 5 O.O.2d 165. Child Support ⚫ 54

Court may order support for child until it attains majority. Josh v. Josh (Ohio 1929) 120 Ohio St. 151, 165 N.E. 717.

The trial court may reinstate support obligations including medical expenses for a handicapped child after prior termination of the order. Bragg v Gorby, No. 86–C–37 (7th Dist Ct App, Columbiana, 6–30–87).

Where a child was injured in an auto accident after he was eighteen, but before graduation, after completing all the requirements for graduation, the duty to support does not continue. Blandon v Blandon, No. CA86–12–173 (12th Dist Ct App, Butler, 6–29–87).

In accordance with public policy and the statutory grant of broad equitable powers, a domestic relations court may order a noncustodial parent to continue child support payments and medical insurance coverage for a child who has reached majority, where the child is severely handicapped and has been under the jurisdiction of the domestic relations division since the age of six or seven. Mullanney v Mullanney, No. C–820944 (1st Dist Ct App, Hamilton, 1–4–84).

Absent specific agreement to pay child support beyond majority in the separation agreement, the term "cost of higher education" means those special costs a student incurs beyond living expenses and cannot include room and board. Frazier v Frazier, No. 2919 (5th Dist Ct App, Licking, 2–14–83).

As part of a separation agreement, the parties may contract for their children to receive education at a parochial school with tuition payment to be made by a designated party. Braun v Braun, No. L–80–156 (6th Dist Ct App, Lucas, 2–20–81).

31. ——— Emancipated children, support award

Trial court did not abuse its discretion in determining that father's child support obligation terminated on date child graduated from high school, and that father was not required to pay support through the entire month in which child graduated, as the common law duty imposed on father to support minor child terminated when child became emancipated, either reaching the age of majority or graduating from high school, such that parties' child became emancipated on date of his graduation. He v. Zeng (Ohio App. 5 Dist., Licking, 05-11-2010) No. 2009-CA-00060, 2010-Ohio-2095, 2010 WL 1918797, Unreported, appeal not allowed 126 Ohio St.3d 1601, 935 N.E.2d 47, 2010-Ohio-4928. Child Support ☞ 393

Trial court's order that former husband's child support obligations continue until child graduated from high school or reached age of 19, the child was otherwise emancipated, or child support order was modified by court indicated that obligation continued after child turned 18 only if child was still in high school and not otherwise emancipated, and thus was proper. Gerlach v. Gerlach (Ohio App. 10 Dist., Franklin, 03-30-2004) No. 03AP-22, No. 03AP-872, 2004-Ohio-1607, 2004 WL 625686, Unreported. Child Support ☞ 223

The fact that a high school offered a student a course of instruction off-campus and with the assistance of other individuals or entities did not render her an emancipated individual for the purpose of child support. Although former division (E) (deleted in 2000) did not define "continuously attends on a full-time basis any recognized and accredited high school," the General Assembly did not intend this section to insist on physical presence at a particular building, to the exclusion of regular, full-time participation in an educational program. Weber v. Weber (Ohio App. 9 Dist., Lorain, 05-23-2001) No. 00CA007722, 2001 WL 542319, Unreported, appeal not allowed 93 Ohio St.3d 1433, 755 N.E.2d 355.

The trial court does not err in finding that a nineteen-year-old daughter is not emancipated and, accordingly, properly denies a motion by the father for termination of child support where the evidence in the record shows that (1) the daughter is a full-time college student, (2) the father and mother pay for nearly all of her expenses including tuition, room, and board, (3) the daughter lives on campus but returns to her mother's home during the summer and on breaks, (4) the daughter works part-

time in a public service related area as a requirement to maintain her scholarship, and (5) there is no indication that the mother has renunciated her right to the care and custody of the daughter nor that the daughter has taken affirmative steps to release herself from parental control. Smyers v. Abramovich (Ohio App. 9 Dist., Summit, 03-07-2001) No. 20124, 2001 WL 222962, Unreported.

An eighteen-year-old student who withdraws from high school and enrolls in the Job Corps where he intends to complete his final year of high school is not emancipated because his mother's continued financial support for clothes, tools and personal items demonstrates that she had not relinquished parental control consistent with her son's emancipation. Johnson v. Johnson (Ohio App. 2 Dist., Montgomery, 12-17-1999) No. 17858, 1999 WL 1206690, Unreported.

A child who quits school when he turns eighteen in March and leaves home in June is emancipated notwithstanding emotional problems and financial assistance from his mother in paying his bills and a court's decision to terminate support for the period after the child quits school and before he leaves home is not an abuse of discretion. Palmer v. Palmer (Ohio App. 2 Dist., Montgomery, 01-22-1999) No. 16986, 1999 WL 22747, Unreported.

Parents can agree to provide post-divorce support for emancipated children by way of an annuity to provide for the children's college education. Strong v. Strong (Ohio App. 6 Dist., Lucas, 02-28-1997) No. L-96-044, 1997 WL 89105, Unreported.

Party seeking relief from child support order bears burden of proving that child is emancipated. Powell v. Powell (Ohio App. 4 Dist., 05-30-1996) 111 Ohio App.3d 418, 676 N.E.2d 556. Child Support ☞ 484

Whether child is emancipated, so as to relieve parent from obligation of support, depends upon particular facts and circumstances of each individual case. Powell v. Powell (Ohio App. 4 Dist., 05-30-1996) 111 Ohio App.3d 418, 676 N.E.2d 556. Child Support ☞ 386; Parent And Child ☞ 16

In determining whether child is emancipated for child support purposes, unique facts and circumstances of each case must be evaluated. Powell v. Powell (Ohio App. 4 Dist., 05-30-1996) 111 Ohio App.3d 418, 676 N.E.2d 556. Child Support ☞ 386

Parents generally have no duty under Ohio law to provide support, including payment for college expenses, to emancipated children. Troha v. Troha (Ohio App. 2 Dist., 06-28-1995) 105 Ohio App.3d 327, 663 N.E.2d 1319. Child Support ☞ 120; Child Support ☞ 386

Parents are obligated to support a minor child until the child reaches the age of majority and is legally emancipated, and where a trial court directs that a father pay child support for his minor daughter until she turns eighteen even though a separation agreement provision requires support until she becomes emancipated or graduates from high school, whichever comes first, and the daughter graduates one month before her eighteenth birthday, the trial court's order does not modify the child support absent a showing of a change of circumstances but rather interprets the separation agreement language to mean that "or graduates from high school" has the same definition as "age of majority," which requires support until the minor child's eighteenth birthday. Dudziak v. Dudziak (Cuyahoga 1992) 81 Ohio App.3d 361, 611 N.E.2d 337.

Where a mother seeks to extend child support payments for the month between a child's high school graduation and her eighteenth birthday, at which time the child becomes emancipated, a motion for relief is unnecessary where the court has continuing jurisdiction and the separation agreement with its child support provision is incorporated into the dissolution agreement and provides for support until the child graduates high school or becomes emancipated, whichever occurs first; the trial court does not have to modify the child support portion of the separation agreement but need only interpret it in light of case law providing for parental obligation of support until the age of majority. Dudziak v. Dudziak (Cuyahoga 1992) 81 Ohio App.3d 361, 611 N.E.2d 337.

A father is obligated to support a child until she reaches majority at age eighteen, at which time she becomes legally emancipated despite a separation agreement stating that the father's support would end when the child graduated high school or became emancipated, whichever came first, where the child graduates one month before her eighteenth birthday. Dudziak v. Dudziak (Cuyahoga 1992) 81 Ohio App.3d 361, 611 N.E.2d 337.

Age of majority in effect at time of entry of dissolution decree that contained child support obligation controlled determination of child's emancipation based on attainment of age of majority. Bauer v. Bauer (Franklin 1989) 57 Ohio App.3d 24, 566 N.E.2d 185. Child Support ⚷ 392

Question of when a child is emancipated so as to relieve a parent from the obligation of support depends upon particular facts and circumstances of each case. Price v. Price (Darke 1983) 12 Ohio App.3d 42, 465 N.E.2d 922, 12 O.B.R. 129. Child Support ⚷ 386; Parent And Child ⚷ 16

Where the age of legal majority is reduced by the legislature, a party to a divorce settlement, under which he is bound to support minor children until they become emancipated, is relieved of any obligation beyond that age designated by the new act. Allison v. Allison (Warren 1975) 44 Ohio App.2d 230, 337 N.E.2d 666, 73 O.O.2d 243.

A father is primarily responsible for the support of his minor children, and that support continues under the law of Ohio until the child is twenty-one years of age or is otherwise emancipated. Burney v. Vance (Ohio Com.Pl. 1969) 17 Ohio Misc. 307, 246 N.E.2d 371, 46 O.O.2d 427.

Where an unrepresented husband/father signed an ambiguous separation agreement which contractually obligated him to pay room and board for his emancipated children, such agreement's ambiguity shall be resolved in favor of the father as being limited to the obligation to pay for educationally related expenses, such as dormitory room and board rather than room and board at the wife's home, as such intention was demonstrated by the limiting word "educational" in the separation agreement. In re Fugazzi, No. 82AP–174 and 82AP–184 (10th Dist Ct App, Franklin, 6-2-83).

32. —— Arrearages, support award

When trial court was faced with the all-too-familiar post-decree situation of ex-wife's earnest claim for reimbursement of children's medical expenses against ex-husband's equity-based assertion of lack of presentation or knowledge of such expenses, trial court did not abuse its discretion in its application of laches in resolving this issue, thereby denying ex-wife reimbursement of the medical bills; ex-wife conceded that she had never presented the bills in question to ex-husband or informed him that they were accruing. Pace v. Pace (Ohio App. 5 Dist., Tuscarawas, 08-02-2010) No. 10 AP 02 0008, 2010-Ohio-3573, 2010 WL 3011083, Unreported. Child Support ⚷ 472

State was not estopped from enforcing against former husband its right to receive child support to which former wife had been entitled, automatically assigned by her upon children's receipt of public assistance payments, by reason of lack of notice to former husband of existence of state's right prior to his entry into agreement with former wife deeming any support arrearages fully satisfied. Monroe Cty. Child Support Enforcement Agency on Behalf of Ullman v. Ullman (Ohio App. 7 Dist., Monroe, 09-06-2005) No. 04-MO-08, 2005-Ohio-4692, 2005 WL 2174005, Unreported. Child Support ⚷ 452; Child Support ⚷ 465

Former husband could not raise equitable defense of laches to bar former wife's claim for child support and spousal support arrears, even though support order was 17 years old, and former husband argued he suffered prejudice as result of former wife's delay because his records of payment had been destroyed in earthquake, where husband came into equity with unclean hands because, instead of making payment to county's bureau of support, former husband voluntarily disobeyed court order by making payments directly to former wife. (Per Farmer, P.J., with one judge concurring separately.) Unger v. Unger (Ohio App. 5 Dist., Stark, 11-01-2004) No. 2003CA00356, 2004-Ohio-5883, 2004 WL 2496435, Unreported. Child Support ⚷ 451; Divorce ⚷ 1054

Laches did not bar former wife's reopening of child support case that sought payment of arrearages from former husband, although element concerning knowledge of the injury or wrong was present, since delay was not unreasonable, excuse for delay in bringing action emanated from former husband's move to California and former wife's unsuccessful efforts to collect child support in California, and former husband had not been prejudiced by delay. Marcum v. Marcum (Ohio App. 7 Dist., Columbiana, 12-19-2003) No. 02 CO 33, 2003-Ohio-7012, 2003 WL 22998229, Unreported. Child Support ☞ 451

A trial court does not err by ordering a father to pay a lump sum support arrearage directly to his daughter after her emancipation where the request for support is properly made prior to the child's emancipation and the motion for support arises out of a court's disposition of unruly charges filed by the father which results in termination of the father's previous status as residential parent; therefore, the father as the non-custodial parent remains responsible for the child's financial support. In re Hollaender (Ohio App. 12 Dist., Warren, 06-19-2000) No. CA99-08-092, 2000 WL 783070, Unreported.

The duty to pay child support is unaffected by any interference with rights of visitation, and no estoppel to claim child support arrears from a father may be inferred from the mother's withholding of visitation with the child. French v. French (Ohio App. 3 Dist., Marion, 05-30-1995) No. 9-95-7, 1995 WL 328110, Unreported, dismissed, appeal not allowed 74 Ohio St.3d 1418, 655 N.E.2d 738.

Awarding ex-wife $21,037.95 in child support arrearages was abuse of discretion, where such figure was based on ex-wife's testimony and, although ex-wife claimed she relied on payment history statement supplied by child support enforcement agency (CSEA) to arrive as such figure, statement indicated arrearages in amount of $21,846.37. Marek v. Marek (Ohio App. 9 Dist., 10-20-2004) 158 Ohio App.3d 750, 822 N.E.2d 410, 2004-Ohio-5556. Child Support ☞ 487

Trial court's entry in which court described and approved magistrate's orders regarding child support arrearages, but which did not set forth orders of court, was not final and appealable order. In re Dortch (Ohio App. 9 Dist., 11-24-1999) 135 Ohio App.3d 430, 734 N.E.2d 434. Child Support ☞ 537

Child support arrearages not incorporated into final decree of divorce are waived and temporary orders are merged into final decree. Brooks v. Brooks (Ohio App. 10 Dist., 12-24-1996) 117 Ohio App.3d 19, 689 N.E.2d 987. Child Support ☞ 223; Child Support ☞ 452

Reviewing court's affirmance of trial court order requiring ex-wife to pay ex-husband's portion of mortgage payments she received upon sale of marital home directly to county child support enforcement agency to pay for ex-husband's arrearage in child support was law of the case and precluded finding that ex-husband was still obligated on entire amount of arrearage without setoff for mortgage payment amounts; however, order did not mention future child support payments and did not preclude holding ex-husband liable for arrearages occurring after date of order. Schneider v. Schneider (Cler-

mont 1992) 83 Ohio App.3d 423, 615 N.E.2d 244. Child Support ☞ 549

The doctrine of laches prevents an award of child support arrearage to a mother who deliberately kept the child from the father for eighteen years where she and her new family moved several times out of state and never requested payment during those years; these actions materially prejudiced the father's rights. Ferree v. Sparks (Warren 1991) 77 Ohio App.3d 185, 601 N.E.2d 568.

Child support arrearages may not be ordered to be paid where the obligor's only source of income is from public assistance received for the benefit of his other children as aid for dependent children benefits are not subject to attachment. Crigger v. Crigger (Franklin 1991) 71 Ohio App.3d 410, 594 N.E.2d 67.

Where a noncustodial parent owes child support arrearages from the date of original decree until the change of custody, a trial court may set off the child support obligation of the new noncustodial parent against the arrearage due the current obligor; however, it is error to only allow one-half of the current obligor's weekly obligation to be set off against the arrearage due. Krause v. Krause (Butler 1987) 35 Ohio App.3d 18, 518 N.E.2d 1221.

The appellate court erred in reversing the trial court's rejection of a defense of laches in a suit to recover child support arrearages where there was substantial disagreement in the evidence regarding both opportunity to bring suit and the question of prejudice. Kinney v. Mathias (Ohio 1984) 10 Ohio St.3d 72, 461 N.E.2d 901, 10 O.B.R. 361.

33. —— Payment to third party, support award

Trial court did not abuse its discretion in failing to give father a child support obligation credit for the cost of trip to Europe for the parties' daughter, where there was no evidence that the trip constituted a need of the parties' child. Onyshko v. Onyshko (Ohio App. 11 Dist., Portage, 03-12-2010) No. 2008-P-0035, 2010-Ohio-969, 2010 WL 891335, Unreported. Child Support ☞ 454

Release agreement ex-wife executed with title company after title company paid money to ex-wife following title company's failure to detect and satisfy ex-wife's judgment lien on ex-husband's real property when it was sold by ex-husband released title company from liability to property buyer for title company's defective title search and in no way satisfied ex-wife's judgment against ex-husband for child support arrearages, where release stated that ex-wife released only her right to enforce her judgment lien on property that was subject of defective title search and that ex-wife was not "waiving or in any manner affecting her lien, charge, or encumbrance upon any land other than land" being sold by ex-husband. Campbell v. Campbell (Ohio App. 9 Dist., Summit, 10-20-2004) No. 21996, 2004-Ohio-5553, 2004 WL 2348173, Unreported. Child Support ☞ 456

Money paid to ex-wife by title company, which failed to detect and satisfy ex-wife's judgment lien on ex-husband's real property when it was sold by ex-husband, did not constitute "gift," within meaning of statute providing that any money paid by person responsible under child support order to person entitled to receive support payments that is not made to child support enforcement agency (CSEA) in accordance with applicable support order shall be deemed gift, where it was undisputed that ex husband did not pay money at issue to ex-wife and there was no evidence that title company paid money at issue on behalf of ex-husband or in satisfaction of ex-wife's judgment lien against ex-husband based on child support arrearages. Campbell v. Campbell (Ohio App. 9 Dist., Summit, 10-20-2004) No. 21996, 2004-Ohio-5553, 2004 WL 2348173, Unreported. Child Support ☞ 454

Trial court did not abuse its discretion in requiring former husband to pay portion of his child support obligation directly to children's parochial school until former wife's outstanding tuition obligation was satisfied. Jefferies v. Stanzak (Ohio App. 12 Dist., 10-18-1999) 135 Ohio App.3d 176, 733 N.E.2d 305. Child Support ☞ 430

For purposes of ex-husband's motion for return of overpayment of child support, payments that he made pursuant to a voluntary agreement with county welfare department after a child was born subsequent to parties' divorce would not be deemed a gift, despite lack of court order mandating those payments; unrefuted evidence showed payments were made to discharge child support obligation, and equitable considerations further supported crediting ex-husband for voluntary expenditures made on behalf of child. Cox v. Cox (Ohio App. 1 Dist., 12-04-1998) 130 Ohio App.3d 609, 720 N.E.2d 946. Child Support ☞ 429

Voluntary payments made by a noncustodial parent directly to a child are not to be considered payments in lieu of support where the divorce decree orders that support payments be made through the court. Evans v. Brown (Franklin 1985) 23 Ohio App.3d 97, 491 N.E.2d 384, 23 O.B.R. 163. Child Support ☞ 425

A supporting parent is not necessarily entitled to credit against arrearages for insurance premium payments made on account of the children but not required by the terms of the support decree. Ferriere v. Ferriere (Cuyahoga 1984) 20 Ohio App.3d 82, 484 N.E.2d 753, 20 O.B.R. 102.

The obligee (the state) can collect only in accordance with Ch 5121; when both parents are obligated under Ch 5121, the question of what share each of two divorced parents will pay is a matter to be determined from the divorce decree. State, Dept. of Mental Health & Mental Retardation, Bureau of Support v. Wiedemann (Ohio App. 12 Dist. 1980) 1 Ohio App.3d 27, 437 N.E.2d 1212, 1 O.B.R. 17. Mental Health ☞ 75

The domestic relations court has clear authority to place the burden of child support as it shall deem best, within the scope of discretion allowed in 3109.05; but this authority does not eliminate or in any way affect the liability of both parents for the support of a minor patient under 5121.06 and the related sections of the Revised Code. State, Dept. of Mental Health & Mental Retardation, Bureau of Support v. Wiedemann (Ohio App. 12 Dist. 1980) 1 Ohio App.3d 27, 437 N.E.2d 1212, 1 O.B.R. 17. Child Support ☞ 11; Mental Health ☞ 75

In an action by a hospital against the parents of a minor child for medical treatment provided to the minor child by the hospital, the mother of the child may not absolve herself of liability to the hospital, a third party, by reason of a provision in the divorce decree requiring the father of the child to pay for all medical expenses incurred by the child. Children's Hospital of Akron v. Johnson (Summit 1980) 68 Ohio App.2d 17, 426 N.E.2d 515, 22 O.O.3d 11.

Where a husband and wife are divorced, the duty to support a minor child is governed by RC 3109.05 and not 3103.03, so that a wife may be required to assume the support of her child which is in the custody of another. Hill v. Hill (Hamilton 1973) 40 Ohio App.2d 1, 317 N.E.2d 250, 69 O.O.2d 1.

Mothers who bring a civil rights action under 42 USC 1983 seeking no monetary relief but requesting that the court permanently enjoin the defendants, various county and state officials responsible for administering child support enforcement services, from failing to provide these services under state law and the Social Security Act, have failed to state a claim upon which relief can be granted; the plaintiffs sought only a "hurry-up" order, and unearthed no acts of noncompliance beyond those already found in an audit by the secretary of health and human services. Carelli v. Howser (C.A.6 (Ohio) 1991) 923 F.2d 1208, rehearing denied.

A divorce decree that appears to contemplate sale of the marital residence and an equal sharing of the net proceeds is dividing property in this respect rather than imposing a support obligation on any party; as a result, a provision calling for the husband to make mortgage payments does not create a support obligation and the obligation may be discharged in the husband's bankruptcy along with any arrearage. In re Shelton (Bkrtcy.S.D.Ohio 1988) 92 B.R. 268.

It is not error to grant a judgment for arrearages for nonpayment of child support for the six year period between emancipation of the child and a final judgment because there was no agreement between the parties that the appellant would not pay child support; also, it was not error to grant interest on the arrearages for that period of time involved. Colister v Colister, No. 43048 (8th Dist Ct App, Cuyahoga, 6-4-81).

34. Evidence

The trial court's determination that the annual cost of daycare would be $15,000 was supported by competent and credible evidence, in divorce proceeding; according to wife's testimony, the cost of daycare for the school year and during summer months would be approximately $15,696, and wife failed to request separate findings of fact as to how the court determined its annual daycare cost. O'Brien v. O'Brien (Ohio App. 12 Dist., Butler,

07-12-2010) No. CA2009-11-289, 2010-Ohio-3258, 2010 WL 2723114, Unreported. Child Support ⚬→ 200

Evidence in post-divorce child support action was sufficient to support order requiring former wife to pay $429.04 per month in child support; although former wife had objected to magistrate's findings that former husband and former wife had stipulated to the $429.04 per month that former wife was to pay for child support, court adopted the findings and attached signed stipulation to judgment entry, and court did not deviate from child support computation worksheet and guidelines when it awarded former husband $429.04 per month in child support. Baddam-Reddy v. Baddam-Reddy (Ohio App. 8 Dist., Cuyahoga, 06-30-2005) No. 85038, 2005-Ohio-3432, 2005 WL 1541080, Unreported, appeal not allowed 107 Ohio St.3d 1423, 837 N.E.2d 1208, 2005-Ohio-6124. Child Support ⚬→ 202

Trial court did not abuse its discretion in formulating award for reimbursement of medical expenses in light of former wife's evidence consisting primarily of her own testimony, dental bills, and her handwritten list of medical expenses as submitted on her federal income tax return. Dunbar v. Dunbar (Ohio, 03-02-1994) 68 Ohio St.3d 369, 627 N.E.2d 532, 1994-Ohio-509. Child Support ⚬→ 487

No direct evidence of value is required to support an award of only $8 per week per child in satisfaction of a father's common-law duty to provide his children with the necessities of life. Kulcsar v. Petrovic (Wayne 1984) 20 Ohio App.3d 104, 484 N.E.2d 1365, 20 O.B.R. 126. Children Out–of–wedlock ⚬→ 67

In a divorce proceeding trial court abused its discretion in awarding child support and alimony payments without requiring evidence of both parties' wages. Geiner v Geiner, No. WD–82–11 (6th Dist Ct App, Wood, 8–13–82).

35. Appeal

Father's potential incarceration as a result of his failure to pay child support affected a substantial right, and thus, judgment of contempt ordering father to serve remainder of 90-day jail sentence previously imposed was appealable, even though father's motion to modify child support remained unresolved. Davis-Wright v. Wright (Ohio App. 4 Dist., Highland, 08-20-2010) No. 09CA1, 2010-Ohio-3984, 2010 WL 3328661, Unreported. Child Support ⚬→ 537

Husband waived for appellate review any challenge against order awarding wife the right to claim dependent child tax credit following divorce; husband failed to object to award at trial and agreed to the tax exemption to wife in the parties' agreement. Warehime v. Warehime (Ohio App. 5 Dist., Guernsey, 06-15-2010) No. 10CA000004, 2010-Ohio-2803, 2010 WL 2474379, Unreported. Child Support ⚬→ 553

3109.051   Parenting time rights

(A) If a divorce, dissolution, legal separation, or annulment proceeding involves a child and if the court has not issued a shared parenting decree, the court shall consider any mediation report filed pursuant to section 3109.052 of the Revised Code and, in accordance with division (C) of this section, shall make a just and reasonable order or decree permitting each parent who is not the residential parent to have parenting time with the child at the time and under the conditions that the court directs, unless the court determines that it would not be in the best interest of the child to permit that parent to have parenting time with the child and includes in the journal its findings of fact and conclusions of law. Whenever possible, the order or decree permitting the parenting time shall ensure the opportunity for both parents to have frequent and continuing contact with the child, unless frequent and continuing contact by either parent with the child would not be in the best interest of the child. The court shall include in its final decree a specific schedule of parenting time for that parent. Except as provided in division (E)(6) of section 3113.31 of the Revised Code, if the court, pursuant to this section, grants parenting time to a parent or companionship or visitation rights to any other person with respect to any child, it shall not require the public children services agency to provide supervision of or other services related to that parent's exercise of parenting time or that person's exercise of companionship or visitation rights with respect to the child. This section does not limit the power of a juvenile court pursuant to Chapter 2151. of the Revised Code to issue orders with respect to children who are alleged to be abused, neglected, or dependent children or to make dispositions of children who are adjudicated abused, neglected, or dependent children or of a common pleas court to issue orders pursuant to section 3113.31 of the Revised Code.

(B)(1) In a divorce, dissolution of marriage, legal separation, annulment, or child support proceeding that involves a child, the court may grant reasonable companionship or visitation rights to any grandparent, any person related to the child by consanguinity or affinity, or any other person other than a parent, if all of the following apply:

(a) The grandparent, relative, or other person files a motion with the court seeking companionship or visitation rights.

(b) The court determines that the grandparent, relative, or other person has an interest in the welfare of the child.

(c) The court determines that the granting of the companionship or visitation rights is in the best interest of the child.

(2) A motion may be filed under division (B)(1) of this section during the pendency of the divorce, dissolution of marriage, legal separation, annulment, or child support proceeding or, if a motion was not filed at that time or was filed at that time and the circumstances in the case have changed, at any time after a decree or final order is issued in the case.

(C) When determining whether to grant parenting time rights to a parent pursuant to this section or section 3109.12 of the Revised Code or to grant companionship or visitation rights to a grandparent, relative, or other person pursuant to this section or section 3109.11 or 3109.12 of the Revised Code, when establishing a specific parenting time or visitation schedule, and when determining other parenting time matters under this section or section 3109.12 of the Revised Code or visitation matters under this section or section 3109.11 or 3109.12 of the Revised Code, the court shall consider any mediation report that is filed pursuant to section 3109.052 of the Revised Code and shall consider all other relevant factors, including, but not limited to, all of the factors listed in division (D) of this section. In considering the factors listed in division (D) of this section for purposes of determining whether to grant parenting time or visitation rights, establishing a specific parenting time or visitation schedule, determining other parenting time matters under this section or section 3109.12 of the Revised Code or visitation matters under this section or under section 3109.11 or 3109.12 of the Revised Code, and resolving any issues related to the making of any determination with respect to parenting time or visitation rights or the establishment of any specific parenting time or visitation schedule, the court, in its discretion, may interview in chambers any or all involved children regarding their wishes and concerns. If the court interviews any child concerning the child's wishes and concerns regarding those parenting time or visitation matters, the interview shall be conducted in chambers, and no person other than the child, the child's attorney, the judge, any necessary court personnel, and, in the judge's discretion, the attorney of each parent shall be permitted to be present in the chambers during the interview. No person shall obtain or attempt to obtain from a child a written or recorded statement or affidavit setting forth the wishes and concerns of the child regarding those parenting time or visitation matters. A court, in considering the factors listed in division (D) of this section for purposes of determining whether to grant any parenting time or visitation rights, establishing a parenting time or visitation schedule, determining other parenting time matters under this section or section 3109.12 of the Revised Code or visitation matters under this section or under section 3109.11 or 3109.12 of the Revised Code, or resolving any issues related to the making of any determination with respect to parenting time or visitation rights or the establishment of any specific parenting time or visitation schedule, shall not accept or consider a written or recorded statement or affidavit that purports to set forth the child's wishes or concerns regarding those parenting time or visitation matters.

(D) In determining whether to grant parenting time to a parent pursuant to this section or section 3109.12 of the Revised Code or companionship or visitation rights to a grandparent, relative, or other person pursuant to this section or section 3109.11 or 3109.12 of the Revised Code, in establishing a specific parenting time or visitation schedule, and in determining other parenting time matters under this section or section 3109.12 of the Revised Code or visitation matters under this section or section 3109.11 or 3109.12 of the Revised Code, the court shall consider all of the following factors:

(1) The prior interaction and interrelationships of the child with the child's parents, siblings, and other persons related by consanguinity or affinity, and with the person who requested companionship or visitation if that person is not a parent, sibling, or relative of the child;

(2) The geographical location of the residence of each parent and the distance between those residences, and if the person is not a parent, the geographical location of that person's residence and the distance between that person's residence and the child's residence;

(3) The child's and parents' available time, including, but not limited to, each parent's employment schedule, the child's school schedule, and the child's and the parents' holiday and vacation schedule;

(4) The age of the child;

(5) The child's adjustment to home, school, and community;

(6) If the court has interviewed the child in chambers, pursuant to division (C) of this section, regarding the wishes and concerns of the child as to parenting time by the parent who is not the residential parent or companionship or visitation by the grandparent, relative, or other person who requested companionship or visitation, as to a specific parenting time or visitation schedule, or as to other parenting time or visitation matters, the wishes and concerns of the child, as expressed to the court;

(7) The health and safety of the child;

(8) The amount of time that will be available for the child to spend with siblings;

(9) The mental and physical health of all parties;

(10) Each parent's willingness to reschedule missed parenting time and to facilitate the other parent's parenting time rights, and with respect to a person who requested companionship or visitation, the willingness of that person to reschedule missed visitation;

(11) In relation to parenting time, whether either parent previously has been convicted of or pleaded guilty to any criminal offense involving any act that resulted in a child being an abused child or a neglected child; whether either parent, in a case in which a child has been adjudicated an abused child or a neglected child, previously has been determined to be the perpetrator of the abusive or neglectful act that is the basis of the adjudication; and whether there is reason to believe that either parent has acted in a manner resulting in a child being an abused child or a neglected child;

(12) In relation to requested companionship or visitation by a person other than a parent, whether the person previously has been convicted of or pleaded guilty to any criminal offense involving any act that resulted in a child being an abused child or a neglected child; whether the person, in a case in which a child has been adjudicated an abused child or a neglected child, previously has been determined to be the perpetrator of the abusive or neglectful act that is the basis of the adjudication; whether either parent previously has been convicted of or pleaded guilty to a violation of section 2919.25 of the Revised Code involving a victim who at the time of the commission of the offense was a member of the family or household that is the subject of the current proceeding; whether either parent previously has been convicted of an offense involving a victim who at the time of the commission of the offense was a member of the family or household that is the subject of the current proceeding and caused physical harm to the victim in the commission of the offense; and whether there is reason to believe that the person has acted in a manner resulting in a child being an abused child or a neglected child;

(13) Whether the residential parent or one of the parents subject to a shared parenting decree has continuously and willfully denied the other parent's right to parenting time in accordance with an order of the court;

(14) Whether either parent has established a residence or is planning to establish a residence outside this state;

(15) In relation to requested companionship or visitation by a person other than a parent, the wishes and concerns of the child's parents, as expressed by them to the court;

(16) Any other factor in the best interest of the child.

(E) The remarriage of a residential parent of a child does not affect the authority of a court under this section to grant parenting time rights with respect to the child to the parent who is not the residential parent or to grant reasonable companionship or visitation rights with respect to the child to any grandparent, any person related by consanguinity or affinity, or any other person.

(F)(1) If the court, pursuant to division (A) of this section, denies parenting time to a parent who is not the residential parent or denies a motion for reasonable companionship or visitation rights filed under division (B) of this section and the parent or movant files a written request for findings of fact and conclusions of law, the court shall state in writing its findings of fact and conclusions of law in accordance with Civil Rule 52.

(2) On or before July 1, 1991, each court of common pleas, by rule, shall adopt standard parenting time guidelines. A court shall have discretion to deviate from its standard parenting time guidelines based upon factors set forth in division (D) of this section.

(G)(1) If the residential parent intends to move to a residence other than the residence specified in the parenting time order or decree of the court, the parent shall file a notice of intent to relocate with the court that issued the order or decree. Except as provided in divisions (G)(2), (3), and (4) of this section, the court shall send a copy of the notice to the parent who is not the residential parent. Upon receipt of the notice, the court, on its own motion or the motion of the parent who is not the residential parent, may schedule a hearing with notice to both parents to determine whether it is in the best interest of the child to revise the parenting time schedule for the child.

(2) When a court grants parenting time rights to a parent who is not the residential parent, the court shall determine whether that parent has been convicted of or pleaded guilty to a violation of section 2919.25 of the Revised Code involving a victim who at the time of the commission of the offense was a member of the family or household that is the subject of the proceeding, has been convicted of or pleaded guilty to any other offense involving a victim who at the time of the commission of the offense was a member of the family or household that is the subject of the proceeding and caused physical harm to the victim in the commission of the offense, or has been determined to be the perpetrator of the abusive act that is the basis of an adjudication that a child is an abused child. If the court determines that that parent has not been so convicted and has not been determined to be the perpetrator of an abusive act that is the basis of a child abuse adjudication, the court shall issue an order stating that a copy of any notice of relocation that is filed with the court pursuant to division (G)(1) of this section will be sent to the parent who is given the parenting time rights in accordance with division (G)(1) of this section.

If the court determines that the parent who is granted the parenting time rights has been convicted of or pleaded guilty to a violation of section 2919.25 of the Revised Code involving a victim who at the time of the commission of the offense was a member of the family or household that is the subject of the proceeding, has been convicted of or pleaded guilty to any other offense involving a victim who at the time of the commission of the offense was a member of the family or household that is the subject of the proceeding and caused physical harm to the victim in the commission of the offense, or has been determined to be the perpetrator of the abusive act that is the basis of an adjudication that a child is an abused child, it shall issue an order stating that that parent will not be given a copy of any notice of relocation that is filed with the court pursuant to division (G)(1) of this section unless the court determines that it is in the best interest of the children to give that parent a copy of the notice of relocation, issues an order stating that that parent will be given a copy of any notice of relocation filed pursuant to division (G)(1) of this section, and issues specific written findings of fact in support of its determination.

(3) If a court, prior to April 11, 1991, issued an order granting parenting time rights to a parent who is not the residential parent and did not require the residential parent in that order to give the parent who is granted the parenting time rights notice of any change of address and if the residential parent files a notice of relocation pursuant to division (G)(1) of this section, the court shall determine if the parent who is granted the parenting time rights has been convicted of or pleaded guilty to a violation of section 2919.25 of the Revised Code involving a victim who at the time of the commission of the offense was a member of the family or household that is the subject of the proceeding, has been convicted of or pleaded guilty to any other offense involving a victim who at the time of the commission of the offense was a member of the family or household that is the subject of the proceeding and caused physical harm to the victim in the commission of the offense, or has been determined to be the perpetrator of the abusive act that is the basis of an adjudication that a child is an abused child. If the court determines that the parent who is granted the parenting time rights has not been so convicted and has not been determined to be the perpetrator of an abusive act that is the basis

of a child abuse adjudication, the court shall issue an order stating that a copy of any notice of relocation that is filed with the court pursuant to division (G)(1) of this section will be sent to the parent who is granted parenting time rights in accordance with division (G)(1) of this section.

If the court determines that the parent who is granted the parenting time rights has been convicted of or pleaded guilty to a violation of section 2919.25 of the Revised Code involving a victim who at the time of the commission of the offense was a member of the family or household that is the subject of the proceeding, has been convicted of or pleaded guilty to any other offense involving a victim who at the time of the commission of the offense was a member of the family or household that is the subject of the proceeding and caused physical harm to the victim in the commission of the offense, or has been determined to be the perpetrator of the abusive act that is the basis of an adjudication that a child is an abused child, it shall issue an order stating that that parent will not be given a copy of any notice of relocation that is filed with the court pursuant to division (G)(1) of this section unless the court determines that it is in the best interest of the children to give that parent a copy of the notice of relocation, issues an order stating that that parent will be given a copy of any notice of relocation filed pursuant to division (G)(1) of this section, and issues specific written findings of fact in support of its determination.

(4) If a parent who is granted parenting time rights pursuant to this section or any other section of the Revised Code is authorized by an order issued pursuant to this section or any other court order to receive a copy of any notice of relocation that is filed pursuant to division (G)(1) of this section or pursuant to court order, if the residential parent intends to move to a residence other than the residence address specified in the parenting time order, and if the residential parent does not want the parent who is granted the parenting time rights to receive a copy of the relocation notice because the parent with parenting time rights has been convicted of or pleaded guilty to a violation of section 2919.25 of the Revised Code involving a victim who at the time of the commission of the offense was a member of the family or household that is the subject of the proceeding, has been convicted of or pleaded guilty to any other offense involving a victim who at the time of the commission of the offense was a member of the family or household that is the subject of the proceeding and caused physical harm to the victim in the commission of the offense, or has been determined to be the perpetrator of the abusive act that is the basis of an adjudication that a child is an abused child, the residential parent may file a motion with the court requesting that the parent who is granted the parenting time rights not receive a copy of any notice of relocation. Upon the filing of the motion, the court shall schedule a hearing on the motion and give both parents notice of the date, time, and location of the hearing. If the court determines that the parent who is granted the parenting time rights has been so convicted or has been determined to be the perpetrator of an abusive act that is the basis of a child abuse adjudication, the court shall issue an order stating that the parent who is granted the parenting time rights will not be given a copy of any notice of relocation that is filed with the court pursuant to division (G)(1) of this section or that the residential parent is no longer required to give that parent a copy of any notice of relocation unless the court determines that it is in the best interest of the children to give that parent a copy of the notice of relocation, issues an order stating that that parent will be given a copy of any notice of relocation filed pursuant to division (G)(1) of this section, and issues specific written findings of fact in support of its determination. If it does not so find, it shall dismiss the motion.

(H)(1) Subject to section 3125.16 and division (F) of section 3319.321 of the Revised Code, a parent of a child who is not the residential parent of the child is entitled to access, under the same terms and conditions under which access is provided to the residential parent, to any record that is related to the child and to which the residential parent of the child legally is provided access, unless the court determines that it would not be in the best interest of the child for the parent who is not the residential parent to have access to the records under those same terms and conditions. If the court determines that the parent of a child who is not the residential parent should not have access to records related to the child under the same terms and conditions as provided for the residential parent, the court shall specify the terms and conditions under which the parent who is not the residential parent is to have access to those records, shall enter its written findings of facts and opinion in the journal, and shall issue an order containing the terms and conditions to both the residential parent and the parent of the child who is not the residential parent. The court shall include in every order issued pursuant to this division notice that any keeper of a record who knowingly fails to comply with the order or division (H) of this section is in contempt of court.

(2) Subject to section 3125.16 and division (F) of section 3319.321 of the Revised Code, subsequent to the issuance of an order under division (H)(1) of this section, the keeper of any record that is related to a particular child and to which the residential parent legally is provided access shall permit the parent of the child who is not the residential parent to have access to the record under the same terms and conditions under which access is provided to the residential parent, unless the residential parent has presented the keeper of the record with a copy of an order issued under division (H)(1) of this section that limits the terms and conditions under which the parent who is not the residential parent is to have access to records pertaining to the child and the order pertains to the record in question. If the residential parent presents the keeper of the record with a copy of that type of order, the keeper of the record shall permit the parent who is not the residential parent to have access to the record only in accordance with the most recent order that has been issued pursuant to division (H)(1) of this section and presented to the keeper by the residential parent or the parent who is not the residential parent. Any keeper of any record who knowingly fails to comply with division (H) of this section or with any order issued pursuant to division (H)(1) of this section is in contempt of court.

(3) The prosecuting attorney of any county may file a complaint with the court of common pleas of that county requesting the court to issue a protective order preventing the disclosure pursuant to division (H)(1) or (2) of this section of any confidential law enforcement investigatory record. The court shall schedule a hearing on the motion and give notice of the date, time, and location of the hearing to all parties.

(I) A court that issues a parenting time order or decree pursuant to this section or section 3109.12 of the Revised Code shall determine whether the parent granted the right of parenting time is to be permitted access, in accordance with section 5104.011 of the Revised Code, to any child day-care center that is, or that in the future may be, attended by the children with whom the right of parenting time is granted. Unless the court determines that the parent who is not the residential parent should not have access to the center to the same extent that the residential parent is granted access to the center, the parent who is not the residential parent and who is granted parenting time rights is entitled to access to the center to the same extent that the residential parent is granted access to the center. If the court determines that the parent who is not the residential parent should not have access to the center to the same extent that the residential parent is granted such access under division (C) of section 5104.011 of the Revised Code, the court shall specify the terms and conditions under which the parent who is not the residential parent is to have access to the center, provided that the access shall not be greater than the access that is provided to the residential parent under division (C) of section 5104.011 of the Revised Code, the court shall enter its written findings of fact and opinions in the journal, and the court shall include the terms and conditions of access in the parenting time order or decree.

(J)(1) Subject to division (F) of section 3319.321 of the Revised Code, when a court issues an order or decree allocating parental rights and responsibilities for the care of a child, the parent of the child who is not the residential parent of the child is entitled to access, under the same terms and conditions under which access is provided to the residential parent, to any student activity that is related to the child and to which the residential parent of the child legally is provided access, unless the court determines that it would not be in the best interest of the child to grant the parent who is not the residential parent access to the student activities under those same terms and conditions. If the court determines that the parent of the child who is not the residential parent should not have access to any student activity that is related to the child under the same terms and conditions as provided for the residential parent, the court shall specify the terms and conditions under which the parent who is not the residential parent is to have access to those student activities, shall enter its written findings of facts and opinion in the journal, and shall issue an order containing the terms and conditions to both the residential parent and the parent of the child who is not the residential parent. The court shall include in every order issued pursuant to this division notice that any school official or employee who knowingly fails to comply with the order or division (J) of this section is in contempt of court.

(2) Subject to division (F) of section 3319.321 of the Revised Code, subsequent to the issuance of an order under division (J)(1) of this section, all school officials and employees shall permit the parent of the child who is not the residential parent to have access to any student activity under the same terms and conditions under which access is provided to the residential parent of the child, unless the residential parent has presented the school official or employee, the board of education of the school, or the governing body of the chartered nonpublic school with a copy of an order issued under division (J)(1) of this section that limits the terms and conditions under which the parent who is not the residential parent is to have access to student activities related to the child and the order pertains to the student activity in question. If the residential parent presents the school official or employee, the board of education of the school, or the governing body of the chartered nonpublic school with a copy of that type of order, the school official or employee shall permit the parent who is not the residential parent to have access to the student activity only in accordance with the most recent order that has been issued pursuant to division (J)(1) of this section and presented to the school official or employee, the board of education of the school, or the governing body of the chartered nonpublic school by the residential parent or the parent who is not the residential parent. Any school official or employee who knowingly fails to comply with division (J) of this section or with any order issued pursuant to division (J)(1) of this section is in contempt of court.

(K) If any person is found in contempt of court for failing to comply with or interfering with any order or decree granting parenting time rights issued pursuant to this section or section 3109.12 of the Revised Code or companionship or visitation rights issued pursuant to this section, section 3109.11 or 3109.12 of the Revised Code, or any other provision of the Revised Code, the court that makes the finding, in addition to any other penalty or remedy imposed, shall assess all court costs arising out of the contempt proceeding against the person and require the person to pay any reasonable attorney's fees of any adverse party, as determined by the court, that arose in relation to the act of contempt, and may award reasonable compensatory parenting time or visitation to the person whose right of parenting time or visitation was affected by the failure or interference if such compensatory parenting time or visitation is in the best interest of the child. Any compensatory parenting time or visitation awarded under this division shall be included in an order issued by the court and, to the extent possible, shall be governed by the same terms and conditions as was the parenting time or visitation that was affected by the failure or interference.

(L) Any parent who requests reasonable parenting time rights with respect to a child under this section or section 3109.12 of the Revised Code or any person who requests reasonable companionship or visitation rights with respect to a child under this section, section 3109.11 or 3109.12 of the Revised Code, or any other provision of the Revised Code may file a motion with the court requesting that it waive all or any part of the costs that may accrue in the proceedings. If the court determines that the movant is indigent and that the waiver is in the best interest of the child, the court, in its discretion, may waive payment of all or any part of the costs of those proceedings.

(M)(1) A parent who receives an order for active military service in the uniformed services and who is subject to a parenting time order may apply to the court for any of the following temporary orders for the period extending from the date of the parent's departure to the date of return:

(a) An order delegating all or part of the parent's parenting time with the child to a relative or to another person who has a close and substantial relationship with the child if the delegation is in the child's best interest;

(b) An order that the other parent make the child reasonably available for parenting time with the parent when the parent is on leave from active military service;

(c) An order that the other parent facilitate contact, including telephone and electronic contact, between the parent and child while the parent is on active military service.

(2)(a) Upon receipt of an order for active military service, a parent who is subject to a parenting time order and seeks an order under division (M)(1) of this section shall notify the other parent who is subject to the parenting time order and apply to the court as soon as reasonably possible after receipt of the order for active military service. The application shall include the date on which the active military service begins.

(b) The court shall schedule a hearing upon receipt of an application under division (M) of this section and hold the hearing not later than thirty days after its receipt, except that the court shall give the case calendar priority and handle the case expeditiously if exigent circumstances exist in the case. No hearing shall be required if both parents agree to the terms of the requested temporary order and the court determines that the order is in the child's best interest.

(c) In determining whether a delegation under division (M)(1)(a) of this section is in the child's best interest, the court shall consider all relevant factors, including the factors set forth in division (D) of this section.

(d) An order delegating all or part of the parent's parenting time pursuant to division (M)(1)(a) of this section does not create standing on behalf of the person to whom parenting time is delegated to assert visitation or companionship rights independent of the order.

(3) At the request of a parent who is ordered for active military service in the uniformed services and who is a subject of a proceeding pertaining to a parenting time order or pertaining to a request for companionship rights or visitation with a child, the court shall permit the parent to participate in the proceeding and present evidence by electronic means, including communication by telephone, video, or internet to the extent permitted by rules of the supreme court of Ohio.

(N) The juvenile court has exclusive jurisdiction to enter the orders in any case certified to it from another court.

(O) As used in this section:

(1) "Abused child" has the same meaning as in section 2151.031 of the Revised Code, and "neglected child" has the same meaning as in section 2151.03 of the Revised Code.

(2) "Active military service" and "uniformed services" have the same meanings as in section 3109.04 of the Revised Code.

(3) "Confidential law enforcement investigatory record" has the same meaning as in section 149.43 of the Revised Code.

(4) "Parenting time order" means an order establishing the amount of time that a child spends with the parent who is not the residential parent or the amount of time that the child is to be physically located with a parent under a shared parenting order.

(5) "Record" means any record, document, file, or other material that contains information directly related to a child, including, but not limited to, any of the following:

(a) Records maintained by public and nonpublic schools;

(b) Records maintained by facilities that provide child care, as defined in section 5104.01 of the Revised Code, publicly funded child care, as defined in section 5104.01 of the Revised Code, or pre-school services operated by or under the supervision of a school district board of education or a nonpublic school;

(c) Records maintained by hospitals, other facilities, or persons providing medical or surgical care or treatment for the child;

(d) Records maintained by agencies, departments, instrumentalities, or other entities of the state or any political subdivision of the state, other than a child support enforcement agency. Access to records maintained by a child support enforcement agency is governed by section 3125.16 of the Revised Code.

(2011 H 121, eff. 6-9-11; 2004 H 11, eff. 5–18–05; 2000 S 180, eff. 3–22–01; 1997 H 408, eff. 10–1–97; 1996 H 274, eff. 8–8–96; 1991 H 155, eff. 7–22–91; 1990 S 3, H 15)

Historical and Statutory Notes

Amendment Note: 2011 H 121 added divisions (M)(1), (M)(1)(a), (M)(1)(b), (M)(1)(c), (M)(2)(a), (M)(2)(b), (M)(2)(c), (M)(2)(d), and (M)(3); redesignated former divisions (M) and (N) as divisions (N) and (O), respectively; added divisions (O)(2), (O)(3), and (O)(4); redesignated former division (N)(2) as division (O)(5); and deleted former division (N)(3).

Amendment Note: 2004 H 11 substituted "care" for "day care" in division (N)(2)(b).

Amendment Note: 2000 S 180 rewrote this section which prior thereto read:

"(A) If a divorce, dissolution, legal separation, or annulment proceeding involves a child and if the court has not issued a shared parenting decree, the court shall consider any mediation report filed pursuant to section 3109.052 of the Revised Code and, in accordance with division (C) of this section, shall make a just and reasonable order or decree permitting each parent who is not the residential parent to visit the child at the time and under the conditions that the court directs, unless the court determines that it would not be in the best interest of the child to permit that parent to visit the child and includes in the journal its findings of fact and conclusions of law. Whenever possible, the order or decree permitting the visitation shall ensure the opportunity for both parents to have frequent and continuing contact with the child, unless frequent and continuing contact by either parent with the child would not be in the best interest of the child. The court shall include in its final decree a specific schedule of visitation for that parent. Except as provided in division (E)(6) of section 3113.31 of the Revised Code, if the court, pursuant to this section, grants any person companionship or visitation rights with respect to any child, it shall not require the public children services agency to provide supervision of or other services related to that person's exercise of companionship or visitation rights with respect to the child. This section does not limit the power of a juvenile court pursuant to Chapter 2151. of the Revised Code to issue orders with respect to children who are alleged to be abused, neglected, or dependent children or to make dispositions of children who are adjudicated abused, neglected, or dependent children or of a common pleas court to issue orders pursuant to section 3113.31 of the Revised Code.

"(B)(1) In a divorce, dissolution of marriage, legal separation, annulment, or child support proceeding that involves a child, the court may grant reasonable companionship or visitation rights to any grandparent, any person related to the child by consanguinity or affinity, or any other person other than a parent, if all of the following apply:

"(a) The grandparent, relative, or other person files a motion with the court seeking companionship or visitation rights.

"(b) The court determines that the grandparent, relative, or other person has an interest in the welfare of the child.

"(c) The court determines that the granting of the companionship or visitation rights is in the best interest of the child.

"(2) A motion may be filed under division (B)(1) of this section during the pendency of the divorce, dissolution of marriage, legal separation, annulment, or child support proceeding or, if a motion was not filed at that time or was filed at that time and the circumstances in the case have changed, at any time after a decree or final order is issued in the case.

"(C) When determining whether to grant companionship or visitation rights to a parent, grandparent, relative, or other person pursuant to this section or section 3109.11 or 3109.12 of the Revised Code, when establishing a specific visitation schedule, and when determining other visitation matters under this section or section 3109.11 or 3109.12 of the Revised Code, the court shall consider any mediation report that is filed pursuant to section 3109.052 of the Revised Code and shall consider all other relevant factors, including, but not limited to, all of the factors listed in division (D) of this section. In considering the factors listed in division (D) of this section for purposes of determining whether to grant visitation rights, establishing a specific visitation schedule, determining other visitation matters under this section or under section 3109.11 or 3109.12 of the Revised Code, and resolving any issues related to the making of any determination with respect to visitation rights or the establishment of any specific visitation schedule, the court, in its discretion, may interview in chambers any or all involved children regarding their wishes and concerns. If the court interviews any child concerning the child's wishes and concerns regarding those visitation matters, the interview shall be conducted in chambers, and no person other than the child, the child's attorney, the judge, any necessary court personnel, and, in the judge's discretion, the attorney of each parent shall be permitted to be present in the chambers during the interview. No person shall obtain or attempt to obtain from a child a written or recorded statement or affidavit setting forth the wishes and concerns of the child regarding those visitation matters. A court, in considering the factors listed in division (D) of this section for purposes of determining whether to grant any visitation rights, establishing a visitation schedule, determining other visitation matters under this section or under section 3109.11 or 3109.12 of the Revised Code, or resolving any issues related to the making of any determination with respect to visitation rights or the establishment of any specific visitation schedule, shall not accept or consider a written or recorded statement or affidavit that purports to set forth the child's wishes or concerns regarding those visitation matters.

"(D) In determining whether to grant companionship or visitation rights to a parent, grandparent, relative, or other person pursuant to this section or section 3109.11 or 3109.12 of the Revised Code, in establishing a specific visitation schedule, and in determining other visitation matters under this section or section 3109.11 or 3109.12 of the Revised Code, the court shall consider all of the following factors:

"(1) The prior interaction and interrelationships of the child with the child's parents, siblings, and other persons related by consanguinity or affinity, and with the person who requested companionship or visitation if that person is not a parent, sibling, or relative of the child;

"(2) The geographical location of the residence of each parent and the distance between those residences, and if the person who requested companionship or visitation is not a parent, the geographical location of that person's residence and the distance between that person's residence and the child's residence;

"(3) The child's and parents' available time, including, but not limited to, each parent's employment schedule, the child's school schedule, and the child's and the parents' holiday and vacation schedule;

"(4) The age of the child;

"(5) The child's adjustment to home, school, and community;

"(6) If the court has interviewed the child in chambers, pursuant to division (C) of this section, regarding the wishes and concerns of the child as to visitation by the parent who is not the residential parent or companionship or visitation by the grandparent, relative, or other person who requested the companionship or visitation, as to a specific visitation schedule, or as to other visitation matters, the wishes and concerns of the child, as expressed to the court;

"(7) The health and safety of the child;

"(8) The amount of time that will be available for the child to spend with siblings;

"(9) The mental and physical health of all parties;

"(10) Each parent's willingness to reschedule missed visitation and to facilitate the other parent's visitation rights, and if the person who requested companionship or visitation is not a parent, the willingness of that person to reschedule missed visitation;

"(11) In relation to visitation by a parent, whether either parent previously has been convicted of or pleaded guilty to any criminal offense involving any act that resulted in a child being an abused child or a neglected child; whether either parent, in a case in which a child has been adjudicated an abused child or a neglected child, previously has been determined to be the perpetrator of the abusive or neglectful act that is the basis of the adjudication; and whether there is reason to believe that either parent has acted in a manner resulting in a child being an abused child or a neglected child;

"(12) In relation to requested companionship or visitation by a person other than a parent, whether the person previously has been convicted of or pleaded guilty to any criminal offense involving any act that resulted in a child being an abused child or a neglected child; whether the person, in a case in which a child has been adjudicated an abused child or a neglected child, previously has been determined to be the perpetrator of the abusive or neglectful act that is the basis of the adjudication; whether either parent previously has been convicted of or pleaded guilty to a violation of section 2919.25 of the Revised Code involving a victim who at the time of the commission of the offense was a member of the family or household that is the subject of the current proceeding; whether either parent previously has been convicted of an offense involving a victim who at the time of the commission of the offense was a member of the family or household that is the subject of the current proceeding and caused physical harm to the victim in the commission of the offense, and whether there is reason to believe that the person has acted in a manner resulting in a child being an abused child or a neglected child;

"(13) Whether the residential parent or one of the parents subject to a shared parenting decree has continuously and willfully denied the other parent's right to visitation in accordance with an order of the court;

"(14) Whether either parent has established a residence or is planning to establish a residence outside this state;

"(15) Any other factor in the best interest of the child.

"(E) The remarriage of a residential parent of a child does not affect the authority of a court under this section to grant visitation rights with respect to the child to the parent who is not the residential parent or to grant reasonable companionship or visitation rights with respect to the child to any grandparent, any person related by consanguinity or affinity, or any other person.

"(F)(1) If the court, pursuant to division (A) of this section, denies visitation to a parent who is not the residential parent or denies a motion for reasonable companionship or visitation rights filed under division (B) of this section and the parent or movant files a written request for findings of fact and conclusions of law, the court shall state in writing its findings of fact and conclusions of law in accordance with Civil Rule 52.

"(2) On or before July 1, 1991, each court of common pleas, by rule, shall adopt standard visitation guidelines. A court shall have discretion to deviate from its standard visitation guidelines based upon factors set forth in division (D) of this section.

"(G)(1) If the residential parent intends to move to a residence other than the residence specified in the visitation order or decree of the court, the parent shall file a notice of intent to relocate with the court that issued the order or decree. Except as provided in divisions (G)(2), (3), and (4) of this section, the court shall send a copy of the notice to the parent who is not the residential parent. Upon receipt of the notice, the court, on its own motion or the motion of the parent who is not the residential parent, may schedule a hearing with notice to both parents to determine whether it is in the best interest of the child to revise the visitation schedule for the child.

"(2) When a court grants visitation or companionship rights to a parent who is not the residential parent, the court shall determine whether that parent has been convicted of or pleaded guilty to a violation of section 2919.25 of the Revised Code involving a victim who at the time of the commission of the offense was a member of the family or household that is the subject of the proceeding, has been convicted of or pleaded guilty to any other offense involving a victim who at the time of the commission of the offense was a member of the family or household that is the subject of the proceeding and caused physical harm to the victim in the commission of the offense, or has been determined to be the perpetrator of the abusive act that is the basis of an adjudication that a child is an abused child. If the court determines that that parent has not been so convicted and has not been determined to be the perpetrator of an abusive act that is the basis of a child abuse adjudication, the court shall issue an order stating that a copy of any notice of relocation that is filed with the court pursuant to division (G)(1) of this section will be sent to the parent who is given the visitation or companionship rights in accordance with division (G)(1) of this section.

"If the court determines that the parent who is granted the visitation or companionship rights has been convicted of or pleaded guilty to a violation of section 2919.25 of the Revised Code involving a victim who at the time of the commission of the offense was a member of the family or household that is the subject of the proceeding, has been convicted of or pleaded guilty to any other offense involving a victim who at the time of the commission of the offense was a member of the family or household that is the subject of the proceeding and caused physical harm to the victim in the commission of the offense, or has been determined to be the perpetrator of the abusive act that is the basis of an adjudication that a child is an abused child, it shall issue an order stating that that parent will not be given a copy of any notice of relocation that is filed with the court pursuant to division (G)(1) of this section unless the court determines that it is in the best interest of the children to give that parent a copy of the notice of relocation, issues an order stating that that parent will be given a copy of any notice of relocation filed pursuant to division (G)(1) of this section, and issues specific written findings of fact in support of its determination.

"(3) If a court, prior to April 11, 1991, issued an order granting visitation or companionship rights to a parent who is not the residential parent and did not require the residential parent in that order to give the parent who is granted the visitation or companionship rights notice of any change of address and if the residential parent files a notice of relocation pursuant to division (G)(1) of this sec-

tion, the court shall determine if the parent who is granted the visitation or companionship rights has been convicted of or pleaded guilty to a violation of section 2919.25 of the Revised Code involving a victim who at the time of the commission of the offense was a member of the family or household that is the subject of the proceeding, has been convicted of or pleaded guilty to any other offense involving a victim who at the time of the commission of the offense was a member of the family or household that is the subject of the proceeding and caused physical harm to the victim in the commission of the offense, or has been determined to be the perpetrator of the abusive act that is the basis of an adjudication that a child is an abused child. If the court determines that the parent who is granted the visitation or companionship rights has not been so convicted and has not been determined to be the perpetrator of an abusive act that is the basis of a child abuse adjudication, the court shall issue an order stating that a copy of any notice of relocation that is filed with the court pursuant to division (G)(1) of this section will be sent to the parent who is granted visitation or companionship rights in accordance with division (G)(1) of this section.

"If the court determines that the parent who is granted the visitation or companionship rights has been convicted of or pleaded guilty to a violation of section 2919.25 of the Revised Code involving a victim who at the time of the commission of the offense was a member of the family or household that is the subject of the proceeding, has been convicted of or pleaded guilty to any other offense involving a victim who at the time of the commission of the offense was a member of the family or household that is the subject of the proceeding and caused physical harm to the victim in the commission of the offense, or has been determined to be the perpetrator of the abusive act that is the basis of an adjudication that a child is an abused child, it shall issue an order stating that that parent will not be given a copy of any notice of relocation that is filed with the court pursuant to division (G)(1) of this section unless the court determines that it is in the best interest of the children to give that parent a copy of the notice of relocation, issues an order stating that that parent will be given a copy of any notice of relocation filed pursuant to division (G)(1) of this section, and issues specific written findings of fact in support of its determination.

"(4) If a parent who is granted visitation or companionship rights pursuant to this section or any other section of the Revised Code is authorized by an order issued pursuant to this section or any other court order to receive a copy of any notice of relocation that is filed pursuant to division (G)(1) of this section or pursuant to court order, if the residential parent intends to move to a residence other than the residence address specified in the visitation or companionship order, and if the residential parent does not want the parent who is granted the visitation or companionship rights to receive a copy of the relocation notice because the parent with visitation or companionship rights has been convicted of or pleaded guilty to a violation of section 2919.25 of the Revised Code involving a victim who at the time of the commission of the offense was a member of the family or household that is the subject of the proceeding, has been convicted of or pleaded guilty to any other offense involving a victim who at the time of the commission of the offense was a member of the family or household that is the subject of the proceeding and caused physical harm to the victim in the commission of the offense, or has been determined to be the perpetrator of the abusive act that is the basis of an adjudication that a child is an abused child, the residential parent may file a motion with the court requesting that the parent who is granted the visitation or companionship rights not receive a copy of any notice of relocation. Upon the filing of the motion, the court shall schedule a hearing on the motion and give both parents notice of the date, time, and location of the hearing. If the court determines that the parent who is granted the visitation or companionship rights has been so convicted or has been determined to be the perpetrator of an abusive act that is the basis of a child abuse adjudication, the court shall issue an order stating that the parent who is granted the visitation or companionship rights will not be given a copy of any notice of relocation that is filed with the court pursuant to division (G)(1) of this section or that the residential parent is no longer required to give that parent a copy of any notice of relocation unless the court determines that it is in the best interest of the children to give that parent a copy of the notice of relocation, issues an order stating that that parent will be given a copy of any notice of relocation filed pursuant to division (G)(1) of this section, and issues specific written findings of fact in support of its determination. If it does not so find, it shall dismiss the motion.

"(H)(1) Subject to division (F)(2) of section 2301.35 and division (F) of section 3319.321 of the Revised Code, a parent of a child who is not the residential parent of the child is entitled to access, under the same terms and conditions under which access is provided to the residential parent, to any record that is related to the child and to which the residential parent of the child legally is provided access, unless the court determines that it would not be in the best interest of the child for the parent who is not the residential parent to have access to the records under those same terms and conditions. If the court determines that the parent of a child who is not the residential parent should not have access to records related to the child under the same terms and conditions as provided for the residential parent, the court shall specify the terms and conditions under which the parent who is not the residential parent is to have access to those records, shall enter its written findings of facts and opinion in the journal, and shall issue an order containing the terms and conditions to both the residential parent and the parent of the child who is not the residential parent. The court shall include in every order issued pursuant to this division notice that any keeper of a record who knowingly fails to comply with the order or division (H) of this section is in contempt of court.

"(2) Subject to division (F)(2) of section 2301.35 and division (F) of section 3319.321 of the Revised Code, subsequent to the issuance of an order under division (H)(1) of this section, the keeper of any record that is related to a particular child and to which the residential parent legally is provided access shall permit the parent of the child who is not the residential parent to have access to the record under the same terms and conditions under which access is provided to the residential parent, unless the residential parent has presented the keeper of the record with a copy of an order issued under division (H)(1) of this section that limits the terms and conditions under which the parent who is not the residential parent is to have access to records pertaining to the child and the order pertains to the record in question. If the residential parent presents the keeper of the record with a copy of that type of order, the keeper of the record shall permit the parent who is not the residential parent to have access to the record only in accordance with the most recent order that has been issued pursuant to division (H)(1) of this section and presented to the keeper by the residential parent or the parent who is not the residential parent. Any keeper of any record who knowingly fails to comply with division (H) of this section or with any order issued pursuant to division (H)(1) of this section is in contempt of court.

"(3) The prosecuting attorney of any county may file a complaint with the court of common pleas of that county requesting the court to issue a protective order preventing the disclosure pursuant to division (H)(1) or (2) of this section of any confidential law enforcement investigatory record. The court shall schedule a hearing on the motion and give notice of the date, time, and location of the hearing to all parties.

"(I) A court that issues a visitation order or decree pursuant to this section, section 3109.11 or 3109.12 of the Revised Code, or any other provision of the Revised Code shall determine whether the parent granted the right of visitation is to be permitted access, in accordance with section 5104.011 of the Revised Code, to any child day-care center that is, or that in the future may be, attended by the children with whom the right of visitation is granted. Unless the court determines that the parent who is not the residential parent should not have access to the center to the same extent that the residential parent is granted access to the center, the parent who is not the residential parent and who is granted visitation or companionship rights is entitled to access to the center to the same extent that the residential parent is granted access to the center. If the court determines that the parent who is not the residential parent should not have access to the center to the same extent that the residential parent is granted such access under division (C) of section 5104.011 of the Revised Code, the court shall specify the terms and conditions under which the parent who is not the residential parent is to have access to the center, provided that the access shall not be greater than the access that is provided to the residential parent under division (C) of section 5104.011 of the Revised Code, the court shall enter its written findings of fact and opinions in the journal, and the court shall include the terms and conditions of access in the visitation order or decree.

"(J)(1) Subject to division (F) of section 3319.321 of the Revised Code, when a court issues an order or decree allocating parental rights and responsibilities for the care of a child, the parent of the child who is not the residential parent of the child is entitled to access, under the same terms and conditions under which access is provided to the residential parent, to any student activity that is related to the child and to which the residential parent of the child legally is provided access, unless the court determines that it would not be in the best interest of the child to grant the parent who is not the residential parent access to the student activities under those same terms and conditions. If the court determines that the parent of the child who is not the residential parent should not have access to any student activity that is related to the child under the same terms and conditions as provided for the residential parent, the court shall specify the terms and conditions under which the parent who is not the residential parent is to have access to those student activities, shall enter its written findings of facts and opinion in the journal, and shall issue an order containing the terms and conditions to both the residential parent and the parent of the child who is not the residential parent. The court shall include in every order issued pursuant to this division notice that any school official or employee who knowingly fails to comply with the order or division (J) of this section is in contempt of court.

"(2) Subject to division (F) of section 3319.321 of the Revised Code, subsequent to the issuance of an order under division (J)(1) of this section, all school officials and employees shall permit the parent of the child who is not the residential parent to have access to any student activity under the same terms and conditions under which access is provided to the residential parent of the child, unless the residential parent has presented the school official or employee, the board of education of the school, or the governing body of the chartered nonpublic school with a copy of an order issued under division (J)(1) of this section that limits the terms and conditions under which the parent who is not the residential parent is to have access to student activities related to the child and the order pertains to the student activity in question. If the residential parent presents the school official or employee, the board of education of the school, or the governing body of the chartered nonpublic school with a copy of that type of order, the school official or employee shall permit the parent who is not the residential parent to have

access to the student activity only in accordance with the most recent order that has been issued pursuant to division (J)(1) of this section and presented to the school official or employee, the board of education of the school, or the governing body of the chartered nonpublic school by the residential parent or the parent who is not the residential parent. Any school official or employee who knowingly fails to comply with division (J) of this section or with any order issued pursuant to division (J)(1) of this section is in contempt of court.

"(K) If any person is found in contempt of court for failing to comply with or interfering with any order or decree granting companionship or visitation rights that is issued pursuant to this section, section 3109.11 or 3109.12 of the Revised Code, or any other provision of the Revised Code, the court that makes the finding, in addition to any other penalty or remedy imposed, shall assess all court costs arising out of the contempt proceeding against the person and require the person to pay any reasonable attorney's fees of any adverse party, as determined by the court, that arose in relation to the act of contempt, and may award reasonable compensatory visitation to the person whose right of visitation was affected by the failure or interference if such compensatory visitation is in the best interest of the child. Any compensatory visitation awarded under this division shall be included in an order issued by the court and, to the extent possible, shall be governed by the same terms and conditions as was the visitation that was affected by the failure or interference.

"(L) Any person who requests reasonable companionship or visitation rights with respect to a child under this section, section 3109.11 or 3109.12 of the Revised Code, or any other provision of the Revised Code may file a motion with the court requesting that it waive all or any part of the costs that may accrue in the proceedings under this section, section 3109.11, or section 3109.12 of the Revised Code. If the court determines that the movant is indigent and that the waiver is in the best interest of the child, the court, in its discretion, may waive payment of all or any part of the costs of those proceedings.

"(M) The juvenile court has exclusive jurisdiction to enter the orders in any case certified to it from another court.

"(N) As used in this section:

"(1) "Abused child" has the same meaning as in section 2151.031 of the Revised Code, and "neglected child" has the same meaning as in section 2151.03 of the Revised Code.

"(2) "Record" means any record, document, file, or other material that contains information directly related to a child, including, but not limited to, any of the following:

"(a) Records maintained by public and nonpublic schools;

"(b) Records maintained by facilities that provide child day-care, as defined in section 5104.01 of the Revised Code, publicly funded child day-care, as defined in section 5104.01 of the Revised Code, or pre-school services operated by or under the supervision of a school district board of education or a nonpublic school;

"(c) Records maintained by hospitals, other facilities, or persons providing medical or surgical care or treatment for the child;

"(d) Records maintained by agencies, departments, instrumentalities, or other entities of the state or any political subdivision of the state, other than a child support enforcement agency. Access to records maintained by a child support enforcement agency is governed by division (F)(2) of section 2301.35 of the Revised Code.

"(3) "Confidential law enforcement investigatory record" has the same meaning as in section 149.43 of the Revised Code."

Amendment Note: 1997 H 408 substituted "division (F)(2) of section 2301.35" for "division (G)(2) of section 2301.35" in divisions (H)(1), (H)(2), and (N)(2)(d); and made changes to reflect gender neutral language.

Amendment Note: 1996 H 274 added the fourth and fifth sentences in division (A); substituted "legal separation" for "alimony" in division (B)(2); and made changes to reflect gender neutral language.

Cross References

Contempt for failure to comply or interference with visitation order, see 2705.031

County children services boards, powers and duties, see 5153.16

Library References

Child Custody ⚖175 to 231, 270 to 329.
Westlaw Topic No. 76D.
C.J.S. Adoption of Persons §§ 140 to 141, 143.

C.J.S. Divorce §§ 988 to 991, 993, 1011 to 1018, 1039.

Research References

ALR Library

80 ALR 5th 1, Child Custody and Visitation Rights Arising from Same-Sex Relationship.
71 ALR 5th 99, Grandparents' Visitation Rights Where Child's Parents Are Living.
69 ALR 5th 1, Grandparents' Visitation Rights Where Child's Parents Are Deceased, or Where Status of Parents is Unspecified.

Encyclopedias

69 Am. Jur. Proof of Facts 3d 281, Grandparent Visitation and Custody Awards.
114 Am. Jur. Proof of Facts 3d 275, Obtaining Child Custody from Citizen Parent and Parent Who Immigrated by Marriage to U.S.
OH Jur. 3d Family Law § 360, Decree of Dissolution--In Cases Involving Minor Children.
OH Jur. 3d Family Law § 922, Effect on Grandparent Visitation.
OH Jur. 3d Family Law § 1041, Relinquishment of Child to Grandparent Through Power of Attorney.
OH Jur. 3d Family Law § 1042, Caretaker Authorization Affidavit.
OH Jur. 3d Family Law § 1044, Hearing.
OH Jur. 3d Family Law § 1053, by Child's Relatives.
OH Jur. 3d Family Law § 1148, Setting Parenting Time Schedule.
OH Jur. 3d Family Law § 1149, Limitation of Parenting Time.
OH Jur. 3d Family Law § 1150, Limitation of Visitation or Parenting Time--Supervision.
OH Jur. 3d Family Law § 1151, Denial of Visitation.
OH Jur. 3d Family Law § 1153, Waiver of Costs for Indigency.

OH Jur. 3d Family Law § 1155, Determination and Effect of Child's Wishes.
OH Jur. 3d Family Law § 1163, Access to Child's Records.
OH Jur. 3d Family Law § 1164, Access to Child's Day Care Center.
OH Jur. 3d Family Law § 1165, Access to Child's Student Activity.
OH Jur. 3d Family Law § 1166, Notice of Residential Parent's Relocation.
OH Jur. 3d Family Law § 1169, Visitation Rights After Divorce or Dissolution.
OH Jur. 3d Family Law § 1170, Visitation Rights Where Parent is Deceased.
OH Jur. 3d Family Law § 1171, Visitation Rights Where Mother is Unmarried.
OH Jur. 3d Family Law § 1173, Determination of Child's Best Interests.
OH Jur. 3d Family Law § 1176, Mediation Report and Costs.
OH Jur. 3d Family Law § 1251, Contempt of Court
OH Jur. 3d Family Law § 1254, Compensatory Visitation.
OH Jur. 3d Family Law § 1536, on Certification from Another Court.
OH Jur. 3d Guardian & Ward § 90, Caretaker Authorization Affidavit; Authority to Execute.
OH Jur. 3d Schools, Universities, & Colleges § 353, School Records and Reports--Confidentiality of Pupil Information.

Forms

Ohio Jurisprudence Pleading and Practice Forms § 101:38, Parenting Time and Companionship Rights.
Ohio Jurisprudence Pleading and Practice Forms § 101:39, Parenting Time and Companionship

Rights--Access to Day Care, Records and School Activities.

Ohio Jurisprudence Pleading and Practice Forms § 101:114, Decree of Dissolution--Children.

Ohio Jurisprudence Pleading and Practice Forms § 101:115, Annulment--Judgment Entry--Dismissal of Annulment Complaint--Grant of Counterclaim for Legal Separation/Divorce.

Ohio Jurisprudence Pleading and Practice Forms § 101:116, Legal Separation--Judgment Entry--Grant.

Ohio Jurisprudence Pleading and Practice Forms § 101:125, Shared Parenting Plan.

Ohio Jurisprudence Pleading and Practice Forms § 101:127, Parenting Time Schedule Schedule.

Treatises and Practice Aids

Klein, Darling, & Terez, Baldwin's Ohio Practice Civil Practice § 24:2, Applicability of Civ. R. 24.

Sowald & Morganstern, Baldwin's Ohio Practice Domestic Relations Law § 9:9, Elements of Agreement--Allocation of Parental Rights and Responsibilities.

Sowald & Morganstern, Baldwin's Ohio Practice Domestic Relations Law § 16:5, Ascertaining the Wishes and Concerns of the Child.

Sowald & Morganstern, Baldwin's Ohio Practice Domestic Relations Law § 18:1, Introduction.

Sowald & Morganstern, Baldwin's Ohio Practice Domestic Relations Law § 18:2, Ohio's Statutory Scheme.

Sowald & Morganstern, Baldwin's Ohio Practice Domestic Relations Law § 18:3, Parenting Time Provisions--Domestic Relations Actions--By a Parent.

Sowald & Morganstern, Baldwin's Ohio Practice Domestic Relations Law § 18:5, Factors in Determining Visitation and Parenting Time Issues.

Sowald & Morganstern, Baldwin's Ohio Practice Domestic Relations Law § 18:6, Additional Considerations.

Sowald & Morganstern, Baldwin's Ohio Practice Domestic Relations Law § 18:7, Constitutional Considerations.

Sowald & Morganstern, Baldwin's Ohio Practice Domestic Relations Law § 18:8, Visitation by Third Parties in Domestic Relations Actions.

Sowald & Morganstern, Baldwin's Ohio Practice Domestic Relations Law § 18:9, The Impact of Adoption.

Sowald & Morganstern, Baldwin's Ohio Practice Domestic Relations Law § 19:2, Jurisdiction Over Child Support.

Sowald & Morganstern, Baldwin's Ohio Practice Domestic Relations Law § 21:2, Parenting Time--Establishing Visitation Order.

Sowald & Morganstern, Baldwin's Ohio Practice Domestic Relations Law § 21:3, Parenting Time--Jurisdiction--In General.

Sowald & Morganstern, Baldwin's Ohio Practice Domestic Relations Law § 21:6, Development of Statutory Requirements.

Sowald & Morganstern, Baldwin's Ohio Practice Domestic Relations Law § 21:8, Enforcement of Parenting Time--Contempt Proceedings in Court.

Sowald & Morganstern, Baldwin's Ohio Practice Domestic Relations Law § 24:3, Jurisdiction.

Sowald & Morganstern, Baldwin's Ohio Practice Domestic Relations Law § 3:35, Effect of Judgment--Allocation of Parental Rights and Responsibilities, Visitation, and Companionship Rights--As Between Parents.

Sowald & Morganstern, Baldwin's Ohio Practice Domestic Relations Law § 3:36, Effect of Judgment--Allocation of Parental Rights and Responsibilities, Visitation, and Companionship Rights--Relatives and Nonparents.

Sowald & Morganstern, Baldwin's Ohio Practice Domestic Relations Law § 9:10, Elements of Agreement--Parenting Time.

Sowald & Morganstern, Baldwin's Ohio Practice Domestic Relations Law § 9:39, Effect of Signed Agreement--Modification.

Sowald & Morganstern, Baldwin's Ohio Practice Domestic Relations Law § 9:59, Separation Agreement--Detailed--Form.

Sowald & Morganstern, Baldwin's Ohio Practice Domestic Relations Law § 11:45, Judgment Entry--Divorce Before a Magistrate With Children--Form.

Sowald & Morganstern, Baldwin's Ohio Practice Domestic Relations Law § 15:55, Award to Third Party--By the Court--Jurisdiction.

Sowald & Morganstern, Baldwin's Ohio Practice Domestic Relations Law § 15:75, Custody in Juvenile Court Proceedings.

Sowald & Morganstern, Baldwin's Ohio Practice Domestic Relations Law § 15:77, Statutory Notices for Parents--Form.

Sowald & Morganstern, Baldwin's Ohio Practice Domestic Relations Law § 16:10, Change of Circumstances--In General.

Sowald & Morganstern, Baldwin's Ohio Practice Domestic Relations Law § 16:11, Change of Circumstances--Relocation and Removal from Jurisdiction.

Sowald & Morganstern, Baldwin's Ohio Practice Domestic Relations Law § 18:10, Procedure--Standard Visitation Guidelines.

Sowald & Morganstern, Baldwin's Ohio Practice Domestic Relations Law § 18:11, Procedure--Relocation Notices, Access to Records, Day Care Facilities, and School Activities.

Sowald & Morganstern, Baldwin's Ohio Practice Domestic Relations Law § 18:12, Procedure--Relocation Notices, Access to Records, Day Care Facilities, and School Activities--Form.

Sowald & Morganstern, Baldwin's Ohio Practice Domestic Relations Law § 18:13, Procedure--Contempt Provisions.

Sowald & Morganstern, Baldwin's Ohio Practice Domestic Relations Law § 18:15, Procedure--Affidavit of Indigency.

Sowald & Morganstern, Baldwin's Ohio Practice Domestic Relations Law § 18:16, Procedure--Separate Cause of Action for Visitation.

Sowald & Morganstern, Baldwin's Ohio Practice Domestic Relations Law § 18:17, Procedure--Restrictions on Visitation.

Sowald & Morganstern, Baldwin's Ohio Practice Domestic Relations Law § 18:22, Modifying Parenting Time--Basis for Modification.

Sowald & Morganstern, Baldwin's Ohio Practice Domestic Relations Law § 18:24, Modifying Parenting Time--Interstate Modification.

Sowald & Morganstern, Baldwin's Ohio Practice Domestic Relations Law § 18:25, Modifying Parenting Time--Attorney Fees.

Sowald & Morganstern, Baldwin's Ohio Practice Domestic Relations Law § 18:29, Visitation Provisions--Domestic Relations Actions--Motion by Third Party to Intervene and Visitation Request--Forms.

Sowald & Morganstern, Baldwin's Ohio Practice Domestic Relations Law § 19:14, Parenting Time.

Sowald & Morganstern, Baldwin's Ohio Practice Domestic Relations Law § 21:14, Enforcement of Parenting Time--Interview of Child.

Sowald & Morganstern, Baldwin's Ohio Practice Domestic Relations Law § 21:26, Civil Sanctions.

Sowald & Morganstern, Baldwin's Ohio Practice Domestic Relations Law § 25:41, Motions Regarding Court Proceedings--Motion for Findings by Court.

Sowald & Morganstern, Baldwin's Ohio Practice Domestic Relations Law § 25:56, Post-Decree Motions--Motion to Modify.

Sowald & Morganstern, Baldwin's Ohio Practice Domestic Relations Law § 25:57, Motions Regarding Attorneys--Motion for Attorney Fees.

Sowald & Morganstern, Baldwin's Ohio Practice Domestic Relations Law § 37:23, Privileged Communication--Allocation of Parental Rights Proceedings.

Sowald & Morganstern, Baldwin's Ohio Practice Domestic Relations Law § 37:32, Privileged Communication--Waiver--Custody and Visitation.

Sowald & Morganstern, Baldwin's Ohio Practice Domestic Relations Law § 37:35, Privileged Communication--Waiver--Child's Privilege.

Sowald & Morganstern, Baldwin's Ohio Practice Domestic Relations Law § 9:124, Parental Rights--Child Not to be Removed from Locale--Form.

Sowald & Morganstern, Baldwin's Ohio Practice Domestic Relations Law § 9:125, Parental Rights--Non-Residential Parent's Right to Records--Form.

Sowald & Morganstern, Baldwin's Ohio Practice Domestic Relations Law § 9:129, Parenting Time--Adopting Court's Guidelines--Form.

Sowald & Morganstern, Baldwin's Ohio Practice Domestic Relations Law § 9:132, Parenting Time--Parents Living Far Apart--Form.

Sowald & Morganstern, Baldwin's Ohio Practice Domestic Relations Law § 9:136, Parenting Time--Procedure When Residential Parent Relocates--Form.

Carlin, Baldwin's Ohio Prac. Merrick-Rippner Probate Law § 99:3, Jurisdiction.

Carlin, Baldwin's Ohio Prac. Merrick-Rippner Probate Law § 106:4, Constitutional Issues.

Carlin, Baldwin's Ohio Prac. Merrick-Rippner Probate Law § 109:9, Parties to Proceedings.

Carlin, Baldwin's Ohio Prac. Merrick-Rippner Probate Law § 99:21, Types of Placement--Stepparent, Guardian, and Grandparent Adoptions.

Carlin, Baldwin's Ohio Prac. Merrick-Rippner Probate Law § 110:15, Visitation Right of Noncustodial Parent and Others.

Carlin, Baldwin's Ohio Prac. Merrick-Rippner Probate Law § 110:31, Parentage Act--Continuing Jurisdiction to Modify or Revoke Judgment.

Adrine & Ruden, Ohio Domestic Violence Law § 15:2, Custody and Visitation Issues; Background Information.

Adrine & Ruden, Ohio Domestic Violence Law § 15:5, Ohio's Legislative Response to Domestic Violence.

Adrine & Ruden, Ohio Domestic Violence Law § 15:6, Ohio's Judicial Response to Domestic Violence.

Adrine & Ruden, Ohio Domestic Violence Law § 15:9, Confidentiality.

Adrine & Ruden, Ohio Domestic Violence Law § 7:13, Collateral Effects of a Guilty Plea or of Being Found Guilty--Custody and Visitation.

Adrine & Ruden, Ohio Domestic Violence Law § 12:15, Remedies--Orders Allocating Parental Rights and Responsibilities.

Adrine & Ruden, Ohio Domestic Violence Law § 15:10, Batterer Access to the Victim and Children.

Adrine & Ruden, Ohio Domestic Violence Law § 15:13, Consideration of Domestic Violence as a Best-Interest Factor--Findings of Fact that Support a Court Decision.

Adrine & Ruden, Ohio Domestic Violence Law § 15:14, Shared Parenting Considerations.

Adrine & Ruden, Ohio Domestic Violence Law § 15:15, Domestic Violence and Visitation Issues.

Adrine & Ruden, Ohio Domestic Violence Law § 15:23, Mediation in Domestic Violence Cases.

Hastings, Manoloff, Sheeran, & Stype, Ohio School Law § 31:5, Parent-Educator Relations.

Hastings, Manoloff, Sheeran, & Stype, Ohio School Law § 23:22, Grandparent Power of Attorney--Form.

Law Review and Journal Commentaries

Arbitration as an Alternative to Divorce Litigation: Redefining the Judicial Role. Andre R. Imbrogno, 31 Cap U L Rev 413 (2003).

Children Born Out Of Wedlock And Nonsupport—Valid Statutory Grounds For Termination Of Parental Rights?, Note. 25 J Fam L 755 (1986–87).

Constitutional questions regarding grandparent visitation and due process standards. 60 Mo L Rev 195 (1995).

Custodial Rights in Non–Traditional Families. Pamela J. MacAdams, 20 Domestic Rel. J. Ohio 53 (July/August 2008).

A Father's Right to Visit His Illegitimate Child, Note. 27 Ohio St L J 738 (Fall 1966).

Grandparent Visitation Rights in Ohio After Grandchild Adoption: Is It Time to Move in a New Direction?, Note. 46 Clev St L Rev 385 (1998).

Grandparent Visitation: The Best Interests of the Grandparent, Child, and Society, Erica L. Strawman. 30 U Tol L Rev 31 (Fall 1998).

Grandparents' Rights in Ohio After H.B. 15, Richard J. Innis. 2 Domestic Rel J Ohio 33 (May/June 1990).

Grandparents' Visitation: Does Troxel v. Grandville Impact Ohio?, Mag. Elaine M. Stoermer. 50 Dayton B Briefs 20 (October 2000).

Grandparents' Visitation Rights in Ohio: A Procedural Quagmire, Comment. 56 U Cin L Rev 295 (1987).

In re Adoption of Ridenour, Note. 18 Ohio N U L Rev 719 (1992).

Is Court-Ordered Non-Parent Visitation in Ohio Unconstitutional in Light of Troxel v. Granville?, Richard L. Innis. 15 Domestic Rel J Ohio 2 (January/February 2003).

Judges' Column, Hon. Francine Bruening. (Ed. note: Judge Bruening discusses the Child Support Reorganization Act of House Bill 352, effective 1–1–98.) 21 Lake Legal Views 1 (June 1998).

Judicial Activism in Domestic Relations Cases, Hon. V. Michael Brigner. (Ed. note: Judge Brigner lists the powers of a judge hearing custody, support, and visitation matters.) 45 Dayton B Briefs 22 (January 1996).

Keeping Kids Out of Court. (Ed. note: Arbitration of custody disputes, but courts reserve the right to review awards.) 19 Nat'l L J B8 (May 5, 1997).

Relocation Issues: Part I—Development of Ohio Law, Hon. Cheryl S. Karner. 5 Domestic Rel J Ohio 37 (May/June 1993).

Sibling Rights to Visitation: A Relationship Too Valuable to Be Denied, Comment. 27 U Tol L Rev 259 (Fall 1995).

There's More than the Wolf Keeping Little Red Riding Hood from Her Grandparents, Hon. Russell A. Steiner. 5 Domestic Rel J Ohio 93 (November/December 1993).

To grandmother's house we go: Examining Troxel, Harrold, and the future of third-party visitation. 74 U Cin L Rev 1549 (Summer 2006).

Visitation Interference: Legal Solutions for Fathers, Hon. V. Michael Brigner. 49 Dayton B Briefs 19 (November 1999).

Visitation Rights of a Grandparent Over the Objection of a Parent: The Best Interests of the Child, Note. 15 J Fam L 51 (1976–77).

Visitation Rights Of An AIDS Infected Parent, Note. 27 J Fam L 715 (1988–89).

Wide–Open Grandparent Visitation Statutes: Is the Door Closing?, Comment. 62 U Cin L Rev 1659 (Spring 1994).

Notes of Decisions

1. Constitutional issues

Trial court that found divorced mother in civil contempt of prior orders concerning visitation could not immediately incarcerate mother without giving her opportunity to purge the contempt; trial court in effect imposed sanctions for criminal contempt without providing the constitutional safeguards applicable to criminal contempt charges. Knisley v. Knisley (Ohio App. 6 Dist., Fulton, 04-29-2005) No. F-04-024, 2005-Ohio-2090, 2005 WL 1007143, Unreported. Child Custody ☞ 874

Prior civil contempt finding against defendant was based on motion alleging her failure to provide her former husband schedules for their children's recreational and extracurricular activities, and, therefore, defendant's subsequent prosecution for perjury for lying to domestic relations court under oath in connection with her testimony about child's dance recital did not constitute double jeopardy. State v. Bell (Ohio App. 12 Dist., Warren, 11-29-2004) No. CA2004-07-082, 2004 WL 3155162, Unreported, appeal not allowed 105 Ohio St.3d 1471, 824 N.E.2d 541, 2005-Ohio-1186. Double Jeopardy ☞ 34

A court's decision to require the residential parent to live close enough to the non-residential parent to facilitate visitation deals with the custody of the parties' children and does not prohibit either party from travelling state to state or relocating; the residential parent is merely prohibited from taking the children with her if she decides to relocate and the prohibition does not violate the residential parent's right to travel. Alvari v. Alvari (Ohio App. 4 Dist., Lawrence, 02-02-2000) No. 99CA05, 2000 WL 133849, Unreported.

A smoker has a constitutional right of privacy to treat his health in whatever manner he chooses, but this right does not include the right to inflict health-destructive secondhand smoke upon other persons, especially children who have no choice in the matter. In re Julie Anne (Ohio Com.Pl., 08-27-2002) 121 Ohio Misc.2d 20, 780 N.E.2d 635, 2002-Ohio-4489. Constitutional Law ☞ 1225

Mother failed to properly invoke the jurisdiction of the court to consider challenge to constitutionality of statute providing standards for considering visitation rights, as record did not indicate that the Attorney General was notified, in any form, that mother was challenging the constitutionality of the statute. Love v. Rable (Ohio App. 3 Dist., 03-16-2001) 147 Ohio App.3d 63, 768 N.E.2d 1185, 2001-Ohio-2174. Constitutional Law ☞ 958

Custody, care and nurture of child reside first with parents, whose primary function and freedom include preparing for obligations the state can neither supply nor hinder. Troxel v. Granville (U.S.Wash., 06-05-2000) 120 S.Ct. 2054, 530 U.S. 57, 147 L.Ed.2d 49. Child Custody ☞ 22

2. Due process

Trial court's decision to suspend father's parenting time with children due to his combativeness during visitation exchanges, which was not conducive to the mental health or safety of the children, was not so indefinite or vague so as to deny father due process, as trial court indicated that once father underwent some sort of professional counseling, he would be able to move to begin receiving parenting time, and trial court, by requiring "some professional intervention" set a low threshold for reconsideration of the issue of parenting time, which should not be difficult for father to meet. Gisslen v. Gisslen (Ohio App. 2 Dist., Montgomery, 06-24-2011) No. 24414, 2011-Ohio-3105, 2011 WL 2520208, Unreported. Child Custody ☞ 550; Child Custody ☞ 577; Constitutional Law ☞ 4396

Child's legal custodian and residential parent received adequate notice and opportunity to defend

against concerns in connection with presence of child's paternal grandfather during visitation between child and child's father, satisfying requirements of due process, despite father's failure to file motion seeking elimination of prohibition of such visitation as established in divorce decree, where no decision below ever expressly permitted visitation between child and child's grandfather, and possibility that child's grandfather would be present during visitation was evident from nature of modifications sought. Arnold v. Arnold (Ohio App. 4 Dist., Athens, 09-27-2005) No. 04CA36, 2005-Ohio-5272, 2005 WL 2416378, Unreported. Child Custody ☞ 606; Constitutional Law ☞ 4396

Grandparent visitation statute and statute referenced in grandparent visitation statute, which enumerated factors for consideration in determining whether to grant grandparent visitation, did not violate father's substantive due process rights as applied to permit maternal grandmother to obtain visitation with children following their mother's death; magistrate accorded special attention and weight to father's wishes and concerns, and magistrate's decision set forth specific findings to support the determination that visitation with maternal grandmother would be in the children's best interest. Crigger v. Crigger (Ohio App. 10 Dist., Franklin, 02-10-2005) No. 04AP-288, 2005-Ohio-519, 2005 WL 314890, Unreported, appeal allowed 106 Ohio St.3d 1411, 830 N.E.2d 345, 2005-Ohio-3154, affirmed 107 Ohio St.3d 100, 836 N.E.2d 1221, 2005-Ohio-5975. Child Custody ☞ 4; Child Custody ☞ 511; Constitutional Law ☞ 4396

Grandparent visitation statute and statute referenced in grandparent visitation statute, which enumerates factors for consideration in determining whether to grant grandparent visitation, did not violate father's substantive due process right, as applied to permit maternal grandmother to obtain visitation with child following mother's death, where trial court afforded father's decision to limit court ordered visitation "special weight," but ultimately decided that grandmother should be granted some visitation rights because it was in child's best interest. Spivey v. Keller (Ohio App. 3 Dist., Allen, 12-13-2004) No. 6-04-09, 2004-Ohio-6667, 2004 WL 2849023, Unreported, appeal allowed 105 Ohio St.3d 1543, 827 N.E.2d 326, 2005-Ohio-2188, affirmed 107 Ohio St.3d 100, 836 N.E.2d 1220, 2005-Ohio-5973, reconsideration denied 108 Ohio St.3d 1418, 841 N.E.2d 321, 2006-Ohio-179. Child Custody ☞ 4; Constitutional Law ☞ 4396

Grandparent visitation statute and statute referenced in grandparent visitation statute, which enumerates factors for consideration in determining whether to grant grandparent visitation, are sufficiently narrowly tailored to promote compelling governmental interest of protecting parents' fundamental right to make decisions concerning child custody and care, and thus, statutes do not on their face violate substantive due process; given range and specificity of statutorily enumerated factors, trial court can not only afford parental decision as to whether to grant grandparent visitation requisite "special weight," but can also take into consideration best interest of child and balance that interest against parent's choice as to grandparent visitation. Spivey v. Keller (Ohio App. 3 Dist., Allen, 12-13-2004) No. 6-04-09, 2004-Ohio-6667, 2004 WL 2849023, Unreported, appeal allowed 105 Ohio St.3d 1543, 827 N.E.2d 326, 2005-Ohio-2188, affirmed 107 Ohio St.3d 100, 836 N.E.2d 1220, 2005-Ohio-5973, reconsideration denied 108 Ohio St.3d 1418, 841 N.E.2d 321, 2006-Ohio-179. Child Custody ⟨⟩ 4; Constitutional Law ⟨⟩ 4396

Trial court's award of visitation to maternal grandparents following death of mother, without affording father's wishes "special weight," violated father's fundamental due process right as a parent to direct the upbringing of his child as he saw fit. Frazier v. Frazier (Ohio App. 4 Dist., Hocking, 02-11-2003) No. 02CA8, 2003-Ohio-1087, 2003 WL 931296, Unreported. Child Custody ⟨⟩ 286; Constitutional Law ⟨⟩ 4396

Language contained in summons and mother's motion for temporary orders was insufficient as a means of providing father with notice that hearing would result in final judgment on issues of custody, child support, and visitation of parties' minor child, and thus, father was denied his constitutional right to due process when hearing was transformed into final hearing on merits of case. Wyatt v. Decsi (Ohio App. 9 Dist., Summit, 12-18-2002) No. 21072, 2002-Ohio-6993, 2002 WL 31828821, Unreported. Child Custody ⟨⟩ 410; Child Support ⟨⟩ 180; Constitutional Law ⟨⟩ 4396

RC 3109.05(B) does not violate the Equal Protection Clause by differentiating between divorced and nondivorced parents in that a court may grant visitation rights to third persons interested in the welfare of a child of divorced parents nor does RC 3109.05(B) violate the Due Process Clause since such visitation rights do not unduly interfere with the home life of the parent or child. Hollingsworth v. Hollingsworth (Franklin 1986) 34 Ohio App.3d 13, 516 N.E.2d 1250.

Due Process Clause of the Fourteenth Amendment, like its Fifth Amendment counterpart, guarantees more than fair process; it also includes substantive component that provides heightened protection against government interference with certain fundamental rights and liberty interests. Troxel v. Granville (U.S.Wash., 06-05-2000) 120 S.Ct. 2054, 530 U.S. 57, 147 L.Ed.2d 49. Constitutional Law ⟨⟩ 3901

Due Process Clause of the Fourteenth Amendment protects fundamental right of parents to make decisions as to care, custody, and control of their children. Troxel v. Granville (U.S.Wash., 06-05-2000) 120 S.Ct. 2054, 530 U.S. 57, 147 L.Ed.2d 49. Constitutional Law ⟨⟩ 4391

Due Process Clause does not permit state to infringe on fundamental right of parents to make child-rearing decisions simply because state judge believes a "better" decision could be made. U.S.C.A. Const.Amend. 14. Troxel v. Granville

(U.S.Wash., 06-05-2000) 120 S.Ct. 2054, 530 U.S. 57, 147 L.Ed.2d 49. Constitutional Law ⟨⟩ 4391

3. Assistance of counsel

Trial counsel's failure to present expert testimony regarding impact of visitation conducted in prison setting, and failure to object to hearsay testimony, was not ineffective assistance of counsel in proceeding in which father, an inmate, sought visitation rights with his two children; father presented no evidence of specific testimony expert would have proffered and failed to demonstrate whether such expert was available, and, although court may have considered hearsay in reaching its decision, father had not demonstrated that there was reasonable probability that court would have reached different result if counsel had objected to testimony. Harris v. Harris (Ohio App. 9 Dist., Lorain, 08-31-2005) No. 04CA008614, 2005-Ohio-4538, 2005 WL 2087836, Unreported. Child Custody ⟨⟩ 500

Mother did not have a constitutional right to effective assistance of counsel during proceeding on father's motion for legal custody of child and mother's motion to suspend father's visitation; there was no constitutional right to counsel in a civil case between individual parents. In re Rosier Lemmon (Ohio App. 5 Dist., Stark, 03-15-2004) No. 2003 CA 00306, 2004-Ohio-1290, 2004 WL 540299, Unreported. Child Custody ⟨⟩ 500

Order in post-divorce proceeding, requiring that father's visitation with parties' three children be supervised and that he attend counseling, did not violate father's First Amendment right to freedom of religion; order addressed visitation issue in context of children's best interests, and not based upon father's religious beliefs, father was still free despite the restrictions to instruct children on his religious beliefs and to teach them as he saw fit, and order did not prohibit or otherwise hinder father from practicing his religious beliefs. Willis v. Willis (Ohio App. 12 Dist., 07-22-2002) 149 Ohio App.3d 50, 775 N.E.2d 878, 2002-Ohio-3716. Child Custody ⟨⟩ 217; Child Custody ⟨⟩ 222; Constitutional Law ⟨⟩ 1409

4. Religious beliefs and issues

While in addition to their free exercise rights, parents have a fundamental right to educate their children, including the right to communicate their moral and religious values, a parent's actions are not insulated from the domestic relations court's visitation inquiry just because they are based upon religious beliefs, especially actions that will harm the child's mental or physical health. Willis v. Willis (Ohio App. 12 Dist., 07-22-2002) 149 Ohio App.3d 50, 775 N.E.2d 878, 2002-Ohio-3716. Child Custody ⟨⟩ 185; Child Custody ⟨⟩ 206; Child Custody ⟨⟩ 207

In deciding visitation issues, a domestic relations court may consider the religious practices of the parents in order to protect the best interests of a child. Willis v. Willis (Ohio App. 12 Dist., 07-22-2002) 149 Ohio App.3d 50, 775 N.E.2d 878, 2002-Ohio-3716. Child Custody ⟨⟩ 185

Visitation rights as to children of divorced parents must be considered without regard to the child's religious training, for all Christian denominations stand on the same footing in the eye of the law. Angel v. Angel (Ohio Com.Pl. 1956) 140 N.E.2d 86, 74 Ohio Law Abs. 531, 2 O.O.2d 136.

Constitutional religious rights are not violated by a child visitation decree giving the noncustodial parent visitation rights on holidays and one Sunday per month, where the custodial parent observes no religious holidays but Sundays. Johnson v Johnson, No. C–830653 (1st Dist Ct App, Hamilton, 7–11–84).

5. In general

After denying former husband's request for shared parenting on expert's recommendation that shared parenting would be problematic, trial court's grant of extended child visitation to husband, such that husband's visitation accounted for more than half of the children's time, was against the manifest weight of the evidence; expert did not recommend extended visitation as an alternative to shared parenting, and expansion of visitation relieved husband of responsibilities of shared parenting while depriving wife of capacity to make decisions which, as residential parent, she alone had authority to make. Livesay v. Livesay (Ohio App. 2 Dist., Montgomery, 12-03-2004) No. 20504, 2004-Ohio-6785, 2004 WL 2903876, Unreported, appeal not allowed 105 Ohio St.3d 1472, 824 N.E.2d 542, 2005-Ohio-1186. Child Custody 421; Child Custody 471

Visitation order which granted father parenting time with parties' out-of-wedlock child every other weekend and alternate Monday and Thursday overnights was not against manifest weight of evidence, in that it was based on mutual agreement between parties. McCage v. Dingess (Ohio App. 5 Dist., Licking, 10-13-2004) No. 03CA111, 2004-Ohio-5692, 2004 WL 2391678, Unreported. Children Out–of–wedlock 20.9

Husband, who was not biological father of child born during husband's marriage to child's biological mother, was not entitled to visitation with child; while child's biological mother and father might not have objected to husband's visitation with child at certain times prior to the hearing, they clearly expressed to the juvenile court at the hearing that they strongly opposed to husband having visitation, and wife/biological mother testified that allowing husband visitation would result in confusion for child and would disrupt child's bonding with his biological father. Collins v. Collins (Ohio App. 12 Dist., Fayette, 10-25-2004) No. CA2003-06-007, 2004-Ohio-5653, 2004 WL 2380992, Unreported. Children Out–of–wedlock 20.9

Father was to undergo transition period of adjustment before he would be entitled to standard overnight visitation of his twin children; twins were in fragile health, twins' therapist testified that increase in father's visitation should be gradual, and father had not indicated an understanding of the necessary precautions, medications, or skills required to care for the twins. Putthoff v. Thompson (Ohio App. 2 Dist., Clark, 01-09-2004) No. 2003CA19, 2004-Ohio-76, 2004 WL 41563, Unreported. Infants 222

Mother's motion to suspend father's visitation, based on claim of sexual abuse, was frivolous, and thus court's $10,000 sanctions award for father's attorney fees was warranted; mother failed to substantiate sexual abuse claim, and mother's actions adversely affected both father and child, as father's visitation was temporarily suspended. Edwards v. Livingstone (Ohio App. 11 Dist., Ashtabula, 08-01-2003) No. 2001-A-0082, No. 2002-A-0060, 2003-Ohio-4099, 2003 WL 21782596, Unreported. Costs 2

Trial court was not required to engage in a consideration of all the facets of statutes governing visitation, child support, and division of marital property, where husband and wife agreed to visitation, child support, and property division which was incorporated into the divorce decree. Zamonski v. Wan (Ohio App. 2 Dist., Montgomery, 02-21-2003) No. 19392, 2003-Ohio-780, 2003 WL 366756, Unreported. Child Custody 203; Child Support 47; Divorce 920

The "direct adverse impact" test, under which the court could consider moral principles when awarding child custody, but only in relation to the direct or probable effect of the parent's conduct on the child, could also be applied in a divorce action when determining nonresidential parent's visitation rights, where the nonresidential parent had admitted to adultery. Anderson v. Anderson (Ohio App. 7 Dist., 03-12-2002) 147 Ohio App.3d 513, 771 N.E.2d 303, 2002-Ohio-1156. Child Custody 192

Trial court's visitation order in divorce action, prohibiting any unrelated male individual from being present during wife's visitation, was improper, even if wife had committed adultery during the marriage and during a previous marriage; trial court had not considered whether presence of an unrelated male individual would have a direct adverse impact on the children, and the broad prohibition of "any" male individual from being present during visitation was not tailored to fit the specific concern the trial court was attempting to address. Anderson v. Anderson (Ohio App. 7 Dist., 03-12-2002) 147 Ohio App.3d 513, 771 N.E.2d 303, 2002-Ohio-1156. Child Custody 219

Father was not liable to mother on her claims for intentional infliction of emotional distress and loss of consortium based upon father's alleged measures to deny mother visitation with parties' two children after parties were divorced and father was awarded custody of children; any emotional distress or loss of consortium incurred by mother resulted from father following orders of domestic relations court, which denied mother visitation with parties' children. Catalano v. Pisani (Ohio App. 11 Dist., 07-23-1999) 134 Ohio App.3d 549, 731 N.E.2d 738. Damages 57.25(1); Parent And Child 7(8)

Nonresidential parent's statutory right to access to records relating to care of child is self-executing, and court needs to take action only if it intends to deny access to records. Badovick v. Badovick (Ohio App. 8 Dist., 05-26-1998) 128 Ohio App.3d 18, 713 N.E.2d 1066. Infants ⟿ 133

Statute governing nonresidential parent's right of access to child's day care facility is not self-executing and places mandatory duty on the court to determine the nonresidential parent's right to access. Badovick v. Badovick (Ohio App. 8 Dist., 05-26-1998) 128 Ohio App.3d 18, 713 N.E.2d 1066. Child Custody ⟿ 175

Although a party exercising visitation rights might gain temporary physical control over the child for that purpose, such control does not constitute "child custody" because the legal authority to make fundamental decisions about the child's welfare remains with the custodial party and because the child eventually must be returned to the more permanent setting provided by that party. Braatz v. Braatz (Ohio, 03-24-1999) 85 Ohio St.3d 40, 706 N.E.2d 1218, 1999-Ohio-203. Child Custody ⟿ 226

Ordinarily, child support and visitation are independent matters. Hamilton v. Hamilton (Ohio App. 6 Dist., 10-27-1995) 107 Ohio App.3d 132, 667 N.E.2d 1256, appeal not allowed 75 Ohio St.3d 1425, 662 N.E.2d 27. Child Custody ⟿ 175; Child Support ⟿ 8

Visitation is a right or privilege that is normally, but not always, granted to nonresidential parent. Hamilton v. Hamilton (Ohio App. 6 Dist., 10-27-1995) 107 Ohio App.3d 132, 667 N.E.2d 1256, appeal not allowed 75 Ohio St.3d 1425, 662 N.E.2d 27. Child Custody ⟿ 182

Because visitation is a right, not a duty, trial court cannot force nonresidential parent to visit his or her child. Hamilton v. Hamilton (Ohio App. 6 Dist., 10-27-1995) 107 Ohio App.3d 132, 667 N.E.2d 1256, appeal not allowed 75 Ohio St.3d 1425, 662 N.E.2d 27. Child Custody ⟿ 182

For purposes of statute providing that court "shall" consider any mediation report filed if divorce proceeding involves child and if court has not issued shared parenting decree, the word "shall" indicates that the statute is mandatory, but statute becomes mandatory only if mediation report is filed. McClure v. McClure (Ohio App. 2 Dist., 10-05-1994) 98 Ohio App.3d 27, 647 N.E.2d 832, appeal not allowed 71 Ohio St.3d 1481, 645 N.E.2d 1260. Alternative Dispute Resolution ⟿ 486; Child Custody ⟿ 419

Reference to 3109.05 was presumed to be intended to refer to 3109.051, in statute providing that whenever court issues child support order, it shall include in order specific provisions for regular, holiday, vacation, and special visitation in accordance with 3109.05, 3109.11, or 3109.12 of the Revised Code or in accordance with any other applicable section of the Revised Code, since 3109.05 deals exclusively with child support, whereas 3109.051 deals exclusively with visitation or companionship rights. Tobens v. Brill (Auglaize 1993)

89 Ohio App.3d 298, 624 N.E.2d 265. Child Support ⟿ 3; Child Support ⟿ 220

Visitation to an incarcerated parent is not prohibited by statute. Tobens v. Brill (Auglaize 1993) 89 Ohio App.3d 298, 624 N.E.2d 265. Child Custody ⟿ 200

Divorce court erred in failing to set forth visitation schedule between father and daughter; although son's custody was contested, daughter's custody was not and there was no evidence upon which court could deny reasonable visitation of father with either child. Frost v. Frost (Franklin 1992) 84 Ohio App.3d 699, 618 N.E.2d 198, motion overruled 66 Ohio St.3d 1489, 612 N.E.2d 1245. Child Custody ⟿ 210

A noncustodial parent may not be denied overnight visitation privileges solely on the grounds of the parent's homosexuality. Conkel v. Conkel (Pickaway 1987) 31 Ohio App.3d 169, 509 N.E.2d 983, 31 O.B.R. 335.

On the evidence the court will not require a child to be sent to her father in another state in the exercise of his rights of visitation. Anonymous v. Anonymous (Ohio Com.Pl. 1962) 180 N.E.2d 205, 88 Ohio Law Abs. 398, 18 O.O.2d 282.

As long as parent adequately cares for his or her children, i.e., is fit, there will normally be no reason for state to inject itself into private realm of the family, in order to further question ability of that parent to make best decisions as to rearing of that parent's children. Troxel v. Granville (U.S.Wash., 06-05-2000) 120 S.Ct. 2054, 530 U.S. 57, 147 L.Ed.2d 49. Parent And Child ⟿ 2.5

Evidence of recklessness was insufficient to sustain father's conviction for violating protection order by leaving a voice mail on mother's pager to arrange visitation with daughter; protection order lent itself to a reasonable interpretation that visitation matters fell outside of the scope of the order and that order authorized him to arrange visitations of daughter with mother. City of Cleveland v. Rogers (Ohio App. 8 Dist., Cuyahoga, 07-11-2002) No. 80430, 2002-Ohio-3547, 2002 WL 1501044, Unreported. Protection Of Endangered Persons ⟿ 98

Trial court may order a noncustodial parent to visit his child, picking her up from her mother for alternate weekends, where such visitation is ordered for the purpose of providing care and maintenance in a nonmonetary form. Bragg v Gorby, No. 86–C–31 (7th Dist Ct App, Columbiana, 6–30–87).

6. Discretion of court

Trial court did not abuse its discretion in suspending father's parenting time with children, as father was, at best, combative with regard to visitation exchanges, in that he videotaped or recorded all exchanges for parenting time and requested the presence of the police at every exchange, his actions during visitation were not conducive to the mental health or safety of the children, and children had stated that they did not feel safe with father due to his actions, and they even began refusing to go with father for parenting time. Gisslen v. Gisslen (Ohio App. 2 Dist., Montgomery, 06-24-2011) No. 24414, 2011-Ohio-3105, 2011 WL 2520208, Unreported. Child Custody ☞ 552; Child Custody ☞ 577

The trial court's order that prohibited mother from having parenting time with child if mother's boyfriend was present was not an abuse of discretion, in post-divorce child custody modification proceeding; child was afraid of mother's boyfriend, boyfriend had allegedly injured child in the past, and mother refused to cooperate with a court order designed to protect child from her boyfriend. Thomas v. Thomas (Ohio App. 2 Dist., Clark, 06-17-2011) No. 2009 CA 88, 2011-Ohio-2977, 2011 WL 2436912, Unreported. Child Custody ☞ 219

Trial court did not abuse its discretion in failing to consider child's health and safety in denying father's motion for expanded parenting time, as father's concerns in this area centered on a difference of opinion he had regarding decision of mother, who was child's residential parent and legal custodian, to enroll child in a part-time versus full-time kindergarten class, which did not involve child's health and safety. Walton v. Walton (Ohio App. 3 Dist., Union, 06-13-2011) No. 14-10-21, 2011-Ohio-2847, 2011 WL 2416292, Unreported. Child Custody ☞ 576

Even if trial court awarded extra visitation rights to father of child born out-of-wedlock in an attempt to make up for mother's previous unwillingness to reschedule missed parenting time, it did not abuse its discretion. Evangelista v. Horton (Ohio App. 7 Dist., Mahoning, 03-22-2011) No. 08 MA 244, 2011 Ohio 1472, 2011 WL 1118474, Unreported. Children Out–of–wedlock ☞ 20.9

Trial court did not abuse its discretion in awarding adjudicated father of child born out-of-wedlock parenting time with child, which consisted of Monday and Wednesday nights from 6:00 p.m. to 8:00 p.m., Fridays during the day from 9:00 a.m. to 3:30 p.m., and alternating weekends beginning on Fridays at 9:00 a.m., and ending on Sundays at 1:00 p.m., without designating a holiday parenting time schedule, but specifying holiday visitation as the parties agree, as parties kept the same work schedule, with father having Fridays off, thus freeing him to spend time with child every Friday, and record demonstrated that parties were willing to and, in fact, had agreed to holiday visitation in the past. Pahl v. Haugh (Ohio App. 3 Dist., Hancock, 03-21-2011) No. 5-10-27, 2011-Ohio-1302, 2011 WL 947016, Unreported. Children Out–of–wedlock ☞ 20.9

Trial court did not abuse its broad discretion in granting husband one week of unsupervised parenting time every other month; husband had attended psychological counseling and was treated with antidepressants, there was no indication of physical harm to child when husband left the state with her, guardian ad litem (GAL) did not believe husband would leave with child again, and GAL had no concerns about husband harming the child or doing anything dangerous. Fordham v. Fordham (Ohio App. 3 Dist., Logan, 04-27-2009) No. 8-08-17, 2009-Ohio-1915, 2009 WL 1110796, Unreported. Child Custody ☞ 210; Child Custody ☞ 217; Child Custody ☞ 421

Trial court did not abuse its discretion in finding mother in contempt for failing to provide phone parenting time to father; divorce decree required mother to facilitate phone contact between father and children during one specific hour each week, mother had knowledge of order, there was evidence that line was busy at time father attempted to call children, and mother's claim that she acted innocently, and not in intentional disregard of court order, was not defense. Valentine v. Valentine (Ohio App. 12 Dist., Butler, 05-16-2005) No. CA2004-01-024, 2005-Ohio-2366, 2005 WL 1131748, Unreported. Child Custody ☞ 854

Trial court visitation order, which deviated from the guidelines and awarded husband two days of visitation with child each month, was not an abuse of discretion, in divorce case; child had a good relationship with wife, child's mother, child's relationship with husband, his father, was strained, child asked that husband not be informed of school events, wife testified that child had nightmares after returning from visitation with husband and that his fingernails would be chewed down, husband fell asleep at the wheel while driving car and child had to yell to wake him up, and husband lived approximately 70 miles away from child. Temple v. Temple (Ohio App. 8 Dist., Cuyahoga, 01-13-2005) No. 83758, No. 83797, 2005-Ohio-92, 2005 WL 77085, Unreported, appeal not allowed 106 Ohio St.3d 1413, 830 N.E.2d 346, 2005-Ohio-3154. Child Custody ☞ 210

Trial court did not commit plain error when it found former husband in contempt for violating parenting time order, notwithstanding his assertion that he had a justifiable cause for doing so, since issue of whether his reasons were justifiable was a matter of discretion. Lamp v. Lamp (Ohio App. 5 Dist., Muskingum, 11-19-2004) No. CT2003-0054, 2004-Ohio-6262, 2004 WL 2674563, Unreported. Child Custody ☞ 904

Parties were entitled to present any additional evidence that could not have been presented to magistrate before the trial court ruled on the objections to magistrate's decision in visitation action, and, in order for trial court to determine whether parties had such evidence, court should have held a hearing and allowed such evidence to be presented for its consideration, and trial court's decision to deny the parties an opportunity to present and/or to proffer evidence for the record constituted an abuse of discretion. Flynn v. Flynn (Ohio App. 10 Dist., Franklin, 07-22-2004) No. 03AP-612, 2004-Ohio-3881, 2004 WL 1631614, Unreported. Child Custody ☞ 504

Trial court's decision allowing father to resume unsupervised visitation with child was not abuse of discretion, even though professionals recommended continuations of supervised visitation based on allegations of fondling, where trial court was free to accept or reject recommendations of professionals in determining whether best interests of child warranted restrictions as to father's visitation by way of supervision. Jackson v. Jackson (Ohio App. 5 Dist., Guernsey, 02-23-2004) No. 03-CA-17, 2004-Ohio-816, 2004 WL 330083, Unreported. Child Custody ☞ 616

Trial court order imposing a visitation schedule and departing from the parties' shared-parenting plan was not an abuse of discretion; father never told mother when he was incarcerated for 30 days for passing a bad check, father lied to mother about his whereabouts during his incarceration, father enrolled child in school without mother's permission, he took child out of state without telling mother or getting her permission, and father was uncooperative in dealing with parenting issues or communicating with mother. Kauble v. Pfeiffer (Ohio App. 3 Dist., Marion, 12-22-2003) No. 9-03-36, 2003-Ohio-6988, 2003 WL 22994559, Unreported. Children Out–of–wedlock ☞ 20.9

Failure to make an order of visitation in divorce case without stating reasons was abuse of discretion. Hayman v. Hayman (Ohio App. 12 Dist., Butler, 01-13-2003) No. CA2001-10-250, No. CA2001-11-268, 2003-Ohio-76, 2003 WL 103413, Unreported. Child Custody ☞ 511

Awarding child visitation to biological father who was never married to mother was not against manifest weight of evidence or abuse of discretion, where mother failed to request separate findings of fact and conclusions of law such that presumption arose that trial court correctly applied law, mother merely challenged magistrate's recommendations adopted by trial court by inviting Court of Appeals to revisit evidence in new light, and record contained some competent, credible evidence going to all essential elements of case. Reynolds v. Nibert (Ohio App. 4 Dist., Scioto, 05-07-2002) No. 01CA2771, 2002-Ohio-6133, 2002 WL 31518183, Unreported. Children Out–of–wedlock ☞ 20.11

Trial court acted within its discretion in requiring father to participate in parenting and anger management classes prior to allowance of any unsupervised visitation with father and mother's two minor children; evidence was presented that father threatened mother in the presence of their children, that father's girlfriend struck one of the children in the face and that father felt that this was justified under certain circumstances, and that father made a threatening gesture to mother while he was on the stand testifying, in the presence of the magistrate. Moog v. Moog (Ohio App. 5 Dist., Tuscarawas, 10-07-2002) No. 2002 AP 04 0030, 2002-Ohio-5482, 2002 WL 31260037, Unreported. Child Custody ☞ 222

Trial court acted within its discretion in awarding father only supervised visitation with father and mother's two minor children; record demonstrated that father showed no appreciation for the danger of allowing children to be on the beach and near the ocean without adult supervision, and father demonstrated by his own testimony that he did not know what his daughter had done while she was visiting with him during the summer. Moog v. Moog (Ohio App. 5 Dist., Tuscarawas, 10-07-2002) No. 2002 AP 04 0030, 2002-Ohio-5482, 2002 WL 31260037, Unreported. Child Custody ☞ 217

In allocating visitation rights a court does not abuse discretion in not requiring a former spouse to share responsibility for transportation of a minor child between Dayton and Indianapolis when her current husband receives a job promotion and transfer which involves a two and one-half hour drive and eliminates weekday visitation; on the contrary, a magistrate achieves an equitable result by ordering the non-custodial parent to transport the child to and from Indianapolis and also orders a reduction of that parent's support obligation by $40 per month to compensate for transportation costs. Brown v. Brown (Ohio App. 2 Dist., Montgomery, 08-29-1997) No. 16039, 1997 WL 531223, Unreported.

Where a child age two years four months hardly knows his father, a visitation order which promotes gradual bonding by way of a six-month period during which father and child have one 48–hour, unsupervised visit per month near the child's home and then allows for seven weeks extended visitation periods in four intervals at the father's home in Texas does not constitute an abuse of discretion. Haudenschield v Brakora, No. 13749, 1993 WL 277846 (2d Dist Ct App, Montgomery, 7–20–93).

Trial court acted within its discretion in ordering a more rigid visitation schedule as to child born out-of-wedlock which reduced father's parenting time, where trial court considered various factors, including physical distance between the parents and parents' inability to cooperate and communicate, parents had interpreted and manipulated the prior visitation order and chose to follow the order only when it met their purposes, father still enjoyed substantial amounts of time with child, and reduction of father's parenting time was necessary to reduce child's travel time and the inconvenience of mid-week visitation with regard to child's school schedule. In re Ross (Ohio App. 1 Dist., 08-22-2003) 154 Ohio App.3d 1, 796 N.E.2d 6, 2003-Ohio-4419. Children Out–of–wedlock ☞ 20.10

In order to further the child's best interest, the trial court has the discretion to limit or restrict visitation rights, and this includes the power to restrict the time and place of visitation, to determine the conditions under which visitation will take place, and to deny visitation rights altogether if visitation would not be in the best interests of the child. Anderson v. Anderson (Ohio App. 7 Dist., 03-12-2002) 147 Ohio App.3d 513, 771 N.E.2d 303, 2002-Ohio-1156. Child Custody ☞ 178; Child Custody ☞ 216; Child Custody ☞ 220

Trial court did not abuse its discretion by deviating from local rule providing for noncustodial parent to receive six weeks of visitation with child during summer months, and instead allowing former husband only two weeks of visitation, where opinion testimony of psychologist and psychology trainee, to which husband did not object, indicated that child's development could regress if she was transferred to husband for the summer months. Badovick v. Badovick (Ohio App. 8 Dist., 05-26-1998) 128 Ohio App.3d 18, 713 N.E.2d 1066. Evidence ☞ 571(1)

Trial court has considerable discretion to decide domestic relations issues, including visitation; discretion requires only that decisions not be unreasonable, arbitrary or unconscionable. Jacobs v. Jacobs (Ohio App. 9 Dist., 04-19-1995) 102 Ohio App.3d 568, 657 N.E.2d 580. Child Custody ☞ 176; Divorce ☞ 184(5)

In divorce action, trial court did not abuse its discretion in entering judgment, in accordance with the apparent agreement of the parties, stating that visitation with child might be granted to father at some future date upon finding by father's treating physician that visitation would be appropriate; father was present in courtroom when attorneys entered into agreement regarding child visitation, father did not object to this agreement, and there was nothing in the record to support father's contention that he did not consent to agreement entered by his attorney. McClure v. McClure (Ohio App. 2 Dist., 10-05-1994) 98 Ohio App.3d 27, 647 N.E.2d 832, appeal not allowed 71 Ohio St.3d 1481, 645 N.E.2d 1260. Child Custody ☞ 203

In divorce action, trial court was not bound to adopt opinion of father's treating physician as to appropriateness of father's visitation with child and thus, trial court would not have abused its discretion in denying father visitation with child even if father had not agreed to waive his visitation; physician diagnosed father with major depression, posttraumatic stress disorder, and multiple personality disorders, physician testified that father's prognosis was fair and that father required continuing psychiatric treatment, and physician stated that posttraumatic stress disorder and personality disorders could be lifelong problems for father. McClure v. McClure (Ohio App. 2 Dist., 10-05-1994) 98 Ohio App.3d 27, 647 N.E.2d 832, appeal not allowed 71 Ohio St.3d 1481, 645 N.E.2d 1260. Evidence ☞ 571(1)

Trial court did not abuse its discretion in granting unsupervised visitation privileges to father after it awarded permanent custody to stepmother, despite contention of relative of child that record contained evidence that father committed domestic violence against stepmother before they were married, and committed domestic violence against woman he lived with after he left stepmother; record contained no evidence that incidents of domestic violence ever had an effect on child who was not present at either incident; moreover, although some witnesses testified that they suspected father abused child, no witness testified that any such abuse had in fact occurred. In re Whaley (Athens 1993) 86 Ohio App.3d 304, 620 N.E.2d 954. Child Custody ☞ 272; Child Custody ☞ 471

Parental rights of visitation are within sound discretion of trial court, and its discretion must be exercised in manner which best protects interest of child. In re Whaley (Athens 1993) 86 Ohio App.3d 304, 620 N.E.2d 954. Child Custody ☞ 176

A visitation order that affords the nonresidential father of two young children two three-week periods of summer visitation does not constitute an abuse of discretion by virtue of the fact that it requires that the children be returned to the residential parent between the visitation periods for one week where the father is a career military officer currently stationed in the United States who may be assigned to an extended tour of service in Europe, even though this will require the children to endure four, rather than two, transatlantic flights. King v. King (Warren 1992) 78 Ohio App.3d 599, 605 N.E.2d 970.

Where there is clear and convincing evidence that a proposed visitation arrangement will be harmful to the welfare of the children, a trial court abuses its discretion in failing to impose sufficient restrictions to ensure the children's well-being. Bodine v. Bodine (Franklin 1988) 38 Ohio App.3d 173, 528 N.E.2d 973. Child Custody ☞ 471

The trial court did not abuse its discretion by limiting a visitation schedule to one week at Christmas and two weeks in the summer, where the child was only three years old and lived approximately two hundred miles distant from the noncustodial parent. In re Marriage of Barber (Cuyahoga 1983) 8 Ohio App.3d 372, 457 N.E.2d 360, 8 O.B.R. 485.

Trial court did not abuse its discretion, in action for divorce and ancillary relief, in granting out-of-state resident husband supervised visitation in-state; trial court specifically referenced its long distance parenting schedule setting forth times for visitation, and took into consideration factors including court-appointed psychologist's determination that husband displayed denial and intolerance, guardian ad litem's recommendation that visitation be supervised and concern that messages and cards husband had left for child were highly critical of wife and distressing to child, and fact that husband was not forthcoming about his residence or housing accommodations. Syslo v. Syslo (Ohio App. 6 Dist., Lucas, 09-30-2002) No. L-01-1273, 2002-Ohio-5205, 2002 WL 31166937, Unreported, appeal not allowed 98 Ohio St.3d 1477, 784 N.E.2d 711, 2003-Ohio-974, certiorari denied 124 S.Ct. 468, 540 U.S. 983, 157 L.Ed.2d 373, on subsequent appeal 2005-Ohio-4870, 2005 WL 2249583. Child Custody ☞ 217

Absent a finding that a noncustodial parent is unfit or that visitation may be harmful to the children, a visitation order which provides for one hour per week visitation in the custodial parent's home and four hours per week visitation in a grandparent's home is punitive on its face and constitutes an abuse of discretion. Harter v Harter, No. CA–8785 (5th Dist Ct App, Stark, 10–26–92).

Where there is a combination of a father's occasional intoxication and his children's multiple school activities, the court may order the father to make arrangements with the children for visitation without abusing its discretion. Kliner v Kliner, No. 81–J–19 (7th Dist Ct App, Jefferson, 2–2–82).

A trial court's failure to provide for any visitation schedule due to a noncustodial parent's current incarceration without exploring options which would allow the incarcerated parent to visit his children prior to his release from incarceration or to establish a schedule effective upon his release constitutes an abuse of discretion and will be reversed and remanded. Tobens v Brill, No. 2-93-3, 1993 WL 312913 (3d Dist Ct App, Auglaize, 8-19-93).

7. Standard orders

Trial court did not abuse its discretion in deviating from the standard order of visitation to grant additional visitation rights to father of child born out-of-wedlock; court retained the discretion to deviate from standard parenting guidelines using the statutory factors for determining visitation. Evangelista v. Horton (Ohio App. 7 Dist., Mahoning, 03-22-2011) No. 08 MA 244, 2011-Ohio-1472, 2011 WL 1118474, Unreported. Children Out–of–wedlock ⚖ 20.9

8. Statutory factors

Error in consideration of statute governing allocation of parental rights and responsibilities for care of children on former wife's motion to modify husband's overnight parenting schedule, rather than statute governing modification of parenting time or visitation, was harmless, where trial court referred to facts that corresponded with "best interests of the child" factors, including interactions between child and husband, child's adjustment to current schedule, and benefits child received as result of overnight parenting time. Banfield v. Banfield (Ohio App. 12 Dist., Clermont, 07-25-2011) No. CA2010-09-066, No. CA2010-09-068, 2011-Ohio-3638, 2011 WL 2989883, Unreported. Child Custody ⚖ 923(4)

Juvenile court exceeded its authority in issuing temporary visitation order granting biological mother's former same-sex partner visitation with child, and, thus, order finding mother in contempt for failing to comply with the visitation order was invalid; statute granted juvenile court the authority to grant visitation to a non-relative in cases involving a divorce, dissolution of marriage, legal separation, annulment, or child support proceeding, but statute did not confer upon a juvenile court the authority to grant visitation to a non-relative in the absence of one of these precipitating events. Rowell v. Smith (Ohio App. 10 Dist., Franklin, 06-09-2011) No. 10AP-675, No. 10AP-708, 2011-Ohio-2809, 2011 WL 2407746, Unreported, stay granted 129 Ohio St.3d 1412, 949 N.E.2d 1006, 2011-Ohio-3386, motion to vacate denied 129 Ohio St.3d 1448, 951 N.E.2d 1045, 2011-Ohio-4217. Children Out–of–wedlock ⚖ 20.9

Trial court's failure to explicitly refer to the statutory factors to be considered when determining

whether a modification of parenting time was in the children's best interest in judgment order that modified father's parenting time did not constitute an abuse of discretion, where trial court did in fact consider the factors, and found a great deal of conflict caused by father during drop-offs and pick-ups surrounding visitation when he would not return children's school materials, sporting equipment, and musical instruments when he returned children to mother after father's visits. Bonner v. Deselm-Bonner (Ohio App. 5 Dist., Guernsey, 05-13-2011) No. 10CA000033, 2011-Ohio-2348, 2011 WL 1944239, Unreported. Child Custody ⚖ 569; Child Custody ⚖ 659

Trial court's failure to explicitly cite to the statutory factors to be used in determining visitation, in deviating from the standard order of visitation to grant additional visitation rights to father of child born out-of-wedlock, did not appear unreasonable, arbitrary, or unconscionable and, thus, did not constitute an abuse of discretion, where the court did contemplate the same underlying concepts as the statutory factors. Evangelista v. Horton (Ohio App. 7 Dist., Mahoning, 03-22-2011) No. 08 MA 244, 2011-Ohio-1472, 2011 WL 1118474, Unreported. Children Out–of–wedlock ⚖ 20.4

Because trial court failed to engage in the required analysis of the factors set forth in statute governing parenting time rights, trial court's judgment with respect to the parenting schedule would be reversed and the case would be remanded to trial court to issue a new judgment that included the required discussion of the statutory factors. Graham v. Harrison (Ohio App. 10 Dist., Franklin, 09-08-2009) No. 08AP-1073, 2009-Ohio-4650, 2009 WL 2872995, Unreported. Child Custody ⚖ 511; Child Custody ⚖ 924

Trial court would not be found in error for failing to specifically reference its consideration of 13 of 16 statutory best-interest factors when considering former wife's motion to modify visitation; the parties narrowed the best-interest factors to be considered by trial court when they negotiated a resolution to the pending motion by agreeing that former husband would submit to psychological testing, there was some evidence that suggested that trial court properly considered the three remaining factors, and former wife failed to request more detailed findings of fact and conclusions of law. Yannitell v. Oaks (Ohio App. 4 Dist., Washington, 11-26-2008) No. 07CA63, 2008-Ohio-6271, 2008 WL 5077646, Unreported. Child Custody ⚖ 659

Father, whose objections to magistrate judge's decision placing restrictions on his child visitation rights did not specifically include contention that magistrate had failed to consider statutory factors, was precluded from asserting that ground on appeal from trial court's adoption of magistrate's decision. Wilms v. Herbert (Ohio App. 9 Dist., Lorain, 01-05-2005) No. 04CA008525, 2005-Ohio-2, 2005 WL 17901, Unreported. Child Custody ⚖ 904

Should trial court decide not to follow local rule governing winter and summer break parenting time, trial court would be required to consider statutory factors regarding parenting time rights in structuring winter and summer break parenting time. Dannaher v. Newbold (Ohio App. 10 Dist., 03-04-2004) 2004-Ohio-1003, 2004 WL 396993. Child Custody ⟜ 210

Trial court in divorce proceedings was required to consider statutory factors regarding parenting time rights in structuring Christmas parenting time, where parents failed to reach agreement as encouraged by local rule. Dannaher v. Newbold (Ohio App. 10 Dist., 03-04-2004) 2004-Ohio-1003, 2004 WL 396993. Child Custody ⟜ 212

A reviewing court will presume that the trial court considered relevant statutory factors when determining parenting time matters absent evidence to the contrary. Quint v. Lomakoski (Ohio App. 2 Dist., 06-16-2006) 167 Ohio App.3d 124, 854 N.E.2d 225, 2006-Ohio-3041, on subsequent appeal 173 Ohio App.3d 146, 877 N.E.2d 738, 2007-Ohio-4722. Child Custody ⟜ 920

Trial court did not abuse its discretion in modifying visitation schedule and not adopting standard visitation schedule applicable to parents living within 150 miles of each other, where RC 3109.051(F)(2) gave trial court authority to deviate from its standard visitation guidelines and trial court considered factors set forth in RC 3109.051(D). Snyder v Snyder, No. S–92–30, 1993 WL 356939 (6th Dist Ct App, Sandusky, 9–17–93).

9. "Best interest" of child

Evidence that seven-year-old child was doing well in school, was involved in many social activities, had many friends in mother's neighborhood, had a close relationship with his brother who resided with mother, that current parenting plan was working well, and that awarding father additional parenting time would create greater instability for child was sufficient to support trial court's finding that it was not in the best interest of the child to grant father additional parenting time. Senesac v. Gray (Ohio App. 12 Dist., Preble, 11-30-2009) No. CA2009-03-010, 2009-Ohio-6237, 2009 WL 4260550, Unreported. Child Custody ⟜ 577

Parenting schedule that did 'not award either mother or father a whole weekend visitation with children was in children's best interest, as Friday and Saturday night were husband's busiest nights at restaurant that he ran, and it was likely that if father was granted whole weekend visitation, he would be forced to hire a babysitter to watch the children for a great deal of the time and would have minimal contact with them, which would neither be conducive to a stable parent-child relationship nor be in the best interest of the children. Lee v. Lee (Ohio App. 5 Dist., Licking, 09-30-2009) No. 2008 CA 112, 2009-Ohio-5250, 2009 WL 3155054, Unreported. Child Custody ⟜ 210

Trial court, in analyzing mother's motion for modification of father's visitation, which was accompanied by her notice of intent to relocate with child to another state, was required to utilize best interest factors set forth in visitation statute, not best interest factors set forth in statute governing custody modification. Campana v. Campana (Ohio App. 7 Dist., Mahoning, 02-20-2009) No. 08 MA 88, 2009-Ohio-796, 2009 WL 428580, Unreported. Child Custody ⟜ 577

Modification of father's parenting time due to mother's requested relocation to another state was not a modification of parental rights and responsibilities that was subject to changed circumstances test or test as to whether harm likely to be caused by change of environment was outweighed by advantages of change of environment to child, both of which are set forth in child custody statutes; rather, modification of father's parenting time was a modification of father's visitation, such that best interest test set forth in visitation statute applied. Campana v. Campana (Ohio App. 7 Dist., Mahoning, 02-20-2009) No. 08 MA 88, 2009-Ohio-796, 2009 WL 428580, Unreported. Child Custody ⟜ 577

Mother was precluded from raising issue on appeal, asserting that juvenile court's conclusion that it was in child's best interests to have contact with individual was against manifest weight of evidence, in proceeding in which individual, who was involved in romantic relationship with mother at time of child's birth, filed motion for companionship or visitation rights, where mother failed to file transcript of proceedings before magistrate. Waszkowski v. Lyons (Ohio App. 11 Dist., Lake, 01-30-2009) No. 2008-L-077, 2009-Ohio-403, 2009 WL 224540, Unreported. Children Out–of–wedlock ⟜ 20.11

Ex-husband was not required to show before the trial court modified its previous order and lifted the supervision restriction on ex-husband's parenting time, and, instead, the trial court only needed to consider the factors set forth in statute governing matters of parenting time and visitation, with the overriding consideration being the best interest of the child. Shafor v. Shafor (Ohio App. 12 Dist., Warren, 01-20-2009) No. CA2008-01-015, 2009-Ohio-191, 2009 WL 119853, Unreported. Child Custody ⟜ 577

Trial court did not abuse its discretion when it lifted the supervision restriction on ex-husband's parenting time with his child; court's decision was not contrary to best interest of the child, purpose of the supervision requirement was no longer at issue, ex-husband had enrolled in, and completed, a parenting class, which was indicative of furthering child's best interest, child was a little over two and a half when supervised parenting order was initiated and was a little over eight when the restriction was lifted, and difference in age, coupled with better ability to articulate any possible problems to ex-wife, counselor, or teachers, played part in lifting the restriction on parenting time. Shafor v. Shafor (Ohio App. 12 Dist., Warren, 01-20-2009) No. CA2008-01-015, 2009-Ohio-191, 2009 WL 119853, Unreported. Child Custody ⟜ 577

Adjudicated natural father, who was incarcerated and allegedly made threats of harm to mother and out-of-wedlock child, failed to demonstrate visitation with child in prison was in the child's best interest. Edwards v. Spraggins (Ohio App. 5 Dist., Licking, 05-17-2005) No. 04CA54, 2005-Ohio-2416, 2005 WL 1163902, Unreported. Children Out–of–wedlock ☞ 20.9

Granting father expanded visitation with nonmarital child was in child's best interest, and thus trial court's decision to change visitation to alternating weeks was warranted; father had no problems transporting child to and from school, child had good relationship with both parents and her extended family, guardian ad litem recommended alternating weeks, mother had attempted to deprive father of court-ordered visitation, and father testified that mother had been verbally abusive to him in child's presence. In re Jones (Ohio App. 12 Dist., Butler, 09-08-2003) No. CA2002-10-256, 2003-Ohio-4748, 2003 WL 22071508, Unreported. Children Out–of–wedlock ☞ 20.10

Trial court did not err by not fully addressing statutory "best interests of the child" factors before rendering its judgment on mother's motion to modify visitation, where court considered statutory factors only eight days earlier in its decision allocating parental rights and visitation. O'Conner v. Patton (Ohio App. 4 Dist., Highland, 03-24-2003) No. 02CA10, 2003-Ohio-2597, 2003 WL 21152852, Unreported, appeal not allowed 99 Ohio St.3d 1469, 791 N.E.2d 984, 2003-Ohio-3669. Child Custody ☞ 659

A visitation award of up to three months in the father's home is not in the best interests of the child where (1) the award conflicts with the court's prior statement in a previous decision that the home may be a danger to the young child, (2) father's seasonal occupation would suffer financial hardship during the time off with his son, (3) the home is lacking potable water, and (4) the grounds are strewn with cars, broken glass and wandering animals. In re Allen (Ohio App. 2 Dist., Montgomery, 06-29-2001) No. 18708, 2001 WL 726698, Unreported.

The burden of proof that visitation would not be in the child's best interest is on the person opposing visitation and there is no requirement to show a change of circumstances in any request to change visitation rights. Matter of Nichols (Ohio App. 12 Dist., Clermont, 06-08-1998) No. CA97-11-102, 1998 WL 295937, Unreported, dismissed, appeal not allowed 84 Ohio St.3d 1406, 701 N.E.2d 1018.

Trial court in divorce proceedings erred in ruling that, if parents could not agree whether father's weekday parenting time would serve child's best interests once she entered first grade, it would conduct a hearing to consider the issue and would employ a rebuttable presumption that father's weekday parenting time would not serve child's best interests; trial court could not establish presumption, apart from statutory requirements, that limited or restricted the right of one parent to advocate a parenting schedule that conformed to child's best interest. Dannaher v. Newbold (Ohio App. 10

Dist., 03-04-2004) 2004-Ohio-1003, 2004 WL 396993. Child Custody ☞ 634

Prior decisions of the Court of Appeals did not vacate earlier parenting plan order and thus mother could be held in contempt for failing to comply with parenting-plan order; first decision remanded the cause to reconsider mother's post-divorce motion for modification of visitation and to determine whether a modification of visitation upon relocation to North Carolina, was in child's best interest, and second decision held that trial court could not modify the order without gathering sufficient facts to make a proper application of the statute. Quint v. Lomakoski (Ohio App. 2 Dist., 09-14-2007) 173 Ohio App.3d 146, 877 N.E.2d 738, 2007-Ohio-4722. Child Custody ☞ 924

A trial court determining parenting time matters must apply the statutory factors and determine the parenting time plan that is in the child's best interest. Quint v. Lomakoski (Ohio App. 2 Dist., 06-16-2006) 167 Ohio App.3d 124, 854 N.E.2d 225, 2006-Ohio-3041, on subsequent appeal 173 Ohio App.3d 146, 877 N.E.2d 738, 2007-Ohio-4722. Child Custody ☞ 177; Child Custody ☞ 178

After making independent review of magistrate's proposed modification of visitation schedule, juvenile court was free to disagree with magistrate's conclusions and to enter its own order, which it found to be in out-of-wedlock child's best interest. In re Ross (Ohio App. 1 Dist., 08-22-2003) 154 Ohio App.3d 1, 796 N.E.2d 6, 2003-Ohio-4419. Children Out–of–wedlock ☞ 20.4

Danger posed to children by secondhand smoke is both a relevant factor and a physical health factor that a family court is mandated to consider under statutory "best interests of the child" analysis for visitation and custody matters. In re Julie Anne (Ohio Com.Pl., 08-27-2002) 121 Ohio Misc.2d 20, 780 N.E.2d 635, 2002-Ohio-4489. Child Custody ☞ 81

When determining best interests of the child in visitation and custody matters, family court has a statutory duty to consider on its own initiative the serious risk of harm of secondhand smoke to children. In re Julie Anne (Ohio Com.Pl., 08-27-2002) 121 Ohio Misc.2d 20, 780 N.E.2d 635, 2002-Ohio-4489. Child Custody ☞ 81

When conducting "best interests of the child" analysis for visitation and custody matters, family courts have an unqualified duty to consider the dangers of secondhand smoke to all children, regardless of the condition of their health. In re Julie Anne (Ohio Com.Pl., 08-27-2002) 121 Ohio Misc.2d 20, 780 N.E.2d 635, 2002-Ohio-4489. Child Custody ☞ 81

In light of its duties under parens patriae doctrine and "best interests of the child" statute, family court would, on its own initiative in child custody and visitation proceeding, restrain mother and father under the penalty of contempt from allowing any person, including themselves, to smoke tobacco anywhere in the presence of minor child, given the scientific evidence demonstrating that secondhand smoke constituted a real and substantial danger to health of children. In re Julie Anne (Ohio Com. Pl., 08-27-2002) 121 Ohio Misc.2d 20, 780 N.E.2d 635, 2002-Ohio-4489. Child Custody ☞ 81; Child Custody ☞ 103; Child Custody ☞ 223

Trial court's failure to schedule visitation by child with former husband on both child's birthday and former husband's birthday, as required by local rules, was improper, and matter would be remanded to allow order to be amended to incorporate visitation, where nothing indicated that court intentionally decided to omit such visitation, and wife did not suggest that such visitation would be against child's best interests. Badovick v. Badovick (Ohio App. 8 Dist., 05-26-1998) 128 Ohio App.3d 18, 713 N.E.2d 1066. Child Custody ☞ 924

Father who sought modification of his child visitation rights under divorce decree was not required to show that there had been change in circumstances; however, trial court was required to consider 15 statutory factors, and, in its sound discretion, determine visitation that was in child's best interest; abrogating *Jacobs v Jacobs*, 102 Ohio App.3d 568, 657 N.E.2d 580. Braatz v. Braatz (Ohio, 03-24-1999) 85 Ohio St.3d 40, 706 N.E.2d 1218, 1999-Ohio-203. Child Custody ☞ 554; Child Custody ☞ 555; Child Custody ☞ 577

Trial court's "decision on divorce" and its "final judgment and decree of divorce" were sufficient to constitute statement of the court's findings of facts and conclusions of law in the case for purposes of statute requiring court to journalize its findings of fact and conclusions of law when court determines that it would not be in best interest of child to permit parent to visit child. McClure v. McClure (Ohio App. 2 Dist., 10-05-1994) 98 Ohio App.3d 27, 647 N.E.2d 832, appeal not allowed 71 Ohio St.3d 1481, 645 N.E.2d 1260. Child Custody ☞ 511

By agreeing to waive his right to visitation with child, father waived his right to statement of trial court's findings of fact and conclusions of law pursuant to statute requiring court to journalize its findings of fact and conclusions of law when court determines that it would not be in best interest of child to permit parent to visit child. McClure v. McClure (Ohio App. 2 Dist., 10-05-1994) 98 Ohio App.3d 27, 647 N.E.2d 832, appeal not allowed 71 Ohio St.3d 1481, 645 N.E.2d 1260. Child Custody ☞ 511

Visitation by two-year-old with her father while father was incarcerated awaiting trial for aggravated murder of child's mother was not in best interests of child, given very limited nature of visitation that could take place between father and child in highly restricted setting, child's young age, and extreme trauma to which she had already been subjected. In re Erica (Ohio Com.Pl. 1994) 65 Ohio Misc.2d 17, 640 N.E.2d 623. Child Custody ☞ 200

Standard court must use in making its decision whether to order visitation is whether visitation is in child's best interest. Holley v. Higgins (Franklin 1993) 86 Ohio App.3d 240, 620 N.E.2d 251. Child Custody ☞ 178

A domestic relations court which granted a divorce retains jurisdiction for the purposes of granting visitation rights as required by the best interest of any children born as issue of the marriage regardless of the existence or venue of a subsequent stepparent adoption proceeding. Bente v. Hill (Clermont 1991) 73 Ohio App.3d 151, 596 N.E.2d 1042, dismissed, jurisdictional motion overruled 62 Ohio St.3d 1422, 577 N.E.2d 1105. Child Custody ☞ 313; Child Custody ☞ 404; Divorce ☞ 154

A trial court may, pursuant to motions to modify and/or enforce visitation and companionship filed following a dissolution, order the parties and their children to undergo mental examinations, as the mental health of the parties and the children is relevant to the children's best interests as to visitation, but the court may order such examinations under Civ R 35(A) only on motion by one of the parties and after evidence has been presented to show good cause for each examination requested; moreover, the court must also specify the time, place, manner, conditions, and scope of any examinations ordered. Brossia v. Brossia (Wood 1989) 65 Ohio App.3d 211, 583 N.E.2d 978.

When a parent seeks to modify a previous visitation arrangement, it is that party who bears the burden of proof as to whether the prior arrangement was not in the best interests of the children; in the same way, the presumption that a parent is fit does not automatically entitle a parent to any visitation schedule desired as the parent must still establish that the schedule is in the children's best interests. Bodine v. Bodine (Franklin 1988) 38 Ohio App.3d 173, 528 N.E.2d 973.

The father of a child born out of wedlock is not entitled to visitation with such child over the objections of the mother, who has legal custody, unless he clearly establishes that such would be in the best interests of the child. In re Connolly (Franklin 1974) 43 Ohio App.2d 38, 332 N.E.2d 376, 72 O.O.2d 194. Children Out-of-wedlock ☞ 20.9

Where a divorce court has by its decree discharged its duty under 3109.05 with respect to the determination of visitation rights of the parent deprived of a minor child's custody, by merely accepting as its order as to visitation that to which the parties have agreed, but without specifically determining what would be for the child's best interest and welfare, and the parents thereafter disagree and a motion for modification is filed by the parent deprived of custody, the court is not bound by the agreement, and, though there are no changed conditions or circumstances which would otherwise justify the court in modifying or changing the previous order, the court must determine that which is for the best interest and welfare of the child and, in the exercise of its discretion, may modify the visitation rights accordingly. Miller v. Miller (Hancock 1966) 7 Ohio App.2d 22, 218 N.E.2d 630, 36 O.O.2d 69.

There is presumption that fit parents act in best interests of their children. Troxel v. Granville (U.S.Wash., 06-05-2000) 120 S.Ct. 2054, 530 U.S. 57, 147 L.Ed.2d 49. Child Custody ☞ 455

In an action for permission to remove a child from the jurisdiction and the noncustodial father, the court determined that the mutual benefit of the father/child visitation right is more in the child's best interests than the mother's change of residence. Jamison v Jamison, No. C–800829 (1st Dist Ct App, Hamilton, 11–10–81).

The trial court did not err in requiring the defendant-appellant determined to be the father in a paternity proceeding to prove that visitation with his child would be in the child's best interest; there is no presumption that a reputed father's visitation would be in the best interests of an illegitimate child. Kuhmer v Gibson, No. 924 (11th Dist Ct App, Geauga, 9–30–81).

10. Age of child

Denial, without hearing, of father's motion for visitation while incarcerated was not arbitrary, unreasonable, or unconscionable; father's incarceration for kidnapping, based on father's unlawful taking of child from state, was "extraordinary circumstance" that would support denial of visitation, and transporting of young child to prison on regular basis to visit with father gave rise to inference of harm to child, and gave rise to presumption that such visitation was not in child's best interest. Moore v. Moore (Ohio App. 5 Dist., Licking, 08-11-2005) No. 04CA111, 2005-Ohio-4151, 2005 WL 1924346, Unreported. Child Custody ☞ 200; Child Custody ☞ 461

Trial court's order leaving visitation with father to child's discretion was not abuse of discretion; child was 14, child did not want contact with father, even if supervised, because of prior abuse, and child had to undergo counseling following alleged abuse. Wilson v. Redmond (Ohio App. 12 Dist., Madison, 07-26-2004) No. CA2003-09-033, 2004-Ohio-3910, 2004 WL 1662259, Unreported. Child Custody ☞ 226

Child's change in age from two and one-half years to nine years, father's desire to spend more time with child, and parties' de facto modification of holiday visitation schedule did not constitute changed circumstances warranting modification of father's visitation schedule as set forth in agreement upon marital dissolution. Jacobs v. Jacobs (Ohio App. 9 Dist., 04-19-1995) 102 Ohio App.3d 568, 657 N.E.2d 580. Child Custody ☞ 574; Child Custody ☞ 577

Change in circumstances supporting modification of visitation order generally should not be predicated upon change in child's age, but child's age is properly considered as relevant factor in determination of child's best interests. Jacobs v. Jacobs (Ohio App. 9 Dist., 04-19-1995) 102 Ohio App.3d 568, 657 N.E.2d 580. Child Custody ☞ 577

Age must be a central consideration in determining when a minor's reluctance in visiting with the noncustodial parent is enough to prevent visitation. Smith v. Smith (Franklin 1980) 70 Ohio App.2d 87, 434 N.E.2d 749, 24 O.O.3d 100. Child Custody ☞ 205

11. Summer parenting

Order requiring father to pay transportation costs of children to visit mother in California for their summer visitation was not ambiguous to degree that father would be required to pay children's transportation costs anywhere in world; order clearly required for payment of transportation costs to California and obligation was limited to summer visitation and did not require father to pay transportation costs if mother wanted to bring children to California any other time. Moshos v. Moshos (Ohio App. 2 Dist., Greene, 09-17-2004) No. 03CA83, 2004-Ohio-4932, 2004 WL 2245087, Unreported. Child Custody ☞ 525

Trial court did not err in failing to include a specific and detailed summer visitation schedule; parenting plan with its standard visitation guidelines and all of the additional agreed judgment entries provided enough detailed information for the parties to conduct proper visitation, and the magistrate produced a comprehensive and effective decision with additional visitation clarification. Kessler v. Warner (Ohio App. 8 Dist., Cuyahoga, 03-27-2003) No. 81532, 2003-Ohio-1515, 2003 WL 1564313, Unreported, appeal not allowed 99 Ohio St.3d 1542, 795 N.E.2d 682, 2003-Ohio-4671. Child Custody ☞ 530

A mother is entitled to reimbursement of daycare costs that she would not have had if the former spouse had exercised his summer visitation pursuant to the parties' shared parenting agreement which states "The father shall be solely responsible for the payment of childcare expenses during the children's period of residence with him." Freed v. Freed (Ohio App. 2 Dist., Greene, 07-07-2000) No. 99 CA 102, 2000 WL 896285, Unreported.

12. Supervised visitation

Former wife was required to comply with trial court's existing visitation order, or face contempt, despite agreed judgment entry which required former husband and former wife to abide by counselor's supervised parenting recommendations. Montgomery v. Montgomery (Ohio App. 4 Dist., Scioto, 12-14-2004) No. 03CA2923, No. 03CA2925, 2004-Ohio-6926, 2004 WL 2940915, Unreported. Child Custody ☞ 854

Two-year-old child's statement that "daddy touched my pee pee," as well as behavioral changes noticed by caregivers, supported trial court's order of supervised visitation, despite testimony of psychologist that he did not believe that child had been sexually molested but that he could not rule it out. In re Anna H.M. (Ohio App. 6 Dist., Wood, 12-12-2003) No. WD-03-033, 2003-Ohio-6746, 2003 WL 22946179, Unreported. Child Custody ☞ 471

Evidence supported trial court order denying father, who was a convicted sex offender, unsupervised visitation with his son, even though two psychologists testified that father posed little physical or sexual threat to son; first psychologist testified that father was violent, exhibited a callous disregard for the rights of others, blamed his daughter for their sexual relationship, and failed to understand the repugnant nature of his sexual molestation of daughter, and both psychologists made no conclusions regarding whether unsupervised visitation would be in son's best interest. In re McCaleb (Ohio App. 12 Dist., Butler, 08-18-2003) No. CA2003-01-012, 2003-Ohio-4333, 2003 WL 21954753, Unreported. Infants ⟺ 175.1

Order in post-divorce proceeding requiring that father's visitation be supervised and that he attend counseling was not against manifest weight of evidence, where trial court found based on testimony of parties and guardian ad litem, psychological evaluator's report, and in-camera interviews of children that father had little comprehension of how children might be harmed by his references to mother as an adulteress or his videotaping of them as he asked them to recant statements they had made to evaluator, and that all three children believed father was unfairly critical of oldest child. Willis v. Willis (Ohio App. 12 Dist., 07-22-2002) 149 Ohio App.3d 50, 775 N.E.2d 878, 2002-Ohio-3716. Child Custody ⟺ 217; Child Custody ⟺ 222

Trial court was required, in ordering in post-divorce proceeding that father's visitation with parties' three children be supervised, to appoint a third party as supervisor after initially ordering that visitation be supervised by father's parents, where father's parents notified father's attorney that they were unwilling to be used in such a fashion. Willis v. Willis (Ohio App. 12 Dist., 07-22-2002) 149 Ohio App.3d 50, 775 N.E.2d 878, 2002-Ohio-3716. Child Custody ⟺ 217

When a county children services board is ordered by a court to provide supervision of visitation in a domestic relations case, the county children services board is obligated to provide that supervision unless and until the order is changed, and the county children services board may not charge the court for costs incurred in carrying out the order, except as provided in the order; refusal to comply with the court's order may be the basis for a contempt proceeding. OAG 92-072.

13. Modification of visitation

Statute governing modification of parenting time or visitation, and not statute governing allocation of parental rights and responsibilities for care of children, governed former wife's motion to modify husband's overnight parenting schedule. Banfield v. Banfield (Ohio App. 12 Dist., Clermont, 07-25-2011) No. CA2010-09-066, No. CA2010-09-068, 2011-Ohio-3638, 2011 WL 2989883, Unreported. Child Custody ⟺ 3

In appealing trial court's overruling of former wife's objection to magistrate's decision to grant former husband's motion to adopt standard order of parenting time in visitation modification proceeding, former wife waived for appellate review any issues concerning protective orders against former husband, former husband's prior criminal charges, completion of required seminar by former wife but not former husband, and children's alleged fear of former husband, where issues were not raised in objection to magistrate's ruling and thus

were not considered by trial court. Eldsonie v. Lewis (Ohio App. 2 Dist., Montgomery, 04-03-2009) No. 22910, 2009-Ohio-1633, 2009 WL 903354, Unreported. Child Custody ⟺ 904

Trial court acted within its discretion in adopting standard order of parenting time in former husband's proceeding to modify visitation, though former husband failed to participate in supervised parenting time that court had provided for former husband pending completion of hearing; divorce decree's provision granting former husband parenting time and visitation rights at all times as parties may agree had proved unworkable, and former husband perceived requirement of supervised visitation as a "slap in the face." Eldsonie v. Lewis (Ohio App. 2 Dist., Montgomery, 04-03-2009) No. 22910, 2009-Ohio-1633, 2009 WL 903354, Unreported. Child Custody ⟺ 217

Trial court order that limited former husband's companionship time with child to two days per week without overnight visits was not an abuse of discretion, in post-divorce proceeding to modify the parties' parenting plan; both parents and the experts agreed that child should spend more time with mother, child was fearful of former husband's angry outbursts, former husband had five guns in the house, and child expressed concern that former husband intended to put her pets to sleep if she lived with former wife. Ilg v. Ilg (Ohio App. 9 Dist., Summit, 12-23-2008) No. 23987, 2008-Ohio-6792, 2008 WL 5340871, Unreported. Child Custody ⟺ 577

Trial court's clarifying judgment modified the domestic violence civil protection order and not the visitation provision in the final judgment of divorce, in that the court reconciled the protection order's no contact provision with the necessity of arranging for the court-ordered visitation provided for in the divorce decree; trial court ordered no change in the visitation established by the divorce decree, and there was no modification of the parties' substantial rights. Davis v. Mendez (Ohio App. 2 Dist., Greene, 11-07-2008) No. 2008 CA 10, No. 2008 CA 21, 2008-Ohio-5768, 2008 WL 4823367, Unreported. Child Custody ⟺ 526; Protection of Endangered Persons ⟺ 70

Trial court acted within its discretion in modifying summer parenting time schedule in manner as to conform children's daycare and extra-curricular activities schedule to father's work schedule and location; mother had arranged for a complex summer activities schedule closer to her residence, and it would have been impossible for father to maintain his summer parenting time schedule while ensuring children's participating in the scheduled activities near mother's home. Daufel v. Daufel (Ohio App. 2 Dist., Montgomery, 08-01-2008) No. 22584, 2008-Ohio-3868, 2008 WL 2942220, Unreported. Child Custody ⟺ 577

Evidence supported trial court's decision to modify custody provisions of divorce decree, so as to increase divorced father's parenting and visitation time with child; both the guardian ad litem and the magistrate made specific findings pertaining to the applicable statutory factors and indicated that an increase in parenting time was in the child's best interests. Elson v. Elson (Ohio App. 3 Dist., Shelby, 06-27-2005) No. 17-04-16, 2005-Ohio-3228, 2005 WL 1503959, Unreported. Child Custody ☞ 577

Conditions upon resumption of visitation imposed by trial court, in parents' action to regain custody of child after voluntarily relinquishing her custody to custodian, were within trial court's broad discretion to modify visitation rights, were not onerous or unjustified, and did not effectively deny parents right to visitation. In re Bailey (Ohio App. 1 Dist., Hamilton, 06-17-2005) No. C-040014, No. C-040479, 2005-Ohio-3039, 2005 WL 1413269, Unreported, appeal not allowed 107 Ohio St.3d 1423, 837 N.E.2d 1208, 2005-Ohio-6124. Infants ☞ 231

Modification of parenting schedule to give father more equal parenting time with parties' out-of-wedlock child was not warranted, where father failed to show substantial change in child's circumstances or that modification would be in child's best interests, and relationship between mother and father was not amicable such that they could cooperate and make decisions jointly with respect to child. McCage v. Dingess (Ohio App. 5 Dist., Licking, 10-13-2004) No. 03CA111, 2004-Ohio-5692, 2004 WL 2391678, Unreported. Children Out–of–wedlock ☞ 20.10

Judgment entry that modified custody by designating father of non-marital child as residential parent and legal custodian was not required to specify terms and conditions of mother's access to school records, where trial court did not determine that mother was not entitled to equal access to records. Haney v. Corbett (Ohio App. 5 Dist., Delaware, 09-02-2004) No. 04CAF01005, 2004-Ohio-4642, 2004 WL 1945642, Unreported. Children Out–of–wedlock ☞ 20.10

Modification of father's weeknight visitation with child, requiring him to both pick up and drop off child at mother's residence, which was located approximately one-and-one-half hours from father's residence, was in child's best interests, in child custody proceeding; it was not in child's best interests for her to be traveling in car for this period of time. Venuto v. Pochiro (Ohio App. 7 Dist., Mahoning, 05-21-2004) No. 02 CA 225, 2004-Ohio-2631, 2004 WL 1152055, Unreported. Child Custody ☞ 577

Given change of circumstances caused by former wife's remarriage and move to another state, child's best interest was served by modifying parenting time but not modifying parental rights and responsibilities; psychologist did not think it was in child's best interest to be moved into father's household, child indicated she wanted to continue to live with former wife and wanted midweek visitation changed so that child would not miss softball practice, and child also indicated she wanted to alternate weeks with former wife and former husband during the summer. (Per Bryant, J., with two Judges concurring in judgment only.) Miller v. Miller (Ohio

App. 3 Dist., Henry, 05-10-2004) No. 7-03-09, 2004-Ohio-2358, 2004 WL 1049158, Unreported. Child Custody ☞ 568; Child Custody ☞ 577

In deciding former wife's motion to relocate minor child to another state, trial court had no authority to prevent relocation; however, if visitation schedule were not modified, former wife would be required to comply with existing visitation schedule or face charges of contempt. (Per Bryant, J., with two Judges concurring in judgment only.) Miller v. Miller (Ohio App. 3 Dist., Henry, 05-10-2004) No. 7-03-09, 2004-Ohio-2358, 2004 WL 1049158, Unreported. Child Custody ☞ 261

Trial court's modification of visitation schedule to allow father to have nightly, 20-minute telephone calls to children was in children's best interest, even though father's visitation was limited to supervised visitation six hours on alternating Sundays, and mother claimed nightly calls placed burden on her; there was no evidence that father had done anything inappropriate with children during visitation, children were available for calls, and children enjoyed time with father. Blasko v. Dyke (Ohio App. 2 Dist., Montgomery, 11-14-2003) No. 19905, 2003-Ohio-6082, 2003 WL 22682124, Unreported. Child Custody ☞ 577

In determining whether to modify father's visitation with nonmarital child, trial court should have made best-interest determination pursuant to factors in statute governing granting parenting time to parent, not statute governing allocating parental rights and responsibilities. In re Jones (Ohio App. 12 Dist., Butler, 09-08-2003) No. CA2002-10-256, 2003-Ohio-4748, 2003 WL 22071508, Unreported. Children Out–of–wedlock ☞ 20.10

Evidence supported trial court's order modifying mother's visitation by changing location of visitation to place near child's home, where there was evidence that mother missed large percentage of her scheduled visitations, she arrived late and left early, she left visits to smoke and to pick up other children and did not always interact with child during visits, which had negative impact on child, and child, who was in first and second grade during time period in question, had been required to travel almost an hour by car, each way, to get to original site of visitation, which resulted in child sometimes missing school, and disruption of child's routine. In re Allen (Ohio App. 12 Dist., Butler, 05-19-2003) No. CA2002-10-238, 2003-Ohio-2548, 2003 WL 21135453, Unreported. Child Custody ☞ 577

Appropriate and applicable standard for considering questions of modification of visitation is set forth in statute governing parenting time rights rather than statute that sets forth the specific rules for determining when a court may modify a custody decree. Flynn v. Flynn (Ohio App. 10 Dist., Franklin, 03-06-2003) No. 02AP-801, 2003-Ohio-990, 2003 WL 759174, Unreported. Child Custody ☞ 577

The residential parent's filing of the statutorily required notice of intent to relocate does not grant to the court the authority to prevent the party's relocation to another state; the court may only modify the visitation schedule to comport with the increased distance between the parties. Spain v. Spain (Ohio App. 3 Dist., Logan, 06-21-1995) No. 8-94-30, 1995 WL 380067, Unreported.

Trial court's error when refusing to modify child visitation, in failing to deem admitted matters contained in mother's requests for admissions, was prejudicial, requiring remand, since matters were material to the issue of modification and court made no findings of fact to support its decision; matters that court erroneously refused to deem admitted were that father was aware of mother and child's move to West Virginia, that father had maintained telephone contact and sporadic in-person contact with the child since then, that for four years father did not seek or exercise any holiday visitation with the child, and that father never exercised his summer visitation or parenting time with the child. Martin v. Martin (Ohio App. 2 Dist., 12-05-2008) 179 Ohio App.3d 805, 903 N.E.2d 1243, 2008-Ohio-6336. Child Custody ⟜ 923(4)

Modification of child visitation is governed by statute that specifically addresses visitation rights, rather than by statute that governs child custody, i.e., "parental rights and responsibilities." Braatz v. Braatz (Ohio, 03-24-1999) 85 Ohio St.3d 40, 706 N.E.2d 1218, 1999-Ohio-203. Child Custody ⟜ 577

Possibility that parties could seek further modification of child visitation order did not justify imposition of midweek visitation which trial court expressly found to be "unfair." Jacobs v. Jacobs (Ohio App. 9 Dist., 04-19-1995) 102 Ohio App.3d 568, 657 N.E.2d 580. Child Custody ⟜ 577

Modification of visitation order to impose court's standard visitation schedule is not per se just and reasonable, as court must consider whether there has been change of circumstances and whether modification is in best interest of child. Jacobs v. Jacobs (Ohio App. 9 Dist., 04-19-1995) 102 Ohio App.3d 568, 657 N.E.2d 580. Child Custody ⟜ 577

Parties' agreement to modify prior visitation schedule may be sufficient change of circumstances to justify court's modification of schedule to conform with that agreement, provided it is in best interest of child; agreement, however, should not be used as change in circumstances that justifies discontinuation of entire visitation schedule without reference to parties' mutually demonstrated desires. Jacobs v. Jacobs (Ohio App. 9 Dist., 04-19-1995) 102 Ohio App.3d 568, 657 N.E.2d 580. Child Custody ⟜ 574; Child Custody ⟜ 577

Modification of visitation rights is governed by RC 3109.05 and the specific rules for determining when a court may modify a custody decree are not equally applicable to modification of visitation rights. Appleby v. Appleby (Ohio 1986) 24 Ohio St.3d 39, 492 N.E.2d 831, 24 O.B.R. 81. Child Custody ⟜ 577

Proof of changed circumstances is not required to support modification of a visitation order. Roudebush v. Roudebush (Franklin 1984) 20 Ohio App.3d 380, 486 N.E.2d 849, 20 O.B.R. 485.

An extended visitation order at issue was not the equivalent of a formal modification of a prior custody decree. State ex rel. Scordato v. George (Ohio 1981) 65 Ohio St.2d 128, 419 N.E.2d 4, 19 O.O.3d 318.

The authority vested in a court by RC 3109.05, in extreme circumstances, includes the authority to give relief, through a just modification of an order of support, to a parent continuously or repeatedly prevented from exercising a right to visit a child by the child's refusal to visit with him; but such jurisdiction should not be exercised until the court first considers whether to make the child a party pursuant to Civ R 75(B)(2). Foster v. Foster (Franklin 1974) 40 Ohio App.2d 257, 319 N.E.2d 395, 69 O.O.2d 250. Child Support ⟜ 306; Child Support ⟜ 324

"Liberal" visitation rights are modified by the pattern of visitation developed by agreement of the parties since the divorce. Hauck v Hauck, No. D-108, 619 (8th Dist Ct App, Cuyahoga, 3-31-83).

14. Interference with visitation

Evidence supported trial court's finding that grant to father of compensatory time for visitation that mother prevented, by modifying visitation schedule to include the missed visitation, was in best interests of child; mother prevented any visitation for an entire six-month period, mother failed to inform father of child's schedule, child was anxious about visitation given mother's efforts to make encounters volatile, and mother had prevented child from forming any familial bond with his father and half-siblings. Clark v. Clark (Ohio App. 11 Dist., Portage, 08-20-2010) No. 2009-P-0096, 2010-Ohio-3967, 2010 WL 3326699, Unreported. Child Custody ⟜ 577

Trial court did not abuse its discretion in denying father's request for modification of standard order of parenting time to give him mid-week overnight visitation with child once school year started, as mother testified that child had difficulty with change in her routine, and she would have to rise earlier on morning following overnight visitation to make trip back to mother's home, and if child stayed overnight with father, she would go to bed at 9:00 p.m., which was the same time that father was required to return child to mother when father's midweek visits were not overnight. Shoenfelt v. Schoenfelt (Ohio App. 2 Dist., Montgomery, 12-11-2009) No. 23497, 2009-Ohio-6594, 2009 WL 4829832, Unreported. Child Custody ⟜ 577

The trial court's allocation of parenting time, which did not award mother and father equal time with out-of-wedlock child and awarded father more time with child, was not an abuse of discretion, in child custody proceeding; mother had an outburst during a visitation exchange in which child was present. McCarty v. Hayner (Ohio App. 4 Dist., Jackson, 08-25-2009) No. 08CA8, 2009-Ohio-4540,

2009 WL 2783427, Unreported. Children Out–of–wedlock ☞ 20.9

Sufficient evidence supported finding that terminating mother's parental rights was in the best interests of her minor son; mother had failed for two years to complete any of the elements of her case plan, particularly treatment for her addiction to drugs and alcohol, son required daily breathing treatments, which mother could not provide, and son had a strong bond with his foster mother, who was interested in adopting him. In re E.S. (Ohio App. 10 Dist., Franklin, 05-20-2004) No. 03AP-869, 2004-Ohio-2572, 2004 WL 1118689, Unreported. Infants ☞ 155; Infants ☞ 159

Issue of child's transportation to and from extra-curricular activities was integral part of parties' visitation order, and thus trial court was authorized to modify manner in which parties had agreed to transport child for purposes of visitation, despite fact that neither party raised issue on former husband's motion to modify visitation; child's increased participation in sports substantially interfered with husband's visitation. Beadle v. Beadle (Ohio App. 4 Dist., Scioto, 03-15-2004) No. 03CA2911, 2004-Ohio-1400, 2004 WL 555443, Unreported. Child Custody ☞ 610

Evidence that custodial unwed mother made unilateral decision to relocate residence of child without prior consultation with father supported finding that she relocated child without requisite advance notice to court and father, even though mother filed a notice of relocation with the court five days before moving to city that was three hours distant by car from former residence. In re Seitz (Ohio App. 11 Dist., Trumbull, 09-26-2003) No. 2002-T-0097, 2003-Ohio-5218, 2003 WL 22234850, Unreported. Children Out–of–wedlock ☞ 20.10

A non-custodial parent is not required as a condition of exercising visitation to present himself at the prescribed time after the custodial parent has made it clear that she will not permit visitation nor is he obliged to seek a reaffirmation of the order when it becomes possible and convenient for him to begin exercising visitation in accordance with its terms. Tangeman v. Tangeman (Ohio App. 2 Dist., Greene, 02-25-2000) No. 99-CA-53, 2000 WL 217284, Unreported.

A trial court abuses its discretion when it orders the suspension of a child support obligation for a period of eighteen months due to the residential parent's noncompliance with the visitation schedule. Roberts v. Roberts (Ohio App. 10 Dist., Franklin, 07-20-1995) No. 95APF01-33, 1995 WL 432612, Unreported.

The duty to pay child support is unaffected by any interference with rights of visitation, and no estoppel to claim child support arrears from a father may be inferred from the mother's withholding of visitation with the child. French v. French (Ohio App. 3 Dist., Marion, 05-30-1995) No. 9-95-7, 1995 WL 328110, Unreported, dismissed, appeal not allowed 74 Ohio St.3d 1418, 655 N.E.2d 738.

Trial court acted within its discretion, when granting parties' divorce, in ordering wife to transport parties' minor child 600 miles to visit husband every time child had three-day weekend from school, where wife had moved outside state during pendency of divorce action without court's permission, and trial court found that wife was attempting to influence child away from husband and that wife may have been able to find comparable job without moving. Corple v. Corple (Ohio App. 7 Dist., 09-26-1997) 123 Ohio App.3d 31, 702 N.E.2d 1234. Child Custody ☞ 213

Broadly drawn order forbidding "visitation in the presence of nonrelative adults of the opposite sex" was necessary to further state's compelling interest in protecting children from myriad possibilities of multiple adulterous relationships and the evidentiary problems associated with establishing the existence or nonexistence of said relationships, and, therefore, order infringed on, but did not violate, husband's constitutional right to freedom of association. Boggs v. Boggs (Ohio App. 5 Dist., 03-03-1997) 118 Ohio App.3d 293, 692 N.E.2d 674. Child Custody ☞ 219; Constitutional Law ☞ 1442

Court's determination that father was not in violation of child visitation order was not against manifest weight of evidence, despite mother's testimony that she had been repeatedly denied telephone access with children and father's admission that he violated visitation order by not being available to answer telephone on several evenings. Davis v. Davis (Ohio App. 7 Dist., 11-20-1996) 115 Ohio App.3d 623, 685 N.E.2d 1292. Child Custody ☞ 970

Custodial parent's interference with visitation by noncustodial parent may be considered as part of "change of circumstances" which would warrant modification of custody. Holm v. Smilowitz (Athens 1992) 83 Ohio App.3d 757, 615 N.E.2d 1047. Child Custody ☞ 555

Question for jury was presented as to whether maternal grandparents had interfered with father's court-ordered visitation with his children, in father's action under interference with possessory interest in minor statute; there was evidence that the grandparents knew that the divorce court had ordered that father have visitation with his children when the grandparents took the grandchildren and their daughter with them to their home in Tennessee. Brown v. Denny (Montgomery 1991) 72 Ohio App.3d 417, 594 N.E.2d 1008. Child Custody ☞ 984

Trial court did not have authority to modify or change mother's custody of children based upon her failure to encourage or implement regular visitation with grandparents as to whom court had provided visitation rights. Truitt v. Truitt (Preble 1989) 65 Ohio App.3d 126, 583 N.E.2d 331. Child Custody ☞ 872

Suspension of a child support obligation pending three undisturbed visitation periods is not a permissible sanction for interference with a visitation order. Fry v. Fry (Paulding 1989) 64 Ohio App.3d 519, 582 N.E.2d 11.

Neither RC 3115.21(B) nor 3109.05(B) authorizes the suspension of a support order or the forgiveness of past due unpaid support because of denial or interference with the obligor's visitation rights. Brown v. Brown (Warren 1984) 16 Ohio App.3d 26, 474 N.E.2d 613, 16 O.B.R. 28.

A custodial parent's denial of visitation rights does not excuse refusal by the supporting parent to obey an order requiring support payments; such denial of visitation rights could be the basis for a motion to reduce support payments. Flynn v. Flynn (Madison 1984) 15 Ohio App.3d 34, 472 N.E.2d 388, 15 O.B.R. 57.

Where a noncustodial parent's delay in re-establishing visitation with his child is due to his inability to locate the child, even though he made diligent efforts to do so, the equitable concept of laches should not be applied to curtail his visitation rights. McGill v. McGill (Montgomery 1982) 3 Ohio App.3d 455, 445 N.E.2d 1163, 3 O.B.R. 535.

If a court establishes a visitation schedule concerning the minor children of the parties, in the absence of proof showing that visitation with the noncustodial parent would cause physical or mental harm to the children or a showing of some justification for preventing visitation, the custodial parent must do more than merely encourage the minor children to visit the noncustodial parent, and until the children can affirmatively and independently decide not to have any visitation with the noncustodial parent, the custodial parent must follow a court order requiring the custodial parent to deliver the children to the noncustodial parent for visitation. Smith v. Smith (Franklin 1980) 70 Ohio App.2d 87, 434 N.E.2d 749, 24 O.O.3d 100. Child Custody ⇐ 181

Where a welfare department does not complete an investigation of alleged abuse by a noncustodial father, within thirty days as required by RC 2151.421 but instead waits nearly one year to close the case because of the complaining mother's refusal to cooperate and the department's failure to take any of the steps available to it to secure cooperation, the father who was deprived of visitation for the entire period should have sought a writ of mandamus ordering the investigation to proceed and cannot sue the department in US district court under 42 USC 1983. Haag v. Cuyahoga County (N.D.Ohio 1985) 619 F.Supp. 262, affirmed 798 F.2d 1414.

Where the noncustodial mother of children moves to another state and refuses to return the children to the custodial father after an extended visitation period in defiance of court orders, the court is within its authority to modify visitation to ensure that the custodial father's rights are not jeopardized. Stehura v Stehura, No. 1333 (11th Dist Ct App, Ashtabula, 2–26–88).

15. Contempt for violation of court ordered visitation

Trial court's order finding mother in contempt for failing to adhere to child visitation schedule was not a final appealable order, where mother was given opportunity to purge herself of the contempt by reasonably complying with the visitation schedule for one year, and the trial court intended to conduct further proceedings before the contempt issue was concluded. Clark v. Clark (Ohio App. 11 Dist., Portage, 08-20-2010) No. 2009-P-0096, 2010-Ohio-3967, 2010 WL 3326699, Unreported. Child Custody ⇐ 902

Clear and convincing evidence showed that ex-wife disobeyed a lawful court order by failing to abide by the terms of the shared parenting agreement regarding vacation and regular summer visitation, and, as a result, ex-wife would be held in contempt for disobeying the court order; however unreasonable ex-wife found the midnight pick-up time to be, ex-husband made his vacation request according to shared parenting plan, and ex-wife failed to communicate her disapproval of ex-husband's stated pick-up time or suggest alternate exchange time, and, thus, when ex-wife denied ex-husband's vacation, she disobeyed the shared parenting plan. Rapp v. Pride (Ohio App. 12 Dist., Butler, 07-06-2010) No. CA2009-12-311, 2010-Ohio-3138, 2010 WL 2653628, Unreported. Child Custody ⇐ 854

Trial court acted within its discretion in finding mother in contempt for violation of parental visitation order, despite father's failure to object at the time of the breaches, where father was entitled to visitation, father complied with notice requirement regarding visitation, and father's visitation time was not fully provided. Schwarzentraub v. Schwarzentraub (Ohio App. 6 Dist., Huron, 02-12-2010) No. H-09-012, 2010-Ohio-472, 2010 WL 497344, Unreported. Child Custody ⇐ 854

Trial court acted within its discretion in finding former wife in civil contempt for denying former husband the opportunity to exercise his court-ordered visitation with their minor child, even though former wife argued that trial court failed to consider extraordinary circumstances and testified that she stopped transporting child for visitation after a friend of child alleged that former husband had engaged in inappropriate behavior with her; child testified that she had a good relationship with former husband, that he had not done anything inappropriate to her, and that, in contrast to the friend's testimony, she had not witnessed any inappropriate behavior between former husband and the friend. Sloat v. James (Ohio App. 5 Dist., Stark, 06-15-2009) No. 2008 CA 00048, 2009-Ohio-2849, 2009 WL 1677850, Unreported. Child Custody ⇐ 870

Mother's defense for preventing father from visiting child, claiming that child had previously sustained injuries while in father's care, was considered by trial court prior to holding mother in civil contempt for violating visitation order; while trial court may not have given the defense the weight mother thought it deserved, the court acted within its discretion by weighing all the facts and circumstances, including the fact that mother had neglected to seek a judicial remedy in light of the child's purported injuries, which assisted trial court in determining whether mother's belief was reasonable and whether she violated the order in a good faith attempt to protect the child. Hensley v. Hensley (Ohio App. 6 Dist., Erie, 04-10-2009) No. E-08-026, 2009-Ohio-1738, 2009 WL 975907, Unreported. Child Custody ☞ 853

Ex-wife violated visitation provision in parties' divorce decree when she chose not to make any attempt to facilitate the court-ordered visitation between ex-husband and parties' son and, instead, actively and intentionally prevented that visitation, and, as such, ex-wife could be held in contempt for violating parties' divorce decree; any reasonable individual in ex-wife's position, once she knew that ex-husband wanted to see his son, could have worked something out regarding the visitation, rather than refusing it and then hiding behind domestic violence civil protection order as an excuse to deny it. Davis v. Mendez (Ohio App. 2 Dist., Greene, 11-07-2008) No. 2008 CA 10, No. 2008 CA 21, 2008-Ohio-5768, 2008 WL 4823367, Unreported. Child Custody ☞ 854

Mother's conduct in walking to father's car to assist in carrying the children's belongings, in violation of court order limiting location of exchanges of children to mother's door, did not injure father or his interest in any way that required or justified the remedial and coercive sanction of civil contempt trial court imposed for mother's conduct. Daufel v. Daufel (Ohio App. 2 Dist., Montgomery, 08-01-2008) No. 22584, 2008-Ohio-3868, 2008 WL 2942220, Unreported. Child Custody ☞ 854

There was insufficient evidence to permit a reasonable finding that former husband was in contempt in failing to provide telephone contact between former wife and their minor child; although wife testified that she called and left a message for child to call her back and he never did, she also testified that she did not know whether husband or child got that message, and husband, who did not recall message, testified that the date in question was his birthday and that he did not recall where he had been or what he was doing. Williamson v. Cooke (Ohio App. 10 Dist., Franklin, 02-06-2007) No. 05AP-936, 2007-Ohio-493, 2007 WL 354147, Unreported, on subsequent appeal 2009-Ohio-6842, 2009 WL 5062118. Child Custody ☞ 870

Even if his conduct was improper and inappropriate, former husband's "setting up" former wife so that she would end up being late in picking up minor child after conclusion of concert did not violate court decree in any manner, such that husband could be held in contempt for his conduct. Williamson v. Cooke (Ohio App. 10 Dist., Franklin, 02-06-2007) No. 05AP-936, 2007-Ohio-493, 2007 WL 354147, Unreported, on subsequent appeal 2009-Ohio-6842, 2009 WL 5062118. Child Custody ☞ 853

Finding former wife not to be in civil contempt for denying former husband his weekend parenting time was not error nor an abuse of discretion, where husband was more than 30 minutes late in arriving to pick up minor child. Williamson v. Cooke (Ohio App. 10 Dist., Franklin, 02-06-2007) No. 05AP-936, 2007-Ohio-493, 2007 WL 354147, Unreported, on subsequent appeal 2009-Ohio-6842, 2009 WL 5062118. Child Custody ☞ 854

Finding former husband in contempt with respect to mid-week visitations, after day for minor child's therapy sessions at speech and hearing clinic was changed from Thursday to Tuesday, was an abuse of trial court's discretion; decree expressly provided mid-week parenting time for husband was to be from 5 to 8 p.m. every Tuesday, but ending time of therapy sessions deprived husband of one-half hour of parenting time, husband's solution was to add the missing half hour at the end of the parenting time, and wife's solution was to ignore the half hour and to shorten husband's parenting time to two and one-half hours, rather than three hours as it would be if decree was strictly followed. Williamson v. Cooke (Ohio App. 10 Dist., Franklin, 02-06-2007) No. 05AP-936, 2007-Ohio-493, 2007 WL 354147, Unreported, on subsequent appeal 2009-Ohio-6842, 2009 WL 5062118. Child Custody ☞ 854

Trial court order suspending former wife's contempt sentence on the condition that former husband was granted more visitation with the parties' children, even though the condition granted husband more visitation than the original visitation order wife was held in contempt for violating, was proper; statute provided that a when a party was found in contempt for failing to comply with an order providing parenting time or visitation the court "may award reasonable compensatory parenting time or visitation to the person whose right of parenting time or visitation was affected." Robinson v. Robinson (Ohio App. 8 Dist., Cuyahoga, 11-23-2005) No. 85980, 2005-Ohio-6240, 2005 WL 3120215, Unreported. Child Custody ☞ 874

Trial court finding that wife was in contempt of court based on her failure to comply with child custody orders, and that wife failed to comply with all of the conditions required to purge civil contempt finding, was not an abuse of discretion, during divorce proceeding; testimony from city police officers and wife herself established that wife failed to comply with the court's child custody orders on numerous occasions, and she went to great lengths to deny father his scheduled parenting rotations, including taking the children out of state. Walton v. Walton (Ohio App. 6 Dist., Wood, 10-28-2005) No. WD-05-002, 2005-Ohio-5734, 2005 WL 2838573, Unreported. Child Custody ☞ 854; Child Custody ☞ 870

Appointment of guardian ad litem was not appropriate in contempt proceeding, seeking to hold ex-wife in contempt for violating court's visitation order; ex-wife's attorney filed a motion for the appointment of a guardian ad litem six months after the contempt proceedings were initiated and only a few days before the hearing was to begin, and the motion was styled as a motion "to suspend visitation and for appointment of guardian," and the contempt proceedings were not the appropriate means by which to request a change in the visitation order. Forrester v. Forrester (Ohio App. 2 Dist., Greene, 09-30-2005) No. 2004 CA 81, 2005-Ohio-5230, 2005 WL 2403955, Unreported. Infants ☞ 78(7)

Former husband's assertion that children told former wife they did not want to visit with her, and that former wife honored children's wishes by voluntarily leaving, was not a valid defense to motion for contempt based upon failure to comply with visitation order, absent any finding that mother was unfit or that visitation would cause harm to children, where visitation order imposed mandatory obligation on former husband irrespective of children's wishes. In re C.P. (Ohio App. 12 Dist., Butler, 07-25-2005) No. CA2004-10-259, 2005-Ohio-3888, 2005 WL 1798269, Unreported. Child Custody ☞ 854

Children's testimony with respect to sleeping arrangements at former wife's house, offered by former husband in contempt proceedings brought by former wife seeking enforcement of visitation order, was properly excluded as irrelevant, in absence of any evidence that visitation with former wife would cause children physical or mental harm, where sleeping arrangements were known to trial court and guardian ad litem, and former husband's defense to motion for contempt was that children, on specified occasions, did not want to visit with former wife, and that former wife acquiesced to children's wishes. In re C.P. (Ohio App. 12 Dist., Butler, 07-25-2005) No. CA2004-10-259, 2005-Ohio-3888, 2005 WL 1798269, Unreported. Child Custody ☞ 866

Even if trial court's findings of facts and conclusions of law in contempt proceeding failed to refer to proceedings held on date contempt hearing commenced, and to mother's witness, any error was harmless in proceeding finding mother to be in contempt for failing to provide father with phone parenting time as required by divorce decree, where record, and trial court's order, when taken as whole, provided adequate basis for Court of Appeals to dispose of all claims and issues presented for review on mother's appeal. Valentine v. Valentine (Ohio App. 12 Dist., Butler, 05 16 2005) No. CA2004-01-024, 2005-Ohio-2366, 2005 WL 1131748, Unreported. Child Custody ☞ 923(1)

Order finding mother in contempt for failing to provide father with phone parenting time as required by divorce decree was not result of bias and prejudice on part of trial court; mother and father had been before same trial court in long string of proceedings related to divorce, trial court repeatedly commented that parties were continually fighting and failing to cooperate, and trial court's comment that jail time would inevitably be imposed was nothing more than isolated remark made after recording numerous observations of interactions between parties. Valentine v. Valentine (Ohio App. 12 Dist., Butler, 05-16-2005) No. CA2004-01-024,

2005-Ohio-2366, 2005 WL 1131748, Unreported. Child Custody ☞ 871

Order finding mother in contempt of court for failure to comply with court-ordered visitation schedule was not final and appealable, where order contained purge provision and no order had been entered finding that mother had failed to purge herself and imposing penalty or sanction. Cooke v. Cooke (Ohio App. 11 Dist., Geauga, 05-06-2005) No. 2005-G-2631, 2005-Ohio-2262, 2005 WL 1075329, Unreported. Child Custody ☞ 902

Magistrate, in child visitation proceedings, acted within his discretion in ordering father to pay costs for the hearing on motion for contempt filed by maternal grandparents, even though trial court denied such motion; although recommending that the motion for contempt be denied, trial court indicated that if he were to allocate fault for the visitation problems, he would place blame on father. Deeslie v. Deeslie (Ohio App. 5 Dist., Licking, 12-29-2004) No. 03CA00114, No. 04CA0035, 2004-Ohio-7273, 2004 WL 3090241, Unreported. Child Custody ☞ 942

Former wife's failure to produce children for several scheduled visitations with former husband warranted finding that she was in contempt of visitation order, despite her excuses for those failures. Montgomery v. Montgomery (Ohio App. 4 Dist., Scioto, 12-14-2004) No. 03CA2923, No. 03CA2925, 2004-Ohio-6926, 2004 WL 2940915, Unreported. Child Custody ☞ 854

Former wife's failure to compel 13-year-old child to visit with former husband warranted finding that she was in contempt of visitation order. Montgomery v. Montgomery (Ohio App. 4 Dist., Scioto, 12-14-2004) No. 03CA2923, No. 03CA2925, 2004-Ohio-6926, 2004 WL 2940915, Unreported. Child Custody ☞ 854

Former wife's contempt of visitation order warranted 60-day jail sentence, since she had engaged in tactics to frustrate former husband's visitation with children for years and she was given the opportunity to avoid that sentence and purge her contempt through future compliance with the visitation order. Montgomery v. Montgomery (Ohio App. 4 Dist., Scioto, 12-14-2004) No. 03CA2923, No. 03CA2925, 2004-Ohio-6926, 2004 WL 2940915, Unreported. Child Custody ☞ 874

Thirty-day jail sentence imposed at time of earlier contempt citation arising from former wife's failure to comply with visitation order could be resuscitated seven years later when wife was again found in contempt of visitation order. Montgomery v. Montgomery (Ohio App. 4 Dist., Scioto, 12-14-2004) No. 03CA2923, No. 03CA2925, 2004-Ohio-6926, 2004 WL 2940915, Unreported. Child Custody ☞ 874

Evidence supported trial court's finding that ex-wife violated the parenting time order; ex-wife's testimony that she did not intend to violate the court order was not a defense, officer testified that ex-wife told him she was not going to turn the children over for visitation and cited several different reasons, and officer testified that he informed ex-wife that, if she did not turn children over, she might be charged with contempt of court. Stephens v. Stephens (Ohio App. 5 Dist., Ashland, 09-02-2004) No. 04-00A-027, 2004-Ohio-4640, 2004 WL 1945664, Unreported. Child Custody ☞ 870

Evidence was insufficient to support mother's allegation that father had physically or sexually abused child, in proceeding in which father sought to have mother held in contempt for failure to abide by visitation order involving parties' children, and mother sought change in custody; emergency room nurse testified that she had examined child, and child had reported that father had punched her in the eye twice, but nurse also conceded that it was not her job to determine how child's injury had occurred, and office manager at pediatrician's office indicated that mother had reported that child had been sexually abused, but manager also indicated that records contained nothing indicating that any doctor had discovered or reported any possible abuse to state. Markel v. Markel (Ohio App. 5 Dist., Ashland, 06-30-2004) No. 04-COA-015, 2004-Ohio-3437, 2004 WL 1465741, Unreported. Child Custody ☞ 637; Child Custody ☞ 870

Trial court's adoption of magistrate's amended decision, which was result of trial court's remand of magistrate's initial decision, was appropriate, in proceeding in which father sought to have mother held in contempt for failure to abide by visitation order involving parties' children; trial court reviewed amended decision, and overruled mother's objections to it, and, when trial court adopted amended decision, all questions regarding whether magistrate had obeyed trial court's instructions on remand had been resolved. Markel v. Markel (Ohio App. 5 Dist., Ashland, 06-30-2004) No. 04-COA-015, 2004-Ohio-3437, 2004 WL 1465741, Unreported. Child Custody ☞ 871

Conduct of magistrate in excusing himself from bench during proffer of evidence by mother's counsel was not erroneous, in contempt proceeding commenced by father, in which he sought to have mother held in contempt for failing to abide by visitation order involving parties' children. Markel v. Markel (Ohio App. 5 Dist., Ashland, 06-30-2004) No. 04-COA-015, 2004-Ohio-3437, 2004 WL 1465741, Unreported. Child Custody ☞ 871

Order that former wife pay former husband's attorney fees following husband's motion for contempt was proper, though neither party submitted evidence regarding attorney fees, no determination was made that wife had ability to pay attorney fees, and no determination was made that either party would be prevented from fully litigating his or her rights; wife was found in contempt for failing to comply with visitation order, and thus attorney fees were automatically assessed, fees charged were nominal in amount, and general statute governing attorney fees in divorce proceedings was not applicable. Beadle v. Beadle (Ohio App. 4 Dist., Scioto, 03-15-2004) No. 03CA2911, 2004-Ohio-1400, 2004 WL 555443, Unreported. Child Custody ☞ 952; Child Custody ☞ 955

Finding of contempt was not warranted regarding former wife's alleged violation of prior court order requiring former wife to permit children to place phone calls to former husband three times per week, since former husband did not bring telephone records to court to support allegations, former husband was out of state and unavailable for telephone calls from children a number of times during period in question, former wife set up three days per week in which children were required to make contact with father, and children often called other times beyond those three days. Beatley v. Beatly (Ohio App. 5 Dist., Delaware, 06-10-2003) No. 02CAF04020, 2003-Ohio-2990, 2003 WL 21350236, Unreported. Child Custody ☞ 853; Child Custody ☞ 870

Trial court did not err in failing to continue in force the provision in parties' visitation guidelines that restricted the parties' attendance at any of the minor child's school functions and at any event, activity or other function solely to the party in possession of the child at the time; based on the contempt citation and the extensive guidance provided in the parenting agreement, the parties had enough information and motivation to attend their child's activities in a mature manner, parties were free to continue to alternate activities based on the prior order that party with possession of the child attend without the other parent, and parties were also free to come up with a mutually agreeable alternative regarding their child's activities. Kessler v. Warner (Ohio App. 8 Dist., Cuyahoga, 03-27-2003) No. 81532, 2003-Ohio-1515, 2003 WL 1564313, Unreported, appeal not allowed 99 Ohio St.3d 1542, 795 N.E.2d 682, 2003-Ohio-4671. Child Custody ☞ 528

Trial court did not abuse its discretion in finding mother in contempt for failure to comply with visitation order; although mother and father offered different explanations for the three incidents that formed basis of contempt finding, the trial court was in the best position to judge the credibility of the witnesses. Patterson v. Patterson (Ohio App. 5 Dist., Stark, 02-03-2003) No. 2002CA00167, 2003-Ohio-517, 2003 WL 231257, Unreported. Child Custody ☞ 854; Child Custody ☞ 871

Trial court was not precluded from fining husband nominal amount of $1.00 for his contempt of the temporary visitation order, which required him to be available during the daytime hours if he began visitation with his minor children the night before; court understood that husband was working on some of the weekdays on which he had the children, that the children were being taken care of by husband's family, and husband testified that he thought the boys were better off with his family during the day than in daycare where the boys would be if they were with his wife. Saltzman v. Saltzman (Ohio App. 3 Dist., Wyandot, 11-27-2002) No. 16-02-10, 2002-Ohio-6490, 2002 WL 31667314, Unreported. Child Custody ☞ 854

It is the absolute duty of the custodial parent to have the children participate in visitation, and parents must immediately attempt to resolve any conflicts that arise through the court or another appropriate party; consequently, a mother who fails to comply with a visitation order and actively interferes with visitation will be found in contempt. Dickard v. Ringenbach (Ohio App. 8 Dist., Cuyahoga, 08-18-1994) No. 66136, 1994 WL 449424, Unreported.

Mother's violations of child visitation scheduling order were not merely technical violations, and thus mother could be found in contempt for violations, even if parties had voluntarily strayed from the schedule over four years since parties' divorce; mother provided only uncorroborated claims of illness to excuse two violations, and offered no excuse for the third. Martin v. Martin (Ohio App. 2 Dist., 12-05-2008) 179 Ohio App.3d 805, 903 N.E.2d 1243, 2008-Ohio-6336. Child Custody ☞ 854

Trial court lacked jurisdiction to decide motion to show cause why mother of child, who was born to mother five months prior to five-year marriage to former husband but shown by paternity testing at time of their divorce not to be former husband's, should not be held in contempt for failure to comply with visitation order that was entered in another county, where trial court declined to adopt previous orders entered in other county. Strope v. Wells (Ohio App. 5 Dist., 04-23-2007) 171 Ohio App.3d 658, 872 N.E.2d 363, 2007-Ohio-1962. Children Out–of–wedlock ☞ 20.4

Finding of contempt was not warranted even though former wife violated parties' out-of-court amended agreement regarding holiday visitation schedule when she sent children to her parents' home during former husband's visitation time; visitation order was in effect, and visitation order could be changed only by court order, not by document signed by parties. Lindman v. Geissler (Ohio App. 5 Dist., 04-23-2007) 171 Ohio App.3d 650, 872 N.E.2d 356, 2007-Ohio-2003. Child Custody ☞ 572; Child Custody ☞ 854

Denial of father's motion in post-divorce proceeding to find mother in contempt for violating schedule governing father's visitation as noncustodial parent was not error, where parties orally and mutually agreed following divorce to modify mother's drop-off times under shared parenting agreement. Willis v. Willis (Ohio App. 12 Dist., 07-22-2002) 149 Ohio App.3d 50, 775 N.E.2d 878, 2002-Ohio-3716. Child Custody ☞ 854

Trial court was precluded from suspending post-divorce proceedings regarding former wife's "visitation contempt action" by reason of husband's military service overseas pursuant to the Soldiers' and Sailors' Civil Relief Act, though husband's commanding officers restricted him from returning to United States during certain months of year, given possibility that husband could return to defend against wife's contempt action during other months of year, husband had instigated proceedings after he had relocated overseas by requesting trial court to "reset" wife's visitation with children, and under trial court's ruling wife was prevented from seeing her children for a substantial period without being able to do anything to vindicate her right pursuant to visitation schedule ordered by the trial court. Henneke v. Young (Ohio App. 2 Dist., 08-10-2001) 145 Ohio App.3d 111, 761 N.E.2d 1140, 2001-Ohio-1504. Armed Services ☞ 34.9(2); Child Custody ☞ 408

Contempt citation was supported by evidence that mother willfully impeded or obstructed court-ordered visitation, even though trial court later conceded that monthly visitation had been rendered impracticable by mother's move with child to another state; fact that judgment may have appeared impracticable in retrospect did not sanction mother's defiance of visitation order. Holm v. Smilowitz (Athens 1992) 83 Ohio App.3d 757, 615 N.E.2d 1047. Child Custody ☞ 854

Modification of a custody order is not among the available sanctions under RC 2705.05(A) as punishment for contempt; a trial court may not as a sanction for contempt of court arising from a custodial parent's interference with a noncustodial parent's visitation rights transfer the authority to the noncustodial parent to grant permission to a minor child to apply for a driver's license or to participate in extracurricular school activities as these changes actually modify custody, which is not a sanction authorized by RC 2705.05(A). Fry v. Fry (Paulding 1989) 64 Ohio App.3d 519, 582 N.E.2d 11.

A court should rigorously use its many powers to discourage a custodial parent from interfering with court-ordered visitation. The custodial parent should be aware that those powers include civil or criminal contempt with fines or imprisonment. Davis v. Davis (Cuyahoga 1988) 55 Ohio App.3d 196, 563 N.E.2d 320. Child Custody ☞ 854

Modification of a visitation order is not an available sanction for a party's contempt of the order by interfering with visitation; modification of a custody order may be accomplished only after a motion invoking the court's continuing jurisdiction, notice, and a hearing on the motion. Andrulis v. Andrulis (Summit 1985) 26 Ohio App.3d 164, 498 N.E.2d 1380, 26 O.B.R. 383.

16. Termination of visitation

Evidence supported trial court's adoption of magistrate's decision denying father's motion to "suspend" mother's visitation time on basis that child was not safe with her mother during visitation; there was no evidence that mother had struck child or harmed her in any way, and, while there was some evidence indicating child sustained slight abrasions on her mouth, lip, hip, and face during mother's visitation time, the record was devoid of any evidence indicating those "injuries" resulted from anything other than the normal playful activity of an outgoing well-developed three-year-old child. Benner v. Benner (Ohio App. 12 Dist., Preble, 01-31-2011) No. CA2010-02-003, 2011-Ohio-416, 2011 WL 334815, Unreported. Child Custody ☞ 577

Trial court did not abuse its discretion in granting husband unsupervised parenting time with his daughter; although husband did not visit with his daughter for approximately seven months, the lack of visitation was not by his choice but, rather, by court order, court found that wife's allegations that husband sexually abused their daughter were false, husband and his daughter needed to re-establish a relationship, and there was no indication that husband ever acted violently towards his daughter, that he ever endangered her as a result of his drinking, or that he got drunk in her presence. Graham v. Graham (Ohio App. 7 Dist., Noble, 12-28-2009) No. 08-NO-353, 2009-Ohio-6876, 2009 WL 5067047, Unreported. Child Custody ⟐ 217

Sufficient evidence supported trial court's finding that visitation modification was in the best interest of the child, so as to support termination of father's telephone privileges and prevention of further contact with child until he could conform his conduct to court's orders; mother and child's guardian ad litem testified regarding father's attempts to alienate child from mother, and guardian ad litem testified that father belittled mother and manipulated child during telephone calls and that she did not think he could abide by court's earlier order not to speak ill of mother in front of child. Lisboa v. Lisboa (Ohio App. 8 Dist., Cuyahoga, 10-01-2009) No. 92321, 2009-Ohio-5228, 2009 WL 3155135, Unreported, appeal not allowed 124 Ohio St.3d 1476, 921 N.E.2d 247, 2010-Ohio-354. Child Custody ⟐ 638

Trial court did not abuse its discretion in determining that children's visitation with father, an inmate, was not in children's best interest; youngest child had virtually no relationship with father and eldest child preferred to wait until father got out of jail to see him, father failed to establish that frequently transporting children to prison was in children's best interest, court's order permitted father to send written correspondence to children, and such interaction, while limited, was appropriate under circumstances. Harris v. Harris (Ohio App. 9 Dist., Lorain, 08-31-2005) No. 04CA008614, 2005-Ohio-4538, 2005 WL 2087836, Unreported. Child Custody ⟐ 200; Child Custody ⟐ 204

Trial court did not abuse its discretion in granting father's motion to temporarily terminate mother's visitation with son, which arose out of juvenile dependency action; caseworker testified at the visitation termination hearing that son was often anxious during his visits with mother, licensed clinical counselor for son testified that son verbalized compelling reasons for terminating visitation, counselor also recommended that it was in son's best interest to temporarily terminate mother's visits, and son's guardian ad litem concurred with counselor's recommendation. In re Unger Children (Ohio App. 5 Dist., Coshocton, 05-12-2005) No. 04 CA 6, 2005-Ohio-2414, 2005 WL 1163915, Unreported. Infants ⟐ 230.1

Trial court error in failing to conduct a hearing prior to granting guardian ad litem's motion to suspend husband's visitation with child was harmless, in divorce case, where divorce trial was conducted, and journal entry awarded husband limited visitation with child. Temple v. Temple (Ohio

App. 8 Dist., Cuyahoga, 01-13-2005) No. 83758, No. 83797, 2005-Ohio-92, 2005 WL 77085, appeal not allowed 106 Ohio St.3d 1413, 830 N.E.2d 346, 2005-Ohio-3154. Child Custody ⟐ 923(3)

Trial court's refusal to amend former wife's and former husband's dissolution decree to terminate former husband's parenting time with child, even though former wife's new husband was the biological father of child and former wife and new husband did not want child to have a relationship with former husband, was proper; former husband had a father-son relationship with child, and former wife and new husband sought to terminate all contact between child and former husband, even though former husband would continue to see child's older sibling. Jennings v. Jennings (Ohio App. 5 Dist., Licking, 05-18-2004) No. 2003-CA-00067, 2004-Ohio-2537, 2004 WL 1109865, Unreported, appeal not allowed 103 Ohio St.3d 1478, 816 N.E.2d 254, 2004-Ohio-5405. Children Out-of–wedlock ⟐ 20.4

Failing to terminate husband's overnight visits with child was not abuse of discretion in divorce proceeding, where guardian ad litem recommended that standard visitation be implemented and family court services evaluator recommended continuation of visits. Arnott v. Arnott (Ohio App. 9 Dist., Summit, 04-30-2003) No. 21291, 2003-Ohio-2152, 2003 WL 1983819, Unreported, motion granted 99 Ohio St.3d 1525, 793 N.E.2d 496, 2003-Ohio-4303, appeal not allowed 99 Ohio St.3d 1545, 795 N.E.2d 683, 2003-Ohio-4671. Child Custody ⟐ 421

Modification of parents' parenting time with child, providing four weeks with father and two weeks with mother, instead of alternating six weeks of parenting time for each party, was not erroneous; trial court noted child's young age, physical distance between parties, child's inability to understand parenting schedule, child's need for stability, and child's interaction and interrelationship with his paternal relatives. Lowry v. Lowry (Ohio App. 5 Dist., Guernsey, 04-24-2003) No. 02CA13, 2003-Ohio-2121, 2003 WL 1958030, Unreported. Child Custody ⟐ 577

Trial court did not abuse its discretion when it decided, during hearing on mother's motion for legal custody of her six-year-old son, not to continue indefinite, court-ordered supervised visitation schedule with mother, where court left door open for mother and legal custodian to work out visitation on their own, and found that visitation was not in child's best interest, as mother was unstable, in that she moved frequently, had no work history, appeared to have no earned income to support either herself or child, received benefits and student loans to which she was not entitled, and threatened caseworkers with physical harm, child had been cared for by custodian for last four of his six years of life and was established in that relationship, and mother and custodian had been unable to amicably work out a visitation schedule that mother would have adhered to. In re Timberlake (Ohio App. 10 Dist., Franklin, 03-13-2003) No. 02AP-792,

2003-Ohio-1183, 2003 WL 1094078, Unreported. Infants ⚭ 222

Denial of mother's request for visitation with child was not abuse of discretion, in child dependency proceeding; mother offered no evidence of any progress in her mental health treatment or condition, or her recent sobriety, to establish that child would not be at risk while with her, father testified that mother showed no interest in trying to keep in contact with child, and mother failed to show that granting her visitation would be in child's best interest. In re DeCara (Ohio App. 11 Dist., Portage, 11-29-2002) No. 2001-P-0088, 2002-Ohio-6584, 2002 WL 31716785, Unreported. Infants ⚭ 222

The fact that a nonresidential parent is imprisoned for a term of years is an extraordinary circumstance which will ordinarily support the denial of visitation, and such visitation is usually presumed not in the best interest of a child unless there is some evidence to the contrary; therefore, where a noncustodial parent is incarcerated for aggravated robbery, a serious offense of violence under Ohio law, and has not demonstrated to the satisfaction of the court that there is any reason whatsoever why visitation with him while he is incarcerated would serve the best interests of the parties' minor children, denial of visitation is not an abuse of discretion. Lowe v. Lowe (Ohio App. 12 Dist., Fayette, 06-23-1997) No. CA97-02-003, 1997 WL 349033, Unreported.

A mother's visitation rights may be suspended due to her physical and emotional harm to her children evidenced by (1) hitting and pinching, (2) pulling the daughter's hair, (3) depriving them of food as punishment of her husband, and (4) physically attacking the husband in front of the children; a court may reinstate visitation after a period free of the mother's negative behavior. Pisani v. Pisani (Ohio App. 8 Dist., Cuyahoga, 01-25-1996) No. 67814, No. 68044, 1996 WL 28572, Unreported, dismissed, appeal not allowed 76 Ohio St.3d 1472, 669 N.E.2d 856.

Trial court abused its discretion in denying all visitation because former husband was incarcerated and then requiring former husband to request visitation upon his release. Tobens v. Brill (Auglaize 1993) 89 Ohio App.3d 298, 624 N.E.2d 265. Child Custody ⚭ 200

Enforcement of a court-approved settlement of a prior visitation modification proceeding terminating the father's visitation rights if the father again engaged in offenses relating to alcohol or drugs is proper where the court determines that termination of visitation rights is in the child's best interest in light of the father's subsequent DWI offenses. Brown v. Brown (Hancock 1992) 78 Ohio App.3d 416, 604 N.E.2d 1380.

Clear and convincing evidence supports the trial court's decision to suspend a father's visitation where (1) the child's intense dislike and fear of his father is shown, (2) there is evidence that a serious problem exists between the father and child due to the child's perceptions of his father's constant fault-finding and lack of empathy with him, and (3) the father has failed to cooperate in therapy and has not acknowledged the existence of a problem. Johntonny v. Malliski (Geauga 1990) 67 Ohio App.3d 709, 588 N.E.2d 200, motion to certify overruled 55 Ohio St.3d 715, 563 N.E.2d 725. Child Custody ⚭ 638

A parent's incarceration for a term of years constitutes an extraordinary circumstance, as do (1) unfitness of the noncustodial parent, and (2) harm to the child caused by visitation. In re Hall (Franklin 1989) 65 Ohio App.3d 88, 582 N.E.2d 1055.

Imprisonment of a parent for a term of years for a violent crime, while an extraordinary circumstance which supports denial of visitation, does not necessarily preclude visitation; visitation may occur, but only if it is in the best interests of the child, a circumstance which must be proven by the incarcerated parent. In re Hall (Franklin 1989) 65 Ohio App.3d 88, 582 N.E.2d 1055. Child Custody ⚭ 200; Child Custody ⚭ 452

Visitation of a noncustodial parent in prison which requires transporting a young child there on a regular frequent basis gives rise to an inference of harm to the child so that this visitation is not in the child's best interest; such an inference should not be drawn only if the incarcerated noncustodial parent proves that visitation at the place of imprisonment is not harmful to the child, but is in the child's best interest. In re Hall (Franklin 1989) 65 Ohio App.3d 88, 582 N.E.2d 1055. Child Custody ⚭ 461

In a proceeding for termination of visitation, where expert testimony establishes that the children would be harmed by knowledge of their father's homosexuality, it is an abuse of discretion not to terminate visitation rights or impose conditions that would guarantee that the children not acquire that knowledge. Roberts v. Roberts (Franklin 1985) 22 Ohio App.3d 127, 489 N.E.2d 1067, 22 O.B.R. 328.

While visitation rights may be entirely denied under extraordinary circumstances, a child's unwillingness and fear to visit the noncustodial parent should be discounted if they result from influence of the custodial parent, or ignorance due to the child's age or lack of familiarity with the noncustodial parent. Pettry v. Pettry (Cuyahoga 1984) 20 Ohio App.3d 350, 486 N.E.2d 213, 20 O.B.R. 454.

Visitation rights may be completely denied only on a showing of such extraordinary circumstances as the unfitness of the noncustodial parent, or that visitation would harm the children, and the burden of proof of such circumstances is on the party contesting visitation privileges. Pettry v. Pettry (Cuyahoga 1984) 20 Ohio App.3d 350, 486 N.E.2d 213, 20 O.B.R. 454.

Where a minor child is less than two years old at the time of the divorce hearing, the mother is still nursing him, the father has difficulty handling the child, and the father has frequently failed to show up for scheduled visitations, the trial court's order granting custody to the mother and limiting the father's visitation rights is not unreasonable, arbitrary, or unconscionable. Lathrop v. Lathrop (Preble 1982) 5 Ohio App.3d 240, 451 N.E.2d 546, 5 O.B.R. 526.

The mere statement of a twelve-year-old child of divorced parents that she did not want to see her father again was insufficient evidence to justify a complete refusal to permit such father to visit her, and a statement by the mother's counsel that defendant had been guilty of misconduct toward his stepdaughter was of no probative value. Marsh v. Marsh (Franklin 1954) 126 N.E.2d 468, 69 Ohio Law Abs. 539.

Termination of incarcerated father's contact with his three children until further order of court was not an abuse of discretion; father failed to file a complaint prior to hearing on motion to terminate, he had notice of hearing, and he was not represented by counsel at hearing, thus giving court no evidence before it that might have supported an order allowing contact, family's caseworker recommended that father have supervised visitation upon release from prison, and guardian ad litem recommended no contact until his release. In re Danielle G. (Ohio App. 6 Dist., Lucas, 09-06-2002) No. L-02-1071, 2002-Ohio-4651, 2002 WL 31002748, Unreported. Infants ☞ 155

Ex-husband's sex change from male to female constituted a substantial change of circumstances that justified temporary termination of a previously ordered right to visitation of minor children until evidence of their growth and maturity could be presented to the trial court. Cisek v Cisek, No. 80-CA-113 (7th Dist Ct App, Mahoning, 7-20-82).

17. Relocation of residential parent

Trial court did not have the authority to prevent mother from relocating with her minor daughter; while express terms of custody statute permitted trial court to schedule hearing "to determine whether it is in the best interest of the child to revise the parenting time schedule for the child," the statute did not give the trial court the authority to prevent the residential parent from relocating with the child, and there were no prior agreements preventing mother from relocating, nor were there any provisions in the dispositional order regarding her ability to relocate. Acus v. Acus (Ohio App. 12 Dist., Madison, 03-08-2010) No. CA2009-08-017, 2010-Ohio-856, 2010 WL 764211, Unreported. Child Custody ☞ 261

Trial court did not abuse its discretion when it decided that the child's mother's remarriage and relocation to another state with child and the resulting modification of father's visitation to court's standard long distance parenting time schedule plus additional time in the summer was in child's best interests; child currently saw father 20 percent of the time during the school year, guardian ad litem recommended allowing child's relocation, moving from an apartment to a home with a yard could be seen as beneficial to child, and modified long distance visitation schedule could be determined to provide sufficient time for bonding with half-sib-

lings and father. Campana v. Campana (Ohio App. 7 Dist., Mahoning, 02-20-2009) No. 08 MA 88, 2009-Ohio-796, 2009 WL 428580, Unreported. Child Custody ☞ 261; Child Custody ☞ 577; Child Custody ☞ 616

Following child custody modification terminating shared parenting agreement and granting father custody of child upon mother's move out of state, trial court's visitation order was not in the best interests of child, where it awarded mother visitation during the second full weekend of every month during the school term from Friday after school until 9:00 Sunday evening, three two-week periods of summer recess, one-half of the spring recess, one-half of the Christmas recess, and Mother's Day; visitation order did not adequately facilitate a relationship between mother and child or address the prior close interaction of the mother and child, the geographic locations of the parties and the child, the parents' available time, and the father's stated desire to cooperate with the mother. In re D.M. (Ohio App. 8 Dist., Cuyahoga, 11-22-2006) No. 87723, 2006-Ohio-6191, 2006 WL 3378429, Unreported, appeal not allowed 113 Ohio St.3d 1468, 864 N.E.2d 654, 2007-Ohio-1722. Child Custody ☞ 577

Determining that best interests of child, who relocated with ex-wife to Texas, would be served by replacing ex-wife's temporary child custody with sole custody was not abuse of discretion, where ex-wife had strong family ties and better prospects of greater financial stability in Texas and, at time initial order was issued related to child custody, ex-husband was unemployed and had not offered plan for housing or schooling of child. Williams v. Williams (Ohio App. 11 Dist., Trumbull, 07-30-2004) No. 2002-T-0101, 2004-Ohio-3992, 2004 WL 1713283, Unreported. Child Custody ☞ 552; Child Custody ☞ 565; Child Custody ☞ 568

Statute governing procedure to be followed when custodial parent files notice of intent to relocate in absence of court order imposing restrictive condition through which trial court retains jurisdiction to review prospective request for relocation did not apply in proceeding in which ex-wife sought to relocate to Texas, where trial court previously ordered that child could not be removed from county without court approval. Williams v. Williams (Ohio App. 11 Dist., Trumbull, 07-30-2004) No. 2002-T-0101, 2004-Ohio-3992, 2004 WL 1713283, Unreported. Child Custody ☞ 261

Ex-wife established that relocating to Texas would be in child's best interest, and thus, granting ex-wife permission to relocate to Texas and replacing ex-wife's sole child custody with temporary custody and setting issue of permanent custody for review in six months was not abuse of discretion, where, at time prior order was issued granting ex-wife sole child custody, ex-husband was unemployed and had not offered plan for housing or schooling of child, and moving to Texas had prospect of greater financial stability for ex-wife and ability to provide child with better housing and schooling. Williams v. Williams (Ohio App. 11 Dist., Trumbull, 07-30-2004) No. 2002-T-0101, 2004-Ohio-3992, 2004 WL 1713283, Unreported. Child Custody ⚓ 568; Child Custody ⚓ 651

While modification of former husband's visitation with minor child was necessary to insure that child had adequate time with husband, after former wife moved child from Ohio to North Carolina, schedule as modified was onerous and unreasonable for former wife and child, who suffered from Tourette's syndrome; trial court awarded husband parenting time at least one three or four day weekend per month coinciding with national holidays, December parenting time consistent with standard order of parenting time, parenting time during child's spring breaks each year, parenting time during second weekend in March, summer parenting time beginning on day after last day of school until one week before school resumed in fall, and parenting time for up to a full weekend any time husband could travel to area where child resided, and, with exception of husband's travel to North Carolina, required wife to be responsible for all travel arrangements and costs. Quint v. Lomakoski (Ohio App. 2 Dist., 06-16-2006) 167 Ohio App.3d 124, 854 N.E.2d 225, 2006-Ohio-3041, on subsequent appeal 173 Ohio App.3d 146, 877 N.E.2d 738, 2007-Ohio-4722. Child Custody ⚓ 577

Where the original decree did not prohibit an out-of-state move by the custodial parent, both parents should bear equally the cost and time of transportation for visitation purposes; the custodial parent should not be penalized for having made the move by being made to bear a disproportionate share of the transportation burden. Pitcher v Pitcher, No. 83AP–530 (10th Dist Ct App, Franklin, 2–28–84).

18. Visitation with grandparents and others—In general

Grandmother's false statements to court, that she had not showered in the nude with her eight-year-old grandson, justified change in visitation; magistrate could conclude that grandmother's false statements indicated that she may not be trustworthy, and, while finding of actual harm was not required for change in visitation, magistrate could also conclude that grandmother's false statements caused grandson emotional harm, in feeling like a liar because grandson was aware that his grandmother was telling a different story than he was. In re A.W.C. (Ohio App. 4 Dist., Washington, 07-29-2010) No. 09CA31, 2010-Ohio-3625, 2010 WL 3064392, Unreported. Child Custody ⚓ 579

Magistrate was free to reconsider his oral decision from first hearing, that he did not have any concern for child's welfare from grandmother's false statements that she had not showered with her eight-year-old grandson, and render subsequent decision to modify visitation; at final hearing, magistrate heard new evidence from child's mother, who testified that child remained in counseling, which indicated the child was still suffering from impact of events, and, because nearly six months had passed since the first hearing and the written decision,

magistrate had more than enough time to reflect on case and reconsider impact of his earlier position. In re A.W.C. (Ohio App. 4 Dist., Washington, 07-29-2010) No. 09CA31, 2010-Ohio-3625, 2010 WL 3064392, Unreported. Child Custody ⚓ 652

Order denying maternal grandparents' motion to intervene in their daughter's divorce proceeding was not a final, appealable order, as denial of motion to intervene did not dispose of merits of grandparents' motion for visitation with children of their daughter and her husband, such that order denying intervention did not affect a substantial right, and visitation motion remained pending. Richardson v. Richardson (Ohio App. 4 Dist., Scioto, 12-09-2009) No. 09CA3293, 2009-Ohio-6492, 2009 WL 4725980, Unreported. Child Custody ⚓ 902

Individual, who was involved in romantic relationship with mother at time of child's birth, had standing to seek companionship and visitation with child; individual did not lack standing merely because he was not biological father, individual was granted, by agreed, temporary judgment entry, parenting time with child, and individual acknowledged paternity of child by filing an affidavit with Central Paternity Registry and was under an administrative support order. Waszkowski v. Lyons (Ohio App. 11 Dist., Lake, 01-30-2009) No. 2008-L-077, 2009-Ohio-403, 2009 WL 224540, Unreported. Children Out–of–wedlock ⚓ 20.4

Trial court, in granting grandmother and aunt visitation of children during child support proceedings, was not required to grant grandmother individual, separate time, but could require aunt and grandmother to share time and encourage aunt and grandmother to cooperate and reach an acceptable division of hours; court's visitation order was reasonable, since trial court weighed appropriate statutory factors, including that aunt and grandmother had been called on frequently to care for children and that children had developed a close bond with aunt and grandmother, but that children had a limited amount of time to spend with their mother, father, aunt, and grandparents. In re J.H. (Ohio App. 2 Dist., Miami, 01-16-2009) No. 08-CA-09, 2009-Ohio-156, 2009 WL 105640, Unreported. Child Custody ⚓ 216

Mother of two children born out of wedlock failed to preserve for appellate review her contention that magistrate erred by failing to consider, in granting grandparent visitation to children's paternal grandmother, an alleged motion made by grandmother on behalf of paternal father to be allowed to take children to visit father in prison, where there was no such motion in trial court record. In re Newsome (Ohio App. 11 Dist., Ashtabula, 05-02-2008) No. 2007-A-0030, 2008-Ohio-2132, 2008 WL 1934428, Unreported. Children Out–of–wedlock ⚓ 20.11

Trial court's suggestion, in denying grandparent's motion to intervene in divorce proceeding, that grandparent participate in her son's telephone calls with children rather than pursue her own telephonic visitation did not constitute a ruling upon the merits of a motion for grandparent visitation. Liming v. Damos (Ohio App. 4 Dist., Athens, 05-16-2006) No. 05CA28, 2006-Ohio-2518, 2006 WL 1382432, Unreported. Child Custody ⟳ 511

Trial court did not act unreasonably, arbitrarily, or unconscionably in declining to exercise its discretionary power to convert grandparent's motion to intervene in her son's divorce proceeding to a motion for grandparent visitation, where grandparent's motion to intervene neither mentioned words "companionship" or "visitation," nor statute authorizing a grandparent to file a motion requesting visitation in a divorce proceeding. Liming v. Damos (Ohio App. 4 Dist., Athens, 05-16-2006) No. 05CA28, 2006-Ohio-2518, 2006 WL 1382432, Unreported. Child Custody ⟳ 413

De facto removal of restriction on visitation between child and child's paternal grandfather, originally established in divorce decree, was properly before court on custodian's motion to modify visitation between child and child's father, where father's disability required inquiry into most appropriate location for visitation and necessity for presence of others during visitation. Arnold v. Arnold (Ohio App. 4 Dist., Athens, 09-27-2005) No. 04CA36, 2005-Ohio-5272, 2005 WL 2416378, Unreported. Child Custody ⟳ 610

Great aunt and uncle failed to satisfy statutory requirements for non-parent visitation rights as to minor children; statutes required either that parent be deceased or that child have been born to unmarried woman or that visitation be sought in divorce or annulment proceeding, and neither child's mother nor father were deceased, mother was married at the time child was born, and great aunt and uncle sought visitation rights in a dependency action commenced by County Children Services in juvenile court. In re E.H. (Ohio App. 9 Dist., Lorain, 04-27-2005) No. 04CA008585, 2005-Ohio-1952, 2005 WL 956967, Unreported. Infants ⟳ 222

In ruling on maternal grandparents' motion seeking increased child visitation, trial court was required to give special weight to custodial father's decision regarding grandparent visitation, even though grandparents' request was intended to provide incarcerated mother increased opportunity for supervised contact with children. Deeslie v. Deeslie (Ohio App. 5 Dist., Licking, 12-29-2004) No. 03CA00114, No. 04CA0035, 2004-Ohio-7273, 2004 WL 3090241, Unreported. Child Custody ⟳ 579

Father's challenge to trial court's approval of grandparents' request for child visitation in the forthcoming summer was moot, where, at time of appeal, grandparents had exercised all of their court-ordered visitation for the summer in question. Deeslie v. Deeslie (Ohio App. 5 Dist., Licking, 12-29-2004) No. 03CA00114, No. 04CA0035, 2004-Ohio-7273, 2004 WL 3090241, Unreported. Child Custody ⟳ 917

Denial of unwed mother's motion to continue proceeding on paternal grandmother's request for visitation was not an abuse of discretion, where five continuances had already been granted, grandmother's request for visitation had been pending for more than a year when mother failed to appear at hearing, and mother's counsel represented that he notified mother of hearing date by letter. In re Washington (Ohio App. 10 Dist., Franklin, 12-21-2004) No. 04AP-429, 2004-Ohio-6981, 2004 WL 2944166, Unreported. Children Out-of-wedlock ⟳ 20.4

Following mother's death, granting maternal grandmother visitation with grandchild pursuant to grandparent visitation statute was not abuse of discretion, where trial court carefully reviewed and applied statutorily enumerated factors for consideration in determining whether to grant grandparent visitation and court found that father's concerns regarding visitation went to nature, quality, and duration of grandparent visitation, rather than to its prohibition. Spivey v. Keller (Ohio App. 3 Dist., Allen, 12-13-2004) No. 6-04-09, 2004-Ohio-6667, 2004 WL 2849023, Unreported, appeal allowed 105 Ohio St.3d 1543, 827 N.E.2d 326, 2005-Ohio-2188, affirmed 107 Ohio St.3d 100, 836 N.E.2d 1220, 2005-Ohio-5973, reconsideration denied 108 Ohio St.3d 1418, 841 N.E.2d 321, 2006-Ohio-179. Child Custody ⟳ 289

Court of Appeals' determination that *Troxel v. Granville*, which held the State of Washington's nonparental visitation statute unconstitutional, did not apply to deny grandparents visitation rights, over father's objection, rendered moot grandparents' contentions on appeal that trial court abused its discretion in denying them visitation and that decision denying them visitation was against the manifest weight of the evidence. Estate of Harrold v. Collier (Ohio App. 9 Dist., Wayne, 08-18-2004) No. 03CA0064, 2004-Ohio-4331, 2004 WL 1837186, Unreported, stay denied 103 Ohio St.3d 1457, 815 N.E.2d 674, 2004-Ohio-5076, motion to certify allowed 104 Ohio St.3d 1407, 818 N.E.2d 709, 2004-Ohio-6364, appeal allowed 104 Ohio St.3d 1408, 818 N.E.2d 710, 2004-Ohio-6364, affirmed 107 Ohio St.3d 44, 836 N.E.2d 1165, 2005-Ohio-5334, certiorari denied 126 S.Ct. 1474, 547 U.S. 1004, 164 L.Ed.2d 248, on subsequent appeal 2006-Ohio-5634, 2006 WL 3055496, appeal not allowed 113 Ohio St.3d 1441, 863 N.E.2d 658, 2007-Ohio-1266. Child Custody ⟳ 917

Troxel v. Granville, which held the State of Washington's nonparental visitation statute unconstitutional as overbroad, did not hold that grandparents' visitation rights, over the objection of a parent, were subject to strict scrutiny and, thus, did not apply to deny grandparents visitation rights, over father's objection. Estate of Harrold v. Collier (Ohio App. 9 Dist., Wayne, 08-18-2004) No. 03CA0064, 2004-Ohio-4331, 2004 WL 1837186, Unreported, stay denied 103 Ohio St.3d 1457, 815 N.E.2d 674, 2004-Ohio-5076, motion to certify allowed 104 Ohio St.3d 1407, 818 N.E.2d 709, 2004-Ohio-6364, appeal allowed 104 Ohio St.3d 1408, 818 N.E.2d 710, 2004-Ohio-6364, affirmed 107 Ohio St.3d 44, 836 N.E.2d 1165, 2005-Ohio-5334, certiorari denied 126 S.Ct. 1474,

547 U.S. 1004, 164 L.Ed.2d 248, on subsequent appeal 2006-Ohio-5634, 2006 WL 3055496, appeal not allowed 113 Ohio St.3d 1441, 863 N.E.2d 658, 2007-Ohio-1266. Child Custody ☜ 286

Issues of denial of grandparents' visitation and interference with religious rights, which trial court did not address in adopting magistrate's decision, could not be the subject matter of appeal from judgment entry adopting magistrate's decision on motions for visitation. Janouk v. Janouk (Ohio App. 7 Dist., Mahoning, 03-15-2004) No. 95-CA-246, No. 99-CA-91, No. 96-CA-206, No. 96-CA-258, 2004-Ohio-1374, 2004 WL 550785, Unreported. Child Custody ☜ 916

Evidence did not support restriction on ex-husband's visitation with children permitting him to allow children to visit their paternal grandparents only once every six weeks, in divorce action; restriction was apparently meant to limit chances that children would come in contact with ex-husband's ex-girlfriend, whose children were children's half-brothers, and, if trial court believed that spending time at grandparents' home was detrimental to children, it should have placed ban on all visits with grandparents. Callender v. Callender (Ohio App. 7 Dist., Carroll, 03-19-2004) No. 03-CA-790, 2004-Ohio-1382, 2004 WL 549484, Unreported. Child Custody ☜ 219

Evidence did not support restricting ex-husband's visitation with children such that he could not allow children to have any contact with their half-brothers, in divorce action; testimony indicated that problems were mostly with half-brother's mother, who was ex-husband's ex-girlfriend, not with half-brothers themselves, children and half-brothers were bound to fight with each other, and, while language half-brother used might be inappropriate, it did not warrant outright bar on contact with children. Callender v. Callender (Ohio App. 7 Dist., Carroll, 03-19-2004) No. 03-CA-790, 2004-Ohio-1382, 2004 WL 549484, Unreported. Child Custody ☜ 219

Sufficient evidence supported restriction that children have no contact with ex-husband's ex-girlfriend during ex-husband's visitation time with children, in divorce action; ex-wife testified that ex-girlfriend had been verbally abusive toward child and tried to manipulate child, during parties' marriage they did not allow children to be around ex-girlfriend, and ex-husband testified that he did not want children to be around ex-girlfriend. Callender v. Callender (Ohio App. 7 Dist., Carroll, 03-19-2004) No. 03-CA-790, 2004-Ohio-1382, 2004 WL 549484, Unreported. Child Custody ☜ 219

Trial court lacked jurisdiction to grant maternal grandfather visitation with mother's child, where a "disruptive precipitating event," such as the death of a parent or a parent filing for divorce, had not occurred, and the juvenile court had never previously exercised jurisdiction over child. Albert v. Lewis (Ohio App. 5 Dist., Morgan, 01-07-2004) No. CA03-001, 2004-Ohio-41, 2004 WL 35469, Unreported. Child Custody ☜ 283

Trial court order granting maternal and paternal grandmothers visitation with minor, who was under the care of county department of jobs and family services (DJFS), was not an abuse of discretion, even though mother of minor objected to the visitation; minor had close relationships with her grandmothers before she was placed in the custody of the DJFS, minor's foster family testified that her manipulative behaviors had lessened, minor requested to visit her grandmothers, and mother admitted that, except for one previous incident each, the grandmothers "took good care" of minor. In re Thompson (Ohio App. 3 Dist., Seneca, 04-16-2003) No. 13-02-45, 2003-Ohio-1909, 2003 WL 1877589, Unreported. Infants ☜ 222

Trial court's interpretation of shared parenting plan to permit grandparents to provide transportation from school to visitation with father was consistent with plain meaning of agreement, which required residential parent to be responsible for transportation of minor children from school and other events, and was not a modification of agreement for which father had to follow statutory procedures. Caldwell v. Caldwell (Ohio App. 4 Dist., Gallia, 04-02-2003) No. 02CA17, 2003-Ohio-1752, 2003 WL 1795247, Unreported. Child Custody ☜ 141; Child Custody ☜ 571

Paternal grandparents who are granted leave to intervene as parties in their son's divorce action solely for the purpose of obtaining visitation with their grandchildren do not have any rights in the determination of custody and placement of the children and no right to notice of dismissal of a motion for reallocation of parental rights and responsibilities. Hughes v. Hughes (Ohio App. 10 Dist., Franklin, 06-11-1996) No. 95APF12-1570, 1996 WL 325486, Unreported.

Restriction upon a father's visitation rights is justified by testimony of the childrens' treating therapists and a record of physical and sexual abuse of the children by the father and his girlfriend. Matter of Lamb (Ohio App. 12 Dist., Butler, 02-12-1996) No. CA95-01-006, 1996 WL 56077, Unreported.

After temporary custody of grandchildren has been awarded to the county children services, the trial court may exercise its discretion and determine whether the grandparents should be allowed to intervene in the proceedings by considering the timeliness of the motion filed by the grandparents, as well as the persuasiveness of the argument the grandparents seek to assert regarding visitation. In re Deleon (Ohio App. 10 Dist., Franklin, 12-22-1994) No. 94APF05-763, 1994 WL 714465, Unreported.

Trial court limited mother's visitation not out of moral or religious concerns but, rather, out of concerns for the safety and welfare of the children, which was a best-interest factor recognized by visitation statute, and, thus, trial court was not required to find a direct adverse impact upon children for purposes of restraining four of mother's family members from having contact with children during mother's visitation. Troyer v. Troyer (Ohio App. 7 Dist., 06-28-2010) 2010 -Ohio- 3276, 2010 WL 2749051. Child Custody ⟐ 219

Any error committed by trial court in failing to specifically refer to the visitation best-interest factors, when making its decision to prohibit four of mother's family members from having contact with children during mother's visitation, was harmless, where many of the visitation best-interest factors had analogues within the custody best-interest factors, trial court analyzed matter under the custody best-interest factors, and trial court's judgment evinced consideration of the relevant visitation factors. Troyer v. Troyer (Ohio App. 7 Dist., 06-28-2010) 2010 -Ohio- 3276, 2010 WL 2749051. Child Custody ⟐ 923(3)

The law does not provide grandparents with inherent legal rights to visit grandchildren, based simply on the family relationship. In re H.W. (Ohio, 06-27-2007) 114 Ohio St.3d 65, 868 N.E.2d 261, 2007-Ohio-2879. Child Custody ⟐ 283

Granting visitation rights to child's cousin was an abuse of discretion, where request was made because child's father was denied any contact with the child because he sexually assaulted his stepdaughter, cousin wanted to maintain contact between child and father's family, visitation decision relied heavily on testimony of licensed clinical counselor who was working with mother and other daughter, counselor's only contact with child in question was in the waiting room when her mother and sister came in for counseling, and counselor had never conducted a formal counseling session with child in question. Love v. Rable (Ohio App. 3 Dist., 03-16-2001) 147 Ohio App.3d 63, 768 N.E.2d 1185, 2001-Ohio-2174. Child Custody ⟐ 271

In addition to the statutory factors in deciding whether to grant third-party visitation, the trial court must consider the extent to which the autonomy of either parent may be undermined, and the impact on the then existing family situation; the strong constitutional protection afforded the right to rear one's children compels this conclusion. Love v. Rable (Ohio App. 3 Dist., 03-16-2001) 147 Ohio App.3d 63, 768 N.E.2d 1185, 2001-Ohio-2174. Child Custody ⟐ 180; Parent And Child ⟐ 2.5

Assuming that adjudicated father's petition for modification of his child support obligation was properly before Juvenile Court, fact that such petition was pending did not vest Juvenile Court with jurisdiction to entertain paternal grandmother's petition for grandparental visitation pursuant to domestic relations statute, where statute setting forth Juvenile Court's jurisdiction in parentage actions did not reference domestic relations statute, and where child's mother was unmarried. Borkosky v. Mihailoff (Ohio App. 3 Dist., 03-03-1999) 132 Ohio App.3d 508, 725 N.E.2d 694. Children Out–of–wedlock ⟐ 20.9

Parental authority of husband who divorced and then remarried was not impermissibly infringed by the granting of grandparent visitation rights with respect to husband's children from his first marriage. Gaffney v. Menrath (Ohio App. 1 Dist., 01-29-1999) 132 Ohio App.3d 113, 724 N.E.2d 507. Child Custody ⟐ 287

Statutory grandparent visitation rights are not limited to situations in which the visitation interests of the parents of the nonresidential parent have been adversely threatened; rather, each set of grandparents has the right to invoke the statute. Gaffney v. Menrath (Ohio App. 1 Dist., 01-29-1999) 132 Ohio App.3d 113, 724 N.E.2d 507. Child Custody ⟐ 283

At common law, grandparents had no right of access to, or constitutional right of association with, their grandchildren. Gaffney v. Menrath (Ohio App. 1 Dist., 01-29-1999) 132 Ohio App.3d 113, 724 N.E.2d 507. Child Custody ⟐ 283; Constitutional Law ⟐ 1443

There is a federal constitutional basis upon which parental autonomy can be asserted, with respect to grandparent visitation. Gaffney v. Menrath (Ohio App. 1 Dist., 01-29-1999) 132 Ohio App.3d 113, 724 N.E.2d 507. Child Custody ⟐ 287

Trial court did not abuse its discretion in granting stepfather visitation rights with ex-wife's child from previous marriage, where guardian ad litem recommended that stepfather be granted visitation rights, and stepfather was only real father child had for six of her 11 years. Shannon v. Shannon (Ohio App. 9 Dist., 08-13-1997) 122 Ohio App.3d 346, 701 N.E.2d 771. Child Custody ⟐ 272

Grandparent visitation rights are statutorily provided and, thus, any changes in this area must be initiated by General Assembly. Beard v. Pannell (Ohio App. 6 Dist., 04-26-1996) 110 Ohio App.3d 572, 674 N.E.2d 1225, appeal not allowed 77 Ohio St.3d 1447, 671 N.E.2d 1285. Child Custody ⟐ 283

Trial court's decision to allow maternal grandmother visitation with granddaughter who was in custody of father was not an abuse of discretion, despite fact that grandmother had previously been convicted of grand theft; grandmother had paid her debt to society more than 16 years ago and record indicated she had been a model citizen and mother since then; moreover, offense for which grandmother was convicted did not result in child abuse or neglect, and thus was not an issue for consideration by trial court under applicable statute. Holley v. Higgins (Franklin 1993) 86 Ohio App.3d 240, 620 N.E.2d 251. Child Custody ⟐ 283

Juvenile court does not have authority to grant paternal grandparents visitation rights with grandchild after grandchild has been adopted by stepfather. Krnac v. Starman (Medina 1992) 83 Ohio App.3d 578, 615 N.E.2d 344, dismissed, jurisdictional motion overruled 66 Ohio St.3d 1485, 612 N.E.2d 1241. Child Custody ⟐ 313

After suspending a father's visitation rights, a trial court may also suspend the paternal grandparents' visitation rights until further court order where the grandparents live only 500 feet from the child's father, the father is at their house every day, and the grandparents do not acknowledge the ill effects of the father's treatment of the child and reinforce the father's conduct. Johntonny v. Malliski (Geauga 1990) 67 Ohio App.3d 709, 588 N.E.2d 200, motion to certify overruled 55 Ohio St.3d 715, 563 N.E.2d 725. Child Custody ☞ 577; Child Custody ☞ 579

In general, grandparental visitation rights do not vest until occurrence of disruptive precipitating event, such as parental death or divorce; absent disruptive event, common law view of deferring to parental autonomy in raising child is observed despite moral or social obligations that encourage contact between grandparents and grandchildren. In re Gibson (Ohio 1991) 61 Ohio St.3d 168, 573 N.E.2d 1074. Child Custody ☞ 285; Child Custody ☞ 289

A trial court's jurisdiction to modify a visitation order and grant visitation rights to any other person includes the authority to add persons not originally parties to the action. Hollingsworth v. Hollingsworth (Franklin 1986) 34 Ohio App.3d 13, 516 N.E.2d 1250. Child Custody ☞ 577

RC 3109.05(B) specifically states that a court in its discretion may grant reasonable companionship or visitation rights "to any other person having an interest in the welfare of the child." This broad category includes any person regardless of the relationship to the custodial or noncustodial parent since the determinative factor in the award is the welfare of the child, not the relationship the person has to or with either parent. Hollingsworth v. Hollingsworth (Franklin 1986) 34 Ohio App.3d 13, 516 N.E.2d 1250. Child Custody ☞ 577

Where a divorced mother of a minor child, having been given custody thereof, has not abandoned the child, has not agreed that the paternal grandparents shall have visitation rights with such child, and where such child has not been living with such grandparents, a court exceeds its authority in granting visitation rights to such grandparents upon a motion for modification of visitation rights filed by the divorced father. Shriver v. Shriver (Union 1966) 7 Ohio App.2d 169, 219 N.E.2d 300, 36 O.O.2d 308.

Whether it will be beneficial to child to have relationship with grandparent is, in any specific case, a decision for parent to make in first instance, and if a fit parent's decision becomes subject to judicial review, court must accord at least some special weight to parent's own determination. Troxel v. Granville (U.S.Wash., 06-05-2000) 120 S.Ct. 2054, 530 U.S. 57, 147 L.Ed.2d 49. Child Custody ☞ 286

A partner in a lesbian relationship does not have an obligation to pay child support insofar as she is not the biological, natural or adoptive mother of her partner's child and her attempt to file a child support proceeding in order to claim visitation rights pursuant to RC 3109.051 must fail. Liston v Pyles, No. 97APF01–137, 1997 WL 467327 (10th Dist Ct App, Franklin, 8–12–97).

Since RC 3109.051 allows an individual related to a child by marriage or any other person other than

a parent to file a motion requesting companionship rights, a trial court errs in dismissing a stepfather as a party by ruling that a stepparent lacks standing to contest any issues regarding companionship rights or the allocation of parental rights and responsibilities. Corn v Corn, No. 15–95–1, 1995 WL 551102 (3d Dist Ct App, Van Wert, 9–15–95).

Although a juvenile court determined that the plaintiff was not the father of a child in a prior proceeding, the domestic relations court errs in determining that it did not have jurisdiction of the plaintiff's claim of visitation and companionship rights since RC 3109.051 expressly permits nonparents to obtain visitation and companionship rights with respect to a minor child in connection with a divorce or legal separation. Cassim v Cassim, No. 94APF12–1771, 1995 WL 546926 (10th Dist Ct App, Franklin, 9–14–95).

19. —— "Best interest of child", visitation with grandparents and others

Trial court did not abuse its discretion in finding that it would not be in children's best interest to have court-ordered visitation with their maternal grandmother, where, since divorce, each parent had the children 50% of the time, children's mother adamantly opposed court-ordered visitation between children and their maternal grandmother, but did not prevent children's father, her ex-spouse, from allowing the children to see maternal grandmother, and, although children's father had permitted the children to visit with maternal grandmother during his parenting time, he did not want the court to require him to do so. Byer v. Byer (Ohio App. 5 Dist., Stark, 08-09-2010) No. 2009-CA-00277, 2010-Ohio-3705, 2010 WL 3159568, Unreported. Child Custody ☞ 286

Under either ordinary "best interest analysis", or "direct adverse impact" test, grandmother's disregard for appropriate physical boundaries between herself and her eight-year-old grandson, by showering nude with grandson, was appropriate basis for reducing grandmother's visitation with child, even though showering incidents had ceased; grandmother's conduct indicated that she might not possess appropriate judgment to take care of the boy, boy had continued to work with counselor to help establish boundaries since incident was revealed to his mother, and grandmother's actions had shattered whatever trust may have existed between herself and boy's mother. In re A.W.C. (Ohio App. 4 Dist., Washington, 07-29-2010) No. 09CA31, 2010-Ohio-3625, 2010 WL 3064392, Unreported. Child Custody ☞ 579

Magistrate was required to consider 16 statutory factors on mother's motion to modify grandmother's visitation rights to determine, in its sound discretion, whether modification was in child's best interest, where magistrate issued detailed decision containing detailed findings of fact and conclusions of law, but did not specifically address every relevant statutory factor. In re A.W.C. (Ohio App. 4 Dist., Washington, 07-29-2010) No. 09CA31,

2010-Ohio-3625, 2010 WL 3064392, Unreported. Child Custody ⚷ 579

Trial court limited mother's visitation not out of moral or religious concerns, but rather out of concerns for the safety and welfare of the children, which was a best-interest factor recognized by visitation statute, and thus, trial court was not required to find a direct adverse impact upon children for purposes of restraining four of mother's family members from having contact with children during mother's visitation; although trial court did not specifically cite to the visitation best interest factors, its judgment, along with the magistrate's decision which it adopted, did evince consideration of the relevant factors. Troyer v. Troyer (Ohio App. 7 Dist., 06-28-2010) No. 09 JE 5, 2010 -Ohio- 3276, 2010 WL 2749051, Unreported. Child Custody ⚷ 219; Child Custody ⚷ 511

Competent and credible evidence established that it was not in children's best interest to have contact with their maternal grandfather during their limited visitation with mother, thus supporting issuance of restraining order prohibiting such contact, in action in which father sought allocation of parental rights and responsibilities; evidence showed that grandfather abused his authority as bishop of local religious community by preventing father from having contact with children for a period of nine months during which he missed the birth of his second child, and other witnesses testified about how they too had been prevented from seeing their loved ones under similar circumstances. Troyer v. Troyer (Ohio App. 7 Dist., 06-28-2010) 188 Ohio App.3d 543, 936 N.E.2d 102, 2010-Ohio-3276. Child Custody ⚷ 219

Competent and credible evidence established that it was not in children's best interest to have contact with their maternal uncle during their limited visitation with mother, thus supporting issuance of restraining order prohibiting such contact, in action in which father sought allocation of parental rights and responsibilities; testimony describing several incidents involving the uncle revealed a tendency on uncle's part to overreact with violence, on one occasion holding his brother down on the ground in freezing temperatures throughout the night while the brother had a psychotic episode. Troyer v. Troyer (Ohio App. 7 Dist., 06-28-2010) No. 09 JE 5, 2010 -Ohio- 3276, 2010 WL 2749051, Unreported. Child Custody ⚷ 219

Competent and credible evidence established that it was not in children's best interest to have contact with their maternal uncle during their limited visitation with mother, thus supporting issuance of restraining order prohibiting such contact, in action in which father sought allocation of parental rights and responsibilities; evidence showed that the uncle had a history of sexually abusing young children in the same religious community in which mother resided, for which he was convicted, sentenced, and classified as a Tier II sex offender. Troyer v. Troyer (Ohio App. 7 Dist., 06-28-2010) No. 09 JE 5, 2010 -Ohio- 3276, 2010 WL 2749051, Unreported. Child Custody ⚷ 219

Trial court did not abuse its discretion when it revised ex-wife's parenting time schedule so as to exclude time on Friday evenings; child cried and protested prior to leaving her paternal great-grandmother's house for parenting time with her mother, court's basic parenting schedule provided for parenting time on alternating weekends beginning at 6:00 p.m. on Friday and ending at 6:00 p.m. on Sunday, with additional visitation each Wednesday, and parenting time provided under the court's basic schedule was not in the best interest of child. Anderson v. Anderson (Ohio App. 12 Dist., Warren, 10-26-2009) No. CA2009-03-033, 2009-Ohio-5636, 2009 WL 3416024, Unreported. Child Custody ⚷ 579

Trial court did not abuse its discretion in adopting magistrate's decision denying motion to suspend mother's visitation with children; evidence was sufficient to support magistrate's finding that continued visitation was in the best interest of the children after considering the health and safety of the children and the mental and physical health of all the parties. Stalnaker v. Peterson (Ohio App. 9 Dist., Summit, 08-27-2008) No. 24071, 2008-Ohio-4329, 2008 WL 3914995, Unreported. Child Custody ⚷ 638

Evidence was sufficient to support magistrate's finding, as adopted by trial court, that it was in the best interest of two children born out of wedlock to permit paternal grandmother's visitation, even though children's mother was opposed to the visitation; children's father was prohibited by protective court order from seeing the children and as a result children did not have contact with paternal relatives, and grandmother was close to the children prior to the time other ceased to permit visitation. In re Newsome (Ohio App. 11 Dist., Ashtabula, 05-02-2008) No. 2007-A-0030, 2008-Ohio-2132, 2008 WL 1934428, Unreported. Children Out–of–wedlock ⚷ 20.9

Grandparent, whose motion to intervene in her son's divorce proceeding was denied, did not have the opportunity to fully and fairly litigate her claim for grandparent visitation, and thus grandparent could file a proper motion for grandparent visitation, where record clearly indicated that trial court did not conduct a hearing, and the parties presented absolutely no evidence upon which the trial court could have properly considered the factors statutorily required to be considered in determining child's best interest. Liming v. Damos (Ohio App. 4 Dist., Athens, 05-16-2006) No. 05CA28, 2006-Ohio-2518, 2006 WL 1382432, Unreported. Divorce ⚷ 171

Juvenile court's decision to grant visitation rights with unmarried mother's minor child to child's maternal grandmother was neither an abuse of discretion nor against the manifest weight of the evidence, despite mother's wishes to the contrary; court noted grandmother's strong, positive bond with child, and her daily care of the child since his birth, and the court also noted that the guardian ad litem recommended that the child's best interests would be served by an award of visitation rights to his grandmother. In re J.F. (Ohio App. 8 Dist., Cuyahoga, 09-15-2005) No. 85242, 2005-Ohio-4816, 2005 WL 2240946, Unreported. Children Out–of–wedlock 20.9

Trial court acted within its discretion in awarding grandparent visitation rights over mother's objection; trial court gave special weight to mother's decisions as a parent but determined that her decisions were over-reactive to grandparents' actions as an attempt to infringe upon her parental rights and responsibilities, and establishing contact with grandparents was in best interests of children. Lobdell v. Lobdell (Ohio App. 5 Dist., Licking, 01-10-2005) No. 2004 CA 0036, 2005-Ohio-80, 2005 WL 66577, Unreported, appeal allowed 105 Ohio St.3d 1561, 828 N.E.2d 116, 2005-Ohio-2447, appeal dismissed as improvidently allowed 107 Ohio St.3d 1201, 836 N.E.2d 1222, 2005-Ohio-5974. Child Custody 286

The constitutional standards, or "standards of legal review," are not different for reviewing a parent's motion for termination of grandparents' visitation as they are for reviewing an original complaint for establishment of grandparents' visitation; in both cases, the best interests of the child are the statutory test. In re Kaiser (Ohio App. 7 Dist., Columbiana, 12-30-2004) No. 04 CO 9, 2004-Ohio-7208, 2004 WL 3090224, Unreported. Child Custody 579

Absent finding that grandparent visitation was in best interest of children, granting maternal grandmother "telephone access" via five minute phone calls every two weeks, after denying her motion to allow visitation, was an abuse of discretion. Moshos v. Moshos (Ohio App. 2 Dist., Greene, 09-17-2004) No. CIV.A. 03CA97, 2004-Ohio-4933, 2004 WL 2245195, Unreported. Child Custody 283

The trial court was required to consider the statutory factors for determining whether to grant paternal grandparents companionship or visitation with out-of-wedlock grandchild, who was the child of their deceased son, before ruling on the issue; the statute did not require a finding that a child was "delinquent, neglected, or abused or that a parent was unfit" before determining whether to grant companionship or visitation to a relative, and statute allowed the court to grant a relative companionship or visitation with a child after the child's parent died if the relative filed a complaint for visitation and the court found that granting companionship rights or visitation was in the best interests of child. In re Talkington (Ohio App. 5 Dist., Stark, 08-09-2004) No. 2003CA00226, 2004-Ohio-4215, 2004 WL 1784603, Unreported. Children Out–of–wedlock 20.3

Trial court did not afford father disproportionate deference, nor otherwise misapply Troxel in a manner as to perfunctorily heed father's request, in vacating interim order, entered following child's adjudication as neglected and dependent child upon mother's incarceration, granting great-grandparents visitation of child, where, although trial court did

afford weight to father's wishes for child's care, it also considered a number of best interest concerns in its examination of case. In re K.M. (Ohio App. 12 Dist., Butler, 04-12-2004) No. CA2002-10-255, 2004-Ohio-1863, 2004 WL 766428, Unreported. Infants 230.1

Trial court considered best interests of child when, on father's motion, it vacated its interim order providing child's great-grandparents visitation, which interim order was entered following child's adjudication as neglected and dependent child upon mother's incarceration; record showed that trial court conducted in camera interview with child to determine her wishes, trial court discussed child's interaction and interrelationship with both father and great-grandparents, and trial court noted that father's motivation for ending great-grandparents' visitation was not malicious or unreasonable, but was intended to reduce child's behavioral problems and stabilize her placement in father's home. In re K.M. (Ohio App. 12 Dist., Butler, 04-12-2004) No. CA2002-10-255, 2004-Ohio-1863, 2004 WL 766428, Unreported. Infants 230.1

Trial court accorded due deference to father's wishes when finding it was in best interest of children to modify non-parents' visitation privileges; children's visitation with non-parents arose by agreement of parties during initial divorce proceedings, court increased non-parents' visitation by reducing mother's companionship time, and, although father opposed such visitation, mother did not. Vitcusky v. Vitcusky (Ohio App. 5 Dist., Richland, 10-15-2003) No. 2002CA083, 2003-Ohio-5486, 2003 WL 22343863, Unreported. Child Custody 578

Trial court did not abuse its discretion in determining that modification of mother's visitation with children was in children's best interest; record demonstrated that court considered issues and pertinent factors as required in statute, and determined that mother's physical and other limitations apparently diminished the quality of time she spent with her children, and that children testified that mother sometimes slept through visits and that visits consisted of watching television. In re Hinkle Children (Ohio App. 12 Dist., Butler, 10-06-2003) No. CA2002-12-309, 2003-Ohio-5282, 2003 WL 22283499, Unreported. Child Custody 577

Statute governing nonparent visitation rights was not unconstitutional as applied to paternal grandparent's petition for visitation contrary to mother's wishes by infringing on mother's fundamental right to make decisions concerning child; trial court accorded due deference to mother's concerns regarding whether allowing visitation was in best interest of child, trial court placed burden of proving that grandmother's visitation was in child's best interest on grandmother, and decision granting visitation was based on careful consideration of statutory factors. Baker v. Baker (Ohio App. 12 Dist., Brown, 02-18-2003) No. CA2002-04-008, 2003-Ohio-731, 2003 WL 356280, Unreported. Child Custody 4

Statute governing nonparent visitation rights did not unconstitutionally impinge on mother's rights by allowing any person, at any time, to request visitation despite mother's wishes; statute permitted consideration of motion only upon precipitating event, petitioning party had to be related to child or show interest in welfare of child, and court was required to consider more than 15 factors to determine whether such visitation is in best interest of child. Baker v. Baker (Ohio App. 12 Dist., Brown, 02-18-2003) No. CA2002-04-008, 2003-Ohio-731, 2003 WL 356280, Unreported. Child Custody ☞ 4

Grandparents are not statutorily entitled to visitation of their grandchildren and a court must consider the factors enumerated in RC 3109.11 as well as the best interest and wishes of the children; consequent denial of visitation to a grandmother is neither an automatic ground for reversal nor an abuse of discretion. In Matter of Skinner (Jennifer, Brittany) (Ohio App. 4 Dist., Adams, 03-23-1994) No. 93CA547, 1994 WL 93149, Unreported.

Competent and credible evidence established that it was not in children's best interest to have contact with their maternal uncle during their limited visitation with mother, thus supporting issuance of restraining order prohibiting such contact, in action in which father sought allocation of parental rights and responsibilities; evidence showed that the uncle had a history of mental health issues, namely a psychotic episode that lasted for several days and was witnessed by young children in the community, including some under the age of ten, and evidence showed that uncle's episodes were usually violent in nature. Troyer v. Troyer (Ohio App. 7 Dist., 06-28-2010) 2010 -Ohio- 3276, 2010 WL 2749051. Child Custody ☞ 219

Competent and credible evidence established that it was not in children's best interest to have contact with their maternal uncle during their limited visitation with mother, thus supporting issuance of restraining order prohibiting such contact, in action in which father sought allocation of parental rights and responsibilities; there was testimony that the uncle acted maliciously towards his brother in the presence of the brother's young children, and uncle admitted holding another brother down on the ground in freezing temperatures throughout the night while the brother had a psychotic episode. Troyer v. Troyer (Ohio App. 7 Dist., 06-28-2010) 188 Ohio App.3d 543, 936 N.E.2d 102, 2010-Ohio-3276. Child Custody ☞ 219

Competent and credible evidence established that it was not in children's best interest to have contact with their maternal uncle during their limited visitation with mother, thus supporting issuance of restraining order prohibiting such contact, in action in which father sought allocation of parental rights and responsibilities; evidence showed that the uncle had a history of mental health issues, namely a psychotic episode that lasted for several days and was witnessed by young children in the community, including some under the age of ten, the uncle threatened life of sheriff three separate times, and

he broke into the home of children's paternal grandfather and assaulted grandfather. Troyer v. Troyer (Ohio App. 7 Dist., 06-28-2010) 188 Ohio App.3d 543, 936 N.E.2d 102, 2010-Ohio-3276. Child Custody ☞ 219

Competent and credible evidence established that it was not in children's best interest to have contact with their maternal uncle during their limited visitation with mother, thus supporting issuance of restraining order prohibiting such contact, in action in which father sought allocation of parental rights and responsibilities; evidence showed that the uncle had a history of sexually abusing young children in the same religious community in which mother resided. Troyer v. Troyer (Ohio App. 7 Dist., 06-28-2010) 188 Ohio App.3d 543, 936 N.E.2d 102, 2010-Ohio-3276. Child Custody ☞ 219

Trial court properly placed burden of proving that visitation would be in the best interest of minor child on maternal grandparents and gave due deference to father's wishes and concerns regarding visitation before determining that it was in child's best interest to grant motion for grandparent visitation, even though trial court did not use the words "special weight" in considering father's wishes. Harrold v. Collier (Ohio, 10-10-2005) 107 Ohio St.3d 44, 836 N.E.2d 1165, 2005-Ohio-5334, certiorari denied 126 S.Ct. 1474, 547 U.S. 1004, 164 L.Ed.2d 248, on subsequent appeal 2006-Ohio-5634, 2006 WL 3055496, appeal not allowed 113 Ohio St.3d 1441, 863 N.E.2d 658, 2007-Ohio-1266. Child Custody ☞ 452; Child Custody ☞ 471; Child Custody ☞ 473

Nonparental visitation statutes, which were narrowly tailored to serve state's compelling interest in protecting child's best interest, did not unconstitutionally infringe on father's fundamental right to make decisions concerning care, custody, and control of his child; statutes limited parties who could petition court for visitation, limited application of statutes to cases where there was specified predicate event or condition, and not only allowed trial court to afford parental decisions the requisite special weight, but also allowed court to take into consideration best interest of child and balance that interest against parent's desires. Harrold v. Collier (Ohio, 10-10-2005) 107 Ohio St.3d 44, 836 N.E.2d 1165, 2005-Ohio-5334, certiorari denied 126 S.Ct. 1474, 547 U.S. 1004, 164 L.Ed.2d 248, on subsequent appeal 2006-Ohio-5634, 2006 WL 3055496, appeal not allowed 113 Ohio St.3d 1441, 863 N.E.2d 658, 2007-Ohio-1266. Child Custody ☞ 4; Child Custody ☞ 270

In addition to the statutory factors for finding that grandparent visitation is in the best interests of the child, the trial court must consider the extent to which the autonomy of either parent may be undermined and the impact on the then-existing family situation. Gaffney v. Menrath (Ohio App. 1 Dist., 01-29-1999) 132 Ohio App.3d 113, 724 N.E.2d 507. Child Custody ☞ 287

In general, grandparent visitation is in child's best interest. Holley v. Higgins (Franklin 1993) 86 Ohio

App.3d 240, 620 N.E.2d 251. Child Custody ☞ 283

A court must decide whether visitation by grandparents is in a child's best interest, and refusal to grant visitation to a grandparent will not be disturbed on appeal where the grandparent has allowed the father to be alone with the child despite an agreement with the father not to do so and where the grandparent is likely to have close contact with the father, who has threatened violence to the child and subjected the child to scenes of extreme violence against the mother. Drennen v. Drennen (Erie 1988) 52 Ohio App.3d 121, 557 N.E.2d 149.

Grandparents may be granted visitation rights under RC 3109.11 and 3109.05(B) if the trial court finds that such visitation is in the child's best interest. In re Whitaker (Ohio 1988) 36 Ohio St.3d 213, 522 N.E.2d 563.

Washington statute providing that any person may petition court for visitation at any time, and that court may order visitation rights for any person when visitation may serve best interest of child, violated substantive due process rights of mother, as applied to permit paternal grandparents, following death of children's father, to obtain increased court-ordered visitation, in excess of what mother had thought appropriate, based solely on state trial judge's disagreement with mother as to whether children would benefit from such increased visitation; at minimum, trial judge had to accord special weight to mother's own determination of her children's best interests. U.S.C.A. Const.Amend. 14; West's RCWA 26.10.160(3). Troxel v. Granville (U.S.Wash., 06-05-2000) 120 S.Ct. 2054, 530 U.S. 57, 147 L.Ed.2d 49. Child Custody ☞ 473; Constitutional Law ☞ 4396

Evidence was sufficient to support finding that best interests of minor child was to continue visitation with her paternal grandparents pursuant to supervised visitation agreement previously reached between child's mother and the grandparents, where trial court specifically addressed every factor listed in statute governing parenting time rights for grandparents and relatives and gave great weight to wishes of the mother; trial court noted that all of mother's visitation requirements had been observed, video tape of visits showed that child and the grandparents had a bond and that child enjoyed her visits, guardian ad litem recommended continuing the visits, and that mother's concerns about the safety of her child with the grandparents during the supervised visits were unfounded. Buehrer v. Lambert (Ohio App. 3 Dist., Henry, 06-18-2002) No. 7-02-03, 2002-Ohio-2980, 2002 WL 1371062, Unreported. Child Custody ☞ 641

Paternal grandmother's visitation rights are terminated where (1) the grandmother permits the child's contact with the father in direct contravention of a court order requiring supervised visits only at the mother's home, (2) the mother has no ulterior motive for stopping visitations, and (3) the trial court finds that the child's mother is fit and presumed to be acting in the best interest of her daughter. In re Sarah V. (Ohio App. 6 Dist., Lucas, 02-08-2002) No. L-01-1250, 2002-Ohio-530, 2002 WL 192085, Unreported.

20. —— Contempt for violation of visitation order, visitation with grandparents and others

Trial court abused its discretion in finding ex-wife in contempt of court for violating trial court's visitation order, which afforded paternal grandmother visitation with child according to detailed schedule; after court's order, parties had entered into verbal agreement regarding visitation and, according to this verbal agreement, because of psychiatric issues concerning child, his therapist was to coordinate visitation with grandmother, parties' actions in entering verbal agreement to allow therapist to coordinate visitation were inconsistent with intent to enforce the court's agreement, and, when grandmother chose not to participate in planned visitation, ex-wife was not on notice as to whether the parties were going to continue to attempt to work through therapist. Myer v. Myer (Ohio App. 5 Dist., Muskingum, 12-28-2009) No. CT2009-0014, 2009-Ohio-6884, 2009 WL 5108489, Unreported. Child Custody ☞ 854

Ex-wife was not entitled to continuance of hearing on paternal grandmother's motion to hold ex-wife in contempt of court for violation of a visitation order; hearing had been continued once due to ex-wife's pregnancy, and although there was letter from ex-wife's doctor stating only that the baby was breastfed and should not travel away from home nor be separated from his mother, no medical reasons were given for the doctor's concern. Myer v. Myer (Ohio App. 5 Dist., Muskingum, 12-28-2009) No. CT2009-0014, 2009-Ohio-6884, 2009 WL 5108489, Unreported. Child Custody ☞ 871

21. —— Termination of visitation, visitation with grandparents and others

Father, who filed a motion to terminate visitation rights previously granted to his son's maternal grandparents, was not required to show a change in circumstances before being entitled to relief. In re Kaiser (Ohio App. 7 Dist., Columbiana, 12-30-2004) No. 04 CO 9, 2004-Ohio-7208, 2004 WL 3090224, Unreported. Child Custody ☞ 579

Juvenile court's finding, in proceeding brought by paternal grandmother and paternal aunt for visitation with children following death of children's father, that mother and father were never married did not require reversal of juvenile court's denial of visitation, even though mother stated in her affidavit that she was married to children's father, and magistrate had found mother and father were married, where father's paternity was not disputed, his paternal rights had never been terminated prior to his death, and finding of marriage was not germane to ultimate issue of whether statutes on visitation by persons other than parents applied retroactively. In re Busdiecker (Ohio App. 12 Dist., Warren, 05-19-2003) No. CA2002-10-104, 2003-Ohio-2556,

2003 WL 21135496, Unreported. Child Custody ☞ 922(6)

Trial court's order, upon custodial father's motion to terminate grandparents' visitation, to reduce visitation and terminate access by grandparents to child's education and medical information was not against the manifest weight of the evidence or abuse of discretion. Fishel v. Fishel (Ohio App. 5 Dist., Tuscarawas, 11-04-2002) No. 2002-AP-03 0023, 2002-Ohio-6178, 2002 WL 31521778, Unreported, appeal not allowed 98 Ohio St.3d 1480, 784 N.E.2d 712, 2003-Ohio-974, reconsideration denied 98 Ohio St.3d 1541, 786 N.E.2d 902, 2003-Ohio-1946. Child Custody ☞ 579

Relatives of parents whose parental rights are terminated have no standing to assert visitation rights. Farley v. Farley (Licking 1992) 85 Ohio App.3d 113, 619 N.E.2d 427. Child Custody ☞ 409

The power given courts by RC 3109.05(B) to grant visitation rights to individuals other than parents is not limited in exercise to the "divorce, dissolution of marriage, alimony, or child support proceeding" provided under RC 3109.05(A); consequently, paternal grandparents may seek visitation rights under RC 3109.05(B) after their son consents to termination of his parental rights and the grandchild is placed for adoption with a maternal uncle. Brandt v DeGroff, No. WMS–85–21 (6th Dist Ct App, Williams, 10–17–86).

22. —— Stepparent adoption, visitation with grandparents and others

Amendments to statutes that created right of grandparent, and other relative, visitation after adoption by stepparent, could not be applied retroactively to children adopted prior to amendments' effective date and, thus, juvenile court did not have authority to grant paternal grandmother and paternal aunt visitation with children after children's father died, and mother's new husband, as stepfather, adopted children; amendments did not include language suggesting they were to be applied retroactively, and adoptive father's duty to support children, and children's right to compel that duty, were vested duties and rights. In re Busdiecker (Ohio App. 12 Dist., Warren, 05-19-2003) No. CA2002-10-104, 2003-Ohio-2556, 2003 WL 21135496, Unreported. Child Custody ☞ 6

The legislature has not provided the juvenile court with the authority to grant visitation rights to biological grandparents following an adoption of a grandchild by a stepparent even where the parental rights of the grandparents' child have been terminated through death. Matter of Apple (Ohio App. 2 Dist., Miami, 09-21-1994) No. 93-VA-59, 1994 WL 515116, Unreported.

Trial court lacked authority to grant paternal grandparents visitation with children of divorced parents after the children were adopted by their stepfather subsequent to their father's death; while a statute preserved the right of grandparent visitation when a surviving spouse remarried, it did not provide for the preservation of visitation rights after

an adoption by a stepparent. Foor v. Foor (Ohio App. 12 Dist., 04-26-1999) 133 Ohio App.3d 250, 727 N.E.2d 618. Child Custody ☞ 313

A trial court has no authority to grant grandparents' visitation rights following a stepparent adoption. Foor v. Foor (Ohio App. 12 Dist., 04-26-1999) 133 Ohio App.3d 250, 727 N.E.2d 618.

Statute permitting court in divorce, dissolution of marriage, legal separation, annulment, or child support proceeding that involves child to grant visitation rights to "any other person other than a parent," does not apply following adoption. State ex rel. Kaylor v. Bruening (Ohio, 10-22-1997) 80 Ohio St.3d 142, 684 N.E.2d 1228, 1997-Ohio-350. Child Custody ☞ 312

Statute providing that marriage of the surviving parent of child does not affect authority of court to grant reasonable companionship or visitation rights to grandparents preserves the right of grandparent visitation when the surviving spouse remarries, but it does not provide for the preservation of grandparent visitation rights after adoption of child by stepparent. Beard v. Pannell (Ohio App. 6 Dist., 04-26-1996) 110 Ohio App.3d 572, 674 N.E.2d 1225, appeal not allowed 77 Ohio St.3d 1447, 671 N.E.2d 1285. Child Custody ☞ 284; Child Custody ☞ 313

Paternal grandparents were divested of visitation and companionship rights with grandchild where their son, child's father, was deceased and mother's new spouse had adopted the child; stepparent adoption terminated child's relationship with paternal grandparents for all purposes and fact that adoption occurred after death of child's father did not change this conclusion. Beard v. Pannell (Ohio App. 6 Dist., 04-26-1996) 110 Ohio App.3d 572, 674 N.E.2d 1225, appeal not allowed 77 Ohio St.3d 1447, 671 N.E.2d 1285. Child Custody ☞ 313

A juvenile court abuses its discretion by ordering that visitation with adopted children's biological grandparents shall continue post-adoption. In re Adoption of Ridenour (Ohio 1991) 61 Ohio St.3d 319, 574 N.E.2d 1055.

RC 3107.15 does not prohibit an order pursuant to RC 3109.05, granting visitation rights to a biological paternal grandparent after adoption of a child by a stepfather, when the biological father's whereabouts are unknown. Welsh v. Laffey (Butler 1984) 16 Ohio App.3d 110, 474 N.E.2d 681, 16 O.B.R. 117.

23. Procedural issues

Action initiated in domestic relations division of court of common pleas on issue of child visitation as to out-of-wedlock child was civil in nature and, thus, father was not entitled to appointment of counsel. Edwards v. Spraggins (Ohio App. 5 Dist., Licking, 05-17-2005) No. 04CA54, 2005-Ohio-2416, 2005 WL 1163902, Unreported. Children Out–of–wedlock ☞ 20.4

Pro se ex-husband's grant of power of attorney to his father did not give father, who was not licensed to practice law, authority to act as an attorney on behalf of ex-husband in proceeding to modify ex-husband's parenting time. Savage v. Savage (Ohio App. 11 Dist., Lake, 11-26-2004) No. 2004-L-024, No. 2004-L-040, 2004-Ohio-6341, 2004 WL 2697281, Unreported. Attorney And Client ⊙ 12(21)

Mother's appeal of visitation order, which required mother to pay therapist's fees in connection with the supervised visitation, was rendered moot, in child dependency case, where the trial court terminated visitation between mother and child. In re Reeher (Ohio App. 7 Dist., Belmont, 02-11-2004) No. 02 BE 68, 2004-Ohio-802, 2004 WL 324760, Unreported. Infants ⊙ 247

While neither provision in divorced parties' agreed entry, nor statute governing parenting time rights, both of which provided that both parents had equal access to records regarding parties' children, granted former husband access to files of guardian ad litem in child custody proceedings, fact that guardian's files did not constitute record under parties' agreed entry or statute did not, standing alone, provide valid reason for quashing former husband's subpoena seeking their disclosure. Hogan v. Hogan (Ohio App. 12 Dist., Butler, 09-08-2003) No. CA2002-09-216, No. CA2002-09-225, 2003-Ohio-4747, 2003 WL 22073132, Unreported. Witnesses ⊙ 16

Costs of psychological examinations for parents and their child, in connection with ex-wife's motion to reduce visitation or for supervised visitation, properly were taxed evenly between ex-wife and ex-husband; the psychological examinations were an integral part of the "investigation" required by the court before the motion for supervised visitation could be determined pursuant to statute providing that court could cause an investigation to be made as to the character, family relations, past conduct, earning ability, and financial worth of each parent and court could tax as costs all or any part of the expenses for each investigation. Tinnel v. Tinnel (Ohio App. 6 Dist., Huron, 03-21-2003) No. H-02-040, 2003-Ohio-1403, 2003 WL 1464081, Unreported. Child Custody ⊙ 940

Mother failed to overcome presumption that trial court followed appropriate statutory scheme applicable to biological father who never married mother in determining whether to award child visitation, rather than statutory scheme applicable to biological father who was married to mother at time child was born, where nowhere in magistrate's recommendation to trial court did magistrate indicate which statutory scheme was used and there was no indication in judgment entry that trial court considered anything other than appropriate statutory scheme. Reynolds v. Nibert (Ohio App. 4 Dist., Scioto, 05-07-2002) No. 01CA2771, 2002-Ohio-6133, 2002 WL 31518183, Unreported. Children Out–of–wedlock ⊙ 20.11

A definite child visitation schedule should be provided by the court where the parties harbor animosity towards one another and are unable to agree upon a summer schedule of visitation for the nonresidential parent; likewise, a trial court errs in failing to award the nonresidential parent six weeks of extended summer visitation with the minor child of the parties as provided by local rule without showing good cause why such visitation should not be permitted. Leas v. Leech (Ohio App. 7 Dist., Jefferson, 08-09-1996) No. 95-J-5, 1996 WL 451374, Unreported.

Telephone visitation between a father and his children is not limited by scheduling his telephone calls to the children and eliminating daily phone calls, which reduces conflict between the parties' households. Darner v. Bach (Ohio App. 12 Dist., Warren, 02-20-1996) No. CA95-06-069, 1996 WL 71490, Unreported.

A residential parent's motion to terminate visitation and the motion of the nonresidential parent to set specific visitation times do not concern custodial issues, and a court errs by granting a motion to modify custody in a case where testimony and evidence do not rise to the level of a substantial change of circumstance but rather indicate the nonresidential parent's increasing demand for additional visitation. David v. Flickinger (Ohio App. 5 Dist., Tuscarawas, 09-19-1995) No. 94AP110077, 1995 WL 557132, Unreported, appeal allowed 75 Ohio St.3d 1410, 661 N.E.2d 758, reversed 77 Ohio St.3d 415, 674 N.E.2d 1159, 1997-Ohio-260.

Because a trial court may modify visitation (as distinguished from custody and support) without a change of circumstances, a judgment fixing visitation is not a final appealable order and an appeal therefrom will be dismissed. Tolerton v Tolerton, No. 92-CA-9, 1993 WL 221254 (5th Dist Ct App, Licking, 6-1-93).

Statute providing that effect of an adoption was to terminate all legal relationships between the adopted child and adopted child's relatives barred juvenile court, after child's adoption, from continuing its prior order of visitation in favor of adoptive mother's former husband, pursuant to statute governing visitation rights to "any other person other than a parent" after a divorce; adoption statute sought to transform the child's collection of relationships and, in effect, give the child a new identity. In re L.H. (Ohio App. 2 Dist., 06-19-2009) 183 Ohio App.3d 505, 917 N.E.2d 829, 2009-Ohio-3046. Child Custody ⊙ 182

Trial court, by accepting jurisdiction for purposes of accepting or rejecting foreign divorce decree, which former wife sought to enforce to gain custody of parties' child, was obligated to allocate parties' parental rights and responsibilities, such that parties were free to seek temporary orders, including order concerning visitation pending outcome of appeal, from trial court. Ronny T. v. Phillip T. (Ohio App. 6 Dist., 09-28-2006) 169 Ohio App.3d 46, 861 N.E.2d 884, 2006-Ohio-5103. Child Custody ⊙ 762

Trial court should have conducted a full evidentiary hearing before issuing judgment entry modifying former husband's visitation with parties' minor son, where Court of Appeals had remanded the matter "for further proceedings." Quint v. Lomakoski (Ohio App. 2 Dist., 06-16-2006) 167 Ohio App.3d 124, 854 N.E.2d 225, 2006-Ohio-3041, on subsequent appeal 173 Ohio App.3d 146, 877 N.E.2d 738, 2007-Ohio-4722. Child Custody ☞ 924

In-camera interviews of children conducted under statute governing visitation rights are confidential and are not to be disclosed to the parents. Willis v. Willis (Ohio App. 12 Dist., 07-22-2002) 149 Ohio App.3d 50, 775 N.E.2d 878, 2002-Ohio-3716. Child Custody ☞ 427

Parents of a child who is the subject of a visitation dispute do not have the right of access to the sealed transcript of in-camera interview between the child and the judge. Willis v. Willis (Ohio App. 12 Dist., 07-22-2002) 149 Ohio App.3d 50, 775 N.E.2d 878, 2002-Ohio-3716. Child Custody ☞ 427

General division of court of common pleas had jurisdiction over mother's claims of intentional infliction of emotional distress and loss of consortium against father based upon father's alleged measures to deny mother visitation with parties' two children, though court did not possess authority to render decision affecting visitation order of domestic relations division; mother was living in county at time when alleged torts were committed, and mother claimed that she suffered emotional distress after suffering extreme scorn, embarrassment, and harassment by members of community, which were claims grounded in tort. Catalano v. Pisani (Ohio App. 11 Dist., 07-23-1999) 134 Ohio App.3d 549, 731 N.E.2d 738. Courts ☞ 50

Trial court that granted wife's first divorce had subject matter jurisdiction over stepfather's motion for visitation with wife's child by first marriage; stepfather properly invoked court's continuing jurisdiction over divorce by filing motion for visitation with original court, rather than with court that granted divorce of stepfather and wife. Shannon v. Shannon (Ohio App. 9 Dist., 08-13-1997) 122 Ohio App.3d 346, 701 N.E.2d 771. Child Custody ☞ 404

Biological father's allegations, that appeal was not complete, beneficial, and speedy, and thus was not adequate remedy to prevent Court of Common Pleas from granting visitation to biological mother following issuance of adoption decree that terminated her parental rights, and that irreparable harm to child and to relationship between biological father would result should visitation proceedings not be stopped, stated cause of action in complaint seeking writ of prohibition. State ex rel. Kaylor v. Bruening (Ohio, 10-22-1997) 80 Ohio St.3d 142, 684 N.E.2d 1228, 1997-Ohio-350. Prohibition ☞ 20

Although Court of Common Pleas had basic statutory jurisdiction to grant visitation to biological parent, it was patently and unambiguously divested by adoption statute of jurisdiction to proceed on biological mother's motions relating to visitation following adoption decree terminating her parental

rights, and writ of prohibition preventing Court from doing so thus was appropriate. State ex rel. Kaylor v. Bruening (Ohio, 10-22-1997) 80 Ohio St.3d 142, 684 N.E.2d 1228, 1997-Ohio-350. Child Custody ☞ 312; Prohibition ☞ 10(2)

Denial of husband's motion for temporary visitation rights in separation action was interlocutory order that was not appealable, and that could not be made appealable by findings that appeal should be undertaken forthwith and that there was no just cause for delay, since that denial did not preclude different judgment upon final determination of case, and denial of motion was not such a distinct portion of action as to constitute separate claim. Cassim v. Cassim (Ohio App. 10 Dist., 11-17-1994) 98 Ohio App.3d 576, 649 N.E.2d 28, on subsequent appeal 1995 WL 546926, dismissed, appeal not allowed 75 Ohio St.3d 1404, 661 N.E.2d 754. Child Custody ☞ 905

Since no mediation report was filed and there was no indication that any mediation occurred, trial court could not have erred by failing to consider mediation report pursuant to statute providing that, if divorce proceeding involves child and if court has not issued shared parenting decree, court shall consider any mediation report filed. McClure v. McClure (Ohio App. 2 Dist., 10-05-1994) 98 Ohio App.3d 27, 647 N.E.2d 832, appeal not allowed 71 Ohio St.3d 1481, 645 N.E.2d 1260. Child Custody ☞ 418

Trial court's allocation of transportation expenses for visitation was unreasonable, insofar as court, in determining parties' income, subtracted father's child support obligation and added the same to mother's income. Gatliff v. Gatliff (Hancock 1993) 89 Ohio App.3d 391, 624 N.E.2d 779. Child Custody ☞ 213

In determining visitation schedule, trial court was not required to continue any temporary arrangements made during pendency of divorce. deLevie v. deLevie (Franklin 1993) 86 Ohio App.3d 531, 621 N.E.2d 594, dismissed, jurisdictional motion overruled 67 Ohio St.3d 1409, 615 N.E.2d 1043. Child Custody ☞ 210

One not a party to an original divorce action may obtain visitation rights through a court's continuing inherent jurisdiction, provided that proper notice is given pursuant to RC 3109.05(B), which provides that "reasonable companionship or visitation rights may be granted to any other person having an interest in the welfare of the child." Hollingsworth v. Hollingsworth (Franklin 1986) 34 Ohio App.3d 13, 516 N.E.2d 1250.

A stepfather may invoke the continuing jurisdiction of the court in a divorce action between the mother and natural father of a child pursuant to Civ R 75(I), in order to obtain an award of visitation rights with a stepchild under RC 3109.05, which permits the court to grant such rights to "any other person having an interest in the welfare of the child." Hutton v. Hutton (Lorain 1984) 21 Ohio App.3d 26, 486 N.E.2d 129, 21 O.B.R. 28.

Trial court erred in denying grandparents post step-parent adoption visitation rights with their grandchildren as the adoption does not prevent them from having standing and they can show an interest in the children's welfare under RC 3109.051. Sweeney v Sweeney, No. CA93–02–004, 1993 WL 414186 (12th Dist Ct App, Fayette, 10–18–93), reversed by 71 Ohio St. 3d 169 (1994).

A court has no jurisdiction to modify a visitation decree where the party was not served pursuant to Civ R 75(I). Jenkins v Jenkins, No. 1504 (4th Dist Ct App, Lawrence, 12–9–81).

Where the father received no notice pursuant to the rules of procedure that the continuing jurisdiction of the court had been invoked to modify his visitation rights, the court of appeals will reverse because the father is entitled to attend such a hearing with a clear understanding of its purpose. Harris v Harris, No. 1593 (2d Dist Ct App, Clark, 10–22–81).

24. In camera interview

Guardian ad litem (GAL) fit within category of "necessary court personnel" under statute identifying the persons who may attend in camera interview of a child during proceedings on a motion to modify visitation; and thus, it was appropriate for GAL to accompany child into judge's chambers and attend the interview session. Moline v. Moline (Ohio App. 11 Dist., Ashtabula, 04-23-2010) No. 2009-A-0013, 2010-Ohio-1799, 2010 WL 1643612, Unreported. Child Custody ⟾ 654; Infants ⟾ 85

An in camera interview of a child may be an appropriate method by which the trial court determines the child's best interest in visitation cases, even if one of the parties objects to such an interview. In re Whitaker (Ohio 1988) 36 Ohio St.3d 213, 522 N.E.2d 563. Child Custody ⟾ 427

25. Continuances

Trial court did not abuse its discretion in proceeding on father's motion to modify visitation and mother's cross-motions for enforcement by denying father's request for a continuance, despite father's contention that continuance was necessary to allow him to obtain new counsel since he himself was subject to a deportation order refusing him entry to the country; father was warned when his counsel withdrew that no continuance would be granted, father was again reminded of the need to obtain counsel or use an alternative method of presenting evidence when his motion to appear via the internet was denied, and father chose to proceed pro se rather than obtain new counsel. Lisboa v. Lisboa (Ohio App. 8 Dist., Cuyahoga, 10-01-2009) No. 92321, 2009-Ohio-5228, 2009 WL 3155135, Unreported, appeal not allowed 124 Ohio St.3d 1476, 921 N.E.2d 247, 2010-Ohio-354. Child Custody ⟾ 651; Child Custody ⟾ 871

Trial court did not abuse its discretion in denying motion for continuance filed by former husband, in contempt proceedings seeking enforcement of visitation order, in order to permit vacationing sheriff's deputy to testify, especially where expected testimony of deputy was largely cumulative and unlikely to have affected court's ultimate decision. In re C.P. (Ohio App. 12 Dist., Butler, 07-25-2005) No. CA2004-10-259, 2005-Ohio-3888, 2005 WL 1798269, Unreported. Child Custody ⟾ 871

Trial court abused its discretion by finding divorced mother in contempt of visitation orders without giving mother an opportunity to fully prepare for contempt hearing; mother learned of the contempt charges only ten days before hearing, and trial court denied mother's request for continuance to prepare and to enable children, who were teenagers, and their psychologist to testify as to the complicated factual causes of the visitation issues. Knisley v. Knisley (Ohio App. 6 Dist., Fulton, 04-29-2005) No. F-04-024, 2005-Ohio-2090, 2005 WL 1007143, Unreported. Child Custody ⟾ 871

Incarcerated ex-husband, who failed to obtain an attorney within four months of his filing of motions to show cause as to why ex-wife should not be held in contempt based on denial of parenting time, was not entitled to a continuance to obtain an attorney. Savage v. Savage (Ohio App. 11 Dist., Lake, 11-26-2004) No. 2004-L-024, No. 2004-L-040, 2004-Ohio-6341, 2004 WL 2697281, Unreported. Child Custody ⟾ 871

Denial of father's request for continuance of hearing on motion for visitation so that he could subpoena critical witnesses was not abuse of discretion; father had plenty of time in between filing motion and hearing to secure witnesses, there was no showing he ensured that attorney had list of witnesses, proposed testimony from witnesses regarding relationship with other son was heard through testimony of father and father's wife, and inconvenience to mother would have been great. Wilson v. Redmond (Ohio App. 12 Dist., Madison, 07-26-2004) No. CA2003-09-033, 2004-Ohio-3910, 2004 WL 1662259, Unreported. Child Custody ⟾ 502

26. Attorney malpractice claim

Client failed to establish that his attorney's alleged negligence in representation of client in connection with client's pursuit of child visitation rights proximately caused his damages, and thus, client could not prevail on legal malpractice claim against attorney; expert testimony regarding client's psychiatric injuries did not link injuries to attorney's conduct, any causal connection was severed by client's own conduct in failing to attend critical appointments and hearings, and evidence did not indicate that client's intervening acts were reasonably foreseeable by attorney. Lytle v. McClain (Ohio App. 9 Dist., Lorain, 09-01-2004) No. 03CA008400, 2004-Ohio-4572, 2004 WL 1932975, Unreported, appeal not allowed 104 Ohio St.3d 1441, 819 N.E.2d 1124, 2004-Ohio-7033. Attorney And Client ⟾ 129(2)

27. Attorney fees

Trial court acted within its discretion in awarding father attorney fees in the amount of $750 in contempt proceedings against mother, in which father alleged that mother had failed to comply with child custody and support order. Mackowiak v. Mackowiak (Ohio App. 12 Dist., Fayette, 06-20-2011) No. CA2010-04-009, 2011-Ohio-3013, 2011 WL 2448997, Unreported, stay denied 129 Ohio St.3d 1503, 955 N.E.2d 386, 2011-Ohio-5358. Child Custody ☞ 943; Child Support ☞ 603

Based on the mandatory language of parenting time rights statute, ex-wife was required to pay attorney fees once court found her in contempt of shared parenting agreement; statute provided that, if any person was found in contempt of court for failing to comply with or interfering with any order or decree granting parenting time rights, the court shall require the person to pay any reasonable attorney fees. Rapp v. Pride (Ohio App. 12 Dist., Butler, 07-06-2010) No. CA2009-12-311, 2010-Ohio-3138, 2010 WL 2653628, Unreported. Child Custody ☞ 943

Because the magistrate did not make any findings and the record contained no evidence regarding attorney fees, the trial court had no factual basis for deciding amount of attorney fees ex-wife, who was found in contempt for violating shared parenting agreement, should pay to ex-husband, and thus, court's decision to award ex-husband $1,500 in attorney fees was an abuse of discretion. Rapp v. Pride (Ohio App. 12 Dist., Butler, 07-06-2010) No. CA2009-12-311, 2010-Ohio-3138, 2010 WL 2653628, Unreported. Child Custody ☞ 955

Trial court's decision to award former husband $1250 in attorney fees after finding former wife in civil contempt for denying former husband the opportunity to exercise his court-ordered visitation with their minor child was not arbitrary, unreasonable, or unconscionable; former husband testified that he incurred $750 in fees to prepare and file the contempt action and an additional $500.00 in fees because the matter proceeded to hearing, former wife testified that she earned seven dollars an hour, and trial court took former wife's financial situation into consideration by allowing her eighteen months to pay the award. Sloat v. James (Ohio App. 5 Dist., Stark, 06-15-2009) No. 2008 CA 00048, 2009-Ohio-2849, 2009 WL 1677850, Unreported. Child Custody ☞ 949

Trial court was not required to inquire into former wife's ability to pay or determine that former husband would be prevented from fully litigating his rights and adequately protecting his interests if attorney fees were not awarded before awarding attorney fees, in case in which former wife was found in contempt for failure to comply with court visitation orders; statute required that a person found in contempt for failure to comply with an order granting parenting time must pay the adverse party's attorney fees that "arose in relation to the act of contempt." Robinson v. Robinson (Ohio App. 8 Dist., Cuyahoga, 11-23-2005) No. 85980,

2005-Ohio-6240, 2005 WL 3120215, Unreported. Child Custody ☞ 943; Child Custody ☞ 954

Order that required mother to pay $5,150.00 in attorney fees, after mother was found in contempt of court for violating the visitation and companionship order, was not an abuse of discretion; statute required a trial court to order the party found in contempt for violating a visitation order to pay the adverse party's reasonable attorney fees arising from the litigation, counsel for mother stipulated to the reasonableness of counsel for father's $200 per hour rate, counsel for father presented a legal bill of $10,300 and stated that 50% of the bill, or $5,150, was allocated to the contempt proceeding, and counsel for mother agreed that 50% of the bill represented services rendered for the contempt motion. Mann v. Mendez (Ohio App. 9 Dist., Lorain, 06-22-2005) No. 04CA008562, 2005-Ohio-3114, 2005 WL 1460045, Unreported. Child Custody ☞ 949

Award of $350 in attorney fees to father in proceeding in which he sought to have mother held in contempt for her failure to abide by visitation order involving parties' children was not supported by record; record contained no itemized statement for services rendered by father's attorney, including time and hourly rates, and no testimony had been offered as to whether services billed for were actually rendered. Markel v. Markel (Ohio App. 5 Dist., Ashland, 06-30-2004) No. 04-COA-015, 2004-Ohio-3437, 2004 WL 1465741, Unreported. Child Custody ☞ 952

Trial court did not err in failing to allow mother the opportunity to purge the $1440 in attorney fees plus court costs assessed in contempt action for mother's failure to comply with visitation order; although mother was entitled to an opportunity to purge sanction for contempt of court, sentence of incarceration which was suspended by the court, not the award of attorney fees and costs, was the sanction for contempt. Patterson v. Patterson (Ohio App. 5 Dist., Stark, 02-03-2003) No. 2002CA00167, 2003-Ohio-517, 2003 WL 231257, Unreported. Child Custody ☞ 957

The court has discretion to award attorney fees in contempt proceedings. In re Contemnor Caron (Ohio Com.Pl., 04-27-2000) 110 Ohio Misc.2d 58, 744 N.E.2d 787. Contempt ☞ 68

Delayed compliance with a court order, even where compliance is effected before a hearing on a contempt motion, does not prevent sanctions or an award of attorney fees. In re Contemnor Caron (Ohio Com.Pl., 04-27-2000) 110 Ohio Misc.2d 58, 744 N.E.2d 787. Contempt ☞ 68; Contempt ☞ 70

Attorney fees may be awarded in a contempt proceeding even where there is no finding of contempt. In re Contemnor Caron (Ohio Com.Pl., 04-27-2000) 110 Ohio Misc.2d 58, 744 N.E.2d 787. Contempt ☞ 68

3109.052 Mediation order; report

(A) If a proceeding for divorce, dissolution, legal separation, annulment, or the allocation of parental rights and responsibilities for the care of a child involves one or more children, if the parents of the children do not agree upon an appropriate allocation of parental rights and responsibilities for the care of their children or do not agree upon a specific schedule of parenting time for their children, the court may order the parents to mediate their differences on those matters in accordance with mediation procedures adopted by the court by local rule. When the court determines whether mediation is appropriate in any proceeding, it shall consider whether either parent previously has been convicted of or pleaded guilty to a violation of section 2919.25 of the Revised Code involving a victim who at the time of the commission of the offense was a member of the family or household that is the subject of the proceeding, whether either parent previously has been convicted of or pleaded guilty to an offense involving a victim who at the time of the commission of the offense was a member of the family or household that is the subject of the proceeding and caused physical harm to the victim in the commission of the offense, and whether either parent has been determined to be the perpetrator of the abusive act that is the basis of an adjudication that a child is an abused child. If either parent has been convicted of or pleaded guilty to a violation of section 2919.25 of the Revised Code involving a victim who at the time of the commission of the offense was a member of the family or household that is the subject of the proceeding, has been convicted of or pleaded guilty to any other offense involving a victim who at the time of the commission of the offense was a member of the family or household that is the subject of the proceeding and caused physical harm to the victim in the commission of the offense, or has been determined to be the perpetrator of the abusive act that is the basis of an adjudication that a child is an abused child, the court may order mediation only if the court determines that it is in the best interests of the parties to order mediation and makes specific written findings of fact to support its determination.

If a court issues an order pursuant to this division requiring mediation, it also may order the parents to file a mediation report within a specified period of time and order the parents to pay the cost of mediation, unless either or both of the parents file a motion requesting that the court waive that requirement. Upon the filing of a motion requesting the waiver of that requirement, the court, for good cause shown, may waive the requirement that either or both parents pay the cost of mediation or may require one of the parents to pay the entire cost of mediation. Any mediation procedures adopted by local court rule for use under this division shall include, but are not limited to, provisions establishing qualifications for mediators who may be employed or used and provisions establishing standards for the conduct of the mediation.

(B) If a mediation order is issued under division (A) of this section and the order requires the parents to file a mediation report, the mediator and each parent who takes part in mediation in accordance with the order jointly shall file a report of the results of the mediation process with the court that issued the order under that division. A mediation report shall indicate only whether agreement has been reached on any of the issues that were the subject of the mediation, and, if agreement has been reached, the content and details of the agreement. No mediation report shall contain any background information concerning the mediation process or any information discussed or presented in the process. The court shall consider the mediation report when it allocates parental rights and responsibilities for the care of children under section 3109.04 of the Revised Code and when it establishes a specific schedule of parenting time under section 3109.051 of the Revised Code. The court is not bound by the mediation report and shall consider the best interest of the children when making that allocation or establishing the parenting time schedule.

(C) If a mediation order is issued under division (A) of this section, the mediator shall not be made a party to, and shall not be called as a witness or testify in, any action or proceeding, other than a criminal, delinquency, child abuse, child neglect, or dependent child action or proceeding, that is brought by or against either parent and that pertains to the mediation process, to any information discussed or presented in the mediation process, to the allocation of parental rights and responsibilities for the care of the parents' children, or to the awarding of parenting time rights in relation to their children. The mediator shall not be made a party to, or be called as a witness or testify in, such an action or proceeding even if both parents give their prior consent to the mediator being made a party to or being called as a witness or to testify in the action or proceeding.

(D) Division (A) of this section does not apply to either of the following:

(1) Any proceeding, or the use of mediation in any proceeding that is not a proceeding for divorce, dissolution, legal separation, annulment, or the allocation of parental rights and responsibilities for the care of a child;

(2) The use of mediation in any proceeding for divorce, dissolution, legal separation, annulment, or the allocation of parental rights and responsibilities for the care of a child, in relation to issues other than the appropriate allocation of parental rights and responsibilities for the care of the parents' children and other than a specific parenting time schedule for the parents' children.

(2000 S 180, eff. 3–22–01; 1990 S 3, eff. 4–11–91)

Historical and Statutory Notes

Amendment Note: 2000 S 180 substituted "parenting time" for "visitation" throughout the section.

Cross References

Communications not subject to privilege, see 2710.05

Disclosure by mediator, see 2710.06
Privileged communications, see 2317.02

Library References

Child Custody ⚖️419.
Westlaw Topic No. 76D.

Research References

Encyclopedias

OH Jur. 3d Alternative Dispute Resolution § 142, Exceptions to Privilege.

OH Jur. 3d Alternative Dispute Resolution § 143, Extent of Mediator's Power to Disclose.

OH Jur. 3d Alternative Dispute Resolution § 156, Domestic Relations.

OH Jur. 3d Alternative Dispute Resolution § 166, Cases Involving Domestic Violence.

OH Jur. 3d Evidence & Witnesses § 736, Privileges Recognized by Statute.

OH Jur. 3d Family Law § 1176, Mediation Report and Costs.

Forms

Ohio Jurisprudence Pleading and Practice Forms § 101:40, Mediation.

Treatises and Practice Aids

Sowald & Morganstern, Baldwin's Ohio Practice Domestic Relations Law § 6:3, Mediation.

Sowald & Morganstern, Baldwin's Ohio Practice Domestic Relations Law § 6:4, Communications Made in Mediation.

Sowald & Morganstern, Baldwin's Ohio Practice Domestic Relations Law § 6:6, Court Order for Mediation--Form.

Sowald & Morganstern, Baldwin's Ohio Practice Domestic Relations Law § 16:1, Jurisdiction.

Sowald & Morganstern, Baldwin's Ohio Practice Domestic Relations Law § 16:9, Mediation.

Sowald & Morganstern, Baldwin's Ohio Practice Domestic Relations Law § 18:6, Additional Considerations.

Sowald & Morganstern, Baldwin's Ohio Practice Domestic Relations Law § 21:2, Parenting Time--Establishing Visitation Order.

Sowald & Morganstern, Baldwin's Ohio Practice Domestic Relations Law § 21:6, Development of Statutory Requirements.

Sowald & Morganstern, Baldwin's Ohio Practice Domestic Relations Law § 21:7, Enforcement of Parenting Time--Comprehensive Parenting Time Order.

Sowald & Morganstern, Baldwin's Ohio Practice Domestic Relations Law § 6:15, High Conflict Families and Parenting Coordination.

Sowald & Morganstern, Baldwin's Ohio Practice Domestic Relations Law § 15:72, Alternate Dispute Resolution--Mediation.

Sowald & Morganstern, Baldwin's Ohio Practice Domestic Relations Law § 18:14, Procedure--Mediation Relating to Visitation.

Sowald & Morganstern, Baldwin's Ohio Practice Domestic Relations Law § 21:18, Practical Methods--Mediation.

Sowald & Morganstern, Baldwin's Ohio Practice Domestic Relations Law § 25:41, Motions Regarding Court Proceedings--Motion for Findings by Court.

Sowald & Morganstern, Baldwin's Ohio Practice Domestic Relations Law § 37:19, Privileged Communication--State Law Privileges--Mediator.

Adrine & Ruden, Ohio Domestic Violence Law § 15:23, Mediation in Domestic Violence Cases.

Law Review and Journal Commentaries

Arbitration as an Alternative to Divorce Litigation: Redefining the Judicial Role. Andre R. Imbrogno, 31 Cap U L Rev 413 (2003).

Can We Talk?, Hon. Francine M. Bruening. (Ed. Note: Mediation is discussed.) 19 Lake Legal Views 1 (June 1996).

Keeping Kids Out of Court. (Ed. note: Arbitration of custody disputes, but courts reserve the right to review awards.) 19 Nat'l L J B8 (May 5, 1997).

Learning From Japan: The Case for Increased Use of Apology in Mediation, Max Bolstad. 48 Clev St L Rev 545 (2000).

Ohio Divorce Mediation, C. Terrence Knapp. 4 Domestic Rel J Ohio 21 (March/April 1992).

Notes of Decisions

Child custody incident to divorce   1

1. Child custody incident to divorce

Mediated settlement agreement between husband and wife concerning child custody incident to divorce was valid and thus enforceable, despite husband's claims after the fact that he was not aware that the agreements reached during mediation were binding, where husband had been in business for 17 years, which required him to negotiate and enter into contracts, and husband knew he could leave the negotiations during the mediation session. Fichthorn v. Fichthorn (Ohio App. 5 Dist., Guern-

sey, 09-28-2009) No. 09-CA-10, 2009-Ohio-5138, 2009 WL 3111922, Unreported. Child Custody ⟻ 419

Husband and wife stipulated in mediated settlement agreement incident to divorce that it was in their child's best interest for wife to be designated as residential custodial parent and, thus, trial court was not required to make finding that mediated settlement agreement with respect to the child custody determination was in the child's best interest. Fichthorn v. Fichthorn (Ohio App. 5 Dist., Guernsey, 09-28-2009) No. 09-CA-10, 2009-Ohio-5138, 2009 WL 3111922, Unreported. Child Custody ⟻ 419

3109.053   Mandatory parenting classes and counseling as condition of allocation of parental rights and responsibilities

In any divorce, legal separation, or annulment proceeding and in any proceeding pertaining to the allocation of parental rights and responsibilities for the care of a child, the court may require, by rule or otherwise, that the parents attend classes on parenting or other related issues or obtain counseling before the court issues an order allocating the parental rights and responsibilities for the care of the minor children of the marriage. If a court in any proceeding requires parents to attend classes on parenting or other related issues or to obtain counseling, the court may require that the parents' children attend the classes or counseling with the parents. If the court orders the parents to attend classes or obtain counseling, the court shall impose the cost of the classes and counseling on, and may allocate the costs between, the parents, except that if the court determines that both parents are indigent, the court shall not impose the cost of the classes or counseling on the parents.

(2000 H 537, eff. 10–5–00; 1996 H 368, eff. 9–10–96)

Historical and Statutory Notes

Amendment Note: 2000 H 537 inserted the second sentence in the section.

Library References

Child Custody ⟻400.
Westlaw Topic No. 76D.

C.J.S. Divorce § 1020.
C.J.S. Parent and Child §§ 94, 203.

Research References

Encyclopedias

OH Jur. 3d Family Law § 1179, Parenting Classes; Counseling.

Forms

Ohio Jurisprudence Pleading and Practice Forms § 101:41, Mandatory Parenting Classes and Counseling.

Treatises and Practice Aids

Sowald & Morganstern, Baldwin's Ohio Practice
Domestic Relations Law § 21:6, Development of
Statutory Requirements.

3109.06 Certification to juvenile court

Except as provided in division (K) of section 2301.03 of the Revised Code, any court, other than a juvenile court, that has jurisdiction in any case respecting the allocation of parental rights and responsibilities for the care of a child under eighteen years of age and the designation of the child's place of residence and legal custodian or in any case respecting the support of a child under eighteen years of age, may, on its own motion or on motion of any interested party, with the consent of the juvenile court, certify the record in the case or so much of the record and such further information, in narrative form or otherwise, as the court deems necessary or the juvenile court requests, to the juvenile court for further proceedings; upon the certification, the juvenile court shall have exclusive jurisdiction.

In cases in which the court of common pleas finds the parents unsuitable to have the parental rights and responsibilities for the care of the child or children and unsuitable to provide the place of residence and to be the legal custodian of the child or children, consent of the juvenile court shall not be required to such certification. This section applies to actions pending on August 28, 1951.

In any case in which a court of common pleas, or other court having jurisdiction, has issued an order that allocates parental rights and responsibilities for the care of minor children and designates their place of residence and legal custodian of minor children, has made an order for support of minor children, or has done both, the jurisdiction of the court shall not abate upon the death of the person awarded custody but shall continue for all purposes during the minority of the children. The court, upon its own motion or the motion of either parent or of any interested person acting on behalf of the children, may proceed to make further disposition of the case in the best interests of the children and subject to sections 3109.42 to 3109.48 of the Revised Code. If the children are under eighteen years of age, it may certify them, pursuant to this section, to the juvenile court of any county for further proceedings. After certification to a juvenile court, the jurisdiction of the court of common pleas, or other court, shall cease, except as to any payments of spousal support due for the spouse and support payments due and unpaid for the children at the time of the certification.

Any disposition made pursuant to this section, whether by a juvenile court after a case is certified to it, or by any court upon the death of a person awarded custody of a child, shall be made in accordance with sections 3109.04 and 3109.42 to 3109.48 of the Revised Code. If an appeal is taken from a decision made pursuant to this section that allocates parental rights and responsibilities for the care of a minor child and designates the child's place of residence and legal custodian, the court of appeals shall give the case calendar priority and handle it expeditiously.

(2010 H 10, eff. 6-17-10; 1999 H 191, eff. 10–20–99; 1990 S 3, eff. 4–11–91; 1990 H 514; 1983 H 93; 1953 H 1; GC 8005–6; Source—GC 8034–1)

Historical and Statutory Notes

Pre–1953 H 1 Amendments: 124 v S 65

Amendment Note: 2010 H 10 substituted "Except as provided in division (K) of section 2301.03 of the Revised Code, any" for "Any" at the beginning of the first undesignated paragraph.

Amendment Note: 1999 H 191 inserted "and subject to sections 3109.42 to 3109.48 of the Revised Code" in the third paragraph; inserted "and 3109.42 to 3109.48" in the fourth paragraph; and made other nonsubstantive changes.

Cross References

Allowance of spousal support modification, see 3105.18

Jurisdiction of juvenile court, see 2151.23

Taking of child into custody by juvenile court, Juv R 6

Library References

Courts ⊕⇒483 to 488(4).
Westlaw Topic No. 106.
C.J.S. Courts §§ 263 to 273.

Research References

Encyclopedias

OH Jur. 3d Family Law § 534, Jurisdiction of Juvenile Court--Certification to Juvenile Court.

OH Jur. 3d Family Law § 723, Effect of Death of Person Awarded Custody.

OH Jur. 3d Family Law § 1097, Death of Residential Parent.

OH Jur. 3d Family Law § 1123, Continuing Jurisdiction of Court; Effect of Death of a Parent.

OH Jur. 3d Family Law § 1124, Certification of Support to Juvenile Court.

OH Jur. 3d Family Law § 1332, Generally; Jurisdiction.

OH Jur. 3d Family Law § 1536, on Certification from Another Court.

OH Jur. 3d Family Law § 1541, Child Custody.

OH Jur. 3d Family Law § 1549, on Certification from Common Pleas.

OH Jur. 3d Family Law § 1550, on Certification from Common Pleas--After Termination of Marriage.

Treatises and Practice Aids

Klein, Darling, & Terez, Baldwin's Ohio Practice Civil Practice § 24:19, Permissive Intervention--Statutory Permissive Intervention--"A Statute of This State Confers a Conditional Right to Intervene".

Sowald & Morganstern, Baldwin's Ohio Practice Domestic Relations Law § 19:2, Jurisdiction Over Child Support.

Sowald & Morganstern, Baldwin's Ohio Practice Domestic Relations Law § 15:54, Award to Third Party--By the Court.

Sowald & Morganstern, Baldwin's Ohio Practice Domestic Relations Law § 15:61, Modifying Allocation of Parental Rights--Death of a Parent.

Sowald & Morganstern, Baldwin's Ohio Practice Domestic Relations Law § 18:21, Modifying Visitation or Parenting Time Orders--Jurisdiction.

Sowald & Morganstern, Baldwin's Ohio Practice Domestic Relations Law § 21:31, Custody to Non-Parent.

Carlin, Baldwin's Ohio Prac. Merrick-Rippner Probate Law § 107:3, Divorce or Alimony Involving Care or Custody of Children.

Carlin, Baldwin's Ohio Prac. Merrick-Rippner Probate Law § 107:11, Certification from Common Pleas Court.

Carlin, Baldwin's Ohio Prac. Merrick-Rippner Probate Law § 107:13, Authority Following Certification.

Carlin, Baldwin's Ohio Prac. Merrick-Rippner Probate Law § 110:35, Civil Support Proceedings--Liability for Child Support.

Carlin, Baldwin's Ohio Prac. Merrick-Rippner Probate Law § 109:120, Appeals--Juvenile Court Judgments--Appeals from Custody Determinations.

Carlin, Baldwin's Ohio Prac. Merrick-Rippner Probate Law § 109:135, Motion to Certify Case to Juvenile Court--Form.

Giannelli & Yeomans, Ohio Juvenile Law § 2:2, Exclusive Original Jurisdiction.

Giannelli & Yeomans, Ohio Juvenile Law § 54:6, Stay of Proceedings.

Giannelli & Yeomans, Ohio Juvenile Law § 34:11, Certification or Transfer from Another Court.

Law Review and Journal Commentaries

The Custody Contest Between a Parent and a Nonparent, Don C. Bolsinger. 2 Domestic Rel J Ohio 51 (July/August 1990).

The Voice of a Child: Independent Legal Representation of Children in Private Custody Disputes

When Sexual Abuse Is Alleged, Kerin S. Bischoff. 138 U Pa L Rev 1383 (May 1990).

Notes of Decisions

Appeal 6
Child support 5
Continuing jurisdiction 1
Death of parent 4
Juvenile court jurisdiction 3
Procedure 2

----

1. Continuing jurisdiction

This section in no wise affects jurisdiction of regular branch of common pleas court to hear, determine and retain jurisdiction in custodial and support orders in divorce cases; however, it authorizes court upon determination of the advisability so to do to relinquish this jurisdiction to the juvenile court, whereupon it is provided that it ceases. Metz v. Metz (Franklin 1934) 17 Ohio Law Abs. 531.

Where in a divorce action custody of a minor child is awarded by the court, that court retains jurisdiction over custody of the child, and in a subsequent divorce action between the custodial parent and a successor spouse, the court hearing that action has no jurisdiction over custody of such child. Loetz v. Loetz (Ohio 1980) 63 Ohio St.2d 1, 406 N.E.2d 1093, 17 O.O.3d 1.

When a parent having legal custody of minor children takes up residence with such children outside the state, an Ohio court has continuing jurisdiction to modify the original custody order. Murck v. Murck (Cuyahoga 1976) 47 Ohio App.2d 292, 353 N.E.2d 917, 1 O.O.3d 355.

When a mother having legal custody of a minor child is domiciled in another state with such child, an Ohio court does not have continuing jurisdiction to modify the original custody order, but if such child resides in Ohio, even though he may be domiciled in another state with the parent having legal custody, the courts of Ohio will have continuing jurisdiction to hear a motion for modification of custody. Heiney v. Heiney (Columbiana 1973) 40 Ohio App.2d 571, 321 N.E.2d 611, 69 O.O.2d 519.

Where a common pleas court, having made an award of custody and an order for the support of a minor child, certifies the same to juvenile court for further proceedings and the jurisdiction of the juvenile court attaches before the minor is eighteen years of age, the jurisdiction of that court continues until the minor attains the age of twenty-one. Slawski v. Slawski (Lucas 1934) 49 Ohio App. 100, 195 N.E. 258, 18 Ohio Law Abs. 515, 1 O.O. 201. Child Custody ☞ 404

RC 3105.21(B) affords a domestic relations court authority to determine custody of a child, as between his parents and another relative, even though that court has dismissed the parent's divorce action; if after dismissing the divorce action, the domestic relations court elects to certify the matter of custody to juvenile court, under RC 3105.21(B) and 3109.04 the domestic relations court must specifically find custody in neither parent to be in the child's best interest, or all jurisdiction over the matter is lost. State ex rel. Easterday v. Zieba (Ohio 1991) 58 Ohio St.3d 251, 569 N.E.2d 1028.

2. Procedure

In case in which father petitioned to modify parenting time, domestic relations court could not certify the case to the juvenile court based on a finding it made, on evidence presented in proceedings on the petition, that one of the children may have been sexually abused by an unknown perpetrator, and therefore, jurisdiction never vested in juvenile court, notwithstanding juvenile court's exclusive jurisdiction over cases concerning allegations of child abuse, where there was no complaint, indictment, or information that contained allegations of abuse, neglect, or dependency, and the domestic relations court did not obtain the juvenile court's consent prior to transfer, and did not make a finding that the parents were unsuitable. Thompson v. Valentine (Ohio App. 12 Dist., 08-30-2010) No. CA2009-09-231, 2010 -Ohio- 4075, 2010 WL 3386235, Unreported. Courts ☞ 488(1)

Where a domestic relations court seeks to transfer a case to juvenile court pursuant to the juvenile court's jurisdiction over cases concerning abused, neglected, or dependent child, it must make finding

that it is in the best interest of child for neither parent to be designated residential parent and legal custodian of the child in order for jurisdiction to vest in the juvenile court. Thompson v. Valentine (Ohio App. 12 Dist., 08-30-2010) 189 Ohio App.3d 661, 939 N.E.2d 1289, 2010 -Ohio- 4075. Courts ☞ 487(1)

The Ohio Rules of Civil Procedure do not apply to a custody proceeding in the juvenile division of a court of common pleas; rather, such proceedings are governed by the Ohio Rules of Juvenile Procedure. Squires v. Squires (Preble 1983) 12 Ohio App.3d 138, 468 N.E.2d 73, 12 O.B.R. 460. Infants ☞ 191

In any case where a court of common pleas has made an award of custody or an order for support, or both, of minor children, that court may certify the case to the juvenile court of any county in the state for further proceedings. Pylant v. Pylant (Huron 1978) 61 Ohio App.2d 247, 401 N.E.2d 940, 15 O.O.3d 407. Courts ☞ 483

Where a court, having acquired jurisdiction over a child by virtue of a divorce action between the child's parents, certifies the matter of the child's custody to a juvenile court, the consent of the juvenile court having been first obtained, the juvenile court has exclusive jurisdiction over the child's custody by virtue of RC 3109.06 and 2151.23(D) and a finding of unfitness of the parents or that there is no suitable relative to have custody is not a necessary prerequisite to such certification, and while such certification shall be deemed to be the complaint in the juvenile court, it does not constitute a complaint in the juvenile court that such child is dependent or neglected and those dispositions provided for under RC 2151.353, 2151.354, and 2151.355 are not applicable to the disposition of such a child, disposition thereof being subject to and controlled by RC 3109.04. In re Height (Van Wert 1975) 47 Ohio App.2d 203, 353 N.E.2d 887, 1 O.O.3d 279. Courts ☞ 472.1

A common pleas court has no jurisdiction to make any order respecting the care and custody or visitation with minor children unless in the prayer of the petition the plaintiff asks for a divorce or alimony. Crum v. Howard (Ohio Com.Pl. 1956) 137 N.E.2d 654, 73 Ohio Law Abs. 111, 1 O.O.2d 399. Child Custody ☞ 404

3. Juvenile court jurisdiction

When a case involving the allocation of parental rights and responsibilities and the place of residence and legal custodianship of children under age eighteen is certified by another court to the juvenile court, the juvenile court has exclusive jurisdiction over it. In re Rutan (Ohio App. 3 Dist., Union, 08-02-2004) No. 14-03-52, 2004-Ohio-4022, 2004 WL 1718160, Unreported. Courts ☞ 488(1)

In case in which father petitioned to modify parenting time, domestic relations court could not certify the case to the juvenile court based on a finding it made, on evidence presented in proceedings on the petition, that one of the children may have been sexually abused by an unknown perpetrator, and, therefore, jurisdiction never vested in juvenile court, where there was no complaint, indictment, or information that contained allegations of abuse, neglect, or dependency, and the domestic relations court did not obtain the juvenile court's consent prior to transfer and did not make a finding that the parents were unsuitable. Thompson v. Valentine (Ohio App. 12 Dist., 08-30-2010) 189 Ohio App.3d 661, 939 N.E.2d 1289, 2010-Ohio-4075. Courts ☞ 488(1)

Failure of common pleas court to make finding that natural parents were unfit custodians of child did not preclude certification of child custody case to juvenile court, where case was certified pursuant to statute giving juvenile court discretion whether to accept certification, rather than statute pursuant to which juvenile court must accept certification based on finding that it is in best interest of child for neither parent to have custody. In re Whaley (Athens 1993) 86 Ohio App.3d 304, 620 N.E.2d 954. Courts ☞ 487(1)

Where a juvenile court grants the temporary custody of a minor child, with the consent of his parents, to a non-relative, after the father had unrestricted custody pursuant to a divorce decree, RC 3109.04(B) and 3109.04(C), as effective September 23, 1974, are not applicable to prevent the court's consideration of a motion filed by the father, in the same court, for the restoration of custody. Leininger v. Leininger (Fulton 1975) 48 Ohio App.2d 21, 355 N.E.2d 508, 2 O.O.3d 15. Child Custody ☞ 6; Child Custody ☞ 578

There is no statutory provision for any juvenile court to certify a case back to the common pleas court; when a case is once certified to a juvenile court, it has exclusive jurisdiction, and the jurisdiction of the common pleas court ceases. Handelsman v. Handelsman (Columbiana 1958) 108 Ohio App. 30, 160 N.E.2d 543, 9 O.O.2d 101.

Express consent of the juvenile court is an essential prerequisite to the acquiring of jurisdiction over children upon certification of an award of custody and support by the common pleas court. Cline v. Cline (Fayette 1955) 137 N.E.2d 633, 73 Ohio Law Abs. 289.

Where common pleas court has, in divorce action, made an order as to custody of minor child, and has certified the case to juvenile court for further proceedings, the common pleas court's jurisdiction ceases and sole jurisdiction is vested in juvenile court under section. In such case, objection to jurisdiction of common pleas court after such certification may be made at any time in further proceedings relating to custody. Agler v. Agler (Franklin 1944) 64 N.E.2d 854, 44 Ohio Law Abs. 289.

Order of common pleas court in divorce case affecting custody of minor is effective until reversed or modified, although case relating to minor is transferred to juvenile court. Sonnenberg v. State (Franklin 1931) 40 Ohio App. 475, 178 N.E. 855, 10 Ohio Law Abs. 271. Child Custody ☞ 523; Child Custody ☞ 531(1)

When orders made in the common pleas court or probate court as to the care and custody of minor children are certified to the juvenile court, the juvenile court may then exercise jurisdiction over said minors in the same manner as in cases originally brought in said juvenile court. No new jurisdiction is conferred except the authority to proceed in said cases, in the same manner, and with the same powers, as if said cases had been adjudicated in the juvenile court. 1925 OAG 2310.

4. Death of parent

Following death of mother to whom trial court had awarded custody in divorce proceeding, dispute over custody of children between father and children's maternal uncle fell within coverage of statute allowing custody to be awarded to relative other than parent "when it is in the best interest of the child," rather than under statute establishing jurisdiction of juvenile courts to determine custody of child not ward of another court of state. Baker v. Baker (Ohio App. 9 Dist., 08-21-1996) 113 Ohio App.3d 805, 682 N.E.2d 661, appeal not allowed 77 Ohio St.3d 1525, 674 N.E.2d 376. Child Custody ☞ 271; Child Custody ☞ 405

Where the parent to whom custody of minor children has been awarded by a divorce court subsequently dies during their minority, custody is to be awarded on the death of that parent as the court may have determined in the best interests of the children; in such event it is not necessary for the court to find that the surviving parent is not a suitable person to have custody before awarding custody to another person. Gordon v. Gordon (Hardin 1973) 33 Ohio App.2d 257, 294 N.E.2d 239, 62 O.O.2d 375. Child Custody ☞ 578; Child Custody ☞ 659

Where the trial court awarded custody of minor children to the father following a divorce action, it had jurisdiction following the death of such father to determine custody upon personal service upon the mother in another state by the local sheriff. Kirkpatrick v. Kirkpatrick (Ohio Com.Pl. 1956) 139 N.E.2d 119, 74 Ohio Law Abs. 14.

5. Child support

Juvenile court's express consent is required before a domestic relations court may transfer a case by certification to the juvenile court on ground that case involves allocation of parental rights and responsibilities for care of minor child or involves support of such child. Thompson v. Valentine (Ohio App. 12 Dist., 08-30-2010) 189 Ohio App.3d 661, 939 N.E.2d 1289, 2010-Ohio-4075. Courts ☞ 487(1)

A trial court has jurisdiction to modify a support order as to future installments, whether or not the right is reserved in the decree; but it has no such jurisdiction to modify unpaid installment support payments which have accrued if the child for whose benefit support was awarded was living and not emancipated at the time of the accrual, unless the right to retrospective modification was specifically reserved in the decree. Wedebrook v. Wedebrook

(Ohio Com.Pl. 1977) 51 Ohio Misc. 81, 367 N.E.2d 937, 5 O.O.3d 342. Child Support ☞ 232; Child Support ☞ 460

Where a parent, against whom an order to pay for the support of a minor child is made, is before the court, the court has the power to order such parent to support such child, even though the child is not physically within the state where the award of support is made. Handelsman v. Handelsman (Columbiana 1958) 108 Ohio App. 30, 160 N.E.2d 543, 9 O.O.2d 101.

6. Appeal

No bond is required in the appeal of a child custody case. Reynolds v. Reynolds (Ross 1964)

200 N.E.2d 890, 94 Ohio Law Abs. 289, 30 O.O.2d 380.

Although it is the general rule that when an appeal is taken from a trial court that court is divested of jurisdiction, except to take action in aid of the appeal, until the case is remanded to it by the appellate court, the best interests of the children sometimes might better be served if the appellate court postpones its resolution of the questions raised by the assignments of error until the juvenile court is re-invested with jurisdiction to review the entire matter of custody in light of the possibility that the passage of some twenty-two months has worked a change in conditions regarding the children's best interest. In the Matter of Wallace, Nos. 360 and 361 (1st Dist Ct App, Clinton, 2–14–79).

3109.07 Appeal to the court of appeals

An appeal to the court of appeals may be had pursuant to the Rules of Appellate Procedure and, to the extent not in conflict with those rules, Chapter 2505. of the Revised Code. (1986 H 412, eff. 3–17–87; 129 v 291; 1953 H 1; GC 8005-7; Source—GC 8035)

Historical and Statutory Notes

Pre–1953 H 1 Amendments: 124 v S 65

Cross References

Relief pending appeal, Civ R 75

Library References

Child Custody ☞903.
Westlaw Topic No. 76D.

C.J.S. Divorce § 1164.
C.J.S. Parent and Child § 148.

Research References

Encyclopedias

OH Jur. 3d Family Law § 1332, Generally; Jurisdiction.

Notes of Decisions

Bond 1
Procedure 2

---

1. Bond

A motion to dismiss an appeal from the overruling of a motion to change the custody of a child will be sustained where no bond is filed within twenty days from the order appealed from. Call v. Call (Franklin 1958) 107 Ohio App. 516, 160 N.E.2d 307, 81 Ohio Law Abs. 243, 9 O.O.2d 54.

An appeal from an order regarding the custody of a child is conditional upon giving bond. Call v. Call (Franklin 1958) 107 Ohio App. 516, 160 N.E.2d 307, 81 Ohio Law Abs. 243, 9 O.O.2d 54.

The giving of the bond specified in RC 3109.07 is a condition precedent to an appeal of the kind provided for therein. Volz v. Volz (Ohio 1957) 167 Ohio St. 141, 146 N.E.2d 734, 4 O.O.2d 136.

Where no bond is filed in an appeal on law and fact from a juvenile court order relating to custody of minor children, the appeal will be retained on questions of law only. Bachtel v. Bachtel (Lucas 1954) 97 Ohio App. 521, 127 N.E.2d 761, 56 O.O. 469. Child Custody ☞ 910

2. Procedure

In proceeding on motion for change of custody, judgment that defers issue of child support for future determination is not "final appealable order." Kouns v. Pemberton (Lawrence 1992) 84 Ohio App.3d 499, 617 N.E.2d 701, motion overruled 66 Ohio St.3d 1489, 612 N.E.2d 1245. Child Custody ☞ 902

Where trial court, as part of final determination of divorce action, found it not to be in best interest of child to award custody to either parent and certified issue of custody to juvenile court, certification order was properly appealable as part of divorce judgment and constituted a final appealable order. Robinson v. Robinson (Franklin 1984) 19 Ohio App.3d 323, 484 N.E.2d 710, 19 O.B.R. 496. Child Custody ⬅ 902

The word "appeal," as used in GC 8005–7 (RC 3109.07), has the meaning specified in subdivision (A) of 2505.01. Volz v. Volz (Ohio 1957) 167 Ohio St. 141, 146 N.E.2d 734, 4 O.O.2d 136.

Where a special statute prescribes the method of appeal from a particular order, such statute is controlling and the general statutes providing for appeal have no application; and compliance with the general statute, but not with the special statute, is not sufficient to perfect such appeal, and hence RC 3109.07 prescribes the only method by which an

appeal may be effected from an order fixing the custody of a child. Gregg v. Mitchell (Scioto 1955) 99 Ohio App. 350, 133 N.E.2d 645, 59 O.O. 133, appeal dismissed 163 Ohio St. 330, 126 N.E.2d 809, 56 O.O. 288. Appeal And Error ⬅ 1

Where custody of minor children is originally granted to the maternal grandparents and a subsequent court order grants custody to the father, both awards of custody constitute final, appealable orders and, therefore, preclude the mother from asserting assignments of error in a proceeding which is not a timely appeal of those orders. Torbeck v Torbeck, No. C–810827 (1st Dist Ct App, Hamilton, 7–21–82).

3109.08   Release of dower rights—Repealed

(1973 S 1, eff. 1–1–74; 130 v S 193)

LIABILITY OF PARENTS

3109.09   Damages recoverable against parent of minor who willfully damages property or commits theft offense; community service

(A) As used in this section, "parent" means one of the following:

(1) Both parents unless division (A)(2) or (3) of this section applies;

(2) The parent designated the residential parent and legal custodian pursuant to an order issued under section 3109.04 of the Revised Code that is not a shared parenting order;

(3) The custodial parent of a child born out of wedlock with respect to whom no custody order has been issued.

(B) Any owner of property, including any board of education of a city, local, exempted village, or joint vocational school district, may maintain a civil action to recover compensatory damages not exceeding ten thousand dollars and court costs from the parent of a minor if the minor willfully damages property belonging to the owner or commits acts cognizable as a "theft offense," as defined in section 2913.01 of the Revised Code, involving the property of the owner. The action may be joined with an action under Chapter 2737. of the Revised Code against the minor, or the minor and the minor's parent, to recover the property regardless of value, but any additional damages recovered from the parent pursuant to this section shall be limited to compensatory damages not exceeding ten thousand dollars, as authorized by this section. A finding of willful destruction of property or of committing acts cognizable as a theft offense is not dependent upon a prior finding that the child is a delinquent child or upon the child's conviction of any criminal offense.

(C)(1) If a court renders a judgment in favor of a board of education of a city, local, exempted village, or joint vocational school district in an action brought pursuant to division (B) of this section, if the board of education agrees to the parent's performance of community service in lieu of full payment of the judgment, and if the parent who is responsible for the payment of the judgment agrees to voluntarily participate in the performance of community service in lieu of full payment of the judgment, the court may order the parent to perform community service in lieu of providing full payment of the judgment.

(2) If a court, pursuant to division (C)(1) of this section, orders a parent to perform community service in lieu of providing full payment of a judgment, the court shall specify in its order the amount of the judgment, if any, to be paid by the parent, the type and number of hours of community service to be performed by the parent, and any other conditions necessary to carry out the order.

(D) This section shall not apply to a parent of a minor if the minor was married at the time of the commission of the acts or violations that would otherwise give rise to a civil action commenced under this section.

(E) Any action brought pursuant to this section shall be commenced and heard as in other civil actions.

(F) The monetary limitation upon compensatory damages set forth in this section does not apply to a civil action brought pursuant to section 2307.70 of the Revised Code.

(1996 H 601, eff. 10–29–96; 1992 H 154, eff. 7–31–92; 1990 S 3; 1988 H 708; 1986 H 158, S 316; 1978 H 456; 1969 S 10; 132 v H 257; 131 v H 159)

Historical and Statutory Notes

Amendment Note: 1996 H 601 added divisions (A) and (A)(1) to (A)(3); redesignated former divisions (A) to (E) as divisions (B) to (F) respectively; substituted "ten thousand dollars" for "six thousand dollars" throughout and "parent of a minor" for "parents who have the parental rights and responsibilities for the care of a minor, and are the residential parents and legal custodians of a minor" in division (B); substituted "This section shall not apply to a parent" for "For purposes of this section, the parents of a minor do not have parental rights and responsibilities for the care of the minor and are not the residential parents and legal custodians of the minor" and "would otherwise give" for "gave" in division (D); changed references from "parents" to "parent" throughout; made changes to reflect gender neutral language; and made other nonsubstantive changes.

Comparative Laws

Ill.—ILCS 740 115/1 et seq.
Ind.—West's A.I.C. 34–31–4–1, 34–31–4–2.

Ky.—Baldwin's KRS 405.025.
Mich.—M.C.L.A. § 600.2913.

Cross References

Vandalism, criminal damaging or endangering, see 2909.05, 2909.06

Victims' rights pamphlet, publication and distribution, see 109.42

Library References

Parent and Child ⬡13.5(2).
Westlaw Topic No. 285.
C.J.S. Parent and Child §§ 191, 310.

Research References

Encyclopedias

OH Jur. 3d Family Law § 208, Intentional Torts.
OH Jur. 3d Family Law § 221, Destructive Acts or Theft.
OH Jur. 3d Family Law § 224, Destructive Acts or Theft--Theft.
OH Jur. 3d Family Law § 226, Who is "Parent" Under Statutes.
OH Jur. 3d Family Law § 227, Parental Rights and Responsibilities of Care.
OH Jur. 3d Family Law § 904, Investigation--Social and Medical Histories.
OH Jur. 3d Family Law § 1719, Notification of Victims.
OH Jur. 3d Insurance § 1015, Coverage or Exclusion of Intentional Injuries or Damages--Particular Policies.
OH Jur. 3d Limitations & Laches § 33, Generally; Injuries to Personal Property.
OH Jur. 3d Negligence § 35, Definitions of Willful and Wanton Misconduct--Legal Effect.

Treatises and Practice Aids

Carlin, Baldwin's Ohio Prac. Merrick-Rippner Probate Law § 109:61, Adjudicatory Hearings--No-

tice to Victims of Crime of Right to Recover Damages and Victim-Impact Statements.
Carlin, Baldwin's Ohio Prac. Merrick-Rippner Probate Law § 110:20, Parentage Act--Jurisdiction and Venue.
Carlin, Baldwin's Ohio Prac. Merrick-Rippner Probate Law § 110:42, Parental Responsibility--Destructive Acts of Children.
Carlin, Baldwin's Ohio Prac. Merrick-Rippner Probate Law § 109:110, Juvenile Court's Authority Over Parents.
Giannelli & Yeomans, Ohio Juvenile Law § 25:3, Responsibilities to Victims and Others.
Giannelli & Yeomans, Ohio Juvenile Law § 47:2, Jurisdiction Over Parents and Others.
Giannelli & Yeomans, Ohio Juvenile Law § 22:13, Restitution.
Hastings, Manoloff, Sheeran, & Stype, Ohio School Law § 38:12, Parental Liability for Property Damage, Theft, or Assault by Children--Statutory Liability.

Law Review and Journal Commentaries

Fundamentally Speaking: Application of Ohio's Domestic Violence Laws in Parental Discipline Cases—A Parental Perspective, Richard Garner. 30 U Tol L Rev 1 (Fall 1998).

Intra–Family Immunities and the Law of Torts in Ohio, John E. Sullivan. 18 W Reserve U L Rev 447 (January 1967).

Liability of Parents for the Willful Torts of Their Children Under Ohio Revised Code Section 3109.09, Stuart A. Laven. 24 Clev St L Rev 1 (Winter 1975).

Motorist Mutual Insurance Co v Bill, 56 OS(2d) 258, 383 NE(2d) 880 (1978): A Limitation on Parental Liability and Willful Acts, Susan J. Scheutzow. 9 Cap U L Rev 749 (Summer 1980).

New student discipline options enacted, Daniel A. Jaffe. 40 Ohio Sch Boards Ass'n J 2 (October 1996).

Parents' Support Obligations to Their Adult Children, Marvin M. Moore. 19 Akron L Rev 183 (Fall 1985).

Property Owner's Civil Action for Minor's Theft, Ron Mount. 4 U Dayton L Rev 539 (1979).

Statutory Vicarious Parental Liability: Review and Reform, Note. 32 Case W Res L Rev 559 (1982).

Student Misconduct—New Weapons for Schools, Richard J. Dickinson. 8 Baldwin's Ohio Sch L J 29 (July/August 1996).

Tort Law: Parental Liability and the Extension of Social Host Liability to Minors—*Huston v. Konieczny*, 52 Ohio St. 3d 214, 556 N.E.2d 505 (1990), Note. 16 U Dayton L Rev 827 (Spring 1991).

Notes of Decisions

In general 1
Attorney fees 8
Emotional distress damages 7
Foster parents negligence 9
Insurance 3
Parent's negligence 6
Strict construction 2
Theft provision 5
Willful damage 4

1. In general

Although no basis existed for imposing liability on parents of teenage children who witnessed but did not report fire started by another teenager, material fact issue existed as to liability of children themselves, precluding summary judgment for them. American Economy Ins. Co. v. Knowles (Ohio App. 2 Dist., 07-26-1996) 113 Ohio App.3d 71, 680 N.E.2d 237. Judgment ☞ 181(33)

Minor's taking of her mother's automobile without permission and her willful driving of automobile without authority or license was not behavior upon which court was to focus in action against mother pursuant to parental liability statute to recover damages arising out of minor's crash of automobile into building but, rather, subsequent act of wrecking automobile was behavior at issue. State Auto. Mut. Ins. Co. v. Newman (Ohio Mun. 1994) 65 Ohio Misc.2d 23, 640 N.E.2d 627. Automobiles ☞ 195(1)

"Willful conduct" under parental liability statute means intentional doing of act which occasions injury and resulting damage; there must be intent to cause injury. State Auto. Mut. Ins. Co. v. Newman (Ohio Mun. 1994) 65 Ohio Misc.2d 23, 640 N.E.2d 627. Parent And Child ☞ 13.5(2)

No statutory authority exists authorizing the payment of guardian ad litem fees from county funds in a civil action involving negligent or intentional acts of an indigent minor in causing fire damage to a rental unit. Nationwide Mut. Ins. Co. v. Wymer (Franklin 1986) 33 Ohio App.3d 318, 515 N.E.2d 987.

In an action brought against a parent and his child for damages caused by a fire in a rental unit, where the court finds the child alone liable for such damages in that the child was responsible for starting the fire, the fees and expenses of a court-appointed guardian ad litem are properly charged to the indigent minor child and not to his parent, as part of the court costs. Nationwide Mut. Ins. Co. v. Wymer (Franklin 1986) 33 Ohio App.3d 318, 515 N.E.2d 987.

When a person trespasses on the lands of another, while the trespass continues, he owes a duty of care to the owner of the premises; such duty includes the obligation to protect the property from harm as a result of the trespass. Wigton v. Lavender (Delaware 1980) 70 Ohio App.2d 241, 436 N.E.2d 1378, 24 O.O.3d 349. Negligence ☞ 210

Where a minor child is validly married, has established his own residence apart from his parents, and is self-supporting, he is no longer within the custody and control of his parents for purposes of establishing liability pursuant to RC 3109.10. Albert v. Ellis (Cuyahoga 1978) 59 Ohio App.2d 152, 392 N.E.2d 1309, 13 O.O.3d 188. Parent And Child ☞ 13.5(2)

The two-year statute of limitations set forth in RC 2305.10 applies to civil actions to recover compensatory damages for injury to property brought under RC 3109.09. Rudnay v. Corbett (Cuyahoga 1977) 53 Ohio App.2d 311, 374 N.E.2d 171, 7 O.O.3d 416.

The Ohio legislature primarily intended RC 3109.09 to establish a civil cause of action, providing for compensatory damages to innocent victims of minor delinquents, against the parents having custody and control of a minor who willfully damages the property of another. Rudnay v. Corbett (Cuyahoga 1977) 53 Ohio App.2d 311, 374 N.E.2d 171, 7 O.O.3d 416.

The Ohio youth commission is not a parent, within the meaning of RC 3109.09, to incarcerated children so as to allow an action in the court of claims for the willful destruction of property. Hahn v. Brown (Franklin 1976) 51 Ohio App.2d 177, 367 N.E.2d 884, 5 O.O.3d 323.

Where two or more children, all covered by RC 3109.09, combine to do damage, the parents are responsible in the amount set forth in the statute for each of said children, and where such acts are committed between October 6, 1965, and October 10, 1965, by four such minor children, the parents are responsible up to the extent of $1,000. Lewis v. Martin (Ohio Com.Pl. 1968) 16 Ohio Misc. 18, 240 N.E.2d 913, 45 O.O.2d 22.

The amendment to RC 3109.09, effective October 24, 1967, which raises the limit of liability of a parent from $250 to $800, is not retroactive, and any damages done prior to that time are limited to the older section, namely, $250. Lewis v. Martin (Ohio Com.Pl. 1968) 16 Ohio Misc. 18, 240 N.E.2d 913, 45 O.O.2d 22.

The parents who are responsible under RC 3109.09 may be joined in the same action with their minor children, and where such children unite in a common willful destruction of property, the minors are jointly and severally liable for the damages, and the parents are jointly and severally liable with said children to the extent of the parents' responsibility under said section. Lewis v. Martin (Ohio Com.Pl. 1968) 16 Ohio Misc. 18, 240 N.E.2d 913, 45 O.O.2d 22.

Under RC 3109.09, a noncustodial parent cannot recover from an ex-spouse and custodial parent for a theft of the noncustodial parent's property by the parties' minor child. Hartford Acc. & Indem. Co. v. Borchers (Franklin 1982) 3 Ohio App.3d 452, 445 N.E.2d 1160, 3 O.B.R. 532.

Neither a county children services board nor a foster parent appointed and certified by a county children services board pursuant to RC 5153.16 and accompanying regulations is a "parent" under RC 3109.09 or 3109.10; accordingly, neither the board nor a foster parent is liable under RC 3109.09 or 3109.10 for the willful damage to or theft of property, or willful or malicious assault of a person, committed by a child in their custody. OAG 87–082.

2. Strict construction

RC 3109.09 is in derogation of the common law and must be strictly construed. Nationwide Ins. Co. v. Love (Lucas 1984) 22 Ohio App.3d 9, 488 N.E.2d 226, 22 O.B.R. 43.

RC 3109.09 creates an exception to the common law principle that liability will not be imposed upon parents for the intentional torts of their minor children, and must be strictly construed and its application limited to those situations involving intentional acts of destruction. Travelers Indem. Co. v. Brooks (Lucas 1977) 60 Ohio App.2d 37, 395 N.E.2d 494, 14 O.O.3d 19.

3. Insurance

Insurer's subrogation claim against minor in which insurer sought to recover for amounts paid to insured as a result of minor's negligent act, allegedly occurring when minor drove insured's vehicle without permission and damaged it, alleged a common law claim for negligence, and thus was independent of insurer's claim against minor's mother brought pursuant to statute that allowed recovery against a parent of minor who willfully damages property or commits a theft offense. Grange Mut. Cas. Co. v. Reynolds (Ohio App. 2 Dist., Montgomery, 01-15-2010) No. 23235, 2010-Ohio-114, 2010 WL 169469, Unreported. Automobiles ☞ 228; Insurance ☞ 3526(1)

Insurer's negligence claim against minor was not barred by minor's mother's bankruptcy filing and eventual discharge; stay and potential discharge to which mother might have been entitled applied to her personal liability to insurer pursuant to statute that allowed recovery against parent of minor who willfully damages property or commits a theft offense, but had no application to minor's liability to insurer on its negligence claim. Grange Mut. Cas. Co. v. Reynolds (Ohio App. 2 Dist., Montgomery, 01-15-2010) No. 23235, 2010-Ohio-114, 2010 WL 169469, Unreported. Bankruptcy ☞ 2396; Bankruptcy ☞ 3412

A homeowner's insurance policy that provides coverage for "property damage caused by an occurrence," which latter term is defined in the policy as "an accident," does not obligate the insurer to pay the claim of an insured under the policy who incurs liability under RC 3109.09 for intentional damage caused by another separately insured under the same policy, absent other clear indicia of such obligation in the insurance contract. Randolf v. Grange Mut. Cas. Co. (Ohio 1979) 57 Ohio St.2d 25, 385 N.E.2d 1305, 11 O.O.3d 110.

A subrogated insurance company may bring an action pursuant to RC 3109.09 for recovery, within the limits of the statute, of amounts paid out under the insurance policy. Peterson v. Slone (Ohio 1978) 56 Ohio St.2d 255, 383 N.E.2d 886, 10 O.O.3d 396.

A subrogated insurer may maintain an action against the parents in custody and control of a minor who willfully damages the property of an owner. Motorists Mut. Ins. Co. v. Bill (Ohio 1978) 56 Ohio St.2d 258, 383 N.E.2d 880, 10 O.O.3d 398.

The homeowners insurance of the parents of a minor wrongdoer is required to defend and/or pay a claim under RC 3109.09. Liberty Mut. Ins. Co. v. Davis (Ohio Mun. 1977) 52 Ohio Misc. 26, 368 N.E.2d 336, 6 O.O.3d 108.

A subrogated insurance company may maintain an action under RC 3109.09 against the parents of a minor wrongdoer. Liberty Mut. Ins. Co. v. Davis (Ohio Mun. 1977) 52 Ohio Misc. 26, 368 N.E.2d 336, 6 O.O.3d 108. Parent And Child ☞ 13.5(2)

4. Willful damage

Willful-acts provision of statute governing imposition of civil liability on parent for property damage caused by minor did not apply to damage to garage and fence that was caused when minor, who did not have driver's license, lost control of third-party's automobile that he took without permission when he was intoxicated; there was no indication that minor intentionally damaged garage and fence. Allstate Ins. Co. v. Jaeger (Ohio App. 9 Dist., Lorain, 11-02-2009) No. 09CA009591, 2009-Ohio-5756, 2009 WL 3531771, Unreported. Parent and Child ☞ 13.5(2)

The father of a minor cannot be held legally accountable on an oral contract made by his son and his son's friends to repair plaintiff's car where there is no finding that the son willfully damaged or stole the car and (1) the son's friend refuses to let the plaintiff see her car when she refuses to give him an additional $100, (2) the owner is forced to have her vehicle towed because the defendants remove the ignition, and (3) the plaintiff is not seeking to recover for the additional damage to the vehicle over and above her claim for contractual damages; therefore, removal of the ignition is not the result of willful damage by the son for which his father can be held legally accountable. Allison v. Boehringer (Ohio App. 2 Dist., Montgomery, 04-12-1995) No. 14862, 1995 WL 225448, Unreported.

Statute that imposes liability upon parents for destructive acts of child only applies to minor who "willfully damages property," which means intentional doing of act that occasions injury and resulting damage. American Economy Ins. Co. v. Knowles (Ohio App. 2 Dist., 07-26-1996) 113 Ohio App.3d 71, 680 N.E.2d 237. Parent And Child ☞ 13.5(2)

When a minor under age steals an automobile, and, in attempting to elude the owner and others seeking to thwart his theft, throws the automobile gears into reverse, floors the gas pedal and precipitously in the darkness on an unfamiliar road backs the automobile over a curb into a tree, damaging the car, such recklessness constitutes "willfully" damaging the property of the "owner" within the meaning of RC 3109.09 and causes the parents having the custody and control of such minor to be liable under such statute for the damage caused by the minor. Central Mut. Ins. Co. v. Rabideau (Lucas 1977) 60 Ohio App.2d 5, 395 N.E.2d 367, 14 O.O.3d 5.

Recovery cannot be had under RC 3109.09 against a minor involved in an automobile accident on the basis that the initial stealing of the automobile was willful. Peterson v. Slone (Ohio 1978) 56 Ohio St.2d 255, 383 N.E.2d 886, 10 O.O.3d 396.

As used in RC 3109.09, "willfully damages property" means the intentional doing of the act which occasions the damage and resulting loss, coupled with the intent or purpose of causing the damage; and in order that parents may be found liable for the tortious acts of their minor children, both the initial act, as well as the subsequent damage, must be found to have been intentional. Motorists Mut. Ins. Co. v. Bill (Ohio 1978) 56 Ohio St.2d 258, 383 N.E.2d 880, 10 O.O.3d 398.

As used in RC 3109.09, the term "damages" is intended to include loss by reason of a theft. Liberty Mut. Ins. Co. v. Davis (Ohio Mun. 1977) 52 Ohio Misc. 26, 368 N.E.2d 336, 6 O.O.3d 108.

"Willful damaging" of property under Ohio statute imposing liability on parents when minor willfully damages property means intentional doing of act which occasions damages and resulting loss, coupled with intent or purpose of causing damage and, to impose liability upon parent, both initial act and subsequent damage must be found to be intentional. Byrd v. Brandeburg (N.D.Ohio, 03-18-1996) 922 F.Supp. 60. Parent And Child ☞ 13.5(2)

5. Theft provision

Under statute governing damages recoverable against parent of minor who willfully commits theft offense, minor driver's father was liable for damage caused to owner's automobile when driver entered and engaged in unauthorized use of automobile; father admitted that he was driver's parent, and driver's acts constituted "theft offense." White v. Westfall (Ohio App. 10 Dist., 09-01-2009) 183 Ohio App.3d 807, 919 N.E.2d 227, 2009-Ohio-4490. Automobiles ☞ 191

Unauthorized use of a motor vehicle by a minor may constitute a theft offense subjecting the minor's parents to liability for damage to an automobile operated without the owner's consent. Evans v. Graham (Franklin 1991) 71 Ohio App.3d 417, 594 N.E.2d 71.

The parents with custody and control of a minor who commits acts cognizable as a "theft offense" and thereby damages the property involved are liable to the property owner under RC 3109.09 regardless of whether the damage was negligent or intentional. West American Ins. Co. v. Carter (Ohio Mun. 1989) 50 Ohio Misc.2d 20, 553 N.E.2d 1099.

The unauthorized use of an automobile is a "theft offense" under RC 2913.01 and therefore grounds under RC 3109.09 for an action by the owner of an automobile against the parents of a child who willfully damages the vehicle while joyriding. Nationwide Ins. Co. v. Love (Lucas 1984) 22 Ohio App.3d 9, 488 N.E.2d 226, 22 O.B.R. 43.

An award of attorney fees in a civil suit under RC 3109.09 against the parents of a minor who damages a stolen automobile while joyriding is without adequate evidentiary support and must be reversed where it is not established that the damage was intentionally inflicted. Nationwide Ins. Co. v. Love (Lucas 1984) 22 Ohio App.3d 9, 488 N.E.2d 226, 22 O.B.R. 43.

Parental liability arises under the "theft provision" of RC 3109.09, as amended by 1978 H 456, eff. 5-23-78, when the child has engaged in conduct which is the equivalent of theft and the property is thereafter damaged, regardless of whether the child acted in a willful or unwillful manner at the time the property was actually damaged. Schirmer v. Losacker (Hamilton 1980) 70 Ohio App.2d 138, 434 N.E.2d 1388, 24 O.O.3d 171. Parent And Child ☞ 13.5(2)

6. Parent's negligence

Mother did not know, nor should she have known, that injury to another was probable consequence of her minor son's behavior and thus did not negligently supervise son, who stole third party's automobile after getting drunk and damaged property owners' garage and fence; mother did not know of any incident when son had used a car, mother spoke to son before son stole car, and mother learned nothing during conversation with son that made mother think that son was misbehaving or that he planned to use a car. Allstate Ins. Co. v. Jaeger (Ohio App. 9 Dist., Lorain, 11-02-2009) No. 09CA009591, 2009-Ohio-5756, 2009 WL 3531771, Unreported. Parent and Child ☞ 13.5(4)

Although parents are generally not liable for wrongful conduct of their children, parent can be liable for his own negligent act when injury caused by child is foreseeable to parent. Boyd v. Watson (Ohio Com.Pl., 07-15-1996) 83 Ohio Misc.2d 88, 680 N.E.2d 251. Parent And Child ☞ 13.5(4)

Parent can be liable for negligent entrustment when he entrusts his child with instrumentality which, because of child's immaturity or lack of experience, may become source of danger to others. Boyd v. Watson (Ohio Com.Pl., 07-15-1996) 83 Ohio Misc.2d 88, 680 N.E.2d 251. Parent And Child ☞ 13.5(4)

Parental liability for negligent entrustment may occur when parent entrusts child with instrumentality that is dangerous per se, or when he entrusts child with instrumentality that is not dangerous per se, but becomes dangerous due to child's immaturity or inexperience. Boyd v. Watson (Ohio Com. Pl., 07-15-1996) 83 Ohio Misc.2d 88, 680 N.E.2d 251. Parent And Child ☞ 13.5(4)

Parent may be liable for negligent supervision when parent fails to exercise proper parental control over his child, and parent knows, or should know from his knowledge of child's habits or tendencies, that failure to exercise such control poses unreasonable risk that child will injure others. Boyd v. Watson (Ohio Com.Pl., 07-15-1996) 83 Ohio Misc.2d 88, 680 N.E.2d 251. Parent And Child ☞ 13.5(4)

Parent may be liable for consenting to, directing, or sanctioning his child's wrongdoing. Boyd v. Watson (Ohio Com.Pl., 07-15-1996) 83 Ohio Misc.2d 88, 680 N.E.2d 251. Parent And Child ☞ 13.5(2)

Statute dealing with parental liability for child's willful damage of property was not basis for imposing liability on parents in connection with fire started by one teenager and witnessed but not reported by parents' teenage children; there was no evidence that parents' children actively participated or

agreed with teenager who started fire to set fire that caused damage to store, or any evidence connecting parents with their children's alleged conduct. American Economy Ins. Co. v. Knowles (Ohio App. 2 Dist., 07-26-1996) 113 Ohio App.3d 71, 680 N.E.2d 237. Parent And Child ☞ 13.5(2)

Fire that was started by teenager in presence of, but without active participation of, parents' teenage children was not foreseeable consequence of any negligent acts of parents such that they could be held liable; parents did not provide their children with dangerous instrumentality, did not direct or sanction any prior wrongdoing, and any parental negligence or lack of supervision and control did not have as foreseeable consequence fire or similar catastrophe. American Economy Ins. Co. v. Knowles (Ohio App. 2 Dist., 07-26-1996) 113 Ohio App.3d 71, 680 N.E.2d 237. Parent And Child ☞ 13.5(4)

There are three situations in which parents might incur liability for conduct of child: (1) when parents negligently entrust child with instrument that becomes source of danger; (2) when parents know of child's wrongdoing and consent to it, direct it, or sanction it; and (3) when parents fail to exercise reasonable control over child when parent knows, or should know, that injury to another is probable consequence. American Economy Ins. Co. v. Knowles (Ohio App. 2 Dist., 07-26-1996) 113 Ohio App.3d 71, 680 N.E.2d 237. Parent And Child ☞ 13.5(2); Parent And Child ☞ 13.5(4)

At common law, parent is not liable for damages caused by child's wrongful conduct, and in order to be excepted from such general proposition, child's alleged misconduct must, at very least, be within reasonable comprehension of alleged negligence of parents. American Economy Ins. Co. v. Knowles (Ohio App. 2 Dist., 07-26-1996) 113 Ohio App.3d 71, 680 N.E.2d 237. Parent And Child ☞ 13.5(2); Parent And Child ☞ 13.5(4)

A parent who negligently fails to supervise his child by permitting the child to violate a municipal curfew may be liable for damages caused during the child's unauthorized use of a motor vehicle if it can be shown that the damage caused by the child is a foreseeable consequence of violation of the curfew. Evans v. Graham (Franklin 1991) 71 Ohio App.3d 417, 594 N.E.2d 71.

At common law, a parent is not ordinarily liable for damages caused by a child's wrongful conduct; however, liability can attach when the injury committed by the child is the foreseeable consequence of a parent's negligent act. In those circumstances, liability arises from the parent's conduct. Huston v. Konieczny (Ohio 1990) 52 Ohio St.3d 214, 556 N.E.2d 505.

A child under seven years of age is incapable, as a matter of law, of committing an intentional tort; therefore, a property owner has no cause of action against the parents of such a child under RC 3109.09 where: (1) the parents had been warned that the child had gone onto the plaintiff's property and thrown objects into a sewer drain; and (2) the child had subsequently committed the same acts, causing serious property damage; however, the property owner may have a cause of action in negligence against the parents. D'Amico v. Burns (Cuyahoga 1984) 13 Ohio App.3d 325, 469 N.E.2d 1016, 13 O.B.R. 402.

Home residents established liability of parents for actions of their minor child under Ohio statute imposing liability when minor "willfully damages" property; evidence that minor was found delinquent of attempted arson, which crime required proof of intent, and unrebutted statements of affiant demonstrated minor's intention to throw Molotov cocktail at residents' home, and use of Molotov cocktail itself demonstrated intention to cause fire damage to home. Byrd v. Brandeburg (N.D.Ohio, 03-18-1996) 922 F.Supp. 60. Parent And Child ⟨⟩ 13.5(2)

Parents who are merely negligent in supervising their children, and in failing to prevent some "willful and malicious injury" by children, are entitled to have any liability arising from such negligent supervision discharged in bankruptcy; "willful and malicious" nature of children's acts is not sufficient to preclude discharge of parents' debt. In re Sintobin (Bkrtcy.N.D.Ohio, 08-08-2000) 253 B.R. 826. Bankruptcy ⟨⟩ 3374(9)

7. Emotional distress damages

Under Ohio parental liability statute, parents of minor defendant who participated in racially-motivated fire bombing of plaintiff's house were liable for property damage caused by incident, but not for plaintiff's emotional distress. Byrd v. Brandeburg (N.D.Ohio, 05-30-1996) 932 F.Supp. 198. Parent And Child ⟨⟩ 13.5(2)

8. Attorney fees

Under Ohio parental liability statute, attorney fees could be collected from parents of minor defendant who participated in racially-motivated bombing of plaintiff's house, where plaintiffs brought action under Fair Housing Act. Byrd v. Brandeburg (N.D.Ohio, 05-30-1996) 932 F.Supp. 198. Civil Rights ⟨⟩ 1480

9. Foster parents negligence

Foster parents of juvenile who shot two people during gas station robbery were not liable in negligence, given absence of evidence that they owed any duty to victims or that they failed to exercise reasonable control over juvenile when they knew or should have known that injury to another was a probable consequence. Cogswell v. Brook (Ohio App. 11 Dist., Geauga, 10-22-2004) No. 2003-G-2511, 2004-Ohio-5639, 2004 WL 2376271, Unreported. Parent And Child ⟨⟩ 15

Foster parents of juvenile who shot two people during gas station robbery did not qualify as "parents," so as to be liable for juvenile's willful conduct. Cogswell v. Brook (Ohio App. 11 Dist., Geauga, 10-22-2004) No. 2003-G-2511, 2004-Ohio-5639, 2004 WL 2376271, Unreported. Parent And Child ⟨⟩ 15

3109.10 Liability of parents for assaults by their children

As used in this section, "parent" has the same meaning as in section 3109.09 of the Revised Code.

Any person is entitled to maintain an action to recover compensatory damages in a civil action, in an amount not to exceed ten thousand dollars and costs of suit in a court of competent jurisdiction, from the parent of a child under the age of eighteen if the child willfully and maliciously assaults the person by a means or force likely to produce great bodily harm. A finding of willful and malicious assault by a means or force likely to produce great bodily harm is not dependent upon a prior finding that the child is a delinquent child.

Any action brought pursuant to this section shall be commenced and heard as in other civil actions for damages.

The monetary limitation upon compensatory damages set forth in this section does not apply to a civil action brought pursuant to section 2307.70 of the Revised Code.

(1996 H 601, eff. 10–29–96; 1995 H 18, eff. 11–24–95; 1990 S 3, eff. 4–11–91; 1986 S 316; 1969 S 11)

Historical and Statutory Notes

Amendment Note: 1996 H 601 inserted the first paragraph; substituted "ten thousand dollars" for "six thousand dollars", deleted "parents who have the parental rights and responsibilities for the care of a child under the age of eighteen, and from any" following "jurisdiction, from the" and "who is the residential parent and legal custodian" preceding "of a child" in the second paragraph; and made other nonsubstantive changes.

Amendment Note: 1995 H 18 substituted "six" for "two", "parent" for "parents", and "custodian" for "custodians"; added "from any parent", "is", and "under the age of eighteen"; and made nonsubstantive changes.

Cross References

Assault, see 2903.11 et seq.
Victims' rights pamphlet, publication and distribution, see 109.42

Library References

Parent and Child ☞13.5(2).
Westlaw Topic No. 285.
C.J.S. Parent and Child §§ 191, 310.

Research References

ALR Library

28 ALR, Federal 2nd Series 179, Claim or Judgment Based on Assault and Battery Other Than Aggravated or Felonious Assault and Battery or Assault or Battery Using Deadly Weapon as Liability for Willful and Malicious Injury Within S523(A)(6) of...

Encyclopedias

OH Jur. 3d Family Law § 225, Assaults.
OH Jur. 3d Family Law § 226, Who is "Parent" Under Statutes.
OH Jur. 3d Family Law § 227, Parental Rights and Responsibilities of Care.
OH Jur. 3d Family Law § 1719, Notification of Victims.

Forms

Ohio Jurisprudence Pleading and Practice Forms § 113:26, Assault of Minor on School Grounds.
Am. Jur. Pl. & Pr. Forms Parent and Child § 107, Introductory Comments.

Treatises and Practice Aids

Sowald & Morganstern, Baldwin's Ohio Practice Domestic Relations Law § 2:16, Capacity to Marry--Legal Age.
Carlin, Baldwin's Ohio Prac. Merrick-Rippner Probate Law § 109:61, Adjudicatory Hearings--Notice to Victims of Crime of Right to Recover Damages and Victim-Impact Statements.
Carlin, Baldwin's Ohio Prac. Merrick-Rippner Probate Law § 110:42, Parental Responsibility--Destructive Acts of Children.
Carlin, Baldwin's Ohio Prac. Merrick-Rippner Probate Law § 109:110, Juvenile Court's Authority Over Parents.
Giannelli & Yeomans, Ohio Juvenile Law § 25:3, Responsibilities to Victims and Others.
Giannelli & Yeomans, Ohio Juvenile Law § 47:2, Jurisdiction Over Parents and Others.
Giannelli & Yeomans, Ohio Juvenile Law § 22:13, Restitution.
Hastings, Manoloff, Sheeran, & Stype, Ohio School Law § 38:12, Parental Liability for Property Damage, Theft, or Assault by Children--Statutory Liability.

Law Review and Journal Commentaries

Statutory Vicarious Parental Liability: Review and Reform, Note. 32 Case W Res L Rev 559 (1982).

Student Misconduct—New Weapons for Schools, Richard J. Dickinson. 8 Baldwin's Ohio Sch L J 29 (July/August 1996).

Notes of Decisions

Act by third person   3
Bankruptcy   8
"Damages" defined   7
Divorced parents   1
Insurance coverage   11
Married child   5
Negligence established   4
Negligence not established   10
"Parent" construed   2
Procedural issues   9
Statute of limitations   6

---

1. Divorced parents

A mother who has custody and control of her seventeen-year-old son is liable for his intentional act of assault and battery arising out of his throwing of a snowball which subsequently hits a person resulting in injury. Labadie v. Semler (Lucas 1990) 66 Ohio App.3d 540, 585 N.E.2d 862.

A father is properly found not to have custody and control of his seventeen-year-old son so as to make him not liable for his son's intentional tort where the evidence shows that (1) the father and mother were divorced, (2) the mother was awarded custody of the son in the divorce proceedings, (3) the father has not lived with the mother and his son for approximately four years, (4) the father did not participate in the disciplining of his son, and (5) the father was not involved in any major decisions made with regard to his son's education. Labadie v. Semler (Lucas 1990) 66 Ohio App.3d 540, 585 N.E.2d 862.

RC 3109.10 does not require a father to submit a legal document to a court showing that he does not have custody of his seventeen-year-old son in an action brought against both him and the child's mother in which an attempt is made to hold them statutorily liable for the intentional acts of their son. Labadie v. Semler (Lucas 1990) 66 Ohio App.3d 540, 585 N.E.2d 862.

2. "Parent" construed

A stepparent, without legal right of custody or obligation of control over a minor, does not constitute a "parent" within the meaning of RC 3109.10. Gosnell v. Middlebrook (Marion 1988) 55 Ohio App.3d 93, 563 N.E.2d 32.

Neither a county children services board nor a foster parent appointed and certified by a county children services board pursuant to RC 5153.16 and accompanying regulations is a "parent" under RC 3109.09 or 3109.10; accordingly, neither the board nor a foster parent is liable under RC 3109.09 or 3109.10 for the willful damage to or theft of property, or willful or malicious assault of a person, committed by a child in their custody. OAG 87–082.

3. Act by third person

Owner of firearm should not be held absolutely liable for any injury that occurs when he permits or leaves firearm accessible to children. Nearor v. Davis (Ohio App. 1 Dist., 03-19-1997) 118 Ohio App.3d 806, 694 N.E.2d 120, appeal not allowed 79 Ohio St.3d 1460, 681 N.E.2d 442. Weapons ☞ 363

A parent is not liable for injuries sustained by a victim of crime where his minor child who is experienced in the handling of firearms lends a firearm to a friend for the stated purpose of lawful hunting but instead the borrower uses the firearm to rob a grocery store and neither the child nor the parent is aware of the borrower's criminal history; in that situation the intervening willful, malicious and criminal act was not intended nor foreseeable by the gun owner. Bilicic v. Brake (Ashtabula 1989) 64 Ohio App.3d 304, 581 N.E.2d 586, motion overruled 49 Ohio St.3d 713, 552 N.E.2d 950.

4. Negligence established

Statutory limitation on a parent's vicarious liability for the torts of his or her children did not apply to claims asserted against father of minor child who was alleged to have sexually assaulted children he was babysitting, where court found that father had acted negligently and wantonly toward plaintiffs, and that father's acts were the direct and proximate cause of injuries for which recovery was sought. Cuervo v. Snell (Ohio App. 10 Dist., 12-01-1998) 131 Ohio App.3d 560, 723 N.E.2d 139, appeal not allowed 85 Ohio St.3d 1460, 708 N.E.2d 1013. Parent And Child ☞ 13.5(4)

Parent's negligent entrustment of gun to child can include not only presenting gun to child, but also having gun accessible to child. Nearor v. Davis (Ohio App. 1 Dist., 03-19-1997) 118 Ohio App.3d 806, 694 N.E.2d 120, appeal not allowed 79 Ohio St.3d 1460, 681 N.E.2d 442. Weapons ☞ 363

Parents of minor child may be liable for torts of child if parents fail to exercise proper parental control over child and parents knew, or should have known, from their knowledge of habits or tendencies of child that failure to exercise such control posed unreasonable risk that child would injure others. Doe v. Kahrs (Ohio Com.Pl., 07-20-1995) 75 Ohio Misc.2d 7, 662 N.E.2d 101. Parent And Child ☞ 13.5(4)

Parents can be held liable for torts of their child when they permit their inexperienced or irresponsible minor child to keep or have access to inherently dangerous instrumentality, under circumstances that should put them on notice that instrumentality may become source of danger to others. Doe v. Kahrs (Ohio Com.Pl., 07-20-1995) 75 Ohio Misc.2d 7, 662 N.E.2d 101. Parent And Child ☞ 13.5(4)

Where parents permit their inexperienced or irresponsible minor child to keep or have access to an inherently dangerous instrumentality, under circumstances which should put them on notice that the instrumentality might become a source of danger to others, reasonable minds could conclude that the parents were negligent in their acquiescence, and that they should be answerable in legal damages for an injury occasioned by the child's use of such instrumentality. McGinnis v. Kinkaid (Cuyahoga 1981) 1 Ohio App.3d 4, 437 N.E.2d 313, 1 O.B.R. 45.

5. Married child

Where a minor child is validly married, has established his own residence apart from his parents, and is self-supporting, he is no longer within the custody and control of his parents for purposes of establishing liability pursuant to RC 3109.10. Albert v. Ellis (Cuyahoga 1978) 59 Ohio App.2d 152, 392 N.E.2d 1309, 13 O.O.3d 188. Parent And Child ☞ 13.5(2)

6. Statute of limitations

The one-year statute of limitation for assault, covered by RC 2305.11, is applicable to RC 3109.10. Liddy v. Smole (Shelby 1978) 56 Ohio App.2d 205, 381 N.E.2d 1335, 10 O.O.3d 203.

7. "Damages" defined

As used in RC 3109.09, the term "damages" is intended to include loss by reason of a theft. Liberty Mut. Ins. Co. v. Davis (Ohio Mun. 1977) 52 Ohio Misc. 26, 368 N.E.2d 336, 6 O.O.3d 108.

8. Bankruptcy

A debt arising from a parent's liability under RC 3109.10 for a willful, malicious assault by his minor child may be discharged in the parent's bankruptcy proceedings, although debts resulting from a willful, malicious injury caused by the debtor cannot be discharged in the debtor's bankruptcy; the minor child's conduct will not be imputed to the parents. In re Whitacre (Bkrtcy.N.D.Ohio 1988) 93 B.R. 584.

9. Procedural issues

Statute which limits a parent's vicarious liability for the torts of his or her children does not protect a parent from liability for his or her own conduct. Cuervo v. Snell (Ohio App. 10 Dist., 12-01-1998) 131 Ohio App.3d 560, 723 N.E.2d 139, appeal not allowed 85 Ohio St.3d 1460, 708 N.E.2d 1013. Parent And Child ☞ 13.5(1)

Claim that judgment entered against defendant in action arising from alleged acts of sexual assault by his minor child while babysitting exceeded statutory limitation on a parent's vicarious liability for assaults by his or her children was waived by defendant's failure to raise issue when court entered the default judgment assessing liability, or when defendant learned that the court had entered a damages judgment against him. Cuervo v. Snell (Ohio App. 10 Dist., 12-01-1998) 131 Ohio App.3d 560, 723 N.E.2d 139, appeal not allowed 85 Ohio St.3d 1460, 708 N.E.2d 1013. Parent And Child 13.5(5)

Minor defendant in tort action is responsible for paying fee of court-appointed guardian ad litem. Thatcher v. Fields (Ohio App. 10 Dist., 01-30-1997) 118 Ohio App.3d 63, 691 N.E.2d 1103. Infants 116

Trial court had no authority to shift, to party that prevailed on his tort claims against minor defendant, the responsibility for paying fee of guardian ad litem appointed to represent minor defendant's interests in tort action. Thatcher v. Fields (Ohio App. 10 Dist., 01-30-1997) 118 Ohio App.3d 63, 691 N.E.2d 1103. Infants 116

Material issue of fact as to whether parents of two minors who allegedly sexually abused another child knew or should have known that at least one of their sons had propensity to engage in aberrant sexual behavior precluded summary judgment for minors' parents in negligent supervision action. Doe v. Kahrs (Ohio Com.Pl., 07-20-1995) 75 Ohio Misc.2d 7, 662 N.E.2d 101. Judgment 181(33)

10. Negligence not established

Father did not have duty to exercise control over his son who was using a water gun at his birthday party, and therefore, father was not liable in negligent supervision action for injuries birthday guests' mother sustained in fall while running to avoid being squirted with water gun by father's son while she was leaving party with her children, even though father saw son point water gun at the mother; son's act was not foreseeable, as son had not been so unruly in past as to put father on notice that son's use of water gun may cause injury to others. Herzberg v. Am. Natl. National Property & Cas. Co. (Ohio App. 10 Dist., Franklin, 12-15-2005) No. 05AP-292, 2005-Ohio-6639, 2005 WL 3435742, Unreported, appeal not allowed 109 Ohio St.3d 1457, 847 N.E.2d 6, 2006-Ohio-2226. Parent And Child 13.5(4)

Parents could not be held liable for negligent supervision of their daughter, who allegedly associated with a violent man and drove getaway car from crime scene, where parents did not provide daughter with a dangerous instrumentality, nor did they consent to her involvement in crime at issue, and they were not on notice of possibility of any criminal activities or vicious propensities of their daughter. Cogswell v. Clark Retail Enterprises, Inc. (Ohio App. 11 Dist., Geauga, 10-22-2004) No. 2003-G-2519, 2004-Ohio-5640, 2004 WL 2376276, Unreported. Parent And Child 13.5(4)

Statute providing that any person is entitled to maintain action to recover compensatory damages in an amount not to exceed $10,000 and costs of suit from parent of a child under age of eighteen if child willfully and maliciously assaults the person by a means or force likely to produce great bodily harm is a "principal offender"-only statute and complicity does not suffice; thus, it did not apply to parents of girl who drove getaway car and who did not personally willfully and maliciously assault plaintiff. Cogswell v. Clark Retail Enterprises, Inc. (Ohio App. 11 Dist., Geauga, 10-22-2004) No. 2003-G-2519, 2004-Ohio-5640, 2004 WL 2376276, Unreported. Parent And Child 13.5(2)

Parents of four-year-old child hit in the eye by a nail failed to establish negligence claim against child who was hammering nail and against his parents; children were engaged in typical backyard play, which was "recreational activity," child who hammered nail acted neither intentionally nor recklessly when nail he was hammering flew out of wood and hit four-year-old child in the eye, and injured child, who stood a few feet away from child hammering nail and watched as he and other boys took turns hammering nails into chair, was a spectator to a recreational activity. Gentry v. Craycraft (Ohio, 02-11-2004) 101 Ohio St.3d 141, 802 N.E.2d 1116, 2004-Ohio-379. Infants 61; Negligence 331; Parent And Child 13.5(2)

Gun being accessible to teenage child does not necessarily constitute danger to others so as to subject parent to liability for negligent entrustment. Nearor v. Davis (Ohio App. 1 Dist., 03-19-1997) 118 Ohio App.3d 806, 694 N.E.2d 120, appeal not allowed 79 Ohio St.3d 1460, 681 N.E.2d 442. Weapons 363

Teenage child's prior instances of misconduct, none of which to parents' knowledge involved firearms, did not make it "foreseeable" that he would fatally shoot his friend with loaded revolver parents had left under their mattress, and thus parents were not liable for negligent entrustment; instances of misconduct included possible involvement in receiving stolen property, possible marijuana use, declining grades at school, disobeying house rule prohibiting visitors when parents were gone, and driving mother's car without her permission and without license or permit. Nearor v. Davis (Ohio App. 1 Dist., 03-19-1997) 118 Ohio App.3d 806, 694 N.E.2d 120, appeal not allowed 79 Ohio St.3d 1460, 681 N.E.2d 442. Weapons 363

Pornographic material was not "dangerous instrumentality," and thus parents of minors who allegedly sexually assaulted minor victim could not be held liable under negligent entrustment claim based on minors' alleged access to such material. Doe v. Kahrs (Ohio Com.Pl., 07-20-1995) 75 Ohio Misc.2d 7, 662 N.E.2d 101. Parent And Child 13.5(4)

Generally, parents cannot be held liable for independent torts of their child unless parents are in some way connected to child's wrongdoing, either actively or passively. Doe v. Kahrs (Ohio Com.Pl.,

07-20-1995) 75 Ohio Misc.2d 7, 662 N.E.2d 101. Parent And Child ⊕ 13.5(2)

Parents cannot be held liable for negligent supervision of their children when parents do not know of children's propensity to engage in sort of conduct that causes plaintiff's injury. Doe v. Kahrs (Ohio Com.Pl., 07-20-1995) 75 Ohio Misc.2d 7, 662 N.E.2d 101. Parent And Child ⊕ 13.5(4)

In absence of any evidence indicating that parents knew or should have known that their son was sexually abusing a minor, parents cannot be held liable for negligent supervision as result of their child's sexually abusing minor plaintiff. Doe v. Kahrs (Ohio Com.Pl., 07-20-1995) 75 Ohio Misc.2d 7, 662 N.E.2d 101. Parent And Child ⊕ 13.5(4)

11. Insurance coverage

Insureds' allegedly negligent supervision of juvenile who murdered his neighbor and their allegedly negligent entrustment of a gun to him were not "occurrences" separate and apart from the underlying intentional tort, and, thus, homeowners' insurance policy provided no liability coverage; the theories were derivative claims arising out of the intentional acts and were not a continuous or repeated exposure to substantially the same general harmful conditions. Offhaus v. Guthrie (Ohio App. 5 Dist., 10-02-2000) 140 Ohio App.3d 90, 746 N.E.2d 685, appeal not allowed 91 Ohio St.3d 1478, 744 N.E.2d 775, reconsideration denied 91 Ohio St.3d 1530, 747 N.E.2d 254. Insurance ⊕ 2275

VISITATION RIGHTS OF RELATIVES

3109.11 Visitation rights of grandparents and other relatives when parent deceased

If either the father or mother of an unmarried minor child is deceased, the court of common pleas of the county in which the minor child resides may grant the parents and other relatives of the deceased father or mother reasonable companionship or visitation rights with respect to the minor child during the child's minority if the parent or other relative files a complaint requesting reasonable companionship or visitation rights and if the court determines that the granting of the companionship or visitation rights is in the best interest of the minor child. In determining whether to grant any person reasonable companionship or visitation rights with respect to any child, the court shall consider all relevant factors, including, but not limited to, the factors set forth in division (D) of section 3109.051 of the Revised Code. Divisions (C), (K), and (L) of section 3109.051 of the Revised Code apply to the determination of reasonable companionship or visitation rights under this section and to any order granting any such rights that is issued under this section.

The remarriage of the surviving parent of the child or the adoption of the child by the spouse of the surviving parent of the child does not affect the authority of the court under this section to grant reasonable companionship or visitation rights with respect to the child to a parent or other relative of the child's deceased father or mother.

If the court denies a request for reasonable companionship or visitation rights made pursuant to this section and the complainant files a written request for findings of fact and conclusions of law, the court shall state in writing its findings of fact and conclusions of law in accordance with Civil Rule 52.

Except as provided in division (E)(6) of section 3113.31 of the Revised Code, if the court, pursuant to this section, grants any person companionship or visitation rights with respect to any child, it shall not require the public children services agency to provide supervision of or other services related to that person's exercise of companionship or visitation rights with respect to the child. This section does not limit the power of a juvenile court pursuant to Chapter 2151. of the Revised Code to issue orders with respect to children who are alleged to be abused, neglected, or dependent children or to make dispositions of children who are adjudicated abused, neglected, or dependent children or of a common pleas court to issue orders pursuant to section 3113.31 of the Revised Code.

(2000 S 180, eff. 3–22–01; 1996 H 274, eff. 8–8–96; 1990 S 3, eff. 4–11–91; 1990 H 15; 1971 H 163)

Historical and Statutory Notes

Amendment Note: 2000 S 180 inserted "or the adoption of the child by the spouse of the surviving parent of the child" in the second paragraph.

Amendment Note: 1996 H 274 added the fourth paragraph; and made changes to reflect gender neutral language.

Cross References

Contempt for failure to comply or interference with visitation order, see 2705.031

County children services boards, powers and duties, see 5153.16

Day care centers, access of parents, see 5104.011

Library References

Child Custody ☞270 to 274, 289.
Westlaw Topic No. 76D.
C.J.S. Divorce § 1015.

Research References

ALR Library

71 ALR 5th 99, Grandparents' Visitation Rights Where Child's Parents Are Living.

69 ALR 5th 1, Grandparents' Visitation Rights Where Child's Parents Are Deceased, or Where Status of Parents is Unspecified.

Encyclopedias

69 Am. Jur. Proof of Facts 3d 281, Grandparent Visitation and Custody Awards.

OH Jur. 3d Family Law § 922, Effect on Grandparent Visitation.

OH Jur. 3d Family Law § 1150, Limitation of Visitation or Parenting Time--Supervision.

OH Jur. 3d Family Law § 1170, Visitation Rights Where Parent is Deceased.

OH Jur. 3d Family Law § 1173, Determination of Child's Best Interests.

OH Jur. 3d Family Law § 1251, Contempt of Court.

Treatises and Practice Aids

Klein, Darling, & Terez, Baldwin's Ohio Practice Civil Practice § 52:4, Findings by the Court--Findings of Fact Required by Statute.

Sowald & Morganstern, Baldwin's Ohio Practice Domestic Relations Law § 18:1, Introduction.

Sowald & Morganstern, Baldwin's Ohio Practice Domestic Relations Law § 18:2, Ohio's Statutory Scheme.

Sowald & Morganstern, Baldwin's Ohio Practice Domestic Relations Law § 18:5, Factors in Determining Visitation and Parenting Time Issues.

Sowald & Morganstern, Baldwin's Ohio Practice Domestic Relations Law § 18:6, Additional Considerations.

Sowald & Morganstern, Baldwin's Ohio Practice Domestic Relations Law § 18:7, Constitutional Considerations.

Sowald & Morganstern, Baldwin's Ohio Practice Domestic Relations Law § 18:8, Visitation by Third Parties in Domestic Relations Actions.

Sowald & Morganstern, Baldwin's Ohio Practice Domestic Relations Law § 18:9, The Impact of Adoption.

Sowald & Morganstern, Baldwin's Ohio Practice Domestic Relations Law § 21:2, Parenting Time--Establishing Visitation Order.

Sowald & Morganstern, Baldwin's Ohio Practice Domestic Relations Law § 21:7, Enforcement of Parenting Time--Comprehensive Parenting Time Order.

Sowald & Morganstern, Baldwin's Ohio Practice Domestic Relations Law § 3:36, Effect of Judgment--Allocation of Parental Rights and Responsibilities, Visitation, and Companionship Rights--Relatives and Nonparents.

Sowald & Morganstern, Baldwin's Ohio Practice Domestic Relations Law § 15:55, Award to Third Party--By the Court--Jurisdiction.

Sowald & Morganstern, Baldwin's Ohio Practice Domestic Relations Law § 18:16, Procedure--Separate Cause of Action for Visitation.

Sowald & Morganstern, Baldwin's Ohio Practice Domestic Relations Law § 18:30, Visitation Provisions--Child of Deceased Parent--Complaint for Visitation--Form.

Sowald & Morganstern, Baldwin's Ohio Practice Domestic Relations Law § 19:14, Parenting Time.

Sowald & Morganstern, Baldwin's Ohio Practice Domestic Relations Law § 21:26, Civil Sanctions.

Carlin, Baldwin's Ohio Prac. Merrick-Rippner Probate Law § 99:3, Jurisdiction.

Carlin, Baldwin's Ohio Prac. Merrick-Rippner Probate Law § 99:8, Suitability of Adoptive Parents--Best Interests of Child.

Carlin, Baldwin's Ohio Prac. Merrick-Rippner Probate Law § 106:4, Constitutional Issues.

Carlin, Baldwin's Ohio Prac. Merrick-Rippner Probate Law § 109:9, Parties to Proceedings.

Carlin, Baldwin's Ohio Prac. Merrick-Rippner Probate Law § 99:21, Types of Placement--Stepparent, Guardian, and Grandparent Adoptions.

Carlin, Baldwin's Ohio Prac. Merrick-Rippner Probate Law § 99:49, Interlocutory and Final Orders.

Carlin, Baldwin's Ohio Prac. Merrick-Rippner Probate Law § 110:15, Visitation Right of Noncustodial Parent and Others.

Adrine & Ruden, Ohio Domestic Violence Law § 12:15, Remedies--Orders Allocating Parental Rights and Responsibilities.

Law Review and Journal Commentaries

The Child's Right to Visit Grandparents, Henry H. Foster and Doris Jonas Freed. 20 Trial (American Trial Lawyers' Assn) 38 (March 1984).

Custodial Rights in Non–Traditional Families. Pamela J. MacAdams, 20 Domestic Rel. J. Ohio 53 (July/August 2008).

Grandparents' Rights in Ohio After H.B. 15, Richard J. Innis. 2 Domestic Rel J Ohio 33 (May/June 1990).

Grandparent Visitation: The Best Interests of the Grandparent, Child, and Society, Erica L. Strawman. 30 U Tol L Rev 31 (Fall 1998).

Grandparents' Visitation Rights in Ohio: A Procedural Quagmire, Comment. 56 U Cin L Rev 295 (1987).

Grandparents' Visitation: Does Troxel v. Grandville Impact Ohio?, Mag. Elaine M. Stoermer. 50 Dayton B Briefs 20 (October 2000).

Is Court-Ordered Non-Parent Visitation in Ohio Unconstitutional in Light of Troxel v. Granville?, Richard L. Innis. 15 Domestic Rel J Ohio 2 (January/February 2003).

Open Adoption: Can Visitation With Natural Family Members Be In The Child's Best Interest?, Note. 30 J Fam L 471 (February 1992).

To grandmother's house we go: Examining Troxel, Harrold, and the future of third-party visitation. 74 U Cin L Rev 1549 (Summer 2006).

Visitation Rights of a Grandparent Over the Objection of a Parent: The Best Interests of the Child, Note. 15 J Fam L 51 (1976–77).

Notes of Decisions

1. Constitutional issues

The constitutional standards, or "standards of legal review," are not different for reviewing a parent's motion for termination of grandparents' visitation as they are for reviewing an original complaint for establishment of grandparents' visitation; in both cases, the best interests of the child are the statutory test. In re Kaiser (Ohio App. 7 Dist., Columbiana, 12-30-2004) No. 04 CO 9, 2004-Ohio-7208, 2004 WL 3090224, Unreported. Child Custody ☞ 579

Troxel v. Granville, which held the State of Washington's nonparental visitation statute unconstitutional as overbroad, did not hold that grandparents' visitation rights, over the objection of a parent, were subject to strict scrutiny and, thus, did not apply to deny grandparents visitation rights, over father's objection. Estate of Harrold v. Collier (Ohio App. 9 Dist., Wayne, 08-18-2004) No. 03CA0064, 2004-Ohio-4331, 2004 WL 1837186, Unreported, stay denied 103 Ohio St.3d 1457, 815 N.E.2d 674, 2004-Ohio-5076, motion to certify allowed 104 Ohio St.3d 1407, 818 N.E.2d 709, 2004-Ohio-6364, appeal allowed 104 Ohio St.3d 1408, 818 N.E.2d 710, 2004-Ohio-6364, affirmed 107 Ohio St.3d 44, 836 N.E.2d 1165, 2005-Ohio-5334, certiorari denied 126 S.Ct. 1474, 547 U.S. 1004, 164 L.Ed.2d 248, on subsequent appeal 2006-Ohio-5634, 2006 WL 3055496, appeal not allowed 113 Ohio St.3d 1441, 863 N.E.2d 658, 2007-Ohio-1266. Child Custody ☞ 286

Court of Appeals' determination that *Troxel v. Granville*, which held the State of Washington's nonparental visitation statute unconstitutional, did not apply to deny grandparents visitation rights, over father's objection, rendered moot grandparents' contentions on appeal that trial court abused its discretion in denying them visitation and that decision denying them visitation was against the manifest weight of the evidence. Estate of Harrold v. Collier (Ohio App. 9 Dist., Wayne, 08-18-2004) No. 03CA0064, 2004-Ohio-4331, 2004 WL 1837186, Unreported, stay denied 103 Ohio St.3d 1457, 815 N.E.2d 674, 2004 Ohio 5076, motion to certify allowed 104 Ohio St.3d 1407, 818 N.E.2d 709, 2004-Ohio-6364, appeal allowed 104 Ohio St.3d 1408, 818 N.E.2d 710, 2004-Ohio-6364, affirmed 107 Ohio St.3d 44, 836 N.E.2d 1165, 2005-Ohio-5334, certiorari denied 126 S.Ct. 1474, 547 U.S. 1004, 164 L.Ed.2d 248, on subsequent appeal 2006-Ohio-5634, 2006 WL 3055496, appeal not allowed 113 Ohio St.3d 1441, 863 N.E.2d 658, 2007-Ohio-1266. Child Custody ☞ 917

Amendments to statutes that created right of grandparent, and other relative, visitation after adoption by stepparent, could not be applied retroactively to children adopted prior to amendments' effective date and, thus, juvenile court did not have authority to grant paternal grandmother and paternal aunt visitation with children after children's father died, and mother's new husband, as stepfather, adopted children; amendments did not include language suggesting they were to be applied retroactively, and adoptive father's duty to support children, and children's right to compel that duty, were vested duties and rights. In re Busdiecker (Ohio App. 12 Dist., Warren, 05-19-2003) No. CA2002-10-104, 2003-Ohio-2556, 2003 WL 21135496, Unreported. Child Custody ☞ 6

Nonparental visitation statutes, which were narrowly tailored to serve state's compelling interest in protecting child's best interest, did not unconstitutionally infringe on father's fundamental right to make decisions concerning care, custody, and control of his child; statutes limited parties who could petition court for visitation, limited application of statutes to cases where there was specified predicate event or condition, and not only allowed trial court to afford parental decisions the requisite special weight, but also allowed court to take into to consideration best interest of child and balance that interest against parent's desires. Harrold v. Collier (Ohio, 10-10-2005) 107 Ohio St.3d 44, 836 N.E.2d 1165, 2005-Ohio-5334, certiorari denied 126 S.Ct. 1474, 547 U.S. 1004, 164 L.Ed.2d 248, on subsequent appeal 2006-Ohio-5634, 2006 WL 3055496, appeal not allowed 113 Ohio St.3d 1441, 863 N.E.2d 658, 2007-Ohio-1266. Child Custody ☞ 4; Child Custody ☞ 270

RC 3109.11, allowing a court to order reasonable companionship and visitation rights with a minor child to relatives of a deceased parent, is not facially unconstitutional. Burton v Jones, Nos. CA86–04–046 and CA86–06–087 (12th Dist Ct App, Butler, 4–27–87).

2. Due process

Grandparent visitation statute and statute referenced in grandparent visitation statute, which enumerated factors for consideration in determining whether to grant grandparent visitation, did not violate father's substantive due process rights as applied to permit maternal grandmother to obtain visitation with children following their mother's death; magistrate accorded special attention and weight to father's wishes and concerns, and magistrate's decision set forth specific findings to support the determination that visitation with maternal grandmother would be in the children's best interest. Crigger v. Crigger (Ohio App. 10 Dist., Franklin, 02-10-2005) No. 04AP-288, 2005-Ohio-519, 2005 WL 314890, Unreported, appeal allowed 106 Ohio St.3d 1411, 830 N.E.2d 345, 2005-Ohio-3154, affirmed 107 Ohio St.3d 100, 836 N.E.2d 1221, 2005-Ohio-5975. Child Custody ☞ 4; Child Custody ☞ 511; Constitutional Law ☞ 4396

Grandparent visitation statute and statute referenced in grandparent visitation statute, which enumerates factors for consideration in determining whether to grant grandparent visitation, did not violate father's substantive due process right, as applied to permit maternal grandmother to obtain visitation with child following mother's death, where trial court afforded father's decision to limit court ordered visitation "special weight," but ultimately decided that grandmother should be granted some visitation rights because it was in child's best interest. Spivey v. Keller (Ohio App. 3 Dist., Allen, 12-13-2004) No. 6-04-09, 2004-Ohio-6667, 2004 WL 2849023, Unreported, appeal allowed 105 Ohio St.3d 1543, 827 N.E.2d 326, 2005-Ohio-2188, affirmed 107 Ohio St.3d 100, 836 N.E.2d 1220, 2005-Ohio-5973, reconsideration denied 108 Ohio St.3d 1418, 841 N.E.2d 321, 2006-Ohio-179. Child Custody ☞ 4; Constitutional Law ☞ 4396

Grandparent visitation statute and statute referenced in grandparent visitation statute, which enumerates factors for consideration in determining whether to grant grandparent visitation, are sufficiently narrowly tailored to promote compelling governmental interest of protecting parents' fundamental right to make decisions concerning child custody and care, and thus, statutes do not on their face violate substantive due process; given range and specificity of statutorily enumerated factors, trial court can not only afford parental decision as to whether to grant grandparent visitation requisite "special weight," but can also take into consideration best interest of child and balance that interest against parent's choice as to grandparent visitation. Spivey v. Keller (Ohio App. 3 Dist., Allen, 12-13-2004) No. 6-04-09, 2004-Ohio-6667, 2004 WL 2849023, Unreported, appeal allowed 105 Ohio St.3d 1543, 827 N.E.2d 326, 2005-Ohio-2188, affirmed 107 Ohio St.3d 100, 836 N.E.2d 1220, 2005-Ohio-5973, reconsideration denied 108 Ohio St.3d 1418, 841 N.E.2d 321, 2006-Ohio-179. Child Custody ☞ 4; Constitutional Law ☞ 4396

Paternal grandparents' due process rights were violated at hearing on guardian ad litem's motion to change paternal grandparents' visitation with children to supervised visitation; paternal grandparents were not given right to rebut allegations of court's witness that children were exposed to unsafe conditions at paternal grandparents' residence, and paternal grandparents were not given opportunity to present evidence. In re Byerly (Ohio App. 11 Dist., Portage, 02-06-2004) No. 2001-P-0158, No. 2001-P-0159, 2004-Ohio-523, 2004 WL 231804, Unreported. Child Custody ☞ 650; Constitutional Law ☞ 4396

Award of visitation to child's paternal grandparents, over express contrary desire of child's mother, was unconstitutional infringement on mother's fundamental due process right to make decisions concerning child's care, custody and control, in absence of any evidence or argument that grandparents' petition arose out of desire to prevent actual or potential harm to child, that mother was unfit parent, or that grandparents had functioned as de facto parents, where grandparents' expressed desire to allow child to have relationship with her father's family did not reflect compelling reason to interfere with mother's fundamental right to care and control. Oliver v. Feldner (Ohio App. 7 Dist., 06-21-2002) 149 Ohio App.3d 114, 776 N.E.2d 499, 2002-Ohio-3209. Child Custody ☞ 286; Constitutional Law ☞ 4396

Nonparental visitation statutes impinged upon fundamental due process right of parents to make decisions concerning care, custody and control of their children, and were thus subject to review under strict scrutiny test in mother's challenge to award of visitation to child's paternal grandparents. Oliver v. Feldner (Ohio App. 7 Dist., 06-21-2002) 149 Ohio App.3d 114, 776 N.E.2d 499, 2002-Ohio-3209. Constitutional Law ☞ 4396

There are at least two hurdles of constitutional due process analysis which must be overcome for a nonparental visitation order to be valid: the first hurdle addresses whether there are compelling and narrowly tailored reasons for a court to be hearing the visitation case at all; the second hurdle addresses whether there are compelling and narrowly tailored reasons for the court to impose a specific visitation order on the parents. Oliver v. Feldner (Ohio App. 7 Dist., 06-21-2002) 149 Ohio App.3d 114, 776 N.E.2d 499, 2002-Ohio-3209. Constitutional Law ☞ 4396

3. Legislative intent

In examining the language of statute granting parents and "other relatives of the deceased father or mother" reasonable companionship or visitation rights with respect to deceased parent's minor child, court had to look at the intent of the legislature when they drafted the statute; in any situation in which children are involved, the legislature acts with the best interests of the child in mind. In re R.V. (Ohio App. 2 Dist., 10-15-2010) 190 Ohio App.3d 313, 941 N.E.2d 1216, 2010 Ohio 5050. Child Custody ☞ 271; Infants ☞ 4

4. Best interest of child

Paternal grandmother was a "relative" of grandchildren's deceased mother and, therefore, was entitled, following mother's death, to seek visitation with grandchildren under statute granting the parents and "other relatives of the deceased father or mother" reasonable companionship or visitation rights with respect to deceased parent's minor child; legislature recognized that, in some situations, a child of the deceased mother may have developed stronger emotional ties with the father's parents than with the deceased mother's parents and that it would be in the child's best interest to continue that relationship with visitation. In re R.V. (Ohio App. 2 Dist., 10-15-2010) 190 Ohio App.3d 313, 941 N.E.2d 1216, 2010 -Ohio- 5050. Child Custody ☞ 289

Trial court properly placed burden of proving that visitation would be in the best interest of minor child on maternal grandparents and gave due deference to father's wishes and concerns regarding visitation before determining that it was in child's best interest to grant motion for grandparent visitation, even though trial court did not use the words "special weight" in considering father's wishes. Harrold v. Collier (Ohio, 10-10-2005) 107 Ohio St.3d 44, 836 N.E.2d 1165, 2005-Ohio-5334, certiorari denied 126 S.Ct. 1474, 547 U.S. 1004, 164 L.Ed.2d 248, on subsequent appeal 2006 Ohio 5634, 2006 WL 3055496, appeal not allowed 113 Ohio St.3d 1441, 863 N.E.2d 658, 2007-Ohio-1266. Child Custody ☞ 452; Child Custody ☞ 471; Child Custody ☞ 473

Trial court in proceeding in which maternal grandmother sought visitation privileges with granddaughter did not abuse its discretion in compelling father who had custody of child to tell child about her mother's death from a drug overdose; it was in child's best interest to know what happened to her mother and such information was best learned from concerned parent rather than from some other source, such as siblings. Holley v. Higgins (Franklin 1993) 86 Ohio App.3d 240, 620 N.E.2d 251. Child Custody ☞ 100

Maternal grandparents may be granted visitation rights, pursuant to RC 3109.11, where the children's father consents to an adoption of the children by their paternal grandparents. The court shall consider the best interest of the children when considering such a request. In re Pennington (Scioto 1988) 55 Ohio App.3d 99, 562 N.E.2d 905.

Grandparents may be granted visitation rights under RC 3109.11 and 3109.05(B) if the trial court finds that such visitation is in the child's best interest. In re Whitaker (Ohio 1988) 36 Ohio St.3d 213, 522 N.E.2d 563.

The companionship and visitation rights vested by RC 3109.11 are neither absolute nor unqualified but are conditioned upon the finding by the proper court that such rights are in the best interest of the child. Graziano v. Davis (Mahoning 1976) 50 Ohio App.2d 83, 361 N.E.2d 525, 4 O.O.3d 55.

The companionship and visitation rights of relatives granted in RC 3109.11 are subservient to the best interests of the minor child. In re Griffiths (Mahoning 1975) 47 Ohio App.2d 238, 353 N.E.2d 884, 1 O.O.3d 307.

In general, the visitation and companionship of a child's grandparents are in a child's best interests, and so where a thirteen year old child, rightly or wrongly, resents or dislikes his grandparents to such a degree that court enforced association cannot be reasonably expected to modify his attitude toward them and can only result in an intensification of his resentment and dislike, the usual benefits of visitation and the necessary elements of companionship do not exist and the best interests of the child require the court to deny visitation rights to such grandparents. In re Griffiths (Mahoning 1975) 47 Ohio App.2d 238, 353 N.E.2d 884, 1 O.O.3d 307.

The companionship and visitation rights vested by RC 3109.11 are neither absolute nor unqualified but are conditioned upon the finding by a court of competent jurisdiction that such rights are in the best interests of the child. In re Griffiths (Mahoning 1975) 47 Ohio App.2d 238, 353 N.E.2d 884, 1 O.O.3d 307. Child Custody ☞ 271

5. Factors

Great aunt and uncle failed to satisfy statutory requirements for non-parent visitation rights as to minor children; statutes required either that parent be deceased or that child have been born to unmarried woman or that visitation be sought in divorce or annulment proceeding, and neither child's mother nor father were deceased, mother was married at the time child was born, and great aunt and uncle sought visitation rights in a dependency action commenced by County Children Services in juvenile court. In re E.H. (Ohio App. 9 Dist., Lorain, 04-27-2005) No. 04CA008585, 2005-Ohio-1952, 2005 WL 956967, Unreported. Infants ☞ 222

Evidence in proceeding on father's motion to terminate visitation rights previously granted to his son's maternal grandparents failed to support juvenile court's finding that father was an unfit parent, even assuming for the sake of argument that the accusations in his motion were incorrect and his motivations were wholly selfish for seeking to terminate grandparents' visitation; there were absolutely no allegations that father was unfit, and, in fact, grandparents admitted he was a good father. In re Kaiser (Ohio App. 7 Dist., Columbiana, 12-30-2004) No. 04 CO 9, 2004-Ohio-7208, 2004 WL 3090224, Unreported. Child Custody ☞ 641

Following mother's death, granting maternal grandmother visitation with grandchild pursuant to grandparent visitation statute was not abuse of discretion, where trial court carefully reviewed and applied statutorily enumerated factors for consideration in determining whether to grant grandparent visitation and court found that father's concerns regarding visitation went to nature, quality, and duration of grandparent visitation, rather than to its prohibition. Spivey v. Keller (Ohio App. 3 Dist., Allen, 12-13-2004) No. 6-04-09, 2004-Ohio-6667, 2004 WL 2849023, Unreported, appeal allowed 105 Ohio St.3d 1543, 827 N.E.2d 326, 2005-Ohio-2188, affirmed 107 Ohio St.3d 100, 836 N.E.2d 1220, 2005-Ohio-5973, reconsideration denied 108 Ohio St.3d 1418, 841 N.E.2d 321, 2006-Ohio-179. Child Custody ☞ 289

The trial court was required to consider the statutory factors for determining whether to grant paternal grandparents companionship or visitation with out-of-wedlock grandchild, who was the child of their deceased son, before ruling on the issue; the statute did not require a finding that a child was "delinquent, neglected, or abused or that a parent was unfit" before determining whether to grant companionship or visitation to a relative, and statute allowed the court to grant a relative companionship or visitation with a child after the child's parent died if the relative filed a complaint for visitation and the court found that granting companionship rights or visitation was in the best interests of child. In re Talkington (Ohio App. 5 Dist., Stark, 08-09-2004) No. 2003CA00226, 2004-Ohio-4215, 2004 WL 1784603, Unreported. Children Out-of-wedlock ☞ 20.3

Juvenile court's finding, in proceeding brought by paternal grandmother and paternal aunt for visitation with children following death of children's father, that mother and father were never married did not require reversal of juvenile court's denial of visitation, even though mother stated in her affidavit that she was married to children's father, and magistrate had found mother and father were married, where father's paternity was not disputed, his paternal rights had never been terminated prior to his death, and finding of marriage was not germane to ultimate issue of whether statutes on visitation by persons other than parents applied retroactively. In re Busdiecker (Ohio App. 12 Dist., Warren, 05-19-2003) No. CA2002-10-104, 2003-Ohio-2556, 2003 WL 21135496, Unreported. Child Custody ☞ 922(6)

Grandparents are not statutorily entitled to visitation of their grandchildren and a court must consider the factors enumerated in RC 3109.11 as well as the best interest and wishes of the children;

consequent denial of visitation to a grandmother is neither an automatic ground for reversal nor an abuse of discretion. In Matter of Skinner (Jennifer, Brittany) (Ohio App. 4 Dist., Adams, 03-23-1994) No. 93CA547, 1994 WL 93149, Unreported.

Due process requirement that a court considering a request for nonparental visitation rights give the wishes of the child's parent "special weight" means that the deference provided to the parent's wishes will only be overcome by some compelling governmental interest and overwhelmingly clear circumstances supporting that governmental interest. Oliver v. Feldner (Ohio App. 7 Dist., 06-21-2002) 149 Ohio App.3d 114, 776 N.E.2d 499, 2002-Ohio-3209. Constitutional Law ☞ 4396

The factors set forth in RC 3109.04(C) with respect to determining the child's best interest in custody cases apply equally to visitation cases. The trial court must weigh these and other relevant factors in determining the child's best interest in visitation cases. In re Whitaker (Ohio 1988) 36 Ohio St.3d 213, 522 N.E.2d 563. Child Custody ☞ 178

6. Adoption

Trial court lacked authority to grant paternal grandparents visitation with children of divorced parents after the children were adopted by their stepfather subsequent to their father's death; while a statute preserved the right of grandparent visitation when a surviving spouse remarried, it did not provide for the preservation of visitation rights after an adoption by a stepparent. Foor v. Foor (Ohio App. 12 Dist., 04-26-1999) 133 Ohio App.3d 250, 727 N.E.2d 618. Child Custody ☞ 313

Statute providing that marriage of the surviving parent of child does not affect authority of court to grant reasonable companionship or visitation rights to grandparents preserves the right of grandparent visitation when the surviving spouse remarries, but it does not provide for the preservation of grandparent visitation rights after adoption of child by stepparent. Beard v. Pannell (Ohio App. 6 Dist., 04-26-1996) 110 Ohio App.3d 572, 674 N.E.2d 1225, appeal not allowed 77 Ohio St.3d 1447, 671 N.E.2d 1285. Child Custody ☞ 284; Child Custody ☞ 313

Where a child's parent dies, the surviving parent remarries, and the surviving parent's new spouse adopts the child, a court may grant visitation rights to relatives of the deceased parent pursuant to RC 3109.11 over the objections of the child's parents, notwithstanding RC 3107.15. In re Thornton (Franklin 1985) 24 Ohio App.3d 152, 493 N.E.2d 977, 24 O.B.R. 241.

The power of the court to order visitation and companionship rights to relatives under RC 3109.11 is not divested or terminated by the adoption of the child of a deceased parent by a stepparent, pursuant to RC 3107.13, and such adoption is merely a factor which the court must consider in determining the best interest of the child under RC 3109.11.

Graziano v. Davis (Mahoning 1976) 50 Ohio App.2d 83, 361 N.E.2d 525, 4 O.O.3d 55.

A relative does not have a preferential right over a pre-adoptive parent in determining who should adopt a child. In re Dickhaus (Ohio Com.Pl. 1974) 41 Ohio Misc. 1, 321 N.E.2d 800, 70 O.O.2d 24.

Trial court has no authority to grant visitation rights to paternal grandparents where the relationship between the father and child has been terminated pursuant to RC 3107.07. In re Adoption of Bitner, No. 81–CA–77 (7th Dist Ct App, Mahoning, 2–24–82).

7. Rights of child

If one parent of an unmarried minor child is deceased, RC 3109.11 vests in the relatives of the deceased parent reasonable companionship and visitation rights to the child during its minority, and vests in the child the right to the companionship and visitation of its relatives. Graziano v. Davis (Mahoning 1976) 50 Ohio App.2d 83, 361 N.E.2d 525, 4 O.O.3d 55. Child Custody ☞ 271

If the father or mother of an unmarried minor child is deceased, RC 3109.11 vests in the relatives of the deceased person reasonable companionship and visitation rights to the minor child during the minority and vests in the minor child the right to the companionship and visitation of its relatives. In re Griffiths (Mahoning 1975) 47 Ohio App.2d 238, 353 N.E.2d 884, 1 O.O.3d 307. Child Custody ☞ 271

8. Procedural issues

Trial court that awarded custody of minor child to biological father was not required to award visitation to deceased mother's surviving husband, to whom mother was married at time she gave birth to child, even though surviving husband had custody of child for first 11 years of child's life, where surviving husband did not file a complaint requesting reasonable visitation or companionship. Lorence v. Goeller (Ohio App. 9 Dist., Lorain, 06-01-2005) No. 04CA008556, 2005-Ohio-2678, 2005 WL 1283713, Unreported. Children Out–of–wedlock ☞ 20.4

Father, who filed a motion to terminate visitation rights previously granted to his son's maternal grandparents, was not required to show a change in circumstances before being entitled to relief. In re Kaiser (Ohio App. 7 Dist., Columbiana, 12-30-2004) No. 04 CO 9, 2004-Ohio-7208, 2004 WL 3090224, Unreported. Child Custody ☞ 579

Trial court did not lose jurisdiction over child custody dispute between maternal and paternal grandparents following dismissal of guardian ad litem's motion to change paternal grandparents' visitation with children to supervised visitation; court retained continuing and exclusive jurisdiction of custody matters. In re Byerly (Ohio App. 11 Dist., Portage, 02-06-2004) No. 2001-P-0158, No. 2001-P-0159, 2004-Ohio-523, 2004 WL 231804, Unreported. Child Custody ☞ 601

Paternal grandparents had right to take deposition of children's psychologist regarding guardian ad litem's motion to change paternal grandparents' visitation with children to supervised visitation; psychologist was only witness called at hearing; and paternal grandparents were entitled to opportunity to dispose a key witness. In re Byerly (Ohio App. 11 Dist., Portage, 02-06-2004) No. 2001-P-0158, No. 2001-P-0159, 2004-Ohio-523, 2004 WL 231804, Unreported. Child Custody ☞ 617

In responding to objection of children's psychologist to turning over his files to paternal grandparents regarding guardian ad litem's motion to change paternal grandparents' visitation with children to supervised visitation, trial court did not abuse its discretion by vacating order requiring disclosure of files and by requiring psychologist to create statement containing summary of files and to file document under seal with court, which would then allow only attorneys to review document. In re Byerly (Ohio App. 11 Dist., Portage, 02-06-2004) No. 2001-P-0158, No. 2001-P-0159, 2004-Ohio-523, 2004 WL 231804, Unreported. Child Custody ☞ 617

Trial court acted within its discretion when it quashed paternal grandparents' subpoena duces tecum for production of children's school records regarding guardian ad litem's motion to change paternal grandparents' visitation with children to supervised visitation; it was within trial court's discretion to determine if school records should be disclosed. In re Byerly (Ohio App. 11 Dist., Portage, 02-06-2004) No. 2001-P-0158, No. 2001-P-0159, 2004-Ohio-523, 2004 WL 231804, Unreported. Privileged Communications And Confidentiality ☞ 410

Trial court did not abuse its discretion when it denied paternal grandparents the opportunity to depose maternal grandparents concerning guardian ad litem's motion to change paternal grandparents' visitation with children to supervised visitation; maternal grandparents did not file motion. In re Byerly (Ohio App. 11 Dist., Portage, 02-06-2004) No. 2001-P-0158, No. 2001-P-0159, 2004-Ohio-523, 2004 WL 231804, Unreported. Child Custody ☞ 617

Following trial court's decision that denied guardian ad litem's motion to change paternal grandparents' visitation with children to supervised visitation but that imposed condition that paternal grandparents seek and maintain counseling, trial court was required to allow paternal grandparents to proffer evidence supporting their defense to preserve issue for review. In re Byerly (Ohio App. 11 Dist., Portage, 02-06-2004) No. 2001-P-0158, No. 2001-P-0159, 2004-Ohio-523, 2004 WL 231804, Unreported. Child Custody ☞ 659; Child Custody ☞ 904

Absent complaint requesting visitation by maternal grandparents, trial court in child custody modification proceeding involving natural father and grandparents was without authority to order visitation rights to grandparents. Harrold v. Collier (Ohio App. 9 Dist., Wayne, 07-31-2002) No. 02CA0005, 2002-Ohio-3864, 2002 WL 1758392, Unreported. Child Custody ☞ 609

3109.12   Visitation rights of grandparents and other relatives when child's mother unmarried

(A) If a child is born to an unmarried woman, the parents of the woman and any relative of the woman may file a complaint requesting the court of common pleas of the county in which the child resides to grant them reasonable companionship or visitation rights with the child. If a child is born to an unmarried woman and if the father of the child has acknowledged the child and that acknowledgment has become final pursuant to section 2151.232, 3111.25, or 3111.821 of the Revised Code or has been determined in an action under Chapter 3111. of the Revised Code to be the father of the child, the father may file a complaint requesting that the court of appropriate jurisdiction of the county in which the child resides grant him reasonable parenting time rights with the child and the parents of the father and any relative of the father may file a complaint requesting that the court grant them reasonable companionship or visitation rights with the child.

(B) The court may grant the parenting time rights or companionship or visitation rights requested under division (A) of this section, if it determines that the granting of the parenting time rights or companionship or visitation rights is in the best interest of the child. In determining whether to grant reasonable parenting time rights or reasonable companionship or visitation rights with respect to any child, the court shall consider all relevant factors, including, but not limited to, the factors set forth in division (D) of section 3109.051 of the Revised Code. Divisions (C), (K), and (L) of section 3109.051 of the Revised Code apply to the determination of reasonable parenting time rights or reasonable companionship or visitation rights under this section and to any order granting any such rights that is issued under this section.

The marriage or remarriage of the mother or father of a child does not affect the authority of the court under this section to grant the natural father reasonable parenting time rights or the parents or relatives of the natural father or the parents or relatives of the mother of the child reasonable companionship or visitation rights with respect to the child.

If the court denies a request for reasonable parenting time rights or reasonable companionship or visitation rights made pursuant to division (A) of this section and the complainant files a written request for findings of fact and conclusions of law, the court shall state in writing its findings of fact and conclusions of law in accordance with Civil Rule 52.

Except as provided in division (E)(6) of section 3113.31 of the Revised Code, if the court, pursuant to this section, grants parenting time rights or companionship or visitation rights with respect to any child, it shall not require the public children services agency to provide supervision of or other services related to that parent's exercise of parenting time rights with the child or that person's exercise of companionship or visitation rights with the child. This section does not limit the power of a juvenile court pursuant to Chapter 2151. of the Revised Code to issue orders with respect to children who are alleged to be abused, neglected, or dependent children or to make dispositions of children who are adjudicated abused, neglected, or dependent children or of a common pleas court to issue orders pursuant to section 3113.31 of the Revised Code.

(2000 S 180, eff. 3–22–01; 1997 H 352, eff. 1–1–98; 1996 H 274, eff. 8–8–96; 1990 S 3, eff. 4–11–91; 1990 H 15)

Historical and Statutory Notes

Amendment Note: 2000 S 180 rewrote this section which prior thereto read:

"(A) If a child is born to an unmarried woman, the parents of the woman and any relative of the woman may file a complaint requesting the court of common pleas of the county in which the child resides to grant them reasonable companionship or visitation rights with the child. If a child is born to an unmarried woman and if the father of the child has acknowledged the child and that acknowledgment has become final pursuant to section 2151.232, 3111.211, or 5101.314 of the Revised Code or has been determined in an action under Chapter 3111. of the Revised Code to be the father of the child, the father, the parents of the father, and any relative of the father may file a complaint requesting the court of common pleas of the county in which the child resides to grant them reasonable companionship or visitation rights with respect to the child.

"(B) The court may grant the companionship or visitation rights requested under division (A) of this section, if it determines that the granting of the companionship or visitation rights is in the best interest of the child. In determining whether to grant any person reasonable companionship or visitation rights with respect to any child, the court shall consider all relevant factors, including, but not limited to, the factors set forth in division (D) of section 3109.051 of the Revised Code. Divisions (C), (K), and (L) of section 3109.051 of the Revised Code apply to the determination of reasonable companionship or visitation rights under this section and to any order granting any such rights that is issued under this section.

"The marriage or remarriage of the mother or father of a child does not affect the authority of the court under this section to grant the natural father, the parents or relatives of the natural father, or the parents or relatives of the mother of the child reasonable companionship or visitation rights with respect to the child.

"If the court denies a request for reasonable companionship or visitation rights made pursuant to division (A) of this section and the complainant files a written request for findings of fact and conclusions of law, the court shall state in writing its findings of fact and conclusions of law in accordance with Civil Rule 52.

"Except as provided in division (E)(6) of section 3113.31 of the Revised Code, if the court, pursuant to this section, grants any person companionship or visitation rights with respect to any child, it shall not require the public children services agency to provide supervision of or other services related to that person's exercise of companionship or visitation rights with respect to the child. This section does not limit the power of a juvenile court pursuant to Chapter 2151. of the Revised Code to issue orders with respect to children who are alleged to be abused, neglected, or dependent children or to make dispositions of children who are adjudicated abused, neglected, or dependent children or of a common pleas court to issue orders pursuant to section 3113.31 of the Revised Code.

Amendment Note: 1997 H 352 inserted "and that acknowledgment has become final" and substituted "2151.232, 3111.211, or 5101.314" for "2105.18" in division (A).

Amendment Note: 1996 H 274 added the fourth paragraph in division (B).

Cross References

Contempt for failure to comply or interference with visitation order, see 2705.031

County children services boards, powers and duties, see 5153.16

Day care centers, access of parents, see 5104.011

Parent and child relationship, effect of judgment determining, see 3111.13

Library References

Children Out-of-Wedlock ☞20.9.
Westlaw Topic No. 76H.

Research References

ALR Library

80 ALR 5th 1, Child Custody and Visitation Rights Arising from Same-Sex Relationship.

71 ALR 5th 99, Grandparents' Visitation Rights Where Child's Parents Are Living.

Encyclopedias

69 Am. Jur. Proof of Facts 3d 281, Grandparent Visitation and Custody Awards.

OH Jur. 3d Family Law § 905, Intervention by Third Party.

OH Jur. 3d Family Law § 1027, Requirements of Support Orders.

OH Jur. 3d Family Law § 1053, by Child's Relatives.

OH Jur. 3d Family Law § 1150, Limitation of Visitation or Parenting Time--Supervision

OH Jur. 3d Family Law § 1151, Denial of Visitation.

OH Jur. 3d Family Law § 1171, Visitation Rights Where Mother is Unmarried.

Forms

Ohio Forms Legal and Business § 28:6, Form Drafting Principles.

Ohio Jurisprudence Pleading and Practice Forms § 111:12, Judgment.

Treatises and Practice Aids

Klein, Darling, & Terez, Baldwin's Ohio Practice Civil Practice § 52:4, Findings by the Court--Findings of Fact Required by Statute.

Sowald & Morganstern, Baldwin's Ohio Practice Domestic Relations Law § 3:8, Jurisdiction and Venue.

Sowald & Morganstern, Baldwin's Ohio Practice Domestic Relations Law § 18:1, Introduction.

Sowald & Morganstern, Baldwin's Ohio Practice Domestic Relations Law § 18:2, Ohio's Statutory Scheme.

Sowald & Morganstern, Baldwin's Ohio Practice Domestic Relations Law § 18:5, Factors in Determining Visitation and Parenting Time Issues.

Sowald & Morganstern, Baldwin's Ohio Practice Domestic Relations Law § 18:6, Additional Considerations.

Sowald & Morganstern, Baldwin's Ohio Practice Domestic Relations Law § 18:7, Constitutional Considerations.

Sowald & Morganstern, Baldwin's Ohio Practice Domestic Relations Law § 18:8, Visitation by Third Parties in Domestic Relations Actions.

Sowald & Morganstern, Baldwin's Ohio Practice Domestic Relations Law § 18:9, The Impact of Adoption.

Sowald & Morganstern, Baldwin's Ohio Practice Domestic Relations Law § 21:2, Parenting Time--Establishing Visitation Order.

Sowald & Morganstern, Baldwin's Ohio Practice Domestic Relations Law § 21:7, Enforcement of Parenting Time--Comprehensive Parenting Time Order.

Sowald & Morganstern, Baldwin's Ohio Practice Domestic Relations Law § 3:36, Effect of Judgment--Allocation of Parental Rights and Responsibilities, Visitation, and Companionship Rights--Relatives and Nonparents.

Sowald & Morganstern, Baldwin's Ohio Practice Domestic Relations Law § 15:55, Award to Third Party--By the Court--Jurisdiction.

Sowald & Morganstern, Baldwin's Ohio Practice Domestic Relations Law § 18:16, Procedure--Separate Cause of Action for Visitation.

Sowald & Morganstern, Baldwin's Ohio Practice Domestic Relations Law § 18:31, Visitation Provisions--Child of Unmarried Mother--Venue Note.

Sowald & Morganstern, Baldwin's Ohio Practice Domestic Relations Law § 18:32, Visitation Provisions--Child of Unmarried Mother--Complaint for Visitation--Form.

Sowald & Morganstern, Baldwin's Ohio Practice Domestic Relations Law § 19:14, Parenting Time.

Sowald & Morganstern, Baldwin's Ohio Practice Domestic Relations Law § 21:26, Civil Sanctions.

Carlin, Baldwin's Ohio Prac. Merrick-Rippner Probate Law § 19:2, Legitimation--Procedure--Acknowledgment of Paternity.

Carlin, Baldwin's Ohio Prac. Merrick-Rippner Probate Law § 106:4, Constitutional Issues.

Carlin, Baldwin's Ohio Prac. Merrick-Rippner Probate Law § 109:9, Parties to Proceedings.

Carlin, Baldwin's Ohio Prac. Merrick-Rippner Probate Law § 99:21, Types of Placement--Stepparent, Guardian, and Grandparent Adoptions.

Carlin, Baldwin's Ohio Prac. Merrick-Rippner Probate Law § 99:49, Interlocutory and Final Orders.

Carlin, Baldwin's Ohio Prac. Merrick-Rippner Probate Law § 110:13, Jurisdiction Over Child Custody Matters--Determination of Custody.

Carlin, Baldwin's Ohio Prac. Merrick-Rippner Probate Law § 110:15, Visitation Right of Noncustodial Parent and Others.

Carlin, Baldwin's Ohio Prac. Merrick-Rippner Probate Law § 110:20, Parentage Act--Jurisdiction and Venue.

Carlin, Baldwin's Ohio Prac. Merrick-Rippner Probate Law § 110:29, Parentage Act--Judgment Determining Existence of Parent-Child Relationship.

Carlin, Baldwin's Ohio Prac. Merrick-Rippner Probate Law § 110:31, Parentage Act--Continuing Jurisdiction to Modify or Revoke Judgment.

Adrine & Ruden, Ohio Domestic Violence Law § 12:15, Remedies--Orders Allocating Parental Rights and Responsibilities.

Law Review and Journal Commentaries

Custodial Rights in Non–Traditional Families. Pamela J. MacAdams, 20 Domestic Rel. J. Ohio 53 (July/August 2008).

Grandparents' Rights in Ohio After H.B. 15, Richard J. Innis. 2 Domestic Rel J Ohio 33 (May/June 1990).

Grandparents' Visitation: Does Troxel v. Grandville Impact Ohio?, Mag. Elaine M. Stoermer. 50 Dayton B Briefs 20 (October 2000).

Is Court-Ordered Non-Parent Visitation in Ohio Unconstitutional in Light of Troxel v. Granville?, Richard L. Innis. 15 Domestic Rel J Ohio 2 (January/February 2003).

To grandmother's house we go: Examining Troxel, Harrold, and the future of third-party visitation. 74 U Cin L Rev 1549 (Summer 2006).

Notes of Decisions

Adjudicated father   6
Constitutional issues   1-2
  Due process   1
  Equal protection   2
Due process, constitutional issues   1
Equal protection, constitutional issues   2
Father, generally   5
Grandparents   3
Procedural issues   8
Statutory factors   7
Visitation rights of unrelated former partner of parent   4

––––––––––

1. Constitutional issues—Due process

Visitation statute which allows grandparents of child born to unmarried woman to seek visitation

rights with child did not violate due process clause on its face, where statute expressly identified parents' wishes and concerns regarding visitation as a factor trial court had to consider in making its determination. In re Washington (Ohio App. 10 Dist., Franklin, 12-21-2004) No. 04AP-429, 2004-Ohio-6981, 2004 WL 2944166, Unreported. Children Out–of–wedlock ⊙ 20.9; Constitutional Law ⊙ 4396

Visitation statute, which allows grandparents of child born to unmarried woman to seek visitation rights with child, was not unconstitutional under due process clause as applied to mother, although mother claimed it was unconstitutional as applied to her when trial court failed to give any special weight to her wishes regarding visitation, where mother did not appear at hearing, and she did not express her wishes concerning visitation with grandmother. In re Washington (Ohio App. 10 Dist., Franklin, 12-21-2004) No. 04AP-429, 2004-Ohio-6981, 2004 WL 2944166, Unreported. Children Out–of–wedlock ⬦ 20.9; Constitutional Law ⬦ 4396

Court of Appeals' determination that *Troxel v. Granville*, which held the State of Washington's nonparental visitation statute unconstitutional, did not apply to deny grandparents visitation rights, over father's objection, rendered moot grandparents' contentions on appeal that trial court abused its discretion in denying them visitation and that decision denying them visitation was against the manifest weight of the evidence. Estate of Harrold v. Collier (Ohio App. 9 Dist., Wayne, 08-18-2004) No. 03CA0064, 2004-Ohio-4331, 2004 WL 1837186, Unreported, stay denied 103 Ohio St.3d 1457, 815 N.E.2d 674, 2004-Ohio-5076, motion to certify allowed 104 Ohio St.3d 1407, 818 N.E.2d 709, 2004-Ohio-6364, appeal allowed 104 Ohio St.3d 1408, 818 N.E.2d 710, 2004-Ohio-6364, affirmed 107 Ohio St.3d 44, 836 N.E.2d 1165, 2005-Ohio-5334, certiorari denied 126 S.Ct. 1474, 547 U.S. 1004, 164 L.Ed.2d 248, on subsequent appeal 2006-Ohio-5634, 2006 WL 3055496, appeal not allowed 113 Ohio St.3d 1441, 863 N.E.2d 658, 2007-Ohio-1266. Child Custody ⬦ 917

Troxel v. Granville, which held the State of Washington's nonparental visitation statute unconstitutional as overbroad, did not hold that grandparents' visitation rights, over the objection of a parent, were subject to strict scrutiny and, thus, did not apply to deny grandparents visitation rights, over father's objection. Estate of Harrold v. Collier (Ohio App. 9 Dist., Wayne, 08-18-2004) No. 03CA0064, 2004-Ohio-4331, 2004 WL 1837186, Unreported, stay denied 103 Ohio St.3d 1457, 815 N.E.2d 674, 2004-Ohio-5076, motion to certify allowed 104 Ohio St.3d 1407, 818 N.E.2d 709, 2004-Ohio-6364, appeal allowed 104 Ohio St.3d 1408, 818 N.E.2d 710, 2004-Ohio-6364, affirmed 107 Ohio St.3d 44, 836 N.E.2d 1165, 2005-Ohio-5334, certiorari denied 126 S.Ct. 1474, 547 U.S. 1004, 164 L.Ed.2d 248, on subsequent appeal 2006-Ohio-5634, 2006 WL 3055496, appeal not allowed 113 Ohio St.3d 1441, 863 N.E.2d 658, 2007-Ohio-1266. Child Custody ⬦ 286

Due process requirement that a court considering a request for nonparental visitation rights give the wishes of the child's parent "special weight" means that the deference provided to the parent's wishes will only be overcome by some compelling governmental interest and overwhelmingly clear circumstances supporting that governmental interest. Oliver v. Feldner (Ohio App. 7 Dist., 06-21-2002) 149 Ohio App.3d 114, 776 N.E.2d 499, 2002-Ohio-3209. Constitutional Law ⬦ 4396

Award of visitation to child's paternal grandparents, over express contrary desire of child's mother, was unconstitutional infringement on mother's fundamental due process right to make decisions concerning child's care, custody and control, in absence of any evidence or argument that grandparents'

petition arose out of desire to prevent actual or potential harm to child, that mother was unfit parent, or that grandparents had functioned as de facto parents, where grandparents' expressed desire to allow child to have relationship with her father's family did not reflect compelling reason to interfere with mother's fundamental right to care and control. Oliver v. Feldner (Ohio App. 7 Dist., 06-21-2002) 149 Ohio App.3d 114, 776 N.E.2d 499, 2002-Ohio-3209. Child Custody ⬦ 286; Constitutional Law ⬦ 4396

Nonparental visitation statutes impinged upon fundamental due process right of parents to make decisions concerning care, custody and control of their children, and were thus subject to review under strict scrutiny test in mother's challenge to award of visitation to child's paternal grandparents. Oliver v. Feldner (Ohio App. 7 Dist., 06-21-2002) 149 Ohio App.3d 114, 776 N.E.2d 499, 2002-Ohio-3209. Constitutional Law ⬦ 4396

There are at least two hurdles of constitutional due process analysis which must be overcome for a nonparental visitation order to be valid: the first hurdle addresses whether there are compelling and narrowly tailored reasons for a court to be hearing the visitation case at all; the second hurdle addresses whether there are compelling and narrowly tailored reasons for the court to impose a specific visitation order on the parents. Oliver v. Feldner (Ohio App. 7 Dist., 06-21-2002) 149 Ohio App.3d 114, 776 N.E.2d 499, 2002-Ohio-3209. Constitutional Law ⬦ 4396

2. —— Equal protection, constitutional issues

Nonparental visitation statutes, which were narrowly tailored to serve state's compelling interest in protecting child's best interest, did not unconstitutionally infringe on father's fundamental right to make decisions concerning care, custody, and control of his child; statutes limited parties who could petition court for visitation, limited application of statutes to cases where there was specified predicate event or condition, and not only allowed trial court to afford parental decisions the requisite special weight, but also allowed court to take into to consideration best interest of child and balance that interest against parent's desires. Harrold v. Collier (Ohio, 10-10-2005) 107 Ohio St.3d 44, 836 N.E.2d 1165, 2005 Ohio 5334, certiorari denied 126 S.Ct. 1474, 547 U.S. 1004, 164 L.Ed.2d 248, on subsequent appeal 2006-Ohio-5634, 2006 WL 3055496, appeal not allowed 113 Ohio St.3d 1441, 863 N.E.2d 658, 2007-Ohio-1266. Child Custody ⬦ 4; Child Custody ⬦ 270

RC 3109.12 violates the Equal Protection Clause in a parties' complaint to establish visitation with their minor half sister who is born to their unmarried mother, who, after the birth, marries the child's natural father; application of RC 3109.12 would result in distinguishing between a child born prior to the marriage of the natural parents and a child born to the same parents after their marriage. Nicoson v Hacker, No. 2000–L–213, 2000 WL 1602666 (11th Dist Ct App, Lake, 12–14–01).

3. Grandparents

Mother of two children born out of wedlock failed to preserve for appellate review her contention that magistrate erred by failing to consider, in granting grandparent visitation to children's paternal grandmother, an alleged motion made by grandmother on behalf of paternal father to be allowed to take children to visit father in prison, where there was no such motion in trial court record. In re Newsome (Ohio App. 11 Dist., Ashtabula, 05-02-2008) No. 2007-A-0030, 2008-Ohio-2132, 2008 WL 1934428, Unreported. Children Out–of–wedlock ☞ 20.11

Evidence was sufficient to support magistrate's finding, as adopted by trial court, that it was in the best interest of two children born out of wedlock to permit paternal grandmother's visitation, even though children's mother was opposed to the visitation; children's father was prohibited by protective court order from seeing the children and as a result children did not have contact with paternal relatives, and grandmother was close to the children prior to the time other ceased to permit visitation. In re Newsome (Ohio App. 11 Dist., Ashtabula, 05-02-2008) No. 2007-A-0030, 2008-Ohio-2132, 2008 WL 1934428, Unreported. Children Out–of–wedlock ☞ 20.9

Juvenile court's decision to grant visitation rights with unmarried mother's minor child to child's maternal grandmother was neither an abuse of discretion nor against the manifest weight of the evidence, despite mother's wishes to the contrary; court noted grandmother's strong, positive bond with child, and her daily care of the child since his birth, and the court also noted that the guardian ad litem recommended that the child's best interests would be served by an award of visitation rights to his grandmother. In re J.F. (Ohio App. 8 Dist., Cuyahoga, 09-15-2005) No. 85242, 2005-Ohio-4816, 2005 WL 2240946, Unreported. Children Out–of–wedlock ☞ 20.9

Consent order between unwed mother and father establishing mother as residential parent and establishing father's visitation, in which mother agreed that paternal grandparents could babysit child during father's visitation time when father worked, and in which parties stipulated that grandparents would not file motion for grandparent visitation unless and until mother failed to abide by terms of consent order, did not create obligation to mother to have grandparents babysit at any other time, and thus, grandparent's remedy for mother's alleged refusal to comply with consent order was not for father to file motion for contempt against mother, but for grandparents to file motion for grandparent visitation. In re Street (Ohio App. 7 Dist., Belmont, 08-25-2005) No. 05 BE 2, 2005-Ohio-4469, 2005 WL 2065120, Unreported. Children Out–of–wedlock ☞ 20.9

Grandparents' visitation rights are granted where the mother's marriage to the biological father after the child is born coupled with the establishment of paternity after the marriage does not vest the parties with the right of parental autonomy which does not apply to a mother and father who have not been married throughout the child's lifetime. Stout v. Kline (Ohio App. 5 Dist., Richland, 03-28-1997) No. 96-CA-71, 1997 WL 219099, Unreported.

Child's step-grandmother had standing to intervene in complaint filed by her son seeking visitation rights with child borne to mother, who was married to son, under statute governing nonparental visitation rights, providing that, if child is born to unmarried woman, the woman's parents and any relative of woman may file complaint for visitation, as the term "relative" included those persons related by affinity, mother was unmarried at time of child's birth, but married son thereafter, and, thus, step-grandmother, as mother's mother-in-law, was a relative by affinity. McFall v. Watson (Ohio App. 4 Dist., 10-02-2008) 178 Ohio App.3d 540, 899 N.E.2d 158, 2008-Ohio-5204. Child Custody ☞ 283; Child Custody ☞ 409

Trial court's order in paternal grandmother's action, against mother, seeking visitation with grandchild, which order denied mother's motion to dismiss and/or for judgment on the pleadings, based on lack of subject matter jurisdiction, was not a final order that was immediately appealable. Digiantonio v. Turnmire (Ohio App. 5 Dist., 11-19-2007) 173 Ohio App.3d 665, 880 N.E.2d 109, 2007-Ohio-6178. Child Custody ☞ 902

Trial court properly placed burden of proving that visitation would be in the best interest of minor child on maternal grandparents and gave due deference to father's wishes and concerns regarding visitation before determining that it was in child's best interest to grant motion for grandparent visitation, even though trial court did not use the words "special weight" in considering father's wishes. Harrold v. Collier (Ohio, 10-10-2005) 107 Ohio St.3d 44, 836 N.E.2d 1165, 2005-Ohio-5334, certiorari denied 126 S.Ct. 1474, 547 U.S. 1004, 164 L.Ed.2d 248, on subsequent appeal 2006-Ohio-5634, 2006 WL 3055496, appeal not allowed 113 Ohio St.3d 1441, 863 N.E.2d 658, 2007-Ohio-1266. Child Custody ☞ 452; Child Custody ☞ 471; Child Custody ☞ 473

Putative paternal grandparents were not qualified to seek court-ordered right to visit their putative biological grandchild, until alleged paternity of grandchild was established by putative father filing legitimation petition or by paternity action to determine if putative father was father of child. In re Martin (Ohio, 02-09-1994) 68 Ohio St.3d 250, 626 N.E.2d 82. Children Out–of–wedlock ☞ 20.4

Even if putative father was father of child, putative paternal grandparents were not entitled to court-ordered right to visit child who had been adopted by maternal grandparents, as statute which provides that adoption of child terminates all legal relationships between adopted child and his relatives does not distinguish between adoption by strangers and nonstrangers. In re Martin (Ohio, 02-09-1994) 68 Ohio St.3d 250, 626 N.E.2d 82. Children Out–of–wedlock ☞ 20.9

In general, grandparental visitation rights do not vest until occurrence of disruptive precipitating event, such as parental death or divorce; absent disruptive event, common-law view of deferring to parental autonomy in raising child is observed despite moral or social obligations that encourage contact between grandparents and grandchildren. In re Gibson (Ohio 1991) 61 Ohio St.3d 168, 573 N.E.2d 1074. Child Custody ☞ 285; Child Custody ☞ 289

Absent complaint requesting visitation by maternal grandparents, trial court in child custody modification proceeding involving natural father and grandparents was without authority to order visitation rights to grandparents. Harrold v. Collier (Ohio App. 9 Dist., Wayne, 07-31-2002) No. 02CA0005, 2002-Ohio-3864, 2002 WL 1758392, Unreported. Child Custody ☞ 609

Trial court was warranted in relying on the best interest test of the minor child, rather than giving deference to mother's determination that non-parent visitation and companionship were not in the best interest of the minor child, in deliberating on mother's motion to terminate paternal grandparents' visitation, where initial judgment entry filed in response to complaint for visitation was a consent order reached by agreement of the mother and grandparents, leaving no need for trial court to make any findings pursuant to the statute governing visitation rights of grandparents, and thus, sole issue before the trial court at termination hearing was whether the visitation should be terminated, not whether it should have been granted originally. Buehrer v. Lambert (Ohio App. 3 Dist., Henry, 06-18-2002) No. 7-02-03, 2002-Ohio-2980, 2002 WL 1371062, Unreported. Child Custody ☞ 579

4. Visitation rights of unrelated former partner of parent

After separation of lesbian couple, non-parent partner had standing to apply to juvenile court for visitation or other parental rights with respect to two children conceived through anonymous artificial insemination and born to mother-partner during partners' committed relationship. In re LaPiana (Ohio App. 8 Dist., Cuyahoga, 08-05-2010) No. 93691, No. 93692, 2010-Ohio-3606, 2010 WL 3042394, Unreported. Children Out of wedlock ☞ 15; Children Out-of-wedlock ☞ 20.9

After separation of lesbian couple, juvenile court had subject matter jurisdiction to determine whether mother-partner, who conceived two children through anonymous artificial insemination during partners' committed relationship, had contractually relinquished sole custody of the children to non parent partner in favor of shared custody, whether it would be in children's best interest to have companionship with non-parent partner, and what that companionship should entail. In re LaPiana (Ohio App. 8 Dist., Cuyahoga, 08-05-2010) No. 93691, No. 93692, 2010-Ohio-3606, 2010 WL 3042394, Unreported. Children Out-of-wedlock ☞ 15; Children Out-of-wedlock ☞ 20.4

Some evidence supported finding that mother-partner, to whom two children were born during lesbian committed relationship with non-parent partner, contractually relinquished sole custody of the children to non-parent partner, in favor of shared custody; mother and partner deliberately planned to have children together during their ten-year relationship, they chose the anonymous donor together, children were given partner's surname, everyone knew the partner as the children's mother, and before birth of first child the mother and the partner entered into written "Agreement to Jointly Raise Our Child" in which they agreed to "jointly and equally parent" and agreed that if they separated, they would share in child's upbringing and the partner with actual physical custody would take all steps necessary to maximize the other's visitation and help make visitation as easy as possible. In re LaPiana (Ohio App. 8 Dist., Cuyahoga, 08-05-2010) No. 93691, No. 93692, 2010-Ohio-3606, 2010 WL 3042394, Unreported. Children Out-of-wedlock ☞ 15; Children Out-of-wedlock ☞ 20.8

Trial court's determination that, six years after separation of lesbian couple, it would be in children's best interests to have companionship with non-parent partner, was not an abuse of discretion, with respect to two children conceived through anonymous artificial insemination of mother-partner and born during partners' ten-year committed relationship; for about five years after separation, mother and partner fully cooperated with each other, took turns picking the children up from school, alternated weekends and holidays with the children, planned and shared children's birthday parties, were flexible on schedules if the other partner had a conflict, and discussed and planned summer camp options for the children, and guardian ad litem testified that the children considered both partners to be their mother and that it would be "devastating" to the children if non-parent was no longer in their lives. In re LaPiana (Ohio App. 8 Dist., Cuyahoga, 08-05-2010) No. 93691, No. 93692, 2010-Ohio-3606, 2010 WL 3042394, Unreported. Children Out-of-wedlock ☞ 15; Children Out-of-wedlock ☞ 20.3

The Defense of Marriage Amendment to the Ohio Constitution did not prohibit a trial court from granting non-parent partner, after separation from mother-partner with whom non-parent had been in a lesbian committed relationship, companionship with two children conceived through anonymous artificial insemination of mother-partner and born during partners' ten-year committed relationship. In re LaPiana (Ohio App. 8 Dist., Cuyahoga, 08-05-2010) No. 93691, No. 93692, 2010-Ohio-3606, 2010 WL 3042394, Unreported. Children Out-of-wedlock ☞ 15; Children Out-of-wedlock ☞ 20.3; Marriage ☞ 54(2)

Step-parent who enjoyed neither an adoptive nor biological relationship with child was nevertheless a relative by affinity who had standing to seek visitation with child; biological mother was unmarried at the time of the child's birth, and, according to statute governing non-parental visitation rights, step-parent, as her husband, was a relative by affinity. McFall v. Watson (Ohio App. 4 Dist., Vinton, 10-02-2008) No. 08CA667, 2008-Ohio-5205, 2008 WL 4456957, Unreported. Child Custody ☞ 272

A partner in a lesbian relationship does not have an obligation to pay child support insofar as she is not the biological, natural or adoptive mother of her partner's child and her attempt to file a child support proceeding in order to claim visitation rights pursuant to RC 3109.051 must fail. Liston v Pyles, No. 97APF01–137, 1997 WL 467327 (10th Dist Ct App, Franklin, 8–12–97).

5. Father, generally

Magistrate's failure to qualify child's counselor as expert witness did not prejudice mother of non-marital child and thus did not amount to reversible error in father's action to establish parent-child relationship; counselor testified at length concerning her treatment of child and gave her opinion as to whether child displayed characteristics of child who was sexually abused, father did not object to any of counselor's testimony that child had suffered trauma and that child's regressive behaviors and emotional outbursts correlated to times when he had regular visitation with father, and magistrate did not attempt to prevent any of mother's questions to counselor. Morehart v. Snider (Ohio App. 9 Dist., Summit, 10-28-2009) No. 24640, 2009-Ohio-5674, 2009 WL 3465746, Unreported. Children Out–of–wedlock ☞ 20.11

Juvenile court acted within its discretion in granting father, a nonresidential parent, standard parenting time with child, who was born out of wedlock; father testified that he and his other two children lived with mother and child for an extended period of time following child's birth, that he supported child during that time by adding the child to his health insurance plan and providing her with clothing, food, and money, and that mother had refused to allow him to see or speak with child despite his numerous requests to do so. Otten v. Tuttle (Ohio App. 12 Dist., Clermont, 06-29-2009) No. CA2008-05-053, 2009-Ohio-3158, 2009 WL 1845249, Unreported. Children Out–of–wedlock ☞ 20.9

The trial court's failure to provide father with child's current address in its parenting order was not an abuse of discretion; the court, after conducting an in camera interview with 16-year-old child, decided to allow child to determine the amount and timing of visitation, child explicitly stated that he did not want to burden his mother with transporting him to the prison, where father was incarcerated, to see father, and that he wanted to wait to visit father until after he obtained his driver's license. In re Frank Brown (Ohio App. 3 Dist., Seneca, 05-11-2009) No. 13-08-46, 2009-Ohio-2192, 2009 WL 1272642, Unreported. Child Custody ☞ 204

Individual, who was involved in romantic relationship with mother at time of child's birth, had standing to seek companionship and visitation with child; individual did not lack standing merely because he was not biological father, individual was

granted, by agreed, temporary judgment entry, parenting time with child, and individual acknowledged paternity of child by filing an affidavit with Central Paternity Registry and was under an administrative support order. Waszkowski v. Lyons (Ohio App. 11 Dist., Lake, 01-30-2009) No. 2008-L-077, 2009-Ohio-403, 2009 WL 224540, Unreported. Children Out–of–wedlock ☞ 20.4

Great aunt and uncle failed to satisfy statutory requirements for non-parent visitation rights as to minor children; statutes required either that parent be deceased or that child have been born to unmarried woman or that visitation be sought in divorce or annulment proceeding, and neither child's mother nor father were deceased, mother was married at the time child was born, and great aunt and uncle sought visitation rights in a dependency action commenced by County Children Services in juvenile court. In re E.H. (Ohio App. 9 Dist., Lorain, 04-27-2005) No. 04CA008585, 2005-Ohio-1952, 2005 WL 956967, Unreported. Infants ☞ 222

After Human Leukocyte Antigen (HLA) tests conclusively excluded plaintiff as father, there was no basis for permitting juvenile court to grant plaintiff visitation rights, where plaintiff had not acknowledged his paternity with probate court following child's birth. Sherburn v. Reichert (Ohio App. 3 Dist., 10-13-1994) 97 Ohio App.3d 120, 646 N.E.2d 255. Children Out–of–wedlock ☞ 20.9

Termination of incarcerated father's contact with his three children until further order of court was not an abuse of discretion; father failed to file a complaint prior to hearing on motion to terminate, he had notice of hearing, and he was not represented by counsel at hearing, thus giving court no evidence before it that might have supported an order allowing contact, family's caseworker recommended that father have supervised visitation upon release from prison, and guardian ad litem recommended no contact until his release. In re Danielle G. (Ohio App. 6 Dist., Lucas, 09-06-2002) No. L-02-1071, 2002-Ohio-4651, 2002 WL 31002748, Unreported. Infants ☞ 155

6. Adjudicated father

Trial court did not abuse its discretion in awarding adjudicated father of child born out-of-wedlock parenting time with child, which consisted of Monday and Wednesday nights from 6:00 p.m. to 8:00 p.m., Fridays during the day from 9:00 a.m. to 3:30 p.m., and alternating weekends beginning on Fridays at 9:00 a.m., and ending on Sundays at 1:00 p.m., without designating a holiday parenting time schedule, but specifying holiday visitation as the parties agree, as parties kept the same work schedule, with father having Fridays off, thus freeing him to spend time with child every Friday, and record demonstrated that parties were willing to and, in fact, had agreed to holiday visitation in the past. Pahl v. Haugh (Ohio App. 3 Dist., Hancock, 03-21-2011) No. 5-10-27, 2011-Ohio-1302, 2011 WL 947016, Unreported. Children Out–of–wedlock ☞ 20.9

Assuming that adjudicated father's petition for modification of his child support obligation was properly before Juvenile Court, fact that such petition was pending did not vest Juvenile Court with jurisdiction to entertain paternal grandmother's petition for grandparental visitation pursuant to domestic relations statute, where statute setting forth Juvenile Court's jurisdiction in parentage actions did not reference domestic relations statute, and where child's mother was unmarried. Borkosky v. Mihailoff (Ohio App. 3 Dist., 03-03-1999) 132 Ohio App.3d 508, 725 N.E.2d 694. Children Out–of–wedlock ⇝ 20.9

Juvenile court of county other than that of child's residence lacked jurisdiction to entertain paternal grandmother's motion for grandparental visitation, where child's mother was unmarried and child's paternity had been established through adjudication. Borkosky v. Mihailoff (Ohio App. 3 Dist., 03-03-1999) 132 Ohio App.3d 508, 725 N.E.2d 694. Child Custody ⇝ 404

7. Statutory factors

Trial court did not abuse its discretion in deviating from the standard order of visitation to grant additional visitation rights to father of child born out-of-wedlock; court retained the discretion to deviate from standard parenting guidelines using the statutory factors for determining visitation. Evangelista v. Horton (Ohio App. 7 Dist., Mahoning, 03-22-2011) No. 08 MA 244, 2011-Ohio-1472, 2011 WL 1118474, Unreported. Children Out–of–wedlock ⇝ 20.9

8. Procedural issues

The trial court's entry of parenting time order as to out-of-wedlock child, without conducting a hearing on the issue, was an abuse of discretion; statutes required that the court consider the best interest of the child, along with certain other issues, including regular, holiday, and vacation time, prior to entering a parenting time order, and the record failed to establish what factors the court considered before it rendered a decision. Jefferson County Child Support Enforcement ex rel. Best v. Scheel (Ohio App. 7 Dist., Jefferson, 06-17-2004) No. 03 JE 35, 2004 Ohio 3210, 2004 WL 1379821, Unreported. Children Out–of–wedlock ⇝ 20.4

The burden of proof that visitation would not be in the child's best interest is on the person opposing visitation and there is no requirement to show a change of circumstances in any request to change visitation rights. Matter of Nichols (Ohio App. 12 Dist., Clermont, 06-08-1998) No. CA97-11-102, 1998 WL 295937, Unreported, dismissed, appeal not allowed 84 Ohio St.3d 1406, 701 N.E.2d 1018.

PREVENTION OF CHILD ABUSE AND CHILD NEGLECT

Cross References

"Abused child," defined, see 2151.031
Child abuse and domestic violence, criminal sanctions, see 2919.22 to 2919.271
Department of human services, division of social administration; care and placement of children, see 5103.12 to 5103.17
Estate taxes, deduction for bequest for prevention of cruelty to children, see 5731.17
Guardian ad litem for abused and neglected children, see 2151.281

Injury or neglect of child, persons required to report, see 2151.421
Neglect, abandonment, or domestic violence, see 3113.01 et seq.
Powers and duties of county children services board, see 5153.16
Protective services for children, see 5101.46

3109.13 Child abuse or neglect prevention programs defined

As used in sections 3109.13 to 3109.18 of the Revised Code:

(A) "Child abuse and child neglect prevention programs" means programs that use primary and secondary prevention strategies that are conducted at the local level and activities and projects of statewide significance designed to strengthen families and prevent child abuse and child neglect.

(B) "Primary prevention strategies" are activities and services provided to the public designed to prevent or reduce the prevalence of child abuse and child neglect before signs of abuse or neglect can be observed.

(C) "Secondary prevention strategies" are activities and services that are provided to a specific population identified as having risk factors for child abuse and child neglect and are designed to intervene at the earliest warning signs of child abuse or child neglect, or whenever a child can be identified as being at risk of abuse or neglect.

(2002 S 121, eff. 3–19–03; 2002 H 248, eff. 4–7–03; 1999 H 283, eff. 1–1–01; 1984 H 319, eff. 12–26–84)

Historical and Statutory Notes

◆**Ed. Note:** The amendment of this section by 2002 S 121, eff. 3–19–03, and 2002 H 248, eff. 4–7–03, was identical. See *Baldwin's Ohio Legislative Service Annotated*, 2002, pages 12/L–2259 and 12/L–2961, or the OH–LEGIS or OH–LEGIS–OLD database on Westlaw, for original versions of these Acts.

Amendment Note: 2002 S 121 rewrote this section, which prior thereto read:

"As used in sections 3109.13 to 3109.18 of the Revised Code, child abuse and child neglect prevention programs means programs designed to prevent child abuse and child neglect, including, but not limited to, any of the following:

"(A) Public awareness programs that pertain to child abuse or child neglect;

"(B) Community–based, family-focused support services and activities that do any of the following:

"(1) Build parenting skills;

"(2) Promote parental behaviors that lead to healthy and positive personal development of parents and children;

"(3) Promote individual, family, and community strengths;

"(4) Provide information, education, or health activities that promote the well-being of families and children.

"(C) Programs that train and place volunteers in programs that pertain to child abuse or child neglect."

Amendment Note: 1999 H 283 rewrote the section, which prior thereto read:

"As used in sections 3109.13 to 3109.18 of the Revised Code, 'child abuse and child neglect prevention programs' means programs designed to prevent child abuse and child neglect, including, but not limited to, any of the following:

"(A) Community–based public awareness programs that pertain to child abuse or child neglect;

"(B) Community–based educational programs that pertain to prenatal care, perinatal bonding, child development, basic child care, care of children with special needs, or coping with family stress;

"(C) Community–based programs that relate to care and treatment in child abuse or child neglect crisis situations; aid to parents who potentially may abuse or neglect their children; child abuse or child neglect counseling; support groups for parents who potentially may abuse or neglect their children, and support groups for their children; or early identification of families in which there is a potential for child abuse or child neglect;

"(D) Programs that train and place volunteers in programs that pertain to child abuse or child neglect;

"(E) Programs that may develop and make available to boards of education curricula and educational materials on basic child care and parenting skills, or programs that would provide both teacher and volunteer training programs."

Ohio Administrative Code References

Child abuse and neglect, supportive services, see OAC Ch 5101:2–39

Library References

Infants ⚷17.
Westlaw Topic No. 211.

C.J.S. Adoption of Persons §§ 10 to 14, 41.
C.J.S. Infants §§ 6, 8 to 9.

Research References

Encyclopedias

OH Jur. 3d Family Law § 1399, Powers and Duties Exercised by Department of Job and Family Services; Generally.

3109.14 Additional fees for birth and death records; children's trust fund

(A) As used in this section, "birth record" and "certification of birth" have the meanings given in section 3705.01 of the Revised Code.

(B)(1) The director of health, a person authorized by the director, a local commissioner of health, or a local registrar of vital statistics shall charge and collect a fee for each certified copy of a birth record, for each certification of birth, and for each copy of a death record. The fee shall be three dollars. The fee is in addition to the fee imposed by section 3705.24 or any other section of the Revised Code. A local commissioner of health or a local registrar of vital statistics may retain an amount of each additional fee collected, not to exceed three per cent of the amount of the additional fee, to be used for costs directly related to the collection of the fee and the forwarding of the fee to the treasurer of state. The additional fees collected, but not retained, under division (B)(1) of this section shall be forwarded to the treasurer of state not later than thirty days following the end of each quarter.

(2) Upon the filing for a divorce decree under section 3105.10 or a decree of dissolution under section 3105.65 of the Revised Code, a court of common pleas shall charge and collect a fee. The fee shall be eleven dollars. The fee is in addition to any other court costs or fees. The county clerk of courts may retain an amount of each additional fee collected, not to exceed three per cent of the amount of the additional fee, to be used for costs directly related to the collection of the fee and the forwarding of the fee to the treasurer of state. The additional fees collected, but not retained, under division (B)(2) of this section shall be forwarded to the treasurer of state not later than twenty days following the end of each month.

(C) The treasurer of state shall deposit the fees forwarded under this section in the state treasury to the credit of the children's trust fund, which is hereby created. A person or government entity that fails to forward the fees in a timely manner, as determined by the treasurer of state, shall forward to the treasurer of state, in addition to the fees, a penalty equal to ten per cent of the fees.

The treasurer of state shall invest the moneys in the fund, and all earnings resulting from investment of the fund shall be credited to the fund, except that actual administrative costs incurred by the treasurer of state in administering the fund may be deducted from the earnings resulting from investments. The amount that may be deducted shall not exceed three per cent of the total amount of fees credited to the fund in each fiscal year, except that the children's trust fund board may approve an amount for actual administrative costs exceeding three per cent but not exceeding four per cent of such amount. The balance of the investment earnings shall be credited to the fund. Moneys credited to the fund shall be used only for the purposes described in sections 3109.13 to 3109.18 of the Revised Code.

(2006 H 530, eff. 6–30–06; 2001 H 94, eff. 9–5–01; 1999 H 283, eff. 1–1–01; 1998 H 426, eff. 7–22–98; 1988 H 790, eff. 3–16–89; 1985 H 201; 1984 H 319)

Historical and Statutory Notes

Amendment Note: 2006 H 530 substituted "the" for "Until October 1, 2001, the fee shall be two dollars. On and after October 1, 2001, the" after "copy of a death record." in division (B)(1); substituted "The" for "Until October 1, 2001, the fee shall be ten dollars. On and after October 1, 2001, the" in division (B)(2); added the last sentence in both division (B)(1) and (B)(2); and rewrote the first sentence of division (C), which prior thereto read:

"The additional fees collected, but not retained, under this section during each month shall be forwarded not later than the tenth day of the immediately following month to the treasurer of state, who shall deposit the fees in the state treasury to the credit of the children's trust fund, which is hereby created."

Amendment Note: 2001 H 94 rewrote divisions (A) and (B) which prior thereto read:

"(A) As used in this section, birth record and certification of birth have the meanings given in section 3705.01 of the Revised Code.

"(B)(1) The director of health, a person authorized by the director, a local commissioner of health, or a local registrar of vital statistics shall charge and collect for each certified copy of a birth record and for each certification of birth a fee of two dollars, and for each copy of a death record a fee of two dollars, in addition to the fee imposed by section

3705.24 or any other section of the Revised Code. A local commissioner of health or a local registrar of vital statistics may retain an amount of each additional fee collected, not to exceed three per cent of the amount of the additional fee, to be used for costs directly related to the collection of the fee and the forwarding of the fee to the treasurer of state.

"(2) Upon the filing for a divorce decree under section 3105.10 or a decree of dissolution under section 3105.65 of the Revised Code, a court of common pleas shall charge and collect a fee of ten dollars in addition to any other court costs or fees. The county clerk of courts may retain an amount of each additional fee collected, not to exceed three per cent of the amount of the additional fee, to be used for costs directly related to the collection of the fee and the forwarding of the fee to the treasurer of state."

Amendment Note: 1999 H 283 designated divisions (A), (B)(1), (B)(2), and (C); inserted "certified" in division (B)(1), substituted "tenth" for "twentieth" and added the second sentence in the first paragraph in division (C); and substituted "3109.13 to 3109.18" for "3109.17 and 3109.18" in the second paragraph in division (C).

Amendment Note: 1998 H 426 substituted "collected" for "that he collects" in the second and third paragraphs; and substituted "twentieth" for "fifth" in the fourth paragraph.

Cross References

Fees and costs, common pleas courts, see 2746.04
Heirloom certifications of birth, fee, see 3705.24

Information supplied from public records, see 3705.23

Library References

Clerks of Courts ☞21.
Health ☞397, 398.
States ☞127.

Westlaw Topic Nos. 79, 198H, 360.
C.J.S. Health and Environment §§ 24, 74.
C.J.S. States §§ 386 to 387.

Research References

Encyclopedias

OH Jur. 3d Family Law § 1399, Powers and Duties Exercised by Department of Job and Family Services; Generally.

Notes of Decisions

Procedure 1

___

1. Procedure

The fees collected by the appropriate clerks of court pursuant to 1984 H 319, eff. 12–26–84, and 1984 S 219, eff. 1–8–85, are to be collected only in cases filed subsequent to the effective dates of those acts. OAG 85–057.

The fee collected pursuant to RC 3109.14 by the county clerk of courts " [u]pon the filing for a divorce decree... or a decree of dissolution" is to be collected upon the filing of the complaint for divorce or the petition for dissolution. OAG 85–057.

The fee collected by the county clerk of courts pursuant to RC 3109.14 must be forwarded to the treasurer of state, irrespective of the subsequent dismissal of the action which generated the fee; further, the fee must be forwarded to the treasurer of state not later than the fifth day of the month immediately following the month in which the fee is collected. OAG 85–057.

3109.15 Children's trust fund board

There is hereby created within the department of job and family services the children's trust fund board consisting of fifteen members. The directors of alcohol and drug addiction services, health, and job and family services shall be members of the board. Eight public members shall be appointed by the governor. These members shall be persons with demonstrated knowledge in programs for children, shall be representative of the demographic composition of this state, and, to the extent practicable, shall be representative of the following categories: the educational community; the legal community; the social work community; the medical community; the voluntary sector; and professional providers of child abuse and child neglect services. Five of these members shall be residents of metropolitan statistical areas as defined by the United States office of management and budget where the population exceeds four hundred thousand; no two such members shall be residents of the same metropolitan statistical area. Two members of the board shall be members of the house of representatives appointed by the speaker of the house of representatives and shall be members of two different political parties. Two members of the board shall be members of the senate appointed by the president of the senate and shall be members of two different political parties. All members of the board appointed by the speaker of the house of representatives or the president of the senate shall serve until the expiration of the sessions of the general assembly during which they were appointed. They may be reappointed to an unlimited number of successive terms of two years at the pleasure of the speaker of the house of representatives or president of the senate. Public members shall serve terms of three years. Each member shall serve until the member's successor is appointed, or until a period of sixty days has elapsed, whichever occurs first. No public member may serve more than two consecutive full terms. All vacancies on the board shall be filled for the balance of the unexpired term in the same manner as the original appointment.

Any member of the board may be removed by the member's appointing authority for misconduct, incompetency, or neglect of duty after first being given the opportunity to be heard in the member's own behalf. Pursuant to section 3.17 of the Revised Code, a member, except a member of the general assembly or a judge of any court in the state, who fails to attend at least three-fifths of the regular and special meetings held by the board during any two-year period forfeits the member's position on the board.

Each member of the board shall serve without compensation but shall be reimbursed for all actual and necessary expenses incurred in the performance of official duties.

At the beginning of the first year of each even-numbered general assembly, the chairperson of the board shall be appointed by the speaker of the house of representatives from among members of the board who are members of the house of representatives. At the beginning of the first year of each odd-numbered general assembly, the chairperson of the board shall be appointed by the president of the senate from among the members of the board who are senate members.

The board shall biennially select a vice-chair from among its nonlegislative members.

(2002 S 121, eff. 3–19–03; 2002 H 248, eff. 4–7–03; 1999 H 471, § 3, eff. 1–1–01; 1999 H 471, § 1, eff. 7–1–00; 1999 H 283, eff. 1–1–01; 1987 H 171, eff. 7–1–87; 1984 H 319)

Uncodified Law

1996 H 670, § 27, as subsequently amended: See Uncodified Law under RC 101.83.

Historical and Statutory Notes

Ed. Note: The amendment of this section by 2002 S 121, eff. 3–19–03, and 2002 H 248, eff. 4–7–03, was identical. See *Baldwin's Ohio Legislative Service Annotated*, 2002, pages 12/L–2260 and 12/L–2962, or the OH–LEGIS or OH–LEGIS–OLD database on Westlaw, for original versions of these Acts.

Amendment Note: 2002 S 121 rewrote the fifth sentence of the first paragraph, which prior thereto read, "Five of these members shall be residents of counties where the population exceeds four hundred thousand; no more than one such member shall be a resident of the same county."; inserted ", or until a period of sixty days has elapsed, whichever occurs first" after "Each member shall serve until the member's successor is appointed" in the first paragraph; inserted "full" before "terms" and deleted ", regardless of whether such terms were full or partial terms" in the first paragraph; and substituted two new final paragraphs for "The speaker of the house of representatives and the president of the senate shall jointly appoint the board chairperson from among the legislative members of the board."

Amendment Note: 2002 H 248 rewrote the fifth sentence of the first paragraph, which prior thereto read, "Five of these members shall be residents of counties where the population exceeds four hundred thousand; no more than one such member shall be a resident of the same county."; inserted ", or until a period of sixty days has elapsed, whichever occurs first" after "Each member shall serve until the member's successor is appointed" in the first paragraph; inserted "full" before "terms" and deleted ", regardless of whether such terms were full or partial terms" in the first paragraph; and substituted two new final paragraphs for "The speaker of the house of representatives and the president of the senate shall jointly appoint the

board chairperson from among the legislative members of the board."

Amendment Note: 1999 H 471, § 3, eff. 1–1–01, substituted "job and family" for "human" twice in the first paragraph.

Amendment Note: 1999 H 471, § 1, eff. 7–1–00, substituted "job and family" for "human" twice in the first paragraph; added the final paragraph; and made changes to reflect gender neutral language and other nonsubstantive changes.

Amendment Note: 1999 H 283 rewrote the section, which prior thereto read:

"There is hereby created within the department of human services the children's trust fund board consisting of thirteen members. The director of health and the director of human services shall be members of the board. Seven public members shall be appointed by the governor. These members shall be persons with demonstrated knowledge in programs for children, shall be representative of the demographic composition of this state, and, to the extent practicable, shall be representative of the following categories: the educational community; the legal community; the social work community; the medical community; the voluntary sector; and professional providers of child abuse and child neglect services. Five of these members shall be residents of counties where the population exceeds four hundred thousand; no more than one such member shall be a resident of the same county. Two members of the board shall be members of the house of representatives appointed by the speaker of the house of representatives and shall be members of two different political parties. Two members of the board shall be members of the senate appointed by the president of the senate and shall be members of two different political parties. All members of the board appointed by the speaker of the house of representatives or the president of the

519

senate shall serve until the expiration of the sessions of the general assembly during which they were appointed. They may be reappointed to an unlimited number of successive terms of two years at the pleasure of the speaker of the house of representatives or president of the senate. Of the public members first appointed, three shall serve for terms of four years; two shall serve for terms of three years; and two shall serve for terms of two years. Thereafter, public members shall serve terms of three years. Each member shall serve until his successor is appointed. No public member may serve more than two consecutive terms, regardless of whether such terms were full or partial terms. All vacancies on the board shall be filled for the balance of the unexpired term in the same manner as the original appointment.

"Any public member of the board may be removed by the governor for misconduct, incompetency, or neglect of duty after first being given the opportunity to be heard in his own behalf.

"Each member of the board shall serve without compensation but shall be reimbursed for all actual and necessary expenses incurred by him in the performance of his official duties.

"The speaker of the house of representatives and the president of the senate shall jointly appoint the board chairman from among the legislative members of the board."

Cross References

Wellness block grant program, administrative agent of, see 121.371

Library References

Infants ⬌17.
Westlaw Topic No. 211.

C.J.S. Adoption of Persons §§ 10 to 14, 41.
C.J.S. Infants §§ 6, 8 to 9.

Research References

Encyclopedias

OH Jur. 3d Family Law § 1399, Powers and Duties Exercised by Department of Job and Family Services; Generally.

Notes of Decisions

Board members' status   1

---

1. Board members' status

The Ohio children's trust fund board is invested with independent power under RC 3109.16 and 3109.17 to allocate public funds and perform other sovereign duties on behalf of the state; its members are accordingly "public officials" for purposes of RC 2921.42. Ethics Op 87–003.

3109.16   Powers and duties

(A) The children's trust fund board, upon the recommendation of the director of job and family services, shall approve the employment of an executive director who will administer the programs of the board.

(B) The department of job and family services shall provide budgetary, procurement, accounting, and other related management functions for the board and may adopt rules in accordance with Chapter 119. of the Revised Code for these purposes. An amount not to exceed three per cent of the total amount of fees deposited in the children's trust fund in each fiscal year may be used for costs directly related to these administrative functions of the department. Each fiscal year, the board shall approve a budget for administrative expenditures for the next fiscal year.

(C) The board may request that the department adopt rules the board considers necessary for the purpose of carrying out the board's responsibilities under this section, and the department may adopt those rules. The department may, after consultation with the board and the executive director, adopt any other rules to assist the board in carrying out its responsibilities under this section. In either case, the rules shall be adopted under Chapter 119. of the Revised Code.

(D) The board shall meet at least quarterly at the call of the chairperson to conduct its official business. All business transactions of the board shall be conducted in public meetings.

Eight members of the board constitute a quorum. A majority of the board members is required to adopt the state plan for the allocation of funds from the children's trust fund. A majority of the quorum is required to make all other decisions of the board.

(E) With respect to funding, all of the following apply:

(1) The board may apply for and accept federal and other funds for the purpose of funding child abuse and child neglect prevention programs.

(2) The board may solicit and accept gifts, money, and other donations from any public or private source, including individuals, philanthropic foundations or organizations, corporations, or corporation endowments.

(3) The board may develop private-public partnerships to support the mission of the children's trust fund.

(4) The acceptance and use of federal and other funds shall not entail any commitment or pledge of state funds, nor obligate the general assembly to continue the programs or activities for which the federal and other funds are made available.

(5) All funds received in the manner described in this section shall be transmitted to the treasurer of state, who shall credit them to the children's trust fund created in section 3109.14 of the Revised Code.

(2011 H 153, eff. 9-29-11; 2006 S 238, eff. 9-21-06; 2002 S 121, eff. 3-19-03; 2002 H 248, eff. 4-7-03; 2000 H 448, § 6, eff. 1-1-01; 1999 H 471, § 3, eff. 1-1-01; 1999 H 471, § 1, eff. 7-1-00; 1999 H 283, eff. 1-1-01; 1994 H 335, eff. 12-9-94; 1987 H 171, eff. 7-1-87; 1985 H 201; 1984 H 319)

Historical and Statutory Notes

Ed. Note: The amendment of this section by 2002 S 121, eff. 3-19-03, and 2002 H 248, eff. 4-7-03, was identical. See *Baldwin's Ohio Legislative Service Annotated*, 2002, pages 12/L-2260 and 12/L-2962, or the OH-LEGIS or OH-LEGIS-OLD database on Westlaw, for original versions of these Acts.

Amendment Note: 2011 H 153 rewrote this section, which prior thereto read:

"The children's trust fund board, upon the recommendation of the director of job and family services, shall approve the employment of an executive director who will administer the programs of the board. The department of job and family services shall provide budgetary, procurement, accounting, and other related management functions for the board and may adopt rules in accordance with Chapter 119. of the Revised Code for these purposes. An amount not to exceed three per cent of the total amount of fees deposited in the children's trust fund in each fiscal year may be used for costs directly related to these administrative functions of the department. Each fiscal year, the board shall approve a budget for administrative expenditures for the next fiscal year.

"The board shall meet at least quarterly at the call of the chairperson to conduct its official business. All business transactions of the board shall be conducted in public meetings. Eight members of the board constitute a quorum. A majority of the board members is required to adopt the state plan for the allocation of funds from the children's trust fund. A majority of the quorum is required to make all other decisions of the board.

"The board may apply for and accept federal and other funds for the purpose of funding child abuse and child neglect prevention programs. In addition, the board may accept gifts and donations from any source, including individuals, philanthropic foundations or organizations, corporations, or corporation endowments. The acceptance and use of federal funds shall not entail any commitment or pledge of state funds, nor obligate the general assembly to continue the programs or activities for which the federal funds are made available. All funds received in the manner described in this section shall be transmitted to the treasurer of state, who shall credit them to the children's trust fund created in section 3109.14 of the Revised Code."

Amendment Note: 2006 S 238 inserted "and may adopt rules in accordance with Chapter 119. of the Revised Code for these purposes" in the second sentence of the first paragraph.

Amendment Note: 2002 S 121 substituted "an executive director who" for "the staff that" in the first paragraph; and rewrote the second paragraph, which prior thereto read:

"The board shall meet at the call of the chairperson to conduct its official business. All business transactions of the board shall be conducted in public meetings. Eight members of the board constitute a quorum. A majority of the quorum is required to approve the state plan for the allocation of funds from the children's trust fund."

Amendment Note: 2002 H 248 substituted "an executive director who" for "the staff that" in the first paragraph; and rewrote the second paragraph, which prior thereto read:

"The board shall meet at the call of the chairperson to conduct its official business. All business transactions of the board shall be conducted in public meetings. Eight members of the board constitute a quorum. A majority of the quorum is required to approve the state plan for the allocation of funds from the children's trust fund."

Amendment Note: 2000 H 448, § 6, substituted "three" for "five" in the first paragraph.

Amendment Note: 1999 H 471, § 3, eff. 1–1–01, substituted "job and family" for "human" twice in the first paragraph.

Amendment Note: 1999 H 471, § 1, eff. 7–1–00, substituted "job and family" for "human" twice in the first paragraph; substituted "chairperson" for "chairman" in the second paragraph; and added the final paragraph.

Amendment Note: 1999 H 283 rewrote the section, which prior thereto read:

"The children's trust fund board, upon the recommendation of the director of human services, shall approve the employment of the staff that will administer the programs of the board. The department of human services shall provide budgetary, procurement, accounting, and other related management functions for the board. An amount not to exceed three per cent of the total amount of fees deposited in the children's trust fund in each fiscal year may be used for costs directly related to these administrative functions of the department. With the approval of the board, an amount exceeding three per cent, but not exceeding four per cent, of the total amount of fees credited to the fund in each fiscal year may be used for costs directly related to these administrative functions.

"The board shall meet at the call of the chairman to conduct its official business. All business transactions of the board shall be conducted in public meetings. The votes of at least seven board members are required to approve the state plan for the allocation of funds from the children's trust fund.

"The board may apply for and accept federal funds for the purposes of sections 3109.13 to 3109.18 of the Revised Code. In addition, the board may accept gifts and donations from any source, including individuals, philanthropic foundations or organizations, corporations, or corporation endowments. The acceptance and use of federal funds shall not entail any commitment or pledge of state funds, nor obligate the general assembly to continue the programs or activities for which the federal funds are made available. All funds received in the manner described in this section shall be transmitted to the treasurer of state, who shall credit them to the children's trust fund created in section 3109.14 of the Revised Code."

Amendment Note: 1994 H 335 inserted "any source, including" and ", corporations, or corporation endowments" in the second sentence in the final paragraph.

Library References

Infants ☞17.
United States ☞82(2).
Westlaw Topic Nos. 211, 393.

C.J.S. Adoption of Persons §§ 10 to 14, 41.
C.J.S. Infants §§ 6, 8 to 9.
C.J.S. United States § 155.

3109.17 State plan for comprehensive child abuse and child neglect prevention; powers and duties of board; reports; list of funding sources

(A) For each fiscal biennium, the children's trust fund board shall establish a biennial state plan for comprehensive child abuse and child neglect prevention. The plan shall be transmitted to the governor, the president and minority leader of the senate, and the speaker and minority leader of the house of representatives and shall be made available to the general public. The board may define in the state plan the term "effective public notice." If the board does not define that term in the state plan, the board shall include in the state plan the definition of "effective public notice" specified in rules adopted by the department of job and family services.

(B) In developing and carrying out the state plan, the children's trust fund board shall, in accordance with rules adopted by the department pursuant to Chapter 119. of the Revised Code, do all of the following:

(1) Ensure that an opportunity exists for assistance through child abuse and child neglect prevention programs to persons throughout the state of various social and economic backgrounds;

(2) Before the thirtieth day of October of each year, notify each child abuse and child neglect prevention advisory board of the amount estimated to be allocated to that advisory board for the following fiscal year;

(3) Develop criteria for county or district local allocation plans, including criteria for determining the plans' effectiveness;

(4) Review, and approve or disapprove, county or district local allocation plans, as described in section 3109.171 of the Revised Code;

(5) Allocate funds to each child abuse and child neglect prevention advisory board for the purpose of funding child abuse and child neglect prevention programs. Funds shall be allocated among advisory boards according to a formula based on the ratio of the number of children under age eighteen in the county or multicounty district to the number of children under age eighteen in the state, as shown in the most recent federal decennial census of population. Subject to the availability of funds and except as provided in section 3109.171 of the Revised Code, each advisory board shall receive a minimum of ten thousand dollars per fiscal year. In the case of an advisory board that serves a multicounty district, the advisory board shall receive, subject to available funds and except as provided in section 3109.171 of the Revised Code, a minimum of ten thousand dollars per fiscal year for each county in the district. Funds shall be disbursed to the advisory boards twice annually. At least fifty per cent of the funds allocated to an advisory board for a fiscal year shall be disbursed to the advisory board not later than the thirtieth day of September. The remainder of the funds allocated to the advisory board for that fiscal year shall be disbursed before the thirty-first day of March.

The board shall specify the criteria child abuse and child neglect prevention advisory boards are to use in reviewing applications under division (F)(3) of section 3109.18 of the Revised Code.

(6) Allocate funds to entities other than child abuse and child neglect prevention advisory boards for the purpose of funding child abuse and child neglect prevention programs that have statewide significance and that have been approved by the children's trust fund board;

(7) Provide for the monitoring of expenditures from the children's trust fund and of programs that receive money from the children's trust fund;

(8) Establish reporting requirements for advisory boards;

(9) Collaborate with appropriate persons and government entities and facilitate the exchange of information among those persons and entities for the purpose of child abuse and child neglect prevention;

(10) Provide for the education of the public and professionals for the purpose of child abuse and child neglect prevention;

(11) Create and provide to each advisory board a children's trust fund grant application form;

(12) Specify the information to be included in a semiannual and an annual report completed by a children's advocacy center for which a child abuse and child neglect prevention advisory board uses funds allocated to the advisory board under section 3109.172 of the Revised Code, and each other person or entity that is a recipient of a children's trust fund grant under division (K)(1) of section 3109.18 of the Revised Code.

(C) The children's trust fund board shall prepare a report for each fiscal biennium that delineates the expenditure of money from the children's trust fund. On or before January 1, 2002, and on or before the first day of January of a year that follows the end of a fiscal biennium of this state, the board shall file a copy of the report with the governor, the president and minority leader of the senate, and the speaker and minority leader of the house of representatives.

(D) The children's trust fund board shall develop a list of all state and federal sources of funding that might be available for establishing, operating, or establishing and operating a children's advocacy center under sections 2151.425 to 2151.428 of the Revised Code. The board periodically shall update the list as necessary. The board shall maintain, or provide for the maintenance of, the list at an appropriate location. That location may be the offices of the department of job and family services. The board shall provide the list upon request to any children's advocacy center or to any person or entity identified in section 2151.426 of the Revised Code as a person or entity that may participate in the establishment of a children's advocacy center.

(2006 S 238, eff. 9–21–06; 2004 S 66, eff. 5–6–05; 2002 S 121, eff. 3–19–03; 2002 H 248, eff. 4–7–03; 1999 H 283, eff. 1–1–01; 1994 H 715, eff. 7–22–94; 1985 H 201, eff. 7–1–85; 1984 H 319)

Historical and Statutory Notes

Ed. Note: The amendment of this section by 2002 S 121, eff. 3–19–03, and 2002 H 248, eff. 4–7–03, was identical. See *Baldwin's Ohio Legislative Service Annotated*, 2002, pages 12/L–2261 and 12/L–2963, or the OH–LEGIS or OH–LEGIS–OLD database on Westlaw, for original versions of these Acts.

Amendment Note: 2006 S 238 inserted "rules adopted by the department pursuant to" in the first paragraph of division (B) and made other nonsubstantive changes.

Amendment Note: 2004 S 66 inserted "may define in the state plan the term 'effective public notice.' If the board does not define that term in the state plan, the board" in division (A); substituted "local" for "comprehensive" in division (B)(3); rewrote division (B)(4), which previously read: "Review county or district comprehensive allocation plans;"; inserted "and except as provided in section 3109.171 of the Revised Code" twice in division (B)(5); deleted the second paragraph of division (B)(5); inserted "that have statewide significance and that have been" and substituted "by the children's trust fund board" for "in the state plan" in division (B)(6); rewrote division (b)(12); added division (D); and made other nonsubstantive changes. Prior to the amendment, the second paragraph of division (B)(5) and (b)(12) read:

"If the children's trust fund board determines, based on county or district performance or on the annual report submitted by an advisory board, that the advisory board is not operating in accordance with the criteria established in division (B)(3) of this section, it may revise the allocation of funds that the advisory board receives.

"(12) Specify the information to be included in an annual report completed by a recipient of a children's trust fund grant under division (K)(1) of section 3109.18 of the Revised Code."

Amendment Note: 2002 S 121 inserted "The board shall include in the state plan the definition of "effective public notice" specified in rules adopted by the department of job and family services." in division (A); substituted "allocated" for "block granted" in division (B)(2); substituted "Allocate funds" for "Make a block grant", "Funds" for "The block grants", "Funds" for "Block grants", "funds" for "amount of the block grant", and "funds" for "block grant" in the first paragraph of division (B)(5); added the new third paragraph to division (B)(5); added new division (B)(6); redesignated former divisions (B)(6) through (B)(9) as (B)(7) through (B)(10); added new divisions (B)(11) and (B)(12); substituted "delineates" for "evaluates" in division (C); and deleted division (D), which prior thereto read:

"(D) In addition to the duties described in this section and in section 3109.16 of the Revised Code, the children's trust fund board shall perform the duties described in section 121.371 of the Revised Code with regard to the wellness block grant program."

Amendment Note: 2002 H 248 inserted "The board shall include in the state plan the definition of "effective public notice" specified in rules adopted by the department of job and family services." in division (A); substituted "allocated" for "block granted" in division (B)(2); substituted "Allocate funds" for "Make a block grant", "Funds" for "The block grants", "Funds" for "Block grants", "funds" for "amount of the block grant", and "funds" for "block grant" in the first paragraph of division (B)(5); added the new third paragraph to division (B)(5); added new division (B)(6); redesignated former divisions (B)(6) through (B)(9) as (B)(7) through (B)(10); added new divisions (B)(11) and (B)(12); substituted "delineates" for "evaluates" in division (C); and deleted division (D), which prior thereto read:

"(D) In addition to the duties described in this section and in section 3109.16 of the Revised Code, the children's trust fund board shall perform the duties described in section 121.371 of the Revised Code with regard to the wellness block grant program."

Amendment Note: 1999 H 283 rewrote the section, which prior thereto read:

"(A) For each fiscal biennium beginning on the first day of July of each odd-numbered year, the children's trust fund board shall establish a biennial state plan for the allocation of funds in the children's trust fund. The plan shall ensure that equal opportunity exists for the establishment of child abuse and child neglect prevention programs and the use of moneys from the fund to provide assistance in all geographic areas of this state and to provide assistance to members of all social and economic groups of this state. The plan shall be transmitted to the governor, the president of the senate, and the speaker of the house of representatives and shall be made available to the general public.

"(B) In developing and carrying out a plan, the children's trust fund board shall, in accordance with Chapter 119. of the Revised Code, do all of the following:

"(1) Develop and adopt the state plan for the allocation of funds and develop criteria, including standards for cost and program effectiveness, for county or district allocation plans and for individual projects in counties or districts that do not have a child abuse and child neglect advisory board;

"(2) Establish criteria, including standards for cost and program effectiveness, for child abuse and child neglect prevention programs;

"(3) Make grants to public or private agencies or schools for the purpose of child abuse and child neglect prevention programs. The board may consider factors such as need, geographic location, diversity, coordination with or improvement of existing services, maintenance of local funding efforts, and extensive use of volunteers. Children's trust fund moneys shall be allocated among all counties according to a formula based on the ratio of the number of children under the age of eighteen in the county to the number of children under the age of eighteen in the state, as shown in the most recent federal decennial census of population; provided, that each county receiving trust fund moneys shall receive a minimum of ten thousand dollars per funding year.

"(4) Approve each county or district allocation plan and individual project in whole or in part if it is in compliance with the criteria established under this section and under section 3109.18 of the Revised Code. If an allocation plan or individual project is rejected in whole or in part, the board shall:

"(a) Cite specific reasons for rejection;

"(b) When appropriate, offer recommendations and technical assistance to bring the plan or project into compliance, holding the funds until the plan or project is finally approved or rejected.

"(5) Notify each advisory board or individual applicant in writing whether the allocation plan or individual project has been approved in whole or in part not later than sixty days after submission of the plan or project to the children's trust fund board;

"(6) Regularly review and monitor the expenditure of moneys from the children's trust fund;

"(7) Consult with appropriate state agencies to help determine the probable effectiveness and fiscal soundness of and need for proposed community-based child abuse and child neglect prevention programs;

"(8) Facilitate the exchange of information between groups concerned with programs for children in this state;

"(9) Provide for statewide educational and public informational conferences and workshops for the purpose of developing appropriate public awareness regarding the problems of families and children, encouraging professional persons and groups to recognize and deal with problems of families and children, making information regarding the problems of families and children and the prevention of these problems available to the general public in order to encourage citizens to become involved in the prevention of such problems, and encouraging the development of community prevention programs;

"(10) Establish a procedure for a written annual internal evaluation of the functions, responsibilities, and performance of the board. The evaluation shall be coordinated with the state plan. The evaluation shall be transmitted to the governor, the president of the senate, and the speaker of the house of representatives and shall be made available to the general public."

Amendment Note: 1994 H 715 rewrote the first sentence of division (A); inserted ", including standards for cost and program effectiveness," in divisions (B)(1) and (B)(2); deleted "substantial" before "compliance" throughout division (B)(4); and deleted "annual" before "state plan" in division (B)(10). Prior to amendment, the first sentence of division (A) read:

"Each year, beginning within one year after the appointment of its first members, the children's trust fund board shall develop a state plan for the allocation of funds in the children's trust fund."

Ohio Administrative Code References

Child abuse and neglect, supportive services, see
OAC Ch 5101:2–39

Library References

Infants ☜17.
States ☜127.
Westlaw Topic Nos. 211, 360.

C.J.S. Adoption of Persons §§ 10 to 14, 41.
C.J.S. Infants §§ 6, 8 to 9.
C.J.S. States §§ 386 to 387.

Research References

Encyclopedias

OH Jur. 3d Family Law § 1399, Powers and Duties Exercised by Department of Job and Family Services; Generally.

Notes of Decisions

Board authority   1

_____

1. Board authority
The children's trust fund board does not have the authority to prohibit schools or school districts

which allow corporal punishment from receiving funds from the children's trust fund. OAG 89–053.

3109.171 Authority of children's trust fund board

(A) On receipt of a local allocation plan from a child abuse and child neglect prevention advisory board submitted pursuant to division (F)(1) of section 3109.18 of the Revised Code, the children's trust fund board may do either of the following:

(1) Approve the plan;

(2) Require that the advisory board make changes to the plan and submit an amended plan to the board.

(B) If an advisory board fails to submit to the children's trust fund board a local allocation plan pursuant to division (F)(1) of section 3109.18 of the Revised Code that is postmarked on or before the first day of April preceding the fiscal year for which the plan is developed, if an advisory board fails to submit an amended plan pursuant to division (A)(2) of this section, or if a plan or an amended plan submitted by an advisory board is not approved by the children's trust fund board, the children's trust fund board may do either of the following for the fiscal year for which the plan was to have been developed:

(1) Deny funding to the advisory board;

(2) Allocate a reduced amount of funds to the advisory board, on a pro-rata daily basis.

(C) If an advisory board fails to submit to the children's trust fund board an annual report pursuant to division (K)(2) of section 3109.18 of the Revised Code not later than the fifteenth day of August following the year for which the report is written, the board, for the following fiscal year, may allocate a reduced amount of funds to the advisory board on a pro-rata daily basis.

(2004 S 66, eff. 5–6–05)

Library References

Infants ⚖17.
Westlaw Topic No. 211.

C.J.S. Adoption of Persons §§ 10 to 14, 41.
C.J.S. Infants §§ 6, 8 to 9.

3109.172 Application for funding to establish children's advocacy centers; restrictions

(A)(1) Each child abuse and child neglect prevention advisory board may request from the children's trust fund board funds in addition to the funds allocated to the advisory board under section 3109.17 of the Revised Code to be used as one-time, start-up costs for the establishment and operation of a children's advocacy center as follows:

(a) If the advisory board serves a single county, the board may request an amount not to exceed five thousand dollars as one-time, start-up costs for the establishment and operation of a children's advocacy center that serves the county.

(b) If the advisory board serves a multicounty district, for each county within the district, the advisory board may request an amount not to exceed five thousand dollars as one-time, start-up costs for the establishment and operation of a children's advocacy center that serves the county in relation to which the use is being made.

(2) Expenditures may be made under division (A)(1) of this section for a children's advocacy center that is established to serve a single county or that is established to serve two or more contiguous counties, provided that the county in relation to which the expenditure is made is served by the center for which the advisory board uses the amount as one-time, start-up costs.

(B) Each children's advocacy center may annually request from the children's trust fund board funds in addition to the funds allocated to the advisory board under section 3109.17 of the Revised Code to conduct primary prevention strategies.

(C) On receipt of a request made pursuant to this section, the children's trust fund board shall review and approve or disapprove the request. If the board disapproves the request, the board shall send to the requestor written notice of the disapproval that states the reasons for the disapproval.

(D) No funds allocated to a child abuse and child neglect prevention advisory board under this section may be used as start-up costs for any children's advocacy center unless the center has as a component a primary prevention strategy.

No child abuse and child neglect advisory board that serves a single county and that, in any fiscal year, uses funds allocated under this section as start-up costs for a children's advocacy center may use any amount out of any funds so allocated to the advisory board for the same center in a different fiscal year or for a different center in any fiscal year. No child abuse and child neglect advisory board that serves a multicounty district and that, in any fiscal year, uses funds so allocated to the advisory board as start-up costs of a children's advocacy center in relation to a particular county within the district may use any amount out of any funds so allocated to the advisory board, in relation to the same county, for the same center in a different fiscal year or for a different center in any fiscal year.

(2004 S 66, eff. 5–6–05)

Library References

Infants ⊙ 17.
States ⊙ 127.
Westlaw Topic Nos. 211, 360.

C.J.S. Adoption of Persons §§ 10 to 14, 41.
C.J.S. Infants §§ 6, 8 to 9.
C.J.S. States §§ 386 to 387.

Research References

Encyclopedias

OH Jur. 3d Family Law § 1461, Children's Advocacy Center.

3109.18 Child abuse and child neglect prevention advisory boards

(A)(1) A board of county commissioners may establish a child abuse and child neglect prevention advisory board or may designate the county family and children first council to serve as the child abuse and child neglect prevention advisory board. The boards of county commissioners of two or more contiguous counties may instead form a multicounty district to be served by a child abuse and child neglect prevention advisory board or may designate a regional family and children first council to serve as the district child abuse and child neglect prevention advisory board. Each advisory board shall meet at least twice a year.

(2) The county auditor is hereby designated as the auditor and fiscal officer of the advisory board. In the case of a multicounty district, the boards of county commissioners that formed the district shall designate the auditor of one of the counties as the auditor and fiscal officer of the advisory board.

(B) Each county that establishes an advisory board or, in a multicounty district, the auditor who has been designated as the auditor and fiscal officer of the advisory board, shall establish a fund in the county treasury known as the county or district children's trust fund. The auditor shall deposit all funds received from the children's trust fund board into that fund, and the auditor shall distribute money from the fund at the request of the advisory board.

(C) Each January, the board of county commissioners of a county that has established an advisory board or, in a multicounty district, the board of county commissioners of the county served by the auditor who has been designated as the auditor and fiscal officer for the advisory board, shall appropriate the amount described in division (B)(2) of section 3109.17 of the Revised Code for distribution by the advisory board to child abuse and child neglect prevention programs.

(D)(1) Except in the case of a county or regional family and children first council that is designated to serve as a child abuse and child neglect prevention advisory board, each advisory board shall consist of an odd number of members from both the public and private sectors, including all of the following:

(a) A representative of an agency responsible for the administration of children's services in the county or district;

(b) A provider of alcohol or drug addiction services or a representative of a board of alcohol, drug addiction, and mental health services that serves the county or district;

(c) A provider of mental health services or a representative of a board of alcohol, drug addiction, and mental health services that serves the county or district;

(d) A representative of a county board of developmental disabilities that serves the county or district;

(e) A representative of the educational community appointed by the superintendent of the school district with largest enrollment in the county or multicounty district.

(2) The following groups and entities may be represented on the advisory board:

(a) Parent groups;

(b) Juvenile justice officials;

(c) Pediatricians, health department nurses, and other representatives of the medical community;

(d) School personnel;

(e) Counselors and social workers;

(f) Head start agencies;

(g) Child care providers;

(h) Other persons with demonstrated knowledge in programs for children.

(3) Of the members first appointed, at least one shall serve for a term of three years, at least one for a term of two years, and at least one for a term of one year. Thereafter, each member shall serve a term of three years. Each member shall serve until the member's successor is appointed. All vacancies on the board shall be filled for the balance of the unexpired term in the same manner as the original appointment.

(E) Each child abuse and child neglect prevention advisory board may incur reasonable costs not to exceed five per cent of the funds allocated to the county or district under section 3109.17 of the Revised Code, for the purpose of carrying out the functions of the advisory board.

(F) Each child abuse and child neglect prevention advisory board shall do all of the following:

(1) For each fiscal biennium, develop a local allocation plan for the purpose of preventing child abuse and child neglect and submit the plan to the children's trust fund board on or before the first day of April preceding the fiscal year for which the plan is developed;

(2) Provide effective public notice, as defined by the children's trust fund board in the state plan or, if the board does not define the term in the state plan, as defined in rules adopted by the department of job and family services, to potential applicants about the availability of funds from the children's trust fund, including an estimate of the amount of money available for grants within each county or district, the date of at least one public hearing, information on obtaining a copy of the grant application form, and the deadline for submitting grant applications;

(3) Review all applications received using criteria specified in the state plan adopted by the board under section 3109.17 of the Revised Code;

(4) Consistent with the local allocation plan developed pursuant to division (F)(1) of this section, make grants to child abuse and child neglect prevention programs.

(5) Establish any reporting requirements for grant recipients, in addition to those specified by the children's trust fund board, and for children's advocacy centers for which funds are used in accordance with section 3109.172 of the Revised Code.

(G) A member of a child abuse and child neglect prevention advisory board shall not participate in the development of a local allocation plan under division (F)(1) of this section if it is reasonable to expect that the member's judgment could be affected by the member's own financial, business, property, or personal interest or other conflict of interest. For purposes of this division, "conflict of interest" means the taking of any action that violates any applicable provision of Chapter 102. or 2921. of the Revised Code. Questions relating to the existence of a conflict of interest pertaining to Chapter 2921. of the Revised Code shall be submitted by the advisory board to the local prosecuting attorney for resolution. Questions relating to the existence of a conflict of interest pertaining to Chapter 102. of the Revised Code shall be submitted by the advisory board to the Ohio ethics commission for resolution.

(H) Each advisory board shall assist the children's trust fund board in monitoring programs that receive money from the children's trust fund and shall perform such other duties for the local administration of the children's trust fund as the children's trust fund board requires.

(I) A children's advocacy center for which a child abuse and child neglect prevention advisory board uses any amount out of the funds allocated to the advisory board under section 3109.172 of the Revised Code, as start-up costs for the establishment and operation of the center, shall use the moneys so received only for establishment and operation of the center in accordance with sections 2151.425 to 2151.428 of the Revised Code. Any other person or entity that is a recipient of a grant from the children's trust fund shall use the grant funds only to fund primary and secondary child abuse and child neglect prevention programs. Any grant funds that are not spent by the recipient of the funds within the time specified by the terms of the grant shall be returned to the county treasurer. Any grant funds returned that are not redistributed by the advisory board within the state fiscal year in which they are received shall be returned to the treasurer of state. The treasurer of state shall deposit such unspent moneys into the children's trust fund to be spent for purposes consistent with the state plan adopted under section 3109.17 of the Revised Code.

(J) Applications for grants from the children's trust fund shall be made to the advisory board on forms prescribed by the children's trust fund board.

(K)(1) Each children's advocacy center for which a child abuse and child neglect prevention advisory board uses any amount out of the funds allocated to the advisory board under section 3109.172 of the Revised Code, as start-up costs for the establishment and operation of the center, and each other person or entity that is a recipient of a children's trust fund grant from an advisory board shall file with the advisory board a copy of a semi-annual and an annual report that includes the information required by the children's trust fund board.

(2) Each advisory board shall file with the children's trust fund board, not later than the fifteenth day of August following the year for which the report is written, a copy of an annual report regarding the county or district local allocation plan that contains the information required by the children's trust fund board, and regarding the advisory board's use of any amount out of the funds allocated to the advisory board under section 3109.172 of the Revised Code as start-up costs for the establishment and operation of a children's advocacy center.

(2009 S 79, eff. 10-6-09; 2004 H 11, eff. 5-18-05; 2004 S 66, eff. 5-6-05; 2002 S 121, eff. 3-19-03; 2002 H 248, eff. 4-7-03; 2000 H 448, § 6, eff. 1-1-01; 1999 H 471, § 3, eff. 1-1-01; 1999 H 471, § 1, eff. 7-1-00; 1999 H 283, eff. 1-1-01; 1987 H 171, eff. 7-1-87; 1986 H 428; 1985 H 201; 1984 H 319)

Uncodified Law

1999 H 283, § 136, eff. 6-30-99, reads:

The amendments to section 3109.18 of the Revised Code by this act shall not affect the term of any member of a child abuse and child neglect advisory board serving on the effective date of this section. Vacancies on the board shall be filled in accordance with section 3109.18 of the Revised Code.

Historical and Statutory Notes

Ed. Note: The amendment of this section by 2002 S 121, eff. 3 19 03, and 2002 H 248, eff. 4-7-03, was identical. See *Baldwin's Ohio Legislative Service Annotated*, 2002, pages 12/L-2262 and 12/L-2964, or the OH-LEGIS or OH-LEGIS-OLD database on Westlaw, for original versions of these Acts.

Amendment Note: 2009 S 79 inserted "county" before "board" and deleted "mental retardation and" after "board of" in division (D)(1)(d).

Amendment Note: 2004 H 11 substituted "care" for "day care" in division (D)(2)(g).

Amendment Note: 2004 S 66 substituted "local" for "comprehensive" in the first sentence of division (G); and rewrote divisions (B), (C), (E), (F), (I), and (K), which prior thereto read:

"(B) Each county that establishes an advisory board or, in a multicounty district, the county the auditor of which has been designated as the auditor and fiscal officer of the advisory board, shall establish a fund in the county treasury known as the county or district children's trust fund. The advisory board shall deposit all funds received from the children's trust fund board into that fund, and the auditor shall distribute money from the fund at the request of the advisory board.

"(C) Each January, the board of county commissioners of a county that has established an advisory board or, in a multicounty district, the board of county commissioners of the county the auditor of which has been designated as the auditor and fiscal officer for the advisory board, shall appropriate the amount described in division (B)(2) of section 3109.17 of the Revised Code for distribution by the advisory board to child abuse and child neglect prevention programs.

"(E) Each board of county commissioners may incur reasonable costs not to exceed five per cent of the funds allocated to the county or district under section 3109.17 of the Revised Code, for the purpose of carrying out the functions of the advisory board.

"(F) Each child abuse and child neglect prevention advisory board shall do all of the following:

"(1) Develop a comprehensive allocation plan for the purpose of preventing child abuse and child neglect and submit the plan to the children's trust fund board;

"(2) Provide effective public notice, as defined in rules adopted by the department of job and family services, to potential applicants about the availability of funds from the children's trust fund, including an estimate of the amount of money available for grants within each county or district, the date of at least one public hearing, information on obtaining a copy of the grant application form, and the deadline for submitting grant applications;

"(3) Review all applications received using criteria specified in the state plan adopted by the board under section 3109.17 of the Revised Code;

"(4) Consistent with the plan developed pursuant to division (F)(1) of this section, make grants to child abuse and child neglect prevention programs. In making grants to child abuse and child neglect prevention programs, the advisory board may consider factors such as need, geographic location, diversity, coordination with or improvement of existing services, maintenance of local funding efforts, and extensive use of volunteers.

"(5) Establish any reporting requirements for grant recipients.

"(I) A recipient of a grant from the children's trust fund shall use the grant funds only to fund primary and secondary child abuse and child neglect prevention programs. Any grant funds that are not spent by the recipient of the funds within the time specified by the terms of the grant shall be returned to the county treasurer. Any grant funds returned that are not redistributed by the advisory board within the state fiscal year in which they are received shall be returned to the treasurer of state. The treasurer of state shall deposit such unspent

moneys into the children's trust fund to be spent for purposes consistent with the state plan adopted under section 3109.17 of the Revised Code.

"(K)(1) Each recipient of a children's trust fund grant from an advisory board shall file with the advisory board a copy of an annual report that includes the information required by the children's trust fund board.

"(2) Each advisory board shall file with the children's trust fund board a copy of an annual report regarding the county or district comprehensive allocation plan that contains the information required by the children's trust fund board."

Amendment Note: 2002 S 121 substituted "officer" for "agent" in divisions (B) and (C); added "and social workers" to division (D)(2)(e); substituted "funds" for "block grant" in division (E); added new division (G); redesignated former divisions (G) through (J) as (H) through (K); inserted "primary and secondary" preceding "child abuse" in new division (I); substituted "state fiscal year in which they are received" for "time specified by the terms of the original grant" in new division (I); substituted "children's trust fund board" for "department of job and family services" in new division (J); substituted "children's trust fund" for "advisory" in new division (K)(1); and rewrote divisions (F)(2) and (F)(3), which prior thereto read:

"(2) Notify potential applicants about the availability of funds from the children's trust fund;

"(3) Review all applications received using any criteria developed by the child abuse and child neglect prevention advisory board;".

Amendment Note: 2002 H 248 substituted "officer" for "agent" in divisions (B) and (C); added "and social workers" to division (D)(2)(e); substituted "funds" for "block grant" in division (E); added new division (G); redesignated former divisions (G) through (J) as (H) through (K); inserted "primary and secondary" preceding "child abuse" in new division (I); substituted "state fiscal year in which they are received" for "time specified by the terms of the original grant" in new division (I); substituted "children's trust fund board" for "department of job and family services" in new division (J); substituted "children's trust fund" for "advisory" in new division (K)(1); and rewrote divisions (F)(2) and (F)(3), which prior thereto read:

"(2) Notify potential applicants about the availability of funds from the children's trust fund;

"(3) Review all applications received using any criteria developed by the child abuse and child neglect prevention advisory board;".

Amendment Note: 2000 H 448, § 6, substituted "five" for "three" in division (E).

Amendment Note: 1999 H 471, § 3, eff. 1–1–01, substituted "job and family" for "human" in division (I).

Amendment Note: 1999 H 471, § 1, eff. 7–1–00, substituted "the member's" for "his" in the second paragraph in division (A); substituted "job and family" for "human" in the introductory paragraph in division (D); and added the final paragraph.

Amendment Note: 1999 H 283 rewrote the section, which prior thereto read:

"(A) Each board of county commissioners in the following counties shall establish a child abuse and child neglect advisory board: Cuyahoga, Franklin, Hamilton, Lucas, Montgomery, and Summit. The boards of county commissioners of the remaining counties may establish a child abuse and child neglect advisory board or the boards of county commissioners of two or more contiguous counties may form a multicounty district to be served by a multicounty child abuse and child neglect advisory board.

"Each child abuse and child neglect advisory board shall consist of an odd number of members who represent both public and private child serving agencies, and persons with demonstrated knowledge in programs for children, such as persons from the educational community, parent groups, juvenile justice, and the medical community. Of the members first appointed, at least one shall serve for a term of three years, at least one for a term of two years, and at least one for a term of one year. Thereafter, each member shall serve a term of three years. Each member shall serve until his successor is appointed. All vacancies on the board shall be filled for the balance of the unexpired term in the same manner as the original appointment. Each board shall meet at least quarterly.

"Each board of county commissioners may incur reasonable costs not to exceed three per cent of the funding allocated to the county or district under section 3109.17 of the Revised Code, for the purpose of carrying out the functions of the advisory board.

"(B) Annually, each child abuse and child neglect advisory board shall:

"(1) Give effective public notice to all potential applicants about the availability of funds from the children's trust fund. The notification shall include an estimate of the amount of money available for grants within each county or district, the date of at least one public hearing, the deadline for submitting applications for grants, and information on obtaining a copy of the application form;

"(2) Review all applications received using criteria established by the children's trust fund board under section 3109.17 of the Revised Code and any criteria developed by the child abuse and child neglect advisory board, and develop an allocation plan for the county or district;

"(3) Submit the allocation plan to the children's trust fund board, with evidence of compliance with this section and with section 3109.17 of the Revised Code;

"(4) Upon notification by the children's trust fund board that the allocation plan is in compliance with the criteria established by the boards, monitor the operation of the allocation plan;

"(5) Establish procedures for evaluating programs in the county or district, including reporting requirements for grant recipients.

"Applicants from counties that are not served by a child abuse and child neglect advisory board shall apply for funding to the children's trust fund board.

"(C) A recipient of a grant from the children's trust fund shall use the grant funds only to fund child abuse and child neglect prevention programs. A recipient of a grant may use the grant funds only for the expansion of existing programs or the creation of new programs.

"Any grant funds that are not spent by the counties or the recipient of the funds within the time specified by the terms of the grant shall be returned to the treasurer of state. The treasurer of state shall deposit such unspent moneys into the children's trust fund to be spent for purposes consistent with the state plan adopted under section 3109.17 of the Revised Code.

"(D) Applications for grants from the children's trust fund shall be on forms prescribed by the department of human services and, after any review required by division (B) of this section, shall be submitted to the children's trust fund board by the date required in the schedule established by rules adopted by the board. Each application shall include at least the following:

"(1) Information showing that the applicant meets the eligibility requirements of section 3109.17 of the Revised Code;

"(2) If the applicant is a corporation, a list of the trustees of the corporation;

"(3) A specification of the amount of money requested;

"(4) A summary of the program that the applicant intends to provide with funds from the grant;

"(5) Any other information required by rules adopted by the children's trust fund board.

"Each recipient of a grant from the children's trust fund shall file two copies of an annual report with the county or district advisory board. If no such board serves the recipient's county of residence, the recipient shall file two copies of an annual report with the children's trust fund board. The annual report shall describe the program provided by the recipient, indicate the manner in which the grant funds were expended, include the results of an independent audit of the funds, and include other information that the granting board or the department may require. If a public agency is a recipient of a grant, the results of the most recent audit of the funds conducted under Chapter 117. of the Revised Code shall be considered to be the results of the independent audit of the funds that must be included in the annual report. The granting boards shall annually file one copy of each annual report with the department, which shall compile the reports received pursuant to this section."

Library References

Infants ⚖17.
States ⚖127.
Westlaw Topic Nos. 211, 360.

C.J.S. Adoption of Persons §§ 10 to 14, 41.
C.J.S. Infants §§ 6, 8 to 9.
C.J.S. States §§ 386 to 387.

Research References

Encyclopedias

OH Jur. 3d Family Law § 1399, Powers and Duties
　Exercised by Department of Job and Family Ser-
　vices; Generally.

3109.19　Duty of parents to support children of unemancipated minor children

(A) As used in this section, "minor" has the same meaning as in section 3107.01 of the Revised Code.

(B)(1) If a child is born to parents who are unmarried and unemancipated minors, a parent of one of the minors is providing support for the minors' child, and the minors have not signed an acknowledgment of paternity or a parent and child relationship has not been established between the child and the male minor, the parent who is providing support for the child may request a determination of the existence or nonexistence of a parent and child relationship between the child and the male minor pursuant to Chapter 3111. of the Revised Code.

(2) If a child is born to parents who are unmarried and unemancipated minors, a parent of one of the minors is providing support for the child, and the minors have signed an acknowledgment of paternity that has become final pursuant to section 2151.232, 3111.25, or 3111.821 of the Revised Code or a parent and child relationship has been established between the child and the male minor pursuant to Chapter 3111. of the Revised Code, the parent who is providing support for the child may file a complaint requesting that the court issue an order or may request the child support enforcement agency of the county in which the child resides to issue an administrative order requiring all of the minors' parents to pay support for the child.

(C)(1) On receipt of a complaint filed under division (B)(2) of this section, the court shall schedule a hearing to determine, in accordance with Chapters 3119., 3121., 3123., and 3125. of the Revised Code, the amount of child support the minors' parents are required to pay, the method of paying the support, and the method of providing for the child's health care needs. On receipt of a request under division (B)(2) of this section, the agency shall schedule a hearing to determine, in accordance with Chapters 3119., 3121., 3123., and 3125. of the Revised Code, the amount of child support the minors' parents are required to pay, the method of paying the support, and the method of providing for the child's health care needs. At the conclusion of the hearing, the court or agency shall issue an order requiring the payment of support of the child and provision for the child's health care needs. The court or agency shall calculate the child support amount using the income of the minors' parents instead of the income of the minors. If any of the minors' parents are divorced, the court or agency shall calculate the child support as if they were married, and issue a child support order requiring the parents to pay a portion of any support imposed as a separate obligation. If a child support order issued pursuant to section 2151.23, 2151.231, 2151.232, 3111.13, or 3111.81 of the Revised Code requires one of the minors to pay support for the child, the amount the minor is required to pay shall be deducted from any amount that minor's parents are required to pay pursuant to an order issued under this section. The hearing shall be held not later than sixty days after the day the complaint is filed or the request is made nor earlier than thirty days after the court or agency gives the minors' parents notice of the action.

(2) An order issued by an agency for the payment of child support shall include a notice stating all of the following: that the parents of the minors may object to the order by filing a complaint pursuant to division (B)(2) of this section with the court requesting that the court issue an order requiring the minors' parents to pay support for the child and provide for the child's health care needs; that the complaint may be filed no later than thirty days after the date of the issuance of the agency's order; and that, if none of the parents of the minors file a complaint pursuant to division (B)(2) of this section, the agency's order is final and enforceable

by a court and may be modified and enforced only in accordance with Chapters 3119., 3121., 3123., and 3125. of the Revised Code.

(D) An order issued by a court or agency under this section shall remain in effect, except as modified pursuant to Chapters 3119., 3121., 3123., and 3125. of the Revised Code until the occurrence of any of the following:

(1) The minor who resides with the parents required to pay support under this section reaches the age of eighteen years, dies, marries, enlists in the armed services, is deported, gains legal or physical custody of the child, or is otherwise emancipated.

(2) The child who is the subject of the order dies, is adopted, is deported, or is transferred to the legal or physical custody of the minor who lives with the parents required to pay support under this section.

(3) The minor's parents to whom support is being paid pursuant to this section is no longer providing any support for the child.

(E) The minor's parents to whom support is being paid under a child support order issued by a court or agency pursuant to this section shall notify, and the minor's parents who are paying support may notify the child support enforcement agency of the occurrence of any event described in division (D) of this section. A willful failure to notify the agency as required by this division is contempt of court with respect to a court child support order. Upon receiving notification pursuant to this division, the agency shall comply with sections 3119.90 to 3119.94 of the Revised Code.

(2000 S 180, eff. 3–22–01; 1997 H 352, eff. 1–1–98; 1995 H 167, eff. 11–15–95)

Historical and Statutory Notes

Amendment Note: 2000 S 180 substituted "3111.25" for "3111.211" and "3111.821" for "5101.314" in division (B)(2); substituted "Chapters 3119., 3121., 3123., and 3125." for "sections 3113.21 to 3113.219" in the first sentence of division (C)(1); substituted "Chapters 3119., 3121., 3123., and 3125." for "sections 3111.23 to 3111.28 and 3113.215" in the second sentence of division (C)(1); deleted "3111.20, 3111.22" and "3111.13" and substituted "3111.81" for "3111.22" in the sixth sentence of division (C)(1); substituted "Chapters 3119., 3121., 3123., and 3125." for "sections 3111.23 to 3111.28 and sections 3113.21 to 3113.219" in division (C)(2); and rewrote divisions (D) and (E). Prior to amendment divisions (D) and (E) read:

"(D) An order issued by a court or agency under this section shall remain in effect, except as modified pursuant to sections 3113.21 to 3113.219 of the Revised Code with respect to a court-issued child support order or pursuant to sections 3111.23 to 3111.28 and 3113.215 of the Revised Code with respect to an administrative child support order, until the occurrence of any of the following:

"(1) The minor who resides with the parents required to pay support under this section reaches the age of eighteen years, dies, marries, enlists in the armed services, is deported, gains legal or physical custody of the child, or is otherwise emancipated.

"(2) The child who is the subject of the order dies, is adopted, is deported, or is transferred to the legal or physical custody of the minor who lives with the parents required to pay support under this section.

"(3) The minor's parents to whom support is being paid pursuant to this section is no longer providing any support for the child.

"(E)(1) The minor's parents to whom support is being paid under a child support order issued by a court pursuant to this section shall notify, and the minor's parents who are paying support may notify the child support enforcement agency of the occurrence of any event described in division (D) of this section. A willful failure to notify the agency as required by this division is contempt of court. Upon receiving notification pursuant to this division, the agency shall comply with division (G)(4) of section 3113.21 of the Revised Code.

"(2) The minor's parents to whom support is being paid under a child support order issued by the agency pursuant to this section shall notify, and the minor's parents who are paying support may notify the child support enforcement agency of the occurrence of any event described in division (D) of this section. Upon receiving notification pursuant to this division, the agency shall comply with division (E)(4) of section 3111.23 of the Revised Code."

Amendment Note: 1997 H 352 inserted "that has become final" and substituted "2151.232, 3111.211, or 5101.314" for "2105.18" in division (A)(2); inserted "and the method of providing for the child's health care needs" twice and "2151.231, 2151.232,", and substituted "3111.211" for "3111.21", in division (C)(1); inserted "and provide for the child's health care needs" in division (C)(2); and made other nonsubstantive changes.

Cross References

Acts in contempt of court, see 2705.02
Contents of support order, see 3119.32
Interfering with action to issue or modify support order, see 2919.231

Release of information to other parent and child support enforcement agency, see 3119.362

Ohio Administrative Code References

Grandparents' request for support for grandchild, see OAC 5101:12–45–15

Library References

Children Out-of-Wedlock ⬤21(1), 34 to 35. Westlaw Topic No. 76H.

C.J.S. Children Out-of-Wedlock §§ 39 to 40, 47, 50, 88 to 96.

Research References

Encyclopedias

OH Jur. 3d Contempt § 19, Statutory List of Contemptuous Acts.

OH Jur. 3d Family Law § 947, Who May Bring an Action.

OH Jur. 3d Family Law § 1025, Hearing; Order.

OH Jur. 3d Family Law § 1134, Separate Order for Providing Health Insurance.

OH Jur. 3d Family Law § 1207, Interfering With Action to Issue or Modify Support Order.

OH Jur. 3d Family Law § 1275, Employer's Compliance With National Medical Support Notice.

Forms

Ohio Jurisprudence Pleading and Practice Forms § 101:63.5, Content of Health Insurance Order.

Treatises and Practice Aids

Katz & Giannelli, Baldwin's Ohio Practice Criminal Law § 109:13, Interfering With Support Actions.

Sowald & Morganstern, Baldwin's Ohio Practice Domestic Relations Law § 22:4, Establishing Parentage.

Sowald & Morganstern, Baldwin's Ohio Practice Domestic Relations Law § 3:10, Judicial Parentage Action--Parties.

Sowald & Morganstern, Baldwin's Ohio Practice Domestic Relations Law § 3:47, Effect of Judgment--Grandparent Duty of Support.

Sowald & Morganstern, Baldwin's Ohio Practice Domestic Relations Law § 3:54, Complaint to Establish Father-Child Relationship--By Grandparent, With Request for Support--Form.

Sowald & Morganstern, Baldwin's Ohio Practice Domestic Relations Law § 11:45, Judgment Entry--Divorce Before a Magistrate With Children--Form.

Carlin, Baldwin's Ohio Prac. Merrick-Rippner Probate Law § 110:35, Civil Support Proceedings--Liability for Child Support.

Carlin, Baldwin's Ohio Prac. Merrick-Rippner Probate Law § 110:45, Parental Responsibility--Duty to Support Children of Unemancipated Minor Children.

Law Review and Journal Commentaries

R.C. 3109.19: Grandparent's Duty to Support Grandchild—Support for Children of Unemancipated Minor Children, Pamela J. MacAdams. 8 Domestic Rel J Ohio 42 (May/June 1996).

Notes of Decisions

Birth expenses, duty to support grandchild 1

---

1. Birth expenses, duty to support grandchild

A grandfather may be ordered to pay birth expenses of a child born to his unmarried and un-

emancipated daughter who is eighteen years of age and enrolled in high school, pursuant to a provision in the parents' decree of dissolution that husband is to pay all medical expenses of the children. Conde v. Conde (Ohio App. 2 Dist., Montgomery, 11-16-2001) No. 18858, 2001 WL 1468894, Unreported.

UNIFORM CHILD CUSTODY JURISDICTION LAW

Comparative Laws

Uniform Child Custody Jurisdiction Act

Table of Jurisdictions Wherein Act Has Been Adopted.

For text of Uniform Act, and variation notes and annotation materials for adopting jurisdictions, see Uniform Laws Annotated, Master Edition, Volume 9, Pt. I.

Jurisdiction	Statutory Citation
Indiana	West's A.I.C. 31–17–3–1 to 31–17–3–25.
Kentucky	KRS 403.400 to 403.350.
Louisiana	LSA–R.S. 13:1700 to 13:1724.
Maryland	Code, Family Law, § 9.5–101 to 9.5–111.
Massachusetts	M.G.L.A. c. 209B, § 1 to 14.
Mississippi	Code 1972, § 93–27–101 to 93–27–112.
Missouri	V.A.M.S. § 452.440 to 452.550.
New Hampshire	RSA 458–A:1 to 458–A:25.
New Jersey	N.J.S.A. 2A:34–53 et seq.
Pennsylvania	23 Pa.C.S.A. § 5402 et seq.
South Carolina	Code 1976, § 20–7–782 to 20–7–830.
South Dakota	SDCL 26–5b–101 to 26–5b–112.
Vermont	15 V.S.A. § 1031 to 1051.
Virgin Islands	16 V.I.C. § 115 to 139.
Wisconsin	W.S.A. 822.01 to 822.25.
Wyoming	Wyo.Stat.Ann., § 20–5–201 to 20–5–212.

Cross References

Divorce, legal separation, and dissolution of marriage actions, child custody provisions, spousal support, see 3105.10, 3105.21, 3105.63, 3105.65

Jurisdiction of juvenile court, see 2151.23

Law Review and Journal Commentaries

A Brief Analysis of the Uniform Child Custody Jurisdiction Act, Charles W. Geron. 51 Ohio St B Ass'n Rep 347 (3–27–78).

Uniform Child Custody Jurisdiction Act: Its Provisions and Effects in Ohio, Note. 7 Cap U L Rev 453 (1977).

3109.21 to 3109.37   Uniform Child Custody Jurisdiction Law—Repealed

(2004 S 185, eff. 4–11–05; 2000 S 180, eff. 3–22–01; 1996 H 274, eff. 8–8–96; 1990 S 3, eff. 4–11–91; 1977 S 135)

Historical and Statutory Notes

Ed. Note: Former RC 3109.27 amended and recodified as RC 3127.23 by 2004 S 185, eff. 4–11–05.

Ed. Note: Former RC 3109.29 amended and recodified as RC 3127.24 by 2004 S 185, eff. 4–11–05.

Ed. Note: Former RC 3109.37 amended and recodified as RC 3127.06 by 2004 S 185, eff. 4–11–05.

TASK FORCE ON FAMILY LAW AND CHILDREN

3109.401   Task force on family law and children; creation

(A) The general assembly finds the following:

(1) That the parent and child relationship is of fundamental importance to the welfare of a child, and that the relationship between a child and each parent should be fostered unless inconsistent with the child's best interests;

(2) That parents have the responsibility to make decisions and perform other parenting functions necessary for the care and growth of their children;

(3) That the courts, when allocating parenting functions and responsibilities with respect to the child in a divorce, dissolution of marriage, legal separation, annulment, or any other proceeding addressing the allocation of parental rights and responsibilities, must determine the child's best interests;

(4) That the courts and parents must take into consideration the following general principles when allocating parental rights and responsibilities and developing appropriate terms for parenting plans:

(a) Children are served by a parenting arrangement that best provides for a child's safety, emotional growth, health, stability, and physical care.

(b) Exposure of the child to harmful parental conflict should be minimized as much as possible.

(c) Whenever appropriate, parents should be encouraged to meet their responsibilities to their children through agreements rather than by relying on judicial intervention.

(d) When a parenting plan provides for mutual decision-making responsibility by the parents but they are unable to make decisions mutually, they should make a good faith effort to utilize the mediation process as required by the parenting plan.

(e) In apportioning between the parents the daily physical living arrangements of the child and the child's location during legal and school holidays, vacations, and days of special importance, a court should not impose any type of standard schedule unless a standard schedule meets the needs of the child better than any proposed alternative parenting plan.

(B) It is, therefore, the purpose of this chapter, when it is in the child's best interest, to foster the relationship between the child and each parent when a court allocates parental rights and responsibilities with respect to the child in a divorce, dissolution, legal separation, annulment, or any other proceeding addressing the allocation of parental rights and responsibilities.

(C) There is hereby created the task force on family law and children consisting of twenty-four members. The Ohio state bar association shall appoint three members who shall be attorneys with extensive experience in the practice of family law. The Ohio association of domestic relations judges shall appoint three members who shall be domestic relations judges. The Ohio association of juvenile and family court judges shall appoint three members who shall be juvenile or family court judges. The chief justice of the supreme court shall appoint eight members, three of whom shall be persons who practice in the field of family law mediation, two of whom shall be persons who practice in the field of child psychology, one of whom shall be a person who represents parent and child advocacy organizations, one of whom shall be a person who provides parenting education services, and one of whom shall be a magistrate employed by a domestic relations or juvenile court. The speaker of the house of representatives shall appoint two members who shall be members of the house of representatives and who shall be from different political parties. The president of the senate shall appoint two members who shall be members of the senate and who shall be from different political parties. The governor shall appoint two members who shall represent child caring agencies. One member shall be the director of job and family services or the director's designee. The chief justice shall designate one member of the task force to chair the task force.

The appointing authorities and persons shall make appointments to the task force on family law and children within thirty days after September 1, 1998. Sections 101.82 to 101.87 of the Revised Code do not apply to the task force.

(D) The task force on family law and children shall do all of the following:

(1) Appoint and fix the compensation of any technical, professional, and clerical employees and perform any services that are necessary to carry out the powers and duties of the task force on family law and children. All employees of the task force shall serve at the pleasure of the task force.

(2) By July 1, 2001, submit to the speaker and minority leader of the house of representatives and to the president and the minority leader of the senate a report of its findings and recommendations on how to create a more civilized and constructive process for the parenting of children whose parents do not reside together. The recommendations shall propose a system to do all of the following:

(a) Put children first;

(b) Provide families with choices before they make a decision to obtain or finalize a divorce, dissolution, legal separation, or annulment;

(c) Redirect human services to intervention and prevention, rather than supporting the casualties of the current process;

(d) Avoid needless conflict between the participants;

(e) Encourage problem solving among the participants;

(f) Force the participants to act responsibly;

(g) Shield both the participants and their children from lasting emotional damage.

(3) Gather information on and study the current state of family law in this state;

(4) Collaborate and consult with entities engaged in family and children's issues including, but not limited to, the Ohio association of child caring agencies, the Ohio family court feasibility study, and the Ohio courts futures commission;

(5) Utilize findings and outcomes from pilot projects conducted by the Ohio family court feasibility study to explore alternatives in creating a more civilized and constructive process for the parenting of children whose parents do not reside together with an emphasis on the areas of mediation and obtaining visitation compliance.

(E) Courts of common pleas shall cooperate with the task force on family law and children in the performance of the task force's duties described in division (D) of this section.
(2000 H 548, eff. 3–22–01; 1999 H 471, eff. 7–1–00; 2000 S 245, eff. 3–30–00; 1998 H 770, eff. 6–17–98; 1998 S 112, eff. 9–1–98)

Uncodified Law

2000 S 245, § 89, eff. 6–30–00, reads, in part:

Sections 169.02, 329.07, 3109.401, 3314.08, 5101.325, 5107.05, 5107.161, 5107.162, and 5111.23 of the Revised Code are amended by this act and also by H.B. 471 of the 123rd General Assembly effective July 1, 2000. The amendments of H.B. 471 are included in this act to confirm the intention to retain them, but they are not intended to be effective until July 1, 2000.

Historical and Statutory Notes

Amendment Note: 2000 H 548 substituted "Sections 101.82 to 101.87" for "Section 101.84"in the second paragraph in division (C); and made other nonsubstantive changes.

Amendment Note: 1999 H 471 substituted "job and family" for "human" in the first paragraph in division (C).

Amendment Note: 2000 S 245 substituted "September 1, 1998" for "the effective date of this section" in the second paragraph in division (C) and "July 1, 2001" for "December 31, 1999" in division (D)(2).

Amendment Note: 1998 H 770 rewrote the second paragraph in division (C); and made other nonsubstantive changes. Prior to amendment, the second paragraph in division (C) read:

"The appointing authorities and persons shall make initial appointments to the task force on family law and children within thirty days after the effective date of this section. Initial appointments to the task force shall be for terms ending July 1, 1999. Thereafter, terms of office shall be for two years, with each term ending on the first day of July of the following odd-numbered year. Members who are members of the general assembly shall hold office until the end of the term for which the member was appointed or until the person ceases to be a member of the general assembly, whichever occurs first. The director of human services shall hold office until the director ceases to be director of human services. Each member shall hold office from the date of the person's appointment until the end of the term for which the member was appointed. Members may be reappointed. Vacancies shall be filled in the manner provided for original appointments. Any member appointed to fill a vacancy occurring prior to the expiration date of the term for which the member's predecessor was appointed shall hold office as a member for the remainder of that term. A member shall continue in office subsequent to the expiration date of the member's term until the member's successor takes office or until a period of sixty days has elapsed, whichever occurs first. Section 101.84 of the Revised Code does not apply to the task force."

Library References

Infants ☜17.
Westlaw Topic No. 211.

C.J.S. Adoption of Persons §§ 10 to 14, 41.
C.J.S. Infants §§ 6, 8 to 9.

PARENT CONVICTED OF KILLING OTHER PARENT

3109.41 Definitions

As used in sections 3109.41 to 3109.48 of the Revised Code:

(A) A person is "convicted of killing" if the person has been convicted of or pleaded guilty to a violation of section 2903.01, 2903.02, or 2903.03 of the Revised Code.

(B) "Custody order" means an order designating a person as the residential parent and legal custodian of a child under section 3109.04 of the Revised Code or any order determining custody of a child under section 2151.23, 2151.33, 2151.353, 2151.354, 2151.415, 2151.417, 2152.16, 2152.17, 2152.19, 2152.21, or 3113.31 of the Revised Code.

(C) "Visitation order" means an order issued under division (B)(1)(c) of section 2151.33 or under section 2151.412, 3109.051, 3109.12, or 3113.31 of the Revised Code.

(2000 S 179, § 3, eff. 1–1–02; 1999 H 191, eff. 10–20–99)

Historical and Statutory Notes

Amendment Note: 2000 S 179, § 3, eff. 1–1–02, deleted "2151.355, 2151.356," before "2151.415," and inserted "2152.16, 2152.17, 2152.19, 2152.21," in division (B).

Library References

Child Custody ⬭61.
Westlaw Topic No. 76D.
C.J.S. Parent and Child § 79.

Research References

Encyclopedias

OH Jur. 3d Family Law § 1038, Denial of Custody Where One Parent is Convicted of Killing the Other.

3109.42 Unavailability of custody for parent convicted of killing other parent

Except as provided in section 3109.47 of the Revised Code, if a parent is convicted of killing the other parent of a child, no court shall issue a custody order designating the parent as the residential parent and legal custodian of the child or granting custody of the child to the parent.

(1999 H 191, eff. 10–20–99)

Library References

Child Custody ⬭61.
Westlaw Topic No. 76D.
C.J.S. Parent and Child § 79.

Research References

Encyclopedias

OH Jur. 3d Family Law § 723, Effect of Death of Person Awarded Custody.

OH Jur. 3d Family Law § 1038, Denial of Custody Where One Parent is Convicted of Killing the Other.

OH Jur. 3d Family Law § 1097, Death of Residential Parent.

OH Jur. 3d Family Law § 1123, Continuing Jurisdiction of Court; Effect of Death of a Parent.

OH Jur. 3d Family Law § 1332, Generally; Jurisdiction.

OH Jur. 3d Family Law § 1549, on Certification from Common Pleas.

3109.43 Unavailability of visitation rights for parent convicted of killing other parent

Except as provided in section 3109.47 of the Revised Code, if a parent is convicted of killing the other parent of a child, no court shall issue a visitation order granting the parent visitation rights with the child.

(1999 H 191, eff. 10–20–99)

Library References

Child Custody ☞200.
Westlaw Topic No. 76D.
C.J.S. Divorce § 1016.

Research References

Encyclopedias

OH Jur. 3d Family Law § 1159, Denial of Visitation Where One Parent is Convicted of Killing the Other.

3109.44 Notice of conviction

Upon receipt of notice that a visitation order is pending or has been issued granting a parent visitation rights with a child or a custody order is pending or has been issued designating a parent as the residential parent and legal custodian of a child or granting custody of a child to a parent prior to that parent being convicted of killing the other parent of the child, the court in which the parent is convicted of killing the other parent shall immediately notify the court that issued the visitation or custody order of the conviction.

(1999 H 191, eff. 10–20–99)

Library References

Child Custody ☞61, 200.
Criminal Law ☞1226(2).
Westlaw Topic Nos. 76D, 110.

C.J.S. Criminal Law §§ 2412 to 2413.
C.J.S. Divorce § 1016.
C.J.S. Parent and Child § 79.

Research References

Encyclopedias

OH Jur. 3d Family Law § 531, Continuing Jurisdiction of Court.

OH Jur. 3d Family Law § 533, Jurisdiction of Juvenile Court.

OH Jur. 3d Family Law § 1038, Denial of Custody Where One Parent is Convicted of Killing the Other.

OH Jur. 3d Family Law § 1159, Denial of Visitation Where One Parent is Convicted of Killing the Other.

3109.45 Termination of visitation order upon receipt of notice of conviction

On receipt of notice under section 3109.44 of the Revised Code, a court that issued a visitation order described in that section shall terminate the order.

(1999 H 191, eff. 10–20–99)

Library References

Child Custody ☞577.
Westlaw Topic No. 76D.
C.J.S. Parent and Child § 143.

Encyclopedias

OH Jur. 3d Family Law § 1159, Denial of Visitation Where One Parent is Convicted of Killing
the Other.

3109.46   Termination of custody order upon receipt of notice of conviction;   deemed new complaint for custody

If the court to which notice is sent under section 3109.44 of the Revised Code is a juvenile court that issued a custody order described in that section, the court shall retain jurisdiction over the order. If the court to which notice is sent is not a juvenile court but the court issued a custody order described in that section, the court shall transfer jurisdiction over the custody order to the juvenile court of the county in which the child has a residence or legal settlement.

On receipt of the notice in cases in which the custody order was issued by a juvenile court or after jurisdiction is transferred, the juvenile court with jurisdiction shall terminate the custody order.

The termination order shall be treated as a complaint filed under section 2151.27 of the Revised Code alleging the child subject of the custody order to be a dependent child. If a juvenile court issued the terminated custody order under a prior juvenile proceeding under Chapter 2151. of the Revised Code in which the child was adjudicated an abused, neglected, dependent, unruly, or delinquent child or a juvenile traffic offender, the court shall treat the termination order as a new complaint.

(1999 H 191, eff. 10–20–99)

3109.47   Custody or visitation order when in best interest of child

(A) A court may do one of the following with respect to a parent convicted of killing the other parent of a child if the court determines, by clear and convincing evidence, that it is in the best interest of the child and the child consents:

(1) Issue a custody order designating the parent as the residential parent and legal custodian of the child or granting custody of the child to that parent;

(2) Issue a visitation order granting that parent visitation rights with the child.

(B) When considering the ability of a child to consent and the validity of a child's consent under this section, the court shall consider the wishes of the child, as expressed directly by the child or through the child's guardian ad litem, with due regard for the maturity of the child.

(1999 H 191, eff. 10–20–99)

Research References

Encyclopedias

OH Jur. 3d Family Law § 1038, Denial of Custody Where One Parent is Convicted of Killing the Other.

OH Jur. 3d Family Law § 1159, Denial of Visitation Where One Parent is Convicted of Killing the Other.

3109.48   Court order and consent of custodian required for visitation

No person, with the child of the parent present, shall visit the parent who has been convicted of killing the child's other parent unless a court has issued an order granting the parent visitation rights with the child and the child's custodian or legal guardian consents to the visit.

(1999 H 191, eff. 10–20–99)

Library References

Child Custody ⚖200.
Westlaw Topic No. 76D.
C.J.S. Divorce § 1016.

Research References

Encyclopedias

OH Jur. 3d Family Law § 723, Effect of Death of Person Awarded Custody.

OH Jur. 3d Family Law § 1097, Death of Residential Parent.

OH Jur. 3d Family Law § 1123, Continuing Jurisdiction of Court; Effect of Death of a Parent.

OH Jur. 3d Family Law § 1159, Denial of Visitation Where One Parent is Convicted of Killing the Other.

OH Jur. 3d Family Law § 1332, Generally; Jurisdiction.

OH Jur. 3d Family Law § 1549, on Certification from Common Pleas.

Notes of Decisions

Constitutional issues   1

___

1.   Constitutional issues

Trial court that ruled on request for visitation filed by father convicted of murdering children's mother lacked jurisdiction over father's subsequently-filed declaratory judgment action seeking to declare statute governing the visitation rights of a parent who kills the other parent unconstitutional, and thus Court of Appeals lacked jurisdiction over father's appeal from trial court's dismissal of declaratory judgment action; trial court's ruling on the visitation request was a final, appealable judgment that deprived trial court of jurisdiction to entertain further motions or claims.   Bozsik v. Burkhart (Ohio App. 9 Dist., Wayne, 07-27-2005) No. 04CA0072, 2005-Ohio-3794, 2005 WL 1763604, Unreported.   Child Custody ⚖ 531(1); Child Custody ⚖ 902;   Declaratory Judgment ⚖ 392.1

GRANDPARENT POWER OF ATTORNEY OR CARETAKER AUTHORIZATION AFFIDAVIT

3109.51   Definitions

As used in sections 3109.52 to 3109.80 of the Revised Code:

(A) "Child" means a person under eighteen years of age.

(B) "Custodian" means an individual with legal custody of a child.

(C) "Guardian" means an individual granted authority by a probate court pursuant to Chapter 2111. of the Revised Code to exercise parental rights over a child to the extent provided in the court's order and subject to the residual parental rights, privileges, and responsibilities of the child's parents.

(D) "Legal custody" and "residual parental rights, privileges, and responsibilities" have the same meanings as in section 2151.011 of the Revised Code.

(2004 H 130, eff. 7–20–04)

Cross References

Jurisdiction of juvenile court, orders for child support, see 2151.23

Pupil to provide certain information, request for records from prior school, notice to police of failure to produce records, notification of power

of attorney or caretaker authorization affidavit, notification of shelter care for victims of domestic violence, see 3313.672

Suspension, expulsion, and removal from premises, see 3313.66

Library References

Powers ⚖7.
Westlaw Topic No. 307.
C.J.S. Powers § 2.

Research References

Treatises and Practice Aids

Sowald & Morganstern, Baldwin's Ohio Practice Domestic Relations Law § 15:53, Award to Third Party--By Parents' Agreement--Power of Attorney.

Carlin, Baldwin's Ohio Prac. Merrick-Rippner Probate Law § 107:2, Original Jurisdiction.

Carlin, Baldwin's Ohio Prac. Merrick-Rippner Probate Law § 61:11, Caretaker Authorization Affidavit--Grandparent and Grandchild.

Adrine & Ruden, Ohio Domestic Violence Law § 12:16, Remedies--Protected Party Concerns.

3109.52   Power of attorney to grandparents for care, physical custody and control of child

The parent, guardian, or custodian of a child may create a power of attorney that grants to a grandparent of the child with whom the child is residing any of the parent's, guardian's, or custodian's rights and responsibilities regarding the care, physical custody, and control of the child, including the ability to enroll the child in school, to obtain from the school district educational and behavioral information about the child, to consent to all school-related matters regarding the child, and to consent to medical, psychological, or dental treatment for the child. The power of attorney may not grant authority to consent to the marriage or adoption of the child. The power of attorney does not affect the rights of the parent, guardian, or custodian of the child in any future proceeding concerning custody of the child or the allocation of parental rights and responsibilities for the care of the child and does not grant legal custody to the attorney in fact.

(2004 H 130, eff. 7–20–04)

Library References

Powers ⚖5 to 7, 17.
Westlaw Topic No. 307.
C.J.S. Powers §§ 2, 8, 15 to 20.

Research References

Encyclopedias

OH Jur. 3d Family Law § 1041, Relinquishment of Child to Grandparent Through Power of Attorney.

OH Jur. 3d Family Law § 1177, Mediator as Party or Witness.

OH Jur. 3d Family Law § 1178, Extent of Court's Power to Order Mediation.

OH Jur. 3d Guardian & Ward § 90, Caretaker Authorization Affidavit; Authority to Execute.

OH Jur. 3d Guardian & Ward § 92, Filing of Power of Attorney or Caretaker Authorization Affidavit With Juvenile Court and Hearing.

Treatises and Practice Aids

Sowald & Morganstern, Baldwin's Ohio Practice Domestic Relations Law § 6:9, Mediator Qualifications.

Carlin, Baldwin's Ohio Prac. Merrick-Rippner Probate Law § 61:11, Caretaker Authorization Affidavit--Grandparent and Grandchild.

Carlin, Baldwin's Ohio Prac. Merrick-Rippner Probate Law App B SPF 15.2, Fiduciary's Acceptance--Guardian.

Hastings, Manoloff, Sheeran, & Stype, Ohio School Law § 23:4, Admission Requirements and Tuition Liability--Special Tuition Exemptions and Waivers.

3109.53 Form and content of power of attorney

To create a power of attorney under section 3109.52 of the Revised Code, a parent, guardian, or custodian shall use a form that is identical in form and content to the following:

POWER OF ATTORNEY

I, the undersigned, residing at..........., in the county of ...., state of.........., hereby appoint the child's grandparent, ..., residing at.........., in the county of.........., in the state of Ohio, with whom the child of whom I am the parent, guardian, or custodian is residing, my attorney in fact to exercise any and all of my rights and responsibilities regarding the care, physical custody, and control of the child,.........., born.........., having social security number (optional).........., except my authority to consent to marriage or adoption of the child.........., and to perform all acts necessary in the execution of the rights and responsibilities hereby granted, as fully as I might do if personally present. The rights I am transferring under this power of attorney include the ability to enroll the child in school, to obtain from the school district educational and behavioral information about the child, to consent to all school-related matters regarding the child, and to consent to medical, psychological, or dental treatment for the child. This transfer does not affect my rights in any future proceedings concerning the custody of the child or the allocation of the parental rights and responsibilities for the care of the child and does not give the attorney in fact legal custody of the child. This transfer does not terminate my right to have regular contact with the child.

I hereby certify that I am transferring the rights and responsibilities designated in this power of attorney because one of the following circumstances exists:

(1) I am: (a) Seriously ill, incarcerated or about to be incarcerated, (b) Temporarily unable to provide financial support or parental guidance to the child, (c) Temporarily unable to provide adequate care and supervision of the child because of my physical or mental condition, (d) Homeless or without a residence because the current residence is destroyed or otherwise uninhabitable, or (e) In or about to enter a residential treatment program for substance abuse;

(2) I am a parent of the child, the child's other parent is deceased, and I have authority to execute the power of attorney; or

(3) I have a well-founded belief that the power of attorney is in the child's best interest.

I hereby certify that I am not transferring my rights and responsibilities regarding the child for the purpose of enrolling the child in a school or school district so that the child may participate in the academic or interscholastic athletic programs provided by that school or district.

I understand that this document does not authorize a child support enforcement agency to redirect child support payments to the grandparent designated as attorney in fact. I further understand that to have an existing child support order modified or a new child support order issued administrative or judicial proceedings must be initiated.

If there is a court order naming me the residential parent and legal custodian of the child who is the subject of this power of attorney and I am the sole parent signing this document, I hereby certify that one of the following is the case:

(1) I have made reasonable efforts to locate and provide notice of the creation of this power of attorney to the other parent and have been unable to locate that parent;

(2) The other parent is prohibited from receiving a notice of relocation; or

(3) The parental rights of the other parent have been terminated by order of a juvenile court.

This POWER OF ATTORNEY is valid until the occurrence of whichever of the following events occurs first: (1) one year elapses following the date this POWER OF ATTORNEY is notarized; (2) I revoke this POWER OF ATTORNEY in writing; (3) the child ceases to reside with the grandparent designated as attorney in fact; (4) this POWER OF ATTORNEY is terminated by court order; (5) the death of the child who is the subject of the power of attorney; or (6) the death of the grandparent designated as the attorney in fact.

WARNING: DO NOT EXECUTE THIS POWER OF ATTORNEY IF ANY STATE-MENT MADE IN THIS INSTRUMENT IS UNTRUE. FALSIFICATION IS A CRIME UNDER SECTION 2921.13 OF THE REVISED CODE, PUNISHABLE BY THE SANC-TIONS UNDER CHAPTER 2929. OF THE REVISED CODE, INCLUDING A TERM OF IMPRISONMENT OF UP TO 6 MONTHS, A FINE OF UP TO $1,000, OR BOTH.

Witness my hand this...... day of............,.....

....
Parent/Custodian/Guardian's signature

....
Parent's signature

....
Grandparent designated as attorney in fact

State of Ohio   )
) ss:
County of ....)

Subscribed, sworn to, and acknowledged before me this...... day of ....,.............

....
Notary Public

Notices:

1. A power of attorney may be executed only if one of the following circumstances exists: (1) The parent, guardian, or custodian of the child is: (a) Seriously ill, incarcerated or about to be incarcerated; (b) Temporarily unable to provide financial support or parental guidance to the child; (c) Temporarily unable to provide adequate care and supervision of the child because of the parent's, guardian's, or custodian's physical or mental condition; (d) Homeless or without a residence because the current residence is destroyed or otherwise uninhabitable; or (e) In or about to enter a residential treatment program for substance abuse; (2) One of the child's parents is deceased and the other parent, with authority to do so, seeks to execute a power of attorney; or (3) The parent, guardian, or custodian has a well-founded belief that the power of attorney is in the child's best interest.
2. The signatures of the parent, guardian, or custodian of the child and the grandparent designated as the attorney in fact must be notarized by an Ohio notary public.
3. A parent, guardian, or custodian who creates a power of attorney must notify the parent of the child who is not the residential parent and legal custodian of the child unless one of the following circumstances applies: (a) the parent is prohibited from receiving a notice of relocation in accordance with section 3109.051 of the Revised Code of the creation of the power of attorney; (b) the parent's parental rights have been terminated by order of a juvenile court pursuant to Chapter 2151. of the Revised Code; (c) the parent cannot be located with reasonable efforts; (d) both parents are executing the power of attorney. The notice must be sent by certified mail not later than five days after the power of attorney is created and must state the name and address of the person designated as the attorney in fact.
4. A parent, guardian, or custodian who creates a power of attorney must file it with the juvenile court of the county in which the attorney in fact resides, or any other court that has jurisdiction over the child under a previously filed motion or proceeding. The power of attorney must be filed not later than five days after the date it is created and be accompanied by a receipt showing that the notice of creation of the power of attorney was sent to the parent who is not the residential parent and legal custodian by certified mail.
5. A parent, guardian, or custodian who creates a second or subsequent power of attorney regarding a child who is the subject of a prior power of attorney must file the power of attorney with the juvenile court of the county in which the attorney in fact resides or any other court that has jurisdiction over the child under a previously filed motion or

proceeding. On filing, the court will schedule a hearing to determine whether the power of attorney is in the child's best interest.

6. This power of attorney does not affect the rights of the child's parents, guardian, or custodian regarding any future proceedings concerning the custody of the child or the allocation of the parental rights and responsibilities for the care of the child and does not give the attorney in fact legal custody of the child.

7. A person or entity that relies on this power of attorney, in good faith, has no obligation to make any further inquiry or investigation.

8. This power of attorney terminates on the occurrence of whichever of the following occurs first: (1) one year elapses following the date the power of attorney is notarized; (2) the power of attorney is revoked in writing by the person who created it; (3) the child ceases to live with the grandparent who is the attorney in fact; (4) the power of attorney is terminated by court order; (5) the death of the child who is the subject of the power of attorney; or (6) the death of the grandparent designated as the attorney in fact.

(If this power of attorney terminates other than by the death of the attorney in fact, the grandparent who served as the attorney in fact shall notify, in writing, all of the following:

(a) Any schools, health care providers, or health insurance coverage provider with which the child has been involved through the grandparent;

(b) Any other person or entity that has an ongoing relationship with the child or grandparent such that the other person or entity would reasonably rely on the power of attorney unless notified of the termination;

(c) The court in which the power of attorney was filed after its creation; and

(d) The parent who is not the residential parent and legal custodian of the child who is required to be given notice of its creation. The grandparent shall make the notifications not later than one week after the date the power of attorney terminates.

9. If this power of attorney is terminated by written revocation of the person who created it, or the revocation is regarding a second or subsequent power of attorney, a copy of the revocation must be filed with the court with which that power of attorney was filed.

Additional information:

To the grandparent designated as attorney in fact:

1. If the child stops living with you, you are required to notify, in writing, any school, health care provider, or health care insurance provider to which you have given this power of attorney. You are also required to notify, in writing, any other person or entity that has an ongoing relationship with you or the child such that the person or entity would reasonably rely on the power of attorney unless notified. The notification must be made not later than one week after the child stops living with you.

2. You must include with the power of attorney the following information:

(a) The child's present address, the addresses of the places where the child has lived within the last five years, and the name and present address of each person with whom the child has lived during that period;

(b) Whether you have participated as a party, a witness, or in any other capacity in any other litigation, in this state or any other state, that concerned the allocation, between the parents of the same child, of parental rights and responsibilities for the care of the child and the designation of the residential parent and legal custodian of the child or that otherwise concerned the custody of the same child;

(c) Whether you have information of any parenting proceeding concerning the child pending in a court of this or any other state;

(d) Whether you know of any person who has physical custody of the child or claims to be a parent of the child who is designated the residential parent and legal custodian of the child or to have parenting time rights with respect to the child or to be a person other than a parent of the child who has custody or visitation rights with respect to the child;

(e) Whether you previously have been convicted of or pleaded guilty to any criminal offense involving any act that resulted in a child being an abused child or a neglected child or previously have been determined, in a case in which a child has been adjudicated an abused child or a neglected child, to be the perpetrator of the abusive or neglectful act that was the basis of the adjudication.

To school officials:

1. Except as provided in section 3313.649 of the Revised Code, this power of attorney, properly completed and notarized, authorizes the child in question to attend school in the district in which the grandparent designated as attorney in fact resides and that grandparent is authorized to provide consent in all school-related matters and to obtain from the school district educational and behavioral information about the child. This power of attorney does not preclude the parent, guardian, or custodian of the child from having access to all school records pertinent to the child.
2. The school district may require additional reasonable evidence that the grandparent lives in the school district.
3. A school district or school official that reasonably and in good faith relies on this power of attorney has no obligation to make any further inquiry or investigation.

To health care providers:

1. A person or entity that acts in good faith reliance on a power of attorney to provide medical, psychological, or dental treatment, without actual knowledge of facts contrary to those stated in the power of attorney, is not subject to criminal liability or to civil liability to any person or entity, and is not subject to professional disciplinary action, solely for such reliance if the power of attorney is completed and the signatures of the parent, guardian, or custodian of the child and the grandparent designated as attorney in fact are notarized.
2. The decision of a grandparent designated as attorney in fact, based on a power of attorney, shall be honored by a health care facility or practitioner, school district, or school official.

(2004 H 130, eff. 7–20–04)

Library References

Powers ☞8.
Westlaw Topic No. 307.
C.J.S. Powers § 3.

Research References

Encyclopedias

OH Jur. 3d Family Law § 1041, Relinquishment of Child to Grandparent Through Power of Attorney.
OH Jur. 3d Guardian & Ward § 88, Form, Notice, and Execution.

Treatises and Practice Aids

Sowald & Morganstern, Baldwin's Ohio Practice Domestic Relations Law § 15:53, Award to Third Party--By Parents' Agreement--Power of Attorney.
Carlin, Baldwin's Ohio Prac. Merrick-Rippner Probate Law § 61:11, Caretaker Authorization Affidavit--Grandparent and Grandchild.

3109.54 Signature and notarization

A power of attorney created pursuant to section 3109.52 of the Revised Code must be signed by the parent, guardian, or custodian granting it and by the grandparent designated as the attorney in fact. For the power of attorney to be effective, the signatures must be notarized. The child's social security number need not appear on the power of attorney for the power of attorney to be effective.

(2004 H 130, eff. 7–20–04)

3109.55 Notice to nonresidential parent and legal custodian; exceptions; method of delivery; contents of notice

(A) A person who creates a power of attorney under section 3109.52 of the Revised Code shall send notice of the creation to the parent of the child who is not the residential parent and legal custodian of the child unless one of the following is the case:

(1) The parent is prohibited from receiving a notice of relocation in accordance with section 3109.051 of the Revised Code.

(2) The parent's parental rights have been terminated by order of a juvenile court pursuant to Chapter 2151. of the Revised Code.

(3) The parent cannot be located with reasonable efforts.

(4) The power of attorney is being created by both parents.

(B) The notice shall be sent by certified mail not later than five days after the power of attorney is created. The notice shall state the name and address of the person designated as the attorney in fact.

(2004 H 130, eff. 7–20–04)

3109.56 Conditions determining execution of power of attorney by one or both parents

When a parent seeks to create a power of attorney pursuant to section 3109.52 of the Revised Code, all of the following apply:

(A) The power of attorney shall be executed by both parents if any of the following apply:

(1) The parents are married to each other and are living as husband and wife.

(2) The child is the subject of a shared parenting order issued pursuant to section 3109.04 of the Revised Code.

(3) The child is the subject of a custody order issued pursuant to section 3109.04 of the Revised Code unless one of the following is the case:

(a) The parent who is not the residential parent and legal custodian is prohibited from receiving a notice of relocation in accordance with section 3109.051 of the Revised Code.

(b) The parental rights of the parent who is not the residential parent and legal custodian have been terminated by order of a juvenile court pursuant to Chapter 2151. of the Revised Code.

(c) The parent who is not the residential parent and legal custodian cannot be located with reasonable efforts.

(B) In all other cases, the power of attorney may be executed only by one of the following persons:

(1) The parent who is the residential parent and legal custodian of the child, as determined by court order or as provided in section 3109.042 of the Revised Code;

(2) The parent with whom the child is residing the majority of the school year in cases in which no court has issued an order designating a parent as the residential parent and legal custodian of the child or section 3109.042 of the Revised Code is not applicable.

(2004 H 130, eff. 7–20–04)

Library References

Powers ⟨key⟩6, 10.
Westlaw Topic No. 307.
C.J.S. Powers § 4.

Research References

Encyclopedias

OH Jur. 3d Family Law § 1041, Relinquishment of Child to Grandparent Through Power of Attorney.
OH Jur. 3d Guardian & Ward § 88, Form, Notice, and Execution.

Treatises and Practice Aids

Carlin, Baldwin's Ohio Prac. Merrick-Rippner Probate Law § 61:11, Caretaker Authorization Affidavit--Grandparent and Grandchild.

3109.57 Conditions required for creation of power of attorney

(A) Except as provided in division (B) of this section and subject to sections 3109.56 and 3109.58 of the Revised Code, a parent, guardian, or custodian may create a power of attorney under section 3109.52 of the Revised Code only under the following circumstances:

(1) The parent, guardian, or custodian of the child is any of the following:

(a) Seriously ill, incarcerated, or about to be incarcerated;

(b) Temporarily unable to provide financial support or parental guidance to the child;

(c) Temporarily unable to provide adequate care and supervision of the child because of the parent's, guardian's, or custodian's physical or mental condition;

(d) Homeless or without a residence because the current residence is destroyed or otherwise uninhabitable;

(e) In or about to enter a residential treatment program for substance abuse.

(2) The parent, guardian, or custodian of the child has a well-founded belief that the power of attorney is in the child's best interest.

(B) In addition to the circumstances described in division (A) of this section and subject to sections 3109.56 and 3109.58 of the Revised Code, a parent may execute a power of attorney if the other parent of the child is deceased.

(2004 H 130, eff. 7–20–04)

Library References

Powers ⟨key⟩5, 10.
Westlaw Topic No. 307.
C.J.S. Powers § 4.

Research References

Encyclopedias

OH Jur. 3d Family Law § 1041, Relinquishment of Child to Grandparent Through Power of Attorney.

Treatises and Practice Aids

Hastings, Manoloff, Sheeran, & Stype, Ohio School Law § 23:4, Admission Requirements and Tu-

ition Liability--Special Tuition Exemptions and Waivers.

3109.58   Certain pending actions prohibiting creation of power of attorney

(A) As used in this section, "temporary custody," "permanent custody," and "planned permanent living arrangement" have the same meanings as in section 2151.011 of the Revised Code.

(B) A power of attorney created pursuant to section 3109.52 of the Revised Code may not be executed with respect to a child while any of the following proceedings are pending regarding the child:

(1) A proceeding for the appointment of a guardian for, or the adoption of, the child;

(2) A juvenile proceeding in which one of the following applies:

(a) The temporary, permanent, or legal custody of the child or the placement of the child in a planned permanent living arrangement has been requested.

(b) The child is the subject of an ex parte emergency custody order issued under division (D) of section 2151.31 of the Revised Code, and no hearing has yet been held regarding the child under division (A) of section 2151.314 of the Revised Code.

(c) The child is the subject of a temporary custody order issued under section 2151.33 of the Revised Code.

(3) A proceeding for divorce, dissolution, legal separation, annulment, or allocation of parental rights and responsibilities regarding the child.

(2004 H 130, eff. 7–20–04)

Library References

Powers ☞10, 31.
Westlaw Topic No. 307.
C.J.S. Powers §§ 4, 25.

Research References

Encyclopedias

OH Jur. 3d Family Law § 1041, Relinquishment of Child to Grandparent Through Power of Attorney.

Treatises and Practice Aids

Carlin, Baldwin's Ohio Prac. Merrick-Rippner Probate Law § 61:11, Caretaker Authorization Affidavit--Grandparent and Grandchild.

3109.59   Termination; filing of revocation of initial power of attorney or subsequent power of attorney

(A) A power of attorney created under section 3109.52 of the Revised Code terminates on the occurrence of whichever of the following events occurs first:

(1) One year elapses following the date the power of attorney is notarized.

(2) The power of attorney is revoked in writing by the person who created it.

(3) The child ceases to reside with the grandparent designated the attorney in fact.

(4) The power of attorney is terminated by court order.

(5) The death of the child who is the subject of the power of attorney.

(6) The death of the grandparent designated as the attorney in fact.

(B) Not later than five days after a power of attorney is terminated pursuant to division (A)(2) of this section, a copy of the revocation of an initial power of attorney or a second or subsequent power of attorney must be filed with the court with which the power of attorney is filed pursuant to section 3109.76 of the Revised Code.

(2004 H 130, eff. 7–20–04)

Library References

Powers ⚷13 to 15.
Westlaw Topic No. 307.
C.J.S. Powers §§ 5 to 7.

Research References

Encyclopedias

OH Jur. 3d Family Law § 1041, Relinquishment of Child to Grandparent Through Power of Attorney.
OH Jur. 3d Family Law § 1044, Hearing.
OH Jur. 3d Guardian & Ward § 89, Termination or Revocation of Power of Attorney.

Treatises and Practice Aids

Carlin, Baldwin's Ohio Prac. Merrick-Rippner Probate Law § 61:11, Caretaker Authorization Affidavit--Grandparent and Grandchild.

Hastings, Manoloff, Sheeran, & Stype, Ohio School Law § 23:4, Admission Requirements and Tuition Liability--Special Tuition Exemptions and Waivers.

3109.60 Notice required upon termination of grandparent's power of attorney

When a power of attorney created pursuant to section 3109.52 of the Revised Code terminates pursuant to division (A)(1), (A)(2), (A)(3), (A)(4), or (A)(5) of section 3109.59 of the Revised Code, the grandparent designated as the attorney in fact shall notify, in writing, all of the following:

(A) The school district in which the child attends school;

(B) The child's health care providers;

(C) The child's health insurance coverage provider;

(D) The court in which the power of attorney was filed under section 3109.74 of the Revised Code;

(E) The parent who is not the residential parent and legal custodian and who is required to be given notice under section 3109.55 of the Revised Code;

(F) Any other person or entity that has an ongoing relationship with the child or grandparent such that the person or entity would reasonably rely on the power of attorney unless notified of the termination.

The grandparent shall make the notifications not later than one week after the date the power of attorney terminates.

(2004 H 130, eff. 7–20–04)

Library References

Powers ⚷13 to 15.
Westlaw Topic No. 307.
C.J.S. Powers §§ 5 to 7.

Research References

Encyclopedias

OH Jur. 3d Family Law § 1041, Relinquishment of Child to Grandparent Through Power of Attorney.

OH Jur. 3d Guardian & Ward § 89, Termination or Revocation of Power of Attorney.

Treatises and Practice Aids

Carlin, Baldwin's Ohio Prac. Merrick-Rippner Pro-
    bate Law § 61:11, Caretaker Authorization Affi-
    davit--Grandparent and Grandchild.

3109.61   Immunity from liability for good faith reliance on power of attorney

A person who, in good faith, relies on or takes action in reliance on a power of attorney created under section 3109.52 of the Revised Code is immune from any criminal or civil liability for injury, death, or loss to persons or property that might otherwise be incurred or imposed solely as a result of the person's reliance or action. The person is not subject to any disciplinary action from an entity that licenses or certifies the person.

Any medical, psychological, or dental treatment provided to a child in reliance on a power of attorney created under section 3109.52 of the Revised Code shall be considered to have been provided in good faith if the person providing the treatment had no actual knowledge of opposition by the parent, guardian, or custodian.

This section does not provide immunity from civil or criminal liability to any person for actions that are wanton, reckless, or inconsistent with the ordinary standard of care required to be exercised by anyone acting in the same capacity as the person.

(2004 H 130, eff. 7–20–04)

Library References

Criminal Law ☞31, 37.20.
Negligence ☞500.
Torts ☞121.
Westlaw Topic Nos. 110, 272, 379.

C.J.S. Criminal Law §§ 53 to 54, 56, 118 to 120, 122.
C.J.S. Negligence §§ 226, 654.
C.J.S. Torts §§ 32 to 33, 37, 40.

Research References

Treatises and Practice Aids

Carlin, Baldwin's Ohio Prac. Merrick-Rippner Pro-
    bate Law § 61:11, Caretaker Authorization Affi-
    davit--Grandparent and Grandchild.

Hastings, Manoloff, Sheeran, & Stype, Ohio School Law § 23:4, Admission Requirements and Tuition Liability--Special Tuition Exemptions and Waivers.

3109.62   Effect of military power of attorney

A military power of attorney executed pursuant to section 574(a) of the "National Defense Authorization Act for Fiscal Year 1994," 107 Stat. 1674 (1993), 10 U.S.C. 1044b, that grants a person's rights and responsibilities regarding the care, custody, and control of the person's child, including the ability to enroll the child in school, to obtain from the school district educational and behavioral information about the child, to consent to all school-related matters regarding the child, and to consent to medical, psychological, or dental treatment for the child shall be considered a power of attorney created pursuant to sections 3109.51 to 3109.61 of the Revised Code, as long as the military power of attorney, according to its terms, remains in effect.

(2004 H 130, eff. 7–20–04)

Library References

Armed Services ☞20.7.
Westlaw Topic No. 34.
C.J.S. Armed Services §§ 1, 67, 71.

Research References

Treatises and Practice Aids

Carlin, Baldwin's Ohio Prac. Merrick-Rippner Pro-
    bate Law § 61:11, Caretaker Authorization Affi-
    davit--Grandparent and Grandchild.

3109.65 Authority of grandparent to execute caretaker authorization affidavit

(A) Except as provided in division (B) of this section, if a child is living with a grandparent who has made reasonable attempts to locate and contact both of the child's parents, or the child's guardian or custodian, but has been unable to do so, the grandparent may obtain authority to exercise care, physical custody, and control of the child including authority to enroll the child in school, to discuss with the school district the child's educational progress, to consent to all school-related matters regarding the child, and to consent to medical, psychological, or dental treatment for the child by executing a caretaker authorization affidavit in accordance with section 3109.67 of the Revised Code.

(B) The grandparent may execute a caretaker authorization affidavit without attempting to locate the following parent:

(1) If paternity has not been established with regard to the child, the child's father.

(2) If the child is the subject of a custody order, the following parent:

(a) A parent who is prohibited from receiving a notice of relocation in accordance with section 3109.051 of the Revised Code;

(b) A parent whose parental rights have been terminated by order of a juvenile court pursuant to Chapter 2151. of the Revised Code.

(2004 H 130, eff. 7–20–04)

Library References

Parent and Child ⊊15.
Westlaw Topic No. 285.
C.J.S. Parent and Child §§ 345 to 350, 357 to 358.

Research References

Encyclopedias

OH Jur. 3d Family Law § 1042, Caretaker Authorization Affidavit.
OH Jur. 3d Guardian & Ward § 90, Caretaker Authorization Affidavit; Authority to Execute.

Treatises and Practice Aids

Carlin, Baldwin's Ohio Prac. Merrick-Rippner Probate Law § 61:11, Caretaker Authorization Affidavit--Grandparent and Grandchild.

Hastings, Manoloff, Sheeran, & Stype, Ohio School Law § 23:4, Admission Requirements and Tuition Liability--Special Tuition Exemptions and Waivers.

3109.66 Form and content of caretaker authorization affidavit

The caretaker authorization affidavit that a grandparent described in section 3109.65 of the Revised Code may execute shall be identical in form and content to the following:

CARETAKER AUTHORIZATION AFFIDAVIT

Use of this affidavit is authorized by sections 3109.65 to 3109.73 of the Ohio Revised Code.

Completion of items 1–7 and the signing and notarization of this affidavit is sufficient to authorize the grandparent signing to exercise care, physical custody, and control of the child who is its subject, including authority to enroll the child in school, to discuss with the school district the child's educational progress, to consent to all school-related matters regarding the child, and to consent to medical, psychological, or dental treatment for the child.

The child named below lives in my home, I am 18 years of age or older, and I am the child's grandparent.

1. Name of child:
2. Child's date and year of birth:
3. Child's social security number (optional):
4. My name:

5. My home address:
6. My date and year of birth:
7. My Ohio driver's license number or identification card number:
8. Despite having made reasonable attempts, I am either:
      (a) Unable to locate or contact the child's parents, or the child's guardian or custodian; or
      (b) I am unable to locate or contact one of the child's parents and I am not required to contact the other parent because paternity has not been established; or
      (c) I am unable to locate or contact one of the child's parents and I am not required to contact the other parent because there is a custody order regarding the child and one of the following is the case:
      (i) The parent has been prohibited from receiving notice of a relocation; or
      (ii) The parental rights of the parent have been terminated.
9. I hereby certify that this affidavit is not being executed for the purpose of enrolling the child in a school or school district so that the child may participate in the academic or interscholastic athletic programs provided by that school or district.

   I understand that this document does not authorize a child support enforcement agency to redirect child support payments. I further understand that to have an existing child support order modified or a new child support order issued administrative or judicial proceedings must be initiated.

WARNING: DO NOT SIGN THIS FORM IF ANY OF THE ABOVE STATEMENTS ARE INCORRECT. FALSIFICATION IS A CRIME UNDER SECTION 2921.13 OF THE REVISED CODE, PUNISHABLE BY THE SANCTIONS UNDER CHAPTER 2929. OF THE REVISED CODE, INCLUDING A TERM OF IMPRISONMENT OF UP TO 6 MONTHS, A FINE OF UP TO $1,000, OR BOTH.

I declare that the foregoing is true and correct:

Signed: .... Date: ....
Grandparent

State of Ohio   )
) ss:
County of ....)

Subscribed, sworn to, and acknowledged before me this...... day of ....,............

....
Notary Public

Notices:

1. The grandparent's signature must be notarized by an Ohio notary public.
2. The grandparent who executed this affidavit must file it with the juvenile court of the county in which the grandparent resides or any other court that has jurisdiction over the child under a previously filed motion or proceeding not later than five days after the date it is executed.
3. A grandparent who executes a second or subsequent caretaker authorization affidavit regarding a child who is the subject of a prior caretaker authorization affidavit must file the affidavit with the juvenile court of the county in which the grandparent resides or any other court that has jurisdiction over the child under a previously filed motion or proceeding. On filing, the court will schedule a hearing to determine whether the caretaker authorization affidavit is in the child's best interest.
4. This affidavit does not affect the rights of the child's parents, guardian, or custodian regarding the care, physical custody, and control of the child, and does not give the grandparent legal custody of the child.

5. A person or entity that relies on this affidavit, in good faith, has no obligation to make any further inquiry or investigation.
6. This affidavit terminates on the occurrence of whichever of the following occurs first: (1) one year elapses following the date the affidavit is notarized; (2) the child ceases to live with the grandparent who signs this form; (3) the parent, guardian, or custodian of the child acts to negate, reverse, or otherwise disapprove an action or decision of the grandparent who signed this affidavit; or (4) the affidavit is terminated by court order; (5) the death of the child who is the subject of the affidavit; or (6) the death of the grandparent who executed the affidavit.

    A parent, guardian, or custodian may negate, reverse, or disapprove a grandparent's action or decision only by delivering written notice of negation, reversal, or disapproval to the grandparent and the person acting on the grandparent's action or decision in reliance on this affidavit.

    If this affidavit terminates other than by the death of the grandparent, the grandparent who signed this affidavit shall notify, in writing, all of the following:
    a) Any schools, health care providers, or health insurance coverage provider with which the child has been involved through the grandparent;
    (b) Any other person or entity that has an ongoing relationship with the child or grandparent such that the person or entity would reasonably rely on the affidavit unless notified of the termination;
    (c) The court in which the affidavit was filed after its creation.

    The grandparent shall make the notifications not later than one week after the date the affidavit terminates.
7. The decision of a grandparent to consent to or to refuse medical treatment or school enrollment for a child is superseded by a contrary decision of a parent, custodian, or guardian of the child, unless the decision of the parent, guardian, or custodian would jeopardize the life, health, or safety of the child.

Additional information:

To caretakers:

1. If the child stops living with you, you are required to notify, in writing, any school, health care provider, or health care insurance provider to which you have given this affidavit. You are also required to notify, in writing, any other person or entity that has an ongoing relationship with you or the child such that the person or entity would reasonably rely on the affidavit unless notified. The notifications must be made not later than one week after the child stops living with you.
2. If you do not have the information requested in item 7 (Ohio driver's license or identification card), provide another form of identification such as your social security number or medicaid number.
3. You must include with the caretaker authorization affidavit the following information:
    (a) The child's present address, the addresses of the places where the child has lived within the last five years, and the name and present address of each person with whom the child has lived during that period;
    (b) Whether you have participated as a party, a witness, or in any other capacity in any other litigation, in this state or any other state, that concerned the allocation, between the parents of the same child, of parental rights and responsibilities for the care of the child and the designation of the residential parent and legal custodian of the child or that otherwise concerned the custody of the same child;
    (c) Whether you have information of any parenting proceeding concerning the child pending in a court of this or any other state;
    (d) Whether you know of any person who has physical custody of the child or claims to be a parent of the child who is designated the residential parent and legal custodian of the child or to have parenting time rights with respect to the child or to be a person other than a parent of the child who has custody or visitation rights with respect to the child;
    (e) Whether you previously have been convicted of or pleaded guilty to any criminal offense involving any act that resulted in a child being an abused child or a neglected child

or previously have been determined, in a case in which a child has been adjudicated an abused child or a neglected child, to be the perpetrator of the abusive or neglectful act that was the basis of the adjudication.

To school officials:

1. This affidavit, properly completed and notarized, authorizes the child in question to attend school in the district in which the grandparent who signed this affidavit resides and the grandparent is authorized to provide consent in all school-related matters and to discuss with the school district the child's educational progress. This affidavit does not preclude the parent, guardian, or custodian of the child from having access to all school records pertinent to the child.
2. The school district may require additional reasonable evidence that the grandparent lives at the address provided in item 5.
3. A school district or school official that reasonably and in good faith relies on this affidavit has no obligation to make any further inquiry or investigation.
4. The act of a parent, guardian, or custodian of the child to negate, reverse, or otherwise disapprove an action or decision of the grandparent who signed this affidavit constitutes termination of this affidavit. A parent, guardian, or custodian may negate, reverse, or disapprove a grandparent's action or decision only by delivering written notice of negation, reversal, or disapproval to the grandparent and the person acting on the grandparent's action or decision in reliance on this affidavit.

To health care providers:

1. A person or entity that acts in good faith reliance on a CARETAKER AUTHORIZA-TION AFFIDAVIT to provide medical, psychological, or dental treatment, without actual knowledge of facts contrary to those stated in the affidavit, is not subject to criminal liability or to civil liability to any person or entity, and is not subject to professional disciplinary action, solely for such reliance if the applicable portions of the form are completed and the grandparent's signature is notarized.
2. The decision of a grandparent, based on a CARETAKER AUTHORIZATION AFFIDA-VIT, shall be honored by a health care facility or practitioner, school district, or school official unless the health care facility or practitioner or educational facility or official has actual knowledge that a parent, guardian, or custodian of a child has made a contravening decision to consent to or to refuse medical treatment for the child.
3. The act of a parent, guardian, or custodian of the child to negate, reverse, or otherwise disapprove an action or decision of the grandparent who signed this affidavit constitutes termination of this affidavit. A parent, guardian, or custodian may negate, reverse, or disapprove a grandparent's action or decision only by delivering written notice of negation, reversal, or disapproval to the grandparent and the person acting on the grandparent's action or decision in reliance on this affidavit.

(2004 H 130, eff. 7–20–04)

Library References

Parent and Child ⌘15.
Westlaw Topic No. 285.
C.J.S. Parent and Child §§ 345 to 350, 357 to 358.

Research References

Encyclopedias

OH Jur. 3d Acknowledgmts, Affid., Oaths, & Notar. § 61, Effect of Notarized Document.

OH Jur. 3d Family Law § 1042, Caretaker Authorization Affidavit.
OH Jur. 3d Guardian & Ward § 90, Caretaker Authorization Affidavit; Authority to Execute.

Treatises and Practice Aids

Carlin, Baldwin's Ohio Prac. Merrick-Rippner Probate Law § 61:11, Caretaker Authorization Affi-
davit--Grandparent and Grandchild.

3109.67 Execution of affidavit

A caretaker authorization affidavit described in section 3109.66 of the Revised Code is executed when the affidavit is completed, signed by a grandparent described in section 3109.65 of the Revised Code, and notarized.

(2004 H 130, eff. 7–20–04)

Cross References

Enrollment of child in school district where grandparent resides, see 3313.649

Library References

Parent and Child ☞15.
Westlaw Topic No. 285.
C.J.S. Parent and Child §§ 345 to 350, 357 to 358.

Research References

Encyclopedias

OH Jur. 3d Acknowledgmts, Affid., Oaths, & No-
tar. § 61, Effect of Notarized Document.
OH Jur. 3d Family Law § 1042, Caretaker Authori-
zation Affidavit.
OH Jur. 3d Guardian & Ward § 90, Caretaker
Authorization Affidavit; Authority to Execute.

OH Jur. 3d Guardian & Ward § 92, Filing of
Power of Attorney or Caretaker Authorization
Affidavit With Juvenile Court and Hearing.

Treatises and Practice Aids

Carlin, Baldwin's Ohio Prac. Merrick-Rippner Probate Law § 61:11, Caretaker Authorization Affi-
davit--Grandparent and Grandchild.

3109.68 Affidavit not permitted when certain proceedings are pending

(A) As used in this section, "temporary custody," "permanent custody," and "planned permanent living arrangement" have the same meanings as in section 2151.011 of the Revised Code.

(B) A caretaker authorization affidavit may not be executed with respect to a child while any of the following proceedings are pending regarding the child:

(1) A proceeding for the appointment of a guardian for, or the adoption of, the child;

(2) A juvenile proceeding in which one of the following applies:

(a) The temporary, permanent, or legal custody of the child or the placement of the child in a planned permanent living arrangement has been requested.

(b) The child is the subject of an ex parte emergency custody order issued under division (D) of section 2151.31 of the Revised Code, and no hearing has yet been held regarding the child under division (A) of section 2151.314 of the Revised Code.

(c) The child is the subject of a temporary custody order issued under section 2151.33 of the Revised Code.

(3) A proceeding for divorce, dissolution, legal separation, annulment, or allocation of parental rights and responsibilities regarding the child.

(2004 H 130, eff. 7–20–04)

Library References

Parent and Child ☞15.
Westlaw Topic No. 285.
C.J.S. Parent and Child §§ 345 to 350, 357 to 358.

Encyclopedias

OH Jur. 3d Guardian & Ward § 90, Caretaker Authorization Affidavit; Authority to Execute.

Treatises and Practice Aids

Hastings, Manoloff, Sheeran, & Stype, Ohio School Law § 23:4, Admission Requirements and Tu-

ition Liability--Special Tuition Exemptions and Waivers.

3109.69 Effect of executed affidavit

Once a caretaker authorization affidavit has been executed under section 3109.67 of the Revised Code, the grandparent may exercise care, physical custody, and control of the child, including enrolling the child in school, discussing with the school district the child's educational progress, consenting to all school-related matters regarding the child, and consenting to medical, psychological, or dental treatment for the child. The affidavit does not affect the rights and responsibilities of the parent, guardian, or custodian regarding the child, does not grant legal custody to the grandparent, and does not grant authority to the grandparent to consent to the marriage or adoption of the child.

(2004 H 130, eff. 7–20–04)

Parent and Child ☞15.
Westlaw Topic No. 285.
C.J.S. Parent and Child §§ 345 to 350, 357 to 358.

Encyclopedias

OH Jur. 3d Family Law § 1042, Caretaker Authorization Affidavit.
OH Jur. 3d Guardian & Ward § 90, Caretaker Authorization Affidavit; Authority to Execute.

Treatises and Practice Aids

Hastings, Manoloff, Sheeran, & Stype, Ohio School Law § 23:4, Admission Requirements and Tuition Liability--Special Tuition Exemptions and Waivers.

3109.70 Termination of affidavit

An executed caretaker authorization affidavit shall terminate on the occurrence of whichever of the following comes first:

(A) One year elapses following the date the affidavit is notarized.

(B) The child ceases to reside with the grandparent.

(C) The parent, guardian, or custodian of the child who is the subject of the affidavit acts, in accordance with section 3109.72 of the Revised Code, to negate, reverse, or otherwise disapprove an action or decision of the grandparent who signed the affidavit with respect to the child.

(D) The affidavit is terminated by court order.

(E) The death of the child who is the subject of the affidavit.

(F) The death of the grandparent who executed the affidavit.

(2004 H 130, eff. 7–20–04)

Parent and Child ☞15.
Westlaw Topic No. 285.
C.J.S. Parent and Child §§ 345 to 350, 357 to 358.

Research References

Encyclopedias

OH Jur. 3d Family Law § 1042, Caretaker Authorization Affidavit.
OH Jur. 3d Family Law § 1044, Hearing.
OH Jur. 3d Guardian & Ward § 91, Caretaker Authorization Affidavit; Termination, Negation, Disapproval, or Reversal.

Treatises and Practice Aids

Hastings, Manoloff, Sheeran, & Stype, Ohio School Law § 23:4, Admission Requirements and Tuition Liability--Special Tuition Exemptions and Waivers.

3109.71 Notice required upon termination of affidavit

When a caretaker authorization affidavit terminates pursuant to division (A), (B), (C), (D), or (E) of section 3109.70 of the Revised Code, the grandparent shall notify, in writing, the school district in which the child attends school, the child's health care providers, the child's health insurance coverage provider, the court in which the affidavit was filed under section 3109.74 of the Revised Code, and any other person or entity that has an ongoing relationship with the child or grandparent such that the person or entity would reasonably rely on the affidavit unless notified of the termination. The grandparent shall make the notifications not later than one week after the date the affidavit terminates.

(2004 H 130, eff. 7–20–04)

Library References

Parent and Child ⟛15.
Westlaw Topic No. 285.
C.J.S. Parent and Child §§ 345 to 350, 357 to 358.

Research References

Encyclopedias

OH Jur. 3d Family Law § 1042, Caretaker Authorization Affidavit.

OH Jur. 3d Guardian & Ward § 91, Caretaker Authorization Affidavit; Termination, Negation, Disapproval, or Reversal.

3109.72 Negation, reversal, or disapproval of action taken pursuant to affidavit

The parent, guardian, or custodian of a child may negate, reverse, or otherwise disapprove any action taken or decision made pursuant to a caretaker authorization affidavit unless negation, reversal, or disapproval would jeopardize the life, health, or safety of the child. A parent, guardian, or custodian may negate, reverse, or disapprove a caretaker's action or decision only by delivering written notice of negation, reversal, or disapproval to the caretaker and the person responding to the caretaker's action or decision in reliance on the affidavit. The act to negate, reverse, or disapprove the action or decision, regardless of whether it is effective, terminates the affidavit.

(2004 H 130, eff. 7–20–04)

Library References

Parent and Child ⟛15.
Westlaw Topic No. 285.
C.J.S. Parent and Child §§ 345 to 350, 357 to 358.

Research References

Encyclopedias

OH Jur. 3d Family Law § 1042, Caretaker Authorization Affidavit.
OH Jur. 3d Guardian & Ward § 91, Caretaker Authorization Affidavit; Termination, Negation, Disapproval, or Reversal.

Treatises and Practice Aids

Hastings, Manoloff, Sheeran, & Stype, Ohio School Law § 23:4, Admission Requirements and Tuition Liability--Special Tuition Exemptions and Waivers.

3109.73 Immunity from liability for good faith reliance on affidavit

A person who, in good faith, relies on or takes action in reliance on a caretaker authorization affidavit is immune from any criminal or civil liability for injury, death, or loss to persons or property that might otherwise be incurred or imposed solely as a result of the reliance or action. The person is not subject to any disciplinary action from an entity that licenses or certifies the person. Any medical, psychological, or dental treatment provided to a child in reliance on an affidavit with respect to the child shall be considered to have been provided in good faith if the the person providing the treatment had no actual knowledge of opposition by the parent, guardian, or custodian.

This section does not provide immunity from civil or criminal liability to any person for actions that are wanton, reckless, or inconsistent with the ordinary standard of care required to be exercised by anyone acting in the same capacity as the person.

(2004 H 130, eff. 7–20–04)

Library References

Criminal Law ⟨=⟩31, 37.20.
Negligence ⟨=⟩500.
Torts ⟨=⟩121.
Westlaw Topic Nos. 110, 272, 379.

C.J.S. Criminal Law §§ 53 to 54, 56, 118 to 120, 122.
C.J.S. Negligence §§ 226, 654.
C.J.S. Torts §§ 32 to 33, 37, 40.

Research References

Encyclopedias

OH Jur. 3d Guardian & Ward § 90, Caretaker Authorization Affidavit; Authority to Execute.

Treatises and Practice Aids

Hastings, Manoloff, Sheeran, & Stype, Ohio School Law § 23:4, Admission Requirements and Tu-

ition Liability--Special Tuition Exemptions and Waivers.

3109.74 Filing of power of attorney or affidavit with juvenile court; accompanying information; report to public children services agency; investigation

(A) A person who creates a power of attorney under section 3109.52 of the Revised Code or executes a caretaker authorization affidavit under section 3109.67 of the Revised Code shall file the power of attorney or affidavit with the juvenile court of the county in which the grandparent designated as attorney in fact or grandparent who executed the affidavit resides or any other court that has jurisdiction over the child under a previously filed motion or proceeding. The power of attorney or affidavit shall be filed not later than five days after the date it is created or executed and may be sent to the court by certified mail.

(B) A power of attorney filed under this section shall be accompanied by a receipt showing that the notice of creation of the power of attorney was sent to the parent who is not the residential parent and legal custodian by certified mail under section 3109.55 of the Revised Code.

(C)(1) The grandparent designated as attorney in fact or the grandparent who executed the affidavit shall include with the power of attorney or the caretaker authorization affidavit the information described in section 3109.27 of the Revised Code.

(2) If the grandparent provides information that the grandparent previously has been convicted of or pleaded guilty to any criminal offense involving any act that resulted in a child being an abused child or a neglected child or previously has been determined, in a case in which a child has been adjudicated an abused child or a neglected child, to be the perpetrator of the abusive or neglectful act that was the basis of the adjudication, the court may report that information to the public children services agency pursuant to section 2151.421 of the Revised Code. Upon the receipt of that information, the public children services agency shall initiate an investigation pursuant to section 2151.421 of the Revised Code.

(3) If the court has reason to believe that a power of attorney or caretaker authorization affidavit is not in the best interest of the child, the court may report that information to the public children services agency pursuant to section 2151.421 of the Revised Code. Upon receipt of that information, the public children services agency shall initiate an investigation pursuant to section 2151.421 of the Revised Code. The public children services agency shall submit a report of its investigation to the court not later than thirty days after the court reports the information to the public children services agency or not later than forty-five days after the court reports the information to the public children services agency when information that is needed to determine the case disposition cannot be compiled within thirty days and the reasons are documented in the case record.

(D) The court shall waive any filing fee imposed for the filing of the power of attorney or caretaker authorization affidavit.

(2004 H 130, eff. 7–20–04)

Cross References

Jurisdiction of juvenile court, orders for child support, see 2151.23

Library References

Parent and Child ⬤15.
Powers ⬤10.
Westlaw Topic Nos. 285, 307.

C.J.S. Parent and Child §§ 345 to 350, 357 to 358.
C.J.S. Powers § 4.

Research References

Encyclopedias

OH Jur. 3d Family Law § 1043, Filing With Juvenile Court.
OH Jur. 3d Guardian & Ward § 92, Filing of Power of Attorney or Caretaker Authorization Affidavit With Juvenile Court and Hearing.

Treatises and Practice Aids

Carlin, Baldwin's Ohio Prac. Merrick-Rippner Probate Law § 107:2, Original Jurisdiction.
Carlin, Baldwin's Ohio Prac. Merrick-Rippner Probate Law § 61:11, Caretaker Authorization Affidavit--Grandparent and Grandchild.

3109.75 Verification of power of attorney or affidavit

On the request of the person in charge of admissions of a school or a person described under division (A)(1)(b) of section 2151.421 of the Revised Code, the court in which the power of attorney or caretaker authorization affidavit was filed shall verify whether a power of attorney or caretaker authorization affidavit has been filed under section 3109.74 of the Revised Code with respect to a child.

(2004 H 130, eff. 7–20–04)

Library References

Parent and Child ⬤15.
Powers ⬤10.
Westlaw Topic Nos. 285, 307.

C.J.S. Parent and Child §§ 345 to 350, 357 to 358.
C.J.S. Powers § 4.

Research References

Encyclopedias

OH Jur. 3d Guardian & Ward § 92, Filing of Power of Attorney or Caretaker Authorization Affidavit With Juvenile Court and Hearing.

3109.76 Requirements regarding subsequent powers of attorney or affidavits

If a second or subsequent power of attorney is created under section 3109.52 of the Revised Code regarding a child who is the subject of a prior power of attorney or a second or subsequent caretaker authorization affidavit is executed under section 3109.67 of the Revised

Code regarding a child who is the subject of a prior affidavit, the person who creates the power of attorney or executes the affidavit must file it with the juvenile court of the county in which the grandparent designated as attorney in fact or the grandparent who executed the affidavit resides or with any other court that has jurisdiction over the child under a previously filed motion or proceeding.

(2004 H 130, eff. 7–20–04)

Library References

Parent and Child ☜15.
Powers ☜10.
Westlaw Topic Nos. 285, 307.

C.J.S. Parent and Child §§ 345 to 350, 357 to 358.
C.J.S. Powers § 4.

Research References

Encyclopedias

OH Jur. 3d Family Law § 1041, Relinquishment of Child to Grandparent Through Power of Attorney.

OH Jur. 3d Guardian & Ward § 92, Filing of Power of Attorney or Caretaker Authorization Affidavit With Juvenile Court and Hearing.

3109.77 Hearing; notice; de novo review

(A) On the filing of a power of attorney or caretaker authorization affidavit under section 3109.76 of the Revised Code, the court in which the power of attorney or caretaker authorization affidavit was filed shall schedule a hearing to determine whether the power of attorney or affidavit is in the child's best interest. The court shall provide notice of the date, time, and location of the hearing to the parties and to the parent who is not the residential parent and legal custodian unless one of the following circumstances applies:

(1) In accordance with section 3109.051 of the Revised Code, that parent is not to be given a notice of relocation.

(2) The parent's parental rights have been terminated by order of a juvenile court pursuant to Chapter 2151. of the Revised Code.

(3) The parent cannot be located with reasonable efforts.

(4) The power of attorney was created by both parents.

(B) The hearing shall be held not later than ten days after the date the power of attorney or affidavit was filed with the court. At the hearing, the parties and the parent who is not the residential parent and legal custodian may present evidence and be represented by counsel.

(C) At the conclusion of the hearing, the court may take any of the following actions that the court determines is in the child's best interest:

(1) Approve the power of attorney or affidavit. If approved, the power of attorney or affidavit shall remain in effect unless otherwise terminated under section 3109.59 of the Revised Code with respect to a power of attorney or section 3109.70 of the Revised Code with respect to an affidavit.

(2) Issue an order terminating the power of attorney or affidavit and ordering the child returned to the child's parent, guardian, or custodian. If the parent, guardian, or custodian of the child cannot be located, the court shall treat the filing of the power of attorney or affidavit with the court as a complaint under section 2151.27 of the Revised Code that the child is a dependent child.

(3) Treat the filing of the power of attorney or affidavit as a petition for legal custody and award legal custody of the child to the grandparent designated as the attorney in fact under the power of attorney or to the grandparent who executed the affidavit.

(D) The court shall conduct a de novo review of any order issued under division (C) of this section if all of the following apply regarding the parent who is not the residential parent and legal custodian:

(1) The parent did not appear at the hearing from which the order was issued.

561

(2) The parent was not represented by counsel at the hearing.

(3) The parent filed a motion with the court not later than fourteen days after receiving notice of the hearing pursuant to division (A) of this section.

(2004 H 130, eff. 7–20–04)

Library References

Parent and Child ⟜15.
Powers ⟜10.
Westlaw Topic Nos. 285, 307.

C.J.S. Parent and Child §§ 345 to 350, 357 to 358.
C.J.S. Powers § 4.

Research References

Encyclopedias

OH Jur. 3d Family Law § 1044, Hearing.
OH Jur. 3d Guardian & Ward § 92, Filing of Power of Attorney or Caretaker Authorization Affidavit With Juvenile Court and Hearing.

Treatises and Practice Aids

Sowald & Morganstern, Baldwin's Ohio Practice Domestic Relations Law § 15:53, Award to Third Party--By Parents' Agreement--Power of Attorney.

3109.78 Creation of power of attorney or affidavit for participation in academic or interscholastic programs prohibited

(A) No person shall create a power of attorney under section 3109.52 of the Revised Code or execute a caretaker authorization affidavit under section 3109.67 of the Revised Code for the purpose of enrolling the child in a school or school district so that the child may participate in the academic or interscholastic athletic programs provided by the school or school district.

(B) A person who violates division (A) of this section is in violation of section 2921.13 of the Revised Code and is guilty of falsification, a misdemeanor of the first degree.

(C) A power of attorney created, or an affidavit executed, in violation of this section is void as of the date of its creation or execution.

(2004 H 130, eff. 7–20–04)

Library References

Parent and Child ⟜15.
Powers ⟜5.

Westlaw Topic Nos. 285, 307.
C.J.S. Parent and Child §§ 345 to 350, 357 to 358.

Research References

Encyclopedias

OH Jur. 3d Guardian & Ward § 90, Caretaker Authorization Affidavit; Authority to Execute.

Treatises and Practice Aids

Hastings, Manoloff, Sheeran, & Stype, Ohio School Law § 23:4, Admission Requirements and Tu-

ition Liability--Special Tuition Exemptions and Waivers.

3109.79 Effect of power of attorney or affidavit on administrative or court child support order

As used in this section, "administrative child support order" and "court child support order" have the same meanings as in section 3119.01 of the Revised Code.

A power of attorney created under section 3109.52 of the Revised Code or a caretaker authorization affidavit executed under section 3109.67 of the Revised Code shall not affect the enforcement of an administrative child support order or court child support order, unless a child support enforcement agency, with respect to an administrative child support order, or a court, with respect to either order, issues an order providing otherwise.

(2004 H 130, eff. 7–20–04)

Library References

Child Support ⚖️440, 465.
Westlaw Topic No. 76E.

C.J.S. Divorce §§ 1121 to 1122, 1133, 1135.
C.J.S. Parent and Child §§ 175, 236, 239 to 240.

Research References

Encyclopedias

OH Jur. 3d Family Law § 1041, Relinquishment of Child to Grandparent Through Power of Attorney.

OH Jur. 3d Family Law § 1042, Caretaker Authorization Affidavit.

OH Jur. 3d Guardian & Ward § 90, Caretaker Authorization Affidavit; Authority to Execute.

Treatises and Practice Aids

Carlin, Baldwin's Ohio Prac. Merrick-Rippner Probate Law § 61:11, Caretaker Authorization Affidavit--Grandparent and Grandchild.

3109.80 Only one power of attorney or affidavit in effect per child

Only one power of attorney created under section 3109.52 of the Revised Code or one caretaker authorization executed under section 3109.67 of the Revised Code may be in effect for a child at one time.

(2004 H 130, eff. 7–20–04)

Cross References

Jurisdiction of juvenile court, orders for child support, see 2151.23
Pupil to provide certain information, see 3313.672

Suspension, expulsion, and removal from premises, see 3313.66

Library References

Parent and Child ⚖️15.
Powers ⚖️10.
Westlaw Topic Nos. 285, 307.

C.J.S. Parent and Child §§ 345 to 350, 357 to 358.
C.J.S. Powers § 4.

Research References

Encyclopedias

OH Jur. 3d Guardian & Ward § 90, Caretaker Authorization Affidavit; Authority to Execute.

Treatises and Practice Aids

Sowald & Morganstern, Baldwin's Ohio Practice Domestic Relations Law § 15:53, Award to Third

Party--By Parents' Agreement--Power of Attorney.

Carlin, Baldwin's Ohio Prac. Merrick-Rippner Probate Law § 107:2, Original Jurisdiction.

Carlin, Baldwin's Ohio Prac. Merrick-Rippner Probate Law § 61:11, Caretaker Authorization Affidavit--Grandparent and Grandchild.

PARENTAGE

PRELIMINARY PROVISIONS

Comparative Laws

Uniform Parentage Act

Table of Jurisdictions Wherein Act Has Been Adopted.

For text of Uniform Act, and variation notes and annotation materials for adopting jurisdictions, see *Uniform Laws Annotated, Master Edition, Volume 9B.*

Jurisdiction	Statutory Citation
California	West's Ann.Cal.Fam. Code, § 7600 to 7730.
Colorado	West's C.R.S.A. § 19–4–101 to 19–4–130.
Hawaii	HRS § 584–1 to 584–26.
Illinois	S.H.A. 750 ILCS 45/1 to 45/28
Kansas	K.S.A. 38–1110 to 38–1138.
Minnesota	M.S.A. § 257.51 to 257.75.
Missouri	V.A.M.S. § 210.817 to 210.854.
Montana	MCA 40–6–101 to 40–6–135.
Nevada	N.R.S. 126.011 to 126.371.
New Jersey	N.J.S.A. 9:17–38 to 9:17–59.
Rhode Island	Gen. Laws 1956, § 15–8–1 to 15–8–27.

Cross References

Action for child support order, existence of parent-child relationship, see 2151.231

Adoption, see 3107.01 et seq.

Capability of children born out of wedlock to inherit, see 2105.17

Children, see 3109.01 et seq.

County court of common pleas, domestic relations divisions, see 2301.03

Duty of parents to support children of unemancipated minor children, see 3109.19

Jurisdiction of juvenile court, orders for child support, see 2151.23

Juvenile courts, action for child support order before acknowledgment becomes final, see 2151.232

Juvenile rules, exceptions, Juv R 1

Parental duty of support, see 3103.031

Reciprocal enforcement of support, adjudication of paternity issue, genetic testing, see 3115.24

Uniform Interstate Family Support Act, duties and powers of responding tribunal, see 3115.16

Uniform Interstate Family Support Act, proceeding to determine parentage, see 3115.52

Vital statistics, birth certificate of legitimatized child, see 3705.09

PRELIMINARY PROVISIONS

3111.01   Definition

(A) As used in sections 3111.01 to 3111.85 of the Revised Code, "parent and child relationship" means the legal relationship that exists between a child and the child's natural or adoptive parents and upon which those sections and any other provision of the Revised Code confer or impose rights, privileges, duties, and obligations. The "parent and child relationship" includes the mother and child relationship and the father and child relationship.

(B) The parent and child relationship extends equally to all children and all parents, regardless of the marital status of the parents

(2000 S 180, eff. 3–22–01; 1992 S 10, eff. 7–15–92; 1986 II 476; 1982 H 245)

Uncodified Law

1992 S 10, § 5, eff. 7–15–92, reads, in part: Sections 3111.01 to 3111.19 of the Revised Code, as enacted or amended by this act, shall apply only to an action brought under sections 3111.01 to 3111.19

of the Revised Code on or after the effective date of this act.

1982 H 245, § 3: See Uncodified Law under 3111.04.

Historical and Statutory Notes

Ed. Note: Former 3111.01 repealed by 1982 H 245, eff. 6–29–82; 1975 S 145; 127 v 1039; 1953 H 1; GC 8006–1; Source—GC 12110.

Pre–1953 H 1 Amendments: 124 v S 65

Amendment Note: 2000 S 180 substituted "3111.85" for "3111.01" in division (A).

Cross References

Adoption, putative father defined, see 3107.01
Adoption, search of putative father registry prior to adoption, exemptions, see 3107.064
Age and schooling certificate, responsibility of parent, see 3331.14
"Child without proper parental care," defined, see 2151.05
Diagnosis and treatment of minor for drug or alcohol related condition, liability of parent for expenses, see 3719.012
DNA database, disclosure of information, see 109.573

Driver's license for minor, obligation of parent, see 4507.07
Duty of married person to support self, spouse, and children, duration of duty to support, see 3103.03
Judges of the divisions of domestic relations, see 2301.03
Liability of parent of minor who willfully damages property or commits theft offense, see 3109.09
Liability of parents for assaults by their children, see 3109.10
Powers of child support enforcement agency in providing service of process of notice or order, see 3125.141

Library References

Parent and Child ⊶1.
Westlaw Topic No. 285.
C.J.S. Parent and Child §§ 1 to 12, 201.

Research References

ALR Library

80 ALR 5th 1, Child Custody and Visitation Rights Arising from Same-Sex Relationship.
90 ALR 5th 1, Construction and Application of Uniform Interstate Family Support Act.
87 ALR 5th 361, Liability of Father for Retroactive Child Support on Judicial Determination of Paternity.

Encyclopedias

OH Jur. 3d Actions § 10, Civil or Criminal.

OH Jur. 3d Decedents' Estates § 81, Illegitimate Blood Relationship--Parentage Act.
OH Jur. 3d Decedents' Estates § 541, as Including Illegitimate Children.
OH Jur. 3d Family Law § 863, Existence and Proof of Relationship.
OH Jur. 3d Family Law § 864, Birth Record of Legitimated Child.
OH Jur. 3d Family Law § 937, Definition of "Parent and Child Relationship".

OH Jur. 3d Family Law § 941, Establishment of Parent and Child Relationship.

OH Jur. 3d Family Law § 942, Interference With Paternity Actions; Penalties.

OH Jur. 3d Family Law § 952, Jurisdiction.

OH Jur. 3d Family Law § 958, Retroactivity of Statute.

OH Jur. 3d Family Law § 971, Burden and Degree of Proof.

OH Jur. 3d Family Law § 981, Fees and Court Costs.

OH Jur. 3d Family Law § 1011, Assumption of Parental Duty of Support.

OH Jur. 3d Family Law § 1016, Action for Support.

OH Jur. 3d Family Law § 1028, Duration of Support; Modification.

OH Jur. 3d Family Law § 1226, Title IV-D Cases.

OH Jur. 3d Family Law § 1318, Service of Withholding or Deduction Notice.

OH Jur. 3d Family Law § 1546, Paternity Actions.

OH Jur. 3d Names § 15, Minors.

Forms

Ohio Forms Legal and Business § 28:2, Definitions.

Ohio Jurisprudence Pleading and Practice Forms § 2:8, Courts of Common Pleas--Juvenile Division.

Ohio Jurisprudence Pleading and Practice Forms § 111:2, Definitions.

Ohio Jurisprudence Pleading and Practice Forms § 111:4, Jurisdiction.

Ohio Jurisprudence Pleading and Practice Forms § 111:5, Standing--Parties.

Ohio Jurisprudence Pleading and Practice Forms § 111:7, Genetic Tests.

Ohio Jurisprudence Pleading and Practice Forms § 96:11, Consent Required.

Ohio Jurisprudence Pleading and Practice Forms § 111:10, Temporary Support Order.

Am. Jur. Pl. & Pr. Forms Bastards § 1, Introductory Comments.

Treatises and Practice Aids

Klein, Darling, & Terez, Baldwin's Ohio Practice Civil Practice § 1:20, Civ. R. 1(C): Exceptions--Effect of Revised Code Section Purporting to Prohibit Application of One or More Civil Rules.

Klein, Darling, & Terez, Baldwin's Ohio Practice Civil Practice § 1:97, Civ. R. 1(C)(7): All Other Special Statutory Proceedings--Revised Code Sections Purporting to Mandate Application of One or More Civil Rules.

Klein, Darling, & Terez, Baldwin's Ohio Practice Civil Practice § 1:98, Civ. R. 1(C)(7): All Other Special Statutory Proceedings--Revised Code Sections Purporting to Prohibit Application of One or More Civil Rules.

Klein, Darling, & Terez, Baldwin's Ohio Practice Civil Practice § 38:15, Right to Jury Trial Under Ohio Statutes--Other Statutes.

Sowald & Morganstern, Baldwin's Ohio Practice Domestic Relations Law § 3:1, Ohio Parentage Act--History and Origin.

Sowald & Morganstern, Baldwin's Ohio Practice Domestic Relations Law § 3:2, Administrative Determination of Parentage--Purpose.

Sowald & Morganstern, Baldwin's Ohio Practice Domestic Relations Law § 3:4, Administrative Determination of Parentage--Acknowledgment, Support Order, and Birth Record.

Sowald & Morganstern, Baldwin's Ohio Practice Domestic Relations Law § 3:5, Administrative Determination of Parentage--No Acknowledgment and Support Order.

Sowald & Morganstern, Baldwin's Ohio Practice Domestic Relations Law § 15:5, Parentage Determinations.

Sowald & Morganstern, Baldwin's Ohio Practice Domestic Relations Law § 19:3, Support Obligations--In General.

Sowald & Morganstern, Baldwin's Ohio Practice Domestic Relations Law § 22:4, Establishing Parentage.

Sowald & Morganstern, Baldwin's Ohio Practice Domestic Relations Law § 3:10, Judicial Parentage Action--Parties.

Sowald & Morganstern, Baldwin's Ohio Practice Domestic Relations Law § 3:14, Judicial Parentage Action--Presumptions of Parentage--Rebutting.

Sowald & Morganstern, Baldwin's Ohio Practice Domestic Relations Law § 3:45, Effect of Judgment--Retrospective Effect.

Sowald & Morganstern, Baldwin's Ohio Practice Domestic Relations Law § 7:20, Relief Incident to Annulment--Children of an Annulled Marriage--Legitimacy of the Child.

Sowald & Morganstern, Baldwin's Ohio Practice Domestic Relations Law § 15:37, Shared Parenting--In General.

Sowald & Morganstern, Baldwin's Ohio Practice Domestic Relations Law § 23:15, In-State Remedies--Determination of Parentage.

Carlin, Baldwin's Ohio Prac. Merrick-Rippner Probate Law § 3:2, Statutory.

Carlin, Baldwin's Ohio Prac. Merrick-Rippner Probate Law § 18:2, Inheritance Rights of Illegitimate Child--Statutory Provisions.

Carlin, Baldwin's Ohio Prac. Merrick-Rippner Probate Law § 18:3, Inheritance Rights of Illegitimate Child--Case Law Affecting Rules of Inheritance Generally.

Carlin, Baldwin's Ohio Prac. Merrick-Rippner Probate Law § 18:6, Inheritance Rights of Illegitimate Child--Will.

Carlin, Baldwin's Ohio Prac. Merrick-Rippner Probate Law § 19:1, Legitimation--Statutory Provisions.

Carlin, Baldwin's Ohio Prac. Merrick-Rippner Probate Law § 19:2, Legitimation--Procedure--Acknowledgment of Paternity.

Carlin, Baldwin's Ohio Prac. Merrick-Rippner Probate Law § 19:4, Legitimation--Historical Provisions.

Carlin, Baldwin's Ohio Prac. Merrick-Rippner Probate Law § 19:5, Legitimation--Insurance Benefits.

Carlin, Baldwin's Ohio Prac. Merrick-Rippner Probate Law § 19:6, Uniform Parentage Act--Jurisdiction of Action to Determine Father-Child Relationship.

Carlin, Baldwin's Ohio Prac. Merrick-Rippner Probate Law § 19:7, Uniform Parentage Act--Presumptions.

Carlin, Baldwin's Ohio Prac. Merrick-Rippner Probate Law § 19:9, Uniform Parentage Act--Res Judicata; Doctrine of Laches.

Carlin, Baldwin's Ohio Prac. Merrick-Rippner Probate Law § 39:4, Interested Persons.

Carlin, Baldwin's Ohio Prac. Merrick-Rippner Probate Law § 99:3, Jurisdiction.

Carlin, Baldwin's Ohio Prac. Merrick-Rippner Probate Law § 99:8, Suitability of Adoptive Parents--Best Interests of Child.

Carlin, Baldwin's Ohio Prac. Merrick-Rippner Probate Law § 107:2, Original Jurisdiction.

Carlin, Baldwin's Ohio Prac. Merrick-Rippner Probate Law § 110:3, Criminal Jurisdiction--Proceedings for Nonsupport.

Carlin, Baldwin's Ohio Prac. Merrick-Rippner Probate Law § 19:10, Uniform Parentage Act--Procedure in Action to Determine Father-Child Relationship.

Carlin, Baldwin's Ohio Prac. Merrick-Rippner Probate Law § 19:13, Uniform Parentage Act--Nonspousal Artificial Insemination; Embryo Donation.

Carlin, Baldwin's Ohio Prac. Merrick-Rippner Probate Law § 19:14, Uniform Parentage Act-Surrogacy Agreement.

Carlin, Baldwin's Ohio Prac. Merrick-Rippner Probate Law § 99:21, Types of Placement--Stepparent, Guardian, and Grandparent Adoptions.

Carlin, Baldwin's Ohio Prac. Merrick-Rippner Probate Law § 99:30, Statutorily Required Consent.

Carlin, Baldwin's Ohio Prac. Merrick-Rippner Probate Law § 99:31, Parties Giving Consent--Biological Parents.

Carlin, Baldwin's Ohio Prac. Merrick-Rippner Probate Law § 99:32, Parties Giving Consent--Putative Father.

Carlin, Baldwin's Ohio Prac. Merrick-Rippner Probate Law § 99:49, Interlocutory and Final Orders.

Carlin, Baldwin's Ohio Prac. Merrick-Rippner Probate Law § 110.13, Jurisdiction Over Child Custody Matters--Determination of Custody.

Carlin, Baldwin's Ohio Prac. Merrick-Rippner Probate Law § 110:15, Visitation Right of Noncustodial Parent and Others.

Carlin, Baldwin's Ohio Prac. Merrick-Rippner Probate Law § 110:19, Parentage Act--Effect.

Carlin, Baldwin's Ohio Prac. Merrick-Rippner Probate Law § 110:20, Parentage Act--Jurisdiction and Venue.

Carlin, Baldwin's Ohio Prac. Merrick-Rippner Probate Law § 110:22, Parentage Act--Presumption of Paternity.

Carlin, Baldwin's Ohio Prac. Merrick-Rippner Probate Law § 110:24, Parentage Act--Genetic Tests, Fees, and Costs.

Carlin, Baldwin's Ohio Prac. Merrick-Rippner Probate Law § 110:26, Parentage Act--Applicability of Civil Rules to Paternity Proceedings.

Carlin, Baldwin's Ohio Prac. Merrick-Rippner Probate Law § 110:27, Parentage Act--Evidence of Paternity.

Carlin, Baldwin's Ohio Prac. Merrick-Rippner Probate Law § 110.28, Parentage Act--Trial of Parentage Action.

Carlin, Baldwin's Ohio Prac. Merrick-Rippner Probate Law § 110:29, Parentage Act--Judgment Determining Existence of Parent-Child Relationship.

Carlin, Baldwin's Ohio Prac. Merrick-Rippner Probate Law § 110:30, Parentage Act--Enforcement of Support Order.

Carlin, Baldwin's Ohio Prac. Merrick-Rippner Probate Law § 110:31, Parentage Act--Continuing Jurisdiction to Modify or Revoke Judgment.

Carlin, Baldwin's Ohio Prac. Merrick-Rippner Probate Law § 110:33, Nonspousal Artificial Insemination and Embryo Donation.

Carlin, Baldwin's Ohio Prac. Merrick-Rippner Probate Law § 110:35, Civil Support Proceedings--Liability for Child Support.

Carlin, Baldwin's Ohio Prac. Merrick-Rippner Probate Law § 110:36, Civil Support Proceedings--Determination of Amount of Support Under Child Support Guidelines.

Carlin, Baldwin's Ohio Prac. Merrick-Rippner Probate Law § 110:38, Civil Support Proceedings--Enforcement of Support Orders.

Carlin, Baldwin's Ohio Prac. Merrick-Rippner Probate Law § 110:39, Civil Support Proceedings--Remedies for Failure to Comply With Support Order.

Carlin, Baldwin's Ohio Prac. Merrick-Rippner Probate Law § 110:40, Civil Support Proceedings--Paternity Compliance Plan.

Carlin, Baldwin's Ohio Prac. Merrick-Rippner Probate Law § 109:141, Complaint in Paternity--Form.

Adrine & Ruden, Ohio Domestic Violence Law § 10:7, Relationships Covered--Persons Who Have a Child in Common.

Law Review and Journal Commentaries

Belsito v Clark: Ohio's Battle with "Motherhood," Dawn Wenk. 28 U Tol L Rev 247 (Fall 1996).

The Contractual Allocation of Procreative Resources and Parental Rights: The Natural Endowment Critique, William J. Wagner. 41 Case W Res L Rev 1 (1990).

The *Davis* Dilemma: How to Prevent Battles over Frozen Preembryos, Note. 41 Case W Res L Rev 543 (1991).

DNA Data Banking: The Dangerous Erosion Of Privacy, E. Donald Shapiro and Michele L. Weinberg. 38 Clev St L Rev 455 (1990).

Enforcement Of Surrogate Mother Contracts: Case Law, The Uniform Acts, and State and Federal Legislation, James T. Flaherty. 36 Clev St L Rev 223 (1988).

Establishing Parentage After Senate Bill 10, Pamela J. MacAdams. 4 Domestic Rel J Ohio 81 (September/October 1992).

Fragmenting and Reassembling the World: Of Flying Squirrels, Augmented Persons, and Other Monsters, Michael H. Shapiro. (Ed. note: The moral dimensions of abortion, genetic engineering, and other products of modern technology are explored.) 51 Ohio St L J 331 (1990).

Frozen Embryos: What They Are And How Should The Law Treat Them?, Comment. 38 Clev St L Rev 585 (1990).

Human Cloning Symposium. 32 U Tol L Rev 321 (Spring 2001).

An Interpretation of Ohio Law on Maternal Status in Gestational Surrogacy Disputes: Belsito v. Clark, Note. 21 U Dayton L Rev 229 (Fall 1995).

Kass v. Kass, Blazing Legal Trails in the Field of Human Reproductive Technology, Kelly Summers. 48 Clev St L Rev 637 (2000).

Legal Implications of In Vitro Fertilization with Donor Eggs: A Research Guide, Note. 13 Legal Reference Serv Q 5 (1994).

Multiplication and Division—New Math for the Courts: New Reproductive Technologies Create Potential Legal Time Bombs, Comment. 95 Dick L Rev 155 (Fall 1990).

New Wine In Old Skins: Using Paternity–Suit Settlements To Facilitate Surrogate Motherhood, Natalie Loder Clark. 25 J Fam L 483 (1986–87).

Prior Agreements for Disposition of Frozen Embryos. 51 Ohio St L J 407 (1990).

Procreative Liberty and the Preembryo Problem: Developing a Medical and Legal Framework to Settle the Disposition of Frozen Preembryos, Note. 52 Case W Res L Rev 721 (Spring 2002).

Regulating Genetic Engineering In An Era Of Increased Judicial Deference: A Proper Balance Of The Federal Powers, William H. von Oehsen III. 40 Admin L Rev 303 (Summer 1988).

Should Indigent Putative Fathers be Provided Court Appointed Counsel in Ohio Paternity Proceedings?, Daniel S. Cade. 10 Ohio N U L Rev 473 (1983).

Stiver v Parker: The Siege on Surrogacy, Note. 22 Cap U L Rev 527 (Spring 1993).

A Surrogacy Agreement that Could Have and Should Have Been Enforced: *R.R. v. M.H.*, 689 N.E.2d 790 (Mass. 1998), Note. 24 U Dayton L Rev 513 (Spring 1999).

Surrogate Parenting: What We Can Learn From Our British Counterparts, Note. 39 Case W Res L Rev 217 (1988–89).

Technology And Motherhood: Legal And Ethical Issues In Human Egg Donation, John A. Robertson. 39 Case W Res L Rev 1 (1988–89).

Would Abolishing the Natural Parent Preference in Custody Disputes Be in Everyone's Best Interest?, Note. 29 J Fam L 539 (1990–91).

Notes of Decisions

Consortium loss through injury 5
Constitutional issues 1
Jurisdiction 6
Mother's marital status 4
Parents 2
Wrongful death action 3

Paternity proceedings brought under RC Ch 3111 are civil in nature and are neither criminal nor quasi-criminal proceedings; consequently, indigent defendants do not have a constitutional right to court-appointed counsel. Sheppard v. Mack (Cuyahoga 1980) 68 Ohio App.2d 95, 427 N.E.2d 522, 22 O.O.3d 104.

1. Constitutional issues

Biological father's claim that trial court denied him his fundamental right to be afforded due process when it dismissed father's motion to intervene in legal father's action against mother for custodial and parenting rights to child to which he had executed acknowledgement of paternity was not ripe for appellate review; biological father was third party to action brought by legal father against mother arising under acknowledgment of paternity, acknowledgement statutes applied only to legal father and mother, biological father had not filed his own paternity action, and biological father had not argued to trial court that any provisions of Uniform Parentage Act violated his constitutional right to care, custody and control of child. Clark v. Malicote (Ohio App. 12 Dist., Clermont, 04-18-2011) No. CA2010-07-049, 2011-Ohio-1874, 2011 WL 1458696, Unreported. Children Out–of–wedlock ⚬ 20.11

2. Parents

"Parent," for the purposes of RC 3109.04 includes only the natural or adoptive parents of a child and a partner in a same-sex female relationship (1) is neither the natural nor the adoptive parent of any of five children, two by adoption and three by artificial insemination, which the partners are raising, (2) is not entitled to an award of parental rights or shared parenting, and (3) is not denied the constitutional right to direct the upbringing of her children by dismissal of the petition for allocation of parental rights and responsibilities; although one partner's decision to co-parent her children with the other partner in a same-sex female relationship may be protected from interference by the state she is not entitled to the benefit of laws that are at present clearly inapplicable to such a "familial" arrangement. In re Ray, Nos. C–000436+, 2001 WL 127666 (1st Dist Ct App, Hamilton, 2–16–01).

3. Wrongful death action

In a wrongful death action against a truck driver and driver's employer involving a collision between the truck driver and a motorist, dismissal is proper on the basis that the plaintiff could not maintain a wrongful death suit on behalf of an alleged minor child of the motorist where the plaintiff and the motorist were not married, the motorist did not in probate court formally acknowledge the child as his with consent of the mother, and the motorist did not designate the child as his heir-at-law, adopt the child, or make provision for the child in his will, and, although a parentage action was brought by the plaintiff and her son, the action was brought after the death of the motorist; thus, as a matter of law, the child cannot inherit from the decedent's estate, including any recovery from the wrongful death action. Hunter–Martin v. Winchester Transp., Inc. (Shelby 1991) 71 Ohio App.3d 273, 593 N.E.2d 383, motion overruled 62 Ohio St.3d 1408, 577 N.E.2d 361.

4. Mother's marital status

Agreed entry in proceeding commenced by putative father of child born out-of-wedlock seeking to establish parent-child relationship, stating that mother and paternal grandparents agreed to share in parenting of child, and that mother was to retain custody of child, was not a "shared parenting plan" between mother and grandparents, for purposes of determining legal standard applicable to grandparents' subsequent motion seeking custody of child; mother and grandparents, as nonparents, could not enter into a shared parenting agreement as a matter of law, as statute governing such agreements provided that they were to be between parents. Purvis v. Hazelbaker (Ohio App. 4 Dist., 02-19-2009) 181 Ohio App.3d 167, 908 N.E.2d 489, 2009-Ohio-765, on subsequent appeal 191 Ohio App.3d 518, 946 N.E.2d 818, 2010-Ohio-6458. Child Custody ☞ 276; Child Custody ☞ 579; Children Out–of–wedlock ☞ 20.4

Indemnification provision in surrogacy contract providing that, in the event that custody of children was awarded to surrogate mother and mother's husband, biological father would be indemnified by surrogate mother and her husband for any and all monies biological father was required to pay for child support, did not violate public policy; this was not abrogation of obligation to support offspring of coital relationship but recognition that, since surrogate was not a parent, if surrogate mother and her husband decided to obtain custody of children, they would become legal parents and surrogacy agreement would terminate, and biological father would be treated as merely the sperm donor and not the parent. J.F. v. D.B. (Ohio App. 9 Dist., 03-15-2006) 165 Ohio App.3d 791, 848 N.E.2d 873, 2006-Ohio-1175, appeal allowed 110 Ohio St.3d 1438, 852 N.E.2d 187, 2006-Ohio-3862, affirmed in part, reversed in part 116 Ohio St.3d 363, 879

N.E.2d 740, 2007-Ohio-6750. Children Out–of–wedlock ☞ 22; Contracts ☞ 108(2)

Since surrogate mother and mother's husband breached surrogacy contract by obtaining custody of children born as result of surrogacy and since surrogacy contract was enforceable, surrogate mother and her husband were liable for restitution of monies paid by biological father, as well as attorney fees, pursuant to surrogacy contract providing that, in event of breach by surrogate mother and her husband, mother and husband shall be liable for any and all monies expended on their behalf, plus attorney fees. J.F. v. D.B. (Ohio App. 9 Dist., 03-15-2006) 165 Ohio App.3d 791, 848 N.E.2d 873, 2006-Ohio-1175, appeal allowed 110 Ohio St.3d 1438, 852 N.E.2d 187, 2006-Ohio-3862, affirmed in part, reversed in part 116 Ohio St.3d 363, 879 N.E.2d 740, 2007-Ohio-6750.

Adulterine bastard is one begotten of the mother's adulterous intercourse, and proceedings ordained by RC 3111.01 et seq. are available to such a child and its mother regardless of the marital status of mother at delivery. Franklin v. Julian (Ohio 1972) 30 Ohio St.2d 228, 283 N.E.2d 813, 59 O.O.2d 264.

Under this section, complainant must be an "unmarried woman" and have been "delivered of or pregnant with a bastard child," but, after birth of still-born child, she cannot comply with these conditions relative to such child, because she has not been "delivered of a bastard child" as word child is commonly used, nor is she pregnant "with a bastard child," and in order for her to maintain action for support, maintenance and necessary expenses caused by pregnancy, complaint must be filed before dead foetus was expelled from mother's womb. Seldenright v Jenkins, 22 Abs 576 (Prob, Tuscarawas 1936).

5. Consortium loss through injury

A minor child has a cause of action for loss of parental consortium against a third-party tortfeasor who negligently or intentionally causes physical injury to the child's parent, based upon prospective application of Gallimore v. Children's Hosp. (1993), 67 Ohio St.3d 244, so that minor children whose mother is injured in a motor vehicle collision have consortium claims against the driver of the vehicle who has caused the collision. Goodrick v Didovic, No. 65093, 1994 WL 173643 (8th Dist Ct App, Cuyahoga, 5-5-94).

6. Jurisdiction

The trial court lacked subject matter jurisdiction to determine the parentage of unborn child, who was the subject of a surrogacy agreement, or issue an order directing the hospital where surrogate mother was expected to deliver child to designate child as the biological child of sperm and egg donors. Nemcek v. Paskey (Ohio Com.Pl., 04-06-2006) 137 Ohio Misc.2d 1, 849 N.E.2d 108, 2006-Ohio-2059. Parent And Child ☞ 20

3111.02   Parent and child relationship; how established; reciprocity

(A) The parent and child relationship between a child and the child's natural mother may be established by proof of her having given birth to the child or pursuant to sections 3111.01 to 3111.18 or 3111.20 to 3111.85 of the Revised Code. The parent and child relationship between a child and the natural father of the child may be established by an acknowledgment of paternity as provided in sections 3111.20 to 3111.35 of the Revised Code, and pursuant to sections 3111.01 to 3111.18 or 3111.38 to 3111.54 of the Revised Code. The parent and child relationship between a child and the adoptive parent of the child may be established by proof of adoption or pursuant to Chapter 3107. of the Revised Code.

(B) A court that is determining a parent and child relationship pursuant to this chapter shall give full faith and credit to a parentage determination made under the laws of this state or another state, regardless of whether the parentage determination was made pursuant to a voluntary acknowledgement of paternity, an administrative procedure, or a court proceeding.

(2000 S 180, eff. 3–22–01; 1997 H 352, eff. 1–1–98; 1994 S 355, eff. 12–9–94; 1992 S 10, eff. 7–15–92; 1986 H 476; 1982 H 245)

Uncodified Law

1994 S 355, § 5: See Uncodified Law under 3111.08.

1992 S 10, § 5: See Uncodified Law under 3111.01.

1982 H 245, § 3: See Uncodified Law under 3111.04.

Historical and Statutory Notes

Ed. Note: Former 3111.02 repealed by 1982 H 245, eff. 6–29–82; 127 v 1039; 1953 H 1; GC 8006–2; Source—GC 12125; see now 3111.04 for provisions analogous to former 3111.02.

Pre–1953 H 1 Amendments: 124 v S 65

Amendment Note: 2000 S 180 rewrote division (A) which prior thereto read:

"(A) The parent and child relationship between a child and the child's natural mother may be established by proof of her having given birth to the child or pursuant to sections 3111.01 to 3111.19 or 3111.20 to 3111.29 of the Revised Code. The parent and child relationship between a child and the natural father of the child may be established

by an acknowledgment of paternity as provided in section 5101.314 of the Revised Code, and pursuant to sections 3111.01 to 3111.19 or 3111.20 to 3111.29 of the Revised Code. The parent and child relationship between a child and the adoptive parent of the child may be established by proof of adoption or pursuant to Chapter 3107. of the Revised Code."

Amendment Note: 1997 H 352 substituted "an acknowledgment of paternity" for "a probate court entering an acknowledgment upon its journal" and "5101.314" for "2105.18" in division (A).

Amendment Note: 1994 S 355 designated division (A) and added division (B).

Cross References

Birth certificates, see 3705.06 et seq.
Records of births, proof, exception to hearsay rule, Evid R 803

Temporary order regarding allocation of parental rights and responsibilities while action pending, see 3109.043

Library References

Adoption ☞17 to 18.
Children Out-of-Wedlock ☞1, 12, 30 to 75.
Westlaw Topic Nos. 17, 76H.

C.J.S. Adoption of Persons §§ 6, 136, 146 to 150.
C.J.S. Children Out-of-Wedlock §§ 1 to 8, 20 to 21, 47 to 53, 71 to 142.

Research References

Encyclopedias

OH Jur. 3d Family Law § 900, Accounting by Petitioner--Purpose; Effect Upon Payments Pursuant to Surrogacy Agreements.
OH Jur. 3d Family Law § 941, Establishment of Parent and Child Relationship.
OH Jur. 3d Family Law § 945, Rebuttal of Presumption.
OH Jur. 3d Family Law § 952, Jurisdiction.

Forms

Ohio Jurisprudence Pleading and Practice Forms § 111:20, to Declare Parent-Child Relationship.

Treatises and Practice Aids

Sowald & Morganstern, Baldwin's Ohio Practice Domestic Relations Law § 3:9, Judicial Parentage Action--Initial Procedure.

Sowald & Morganstern, Baldwin's Ohio Practice Domestic Relations Law § 3:10, Judicial Parentage Action--Parties.

Sowald & Morganstern, Baldwin's Ohio Practice Domestic Relations Law § 3:46, Effect of Judgment--Inheritance.

Sowald & Morganstern, Baldwin's Ohio Practice Domestic Relations Law § 23:15, In-State Remedies--Determination of Parentage.

Carlin, Baldwin's Ohio Prac. Merrick-Rippner Probate Law § 18:2, Inheritance Rights of Illegitimate Child--Statutory Provisions.

Carlin, Baldwin's Ohio Prac. Merrick-Rippner Probate Law § 19:1, Legitimation--Statutory Provisions.

Carlin, Baldwin's Ohio Prac. Merrick-Rippner Probate Law § 19:4, Legitimation--Historical Provisions.

Carlin, Baldwin's Ohio Prac. Merrick-Rippner Probate Law § 19:6, Uniform Parentage Act--Jurisdiction of Action to Determine Father-Child Relationship.

Carlin, Baldwin's Ohio Prac. Merrick-Rippner Probate Law § 19:7, Uniform Parentage Act--Presumptions.

Carlin, Baldwin's Ohio Prac. Merrick-Rippner Probate Law § 99:2, History.

Carlin, Baldwin's Ohio Prac. Merrick-Rippner Probate Law § 19:10, Uniform Parentage Act--Procedure in Action to Determine Father-Child Relationship.

Carlin, Baldwin's Ohio Prac. Merrick-Rippner Probate Law § 99:31, Parties Giving Consent--Biological Parents.

Carlin, Baldwin's Ohio Prac. Merrick-Rippner Probate Law § 99:40, Consent Not Required--Putative Father.

Carlin, Baldwin's Ohio Prac. Merrick-Rippner Probate Law § 99:49, Interlocutory and Final Orders.

Carlin, Baldwin's Ohio Prac. Merrick-Rippner Probate Law § 109:41, Prehearing Procedures in Juvenile Court--Temporary Orders Pending Hearing.

Carlin, Baldwin's Ohio Prac. Merrick-Rippner Probate Law § 110:13, Jurisdiction Over Child Custody Matters--Determination of Custody.

Carlin, Baldwin's Ohio Prac. Merrick-Rippner Probate Law § 110:19, Parentage Act--Effect.

Carlin, Baldwin's Ohio Prac. Merrick-Rippner Probate Law § 110:20, Parentage Act--Jurisdiction and Venue.

Carlin, Baldwin's Ohio Prac. Merrick-Rippner Probate Law § 110:29, Parentage Act--Judgment Determining Existence of Parent-Child Relationship.

Carlin, Baldwin's Ohio Prac. Merrick-Rippner Probate Law § 110:34, Parentage Act--Administrative Support Orders.

Adrine & Ruden, Ohio Domestic Violence Law § 10:7, Relationships Covered--Persons Who Have a Child in Common.

Law Review and Journal Commentaries

Anna J. v. Mark C.: Proof Of The Imminent Need For Surrogate Motherhood Regulation, Note. 30 J Fam L 493 (February 1992).

Enforcement Of Surrogate Mother Contracts: Case Law, The Uniform Acts, and State and Federal Legislation, James T. Flaherty. 36 Clev St L Rev 223 (1988).

Kass v. Kass, Blazing Legal Trails in the Field of Human Reproductive Technology, Kelly Summers. 48 Clev St L Rev 637 (2000).

Modern Reproductive Technology and Motherhood: The Search for Common Ground and the Recognition of Difference, Comment. 62 U Cin L Rev 1623 (Spring 1994).

Practice Pointer Effects of 1994 Am. S B 355, Richard L. Innis. 7 Domestic Rel J Ohio 6 (January/February 1995).

Procreative Liberty and the Preembryo Problem: Developing a Medical and Legal Framework to Settle the Disposition of Frozen Preembryos, Note. 52 Case W Res L Rev 721 (Spring 2002).

Surrogate Parenting: What We Can Learn From Our British Counterparts, Note. 39 Case W Res L Rev 217 (1988–89).

Technology And Motherhood: Legal And Ethical Issues In Human Egg Donation, John A. Robertson. 39 Case W Res L Rev 1 (1988–89).

Notes of Decisions

In general 1
Action by child 4
Action by husband 3
Construction with other laws 2
In loco parentis 9
Jurisdiction 10
Natural father 6
Natural mother 7
Natural parents 8

Surrogacy agreement 5

---

1. In general

Cohabiting, unmarried female same-sex partner of children's mother was not a "parent," for purposes of entering into a shared parenting agreement. In re Bonfield (Ohio, 08-28-2002) 96 Ohio St.3d 218, 773 N.E.2d 507, 2002-Ohio-4182, opinion superseded on reconsideration 97 Ohio St.3d 387, 780 N.E.2d 241, 2002-Ohio-6660. Child Custody ⊕ 125; Child Custody ⊕ 274

2. Construction with other laws

RC 3111.02 to 3111.04, 3111.09, and 3111.10 are in pari materia and must be construed together. Hulett v. Hulett (Ohio 1989) 45 Ohio St.3d 288, 544 N.E.2d 257.

R.C. Chapter 3111 paternity proceedings or adoption are not the exclusive methods by which paternity may be determined. In re Custody of Davis (Guernsey 1987) 41 Ohio App.3d 81, 534 N.E.2d 945. Children Out–of–wedlock ☞ 1

3. Action by husband

Prior decision of the Court of Appeals, holding that res judicata barred former husband's action seeking a determination of paternity, amounted to an "admission on file" for purposes of summary judgment in a subsequent paternity action, where trial court deemed prior appellate decision admitted as true and genuine by husband, and husband did not challenge that ruling. Donnelly v. Kashnier (Ohio App. 9 Dist., Medina, 02-12-2003) No. 02CA0051-M, 2003-Ohio-639, 2003 WL 294413, Unreported. Children Out–of–wedlock ☞ 64

Prior trial court finding that former husband knew himself not to be the father of child for whom he was ordered to pay child support before he acknowledged himself to be the father in a dissolution proceeding was law of the case, precluding father from subsequently challenging paternity. Donnelly v. Kashnier (Ohio App. 9 Dist., Medina, 02-12-2003) No. 02CA0051-M, 2003-Ohio-639, 2003 WL 294413, Unreported. Courts ☞ 99(6)

Parent and child relationship could not be established between husband and wife's child for purposes of establishing husband's child support obligation pursuant to a divorce, even though husband adopted child in another country; parent and child relationship could only be established on basis of foreign adoption of child by husband, and court could not recognize foreign adoption without verification and approved by the Immigration and Naturalization Service. Walsh v. Walsh (Ohio App. 11 Dist., 09-24-2001) 146 Ohio App.3d 48, 764 N.E.2d 1103, 2001-Ohio-4315. Adoption ☞ 20

Where a man expressly acknowledges paternity of a child in a separation agreement incorporated into a judgment for dissolution, both parties to the separation agreement were represented by counsel, and the parties agreed to the man's child support obligation, a subsequent paternity action to establish that the man is not the child's biological father is barred by res judicata. Kashnier v. Donelly (Medina 1991) 81 Ohio App.3d 154, 610 N.E.2d 519.

A judgment entry in a divorce action finding that a child was born during the marriage and ordering the husband to pay child support is not conclusive as to the paternity of the child where the husband had denied such paternity in the divorce action and the decree did not explicitly find that a parent and child relationship existed; res judicata is inapplicable in a subsequent paternity action filed by the putative father absent a specific finding that a parent and child relationship existed; therefore, a

juvenile court errs in dismissing the subsequent paternity action. LaBonte v. LaBonte (Meigs 1988) 61 Ohio App.3d 209, 572 N.E.2d 704, motion overruled 42 Ohio St.3d 709, 538 N.E.2d 122.

The two methods for a father to secure companionship rights with an illegitimate child are (1) to acknowledge his paternity or (2) have his paternity determined in an action pursuant to RC Ch 3111; where it is undisputed that a putative father who seeks visitation rights, did not acknowledge his paternity with the probate court following the child's birth and HLA tests conclusively exclude him as the father, there is no statutory basis permitting the juvenile court to order visitation rights. Sherburn v Reichert, No. 15–94–3, 1994 WL 581539 (3d Dist Ct App, Van Wert, 10–13–94).

4. Action by child

Minor child has cause of action for loss of parental consortium against third-party tort-feasor who negligently or intentionally injures child's parent. Coleman v. Sandoz Pharmaceuticals Corp. (Ohio, 02-14-1996) 74 Ohio St.3d 492, 660 N.E.2d 424, 1996-Ohio-292. Parent And Child ☞ 7.5

Derivative claim for loss of parental consortium that is filed by intervening minor child can be brought against additional defendants in event that parent's case in chief has only one defendant. Coleman v. Sandoz Pharmaceuticals Corp. (Ohio, 02-14-1996) 74 Ohio St.3d 492, 660 N.E.2d 424, 1996-Ohio-292. Parent And Child ☞ 7.5

Child has statutory right to bring paternity action and has separate and distinct claim from that of his mother. Rees v. Heimberger (Cuyahoga 1989) 60 Ohio App.3d 45, 573 N.E.2d 189, dismissed 47 Ohio St.3d 702, 547 N.E.2d 986, rehearing denied 48 Ohio St.3d 707, 550 N.E.2d 483, certiorari denied 110 S.Ct. 1827, 494 U.S. 1088, 108 L.Ed.2d 956. Children Out–of–wedlock ☞ 34

5. Surrogacy agreement

Surrogacy agreement was valid and enforceable under which a gestational surrogate agreed to relinquish, to the intended mother, physical custody and any and all rights to child born from embryo formed outside the womb by anonymously donated egg and sperm, and therefore, the intended mother rebutted presumption that surrogate, as woman who gave birth to child, was the child's legal and natural mother under the Parentage Act; the agreement set forth in writing following extensive negotiations, the agreement included an acknowledgement that the parties entered into it voluntarily and with the aid of counsel, and, in consideration, intended mother paid for gestational surrogate's unreimbursed medical costs, the cost of a $200,000 term life insurance policy, and an additional $15,000 for living expenses. S.N. v. M.B. (Ohio App. 10 Dist., 06-10-2010) 188 Ohio App.3d 324, 935 N.E.2d 463, 2010-Ohio-2479, cause dismissed 126 Ohio St.3d 1525, 931 N.E.2d 126, 2010-Ohio-3583. Children Out–of–wedlock ☞ 15

Intended mother's voluntary acknowledgement of maternity, as set forth in a surrogacy agreement setting forth terms by which surrogate mother would carry and give birth to embryos formed outside the womb by donor egg and sperm, was sufficient under the Parentage Act, consistent with cases concerning voluntary acknowledgements of paternity, to rebut the presumption that surrogate mother was the "natural mother" of resulting child by reason of her having given birth to the child. S.N. v. M.B. (Ohio App. 10 Dist., 06-10-2010) 188 Ohio App.3d 324, 935 N.E.2d 463, 2010-Ohio-2479, cause dismissed 126 Ohio St.3d 1525, 931 N.E.2d 126, 2010-Ohio-3583. Children Out–of–wedlock ☞ 15

Ohio's Parentage Act facially applies to any parentage determination, including cases in which a child's maternity is at issue due to a surrogacy arrangement, and where neither party is biologically related to the child. S.N. v. M.B. (Ohio App. 10 Dist., 06-10-2010) 188 Ohio App.3d 324, 935 N.E.2d 463, 2010-Ohio-2479, cause dismissed 126 Ohio St.3d 1525, 931 N.E.2d 126, 2010-Ohio-3583. Children Out–of–wedlock ☞ 15

6. Natural father

Former husband of child's mother was presumed natural father of child born during the marriage, precluding husband from subsequently challenging paternity. Donnelly v. Kashnier (Ohio App. 9 Dist., Medina, 02-12-2003) No. 02CA0051-M, 2003-Ohio-639, 2003 WL 294413, Unreported. Children Out–of–wedlock ☞ 3

Indemnification provision in surrogacy contract providing that, in the event that custody of children was awarded to surrogate mother and mother's husband, biological father would be indemnified by surrogate mother and her husband for any and all monies biological father was required to pay for child support, did not violate public policy; this was not abrogation of obligation to support offspring of coital relationship but recognition that, since surrogate was not a parent, if surrogate mother and her husband decided to obtain custody of children, they would become legal parents and surrogacy agreement would terminate, and biological father would be treated as merely the sperm donor and not the parent. J.F. v. D.B. (Ohio App. 9 Dist., 03-15-2006) 165 Ohio App.3d 791, 848 N.E.2d 873, 2006-Ohio-1175, appeal allowed 110 Ohio St.3d 1438, 852 N.E.2d 187, 2006-Ohio-3862, affirmed in part, reversed in part 116 Ohio St.3d 363, 879 N.E.2d 740, 2007-Ohio-6750. Children Out–of–wedlock ☞ 22; Contracts ☞ 108(2)

Since surrogate mother and mother's husband breached surrogacy contract by obtaining custody of children born as result of surrogacy and since surrogacy contract was enforceable, surrogate mother and her husband were liable for restitution of monies paid by biological father, as well as attorney fees, pursuant to surrogacy contract providing that, in event of breach by surrogate mother and her husband, mother and husband shall be liable for any and all monies expended on their behalf, plus attorney fees. J.F. v. D.B. (Ohio App. 9 Dist., 03-15-2006) 165 Ohio App.3d 791, 848 N.E.2d 873,

2006-Ohio-1175, appeal allowed 110 Ohio St.3d 1438, 852 N.E.2d 187, 2006-Ohio-3862, affirmed in part, reversed in part 116 Ohio St.3d 363, 879 N.E.2d 740, 2007-Ohio-6750.

7. Natural mother

Under statute governing establishment of parent and child relationship, maternity can be established by identifying natural mother through birth process or by other means, including DNA blood tests. Belsito v. Clark (Ohio Com.Pl. 1994) 67 Ohio Misc.2d 54, 644 N.E.2d 760. Children Out–of–wedlock ☞ 5; Parent And Child ☞ 1

8. Natural parents

When child is delivered by gestational surrogate who has been impregnated through process of in vitro fertilization, natural parents of child shall be identified by determination as to which individuals have provided genetic imprint for that child, and if individuals who have been identified as genetic parents have not relinquished or waived their rights to assume legal status of natural parents, they shall be considered natural and legal parents of that child. Belsito v. Clark (Ohio Com.Pl. 1994) 67 Ohio Misc.2d 54, 644 N.E.2d 760. Parent And Child ☞ 20

9. In loco parentis

When person accepts custody of child, that person stands in loco parentis to child, accepting all rights and responsibilities that go with that status. Evans v. Ohio State Univ. (Ohio App. 10 Dist., 07-23-1996) 112 Ohio App.3d 724, 680 N.E.2d 161, appeal not allowed 77 Ohio St.3d 1494, 673 N.E.2d 149. Parent And Child ☞ 15

Key factors of "in loco parentis" relationship are intentional assumption of obligations incidental to parental relationship, especially support and maintenance. Evans v. Ohio State Univ. (Ohio App. 10 Dist., 07-23-1996) 112 Ohio App.3d 724, 680 N.E.2d 161, appeal not allowed 77 Ohio St.3d 1494, 673 N.E.2d 149. Parent And Child ☞ 15

"In loco parentis" is relationship which person assumes toward child not his own, holding him out to world as member of his family toward whom he owes discharge of parental duties; person standing in loco parentis to child is one who put himself in position of lawful parent assuming obligations incident to parental relation, without going through formalities necessary to legal adoption. Evans v. Ohio State Univ. (Ohio App. 10 Dist., 07-23-1996) 112 Ohio App.3d 724, 680 N.E.2d 161, appeal not allowed 77 Ohio St.3d 1494, 673 N.E.2d 149. Parent And Child ☞ 15

10. Jurisdiction

Juvenile court had jurisdiction to determine the surname by which child would be known after establishment of the existence of the parent and child relationship and a showing that the name determination was in the best interest of child. Wood v. Palomba (Ohio App. 5 Dist., Tuscarawas, 05-12-2009) No. 2008 AP 08 0054, 2009-Ohio-2236,

2009 WL 1317508, Unreported. Children Out–of–wedlock ⬤ 1

The trial court lacked subject matter jurisdiction to determine the parentage of unborn child, who was the subject of a surrogacy agreement, or issue an order directing the hospital where surrogate mother was expected to deliver child to designate child as the biological child of sperm and egg donors. Nemcek v. Paskey (Ohio Com.Pl., 04-06-2006) 137 Ohio Misc.2d 1, 849 N.E.2d 108, 2006-Ohio-2059. Parent And Child ⬤ 20

3111.03 Presumptions as to father and child relationship

(A) A man is presumed to be the natural father of a child under any of the following circumstances:

(1) The man and the child's mother are or have been married to each other, and the child is born during the marriage or is born within three hundred days after the marriage is terminated by death, annulment, divorce, or dissolution or after the man and the child's mother separate pursuant to a separation agreement.

(2) The man and the child's mother attempted, before the child's birth, to marry each other by a marriage that was solemnized in apparent compliance with the law of the state in which the marriage took place, the marriage is or could be declared invalid, and either of the following applies:

(a) The marriage can only be declared invalid by a court and the child is born during the marriage or within three hundred days after the termination of the marriage by death, annulment, divorce, or dissolution;

(b) The attempted marriage is invalid without a court order and the child is born within three hundred days after the termination of cohabitation.

(3) An acknowledgment of paternity has been filed pursuant to section 3111.23 or former section 5101.314 of the Revised Code and has not become final under former section 3111.211 or 5101.314 or section 2151.232, 3111.25, or 3111.821 of the Revised Code.

(B) A presumption that arises under this section can only be rebutted by clear and convincing evidence that includes the results of genetic testing, except that a presumption that is conclusive as provided in division (A) of section 3111.95 or division (B) of section 3111.97 of the Revised Code cannot be rebutted. An acknowledgment of paternity that becomes final under section 2151.232, 3111.25, or 3111.821 of the Revised Code is not a presumption and shall be considered a final and enforceable determination of paternity unless the acknowledgment is rescinded under section 3111.28 or 3119.962 of the Revised Code. If two or more conflicting presumptions arise under this section, the court shall determine, based upon logic and policy considerations, which presumption controls.

(C)(1) Except as provided in division (C)(2) of this section, a presumption of paternity that arose pursuant to this section prior to March 22, 2001, shall remain valid on and after that date unless rebutted pursuant to division (B) of this section. This division does not apply to a determination described in division (B)(3) of this section as division (B)(3) of this section existed prior to March 22, 2001.

(2) A presumption of paternity that arose prior to March 22, 2001, based on an acknowledgment of paternity that became final under former section 3111.211 or 5101.314 or section 2151.232 of the Revised Code is not a presumption and shall be considered a final and enforceable determination of paternity unless the acknowledgment is rescinded under section 3111.28 or 3119.962 of the Revised Code.

(2006 H 102, eff. 6–15–06; 2000 S 180, eff. 3–22–01; 1999 H 471, eff. 7–1–00; 1997 H 352, eff. 1–1–98; 1992 S 10, eff. 7–15–92; 1990 S 3; 1988 H 790; 1986 H 476; 1982 H 245)

Uncodified Law

1992 S 10, § 5: See Uncodified Law under 3111.01.

1982 H 245, § 3: See Uncodified Law under 3111.04.

Historical and Statutory Notes

Ed. Note: 3111.03 contains provisions analogous to former 3105.13 and 3105.33, repealed by 1982 H 245, eff. 6–29–82.

Ed. Note: Former 3111.03 repealed by 1982 H 245, eff. 6–29–82; 1953 H 1; GC 8006–3; Source—GC 12134; see now 3111.04 for provisions analogous to former 3111.03.

Pre-1953 H 1 Amendments: 124 v S 65

Amendment Note: 2006 H 102 inserted "or division (B) of section 3111.97" in division (B); and substituted "March 22, 2001," for "the effective date of this amendment" in division (C).

Amendment Note: 2000 S 180 rewrote this section which prior thereto read:

"(A) A man is presumed to be the natural father of a child under any of the following circumstances:

"(1) The man and the child's mother are or have been married to each other, and the child is born during the marriage or is born within three hundred days after the marriage is terminated by death, annulment, divorce, or dissolution or after the man and the child's mother separate pursuant to a separation agreement.

"(2) The man and the child's mother attempted, before the child's birth, to marry each other by a marriage that was solemnized in apparent compliance with the law of the state in which the marriage took place, the marriage is or could be declared invalid, and either of the following applies:

"(a) The marriage can only be declared invalid by a court and the child is born during the marriage or within three hundred days after the termination of the marriage by death, annulment, divorce, or dissolution;

"(b) The attempted marriage is invalid without a court order and the child is born within three hundred days after the termination of cohabitation.

"(3) The man and the child's mother, after the child's birth, married or attempted to marry each other by a marriage solemnized in apparent compliance with the law of the state in which the marriage took place, and either of the following occurs:

"(a) The man has acknowledged his paternity of the child in a writing sworn to before a notary public,

"(b) The man is required to support the child by a written voluntary promise or by a court order.

"(4) An acknowledgment of paternity filed with the division of child support in the department of job and family services becomes final pursuant to section 2151.232, 3111.211, or 5101.314 of the Revised Code.

"(5) A court or administrative body, pursuant to section 3111.09, 3111.22, or 3115.52 of the Revised Code or otherwise, has ordered that genetic tests be conducted or the natural mother and alleged natural father voluntarily agreed to genetic testing pursuant to former section 3111.21 of the Revised Code to determine the father and child relationship and the results of the genetic tests indicate a proba-

bility of ninety-nine per cent or greater that the man is the biological father of the child.

"(B)(1) A presumption arises under division (A)(3) of this section regardless of the validity or invalidity of the marriage of the parents. A presumption that arises under this section can only be rebutted by clear and convincing evidence that includes the results of genetic testing, except that a presumption that arises under division (A)(1) or (2) of this section is conclusive as provided in division (A) of section 3111.37 of the Revised Code and cannot be rebutted. If two or more conflicting presumptions arise under this section, the court shall determine, based upon logic and policy considerations, which presumption controls. If a determination described in division (B)(3) of this section conflicts with a presumption that arises under this section the determination is controlling.

"(2) Notwithstanding division (B)(1) of this section, a presumption that arises under division (A)(4) of this section may only be rebutted as provided in division (B)(2) of section 5101.314 of the Revised Code.

"(3) Notwithstanding division (A)(5) of this section, a final and enforceable determination finding the existence of a father and child relationship pursuant to former section 3111.21 or section 3111.22 of the Revised Code that is based on the results of genetic tests ordered pursuant to either of those sections, is not a presumption.

"(C) A presumption of paternity that arose pursuant to this section prior to January 1, 1998, shall remain valid on and after that date unless rebutted pursuant to division (B) of this section. This division does not apply to a determination described in division (B)(3) of this section."

Amendment Note: 1999 H 471 substituted "job and family" for "human" in division (A)(4); and substituted "January 1, 1998" for "the effective date of this amendment" in division (C).

Amendment Note: 1997 H 352 deleted former division (A)(3)(b); redesignated former division (A)(3)(c) as new division (A)(3)(b); deleted former division (A)(4); redesignated former divisions (A)(5) and (A)(6) as new divisions (A)(4) and (A)(5) and rewrote those divisions; designated division (B)(1) and added the fourth sentence therein; added divisions (B)(2), (B)(3), and (C); and made other nonsubstantive changes. Prior to amendment, former divisions (A)(3)(b) and (A)(4) through (A)(6) read:

"(b) The man, with his consent, is named as the child's father on the child's birth certificate;"

"(4) The man, with his consent, signs the child's birth certificate as an informant as provided in section 3705.09 of the Revised Code.

"(5) A court enters upon its journal an acknowledgment of paternity pursuant to section 2105.18 of the Revised Code.

"(6) A court or administrative body, pursuant to section 3111.09 or 3115.24 of the Revised Code or otherwise, has ordered that genetic tests be conducted or the natural mother and alleged natural father voluntarily agreed to genetic testing pursuant to section 3111.21 or 3111.22 of the Revised Code

to determine the father and child relationship and the results of the genetic tests indicate a probability of ninety-five per cent or greater that the man is the biological father of the child."

Cross References

Hospital staff sending signed and notarized acknowledgment of paternity to child support division, see 3727.17

Non-spousal insemination, effect of physician's failure to comply with statutes, see 3111.38

Presumptions in general in civil actions and proceedings, Evid R 301

Registrar sending signed and notarized acknowledgment of paternity to child support division, see 3705.091

Solemnization of marriage, see 3101.08 to 3101.13

Ohio Administrative Code References

Conducting the administrative support hearing, see OAC 5101:12–45–05.2

Presumption of paternity, see OAC 5101:12–40–10

Support order establishment process, see OAC 5101:12–45–05

Library References

Children Out-of-Wedlock ⌐3, 43.
Westlaw Topic No. 76H.
C.J.S. Children Out-of-Wedlock §§ 10 to 14, 109.

Research References

Encyclopedias

OH Jur. 3d Family Law § 863, Existence and Proof of Relationship.

OH Jur. 3d Family Law § 900, Accounting by Petitioner--Purpose; Effect Upon Payments Pursuant to Surrogacy Agreements.

OH Jur. 3d Family Law § 944, Statutory Presumptions.

OH Jur. 3d Family Law § 945, Rebuttal of Presumption.

OH Jur. 3d Family Law § 952, Jurisdiction.

OH Jur. 3d Family Law § 956, Pretrial Procedures.

OH Jur. 3d Family Law § 987, Legitimation by Marriage.

OH Jur. 3d Family Law § 988, Legitimation by Acknowledgment of Paternity.

OH Jur. 3d Family Law § 997, Status of Husband and Donor.

OH Jur. 3d Family Law § 1016, Action for Support.

OH Jur. 3d Family Law § 1019, Child Support Action in Juvenile Court; Other Courts With Jurisdiction.

OH Jur. 3d Family Law § 1020, Request for Administrative Order.

OH Jur. 3d Health & Sanitation § 67, Births--Paternity Concerns.

Forms

Ohio Forms Legal and Business § 28:4, Introduction.

Ohio Forms Legal and Business § 28:7, Acknowledgment of Paternity.

Ohio Forms Legal and Business § 28:9, Request to Amend Birth Certificate--Out-Of-Wedlock Child--Marriage After Child's Birth.

Ohio Forms Legal and Business § 28:12, Consent to Artificial Insemination of Wife.

Ohio Jurisprudence Pleading and Practice Forms § 111:5, Standing--Parties.

Ohio Jurisprudence Pleading and Practice Forms § 111:6, Presumptions.

Ohio Jurisprudence Pleading and Practice Forms § 111:11, Evidence.

Ohio Jurisprudence Pleading and Practice Forms § 111:29, Report of Referee--Child Support--Default.

Treatises and Practice Aids

Sowald & Morganstern, Baldwin's Ohio Practice Domestic Relations Law § 7:4, Annulment Versus Divorce.

Sowald & Morganstern, Baldwin's Ohio Practice Domestic Relations Law § 11:9, Grounds--Spouse Living at Time of Marriage.

Sowald & Morganstern, Baldwin's Ohio Practice Domestic Relations Law § 2:58, Void and Voidable Marriages--Definitions.

Sowald & Morganstern, Baldwin's Ohio Practice Domestic Relations Law § 22:4, Establishing Parentage.

Sowald & Morganstern, Baldwin's Ohio Practice Domestic Relations Law § 22:7, Establishing Support Order.

Sowald & Morganstern, Baldwin's Ohio Practice Domestic Relations Law § 3:10, Judicial Parentage Action--Parties.

Sowald & Morganstern, Baldwin's Ohio Practice Domestic Relations Law § 3:13, Judicial Parentage Action--Presumptions of Parentage--Creating.

Sowald & Morganstern, Baldwin's Ohio Practice Domestic Relations Law § 3:14, Judicial Parentage Action--Presumptions of Parentage--Rebutting.

Sowald & Morganstern, Baldwin's Ohio Practice Domestic Relations Law § 3:15, Evidence--In General.

Sowald & Morganstern, Baldwin's Ohio Practice Domestic Relations Law § 3:17, Evidence--Genetic Tests--Background.

Sowald & Morganstern, Baldwin's Ohio Practice Domestic Relations Law § 3:22, Burden of Proof and Weight of the Evidence.

Sowald & Morganstern, Baldwin's Ohio Practice Domestic Relations Law § 3:30, Res Judicata and Vacation of Parentage Orders.

Sowald & Morganstern, Baldwin's Ohio Practice Domestic Relations Law § 3:31, Relief from Paternity or Support Judgment, Under RC 3119.961.

Sowald & Morganstern, Baldwin's Ohio Practice Domestic Relations Law § 3:46, Effect of Judgment--Inheritance.

Sowald & Morganstern, Baldwin's Ohio Practice Domestic Relations Law § 3:50, Related Issues--Artificial Insemination and Surrogate Mothers.

Sowald & Morganstern, Baldwin's Ohio Practice Domestic Relations Law § 7:20, Relief Incident to Annulment--Children of an Annulled Marriage--Legitimacy of the Child.

Sowald & Morganstern, Baldwin's Ohio Practice Domestic Relations Law § 23:16, In-State Remedies--Determination of Support.

Snyder & Giannelli, Baldwin's Ohio Practice Evidence § 301.15, Selected Presumptions.

Carlin, Baldwin's Ohio Prac. Merrick-Rippner Probate Law § 8:2, Appeal--Final Appealable Orders.

Carlin, Baldwin's Ohio Prac. Merrick-Rippner Probate Law § 12:1, Scope of RC Ch. 2125.

Carlin, Baldwin's Ohio Prac. Merrick-Rippner Probate Law § 12:7, Status of Beneficiaries Fixed at Death of Decedent.

Carlin, Baldwin's Ohio Prac. Merrick-Rippner Probate Law § 12:8, Afterborn Beneficiary; Next of Kin.

Carlin, Baldwin's Ohio Prac. Merrick-Rippner Probate Law § 19:1, Legitimation--Statutory Provisions.

Carlin, Baldwin's Ohio Prac. Merrick-Rippner Probate Law § 19:2, Legitimation--Procedure--Acknowledgment of Paternity.

Carlin, Baldwin's Ohio Prac. Merrick-Rippner Probate Law § 19:7, Uniform Parentage Act--Presumptions.

Carlin, Baldwin's Ohio Prac. Merrick-Rippner Probate Law § 19:9, Uniform Parentage Act--Res Judicata; Doctrine of Laches.

Carlin, Baldwin's Ohio Prac. Merrick-Rippner Probate Law § 12:18, "Parent" Construed.

Carlin, Baldwin's Ohio Prac. Merrick-Rippner Probate Law § 15:27, Child Without Issue Predeceasing Parent.

Carlin, Baldwin's Ohio Prac. Merrick-Rippner Probate Law § 15:30, Child Born Out of Wedlock.

Carlin, Baldwin's Ohio Prac. Merrick-Rippner Probate Law § 19:10, Uniform Parentage Act--Procedure in Action to Determine Father-Child Relationship.

Carlin, Baldwin's Ohio Prac. Merrick-Rippner Probate Law § 19:13, Uniform Parentage Act--Nonspousal Artificial Insemination; Embryo Donation.

Carlin, Baldwin's Ohio Prac. Merrick-Rippner Probate Law § 99:30, Statutorily Required Consent.

Carlin, Baldwin's Ohio Prac. Merrick-Rippner Probate Law § 99:31, Parties Giving Consent--Biological Parents.

Carlin, Baldwin's Ohio Prac. Merrick-Rippner Probate Law § 99:49, Interlocutory and Final Orders.

Carlin, Baldwin's Ohio Prac. Merrick-Rippner Probate Law § 99:71, Acknowledgment of Paternity Affidavit--Form.

Carlin, Baldwin's Ohio Prac. Merrick-Rippner Probate Law § 110:13, Jurisdiction Over Child Custody Matters--Determination of Custody.

Carlin, Baldwin's Ohio Prac. Merrick-Rippner Probate Law § 110:19, Parentage Act--Effect.

Carlin, Baldwin's Ohio Prac. Merrick-Rippner Probate Law § 110:20, Parentage Act--Jurisdiction and Venue.

Carlin, Baldwin's Ohio Prac. Merrick-Rippner Probate Law § 110:22, Parentage Act--Presumption of Paternity.

Carlin, Baldwin's Ohio Prac. Merrick-Rippner Probate Law § 110:23, Parentage Act--Parties in Parentage Action.

Carlin, Baldwin's Ohio Prac. Merrick-Rippner Probate Law § 110:27, Parentage Act--Evidence of Paternity.

Carlin, Baldwin's Ohio Prac. Merrick-Rippner Probate Law § 110:31, Parentage Act--Continuing Jurisdiction to Modify or Revoke Judgment.

Carlin, Baldwin's Ohio Prac. Merrick-Rippner Probate Law § 110:33, Nonspousal Artificial Insemination and Embryo Donation.

Carlin, Baldwin's Ohio Prac. Merrick-Rippner Probate Law § 110:34, Parentage Act--Administrative Support Orders.

Adrine & Ruden, Ohio Domestic Violence Law § 10:7, Relationships Covered--Persons Who Have a Child in Common.

Adrine & Ruden, Ohio Domestic Violence Law § 11:14, Ex Parte Protection Orders--Available Relief--Orders to Vacate or Evict.

Restatement (3d) Property (Wills & Don. Trans.) § 2.5, Parent and Child Relationship.

Law Review and Journal Commentaries

Acknowledgement of Paternity—Changes in Statutes and Forms, Angela G. Carlin. 10 Prob L J Ohio 10 (September/October 1999).

Artificial Insemination: Donor Rights In Situations Involving Unmarried Recipients, Note. 26 J Fam L 793 (1987–88).

The Biological Father's Right to Require a Pregnant Woman to Undergo Medical Treatment Necessary to Sustain Fetal Life, Comment. 94 Dick L Rev 199 (Fall 1989).

The Burden of Proof in a Paternity Proceeding, Note. 25 J Fam L 357 (1986–87).

The DNA Paternity Test: Legislating the Future Paternity Action, E. Donald Shapiro, Stewart Reifler, Claudia L. Psome. 7 J L & Health 1 (1992–93).

Enforcement Of Surrogate Mother Contracts: Case Law, The Uniform Acts, and State and Federal Legislation, James T. Flaherty. 36 Clev St L Rev 223 (1988).

The Need for Statutes Regulating Artificial Insemination by Donors, Note. 46 Ohio St L J 1055 (1986).

Paternity: Rebuttable Presumption, Lawrence G. Sheehe, Jr. 63 Law & Fact 10 (November–December 1989).

Pena v. Mattow: The Parental Rights of a Statutory Rapist, Angela D. Luchese. 36 J Fam L 285 (1997–98).

The Presumption of Paternity in Child Support Cases: A Triumph of Law over Biology, Comment. 70 U Cin L Rev 1151 (Spring 2002).

Procreative Liberty and the Preembryo Problem: Developing a Medical and Legal Framework to Settle the Disposition of Frozen Preembryos, Note. 52 Case W Res L Rev 721 (Spring 2002).

Protecting a Husband's Parental Rights When His Wife Disputes the Presumption of Legitimacy, Note. 28 J Fam L 115 (1989–90).

Smith v. Cole: Triumph in Family Court, Comment. 40 Case W Res L Rev 1157 (1989–90).

When Does Divorce Decree Bar Parentage Action?, Pamela J. MacAdams. 8 Domestic Rel J Ohio 95 (November/December 1996).

Notes of Decisions

In general   1
Admissibility of evidence   9
Appeals   12
Artificial insemination   8
Burden of proof, presumption of paternity   5
Due process   2
Judgment of paternity   11
Marriage during pregnancy, presumption of paternity   4
Presumption of paternity   3-6
    In general   3
    Burden of proof   5
    Marriage during pregnancy   4
    Rebuttal   6
Rebuttal, presumption of paternity   6
Res judicata/estoppel   10
Wrongful death   7

1. In general

Juvenile Court lacked jurisdiction to order retroactive child support, in paternity proceedings, when the first claim for support was made after the child reached the age of majority and the duty to support had elapsed. Carnes v. Kemp (Ohio App. 3 Dist., Auglaize, 11-03-2003) No. 2-03-10, 2003-Ohio-5884, 2003 WL 22473582, Unreported, stay denied 101 Ohio St.3d 1419, 802 N.E.2d 152, 2004-Ohio-123, motion to certify allowed 101 Ohio St.3d 1465, 804 N.E.2d 39, 2004-Ohio-819, appeal allowed 101 Ohio St.3d 1466, 804 N.E.2d 40, 2004-Ohio-819, motion granted 103 Ohio St.3d 1419, 814 N.E.2d 63, 2004-Ohio-4504, reversed 104 Ohio St.3d 629, 821 N.E.2d 180, 2004-Ohio-7107. Children Out–of–wedlock ⚭ 67

Intended mother's voluntary acknowledgement of maternity, as set forth in a surrogacy agreement setting forth terms by which surrogate mother would carry and give birth to embryos formed outside the womb by donor egg and sperm, was sufficient under the Parentage Act, consistent with cases concerning voluntary acknowledgements of paternity, to rebut the presumption that surrogate mother was the "natural mother" of resulting child by reason of her having given birth to the child. S.N. v. M.B. (Ohio App. 10 Dist., 06-10-2010) 188 Ohio App.3d 324, 935 N.E.2d 463, 2010-Ohio-2479, cause dismissed 126 Ohio St.3d 1525, 931 N.E.2d 126, 2010-Ohio-3583. Children Out–of–wedlock ⚭ 15

Ohio's Parentage Act facially applies to any parentage determination, including cases in which a child's maternity is at issue due to a surrogacy arrangement, and where neither party is biologically related to the child. S.N. v. M.B. (Ohio App. 10 Dist., 06-10-2010) 188 Ohio App.3d 324, 935 N.E.2d 463, 2010-Ohio-2479, cause dismissed 126 Ohio St.3d 1525, 931 N.E.2d 126, 2010-Ohio-3583. Children Out–of–wedlock ⚭ 15

The trial court lacked subject matter jurisdiction to determine the parentage of unborn child, who was the subject of a surrogacy agreement, or issue an order directing the hospital where surrogate mother was expected to deliver child to designate child as the biological child of sperm and egg donors. Nemcek v. Paskey (Ohio Com.Pl., 04-06-2006) 137 Ohio Misc.2d 1, 849 N.E.2d 108, 2006-Ohio-2059. Parent And Child ⚭ 20

Genetic tests indicating greater than 95% probability that putative father was not child's biological father gave rise to presumption of nonpaternity. Riddle v. Riddle (Ohio Com.Pl. 1992) 63 Ohio Misc.2d 43, 619 N.E.2d 1201. Children Out–of–wedlock ⚭ 43

RC 3111.02 to 3111.04, 3111.09, and 3111.10 are in pari materia and must be construed together. Hulett v. Hulett (Ohio 1989) 45 Ohio St.3d 288, 544 N.E.2d 257.

A presumption of paternity does not arise under RC 3111.03(A)(3)(a) when a man states he is the natural father of a child in an affidavit supporting a change of name for the child if the man does not marry the child's mother afterwards. McMullen v. Muir (Cuyahoga 1986) 34 Ohio App.3d 241, 517 N.E.2d 1381.

Trial court properly dismissed for failure to state a claim for relief plaintiff's suit to be declared father of a minor child where the defendant-parents were lawfully married at the time of such child's conception. N.J. v B.A, No. CA–6088 (5th Dist Ct App, Stark, 8–15–83).

2. Due process

A provision of a state evidence code which presumes that a child born to a married woman living with her husband, who is neither impotent nor sterile, is a child of the marriage does not violate the due process rights of a man who wishes to establish his paternity of a child born to the wife of another man nor infringe upon the constitutional right of the child to maintain a relationship with her natural father. (Ed. note: California law construed in light of federal constitution.) Michael H. v. Gerald D. (U.S.Cal. 1989) 109 S.Ct. 2333, 491 U.S. 110, 105 L.Ed.2d 91, rehearing denied 110 S.Ct. 22, 492 U.S. 937, 106 L.Ed.2d 634, rehearing denied 111 S.Ct. 1645, 499 U.S. 984, 113 L.Ed.2d 739, motion to amend denied 112 S.Ct. 1931, 504 U.S. 905, 118 L.Ed.2d 538.

3. Presumption of paternity—In general

A man's act of signing the child's birth certificate or consenting to being named as the child's father on the birth certificate is not listed among the circumstances giving rise to statutory presumption of father and child relationship. In re Adoption of G.B. (Ohio App. 3 Dist., Seneca, 10-18-2010) No. 13-10-01, 2010-Ohio-5059, 2010 WL 4055551, Unreported. Children Out–of–wedlock ☞ 3; Children Out–of–wedlock ☞ 12

Act of prospective stepfather in signing the child's birth certificate did not result in a presumption that he was the child's father and, consequently, he was not the child's presumed father at the time he filed his petition to adopt the child so as to render the petition a nullity. In re Adoption of G.B. (Ohio App. 3 Dist., Seneca, 10-18-2010) No. 13-10-01, 2010-Ohio-5059, 2010 WL 4055551, Unreported. Adoption ☞ 4; Children Out–of–wedlock ☞ 3

Formal acknowledgement of paternity entered into by mother and putative father could not be rebutted by results of subsequent genetic testing that showed putative father was not child's biological father, where formal acknowledgement of paternity rose above level of presumption, and was final and conclusive determination of paternity. Thomas v. Cruz (Ohio App. 9 Dist., Lorain, 11 12 2003) No. 03CA008247, 2003-Ohio-6011, 2003 WL 22657864, Unreported. Children Out–of–wedlock ☞ 33

False testimony of an adverse party in a divorce proceeding, that the husband was the father of a child fourteen years before, does not warrant a finding of fraud upon the court; this is intrinsic fraud, time-barred by the one-year statute of limitations of Civ 60(B)(3). Still v. Still (Ohio App. 4

Dist., Gallia, 06-25-1996) No. 95CA15, 1996 WL 362259, Unreported.

Statutes permitting severance of a parent-child relationship because the parent and child were mistaken about their joint genetic heritage are unconstitutional; statutes overlook complexity of the parent-child relationship and represent an attempt to write a new rule allowing relief from judgment for mistakes, inadvertence, excusable neglect, newly discovered evidence, or fraud. Van Dusen v. Van Dusen (Ohio App. 10 Dist., 01-28-2003) 151 Ohio App.3d 494, 784 N.E.2d 750, 2003-Ohio-350. Infants ☞ 132

Best interests of children born out of wedlock weighed against allowing putative father to disestablish paternity through genetic testing, where putative father and mother lived together for approximately six years, during which period both children were conceived and born, mother did not have sexual relations with anyone other than putative father for entire period they lived together, putative father always treated children as his own and held himself out in community as their natural father, and putative father did not begin to assert nonpaternity until mother left him and sought child support. Crago v. Kinzie (Ohio Com.Pl., 06-01-2000) 106 Ohio Misc.2d 51, 733 N.E.2d 1219. Children Out–of–wedlock ☞ 7

Statutory presumption of paternity of child conceived in wedlock but born after parents' divorce did not apply, and mother's former husband was not required to be joined as party defendant in parentage action, where trial court expressly stated by interlineation in decree of divorce that mother was pregnant and that former husband was not child's father. Nwabara v. Willacy (Ohio App. 8 Dist., 08-09-1999) 135 Ohio App.3d 120, 733 N.E.2d 267, dismissed, appeal not allowed 87 Ohio St.3d 1451, 719 N.E.2d 967. Children Out–of–wedlock ☞ 3; Children Out–of–wedlock ☞ 35

Putative father waived appellate review of his claims that jury was inaccurately instructed that presumption of paternity arose against him by virtue of DNA test result showing likelihood greater than 95% that he was the father, that he had burden to rebut such presumption of paternity, and that degree of proof required to rebut presumption was by clear and convincing evidence, where defense counsel, given opportunity to correct or add to jury instructions, took no steps to do so in manner of objection. Nwabara v. Willacy (Ohio App. 8 Dist., 08-09-1999) 135 Ohio App.3d 120, 733 N.E.2d 267, dismissed, appeal not allowed 87 Ohio St.3d 1451, 719 N.E.2d 967. Children Out–of–wedlock ☞ 73

Laches is equitable defense to paternity action. Seegert v. Zietlow (Ohio App. 8 Dist., 08-15-1994) 95 Ohio App.3d 451, 642 N.E.2d 697. Children Out–of–wedlock ☞ 38

The presumption that a child conceived during wedlock is legitimate can be overcome by evidence which is strong and convincing. Quasion v. Friedman (Montgomery 1959) 110 Ohio App. 166, 169

N.E.2d 28, 12 O.O.2d 430. Children Out–of–wed-lock ☞ 3

4. ——— Marriage during pregnancy, presumption of paternity

Civ R 60 relief from agreed judgment entry stipulating that parties in divorce had no issue born of the marriage was proper where, once the stipula-tion is disregarded, the husband claims the child born to his wife is his daughter. Wingenfeld v Wingenfeld, No. 63942, 1993 WL 497074 (8th Dist Ct App, Cuyahoga, 12–2–93).

Ordinarily, a child born during a marriage is presumed to be the child of the husband. J.F. v. D.B. (Ohio App. 9 Dist., 03-15-2006) 165 Ohio App.3d 791, 848 N.E.2d 873, 2006-Ohio-1175, ap-peal allowed 110 Ohio St.3d 1438, 852 N.E.2d 187, 2006-Ohio-3862, affirmed in part, reversed in part 116 Ohio St.3d 363, 879 N.E.2d 740, 2007-Ohio-6750. Children Out–of–wedlock ☞ 3

Under common law, child was "child of the marriage" of parties, where child was born during marriage and parties continued to live together for slightly less than one year after child was born. Cassim v. Cassim (Ohio App. 10 Dist., 11-17-1994) 98 Ohio App.3d 576, 649 N.E.2d 28, on subsequent appeal 1995 WL 546926, dismissed, appeal not allowed 75 Ohio St.3d 1404, 661 N.E.2d 754. Child Custody ☞ 75

Term "child of the marriage," as used in rules and statute with respect to divorce and separation, includes child who is born to wife during marriage and, thus, who is presumptively the child of the husband. Cassim v. Cassim (Ohio App. 10 Dist., 11-17-1994) 98 Ohio App.3d 576, 649 N.E.2d 28, on subsequent appeal 1995 WL 546926, dismissed, ap-peal not allowed 75 Ohio St.3d 1404, 661 N.E.2d 754. Child Custody ☞ 75; Children Out–of–wed-lock ☞ 3

Presumption of paternity created by putative fa-ther's marriage to mother at time of child's birth and his signature on birth certificate conflicted with presumption of nonpaternity created by genetic test results indicating more than 95% probability of nonpaternity, requiring use of logic and analysis of policy considerations in determining what presump-tion should control. Riddle v. Riddle (Ohio Com. Pl. 1992) 63 Ohio Misc.2d 43, 619 N.E.2d 1201. Children Out–of–wedlock ☞ 43

A man who marries a pregnant woman can rebut the presumption of paternity by presenting clear and convincing evidence of fraud and nonpaternity. Carson v. Carson (Brown 1989) 62 Ohio App.3d 670, 577 N.E.2d 391, motion overruled 46 Ohio St.3d 716, 546 N.E.2d 1334. Children Out–of–wedlock ☞ 3

Pursuant to RC 3111.03(A)(1), a man is pre-sumed to be the natural father of a child where the man and the child's mother are or have been married to each other and the child is born during the marriage; however, such presumption may be rebutted by clear and convincing evidence to the contrary. Hulett v. Hulett (Ohio 1989) 45 Ohio St.3d 288, 544 N.E.2d 257.

Where a child is conceived and born during the marriage of a husband and wife, the husband is presumed to be the father of the child even though the husband had a vasectomy prior to the concep-tion of the child, since the husband failed to return for a sperm test after the vasectomy, and even though the wife admits having had a sexual rela-tionship with another man. Walkup v. Walkup (Brown 1986) 31 Ohio App.3d 248, 511 N.E.2d 119, 31 O.B.R. 532.

A man who marries a woman while she is preg-nant is presumed to be the natural father of any child born from the pregnancy; however, this pre-sumption can be rebutted by clear and convincing evidence. Johnson v. Adams (Ohio 1985) 18 Ohio St.3d 48, 479 N.E.2d 866, 18 O.B.R. 83. Children Out–of–wedlock ☞ 3

While every child conceived in wedlock is pre-sumed legitimate, such presumption is not conclu-sive and may be rebutted by clear and convincing evidence that there were no sexual relations be-tween husband and wife during the time in which the child must have been conceived, and a com-plaint for determination of paternity is sufficient if the plaintiff alleges he is the natural father of the child. Joseph v. Alexander (Ohio 1984) 12 Ohio St.3d 88, 465 N.E.2d 448, 12 O.B.R. 77. Children Out–of–wedlock ☞ 3

In a custody action involving a child conceived and born while the parties were married, a stipula-tion and affidavit to the effect that the husband is not the father of the child are insufficient as a matter of law to overcome the presumption of legitimacy of such child. Nelson v. Nelson (Frank-lin 1983) 10 Ohio App.3d 36, 460 N.E.2d 653, 10 O.B.R. 44.

The biological father of a child cannot be held for her support where the mother, during pregnan-cy, contracts marriage with another man, who mar-ries her with full knowledge of her condition and thereby consents to stand in loco parentis to such child and to being the father of the child. Hall v. Rosen (Ohio 1977) 50 Ohio St.2d 135, 363 N.E.2d 725, 4 O.O.3d 336. Children Out–of–wedlock ☞ 33

Where a man marries a woman who is pregnant by another man, and there is no showing of fraud in the inception of the marriage, the husband is con-clusively presumed to be the father of the child. Burse v. Burse (Hamilton 1976) 48 Ohio App.2d 244, 356 N.E.2d 755, 2 O.O.3d 197. Children Out–of–wedlock ☞ 3

Where a man marries a woman with full knowl-edge that she is pregnant by another, and the child is born during their marriage, and subsequently the woman obtains a divorce, the divorced husband may be ordered to support such minor child, inas-much as by such marriage the husband deprives the wife of the right to institute a bastardy action against the child's natural father. Gustin v. Gustin (Montgomery 1958) 108 Ohio App. 171, 161 N.E.2d

68, 9 O.O.2d 204. Child Support ⟵ 30; Children Out–of–wedlock ⟵ 21(1)

A motion to terminate a child support decree will be denied where a man marries a pregnant woman with full knowledge of her condition, because the law conclusively presumes that he is father of the child, and even a failure to permit or admit blood tests to disprove paternity is not in error. Humphrey v Humphrey, No. C–800312 (1st Dist Ct App, Hamilton, 5–6–81).

5. —— Burden of proof, presumption of paternity

Exclusion as the father through genetic testing constitutes clear and convincing evidence that overcomes the presumption of paternity created under RC 3111.03 and where the defendant is excluded as the father there is no minor issue of the marriage and RC 3109.04 no longer provides the court of common pleas with subject matter jurisdiction to make a ruling on custody; instead the issue of custody becomes subject matter exclusive to the juvenile court pursuant to RC 2151.23, and consequently, the "best interest of the child" standard in determining custody does not apply. Thompson v. Thompson (Ohio App. 4 Dist., Highland, 08-10-1995) No. 94CA859, 1995 WL 481480, Unreported.

Evidence a defendant had sexual relations with a child's mother approximately nine months prior to the birth of the child, HLA test results producing a 99.93% probability the defendant is the father of the child, and testimony the mother's husband was incarcerated with no access to an intimate relationship with the mother for months prior to and after the approximate time of conception constitutes clear and convincing evidence rebutting the presumption that the mother's husband is the father of the child and a failure to obtain an HLA test of the husband does not preclude a judgment finding the defendant to be the natural father of the child. Feister v Lee, No. 93AP060037, 1993 WL 472868 (5th Dist Ct App, Tuscarawas, 11–1–93).

Presumption of paternity resulting from genetic testing may only be rebutted by clear and convincing evidence. Filkins v. Cales (Logan 1993) 86 Ohio App.3d 61, 619 N.E.2d 1156, motion overruled 67 Ohio St.3d 1422, 616 N.E.2d 506. Children Out–of–wedlock ⟵ 43

Mother established prima facie parent-child relationship between putative father and daughter by preponderance of evidence in view of fact that genetic test disclosed 98.5% probability that he was biological father of child, that mother had sexual intercourse with putative father twice during alleged month of conception, that, although she had sexual intercourse with one other man during that month, genetic blood testing excluded him as biological father of child, and that putative father admitted under cross-examination that it was possible that he had sexual intercourse with child's mother during month of conception and they did not use any form of contraceptive. Filkins v. Cales (Logan 1993) 86 Ohio App.3d 61, 619 N.E.2d 1156,

motion overruled 67 Ohio St.3d 1422, 616 N.E.2d 506. Children Out–of–wedlock ⟵ 53

Clear and convincing evidence sufficient to overcome the presumption of paternity contained in RC 3111.03(A)(1) may be adduced through any or all of the enumerated methods prescribed by RC 3111.10, including the submission of genetic test results. Hulett v. Hulett (Ohio 1989) 45 Ohio St.3d 288, 544 N.E.2d 257.

RC 3111.03 abolishes the conclusive presumption of paternity established by Hall v Rosen, 50 OS(2d) 135 (1977), and provides that the presumption of paternity may be refuted by clear and convincing evidence; this provision should be applied retroactively. Johnson v Adams, No. 81 X 29 (4th Dist Ct App, Washington, 2–3–84), affirmed by 18 OS(3d) 48, 18 OBR 83, 479 NE(2d) 866 (1985).

The presumption of paternity set forth in RC 3111.03 is overcome by clear and convincing evidence, such as the birth of a biracial child to a married couple of the same race. Murph v Murph, No. 10262 (2d Dist Ct App, Montgomery, 7–16–87).

Appellate court distinguished an "alleged" father from a "presumed" father. Where there is clear and convincing evidence of sexual relations between husband and wife during possible conception period, the presumption of RC 3111.03 becomes essentially conclusive and not rebutted by genetic tests which are to be used only with respect to an alleged father, not a presumed father. Hulett v Hulett, No. 87AP–330 (10th Dist Ct App, Franklin, 11–17–87).

A complainant mother in a bastardy action, who was married at the time of her child's conception, must establish, by clear and convincing evidence, that her husband was not the father of the child, and, by a preponderance of the evidence, that the defendant was the father of the child, and in such case, a verdict for the complainant mother finding the defendant to be the father of such child is against the manifest weight of the evidence where such evidence shows that complainant's husband had actual physical access to complainant at the time of the child's conception, and that, following the husband's subsequent divorce from complainant, he took her into his home and, when the child was born, took her to the hospital, visited her there frequently, did not protest the use of his name as the father of the child, and brought the mother and child to his home after their release from the hospital. State ex rel. Satterfield v. Sullivan (Franklin 1962) 115 Ohio App. 347, 185 N.E.2d 47, 20 O.O.2d 419.

6. —— Rebuttal, presumption of paternity

A presumption that the husband is the natural father of a child is rebutted by genetic testing that indicates a 99.96 per cent probability that the mother's live-in boyfriend is the child's father and by testimony of the mother indicating (1) the child's baby picture is identical to that of the boyfriend, (2) the threesome functions as a family, (3) the friend keeps the child when the mother works evenings and visits the child every weekend, and (4) the husband was involved in three other marriages without bearing children and doctors advise him that he is unable to produce a child. Chenoweth v. Chenoweth (Ohio App. 2 Dist., Montgomery, 03-20-1998) No. 16700, 1998 WL 127591, Unreported.

A husband's paternity is rebuttable by a genetic test and a putative father may bring a parentage action where the mother was, and continues to be, married to another man at the time the child was conceived. Crawford County Child Support Enforcement Agency v. Sprague (Ohio App. 3 Dist., Crawford, 12-05-1997) No. 3-97-13, 1997 WL 746770, Unreported.

Evidence in parentage proceeding was sufficient to rebut statutory presumption that mother's former husband was natural father of child born within 300 days of divorce decree; mother testified that putative father was child's natural father, results of DNA test, testified to by expert witness, indicated putative father's paternity with 99.95 percent probability and excluded all other men by probability of .05 percent. Nwabara v. Willacy (Ohio App. 8 Dist., 08-09-1999) 135 Ohio App.3d 120, 733 N.E.2d 267, dismissed, appeal not allowed 87 Ohio St.3d 1451, 719 N.E.2d 967. Children Out–of–wedlock ☞ 53

Doctor's inconsistent testimony that child's estimated gestational age at birth was about 34 weeks, which would have placed probable date of conception one month before mother and putative father had intercourse, did not rise to level of clear and convincing evidence required to rebut presumption of paternity established by genetic test results which disclosed that there was 98.5% probability that putative father was biological father of child. Filkins v. Cales (Logan 1993) 86 Ohio App.3d 61, 619 N.E.2d 1156, motion overruled 67 Ohio St.3d 1422, 616 N.E.2d 506. Children Out–of–wedlock ☞ 43

The presumption that a child conceived in wedlock is legitimate cannot be rebutted except by evidence that the spouses had no sexual relations during the time in which the child was conceived. Joseph v Alexander, No. CA–6781 (5th Dist Ct App, Stark, 5–5–86).

7. Wrongful death

Putative father of minor child who had died in automobile accident was entitled to receive wrongful death proceeds awarded as result of child's death, even though putative father had failed to satisfy technical requirements for establishing parent-child relationship, where following child's death both mother and putative father testified that he was in fact child's natural father. In re Estate of Pulford (Ohio App. 11 Dist., 07-28-1997) 122 Ohio App.3d 92, 701 N.E.2d 58. Death ☞ 101

In a wrongful death action against a truck driver and driver's employer involving a collision between the truck driver and a motorist, dismissal is proper on the basis that the plaintiff could not maintain a wrongful death suit on behalf of an alleged minor child of the motorist where the plaintiff and the motorist were not married, the motorist did not in probate court formally acknowledge the child as his

with consent of the mother, and the motorist did not designate the child as his heir-at-law, adopt the child, or make provision for the child in his will, and, although a parentage action was brought by the plaintiff and her son, the action was brought after the death of the motorist; thus, as a matter of law, the child cannot inherit from the decedent's estate, including any recovery from the wrongful death action. Hunter–Martin v. Winchester Transp., Inc. (Shelby 1991) 71 Ohio App.3d 273, 593 N.E.2d 383, motion overruled 62 Ohio St.3d 1408, 577 N.E.2d 361.

8. Artificial insemination

Indemnification provision in surrogacy contract providing that, in the event that custody of children was awarded to surrogate mother and mother's husband, biological father would be indemnified by surrogate mother and her husband for any and all monies biological father was required to pay for child support, did not violate public policy; this was not abrogation of obligation to support offspring of coital relationship but recognition that, since surrogate was not a parent, if surrogate mother and her husband decided to obtain custody of children, they would become legal parents and surrogacy agreement would terminate, and biological father would be treated as merely the sperm donor and not the parent. J.F. v. D.B. (Ohio App. 9 Dist., 03-15-2006) 165 Ohio App.3d 791, 848 N.E.2d 873, 2006-Ohio-1175, appeal allowed 110 Ohio St.3d 1438, 852 N.E.2d 187, 2006-Ohio-3862, affirmed in part, reversed in part 116 Ohio St.3d 363, 879 N.E.2d 740, 2007-Ohio-6750. Children Out–of–wedlock ☞ 22; Contracts ☞ 108(2)

Since surrogate mother and mother's husband breached surrogacy contract by obtaining custody of children born as result of surrogacy and since surrogacy contract was enforceable, surrogate mother and her husband were liable for restitution of monies paid by biological father, as well as attorney fees, pursuant to surrogacy contract providing that, in event of breach by surrogate mother and her husband, mother and husband shall be liable for any and all monies expended on their behalf, plus attorney fees. J.F. v. D.B. (Ohio App. 9 Dist., 03-15-2006) 165 Ohio App.3d 791, 848 N.E.2d 873, 2006-Ohio-1175, appeal allowed 110 Ohio St.3d 1438, 852 N.E.2d 187, 2006-Ohio-3862, affirmed in part, reversed in part 116 Ohio St.3d 363, 879 N.E.2d 740, 2007-Ohio-6750.

Failure to comply with medical requirements of artificial insemination statutes would prevent mother from invoking nonspousal artificial insemination statute to obtain dismissal of sperm donor's complaint to determine paternity, custody, support, and visitation. C.O. v. W.S. (Ohio Com.Pl., 03-01-1994) 64 Ohio Misc.2d 9, 639 N.E.2d 523 Children Out–of–wedlock ☞ 15

Even if artificial insemination statute establishing legal relationship between donor and mother applied, statute was unconstitutional as applied to donor and child insofar as it could be read to absolutely extinguish donor's efforts to assert rights and responsibilities of being father in case in which mother had solicited participation of donor, who was known to her, and donor and mother agreed that there would be relationship between donor and child. C.O. v. W.S. (Ohio Com.Pl., 03-01-1994) 64 Ohio Misc.2d 9, 639 N.E.2d 523 Children Out-of-wedlock ☞ 15

Artificial insemination statute establishing legal relationship between donor and mother would not apply to prevent paternity adjudication where unmarried woman solicited participation of donor, who was known to her, and where donor and woman agreed that there would be relationship between donor and child. C.O. v. W.S. (Ohio Com.Pl., 03-01-1994) 64 Ohio Misc.2d 9, 639 N.E.2d 523 Children Out-of-wedlock ☞ 15

Where a husband and wife agree to conceive a child by means of artificial insemination, and a child so conceived is born to the parties, it is against public policy for a court to enter a judgment establishing the husband's non-paternity in connection with a divorce of the parties and the remarriage of the mother. Brooks v. Fair (Van Wert 1988) 40 Ohio App.3d 202, 532 N.E.2d 208.

Where a husband and wife agree to conceive a child by means of artificial insemination, and a child so conceived is born to the parties, it is against public policy for a court to enter a judgment establishing the husband's non-paternity in connection with a divorce of the parties and the remarriage of the mother. Brooks v. Fair (Van Wert 1988) 40 Ohio App.3d 202, 532 N.E.2d 208.

9. Admissibility of evidence

Trial court had authority to enforce shared parenting agreement, even though child's putative father was determined not to be child's biological father, where evidence established that parent and child relationship existed between putative father and child; putative father was listed as father on child's birth certificate, mother and putative father went to Child Support Enforcement Agency (CSEA) and signed acknowledgement of paternity, administrative order that required putative father to pay child support and provide health insurance for child indicated that basis of support duty was acknowledgement of paternity filed with central paternity registry, and there was no evidence either party had attempted to rescind acknowledgment of paternity. Thomas v. Cruz (Ohio App. 9 Dist., Lorain, 11-12-2003) No. 03CA008247, 2003-Ohio-6011, 2003 WL 22657864, Unreported. Children Out-of-wedlock ☞ 20.9

Genetic test results are admissible without the need for foundation testimony or further proof of authenticity or accuracy where the biological father fails to file a written objection to the report of the court-ordered genetic test results and does not dispute that he received a copy. Joy B. v. Glen D. (Ohio App. 6 Dist., Wood, 08-06-1999) No. OT-99-002, 1999 WL 575945, Unreported.

10. Res judicata/estoppel

Under doctrine of res judicata, putative father's second motion for relief from judgment of paternity, based on results of genetic blood test which excluded him from being father of child, was barred by virtue of denial of his first motion for relief from judgment which had been specifically based on ground of newly discovered evidence; grounds for both motions were identical, i.e., newly discovered evidence. Matter of Kay B. v. Timothy C. (Ohio App. 6 Dist. 1997) 117 Ohio App.3d 598, 690 N.E.2d 1366.

Finding in original divorce decree that child born during parties' marriage was former husband's child was res judicata as to father's motion to have himself declared as not the child's biological father because DNA (deoxyribonucleic acid) test results indicated that father and child were not genetically linked. Van Dusen v. Van Dusen (Ohio App. 10 Dist., 01-28-2003) 151 Ohio App.3d 494, 784 N.E.2d 750, 2003-Ohio-350. Divorce ☞ 172

Under version of presumption statute in effect at time of children's out-of-wedlock births, court had discretion to balance equities in determining whether putative father was estopped from seeking genetic testing in attempt to disestablish paternity, where putative father's act in signing their birth certificates created presumption of paternity, and genetic testing was not mentioned in statute. Crago v. Kinzie (Ohio Com.Pl., 06-01-2000) 106 Ohio Misc.2d 51, 733 N.E.2d 1219. Children Out-of-wedlock ☞ 7

Putative father's representation of himself as child's natural father causes certain benefits to flow to father and certain detriments to flow to child, and may warrant application of doctrine of equitable estoppel to preclude admission of genetic test results in parentage action. Crago v. Kinzie (Ohio Com.Pl., 06-01-2000) 106 Ohio Misc.2d 51, 733 N.E.2d 1219. Children Out-of-wedlock ☞ 58

Legitimation order filed in probate court with consent of mother did not bar subsequent parentage action wherein mother sought child support arrearages; application of doctrine of res judicata would violate state's strong public policy favoring protection of children and their support, health, maintenance and welfare, and would also violate equal protection. Lewis v. Chapin (Ohio App. 8 Dist., 03-21-1994) 93 Ohio App.3d 695, 639 N.E.2d 848 Children Out-of-wedlock ☞ 33; Constitutional Law ☞ 3192

Child was not barred under doctrine of res judicata from pursuing parentage action on basis that father acknowledged existence of parent-child relationship and that mother consented to filing of legitimacy order, as child was not a party or in privity with a party to the legitimacy order. Lewis v. Chapin (Ohio App. 8 Dist., 03-21-1994) 93 Ohio App.3d 695, 639 N.E.2d 848 Children Out-of-wedlock ☞ 33

Doctrines of laches and equitable estoppel precluded mother from claiming that putative father, who was married to her at time of birth and had signed birth certificate, was not child's biological father based on genetic results; mother had allowed putative father to believe that he was child's father for more than five years, allowed him to financially contribute to care and support of child, participated in development of intimate father/son relationship, and represented to putative father's parents that they were child's grandparents and allowed them to develop relationship with child. Riddle v. Riddle (Ohio Com.Pl. 1992) 63 Ohio Misc.2d 43, 619 N.E.2d 1201. Children Out–of–wedlock ☞ 1

Common Pleas Court has inherent authority, when considering best interests of minor child, to estop mother from using genetic testing to disestablish child's paternity with his or her presumed father. Riddle v. Riddle (Ohio Com.Pl. 1992) 63 Ohio Misc.2d 43, 619 N.E.2d 1201. Children Out–of–wedlock ☞ 1

An appellant in a divorce action may not raise the issue of paternity fifteen months after the decree, stating that another man fathered his children, by claiming that genetic testing was not available under prior law when he had offered no clear and convincing evidence on the issue. Weber v. Weber (Fulton 1991) 74 Ohio App.3d 396, 599 N.E.2d 288.

A judgment entry in a divorce action finding that a child was born during the marriage and ordering the husband to pay child support is not conclusive as to the paternity of the child where the husband had denied such paternity in the divorce action and the decree did not explicitly find that a parent and child relationship existed; res judicata is inapplicable in a subsequent paternity action filed by the putative father absent a specific finding that a parent and child relationship existed; therefore, a juvenile court errs in dismissing the subsequent paternity action. LaBonte v. LaBonte (Meigs 1988) 61 Ohio App.3d 209, 572 N.E.2d 704, motion overruled 42 Ohio St.3d 709, 538 N.E.2d 122.

Duly notorized declaration of paternity signed by one putative father did not have force of final judgment and did not bar, on res judicata grounds, subsequent legitimation action against second putative father; declaration of paternity had never been filed with probate court. Collett v. Cogar (Ohio 1988) 35 Ohio St.3d 114, 518 N.E.2d 1202. Children Out–of–wedlock ☞ 13

The doctrine of res judicata can be invoked to give conclusive effect to determination of parentage contained in dissolution decree or legitimation order, thereby barring a subsequent paternity action brought pursuant to parentage statute. In re Gilbraith (Ohio 1987) 32 Ohio St.3d 127, 512 N.E.2d 956. Child Support ☞ 225; Children Out–of–wedlock ☞ 13; Children Out–of–wedlock ☞ 21(2)

11. Judgment of paternity

Putative father's motion for relief from judgment of paternity, based on recently obtained results of genetic blood test which excluded him from being

father of child, was based on newly discovered evidence and, therefore, was untimely when it was filed more than one year after entry of judgment. Matter of Kay B. v. Timothy C. (Ohio App. 6 Dist. 1997) 117 Ohio App.3d 598, 690 N.E.2d 1366.

Statements of counsel indicating that the client concedes he is the father and "there is no dispute that the child in question is the defendant's" and that he is the father of the child conceived by him and the victim of his attack are sufficient for conviction of domestic violence based upon an admitted fact and not upon a presumption of paternity. State v. Rowland (Ohio App. 2 Dist., Greene, 08-08-1997) No. 96 CA 135, 1997 WL 446861, Unreported.

In divorce action involving pregnant wife, parties' agreed entry, pursuant to which wife dropped any claim against husband with regard to unborn child, was insufficient to overcome statutory presumption of legitimacy, where domestic relations court adopted the agreed entry without holding hearing and receiving evidence to rebut presumption of legitimacy, divorce decree made finding of nonpaternity, and husband did not undertake obligation for child support. Fitzpatrick v. Fitzpatrick (Ohio App. 12 Dist., 03-02-1998) 126 Ohio App.3d 476, 710 N.E.2d 778, dismissed, appeal not allowed 82 Ohio St.3d 1441, 695 N.E.2d 264. Children Out–of–wedlock ☞ 3

A judgment pursuant to former RC 3111.17 which sets visitation rights and support duties of a man who has signed a birth certificate as informant, even though both he and the mother admit he is not the natural father, may be properly vacated to relieve the child and mother from the determination of paternity implicit in the judgment. In re Smith (Miami 1984) 16 Ohio App.3d 75, 474 N.E.2d 632, 16 O.B.R. 79.

A determination of a "reputed father" under RC 3111.17 does not convert that finding into a finding of a "natural father" under RC 2105.18, nor does such a determination give the mother authority either as agent for the father or by operation of law to file an application for legitimation under RC 2105.18 and acknowledge that the alleged father is the natural father of the child. In re Minor of Martin (Cuyahoga 1977) 51 Ohio App.2d 21, 365 N.E.2d 892, 5 O.O.3d 141.

12. Appeals

A divorce decree that entered judgment on the custody and support of an older child but deferred the question of support for an unborn child pending a determination of paternity is a final appealable order where a speedy determination and review of the custody question for the older child outweighed the danger of piecemeal appeals or harm to the prompt and orderly disposition of litigation, and the court expressly found that there was no just reason for delay. Evicks v. Evicks (Lawrence 1992) 79 Ohio App.3d 657, 607 N.E.2d 1090.

PRACTICE AND PROCEDURE

3111.04   Action to determine father and child relationship

(A) An action to determine the existence or nonexistence of the father and child relationship may be brought by the child or the child's personal representative, the child's mother or her personal representative, a man alleged or alleging himself to be the child's father, the child support enforcement agency of the county in which the child resides if the child's mother, father, or alleged father is a recipient of public assistance or of services under Title IV–D of the "Social Security Act," 88 Stat. 2351 (1975), 42 U.S.C.A. 651, as amended, or the alleged father's personal representative.

(B) An agreement does not bar an action under this section.

(C) If an action under this section is brought before the birth of the child and if the action is contested, all proceedings, except service of process and the taking of depositions to perpetuate testimony, may be stayed until after the birth.

(D) A recipient of public assistance or of services under Title IV D of the "Social Security Act," 88 Stat. 2351 (1975), 42 U.S.C.A. 651, as amended, shall cooperate with the child support enforcement agency of the county in which a child resides to obtain an administrative determination pursuant to sections 3111.38 to 3111.54 of the Revised Code, or, if necessary, a court determination pursuant to sections 3111.01 to 3111.18 of the Revised Code, of the existence or nonexistence of a parent and child relationship between the father and the child. If the recipient fails to cooperate, the agency may commence an action to determine the existence or nonexistence of a parent and child relationship between the father and the child pursuant to sections 3111.01 to 3111.18 of the Revised Code.

(E) As used in this section, "public assistance" means all of the following:

(1) Medicaid under Chapter 5111. of the Revised Code;

(2) Ohio works first under Chapter 5107. of the Revised Code;

(3) Disability financial assistance under Chapter 5115. of the Revised Code.

(2011 H 153, eff. 10-1-11; 2009 H 1, eff. 10-16-09; 2008 H 562, eff. 9–23–08; 2006 H 136, eff. 5–17–06; 2003 H 95, eff. 6–26–03; 2000 S 180, eff. 3–22–01; 1997 H 352, eff. 1–1–98; 1992 S 10, eff. 7–15–92; 1982 H 245)

Uncodified Law

1992 S 10, § 5: See Uncodified Law under 3111.01.

1982 H 245, § 3, eff. 6–29–82, reads: An action may be commenced pursuant to sections 3111.01 to 3111.19 of the Revised Code, as enacted by Section 1 of this act, to establish the father and child relationship, or the mother and child relationship, irrespective of whether a child is born prior to, or on or after, the effective date of this act.

Historical and Statutory Notes

Ed. Note: Former 3111.04 repealed by 1982 H 245, eff. 6–29–82; 127 v 1039; 125 v 184; 1953 H 1; GC 8006–4; Source—GC 12111. 3111.04 contains provisions analogous to former 3111.02 and 3111.03, repealed by 1982 H 245, eff. 6–29–82.

Pre–1953 H 1 Amendments: 124 v S 65

Amendment Note: 2011 H 153 deleted division (E)(4), which prior thereto read:

"(4) Children's buy-in program under sections 5101.5211 to 5101.5216 of the Revised Code."

Amendment Note: 2009 H 1 deleted former division (E)(4); and made harmonizing changes to division designations. Prior to amendment, former division (E)(4) read:

"(4) Disability medical assistance under Chapter 5115. of the Revised Code;"

Amendment Note: 2008 H 562 rewrote division (E), which prior to amendment read:

"(E) As used in this section, 'public assistance' means medical assistance under Chapter 5111. of the Revised Code, assistance under Chapter 5107. of the Revised Code, disability financial assistance under Chapter 5115. of the Revised Code, or disability medical assistance under Chapter 5115. of the Revised Code."

Amendment Note: 2006 H 136 inserted ", father, or alleged father" in division (A).

Amendment Note: 2003 H 95 substituted "disability financial assistance" for "or disability assistance", and inserted ", or disability medical assistance under Chapter 5115. of the Revised Code", in Subdivision (E).

Amendment Note: 2000 S 180 substituted "sections 3111.38 to 3111.54" for "section 3111.22" and "3111.18" for "3111.19" twice in division (D).

Amendment Note: 1997 H 352 rewrote this section, which prior thereto read:

"(A) An action to determine the existence or nonexistence of the father and child relationship may be brought by the child or the child's personal representative, the child's mother or her personal representative, a man alleged or alleging himself to be the child's father, the child support enforcement agency of the county in which the child resides if the child's mother is a recipient of public assistance as defined in section 2301.351 of the Revised Code or of services under Title IV–D of the "Social Security Act," 88 Stat. 2351 (1975), 42 U.S.C.A. 651, as amended, or the alleged father's personal representative.

"(B) An agreement does not bar an action under this section.

"(C) If an action under this section is brought before the birth of the child and if the action is contested, all proceedings, except service of process and the taking of depositions to perpetuate testimony, may be stayed until after the birth.

"(D) A recipient of public assistance as defined in section 2301.351 of the Revised Code or of services under Title IV–D of the "Social Security Act," 88 Stat. 2351 (1975), 42 U.S.C.A. 651, as amended, shall request the child support enforcement agency of the county in which a child resides to make an administrative determination of the existence or nonexistence of a parent and child relationship between the father and the child pursuant to section 3111.22 of the Revised Code before the recipient commences an action to determine the existence or nonexistence of that parent and child relationship."

Cross References

Guardian of the person or the estate, see 2111.06

Reciprocal enforcement of support, defense of non-paternity, adjudication of paternity issue, see 3115.24

Ohio Administrative Code References

Paternity establishment, see OAC 5101:12–40–05

Library References

Children Out-of-Wedlock ☞30, 33 to 34.
Social Security and Public Welfare ☞4.16.
Westlaw Topic Nos. 76H, 356A.
C.J.S. Children Out-of-Wedlock §§ 47, 50, 71, 80 to 83, 88 to 97.

C.J.S. Social Security and Public Welfare §§ 28 to 33, 52 to 53.

Research References

Encyclopedias

OH Jur. 3d Family Law § 909, Final Decree or Interlocutory Order.
OH Jur. 3d Family Law § 945, Rebuttal of Presumption.
OH Jur. 3d Family Law § 947, Who May Bring an Action.
OH Jur. 3d Family Law § 948, Who May Bring an Action--Child Support Enforcement Agency.
OH Jur. 3d Family Law § 949, Stay of Action Until Birth of Child.
OH Jur. 3d Family Law § 952, Jurisdiction.

Forms

Ohio Jurisprudence Pleading and Practice Forms § 111:3, Limitation of Actions.
Ohio Jurisprudence Pleading and Practice Forms § 111:5, Standing--Parties.

Treatises and Practice Aids

Sowald & Morganstern, Baldwin's Ohio Practice Domestic Relations Law § 3:8, Jurisdiction and Venue.

Sowald & Morganstern, Baldwin's Ohio Practice Domestic Relations Law § 3:9, Judicial Parentage Action--Initial Procedure.
Sowald & Morganstern, Baldwin's Ohio Practice Domestic Relations Law § 18:8, Visitation by Third Parties in Domestic Relations Actions.
Sowald & Morganstern, Baldwin's Ohio Practice Domestic Relations Law § 3:10, Judicial Parentage Action--Parties.
Sowald & Morganstern, Baldwin's Ohio Practice Domestic Relations Law § 3:14, Judicial Parentage Action--Presumptions of Parentage--Rebutting.
Sowald & Morganstern, Baldwin's Ohio Practice Domestic Relations Law § 3:50, Related Issues--Artificial Insemination and Surrogate Mothers.
Carlin, Baldwin's Ohio Prac. Merrick-Rippner Probate Law § 17:2, Designation--Effect.
Carlin, Baldwin's Ohio Prac. Merrick-Rippner Probate Law § 19:4, Legitimation--Historical Provisions.
Carlin, Baldwin's Ohio Prac. Merrick-Rippner Probate Law § 19:6, Uniform Parentage Act--Jurisdiction of Action to Determine Father-Child Relationship.

Carlin, Baldwin's Ohio Prac. Merrick-Rippner Probate Law § 19:7, Uniform Parentage Act--Presumptions.

Carlin, Baldwin's Ohio Prac. Merrick-Rippner Probate Law § 19:8, Uniform Parentage Act--Support Order.

Carlin, Baldwin's Ohio Prac. Merrick-Rippner Probate Law § 19:9, Uniform Parentage Act--Res Judicata; Doctrine of Laches.

Carlin, Baldwin's Ohio Prac. Merrick-Rippner Probate Law § 19:10, Uniform Parentage Act--Procedure in Action to Determine Father-Child Relationship.

Carlin, Baldwin's Ohio Prac. Merrick-Rippner Probate Law § 99:49, Interlocutory and Final Orders.

Carlin, Baldwin's Ohio Prac. Merrick-Rippner Probate Law § 110:20, Parentage Act--Jurisdiction and Venue.

Carlin, Baldwin's Ohio Prac. Merrick-Rippner Probate Law § 110:22, Parentage Act--Presumption of Paternity.

Carlin, Baldwin's Ohio Prac. Merrick-Rippner Probate Law § 110:23, Parentage Act--Parties in Parentage Action.

Carlin, Baldwin's Ohio Prac. Merrick-Rippner Probate Law § 110:34, Parentage Act--Administrative Support Orders.

Carlin, Baldwin's Ohio Prac. Merrick-Rippner Probate Law § 110:35, Civil Support Proceedings--Liability for Child Support.

Law Review and Journal Commentaries

Bankruptcy Reform Act of 1994—What the Bankruptcy Code Giveth, Domestic Relations Courts (and Congress) Taketh Away, C.R. "Chip" Bowles. 8 Domestic Rel J Ohio 17 (March/April 1996).

The Burden of Proof in a Paternity Proceeding, Note. 25 J Fam L 357 (1986–87).

The Constitutional Rights of Unwed Fathers Before and After *Lehr v. Robertson*, Elizabeth Buchanan. 45 Ohio St L J 313 (1984).

Fathers, Biological and Anonymous, and Other Legal Strangers: Determination of Parentage and Artificial Insemination by Donor Under Ohio Law, Susan Garner Eisenman. 45 Ohio St L J 383 (1984).

Finality in Parentage Findings: Perfection or Finality?, Pamela J. MacAdams. 10 Domestic Rel J Ohio 19 (March/April 1998).

Gideon's Trumpet Revisited: Protecting the Rights of Indigent Defendants in Paternity Actions, Mark D. Esterle. 24 J Fam L 1 (1985–86).

The Inheritance Rights (or Lack Thereof) of Legitimated Children in Ohio. Angela G. Carlin, 11 Prob L J Ohio 109 (July/August 2001).

Looking to Unwed Dads to Fill the Public Purse: A Disturbing Wave in Welfare Reform, Roger J.R. Levesque. 32 J Fam L 1 (Winter 1994).

Should Indigent Putative Fathers be Provided Court Appointed Counsel in Ohio Paternity Proceedings?, Daniel S. Cade. 10 Ohio N U L Rev 473 (1983).

Symposium: The Implications of Welfare Reform for Children. 60 Ohio St L J 1177 (1999).

Usefulness of Polygraph Results in Paternity Investigations when Used In Conjunction With Exclusionary Blood Tests and a Sixty–Day Conception Period, Richard J. Phannenstill. 21 J Fam L 69 (1982–83).

Notes of Decisions

---

1. Validity

Paternity statute, which granted putative fathers standing to assert paternity when there was presumption of legitimacy, was unconstitutional infringement on fundamental interests of family of child born during mother's marriage to her husband without sufficient governmental purpose to justify the infringement for due process purposes, where putative father had no relationship with child, and mother and husband intended to nurture and raise child in their unitary family. Merkel v. Doe (Ohio Com.Pl., 06-16-1993) 63 Ohio Misc.2d 490, 635 N.E.2d 70. Children Out–of–wedlock ☞ 31; Constitutional Law ☞ 4392

2. Constitutional issues

Even if Parentage Act precluded illegitimate children from claiming inheritance rights from and through their natural fathers absent inter vivos adjudication of paternity, inheritance scheme would not violate equal protection as to illegitimate children, as illegitimate child had several options through which to effectuate inheritance rights during father's lifetime, including acknowledgment, legitimation and right of action by child to establish paternity. Brookbank v. Gray (Ohio, 01-17-1996) 74 Ohio St.3d 279, 658 N.E.2d 724, 1996-Ohio-135. Children Out–of–wedlock ☞ 82; Constitutional Law ☞ 3184

Rules that state is constitutionally required to provide appointed counsel and blood grouping tests to indigent putative father who faces state as adversary in paternity proceedings are to be applied retroactively. Keeney v. Lawson (Hamilton 1984) 19 Ohio App.3d 318, 484 N.E.2d 745, 19 O.B.R. 491. Courts ☞ 100(1)

3. Due process

Denial of court-appointed counsel for indigent paternity defendant who faced state as adversary, when complainant mother and her child were recipients of public assistance, violated due process guarantees of State and Federal Constitutions, as private interests of both putative father and child were substantial, substantial interest and integrity of paternity determination itself could be damaged were defendant to be denied counsel during proceedings, and state's financial stake in providing defendant with court-appointed counsel was insignificant relative to private interests involved. State ex rel. Cody v. Toner (Ohio 1983) 8 Ohio St.3d 22, 456 N.E.2d 813, 8 O.B.R. 255, certiorari denied 104 S.Ct. 1912, 466 U.S. 938, 80 L.Ed.2d 461. Constitutional Law ☞ 4020

4. Equal protections

Statute which did not expressly prohibit mother from bringing parentage action after child became adult and father's right to visitation had expired did not violate father's right to equal protection; father's failure to obtain visitation rights resulted from his own inaction rather than from parentage statutes, and, moreover, mother's action was barred under doctrine of laches. Park v. Ambrose (Ross 1993) 85 Ohio App.3d 179, 619 N.E.2d 469, dismissed, jurisdictional motion overruled 67 Ohio St.3d 1409, 615 N.E.2d 1043. Children Out–of–wedlock ☞ 31; Constitutional Law ☞ 3192

Ohio Wrongful Death Statute did not violate equal protection by requiring that formal acknowledgment of paternity be made for children born out of wedlock to have standing to bring suit; requirement of formal acknowledgement of paternity is rationally related to legitimate state interest in avoiding spurious wrongful death claim, and children born out of wedlock were not discriminated against per se. Martin v. Daily Express, Inc. (N.D.Ohio, 02-28-1995) 878 F.Supp. 91. Constitutional Law ☞ 3195; Death ☞ 9

It is a violation of the equal protection clauses of the United States and Ohio constitutions to allow the aid and support of the child support enforcement agency in an action for child support brought by parents who have established their parentage through the probate court and residential parents who are on public assistance while denying the aid and support of the child support enforcement agency to parents who have established their parentage through the administrative process. Cuyahoga County Support Enforcement Agency v Lozada, Nos. 67463+, 1995 WL 386965 (8th Dist Ct App, Cuyahoga, 6–29–95).

5. In general

Trial court's dismissal of alleged father's complaint for parentage and custody without prejudice was not a final order and, thus, was not appealable. In re Thigpen (Ohio App. 2 Dist., Montgomery, 08-22-2003) No. 19726, 2003-Ohio-4431, 2003 WL 21995299, Unreported. Children Out–of–wedlock ☞ 73

In a parentage action in juvenile court to establish paternity and to recover past child support, an award of "arrearages" of $4000 for ten and one-half years for a total of $42,000 is an abuse of discretion where the child support worksheet imputes to the father an income of $50,000 per year since the birth of the child, tax returns indicate past income levels considerably less than the imputed amount, and the worksheet does not reflect support payments the father has already made. Harris v Knights, No. 64268, 1994 WL 50699 (8th Dist Ct App, Cuyahoga, 2–17–94).

Father fails to allege a basis for relief under Civ R 60(B) by his failure to allege fraud after blood tests showed that he could not be the child's biological father. In re Belden, No. 92 CA 21, 1993 WL 179254 (2d Dist Ct App, Miami, 5–25–93).

Former husband was required to comply with child support orders until paternity claim was resolved. In re Contemnor Caron (Ohio Com.Pl., 04-27-2000) 110 Ohio Misc.2d 58, 744 N.E.2d 787. Child Support ☞ 375

A court order mandating payment of child support is not stayed by the filing of a companion parentage action to disestablish paternity. In re Contemnor Caron (Ohio Com.Pl., 04-27-2000) 110 Ohio Misc.2d 58, 744 N.E.2d 787. Child Support ☞ 244

Court deciding whether adjudicated father should be estopped from challenging relationship by means of motion for relief from parentage determination may examine factors including: whether adjudicated father had reason to suspect parentage and whether he acted reasonably after first developing his suspicions; whether adjudicated father established relationship with child and nature of parties' relationship; likely future of any relationship; and chance of finding and establishing relationship with child's biological father. Leguillon v. Leguillon (Ohio App. 12 Dist., 01-12-1998) 124 Ohio App.3d 757, 707 N.E.2d 571. Children Out–of–wedlock ☞ 1

Absent showing that alleged father requested leave, stay of paternity and child support proceedings was not required, under Soldiers' and Sailors' Civil Relief Act, by reason of alleged father's military service. Phelps v. Fowler (Ohio App. 8 Dist.,

11-13-1995) 107 Ohio App.3d 263, 668 N.E.2d 558, appeal not allowed 75 Ohio St.3d 1452, 663 N.E.2d 332. Armed Services ⟿ 34.9(2); Children Out–of–wedlock ⟿ 57

While Ohio Department of Human Resources (ODHR) has authority to seek recoupment for its monetary expenditures for support of its recipients, proper procedure must be employed to recover such expenditures. Dorsett v. Wheeler (Ohio App. 3 Dist., 03-16-1995) 101 Ohio App.3d 716, 656 N.E.2d 698. Social Security And Public Welfare ⟿ 11

Legal custodians of child, who obtained custody from child's mother, were in privity with mother, and so were barred by res judicata from litigating issue of paternity of child that had been decided in divorce decree. Broxterman v. Broxterman (Ohio App. 1 Dist., 03-15-1995) 101 Ohio App.3d 661, 656 N.E.2d 394. Children Out–of–wedlock ⟿ 33; Divorce ⟿ 172

Child was not in privity with his mother in divorce action, and so was not barred by res judicata from bringing paternity action, even though paternity had been decided in divorce decree; although interests of child and mother coincided over support, their interests may have diverged on child's right to know identity of his biological father, and his potential rights of inheritance from his biological father. Broxterman v. Broxterman (Ohio App. 1 Dist., 03-15-1995) 101 Ohio App.3d 661, 656 N.E.2d 394. Child Support ⟿ 225; Children Out–of–wedlock ⟿ 21(2); Children Out–of–wedlock ⟿ 33

Legitimation of child granted pursuant to code section in effect at time of legitimation was sufficient to trigger one-year period of nonsupport found in subsequently adopted code section which obviated need to obtain parental consent to adoption, as language in new code section did not change or modify law, but merely clarified it. In re Adoption of Lassiter (Ohio App. 2 Dist., 02-24-1995) 101 Ohio App.3d 367, 655 N.E.2d 781, dismissed, appeal not allowed 73 Ohio St.3d 1410, 651 N.E.2d 1308. Adoption ⟿ 7.4(6)

In action to determine father and child relationship with minor child, after successful final determination in that case establishing existence of father-child relationship, father was not entitled as a matter of right to file motion in that proceeding seeking visitation rights with minor child. Burns v. Darnell (Ohio App. 10 Dist., 01-26-1995) 100 Ohio App.3d 419, 654 N.E.2d 169. Children Out–of–wedlock ⟿ 20.9

Putative father could not challenge paternity order more than 30 days after administrative determination and did not have right to HLA testing. State ex rel. Fulton Cty. Dept. of Human Serv. v. Kenneth J. (Ohio App. 6 Dist., 12-23-1994) 99 Ohio App.3d 475, 651 N.E.2d 27. Children Out–of–wedlock ⟿ 58; Children Out–of–wedlock ⟿ 68

Legitimation order filed in probate court with consent of mother did not bar subsequent parentage action wherein mother sought child support

arrearages; application of doctrine of res judicata would violate state's strong public policy favoring protection of children and their support, health, maintenance and welfare, and would also violate equal protection. Lewis v. Chapin (Ohio App. 8 Dist., 03-21-1994) 93 Ohio App.3d 695, 639 N.E.2d 848 Children Out–of–wedlock ⟿ 33; Constitutional Law ⟿ 3192

Assuming that probate court's finding that woman was intestate's biological child was supported by competent, credible evidence, woman failed to establish that she was "legitimized" in one of recognized manners and thus had no right to intestate's estate; only method by which woman could affirmatively seek relief would have been under Parentage Act which required that parentage action be brought in juvenile court which woman had failed to do. In re Estate of Hicks (Ohio App. 6 Dist., 09-30-1993) 90 Ohio App.3d 483, 629 N.E.2d 1086. Children Out–of–wedlock ⟿ 86

Parentage must be determined prior to death of putative father to the extent that parent-child relationship is being established under chapter governing descent and distribution; however, parent-child relationship may be established after death of putative father under chapter governing paternity actions. In re Estate of Hicks (Ohio App. 6 Dist., 09-30-1993) 90 Ohio App.3d 483, 629 N.E.2d 1086. Children Out–of–wedlock ⟿ 33; Children Out–of–wedlock ⟿ 86

When the state acts on a paternity complaint, a court should at the outset of the case determine whether the defendant is indigent and whether counsel should be appointed in his behalf. Rees v. Heimberger (Cuyahoga 1989) 60 Ohio App.3d 45, 573 N.E.2d 189, dismissed 47 Ohio St.3d 702, 547 N.E.2d 986, rehearing denied 48 Ohio St.3d 707, 550 N.E.2d 483, certiorari denied 110 S.Ct. 1827, 494 U.S. 1088, 108 L.Ed.2d 956. Children Out–of–wedlock ⟿ 57

A judgment entry in a divorce action finding that a child was born during the marriage and ordering the husband to pay child support is not conclusive as to the paternity of the child where the husband had denied such paternity in the divorce action and the decree did not explicitly find that a parent and child relationship existed; res judicata is inapplicable in a subsequent paternity action filed by the putative father absent a specific finding that a parent and child relationship existed; therefore, a juvenile court errs in dismissing the subsequent paternity action. LaBonte v. LaBonte (Meigs 1988) 61 Ohio App.3d 209, 572 N.E.2d 704, motion overruled 42 Ohio St.3d 709, 538 N.E.2d 122.

Although a proper party may intervene in an existing parentage action brought under RC 3111.04, a proper party may not bring a Civ R 60(B) motion to vacate a judgment in an action to which he was never a party. Hardman v. Chiaramonte (Summit 1987) 39 Ohio App.3d 9, 528 N.E.2d 1270.

The doctrine of res judicata can be invoked to give conclusive effect to a determination of parentage contained in a dissolution decree or a legitimation order, thereby barring a subsequent paternity action brought pursuant to RC Ch 3111. In re Gilbraith (Ohio 1987) 32 Ohio St.3d 127, 512 N.E.2d 956. Child Support ☞ 225; Children Out-of–wedlock ☞ 13; Children Out–of–wedlock ☞ 21(2)

Under Uniform Parentage Act, child, child's mother, alleged father of child, or their personal representatives may bring action in juvenile court to effect determination of paternity and to provide for custody and support. Manley v. Howard (Marion 1985) 25 Ohio App.3d 1, 495 N.E.2d 436, 25 O.B.R. 30. Children Out–of–wedlock ☞ 34

The decisions of State ex rel Cody v Toner, 8 OS(3d) 22, 8 OBR 255, 456 NE(2d) 813 (1983), cert denied 466 US 938, 104 SCt 1912, 80 LEd(2d) 461 (1984), and Anderson v Jacobs, 68 OS(2d) 67, 428 NE(2d) 419 (1981), that the state must provide appointed counsel and blood grouping tests to indigent defendants who face the state as an adversary in paternity proceedings are to be applied retroactively and may therefore be the basis for vacation of judgment pursuant to Civ R 60(B). Keeney v. Lawson (Hamilton 1984) 19 Ohio App.3d 318, 484 N.E.2d 745, 19 O.B.R. 491.

RC Ch 3111, as re-enacted by 1982 H 245, eff. 6–29–82, has no application to paternity actions in which judgment was entered prior to that date. Johnson v. Adams (Ohio 1985) 18 Ohio St.3d 48, 479 N.E.2d 866, 18 O.B.R. 83. Children Out–of–wedlock ☞ 31

In a paternity proceeding brought in juvenile court pursuant to RC Ch 3111, a motion for summary judgment will not lie. De Salvo v. Sukalski (Geauga 1983) 8 Ohio App.3d 337, 457 N.E.2d 349, 8 O.B.R. 448. Judgment ☞ 180

Determination of paternity in a bastardy proceeding is not a prerequisite to the prosecution of a parent under RC 2903.08 for nonsupport of an illegitimate child. State v. Medley (Miami 1960) 111 Ohio App. 352, 172 N.E.2d 143, 14 O.O.2d 328. Child Support ☞ 653; Children Out–of–wedlock ☞ 21(2)

The action provided by the statutes of Ohio whereby the mother may institute proceedings against the father of an illegitimate child is found in this section, which action may be maintained only by an unmarried woman. Sullivan v. Wilkoff (Mahoning 1939) 63 Ohio App. 269, 26 N.E.2d 460, 17 O.O. 32. Children Out–of–wedlock ☞ 30; Children Out–of–wedlock ☞ 34

A creditor has no civil cause of action against a reputed father for necessaries furnished a bastard child. Hoffer v. White (Warren 1935) 53 Ohio App. 187, 4 N.E.2d 595, 20 Ohio Law Abs. 288, 5 O.O. 73.

Bastardy action does not abate because complainant gave birth to still-born child, as complaint was filed long before dead fetus was born, and complainant is entitled to trial to determine whether she is entitled to judgment "for support, maintenance and necessary expenses caused by pregnan-

cy," as provided for under this section. Seldenright v. Jenkins (Ohio Prob. 1936) 3 Ohio Supp. 36, 22 Ohio Law Abs. 576, 7 O.O. 127.

Bastardy proceedings are governed wholly by statute, and under the provisions of the general code, a woman, to make a valid complaint in bastardy, must have been unmarried at the time of the birth of the alleged bastard child. State ex rel. Hoerres v. Wilkoff (Ohio 1952) 157 Ohio St. 286, 105 N.E.2d 39, 47 O.O. 174.

Right of action exists under the statute irrespective of whether the child is stillborn or born alive. State ex rel. Discus v. Van Dorn (Crawford 1937) 56 Ohio App. 82, 10 N.E.2d 14, 24 Ohio Law Abs. 104, 8 O.O. 393.

The presumption that a child conceived in wedlock is legitimate cannot be rebutted except by evidence that the spouses had no sexual relations during the time in which the child was conceived. Joseph v Alexander, No. CA–6781 (5th Dist Ct App, Stark, 5–5–86).

The trial court properly refused to apply a ten-year statute of limitations to a legitimization proceeding since such is a special proceeding rather than a civil action. Moore v Bailey, No. 13–82–16 (3d Dist Ct App, Seneca, 8–5–83).

A child should be appointed a guardian ad litem and made a party to a legitimization proceeding, when it is clear that the mother, as natural guardian, has an adverse interest in the proceeding. Blackburn v Ludden, 1 OBR 340 (App, Trumbull 1982).

In parentage proceedings where the complainant-mothers and their children are recipients of public assistance, the state public defender must, in accordance with RC 120.18, 120.28, and 120.33, partially reimburse the counties for the cost of representing indigent paternity defendants who face the state as an adversary. OAG 85–090.

6. Construction with other laws

The portion of RC 2105.18 unqualifiedly requiring the mother's consent to an application for legitimization is unconstitutional in that it violates the equal protection clause; however, the remaining portions of the statute are constitutional and severable. Moore v Bailey, No. 13–82–16 (3d Dist Ct App, Seneca, 8–5–83).

A county department of human services has no standing to (1) initiate a law suit to determine parentage after a mother assigned her right to receive child support to the agency to receive ADC, or (2) declare RC 3111.14 unconstitutional for not protecting the rights of illegitimate children because there is no general public interest in pecuniary reimbursement. State ex rel. Athens Cty. Dept. of Human Serv. v. Wolf (Athens 1991) 77 Ohio App.3d 619, 603 N.E.2d 252.

7. Nature of action

A husband's paternity is rebuttable by a genetic test and a putative father may bring a parentage action where the mother was, and continues to be, married to another man at the time the child was conceived. Crawford County Child Support Enforcement Agency v. Sprague (Ohio App. 3 Dist., Crawford, 12-05-1997) No. 3-97-13, 1997 WL 746770, Unreported.

Paternity is a special proceeding under RC 2505.02, but a judgment related to paternity, in itself, does not affect a substantial right until the trial court issues a support order based upon the judgment of defendant's paternity, so that a defendant's motion to vacate the judgment, filed thirty-three days after the final order, entitles the defendant to a hearing on the merits of his motion. Adams v. Jett (Ohio App. 2 Dist., Montgomery, 02-08-1995) No. 14636, 1995 WL 51060, Unreported.

Various parentage statutes encourage and accommodate establishment of parent-child relationships regardless of whether genetic relationship is conclusively established, and legislature has not specified that establishment of genetic relationship is prerequisite to establishment of parent-child relationship. Leguillon v. Leguillon (Ohio App. 12 Dist., 01-12-1998) 124 Ohio App.3d 757, 707 N.E.2d 571. Children Out–of–wedlock ☞ 1

RC 3111.02 to 3111.04, 3111.09, and 3111.10 are in pari materia and must be construed together. Hulett v. Hulett (Ohio 1989) 45 Ohio St.3d 288, 544 N.E.2d 257.

Proceedings under RC Ch 3111 and adoption are not the exclusive legal mechanisms by which paternity may be determined to provide a basis for child support and custody orders; an acknowledgment of paternity under RC 2105.18 provides a sufficient legal basis for such orders. In re Custody of Davis (Guernsey 1987) 41 Ohio App.3d 81, 534 N.E.2d 945.

RC 3111.04(A) may not be used to determine the nonexistence of a parent-child relationship retroactively, although it may be applied retroactively to establish the existence of such relationship. Brooks v. Fair (Van Wert 1988) 40 Ohio App.3d 202, 532 N.E.2d 208.

Where a husband and wife agree to conceive a child by means of artificial insemination, and a child so conceived is born to the parties, it is against public policy for a court to enter a judgment establishing the husband's non-paternity in connection with a divorce of the parties and the remarriage of the mother. Brooks v. Fair (Van Wert 1988) 40 Ohio App.3d 202, 532 N.E.2d 208.

A complainant/mother in an appeal from civil paternity proceedings is not entitled to a court-appointed counsel or a transcript provided at public expense because there is no possibility of the mother or child involved being deprived of their physical liberty should the appeal fail. State ex rel. Armstrong v. Hall (Marion 1986) 33 Ohio App.3d 1, 514 N.E.2d 424.

8. Acknowledgment

Mother's failure to rescind acknowledgement of paternity executed by claimed father did not affect her ability to bring a paternity action, as claimed father failed to prove that acknowledgement had been filed with office of child support, which was required by statute for acknowledgement to be final and enforceable. Jennifer C. v. Tony M.D. (Ohio App. 12 Dist., Clermont, 09-26-2005) No. CA2005-01-005, 2005-Ohio-5050, 2005 WL 2335332, Unreported. Children Out–of–wedlock ☞ 34

While GC 8591 (RC 2105.18) requires both proof of parentage and acknowledgment of children of parent after his marriage, yet if evidence of acknowledgment before marriage is abundant, and proof of parentage clear, slight evidence of acknowledgment on part of parent after marriage, will be sufficient to establish legitimacy of child. (See also Siegel v Lowe, 11 Abs 140 (1931).) Stradling v. Printz (Champaign 1931) 10 Ohio Law Abs. 134.

Father assumed duty of supporting son, and one-year period of nonsupport obviating need to obtain parental consent to adoption began to run, when father acknowledged paternity and trial court granted legitimacy. In re Adoption of Lassiter (Ohio App. 2 Dist., 02-24-1995) 101 Ohio App.3d 367, 655 N.E.2d 781, dismissed, appeal not allowed 73 Ohio St.3d 1410, 651 N.E.2d 1308. Adoption ☞ 7.4(6)

An acknowledgment of paternity under RC 2105.18 functions as an admission and a probate court's order of legitimacy based on such acknowledgment pursuant to RC 2105.18 is a judicial determination of parentage or paternity which establishes a full parent-child relationship for all legal purposes. In re Custody of Davis (Guernsey 1987) 41 Ohio App.3d 81, 534 N.E.2d 945.

Proceedings under RC Ch 3111 and adoption are not the exclusive legal mechanisms by which paternity may be determined to provide a basis for child support and custody orders; an acknowledgment of paternity under RC 2105.18 provides a sufficient legal basis for such orders. In re Custody of Davis (Guernsey 1987) 41 Ohio App.3d 81, 534 N.E.2d 945.

The validity of an RC 2105.18 acknowledgment of paternity may not be attacked in defending an action for custody and support. In re Custody of Davis (Guernsey 1987) 41 Ohio App.3d 81, 534 N.E.2d 945. Children Out–of–wedlock ☞ 12

Duly notarized declaration of paternity signed by one putative father did not have force of final judgment and did not bar, on res judicata grounds, subsequent legitimation action against second putative father; declaration of paternity had never been filed with probate court. Collett v. Cogar (Ohio 1988) 35 Ohio St.3d 114, 518 N.E.2d 1202. Children Out–of–wedlock ☞ 13

A judgment pursuant to former RC 3111.17 which sets visitation rights and support duties of a man who has signed a birth certificate as informant, even though both he and the mother admit he is not the natural father, may be properly vacated to relieve the child and mother from the determination of paternity implicit in the judgment. In re Smith (Miami 1984) 16 Ohio App.3d 75, 474 N.E.2d 632, 16 O.B.R. 79.

Court of appeals erred when it summarily granted custody of an illegitimate child to the natural mother in a dispute with the natural father in a habeas corpus proceeding. Pruitt v. Jones (Ohio 1980) 62 Ohio St.2d 237, 405 N.E.2d 276, 16 O.O.3d 276.

RC 2105.18 affords every illegitimate child the opportunity to become legitimated by filing an application for legitimation and by proving by clear and convincing evidence the identity of the child's natural father. If the probate court is satisfied that the person named in the application for legitimation is the child's natural father and that establishment of this relationship is for the best interest of the child, the court shall enter that finding of fact upon its journal and thereafter the child is the child of the person named in the application as though born to him in lawful wedlock. In re Minor of Martin (Cuyahoga 1977) 51 Ohio App.2d 21, 365 N.E.2d 892, 5 O.O.3d 141.

A determination of a "reputed father" under RC 3111.17 does not convert that finding into a finding of a "natural father" under RC 2105.18, nor does such a determination give the mother authority either as agent for the father or by operation of law to file an application for legitimation under RC 2105.18 and acknowledge that the alleged father is the natural father of the child. In re Minor of Martin (Cuyahoga 1977) 51 Ohio App.2d 21, 365 N.E.2d 892, 5 O.O.3d 141.

An illegitimate child may be legitimated if the natural father of the child files an application in the appropriate probate court acknowledging that the child is his and the mother of the child consents to the legitimation. If the probate court is satisfied that the applicant is the natural father and that establishment of this relationship is for the best interest of the child, the probate court shall enter the finding of fact upon its journal and thereafter the child is the child of the applicant as though born to him in lawful wedlock. In re Minor of Martin (Cuyahoga 1977) 51 Ohio App.2d 21, 365 N.E.2d 892, 5 O.O.3d 141.

An illegitimate child cannot inherit from or through his natural father unless the father takes some steps during his lifetime to permit such inheritance, such as acknowledgment pursuant to RC 2105.18, designating the illegitimate as an heir pursuant to RC 2105.15, adopting the illegitimate, or providing for the illegitimate in his will. Moore v. Dague (Franklin 1975) 46 Ohio App.2d 75, 345 N.E.2d 449, 75 O.O.2d 68. Children Out–of–wedlock ☞ 86; Children Out–of–wedlock ☞ 90

The rule that an acknowledgment by a husband after marriage recognizing a child born out of wedlock as his is sufficient to establish parentage does not apply to establish the legitimacy of such child where there is probative evidence to the contrary. Comer v. Comer (Logan 1962) 119 Ohio App. 529, 200 N.E.2d 656, 28 O.O.2d 142, affirmed 175 Ohio St. 313, 194 N.E.2d 572, 25 O.O.2d 182.

There is a presumption that the best interests of a bastard child require it to be in its mother's custody, and the burden is upon the person disputing such mother's right to custody to prove that such child should not be in its mother's custody. In re Gary (Cuyahoga 1960) 112 Ohio App. 331, 167 N.E.2d 509, 83 Ohio Law Abs. 486, 14 O.O.2d 431.

Illegitimate, posthumous child unacknowledged by putative father held not dependent "child" and not entitled to compensation for putative father's death. Staker v. Industrial Commission of Ohio (Ohio 1933) 127 Ohio St. 13, 186 N.E. 616, 38 Ohio Law Rep. 480. Children Out–of–wedlock ☞ 80; Workers' Compensation ☞ 420.26

To prove legitimacy of a child born out of wedlock, there must be proved not only the acknowledgment by the husband after marriage, but also that the husband is in fact the father; an acknowledgment clearly showing recognition of such child as his is sufficient. Eichorn v. Zedaker (Ohio 1922) 109 Ohio St. 609, 144 N.E. 258, 19 Ohio Law Rep. 588, 19 Ohio Law Rep. 633.

On the evidence children of deceased wage earner were entitled to social security benefits on the ground that said decedent had acknowledged them to be his children. Folsom v. Furber (C.A.6 (Ohio) 1958) 256 F.2d 120, 83 Ohio Law Abs. 42, 6 O.O.2d 509.

Designation by a soldier of his wife by a void marriage as beneficiary of his war-risk insurance together with recognition by him of a child of such void marriage is not sufficient to show that his designation of the mother was intended to be in trust for the child. Elliott v. U.S. (N.D.Ohio 1920) 271 F. 1001. Armed Services ☞ 77(7); Insurance ☞ 3465

A child of a marriage void because both parents have other spouses living and undivorced is entitled to inherit from its father where it had been recognized by the father before his death. Elliott v. U.S. (N.D.Ohio 1920) 271 F. 1001.

Decedent's supplying minors with money, allowing them to visit on weekends, and allowing them to call him dad was not formal acknowledgment of child in probate court and could not be basis for children born out of wedlock to establish standing under Ohio Wrongful Death Statute. Martin v. Daily Express, Inc. (N.D.Ohio, 02-28-1995) 878 F.Supp. 91. Death ☞ 31(8)

Naming children born out of wedlock as devisees, without suggesting that children were testator's, was not formal acknowledgment of paternity needed for children to have standing to bring suit for death of testator under Ohio Wrongful Death Statute. Martin v. Daily Express, Inc. (N.D.Ohio, 02-28-1995) 878 F.Supp. 91. Death ☞ 31(8)

Probate court order declaring heirship did not establish standing of minor children born out of wedlock to bring suit under Ohio Wrongful Death Statute for death of alleged father; decedent did not acknowledge paternity, mother did not consent to alleged acknowledgment, and no action to establish paternity was taken during decedent's life. Martin v. Daily Express, Inc. (N.D.Ohio, 02-28-1995) 878 F.Supp. 91. Death ☞ 31(8)

Probate court had jurisdiction to consider whether acknowledgment of paternity improperly purported to change child's name. In re Mantia–Allen (Montgomery 1996) 108 Ohio App.3d 302, 670 N.E.2d 570.

The two methods for a father to secure companionship rights with an illegitimate child are (1) to acknowledge his paternity or (2) have his paternity determined in an action pursuant to RC Ch 3111; where it is undisputed that a putative father who seeks visitation rights, did not acknowledge his paternity with the probate court following the child's birth and HLA tests conclusively exclude him as the father, there is no statutory basis permitting the juvenile court to order visitation rights. Sherburn v Reichert, No 15–94–3, 1994 WL 581539 (3d Dist Ct App, Van Wert, 10–13–94).

In a wrongful death action against a truck driver and driver's employer involving a collision between the truck driver and a motorist, dismissal is proper on the basis that the plaintiff could not maintain a wrongful death suit on behalf of an alleged minor child of the motorist where the plaintiff and the motorist were not married, the motorist did not in probate court formally acknowledge the child as his with consent of the mother, and the motorist did not designate the child as his heir-at-law, adopt the child, or make provision for the child in his will, and, although a parentage action was brought by the plaintiff and her son, the action was brought after the death of the motorist; thus, as a matter of law, the child cannot inherit from the decedent's estate, including any recovery from the wrongful death action. Hunter–Martin v. Winchester Transp., Inc. (Shelby 1991) 71 Ohio App.3d 273, 593 N.E.2d 383, motion overruled 62 Ohio St.3d 1408, 577 N.E.2d 361.

9. Children of marriage

Finding in original divorce decree that child born during parties' marriage was former husband's child was res judicata as to father's motion to have himself declared as not the child's biological father because DNA (deoxyribonucleic acid) test results indicated that father and child were not genetically linked. Van Dusen v. Van Dusen (Ohio App. 10 Dist., 01-28-2003) 151 Ohio App.3d 494, 784 N.E.2d 750, 2003-Ohio-350. Divorce ☞ 172

Where plaintiff and defendant in divorce action both alleged that two children were born as issue of the marriage, and uncontradicted facts showed that first child was born three months prior to the marriage, first born child was a legitimate child of the parties, and court should have so found. De Garmo v. De Garmo (Champaign 1949) 92 N.E.2d 414, 56 Ohio Law Abs. 357. Children Out–of–wedlock ☞ 11

Under RC 2105.18 if there would have been a valid common law marriage between the parents of a child, but for the existing marriage of one of the parents, although this fact was known to both parents when they purported to effect the common law marriage, such is a marriage "null in law" and the child is legitimate. Wolf v. Gardner (C.A.6 (Ohio)

1967) 15 Ohio Misc. 161, 386 F.2d 295, 43 O.O.2d 179.

A woman whose child was conceived and born during lawful marriage may, after death of her husband and while unmarried, institute and maintain a bastardy proceeding under the statute, charging another than her former husband with being the father of the child. (See also State ex rel Hoerres v Wilkoff, 157 OS 286, 105 NE(2d) 39 (1952); overruled by Franklin v Julian, 30 OS(2d) 228, 283 NE(2d) 813 (1972).) State ex rel. Sprungle v. Bard (Cuyahoga 1950) 98 N.E.2d 63, 59 Ohio Law Abs. 129.

10. Admission of paternity

Putative father's claim that his admission of paternity in prior proceeding was invalid was not cognizable on appeal from court order requiring putative father to pay child support arrears and maternity expenses, where putative father did not appeal from original paternity proceedings. CSEA ex rel. E.T. v. H.S. (Ohio App. 8 Dist., Cuyahoga, 05-06-2004) No. 82820, 2004-Ohio-2343, 2004 WL 1047831, Unreported, as amended nunc pro tunc. Children Out–of–wedlock ☞ 73

Prior decision of the Court of Appeals, holding that res judicata barred former husband's action seeking a determination of paternity, amounted to an "admission on file" for purposes of summary judgment in a subsequent paternity action, where trial court deemed prior appellate decision admitted as true and genuine by husband, and husband did not challenge that ruling. Donnelly v. Kashnier (Ohio App. 9 Dist., Medina, 02-12-2003) No. 02CA0051-M, 2003-Ohio-639, 2003 WL 294413, Unreported. Children Out–of–wedlock ☞ 64

A forty-two year old man who voluntarily files a petition to be declared the father, even though he knows that he may be infertile, is not entitled to Civ R 60(B) relief from the agreed order declaring him to be the father where the sole ground for relief is the infertility which he knew about since he was nineteen years old. Snyder v. Fulkrod (Ohio App. 9 Dist., Summit, 12-13-1995) No. 17225, 1995 WL 734021, Unreported, appeal not allowed 75 Ohio St.3d 1511, 665 N.E.2d 681.

Putative father's voluntary and unequivocal actions taken at the births of his two children constituted binding acknowledgments of paternity, estopping him from subsequently attempting to establish the contrary in context of mother's action for child support; putative father signed birth certificates of both children along with mother, lived with mother during entire period during which both children were conceived and born, and held children out as his own until mother left him and sought child support. Crago v. Kinzie (Ohio Com.Pl., 06-01-2000) 106 Ohio Misc.2d 51, 733 N.E.2d 1219. Children Out–of–wedlock ☞ 12

The presumption of paternity of a man signing a birth certificate as informant pursuant to RC 3705.14 may be overcome by the admissions of the man and the mother that he is not the natural father. In re Smith (Miami 1984) 16 Ohio App.3d 75, 474 N.E.2d 632, 16 O.B.R. 79.

There is a distinction between a "putative" father and a father who has been adjudicated as such by his own admission, in that a father adjudicated as such by his own admission has legal standing to seek custody of his illegitimate child against the world, including the mother. In re Wright (Ohio Com.Pl. 1977) 52 Ohio Misc. 4, 367 N.E.2d 931, 6 O.O.3d 31.

11. Child support enforcement agencies

Prospective adoptive parents were not necessary parties to putative father's paternity action; statute described the necessary parties to a paternity action as the birth mother, all presumed fathers, and the child. B.W. v. D.B.-B. (Ohio App. 6 Dist., 06-10-2011) 193 Ohio App.3d 637, 953 N.E.2d 369, 2011-Ohio-2813. Children Out–of–wedlock ⟋ 34

In paternity action filed by Child Support Enforcement Agency (CSEA) on behalf of mother and children, father could not be required to reimburse CSEA for governmental financial assistance given to mother and her children, where CSEA was never made party to action and there was no evidence in record to support amount awarded to CSEA. Dorsett v. Wheeler (Ohio App. 3 Dist., 03-16-1995) 101 Ohio App.3d 716, 656 N.E.2d 698. Children Out–of–wedlock ⟋ 67

In paternity action filed by Child Support Enforcement Agency (CSEA), trial court, if not CSEA's attorney, had affirmative duty to inquire into status of mother's legal representation, though CSEA's complaint named mother and children as plaintiffs, as CSEA's attorney did not represent mother's interests during hearing and trial court expressly found that mother appeared without counsel. Dorsett v. Wheeler (Ohio App. 3 Dist., 03-16-1995) 101 Ohio App.3d 716, 656 N.E.2d 698. Children Out–of–wedlock ⟋ 57

In paternity action filed by Child Support Enforcement Agency (CSEA), record supported finding of paternity, where father admitted paternity at hearing and blood tests of parties concluded probability of paternity at approximately 99 percent. Dorsett v. Wheeler (Ohio App. 3 Dist., 03-16-1995) 101 Ohio App.3d 716, 656 N.E.2d 698. Children Out–of–wedlock ⟋ 53

County Support Enforcement Agency has no independent authority to initiate action to establish putative father's parentage without mother's initial request for administrative determination. State ex rel. Gillion v. Reese (Ohio App. 8 Dist., 09-06-1994) 97 Ohio App.3d 315, 646 N.E.2d 852, appeal not allowed 71 Ohio St.3d 1466, 644 N.E.2d 1388. Children Out–of–wedlock ⟋ 34

12. Agreement between parties

A justice of the peace has no authority to discharge accused in a bastardy proceeding on ground that it appears from an examination of the complainant that prior to the filing of her complaint she and accused had entered into a private agreement by which accused had paid her an amount equal to

the amount the common pleas court would charge the reputed father for maintenance of child. Walker v. Chandler (Ohio App. 7 Dist. 1921) 15 Ohio App. 292. Children Out–of–wedlock ⟋ 33

Alleged agreement between mother and putative father concerning child support did not prevent mother from pursuing paternity action. Spain v. Hubbard (Ohio App. 7 Dist., Belmont, 05-12-2003) No. 02BA15, 2003-Ohio-2555, 2003 WL 21134700, Unreported. Children Out–of–wedlock ⟋ 33

After decree of divorce or dissolution has been entered which includes adjudication or agreement as to parentage and parental rights and obligations, postdecree paternity action on child's behalf is subject to overriding consideration of child's best interest. Leguillon v. Leguillon (Ohio App. 12 Dist., 01-12-1998) 124 Ohio App.3d 757, 707 N.E.2d 571. Child Support ⟋ 224; Children Out–of–wedlock ⟋ 21(2); Children Out–of–wedlock ⟋ 33

Determination of parentage in agreed dissolution decree or legitimation order will bar subsequent paternity action. Cornell v. Brumfield (Ohio App. 4 Dist., 10-10-1996) 115 Ohio App.3d 259, 685 N.E.2d 270.

Agreed settlement entry of previous parentage action between parents of minor child and judgment of support entered as result of action brought by child to establish parent-child relationship were not mutually exclusive and were capable of simultaneous enforcement, as parentage claims of child and his mother were separate and distinct. Cornell v. Brumfield (Ohio App. 4 Dist., 10-10-1996) 115 Ohio App.3d 259, 685 N.E.2d 270.

Mother's compromise agreement with alleged father did not bar later paternity action brought on behalf of child to recover prospective support and by Department of Human Services to recover birthing expenses, where child was not party to compromise agreement. Payne v. Cartee (Ohio App. 4 Dist., 06-10-1996) 111 Ohio App.3d 580, 676 N.E.2d 946, appeal not allowed 77 Ohio St.3d 1482, 673 N.E.2d 143. Children Out–of–wedlock ⟋ 33

After decree of divorce or dissolution has been entered which includes adjudication or agreement as to parentage and parental rights and obligations, postdecree paternity action cannot be brought on child's behalf absent express determination by court that such action is in best interest of child. Broxterman v. Broxterman (Ohio App. 1 Dist., 03-15-1995) 101 Ohio App.3d 661, 656 N.E.2d 394. Child Custody ⟋ 532; Child Support ⟋ 224; Children Out–of–wedlock ⟋ 21(2); Children Out–of–wedlock ⟋ 33

In an application for legitimation, evidence of a prior agreement between the natural mother and the applicant as to child support and visitation rights is sufficient to constitute consent by the natural mother to the legitimation. In re Legitimation of Conn (Franklin 1982) 7 Ohio App.3d 241, 455 N.E.2d 16, 7 O.B.R. 303.

Former RC 2105.18 is silent concerning the manner in which consent by the natural mother to the legitimazation of her child is to be received; therefore, an agreement by the mother to the father's legitimazation of the child, which was entered in the domestic relations court in connection with an order of support is sufficient to constitute consent pursuant to RC 2105.18. In re Legitimation of Conn (Franklin 1982) 7 Ohio App.3d 241, 455 N.E.2d 16, 7 O.B.R. 303.

The natural father of a child has no legal right to disaffirm or revoke a written agreement of permanent surrender of custody of a child executed by the natural and unmarried mother prior to her marriage to the father. Ex parte Combs (Ohio Com.Pl. 1958) 150 N.E.2d 505, 77 Ohio Law Abs. 458.

13. Surrogates

Once trial court determined that biological mother was natural mother of twins born to surrogate mother under surrogacy contract, trial court was then required to determine whether biological mother waived rights to assume legal status as natural mother before making determination of parent-child relationship between biological mother and triplets. Rice v. Flynn (Ohio App. 9 Dist., Summit, 09-07-2005) No. 22416, 2005-Ohio-4667, 2005 WL 2140576, Unreported. Children Out–of–wedlock ∞ 1

Surrogate mother's claim on appeal from order declaring that parent-child relationship existed between biological father and triplets and biological mother and triplets, that trial court lacked jurisdiction to make parenting decisions, was not ripe for review, where order merely established parentage with respect to triplets and did not establish parenting or allocate parental rights and responsibilities for triplets. Rice v. Flynn (Ohio App. 9 Dist., Summit, 09-07-2005) No. 22416, 2005 Ohio 4667, 2005 WL 2140576, Unreported. Children Out–of–wedlock ∞ 1

The trial court lacked subject matter jurisdiction to determine the parentage of unborn child, who was the subject of a surrogacy agreement, or issue an order directing the hospital where surrogate mother was expected to deliver child to designate child as the biological child of sperm and egg donors. Nemcek v. Paskey (Ohio Com.Pl., 04-06-2006) 137 Ohio Misc.2d 1, 849 N.E.2d 108, 2006-Ohio-2059. Parent And Child ∞ 20

14. Laches

On public-policy grounds, laches is not available as defense to paternity claim, though father was not informed he was child's father until child was more than 15 years old; parent-child relationship could be established through court-ordered visitation, and father would have ability to become involved in child's life. Still v. Hayman (Ohio App. 7 Dist., 07-30-2003) 153 Ohio App.3d 487, 794 N.E.2d 751, 2003-Ohio-4113. Children Out–of–wedlock ∞ 38

Assuming that on public policy grounds laches was available as defense to paternity claim, delay in seeking to establish paternity was unreasonable, as element favoring application of laches defense; mother did not reveal father's true identity to father and to county child support enforcement agen-

cy (CSEA) until child was more than 15 years old, and mother's claim that she did not reveal father's name earlier because he had raped her was not credible. Still v. Hayman (Ohio App. 7 Dist., 07-30-2003) 153 Ohio App.3d 487, 794 N.E.2d 751, 2003-Ohio-4113. Children Out-of-wedlock ∞ 38

Mother's "dilatory" conduct did not amount to unexplained or unreasonable delay and, thus, laches did not bar her paternity action against putative father; mother testified that she notified putative father in person when she was pregnant, mother instituted parentage action eight months after giving birth, action was voluntarily dismissed five and one-half years later for failure to serve summons on putative father within one year of filing action and mother refiled action only two months later. Seegert v. Zietlow (Ohio App. 8 Dist., 08-15-1994) 95 Ohio App.3d 451, 642 N.E.2d 697. Children Out–of–wedlock ∞ 38

Putative father was not "materially prejudiced" by mother's alleged dilatory conduct in bringing paternity proceedings and, thus, laches did not bar that action; putative father's generic assertion of hardship arising from allegedly excessive award was insufficient to rise to level of material prejudice, and, despite putative father's claim that he had lost all rights of visitation, custody and participation in direction of child's growth and development during her formative years, child was nine years old and had many formative years remaining. Seegert v. Zietlow (Ohio App. 8 Dist., 08-15-1994) 95 Ohio App.3d 451, 642 N.E.2d 697. Children Out–of–wedlock ∞ 38

15. Child's action

Adult child who had learned of identity of her birth father as an adult was not entitled to award of retroactive support, where at time of child's birth, child's mother and her husband, who could not conceive a child, mutually agreed with birth father, whose affair with mother had resulted in child's conception, that child would be raised by mother and her husband as if child were their natural child, husband remained committed to child throughout her childhood, and child was raised in a middle-class lifestyle with all of her basic needs met. Hugershoff v. Loecy (Ohio Com.Pl., 09-28-1999) 103 Ohio Misc.2d 58, 725 N.E.2d 378. Children Out–of–wedlock ∞ 21(2)

Right of a child to bring an action to establish paternity is separate and distinct from its mother's right to bring such an action, and a mother's agreement not to establish paternity cannot bind the child. Snider v. Lillie (Ohio App. 1 Dist., 10-17-1997) 131 Ohio App.3d 444, 722 N.E.2d 1036, dismissed, appeal not allowed 81 Ohio St.3d 1452, 690 N.E.2d 546. Children Out–of–wedlock ∞ 34

Former wife's child, who was born after former wife and former husband divorced, was not bound by domestic relations court's finding of illegitimacy in divorce decree, and he could bring separate paternity action against former husband. Fitzpatrick v. Fitzpatrick (Ohio App. 12 Dist., 03-02-1998) 126 Ohio App.3d 476, 710 N.E.2d 778, dismissed, appeal not allowed 82 Ohio St.3d 1441, 695 N.E.2d 264. Child Custody ☞ 533; Children Out–of–wedlock ☞ 33

The right of a child to bring an action to establish paternity is separate and distinct from a mother's right to bring such an action. Fitzpatrick v. Fitzpatrick (Ohio App. 12 Dist., 03-02-1998) 126 Ohio App.3d 476, 710 N.E.2d 778, dismissed, appeal not allowed 82 Ohio St.3d 1441, 695 N.E.2d 264. Children Out–of–wedlock ☞ 34

Where a mother enters into agreement not to establish paternity with an alleged father, the child is not bound by the agreement and may subsequently bring a paternity action against the alleged father. Fitzpatrick v. Fitzpatrick (Ohio App. 12 Dist., 03-02-1998) 126 Ohio App.3d 476, 710 N.E.2d 778, dismissed, appeal not allowed 82 Ohio St.3d 1441, 695 N.E.2d 264. Children Out–of–wedlock ☞ 33

Res judicata did not bar former wife's child, who was found in divorce decree to be illegitimate, from bringing parentage action in juvenile court; child was not party to divorce action, and child was not in privity with former wife. Fitzpatrick v. Fitzpatrick (Ohio App. 12 Dist., 03-02-1998) 126 Ohio App.3d 476, 710 N.E.2d 778, dismissed, appeal not allowed 82 Ohio St.3d 1441, 695 N.E.2d 264. Children Out–of–wedlock ☞ 33

Child's claim in parentage action is separate and distinct from that of the mother. State ex rel. Donovan v. Zajac (Ohio App. 11 Dist., 01-02-1998) 125 Ohio App.3d 245, 708 N.E.2d 254, dismissed, appeal not allowed 81 Ohio St.3d 1521, 692 N.E.2d 1023. Children Out–of–wedlock ☞ 30

Child is not barred by paternity adjudication from bringing action to determine existence or nonexistence of father-child relationship; although adjudication may bar father from challenging relationship under doctrine of res judicata, child may still challenge relationship since he or she was arguably not in privity with parties to original action. Leguillon v. Leguillon (Ohio App. 12 Dist., 01-12-1998) 124 Ohio App.3d 757, 707 N.E.2d 571. Children Out–of–wedlock ☞ 33; Children Out–of–wedlock ☞ 68

Court determining whether to permit child to bring his or her own action to seek or challenge adjudication of paternity should consider appointment of guardian ad litem to aid in determining child's best interests. Leguillon v. Leguillon (Ohio App. 12 Dist., 01-12-1998) 124 Ohio App.3d 757, 707 N.E.2d 571. Infants ☞ 78(1)

Juvenile court did not abuse its discretion by permitting mother to proceed as child's next friend in his paternity action, where such action was prosecuted solely on son's behalf, there was no showing that she might fail to vigorously pursue child's action, and guardian ad litem was appointed three days after determination that alleged father was, in fact, child's father. Payne v. Cartee (Ohio App. 4 Dist., 06-10-1996) 111 Ohio App.3d 580, 676 N.E.2d 946, appeal not allowed 77 Ohio St.3d 1482, 673 N.E.2d 143. Infants ☞ 81

Mother's claim is distinct and separate from that of child for purposes of determining whether judgment in mother's paternity action presents res judicata bar to later action by child. Payne v. Cartee (Ohio App. 4 Dist., 06-10-1996) 111 Ohio App.3d 580, 676 N.E.2d 946, appeal not allowed 77 Ohio St.3d 1482, 673 N.E.2d 143. Children Out–of–wedlock ☞ 33; Children Out–of–wedlock ☞ 68

Child was not in privity with mother with regard to compromise agreement reached in mother's paternity action, and, therefore, doctrine of equitable estoppel did not apply to a child's paternity action, regardless of whether alleged father relied on any of mother's representations with regard to effect of compromise. Payne v. Cartee (Ohio App. 4 Dist., 06-10-1996) 111 Ohio App.3d 580, 676 N.E.2d 946, appeal not allowed 77 Ohio St.3d 1482, 673 N.E.2d 143. Children Out–of–wedlock ☞ 33

Doctrine of laches did not apply to child's paternity action, even though alleged father had dramatically changed his obligations in life by getting married and having a new family, absent showing that alleged father incurred these new family obligations in reliance on terms of compromise agreement with mother. Payne v. Cartee (Ohio App. 4 Dist., 06-10-1996) 111 Ohio App.3d 580, 676 N.E.2d 946, appeal not allowed 77 Ohio St.3d 1482, 673 N.E.2d 143. Children Out–of–wedlock ☞ 38

Child was not party to his mother's prior divorce action, so as to bar subsequent paternity action on res judicata grounds. State ex rel. Smith v. Smith (Ohio App. 8 Dist., 04-08-1996) 110 Ohio App.3d 336, 674 N.E.2d 398, appeal not allowed 76 Ohio St.3d 1496, 670 N.E.2d 243. Child Custody ☞ 532; Children Out–of–wedlock ☞ 33

Assuming that probate court's finding that woman was intestate's biological child was supported by competent, credible evidence, woman failed to establish that she was "legitimized" in one of recognized manners and thus had no right to intestate's estate; only method by which woman could affirmatively seek relief would have been under Parentage Act which required that parentage action be brought in juvenile court which woman had failed to do. In re Estate of Hicks (Ohio App. 6 Dist., 09-30-1993) 90 Ohio App.3d 483, 629 N.E.2d 1086. Children Out–of–wedlock ☞ 86

Implied agreement between mother and father, if any, did not bar award of child support in child's action to establish paternity. Park v. Ambrose (Ross 1993) 85 Ohio App.3d 179, 619 N.E.2d 469, dismissed, jurisdictional motion overruled 67 Ohio St.3d 1409, 615 N.E.2d 1043. Children Out–of–wedlock ☞ 33

Pursuant to RC 3111.04, a child has a right to bring a paternity action in his own name; thus, a child's claim is separate and distinct from that of his mother. Rees v. Heimberger (Cuyahoga 1989) 60 Ohio App.3d 45, 573 N.E.2d 189, dismissed 47 Ohio St.3d 702, 547 N.E.2d 986, rehearing denied 48 Ohio St.3d 707, 550 N.E.2d 483, certiorari denied 110 S.Ct. 1827, 494 U.S. 1088, 108 L.Ed.2d 956. Children Out–of–wedlock ☞ 34

A child born out of wedlock may seek to inherit from his natural father by establishing paternity through RC 3111.04 or by the procedures established under RC Ch 2105. Garrison v. Smith (Lucas 1988) 55 Ohio App.3d 14, 561 N.E.2d 1041. Children Out–of–wedlock ⬤ 86

A testator's illegitimate child can contest the will if a parent-child relationship was established during the testator's life. Birman v. Sproat (Miami 1988) 47 Ohio App.3d 65, 546 N.E.2d 1354.

Where there is no prior judgment of paternity, the doctrine of res judicata does not act as a bar to a legitimation action subsequently brought by or on behalf of a child under RC Ch 3111. Collett v. Cogar (Ohio 1988) 35 Ohio St.3d 114, 518 N.E.2d 1202. Children Out–of–wedlock ⬤ 13

An illegitimate child may bring a civil action under common-law against his father for support and maintenance, and mother of the illegitimate child may maintain a separate cause of action against father for cost of past support of the child as well as for future support. Kulcsar v. Petrovic (Wayne 1984) 20 Ohio App.3d 104, 484 N.E.2d 1365, 20 O.B.R. 126. Children Out–of–wedlock ⬤ 30; Children Out–of–wedlock ⬤ 34

A child born out of wedlock may not bring a paternity proceeding under RC Ch 3111, but such child does have the same common law right to bring a civil action against his father for support and maintenance as does a legitimate child, incident to which the court shall make a determination on the issue of paternity, and so the unmarried mother's dismissal of her action under RC Ch 3111 with prejudice is not a bar to the minor child's separate common law action for support and maintenance from his putative father. Johnson v. Norman (Ohio 1981) 66 Ohio St.2d 186, 421 N.E.2d 124, 20 O.O.3d 196.

An adulterine bastard is one begotten of the mother's adulterous intercourse and the proceedings ordained by RC 3111.01 et seq. (bastardy proceedings) are available to such a child and its mother regardless of the marital status of the mother at delivery. Franklin v. Julian (Ohio 1972) 30 Ohio St.2d 228, 283 N.E.2d 813, 59 O.O.2d 264.

RC 2151.42, which makes it a criminal offense for the father of an illegitimate child to fail to support such a child, does not give rise to a civil action for support on behalf of such child. Baston v. Sears (Ohio 1968) 15 Ohio St.2d 166, 239 N.E.2d 62, 44 O.O.2d 144.

Where a minor commences an action under RC 3111.01 and no attack is made upon her capacity to sue until after a verdict is rendered finding the defendant guilty, the trial court has the power to permit the minor to amend her complaint to show her minority by adding the affidavit of her mother, as next friend, to the complaint and to conform the complaint and proceedings to the facts proved when the amendment does not substantially change the claim, and failure to do so constitutes error. Taylor v. Scott (Ohio 1959) 168 Ohio St. 391, 155

N.E.2d 884, 7 O.O.2d 243. Children Out–of–wedlock ⬤ 41

To determine the rights, status, and legal relations of an illegitimate child in regard to the alleged father, such child may, by his next friend, maintain an action for declaratory judgment. Maiden v. Maiden (Ohio Com.Pl. & Juv. 1955) 153 N.E.2d 460, 78 Ohio Law Abs. 551, 11 O.O.2d 362.

A minor cannot bring a bastardy action. State ex rel. Love v. Jones (Hamilton 1953) 98 Ohio App. 45, 128 N.E.2d 228, 57 O.O. 161.

RC 2105.06 does not apply to a person who dies testate; therefore someone born out of wedlock who contests the will and seeks a petition to determine heirship may not utilize RC Ch 3111 to establish paternity post mortem in order to inherit from the deceased who dies testate without taking any affirmative measures at his disposal to leave an inheritance to the child born out of wedlock. Rushford v Caines, No. 00AP–1072, 2001 WL 310006 (10th Dist Ct App, Franklin, 3–30–01).

A minor child is not barred from instituting a later action to determine paternity when a prior action brought in her name has reached judgment through a stipulated agreement. Ransome v Lampman, Nos. 94-CA-20+, 1995 WL 136983, 2d Dist Ct App, Miami, 3-31-95).

A bastardy proceeding cannot be instituted and maintained by the state of Ohio, nor by a complainant while she is a minor. State ex rel. Love v. Jones (Ohio Com.Pl. 1953) 111 N.E.2d 607, 65 Ohio Law Abs. 595, 50 O.O. 249, affirmed 98 Ohio App. 45, 128 N.E.2d 228, 57 O.O. 161.

An individual may file a paternity action against the estate of a deceased putative parent, as the action is not barred by the death of the alleged parent. Martin v Davidson; vacated by 53 OS(3d) 240, 559 NE(2d) 1348 (1990), No. 13840 (9th Dist Ct App, Summit, 4–19–89).

16. Standing

County child support enforcement agency (CSEA) had standing to file paternity complaint, even though mother of child was not recipient of public assistance or of services under Title IV-D of Social Security Act; state statute on bringing of paternity actions merely clarified which county CSEA would handle particular parentage action in event that neither mother nor alleged father would voluntarily take on role of plaintiff. Shockley v. Hedges (Ohio App. 5 Dist., Fairfield, 12-22-2005) No. 05 CA 49, 2005-Ohio-6948, 2005 WL 3537682, Unreported. Children Out–of–wedlock ⬤ 34

A prior divorce decree does not bar a child support enforcement agency from initiating its own action to establish a parent-child relationship between a minor child and the former husband and to request the court order the former husband to pay current and future child support, including health insurance. State ex rel. Smith v. Smith (Ohio App. 8 Dist., 04-08-1996) 110 Ohio App.3d 336, 674 N.E.2d 398, appeal not allowed 76 Ohio St.3d 1496, 670 N.E.2d 243.

County child support enforcement agency was not in privity with mother in prior divorce proceeding, so as to bar agency from bringing subsequent paternity action on grounds of res judicata; agency would not succeed to estate or interest formerly held by mother, but had interest in determining existence of parent-child relationship between child who was not named in divorce decree and mother's former husband. State ex rel. Smith v. Smith (Ohio App. 8 Dist., 04-08-1996) 110 Ohio App.3d 336, 674 N.E.2d 398, appeal not allowed 76 Ohio St.3d 1496, 670 N.E.2d 243. Child Custody ⬤➡ 532; Children Out–of–wedlock ⬤➡ 33

Alleged father lacked standing to argue that conflict of interest resulted from joint representation of mother, child, and the Department of Health and Human Services in suit to determine paternity and past-due child support. Phelps v. Fowler (Ohio App. 8 Dist., 11-13-1995) 107 Ohio App.3d 263, 668 N.E.2d 558, appeal not allowed 75 Ohio St.3d 1452, 663 N.E.2d 332. Attorney And Client ⬤➡ 21.20

Unlike a custody proceeding under RC 3109.27, there is no statutory requirement that a party bringing an RC Ch 3111 parentage action provide notice of related proceedings in other courts. Hardman v. Chiaramonte (Summit 1987) 39 Ohio App.3d 9, 528 N.E.2d 1270. Children Out–of–wedlock ⬤➡ 39

Husband of mother of natural father's children did not have standing to maintain action to determine existence and nonexistence of father and child relationship between children and natural father. Weinman v. Larsh (Ohio 1983) 5 Ohio St.3d 85, 448 N.E.2d 1384, 5 O.B.R. 138. Children Out–of–wedlock ⬤➡ 34

Although a county department of human services may intervene in a parentage action for purposes of collecting or recovering support, a county department of human services does not have standing to initiate a parentage action. State ex rel Athens County Human Services Dept v Wolf, No. 1462 (4th Dist Ct App, Athens, 10–9–91).

17. Legal effect of finding; inheritance

Issue of a slave marriage, though their parents died before the Emancipation Proclamation, are lawful heirs of their father as to land in this state. Morris v. Williams (Ohio 1883) 39 Ohio St. 554, 10 W.L.B. 445. Descent And Distribution ⬤➡ 26; Slaves ⬤➡ 14

Under statute of descent of 1861, providing that "the issue of marriage deemed null in law, shall nevertheless be legitimate," the children of de facto marriage may inherit from father. Wright v. Lore (Ohio 1861) 12 Ohio St. 619.

Legislative divorces were void, but courts held second marriages valid on account of consequences resulting from declaring them void, such as rendering illegitimate the issue of second marriages. Bingham v. Miller (Ohio 1848) 17 Ohio 445, 49 Am.Dec. 471.

Child born out of wedlock was an heir-at-law of deceased father, where parent-child relationship was established under the Parentage Act prior to

father's death. Stima v. Armatrout (Ohio App. 3 Dist., Seneca, 10-11-2002) No. 13-02-26, 2002-Ohio-5493, 2002 WL 31268408, Unreported. Children Out–of–wedlock ⬤➡ 86

Marriage of mother of child by defendant at time when he must have known she was enceinte, living with her and child as husband and father and providing for their maintenance and support for about a year, finding of trial court that child was child of parties in divorce decree undenied and uncontradicted made proof of acknowledgment by defendant that child was his child and therefore legitimate. Craner v. State (Montgomery 1936) 21 Ohio Law Abs. 260. Child Support ⬤➡ 214; Child Support ⬤➡ 663; Children Out–of–wedlock ⬤➡ 21(2)

A juvenile court admission of paternity pursuant to former statute is not the equivalent of an acknowledgement of paternity sufficient to operate under former statute to vest a child born out of wedlock with rights of inheritance from the natural father. In re Estate of Vaughan (Ohio, 01-17-2001) 90 Ohio St.3d 544, 740 N.E.2d 259, 2001-Ohio-222. Children Out–of–wedlock ⬤➡ 90

Admission of paternity by putative father during 1981 juvenile court proceeding, in which mother sought determination of paternity and financial support, did not constitute an adjudication of a natural parent-child relationship sufficient to vest child with rights of inheritance by and through father under then-applicable statutes; under former scheme, juvenile court lacked jurisdiction to determine identity of "natural" father, and could only hold proceedings allowing mother to obtain support and maintenance for child, and any necessary expenses for pregnancy and childbirth. In re Estate of Vaughan (Ohio, 01-17-2001) 90 Ohio St.3d 544, 740 N.E.2d 259, 2001-Ohio-222. Children Out–of–wedlock ⬤➡ 90

A testator's illegitimate child can contest the will if a parent-child relationship was established during the testator's life. Birman v. Sproat (Miami 1988) 47 Ohio App.3d 65, 546 N.E.2d 1354.

An acknowledgment of paternity under RC 2105.18 functions as an admission and a court order of legitimacy pursuant to RC 2105.18 establishes a full legal father-child relationship that can be the basis for child support and custody orders. In re Custody of Davis (Guernsey 1987) 41 Ohio App.3d 81, 534 N.E.2d 945.

After a man is adjudged a putative father and ordered to pay support until the child is eighteen, pursuant to former RC 3111.17, if the man acknowledges paternity under RC 2105.18, he assumes the obligation imposed by RC 3103.03 to support the child throughout its minority, as minority is defined by RC 3109.01, subject to subsequent amendments to RC 3109.01 and RC 3103.03. Zweifel v. Price (Franklin 1985) 24 Ohio App.3d 101, 493 N.E.2d 300, 24 O.B.R. 171.

The second paragraph of RC 2105.18 was intended to provide an avenue for determining the descent and distribution rights of a previously illegitimate child by allowing for that child's legitimation, and not to provide an individual with the means for challenging the paternity of an already legitimate child. In re Mancini (Lorain 1981) 2 Ohio App.3d 124, 440 N.E.2d 1232, 2 O.B.R. 138.

The Ohio laws of descent and distribution denying a right of an illegitimate child to inherit from a natural father unless the father has taken certain steps such as marrying the mother, acknowledging the child, designating the child as an heir-at-law, adoption, or making a provision in a will, are valid. White v. Randolph (Ohio 1979) 59 Ohio St.2d 6, 391 N.E.2d 333, 13 O.O.3d 3, appeal dismissed 100 S.Ct. 1000, 444 U.S. 1061, 62 L.Ed.2d 743. Children Out–of–wedlock ☞ 82; Constitutional Law ☞ 3184

Although a man, after marrying a child's mother, signs a declaration of paternity indicating he is the father of such child and a birth certificate is issued reflecting this contention, he obtains no rights to custody or visitation after a decree of divorce has been entered, where it is undisputed that another is the biological father. Chatman v. Chatman (Franklin 1977) 54 Ohio App.2d 6, 374 N.E.2d 433, 8 O.O.3d 24. Child Support ☞ 31

An illegitimate child whose paternity has been established during the lifetime of the natural father is entitled to a year's allowance for support from the father's estate. In re Estate of Holley (Ohio Com.Pl. 1975) 44 Ohio Misc. 78, 337 N.E.2d 675, 73 O.O.2d 265. Children Out–of–wedlock ☞ 90

A man who marries a woman while she is pregnant is presumed in law to be the father of the child, and no formal acknowledgment under RC 2105.18 by father is required in order for such child to inherit. Romweber v. Martin (Ohio 1972) 30 Ohio St.2d 25, 282 N.E.2d 36, 59 O.O.2d 58. Children Out–of–wedlock ☞ 86

A child conceived out of wedlock, but born during wedlock, inherits property from and through his natural father as the issue of such marriage. Romweber v. Martin (Ohio 1972) 30 Ohio St.2d 25, 282 N.E.2d 36, 59 O.O.2d 58. Children Out–of–wedlock ☞ 86

The illegitimate child of the widow of a testator is not his heir-at-law and, therefore, does not have sufficient interest to maintain a will contest, even though the testator married the child's mother after its birth and acknowledged the child as his own, unless he was in fact the father of the child. Comer v. Comer (Ohio 1963) 175 Ohio St. 313, 194 N.E.2d 572, 25 O.O.2d 182.

As used in GC 1465–82 (RC 4123.59), "children" includes legitimate children, adopted children, and illegitimate children legitimatized in the manner provided by statute, but not illegitimate children. Miller v. Industrial Commission (Ohio 1956) 165 Ohio St. 584, 138 N.E.2d 672, 60 O.O. 522.

A child born out of wedlock after the death of the reputed father may not have a recovery in a wrongful death action. Bonewit v. Weber (Summit 1952) 95 Ohio App. 428, 120 N.E.2d 738, 54 O.O. 20.

In a proceeding for determination of heirship, where petitioner, claiming to be the natural child of the decedent, was born while his mother was married to a person other than the decedent who later married the mother, evidence of admission by decedent, not in presence of third person, that petitioner is his child is admissible, and in such case, the presumption that petitioner is the child of the first husband must be overcome by clear and convincing evidence and not by a mere preponderance. Snyder v. McClelland (Franklin 1948) 83 Ohio App. 377, 81 N.E.2d 383, 51 Ohio Law Abs. 600, 38 O.O. 434.

This section removes the stamp of illegitimacy from a child whose father acknowledges it and intermarries with its mother either before or after the birth of the child, and such issue is the legitimate child of the father within purview of Workmen's Compensation Act, though the accidental death of the father occurred two weeks prior to the birth of the child. Garner v. B. F. Goodrich Co. (Ohio 1940) 136 Ohio St. 397, 26 N.E.2d 203, 16 O.O. 568.

Daughter of married man and paramour intermarrying and acknowledging daughter, held legitimate, regardless of date of daughter's birth notwithstanding nullity of marriage, and daughter was aunt's "niece" and "child" of aunt's brother within aunt's will. Clinton County Nat. Bank & Trust Co. of Wilmington v. Todhunter (Clinton 1931) 43 Ohio App. 289, 183 N.E. 88, 11 Ohio Law Abs. 450, 37 Ohio Law Rep. 279. Children Out–of–wedlock ☞ 12; Wills ☞ 499

An agreement of marriage followed by living together as husband and wife, establishes a valid marriage at common law. Umbenhower v. Labus (Ohio 1912) 85 Ohio St. 238, 97 N.E. 832, 9 Ohio Law Rep. 554. Common Law ☞ 14; Marriage ☞ 20(1)

A child by parents who could not then marry, may be legitimatized by the subsequent marriage of its parents. Ives v. McNicoll (Ohio 1899) 59 Ohio St. 402, 41 W.L.B. 180, 53 N.E. 60, 69 Am.St.Rep. 780.

One marrying the mother of a bastard is in law presumed to be its father and this presumption is conclusive. Ives v. McNicoll (Ohio 1899) 59 Ohio St. 402, 41 W.L.B. 180, 53 N.E. 60, 69 Am.St.Rep. 780.

A child adopted in a foreign state may inherit here. Simpson v. Simpson (Ohio Cir. 1906) 19 Ohio C.D. 503, 9 Ohio C.C.N.S. 137. Adoption ☞ 21; Adoption ☞ 25

If the father and mother of a bastard subsequently marry and the father acknowledges the child as his, it will take under a devise "to the heirs of the father's body." (See also Ives v McNicoll, 12 CC 297, 5 CD 555 (Hamilton 1896), affirmed by 59 OS 402, 53 NE 60 (1899).) Kniffin v. Schaffer (Ohio Cir. 1894) 4 Ohio C.D. 62.

"Legitimate" in this section means to legitimatize a bastard. McNicoll v. Ives (Ohio Com.Pl. 1895) 4 Ohio Dec. 75, 3 Ohio N.P. 6, affirmed 5 Ohio C.D.

555, affirmed 59 Ohio St. 402, 41 W.L.B. 180, 53 N.E. 60, 69 Am.St.Rep. 780.

Surviving child insurance benefits were not payable to an illegitimate child of a father who took no steps to acknowledge paternity during his lifetime, in the absence of proof that before his death, father contributed to the child's support. Kohut v. Secretary of Health, Ed. and Welfare (C.A.6 (Ohio) 1981) 664 F.2d 120.

An illegitimate child who has not been legitimatized in accordance with statute may not share in the proceeds of an insurance policy that designates as beneficiaries "employee's children who survive the employee." Aetna Life Ins. Co., Hartford, Conn. v. McMillan (N.D.Ohio 1958) 171 F.Supp. 111, 89 Ohio Law Abs. 208, 13 O.O.2d 100. Insurance ☞ 3480

The filing of the acknowledgement of paternity pursuant to RC 2105.18 accompanied by the filing of an objection to adoption pursuant to RC 3107.06(F)(4) is sufficient to place the father within the purview of RC 3107.07(A) as a parent and not within RC 3107(B). In re Adoption of Dickson, No. 94–CA–57, 1995 WL 495450 (5th Dist Ct App, Fairfield, 5–19–95).

18. Effect of paternity proceeding on stepfather's adoption petition

The probate court was required to refrain from proceeding with stepfather's petition to adopt child while biological father's paternity proceeding was pending in juvenile court. In re Adoption of P.A.C. (Ohio, 07-22-2010) 126 Ohio St.3d 236, 933 N.E.2d 236, 2010-Ohio-3351, reconsideration denied 126 Ohio St.3d 1592, 934 N.E.2d 939, 2010-Ohio-4880. Adoption ☞ 9.1

19. Jurisdiction

Trial court lacked jurisdiction to issue order for visitation between adjudicated father and child pursuant to Uniform Interstate Family Support Act (UIFSA), where mere filing of action under such statute did not confer jurisdiction over nonresident mother and child in regard to separate visitation proceeding. Homler v. Homler (Ohio App. 9 Dist., Lorain, 05-24-2006) No. 05CA008752, 2006-Ohio-2556, 2006 WL 1409801, Unreported, appeal not allowed 111 Ohio St.3d 1431, 855 N.E.2d 496, 2006-Ohio-5351. Children Out–of–wedlock ☞ 20.13

Trial court lacked jurisdiction to issue order for visitation between adjudicated father and child, upon adjudicated father's oral raising of issue in action brought by county Child Support Enforcement Agency (CSEA), mother, and child to establish child's parentage, where applicable statute provided for bringing of custody action separate from action to establish paternity, and adjudicated father did not file petition for custody or parenting time. Homler v. Homler (Ohio App. 9 Dist., Lorain, 05-24-2006) No. 05CA008752, 2006-Ohio-2556, 2006 WL 1409801, Unreported, appeal not allowed 111 Ohio St.3d 1431, 855 N.E.2d 496,

2006-Ohio-5351. Children Out–of–wedlock ☞ 20.4

Probate court, and not common pleas court, had exclusive jurisdiction over mother's motion to change child's surname, where mother did not file motion in context of parentage action, and parentage had already been established and was not in dispute. Porter v. Walker (Ohio App. 9 Dist., Lorain, 06-15-2005) No. 04CA008575, 2005-Ohio-2972, 2005 WL 1398901, Unreported. Courts ☞ 472.4(8); Courts ☞ 472.5

The probate court lacked jurisdiction to hear action filed by testator's siblings challenging the parentage of testator's child, after testator's will was admitted to probate; probate courts lacked jurisdiction to hear paternity actions. Dircksen v. Dircksen (Ohio App. 3 Dist., Shelby, 12-27-2004) No. 17-04-08, 2004-Ohio-7041, 2004 WL 2980658, Unreported. Children Out–of–wedlock ☞ 88

Prospective adoptive parents waived their appellate arguments that challenged the juvenile court's personal jurisdiction determination in paternity proceeding filed by putative father, where adoptive parents failed to present any argument on appeal that challenged the juvenile court's determination of personal jurisdiction. B.W. v. D.B.-B. (Ohio App. 6 Dist., 06-10-2011) 193 Ohio App.3d 637, 953 N.E.2d 369, 2011-Ohio-2813. Children Out–of–wedlock ☞ 73

The juvenile court had subject matter jurisdiction to consider putative father's paternity action prior to the probate court's adjudication of prospective adoptive parents' action to adopt child. B.W. v. D.B.-B. (Ohio App. 6 Dist., 06-10-2011) 193 Ohio App.3d 637, 953 N.E.2d 369, 2011-Ohio-2813. Courts ☞ 475(1)

A final decree of adoption does not patently and unambiguously divest a juvenile court of jurisdiction to determine paternity solely for the limited purpose of allowing the putative father to establish that he is the biological father so that he can exercise his statutory rights to provide information regarding his social and medical history for placement in the child's adoption records. State ex rel. Furnas v. Monnin (Ohio, 10-30-2008) 120 Ohio St.3d 279, 898 N.E.2d 573, 2008-Ohio-5569. Adoption ☞ 14

Primary jurisdiction over issue of paternity of child with whom mother had been pregnant at time of her divorce was properly exercised in juvenile court, in which child, through his mother, exercised his separate right to bring paternity action against putative father. Nwabara v. Willacy (Ohio App. 8 Dist., 08-09-1999) 135 Ohio App.3d 120, 733 N.E.2d 267, dismissed, appeal not allowed 87 Ohio St.3d 1451, 719 N.E.2d 967. Children Out–of–wedlock ☞ 36

Despite mother's contention that father's failure to participate in administrative determination of parentage precluded court of common pleas from exercising jurisdiction over parentage action, given apparent conflict in jurisdictional statutes, court of common pleas was not so patently and unambiguously devoid of subject matter jurisdiction that

Court of Appeals would issue writ of prohibition prohibiting court of common pleas from exercising jurisdiction while final judgment was pending. State ex rel. Dixon v. Clark Cty. Court of Common Pleas, Juv. Div. (Ohio App. 2 Dist., 05-17-1995) 103 Ohio App.3d 523, 660 N.E.2d 486. Prohibition ☞ 10(2)

Fact that prosecutor from child support enforcement agency signed paternity complaint did not establish that action was brought by the agency rather than mother so that court was without jurisdiction. Ransome v. Lampman (Ohio App. 2 Dist., 03-31-1995) 103 Ohio App.3d 8, 658 N.E.2d 313, dismissed, appeal not allowed 73 Ohio St.3d 1449, 654 N.E.2d 985. Children Out–of–wedlock ☞ 36

Trial court had subject matter jurisdiction to award child support retroactive to child's date of birth in paternity proceeding brought more than 20 years after child was born. Park v. Ambrose (Ross 1993) 85 Ohio App.3d 179, 619 N.E.2d 469, dismissed, jurisdictional motion overruled 67 Ohio St.3d 1409, 615 N.E.2d 1043. Children Out–of–wedlock ☞ 38; Children Out–of–wedlock ☞ 67

A probate judge in common pleas court has no subject matter jurisdiction to determine paternity as an ancillary claim to heirship against the estate of his alleged father. Martin v. Davidson (Ohio 1990) 53 Ohio St.3d 240, 559 N.E.2d 1348. Children Out–of–wedlock ☞ 33

A plaintiff claiming to be the natural father of a child born to a woman while she was married to another man may assert that claim in an action brought pursuant to the Uniform Parentage Act, RC Ch 3111, even though the child was determined to be the issue of the marriage during an earlier divorce suit in which the plaintiff was not a party, and the juvenile court has jurisdiction over the

plaintiff's claim. Gatt v. Gedeon (Cuyahoga 1984) 20 Ohio App.3d 285, 485 N.E.2d 1059, 20 O.B.R. 376.

20. Presumption of paternity

While every child conceived in wedlock is presumed legitimate, such presumption is not conclusive and may be rebutted by clear and convincing evidence that there were no sexual relations between husband and wife during the time in which the child must have been conceived, and a complaint for determination of paternity is sufficient if the plaintiff alleges he is the natural father of the child. Joseph v. Alexander (Ohio 1984) 12 Ohio St.3d 88, 465 N.E.2d 448, 12 O.B.R. 77. Children Out–of–wedlock ☞ 3

21. Review

Court of Appeals was unable to conclude that the trial court independently, and without deference to the magistrate, reviewed the matter before it and, as such, case would be remanded to allow trial court to independently review the objections to the magistrate's decision in paternity proceedings that it was in the child's best interest to change out-of-wedlock child's surname from that of mother to father; trial court's language, stating that the magistrate's decision did not indicate an abuse of discretion and that magistrate's decision was not unreasonable, unconscionable, or arbitrary, implied the trial court used the appellate abuse of discretion standard in reviewing the magistrate's decision, whether or not it was the trial court's intent to do so. Jones v. Smith (Ohio App. 4 Dist., 01-13-2010) 187 Ohio App.3d 145, 931 N.E.2d 592, 2010-Ohio-131. Children Out–of–wedlock ☞ 1; Children Out–of–wedlock ☞ 73

3111.05 Limitation of action

An action to determine the existence or nonexistence of the father and child relationship may not be brought later than five years after the child reaches the age of eighteen. Neither section 3111.04 of the Revised Code nor this section extends the time within which a right of inheritance or a right to a succession may be asserted beyond the time provided by Chapter 2105., 2107., 2113., 2117., or 2123. of the Revised Code.

(1982 H 245, eff. 6–29–82)

Uncodified Law

1992 S 10, § 5: See Uncodified Law under 3111.01.

1982 H 245, § 3: See Uncodified Law under 3111.04.

Historical and Statutory Notes

Ed. Note: Former 3111.05 repealed by 1982 H 245, eff. 6–29–82; 127 v 1039; 125 v 184; 1953 H 1; GC 8006–5; Source—GC 12112.

Pre–1953 H 1 Amendments 124 v S 65

Library References

Children Out-of-Wedlock ☞38.
Westlaw Topic No. 76H.
C.J.S. Children Out-of-Wedlock §§ 49, 84 to 85.

Research References

ALR Library

87 ALR 5th 361, Liability of Father for Retroactive Child Support on Judicial Determination of Paternity.

86 ALR 5th 637, Right of Illegitimate Child to Maintain Action to Determine Paternity.

Encyclopedias

OH Jur. 3d Family Law § 950, Limitation of Actions.

OH Jur. 3d Family Law § 979, Child Support Judgments or Orders--Period During Which Duty Owed.

Forms

Ohio Jurisprudence Pleading and Practice Forms § 111:3, Limitation of Actions.

Ohio Jurisprudence Pleading and Practice Forms § 12:11, Checklist--Statutes of Limitations.

Treatises and Practice Aids

Sowald & Morganstern, Baldwin's Ohio Practice Domestic Relations Law § 19:2, Jurisdiction Over Child Support.

Sowald & Morganstern, Baldwin's Ohio Practice Domestic Relations Law § 3:24, Defenses--Statute of Limitations.

Sowald & Morganstern, Baldwin's Ohio Practice Domestic Relations Law § 3:39, Effect of Judgment--Child Support--Past Care--Claim Brought After Child is Emancipated.

Carlin, Baldwin's Ohio Prac. Merrick-Rippner Probate Law § 17:2, Designation--Effect.

Carlin, Baldwin's Ohio Prac. Merrick-Rippner Probate Law § 19:8, Uniform Parentage Act--Support Order.

Carlin, Baldwin's Ohio Prac. Merrick-Rippner Probate Law § 107:8, Age Jurisdiction.

Carlin, Baldwin's Ohio Prac. Merrick-Rippner Probate Law § 19:10, Uniform Parentage Act--Procedure in Action to Determine Father-Child Relationship.

Carlin, Baldwin's Ohio Prac. Merrick-Rippner Probate Law § 99:40, Consent Not Required--Putative Father.

Carlin, Baldwin's Ohio Prac. Merrick-Rippner Probate Law § 110:21, Parentage Act--Statute of Limitations.

Carlin, Baldwin's Ohio Prac. Merrick-Rippner Probate Law § 110:29, Parentage Act--Judgment Determining Existence of Parent-Child Relationship.

Carlin, Baldwin's Ohio Prac. Merrick-Rippner Probate Law § 110:30, Parentage Act--Enforcement of Support Order.

Carlin, Baldwin's Ohio Prac. Merrick-Rippner Probate Law § 110:35, Civil Support Proceedings--Liability for Child Support.

Law Review and Journal Commentaries

Practice Pointer—Application of the Doctrine of Laches in Parentage Actions, Pamela J. MacAdams. 9 Domestic Rel J Ohio 9 (January/February 1997).

Notes of Decisions

Adult children 7
Constitutional issues 1
Construction with other laws 2
Jurisdiction 8
Laches 4
Limit for bringing action 6
Public policy 3
Res judicata 5

-----

1. Constitutional issues

A limitations period of six years for bringing paternity suits claiming the defendant is the father of an illegitimate child is held "not substantially related to [the state] interest in avoiding the litigation of stale or fraudulent claims" and held to deny the equal Protection of the laws secured by the Fourteenth Amendment to the federal constitution, in view of the state's law allowing legitimate children to seek support from their parents at any time. (Ed. note: Pennsylvania statute construed in light of federal constitution.) Clark v. Jeter (U.S.Pa. 1988) 108 S.Ct. 1910, 486 U.S. 456, 100 L.Ed.2d 465.

The provision of RC 3111.05 limiting actions to determine paternity to five years after the child reaches eighteen is not unconstitutional on its face. Pound v Fracker, No. CA–3018 (5th Dist Ct App, Licking, 5–22–84).

2. Construction with other laws

The four-year statute of limitations of RC 2305.09(D) is inapplicable to a parentage action; rather, RC 3111.05, providing that a parentage action shall not be brought later than five years following a child reaching the age of eighteen, is controlling, even if the child was born before the effective date of RC 3111.05. Marcy v. McCommons (Ashtabula 1988) 55 Ohio App.3d 191, 563 N.E.2d 315.

The limitation of actions brought under RC Ch 3111 is governed by RC 3111.05, and not by RC 2305.09. Manley v. Howard (Marion 1985) 25 Ohio App.3d 1, 495 N.E.2d 436, 25 O.B.R. 30.

An action for support brought by a mother of an illegitimate child which was time-barred by RC 2305.09 before the enactment of RC Ch 3111 by 1982 H 245, eff. 6–29–82, is not revived by that enactment. Manley v. Howard (Marion 1985) 25 Ohio App.3d 1, 495 N.E.2d 436, 25 O.B.R. 30.

RC 2105.06 does not apply to a person who dies testate; therefore someone born out of wedlock who contests the will and seeks a petition to determine heirship may not utilize RC Ch 3111 to establish paternity post mortem in order to inherit from the deceased who dies testate without taking any affirmative measures at his disposal to leave an inheritance to the child born out of wedlock. Rushford v Caines, No. 00AP–1072, 2001 WL 310006 (10th Dist Ct App, Franklin, 3–30–01).

3. Public policy

Assuming that on public-policy grounds laches was available as defense to paternity claim, delay of more than 15 years in seeking to establish paternity was not prejudicial to father, as element precluding application of laches; father-child relationship could be established through court-ordered visitation, and father would have ability to become involved in child's life. Still v. Hayman (Ohio App. 7 Dist., 07-30-2003) 153 Ohio App.3d 487, 794 N.E.2d 751, 2003 Ohio 4113. Children Out of wedlock ☞ 38

On public-policy grounds, laches is not available as defense to paternity claim, though father was not informed he was child's father until child was more than 15 years old; parent-child relationship could be established through court-ordered visitation, and father would have ability to become involved in child's life. Still v. Hayman (Ohio App. 7 Dist., 07-30-2003) 153 Ohio App.3d 487, 794 N.E.2d 751, 2003-Ohio-4113. Children Out–of–wedlock ☞ 38

Assuming that on public policy grounds laches was available as defense to paternity claim, delay in seeking to establish paternity was unreasonable, as element favoring application of laches defense; mother did not reveal father's true identity to father and to county child support enforcement agency (CSEA) until child was more than 15 years old, and mother's claim that she did not reveal father's name earlier because he had raped her was not credible. Still v. Hayman (Ohio App. 7 Dist., 07-30-2003) 153 Ohio App.3d 487, 794 N.E.2d 751, 2003-Ohio-4113. Children Out-of-wedlock ☞ 38

4. Laches

Divorced father against whom county child support enforcement agency attempted to enforce child support order 38 years after it was entered was not prejudiced in his defense by destruction of agency's case file due to inactivity in the case, for purposes of determining whether action was barred by doctrine of laches; father admitted he never made any payments toward his obligation, calculation of total amount owed was evident from child support order and date youngest child became emancipated, father did not claim that evidence of payments by military allotment was now unavailable, and other records were available from which to calculate amount of tax refunds intercepted by agency. Watson v. Watson (Ohio App. 2 Dist., Clark, 08-12-2005) No. 04CA0066, 2005-Ohio-4195, 2005 WL 1939815, Unreported. Child Support ☞ 451

Laches is not a defense in an action for paternity and child support brought fourteen years after the child's birth where the defendant (1) is contacted by the county child support enforcement agency before the child's birth and informed of his putative parentage, (2) is informed by his own mother, shortly after the birth, that the child's mother had advised her that he was the putative father, (3) makes no attempt to verify whether or not he is the father, and (4) is not materially prejudiced by delay in bringing the action. Cooper v. Russell (Ohio App. 12 Dist., Warren, 09-05-1995) No. CA94-11-095, 1995 WL 520773, Unreported.

Laches barred county child support enforcement agency (CSEA) from recovering from father reimbursement of Aid to Dependent Children (ADC) benefits, and barred father from being liable for retroactive child support, where father was not told he was child's father until child was 13 years old; mother, by deliberately lying for 15 years to father and to agency regarding true identity of child's father, deprived father of opportunity to become involved in child's life. Still v. Hayman (Ohio App. 7 Dist., 07-30-2003) 153 Ohio App.3d 487, 794 N.E.2d 751, 2003-Ohio-4113. Child Support ☞ 150; Social Security And Public Welfare ☞ 194.19

Key rules of equity, equitable estoppel, and laches contain "unreasonable passage of time" and "reliance" components, and passage of substantial amount of time without putative father contesting paternity, after child's birth and his acknowledgment of parentage, relied upon by mother and child, would render subsequent attempt to disestablish paternity burdensome on child, mother, the public, and the courts, and would likely result in estrangement of children from fathers and increased burden of child support on taxpayers, contrary to public policy. Crago v. Kinzie (Ohio Com. Pl., 06-01-2000) 106 Ohio Misc.2d 51, 733 N.E.2d 1219. Children Out–of–wedlock ☞ 7

Parentage action in juvenile court was not barred by doctrine of laches, despite mother's failure to name putative father as party in her divorce action and despite delay of years in bringing parentage action, where jurisdiction over issue of child's parentage was properly in juvenile court and parentage action was brought by virtue of child's statutory right rather than mother's. Nwabara v. Willacy (Ohio App. 8 Dist., 08-09-1999) 135 Ohio App.3d 120, 733 N.E.2d 267, dismissed, appeal not allowed 87 Ohio St.3d 1451, 719 N.E.2d 967. Children Out–of–wedlock ☞ 38

Complaint seeking adjudication of paternity and back child support, brought one month prior to child's attaining age of majority, was not barred by doctrine of laches, as putative father was not materially prejudiced by delay; adjudicated father did not claim loss of evidence helpful to his case or change in his position that would not have occurred had child's mother not delayed in asserting her rights, and had been aware of child's existence and likelihood of his paternity since her birth. State ex rel. Donovan v. Zajac (Ohio App. 11 Dist., 01-02-1998) 125 Ohio App.3d 245, 708 N.E.2d 254, dismissed, appeal not allowed 81 Ohio St.3d 1521, 692 N.E.2d 1023. Children Out–of–wedlock ⬡ 38

Laches may be applicable in parentage actions filed prior to the expiration of the statute of limitations, but only if the defendant can show material prejudice. Wright v. Oliver (Ohio 1988) 35 Ohio St.3d 10, 517 N.E.2d 883. Children Out–of–wedlock ⬡ 38

5. Res judicata

Prior decision of the Court of Appeals, holding that res judicata barred former husband's action seeking a determination of paternity, amounted to an "admission on file" for purposes of summary judgment in a subsequent paternity action, where trial court deemed prior appellate decision admitted as true and genuine by husband, and husband did not challenge that ruling. Donnelly v. Kashnier (Ohio App. 9 Dist., Medina, 02-12-2003) No. 02CA0051-M, 2003-Ohio-639, 2003 WL 294413, Unreported. Children Out–of–wedlock ⬡ 64

Finding in original divorce decree that child born during parties' marriage was former husband's child was res judicata as to father's motion to have himself declared as not the child's biological father because DNA (deoxyribonucleic acid) test results indicated that father and child were not genetically linked. Van Dusen v. Van Dusen (Ohio App. 10 Dist., 01-28-2003) 151 Ohio App.3d 494, 784 N.E.2d 750, 2003-Ohio-350. Divorce ⬡ 172

Legitimation order filed in probate court with consent of mother did not bar subsequent parentage action wherein mother sought child support arrearages; application of doctrine of res judicata would violate state's strong public policy favoring protection of children and their support, health, maintenance and welfare, and would also violate equal protection. Lewis v. Chapin (Ohio App. 8 Dist., 03-21-1994) 93 Ohio App.3d 695, 639 N.E.2d 848 Children Out–of–wedlock ⬡ 33; Constitutional Law ⬡ 3192

Child was not barred under doctrine of res judicata from pursuing parentage action on basis that father acknowledged existence of parent-child relationship and that mother consented to filing of legitimacy order, as child was not a party or in privity with a party to the legitimacy order. Lewis v. Chapin (Ohio App. 8 Dist., 03-21-1994) 93 Ohio App.3d 695, 639 N.E.2d 848 Children Out–of–wedlock ⬡ 33

The doctrine of res judicata can be invoked to give conclusive effect to a determination of parentage contained in a dissolution decree or a legitimation order, thereby barring a subsequent paternity action brought pursuant to RC Ch 3111. In re Gilbraith (Ohio 1987) 32 Ohio St.3d 127, 512 N.E.2d 956. Child Support ⬡ 225; Children Out–of–wedlock ⬡ 13; Children Out–of–wedlock ⬡ 21(2)

6. Limit for bringing action

Juvenile court has jurisdiction to award retroactive child support payments to an adult emancipated child if a parentage action is filed prior to the child's twenty-third birthday. Carnes v. Kemp (Ohio, 12-30-2004) 104 Ohio St.3d 629, 821 N.E.2d 180, 2004-Ohio-7107. Children Out–of–wedlock ⬡ 67

Child has up until the age of 23 to file a parentage action. Carnes v. Kemp (Ohio, 12-30-2004) 104 Ohio St.3d 629, 821 N.E.2d 180, 2004-Ohio-7107. Children Out–of–wedlock ⬡ 38

Court lacked authority to order biological father to provide present and future child support to child who had reached age of majority and was emancipated, even though paternity action had been timely filed within five years after child reached age 18. Snider v. Lillie (Ohio App. 1 Dist., 10-17-1997) 131 Ohio App.3d 444, 722 N.E.2d 1036, dismissed, appeal not allowed 81 Ohio St.3d 1452, 690 N.E.2d 546. Children Out–of–wedlock ⬡ 21(2); Children Out–of–wedlock ⬡ 67

Time in which to bring a claim to establish paternity is five years longer than period of father's duty to support, which expires when child reaches age 18. Snider v. Lillie (Ohio App. 1 Dist., 10-17-1997) 131 Ohio App.3d 444, 722 N.E.2d 1036, dismissed, appeal not allowed 81 Ohio St.3d 1452, 690 N.E.2d 546. Children Out–of–wedlock ⬡ 38

Child may bring action to establish paternity and pursue past support obligation even after any present support obligation has been eliminated due to child's reaching majority. Hudgins v. Mitchell (Ohio App. 9 Dist., 06-17-1998) 128 Ohio App.3d 403, 715 N.E.2d 213. Child Support ⬡ 177; Children Out–of–wedlock ⬡ 21(1)

Putative daughter was entitled to establish her paternity for purposes of inheritance, despite death of her alleged father. Meckstroth v. Robinson (Ohio Com.Pl., 04-05-1996) 83 Ohio Misc.2d 57, 679 N.E.2d 744. Children Out–of–wedlock ⬡ 34

Statute of limitations for parentage action does not begin to run until child reaches age of majority. Lewis v. Chapin (Ohio App. 8 Dist., 03-21-1994) 93 Ohio App.3d 695, 639 N.E.2d 848 Children Out–of–wedlock ⬡ 38; Limitation Of Actions ⬡ 72(1)

Failure of temporary administrator of intestate's estate to assert that alleged biological daughter of intestate should have been barred by statute of limitations provision applicable to paternity actions from establishing parentage for purposes of descent and distribution resulted in waiver of that defense. In re Estate of Hicks (Ohio App. 6 Dist., 09-30-1993) 90 Ohio App.3d 483, 629 N.E.2d 1086. Limitation Of Actions ⬡ 182(5)

Parentage action brought by adult child within five years after she reached majority was timely regardless of limitations period in effect when child was born. Park v. Ambrose (Ross 1993) 85 Ohio App.3d 179, 619 N.E.2d 469, dismissed, jurisdictional motion overruled 67 Ohio St.3d 1409, 615 N.E.2d 1043. Limitation Of Actions ⬡ 6(11)

Limitations period for parentage actions is five years after child reaches 18 years of age regardless of whether prior parentage statutes in effect when child was born would otherwise have barred action.

Park v. Ambrose (Ross 1993) 85 Ohio App.3d 179, 619 N.E.2d 469, dismissed, jurisdictional motion overruled 67 Ohio St.3d 1409, 615 N.E.2d 1043. Limitation Of Actions ⛐ 6(11)

The statute of limitations of RC 3111.05 is properly applied to an action commenced under RC Ch 2105 to determine heirship, where the action is essentially a paternity action. Garrison v. Smith (Lucas 1988) 55 Ohio App.3d 14, 561 N.E.2d 1041.

7. Adult children

Mother of adult child was barred by doctrine of laches from pursuing claim for child support and other statutory relief arising out of parentage action against estate of deceased father, where mother, her husband, and father were aware early on of father's paternity, but had entered mutual understanding that child would be raised by mother and her husband without any interference from father, and mother, after initially making decision not to pursue child support, had waited for over 23 years before bringing suit. Hugershoff v. Loecy (Ohio Com.Pl., 09-28-1999) 103 Ohio Misc.2d 58, 725 N.E.2d 378. Children Out-of-wedlock ⛐ 38

Adult child born out of wedlock was not barred by doctrine of laches from seeking support and other statutory relief from father, even though such a claim by child's mother was barred due to her initial decision not to seek child support, and delay of over 23 years in asserting such a claim, where child did not unreasonably delay in bringing claim after becoming aware of her birth father's identity.

Hugershoff v. Loecy (Ohio Com.Pl., 09-28-1999) 103 Ohio Misc.2d 58, 725 N.E.2d 378. Child Support ⛐ 177; Children Out-of-wedlock ⛐ 21(2)

8. Jurisdiction

Juvenile Court lacked jurisdiction to order retroactive child support, in paternity proceedings, when the first claim for support was made after the child reached the age of majority and the duty to support had elapsed. Carnes v. Kemp (Ohio App. 3 Dist., Auglaize, 11-03-2003) No. 2-03-10, 2003-Ohio-5884, 2003 WL 22473582, Unreported, stay denied 101 Ohio St.3d 1419, 802 N.E.2d 152, 2004-Ohio-123, motion to certify allowed 101 Ohio St.3d 1465, 804 N.E.2d 39, 2004-Ohio-819, appeal allowed 101 Ohio St.3d 1466, 804 N.E.2d 40, 2004-Ohio-819, motion granted 103 Ohio St.3d 1419, 814 N.E.2d 63, 2004-Ohio-4504, reversed 104 Ohio St.3d 629, 821 N.E.2d 180, 2004-Ohio-7107. Children Out-of-wedlock ⛐ 67

Juvenile court had jurisdiction to award retroactive child support payments to adult emancipated child who filed paternity action before her twenty-third birthday; statute governing paternity actions expressly provided that child was entitled to commence paternity action up to age of 23, and child support statute provided that juvenile court had authority to make support order once parentage determination was made. Carnes v. Kemp (Ohio, 12-30-2004) 104 Ohio St.3d 629, 821 N.E.2d 180, 2004-Ohio-7107. Children Out-of-wedlock ⛐ 67

3111.06 Jurisdiction

(A) Except as otherwise provided in division (B) or (C) of section 3111.381 of the Revised Code, an action authorized under sections 3111.01 to 3111.18 of the Revised Code may be brought in the juvenile court or other court with jurisdiction under section 2101.022 or 2301.03 of the Revised Code of the county in which the child, the child's mother, or the alleged father resides or is found or, if the alleged father is deceased, of the county in which proceedings for the probate of the alleged father's estate have been or can be commenced, or of the county in which the child is being provided support by the county department of job and family services of that county. An action pursuant to sections 3111.01 to 3111.18 of the Revised Code to object to an administrative order issued pursuant to former section 3111.21 or 3111.22 or sections 3111.38 to 3111.54 of the Revised Code determining the existence or nonexistence of a parent and child relationship that has not become final and enforceable, may be brought only in the juvenile court or other court with jurisdiction of the county in which the child support enforcement agency that issued the order is located. If an action for divorce, dissolution, or legal separation has been filed in a court of common pleas, that court of common pleas has original jurisdiction to determine if the parent and child relationship exists between one or both of the parties and any child alleged or presumed to be the child of one or both of the parties.

(B) A person who has sexual intercourse in this state submits to the jurisdiction of the courts of this state as to an action brought under sections 3111.01 to 3111.18 of the Revised Code with respect to a child who may have been conceived by that act of intercourse. In addition to any other method provided by the Rules of Civil Procedure, personal jurisdiction may be acquired by personal service of summons outside this state or by certified mail with proof of actual receipt.

(2006 H 136, eff. 5–17–06; 2000 S 180, eff. 3–22–01; 1999 H 471, eff. 7–1–00; 1997 H 352, eff. 1–1–98; 1990 H 514, eff. 1–1–91; 1986 H 476; 1982 H 245)

Uncodified Law

1992 S 10, § 5: See Uncodified Law under 3111.01.

1982 H 245, § 3: See Uncodified Law under 3111.04.

Historical and Statutory Notes

Ed. Note: Former 3111.06 repealed by 1982 H 245, eff. 6–29–82; 127 v 1039; 125 v 184; 1953 H 1; GC 8006–6; Source—GC 12113. 3111.06 contains provisions analogous to former 3111.08, repealed by 1982 H 245, eff. 6–29–82.

Pre–1953 H 1 Amendments: 124 v S 65

Amendment Note: 2006 H 136 substituted "Except as otherwise provided in division (B) or (C) of section 3111.381 of the Revised Code, an" for "An" in the first sentence of division (A).

Amendment Note: 2000 S 180 rewrote division (A) and substituted "3111.18" for "3111.19" in division (B). Prior to amendment division (A) read:

"(A) The juvenile court has original jurisdiction of any action authorized under sections 3111.01 to 3111.19 of the Revised Code. An action may be brought under those sections in the juvenile court of the county in which the child, the child's mother, or the alleged father resides or is found or, if the alleged father is deceased, of the county in which proceedings for the probate of the alleged father's estate have been or can be commenced, or of the county in which the child is being provided support by the county department of job and family services of that county. An action pursuant to sections 3111.01 to 3111.19 of the Revised Code to object to an administrative order issued pursuant to former section 3111.21 or section 3111.22 of the Revised Code determining the existence or nonexistence of a parent and child relationship that has not become final and enforceable, may be brought only in the juvenile court of the county in which the child support enforcement agency that issued the order is located. If an action for divorce, dissolution, or legal separation has been filed in a court of common pleas, that court of common pleas has original jurisdiction to determine if the parent and child relationship exists between one or both of the parties and any child alleged or presumed to be the child of one or both of the parties."

Amendment Note: 1999 H 471 substituted "county department of job and family services" for "department of human services" in division (A).

Amendment Note: 1997 H 352 added the third sentence in division (A); and made changes to reflect gender neutral language.

Cross References

Jurisdiction of juvenile court, see 2151.23
Service of process, Civ R 4 to 4.6

Library References

Children Out-of-Wedlock ⏝36.
Westlaw Topic No. 76H.
C.J.S. Children Out-of-Wedlock §§ 48, 86.

Research References

Encyclopedias

OH Jur. 3d Family Law § 909, Final Decree or Interlocutory Order.
OH Jur. 3d Family Law § 952, Jurisdiction.

Forms

Ohio Jurisprudence Pleading and Practice Forms § 111:4, Jurisdiction.

Treatises and Practice Aids

Klein, Darling, & Terez, Baldwin's Ohio Practice Civil Practice § 4.3:14, Fourteenth Amendment Due Process Restrictions on Exercise of Personal Jurisdiction by State Courts--Contacts as Constitutionally Permissible Basis of State Court Personal Jurisdiction--Decis...
Klein, Darling, & Terez, Baldwin's Ohio Practice Civil Practice § 4.3:23, Primary Ohio Long-Arm Provisions in General--The Various Ohio Long-Arm Provisions.

Sowald & Morganstern, Baldwin's Ohio Practice Domestic Relations Law § 3:8, Jurisdiction and Venue.
Sowald & Morganstern, Baldwin's Ohio Practice Domestic Relations Law § 15:5, Parentage Determinations.
Sowald & Morganstern, Baldwin's Ohio Practice Domestic Relations Law § 19:2, Jurisdiction Over Child Support.
Sowald & Morganstern, Baldwin's Ohio Practice Domestic Relations Law § 21:3, Parenting Time--Jurisdiction--In General.
Sowald & Morganstern, Baldwin's Ohio Practice Domestic Relations Law § 22:4, Establishing Parentage.
Sowald & Morganstern, Baldwin's Ohio Practice Domestic Relations Law § 23:3, Impediments to Interstate Support Actions--Personal Jurisdiction--Constitutional Requirements.
Sowald & Morganstern, Baldwin's Ohio Practice Domestic Relations Law § 23:7, Impediments to

Interstate Support Actions--Personal Jurisdiction--Ohio Civil Rules--Parentage Determinations.

Sowald & Morganstern, Baldwin's Ohio Practice Domestic Relations Law § 3:39, Effect of Judgment--Child Support--Past Care--Claim Brought After Child is Emancipated.

Sowald & Morganstern, Baldwin's Ohio Practice Domestic Relations Law § 3:52, Complaint to Establish Father-Child Relationship--By Mother--Form.

Carlin, Baldwin's Ohio Prac. Merrick-Rippner Probate Law § 19:4, Legitimation--Historical Provisions.

Carlin, Baldwin's Ohio Prac. Merrick-Rippner Probate Law § 19:6, Uniform Parentage Act--Juris-

diction of Action to Determine Father-Child Relationship.

Carlin, Baldwin's Ohio Prac. Merrick-Rippner Probate Law § 39:4, Interested Persons.

Carlin, Baldwin's Ohio Prac. Merrick-Rippner Probate Law § 19:10, Uniform Parentage Act--Procedure in Action to Determine Father-Child Relationship.

Carlin, Baldwin's Ohio Prac. Merrick-Rippner Probate Law § 99:49, Interlocutory and Final Orders.

Carlin, Baldwin's Ohio Prac. Merrick-Rippner Probate Law § 110:20, Parentage Act--Jurisdiction and Venue.

Carlin, Baldwin's Ohio Prac. Merrick-Rippner Probate Law § 110:26, Parentage Act--Applicability of Civil Rules to Paternity Proceedings.

Law Review and Journal Commentaries

Service of Process on Out-of-State Obligors, Don C. Bolsinger. 3 Domestic Rel J Ohio 1 (January/February 1991).

Notes of Decisions

Constitutional issues 1
Personal jurisdiction 3
Subject matter jurisdiction 2

---

1. Constitutional issues

An order establishing parentage is vacated and a motion for back child support is dismissed based upon the absence of due process where the conception and birth of a child takes place in a state other than Ohio and the parties never lived in a marital relationship in Ohio either before or after the child's birth. State ex rel. Wayne Cty. Child Support Enforcement Agency v. Tanner (Ohio App. 9 Dist., 11-07-2001) 146 Ohio App.3d 765, 768 N.E.2d 679, 2001-Ohio-1722, appeal not allowed 94 Ohio St.3d 1487, 763 N.E.2d 1185.

2. Subject matter jurisdiction

Trial court had jurisdiction to hear and determine merits of nonmarital child's request for retroactive child support against mother in parentage action, even though child was emancipated; juvenile court had jurisdiction over a parentage action, and the court could consider a claim for support after it determined parentage. Elzey v. Springer (Ohio App. 12 Dist., Fayette, 03-22-2004) No. CA2003-04-005, 2004-Ohio-1373, 2004 WL 549805, Unreported. Children Out–of–wedlock ☞ 36

Juvenile court had subject matter jurisdiction over underlying action brought by father to allocate parental rights and responsibilities and obtain legal custody of his child, and also had authority to include prospective adoptive parents as parties in underlying action. Callahan v. Court of Common Pleas of Pickaway County (Ohio App. 4 Dist., Pickaway, 09-26-2002) No. 02CA4, 2002-Ohio-5418, 2002 WL 31248607, Unreported. Child Custody ☞ 404; Child Custody ☞ 409

A final decree of adoption does not patently and unambiguously divest a juvenile court of jurisdiction to determine paternity solely for the limited purpose of allowing the putative father to establish that he is the biological father so that he can exercise his statutory rights to provide information regarding his social and medical history for placement in the child's adoption records. State ex rel. Furnas v. Monnin (Ohio, 10-30-2008) 120 Ohio St.3d 279, 898 N.E.2d 573, 2008-Ohio-5569. Adoption ☞ 14

Primary jurisdiction over issue of paternity of child with whom mother had been pregnant at time of her divorce was properly exercised in juvenile court, in which child, through his mother, exercised his separate right to bring paternity action against putative father. Nwabara v. Willacy (Ohio App. 8 Dist., 08-09-1999) 135 Ohio App.3d 120, 733 N.E.2d 267, dismissed, appeal not allowed 87 Ohio St.3d 1451, 719 N.E.2d 967. Children Out–of–wedlock ☞ 36

Following entry of divorce decree, domestic relations court did not have original or continuing jurisdiction to consider issue of paternity raised by former wife's child, who was born after the divorce. Fitzpatrick v. Fitzpatrick (Ohio App. 12 Dist., 03-02-1998) 126 Ohio App.3d 476, 710 N.E.2d 778, dismissed, appeal not allowed 82 Ohio St.3d 1441, 695 N.E.2d 264. Children Out–of–wedlock ☞ 36

Domestic relations courts have original jurisdiction to consider parentage issues during pendency of divorce, dissolution, or legal separation actions. Leguillon v. Leguillon (Ohio App. 12 Dist., 01-12-1998) 124 Ohio App.3d 757, 707 N.E.2d 571. Children Out–of–wedlock ☞ 36

Juvenile division had jurisdiction over child's paternity action filed after mother's paternity action was dismissed with prejudice by general division and before alleged father filed motion to reopen the action in the general division. Payne v. Cartee

(Ohio App. 4 Dist., 06-10-1996) 111 Ohio App.3d 580, 676 N.E.2d 946, appeal not allowed 77 Ohio St.3d 1482, 673 N.E.2d 143. Children Out–of–wedlock ☞ 36

General division of Common Pleas Court exhausted its exclusive jurisdiction over paternity action by dismissing action with prejudice, and, therefore, juvenile division had concurrent jurisdiction over child's later filed paternity action against same alleged father. Payne v. Cartee (Ohio App. 4 Dist., 06-10-1996) 111 Ohio App.3d 580, 676 N.E.2d 946, appeal not allowed 77 Ohio St.3d 1482, 673 N.E.2d 143. Courts ☞ 50

Juvenile courts have original jurisdiction over parentage actions. State ex rel. Willacy v. Smith (Ohio, 03-19-1997) 78 Ohio St.3d 47, 676 N.E.2d 109, 1997-Ohio-244. Children Out–of–wedlock ☞ 36

Postjudgment appeal was adequate remedy at law in juvenile court parentage action, precluding putative father from challenging juvenile court's exercise of subject matter jurisdiction by seeking writ of prohibition or mandamus, absent patent and unambiguous lack of jurisdiction, despite numerous interlocutory orders and alleged absence of mechanism to guarantee reimbursement of putative father's temporary child support payments. State ex rel. Willacy v. Smith (Ohio, 03-19-1997) 78 Ohio St.3d 47, 676 N.E.2d 109, 1997-Ohio-244. Mandamus ☞ 4(4); Prohibition ☞ 3(3)

Jurisdiction was not patently and unambiguously lacking in juvenile court parentage action brought by natural mother against child's putative father, barring putative father's mandamus and prohibition action challenging juvenile court's subject matter jurisdiction, although mother was married to another man at time child was born; mother's complaint sufficiently alleged that child was born out of wedlock by stating that his conception and birth resulted from her affair with putative father, giving juvenile court basic statutory jurisdiction to proceed. State ex rel. Willacy v. Smith (Ohio, 03-19-1997) 78 Ohio St.3d 47, 676 N.E.2d 109, 1997-Ohio-244. Mandamus ☞ 31; Prohibition ☞ 5(3)

Where divorce action is no longer pending, domestic relations court does not have necessary jurisdiction to hear paternity action. State ex rel. Smith v. Smith (Ohio App. 8 Dist., 04-08-1996) 110 Ohio App.3d 336, 674 N.E.2d 398, appeal not allowed 76 Ohio St.3d 1496, 670 N.E.2d 243. Children Out–of–wedlock ☞ 36; Courts ☞ 475(15)

Paternity action brought by state after final judgment was entered in mother's divorce action was required to be brought in Juvenile Court, rather than in Domestic Relations Division of the common pleas court. State ex rel. Smith v. Smith (Ohio App. 8 Dist., 04-08-1996) 110 Ohio App.3d 336, 674 N.E.2d 398, appeal not allowed 76 Ohio St.3d 1496, 670 N.E.2d 243. Courts ☞ 475(15)

Court of common pleas has jurisdiction to determine paternity of child born out of wedlock in conjunction with wrongful death claim; juvenile court's jurisdiction over such issues is not exclusive.

Brookbank v. Gray (Ohio, 01-17-1996) 74 Ohio St.3d 279, 658 N.E.2d 724, 1996-Ohio-135. Children Out–of–wedlock ☞ 36; Courts ☞ 472.1

Legal custodians of child, who obtained custody from child's mother, were in privity with mother, and so were barred by res judicata from litigating issue of paternity of child that had been decided in divorce decree. Broxterman v. Broxterman (Ohio App. 1 Dist., 03-15-1995) 101 Ohio App.3d 661, 656 N.E.2d 394. Children Out–of–wedlock ☞ 33; Divorce ☞ 172

Although divorce action was completed, jurisdiction over paternity action that was brought as post-decree motion was proper in Court of Domestic Relations, not solely in Juvenile Court, since other postdecree matters were still pending. Broxterman v. Broxterman (Ohio App. 1 Dist., 03-15-1995) 101 Ohio App.3d 661, 656 N.E.2d 394. Courts ☞ 475(15)

When divorce action is pending between the putative parents of child, court considering that action has original jurisdiction to determine whether parent-child relationship exists between a party and the child; however, divorce action is not subject to statutory genetic testing mandates until jurisdiction of the court to determine paternity is invoked by pleadings which put existence or nonexistence of father-child relationship in issue. McClure v. McClure (Ohio App. 2 Dist., 10-05-1994) 98 Ohio App.3d 27, 647 N.E.2d 832, appeal not allowed 71 Ohio St.3d 1481, 645 N.E.2d 1260. Divorce ☞ 59; Divorce ☞ 86; Divorce ☞ 108

Juvenile court, in determining paternity, had jurisdiction to decide state's action for aid furnished by state for support and medical expenses of children born out-of-wedlock. Brightwell v. Easter (Ohio App. 9 Dist., 03-09-1994) 93 Ohio App.3d 425, 638 N.E.2d 1067. Social Security And Public Welfare ☞ 194.19

Trial court did not have jurisdiction, after filing of appeal, to modify qualified domestic relations order (QDRO) in paternity action to take into account tax consequences that had not been previously considered; trial court modified judgment on appeal by changing amount of judgment, and, thus, interfered with Court of Appeals' ability to affirm, modify or reverse judgment on appeal. Albertson v. Ryder (Lake 1993) 85 Ohio App.3d 765, 621 N.E.2d 480. Children Out–of–wedlock ☞ 73

Trial court had subject matter jurisdiction to award child support retroactive to child's date of birth in paternity proceeding brought more than 20 years after child was born. Park v. Ambrose (Ross 1993) 85 Ohio App.3d 179, 619 N.E.2d 469, dismissed, jurisdictional motion overruled 67 Ohio St.3d 1409, 615 N.E.2d 1043. Children Out–of–wedlock ☞ 38; Children Out–of–wedlock ☞ 67

Both general division of Court of Common Pleas, in dissolution action, and juvenile division, in paternity action, have authority to decide paternity issue. LaBonte v. LaBonte (Meigs 1988) 61 Ohio App.3d

209, 572 N.E.2d 704, motion overruled 42 Ohio St.3d 709, 538 N.E.2d 122. Courts ☜ 50

A probate judge in common pleas court has no subject matter jurisdiction to determine paternity as an ancillary claim to heirship against the estate of his alleged father. Martin v. Davidson (Ohio 1990) 53 Ohio St.3d 240, 559 N.E.2d 1348. Children Out–of–wedlock ☜ 33

A plaintiff claiming to be the natural father of a child born to a woman while she was married to another man may assert that claim in an action brought pursuant to the Uniform Parentage Act, RC Ch 3111, even though the child was determined to be the issue of the marriage during an earlier divorce suit in which the plaintiff was not a party, and the juvenile court has jurisdiction over the plaintiff's claim. Gatt v. Gedeon (Cuyahoga 1984) 20 Ohio App.3d 285, 485 N.E.2d 1059, 20 O.B.R. 376.

A juvenile court's original jurisdiction over parentage actions does not exclude the jurisdiction of a court of common pleas. Standifer v. Arwood (Warren 1984) 17 Ohio App.3d 241, 479 N.E.2d 304, 17 O.B.R. 508.

A domestic relations court is the proper forum to determine matters of paternity during the pendency of a divorce action. Roebuck v Roebuck, No. 54986 (8th Dist Ct App, Cuyahoga, 2–2–89).

3. Personal jurisdiction

Common pleas court was not entitled to exercise personal jurisdiction over putative father in paternity action, pursuant to statute providing that person who had sexual intercourse in state submitted to jurisdiction of court as to action brought, with respect to child who may have been conceived, where child was not conceived in state. State ex rel. Wayne Cty. Child Support Enforcement Agency v. Tanner (Ohio App. 9 Dist., 11-07-2001) 146 Ohio App.3d 765, 768 N.E.2d 679, 2001-Ohio-1722, appeal not allowed 94 Ohio St.3d 1487, 763 N.E.2d 1185. Children Out–of–wedlock ☜ 36

Ohio courts did not have long-arm jurisdiction over putative father in paternity case; mother acknowledged that conception had occurred in Texas, and putative father had never entered state or had any contacts with Ohio. Gaisford v. Swanson

(Paulding 1992) 83 Ohio App.3d 457, 615 N.E.2d 266. Children Out–of–wedlock ☜ 36

Insufficient contacts with Ohio are present to confer personal jurisdiction over a defendant in an Ohio court in a paternity action where the child was not conceived in Ohio and the parties did not live in a marital relationship in Ohio, although the defendant transported the mother to Ohio prior to the child's birth, visited the mother and child in Ohio, and sent support payments to Ohio. Massey–Norton v. Trammel (Franklin 1989) 61 Ohio App.3d 394, 572 N.E.2d 821, dismissed 44 Ohio St.3d 714, 542 N.E.2d 1110.

Where paternity proceedings are instituted by a plaintiff who claims to be the biological father of an illegitimate child, the mother's claim that she did not consent to sexual intercourse at the time the child was conceived is irrelevant to obtaining personal jurisdiction over her under RC 3111.06. Van Pham v. Redle (Summit 1985) 29 Ohio App.3d 213, 504 N.E.2d 1147, 29 O.B.R. 258.

Court rejected state's argument that failure to support an illegitimate child constitutes a tortious act which would extend personal jurisdiction over a nonresident defendant in a parental action when the defendant had never been in Ohio. State ex rel. Stone v. Court of Common Pleas of Cuyahoga County, Juvenile Div. (Ohio 1984) 14 Ohio St.3d 32, 470 N.E.2d 899, 14 O.B.R. 333.

A bastardy action may be brought against an Ohio defendant by a woman who is not a resident of Ohio. (Annotation from former RC 3111.01.) Smith v. Smith (Ohio Com.Pl. 1965) 11 Ohio Misc. 25, 224 N.E.2d 925, 40 O.O.2d 136.

A bastardy proceeding can be maintained against an Ohio resident notwithstanding that the child was conceived and born in another state and that the mother and child were never residents of Ohio, regardless of the laws of the other state. (Annotation from former RC 3111.08.) Yuin v. Hilton (Ohio 1956) 165 Ohio St. 164, 134 N.E.2d 719, 59 O.O. 219.

Refusing or failing to pay necessary monetary support for dependent, minor children is a tortious "act or omission in this state" sufficient to create a basis for in personam jurisdiction under Civ R 4.3(A)(3). Upole v Caldwell, No. WD–84–23 (6th Dist Ct App, Wood, 9–14–84).

3111.07 Necessary parties; intervenors

(A) The natural mother, each man presumed to be the father under section 3111.03 of the Revised Code, and each man alleged to be the natural father shall be made parties to the action brought pursuant to sections 3111.01 to 3111.18 of the Revised Code or, if not subject to the jurisdiction of the court, shall be given notice of the action pursuant to the Rules of Civil Procedure and shall be given an opportunity to be heard. The child support enforcement agency of the county in which the action is brought also shall be given notice of the action pursuant to the Rules of Civil Procedure and shall be given an opportunity to be heard. The court may align the parties. The child shall be made a party to the action unless a party shows good cause for not doing so. Separate counsel shall be appointed for the child if the court finds that the child's interests conflict with those of the mother.

If the person bringing the action knows that a particular man is not or, based upon the facts and circumstances present, could not be the natural father of the child, the person bringing the action shall not allege in the action that the man is the natural father of the child and shall not make the man a party to the action.

(B) If an action is brought pursuant to sections 3111.01 to 3111.18 of the Revised Code and the child to whom the action pertains is or was being provided support by the department of job and family services, a county department of job and family services, or another public agency, the department, county department, or agency may intervene for purposes of collecting or recovering the support.

(2006 H 136, eff. 5–17–06; 2000 S 180, eff. 3–22–01; 1999 H 471, eff. 7–1–00; 1997 H 352, eff. 1–1–98; 1992 S 10, eff. 7–15–92; 1990 H 591; 1986 H 428, H 476; 1982 H 245)

Uncodified Law

1992 S 10, § 5: See Uncodified Law under 3111.01.

1982 H 245, § 3: See Uncodified Law under 3111.04.

Historical and Statutory Notes

Ed. Note: Former 3111.07 repealed by 1982 H 245, eff. 6–29–82; 127 v 1039; 125 v 184; 1953 H 1; GC 8006–7; Source—GC 12114; see now 3111.19 for provisions analogous to former 3111.07.

Pre–1953 H 1 Amendments: 124 v S 65

Amendment Note: 2006 H 136 rewrote the first paragraph of division (A) which prior thereto read:

"(A) The natural mother, each man presumed to be the father under section 3111.03 of the Revised Code, each man alleged to be the natural father, and, if the party who initiates the action is a recipient of public assistance as defined in section 3111.04 of the Revised Code or if the responsibility for the collection of support for the child who is the subject of the action has been assumed by the child support enforcement agency under Title IV–D of the "Social Security Act," 88 Stat. 2351 (1975), 42 U.S.C.A. 651, as amended, the child support enforcement agency of the county in which the child resides shall be made parties to the action brought pursuant to sections 3111.01 to 3111.18 of the Revised Code or, if not subject to the jurisdiction of the court, shall be given notice of the action pursuant to the Rules of Civil Procedure and shall be given an opportunity to be heard. The court may align the parties. The child shall be made a party to the action unless a party shows good cause for not doing so. Separate counsel shall be appointed for the child if the court finds that the child's interests conflict with those of the mother."

Amendment Note: 2000 S 180 substituted "3111.18" for "3111.19" in divisions (A) and (B).

Amendment Note: 1999 H 471 substituted "job and family" for "human" twice in division (B).

Amendment Note: 1997 H 352 substituted "3111.04" for "2301.351" in the first paragraph in division (A).

Cross References

Compulsory joinder, Civ R 19.1
Guardian of the person or the estate, see 2111.06
Guardians ad litem, see 2151.281

Juvenile court proceedings, right to counsel, guardian ad litem, Juv R 4
Service of process, Civ R 4 to 4.6

Library References

Children Out-of-Wedlock ⟰30, 34.
Westlaw Topic No. 76H.

C.J.S. Children Out-of-Wedlock §§ 47, 50, 71, 88 to 97.

Research References

ALR Library

86 ALR 5th 637, Right of Illegitimate Child to Maintain Action to Determine Paternity.

Encyclopedias

OH Jur. 3d Family Law § 953, Necessary Parties.
OH Jur. 3d Family Law § 954, Intervenors.

Forms

Ohio Jurisprudence Pleading and Practice Forms § 111:5, Standing--Parties.

Treatises and Practice Aids

Sowald & Morganstern, Baldwin's Ohio Practice Domestic Relations Law § 22:4, Establishing Parentage.
Sowald & Morganstern, Baldwin's Ohio Practice Domestic Relations Law § 3:10, Judicial Parentage Action--Parties.
Sowald & Morganstern, Baldwin's Ohio Practice Domestic Relations Law § 3:32, Right to Counsel.
Sowald & Morganstern, Baldwin's Ohio Practice Domestic Relations Law § 3:43, Effect of Judgment--Compromise Settlements.

Sowald & Morganstern, Baldwin's Ohio Practice Domestic Relations Law § 3:54, Complaint to Establish Father-Child Relationship--By Grandparent, With Request for Support--Form.

Sowald & Morganstern, Baldwin's Ohio Practice Domestic Relations Law § 22:24, Role of CSEA Attorneys and Party Status of CSEA.

Carlin, Baldwin's Ohio Prac. Merrick-Rippner Probate Law § 19:4, Legitimation--Historical Provisions.

Carlin, Baldwin's Ohio Prac. Merrick-Rippner Probate Law § 19:6, Uniform Parentage Act--Jurisdiction of Action to Determine Father-Child Relationship.

Carlin, Baldwin's Ohio Prac. Merrick-Rippner Probate Law § 19:8, Uniform Parentage Act--Support Order.

Carlin, Baldwin's Ohio Prac. Merrick-Rippner Probate Law § 19:10, Uniform Parentage Act--Procedure in Action to Determine Father-Child Relationship.

Carlin, Baldwin's Ohio Prac. Merrick-Rippner Probate Law § 99:49, Interlocutory and Final Orders.

Carlin, Baldwin's Ohio Prac. Merrick-Rippner Probate Law § 109:45, Adjudicatory Hearings--Parties' Right to Counsel.

Carlin, Baldwin's Ohio Prac. Merrick-Rippner Probate Law § 110:23, Parentage Act--Parties in Parentage Action.

Carlin, Baldwin's Ohio Prac. Merrick-Rippner Probate Law § 110:25, Parentage Act--Right to Counsel for Indigent Paternity Defendant.

Notes of Decisions

Adoptive parents 5
Agency as a party 4
Alleged father as defendant 2
Child as a party 1
Intervenor 3

---

1. Child as a party

Failure to name child as a party in proceeding in which claimant challenged administrative order establishing nonexistence of parent-child relationship and sought to establish parent-child relationship between himself and child resulted in harmless error; even if child was named a party to action, appointment of counsel would not have been required. E.B. v. T.J. (Ohio App. 8 Dist., Cuyahoga, 02-02-2006) No. 86399, 2006-Ohio-441, 2006 WL 242507, Unreported, appeal not allowed 109 Ohio St.3d 1507, 849 N.E.2d 1028, 2006-Ohio-2998, reconsideration denied 110 Ohio St.3d 1468, 852 N.E.2d 1216, 2006-Ohio-4288, certiorari denied 127 S.Ct. 1266, 549 U.S. 1215, 167 L.Ed.2d 91. Children Out–of–wedlock ☞ 73

Failure to name child as a party was fault of claimant, rather than trial court, in proceeding in which claimant challenged administrative order establishing nonexistence of parent-child relationship and sought to establish parent-child relationship between himself and child; although child was subject of proceeding and was required to be named as a party, claimant filed complaint and neither named nor served child with complaint. E.B. v. T.J. (Ohio App. 8 Dist., Cuyahoga, 02-02-2006) No. 86399, 2006-Ohio-441, 2006 WL 242507, Unreported, appeal not allowed 109 Ohio St.3d 1507, 849 N.E.2d 1028, 2006-Ohio-2998, reconsideration denied 110 Ohio St.3d 1468, 852 N.E.2d 1216, 2006-Ohio-4288, certiorari denied 127 S.Ct. 1266, 549 U.S. 1215, 167 L.Ed.2d 91. Children Out–of–wedlock ☞ 41

Any error was harmless as to trial court's failure to name child as party to paternity and child support action and its failure to appoint counsel for child, where child's interest did not appear to conflict with mother's interests. Still v. Hayman (Ohio App. 7 Dist., 07-30-2003) 153 Ohio App.3d 487, 794

N.E.2d 751, 2003-Ohio-4113. Child Support ☞ 558(1); Children Out–of–wedlock ☞ 72.1

Child's interests conflicted with the interests of her mother, and trial court's failure to appoint separate counsel for child in adjudicated father's proceedings to terminate the parent-child relationship, child support, and child support arrears, based on contention that genetic testing established he was not child's father, was reversible error, where mother repeatedly failed to appear for scheduled hearings, and, through counsel, waived her right to child support arrears; child's best interests were not automatically served by severing parent-child relationship just because parent and child were mistaken about their joint genetic heritage. Boggs v. Brnjic (Ohio App. 8 Dist., 05-08-2003) 153 Ohio App.3d 399, 794 N.E.2d 684, 2003-Ohio-2318. Child Support ☞ 491; Child Support ☞ 558(4); Children Out–of–wedlock ☞ 57; Children Out–of–wedlock ☞ 73

The purpose of a paternity proceeding under RC Ch 3111 is to provide a remedy for the unmarried mother of a minor child born out of wedlock, and the action may be commenced only by the unmarried mother or her legal representative; the child born out of wedlock is not a party to such action. Johnson v. Norman (Ohio 1981) 66 Ohio St.2d 186, 421 N.E.2d 124, 20 O.O.3d 196.

A child born out of wedlock may not bring a paternity proceeding under RC Ch 3111, but such child does have the same common-law right to bring a civil action against his father for support and maintenance as does a legitimate child, incident to which the court shall make a determination on the issue of paternity, and so the unmarried mother's dismissal of her action under RC Ch 3111 with prejudice is not a bar to the minor child's separate common-law action for support and maintenance from his putative father. Johnson v. Norman (Ohio 1981) 66 Ohio St.2d 186, 421 N.E.2d 124, 20 O.O.3d 196.

Bastardy proceedings are governed by the procedure provided for the trial of civil cases, and an action brought by a minor must comply with RC

2307.11. Taylor v. Scott (Ohio 1959) 168 Ohio St. 391, 155 N.E.2d 884, 7 O.O.2d 243.

A compromise agreement establishing paternity and child support entered pursuant to former RC 3111.07 is dispositive between the mother and father only and does not bar a support modification action brought on behalf of the child; as the child's action is not barred, use of RC 3113.215 in the modification proceeding is proper. Carpenter v Digman, No. 91–CA–4 (5th Dist Ct App, Knox, 7–22–91).

2. Alleged father as defendant

Statutory presumption of paternity of child conceived in wedlock but born after parents' divorce did not apply, and mother's former husband was not required to be joined as party defendant in parentage action, where trial court expressly stated by interlineation in decree of divorce that mother was pregnant and that former husband was not child's father. Nwabara v. Willacy (Ohio App. 8 Dist., 08-09-1999) 135 Ohio App.3d 120, 733 N.E.2d 267, dismissed, appeal not allowed 87 Ohio St.3d 1451, 719 N.E.2d 967. Children Out–of–wedlock ⟜ 3; Children Out–of–wedlock ⟜ 35

Jury instructions as to presumption of paternity with respect to child born within 300 days of divorce decree and as to requirement that mother's former husband be joined as party defendant by virtue of such presumption were not warranted in parentage action, where divorce court's finding that mother's former husband was not child's father, supported by clear and convincing evidence, was res judicata on issue of former husband's presumed paternity. Nwabara v. Willacy (Ohio App. 8 Dist., 08-09-1999) 135 Ohio App.3d 120, 733 N.E.2d 267, dismissed, appeal not allowed 87 Ohio St.3d 1451, 719 N.E.2d 967. Children Out–of–wedlock ⟜ 60

Jurisdiction was not patently and unambiguously lacking in juvenile court parentage action brought by natural mother against child's putative father, barring putative father's mandamus and prohibition action challenging juvenile court's subject matter jurisdiction, although mother was married to another man at time child was born; mother's complaint sufficiently alleged that child was born out of wedlock by stating that his conception and birth resulted from her affair with putative father, giving juvenile court basic statutory jurisdiction to proceed. State ex rel. Willacy v. Smith (Ohio, 03-19-1997) 78 Ohio St.3d 47, 676 N.E.2d 109, 1997-Ohio-244. Mandamus ⟜ 31; Prohibition ⟜ 5(3)

In action to establish parent and child relationship, only proper parties are natural mother, presumed father, and alleged natural father. Vance v. Banks (Cuyahoga 1994) 94 Ohio App.3d 475, 640 N.E.2d 1214, appeal not allowed 70 Ohio St.3d 1447, 639 N.E.2d 115, certiorari denied 115 S.Ct. 1144, 513 U.S. 1170, 130 L.Ed.2d 1103. Children Out–of–wedlock ⟜ 30; Children Out–of–wedlock ⟜ 34

A woman who is unmarried (not having a lawful husband) and pregnant may, under the statute, institute a bastardy proceeding charging another than her former husband with being the father of the child, even though child was conceived during the existence of a lawful marriage. State ex rel. Walker v. Clark (Ohio 1944) 144 Ohio St. 305, 58 N.E.2d 773, 29 O.O. 450.

Where the trial court determined that a minor child was conclusively presumed to be the child of the parties who were married to each other at her birth, but neither the child nor the man alleged by the husband to be the father of the child were joined as parties, the judgment is not binding since all necessary parties were not before the court. Corder v Corder, No. CA–1591 (5th Dist Ct App, Tuscarawas, 9–13–82).

3. Intervenor

Trial court was not required to enter judgment in favor of Department of Human Services (DHS) in mother's action for determination of paternity and for back child support, where DHS was not named as party and did not intervene to recover amounts paid in public assistance to mother and child; better practice, however, would have been for DHS to intervene rather than to bring separate action. State ex rel. Donovan v. Zajac (Ohio App. 11 Dist., 01-02-1998) 125 Ohio App.3d 245, 708 N.E.2d 254, dismissed, appeal not allowed 81 Ohio St.3d 1521, 692 N.E.2d 1023. Social Security And Public Welfare ⟜ 194.19

Derivative claim for loss of parental consortium that is filed by intervening minor child can be brought against additional defendants in event that parent's case in chief has only one defendant. Coleman v. Sandoz Pharmaceuticals Corp. (Ohio, 02-14-1996) 74 Ohio St.3d 492, 660 N.E.2d 424, 1996-Ohio-292. Parent And Child ⟜ 7.5

Attorney violates disciplinary rule prohibiting attorney from giving advice to person who is not represented by lawyer and whose interests may conflict with those of attorney's client by arranging for appointment of guardian ad litem for child allegedly fathered by client and arranging for guardian to sign, on behalf of child, consent judgment entry dismissing parentage action with prejudice. Disciplinary Counsel v. Rich (Ohio 1994) 69 Ohio St.3d 470, 633 N.E.2d 1114. Attorney And Client ⟜ 44(1)

Public reprimand, rather than one-year suspension, is warranted by attorney's violation of disciplinary rule prohibiting him from giving advice to person who is not represented by lawyer and whose interests may conflict with those of his client, where violation consists of arranging for appointment of guardian ad litem for child allegedly fathered by client and arranging for guardian to sign, on behalf of child, consent judgment entry dismissing parentage action with prejudice. Disciplinary Counsel v. Rich (Ohio 1994) 69 Ohio St.3d 470, 633 N.E.2d 1114. Attorney And Client ⟜ 59.8(1)

Although a proper party may intervene in an existing parentage action brought under RC 3111.04, a proper party may not bring a Civ R 60(B) motion to vacate a judgment in an action to which he was never a party. Hardman v. Chiaramonte (Summit 1987) 39 Ohio App.3d 9, 528 N.E.2d 1270.

Although a county department of human services may intervene in a parentage action for purposes of collecting or recovering support, a county department of human services does not have standing to initiate a parentage action. State ex rel Athens County Human Services Dept v Wolf, No. 1462 (4th Dist Ct App, Athens, 10-9-91).

4. Agency as a party

The child support enforcement agency is to be considered a proper party to all actions for the collection of child support and dismissal of the agency violates the constitutional guarantee of equal protection. State, Cuyahoga Child Support Enforcement Agency v. Sea ls (Ohio App. 8 Dist., Cuyahoga, 05-09-1996) No. 69249, 1996 WL 239886, Unreported.

County child support enforcement agency was entitled to participate in parentage action following admission of paternity and in absence of evidence of past child support, as agency was necessary party and adjudicated father suffered no prejudice from agency's participation. State ex rel. Donovan v. Zajac (Ohio App. 11 Dist., 01-02-1998) 125 Ohio App.3d 245, 708 N.E.2d 254, dismissed, appeal not allowed 81 Ohio St.3d 1521, 692 N.E.2d 1023. Children Out–of–wedlock ☞ 34

Trial court's dismissal of child support enforcement agency as party in five child support actions where parentage was established through administrative proceedings violated equal protection clauses of State and Federal Constitutions; statutory scheme, which permits agency to be party in support actions where parentage is established through probate court and where parents are on public assistance, but which does not specifically permit agency to be party when parentage is established through administrative proceedings, did not have rational basis, since enforcement agency can only effectuate its duty to protect best interests of child and public fisc by being joined as party in all child support enforcement actions. Cuyahoga Cty. Support Enforcement Agency v. Lozada (Ohio App. 8 Dist., 07-10-1995) 102 Ohio App.3d 442, 657 N.E.2d 372. Child Support ☞ 473; Constitutional Law ☞ 3455

5. Adoptive parents

Prospective adoptive parents were not necessary parties to putative father's paternity action; statute described the necessary parties to a paternity action as the birth mother, all presumed fathers, and the child. B.W. v. D.B.-B. (Ohio App. 6 Dist., 06-10-2011) 193 Ohio App.3d 637, 953 N.E.2d 369, 2011-Ohio-2813. Children Out–of–wedlock ☞ 34

3111.08 Civil nature of action to establish father and child relationship; judgment; default judgment

(A) An action brought pursuant to sections 3111.01 to 3111.18 of the Revised Code to declare the existence or nonexistence of the father and child relationship is a civil action and shall be governed by the Rules of Civil Procedure unless a different procedure is specifically provided by those sections.

(B) If an action is brought against a person to declare the existence or nonexistence of the father and child relationship between that person and a child and the person in his answer admits the existence or nonexistence of the father and child relationship as alleged in the action, the court shall enter judgment in accordance with section 3111.13 of the Revised Code. If the person against whom the action is brought fails to plead or otherwise defend against the action, the opposing party may make an oral or written motion for default judgment pursuant to the Rules of Civil Procedure. The court shall render a judgment by default against the person after hearing satisfactory evidence of the truth of the statements in the complaint.

(2000 S 180, eff. 3–22–01; 1994 S 355, eff. 12–9–94; 1992 S 10, eff. 7–15–92; 1990 H 591; 1986 H 476; 1982 H 245)

Uncodified Law

1994 S 355, § 5, eff. 12–9–94, reads: The provisions of this act that apply to actions brought under Chapter 3111. of the Revised Code to determine paternity apply only to actions initiated on or after the effective date of this act.

1992 S 10, § 5: See Uncodified Law under 3111.01.

1982 H 245, § 3: See Uncodified Law under 3111.04.

Historical and Statutory Notes

Ed. Note: Former 3111.08 repealed by 1982 H 245, eff. 6–29–82; 1976 H 390; 127 v 1039; 1953 H 1; GC 8006–8; Source—GC 12115; see now 3111.06 for provisions analogous to former 3111.08.

Pre–1953 H 1 Amendments: 124 v S 65

Amendment Note: 2000 S 180 substituted "3111.18" for "3111.19" in division (A).

Amendment Note: 1994 S 355 rewrote division (B), which previously read:

"(B) If an action is brought against a person to declare the existence or nonexistence of the father and child relationship between that person and a child and the person in his answer admits the existence or nonexistence of the father and child relationship as alleged in the action, the court shall enter judgment in accordance with section 3111.13 of the Revised Code. If the person against whom the action is brought does not admit the existence or nonexistence of the father and child relationship, the court, upon its own motion, may order, and, upon the motion of any party to the action, shall order genetic tests to be taken in accordance with section 3111.09 of the Revised Code. If genetic tests are ordered upon the motion of a party or the court, the court shall order that the child's mother, the child, the alleged father, and any other defen-

dant submit to the genetic tests in accordance with section 3111.09 of the Revised Code. A willful failure to submit to genetic tests as ordered by the court is contempt of court. If the person against whom the action is brought does not appear personally or by counsel at a pretrial hearing scheduled under section 3111.11 of the Revised Code, the opposing party may file a written motion for default judgment against the person. The motion, along with a notice of the date and time when it is to be heard, shall be served upon the person in the same manner as is provided for service of a complaint under the Rules of Civil Procedure. The court may render a judgment by default against the person after hearing satisfactory evidence of the truth of the statements in the complaint."

Cross References

Default judgment, Civ R 55
Service of process, Civ R 4 to 4.6

Library References

Children Out-of-Wedlock ⟂30, 63.
Westlaw Topic No. 76H.

C.J.S. Children Out-of-Wedlock §§ 47, 71, 94, 96 to 97, 121 to 128.

Research References

Encyclopedias

OH Jur. 3d Family Law § 939, Civil Nature of Proceedings.
OH Jur. 3d Family Law § 955, Admissions; Default.
OH Jur. 3d Family Law § 974, Jury Trial.

Forms

Ohio Jurisprudence Pleading and Practice Forms § 111:7, Genetic Tests.
Ohio Jurisprudence Pleading and Practice Forms § 111:9, Pretrial Hearing and Trial.
Ohio Jurisprudence Pleading and Practice Forms § 111:33, Report of Referee--Set for Default Hearing.

Treatises and Practice Aids

Klein, Darling, & Terez, Baldwin's Ohio Practice Civil Practice § 1:20, Civ. R. 1(C): Exceptions--Effect of Revised Code Section Purporting to Prohibit Application of One or More Civil Rules.
Klein, Darling, & Terez, Baldwin's Ohio Practice Civil Practice § 1:88, Civ. R. 1(C)(7): All Other Special Statutory Proceedings--Matters Held to be Other Special Statutory Proceedings--Parentage Action (RC 3111.04).
Klein, Darling, & Terez, Baldwin's Ohio Practice Civil Practice § 1:97, Civ. R. 1(C)(7): All Other Special Statutory Proceedings--Revised Code Sections Purporting to Mandate Application of One or More Civil Rules.
Klein, Darling, & Terez, Baldwin's Ohio Practice Civil Practice § 1:98, Civ. R. 1(C)(7): All Other Special Statutory Proceedings--Revised Code

Sections Purporting to Prohibit Application of One or More Civil Rules.
Sowald & Morganstern, Baldwin's Ohio Practice Domestic Relations Law § 23:7, Impediments to Interstate Support Actions--Personal Jurisdiction--Ohio Civil Rules--Parentage Determinations.
Sowald & Morganstern, Baldwin's Ohio Practice Domestic Relations Law § 3:12, Judicial Parentage Action--Procedure Before Hearing.
Sowald & Morganstern, Baldwin's Ohio Practice Domestic Relations Law § 3:22, Burden of Proof and Weight of the Evidence.
Sowald & Morganstern, Baldwin's Ohio Practice Domestic Relations Law § 3:29, Resolution Without Trial.
Carlin, Baldwin's Ohio Prac. Merrick-Rippner Probate Law § 19:6, Uniform Parentage Act--Jurisdiction of Action to Determine Father-Child Relationship.
Carlin, Baldwin's Ohio Prac. Merrick-Rippner Probate Law § 19:10, Uniform Parentage Act--Procedure in Action to Determine Father-Child Relationship.
Carlin, Baldwin's Ohio Prac. Merrick-Rippner Probate Law § 99:39, Consent Not Required--Noncommunication and Nonsupport.
Carlin, Baldwin's Ohio Prac. Merrick-Rippner Probate Law § 110:20, Parentage Act--Jurisdiction and Venue.
Carlin, Baldwin's Ohio Prac. Merrick-Rippner Probate Law § 110:26, Parentage Act--Applicability of Civil Rules to Paternity Proceedings.

Notes of Decisions

1. Constitutional issues

Indigent paternity defendant has a constitutional right to appointed counsel when the state is a plaintiff in a paternity action. Douglas v. Boykin (Ohio App. 12 Dist., 07-07-1997) 121 Ohio App.3d 140, 699 N.E.2d 123. Children Out–of–wedlock ☞ 57

Putative father validly waived his right to counsel at paternity hearing, despite the absence of a transcript, where magistrate made handwritten notation that putative father was advised of his right to counsel and blood testing and that he waived those rights, and putative father signed report. Douglas v. Boykin (Ohio App. 12 Dist., 07-07-1997) 121 Ohio App.3d 140, 699 N.E.2d 123. Children Out–of–wedlock ☞ 57

The requirement to submit to the withdrawal of blood to determine paternity is not susceptible to a right of privacy challenge, and as such, a court may find one who refuses to comply with such an order in contempt. McCarty v. Kimmel (Montgomery 1989) 62 Ohio App.3d 775, 577 N.E.2d 665.

The ruling that RC 3111.17 and 3111.18 are unconstitutional as a denial of the equal protection clause of the US Const Am 14 insofar as the sections provide for the imprisonment of an indigent defendant adjudged to be the reputed father of plaintiff's illegitimate child solely because of his inability to pay the award ordered by the court removed the last vestige of a criminal or quasi-criminal case from paternity proceedings. Bigsby v. Bates (Ohio Com.Pl. 1978) 59 Ohio Misc. 51, 391 N.E.2d 1384, 11 O.O.3d 262, 13 O.O.3d 260.

An agreed judgment entry which finds a defendant to be the "reputed father" of a child and orders support does not constitute a valid legal determination of paternity and does not give rise to a statutory obligation of support; therefore, an order for support without a prior valid determination of paternity must be vacated and remanded. Glass v Campbell, No. 15–92–18 (3d Dist Ct App, Van Wert, 5–27–93).

2. Construction with other laws

In an action to establish a father-child relationship where the mother, prior to her pregnancy, enlists in the United States Navy and is on active duty during the time of default proceedings which result in an order that she pay child support, the trial court fails to comply with the protections of the Soldiers' and Sailors' Civil Relief Act by allowing her attorney to withdraw prior to the default proceeding, leaving her without representation, and despite the fact that she had notice of the action, the Soldiers' and Sailors' Act affords active duty service persons entitlement to legal representation which is separate and apart from the notice issue. State ex rel Burden v Smith, No. 94APF06-877, 1994 WL 714505 (10th Dist Ct App, Franklin, 12-22-94).

An unmarried parent is subject to the support obligation to which RC 3107.07(A) refers only where a paternity determination has been rendered pursuant to RC 3111.08(B) or 3111.12. In re Adoption of Sunderhaus (Ohio 1992) 63 Ohio St.3d 127, 585 N.E.2d 418, rehearing denied 63 Ohio St.3d 1442, 589 N.E.2d 46. Adoption ☞ 7.4(6)

3. Nature of action

Adjudicated father was entitled to hearing on his motion for relief from judgment of paternity, where adjudicated father had been diagnosed as paranoid and schizophrenic and was apparently unable to file his own affidavit in support of motion, and where his mother and legal guardian submitted uncontroverted affidavit in support of motion to effect that he had never lived at address on file with post office, at which notice of proceedings was properly served. Christy L.W. v. Chazarea E.S. (Ohio App. 6 Dist., Ottawa, 01-31-2003) No. OT-02-019, 2003-Ohio-483, 2003 WL 220419, Unreported. Children Out–of–wedlock ☞ 64

Claim for support and other statutory relief from father by child born out of wedlock is separate and distinct from that of her mother. Hugershoff v. Loecy (Ohio Com.Pl., 09-28-1999) 103 Ohio Misc.2d 58, 725 N.E.2d 378. Children Out–of–wedlock ☞ 21(2)

Statute allowing parties in paternity action to enter compromise agreement subject to court approval supersedes rule allowing dismissal by stipulation without court approval. State ex rel. Fowler v. Smith (Ohio, 02-23-1994) 68 Ohio St.3d 357, 626 N.E.2d 950, 1994-Ohio-302. Children Out–of–wedlock ☞ 33

Although a parentage action brought by a natural mother takes place in a juvenile division of the common pleas court, the civil rules apply rather than the juvenile rules; thus, a motion for judgment on the pleadings under Civ R 12(C) is permissible in a parentage action. Nelson v. Pleasant (Lawrence 1991) 73 Ohio App.3d 479, 597 N.E.2d 1137.

Actions under RC 3111.01 to 3111.24 relating to paternity proceedings are, unless specified otherwise therein, governed by the Rules of Civil Procedure. Bigsby v. Bates (Ohio Com.Pl. 1978) 59 Ohio Misc. 51, 391 N.E.2d 1384, 11 O.O.3d 262, 13 O.O.3d 260. Children Out–of–wedlock ⊂⇒ 30

A bastardy action is essentially civil in nature, and the failure of the defendant in such action to testify may be the subject of comment to the jury. Smith v. Lautenslager (Hamilton 1968) 15 Ohio App.2d 212, 240 N.E.2d 109, 44 O.O.2d 371.

Bastardy proceedings are governed by the procedure provided for the trial of civil cases, and an action brought by a minor must comply with RC 2307.11. Taylor v. Scott (Ohio 1959) 168 Ohio St. 391, 155 N.E.2d 884, 7 O.O.2d 243.

While some of the procedure in a bastardy case is similar to that in a criminal case, the proceeding is a civil one. Durst v. Griffith (Hocking 1932) 43 Ohio App. 44, 182 N.E. 519, 12 Ohio Law Abs. 522, 37 Ohio Law Rep. 183.

Bastardy proceeding is quasi-criminal proceeding, but is so far civil that, where verdict of three-fourths of jurors is allowed in any civil case, it is also allowed in such proceeding, and it is not necessary to furnish proof beyond reasonable doubt, preponderance of evidence being sufficient. Schneider v. State (Cuyahoga 1929) 33 Ohio App. 125, 168 N.E. 568.

Bastardy proceeding has for its primary object fixing of sum of money to be paid by accused to complainant "for her support, maintenance, and necessary expenses caused by pregnancy and childbirth." Seldenright v. Jenkins (Ohio Prob. 1936) 3 Ohio Supp. 36, 22 Ohio Law Abs. 576, 7 O.O. 127. Children Out–of–wedlock ⊂⇒ 30

Prosecutions of complaints relating to bastardy are, unless specified otherwise therein, governed by the procedure provided for the trial of civil cases. State ex rel. Wise v. Chand (Ohio 1970) 21 Ohio St.2d 113, 256 N.E.2d 613, 50 O.O.2d 322.

4. Genetic testing

Common pleas court has inherent power to estop mother from using genetic testing to disestablish child's paternity with his or her presumed father under doctrine of laches, but there must be finding of material prejudice to invoke the doctrine. Sherburn v. Reichert (Ohio App. 3 Dist., 10-13-1994) 97 Ohio App.3d 120, 646 N.E.2d 255. Children Out–of–wedlock ⊂⇒ 45

Eligibility for genetic test in paternity action is not guaranteed, and court can find defendant has fathered child without genetic test results if defendant fails to submit to blood test. Harvey v. Mynatt (Summit 1994) 94 Ohio App.3d 619, 641 N.E.2d 291. Children Out–of–wedlock ⊂⇒ 58

Assuming that putative father's request for blood testing in letter sent to court after receiving complaint in paternity action could be considered motion for genetic test, motion was not made in timely fashion, where letter was sent to court two days after father's answer to paternity complaint was due and court did not receive letter until one week after answer was due. Harvey v. Mynatt (Summit 1994)

94 Ohio App.3d 619, 641 N.E.2d 291. Children Out–of–wedlock ⊂⇒ 58

Mother established prima facie parent-child relationship between putative father and daughter by preponderance of evidence in view of fact that genetic test disclosed 98.5% probability that he was biological father of child, that mother had sexual intercourse with putative father twice during alleged month of conception, that, although she had sexual intercourse with one other man during that month, genetic blood testing excluded him as biological father of child, and that putative father admitted under cross-examination that it was possible that he had sexual intercourse with child's mother during month of conception and they did not use any form of contraceptive. Filkins v. Cales (Logan 1993) 86 Ohio App.3d 61, 619 N.E.2d 1156, motion overruled 67 Ohio St.3d 1422, 616 N.E.2d 506. Children Out–of–wedlock ⊂⇒ 53

5. Pleadings

Father was not entitled to set aside trial court's judgment dismissing his action to establish paternity, child support, and parenting time under catch-all provision of rule of civil procedure reflecting inherent power to court to relieve person from unjust operation of judgment; although father argued court, when existence of father-child relationship was admitted in pleadings, had duty to prepare and journalize separate entry establishing existence of relationship, father, as party to action, was responsible for preparation of entries. In re Adoption of A.N.L. (Ohio App. 12 Dist., Warren, 08-16-2005) No. CA2004-11-131, No. CA2005-04-046, 2005-Ohio-4239, 2005 WL 1949678, Unreported. Children Out–of–wedlock ⊂⇒ 20.4; Children Out–of–wedlock ⊂⇒ 64

The Ohio Rules of Civil Procedure apply to parentage actions; thus, an answer must be filed by the person against whom the action is brought, and a failure to properly plead the affirmative defense of laches bars its defense at trial. Eppley v. Bratton (Ohio App. 5 Dist., Coshocton, 11-07-1994) No. 94 CA 7, 1994 WL 668111, Unreported, appeal not allowed 71 Ohio St.3d 1494, 646 N.E.2d 469.

When divorce action is pending between the putative parents of child, court considering that action has original jurisdiction to determine whether parent-child relationship exists between a party and the child; however, divorce action is not subject to statutory genetic testing mandates until jurisdiction of the court to determine paternity is invoked by pleadings which put existence or non-existence of father-child relationship in issue. McClure v. McClure (Ohio App. 2 Dist., 10-05-1994) 98 Ohio App.3d 27, 647 N.E.2d 832, appeal not allowed 71 Ohio St.3d 1481, 645 N.E.2d 1260. Divorce ⊂⇒ 59; Divorce ⊂⇒ 86; Divorce ⊂⇒ 108

6. Jurisdiction

Trial court obtained personal jurisdiction over putative father by virtue of county's properly served complaint and by virtue of putative father's answer, and, therefore, court had jurisdiction to enter default judgment against putative father despite his contention that he was never properly served with motion for default judgment. Austin v. Payne (Ohio App. 9 Dist., 12-20-1995) 107 Ohio App.3d 818, 669 N.E.2d 543. Children Out–of–wedlock ☞ 36; Children Out–of–wedlock ☞ 64

Juvenile court, in determining paternity, had jurisdiction to decide state's action for aid furnished by state for support and medical expenses of children born out-of-wedlock. Brightwell v. Easter (Ohio App. 9 Dist., 03-09-1994) 93 Ohio App.3d 425, 638 N.E.2d 1067. Social Security And Public Welfare ☞ 194.19

7. Res judicata

Prior decision of the Court of Appeals, holding that res judicata barred former husband's action seeking a determination of paternity, amounted to an "admission on file" for purposes of summary judgment in a subsequent paternity action, where trial court deemed prior appellate decision admitted as true and genuine by husband, and husband did not challenge that ruling. Donnelly v. Kashnier (Ohio App. 9 Dist., Medina, 02-12-2003) No. 02CA0051-M, 2003-Ohio-639, 2003 WL 294413, Unreported. Children Out–of–wedlock ☞ 64

Parentage action in juvenile court was not barred by application of res judicata, despite fact that mother had been pregnant with subject child at time of her divorce, where domestic relations court entered finding that mother's husband was not child's biological father but made no finding as to identity of child's biological father, and neither child nor putative father was a party to divorce action. Nwabara v. Willacy (Ohio App. 8 Dist., 08-09-1999) 135 Ohio App.3d 120, 733 N.E.2d 267, dismissed, appeal not allowed 87 Ohio St.3d 1451, 719 N.E.2d 967. Children Out–of–wedlock ☞ 33

8. Defendants

When the state acts on a paternity complaint, a court should at the outset of the case determine whether the defendant is indigent and whether counsel should be appointed in his behalf. Rees v. Heimberger (Cuyahoga 1989) 60 Ohio App.3d 45, 573 N.E.2d 189, dismissed 47 Ohio St.3d 702, 547 N.E.2d 986, rehearing denied 48 Ohio St.3d 707, 550 N.E.2d 483, certiorari denied 110 S.Ct. 1827, 494 U.S. 1088, 108 L.Ed.2d 956. Children Out–of–wedlock ☞ 57

The court of domestic relations of Franklin County has authority, under this section, to issue its warrant for the arrest of a nonresident of the county charged with being the father of a bastard child, conceived and born in another state, and to serve such warrant upon the person named therein in a sister county of the state and bring such person into Franklin County for trial. Barnett v. Boice (Franklin 1930) 37 Ohio App. 549, 175 N.E. 620, 10 Ohio Law Abs. 157.

An unmarried, pregnant woman may institute a bastardy proceeding charging one other than her former husband with being the father of the child, even though such child was conceived during the existence of a lawful marriage. State ex rel. Sprungle v. Bard (Cuyahoga 1950) 98 N.E.2d 63, 59 Ohio Law Abs. 129.

9. Parties

Although a proper party may intervene in an existing parentage action brought under RC 3111.04, a proper party may not bring a Civ R 60(B) motion to vacate a judgment in an action to which he was never a party. Hardman v. Chiaramonte (Summit 1987) 39 Ohio App.3d 9, 528 N.E.2d 1270.

The caption or title of an action or proceeding instituted by the filing of a complaint under the bastardy act and dealing with an award to the complainant should contain only the names of the complainant and accused. State ex rel. Love v. Jones (Hamilton 1953) 98 Ohio App. 45, 128 N.E.2d 228, 57 O.O. 161.

10. Presumptions and burden of proof

Mother's burden of proof in paternity action was to establish existence of parent-child relationship between putative father and daughter by preponderance of evidence. Filkins v. Cales (Logan 1993) 86 Ohio App.3d 61, 619 N.E.2d 1156, motion overruled 67 Ohio St.3d 1422, 616 N.E.2d 506. Children Out–of–wedlock ☞ 52

Paternity of a child is proven by a preponderance of the evidence where (1) evidence is introduced of sexual intercourse within the period of conception; (2) expert testimony is given concerning the probability of defendant's paternity based on genetic testing; and (3) expert testimony is given regarding the probability of defendant's paternity based on the physical characteristics and ethnic ancestry of the parties. Grove v. Mattison (Franklin 1988) 61 Ohio App.3d 252, 572 N.E.2d 731, dismissed 42 Ohio St.3d 706, 537 N.E.2d 226.

The standard of proof of paternity is a preponderance of the evidence. Domigan v. Gillette (Clark 1984) 17 Ohio App.3d 228, 479 N.E.2d 291, 17 O.B.R. 494.

To overcome the presumption that a child born during a marriage is a child of the husband, the evidence must be clear and convincing that the spouses had no sexual relations during the possible period of conception. Joseph v. Alexander (Ohio 1984) 12 Ohio St.3d 88, 465 N.E.2d 448, 12 O.B.R. 77.

In bastardy proceedings burden of proof is on defendant to prove that complainant had entered into common law marriage at time of filing of affidavit. State ex rel. Allen v. Wagoner (Trumbull 1961) 182 N.E.2d 328, 88 Ohio Law Abs. 218.

11. Sufficiency of evidence

Father fails to allege a basis for relief under Civ R 60(B) by his failure to allege fraud after blood tests showed that he could not be the child's biological father. In re Belden, No. 92 CA 21, 1993 WL 179254 (2d Dist Ct App, Miami, 5–25–93).

Juvenile court may enter judgment in paternity action upon satisfactory evidence of paternity. Lewis v. Chapin (Ohio App. 8 Dist., 03-21-1994) 93 Ohio App.3d 695, 639 N.E.2d 848 Children Out–of–wedlock ⚖ 53

12. Default judgment

Juvenile court improperly applied standard for deciding motions for relief from judgment to adjudicated father's motion for relief from default adjudication of paternity, where adjudicated father alleged that he was never properly served with process in parentage action and that judgment on complaint was thus void ab initio. Christy L.W. v. Chazarea E.S. (Ohio App. 6 Dist., Ottawa, 01-31-2003) No. OT-02-019, 2003-Ohio-483, 2003 WL 220419, Unreported. Children Out–of–wedlock ⚖ 64

Failure to inform putative father of court's intent to enter finding of paternity on his refusal to submit to genetic testing precluded finding of paternity by default, where putative father appeared before trial court for purpose of contesting paternity; adjudication was available only as sanction for willful refusal to submit to genetic testing, and not under statutory provision governing default paternity judgments. Marsh v. Clay (Ohio App. 8 Dist., 02-02-1998) 125 Ohio App.3d 518, 708 N.E.2d 1073, on subsequent appeal 2000 WL 1900333. Children Out–of–wedlock ⚖ 64

Trial court was not required to allow putative father to receive genetic test to determine if he was father of child born out of wedlock prior to entering default judgment in paternity action brought by county child support enforcement agency, despite putative father's request for blood test in letter sent to court after father received copy of paternity complaint, where letter was sent after father's answer to complaint was due, and father failed to appear and contest motion for default judgment after receipt of notice of default hearing. Harvey v. Mynatt (Summit 1994) 94 Ohio App.3d 619, 641 N.E.2d 291. Children Out–of–wedlock ⚖ 58

Defendant who was in default of answer and had failed to appear in parentage action was not entitled to notice of filing of motion for default. Long v. Bartlett (Franklin 1992) 73 Ohio App.3d 764, 598 N.E.2d 197. Children Out–of–wedlock ⚖ 64

Where no answer is filed to a complaint alleging paternity, the trial court errs in entering judgment by default without first conducting the pretrial hearing provided under RC 3111.11. Potts v Wilson, No. 409 (4th Dist Ct App, Adams, 5–30–85).

13. Summary judgement

Motion for summary judgment is available in paternity actions under statute to declare the existence or nonexistence of the father and child relationship. Sexton v. Conley (Ohio App. 4 Dist., Scioto, 11-12-2002) No. 01CA2823,

2002-Ohio-6346, 2002 WL 31630766, Unreported. Children Out–of–wedlock ⚖ 64

A motion for summary judgment may lie in paternity proceedings in juvenile court. State, Cuyahoga Child Support Enforcement Agency ex rel. Drews v. Ambrosi (Ohio App. 8 Dist., Cuyahoga, 09-03-1998) No. 73761, 1998 WL 563993, Unreported, dismissed, appeal not allowed 84 Ohio St.3d 1484, 705 N.E.2d 365, on reconsideration 85 Ohio St.3d 1428, 707 N.E.2d 517.

A person is not entitled to relief under Civ R 60(B)(2) or (5) from a judgment of paternity and child support where he signed the child's birth certificate and an administrative order indicating he was the child's biological father even though he knew he was not the biological father because the mother was two months pregnant when he began dating her, and therefore a recent DNA test result showing a 0.00 chance he was the father is not "new evidence" under Civ R 60(B)(2), the specific provision of the rule that prevails over the more general section, (B)(5); although it may appear unfair to require an individual to pay child support for a child not biologically his own, there must be some finality to a judgment and one cannot choose to be a parent and then change his or her mind when the relationship is dissolved. Shaffer v. Rusnak (Ohio App. 5 Dist., Guernsey, 07-01-1998) No. 97 CA 26, 1998 WL 429624, Unreported, dismissed, appeal not allowed 84 Ohio St.3d 1408, 701 N.E.2d 1018.

Motion for summary judgment does not lie in a paternity proceeding in juvenile court. De Salvo v. Sukalski (Geauga 1983) 8 Ohio App.3d 337, 457 N.E.2d 349, 8 O.B.R. 448. Judgment ⚖ 180

14. Appeals

An order mandating genetic testing in a parentage action is not a final appealable order as it is not determinative of the parentage action. McCarty v. Kimmel (Montgomery 1989) 62 Ohio App.3d 775, 577 N.E.2d 665. Children Out–of–wedlock ⚖ 73

15. Plain error

In a parentage action, a trial court commits plain error when it considers a document submitted by the county support enforcement agency entitled "Plaintiff's Written Interrogatories for Oral Deposition," where the document does not comprise (1) an interrogatory because it was served on a nonparty, (2) a deposition because the defendant did not receive notice as required by Civ R 31, and (3) an affidavit because the answers were not given under oath. Stilwell v. Vanmeter (Ohio App. 2 Dist., Clark, 01-24-1996) No. 95-CA-66, 1996 WL 27846, Unreported.

The trial court errs in affirming the order of parentage where the notice of the order is not properly served, thereby denying the parties the thirty days from the date of the order to object. Howard v. Heineman (Ohio App. 5 Dist., Delaware, 06-30-1995) No. 94CAF12039, 1995 WL 495483, Unreported.

3111.09   Genetic tests and DNA records

(A)(1) In any action instituted under sections 3111.01 to 3111.18 of the Revised Code, the court, upon its own motion, may order and, upon the motion of any party to the action, shall order the child's mother, the child, the alleged father, and any other person who is a defendant in the action to submit to genetic tests.   Instead of or in addition to genetic testing ordered pursuant to this section, the court may use the following information to determine the existence of a parent and child relationship between the child and the child's mother, the alleged father, or another defendant:

(a) A DNA record of the child's mother, the child, the alleged father, or any other defendant that is stored in the DNA database pursuant to section 109.573 of the Revised Code;

(b) Results of genetic tests conducted on the child, the child's mother, the alleged father, or any other defendant pursuant to former section 3111.21 or 3111.22 or sections 3111.38 to 3111.54 of the Revised Code.

If the court intends to use the information described in division (A)(1)(a) of this section, it shall order the superintendent of the bureau of criminal identification and investigation to disclose the information to the court.   If the court intends to use the genetic test results described in division (A)(1)(b) of this section, it shall order the agency that ordered the tests to provide the report of the genetic test results to the court.

(2) If the child support enforcement agency is not made a party to the action, the clerk of the court shall schedule the genetic testing no later than thirty days after the court issues its order.   If the agency is made a party to the action, the agency shall schedule the genetic testing in accordance with the rules adopted by the director of job and family services pursuant to section 3111.611 of the Revised Code.   If the alleged father of a child brings an action under sections 3111.01 to 3111.18 of the Revised Code and if the mother of the child willfully fails to submit to genetic testing or if the mother is the custodian of the child and willfully fails to submit the child to genetic testing, the court, on the motion of the alleged father, shall issue an order determining the existence of a parent and child relationship between the father and the child without genetic testing.   If the mother or other guardian or custodian of the child brings an action under sections 3111.01 to 3111.18 of the Revised Code and if the alleged father of the child willfully fails to submit himself to genetic testing or, if the alleged father is the custodian of the child and willfully fails to submit the child to genetic testing, the court shall issue an order determining the existence of a parent and child relationship between the father and the child without genetic testing.   If a party shows good cause for failing to submit to genetic testing or for failing to submit the child to genetic testing, the court shall not consider the failure to be willful.

(3) Except as provided in division (A)(4) of this section, any fees charged for the tests shall be paid by the party that requests them, unless the custodian of the child is represented by the child support enforcement agency in its role as the agency providing enforcement of child support orders under Title IV–D of the "Social Security Act," 88 Stat. 2351 (1975), 42 U.S.C. 651, as amended, the custodian is a participant in Ohio works first under Chapter 5107. of the Revised Code for the benefit of the child, or the defendant in the action is found to be indigent, in which case the child support enforcement agency shall pay the costs of genetic testing.   The child support enforcement agency, within guidelines contained in that federal law, shall use funds received pursuant to Title IV–D of the "Social Security Act," 88 Stat. 2351 (1975), 42 U.S.C. 651, as amended, to pay the fees charged for the tests.

Except as provided in division (A)(4) of this section, if there is a dispute as to who shall pay the fees charged for genetic testing, the child support enforcement agency shall pay the fees, but neither the court nor the agency shall delay genetic testing due to a dispute as to who shall pay the genetic testing fees.   The child support enforcement agency or the person who paid the fees charged for the genetic testing may seek reimbursement for the genetic testing fees from the person against whom the court assesses the costs of the action.   Any funds used in accordance with this division by the child support enforcement agency shall be in addition to any other funds that the agency is entitled to receive as a result of any contractual provision for specific funding allocations for the agency between the county, the state, and the federal government.

(4) If, pursuant to former section 3111.21 or 3111.22 or sections 3111.38 to 3111.54 of the Revised Code, the agency has previously conducted genetic tests on the child, child's mother, alleged father, or any other defendant and the current action pursuant to section 3111.01 to 3111.18 of the Revised Code has been brought to object to the result of those previous tests, the agency shall not be required to pay the fees for conducting genetic tests pursuant to this section on the same persons.

(B)(1) The genetic tests shall be made by qualified examiners who are authorized by the court or the department of job and family services. An examiner conducting a genetic test, upon the completion of the test, shall send a complete report of the test results to the clerk of the court that ordered the test or, if the agency is a party to the action, to the child support enforcement agency of the county in which the court that ordered the test is located.

(2) If a court orders the superintendent of the bureau of criminal identification and investigation to disclose information regarding a DNA record stored in the DNA database pursuant to section 109.573 of the Revised Code, the superintendent shall send the information to the clerk of the court that issued the order or, if the agency is a party to the action, to the child support enforcement agency of the county in which the court that issued the order is located.

(3) If a court orders the child support enforcement agency to provide the report of the genetic test results obtained pursuant to former section 3111.21 or 3111.22 or sections 3111.38 to 3111.54 of the Revised Code, the agency shall send the information to the person or government entity designated by the court that issued the order.

(4) The clerk, agency, or person or government entity under division (B)(3) of this section that receives a report or information pursuant to division (B)(1), (2), or (3) of this section shall mail a copy of the report or information to the attorney of record for each party or, if a party is not represented by an attorney, to the party. The clerk, agency, or person or government entity under division (B)(3) of this section that receives a copy of the report or information shall include with the report or information sent to an attorney of record of a party or a party a notice that the party may object to the admission into evidence of the report or information by filing a written objection as described in division (D) of section 3111.12 of the Revised Code with the court that ordered the tests or ordered the disclosure of the information no later than fourteen days after the report or information was mailed to the attorney of record or to the party. The examiners may be called as witnesses to testify as to their findings. Any party may demand that other qualified examiners perform independent genetic tests under order of the court. The number and qualifications of the independent examiners shall be determined by the court.

(C) Nothing in this section prevents any party to the action from producing other expert evidence on the issue covered by this section, but, if other expert witnesses are called by a party to the action, the fees of these expert witnesses shall be paid by the party calling the witnesses and only ordinary witness fees for these expert witnesses shall be taxed as costs in the action.

(D) If the court finds that the conclusions of all the examiners are that the alleged father is not the father of the child, the court shall enter judgment that the alleged father is not the father of the child. If the examiners disagree in their findings or conclusions, the court shall determine the father of the child based upon all the evidence.

(E) As used in sections 3111.01 to 3111.85 of the Revised Code:

(1) "Genetic tests" and "genetic testing" mean either of the following:

(a) Tissue or blood tests, including tests that identify the presence or absence of common blood group antigens, the red blood cell antigens, human lymphocyte antigens, serum enzymes, serum proteins, or genetic markers;

(b) Deoxyribonucleic acid typing of blood or buccal cell samples.

"Genetic test" and "genetic testing" may include the typing and comparison of deoxyribonucleic acid derived from the blood of one individual and buccal cells of another.

(2) "DNA record" and "DNA database" have the same meanings as in section 109.573 of the Revised Code.

(2000 S 180, eff. 3–22–01; 1999 H 471, eff. 7–1–00; 1997 H 352, eff. 1–1–98; 1997 H 408, eff. 10–1–97; 1996 H 357, eff. 9–19–96; 1995 H 5, eff. 8–30–95; 1994 S 355, eff. 12–9–94; 1992 S 10, eff. 7–15–92; 1990 H 591; 1988 H 708; 1987 H 231; 1986 H 476; 1982 H 245)

Uncodified Law

1994 S 355, § 5: See Uncodified Law under 3111.08.

1992 S 10, § 5: See Uncodified Law under 3111.01.

1982 H 245, § 3: See Uncodified Law under 3111.04.

Historical and Statutory Notes

Ed. Note: RC 3111.09 contains provisions analogous to former RC 3111.16, repealed by 1982 H 245, eff. 6–29–82.

Ed. Note: Former RC 3111.09 repealed by 1982 H 245, eff. 6–29–82; 1953 H 1; GC 8006–9; Source—GC 12116.

Pre–1953 H 1 Amendments: 124 v S 65

Amendment Note: 2000 S 180 substituted "3111.18" for "3111.19" once in division (A)(1), twice in division (A)(2), and once in division (A)(4); inserted "or sections 3111.38 to 3111.54" in division (A)(1)(b), (A)(4), and (B)(3); substituted "3111.611" for "2301.35" in division (A)(2); substituted "3111.85" for "3111.29" in division (E); and made other nonsubstantive changes.

Amendment Note: 1999 H 471 substituted "director of job and family services" for "department of human services" in division (A)(2); and substituted "job and family" for "human" in division (B)(1).

Amendment Note: 1997 H 352 split division (A) into paragraphs; designated division (A)(1) and rewrote that division; designated division (A)(2) and inserted "on the motion of the alleged father" therein; designated division (A)(3) and inserted "Except as provided in division (A)(4) of this section," at the beginning thereof; added division (A)(4) and new division (B)(3); redesignated former division (B)(3) as new division (B)(4) and inserted "or person or government entity under division (B) of this section" twice and ", (2), or (3)" therein; deleted "or jury" before "shall determine"

in division (D); and made other nonsubstantive changes.

Amendment Note: 1997 H 408 split the paragraphs in division (A); and substituted "participant in Ohio works first" for "recipient of aid to dependent children" in the second paragraph in division (A).

Amendment Note: 1996 H 357 substituted "either of the following" for "a series of serological" in division (E)(1); designated and rewrote division (E)(1)(a); and added division (E)(1)(b) and the final paragraph in division (E)(1). Prior to amendment, the provisions now contained in division (E)(1)(a) read "tests, that are either immunological or biochemical or both immunological and biochemical in nature, and that are specifically selected because of their known genetic transmittance. 'Genetic tests' and 'genetic testing' include, but are not limited to, tests for the presence or absence of the common blood group antigens, the red blood cell antigens, human lymphocyte antigens, serum enzymes, and serum proteins and for the comparison of the deoxyribonucleic acid."

Amendment Note: 1995 H 5 added the third sentence in division (A); designated division (B)(1); added division (B)(2); designated division (B)(3); added all references to DNA record information and deleted "(1)" after "(D)" in the second sentence in division (B)(3); designated division (E)(1); added division (E)(2); and made other nonsubstantive changes.

Amendment Note: 1994 S 355 added the second through the fourth sentence in division (D).

Cross References

Hearsay exceptions, records of vital statistics, Evid
  R 803
Testimony by experts, Evid R 702

Ohio Administrative Code References

Court order for genetic testing, see OAC
  5101:12–40–25

Reimbursement for cost of genetic testing, see
  OAC 5101:12–40–36

Library References

Children Out-of-Wedlock ⊜45, 58.
Westlaw Topic No. 76H.
C.J.S. Children Out-of-Wedlock §§ 76 to 79.

Research References

ALR Library

77 ALR 5th 201, Authentication of Blood Sample Taken from Human Body for Purposes Other Than Determining Blood Alcohol Content.

Encyclopedias

OH Jur. 3d Criminal Law: Substantive Principles and Offenses § 165, Dna Laboratory and Database.

OH Jur. 3d Family Law § 945, Rebuttal of Presumption.

OH Jur. 3d Family Law § 952, Jurisdiction.

OH Jur. 3d Family Law § 958, Retroactivity of Statute.

OH Jur. 3d Family Law § 961, Who Must Pay.

OH Jur. 3d Family Law § 962, Who May Perform.

OH Jur. 3d Family Law § 963, Use of Results.

Forms

Ohio Jurisprudence Pleading and Practice Forms § 41:6, Scope and Manner of Examination--Blood Tests.

Ohio Jurisprudence Pleading and Practice Forms § 60:4, Admissibility.

Ohio Jurisprudence Pleading and Practice Forms § 111:2, Definitions.

Ohio Jurisprudence Pleading and Practice Forms § 111:7, Genetic Tests.

Ohio Jurisprudence Pleading and Practice Forms § 111:9, Pretrial Hearing and Trial.

Ohio Jurisprudence Pleading and Practice Forms § 111:22, Genetic Testing.

Ohio Jurisprudence Pleading and Practice Forms § 111:30, Report of Referee--Genetic Testing.

Treatises and Practice Aids

Sowald & Morganstern, Baldwin's Ohio Practice Domestic Relations Law § 22:4, Establishing Parentage.

Sowald & Morganstern, Baldwin's Ohio Practice Domestic Relations Law § 3:17, Evidence--Genetic Tests--Background.

Sowald & Morganstern, Baldwin's Ohio Practice Domestic Relations Law § 3:18, Evidence--Genetic Tests--Testing Procedure.

Sowald & Morganstern, Baldwin's Ohio Practice Domestic Relations Law § 3:19, Evidence--Genetic Tests--Results of Test.

Sowald & Morganstern, Baldwin's Ohio Practice Domestic Relations Law § 3:20, Evidence--Genetic Tests--Costs of Testing.

Sowald & Morganstern, Baldwin's Ohio Practice Domestic Relations Law § 3:22, Burden of Proof and Weight of the Evidence.

Sowald & Morganstern, Baldwin's Ohio Practice Domestic Relations Law § 3:30, Res Judicata and Vacation of Parentage Orders.

Sowald & Morganstern, Baldwin's Ohio Practice Domestic Relations Law § 3:45, Effect of Judgment--Retrospective Effect.

Carlin, Baldwin's Ohio Prac. Merrick-Rippner Probate Law § 18:2, Inheritance Rights of Illegitimate Child--Statutory Provisions.

Carlin, Baldwin's Ohio Prac. Merrick-Rippner Probate Law § 19:6, Uniform Parentage Act--Jurisdiction of Action to Determine Father-Child Relationship.

Carlin, Baldwin's Ohio Prac. Merrick-Rippner Probate Law § 19:7, Uniform Parentage Act--Presumptions.

Carlin, Baldwin's Ohio Prac. Merrick-Rippner Probate Law § 19:9, Uniform Parentage Act--Res Judicata; Doctrine of Laches.

Carlin, Baldwin's Ohio Prac. Merrick-Rippner Probate Law § 108:5, Juvenile Court Jurisdiction--Delinquent Child--Dna Testing of Certain Delinquent Children.

Carlin, Baldwin's Ohio Prac. Merrick-Rippner Probate Law § 19:10, Uniform Parentage Act--Procedure in Action to Determine Father-Child Relationship.

Carlin, Baldwin's Ohio Prac. Merrick-Rippner Probate Law § 110:19, Parentage Act--Effect.

Carlin, Baldwin's Ohio Prac. Merrick-Rippner Probate Law § 110:22, Parentage Act--Presumption of Paternity.

Carlin, Baldwin's Ohio Prac. Merrick-Rippner Probate Law § 110:24, Parentage Act--Genetic Tests, Fees, and Costs.

Carlin, Baldwin's Ohio Prac. Merrick-Rippner Probate Law § 110:26, Parentage Act--Applicability of Civil Rules to Paternity Proceedings.

Carlin, Baldwin's Ohio Prac. Merrick-Rippner Probate Law § 110:27, Parentage Act--Evidence of Paternity.

Carlin, Baldwin's Ohio Prac. Merrick-Rippner Probate Law § 110:28, Parentage Act--Trial of Parentage Action.

Restatement (3d) Property (Wills & Don. Trans.) § 2.5, Parent and Child Relationship.

Law Review and Journal Commentaries

DNA Data Banking: The Dangerous Erosion Of Privacy, E. Donald Shapiro and Michele L. Weinberg. 38 Clev St L Rev 455 (1990).

DNA Database Statutes & Privacy in the Information Age, Note. 10 Health Matrix: J Law-Medicine 119 (Winter 2000).

DNA Identification Testing: Assessing The Threat To Privacy, Dan L. Burke. 24 U Tol L Rev 87 (Fall 1992).

The DNA Paternity Test: Legislating the Future Paternity Action, E. Donald Shapiro, Stewart Reifler, Claudia L. Psome. 7 J L & Health 1 (1992–93).

An Interpretation of Ohio Law on Maternal Status in Gestational Surrogacy Disputes: Belsito v. Clark, Note. 21 U Dayton L Rev 229 (Fall 1995).

A Layman's Guide to the Use of Blood Group Analysis in Paternity Testing, E. G. Reisner and T. A. Bolk. 20 J Fam L 657 (1981–82).

Patenting of Human DNA Sequences—Implications for Prenatal Genetic Testing, Note. 36 J Fam L 267 (1997–98).

A Surrogacy Agreement that Could Have and Should Have Been Enforced: *R.R. v. M.H.*, 689 N.E.2d 790 (Mass. 1998), Note. 24 U Dayton L Rev 513 (Spring 1999).

Uniform Parentage Act: Ohio Recognizes Genetic Testing's Validity To Rebut The Presumption That The Natural Mother's Husband Is Not The Father—Hulett v. Hulett, 45 Ohio St. 3d 288, 544 N.E. 2d 257 (1989), Note. 16 U Dayton L Rev 497 (Winter 1991).

Usefulness of Polygraph Results in Paternity Investigations When Used In Conjunction With Exclusionary Blood Tests and a Sixty–Day Conception Period, Richard J. Phannenstill. 21 J Fam L 69 (1982–83).

Notes of Decisions

1. Due process

The putative father in a paternity proceeding is denied due process where the referee grants him approximately five weeks in which to have genetic blood tests done at the putative father's expense; this period of time is insufficient to permit the putative father with an income of $300 per week to accumulate funds to defray the $280 cost of the tests. Hamilton County Dept. of Human Services v. Ball (Hamilton 1986) 36 Ohio App.3d 89, 521 N.E.2d 462.

The denial of blood grouping tests to an indigent paternity defendant, who is unable to prepay for such tests, and who faces the state as an adversary when the complainant-mother and her child are recipients of public assistance, violates the due process guarantee of US Const Am 14. Anderson v. Jacobs (Ohio 1981) 68 Ohio St.2d 67, 428 N.E.2d 419, 22 O.O.3d 268. Children Out–of–wedlock ☞ 58; Constitutional Law ☞ 4020

2. Equal protection

The state of Ohio having granted by statute to all defendants in bastardy proceedings, which are "quasi criminal" in nature, the right to a blood test to determine paternity, cannot deny this right to those defendants who are unable to pay the required fee in advance, without violating the equal protection clause of the United States Constitution, because such a defendant's ability to pay in advance bears no rational relationship to his guilt or innocence, and to discriminate upon this basis constitutes that type of invidious discrimination which is constitutionally prohibited; it is mandatory that the

trial court tax as costs the expense of a blood test requested by appropriate motion by an indigent in a bastardy action. Walker v. Stokes (Cuyahoga 1975) 45 Ohio App.2d 275, 344 N.E.2d 159, 74 O.O.2d 402.

3. In general

If an adjudicated father failed to seek genetic testing despite knowledge of the reasonable likelihood he was not the biological father, he makes a voluntary, deliberate choice that a motion for equitable relief from a child support judgment cannot undo. Dunkle v. Dunkle (Ohio App. 4 Dist., 11-08-1999) 135 Ohio App.3d 669, 735 N.E.2d 469. Child Support ☞ 250; Children Out–of–wedlock ☞ 21(1)

Common pleas court has inherent power to estop mother from using genetic testing to disestablish child's paternity with his or her presumed father under doctrine of laches, but there must be finding of material prejudice to invoke the doctrine. Sherburn v. Reichert (Ohio App. 3 Dist., 10-13-1994) 97 Ohio App.3d 120, 646 N.E.2d 255. Children Out–of–wedlock ☞ 45

"Natural parent" refers to child and parent being of same blood or related by blood or genetics. Belsito v. Clark (Ohio Com.Pl. 1994) 67 Ohio Misc.2d 54, 644 N.E.2d 760. Parent And Child ☞ 1

Statutes addressing rescission of paternity acknowledgements, temporary child support orders, and notification of paternity test results, all of which were enacted after entry of paternity and support orders, could not serve as basis for challenging orders. Norris v. Norris (Ohio App. 5 Dist., Ashland, 09-27-2002) No. 02 COA 016, 2002-Ohio-5285, 2002 WL 31185798, Unreported. Children Out–of–wedlock ☞ 31

4. Construction with other laws

RC 3111.02 to 3111.04, 3111.09, and 3111.10 are in pari materia and must be construed together. Hulett v. Hulett (Ohio 1989) 45 Ohio St.3d 288, 544 N.E.2d 257.

RC 3111.09 and 3111.10, as enacted by 1982 H 245, eff. 6–29–82, do not affect substantive rights, and thus may be applied retrospectively to abrogate the usage of the provision under former RC 3111.16 that test results be receivable in evidence only when favorable to the defendant. Standifer v.

Arwood (Warren 1984) 17 Ohio App.3d 241, 479 N.E.2d 304, 17 O.B.R. 508.

5. Purpose

One obvious goal of various parentage statutes is to accommodate genetic evidence to ensure that correct parentage determination is made from the outset; duty to support children applies to "biological or adoptive parent," and statutes give precedence to genetic testing over any presumption of legitimacy. Leguillon v. Leguillon (Ohio App. 12 Dist., 01-12-1998) 124 Ohio App.3d 757, 707 N.E.2d 571. Child Support ☞ 5; Children Out-of-wedlock ☞ 21(1)

6. Nature of action

As a paternity proceeding is neither a criminal nor a quasi-criminal action, it is not a denial of due process or equal protection of the law as guaranteed by the US Const Am 14, to require by rule of court that the defendant pay in advance for the costs of blood grouping tests granted pursuant to the defendant's motion. Bigsby v. Bates (Ohio Com.Pl. 1978) 59 Ohio Misc. 51, 391 N.E.2d 1384, 11 O.O.3d 262, 13 O.O.3d 260.

7. Discretion of court

Trial court did not abuse its discretion in overruling inmate's motion to convey, in proceeding in which inmate challenged administrative order establishing nonexistence of parent-child relationship and sought to establish parent-child relationship between himself and child; inmate had no chance of success on merits of his claims since genetic tests confirmed zero percent probability of parent-child relationship, and court was not required to convey inmate to courtroom to discuss his conspiracy theories regarding why genetic test resulted in showing of no parent-child relationship. E.B. v. T.J. (Ohio App. 8 Dist., Cuyahoga, 02-02-2006) No. 86399, 2006-Ohio-441, 2006 WL 242507, Unreported, appeal not allowed 109 Ohio St.3d 1507, 849 N.E.2d 1028, 2006-Ohio-2998, reconsideration denied 110 Ohio St.3d 1468, 852 N.E.2d 1216, 2006-Ohio-4288, certiorari denied 127 S.Ct. 1266, 549 U.S. 1215, 167 L.Ed.2d 91. Prisons ☞ 310

It is an abuse of discretion to assess the costs of human leukocyte antigen testing, incurred in a paternity proceeding, against an indigent putative father whose test results definitively exclude him as the biological father of the child. Little v. Stoops (Clinton 1989) 65 Ohio App.3d 758, 585 N.E.2d 475.

8. Genetic testing

Trial court did not violate claimant's constitutional rights when it denied his request for additional genetic testing, in proceeding in which claimant challenged administrative order establishing nonexistence of parent-child relationship and sought to establish parent-child relationship between himself and child; claimant filed for determination of paternity, and, pursuant to statute, county support enforcement agency conducted genetic testing of child, mother, and claimant and determined there was zero percent probability of paternity, and thus,

it was no longer responsibility of agency or court to pay for additional genetic testing. E.B. v. T.J. (Ohio App. 8 Dist., Cuyahoga, 02-02-2006) No. 86399, 2006-Ohio-441, 2006 WL 242507, Unreported, appeal not allowed 109 Ohio St.3d 1507, 849 N.E.2d 1028, 2006-Ohio-2998, reconsideration denied 110 Ohio St.3d 1468, 852 N.E.2d 1216, 2006-Ohio-4288, certiorari denied 127 S.Ct. 1266, 549 U.S. 1215, 167 L.Ed.2d 91. Children Out-of-wedlock ☞ 30; Children Out-of-wedlock ☞ 58

Mother's failure to submit samples of children for genetic testing warranted rescission of alleged father's acknowledgement of paternity. McGrath v. Saret (Ohio App. 5 Dist., Fairfield, 01-13-2005) No. 04 CA 27, 2005-Ohio-217, 2005 WL 121713, Unreported. Children Out-of-wedlock ☞ 7

Failure to inform putative father of court's intent to enter finding of paternity on his refusal to submit to genetic testing precluded finding of paternity by default, where putative father appeared before trial court for purpose of contesting paternity; adjudication was available only as sanction for willful refusal to submit to genetic testing, and not under statutory provision governing default paternity judgments. Marsh v. Clay (Ohio App. 8 Dist., 02-02-1998) 125 Ohio App.3d 518, 708 N.E.2d 1073, on subsequent appeal 2000 WL 1900333. Children Out-of-wedlock ☞ 64

Some form of adversarial hearing is required before trial court may make paternity determination based upon putative father's willful refusal to submit to genetic testing; statute provides party opportunity to explain why refusal to submit to genetic testing was not willful. Marsh v. Clay (Ohio App. 8 Dist., 02-02-1998) 125 Ohio App.3d 518, 708 N.E.2d 1073, on subsequent appeal 2000 WL 1900333. Children Out-of-wedlock ☞ 57

Putative father would not be allowed, three years after judgment finding him to be child's father, which adjudication he had originally sought, to dismiss complaint or to have genetic testing done to determine whether he was biological father, notwithstanding physician's statement in affidavit that it was highly unlikely that plaintiff could be child's father; there would be no current benefit to child to change her position as plaintiff's daughter, procedural rule did not contemplate dismissal of action, at plaintiff's request, three years after rendering of final appealable order in plaintiff's favor, and plaintiff had failed to request genetic testing when he could have properly done so, at which time request would have been granted. Frederick v. Alltop (Ohio Com.Pl., 05-16-1996) 80 Ohio Misc.2d 13, 672 N.E.2d 1123. Children Out-of-wedlock ☞ 68

Once Human Leukocyte Antigen (HLA) test excluded plaintiff as father, juvenile court lacked discretion to consider other evidence of paternity, such as mother's misleading plaintiff into believing he was the natural father, and was required to enter judgment that plaintiff was not the father. Sherburn v. Reichert (Ohio App. 3 Dist., 10-13-1994) 97

Ohio App.3d 120, 646 N.E.2d 255. Children Out-of-wedlock ⟋ 46

Results of Human Leukocyte Antigen (HLA) test excluding plaintiff as father were correctly before juvenile court for its review, where court had sua sponte ordered the test. Sherburn v. Reichert (Ohio App. 3 Dist., 10-13-1994) 97 Ohio App.3d 120, 646 N.E.2d 255. Children Out–of–wedlock ⟋ 58

Eligibility for genetic test in paternity action is not guaranteed, and court can find defendant has fathered child without genetic test results if defendant fails to submit to blood test. Harvey v. Mynatt (Summit 1994) 94 Ohio App.3d 619, 641 N.E.2d 291. Children Out–of–wedlock ⟋ 58

Trial court was not required to allow putative father to receive genetic test to determine if he was father of child born out of wedlock prior to entering default judgment in paternity action brought by county child support enforcement agency, despite putative father's request for blood test in letter sent to court after father received copy of paternity complaint, where letter was sent after father's answer to complaint was due, and father failed to appear and contest motion for default judgment after receipt of notice of default hearing. Harvey v. Mynatt (Summit 1994) 94 Ohio App.3d 619, 641 N.E.2d 291. Children Out–of–wedlock ⟋ 58

Assuming that putative father's request for blood testing in letter sent to court after receiving complaint in paternity action could be considered motion for genetic test, motion was not made in timely fashion, where letter was sent to court two days after father's answer to paternity complaint was due and court did not receive letter until one week after answer was due. Harvey v. Mynatt (Summit 1994) 94 Ohio App.3d 619, 641 N.E.2d 291. Children Out–of–wedlock ⟋ 58

Results of human leukocyte antigen blood test are admissible to determine paternity. Strack v. Pelton (Ohio 1994) 70 Ohio St.3d 172, 637 N.E.2d 914. Children Out–of–wedlock ⟋ 45

Motion for relief from paternity determination in divorce judgment based on genetic test results showing that husband was not father of child was untimely when made nearly nine years after judgment became final and five years after results of test became admissible; fact that motion was filed shortly after receiving results of genetic testing was irrelevant. Strack v. Pelton (Ohio 1994) 70 Ohio St.3d 172, 637 N.E.2d 914. Child Support ⟋ 220; Children Out–of–wedlock ⟋ 21(2)

Genetic tests indicating greater than 95% probability that putative father was not child's biological father gave rise to presumption of nonpaternity. Riddle v. Riddle (Ohio Com.Pl. 1992) 63 Ohio Misc.2d 43, 619 N.E.2d 1201. Children Out–of–wedlock ⟋ 43

Results from genetic testing which could have been made available prior to final judgment and are not made available until after final judgment are not newly discovered evidence for purposes of Civ

R 60(B)(2). Hardman v. Chiaramonte (Summit 1987) 39 Ohio App.3d 9, 528 N.E.2d 1270.

Human leukocyte antigen (HLA) tests are basically genetic comparison examinations rather than blood grouping tests, and constitute relevant evidence to establish the probability of paternity. Owens v. Bell (Ohio 1983) 6 Ohio St.3d 46, 451 N.E.2d 241, 6 O.B.R. 65.

Where blood-grouping tests may be required to determine whether a party or any person involved can be excluded as being the father of a child and law authorizes admission of such evidence only where results of test establish nonpaternity, the results of such blood-grouping tests, where a mere possibility of parentage is thereby disclosed, are not competent, and their admission is prejudicial. State ex rel. Freeman v. Morris (Ohio 1951) 156 Ohio St. 333, 102 N.E.2d 450, 46 O.O. 188.

9. Best interests of children

Performing genetic testing to determine whether former husband was biological father of child born during marriage was not in best interest of child, and thus trial court properly denied former wife's request for such testing on her motion for relief from the decree of divorce which adjudicated former husband the father of her son; former wife failed to raise paternity issue during divorce, child had been in former husband's custody since marriage ended, former wife had not taken care of child on regular basis, and child had bonded with former husband. Hittle v. Palbas (Ohio App. 2 Dist., Greene, 10-31-2003) No. 2003CA52, 2003-Ohio-5843, 2003 WL 22462141, Unreported. Child Custody ⟋ 526

Common Pleas Court has inherent authority, when considering best interests of minor child, to estop mother from using genetic testing to disestablish child's paternity with his or her presumed father. Riddle v. Riddle (Ohio Com.Pl. 1992) 63 Ohio Misc.2d 43, 619 N.E.2d 1201. Children Out–of–wedlock ⟋ 1

10. Indigent defendant

The decisions of State ex rel Cody v Toner, 8 OS(3d) 22, 8 OBR 255, 456 NE(2d) 813 (1983), cert denied 466 US 938, 104 SCt 1912, 80 LEd(2d) 461 (1984), and Anderson v Jacobs, 68 OS(2d) 67, 428 NE(2d) 419 (1981), that the state must provide appointed counsel and blood grouping tests to indigent defendants who face the state as an adversary in paternity proceedings are to be applied retroactively and may therefore be the basis for vacation of judgment pursuant to Civ R 60(B). Keeney v. Lawson (Hamilton 1984) 19 Ohio App.3d 318, 484 N.E.2d 745, 19 O.B.R. 491.

Where the defendant in a paternity action knowingly and voluntarily plead guilty, never requested genetic tests, and did not tell the court that he was indigent, the trial court was not required to inform the defendant of his constitutional right to the state's prepayment of the cost of the genetic tests. Edwards v. Porter (Lorain 1983) 8 Ohio App.3d 277, 456 N.E.2d 1347, 8 O.B.R. 370.

11. Newly discovered evidence

Genetic test results obtained after entry of divorce decree establishing former husband's child support obligation was not "newly discovered evidence," for purposes of motion for relief from judgment, even though test results revealed a zero percent probability that husband was child's father. Dunkle v. Dunkle (Ohio App. 4 Dist., 11-08-1999) 135 Ohio App.3d 669, 735 N.E.2d 469. Child Support 🔗 220

For purposes of the rule providing for relief from judgment based on newly discovered evidence, results of a paternity test, not obtained and thus not provided until after an adjudication of the existence of a parent-and-child relationship are not "newly discovered evidence." Cuyahoga Support Enforcement Agency v. Guthrie (Ohio, 02-17-1999) 84 Ohio St.3d 437, 705 N.E.2d 318, 1999-Ohio-362. Children Out–of–wedlock 🔗 68

12. Admissibility of evidence

Genetic test results are admissible without the need for foundation testimony or further proof of authenticity or accuracy where the biological father fails to file a written objection to the report of the court-ordered genetic test results and does not dispute that he received a copy. Joy B. v. Glen D. (Ohio App. 6 Dist., Wood, 08-06-1999) No. OT-99-002, 1999 WL 575945, Unreported.

Admissibility of results of genetic testing of mother, child, and putative father, performed upon agreement of mother and putative father and without order of court, was governed by relevancy standard for scientific evidence rather than statutory standard for results of genetic testing. Nwabara v. Willacy (Ohio App. 8 Dist., 08-09-1999) 135 Ohio App.3d 120, 733 N.E.2d 267, dismissed, appeal not allowed 87 Ohio St.3d 1451, 719 N.E.2d 967. Children Out–of–wedlock 🔗 45

Juvenile court must consider genetic evidence regarding paternity of child, even in absence of proffer by the parties. Sherburn v. Reichert (Ohio App. 3 Dist., 10-13-1994) 97 Ohio App.3d 120, 646 N.E.2d 255. Children Out–of–wedlock 🔗 58

While the scientific laws of blood-grouping are not "immutable," where the testifying expert was qualified, the testing procedures were technologically correct, the results were consistent and the interpretation sound, this evidence may be considered and may be given sufficient weight to overcome lay testimony to the contrary, including the testimony of the parties. Garrett v. Garrett (Hamilton 1977) 54 Ohio App.2d 25, 374 N.E.2d 654, 8 O.O.3d 41. Evidence 🔗 508; Evidence 🔗 574

On trial of a bastardy proceeding instituted by unmarried woman whose child was conceived during existence of a prior marital relation, plaintiff, to establish the nonpaternity of her former husband, may call as a witness a qualified expert who may be permitted to testify that the findings and result of a standard and recognized blood-grouping test made by him from blood of plaintiff, the child, and her former husband, excluded the former husband as the father of the child; findings and result of such

test admitted in evidence are not conclusive of nonpaternity, but may be considered for whatever weight they may have in proving that fact. State ex rel. Walker v. Clark (Ohio 1944) 144 Ohio St. 305, 58 N.E.2d 773, 29 O.O. 450.

Where alleged father of a bastard child offers in evidence the testimony of an expert witness who made what is known as the Landsteiner–Bernstein blood group testing of the blood of the mother and child and the reputed father, which disclosed that the reputed father could not be the father of the child, it is not error for court to refuse the admission of such testimony as conclusive evidence, but to admit it along with other evidence for whatever weight it may have to prove the nonpaternity of the alleged father. State ex rel. Slovak v. Holod (Guernsey 1939) 63 Ohio App. 16, 24 N.E.2d 962, 16 O.O. 257.

13. Presumption and burden of proof

Putative father whose nonpaternity was conclusively established by genetic testing conducted more than one year after entry of paternity judgment was not entitled to relief from that judgment on ground that it was no longer equitable to enforce it; putative father was aware of parentage proceedings against him and that genetic testing could be performed, but he chose to ignore these initial proceedings and, in doing so, made voluntary, deliberate choice not to seek genetic testing until after finding of parentage and until after he was notified of support arrearage. Cuyahoga Support Enforcement Agency v. Guthrie (Ohio, 02-17-1999) 84 Ohio St.3d 437, 705 N.E.2d 318, 1999-Ohio-362. Children Out–of–wedlock 🔗 68

Presumption of paternity created by putative father's marriage to mother at time of child's birth and his signature on birth certificate conflicted with presumption of nonpaternity created by genetic test results indicating more than 95% probability of nonpaternity, requiring use of logic and analysis of policy considerations in determining what presumption should control. Riddle v. Riddle (Ohio Com. Pl. 1992) 63 Ohio Misc.2d 43, 619 N.E.2d 1201. Children Out–of–wedlock 🔗 43

Paternity of a child is proven by a preponderance of the evidence where (1) evidence is introduced of sexual intercourse within the period of conception; (2) expert testimony is given concerning the probability of defendant's paternity based on genetic testing; and (3) expert testimony is given regarding the probability of defendant's paternity based on the physical characteristics and ethnic ancestry of the parties. Grove v. Mattison (Franklin 1988) 61 Ohio App.3d 252, 572 N.E.2d 731, dismissed 42 Ohio St.3d 706, 537 N.E.2d 226.

14. Contempt

Trial court's statement to putative father that his failure to submit to genetic testing might result in contempt citation punishable by either fine or imprisonment did not in any way constitute notice that his failure to submit to genetic testing would result in paternity determination, as prerequisite to entry of paternity determination as sanction for willful refusal to submit to testing. Marsh v. Clay (Ohio App. 8 Dist., 02-02-1998) 125 Ohio App.3d 518, 708 N.E.2d 1073, on subsequent appeal 2000 WL 1900333. Children Out–of–wedlock ☞ 64

The requirement to submit to the withdrawal of blood to determine paternity is not susceptible to a right of privacy challenge, and as such, a court may find one who refuses to comply with such an order in contempt. McCarty v. Kimmel (Montgomery 1989) 62 Ohio App.3d 775, 577 N.E.2d 665.

Sanctions other than dismissal of paternity proceeding would have been more appropriate when mother failed to appear at center for genetic testing, especially where there was no showing that delay was intentional, and neither state nor child could control mother's conduct; trial court could have found mother in contempt of court, rescheduled test, and had her pay cost of testing. Dukes v. Cole (Lorain 1985) 23 Ohio App.3d 65, 491 N.E.2d

374, 23 O.B.R. 110. Children Out–of–wedlock ☞ 58

15. Appeals

Child Support Enforcement Agency (CSEA) waived right to contend on appeal that trial court lacked authority to grant adjudicated father's motion for genetic testing, which was filed under statute determining parent-child relationship, as opposed to the statute providing relief from judgment, where CSEA did not object on this ground to trial court, and CSEA requested a genetic test of the parties on its own motion. Boggs v. Brnjic (Ohio App. 8 Dist., 05-08-2003) 153 Ohio App.3d 399, 794 N.E.2d 684, 2003-Ohio-2318. Child Support ☞ 539; Child Support ☞ 553; Children Out–of–wedlock ☞ 73

An order mandating genetic testing in a parentage action is not a final appealable order as it is not determinative of the parentage action. McCarty v. Kimmel (Montgomery 1989) 62 Ohio App.3d 775, 577 N.E.2d 665. Children Out–of–wedlock ☞ 73

3111.10 Admissible evidence

In an action brought under sections 3111.01 to 3111.18 of the Revised Code, evidence relating to paternity may include:

(A) Evidence of sexual intercourse between the mother and alleged father at any possible time of conception;

(B) An expert's opinion concerning the statistical probability of the alleged father's paternity, which opinion is based upon the duration of the mother's pregnancy;

(C) Genetic test results, weighted in accordance with evidence, if available, of the statistical probability of the alleged father's paternity;

(D) Medical evidence relating to the alleged father's paternity of the child based on tests performed by experts. If a man has been identified as a possible father of the child, the court may, and upon the request of a party shall, require the child, the mother, and the man to submit to appropriate tests. Any fees charged for the tests shall be paid by the party that requests them unless the court orders the fees taxed as costs in the action.

(E) All other evidence relevant to the issue of paternity of the child.

(2000 S 180, eff. 3–22–01; 1986 H 476, eff. 9–24–86; 1982 H 245)

Uncodified Law

1992 S 10, § 5: See Uncodified Law under 3111.01.

1982 H 245, § 3: See Uncodified Law under 3111.04.

Historical and Statutory Notes

Ed. Note: Former 3111.10 repealed by 1982 H 245, eff. 6–29–82; 127 v 1039; 1953 H 1; GC 8006–10; Source—GC 12117.

Pre–1953 H 1 Amendments: 124 v S 65

Amendment Note: 2000 S 180 substituted "3111.18" for "3111.19" in the first sentence of the section.

Cross References

Relevancy and its limits, Evid R 401 to 411

Library References

Children Out-of-Wedlock ☞44 to 51. Westlaw Topic No. 76H.

C.J.S. Children Out-of-Wedlock §§ 76 to 79, 102 to 108.

Research References

ALR Library

77 ALR 5th 201, Authentication of Blood Sample Taken from Human Body for Purposes Other Than Determining Blood Alcohol Content.

Encyclopedias

OH Jur. 3d Family Law § 900, Accounting by Petitioner--Purpose; Effect Upon Payments Pursuant to Surrogacy Agreements.

OH Jur. 3d Family Law § 945, Rebuttal of Presumption.

OH Jur. 3d Family Law § 952, Jurisdiction.

Forms

Ohio Jurisprudence Pleading and Practice Forms § 41:6, Scope and Manner of Examination--Blood Tests.

Ohio Jurisprudence Pleading and Practice Forms § 60:4, Admissibility.

Ohio Jurisprudence Pleading and Practice Forms § 111:11, Evidence.

Treatises and Practice Aids

Sowald & Morganstern, Baldwin's Ohio Practice Domestic Relations Law § 3:13, Judicial Parentage Action--Presumptions of Parentage--Creating.

Sowald & Morganstern, Baldwin's Ohio Practice Domestic Relations Law § 3:15, Evidence--In General.

Sowald & Morganstern, Baldwin's Ohio Practice Domestic Relations Law § 3:17, Evidence--Genetic Tests--Background.

Sowald & Morganstern, Baldwin's Ohio Practice Domestic Relations Law § 3:21, Evidence--Other Types of Evidence.

Sowald & Morganstern, Baldwin's Ohio Practice Domestic Relations Law § 3:45, Effect of Judgment--Retrospective Effect.

Snyder & Giannelli, Baldwin's Ohio Practice Evidence R 702, Testimony by Experts.

Carlin, Baldwin's Ohio Prac. Merrick-Rippner Probate Law § 19:7, Uniform Parentage Act--Presumptions.

Carlin, Baldwin's Ohio Prac. Merrick-Rippner Probate Law § 19:10, Uniform Parentage Act--Procedure in Action to Determine Father-Child Relationship.

Carlin, Baldwin's Ohio Prac. Merrick-Rippner Probate Law § 110:19, Parentage Act--Effect.

Carlin, Baldwin's Ohio Prac. Merrick-Rippner Probate Law § 110:22, Parentage Act--Presumption of Paternity.

Carlin, Baldwin's Ohio Prac. Merrick-Rippner Probate Law § 110:26, Parentage Act--Applicability of Civil Rules to Paternity Proceedings.

Carlin, Baldwin's Ohio Prac. Merrick-Rippner Probate Law § 110:27, Parentage Act--Evidence of Paternity.

Law Review and Journal Commentaries

Chromosome Testing—New, Improved Paternity Tests?, Note. 28 J Fam L 753 (1989–90).

DNA Data Banking: The Dangerous Erosion Of Privacy, E. Donald Shapiro and Michele L. Weinberg. 38 Clev St L Rev 455 (1990).

"Genetically" Altered Admissibility: Legislative Notice Of DNA Typing, Note. 39 Clev St L Rev 415 (1991).

The Need for Statutes Regulating Artificial Insemination by Donors, Note. 46 Ohio St L J 1055 (1986).

Patenting of Human DNA Sequences—Implications for Prenatal Genetic Testing, Note. 36 J Fam L 267 (1997–98).

Notes of Decisions

Construction and application   1
HLA tests   2
Other relevant evidence   3
Presumptions and burden of proof   5
Sexual intercourse with others   4

---

1. Construction and application

RC 3111.02 to 3111.04, 3111.09, and 3111.10 are in pari materia and must be construed together. Hulett v. Hulett (Ohio 1989) 45 Ohio St.3d 288, 544 N.E.2d 257.

RC 3111.09 and 3111.10, as enacted by 1982 H 245, eff. 6–29–82, do not affect substantive rights, and thus may be applied retrospectively to abrogate the usage of the provision under former RC 3111.16 that test results be receivable in evidence only when favorable to the defendant. Standifer v.

Arwood (Warren 1984) 17 Ohio App.3d 241, 479 N.E.2d 304, 17 O.B.R. 508.

2. HLA tests

The plaintiff in a paternity action must present proper foundational evidence to introduce results of court-ordered Human Leukocyte Antigen (HLA) blood testing, such as evidence that the blood tested was actually that of the defendant, the mother and the child, since there is no special statutory provision exempting the admission of HLA tests from the basic foundational requirements set forth in the Ohio Rules of Evidence. McElroy v Gilbert, No. 92 CA 9, 1994 WL 527119 (7th Dist Ct App, Mahoning, 9–27–94).

Results of Human Leukocyte Antigen (HLA) test excluding plaintiff as father were correctly before juvenile court for its review, where court had sua sponte ordered the test. Sherburn v. Reichert (Ohio App. 3 Dist., 10-13-1994) 97 Ohio App.3d

120, 646 N.E.2d 255. Children Out–of–wedlock ☞ 58

Results of human leukocyte antigen blood test are admissible to determine paternity. Strack v. Pelton (Ohio 1994) 70 Ohio St.3d 172, 637 N.E.2d 914. Children Out–of–wedlock ☞ 45

Human leukocyte antigen blood test results are admissible in an action to determine paternity where the following foundational requirements have been established: (1) the blood tested was in fact that of the defendant, the plaintiff, and the child; (2) the test results were based upon reliable blood samples; and (3) there was an unbroken chain of custody from the time the samples were taken to the time they were analyzed. Camden v. Miller (Clark 1986) 34 Ohio App.3d 86, 517 N.E.2d 253. Children Out–of–wedlock ☞ 45

Human leukocyte antigen (HLA) tests are basically genetic comparison examinations rather than blood grouping tests, and constitute relevant evidence to establish the probability of paternity. Owens v. Bell (Ohio 1983) 6 Ohio St.3d 46, 451 N.E.2d 241, 6 O.B.R. 65.

3. Other relevant evidence

Intended mother's voluntary acknowledgement of maternity, as set forth in a surrogacy agreement setting forth terms by which surrogate mother would carry and give birth to embryos formed outside the womb by donor egg and sperm, was sufficient under the Parentage Act, consistent with cases concerning voluntary acknowledgements of paternity, to rebut the presumption that surrogate mother was the "natural mother" of resulting child by reason of her having given birth to the child. S.N. v. M.B. (Ohio App. 10 Dist., 06-10-2010) 188 Ohio App.3d 324, 935 N.E.2d 463, 2010-Ohio-2479, cause dismissed 126 Ohio St.3d 1525, 931 N.E.2d 126, 2010-Ohio-3583. Children Out–of–wedlock ☞ 15

Juvenile court must consider genetic evidence regarding paternity of child, even in absence of proffer by the parties. Sherburn v. Reichert (Ohio App. 3 Dist., 10-13-1994) 97 Ohio App.3d 120, 646 N.E.2d 255. Children Out–of–wedlock ☞ 58

Under RC 3111.10(E), a jury view of the child whose paternity is disputed, for purposes of comparing its physical characteristics and appearances with the alleged father, is permissible. Domigan v. Gillette (Clark 1984) 17 Ohio App.3d 228, 479 N.E.2d 291, 17 O.B.R. 494.

A proposed witness in a paternity action need not be rejected or grounds of public policy when such witness is the child whose paternity is under inquiry. Philpot v. Williams (Hamilton 1983) 8 Ohio App.3d 241, 456 N.E.2d 1315, 8 O.B.R. 314

In a prosecution for nonsupport of an illegitimate child, an adjudication of paternity in a bastardy action is admissible, but does not constitute conclusive proof. State v. Lockwood (Cuyahoga 1959) 160 N.E.2d 131, 84 Ohio Law Abs. 257.

Evidence obtained by accused under the statute must be considered as defensive matter; if accused wishes to introduce such, he must offer it during the presentation of his own case. State ex rel. Brannon v. Turner (Franklin 1947) 81 Ohio App. 47, 77 N.E.2d 255, 49 Ohio Law Abs. 446, 36 O.O. 359.

Proper interpretation of this section is that accused shall be permitted to ask complainant any question which within rules of evidence is competent, relevant or material to complaint of prosecuting witness or which under such rules may have any tendency to establish defense. Mabra v. State ex rel. Settles (Clark 1935) 21 Ohio Law Abs. 190.

4. Sexual intercourse with others

Evidence in a bastardy action of complainant's sexual relations with other persons at a time which could not have resulted in the conception complained or of her bad character in general is inadmissible. Taylor v. Mosley (Ohio Juv. 1961) 178 N.E.2d 55, 87 Ohio Law Abs. 335, 17 O.O.2d 439.

5. Presumptions and burden of proof

Paternity of a child is proven by a preponderance of the evidence where (1) evidence is introduced of sexual intercourse within the period of conception; (2) expert testimony is given concerning the probability of defendant's paternity based on genetic testing; and (3) expert testimony is given regarding the probability of defendant's paternity based on the physical characteristics and ethnic ancestry of the parties. Grove v. Mattison (Franklin 1988) 61 Ohio App.3d 252, 572 N.E.2d 731, dismissed 42 Ohio St.3d 706, 537 N.E.2d 226.

Clear and convincing evidence sufficient to overcome the presumption of paternity contained in RC 3111.03(A)(1) may be adduced through any or all of the enumerated methods prescribed by RC 3111.10, including the submission of genetic test results. Hulett v. Hulett (Ohio 1989) 45 Ohio St.3d 288, 544 N.E.2d 257.

The facts upon which a hypothetical question to an expert witness is premised must be established by the party calling the witness by a preponderance of the evidence; it is up to the jury to determine whether the preponderance test has been met. Camden v. Miller (Clark 1986) 34 Ohio App.3d 86, 517 N.E.2d 253. Evidence ☞ 553(4)

A state statute establishing the burden of proof in civil paternity actions as a preponderance of the evidence rather than clear and convincing evidence does not deprive the defendant of due process of law. (Ed. note: Pennsylvania statute construed in light of federal constitution.) Rivera v. Minnich (U.S.Pa. 1987) 107 S.Ct. 3001, 483 U.S. 574, 97 L.Ed.2d 473.

3111.11 Pretrial procedures

If the person against whom an action is brought pursuant to sections 3111.01 to 3111.18 of the Revised Code does not admit in his answer the existence or nonexistence of the father and child relationship, the court shall hold a pretrial hearing, in accordance with the Civil Rules, at a time set by the court. At the pretrial hearing, the court shall notify each party to the action that the party may file a motion requesting the court to order the child's mother, the alleged father, and any other person who is a defendant in the action to submit to genetic tests and, if applicable, to the appropriate tests referred to in section 3111.10 of the Revised Code. When the court determines that all pretrial matters have been completed, the action shall be set for trial.

(2000 S 180, eff. 3–22–01; 1986 H 476, eff. 9–24–86; 1982 H 245)

Uncodified Law

1992 S 10, § 5: See Uncodified Law under 3111.01.

1982 H 245, § 3: See Uncodified Law under 3111.04.

Historical and Statutory Notes

Ed. Note: Former 3111.11 repealed by 1982 H 245, eff. 6–29–82; 1953 H 1; GC 8006–11; Source—GC 12118.

Pre–1953 H 1 Amendments: 124 v S 65

Amendment Note: 2000 S 180 substituted "3111.18" for "3111.19" in the first sentence of the section.

Library References

Children Out-of-Wedlock ☞39, 58.
Westlaw Topic No. 76H.
C.J.S. Children Out-of-Wedlock §§ 51, 73 to 79, 98.

Research References

Encyclopedias

OH Jur. 3d Family Law § 956, Pretrial Procedures.

Forms

Ohio Jurisprudence Pleading and Practice Forms § 111:9, Pretrial Hearing and Trial.

Treatises and Practice Aids

Sowald & Morganstern, Baldwin's Ohio Practice Domestic Relations Law § 3:12, Judicial Parentage Action--Procedure Before Hearing.

Carlin, Baldwin's Ohio Prac. Merrick-Rippner Probate Law § 19:10, Uniform Parentage Act--Procedure in Action to Determine Father-Child Relationship.

Carlin, Baldwin's Ohio Prac. Merrick-Rippner Probate Law § 110:26, Parentage Act--Applicability of Civil Rules to Paternity Proceedings.

Notes of Decisions

Default judgment   2
Res judicata   1
Waiver of defenses   3

-----

1.   Res judicata

Legal custodians of child, who obtained custody from child's mother, were in privity with mother, and so were barred by res judicata from litigating issue of paternity of child that had been decided in divorce decree. Broxterman v. Broxterman (Ohio App. 1 Dist., 03-15-1995) 101 Ohio App.3d 661, 656 N.E.2d 394. Children Out–of–wedlock ☞ 33; Divorce ☞ 172

Child was not in privity with his mother in divorce action, and so was not barred by res judicata from bringing paternity action, even though paternity had been decided in divorce decree; although interests of child and mother coincided over support, their interests may have diverged on child's

right to know identity of his biological father, and his potential rights of inheritance from his biological father. Broxterman v. Broxterman (Ohio App. 1 Dist., 03-15-1995) 101 Ohio App.3d 661, 656 N.E.2d 394. Child Support ☞ 225; Children Out–of–wedlock ☞ 21(2); Children Out–of–wedlock ☞ 33

The doctrine of res judicata can be invoked to give conclusive effect to a determination of parentage contained in a dissolution decree or a legitimation order, thereby barring a subsequent paternity action brought pursuant to RC Ch 3111. In re Gilbraith (Ohio 1987) 32 Ohio St.3d 127, 512 N.E.2d 956. Child Support ☞ 225; Children Out–of–wedlock ☞ 13; Children Out–of–wedlock ☞ 21(2)

2.   Default judgment

Defendant who was in default of answer and had failed to appear in parentage action was not entitled to notice of filing of motion for default. Long

v. Bartlett (Franklin 1992) 73 Ohio App.3d 764, 598 N.E.2d 197. Children Out–of–wedlock ☞ 64

Where no answer is filed to a complaint alleging paternity, the trial court errs in entering judgment by default without first conducting the pretrial hearing provided under RC 3111.11. Potts v Wilson, No. 409 (4th Dist Ct App, Adams, 5–30–85).

3. Waiver of defenses

The Ohio Rules of Civil Procedure apply to parentage actions; thus, an answer must be filed by the person against whom the action is brought, and a failure to properly plead the affirmative defense of laches bars its defense at trial. Eppley v. Bratton (Ohio App. 5 Dist., Coshocton, 11-07-1994) No. 94 CA 7, 1994 WL 668111, Unreported, appeal not allowed 71 Ohio St.3d 1494, 646 N.E.2d 469.

3111.111 Temporary support order pending action objecting to parentage determination

If an action is brought pursuant to sections 3111.01 to 3111.18 of the Revised Code to object to a determination made pursuant to former section 3111.21 or 3111.22 or sections 3111.38 to 3111.54 of the Revised Code that the alleged father is the natural father of a child, the court, on its own motion or on the motion of either party, shall issue a temporary order for the support of the child pursuant to Chapters 3119., 3121., 3123., and 3125. of the Revised Code requiring the alleged father to pay support to the natural mother or the guardian or legal custodian of the child. The order shall remain in effect until the court issues a judgment in the action pursuant to section 3111.13 of the Revised Code that determines the existence or nonexistence of a father and child relationship. If the court, in its judgment, determines that the alleged father is not the natural father of the child, the court shall order the person to whom the temporary support was paid under the order to repay the alleged father all amounts paid for support under the temporary order.

(2000 S 180, eff. 3–22–01; 1997 H 352, eff. 1–1–98)

Historical and Statutory Notes

Amendment Note: 2000 S 180 substituted "3111.18" for "3111.19"; inserted "or sections 3111.38 to 3111.54"; substituted "Chapters 3119., 3121., 3123., and 3125." for "section 3113.21 to 3113.219"; and made other nonsubstantive changes.

Library References

Children Out-of-Wedlock ☞67.
Westlaw Topic No. 76H.
C.J.S. Children Out-of-Wedlock §§ 123 to 126.

Research References

Encyclopedias

OH Jur. 3d Family Law § 957, Temporary Child Support Order.
OH Jur. 3d Family Law § 958, Retroactivity of Statute.

Forms

Ohio Jurisprudence Pleading and Practice Forms § 111:10, Temporary Support Order.

Treatises and Practice Aids

Sowald & Morganstern, Baldwin's Ohio Practice Domestic Relations Law § 3:42, Effect of Judgment--Child Support--Temporary Support Order.
Carlin, Baldwin's Ohio Prac. Merrick-Rippner Probate Law § 19:10, Uniform Parentage Act--Pro-

cedure in Action to Determine Father-Child Relationship.
Carlin, Baldwin's Ohio Prac. Merrick-Rippner Probate Law § 19:11, Uniform Parentage Act--Temporary Support Pending Action Objecting to Parentage Determination.
Carlin, Baldwin's Ohio Prac. Merrick-Rippner Probate Law § 110:26, Parentage Act--Applicability of Civil Rules to Paternity Proceedings.
Carlin, Baldwin's Ohio Prac. Merrick-Rippner Probate Law § 110:30, Parentage Act--Enforcement of Support Order.
Carlin, Baldwin's Ohio Prac. Merrick-Rippner Probate Law § 110:35, Civil Support Proceedings--Liability for Child Support.

Notes of Decisions

Procedural issues   1

1. Procedural issues

Biological father in paternity and child support case waived objection to any lack of personal jurisdiction over him that resulted from defective service by entering voluntary appearance in the case and arguing the merits of default judgment previously entered against him, including filing of motions for genetic testing and reduction of child support, even though father argued that criminal charges pending against him for nonpayment of child support made the genetic testing urgent; father waited for many months after filing the motions on the merits before moving to vacate default judgment for lack of personal jurisdiction. State ex rel. Athens Cty. Dept. of Job & Family Servs. v. Martin (Ohio App. 4 Dist., Athens, 04-14-2008) No. 07CA11, 2008-Ohio-1849, 2008 WL 1758896, Unreported, appeal not allowed 119 Ohio St.3d 1448, 893 N.E.2d 518, 2008-Ohio-4487. Children Out–of–wedlock ☞ 64

Biological father failed to preserve for appellate review his argument that trial court erred in adopting magistrate's decision to deny the motion to vacate default judgment entered against him in paternity and child support case on the basis that magistrate relied on untimely filed memoranda from county child support enforcement agency, where biological father did not object to magistrate's scheduling order permitting memoranda until day before hearing and did not request additional time to file a reply. State ex rel. Athens Cty. Dept. of Job & Family Servs. v. Martin (Ohio App. 4 Dist., Athens, 04-14-2008) No. 07CA11, 2008-Ohio-1849, 2008 WL 1758896, Unreported, appeal not allowed 119 Ohio St.3d 1448, 893 N.E.2d 518, 2008-Ohio-4487. Children Out–of–wedlock ☞ 73

Statutes addressing rescission of paternity acknowledgements, temporary child support orders, and notification of paternity test results, all of which were enacted after entry of paternity and support orders, could not serve as basis for challenging orders. Norris v. Norris (Ohio App. 5 Dist., Ashland, 09-27-2002) No. 02 COA 016, 2002-Ohio-5285, 2002 WL 31185798, Unreported. Children Out–of–wedlock ☞ 31

3111.12   Testimony; admissibility of genetic test results or DNA records

(A) In an action under sections 3111.01 to 3111.18 of the Revised Code, the mother of the child and the alleged father are competent to testify and may be compelled to testify by subpoena. If a witness refuses to testify upon the ground that the testimony or evidence of the witness might tend to incriminate the witness and the court compels the witness to testify, the court may grant the witness immunity from having the testimony of the witness used against the witness in subsequent criminal proceedings.

(B) Testimony of a physician concerning the medical circumstances of the mother's pregnancy and the condition and characteristics of the child upon birth is not privileged.

(C) Testimony relating to sexual access to the mother by a man at a time other than the probable time of conception of the child is inadmissible in evidence, unless offered by the mother.

(D) If, pursuant to section 3111.09 of the Revised Code, a court orders genetic tests to be conducted, orders disclosure of information regarding a DNA record stored in the DNA database pursuant to section 109.573 of the Revised Code, or intends to use a report of genetic test results obtained from tests conducted pursuant to former section 3111.21 or 3111.22 or sections 3111.38 to 3111.54 of the Revised Code, a party may object to the admission into evidence of any of the genetic test results or of the DNA record information by filing a written objection with the court that ordered the tests or disclosure or intends to use a report of genetic test results. The party shall file the written objection with the court no later than fourteen days after the report of the test results or the DNA record information is mailed to the attorney of record of a party or to a party. The party making the objection shall send a copy of the objection to all parties.

If a party files a written objection, the report of the test results or the DNA record information shall be admissible into evidence as provided by the Rules of Evidence. If a written objection is not filed, the report of the test results or the DNA record information shall be admissible into evidence without the need for foundation testimony or other proof of authenticity or accuracy.

(E) If a party intends to introduce into evidence invoices or other documents showing amounts expended to cover pregnancy and confinement and genetic testing, the party shall notify all other parties in writing of that intent and include copies of the invoices and documents. A party may object to the admission into evidence of the invoices or documents by filing a written objection with the court that is hearing the action no later than fourteen days after the notice and the copies of the invoices and documents are mailed to the attorney of record of each party or to each party.

If a party files a written objection, the invoices and other documents shall be admissible into evidence as provided by the Rules of Evidence. If a written objection is not filed, the invoices or other documents are admissible into evidence without the need for foundation testimony or other evidence of authenticity or accuracy.

(F) A juvenile court or other court with jurisdiction under section 2101.022 or 2301.03 of the Revised Code shall give priority to actions under sections 3111.01 to 3111.18 of the Revised Code and shall issue an order determining the existence or nonexistence of a parent and child relationship no later than one hundred twenty days after the date on which the action was brought in the juvenile court or other court with jurisdiction.

(2000 S 180, eff. 3–22–01; 1997 H 352, eff. 1–1–98; 1995 H 5, eff. 8–30–95; 1994 S 355, eff. 12–9–94; 1992 S 10, eff. 7–15–92; 1986 H 476; 1982 H 245)

Uncodified Law

1994 S 355, § 5: See Uncodified Law under 3111.08.

1992 S 10, § 5: See Uncodified Law under 3111.01.

1982 H 245, § 3: See Uncodified Law under 3111.04.

Historical and Statutory Notes

Ed. Note: RC 3111.12 contains provisions analogous to former RC 3111.15, repealed by 1982 H 245, eff. 6–29–82.

Ed. Note: Former RC 3111.12 repealed by 1982 H 245, eff. 6–29–82; 1953 H 1; GC 8006–12; Source—GC 12119.

Pre–1953 H 1 Amendments: 124 v S 65

Amendment Note: 2000 S 180 substituted "3111.18" for "3111.19" in division (A); inserted "or sections 3111.38 to 3111.54" in division (D); rewrote division (F); and made other nonsubstantive changes. Prior to amendment division (F) read:

"(F) A juvenile court shall give priority to actions under sections 3111.01 to 3111.19 of the Revised Code and shall issue an order determining the existence or nonexistence of a parent and child relationship no later than one hundred twenty days after the date on which the action was brought in the juvenile court."

Amendment Note: 1997 H 352 rewrote divisions (D) and (E), which prior thereto read:

"(D) If, pursuant to section 3111.09 of the Revised Code, a court orders genetic tests to be conducted or orders disclosure of information regarding a DNA record stored in the DNA database pursuant to section 109.573 of the Revised Code, a party may object to the admission into evidence of the report of the test results or of the DNA record information by filing a written objection with the court that ordered the tests or disclosure. The

party shall file the written objection with the court no later than fourteen days after the report of the test results or the DNA record information is mailed to the attorney of record of a party or to a party. The party making the objection shall send a copy of the objection to all parties.

"If a party files a written objection, the report of the test results or the DNA record information shall be admissible into evidence as provided by the Rules of Evidence. If a written objection is not filed, the report of the test results or the DNA record information shall be admissible into evidence without the need for foundation testimony or other proof of authenticity or accuracy.

"(E) Any party to an action brought pursuant to sections 3111.01 to 3111.19 of the Revised Code may demand a jury trial by filing the demand within three days after the action is set for trial. If a jury demand is not filed within the three-day period, the trial shall be by the court.

"If the action is tried to a jury, the verdict of the jury is limited only to the parentage of the child, and all other matters involved in the action shall be determined by the court following the rendering of the verdict."

Amendment Note: 1995 H 5 added all references to DNA record information in division (D); and made changes to reflect gender neutral language.

Amendment Note: 1994 S 355 added division (D); and redesignated former divisions (D) and (E) as divisions (E) and (F).

Cross References

Common pleas court to grant transactional immunity, procedure, exceptions, see 2945.44

Jury trial of right, Civ R 38

Reciprocal enforcement of support proceedings, self-incrimination, immunity, see 3115.19
Right against compulsory self-incrimination, see O Const Art I §10

Right of trial by jury, see O Const Art I §5
Testimony regarding witness credibility, not waiver of privilege against self-incrimination, Evid R 608

Library References

Children Out-of-Wedlock ⬥45 to 46, 50, 58, 65.
Criminal Law ⬥42.
Witnesses ⬥8, 83.
Westlaw Topic Nos. 76H, 110, 410.

C.J.S. Children Out-of-Wedlock §§ 76 to 79, 103 to 104, 107.
C.J.S. Criminal Law §§ 65, 97 to 112.
C.J.S. Witnesses §§ 2, 20 to 22, 25, 204.

Research References

Encyclopedias

OH Jur. 3d Family Law § 950, Limitation of Actions.
OH Jur. 3d Family Law § 963, Use of Results.
OH Jur. 3d Family Law § 972, Testimony.

Forms

Ohio Jurisprudence Pleading and Practice Forms § 111:11, Evidence.

Treatises and Practice Aids

Klein, Darling, & Terez, Baldwin's Ohio Practice Civil Practice § 1:88, Civ. R. 1(C)(7): All Other Special Statutory Proceedings--Matters Held to be Other Special Statutory Proceedings--Parentage Action (RC 3111.04).
Klein, Darling, & Terez, Baldwin's Ohio Practice Civil Practice § 38:2, Applicability of Civ. R. 38.
Klein, Darling, & Terez, Baldwin's Ohio Practice Civil Practice § 38:15, Right to Jury Trial Under Ohio Statutes--Other Statutes.
Sowald & Morganstern, Baldwin's Ohio Practice Domestic Relations Law § 3:12, Judicial Parentage Action--Procedure Before Hearing.
Sowald & Morganstern, Baldwin's Ohio Practice Domestic Relations Law § 3:15, Evidence--In General.
Sowald & Morganstern, Baldwin's Ohio Practice Domestic Relations Law § 3:16, Evidence--Witnesses.
Sowald & Morganstern, Baldwin's Ohio Practice Domestic Relations Law § 3:19, Evidence--Genetic Tests--Results of Test.
Sowald & Morganstern, Baldwin's Ohio Practice Domestic Relations Law § 3:20, Evidence--Genetic Tests--Costs of Testing.
Sowald & Morganstern, Baldwin's Ohio Practice Domestic Relations Law § 3:40, Effect of Judgment--Child Support--Other Remedies.

Carlin, Baldwin's Ohio Prac. Merrick-Rippner Probate Law § 18:2, Inheritance Rights of Illegitimate Child--Statutory Provisions.
Carlin, Baldwin's Ohio Prac. Merrick-Rippner Probate Law § 19:6, Uniform Parentage Act--Jurisdiction of Action to Determine Father-Child Relationship.
Carlin, Baldwin's Ohio Prac. Merrick-Rippner Probate Law § 19:7, Uniform Parentage Act--Presumptions.
Carlin, Baldwin's Ohio Prac. Merrick-Rippner Probate Law § 19:8, Uniform Parentage Act--Support Order.
Carlin, Baldwin's Ohio Prac. Merrick-Rippner Probate Law § 108:5, Juvenile Court Jurisdiction--Delinquent Child--Dna Testing of Certain Delinquent Children.
Carlin, Baldwin's Ohio Prac. Merrick-Rippner Probate Law § 19:10, Uniform Parentage Act--Procedure in Action to Determine Father-Child Relationship.
Carlin, Baldwin's Ohio Prac. Merrick-Rippner Probate Law § 99:39, Consent Not Required--Noncommunication and Nonsupport.
Carlin, Baldwin's Ohio Prac. Merrick-Rippner Probate Law § 110:20, Parentage Act--Jurisdiction and Venue.
Carlin, Baldwin's Ohio Prac. Merrick-Rippner Probate Law § 110:22, Parentage Act--Presumption of Paternity.
Carlin, Baldwin's Ohio Prac. Merrick-Rippner Probate Law § 110:24, Parentage Act--Genetic Tests, Fees, and Costs.
Carlin, Baldwin's Ohio Prac. Merrick-Rippner Probate Law § 110:26, Parentage Act--Applicability of Civil Rules to Paternity Proceedings.
Carlin, Baldwin's Ohio Prac. Merrick-Rippner Probate Law § 110:27, Parentage Act--Evidence of Paternity.
Carlin, Baldwin's Ohio Prac. Merrick-Rippner Probate Law § 110:28, Parentage Act--Trial of Parentage Action.

Law Review and Journal Commentaries

DNA Database Statutes & Privacy in the Information Age, Note. 10 Health Matrix: J Law-Medicine 119 (Winter 2000).

Notes of Decisions

Admissibility of evidence   5   **Burden of proof   4**

----

1. Support obligation

An unmarried parent is subject to the support obligation to which RC 3107.07(A) refers only where a paternity determination has been rendered pursuant to RC 3111.08(B) or 3111.12. In re Adoption of Sunderhaus (Ohio 1992) 63 Ohio St.3d 127, 585 N.E.2d 418, rehearing denied 63 Ohio St.3d 1442, 589 N.E.2d 46. Adoption ⬤➡ 7.4(6)

Since, under this section, as amended effective April 5, 1923, bastardy complaint by mother is not bar to prosecution of father for failure to support child, charge that proceeding by mother was not wholly in her interest, but was also to protect state from care of child, constituted prejudicial error. Pummell v. State (Vinton 1926) 22 Ohio App. 340, 154 N.E. 745, 5 Ohio Law Abs. 293.

2. Nature of action

RC 3111.12(F) is directory in nature in that parentage cases are to be decided in one hundred and twenty (120) days and does not provide for an express dismissal of the case if that time frame is not met. State ex rel. Lawrence County Child Support Enforcement Agency v. Ward (Ohio App. 4 Dist., Lawrence, 11-18-1996) No. 95CA40, 1996 WL 668832, Unreported.

The trial of an action in bastardy is governed by the code of civil procedure, so far as it is applicable, and the complainant has the right under the Constitution and statutes to have the issues raised therein tried by a jury. State ex rel. Wonderland v. Shuba (Lucas 1951) 91 Ohio App. 64, 107 N.E.2d 407, 48 O.O. 240.

Bastardy statutes do not contemplate the punishment of criminal act but only enforcement of moral duty of reimbursing complainant for expense of and maintaining child; verdict of guilty against putative father may be rendered upon the concurrence of three-fourths or more members of jury. State ex rel. Gill v. Volz (Ohio 1951) 156 Ohio St. 60, 100 N.E.2d 203, 45 O.O. 63.

3. Jury trial

The language in RC 3111.12(D) requiring a jury demand in a paternity suit to be made "within three days after the action is set for trial" means "not later than" three days after a trial date is set and does not require that the demand be filed within the three-day period, and a jury demand was timely and proper when it was filed months before a trial date was set. Abbott v. Potter (Jackson 1992) 78 Ohio App.3d 335, 604 N.E.2d 804.

The requirement in RC 3111.12(D) that a jury demand in a paternity suit be made not later than three days after a trial date is set does not clearly conflict with the requirement in Civ R 38(B) that a jury demand be made not later than fourteen days after service of the last pleading directed to the

issue, and in such case the statute rather than the rule controls the time within which to make a jury demand. Abbott v. Potter (Jackson 1992) 78 Ohio App.3d 335, 604 N.E.2d 804.

The trial court abuses its discretion by refusing a defendant in a paternity action a jury trial when his request had been granted at pretrial, even though his payment of a jury deposit was not made within the time period prescribed by local rule and the court did not return the deposit but applied it to costs. Wade v. Oglesby (Huron 1991) 74 Ohio App.3d 560, 599 N.E.2d 748.

The granting of a new trial in a bastardy case is not an abuse of discretion as being unreasonable, arbitrary or unconscionable, where, after verdict and judgment, it is discovered that one of the jurors had previously been a defendant in a paternity suit and had remained silent when the jury was asked on voir dire examination whether any one of them had ever "been involved in a paternity case." Strader v. Mendenhall (Clark 1959) 110 Ohio App. 231, 167 N.E.2d 504, 83 Ohio Law Abs. 23, 13 O.O.2d 13.

Unless otherwise specified, paternity actions are governed by the Ohio rules of civil procedure and, thus, a defendant who fails to demand a jury trial pursuant to Civ R 38, but instead makes a request for the first time on the day of trial, waives his right to a jury trial. Lent v Stull, No. 81 X 7 (4th Dist Ct App, Washington, 2–25–82).

4. Burden of proof

Finding in divorce action that husband is father of two children born during marriage may not be used to resolve disputed paternity issue involving those two children in subsequent criminal nonsupport trial. State v. Cole (Ohio App. 1 Dist., 03-23-1994) 94 Ohio App.3d 629, 641 N.E.2d 732, appeal not allowed 70 Ohio St.3d 1416, 637 N.E.2d 12. Divorce ⬤➡ 172

RC 3111.12(C) does not impermissibly shift the burden of proof to defendants in paternity actions. Grove v. Mattison (Franklin 1988) 61 Ohio App.3d 252, 572 N.E.2d 731, dismissed 42 Ohio St.3d 706, 537 N.E.2d 226.

5. Admissibility of evidence

Genetic test results are admissible without the need for foundation testimony or further proof of authenticity or accuracy where the biological father fails to file a written objection to the report of the court-ordered genetic test results and does not dispute that he received a copy. Joy B. v. Glen D. (Ohio App. 6 Dist., Wood, 08-06-1999) No. OT-99-002, 1999 WL 575945, Unreported.

6. Testimony

In paternity action, child whose paternity is under inquiry is not incompetent to testify. Philpot v. Williams (Hamilton 1983) 8 Ohio App.3d 241, 456 N.E.2d 1315, 8 O.B.R. 314. Witnesses ⬤➡ 92

An accused in a bastardy case may be called by counsel for complainant, and, over defendant's objection, be compelled to testify under cross-examination, either orally or by deposition, but cannot be forced to testify or to give evidence in such proceeding, when to do so would tend to incriminate him. Taylor v. Mosley (Ohio Juv. 1961) 178 N.E.2d 55, 87 Ohio Law Abs. 335, 17 O.O.2d 439.

In a bastardy proceeding where there is a direct conflict in the evidence as to whether complainant and defendant had sexual relations about the time the child was conceived, the question is one for the jury, and it is the jury's prerogative to believe the complainant and disbelieve the defendant. Wells v.

Fulton (Montgomery 1953) 96 Ohio App. 178, 121 N.E.2d 437, 54 O.O. 171, 54 O.O. 240.

Where a defendant in a bastardy action testified on cross-examination but not on direct, plaintiff was not entitled to an instruction that the jury could take into consideration such failure to testify. State ex rel. Johnson v. Mooney (Cuyahoga 1961) 171 N.E.2d 918, 86 Ohio Law Abs. 105.

A defendant in a bastardy action may be compelled to testify against himself. State ex rel. Hetzler v. Snyder (Ohio Mun. 1950) 109 N.E.2d 54, 63 Ohio Law Abs. 42.

3111.13 Effects of judgment; support orders; contempt; prohibitions on certain arrearages

(A) The judgment or order of the court determining the existence or nonexistence of the parent and child relationship is determinative for all purposes.

(B) If the judgment or order of the court is at variance with the child's birth record, the court may order that a new birth record be issued under section 3111.18 of the Revised Code.

(C) Except as otherwise provided in this section, the judgment or order may contain, at the request of a party and if not prohibited under federal law, any other provision directed against the appropriate party to the proceeding, concerning the duty of support, the payment of all or any part of the reasonable expenses of the mother's pregnancy and confinement, the furnishing of bond or other security for the payment of the judgment, or any other matter in the best interest of the child. After entry of the judgment or order, the father may petition that he be designated the residential parent and legal custodian of the child or for parenting time rights in a proceeding separate from any action to establish paternity. Additionally, if the mother is unmarried, the father may file a complaint requesting the granting of reasonable parenting time rights, and the parents of the father, any relative of the father, the parents of the mother, and any relative of the mother may file a complaint requesting the granting of reasonable companionship or visitation rights, with the child pursuant to section 3109.12 of the Revised Code.

The judgment or order shall contain any provision required by section 3111.14 of the Revised Code.

(D) Support judgments or orders ordinarily shall be for periodic payments that may vary in amount. In the best interest of the child, the purchase of an annuity may be ordered in lieu of periodic payments of support if the purchase agreement provides that any remaining principal will be transferred to the ownership and control of the child on the child's attainment of the age of majority.

(E) In determining the amount to be paid by a parent for support of the child and the period during which the duty of support is owed, a court enforcing the obligation of support shall comply with Chapters 3119., 3121., 3123., and 3125. of the Revised Code.

(F)(1) Any court that makes or modifies an order for child support under this section shall comply with Chapters 3119., 3121., 3123., and 3125. of the Revised Code. If any person required to pay child support under an order made under this section on or after April 15, 1985, or modified on or after December 1, 1986, is found in contempt of court for failure to make support payments under the order, the court that makes the finding, in addition to any other penalty or remedy imposed, shall assess all court costs arising out of the contempt proceeding against the person and require the person to pay any reasonable attorney's fees of any adverse party, as determined by the court, that arose in relation to the act of contempt.

(2) When a court determines whether to require a parent to pay an amount for that parent's failure to support a child prior to the date the court issues an order requiring that parent to pay an amount for the current support of that child, it shall consider all relevant factors, including, but not limited to, any monetary contribution either parent of the child made to the support of the child prior to the court issuing the order requiring the parent to pay an amount for the current support of the child.

(3)(a) A court shall not require a parent to pay an amount for that parent's failure to support a child prior to the date the court issues an order requiring that parent to pay an amount for the current support of that child or to pay all or any part of the reasonable expenses of the mother's pregnancy and confinement, if both of the following apply:

(i) At the time of the initial filing of an action to determine the existence of the parent and child relationship with respect to that parent, the child was over three years of age.

(ii) Prior to the initial filing of an action to determine the existence of the parent and child relationship with respect to that parent, the alleged father had no knowledge and had no reason to have knowledge of his alleged paternity of the child.

(b) For purposes of division (F)(4)(a)(ii) of this section, the mother of the child may establish that the alleged father had or should have had knowledge of the paternity of the child by showing, by a preponderance of the evidence, that she performed a reasonable and documented effort to contact and notify the alleged father of his paternity of the child.

(c) A party is entitled to obtain modification of an existing order for arrearages under this division regardless of whether the judgment, court order, or administrative support order from which relief is sought was issued prior to, on, or after October 27, 2000.

(G) As used in this section, "birth record" has the same meaning as in section 3705.01 of the Revised Code.

(H) Unless the court has reason to believe that a person named in the order is a potential victim of domestic violence, any order issued pursuant to this section finding the existence of a parent and child relationship shall contain the full names, addresses, and social security numbers of the mother and father of the child and the full name and address of the child.

(2000 S 180, eff. 3–22–01; 2000 H 242, eff. 10–27–00; 1997 H 352, eff. 1–1–98; 1993 H 173, eff. 12–31–93; 1993 S 115; 1992 S 10; 1990 S 3, H 591, H 15; 1988 H 790, H 708; 1987 H 231; 1986 H 509; 1984 H 614; 1982 H 245)

Uncodified Law

2000 H 242, § 3, eff. 10–27–00, reads:

The General Assembly hereby declares that it is a person's or male minor's substantive right to obtain relief from a final judgment, court order, or administrative determination or order that determines that the person or male minor is the father of a child or that requires the person or male minor to pay child support for a child. The person or male minor may obtain relief from a final judg-ment, court order, or administrative determination or order only if relief is granted based on genetic evidence that the person or male minor is not the father of the child who is the subject of the judg-ment, order, or determination.

1992 S 10, § 5: See Uncodified Law under 3111.01.

1982 H 245, § 3: See Uncodified Law under 3111.04.

Historical and Statutory Notes

Ed. Note: RC 3111.13 contains provisions anal-ogous to former RC 3111.17, repealed by 1982 H 245, eff. 6–29–82.

Ed. Note: Former RC 3111.13 repealed by 1982 H 245, eff. 6–29–82; 1953 H 1; GC 8006–13; Source—GC 12120; see now RC 3119.86 for provi-sions analogous to former RC 3111.13(F)(2), which related to the duration of support orders.

Pre–1953 H 1 Amendments: 124 v S 65

Amendment Note: 2000 S 180 rewrote this sec-tion which prior thereto read:

"(A) The judgment or order of the court deter-mining the existence or nonexistence of the parent and child relationship is determinative for all pur-poses.

"(B) If the judgment or order of the court is at variance with the child's birth record, the court may order that a new birth record be issued under section 3111.18 of the Revised Code.

"(C) Except as otherwise provided in this sec-tion, the judgment or order may contain any other provision directed against the appropriate party to the proceeding, concerning the duty of support, the furnishing of bond or other security for the pay-ment of the judgment, or any other matter in the best interest of the child. The judgment or order shall direct the father to pay all or any part of the reasonable expenses of the mother's pregnancy and confinement. After entry of the judgment or or-der, the father may petition that he be designated the residential parent and legal custodian of the child or for visitation rights in a proceeding sepa-rate from any action to establish paternity. Addi-tionally, if the mother is unmarried, the father, the parents of the father, any relative of the father, the parents of the mother, and any relative of the mother may file a complaint pursuant to section 3109.12 of the Revised Code requesting the granting under that section of reasonable companionship or visitation rights with respect to the child.

"The judgment or order shall contain any provision required by section 3111.14 of the Revised Code.

"(D) Support judgments or orders ordinarily shall be for periodic payments that may vary in amount. In the best interest of the child, a lump-sum payment or the purchase of an annuity may be ordered in lieu of periodic payments of support.

"(E) In determining the amount to be paid by a parent for support of the child and the period during which the duty of support is owed, a court enforcing the obligation of support shall comply with sections 3113.21 to 3113.219 of the Revised Code.

"(F)(1) Each order for child support made or modified under this section shall include as part of the order a general provision, as described in division (A)(1) of section 3113.21 of the Revised Code, requiring the withholding or deduction of income or assets of the obligor under the order as described in division (D) or (H) of section 3113.21 of the Revised Code, or another type of appropriate requirement as described in division (D)(3), (D)(4), or (H) of that section, to ensure that withholding or deduction from the income or assets of the obligor is available from the commencement of the support order for collection of the support and of any arrearages that occur; a statement requiring all parties to the order to notify the child support enforcement agency in writing of their current mailing address, current residence address, current residence telephone number, current driver's license number, and any changes to that information; and a notice that the requirement to notify the agency of all changes to that information continues until further notice from the court. Any court that makes or modifies an order for child support under this section shall comply with sections 3113.21 to 3113.219 of the Revised Code. If any person required to pay child support under an order made under this section on or after April 15, 1985, or modified on or after December 1, 1986, is found in contempt of court for failure to make support payments under the order, the court that makes the finding, in addition to any other penalty or remedy imposed, shall assess all court costs arising out of the contempt proceeding against the person and require the person to pay any reasonable attorney's fees of any adverse party, as determined by the court, that arose in relation to the act of contempt.

"(2) Notwithstanding section 3109.01 of the Revised Code, if a court issues a child support order under this section, the order shall remain in effect beyond the child's eighteenth birthday as long as the child continuously attends on a full-time basis any recognized and accredited high school or the order provides that the duty of support of the child continues beyond the child's eighteenth birthday. Except in cases in which the order provides that the duty of support continues for any period after the child reaches nineteen years of age, the order shall not remain in effect after the child reaches age nineteen. Any parent ordered to pay support under a child support order issued under this section shall continue to pay support under the order, including during seasonal vacation periods, until the order terminates.

"(3) When a court determines whether to require a parent to pay an amount for that parent's failure to support a child prior to the date the court issues an order requiring that parent to pay an amount for the current support of that child, it shall consider all relevant factors, including, but not limited to, any monetary contribution either parent of the child made to the support of the child prior to the court issuing the order requiring the parent to pay an amount for the current support of the child.

"(4)(a) A court shall not require a parent to pay an amount for that parent's failure to support a child prior to the date the court issues an order requiring that parent to pay an amount for the current support of that child or to pay all or any part of the reasonable expenses of the mother's pregnancy and confinement, if both of the following apply:

"(i) At the time of the initial filing of an action to determine the existence of the parent and child relationship with respect to that parent, the child was over three years of age.

"(ii) Prior to the initial filing of an action to determine the existence of the parent and child relationship with respect to that parent, the alleged father had no knowledge and had no reason to have knowledge of his alleged paternity of the child.

"(b) For purposes of division (F)(4)(a)(ii) of this section, the mother of the child may establish that the alleged father had or should have had knowledge of the paternity of the child by showing, by a preponderance of the evidence, that she performed a reasonable and documented effort to contact and notify the alleged father of his paternity of the child.

"(c) A party is entitled to obtain modification of an existing order for arrearages under this division regardless of whether the judgment, court order, or administrative support order from which relief is sought was issued prior to, on, or after the effective date of this amendment.

"(G) As used in this section, "birth record" has the same meaning as in section 3705.01 of the Revised Code.

"(H) Unless the court has reason to believe that a person named in the order is a potential victim of domestic violence, any order issued pursuant to this section finding the existence of a parent and child relationship shall contain the full names, addresses, and social security numbers of the mother and father of the child and the full name and address of the child."

Amendment Note: 2000 H 242 substituted "Except as otherwise provided in this section, the" for "the" in division (C); and added new division (F)(4).

Amendment Note: 1997 H 352 deleted "division (B) of" before "section 3111.14" in the second paragraph in division (C); deleted "on or after December 31, 1993," before "shall include", substituted "income" for "wages" twice and "(D)(3), (D)(4)" for "(D)(6), (D)(7)", inserted "current residence telephone number, current driver's license number,", and deleted "on or after April 12, 1990," before "shall comply", in division (F)(1); inserted "or the order provides that the duty of support of the child continues beyond the child's eighteenth birthday" and added the second sentence in division (F)(2); added division (H); and made other nonsubstantive changes.

Amendment Note: 1993 H 173 rewrote division (F)(1) before the first semi-colon, which previously read:

"(F)(1) Each order for child support made or modified under this section on or after December 1, 1986, shall be accompanied by one or more orders described in division (D) or (H) of section 3113.21 of the Revised Code, whichever is appropriate under the requirements of that section".

Amendment Note: 1993 S 115 rewrote division (E), which previously read:

"(E) In determining the amount to be paid by a parent for support of the child and the period during which the duty of support is owed, a court enforcing the obligation of support shall comply with sections 3113.21 to 3113.219 of the Revised Code, and shall consider all relevant factors, including, but not limited to, all of the following:

"(1) The physical and emotional condition and needs of the child;

"(2) The standard of living and circumstances of each parent and the standard of living the child would have enjoyed had the parents been married;

"(3) The relative financial resources, other assets and resources, and needs of each parent;

"(4) The earning ability of each parent;

"(5) The need and capacity of the child for education, and the educational opportunities that would have been available to him had the parents been married;

"(6) The age of the child;

"(7) The financial resources and the earning ability of the child;

"(8) The responsibility of each parent for the support of others;

"(9) The value of services contributed by the parent who is the residential parent and legal custodian."

Cross References

Contempt action for failure to pay support, see 2705.031, 2705.05
Criminal nonsupport of dependents, see 2919.21
Duty of parents to support children of unemancipated minor children, see 3109.19
Interfering with action to issue or modify support order, see 2919.231

Lottery winner to state under oath whether or not he is in default of support order, hearing, deduction order, see 3770.071
Vital statistics, birth record of legitimatized child, see 3705.09

Ohio Administrative Code References

Support order establishment process, see OAC 5101:12–45–05

Library References

Children Out-of-Wedlock ⚖68, 69.
Westlaw Topic No. 76H.
C.J.S. Children Out-of-Wedlock §§ 127 to 130.

Research References

ALR Library

87 ALR 5th 361, Liability of Father for Retroactive Child Support on Judicial Determination of Paternity.
40 ALR 5th 697, Rights and Remedies of Parents Inter Se With Respect to the Names of Their Children.

Encyclopedias

OH Jur. 3d Constitutional Law § 479, Application of Prohibition.
OH Jur. 3d Constitutional Law § 480, Test for Substantive Nature of Legislation.

OH Jur. 3d Family Law § 938, Purpose of Proceedings.
OH Jur. 3d Family Law § 955, Admissions; Default.
OH Jur. 3d Family Law § 977, Child Support Judgments or Orders.
OH Jur. 3d Family Law § 978, Child Support Judgments or Orders--Amount and Form of Support Order.
OH Jur. 3d Family Law § 979, Child Support Judgments or Orders--Period During Which Duty Owed.
OH Jur. 3d Family Law § 983, New Birth Record.

OH Jur. 3d Family Law § 1025, Hearing; Order.

OH Jur. 3d Family Law § 1027, Requirements of Support Orders.

OH Jur. 3d Family Law § 1028, Duration of Support; Modification.

OH Jur. 3d Family Law § 1029, Determination of Amount of Support.

OH Jur. 3d Family Law § 1184, Annuity in Lieu of Periodic Support Payments.

OH Jur. 3d Family Law § 1207, Interfering With Action to Issue or Modify Support Order.

OH Jur. 3d Names § 15, Minors.

Forms

Ohio Forms Legal and Business § 28:6, Form Drafting Principles.

Ohio Jurisprudence Pleading and Practice Forms § 99:1, Introduction.

Ohio Jurisprudence Pleading and Practice Forms § 111:12, Judgment.

Treatises and Practice Aids

Katz & Giannelli, Baldwin's Ohio Practice Criminal Law § 109:10, Nonsupport.

Katz & Giannelli, Baldwin's Ohio Practice Criminal Law § 109:13, Interfering With Support Actions.

Sowald & Morganstern, Baldwin's Ohio Practice Domestic Relations Law § 3:1, Ohio Parentage Act--History and Origin.

Sowald & Morganstern, Baldwin's Ohio Practice Domestic Relations Law § 19:2, Jurisdiction Over Child Support.

Sowald & Morganstern, Baldwin's Ohio Practice Domestic Relations Law § 19:4, Support Obligations--Duration.

Sowald & Morganstern, Baldwin's Ohio Practice Domestic Relations Law § 21:3, Parenting Time--Jurisdiction--In General.

Sowald & Morganstern, Baldwin's Ohio Practice Domestic Relations Law § 21:9, Enforcement of Parenting Time--Self-Help Efforts.

Sowald & Morganstern, Baldwin's Ohio Practice Domestic Relations Law § 3:11, Judicial Parentage Action--Pleading.

Sowald & Morganstern, Baldwin's Ohio Practice Domestic Relations Law § 3:31, Relief from Paternity or Support Judgment, Under RC 3119.961.

Sowald & Morganstern, Baldwin's Ohio Practice Domestic Relations Law § 3:35, Effect of Judgment--Allocation of Parental Rights and Responsibilities, Visitation, and Companionship Rights--As Between Parents.

Sowald & Morganstern, Baldwin's Ohio Practice Domestic Relations Law § 3:36, Effect of Judgment--Allocation of Parental Rights and Responsibilities, Visitation, and Companionship Rights--Relatives and Nonparents.

Sowald & Morganstern, Baldwin's Ohio Practice Domestic Relations Law § 3:37, Effect of Judgment--Child Support--In General.

Sowald & Morganstern, Baldwin's Ohio Practice Domestic Relations Law § 3:38, Effect of Judgment--Child Support--Past Care.

Sowald & Morganstern, Baldwin's Ohio Practice Domestic Relations Law § 3:39, Effect of Judgment--Child Support--Past Care--Claim Brought After Child is Emancipated.

Sowald & Morganstern, Baldwin's Ohio Practice Domestic Relations Law § 3:40, Effect of Judgment--Child Support--Other Remedies.

Sowald & Morganstern, Baldwin's Ohio Practice Domestic Relations Law § 3:45, Effect of Judgment--Retrospective Effect.

Sowald & Morganstern, Baldwin's Ohio Practice Domestic Relations Law § 3:51, Related Issues--Name.

Sowald & Morganstern, Baldwin's Ohio Practice Domestic Relations Law § 3:52, Complaint to Establish Father-Child Relationship--By Mother--Form.

Sowald & Morganstern, Baldwin's Ohio Practice Domestic Relations Law § 3:60, Complaint for Custody, Support, and Visitation--Form.

Sowald & Morganstern, Baldwin's Ohio Practice Domestic Relations Law § 3:61, Answer and Counterclaim to Complaint for Custody, Support, and Visitation--Form.

Sowald & Morganstern, Baldwin's Ohio Practice Domestic Relations Law § 19:26, Contempt.

Carlin, Baldwin's Ohio Prac. Merrick-Rippner Probate Law § 18:2, Inheritance Rights of Illegitimate Child--Statutory Provisions.

Carlin, Baldwin's Ohio Prac. Merrick-Rippner Probate Law § 19:2, Legitimation--Procedure--Acknowledgment of Paternity.

Carlin, Baldwin's Ohio Prac. Merrick-Rippner Probate Law § 19:8, Uniform Parentage Act--Support Order.

Carlin, Baldwin's Ohio Prac. Merrick-Rippner Probate Law § 19:9, Uniform Parentage Act--Res Judicata; Doctrine of Laches.

Carlin, Baldwin's Ohio Prac. Merrick-Rippner Probate Law § 100:5, Minor--Jurisdiction of Probate Court.

Carlin, Baldwin's Ohio Prac. Merrick-Rippner Probate Law § 100:8, Minor--Best Interests of Minor.

Carlin, Baldwin's Ohio Prac. Merrick-Rippner Probate Law § 107:8, Age Jurisdiction.

Carlin, Baldwin's Ohio Prac. Merrick-Rippner Probate Law § 110:1, Criminal Jurisdiction.

Carlin, Baldwin's Ohio Prac. Merrick-Rippner Probate Law § 19:10, Uniform Parentage Act--Procedure in Action to Determine Father-Child Relationship.

Carlin, Baldwin's Ohio Prac. Merrick-Rippner Probate Law § 99:39, Consent Not Required--Noncommunication and Nonsupport.

Carlin, Baldwin's Ohio Prac. Merrick-Rippner Probate Law § 110:13, Jurisdiction Over Child Custody Matters--Determination of Custody.

Carlin, Baldwin's Ohio Prac. Merrick-Rippner Probate Law § 110:15, Visitation Right of Noncustodial Parent and Others.

Carlin, Baldwin's Ohio Prac. Merrick-Rippner Probate Law § 110:20, Parentage Act--Jurisdiction and Venue.

Carlin, Baldwin's Ohio Prac. Merrick-Rippner Probate Law § 110:21, Parentage Act--Statute of Limitations.

Carlin, Baldwin's Ohio Prac. Merrick-Rippner Probate Law § 110:22, Parentage Act--Presumption of Paternity.

Carlin, Baldwin's Ohio Prac. Merrick-Rippner Probate Law § 110:26, Parentage Act--Applicability of Civil Rules to Paternity Proceedings.

Carlin, Baldwin's Ohio Prac. Merrick-Rippner Probate Law § 110:29, Parentage Act--Judgment Determining Existence of Parent-Child Relationship.

Carlin, Baldwin's Ohio Prac. Merrick-Rippner Probate Law § 110:30, Parentage Act--Enforcement of Support Order.

Carlin, Baldwin's Ohio Prac. Merrick-Rippner Probate Law § 110:31, Parentage Act--Continuing Jurisdiction to Modify or Revoke Judgment.

Carlin, Baldwin's Ohio Prac. Merrick-Rippner Probate Law § 110:32, Parentage Act--Compromise Agreement Between Alleged Father and Mother.

Carlin, Baldwin's Ohio Prac. Merrick-Rippner Probate Law § 110:35, Civil Support Proceedings--Liability for Child Support.

Carlin, Baldwin's Ohio Prac. Merrick-Rippner Probate Law § 110:38, Civil Support Proceedings--Enforcement of Support Orders.

Carlin, Baldwin's Ohio Prac. Merrick-Rippner Probate Law § 109:141, Complaint in Paternity--Form.

Adrine & Ruden, Ohio Domestic Violence Law § 17:4, Confidentiality and Privilege.

Adrine & Ruden, Ohio Domestic Violence Law § 15:10, Batterer Access to the Victim and Children.

Giannelli & Yeomans, Ohio Juvenile Law § 45:11, Permanent Custody--Best Interest Factors.

Law Review and Journal Commentaries

Family Law—Support—The Natural Father of a Child Born Out of Wedlock May Not Assert as a Defense Against His Support Obligation the Mother's Deliberate Misrepresentation That She Was Using Contraception, Note. 29 Vill L Rev 185 (1983–84).

Looking to Unwed Dads to Fill the Public Purse: A Disturbing Wave in Welfare Reform, Roger J.R. Levesque. 32 J Fam L 1 (Winter 1994).

Practice Pointer: Nonmodifiable Child Support Via Annuity, Pamela J. MacAdams. 2 Domestic Rel J Ohio 70 (September/October 1990).

Support Issues in Paternity Cases, Pamela J. MacAdams. 7 Domestic Rel J Ohio 81 (November/December 1995).

Notes of Decisions

In general 3
Acknowledgement 7
Amount of support payments 12
Attorney fees 18
Constitutional issues 1
Construction and application 2
Contempt 16
Custody determinations 8
Defenses 14
Father's surname 6
Federal tax 15
Final or appealable 17
Jurisdiction 9
Parties 10
Purpose 4
Retroactive child support 5
Standing 11
Time of liability for support 13

---

1. Constitutional issues

Alleged father had constitutional right to the assistance of counsel in proceedings to establish paternity and determine child support obligations, and thus trial court's refusal to grant alleged father a continuance of trial in order to obtain new counsel one day after granting former counsel's motion to withdraw required reversal of trial court's order establishing paternity and awarding mother past and current child support; substantial pecuniary interests of alleged father were at stake. Post v.

Caycedo (Ohio App. 9 Dist., Summit, 01-19-2005) No. 21954, 2005-Ohio-161, 2005 WL 100785, Unreported. Children Out–of–wedlock ⚬ 57, Children Out–of–wedlock ⚬ 73

A person is not entitled to relief under Civ R 60(B)(2) or (5) from a judgment of paternity and child support where he signed the child's birth certificate and an administrative order indicating he was the child's biological father even though he knew he was not the biological father because the mother was two months pregnant when he began dating her, and therefore a recent DNA test result showing a 0.00 chance he was the father is not "new evidence" under Civ R 60(B)(2), the specific provision of the rule that prevails over the more general section, (B)(5); although it may appear unfair to require an individual to pay child support for a child not biologically his own, there must be some finality to a judgment and one cannot choose to be a parent and then change his or her mind when the relationship is dissolved. Shaffer v. Rusnak (Ohio App. 5 Dist., Guernsey, 07-01-1998) No. 97 CA 26, 1998 WL 429624, Unreported, dismissed, appeal not allowed 84 Ohio St.3d 1408, 701 N.E.2d 1018.

Statutory amendment allowing for modification of existing orders for payment of child support arrearages, when parentage action was not initiated before child attained age of three years and alleged father did not know or have reason to know of his paternity, was a "substantive statute," as element for determining whether amendment violated constitutional provision prohibiting General Assembly from passing retroactive laws; mother had vested right in pre-amendment court order for father's payment of child support arrearages, and statute impaired that vested right. Smith v. Smith (Ohio, 05-31-2006) 109 Ohio St.3d 285, 847 N.E.2d 414, 2006-Ohio-2419. Children Out–of–wedlock ☞ 31; Children Out–of–wedlock ☞ 69(6); Statutes ☞ 278.32

General Assembly intended retroactive application of statutory amendment, as element for determining whether constitutional provision prohibiting retroactive laws was violated by statutory amendment allowing for modification of existing orders for payment of child support arrearages when parentage action was not initiated before child attained age of three years and alleged father did not know or have reason to know of his paternity; General Assembly expressly stated that a party was entitled to modification of judgment issued "prior to" effective date of statutory amendment. Smith v. Smith (Ohio, 05-31-2006) 109 Ohio St.3d 285, 847 N.E.2d 414, 2006-Ohio-2419. Children Out–of–wedlock ☞ 31; Children Out–of–wedlock ☞ 69(6); Statutes ☞ 278.32

Statutory amendment allowing for modification of existing orders for payment of child support arrearages, when parentage action was not initiated before child attained age of three years and alleged father did not know or have reason to know of his paternity, violated constitutional provision prohibiting General Assembly from passing retroactive laws, as applied to order for payment of child support arrearages that existed before enactment of statutory amendment. Smith v. Smith (Ohio, 05-31-2006) 109 Ohio St.3d 285, 847 N.E.2d 414, 2006-Ohio-2419. Children Out–of–wedlock ☞ 31; Children Out–of–wedlock ☞ 69(6); Statutes ☞ 278.32

Statute regarding retroactive child support was not unconstitutional under constitution section prohibiting retroactive laws. Pier v. Gilbert (Ohio Com.Pl., 11-25-2002) 126 Ohio Misc.2d 91, 804 N.E.2d 106, 2002-Ohio-7484. Child Support ☞ 4

Right of indigent putative father to court-appointed counsel in paternity case does not extend to hearings to determine amount of support once paternity has been established. Geauga Cty. Dept. of Human Serv. v. Hall (Ohio Com.Pl., 01-05-1995) 68 Ohio Misc.2d 75, 647 N.E.2d 579. Children Out–of–wedlock ☞ 69(6)

Statute which did not expressly prohibit mother from bringing parentage action after child became adult and father's right to visitation had expired did not violate father's right to equal protection; father's failure to obtain visitation rights resulted from his own inaction rather than from parentage statutes, and, moreover, mother's action was barred under doctrine of laches. Park v. Ambrose (Ross 1993) 85 Ohio App.3d 179, 619 N.E.2d 469, dismissed, jurisdictional motion overruled 67 Ohio St.3d 1409, 615 N.E.2d 1043. Children Out–of–wedlock ☞ 31; Constitutional Law ☞ 3192

To the extent that an expense is incurred due to a custodial parent's decision to raise a minor in a particular religion, a support order which includes such expense does not impinge upon the rights guaranteed by the Establishment Clause of the First Amendment. However, while it is reasonable to assume, absent evidence to the contrary, that one-half of a parent's ordinary expenses for food, shelter, clothing, transportation, and so forth is expended for the support of a minor, there is no such presumption with respect to extraordinary expenses such as religious or charitable donations. These discretionary expenditures must be supported by evidence which tends to establish that the expenses are incurred on behalf of the child. Dunson v. Aldrich (Franklin 1988) 54 Ohio App.3d 137, 561 N.E.2d 972.

The obligation created by the statute is not a debt within the meaning of O Const Art I §15. Belding v. State (Ohio 1929) 121 Ohio St. 393, 169 N.E. 301, 8 Ohio Law Abs. 28, 30 Ohio Law Rep. 546.

2. Construction and application

Term "child" as used in descent and distribution statute R.C. §2105.06, providing that "child" could inherit property from parent, includes child born out-of-wedlock as well as legitimate child, if parent-child relationship has been established prior to death of father under procedures for determination of paternity under Parentage Act. Beck v. Jolliff (Knox 1984) 22 Ohio App.3d 84, 489 N.E.2d 825, 22 O.B.R. 237. Children Out–of–wedlock ☞ 86

The word "children," as it appears in the substitute beneficiary clause of a group life insurance policy, is to be construed to mean all offspring, regardless of whether they are born in or out of wedlock. Butcher v. Pollard (Cuyahoga 1972) 32 Ohio App.2d 1, 288 N.E.2d 204, 61 O.O.2d 1. Insurance ☞ 3480

3. In general

Father was not entitled to set aside trial court's judgment dismissing his action to establish paternity, child support, and parenting time under catch-all provision of rule of civil procedure reflecting inherent power to court to relieve person from unjust operation of judgment; although father argued court, when existence of father-child relationship was admitted in pleadings, had duty to prepare and journalize separate entry establishing existence of relationship, father, as party to action, was responsible for preparation of entries. In re Adoption of A.N.L. (Ohio App. 12 Dist., Warren, 08-16-2005) No. CA2004-11-131, No. CA2005-04-046, 2005-Ohio-4239, 2005 WL 1949678, Unreported. Children Out–of–wedlock ☞ 20.4; Children Out–of–wedlock ☞ 64

Finding that adjudicated father had knowledge of his father-son relationship to the minor child was supported by evidence that mother informed father that he was the biological father prior and subsequent to child's birth, that father desired to establish visitation and paternity prior to establishment of paternity, and that child was over the age of three at time of initial filing of paternity complaint, and finding satisfied statutory requirements for awarding retroactive child support to mother. Pfeifer v. Shannon (Ohio App. 11 Dist., Portage, 12-23-2004) No. 2003-P-0117, 2004-Ohio-7241, 2004 WL 3090215, Unreported. Children Out–of–wedlock ⚬ 53; Children Out–of–wedlock ⚬ 67

The trial court could consider parenting time issues during paternity proceeding; statute regarding the effects of a paternity judgment did not mandate a separate proceeding to determine visitation, rather, it granted permission for a father to petition for visitation in a proceeding separate from the paternity proceeding. Jefferson County Child Support Enforcement ex rel. Best v. Scheel (Ohio App. 7 Dist., Jefferson, 06-17-2004) No. 03 JE 35, 2004-Ohio-3210, 2004 WL 1379821, Unreported. Children Out–of–wedlock ⚬ 20.9

After former wife assigned portion of child support arrearages owed by former husband to County Child Support Enforcement Agency (CSEA), only CSEA had legal right to waive arrearages, and record contained no evidence that CSEA waived arrearages. Utt v. Utt (Ohio App. 4 Dist., Washington, 12-17-2003) No. 03CA38, 2003-Ohio-7043, 2003 WL 23000154, Unreported. Child Support ⚬ 452

Juvenile court improperly applied standard for deciding motions for relief from judgment to adjudicated father's motion for relief from default adjudication of paternity, where adjudicated father alleged that he was never properly served with process in parentage action and that judgment on complaint was thus void ab initio. Christy L.W. v. Chazarea E.S. (Ohio App. 6 Dist., Ottawa, 01-31-2003) No. OT-02-019, 2003-Ohio-483, 2003 WL 220419, Unreported. Children Out–of–wedlock ⚬ 64

Adjudicated father was entitled to hearing on his motion for relief from judgment of paternity, where adjudicated father had been diagnosed as paranoid and schizophrenic and was apparently unable to file his own affidavit in support of motion, and where his mother and legal guardian submitted uncontroverted affidavit in support of motion to effect that he had never lived at address on file with post office, at which notice of proceedings was properly served. Christy L.W. v. Chazarea E.S. (Ohio App. 6 Dist., Ottawa, 01-31-2003) No. OT-02-019, 2003-Ohio-483, 2003 WL 220419, Unreported. Children Out–of–wedlock ⚬ 64

After a court establishes paternity, it may, but is not required to, award support to an adult emancipated child. Sexton v. Conley (Ohio App. 4 Dist., Scioto, 11-12-2002) No. 01CA2823, 2002-Ohio-6346, 2002 WL 31630766, Unreported. Children Out–of–wedlock ⚬ 67

The juvenile court's authority to order payment of back child support is not defeated by subsequent adoption of the child; however, the court errs by ordering the father to pay support for five months after the child is adopted by the mother's husband.

Black v. Hart (Ohio App. 9 Dist., Summit, 06-05-1996) No. 17524, 1996 WL 304284, Unreported.

Trial court's error in divorce action in relying on statute which specifically pertained to parentage actions when ordering husband to purchase an annuity in lieu of periodic child support payments was harmless error, as court was within its discretion in determining that the purchase of an annuity was in the best interest of the children. Moore v. Moore (Ohio App. 6 Dist., 01-25-2008) 175 Ohio App.3d 1, 884 N.E.2d 1113, 2008-Ohio-255, appeal not allowed 118 Ohio St.3d 1506, 889 N.E.2d 1025, 2008-Ohio-3369. Child Support ⚬ 558(2)

Statute allowing a trial court to order the purchase of an annuity in lieu of child support payments specifically pertained to parentage actions and thus did not support trial court's decision in divorce action to require husband to purchase an annuity in lieu of periodic child support payments. Moore v. Moore (Ohio App. 6 Dist., 01-25-2008) 175 Ohio App.3d 1, 884 N.E.2d 1113, 2008-Ohio-255, appeal not allowed 118 Ohio St.3d 1506, 889 N.E.2d 1025, 2008-Ohio-3369. Child Support ⚬ 155

Once a father-child relationship is established, a trial court has the authority to order support. Carnes v. Kemp (Ohio, 12-30-2004) 104 Ohio St.3d 629, 821 N.E.2d 180, 2004-Ohio-7107. Children Out–of–wedlock ⚬ 67

Likely future of any parent-child relationship and/or the chance that the child may establish a relationship with her biological father are relevant factors in determining timeliness of a motion for equitable relief from a child support order, based on issue of nonpaternity. Dunkle v. Dunkle (Ohio App. 4 Dist., 11-08-1999) 135 Ohio App.3d 669, 735 N.E.2d 469. Child Support ⚬ 323; Children Out–of–wedlock ⚬ 21(1)

Dismissal of paternity action without prejudice was proper upon mother's failure to prosecute, where dismissal with prejudice would have foreclosed valid claim of county child support enforcement agency for reimbursement of monies expended for child support. State ex rel. Cody v. Bradley (Ohio App. 2 Dist., 09-30-1997) 123 Ohio App.3d 397, 704 N.E.2d 307. Children Out–of–wedlock ⚬ 54

Trial court did not abuse its discretion in denying putative father's motion for relief from judgment for child support arrearages, even though court granted relief from judgment of paternity and for future support, where motion was based on newly discovered evidence in form of genetic tests that excluded him as father and that he was impotent, and motion was made more than one year after judgment was entered. Douglas v. Boykin (Ohio App. 12 Dist., 07-07-1997) 121 Ohio App.3d 140, 699 N.E.2d 123. Children Out–of–wedlock ⚬ 69(6)

Subsequent to order establishing paternity, father must file separate complaint in separate action if he wishes to seek visitation with the child, and father cannot merely file motion for visitation in paternity proceedings. Burns v. Darnell (Ohio App. 10 Dist., 01-26-1995) 100 Ohio App.3d 419, 654 N.E.2d 169. Children Out–of–wedlock ☞ 20.4

Trial court in paternity action did not err in overruling motion to transfer father's request for visitation where denial was predicated upon failure of father-plaintiff to file separate action seeking visitation, rather than because motion was filed in wrong county. Burns v. Darnell (Ohio App. 10 Dist., 01-26-1995) 100 Ohio App.3d 419, 654 N.E.2d 169. Children Out–of–wedlock ☞ 20.4

Juvenile court may enter judgment in paternity action upon satisfactory evidence of paternity. Lewis v. Chapin (Ohio App. 8 Dist., 03-21-1994) 93 Ohio App.3d 695, 639 N.E.2d 848 Children Out–of–wedlock ☞ 53

Trial court which adopted shared-parenting plan granting residential status to father during school year and to mother during summer months could properly determine that strict application of child support guidelines would be inappropriate and accordingly deny child support to father under circumstances that parties stipulated that cost of children's parochial education would be shared in proportion to their relative incomes, both parties were required to carry medical insurance for children, and parties were required to share cost of clothing, school supplies and other ordinary expenses. Eickelberger v. Eickelberger (Ohio App. 12 Dist., 02-22-1994) 93 Ohio App.3d 221, 638 N.E.2d 130. Child Support ☞ 148

Shared-parenting order in divorce action was not improper on theory it encouraged excessive entanglement between parties in requiring parties to cooperate and communicate by sharing expenses. Eickelberger v. Eickelberger (Ohio App. 12 Dist., 02-22-1994) 93 Ohio App.3d 221, 638 N.E.2d 130. Child Custody ☞ 127

It is court, and not county department of human services, that is charged with determining child support and related payments by parent following parentage action with respect to child receiving Aid to Families with Dependent Children (AFDC). Gilpen v. Justice (Fayette 1993) 85 Ohio App.3d 86, 619 N.E.2d 94, motion overruled 67 Ohio St.3d 1410, 615 N.E.2d 1044. Children Out–of–wedlock ☞ 67

A party who fails to answer a paternity complaint has no right to notice prior to entry of a default judgment. Long v. Bartlett (Franklin 1992) 73 Ohio App.3d 764, 598 N.E.2d 197.

A parentage action brought by a natural mother against a putative father is barred by res judicata where the parties have previously entered into an agreement signed and journalized by the court, providing for the father to pay the mother $20 a week until the minor child's eighteenth birthday and for the mother to release the father from all claims against him; the fact that the agreement failed to determine the parent/child relationship did not render it void since RC 3111.19 expressly provides that the agreement need not make such a

determination. Nelson v. Pleasant (Lawrence 1991) 73 Ohio App.3d 479, 597 N.E.2d 1137.

Amended sections of R.C. §3111.01 et seq., governing paternity proceedings, that became effective on or after June 29, 1982, have no application to paternity actions in which a judgment was entered prior to effective date. Johnson v. Adams (Ohio 1985) 18 Ohio St.3d 48, 479 N.E.2d 866, 18 O.B.R. 83. Children Out–of–wedlock ☞ 31

While every child conceived in wedlock is presumed legitimate, such presumption is not conclusive and may be rebutted by clear and convincing evidence that there were no sexual relations between husband and wife during the time in which the child must have been conceived, and a complaint for determination of paternity is sufficient if the plaintiff alleges he is the natural father of the child. Joseph v. Alexander (Ohio 1984) 12 Ohio St.3d 88, 465 N.E.2d 448, 12 O.B.R. 77. Children Out–of–wedlock ☞ 3

An action which alleges that a woman has conceived, during wedlock, an illegitimate child by a man other than her husband may not be maintained by the husband as an action for past necessaries furnished, against the alleged natural father of such child. Weinman v. Larsh (Ohio 1983) 5 Ohio St.3d 85, 448 N.E.2d 1384, 5 O.B.R. 138.

The support and maintenance award under RC 3111.17 is dependent on both the mother's needs and the father's ability to pay. Edwards v. Sadusky (Summit 1982) 4 Ohio App.3d 297, 448 N.E.2d 506, 4 O.B.R. 548. Children Out–of–wedlock ☞ 67

The provision in RC 3111.17 for a court order requiring the reputed father to give security for support payments is one of several remedies available to secure payment of the judgment and it is within the sound discretion of the juvenile court. Edwards v. Sadusky (Summit 1982) 4 Ohio App.3d 297, 448 N.E.2d 506, 4 O.B.R. 548. Children Out–of–wedlock ☞ 70

Determination of paternity in a bastardy proceeding is not a prerequisite to the prosecution of a parent under RC 2903.08 for nonsupport of an illegitimate child. State v. Medley (Miami 1960) 111 Ohio App. 352, 172 N.E.2d 143, 14 O.O.2d 328. Child Support ☞ 653; Children Out–of–wedlock ☞ 21(2)

An adjudication in a bastardy proceeding is not conclusive upon the state unless expressly made so by statute, and the state has power to prosecute criminal proceedings for nonsupport of an illegitimate child at any time before, after and independently of an adjudication in a bastardy proceeding, and wholly independently of any finding therein made, or judgment therein rendered, with respect to the question of paternity. State v. Schwartz (Ohio 1940) 137 Ohio St. 371, 30 N.E.2d 551, 19 O.O. 90. Children Out–of–wedlock ☞ 68

Establishment of paternity pursuant to RC Ch 3111 confers upon a child born out of wedlock the same rights of inheritance under RC 2105.06(A) as a child born within wedlock. Beck v Jolliff, 20 OBR 129 (App, Knox 1984).

An agreed judgment entry which finds a defendant to be the "reputed father" of a child and orders support does not constitute a valid legal determination of paternity and does not give rise to a statutory obligation of support; therefore, an order for support without a prior valid determination of paternity must be vacated and remanded. Glass v Campbell, No. 15–92–18 (3d Dist Ct App, Van Wert, 5–27–93).

The reputed father who has paid or given security as ordered by court for maintenance of the child, under this section, is not liable to proceedings under GC 13008 (RC 3113.01), for nonsupport. 1917 (Pt 2) OAG 601.

4. Purpose

Prior decision of the Court of Appeals, holding that res judicata barred former husband's action seeking a determination of paternity, amounted to an "admission on file" for purposes of summary judgment in a subsequent paternity action, where trial court deemed prior appellate decision admitted as true and genuine by husband, and husband did not challenge that ruling. Donnelly v. Kashnier (Ohio App. 9 Dist., Medina, 02-12-2003) No. 02CA0051-M, 2003-Ohio-639, 2003 WL 294413, Unreported. Children Out–of–wedlock ☞ 64

Trial court was required to consider support being paid by father of minor child to child's mother pursuant to agreed settlement entry of previous parentage action in calculating support payable under judgment entered in child's subsequent action to establish parent-child relationship; while prior action was not res judicata with respect to issue of support, both actions served same purpose in that they required payment of money for benefit of child, and child was only entitled to single "support." Cornell v. Brumfield (Ohio App. 4 Dist., 10-10-1996) 115 Ohio App.3d 259, 685 N.E.2d 270.

Mother's claim against alleged father was distinct from Department of Human Services' claim for reimbursement of birthing expenses, for purposes of determining whether judgment rendered in mother's paternity action barred Department's later claim. Payne v. Cartee (Ohio App. 4 Dist., 06-10-1996) 111 Ohio App.3d 580, 676 N.E.2d 946, appeal not allowed 77 Ohio St.3d 1482, 673 N.E.2d 143. Children Out–of–wedlock ☞ 33; Children Out–of–wedlock ☞ 68

Purpose of paternity statute is to compel father of illegitimate child to bear expenses of childbirth and child support so that mother will not be solely responsible for that support and so that child will not be financial burden on state. Seegert v. Zietlow (Ohio App. 8 Dist., 08-15-1994) 95 Ohio App.3d 451, 642 N.E.2d 697. Children Out–of–wedlock ☞ 31

5. Retroactive child support

Trial court's conclusion that unmarried father knew or had reason to know of his alleged paternity of child, so as to enable mother to seek retroactive child support upon establishing father's paternity, was not against the manifest weight of the evidence;

father and mother discussed mother's pregnancy and their options when mother became pregnant, and mother made occasional attempts to contact father thereafter, including leaving messages with his roommate and searching for his contact information approximately twice a year. Osgood v. Dzikowski (Ohio App. 10 Dist., Franklin, 09-30-2008) No. 08AP-105, 2008-Ohio-5065, 2008 WL 4416653, Unreported. Children Out–of–wedlock ☞ 67

Statute allowing a mother who seeks retroactive child support to establish that the father knew or had reason to know of his alleged paternity of child by showing that she made a "reasonable and documented effort to contact and notify the alleged father of his paternity" did not require such effort to be supported by written documentation, and thus unmarried mother's testimony as to her efforts to contact father was sufficient to support trial court's conclusion that mother's efforts were reasonable and documented; purpose of the documentation requirement was to require an explanation detailed enough to be susceptible of meaningful challenge. Osgood v. Dzikowski (Ohio App. 10 Dist., Franklin, 09-30-2008) No. 08AP-105, 2008-Ohio-5065, 2008 WL 4416653, Unreported. Children Out–of–wedlock ☞ 67

Trial court had jurisdiction to hear and determine merits of nonmarital child's request for retroactive child support against mother in parentage action, even though child was emancipated; juvenile court had jurisdiction over a parentage action, and the court could consider a claim for support after it determined parentage. Elzey v. Springer (Ohio App. 12 Dist., Fayette, 03-22-2004) No. CA2003-04-005, 2004-Ohio-1373, 2004 WL 549805, Unreported. Children Out–of–wedlock ☞ 36

Laches and equitable considerations barred mother's claim against father for retroactive child support, where mother delayed case for 10 years with no apparent reason, father did not know he was father and mother concealed that fact even though father was nearby, mother had not seemed concerned about father's lack of support, father suffered loss of love and companionship of child for 10-year period, child did not appear to have been neglected, penalized, or harmed any more than any other fatherless child, and father had agreed to pay substantial prospective award of support. Pier v. Gilbert (Ohio Com.Pl., 11-25-2002) 126 Ohio Misc.2d 91, 804 N.E.2d 106, 2002-Ohio-7484. Children Out–of–wedlock ☞ 38

Father did not have knowledge of paternity, and mother failed to make reasonable and documented effort to inform father of paternity, for purposes of retroactive child support; there was more than one other potential father, and mother had only one or two conversations with father in nine-year period prior to action for child support. Pier v. Gilbert (Ohio Com.Pl., 11-25-2002) 126 Ohio Misc.2d 91, 804 N.E.2d 106, 2002-Ohio-7484. Children Out–of–wedlock ☞ 67

Juvenile court has jurisdiction in parentage action to award retroactive or back child support for period of time prior to date upon which parent-child relationship is judicially established. Seegert v. Zietlow (Ohio App. 8 Dist., 08-15-1994) 95 Ohio App.3d 451, 642 N.E.2d 697. Children Out–of–wedlock ⊜ 67

Mother's inaction during child's minority did not bar adult child's claim for retroactive support in parentage action brought by child. Park v. Ambrose (Ross 1993) 85 Ohio App.3d 179, 619 N.E.2d 469, dismissed, jurisdictional motion overruled 67 Ohio St.3d 1409, 615 N.E.2d 1043. Children Out–of–wedlock ⊜ 38

6. Father's surname

Court of common pleas, in context of paternity action, may determine surname by which child shall be known after establishment of existence of parent and child relationship, and showing that name determination is in best interest of child. Eagleson v. Hall (Ohio App. 5 Dist., Guernsey, 07-22-2008) No. 2007-CA-28, 2008-Ohio-3647, 2008 WL 2840602, Unreported. Children Out–of–wedlock ⊜ 1

Unmarried father's claims that he had made several attempts to support and spend time with child and that it was more meaningful to father that child's surname be changed to match father's surname were not appropriate bases for name change. In re Dayton (Ohio App. 7 Dist., 11-28-2003) 155 Ohio App.3d 407, 801 N.E.2d 531, 2003-Ohio-6397. Children Out–of–wedlock ⊜ 1

In determining whether change of surname is in best interest of child of unmarried parents, trial court shall consider: effect of change on preservation and development of child's relationship with each parent; identification of child as part of family unit; length of time that child has used surname; child's preference if child is of sufficient maturity to express a meaningful preference; whether child's surname is different from surname of child's residential parent; embarrassment, discomfort, or inconvenience that may result when child bears surname different from residential parent's; parental failure to maintain contact with and support of child; and any other factor relevant to child's best interest. In re Dayton (Ohio App. 7 Dist., 11-28-2003) 155 Ohio App.3d 407, 801 N.E.2d 531, 2003-Ohio-6397. Children Out–of–wedlock ⊜ 1

A court of common pleas may determine surname by which child of unmarried parents shall be known after establishment of parent and child relationship, and may change child's surname upon a showing that name change is in best interest of child. In re Dayton (Ohio App. 7 Dist., 11-28-2003) 155 Ohio App.3d 407, 801 N.E.2d 531, 2003-Ohio-6397. Children Out–of–wedlock ⊜ 1

Unmarried father failed to demonstrate how changing surname of child from that of mother, who was residential parent, to that of father would be in child's best interest; father's claims that child was only six months old and was too young to express preference, that name change would not affect mother's relationship to child and would not

be inconvenienced by name change, that child had no friends that would have referred to him by mother's surname, and that name change would not cause real inconvenience only showed name change would not be harmful to child. In re Dayton (Ohio App. 7 Dist., 11-28-2003) 155 Ohio App.3d 407, 801 N.E.2d 531, 2003-Ohio-6397. Children Out–of–wedlock ⊜ 1

In paternity action filed by Child Support Enforcement Agency (CSEA), trial court could not change surnames of children without first determining whether name change was in best interests of children. Dorsett v. Wheeler (Ohio App. 3 Dist., 03-16-1995) 101 Ohio App.3d 716, 656 N.E.2d 698. Children Out–of–wedlock ⊜ 1

In determining the best interest of the child concerning the surname to be used when parents who have never been married contest a surname, the court should consider: (1) the length of time that the child has used a surname; (2) the effect of a name change on the father-child relationship and on the mother-child relationship; (3) the identification of the child as part of a family unit; (4) the embarrassment, discomfort, or inconvenience that may result when a child bears a surname different from the custodial parent's; (5) the preference of the child if the child is of an age and maturity to express a meaningful preference; and (6) any other factor relevant to the child's best interest. Courts should consider only those factors present in the particular circumstances of each case. Bobo v. Jewell (Ohio 1988) 38 Ohio St.3d 330, 528 N.E.2d 180. Children Out–of–wedlock ⊜ 1

Pursuant to RC 3111.13(C), a court of common pleas may determine the surname by which the child shall be known after establishment of the existence of the parent and child relationship, and a showing that the name determination is in the best interest of the child. Bobo v. Jewell (Ohio 1988) 38 Ohio St.3d 330, 528 N.E.2d 180. Children Out–of–wedlock ⊜ 1

7. Acknowledgement

Ex-boyfriend, who had previously acknowledged paternity of ex-girlfriend's child, was not entitled to have his child support arrearages to state, which provided assistance to child, set aside after genetic testing, conducted several years later, confirmed he was not child's father; ex-boyfriend's voluntary acknowledgment of parentage effectively prevented state from identifying true biological father in a timely manner and pursuing reimbursement from him, state was now precluded from collecting back support from the child's biological father, and record demonstrated that state justifiably relied upon ex-boyfriend's acknowledgement of parentage. Newton v. Dunn (Ohio App. 4 Dist., Ross, 10-08-2003) No. 03CA2701, 2003-Ohio-5523, 2003 WL 22369276, Unreported. Children Out–of–wedlock ⊜ 69(6)

Prior trial court finding that former husband knew himself not to be the father of child for whom he was ordered to pay child support before he acknowledged himself to be the father in a dissolution proceeding was law of the case, precluding father from subsequently challenging paternity. Donnelly v. Kashnier (Ohio App. 9 Dist., Medina, 02-12-2003) No. 02CA0051-M, 2003-Ohio-639, 2003 WL 294413, Unreported. Courts ☞ 99(6)

While generally some adjudication or acknowledgement of paternity is necessary for court to invoke its statutory power to order child support, the right to find out who one's father is (or is not) is separate and distinct from the right to support from one's father. Snider v. Lillie (Ohio App. 1 Dist., 10-17-1997) 131 Ohio App.3d 444, 722 N.E.2d 1036, dismissed, appeal not allowed 81 Ohio St.3d 1452, 690 N.E.2d 546. Children Out-of-wedlock ☞ 30

8. Custody determinations

Pursuant to a parentage action where the issue of who would have custody of the child is never before the court or addressed in an agreement between the parties, it is error for the trial court to address issues of child support and visitation without first making a determination as to which parent will have custody. State ex rel. Ellen v. Deal (Ohio App. 10 Dist., Franklin, 12-27-1994) No. 94APF04-549, 1994 WL 723377, Unreported.

The validity of an former RC 2105.18 acknowledgment of paternity may not be attacked in defending an action for custody and support. In re Custody of Davis (Guernsey 1987) 41 Ohio App.3d 81, 534 N.E.2d 945. Children Out-of-wedlock ☞ 12

A judgment establishing paternity and imposing a duty to support on the father may also imply a determination of custody to the mother, so that a motion to determine custody filed years later by the father should be determined according to the standards for change in custody set forth in RC 3109.04(B)(1). In re Brazell (Ohio Com.Pl. 1986) 27 Ohio Misc.2d 7, 499 N.E.2d 925, 27 O.B.R. 68.

A judgment in a paternity action has the effect of a prior determination of custody; therefore, a subsequent change of custody pursuant to a petition by the natural father must be based on a finding of changed circumstances. In re Yates (Franklin 1984) 18 Ohio App.3d 95, 481 N.E.2d 646, 18 O.B.R. 458.

When the alleged natural father of an illegitimate child, who has participated in the nurturing process of the child, files a complaint seeking custody of the child under RC 2151.23(A)(2), and the mother admits that he is the natural father of the child, the natural father has equality of standing with the mother with respect to the custody of the child, and the court shall determine which parent shall have the legal custody of the child, taking into account what would be in the best interests of the child. In re Byrd (Ohio 1981) 66 Ohio St.2d 334, 421 N.E.2d 1284, 20 O.O.3d 309. Children Out-of-wedlock ☞ 20.4

There is a distinction between a "putative" father and a father who has been adjudicated as such by his own admission, in that a father adjudicated as such by his own admission has legal standing to seek custody of his illegitimate child against the world, including the mother. In re Wright (Ohio Com.Pl. 1977) 52 Ohio Misc. 4, 367 N.E.2d 931, 6 O.O.3d 31.

The mother of an illegitimate child has a right of custody that is superior to that of the putative father. In re H. (Ohio Com.Pl. 1973) 37 Ohio Misc. 123, 305 N.E.2d 815, 66 O.O.2d 178, 66 O.O.2d 368.

The custody of an illegitimate child will not be taken from the mother and awarded to the father merely upon the basis that the wife has contracted an interracial marriage. In re H. (Ohio Com.Pl. 1973) 37 Ohio Misc. 123, 305 N.E.2d 815, 66 O.O.2d 178, 66 O.O.2d 368.

The mother of a bastard child is its natural guardian, has the legal right to its custody, and is legally responsible for its care and support. In re Gary (Cuyahoga 1960) 112 Ohio App. 331, 167 N.E.2d 509, 83 Ohio Law Abs. 486, 14 O.O.2d 431. Children Out-of-wedlock ☞ 20.1; Children Out-of-wedlock ☞ 21(3)

9. Jurisdiction

Trial court had jurisdiction in paternity proceeding to order that claimed father's name be removed from child's birth certificate and that child's last name be changed to that of mother, after it excluded claimed father as child's biological father based on genetic testing, as paternity statute permitted trial court to modify birth certificate and decide issue of name change at time parentage was established. Jennifer C. v. Tony M.D. (Ohio App. 12 Dist., Clermont, 09-26-2005) No. CA2005-01-005, 2005-Ohio-5050, 2005 WL 2335332, Unreported. Children Out-of-wedlock ☞ 1; Children Out-of-wedlock ☞ 64; Health ☞ 397

Issue of trial court's subject matter jurisdiction over mother's petition to change name of child could not be waived. Porter v. Walker (Ohio App. 9 Dist., Lorain, 06-15-2005) No. 04CA008575, 2005-Ohio-2972, 2005 WL 1398901, Unreported. Names ☞ 20

Juvenile court had subject matter jurisdiction to determine putative father's parental rights with respect to child, after court determined paternity, even though a separate proceeding to establish parental rights was not filed by father; failure to proceed in a separate proceeding to determine parental rights did not constitute a jurisdictional defect affecting power of court to issue judgment as to parental rights. B.W. v. D.B.-B. (Ohio App. 6 Dist., 06-10-2011) 193 Ohio App.3d 637, 953 N.E.2d 369, 2011-Ohio-2813. Children Out-of-wedlock ☞ 20.4

Juvenile court's statutory jurisdiction to render final judgment in parentage action includes power to enter order of paternity and order of child support, and also to determine issues of custody and visitation arising from parentage action. Borkosky v. Mihailoff (Ohio App. 3 Dist., 03-03-1999) 132 Ohio App.3d 508, 725 N.E.2d 694. Child

Support ☞ 11; Children Out–of–wedlock ☞ 20.4; Children Out–of–wedlock ☞ 36

Court in which paternity proceeding is pending had subject matter jurisdiction to award back child support to an adult child. Hugershoff v. Loecy (Ohio Com.Pl., 08-26-1998) 103 Ohio Misc.2d 55, 725 N.E.2d 376. Children Out–of–wedlock ☞ 36

Juvenile court possessed jurisdiction to make custody and visitation order in paternity judgment, under statute allowing order determining existence of parent and child relationship to contain any other provision directed against appropriate party to proceeding, concerning matter in best interest of child. Pegan v. Crawmer (Ohio, 07-24-1996) 76 Ohio St.3d 97, 666 N.E.2d 1091, 1996-Ohio-419. Children Out–of–wedlock ☞ 20.4

Juvenile court, in determining paternity, had jurisdiction to decide state's action for aid furnished by state for support and medical expenses of children born out-of-wedlock. Brightwell v. Easter (Ohio App. 9 Dist., 03-09-1994) 93 Ohio App.3d 425, 638 N.E.2d 1067. Social Security And Public Welfare ☞ 194.19

Mother's laches will not be imputed to child so as to bar child's claim for support in parentage action. Park v. Ambrose (Ross 1993) 85 Ohio App.3d 179, 619 N.E.2d 469, dismissed, jurisdictional motion overruled 67 Ohio St.3d 1409, 615 N.E.2d 1043. Children Out–of–wedlock ☞ 38

Child's claim for support in parentage action is separate and distinct from claim of mother. Park v. Ambrose (Ross 1993) 85 Ohio App.3d 179, 619 N.E.2d 469, dismissed, jurisdictional motion overruled 67 Ohio St.3d 1409, 615 N.E.2d 1043. Children Out–of–wedlock ☞ 67

An order designating paternal grandparents as legal custodians is void ab initio where the action seeking custody is initiated by a motion in a parentage proceeding; furthermore, RC 3111.13 contemplates an entirely new proceeding after the determination of paternity by which the father would be the named plaintiff and the mother would be the named defendant and where the mother is never served with a summons and copies of a complaint seeking custody the trial court does not have personal jurisdiction over her and does not have the authority to render the custody determination. Mary B. v Zollie M, No. L–96–120, 1997 WL 90612 (6th Dist Ct App, Lucas, 2–28–97).

10. Parties

Evidence supported finding that prospective adoptive parents were not parties to putative father's proceeding to determine parental rights; juvenile rule defined a party to a hearing governing the legal custody of a child as the child who was subject to the proceeding, the child's parents or guardians, or the grandparents, in appropriate cases. B.W. v. D.B.-B. (Ohio App. 6 Dist., 06-10-2011) 193 Ohio App.3d 637, 953 N.E.2d 369, 2011-Ohio-2813. Children Out–of–wedlock ☞ 20.4

11. Standing

Child and Department of Human Services were not in privity with mother, and, therefore, judgment rendered in mother's paternity action did not present res judicata bar to later action by child and Department. Payne v. Cartee (Ohio App. 4 Dist., 06-10-1996) 111 Ohio App.3d 580, 676 N.E.2d 946, appeal not allowed 77 Ohio St.3d 1482, 673 N.E.2d 143. Children Out–of–wedlock ☞ 33; Children Out–of–wedlock ☞ 68

12. Amount of support payments

Amount of retroactive child support to be awarded mother, in paternity action father brought six years after child was born, was to be based on mother's actual income figures, rather than minimum wage; father submitted employment application of mother that indicated she earned more than minimum wage at some of her jobs, and mother also testified that she earned $15/hour for eight months working for a steel company. Walk v. Bryant (Ohio App. 4 Dist., Lawrence, 03-12-2004) No. 03CA7, 2004-Ohio-1295, 2004 WL 540919, Unreported. Children Out–of–wedlock ☞ 67

Trial court's decision to award mother retroactive child support was not unreasonable, unconscionable or arbitrary, in paternity action brought by father six years after child was born, where father had reason to believe he was child's father, father had remained active in child's life as his father for a period of four years after child's birth, and father had not provided regular support for child's needs. Walk v. Bryant (Ohio App. 4 Dist., Lawrence, 03-12-2004) No. 03CA7, 2004-Ohio-1295, 2004 WL 540919, Unreported. Children Out–of–wedlock ☞ 67

Purge conditions as noted in journal entry requiring father to pay $2,762.11 towards total child support arrearage, to pay $35.12 per week plus processing fee, and to pay $20 per month toward remaining arrearage were unreasonable, insofar as father, who was unemployed, had no driver's license, and was partially disabled, was required to meet purge conditions within five days of filing entry. Schuman v. Cranford (Ohio App. 4 Dist., Vinton, 04-23-2003) No. 02CA571, 2003-Ohio-2117, 2003 WL 1958021, Unreported. Child Support ☞ 445

Temporary child support award to mother of $200 per week was not abuse of trial court's discretion in parentage action; adjudicated father's annual income was $105,000, mother's annual income was $35,000, mother had child care expenses of approximately $600 per month, and court ordered parties to submit additional financial information within 30 days to permit review of propriety of award in greater detail. Nwabara v. Willacy (Ohio App. 8 Dist., 08-09-1999) 135 Ohio App.3d 120, 733 N.E.2d 267, dismissed, appeal not allowed 87 Ohio St.3d 1451, 719 N.E.2d 967. Children Out–of–wedlock ☞ 21(2)

Amount of trial court's award to mother of past care was not abuse of discretion, where court had at its disposal in calculating such award adequate financial information as to both parties and child support schedules and worksheets required by statute, and where adjudicated father did not specify any specific items of past care he found objectionable or what amount he found excessive. Nwabara v. Willacy (Ohio App. 8 Dist., 08-09-1999) 135 Ohio App.3d 120, 733 N.E.2d 267, dismissed, appeal not allowed 87 Ohio St.3d 1451, 719 N.E.2d 967. Child Support ⟨⟩ 199

Child born out of wedlock was not entitled to half of award of back child support owed by her adjudicated father, and entire award was required to go to mother, in absence of any evidence that mother had not spent funds awarded on necessities for raising child and where mother's action for back child support was not barred by laches. State ex rel. Donovan v. Zajac (Ohio App. 11 Dist., 01-02-1998) 125 Ohio App.3d 245, 708 N.E.2d 254, dismissed, appeal not allowed 81 Ohio St.3d 1521, 692 N.E.2d 1023. Children Out–of–wedlock ⟨⟩ 67

Parent obliged to make periodic payments of child support cannot also be required to fund future needs trust for child's benefit; while court may require that parent make lump-sum payment or purchase annuity for child's benefit, such payment or annuity is in lieu of periodic support payments. Frazier v. Daniels (Ohio App. 1 Dist., 02-26-1997) 118 Ohio App.3d 425, 693 N.E.2d 289. Child Support ⟨⟩ 223

Juvenile court did not abuse its discretion in parentage action by calculating back child support owed for each year of child's life by use of worksheets with reference to applicable law for each given year, due to dramatic changes in parties' financial situations since child's birth. Seegert v. Zietlow (Ohio App. 8 Dist., 08-15-1994) 95 Ohio App.3d 451, 642 N.E.2d 697. Children Out–of–wedlock ⟨⟩ 67

Father failed to demonstrate abuse of discretion by juvenile court in parentage proceeding in awarding $3,900 in current child support for year of 1993; pursuant to statutory guidelines, "rebuttably presumed" correct amount was $4,542 for 1993 and, despite father's claims to contrary, his disposable income exceeded amount of child support for that year. Seegert v. Zietlow (Ohio App. 8 Dist., 08-15-1994) 95 Ohio App.3d 451, 642 N.E.2d 697. Children Out–of–wedlock ⟨⟩ 67

Juvenile court was required to award to state in paternity actions full amount of past aid provided to children born out of wedlock, and award of amount less than all aid furnished to children was improper. Brightwell v. Easter (Ohio App. 9 Dist., 03-09-1994) 93 Ohio App.3d 425, 638 N.E.2d 1067. Social Security And Public Welfare ⟨⟩ 194.19

Awards against fathers of children born out-of-wedlock to state for reimbursement of support and medical expenses paid on behalf of children were not modifiable. Brightwell v. Easter (Ohio App. 9 Dist., 03-09-1994) 93 Ohio App.3d 425, 638 N.E.2d 1067. Social Security And Public Welfare ⟨⟩ 194.19

Social security payments for a child's benefit must be considered in connection with child support payments ordered to be made by the parent whose retirement triggers the payments, but this does not justify crediting the entire monthly benefit amount to child support, nor is the determination of necessary child support unaffected by the receipt of the benefits; the proper method is to deduct all or part of the benefit amount from the guideline-determined necessary support based on the child's best interest and equity to both parents. McNeal v. Cofield (Franklin 1992) 78 Ohio App.3d 35, 603 N.E.2d 436.

Trial court abused its discretion by setting up savings account for child born out-of-wedlock to be funded by father and be disbursed as court ordered, where account was not based on child's current needs or support. Bailey v. Mitchell (Cuyahoga 1990) 67 Ohio App.3d 441, 587 N.E.2d 358. Children Out–of–wedlock ⟨⟩ 67

A juvenile court does not impermissibly order a father to pay child support without consideration of the applicable statutory provisions and child support guidelines issued by the state supreme court where the statement of proceedings shows that the court inquired of counsel and the parties regarding the subjects required by the statutory provisions and the guidelines and that it, based on its inquiries, found the parties' circumstances had sufficiently changed to order a modification of support. Miller v. Barker (Cuyahoga 1989) 64 Ohio App.3d 649, 582 N.E.2d 647.

Where evidence of a defendant's monthly child support expenses from a prior marriage are before the court, absent evidence to the contrary, a reviewing court will presume that the court properly considered the evidence in fashioning a child support award pursuant to RC 3111.13. Dunson v. Aldrich (Franklin 1988) 54 Ohio App.3d 137, 561 N.E.2d 972. Child Support ⟨⟩ 555

An award of child support made pursuant to RC 3111.13(E) must countenance both parents' financial status and the father's ability to pay. In making this award, it is appropriate for the trial court to first ascertain the amount necessary to support the child and then to fashion an award which is reasonable in light of the factors listed in RC 3111.13(E). Dunson v. Aldrich (Franklin 1988) 54 Ohio App.3d 137, 561 N.E.2d 972. Child Support ⟨⟩ 62; Child Support ⟨⟩ 143

In the absence of evidence to the contrary, it is not an abuse of discretion for the court to assume that one-half of the plaintiff-mother's necessary monthly expenses are incurred on behalf of her child. Dunson v. Aldrich (Franklin 1988) 54 Ohio App.3d 137, 561 N.E.2d 972. Child Support ⟨⟩ 194

The phrase "support and maintenance," as it was used in RC 3111.17(Repealed), did not include within its meaning lost wages as a consequence of a pregnancy. Jelen v. Price (Cuyahoga 1983) 9 Ohio App.3d 174, 458 N.E.2d 1267, 9 O.B.R. 284. Children Out–of–wedlock ⟨⟩ 67

In paternity proceedings, the juvenile court may consider insurance payments and disability benefits received by the mother of an illegitimate child in determining her need for medical expenses and support during pregnancy, delivery, and post-natal convalescence. Edwards v. Sadusky (Summit 1982) 4 Ohio App.3d 297, 448 N.E.2d 506, 4 O.B.R. 548. Children Out–of–wedlock ☞ 67

Trial court award of retroactive child support from when father stopped voluntarily providing support, rather than from the date of child's birth, was not an abuse of discretion; father had voluntarily been providing support for child since shortly after child's birth, and father provided money to purchase an air conditioner to maintain child's health. Evans v. Richardson (Ohio App. 10 Dist., Franklin, 07-11-2002) No. 01AP-1328, 2002-Ohio-3555, 2002 WL 1477358, Unreported. Child Support ☞ 150

Under section, the obligation of the bond therein prescribed is confined to payment of support, maintenance, and necessary expenses of the complainant caused by the pregnancy and childbirth together with the cost of prosecution, and does not run to any reasonable sum fixed by the court for support and maintenance of the child until it becomes eighteen years of age. State ex rel. Adkins v. Mefford (Hamilton 1944) 75 Ohio App. 215, 61 N.E.2d 635, 43 Ohio Law Abs. 349, 30 O.O. 554.

A juvenile court must use the child support guidelines when determining the amount of child support to be awarded. In re Stewart, No. 88 CA 15 (2d Dist Ct App, Greene, 11–23–88).

Where a father has been disabled and unemployed for four years preceding a support hearing, and has no income at the time of the hearing, it is consistent with RC 3111.13 for the court to decline to order support payments, with the proviso that if the father were to become employed or obtain a source of income, a hearing would be held at such time to determine support payments. Fedor v DiBacco, No. 83 CA 46 (7th Dist Ct App, Mahoning, 1–11–84).

13. Time of liability for support

Wife failed to establish that she was entitled to retroactive child support from the filing date of the divorce; magistrate ordered child support to start the month after he issued his decision, and there was no evidence on the record that mother filed a motion for child support prior to the final divorce hearing. Longo v. Longo (Ohio App. 11 Dist., Geauga, 04-29-2005) No. 2004-G-2556, 2005-Ohio-2069, 2005 WL 1007248, Unreported, appeal not allowed 106 Ohio St.3d 1555, 836 N.E.2d 581, 2005-Ohio-5531. Child Support ☞ 150

Doctrine of laches could be applied in action brought by Child Support Enforcement Agency (CESA), on mother's behalf, seeking child support arrears and maternity expenses; although Supreme Court has stated that doctrine generally is not applied to government, issues in proceeding were private in character, rather than public, as amounts

of money were to be paid to mother, rather than government. CSEA ex rel. E.T. v. H.S. (Ohio App. 8 Dist., Cuyahoga, 05-06-2004) No. 82820, 2004-Ohio-2343, 2004 WL 1047831, Unreported, as amended nunc pro tunc. Children Out–of–wedlock ☞ 69(6)

Putative father adequately raised defense of laches in proceeding brought by Child Support Enforcement Agency (CESA), on mother's behalf, seeking child support arrears and maternity expenses, where putative father argued in trial court that he had right to timely institution of enforcement proceedings, that he was prejudiced by delay, and that "38 years was far too long to be persecuted under so-called colors of law." CSEA ex rel. E.T. v. H.S. (Ohio App. 8 Dist., Cuyahoga, 05-06-2004) No. 82820, 2004-Ohio-2343, 2004 WL 1047831, Unreported, as amended nunc pro tunc. Children Out–of–wedlock ☞ 69(6)

Trial court abused its discretion, in paternity action father brought six years after child was born, by ordering father to pay half of $2,348 in past due birthing expenses, though mother testified that such amount was still owing, where documentary evidence submitted by mother indicated that mother was only charged $1,500 by physician for birthing expenses. Walk v. Bryant (Ohio App. 4 Dist., Lawrence, 03-12-2004) No. 03CA7, 2004-Ohio-1295, 2004 WL 540919, Unreported. Children Out–of–wedlock ☞ 67

Trial court did not abuse its discretion, in paternity action brought by father, by finding that mother did not waive her right to seek birthing expenses and retroactive child support, though mother never asked father for birthing expenses and retroactive child support and only asserted claims in paternity action father brought six years after child was born; mother's lack of diligence was not inconsistent with an assertion of her right to child support. Walk v. Bryant (Ohio App. 4 Dist., Lawrence, 03-12-2004) No. 03CA7, 2004-Ohio-1295, 2004 WL 540919, Unreported. Children Out–of–wedlock ☞ 33

Trial court did not abuse its discretion by finding that father was not materially prejudiced by mother's delay in asserting her claims for birthing expenses and retroactive child support, and thus that mother's claims were not barred by laches, in action brought by father to establish paternity six years after child was born, though father did not maintain records to document support he had provided up until time his relationship with mother was terminated, as any prejudice father suffered resulted not from mother's delay but from his own actions. Walk v. Bryant (Ohio App. 4 Dist., Lawrence, 03-12-2004) No. 03CA7, 2004-Ohio-1295, 2004 WL 540919, Unreported. Children Out–of–wedlock ☞ 38

Trial court order which maintained that father was liable for child support arrearage owed to the State, even though genetic testing revealed that father was not the biological father of 14-year-old child, was not an abuse of discretion; father admitted that when child was born he was not sure he was child's biological father, when State initiated paternity proceedings father admitted he was child's biological father, State provided public assistance on behalf of child and was owed almost $17,000.00, and the State was precluded from collecting support from child's biological father. Garst v. Hopkins (Ohio App. 2 Dist., Clark, 03-28-2003) No. 2002-CA-50, 2003-Ohio-1557, 2003 WL 1571704, Unreported. Children Out–of–wedlock ⬤ 21(1); Social Security And Public Welfare ⬤ 11

So long as a child commences a paternity action prior to the twenty-third birthday, a court may award retroactive child support, or any other applicable remedy upon finding existence of parent-child relationship. Sexton v. Conley (Ohio App. 4 Dist., Scioto, 11-12-2002) No. 01CA2823, 2002-Ohio-6346, 2002 WL 31630766, Unreported. Children Out–of–wedlock ⬤ 67

In a parentage action a trial court may order the payment of child support retroactive to the time of the child's birth provided that the action for parentage is brought within five years after the child has reached the age of majority. State ex rel. Donovan v. Zajac (Ohio App. 11 Dist., Geauga, 06-23-2000) No. 98-G-2199, 2000 WL 816249, Unreported.

An award of child support retroactive to the child's date of birth is denied where the mother (1) repeatedly prevents the father from having access to the child, (2) refuses to return telephone calls, (3) neglects to provide the father pictures or information of the child's well-being, and (4) states she does not believe the father deserves information about or contact with the child. Tod W. v. Erika P. (Ohio App. 6 Dist., Wood, 09-17-1999) No. WD-99-013, 1999 WL 728087, Unreported.

A parent who makes significant financial contributions towards the care of his son for nine years prior to the date the complaint for support is filed is relieved of his support obligation for the nine year period where (1) the child has had severe mental and physical disabilities since birth and is confined to a wheelchair, (2) a good faith relationship exists between the mother and father before the support complaint is filed such that the child's financial needs were apparently met, and (3) there is reason to expect that the father's support obligation may last well beyond the time that the child reaches the age of majority. Shockey v. Blackburn (Ohio App. 12 Dist., Warren, 05-17-1999) No. CA98-07-085, 1999 WL 326174, Unreported.

A minor has a right to an award of retroactive child support independent of his mother's claim. Crawley-Kinley v. Price (Ohio App. 1 Dist., Hamilton, 03-13-1996) No. C-940920, 1996 WL 107569, Unreported.

Juvenile court has jurisdiction to award retroactive child support payments to an adult emancipated child if a parentage action is filed prior to the child's twenty-third birthday. Carnes v. Kemp (Ohio, 12-30-2004) 104 Ohio St.3d 629, 821 N.E.2d 180, 2004-Ohio-7107. Children Out–of–wedlock ⬤ 67

Juvenile court had jurisdiction to award retroactive child support payments to adult emancipated child who filed paternity action before her twenty-third birthday; statute governing paternity actions expressly provided that child was entitled to commence paternity action up to age of 23, and child support statute provided that juvenile court had authority to make support order once parentage determination was made. Carnes v. Kemp (Ohio, 12-30-2004) 104 Ohio St.3d 629, 821 N.E.2d 180, 2004-Ohio-7107. Children Out–of–wedlock ⬤ 67

When there has never been a meaningful relationship between the child and the adjudicated father, a two-year period between the initial parentage adjudication and a motion for relief from a child support order may not be per se unreasonable; however, the reasonable time period may have elapsed where the child and the adjudicated "father" have established a relationship. Dunkle v. Dunkle (Ohio App. 4 Dist., 11-08-1999) 135 Ohio App.3d 669, 735 N.E.2d 469. Child Support ⬤ 323; Children Out–of–wedlock ⬤ 21(1)

Trial court's reliance on mere passage of time as the only factor in determining that two years between entry of divorce judgment and former husband's motion for relief from child support obligation was unreasonable was an abuse of discretion; neither party contended that husband knew of his nonpaternity at the time of the divorce, which raised additional relevant factors, including when husband first suspected he was not child's biological father and what the nature of the relationship was between husband and child. Dunkle v. Dunkle (Ohio App. 4 Dist., 11-08-1999) 135 Ohio App.3d 669, 735 N.E.2d 469. Child Support ⬤ 220, Child Support ⬤ 323

Trial court did not abuse its statutory discretion, in parentage and support action, in ordering adjudicated father to pay child support commencing two days after conclusion of jury trial, where court's statutory discretion was broad enough to have permitted it to order support from child's birth forward, and child was two years old at conclusion of jury trial. Nwabara v. Willacy (Ohio App. 8 Dist., 08-09-1999) 135 Ohio App.3d 120, 733 N.E.2d 267, dismissed, appeal not allowed 87 Ohio St.3d 1451, 719 N.E.2d 967. Children Out–of–wedlock ⬤ 21(2)

Court is not required to award child support retroactively from the time paternity is determined, and discretion is left with the court. Hugershoff v. Loecy (Ohio Com.Pl., 09-28-1999) 103 Ohio Misc.2d 58, 725 N.E.2d 378. Children Out–of–wedlock ⬤ 21(2)

Trial court calculating adjudicated father's back child support obligation with respect to child born in October erred in including payments for January through September of year of child's birth in calculation, because there was no duty to support child before her birth. State ex rel. Donovan v. Zajac (Ohio App. 11 Dist., 01-02-1998) 125 Ohio App.3d 245, 708 N.E.2d 254, dismissed, appeal not allowed

81 Ohio St.3d 1521, 692 N.E.2d 1023. Children Out–of–wedlock ☞ 67

Trial court erred in requiring adjudicated father to pay back child support, covering period of 21 years, in lump sum payment; father was entitled to payment schedule over reasonable period of time, not less than three years. State ex rel. Donovan v. Zajac (Ohio App. 11 Dist., 01-02-1998) 125 Ohio App.3d 245, 708 N.E.2d 254, dismissed, appeal not allowed 81 Ohio St.3d 1521, 692 N.E.2d 1023. Children Out–of–wedlock ☞ 67

Remand for recalculation of adjudicated father's back child support obligation was required, where trial court erroneously applied guidelines enacted when child was nine years old to calculate father's obligation as of her date of birth. State ex rel. Donovan v. Zajac (Ohio App. 11 Dist., 01-02-1998) 125 Ohio App.3d 245, 708 N.E.2d 254, dismissed, appeal not allowed 81 Ohio St.3d 1521, 692 N.E.2d 1023. Children Out–of–wedlock ☞ 73

Trial court clearly has discretion to award support from date of child's birth. Frazier v. Daniels (Ohio App. 1 Dist., 02-26-1997) 118 Ohio App.3d 425, 693 N.E.2d 289. Children Out–of–wedlock ☞ 69(6)

Back child support may be ordered in paternity proceeding to date of child's birth. Beach v. Poole (Ohio App. 5 Dist., 06-17-1996) 111 Ohio App.3d 710, 676 N.E.2d 1254, appeal not allowed 77 Ohio St.3d 1482, 673 N.E.2d 143. Children Out–of–wedlock ☞ 67

While trial court does not have authority to order child support until there is legal determination of parentage, once that determination is made, putative father can be ordered to pay support retroactive to date of child's birth; date of judicial establishment of parentage is not date putative father became child's father, as putative father was child's natural father from date of child's birth. Beach v. Poole (Ohio App. 5 Dist., 06-17-1996) 111 Ohio App.3d 710, 676 N.E.2d 1254, appeal not allowed 77 Ohio St.3d 1482, 673 N.E.2d 143. Children Out–of–wedlock ☞ 67

In parentage action, absent a defense, court may award child support from date of child's birth to date of paternity adjudication. Lewis v. Chapin (Ohio App. 8 Dist., 03-21-1994) 93 Ohio App.3d 695, 639 N.E.2d 848 Children Out–of–wedlock ☞ 67

Trial court had subject matter jurisdiction to award child support retroactive to child's date of birth in paternity proceeding brought more than 20 years after child was born. Park v. Ambrose (Ross 1993) 85 Ohio App.3d 179, 619 N.E.2d 469, dismissed, jurisdictional motion overruled 67 Ohio St.3d 1409, 615 N.E.2d 1043. Children Out–of–wedlock ☞ 38; Children Out–of–wedlock ☞ 67

Mother's claim for retroactive child support was barred under doctrine of laches, where mother failed to seek support until child was adult and had not permitted father to have any input in child's upbringing. Park v. Ambrose (Ross 1993) 85 Ohio App.3d 179, 619 N.E.2d 469, dismissed, jurisdictional motion overruled 67 Ohio St.3d 1409, 615 N.E.2d 1043. Children Out–of–wedlock ☞ 38

A natural father's duty to support a child arises at birth, particularly where he acknowledges paternity, and where the natural father unjustifiably fails to communicate with or support a child for one year prior to the filing of an adoption petition, his consent to the adoption of his illegitimate child is unnecessary. In re Adoption of Taylor (Medina 1989) 61 Ohio App.3d 500, 573 N.E.2d 156, motion overruled 43 Ohio St.3d 712, 541 N.E.2d 78.

In the absence of a specific finding that the equitable amount that a paternity defendant should pay toward child support has not varied since the birth of the child, it is inappropriate for a court to utilize the current finding as to appropriate child support and arbitrarily determine the amount due for support since the birth of the child by multiplying the number of weeks involved by the current child support amount. Dunson v. Aldrich (Franklin 1988) 54 Ohio App.3d 137, 561 N.E.2d 972. Children Out–of–wedlock ☞ 67

Child support must be awarded from the date of the child's birth to the date of the paternity adjudication. Edwards v. Sadusky (Summit 1982) 4 Ohio App.3d 297, 448 N.E.2d 506, 4 O.B.R. 548.

Where support payments for the period from the date of a child's birth to the date of adjudication are prayed for and proved, the court abuses its discretion by failing to make an award of child support for that period, unless there is an affirmative demonstration of some circumstance which reasonably could relieve the father of this obligation and the child of this entitlement. Baugh v. Carver (Hamilton 1981) 3 Ohio App.3d 139, 444 N.E.2d 58, 3 O.B.R. 157. Children Out–of–wedlock ☞ 67

The court in a bastardy action has jurisdiction to order support payments to commence with the birth of the child, even though the complaint was filed subsequent to the birth of the child. Weaver v. Chandler (Franklin 1972) 31 Ohio App.2d 243, 287 N.E.2d 917, 60 O.O.2d 405. Children Out–of–wedlock ☞ 67

A person adjudged to be the reputed father of an illegitimate child before such child attains the age of eighteen years is liable for support of the child from the time of its birth until such adjudication. Willis v. Wilson (Lawrence 1947) 83 Ohio App. 311, 80 N.E.2d 175, 51 Ohio Law Abs. 122, 38 O.O. 1.

RC 3111.13(C) confers jurisdiction on the court to determine whether an order of retroactive support is appropriate when brought after the child is emancipated. Spires v Moore, No. CT98–0040, 2000 WL 1545 (5th Dist Ct App, Muskingum, 11–24–99).

Where an order of paternity has been vacated after a subsequent HLA test, it is error for the court to order relief from the support obligation retroactive to the date of the original order when the adjudged father failed to obtain appropriate HLA testing for three years after the original order.

Haney v Feltner, No. C–830715 (1st Dist Ct App, Hamilton, 7–3–84).

Payment for the support of an illegitimate child starts from the time of the child's birth. State ex rel. Raydel v. Raible (Ohio Com.Pl. 1953) 112 N.E.2d 568, 64 Ohio Law Abs. 438, affirmed 117 N.E.2d 480, 69 Ohio Law Abs. 356, appeal dismissed 162 Ohio St. 74, 120 N.E.2d 590, 54 O.O. 18.

14. Defenses

Trial court determination that the doctrine of laches did not apply as a defense to all child support that accrued before a temporary child support order was issued was not an abuse of discretion, in proceeding to establish paternity, even though child was a teenager when paternity proceeding was initiated; father obtained child's birth certificate shortly after child's birth to see if he had been listed as child's father, father was aware that mother told her friends that father was child's biological father, child grew up knowing that father was his biological father, and mother testified that she told father that he was the biological father of child and he chose not to establish a relationship with child. Zartman v. Swad (Ohio App. 5 Dist., Fairfield, 07-28-2003) No. 02CA86, 2003-Ohio-4140, 2003 WL 21804426, Unreported, appeal not allowed 100 Ohio St.3d 1508, 799 N.E.2d 187, 2003-Ohio-6161. Child Support ⟜ 177

Statutory laches defense did not apply as a defense to father's obligation to pay child support for the period prior to the entry of a temporary child support order, in proceeding to establish parentage; statutory laches defense applied only if the father had no knowledge or reason to know of the child, father admitted that he obtained child's birth certificate shortly after child's birth to see if he was listed as child's father, and mother testified that she told father that he was child's biological father shortly after child's birth and father chose not to be involved in child's life. Zartman v. Swad (Ohio App. 5 Dist., Fairfield, 07-28-2003) No. 02CA86, 2003-Ohio-4140, 2003 WL 21804426, Unreported, appeal not allowed 100 Ohio St.3d 1508, 799 N.E.2d 187, 2003-Ohio-6161. Child Support ⟜ 177

15. Federal tax

Income tax exemption for child out-of-wedlock would alternate yearly between mother and father pursuant to temporary agreement. Pier v. Gilbert (Ohio Com.Pl., 11-25-2002) 126 Ohio Misc.2d 91, 804 N.E.2d 106, 2002-Ohio-7484. Children Out–of–wedlock ⟜ 67; Internal Revenue ⟜ 3297; Taxation ⟜ 3501

Birthing expenses, which are defined in state statute as proper part of child support order, may be recouped from parent's federal tax refund under federal statute requiring past-due child support to be withheld from federal income tax refunds. Gladysz v. King (Ohio App. 2 Dist., 03-31-1995) 103 Ohio App.3d 1, 658 N.E.2d 309, appeal not allowed

73 Ohio St.3d 1428, 652 N.E.2d 801. Internal Revenue ⟜ 4973

County child support enforcement agency could not collect monies pursuant to federal statute requiring past-due child support to be withheld from obligor's federal income tax refunds as there was no "past due" child support where father was not in default of obligation fixed by court to pay one-half expenses of mother's pregnancy despite fact that father had not yet extinguished that debt. Gladysz v. King (Ohio App. 2 Dist., 03-31-1995) 103 Ohio App.3d 1, 658 N.E.2d 309, appeal not allowed 73 Ohio St.3d 1428, 652 N.E.2d 801. Children Out–of–wedlock ⟜ 69(6); Internal Revenue ⟜ 4973

Trial court did not err in splitting children's tax exemptions between father and mother even though father, pursuant to shared-parenting plan, was residential parent of children for nine months of year. Eickelberger v. Eickelberger (Ohio App. 12 Dist., 02-22-1994) 93 Ohio App.3d 221, 638 N.E.2d 130. Child Support ⟜ 141

16. Contempt

Father's failure to maintain dental insurance for the benefit of his children as he was previously ordered to do warranted finding of contempt, despite father's argument that he attempted to provide for the children's dental needs by means other than by insurance. O'Connor v. O'Connor (Ohio App. 10 Dist., Franklin, 05-01-2008) No. 07AP-248, 2008-Ohio-2276, 2008 WL 2025267, Unreported. Child Support ⟜ 444

Trial court acted within its discretion by entering purge order permitting father to purge himself of a second finding of contempt, for failing to pay children's dental insurance as previously ordered, by paying for certain orthodontia expenses incurred by the children; the order did not arise from a determination that the orthodontia expenses were included in the dental insurance coverage, and was not a child support order, but rather, provided father a short-term alternative to incarceration. O'Connor v. O'Connor (Ohio App. 10 Dist., Franklin, 05-01-2008) No. 07AP-248, 2008-Ohio-2276, 2008 WL 2025267, Unreported. Child Support ⟜ 445

There was some competent, credible evidence to support trial court's findings regarding child support or child expense payments made by father, supporting finding of contempt arising from father's failure to make such payments as previously ordered by court, even though father alleged that trial court erred in excluding certain undated invoices and other undocumented claims of payment. O'Connor v. O'Connor (Ohio App. 10 Dist., Franklin, 05-01-2008) No. 07AP-248, 2008-Ohio-2276, 2008 WL 2025267, Unreported. Child Support ⟜ 487

Father violated court order when he failed to pay County Children Services Enforcement Agency for birth services rendered by County Department of Human Services, for purposes of determination of contempt, even if father paid restitution to County for mother's welfare fraud; father was ordered by court to make payments for his own obligation and failed to do so. McKinnis v. Parlier (Ohio App. 12 Dist., Clermont, 06-14-2004) No. CA2003-06-050, 2004-Ohio-3010, 2004 WL 1300160, Unreported. Child Support ⚖ 444

Child support obligor who fails to comply with child support order has burden to prove inability to pay, and it is not prerequisite to finding of contempt that violation be purposeful, willing, or intentional. Watson v. Wolsonovich (Ohio App. 7 Dist., 07-12-1996) 112 Ohio App.3d 565, 679 N.E.2d 350. Child Support ⚖ 445; Child Support ⚖ 484

17. Final or appealable

Juvenile court order establishing father's paternity and ordering father to pay permanent child support was a final order, although father's complaint to establish visitation was pending, and thus mother was required to file notice of appeal within 30 days of order. O'Neill v. Crawford (Ohio App. 8 Dist., Cuyahoga, 11-10-2004) No. 84307, 2004-Ohio-6023, 2004 WL 2579001, Unreported. Children Out–of–wedlock ⚖ 73

Juvenile court's judgment establishing paternity and setting visitation but not addressing issue of support was not final, as would support extraordinary writ of prohibition, where issue of support was before juvenile court. State ex rel. Dixon v. Clark Cty. Court of Common Pleas, Juv. Div. (Ohio App. 2 Dist., 05-17-1995) 103 Ohio App.3d 523, 660 N.E.2d 486. Prohibition ⚖ 3(1)

18. Attorney fees

Award to child's mother of $5,000 in attorney fees, in form of child support, was within trial court's statutory authority, given adjudicated father's dilatory tactics and evasion of his support obligation. Nwabara v. Willacy (Ohio App. 8 Dist., 08-09-1999) 135 Ohio App.3d 120, 733 N.E.2d 267, dismissed, appeal not allowed 87 Ohio St.3d 1451, 719 N.E.2d 967. Child Support ⚖ 603; Children Out–of–wedlock ⚖ 21(2)

A juvenile court errs in not entertaining evidence on the issue of attorney fees and in failing, within its sound discretion, to make a reasonable award of attorney fees under the mandate of RC 3111.13(F) to a mother after it has found a father in contempt for nonpayment of child support. Miller v. Barker (Cuyahoga 1989) 64 Ohio App.3d 649, 582 N.E.2d 647.

A court is not granted authority by RC Ch 3111 to award attorney fees in a paternity proceeding. Dunson v. Aldrich (Franklin 1988) 54 Ohio App.3d 137, 561 N.E.2d 972. Children Out–of–wedlock ⚖ 75

3111.14 Fees for experts; court costs

The court may order reasonable fees for experts and other costs of the action and pretrial proceedings, including genetic tests, to be paid by the parties in proportions and at times determined by the court. The court may order the proportion of any party to be paid by the court, and, before or after payment by any party or the county, may order all or part of the fees and costs to be taxed as costs in the action.

(1992 S 10, eff. 7–15–92; 1990 H 591; 1982 H 245)

Uncodified Law

1992 S 10, § 5: See Uncodified Law under 3111.01.

1982 H 245, § 3: See Uncodified Law under 3111.04.

Historical and Statutory Notes

Ed. Note: RC 3111.14 contains provisions analogous to former RC 3111.17, repealed by 1982 H 245, eff. 6–29–82.

Ed. Note: Former RC 3111.14 repealed by 1982 H 245, eff. 6–29–82; 1953 H 1; GC 8006–14; Source—GC 12121.

Pre–1953 H 1 Amendments: 124 v S 65

Cross References

Board of county commissioners may pay expert witness fee, see 307.52

Library References

Children Out-of-Wedlock ⚖75.
Westlaw Topic No. 76H.

C.J.S. Children Out-of-Wedlock §§ 53, 76, 139 to 142.

Research References

Encyclopedias

OH Jur. 3d Family Law § 981, Fees and Court Costs.

OH Jur. 3d Family Law § 1027, Requirements of Support Orders.

Forms

Ohio Jurisprudence Pleading and Practice Forms § 111:12, Judgment.

Treatises and Practice Aids

Sowald & Morganstern, Baldwin's Ohio Practice Domestic Relations Law § 3:20, Evidence--Genetic Tests--Costs of Testing.

Sowald & Morganstern, Baldwin's Ohio Practice Domestic Relations Law § 3:33, Attorney Fees and Costs.

Carlin, Baldwin's Ohio Prac. Merrick-Rippner Probate Law § 19:12, Uniform Parentage Act--Costs and Appointed Counsel.

Carlin, Baldwin's Ohio Prac. Merrick-Rippner Probate Law § 110:24, Parentage Act--Genetic Tests, Fees, and Costs.

Carlin, Baldwin's Ohio Prac. Merrick-Rippner Probate Law § 110:29, Parentage Act--Judgment Determining Existence of Parent-Child Relationship.

Notes of Decisions

Attorney fees   6
Bankruptcy effect   3
Expert witness fees   5
Guardian ad litem fees   4
HLA tests   2
Indigent defendant   1

1. Indigent defendant

Where the defendant in a paternity action knowingly and voluntarily plead guilty, never requested genetic tests, and did not tell the court that he was indigent, the trial court was not required to inform the defendant of his constitutional right to the state's prepayment of the cost of the genetic tests. Edwards v. Porter (Lorain 1983) 8 Ohio App.3d 277, 456 N.E.2d 1347, 8 O.B.R. 370.

The denial of blood grouping tests to an indigent paternity defendant, who is unable to prepay for such tests, and who faces the state as an adversary when the complainant-mother and her child are recipients of public assistance, violates the due process guarantee of US Const Am 14. Anderson v. Jacobs (Ohio 1981) 68 Ohio St.2d 67, 428 N.E.2d 419, 22 O.O.3d 268. Children Out–of–wedlock ⇨ 58; Constitutional Law ⇨ 4020

GC 12123 (RC 3111.17) did not authorize an award of attorney's fees. State ex rel. Raydel v. Raible (Cuyahoga 1954) 117 N.E.2d 480, 69 Ohio Law Abs. 356, appeal dismissed 162 Ohio St. 74, 120 N.E.2d 590, 54 O.O. 18.

2. HLA tests

In paternity action in which results of genetic testing clearly excluded indigent putative father as natural father of child, costs of genetic testing were properly taxable against mother and would thus be paid by county child support agency under statute authorizing payment of court costs by local social service agency when custodian was recipient of Aid for Dependent Children and defendant was found to be indigent. Little v. Stoops (Clinton 1989) 65 Ohio App.3d 758, 585 N.E.2d 475. Children Out–of–wedlock ⇨ 75; Counties ⇨ 138

The cost of an HLA test to determine paternity is a necessary litigating expense and it is reversible error not to tax such cost to a nonindigent plaintiff who does not prevail at trial. Reed v Pace, No. 48612 (8th Dist Ct App, Cuyahoga, 4–18–85).

3. Bankruptcy effect

Although bankruptcy matters are inherently proceedings in equity and must foster equitable results, bankruptcy court would not second-guess judgment rendered by state court in establishing Chapter 7 debtor-biological father's debt for paternity action expenses where debtor was not placed in any worse position than that which existed before bankruptcy and debtor had opportunity to argue merits of debt allocation before the state court. In re Lamb (Bkrtcy.N.D.Ohio, 05-08-1996) 198 B.R. 511. Bankruptcy ⇨ 2125; Bankruptcy ⇨ 3409

4. Guardian ad litem fees

While RC 3111.14 does not expressly mention guardian ad litem fees, such fees may be awarded if they are found to constitute "reasonable fees for experts" or "other costs of the action." Sutherland v. Sutherland (Franklin 1989) 61 Ohio App.3d 154, 572 N.E.2d 215.

5. Expert witness fees

Trial court did not abuse its discretion in requiring adjudicated father to pay one-half of DNA expert witness' fee as costs, where expert witness was procured jointly by parties prior to action and the witness testified at trial. Nwabara v. Willacy (Ohio App. 8 Dist., 08-09-1999) 135 Ohio App.3d 120, 733 N.E.2d 267, dismissed, appeal not allowed 87 Ohio St.3d 1451, 719 N.E.2d 967. Children Out–of–wedlock ⇨ 75

6. Attorney fees

Failure of legislature to include in parentage act a provision for payment of attorney fees as "costs" in paternity actions involving child support orders denied unmarried mother equal protection of the law because payment of attorney fees as "costs" was statutorily available in divorce proceedings. McQueen v. Hawkins (Lucas 1989) 63 Ohio App.3d 243, 578 N.E.2d 539. Children Out–of–wedlock ⇨ 31; Constitutional Law ⇨ 3467

RC 3111.14 does not provide for an award of attorney fees. Sutherland v. Sutherland (Franklin 1989) 61 Ohio App.3d 154, 572 N.E.2d 215.

A court is not granted authority by RC Ch 3111 to award attorney fees in a paternity proceeding.

Dunson v. Aldrich (Franklin 1988) 54 Ohio App.3d 137, 561 N.E.2d 972. Children Out–of–wedlock ⬤ 75

3111.15 Enforcement of support order

(A) If the existence of the father and child relationship is declared or if paternity or a duty of support has been adjudicated under sections 3111.01 to 3111.18 of the Revised Code or under prior law, the obligation of the father may be enforced in the same or other proceedings by the mother, the child, or the public authority that has furnished or may furnish the reasonable expenses of pregnancy, confinement, education, support, or funeral, or by any other person, including a private agency, to the extent that any of them may furnish, has furnished, or is furnishing these expenses.

(B) The court may order support payments to be made to the mother, the clerk of the court, or a person or agency designated to administer them for the benefit of the child under the supervision of the court.

(C) Willful failure to obey the judgment or order of the court is a civil contempt of the court.

(2000 S 180, eff. 3–22–01; 1986 H 476, eff. 9–24–86; 1982 H 245)

Uncodified Law

1992 S 10, § 5: See Uncodified Law under 3111.01.

1982 H 245, § 3: See Uncodified Law under 3111.04.

Historical and Statutory Notes

Ed. Note: Former 3111.15 repealed by 1982 H 245, eff. 6–29–82; 125 v 184; 1953 H 1; GC 8006–15; Source—GC 12122; see now 3111.12 for provisions analogous to former 3111.15. 3111.15 contains provisions analogous to former 3111.17, repealed by 1982 S 245, eff. 6–29–82.

Pre–1953 H 1 Amendments: 124 v S 65

Amendment Note: 2000 S 180 substituted "3111.18" for "3111.19" in division (A).

Cross References

Contempt action for failure to pay support, see 2705.031, 2705.05
Criminal nonsupport of dependents, see 2919.21
Lottery winner to state under oath whether or not he is in default of support order, hearing, deduction order, see 3770.071

Small loans; assignment or order of wages for support, see 1321.32, 1321.33

Ohio Administrative Code References

Child support program, see OAC Ch 5101:1–29

Library References

Children Out-of-Wedlock ⬤69.
Westlaw Topic No. 76H.
C.J.S. Children Out-of-Wedlock §§ 129 to 130.

Research References

ALR Library

87 ALR 5th 361, Liability of Father for Retroactive Child Support on Judicial Determination of Paternity.

Encyclopedias

OH Jur. 3d Family Law § 1028, Duration of Support; Modification.

Forms

Ohio Forms Legal and Business § 28:4, Introduction.

Ohio Jurisprudence Pleading and Practice Forms § 111:13, Enforcement.

Treatises and Practice Aids

Sowald & Morganstern, Baldwin's Ohio Practice Domestic Relations Law § 3:37, Effect of Judgment--Child Support--In General.

Carlin, Baldwin's Ohio Prac. Merrick-Rippner Probate Law § 19:8, Uniform Parentage Act--Support Order.

Carlin, Baldwin's Ohio Prac. Merrick-Rippner Probate Law § 19:9, Uniform Parentage Act--Res Judicata; Doctrine of Laches.

Carlin, Baldwin's Ohio Prac. Merrick-Rippner Probate Law § 110:30, Parentage Act--Enforcement of Support Order.

Carlin, Baldwin's Ohio Prac. Merrick-Rippner Probate Law § 110:31, Parentage Act--Continuing Jurisdiction to Modify or Revoke Judgment.

Carlin, Baldwin's Ohio Prac. Merrick-Rippner Probate Law § 110:35, Civil Support Proceedings--Liability for Child Support.

Law Review and Journal Commentaries

Bankruptcy Reform Act of 1994—What the Bankruptcy Code Giveth, Domestic Relations Courts (and Congress) Taketh Away, C.R. "Chip" Bowles. 8 Domestic Rel J Ohio 17 (March/April 1996).

Into the Red to Stay in the Pink: The Hidden Cost of Being Uninsured. Hugh F. "Trey" Daly III, Leslie M. Oblak, Robert W. Seifert, and Kimberly Shellenberger, 12 Health Matrix: J Law-Medicine 39 (Winter 2002).

Notes of Decisions

Bankruptcy 9
Construction and application 1
Discretion of court 3
Duty to support 6
Imprisonment of defendant 7
Indigent defendants 10
Jurisdiction 4
Proper parties 5
Purpose 2
Right of action 8

1. Construction and application

Use of the words "father" and "mother" as respective equivalents to obligor and obligee, in statute governing awards of retroactive child support in paternity actions, did not serve to preclude entry of order requiring biological father to pay presumed father retroactive child support for the six-year period in which presumed father enjoyed residential and legal custody of child, as it was clear from the language of the statute that "any other person" that furnished expenses for the support of a child could seek enforcement of a support order against the adjudicated father. Dawson v. Dawson (Ohio App. 3 Dist., Union, 11-16-2009) No. 14-09-08, No. 14-09-12, No. 14-09-10, No. 14-09-11, 2009-Ohio-6029, 2009 WL 3806251, Unreported, appeal not allowed 124 Ohio St.3d 1521, 923 N.E.2d 622, 2010-Ohio-1075. Children Out–of–wedlock ☞ 67

2. Purpose

Purpose of paternity statute is to compel father of illegitimate child to bear expenses of childbirth and child support so that mother will not be solely responsible for that support and so that child will not be financial burden on state. Seegert v. Zietlow (Ohio App. 8 Dist., 08-15-1994) 95 Ohio App.3d 451, 642 N.E.2d 697. Children Out–of–wedlock ☞ 31

3. Discretion of court

Trial court clearly has discretion to award support from date of child's birth. Frazier v. Daniels (Ohio App. 1 Dist., 02-26-1997) 118 Ohio App.3d 425, 693 N.E.2d 289. Children Out–of–wedlock ☞ 69(6)

4. Jurisdiction

Juvenile court has jurisdiction in parentage action to award retroactive or back child support for period of time prior to date upon which parent-child relationship is judicially established. Seegert v. Zietlow (Ohio App. 8 Dist., 08-15-1994) 95 Ohio App.3d 451, 642 N.E.2d 697. Children Out–of–wedlock ☞ 67

Juvenile court, in determining paternity, had jurisdiction to decide state's action for aid furnished by state for support and medical expenses of children born out-of-wedlock. Brightwell v. Easter (Ohio App. 9 Dist., 03-09-1994) 93 Ohio App.3d 425, 638 N.E.2d 1067. Social Security And Public Welfare ☞ 194.19

5. Proper parties

Child and Department of Human Services were not in privity with mother, and, therefore, judgment rendered in mother's paternity action did not present res judicata bar to later action by child and Department. Payne v. Cartee (Ohio App. 4 Dist., 06-10-1996) 111 Ohio App.3d 580, 676 N.E.2d 946, appeal not allowed 77 Ohio St.3d 1482, 673 N.E.2d 143. Children Out–of–wedlock ☞ 33; Children Out–of–wedlock ☞ 68

Department of Human Services (DHS), as only entity which provided support for minor children, was only public authority that could bring suit against putative fathers for reimbursement; county Support Enforcement Agency could not bring suit for reimbursement on behalf of DHS. State ex rel. Gillion v. Reese (Ohio App. 8 Dist., 09-06-1994) 97 Ohio App.3d 315, 646 N.E.2d 852, appeal not allowed 71 Ohio St.3d 1466, 644 N.E.2d 1388. Social Security And Public Welfare ⟜ 194.19

Determination that mother who received aid to dependent children from county department of human services had no right to bring action to enforce father's child support obligation did not deprive mother of her right to be heard and to access to courts; courts remained open to mother when she had legitimate gripe against system. Vance v. Banks (Cuyahoga 1994) 94 Ohio App.3d 475, 640 N.E.2d 1214, appeal not allowed 70 Ohio St.3d 1447, 639 N.E.2d 115, certiorari denied 115 S.Ct. 1144, 513 U.S. 1170, 130 L.Ed.2d 1103. Children Out–of–wedlock ⟜ 34; Constitutional Law ⟜ 2314

In action to establish parent and child relationship, neither county department of human services nor any state agency can be proper party for purpose of initiating action, but can only intervene for limited purpose of collecting or recovering support if it is support provider. Vance v. Banks (Cuyahoga 1994) 94 Ohio App.3d 475, 640 N.E.2d 1214, appeal not allowed 70 Ohio St.3d 1447, 639 N.E.2d 115, certiorari denied 115 S.Ct. 1144, 513 U.S. 1170, 130 L.Ed.2d 1103. Children Out–of–wedlock ⟜ 34

6. Duty to support

Back child support may be ordered in paternity proceeding to date of child's birth. Beach v. Poole (Ohio App. 5 Dist., 06-17-1996) 111 Ohio App.3d 710, 676 N.E.2d 1254, appeal not allowed 77 Ohio St.3d 1482, 673 N.E.2d 143. Children Out–of–wedlock ⟜ 67

While trial court does not have authority to order child support until there is legal determination of parentage, once that determination is made, putative father can be ordered to pay support retroactive to date of child's birth; date of judicial establishment of parentage is not date putative father became child's father, as putative father was child's natural father from date of child's birth. Beach v. Poole (Ohio App. 5 Dist., 06-17-1996) 111 Ohio App.3d 710, 676 N.E.2d 1254, appeal not allowed 77 Ohio St.3d 1482, 673 N.E.2d 143. Children Out–of–wedlock ⟜ 67

Any right by mother to receive $50 from father's monthly child support obligation, which was to be paid to county department of human services, did not confer upon mother right to enforce father's child support obligation, which had been assigned to department by operation of law due to mother's receipt of aid to dependent children; mother's right to receive certain amount from amount collected required satisfaction of certain conditions and could be enforced only after amount had been collected. Vance v. Banks (Cuyahoga 1994) 94 Ohio App.3d 475, 640 N.E.2d 1214, appeal not allowed 70 Ohio St.3d 1447, 639 N.E.2d 115, certiorari denied 115 S.Ct. 1144, 513 U.S. 1170, 130 L.Ed.2d 1103. Children Out–of–wedlock ⟜ 34

Motion for order to show cause why parent should not be held in contempt for failure to comply with court order to support child can be enforced only by party who provided or provides support. Vance v. Banks (Cuyahoga 1994) 94 Ohio App.3d 475, 640 N.E.2d 1214, appeal not allowed 70 Ohio St.3d 1447, 639 N.E.2d 115, certiorari denied 115 S.Ct. 1144, 513 U.S. 1170, 130 L.Ed.2d 1103. Child Support ⟜ 473

Awards against fathers of children born out-of-wedlock to state for reimbursement of support and medical expenses paid on behalf of children were not modifiable. Brightwell v. Easter (Ohio App. 9 Dist., 03-09-1994) 93 Ohio App.3d 425, 638 N.E.2d 1067. Social Security And Public Welfare ⟜ 194.19

A natural father's duty to support a child arises at birth, particularly where he acknowledges paternity, and where the natural father unjustifiably fails to communicate with or support a child for one year prior to the filing of an adoption petition, his consent to the adoption of his illegitimate child is unnecessary. In re Adoption of Taylor (Medina 1989) 61 Ohio App.3d 500, 573 N.E.2d 156, motion overruled 43 Ohio St.3d 712, 541 N.E.2d 78.

Where the father is ordered to pay as support ten per cent of any and all commissions, overrides and bonuses, such an order is in conformity with RC 3111.17. Misquitta v Misquitta, No. 1188 (7th Dist Ct App, Columbiana, 8–17–78).

7. Imprisonment of defendant

A jail sentence for failure to pay child support or spousal support is not imprisonment for a debt and is not prohibited by the state constitution. In re Contemnor Caron (Ohio Com.Pl., 04-27-2000) 110 Ohio Misc.2d 58, 744 N.E.2d 787. Child Support ⟜ 496; Constitutional Law ⟜ 1106; Divorce ⟜ 1101

The language of RC 3111.17 providing that the defendant shall be jailed if he "neglects or refuses" to pay the award ordered by the court does not authorize the jailing of an indigent defendant; before the defendant can be jailed because he "neglects or refuses" to pay or secure the award ordered by the court, he must be accorded the opportunity to prove that he is unable to pay or secure the award. Bigsby v. Bates (Ohio Com.Pl. 1978) 59 Ohio Misc. 51, 391 N.E.2d 1384, 11 O.O.3d 262, 13 O.O.3d 260. Children Out–of–wedlock ⟜ 69(5)

The provisions of RC 3111.17 and 3111.18 are unconstitutional as a denial of the Equal Protection Clause guaranteed by US Const Am XIV, insofar as these sections provide for the imprisonment of an indigent defendant adjudged to be the reputed father of the plaintiff's illegitimate child solely because of his inability to pay the support award ordered by the court. Walker v. Stokes (Cuyahoga 1977) 54 Ohio App.2d 119, 375 N.E.2d 1258, 8 O.O.3d 237. Children Out–of–wedlock ⟜ 31; Constitutional Law ⟜ 3738

A defendant who fails to pay an award for maternity expenses in a bastardy action may be committed to jail. Crawford v. Hasberry (Ohio Juv. 1962)

186 N.E.2d 522, 90 Ohio Law Abs. 205, 21 O.O.2d 350.

8. Right of action

County child support enforcement agency was entitled to participate in parentage action following admission of paternity and in absence of evidence of past child support, as agency was necessary party and adjudicated father suffered no prejudice from agency's participation. State ex rel. Donovan v. Zajac (Ohio App. 11 Dist., 01-02-1998) 125 Ohio App.3d 245, 708 N.E.2d 254, dismissed, appeal not allowed 81 Ohio St.3d 1521, 692 N.E.2d 1023. Children Out–of–wedlock ☞ 34

Mother's claim against alleged father was distinct from Department of Human Services' claim for reimbursement of birthing expenses, for purposes of determining whether judgment rendered in mother's paternity action barred Department's later claim. Payne v. Cartee (Ohio App. 4 Dist., 06-10-1996) 111 Ohio App.3d 580, 676 N.E.2d 946, appeal not allowed 77 Ohio St.3d 1482, 673 N.E.2d 143. Children Out–of–wedlock ☞ 33; Children Out–of–wedlock ☞ 68

Mother who received aid to dependent children from county department of human services had no right to bring action against father to recover child support, as any such right was assigned to county department of human services by operation of law. Vance v. Banks (Cuyahoga 1994) 94 Ohio App.3d 475, 640 N.E.2d 1214, appeal not allowed 70 Ohio St.3d 1447, 639 N.E.2d 115, certiorari denied 115 S.Ct. 1144, 513 U.S. 1170, 130 L.Ed.2d 1103. Children Out–of–wedlock ☞ 34

Mother's right to initiate action against child's natural father to establish parent and child relationship did not also give her right to enforce parental obligation to support child, where mother received aid to dependent children from county department of human services; right to enforce parental obligation to support depended entirely on who was support provider of child. Vance v. Banks (Cuyahoga 1994) 94 Ohio App.3d 475, 640 N.E.2d 1214, appeal not allowed 70 Ohio St.3d 1447, 639 N.E.2d 115, certiorari denied 115 S.Ct. 1144, 513 U.S. 1170, 130 L.Ed.2d 1103. Children Out–of–wedlock ☞ 34

Plaintiff's action against the biological father seeking reimbursement for necessaries furnished to plaintiff's wife's children born during his marriage is properly dismissed when it is clear from the record that such action was not brought for the benefit of, nor out of concern for, the children involved. Weinman v Larsh, No. C-810383 (1st Dist Ct App,

Hamilton, 3-31-82), affirmed by 5 OS(3d) 85, 5 OBR 138, 448 NE(2d) 1384 (1983).

9. Bankruptcy

Although bankruptcy matters are inherently proceedings in equity and must foster equitable results, bankruptcy court would not second-guess judgment rendered by state court in establishing Chapter 7 debtor-biological father's debt for paternity action expenses where debtor was not placed in any worse position than that which existed before bankruptcy and debtor had opportunity to argue merits of debt allocation before the state court. In re Lamb (Bkrtcy.N.D.Ohio, 05-08-1996) 198 B.R. 511. Bankruptcy ☞ 2125; Bankruptcy ☞ 3409

Medical expenses arising from paternity action typically are not dischargeable. In re Lamb (Bkrtcy.N.D.Ohio, 05-08-1996) 198 B.R. 511. Bankruptcy ☞ 3365(8)

Chapter 7 debtor opposing nondischargeability of debt arising from paternity judgment failed to establish that government engaged in affirmative misconduct, and thus failed to meet burden upon summary judgment to show genuine issue of fact regarding equitable estoppel argument, where debtor alleged that county department of human services delayed in sending medical invoices to debtor's third-party insurance carrier, but debtor offered no proof in support of his claims and did not allege that he either changed his position or detrimentally relied upon any representation by department that it would expeditiously remit bills. In re Lamb (Bkrtcy.N.D.Ohio, 05-08-1996) 198 B.R. 511. Bankruptcy ☞ 2164.1; Estoppel ☞ 62.3

An $11,000 obligation resulting from the compromise of a paternity action is a support payment to the child that cannot be discharged in the father's bankruptcy action where the amount was based on analysis of what would have been required for support had a declaration of paternity applied from the date of birth to the time of the agreement and from certain medical expenses relating to the birth. In re Wilson (Bkrtcy.S.D.Ohio 1989) 109 B.R. 283. Bankruptcy ☞ 3365(13)

10. Indigent defendants

In parentage proceedings where the complainant-mothers and their children are recipients of public assistance, the state public defender must, in accordance with RC 120.18, RC 120.28, and RC 120.33, partially reimburse the counties for the cost of representing indigent paternity defendants who face the state as an adversary. OAG 85–090.

3111.16 Continuing jurisdiction

The court has continuing jurisdiction to modify or revoke a judgment or order issued under sections 3111.01 to 3111.18 of the Revised Code to provide for future education and support and a judgment or order issued with respect to matters listed in divisions (C) and (D) of section 3111.13 and division (B) of section 3111.15 of the Revised Code, except that a court entering a judgment or order for the purchase of an annuity under division (D) of section 3111.13 of the Revised Code may specify that the judgment or order may not be modified or revoked.

(2000 S 180, eff. 3–22–01; 1986 H 476, eff. 9–24–86; 1982 H 245)

Uncodified Law

1992 S 10, § 5: See Uncodified Law under
3111.01.

1982 H 245, § 3: See Uncodified Law under
3111.04.

Historical and Statutory Notes

Ed. Note: Former 3111.16 repealed by 1982 H
245, eff. 6–29–82; 1975 S 145; 1953 H 1; GC
8006–16; Source—GC 12122–1; see now 3111.09
for provisions analogous to former 3111.16.

Pre–1953 H 1 Amendments: 124 v S 65

Amendment Note: 2000 S 180 substituted
"3111.18" for "3111.19"; and deleted "the payment
of a lump sum or" before "the purchase of an
annuity".

Library References

Children Out-of-Wedlock ☞64.
Westlaw Topic No. 76H.
C.J.S. Children Out-of-Wedlock §§ 121 to 122.

Research References

Encyclopedias

OH Jur. 3d Family Law § 985, Continuing Jurisdiction.

OH Jur. 3d Family Law § 1028, Duration of Support; Modification.

Treatises and Practice Aids

Markus, Baldwin's Ohio Handbook Series -- Trial
Handbook § 25:14, Expert Testimony--Paternity.

Sowald & Morganstern, Baldwin's Ohio Practice
Domestic Relations Law § 20:8, Continuing Jurisdiction--In General.

Sowald & Morganstern, Baldwin's Ohio Practice
Domestic Relations Law § 24:6, Parentage.

Sowald & Morganstern, Baldwin's Ohio Practice
Domestic Relations Law § 3:17, Evidence--Genetic Tests--Background.

Sowald & Morganstern, Baldwin's Ohio Practice
Domestic Relations Law § 3:30, Res Judicata
and Vacation of Parentage Orders.

Sowald & Morganstern, Baldwin's Ohio Practice
Domestic Relations Law § 3:40, Effect of Judgment--Child Support--Other Remedies.

Carlin, Baldwin's Ohio Prac. Merrick-Rippner Probate Law § 19:9, Uniform Parentage Act--Res
Judicata; Doctrine of Laches.

Carlin, Baldwin's Ohio Prac. Merrick-Rippner Probate Law § 110:26, Parentage Act--Applicability
of Civil Rules to Paternity Proceedings.

Carlin, Baldwin's Ohio Prac. Merrick-Rippner Probate Law § 110:27, Parentage Act--Evidence of
Paternity.

Carlin, Baldwin's Ohio Prac. Merrick-Rippner Probate Law § 110:31, Parentage Act--Continuing
Jurisdiction to Modify or Revoke Judgment.

Carlin, Baldwin's Ohio Prac. Merrick-Rippner Probate Law § 109:114, Proceedings After Judgment: Continuing Jurisdiction of Juvenile Court.

Notes of Decisions

Support modification   1
Vacation of decree   2

_____

1. Support modification

A simple assertion of non-paternity is insufficient
to invoke the trial court's continuing jurisdiction to
modify its child support and health insurance orders. Clippinger v. Clippinger (Ohio App. 12 Dist.,
Preble, 01-12-1998) No. CA97-05-010, 1998 WL
8682, Unreported.

Court retains continuing jurisdiction over its orders concerning custody, care and support of children, even when court's initial order was based on
agreement by parents of the child; child affected by
such an order is considered a ward of the court,
which may always reconsider and modify its rulings
when changed circumstances require it during
child's minority. Singer v. Dickinson (Ohio 1992)
63 Ohio St.3d 408, 588 N.E.2d 806. Child Custody

☞ 555; Child Custody ☞ 574; Child Support ☞
239

Courts have continuing jurisdiction to modify
orders for the support of illegitimate children even
though the power is not reserved in the original
order. State ex rel. Niven v. Tomblin (Summit
1948) 82 Ohio App. 376, 81 N.E.2d 637, 38 O.O.
51.

In a bastardy action a court has continuing jurisdiction until the child involved reaches eighteen,
and is not barred from reducing delinquent installments to a lump-sum judgment by any statute of
limitations. State ex rel. Marshall v. Steinbaugh
(Ohio Juv. 1939) 138 N.E.2d 252, 73 Ohio Law
Abs. 509.

The jurisdiction of the court is continuing as it
relates to illegitimate children and an order for
support is subject to modification. State ex rel.
Raydel v. Raible (Ohio Com.Pl. 1953) 112 N.E.2d
568, 64 Ohio Law Abs. 438, affirmed 117 N.E.2d
480, 69 Ohio Law Abs. 356, appeal dismissed 162
Ohio St. 74, 120 N.E.2d 590, 54 O.O. 18.

2. Vacation of decree

Child support obligor was not entitled to termination of support arrearages following vacation of judgment of parentage based upon results of genetic testing, where arrearage was result of obligor's own inexcusable conduct; obligor initially declined to pursue genetic testing and agreed that he was subject child's biological father, and did not avail himself of opportunity to seek vacation of consent finding of paternity until child was a teenager. Jennifer H. v. Harold J.D. (Ohio App. 6 Dist., Lucas, 02-04-2005) No. L-04-1053, 2005-Ohio-407, 2005 WL 279949, Unreported. Children Out–of–wedlock ⟜ 69(6)

Juvenile court's continuing jurisdiction over paternity matter authorized court to vacate initial finding of paternity and interim order of child support in light of postjudgment genetic testing which conclusively established putative father's nonpaternity. Cuyahoga Support Enforcement Agency v. Guthrie (Ohio, 02-17-1999) 84 Ohio St.3d 437,

705 N.E.2d 318, 1999-Ohio-362. Children Out–of–wedlock ⟜ 67; Children Out–of–wedlock ⟜ 68

Although initial judgment of parentage and order requiring putative father to pay future child support were properly vacated in light of postjudgment genetic tests which conclusively established putative father's nonpaternity, he was not entitled to avoid all arrearages that existed due to his own inexcusable neglect; putative father voluntarily and deliberately disregarded initial parentage proceedings, thereby causing delay of finding of nonpaternity. Cuyahoga Support Enforcement Agency v. Guthrie (Ohio, 02-17-1999) 84 Ohio St.3d 437, 705 N.E.2d 318, 1999-Ohio-362. Children Out–of–wedlock ⟜ 68; Children Out–of–wedlock ⟜ 69(6)

Where HLA test results exclude as the probable father of the child the man adjudged the father of a child in a prior paternity proceeding, the court has continuing jurisdiction to vacate the order of paternity. Haney v Feltner, No. C–830715 (1st Dist Ct App, Hamilton, 7–3–84).

3111.17 Action to determine mother and child relationship

Any interested party may bring an action to determine the existence or nonexistence of a mother and child relationship. Insofar as practicable, the provisions of sections 3111.01 to 3111.18 of the Revised Code that are applicable to the father and child relationship shall apply to an action brought under this section.

(2000 S 180, eff. 3–22–01; 1986 H 476, eff. 9–24–86; 1982 H 245)

Uncodified Law

1992 S 10, § 5: See Uncodified Law under 3111.01.

1982 H 245, § 3: See Uncodified Law under 3111.04.

Historical and Statutory Notes

Ed. Note: Former 3111.17 repealed by 1982 H 245, eff. 6–29–82; 1975 S 145; 1970 S 460; 125 v 184; 1953 H 1; GC 8006–17; Source—GC 12123; see now 3111.13 to 3111.15 for provisions analogous to former 3111.17, and 3111.03, 3111.04, and 3111.15 for annotations from former 3111.17.

Pre–1953 H 1 Amendments: 124 v S 65

Amendment Note: 2000 S 180 substituted "3111.18" for "3111.19".

Library References

Children Out-of-Wedlock ⟜1, 30 to 75.
Westlaw Topic No. 76H.

C.J.S. Children Out-of-Wedlock §§ 1 to 8, 47 to 53, 71 to 142.

Research References

ALR Library

87 ALR 5th 361, Liability of Father for Retroactive Child Support on Judicial Determination of Paternity.
77 ALR 5th 567, Determination of Status as Legal or Natural Parents in Contested Surrogacy Births.

Encyclopedias

OH Jur. 3d Family Law § 900, Accounting by Petitioner--Purpose; Effect Upon Payments Pursuant to Surrogacy Agreements.
OH Jur. 3d Family Law § 938, Purpose of Proceedings.

OH Jur. 3d Family Law § 941, Establishment of Parent and Child Relationship.
OH Jur. 3d Family Law § 952, Jurisdiction.
OH Jur. 3d Family Law § 991, Inheritance from Father.

Forms

Ohio Forms Legal and Business § 28:4, Introduction.

Treatises and Practice Aids

Sowald & Morganstern, Baldwin's Ohio Practice Domestic Relations Law § 3:10, Judicial Parentage Action--Parties.

Sowald & Morganstern, Baldwin's Ohio Practice Domestic Relations Law § 3:31, Relief from Paternity or Support Judgment, Under RC 3119.961.

Sowald & Morganstern, Baldwin's Ohio Practice Domestic Relations Law § 3:33, Attorney Fees and Costs.

Sowald & Morganstern, Baldwin's Ohio Practice Domestic Relations Law § 20:71, Criminal Nonsupport.

Carlin, Baldwin's Ohio Prac. Merrick-Rippner Probate Law § 18:2, Inheritance Rights of Illegitimate Child--Statutory Provisions.

Carlin, Baldwin's Ohio Prac. Merrick-Rippner Probate Law § 19:4, Legitimation--Historical Provisions.

Carlin, Baldwin's Ohio Prac. Merrick-Rippner Probate Law § 19:10, Uniform Parentage Act--Procedure in Action to Determine Father-Child Relationship.

Carlin, Baldwin's Ohio Prac. Merrick-Rippner Probate Law § 110:20, Parentage Act--Jurisdiction and Venue.

Carlin, Baldwin's Ohio Prac. Merrick-Rippner Probate Law § 110:23, Parentage Act--Parties in Parentage Action.

Carlin, Baldwin's Ohio Prac. Merrick-Rippner Probate Law § 110:29, Parentage Act--Judgment Determining Existence of Parent-Child Relationship.

Carlin, Baldwin's Ohio Prac. Merrick-Rippner Probate Law § 110:31, Parentage Act--Continuing Jurisdiction to Modify or Revoke Judgment.

Law Review and Journal Commentaries

Kass v. Kass, Blazing Legal Trails in the Field of Human Reproductive Technology, Kelly Summers. 48 Clev St L Rev 637 (2000).

Modern Reproductive Technology and Motherhood: The Search for Common Ground and the Recognition of Difference, Comment. 62 U Cin L Rev 1623 (Spring 1994).

Notes of Decisions

Child support obligation   **1**
Jurisdiction   **2**
Sufficiency of evidence   **3**

---

1. Child support obligation

Lesbian mother's agreement, to accept full financial responsibility for children in exchange for father impregnating mother, was circumstance "which ought reasonably to relieve father" of child support obligation between date of birth and date amicable and cooperative parenting arrangement broke down and, thus, trial court's refusal to order child support to commence at birth was not an abuse of discretion. Myers v. Moschella (Ohio App. 1 Dist., 06-26-1996) 112 Ohio App.3d 75, 677 N.E.2d 1243. Children Out–of–wedlock ☞ 22; Children Out–of–wedlock ☞ 67

Since father's child support payments were past due, trial court was required to grant state's motion to reduce support arrearages to lump-sum judgment, and court improperly relied on equitable principles to deny state's motion, where state's motion encompassed only unpaid child support; even if trial court believed that order finding paternity was inequitable, fairness of that order was not before court. State ex rel. LaMar v. Stabile (Ohio App. 9 Dist., 08-25-1993) 90 Ohio App.3d 54, 627 N.E.2d 1076. Children Out–of–wedlock ☞ 69(6)

2. Jurisdiction

The trial court lacked subject matter jurisdiction to determine the parentage of unborn child, who was the subject of a surrogacy agreement, or issue an order directing the hospital where surrogate mother was expected to deliver child to designate child as the biological child of sperm and egg donors. Nemcek v. Paskey (Ohio Com.Pl., 04-06-2006) 137 Ohio Misc.2d 1, 849 N.E.2d 108, 2006-Ohio-2059. Parent And Child ☞ 20

3. Sufficiency of evidence

Establishing parent-child relationship between putative father and non-marital child was warranted in mother's paternity action, although mother's husband was listed on birth certificate as the father, and although putative father did not desire relationship with child; parties were aware at time of birth that putative father was the biological father, genetic testing confirmed that putative father was biological father, and there was no evidence that rebutting presumption that mother's husband was natural father was not in child's best interests. H.N.H. v. H.M.F. (Ohio App. 8 Dist., Cuyahoga, 04-21-2005) No. 84642, 2005-Ohio-1869, 2005 WL 927004, Unreported. Children Out–of–wedlock ☞ 53

Intended mother's voluntary acknowledgement of maternity, as set forth in a surrogacy agreement setting forth terms by which surrogate mother would carry and give birth to embryos formed outside the womb by donor egg and sperm, was sufficient under the Parentage Act, consistent with cases concerning voluntary acknowledgements of paternity, to rebut the presumption that surrogate mother was the "natural mother" of resulting child by reason of her having given birth to the child. S.N. v. M.B. (Ohio App. 10 Dist., 06-10-2010) 188 Ohio App.3d 324, 935 N.E.2d 463, 2010-Ohio-2479, cause dismissed 126 Ohio St.3d 1525, 931 N.E.2d 126, 2010-Ohio-3583. Children Out–of–wedlock ☞ 15

In paternity proceedings, the juvenile court may consider insurance payments and disability benefits received by the mother of an illegitimate child in determining her need for medical expenses and support during pregnancy, delivery, and post-natal convalescence. Edwards v. Sadusky (Summit 1982)

4 Ohio App.3d 297, 448 N.E.2d 506, 4 O.B.R. 548. Children Out–of–wedlock ☞ 67

3111.18   New birth record

As used in this section, "birth record" has the meaning given in section 3705.01 of the Revised Code.

Upon the order of a court of this state or upon the request of a court of another state, the department of health shall prepare a new birth record consistent with the findings of the court and shall substitute the new record for the original birth record.

(1988 H 790, eff. 3–16–89; 1982 H 245)

Uncodified Law

1992 S 10, § 5: See Uncodified Law under 3111.01.

1982 H 245, § 3: See Uncodified Law under 3111.04.

Historical and Statutory Notes

Ed. Note: Former 3111.18 repealed by 1982 H 245, eff. 6–29–82; 1953 H 1; GC 8006–18; Source GC 12124.

Pre–1953 H 1 Amendments: 124 v S 65

Cross References

Action for child support order before acknowledgment becomes final, see 2151.232
Juvenile court jurisdiction, see 2151.23

Parental duty of support, see 3103.031
Vital statistics, birth record of legitimatized child, see 3705.09

Library References

Health ☞397.
Westlaw Topic No. 198H.
C.J.S. Health and Environment §§ 24, 74.

Research References

Encyclopedias

OH Jur. 3d Family Law § 941, Establishment of Parent and Child Relationship.
OH Jur. 3d Family Law § 952, Jurisdiction.
OH Jur. 3d Family Law § 981, Fees and Court Costs.
OH Jur. 3d Family Law § 983, New Birth Record.
OH Jur. 3d Family Law § 1011, Assumption of Parental Duty of Support.
OH Jur. 3d Family Law § 1016, Action for Support.
OH Jur. 3d Family Law § 1027, Requirements of Support Orders.
OH Jur. 3d Family Law § 1028, Duration of Support; Modification.
OH Jur. 3d Family Law § 1226, Title IV-D Cases.
OH Jur. 3d Family Law § 1546, Paternity Actions.

Forms

Ohio Forms Legal and Business § 28:6, Form Drafting Principles.
Ohio Jurisprudence Pleading and Practice Forms § 2:8, Courts of Common Pleas--Juvenile Division.
Ohio Jurisprudence Pleading and Practice Forms § 111:4, Jurisdiction.

Ohio Jurisprudence Pleading and Practice Forms § 111:5, Standing--Parties.
Ohio Jurisprudence Pleading and Practice Forms § 111:7, Genetic Tests.
Ohio Jurisprudence Pleading and Practice Forms § 96:11, Consent Required.
Ohio Jurisprudence Pleading and Practice Forms § 111:10, Temporary Support Order.
Ohio Jurisprudence Pleading and Practice Forms § 111:12, Judgment.

Treatises and Practice Aids

Klein, Darling, & Terez, Baldwin's Ohio Practice Civil Practice § 60:8, Civ. R. 60(B)--In General--Tension Between Accuracy and Finality.
Klein, Darling, & Terez, Baldwin's Ohio Practice Civil Practice § 60:45, Civ. R. 60(B)(2)--In General.
Klein, Darling, & Terez, Baldwin's Ohio Practice Civil Practice § 60:54, Civ. R. 60(B)(4)--In General.
Klein, Darling, & Terez, Baldwin's Ohio Practice Civil Practice § 60:63, Civ. R. 60(B)(5)--Any Other Reason Justifying Relief from Judgment--Civ. R. 60(B)(5) Not Applicable If One of More Specific Civ. R. 60(B) Grounds Applies.

Sowald & Morganstern, Baldwin's Ohio Practice Domestic Relations Law § 3:2, Administrative Determination of Parentage--Purpose.

Sowald & Morganstern, Baldwin's Ohio Practice Domestic Relations Law § 3:4, Administrative Determination of Parentage--Acknowledgment, Support Order, and Birth Record.

Sowald & Morganstern, Baldwin's Ohio Practice Domestic Relations Law § 3:5, Administrative Determination of Parentage--No Acknowledgment and Support Order.

Sowald & Morganstern, Baldwin's Ohio Practice Domestic Relations Law § 3:51, Related Issues--Name.

Sowald & Morganstern, Baldwin's Ohio Practice Domestic Relations Law § 23:15, In-State Remedies--Determination of Parentage.

Carlin, Baldwin's Ohio Prac. Merrick-Rippner Probate Law § 18:2, Inheritance Rights of Illegitimate Child--Statutory Provisions.

Carlin, Baldwin's Ohio Prac. Merrick-Rippner Probate Law § 18:3, Inheritance Rights of Illegitimate Child--Case Law Affecting Rules of Inheritance Generally.

Carlin, Baldwin's Ohio Prac. Merrick-Rippner Probate Law § 19:1, Legitimation--Statutory Provisions.

Carlin, Baldwin's Ohio Prac. Merrick-Rippner Probate Law § 19:2, Legitimation--Procedure--Acknowledgment of Paternity.

Carlin, Baldwin's Ohio Prac. Merrick-Rippner Probate Law § 19:4, Legitimation--Historical Provisions.

Carlin, Baldwin's Ohio Prac. Merrick-Rippner Probate Law § 19:6, Uniform Parentage Act--Jurisdiction of Action to Determine Father-Child Relationship.

Carlin, Baldwin's Ohio Prac. Merrick-Rippner Probate Law § 19:7, Uniform Parentage Act--Presumptions.

Carlin, Baldwin's Ohio Prac. Merrick-Rippner Probate Law § 99:3, Jurisdiction.

Carlin, Baldwin's Ohio Prac. Merrick-Rippner Probate Law § 99:8, Suitability of Adoptive Parents--Best Interests of Child.

Carlin, Baldwin's Ohio Prac. Merrick-Rippner Probate Law § 107:2, Original Jurisdiction.

Carlin, Baldwin's Ohio Prac. Merrick-Rippner Probate Law § 110:3, Criminal Jurisdiction--Proceedings for Nonsupport.

Carlin, Baldwin's Ohio Prac. Merrick-Rippner Probate Law § 19:10, Uniform Parentage Act--Procedure in Action to Determine Father-Child Relationship.

Carlin, Baldwin's Ohio Prac. Merrick-Rippner Probate Law § 19:13, Uniform Parentage Act--Nonspousal Artificial Insemination; Embryo Donation.

Carlin, Baldwin's Ohio Prac. Merrick-Rippner Probate Law § 99:21, Types of Placement--Stepparent, Guardian, and Grandparent Adoptions.

Carlin, Baldwin's Ohio Prac. Merrick-Rippner Probate Law § 99:30, Statutorily Required Consent.

Carlin, Baldwin's Ohio Prac. Merrick-Rippner Probate Law § 99:31, Parties Giving Consent--Biological Parents.

Carlin, Baldwin's Ohio Prac. Merrick-Rippner Probate Law § 99:32, Parties Giving Consent--Putative Father.

Carlin, Baldwin's Ohio Prac. Merrick-Rippner Probate Law § 99:49, Interlocutory and Final Orders.

Carlin, Baldwin's Ohio Prac. Merrick-Rippner Probate Law § 110:13, Jurisdiction Over Child Custody Matters--Determination of Custody.

Carlin, Baldwin's Ohio Prac. Merrick-Rippner Probate Law § 110:15, Visitation Right of Noncustodial Parent and Others.

Carlin, Baldwin's Ohio Prac. Merrick-Rippner Probate Law § 110:19, Parentage Act--Effect.

Carlin, Baldwin's Ohio Prac. Merrick-Rippner Probate Law § 110:20, Parentage Act--Jurisdiction and Venue.

Carlin, Baldwin's Ohio Prac. Merrick-Rippner Probate Law § 110:24, Parentage Act--Genetic Tests, Fees, and Costs.

Carlin, Baldwin's Ohio Prac. Merrick-Rippner Probate Law § 110:26, Parentage Act--Applicability of Civil Rules to Paternity Proceedings.

Carlin, Baldwin's Ohio Prac. Merrick-Rippner Probate Law § 110:27, Parentage Act--Evidence of Paternity.

Carlin, Baldwin's Ohio Prac. Merrick-Rippner Probate Law § 110:28, Parentage Act--Trial of Parentage Action.

Carlin, Baldwin's Ohio Prac. Merrick-Rippner Probate Law § 110:29, Parentage Act--Judgment Determining Existence of Parent-Child Relationship.

Carlin, Baldwin's Ohio Prac. Merrick-Rippner Probate Law § 110:30, Parentage Act--Enforcement of Support Order.

Carlin, Baldwin's Ohio Prac. Merrick-Rippner Probate Law § 110:31, Parentage Act--Continuing Jurisdiction to Modify or Revoke Judgment.

Carlin, Baldwin's Ohio Prac. Merrick-Rippner Probate Law § 110:35, Civil Support Proceedings--Liability for Child Support.

Carlin, Baldwin's Ohio Prac. Merrick-Rippner Probate Law § 110:39, Civil Support Proceedings--Remedies for Failure to Comply With Support Order.

Adrine & Ruden, Ohio Domestic Violence Law § 10:7, Relationships Covered--Persons Who Have a Child in Common.

3111.19 Interference with parentage action

No person, by using physical harassment or threats of violence against another person, shall interfere with the other person's initiation or continuance of, or attempt to prevent the other person from initiating or continuing, an action under sections 3111.01 to 3111.18 of the Revised Code.

(2000 S 180, eff. 3–22–01)

Uncodified Law

1992 S 10, § 5: See Uncodified Law under 3111.01.

1982 H 245, § 3: See Uncodified Law under 3111.04.

Historical and Statutory Notes

Ed. Note: 3111.19 is former 3111.29, amended and recodified by 2000 S 180, eff. 3–22–01; 1992 S 10, eff. 7–15–92.

Ed. Note: Former 3111.19 repealed by 2000 S 180, eff. 3–22–01; 1993 S 115, eff. 10–12–93; 1982 H 245.

Ed. Note: Prior 3111.19 repealed by 1982 H 245, eff. 6–29–82; 127 v 1039; 1953 H 1; GC 8006–19; Source—GC 12128.

Pre–1953 H 1 Amendments: 124 v S 65

Amendment Note: 2000 S 180 substituted "3111.18" for "3111.19"; and made changes to reflect gender neutral language.

Cross References

Penalty: 3111.99(B)
Support orders, interfering with action to issue or modify, see 2919.231

Library References

Obstructing Justice ⚷6.
Westlaw Topic No. 282.
C.J.S. Obstructing Justice or Governmental Administration §§ 3 to 8, 37 to 38.

Research References

ALR Library

90 ALR 5th 1, Construction and Application of Uniform Interstate Family Support Act.

Encyclopedias

OH Jur. 3d Family Law § 942, Interference With Paternity Actions; Penalties.
OH Jur. 3d Family Law § 1207, Interfering With Action to Issue or Modify Support Order.

Forms

Ohio Forms Legal and Business § 15:6, Checklist--Drafting Compromise and Settlement Agreements.
Ohio Forms Legal and Business § 28:11, Agreement for Support of Illegitimate Child.
Ohio Forms Legal and Business § 28:12, Consent to Artificial Insemination of Wife.
Ohio Jurisprudence Pleading and Practice Forms § 111:9, Pretrial Hearing and Trial.

Treatises and Practice Aids

Klein, Darling, & Terez, Baldwin's Ohio Practice Civil Practice § 1:20, Civ. R. 1(C): Exceptions--Effect of Revised Code Section Purporting to Prohibit Application of One or More Civil Rules.
Klein, Darling, & Terez, Baldwin's Ohio Practice Civil Practice § 1:97, Civ. R. 1(C)(7): All Other Special Statutory Proceedings--Revised Code Sections Purporting to Mandate Application of One or More Civil Rules.
Klein, Darling, & Terez, Baldwin's Ohio Practice Civil Practice § 1:98, Civ. R. 1(C)(7): All Other Special Statutory Proceedings--Revised Code Sections Purporting to Prohibit Application of One or More Civil Rules.
Klein, Darling, & Terez, Baldwin's Ohio Practice Civil Practice § 38:15, Right to Jury Trial Under Ohio Statutes--Other Statutes.
Katz & Giannelli, Baldwin's Ohio Practice Criminal Law § 109:13, Interfering With Support Actions.
Sowald & Morganstern, Baldwin's Ohio Practice Domestic Relations Law § 15:5, Parentage Determinations.
Sowald & Morganstern, Baldwin's Ohio Practice Domestic Relations Law § 19:3, Support Obligations--In General.
Sowald & Morganstern, Baldwin's Ohio Practice Domestic Relations Law § 22:4, Establishing Parentage.
Sowald & Morganstern, Baldwin's Ohio Practice Domestic Relations Law § 3:10, Judicial Parentage Action--Parties.
Sowald & Morganstern, Baldwin's Ohio Practice Domestic Relations Law § 3:23, Criminal Interference With Establishment of Paternity.
Sowald & Morganstern, Baldwin's Ohio Practice Domestic Relations Law § 3:30, Res Judicata and Vacation of Parentage Orders.
Sowald & Morganstern, Baldwin's Ohio Practice Domestic Relations Law § 3:40, Effect of Judgment--Child Support--Other Remedies.
Sowald & Morganstern, Baldwin's Ohio Practice Domestic Relations Law § 3:43, Effect of Judgment--Compromise Settlements.
Sowald & Morganstern, Baldwin's Ohio Practice Domestic Relations Law § 3:45, Effect of Judgment--Retrospective Effect.
Carlin, Baldwin's Ohio Prac. Merrick-Rippner Probate Law § 19:1, Legitimation--Statutory Provisions.

Carlin, Baldwin's Ohio Prac. Merrick-Rippner Probate Law § 19:2, Legitimation--Procedure--Acknowledgment of Paternity.

Carlin, Baldwin's Ohio Prac. Merrick-Rippner Probate Law § 19:4, Legitimation--Historical Provisions.

Carlin, Baldwin's Ohio Prac. Merrick-Rippner Probate Law § 19:5, Legitimation--Insurance Benefits.

Carlin, Baldwin's Ohio Prac. Merrick-Rippner Probate Law § 19:6, Uniform Parentage Act--Jurisdiction of Action to Determine Father-Child Relationship.

Carlin, Baldwin's Ohio Prac. Merrick-Rippner Probate Law § 19:9, Uniform Parentage Act--Res Judicata; Doctrine of Laches.

Carlin, Baldwin's Ohio Prac. Merrick-Rippner Probate Law § 39:4, Interested Persons.

Carlin, Baldwin's Ohio Prac. Merrick-Rippner Probate Law § 99:31, Parties Giving Consent--Biological Parents.

Carlin, Baldwin's Ohio Prac. Merrick-Rippner Probate Law § 99:32, Parties Giving Consent--Putative Father.

Carlin, Baldwin's Ohio Prac. Merrick-Rippner Probate Law § 110:19, Parentage Act--Effect.

Carlin, Baldwin's Ohio Prac. Merrick-Rippner Probate Law § 110:20, Parentage Act--Jurisdiction and Venue.

Carlin, Baldwin's Ohio Prac. Merrick-Rippner Probate Law § 110:26, Parentage Act--Applicability of Civil Rules to Paternity Proceedings.

Carlin, Baldwin's Ohio Prac. Merrick-Rippner Probate Law § 110:32, Parentage Act--Compromise Agreement Between Alleged Father and Mother.

Notes of Decisions

Action to set aside agreement 3
Bankruptcy 1
Res judicata 2

---

1. Bankruptcy

An obligation for child support arrearages will be discharged in bankruptcy, as between the debtor and the mother, where the obligation arose by agreement in settlement of a paternity proceeding in which the debtor denied paternity, and where no evidence of paternity is before the bankruptcy court. Matter of Gray (Bkrtcy.S.D.Ohio 1984) 41 B.R. 759.

2. Res judicata

Trial court was required to consider support being paid by father of minor child to child's mother pursuant to agreed settlement entry of previous parentage action in calculating support payable under judgment entered in child's subsequent action to establish parent-child relationship; while prior action was not res judicata with respect to issue of support, both actions served same purpose in that they required payment of money for benefit of child, and child was only entitled to single "support." Cornell v. Brumfield (Ohio App. 4 Dist., 10-10-1996) 115 Ohio App.3d 259, 685 N.E.2d 270.

Issues of paternity and support determined in compromise agreement reached by child's parents in parentage action initiated by child's mother were not res judicata with respect to subsequent action against father by child to establish parent-child relationship, despite fact that second action was also initiated by child's mother, in her capacity as child's next friend; mother's status as plaintiff was mere pleading formality, mother and child were not in privity, and child was never party to previous parentage action. Cornell v. Brumfield (Ohio App. 4 Dist., 10-10-1996) 115 Ohio App.3d 259, 685 N.E.2d 270.

Agreed entry in parentage action bars any subsequent relitigation of same issues in second parentage case between same parties. Cornell v. Brum-

field (Ohio App. 4 Dist., 10-10-1996) 115 Ohio App.3d 259, 685 N.E.2d 270.

Legitimation order filed in probate court with consent of mother did not bar subsequent parentage action wherein mother sought child support arrearages; application of doctrine of res judicata would violate state's strong public policy favoring protection of children and their support, health, maintenance and welfare, and would also violate equal protection. Lewis v. Chapin (Ohio App. 8 Dist., 03-21-1994) 93 Ohio App.3d 695, 639 N.E.2d 848 Children Out–of–wedlock ⟐ 33; Constitutional Law ⟐ 3192

A parentage action brought by a natural mother against a putative father is barred by res judicata where the parties have previously entered into an agreement signed and journalized by the court, providing for the father to pay the mother $20 a week until the minor child's eighteenth birthday and for the mother to release the father from all claims against him; the fact that the agreement failed to determine the parent/child relationship did not render it void since RC 3111.19 expressly provides that the agreement need not make such a determination. Nelson v. Pleasant (Lawrence 1991) 73 Ohio App.3d 479, 597 N.E.2d 1137.

An illegitimate child may not bring a declaratory judgment action asking that the defendant be found to be his putative father and thereby obtain financial support for himself, and also the right to have his surname changed to that of the defendant, where the mother of the child entered into a compromise agreement under RC 3111.07. In re Paternity (Ohio Com.Pl. 1965) 4 Ohio Misc. 193, 211 N.E.2d 894, 33 O.O.2d 299.

3. Action to set aside agreement

Where a mother enters into agreement not to establish paternity with an alleged father, the child is not bound by the agreement and may subsequently bring a paternity action against the alleged father. Fitzpatrick v. Fitzpatrick (Ohio App. 12 Dist., 03-02-1998) 126 Ohio App.3d 476, 710 N.E.2d 778, dismissed, appeal not allowed 82 Ohio

St.3d 1441, 695 N.E.2d 264. Children Out–of–wedlock ☞ 33

Mother's compromise agreement with alleged father did not bar later paternity action brought on behalf of child to recover prospective support and by Department of Human Services to recover birthing expenses, where child was not party to compromise agreement. Payne v. Cartee (Ohio App. 4 Dist., 06-10-1996) 111 Ohio App.3d 580, 676 N.E.2d 946, appeal not allowed 77 Ohio St.3d 1482, 673 N.E.2d 143. Children Out–of–wedlock ☞ 33

Overruling stipulation for dismissal of paternity action for past child support, as not in best interests of child, was not an abuse of discretion in light of absence of evidence on alleged father's ability to pay and emancipated child's need for past support. Phelps v. Fowler (Ohio App. 8 Dist., 11-13-1995) 107 Ohio App.3d 263, 668 N.E.2d 558, appeal not allowed 75 Ohio St.3d 1452, 663 N.E.2d 332. Stipulations ☞ 13

Trial court obtained jurisdiction to proceed with adjudication of paternity, notwithstanding prior stipulation for dismissal. Phelps v. Fowler (Ohio App. 8 Dist., 11-13-1995) 107 Ohio App.3d 263, 668 N.E.2d 558, appeal not allowed 75 Ohio St.3d 1452, 663 N.E.2d 332. Stipulations ☞ 14(6)

Parties to a paternity action may enter into settlement agreement concerning the action. Ransome v. Lampman (Ohio App. 2 Dist., 03-31-1995) 103 Ohio App.3d 8, 658 N.E.2d 313, dismissed, appeal not allowed 73 Ohio St.3d 1449, 654 N.E.2d 985. Children Out–of–wedlock ☞ 22

As binding contracts, settlement agreements, including those in paternity action, may be enforced through breach of contract action. Ransome v Lampman (Ohio App. 2 Dist., 03-31-1995) 103 Ohio App.3d 8, 658 N.E.2d 313, dismissed, appeal not allowed 73 Ohio St.3d 1449, 654 N.E.2d 985. Children Out–of–wedlock ☞ 22

Mother had remedy by way of breach of contract complaint for putative father's failure to make support payments in accordance with settlement of paternity action, and thus was not entitled to relief from judgment approving the settlement. Ransome v. Lampman (Ohio App. 2 Dist., 03-31-1995) 103 Ohio App.3d 8, 658 N.E.2d 313, dismissed, appeal not allowed 73 Ohio St.3d 1449, 654 N.E.2d 985. Children Out–of–wedlock ☞ 22

Where court properly approved compromise agreement entered into by parties to paternity action and there was no indication that mother was forced or coerced into the agreement or that she did not understand the ramifications of entering the agreement, mother was not entitled to relief from judgment under catchall provision, even though she was not experienced in legal matters. Ransome v. Lampman (Ohio App. 2 Dist., 03-31-1995) 103 Ohio App.3d 8, 658 N.E.2d 313, dismissed, appeal not allowed 73 Ohio St.3d 1449, 654 N.E.2d 985. Children Out–of–wedlock ☞ 22

Fact that child was not represented by guardian ad litem in paternity proceedings was not sufficient reason to relieve mother from settlement agreement. Ransome v. Lampman (Ohio App. 2 Dist., 03-31-1995) 103 Ohio App.3d 8, 658 N.E.2d 313, dismissed, appeal not allowed 73 Ohio St.3d 1449, 654 N.E.2d 985. Children Out–of–wedlock ☞ 22

Mother's motion for relief from judgment approving settlement of paternity action was not timely under catchall provision where it was brought eight years after the judgment and most of the reasons cited in support of motion were in existence immediately after judgment was entered. Ransome v. Lampman (Ohio App. 2 Dist., 03-31-1995) 103 Ohio App.3d 8, 658 N.E.2d 313, dismissed, appeal not allowed 73 Ohio St.3d 1449, 654 N.E.2d 985. Child Support ☞ 323; Children Out–of–wedlock ☞ 22

Child's interests in paternity action conflicted with those of her mother, so that child was entitled to relief from settlement even though mother was not, where it was likely in prosecutor's interest to have a compromise agreement entered into by the parties and mother's motivation in compromising the action may have been merely to cooperate with public authorities so that she might continue to receive public support, whereas child's interests included right to know the identity of her father so that she might enjoy the physical, mental, and emotional support of both of her parents during her lifetime, as well as the bundle of rights which accompany the determination of parentage. Ransome v. Lampman (Ohio App. 2 Dist., 03-31-1995) 103 Ohio App.3d 8, 658 N.E.2d 313, dismissed, appeal not allowed 73 Ohio St.3d 1449, 654 N.E.2d 985. Child Support ☞ 324; Children Out–of–wedlock ☞ 22; Children Out–of–wedlock ☞ 33

Child was entitled to relief from judgment approving settlement of paternity action without determination of paternity even though judgment was entered nearly eight years earlier, as child was quite young and could not have been expected to have sought relief in the interim period. Ransome v. Lampman (Ohio App. 2 Dist., 03-31-1995) 103 Ohio App.3d 8, 658 N.E.2d 313, dismissed, appeal not allowed 73 Ohio St.3d 1449, 654 N.E.2d 985. Child Support ☞ 323; Children Out–of–wedlock ☞ 22; Children Out–of–wedlock ☞ 33

Order of juvenile court, by agreement of parties, awarding custody of child to natural mother and giving support duties and visitation privileges to natural mother's brother-in-law as putative father should not have been made without consideration of best interest of child and vacation of such order on basis that it was unjust was not an abuse of the trial court's discretion. In re Smith (Miami 1984) 16 Ohio App.3d 75, 474 N.E.2d 632, 16 O.B.R. 79. Children Out–of–wedlock ☞ 20.3

Where a plaintiff brought an action to set aside a settlement agreement entered into in a bastardy proceeding and the defendant filed motions and obtained subpoenas duces tecum ordering the plaintiff to appear for a taking of his deposition, and plaintiff failed to do so, a trial court acted properly in ordering him to appear. Raible v.

Raydel (Cuyahoga 1952) 110 N.E.2d 431, 63 Ohio Law Abs. 591, appeal dismissed 158 Ohio St. 328, 109 N.E.2d 319, 49 O.O. 180.

Statute allowing parties in paternity action to enter compromise agreement subject to court approval supersedes rule allowing dismissal by stipulation without court approval. State ex rel. Fowler

v. Smith (Ohio 1994) 68 Ohio St.3d 357, 626 N.E.2d 950.

A minor child is not barred from instituting a later action to determine paternity when a prior action brought in her name has reached judgment through a stipulated agreement. Ransome v Lampman, Nos. 94–CA–20+, 1995 WL 136983, 2d Dist Ct App, Miami, 3–31–95).

ACKNOWLEDGMENT OF PATERNITY

3111.20   Birth record

As used in sections 3111.21 to 3111.85 of the Revised Code, "birth record" has the same meaning as in section 3705.01 of the Revised Code.

(2000 S 180, eff. 3–22–01)

Uncodified Law

2001 S 99, § 4, eff. 10–31–01, reads:

Section 3121.01 of the Revised Code, as presented in this act, includes matter that was amended into former sections 3111.20 and 3113.21 of the Revised Code by Sub. H.B. 535 of the 123rd General Assembly. Paragraphs of former sections 3111.20 and 3113.21 of the Revised Code containing H.B. 535 amendments were transferred to section 3121.01 of the Revised Code by Am. Sub. S.B. 180 of the 123rd General Assembly as part of its

general revision of the child support laws. Inclusion of the H.B. 535 amendments in section 3121.01 of the Revised Code is in recognition of the principle stated in division (B) of section 1.52 of the Revised Code that amendments are to be harmonized if capable of simultaneous operation. The version of section 3121.01 of the Revised Code presented in this act therefore is the resulting version in effect prior to the effective date of the section in this act.

Historical and Statutory Notes

Ed. Note: RC 3111.20 contains provisions analogous to former RC 5101.314(F), repealed by 2000 S 180, eff. 3–22–01.

Ed. Note: Former 3111.20 repealed by 2000 S 180, eff. 3–22–01; 2000 H 535, eff. 4–1–01; 2000 H 509, eff. 9–21–00; 1999 H 471, eff. 7–1–00; 1999 H 222, eff. 11–2–99; 1997 H 352, eff. 1–1–98; 1997 H 408, eff. 10–1–97; 1996 H 710, § 7, eff. 6–11–96; 1995 H 167, eff. 6–11–96; 1992 S 10, eff. 7–15–92.

Ed. Note: Former RC 3111.20(A) contained definitions related to the parental obligation of support. See now RC 3119.01; 3121.01; 3123.01; 3125.01 for provisions analogous to former RC 3111.20(A).

Ed. Note: Former RC 3111.20(B) related to the duty of support of a presumed father. See now RC

3111.77 for provisions analogous to former RC 3111.20(B).

Ed. Note: Former RC 3111.20(C) and (D) related to administrative support actions. See now RC 3111.78; 3111.80; 3111.81; 3111.82; 3111.821 for provisions analogous to former RC 3111.20(C).

Ed. Note: Prior 3111.20 repealed by 1982 H 245, eff. 6–29–82; 1975 S 145; 127 v 1039; 1953 H 1; GC 8006–20; Source—GC 12129.

Ed. Note: The effective date of the amendment of this section by 1995 H 167 was changed from 11–15–96 to 6–11–96 by 1996 H 710, § 7, eff. 6–11–96.

Pre–1953 H 1 Amendments: 124 v S 65

Library References

Health ☜397.
Westlaw Topic No. 198H.
C.J.S. Health and Environment §§ 24, 74.

Research References

Encyclopedias

OH Jur. 3d Family Law § 941, Establishment of Parent and Child Relationship.
OH Jur. 3d Family Law § 1011, Assumption of Parental Duty of Support.

Forms

Ohio Jurisprudence Pleading and Practice Forms § 100:6, Classifications of Contempt--Indirect.
Ohio Jurisprudence Pleading and Practice Forms § 96:11, Consent Required.

Treatises and Practice Aids

Sowald & Morganstern, Baldwin's Ohio Practice Domestic Relations Law § 3:3, Administrative Determination of Parentage--Initial Procedure.

Sowald & Morganstern, Baldwin's Ohio Practice Domestic Relations Law § 19:3, Support Obligations--In General.

Sowald & Morganstern, Baldwin's Ohio Practice Domestic Relations Law § 20:3, Statutory History--1992 Senate Bill 10, The "Poster Bill".

Sowald & Morganstern, Baldwin's Ohio Practice Domestic Relations Law § 3:10, Judicial Parentage Action--Parties.

Sowald & Morganstern, Baldwin's Ohio Practice Domestic Relations Law § 3:13, Judicial Parentage Action--Presumptions of Parentage--Creating.

Carlin, Baldwin's Ohio Prac. Merrick-Rippner Probate Law § 18:2, Inheritance Rights of Illegitimate Child--Statutory Provisions.

Carlin, Baldwin's Ohio Prac. Merrick-Rippner Probate Law § 19:1, Legitimation--Statutory Provisions.

Carlin, Baldwin's Ohio Prac. Merrick-Rippner Probate Law § 19:2, Legitimation--Procedure--Acknowledgment of Paternity.

Carlin, Baldwin's Ohio Prac. Merrick-Rippner Probate Law § 19:4, Legitimation--Historical Provisions.

Carlin, Baldwin's Ohio Prac. Merrick-Rippner Probate Law § 19:8, Uniform Parentage Act--Support Order.

Carlin, Baldwin's Ohio Prac. Merrick-Rippner Probate Law § 110:3, Criminal Jurisdiction--Proceedings for Nonsupport.

Carlin, Baldwin's Ohio Prac. Merrick-Rippner Probate Law § 15:20, Children or Lineal Descendants--In General.

Carlin, Baldwin's Ohio Prac. Merrick-Rippner Probate Law § 19:10, Uniform Parentage Act--Procedure in Action to Determine Father-Child Relationship.

Carlin, Baldwin's Ohio Prac. Merrick-Rippner Probate Law § 99:31, Parties Giving Consent--Biological Parents.

Carlin, Baldwin's Ohio Prac. Merrick-Rippner Probate Law § 99:32, Parties Giving Consent--Putative Father.

Carlin, Baldwin's Ohio Prac. Merrick-Rippner Probate Law § 110:13, Jurisdiction Over Child Custody Matters--Determination of Custody.

Carlin, Baldwin's Ohio Prac. Merrick-Rippner Probate Law § 110:19, Parentage Act--Effect.

Carlin, Baldwin's Ohio Prac. Merrick-Rippner Probate Law § 110:20, Parentage Act--Jurisdiction and Venue.

Carlin, Baldwin's Ohio Prac. Merrick-Rippner Probate Law § 110:23, Parentage Act--Parties in Parentage Action.

Carlin, Baldwin's Ohio Prac. Merrick-Rippner Probate Law § 110:29, Parentage Act--Judgment Determining Existence of Parent-Child Relationship.

Carlin, Baldwin's Ohio Prac. Merrick-Rippner Probate Law § 110:31, Parentage Act--Continuing Jurisdiction to Modify or Revoke Judgment.

Carlin, Baldwin's Ohio Prac. Merrick-Rippner Probate Law § 110:35, Civil Support Proceedings--Liability for Child Support.

Law Review and Journal Commentaries

Bankruptcy Reform Act of 1994—What the Bankruptcy Code Giveth, Domestic Relations Courts (and Congress) Taketh Away, C.R. "Chip" Bowles. 8 Domestic Rel J Ohio 17 (March/April 1996).

Finality in Parentage Findings: Perfection or Finality?, Pamela J. MacAdams. 10 Domestic Rel J Ohio 19 (March/April 1998).

Should Children be Penalized Because Their Parents Did Not Marry? A Constitutional Analysis of Section 516 of the New York Family Court Act, Allan E. Mayefsky and Gary von Stange. 26 U Tol L Rev 957 (Summer 1995).

Notes of Decisions

In general 1
Administrative proceedings 2

1. In general

County support enforcement agency lacked statutory authority to bring action in its own name against relator's husband for child support when relator and husband were married, did not dispute parentage, and did not receive public assistance; two statutory exceptions permitting agency to bring action in its own name, when probate court enters acknowledgement of paternity upon its journal and when father voluntarily signs birth certificate as informant pursuant to statute, did not apply. In re Owens (Ohio App. 8 Dist., 07-05-1994) 104 Ohio App.3d 201, 661 N.E.2d 765, appeal allowed 71 Ohio St.3d 1422, 642 N.E.2d 387, appeal dismissed as improvidently allowed 74 Ohio St.3d 1280, 658 N.E.2d 304, 1996-Ohio-273. Child Support ☞ 179

The statutory language from RC 3111.20(C) is broad enough to authorize a juvenile court to award child support retroactive to the date of the birth of the child. State ex rel Summit County Human Services Dept v Paynter, No. 16657, 1994 WL 665512 (9th Dist Ct App, Summit, 11–30–94).

A person is not entitled to relief under Civ R 60(B)(2) or (5) from a judgment of paternity and child support where he signed the child's birth certificate and an administrative order indicating he was the child's biological father even though he knew he was not the biological father because the mother was two months pregnant when he began dating her, and therefore a recent DNA test result showing a 0.00 chance he was the father is not "new evidence" under Civ R 60(B)(2), the specific provision of the rule that prevails over the more general section, (B)(5); although it may appear unfair to require an individual to pay child support for a child not biologically his own, there must be some finality to a judgment and one cannot choose to be a parent and then change his or her mind when the relationship is dissolved. Shaffer v Rusnak, No. 97 CA 26, 1998 WL 429624 (5th Dist Ct App, Guernsey, 7–1–98).

2. Administrative proceedings

Despite mother's contention that father's failure to participate in administrative determination of parentage precluded court of common pleas from exercising jurisdiction over parentage action, given apparent conflict in jurisdictional statutes, court of common pleas was not so patently and unambiguously devoid of subject matter jurisdiction that Court of Appeals would issue writ of prohibition prohibiting court of common pleas from exercising jurisdiction while final judgment was pending. State ex rel. Dixon v. Clark Cty. Court of Common Pleas, Juv. Div. (Clark 1995) 103 Ohio App.3d 523, 660 N.E.2d 486.

3111.21 Signing and notarizing of acknowledgment

If the natural mother and alleged father of a child sign an acknowledgment of paternity affidavit prepared pursuant to section 3111.31 of the Revised Code with respect to that child at a child support enforcement agency, the agency shall provide a notary public to notarize the acknowledgment.

(2000 S 180, eff. 3–22–01)

Historical and Statutory Notes

Ed. Note: Former 3111.21 repealed by 2000 S 180, eff. 3–22–01; 1999 H 471, eff. 7–1–00; 1997 H 352, eff. 1–1–98.

Ed. Note: Former RC 3111.21 contained provisions specifying CSEA actions upon receipt of a notarized acknowledgement of paternity. See now RC 3111.22 for provisions analogous to those deleted from current RC 3111.21, as amended by 2000 S 180, eff. 3–22–01.

Ed. Note: Prior 3111.21 repealed by 1997 H 352, eff. 1–1–98; 1996 H 710, § 7, eff. 6–11–96; 1995 H 167, eff. 6–11–96; 1992 S 10, eff. 7–15–92.

Ed. Note: Prior 3111.21 repealed by 1982 H 245, eff. 6–29–82; 1953 H 1; GC 8006–21; Source—GC 12130.

Ed. Note: The effective date of the amendment of this section by 1995 H 167 was changed from 11–15–96 to 6–11–96 by 1996 H 710, § 7, eff. 6–11–96.

Pre–1953 H 1 Amendments: 124 v S 65

Cross References

Action for child support order, existence of parent-child relationship, see 2151.231
Contempt of court, see 2705.02
Duty of parents to support children of unemancipated minor children, see 3109.19

Hospitals, staff to meet with unmarried mothers, see 3727.17

Library References

Children Out-of-Wedlock ⊚21(2).
Westlaw Topic No. 76H.
C.J.S. Children Out-of-Wedlock §§ 41 to 44.

Research References

Encyclopedias

OH Jur. 3d Family Law § 882, Putative Father Registry.
OH Jur. 3d Family Law § 958, Retroactivity of Statute.

Forms

Ohio Jurisprudence Pleading and Practice Forms § 111:4, Jurisdiction.
Ohio Jurisprudence Pleading and Practice Forms § 111:7, Genetic Tests.

Ohio Jurisprudence Pleading and Practice Forms § 111:10, Temporary Support Order.

Treatises and Practice Aids

Sowald & Morganstern, Baldwin's Ohio Practice Domestic Relations Law § 18:8, Visitation by Third Parties in Domestic Relations Actions.
Sowald & Morganstern, Baldwin's Ohio Practice Domestic Relations Law § 20:3, Statutory History--1992 Senate Bill 10, The "Poster Bill".

Sowald & Morganstern, Baldwin's Ohio Practice Domestic Relations Law § 3:18, Evidence--Genetic Tests--Testing Procedure.

Sowald & Morganstern, Baldwin's Ohio Practice Domestic Relations Law § 3:20, Evidence--Genetic Tests--Costs of Testing.

Sowald & Morganstern, Baldwin's Ohio Practice Domestic Relations Law § 3:42, Effect of Judgment--Child Support--Temporary Support Order.

Carlin, Baldwin's Ohio Prac. Merrick-Rippner Probate Law § 19:4, Legitimation--Historical Provisions.

Carlin, Baldwin's Ohio Prac. Merrick-Rippner Probate Law § 19:7, Uniform Parentage Act--Presumptions.

Carlin, Baldwin's Ohio Prac. Merrick-Rippner Probate Law § 19:10, Uniform Parentage Act--Procedure in Action to Determine Father Child Relationship.

Carlin, Baldwin's Ohio Prac. Merrick-Rippner Probate Law § 19:11, Uniform Parentage Act--Temporary Support Pending Action Objecting to Parentage Determination.

Carlin, Baldwin's Ohio Prac. Merrick-Rippner Probate Law § 99:30, Statutorily Required Consent.

Carlin, Baldwin's Ohio Prac. Merrick-Rippner Probate Law § 99:32, Parties Giving Consent--Putative Father.

Carlin, Baldwin's Ohio Prac. Merrick-Rippner Probate Law § 99:38, Consent Not Required--Statutory Scheme.

Carlin, Baldwin's Ohio Prac. Merrick-Rippner Probate Law § 110:24, Parentage Act--Genetic Tests, Fees, and Costs.

Carlin, Baldwin's Ohio Prac. Merrick-Rippner Probate Law § 110:26, Parentage Act--Applicability of Civil Rules to Paternity Proceedings.

Carlin, Baldwin's Ohio Prac. Merrick-Rippner Probate Law § 110:28, Parentage Act--Trial of Parentage Action.

Carlin, Baldwin's Ohio Prac. Merrick-Rippner Probate Law § 110:30, Parentage Act--Enforcement of Support Order.

Carlin, Baldwin's Ohio Prac. Merrick-Rippner Probate Law § 110:34, Parentage Act--Administrative Support Orders.

Carlin, Baldwin's Ohio Prac. Merrick-Rippner Probate Law § 110:35, Civil Support Proceedings--Liability for Child Support.

Adrine & Ruden, Ohio Domestic Violence Law § 10:7, Relationships Covered--Persons Who Have a Child in Common.

Law Review and Journal Commentaries

Basics of the Ohio putative father registry. Erik L. Smith, 19 Ohio Law 6 (March/April 2005).

Notes of Decisions

Administrative order 2
Constitutional issues 1
Surrogacy agreement 3

---

1. Constitutional issues

It is a violation of the equal protection clauses of the United States and Ohio constitutions to allow the aid and support of the child support enforcement agency in an action for child support brought by parents who have established their parentage through the probate court and residential parents who are on public assistance while denying the aid and support of the child support enforcement agency to parents who have established their parentage through the administrative process. Cuyahoga County Support Enforcement Agency v Lozada, Nos. 67463+, 1995 WL 386965 (8th Dist Ct App, Cuyahoga, 6–29–95).

Dismissal of the child support enforcement agency (CSEA) as a party in an action for child support under RC 3111.21 via RC 2151.231 violates the Ohio and federal Equal Protection Clauses when a similarly situated residential parent who legitimizes a child through probate court is entitled to have the CSEA advocate for a proper child support order in the juvenile court under RC 3111.20, by way of RC 2151.231. Cuyahoga County Support Enforcement Agency v Lozada, No. 67463+, 1995 WL 386965 (8th Dist Ct App, Cuyahoga, 6–29–95).

2. Administrative order

A person is not entitled to relief under Civ R 60(B)(2) or (5) from a judgment of paternity and child support where he signed the child's birth certificate and an administrative order indicating he was the child's biological father even though he knew he was not the biological father because the mother was two months pregnant when he began dating her, and therefore a recent DNA test result showing a 0.00 chance he was the father is not "new evidence" under Civ R 60(B)(2), the specific provision of the rule that prevails over the more general section, (B)(5); although it may appear unfair to require an individual to pay child support for a child not biologically his own, there must be some finality to a judgment and one cannot choose to be a parent and then change his or her mind when the relationship is dissolved. Shaffer v Rusnak, No. 97 CA 26, 1998 WL 429624 (5th Dist Ct App, Guernsey, 7–1–98).

A person is not entitled to relief under Civ R 60(B)(2) or (5) from a judgment of paternity and child support where he signed the child's birth certificate and an administrative order indicating he was the child's biological father even though he knew he was not the biological father because the mother was two months pregnant when he began dating her, and therefore a recent DNA test result showing a 0.00 chance he was the father is not "new evidence" under Civ R 60(B)(2), the specific provision of the rule that prevails over the more general section, (B)(5); although it may appear unfair to require an individual to pay child support for a child not biologically his own, there must be some finality to a judgment and one cannot choose to be a parent and then change his or her mind when the relationship is dissolved. Shaffer v Rusnak, No. 97 CA 26, 1998 WL 429624 (5th Dist Ct App, Guernsey, 7–1–98).

3. Surrogacy agreement

Surrogacy agreement was valid and enforceable under which a gestational surrogate agreed to relinquish, to the intended mother, physical custody and any and all rights to child born from embryo formed outside the womb by anonymously donated egg and sperm, and therefore, the intended mother

rebutted presumption that surrogate, as woman who gave birth to child, was the child's legal and natural mother under the Parentage Act; the agreement set forth in writing following extensive negotiations, the agreement included an acknowledgement that the parties entered into it voluntarily and with the aid of counsel, and, in consideration, intended mother paid for gestational surrogate's unreimbursed medical costs, the cost of a $200,000 term life insurance policy, and an additional $15,000 for living expenses. S.N. v. M.B. (Ohio App. 10 Dist., 06-10-2010) 188 Ohio App.3d 324, 935 N.E.2d 463, 2010-Ohio-2479, cause dismissed 126 Ohio St.3d 1525, 931 N.E.2d 126, 2010-Ohio-3583. Children Out–of–wedlock ⟜ 15

3111.211 Administrative support order before acknowledgment becomes final—Repealed

(2000 S 180, eff. 3–22–01; 1999 H 471, eff. 7–1–00; 1997 H 352, eff. 1–1–98)

Historical and Statutory Notes

Ed. Note: Former RC 3111.211(A) related to paternity issues in administrative support hearings.

See now RC 3111.82; 3111.821 for provisions analogous to former RC 3111.211(A).

3111.22 Signed and notarized acknowledgment of paternity to be sent to office of child support

A child support enforcement agency shall send a signed and notarized acknowledgment of paternity to the office of child support in the department of job and family services pursuant to section 3111.23 of the Revised Code. The agency shall send the acknowledgment no later than ten days after it has been signed and notarized. If the agency knows a man is presumed under section 3111.03 of the Revised Code to be the father of the child and the presumed father is not the man who signed an acknowledgment with respect to the child, the agency shall not notarize or send the acknowledgment with respect to the child pursuant to this section.
(2000 S 180, eff. 3–22–01)

Historical and Statutory Notes

Ed. Note: RC 3111.22 contains provisions analogous to those deleted from current RC 3111.21, as amended by 2000 S 180, eff. 3–22–01.

Ed. Note: Former 3111.22 repealed by 2000 S 180, eff. 3–22–01; 1999 H 471, eff. 7–1–00; 1997 H 352, eff. 1–1–98; 1996 H 710, § 7, eff. 6–11–96; 1995 H 167, eff. 6–11–96; 1992 S 10, eff. 7–15–92.

Ed. Note: Former RC 3111.22(A) related to availability of de novo court actions to determine paternity. See now RC 3111.381 for provisions analogous to former RC 3111.22(A).

Ed. Note: Former RC 3111.22(B) related to requests for administrative paternity determinations. See now RC 3111.38; 3111.39; 3111.40 for provisions analogous to former RC 3111.22(B).

Ed. Note: Former RC 3111.22(C) related to notice, order and testing procedures for paternity testing in administrative proceedings. See now RC 3111.41; 3111.42; 3111.421; 3111.44; 3111.45; 3111.46; 3111.48 for provisions analogous to former 3111.22(C).

Ed. Note: Former RC 3111.22(D) related to appeal of conclusive paternity determination. See now RC 3111.49 for provisions analogous to former RC 3111.22(D).

Ed. Note: Former RC 3111.22(E) related to administrative support orders based on administrative paternity determinations. See now RC 3111.80; 3111.81 for provisions analogous to former RC 3111.22(E).

Ed. Note: Former RC 3111.22(F) related to paternity determinations deemed inconclusive due to failure to submit to testing. See now RC 3111.47; 3111.50 for provisions analogous to former RC 3111.22(F).

Ed. Note: Former RC 3111.22(G) related to the contents of administrative paternity orders, including name changes. See now RC 3111.51; 3111.52 for provisions analogous to former RC 3111.22(G).

Ed. Note: Former RC 3111.22(H) related to the effect of prior administrative paternity determinations. See now RC 3111.85 for provisions analogous to former RC 3111.22(H).

Ed. Note: Prior 3111.22 repealed by 1982 H 245, eff. 6–29–82; 1953 H 1; GC 8006–22; Source—GC 12131.

Ed. Note: The effective date of the amendment of this section by 1995 H 167 was changed from 11–15–96 to 6–11–96 by 1996 H 710, § 7, eff. 6–11–96.

Pre–1953 H 1 Amendments: 124 v S 65

Ohio Administrative Code References

Acknowledgment of paternity, see OAC 5101:12–40–15
Central paternity registry, see OAC 5101:12–40–30

Library References

Children Out-of-Wedlock ⚎21(2).
Westlaw Topic No. 76H.
C.J.S. Children Out-of-Wedlock §§ 41 to 44.

Research References

Encyclopedias

OH Jur. 3d Family Law § 965, Blood Tests.

Forms

Ohio Jurisprudence Pleading and Practice Forms § 100:6, Classifications of Contempt--Indirect.
Ohio Jurisprudence Pleading and Practice Forms § 111:4, Jurisdiction.
Ohio Jurisprudence Pleading and Practice Forms § 111:7, Genetic Tests.
Ohio Jurisprudence Pleading and Practice Forms § 111:10, Temporary Support Order.

Treatises and Practice Aids

Sowald & Morganstern, Baldwin's Ohio Practice Domestic Relations Law § 3:3, Administrative Determination of Parentage--Initial Procedure.
Sowald & Morganstern, Baldwin's Ohio Practice Domestic Relations Law § 3:8, Jurisdiction and Venue.
Sowald & Morganstern, Baldwin's Ohio Practice Domestic Relations Law § 3:9, Judicial Parentage Action--Initial Procedure.
Sowald & Morganstern, Baldwin's Ohio Practice Domestic Relations Law § 22:4, Establishing Parentage.
Sowald & Morganstern, Baldwin's Ohio Practice Domestic Relations Law § 3:18, Evidence--Genetic Tests--Testing Procedure.
Sowald & Morganstern, Baldwin's Ohio Practice Domestic Relations Law § 3:20, Evidence--Genetic Tests--Costs of Testing.
Sowald & Morganstern, Baldwin's Ohio Practice Domestic Relations Law § 3:42, Effect of Judgment--Child Support--Temporary Support Order.
Carlin, Baldwin's Ohio Prac. Merrick-Rippner Probate Law § 19:2, Legitimation--Procedure--Acknowledgment of Paternity.
Carlin, Baldwin's Ohio Prac. Merrick-Rippner Probate Law § 19:6, Uniform Parentage Act--Jurisdiction of Action to Determine Father-Child Relationship.

Carlin, Baldwin's Ohio Prac. Merrick-Rippner Probate Law § 19:10, Uniform Parentage Act--Procedure in Action to Determine Father-Child Relationship.
Carlin, Baldwin's Ohio Prac. Merrick-Rippner Probate Law § 19:11, Uniform Parentage Act--Temporary Support Pending Action Objecting to Parentage Determination.
Carlin, Baldwin's Ohio Prac. Merrick-Rippner Probate Law § 110:13, Jurisdiction Over Child Custody Matters--Determination of Custody.
Carlin, Baldwin's Ohio Prac. Merrick-Rippner Probate Law § 110:19, Parentage Act--Effect.
Carlin, Baldwin's Ohio Prac. Merrick-Rippner Probate Law § 110:20, Parentage Act--Jurisdiction and Venue.
Carlin, Baldwin's Ohio Prac. Merrick-Rippner Probate Law § 110:23, Parentage Act--Parties in Parentage Action.
Carlin, Baldwin's Ohio Prac. Merrick-Rippner Probate Law § 110:24, Parentage Act--Genetic Tests, Fees, and Costs.
Carlin, Baldwin's Ohio Prac. Merrick-Rippner Probate Law § 110:26, Parentage Act--Applicability of Civil Rules to Paternity Proceedings.
Carlin, Baldwin's Ohio Prac. Merrick-Rippner Probate Law § 110:28, Parentage Act--Trial of Parentage Action.
Carlin, Baldwin's Ohio Prac. Merrick-Rippner Probate Law § 110:29, Parentage Act--Judgment Determining Existence of Parent-Child Relationship.
Carlin, Baldwin's Ohio Prac. Merrick-Rippner Probate Law § 110:30, Parentage Act--Enforcement of Support Order.
Carlin, Baldwin's Ohio Prac. Merrick-Rippner Probate Law § 110:31, Parentage Act--Continuing Jurisdiction to Modify or Revoke Judgment.
Carlin, Baldwin's Ohio Prac. Merrick-Rippner Probate Law § 110:34, Parentage Act--Administrative Support Orders.
Carlin, Baldwin's Ohio Prac. Merrick-Rippner Probate Law § 110:35, Civil Support Proceedings--Liability for Child Support.

Law Review and Journal Commentaries

Acknowledgement of Paternity—Changes in Statutes and Forms, Angela G. Carlin. 10 Prob L J Ohio 10 (September/October 1999).

Bankruptcy Reform Act of 1994—What the Bankruptcy Code Giveth, Domestic Relations Courts (and Congress) Taketh Away, C.R. "Chip" Bowles. 8 Domestic Rel J Ohio 17 (March/April 1996).

Basics of the Ohio putative father registry. Erik L. Smith, 19 Ohio Law 6 (March/April 2005).

Establishing Parentage After Senate Bill 10, Pamela J. MacAdams. 4 Domestic Rel J Ohio 81 (September/October 1992).

Notes of Decisions

In general 2
Constitutional issues 1
Jurisdiction 3

---

1. Constitutional issues

Trial court's dismissal of child support enforcement agency as party in five child support actions where parentage was established through administrative proceedings violated equal protection clauses of State and Federal Constitutions; statutory scheme, which permits agency to be party in support actions where parentage is established through probate court and where parents are on public assistance, but which does not specifically permit agency to be party when parentage is established through administrative proceedings, did not have rational basis, since enforcement agency can only effectuate its duty to protect best interests of child and public fisc by being joined as party in all child support enforcement actions. Cuyahoga Cty. Support Enforcement Agency v. Lozada (Ohio App. 8 Dist., 07-10-1995) 102 Ohio App.3d 442, 657 N.E.2d 372. Child Support ☞ 473; Constitutional Law ☞ 3455

It is a violation of the equal protection clauses of the United States and Ohio constitutions to allow the aid and support of the child support enforcement agency in an action for child support brought by parents who have established their parentage through the probate court and residential parents who are on public assistance while denying the aid and support of the child support enforcement agency to parents who have established their parentage through the administrative process. Cuyahoga County Support Enforcement Agency v Lozada, Nos. 67463+, 1995 WL 386965 (8th Dist Ct App, Cuyahoga, 6–29–95).

2. In general

Surrogacy agreement was valid and enforceable under which a gestational surrogate agreed to relinquish, to the intended mother, physical custody and any and all rights to child born from embryo formed outside the womb by anonymously donated egg and sperm, and therefore, the intended mother rebutted presumption that surrogate, as woman who gave birth to child, was the child's legal and natural mother under the Parentage Act; the agreement set forth in writing following extensive negotiations, the agreement included an acknowledgement that the parties entered into it voluntarily and

with the aid of counsel, and, in consideration, intended mother paid for gestational surrogate's unreimbursed medical costs, the cost of a $200,000 term life insurance policy, and an additional $15,000 for living expenses. S.N. v. M.B. (Ohio App. 10 Dist., 06-10-2010) 188 Ohio App.3d 324, 935 N.E.2d 463, 2010-Ohio-2479, cause dismissed 126 Ohio St.3d 1525, 931 N.E.2d 126, 2010-Ohio-3583. Children Out–of–wedlock ☞ 15

Father's duty to support child did not begin until date administrative parentage determination became final, nearly a month after mother and stepfather petitioned to adopt child, and, therefore, father's earlier failure to support child did not obviate need to obtain father's consent to adoption. In re Adoption of Hudnell (Ohio App. 4 Dist., 08-06-1996) 113 Ohio App.3d 296, 680 N.E.2d 1055. Adoption ☞ 7.4(6); Children Out–of–wedlock ☞ 21(2)

Paternity suit judgments are nondischargeable under provision of Bankruptcy Code rendering nondischargeable a debt to spouse, former spouse, or child of debtor for alimony to, maintenance for, or support of such spouse or child, in connection with separation agreement, divorce decree or "other order of a court of record." In re Oberley (Bkrtcy. N.D.Ohio 1993) 153 B.R. 179. Bankruptcy ☞ 3365(13); Bankruptcy ☞ 3368

Statutes addressing rescission of paternity acknowledgements, temporary child support orders, and notification of paternity test results, all of which were enacted after entry of paternity and support orders, could not serve as basis for challenging orders. Norris v. Norris (Ohio App. 5 Dist., Ashland, 09-27-2002) No. 02 COA 016, 2002-Ohio-5285, 2002 WL 31185798, Unreported. Children Out–of–wedlock ☞ 31

A person is not entitled to relief under Civ R 60(B)(2) or (5) from a judgment of paternity and child support where he signed the child's birth certificate and an administrative order indicating he was the child's biological father even though he knew he was not the biological father because the mother was two months pregnant when he began dating her, and therefore a recent DNA test result showing a 0.00 chance he was the father is not "new evidence" under Civ R 60(B)(2), the specific provision of the rule that prevails over the more general section, (B)(5); although it may appear unfair to require an individual to pay child support for a child not biologically his own, there must be some finality to a judgment and one cannot choose to be a parent and then change his or her mind when the relationship is dissolved. Shaffer v Rusnak, No. 97 CA 26, 1998 WL 429624 (5th Dist Ct App, Guernsey, 7–1–98).

A motion for summary judgment may lie in paternity proceedings in juvenile court. State ex rel Drews v Ambrosi, No. 73761, 1998 WL 563993 (8th Dist Ct App, Cuyahoga, 9–3–98).

3. Jurisdiction

Fact that adjudicated father's motion for modification of child support was pending before Juvenile Court did not give Juvenile Court jurisdiction to entertain paternal grandmother's petition for grandparental visitation, where child support obligation was established by virtue of administrative order, over modification of which Juvenile Court lacked jurisdiction. Borkosky v. Mihailoff (Ohio App. 3 Dist., 03-03-1999) 132 Ohio App.3d 508, 725 N.E.2d 694. Child Custody ☞ 404

Domestic relations courts have original jurisdiction to consider parentage issues during pendency of divorce, dissolution, or legal separation actions. Leguillon v. Leguillon (Ohio App. 12 Dist., 01-12-1998) 124 Ohio App.3d 757, 707 N.E.2d 571. Children Out–of–wedlock ☞ 36

Despite mother's contention that father's failure to participate in administrative determination of parentage precluded court of common pleas from exercising jurisdiction over parentage action, given apparent conflict in jurisdictional statutes, court of common pleas was not so patently and unambiguously devoid of subject matter jurisdiction that Court of Appeals would issue writ of prohibition prohibiting court of common pleas from exercising jurisdiction while final judgment was pending. State ex rel. Dixon v. Clark Cty. Court of Common Pleas, Juv. Div. (Clark 1995) 103 Ohio App.3d 523, 660 N.E.2d 486.

3111.221 Preparation of new birth record pursuant to determination of parent and child relationship—Repealed

(2000 S 180, eff. 3–22–01; 1997 H 352, eff. 1–1–98)

Historical and Statutory Notes

Ed. Note: Former 3111.221 amended and recodified as 3111.58 by 2000 S 180, eff. 3–22–01.

3111.23 Acknowledgment of paternity

The natural mother, the man acknowledging he is the natural father, or the other custodian or guardian of a child, a child support enforcement agency pursuant to section 3111.22 of the Revised Code, a local registrar of vital statistics pursuant to section 3705.091 of the Revised Code, or a hospital staff person pursuant to section 3727.17 of the Revised Code, in person or by mail, may file an acknowledgment of paternity with the office of child support in the department of job and family services, acknowledging that the child is the child of the man who signed the acknowledgment. The acknowledgment of paternity shall be made on the affidavit prepared pursuant to section 3111.31 of the Revised Code, shall be signed by the natural mother and the man acknowledging that he is the natural father, and each signature shall be notarized. The mother and man may sign and have the signature notarized outside of each other's presence. An acknowledgment shall be sent to the office no later than ten days after it has been signed and notarized. If a person knows a man is presumed under section 3111.03 of the Revised Code to be the father of the child described in this section and that the presumed father is not the man who signed an acknowledgment with respect to the child, the person shall not notarize or file the acknowledgment pursuant to this section.

(2000 S 180, eff. 3–22–01)

Historical and Statutory Notes

Ed. Note: RC 3111.23 contains provisions analogous to former RC 5101.314(A)(1), repealed by 2000 S 180, eff. 3–22–01.

Ed. Note: Former 3111.23 repealed by 2000 S 180, eff. 3–22–01; 1999 H 471, eff. 7–1–00; 1998 S 170, eff. 3–30–99; 1997 H 352, eff. 1–1–98; 1997 H 408, eff. 10–1–97; 1996 S 292, eff. 11–6–96; 1996 H 710, § 7, eff. 6–11–96; 1995 H 167, eff. 6–11–96; 1993 H 173, eff. 12–31–93; 1992 S 10.

Ed. Note: Former RC 3111.23(A) contained various provisions relating to the issuance of with-

holding/deduction orders. See now RC 3121.02; 3121.0311; 3121.032; 3121.035; 3121.27; 3121.33; 3121.34 for provisions analogous to former RC 3111.23(A).

Ed. Note: Former RC 3111.23(B) related to the required contents of withholding/deduction notices. See now RC 3121.03; 3121.036; 3121.037 for provisions analogous to former 3111.23(B).

Ed. Note: Former RC 3111.23(C) related to the number of notices or orders required. See now RC

3121.033 for provisions analogous to former RC 3111.23(C).

Ed. Note: Former RC 3111.23(D) related to priority among multiple withholding/deduction notices. See now RC 3121.034 for provisions analogous to former RC 3111.23(D).

Ed. Note: Former RC 3111.23(E) related to service and notice requirements, including termination. See now RC 3121.23; 3121.24; 3121.29; 3119.87; 3119.88; 3119.89; 3119.90; 3119.93; 3119.94 for provisions analogous to former RC 3111.23(E).

Ed. Note: Former RC 3111.23(F) related to disposition of lump sum payments. See now RC 3121.12 for provisions analogous to former RC 3111.23(F).

Ed. Note: Former RC 3111.23(G) related to specific contents of withholding/deduction orders.

See now RC 3121.30; 3121.039; 3121.038 for provisions analogous to former RC 3111.23(G).

Ed. Note: Former RC 3111.23(H) related to termination by payment of arrearages. See now 3123.13 for provisions analogous to former RC 3111.23(H).

Ed. Note: Former RC 3111.23(I) related to payment of arrearages to ODHS. See now RC 3123.19 for provisions analogous to former RC 3111.23(I).

Ed. Note: Prior 3111.23 repealed by 1982 H 245, eff. 6–29–82; 1953 H 1; GC 8006–23; Source—GC 12132.

Ed. Note: The effective date of the amendment of this section by 1995 H 167 was changed from 11–15–96 to 6–11–96 by 1996 H 710, § 7, eff. 6–11–96.

Pre–1953 H 1 Amendments: 124 v S 65

Cross References

Penalty: 3111.99(C), (D)
Action for child support order before acknowledgment becomes final, see 2151.232
Alternative retirement plans for employees of public institutions of higher education, exemption from legal process, applicability, see 3305.08
Duty of parents to support children of unemancipated minor children, see 3109.19

Income and benefits subject to withholding, see 145.56, 742.47, 3307.71, 3309.66, 3770.07, 5505.22
Public employees retirement board, required information, see 145.27
School employees retirement board, required information, see 3309.22
Teachers retirement board, required information, see 3307.21

Library References

Children Out-of-Wedlock ⬤21(2).
Westlaw Topic No. 76H.
C.J.S. Children Out-of-Wedlock §§ 41 to 44.

Research References

Encyclopedias

OH Jur. 3d Family Law § 864, Birth Record of Legitimated Child.
OH Jur. 3d Family Law § 944, Statutory Presumptions.
OH Jur. 3d Family Law § 958, Retroactivity of Statute.
OH Jur. 3d Family Law § 988, Legitimation by Acknowledgment of Paternity.
OH Jur. 3d Family Law § 1016, Action for Support.
OH Jur. 3d Family Law § 1230, Payment of Support by Obligor to Child Support Enforcement Agency.

Forms

Ohio Forms Legal and Business § 28:6, Form Drafting Principles.
Ohio Forms Legal and Business § 28:7, Acknowledgment of Paternity.
Ohio Forms Legal and Business § 28:10, Request to Amend Birth Certificate--Acknowledgment of Paternity Filed.
Ohio Jurisprudence Pleading and Practice Forms § 100:6, Classifications of Contempt--Indirect.

Ohio Jurisprudence Pleading and Practice Forms § 111:19, to Income Provider--Withhold Obligor Income, Assets.

Treatises and Practice Aids

Sowald & Morganstern, Baldwin's Ohio Practice Domestic Relations Law § 3:2, Administrative Determination of Parentage--Purpose.
Sowald & Morganstern, Baldwin's Ohio Practice Domestic Relations Law § 3:8, Jurisdiction and Venue.
Sowald & Morganstern, Baldwin's Ohio Practice Domestic Relations Law § 3:9, Judicial Parentage Action--Initial Procedure.
Sowald & Morganstern, Baldwin's Ohio Practice Domestic Relations Law § 3:10, Judicial Parentage Action--Parties.
Sowald & Morganstern, Baldwin's Ohio Practice Domestic Relations Law § 3:13, Judicial Parentage Action--Presumptions of Parentage--Creating.
Sowald & Morganstern, Baldwin's Ohio Practice Domestic Relations Law § 3:42, Effect of Judgment--Child Support--Temporary Support Order.
Sowald & Morganstern, Baldwin's Ohio Practice Domestic Relations Law § 3:49, Related Issues--Adoption.

Sowald & Morganstern, Baldwin's Ohio Practice Domestic Relations Law § 23:15, In-State Remedies--Determination of Parentage.

Carlin, Baldwin's Ohio Prac. Merrick-Rippner Probate Law § 18:3, Inheritance Rights of Illegitimate Child--Case Law Affecting Rules of Inheritance Generally.

Carlin, Baldwin's Ohio Prac. Merrick-Rippner Probate Law § 19:2, Legitimation--Procedure--Acknowledgment of Paternity.

Carlin, Baldwin's Ohio Prac. Merrick-Rippner Probate Law § 19:4, Legitimation--Historical Provisions.

Carlin, Baldwin's Ohio Prac. Merrick-Rippner Probate Law § 19:5, Legitimation--Insurance Benefits.

Carlin, Baldwin's Ohio Prac. Merrick-Rippner Probate Law § 19:7, Uniform Parentage Act Presumptions.

Carlin, Baldwin's Ohio Prac. Merrick-Rippner Probate Law § 93:1, Property Subject to Sale--General Rule.

Carlin, Baldwin's Ohio Prac. Merrick-Rippner Probate Law § 99:32, Parties Giving Consent--Putative Father.

Carlin, Baldwin's Ohio Prac. Merrick-Rippner Probate Law § 99:49, Interlocutory and Final Orders.

Carlin, Baldwin's Ohio Prac. Merrick-Rippner Probate Law § 110:13, Jurisdiction Over Child Custody Matters--Determination of Custody.

Carlin, Baldwin's Ohio Prac. Merrick-Rippner Probate Law § 110:19, Parentage Act--Effect.

Carlin, Baldwin's Ohio Prac. Merrick-Rippner Probate Law § 110:20, Parentage Act--Jurisdiction and Venue.

Carlin, Baldwin's Ohio Prac. Merrick-Rippner Probate Law § 110:22, Parentage Act--Presumption of Paternity.

Carlin, Baldwin's Ohio Prac. Merrick-Rippner Probate Law § 110:23, Parentage Act--Parties in Parentage Action.

Carlin, Baldwin's Ohio Prac. Merrick-Rippner Probate Law § 110:31, Parentage Act--Continuing Jurisdiction to Modify or Revoke Judgment.

Carlin, Baldwin's Ohio Prac. Merrick-Rippner Probate Law § 110:34, Parentage Act--Administrative Support Orders.

Law Review and Journal Commentaries

Bankruptcy Reform Act of 1994—What the Bankruptcy Code Giveth, Domestic Relations Courts (and Congress) Taketh Away, C.R. "Chip" Bowles. 8 Domestic Rel J Ohio 17 (March/April 1996).

Basics of the Ohio putative father registry. Erik L. Smith, 19 Ohio Law 6 (March/April 2005).

BWC and Self–Insured Employer Liability for Spousal and Child Support, C. Jeffrey Waite, Jo Ann Wasil and Mark E. Mastrangelo. 14 Workers' Compensation J Ohio 1 (January/February 1999).

BWC and Self–Insured Employer Liability for Spousal and Child Support, C. Jeffrey Waite. 11 Domestic Rel J Ohio 17 (March/April 1999).

The Inheritance Rights (or Lack Thereof) of Legitimated Children in Ohio. Angela G. Carlin, 11 Prob L J Ohio 109 (July/August 2001).

Looking to Unwed Dads to Fill the Public Purse: A Disturbing Wave in Welfare Reform, Roger J.R. Levesque. 32 J Fam L 1 (1993–94).

Notes of Decisions

Acknowledgement in probate court 1
Administrative proceedings 3
Surrogacy agreements 2

1. Acknowledgement in probate court

County support enforcement agency lacked statutory authority to bring action in its own name against relator's husband for child support when relator and husband were married, did not dispute parentage, and did not receive public assistance; two statutory exceptions permitting agency to bring action in its own name, when probate court enters acknowledgement of paternity upon its journal and when father voluntarily signs birth certificate as informant pursuant to statute, did not apply. In re Owens (Ohio App. 8 Dist., 07-05-1994) 104 Ohio App.3d 201, 661 N.E.2d 765, appeal allowed 71 Ohio St.3d 1422, 642 N.E.2d 387, appeal dismissed as improvidently allowed 74 Ohio St.3d 1280, 658 N.E.2d 304, 1996-Ohio-273. Child Support ☞ 179

2. Surrogacy agreements

Surrogacy agreement was valid and enforceable under which a gestational surrogate agreed to relin-

quish, to the intended mother, physical custody and any and all rights to child born from embryo formed outside the womb by anonymously donated egg and sperm, and therefore, the intended mother rebutted presumption that surrogate, as woman who gave birth to child, was the child's legal and natural mother under the Parentage Act; the agreement set forth in writing following extensive negotiations, the agreement included an acknowledgement that the parties entered into it voluntarily and with the aid of counsel, and, in consideration, intended mother paid for gestational surrogate's unreimbursed medical costs, the cost of a $200,000 term life insurance policy, and an additional $15,000 for living expenses. S.N. v. M.B. (Ohio App. 10 Dist., 06-10-2010) 188 Ohio App.3d 324, 935 N.E.2d 463, 2010-Ohio-2479, cause dismissed 126 Ohio St.3d 1525, 931 N.E.2d 126, 2010-Ohio-3583. Children Out–of–wedlock ☞ 15

3. Administrative proceedings

Despite mother's contention that father's failure to participate in administrative determination of parentage precluded court of common pleas from exercising jurisdiction over parentage action, given apparent conflict in jurisdictional statutes, court of common pleas was not so patently and unambiguously devoid of subject matter jurisdiction that Court of Appeals would issue writ of prohibition prohibiting court of common pleas from exercising jurisdiction while final judgment was pending. State ex rel. Dixon v. Clark Cty. Court of Common Pleas, Juv. Div. (Clark 1995) 103 Ohio App.3d 523, 660 N.E.2d 486.

3111.231 Administrative order requiring obligor to seek employment or participate in work activity—Repealed

(2000 S 180, eff. 3–22–01; 1999 H 471, eff. 7–1–00; 1997 H 352, eff. 1–1–98)

Historical and Statutory Notes

Ed. Note: Former RC 3111.231 related to administrative orders directing obligor to seek employment. See now RC 3121.03 for provisions analogous to former RC 3111.231.

3111.24 Examination of acknowledgment; return of incorrect acknowledgment; entry of acknowledgment information into birth registry

(A) On the filing of an acknowledgment, the office of child support shall examine the acknowledgment to determine whether it is completed correctly. The office shall make the examination no later than five days after the acknowledgment is filed. If the acknowledgment is completed correctly, the office shall comply with division (B) of this section. If the acknowledgment is not completed correctly, the office shall return it to the person or entity that filed it. The person or entity shall have ten days from the date the office sends the acknowledgment back to correct it and return it to the office. The office shall send, along with the acknowledgment, a notice stating what needs to be corrected and the amount of time the person or entity has to make the corrections and return the acknowledgment to the office.

If the person or entity returns the acknowledgment in a timely manner, the office shall examine the acknowledgment again to determine whether it has been correctly completed. If the acknowledgment has been correctly completed, the office shall comply with division (B) of this section. If the acknowledgment has not been correctly completed the second time or if the acknowledgment is not returned to the office in a timely manner, the acknowledgment is invalid and the office shall return it to the person or entity and shall not enter it into the birth registry. If the office returns an acknowledgment the second time, it shall send a notice to the person or entity stating the errors in the acknowledgment and that the acknowledgment is invalid.

(B) If the office determines an acknowledgment is correctly completed, the office shall enter the information on the acknowledgment into the birth registry pursuant to sections 3111.64 and 3111.65 of the Revised Code. After entering the information in the registry, the office shall send the acknowledgment to the department of health for storage pursuant to section 3705.091 of the Revised Code. The office may request that the department of health send back to the office any acknowledgment that is being stored by the department of health pursuant to that section.

(2000 S 180, eff. 3–22–01)

Historical and Statutory Notes

Ed. Note: RC 3111.24 contains provisions analogous to former RC 5101.314(A)(2), repealed by 2000 S 180, eff. 3–22–01.

Ed. Note: Former 3111.24 repealed by 2000 S 180, eff. 3–22–01; 1999 H 471, eff. 7–1–00; 1997 H 352, eff. 1–1–98; 1993 H 173, eff. 12–31–93; 1992 S 10.

Ed. Note: Former RC 3111.24 related to collection and disbursement procedures pursuant to withholding/deduction orders. See now RC 3121.18; 3121.19; 3121.20; 3121.21; 3121.50 for provisions analogous to former RC 3111.24.

Ed. Note: Prior 3111.24 repealed by 1982 H 245, eff. 6–29–82; 1953 H 1; GC 8006–24; Source—GC 12133.

Pre–1953 H 1 Amendments: 124 v S 65

Cross References

Action for child support order before acknowledgment becomes final, see 2151.232

Ohio Administrative Code References

Support order establishment process, see OAC 5101:12–45–05

Library References

Children Out-of-Wedlock ☞21(2).
Health ☞397.
Westlaw Topic Nos. 76H, 198H.

C.J.S. Children Out-of-Wedlock §§ 41 to 44.
C.J.S. Health and Environment §§ 24, 74.

Research References

Encyclopedias

OH Jur. 3d Family Law § 988, Legitimation by Acknowledgment of Paternity.
OH Jur. 3d Family Law § 1016, Action for Support.

Treatises and Practice Aids

Carlin, Baldwin's Ohio Prac. Merrick-Rippner Probate Law § 19:2, Legitimation--Procedure--Acknowledgment of Paternity.

Carlin, Baldwin's Ohio Prac. Merrick-Rippner Probate Law § 19:4, Legitimation--Historical Provisions.
Carlin, Baldwin's Ohio Prac. Merrick-Rippner Probate Law § 110:13, Jurisdiction Over Child Custody Matters--Determination of Custody.
Carlin, Baldwin's Ohio Prac. Merrick-Rippner Probate Law § 110:20, Parentage Act--Jurisdiction and Venue.
Carlin, Baldwin's Ohio Prac. Merrick-Rippner Probate Law § 110:35, Civil Support Proceedings--Liability for Child Support.

Law Review and Journal Commentaries

The Inheritance Rights (or Lack Thereof) of Legitimated Children in Ohio. Angela G. Carlin, 11 Prob L J Ohio 109 (July/August 2001).

3111.241, 3111.242 Health insurance coverage for children; Contempt—Repealed

(2000 S 180, eff. 3–22–01; 1997 H 352, eff. 1–1–98; 1997 S 67, eff. 6–4–97; 1996 H 710, § 7, eff. 6–11–96; 1995 H 167, eff. 6–11–96; 1995 H 249, eff. 7–17–95; 1992 S 10, eff. 7–15–92)

Historical and Statutory Notes

Ed. Note: Former RC 3111.241 related to health insurance required by child support orders. See now RC 3119.01; 3119.30; 3119.301; 3119.31; 3119.40; 3119.41; 3119.44; 3119.45; 3119.47; 3119.48; 3119.49; 3119.50; 3119.51; 3119.52; 3119.53; 3119.54; 3119.56; 3119.57 for provisions analogous to former RC 3111.241.

Ed. Note: Former RC 3111.242 related to contempt as a means of enforcing administrative testing and support orders. See now RC 3121.37; 3121.54 for provisions analogous to former RC 3111.242.

Ed. Note: The effective date of the amendment of these sections by 1995 H 167 was changed from 11–15–96 to 6–11–96 by 1996 H 710, § 7, eff. 6–11–96.

3111.25 Final and enforceable acknowledgment

An acknowledgment of paternity is final and enforceable without ratification by a court when the acknowledgment has been filed with the office of child support, the information on the acknowledgment has been entered in the birth registry, and the acknowledgment has not been rescinded and is not subject to possible recission [*sic*] pursuant to section 3111.27 of the Revised Code.

(2000 S 180, eff. 3–22–01)

Historical and Statutory Notes

Ed. Note: RC 3111.25 contains provisions analogous to former RC 5101.314(A)(3)(a) and (b), repealed by 2000 S 180, eff. 3–22–01.

Ed. Note: Former 3111.25 repealed by 2000 S 180, eff. 3–22–01; 1999 H 471, eff. 7–1–00; 1997 H 352, eff. 1–1–98; 1993 H 173, eff. 12–31–93; 1992 S 10.

Ed. Note: Former RC 3111.25 related to restrictions on employers of obligors. See now RC 3121.38; 3121.39 for provisions analogous to former RC 3111.25.

Cross References

Action for child support order, see 2151.231
Action for child support order before acknowledgment becomes final, see 2151.232

Ohio Administrative Code References

Acknowledgment of paternity, see OAC 5101:12–40–15

Support order establishment process, see OAC 5101:12–45–05

Library References

Children Out-of-Wedlock ☞21(2).
Westlaw Topic No. 76H.
C.J.S. Children Out-of-Wedlock §§ 41 to 44.

Research References

Encyclopedias

OH Jur. 3d Family Law § 881, Who Must Consent.
OH Jur. 3d Family Law § 944, Statutory Presumptions.
OH Jur. 3d Family Law § 988, Legitimation by Acknowledgment of Paternity.
OH Jur. 3d Family Law § 1011, Assumption of Parental Duty of Support.
OH Jur. 3d Family Law § 1016, Action for Support.
OH Jur. 3d Family Law § 1019, Child Support Action in Juvenile Court; Other Courts With Jurisdiction.
OH Jur. 3d Family Law § 1020, Request for Administrative Order.
OH Jur. 3d Family Law § 1053, by Child's Relatives.
OH Jur. 3d Family Law § 1171, Visitation Rights Where Mother is Unmarried.

Forms

Ohio Jurisprudence Pleading and Practice Forms § 96:9, Putative Father Registry.
Ohio Jurisprudence Pleading and Practice Forms § 111:6, Presumptions.

Treatises and Practice Aids

Sowald & Morganstern, Baldwin's Ohio Practice Domestic Relations Law § 3:8, Jurisdiction and Venue.
Sowald & Morganstern, Baldwin's Ohio Practice Domestic Relations Law § 21:2, Parenting Time--Establishing Visitation Order.
Sowald & Morganstern, Baldwin's Ohio Practice Domestic Relations Law § 22:4, Establishing Parentage.

Sowald & Morganstern, Baldwin's Ohio Practice Domestic Relations Law § 3:13, Judicial Parentage Action--Presumptions of Parentage--Creating.
Sowald & Morganstern, Baldwin's Ohio Practice Domestic Relations Law § 3:30, Res Judicata and Vacation of Parentage Orders.
Sowald & Morganstern, Baldwin's Ohio Practice Domestic Relations Law § 3:31, Relief from Paternity or Support Judgment, Under RC 3119.961.
Carlin, Baldwin's Ohio Prac. Merrick-Rippner Probate Law § 19:2, Legitimation--Procedure--Acknowledgment of Paternity.
Carlin, Baldwin's Ohio Prac. Merrick-Rippner Probate Law § 19:4, Legitimation--Historical Provisions.
Carlin, Baldwin's Ohio Prac. Merrick-Rippner Probate Law § 19:7, Uniform Parentage Act--Presumptions.
Carlin, Baldwin's Ohio Prac. Merrick-Rippner Probate Law § 110:3, Criminal Jurisdiction--Proceedings for Nonsupport.
Carlin, Baldwin's Ohio Prac. Merrick-Rippner Probate Law § 99:30, Statutorily Required Consent.
Carlin, Baldwin's Ohio Prac. Merrick-Rippner Probate Law § 99:32, Parties Giving Consent--Putative Father.
Carlin, Baldwin's Ohio Prac. Merrick-Rippner Probate Law § 99:34, Parties Giving Consent--Agency.
Carlin, Baldwin's Ohio Prac. Merrick-Rippner Probate Law § 99:49, Interlocutory and Final Orders.
Carlin, Baldwin's Ohio Prac. Merrick-Rippner Probate Law § 110:13, Jurisdiction Over Child Custody Matters--Determination of Custody.

Carlin, Baldwin's Ohio Prac. Merrick-Rippner Probate Law § 110:15, Visitation Right of Noncustodial Parent and Others.

Carlin, Baldwin's Ohio Prac. Merrick-Rippner Probate Law § 110:20, Parentage Act--Jurisdiction and Venue.

Carlin, Baldwin's Ohio Prac. Merrick-Rippner Probate Law § 110:22, Parentage Act--Presumption of Paternity.

Carlin, Baldwin's Ohio Prac. Merrick-Rippner Probate Law § 110:26, Parentage Act--Applicability of Civil Rules to Paternity Proceedings.

Carlin, Baldwin's Ohio Prac. Merrick-Rippner Probate Law § 110:31, Parentage Act--Continuing Jurisdiction to Modify or Revoke Judgment.

Carlin, Baldwin's Ohio Prac. Merrick-Rippner Probate Law § 110:35, Civil Support Proceedings--Liability for Child Support.

Law Review and Journal Commentaries

Bankruptcy Reform Act of 1994—What the Bankruptcy Code Giveth, Domestic Relations Courts (and Congress) Taketh Away, C.R. "Chip" Bowles. 8 Domestic Rel J Ohio 17 (March/April 1996)

Basics of the Ohio putative father registry. Erik L. Smith, 19 Ohio Law 6 (March/April 2005).

The Inheritance Rights (or Lack Thereof) of Legitimated Children in Ohio. Angela G. Carlin, 11 Prob L J Ohio 109 (July/August 2001).

Notes of Decisions

Filing acknowledgment   1

---

1. Filing acknowledgment

Once timeframe for filing an action to rescind final and enforceable acknowledgement of paternity lapsed, man who signed acknowledgement was deemed to be child's legal father, even though he signed acknowledgement knowing it to be false. In re Guardianship of Elliott (Ohio App. 3 Dist., Putnam, 11-08-2010) No. 12-10-02, 2010-Ohio-5405, 2010 WL 4471277, Unreported. Children Out–of–wedlock ⟨key⟩ 12

Question of law of whether trial court erred in its determination that the legal effect of man's acknowledgement of paternity was negated by man's

signing an affidavit that he knew to be false was subject to de novo review. In re Guardianship of Elliott (Ohio App. 3 Dist., Putnam, 11-08-2010) No. 12-10-02, 2010-Ohio-5405, 2010 WL 4471277, Unreported. Guardian and Ward ⟨key⟩ 13(8)

Trial court did not err in excluding claimed father as child's biological father, notwithstanding existence of acknowledgment of paternity, as claimed father failed to show that acknowledgement had been filed with office of child support, which was required by statute for acknowledgement to be final and enforceable. Jennifer C. v. Tony M.D. (Ohio App. 12 Dist., Clermont, 09-26-2005) No. CA2005-01-005, 2005-Ohio-5050, 2005 WL 2335332, Unreported. Children Out–of–wedlock ⟨key⟩ 35

3111.26 Effect of final and enforceable acknowledgment

After an acknowledgment of paternity becomes final and enforceable, the child is the child of the man who signed the acknowledgment of paternity, as though born to him in lawful wedlock. If the mother is unmarried, the man who signed the acknowledgment of paternity may file a complaint requesting the granting of reasonable parenting time with the child under section 3109.12 of the Revised Code and the parents of the man who signed the acknowledgment of paternity, any relative of the man who signed the acknowledgment of paternity, the parents of the mother, and any relative of the mother may file a complaint pursuant to that section requesting the granting of reasonable companionship or visitation rights with the child. Once the acknowledgment becomes final the man who signed the acknowledgment of paternity assumes the parental duty of support.

(2000 S 180, eff. 3–22–01)

Historical and Statutory Notes

Ed. Note: RC 3111.26 contains provisions analogous to portions of former RC 5101.314(A)(4)(a), repealed by 2000 S 180, eff. 3–22–01.

Ed. Note: Former 3111.26 repealed by 2000 S 180, eff. 3–22–01; 1997 H 352, eff. 1–1–98; 1992 S 10, eff. 7–15–92.

Ed. Note: Former RC 3111.26 related to contingency if unable to obtain service. See now RC 3111.43 for provisions analogous to former RC 3111.26.

Library References

Children Out-of-Wedlock ⟨key⟩20.2, 21(2). Westlaw Topic No. 76H.

C.J.S. Children Out-of-Wedlock §§ 37 to 38, 41 to 44.

Research References

Encyclopedias

OH Jur. 3d Family Law § 988, Legitimation by Acknowledgment of Paternity.

Treatises and Practice Aids

Sowald & Morganstern, Baldwin's Ohio Practice Domestic Relations Law § 22:4, Establishing Parentage.

Carlin, Baldwin's Ohio Prac. Merrick-Rippner Probate Law § 19:2, Legitimation--Procedure--Acknowledgment of Paternity.

Carlin, Baldwin's Ohio Prac. Merrick-Rippner Probate Law § 19:4, Legitimation--Historical Provisions.

Carlin, Baldwin's Ohio Prac. Merrick-Rippner Probate Law § 110:13, Jurisdiction Over Child Custody Matters--Determination of Custody.

Carlin, Baldwin's Ohio Prac. Merrick-Rippner Probate Law § 110:15, Visitation Right of Noncustodial Parent and Others.

Law Review and Journal Commentaries

Basics of the Ohio putative father registry. Erik L. Smith, 19 Ohio Law 6 (March/April 2005).

The Inheritance Rights (or Lack Thereof) of Legitimated Children in Ohio. Angela G. Carlin, 11 Prob L J Ohio 109 (July/August 2001).

3111.27 Rescission of acknowledgment

(A) Except as provided in section 2151.232 or 3111.821 of the Revised Code, for an acknowledgment of paternity filed with the office of child support to be rescinded both of the following must occur:

(1) Not later than sixty days after the date of the latest signature on the acknowledgment, one of the persons who signed it must do both of the following:

(a) Request a determination under section 3111.38 of the Revised Code of whether there is a parent and child relationship between the man who signed the acknowledgment and the child who is the subject of it;

(b) Give the office written notice of having complied with division (A)(1)(a) of this section and include in the notice the name of the child support enforcement agency conducting genetic tests to determine whether there is a parent and child relationship;

(2) An order must be issued under section 3111.46 of the Revised Code determining whether there is a parent and child relationship between the man and the child.

(B) Not later than the end of the business day following the business day on which the office receives a notice under division (A)(1)(b) of this section, it shall contact the agency indicated in the notice to verify that the person sending it has complied with division (A)(1) of this section. If the office verifies compliance, and the notice was sent within the time limit required by this section, the office shall note in its records the date the notice was received and that the acknowledgment to which the notice pertains is subject to recission [*sic*]. The office shall direct the agency to notify the office of the agency's issuance of an order described in division (A)(2) of this section. On receipt from an agency of notice that an order described in division (A)(2) of this section has been issued, the acknowledgment to which the order pertains shall be rescinded as of the date.

If the office is unable to verify compliance with division (A)(1) of this section, it shall note in its records the date the notice under division (A)(1)(b) of this section was received and that compliance with division (A)(1) of this section was not verified.

(2000 S 180, eff. 3–22–01)

Historical and Statutory Notes

Ed. Note: RC 3111.27 contains provisions analogous to former RC 5101.314(B)(1)(a) and (b), repealed by 2000 S 180, eff. 3–22–01.

Ed. Note: Former 3111.27 repealed by 2000 S 180, eff. 3–22–01; 1999 H 471, eff. 7–1–00; 1997 H 352, eff. 1–1–98; 1996 H 710, § 7, eff. 6–11–96; 1995 H 167, eff. 6–11–96; 1992 S 10, eff. 7–15–92.

Ed. Note: Former RC 3111.27 related to administrative review of support orders. See now RC 3119.60; 3119.61; 3119.72; 3119.73; 3119.76 for provisions analogous to former RC 3111.27.

Ed. Note: The effective date of the amendment of this section by 1995 H 167 was changed from

11–15–96 to 6–11–96 by 1996 H 710, § 7, eff. 6–11–96.

Ohio Administrative Code References

Rescinding an acknowledgment of paternity, see OAC 5101:12–40–17

Library References

Children Out-of-Wedlock ⚖21(2).
Westlaw Topic No. 76H.
C.J.S. Children Out-of-Wedlock §§ 41 to 44.

Research References

Encyclopedias

OH Jur. 3d Family Law § 863, Existence and Proof of Relationship.
OH Jur. 3d Family Law § 988, Legitimation by Acknowledgment of Paternity.

Treatises and Practice Aids

Sowald & Morganstern, Baldwin's Ohio Practice Domestic Relations Law § 3:5, Administrative Determination of Parentage--No Acknowledgment and Support Order.
Sowald & Morganstern, Baldwin's Ohio Practice Domestic Relations Law § 22:4, Establishing Parentage.
Sowald & Morganstern, Baldwin's Ohio Practice Domestic Relations Law § 22:5, Establishing Parentage--Timely Rescission.
Sowald & Morganstern, Baldwin's Ohio Practice Domestic Relations Law § 22:6, Establishing Parentage--Rescission After Final Acknowledgment.
Sowald & Morganstern, Baldwin's Ohio Practice Domestic Relations Law § 3:13, Judicial Parentage Action--Presumptions of Parentage--Creating.
Sowald & Morganstern, Baldwin's Ohio Practice Domestic Relations Law § 22.15, Support Modification--Overview.
Carlin, Baldwin's Ohio Prac. Merrick-Rippner Probate Law § 19:2, Legitimation--Procedure--Acknowledgment of Paternity.
Carlin, Baldwin's Ohio Prac. Merrick-Rippner Probate Law § 19:4, Legitimation--Historical Provisions.
Carlin, Baldwin's Ohio Prac. Merrick-Rippner Probate Law § 110:13, Jurisdiction Over Child Custody Matters--Determination of Custody.
Carlin, Baldwin's Ohio Prac. Merrick-Rippner Probate Law § 110:20, Parentage Act--Jurisdiction and Venue.
Carlin, Baldwin's Ohio Prac. Merrick-Rippner Probate Law § 110:31, Parentage Act--Continuing Jurisdiction to Modify or Revoke Judgment.
Carlin, Baldwin's Ohio Prac. Merrick-Rippner Probate Law § 110:34, Parentage Act--Administrative Support Orders.

Law Review and Journal Commentaries

The Inheritance Rights (or Lack Thereof) of Legitimated Children in Ohio. Angela G. Carlin, 11 Prob L J Ohio 109 (July/August 2001).

Notes of Decisions

Procedural issues   1

---

1. Procedural Issues

Mother's failure to rescind acknowledgement of paternity executed by claimed father did not affect her ability to bring a paternity action, as claimed father failed to prove that acknowledgement had been filed with office of child support, which was required by statute for acknowledgement to be final and enforceable. Jennifer C. v. Tony M.D. (Ohio App. 12 Dist., Clermont, 09-26-2005) No. CA2005-01-005, 2005-Ohio-5050, 2005 WL 2335332, Unreported. Children Out–of–wedlock ⚖ 34

Pursuant to RC 3111.27, the department of human services adopts OAC 5101:1–32–15 and reviewing RC 3111.27 and OAC 5101:1–32–15 and construing them in pari materia, the appeals court concludes (1) after the thirty-two-day period for filing objections to the administrative support order has passed, a party can only seek modification of their order by first filing a request for an administrative review of the order with the CSEA; (2) if the CSEA determines that a modification is necessary and in the best interest of the child, the CSEA shall recalculate the support order by utilizing the child support guidelines set forth in RC 3113.215 and shall modify the order whenever the recalculated support amount has changed by more than ten per cent; (3) moreover, the CSEA shall not deviate from the guidelines in recalculating support; (4) if the CSEA modifies the administrative support order, the obligor or obligee may object to the modified order by initiating an action pursuant to RC

2151.231 in the juvenile court; and (5) objections to the modified administrative support order, however, are not limited by a thirty-day requirement.

Kruse v Pinniger, No. L–95–029, 1995 WL 703917 (6th Dist Ct App, Lucas, 12–1–95).

3111.28 Rescission of acknowledgment for fraud, duress, or material mistake of fact

After an acknowledgment becomes final pursuant to section 2151.232, 3111.25, or 3111.821 of the Revised Code, a man presumed to be the father of the child pursuant to section 3111.03 of the Revised Code who did not sign the acknowledgment, either person who signed the acknowledgment, or a guardian or legal custodian of the child may bring an action to rescind the acknowledgment on the basis of fraud, duress, or material mistake of fact. The court shall treat the action as an action to determine the existence or nonexistence of a parent and child relationship pursuant to sections 3111.01 to 3111.18 of the Revised Code. An action pursuant to this section shall be brought no later than one year after the acknowledgment becomes final. The action may be brought in one of the following courts in the county in which the child, the guardian or custodian of the child, or either person who signed the acknowledgment resides: the juvenile court or the domestic relations division of the court of common pleas that has jurisdiction pursuant to section 2101.022 or 2301.03 of the Revised Code to hear and determine cases arising under Chapter 3111. of the Revised Code.

(2000 S 180, eff. 3–22–01)

Historical and Statutory Notes

Ed. Note: RC 3111.28 contains provisions analogous to former RC 5101.314(B)(2), repealed by 2000 S 180, eff. 3–22–01.

Ed. Note: Former 3111.28 repealed by 2000 S 180, eff. 3–22–01; 1997 H 352, eff. 1–1–98; 1996 H 710, § 7, eff. 6–11–96; 1995 H 167, eff. 6–11–96; 1993 H 173, eff. 12–31–93; 1992 S 10.

Ed. Note: Former RC 3111.28 related to failure by payor or obligor to cooperate in administrative

review. See now RC 3119.72 for provisions analogous to former RC 3111.28.

Ed. Note: The effective date of the amendment of this section by 1995 H 167 was changed from 11–15–96 to 6–11–96 by 1996 H 710, § 7, eff. 6–11–96.

Cross References

Juvenile court jurisdiction, see 2151.23

Ohio Administrative Code References

Rescinding an acknowledgment of paternity, see OAC 5101:12–40–17

Library References

Children Out-of-Wedlock ⊜21(2).
Westlaw Topic No. 76H.
C.J.S. Children Out-of-Wedlock §§ 41 to 44.

Research References

Encyclopedias

OH Jur. 3d Family Law § 863, Existence and Proof of Relationship.
OH Jur. 3d Family Law § 944, Statutory Presumptions.

Forms

Ohio Jurisprudence Pleading and Practice Forms § 2:8, Courts of Common Pleas--Juvenile Division.
Ohio Jurisprudence Pleading and Practice Forms § 111:6, Presumptions.

Treatises and Practice Aids

Sowald & Morganstern, Baldwin's Ohio Practice Domestic Relations Law § 3:4, Administrative Determination of Parentage--Acknowledgment, Support Order, and Birth Record.
Sowald & Morganstern, Baldwin's Ohio Practice Domestic Relations Law § 20:3, Statutory History--1992 Senate Bill 10, The "Poster Bill".
Sowald & Morganstern, Baldwin's Ohio Practice Domestic Relations Law § 22:4, Establishing Parentage.
Sowald & Morganstern, Baldwin's Ohio Practice Domestic Relations Law § 22:6, Establishing

Parentage--Rescission After Final Acknowledgment.

Sowald & Morganstern, Baldwin's Ohio Practice Domestic Relations Law § 3:13, Judicial Parentage Action--Presumptions of Parentage--Creating.

Carlin, Baldwin's Ohio Prac. Merrick-Rippner Probate Law § 19:2, Legitimation--Procedure--Acknowledgment of Paternity.

Carlin, Baldwin's Ohio Prac. Merrick-Rippner Probate Law § 19:4, Legitimation--Historical Provisions.

Carlin, Baldwin's Ohio Prac. Merrick-Rippner Probate Law § 19:6, Uniform Parentage Act--Jurisdiction of Action to Determine Father-Child Relationship.

Carlin, Baldwin's Ohio Prac. Merrick-Rippner Probate Law § 19:7, Uniform Parentage Act--Presumptions.

Carlin, Baldwin's Ohio Prac. Merrick-Rippner Probate Law § 107:2, Original Jurisdiction.

Carlin, Baldwin's Ohio Prac. Merrick-Rippner Probate Law § 99:49, Interlocutory and Final Orders.

Carlin, Baldwin's Ohio Prac. Merrick-Rippner Probate Law § 110:20, Parentage Act--Jurisdiction and Venue.

Carlin, Baldwin's Ohio Prac. Merrick-Rippner Probate Law § 110:22, Parentage Act--Presumption of Paternity.

Carlin, Baldwin's Ohio Prac. Merrick-Rippner Probate Law § 110:23, Parentage Act--Parties in Parentage Action.

Carlin, Baldwin's Ohio Prac. Merrick-Rippner Probate Law § 110:31, Parentage Act--Continuing Jurisdiction to Modify or Revoke Judgment.

Law Review and Journal Commentaries

Bankruptcy Reform Act of 1994 What the Bankruptcy Code Giveth, Domestic Relations Courts (and Congress) Taketh Away, C.R. "Chip" Bowles. 8 Domestic Rel J Ohio 17 (March/April 1996).

The Inheritance Rights (or Lack Thereof) of Legitimated Children in Ohio. Angela G. Carlin, 11 Prob L J Ohio 109 (July/August 2001).

Notes of Decisions

Procedural issues 1

1. Procedural issues

Once timeframe for filing an action to rescind final and enforceable acknowledgement of paternity lapsed, man who signed acknowledgement was deemed to be child's legal father, even though he signed acknowledgement knowing it to be false. In re Guardianship of Elliott (Ohio App. 3 Dist., Putnam, 11-08-2010) No. 12-10-02, 2010-Ohio-5405, 2010 WL 4471277, Unreported. Children Out-of-wedlock ⬌ 12

Question of law of whether trial court erred in its determination that the legal effect of man's acknowledgment of paternity was negated by man's

signing an affidavit that he knew to be false was subject to de novo review. In re Guardianship of Elliott (Ohio App. 3 Dist., Putnam, 11-08-2010) No. 12-10-02, 2010-Ohio-5405, 2010 WL 4471277, Unreported. Guardian and Ward ⬌ 13(8)

Mother's failure to rescind acknowledgement of paternity executed by claimed father did not affect her ability to bring a paternity action, as claimed father failed to prove that acknowledgement had been filed with office of child support, which was required by statute for acknowledgement to be final and enforceable. Jennifer C. v. Tony M.D. (Ohio App. 12 Dist., Clermont, 09-26-2005) No. CA2005-01-005, 2005-Ohio-5050, 2005 WL 2335332, Unreported. Children Out-of-wedlock ⬌ 34

3111.29 Complaint for child support

Once an acknowledgment of paternity becomes final under section 3111.25 of the Revised Code, the mother or other custodian or guardian of the child may file a complaint pursuant to section 2151.231 of the Revised Code in the juvenile court or other court with jurisdiction under section 2101.022 or 2301.03 of the Revised Code of the county in which the child or the guardian or legal custodian of the child resides requesting that the court order the father to pay an amount for the support of the child, may contact the child support enforcement agency for assistance in obtaining the order, or may request that an administrative officer of a child support enforcement agency issue an administrative order for the payment of child support pursuant to section 3111.81 of the Revised Code.

(2000 S 180, eff. 3–22–01)

Historical and Statutory Notes

Ed. Note: RC 3111.29 contains provisions analogous to former RC 5101.314(A)(4)(b), repealed by 2000 S 180, eff. 3–22–01.

Ed. Note: Former 3111.29 amended and recodified as 3111.19 by 2000 S 180, eff. 3–22–01; 1992 S 10, eff. 7–15–92.

Library References

Children Out-of-Wedlock ☜21(2), 30, 32.
Westlaw Topic No. 76H.

C.J.S. Children Out-of-Wedlock §§ 41 to 44, 47, 71, 94, 96 to 97.

Research References

Encyclopedias

OH Jur. 3d Family Law § 1016, Action for Support.

OH Jur. 3d Family Law § 1019, Child Support Action in Juvenile Court; Other Courts With Jurisdiction.

OH Jur. 3d Family Law § 1020, Request for Administrative Order.

OH Jur. 3d Family Law § 1021, Hearing on Request; Determination of Support.

Forms

Ohio Jurisprudence Pleading and Practice Forms § 96:11, Consent Required.

Treatises and Practice Aids

Sowald & Morganstern, Baldwin's Ohio Practice Domestic Relations Law § 19:3, Support Obligations--In General.

Sowald & Morganstern, Baldwin's Ohio Practice Domestic Relations Law § 3:10, Judicial Parentage Action--Parties.

Sowald & Morganstern, Baldwin's Ohio Practice Domestic Relations Law § 3:40, Effect of Judgment--Child Support--Other Remedies.

Sowald & Morganstern, Baldwin's Ohio Practice Domestic Relations Law § 27:21, Subject Matter Jurisdiction--Jurisdiction for Child Support.

Carlin, Baldwin's Ohio Prac. Merrick-Rippner Probate Law § 19:1, Legitimation--Statutory Provisions.

Carlin, Baldwin's Ohio Prac. Merrick-Rippner Probate Law § 19:2, Legitimation--Procedure--Acknowledgment of Paternity.

Carlin, Baldwin's Ohio Prac. Merrick-Rippner Probate Law § 19:4, Legitimation--Historical Provisions.

Carlin, Baldwin's Ohio Prac. Merrick-Rippner Probate Law § 99:31, Parties Giving Consent--Biological Parents.

Carlin, Baldwin's Ohio Prac. Merrick-Rippner Probate Law § 110:19, Parentage Act--Effect.

Carlin, Baldwin's Ohio Prac. Merrick-Rippner Probate Law § 110:20, Parentage Act--Jurisdiction and Venue.

Carlin, Baldwin's Ohio Prac. Merrick-Rippner Probate Law § 110:34, Parentage Act--Administrative Support Orders.

Law Review and Journal Commentaries

The Inheritance Rights (or Lack Thereof) of Legitimated Children in Ohio. Angela G. Carlin, 11 Prob L J Ohio 109 (July/August 2001).

3111.30 Department of health to receive notice of acknowledgment; preparation of new birth certificate consistent with acknowledgment

Once an acknowledgment of paternity becomes final, the office of child support shall notify the department of health of the acknowledgment. If the original birth record is inconsistent with the acknowledgment, on receipt of the notice, the department of health shall, in accordance with section 3705.09 of the Revised Code, prepare a new birth record consistent with the acknowledgment and substitute the new record for the original birth record.

(2000 S 180, eff. 3–22–01)

Historical and Statutory Notes

Ed. Note: RC 3111.30 contains provisions analogous to former RC 5101.314(A)(4)(c), repealed by 2000 S 180, eff. 3–22–01.

Ed. Note: Former 3111.30 amended and recodified as 3111.88 by 2000 S 180, eff. 3–22–01; 1986 H 476, eff. 9–24–86.

Ohio Administrative Code References

Modifying the birth record, see OAC 5101:12–40–27

Library References

Health ☞397.
Westlaw Topic No. 198H.
C.J.S. Health and Environment §§ 24, 74.

Research References

Encyclopedias

OH Jur. 3d Health & Sanitation § 67, Births--
Paternity Concerns.

Treatises and Practice Aids

Carlin, Baldwin's Ohio Prac. Merrick-Rippner Probate Law § 18:2, Inheritance Rights of Illegitimate Child--Statutory Provisions.

Carlin, Baldwin's Ohio Prac. Merrick-Rippner Probate Law § 19:2, Legitimation--Procedure--Ac-
knowledgment of Paternity

Carlin, Baldwin's Ohio Prac. Merrick-Rippner Probate Law § 19:13, Uniform Parentage Act--Non-
spousal Artificial Insemination; Embryo Donation.

Carlin, Baldwin's Ohio Prac. Merrick-Rippner Probate Law § 110:31, Parentage Act--Continuing
Jurisdiction to Modify or Revoke Judgment.

Law Review and Journal Commentaries

Basics of the Ohio putative father registry. Erik
L. Smith, 19 Ohio Law 6 (March/April 2005).

The Inheritance Rights (or Lack Thereof) of
Legitimated Children in Ohio. Angela G. Carlin, 11
Prob L J Ohio 109 (July/August 2001).

3111.31   Acknowledgment of paternity affidavit

The department of job and family services shall prepare an acknowledgment of paternity affidavit that includes in boldface type at the top of the affidavit the rights and responsibilities of and the due process safeguards afforded to a person who acknowledges that he is the natural father of a child, including that if an alleged father acknowledges a parent and child relationship he assumes the parental duty of support, that both signators waive any right to bring an action pursuant to sections 3111.01 to 3111.18 of the Revised Code or make a request pursuant to section 3111.38 of the Revised Code, other than for purposes of rescinding the acknowledgment pursuant to section 3111.27 of the Revised Code in order to ensure expediency in resolving the question of the existence of a parent and child relationship, that either parent may rescind the acknowledgment pursuant to section 3111.27 of the Revised Code, that an action may be brought pursuant to section 3111.28 of the Revised Code, or a motion may be filed pursuant to section 3119.961 of the Revised Code, to rescind the acknowledgment, and that the natural father has the right to petition a court pursuant to section 3109.12 of the Revised Code for an order granting him reasonable parenting time with respect to the child and to petition the court for custody of the child pursuant to section 2151.23 of the Revised Code.   The affidavit shall include all of the following:

(A) Basic instructions for completing the form, including instructions that both the natural father and the mother of the child are required to sign the statement, that they may sign the statement without being in each other's presence, and that the signatures must be notarized;

(B) Blank spaces to enter the full name, social security number, date of birth and address of each parent;

(C) Blank spaces to enter the full name, date of birth, and the residence of the child;

(D) A blank space to enter the name of the hospital or department of health code number assigned to the hospital, for use in situations in which the hospital fills out the form pursuant to section 3727.17 of the Revised Code;

(E) An affirmation by the mother that the information she supplied is true to the best of her knowledge and belief and that she is the natural mother of the child named on the form and assumes the parental duty of support of the child;

(F) An affirmation by the father that the information he supplied is true to the best of his knowledge and belief, that he has received information regarding his legal rights and responsibilities, that he consents to the jurisdiction of the courts of this state, and that he is the natural father of the child named on the form and assumes the parental duty of support of the child;

(G) Signature lines for the mother of the child and the natural father;

(H) Signature lines for the notary public;

(I) An instruction to include or attach any other evidence necessary to complete the new birth record that is required by the department by rule.

(2000 S 180, eff. 3–22–01)

Historical and Statutory Notes

Ed. Note: RC 3111.31 contains provisions analogous to former RC 5101.324(D)(1), repealed by 2000 S 180, eff. 3–22–01.

Ed. Note: Former 3111.31 amended and recodified as 3111.89 by 2000 S 180, eff. 3–22–01; 1986 H 476, eff. 9–24–86.

Library References

Children Out-of-Wedlock ⊚21(2).
Infants ⊚17.
Westlaw Topic Nos. 76H, 211.

C.J.S. Adoption of Persons §§ 10 to 14, 41.
C.J.S. Children Out-of-Wedlock §§ 41 to 44.
C.J.S. Infants §§ 6, 8 to 9.

Research References

Encyclopedias

OH Jur. 3d Family Law § 988, Legitimation by Acknowledgment of Paternity.
OH Jur. 3d Family Law § 1016, Action for Support.

Forms

Ohio Forms Legal and Business § 28:5, Child Born as Result of Artificial Insemination.
Ohio Jurisprudence Pleading and Practice Forms § 111:10, Temporary Support Order.

Treatises and Practice Aids

Sowald & Morganstern, Baldwin's Ohio Practice Domestic Relations Law § 3:5, Administrative Determination of Parentage--No Acknowledgment and Support Order.
Sowald & Morganstern, Baldwin's Ohio Practice Domestic Relations Law § 22:4, Establishing Parentage.

Carlin, Baldwin's Ohio Prac. Merrick-Rippner Probate Law § 19:1, Legitimation--Statutory Provisions.
Carlin, Baldwin's Ohio Prac. Merrick-Rippner Probate Law § 19:2, Legitimation--Procedure--Acknowledgment of Paternity.
Carlin, Baldwin's Ohio Prac. Merrick-Rippner Probate Law § 19:4, Legitimation--Historical Provisions.
Carlin, Baldwin's Ohio Prac. Merrick-Rippner Probate Law § 110:1, Criminal Jurisdiction.
Carlin, Baldwin's Ohio Prac. Merrick-Rippner Probate Law § 110:13, Jurisdiction Over Child Custody Matters--Determination of Custody.
Carlin, Baldwin's Ohio Prac. Merrick-Rippner Probate Law § 110:19, Parentage Act--Effect.
Carlin, Baldwin's Ohio Prac. Merrick-Rippner Probate Law § 110:20, Parentage Act--Jurisdiction and Venue.
Carlin, Baldwin's Ohio Prac. Merrick-Rippner Probate Law § 110:23, Parentage Act--Parties in Parentage Action.

Law Review and Journal Commentaries

Basics of the Ohio putative father registry. Erik L. Smith, 19 Ohio Law 6 (March/April 2005).

Procreative Liberty and the Preembryo Problem: Developing a Medical and Legal Framework to Settle the Disposition of Frozen Preembryos, Note. 52 Case W Res L Rev 721 (Spring 2002).

Notes of Decisions

Administrative proceedings 4
Due process 1
Probate court 5
Proper parties 2
Support obligations 3

———

1. Due process

It is a violation of the equal protection clauses of the United States and Ohio constitutions to allow the aid and support of the child support enforcement agency in an action for child support brought by parents who have established their parentage through the probate court and residential parents who are on public assistance while denying the aid and support of the child support enforcement agency to parents who have established their parentage through the administrative process. Cuyahoga County Support Enforcement Agency v Lozada, Nos. 67463+, 1995 WL 386965 (8th Dist Ct App, Cuyahoga, 6–29–95).

2. Proper parties

County support enforcement agency lacked statutory authority to bring action in its own name against relator's husband for child support when relator and husband were married, did not dispute parentage, and did not receive public assistance; two statutory exceptions permitting agency to bring action in its own name, when probate court enters acknowledgement of paternity upon its journal and when father voluntarily signs birth certificate as informant pursuant to statute, did not apply. In re Owens (Ohio App. 8 Dist., 07-05-1994) 104 Ohio App.3d 201, 661 N.E.2d 765, appeal allowed 71 Ohio St.3d 1422, 642 N.E.2d 387, appeal dismissed as improvidently allowed 74 Ohio St.3d 1280, 658 N.E.2d 304, 1996-Ohio-273. Child Support ☞ 179

Dismissal of the child support enforcement agency (CSEA) as a party in an action for child support under RC 3111.21 via RC 2151.231 violates the Ohio and federal Equal Protection Clauses when a similarly situated residential parent who legitimizes a child through probate court is entitled to have the CSEA advocate for a proper child support order in the juvenile court under RC 3111.20, by way of RC 2151.231. Cuyahoga County Support Enforcement Agency v Lozada, No. 67463+, 1995 WL 386965 (8th Dist Ct App, Cuyahoga, 6–29–95).

3. Support obligations

Laches barred county child support enforcement agency (CSEA) from recovering from father reimbursement of Aid to Dependent Children (ADC) benefits, and barred father from being liable for retroactive child support, where father was not told he was child's father until child was 15 years old; mother, by deliberately lying for 15 years to father and to agency regarding true identity of child's father, deprived father of opportunity to become involved in child's life. Still v. Hayman (Ohio App. 7 Dist., 07-30-2003) 153 Ohio App.3d 487, 794 N.E.2d 751, 2003-Ohio-4113. Child Support ☞ 150; Social Security And Public Welfare ☞ 194.19

An obligor who deliberately redirects part of his income to his new wife to avoid child support obligations perpetrates a fraud upon the court which consequently awards retroactive support payments to remedy the results of the scheme to defraud the court. Leffel v Leffel, No. 97–CA–20, 1997 WL 666102 (2d Dist Ct App, Clark, 10–24–97).

4. Administrative proceedings

Trial court's dismissal of child support enforcement agency as party in five child support actions where parentage was established through administrative proceedings violated equal protection clauses of State and Federal Constitutions; statutory scheme, which permits agency to be party in support actions where parentage is established through probate court and where parents are on public assistance, but which does not specifically permit agency to be party when parentage is established through administrative proceedings, did not have rational basis, since enforcement agency can only effectuate its duty to protect best interests of child and public fisc by being joined as party in all child support enforcement actions. Cuyahoga Cty. Support Enforcement Agency v. Lozada (Ohio App. 8 Dist., 07-10-1995) 102 Ohio App.3d 442, 657 N.E.2d 372. Child Support ☞ 473; Constitutional Law ☞ 3455

Despite mother's contention that father's failure to participate in administrative determination of parentage precluded court of common pleas from exercising jurisdiction over parentage action, given apparent conflict in jurisdictional statutes, court of common pleas was not so patently and unambiguously devoid of subject matter jurisdiction that Court of Appeals would issue writ of prohibition prohibiting court of common pleas from exercising jurisdiction while final judgment was pending. State ex rel. Dixon v. Clark Cty. Court of Common Pleas, Juv. Div. (Clark 1995) 103 Ohio App.3d 523, 660 N.E.2d 486.

5. Probate court

It is a violation of the equal protection clauses of the United States and Ohio constitutions to allow the aid and support of the child support enforcement agency in an action for child support brought by parents who have established their parentage through the probate court and residential parents who are on public assistance while denying the aid and support of the child support enforcement agency to parents who have established their parentage through the administrative process. Cuyahoga County Support Enforcement Agency v Lozada, Nos. 67463+, 1995 WL 386965 (8th Dist Ct App, Cuyahoga, 6–29–95).

3111.32 Pamphlets

The department of job and family services shall prepare pamphlets that discuss the benefit of establishing a parent and child relationship, the proper procedure for establishing a parent and child relationship between a father and his child, and a toll-free telephone number that interested persons may call for more information regarding the procedures for establishing a parent and child relationship.

(2000 S 180, eff. 3–22–01)

Historical and Statutory Notes

Ed. Note: RC 3111.32 contains provisions analogous to portions of former RC 5101.324(C), repealed by 2000 S 180, eff. 3–22–01.

Ed. Note: Former 3111.32 recodified as 3111.90 by 2000 S 180, eff. 3–22–01; 1986 H 476, eff. 9–24–86.

Ohio Administrative Code References

Distribution of paternity acknowledgement affidavit
  and brochure, see OAC 5101:12–40–01

Library References

Infants ⟊17.
Westlaw Topic No. 211.

C.J.S. Adoption of Persons §§ 10 to 14, 41.
C.J.S. Infants §§ 6, 8 to 9.

Research References

Forms

Ohio Forms Legal and Business § 28:12, Consent
  to Artificial Insemination of Wife.

Law Review and Journal Commentaries

Basics of the Ohio putative father registry. Erik
L. Smith, 19 Ohio Law 6 (March/April 2005).

3111.33 Availability of pamphlets and acknowledgment of paternity affidavits

The department of job and family services shall make available the pamphlets and the acknowledgment of paternity affidavits and statements to the department of health, to each hospital it has a contract with pursuant to section 3727.17 of the Revised Code, and to any individual who requests a pamphlet. The department of job and family services shall make available the affidavit acknowledging paternity to each county child support enforcement agency, the department of health, and any other person or agency that requests copies.
(2000 S 180, eff. 3–22–01)

Historical and Statutory Notes

Ed. Note: RC 3111.33 contains provisions analogous to portions of former RC 5101.324(C) and (D)(3), repealed by 2000 S 180, eff. 3–22–01.

Ed. Note: Former 3111.33 recodified as 3111.91 by 2000 S 180, eff. 3–22–01; 1986 H 476, eff. 9–24–86.

Ohio Administrative Code References

Distribution of paternity acknowledgement affidavit
  and brochure, see OAC 5101:12–40–01

Library References

Infants ⟊17.
Westlaw Topic No. 211.

C.J.S. Adoption of Persons §§ 10 to 14, 41.
C.J.S. Infants §§ 6, 8 to 9.

Research References

Encyclopedias

50 Am. Jur. Trials 1, Liability of Sperm Banks.

Law Review and Journal Commentaries

Procreative Liberty and the Preembryo Problem: Developing a Medical and Legal Framework to Settle the Disposition of Frozen Preembryos, Note. 52 Case W Res L Rev 721 (Spring 2002).

3111.34 Rules specifying additional evidence for new birth certificate

The director of job and family services, in consultation with the department of health, shall adopt rules specifying additional evidence necessary to complete a new birth record that is required to be included with an acknowledgment of paternity affidavit.

(2000 S 180, eff. 3–22–01)

Historical and Statutory Notes

Ed. Note: RC 3111.34 contains provisions analogous to former RC 5101.324(D)(2), repealed by 2000 S 180, eff. 3–22–01.

Ed. Note: Former 3111.34 amended and recodified as 3111.92 by 2000 S 180, eff. 3–22–01; 1986 H 476, eff. 9–24–86.

Ohio Administrative Code References

Modifying the birth record, see OAC 5101:12–40–27

Library References

Health ☞397.
Westlaw Topic No. 198H.
C.J.S. Health and Environment §§ 24, 74.

Law Review and Journal Commentaries

Procreative Liberty and the Preembryo Problem: Developing a Medical and Legal Framework to

Settle the Disposition of Frozen Preembryos, Note. 52 Case W Res L Rev 721 (Spring 2002).

3111.35 Rules

The director of job and family services shall adopt rules pursuant to Chapter 119. of the Revised Code to implement sections 3111.20 to 3111.34 of the Revised Code that are consistent with Title IV–D of the "Social Security Act," 88 Stat. 2351, 42 U.S.C. 651 et seq., as amended.

(2000 S 180, eff. 3–22–01)

Historical and Statutory Notes

Ed. Note: RC 3111.35 contains provisions analogous to former RC 5101.314(E), repealed by 2000 S 180, eff. 3–22–01.

Ed. Note: Former 3111.35 amended and recodified as 3111.93 by 2000 S 180, eff. 3–22–01; 1986 H 476, eff. 9–24–86.

Ohio Administrative Code References

Acknowledgment of paternity, see OAC 5101:12–40–15

Library References

Infants ☞17.
Social Security and Public Welfare ☞194 to 194.1.
Westlaw Topic Nos. 211, 356A.
C.J.S. Adoption of Persons §§ 10 to 14, 41.

C.J.S. Infants §§ 6, 8 to 9.
C.J.S. Social Security and Public Welfare §§ 206, 209 to 213, 215, 227, 229.

Research References

Encyclopedias

OH Jur. 3d Family Law § 882, Putative Father Registry.
OH Jur. 3d Family Law § 941, Establishment of Parent and Child Relationship.

Treatises and Practice Aids

Carlin, Baldwin's Ohio Prac. Merrick-Rippner Probate Law § 19:1, Legitimation--Statutory Provisions.
Carlin, Baldwin's Ohio Prac. Merrick-Rippner Probate Law § 19:2, Legitimation--Procedure--Acknowledgment of Paternity.
Carlin, Baldwin's Ohio Prac. Merrick-Rippner Probate Law § 19:4, Legitimation--Historical Provisions.

Carlin, Baldwin's Ohio Prac. Merrick-Rippner Probate Law § 15:20, Children or Lineal Descendants--In General.
Carlin, Baldwin's Ohio Prac. Merrick-Rippner Probate Law § 99:30, Statutorily Required Consent.
Carlin, Baldwin's Ohio Prac. Merrick-Rippner Probate Law § 99:31, Parties Giving Consent--Biological Parents.
Carlin, Baldwin's Ohio Prac. Merrick-Rippner Probate Law § 99:32, Parties Giving Consent--Putative Father.
Carlin, Baldwin's Ohio Prac. Merrick-Rippner Probate Law § 99:38, Consent Not Required--Statutory Scheme.

Carlin, Baldwin's Ohio Prac. Merrick-Rippner Probate Law § 110:13, Jurisdiction Over Child Custody Matters--Determination of Custody.

Carlin, Baldwin's Ohio Prac. Merrick-Rippner Probate Law § 110:19, Parentage Act--Effect.

Carlin, Baldwin's Ohio Prac. Merrick-Rippner Probate Law § 110:20, Parentage Act--Jurisdiction and Venue.

Carlin, Baldwin's Ohio Prac. Merrick-Rippner Probate Law § 110:23, Parentage Act--Parties in Parentage Action.

Carlin, Baldwin's Ohio Prac. Merrick-Rippner Probate Law § 110:29, Parentage Act--Judgment Determining Existence of Parent-Child Relationship.

Carlin, Baldwin's Ohio Prac. Merrick-Rippner Probate Law § 110:31, Parentage Act--Continuing Jurisdiction to Modify or Revoke Judgment.

Adrine & Ruden, Ohio Domestic Violence Law § 10:7, Relationships Covered--Persons Who Have a Child in Common.

Notes of Decisions

Consent 1

---

1. Consent

Although physician should have obtained ex-husband's written consent to ex-wife's artificial insemination by donor (AID) prior to proceeding with insemination, physician's failure to do so did not affect legal rights of children subsequently born to ex-wife as result of procedure or legal rights and obligations of ex-husband. Jackson v. Jackson (Ohio App. 2 Dist., 05-26-2000) 137 Ohio App.3d 782, 739 N.E.2d 1203. Children Out-of-wedlock ⊜ 15; Parent And Child ⊜ 20

3111.36, 3111.37 Physician's files; confidential information; donor information; action for file inspection; Husband rather than donor regarded as natural father of child—Repealed

(2000 S 180, eff. 3–22–01; 2000 H 242, eff. 10–27–00; 1997 H 352, eff. 1–1–98; 1986 H 476, eff. 9–24–86)

Historical and Statutory Notes

Ed. Note: Former 3111.36 and 3111.37 amended and recodified as 3111.94 and 3111.95, respectively, by 2000 S 180, eff. 3–22–01.

ADMINISTRATIVE DETERMINATION OF EXISTENCE OR NONEXISTENCE OF PARENT AND CHILD RELATIONSHIP

3111.38 Existence or nonexistence of parent and child relationship

At the request of a person described in division (A) of section 3111.04 of the Revised Code the child support enforcement agency of the county in which a child resides or in which the guardian or legal custodian of the child resides shall determine the existence or nonexistence of a parent and child relationship between an alleged father and the child.

(2000 S 180, eff. 3–22–01)

Historical and Statutory Notes

Ed. Note: RC 3111.38 contains provisions analogous to portions of former RC 3111.22(B), repealed by 2000 S 180, eff. 3–22–01.

Ed. Note: Former 3111.38 amended and recodified as 3111.96 by 2000 S 180, eff. 3–22–01; 1986 H 476, eff. 9–24–86.

Ohio Administrative Code References

Administrative determination of the existence or non-existence of a father and child relationship, see OAC 5101:12–40–20

Library References

Children Out-of-Wedlock ⊜30.
Westlaw Topic No. 76H.

C.J.S. Children Out-of-Wedlock §§ 47, 71, 94, 96 to 97.

Research References

Encyclopedias

OH Jur. 3d Family Law § 939, Civil Nature of Proceedings.

OH Jur. 3d Family Law § 941, Establishment of Parent and Child Relationship.

OH Jur. 3d Family Law § 1016, Action for Support.

Forms

Ohio Jurisprudence Pleading and Practice Forms § 111:4, Jurisdiction.

Ohio Jurisprudence Pleading and Practice Forms § 111:5, Standing--Parties.

Ohio Jurisprudence Pleading and Practice Forms § 111:7, Genetic Tests.

Ohio Jurisprudence Pleading and Practice Forms § 111:10, Temporary Support Order.

Treatises and Practice Aids

Sowald & Morganstern, Baldwin's Ohio Practice Domestic Relations Law § 3:2, Administrative Determination of Parentage--Purpose.

Sowald & Morganstern, Baldwin's Ohio Practice Domestic Relations Law § 3:3, Administrative Determination of Parentage--Initial Procedure.

Sowald & Morganstern, Baldwin's Ohio Practice Domestic Relations Law § 3:9, Judicial Parentage Action--Initial Procedure.

Sowald & Morganstern, Baldwin's Ohio Practice Domestic Relations Law § 22:4, Establishing Parentage.

Sowald & Morganstern, Baldwin's Ohio Practice Domestic Relations Law § 3:10, Judicial Parentage Action--Parties

Sowald & Morganstern, Baldwin's Ohio Practice Domestic Relations Law § 3:42, Effect of Judgment--Child Support--Temporary Support Order.

Sowald & Morganstern, Baldwin's Ohio Practice Domestic Relations Law § 3:45, Effect of Judgment--Retrospective Effect.

Sowald & Morganstern, Baldwin's Ohio Practice Domestic Relations Law § 3:46, Effect of Judgment--Inheritance

Sowald & Morganstern, Baldwin's Ohio Practice Domestic Relations Law § 3:61, Answer and Counterclaim to Complaint for Custody, Support, and Visitation--Form.

Sowald & Morganstern, Baldwin's Ohio Practice Domestic Relations Law § 23:15, In-State Remedies Determination of Parentage.

Carlin, Baldwin's Ohio Prac. Merrick-Rippner Probate Law § 18:2, Inheritance Rights of Illegitimate Child--Statutory Provisions.

Carlin, Baldwin's Ohio Prac. Merrick-Rippner Probate Law § 19:1, Legitimation--Statutory Provisions.

Carlin, Baldwin's Ohio Prac. Merrick-Rippner Probate Law § 19:2, Legitimation--Procedure--Acknowledgment of Paternity.

Carlin, Baldwin's Ohio Prac. Merrick-Rippner Probate Law § 19:4, Legitimation--Historical Provisions.

Carlin, Baldwin's Ohio Prac. Merrick-Rippner Probate Law § 19:6, Uniform Parentage Act--Jurisdiction of Action to Determine Father-Child Relationship.

Carlin, Baldwin's Ohio Prac. Merrick-Rippner Probate Law § 19:10, Uniform Parentage Act--Procedure in Action to Determine Father-Child Relationship.

Carlin, Baldwin's Ohio Prac. Merrick-Rippner Probate Law § 19:11, Uniform Parentage Act--Temporary Support Pending Action Objecting to Parentage Determination.

Carlin, Baldwin's Ohio Prac. Merrick-Rippner Probate Law § 19:13, Uniform Parentage Act--Nonspousal Artificial Insemination; Embryo Donation.

Carlin, Baldwin's Ohio Prac. Merrick-Rippner Probate Law § 99:30, Statutorily Required Consent.

Carlin, Baldwin's Ohio Prac. Merrick-Rippner Probate Law § 99:31, Parties Giving Consent--Biological Parents.

Carlin, Baldwin's Ohio Prac. Merrick-Rippner Probate Law § 110:13, Jurisdiction Over Child Custody Matters--Determination of Custody.

Carlin, Baldwin's Ohio Prac. Merrick-Rippner Probate Law § 110:19, Parentage Act--Effect.

Carlin, Baldwin's Ohio Prac. Merrick-Rippner Probate Law § 110:20, Parentage Act--Jurisdiction and Venue.

Carlin, Baldwin's Ohio Prac. Merrick-Rippner Probate Law § 110:24, Parentage Act--Genetic Tests, Fees, and Costs.

Carlin, Baldwin's Ohio Prac. Merrick-Rippner Probate Law § 110:26, Parentage Act--Applicability of Civil Rules to Paternity Proceedings.

Carlin, Baldwin's Ohio Prac. Merrick-Rippner Probate Law § 110:28, Parentage Act--Trial of Parentage Action.

Carlin, Baldwin's Ohio Prac. Merrick-Rippner Probate Law § 110:29, Parentage Act--Judgment Determining Existence of Parent-Child Relationship.

Carlin, Baldwin's Ohio Prac. Merrick-Rippner Probate Law § 110:30, Parentage Act--Enforcement of Support Order.

Carlin, Baldwin's Ohio Prac. Merrick-Rippner Probate Law § 110:31, Parentage Act--Continuing Jurisdiction to Modify or Revoke Judgment.

Carlin, Baldwin's Ohio Prac. Merrick-Rippner Probate Law § 110:34, Parentage Act--Administrative Support Orders.

Carlin, Baldwin's Ohio Prac. Merrick-Rippner Probate Law § 110:35, Civil Support Proceedings--Liability for Child Support.

Notes of Decisions

Consent   1

_____

1. Consent

Administrative proceeding initiated by Child Support Enforcement Agency (CSEA), resulting in issuance of administrative order establishment of paternity and finding that parent-child relationship existed between adjudicated father and child, was sufficient to establish paternity, for purposes of statutes establishing requirements for consent to adoption. In re Adoption of Law (Ohio App. 3 Dist., Allen, 02-13-2006) No. 1-05-64,

2006-Ohio-600, 2006 WL 319141, Unreported. Adoption ☞ 7.2(3)

Although physician should have obtained ex-husband's written consent to ex-wife's artificial insemination by donor (AID) prior to proceeding with insemination, physician's failure to do so did not affect legal rights of children subsequently born to ex-wife as result of procedure or legal rights and obligations of ex-husband. Jackson v. Jackson (Ohio App. 2 Dist., 05-26-2000) 137 Ohio App.3d 782, 739 N.E.2d 1203. Children Out–of–wedlock ☞ 15; Parent And Child ☞ 20

3111.381   Requirements to bring action; jurisdiction

(A) Except as provided in divisions (B), (C), (D), and (E) of this section, no person may bring an action under sections 3111.01 to 3111.18 of the Revised Code unless the person has requested an administrative determination under section 3111.38 of the Revised Code of the existence or nonexistence of a parent and child relationship.

(B) An action to determine the existence or nonexistence of a parent and child relationship may be brought by the child's mother in the appropriate division of the court of common pleas in the county in which the child resides, without requesting an administrative determination, if the child's mother brings the action in order to request an order to determine the allocation of parental rights and responsibilities, the payment of all or any part of the reasonable expenses of the mother's pregnancy and confinement, or support of the child. The clerk of the court shall forward a copy of the complaint to the child support enforcement agency of the county in which the complaint is filed.

(C) An action to determine the existence or nonexistence of a parent and child relationship may be brought by the putative father of the child in the appropriate division of the court of common pleas in the county in which the child resides, without requesting an administrative determination, if the putative father brings the action in order to request an order to determine the allocation of parental rights and responsibilities. The clerk of the court shall forward a copy of the complaint to the child support enforcement agency of the county in which the complaint is filed.

(D) If services are requested by the court, under divisions (B) and (C) of this section, of the child support enforcement agency to determine the existence or nonexistence of a parent and child relationship, a Title IV–D application must be completed and delivered to the child support enforcement agency.

(E) If the alleged father of a child is deceased and proceedings for the probate of the estate of the alleged father have been or can be commenced, the court with jurisdiction over the probate proceedings shall retain jurisdiction to determine the existence or nonexistence of a parent and child relationship between the alleged father and any child without an administrative determination being requested from a child support enforcement agency.

If an action for divorce, dissolution of marriage, or legal separation, or an action under section 2151.231 or 2151.232 of the Revised Code requesting an order requiring the payment of child support and provision for the health care of a child, has been filed in a court of common pleas and a question as to the existence or nonexistence of a parent and child relationship arises, the court in which the original action was filed shall retain jurisdiction to determine the existence or nonexistence of the parent and child relationship without an administrative determination being requested from a child support enforcement agency.

If a juvenile court or other court with jurisdiction under section 2101.022 or 2301.03 of the Revised Code issues a support order under section 2151.231 or 2151.232 of the Revised Code relying on a presumption under section 3111.03 of the Revised Code, the juvenile court or other court with jurisdiction that issued the support order shall retain jurisdiction if a question as to the existence of a parent and child relationship arises.

(2006 H 136, eff. 5–17–06; 2000 S 180, eff. 3–22–01)

Historical and Statutory Notes

Ed. Note: RC 3111.381 contains provisions analogous to former RC 3111.22(A), repealed by 2000 S 180, eff. 3–22–01.

Amendment Note: 2006 H 136 inserted references to divisions (C), (D), and (E) in division (A);

added new divisions (B), (C), and (D); redesignated former division (B) as (E); and made other nonsubstantive changes.

Library References

Children Out-of-Wedlock ⊕33, 36.
Westlaw Topic No. 76H.

C.J.S. Children Out-of-Wedlock §§ 47 to 48, 80 to 83, 86.

Research References

Encyclopedias

OH Jur. 3d Family Law § 947, Who May Bring an Action.

OH Jur. 3d Family Law § 952, Jurisdiction.

Treatises and Practice Aids

Sowald & Morganstern, Baldwin's Ohio Practice Domestic Relations Law § 3:2, Administrative Determination of Parentage--Purpose.

Sowald & Morganstern, Baldwin's Ohio Practice Domestic Relations Law § 3:4, Administrative Determination of Parentage--Acknowledgment, Support Order, and Birth Record.

Sowald & Morganstern, Baldwin's Ohio Practice Domestic Relations Law § 15:5, Parentage Determinations.

Sowald & Morganstern, Baldwin's Ohio Practice Domestic Relations Law § 22:4, Establishing Parentage.

Sowald & Morganstern, Baldwin's Ohio Practice Domestic Relations Law § 3:53, Complaint to Establish Father-Child Relationship--By Father--Form.

Sowald & Morganstern, Baldwin's Ohio Practice Domestic Relations Law § 3:54, Complaint to

Establish Father-Child Relationship--By Grandparent, With Request for Support--Form.

Sowald & Morganstern, Baldwin's Ohio Practice Domestic Relations Law § 23:15, In-State Remedies--Determination of Parentage.

Carlin, Baldwin's Ohio Prac. Merrick-Rippner Probate Law § 19:4, Legitimation--Historical Provisions.

Carlin, Baldwin's Ohio Prac. Merrick-Rippner Probate Law § 19:6, Uniform Parentage Act--Jurisdiction of Action to Determine Father-Child Relationship.

Carlin, Baldwin's Ohio Prac. Merrick-Rippner Probate Law § 19:10, Uniform Parentage Act--Procedure in Action to Determine Father-Child Relationship.

Carlin, Baldwin's Ohio Prac. Merrick-Rippner Probate Law § 99:49, Interlocutory and Final Orders.

Carlin, Baldwin's Ohio Prac. Merrick-Rippner Probate Law § 110:20, Parentage Act--Jurisdiction and Venue.

Carlin, Baldwin's Ohio Prac. Merrick-Rippner Probate Law § 110:34, Parentage Act--Administrative Support Orders.

Notes of Decisions

Administrative determination of parentage 1

1. Administrative determination of parentage

Failure of mother, child, and county child support enforcement agency to obtain administrative determination of parentage did not deprive trial court of jurisdiction to entertain paternity action and award current and past child support; statute

only required a "request" for an administrative determination be made before an action is commenced, and father had admitted paternity. (Per Evans, J., with two judges concurring in the judgment). State ex rel. Jackson County Child Support Enforcement Agency v. Long (Ohio App. 4 Dist., Jackson, 04-22-2004) No. 03CA1, 2004-Ohio-2184, 2004 WL 914640, Unreported. Children Out–of–wedlock ⊕ 36

3111.39 Multiple requests for determination of existence or nonexistence of parent and child relationship

If more than one child support enforcement agency receives a request to determine the existence or nonexistence of a parent and child relationship concerning the same child and each agency is an appropriate agency for the filing of the request as provided in section 3111.38 of the Revised Code, the agency that receives the request first shall act on the request. If an agency that receives a request is not the appropriate agency for the filing of the request, the agency shall forward the request to the agency of the county in which the child or the guardian or legal custodian of the child resides, and the latter agency shall proceed with the request.

(2000 S 180, eff. 3–22–01)

Historical and Statutory Notes

Ed. Note: RC 3111.39 contains provisions analogous to portions of former RC 3111.22(B), repealed by 2000 S 180, eff. 3–22–01.

Library References

Children Out-of-Wedlock ⊸30.
Westlaw Topic No. 76H.

C.J.S. Children Out-of-Wedlock §§ 47, 71, 94, 96 to 97.

3111.40 Contents of request for administrative determination of existence or nonexistence of parent and child relationship

A request for an administrative determination of the existence or nonexistence of a parent and child relationship shall contain all of the following:

(A) The name, birthdate, and current address of the alleged father of the child;

(B) The name, social security number, and current address of the mother of the child;

(C) The name and last known address of the alleged father of the child;

(D) The name and birthdate of the child.

(2000 S 180, eff. 3–22–01)

Historical and Statutory Notes

Ed. Note: RC 3111.40 contains provisions analogous to former RC 3111.22(B)(1) to (4), repealed by 2000 S 180, eff. 3–22–01.

Ohio Administrative Code References

Administrative determination of the existence or non-existence of a father and child relationship, see OAC 5101:12–40–20

Library References

Children Out-of-Wedlock ⊸30.
Westlaw Topic No. 76H.

C.J.S. Children Out-of-Wedlock §§ 47, 71, 94, 96 to 97.

Research References

Treatises and Practice Aids

Sowald & Morganstern, Baldwin's Ohio Practice Domestic Relations Law § 3:3, Administrative Determination of Parentage--Initial Procedure.

Carlin, Baldwin's Ohio Prac. Merrick-Rippner Probate Law § 19:10, Uniform Parentage Act--Procedure in Action to Determine Father-Child Relationship.

3111.41 Administrative office to consider request; order; genetic tests

On receiving a request for a determination of the existence or nonexistence of a parent and child relationship, a child support enforcement agency shall assign an administrative officer to consider the request. The officer shall issue an order requiring the child, mother, and alleged father to submit to genetic testing. The order shall specify the date of the genetic tests for the mother, alleged father, and child, which shall be no later than forty-five days after the date of assignment of the administrative officer. The tests shall be conducted in accordance with the rules adopted by the director of job and family services under section 3111.611 of the Revised Code.

(2000 S 180, eff. 3–22–01)

Historical and Statutory Notes

Ed. Note: RC 3111.41 contains provisions analogous to portions of former RC 3111.22(C)(1), repealed by 2000 S 180, eff. 3–22–01.

Ohio Administrative Code References

Scheduling and conducting genetic tests, see OAC 5101:12–40–20.1

Library References

Children Out-of-Wedlock ⟨⟩30.
Westlaw Topic No. 76H.

C.J.S. Children Out-of-Wedlock §§ 47, 71, 94, 96 to 97.

Research References

Treatises and Practice Aids

Sowald & Morganstern, Baldwin's Ohio Practice Domestic Relations Law § 22:4, Establishing Parentage.

Sowald & Morganstern, Baldwin's Ohio Practice Domestic Relations Law § 23:15, In-State Remedies--Determination of Parentage.

3111.42 Notice to accompany order for genetic testing; contents

A child support enforcement agency shall attach a notice to each order for genetic testing and send both to the mother and the alleged father. The notice shall state all of the following:

(A) That the agency has been asked to determine the existence of a parent and child relationship between a child and the alleged named father;

(B) The name and birthdate of the child of which the man is alleged to be the natural father;

(C) The name of the mother and the alleged natural father;

(D) The rights and responsibilities of a parent;

(E) That the child, the mother, and the alleged father must submit to genetic testing at the date, time, and place determined by the agency in the order issued pursuant to section 3111.41 of the Revised Code;

(F) The administrative procedure for determining the existence of a parent and child relationship;

(G) That if the alleged father or natural mother willfully fails to submit to genetic testing, or the alleged father, natural mother, or the custodian of the child willfully fails to submit the child to genetic testing, the agency will issue an order that it is inconclusive whether the alleged father is the child's natural father;

(H) That if the alleged father or natural mother willfully fails to submit to genetic testing, or the alleged father, natural mother, or custodian of the child willfully fails to submit the child to genetic testing, they may be found in contempt of court.

(2000 S 180, eff. 3–22–01)

Historical and Statutory Notes

Ed. Note: RC 3111.42 contains provisions analogous to portions of former RC 3111.22(C)(1), repealed by 2000 S 180, eff. 3–22–01.

Library References

Children Out-of-Wedlock ⟨⟩30.
Westlaw Topic No. 76H.

C.J.S. Children Out-of-Wedlock §§ 47, 71, 94, 96 to 97.

Research References

Treatises and Practice Aids

Sowald & Morganstern, Baldwin's Ohio Practice Domestic Relations Law § 3:3, Administrative Determination of Parentage--Initial Procedure.

Sowald & Morganstern, Baldwin's Ohio Practice Domestic Relations Law § 22:4, Establishing Parentage.

3111.421 Rules of civil procedure to apply

The notice and order described in section 3111.42 of the Revised Code shall be sent in accordance with the provisions of the Rules of Civil Procedure that govern service of process, except to the extent that the provisions of the Civil Rules by their nature are clearly inapplicable and except that references in the provisions of the Civil Rules to the court or to the clerk of the court shall be construed as being references to the child support enforcement agency or the administrative officer.

(2000 S 180, eff. 3–22–01)

Historical and Statutory Notes

Ed. Note: RC 3111.421 contains provisions analogous to portions of former RC 3111.22(C)(1), repealed by 2000 S 180, eff. 3–22–01.

Library References

Children Out-of-Wedlock ⚷30.
Westlaw Topic No. 76H.

C.J.S. Children Out-of-Wedlock §§ 47, 71, 94, 96 to 97.

Research References

Treatises and Practice Aids

Sowald & Morganstern, Baldwin's Ohio Practice Domestic Relations Law § 3:3, Administrative Determination of Parentage--Initial Procedure.

3111.43 Notice of request to determine existence or nonexistence of parent and child relationship

If a child support enforcement agency is asked to determine the existence or nonexistence of a parent and child relationship, the administrative officer shall provide notice of the request pursuant to the Rules of Civil Procedure to the natural mother of the child who is the subject of the request, each man presumed under section 3111.03 of the Revised Code to be the father of the child, and each man alleged to be the natural father. If the agency is unable to obtain service of process on the presumed father, alleged father, or natural mother within the time prescribed by section 3111.41 of the Revised Code, the agency shall proceed with genetic testing of all of those persons who are present on the date scheduled for the testing.

(2000 S 180, eff. 3–22–01)

Historical and Statutory Notes

Ed. Note: RC 3111.43 contains provisions analogous to former RC 3111.26, repealed by 2000 S 180, eff. 3–22–01.

Library References

Children Out-of-Wedlock ⚷30.
Westlaw Topic No. 76H.

C.J.S. Children Out-of-Wedlock §§ 47, 71, 94, 96 to 97.

Research References

Encyclopedias

OH Jur. 3d Family Law § 948, Who May Bring an
   Action--Child Support Enforcement Agency.

OH Jur. 3d Family Law § 956, Pretrial Procedures.

3111.44 Conference; genetic testing

After issuing a genetic testing order, the administrative officer may schedule a conference with the mother and the alleged father to provide information. If a conference is scheduled and no other man is presumed to be the father of the child under section 3111.03 of the Revised Code, the administrative officer shall provide the mother and alleged father the opportunity to sign an acknowledgment of paternity affidavit prepared pursuant to section 3111.31 of the Revised Code. If they sign an acknowledgment of paternity, the administrative officer shall cancel the genetic testing order the officer had issued. Regardless of whether a conference is held, if the mother and alleged father do not sign an acknowledgment of paternity affidavit or if an affidavit cannot be notarized or filed because another man is presumed under section 3111.03 of the Revised Code to be the father of the child, the child, the mother, and the alleged father shall submit to genetic testing in accordance with the order issued by the administrative officer.

(2000 S 180, eff. 3–22–01)

Historical and Statutory Notes

Ed. Note: RC 3111.44 contains provisions analogous to portions of former RC 3111.22(C)(1),
repealed by 2000 S 180, eff. 3–22–01.

Library References

Children Out-of-Wedlock ⚫30.
Westlaw Topic No. 76H.

C.J.S. Children Out-of-Wedlock §§ 47, 71, 94, 96 to
   97.

Research References

Encyclopedias

OH Jur. 3d Family Law § 956, Pretrial Procedures.

Treatises and Practice Aids

Sowald & Morganstern, Baldwin's Ohio Practice
   Domestic Relations Law § 3:3, Administrative
   Determination of Parentage--Initial Procedure.
Sowald & Morganstern, Baldwin's Ohio Practice
   Domestic Relations Law § 3:4, Administrative

Determination of Parentage--Acknowledgment,
   Support Order, and Birth Record.
Sowald & Morganstern, Baldwin's Ohio Practice
   Domestic Relations Law § 3:5, Administrative
   Determination of Parentage--No Acknowledg-
   ment and Support Order.
Sowald & Morganstern, Baldwin's Ohio Practice
   Domestic Relations Law § 22:4, Establishing
   Parentage.

3111.45 Qualified examiner to conduct genetic testing; report of test results

The genetic testing required under an administrative genetic testing order shall be conducted by a qualified examiner authorized by the department of job and family services. On completion of the genetic tests, the examiner shall send a complete report of the test results to the agency.

(2000 S 180, eff. 3–22–01)

Historical and Statutory Notes

Ed. Note: RC 3111.45 contains provisions analogous to portions of former RC 3111.22(C)(2),
repealed by 2000 S 180, eff. 3–22–01.

Ohio Administrative Code References

Scheduling and conducting genetic tests, see OAC
   5101:12–40–20.1

Statewide genetic testing contract, see OAC
   5101:12–1–85

Library References

Children Out-of-Wedlock ⊝30.
Westlaw Topic No. 76H.

C.J.S. Children Out-of-Wedlock §§ 47, 71, 94, 96 to 97.

Research References

Encyclopedias

OH Jur. 3d Family Law § 962, Who May Perform.

3111.46 Duties of administrative officer upon receipt of test results

On receipt of the genetic test results, the administrative officer shall do one of the following:

(A) If the results of the genetic testing show a ninety-nine per cent or greater probability that the alleged father is the natural father of the child, the administrative officer of the agency shall issue an administrative order that the alleged father is the father of the child who is the subject of the proceeding.

(B) If the results of genetic testing show less than a ninety-nine per cent probability that the alleged father is the natural father of the child, the administrative officer shall issue an administrative order that the alleged father is not the father of the child who is the subject of the proceeding.

An order issued pursuant to this section shall be sent to parties in accordance with the Civil Rule governing service and filing of pleadings and other papers subsequent to the original complaint.

(2000 S 180, eff. 3–22–01)

Historical and Statutory Notes

Ed. Note: RC 3111.46 contains provisions analogous to former RC 3111.22(C)(2)(a) to (c), repealed by 2000 S 180, eff. 3–22–01.

Ohio Administrative Code References

Administrative paternity orders, see OAC 5101:12–40–20.2

Library References

Children Out-of-Wedlock ⊝30.
Westlaw Topic No. 76H.

C.J.S. Children Out-of-Wedlock §§ 47, 71, 94, 96 to 97.

Research References

Encyclopedias

OH Jur. 3d Family Law § 956, Pretrial Procedures.
OH Jur. 3d Family Law § 1021, Hearing on Request; Determination of Support.

Treatises and Practice Aids

Sowald & Morganstern, Baldwin's Ohio Practice Domestic Relations Law § 3:3, Administrative Determination of Parentage--Initial Procedure.
Sowald & Morganstern, Baldwin's Ohio Practice Domestic Relations Law § 3:5, Administrative

Determination of Parentage--No Acknowledgment and Support Order.
Sowald & Morganstern, Baldwin's Ohio Practice Domestic Relations Law § 23:15, In-State Remedies--Determination of Parentage.
Carlin, Baldwin's Ohio Prac. Merrick-Rippner Probate Law § 19:2, Legitimation--Procedure--Acknowledgment of Paternity.
Carlin, Baldwin's Ohio Prac. Merrick-Rippner Probate Law § 110:34, Parentage Act--Administrative Support Orders.

3111.47 Failure to submit to genetic testing

If the alleged natural father or the natural mother willfully fails to submit to genetic testing or if either parent or any other person who is the custodian of the child willfully fails to submit the child to genetic testing, the agency shall enter an administrative order stating that it is inconclusive as to whether the alleged natural father is the natural father of the child.
(2000 S 180, eff. 3–22–01)

Historical and Statutory Notes

Ed. Note: RC 3111.47 contains provisions analogous to portions of former RC 3111.22(F), repealed by 2000 S 180, eff. 3–22–01.

Ohio Administrative Code References

Administrative paternity orders, see OAC 5101:12 40 20.2

Library References

Children Out-of-Wedlock ⊗⟶30.
Westlaw Topic No. 76H.

C.J.S. Children Out-of-Wedlock §§ 47, 71, 94, 96 to 97.

Research References

Treatises and Practice Aids

Sowald & Morganstern, Baldwin's Ohio Practice Domestic Relations Law § 3:3, Administrative Determination of Parentage--Initial Procedure.
Sowald & Morganstern, Baldwin's Ohio Practice Domestic Relations Law § 3:4, Administrative Determination of Parentage Acknowledgment, Support Order, and Birth Record.

Sowald & Morganstern, Baldwin's Ohio Practice Domestic Relations Law § 3:7, Administrative Determination of Parentage--Dismissal.
Sowald & Morganstern, Baldwin's Ohio Practice Domestic Relations Law § 23:15, In-State Remedies--Determination of Parentage.

3111.48 Notice of right to bring actions

An administrative officer shall include in an order issued under section 3111.46 of the Revised Code a notice that contains the information described in section 3111.49 of the Revised Code informing the mother, father, and the guardian or legal custodian of the child of the right to bring an action under sections 3111.01 to 3111.18 of the Revised Code and of the effect of failure to timely bring the action.

An agency shall include in an administrative order issued under section 3111.47 of the Revised Code a notice that contains the information described in section 3111.50 of the Revised Code informing the parties of their right to bring an action under sections 3111.01 to 3111.18 of the Revised Code.

(2000 S 180, eff. 3–22–01)

Historical and Statutory Notes

Ed. Note: RC 3111.48 contains provisions analogous to portions of former RC 3111.22(C)(2), repealed by 2000 S 180, eff. 3–22–01.

Library References

Children Out-of-Wedlock ⊗⟶30.
Westlaw Topic No. 76H.

C.J.S. Children Out-of-Wedlock §§ 47, 71, 94, 96 to 97.

Research References

Treatises and Practice Aids

Carlin, Baldwin's Ohio Prac. Merrick-Rippner Probate Law § 110.31, Parentage Act--Continuing Jurisdiction to Modify or Revoke Judgment.

3111.49 Objection to administrative order; finality of order

The mother, alleged father, and guardian or legal custodian of a child may object to an administrative order determining the existence or nonexistence of a parent and child relationship by bringing, within thirty days after the date the administrative officer issues the order, an action under sections 3111.01 to 3111.18 of the Revised Code in the juvenile court or other court with jurisdiction under section 2101.022 or 2301.03 of the Revised Code in the county in which the child support enforcement agency that employs the administrative officer who issued the order is located. If the action is not brought within the thirty-day period, the administrative order is final and enforceable by a court and may not be challenged in an action or proceeding under Chapter 3111. of the Revised Code.

(2000 S 180, eff. 3–22–01)

Historical and Statutory Notes

Ed. Note: RC 3111.49 contains provisions analogous to former RC 3111.22(D), repealed by 2000 S 180, eff. 3–22–01.

Ohio Administrative Code References

Support order establishment process, see OAC 5101:12–45–05

Library References

Children Out-of-Wedlock ⚯30.
Westlaw Topic No. 76H.

C.J.S. Children Out-of-Wedlock §§ 47, 71, 94, 96 to 97.

Research References

Encyclopedias

OH Jur. 3d Family Law § 950, Limitation of Actions.

Treatises and Practice Aids

Sowald & Morganstern, Baldwin's Ohio Practice Domestic Relations Law § 3:4, Administrative Determination of Parentage--Acknowledgment, Support Order, and Birth Record.
Sowald & Morganstern, Baldwin's Ohio Practice Domestic Relations Law § 3:5, Administrative

Determination of Parentage--No Acknowledgment and Support Order.
Sowald & Morganstern, Baldwin's Ohio Practice Domestic Relations Law § 3:6, Administrative Determination of Parentage--Finality.
Sowald & Morganstern, Baldwin's Ohio Practice Domestic Relations Law § 22:2, CSEA Service Delivery.
Carlin, Baldwin's Ohio Prac. Merrick-Rippner Probate Law § 110:31, Parentage Act--Continuing Jurisdiction to Modify or Revoke Judgment.

Notes of Decisions

Appeal   1

------

1. Appeal

Prospective adoptive parents were barred from raising on appeal in adoption case issue that administrative order establishment of paternity was insufficient to create parent-child relationship between

incompetent adjudicated father and child due to failure of Child Support Enforcement Agency (CSEA) to comply with its statutory chain of duties, where prospective adoptive parents did not object to initial administrative finding of paternity in paternity case. In re Adoption of Law (Ohio App. 3 Dist., Allen, 02-13-2006) No. 1-05-64, 2006-Ohio-600, 2006 WL 319141, Unreported. Adoption ⚯ 15

3111.50   Inconclusive administrative orders; action to establish parent and child relationship

If a child support enforcement agency issues an administrative order stating that it is inconclusive as to whether the alleged natural father is the natural father of the child, any of the parties may bring an action under sections 3111.01 to 3111.18 of the Revised Code to establish a parent and child relationship.

(2000 S 180, eff. 3–22–01)

Historical and Statutory Notes

Ed. Note: RC 3111.50 contains provisions analogous to portions of former RC 3111.22(F), repealed by 2000 S 180, eff. 3–22–01.

Library References

Children Out-of-Wedlock ☞34.
Westlaw Topic No. 76H.
C.J.S. Children Out-of-Wedlock §§ 50, 88 to 96.

Research References

Treatises and Practice Aids

Sowald & Morganstern, Baldwin's Ohio Practice Domestic Relations Law § 22:2, CSEA Service Delivery.
Sowald & Morganstern, Baldwin's Ohio Practice Domestic Relations Law § 22:4, Establishing Parentage.

Carlin, Baldwin's Ohio Prac. Merrick-Rippner Probate Law § 110:3, Criminal Jurisdiction--Proceedings for Nonsupport.

3111.51   Contents of administrative orders; exceptions

Unless the child support enforcement agency has reason to believe that a person named in the order is a potential victim of domestic violence, any administrative order finding the existence of a parent and child relationship shall contain the full names, addresses, and social security numbers of the mother and father of the child who is the subject of the order and the full name and address of the child.

(2000 S 180, eff. 3–22–01)

Historical and Statutory Notes

Ed. Note: RC 3111.51 contains provisions analogous to portions of former RC 3111.22(G), repealed by 2000 S 180, eff. 3–22–01.

Ohio Administrative Code References

Administrative paternity orders, see OAC 5101:12–40–20.2

Library References

Children Out-of-Wedlock ☞30.
Westlaw Topic No. 76H.

C.J.S. Children Out-of-Wedlock §§ 47, 71, 94, 96 to 97.

Research References

Treatises and Practice Aids

Adrine & Ruden, Ohio Domestic Violence Law § 17:4, Confidentiality and Privilege.

Adrine & Ruden, Ohio Domestic Violence Law § 15:10, Batterer Access to the Victim and Children.

3111.52   Change of child's surname

The child support enforcement agency, as part of an administrative order determining the existence of a parent and child relationship, may order the surname of the child subject to the determination to be changed and order the change to be made on the child's birth record consistent with the order if both the parties agree to the change.

(2000 S 180, eff. 3–22–01)

Historical and Statutory Notes

Ed. Note: RC 3111.52 contains provisions analogous to portions of former RC 3111.22(G), repealed by 2000 S 180, eff. 3–22–01.

Ohio Administrative Code References

Modifying the birth certificate, see OAC 5101:12–40–20.3

Modifying the birth record, see OAC 5101:12–40–27

Library References

Children Out-of-Wedlock ⚌1, 30.
Health ⚌397.
Westlaw Topic Nos. 76H, 198H.

C.J.S. Children Out-of-Wedlock §§ 1 to 8, 47, 71, 94, 96 to 97.
C.J.S. Health and Environment §§ 24, 74.

Research References

Treatises and Practice Aids

Sowald & Morganstern, Baldwin's Ohio Practice Domestic Relations Law § 3:4, Administrative Determination of Parentage--Acknowledgment, Support Order, and Birth Record.

Sowald & Morganstern, Baldwin's Ohio Practice Domestic Relations Law § 3:51, Related Issues--Name.

3111.53 Administrative officers

(A) A child support enforcement agency, in accordance with the rules adopted by the director of job and family services pursuant to division (B) of this section, shall employ an administrative officer, contract with another entity to provide an administrative officer, or contract with an individual to serve as an administrative officer to issue administrative orders determining the existence or nonexistence of a parent and child relationship, requiring the payment of child support, or both.

(B) The director of job and family services shall adopt rules in accordance with Chapter 119. of the Revised Code regulating administrative officers who issue administrative orders described in division (A) of this section, including the following:

(1) The qualifications of the administrative officer;

(2) Any other procedures, requirements, or standards necessary for the employment of the administrative officer.

(2000 S 180, eff. 3–22–01)

Historical and Statutory Notes

Ed. Note: 3111.53 is former 2301.358, amended and recodified by 2000 S 180, eff. 3–22–01; 1999 H 471, eff. 7–1–00; 1997 H 352, eff. 1–1–98; 1996 H 710, § 7, eff. 6–11–96; 1995 H 167, eff. 6–11–96; 1992 S 10, eff. 7–15–92.

Ed. Note: The effective date of the amendment of this section by 1995 H 167 was changed from 11–15–96 to 6–11–96 by 1996 H 710, § 7, eff. 6–11–96.

Amendment Note: 2000 S 180 rewrote this section which prior thereto read:

"(A) A child support enforcement agency, in accordance with the rules adopted by the director of job and family services pursuant to division (B) of this section, shall employ an administrative officer, contract with another entity to provide an administrative officer, or contract with an individual to serve as an administrative officer to issue, in accordance with sections 3111.22 to 3111.29 and 3113.215 of the Revised Code, administrative orders determining the existence or nonexistence of a parent and child relationship and requiring the payment of child support, or in accordance with sections 3111.20, 3111.23 to 3111.29, and 3113.215

of the Revised Code, administrative orders requiring the payment of child support.

"(B) The director of job and family services shall adopt rules in accordance with Chapter 119. of the Revised Code regulating administrative officers who issue administrative orders described in division (A) of this section, including, but not limited to:

"(1) The qualifications of the administrative officer;

"(2) Any other procedures, requirements, or standards necessary for the employment of the administrative officer. "

Amendment Note: 1999 H 471 substituted "director of job and family services" for "department of human services" in division (A) and in the introductory paragraph in division (B).

Amendment Note: 1997 H 352 substituted "3111.22" for "3111.21".

Amendment Note: 1995 H 167 inserted ", or in accordance with sections 3111.20, 3111.23 to 3111.29, and 3113.215 of the Revised Code, administrative orders requiring the payment of child support" in division (A); deleted ", in accordance with sections 3111.21 to 3111.29 and 3113.215 of the Revised Code" before "administrative orders" in division (B); and substituted "described in division (A) of this section" for "determining the existence or nonexistence of a parent and child relationship and requiring the payment of child support" in division (B).

Library References

Infants ⚎17.
Westlaw Topic No. 211.

C.J.S. Adoption of Persons §§ 10 to 14, 41.
C.J.S. Infants §§ 6, 8 to 9.

Research References

Encyclopedias

OH Jur. 3d Family Law § 1216, Child Support Enforcement Agency Review of Administrative Child Support Order.

Notes of Decisions

Personal bias or prejudice   2
Representing multiply agencies   1

---

1. Representing multiply agencies

Trial court erred in declining to enforce administrative child support order obtained by county child support enforcement agency for child born out of wedlock on ground that administrative hearing was conducted by an employee of county agency, where no one objected to or appealed administrative order, and record was devoid of any indication that hearing officer was unqualified. Jefferson County Child Support Enforcement Agency ex rel. Harris v. Ross (Ohio App. 7 Dist., Jefferson, 02-14-2003) No. 02-JE-24, 2003-Ohio-699, 2003 WL 352417, Unreported. Child Support ⚎ 465

Child support enforcement agency staff attorney may not represent state in contempt action or other actions involving matter in which attorney served as hearing officer and issued administrative orders, but is not barred from representing state in matter solely because party once appeared in other matter before attorney serving as hearing officer. Bd. of Commrs. on Grievances & Discipline Op. 2006–6 (6–9–06).

A person may serve as a part-time administrative hearing officer for a county child support enforcement agency and part-time magistrate of a court of common pleas in an adjacent county, provided that as a magistrate she does not preside over cases involving the child support enforcement agency that employs her as an administrative hearing officer. OAG 05–022.

An individual may hold simultaneously the positions of assistant county prosecuting attorney and administrative hearing officer for a child support enforcement agency (CSEA) that is within the county department of human services, provided that the individual, as an administrative hearing officer, does not preside over a hearing in which one of the parties is represented by the county prosecuting attorney who employs him as an assistant county prosecuting attorney or sit in judgment of his own professional work for, and legal advice to, the county department of human services or the CSEA. In addition, the individual, as an assistant county prosecuting attorney, may not conduct civil or criminal proceedings, under RC 117.27 to 117.29, 309.12, 2733.04, and 2733.05, against officers of the county department of human services or the CSEA that appoints him as an administrative hearing officer, or initiate criminal or civil proceedings against defendants who fail to comply with child support orders. OAG 97–044.

2. Personal bias or prejudice

Trial court's refusal to register administrative child support order by finding it invalid because the administrative hearing was not conducted by a detached magistrate was without basis; no one objected to the order, and there was no indication in the record or the transcript that administrative hearing officer was either biased, prejudiced, or unqualified for the position. Jefferson County Child Support Enforcement Agency ex rel. Toma v. Harris (Ohio App. 7 Dist., Jefferson, 01-29-2003) No. 02JE22, 2003-Ohio-496, 2003 WL 220415, Unreported. Child Support ⚎ 465

3111.54 Finding of contempt

If an alleged father or natural mother willfully fails to submit to genetic testing, or if the alleged father, natural mother, or any other person who is the custodian of the child willfully fails to submit the child to genetic testing, as required by an order for genetic testing issued under section 3111.41 of the Revised Code, the child support enforcement agency that issued the order may request that the juvenile court or other court with jurisdiction under section 2101.022 or 2301.03 of the Revised Code of the county in which the agency is located find the alleged father, natural mother, or other person in contempt pursuant to section 2705.02 of the Revised Code.

(2000 S 180, eff. 3–22–01)

Historical and Statutory Notes

Ed. Note: RC 3111.54 contains provisions analogous to former RC 3111.242(B), repealed by 2000 S 180, eff. 3–22–01.

Ohio Administrative Code References

Administrative paternity orders, see OAC 5101:12–40–20.2

Library References

Administrative Law and Procedure ☞937.
Children Out-of-Wedlock ☞30.
Infants ☞17.
Westlaw Topic Nos. 15A, 76H, 211.
C.J.S. Adoption of Persons §§ 10 to 14, 41.

C.J.S. Children Out-of-Wedlock §§ 47, 71, 94, 96 to 97.
C.J.S. Infants §§ 6, 8 to 9.
C.J.S. Public Administrative Law and Procedure § 501.

Research References

Encyclopedias

OH Jur. 3d Family Law § 941, Establishment of Parent and Child Relationship.

Forms

Ohio Jurisprudence Pleading and Practice Forms § 111:4, Jurisdiction.
Ohio Jurisprudence Pleading and Practice Forms § 111:5, Standing--Parties.
Ohio Jurisprudence Pleading and Practice Forms § 111:7, Genetic Tests.
Ohio Jurisprudence Pleading and Practice Forms § 111:10, Temporary Support Order.

Treatises and Practice Aids

Sowald & Morganstern, Baldwin's Ohio Practice Domestic Relations Law § 3:4, Administrative Determination of Parentage--Acknowledgment, Support Order, and Birth Record.
Sowald & Morganstern, Baldwin's Ohio Practice Domestic Relations Law § 3:42, Effect of Judgment--Child Support--Temporary Support Order.
Carlin, Baldwin's Ohio Prac. Merrick-Rippner Probate Law § 18:2, Inheritance Rights of Illegitimate Child--Statutory Provisions.
Carlin, Baldwin's Ohio Prac. Merrick-Rippner Probate Law § 19:1, Legitimation--Statutory Provisions.
Carlin, Baldwin's Ohio Prac. Merrick-Rippner Probate Law § 19:2, Legitimation--Procedure--Acknowledgment of Paternity.
Carlin, Baldwin's Ohio Prac. Merrick-Rippner Probate Law § 19:4, Legitimation--Historical Provisions.
Carlin, Baldwin's Ohio Prac. Merrick-Rippner Probate Law § 19:6, Uniform Parentage Act--Jurisdiction of Action to Determine Father-Child Relationship.
Carlin, Baldwin's Ohio Prac. Merrick-Rippner Probate Law § 19:10, Uniform Parentage Act--Procedure in Action to Determine Father-Child Relationship.
Carlin, Baldwin's Ohio Prac. Merrick-Rippner Probate Law § 19:11, Uniform Parentage Act--Temporary Support Pending Action Objecting to Parentage Determination.
Carlin, Baldwin's Ohio Prac. Merrick-Rippner Probate Law § 19:13, Uniform Parentage Act--Nonspousal Artificial Insemination; Embryo Donation.
Carlin, Baldwin's Ohio Prac. Merrick-Rippner Probate Law § 99:30, Statutorily Required Consent.
Carlin, Baldwin's Ohio Prac. Merrick-Rippner Probate Law § 99:31, Parties Giving Consent--Biological Parents.
Carlin, Baldwin's Ohio Prac. Merrick-Rippner Probate Law § 110:13, Jurisdiction Over Child Custody Matters--Determination of Custody.
Carlin, Baldwin's Ohio Prac. Merrick-Rippner Probate Law § 110:19, Parentage Act--Effect.
Carlin, Baldwin's Ohio Prac. Merrick-Rippner Probate Law § 110:20, Parentage Act--Jurisdiction and Venue.
Carlin, Baldwin's Ohio Prac. Merrick-Rippner Probate Law § 110:24, Parentage Act--Genetic Tests, Fees, and Costs.
Carlin, Baldwin's Ohio Prac. Merrick-Rippner Probate Law § 110:26, Parentage Act--Applicability of Civil Rules to Paternity Proceedings.
Carlin, Baldwin's Ohio Prac. Merrick-Rippner Probate Law § 110:28, Parentage Act--Trial of Parentage Action.
Carlin, Baldwin's Ohio Prac. Merrick-Rippner Probate Law § 110:29, Parentage Act--Judgment Determining Existence of Parent-Child Relationship.
Carlin, Baldwin's Ohio Prac. Merrick-Rippner Probate Law § 110:30, Parentage Act--Enforcement of Support Order.
Carlin, Baldwin's Ohio Prac. Merrick-Rippner Probate Law § 110:35, Civil Support Proceedings--Liability for Child Support.

3111.58 Preparation of new birth record pursuant to determination of parent and child relationship

If an administrative order determining the existence or nonexistence of a parent and child relationship includes a finding that the child's father is a man other than the man named in the child's birth record as the father or is otherwise at variance with the child's birth record, the agency that made the determination shall notify the department of health of the determination as soon as any period for objection to the determination provided for in former section 3111.21 or 3111.22 or section 3111.49 of the Revised Code has elapsed.

On receipt of notice under this section or notice from an agency of another state with authority to make paternity determinations that has made a determination of the existence or nonexistence of a parent and child relationship, the department of health shall prepare a new birth record consistent with the agency's determination and substitute the new record for the original birth record.

(2000 S 180, eff. 3–22–01)

Historical and Statutory Notes

Ed. Note: 3111.58 is former 3111.221, amended and recodified by 2000 S 180, eff. 3–22–01; 1997 H 352, eff. 1–1–98.

Amendment Note: 2000 S 180 deleted the first paragraph of the section; inserted "3111.22 or" in the new first paragraph; and substituted "3111.49" for "3111.22" in the new first paragraph. Prior to deletion the former first paragraph read:

"As used in this section, "birth record" has the same meaning as in section 3705.01 of the Revised Code."

Cross References

Administrative child support orders, birth record defined, see 3705.01

Ohio Administrative Code References

Modifying the birth certificate, see OAC 5101:12–40–20.3

Modifying the birth record, see OAC 5101:12–40–27

Library References

Health ☞397.
Westlaw Topic No. 198H.
C.J.S. Health and Environment §§ 24, 74.

Research References

Treatises and Practice Aids

Sowald & Morganstern, Baldwin's Ohio Practice Domestic Relations Law § 3:4, Administrative

Determination of Parentage--Acknowledgment, Support Order, and Birth Record.

3111.61 Collection of samples and genetic testing

If a child support enforcement agency is made a party to an action brought to establish a parent and child relationship under sections 3111.01 to 3111.18 of the Revised Code and the court orders the parties to the action to submit to genetic testing or the agency orders the parties to submit to genetic testing under section 3111.41 of the Revised Code, the agency shall provide for collection of samples and performance of genetic testing in accordance with generally accepted medical techniques. If a court ordered the genetic testing, the agency shall inform the court of the procedures for collecting the samples and performing the genetic tests, in accordance with the rules governing on-site genetic testing adopted by the director of job and family services pursuant to section 3111.611 of the Revised Code.

(2000 S 180, eff. 3–22–01)

Historical and Statutory Notes

Ed. Note: 3111.61 is former 2301.356, amended and recodified by 2000 S 180, eff. 3–22–01; 1999 H 471, eff. 7–1–00; 1997 H 352, eff. 1–1–98; 1996 H 357, eff. 9–19–96; 1992 S 10, eff. 7–15–92.

Amendment Note: 2000 S 180 substituted "3111.18" for "3111.19", "section 3111.41" for "sections 3111.22 to 3111.29", and "3111.611" for "2305.35".

Amendment Note: 1999 H 471 substituted "director of job and family services" for "department of human services".

Amendment Note: 1997 H 352 substituted "the agency orders the parties to submit to" for "if the natural mother and alleged natural father voluntarily agree to be bound by" and "3111.22" for

"3111.21"; and made other nonsubstantive changes.

Amendment Note: 1996 H 357 substituted "provide for collection of samples and performance of genetic testing in accordance with generally accepted medical techniques. If" for "make available a medically trained phlebotomist to withdraw the necessary blood samples and an authorized examiner to perform the genetic tests. The agency shall provide the phlebotomist, the examiner, and a location to withdraw the blood samples, and, if"; inserted "the agency" and substituted "collecting the samples" for "withdrawing the blood samples" in the final sentence; and made other nonsubstantive changes.

Library References

Children Out-of-Wedlock ⬉58.
Westlaw Topic No. 76H.
C.J.S. Children Out-of-Wedlock §§ 76 to 79.

3111.611   Rules governing establishment of on-site genetic testing programs

The director of job and family services shall adopt in accordance with Chapter 119. of the Revised Code rules governing the establishment by child support enforcement agencies of on-site genetic testing programs to be used in actions under sections 3111.01 to 3111.18 of the Revised Code and in administrative procedures under sections 3111.38 to 3111.54 of the Revised Code. The rules shall include provisions relating to the environment in which a blood or buccal cell sample may be drawn, the medical personnel who may draw a sample, the trained personnel who may perform the genetic comparison, the types of genetic testing that may be performed on a sample, and the procedure for notifying the court of the location at which the sample will be drawn, who will draw the sample, and who will perform the genetic testing on the sample, and any other procedures or standards the director determines are necessary for the implementation of on-site genetic testing.

(2000 S 180, eff. 3–22–01)

Historical and Statutory Notes

Ed. Note: RC 3111.611 contains provisions analogous to former RC 2301.35(D)(2), repealed by 2000 S 180, eff. 3–22–01.

Ohio Administrative Code References

Scheduling and conducting genetic tests, see OAC
  5101:12–40–20.1

Library References

Children Out-of-Wedlock ⬉58.
Infants ⬉17.
Westlaw Topic Nos. 76H, 211.

C.J.S. Adoption of Persons §§ 10 to 14, 41.
C.J.S. Children Out-of-Wedlock §§ 76 to 79.
C.J.S. Infants §§ 6, 8 to 9.

BIRTH REGISTRY AND PUTATIVE FATHER REGISTRY

3111.64   Birth registry

The office of child support in the department of job and family services shall establish and maintain a birth registry that shall contain all of the following information contained in orders determining the existence of a parent and child relationship and acknowledgments of paternity required to be filed with the office:

(A) The names of the parents of the child subject to the order or acknowledgment;

(B) The name of the child;

(C) The resident address of each parent and each parent's social security number.

(2000 S 180, eff. 3–22–01)

Historical and Statutory Notes

Ed. Note: RC 3111.64 contains provisions analogous to former RC 5101.314(D)(1), repealed by 2000 S 180, eff. 3–22–01.

Ohio Administrative Code References

Central paternity registry, see OAC 5101:12–40–30

Library References

Health ⚷397.
Infants ⚷17.
Westlaw Topic Nos. 198H, 211.

C.J.S. Adoption of Persons §§ 10 to 14, 41.
C.J.S. Health and Environment §§ 24, 74.
C.J.S. Infants §§ 6, 8 to 9.

Research References

Treatises and Practice Aids

Sowald & Morganstern, Baldwin's Ohio Practice Domestic Relations Law § 19:3, Support Obligations--In General.
Sowald & Morganstern, Baldwin's Ohio Practice Domestic Relations Law § 22:29, Parent Location.

Carlin, Baldwin's Ohio Prac. Merrick Rippner Probate Law § 19:2, Legitimation--Procedure--Acknowledgment of Paternity.
Carlin, Baldwin's Ohio Prac. Merrick-Rippner Probate Law § 110:20, Parentage Act--Jurisdiction and Venue.

3111.65 Maintenance and accessibility of birth registry

The birth registry shall be maintained as part of and be accessible through the automated system created pursuant to section 3125.07 of the Revised Code. The office of child support shall make comparisons of the information in the registry with the information maintained by the department of job and family services pursuant to sections 3107.062 and 3121.894 of the Revised Code. The office shall make the comparisons in the manner and in the time intervals required by the rules adopted pursuant to section 3111.67 of the Revised Code.

(2000 S 180, eff. 3–22–01)

Historical and Statutory Notes

Ed. Note: RC 3111.65 contains provisions analogous to former RC 5101.314(D)(2), repealed by 2000 S 180, eff. 3–22–01.

Library References

Health ⚷397.
Infants ⚷17.
Westlaw Topic Nos. 198H, 211.

C.J.S. Adoption of Persons §§ 10 to 14, 41.
C.J.S. Health and Environment §§ 24, 74.
C.J.S. Infants §§ 6, 8 to 9.

Research References

Treatises and Practice Aids

Carlin, Baldwin's Ohio Prac. Merrick-Rippner Probate Law § 19:2, Legitimation--Procedure--Acknowledgment of Paternity.

Carlin, Baldwin's Ohio Prac. Merrick-Rippner Probate Law § 110:20, Parentage Act--Jurisdiction and Venue.

3111.66 Filing of orders

A court or child support enforcement agency, whichever is applicable, shall file the following with the office of child support:

(A) An order issued pursuant to section 3111.13 of the Revised Code on or after January 1, 1998;

(B) An order issued pursuant to section 3111.22 of the Revised Code on or after January 1, 1998, that has become final and enforceable;

(C) An order issued pursuant to section 3111.46 of the Revised Code on or after the effective date of this section.

On the filing of an order pursuant to this section, the office shall enter the information on the order in the birth registry.

(2000 S 180, eff. 3–22–01)

Historical and Statutory Notes

Ed. Note: RC 3111.66 contains provisions analogous to former RC 5101.314(C), repealed by 2000 S 180, eff. 3–22–01.

Library References

Children Out-of-Wedlock ☞63.
Records ☞3.

Westlaw Topic Nos. 76H, 326.
C.J.S. Children Out-of-Wedlock §§ 121 to 128.

3111.67 Rules for birth registry

The director of job and family services shall adopt rules pursuant to Chapter 119. of the Revised Code to implement the requirements of sections 3111.64 to 3111.66 of the Revised Code that are consistent with Title IV–D of the "Social Security Act," 88 Stat. 2351, 42 U.S.C. 651 et seq., as amended.

(2000 S 180, eff. 3–22–01)

Historical and Statutory Notes

Ed. Note: RC 3111.67 contains provisions analogous to former RC 5101.314(E), repealed by 2000 S 180, eff. 3–22–01.

Library References

Health ☞397.
Infants ☞17.
Social Security and Public Welfare ☞194 to 194.1.
Westlaw Topic Nos. 198H, 211, 356A.
C.J.S. Adoption of Persons §§ 10 to 14, 41.

C.J.S. Health and Environment §§ 24, 74.
C.J.S. Infants §§ 6, 8 to 9.
C.J.S. Social Security and Public Welfare §§ 206, 209 to 213, 215, 227, 229.

Research References

Treatises and Practice Aids

Sowald & Morganstern, Baldwin's Ohio Practice Domestic Relations Law § 22:29, Parent Location.

3111.69 Examining putative father registry

The office of child support in the department of job and family services and a child support enforcement agency may examine the putative father registry established under section 3107.062 of the Revised Code to locate an absent parent for the purpose of the office or agency carrying out its duties under the child and spousal support enforcement programs established under Chapter 3125. of the Revised Code. Neither the office nor an agency shall use the information it receives from the registry for any purpose other than child and spousal support enforcement.

(2000 S 180, eff. 3–22–01)

Historical and Statutory Notes

Ed. Note: 3111.69 is former 5101.313, amended and recodified by 2000 S 180, eff. 3–22–01; 1999 H 471, eff. 7–1–00; 1996 H 419, eff. 9–18–96.

Amendment Note: 2000 S 180 substituted "office" for "division" three times and "Chapter 3125" for "section 5101.31".

Cross References

Availability of state government public records, public records defined, see 149.43

Personal information systems, right to inspection, see 1347.08

Library References

Children Out-of-Wedlock ☞30.
Infants ☞17.
Westlaw Topic Nos. 76H, 211.
C.J.S. Adoption of Persons §§ 10 to 14, 41.

C.J.S. Children Out-of-Wedlock §§ 47, 71, 94, 96 to 97.
C.J.S. Infants §§ 6, 8 to 9.

Research References

Encyclopedias

OH Jur. 3d Defamation & Privacy § 183, Exceptions.
OH Jur. 3d Family Law § 882, Putative Father Registry.
OH Jur. 3d Family Law § 1228, Restrictions on Use of Information; Confidentiality.

OH Jur. 3d Family Law § 1247, Access to Information; Restrictions on Use and Confidentiality.

Treatises and Practice Aids

Gotherman & Babbit, Ohio Municipal Law § 6:12, Exceptions to General Rule.

MISCELLANEOUS PROVISIONS

3111.71 Contracts with local hospitals for staff to meet with certain unmarried women

The department of job and family services shall enter into a contract with local hospitals for the provision of staff by the hospitals to meet with unmarried women who give birth in or en route to the particular hospital. On or before April 1, 1998, each hospital shall enter into a contract with the department of job and family services pursuant to this section regarding the duties imposed by this section and section 3727.17 of the Revised Code concerning paternity establishment. A hospital that fails to enter into a contract shall not receive the fee from the department for correctly signed and notarized affidavits submitted by the hospital.

(2000 S 180, eff. 3–22–01)

Historical and Statutory Notes

Ed. Note: RC 3111.71 contains provisions analogous to portions of former 2301.357(B), repealed by 2000 S 180, eff. 3–22–01.

Library References

Health ☞256.
Infants ☞17.
Westlaw Topic Nos. 198H, 211.

C.J.S. Adoption of Persons §§ 10 to 14, 41.
C.J.S. Hospitals § 18.
C.J.S. Infants §§ 6, 8 to 9.

Research References

Treatises and Practice Aids

Carlin, Baldwin's Ohio Prac. Merrick-Rippner Probate Law § 19:1, Legitimation--Statutory Provisions.

3111.72 Requirements of contract

The contract between the department of job and family services and a local hospital shall require all of the following:

(A) That the hospital provide a staff person to meet with each unmarried mother who gave birth in or en route to the hospital within twenty-four hours of the birth or before the mother is released from the hospital;

(B) That the staff person attempt to meet with the father of the unmarried mother's child if possible;

(C) That the staff person explain to the unmarried mother and the father, if he is present, the benefit to the child of establishing a parent and child relationship between the father and the child and the various proper procedures for establishing a parent and child relationship;

(D) That the staff person present to the unmarried mother and, if possible, the father, the pamphlet or statement regarding the rights and responsibilities of a natural parent that is prepared and provided by the department of job and family services pursuant to section 3111.32 of the Revised Code;

(E) That the staff person provide the mother and, if possible, the father, all forms and statements necessary to voluntarily establish a parent and child relationship, including, but not limited to, the acknowledgment of paternity affidavit prepared by the department of job and family services pursuant to section 3111.31 of the Revised Code;

(F) That the staff person, at the request of both the mother and father, help the mother and father complete any form or statement necessary to establish a parent and child relationship;

(G) That the hospital provide a notary public to notarize an acknowledgment of paternity affidavit signed by the mother and father;

(H) That the staff person present to an unmarried mother who is not participating in the Ohio works first program established under Chapter 5107. or receiving medical assistance under Chapter 5111. of the Revised Code an application for Title IV–D services;

(I) That the staff person forward any completed acknowledgment of paternity, no later than ten days after it is completed, to the office of child support in the department of job and family services;

(J) That the department of job and family services pay the hospital twenty dollars for every correctly signed and notarized acknowledgment of paternity affidavit from the hospital.
(2000 S 180, eff. 3–22–01)

Historical and Statutory Notes

Ed. Note: RC 3111.72 contains provisions analogous to portions of former 2301.357(B), repealed by 2000 S 180, eff. 3–22–01.

Library References

Health ☞256.
Infants ☞17.
Westlaw Topic Nos. 198H, 211.

C.J.S. Adoption of Persons §§ 10 to 14, 41.
C.J.S. Hospitals § 18.
C.J.S. Infants §§ 6, 8 to 9.

3111.73   Reports

Not later than July 1, 1998, and the first day of each July thereafter, the department of job and family services shall complete a report on the hospitals that have not entered into contracts described in this section. The department shall submit the report to the chairperson and ranking minority member of the committees of the house of representatives and senate with primary responsibility for issues concerning paternity establishment.
(2000 S 180, eff. 3–22–01)

Historical and Statutory Notes

Ed. Note: RC 3111.73 contains provisions analogous to former 2301.357(C), repealed by 2000 S 180, eff. 3–22–01.

3111.74 Requirements when presumed father is not man who signed or is attempting to sign acknowledgment

If the hospital knows or determines that a man is presumed under section 3111.03 of the Revised Code to be the father of a child and that the presumed father is not the man who signed or is attempting to sign an acknowledgment with respect to the child, the hospital shall take no further action with regard to the acknowledgment and shall not send the acknowledgment to the office of child support.

(2000 S 180, eff. 3–22–01)

Historical and Statutory Notes

Ed. Note: RC 3111.74 contains provisions analogous to former 2301.357(D), repealed by 2000 S 180, eff. 3–22–01.

PARENTAL SUPPORT

3111.77 Duty of parental support

A man who is presumed to be the natural father of a child pursuant to section 3111.03 of the Revised Code assumes the parental duty of support with respect to the child as provided in section 3103.031 of the Revised Code.

(2000 S 180, eff. 3–22–01)

Historical and Statutory Notes

Ed. Note: RC 3111.77 contains provisions analogous to former RC 3111.20(B), repealed by 2000 S 180, eff. 3–22–01.

Ohio Administrative Code References

Conducting the administrative support hearing, see
   OAC 5101:12–45–05.2

Research References

Encyclopedias

OH Jur. 3d Family Law § 863, Existence and Proof of Relationship.

Treatises and Practice Aids

Sowald & Morganstern, Baldwin's Ohio Practice Domestic Relations Law § 20:3, Statutory History--1992 Senate Bill 10, The "Poster Bill".

Carlin, Baldwin's Ohio Prac. Merrick-Rippner Probate Law § 19:1, Legitimation--Statutory Provisions.

Notes of Decisions

Discretion of court   2
Jurisdiction   3
Retroactive support   1

1. Retroactive support

Father waived his request for retroactive child support against mother in parentage action, where father had notice of emancipated child's petition for retroactive child support against mother, and father failed to assert any right to retroactive support. Elzey v. Springer (Ohio App. 12 Dist., Fayette,   03-22-2004)   No.   CA2003-04-005, 2004-Ohio-1373, 2004 WL 549805, Unreported. Children Out–of–wedlock ☞ 41

Order awarding father retroactive child support in parentage action was improper; emancipated nonmarital son, not the father, requested retroactive support, and thus support should be paid to emancipated son. Elzey v. Springer (Ohio App. 12 Dist., Fayette, 03-22-2004) No. CA2003-04-005, 2004-Ohio-1373, 2004 WL 549805, Unreported. Children Out–of–wedlock ☞ 67

2. Discretion of court

Trial court did not abuse discretion in ordering father to pay retroactive child support for nine-year-old child, even though laches barred mother's claim for support, where laches did not bar child's claim, father had waived his rights as a father by failing to timely assert them even though he suspected he was child's father, and father still had opportunity to be involved in child's life. (Per Evans, J., with two judges concurring in the judgment). State ex rel. Jackson County Child Support Enforcement Agency v. Long (Ohio App. 4 Dist., Jackson, 04-22-2004) No. 03CA1, 2004-Ohio-2184,

2004 WL 914640, Unreported. Children Out–of–wedlock ☞ 67

Juvenile court did not abuse its discretion in parentage action by calculating back child support owed for each year of child's life by use of worksheets with reference to applicable law for each given year, due to dramatic changes in parties' financial situations since child's birth. Seegert v. Zietlow (Ohio App. 8 Dist., 08-15-1994) 95 Ohio App.3d 451, 642 N.E.2d 697. Children Out–of–wedlock ☞ 67

3. Jurisdiction

Trial court had jurisdiction to hear and determine merits of nonmarital child's request for retroactive child support against mother in parentage action, even though child was emancipated; juvenile court had jurisdiction over a parentage action, and the court could consider a claim for support after it determined parentage. Elzey v. Springer (Ohio App. 12 Dist., Fayette, 03-22-2004) No. CA2003-04-005, 2004-Ohio-1373, 2004 WL 549805, Unreported. Children Out–of–wedlock ☞ 36

Juvenile Court lacked jurisdiction to order retroactive child support, in paternity proceedings, when the first claim for support was made after the child reached the age of majority and the duty to support had elapsed. Carnes v. Kemp (Ohio App. 3 Dist., Auglaize, 11-03-2003) No. 2-03-10, 2003-Ohio-5884, 2003 WL 22473582, Unreported, stay denied 101 Ohio St.3d 1419, 802 N.E.2d 152, 2004-Ohio-123, motion to certify allowed 101 Ohio St.3d 1465, 804 N.E.2d 39, 2004-Ohio-819, appeal allowed 101 Ohio St.3d 1466, 804 N.E.2d 40, 2004-Ohio-819, motion granted 103 Ohio St.3d 1419, 814 N.E.2d 63, 2004-Ohio-4504, reversed 104 Ohio St.3d 629, 821 N.E.2d 180, 2004-Ohio-7107. Children Out–of–wedlock ☞ 67

3111.78 Actions permitted to require man to pay support and provide for health care needs

A parent, guardian, or legal custodian of a child, the person with whom the child resides, or the child support enforcement agency of the county in which the child, parent, guardian, or legal custodian of the child resides may do the following to require a man to pay support and provide for the health care needs of the child if the man is presumed to be the natural father of the child under section 3111.03 of the Revised Code:

(A) If the presumption is not based on an acknowledgment of paternity, file a complaint pursuant to section 2151.231 of the Revised Code in the juvenile court or other court with jurisdiction under section 2101.022 or 2301.03 of the Revised Code of the county in which the child, parent, guardian, or legal custodian resides;

(B) Ask an administrative officer of a child support enforcement agency to issue an administrative order pursuant to section 3111.81 of the Revised Code;

(C) Contact a child support enforcement agency for assistance in obtaining an order for support and the provision of health care for the child.

(2000 S 180, eff. 3–22–01)

Historical and Statutory Notes

Ed. Note: RC 3111.78 contains provisions analogous to portions of former RC 3111.20(C), repealed by 2000 S 180, eff. 3–22–01.

Ohio Administrative Code References

Support order establishment process, see OAC 5101:12–45–05

Library References

Children Out-of-Wedlock ⟨⟩30, 34.
Westlaw Topic No. 76H.

C.J.S. Children Out-of-Wedlock §§ 47, 50, 71, 88 to 97.

Research References

Encyclopedias

OH Jur. 3d Family Law § 1016, Action for Support.

OH Jur. 3d Family Law § 1019, Child Support Action in Juvenile Court; Other Courts With Jurisdiction.

OH Jur. 3d Family Law § 1020, Request for Administrative Order.

OH Jur. 3d Family Law § 1021, Hearing on Request; Determination of Support.

Treatises and Practice Aids

Sowald & Morganstern, Baldwin's Ohio Practice Domestic Relations Law § 19:2, Jurisdiction Over Child Support.

Sowald & Morganstern, Baldwin's Ohio Practice Domestic Relations Law § 20:3, Statutory History--1992 Senate Bill 10, The "Poster Bill".

Sowald & Morganstern, Baldwin's Ohio Practice Domestic Relations Law § 22:7, Establishing Support Order.

Sowald & Morganstern, Baldwin's Ohio Practice Domestic Relations Law § 23:16, In-State Remedies--Determination of Support.

Carlin, Baldwin's Ohio Prac. Merrick-Rippner Probate Law § 110:34, Parentage Act--Administrative Support Orders.

Notes of Decisions

Legal custody   2
Personal bias or prejudice   1

----

1.   Personal bias or prejudice

Trial court's refusal to register administrative child support order by finding it invalid because the administrative hearing was not conducted by a detached magistrate was without basis; no one objected to the order, and there was no indication in the record or the transcript that administrative hearing officer was either biased, prejudiced, or unqualified for the position. Jefferson County Child Support

Enforcement Agency ex rel. Toma v. Harris (Ohio App. 7 Dist., Jefferson, 01-29-2003) No. 02JE22, 2003-Ohio-496, 2003 WL 220415, Unreported. Child Support ⟨⟩ 465

2.   Legal custody

Child support order could not be administratively set, nor adopted by the court, on behalf of a caretaker who did not have legal custody of child. Tuscarawas County CSEA v. Sanders (Ohio App. 5 Dist., Tuscarawas, 10-15-2003) No. 2003AP030020, 2003-Ohio-5624, 2003 WL 22400729, Unreported. Child Support ⟨⟩ 189

3111.80   Administrative hearings

If a request for issuance of an administrative support order is made under section 3111.29 or 3111.78 of the Revised Code or an administrative officer issues an administrative order determining the existence of a parent and child relationship under section 3111.46 of the Revised Code, the administrative officer shall schedule an administrative hearing to determine, in accordance with Chapters 3119. and 3121. of the Revised Code, the amount of child support any parent is required to pay, the method of payment of child support, and the method of providing for the child's health care.

The administrative officer shall send the mother and the father of the child notice of the date, time, place, and purpose of the administrative hearing. With respect to an administrative hearing scheduled pursuant to an administrative order determining, pursuant to section 3111.46 of the Revised Code, the existence of a parent and child relationship, the officer shall attach the notice of the administrative hearing to the order and send it in accordance with that section.   The Rules of Civil Procedure shall apply regarding the sending of the notice, except to the extent the civil rules, by their nature, are clearly inapplicable and except that references in the civil rules to the court or the clerk of the court shall be construed as being references to the child support enforcement agency or the administrative officer.

The hearing shall be held no later than sixty days after the request is made under section 3111.29 or 3111.78 of the Revised Code or an administrative officer issues an administrative order determining the existence of a parent and child relationship under section 3111.46 of the Revised Code.   The hearing shall not be held earlier than thirty days after the officer gives the mother and father notice of the hearing.

(2000 S 180, eff. 3–22–01)

Historical and Statutory Notes

Ed. Note: RC 3111.80 contains provisions analogous to former RC 3111.22(E)(1), and provisions analogous to portions of former RC 3111.20(D), both repealed by 2000 S 180, eff. 3–22–01.

Ohio Administrative Code References

Administrative paternity orders, see OAC 5101:12–40–20.2

Scheduling the administrative support hearing, see OAC 5101:12–45–05.1

Library References

Children Out-of-Wedlock ⇐30.
Westlaw Topic No. 76H.

C.J.S. Children Out-of-Wedlock §§ 47, 71, 94, 96 to 97.

Research References

Encyclopedias

OH Jur. 3d Family Law § 1021, Hearing on Request; Determination of Support.
OH Jur. 3d Family Law § 1022, Order for Support.

Forms

Ohio Forms Legal and Business § 28:5, Child Born as Result of Artificial Insemination.
Ohio Forms Legal and Business § 28:12, Consent to Artificial Insemination of Wife.

Treatises and Practice Aids

Sowald & Morganstern, Baldwin's Ohio Practice Domestic Relations Law § 3:4, Administrative Determination of Parentage--Acknowledgment, Support Order, and Birth Record.

Sowald & Morganstern, Baldwin's Ohio Practice Domestic Relations Law § 3:5, Administrative Determination of Parentage--No Acknowledgment and Support Order.
Sowald & Morganstern, Baldwin's Ohio Practice Domestic Relations Law § 20:3, Statutory History--1992 Senate Bill 10, The "Poster Bill".
Sowald & Morganstern, Baldwin's Ohio Practice Domestic Relations Law § 3:41, Effect of Judgment--Child Support--Administrative Support Order.
Carlin, Baldwin's Ohio Prac. Merrick-Rippner Probate Law § 110:34, Parentage Act--Administrative Support Orders.
Carlin, Baldwin's Ohio Prac. Merrick-Rippner Probate Law § 110:35, Civil Support Proceedings-- · Liability for Child Support.

3111.81   Administrative order for payment of support and provision for child's health care

After the hearing under section 3111.80 of the Revised Code is completed, the administrative officer may issue an administrative order for the payment of support and provision for the child's health care.   The order shall do all of the following:

(A) Require periodic payments of support that may vary in amount, except that, if it is in the best interest of the child, the administrative officer may order the purchase of an annuity in lieu of periodic payments of support if the purchase agreement provides that any remaining principal will be transferred to the ownership and control of the child on the child's attainment of the age of majority;

(B) Require the parents to provide for the health care needs of the child in accordance with sections 3119.29 to 3119.56 of the Revised Code;

(C) Include a notice that contains the information described in section 3111.84 of the Revised Code informing the mother and the father of the right to object to the order by bringing an action for the payment of support and provision of the child's health care under section 2151.231 of the Revised Code and the effect of a failure to timely bring the action. (2002 H 657, eff. 12–13–02; 2000 S 180, eff. 3–22–01)

Historical and Statutory Notes

Ed. Note: RC 3111.81 contains provisions analogous to former RC 3111.20(D)(1) and (2), and provisions analogous to former RC 3111.22(E)(1)(a) to (c), repealed by 2000 S 180, eff. 3–22–01.

Amendment Note: 2002 H 657 substituted "3119.29" for "3119.30" and "3119.56" for "3119.58" in division (B); and made other nonsubstantive changes.

Cross References

Acts in contempt of court, see 2705.02

Ohio Administrative Code References

Administrative support order, see OAC 5101:12–45–05.3

Library References

Children Out-of-Wedlock ⬧30.
Westlaw Topic No. 76H.

C.J.S. Children Out-of-Wedlock §§ 47, 71, 94, 96 to 97.

Research References

Encyclopedias

OH Jur. 3d Contempt § 19, Statutory List of Contemptuous Acts.
OH Jur. 3d Family Law § 1016, Action for Support.
OH Jur. 3d Family Law § 1020, Request for Administrative Order.
OH Jur. 3d Family Law § 1022, Order for Support.
OH Jur. 3d Family Law § 1025, Hearing; Order.

Treatises and Practice Aids

Sowald & Morganstern, Baldwin's Ohio Practice Domestic Relations Law § 20:3, Statutory History--1992 Senate Bill 10, The "Poster Bill".
Sowald & Morganstern, Baldwin's Ohio Practice Domestic Relations Law § 22:7, Establishing Support Order.

Sowald & Morganstern, Baldwin's Ohio Practice Domestic Relations Law § 23:16, In-State Remedies--Determination of Support.
Carlin, Baldwin's Ohio Prac. Merrick-Rippner Probate Law § 19:2, Legitimation--Procedure--Acknowledgment of Paternity.
Carlin, Baldwin's Ohio Prac. Merrick-Rippner Probate Law § 110:13, Jurisdiction Over Child Custody Matters--Determination of Custody.
Carlin, Baldwin's Ohio Prac. Merrick-Rippner Probate Law § 110:20, Parentage Act--Jurisdiction and Venue.
Carlin, Baldwin's Ohio Prac. Merrick-Rippner Probate Law § 110:29, Parentage Act--Judgment Determining Existence of Parent-Child Relationship.
Carlin, Baldwin's Ohio Prac. Merrick-Rippner Probate Law § 110:34, Parentage Act--Administrative Support Orders.

Notes of Decisions

In general   1

1. In general

County child support enforcement agency did not have authority to administratively create a child support order where none previously existed, and thus, trial court erred as a matter of law when it affirmed agency's findings establishing a child support obligation against divorced mother. Rieger v. Rieger (Ohio App. 9 Dist., Lorain, 12-18-2002) No. 02CA008035, 2002-Ohio-6991, 2002 WL 31828741, Unreported. Child Support ⬧ 189

Pursuant to RC 3111.80–.81, an administrative child support order issued by an administrative officer of a child support enforcement agency may, regardless of the marital status and living arrangements of a child's parents, establish the amount of child support an emancipated woman who is the biological mother of a child is required to pay when the child resides with a third party who is the legal custodian of the child. OAG 06–002.

3111.82   Party may raise existence or nonexistence of relationship

A party to a request made under section 3111.78 of the Revised Code for an administrative support order may raise the issue of the existence or nonexistence of a parent and child relationship.

(2000 S 180, eff. 3–22–01)

Historical and Statutory Notes

Ed. Note: RC 3111.82 contains provisions analogous to portions of former RC 3111.20(C) and former RC 3111.211(A), both repealed by 2000 S 180, eff. 3–22–01.

Ohio Administrative Code References

Conducting the administrative support hearing, see
  OAC 5101:12–45–05.2

Library References

Children Out-of-Wedlock ⚮30.
Westlaw Topic No. 76H.

C.J.S. Children Out-of-Wedlock §§ 47, 71, 94, 96 to 97.

Research References

Encyclopedias

OH Jur. 3d Family Law § 1016, Action for Support.

Treatises and Practice Aids

Sowald & Morganstern, Baldwin's Ohio Practice Domestic Relations Law § 19:3, Support Obligations--In General.

Sowald & Morganstern, Baldwin's Ohio Practice Domestic Relations Law § 3:13, Judicial Parentage Action--Presumptions of Parentage--Creating.

3111.821   Determination of existence of parent and child relationship

If a request is made pursuant to section 3111.78 of the Revised Code for an administrative support order and the issue of the existence or nonexistence of a parent and child relationship is raised, the administrative officer shall treat the request as a request made pursuant to section 3111.38 of the Revised Code and determine the issue in accordance with that section. If the request made under section 3111.78 of the Revised Code is made based on an acknowledgment of paternity that has not become final, the administrative officer shall promptly notify the office of child support in the department of job and family services when the officer issues an order determining the existence or nonexistence of a parent and child relationship with respect to the child who is the subject of the acknowledgment of paternity. On receipt of the notice by the office, the acknowledgment of paternity shall be considered rescinded.

If the parties do not raise the issue of the existence or nonexistence of a parent and child relationship pursuant to the request made under section 3111.78 of the Revised Code and an administrative order is issued pursuant to section 3111.81 of the Revised Code prior to the date the acknowledgment of paternity becomes final, the acknowledgment shall be considered final as of the date of the issuance of the order. An administrative order issued pursuant to section 3111.81 of the Revised Code shall not affect an acknowledgment that becomes final prior to the issuance of the order.

(2000 S 180, eff. 3–22–01)

Historical and Statutory Notes

Ed. Note: RC 3111.821 contains provisions analogous to portions of former RC 3111.20(C) and former RC 3111.211(A), both repealed by 2000 S 180, eff. 3–22–01.

Cross References

Action for child support order, see 2151.231
Parental duty of support, see 3103.031

Ohio Administrative Code References

Conducting the administrative support hearing, see OAC 5101:12–45–05.2

Support order establishment process, see OAC 5101:12–45–05

Library References

Children Out-of-Wedlock ⬤30.
Westlaw Topic No. 76H.

C.J.S. Children Out-of-Wedlock §§ 47, 71, 94, 96 to 97.

Research References

Encyclopedias

OH Jur. 3d Family Law § 944, Statutory Presumptions.

OH Jur. 3d Family Law § 1011, Assumption of Parental Duty of Support.

OH Jur. 3d Family Law § 1016, Action for Support.

OH Jur. 3d Family Law § 1053, by Child's Relatives.

OH Jur. 3d Family Law § 1171, Visitation Rights Where Mother is Unmarried.

Forms

Ohio Jurisprudence Pleading and Practice Forms § 96:9, Putative Father Registry.

Ohio Jurisprudence Pleading and Practice Forms § 111:6, Presumptions.

Ohio Jurisprudence Pleading and Practice Forms § 96:11, Consent Required.

Treatises and Practice Aids

Sowald & Morganstern, Baldwin's Ohio Practice Domestic Relations Law § 21:2, Parenting Time--Establishing Visitation Order.

Sowald & Morganstern, Baldwin's Ohio Practice Domestic Relations Law § 3:13, Judicial Parentage Action--Presumptions of Parentage--Creating.

Sowald & Morganstern, Baldwin's Ohio Practice Domestic Relations Law § 3:30, Res Judicata and Vacation of Parentage Orders.

Sowald & Morganstern, Baldwin's Ohio Practice Domestic Relations Law § 3:31, Relief from Paternity or Support Judgment, Under RC 3119.961.

Sowald & Morganstern, Baldwin's Ohio Practice Domestic Relations Law § 3:52, Complaint to Establish Father-Child Relationship--By Mother--Form.

Carlin, Baldwin's Ohio Prac. Merrick-Rippner Probate Law § 19:1, Legitimation--Statutory Provisions.

Carlin, Baldwin's Ohio Prac. Merrick-Rippner Probate Law § 19:2, Legitimation--Procedure--Acknowledgment of Paternity.

Carlin, Baldwin's Ohio Prac. Merrick-Rippner Probate Law § 19:7, Uniform Parentage Act--Presumptions.

Carlin, Baldwin's Ohio Prac. Merrick-Rippner Probate Law § 110:3, Criminal Jurisdiction--Proceedings for Nonsupport.

Carlin, Baldwin's Ohio Prac. Merrick-Rippner Probate Law § 99:30, Statutorily Required Consent.

Carlin, Baldwin's Ohio Prac. Merrick-Rippner Probate Law § 99:32, Parties Giving Consent--Putative Father.

Carlin, Baldwin's Ohio Prac. Merrick-Rippner Probate Law § 99:34, Parties Giving Consent--Agency.

Carlin, Baldwin's Ohio Prac. Merrick-Rippner Probate Law § 99:49, Interlocutory and Final Orders.

Carlin, Baldwin's Ohio Prac. Merrick-Rippner Probate Law § 110:20, Parentage Act--Jurisdiction and Venue.

Carlin, Baldwin's Ohio Prac. Merrick-Rippner Probate Law § 110:22, Parentage Act--Presumption of Paternity.

Carlin, Baldwin's Ohio Prac. Merrick-Rippner Probate Law § 110:26, Parentage Act--Applicability of Civil Rules to Paternity Proceedings.

Carlin, Baldwin's Ohio Prac. Merrick-Rippner Probate Law § 110:31, Parentage Act--Continuing Jurisdiction to Modify or Revoke Judgment.

Carlin, Baldwin's Ohio Prac. Merrick-Rippner Probate Law § 110:34, Parentage Act--Administrative Support Orders.

Carlin, Baldwin's Ohio Prac. Merrick-Rippner Probate Law § 110:35, Civil Support Proceedings--Liability for Child Support.

3111.83 Registration of order

An administrative officer who issues an administrative support order for the payment of support and provision for a child's health care shall register the order or cause the order to be registered in the system established under section 3111.831 of the Revised Code or with the clerk of the court of appropriate jurisdiction of the county served by the administrative officer's child support enforcement agency.

(2000 S 180, eff. 3–22–01)

Ohio Administrative Code References

Administrative support order, see OAC
5101:12–45–05.3

Library References

Children Out-of-Wedlock ☜30.
Westlaw Topic No. 76H.

C.J.S. Children Out-of-Wedlock §§ 47, 71, 94, 96 to
97.

Research References

Treatises and Practice Aids

Sowald & Morganstern, Baldwin's Ohio Practice
Domestic Relations Law § 22:14, Support Collection and Distribution.

3111.831 Development of system and procedure for safekeeping and retrieval of orders

Each child support enforcement agency may develop a system and procedure for the
organized safekeeping and retrieval of administrative support orders for the payment of
support and provision for the child's health care.

(2000 S 180, eff. 3–22–01)

Ohio Administrative Code References

Administrative support order, see OAC
5101:12–45–05.3

Library References

Infants ☜17.
Westlaw Topic No. 211.

C.J.S. Adoption of Persons §§ 10 to 14, 41.
C.J.S. Infants §§ 6, 8 to 9.

Research References

Treatises and Practice Aids

Sowald & Morganstern, Baldwin's Ohio Practice
Domestic Relations Law § 22:14, Support Collection and Distribution.

3111.832 Fee not to be charged

If an administrative support order is registered with the clerk of a court of appropriate
jurisdiction, the clerk shall not charge a fee for the registration and shall assign the order a case
number.

(2000 S 180, eff. 3–22–01)

Ohio Administrative Code References

Administrative support order, see OAC
5101:12–45–05.3

Library References

Clerks of Courts ☜18, 67.
Westlaw Topic No. 79.
C.J.S. Courts § 340.

Research References

Treatises and Practice Aids

Sowald & Morganstern, Baldwin's Ohio Practice
  Domestic Relations Law § 22:14, Support Collection and Distribution.

3111.84 Action for payment of support and provision for child's health care

The mother or father of a child who is the subject of an administrative support order may object to the order by bringing an action for the payment of support and provision for the child's health care under section 2151.231 of the Revised Code in the juvenile court or other court with jurisdiction under section 2101.022 or 2301.03 of the Revised Code of the county in which the child support enforcement agency that employs the administrative officer is located. The action shall be brought not later than thirty days after the date of the issuance of the administrative support order. If neither the mother nor the father brings an action for the payment of support and provision for the child's health care within that thirty-day period, the administrative support order is final and enforceable by a court and may be modified only as provided in Chapters 3119., 3121., and 3123. of the Revised Code.

(2000 S 180, eff. 3–22–01)

Ohio Administrative Code References

Administrative support order, see OAC 5101:12–45–05.3

Objecting to the administrative support order, see OAC 5101:12–45–05.4

Library References

Children Out-of-Wedlock ⬤30, 34, 38.
Westlaw Topic No. 76H.

C.J.S. Children Out-of-Wedlock §§ 47, 49 to 50, 71, 84 to 85, 88 to 97.

Research References

Encyclopedias

OH Jur. 3d Family Law § 1022, Order for Support.
OH Jur. 3d Family Law § 1023, Objection to Administrative Order.

Treatises and Practice Aids

Sowald & Morganstern, Baldwin's Ohio Practice
  Domestic Relations Law § 20:3, Statutory Histo-
  ry--1992 Senate Bill 10, The "Poster Bill".
Sowald & Morganstern, Baldwin's Ohio Practice
  Domestic Relations Law § 22:4, Establishing
  Parentage.

Sowald & Morganstern, Baldwin's Ohio Practice
  Domestic Relations Law § 22:7, Establishing
  Support Order.
Sowald & Morganstern, Baldwin's Ohio Practice
  Domestic Relations Law § 23:16, In-State Reme-
  dies--Determination of Support.
Carlin, Baldwin's Ohio Prac. Merrick-Rippner Pro-
  bate Law § 110:34, Parentage Act--Administra-
  tive Support Orders.

3111.85 Effect of support orders issued under former R.C. 3111.21 prior to January 1, 1998

An administrative support order issued pursuant to former section 3111.21 of the Revised Code prior to January 1, 1998, that is in effect on the effective date of this section shall remain in effect on and after the effective date of this section and shall be considered an administrative support order issued pursuant to section 3111.81 of the Revised Code for all purposes.

(2000 S 180, eff. 3–22–01)

Historical and Statutory Notes

Ed. Note: RC 3111.85 contains provisions analogous to former RC 3111.22(H), repealed by 2000 S 180, eff. 3–22–01.

Cross References

Parental duty of support, see 3103.031

Library References

Children Out-of-Wedlock ⚖31.
Westlaw Topic No. 76H.
C.J.S. Children Out-of-Wedlock §§ 47, 72.

Research References

Encyclopedias

OH Jur. 3d Actions § 10, Civil or Criminal.
OH Jur. 3d Family Law § 1011, Assumption of Parental Duty of Support.

Treatises and Practice Aids

Carlin, Baldwin's Ohio Prac. Merrick-Rippner Probate Law § 18:2, Inheritance Rights of Illegitimate Child--Statutory Provisions.
Carlin, Baldwin's Ohio Prac. Merrick-Rippner Probate Law § 19:1, Legitimation--Statutory Provisions.
Carlin, Baldwin's Ohio Prac. Merrick-Rippner Probate Law § 19:4, Legitimation--Historical Provisions.

Carlin, Baldwin's Ohio Prac. Merrick-Rippner Probate Law § 19:10, Uniform Parentage Act--Procedure in Action to Determine Father-Child Relationship.
Carlin, Baldwin's Ohio Prac. Merrick-Rippner Probate Law § 99:31, Parties Giving Consent--Biological Parents.
Carlin, Baldwin's Ohio Prac. Merrick-Rippner Probate Law § 99:32, Parties Giving Consent--Putative Father.
Carlin, Baldwin's Ohio Prac. Merrick-Rippner Probate Law § 110:13, Jurisdiction Over Child Custody Matters--Determination of Custody.
Carlin, Baldwin's Ohio Prac. Merrick-Rippner Probate Law § 110:19, Parentage Act--Effect.

NON–SPOUSAL ARTIFICIAL INSEMINATION

3111.88   Definitions

As used in sections 3111.88 to 3111.96 of the Revised Code:

(A) "Artificial insemination" means the introduction of semen into the vagina, cervical canal, or uterus through instruments or other artificial means.

(B) "Donor" means a man who supplies semen for a non-spousal artificial insemination.

(C) "Non–spousal artificial insemination" means an artificial insemination of a woman with the semen of a man who is not her husband.

(D) "Physician" means a person who is licensed pursuant to Chapter 4731. of the Revised Code to practice medicine or surgery or osteopathic medicine or surgery in this state.

(E) "Recipient" means a woman who has been artificially inseminated with the semen of a donor.

(2000 S 180, eff. 3–22–01)

Historical and Statutory Notes

Ed. Note: 3111.88 is former 3111.30, amended and recodified by 2000 S 180, eff. 3–22–01; 1986 H 476, eff. 9–24–86.

Amendment Note: 2000 S 180 substituted "3111.88" for "3111.30" and "3111.96" for "3111.38" in the first sentence of the section.

Research References

Forms

Ohio Jurisprudence Pleading and Practice Forms § 111:15, Definitions.

Treatises and Practice Aids

Sowald & Morganstern, Baldwin's Ohio Practice Domestic Relations Law § 3:31, Relief from Paternity or Support Judgment, Under RC 3119.961.

Carlin, Baldwin's Ohio Prac. Merrick-Rippner Probate Law § 18:2, Inheritance Rights of Illegitimate Child--Statutory Provisions.
Carlin, Baldwin's Ohio Prac. Merrick-Rippner Probate Law § 19:13, Uniform Parentage Act--Nonspousal Artificial Insemination; Embryo Donation.
Carlin, Baldwin's Ohio Prac. Merrick-Rippner Probate Law § 110:19, Parentage Act--Effect.

Carlin, Baldwin's Ohio Prac. Merrick-Rippner Probate Law § 110:22, Parentage Act--Presumption of Paternity.

Carlin, Baldwin's Ohio Prac. Merrick-Rippner Probate Law § 110:31, Parentage Act--Continuing Jurisdiction to Modify or Revoke Judgment.

Carlin, Baldwin's Ohio Prac. Merrick-Rippner Probate Law § 110:33, Nonspousal Artificial Insemination and Embryo Donation.

Law Review and Journal Commentaries

Artificial insemination: In the child's best interest? 5 Alb L J Sci & Tech 321 (1996).

Surrogate Parenting: What We Can Learn From Our British Counterparts, Note. 39 Case W Res L Rev 217 (1988–89).

Notes of Decisions

Artificial insemination   1
Paternity action by donor   2

1. Artificial insemination

Even if artificial insemination statute establishing legal relationship between donor and mother applied, statute was unconstitutional as applied to donor and child insofar as it could be read to absolutely extinguish donor's efforts to assert rights and responsibilities of being father in case in which mother had solicited participation of donor, who was known to her, and donor and mother agreed that there would be relationship between donor and child. C.O. v. W.S. (Ohio Com.Pl., 03-01-1994) 64 Ohio Misc.2d 9, 639 N.E.2d 523   Children Out-of–wedlock ☞ 15

2. Paternity action by donor

Failure to comply with medical requirements of artificial insemination statutes would prevent mother from invoking nonspousal artificial insemination statute to obtain dismissal of sperm donor's complaint to determine paternity, custody, support, and visitation. C.O. v. W.S. (Ohio Com.Pl., 03-01-1994) 64 Ohio Misc.2d 9, 639 N.E.2d 523   Children Out-of–wedlock ☞ 15

Artificial insemination statute establishing legal relationship between donor and mother would not apply to prevent paternity adjudication where unmarried woman solicited participation of donor, who was known to her, and where donor and woman agreed that there would be relationship between donor and child. C.O. v. W.S. (Ohio Com.Pl., 03-01-1994) 64 Ohio Misc.2d 9, 639 N.E.2d 523   Children Out-of–wedlock ☞ 15

3111.89   Sections applicable to non-spousal artificial insemination

Sections 3111.88 to 3111.96 of the Revised Code deal with non-spousal artificial insemination for the purpose of impregnating a woman so that she can bear a child that she intends to raise as her child. These sections do not deal with the artificial insemination of a wife with the semen of her husband or with surrogate motherhood.

(2000 S 180, eff. 3–22–01)

Historical and Statutory Notes

Ed. Note: 3111.89 is former 3111.31, amended and recodified by 2000 S 180, eff. 3–22–01; 1986 H 476, eff. 9–24–86.

Amendment Note: 2000 S 180 substituted "3111.88" for "3111.30" and "3111.96" for "3111.38" in the first sentence of the section.

Library References

Children Out-of-Wedlock ☞1.
Westlaw Topic No. 76II.
C.J.S. Children Out-of-Wedlock §§ 1 to 8.

Research References

Forms

Ohio Forms Legal and Business § 28:5, Child Born as Result of Artificial Insemination.

Treatises and Practice Aids

Sowald & Morganstern, Baldwin's Ohio Practice Domestic Relations Law § 3:50, Related Issues--Artificial Insemination and Surrogate Mothers.

Carlin, Baldwin's Ohio Prac. Merrick-Rippner Probate Law § 110:33, Nonspousal Artificial Insemination and Embryo Donation.

Law Review and Journal Commentaries

Belsito v Clark: Ohio's Battle with "Motherhood," Dawn Wenk. 28 U Tol L Rev 247 (Fall 1996).

3111.90 Supervision by physician

A non-spousal artificial insemination shall be performed by a physician or a person who is under the supervision and control of a physician. Supervision requires the availability of a physician for consultation and direction, but does not necessarily require the personal presence of the physician who is providing the supervision.

(2000 S 180, eff. 3–22–01)

Historical and Statutory Notes

Ed. Note: 3111.90 is former 3111.32, recodified by 2000 S 180, eff. 3–22–01; 1986 H 476, eff. 9–24–86.

Library References

Health ☞192.
Westlaw Topic No. 198H.

C.J.S. Physicians, Surgeons, and Other Health Care Providers §§ 71 to 73.

Research References

Forms

Treatises and Practice Aids

Ohio Jurisprudence Pleading and Practice Forms § 111:16, Medical History and Examination of Donor.

Carlin, Baldwin's Ohio Prac. Merrick-Rippner Probate Law § 110:33, Nonspousal Artificial Insemination and Embryo Donation.

3111.91   Fresh semen; frozen semen; medical history of donor; laboratory studies

(A) In a non-spousal artificial insemination, fresh or frozen semen may be used, provided that the requirements of division (B) of this section are satisfied.

(B)(1) A physician, physician assistant, clinical nurse specialist, certified nurse practitioner, certified nurse-midwife, or person under the supervision and control of a physician may use fresh semen for purposes of a non-spousal artificial insemination, only if within one year prior to the supplying of the semen, all of the following occurred:

(a) A complete medical history of the donor, including, but not limited to, any available genetic history of the donor, was obtained by a physician, a physician assistant, a clinical nurse specialist, or a certified nurse practitioner.

(b) The donor had a physical examination by a physician, a physician assistant, a clinical nurse specialist, or a certified nurse practitioner.

(c) The donor was tested for blood type and RH factor.

(2) A physician, physician assistant, clinical nurse specialist, certified nurse practitioner, certified nurse-midwife, or person under the supervision and control of a physician may use frozen semen for purposes of a non-spousal artificial insemination only if all the following apply:

(a) The requirements set forth in division (B)(1) of this section are satisfied;

(b) In conjunction with the supplying of the semen, the semen or blood of the donor was the subject of laboratory studies that the physician involved in the non-spousal artificial insemination considers appropriate. The laboratory studies may include, but are not limited to, venereal disease research laboratories, karotyping, GC culture, cytomegalo, hepatitis, kemzyme, Tay–Sachs, sickle-cell, ureaplasma, HLTV–III, and chlamydia.

(c) The physician involved in the non-spousal artificial insemination determines that the results of the laboratory studies are acceptable results.

(3) Any written documentation of a physical examination conducted pursuant to division (B)(1)(b) of this section shall be completed by the individual who conducted the examination.

(2002 S 245, eff. 3–31–03; 2000 S 180, eff. 3–22–01)

Historical and Statutory Notes

Ed. Note: 3111.91 is former 3111.33, recodified by 2000 S 180, eff. 3–22–01; 1986 H 476, eff. 9–24–86.

Amendment Note: 2002 S 245 added ", physician assistant, clinical nurse specialist, certified nurse practitioner, certified nurse-midwife," to division (B)(2); added division (B)(3); and rewrote division (B)(1), which prior thereto read:

"(B)(1) A physician or person under the supervision and control of a physician may use fresh semen for purposes of a non-spousal artificial insemination, only if within one year prior to the supplying of the semen, a complete medical history of the donor, including, but not limited to, any available genetic history of the donor, was obtained by a physician, the donor had a physical examination by a physician, and the donor was tested for blood type and RH factor."

Library References

Health ☞192.
Westlaw Topic No. 198H.

C.J.S. Physicians, Surgeons, and Other Health Care Providers §§ 71 to 73.

Research References

Forms

Ohio Jurisprudence Pleading and Practice Forms § 111:16, Medical History and Examination of Donor.

Treatises and Practice Aids

Carlin, Baldwin's Ohio Prac. Merrick-Rippner Probate Law § 110:33, Nonspousal Artificial Insemination and Embryo Donation.

Law Review and Journal Commentaries

Artificial insemination: In the child's best interest? 5 Alb L J Sci & Tech 321 (1996).

Federal Regulation of Artificial Insemination Donor Screening Practices: An Opportunity for Law to Co–Evolve with Medicine, Comment. 96 Dick L Rev 37 (Fall 1991).

3111.92   Consents to non-spousal insemination of married woman

The non-spousal artificial insemination of a married woman may occur only if both she and her husband sign a written consent to the artificial insemination as described in section 3111.93 of the Revised Code.

(2000 S 180, eff. 3–22–01)

Historical and Statutory Notes

Ed. Note: 3111.92 is former 3111.34, amended and recodified by 2000 S 180, eff. 3–22–01; 1986 H 476, eff. 9–24–86.

Amendment Note: 2000 S 180 substituted "3111.93" for "3111.35".

Library References

Health ☞905.
Westlaw Topic No. 198H.
C.J.S. Physicians, Surgeons, and Other Health Care Providers §§ 118 to 120.

C.J.S. Right to Die §§ 47, 49, 52.

Research References

Encyclopedias

OH Jur. 3d Family Law § 995, Consent.

Forms

Ohio Forms Legal and Business § 28:5, Child Born as Result of Artificial Insemination.

Ohio Forms Legal and Business § 28:12, Consent to Artificial Insemination of Wife.
Ohio Jurisprudence Pleading and Practice Forms § 111:17, Confidentiality.

Treatises and Practice Aids

Carlin, Baldwin's Ohio Prac. Merrick-Rippner Probate Law § 110:33, Nonspousal Artificial Insemination and Embryo Donation.

Notes of Decisions

Consent 1

───────

1. Consent

Although physician should have obtained ex-husband's written consent to ex-wife's artificial insemination by donor (AID) prior to proceeding with insemination, physician's failure to do so did not affect legal rights of children subsequently born to ex-wife as result of procedure or legal rights and obligations of ex-husband. Jackson v. Jackson (Ohio App. 2 Dist., 05-26-2000) 137 Ohio App.3d 782, 739 N.E.2d 1203. Children Out–of–wedlock ☞ 15; Parent And Child ☞ 20

Trial court's conclusion that ex-husband consented to his ex-wife's initial artificial insemination by donor (AID) procedure and did not withdraw his consent prior to ex-wife's second AID procedure, which resulted in birth of twins, was not against manifest weight of the evidence; ex–husband's co-worker testified that ex-wife told him that ex-husband was not in favor of pregnancy, but co-worker could not remember if this conversation took place before or after ex-wife became pregnant, other co-worker testified that ex-wife never made a specific statement that her ex-husband did not want children, and witness testified that ex-husband had consented in the past to AID. Jackson v. Jackson (Ohio App. 2 Dist., 05-26-2000) 137 Ohio App.3d 782, 739 N.E.2d 1203. Parent And Child ☞ 20

Although statute requiring a physician to obtain husband's consent prior to performing artificial insemination by nonspousal donor provided no remedy for its breach, husband could maintain claim against physician for fraud. Kerns v. Schmidt (Ohio App. 10 Dist., 06-09-1994) 94 Ohio App.3d 601, 641 N.E.2d 280. Fraud ☞ 31

Husband stated claim of fraud, independent of any claim of malpractice, against physician by asserting that physician performed artificial insemination by nonspousal donor on his wife without first obtaining his consent; husband alleged that physician assured him there would be no artificial insemination without his consent, that physician breached statutory duty to refrain from performing nonspousal artificial insemination without husband's consent, that physician knew he needed to obtain such consent yet disregarded that requirement with intent to mislead husband, that husband justifiably relied upon physician's assurances, and that husband was damaged by physician's conduct. Kerns v. Schmidt (Ohio App. 10 Dist., 06-09-1994) 94 Ohio App.3d 601, 641 N.E.2d 280. Fraud ☞ 31

Claim that physician was negligent per se for performing artificial insemination by nonspousal donor on his wife without first obtaining statutorily required consent of husband was subject to statute of limitations for medical claim. Kerns v. Schmidt (Ohio App. 10 Dist., 06-09-1994) 94 Ohio App.3d 601, 641 N.E.2d 280. Health ☞ 923

3111.93 Recipient information and statements; date of insemination to be recorded

(A) Prior to a non-spousal artificial insemination, the physician associated with it shall do the following:

(1) Obtain the written consent of the recipient on a form that the physician shall provide. The written consent shall contain all of the following:

(a) The name and address of the recipient and, if married, her husband;

(b) The name of the physician;

(c) The proposed location of the performance of the artificial insemination;

(d) A statement that the recipient and, if married, her husband consent to the artificial insemination;

(e) If desired, a statement that the recipient and, if married, her husband consent to more than one artificial insemination if necessary;

(f) A statement that the donor shall not be advised by the physician or another person performing the artificial insemination as to the identity of the recipient or, if married, her husband and that the recipient and, if married, her husband shall not be advised by the physician or another person performing the artificial insemination as to the identity of the donor;

(g) A statement that the physician is to obtain necessary semen from a donor and, subject to any agreed upon provision as described in division (A)(1)(n) of this section, that the recipient and, if married, her husband shall rely upon the judgment and discretion of the physician in this regard;

(h) A statement that the recipient and, if married, her husband understand that the physician cannot be responsible for the physical or mental characteristics of any child resulting from the artificial insemination;

(i) A statement that there is no guarantee that the recipient will become pregnant as a result of the artificial insemination;

(j) A statement that the artificial insemination shall occur in compliance with sections 3111.88 to 3111.96 of the Revised Code;

(k) A brief summary of the paternity consequences of the artificial insemination as set forth in section 3111.95 of the Revised Code;

(*l*) The signature of the recipient and, if married, her husband;

(m) If agreed to, a statement that the artificial insemination will be performed by a person who is under the supervision and control of the physician;

(n) Any other provision that the physician, the recipient, and, if married, her husband agree to include.

(2) Upon request, provide the recipient and, if married, her husband with the following information to the extent the physician has knowledge of it:

(a) The medical history of the donor, including, but not limited to, any available genetic history of the donor and persons related to him by consanguinity, the blood type of the donor, and whether he has an RH factor;

(b) The race, eye and hair color, age, height, and weight of the donor;

(c) The educational attainment and talents of the donor;

(d) The religious background of the donor;

(e) Any other information that the donor has indicated may be disclosed.

(B) After each non-spousal artificial insemination of a woman, the physician associated with it shall note the date of the artificial insemination in the physician's records pertaining to the woman and the artificial insemination, and retain this information as provided in section 3111.94 of the Revised Code.

(2000 S 180, eff. 3–22–01)

Historical and Statutory Notes

Ed. Note: 3111.93 is former 3111.35, amended and recodified by 2000 S 180, eff. 3–22–01; 1986 H 476, eff. 9–24–86.

Amendment Note: 2000 S 180 substituted "3111.88" for "3111.30" and "3111.96" for "3111.38" in division (A)(1)(j); substituted "3111.95" for "3111.37" in division (A)(1)(k); substituted "3111.94" for "3111.36" in division (B); and made changes to reflect gender neutral language.

Library References

Health ⚕905 to 906.
Westlaw Topic No. 198H.
C.J.S. Physicians, Surgeons, and Other Health Care
    Providers §§ 118 to 120.

C.J.S. Right to Die §§ 47, 49, 52.

Research References

Encyclopedias

OH Jur. 3d Family Law § 995, Consent.

Forms

Ohio Forms Legal and Business § 28:12, Consent
    to Artificial Insemination of Wife.

Ohio Jurisprudence Pleading and Practice Forms
    § 111:17, Confidentiality.

Treatises and Practice Aids

Carlin, Baldwin's Ohio Prac. Merrick-Rippner Probate Law § 110:33, Nonspousal Artificial Insemination and Embryo Donation.

3111.94 Physician's files; confidential information; donor information; action for file inspection

(A) The physician who is associated with a non-spousal artificial insemination shall place the written consent obtained pursuant to division (A)(1) of section 3111.93 of the Revised Code, information provided to the recipient and, if married, her husband pursuant to division (A)(2) of that section, other information concerning the donor that the physician possesses, and other matters concerning the artificial insemination in a file that shall bear the name of the recipient. This file shall be retained by the physician in the physician's office separate from any regular medical chart of the recipient, and shall be confidential, except as provided in divisions (B) and (C) of this section. This file is not a public record under section 149.43 of the Revised Code.

(B) The written consent form and information provided to the recipient and, if married, her husband pursuant to division (A)(2) of section 3111.93 of the Revised Code shall be open to inspection only until the child born as the result of the non-spousal artificial insemination is twenty-one years of age, and only to the recipient or, if married, her husband upon request to the physician.

(C) Information pertaining to the donor that was not provided the recipient and, if married, her husband pursuant to division (A)(2) of section 3111.93 of the Revised Code and that the physician possesses shall be kept in the file pertaining to the non-spousal artificial insemination for at least five years from the date of the artificial insemination. At the expiration of this period, the physician may destroy such information or retain it in the file.

The physician shall not make this information available for inspection by any person during the five-year period or, if the physician retains the information after the expiration of that period, at any other time, unless the following apply:

(1) A child is born as a result of the artificial insemination, an action is filed by the recipient, her husband if she is married, or a guardian of the child in the domestic relations division or, if there is no domestic relations division, the general division of the court of common pleas of the county in which the office of the physician is located, the child is not twenty-one years of age or older, and the court pursuant to division (C)(2) of this section issues an order authorizing the inspection of specified types of information by the recipient, husband, or guardian;

(2) Prior to issuing an order authorizing an inspection of information, the court shall determine, by clear and convincing evidence, that the information that the recipient, husband, or guardian wishes to inspect is necessary for or helpful in the medical treatment of the child born as a result of the artificial insemination, and shall determine which types of information in the file are germane to the medical treatment and are to be made available for inspection by the recipient, husband, or guardian in that regard. An order only shall authorize the inspection of information germane to the medical treatment of the child.

(2000 S 180, eff. 3–22–01)

Historical and Statutory Notes

Ed. Note: 3111.94 is former 3111.36, amended and recodified by 2000 S 180, eff. 3–22–01; 1986 H 476, eff. 9–24–86.

Amendment Note: 2000 S 180 substituted "3111.93" for "3111.35" in divisions (A), (B), and (C); and made changes to reflect gender neutral language.

Library References

Health ☞196.
Westlaw Topic No. 198H.

C.J.S. Physicians, Surgeons, and Other Health Care Providers §§ 71, 77.

Research References

Encyclopedias

OH Jur. 3d Family Law § 996, Retention of Information.

Forms

Ohio Forms Legal and Business § 28:12, Consent to Artificial Insemination of Wife.

Ohio Jurisprudence Pleading and Practice Forms
§ 111:17, Confidentiality.

Treatises and Practice Aids

Carlin, Baldwin's Ohio Prac. Merrick-Rippner Probate Law § 110:33, Nonspousal Artificial Insemination and Embryo Donation.

3111.95   Husband rather than donor regarded as natural father of child

(A) If a married woman is the subject of a non-spousal artificial insemination and if her husband consented to the artificial insemination, the husband shall be treated in law and regarded as the natural father of a child conceived as a result of the artificial insemination, and a child so conceived shall be treated in law and regarded as the natural child of the husband. A presumption that arises under division (A)(1) or (2) of section 3111.03 of the Revised Code is conclusive with respect to this father and child relationship, and no action or proceeding under sections 3111.01 to 3111.18 or sections 3111.38 to 3111.54 of the Revised Code shall affect the relationship.

(B) If a woman is the subject of a non-spousal artificial insemination, the donor shall not be treated in law or regarded as the natural father of a child conceived as a result of the artificial insemination, and a child so conceived shall not be treated in law or regarded as the natural child of the donor. No action or proceeding under sections 3111.01 to 3111.18 or sections 3111.38 to 3111.54 of the Revised Code shall affect these consequences.

(2000 S 180, eff. 3–22–01)

Historical and Statutory Notes

Ed. Note: 3111.95 is former 3111.37, amended and recodified by 2000 S 180, eff. 3–22–01; 2000 H 242, eff. 10–27–00; 1997 H 352, eff. 1–1–98; 1986 H 476, eff. 9–24–86.

Amendment Note: 2000 S 180 substituted "3111.18" for "3111.19" and "sections 3111.38 to 3111.54" for "section 3111.22 or 3113.2111" in division (A); and substituted "3111.18" for "3111.19"

and "sections 3111.38 to 3111.54" for "section 3111.22".

Amendment Note: 2000 H 242 inserted "or 3113.2111".

Amendment Note: 1997 H 352 inserted "or proceeding" and "or section 3111.22" in divisions (A) and (B).

Ohio Administrative Code References

Conducting the administrative support hearing, see OAC 5101:12–45–05.2
Presumption of paternity, see OAC 5101:12–40–10

Support order establishment process, see OAC 5101:12–45–05

Library References

Children Out-of-Wedlock ☞3, 10, 35.
Westlaw Topic No. 76H.

C.J.S. Children Out-of-Wedlock §§ 10 to 14, 47, 50, 95.

Research References

Encyclopedias

OH Jur. 3d Family Law § 944, Statutory Presumptions.
OH Jur. 3d Family Law § 997, Status of Husband and Donor.

Forms

Ohio Forms Legal and Business § 28:5, Child Born as Result of Artificial Insemination.
Ohio Jurisprudence Pleading and Practice Forms § 111:6, Presumptions.

Treatises and Practice Aids

Sowald & Morganstern, Baldwin's Ohio Practice Domestic Relations Law § 3:50, Related Issues--Artificial Insemination and Surrogate Mothers.

Carlin, Baldwin's Ohio Prac. Merrick-Rippner Probate Law § 18:2, Inheritance Rights of Illegitimate Child--Statutory Provisions.
Carlin, Baldwin's Ohio Prac. Merrick-Rippner Probate Law § 19:7, Uniform Parentage Act--Presumptions.
Carlin, Baldwin's Ohio Prac. Merrick-Rippner Probate Law § 19:13, Uniform Parentage Act--Nonspousal Artificial Insemination; Embryo Donation.
Carlin, Baldwin's Ohio Prac. Merrick-Rippner Probate Law § 99:49, Interlocutory and Final Orders.
Carlin, Baldwin's Ohio Prac. Merrick-Rippner Probate Law § 110:19, Parentage Act--Effect.

Carlin, Baldwin's Ohio Prac. Merrick-Rippner Probate Law § 110:22, Parentage Act--Presumption of Paternity.

Carlin, Baldwin's Ohio Prac. Merrick-Rippner Probate Law § 110:31, Parentage Act--Continuing Jurisdiction to Modify or Revoke Judgment.

Carlin, Baldwin's Ohio Prac. Merrick-Rippner Probate Law § 110:33, Nonspousal Artificial Insemination and Embryo Donation.

Law Review and Journal Commentaries

In re T.R.: Not In Front of the Children, Bill Dickhaut. I Ky Children's Rts J 10 (July 1991).

Notes of Decisions

Child support obligation 3
Custody in divorce actions 2
Public policy 1

----

1. Public policy

Where a husband and wife agree to conceive a child by means of artificial insemination, and a child so conceived is born to the parties, it is against public policy for a court to enter a judgment establishing the husband's non-paternity in connection with a divorce of the parties and the remarriage of the mother. Brooks v. Fair (Van Wert 1988) 40 Ohio App.3d 202, 532 N.E.2d 208.

2. Custody in divorce actions

Legal parentage, not to be confused with biological parentage, must be established before the issue of custody can properly be decided where the child is the product of artificial insemination of a married woman by a man not her husband. In re Adoption of Reams (Franklin 1989) 52 Ohio App.3d 52, 557 N.E.2d 159, dismissed 50 Ohio St.3d 707, 553 N.E.2d 684. Adoption ☞ 7.1

3. Child support obligation

Father who had donated sperm to gay mother and her domestic partner, resulting in conception and birth of child, was precluded by operation of res judicata from challenging paternity and consequential demand for child support under nonspousal artificial insemination statute, where, after child's birth, father himself instituted administrative proceedings to establish paternity, which resulted in issuance of administrative determination of paternity that went unchallenged for approximately six years until institution of support proceedings. Curtis v. Prince (Ohio App. 9 Dist., Summit, 12-08-2010) No. 25194, 2010-Ohio-5999, 2010 WL 5071195, Unreported, appeal not allowed 128 Ohio St.3d 1429, 943 N.E.2d 574, 2011-Ohio-1049. Children Out–of–wedlock ☞ 15; Children Out–of–wedlock ☞ 68

Ex-husband had duty to support twins born to ex-wife during parties' marriage as result of artificial insemination by donor (AID) procedure, despite fact that ex-husband never provided his written consent to AID procedure; ex–wife met her burden of establishing that ex-husband orally consented to AID procedure, and ex-husband failed to prove by preponderance of the evidence that he withdrew his consent prior to time ex-wife underwent AID procedure which resulted in the twins' birth. Jackson v. Jackson (Ohio App. 2 Dist., 05-26-2000) 137 Ohio App.3d 782, 739 N.E.2d 1203. Child Support ☞ 63

3111.96 Effect of physician's failure to comply with statutes

The failure of a physician or person under the supervision and control of a physician to comply with the applicable requirements of sections 3111.88 to 3111.95 of the Revised Code shall not affect the legal status, rights, or obligations of a child conceived as a result of a nonspousal artificial insemination, a recipient, a husband who consented to the non-spousal artificial insemination of his wife, or the donor. If a recipient who is married and her husband make a good faith effort to execute a written consent that is in compliance with section 3111.93 of the Revised Code relative to a non-spousal artificial insemination, the failure of the written consent to so comply shall not affect the paternity consequences set forth in division (A) of section 3111.95 of the Revised Code.

(2000 S 180, eff. 3–22–01)

Historical and Statutory Notes

Ed. Note: 3111.96 is former 3111.38, amended and recodified by 2000 S 180, eff. 3–22–01; 1986 H 476, eff. 9–24–86.

Amendment Note: 2000 S 180 substituted "3111.88" for "3111.30", "3111.95" for "3111.37" twice, and "3111.93" for "3111.35".

Library References

Children Out-of-Wedlock ☞3, 10, 35.
Health ☞905 to 906.
Westlaw Topic Nos. 76H, 198H.
C.J.S. Children Out-of-Wedlock §§ 10 to 14, 47, 50, 95.

C.J.S. Physicians, Surgeons, and Other Health Care Providers §§ 118 to 120.
C.J.S. Right to Die §§ 47, 49, 52.

Research References

Forms

Ohio Forms Legal and Business § 28:5, Child Born as Result of Artificial Insemination.
Ohio Forms Legal and Business § 28:12, Consent to Artificial Insemination of Wife.

Treatises and Practice Aids

Carlin, Baldwin's Ohio Prac. Merrick-Rippner Probate Law § 18:2, Inheritance Rights of Illegitimate Child--Statutory Provisions.
Carlin, Baldwin's Ohio Prac. Merrick-Rippner Probate Law § 19:13, Uniform Parentage Act--Non-

spousal Artificial Insemination; Embryo Donation.
Carlin, Baldwin's Ohio Prac. Merrick-Rippner Probate Law § 110:19, Parentage Act--Effect.
Carlin, Baldwin's Ohio Prac. Merrick-Rippner Probate Law § 110:22, Parentage Act--Presumption of Paternity.
Carlin, Baldwin's Ohio Prac. Merrick-Rippner Probate Law § 110:31, Parentage Act--Continuing Jurisdiction to Modify or Revoke Judgment.
Carlin, Baldwin's Ohio Prac. Merrick-Rippner Probate Law § 110:33, Nonspousal Artificial Insemination and Embryo Donation.

EMBRYO DONATION

3111.97   Birth mother regarded as natural mother; effect of husband's consent

(A) A woman who gives birth to a child born as a result of embryo donation shall be treated in law and regarded as the natural mother of the child, and the child shall be treated in law and regarded as the natural child of the woman. No action or proceeding under this chapter shall affect the relationship.

(B) If a married woman gives birth to a child born as a result of embryo donation to which her husband consented, the husband shall be treated in law and regarded as the natural father of the child, and the child shall be treated in law and regarded as the natural child of the husband. A presumption that arises under division (A)(1) or (2) of section 3111.03 of the Revised Code is conclusive with respect to this father and child relationship, and no action or proceeding under this chapter shall affect the relationship.

(C) If a married woman gives birth to a child born as a result of embryo donation to which her husband has not consented, a presumption that arises under division (A)(1) or (2) of section 3111.03 of the Revised Code that the husband is the father of the child may be rebutted by clear and convincing evidence that includes the lack of consent to the embryo donation.

(D) As used in this division, "donor" means an individual who produced genetic material used to create an embryo, consents to the implantation of the embryo in a woman who is not the individual or the individual's wife, and at the time of the embryo donation does not intend to raise the resulting child as the individual's own.

If an individual who produced genetic material used to create an embryo dies, the other person who produced genetic material used to create the embryo may consent to donate the embryo. In such a case, the deceased person shall be deemed a donor for the purposes of this section.

A donor shall not be treated in law or regarded as a parent of a child born as a result of embryo donation. A donor shall have no parental responsibilities and shall have no right, obligation, or interest with respect to a child resulting from the donation.

(E) This section deals with embryo donation for the purpose of impregnating a woman so that she can bear a child that she intends to raise as her child.

(2006 H 102, eff. 6–15–06)

Research References

Encyclopedias

OH Jur. 3d Family Law § 944, Statutory Presumptions.

Treatises and Practice Aids

Carlin, Baldwin's Ohio Prac. Merrick-Rippner Probate Law § 19:13, Uniform Parentage Act--Non-

spousal Artificial Insemination; Embryo Donation.

Carlin, Baldwin's Ohio Prac. Merrick-Rippner Probate Law § 110:22, Parentage Act--Presumption of Paternity.

Carlin, Baldwin's Ohio Prac. Merrick-Rippner Probate Law § 110:33, Nonspousal Artificial Insemination and Embryo Donation.

Law Review and Journal Commentaries

Are you my mommy? A call for regulation of embryo donation. Michelle L. Anderson, 35 Cap. U. L. Rev. 589 (Winter 2006).

The legal status of the ex utero embryo: Implications for adoption law. Katheryn D. Katz, 35 Cap. U. L. Rev 303 (Winter 2006).

What do we tell the children? Ellen Waldman, 35 Cap. U. L. Rev. 517 (Winter 2006).

What the Erie "Surrogate Triplets" Can Teach State Legislatures about the Need to Enact Article 8 of the Uniform Parentage Act (2000). Robert E. Rains, 56 Clev. St. L. Rev. 1 (2008).

What's my place in this world? Lynne Marie Kohm, 35 Cap. U. L. Rev. 563 (Winter 2006).

Notes of Decisions

Contract rights   1

---

1. Contract rights

No public policy of Ohio is violated when a gestational-surrogacy contract is entered into, even

when one of the provisions prohibits the gestational surrogate from asserting parental rights regarding children she bears that are of another woman's artificially inseminated egg. J.F. v. D.B. (Ohio, 12-20-2007) 116 Ohio St.3d 363, 879 N.E.2d 740, 2007-Ohio-6750. Parent And Child ⟳ 20

PENALTIES

3111.99   Penalties

Whoever violates section 3111.19 of the Revised Code is guilty of interfering with the establishment of paternity, a misdemeanor of the first degree.

(2000 S 180, eff. 3–22–01; 1999 H 471, eff. 7–1–00; 1997 H 352, eff. 1–1–98; 1996 H 710, § 7, eff. 6–11–96; 1995 H 167, eff. 6–11–96; 1995 S 2, eff. 7–1–96; 1992 S 10, eff. 7–15–92)

Uncodified Law

1996 H 710, § 15, eff. 6–11–96, reads, in part:

(A) The amendments to sections 2151.231, 2301.34, 2301.35, 2301.351, 2301.358, 2705.02, 3111.20, 3111.21, 3111.22, 3111.23, 3111.241, 3111.242, 3111.27, 3111.28, 3111.99, 3113.21, 3113.214, 3113.215, 3113.99, 4723.07, and 4723.09

of the Revised Code by Sub. H.B. 167 of the 121st General Assembly take effect, and their existing interim versions are correspondingly repealed, on the date this act takes effect and not on November 15, 1996 [.]

Historical and Statutory Notes

Ed. Note: Former RC 3111.99 related to penalties for non-compliance with support orders. See now RC 3121.99; 3121.59 for provisions analogous to former RC 3111.99.

Ed. Note: The effective date of the amendment of this section by 1995 H 167 was changed from 11–15–96 to 6–11–96 by 1996 H 710, § 7, eff. 6–11–96.

Amendment Note: 2000 S 180 rewrote this section which prior thereto read:

"(A) For purposes of this section, "administrative support order" and "obligor" have the same meaning as in section 3111.20 of the Revised Code.

"(B) Whoever violates section 3111.29 of the Revised Code is guilty of interfering with the establishment of paternity, a misdemeanor of the first degree.

"(C) An obligor who violates division (B)(1)(c) of section 3111.23 of the Revised Code shall be fined not more than fifty dollars for a first offense, not more than one hundred dollars for a second offense, and not more than five hundred dollars for each subsequent offense.

"(D) An obligor who violates division (E)(2) of section 3111.23 of the Revised Code shall be fined not more than fifty dollars for a first offense, not more than one hundred dollars for a second offense, and not more than five hundred dollars for each subsequent offense.

"(E) A fine imposed pursuant to division (C) or (D) of this section shall be paid to the division of child support in the department of job and family services or, pursuant to division (H)(4) of section 2301.35 of the Revised Code, the child support enforcement agency. The amount of the fine that does not exceed the amount of arrearage the obligor owes under the administrative support order shall be disbursed in accordance with the support order. The amount of the fine that exceeds the amount of the arrearage under the support order shall be called program income and shall be collected in accordance with section 5101.325 of the Revised Code."

Amendment Note: 1999 H 471 substituted "job and family" for "human" in division (E).

Amendment Note: 1997 H 352 substituted "division of child support in the department of human services or, pursuant to division (H) of section 2301.35 of the Revised Code, the child support enforcement agency" for "child support enforcement agency administering the obligor's child support order" and "called program income and shall be collected in accordance with section 5101.325 of the Revised Code" for "used by the agency for the administration of its program for child support enforcement" in division (E).

Amendment Note: 1995 S 2 deleted the former second sentence, which read:

"If the offender previously has been convicted of or pleaded guilty to a violation of section 3111.29 or 2919.231 of the Revised Code, interfering with the establishment of paternity is a felony of the fourth degree."

Amendment Note: 1995 H 167 added division (A); designated division (B); and added divisions (C), (D), and (E).

Library References

Obstructing Justice ⚖6, 21.
Westlaw Topic No. 282.

C.J.S. Obstructing Justice or Governmental Administration §§ 3 to 8, 37 to 38, 47.

Research References

Encyclopedias

OH Jur. 3d Decedents' Estates § 541, as Including Illegitimate Children.
OH Jur. 3d Family Law § 942, Interference With Paternity Actions; Penalties.
OH Jur. 3d Family Law § 1230, Payment of Support by Obligor to Child Support Enforcement Agency.

Treatises and Practice Aids

Sowald & Morganstern, Baldwin's Ohio Practice Domestic Relations Law § 3:23, Criminal Interference With Establishment of Paternity.
Carlin, Baldwin's Ohio Prac. Merrick-Rippner Probate Law § 19:4, Legitimation--Historical Provisions.

Carlin, Baldwin's Ohio Prac. Merrick-Rippner Probate Law § 110:19, Parentage Act--Effect.
Carlin, Baldwin's Ohio Prac. Merrick-Rippner Probate Law § 110:35, Civil Support Proceedings--Liability for Child Support.
Carlin, Baldwin's Ohio Prac. Merrick-Rippner Probate Law § 110:36, Civil Support Proceedings--Determination of Amount of Support Under Child Support Guidelines.
Carlin, Baldwin's Ohio Prac. Merrick-Rippner Probate Law § 110:38, Civil Support Proceedings--Enforcement of Support Orders.
Carlin, Baldwin's Ohio Prac. Merrick-Rippner Probate Law § 110:40, Civil Support Proceedings--Paternity Compliance Plan.

INDEX

See Volume containing end of Title 31

END OF VOLUME